James W. McCollum

Baker Theological Dictionary of the Bible

Baker Theological Dictionary of the Bible

Walter A. Elwell
Editor

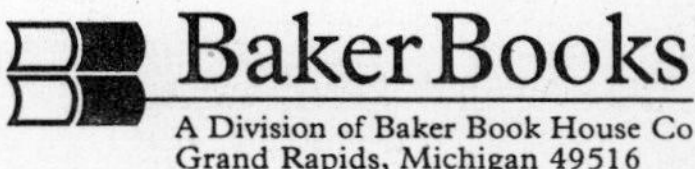

Published by Baker Books
a division of Baker Book House Company
P.O. Box 6287, Grand Rapids, MI 49516-6287

Previously published as *Evangelical Dictionary of Biblical Theology*
Published in 2000 as *Baker Theological Dictionary of the Bible*

Printed in the United States of America

ISBN 0-8010-2256-8

For current information about all releases from Baker Book House, visit our web site:
http://www.bakerbooks.com

Introduction

In these increasingly post-Christian and post-modern days there is a virtual illiteracy not only about the historical or factual content of the Bible but also about what the Bible teaches theologically. This began in the early part of this century, with Alfred North Whitehead lamenting it as early as the 1930s. It has continued unabated into our own time so that now, even in Christian colleges where students at least have a church background, there is only a rudimentary biblical or theological understanding to be found. But this is also a day of information explosion, and many people are not satisfied with knowing more about the Chicago Cubs or the lastest trends in Hollywood than they do about the theology of the Bible. Although good books are available to help rectify this situation, such as *The New International Dictionary of New Testament Theology* (3 vols.) or *The Theological Wordbook of the Old Testament* (2 vols.) unfortunately, they require a knowledge of Hebrew and Greek and hence are inaccessible to most people. It was for this reason that Baker Book House decided to produce a convenient, one-volume work that covered both the Old and the New Testaments but did not require a knowledge of the original languages. The research was in fact done in the Hebrew and Greek texts of the Bible, but it was written in such a way that virtually anyone could understand it.

The present volume is intended to make available to interested pastors, students, teachers, and lay people the biblical teaching on a wide variety of topics, ranging from the individual books of the Bible (such as the theological teaching of Isaiah) to specifically theological ideas (such as atonement or prophecy) to individual ideas that might appear only a few times or even once in the Scriptures (such as abyss or Armageddon). In every instance an attempt has been made to emphasize the theological significance rather than focus on the historical, social, geographical, or biographical elements involved. The writers were also instructed to steer away from the complexities of current academic debate on these subjects because of the rapidly changing and rather esoteric nature of some of these debates, as well as the limited space available in a one-volume work. It was thought better to deal with the subject as understood from the Bible than to deal with all of those technical issues that led to that understanding. For all practical purposes, those issues are of little interest to most people (much as we scholars are loath to admit it).

This work is also defined as "Evangelical," meaning that the full integrity and trustworthiness of the Scriptures are affirmed. All the writers honor the Scriptures as the Written Word of God and not only write with that understanding but live their lives according to it.

Bibliographies are appended to the larger articles, and again, they are designed for the reader. Books and articles referred to are almost all currently available, written in English and readable by most people. Some bibliographical entries depart from this goal, but only when deemed necessary.

It is the supreme desire and prayer of the writers of this volume that the reader will be edified both intellectually and spiritually by the use of it. What the Scriptures teach us is the most vitally needed thing today. These are in fact God's very words to us and are profitable for correction, reproof, and instruction in righteousness. If this present volume helps in that regard by making clear what the Bible is saying on any given topic, then the prayers of the writers will have been answered.

I would also like to thank those people who have had a hand in producing this work, so much of it behind the scenes. I would especially like to thank my wife Barbara, Allan Fisher, Jim Weaver, Maria den Boer, Cindy Ingrum, Rebecca Cooper, Bruce Paulson, and J. D. Douglas, whose sharp eye for detail seldom fails.

WALTER A. ELWELL

Abbreviations

ABD — *Anchor Bible Dictionary*, ed. D. N. Freeman
AJSL — *American Journal of Semitic Languages and Literature*
ATR — *Anglican Theological Review*
AV — Authorized Version
BA — *Biblical Archaeologist*
BAR — *Biblical Archaeologist Reader*
BASOR — *Bulletin of the American Schools of Oriental Research*
BDT — *Baker Dictionary of Theology*, ed. E. F. Harrison
BEB — *Baker Encyclopedia of the Bible*, ed. W. A. Elwell
Bib — *Biblica*
BJRL — *Bulletin of the John Rylands University Library of Manchester*
BSac — *Bibliotheca Sacra*
BT — *The Bible Translator*
BTB — *Biblical Theology Bulletin*
CBQ — *Catholic Biblical Quarterly*
ChrEdJ — *Christian Education Journal*
CTJ — *Calvin Theological Journal*
CTR — *Criswell Theological Review*
DAC — *Dictionary of the Apostolic Church*, ed. J. Hastings
DJG — *Dictionary of Jesus and the Gospels*, ed. J. B. Green, S. McKnight, and I. H. Marshall
DNTT — *Dictionary of New Testament Theology*
DPL — *Dictionary of Paul and His Letters*, ed. G. F. Hawthorne, R. P. Martin, and D. G. Reid
EDNT — *Exegetical Dictionary of the New Teatament*, ed. H. Balz and G. Schneider
EDT — *Evangelical Dictionary of Theology*, ed. W. A. Elwell
EvQ — *Evangelical Quarterly*
EvRTh — *Evangelical Review of Theology*
EvTh — *Evangelische Theologie*
ExpT — *Expository Times*
Gk. — Greek
GraceThJ — *Grace Theological Journal*
HBD — *Harper's Bible Dictionary*, ed. M. S. Miller and J. L. Miller
Heb. — Hebrew
HTR — *Harvard Theological Review*
HUCA — *Hebrew Union College Annual*
IB — *Interpreter's Bible*, ed. G. A. Buttrick
IBD — *Illustrated Bible Dictionary*
IDB — *The Interpreter's Dictionary of the Bible*, ed. G. A. Buttrick
Int — *Interpretation*
ISBE — *The International Standard Bible Encyclopedia*, ed. G. W. Bromiley
ITQ — *Irish Theological Quarterly*
JAAR — *Journal of the American Academy of Religion*
JAOS — *Journal of the American Oriental Society*
JBL — *Journal of Biblical Literature*
JETS — *Journal of the Evangelical Theological Society*
JJS — *Journal of Jewish Studies*
JNES — *Journal of Near Eastern Studies*
JRE — *Journal of Religious Ethics*
JSNT — *Journal for the Study of the New Testament*
JSOT — *Journal for the Study of the Old Testament*
JSS — *Journal of Semitic Studies*
JTS — *Journal of Theological Studies*
LuthThJ — *Lutheran Theological Journal*
KJV — King James Version
Lat. — Latin
LXX — Septuagint
NASB — New American Standard Bible
NBD — *New Bible Dictionary*, ed. J. D. Douglas et al.
NEB — New English Bible
Neot — *Neotestimentica*
NIDNTT — *The New International Dictionary of New Testament Theology*, ed. C. Brown
NIV — New International Version
NovT — *Novum Testamentum*
NRSV — New Revised Standard Version
NTS — *New Testament Studies*
OED — *Oxford English Dictionary*
par./pars. — parallel/parallels
RefThR — *Reformed Theological Review*
RevExp — *Review and Expositor*
RSV — Revised Standard Version
SBLSP — *Society of Biblical Literature Seminar Papers*
Scr — *Scripture*
SJT — *Scottish Journal of Theology*
St — *Studia theologica*
SWJTh — *Southwestern Journal of Theology*
TAB — *Topical Analysis of the Bible*, ed. W. A. Elwell
TAPS — *Transactions of the American Philosophical Society*
TDNT — *Theological Dictionary of the New Testament*, ed. G. Kittel and G. Friedrich
TDOT — *Theological Dictionary of the Old Testament*, ed. G. J. Botterweck and H. Ringgren
TEV — Today's English Version
TrinityJ — *Trinity Journal*
TWOT — *Theological Wordbook of the Old Testament*, ed. R. L. Harris, G. L. Archer, Jr., and B. K. Waltke
TrinityJ — *Trinity Journal*
TynBul — *Tyndale Bulletin*
VoxEv — *Vox Evangelica*
VT — *Vetus Testamentum*
WTJ — *Westminster Theological Journal*
ZAW — *Zeitschrift für die alttestamentliche Wissenschaft*
ZPED — *The Zondervan Pictorial Encyclopedia of the Bible*, ed. M. C. Tenney

Contributors

Adams, Eric W. M.A., Wheaton College Graduate School.

Akin, Daniel L. Ph.D., University of Texas at Arlington. Associate Professor of Theology, Southeastern Baptist Theological Seminary, Wake Forest, North Carolina.

Alexander, Ralph H. Th.D., Dallas Theological Seminary.

Arnold, Bill T. Ph.D., Hebrew Union College. Professor of Old Testament and Semitic Languages, Asbury Theological Seminary, Wilmore, Kentucky.

Averbeck, Richard E. Ph.D., Dropsie College, Annenberg Research Institute. Associate Professor of Old Testament and Semitic Languages, Trinity Evangelical Divinity School, Deerfield, Illinois.

Baker, David W. Ph.D., University of London. Professor of Old Testament and Semitic Languages; Chair, Department of Biblical Studies, Ashland Theological Seminary, Ashland, Ohio.

Beyer, Bryan E. Ph.D., Hebrew Union College. Dean of the Bible College, Columbia International University, Columbia, South Carolina.

Blomberg, Craig L. Ph.D., University of Aberdeen. Professor of New Testament, Denver Seminary, Denver, Colorado.

Bock, Darrell L. Ph.D., University of Aberdeen. Research Professor of New Testament Studies, Dallas Theological Seminary, Dallas, Texas.

Borchert, Gerald L. Ph.D., Princeton Theological Seminary. T. Rupert and Lucille Coleman Professor of New Testament Interpretation, Southern Baptist Theological Seminary, Louisville, Kentucky.

Bramer, Stephen J. Ph.D. candidate, Dallas Theological Seminary. Professor of Biblical Studies, Briercrest Bible College and Biblical Seminary.

Bridges, Carl B., Jr. Ph.D., Union Theological Seminary in Virginia. Professor of New Testament, Johnson Bible College, Knoxville, Tennessee.

Brown, William E. Th.D., Dallas Theological Seminary. President, Bryan College.

Buckwalter, H. Douglas. Ph.D., University of Aberdeen. Assistant Professor of New Testament, Evangelical School of Theology, Myerstown, Pennsylvania.

Bullock, C. Hassell. Ph.D., Hebrew Union College. Franklin S. Dyrness Professor of Biblical Studies, Wheaton College, Wheaton, Illinois.

Burge, Gary M. Ph.D., King's College, University of Aberdeen. Professor of New Testament, Wheaton College, Wheaton, Illinois.

Cameron, Nigel M. de S. Ph.D., Edinburgh. Senior Vice President of Academic Planning and Professor of Theology and Culture, Trinity International University, Deerfield, Illinois.

Chamblin, J. Knox. Th.D., Union Theological Seminary. Professor of New Testament, Reformed Theological Seminary, Jackson, Mississippi.

Chavalas, Mark W. Ph.D., UCLA. Assistant Professor of History, University of Wisconsin, La Crosse, Wisconsin.

Davidson, Richard M. Ph.D., Andrews University. Professor of Old Testament Interpretation, Andrews University, Berrien Springs, Michigan.

Davis, Thomas W. Ph.D., University of Arizona. Senior Project Manager, Archaeology, R. Christopher Goodwin and Associates Inc.

Deasley, A. R. G. Ph.D., University of Manchester. Professor of New Testament, Nazarene Theological Seminary, Kansas City, Missouri.

Dempster, Stephen G. Ph.D., Associate Professor of Religious Studies, Atlantic Baptist College, Moncton, New Brunswick, Canada.

Dickens, Owen. Ph.D., Brandeis. Associate Professor of Religion, Asbury College, Wilmore, Kentucky.

Dillard, Raymond B. Ph.D., Former Professor of Old Testament Language and Literature, Westminster Theological Seminary, Philadelphia, Pennsylvania. Deceased.

Dockery, David S. Ph.D., University of Texas. Vice President for Academic Administration and Professor of New Testament Theology, Southern Baptist Theological Seminary, Louisville, Kentucky.

Doriani, Daniel. Ph.D., Westminster Theological Seminary. Associate Professor of New Testament, Covenant Theological Seminary, St. Louis, Missouri.

Duke, Rodney K. Ph.D., Emory University. Assistant Professor of Philosophy and Religion, Appalachian State University, Boone, North Carolina.

Dunnett, Walter M. Ph.D., Case-Western Reserve University. Priest Associate, Church of the Messiah (Episcopal), St. Paul, Minnesota.

Elwell, Walter A. Ph.D., University of Edinburgh. Professor of Bible and Theology, Wheaton College Graduate School, Wheaton, Illinois.

Engelhard, David H. Ph.D., Brandeis University. General Secretary, Christian Reformed Church in North America, Grand Rapids, Michigan.

Enlow, Ralph E., Jr. Ed.D., Vanderbilt University. Vice President for Academic Affairs, Columbia International University, Columbia, South Carolina.

Ericson, Norman R. Ph.D., University of Chicago. Professor of New Testament Studies, Wheaton College, Wheaton, Illinois.

Farrell, Hobert K. Ph.D., Boston University. Professor and Coordinator of Biblical Studies, LeTourneau University, Longview, Texas.

Ferguson, Paul. Ph.D., Professor of Old Testament, Christian Life College, Mount Prospect, Illinois.

Finley, Harvey E. Ph.D., Oriental Seminary—The Johns Hopkins University. Professor Emeritus of Old Testament, Nazarene Theological Seminary, Kansas City, Missouri.

Fisk, Bruce N. Ph.D. candidate, Duke University. Instructor in New Testament, Briercrest Bible College, Caronport, Saskatchewan, Canada.

Foulkes, Francis. M.A., Oxford. Formerly Warden, St. John's Theological College, Auckland, New Zealand.

Franz, Gordon. M.A., Columbia Biblical Seminary. Field trip instructor, Institute of Holy Land Studies, Jerusalem, Israel.

Garrett, Duane A. Ph.D., Baylor University. Professor of Hebrew and Old Testament, Canadian Southern Baptist Seminary, Cochrane, Alberta, Canada.

Gerig, Wesley L. Ph.D., University of Iowa. Professor of Bible, Taylor University, Fort Wayne, Indiana.

Goldberg, Louis. Th.D., Grace Theological Seminary. Professor of Theology and Jewish Studies, Moody Bible Institute, Chicago, Illinois.

Gruenler, Royce Gordon. Ph.D., University of Aberdeen. Professor of New Testament, Gordon-Conwell Theological Seminary, South Hamilton, Massachusetts.

Hagan, G. Michael. Ph.D., UCLA. Vice President for Academic Affairs and Professor of Old Testament, North American Baptist Seminary, Sioux Falls, South Dakota.

Hamstra, Sam, Jr. Ph.D., Marquette University. Director of Campus Ministry, Trinity Christian College, Palos Heights, Illinois.

Harrison, R. K. Ph.D., University of London. Former Professor of Old Testament, Wycliffe College, Toronto. Deceased.

Harvey, John D. Th.D., candidate, Toronto School of Theology. Assistant Professor of New Testament and Greek, Columbia Biblical Seminary and Graduate School of Missions, Columbia, South Carolina.

Hawthorne, Gerald F. Ph.D., University of Chicago. Professor of Greek, emeritus, Wheaton College, Wheaton, Illinois.

Hess, Richard S. Ph.D., Hebrew Union College. Reader in Old Testament Studies, Roehampton Institute, London.

Hiebert, Robert J. V. Ph.D., University of Toronto. Professor of Old Testament, Ontario Bible College, Willowdale, Ontario, Canada.

Hildebrand, David. Ph.D., The University of St. Michael's College, Toronto School of Theology. Professor of Old Testament and Hebrew, Briercrest Bible College, Caronport, Saskatchewan, Canada.

Hill, Andrew E. Ph.D., University of Michigan. Associate Professor of Old Testament, Wheaton College, Wheaton, Illinois.

Hoch, Carl B., Jr. Th.D., Dallas Theological Seminary. Professor of New Testament, Grand Rapids Baptist Seminary, Grand Rapids, Michigan.

Huttar, David K. Ph.D., Brandeis University. Professor of Bible, Nyack College, Nyack, New York.

Jervis, L. Ann., Th.D., Assistant Professor of New Testament, Wycliffe College, Toronto, Ontario, Canada.

Kaiser, Walter C., Jr. Ph.D., Brandeis University. Colman M. Mockler Distinguished Professor of Old Testament and Director of Foundation for Biblical Ethics, Gordon-Conwell Theological Seminary, South Hamilton, Massachusetts.

Karlberg, Mark W. Th.D., Westminster Theological Seminary. Theological writer and teacher.

Keefer, Luke L., Jr. Ph.D., Temple University. Professor of Church History and Theology, Ashland Theological Seminary, Ashland, Ohio.

Kelhoffer, James A. M.A., Wheaton College Graduate Student, Univerisity of Chicago.

Keylock, Leslie R. Ph.D., Trinity International University. Professor of Bible and Theology, Moody Bible Institute, Chicago, Illinois.

Klein, George L. Ph.D., Dropsie College/Annenberg Research Institute. Academic Dean and Professor of Old Testament, The Criswell College, Dallas, Texas.

Larkin, William J., Jr. Ph.D., University of Durham. Professor of New Testament and Greek, Columbia Biblical Seminary and Graduate School of Missions, Columbia, South Carolina.

Lawlor, John I. Ph.D., Drew University. Professor of Old Testament Studies, Baptist Bible Seminary, Clarks Summit, Pennsylvania.

Longman, Tremper, III. Ph.D., Yale University. Professor and Chair, Old Testament. Westminster Theological Seminary, Philadelphia, Pennsylvania.

Mare, W. Harold. Ph.D., University of Pennsylvania. Professor of New Testament, Covenant Theological Seminary, St. Louis, Missouri.

Martens, Elmer A. Ph.D., Claremont Graduate School. Professor of Old Testament, Mennonite Brethren Biblical Seminary, Fresno, California.

McKnight, Scot. Ph.D., University of Nottingham. Karl A. Olsson Professor in Religious Studies, North Park College, Chicago, Illinois.

McLean, Mark D. Ph.D., Harvard University. Professor of Biblical Studies and Philosophy, Evangel College, Springfield, Missouri.

McRay, John. Ph.D., University of Chicago. Professor of New Testament and Archaeology, Wheaton College, Wheaton, Illinois.

Meadors, Gary T. Th.D., Grace Theological Seminary. Professor of New Testament, Grand Rapids Baptist Seminary, Grand Rapids, Michigan.

Meier, Samuel A. Ph.D., Associate Professor of Hebrew, The Ohio State University, Columbus, Ohio.

Merrill, Eugene H. Ph.D., Columbia University. Professor of Old Testament Studies, Dallas Theological Seminary, Dallas, Texas.

Moo, Douglas J. Ph.D., University of St. Andrews. Professor of New Testament, Trinity Evangelical Divinity School, Deerfield, Illinois.

Moreau, A. Scott. D.Miss., Trinity Evangelical Divinity School. Associate Professor of Missions and Intercultural Studies, Wheaton College, Wheaton, Illinois.

Morley, Brian K. Ph.D., Claremont. Assistant Professor, The Master's College.

Morris, Leon L. Ph.D., University of Cambridge. Retired.

Motyer, Stephen. Ph.D., King's College. Lecturer and Tutor, London Bible College, Northwood, Middlesex, England.

Mullen, Bradford A. Ph.D., Boston University. Associate Professor of Theology, Columbia Biblical Seminary, Columbia, South Carolina.

Nelson, William B., Jr. Ph.D., Harvard University. Associate Professor of Old Testament, Westmont College, Santa Barbara, California.

Okholm, Dennis L. Ph.D., Princeton Theological Seminary. Associate Professor of Theology, Wheaton College, Wheaton, Illinois.

Oswalt, John N. Ph.D., Brandeis. Professor of Old Testament and Semitic Languages, Asbury Theological Seminary, Wilmore, Kentucky.

Parsons, Greg W. Th.D., Dallas Theological Seminary. Professor of Biblical Studies, Baptist Missionary Association Theological Seminary, Jacksonville, Texas.

Pate, C. Marvin. Ph.D., Marquette University. Professor of Bible, Moody Bible Institute, Chicago, Illinois.

Payne, Philip Barton. Ph.D., Cambridge University. President, Linguists' Software, Inc.

Peterson, Robert A. Ph.D., Drew University. Professor of Systematic Theology, Covenant Theological Seminary, St. Louis, Missouri.

Petrotta, Anthony J. Ph.D., University of Sheffield.

Phillips, Timothy R. Ph.D., Vanderbilt University. Associate Professor of Systematic and Historical Theology.

Rainbow, Paul Andrew. D.Phil., Oxford University. Professor of New Testament, North American Baptist Seminary, Sioux Falls, South Dakota.

Rightmire, R. David. Ph.D., Marquette University. Professor of Bible and Theology, Asbury College, Wilmore, Kentucky.

Scaer, David P. Th.D., Concordia Seminary. Professor of Systematic Theology and New Testament, Concordia Theological Seminary, Fort Wayne, Indiana.

Schaefer, Glenn E. Ph.D., The Southern Baptist Theological Seminary. Professor of Old Testament and Chairman of the Division of World Ministries, Simpson College, Redding, California.

Schmidt, Thomas E. Ph.D., Cambridge University. Professor of New Testament, Westmont College, Santa Barbara, California.

Schoville, Keith N. Ph.D., University of Wisconsin. Professor of Hebrew and Semitic Studies, University of Wisconsin, Madison, Wisconsin.

Schultz, Carl. Ph.D., Brandeis University. Professor of Old Testament and Chair of the Department of Religion and Philosophy, Houghton College, Houghton, New York.

Scott, J. Julius, Jr. Ph.D., University of Manchester. Professor of Biblical and Historical Studies, Wheaton College Graduate School, Wheaton, Illinois.

Shoemaker, Melvin H. M.Phil., Drew University. Associate Professor of New Testament, C. P. Haggard School of Theology, Azusa Pacific University, Azusa, California.

Shogren, Gary Steven. Ph.D., Aberdeen University. Professor of New Testament, Biblical Theological Seminary, Hatfield, Pennsylvania.

Silva, Moisés. Ph.D., University of Manchester. Professor of New Testament, Westminster Theological Seminary, Philadelphia, Pennsylvania.

Simmons, William A. Ph.D., University of St. Andrews. Associate Professor, Lee College, Cleveland, Tennessee.

Slane Craig J. Th.D., Lutheran School of Theology. Professor of Bible and Theology, Simpson College, Redding, California.

Smith, Andrew L. Ph.D., Boston University. Assistant Professor of Bible, Grand Rapids Baptist College, Grand Rapids, Michigan.

Smith, Barry D. Ph.D., McMaster University. Associate Professor of Religious Studies, Atlantic Baptist College, Moncton, New Brunswick, Canada.

Spender, Robert D. Ph.D., Dropsie College for Hebrew and Cognate Learning.

Sprinkle, Joe M. Ph.D., Hebrew Union College—Jewish Institute of Religion. Assistant Professor of Old Testament, Toccoa Falls College, Toccoa Falls, Georgia.

Stein, Robert H. Ph.D., Princeton University. Professor of New Testament, Bethel Theological Seminary, St. Paul, Minnesota.

Stek, John H. Th.M., Westminster Theological Seminary. Associate Professor of Old Testament, Emeritus, Calvin Theological Seminary, Grand Rapids, Michigan.

Swartz, Herbert L. Th.D., Victoria University. Professor of Biblical Studies, Eastern Mennonite University, Harrisonburg, Virginia.

Thielman, Frank. Ph.D., Duke University. Associate Professor of Divinity, Beeson Divinity School, Birmingham, Alabama.

Toon, Peter. D. Phil., Oxford. Professor of Anglican Studies, Philadelphia Theological Seminary, Philadelphia, Pennsylvania.

Towner, Philip H. Ph.D., University of Aberdeen. Research Fellow, Department of New Testament, University of Aberdeen, Aberdeen, Scotland.

Trafton, Joseph L. Ph.D., Duke University. Professor of Christian Origins, Western Kentucky University, Bowling Green, Kentucky.

Trebilco, Paul. Ph.D., University of Durham. Professor of New Testament Studies, Knox Theological Hall, Dunedin, New Zealand.

Trotter, Andrew H., Jr. Ph.D., University of Cambridge. Executive Director, Center for Christian Study.

Turner, David L. Th.D., Grace Theological Seminary. Professor of New Testament, Grand Rapids Baptist Seminary, Grand Rapids, Michigan.

Ury, M. William. Ph.D., Drew University. Associate Professor of Systematic and Historical Theology, Wesley Biblical Seminary, Jackson, Mississippi.

Van Dam, Cornelis. Th.D., Theologische Universiteit. Professor of Old Testament, Theological College of the Canadian Reformed Churches, Hamilton, Ontario, Canada.

Van Groningen, Gerard. Ph.D., University of Melbourne. Adjunct Professor of Old Testament, Covenant Theological Seminary, St. Louis, Missouri.

Vannoy, J. Robert. Th.D., Free University. Professor of Old Testament, Biblical Theological Seminary, Hatfield, Pennsylvania.

Wallmark, Leonard S. D.Min., Golden Gate Baptist Theological Seminary. Professor of Bible and Theology, Simpson College, Redding, California.

Waltke, Bruce K. Ph.D., Harvard University. Marshall Sheppard Professor of Biblical Studies, Regent College, Vancouver, British Columbia, Canada.

Wegner, Paul D. Ph.D., University of London. Assistant Professor, Moody Bible Institute, Chicago, Illinois.

White, R. E. O. B.D., London. Former Principal, Scottish Baptist College, Glasgow, United Kingdom.

Wilkins, Michael J. Ph.D., Fuller Theological Seminary. Dean of the Faculty; Chair and Professor in the Department of New Testament Language and Literature, Talbot School of Theology, La Mirada, California.

Williams, William C. Ph.D., New York University. Professor of Old Testament, Southern California College, Costa Mesa, California.

Winkler, Alan N. Th.M., Dallas Theological Seminary. Professor Emeritus, Bryan College, Dayton, Tennessee.

Wolf, Herbert M. Ph.D., Brandeis. Professor of Old Testament, Wheaton College Graduate School, Wheaton, Illinois.

Woodruff, William J. M.Th., Asbury Theological Seminary. Retired, Olivet Nazarene University, Kankakee, Illinois.

Yarbrough, Robert W. Ph.D., University of Aberdeen. Associate Professor of New Testament Studies, Covenant Theological Seminary, St. Louis, Missouri.

Aa

Aaron. Aaron had the distinctive privilege of being Moses' close associate and also the one selected as the first high priest of God's people. He and the firstborn son of each generation of his lineage were dedicated in a special anointing ceremony to officiate before God and on behalf of God's people as high priests.

Aaron, the first priest of ancient Israel, was the older brother of Moses. His parents Amram and Jochebed were Kohathites of the tribe of Levi. Two aspects of Aaron's earlier years provided a matrix out of which he responded to God's call to help Moses when he returned to Egypt. First, Aaron was committed to the God of the "fathers"—Abraham, Isaac, and Jacob (Exod. 3:1–6). Second, he understood that God had made a covenant with Abraham that included him and the people of Israel.

Pre-Sinai. Aaron agreed to help his brother Moses in the cause of seeking the release of his people from bondage. He and Moses were Yahweh's human instruments, carrying out Yahweh's mighty, unprecedented salvation-acts.

First, he accepted God's call to be Moses' mouthpiece before Pharaoh (Exod. 4:10–17; 5:1–13; 6:10–13; 6:28–7:7), a risky assignment. Both he and Moses were to be Yahweh's messengers in a hostile, polytheistic setting.

Second, as Moses' prophet (Exod. 7:1) he was an important proclaimer of God's word to Pharaoh and the other Egyptians. He fulfilled his priestly role by serving as mediator and intercessor on behalf of the people of Israel.

Third, like Moses he was moved by the Spirit of God and was used to effect miracles a number of times on the way to Sinai.

At Sinai. God graciously granted both Moses and Aaron new revelation during Israel's encampment at Sinai.

First, they were granted an unparalleled privilege. Moses and Aaron were allowed to enter into God's holy presence on Sinai (Exod. 19:24; 24:9–10).

Second, Aaron and Moses were leader-participants in the covenant Yahweh made between himself and the people of Israel.

Third, Yahweh delivered specific instructions to Aaron and Moses at Sinai about how they were to lead Israel to become his holy nation and kingdom of priests.

The Break in Loyalty. Aaron was directly responsible for a grave offense against God when Moses was on Mount Sinai receiving the written law of Israel (Exod. 32:1–10). He gave in to the demands of the people, collecting the necessary materials and supervising the making of a golden calf. He then told the people, "These are your gods, O Israel, who brought you up out of Egypt." Aaron then set up an altar and proceeded to lead the people in worshiping the calf.

Aaron acted against what he knew God wanted. Perhaps he had not completely detached himself from the Apis-bull worship of Egypt or from some insidious feature of Baal worship present in Egypt. In spite of his sin, Aaron was restored to his position of high priest. This is a most remarkable incident demonstrating the grace and compassion of God.

High Priest of God Most High. Aaron was duly attired and dedicated as God's priest (Lev. 8–9). He ministered before Yahweh, whose presence-cloud dwelt above the mercy seat over the ark of the covenant in the Most Holy Place of the tabernacle (Exod. 40:38).

Aaron was chief as he ministered with other priests in presenting offerings and sacrifices to Yahweh for himself and for the people of Israel. He was an intercessor and mediator before Yahweh among his people. His priestly vestments, especially the ephod and breastplate adorned with precious stones inscribed with the names of the tribes, emphasized in a special way this ministry before God on behalf of the people. HARVEY E. FINLEY

See also OFFERINGS AND SACRIFICES; PRIEST, PRIESTHOOD.

Bibliography. W. F. Albright, *History, Archaeology and Christian Humanism;* O. T. Allis, *ZPEB,* 1:1–4; B. S. Childs, *The Book of Exodus;* L. G. Cox, *Exodus;* C. F. H. Henry, *God Who Speaks and Shows;* J. P. Hyatt, *Exodus;* C. F. Keil and F. Delitzsch, *The Pentateuch;* D. F. Kinlaw, *Leviticus.*

Abaddon. In the Book of Revelation (9:1–11), when John sees his vision of the fifth trumpet blowing, a vast horde of demonic horsemen is seen arising from the newly opened abyss. They are sent forth to torment the unfortunate inhabitants of earth, but not to kill them. They have a ruler over them, called a king (*basileia*), the angel of the abyss, whose name is given in both Hebrew and Greek. In Hebrew it is Abaddon and in Greek Apollyon, both words meaning Destroyer or Destruction.

The word only occurs once in the New Testament (Rev. 9:11) and five times in the Old Testament (Job 26:6; 28:22; 31:12; Ps. 88:11; Prov. 15:11). In Psalm 88:11 Destruction is parallel to the grave; in Job 26:6 and Proverbs 26:6 it is parallel to Sheol; in Job 28:22 it is parallel to Death. Job 31:12 says sin is a fire that burns to destruction. So in the Old Testament Abaddon means the place of utter ruin, death, desolation, or destruction.

The angel of the abyss is called Destruction or Destroyer because his task is to oversee the devastation of the inhabitants of the earth, although it is curious that his minions are allowed only to torture and not to kill. His identity is a matter of dispute. Some make him Satan himself, while others take him to be only one of Satan's many evil subordinates. WALTER A. ELWELL

Abba. *See* FATHERHOOD OF GOD.

Abomination That Causes Desolation, the. An expression that occurs three times in the Septuagint of Daniel (9:27; 11:31; 12:11) and twice in the words of Jesus (Matt. 24:15; Mark 13:14), where slight linguistic variation exists. Luke's account of this prophecy (21:20) is more general and speaks of armies surrounding Jerusalem. First Maccabees, quoting Daniel, refers these words to the sacrifice of swine's flesh on the altar in Jerusalem by Antiochus IV, Epiphanes, in 168 B.C. (1:54). Josephus, without referring to Daniel, recounts this episode in detail (*Antiq*. 7.5.4). Jesus, in using these cryptic words of Daniel, is also predicting a desecration of the temple, or at lest the temple area, which will parallel the catastrophic event of the past, so well remembered by the Jews of his day.

There have been numerous suggestions as to precisely what Jesus meant by this prophecy. It should be noted that for Jesus, the Abomination has become a personal force rather than an event—*he* stands (in the holy place [Matt. 24:15] where he does not belong [Mark 13:14]). This has caused some to look for a particular historical act by an individual for fulfillment (variously, Pilate, Caligula, or Hadrian, more proximately, or more remotely the Antichrist himself in the endtimes) as the ultimate Abomination. Others have argued, especially in light of Luke 21:20 and Daniel's words, that either the destruction of Jerusalem in A.D. 70 or the desecration of the temple at that time, whether by the apostate Jews beforehand or the Romans afterward, fulfilled Jesus' prophetic words.

Given the nature of prophetic utterance, which often includes a more proximate and remote fulfillment, there is no reason why there could not be truth in both of these approaches. Jesus could very well be referring to the end of the age—he was, after all, answering the questions of "when will this happen" (i.e., the destruction of the temple) and "what will be the sign of your coming and the end of the age?" (Matt. 24:3)—as well as to the destruction of Jerusalem in A.D. 70. If this is so, then the early Christians were right when they fled Jerusalem in obedience to Jesus' words (Matt. 24:16–20), but were also right when they looked for yet another, more cataclysmic fulfillment in the more distant future that would constitute the end of the age. WALTER A. ELWELL

Abortion. ***Humankind as God's Unique Image-Bearer.*** Although only a handful of Old Testament texts, all in Genesis, explicitly portray humankind as God's image-bearer, this handful can hardly be described as insignificant. Key Hebrew terms in this connection include *ṣelem* (image, likeness; Gen. 1:26, 27a, b; 9:6) and *dĕmût* (form, shape, likeness; Gen. 1:26; 5:1). These terms designate humanity, over and against the rest of creation, as somehow modeled after God.

Attempts to articulate precisely the way in which humankind reflects God's image have yielded a bewildering array of proposals, keying on human qualities such as reason, volition, moral responsibility, sexual duality (Gen. 1:27b), physical form, and capacity to govern (Gen. 1:28) or enter into relationships (Gen. 1:26; 2:18). But pinpointing the location of this image may be neither possible nor helpful. As James Barr has shown, the writer's choice of *ṣelem* is, in part, a choice to reject several other more loaded terms that would carry overtones of idolatry or introduce unacceptable ideas about God. Most likely, the declaration of divine-human resemblance in Genesis 1 is generic, serving to set humanity not only apart from other creatures but also over them. There is a fundamental discontinuity between humankind and the animal realm (Gen. 1:24–28; cf. 2:7 with 2:19), a discontinuity reiterated when, after the flood, God affirms the killing and eating of animals but prohibits murder (Gen. 9:6).

Many point out that the Old Testament characteristically views people as a whole, without separating them into physical and spiritual components. Accordingly, an understanding of the divine image that is limited to certain spiritual or psychological qualities, divorced from the physical dimension, is too confining. Rather, this likeness belongs to people as people; it is intrinsic to being human. To locate human life is to locate a divine likeness. Nothing in Genesis suggests that human disobedience has eradicated the image (Gen. 9:6; cf. 1 Cor. 11:7; James 3:9); neither does Scripture support equating the divine-human resemblance with capacities not present until later stages of human development. Typically, developmental models find the image of God fully manifest only in rational, self-conscious persons, but this requires importing foreign categories and concepts. Personhood, however defined, may be a useful category, but it is not a biblical one.

The psalmist's portrait of humanity, as distinguished from the rest of creation, employs language of dignity, honor, and lofty position, rather than of divine image (Ps. 8:3–8). Whether humankind is made a little lower than God (8:5 NASB) or the heavenly beings (NIV; cf. LXX; Heb. 2:7, 9), the point remains the same: Among earth's creatures humankind is unique, and over earth's creatures humankind is supreme. At the same time, the psalms carefully preserve the infinite distance between humanity and its Creator; divine likeness is never confused with divinity (8:4; 113:1–9; 144:3–4).

On several occasions, in widely divergent contexts, New Testament authors endorse this depiction of human dignity and God-likeness. In 1 Corinthians 11:7, Paul weaves together strands from Genesis 1, Psalm 8, and Exodus 34 to establish that men, in corporate worship, should not cover their heads, because man is the image of God. Acts 17:28 finds Paul enlisting Stoic support to establish essential links between God and humankind, in order to demonstrate the absurdity of likening God to inanimate objects. James 3:9 underlines the tongue's hypocrisy when it praises God while cursing God's image-bearers. Elsewhere, Christ is the quintessential divine image-bearer according to whose pattern redeemed humanity is being recreated (Col. 1:15; 3:10; Heb. 2:6–10; cf. Rom. 8:29; 2 Cor. 3:18; 4:4).

A predictable corollary of Scripture's portrayal of humankind's dignity and God-likeness is the prohibition of murder. It underlies God's curse of Cain (Gen. 4:10–11), is explained in God's covenant with Noah (Gen. 9:5–6), is exemplified in the lives of Jacob (Gen. 27:41–42; 32:11–12), Joseph (Gen. 37:21, 22, 27; 42:22), and Moses (Exod. 2:12–14), and finally is encoded as the sixth commandment (Exod. 20:13; Deut. 5:17). Numerous laws explain how it was to be understood and enforced and how to distinguish murder from accidental killing. But with this prohibition of murder came also mandatory capital punishment (Gen. 9:5–6), even for such offenses as cursing one's parents (Exod. 21:17) or committing adultery (Deut. 22:22). And God himself, on many occasions, intervened to destroy human lives. Thus, although Mosaic law would not tolerate the cheapening of human life, it was not because human beings have infinite value and therefore must live, but because human life is a gracious gift from God, images God, and therefore deserves high honor. Strictly speaking, there was (and is) no *right to life;* only when I accept that my own life is neither required nor indispensable, and that I live only by God's mercy, can I gain the perspective needed to show mercy to others and to offer them protection.

Conception as a Sign of God's Blessing. Numerous narrative texts, especially in Genesis, depict God's active role in conception and childbirth. Two themes emerge. First, conception and childbirth are gifts from God. Genesis 1:28 is less a set of divinely imposed obligations—to populate and to rule—than it is a revelation of God-given privileges: "God blessed them and said to them, 'Be fruitful and increase in number.'" This manifestation of divine blessing in the form of posterity is echoed in God's judgment upon the serpent (Gen. 3:15), and continues as the heart of God's commitments to Abraham (Gen. 17:6, 16; 21:1–2), Isaac (26:3–4, 24), Jacob (28:14; 30:18, 20; 33:5) and Israel (Deut. 7:13); as the reward to Shiphrah and Puah, the Hebrew midwives, for their refusal to commit infanticide (Exod. 1:20–21); and as an assurance to wives who, being falsely accused of unfaithfulness, pass the ritual test for impurity (Num. 5:28). Job's restoration is marked by the blessing of offspring (42:12–17); and the psalmist depicts the blessing, particularly of sons, in terms of inheritance and divine reward, legal protection, and prestige (127:3–5; cf. 113:9; 128:3–4). In the New Testament, Luke portrays Elizabeth's remarkable conception of John the Baptist as a sign of the Lord's magnified mercy toward her (1:25, 58), and in the angel's words to Mary foretelling the conception of "the Son of the Most High," blessings of the Messiah's arrival and of promised fertility stand together (Luke 1:28–38). In our own age, characterized as it is by overpopulation, birth control, and increasingly fragmented families, the biblical portrait of the child as divine blessing may appear quaint to some and even oppressive to others. Nevertheless, it would be unwise to dismiss outright so consistent a testimony; pregnancy is never seen as a curse, nor children as divine punishment for sexual promiscuity.

A second, related theme, most prominent once again in the Genesis narratives, portrays God directly involved in both causing and preventing fertility. More than once, God's merciful intervention stands out against a backdrop of barrenness and despair. Most striking are the accounts of the three mothers of the Jewish nation, Sarah, Rebekah, and Rachel, each of whom saw barrenness give way to fruitfulness as God set out to fulfill his promises to Abraham. Sometimes, the

Lord's intervention is noted in passing, without explanation (Gen. 4:1; Ruth 4:13), but other times God's bestowal of fertility or infertility is in direct response to obedience or disobedience (Exod. 23:26; Lev. 20:20–21; Deut. 7:13–14; 30:5, 9; Hos. 9:11). Biblical evidence stops short of suggesting that every conception is a direct act of divine causation; neither is barrenness infallibly linked with divine displeasure. Nevertheless God's initiative, causing or preventing conception or stillbirth, surely establishes this domain as one in which God is intensely interested and over which God is ultimately sovereign.

The silence of the Old Testament on abortion is indeed perplexing. But within a cultural context that valued childbirth and children so highly as a tangible sign of God's blessing it is more likely that, for the Jewish family, the intentional termination of pregnancy was unknown, distasteful, or even unconscionable than that their stance was casual, tolerant, or positive toward the practice. Clearly, many elements of the Mosaic code targeted directly Israel's inclination to adopt immoral practices deeply ingrained in Canaanite culture, including the abhorrent ritual of child sacrifice. Thus, while Old Testament law addressed explicitly offensive cultic practices that posed an obvious threat, abortion was not pervasive or popular enough to qualify. Subsequent Jewish literature abundantly confirms Israel's widespread rejection of both exposure and induced abortion.

The New Testament silence on abortion is also curious, since abortion was well known in the first-century Greco-Roman world. The mystery is not solved by appealing to condemnations of sorcery (*pharmakeia;* Gal. 5:20; Rev. 9:21; 18:23; 21:8; 22:15); this evidence is neither clear nor convincing. Neither do texts on infanticide settle the question (Matt. 2:16–18; Acts 7:17–19). As in the Old Testament, the answer probably has more to do with the occasional nature of New Testament documents and the moral framework the church inherited from Judaism. Although many pagan practices made their way into the early church, some were considered idolatrous or so morally repugnant that they remained outside. For these, no teaching was required. In the second and third centuries, as the church's Jewish heritage was matched or surpassed by Roman and pagan influences, explicit condemnations of abortion became necessary.

The Unborn as God's Handiwork. Another important biblical theme, most prominent in Old Testament poetic and prophetic literature, relates to God's direct interest in the development of the fetus during pregnancy. Within the body of Mosaic legislation, the most explicit discussion of the unborn child occurs in Exodus 21:22–25, which describes premature delivery caused by a blow, almost certainly accidental, to a pregnant woman. The gap between this scenario and an act of premeditated abortion is a wide one, but it does provide important clues regarding the nature and extent of Israel's concern for the fetus. Unfortunately, certain textual ambiguities threaten to obscure whatever contribution it might offer. First, is the premature delivery a miscarriage or a live birth? The crucial phrase, *wĕyāṣʾ û yĕlādĕāh* (lit. "and her children come forth"), is rendered by the RSV "so that she has a miscarriage" (cf. NASB, TEV) whereas the NIV has "and she gives birth prematurely." Both renderings are necessarily interpretive. Although the versatile *yāṣāʾ* (go out, come out, come forth) routinely describes normal, live birth (Gen. 25:25–26; 38:28–30; Job 1:21; 3:11; Eccles. 5:15; Jer. 1:5; 20:18; cf. Deut. 28:57; Job 38:8, 29), it may on occasion refer to stillbirth (Num. 12:12); the flexibility of the term allows for both. But given that *yāṣāʾ* is linked with *yeled,* the common Hebrew word for child, and that another word, *šĕkôl,* is available if the writer wants to point clearly to the bereavement of miscarriage, live birth seems slightly more likely.

A second ambiguity builds upon the first and concerns the harm or injury envisioned in verses 22–23. Versions like the NASB that speak of "any *further* injury" imply that the fetus is already dead, and that only harm done to the mother is in view. According to this reading, maternal injury or death requires parallel retribution while fetal death incurs only a fine. The alternative is reflected in the NIV, according to which the harm may be suffered by mother or child, ranging from minor trauma to death. In this case, fetal and maternal death are treated equally, implying that fetus and mother have the same legal status. Supporters of this view point out that the opposition in the text is, technically, between premature delivery and harm, not between fetal death and further harm. Moreover, the author could have added "to her" if the harm in view was only the mother's. While neither view is without problems, this second alternative seems more natural. But even if Exodus 21 is taken to grant the mother more protection than her unborn child, it also establishes that causing the death of the unborn, even accidentally, is morally culpable. Plainly, no authority to perform abortion is granted.

In biblical poetry, descriptions of life in the womb occur in a variety of settings. Job, with powerful rhetorical flourish, laments his present plight by cursing the day of his birth (3:1–19; 10:18–19; cf. Jer. 20:14–18). Better, it would seem, to be stillborn than to live and endure such suffering; quality of life, not quantity, is paramount. Obviously, these bitter lamentations of the lead character do not represent the perspectives of God or the author. Circumstances have obscured his vision. The reader knows the end of the story and feels compelled to challenge Job's quality of life argument, as do other passages, which confirm that God's people will not and cannot escape suffering in this life. Prior to the final restoration, various degrees of imperfect, painful existence are inevitable.

The psalmist sometimes recalls God's shelter and provision during the earliest stages of life when making requests for God's ongoing protection and guidance (22:9–10; 71:6; 119:73). Since there is substantial continuity between fetal and adult life (51:5; 139:13; cf. Jer. 1:5), God's care for the former assures his continued care for the latter. In other contexts, God's interest in prenatal development demonstrates his greatness and inscrutability (139:13–16; cf. Eccles. 11:5). Not only is God involved in forming the unborn child (139:13–14), but God's knowledge of every detail of the child's form (v. 15) and lifespan (v. 16) knows no limits. Various elements here do not pretend to be reasoned descriptions of cosmic or biological reality, but have instead a primarily rhetorical or emotive function, proclaiming forcefully that the infinite God cares profoundly for human individuals, whenever, wherever, and however they may be found. Accordingly, when human formation is said first to occur in the womb (v. 13) and then in the depths of the earth (v. 15; cf. Gen. 2:7), the crucial point—that God's creative power is working from the earliest points—is only strengthened. And when verse 16 pushes back to the very earliest, unformed stages of life (*gōlem*, embryo, formless thing), and perhaps even earlier, it is to celebrate God's limitless foreknowledge and providential involvement with each individual. Even before God acts to create, God knows and cares for his creatures.

When Isaiah considers the early stages of Israel's history and his own commission as a prophet, he takes up images of life in the womb, declaring powerfully that, like the unborn child, God's people at all stages rest solidly within the realm of God's watchful care and concern (44:2, 21, 24; 46:3; 49:1–5). And Jeremiah's prophetic commission originates before birth—even before conception (1:4–5).

Both Testaments refer to the fetus in terms routinely applied to the young child (Gen. 25:22; 38:27–30; Job 1:21; 3:3, 11–16; 10:18–19; 31:15; Ps. 51:5; Isa. 49:5; Jer. 20:14–18; Hos. 12:3; Luke 1:15, 41, 44; Rom. 9:10–11), implying continuity between the two and distinct individuality for the fetus. Alongside birth, conception and gestation stand as important parts of one's personal history. Nowhere is this more clearly shown than in the prebirth rivalry between Jacob and Esau, and in the encounter between John and Jesus recorded in Luke's birth narrative. Jacob's struggle with Esau in the womb prophetically anticipated events later in life (Gen. 25:21–26), and when John the Baptist, as a fetus of six months, leapt in the presence of the newly conceived Jesus, he inaugurated his witness to the One who is to come (Luke 1:39–45). Finally, there is evidence from the incarnation itself. As the Word become flesh (John 1:14) and the last Adam (1 Cor. 15:45; cf. v. 22; Rom. 5:14), Jesus fully embraced humanity to redeem it. But unlike the first Adam who emerged fully formed from the earth, Jesus' entrance into humanity was as a zygote in Mary's womb. The incarnation took place not in a Bethlehem stable but nine months earlier in Nazareth, as the Holy Spirit caused a virgin to conceive.

All of this strongly affirms the humanity of the unborn and portrays a God hard at work forming and protecting preborn life. Attempts to thwart this divine process would clearly be attempts to usurp God's role by destroying the human life God has begun to create and hence morally wrong.

God as Defender of the Defenseless. Another useful line of investigation concerns biblical attitudes toward the weak, defenseless members of society. Clearly, the central participants in a crisis pregnancy—mother and fetus—would belong to such a group. In the Old Testament, both orphan (or fatherless; *yātôm*) and widow (*ʾalmānâ*) were singled out for special care, due to their unique needs and intense vulnerability. God takes up their cause and warns of dire consequences for their oppressors. Laws established to ensure their well-being (Deut. 14:29; 24:17–21; 26:12–13; cf. 16:11, 14) were echoed by prophets whose demands for social justice showed they considered orphans, widows, and the like particularly defenseless. Job contended strenuously, against the charges of Eliphaz (22:9), that his conduct toward orphans and widows had been exemplary (29:12–13; 31:16–23). Further testimony to this profound interest in society's least protected is heard from texts that single out the destruction of pregnant women and children among the atrocities perpetrated by enemy troops (2 Kings 8:12; 15:16; Hos. 10:14–15; Nah. 3:10; cf. Matt. 2:16). More inhumane acts could scarcely be imagined.

The New Testament echoes many of the same themes, but perhaps in a higher key for, alongside unambiguous texts like James 1:27 and 1 Timothy 5:3–16, several Synoptic sayings move well beyond concern for children's needs; the child becomes the paradigm for entrance into, and life within, the kingdom (Matt. 18:1–6 and parallels; 19:13–15 and parallels). In Jesus' rejection of human standards of greatness, he not only turns on its head the conventional wisdom of the day, but also affords children unprecedented worth and dignity.

In all of this it is hard to ignore the persistent call for profound compassion and practical concern for the most vulnerable and least influential members of the community. A just society will shape its laws to protect, in particular, pregnant women and unborn children, and will provide refuge for both in times of crisis. BRUCE N. FISK

Bibliography. J. Barr, *Bulletin of the John Rylands University Library of Manchester* 51 (1968–69): 11–26; M. Belz, *Suffer the Little Children: Christians, Abortion, and Civil Disobedience;* G. Bray, *TB* 42/2 (1991): 195–225; H. O. J. Brown, *Death Before Birth;* J. J. Davis, *Abortion and the Christian;* P. B. Fowler, *Abortion: Toward an Evangelical Consensus;* J. Frame, *Thou Shalt Not Kill;* M. J. Gorman, *Abortion and the Early Church: Christian, Jewish and Pagan Attitudes in the Greco-Roman World;* G. Grisez, *Abortion: The Myths, the Realities, and the Arguments;* J. K. Hoffmeier, ed., *Abortion: A Christian Understanding and Response;* H. W. House, *WTJ* 41 (1978): 108–23; B. S. Jackson, *VT* 23 (1973): 273–304; D. G. Jones, *Brave New People: Ethical Issues at the Commencement of Life;* O. O'Donovan, *Begotten or Made;* J. B. Pritchard, *Ancient Near Eastern Texts Relating to the Old Testament;* P. Ramsey, *The Ethics of Fetal Research;* F. A. Schaeffer, *A Christian Manifesto;* R. J. Sider, *Completely Pro-Life: Building a Consistent Stance on Abortion, the Family, Nuclear Weapons, the Poor;* J. Stott, *Decisive Issues Facing Christians Today;* R. N. Wennberg, *Life in the Balance: Exploring the Abortion Controversy;* C. Young, *The Least of These.*

Abraham. ***The Old Testament.*** This man, whose name may mean "the father is exalted," was the first of the great patriarchs of Israel. In the ancient Near East a patriarch was the leader or ancestor of a family, but Abraham exceeded this status by becoming the progenitor of one specific nation, the Hebrews, as well as of other peoples. The story of his life (Gen. 11:27b–25:12) appears to comprise one of eleven Mesopotamian tablets underlying Genesis, and in typical fashion probably had a title ("Abram, Nahor and Haran," 11:27b) and a concluding colophon "these are the generations of" (KJV), that is, "family histories of" (25:12). The material was apparently compiled in the time of Isaac at Beer Lahai Roi (Gen. 25:11), the finished unit probably comprising a group of smaller tablets linked in a series.

The date of Abraham's birth in Ur "of the Chaldees" (i.e., southern Ur) is not known, but can be computed roughly from archeological evidence at Bab-edh-Dhra, near Sodom. The latter was destroyed about 1900 B.C. No monuments to him have survived, but discoveries at Mari, Nuzi, and elsewhere have shown that his activities were consistent with Middle Bronze Age Mesopotamian life (ca. 2000–1500 B.C.). As such, Abraham emerged from a background of high culture, and was not the illiterate shepherd envisaged by some nineteenth-century literary critics.

Abraham is of profound religious significance because he was the historic ancestor of the twelve tribes, the "seed of Abraham," who regularly described their God as "the God of Abraham." By virtue of being children of divine promise (Gen. 12:2), the Israelites were living proof of God's existence and power in human society. This general promise was made specific by means of a covenant between God and Abraham (Gen. 15:8–18; 17:1–14), which provided the offspring of the patriarch with a large tract of territory. Abraham was to father many nations (Gen. 17:5), and the covenant that was to be established with him and his seed was to be perpetual in nature.

The idea of a covenant, or binding agreement between two parties, was already familiar in the early Middle Bronze Age, and by mutual agreement involved penalties if one of the participants defaulted. It was normally marked by some form of ritual (Gen. 15:9–17), which emphasized the solemnity and significance of the occasion. Abraham was instructed to keep the covenant obligations, and as a material token the institution of circumcision was imposed upon him and his descendants. When performed, this procedure constituted formal indication of membership within the Israelite community.

Although coming from a background of polytheism and idolatry at Ur, Abraham had been reared in the faith of the one true God by his father Terah. But when he received the Lord's call at a mature stage of his life, he recognized that he had been chosen to implement a specific part of God's plan for human destiny. He was not to fulfill it alone, because the Lord undertook to go with him (Gen. 12:4). He was required to be consistently obedient to God's will, however difficult that might be, and to trust without question the guidance he would receive against the background of the covenant framework. It should be noted that Abraham was not asked to be obedient as a condition of the covenant. Rather, his response in faith was based upon what he already knew about the God of his ancestors, and was thus a matter of free choice. The importance of strict obedience to the Lord's injunctions assumes early prominence in Old Testament theology. Put simply, without unquestioning submission to God's stipulations there could be neither fellowship with the Lord nor blessings poured out upon the covenant people.

The continuing faith Abraham had can be illustrated by reference to four specific occasions in his life. The first was God's command to leave both family and homeland and migrate to a strange country (Gen. 12:1). The severing of emotional ties was bound to be costly, yet Abraham went forward without once questioning God's directives, believing instead in God's power to fulfill his promises.

The second occasion actually completed the first, consisting of Abraham's parting company with his nephew Lot (Gen. 13:1–16) because of friction between their herdsmen. Although doubtless distressed at withdrawing from a relative, Abraham behaved generously in allowing Lot to choose the territory that he preferred (Gen. 13:8–11), whereupon God renewed his promises of land and offspring to the childless Abraham.

The third was yet another occasion when the covenant was confirmed, this time in greater detail (Gen. 17:1–27). God promised Abraham a son who would be named Isaac (Gen. 17:16), and who would be the inheritor of the everlasting covenant (Gen. 17:19, 21). It seems that Abraham assumed that Ishmael was to function in that capacity, but when this was denied he acknowledged the Lord's will obediently, and awaited in faith the fulfillment of the promise that all the nations of the earth would be blessed in him (Gen. 18:18).

Perhaps the most serious test of Abraham's obedience and faith came when God ordered him to offer up in sacrifice the very one through whom the covenant was to be perpetuated: his son Isaac (Gen. 22:1–2). Dutifully and without questioning, Abraham followed the ritual procedure, and at the climactic moment God intervened on behalf of Isaac (Gen. 22:11), stating that Abraham had passed the divinely imposed test of submission and faith (Gen. 22:12). For such implicit obedience Abraham was to become an example of covenant fidelity. In 2 Chronicles 20:7 (cf. James 2:23) Abraham is described as the "friends" of God. As late as New Testament times, he and Sarah were lauded as people who lived and died in an attitude of faith (Heb. 11:8–18).

The New Testament. If God's plan for human salvation was to be implemented, the Lord had to be able to trust those whom he called and empowered for this task. Only after testing under difficult conditions did the relative trustworthiness of the servant become apparent. In Abraham's case, his unwavering faith accomplished the fulfillment of the covenant promises in terms of a great nation that would honor him through the centuries as "their father" (John 8:39; Rom. 4:16). This privilege, however, was not to be restricted to the Jews, but was also shared by adherents to the world religions of Christianity and Islam.

The prophecy whereby all human families would be blessed (or "bless themselves") came to fruition in the work of Jesus Christ, the Messiah of God, who was the long-promised descendant of Abraham (Matt. 1:1; Gal. 3:16). His atoning death broke the power of sin over human beings and enabled them to be reconciled to God through penitence and faith. The saving work of Christ ushered in the new covenant prophesied by Jeremiah (31:31) and was given definitive shape in the Christian church, a body of believers committed to serve Jesus as king and lord through acts of obedience and faith. This privileged group is blessed by the assurance of God's love and his saving power that sustain all who trust in him. But while being a recipient of blessing, the Christian church is commanded to fulfill covenant responsibilities (Matt. 28:14) in a manner unknown to the covenant people of Old Testament times. It is by this means, however, that the Abrahamic blessings come into effect when both Jewish and Gentile sinners find forgiveness and spiritual rebirth in Christ through the proclamation of the gospel.

The Christian faith thus stands in an unbroken chain of spirituality that has come down through the ages. The new covenant on which the Christian church is founded is based upon an individual's relationship with God in Christ, and not upon the response of a group such as a tribe to the Lord's commands. The atoning work of Christ on Calvary, achieved by a man as fully obedient to God's commands (Phil. 2:8) as Abraham ever was, has released a flood of divine grace upon an undeserving world, and has brought the blessed fruit of the Spirit (Gal. 5:22–23) into the believer's life.

Paul stressed that the children of God by faith in Jesus were in fact members of Abraham's offspring, and thus heirs according to the promise (Gal. 3:26–29). Thus Christians can speak confidently of Abraham as "the father of the faithful," and praise a merciful God because it was through his fidelity in remote ages that our eternal salvation has become an actuality. Abraham, Sarah, Isaac, and others are no longer shadowy images which, in an earlier age of biblical criticism, were often dismissed as legendary or even mythological. Instead, the participants in the Abrahamic covenant are seen as real persons with whom modern Christians are privileged to join in witness to God's power and his plan of salvation through Christ. While Christians can rejoice in the realization that the blessings of Abraham's covenant have become their very own, it is important for them to remember that, as Jesus taught, the true children of Abraham perform the deeds of Abraham (John 8:39).

Dynamic though Abraham's covenant was, sheer physical descent from the revered patriarch did not of itself guarantee an individual's salvation, as John the Baptist pointed out (Matt. 3:9). Nor did it imply that there were no unbelievers in ancient Israel (Rom. 9:6). Only those members whose lives manifested the obedience and trust of the patriarch would participate in covenant blessings. The man who for Paul was the exemplar of faith (Rom. 4:16–22; Gal. 3:6–12) was understood by James to demonstrate that justification by faith is proved in works that issue from such a faith (James 2:20–24). The emphasis, however, is upon the genuine nature of the faith rather than such deeds as may result.

R. K. Harrison

See also Israel.

Bibliography. G. Bush, *Notes on Genesis;* D. Kidner, *Genesis;* K. A. Kitchen, *Ancient Orient and Old Testament;* F. B. Meyer, *Abraham: The Obedience of Faith;* C. F. Pfeiffer, *The Patriarchal Age;* A. R. Millard and D. J. Wiseman, *Essays on the Patriarchal Narratives.*

Abraham's Bosom. Unique phrase found in a parable of Jesus describing the place where

Lazarus went after death (Luke 16:19–31). It is a figurative phrase that appears to have been drawn from a popular belief that the righteous would rest by Abraham's side in the world to come, an opinion described in Jewish literature at the time of Christ. The word *kolpos* literally refers to the side or lap of a person. Figuratively, as in this case, it refers to a place of honor reserved for a special guest, similar to its usage in John 13:23. In the case of Lazarus, the reserved place is special because it is beside Abraham, the father of all the righteous. The phrase may be synonymous to the paradise promised to the thief on the cross (Luke 23:43). Together these passages support the conviction that a believer enjoys immediate bliss at the moment of physical death. SAM HAMSTRA, JR.

See also HADES; PARADISE; SHEOL.

Abstain, Abstinence. Forbearance of certain activities as a matter of command and voluntary practice for moral and religious purposes. The word-group "to abstain," under which popular discussions of negation often take place, is actually rare in English translation. The King James Version never uses this group in the Old Testament and only seven times in the New Testament. The New International Version has three occurrences in the Old Testament (Exod. 19:15; 31:17; Num. 6:3) and a similar group in the New Testament. The semantic domain New Testament lexicon by Louw and Nida does not assign an "abstain" domain. The concept of abstinence, therefore, is addressed by considering a variety of biblical categories that prohibit certain behavioral patterns.

The biblical concept of abstinence is predominately a moral issue. Even in the pristine garden of Eden God told Adam to abstain from eating the fruit of a certain tree. God's moral law, characterized in the Ten Commandments (Exod. 20), expects his people to abstain from whatever he identifies as evil or out of bounds. There is a continuum of continuity and discontinuity between the Old Testament and New Testament in this regard. The New Testament upholds the normative moral codes of the Old Testament and exhorts believers to abstain from practices that would violate those codes (cf. 1 Thess. 4:3; 5:22; 1 Peter 2:11). On the other hand, the Old Testament places food laws (Lev. 11; signified codes of holiness in contradistinction to other nations) and Sabbath observance into the moral realm. God had given stipulations of prohibition for these categories and to violate those regulations was constituted as disobedience. Stipulated foods and activities on the Sabbath were not intrinsically evil, but they were legally stipulated to be so. Old Testament ceremonial regulations (e.g., rules to regulate what was considered clean or unclean in relation to religious practices) were treated as moral issues in humankind's relationship to God. The New Testament, however, abrogated the food law distinctions and did not perpetuate prohibitions concerning the Sabbath and rules of uncleanness.

Voluntary aspects of abstinence provide opportunities for God's people to demonstrate their commitment to the divine program above and beyond the call of duty. The category of vows in the Old Testament provides an occasion for believers to demonstrate special dedication to God. Making vows was never imposed upon an Old Testament believer as an obligation (Deut. 23:22), but once a vow was made, it was a solemn and binding duty to keep it (Deut. 23:21–23; Mal. 1:14; cf. Jesus' condemnation of vow abuse, Matt. 15:4–6; Mark 7:10–13). Vows could not be made in relation to obligatory religious duties (Lev. 27, esp. vv. 26–28) but in regard to special areas of promises made to God or others. Paul's unique use of a Jewish vow in Acts 18:18 (cf. 21:23–24) illustrates the amoral and religious transcultural nature of a vow during that period. Most Old Testament vows were of a positive nature, but the vow also could be a promise to abstain from some normally acceptable activity for a religious purpose. The Nazirite vow was a special category (Num. 6:1–21) that pertained to a person's lifestyle rather than one specified activity or promise. The most famous Nazirites of biblical history were Samson (Judg. 13) and Samuel (1 Sam. 1:11). Samson was stipulated as a Nazirite by God's message to his parents before he was born. Hannah vowed to give her son as a Nazirite if God would only make her fertile. The Nazirite was to distinguish himself or herself (cf. Num. 6:2) by abstaining from the normal practices of cutting the hair and drinking wine or other fermented beverages. John the Baptist portrays some of the traits of a Nazirite, but it is not certain that he lived under that vow.

The practice of fasting was another major form of abstinence in biblical history. Fasting in the Old Testament was only required by law on the Day of Atonement (Lev. 16:29). Its practice was more widespread and was particularly connected with religious festivals. Zechariah 8:19 notes four fasting periods in a positive way. The relative frequency of the vocabulary for fasting is well balanced between the Old Testament and New Testament and indicates that it was a common religious practice. Many of the references, however, address the abuse of fasting. This religious practice had become for many a mere externalistic form naively utilized as a way of manipulating God to perform their wishes. Jesus condemned empty formalism, but did not abrogate fasting as a religious practice (cf. Matt. 9:14–15). Fasting is practiced in the Book of Acts by believers making important decisions (cf. 13:2–3). While there is no instruction in the Epistles concerning fasting as a religious practice to enhance one's spirituality, the use of positive biblical models of fasting are not prohibited. Scripture never promotes asceticism as a means to an end, but it does encourage voluntary symbols of dedication to God that proceed from proper motives.

The term "abstinence" is often identified with the question of the use or nonuse of alcoholic beverages. The Bible consistently condemns drunkenness, but it cannot be viewed as teaching total abstinence from fermented wine. The linguistic, historical-cultural, and contextual aspects of Scripture are often abused by those who claim that the Bible requires total abstinence. The primary Hebrew terms are *yayin, tîrôš,* and *ʿāsîm.* All three may refer to fermented wine in a negative connotation (cf. in order Prov. 23:31; Hos. 4:11; Isa. 49:26) and all three refer to the expected positive use of fermented wine (*yayin* = Lev. 23:13; Num. 6:20; 28:14; Deut. 14:26; Ps. 104:15; Isa. 55:1; *tîrôš* = Deut. 14:23; *ʿāsîm* = Joel 3:18). All three are used interchangeably and no hard-line distinctions for a linguistic reference to unfermented as opposed to fermented wine can be sustained for any term. The Greek word *oinos* commonly translates all three terms in the Septuagint and is the common term for wine in the Greek period and in the New Testament. Paul cites *oinos* as a nonissue equivalent to the meat offered to idols in Romans 14:21. The less-used Greek term *gleukos,* "new wine," may also mean fermented (cf. Acts 2:13). The ancient world often diluted wine with water for a more or less fermented effect, although this could be viewed as an insult (cf. Isa. 1:22).

The historical setting of Israel as one of the leading and most respected wine-producing nations in their part of the ancient world is well documented. The blessings of this product are recorded in the Bible along with the evils that come from its abuse. Wine is a major image of joy and blessing (cf. Gen. 27:28; Ps. 104:14–15). The messianic era is depicted as a time of great blessing via this imagery (Joel 3:18; Amos 9:13; Zech. 9:17). The destruction of wine is noted as a calamity in the life of Israel (Deut. 28:30–39; Isa. 62:8; 65:21; Mic. 6:15; Zeph. 1:13).

Believers in any given time period or geographical location may choose total abstinence from alcoholic beverages for numerous reasons. One may use certain passages of Scripture to warn against abuse just like ancient Israel did. The abuse of strong drink has plagued all cultures and reasons to abstain abound. Careful biblical interpretation, however, requires that the choice to abstain be made for reasons other than the demand of the biblical pattern.

GARY T. MEADORS

Bibliography. B. L. Bandstra, *ISBE,* 4:1068–72; R. Pierard, *EDT,* pp. 27–29.

Abyss. In our English Bibles, the Greek word *abyssos* is transliterated as "abyss" (RSV "bottomless pit") in every instance except Romans 10:7, where it is translated "the deep." In the Septuagint *abyssos* translates *Tehom* almost exclusively, but in rare instances *Shula* (Isa. 44:27), *Meshula* (Job 41:22), and *Racha* (Job 36:16).

In the Old Testament *abyssos* is invariably descriptive of the watery depths of the earth, whether oceans or springs, in contradistinction to the land (e.g., Pss. 77:16; 78:15; 106:9; Isa. 51:10; Amos 7:4), although in Psalm 71:20, "the depths of the earth" are spoken of in a manner almost signifying death (however, it probably means no more than the depths of one's troubles on earth). *Abyssos* never translates *Sheol,* so in the Old Testament it never carries the idea of the realm of the dead or the afterlife. In Genesis 1:2 the total inchoate earth is called "the deep," over which the Spirit of God hovered.

During the intertestamental period the situation began to change and the meaning of *abyssos* broadened to include the idea of death as well as the realm of demonic spirits (e.g., Jub. 5:6; 1 Enoch 10:4, 11).

In the New Testament the changeover is complete. *Abyssos* is never used to refer to the waters of the earth. Here it is used in two ways. First, in Romans 10:7 Paul uses it specifically to mean "the realm of the dead," drawing from Deuteronomy 30:12–14, but not quoting exactly. He contrasts "ascent into heaven" with "descent into the abyss," but because Christ was there, the abyss should not be conceived as an evil or demonic realm. Second, Luke (8:31) and John (Rev. 9:1–2; 11:7; 17:8; 20:1, 3) describe the abyss specifically as the dwelling place of demons and the beast and as a place of confinement unto judgment that is under God's control. In Luke 8:31 the demons beg Jesus not to send them into the abyss, knowing that they will no longer be free to wreak havoc on the earth. Here, *abyssos* is similar to *tartarus* in 2 Peter 2:4, where the angels that sinned are confined until the judgment. In John's vision of the fifth trumpet (Rev. 9:1–11), the shaft leading to the abyss is opened, releasing the demonic hoard of locusts. Their ruler is "the angel of the abyss," whose name is Destruction (Heb. Abaddon; Gk. Appolyon). The beast who ascends from the abyss (Rev. 11:7; 17:8) presents a complex picture. Combined, it represents the antichrist, demonic power, Rome (i.e., political power as supportive of the harlot), and ultimate evil. This beast is to be thrown alive into the "fiery lake of burning sulphur" (Rev. 19:20). Satan is chained in the abyss for a thousand years (Rev. 20:1, 3), until he, too, is thrown into the lake of fire (Rev. 20:10).

WALTER A. ELWELL

See also ABADDON; REVELATION, THEOLOGY OF.

Accountability. *See* RESPONSIBILITY.

Accursed. *See* CURSE, ACCURSED.

Accuser. *See* SATAN.

Acknowledge. *See* CONFESS, CONFESSION.

Acts, Theology of. *See* LUKE–ACTS, THEOLOGY OF.

Adam. "Adam" is both the proper name of the first human and a designation for humankind. God himself gave this appellation to Adam and Eve (Gen. 5:1–2). The color red lies behind the Hebrew root *ʾādām*. This may reflect the red soil from which he was made.

Adam was formed from the ground (Gen. 2:7). Word play between "Adam" and "ground" (*ădāmâ*) is unmistakable. It is important that Adam is identified with humankind rather than any particular nationality. The country from which the dust was taken is not specified. Rabbis believed it came from all over the earth so no one could say, "My father is greater than yours."

The word "formed" suggests the careful work of a potter making an exquisite art-piece. Into this earthen vessel God breathed the breath of life (Gen. 2:7). These words describe vivid intimacy between God and man not shared by animals.

Adam was made a little lower than "angels" (or "God") at his creation and "crowned with glory and honor" (Ps. 8:5). (Rabbis speculated the glory of Adam's heel outshone the sun.) He was commissioned as a vassal king to rule over God's creation. The words "subdue," "rule," "under his feet" (Gen. 1:28; Ps. 8:6) suggest kingship over nature but not over his fellow man.

Many elements present in Mesopotamian creation stories like Enuma Elish are absent. There is nothing about autocratic king ship lowered from heaven. No brick mold is given. Adam is not laden with the task of building temples and cities. He was not created to relieve Gods of tedious labor but to reflect God's care of the world of nature. God did not appoint death for Adam and keep life exclusively for himself as in the Gilgameth epic.

No shrub or cultivated plant had yet grown where Adam was created. He awoke to a barren landscape (Gen. 2:5–7). His first sight may have been God planting a garden for him. He could clearly see that all good and perfect gifts come from the Lord God.

Man was placed into this beauty to "work it and take care of it" (Gen. 2:15). Unlike the Sumerian garden story of Enki and Ninhursag, there was no gardener working for Adam. Meaningful, productive activity was always part of paradise. Adam was not placed there to be a vegetable but to grow them. Man was not created to be waited on but to join God in preserving and propagating creation.

Man was furnished with every pleasant, nourishing experience God could provide. He was warned about the tree of knowledge of good and evil (2:17). The Hebrew word for "know" includes the idea of knowing by experience. The forbidden tree contained the option of experiencing the opposite of what comes from the hand of God. God wished to spare Adam from pain and death but at the same time left him freedom of choice for options beyond the sphere of his provision.

Adam was not only a laborer but a thinker. God brought him all the animals to see what he would call them. Included in ancient ideas of naming would also be sovereignty over the item named. (Note that Hebrews brought before the king are renamed in Dan. 1:7.)

The first lesson Adam learned was that his work was too big to do alone. His inspection of the animal kingdom revealed no suitable helper. The one who would make his life complete came from his own rib. They would become one flesh (Gen. 2:18–24). This is a far different scenario from the sexual escapades of Enki (= "lord of the earth") in the Sumerian garden story.

The most intelligent animal confronted humankind under whose feet he had been placed (Gen. 1:28; 3:1). Was Eve selected because she would in some way be easier to deceive? Or was the more difficult subject taken first? It is noteworthy that no special efforts to persuade Adam are recorded. He seems to eat what he is offered without objection (3:6). It is, however, important to observe that Adam was called first as the one whose position of leadership made him responsible for the act (3:9).

The anticipation of being like God never materialized. Adam and Eve's state of existence was not enhanced but filled with misery and death. They would have to leave the garden to experience what life would be outside God's perfect will.

PAUL FERGUSON

See also EVE; FALL, THE; GENESIS, THEOLOGY OF.

Bibliography. W. Brueggemann, *Genesis;* J. Davis, *Paradise to Prison;* L. Harris, *Man—God's Eternal Creation;* A Ross, *Creation and Blessing.*

Adam, the Second. Christ is the "image of the invisible God, the firstborn over all creation" (Col. 1:15). Like the first Adam, he is the "ruler of . . . creation" (Rev. 3:14). He is its author and perfecter (Heb. 12:2). Anyone in Christ is a "new creation" (2 Cor. 5:17).

He existed in the form of God, yet did not consider equality with God something to be grasped (Phil. 2:6). He did not desire to be more than man (2:7–8). He was "made like his brothers in every way" so that "by his death he might destroy him who holds the power of death" and free those held in slavery by fear of death (Heb. 2:14, 17).

Christ was crowned with glory and honor over the world to come (Heb. 2:5–7). The first Adam lost his crown and gained death. The second Adam was crowned because he tasted death for every man (2:8–9). Sin and death upon all men entered the world through one man. By the obedience of the second Adam life abounds to many (Rom. 5:12–19).

He was tempted in every way, as was Adam, yet was without sin (Matt. 4:1–11; Heb. 4:15). Like the serpent he says, "Take and eat" (Matt. 26:26), but this food brings life to the world (John 6:33). Christ and Adam are both sons of God (Matt. 1:1; Luke 3:37). Both have their sonship by his power (Gen. 2:7; Luke 1:35; Rom. 1:4). God breathed into Adam the breath of life. Jesus breathed on his disciples and said, "Receive the Holy Spirit" (John 20:22).

"As in Adam all die, so in Christ all will be made alive" (1 Cor. 15:22). Adam was a pattern of the one to come (Rom. 5:14). One of the greatest things to be said for the first Adam was that he became "a living being." Christ, however, became "a life-giving spirit" (1 Cor. 15:45). This spiritual life force does not make us slaves again to fear but the spirit of the Son comes into our hearts crying "*Abba,* Father" (Rom. 8:15; Gal. 4:6–7).

The first Adam came from the dust. The second Adam came from heaven (1 Cor. 15:47). He came down from heaven not to do his own will but the will of him who sent him (John 6:38). God called the first man by name out of hiding (Gen. 3:9). The second Adam calls his own by name and they hear his voice (John 10:3). One day the dead will hear the voice of the Son of God. Those who hear will live (John 5:25).

We have borne the likeness of the earthly man, the first Adam. In the resurrection we will bear the likeness of the man from heaven (1 Cor. 15:49). By the power that enables him to bring everything under his control, he will transform our lowly bodies so they will be like his glorious body. The last enemy placed under the feet of the second Adam is death (Ps. 110:1; 1 Cor. 15:26). He will not reach out and try to grasp more but will turn everything over to God who will be all in all (15:28).

PAUL FERGUSON

See also CHRIST, CHRISTOLOGY; JESUS CHRIST, NAME AND TITLES OF.

Bibliography. C. K. Barrett, *From First Adam to Last;* W. D. Davies, *Paul and Rabbinic Judaism;* J. D. G. Dunn, *Christology in the Making;* H. Ridderbos, *Paul;* R. Scroggs, *The Last Adam.*

Adoption. Act of leaving one's natural family and entering into the privileges and responsibilities of another. In the Bible, adoption is one of several family-related terms used to describe the process of salvation and its subsequent benefits. God is a father who graciously adopts believers in Christ into his spiritual family and grants them all the privileges of heirship. Salvation is much more than forgiveness of sins and deliverance from condemnation; it is also a position of great blessing. Believers are children of God.

Old Testament. Legal adoption was not prescribed in Jewish law or practiced by the Israelites. In fact, the term "adoption" does not occur in the Old Testament. While there are several possible allusions to adoption, such as Moses (Exod. 2:10), Genubath (1 Kings 11:20), and Esther (Esther 2:7), the incidents recorded take place in foreign societies (Egyptian and Persian) and there is no evidence that legal adoptions were enacted.

The adoption metaphor was not lost to Israel, however. God declares that he is the Father of the nation Israel, whom he loves as his child (Isa. 1:2; Hos. 11:1). He tells Pharaoh, "Israel is my firstborn son" (Exod. 4:22). More specifically, he says to David (and the Messiah), "You are my son; today I have become your Father" (Ps. 2:7); and of David's descendant, "I will be his father, and he will be my son" (2 Sam. 7:14). Although not precisely adoption passages, the instances of declared sonship in the Old Testament provide a theological foundation for Israel's designation as the children of God.

New Testament. The New Testament cultural environment was much different from that of the Old since elaborate laws and ceremonies for adoption were part of both Greek and Roman society. To people with this background, the adoption metaphor in the New Testament was particularly meaningful.

The Greek word for adoption (*huiothesia*) means to "place as a son" and is used only by Paul in the New Testament. Each of the five occurrences in his letters is to readers of a decidedly Roman background. In one instance Paul refers to the Old Testament idea of Israel's special position as the children of God—"Theirs is the adoption as sons" (Rom. 9:4). The remaining four references describe how New Testament believers become children of God through his gracious choice. The full scope of God's work of salvation—past, present, and future—is seen in adoption.

The believer's adoption as a child of God was determined by God from eternity: God "predestined us to be adopted as his sons through Jesus Christ" (Eph. 1:5). This adoption is not the result of any merit on the part of the believer, but solely the outworking of God's love and grace (Eph. 1:5, 7).

The present reality of the believer's adoption into the family of God is release from the slavery of sin and the law and a new position as a free heir of God. Entering into salvation brings the rights and privileges of free sonship: "For you did not receive a spirit that makes you a slave again to fear, but you received the Spirit of sonship.

And by him we cry, *'Abba,* Father'" (Rom. 8:15). Paul tells the Galatians that Christians were redeemed from the law so that they might receive adoption as sons. As a result the Holy Spirit comes into the believer's heart crying, *"Abba,* Father" (Gal. 4:5). The intimacy of a relationship with God the Father in contrast to the ownership of slavery is a remarkable feature of salvation.

Like many aspects of salvation, there is an eschatological component of adoption. Believers "wait eagerly for our adoption as sons, the redemption of our bodies" (Rom. 8:23). The full revelation of the believer's adoption is freedom from the corruption present in the world. Being a member of God's family includes the ultimate privilege of being like him (1 John 3:2) and being conformed to the glorious body of Christ (Phil. 3:21). This is part of the promised inheritance for all God's children (Rom. 8:16–17). WILLIAM E. BROWN

See also CHRISTIANS, NAMES OF.

Bibliography. G. Braumann, *NIDNTT,* 1:287–90; A. H. Leitch, *ZPEB,* 1:63–65; F. Lyall, *Slaves, Citizens, Sons: Legal Metaphors in the Epistles.*

Adultery. *See* IMMORALITY, SEXUAL.

Adversary. *See* SATAN.

Advocate. Translation (consistently in NRSV and JB) of the Greek work *paraklētos,* which is used five times in the New Testament. *Paraklētos* is found in John 14:16, 26; 15:26; and 16:7 in the words of Jesus with reference to the Holy Spirit. In 1 John 2:1 it refers to Christ. Most English translations have "advocate" in 1 John 2:1, although the New International Version renders it as "one who speaks in our defense." To determine the meaning we need to consider the word's etymology, its usage outside the New Testament, and its context in the New Testament passages. By derivation the word means "one called alongside," but the Gospel emphasizes that the Holy Spirit, as *Paraklētos,* is "sent" from the Father. In earlier Greek the word signified one called in to a person's defense, a helper in court. In two Greek translations of Job (16:2) it is used for Job's "comforters." Clearly the work of the Holy Spirit is more than either of these: the Spirit is more than a "Counselor" and stronger than a "Comforter" (in our modern sense of the word). The Gospel passages certainly mean that the Holy Spirit is Helper, "another" *Paraklētos* (John 14:16), because Jesus had truly been that. The Spirit was promised to remain with Jesus' disciples always (14:16), to "teach" (14:26), to "testify" about Christ and to enable them to testify (15:26), and to "convict the world of guilt" (16:7). Then 1 John 2:1 speaks of Jesus as our continuing advocate with the Father, because we who are sinful find in him the atoning sacrifice for our sins, and thus have our acceptance with the Father. FRANCIS FOULKES

See also HOLY SPIRIT.

Bibliography. J. Behm, *TDNT,* 5:800–14; G. Braumann, *NIDNTT,* 1:88–91; L. Morris, *The Gospel according to John.*

Affliction. *See* PERSECUTION; SUFFERING.

Age, Ages. The Greek *aiōn* in the Septuagint and New Testament corresponds to the Hebrew *ʿolām* of the Old Testament. Both words usually depend on a preposition (for example, *ʿad ʿôlām* and *eis ton aiōnon* are rendered "forever"). In some contexts *ʿolām* and *aiōn* are translated "age" ("world" in the AV); the Greek *chronoi* may also mean "ages."

Ages as Epochs of Time. Both Testaments speak of "ages" as undefined periods of history over which God rules (Ps. 90:2; 1 Tim. 1:17; Jude 25). As with much intertestamental literature, the Apocalypse of Weeks goes farther, in this case dividing history into ten epochs of varying lengths (1 Enoch 91:12–17; 93:1–10). But the canonical writers do not try to calculate when successive ages will begin or end.

The Bible may refer to past ages in order to exalt God's knowledge as Creator in comparison with human ignorance (Isa. 64:4; cf. Deut. 4:32). In the New Testament the hidden wisdom of God is repeatedly connected with the gospel, a mystery that he has chosen to reveal after long ages (*aiōn* in 1 Cor. 2:7; Eph. 3:9; Col. 1:26; *chronoi* in Rom. 16:25; 2 Tim. 1:9; Titus 1:2).

According to 1 Corinthians 10:11, Hebrews 9:26, and 1 Peter 1:20, the present era is the end of the ages. Even while the church anticipates the future consummation, it lives already in the time in which God's plan of redemption is being fulfilled (cf. 2 Cor. 1:20).

The boundless future may also be regarded as a series of ages. Normally the "ages to come" are invoked by the prophets to underscore God's unending blessings for his people (Isa. 45:17; Dan. 7:18). This theme is later taken up by Paul in Ephesians 2:7: "that in the coming ages he might show the incomparable riches of his grace, expressed in his kindness to us in Christ Jesus."

This Age and the Age to Come. The Old Testament predicts the future coming of God or the Messiah; most forms of postbiblical Judaism (see esp. 2 Esdras) go further and differentiate this age from the age to come, which is also known as the kingdom of God. This two-age schema is echoed in Matthew 12:32 and Ephesians 1:21, but the New Testament transforms the traditional pattern: with the coming of Christ, the blessings of the future are manifested among God's people in the present age (cf. Heb. 6:5).

In terms of this age as a time of sin and darkness, *aiōn* is sometimes synonymous with *kosmos* or "the world" (cf. Mark 4:19; Rom. 12:2; 1 Cor. 1:20). During this time, Satan appears as the "god" of this age (2 Cor. 4:4) and sin prevails (Gal. 1:4; 2 Tim. 4:10; Titus 2:12). The citizens of this age are living in darkness and must rely on the devices of their own human wisdom (Luke 16:8; 1 Cor. 1:20; 2:6, 8; 3:18). But so long as Christians remain in the world, they are cheered by the spiritual presence of Jesus until the close of this age (Matt. 28:20).

Cataclysmic signs will signal the close of the present era (*synteleia* [*tou*] *aiōnos,* Matt. 24:3). According to the New Testament, the end of the age will bring the return of Christ and the judgment of the wicked (Matt. 13:39–40, 49).

When the age to come arrives, the dead will rise to inherit eternal life (Luke 20:34–35). Jewish and later Christian apocalypticists loved to speculate about the blessings of this future age, but the simple message of the Bible is that the coming age will bring a good inheritance (Mark 10:30; Luke 18:30). Paul's advice to Christians is to invest for the age to come by practicing generosity and good deeds in this present age (1 Tim. 6:17–19). Gary Steven Shogren

Bibliography. J. Barr, *Biblical Words for Time;* O. Cullmann, *Christ and Time;* J. Guhrt, *NIDNTT,* 3:826–33; A. A. MacRae, *TWOT,* 2:672–73; D. S. Russell, *The Method and Message of Jewish Apocalyptic;* H. Sasse, *TDNT,* 1:197–209.

Age, Old (the Aged). Though the Bible seldom discusses old age directly, there are several terms that relate to this topic. The most common Hebrew expression for age, *zāqēn,* is often a simple designation of advanced age. After Abraham is said to be old (*zāqēn*), an explanatory phrase is used: "well advanced in years" (lit. "days," Gen. 24:1). This phrase illustrates the Hebrew practice of indicating age by marking the passage of time, usually employing the word "day" or "year." As Jacob approached death, his 147 years were summarized as "the years of his life" (Gen. 47:28). A rich, full life is one that is satiated in time, as Job was "full of years" (Job 42:17; cf. Abraham in Gen. 25:8).

The adjective *zāqēn,* "elder, old," is applied to various offices in the Old Testament, always as an indication of one's nobility. It could refer to the oldest servant of one's household (Gen. 24:2) or to the officers of the Egyptian royal court (Gen. 50:7). The office of "elder" took on political connotations when it referred to David's chief servants (2 Sam. 12:17), as well as to the elders of Egypt, Moab, or Midian (Gen. 50:7; Num. 22:7). During the time of Moses, "the elders of Israel" were an important group of leaders who accompanied him on his first meeting with Pharaoh (Exod. 3:18), served as intermediaries with the nation (Exod. 19:7), assisted Moses at the ratification of the Sinai covenant (Exod. 24:1), and assisted Moses in many other ways throughout his lifetime (Exod. 17:5; Num. 11:16–17).

The Old Testament also uses "gray head" (*śêbâ*) as a synonym for advanced age. In the famous covenant ceremony of Genesis 15, God assured Abraham that he would die in peace and that he would be buried in "a good old age" (*śêbâ ṭôbâ,* v. 15; cf. 25:8). Likewise David died "at a good old age, having enjoyed long life, wealth and honor" (1 Chron. 29:28). A "gray head" was looked on as a crown of glory attained through righteous living (Prov. 16:31). A similar picture occurs in Daniel's vision of the Ancient of Days, whose hair was like pure lamb's wool (Dan. 7:9).

The term *yāšēš* can refer to an aged and decrepit person who is helpless or defenseless. Nebuchadnezzar had no compassion on the aged or the feeble (2 Chron. 36:17). This term's derivative (*yāšîš*) designates those worthy of respect due to their age (Job 15:10; 32:6). Hebrew also uses *kelah,* which usually connotes "wealth," for ripe old age (NIV's "full vigor," Job 5:26). The Old Testament places high value on the elderly, as is evident from the command in Leviticus 19:32: "Rise in the presence of the aged (*śêbâ*), show respect for the elderly (*zāqēn*) and revere your God."

As in the Old Testament, the New Testament term "elder" (*presbytēs*) can denote simply a person of advanced age. Zechariah uses the term to describe himself as nearing the end of child-bearing years (Luke 1:18). Paul uses this term to refer to himself as "an old man" (Philemon 9). He also gave instruction to Timothy regarding his speech to older men and women (1 Tim. 5:1–2; cf. Titus 2:2–3). But more commonly, the term is used to describe the leadership of the people (*presbyteroi,* Matt. 21:23). The "elders" were apparently an unofficial political group that played an active role in public affairs. They appear frequently in association with the chief priests and scribes.

Later in the New Testament period, the "elders" became the official religious leadership in the early church. Though the specific origins of eldership in the early church are uncertain, it seems clear that the office was based on the Old Testament and early Jewish custom of bestowing honor and respect to members of the community of advanced age. As the fledgling church began to grow, elders were appointed or ordained as overseers for each local congregation (Acts 14:23). Early in the history of the church, they were seen as an established class of officials, who were leaders of the church in Jerusalem (Acts 11:30). They appear along with "the apostles" at the Jerusalem Council to settle the dispute about Gentile converts (Acts 15:2, 4, 22).

The officers known as "elders" in the early church are also sometimes called "bishops" ("overseers," *episkopos*). The two terms are interchangeable in Titus 1:5 and 7. "Elder" and "bishop" appear to overlap in 1 Timothy, where the instructions concerning "elders" (5:17) probably refer to both the bishops of 3:1 and the deacons of 3:8. So the elders of the early church were overseers (or "bishops," Acts 20:28), pastors (Eph. 4:11), and leaders (Heb. 13:7), who had authority over the flock of God (1 Thess. 5:12). They were called on for prayer (James 5:14) and teaching the Word (1 Tim. 5:17). Elders were protected from malicious accusations, but if they persisted in sin, they were to be rebuked publicly as an example for all believers (1 Tim. 5:19–20). A church without an elder appointed over it meant the work of the missionary was "left unfinished" (Titus 1:5). Qualifications for the office of elder included a righteous lifestyle, monogamy, and humility.

The New Testament term *gēras* (and related verb *gēraskō*) refers to old age in general. The angel Gabriel told Mary that Elizabeth had conceived a son "in her old age" (Luke 1:36). The author of Hebrews proclaims that something that is obsolete and "aging" will soon disappear (8:13).

In tribal societies of the ancient Near East, reverence and respect were accorded to the aged. In the Bible, longevity is considered a reward for a virtuous and righteous life, and the aged were thought of as mature in wisdom and experience. The Old Testament custom of honoring the aged with positions of favor politically and socially was continued in the New Testament practice of conferring leadership roles on the "elders."

Finally, we may note that the modern concept of "retirement" is unknown in the Bible. The Levites retired from official service at age fifty, but they then assisted younger priests (Num. 8:24–26). Zechariah, in the New Testament period, considered himself old, but he continued his service in the temple (Luke 1:18–25). Without doubt, in ancient agricultural societies, the nature of physical labor meant cessation from work at a relatively early age. But retirees were then responsible for training their grandchildren and became advisors for the younger generation. The Bible has no concept of ending one's life-work in order to spend the remainder of one's days in leisure. William T. Arnold

See also Death, Mortality.

Bibliography. J. G. Harris, *Biblical Perspectives on Aging: God and the Elderly;* R. K. Harrison, *ISBE*, 3:587.

Alien. *See* Foreigner.

Allegory. A popular form of literature in which a story points to a hidden or symbolic parallel meaning. Certain elements, such as people, things, and happenings in the story, point to corresponding elements in another realm or level of meaning. The closer the resemblances between the two realms, the more detailed is the allegory. The best allegories are interesting, coherent stories in their own right and through the story provide new insight into the realm they depict (e.g., *Pilgrim's Progress* and *The Narnia Chronicles*). Semitic parables, including the Gospel parables, have varying amounts of allegorical elements. Those with many corresponding elements in both realms are properly called allegories.

Allegorical interpretation, sometimes called allegorizing, is interpretation of texts that treats them as allegorical, whether or not their author intended them to be allegories. Allegorical interpretations even of true allegories can be misleading, either in incorrectly identifying the corresponding elements in the referent or in identifying corresponding elements where no correspondence was originally intended. Either allegorizing error usually detracts from the coherence of the message the author intended. Such unwarranted allegorizing was prevalent in the later church fathers and often ludicrous in gnostic circles.

Nathan's parable of the rich man who slew a poor man's beloved pet lamb in 2 Samuel 12:1–4 has allegorical reference to David's actions in causing Uriah's death in order to take his wife. But it was just different enough that David did not initially recognize the referent and pronounced judgment on the wicked rich man. Nathan's "You are the man!" struck David to the quick precisely because he recognized the parallels between his actions and the rich man's, between Uriah and the poor man, and between Uriah's wife and the ewe lamb. The allegory told by the wise woman of Tekoa in 2 Samuel 14:4–7 similarly opened David's eyes to a new perspective and caused him to spare the life of Absalom. (Other Old Testament allegories include Isa. 5:1–6; Ezek. 17:1–24; 24:3–14; Dan. 2:31–45; 4:10–33; 7:1–28; 8:1–27.)

The parables of Jesus have a wide range of degrees of allegorical reference. The parable of the sower is followed by an allegorical interpretation (Mark 4:14–20) that has been widely criticized, but on examination, the common objections turn out to support authenticity. For example, birds as a symbol for Satan, rather than being alien were commonly used to depict Satan in rabbinic literature (e.g., Jub. 11:5–24), where birds devour seed in the process of sowing. If the Gospel tradition progressively allegorized the parables, as many allege, it is surely odd that the earliest Gospels (Mark, Matthew) contain the most allegorical elements, whereas the later Gospels contain progressively less (Luke, John).

In Galatians 4:21–31 Paul uses the story of the children of Sarah (Isaac) and Hagar (Ishmael) and the images of Jerusalem above and Mount

Sinai as a double allegory, both pairs contrasting the covenant of freedom and the covenant of slavery. This allegory adds an earthy, emotional appeal to Paul's arguments for freedom in Christ.

PHILIP BARTON PAYNE

See also PARABLE.

Bibliography. P. B. Payne, *Gospel Perspectives*, pp. 163–207.

Almighty. *See* GOD, NAMES OF.

Almsgiving. *See* CONTRIBUTION.

Altar. Structure on which offerings are made to a deity. The Hebrew word for altar is *mizbēah,* from a verbal root meaning "to slaughter." Greek renders this word as *thusiastērion,* "a place of sacrifice." In the developed temple ritual, the same word is used for both the altar of holocausts and the altar of incense. Thus, an altar is a place where sacrifice is offered, even if it is not an event involving slaughter.

Altars could be natural objects or man-made constructs. Four materials are recorded as being used in altars: stone, earth, metal, and brick. Archaeology has provided numerous examples of altars from Palestine dating back to approximately 3000 B.C. Natural rocks were also used (Judges 6:20). An altar could stand alone, or it was located in the courtyard of a shrine.

Their Jerusalem temple had two altars: the altar of incense and the altar of holocausts. The altar of incense was placed inside the sanctuary in front of the curtain screening the Holy of Holies. It was made of gold-covered wood. It stood upright and measured 1 x 1 x 2 cubits. Archaeological data indicate that all four corners of the upper surface were slightly peaked. Twice a day, incense was burned on the altar.

The altar of holocausts stood in the courtyard of the temple. Like the other objects in the courtyard, the altar was made of bronze. It measured 20 x 20 x 10 cubits (2 Chron. 4). Ahaz replaced this altar with one modeled on an alter he had seen in Damascus (2 Kings 16). He moved the old altar, using it for divination. In Ezekiel's vision the courtyard altar also was horned (Ezek. 43:15).

Altars were places where the divine and human worlds interacted. Altars were places of exchange, communication, and influence. God responded actively to altar activity. The contest between Elijah and the prophets of Baal involving an altar demonstrated interaction between Yahweh and Baal. Noah built an altar and offered a sacrifice to Yahweh. God smelled the aroma and found it pleasing. He responded to Noah's action by declaring that he would never again destroy all living things through a flood. In the patriarchal period, altars were markers of place, commemorating an encounter with God (Gen. 12:7), or physical signs of habitation. Abraham built an altar where he pitched his tent between Bethel and Ai. Presumably at that altar he "called on the name of the LORD" (Gen. 12:8). Interestingly, we are not told if there was a response. In the next passage, however, Abraham went to Egypt and fell into sin, lying about Sarah out of fear of Pharaoh. Perhaps there was no true communication at the altar between Bethel and Ai.

Sacrifices were the primary medium of exchange in altar interactions. The priestly code of Leviticus devotes a great deal of space to proper sacrificial procedure, and to what sacrifices are appropriate in various circumstances. Sacrifice was the essential act of external worship. Unlike the divinities of the nations surrounding ancient Israel, Yahweh did not need sacrifices to survive. The Israelites, however, needed to perform the act of sacrifice in order to survive (Exod. 30:21). The act of sacrifice moved the offering from the profane to the sacred, from the visible to the invisible world. By this action the worshiper sealed a contract with God. Blood, believed to contain the "life" of an animal (or a human being), was particularly important in the sacrificial ritual. It was sprinkled against the altar (Lev. 1); once a year, blood was smeared on the horns of the incense altar.

The horns of the altar may have functioned as boundary markers, setting apart the sacred space that was the actual place of intersection of the divine and human spheres. In the stark and moving story of Abraham's encounter with God at Moriah, Abraham built an altar and arranged the wood on it (Gen. 22:9). After Isaac was laid on the altar, but *before* he was sacrificed, God proclaimed his recognition that Isaac had "not [been] withheld." By placing Isaac on the altar, Abraham transferred him from the profane to the sacred.

This sacred altar and its horns, where the atoning blood was splashed, provided a place of sanctuary. The altar was a place where an unintentional murderer could gain a haven (Exod. 21:13–14). If the murder was premeditated, however, then the altar was clearly profaned by the murderer's presence and the individual could be taken away and killed. Joab was denied the sanctuary of the horns because he had conspired to kill Amasa and Abner. In an oracle against Israel (Amos 3:14), God declared that "the horns of the altar will be cut off and fall to the ground." The message is clear: There will be no place to intercede with God, and no place to claim his sanctuary.

After the exile, the first thing to be rebuilt was the altar. Then the temple was reconstructed. The temple was ultimately secondary to the altar. In chastising the religious establishment, Jesus underlined the sacredness of the altar, making clear his understanding that the altar "makes the gift sacred" (Matt. 23:19). In Revelation the altar in the heavenly temple shelters martyred souls and even speaks (Rev. 16:7). The New Testament writer of Hebrews (13:10) implies that the ultimate altar is the cross. Here divine and human interchange is consummated. The cross becomes the sanctuary of the believer, providing protection from the penalties of sin. THOMAS W. DAVIS

See also OFFERINGS AND SACRIFICES; PRIEST, PRIESTHOOD.

Bibliography. R. de Vaux, *Ancient Israel;* M. Haran, *Temples and Temple Service in Ancient Israel;* C. L. Meyers, *HBD*, pp. 22–25.

Amen. In current usage, the term "amen" has become little more than a ritualized conclusion to prayers. Yet the Hebrew and Greek words for amen appear hundreds of times in the Bible and have several uses. Amen is a transliteration of the Hebrew word *ʾāmēn.* The verb form occurs more than one hundred times in the Old Testament and means to take care, to be faithful, reliable or established, or to believe someone or something. The idea of something that is faithful, reliable, or believable seems to lie behind the use of amen as an exclamation on twenty-five solemn occasions in the Old Testament. Israel said "amen" to join in the praises of God (1 Chron. 16:36; Neh. 8:6; and at the end of each of the first four books of Psalms, at 41:13; 72:19; 89:52; 106:48).

Amen is never used solely to confirm a blessing in the Old Testament, but Israel did accept the curse of God on sin by it (twelve times in Deut. 27, and in Neh. 5:13), and once Jeremiah affirms God's statements of the blessings and the curses of the covenant with an amen (Jer. 11:5). It can also confirm a statement made by people (Num. 5:22; 1 Kings 1:36; Neh. 5:13). These kinds of uses lie behind the popular, basically correct, dictum that amen means "So be it."

Amen has other uses. Jeremiah mocks the words of a false prophet with an amen (28:6). Because God is trustworthy, Isaiah can call him "the God of amen," in whose name his servants should invoke blessings and take oaths (Isa. 65:16; see also Rev. 3:14). But Jesus' use of amen is the most striking innovation.

Jesus introduces his teaching by saying *amēn legō humin,* that is, "truly I say to you," on nearly seventy occasions in the Gospels (thirty times in Matthew, thirteen in Mark, six in Luke, and twenty in John, where the amen is always doubled). Where the prophets often said, "Thus says the Lord," Jesus often says, "Amen *I* say to you." Although some scholars see the formula merely as a method of giving emphasis to a statement, in actuality it constitutes a significant part of Jesus' implicit teaching about himself. We ought to consider Jesus' use of the term "amen" alongside his other implicit claims to deity, such as his claim of the right to forgive sins and to judge humankind, and his custom of performing miracles on his own authority. No mere human has the right to forgive sins, yet Jesus forgave sins. God is the judge of humankind, yet Jesus judges. God's agents ascribe the will and the glory to God when they perform miracles, yet Jesus performed miracles on his own authority. Likewise, prophets never spoke on their own authority. They say, "Thus says the Lord." Or, like Paul, they say they received a revelation from heaven. But Jesus says, "Truly I say to you" dozens of times, asserting that his words are certainly true because *he* says them.

Jesus often uses the formula when he corrects errors or is engaged in disputes. When Jesus instructed Nicodemus, for example, he appealed not to Scripture but to his own authority, saying "*Amēn, amēn,* I say to you" (John 3:3, 5; see also Matt. 6:2, 5, 16; 18:3; Luke 13:35; John 5:19, 24, 25; 6:26, 32, 47, 53). *Amēn legō humin* also punctuates the teaching of truths unknown in the Old Testament, and seasons startling sayings for which Jesus offers no proof other than his own authority. Here the amen implies that Jesus' words, like the Father's, are true merely because he utters them (Matt. 24:34; 26:13; Mark 3:28; Luke 12:37; John 10:1). So in Matthew 5 Jesus comments on the Old Testament or Jewish interpretations of it six times in the chapter, saying, "You have heard that it was said . . . , but I tell you." He concludes the first section with the amen in 5:26, and by so doing asserts that his authority exceeds the Jewish interpreters', and even brings a revelation that surpasses that of the Old Testament law itself.

In this way, whenever Jesus says *"amēn legō humin,"* he shows awareness of his authority, his deity. This evidence of Jesus' messianic self-consciousness is important because it resists skeptical attacks on the faith. Critics try to exclude many texts that present Christ's deity on the grounds that they are unauthentic. But implicit claims to deity, whether they be Jesus' use of the amen or other ones, appear in virtually every paragraph of the Gospels, and cannot be explained away.

Paul's use of amen returns to the Old Testament world, except that he utters amen only to bless, not to curse. Many times Paul's letters burst into praise of God the Father or God the Son and seal the confession with the amen (Rom. 1:25; 9:5; 11:36; Gal. 1:3–5; Eph. 3:21; Phil. 4:20; 1 Tim. 1:17; 6:16; 2 Tim. 4:18). A doxology appears at or near the end of several letters, and all close with the amen. Other letters end with a blessing on his readers, again completed with amen (1 Cor. 16:23–24; Gal. 6:18). Paul also invites his readers to say amen to the promises of God (2 Cor. 1:20; see also Rev. 22:20). Amen also closes spontaneous doxologies in Revelation;

there, however, the object of praise is more often the Son than the Father (1:6–7; 5:14; 7:12; 19:4). In all this Paul and Revelation resemble the Jewish custom of the day, in which Jews said amen when they heard another bless the Lord whether in private prayer (Tobit 8:8) or in worship. But they surpass it in the sheer spontaneity and enthusiasm of their praises.

Several other New Testament epistles follow Paul by praising God and/or calling on him to bestow the grace the readers need (Heb. 13:20–21; 1 Pet. 4:11; 5:10–11; 2 Pet. 3:17–18; Jude 24–25; Rev. 22:21). As in Paul, these final words often recapitulate the main themes of the letter, which the writer seals with the amen that both declare and pleads, "So be it! May God indeed be praised for bestowing the gifts his people need."

DANIEL DORIANI

Amos, Theology of. Like all biblical prophets, Amos spoke the oracles of Yahweh, Israel's God, to people in a particular context. In order to comprehend the theology of the book that bears his name, one must have a basic understanding of that context.

The original recipients of Amos's message were the citizens of the northern kingdom of Israel in approximately 760 B.C. That Yahweh would call Amos to prophesy to them was, in itself, rather remarkable because he was neither a religious professional nor a northerner, but a farmer from Tekoa in Judah (1:1; 7:14–15). What this signified, to any who might be attuned to perceive it, was that Yahweh was not the sort of God who felt constrained by convention when choosing an individual for the task at hand, even if that person should appear to be unqualified. His task for this layman from the south was that he travel to what was essentially a foreign country and speak a hard message to people living in relative ease.

Israel, during the reign of Jeroboam II (793–753) was propelled to heights of power and prosperity unmatched since the days of David and Solomon. Many were buoyed by a sense of well-being and felt optimistic about the future. While the military was strong and the gross national product was high, however, the nation was in an advanced state of social, moral, and spiritual decay. Shocking extremes of privilege and powerlessness, wealth and want had emerged. Judges could be bribed. Religion was a syncretistic mix of ritualistic devotion to Yahweh and various pagan deities. The fact that Yahweh had to summon Amos to address this situation was a damning indictment of Israel's leaders, both religious and secular, who lacked the requisite ethical fiber. A notable exception was Hosea, whose denunciation of Israel's spiritual apostasy complemented Amos's devastating exposé of her tattered social and moral fabric.

Yahweh. Any discussion of the theology of the Book of Amos must begin with its portrait of Yahweh. One catches glimpses of many aspects of his character and activity. The three most prominent features of that portrait are his sovereignty, justice, and grace.

Throughout the book, in utterances that contain a remarkable number of first-person singular forms, Yahweh indicates his sovereignty by repeatedly asserting that he initiates things. Events—both past (2:9–11; 4:6–11; 9:7) and future (1:4–5; 2:13–16; 5:27; 6:14; 9:11–15)—are not the products of chance but Yahweh's inventions. Furthermore, he reports effects, of which he himself is the cause, in advance of their occurrence (3:6–8).

The prophecy of Amos highlights two major spheres in which Yahweh manifests his sovereignty: nature and the nations. In some passages his lordship over nature is demonstrated in both his role as its creator (4:13; 5:8) and his harnessing of its awesome forces for his own purposes (4:6–11; 5:8–9; 7:1–6; 8:7–14; 9:5–6). These and other parts of the book (1:2; 3:8) reveal the great power and terrible majesty of the God with whom Israel must deal.

Yahweh also manifests his supreme authority over the nations. As might be expected, Amos shows that Yahweh is Israel's sovereign. It is he who elected or chose the people of Israel for a special covenant relationship with himself, who rescued them from slavery in Egypt, and who led them through the blistering wilderness to their territorial inheritance, which he wrested from the Amorites (2:9–10; 3:1–2; cf. Gen. 15:12–16). Yahweh now declares that he will punish and disperse the present covenant community, which has been unfaithful to him (2:13; 3:14; 5:26–27). Ultimately he will restore Israel (9:11–15).

However, insists Amos, Yahweh not only rules in Israel's affairs; he also controls the movements of other peoples (9:7), summons other nations to do his bidding (6:14), and judges other states in accordance with the standards he has set for them (1:3–2:3).

Another important feature in Amos's portrait of Yahweh is his justice. Yahweh's justice is a corollary to his holiness and righteousness—attributes that reflect his very essence and that he expects will distinguish those who name him as their God (Exod. 19:5–6; Lev. 11:44–45; 20:7; Amos 5:14–15, 24). As already indicated, the basis on which Yahweh relates to the Israelites is his covenant with them. In that covenant he sets forth his expectations regarding the way in which they ought to relate to him and to each other. These relationships are to be characterized by the sort of love that manifests itself in loyalty and faithfulness to him (Deut. 6:4–14; Amos 5:4–6) and justice and compassion to their neighbors (Lev. 19:9–18; Amos 5:15, 24). He also spells out, in terms reminiscent of the treaties between ancient suzerains and their vassal states, the consequences of fulfilling (blessing) and falling short (judgment) of those expectations (Lev. 26:3–39; Deut. 28:1–68; 29:22–28). He blesses in accordance with the promises of the covenant (Deut. 30:1–10; Amos 9:11–15). He judges not as a surly deity who from time to time lashes out at his people in arbitrary and petulant outbursts, but as one who causes the covenantal curses to take effect (Amos 7:1–9). This is evident in the references to famine and hunger (4:6; 8:11–12; cf. Lev. 26:26; Deut. 28:48, 51–57), drought and thirst (4:7–8; 8:13–14; cf. Lev. 26:19–20; Deut. 28:22–24, 48), disease and plagues (4:9–10; cf. Lev. 26:16, 25; Deut. 28:21–22, 27, 35, 38–40, 42, 59–61), disaster (4:11; cf. Deut. 29:22–23), military defeat and destruction (2:14–16; 3:11, 14–15; 4:10; 5:3; 6:11, 14; 7:9, 17; 8:3; 9:1, 8, 10; cf. Lev. 26:17, 25, 30–33; Deut. 28:25, 48–57), and exile (4:2–3; 5:5, 27; 6:7; 7:11, 17; 9:4; cf. Lev. 26:33–39; Deut. 28:36–37, 41, 63–68).

Yahweh's justice is observable, as well, in his dealings with other nations. They are expected to act in conformity with the basic ethical and moral standards that are part of general revelation. These standards are imprinted on the consciences of even those humans who do not have access to Israel's legal code (Ps. 19:1–4; Acts 14:17; 17:24–28; Rom. 1:18–32; 2:14–15). When nations fail to measure up to the basic standards, Yahweh sees to it that they experience appropriate retribution (Amos 1:3–2:3).

The Book of Amos also gives clear indication of Yahweh's grace, that is, the lovingkindness and mercy that he lavishes on people without regard to merit. This grace is evident, first of all, in his election of Israel (Amos 3:2a; cf. Exod. 19:3–8). Elsewhere, Yahweh assures his people that this privilege was not given to them because they were so numerous or righteous, for they were neither. He chose them and gave them the land that he had promised because of his love for them, his loyalty to the patriarchs, and his revulsion at the wickedness of that land's previous inhabitants (Deut. 7:6–9; 9:4–6). Throughout Israel's history he has demonstrated his loving concern for the people by his mighty acts and marvelous provisions. But they have responded with unfaithfulness and rejection of those whom he has sent to point the way back to himself (Amos 2:6–12; 7:12–16). He has sought to jolt them out of their spiritual lethargy and to bring them to repentance by sending calamities of the sort described in the covenant curses, but to no avail (4:6–11). Yet he continues to invite them to seek him and live as they should (5:4–6, 14–15, 24). Although the situation deteriorates to the point that he can no longer spare the nation (7:1–8; 8:1–2), he still talks in terms of a surviving remnant of the people (5:15; 9:8–10). He also looks beyond the gloom of punishment to a time when he will rejuvenate the land and establish the remnant there (9:11–15). Yahweh's grace is evident not just in his blessings but also in his judgments.

Israel. The focus of Amos's prophecy is, of course, the Israelite nation. As already indicated, Amos asserts the fact of Israel's election. But the prophet goes on to say that the privilege of election brings with it a high degree of accountability to the God with whom Israel is in relationship. The standard by which she is judged is more stringent than that for other nations. She is thus especially liable to judgment (3:2) and yet, paradoxically, in judgment she becomes like those other nations (1:3–2:16; 9:7–8).

The basis for Israel's judgment is her unfaithfulness to Yahweh. That infidelity is manifested in a number of ways, but intrinsic to each is the fact that she fails to measure up to Yahweh's expectations for her (7:7–8). Instead of reflecting the humanitarian and egalitarian character of much pentateuchal legislation (Exod. 23:9; Lev. 19:15; 25:35–43; Deut. 17:18–20; 24:14–18), Israelite society is fractured into classes defined by economics and political influence (Amos 2:6–8; 3:9–10, 15; 4:1; 5:11–12; 6:1, 4–7, 11; 7:1; 8:4–6). In the face of detailed covenantal provisions for the care of the poor and disadvantaged (Exod. 22:22–27; 23:10–11; Lev. 19:9–10; 25:35–55; Deut. 10:17–19; 15:7–15; 24:19–22), Israelites with power and wealth oppress those who have neither, further enriching themselves at the expense of these unfortunates (Amos 2:6–8; 3:9–10; 4:1; 5:11–12; 8:4, 6). Despite Yahweh's insistence that justice be meted out in an atmosphere of fairness, truthfulness, and impartiality (Exod. 23:1–3, 6–8; Deut. 10:17–18; 19:15–19; 25:1–3), Israel's courts dispense lies, exploitation, and verdicts favorable to those with the means to purchase them (Amos 2:6–8; 5:7, 10–12; 6:12; 8:6). In defiance of explicit instructions to conduct honest business transactions (Lev. 19:35–36; Deut. 25:13–16), greedy merchants cheat their customers by selling goods of inferior quality at inflated prices (Amos 8:4–6).

What makes this litany of avarice and corruption even worse is the fact that it describes a nation of people who are known for—and in fact take pride in—their religious involvement (Amos 4:4–5; 5:21–23; 8:10). Furthermore, they have the audacity to claim that Yahweh is with them (5:14). Undoubtedly, those who enjoy the benefits of the nation's power and wealth interpret them as evidences of Yahweh's favor and blessing, which they presume will continue indefinitely (9:10). Amos blasts the advocates of this perverse prosperity gospel for their smug complacency, false sense of security, and pride (6:1–14; 8:7). They are not living in the light of Yahweh's benevolent smile, as they suppose, but in the lull before the storm of judgment (2:13–16; 6:11; 7:7–9; 8:1–2). Obviously to this, some speak longingly of the day of Yahweh (5:18a), a day on which the messianic kingdom (in which they undoubtedly think they will play a prominent part) will violently displace the present order (5:18b–20; 9:8–15). The religion on which they rely to secure a place for themselves in that kingdom, however, is clearly a hollow one that features much ritual and cultic activity designed to appease or manipulate the deity. But it has no appreciable impact on the everyday conduct of its adherents (8:4–6). Beneath the surface, it is not the pure form of the worship of Yahweh envisioned in the Pentateuch with its exclusive devotion to Israel's God and its centralized cult (Exod. 20:2–6; Deut. 5:6–10; 6:4–5; 12:1–13:18). Rather, it is characterized by a multiplicity of shrines and susceptibility to incursions by pagan deities and their frequently licentious rites (Amos 2:7b–8; 3:14; 4:4; 5:5, 26; 7:9; 8:14). This kind of religion is odious to Yahweh and it provokes him to explode with indignation (5:21–24).

Israel's doom is sealed (3:11; 5:27; 8:1–3) because she has passed up repeated chances to be reconciled to the God of the covenant (4:6–11; 5:4–6, 14–15, 24). Nothing else remains to be done or said except to issue a warning for the nation to prepare to meet the God who is coming in judgment (4:12).

The Nations. Although Israel is the focus of Amos's prophecy, he says significant things about the peoples that surround her as well. In this he is comparable to other prophets whose utterances include oracles about foreign nations (cf. Isa. 13–23; Jer. 46–51; Ezek. 25–32; Zeph. 2:4–15). Most of these oracles are judgment pronouncements. Underlying them all is the understanding that Yahweh's sovereignty extends beyond the borders of Israel, that he controls the destinies of the peoples in those foreign regions, and that they are accountable to him for their actions.

The accountability of the nations to Yahweh appears to be based on a covenant relationship analogous to the one between Yahweh and Israel. This flows naturally from the idea of Yahweh's sovereignty over the nations, whose origins, movements, and destinies, like Israel's, are under his control (Amos 1:3–2:5; 2:9–10; 4:10–11; 6:14; 9:7, 11–12).

Taking a different tack, one may observe that the inhabitants of the nations singled out for special attention in Amos 1–2 could be regarded as Yahweh's subjects. Their respective territories were originally included within the borders of the land that he promised to Abram's descendants (Gen. 15:18). Subsequently, these territories were controlled by David (2 Sam. 8:1–14) and Solomon (1 Kings 4:21, 24) and, ultimately, they will be included in the messianic kingdom envisioned by the prophets. Furthermore, Edom (Gen. 25:21–26; 36:1, 8), Ammon, and Moab (Gen. 19:36–38) have a common ancestry with Israel. Thus all of the groups mentioned above could be considered to be connected to each other and bound to Yahweh in covenant.

In one way or another, all of these nations have demonstrated persistent disloyalty to Yahweh. With the words, "I will not turn back my wrath" (Amos 1:3, 6, 9, 11, 13; 2:1, 4, 6), he announces either his intention not to revoke the thundering pronouncement of judgment against each covenant-breaking nation (1:2), or his decision not to take such a nation back to himself as a covenant partner in good standing. In either case, each will suffer the fate that any vassal state can expect at the hands of the suzerain against whom it has rebelled—devastating military reprisals, including the razing of its principal cities.

Amos's purpose in uttering oracles about nations beyond the borders of eighth-century Israel is not only to declare the impending punishment of others who have been disloyal to Yahweh. In fact, these pronouncements will never be heard by those about whom they are made except, in the course of time, by the people of Judah. The original intended audience for all these utterances is Israel (1:1). As Amos solemnly proclaims the destruction of her nearest adversaries, he undoubtedly gains the sympathetic attention of the people to whom he has been sent to deliver a word from Yahweh. Their expectation is that when, at last, he does speak about their nation, the message will be one of vindication and salvation. But when he proceeds to expose their transgressions just as he has exposed those of their neighbors, he reveals that his strategy all along has been to hem Israel in on every side with the fires of judgment (1:4, 7, 10, 12, 14; 2:2, 5). She now stands isolated as the last victim of Yahweh's wrath. His patience with her, as with the other nations, has run out (2:6–13).

Judgment. The Book of Amos provides some significant insights into the theme of judgment. Yahweh sends retribution on both Israel and the nations for their deliberate and repeated covenant violations. He does not act precipitously in this, but mingles wrath with grace in the hope that the offending party will repent and avoid ultimate destruction. Three additional observations with respect to the prophet's theology of judgment may be highlighted.

First, Yahweh's judgment is frequently talionic. It is just retribution or judgment in kind. Thus those who oppress others and enrich themselves at the expense of the disadvantaged will not get to enjoy the fruits of their treachery (5:11–12). Plunderers and looters will themselves be plundered (3:10–11). The mighty who rely on their physical prowess and boast about military exploits will be bettered on those counts by others who are more capable (2:14–16; 6:13–14). The foremost in Israelite society, complacent and secure, will be among the first to go into exile (6:1, 7). People who have rejected the ministry of Yahweh's prophets will experience a famine for the word of Yahweh and will search for it everywhere, but without success (2:12; 7:12–16; 8:11–12). Those who worship the gods of the nations will be exiled to such nations (5:26–27).

Second, Yahweh's judgment, when untempered by his mercy, is comprehensive and relentless. It will be felt throughout the land (1:2; 5:16–17; 6:14). No one will elude the tireless "Hound of Heaven" (9:1–4). By the time Yahweh's wrath has been sated, there will be pathetically little left of the nation (3:12).

Third, the judgment of Israel and the eschatological day of Yahweh are related events. Israelites in Amos's time are looking forward to that day (5:18), evidently expecting that the Gentile nations will be vanquished and Israel will be elevated to a place of preeminence among the nations because of her special relationship with Yahweh. But Amos brings them up short by pointing out that Yahweh is going to settle his accounts with Israel as well, and not just with other nations (2:13–16; 5:18–20; 8:1–3, 9–14). Amos's association of Israel's soon-coming judgment with the day of Yahweh forcefully drives home the point that this will be the nation's ultimate encounter with him.

Hope and Restoration. The message of Amos is largely a gloomy one, but not exclusively so. Even in some of Yahweh's dark pronouncements of retribution against Israel there are glimmers of hope regarding the survival of a remnant of the people (3:12; 5:3, 15; 9:8–10). These passages set the stage for the last five verses of the book, which are so different in tone and perspective that most biblical scholars feel they constitute a later addition. The tone of 9:11–15 is completely positive with no hint of judgment. The perspective seems to be that of an exile from Judah; there are references to returning from captivity (v. 14; cf. Deut. 30:1–3; Jer. 30:3), repairing and rebuilding of ruins (vv. 11, 14), and possessing the remnant of Edom (v. 12). While it is true that this promise concerning the subjugation of Edom and other nations is to be seen in the context of Israel's longstanding expectation of a restored Davidic kingdom (v. 11; cf. Isa. 9:1–7; 11:10–16), the singling out of a presumably chastened remnant of Edom in Amos 9:12 calls to mind a number of biblical invectives against the descendants of Esau for their gleeful complicity with the Babylonian conquerors of Judah in 586 B.C. (Ps. 137:7; Lam. 4:21–22; Ezek. 25:12–14; Obad. 5–21). Whether or not the last section of the Book of Amos comes directly from the prophet of that name, there is no more reason for believers to doubt its place within the inspired canon of Scripture than one would any of the biblical books for which the question of authorship remains open.

The phrase that introduces this section, "In that day" (9:11), associates the events described in this salvation oracle with the eschatological day of Yahweh. Here is portrayed the bright side of that day, the light of which will never dawn on the intransigent Israelites to whom Amos ministers. It will be a day of weal or woe depending on the state of one's relationship with Yahweh (cf. Joel 3:12–21; Obad. 15–21; Zech. 12:1–9; 14:1–21; Mal. 4:1–6).

Two main themes form the backdrop for Amos's description of the establishment of Yahweh's everlasting kingdom. The first, alluded to earlier, is a return to the golden age of Israel's history—the time of David's rule (vv. 11–12). Seemingly implied in verse 11 is what other prophets state explicitly, namely, that Yahweh will restore a united kingdom over which an eschatological David will preside (cf. Isa. 11:10–14; Jer. 33:23–26; Ezek. 37:15–28; Hos. 1:11; 3:4–5). In verse 12 we read of the recovery of the territory that once belonged to the Davidic empire. Yahweh will thus reestablish his claim to those nations that were, in David's day, under the aegis of his covenant with Israel. What, in the context of that covenant, is described in imperialistic terms becomes, in the new covenant context, a description of the establishment of Christ's universal church (Acts 15:5–17).

The second major theme of this section is the reversal of the covenant curses (vv. 13–15). This scenario is played out in the land that Yahweh originally gave to the patriarchs and their descendants (Gen. 13:14–17; 26:2–3; 28:10–13), but which Israel lost because of her unfaithfulness to him (Lev. 18:24–28; 26:27–39; 2 Kings 17:3–23; 21:1–16; 23:26–27; 24:1–4; 2 Chron. 36:11–21). The prophet anticipates a time of unprecedented revitalization. Returning exiles will be securely reestablished in the land as they rebuild its ruins and enjoy its lavish bounty. This renewed existence is described in terms that suggest a restored Eden and a new creation (cf. Isa. 65:17–25; Ezek. 47:1–12; Joel 3:18). It becomes clear that, just as impending manifestations of Yahweh's wrath are seen to be related to his final day of judgment, so also the imminent restoration of the exiles represents the first stage in the establishment of his eternal kingdom. Thus a book whose message is, for the most part, characterized by such foreboding concludes with the kind of hope to which the faithful of all the ages are attuned.

ROBERT J. V. HIEBERT

Bibliography. M. L. Barré, *JBL* 105 (1986): 611–31; R. Clements, *When God's Patience Runs Out: the Truth of Amos for Today;* P. C. Craigie, *The Twelve Prophets;* R. S. Cripps, *A Critical and Exegetical Commentary on the Book of Amos;* E. Hammershaimb, *The Book of Amos: A Commentary;* J. H. Hayes, *Amos, the Eighth-Century Prophet: His Times and Preaching;* P. J. King, *Amos, Hosea, Micah—An Archaeological Commentary;* J. Marsh, *Amos and Micah: Introduction and Commentary;* J. L. Mays, *Amos;* J. A. Motyer, *The Message of*

Amos; D. Stuart, *Hosea–Jonah;* J. A. Ward, *Amos, Hosea;* H. W. Wolff, *Joel and Amos.*

Anathema. *See* CURSE, ACCURSED.

Angel. Superhuman or heavenly being who serves as God's messenger. Both the Hebrew *malʾāk* and the Greek *angelos* indicate that these beings also act decisively in fulfilling God's will in the world. But these two terms also apply to human beings as messengers (1 Kings 19:2; Hag. 1:13; Luke 7:24). "Angels" are mentioned almost three hundred times in Scripture, and are only noticeably absent from books such as Ruth, Nehemiah, Esther, the letters of John, and James.

The Old Testament. From the beginning, angels were part of the divine hierarchy. They were created beings (Ps. 148:2, 5), and were exuberant witnesses when God brought the world into being (Job 38:7). By nature they were spiritual entities, and thus not subject to the limitations of human flesh. Although holy, angels could sometimes behave foolishly (Job 4:18), and even prove to be untrustworthy (Job 15:15). Probably these qualities led to the "fall" of some angels, including Satan, but the Bible contains no description of that event. When angels appeared in human society they resembled normal males (Gen. 18:2, 16; Ezek. 9:2), and never came dressed as women.

In whatever form they occurred, however, their general purpose was to declare and promote God's will. On infrequent occasions they acted as agents of destruction (Gen. 19:13; 2 Sam. 24:16; 2 Kings 19:35, etc.). Sometimes angels addressed people in dreams, as with Jacob (Gen. 28:12; 31:11), and could be recognized by animals before human beings became aware of them, as with Balaam (Num. 22:22). Collectively the divine messengers were described as the "angelic host" that surrounded God (1 Kings 22:19) and praised his majesty constantly (Ps. 103:21). The Lord, their commander, was known to the Hebrews as the "Lord of hosts." There appears to have been some sort of spiritual hierarchy among them. Thus the messenger who instructed Joshua was a self-described "commander of the Lord's army" (Josh. 5:14–15), although this designation could also mean that it was God himself who was speaking to Joshua.

In Daniel, two angels who interpreted visions were unnamed (7:16; 10:5), but other visions were explained to Daniel by the angel Gabriel, who was instructed by a "man's voice" to undertake this task (8:15–16). When a heavenly messenger appeared to Daniel beside the river Hiddekel (Tigris), he spoke of Michael as "one of the chief princes" (10:13, 21). This mighty angel would preside over the fortunes of God's people in the latter time (12:1). Thereafter he was regarded by the Hebrews as their patron angel. In the postexilic period the term "messenger" described the teaching functions of the priest (Mal. 2:7), but most particularly the individual who was to prepare the way for the Lord's Messiah (Mal. 3:1).

Two other terms relating to spiritual beings were prominent at various times in Israel's history. The first was "cherubim," a plural form, conceived of as winged creatures (Exod. 25:20), and mentioned first in connection with the expulsion of Adam and Eve from Eden (Gen. 3:24). Apart from their functions as guardians, however, nothing is said about their character. When the wilderness tabernacle was being fashioned, God ordered two gold cherubim to be placed on top of the "mercy seat" or lid of the covenant ark to screen it. These came to be known as the "cherubim of the Glory" (Heb. 9:5). Cherubim designs were also incorporated into the fabric of the inner curtain (Ezek. 26:1) and the veil of the tabernacle (Exod. 26:31).

Solomon placed two wooden cherubim plated with gold leaf in the Most Holy Place of the temple, looking toward the Holy Place. They stood ten cubits (about fourteen feet) high and their wings were five cubits (about seven feet) long. Near Eastern archeological excavations have shown how popular the concept of winged creatures was in antiquity. The throne of Hiram at Byblos (ca. 1200 B.C.) was supported by a pair of creatures with human faces, lions' bodies, and large protective wings. It was above the cherubim that the Lord of hosts sat enthroned (1 Sam. 4:4).

The seraphim were also thought of as winged, and in Isaiah's vision they were stationed above the Lord's throne (6:1–2). They seemed to possess a human figure, and had voices, faces, and feet. According to the vision their task was to participate in singing God's praises antiphonally. They also acted in some unspecified manner as mediums of communication between heaven and earth (Isa. 6:6). The living creatures of Ezekiel 1:5–14 were composites of human and animal parts, which was typically Mesopotamian in character, and they seem to have depicted the omnipotence and omniscience of God.

The Apocrypha. In the late postexilic period angelology became a prominent feature of Jewish religion. The angel Michael was deemed to be Judaism's patron, and the apocryphal writings named three other archangels as leaders of the angelic hierarchy. Chief of these was Raphael, who was supposed to present the prayers of pious Jews to God (Tobit 12:15). Uriel explained to Enoch many of his visions (1 Enoch 21:5–10; 27:2–4), interpreted Ezra's vision of the celestial Jerusalem (2 Esdras 10:28–57), and explained the fate of the fallen angels who supposedly married human women (1 Enoch 19:1–9; cf. Gen. 6:2). Gabriel, Michael, Raphael, and Uriel (1 Enoch 40:3, 6) reported to God about the depraved state of humanity, and received appropriate instructions. According to contemporary thought, Gabriel sat on God's left, while Michael sat on the right side (2 Enoch 24:1). The primary concern of these two angels, however, was supposedly with missions on earth and affairs in heaven, respectively. In rabbinic Judaism they assumed a character which, while sometimes dramatic, had no factual basis in divine revelation.

The New Testament. Against this background of belief in angels who were involved in human affairs, it was not surprising that the angel Gabriel should be chosen to visit Zechariah, the officiating priest in the temple, to inform him that he was to become a father, and that he had to name his son John (Luke 1:11–20). Gabriel was not referred to here as an archangel, the Greek term *archangelos,* appearing only in 1 Thessalonians 4:16 to describe an otherwise unnamed executive angel, and also in Jude 9, which refers to "Michael the archangel." Six months after his announcement to Zechariah, Gabriel appeared to Mary to inform her that God had selected her to become the mother of Jesus, the promised Messiah (Luke 1:26–33).

Nothing in Gabriel's behavior is inconsistent with Old Testament teachings about angels. It has been pointed out frequently that, just as they were active when the world began, so angels were correspondingly prominent when the new era of divine grace dawned with the birth of Jesus. On three occasions an angel visited Joseph in a vision concerning Jesus (Matt. 1:20; 2:13, 19). On the first two occasions the celestial visitor is described as "the angel of the Lord," which could possibly be a way of describing God himself. On the last visit the heavenly messenger was described simply as "an angel of the Lord." In the end, however, the celestial beings were most probably of the same order, and were fulfilling among humans those duties normally assigned to such angels as Gabriel (Luke 1:19).

There is nothing recorded about the actual form of the latter, but Zechariah appears to have recognized the angel immediately as a celestial being, and was terrified (Luke 1:12). His penalty for not having learned anything from his ancestor Abraham's experience (Luke 1:18; cf. Gen. 17:17) would only be removed when his son John was born (Luke 1:20). When Gabriel announced to Mary that she would bear Jesus (Luke 31), she seems to have been more disturbed by his message than his appearance. The birth of Jesus was announced to Bethlehem shepherds by the angel of the Lord, and since he was accompanied by the divine glory he may well have been the Lord himself. The message of joy having been proclaimed, the heavenly host of angels praised and glorified God (Luke 2:13–14) for a short period, as they had done at the creation of the world (Job 38:7), after which they departed.

During his ministry, angels came and ministered to Jesus after he had resisted the devil's temptations (Matt. 4:11). Again, when Jesus was submitting himself to God's will in the garden of Gethsemane (Luke 22:40–44), an angel came from heaven to strengthen him. At the resurrection, the angel of the Lord rolled back the stone from Jesus' burial place (Matt. 28:2), and he was described as having a countenance like lightning and garments as white as snow (Matt. 28:3). Again, this celestial being performed a service of reassurance and love for Mary and Mary of Magdala, who subsequently reported seeing "a vision of angels" (Luke 24:23). In John's Gospel Mary Magdalene saw two angels in white clothing, sitting in the empty tomb, just before she met the risen Lord (John 20:12–16).

In Acts, the imprisoned apostles were released by an angel (5:19). Philip was ordered by an angel to meet an Ethiopian official (8:26–28), while another celestial being appeared to Cornelius (10:3). The angel of the Lord released Peter from prison (12:7–11), and subsequently afflicted Herod with a fatal illness (12:23). When Paul and his companions were about to be shipwrecked the apostle assured them of the presence of a guardian angel (27:23–24).

Paul referred subsequently to angelic hierarchies ("thrones, powers, rulers, or authorities") when proclaiming the cosmic supremacy of Jesus (Col. 1:15–16; cf. 1 Peter 3:22), and prohibited the worship of angels in the Colossian church (Col. 2:18) in an attempt to avoid unorthodox practices. His reference to "angels" in 1 Corinthians 11:10 may have been a warning that such things observe humans at worship, and thus the Corinthians should avoid improper conduct or breaches of decency.

The angelology of 2 Peter and Jude reflects some of the intertestamental Jewish traditions concerning "wicked angels." In Revelation there are numerous symbolic allusions to angels, the worship of which is forbidden (22:8–9). The "angels of the seven churches" (1:20) are the specific spiritual representations or personifications of these Christian groups. A particularly sinister figure was Abaddon (Apollyon in Greek), the "angel of the bottomless pit" (9:11), who with his minions was involved in a fierce battle with Michael and his angels (12:7–9).

Jesus accepted as valid the Old Testament references to angels and their functions (Matt. 22:30), but spoke specifically of the "devil and his angels" (Matt. 25:41) as destined for destruction. He fostered the idea of angels ministering to believers (cf. Heb. 1:14), and as being concerned for the welfare of children (Matt. 18:10). He described angels as holy creatures (Mark 8:38) who could rejoice when a sinner repented (Luke 15:10). Angels were devoid of sexual characteristics (Matt. 22:30), and although they were highly intelligent ministers of God's will they were not omniscient (Matt. 24:36).

Christ claimed at his arrest in Gethsemane that more than twelve legions of angels (numbering about 72,000) were available to deliver him, had he wanted to call upon them for assistance (Matt. 26:53). He taught that angels would be with him when he returned to earth at the second coming (Matt. 25:31), and that they would be involved significantly in the last judgment (Matt. 13:41, 49). Finally, angels set a model of obedience to God's will in heaven to which the Christian church should aspire (cf. Matt. 6:10).

Some writers contrast the celestial beings with "fallen angels," of which there are two varieties. The first consists of unimprisoned, evil beings working under Satan's leadership, and generally regarded as demons (Luke 4:35; 11:15; John 10:21). The second were imprisoned (2 Peter 2:4; Jude 6) spirits because they forsook their original positions in heaven. For New Testament writers they were particularly dangerous. The precise difference in function and character is not explained in Scripture, but some have thought that the latter were the "sons of God" who cohabited with mortal women (Gen. 6:1–2). This view, however, is strictly conjectural. Presumably the imprisoned angels are the ones who will be judged by the saints (1 Cor. 6:3).

In a material world that is also populated by good and evil spirits, the Bible teaches that the heavenly angels set an example of enthusiastic and resolute fulfillment of God's will. They acknowledge Jesus as their superior, and worship him accordingly. Angels continue to perform ministering duties among humans, and this function has led to the concept of "guardian angels," perhaps prompted by Christ's words in Matthew 18:10. It is not entirely clear whether each individual has a specific angelic guardian, but there is certainly no reason for doubting that an angel might well be assigned to care for the destinies of groups of individuals such as families. These celestial ministries will be most effective when the intended recipients are receptive to the Lord's will for their lives.

R. K. Harrison

Bibliography. G. B. Caird, *Principalities and Powers;* A. C. Gaebelein, *The Angels of God;* B. Graham, *Angels: God's Secret Agents;* H. Lockyer, *The Mystery and Ministry of Angels;* A. Whyte, *The Nature of Angels.*

Angel of the Lord (Heb. *mal'ak yehwah).* Supernatural being who bears a message on behalf of God. In many passages in the Old Testament, the angel of the Lord is identified with God, while in other instances a distinction is made between the Lord and the angel. In general, however, the terms "the angel of the Lord," "the Lord," and "God" are interchangeable.

The angel of the Lord is the messenger of both good and evil. He comes to Hagar after she has fled from the abusive Sarai (Gen. 16:7–14) to assure her that God has heard about her misery and that her descendants will be too numerous to count. She names him "You are the God who sees me" (v. 13). The angel of the Lord pronounces a curse on the people of Meroz, because they refused to come to the help of the Lord (Judg. 5:23).

The angel of the Lord executes judgment on behalf of the Lord. He puts to death 185,000 Assyrian soldiers in their camp, thereby saving Jerusalem from decimation (2 Kings 19:35).

The angel of the Lord both commissions and commends God's servants. The commander of the Lord's army commissions Joshua to undertake the Lord's battles for Canaan, just as Moses had been commissioned to confront Pharaoh (Josh. 5:13–15; cf. Exod. 3:5). The angel of the Lord appears to Abraham. He stops Abraham from sacrificing Isaac and commends him because he has not withheld his only son from God (Gen. 22:11–18). Abraham identifies the angel as God, calling the place "The Lord Will Provide."

The angel of the Lord carries out a ministry of reconciliation. He asks how long God will withhold mercy from Jerusalem and Judah (Zech. 1:12).

The connection between the angel of the Lord and the preincarnate appearance of the Messiah cannot be denied. Manoah meets the angel of the Lord, and declares that he has seen God. The angel accepts worship from Manoah and his wife as no mere angel, and refers to himself as "Wonderful," the same term applied to the coming deliverer in Isaiah 9:6 (Judg. 13:9–22). The functions of the angel of the Lord in the Old Testament prefigure the reconciling ministry of Jesus. In the New Testament, there is no mention of the angel of the Lord; the Messiah himself is this person.

Louis Goldberg

See also Theophany.

Bibliography. A. Bowling, *TWOT,* 1:464–65; G. B. Funderburk, *ZPEB,* 1:160–66; J. B. Payne, *Theology of the Older Testament.*

Anger. Strong emotional reaction of displeasure, often leading to plans for revenge or punishment. There are many words for anger in Hebrew; in Greek *orgē* and *thumos* are used more or less interchangeably.

The Anger of God. Unlike pagan gods, whose tirades reflect the fickleness of their human creators, Yahweh "expresses his wrath every day" because he is a righteous judge (Ps. 7:11). At the same time, God is merciful and not easily provoked to anger (Exod. 34:6; Ps. 103:8–9).

God may choose to display his wrath within historical events, as in Israel's wilderness wanderings (Ps. 95:10–11) or the Babylonian exile (Lam. 2:21–22). But his wrath will be fully expressed on the *dies irae,* the day of wrath at the end of the age, when all wrongs will be punished (Zeph. 1:14–18).

John the Baptist warns of God's fiery judgment (Matt. 3:7). Jesus will execute God's wrath at his second coming (Rev. 6:15–17). While the wicked already stand under God's condemnation (John 3:36; Eph. 2:3), by sinning, they continue to store up wrath (Rom. 2:5; 9:22). But God in his mercy sent Jesus to turn away his anger by a sacrifice of propitiation (Rom. 3:25; 5:9; 1 John 2:2; 4:10).

Some have doubted whether a God of love can experience anger toward his creatures. The Jewish philosopher Philo championed the Stoic idea that a perfect being by definition could not become angry. In the twentieth century, C. H. Dodd held that "wrath of God" is merely symbolic of the fact that sin has consequences. But such viewpoints reveal more about the writers' theological assumptions than the consistent teaching of the Bible.

Human Anger. The Bible usually portrays human anger as sinful. Cain's ire would have been turned to good if he had repented and offered an acceptable sacrifice. But by nursing his wrath against a holy God and the righteous Abel, he ends up committing murder (Gen. 4:3–8).

"Refrain from anger and turn from wrath"—so warns Psalm 37:8. In contrast with our modern emphasis on the constructive uses of anger, Proverbs urges us to think carefully before expressing anger (12:16; 14:29; 19:11), to be patient (16:32), and to show restraint (29:11). Angry people cause conflicts (29:22; 30:33) and continually get themselves into trouble (19:19); they should be avoided (22:24–25). In biblical history, Saul stands out as the embodiment of sinful rage (see 1 Sam. 19:9–10; 20:30–34). On the other hand, Job and many psalmists display anger and frustration with their situation—and at times even with God himself. In the end Job is rebuked because he has doubted God's justice (chaps. 35–36), but the psalmists' prayers are acceptable apparently because they are viewing the world from God's perspective; since God knows the heart, it is better for them to voice their anger than it is to deny it.

Jesus warns that angry people will face God's judgment (Matt. 5:22; cf. Gal. 5:20; Col. 3:6–8). James reflects the wisdom of the Old Testament when he tells his readers to "be quick to listen, slow to speak and slow to become angry" (1:9). According to Ephesians 4:25–27, people should speak truthfully, but their anger should be restrained, short-lived, and used for righteous ends. Provoking another person to anger without reason is in itself a sin (Eph. 6:4). Anger can divide a church (2 Cor. 12:20) and frustrate prayer (1 Tim. 2:8); an elder must not be "quick-tempered" (Titus 1:7).

People may, however, react to sin in the way that God does—in holiness and without desire for personal vengeance (Rom. 12:19–21). Moses was therefore justly angry with Pharaoh (Exod. 11:8). But Jesus the God-Man gives us the best example of how to express righteous anger (Matt. 23:1–36; Mark 3:5; 11:15–17; John 2:13–17).

At the same time, people may believe that their anger is warranted when it is not; such anger is usually rooted in a desire to justify oneself. Simeon and Levi's slaughter of the Shechemites goes well beyond righteous anger (Gen. 34:1–31; 49:5–7). Jonah believes that he is right to be angry when God spares the wicked (chap. 4). Those who angrily oppose Jesus think that God is on their side (Matt. 21:15–16). Even the disciples are self-righteously angry with James and John (Matt. 20:24) and with the woman who anointed Jesus with costly ointment (Mark 14:4–5).

GARY STEVEN SHOGREN

See also WRATH OF GOD.

Bibliography. G. C. Berkhouwer, *Studies in Dogmatics: Sin;* F. Büchsel, *TDNT,* 3:167–68; H. C. Hahn, *NIDNTT,* 1:105–13; H. Kleinknecht et al., *TDNT,* 5:382–447.

Animals. ***God as Creator and Sustainer.*** Animals, like the rest of the universe, are created by God. In Genesis 1, God's approval of the created world is regularly expressed by the phrase "and God saw that it was good." God blesses the animals (v. 22) and at the end of the sixth day "God saw all that he had made, and it was very good" (v. 31). It was very good for waters, air, and land to teem with living creatures. Clearly, animals are valued by God in and for themselves, and God expresses pleasure and delight in them. Animals are not primarily created for the benefit of humanity, and deserve respect because they are God's very good work. God answers Job's complaint by speaking of the mountain goat, lion, eagle, and the mysterious Leviathan and Behemoth (Job 39:1–41:34). These animals are wild and outside human usefulness and understanding, yet God knows tham intimately and delights in them for their own sake.

As Psalm 104 makes clear, God sustains all of life, so that all creatures, including humanity, are alike in their dependence on God. In this psalm, animals are pictured in creation alongside humanity, not beneath it; nor do they exist for the sake of humans. Animals are seen as valuable to God, who make them in their uniqueness for his own purposes, sustains them, and rejoices over them (cf. Job 12:10; Pss. 36:6; 145:16; Jonah 4:11; Luke 12:24). Jesus reaffirms the value of the animal world in Luke 12:6: "Are not five sparrows sold for two pennies? Yet not one of them is forgotten by God."

As Creator, God is Lord over the world, including animals, for, "The earth is the Lord's and everything in it" (1 Cor. 10:26; cf. 1 Chron. 29:11; Pss. 74:13–14; 89:11). Thus the psalmist can say of God, "every animal of the forest is mine, and the cattle on a thousand hills. I know every bird in the mountains, and the creatures of the field are mine" (Ps. 50:10–11; cf. Exod. 13:12; Job 41:11). Because they are created by God, all creation, including animals, should praise God (Pss. 148:7–10; 150:6; cf. Rev. 5:13). Christ's work of creating, sustaining, and reconciling all things also includes the animal world (Col. 1:16–17).

Animals and the Hope of Future Transformation. The hope of future transformation includes animals. Isaiah speaks of the day of the Lord in the following terms: "The wolf will live with the lamb, the leopard will lie down with the goat, the calf and the lion and the yearling together; and a little child will lead them" (Isa. 11:6). This is a vision of future transformation and harmony, when all creation will be renewed (cf. Isa. 35:9; 65:17, 25; 66:22; Hos. 2:18; Joel 2:22; Eph. 1:9–10; Rev. 21:1–4). In Romans 8:19–22 Paul speaks of the groaning of the whole creation and of the hope that creation itself will be liberated from its bondage to decay. Human salvation is inseparable from the liberation of the created world, including animals. Humanity is to be redeemed with creation, not apart from it. Yet the future reality of a new creation has already begun in Christ. Christians must now live in a way that is consistent with the kingdom, and so are called to embrace kingdom values and goals, including harmony with creation, and so are to act to preserve and enhance the created order.

Humanity and Animals. God has given humanity dominion over "the fish of the sea and the birds of the air and over every living creature that moves on the ground" (Gen. 1:28; cf. Ps. 8:6–8). The king of Israel had dominion over the nation, but was expected to act as a shepherd, who ensured the welfare of those entrusted to his care (Deut. 17:14–20; 2 Sam. 5:2; Ps. 72). The concept of dominion in Genesis 1:28 involves wise stewardship and rsponsible care for the animal world. Humanity is vegetarian in Genesis 1:29; human dominion in Genesis 1 does not produce any unpleasant consequences for animals. Further, humanity is responsible to God with respect to this stewardship, for the created world remains God's world. Thus, dominion is not a license for the unbridled exploitation of animals and nature. Yet the exercise of dominion has been flawed by sin and the harmony and peace of creation have been shattered (Gen. 3:14–15, 17–19).

In Genesis 1 humanity is unique, in that only humanity is made in the image of God. In Genesis 2:20 animals are not suitable companions for Adam. However, a very strong link exists between the animal world and humanity since in Genesis 1:24–31 both are created on the same day, and in Genesis 2:7, 19 both the man and the animals are formed from the ground. Humanity is thus not independent of the created order. Because of this closeness between humanity and animals, the condition of the two groups is often spoken of in similar terms. For example, both animals and people are dependent on the providence of God (Ps. 104:10–30; Luke 12:22–24) and animals bear the consequences of God's judgment along with people (Gen. 6:7; Exod. 9:1–7; Jer. 14:5–6; Zeph. 1:2–3).

The Use and Treatment of Animals. Animals are of service to people, for example, for transport (1 Sam. 16:20; Esther 8:10, 14) or for clothing (Gen. 3:21). They are also a sign of wealth (Gen. 24:35; Job 1:13–21). In Genesis 1:29 only plants were given as food for people, and the picture of the garden in Genesis 2 is one of peace between animals and Adam. It is only after the fall and the flood that God gave all living things, except their blood, to Noah and his family for food (Gen. 9:1–4). Only clean animals could be eaten (Lev. 11), but Jesus declared all food clean (Mark 7:17–23; cf. Acts 10:10–16). Vegetarianism is neither commanded nor forbidden and it is clear that Paul considered meat-eating to be acceptable for Christians (Rom. 14:1–4; 1 Cor. 8:7–10). God is well aware of the destructive tendencies of fallen humanity, and so in Genesis 9:8–17 makes a covenant with all living things, including animals. This shows God's continuing commitment to all of creation.

In the Old Testament, sacrifices involved the offering of certain unblemished animals (Exod. 12:1–8; Lev. 4, 16), or their blood was used on other occasions such as the consecration of priests (Exod. 29).

There are a number of injunctions that concern the welfare of animals. Animals share some of the privileges of God's people, and so the Sabbath rest applies equally to them: "Six days do your work, but on the seventh day do not work, so that your ox and your donkey may rest" (Exod. 23:12; cf. Lev. 25:7; Deut. 5:14). Further, an ox treading the corn was not to be muzzled (Deut. 25:4; quoted in 1 Cor. 9:9 and 1 Tim. 5:18, where it is applied to people) and a fallen ox was to be helped to its feet (Deut. 22:4; cf. Lev. 22:27–28: Deut. 22:6–7, 10). Jesus also pointed to the humanitarian treatment of animals on the Sabbath (Matt. 12:11–12; Luke 13:15; 14:5) and argued from this that he should free people from illness on the Sabbath. This sense of responsibility for the welfare of animals is summed up in Proverbs 12:10: "A righteous man cares for the needs of his animal." Thus, animals are owed some of the basic obligations we extend to fellow human beings.

Illustrations from the Animal World. Since the people of the Bible interacted regularly with animals they often used images from the animal world as illustrations. This use of images derived from animals often makes a passage very vivid.

Pertinent characteristics of animals are often used as images for God's activity. In Hosea 13:7–8 we read that God will come upon Israel "like a lion, like a leopard I will lurk by the path. Like a bear robbed of her cubs, I will attack them and rip them open." In Isaiah 31:5 we read: "Like birds hovering overhead, the LORD Almighty will shield Jerusalem." Illustrations from animal husbandry are used for God. For example, in Isaiah 40:11 we read: "he tends his flock like a shepherd: He gathers the lambs in his arms and carries them close to his heart; he gently leads those that have young" (cf. Ps. 23). In John 10:14 Jesus says "I am the good shepherd; I know my sheep and my sheep know me." Leaders of God's people can also be described as shepherds (Ezek. 34; Acts 20:28; cf. 1 Peter 5:1–4).

People are consistently seen as like sheep, mainly because sheep are easily led astray and lost and are unable to fend for themselves or to find their way home. In Isaiah 53:6 we read: "All we like sheep, have gone astray; we have all turned to our own way." Similarly, the people of Israel are spoken of as God's sheep (Pss. 74:1; 100:3; Jer. 23:1; Matt. 9:36; John 21:15). The image is used in another way in John 1:29: "Look, the Lamb of God, who takes away the sin of the world!" In Revelation Jesus is regularly spoken of as the Lamb.

Often animals know the right thing to do, and thus discredit humans. Thus note Isaiah 1:3 ("The ox knows his master, the donkey his owner's manger, but Israel does not know, my people do not understand") and Jeremiah 8:7 ("Even the stork in the sky knows her appointed seasons, and the dove, the swift and the thrush observe the time of their migration. But my people do not know the requirements of the LORD").

The characteristis of an animal can be used as a metaphor for a person. The lion is used as a metaphor for strength (Ps. 17:12; Ezek. 19:2–6; Amos 3:12; Rev. 5:5); the wild bear for ferocity (2 Sam. 17:8); the heifer for stubbornness (Hos. 4:16); the lamb for gentleness, particularly when it is led to the slaughter (Isa. 53:7; Jer. 11:19; Acts 8:32); the deer for stability in trying situations (2 Sam. 22:34; Ps. 18:33); the "beast" as an embodiment of evil (Rev. 11:7; 13:1–3). Dogs are generally used metaphorically for something negative, since they were scavengers who carried disease (1 Kings 21:23–24; Matt. 7:6; Phil. 3:2; Peter 2:22; Rev. 22:15). Glory can fly away like a bird (Hos. 9:11); animals can be tamed, but not the human tongue (James 3:3, 5, 7–8). A colt symbolizes peace, and so Jesus rode into Jerusalem on a colt rather than a horse, which was associated with war.

Similarly, Jesus used illustrations from the animal world in his parables and teaching. In Matthew 10:16 Jesus said: "I am sending you out like sheep among wolves. Therefore be shrewd as snakes and as innocent as doves." In his lament over Jerusalem Jesus said, "How often I have longed to gather your children together, as a hen gathers her chicks under her wings" (Matt. 23:37). In Matthew 25:31–46 Jesus' teaching hinges on the fact that sheep and goats were often very difficult to distinguish from one another. PAUL TREBILCO

Bibliography. S. Bishop, *Themelios* 16:3 (1991): 8–14; F. S. Bodenheimer, *Animal and Man in Bible Lands;* F. Bridger, *Tyn Bul* 41 (1990): 290–301; G. S. Cansdale, *Animals of Bible Lands;* T. Cooper, *Green Christianity: Caring for the Whole Creation;* W. Granberg-Michaelson, *Tending the Garden: Essays on the Gospel and the Earth;* R. Griffiths, *The Human Use of Animals;* A. Linzey, *Christianity and the Rights of Animals;* A. Linzey and T. Regan, *Animals and Christianity: A Book of Readings;* R. Murray, *The Cosmic Covenant: Biblical Themes of Justice, Peace and the Integrity of Creation.*

Anoint. To smear or rub with oil or perfume for either private or religious purposes. The Hebrew term for "anoint," *māšaḥ,* has secular connotations, such as rubbing a shield with oil (Isa. 21:5), smearing paint on a house (Jer. 22:14), or anointing the body with oil (Amos 6:6). The theological meaning of *māšaḥ* is fourfold. First, an individual or object set apart for divine use is said to be "anointed." Solomon was anointed ruler over Israel (1 Chron. 29:22); this anointing made him both responsible for and accountable to the people. Anointed kings sometimes failed in their tasks, and were reminded of their accountability (1 Sam. 15:17; 2 Sam. 12:7). Second, when people were anointed, God empowered them to accomplish his tasks (1 Sam. 10:6; 16:13). Third, no one was allowed to harm God's anointed (1 Sam. 24:10; 26:9). Finally, the term *māšîaḥ* derived from *māšaḥ,* refers to Israel's Messiah who was to come from the house of David (Pss. 84:9; 89:38, 51). In the New Testament, Christ is portrayed as the Messiah. Jesus is the promised deliverer (John 1:41; 4:25), anointed with the Holy Spirit and with power (Acts 10:38).

LOUIS GOLDBERG

See also JESUS CHRIST, NAME AND TITLES OF; MESSIAH.

Bibliography. H. L. Ellison, *The Centrality of the Messianic Idea for the Old Testament;* V. P. Hamilton, *TWOT,* 1:1255–56; J. B. Payne, *Theology of the Older Testament.*

Anointed One. *See* JESUS CHRIST, NAME AND TITLES OF.

Anthropomorphism (Gk. *anthrōpos* [human] + *morphē* [form]). Assignment of human attributes to nonhuman things. Biblical anthropomorphisms are used primarily in reference to God, who is neither visible (John 1:18) nor human (Num. 23:19; 1 Sam. 15:29). They are also used to assign human characteristics to angels (Gen. 16:7; 18:1–19:1), Satan (1 Chron. 21:1; Luke 13:16), and demons (Luke 8:32). Evil is also personified, depicted as slaying (Ps. 34:21) and pursuing (Prov. 13:21). Infrequently, human qualities are attributed to animals (Num. 22:28–30) or vegetation (Judg. 9:7–15).

The use of human terminology to talk about God is necessary when we, in our limitations, wish to express truths about the Deity who by his very nature cannot be described or known. From biblical times to the present, people have felt compelled to explain what God is like, and no expressions other than human terms are able to convey any semblance of meaning to the indescribable. Thus, in Genesis alone God creates (1:1), moves (1:2), speaks (1:3), sees (1:4), divides (1:4), places (1:17), blesses (1:22), plants (2:8), walks (3:8), shuts (7:16), smells (8:21), descends (11:5), scatters (11:8), hears (21:17), tests (22:1), and judges (30:6).

Perhaps the most profound anthropomorphism is the depiction of God establishing a covenant, for the making of covenants is a very human activity. God enters into an agreement (covenant) with Israel at Sinai (Exod. 19:5–6), an outgrowth of an earlier covenant he had made with Abraham (Gen. 17:1–18). Later, this agreement is transformed into a new covenant through Jesus Christ (Matt. 26:26–29). Theologically, the legal compact initiated by God becomes the instrument through which he established an intimate and personal relationship with the people, both collectively and individually. Without anthropomorphic expressions, this theological reality would remain virtually inexplicable.

Anthropomorphisms also attribute human form and shape to God. God redeems Israel from Egyptian bondage with an outstretched arm (Exod. 6:6). Moses and his companions see God, and they eat and drink with him (Exod. 24:10–11). Other texts refer to the back, face, mouth, lips, ears, eyes, hand, and finger of God. The expression, "the Lord's anger burned" (Exod. 4:14) is interesting. A literal translation of the Hebrew is "the nose of the Lord burned."

Indirect anthropomorphic expressions also appear, such as the sword and arrows of the Lord and the throne and footstool of God.

Akin to anthropomorphisms are anthropopathisms (Gk. *anthrōpos + pathos* [passion]), used to refer to God's emotions. God is a jealous God (Exod. 20:5) who hates (Amos 5:21) and becomes angry (Jer. 7:20), but he also loves (Exod. 20:6) and is pleased (Deut. 28:63).

Anthropomorphisms and anthropopathisms are figures of speech that transmit theological truths about God to humankind. Only when taken literally are they misconstrued. Taken as metaphorical expressions, they provide by analogy a conceptual framework by which the God who is beyond our comprehension becomes a person—a person whom we can love. In the New Testament the analogy becomes reality in the mystery of the incarnation (John 1:1–18).

Keith N. Schoville

Bibliography. J. Barr, *HBD*, p. 32; E. W. Bullinger, *Figures of Speech Used in the Bible;* M. Eliade, ed., *The Encyclopedia of Religion*, vol. 1; W. E. Miles, ed., *Mercer Dictionary of the Bible.*

Antichrist. The term "antichrist" occurs only in 1 and 2 John, and there in both singular and plural forms. It is part of a complex of images and figures that represent the activity and power of evil—of those forces that are hostile to God. The Old Testament uses the figure of a dragon to symbolize evil's conflict with God existing from the time of creation to God's final triumph (Isa. 27:1; cf. Gen 1:21; see also the reference to Rahab the dragon/sea monster defeated at the time of creation, Ps. 89:9–10; cf. Job 9:13; 26:12). The dragon figure is applied to earthly powers who are enemies of God, such as Nebuchadnezzer (Jer. 51:34) and Pharoah (Ezek. 32:2). The figure of the beast also denotes forces (specifically political powers) hostile to God (Dan. 7). Both these figures reappear in the New Testament, particularly in Revelation. The dragon is used twelve times in Revelation and designates the devil and Satan and the enemy of God's Messiah. The beast is a central image in Revelation used to symbolize that which opposes and parodies God.

The New Testament indicates the presence of cosmic opposition to God through reference primarily to forces, people, or a person who seek to deceive those who already know God's Messiah. The cosmic struggle with evil is now chiefly localized in the church. So the spirit of antichrist (1 John 4:3), the false Christs (Mark 13:22) and antichrists (1 John 2:18), the antichrist (1 John 2:18, 22; 4:3; 2 John 7), the man of lawlessness (2 Thess. 2:3), and the "desolating sacrilege" (Mark 13:14—the masculine participle suggesting a person such as the antichrist) all concentrate their activity on the elect or the community of faith. These figure(s) lie and deny Christ (1 John 2:22; 2 John 7; cf. 1 John 4:3), lead astray (Mark 13:22), oppose and even declare himself as God in the temple (2 Thess. 2:4, cf. Mark 13:14).

In both Testaments these figures function not only to describe the magnitude and threat of evil but to affirm God's control over creation. In the Old Testament and New Testament the image of the beast is used to describe both the power and intensity of evil and to declare God's ultimate victory. The figure of the antichrist and the man of lawlessness do not occur in the Old Testament, although their New Testament use is replete with Old Testament allusions. In the New Testament these figures function in line with the Old Testament conviction that God will ultimately defeat the forces of evil.

The predominant venue for these figures in the Bible is in the context of discussion of the last days. The eschaton is recognizable because of the unleashing of evil and will be characterized by a particularly vivid and horrific confrontation between God and his enemy (2 Thess. 2; 1 John 2:18). This expectation accords with that of Jewish apocalyptic literature (Sybilline Oracles, Book 3; IV Esdras 5.6) and early Catholic Christianity (Didache 16:1–4). The constant biblical conviction is that God will ultimately triumph over every opposition to him and his people, whether such enmity is manifested in earthly or supernatural powers. The last battle will be won by God and the beneficiaries will be God's people. L. ANN JERVIS

Bibliography. M. D. Hooker, *BJRL* 65 (1982):78–99; H. K. Larondelle, *Andrews University Seminary Studies* 21 (1983):61–69.

Anxiety. Uneasy feeling of uncertainty, agitation, dread, or fear. The most common words in Scripture translated as "anxious" or "anxiety" are the Hebrew *dĕʾāgâ,* (ten times in either the verbal or noun form) and the Greek *merimma* (twelve times in either the verbal or noun form). Older English versions of the Bible often render these words as "thought," "worry," or "care."

In the Bible anxiety is frequently depicted as the common human reaction to stressful circumstances. Saul's father was anxious about his lost donkeys, and then about Saul's failure to return from looking for them (1 Sam. 9:5; 10:2). The psalmist confesses that anxiety is "great" within him (Ps. 94:19). Anxiety is portrayed in the Scripture as being inconsistent with trust in God. David prays: "Search me, O God, and know my heart; test me and know my anxious thought" (Ps. 139:23). Jesus' command, "do not worry," which occurs six times in the Sermon on the Mount (Matt. 6:25–33), is coupled with admonitions to trust in the heavenly Father. Paul urges: "Do not be anxious about anything, but in everything, by prayer and petition, with thanksgiving, present your requests to God" (Phil. 4:6). Anxiety frequently manifests itself in ungodly concern about provision, performance, or reputation, and appears to be rooted in incomplete knowledge, lack of control over circumstances, or failure to take an "eternal" perspective on things (Matt. 6:25–34; 10:19; Mark 13:11; Luke 12:11–12, 22–34). Occasionally, anxiety is a symptom of guilt (Ps. 38:18).

Freedom from anxiety begins with confession that it is not God's will. In fact, anxiety is a subtle insinuation that God is either unable or disinclined to see to our welfare. Other remedial measures include recognizing the futility of worry (Matt. 6:27; Luke 12:25); cultivating a growing understanding of God's power and fatherly disposition (Matt. 6:26; Luke 12:30); entrusting to God the things that we cannot control (1 Peter 5:7); increasingly viewing things in eternal perspective (Matt. 6:32–34; Luke 12:30–34); and substituting prayer for worry (Phil. 4:6). RALPH E. ENLOW, JR.

See also CARE.

Apocalyptic. Type of biblical literature that emphasizes the lifting of the veil between heaven and earth and the revelation of God and his plan for the world. Apocalyptic writings are marked by distinctive literary features, particularly prediction of future events and accounts of visionary experiences or journeys to heaven, often involving vivid symbolism. Later apocalypses often build upon and elaborate the symbolism employed by earlier ones. This is particularly the case in the Book of Revelation, in which not only earlier apocalypses but the whole Old Testament is plundered for ideas and symbols. Readers need to be alert to discern allusions.

It has often been argued that apocalyptic is a response to distress, enabling suffering people to see that God is in control of their circumstances and that ultimate deliverance is assured. There is certainly truth in this. However, as a total explanation it may be questioned. Apocalyptic is not the only biblical response to suffering, and therefore other factors must prompt it as well. Furthermore, the apocalyptic movement seems to have flourished also at times when particular suffering was not experienced. It is not clear, for instance, that Revelation is a response *to* suffering, although suffering is predicted in it (2:10; 13:10). Sociologically, it seems better to say that apocalyptic is the product of a prophetic movement, which claims to reveal the way things really are, both in heaven and on earth (the term "apocalypse," the Greek name of the Book of Revelation, means "unveiling").

The biblical apocalyptic writings are characterized by certain distinctive theological ideas, which we will survey below. These concern particularly the relation between heaven and earth, the rule of God over both, and his ultimate victory over evil. However, these ideas are not found only in apocalyptic, but are themes of the whole biblical testimony in different ways. The mere appearance of these themes, therefore, cannot provide us with an adequate definition of apocalyptic. It is their appearance in this distinctive literary form, arising from this distinctive prophetic movement, which makes apocalyptic what it is.

The Bible contains two great examples of apocalyptic: Daniel and Revelation. But just as the distinctive themes of apocalyptic appear throughout the Scriptures, so we find that its literary forms have walk-on parts in many other books (Ezek. 1–3; Zech. 1–6; Matt. 24; Eph. 1:15–23; Heb. 12:22–24). Extrabiblical apocalyptic works like 1 Enoch (first century B.C. plus later additions) and 4 Ezra and 2 Baruch (both first century A.D.) are matched by apocalyptic passages in many other works. There was a flowering of apocalyptic in the late first century A.D., following the destruction of the temple and Jerusalem, as Jews sought revelation from God to explain that horrifying disaster. It is interesting that this is when the Book of Revelation is usually dated—undoubtedly the greatest example of apocalyptic.

Within Judaism apocalyptic faded out, but an apocalyptic visionary tradition has remained alive within Christianity ever since. No subsequent work, however, ancient or modern, attains the grandeur and power of the canonical Book of Revelation.

Apocalyptic and Revelation. The fundamental conviction of apocalyptic is that the world may be understood, but only by revelation that enables understanding. The mode of revelation varies. Daniel usually receives visionary dreams in his sleep (2:19; 7:1), but he also has day-time visions (10:4–5) and is able to pass on words from God like a traditional prophet (5:25–28). John receives his revelation while "in the Spirit" (Rev. 1:10), which seems in his case to indicate an out-of-body journey to heaven (4:1—something claimed in other apocalypses of the period).

Apocalyptic is distinguished from other forms of prophecy in that God himself rarely speaks. The revelation is communicated through angels or other heavenly figures. Both Daniel and Revelation are full of speech, but in both books the only occasion on which the voice of God is unequivocally heard is Revelation 21:5–8, a passage all the more climactic because of this rarity. In both books a particular angel acts as a guide and instructor (Dan. 9:21; Rev. 17:1; 22:8).

One interesting difference between Revelation and all other apocalypses is the extent to which it leaves visions unexplained. The usual pattern, both in Daniel and in the extrabiblical apocalypses, is that a vision is followed by an explanation of the symbolism (Dan. 7:15–27; Zech. 1:7–21), rather like the instances in which a parable of Jesus is followed by an interpretation (Matt. 13:24–30, 36–43; Mark 4:1–20).

This is only occasionally the case in Revelation. In 7:13 a heavenly figure actually asks John for an explanation of what he has just seen (but then provides it for him). In most cases the visions are just related, so that the reader is challenged to provide the interpretation, as in the case of the majority of Jesus' parables. It is not by accident that each of the letters to the churches ends with the appeal associated with the parables: "He who has an ear, let him hear." Right interpretation demands spiritual capacity and insight.

The Interconnectedness of Heaven and Earth. This follows as much from the mode of revelation as from the fact of it. John's entry into heaven is a token of the closeness of heaven to earth. Having entered it, he is able from that vantage-point to survey both heaven and earth and to see how, really, earth can only be understood when it is seen as one-half of a much greater reality. The same is true, though less clearly, in Daniel.

This interconnectedness is expressed in various ways. There are heavenly counterparts of earthly realities, like the "angels of the seven churches" (Rev. 1:20), and the four living creatures by the throne (Rev. 4:6), and the "son of man" of Daniel 7:13, who to some extent represents God's people in heaven (Dan. 7:18). Similarly there are earthly counterparts of heavenly realities, seen for instance in the ghastly pairing of the two women who are also cities in Revelation 17–21: on the one hand the Great Whore, who enslaves the world by war and commerce, and on the other the Bride of Christ, who brings healing to the nations.

There is mutual penetration, expressed both by the presence of the risen Christ in and with his church (Rev. 1–3), and also by the way in which earthly powers are seen as nurtured by the power of the beast (Rev. 17). Life on earth is determined from heaven: Decrees are issued from the throne that affect the earth (Rev. 16:1; cf. Dan. 7:26), and events in heaven have a radical effect on earth (such as the ejection of the defeated dragon from heaven, Rev. 12:9, 12).

Although earth is the sphere of the dragon and the beast, yet heaven and earth are seen as a single organism. This appears vividly in the compelling vision of universal worship in Revelation 5, where John sees (and hears) the worship spreading from the throne in concentric circles outward, from the living creatures to the twenty-four elders, then to the myriads of angels (v. 11), and finally to "every created thing in heaven and on earth and under the earth" (v. 13), with this final shout of praise echoed by an "Amen!" back at the center. At the end heaven and earth will be recreated together (Rev. 21:1).

God's Rule over a Chaotic World. The basic message of Daniel 2–5 is that "the Most High God is sovereign over the kingdoms of men and sets over them anyone he wishes" (Dan. 5:21). Similarly, but by very different means, the seals visions in Revelation 6 teach that the decree of God underlies all the chaotic horrors of human experience, including imperial conquest (6:2), war (6:3), violent and premature death (6:7), and the supreme (inexplicable?) injustice of being murdered for loyalty to the Creator (6:9–11).

As in the Book of Job, no reason is given for the presence of such things in God's world, but a profound answer is provided nonetheless: All these things issue from the scroll that only the slain Lamb is worthy to open (5:1–10). Such evils are permitted to exist in the world only because the Lamb—God himself in Christ—has suffered them all firsthand (especially the final one).

Ultimately, God's rule over the world is to be expressed by the overthrow of the powers that produce such evils (Rev. 6:15–17—foreshadowing the climactic overthrow of Babylon the Great in chapters 17–19).

The Protection of God's People. The presentation of the "son of man" before God assures the status and security of "the people of the Most High" (Dan. 7:13, 22). This does not mean that they are preserved from suffering. The great beast, whose power Daniel sees being transferred to the "son of man," will still wage war on the saints and prevail over them (7:21, 25). But because the vision has been given in which the power of the beast has already been destroyed, God's people can be assured that they will be kept safe under its rule.

In Revelation the same idea is conveyed immediately by the vision of the risen Christ patrolling among the lampstands that represent the seven churches (1:20), and by his direct messages of warning and encouragement. He holds their "angels" in his hand. This is also the function of the dramatic interludes that intrude into the structural pattern of repeated "sevens." Between the sixth and seventh seals, John witnesses the "sealing" (play on words) of "the servants of our God" (7:3), so that they will not be harmed by the calamities he has just seen. A mark of ownership is set upon them, not to save them from the experience of war, famine, and disease, but to ensure that they will be among those who "come out of the great tribulation" (7:14), and who will no longer hunger or thirst (7:16).

Similarly between the sixth and seventh trumpets another interlude occurs (Rev. 10:8–11:13) that concerns the preaching of the gospel before a hostile world. While they give their testimony, the two witnesses are kept safe, even though they are defeated by "the beast from the abyss" and follow their Lord through death and resurrection (11:5–12).

The message of the book is that, even though we cannot avoid bearing the mark of the beast as inhabitants of this world-order (13:16), yet, viewed from heaven, we also bear the name of God and of the Lamb on our foreheads, and are secure with him (14:1–5).

The Ultimate Victory of God. This is the theme that unites the biblical apocalypses with all others of the same period. The powers of this world will be overthrown and replaced by the kingdom of God. This means both secular world powers and the power of evil that lie behind them. The vision that energizes apocalyptic is the day when "the kingdom of the world has become the kingdom of our Lord and of his Christ" (Rev. 11:15).

STEPHEN MOTYER

See also REVELATION, THEOLOGY OF.

Bibliography. J. Bloch, *On the Apocalyptic in Judaism;* F. C. Burkitt, *Jewish and Christian Apocalypses;* R. H. Charles, *The Book of Enoch;* idem, *Testaments of the Twelve Patriarchs;* S. B. Frost, *Old Testament Apocalyptic;* D. Guthrie, *The Relevance of John's Apocalypse;* J. R. Harris, *The Odes;* idem, *Psalms of Solomon;* P. S. Minear, *New Testament Apocalyptic;* F. C. Porter, *The Message of the Apocalyptical Writers;* C. Rowland, *The Open Heaven: A Study of Apocalyptic in Judaism and Early Christianity;* H. H. Rowley, *Jewish Apocalyptic and the Dead Sea Scrolls;* idem, *The Relevance of Apocalyptic;* D. S. Russell, *The Method and Message of Jewish Apocalyptic;* L. L. Thompson, *The Book of Revelation.*

Apocrypha. "Apocrypha" comes from the Greek word *apokrypha,* which means "things that are hidden, secret." "The Apocrypha" refers to two collections of ancient Jewish and Christian writings that have certain affinities with the various books of the Old Testament and New Testament but were not canonized by Christians as a whole: the Old Testament Apocrypha, which are still viewed as canonical by some Christians, and the New Testament Apocrypha, which are not.

The Old Testament Apocrypha, often referred to simply as "the Apocrypha," is a collection of Jewish books that are included in the Old Testament canons of Roman Catholic and Eastern Orthodox Christians, but not of Protestants. Most of the books were composed in Hebrew prior to the Christian era, but they apparently never were accepted by the Jews as part of the Hebrew canon. At an early date they were translated into Greek and in this form came to be used by Christians as early as the end of the first century A.D. They were eventually included in Christian copies of the Greek Old Testament and, later, the Latin Vulgate. The Protestant Reformers, while affirming the unique authority of the Hebrew canon, allowed that the books of the Apocrypha were useful for reading. Over time, however, the Apocrypha has fallen into disuse among Protestants.

The Roman Catholic Apocrypha consists of Tobit, Judith, the Additions to Esther, the Additions to Daniel (the Prayer of Azariah and the Three Young Men, Susanna, and Bel and the Dragon), the Wisdom of Solomon, Ecclesiasticus (also called Sirach), Baruch (also called 1 Baruch), the Letter of Jeremiah, 1 Maccabees, and 2 Maccabees. The Greek Orthodox Church adds 1 Esdras, Psalm 151, the Prayer of Manasseh, and 3 Maccabees, with 4 Maccabees in an appendix. The Russian Orthodox Church adds 1 Esdras, 2 Esdras, Psalm 151, and 3 Maccabees. The Roman Catholic canon places the Prayer of Manasseh, 1 Esdras, and 2 Esdras in an appendix without implying canonicity.

Several of these writings are tied closely to Old Testament books. First Esdras, for example, is primarily a retelling of the material found in 2 Chronicles 35:1–36:23, Ezra, and Nehemiah 7:6–8:12; Psalm 151 purports to be an additional psalm of David. More interesting are the Additions to Esther. Inserted at strategic points, these clearly secondary additions, which include among other things prayers by Mordecai and Esther, serve to give a distinctively religious slant to the Book of Esther, otherwise noted for its failure to mention God or even prayer. The Additions to Daniel have a less unified purpose. Susanna (chapter 13 of the Greek Daniel) is a delightful little story affirming God's vindication of those who hope in him, and Bel and the Dragon (chapter 14 of the Greek Daniel) exposes the folly of idolatry. The Prayer of Azariah and the Three Young Men, placed after Daniel 3:23, is a prayer of trust in God offered up by Azariah (i.e., Abednego—Dan. 1:7) and his companions (Shadrach and Meshach) in the fiery furnace. It is noteworthy for its expression of confidence that God will accept the sacrifice of a contrite heart and a humble spirit. Another noteworthy (and secondary) prayer is the Prayer of Manasseh, apparently composed to give content to the prayer of repentance offered by Manasseh that is mentioned in 2 Chronicles 33:12–13. It includes a powerful expression of contrition for sin and trust in the grace of God. Two books are associated with Jeremiah: the Letter of Jeremiah is an attack on idolatry, and Baruch, attributed to Jeremiah's secretary (cf. Jer. 36:4–8), extols the virtues of Wisdom, which is identified with the Law.

Two other Wisdom books are contained in the Apocrypha. The Wisdom of Solomon, ostensibly related to Solomon, deliberates on the future reward of the righteous and punishment of the ungodly, sings the praises of Wisdom, and, through a retelling of the exodus story, celebrates God's exaltation of Israel through the very things by which her enemies were punished. Affirmations, among other things, of the preexistence and immortality of the soul indicate a considerable degree of Greek influence upon the author. Ecclesiasticus contains the teachings, in a form resembling that of the Book of Proverbs, of a second century B.C. Jewish teacher named Jesus ben Sira. The author praises and personifies (cf. Prov. 8:22–31) Wisdom, whom he identifies with the Law, and provides practical precepts for everyday living. The book contains numerous parallels to the ethical sections of the New Testament, especially the Book of James.

Two of the most popular books in the Apocrypha tell the stories, undoubtedly legendary, of two otherwise unknown Jews. Set in the time of Nebuchadnezzar, Judith is a vivid and dramatic narrative of a beautiful Jewish widow, who, through a combination of extraordinary courage and trust in God, delivers her people in a time of crisis. Tobit, purportedly from the time of the Assyrian exile, combines the themes of quest, romance, and overcoming the demonic in a story of God's healing of his faithful servant Tobit and deliverance of the unfortunate widow Sarah. It testifies to a developing demonology and angelology within Judaism, and emphasizes the importance of charitable deeds, containing some striking parallels to the ethical teaching in the New Testament, including a negative form of the Golden Rule (cf. Matt. 7:12).

Four books are associated, in name at least, with the Maccabees, those Jewish heroes who, led by Judas Maccabeus, waged the Maccabean Revolt in the second century B.C. against the Greek tyrant Antiochus IV, who attempted to ban the practice of Judaism. First Maccabees, the longest and most detailed account, is an especially important historical source for the revolt. Apart from his obvious support of the revolt and opposition to the hellenization of Judaism that preceded it, the author's primary religious perspective seems to be that God—or, rather, heaven—helps those who take initiative and trust in him. Second Maccabees is more openly theological and affirms such ideas as the glories of martyrdom, the sufferings of the martyr as being expiatory for the sins of the nation, the resurrection of the body, prayer for the dead, and the intercession of the saints. Both books are of first importance for understanding the historical setting for Hanukkah, the Jewish festival of rededication of the temple, which originates from the Maccabean Revolt.

Fourth Maccabees, an imaginative elaboration on the martyrdoms in 2 Maccabees, is a distinctive melding of Greek and Jewish ideas. Affirming the immortality of the righteous and the eternal punishment of the wicked, the author seeks to demonstrate that inspired reason, guided by the Law, is supreme ruler over the passions. Third Maccabees tells not of the Maccabees, but of the plight of Egyptian Jews near the end of the third century B.C.; its focus is on God's faithfulness to his people.

Second Esdras, purportedly composed by Ezra, was written in response to the destruction of Jerusalem by the Romans in A.D. 70. Second Esdras centers around the theme of God's justice in the light of the devastating defeat of his people Israel by a godless nation. It includes significant discussions on the nature of sin and its connection with Adam (cf. Rom. 5), the limitations of human understanding, the signs of the end, the final judgment, the intermediate state between death and the final judgment, the destruction of the Roman Empire, and the coming Messiah. Both in its overall orientation and in many of its details, 2 Esdras contains a number of striking parallels to the Book of Revelation, with which it is contemporary.

The Jews wrote numerous other works that are not included in any Christian canon. Many of them were attributed to major Old Testament figures; they are called the Pseudepigrapha. Although the literature is too vast and varied to summarize here, many Pseudepigrapha contain visionary journeys through heaven (or a series of heavens) and hell, an increased interest in angels and demons, speculations on the origins of sin and the nature of the final judgment, various expectations of a Messiah, predictions of the end of time, and ethical exhortations. The Pseudepigrapha attest to the rich theological diversity within Judaism during the intertestamental period.

The New Testament Apocrypha is an amorphous collection of writings that are for the most part either about, or pseudonymously attributed to, New Testament figures. These books are generally modeled after the literary forms found in the New Testament: there are apocryphal gospels, acts, letters, and revelations. Unlike the Old Testament Apocrypha, the New Testament Apocrypha have never been viewed as canonical by any of the major branches of Christianity, nor is there any reason to believe that the traditions they record have any historical validity. Nonetheless, some of these books were widely used by Christians throughout the Middle Ages and have left their mark on the church.

Numerous apocryphal gospels were produced by early Christians. Many of them, such as the Gospel of Thomas, the Gospel of Mary, and the Dialogue of the Savior, were composed by heretical groups like the Gnostics and purport to give "secret," unorthodox teachings of Jesus. Others fill in gaps in the New Testament Gospels, usually with a heightened sense of the miraculous. The Protevangelium of James, for example, tells the story of Mary's birth, childhood, and eventual marriage to Joseph (a widower with children), culminating in a detailed account of the birth of Jesus (in a cave) and a strong affirmation of Mary's virginity. The Infancy Gospel of Thomas narrates Jesus' childhood from age five to age twelve, with the child Jesus performing numerous miracles, sometimes to the point of absurdity (e.g., bringing clay sparrows to life). The Gospel of Nicodemus (also called the Acts of Pilate), provides a detailed account of Jesus' trial and descent into hell. The Gospel of Peter presents, after an otherwise straightforward account of the crucifixion, a vivid narration of the resurrection of Jesus: two angels come down from heaven, enter the tomb, and exit with Jesus, followed by a talking Cross.

The apocryphal acts (Acts of Andrew, Acts of John, Acts of Paul, Acts of Peter, and Acts of Thomas) purport to trace the journeys of the apostles, with Thomas going all the way to India. Three features in these books stand out. First, they are filled with supernatural deeds: miracles abound, especially the raising of the dead, and even a talking lion gets baptized. Second, they promote a celibate lifestyle, even among husbands and wives. Third, they glorify martyrdom, especially among the apostles: Andrew is crucified, Paul is beheaded, Peter is crucified upside down, and Thomas is executed with spears; only John is spared a martyr's death.

There are also apocryphal letters (e.g., 3 Corinthians, Letter to the Laodiceans [cf. Col. 4:16], and Pseudo-Titus), which tend to reflect heretical notions, and apocryphal apocalypses (e.g., Apocalypse of Peter and Apocalypse of Paul). The latter present, in contrast to the relatively reserved statements in the New Testament, vivid descriptions of hell, where sinners are punished in accordance with their sins: blasphemers, for example, hang by their tongues over a blazing fire. In addition, the Apocalypse of Paul purports to give a detailed narration of Paul's rapture to the third heaven (cf. 2 Cor. 12:2).

Apart from the issue of canonicity, the Old Testament Apocrypha has had a pronounced and pervasive influence on Western culture. The stories, themes, and language of these books (especially Judith, Tobit, Susanna, the Maccabees, Ecclesiasticus, and the Wisdom of Solomon) have been utilized by literary figures such as Shakespeare, Milton, and Longfellow, composers such as Charles Wesley, Handel, and Rubinstein, and artists such as Michaelangelo, Rembrandt, and van Dyck. The New Testament Apocrypha, though less influential, has contributed to the traditions about Jesus and the travels and fate of the apostles, not to mention the development of the Christian concept of hell, most notably through the *Inferno* of Dante.

Joseph L. Trafton

See also Bible, Canon of the.

Bibliography. J. H. Charlesworth, ed., *The Old Testament Pseudepigrapha;* J. K. Elliott, ed., *The Apocryphal New Testament;* E. Hennecke and W. Schneemelcher, eds., *New Testament Apocrypha;* B. M. Metzger, *An Introduction to the Apocrypha;* G. W. E. Nickelsburg, *Jewish Literature Between the Bible and the Mishnah;* E. Schürer, *The History of the Jewish People in the Age of Jesus Christ;* H. F. D. Sparks, ed., *The Apocryphal Old Testament;* M. E. Stone, ed., *Jewish Writings of the Second Temple Period.*

Apollyon. *See* Abaddon.

Apostasy. (Heb. *měšûbâ,;* Gk. *parapiptō, aphistēmi, apostasia).* Defection from the faith, an act of unpardonable rebellion against God and his truth. The sin of apostasy results in the abandonment of Christian doctrine and conduct. With respect to the covenant relationship established through prior profession of faith (passive profession in the case of baptized infants), apostates place themselves under the curse and wrath of God as covenant breakers, having entered into a state of final and irrevocable condemnation. Those who apostatize are thus numbered among the reprobate. Since the resurrection of Christ, there is no distinction between blasphemy against Christ and blasphemy against the Holy Spirit (cf. Matt. 12:31–32; Heb. 6:4–6; 10:26–29; 1 John 5:16–17). G. C. Berkouwer comments: "We must underscore the deep seriousness of the biblical warning against apostasy 'after enlightenment' and 'after the knowledge of the truth.' This is the apostasy which reviles the Spirit of grace and despises the Son of God and crucifies the Man of Sorrows anew" (p. 343). Berkouwer is correct to refute the idea that this sin against the Holy Spirit is a *mysterium iniquitatis* ("a mystery of sin"), a sin difficult, if at all possible, to define precisely in the Bible.

Apostatizing from God's redemptive covenant is an act of unpardonable transgression and rebellion. All other sins are forgiven on true repentance and faith. Those who fall out of fellowship with the saints are restored to full communion through confession of sin and reaffirmation of faith in Jesus Christ. Excommunication, as a final step in the process of ecclesiastical discipline, is undertaken in the hope of restoring the wayward sinner who has fallen into grievous sin (1 Cor. 5:1–5).

Israel of old repeatedly broke covenant with God. By impugning the name and works of Yahweh, Israel despised her calling and proved to be a stubborn and disobedient nation. Pentateuchal law identifies covenantal faithlessness as apostasy (see, e.g., the curses of the covenant pronounced on Mount Ebal by the Israelites in Deut. 27:9–26). With respect to temporal blessing in the land of promise, restoration of Israel to divine favor after covenant breaking was always a consequence of divine grace and mercy, not because of meritorious works on Israel's part.

In biblical prophecy apostasy is an eschatological sign of the impending day of the Lord, a precursor of the final day of judgment. Ancient Israel's experience of divine wrath and displeasure served as typological foreshadowings of that latter day. The increase in apostasy in these last days of the church's wilderness experience is associated with the appearance of the "man of lawlessness" (2 Thess. 2:1–3).

MARK W. KARLBERG

See also BACKSLIDING; BLASPHEMY AGAINST THE HOLY SPIRIT; DENIAL.

Bibliography. G. C. Berkouwer, *Sin;* idem, *The Return of Christ;* A. A. Hoekema, *The Bible and the Future;* H. Ridderbos, *Paul: An Outline of His Theology.*

Apostle (Gk. *apostolos*). Envoy, ambassador, or messenger commissioned to carry out the instructions of the commissioning agent.

Etymology and Usage of the Term. Pre-Christian use of *apostolos* in the sense of messenger is rare. More common is the verb *apostellō,* referring to the sending of a fleet or an embassy. Only in Herodotus (1.21; 5.38) is it used of a personal envoy. Josephus employs it once *(Antiquities* 17.11.1) in the classical sense of an embassy. Epictetus *(Discourse* 3.22) speaks of the ideal Cynic teacher as one "sent by Zeus" to be a messenger of the gods and an "overseer" of human affairs.

The Septuagint uses *apostellō* or *exapostellō* some seven hundred times to translate the Hebrew *šālaḥ* ("stretch out," "send"). More than the act of sending, this word includes the idea of the authorization of a messenger. The noun *apostolos* is found only in 1 Kings 14:6, where the commissioning and empowering of the prophet are clearly in mind. Thus, the Septuagint uses the *apostellō* word-group to denote the authorization of an individual to fulfill a particular function, with emphasis on the one who sends, not on the one who is sent.

The noun *apostolos* appears seventy-nine times in the New Testament (ten in the Gospels; twenty-eight in Acts; thirty-eight in the Epistles; and three in Revelation). The vast majority of these occurrences are found in Luke–Acts (thirty-four) and in the Pauline epistles (thirty-four), and refer to those appointed by Christ for a special function in the church. Their unique place is based not only on having witnessed the resurrection, but also on having been commissioned and empowered by the resurrected Lord to proclaim the gospel to all nations.

In the New Testament *apostolos* is applied to Jesus as the Sent One of God (Heb. 3:1), to those sent by God to preach to Israel (Luke 11:49), to those sent by churches (2 Cor. 8:23; Phil. 2:25), and most often, to the individuals who had been appointed by Christ to preach the gospel of the kingdom. This latter category, however, is understood differently by New Testament writers. For example, Luke–Acts uses the term "apostle" to refer almost exclusively to the Twelve, while Paul uses it in relation to a broader group of individuals. The expression "all the apostles" in 1 Corinthians 15:7 seems to include more than the twelve referred to in verse 5. James is considered here, and in Galatians 1:19, to be an apostle. Barnabas is referred to as an apostle in Acts 14:14 (cf. 11:22–24; 13:1–4). Paul calls Andronicus and Junias apostles in Romans 16:7. In this broader sense, an apostle was a witness to the resurrection of Christ, sent by him to make disciples of all nations.

Christ the Apostle. Although there is only one explicit reference to Jesus as an apostle (Heb. 3:1), implicit references to his having been "sent" by the Father are found throughout the New Testament. Nowhere is this more pronounced than in the Gospel of John, where Christ's entire ministry is qualified by the term *apostellō* ("send"). As the Father sent his Son into the world (3:17, 34; 5:36–38; 6:29, 57; 10:36; 17:3, 8, 18, 21, 23; 20:21), Jesus in turn "sends out" his disciples (4:38; 17:18) to continue and extend his mission. Thus, all apostleship finds its meaning in Jesus the Apostle, sent by God to be the Savior of the world (1 John 4:14).

The Twelve. Jesus had a large number of disciples during his ministry, but not all of them were apostles. The Twelve were chosen out of a wider group both to be with Jesus as disciples and to be sent out to preach and teach as apostles. There are four lists of the Twelve in the New Testament, one in each of the three Synoptic Gospels (Matt. 10:1–4; Mark 3:13–19; Luke 6:12–16) and one in Acts (1:13). These lists are roughly the same, representing four variant forms of a single early oral tradition.

Matthew and Mark identify the Twelve as apostles only once, and in each case, in the context of a missionary journey (Matt. 10:2; Mark 6:30). Here the word designates function rather than status. Luke, however, frequently and almost exclusively calls the Twelve "apostles" (6:13; 9:10; 17:5; 22:14; 24:10; Acts 1:26; 2:43; 4:35, 36, 37; 5:2, 12, 18; 8:1). Except for Luke 11:49 and Acts 14:14, Luke applies *apostolos* only to the Twelve. Because they had been called by Jesus, had been with Jesus throughout his ministry, and had witnessed his resurrection, they possessed the best possible knowledge of what Jesus had said and done. Commissioned by the risen Christ and empowered by the Holy Spirit, they became witnesses to the saving work of God in Christ. The identification of the Twelve as apostles finds its basis not only in the use of this title for them in the Gospel narrative, but also in the post-Easter task given to them by Jesus (Matt. 28:19–20; Mark 16:15–18; Luke 24:48–49; John 20:21–23; Acts 1:8). Thus, the essential qualification of an apostle is being called and sent by Christ. In the case of Matthias, additional qualifications come to light. In addition to the divine call, the person must have been a disciple of Jesus from John's baptism to the ascension, and specifically a witness of the resurrection (Acts 1:21–22).

Jesus' choice of twelve disciples to form an inner circle of followers served to symbolize the truth that he had come to build a new house of Israel. The Twelve formed the nucleus of this new people of God, corresponding to the twelve tribes of Israel, and signifying God's saving activity at work in Jesus and his followers. Their number implies that they were destined primarily to work among the children of Israel. Although not confined to the Jews, the mission of the Twelve had special relation to the twelve tribes of Israel, as emphasized in the promise of Matthew 19:28.

Paul the Apostle. Since Paul had not accompanied Jesus during his earthly ministry, he did not meet the apostolic criteria of Acts 1:21–22. It is clear, however, that he considered himself to be an apostle. Even though the only place in the Book of Acts where Paul is called an apostle is in reference to the apostles of the church in Antioch (14:4, 14), Luke's portrayal of Paul's ministry as paradigmatic for the church gives implicit support to his apostolic claims. Not only does Acts depict Paul as manifesting the signs of an apostle, but in its three accounts of the Damascus Road encounter, his apostolic task is presented as the direct action of the risen Christ (9:3–5; 22:6–8; 26:12–18; cf. 2 Cor. 4:6; Gal. 1:16).

Paul's own claim to apostleship is likewise based on the divine call of Christ (Rom. 1:1; 1 Cor. 1:1; Gal. 1:1, 15; cf. 2 Cor. 1:1; Eph. 1:1; Col. 1:1; 1 Tim. 1:1; 2 Tim. 1:1; Titus 1:1). He is an apostle, "not from men nor by man, but by Jesus Christ and God the Father, who raised him from the dead" (Gal. 1:1). His encounter with the resurrected Jesus served as the basis for his unique claim to be an "apostle to the Gentiles" (Rom. 11:13). Paul bases his apostleship on the grace of God, not on ecstatic gifts or the signs of an apostle (2 Cor. 12). His apostolic commission is to serve God primarily through preaching the gospel (Rom. 1:9; 15:19; 1 Cor. 1:17).

Paul uses the word "apostle" in more than one sense. At times he employs the term in the broader sense of messenger or agent (2 Cor. 8:23; Phil. 2:25). More often, however, Paul uses the term to refer to those who had been commissioned by the risen Lord to the apostolic task. Included in this category are the Twelve (although he never explicitly applies the title of apostle to them as a group), Peter (Gal. 1:18), Paul himself (Rom. 1:1; 1 Cor. 1:1; 9:1–2; 15:8–10; Gal. 2:7–8), James the brother of Jesus (Gal. 1:19; cf. Acts 15:13), Barnabas (1 Cor. 9:1–6; Gal. 2:9; cf. Acts 14:4, 14), and possibly others (Rom. 16:7). In addition to understanding apostleship in terms of its basis in a divine call, Paul views the life of an apostle as being one of self-sacrificial service that entails suffering (1 Cor. 4:9–13; 15:30–32; 2 Cor. 4:7–12; 11:23–29).

Apostles and the Spirit. The primary function of the apostles was to witness to Christ. The Twelve had intimate knowledge of his life, and a wider group had been witnesses to his resurrection. Their commissioning by the risen Lord to worldwide witness (Acts 1:8), however, was incomplete without the anointing of the Spirit. Only after Pentecost were they empowered by the Spirit for their ministry of word and deed. Their witness to Christ was not only empowered, but also guided and validated by the Spirit (John 14:26). Thus, their full apostolic vocation was realized only in the Spirit (John 14–17). Paul viewed apostleship as a gift of the Spirit (1 Cor. 12:28), which was often accompanied by miraculous signs and mighty works (2 Cor. 12:12). Such signs and wonders, however, were clearly secondary to the apostolic functions of preaching and teaching.

Apostolic Authority. Having direct knowledge of the incarnate Word, and being sent out as authorized agents of the gospel, the apostles provided the authentic interpretation of the life and teaching of Jesus. Because their witness to Christ was guided by the Spirit (John 15:26–27), the apostles' teaching was considered normative for the church. They were regarded as the "pillars" (Gal. 2:9) and "foundation" (Eph. 2:20; cf. Rev. 21:14) of the church, and their teaching became the norm for Christian faith and practice. The deposit of revelation transmitted by the apostles and preserved in its written form in the New Testament thus forms the basis of postapostolic preaching and teaching in the church.

It is evident that the apostles formed the nucleus of primitive Christianity. The New Testament highlights their function as apostles, without delineating in detail the authoritative nature of their office in relation to the church. What is emphasized is that their apostolic commission authorized them to preach (1 Cor. 1:17); to be ambassadors for Christ (2 Cor. 5:20; Eph. 6:20); to be witnesses to all nations (Luke 24:48); and to make disciples of all peoples (Matt. 28:19).

R. David Rightmire

Bibliography. F. Agnew, *JBL* 105 (1986): 75–96; C. K. Barrett, *Signs of an Apostle;* W. Baur, *New Testament Apocrypha* 2 (1965): 35–74; O. Cullmann, *Early Church;* E. J. Goodspeed, *The Twelve;* L. Goppelt, *Apostolic and Post-Apostolic Times;* J. B. Lightfoot, *Galatians,* pp. 92–101; H. Mosbech, *ST* 2 (1948): 166–200; D. Müller, *NIDNTT,* 1:126–33; J. Munck, *ST* 3 (1949): 96–100; K. Rengstorf, *TDNT,* 1:398–447; W. Schneemelcher, *New Testament Apocrypha* 2 (1965): 25–34; R. Schnackenburg, *Apostolic History and the Gospel,* pp. 287–303.

Apostleship, Gift of. *See* Holy Spirit, Gifts of.

Appear, Appearance. ***The Old Testament.*** The Hebrew word most commonly used for appearance in the Old Testament is *rāʾâ.* The seeing of God leads to an understanding of his nature and his purposes for Israel. When people appear before God, their loyalty and obedience to God are disclosed.

The Appearing of God. One of the defining characteristics of God in the Old Testament is that he is the one who appears (Exod. 6:3). The salvation history of Israel is punctuated with and propelled by appearances from God. God appeared to Abram (Gen. 12:7), Isaac (Gen. 26:2), and Jacob (Gen. 28:12–17), promising that their descendants were chosen by him. Subsequently he appeared to Moses, promising deliverance (Exod. 3:2) and establishing a covenant with Israel (Exod. 19–24). Stephen refers to this central feature of Jewish religion (Acts 7:2). Appearing by its very nature requires one or more people to perceive/receive the appearance. While later rabbinic texts hold that a direct vision of God is reserved for the righteous in the age to come, the Pentateuch in particular recounts that God was visible (in various forms) at certain moments to certain people.

God appears for specific purposes, so those who receive his appearances also receive some sort of commission. The appearance of God both validates a person's role (Exod. 4:5) and initiates a new stage in God's revelation of himself and his purposes for Israel. A common pattern in the Old Testament is that through his appearance to one person God subsequently reveals himself to all of Israel (Lev. 9:23). In the psalms God's appearance in Zion is for the general benefit of those who are faithful (Ps. 84:7). The religious significance and historical reality of appearances of God are signified by commemorative sites, such as El-bethel, Shechem, and Shiloh.

God appears in the Old Testament to reveal his character, identity, and purposes for Israel. This quality of disclosure is seen in the fact that an appearance of God is typically connected with a revelation of his glory (Exod. 16:10) or with a "word of the Lord" (Gen. 15:1). At his appearances God reveals himself as one who listens and responds (Judg. 13; 1 Kings 9:2–3), who comforts and cares (2 Chron. 1:7). God's appearances make clear that his purpose for Israel is both her deliverance and her loyalty to him (e.g., Num. 14:10–12). God's appearing functions also as a reward for obedience (Lev. 9:6). The appearing of the righteous God can be threatening and terrifying (Judg. 13), but generally God's appearances provide hope. Remembrance of God's appearances provides the basis for trust in God's faithfulness and love (Jer. 31:3).

God makes his appearances in various forms, most typically through an angel (who can look very human [Gen. 18:2; Judg. 13:6]), in visions, and in dreams.

While the majority of Old Testament references to God's appearances tell of specific historical moments, there is also expectation of future appearances. The future appearance of God or God's messenger entails judgment (Mal. 3:1–5) but also the vindication of belief in him (Pss. 84:7; 102:16). One of the most profound expressions of religious longing is the hope for a vision of God (Ps. 42:2). Just as several of God's past appearances are connected with specific places, so future appearances are expected in religiously significant locales, particularly the temple and Zion.

People Appear before God. There are several references to God's people appearing before him (e.g., Exod. 23:17; 34:20; Deut. 31:11; Isa. 1:12). Such references speak not just of an obedient response to the kingly authority of God or of cultic observances but of Israel's requirement to be conscious of and accountable for what she knows of the revealed truth about God. Just as God's appearances are a self-disclosure, so Israel's appearance before God discloses the adequacy or inadequacy of her response to God's self-revelation. Appearing in the presence of God is part of establishing (1 Sam. 1:22) and maintaining (Deut. 16:16) a special relationship with the God of Israel.

The New Testament. *Appearing of God, His Purposes and Gifts.* Reference to the appearance of God (in the form of an angel) occurs primarily in the birth and resurrection narratives of the Gospels (Matt. 1:20–21; 28:2–7; Mark 16:5; Luke 1:11; 22:43). These appearances announce and confirm the good news of God's deliverance in Jesus Christ. As in the Old Testament God's appearances serve to direct

(Matt. 2:13) and disclose his purposes (Matt. 17:1; Mark 9:4; Luke 9:31). God's gift of eternal life is made manifest in Christ for those who believe (1 John 1:1–2).

Appearing of Christ. While reference is made to Christ's presently appearing before God in a priestly capacity on behalf of believers (Heb. 9:24), the major referent is to the post-resurrection earthly appearances of Jesus Christ. In the Gospels, Acts, and writings of Paul the resurrection is confirmed when the risen Christ's appearance is perceived by the disciples (e.g., Luke 24:34, 36–45; cf. John 21:14). Such appearances occur only before Christ's ascension (John 20:17). Their import is to reveal the meaning of his life, death, and resurrection (Luke 24:25–27) to those who would witness to him. Seeing the risen Jesus confirms that he is to be worshiped (Matt. 28:17). The appearance of the risen Lord in bodily form is a distinctive and definitive type of appearance that signifies the dawn of the new age of salvation.

Just as the authority of an Old Testament prophet or leader involved having received an appearance from God, so an essential requirement for apostleship in the New Testament is having received an appearance from the risen Christ. Again as in the Old Testament the appearance of God is purposeful and those who receive it also receive a commission (Acts 10:40–42). The connection between commission and appearance is especially clear in Paul's life. Luke recounts that the Lord Jesus appeared to Saul (Acts 9:17) for the purpose of appointing him to bear witness to the Gentiles (Acts 26:16). Paul regards this appearance as both a validation of his apostleship and as central to the message of the gospel (1 Cor. 15:3–8).

The centrality to the Christian faith of belief in Christ's appearance may be the background to the Pastorals' use. There the concept of Christ appearing includes his incarnation and work of salvation. Christ's appearing is spoken of in the abstract as something that the writer and his readers share and understand (1 Tim. 3:16). While Christ's appearing is connected with the abolition of death (2 Tim. 1:10), it is not a confirmation of the resurrection so much as of the truth of the gospel and the worthwhileness of witnessing to Jesus Christ (2 Tim. 4:1). Rather than using the concept of appearing in connection with historical moments, it has become shorthand for the continuing salvific work of Christ (Titus 2:11; 3:4).

The Gospel of John refers to the appearing (*emphanizō* or *phaneroō*) of Christ also in this more abstract way. The Fourth Gospel speaks not only of the bodily appearance of the resurrected Christ, but also of his revelation to Israel (1:31) and to the people God gave him (John 17:6). Christ's identity appears through his signs (2:11) and as believers love him (14:21–24).

The New Testament does not just proclaim that Christ has appeared but hopes for a second appearance. This is implicit in Jesus' promise to his disciples in Mark 16:7 and may be the proper referent for Jesus' words in Matthew 24:30. Other New Testament writings speak of the time when Christ will be revealed or appear again (Col. 3:4; 1 Tim. 6:14; Titus 2:13; 1 John 2:28). The expected appearing of Christ is a warning to believers (1 John 2:28), a promise of defeat of the enemy (2 Thess. 2:8), and an encouragement (1 Peter 5:4). At that second appearing God will reward those who have believed in him (Heb. 9:28).

Christ's first appearance in all of its facets (incarnation, death, and resurrection) served to express God's concern for and deliverance of all people. It is visible to those with eyes to see. Christians hope for a second appearance when all the promises entailed in the first appearance will be delivered and when God's character and purposes and their identity as the faithful ones will be fully manifest.

Appearance of People. As in the Old Testament, the New Testament refers to people appearing before God—at the judgment seat (2 Cor. 5:10). The most interesting referent, however, has to do with the revelation of believers at the end. When Christ appears so too will those who have believed in him (Col. 3:4; cf. Rom. 8:19).

L. Ann Jervis

Appoint. ***The Old Testament.*** The basic meaning of "appoint" is either "visit" or "establish or set in authority." The extension of visit carries the idea of appointment, meaning to set in place (as a time, place, or event). The theological importance focuses on the appointing, consecrating, or commissioning of persons for special service to the Lord and his people. It can also carry implications for God's providence or the establishment of laws or principles.

Consecration for Service. Consecration is a special type of appointment. Four examples can be noted: (1) the consecration of Aaron and his sons (Exod. 28–29); (2) the appointment of Levites as servants of God (Num. 3–8); (3) the naming of seventy elders to assist Moses (Num. 11, 24–25); and (4) the commissioning of Moses' successor (Num. 27).

The appointment of the seventy to assist Moses was at God's initiative. Their ordination involved standing with Moses to receive the Spirit that rested upon Moses (Num. 11:17–25). Joshua's ordination consisted of receiving commissioning while standing before the priest and the congregation (Num. 27:18–23). Moses laid his hand on Joshua as a symbol of the transference of authority.

Of primary significance is the ordination of Aaron and the Levites. Aaron and his sons alone were to serve as priests (Exod. 28:1), to offer sacrifices (Num. 8:1–7), and to bless the people (Num. 6:22–27). Aaron was anointed (Lev. 8:12) and the special vestments previewed those worn by preexilic monarchs (see Exod. 28). Because it marked the beginning of the priesthood in Israel, the consecration of Aaron to this office was of special significance. The entire event and its accompanying instructions were completely detailed.

As an extension of the appointment of Aaron and his sons, they were to bless the people (Num. 6:22–27). In reality, it is God's own blessing of his people. God himself commanded Aaron and his sons to place the Lord's name on the Israelites (6:27).

The Synoptic Gospels. Foundational to the understanding of "appoint" in the New Testament is Jesus' statement about the kingdom that he has appointed to his followers (Luke 9–10). The New Testament practice is often associated with the laying on of hands.

Jesus appointed twelve disciples to be with him and that he could send out to preach (Mark 3:14). The Great Commission was given on the basis of Jesus' authority (Matt. 28:18–20). The One who appointed the kingdom to Jesus, who granted him authority, was God the Father Almighty.

Acts. Matthias was appointed by the casting of lots to replace Judas among the Twelve (1:12–26). Most significant is the reference to Barnabas and Paul and their appointment of elders in every church after prayer and fasting (14:23).

At the conclusion of the first missionary journey Paul and Barnabas established leadership in the new congregations. There remains a question in Acts 14:23 regarding who appointed the elders—the apostles or the congregation. The most natural reading of the passage suggests that Paul and Barnabas did. Perhaps in these settings the apostles' wisdom was necessary to establish leadership, though the apostles' selection may have been confirmed by vote of the congregations (see also Titus 1:5).

In Acts 26:16 Paul recounts his experience with the risen Christ. God appointed or placed Paul into service. The statement is extremely forceful, offering the mental picture of God picking up Paul and pointing him in the divinely intended direction. DAVID S. DOCKERY

Archangel. *See* ANGEL.

Ark. Gold-covered acacia wood box measuring 2.5 x 1.5 x 1.5 cubits that for the Israelite people symbolized the presence of God. It is first mentioned in Exodus 25:10–22 among the furnishings of the tabernacle. The ark's top cover supported two winged creatures called cherubim. They faced each other across the top of the ark and their outstretched wings touched at the tips. The mobility of the ark was insured by two permanently attached carrying poles, reflecting the fact that the people of Israel and their God had no fixed dwellingplace. Even when the ark was permanently located in the Holy of Holies, the poles remained (1 Kings 8), a visible reminder that God was "tenting" among his people, but that his presence could be withdrawn.

The practical function of the ark was to protect and preserve various sacred objects. In the early accounts of the ark only the Mount Sinai covenant tablets are so protected, giving rise to the common epithet, the "ark of the covenant" (Exod. 25:16; 1 Kings 8:9), or a variant, "ark of the LORD's covenant" (Num. 14:44). Later traditions also mentioned a portion of preserved manna and Aaron's rod as being in the ark (Heb. 9:4). The ark also had a military role, leading the march of the people of Israel in the wilderness (Num. 10:33), circling the walls of Jericho (Josh. 4:6), and going forth to battle against the Philistines (1 Sam. 4:5).

Scripture associates God's physical presence with the ark. Moses addressed the ark as "the LORD" in the wilderness (Num. 10:35). The ark was sacred, indeed, dangerous to friends and foes alike. The Philistines recognized its holiness, and to neutralize its power they placed it in the temple of Dagon, to Dagon's distress (1 Sam. 5:8). The awesome holiness of the ark was demonstrated when Uzzah was killed for touching the ark when he tried to prevent it from falling (1 Chron. 13:10).

In the temple, the ark occupied the Holy of Holies. With a permanent location, the theological understanding of the ark changed. The cover of the ark was seen as the throne of God with the cherubim supporting him and setting aside the space between their wings as his seat. Interestingly, Solomon placed huge cherubim to flank the ark in the temple, thus setting apart the entire ark and its surrounding space as God's seat. Solomon aimed to make a place where God could "dwell forever" (1 Kings 8:13). Hezekiah, seeking divine aid against the Assyrians, called on the "God of Israel, enthroned between the cherubim" (2 Kings 19:15).

The ark disappears from post-Solomonic biblical history except for a passing reference in 2 Chronicles 35:3, where the Levites are charged by Josiah no longer to carry the ark about. This may be as much a reflection of a postexilic understanding of Josiah (the new David who would correct the behavior of the Levites) as that of the actual ark itself.

In the return, according to the prophet Jeremiah, the ark would not be remembered or replaced, because Jerusalem would be "The Throne of the Lord" (3:16; the only prophetic mention of the ark). In the new temple envisioned by Ezekiel, no ark is mentioned. There will be no ark because in the new kingdom God will no longer be just a God of Israel, dwelling in a limited space, but will reveal himself as the God of all nations ruling with a new covenant. In Revelation 11:19 (the only New Testament mention) the ark has returned to the direct care of God, sacred, but no longer functional. In the New Testament, Christ himself is the bearer of the new covenant and the focus of God's presence.

Thomas W. Davis

Bibliography. R. G. Boling and G. E. Wright, *Joshua;* R. de Vaux, *Ancient Israel;* M. Haran, *Temple and Temple Service in Ancient Israel.*

Armageddon. A name occurring only once in the Bible and designating the place where the last great battle of the ages will take place (Rev. 16:16). It will coincide with the second coming of Christ (Rev. 16:15) and there all of the hosts of evil will be defeated (Rev. 19:11–21).

Armageddon is a Hebrew word, although it does not occur in the Old Testament. Its meaning is not exactly clear, but it is best taken to mean Mount Megiddo, since "Har" in Hebrew means mountain and "Mageddon" is the place-name of Megiddo.

In Old Testament history Megiddo was a place of numerous decisive battles because of the broad plain that stood before it. Deborah and Barak defeated Sisera and his Canaanite army there (Judg. 4–5), Gideon drove off the Midianites and Amalekites (Judg. 6), Saul and the army of Israel were defeated because of their failure to trust in God (1 Sam. 31), and the Egyptian army under Pharaoh Neco killed Josiah, king of Judah (2 Kings 23:29). Although these decisive battles were fought before Megiddo, the place-name never became fixed in Jewish tradition as designating the place of decisive battle. However, given the fact that it was such a place, it is natural that John should use it to locate the final great battle on earth.

Some interpreters take John's designation literally, expecting the armies of the earth to gather against God in the endtimes below the remains of Old Testament Megiddo; others see in it a more figurative element. They point out that Megiddo was not really a mountain at all and that the battle will take place in the plain. Perhaps John designated it Mount Megiddo as a clue to its symbolic meaning, drawing together the historic place of conflict in Israel's history with the prophecies of Ezekiel that speak of the great eschatological conflict taking place in the mountains of Israel (Ezek. 39:2, 4, 17).

In any case, John sees the final triumph of God at Armageddon and offers that to the persecuted Christians as a word of comfort and hope that evil will not win, but is doomed to ultimate destruction.

Walter A. Elwell

Armor. Scripture frequently employs the imagery of armor as a metaphor for spiritual defense and protection. Old Testament symbolism emphasizes that God himself is the protector of his people. In Genesis 15, God prefaces his reiteration of the Abrahamic covenant with the assurance, "I am your shield, and your very great reward." Thereafter, the shield becomes perhaps the most common symbol of God's steadfast love and protection in the Old Testament. The metaphor is employed twenty-four times. It is a favorite device of David, who invokes this symbolism fifteen times, as in 2 Samuel 22:31, "He [the Lord] is a shield for all who take refuge in him." In Psalm 91:4, David reveals that security is grounded specifically on the absolute faithfulness of God. In light of God's unfailing fidelity, believers are exhorted to trust in the Lord and take refuge behind him as their protective shield (Ps. 115:9–11).

In the New Testament, the imagery of armor is invoked less frequently. Whereas Old Testament symbolism emphasizes the personification of God as shield, the New Testament reveals various aspects of God's redemptive provision as the means by which the believer may lay hold of God's protection. Such symbolism is employed by Paul (Rom. 13:12; Eph. 6:10–18; 1 Thess. 5:8). The most comprehensive and familiar, of course, is Paul's exhortation to the Ephesian believers to "put on the full armor of God." Paul's use of the Greek word *panoplia* in this connection refers to the basic outfit of a Roman soldier of his day. Believers are warned to take up each element of the armor provided because of the reality of opposition in the spiritual realm (Eph. 6:12) and because of the imminence of the day of the Lord (Rom. 13:12; 1 Thess. 5:8). Every Pauline reference to the symbolism of armor is accompanied by the command to "put on" the armor. This injunction implies that believers should consciously appropriate elements of God's redemptive provision needed for every area of vulnerability to spiritual attack.

Ralph E. Enlow, Jr.

Army. *See* War, Holy War.

Arrogance. *See* Pride.

Artemis. *See* Gods and Goddesses, Pagan.

Ascension of Jesus Christ. Event, recorded most fully in Acts 1:1–11, by which Christ concluded his postresurrection appearances, left the earth, and was taken up into heaven, not to return physically until his second advent. The New Testament authors theologically distinguish the event by connecting it to the atoning work of Jesus on the cross, the high priestly ministry of the exalted Christ, the regaining of Christ's glory with the Father, the sending of the Holy Spirit, the present power of Christ as ruler over all authorities and dominions in heaven and earth, and the fact that Jesus ascends for the benefit of his people.

The Old Testament. The Old Testament contains several stories of, and references to, "ascension" that may prefigure the ascension of Jesus. While the Old Testament contains stories of ascension that take place in dreams or visions (Gen. 28:12), straightforward narratives like that of the angel of the Lord ascending in the flame of the altar while Manoah and his wife look on (Judg. 13:20), and particularly of Elijah ascending to heaven in a whirlwind (2 Kings 2:11–12), although not related directly in the New Testament to the ascension of Jesus, are rightly seen as fundamental to the New Testament understanding that Jesus physically came down from heaven and returned there. Most of the Old Testament references to ascension into heaven emphasize that it is a divine act done only by God's power and not to be thought of as possible by mere humanity (Deut. 30:11–12; Prov. 30:4; Isa. 14:12–15).

The New Testament. There is very little reference to the ascension in the New Testament, although reference abounds to the exaltation of Christ. In virtually all these passages, a literal ascension from earth to heaven seems assumed, although some scholars have challenged whether Paul believed in such an ascension because of his movement from resurrection directly to exaltation in such passages as Romans 1:4; 8:34; and 1 Corinthians 15:12–28. Ephesians 4:10 and 1 Timothy 3:16 contradict this opinion, and it can be safely said that, given the clear references to Christ's ascension in other New Testament documents and the plain and relatively uniform witness of the New Testament to a bodily resurrection of Christ, that Paul and indeed all the New Testament authors would agree with Luke that after forty days of appearances to his disciples, Jesus experienced a literal, physical ascension into heaven, albeit in his "spiritual body" as the firstfruits of the final resurrection that is envisioned for us all at the end of time (cf. 1 Cor. 15:20–28; 1 Thess. 4:13–18).

Clear references to the ascension are found scattered throughout the New Testament so that it cannot be claimed that only Luke believed it happened. The most important passages are of course in Luke's writings: Luke 24:51 (textually in some dispute, but generally accepted) and Acts 1:1–11 recount the event in historical narrative, and Acts 2:31–35 assumes it. The Johannine references (John 3:13; 6:62; 14:3–4; 16:5–7; 20:17), when taken as a whole, clearly teach it, as do Hebrews 4:14; 6:20; and 1 Peter 3:21–22. Whatever theological conclusions are made by the New Testament authors about the ascension, they are made in the context of a belief in a historical event.

Ascension and Atonement. Particularly for the author of Hebrews, the ascension bridges the gap between the earthly work of Jesus Christ on the cross and his heavenly ministry as high priest, offering his sacrifice on the altar before the throne of God. This high priest is now seated "at the right hand of the throne of the Majesty in heaven" (8:1), signifying that there is no more act of sacrifice necessary; he neither sacrifices perpetually in heaven, nor is there any sacrifice on earth that can add to his death on the cross (10:11–14). The ascension is, however, viewed in some respects as the completion of that atoning work: it was necessary for Christ to "enter heaven . . . to appear . . . once for all at the end of the ages to do away with sin by the sacrifice of himself" (9:24–26). The author of Hebrews does not deny the significance of the historical crucifixion but argues that it is not complete until the blood is brought into the Most Holy Place and sprinkled in the appropriate way before the altar of God. Thus the ascension becomes an essential part of the atonement, allowing the historical Jesus who is now the reigning Priest/King to finish in heaven, the "true tabernacle," the sacrificial work necessary to accomplish our redemption.

Other New Testament authors explore this connection. The use of *anapherein* in Luke 24:51 may be theologically motivated to connect the ascension with the atonement. Acts 1:22 ties the whole earthly work of Jesus into a period between Jesus' baptism and the ascension. John, while not emphasizing the connection, nevertheless refers to it in John 3:13–14 and strongly teaches it through the idea of Jesus' being glorified both on the cross and in his return to the Father (John 7:39; 12:20–33; 17:5). The mention of extremes in Paul's use of the descent/ascent motif in Ephesians 4:10–11 calls to mind Paul's view that the nadir of Christ's descent was certainly the cross (Phil. 2:8); this "descent" is then connected in the passage with its opposite, his ascending "higher than all the heavens" to emphasize that Christ has the right to give gifts to men because he paid the price for them (cf. 1 Cor. 6:20). Romans 8:34 connects the present intercessory work of Christ with his work on the cross, viewing the death, resurrection, and exaltation (implying the ascension) of Jesus as one continuous event.

Ascension and Power. Clearly the greatest theological emphasis of the New Testament regarding the ascension is that Christ now regains the glory he had with the Father before the world began, is now able to send his powerful Spirit into the world, and reigns from heaven over every authority and power in heaven and earth. Thus, in John, Jesus connects attaining his glory and the sending of the Spirit with ascending to the Father (6:61–63; 7:39; 12:12–16; 16:5–11). Similarly, Acts 2:33–36 presents the ascended Jesus as the one who has been placed on the throne of David; the appearances of the ascended Christ are exclusively in Acts those of a powerful, enthroned Christ (Acts 7:56; 9:3–9 and pars.). Paul writes that God put his "mighty strength" to work "in Christ when he . . . seated him at his right hand in the heavenly realms, far above all rule and authority, power and dominion, and every title that can be given, not only in the present age but also in the one to come" (Eph. 1:20–21). It is from this exalted position that he "gave gifts to men" (Eph. 4:8–10). Peter, too, emphasizes the power that is now Christ's because of the ascension: "[He] has gone into heaven and is at God's right hand—with angels, authorities and powers in submission to him" (1 Peter 3:21–22).

The author of Hebrews shows this in his unique analogy between the exalted Son of God (4:14) who has "entered the inner sanctuary" and the priest/king Melchizedek (6:16–20). Melchizedek blessed Abraham, was king of righteousness and peace, and was without father, mother, genealogy, beginning of days or end of life (7:1–3). Only the ascended Jesus is powerful enough as the one who, like Melchizedek, has the power of an indestructible life (7:16) to enter before the throne of grace as a high priest who is "exalted above the heavens" to offer himself once for all (7:26–27).

The theological emphasis of the ascension story itself also lies in the concept of the newly gained power of the risen Son of God (Acts 1:1–11). The story's setting is one in which Jesus has been speaking to his disciples of the kingdom (1:3). He now appears in Jerusalem, the Old Testament seat of God's power and presence, in order to take final leave of them. They ask him if this is the time that he will restore the kingdom to Israel. His answer is his commission to them to be his witnesses, followed by his ascension. His authority over them is emphasized by the abundance of imperatives and promises in his brief dialogue with them: Six times in four sentences he either commands them to do something or promises something will happen to them (1:4–5, 7–8), and his chief promise to them is one of power (1:8).

The actual event itself demonstrates his power at every turn. He ascends in a cloud, echoing Daniel 7:13 with its connotations of power (Acts 1:9). The "intense gaze" (*atenizein*) of the apostles emphasizes the awe of the moment and contrasts the power of Jesus with their humility (1:10), as does their rebuke by the two men dressed in white (1:11). Finally, the link with the second coming of Jesus both in the way Jesus ascends (in a cloud) and in the words of the two men ("This same Jesus, who has been taken from you into heaven, will come back in the same way") describes the ascension of an exalted, seated King of heaven who will come back "in power and great glory" (Mark 13:26).

Ascension and Love. A little noticed aspect of the New Testament's theology of the ascension is the emphasis placed on Jesus' ascending *for his people.* This love manifests itself in the sending of his Spirit, an act dependent upon Jesus' ascension. Thus, in John, he tells the disciples that he goes to prepare a place "for you" (14:3) and that "it is for your good that I am going away. Unless I go away, the Counselor will not come to you; but if I go, I will send him to you" (16:7). The references to the ascension in Acts 1 and 2 both come in the context of a giving Christ who bestows the Spirit on his people, as does the reference in Ephesians 4:8–10. Hebrews emphasizes that his going into the "inner shrine" was "on our behalf" (6:20; 9:24 NRSV), and that since we have "a great high priest who has passed through the heavens . . . let us hold fast to our confession" (4:14 NRSV). These references to Jesus ascending "on our behalf" further connect the ascension with Jesus' atoning work, implying that, far from being a self-oriented, power-seeking act, the ascension is to be viewed as flowing from the same self-sacrificial love Jesus demonstrated for his people in his incarnation (2 Cor. 8:9) and crucifixion (Rom. 5:6–8). ANDREW H. TROTTER, JR.

See also JESUS CHRIST.

Bibliography. J. G. Davies, *He Ascended into Heaven;* W. Milligan, *The Ascension and Heavenly Priesthood of Our Lord;* G. C. Nicholson, *Death as Departure;* M. C. Parsons, *The Departure of Jesus in Luke–Acts;* H. B. Swete, *The Ascended Christ;* K. C. Thompson, *Received Up into Glory;* P. Toon, *The Ascension of Our Lord.*

Ashamed. *See* SHAME.

Asherah. *See* GODS AND GODDESSES, PAGAN.

Ashtoreth. *See* GODS AND GODDESSES, PAGAN.

Assembly. *See* CHURCH, THE; ISRAEL.

Assurance. In the midst of a world filled with uneasiness and insecurity, assurance of a person's security in God is one of the hallmarks of the authentic Christian life. Such assurance is not based on human resources, abilities, or ingenuity, but on confidence in the caring power of God for believers.

Such divine concern in the life of an individual or a community of faith is not to be likened to some superficial good luck charm or magical incantation that protects a person against the traumas and tragedies of human existence. Instead, assurance in God provides an anchor of confidence and hope (Heb. 6:18) in the midst of pain and sorrow, because the believer has learned the secret of casting all worries and cares on God, who is genuinely concerned for people (1 Peter 5:7).

Assurance can be linked to faith and faithfulness (Heb. 10:22), because it is one of the ways that the biblical writers describe an authentic relationship with God. While reliance on God is accompanied by the confidence that God is intimately involved in the lives of believers (1 John 5:14), faith in God does not *earn* a sense of security or assurance. Moreover, it cannot be achieved by attendance at church, by works of kindness, or by ecclesiastical pardon. The foundation for the assurance of one's salvation or well-being with God is rooted in a divine gift. God is the provider of salvation in Jesus Christ (John 3:16; 2 Cor. 5:18–19). Moreover, it is God who will bring to completion this divine gift (Phil. 1:6). It is this assurance that God continues to work in the lives of believers that is the basis for the Christian doctrine of perseverance—endurance or continuing response to God's leading (Eph. 6:18; Heb. 12:1; James 1:25). Assurance and perseverance are two sides of the same message.

Assurance of a relationship with God in Christ is the way believers express the mysterious connection between the infinite nature of God and the fallible nature of humanity. Life with God (whether in ancient Israel or in Christianity) is a dynamic reality, not some chess game in which God moves all the pawns and kings without reference to human response (note the amazing conditional statement in Jer. 18:7–10). Resisting temptation (with divine help; cf. Matt. 6:13; 1 John 5:14) is a key to sense of security in God (cf. 1 Cor. 10:13; James 4:7). Evil and the devil are not some toys with which believers can play (1 Peter 5:8–9).

But believers are not left to their own resources. The presence of the Holy Spirit in the lives of believers is a guarantee or assurance that God is at work in believers' lives (2 Cor. 1:22; 5:5). It is through the Spirit that believers know the reality of God's presence in their lives (1 John 4:13). Forces external to them will never be able to separate them from the love of God in Christ Jesus (Rom. 8:35–39); no power (symbolized by robber or wolf) is able to steal believers (symbolized by sheep) out of the loving arms of God's Son (John 10:28).

This sense of assurance for believers is not merely limited to the present era on earth, but the resurrection of Jesus assures Christians that they are not deluded in their expectation of a future hope with their Lord (1 Cor. 15:17–20). The resurrection of Jesus is the powerful guarantee that Christian preaching and faith are not in vain (v. 14). The Holy Spirit's presence provides assurance that Christians will receive their promised inheritance with God (Eph. 1:14).

GERALD L. BORCHERT

See also CONFIDENCE; ENDURANCE.

Bibliography. G. L. Borchert, *Assurance and Warning;* D. A. Carson, *Divine Sovereignty and Human Responsibility;* I. H. Marshall, *Kept by the Power.*

Astrology. In the early history of humanity, astrology and astronomy were closely related. The latter dealt with the movements of heavenly bodies, while the former attempted to interpret the possible effects that these might have upon earth's inhabitants. In Babylonia, where astrology had its origins, considerable importance was attached to such phenomena as eclipses and meteors, to say nothing of planetary movements. Individual stars and constellations were given names, and when they began to be worshiped as gods, the way was opened for astrologers to make predictions as to how people on earth might be affected.

In the second millennium B.C., Babylonian astrologers drew up horoscopes indicating what might be expected to happen in each month. Once twelve of these menologies had been compiled, they were used year after year without change. The superstitious Babylonians also devised the zodiac, a division of the celestial sphere into twelve equal parts known as signs or houses, which were named after the sun, moon, and principal planets. By the late fourth century B.C., Mesopotamian astrology had spread to Greece, and about a century later was adopted widely by the Egyptians. When Greek culture was absorbed by the Romans, astrology assumed the form of a religion, and its practitioners began to design individual horoscopes.

The Old Testament. While some have asserted that the twelvefold blessing pronounced by Jacob on his sons (Gen. 49:1–28) had some astrological significance, there is nowhere in the material any mention of the possible influence of heavenly bodies. The Israelites were forbidden to worship stars (Deut. 9:14), this being seen as an offshoot of astrological speculation. Several centuries later, the influence of Mesopotamian star adulation was being experienced in Israel, causing Amos to condemn the northern kingdom's worship of Saturn (5:26). Jeremiah also referred to the pagan veneration of Ishtar or Venus (7:18; 44:17–19) as well as celestial bodies generally (8:2; 19:13). Isaiah was the first to refer specifically to astrologers and their activities (47:13), and in his prophecy he predicted their destruction, saying that "the fire will burn them up" (47:14).

Daniel seems to have been familiar with astrologers (2:27; 4:7) and with their inability to interpret the king's dreams. Some writers have suggested that the term "Chaldean," used to describe the wise men of Babylon who acted as astrologers, had actually been written *galdu,* "astrologers," by Daniel, but later on was transcribed incorrectly as *kaldu,* since by then Chaldea (*mat Kaldu*) had become known as the place where they flourished. Daniel repudiated their supposed abilities by declaring that only God can be regarded as the true source of revelations concerning the future (5:14–16).

Some two centuries before Christ was born, astrology gained a foothold in Jewish religion, when identification of certain angels with stars and planets came into vogue. Although the tradition was repudiated in Wisdom 13:1–4, it had already become impossible to halt the Jewish fascination with astrology. The remains of a Byzantine synagogue floor, unearthed at sixth-century A.D. levels at Beth Alpha in Palestine, included a mosaic in the form of a zodiac, thus showing the extent to which astrology had infiltrated religious architecture.

The New Testament. It is against the intertestamental period's concern with angels and elemental spirits that the influence of astrology on early Christianity must be assessed. What may have been an example of celestial phenomena being given an astrological interpretation involved the appearance of an unusual star in the heavens. Such occurrences were not entirely unknown in antiquity, and sometimes were taken as pointing to the birth of a famous person, such as Alexander the Great. Thus the Mesopotamian magi (Matt. 2:1–2), who were most probably professional astrologers, were able to both reassure and alarm Herod by offering him astrological reasons for their journey. The star has been a matter of debate also. The magi spoke of it as a single entity, but some scholars have regarded it as a conjunction of Jupiter, Mars, and Saturn. Others prefer the translation "in its ascendancy" to the traditional "in the east." If the star was a single celestial body, it could possibly have been a nova in its final stage of existence, but this cannot be demonstrated. The Greek word *magoi* appears again in Acts 8:9 and 13:6–8, to describe magicians rather than astrologers.

There could possibly be a reference to the worship of angelic beings in some of Paul's writings, notably in Galatians 4:3 and Colossians 2:15, 20, where the veneration of celestial bodies, particularly among Colossian Christians, was being condemned. Less probably is the speculation that the depth (Gk. *bathos*) and height (Gk. *hypsōma*) as in Romans 8:39 can be interpreted astrologically. If anything, they are astronomical terms intended to denote space in relation to the earth. It would thus appear that the New Testament contains no explicit statements that would support the practice of astrology. While some have argued that the magi's visit to Bethlehem gives proper credence to the value of astrology, the fact is that, from a theological perspective, the obedient believer is led in life by the Holy Spirit, who was promised by Christ as the one who would guide the godly into all truth (John 16:13).

Anthropologists and others have observed that when religion declines in a culture it is replaced by superstition. Consequently, it is only to be expected that when people fall away from the faith once delivered to the saints they will place increasing trust in such astrological devices as horoscopes. Part of the popularity of these ancient Mesopotamian devices is that they are seen to afford a possible glimpse into the immediate future. It is unhappily true that they are immensely popular among superstitious persons, and are given wide circulation in the press. It is almost unbelievable that some scientists, who above all others insist upon a pragmatic, empirical approach to their work that is devoid of any possible religious influence, should consult their horoscopes each morning before undertaking the day's responsibilities.

Many of those in bondage to horoscopes argue that nowadays the stars are not consulted, but that instead the predictions are formulated mathematically, and customized to accommodate the latitude and longitude of particular individuals. Christians need to reject such spurious "science," and commit their way consistently to the continual guidance of the Holy Spirit. R. K. HARRISON

See also DIVINATION.

Bibliography. R. Gleadow, *The Origin of the Zodiac;* L. MacNeice, *Astrology.*

Atonement. That the Bible's central message is atonement, that is, that God has provided a way for humankind to come back into harmonious relation with him, is everywhere apparent in Scripture. From the first stories in Genesis to the last visions of Revelation, God seeks to reconcile his people to himself. Atonement, however, cannot be usefully discussed in this way, and translators have settled on it, and its cognate expressions, as a translation for a relatively circumscribed number of nouns and verbs in the Bible.

The Old Testament. In the Old Testament atonement, and related phrases, such as sacrifice of atonement, most often translates the Hebrew piel verb *kipper* and two related nouns, one, *kippurîm,* found always in the plural and signifying the noun equivalent of *kipper,* and the other, *kapporeth,* meaning the so-called mercy-seat or the place where the sacrifice of atonement happens. These occur with meanings related to atonement around 140 times, almost always in the context of the cultus, as a sacrifice for sins and to provide reconciliation to God.

The breadth of the use of the concept in the Old Testament is striking. Atonement is provided for inanimate objects such as a mildewing house, the altar in the temple, the sanctuary (i.e., the Holy of Holies within the Tent of Meeting), the holy place, and the tent of meeting/temple itself. In one place atonement is also provided for an animal, the scapegoat used in the atonement rituals found in Leviticus 16. Sacrifice accomplishes atonement "for sins" in many places, though these passages always mean atonement for people "because of" their sins rather than atonement "on behalf of" sins, as if sins were being personified and therefore in need of redemption. Of course, the majority of all the references are to atonement on behalf of people, either individually or as members of the community of Israel.

Atonement for inanimate objects is found twelve places in the Old Testament: Exod. 29:36–37; 30:10; Lev. 8:15; 14:53; 16:10, 16, 18, 20; Ezek. 43:20, 26; 45:20. Eleven of these passages refer to cleansing either the tent/temple, one of its rooms, or the altar inside it. The lone exception refers to the cleansing of a contaminated house. In one of the stranger passages of the Law, God instructs Moses and Aaron about the purification rites they are to apply to a house that has "a spreading mildew" and declares that, if a house responds to the treatment, then it can be declared clean (Lev. 14:33–53). The priest cleanses the house by sacrificing a bird, and dipping cedar wood, hyssop, scarlet yarn, and a live bird in the blood of the dead bird, then sprinkling the blood on the house seven times. He then is to release the live bird into the open fields outside the town. "In this way he will make atonement for the house, and it will be clean" (Lev. 14:53).

The entire passage significantly echoes the preceding passage in which a human being undergoes the same investigations and purifications for infectious skin diseases, and it anticipates the important regulations of Leviticus 16 concerning the Day of Atonement, the most important sacrifice of all, when sacrifice is made for the cleansing of the sins of all the people. The point is apparently that the surface of the skin can demonstrate a deeper sickness underneath as can the surface of a house; both need to be cleansed of that deeper sickness as does the human heart of its sin.

Far more important are the references to the atonement of the Tent of Meeting, the temple, the holy place, the sanctuary, and the altar. These take place in the contexts of the ordination of priests (Exod. 29:35–37; Lev. 8:15), God's instructions for the building of the eschatological temple in the later chapters of Ezekiel (43:20, 26; 45:20), and the Day of Atonement itself (Lev. 16:16, 18, 20). The need for cleansing the buildings, the altar and the sanctuaries is due to the fact that these are the meeting places of the divine, Holy One with his people. The holiness and purity of God are so emphasized that not only does he and the one who approaches him have to be pure, but even the means of their communication and relationship must be covered by the blood of an atoning sacrifice because of its contamination by sin.

It is perhaps important that this cleansing of inanimate objects, with the lone exception of the house (which seems to serve as an analog to human cleansing), is limited to the house of God and its parts. There is no sense that the world is God's place of meeting and in need of a cleansing sacrifice of atonement, but rather that the special cultic and covenantal relationship that God has with his people is what is in need of purification. This is not to deny that the world has been infected by sin, just that the particular relationship of redemption that God has with his covenant people is not extended to the whole world, but simply to the people of Israel, and even that is vicarious, that is, through the priests and their cultic duties.

Primary among the objects of atonement in the Old Testament are the people of God, but the means of atonement can vary. Goats, sheep, and birds are listed among the acceptable animals to be sacrificed, but there were also grain, oil, and drink offerings. Ransom money can provide atonement for the lives of the people; God commands at least one census to be made of the people at which each participant pays the same amount to buy his life and the lives of his family from God, who promises no plague will harm them when they do pay (Exod. 30:11–16). Significantly, the money is to be used to support the services of the Tent of Meeting, hence tying it to the sacrifice of blood for atonement, if only in a tangential way. The other nonanimal sacrifices are often equally tied to atonement by blood.

Certainly the most frequently mentioned means of atonement in the Old Testament were the blood sacrifices, dominating the use of the term by constant reference in the books of Leviticus and Numbers. Atonement needed to be made for everything from heinous crimes like idolatry (Num. 16:47) to mistakes of intent, when the only sin was ignorance or error, not willful disobedience (Num. 15:22–29).

Perhaps the heart of the Old Testament teaching on atonement is found in Leviticus 16, where the regulations for the Day of Atonement occur. Five characteristics relating to the ritual of the Day of Atonement are worthy of note because they are generally true of atonement as it is found throughout Scripture: (1) the sovereignty of God in atonement; (2) the purpose and result of making atonement; (3) the two goats emphasize two different things, and the burning another, about the removal of sin; (4) that Aaron had to make special sacrifice for himself; (5) the comprehensive quality of the act.

Atonement is clearly the action of God and not of man throughout the Bible, but especially in Leviticus 16. Aaron's two sons, Nadab and Abihu, had been recently put to death by the Lord for disobeying his command by offering "unauthorized fire" before the Lord (Lev. 10:1–3). Here God gives Aaron precise instructions concerning how he wants the sacrifices to be made, down to the clothes Aaron is to wear, the bathing rituals in which he is to engage, and the types of sacrificial animals he is to bring. His sovereignty is further emphasized by the fact that the lot is used to choose which goat will be sacrificed and which goat will serve as the scapegoat.

The purpose for the ritual is made very clear in several places. It is to cleanse you "from all your sins" (Lev. 16:30). Other passages make it clear that such cleansing results in saving the life of the participant (cf., e.g., Lev. 17:11). The restoring of pure relationship is an important result, too, since the atonement is for all "uncleanness and rebellion of the Israelites, whatever their sins have been" (Lev. 16:16). Thus Israel is reunited in purity to its God by the atoning sacrifice for sins.

The symbolic import of the sacrifices is so detailed that three different actions were necessary to display everything that God apparently intended us to understand about the way he was to deal with sin. The sacrificial death of the first goat showed clearly that the offense of sin requires the punishment of death (Ezek. 18:4). The sending of the second goat into the wilderness with the sins laid on the top of its head emphasizes that sin will be removed from the person and the community "as far as the east is from the west" (Ps. 103:12). The burning of the sacrifice so that it is consumed shows the power of God over sin, completely destroying it so that it can bother the supplicant no more.

Particularly important for the full biblical picture of atonement as it is found in Christ is the sacrifice Aaron makes for himself and his family (Lev. 16:11–14). Everyone, even the high priest, is guilty and needs atonement that can only be provided by God himself. The author of Hebrews emphasizes this point to make clear his doctrine of the purity of Christ as both the true and perfect sacrifice and the true and perfect priest who performs the ritual of atonement (8:3–6; 9:6–15). The Old Testament sacrifices are shown to be but shadows of the real sacrifice of Christ on the cross by the fact of Aaron's sinfulness; an imperfect high priest cannot offer a true sacrifice, just as the blood of bulls and goats could never truly pay for the offense of human sin or substitute for the shedding of human blood.

Lastly, atonement covers all the sins—intentional, unintentional, heinous, trivial—of those for whom it is intended. No one was to enter the Tent of Meeting until the ritual was over because what was taking place there was for the whole of the community of Israel (Lev. 16:17), presumably because any interference with the sovereign action of God's cleansing might bring an impurity into the equation that would nullify the purificatory act. The comprehensive nature of the sacrifice of atonement prefigures the comprehensiveness of the shedding of Christ's blood on the cross, but it limits its effects in the same way the Old Testament limits the effects of its sacrifice on the day of atonement—to the people whom God has elected to call his own and them alone.

The New Testament. The so-called ransom saying, found in the Gospel of Mark (10:45; cf. the parallel saying at Matt. 20:28), has been much disputed as to its authenticity, but its theological content is clear. Speaking in the context of the apostles' dispute over which of them is the greatest, Jesus relates his mission to two things: serving all and giving his life as a ransom for many. Like many of the teachings of Jesus, the saying dramatically extends the answer to an immediate question or problem (that of the selfishness and pride of the apostles) to include something that no one would have linked to that problem (the ransom nature of the cross). The saying of course primarily relates the death of Christ to the metaphor of service; giving his life is the greatest example of servanthood that can be imagined. The fact that his death is also a ransom links the idea of atonement to the servant spirit of the Christ, probably in the light of the famous servant song of Isaiah 53.

The second Gospel passage relating to atonement appears in the eucharistic words of Jesus recorded in all three Gospels (Matt. 26:26–29 = Mark 14:22–25 = Luke 22:15–20). At Luke 22:19–20, Jesus asserts that both the bread and the wine symbolize the fact that his death would be "for you" (*huper humōn*), a phrase not found in the other Gospels (though the notion of the blood of Christ being "poured out for many" is found in both Matthew and Mark). The key element linking the passage in all three Gospels to atonement is the sacrificial nature of the language; the poured-out blood is the blood of the lamb of Leviticus 16, sacrificed "for the forgiveness of sins" (Matt. 26:28).

To discuss Paul on atonement is, again, to make a choice between a thorough discussion of Paul's soteriology and limiting oneself to a discussion of the meaning of *hilasterion* in Romans 3:25. Space does not even allow for a full evaluation of the latter in this article. The preponderance of the evidence weighs in favor of a translation that recognizes the background of Leviticus 16 in the crucial passage. Some now argue that Paul intends a quite specific reference to the mercy seat of the Ark of the Covenant and that *hilasterion* should be translated "mercy seat."

In any case the passage occurs in a clear context of God's righteous, wrathful judgment against the sins of humankind (Rom. 1:18–3:31; cf. esp. 1:18; 2:5) and declares God's merciful action of atonement on behalf of his people. He takes an action that is rightly called "substitutionary," putting his Son in our place and so remaining just but also demonstrating his mercy (3:25–26). This shuts out any possibility for humankind to boast of its having saved itself (3:27). Thus the themes of sovereignty, mercy, and comprehensiveness that we saw present in Leviticus 16 are paramount in the mind of Paul too.

The same applies to the rest of the references to *hilasterion* and its cognates (*hilaskomai, hilasmos*) in the New Testament. Hebrews 2:17 points squarely at Jesus as the high priests of Leviticus 16 who offers a sacrifice of atonement (*hilaskomai*) for his brothers and is therefore a merciful and faithful high priest, but who is of course also the very sacrifice he offers, suffering so that he is able to help those who are tempted in their time of need. The oneness both between Jesus and the redeemed and between God and humanity is emphasized by the family metaphor used throughout the context of the passage (Heb. 2:10–17). Similarly, in 1 John 2:2 Jesus' sacrifice of atonement (*hilasmos*) is powerful enough to heal the sins of the whole world and unite it to God, but it is only "Jesus Christ, the Righteous One" (1 John 2:1) who can accomplish this. God's sovereignty and love in atonement are clearly seen in 1 John 4:10 and cap the New Testament teaching on this essential doctrine: our love for God is not the issue, but rather his for us and it is this love that has both motivated and produced the sacrifice of atonement (*hilasmos*) necessary for healing the relationship of God to man. So the biblical teaching about atonement is summed up: "This is love: not that we loved God, but that he loved us and sent his Son as an atoning sacrifice for our sins" (1 John 4:10). ANDREW H. TROTTER, JR.

See also CROSS, CRUCIFIXION; DEATH OF CHRIST.

Bibliography. C. Brown, H.-G. Link, and H. Vorländer, *NIDNTT,* 3:145–76; W. Elwell, *EDT,* pp. 98–100; J. B. Green, *DPL,* pp. 201–9; idem, *EDT,* pp. 146–63; J. M. Gundry-Volf, *DPL,* pp. 279–84; M. Hengel, *The Atonement: The Origins of Doctrine in the New Testament;* A. McGrath, *DPL,* pp. 192–97; L. Morris, *The Apostolic Preaching of the Cross;* idem, *EDT,* pp. 97, 100–102; S. Page, *EDT,* pp. 660–62; V. Taylor, *The Atonement in New Testament Teaching;* R. Wallace, *The Atoning Death of Christ;* H.-R. Weber, *The Cross: Tradition and Interpretation.*

Atonement, Day of. *See* FEASTS AND FESTIVALS OF ISRAEL.

Atoning Sacrifice. *See* ATONEMENT.

Authorities. *See* POWERS.

Authority. The concept of authority seldom appears in the Old Testament. It is used predominantly in the New Testament, where the word *exousia* functions in at least four ways.

First, authority is the freedom to decide or a right to act without hindrance. All such authority begins with God, for there is no authority except from God (Rom. 13:1). God has the right to mold the clay as he wishes (Rom. 9:21) and to set times and dates (Acts 1:7). God gave Paul the right to preach the gospel (1 Cor. 9:18). Believers have the right to become children of God (John 1:12), and they have freedom with respect to the law (1 Cor. 8:9). While authority is valueless without the power to make it effective, we can make a fine distinction between the two concepts. This first understanding of authority, then, is distinct from power and refers primarily to a prerogative.

Second, the concept of authority refers to the power, ability, or capability to complete an action. Jesus was given the authority to forgive sins (Matt. 9:6–8) and to drive out spirits (Mark 6:7). Jesus gave seventy-two disciples the authority to trample on snakes and scorpions (Luke 10:19). Simon sought power to grant the Holy Spirit (Acts 8:19). Satan has authority to function within the parameters established by God (Acts 26:18).

Third, the word "authority" is used with reference to delegated authority in the form of a warrant, license, or authorization to perform. Jesus was asked by whose authorization he taught (Matt. 21:23). He was granted authority for his ministry from God the Father (John 10:18). Saul was sent to Damascus to persecute Christians by warrant of the priests (Acts 26:12). God gave the apostles license to build up the church (2 Cor. 10:8).

Fourth, by a natural extension of meaning, *exousia* sometimes denotes the sphere in which authority is exercised. God has established spheres of authority in the world, such as civil government. Jesus was handed over to the official power of the governor (Luke 20:20). When Pilate learned that Jesus was under Herod's jurisdiction or authority, the governor sent him to Herod (Luke 23:7). Rulers and kings have their spheres of influence (Rom. 13:1), as does Satan (Col. 1:13), but Christ has been placed above all realms of authority (Eph. 1:21). More often *exousia* refers to the power employed by rulers or others in high positions by virtue of their office, such as civil magistrates (Titus 3:1). This use of authority indicates a social relation between at least two individuals where one is the ruler. The subordinate in the relationship accepts the ruler's orders, not by external constraint but out of the conviction that the ruler is entitled to give orders and that it is the duty of the subject to obey and recognize the authenticity of the ruler's position and orders.

From a theological perspective the fourth use of authority is most significant. The question of authority is a fundamental issue facing every person, especially the believer. Its significance cannot be overestimated. Every person has an authority in life that he or she submits to as a subordinate, not by constraint but by conviction. Furthermore, God has created human beings to live under his authority. When they choose to live under a different rule, that of self or an idol, they sin. This is, in a simple summary, the teaching of Genesis 1–3. That portion of Scripture illustrates the human tendency, moved by pride, to seek independence from external authority and to establish self as the final authority in life.

How, then, does God exercise his authority over creation and his creatures? The testimony of Scripture is that God has established three fundamental spheres of authority within which he delegates authority to individuals. These spheres are civil government, the home, and the church. The believer is obliged to obey those holding authority in those realms. Citizens are to submit to the governing authorities (1 Peter 2:13–14). Children are to obey parents (Eph. 6:1–2). Believers were to honor spiritual authorities such as apostles who demanded compliance on the basis of their commission from the Lord. There are exceptions. When a person in authority violates the trust granted by God, the source of all authority, the subordinate is free, indeed mandated, "to obey God rather than man" (Acts 5:29). The apostle Peter provides the clearest example of what is called civil disobedience. In his epistle he encourages disciples of Christ to submit to governing authorities (1 Peter 2:13). According to Luke, however, when the governing authorities commanded Peter to cease preaching, he disobeyed (Acts 5:29).

The issue facing contemporary Christians is how God exercises his authority in the spiritual realm, that is, the church. In the Old Testament, the answer was clear. God exercised his authority through prophets, priests, and kings. At the time of Christ, the disciples submitted to the lordship of God the Father through obedience to Jesus. Christ, then, delegated authority to the apostles, who directed the affairs of the primitive church. When Christ comes again, he will reign from a new throne in the new city. How does God in Christ exercise his authority in the dispensation between his comings?

Has the authority of the apostles been transmitted through the tradition or by episcopal consecration? The evangelical response to that question, uncovered in the Protestant Reformation, is *sola Scriptura*. Evangelical theology appeals to the authority of Scripture because it views the Bible as the written Word of God, pointing beyond itself to the absolute authority, the living and transcendent Word of God. God exercises authority over the church through the Scriptures, which impart authoritative truth. The Bible issues definitive directives. It offers an authoritative norm by which all doctrine and principles must be shaped for both individual believers and the church. The Bible is a record and explanation of divine revelation that is both complete (sufficient) and comprehensible (perspicuous); that is to say, it contains all that the church needs to know in this world for its guidance in the way of salvation and service.

Sam Hamstra, Jr.

Bibliography. B. Holmberg, *Paul and Power: The Structure of Authority in the Primitive Church.*

Avenger of Blood. *See* Kinsman-Redeemer.

Awe, Awesome. Webster's dictionary defines awe as mingled dread, veneration, and wonder. English Bible translations employ the words "awe" or "awesome" almost exclusively to refer to the person or work of God. While the word "awe" appears only rarely in the KJV, modern English versions such as the NASB and NIV translate as many as six different Hebrew words and three different Greek words as "awe" or "awesome." The most common Hebrew word, *yārēʾ*, occurs in various forms over 400 times in the Old Testament, and is commonly translated "fear." Both the NIV and NASB, however, often render "awe" (e.g., Exod. 15:11; 1 Sam. 12:18; Ps. 119:120; Hab. 3:2).

In the Gospels and Acts, the Greek *phobos,* the common word for fear, is occasionally translated "awe," or "filled with awe." It describes people's reaction to astonishing works of God such as Jesus' demonstration of authority to forgive sins (Luke 5:26), the raising of the widow's son (Luke 7:16), or the outpouring of the Holy Spirit in the early church (Acts 2:43).

When confronted with God's awesome presence the inevitable human response is to quiver and cower. In fact, the Bible never records a direct personal encounter with God in which the individual was not visibly shaken by God's awesomeness. When God appeared to Moses in the burning bush, Moses hid his face and trembled before God (Exod. 3:6). When Isaiah saw the Lord in his glory and majesty, he cried, "Woe is me, I am ruined!" (6:5). When the risen Christ appeared to Saul the persecutor on the Damascus road, Saul prostrated himself in fear and trembling (Acts 9:3). The Bible emphasizes, however, that genuine awe is primarily a disposition rather than merely an emotional state. God's person and his works of creation, providence, redemption, and judgment are astounding and demand both sober contemplation and humble submission. God's people are commanded to show proper regard for his power and dominion—his absolute authority to rule (Job 25:2; Jer. 33:9) and his power to perform what he will (Deut. 4:34; 34:12; 1 Sam. 12:18; Hab. 3:2). On the other hand, the Bible makes it clear that there will come a day when persons who refuse to acknowledge God's awesomeness will tremble and wail before his vengeful presence and his righteous judgement (Jer. 2:19; Zeph. 2:11).

Ralph Enlow

See also Fear.

Bb

Baal. *See* Gods and Goddesses, Pagan.

Baal-Zebub. *See* Gods and Goddesses, Pagan.

Babylon. Capital of the Neo-Babylon Empire of the mid-first millennium B.C. Babylon has both a historic role and a theological role in the Bible. Certain themes become associated with it. In the Book of Revelation, these themes culminate in the image of the whore of Babylon. As a result of this biblical imagery, Babylon has transcended its historical significance to become synonymous with sin and pride in Western art and literature.

Babylon first appears in the Bible under the guise of the tower of Babel (Gen. 11). The Hebrew word for "confused" in verse 9 is *babal*, which sounds like *babel* (Babylon). The great evil of the tower builders is their sinful pride against the rule of God. This theme will reappear in the prophetic writings against the city.

During the reign of Hezekiah, envoys from Babylon came to Jerusalem (2 Kings 20:12–19). The prophet Isaiah chastised the king for showing off the treasures of Judah and predicted that Babylon would some day carry these riches off. This was a startling revelation, for Assyria was the great power of the day and seemingly unassailable. The visit was probably an attempt by Babylon to foment problems for Assyria in the west, thereby diverting attention from Babylon. The postexilic reader would have seen the roots of the destruction of Jerusalem in the foolish pride of Hezekiah and in the greed of Babylon.

The prophets describe Babylon as a city of pride and idolatry. Yet the destruction of Jerusalem by Babylon presents the prophets with a dilemma. If God is sovereign and makes use of Babylon to punish Judah, can Babylon—as a tool in the hand of its Master—be blamed for its behavior? Isaiah addresses this problem by portraying Babylon as a woman, the queen of kingdoms (47:5), who should be tender and delicate but is not. God gave his people over into her power, but rather than caring for them she has shown them no mercy. This is a result of her overweening pride, evidenced in her statement that "I am, and there is none besides me" (v. 8). Although the conquest of Jerusalem is in keeping with the will of God, the brutality and greed of the conquerors—the fruit of Babylon's idolatry and failure to recognize the kingship of God—are not. Because of Babylon's pride, she will be destroyed. Psalm 137 personifies Babylon as a woman who is doomed to destruction and whose infant children will be savagely killed.

Jeremiah sees the future destruction of Babylon as a punishment because the Babylonians rejoiced at the destruction of Judah and ruthlessly plundered the people of God (50:11). Babylon herself will become a "heap of ruins" (51:37). Daniel reinforces the picture of Babylon as full of pride and defiance toward God. Nebuchadnezzar, king of Babylon, is punished with madness because he denied God's control over "Babylon the Great" (4:30).

Centuries after the destruction of the Neo-Babylonian state by Cyrus of Persia, Babylon reappears in a dramatic role in the Book of Revelation—a role marked by numerous references to Old Testament imagery. Pride, idolatry, cruelty, and greed are associated with the city.

The dominant image of Babylon in Revelation is the city's personification of a rich woman, the "mother of prostitutes" (17:5). Babylon is a great city that rules over the earth.

Babylon, the historic oppressor of God's people, represents the new oppressor of Christ's church. Like the Mesopotamian city, the "great city" (Rome) will be judged and will become a desolate wilderness. The metaphor extends beyond the physical Rome to the entire world, "intoxicated with the wine of her adulteries" (17:2). The people of God, however, will be delivered from the grasp of the prophetic Babylon just as Ezekiel foretold for the exiles held captive in the historic Babylon. Thomas W. Davis

Bibliography. J. M. Ford, *Revelation;* R. E. Clemens, *Jeremiah;* G. E. Wright, *The Book of Jonah.*

Backsliding. Condition that results from spiritual apathy or disregard for the things of God, whether on the part of an individual or a group bound by a prior covenantal pledge of commitment to uphold the doctrine and commandments of the Lord. Backsliding includes departure from a good confession of faith and from the ethical standards prescribed for God's people in the Scriptures. To varying degrees, depending on the extent of neglect of God and his commandments, the spiritually wayward experience a season of estrangement and abandonment from God and his people. In instances of apostasy when one spurns the grace of God by renouncing the blessings of the covenant, there is no possibility of repentance for sin, only a divine sealing unto the day of judgment (Heb. 6:4–6; 10:26–31).

The sin of backsliding raises the important theological question concerning the relation between faith and perseverance. In cases of temporary backsliding, how do we understand the spiritual condition of the true son or daughter of God? Can one who is united to Christ (i.e., one who is regenerated by God and justified by grace through faith) fall again under the dominion of sin? Reformed theologians have maintained that the sinner redeemed by grace has been delivered once-for-all from bondage to sin. For such (elect) individuals, consequently, backsliding does not entail a fall from grace, whereby one is placed once more under sin's dominion. When a former disciple renounces Christian faith and conduct, however, that person is not a true son or daughter of God, and thus is not numbered among God's elect. Genuine development in the life history of everyone born into the world reveals the unfolding of God's decretive purpose in the salvation of the elect and the condemnation of the reprobate who remain under the wrath of God (John 3:18–21, 36; 5:24–29). History is the process of differentiation between the two seeds: the seed of the woman and the seed of the serpent (Gen. 3:15).

The frequent occurrence and gravity of backsliding among the people of God is vividly portrayed in the corporate life of Israel during the Mosaic epoch of redemptive history. The house of Israel was guilty of committing the sin of backsliding on numerous occasions. In the speech of Hezekiah, the Chronicler highlights Israel's history as a lengthy period of disobedience. "Our fathers were unfaithful; they did evil in the eyes of the LORD our God and forsook him. They turned their faces away from the LORD's dwelling place and turned their backs on him" (2 Chron. 29:6; cf. 36:14). The cause of Israel's backslidings was her stubbornness of heart. Repeatedly the prophets addressed Israel's waywardness and unfaithfulness. As agents of God's covenant lawsuit against the obstinate and stiff-necked people, the prophets pleaded with Israel to repent of her sins and return to God in true faith and holiness. Failing to heed the warning, Israel suffered the full displeasure and abandonment of God in the Babylonian deportation and exile. Hosea describes Israel in particularly graphic terms as an adulterous people (2:5; 4:12; 5:7; 9:1). Her sins of prostitution and sexual immorality, indicative of her spiritual condition, drove her away from God, causing her to apostasize from the faith. Rather than consecrating their life and temporal blessings to the glory of God, the Israelites profaned the name and works of God. "Like Adam, they have broken the covenant—they were unfaithful to me there" (Hos. 6:7).

Israel's backsliding was both a divine chastisement and a rebuke for sin (Jer. 2:19). Only the mercy and compassion of Yahweh could restore Israel to favor (Jer. 3:22; 14:7). The restoration of Israel from exile, however, required the making of a new and better covenant, one that could not be broken (Jer. 31:22–34). Through divine cleansing Israel would once again become the people of God (Hos. 2:23). "They will no longer defile themselves with their idols and vile images or with any of their offenses, for I will save them from all their sinful backsliding, and I will cleanse them. They will be my people, and I will be their God" (Ezek. 37:23).

Israel serves as an example to us. In the teachings of Christ and his apostles the people of God are exhorted to persevere in righteousness and holiness, so as not to fall under divine condemnation. The sin of apostasy is real for covenant confessors. Accordingly, the angel of the church in Ephesus warns those who have forsaken their first love: "Remember the height from which you have fallen! Repent and do the things you did at first" (Rev. 2:5). The saints are to persevere in doing the will of God, remembering the covenant he has made with us in his Son, Jesus Christ. The grace of perseverance is one of the benefits of Christ's atoning sacrifice for our sins. Thus our Lord instructs: "I am the vine; you are the branches. If a man remains in me and I in him, he will bear much fruit; apart from me you can do nothing. . . . If you obey my commands, you will remain in my love, just as I have obeyed my Father's commands and remain in his love" (John 15:5, 10). The cure for backsliding is found in the abiding love and mercy of God who remains faithful to his promise of grace in Christ Jesus, whose righteousness and salvation is apprehended through true faith and repentance.

MARK W. KARLBERG

See also APOSTASY; DENIAL; SANCTIFICATION.

Bibliography. A. A. Hoekema, *Saved by Grace;* J. Murray, *Redemption: Accomplished and Applied;* B. B. Warfield, *The Plan of Salvation.*

Ban. *See* DEVOTE, DEVOTED.

Baptism for the Dead. First Corinthians 15:29 remains an enigma, although over thirty "explanations" have been suggested. Substituting alternative phrases—baptism for "the spiritually dead," "the dying," "in memory of the departed," or others—merely multiplies problems. Vicarious baptisms for the benefit of the dead, practiced on the fringe of Christianity from the second century, illustrate the influence of this verse, but not Paul's meaning. Paul is arguing that if Jesus has not risen, then Christian faith, preaching, remission, hope, are all vain; so is "baptism for the dead." He cannot mean Christian baptism, for none of its conditions or benefits, as Paul expounds them, can be affirmed of the dead. Besides, the following phrase ("And as for us . . ." NIV; "And we ourselves . . ." NEB) dissociates Paul and his colleagues from the practice.

If docetic type Christians infected the church at Corinth, they may have accepted baptism for departed *souls*: but how would that prove *bodily* resurrection? Similarly, some Dionysian rites and some practices of the mystery religions were held to ensure access, and safe journeying, in the spiritual world, even for those already dead. And Paul could argue from pagan parallels without immediately condemning them (see, e.g., 1 Cor. 10:20–22). But this analogy again does not necessarily imply bodily resurrection.

Yet even as a Pharisee Paul could not conceive a disembodied immortality, leaving the surviving personality incomplete (see 2 Cor. 5:1–4). Is he then arguing that even pagans, if their baptism for the dead be properly understood, testify unconsciously to a bodily resurrection?

R. E. O. WHITE

Bibliography. M. Brauch, *Hard Sayings of Paul.*

Baptism of Fire. As John the Baptist preached in the Judean wilderness, he declared, "I baptize you with water for repentance. But after me will come one who . . . will baptize you with the Holy Spirit and with fire" (Matt. 3:11; cf. Luke 3:16).

Throughout Scripture, fire often represents judgment (Gen. 19:24; 2 Kings 1:10; Amos 1:4–7; Matt. 7:19; 2 Thess. 1:8; James 5:3), including everlasting punishment (Matt. 18:8; Jude 7). But it can also have a positive, purifying effect on God's people (Isa. 1:25; Zech. 13:9; Mal. 3:2–3; 1 Cor. 3:13–15; 1 Peter 1:7; Rev. 3:18).

In the context of John's preaching, it is natural to associate the baptism of fire with judgment (cf. Matt. 3:10, 12; Luke 3:9, 17). On the other hand, John is first of all addressing believers—those who are receiving his water-baptism. So some think of the fiery tongues at Pentecost as the fulfillment of his prediction. But the grammatical construction in Greek (the use of one preposition to govern two objects) is most naturally taken as referring to only one baptism that involves both blessing and judgment (cf. esp. Isa. 4:4). Pentecost may well represent the firstfruits of purgation for believers, but the baptism is not complete until all people experience final judgment.

CRAIG L. BLOMBERG

See also BAPTISM OF THE HOLY SPIRIT; HOLY SPIRIT; HOLY SPIRIT, GIFTS OF.

Bibliography. J. D. G. Dunn, *Baptism in the Holy Spirit; NIDNTT,* 1:652–57.

Baptism of the Holy Spirit. Seven New Testament passages speak of baptism of/in/with/by the Holy Spirit. The varying prepositions reflect the fact that the Spirit is both the agent and sphere of this baptism. Six of these passages refer to John the Baptist's teaching, contrasting his baptism in water with Jesus' future baptism in the Holy Spirit. The seventh is 1 Corinthians 12:13, which refers to the initiation of all the Corinthian Christians into the church.

In Matthew 3:11 and Luke 3:16, John predicts that the Messiah who will come after him will baptize with the Spirit and fire. This expression is best taken as referring to the one purifying action of the Spirit that blesses believers and condemns unbelievers, and which embraces the entire work of the Spirit from Pentecost on, culminating in final judgment. Mark 1:8 and John 1:33 reflect this identical utterance of John, but mention only the baptism of the Spirit. It is unlikely that anybody in John's original audience knew exactly what he meant by these predictions.

In Acts 1:5, however, as Jesus prepares to ascend into heaven, he refers back to John's words and predicts their fulfillment within "a few days." In just a little over a week, the disciples celebrate Pentecost and receive the outpouring of the Holy Spirit in fulfillment of the prophecy of Joel 2:28–32 (Acts 2:1–41, esp. vv. 17–21). A number of years later, when Peter is ministering to Cornelius, the Spirit again manifests itself in dramatically similar ways (leading to the common labeling of this event as the "Gentile Pentecost"). These similarities lead Peter to reflect on Jesus' parting words again and to quote them to the Jewish-Christian leaders in Jerusalem in defense of his "scandalous" association with Gentiles (Acts 11:16).

It is clear that all six of these references to the baptism of the Holy Spirit have Pentecost-like experiences primarily in view. In 1 Corinthians 12:13, however, it is not stated that all the Corinthians had experienced some dramatic, visible manifestation of the Spirit when they were baptized. The common phenomenon seems rather to be that of initiation. Just as baptism in water was the initiation rite symbolizing repentance and faith in Christ, entrance into the community of believers, and incorporation into Christ's body, so "baptism in the Spirit" referred to that moment in which the Spirit first began to operate in believers' lives. No particular style of the Spirit's arrival is paradigmatic; he may come quietly and almost imperceptibly or dramatically and tangibly.

The experience of the disciples at Pentecost is further complicated by the fact that they lived through the transitional period from the old covenant age to the time of the new covenant, which the complex of events beginning with the crucifixion and resurrection and culminating with Christ's exaltation and sending of the Spirit at Pentecost inaugurated. It is important to note that Pentecost was not the disciples' first experience of the Holy Spirit (John 14:17; 20:22), but that does not necessarily justify the generalization that the "baptism of the Spirit" will ever again be a "second blessing"—a deeper experience of the Spirit subsequent to conversion. Pentecost was a second blessing for the disciples because they were followers of Jesus both before and after his death. But there is no indication that Cornelius and his friends underwent any second experience of the Spirit. Their Spirit-baptism was simultaneous with their conversion to Christ. So too nothing is said about the Corinthians having any two-stage experience. If the entire church had been baptized in the Spirit, including the large number of "carnal" Christians Paul elsewhere rebukes (1 Cor. 3:1–4), then clearly Spirit-baptism cannot guarantee a certain level of Christian maturity or holiness. And if no one spiritual gift was held by all Corinthian believers (1 Cor. 12:29–30), then neither may Spirit-baptism be uniformly equated with the reception of any particular gift of the Spirit.

None of this is to deny that Christians often receive a renewed sense of the Spirit's presence or power one or more times after conversion. Luke employs the expression, "the filling of the Holy Spirit," to refer to these occasions, particularly when bold proclamation of the gospel quickly follows (e.g., Acts 2:4; 4:8, 31; 13:9). When one of these events seems particularly constitutive for a new stage of Christian experience, it may be appropriate, as Green suggests, to speak of a "release in the Spirit." But if one wishes to be faithful to biblical usage, one will reserve the expression "baptism in the Spirit" for the indwelling of God through his Holy Spirit at the moment of a believer's salvation. As Green, himself a charismatic, lucidly concludes (p. 134), all seven scriptural references "point not to a second experience, but to an unrepeatable, if complex, plunging into Christ, with repentance and faith, justification and forgiveness, sonship and public witness, the gift of the Holy Spirit and the seal of belonging, all being part of initiation into Christ," even if "some parts of the whole [may be] seen sooner than others."

It is sometimes argued that certain passages that refer to baptism, without any further qualification, also teach about Spirit-baptism (e.g., Rom. 6:4; Gal. 3:27; Col. 2:12; 1 Peter 3:21). This interpretation is usually designed to protect these texts against a view that takes them to teach baptismal regeneration. But, in fact, the early church consistently used "baptism" without any qualifiers to refer to water-baptism. None of these passages, even when taken to refer to immersion in water, implies baptismal regeneration, but they do demonstrate how closely linked water-baptism and conversion were (and hence Spirit-baptism as well) in New Testament times.

CRAIG L. BLOMBERG

See also BAPTISM OF FIRE; BAPTIZE, BAPTISM; HOLY SPIRIT; HOLY SPIRIT, GIFTS OF.

Bibliography. G. R. Beasley-Murray, *Baptism in the New Testament;* J. D. G. Dunn, *Baptism in the Holy Spirit; EDT,* pp. 121–22; H. M. Ervin, *Conversion-Initiation and the Baptism in the Holy Spirit;* M. Green, *Baptism.*

Baptize, Baptism. The Greek root-word *baptizein* means to plunge, immerse, sink; hence to wash; to be immersed, overwhelmed (in trouble). From Jewish rules of purification concerning ritual uncleanness the word gained a technical religious connotation implying "purification" from all that might exclude from God's presence.

When, at the diaspora, numerous Gentiles sought admission to Israel, the required public repentance and acceptance of Mosaic Law was accompanied by immersion in water, symbolizing and effecting religious, moral, and ritual cleansing from the defilements of paganism. Ancient Jewish discussions (echoed in 1 Cor. 10:2) support a pre-Christian date for this proselyte baptism. This is why John's baptism needed no explanation, though his authority to perform it was challenged and his demand for purification of "children of Abraham" gave deep offense (Matt. 3:7–9; John 1:19–24).

John's practice added to proselyte baptism a still stronger emphasis on repentance, a firm background of moral teaching (Luke 3:3, 10–14, 33), and initiation into a community ("John's disciples") preparing for Messiah's advent (Luke 3:16–17).

The rite gained yet deeper meanings and greater authority from Jesus' example and experience. Why Jesus, being sinless, received a "baptism of repentance" is debatable. Some think Jesus was already aware of his role as Servant-Messiah, "numbered with the transgressors" (Isa. 53:12). But Mark 1:10–11 shows that assurance was finally given to him, in words from Psalm 2:7 and Isaiah 42:1, when he came up out of the water. Since Jesus held John's movement and practice to be "from heaven," to identify himself with it was an act of "righteousness" which it was "fitting" to fulfill (Matt. 3:15; 21:25).

With assurance of Jesus' sonship came the enduement of the Holy Spirit for his task. Jesus never returned to the secluded life of Nazareth, but was "driven" by the Spirit into the wilderness, where his sonship was tested (Matt. 4:3, 6) and his messianic work was prepared for.

The earlier Gospels do not record that Jesus himself baptized. Peter's invitation at Pentecost, Luke's record (in Acts) of fifteen baptisms, and the teaching of Paul, Peter, and John leave no doubt, however, that the first disciples believed that baptism possessed Christ's authority, as Matthew declares (28:19–20).

Luke's account of apostolic baptism assumes the rite's original association with repentance and remission (Acts 2:38), with washing away sin (22:16), and with admission to the religious community. But his emphasis falls on baptism's new features. Though the gospel era dates from the baptism John preached (1:22; 10:37), Christian baptism, as conferring the Holy Spirit, is contrasted with John's (attributed to John in each Gospel, to Jesus at Acts 1:5; 11:16). This is emphasized at 18:25 and 19:1–7, and leads to rebaptism with water and the (exceptional) laying on of hands, before the Spirit is conferred. On the other hand, that Cornelius and his friends *have* received the Spirit becomes Peter's justification for their subsequent baptism (10:47; 11:17; cf. 8:14–17). No formal pattern of initiation is yet evident: Order varies with circumstances and preparation. But the association of water baptism with Spirit possession gave rise to the curious phrase "baptism in/with Holy Spirit" (Mark 1:8; Acts 1:5).

In nine instances Luke represents baptism as the expected response to hearing and receiving the gospel. In four of these, kinsmen, close friends, or a household hear and respond; at 16:14–15 and 18:8 it is not stated that the household believed.

This response was to the gospel of Jesus, Son of God and Savior, who was crucified, rose again, forgives sins, bestows the Spirit, and will come again as Judge, all summarized succinctly but clearly in baptism in or into the name of Jesus as Christ, Lord, Son of God (8:37). "In the name" implied Jesus' authority for the rite; "into the name" (8:16; 19:5) indicated passing into Jesus' ownership, as one "redeemed." James 2:7 suggests an invocation of Jesus (to be present?); elsewhere, the irrevocable public confession of Christ as Lord (Rom. 10:9–13; 14:9; Phil. 2:11) marks the decisive commitment of the baptized to all the privileges and obligations of Christian life. Such baptismal confession became the germ of later creeds; the trinitarian formulation in Matthew 28:18–20 may well represent an early stage in credal development.

Reflection on the church's practice enriched further the theological and ethical significance of baptism, without varying its conditions or abandoning its original meaning.

Thus Paul, baptized within three days of his dramatic conversion, was evidently familiar with the need, despite the Pharisees' hostility toward it (John 1:24–25). He gives it surprising prominence among essentials that unite the church (Eph. 4:4; the Eucharist is not included). He administered, or authorized, baptism throughout his missions, yet would not boast of baptizing anyone and resented baptism being made a badge of partisanship (1 Cor. 1:13–17). And he assumes that baptism is understood in churches he had not visited (Rome, Colossae).

So, too, Paul assumes the original method of immersion (Rom. 6) and the accompanying confession of Christ's lordship (Rom. 10:9–13), which in 1 Corinthians 1:12–13, 6:19–20, and Galatians 3:29, 5:24 clearly implies belonging to Christ. But he adds the idea of being "sealed" with the purchaser's mark, as property awaiting collection (Rom. 8:23; 2 Cor. 1:22; Eph. 4:30). This "good confession" (1 Tim. 6:12) made at baptism responds to Paul's gospel of a suffering and risen Lord, presented through the gracious initiative of God and offered to faith, trust, and obedience. Paul insists that none are saved by their own good works, not even by the good work of baptism, but only by faith in Christ (Rom. 3:20; 4:4–5; Gal. 3:2, 11; Eph. 2:8).

Paul retained, too, the original interpretation of baptism as entrance to the religious community: "We were all baptized . . . into one body" (1 Cor. 12:13). Some think that Paul means this by the phrase "baptized into Christ" (Gal. 3:27). They understand his description of the Christian as "in Christ" as an ecclesiological formula—the believer is baptized into "the whole Christ," of which the risen Lord is head and the church is the body. Others interpret "in Christ" as a more individual, mystical relationship. Doubtless Paul would affirm that a true baptism introduced the convert to both privileges.

Again, Paul continues to emphasize the connection of baptism with enduement by the Spirit. It is "by the Spirit" that the baptized is initiated into the church, made to drink of one Spirit, and sealed for ultimate redemption. Paul regularly refers to the believer's reception of the Spirit in a tense signifying a certain point in time ("baptismal aorists"), speaks of baptism as being "washed . . . in the Spirit" (1 Cor. 6:11), and so can assume that everyone baptized "has" the Spirit (Rom. 8:9). Yet he nowhere argues this, as by recalling Jesus' baptismal enduement; he takes reception of the Spirit in baptism for granted and life under the rule of the Spirit as the norm of Christian experience (Rom. 8:2–5). Even so, the Spirit given at baptism is but an earnest, a down payment, guaranteeing immeasurable future blessings (2 Cor. 1:22; 5:5).

Paul retains also the earliest interpretation of baptism as a washing away of sin, a "washing of rebirth and renewal by the Holy Spirit" as Titus 3:5 describes it, a cleansing of the bride-church "by the washing of water with the Word" (1 Cor. 6:11; Eph. 5:26). The precise relation of water, Word, and Spirit in this cleansing experience is not defined; they are concomitant elements in a rite mediating to penitent hearts the divine remission.

The implied total change of attitude and relationship could be expressed metaphorically in two ways. The disrobing and rerobing metaphor of Colossians 3:8–14 (and six parallels) echoes the catechetical instruction already familiar to the first readers, and alludes directly to physical arrangements for baptismal "bathing." The second metaphor relates to circumcision, another "cleansing" required of Jewish proselytes, sometimes explained as "a putting off of the flesh." Paul assures the Gentile converts at Colossae that they do not need Jewish circumcision, as certain Judaists were insisting: "In [Christ] you were also circumcised in the putting off of the sinful nature, not with a circumcision done by the hands of men but with the circumcision done by Christ, having been buried with him in baptism" (Col. 2:11–12). That is Paul's only reference to baptism's accomplishing what circumcision portrayed. He turns from it at once to describe the change that baptism signifies in the language he prefers: "buried with him in baptism . . . raised with him through . . . faith in the power of God."

This conception of the baptismal pool as a grave in which the pre-Christian self and its ways are buried once and for all and from which a new self rises to a new quality of living appears to be Paul's own. It looks back to one of Jesus' metaphors for repentance, self-crucifixion (Mark 8:34; Gal. 2:20; 6:14), and recognizes in baptism the moment when the convert does indeed, publicly, take up his or her cross, dying with Christ to self, to sin, and to the world, and rising with him to a life constantly renewed by his resurrection power (Rom. 6:1–11).

Such a death and resurrection with Christ is implied in accepting the gospel. In Romans, Paul repudiates the suggestion that if man is justified by faith alone, he may go on sinning so long as he goes on exercising faith. Paul replies that one cannot consistently accept Christ's death for one's sins and act as though sin did not matter. The repentant faith that grasps salvation commits the believer, inescapably, to a faith-union with Christ in which he or she dies with Christ to sin and rises with Christ to sin-renouncing life. This baptism expresses, illustrates, and finalizes.

Paul certainly means that, *given repentance and faith,* the act of baptism (which can never be undone) accomplishes all it represents—commitment to the Lord's possession, admission to the church, enduement with the Spirit, remission and repudiation of sin. But Paul is equally clear that what is declared in baptism must be sustained thereafter. The baptized must obey their newfound Lord, be loyal to the church they join (Phil. 2:1–4), walk in the Spirit and bear the Spirit's fruit (Gal. 5:16–25), count themselves dead to sin, not letting sin reign (Rom. 6:11–12; 8:5–8; Col. 3:5–6). The baptized will rejoice greatly in what *has* happened, and maintain their baptismal attitude for the remainder of their lives, repenting deeply for every failure to do so.

Many scholars are persuaded that the basis of 1 Peter was a sermon to the newly baptized. Certainly the message is appropriately addressed for this purpose (1:14, 23; 2:2–3, 10, 25), with suitable admonition to existing and incoming church members (5:1–5). It has much to say about the gospel, faith, new birth, purification, putting aside the flesh, the Spirit, admission to the community, reverencing Christ as Lord—echoing much of the baptismal thinking already noticed.

Peter's new contribution (3:21–22) raises innumerable questions. The strong declaration "baptism that now saves you" recalls Mark 16:16 as well as Peter's "command" to baptize (Acts 10:48). But the precise meaning needs care. It is as an appeal for a "clear conscience," and through the triumphant resurrection and ascension of Christ above all "authorities," that baptism achieves *this* "salvation."

The readers' situation is outlined in 3:13–17, 4:1–5, where again "a clear conscience" is urged and explained. The threat of persecution recurs in 4:12–19, and again is to be met by good social behavior. Against this background, baptism is no merely physical washing (as in Judaist, Essene, or pagan circles), but "the pledge of a good conscience towards God" and threatening civic authorities, ensuring innocent social conduct. This will not guarantee safety, as Christ's suffering shows (3:18); Christians must still arm themselves to suffer unjustly. But as he triumphed so can they, in his power and protection.

This unexpected exhortation is not unsupported. At Pentecost Peter had urged his hearers to save themselves by baptism from "this crooked generation." The Baptist had called his hearers to a baptism of repentance as the way of escape from a world under judgment. Now Peter cites Noah and his pitiful minority amid another evil generation; only eight souls saved *by* the flood from God's judgment upon that sinful age. In such far-ranging thoughts Peter extends the meaning of baptism to include a promise of social responsibility, and assured support and protection, now, in face of evils that threaten new converts, and ultimate victory. The baptized have enlisted in the eternal warfare of good and evil, but their Lord has already overcome.

So much has been made of John's "sacramentalism" that it is imperative to emphasize that for him, too, salvation comes through "believing" (over fifty times in John, 1 John) in the historic Christ (stressed fifteen times), "sent" by the loving initiative of God (over fifty references) to those chosen. The operation of the Spirit in baptism, and the implied entrance to the Christian community, are as clear in John as in the earlier sources (John 3:5–6; 17).

But John does insist rather more strongly on the necessity of baptism (John 3:5; 13:8–9), on Christ's authorizing baptism (John 3:22, 26; 4:1–2), and on the superiority of Christian baptism to that of the Baptist (John 1:26–33; 3:25–30). By omitting any description of Jesus' baptism, John plays down any "memorial" or imitative baptism, in order to stress that in baptism it is the believer's experience that matters.

Without a new birth of water and Spirit, none can see or enter the kingdom or attain a spiritual nature. The healing of blindness by washing at Christ's command (John 9:11) led the church later to call baptism "the enlightenment." John 19:34, so solemnly underlined, suggests that one purpose of Christ's death was precisely to provide the sacramental water and blood by which Christian experience would be transmitted and nourished. First John 5:6–12 is the converse: The continuing witness of the Spirit and the sacraments in the ongoing experience of the church testify (against Gnostic denials) that Christ did come in the flesh, and die, that we might live.

By the time John wrote, Christian baptism was long established and its spiritual significance and power fully understood. But there is no tension between John's sacramentalism and faith as the means of initiating Christian life. The sacrament is a faith-sacrament, rooted in history, and conveying what it represents not by magic but by divine action in believing and receptive hearts.

Christian baptism thus preserves the covenantal basis of biblical thought: God first offers in grace, human beings then respond in gratitude, deserving nothing. In the gospel, God offers through Christ forgiveness, life, the Spirit: the baptismal response, hallowed by Christ, *expresses* faith in the dying and rising Savior-Lord, and *registers* the resolve to die to former sinfulness and rise to new life. God does not ignore such aspiration: He fulfills for the believing heart all the promises of the gospel it is ready to receive.

R. E. O. White

See also Baptism of Fire; Baptism of the Holy Spirit; Holy Spirit, Gifts of.

Bibliography. K. Barth, *Teaching of the Church regarding Baptism;* O. Cullmann, *Baptism in the New Testament;* G. R. Beasley-Murray, *Baptism in the New Testament;* M. B. Green, *Baptism;* P. Ch. Marcel, The *Biblical Doctrine of Infant Baptism;* R. E. O. White, *The Biblical Doctrine of Initiation.*

Beast. *See* Antichrist.

Beatitude. *See* Blessedness.

Beatitudes (Lat. *beatitudo*)**.** Condition or statement of blessedness. In the Latin of the Vulgate, *beatus,* the word for blessed, happy, or fortunate, begins certain verses such as Psalm 1:1: "Blessed is the man who does not walk in the counsel of the wicked." Old Testament beatitudes begin with the Hebrew word *ʾašrê* and the New Testament beatitudes with the Greek word *makarios.* They are used of people, not of God. Some English Bibles translate *eulogētos* as "blessed" ("Blessed be the Lord God of Israel" [Luke 1:68, KJV]), but without the characteristic *makarios,* phrases containing this term are not beatitudes. Old Testament beatitudes, found most frequently in the psalms (e.g., 2:12; 32:2; 40:4; 41:1; 65:4; 84:4–5; 106:3; 112:1; 128:1), are also located in Proverbs 8:32; Isaiah 32:20; 56:2; and Daniel 12:12. The plural proper noun, the Beatitudes, is the common designation for Matthew 5:3–10. Luke's parallel (6:20b–26), with four statements of blessedness and four maledictions, is called the Beatitudes and Woes. Statements of blessing are also found in Matthew 13:16; John 20:29; and Revelation 1:3; 14:13; 16:15; 19:9; 20:6; 22:7, 14.

The classical New Testament beatitude has three parts: (1) the adjective "blessed"; (2) the identification of the "blessed" person(s) by a descriptive clause or participle; and (3) the condition assuring "blessedness." Thus in Matthew's first beatitude (5:3), "Blessed are the poor in spirit, for theirs is the kingdom of heaven," the "blessed" persons are identified as the "poor in spirit" and are "blessed" because "theirs is the kingdom of heaven." As the first word in the psalms (1:1), blessed is applied generally to all those within God's redemptive covenant established with Abraham. The believer praying Psalm 1:1 becomes the beatitude's subject. His blessedness comes within his relationship to God in which he accomplishes the divine will and keeps himself separate from God's enemies (1:1–2). The Torah, God's written revelation, is his constant occupation (v. 2). Unbelievers are destined to destruction (vv. 4–6), but the "blessed" is promised life with God (v. 3). Psalm 32 sees the "blessed" as one "whose transgressions are forgiven" and "whose sin the Lord does not count against him." The sinner's iniquity is imputed by God to the Suffering Servant (Isa. 53:6).

The concept of blessedness is not easily translated into English. "Happy," "fortunate," and "favored" have all been offered as less than completely satisfactory translations. "Happy" focuses narrowly on emotional well-being, not taking into account that within relationship to God sin is confessed (Ps. 32:3–5). "Fortunate" is derived from the Latin word for chance or luck and was used also for the Roman goddess who determined arbitrarily and capriciously each person's destiny. It still means a haphazard random selection, success, collective possessions and wealth, not given others. Since the poor (Luke 6:20), those who confess sin (Ps. 32:3–5), and the dead (Rev. 14:13) are subjects of the beatitudes, "happy" and "fortunate" seem inappropriate. *Favor* is the Latin word for grace; to avoid confusion "favored" should not be used. "Blessed" should be used in all cases, so that the English reader will recognize that these passages are related as beatitudes. Blessedness should not be seen as a reward for religious accomplishments, but as an act of God's grace in believers' lives. Rather than congratulating them on spiritual or moral achievements, the beatitude underscores the fact that sinners stand within a forgiving relationship made possible by Christ's atonement.

Scholars debate the connections between Matthew's and Luke's beatitudes. The two-source (Mark and "Q", standing for *Quelle,* the German word for source) hypothesis holds that there are "Q" beatitudes, from which Matthew and Luke took theirs. These "Q" beatitudes are a reconstructed abridgement of Luke's four statements, which Matthew expanded with five additional ones. Another view suggests that each independently took over oral tradition, as he knew it directly (Matthew) or obtained it from others (Luke). Still another holds that one evangelist was first and that the other worked with his beatitudes. This issue cannot be resolved to everyone's satisfaction. It should be noted that Matthew's version was most widespread in the postapostolic fathers and remains the best known. Luke's use of the second person plural in each of his four beatitudes may suggest a dependency on Matthew's ninth beatitude, where he introduces this form for the first time (5:11).

The similarity between Matthew's Sermon on the Mount (5–7) and Luke's Sermon on the Plain (6:17–49), in which both place their beatitudes, points to a specific occasion in Jesus' ministry, probably near Capernaum, without ruling out the possibility that they were basic to his ordinary preaching at other times (see Matt. 4:23–25). Matthew's arrangement, matching the first and eighth of his nine beatitudes and Luke's four beatitudes and four woes, points to each evangelist's arrangement of the material.

The beatitudes are descriptive of all Christians and do not single out separate groups as distinct from each other. Thus the blessings are applicable to all. The "poor in spirit" are also "those who mourn" (Matt. 5:4) or "hunger and thirst for righteousness" (5:6). Each beatitude looks at the Christian life from a different perspective. Matthew's first beatitude with its "the poor in spirit" (5:3) is the best known and perhaps the most difficult to interpret. With the omission of "in spirit" (6:20b), Luke points to the economically poor, a recognized theme in his Gospel. He includes the personal "yours" in promising them "the kingdom of God," his substitute for Matthew's "kingdom of heaven." Matthew's "in spirit" indicates that these "poor" make no claim on God. The tension between Matthew's spiritual poor and Luke's economic poor should not be overdrawn, since the latter uses those who are financially deprived as examples of those who depend on God, a common theme of all the beatitudes. Matthew's remaining eight beatitudes expand on the first. The mourners will experience God's comfort (v. 4). The meek demonstrate a Christ-like attitude that demands nothing for itself. Thus the meek with Jesus shall inherit the earth (v. 5). Those who "hunger and thirst for righteousness" (v. 6) desire God's saving righteousness in Christ. The mercy Christians show to others (v. 7) must be that of Christ, who showed mercy to his tormentors (Luke 23:34). In the fifth petition of the Lord's Prayer Christians pray that God will forgive them, just as they forgive others (Matt. 6:12). Seeing God is reserved to Christ (John 1:18), but now the pure in heart will see God with him (v. 8). The Gospels reserve the phrase "Son of God" to Jesus alone, but the peacemakers show themselves to be reconciled to God, and all people are now entitled to a like honor in being called the sons of God (v. 9). The eighth beatitude follows the first with its promise of the kingdom of heaven, Christ's pledge that they will participate in his suffering and glory. Here the "poor in spirit" are defined as "persecuted because of righteousness" (v. 10). The ninth and final beatitude (v. 11), by adding the specific "you" and "account of me," places Christ in the center of the Beatitudes and sees the believers' state of blessedness in their persecution for his sake. The Beatitudes are christological because he spoke them and they reach their perfection in him. In his perfection they are descriptive of the church's promised holiness.

Luke 1:48 and Matthew 16:17 differ from other beatitudes in singling out specific persons. The recognition of Mary's blessedness by succeeding generations rests in the Lord's selection of her as his mother and not in the morally superior accomplishment of her will. Peter is blessed because God has revealed to him that Jesus is the Christ, the Son of God, a faith unobtainable through his own effort. Thus he becomes a prototype of all believers in Christ. The beatitudes of the Book of Revelation concentrate on the victory promised Christians dying in the faith. Their condition is certain: "Blessed are the dead who die in the Lord . . . they will rest from their labor, for their deeds will follow them" (14:13). Their blessedness is seen that in death God gives them rest.

DAVID P. SCAER

See also JESUS CHRIST; SERMON ON THE MOUNT.

Bibliography. I. W. Batdorf, *Interpreting the Beatitudes;* D. Hamm, *The Beatitudes in Context;* J. Lambrecht, *The Sermon on the Mount.* J. M. Boice *The Sermon on the Mount.*

Beauty. ***Old Testament Significance.*** Appreciation for beauty is a consistent theme throughout the Bible. The Bible also has a full-orbed doctrine of beauty. Thus, beauty for beauty's sake is not addressed. The Old Testament Scriptures are particularly appreciative of nature. God announced that creation was good (Gen. 1). The psalms reveal an appreciation for God's handiwork (Pss. 8; 19:1; 29; 104). God made his world good by causing the springs to gush forth in the valleys, the grass to grow for the cattle, and the moon to mark the seasons. The Hebrew mind that reflected on God's goodness in nature was in contrast to the pagan mind-set of the surrounding nations, which often went so far as to declare that the world was totally evil.

Human Attractiveness. Both women and men are described as attractive. Human beings at times used cosmetics to make themselves more beautiful (Isa. 3:18–24). Sarah (Gen. 12:11), Rebekah (Gen. 24:16), Abigail (1 Sam. 25:3), Rachel, Abishag, Bathsheba, and Esther are singled out for their beauty. Yet physical beauty was secondary to piety and resourcefulness (Prov. 31:10–31; also see 1 Tim. 2:9–10; 1 Peter 3:3–5). The writer of the Song of Solomon portrays his love for his bride as beautiful. Though the Hebrews did not exalt the human form as did the ancient Greeks, some men are referred to as exceedingly handsome: David (1 Sam. 16:12), Absalom (2 Sam. 14:25), Daniel (Dan. 1:15), Joseph, Jonathan, and even Moses as a child (Exod. 1). Clothing also had esthetic appeal (see Gen. 41:42; 45:22; Exod. 26:36; 28:2; Rev. 3:4).

Divine Descriptions. Scripture presents an implicit theology of beauty as a concomitant of divine creativity and eschatological redemption. The Lord's favor is beautiful and his hopeful promises offer "beauty for ashes" for his people (Ps. 90:17; Isa. 61:3). God is a diadem of beauty for the faithful Israelite remnant (Isa. 28:5).

God is a God of glory, and his Shekinah glory is ever present among his people (Exod. 16:7; 24:16; 40:34; Lev. 9:6; Num. 14:10; Deut. 5:24). The promised Messiah was prophesied to be a beautiful king (Isa. 33:17). Yet the prophet also said that the suffering Messiah would have "no beauty or majesty to attract us to him" (Isa. 53:2).

Johannine Significance. It should hardly surprise us that beauty plays such an important role in the Bible's eschatological drama. The Book of Revelation avoids anthropomorphic representations of God. God is described in undeniable splendor. The concept of beauty thus is more significant than simple attractiveness. Beauty is similar, if not synonymous, with God's glory. The one who sits on the throne of the universe "had the appearance of jasper . . . and a rainbow, resembling an emerald, encircled the throne" (Rev. 4:3). The Holy City, the final estate prepared for God's people, is gloriously adorned as a bride for her husband (Rev. 21:2).

Pauline Significance. In the present period, believers are exhorted to live in a manner that will make the teaching of the Lord beautiful and attractive before unbelievers (Titus 2:10). Those who preach the gospel can be described as beautiful (Rom. 10:15).

DAVID S. DOCKERY

Beelzebub. *See* GODS AND GODDESSES, PAGAN.

Belief, Believe. *See* FAITH.

Benediction. *See* THANKFULNESS, THANKSGIVING.

Bible, Authority of the. The central question that runs through the Bible is that of the authority of God. His authority is majestically displayed in Genesis 1, where the words "and God said" puncture the darkness of chaos and speak the cosmos into being. It is supremely challenged by a creature of his own making in Genesis 3: "Yea, hath God said . . . ?" asks the serpent of the woman (3:1 KJV), and the question reverberates down through the centuries that follow, all the way to the Book of Revelation, where the Almighty God "hath on his vesture and on his thigh a name written, KING OF KINGS AND LORD OF LORDS," and "death and hell were cast into the lake of fire. This is the second death," as the Lord God Omnipotent's reign is eschatologically established and every challenge to his authority destroyed (19:16; 20:14 KJV). This is the theological context for the question of the authority of the Bible, because as God's written ("inscripturated") revelation its authority is the authority of God; for what Scripture says, God says.

The serpent's question in Genesis 3 is not simply the most striking example of a challenge to the authority of God; it is the fruit of the challenge of Lucifer who as the devil stands behind, or within, the serpent. And it is the challenge that leads Eve, and then Adam, into their definitive act of rebellion. It should be noted that the serpent's challenge "Hath God said?" is, in particular, a challenge to the authority of the word of God, a claim to know better than the word that God has spoken. This focus in the original act of sin on challenge to the authority of God in his word underlines from the outset the closeness of the connection between the person and the word of a God who is characterized as God who speaks. "When the woman saw that the fruit of the tree was good for food and pleasing to the eye, and also desirable for gaining wisdom, she took some and ate it. She also gave some to her husband, and he ate it. . . . Then the LORD God said to the woman, 'What is this you have done?'" (3:6, 13). The consequences are extraordinary.

So it is vital to understand that this doctrine, far from playing a minor role on the fringes of Christian belief, brings us face to face with the authority of God himself. What is at stake in the authority of Holy Scripture is the authority of its divine author. And, in light of the fact that every doctrine believed by the church is in turn authorized by appeal to Holy Scripture (theological proposals are grounded "according to the Scriptures," in the words of the creed), it is no exaggeration to say that the entire structure of Christian theology stands or falls by the authority of Scripture, the major premise for every theological statement that would claim the allegiance of the canonical community that is the church of Jesus Christ. This is still widely admitted in contemporary theological discussion, both implicitly (for every theologian, orthodox or not, quotes Scripture to bolster theological argument), and sometimes in so many words.

That immensely significant fact offers the context for the realization that the doctrine of the authority of the Bible is, uniquely, *reflective* in character. That is, though its subject is the Bible, it is a biblical doctrine like other biblical doctrines. Yet unlike other matters of Christian belief and practice on which the Bible speaks—Christology, eschatology, the nature of God, the Christian life—we are here concerned with what the Bible says about itself. It is sometimes suggested that this invalidates the Bible's testimony to its own authority, though it is a matter of logic that the highest authority must be its own authority. If the Bible is the "supreme rule of faith and life," none can be higher. Moreover, the Bible's self-testimony is pluriform and, in turn, sustained by the testimony of others; especially, the internal testimony of the Holy Spirit. Let us briefly review each of these factors, because they have special relevance to the significance of the reflexive character of the doctrine.

First, the pluriform character of the Bible's self-testimony. As we shall shortly be reminded, what we find in Holy Scripture is not some bald claim to raw authority but a collation of many testimonies on behalf of Holy Scripture as a book. The canonical claim takes the form of interlocking claims and evidences that include the phenomena of the divine speech, the particular testimony of Jesus Christ to the character of what we call the Old Testament, and the authoritative use of canonical books by the writers of others. Second, the Bible's testimony is sustained by the use of the Bible in the church, as its authority has been recognized and found to be effective for the definition of doctrine and ethics, the public preaching of the gospel, and private devotion. Third, the chief ground of the believer's and the church's confidence in the authority of Holy Scripture lies in the internal testimony of the Holy Spirit in the heart of the Christian. That is to say, though the Scripture seems to be self-attesting, it is the divine author of Scripture, the Holy Spirit of God, who inspired the writing of that same Scripture, who is its final witness. He assures the believer that this canonical Scripture is verily the word of God written. That is, God offers his own witness to his word.

Yet the authority of Scripture is also a biblical doctrine like any other. It is the plainest of all biblical teachings, assumed as the starting point of the Bible in its role as a teaching book just as it has been assumed as the major premise of every use of the Bible since, lying behind the very possibility of biblical theology. Among the theological disciplines, "Bibliology" is both prolegomenon, part of the prelude to theology proper, and one among the articles that follow.

The Biblical Testimony. Perhaps the most striking, if often least noticed, testimony is the sustained interweaving of the direct speech of God in the text of the canonical Scriptures of the Old and New Testament. While serving as chief illustration and paradigm of revelation, the direct speech of the Creator-Redeemer resonates throughout the Scriptures and imparts its own stamp of authority to those books in which it is found. It is thus that the Book of Genesis begins with a chapter-long listing of the creative words of God, "And God said. . . ." Chapters 2 and 3 narrate the interlocution of the Lord God and Adam and Eve in the garden. In chapter 4 the Lord engages Cain in interrogation, and curse, and finally grace. And the pattern continues through the flood and the covenant with Noah, and into the call of Abra(ha)m and the long account of the patriarchal discipleship (and the later historical books). In Exodus this narrative leads to the giving of the law on Sinai, and alongside the Ten Commandments, written by the finger of God, we read the mass of first-person instruction that became the basis of the civil and ceremonial practice of the Hebrews. The prophetic books, of course, consist in large measure of discourse from the mouth of God. As we later read, "In the past God spoke to our forefathers through the prophets at many times and in various ways" (Heb. 1:1).

In the New Testament there is some similarity, especially in the Book of Revelation, which repeatedly records the words of God. But there is also a fundamental difference: On page after page of the four Gospels, the incarnate Son of God speaks in human flesh the words of God. "In these last days he has spoken to us by his Son" (Heb. 1:2). As is so apparent in a red-letter testament, Matthew, Mark, Luke, and John record the very words of Jesus in an extensive fashion.

Of course, it is possible to conclude that such claims to divine authority in particular portions of Holy Scripture need not extend to the whole. A general regard for the trustworthiness of Scripture is all that is needed to sustain the divine authority of sayings placed in the mouth of God. Indeed, is not the implication of "Thus says the Lord" that those other sayings recorded by the prophet fall short of divine authority? Should not the quoted speech of Jesus of Nazareth be taken to have an authority to which the letters of Saul of Tarsus could never aspire?

As it happens, the Scriptures themselves tell another story. For the teaching of Jesus Christ extends to the question of bibliology. This is evident in all four Gospels, and the evidence is overwhelming. In John 10:34 we read that Jesus said "The Scripture cannot be broken." In Mark 12:36, of Psalm 110, he states that David is speaking by the Holy Spirit. One of the most significant of all the many New Testament uses of the Old is found in Matthew 19. We read: "Some Pharisees came to him to test him. They asked, 'Is it lawful for a man to divorce his wife for any and every reason?' 'Haven't you read,' he replied, 'that at the beginning the Creator "made them male and female," and said, "for this reason a man will leave his father and mother and be united to his wife, and the two will become one flesh"?'" (4–5). The importance of this reference lies in the fact that in Genesis 2:24, where we find this statement about leaving parents to become one flesh with a wife, the comment is simply attributed to the narrator. It is Jesus who puts it into the mouth of the one who "made them male and female." And the implication is strong: that what Scripture says, God says, whether Scripture places it in the divine speech or as narration and commentary.

The second thread of internal testimony within Scripture may be traced through apostolic use of other canonical books. There is of course extensive New Testament use of the Old in a manner consonant with that which we find in the teaching of Jesus. In 2 Peter 3:15–16 we find this principle carried through into the New Testament Scriptures themselves, as the writings of the apostle Paul are placed on a level with Holy Scripture: "Bear in mind that our Lord's patience means salvation, just as our dear brother Paul also wrote to you with the wisdom that God gave him. He writes the same way in all his letters, speaking in them of these matters. His letters contain some things that are hard to understand, which ignorant and unstable people distort, as they do the other Scriptures, to their own destruction."

The Use of Scripture in the Church. The central place of Holy Scripture in the life and history of the church in every age offers telling evidence of its authority. We do not believe its authority stems from the teaching of the church. But we note the authority which Scripture has, from the start, exercised in all the churches, as believers in the first century and the twentieth have done homage to the written Word of God as rule for their minds, their hearts, and their lives. Here we unite the devotional and doctrinal use of Scripture, its place in preaching, private reading, the great doctrinal controversies, and the anguish of the believer persecuted or bereft who turns to the Word of God for comfort from God himself. It is through Scripture that God has ruled the mind and heart of the church and the Christian.

The Testimony of the Holy Spirit. Central to Christian confidence in the authority of Scripture lies the conviction that behind every argument and experience that lead the believer to trust the Bible there is another witness to be discerned; that of God the Holy Spirit, himself inspirer and interpreter of Scripture, as he testifies to that Word of God. We have noted that it is not possible for a supreme authority to find final testimony in anything lesser. So it is in God only that Scripture can be attested. As Calvin puts it, "For as God alone is a fit witness of himself in his Word, so also the Word will not find acceptance in men's hearts before it is scaled by the inward testimony of the Spirit. That same Spirit, therefore, who has spoken through the mouths of the prophets must penetrate into our hearts to persuade us that they faithfully proclaimed what had been divinely commanded" (*Inst.* 1.7.4).

The near-universal acceptance of biblical authority in the church, liberal and conservative alike, is not coincidental. It draws our attention to the character of the church of Jesus Christ as a canonical community—the people of the book. Yet one implication of this wide assumption that theology should be done "according to the Scriptures" is that the tail comes to wag the dog; because it is necessary to justify theological proposals with reference to Scripture, persons of all theological persuasions seek to find some way to connect their conclusions, on whatever ground they may have been reached, with Scripture. This has led to growing uncertainty about what it means to say that the Bible has authority. To what does that authority extend? Several points of focus have emerged in this discussion. The task of *contextualizing* the teaching of Holy Scripture in the cultures of every century has demanded the best scholars and exegetes at the disposal of the church. It also raises the question of the *extent* of biblical authority. Does it indeed extend to the Pauline condemnation of homosexuality? Growing disagreement among evangelicals has focused on issues of *hermeneutics,* and the nature of authoritative inspiration—whether it implies *inerrancy.* The Chicago Statement on Biblical Inerrancy is widely accepted as a consensus statement of the biblical position, and begins with an affirmation that "recognition of the total truth and trustworthiness of Holy Scripture is essential to a full grasp and adequate confession of its authority." That is to say, acknowledgment of the authority of Holy Scripture is no mere *pro forma* indication of respect, but involves confidence in its inerrancy. "The following Statement affirms this inerrancy of Scripture afresh, making clear our understanding of it and warning against its denial. We are persuaded that to deny it is to set aside the witness of Jesus Christ and of the Holy Spirit and to refuse that submission to the claims of God's own Word which marks true Christian faith." The heart of the confession that follows is found in this paragraph: "Holy Scripture, being God's own Word, written by men prepared and superintended by His Spirit, is of infallible divine authority in all matters upon which it touches: it is to be believed, as God's instruction, in all that it affirms; obeyed, as God's command, in all that it requires; embraced, as God's pledge, in all that it promises." NIGEL M. DE S. CAMERON

See also BIBLE, CANON OF THE; BIBLE, INSPIRATION OF THE.

Bibliography. C. F. H. Henry, *God, Revelation, and Authority;* J. I. Packer, *Fundamentalism and the Word of God;* B. B. Warfield, *The Inspiration and Authority of the Bible;* J. D. Woodbridge, *Biblical Authority: A Critique of the Rogers/McKim Proposal.*

Bible, Canon of the. The word "canon" derives from the Hebrew term *qāneh* and the Greek term *kanōn*, both of which refer to a measuring rod. It designates the exclusive collection of documents in the Judeo-Christian tradition that have come to be regarded as Scripture. The Jewish canon was written in both Hebrew and Aramaic, while the Christian canon was written in Greek.

Theology and Criteria of Canonicity. The historic Christian belief is that the Holy Spirit who inspired the writing of the books also controlled their selection and that this is something to be discerned by spiritual insight rather than by historical research. It is felt that statements in the writings themselves (such as 1 Cor. 2:13; 14:37; Gal. 1:8–9; 1 Thess. 2:13) would cause local churches to preserve them and eventually collect them in a general canon.

A number of criteria were involved in the church's choice of the books it acknowledged as genuine and used in worship services. Irenaeus and other authors of the first three centuries, who wrote against heretical movements and their literature, reveal some of the criteria that the early church used in evaluating its literature.

- The basic criterion of acceptance was *apostolicity*: Was a document written by an apostle? Books known to have been written by apostles were eagerly embraced and churches that knew the legacy of books written by men who were not apostles, such as Mark and Luke, accepted them as well. But other churches, which were not familiar with this legacy, were hesitant to receive such books, especially those that did not contain the name of an author, such as the Gospels, Acts, and Hebrews.
- A second and related question, then, was asked. If a book was not written by an apostle, is its *content apostolic*? This was an early problem with Revelation, because its theological content was difficult to discern. Tertullian valued Hebrews highly, but thought it was written by Barnabas.
- A third criterion was the claim to inspiration. Does the author *claim inspiration*? Some did not.
- A fourth question was: Is it *accepted by loyal churches*? This was a *very* important consideration. What was the attitude of the church in the city to which it was originally written?
- People of every generation have inherently asked about each book of the Bible: Does it have the *"ring of genuineness"*? The testimony of the Spirit was important. In the Old Testament canon there were questions about Esther for a period of time because it does not contain the name of God. Many questioned Revelation in those early years because it did not have this "ring of genuineness."

The Old Testament Canon. Although Christians include both Old and New Testaments in their canon, Jews do not accept a "New" Testament and repudiate the identification of their canon as the "Old" Testament. The proper designation for the Jewish Bible is Tanak, an acronym constituted from the initial letters of the three divisions of that canon—Law (Torah), Prophets (Naviim), and Writings (Kethubim).

The terms "obsolete" and "aging" are used in Hebrews 8:13 with reference to the Jewish covenant. However, early church writers before the latter part of the second century do not use the terms "old" and "new" to designate two different covenants. They considered the second covenant to be a continuation of the first. It was new in the sense of fresh, not in the sense of different. Even in the third century, authors such as Clement of Alexandria and Origen used the expression "new covenant" to refer to the covenant rather than to the documents containing it.

There are also important differences in the content and order of the early canons. Extant Greek Old Testament manuscripts, whose text is quoted often in the New Testament, contain apocryphal books. But the Hebrew Old Testament canon recognized by Palestinian Jews (Tanak) did not include the fourteen books of the Apocrypha. Since the Hebrew Bible was preferred by the Reformers during the Protestant Reformation in their struggle against the Catholic Church, whose Bible contained the Apocrypha, translators of Protestant Bibles excluded the Apocrypha. Thus Protestant and evangelical Bibles duplicate the content of the Hebrew Bible (the current thirty-nine books).

However, the arrangement of books is that of the Latin Vulgate, from which the earliest English translations were made, including the first English translation by John Wycliffe. Even though the New Testament was written in Greek, Protestant and evangelical Bibles do not embrace either the content or the arrangement of the Greek Old Testament. Greek Old Testament manuscripts typically preserve the Alexandrian order, which arranged books according to their subject matter (narrative, history, poetry, and prophecy). Apocryphal books were appropriately interspersed into these categories. The arrangement of the books in the Hebrew Bible is different from both the Greek and the Latin.

According to the testimony of Talmudic and rabbinic sources, the thirty-nine books of the Hebrew Bible were originally divided into only twenty-four. This included three categories embracing five books of Law (Torah), eight Prophets, and eleven Writings. The Law contained the first five books, the Penteteuch. The eight Prophets included Joshua, Judges, Samuel (1 and 2), Kings (1 and 2), Isaiah, Jeremiah, Ezekiel, and the Minor Prophets (12). The eleven books of the Writings contained the subdivisions of poetry (Psalms, Proverbs, Job), the five Megilloth or Rolls (Song of Songs, Ruth, Lamentations, Ecclesiastes, Esther), and the three books of history (Daniel, Ezra-Nehemiah, and Chronicles 1–2).

The Hebrew canon was a thousand years in formation and nothing is known about this process. The Torah of Moses, the oldest portion, was probably written in the fifteenth century B.C., and Malachi, the latest portion, was produced in the fifth century B.C. Some date Daniel in the second century. The Torah or Pentateuch was immediately acknowledged as authoritative and never questioned thereafter. The Prophets and Writings were produced over a period of centuries and gradually won their place in the hearts of the people. Therefore, the Jewish people of Bible times never had the complete Old Testament as we know it.

The Old Testament refers to about fifteen books not contained in it, such as the Book of Jashar (Josh. 10:13) and the Book of the Annals of Solomon (1 Kings 11:41). Although some books of the Old Testament were discussed in Judea at the Pharisaic Council of Jamnia in A.D. 90, the canon itself was not a topic of consideration and this group had no decision-making power. Historically, Jewish scholars have considered the canon closed since the time of Malachi, and have not included the Apocrypha, which was written in subsequent times.

The New Testament Canon. The formation of the New Testament canon, like the Old, was a process rather than an event. Analysis of the process is more historical than biblical, since the church of the New Testament, like the Israel of the Old Testament, never had the complete canon during the time spanned by its canonical literature. However, an occasional indication of the attitude of first-century Christians about their literature is found in the New Testament. Second Peter 3:16 refers to Paul's letters as being misapplied, presumably using the word "scripture" in its usual biblical sense as the Scripture.

Paul refers to a previous letter he wrote to Corinth (1 Cor. 5:9) and to a letter to the Laodiceans (Col. 4:16), neither of which the early church preserved in its canon. The followers of inspired men of God would have regarded everything written by them as authoritative, but not all of their writings were equally useful to the church throughout the ancient world, and so not all of them found universal acceptance. This is what is meant by the term "canon"—that which was finally accepted on an empirewide basis.

Throughout the Roman Empire there existed local canons that often represented no wider usage than that of a particular city and its immediate surroundings. Two of our earliest and best manuscripts of the Greek Testament contain books not accepted by the church as a whole. Codex Sinaiticus (ca. A.D. 350) contained the books Hermas and Barnabas, and Codex Alexandrinus (ca. A.D. 450) contained 1 and 2 Clement. These probably represented only the environs of Alexandria. The Muratorian Canon, probably representative of the church in Rome in the second century, includes books not in our canon, and differentiates those that can be read in public to the whole church from those which are to be read only in private devotion.

Evidence of a collection of Paul's letters is found as early as 2 Peter 3:16, and Paul instructed the churches in Colossae and Laodicea to exchange his letters to them for public reading. This indicates that some letters were intended to be circulated among the churches from the day they were received. The seven churches of Asia were clearly all expected to receive a copy of the Revelation of John for reading in their assemblies.

Thus, the process of collecting and preserving documents would have been underway from the very beginning. Every church receiving such literature would have asked questions concerning authenticity. Such is the process of canonization. Local canons, which often contained some books not utilized by other local churches, were eventually replaced by those lists that represented the general usage of churches throughout the empire.

Of necessity, the process was gradual. It was initially motivated by the desire of various churches to have as many authentic documents of apostolic men as possible, and later motivated by the interaction of church leaders struggling with the question of which books could be appealed to in their debates about the nature of Christ and the church. These discussions began as early as the second century and escalated in the christological controversies of the fourth century, when we have our first full lists of canonical New Testament books.

There are no extant lists from the third century, and only the Muratorian Canon remains from the second, although its form is only a discussion of various books and not a canon in the proper sense of the term. The earliest known collection of Paul's letters is in the Chester Beatty Papyri, which gives us clear evidence of a collection of Paul's letters at the end of the second century.

The earliest extant use of the term "canon" is from the fourth century in the *Ecclesiastical History* of Eusebius of Caesarea (6.25; cf. related words in 3.3.1; 3.25.1–6; 3.31.6). Correspondingly, the first record of discussions about the canon and the differentiation of various categories within it is from this century.

Eusebius distinguishes four groups of books: (1) *accepted* (most of our twenty-seven), (2) *disputed* (James, Jude, 2 Peter, 2 and 3 John), (3) *rejected* (various apocryphal New Testament books), and (4) *heretical* (primarily pseudepigraphical books). He has Revelation in both the accepted and rejected categories, saying opinion on it at the time was divided.

The first exclusive list of our twenty-seven books is in the festal letter #96 of Athanasius (A.D. 367). However, the order is different with the General Epistles following Acts and Hebrews following 2 Thessalonians. The first exclusive list of our twenty-seven books in their current familiar order is in the writings of Amphilocius of Iconium in A.D. 380.

There is no "proper" order of New Testament books; several different arrangements exist in early manuscripts. More than 284 different sequences of biblical books (Old and New Testament) have been found in Latin manuscripts alone, and more than twenty different arrangements of Paul's letters have been found in ancient authors and manuscripts.

Division of individual books of the canon into smaller sections is first indicated in the fourth century, in Codex Vaticanus, which uses paragraph divisions, somewhat comparable to the Hebrew Bible. Our familiar chapter and verse divisions were introduced into the Bible quite late in the history of the canon. Stephen Langton introduced the chapters into the Latin Bible prior to his death in 1228, and Stephanus added the verses in the New Testament in 1551 and his publication of a Greek and Latin edition of the New Testament. Verses are attested in the Hebrew Bible as far back as the Mishnah (Megillah 4:4). The first English Bible to include verse divisions was the Geneva Bible of 1560. Thus, our English translations reflect the divisions as well as the order of the Latin Vulgate. JOHN MCRAY

See also APOCRYPHA; BIBLE, AUTHORITY OF THE; BIBLE, INSPIRATION OF THE.

Bibliography. F. F. Bruce, *The Canon of Scripture;* idem, *The Books and the Parchments;* H. von Campenhausen, *The Formation of the Christian Bible;* B. S. Childs, *The New Testament as Canon;* E. J. Goodspeed, *The Formation of the New Testament;* R. M. Grant, *The Formation of the New Testament;* B. Metzger, *The Canon of the New Testament;* H. E. Ryle, *The Canon of the Old Testament;* J. Sanders, *Torah and Canon;* B. F. Westcott, *The Canon of the New Testament.*

Bible, Inspiration of the. The cornerstone of evangelical theology lies in its confession of the inspiration and authority of the Bible, as the revealed "Word of God Written." Since the term "inspired" is used of the Bible in different ways, it is important to clarify the particular sense in which it should be employed, not because evangelicals have coined a new meaning for inspiration, but rather to make clear their adherence to the sense in which the Church has historically confessed her faith in Holy Scripture. We should also note that by calling inspiration the cornerstone of evangelical theology we deny the strange charge, often leveled against conservative Christians, that they are "bibliolators," worshiping the Scriptures in the place of God. The seriousness with which evangelicals take the inspiration of Holy Scriptures derives exclusively from their conviction that when they read it they read the very words of God. It is only by attending to those inspired words that believers may properly hear what he has said. Evangelical biblio*logy* (the doctrine of Scripture that centers on its inspiration), far from leading to biblio*latry* (the worship of Scripture), lies at the heart of true worship of God. For the doctrine, though itself a biblical doctrine, points beyond itself and does nothing other than direct our attention most carefully to everything Scripture says. It assures us that what Scripture says, God says. We may therefore say that this doctrine serves as the point of connection between the canon of Holy Scripture and the God who is its author; it is the ground of Scripture's authority that itself entails its revelatory character.

In 2 Peter 1:19–21, we read that "no prophecy of Scripture came about by the prophet's own interpretation. For prophecy never had its origin in the will of man, but men spoke from God as they were carried along by the Holy Spirit." The scope of prophecy here is uncertain: It may refer simply to the corpus of the writing prophets, or more broadly to the historical books of the Old Testament also, or indeed (as Warfield argues) to the whole Old Testament. Certainly it speaks precisely of the divine origin of that portion of Scripture to which it refers, and of the role of the Holy Spirit in "carrying along" the human writers, such that the "word of the prophets" may be "made more certain" (1:19).

The Bible's View of Itself. Every Christian doctrine is founded in Holy Scripture—the creeds and confessions of the church, as surely as the pastor's message, find their justification in one place alone: the teaching of Holy Scripture. It is in the course of conveying teaching on every other subject that Scripture also teaches about itself. It is important to note that texts like 2 Timothy 3:16 and 2 Peter 1:19–21 are not isolated statements but articulate a doctrine taught throughout Holy Scripture. What is recorded in Scripture comes from God; the very recording has taken place under a divine superintendence.

Substantial portions of the Pentateuch are *directly* attributed to God. The plainest passage is Exodus 20, in which the Ten Commandments are recorded; we later learn (31:18; 32:15–16) that they were written on two tablets of stone, "inscribed on both sides, front and back. The tablets were the work of God; the writing was the writing of God, engraved on the tablets." But the context of these laws written by the finger of God is the mass of legislation in Exodus, Leviticus, Numbers, and Deuteronomy, in which the constant reiteration of "The LORD said to Moses" culminates in Deuteronomy 31:9: "So Moses wrote down this law and gave it to the priests . . . and to all the elders of Israel."

The prophetic books of the Old Testament are largely composed of extended passages placed by the writer in the mouth of God. "The word of the LORD came to me, saying . . ." is the constant refrain of the writing prophets, offering the most explicit endorsement of the apostle Peter's model of prophetic inspiration, as Isaiah and Jeremiah and Ezekiel were "carried along by the Holy Spirit."

Simply to focus on those occasions when the biblical writers explicitly attribute elements in their literary product to God's special work might be taken to imply the contrary of the position we are developing; that parts of Scripture have this special status while other parts do not. The evidence of the New Testament (and, indeed, of the development of Jewish attitudes to the books of the Old Testament before that time) suggests something very different: that these books had been accorded the status of inspired Scripture. And the argument is not merely historical, showing what the first Christians believed. Second Timothy 3:16 and 2 Peter 1:21 indicate a settled view of Scripture on the part of the church, which the Gospels demonstrate was in harmony with the teaching of Jesus himself. The Gospel pages are peppered with his question "Have you not read . . . ?" and Jesus' confident assertion, "It is written . . ." (that is, "The Bible says . . ."). That the incarnate Son of God should treat the Old Testament in this fashion offers the strongest possible endorsement of the divine inspiration of Holy Scripture, neatly illustrated in Matthew 19:4–5 were Jesus quotes Genesis 2:24 ("For this reason a man will leave his father and mother . . ."). In Genesis this is a comment by the narrator. Jesus puts it directly into the mouth of God: "The Creator 'made them male and female,' and said, 'For this reason . . .'" Since this example fits so well into Jesus' other use of Scripture, its significance is beyond doubt: He regarded all of Scripture as that which God has spoken.

When Jesus promised the Holy Spirit to the disciples he told them that they would be led by the Spirit "into all truth" (John 16:13). By analogy with the Old Testament, we might anticipate that the Spirit would ensure a further canonical record of the work of God in Christ. And we are not mistaken. As early as the later New Testament documents themselves, there is a recognition of this process. In 2 Peter 3:16 we read that Paul's "letters contain some things that are hard to understand, which ignorant and unstable people distort, as they do the other Scriptures." Already, within the pages of the New Testament, Paul's letters are accorded the status of Scripture, setting the pattern for the recognition of all the books of the second Testament as inspired and therefore canonical for the church of Jesus Christ.

NIGEL M. DE S. CAMERON

See also BIBLE, AUTHORITY OF THE; BIBLE, CANON OF THE.

Bibliography. G. C. Berkouwer, *Holy Scripture;* D. A. Carson and J. W. Woodbridge, eds., *Scripture and Truth;* idem, *Hermeneutics, Authority, and Canon;* C. F. H. Henry, *God, Revelation, and the Bible;* R. Pache, *The Inspiration and Authority of Scripture;* I. Packer, *Fundamentalism and the Word of God;* B. B. Warfield, *The Inspiration and Authority of the Bible.*

Biblical Theology. Study of the Bible that seeks to discover what the biblical writers, under divine guidance, believed, described, and taught in the context of their own times.

Relation to Other Disciplines. Biblical theology is related to but different from three other major branches of theological inquiry. Practical theology focuses on pastoral application of biblical truths in modern life. Systematic theology articulates the biblical outlook in a current doctrinal or philosophical system. Historical theology investigates the development of Christian thought in its growth through the centuries since biblical times.

Biblical theology is an attempt to articulate the theology that the Bible contains as its writers addressed their particular settings. The Scriptures came into being over the course of many centuries, from different authors, social settings, and geographical locations. They are written in three different languages and numerous literary forms (genres). Therefore analytic study leading to synthetic understanding is required to grasp their overarching themes and underlying unities. Biblical theology labors to arrive at a coherent synthetic overview without denying the fragmentary nature of the light the Bible sheds on some matters, and without glossing over tensions that may exist as various themes overlap (e.g., God's mercy and God's judgment; law and grace).

Preliminary Assumptions. Study of any object calls for assumptions appropriate to that object. An African witch doctor's assumptions would probably not yield many empirically valid observations regarding the cause and cure of whooping cough. Likewise, biblical theology calls for certain assumptions without which valid observations about the meaning of the Bible's parts and whole are sure to elude the observer.

Inspiration. The whole Bible is given by God. While it unabashedly affirms and reflects its human authorship, it is no less insistent on its divine origin and message. Attempts to separate God's word from Scripture's words, a feature of academic biblical theology since its inception in Germany in 1787, have often resulted in the interpreter airing personal critical convictions rather than laying bare the theology of the writings themselves.

Unity. While contrasts and tensions exist within the biblical corpus due to the local and temporal soil from which its components first sprang, a solidarity underlies them. This solidarity is grounded in the oneness of God's identity and redemptive plan. It is also rooted in humankind's sinful solidarity in the wake of Adam's fall. Scripture's undeniable diversity, commonly overplayed in current critical discussion, complements rather than obliterates its profound unity. Scripture is its own best interpreter, and uncertainties raised by one portion are often legitimately settled by appeal to another.

Reliability. Since God is the ultimate author of the Bible, and since truthfulness characterizes his communication to person, biblical theology is justified in upholding the full reliability of the Bible rightly interpreted. Scholars indifferent or hostile to the Bible's truth claims have impugned its integrity from earliest times. In the modern era a panoply of critical methods, with their underlying assumptions, makes skepticism toward the Bible as historically understood in the church the accepted order of the day. But thinkers of stature remain convinced that the Bible contains no material errors, although it does present conundrums that do not yet admit of universally accepted answers. Even critical tools, when employed judiciously rather than only skeptically, have helped confirm to many that assuming the veracity of the biblical text and message may not be any more uncritical than wholesale rejection of it.

Christ the Center. Jesus explicitly stated that the Scriptures point to him (Luke 24:27, 44; John 5:39). The New Testament writers follow Jesus in this conviction. The Old Testament writers are aware of a future fulfillment to Yahweh's present promises to his people; that fulfillment, while multifaceted, is summed up in Jesus messianic ministry. While biblical theology can err in overstating the ways the Old Testament foreshadows and predicts the Messiah, and the ways in which the New Testament finds its meaning in Jesus Christ, it may likewise err in denying him his central place in the grand drama of both biblical and world history.

Overview of Biblical Theology. Biblical theologians have proposed various methods of going about their task. Some stress the Bible's key integrating themes: covenant, the exodus, the kingdom of God, promise and fulfillment, God's glory, reconciliation, and many others. Some stress the relationship of Scripture's various parts to Jesus Christ. Some see the proper center of biblical theology as being God himself or his mighty acts of deliverance. Still others stress the similarities between biblical statements of the past and confessional statements that have arisen in the history of the church.

While there are strengths to each of these approaches, there are also limitations. None alone is adequate. This is not surprising, since God, his ways, and the writings that convey knowledge of him defy reduction to even the most skilled human organization and exposition. Many would agree that the best method must be multiplex in nature.

Moreover, any approach must factor in the progressive and historical dimension of the Bible's theology. What God brought about, he accomplished gradually over the course of time. The theology of the Bible unfolds in the course of the events it describes and sometimes precipitates. Below is a survey of biblical theology centering on its historical rise and progression.

Creation and Fall. The early chapters of Genesis, corroborated by subsequent statements in both Old Testament and New Testament, affirm that God created the world by fiat decree ("And God said . . . ; cf. Heb. 11:3), not out of preexisting matter. God alone is eternal; matter is not. In its primordial state the created order was pristine and unspoiled—"very good" (Gen. 1:31).

Crowning six days (whether literal or metaphorical) of creative activity, God brought humankind into being. Both male and female were part of God's creative intention from the beginning (1:27), yet Adam was created first and then Eve as his companion (2:18). Their complementary (not interchangeable) natures and roles precede rather than rise out of the sin into which they fell.

Evil's origin is shrouded in considerable (not utter) mystery, but it was personified in a serpentine figure of intelligence and beauty who beguiled both human inhabitants of Eden (chap. 3). The outcome was estrangement from God and a future marked with pain and woe. Yet the curse of sin is ameliorated from the start by a God who seeks sinners to redeem them (3:9). His majesty in creation is, if anything, exceeded by his graciousness in redemption.

Covenant and Captivity. Genesis 4–11 moves rapidly through the vicissitudes of early humankind to the time of Noah. Humankind becomes so corrupt that a sweeping response is called for. Despite Noah's faithful preaching (2 Peter 2:5), few repent in view of the coming flood. Nearly universal loss of human life results. God covenants—establishes terms under which redemptive relationship to him rather than judgment are possible—with the remnant, Noah and his kin (Gen. 9:1–17), foreshadowing the covenant par excellence with Abraham lying yet in the future.

Despite God's covenant initiative, the debacle at Babel (11:1–9) documents humankind's continued disposition to rebellion. Yet God's disposition to save is greater still. He chooses Abram through whom to redeem a people, thereby blessing all the nations of the earth (12:3). To Abram, later called Abraham (17:5), the Hebrew people trace their ancestry. Subsequently this people becomes known as the Jews, from whom Christ is descended. The line from Abraham to the Savior of humankind is in that sense direct.

Abraham is saved through his trust in God's saving mercy alone, as atonement for sin and hope for the future (15:6). This trust does not exclude but rather presupposes his obedient responsiveness to God's revealed will (22:18); "faith" and "faithfulness" are mutually conditioning. Abraham's sacrifice of Isaac, halted by an angel, foreshadows God's own sacrifice for sin millennia hence, just as his wife Sarah's conception of a son at the age of ninety prefigures resurrection from the dead (Rom. 4:17–25).

Abraham's descendants (Isaac, Jacob) bear the responsibility of the covenant God made with their father, but they seldom rise to his level of integrity in seeking the Lord. From Jacob's, or Israel's (35:10) sons come heads of Israel's twelve tribes. One of the youngest of these, Joseph, is preserved by God through kidnapping and imprisonment in Egypt. His rise to power there as adjutant second only to Pharaoh himself sets the stage for a captivity of Israel's descendants some four centuries in length, in keeping with God's promise to Abraham (15:16). The closing chapters of Genesis and the beginning of Exodus chronicle this saga.

Torah and Theocracy. By God's own initiative and power, Moses arises to lead God's people out of their bondage. Their deliverance is a direct result of God's covenant with Abraham (Exod. 2:24). Following revelation of his own name for himself (Yahweh) to Moses (3:14), God breaks Pharaoh's stranglehold on the hapless Israelites. The first Passover (chap. 12) averts the death angel's visitation. It also sets the stage for the dramatic exodus from Egypt through the Red (or Reed) Sea (13:17–22), a historical precedent and enduring symbol of divine deliverance by God's own hand in all ages since.

While knowledge of God's moral character and will was not unknown among God's people prior to Moses, it is revealed in fuller and more definite form, and in a more discrete social context, at Mount Sinai (chap. 19). This instruction, epitomized by the Decalogue or Ten Commandments, does not set aside, but rather, gives a vehicle for living within the Abrahamic covenant. In the law Israel receives a moral, social, and religious charter through which God will further his redemptive will for centuries to come. His aim to bless all nations in keeping with his promise to Abraham is still at work. While parts of this law appear to have their fulfillment primarily in their own day and time, others are restated in the New Testament, and all retain value and relevance (Rom. 15:4; 1 Cor. 10:11). The basic dynamic of God's people honoring their Lord through fidelity to his revealed written word is basic to the faith that both Old Testament and New Testament model and prescribe.

Along with Moses—a precursor of the Messiah (Exod. 18:18; cf. Acts 3:20–23)—and the law, come Aaron and the priesthood. Bloody sacrifices could not in themselves furnish atonement for sins any more than legal adherence to the Mosaic moral code. Yet both sacrificial cult and legal requirement were continual reminders of God's disapproval of sin and his offer of reconciliation to the contrite of heart. As such they pointed to the perfect sacrifice and fulfiller of the law, Jesus Christ.

The five Old Testament books of Moses, the Pentateuch, set forth a lofty practical and spiritual agenda. The Israelites in Moses' wake at first uphold God's honor, crossing the Jordan under divine leadership as administered by Joshua. They then submit to circumcision (Josh. 5), a reaffirmation of submission to the Lord revealed at Sinai in contrast to their parents' chronic disbelief (1 Cor. 10:5; Heb. 3:19). Yet even as Joshua passes from the scene, the Israelites succumb to the idolatry of the lands they have conquered. A pattern of spiritual degeneration and periodic divine deliverance marks the era described by the Book of Judges.

God's tenacious striving with his people for their deliverance takes a new turn in the time of

Samuel. As a prophet, one especially called and enabled by God to speak on his behalf, it falls to him to appoint Israel's first earthly king, Saul.

Monarchy and Apostasy. From the time of Saul (ca. 1020 B.C.) to the fall of Jerusalem (586 B.C.), God works through kings and their subject peoples to achieve his ends. R. Bultmann's quip that the Old Testament is not a history of redemption but of disaster (*Unheilsgeschichte*) is overly dour, yet captures an important dimension of this segment of Old Testament history and thus its theology. God faithfully raises up and blesses leaders who are charged with guiding God's people in God's ways. There are signal successes, but the general drift is lower than the high calling God extends.

David is the central figure, his reign prefiguring the messianic kingdom itself. His hymns of praise, contrition, and instruction (the psalms, not all attributable to David) are timely yet timeless models of spiritual insight and thus central to the focus of biblical theology. Likewise the wisdom (given explicitly by God: 1 Kings 3:12) of his son Solomon stands at the center of an equally weighty literary corpus for biblical-theological work, the so-called wisdom literature. This material furnishes a gnomic counterpart to the more prevalent Old Testament literary forms of narrative and law. Biblical theology minimizes the theology distinct to any of these Old Testament forms at the peril of attenuating Scripture's full message.

During the monarchy, as already in centuries previous, prophets consistently warn of drifting away from the Lord and toward the religious though godless ways of Israel's neighbors. Nathan rebukes David; Ahijah and Iddo speak to Solomon's times; Elijah and Elisha minister to the northern kingdom of Israel after its split from Judah to the south following Solomon's reign. The office of prophet is central to the Old Testament. Like the Old Testament office of priest and king, it not only actualizes God's redemptive work in Old Testament times but also foreshadows the offices fulfilled by the Messiah yet to come.

The drift that God's prophets decry is documented by writing prophets like Isaiah, Hosea, Micah, and Amos. The northern kingdom falls into apostasy and finally judgment at the hand of Assyria (722 B.C.). The southern kingdom is favored with spiritual renewals under noble kings like Hezekiah and Josiah. Yet it, too, fails to give God his due, as Jeremiah particularly makes clear. In 587 B.C. Babylonia appears to shatter forever the regnancy of the line of David. Jeremiah's doleful lamentations bespeak the despondency of those who await, now with virtually no visible consolation, the deliverance and glory promised to their forefathers since Abraham.

Restoration and Remnant. Jeremiah's hope (Jer. 31), grounded in God's revelation to previous prophets like Moses, David, and Isaiah, finds eloquent expression in Ezekiel and Daniel. They too experience the ravages of deportation to Babylon but cling to and proclaim the continued validity of God's earlier promises. Inspired no doubt by this prophetic guidance, small bands begin to return from Babylon to rebuild Jerusalem (ca. 520 B.C.), spurred on by Haggai and Zechariah. Other waves of repatriates under Nehemiah and Ezra give a boost to the work some decades later (ca. 450 B.C.). The final book of the Old Testament testifies to their labor, yet decries a people still divided in their loyalties between God and their own willfulness. That same book upholds the promise of vindication for all who turn to the covenant God in repentance, and pliant trust in a coming deliverer (Mal. 4) whose work will furnish the means of their vindication. That deliverer will also mete out eternal judgment to those hostile or indifferent to the covenant God.

The truly faithful few—their number seems seldom if ever to constitute a hegemony among Abraham's physical descendants throughout Old Testament history—appear to dwindle steadily once the Old Testament period proper ends. The children of Abraham and the land of promise languish under the rule of Persia, which is terminated abruptly by the Greeks in the 320s B.C., who are in turn succeeded by Egyptian and then Syrian overlords. During these decades the religious forms and theological idioms of the Old Testament, diverse in themselves, are transformed into patterns that give Judaism as seen in New Testament times its distinctive faces. A period of Jewish independence (165–163 B.C.) is cut off by the Romans, who appoint Herod the Great as administrator of Galilee, Judea, and their environs around 38 B.C.

Isaiah had spoken of a time of great darkness when the Lord himself would visit his people (9:1–7). A biblical-theological survey of the Old Testament and its aftermath finds that time to have arrived in the days of Jesus' birth.

Fulfillment and Deliverance. The genealogies of both Matthew and Luke testify to the intrinsic connection of Jesus' coming with God's purpose and work in previous epochs. Luke 1–2 describes the Old Testament hopes of figures like Zechariah, Elizabeth, Mary, Simeon, and Anna as these all voice confidence in the fidelity of God to his Old Testament promises.

In Jesus of Nazareth God's deliverance and fulfillment arrive. God's reign, graphically and variously prefigured in Old Testament events and institutions, is actually at hand. John the Baptist electrifies a religiously fragmented and politically oppressed nation as the divine voice echoes once again through the prophetic ministry. Jesus, who is also seen as a prophet (Mark 8:28), reaps the benefit of this excitement. Like John, he preaches repentance and the imminence of God's kingdom. Unlike John, who pointed to another, Jesus calls men and women to himself.

Over a span of some three years Jesus traverses the lands of Galilee, Judea, Samaria, and adjoining districts. He devotes special attention to a group of twelve who will carry on his work once he departs, but he also issues a call and instruction to the (predominantly but not exclusively Jewish) masses. His message targets ethnic Israel but has application to all peoples, even during his lifetime. His teachings, sublime by any reckoning, cannot by separated from a consciousness of unique filial relationship to God. He appeared to be asserting that he was in some sense God's equal. His teaching must also be seen in the light of his insistence that he came to bring deliverance, not through mastery of knowledge he transmits, but through personal trust in the sacrificial, saving death he undergoes (Mark 8:31; 10:32–34, 45). The four Gospels concur in presenting the climax of Jesus' coming, not in his miracles, wisdom, or ethics, great as these are, but in his atoning death and vindicating resurrection.

Jesus' ministry, then, is the culmination of God's saving plan established in Old Testament times. His call to repentance and offer of new life fulfills the prophetic office; his sacrificial death and mediatorial role fulfill the role of an eternal high priest; the rule he possesses (John 18:37) in David's train establishes him as King of kings, the invisible God's incarnate regent over all space, time, and history. The messianic deliverance already foretold in Eden (Gen. 3:15) finds definitive expression in the Messiah Jesus. But his story outlives his earthly life.

The Age to Come. Not clearly foreseen, apparently, by either Old Testament prophets or the earliest New Testament disciples, was the already–not yet complexion of the messianic age. While it dawned with Jesus' advent, and in particular with his resurrection, the full sun of the heavenly day awaits his return.

Jesus established the church as the focus of the Father's ongoing redemptive presence, through the Spirit, until the time of the Son's return. While all the New Testament writings play a role in testifying to this, Acts describes how it was lived out in the first three decades following Christ, while the New Testament Epistles instruct and steer the postresurrection people of God in those same generations—and beyond.

Original disciples of Jesus, like Peter and John, play central roles in the church's early rise, but in retrospect pride of place belongs to Paul in important respects. The clarity of his God-given insights into the apostolic office, the nature of life "in Christ," justification by grace through faith, the mission of the church to Jew and Gentile alike, the ongoing place of ethnic Israel in the divine plan, the sanctity of marriage and the sex roles God ordained, the practical outworkings of Christ's Spirit—all these and more are the priceless heirlooms granted to the church, largely Gentile since first-century times, through Paul, an ex-Pharisee. He not only proclaimed but was perhaps the most notable example of the efficacy of the cross of Christ he preached.

Meanwhile, the spiritual descendants of the apostles still look for the full manifestation of the kingdom Jesus promised to establish at his second coming. They await that day in ongoing worship, sacrificial regard for one another (love), growth in the grace and knowledge that Christ and Scripture impart, and outreach to a world both hungry for and hostile toward the gospel. Eschatologically oriented portions of both Old Testament and New Testament, in particular the Book of Revelation, furnish rich resources for reflection and guidance.

Past and Future of the Discipline. The role of the Bible in Christian thought over the centuries has varied widely. Until relatively recently biblical theology as a distinct discipline did not exist. Theology drew its verities directly from the biblical text, often with little linguistic, historical, and hermeneutical sophistication. The theological (and sometimes political or philosophical) commitments of church leaders dominated the way the Bible was read. This too seldom resulted in interpretation that was sensitive to the Bible's original meaning in its setting.

With the rise of critical thought associated with Descartes (1596–1650) and Kant (1724–1804), the teaching of the church (as well as the Bible) was seen in a new light. Critical rationality could separate the temporal husk of the biblical writings from their enduring kernel. Thus one dogma, that of the church, was replaced by another—that of Enlightenment rationalism and its progeny. It was at this time that biblical theology as a distinct discipline made its appearance.

Since that time biblical theology has tended to draw its certainties from trends in the larger academic world. Most biblical scholars "have allowed their world-view and historical method to be given them by their culture" (R. Morgan). For much of the twentieth century Bultmann's existentialist reading of the New Testament has dominated. In Old Testament theology, works by luminaries like Procksch, Eichrodt, Vriezen, Jacob, and von Rad have commanded attention. Yet both Old Testament and New Testament theology, like mainline theological thought generally, are currently in disarray. Many Old Testament and New Testament scholars openly reject classic Christian understanding of the Bible, finding neither unity nor a saving message in it—and certainly not definitive truth. Some even reject the possibility of Old Testament or New Testament theology, let alone biblical theology as a combination of the two, convinced that critical analysis of the Bible can result in nothing more than what ephemeral and disputed literary or social science methods yield.

Many scholars will continue to walk in the lights, or shadows, of the disintegrative, pluralistic, and deconstructive impulses that characterize Western thought at the end of the millennium. Evangelical thinkers can learn much about the Bible from their observations and even more about articulating the Bible's message in the idioms of the age.

Yet biblical theology has suffered enough at the hands of idioms that have garbled the Bible's message through the enthronement of conceptualities foreign to it. In 1787 J. P. Gabler inaugurated the discipline, calling for it to rescue the Bible from the dogmatic chains of the church. Today the dogmatic bonds of modernity—atheism, post- and Neo-Marxism, relativism and reductionism, selfish materialism, narcissistic individualism, New Age spiritism, feminism—are as destructive of biblical theology as any chains ever imposed by the church.

To avoid furthering merely one more -ism, interpreters faithful to the biblical subject matter need to let the sources' certainties furnish them with their own. (With all due respect to current critiques of foundationalism, if all statements are ultimately functions of selves wrapped up in their basic beliefs, then all human expression is solipsism, and the possibility of not only biblical theology but all rational inquiry is called in question.)

Biblical theology will move forward, if it does, as its practitioners know, love, and submit to the God of the Bible rather than the ideologies of the age. God is not a composite of the latest critical theories. This is not to denigrate scholarship but to recognize that God's word, if living and true, calls for substantially (not totally) different approaches to it than post-Enlightenment academic theology in its present forms furnishes. Biblical literacy in the church, to say nothing of biblical redemption in the world, is at stake. Both church and world could gain transforming conviction from the fruit of a discipline humble enough to discern, and brave enough to advocate, the ancient yet contemporary verities that biblical theology is charged to bring to light.

ROBERT W. YARBROUGH

Bibliography. W. Eichrodt, *Theology of the Old Testament,* 2 vols.; D. Guthrie, *New Testament Theology;* G. Hasel, *Old Testament Theology: Basic Issues in the Current Debate* and *New Testament Theology: Basic Issues in the Current Debate;* B. Ollenburger et al., eds., *The Flowering of Old Testament Theology;* R. Muller, *The Study of Theology;* H. Räisänen, *Beyond New Testament Theology;* A. Schlatter, *The Nature of New Testament Theology;* K. Scholder, *The Birth of Modern Critical Theology;* G. Vos, *Biblical Theology.*

Birth, New. See NEW BIRTH.

Birth of Jesus. *See* VIRGIN BIRTH.

Bishop. *See* OVERSEER.

Blameless. ***The Old Testament.*** The concept of blamelessness carries with it two different, yet not dissimilar ideas. The first refers to sacrificial animals that were "without defect" (Lev. 1:3; 3:1, 6; Num. 6:14). Only animals that were undefiled physically were worthy of being offered to the Lord. Sacrificing blemished animals was a violation of biblical law and a demonstration of brazen disrespect for God (Mal. 1:6–14).

From this religious ritual idea comes the notion of moral perfection for individuals. "Blameless" people are those who cannot be accused of wrongdoing before people or God (Pss. 15:2; 18:23). David prays, "Keep your servant also from willful sin. . . . Then will I be blameless" (Ps. 19:13). David is seeking blamelessness not in a physical but in a moral sense.

The New Testament. The concept of moral blamelessness is heightened in the New Testament and employed almost exclusively as a characteristic of Christ and his followers. The sacrificial terminology is applied to the work of Jesus Christ when he is described as "a lamb without blemish or defect" (1 Peter 1:19), who "through the eternal Spirit offered himself unblemished to God" (Heb. 9:14). The blameless character of Christ is seen in his continuing work as the believer's high priest who "meets our need—one who is holy blameless, pure, set apart from sinners, exalted above the heavens" (Heb. 7:26).

When applied to Christians, the quality of blamelessness is both a positional benefit of salvation and a moral character to be achieved. Each person is worthy of accusation in the sight of God. The blameless character of Christians, however, is the intention of God, who "chose us in him before the creation of the world to be holy and blameless in his sight" (Eph. 1:4). Christ's love and sacrifice for the church were such that he could present her to himself "without stain or wrinkle or any other blemish, but holy and blameless" (Eph. 5:27).

This positional quality of blamelessness is not earned by personal gain, but imputed by the death and resurrection of Christ (Col. 1:22). God's power and protection ensure that the believer maintains a blameless status until the final judgment (1 Cor. 1:8; Jude 24). In these occurrences, the legal connotation of deliverance from accusation is clearly seen. God alone has the power and right to accuse the believer and pronounce condemnation, but through his grace and power he renders the believer blameless in his sight.

In light of the positional reality, the believer is called to live in such a way as to attain the quality of blamelessness. In these cases, it is evident that blamelessness refers to public respectability as an outgrowth of private moral character. Christians must "make every effort to be found spotless, blameless and at peace with him" (2 Peter 3:14). By growing in discernment and avoiding a critical spirit, believers can become "pure and blameless" in an age marked by wickedness (Phil. 1:10; 2:14–15).

The importance of a blameless character for the church is seen in the qualifications for church leaders who must be blameless and above reproach (1 Tim. 3:10; Titus 1:6). The Scriptures further define the sphere of the Christian's blameless behavior as including godly service (James 1:27) and the marriage bed (Heb. 13:4). The characteristic of blamelessness thus should define the believer's private and public life as a reflection of the transforming work of God's grace in salvation. WILLIAM E. BROWN

Bibliography. R. Earle, *Word Meanings in the New Testament;* W. E. Vine, M. F. Unger, and W. White, Jr., *Vine's Expository Dictionary of Biblical Words.*

Blasphemy. ***Definition.*** In English "blasphemy" denotes any utterance that insults God or Christ (or Allah, or Muhammed) and gives deeply felt offense to their followers. In several states in the United States and in Britain, blasphemy is a criminal offense, although there have been few prosecution in this century. In Islamic countries generally no distinction is made between blasphemy and heresy, so that any perceived rejection of the Prophet or his message, by Muslims or non-Muslims, is regarded as blasphemous.

The biblical concept is very different. There is no Hebrew word equivalent to the English "blasphemy," and the Greek root *blasphēm-*, which is used fifty-five times in the New Testament, has a wide meaning. In both Testaments the idea of blasphemy as something that offends the religious sensibilities of others is completely absent.

The Old Testament. At least five different Hebrew verbs are translated "blaspheme" in English translations. Translators choose "blaspheme" when, for instance, the verbs "curse" (*qālal*), "revile" (*gādap*), or "despise" (*hērēp*) are used with God as the object. No special verb is reserved for cursing or insults directed at God.

However, to curse or insult God is an especially grave sin. It can be done by word or by deed. There is little distinction between the sinner who deliberately abuses the name of the Lord (Lev. 24:10–16), and the one who deliberately flouts his commandments (Num. 15:30–31). For both, the death penalty is prescribed. Similarly, the prayer of the Levites in Nehemiah 9 calls "awful blasphemies" all that Israelites did when they made the golden calf (9:18).

David's flagrant sin with Bathsheba may be called a blasphemy (2 Sam. 12:14), but a more likely translation is that David has "made the enemies of the Lord show utter contempt" (NIV). Instead of testifying by lifestyle to the character of the Lord, David's action confirms the blasphemous belief of the nations that the Lord is no different from any other national god.

The New Testament. The Greek root *blasphēm-* can be used of strong insults thrown at other people (Mark 15:29; Acts 13:45; Eph. 4:31; 1 Peter 4:4), or even unjust accusations (Rom. 3:8), but it is more usually used of insults offered to God (e.g., Rev. 13:6; 16:9). Jesus is accused of blasphemy for pronouncing forgiveness and for claiming a unique relationship with God (Matt. 26:65; Mark 2:7; John 10:33).

Jesus picks up the Numbers 15 passage about blasphemy in his famous saying about blasphemy against the Holy Spirit (Matt. 12:31–32; Mark 3:28–29; Luke 12:10). Numbers 15:22–31 distinguishes between unintentional sin committed in ignorance (for which forgiveness is possible), and defiant sin, called blasphemy, for which there is no forgiveness. Jesus teaches that the blasphemy for which there is no forgiveness is that against the Holy Spirit; all other blasphemies, particularly those against "the Son of Man," may be forgiven. Insults thrown at "the Son of Man" may be forgiven because they are committed in ignorance of who he really is: his heavenly glory does not appear on earth. But to ascribe obvious manifestations of the Spirit to the devil's agency is a much more serious offense not committed in ignorance.

This downgrading of the significance of blasphemy against Christ marks an important difference between Christianity and Islam. Whereas Muslims are bound to defend the honor of the Prophet, for Christians Jesus is the one who says, "The insults of those who insult you have fallen on me" (Rom. 15:3, quoting Ps. 69:9). He deliberately accepts the vilification of others and prays for the forgiveness of those who insult him (Luke 23:34). In this, he sets an example for Christians to follow. According to Peter (1 Peter 2:19–25), they must accept insult and blasphemy without retaliation, as he did.

There is only one kind of blasphemy that Christians must resist: the blasphemy they will bring on themselves if they cause a fellow believer to stumble through the thoughtless exercise of their freedom (Rom. 14:15–16; 1 Cor. 10:28–30).

STEPHEN MOTYER

Bibliography. I. Howard Marshall, *Theology* 67 (1964): 65–67; R. Simpson. *Blasphemy and the Law in a Plural Society.*

Blasphemy Against the Holy Spirit. Overt, verbal, and conscious repudiation of the fact that God is at work in Jesus Christ accomplishing his designs through the power of the Holy Spirit. Exactly what is being described by this expression, found in Mark 3:29 (par. Matt. 12:32; Luke 12:10), has vexed both scholars and ordinary Christians for centuries.

Several observations are in order. First, the *object* of this "blasphemy" is the Holy Spirit, who is clearly distinguished in the context from Jesus

Christ, the Son of Man, who may be blasphemed by someone who yet is forgiven (Matt. 12:32). While the Spirit is the object, however, it is the Spirit's work *in Jesus Christ* that is the focus of the passage. Second, the *result* of this blasphemy is that the blasphemer cannot be forgiven by God. Third, the *consequence* of this blasphemy is eternal unforgivability. Mark calls this the "eternal sin," a term found in modern translations; the KJV has "eternal judgment." Finally, the *circumstances* of Jesus' pronouncement include the attribution of his powers to demonic sources (Mark 3:22).

What is this sin? Both Mark and Luke use the term "blaspheme" while Matthew has the more ordinary "speaks against," showing that all three have in mind some kind of verbal repudiation or denunciation of the Spirit of God in the ministry of Jesus. Ancients believed in the power of words and uttering imprecations, curses, and blasphemies were taken seriously. The verb "blaspheme" means to speak abusively or insultingly of someone or something (Acts 18:6; Rom. 14:16). In the Old Testament the term was used specially for derisive language and attitudes toward the God of the covenant with Israel (2 Kings 19:4; 6, 22; Isa. 66:3; Ezek. 35:12–13). The fundamental notion inherited by New Testament authors, and Jesus in particular, is expressed in Leviticus 24:15–16: "Whoever curses (*q̄alal; katareō*) his God shall bear his sin. He who blasphemes (*nāqab; onomazō*) the name of the Lord shall be put to death; all the congregation shall stone him; the sojourner as well as the native, when he blasphemes (*nāqab; onomazō*) the Name, shall be put to death" (RSV; cf. Lev. 24:10–23 for the blasphemer).

Furthermore, the Spirit is the sign of the new age and the reception of the Spirit is the focus of hope in some Old Testament visions. Thus, Isaiah 63:7–64:11 speaks of God's covenantal faithfulness to his people, led by Moses, even when they grieved the Holy Spirit (63:10). The prayer is that God would rend his heavens and come down to his people and make his name great among the nations (64:1–2). One suspects that the advent of the Holy Spirit at the baptism of Jesus fulfills this Old Testament hope, and yet Israel remains hardened and grieves the Spirit once again (cf. 63:10; Mark 3:29). What we find then is double accountability: Old Testament disobedience, followed by God's promised restoration in sending the Spirit, and now once again the same rejection.

Consequently, when we come to the text of the Synoptic Gospels there is a history of interpretation and applications that prohibit anyone (Lev. 24:15–16 includes the sojourner) from denouncing the God of Israel, repudiating his claims, and insulting his honor. What Jesus claims is that a similar type of sin is being committed whenever one speaks against the Holy Spirit as revealed powerfully in his ministry. What caused stoning in the Old Testament, now incurs eternal condemnation; such a sin is unforgivable.

What are the specific symptoms of this sin? There have been many suggestions in the history of interpretation, including breaking the third commandment (Exod. 20:7: taking the Lord's name in vain) or the seventh commandment (Exod. 20:14: adultery; cf. 1 Cor. 6:18), postbaptismal sins (Origen), post-Pentecost rejection of the Spirit, and the attempt to achieve meritorious righteousness before God. Others have given up on finding the meaning. While the various proposals may have some merit, it is best to examine "blasphemy against the Spirit" in the Gospels themselves to see what light they shed on what is being addressed.

The contexts of the Gospels provide the important clues. In Mark and Matthew, the context is Jesus' exorcisms by the power of God's Spirit (Matt. 12:22–24; cf. Mark 3:22). While Jesus contends that one might miss the revelation of God in his lowly person (Matt. 12:32a), no one can miss the power of God at work in his ability to exorcize demons (Matt. 12:32b; Mark 3:29). Thus, the unforgivable sin is repudiation of the work of God, seen in Jesus' powerful acts of exorcism.

Luke puts this same saying in a slightly different context: the public acknowledgment of Jesus Christ. Jesus says it is one thing to deny him publicly; it is quite another thing to repudiate the power of the Holy Spirit (Luke 12:8–10). Thus, the unforgivable sin here seems to be public repudiation of the power of the Spirit in the ministry of the apostles of Jesus. What we see here is probably an application: inasmuch as it is blasphemous to reject the Spirit in the ministry of Jesus, so it is also blasphemous to reject the Spirit in the ministry of the Twelve (since they are personal agents of Jesus). After all, the Spirit purifies and enables holiness (Ps. 51:11–13; Ezek. 36:25–27). In summary, we may confidently conclude that "blasphemy against the Spirit" is overt, even verbal, repudiation of the presence of God's Spirit in the ministry of Jesus and those whom he has sent.

After the earthly ministry and death of Christ, the emphasis on the Spirit as the object of the blasphemous words and attitudes will give way to an emphasis on Jesus Christ (cf. James 2:7). Hence, we find Paul's preaching of Christ crucified being repudiated; this would appear to be "blasphemy against the Spirit" as well (Acts 13:8, 45; 14:2; 18:6; 19:13–16).

Blasphemy against the Spirit and apostasy are related. Apostasy, whether defined in the Calvinistic or Arminian sense, is committed by those who have had some relationship to God through Christ. Thus, apostasy is acceptance followed by repudiation of Jesus Christ (Heb. 6:4–6; 10:29–39; 1 John 5:16–17); blasphemy against the

Spirit is not preceded by acceptance. It describes overt repudiation before any kind of commitment is made. While we may distinguish these two sins in this manner, it also needs to be observed that the two sins amount to largely the same stance. For both involve an overt repudiation of God's work in Christ. SCOT MCKNIGHT

See also HOLY SPIRIT; "SIN UNTO DEATH."

Bibliography. C. K. Barrett, *The Holy Spirit and the Gospel Tradition;* G. C. Berkouwer, *Sin;* H. W. Beyer, *TDNT,* 1:621–25; O. Hofius, *EDNT,* 1:219–21; W. D. Davies and D. C. Allison, Jr., *The Gospel according to Saint Matthew;* A. Richardson, *An Introduction to the Theology of the New Testament;* N. Turner, *Christian Words;* G. H. Twelftree, *Dictionary of Jesus and the Gospels,* pp. 75–77; H. Währisch, W. Mundle, and C. Brown, *NIDNTT,* 3.340–47.

Blessedness. Condition or state of being in God's grace or favor. The Bible contains the words "bless," "blessing," and "blessed," but not the noun "blessedness," although the idea of a spiritual state of beatitude in which believers enjoy God's fellowship permeates the Bible. Bless translates the Hebrew *ʾašrê* and *barûk* and the Greek *eulogētos* and *makarios*. All are used of believers, but only *barûk* and *eulogētos* of God. These words suggest divine protection, evoking believers' trust in their benefactor. They know God as the origin of every good thing in both this life and the next. The English word "blessedness" is derived from the root word for "blood" and suggests something set aside through sacrifice and in the Bible through Christ's sacrificial death for sins. Every aspect of the Christian life is embraced by blessedness with no credit assumed by the person experiencing it. It is purely God's grace.

In the Old Testament this blessedness may involve material things, but forgiveness is foremost (Ps. 32:1). All Christians are blessed simply by believing in Christ and hearing and keeping his word (Luke 11:28) and their perseverance in the face of trial (Matt. 11:6). Blessedness can apply to special endowments. Abraham (Gen. 12:1–3) and Peter (Matt. 16:17) are blessed because they stand at the head of God's people in each Testament and are channels of God's blessedness to others. Elizabeth, as following generations, recognizes Mary's blessedness as the Lord's mother (Luke 1:42, 48). Perfected blessedness belongs to the dead in Christ (Rev. 14:13). Whereas holiness refers to God's unapproachability and moral demands, blessedness focuses on what God does for the believer. From eternity he is blessed (*eulogētos*) in acting graciously, bestowing blessings and good things upon his people (Eph. 1:3–4). Blessedness means God's bringing his promises to David to fulfillment in raising up Jesus as the Christ (Luke 1:68–70). The original experience of Adam and Eve in Eden is a blessedness derived from a creation in which God provides for their spiritual well-being with his companionship and their physical needs with the garden's trees (Gen. 2). The lost blessedness is replaced by cursed ground (Gen. 3:17). No longer does man know God as benefactor, but rather malefactor, responsible for every evil experienced (Gen. 3:12–13). While some like Abel, Seth, Noah, and the patriarchs regain blessedness, others like Cain (Gen. 4:11) and Canaan (Gen. 9:25) fall under God's disfavor. The lost blessedness of the original paradise is fully restored by the cross and is now associated with the redemption (Luke 23:43). On that account Jesus is called blessed (Matt. 23:39; Luke 1:42; 19:38).

The patriarchs live in a state of unperfected blessedness with their weaknesses removed at death (Heb. 11:13). Blessedness for Israel was dependent on their keeping the covenant by which God established them as his people. It required their worship of him as the only God. Idolatry deprived them of their blessedness. Blessedness in the Old Testament at times assures certain material blessings (Gen. 39:5). Canaan is given as a land of inheritance to Israel and military conquest and physical prosperity follow (1 Kings 4:20). The psalms focus on the individual, often with physical prosperity given to God's enemies. Blessedness entails the believer's continual occupation with God's word, the avoidance of the wicked, and perseverance and final flourishing (Ps. 1). This psalm's first words, "blessed" (*ʾašrê*), serve to introduce the others. They reflect on a blessedness in which believers suffer abandonment by God (Ps. 22), material deprivation, and seeing the wicked flourish, but are finally victorious (Ps. 2). Israel's persecuted prophets lived in the same unresolved dilemma, one now promised Christians (Matt. 5:12). Blessedness is seen not in how God materially rewarded the prophets, but in their perseverance (James 5:11). The occasional Old Testament association of blessedness with material advantages is reversed in the New Testament and is linked with financial destitution. The poor (Luke 6:20) and the poor in spirit (Matt. 5:3) have already gotten their blessedness in attaining the kingdom of God. Jesus is despised by others (Isa. 53:3) and the poorest of men and still in him blessedness comes to its highest expression (2 Cor. 8:9). The blessedness of the righteous is seen in their persecution by God's enemies (Matt. 5:11–12). The apostles are blessed in seeing what prophets could only long for (Matt. 13:16) and rejoice because they are allowed to suffer for Christ (Acts 5:41). Suffering brings martyrs into a state of blessedness (Rev. 14:13). The martyrs have attained blessedness and are called "saints," not because of their moral perfection, but because their deaths identify them with Christ.

DAVID P. SCAER

Bibliography. C. W. Mitchell, *The Meaning of b r k "to bless" in the Old Testament;* C. Westermann, *Blessing in the Bible and the Life of the Church.*

Blessing. God's intention and desire to bless humanity is a central focus of his covenant relationships. For this reason, the concept of blessing pervades the biblical record. Two distinct ideas are present. First, a blessing was a public declaration of a favored status with God. Second, the blessing endowed power for prosperity and success. In all cases, the blessing served as a guide and motivation to pursue a course of life within the blessing.

The Old Testament. Terms for blessing abound in the Old Testament, occurring over 600 times. The major terms are related to the word meaning "to kneel," since in earlier times one would kneel to receive a blessing.

The history of Israel begins with the promise of blessing. The curse, which had dominated the early chapters of the biblical story (Gen. 3:14, 17; 4:11; 5:29; 9:25), was countered by God's promise to Abraham that "all peoples on earth will be blessed through you" (Gen. 12:3). The record of Israel's past is best understood as an outworking of blessing and cursing (Deut. 27:1–28:68).

The institutions of society—the family, government, and religion—were the means by which ceremonial blessings were received. Within the family the father blessed his wife and children (Gen. 27:27–29; 49:25–26; 1 Sam. 2:20). In the government context, the ruler blessed his subjects (2 Sam. 6:18; 1 Kings 8:14, 55). Those who possessed a priestly role were bestowed with the privilege of blessing (Gen. 14:19; Lev. 9:22). The tribe of Levi was set apart "to pronounce blessings in his [the LORD's] name" (Deut. 10:8; 21:5).

Three common themes are present in formal Old Testament blessings. First, the greater blesses the lesser, a fact picked up by the writer of Hebrews to demonstrate the superiority of Melchizedek to Abraham (Heb. 7:6–7). Second, the blessing is a sign of special favor that is intended to result in prosperity and success (Deut. 28:3–7). Third, the blessing is actually an invocation for God's blessing: "May God Almighty bless you and make you fruitful" (Gen. 28:3).

In a less ceremonial sense, the Scriptures declare a general blessing on the righteous. Those who are obedient to God's commands are blessed with affluence and victory (Deut. 28:1–14). On the other hand, those who are disobedient are cursed (Deut. 28:15–68) and suffer the consequences of drought, disease, and deprivation.

It is also possible for a person to "bless" God. The terminology arises as a response to the blessings bestowed by God: "Bless the LORD, O my soul, and forget not all his benefits" (Ps. 103:2 KJV). These occurrences of "bless" are usually translated "praise" or "extol" in modern versions.

The New Testament. The parallels between the Old and New Testament usages of blessing are striking. To be blessed is to be granted special favor by God with resulting joy and prosperity. In the New Testament, however, the emphasis is more on spiritual rather than on material blessings.

God's promise to Abraham again serves as a foundation for blessings. The pledge that "all peoples on earth shall be blessed" (Gen. 12:3) is fulfilled in the person and work of Jesus Christ (Gal. 3:8–14). He has borne the consequences of the curse for believers (Gal. 3:13) and blessed them with the forgiveness of sins (Rom. 4:6–9; see Ps. 32:1–2). Believers are "blessed . . . with every spiritual blessing in Christ" (Eph. 1:3) and now inherit the blessings promised through the patriarchs (Heb. 6:12, 15; 12:17; 1 Peter 3:9). As a result of receiving God's blessings in Christ, believers are called to be a source of blessing to the world, especially in response to those who persecute them (Luke 6:27–28; Rom. 12:14; 1 Cor. 4:12; 1 Peter 3:9; cf. Isa. 19:24; Zech. 8:13).

In a general sense, the terms for blessing in the New Testament are used to designate that one is favored by God. Included among these are Jesus (Mark 11:9–10); children (Mark 10:13–16); Mary (Luke 1:42, 48); the disciples (Luke 24:50); those who "have not seen and yet have believed" (John 20:29); and those who endure trials (James 1:12; 5:11). As in the Old Testament, when these words are ascribed to God they are rendered "praise" (Rom. 1:25; 9:5; 2 Cor. 11:31).

The most recognizable references to blessing come from the teachings of Jesus. He declares that in spite of difficulties at the present time, the promises of God's salvation and coming kingdom bring a state of happiness and recognized favor with God (Matt. 5:3–10; Luke 6:20–22). The culmination of the Scriptures proclaims the end of the curse (Rev. 22:3) and the eternal blessedness of the people of God (Rev. 20:6; 22:7).

WILLIAM E. BROWN

Bibliography. W. Eichrodt, *Theology of the Old Testament;* H.-G. Link and U. Becker, *NIDNTT,* 3:206–18.

Blindness. Scripture often employs the imagery of blindness to describe the spiritual condition of persons who are either unable or unwilling to perceive divine revelation. The things of God are perceived not by observation and inquiry, but by revelation and illumination (Matt. 11:25–27; 1 Cor. 1:21; 2 Peter 1:19–21). It is the Lord who "gives sight to the blind" (Ps. 146:8; Isa. 42:16).

The figure of blindness is a favorite device of Isaiah, who repeatedly announces to rebellious Israel that God has afflicted them and their apostate prophets, priests, and rules with blindness (43:8; 56:10; 59:10). Zephaniah reveals that this condition is divinely imposed upon the hardhearted (1:17). Appropriately, then, the Messiah's ministry would be marked by opening the eyes of the spiritually blind (Isa. 42:7, 16, 18). At the outset of his public ministry, Jesus lay claim to the messianic office by revealing that he would fulfill

Isaiah's prophetic promise to proclaim "recovery of sight to the blind" (Luke 4:18).

Some of Jesus' strongest outbursts were directed at the Pharisees, who masqueraded their superficial conformity to Jewish ceremonial laws as sincere and sufficient righteousness in the sight of God. Jesus follows the form of Isaiah in castigating the Pharisees as "blind guides of the blind" (Matt. 15:14; cf. 23:16–26; John 9:39–41). He announces that he will impose judgment on these self-righteous legalists, "so that the blind will see and those who see will become blind" (John 9:39).

Paul tells the Corinthian believers that blindness aptly describes the spiritual state of pagan unbelievers. He points out that this blindness is inflicted by the "god of this age [who] has blinded the minds of unbelievers, so that they cannot see the light of the gospel of the glory of Christ, who is the image of God" (2 Cor. 4:4). The New Testament reveals that believers are subject to spiritual blindness. Peter deems those who fail increasingly to exhibit diligence in pursuit of spiritual virtue as blind or nearsighted (2 Peter 1:9). And the exalted Lord of the church views the lukewarm but haughty Laodicean church as wretched, pitiful, poor, blind, and naked (Rev. 3:17).

Spiritual blindness, then, refers in some instances to the inability of unbelievers to comprehend spiritual truth, specifically failure to recognize the true identity of the incarnate Word, Jesus Christ. It is vital, therefore, to conduct all Christian witness in dependence on the Holy Spirit, who works to counteract the cataracts of Satan and to reveal the truth of God. But spiritual blindness can also afflict believers who fail to perceive their true spiritual condition. To avoid the plague of spiritual blindness and escape the condemnation of leading others into spiritual ruin, believers must be quick to appropriate and obey the Word of God.

Ralph E. Enlow, Jr.

Boasting. The concept of boasting is found frequently in both the Old and the New Testaments. The object of boasting determines its nature. If it is God or the commendable qualities of others, then boasting can be described as proper; if it is wrongly applied to oneself, then it is improper. The Hebrew word *halel* is sometimes translated "boast." The basic meaning of the word is "to praise," as in the English word "hallelujah," which means "praise Jehovah." The Greek word *kauchaomai* ("to vaunt oneself") is used in the New Testament. Like its Hebrew counterpart, it is used in both a good and a bad sense.

Proper Boasting. In Psalm 44:8 the sons of Korah confess, "In God we make our boast all day long." There is no higher or more appropriate form of boasting than this. The Hebrew word *halel* also conveys the idea of chanting loud praises. Some scholars have suggested that the loudness of the praise was intended to drive away evil spirits, but that is unlikely. The hampering of Satan, however, may be a byproduct of praise since Satan cannot accomplish his purposes where God is exalted. It should also be pointed out that included in praising God is the joy that we experience in doing so.

Boasting about God is one of humankind's most profitable activities. Jesus told the woman at the well that the Father seeks our worship (John 4:23). Both anthropologists and psychologists tell us that human beings invariably imitate what they worship, so the end result of boasting in God is the sincere aspiration to be like him (2 Cor. 4:18).

The Scriptures encourage us to engage in proper boasting or praise of other human beings: "Let another praise you, and not your own mouth" (Prov. 27:2); "a woman who fears the Lord is to be praised" (Prov. 31:30). Paul boasts in the churches when he can (2 Cor. 7:14), and our Lord himself commends six of the seven churches to whom he speaks in the Book of Revelation. Proper boasting in others is a source of encouragement in the body of Christ. In addition to boasting in others, Paul also boasts in hope of the glory of God (Rom. 5:2), sufferings (Rom. 5:3), God (Rom. 5:11), the Lord (Christ) (1 Cor. 1:31; Phil. 3:3), his infirmities (2 Cor. 12:9), and the cross (Gal. 6:14). These uses of *kauchaomai* basically convey the idea of "rejoicing" or "glorifying" as the word is translated in most versions.

Improper Boasting. The wrong way to boast is to boast in ourselves. After saying that we have received everything from God, Paul poses the question, "Why do you boast as though you did not?" (1 Cor. 4:7), clearly implying that any time we boast in ourselves we are taking praise that belongs to God alone. Paul also mentions the fact that we should not boast in other people (1 Cor. 3:21), in the sense of putting them above Christ. We should also not boast in appearances rather than what is in the heart (2 Cor. 5:12). We are warned not to boast beyond proper limits (2 Cor. 10:13). We must refrain from presenting an exaggerated description of ourselves. In the great passage on grace as the means of salvation Paul describes salvation as not being "by works." Because it is God's gift, "no one can boast" (Eph. 2:9). Therefore, we are not to boast as if we were self-sufficient. James reminds us that all arrogant boasting is evil (4:16).

Boasting in oneself is an expression of pride. Those who sin express arrogance by implying that they can successfully violate the laws of Almighty God. Paul describes the arrogant and boastful as "God-haters" (Rom. 1:30). Humility is defined as the absence of arrogance and boasting and is characterized by submission to God's will. The absence of self-exaltation and the attitude of humility place one in a position of being blessed by God (Isa. 66:2).

In his discussion on the sinfulness of the human race Paul concludes that boasting is excluded on the principle of faith (Rom. 3:27). The entire scope of biblical teaching about boasting is best summarized in a statement made by Jeremiah and later quoted by Paul: "Let him who boasts boast in the Lord" (Jer. 9:24; 1 Cor. 1:31).

Alan N. Winkler

Body. ***Old Testament.*** The doctrine of creation sets forth the essential corporeality of human existence. When God created Adam and Eve, he provided them with physical bodies (Gen. 2:7, 22). The fact that God formed the physical body first and then breathed into it the breath of life means that we are living bodies, not simply incarnated souls. This holistic relationship between body and soul undermines any thought that a human being is simply the sum of its parts (i.e., mind + soul + body, etc.). One does not *have* a body, one *is* a body.

Bodily existence is not only an essential aspect of being human, it is also God's perfect will. In the beginning God pronounces that all of his creation is "very good" (Gen. 1:31). So to be truly human is to exist bodily. This divine affirmation of physical existence is diametrically opposed to any notion that the body is inferior to the spirit. Unlike the Gnostics of the second and third centuries A.D., the Scriptures never represent the physical body as a prison from which the spirit must be freed. There is absolutely nothing inherently evil about the human body. Throughout the Old Testament, the body is presented as a marvelous gift from God, which evidences his indescribable wisdom and power (Ps. 139:14–16). It is never represented as an impediment to communion, service, or worship of God. Prior to the fall, Adam and Eve enjoyed perfect fellowship with God, and that fellowship was experienced in the body (Gen. 1:27–31). This integration of body and soul constitutes an internal dynamic that is truly remarkable. The body becomes the expression of the soul. The voice articulates prayer, raised hands express praise, bowing low reflects humble adoration and worship.

This essential relationship of body and soul provides for an extraordinary integration of the material and spiritual realms. For example, the sin of Adam and Eve not only affected their spiritual status before God, but had physical consequences as well. They died and the earth from which the body was formed was cursed (Gen. 2:17; 3:17–19). With regard to the final disposition of the body the principle of "dust to dust" holds true (Gen. 3:19; Job 10:9; Ps. 104:29; Eccles. 3:20; 12:7). The body is folded as a tent and returns to the earth from which it came (Ps. 146:4; Isa. 38:12). Job declares that despite the natural decomposition of his body, he will see God with his own eyes, in his own flesh (19:26–27). The psalmist rejoices that God will not allow his holy one to see corruption (Ps. 16:10). Isaiah speaks of the earth casting out the dead and Daniel prophesies that those who sleep in dust shall awake (Isa. 26:19; Dan. 12:2). Throughout the intertestamental period, the belief in the future resurrection and glorification of the body became even more developed (1 Enoch 20:8; 22:13; 2 Baruch 50:3–4; 2 Macc. 7:9, 36).

New Testament. The essential corporeality of human existence is supremely set forth in the New Testament. The incarnation is God's ultimate endorsement of the physical body (Matt. 1:20–25; Luke 1:26–35; Rom. 1:3; Gal. 4:4; 1 Tim. 3:16; 1 John 4:2–3). Complete redemption means the reclamation of humanness in the most comprehensive sense, and this mandates the "in fleshing" of the Word (John 1:14). Jesus' body becomes the locus for God's redemptive activity in the world. Indeed his body is both temple and sacrifice in that it manifests the glory of God and atones for the sins of the world (Mark 14:22; Luke 22:19; John 1:14; 2:21; Rom. 3:24–25; Heb. 9:14; 1 Peter 2:19, 24). The physical resurrection of his body not only served as the Father's "amen" to the life and ministry of Jesus, but also as a kind of "firstfruits" of the resurrection of all believers (1 Cor. 15:20–23).

The bodies of the regenerated are also the arena of faith and practice. The primary allegiance of the body is not to the things of this world or to the sinful desires of the flesh (Rom. 6:12–23). On the contrary, the body is the Lord's and the Lord is to be glorified in the body (1 Cor. 6:13, 20). The body is the temple of the Holy Spirit (1 Cor. 6:19). Through the indwelling of the Spirit, the body becomes the place of kingdom expression in this present age. This special presence of God constitutes a community of faith whose identity cannot be confined to this world. In a very real sense, the church is the body of Christ (Rom. 12:4–5; 1 Cor. 6:15; 12:12–31; Eph. 4:4–13).

All of these things are a proleptic realization of greater glory yet to come. At the second coming, all in Christ will receive a glorified body designed to exist in a heavenly realm (1 Cor. 15; 2 Cor. 5:1–5; Phil. 3:21; 1 Thess. 4:13–18). Just as the fall of Adam brought a curse on the earth, the resurrection of the body has consequences of cosmic proportions. The redemption of our bodies ushers in the liberation of the entire creation, breaking the bondage of suffering and death forever (Rom. 8:18–25).

William A. Simmons

See also Person, Personhood.

Bibliography. R. S. Anderson, *On Being Human: Essays in Theological Anthropology;* G. H. Clark, *The Biblical Doctrine of Man;* R. W. A. McKinney, *Creation, Christ and Culture: Studies in Honor of T. F. Torrance;* J. A. T. Robinson, *The Body: A Study in Pauline Theology;* E. C. Rust, *RevExp* 58 (1961): 296–311; A. A. Vogel, *Body Theology: God's Presence in Man's World.*

Body of Christ. The body metaphor for the people of God is a powerful image that bespeaks the new historical reality brought about in Christ. It surfaces in only four New Testament epistles, but in a bewildering array of associations.

Relational Unity in Romans and 1 Corinthians. Romans (12:4–5) and 1 Corinthians (10:17; 11:29; 12:12–27) reflect an earlier stage of usage. Paul's fullest treatment of the theme (1 Cor. 12:12–27) consists of an extended comparison between the human body (*sōma*) and the church in order to emphasize horizontal union among the members of Christ's body and to demonstrate dramatically both diversity within unity (12:12a, 14–19) and unity out of diversity (12:12b, 20–27). A church that was well known both for the giftedness of its members (1 Cor. 1:7) and its toleration of divisions (1 Cor. 1:10–13; 3:3; 4:6; 6:6; 11:17–22; 12:25) needed to heed warnings against both groundless inferiority (12:14–19) and disdainful superiority (12:21–25). Each member of the body has an important (vv. 17, 22), although not always glamorous (vv. 23–24), contribution to make, and no member experiences humiliation or honor without somehow affecting the rest (v. 26; cf. 2 Cor. 11:28–29).

Similar injunctions come in Romans 12. Instead of displays of arrogance (vv. 3, 16), each member of the body is called to employ his or her gift(s) in brotherly love (v. 10), recognizing both the diversity (vv. 4–5a) and the unity (v. 5b) that define their place in Christ. For Paul, the urgent need for humility, interdependence, and love within the Christian community is grounded in this dynamic horizontal unity between members of the body of Christ, a union that overcomes even the most imposing racial and social barriers (1 Cor. 12:13; cf. Gal. 3:28; Eph. 2:16). But it is not at all clear that Paul took up the body metaphor simply as a memorable way to describe relations within the community. Horizontal, social relations between members are grounded in the vertical union each member enjoys with Christ (Rom. 12:5; 1 Cor. 10:16–17; 12:13). That body of Christ language could apply both to the local congregation (1 Cor. 12:27) and to something more universal (1 Cor. 12:13) not only attests to the flexibility of the metaphor but also reflects an important element in Paul's ecclesiology: the local church is a localized manifestation of the church universal (1 Cor. 1:2; 2 Cor. 1:1).

Union with Christ in Ephesians and Colossians. Ephesians and Colossians reflect a further stage of development. The imagery shifts from horizontal unity among members (one out of many) to vertical union with Christ (the many in the One). No longer is the head merely one body part among many, but Christ's role as head over the church entails organic unity (Eph. 4:15–16; Col. 2:19), authority and supremacy (Eph. 1:22; 5:24; Col. 1:18), self-sacrifice (Eph. 5:25), origination (Col. 1:17–18), provision of life (Col. 2:19; cf. 3:3–4), and enablement of growth and sanctification (Eph. 4:16; 5:26–30; Col. 2:19). Moreover, this head-body relationship between Christ and the church stands at the center of God's plan for the entire cosmos over which Christ has been established as sovereign (Eph. 1:20–23). But whereas Christ fills the cosmos in terms of his ultimate sovereignty, he fills his body, the church, as he supplies power (1:19), infuses life (2:5), secures exaltation (2:6), and showers kindness (2:7). Only the church is called Christ's fullness (1:23), and as the body of Christ, the church shares Christ's exaltation and session at God's right hand in the heavenly places (Eph. 1:20; 2:6).

Related Themes and Possible Influences. Attempts to identify the background and antecedents of New Testament body imagery have not been totally successful. Least likely influences include Gnostic mythology (Schlier, Käsemann, Bultmann), ancient political theory (which drew parallels between the city or state and the human body; E. A. Judge, F. Müssner, W. L. Knox; J. C. Beker), and rabbinic speculation about the nature of Adam's body (W. D. Davies). Luke's description of Paul's experience outside Damascus (Acts 9:4–5) suggests a close association between the exalted Jesus and his followers on earth, but actual "body" language is entirely absent. Similarly, Old Testament portrayals of God as bridegroom and Israel as bride do not stress unity nor do they portray the marriage as a "one flesh" relationship. And even when Christ's roles as head and bridegroom of the church converge (Eph. 5:23–32), the metaphors function independently.

A stronger case can be made for the influence of the Old Testament principle of corporate representation (Ridderbos, Clowney). If a representative could act on behalf of his group, it would be natural to identify the group with that representative. (H. W. Robinson's more complex notion of corporate personality, which all but obliterates the sense of individuality in ancient Hebrew culture, should finally be laid to rest.) Clearly, the New Testament ties the destiny of God's people to the faithful and selfless act of Messiah, and identification with Christ in his death is indispensable for Paul (Rom. 6:8; Gal. 2:20; 5:24; and his "in Christ" formula). Nevertheless, clear indications that Old Testament representation was the formative influence in Paul's concept of the body of Christ are lacking. Indeed, the idea that the one can represent the many is not at all limited to Hebrew culture (M. Barth, *Ephesians*, 195f.; S. Porter, 298). In the end, it is best to imagine Paul enlisting various themes and background ideas while forging a unique and versatile metaphor that served his own ecclesiological and christological purposes.

The Church and the Death of Jesus. Significantly, in both 1 Corinthians and Ephesians, the metaphorical body of Christ is tied tightly to the physical body of Jesus in its death on the cross. Jesus' body is represented by the bread of the Eucharist (1 Cor. 10:16–17; cf. 11:29?) so that those who share the single loaf of communion constitute a single body; their actions demonstrate both corporate inclusion into Christ and their membership in the Christian community that Christ's death brought into existence. But it is connection to Christ and his death that establishes connection to his people. In Ephesians, the bodily death of Jesus on the cross is what abolishes the enmity between Jew and Gentile (2:13–15), and replaces it with reconciliation and unity (2:16). Whether in one body (*en heni sōmati*) refers to the physical, bodily death of Jesus or, more likely, to the church that constitutes a unity, the effect is accomplished through the cross. And Christ's role as Savior of the body (5:23) is explained in terms of his sacrificial death on behalf of the church (5:25; cf. 5:2). In Colossians, the relationship between the physical death of Christ and the church as the body of Christ is less explicit, but foundational nonetheless (1:18–24; 2:12–3:4). The redemptive work of Christ, accomplished bodily on the cross, established unity among God's people. To call those people the body of Christ was to highlight dramatically the event and the person responsible for their very life and final destiny.

BRUCE N. FISK

See also CHURCH, THE.

Bibliography. R. Banks, *Paul's Idea of Community;* J. C. Beker, *Paul the Apostle: The Triumph of God in Life and Thought;* E. Best, *One Body in Christ;* E. P. Clowney, *Biblical Interpretation and the Church: The Problem of Contextualization;* W. D. Davies, *Paul and Rabbinic Judaism;* R. Y. K. Fung, *EvQ* 53 (1981): 89–107; R. H. Gundry, Soma *in the New Testament;* A. T. Lincoln, *Paradise Now and Not Yet;* P. S. Minear, *Images of the Church in the New Testament;* S. E. Porter, *SJT* 43 (1990): 289–307; H. Ridderbos, *Paul: An Outline of His Theology;* H. Rikhof, *The Concept of Church: A Methodological Inquiry into the Use of Metaphors in Ecclesiology;* H. W. Robinson, *The Christian Doctrine of Man;* J. A. T. Robinson, *The Body: A Study in Pauline Theology;* R. Schnackenburg, *The Church in the New Testament;* E. Schweizer, *TDNT,* 7:1067–80.

Book, Book of Life. The written word was a powerful creation in the ancient Near East. Both Egyptians and Babylonians saw writing as sacred, a direct gift of the gods. Although Yahweh did not make writing a specific gift to the people of Israel, he did employ writing in his dealings with people. He used writing to communicate directly in specific instances, such as the Ten Commandments and at Balthasar's feast. The biblical writers also record that God shared with humanity the employment of writing in an "economic" role. The balance book of God is named "the Book of Life."

An anguished interchange between a wrathful Yahweh and a pleading Moses after the discovery of the golden calf illustrates the Old Testament understanding of the Book of Life. Moses asks that God either forgive the people or "blot me out of the book you have written" (Exod. 32:32). Yahweh responds that he will blot out whoever has sinned; the punishment is immediate. The Book of Life is a list of the righteous. In the Old Testament focus on divine reward and punishment in this life, the blessed on the list receive their blessings here and now and those stricken from the book suffer in this life, not in some eternal future. The psalmist understands this when he asks God to "list my tears on your scroll" (56:8) and have his enemies "blotted out of the book of life" (69:28).

The New Testament transforms this balance book into an eternal ledger of heavenly citizenship. Within the classical world, citizenship was not an automatic right, but a strictly protected honor. Citizens were specifically enrolled, and the franchise was strictly limited. In the Gospel story of the seventy sent out into the world, Jesus assures these disciples that their names will be written in heaven (Luke 10:20). In the letter to the church at Sardis, heavenly citizenship, exemplified by listing in the Book of Life, is promised to those who overcome the world (Rev. 3:5). At the last judgment, anyone whose name is not written in the Book of Life is thrown into the Lake of Fire (Rev. 20:15). THOMAS W. DAVIS

Bibliography. A. A. Anderson, *Psalms (1–72);* A. Mazar, *Archaeology of the Land of the Bible 10,000–586 B.C.E.*

Born Again. *See* NEW BIRTH.

Bought. *See* REDEEM, REDEMPTION.

Branch. Many figures of speech in Scripture used to illustrate spiritual truth are taken from agriculture. One such set of ideas has to do with limbs, secondary stems, or new growth on vines, bushes, and trees. More than twenty Hebrew and Greek words are employed to connote this growth; they have been translated variously as a "branch," "shoot," "sprout," "tendril," or "twig."

When olive trees, indigenous to Israel, are cut down, new trees grow from the shoots that sprout from the base and root system. It was not uncommon for the prophets to depict the Messiah as a new shoot or branch growing from David's stock, even though that "tree" would be cut off. Isaiah proclaims that "A shoot will come up from the stump of Jesse; from his roots a Branch will bear fruit" (11:1). Jeremiah announces that one day in the future the Lord will raise up for David a "righteous Branch," who will reign as the rightful heir to the throne (23:5). Zechariah notes that this royal Branch will be the one who will rebuild the temple (6:12–13).

Israel is often referred to as a vine. The Lord brought Israel, the vine, out of Egypt and planted it in the promised land. As the Lord blessed the vine, it prospered and "sent out its boughs to the Sea, its shoots as far as the River" (Ps. 80:11). The fruit that the vine produced, however, was an embarrassment to the Lord and steps were taken against it (see Isa. 5:1–7). More often, however, the prophets use the analogy of the vine and branches to describe Israel's future restoration (Isa. 60:21; Hos. 14:6).

Jesus uses the analogy of the relationship of the vine to the branches to describe his relationship with his disciples: "I am the vine; you are the branches" (John 15:5). The branches derive their very existence and ability to produce fruit from the vine. Detached, the branches cease to live or produce. Likewise, apart from Christ, an individual has neither spiritual life nor fruit.

In Romans 11 Paul draws attention to grafting a branch into a stock. Normally, a farmer takes a wild root or stock and grafts into it a cultivated scion. That was not the case with Israel, the cultivated olive tree; the branches broken off were replaced by wild olive shoots, in other words, Gentile believers. When the Deliverer from Zion comes, however, it will be easy for him to restore Israel to its rightful position (vv. 25–27).

GLENN E. SCHAEFER

See also JESUS CHRIST, NAME AND TITLES OF; MESSIAH.

Bibliography. W. J. Beecher, *The Prophets and the Promise;* R. Brown, *The Gospel According to John;* R. L. Harris, *Baker's Dictionary of Theology;* W. Kaiser, *Toward an Old Testament Theology;* S. Mowinckel, *He That Cometh.*

Bread, Bread of Presence. Bread was the essential food of the ancient Israelites. Indeed, the very word "bread" could be used generically for any kind of food. Meat was eaten by peasants only at festival occasions, and other foods supplemented bread. As the mainstay of life, bread came to be a primary metaphor for life and sustenance.

Bread in the Bible functions as a social bond. The giving of bread to another is a major element of hospitality and serves as a sign of respect and concern (Gen. 14:18; 18:6; 19:3; Deut. 23:4; Ruth 2:14; 1 Sam. 25:18; 28:24; 2 Sam. 16:1–2). Conversely, to take someone's bread and then turn against that person is to commit a heinous offense of ingratitude and betrayal, as in the case of Judas Iscariot (Ps. 41:9; John 13:18–30).

Metaphorically, eating the "bread of idleness" is to indulge oneself without doing one's household duty (Prov. 31:27). Also, bread can symbolize a financial investment (Eccles. 11:1).

The ritual and theological texts of the Bible often refer to bread. It played a role in the consecration of the Aaronic priests (Exod. 29:2–3). Bread was also used as part of an offering of thanksgiving to God (Lev. 7:12–13). Of particular importance in Israel's worship is unleavened bread. In the first Passover, the eating of unleavened bread typified the haste of Israel's departure from Egypt (Exod. 12:8–11), although there are already indications that leaven is associated with the pervasive influence of evil (Exod. 12:14–20). So important was this concept that a special festival of unleavened bread was instituted (Lev. 23:6).

The association of leaven with evil underlines the fact that bread or leaven can represent temptation, false teaching, or materialism. Human life is not sustained by bread alone (physical provision), but requires the spiritual provision of the Word of God (Deut. 8:3; Job 23:12). This concept enabled Jesus to reject the temptations of Satan (Matt. 4:3–4; Luke 4:3–4), and also underlies the practice of fasting, that is, refraining from eating bread during periods of intense focus on an encounter with God (Exod. 34:28; Deut. 9:9; 2 Sam. 3:35). In Matthew 16:5–12, leaven represents the doctrine of the Sadducees and Pharisees.

More positively, bread frequently stands for God's provision for his people. The practice of setting the bread of the Presence before God expresses this concept. Every Sabbath the priests put twelve loaves of bread on the table of the bread of the Presence in the temple (Exod. 25:23–30; 35:13; 39:36; Lev. 24:5–9). In contrast to the religious ideas of the surrounding nations, the Bible does not imply that the bread was meant as food for God (Ps. 50:12–15). Instead, the bread was placed before Yahweh as a token of gratitude for his provision for his people. For Jesus, David's eating of the bread of the Presence suggests that human need can at times overrule ritual prohibition (1 Sam. 21:4–6; Mark 2:26).

The manna in the wilderness is the quintessential example of bread as a provision of God. The Israelites were to gather just enough for each day and not hoard, since they needed to learn to depend on God for each day's supply (Exod. 16:4–5). Similarly, the Christian prays for "daily" bread (Matt. 6:11). Such provision spares one from the dangers of both poverty and wealth (Prov. 30:8). Jesus teaches that God feeds his people as a father does his children (Matt. 7:9), and dramatically illustrates this truth in the miraculous feeding of the crowds (Matt. 14:15–21; 15:32–38). The disciples were thus not to be concerned about where they would obtain bread when they went out to serve God (Luke 9:3; cf. Ps. 37:25). At the same time, the Christian is not to rely on the charity of the church for bread but earn it (2 Thess. 3:12). The failure of the bread supply is a mark of judgment (Lev. 26:26; Lam. 1:11; 2:12; 4:4; 5:6; Amos 4:6).

The New Testament uses bread as a rich theological metaphor. As God supplies bread, so he will also supply righteousness to his people (2 Cor. 9:10). Above all, Jesus himself is the bread of life; he is the sustenance from God that gives eternal life (John 6:25–59). Christians thus partake of Christ's body in the bread of the Lord's Supper. In this, they remember his sacrificial death and celebrate the eternal life he supplies (Matt. 26:26–29). After the resurrection, Jesus' eating of bread with the disciples was a token of his victory over death (Luke 24:30, 35; John 21:13), and Christians after that met on the first of the week for the breaking of bread (Acts 20:7).

DUANE A. GARRETT

Breaking of Bread. *See* LORD'S SUPPER, THE.

Bride. *See* CHURCH, THE; MARRIAGE.

Bridegroom. *See* MARRIAGE.

Brother. *See* CHRISTIANS, NAMES OF; FAMILY LIFE AND RELATIONS.

Build Up. The work of building up is almost always seen in a positive light in the Scriptures. The Hebrew word *bānâ* is used of building a physical structure. It is used to describe the building up of Jerusalem (Ps. 147:2). It is interestingly used to describe God's fashioning of Adam's rib into a woman (Gen. 2:22). This word also denotes the place that Rachel and Leah had in "building" the house (family) of Israel.

To build up is often used in the sense of strengthening, establishing, and causing to prosper. "If you return to the Almighty, you will be restored" (Job 22:23). "God will . . . rebuild the cities of Judah" (Ps. 69:35). Jeremiah spoke of God's intention to build up and plant a kingdom (18:9). He also describes God's intentions for the nation after the captivity (24:6). This condition will also be realized in God's purpose for Israel in the last days (31:4; 33:7). The poetic books speak of a person being built up in wisdom (24:3).

In the New Testament we find several compound Greek verbs that are based on the root verb *domeō,* meaning "to build." Paul uses *epoikodomeō* to describe himself as an expert builder in 1 Corinthians 3:10, and then encourages others to be careful how they build upon the foundation he laid. The teachers who follow after Paul should build up their pupils in the knowledge of Christ. Paul emphasizes that Christ is the only foundation (v. 11), but there are many ways of building upon it (v. 12). From the passage it seems clear that even saved people can spend their lives building in areas that do not count for eternity. Those who build in eternal values that will stand the test of fire will be rewarded (v. 14).

This same verb is found in Ephesians 2, describing the mystical body of Christ into which the Gentile believers are "built on the foundation of the apostles and prophets" (v. 20). The Gentiles are also "being built together to become a dwelling in which God lives by his Spirit" (v. 22). This indicates that the Holy Spirit is continuing to build the church.

Jude uses this word to encourage believers to build themselves up in their faith (v. 20). Believers are to be grounded in the body of truth that constitutes faith; and then they are built up by continuing prayer. God builds us by the Holy Spirit. Teachers are sometimes his instruments but we are responsible individually to allow conditions to be present that bring about this building up. *Epoidomeō* is also used in a negative sense in 1 Corinthians 8:10 in reference to a weaker brother who is emboldened to eat things sacrificed to idols.

The other Greek verb that is germane to this topic is *oikodomeō.* It is used to describe the construction of a building (1 Peter 2:7). It is also used of the church being built up (Acts 9:31). In 1 Corinthians 14:4 it is translated as "edifies." The main use of the word seems to center on actions of believers toward each other as in 1 Corinthians 10:23, "'Everything is permissible'—but not everything is constructive." This concept of edifying is further explained in Ephesians 4:12–16. Spiritual gifts are not given for self-aggrandizement but for the building up of the body of Christ (v. 12). The church working together as a team is to be striving to build itself up in love (v. 16).

ALAN N. WINKLER

Bibliography. A. T. Robertson, *Word Pictures in the New Testament.*

Building. ***From Sacred Space to Holy House.*** The localized presence of God and God's glory among his people is central to the unfolding story of the Old Testament. This "sacred geography" includes Eden (Gen. 2:8), Bethel (Gen. 28:10–22), Sinai (Exod. 3:5–6; 19:18–20; 24:16; 34:5; Deut. 4:12; 5:24; Ps. 68:8; cf. Heb. 12:18–21), and Shiloh (Judg. 18:31; 1 Sam. 3:21; Ps. 78:60; Jer. 7:12). God's glory rested over the ark of the covenant (Exod. 25:22), in the tabernacle (Exod. 40:34–38; Num. 9:15; 2 Sam. 7:5–7, 13), and in Solomon's temple, God's house (1 Kings 8:10–21; Pss. 26:8; 27:4; 84:1–4; Ezek. 10:18), and in Jerusalem (Pss. 50:1–2; 76:2; 132:13–14; Ezek. 48:35). Although Israel knew well that God could not be confined to this earth, much less a man-made dwelling (1 Kings 8:27, 30, 39, 43, 49; 2 Chron. 2:6; 6:18; Isa. 66:1; cf. Ps. 2:4; 11:4; Acts 7:48–50), they experienced God among them in specific, holy places. Such encounters demonstrated their unique position as a people (Exod. 19:4–6; Deut. 8:6–11), and demanded ritual purity (Exod. 29:29–30; Num. 8:5–22; Isa. 52:11; Mal. 3:1–4) and separateness from foreigners (Exod. 23:20–33). Israel's prophets looked forward to a day when God's sanctuary would be forever among his people (Ezek. 37:26–28; 43:1–7; Mic. 4:1–2; Hag. 2:7; Zech. 2; 6:11–15; 8:3, 23; 14:4). In other contexts, images of reconstruction and rebuilding symbolize God's postexilic restoration of Israel (Jer. 24:4–7; 31:4, 27–40; 33:7; 42:10; Ezek. 36:33–36; Amos 9:11–15). This language was both literal, referring to their homes and cities, and metaphorical, referring to the nation and its fortunes. Both these themes, of God *dwelling among* his people and God *building up* his people, are taken up in the New Testament as images for the new covenant community.

From Solomon's Temple to Something Greater. In the Gospels, especially Luke, temple worship figures prominently (1:9; 2:27, 46; 19:47; 21:37; 24:53), and Jesus affirms the continuing sanctity of the temple as the dwelling-place of God (Matt. 23:21; cf. John 2:17). Nevertheless, as the drama unfolds, Jesus is revealed to be greater than the temple (Matt. 12:6); he is driven to purify it (Mark 11:15–18; cf. Mal. 3:1–3), foresees its destruction (Matt. 24:2; Mark 13:2; John 4:21), and is tried, in part, for his alleged antitemple stance (Matt. 26:61). Jesus' promise to build his church echoes God's promise to Israel in the Old Testament (Matt. 16:18; cf. Acts 15:14–18). For John, Jesus is the new tabernacle (1:14) and temple (2:19–21) of God. Although the early Christians continued to worship at the temple (Acts 2:46; 5:42), Stephen's apology, echoing both Jesus and Isaiah 66, betrayed a shifting perspective on the locus of God's presence with his people (Acts 6:14; 7:48–50; cf. John 4:21–24; Heb. 10:19–22).

Internal Disunity, External Defilement, and Inter-racial Enmity. In several passages Paul identifies the church as the eschatological dwelling of God. God is not only present among, but actually dwells within, his people. First Corinthians 3:9b–17, as a sober warning to the divisive, describes the church as a building (*oikodomē*) established upon the foundation of Jesus Christ, built up by Paul and other laborers, and jealously guarded by God against all who would cause it harm (3:13–15, 17). The church is under construction, and God functions to oversee and protect the project (3:10; Ps. 127:1) until it is finally complete. The church is also, however, a fully occupied dwelling, the temple of God's Holy Spirit (*naos theou;* 3:16). The first image highlights the need for diligent, responsible human effort; the second, the reality of God's holy presence and impending judgment (cf. 1 Sam. 5:7; 2 Sam. 6:7; 1 Peter 4:17).

In 2 Corinthians 6:16–7:1 the church is called the temple of the living God (*naos theou zōntos*) in stark contrast to a world characterized by lawlessness, darkness, disbelief, and idolatry. It is God's dwelling-place and consists of God's people. The call to purity and separateness here, drawn from Israel's scriptures (Exod. 29:45; Lev. 26:11–12; 2 Sam. 7:14; Isa. 52:11; Ezek. 37:26–28), ha sin mind primarily the defilement of pagan religious practices (cf. 1 Cor. 10:19–22); as God's restored temple, God's people must commit themselves to holy living (2 Cor. 7:1). Appropriate conduct is also the focus of 1 Timothy 3:15, where the church is the established and unmovable house of God (*oikos theou*).

As a celebration of Jew-Gentile unity and equality in Christ, Ephesians 2:20–22 portrays the church as building (*oikodomē*), holy temple (*naos hagios*), and dwelling-place of God (*katoikētērion tou theou*). Within this structure, Christ's preeminent role as the cornerstone establishes unity between Jew and Gentile (cf. Ps. 118:22; Isa. 28:16; Matt. 21:42; Acts 4:11; 1 Peter 2:7) and provides the whole with life and growth (Eph. 2:21), while the apostles and New Testament prophets provide a solid foundation (2:20; cf. Rev. 3:12; 21:14). Images of nation, building, body, and temple converge but the central message is clear: Because Christ's death has established peace, union with Christ dissolves all barriers between Jew and Gentile.

A Spiritual House of Living Stones and Holy Priests. The spiritual house (*oikos pneumatikos*) of 1 Peter 2:4–5 is clearly a temple. Christ, who was once rejected by humankind (Ps. 118:22), is now a choice, living stone in God's temple (Isa. 28:16), sharing his life and bringing unity to all who come to him. But the writer's focus shifts quickly from the building itself to the activities within; not only are believers living stones in God's house, but the church corporately is called to perform priestly service and offer holy sacrifices (1 Peter 2:5, 9; cf. 4:17; Rom. 12:1).

Heavenly Houses for God's People. The resurrection body of the believer can also be called a dwelling. In 2 Corinthians 5:1–4, this house (*oikodomē, oikia, oikētērion*) is designed and built by God, not by human hands (cf. Mark 14:58; Col. 2:11), and it far surpasses the earthly tent of this life, which is subject to decay and death (2 Cor. 4:16; 5:1; cf. 2 Peter 1:13–14). This heavenly house is not so much a temple for the Spirit (cf. 1 Cor. 6:19) as it is the residence of the glorified believer and that which overcomes earthly affliction, mortality, and the nakedness of the intermediate state (2 Cor. 5:3–4). In the event of death, the new house *replaces* the old (v. 1); for those who survive until the parousia, the old is transformed *into* the new (vv. 2, 4).

Bruce N. Fisk

See also Church, the; Tabernacle; Temple.

Bibliography. E. P. Clowney, *Biblical Interpretation and the Church: The Problem of Contextualization;* R. Y. K. Fung, *EvQ* 53 (1981): 89–107; M. J. Harris, *From Grave to Glory: Resurrection in the New Testament;* A. T. Lincoln, *Paradise Now and Not Yet;* R. J. McKelvey, *The New Temple: The Church in the New Testament;* P. S. Minear, *Images of the Church in the New Testament;* H. Ridderbos, *Paul: An Outline of His Theology;* B. Witherington, *Jesus, Paul and the End of the World.*

Burden. In the Old Testament the English word "burden" is translated from the Hebrew word *maśśāʾ*. It is used of a donkey's burden (Exod. 23:5). In Numbers 4:15 it is used of the items the sons of Kohath carried as they moved the tabernacle from place to place in the wilderness. Another kind of burden is described in Numbers 11:11, 17, where Moses is bearing the burden of the people and the Lord tells him to gather the seventy elders so that "they will help you carry the burden of the people." In that instance, the burden is not physical but psychological and spiritual. David uses the word in the same way when he is leaving Jerusalem and says to Hushai, "If you go with me, you will be a burden to me" (2 Sam. 15:33). Job asks God if he has become a burden to him (7:20).

The same Hebrew word is used in reference to a prophetic utterance describing a threat or punishment on a nation or people. Isaiah uses the term in chapters 13 through 23. Ezekiel, Jeremiah, and Zechariah all have similar sections. Recent translations have tended to render the word "oracle" instead of "burden." The basic concept seems to be that Israel's sinful actions have caused God to be burdened. Therefore, in righteousness he is compelled to judge them.

In the New Testament *phortion*, the Greek word used for burden, denotes the troubles of this life. In Matthew 23:4 Jesus describes the heavy burdens the Pharisees laid upon the people "but they themselves are not willing to lift a finger to move them." Obviously this is a burden of legalism. This same Greek word is used to describe a man's load of imperfections and sins in Galatians 6:5. Jesus uses the same word to describe his burden in Matthew 11:30: "My yoke is easy and my burden is light." The reason for having a light burden is described in the previous verse: "I am gentle and humble in heart." Burdens will come in this life but they will be light if we have Jesus' approach to life.

Another Greek word, *baros*, is used to describe the decision of the first church council in Jerusalem: "We will not place upon you any greater burden than these" (Acts 15:28). *Baros* is also used in Galatians 6:2 to describe our Christian responsibility.

Alan N. Winkler

Burial. Burial was a matter of great importance in the Old Testament. The story of Abraham's negotiation to purchase a cave for Sarah's burial is told in detail (Gen. 23). Graves were sometimes marked with pillars (Gen. 35:20; 2 Kings 23:17), and places where famous Old Testament figures were buried were known for generations to come (Acts 2:29) and were even adorned by them (Matt. 23:29). The Old Testament writers routinely describe the burials of the major characters in the narrative (for a number of the judges little is recorded about them *except* where they were buried—cf. Judg. 10:1–2, 3–5; 12:8–10, 11–12, 13–15); indeed, that the site of Moses' grave is unknown is so unusual as to require special comment (Deut. 34:6). On the other hand, not receiving a proper burial was a matter of great shame (Isa. 14:18–20; Jer. 16:4).

The strong emphasis in the Old Testament on burial serves to bind the dead with their ancestors, and, hence, the Jews together as a people. Typical burial expressions include "he was gathered to his people" (Gen. 35:29; 49:33) and "he rested with his fathers" (1 Kings 2:10; 11:43). Indeed, families were buried together (Gen. 49:29–33), even if it meant traveling a great distance to do so (Gen. 50:12–13). That burial resulted in the corruption of the body was understood (Gen. 3:19; Job 17:13–16; Ps. 16:10; Acts 13:36), but it was precisely against that common recognition of the fate of the dead that the hope of resurrection was born (Isa. 26:19; Dan. 12:2).

The Jewish practice of burying the dead is carried forward into the New Testament period. John the Baptist's disciples buried his body (Matt. 14:12), and Joseph of Arimathea buried Jesus (Matt. 27:57–60; Mark 15:42–46; Luke 23:50–53; John 19:38–42 [accompanied by Nicodemus]). With the money paid to Judas the chief priests purchased a field to use as a burial place for foreigners (Matt. 27:5–7). The earliest Christians, being Jews, continued the practice, burying Ananias and Sapphira (Acts 5:6–10) and Stephen (Acts 8:2).

Jesus' burial is especially important, of course, because it is followed by his resurrection. In addition to all four Gospel writers recording the tomb being found empty (Matt. 28:1–7; Mark 16:1–7; Luke 24:1–12; John 20:1–12), Matthew notes the care to which the chief priests and the Pharisees went to make Jesus' tomb secure (27:6–66) and the subsequent rumor they spread when their efforts failed (28:11–15). Paul, in his recitation of the resurrection tradition that he had passed on to the Corinthians, notes that Christ "was buried" (1 Cor. 15:4). The early Christians, therefore, came to understand Jesus' burial as a necessary (but temporary!) prelude to his resurrection.

Paul presses the connection between burial and resurrection one step further by applying it to baptism. In both Romans (6:4) and Colossians

(2:12) he presents baptism as a symbol of being buried with Christ. Through faith Christians are then raised with Christ to live a new life. Thus, burial comes to be connected not just with the hope of a future resurrection secured by the resurrection of Jesus (1 Cor. 15:20–23; 1 Thess. 4:14), but also with the reality of new life in Christ in the present.

The Bible contains other metaphorical uses of burial terminology. The corruption of the body in the grave provides a natural link to corrupt speech (Ps. 5:9; Rom. 3:13) and to people who are corrupt within (Matt. 23:27). Similarly, Jesus uses Isaiah's mention of the worm that does not die in its assault on a corpse as a picture of hell (Mark 9:48). Jesus also speaks of burying the dead as a spiritual antithesis to following him (Matt. 8:21–22; Luke 9:59–60).

JOSEPH L. TRAFTON

See also BAPTIZE, BAPTISM.

Bibliography. R. Hachili, *Anchor Bible Dictionary,* 1:785–94; S. Safrai, *The Jewish People in the First Century,* 2:773–87.

Burnt Offering. *See* OFFERINGS AND SACRIFICES.

Buy. *See* REDEEM, REDEMPTION.

Cc

Calf-Idol. *See* Idol, Idolatry.

Call, Calling. This prominent biblical term is used with particular theological significance in three ways: in connection with worship, with election, and with vocation.

Worship. To "call on" God or the Lord is a frequent biblical expression: it occurs fifty-six times in total (Old Testament, 45; New Testament, 11); on four occasions it is applied to other gods. It often appears in the fuller form, "call on the name of" (31 times). The highest concentration is in the psalms (16 times).

Across the range of its occurrences this expression acquires several nuances. The basic meaning, always present, is simply to utter the name of God (Ps. 116:4; Zech. 13:9). But it can mean more broadly to pray (Ps. 17:6; Jon. 1:6; Matt. 26:53), and indeed can signify a whole act of cultic worship (Gen. 12:8; 1 Chron. 21:26). More particularly, to call on God's name can mean to appeal to his mercy and power from a situation of weakness and need (2 Kings 5:11; Ps. 116:4; Lam. 3:55; Matt. 26:53), but more often it connotes a basic commitment to the Lord as opposed to other gods (1 Kings 18:24; Ps. 79:6; Zech. 13:9; Acts 9:14), sometimes an initial commitment (Gen. 4:26; Acts 22:16). With this thought of commitment prominent, calling on the Lord can even have a proclamatory flavor: "Give thanks to the Lord, call on his name; make known among the nations what he has done" (1 Chron. 16:8; cf. Ps. 116:13; Isa. 12:4).

The New Testament use of this expression is remarkable for the way in which it is applied to Jesus. Joel 2:32 is quoted in both Acts 2:21 and Romans 10:13, but in both places "the Lord" is then identified as Jesus (Acts 2:36; Rom. 10:14). The dramatic conviction of the first (Jewish) Christians was that Israel's worship needed to be redirected: people could no longer be saved by calling on Yahweh/Jehovah, the Old Testament name of God, but only on that of Jesus: "there is no other name under heaven given to men by which we must be saved" (Acts 4:12). To "call on the name of our Lord Jesus Christ" (1 Cor. 1:2) therefore means worshiping him with divine honors.

Election. "Call" is one of the biblical words associated with the theme of election. In both Hebrew and Greek, "call" can be used in the sense of "naming" (Gen. 2:19; Luke 1:13), and in biblical thought to give a name to something or someone was to bestow an identity. Names often encapsulated a message about the person concerned (Ruth 1:20–21; John 1:42; cf. Matt. 16:18). When God is the one who bestows names, the action is almost equivalent to creation: "Who created all these? He who brings out the starry host one by one, and calls them each by name. Because of his great power and mighty strength, not one of them is missing" (Isa. 40:26).

This theme is developed particularly in Isaiah 40–55, which forms an important background to the New Testament use of the term. The creative "calling" of the stars is matched by the "calling" of Abraham, which meant both the summons to leave Ur and the call to be the father of Israel: "When I called him he was but one, and I blessed him and made him many" (51:2). Similarly Israel the nation has been called—"I took you from the ends of the earth, from its farthest corners I called you" (41:9; cf. 48:12)—and this means that they are "called by my name . . . created for my glory" (43:7; cf. Hos. 1:10). God has bestowed his own name upon Israel as part of the creative act that made Israel his own elect people. Now also the Servant of the Lord has been "called" to be the Savior of the world (42:6; 49:1); and so has Cyrus, to be the instrument of judgment of Babylon (48:15).

Thus in Isaiah "call" brings together the ideas of naming, election, ownership, and appointment, as the word is used with different nuances in different contexts. It connotes the creative word of God, by which he acts effectively within the world.

The New Testament picks up all these ideas and takes them further. The influence of Isaiah is seen particularly in the writings of Paul and Peter, who use "call" as a semitechnical term denoting God's effective summons of people to faith in Christ; verb and noun together are used approximately forty-three times with this general denotation. However, within this overall usage various shades of meaning of and nuances may be discerned:

Initiation. "Were you a slave when you were called?" (1 Cor. 7:21). In this verse and many other places "called" is almost equivalent to "converted," pointing to the moment of initiation when faith was born. But it means more than "converted," for it points beyond a change of mind and heart to the action of God. This theological hinterland comes out clearly in Romans 8:30: "those he predestined, he also called; those he called, he also justified." Here the creative word of God is clearly visible. This is not a "call" that can be ignored: It comes from one who "gives life to the dead and calls things that are not as though they were" (Rom. 4:17). By such a creative act God, says Peter, has "called you out of darkness into his wonderful light" and thus formed "a chosen people, a royal priesthood, a holy nation, a people belonging to God" (1 Peter 2:9).

Naming. To be "called" by God means to be "called" something different: the new name "sons of living God" is given to those whom God has called, both Jews and Gentiles (Rom. 9:24–26). Here the notion that God's people bear his own name receives a new shape. In baptism converts were washed, sanctified, justified in the name of the Lord Jesus Christ (1 Cor. 6:11), so that his is "the noble name of him to whom you belong" (James 2:7). Because they bear his name, Paul prays that "the name of our Lord Jesus may be glorified in you" (2 Thess. 1:12).

Destiny. In a string of references "call" and "calling" connote the ultimate destiny of believers. The moment at which they were called points ahead to the final goal to which they are called by God (1 Cor. 1:9; Eph. 4:4; Phil. 3:14; 1 Thess. 5:24; 1 Tim. 6:12; Heb. 3:1; 1 Peter 5:10).

Holiness. "We constantly pray for you, that our God may count you worthy of his calling" (2 Thess. 1:11). The fact of God's call, and the destiny it involves, has moral consequences now. Believers are called to be holy (Rom. 1:7; 1 Cor. 1:2), and must walk worthy of their calling (Eph. 4:1). Peter twice uses the phrase "to this you were called" with reference to the meekness Christians must show their opponents, following the example of Jesus (1 Peter 2:21; 3:9).

Vocation. The notion of appointment to office, which we observed in Isaiah, is also taken up in the New Testament. When Paul was "called by grace," it meant not just his conversion but also his appointment as apostle to the Gentiles (Gal. 1:15). He is therefore "called to be an apostle" (Rom. 1:1; 1 Cor. 1:1).

Apostleship is the only spiritual gift in connection with which the word "call" is used, and it may be that this reflects the uniqueness of the office in Paul's mind. However, from another perspective he regards all spiritual gifts as equally "the work of one and the same Spirit, and he gives them to each one, just as he determines" (1 Cor. 12:11), and therefore it would probably not be biblically inappropriate to extend the idea of vocation to all ministries within the church. The exercise of whatever gifts we possess is a "call" from God (vocation is not just to the "ordained" ministry!).

May we extend the idea of vocation also to cover secular employment? Luther took this step, radically teaching that any work may be a "calling" from God. Some have argued that Paul uses the word "calling" in something like this sense in 1 Corinthians 1:26 and 7:17, 20: "each one should remain in the situation which he was in when God called him" (7:20). Here "called" clearly refers to conversion, but "calling" could refer to the socioeconomic state of the convert (here, slave or freed).

Since Paul is happy for this state to be changed, if opportunity presents (7:21), it seems unlikely that he would regard it alone as a full "calling" from God. Probably he is using the word in a broad sense: "Let everyone remain loyal to God's call, which means living as a Christian in whatever situation you find yourself."

However, even if "calling" is not used in this way in the Bible, it is surely biblical to regard all work as an opportunity to glorify God and to serve him. STEPHEN MOTYER

Bibliography. G. W. Bromiley, *ISBE*, 1:580–82; A. A. Hoekema, *Saved by Grace;* D. Peterson, *Engaging with God: A Biblical Theology of Worship.*

Canaan. *See* LAND (OF ISRAEL).

Canon. *See* BIBLE, CANON OF THE.

Capstone. An architectural term denoting the top stone in a building or wall. If it caps an arch it is called a keystone. The expression is used twice in the Old Testament (Ps. 118:22; Zech. 4:7). In Zechariah 4:7 it is clearly the capstone of the temple that is in view. The meaning in Psalm 118:22 is less clear ("keystone" JB; "capstone" NIV; "cornerstone" NRSV). The Hebrew is translated by the Septuagint as *kephalēn gōnias,* literally, "the head of the corner." This term has made its way into the New Testament five times (Matt. 21:42; Mark 12:10; Luke 20:17; Acts 4:11; 1 Peter 2:7). Psalm 118:22 evidently refers to the king who was disallowed, but then acknowledged to be the rightful ruler. Jesus makes use of this psalm in a parable referring to Israel and its rejection of him as Messiah (Matt. 21:33–44, and parallels). In Acts 4:11 Peter makes use of Psalm 118:22 to defend himself against his Jewish detractors.

In all these passages it must be acknowledged that "capstone" or "cornerstone" would make an equally good translation. It is 1 Peter 2:7 that tips the scales toward "cornerstone." These three passages (Ps. 118:22; Isa. 8:14; 28:16) are used together to make the point that Christ is supreme, and two of these passages (Isa. 28:16; 8:14) clearly refer to a cornerstone.

So the Zechariah 4:7 passage is clearly "capstone" but the remainder are probably best taken as "cornerstone," with the point being that Jesus was rejected by the ones who ought to have known him (builders = Jewish leadership), but God has exalted him to be the chief stone above all, the very head of the corner, on which all else depends.

WALTER A. ELWELL

See also CORNERSTONE.

Care. In the Old Testament several Hebrew words are translated as "care" or a similar word (e.g., "worry" or "anxious"). In 1 Samuel 10:2, when Samuel anoints Saul as king, a series of signs are predicted by Samuel to prove God's favor on Saul, culminating in the indwelling of God's Spirit. The first sign is that two men will say to Saul, "The donkeys that you went to seek are found, and now your father has stopped worrying about them and is worrying about you" (NRSV).

The connotation of caring about something to the point of "worrying" about it is picked up in the New Testament. As in the Old Testament, the undertone can be positive or negative. In the New Testament, the principal utilization is negative. The most common Greek word that is translated "care" is the noun *merimna* (or the verb *merimnaō*).

In Matthew 13:22 in Christ's parable of the four seeds, the third person is represented by the seed that was choked out by the "cares of the world." The enigmatic meaning of the parable is that preoccupation with the world depletes one's devotion to God. Because the world is temporal, inordinate care for the world causes preoccupation with the result of not caring for eternal things; consequently, the Word does not become deeply implanted.

In Luke 21:34 believers are warned to be watchful of the Lord's return and not to be "weighed down with . . . the worries of this life" (NRSV). In 2 Corinthians 11:28 Paul lists his sufferings as his glory in his defense against the "superapostles." Besides his external sufferings, his care for all the churches and the subsequent heartache because of an intense concern for those he loved is Paul's mark of true apostleship. It can be seen that care to the point of burden is intended.

Another Greek word for "care" is *melō*. It, too, can denote anxiety or earnest concern, depending on the context. In 1 Peter 5:7 both the verb *melō* and the noun *merimna* are used: "Cast all your anxiety (*merimna*) on him, because he cares (*melō*) for you" (NRSV).

Care to the point of anxiety is seen as harmful and as contrary to faith in God. Matthew 6:25 says, "Do not worry about your life." It is necessary that a person gives basic attention to having food and shelter. The fact that the same words for "care" are also translated "anxiety" or "worry" shows that the derivation of anxiety could be a reasonable care turned awry. When one's desires are inordinate with the result being a focus on temporal existence instead of eternal life, the consequence can be harmful. For example, the negative effects of anxiety can be seen in one's health status. Too much stress can cause manifold health problems. Worry cannot add a single hour to our life span, according to Matthew 6:27, and therefore, it is a waste of time. Trusting in God when one cannot change a situation is biblical faith. Inactive, worrisome reasoning is diametrically opposed to the Jewish and Christian concept of faith.

Paul says in Philippians 4:6, "Do not worry about anything" (NRSV). The word *merimnao* does not mean "do not 'care' about anything." Rather, Paul wants the Philippians to "in everything by prayer and supplication with thanksgiving let your requests be made known to God." In other words, thankfulness, which is a part of faith, resolves the quandary of anxiety. ERIC W. ADAMS

See also ANXIETY.

Bibliography. G. R. Collins, *Overcoming Anxiety;* B. Narramore and B. Counts, *Freedom from Guilt;* C. Osborn, *Release from Fear and Anxiety;* P. Tournier, *Guilt and Grace.*

Celebrate, Celebration. The word "celebrate" and its derivatives are used only three times in the KJV, but the NIV uses them eighty-three times. The word "celebrate" is the translation of the Hebrew verb *ḥāgag,* which means to prepare, keep, or observe a feast or festival; the noun *ḥag,* which indicates a feast or festival; and the verb *ʿāśâ,* which means to do, make, or celebrate. These words are used to describe the celebration of the three main pilgrimage feasts—the Passover, the Feast of Firstfruits, and the Feast of Tabernacles—and other special events in the life of Israel.

Passover was first instituted by Moses. He asked for Pharaoh's permission to go into the desert "to celebrate a festival to the LORD" (Exod. 10:9). The celebration of Passover is spelled out fully in Exodus 12:3–40. God sent a plague that took the lives of the firstborn children in the Egyptian homes but passed over the homes of the Israelites. Passover marks the passing from slavery in Egypt to freedom in the promised land.

Exodus 12:14 gives the guidelines: "This is a day you are to commemorate, for the generations to come you shall celebrate it as a festival to the LORD—a lasting ordinance." It is also known as the Feast of Unleavened Bread, because "it was on this very day that I brought your divisions out of Egypt. Celebrate this day as a lasting ordinance for the generations to come" (Exod. 12:17).

The celebration of the Passover was for a perpetual remembrance, to keep alive for future generations what God had done for the Israelites in redeeming them from bondage in Egypt and guaranteeing freedom for subsequent generations. Passover was an important aspect of the instruction of the children. When they asked, "What does this ceremony mean to you?" they were taught that "It is the Passover sacrifice to the LORD, who passed over the houses of the Israelites . . . when he struck down the Egyptians" (Exod. 12:26–27). When the Israelites heard this, they worshiped. This celebration has been passed on from generation to generation, and the Haggada, the telling of the story, has become a vital part of the celebration. It is a constant reminder of what God has done in order to encourage religious devotion. It bonds people to God and to each other in the family unit.

Celebration is centered around a feast or festival, with eating, singing, and the playing of instruments. When Jerusalem became the capital and the temple had been built, then celebration took place in and around the temple, which was the center of worship. But celebration took place more often than at the appointed times of the religious observances. When the walls of Jerusalem were finished under Nehemiah's supervision, the Levites were brought to Jerusalem to lead in the celebration and to dedicate the completed walls. It was a time of joyful celebration (Neh. 12:27–28).

Jesus celebrated the Passover many times in Jerusalem. But when he celebrated the Passover for the last time, he gave it a new content. It is now called the Lord's Supper or communion, and is celebrated at various times in Christian churches.

WILLIAM J. WOODRUFF

See also FEASTS AND FESTIVALS OF ISRAEL.

Ceremonial Law. *See* LAW.

Chemosh. *See* GODS AND GODDESSES, PAGAN.

Cherub, Cherubim. *See* ANGEL.

Child, Children. *See* FAMILY LIFE AND RELATIONS.

Children of God. *See* ADOPTION.

Choose. *See* ELECT, ELECTION.

Chosen One. *See* JESUS CHRIST, NAME AND TITLES OF.

Christ as King. *See* KING, CHRIST AS.

Christ as Priest. *See* PRIEST, CHRIST AS.

Christ as Prophet. *See* PROPHET, CHRIST AS.

Christ, Christology. Jesus Christ is the central figure whom the Old Testament foreshadows and the New Testament proclaims as prophecy become fact. It is accordingly of first importance to understand the biblical portrayal of the Messiah (Heb. *māšîaḥ*; Gk. *christos,* from *chriō*, to anoint), whom God has anointed to redeem his people and creation.

A key passage that summarizes the risen Christ's own interpretation of his completed messiahship is the Emmaus saying of Luke 24:25–27: "'How foolish you are, and how slow of heart to believe all that the prophets have spoken! Did not the Christ have to suffer these things and then enter his glory?' And beginning with Moses and all the Prophets, he explained to them what was said in all the Scriptures concerning himself." In Luke's abbreviated account abstracted from a longer and more detailed story circulated among eyewitnesses in the early church, Jesus claims the Old Testament as prelude to his role as the Christ/Messiah, highlighting his redemptive suffering and triumphal glorification. He attests the continuity of the old and the new and invites his followers to see "in all the Scriptures the things concerning himself." Jesus also promises that his disciples will receive the gift of reliable remembrance and accurate interpretation ("All this I have spoken while still with you. But the Counselor, the Holy Spirit, whom the Father will send in my name, will teach you all things and will remind you of everything I have said to you" (John 14:25–26; cf. 15:26–27).

Old Testament Images of Christ. In the Old Testament anointing with oil was associated with the Lord's appointing a person to the office of priest, king, or prophet to save and preserve Israel. To fill the priestly office Moses was directed by the Lord to anoint Aaron and his sons: "anoint them and ordain them. Consecrate them so that they may serve me as priests" (Exod. 28:41). For the kingly office Samuel anointed Saul and said, "Has not the LORD anointed you leader over his inheritance?" (1 Sam. 10:1). After Saul's failure, the Lord commanded Samuel to anoint David: "So Samuel took the horn of oil and anointed him in the presence of his brothers, and from that day on the Spirit of the LORD came upon David in power" (1 Sam. 16:13). King and priest were anointed together at the formal installation of Solomon as king and Zadok as priest (1 Chron.

29:22). Of Solomon, the Chronicler remarks, "The LORD highly exalted Solomon in the sight of all Israel and bestowed on him royal splendor such as no king over Israel ever had before" (1 Chron. 29:25). These texts underscore several composite characteristics of the messianic figure. As king, he is appointed by the Lord and in being separated for service receives the powerful Spirit of the Lord, reigns over the people of the Lord, and serves them by delivering them from the hand of their enemies (cf. Ps. 2:1–12). As priest, he is clothed with salvation for the joy of the saints as he atones for the people's sins (cf. Ps. 132:16). These typological offices notably describe Jesus' royal messiahship, which inaugurates the saving reign of God by the anointing of the Spirit and the invasion of satanic territory. They also describe his priestly office in atoning for the sins of the people by his suffering as the final and perfect sacrifice, accompanied by majesty and glory. These are the themes Jesus encapsulates in his Emmaus address.

The prophets, too, were anointed, and Jesus fulfills their role as the superior messianic prophet. To Elijah God gives the command, "and anoint Elisha . . . to succeed as prophet" (1 Kings 19:16b). God says of his anointed prophets, "Do not touch my anointed ones; do my prophets no harm" (Ps. 105:15). In the prophetic literature Isaiah foresees the coming of a royal servant figure who will embody the true Israel and gather to himself not only sinful Israel but will be a light to the nations of the Gentiles as well. He will be a despised servant ruler before whom kings and princes will prostrate themselves (Isa. 49:5–7), a figure who will take prey from the mighty (vv. 24–25) as Jesus will invade demonic strongholds and plunder Satan's goods (Matt. 12:28–29). The messianic servant will make himself an offering for sin and make many to be accounted righteous; he will bear their iniquities and so be glorified and divide the spoil with the strong because he poured out his soul to death and was numbered with the transgressors (Isa. 53). Jesus as anointed Messiah embodies these royal and priestly functions and consciously sets his vision on fulfilling Old Testament suffering and glorification typologies in the cross and resurrection (Matt. 16:21). At the failure of the princely and priestly shepherd of Israel Ezekiel prophesies that the Lord God himself will come as shepherd: "As a shepherd looks after his scattered flock when he is with them, so will I look after my sheep. . . . I myself will tend my sheep and have them lie down, declares the Sovereign LORD. I will search for the lost and bring back the strays. I will bind up the injured and strengthen the weak, but the sleek and the strong I will destroy. I will shepherd the flock with justice" (34:12, 15–16). Jesus similarly uses the personal pronoun "I" in claiming to fulfill Ezekiel's prophecy: "I am the good shepherd. The good shepherd lays down his life for the sheep" (John 10:11). Daniel foresees one like a Son of man who receives from the Ancient of Days authority, glory, and sovereign power and an everlasting dominion that will never pass away (Dan. 7:13–14). Jesus claims to be the Son of man who has authority as Lord of the Sabbath and of the endtimes (Matt. 12:3–7; 16:21–28). Haggai foretells the glorious overthrow of the kingdoms of the nations with their chariots and riders by the victorious servant king anointed by the Lord of hosts (2:21–23); Jesus claims to be the victorious king of the kingdom of God who is binding Satan by the power of the Spirit (Matt. 12:28–29). Zechariah foresees the coming victorious king, humble and riding on an ass, whose dominion will be from sea to sea, who will set the captives free by the blood of the covenant (9:9–11); Jesus fulfills the prophecy with his ministry of passion and promise of final redemption and judgment (Matt. 21:1–46; 24:27–31; 26:26–29).

Images of Christ in the Gospels. Jesus evinces a characteristic eschatological power that reveals his messianic self-understanding: in him the reign of God is personified; he is acting as the anointed agent in a powerful invasion to rescue Satan's prisoners, one by one.

The parables of the kingdom shed further light on Jesus' Christology of inaugurated eschatology, since a true metaphor is more than a sign because it bears the reality to which it refers. The following sayings describe Jesus' messianic understanding as he sees the power of God at work in his own ministry and in those who accept him. In the parable of the children in the marketplace (Matt. 11:16–19) Jesus declares with authority his right to invite outcasts to open table fellowship, thereby going beyond nationalist and ethnic interests to include all who will eat with this friend of tax collectors and sinners (implicitly fulfilling the vision of Isa. 49:5–13). In the twin parables of the treasure hidden in a field and the pearl of great price (Matt. 13:44–46) Jesus describes the surprise and joy of discovering and acquiring great treasure, implying that the saving reign of God is present to be discovered and acquired. Only one who is supremely confident that he is anointed to speak with divine authority could make such a radical announcement. Astounding is Jesus' announcement that forgiveness of sins is present in response to himself, and still more startling is that lost Gentile sinners (including Jews who have made themselves like Gentiles) are forgiven and welcomed into table fellowship. In the parable of the prodigal son (Luke 15:11–32) the reprobate who has become like a Gentile is forgiven and restored to the father's table, in reversal of traditional theology that the son was "dead."

We need to ask what opinion Jesus must have had of himself to speak as he did against the traditional viewpoint of religious authority. Jesus exhibits a decisive Christology that exceeds the messianic views of Judaism. Jesus appears to speak as the voice of God in announcing the inauguration of the eschatological time when the unforgivable sinner is forgiven. No other explanation can satisfactorily account for the phenomenon (the rejecting Pharisees, on the other hand, see Jesus as demonically possessed and heretically mad, Matt. 12:24). The parables of the lost sheep and the lost coin (Luke 15:3–10) bear out the same theme of searching, finding, and rejoicing that characterizes Jesus' inauguration of the messianic time of salvation, as do the parables of the great supper (Matt. 22:1–14; Luke 14:16–24) and the unjust steward (Luke 16:1–9), which emphasize the importance of immediate decision. So also the laborers in the vineyard (Matt. 20:1–16), the two sons (Matt. 21:28–31), and the Pharisee and the tax collector (Luke 18:9–14a), which note that preconceived ideas may blind one to the present challenge. The good Samaritan (Luke 10:29–37), the unmerciful servant (Matt. 18:23–35), the tower builder and the king going to war (Luke 14:28–32) describe the necessary response to the challenge; the friend at midnight (or importunate friend, Luke 11:5–8) and the unjust judge (the importuned judge, Luke 18:1–8) underscore the importance of confidence in God in the present messianic moment and of "pestering" God with petitions.

The critical consensus of those sayings that imply Jesus' messianic self-understanding also includes his appeal to discipleship, typical of which is Luke 9:62: "No one who puts his hand to the plow and looks back is fit for service in the kingdom of God." Scholars note "the radical nature of the demand," in view of which it should be asked what sort of person would make such a claim except one who is certain of his divine calling and the presence of God's reign in his ministry. While the idiom of entering the kingdom of God is found in both Judaism and the early church, Jesus' attitude toward riches and the kingdom is more radical than that of the rabbis. Jesus says, "How hard it is for the rich to enter the kingdom of God! . . . It is easier for a camel to go through the eye of a needle than for a rich man to enter the kingdom of God" (Mark 10:23b, 25). The saying would lead one to conclude that the challenge of the proclamation arises from the intention of Jesus the proclaimer. In making such an absolute demand of his hearers, Jesus implies that he considers himself absolutely worth following. This is borne out in the unusual saying of Luke 9:60, "Let the dead bury their own dead, but you go and proclaim the kingdom of God"; and the exhortation of Matthew 7:13a (cf. Luke 13:24), "Enter through the narrow gate . . . ," which underscores the radical nature of Jesus' demand and points to his sense of messianic confidence. A similar point is made in the saying in Luke 14:11, "For everyone who exalts himself will be humbled, and he who humbles himself will be exalted," which implies that only one who is conscious of speaking with the authority of God can announce that all must and will be in accordance with the values of God.

The sayings of Jesus agreed on by a consensus of scholars as historically authentic continue with three attitude utterances. In Mark 10:15, "I tell you the truth, anyone who will not receive the kingdom of God like a little child will never enter it," Jesus presents the unforgettable image that one must bring to the announcement of the messianic activity of God the ready trust and instinctive obedience of a child. The originality of Jesus is implicit in the saying and can come only from one who is convinced that he has the authority to challenge traditional ways of thinking. Jesus' use of the personal pronoun "I" in the formula "I tell you the truth" lends additional weight not only to the demand but to the view that Jesus is indwelling the saying with an intentional authority as he understands himself to have the right to make demands that only God has the right to make. Matthew 5:39b–41 also substitutes unusual teaching for the traditional Jewish understanding of the messianic age: "If someone strikes you on the right cheek, turn to him the other also. And if someone wants to sue you and take your tunic, let him have your cloak as well. If someone forces you to go one mile, go with him two miles." In this excerpt from Jesus' larger manual for mission in the Sermon on the Mount he is presenting the proper attitude of discipleship in the inaugurated age of evangelization when the disciples, following the example of their Messiah, place themselves at the disposal of sinners to bring them to salvation. Jesus does not emphasize personal rights or prudential self-interest but mission servanthood in this messianic endtime. The daring that motivates Jesus to contrast the present with the past and to place himself in authority over Moses indicates that he is speaking with divine authority. He claims to supersede the teachings of Moses by the formula, "You have heard that it was said . . . But I tell you," (Matt. 5:21–22, 27–28, 31–32, 33–34, 38–39, 43–44) as he presses to the intent of the Law in preparing the disciples for the mission of the messianic age.

Yet another of the contrasts generally accepted as genuine is Jesus' saying, "Love your enemies and pray for those who persecute you" (Matt. 5:44). This mandate for mission implies that Jesus consciously mediates messianic love in his word of forgiveness and table fellowship with sinners. Internal attitudes are emphasized more intensely by Jesus in the new messianic time than they were in the Old Testament typologies: "Nothing outside a man can make him 'unclean' by going into him. Rather, it is what comes out of a man that makes him 'unclean'" (Mark 7:15). This saying goes against the grain of rabbinic and sectarian Judaism by insisting that it is one's own attitudes and behavior, not external practices relating to foods, which defile a person. It is one of the most remarkable statements of Jesus and is coherent with Jesus' attitude and behavior toward tax collectors and sinners. When the saying is placed in the context of Jesus' inaugurated kingdom proclamation, one sees that the kingly Messiah requires a new attitude and conversion of thought in regard to himself. There is no longer clean and unclean according to the old typologies of food and ethnic priorities, but equality between Jew and Gentile through the far-reaching forgiveness of the Messiah that brings inner transformation. By forgiving sinners and by fellowshiping with them in joyous feasting Jesus personifies the kingly messianic activity of God. Thus the petition in the Lord's Prayer, "Forgive us our sins, as we ourselves herewith forgive everyone who has sinned against us" implies not only the presence of forgiveness in Jesus the Messiah but acknowledges that his disciples are to carry on the messianic mission by sharing the good news of forgiveness with others.

The texts examined above imply the present work of the Messiah. A number of "consensus" passages also imply confidence in the future dimension of the Messiah's inaugurated work. The parable of the sower (Mark 4:3–9) contrasts the small amount of seed and the bountiful harvest. Forgiveness and table fellowship, like the seed, are planted and taking root and anticipate rich blessings to come as the fruition of Jesus' messianic work. Only one who is supremely self-confident about what is coming to pass through his present words and acts, and about what will be brought to fruition in the future, could utter such sayings as those of the mustard seed (Mark 4:30–32), the leaven (Matt. 13:33), the seed growing of itself (Mark 4:26–29), the petition "your kingdom come" (Matt. 6:10), and the prophecy "I say to you that many will come from the east and the west, and will take their places at the feast with Abraham, Isaac and Jacob in the kingdom of heaven" (Matt. 8:11). What is remarkable about all these sayings is the implied declaration of small beginnings, big endings. Already seeds are being sown and are taking root, bread is rising, the reign of God is inaugurated, the banquet has already begun as converted sinners begin to feast at the gracious Messiah's table, and all will be brought to fulfillment at the end of the age.

Jesus claims that in his ministry both the prophetic and wisdom traditions of the Old Testament are superseded: "and now one greater than Jonah is here . . . , now one greater than Solomon is here" (Matt. 12:41–42). He says to his hearers, "But blessed are your eyes because they see, and your ears because they hear. For I tell you the truth, many prophets and righteous men longed to see what you see but did not see it, and to hear what you hear but did not hear it" (Matt. 13:17). Jesus sees himself as the Messiah who inaugurates the reign of God and phases out the old era of the prophets represented by John the Baptist. In a passage that is distinctly messianic, John the Baptist, hearing in prison what Christ was doing, inquires of Jesus through his disciples, "Are you the one who was to come, or should we expect someone else?" (Matt. 11:2–3). Jesus presents as evidence his works of miracles and preaching and remarks, "I tell you the truth: Among those born of women there has not arisen anyone greater than John the Baptist; yet he who is least in the kingdom of heaven is greater than he. From the days of John the Baptist until now, the kingdom of heaven has been forcefully advancing, and forceful men lay hold of it" (Matt. 11:11–12). The new and forceful arrival of the redemptive reign of God is embodied in the ministry of Jesus, who binds Satan and plunders his stronghold, releasing his prisoners: "But if I drive out demons by the Spirit of God, then the kingdom of God has come upon you. Or again, how can anyone enter a strong man's house and carry off his possessions unless his first ties up the strong man? Then he can rob his house" (Matt. 12:28–29). In these declarations of messianic intention Jesus shows that he is conscious of being the stronger man who, with the Father and the Spirit, is despoiling satanic power and redeeming prisoners from spiritual bondage.

Peter is inspired by the Father to utter an affirmation of Jesus' messiahship: "You are the Christ, the Son of the living God" (Matt. 16:16). In this confession Jesus is affirmed as divine through the title "Son of the living God" and as the Christ who fulfills the messianic prophecies of the Old Testament. Jesus then discloses that he is the suffering Messiah whose work will culminate in his death and resurrection (Matt. 16:21), countermanding Peter's objections that stem from the traditional view of messiahship as something tied to ethnic and nationalistic aspirations. The older typology is condemned as obsolete, and even as demonic ("Get behind me, Satan!"), now that Christ has come in fulfillment of Old Testament prophecy (Matt. 16:22–23). Yet, while Jesus has inaugurated the messianic age and his mission is unfolding, the time is not yet ripe for a full declaration of his identity until he has completed his redemptive work. Hence the significance of the messianic secret voiced in Matthew 16:20. When his role as Christ draws to fulfillment during the final days in Jerusalem, he increasingly claims the space of the religious leaders by exegeting them into silence (Matt. 22:41–46). To the Pharisees he puts the question, "What do you think about the Christ? Whose son is he?"—presenting them with a problem text they cannot solve. The answer lies in the fact that Jesus is both David's son and David's Lord. Critiquing the Pharisees before the crowds and his disciples, he claims to be the Christ who has authority as their teacher, leader, and master (the triple meaning of *kathēgētēs,* Matt. 23:10).

In the eschatological discourse on the Mount of Olives Jesus warns his followers of deceivers who will falsely announce the Christ or claim to be Christ, a title only he can rightfully claim. In his trial before the Sanhedrin (Matt. 26:63–64) Jesus responds to the high priest's question, "Tell us if you are the Christ, the Son of God," by affirming, "Yes, it is as you say," attesting his consciousness of being the messianic God-man with the further prophecy, "But I say to all of you: In the future you will see the Son of Man sitting at the right hand of the Mighty One and coming on the clouds of heaven." The high priest correctly understands this as a claim to messiahship and divinity, but ironically misconstrues it as blasphemy worthy of death because he does not accept Jesus' credentials as Messiah (vv. 65–66). Nonetheless the incident attests the fact that Jesus made the claim, as does the reaction of the Sanhedrin, which insults him with blows and taunts him with the words, "Prophesy to us, Christ. Who hit you?" (vv. 67–68). Their taunting continues at the cross, according to the Markan account (Mark 15:32), confirming that Jesus had claimed to be Christ and King: "Let this Christ, this King of Israel, come down now from the cross, that we may see and believe." The fact that Jesus had claimed the title "Christ," however falsely in the eyes of his accusers, is further attested in the account of his trial before Pilate. To the governor's question, "Are you the king of the Jews?" Jesus replies, "Yes, it is as you say" (Matt. 27:11), affirming that he is the reigning Messiah, whereupon Pilate refers to him before the crowds as "Jesus who is called Christ" (vv. 17, 22).

In Luke's account of Jesus' ministry the affirmation of Jesus' messiahship is made early on by John the Baptist, who answers those who wonder whether he might possibly be the Christ (Luke 3:15–17). John defers to Jesus as the mightier one who is to baptize with the Holy Spirit and fire; he, in contrast, baptizes only in a preliminary way with the water of repentance. Luke notes the continuity of John's early prophecy and Jesus' finished work when the risen Jesus refers his superior baptism to Pentecost and to the community's coming proclamation of his saving messianic ministry (Acts 1:5, 8). Overall, Luke's account of Jesus' messianic claims are parallel to those in Matthew and Mark. He closes his Gospel account with the risen Lord's claim to be the suffering and glorified Christ who fulfills Old Testament prophecy (Luke 24:26–27, 44–47: "Everything must be fulfilled that is written about me in the Law of Moses, the Prophets and the Psalms"). In Luke's portrait of the Messiah Jesus knows throughout his ministry that he is the Christ.

Jesus' messianic self-understanding is corroborated by the Fourth Gospel, which John drew from the original pool of his personal remembrances and wrote in the late 50s or early 60s as complementary to the Synoptic Gospels, of which he was aware. The Gospel of John is therefore a valuable source of Jesus' historical claims to messiahship throughout his ministry. Among the numerous references to *christos* in John several suffice to illustrate Jesus' conscious claim to messiahship. To the Samaritan woman at the well who confesses her belief that Messiah is coming, Jesus replies, "I who speak to you am he" (4:25–26). Jesus responds to the skeptical in Jerusalem with the declaration that he has been sent from the Father. Many put their faith in him and ask, "When the Christ comes, will he do more miraculous signs than this man?" (7:25–31). In his prayer to the Father Jesus asserts that "this is eternal life: that they may know you, the only true God, and Jesus Christ, whom you have sent" (17:3). Near the end of his account John explains that his reason for writing his Gospel is to encourage belief that "Jesus is the Christ, the Son of God, and that by believing you may have life in his name" (20:31). This forms an inclusio with the christological claim in the prologue that Jesus is superior to Moses and to John the Baptist, since both are preparatory to Christ (1:15–18, 19–27). Throughout the Gospel of John there are many implications of messiahship in language of intimate relationship with the Father. Jesus is the Son who represents the Father and to whom divine judgment and honor have been given, so that whoever "does not honor the Son does not honor the Father, who sent him" (5:23). All are claims of Jesus that explain his confrontation with those who refuse to move from the older shadowy typologies to Jesus the messianic Reality. His conscious claim to preexistence is affirmed in 8:58 ("Before Abraham was born, I am"), further attesting his conscious superiority to father Abraham and his opposition to those who would prefer the past to the present, the shadow to the Reality.

The four Gospels therefore present complementary portraits of Jesus, whose self-interpretation goes far beyond popular expectations of a political Davidic figure. Jesus the Messiah asserts that he is both human and divine and is the one who alone can atone for sin, provide eternal life, and qualify for glorification as the anointed and faithful image bearer of God. The Gospels thus present a high Christology that is to be traced to Jesus himself.

Images of Christ in the Apostolic Writings. The Book of Acts and the letters of Paul demonstrate how Jesus' earliest followers proclaimed his saving work as the Christ. The early chapters of Acts form an important bridge between Jesus and the early church and give details of the community's kerygma. There is a noticeable focus on *christos* terminology in this proclamation of Jesus as the Christ. The oblique messianic terms "kingdom of God" and "Son of man" Jesus used virtually drop out of apostolic usage. The church early on realized that to preach the kingdom was to preach Christ, who is the redeeming and glorified King of the kingdom. The three points of Jesus' opening kergyma in Mark 1:15 are matched by the three points of Peter's kergyma on Pentecost (Acts 2:22–36), except that the second is replaced by the reality of the crucified, risen, and exalted Christ who reigns on the throne of David.

This simple outline of the early apostolic kerygma, with its focus on Jesus as the Christ, is further attested by Peter's proclamation at Solomon's Colonnade (3:11–26), before the Sanhedrin (4:8–12), upon the apostles' release from prison (4:23–30), and in regular witnessing in Jerusalem (5:42). The unfolding fulfillment of the risen Christ's prophecy to the disciples in Acts 1:8 ("you will be my witnesses in Jerusalem, and in all Judea and Samaria, and to the ends of the earth") continues with Luke's noting that "Philip went down to a city in Samaria and proclaimed the Christ there" (8:5), presumably using the common kerygmatic outline of Jesus as Messiah. Luke comments that following Saul's conversion the former persecutor of the church gave witness in Damascus that "Jesus is the Son of God" and says that "Saul grew more and more powerful and baffled the Jews living in Damascus by proving that Jesus is the Christ" (9:20–22).

Luke also recounts the story of Cornelius's conversion and the extension of the gospel to the Gentiles, including Peter's witness to Jesus' messianic ministry on that occasion, providing an early summary statement on Christology (10:36–43). Peter's proclamation informs us of the solid bridge in early apostolic Christology between Old Testament prophecy and Jesus, and between the healing and suffering ministry of Jesus and his exaltation in his resurrection, and his role as eschatological judge of the living and the dead. In addition, it points to the veracity of apostolic reportage that the facts are accredited by eyewitnesses, and describes the main purpose of Jesus' messianic ministry and the witnesses of his work, namely, that those who hear the message might believe in the name of Jesus and receive forgiveness of sins. Peter's proclamation also provides a bridge between the early apostolic witness to Christ and the Christology of the letters that are written by Peter and Paul as the mission of the church expands in fulfillment of the prophecy of the risen Christ.

Galatians is very likely the earliest of the apostolic letters, with the possible exception of James, which is devoted almost entirely to in-house *parenesis* or teaching about the ethical implications of Christology, also a concern of Paul in the latter sections of his letters. Probably written in A.D. 48 prior to the Jerusalem Council (Acts 15), Galatians focuses on a christological matter central to the survival of Christianity, namely, the sufficiency of the person and work of Christ. Like Hebrews, written by an anonymous acquaintance of Paul during Nero's persecution of Christians in the mid-60s, Galatians makes the strong christological point that Christ fulfills the old messianic shadows and is therefore the superior Reality who serves as the final identity marker of the believing community. The Old Testament messianic typologies have found their fulfillment in him and thus have come to a functional end. The Judaizers, who are working on Paul's recent converts in Galatia, are teaching otherwise. Gentile Christians, they insist, must first become Jews and follow Old Testament typologies (such as circumcision) in order to become God's true people. Paul's uncompromising response is that a Christ who has not completely fulfilled the Old Testament typologies is not a Christ worth worshiping. Such teachers as the Judaizers do not represent the Messiah's completed work of salvation and are therefore to be condemned (1:8–9) because they patch the shadows onto the Reality, thereby subtracting from the complete and perfect salvation accomplished by Jesus the Messiah. As J. Gresham Machen aptly observed, it was Paul who steered the early church away from a weakening compromise with Judaism when even Peter momentarily succumbed to the temptation at Antioch, as Paul records in Galatians 2:11–16. While believers in Israel during the Old Testament period were saved by accepting God's grace as mediated by the typologies of the Torah, the same God of grace now redeems his people through Jesus Christ his Son, and through him alone, for all the former symbols point to him. In one of Paul's great christological declarations the apostle affirms that believing Jews like himself "have put our faith in Christ Jesus that we may be justified by faith in Christ and not by observing the law, because by observing the law no one will be justified" (v. 16). Paul's point is not that believers are now saved by grace whereas in the Old Testament they were saved by works, but rather that what now mediates grace and identifies God's people is Jesus Christ the Lord and author of the Torah. In the Old Testament God's grace was mediated by a set of prophetic symbols, and it was Israel's faith in God's grace attested by their active faithfulness to the identity symbols of the Torah that saved them. In Paul's Christology it is Christ who is the mediator of grace, not any longer the Torah, now that the fullness of time has come (4:4). The symbolism of the Torah is now absorbed into the Reality of Christ. Christ the ultimate Reality is no longer mediated by the temporary symbols.

The same point is powerfully articulated in Hebrews, written near the end of the apostolic era. Because of Nero's persecution of Christians, Jewish believers were tempted to fall back into the typologies of the Old Testament for temporary security. The writer demonstrates the superiority of Jesus over Moses as that of a son over a servant. While Moses was faithful in God's house as a servant, he testified to what would be said in the future: "But Christ is faithful as a son over God's house" (3:1–6). Christ did not take on the limited and temporal glory of the Aaronic priesthood but as Son of the Father was designated "a priest forever in the order of Melchizedek" (5:4–6). Christ as the final and superior high priest has fulfilled the sacrificial symbolism of the Old Testament tabernacle once for all (9:11–14). Thus in the opening hymn to the Son (1:2–3), Christ is extolled as the heir of all things, the creator of the universe, "the radiance of God's glory and the exact representation of his being, sustaining all things by his powerful word. After he had provided purification for sins, he sat down at the right hand of the Majesty in heaven." Christ is accordingly the best; there is no going back to the Old Testament typologies, which in their appointed time were good but now become bad if they are added to the finished and perfect work of Christ.

In between the first and last great warning letters of Galatians and Hebrews during the apostolic period lie the other canonical writings, which are consistent with the high Christology of Jesus and his early interpreters. In his correspondence with the Corinthians in the early 60s Paul contends that the substance of his message is Christ, who was not only crucified but is "the power of God and the wisdom of God" (1 Cor. 1:23–24); he is the only foundation (3:11), for he is of God (3:23); he was the spiritual rock that accompanied Israel in the wilderness (10:4), and thus the Reality that indwelled the typological symbols of the Old Testament. In Paul's Christology of the Lord's Supper, the cup of thanksgiving and the broken bread are a higher participation in the blood and body of Christ (10:16; so also 11:23–26), for now the symbol is in the Reality, not the Reality in the symbol, as in the old epoch. Believers themselves participate in the body of Christ, since God's children (like the symbols) now indwell the highest Reality (12:12, 27). Christ is the Messiah of the new society; he has inaugurated the new family of God by his saving ministry, beginning with the apostles (15:3–11). The societal mission of Christ is grounded in the fact of his historical resurrection, which attests the deity and humanity of Christ the Messiah (15:12–23).

The truth that Christ is the anointed one who creates the new family of God is confirmed by Paul in 2 Corinthians. There he writes of the overflowing of the sufferings of Christ into our lives so that we comfort one another and share a common salvation (1:3–7) as those who are anointed with God's Yes in Christ, are set with the seal of his ownership, and are given the Spirit in our hearts as a deposit of things to come (1:18–22). The family responsibility of ownership means that we share in Christ's anointing as we march in triumphal procession with him and as he spreads through us the fragrance of the knowledge of him everywhere (2:14–16). We do not live in the gospel, but the gospel lives in us, who live in Christ. Paul's Christology accordingly carries on the Christology of Jesus; we are seen to be "in Christ," a figure Paul uses over 125 times in his letters and that connotes the fact that we represent the Reality of God because we dwell in the Reality of Christ. We are a letter of Christ who is written on our hearts, thereby making us competent to be ministers of a new covenant that works not as a distant and fading glory as with Moses, but with the surpassing glory of Christ who ministers through us by the Spirit of freedom, as we are "being transformed into his likeness with ever-increasing glory" (3:2–18).

The participation of believers in the sufferings and glory of Christ and therefore in his ministry of reconciliation that builds the family of God, is accordingly essential to Paul's Christology (5:14–21). This mission-evangelism theme is undoubtedly what Paul has in mind when he speaks of filling up "what is still lacking in regard to Christ's afflictions" (Col. 1:24). This is not in any sense our adding to Christ's atoning work, but our suffering as servants to proclaim the message to those whom God is calling into his family. Since Christ is the goal and end of the Old Testament Law, so "faith comes from hearing the message, and the message is heard through the word of Christ" (Rom. 10:17), as faithful believers in Christ proclaim the Messiah's saving work, participate in messianic glory, and invite others to do the same. ROYCE GORDON GRUENLER

See also JESUS CHRIST; JESUS CHRIST, NAME AND TITLES OF; KING, CHRIST AS; MESSIAH; PRIEST, CHRIST AS; PROPHET, CHRIST AS.

Bibliography. M. Bockmuehl, *This Jesus: Martyr, Lord, Messiah;* J. Charlesworth, ed., *The Messiah: Developments in Earliest Judaism and Christianity;* O. Cullmann, *The Christology of the New Testament;* M. J. Harris, *Jesus as God;* L. D. Hurst and N.T. Wright, eds., *The Glory of Christ in the New Testament;* I. H. Marshall, *The Origins of the New Testament Christology;* C. F. D. Moule, *The Origin of Christology;* J. Smith, *The Promised Messiah; TAB,* pp. 69–134; V. Taylor, *The Person of Christ in New Testament Teaching;* J. Wenham, *Redating Matthew, Mark and Luke;* N. T. Wright, *The Climax of the Covenant.*

Christ Messiah. *See* JESUS CHRIST, NAME AND TITLES OF; MESSIAH.

Christophany. *See* ANGEL OF THE LORD; THEOPHANY.

Christians, Names of. The New Testament contains over 175 names, descriptive titles, and figures of speech referring to Christians, applicable to both the individual and the group. The origin of these names is traceable to the Old Testament, Jesus' teaching, the church, and nonbelievers. Few of them appear as static proper names; instead, the New Testament contexts in which they occur largely determine their meaning.

These names are rich in theological detail. The giving of personal names in biblical times often signified a religious conviction about their recipients or something that would be done through these people. The giving of Christian names, likewise, expresses something about the religious status and character of the person and group named and something about what God has done, is doing, and will do in and through them. These names, in effect, provide us with a first-century compendium of Christian belief. They describe, in part, the Old Testament Jewish roots of Christianity, the role of the Godhead within Christianity, the union of believers with God and Christ, the nature of Christian life and conduct, and the importance of the gospel.

Names Associated with Old Testament Israel. Comparable to the Old Testament's depiction of national Israel as Abraham's physical descendants, the New Testament depicts the church as his spiritual heirs. Jesus appears in the New Testament as the means through which God has fulfilled his promise to make Abraham "the father of many nations." On the basis of the believer's union with Christ, the church stands as its direct fulfillment. Abraham's faith, in this regard, models Christian belief. His faith in God's promises was "credited to him as righteousness" (Gen. 15:6); this holds true as well for anyone who places faith in Jesus (Rom. 4). For this reason, Paul stresses that *all* believers—Jew and Gentile—legitimately stand as Abraham's offspring (Rom. 4:16; 9:8), seed (Gal. 3:29), Abraham's children (Rom. 9:7; Gal. 3:7), and children of the free woman (Gal. 4:31) and the promise (Rom. 9:8; Gal. 4:28).

The New Testament posits a high degree of continuity between Old Testament Israel and the church. The way in which Christians have frequently taken over and adapted Old Testament names and terms relating to Israel to describe themselves particularly strengthens this link. This is evident in various descriptive titles (such as "chosen people" [1 Peter 2:9; cf. Isa. 45:4]), figures of speech (like flock [John 10:16; cf. Jer. 31:10]), and the imaging of divine qualities (e.g., a "holy people" [Eph. 5:3; cf. Deut. 28:9]). The church made a deliberate effort to identify themselves with believing Israel. The church now appears as its successor, as the new Israel or true Israel. (But this present status of the church does not necessarily exclude a future response in faith by ethnic Israel as a whole [see esp. Rom. 11:25–32]). Biblical writers describe both believing Israel and the church as a creative work of God (Isa. 60:21; 64:8; Eph. 2:10), further strengthening this continuity. God's revelation in Christ is not the negation of his revelation through Moses, but its perfect and final fulfillment.

The temple appears in Israel's history, from the early monarchy period on, as the center of worship. Here God's presence visibly dwells and priests intercede before him on behalf of the people by means of offerings and sacrifices. The New Testament spiritualizes this religious focal point with respect to believers.

Believers are the holy temple of the Holy Spirit (1 Cor. 6:19) and the living God (1 Cor. 3:16–17); they are its living stones (1 Peter 2:5) and golden lampstands (Rev. 1:12–13, 20). As living stones, believers are being built up by Christ into a spiritual house, a temple, which stands in marked contrast to the physical temple built with dead stones. As God's temple, all believers have his Spirit living in them—a pervasive divine indwelling unknown to Old Testament Israel.

Believers consider themselves a holy and royal priesthood (1 Peter 2:5, 9), a kingdom of priests (Rev. 1:5–6; 5:10), and priests of God and Christ (Rev. 20:6). Thus, like Old Testament Israel, the church appears as a kingdom of priests. But unlike Old Testament Israel, they become ministers of a new covenant (2 Cor. 3:6). This new work does not, however, mark the abrogation of the Mosaic law, but its ultimate fulfillment in Christ. Whereas the old covenant was external and written on stone tablets, and resulted in condemnation when people failed to keep the law, the new covenant is internal and written on the hearts of people, who, through faith, are redeemed by Christ and regenerated by the Holy Spirit.

Believers also visualize themselves as an aroma of Christ (2 Cor. 2:15), firstfruits of all God's creation (James 1:18), and firstfruits to God and the Lamb (Rev. 14:1–4). Paul exhorts believers to offer themselves to God continually as living sacrifices in the form of thanksgiving or dedicatory offerings (Rom. 6:13; 12:1–2).

Old Testament writers frequently describe Jerusalem as the city of God's presence, the city of God (Pss. 48:1, 8; 87:3), and the holy place where the Most High dwells (Ps. 46:4). In the New Testament, this relation is applied to the church. John, in the Book of Revelation, depicts the church as the bride of the Lamb, descending from heaven as the city of God (3:12), the Holy City (21:2, 10; 22:19), and the new Jerusalem (3:12; 21:2, 10). Here the image of the heavenly city symbolizes the perfect and enduring presence of God (and

Christ) among all his people. This same relation is also portrayed in Hebrews 12:22, where the heavenly city is described as the city of the living God, heavenly Jerusalem, and Mount Zion.

Names Associated with the Godhead. The New Testament names, the called (Rev. 17:14), the chosen (Col. 3:12; 1 Peter 2:9; Rev. 17:14), and the elect (Mark 13:20, 22, 27; Titus 1:1; 1 Peter 1:1), clearly indicate that believers are joined to God by his sovereign election to salvation. The first Christians experienced an identity crisis. Was it Christianity or Judaism that stood directly in line with the Old Testament promises of God? This dilemma was resolved through the realization that Christians too were predestined to share in God's plan of salvation. Peter's description of believers as a people belonging to God (1 Pet. 2:9–10) is reminiscent of Hosea 1:6–10 (cf. also Rom. 9:25–26; 10:19) and intended to resolve any uncertainty in this regard.

Names of Christians also reveal that believers identify themselves with divine qualities and exhort one another to image them in conduct. Jesus says, "Anyone who has seen me has seen the Father" (John 14:9; see also 12:45; 2 Cor. 4:4; Col. 1:15; Heb. 1:3). Jesus images God. As God's children, believers are similarly to image something of God and Christ's character, both individually and as a group. Their ability to do so is based solely on the new life won for them in Christ, through which they have been made the "righteousness of God" (2 Cor. 5:21), and on the provision of the Spirit as their divine resource for achieving this standard in living. Therefore, as these names suggest, to see believers was (and still should be), in effect, to see something of God and Christ.

In a more restricted sense, New Testament writers refer to believers as witnesses. The majority of instances occur in Luke's Gospel (1:2; 24:48) and Acts (1:8, 22; 2:32; 3:15; 5:32; 10:39, 41; 13:31; 26:16), with two in the Petrine letters (1 Peter 5:1; 2 Peter 1:16–18). The term "witness" (*marturia*) refers to eyewitness testimony to Jesus, to one who presents evidence of the gospel message on the basis of firsthand knowledge of Jesus' life, death, and resurrection (Acts 1:22). As Luke clarifies in Acts, the historical reliability of the gospel message is as important as the message itself, for its authenticity is what provides listeners (and readers) with the need and urgency to respond to it. The basic assumption here is the historicity of Jesus' life, ministry, and passion as reported by Luke and, more broadly, by the New Testament itself. A number of other names of believers—-Christians (Acts 11:26; 26:28; 1 Peter 4:16), disciples (John 13:35; Acts 6:1–2; 11:26; 14:21–22; 18:27), followers of the Way (Acts 9:1–2; 19:9, 23; 22:4; 24:14, 22), and Nazarenes (Acts 24:5)—seem closely tied to the historical Jesus.

Names Associated with the Believer's Union with God and Christ. New Testament writers use a number of different family-related concepts to describe, positionally, the believer's standing with God and Christ. In general terms, believers are members of God's family (Eph. 3:14–15; 1 Peter 4:17) and household (Eph. 2:19–20; 1 Tim. 3:15). Believers are frequently pictured as God's offspring. Their sonship is predestined by God (Rom. 8:23), entered into by faith (Gal. 3:26–28), attested to by God's Spirit (Rom. 8:15–16), and qualifies them as heirs of God (Rom. 8:17; Gal. 3:29; 4:7).

In marital terms, believers will be presented to Christ, their husband, as pure virgins (2 Cor. 11:2) and his bride (Rev. 19:7–8; 21:2, 9; 22:17). These images portray the complete and perfect union of Christ and his people.

Believers are Christ's intimates; they are brothers (Rom. 8:29; Heb. 2:11–12, 17) and friends (John 15:13–15)—a relation freely granted to them by Christ based on his redeeming work.

The New Testament reflects a strong family bond among believers. They call each other brother (Acts 9:17; 14:2; 15:36), a brotherhood of believers (1 Peter 2:17), family (Gal. 6:10), and friends (3 John 14).

New Testament names of Christians, such as believers (Acts 4:32; 2 Cor. 6:15; 1 Tim. 4:12), followers of the Way (Acts 9:1–2), and slaves and servants of God and Christ (2 Cor. 6:4; Eph. 6:6), reflect a new Spirit-inspired and Spirit-guided allegiance to God and Christ. As these names suggest, this kind of commitment aims at a complete renunciation of any mental or physical allegiance to persons or things that would impinge on a faithful reliance on God and Christ.

The New Testament contains many names of Christians that explicitly identify believers with God and Christ. Perhaps the most expressive of these is the body of Christ imagery. All believers are united to Christ (1 Cor. 6:15–17), with Christ as the head (Eph. 1:22–23; Col. 1:18) and the church as his body (1 Cor. 12:27; Eph. 1:22–23; Col. 1:24). The body, in turn, is made up of many parts (Rom. 12:4–5; 1 Cor. 12:12, 14, 20), each having distinguishable but interdependent, God-appointed tasks (1 Cor. 12:15–19, 21–26).

Names Associated with Christian Life and Conduct. According to the New Testament, moral purity is a distinguishing feature of Christian life and conduct. Names patterned after the day-night and light-darkness contrasts particularly illustrate this. Believers are sons of the day (1 Thess. 5:5), children of light (Eph. 5:8), light in the Lord (Eph. 5:8), light of the world (Matt. 5:14–16), and sons of the light (John 12:35–36, 46; 1 Thess. 5:5). These designations stand in marked contrast to ones depicting their former sinful life in darkness and night (Eph. 5:8; 1 Thess. 5:5). Names such as the blameless (1 Thess. 3:13; Rev. 14:4–5), the holy (Eph. 2:19–21;

5:3; 1 Thess. 3:13), instruments for noble purposes (2 Tim. 2:21), obedient children (1 Peter 1:13–16), the righteous (1 Peter 3:12; 4:18), and saints (Acts 26:10; Rom. 8:27; 1 Cor. 6:1–2) reiterate our continuing responsibility to reflect in life and practice this new moral standing with God.

The term "world" (*kosmos*) in the New Testament often denotes unbelievers and their sinful way of life. The New Testament graphically affirms that believers are not of the world. They are aliens and strangers (1 Peter 1:1, 17; 2:11). The world perceives preachers of the gospel as fools for Christ (1 Cor. 4:10), and refuse of the world and scum of the earth (1 Cor. 4:13). Yet as salt of the earth (Matt. 5:13), believers ultimately strive, despite hostility, to win the world to Christ.

Names of Christians also indicate a number of important responsibilities the Christian has. As priests (1 Pet. 2:9; Rev. 1:5–6), believers are to offer themselves continually in spiritual service and worship to God. Believers are to love the lost. Christians are servants of the gospel (Eph. 3:7), chosen instruments taking the gospel to Jew and Gentile (Acts 9:15), and salt of the earth (Matt. 5:13). As ambassadors of Christ (2 Cor. 5:20), they, in fact, serve as Christ's representatives through whom Christ (and God) delivers his message of reconciliation to the world.

Believers are to desire personal piety. The images of athletes (2 Tim. 2:5), doers of the Word (James 1:22–25), hardworking farmers (2 Tim. 2:6), obedient children (1 Peter 1:14–16), runners in a race (1 Cor. 9:24–27; Heb. 12:1), and soldiers (2 Tim. 2:3–4) indicate that perseverance, obedience, discipline, single-mindedness, and the putting into practice of biblical teaching should typify the life of all believers.

Names Associated with the Gospel. Understood in the names of Christians, as Abraham's descendants and heirs to the promises God made to him, is the gospel's universal mandate. It is for *all* people. Through Christ, Abraham has become the "father of all nations," the one through whom "all peoples on the earth will be blessed" (Gen. 12:3).

The hope of the gospel is the hope of eternal life. In Jesus' teaching, children of God are children of the resurrection (Luke 20:35–36). Believers are heirs to the promise of the gospel, the hope of eternal life (Rom. 8:17; Titus 3:7).

In Revelation 3:12, Jesus promises to give believers the name of God, the name of the city of God (the new Jerusalem), and his own new name. This means nothing short of an inseparable identification and perfect union of all believers eternally with God and the Lord Jesus Christ.

H. Douglas Buckwalter

Bibliography. H. J. Cadbury, *The Beginnings of Christianity,* 5:375–92; R. S. Rayburn, *EDT,* pp. 216–18; *BEB,* 1:431–34; *TAB,* pp. 537–42.

Chronicles, Theology of. ***Chronicles' Perspective on Israel's Past.*** Chronicles re-presents the historical traditions of Israel from a different perspective and for different purposes than those found in Samuel–Kings. Samuel–Kings looks at the past from the perspective of the nation's exile in Babylon (586–538 B.C.), a time when the very existence of Israel seemed to have drawn to an end. The Israelites had lost not only the temple of Yahweh and self-rule through their Davidic king, but also the promised land itself. They sought to maintain their identity as the people of Yahweh within communities transplanted in a foreign land. Samuel–Kings, teaches the community that the exile was not the result of God's unfaithfulness to them, but the product of Israel's own repeated violations of God's covenant. It emphasizes Israel's almost fatalistic "downhill slide" to exile.

By contrast, Chronicles was written at some point in time after the Babylonian exile. In continuing faithfulness, God had restored the people to the promised land in 538 B.C. through the agency of Cyprus, the founder of the Persian Empire. The activities of sacrificial worship once again resounded in the reconstructed temple at Jerusalem. Life had begun anew for those who had returned home, although they still lived under foreign rule and without their Israelite king. Chronicles, in light of the experience of God's mercy in restoring Israel, presents a new perspective on Israel's past. The same historical panorama provides new insights into God's ways of interacting with Israel, and new lessons for the community of faith. Chronicles provides details about the exile and other disasters, an explanation of the return from exile and other blessings, a defense of certain religious and political institutions, and an implicit call for the community to behave faithfully toward Yahweh.

As a result of this perspective, the re-presentation of the past differs from that of Samuel–Kings in some key respects. First, Chronicles illustrates more fully how Israel's prosperity and success are the results of Yahweh's blessing. Second, although Israel's disasters are presented as the result of God's judgment on Israel's unfaithfulness, that unfaithfulness is described differently. Samuel–Kings portrays Israel's unfaithfulness as idolatry and failure to keep God's statutes (2 Kings 17:7–18). Chronicles probes more deeply and delineates Israel's unfaithfulness more specifically. In Chronicles, Israel's unfaithfulness is identified as "forsaking Yahweh," or not properly "seeking Yahweh." "Seeking Yahweh" implies a total response to God. In order to "seek Yahweh" one turns to, prays to, inquires of, trusts, praises, and worships Yahweh and no other god. Most important, one does so through the proper religious means and in the proper place, that is, in the presence of the ark of Yahweh or the temple. On the other hand, "forsaking Yahweh" entails the opposite. More than idolatry, it is unfaithfulness demonstrated by failing to turn to Yahweh, neglecting God's temple, and ignoring God's ordained religious and political institutions, the levitical priesthood, and the Davidic king. Third, Chronicles shows that reversals in Israel's fortunes could and did take place from generation to generation. If the king and people, suffering the consequences of forsaking God, humbled themselves and sought God, then they would be restored. But, if they were experiencing the blessings of God and forsook God, then they would be cursed.

The Structure of Chronicles. Chronicles opens with genealogical materials and lists (1 Chron. 1–9) which usher the reader into the subject matter and worldview of the main narrative. Beginning with creation (Adam), the focus quickly narrows temporally, geographically, and nationally to the tribes of Israel (chaps. 2–8). Emphasis is placed on (1) the tribe of Levi and the levitical priesthood; (2) the tribe of Judah and the Davidic monarchy; and (3) the tribe of Benjamin, from which came the first Israelite king, with whom the narrative proper begins in chapter 10. In 9:2–21, genealogical lists record the first exiles who resettled the land, an event alluded to at the close of Chronicles (2 Chron. 36:2–23). Brief narrative comments are interspersed among these lists, which reveal Yahweh's interactions with those who trust him (4:10; 5:20–22) and with those who are unfaithful (2:3; 5:25–26; 9:1). The narrative proper then begins at 1 Chronicles 10.

The main historical principle or pattern is established in the discussion of the reigns of the first three kings: Saul, David, and Solomon (1 Chron. 10–2 Chron. 9). When a king seeks Yahweh, he is blessed; when a king forsakes Yahweh, he comes to grief. A brief negative portrayal of Saul stands in contrast to the positive portrayals of David and Solomon. Saul died and his kingdom was turned over to David, because Saul sought advice through a medium, the witch of Endor (cf. 1 Sam. 28), and not from Yahweh (10:13–14). While Chronicles devotes much material to David, little is said about David the man, about his shortcomings, his thoughts, his feelings. Rather, one reads almost exclusively about David's positive interactions with Yahweh. Through the juxtaposition of contrasting scenes, the story presents a reciprocal relationship between David (with all Israel) and Yahweh. This relationship demonstrates the principle of seeking Yahweh. Yahweh establishes the kingdom of David, granting popular support, military victory, and a lasting dynasty (chaps. 11–12, 14, 17–20). David, in turn, establishes the proper worship of Yahweh in regard to the ark, the appointment of religious officials, and preparations for the temple (chaps. 13, 15–16, 21–29). In David's closing speeches, Chronicles clearly spells out the principle of seeking: "If you seek him, he will be found by you; but if you forsake him, he will reject you forever" (28:9; see 22:6–16, 17–19; 28:1–10). Chronicles then shows Solomon as one who followed the pattern initiated by David. Solomon established the proper worship of Yahweh, carrying out the construction of the temple. Yahweh established him, granting him wisdom, peace, and prosperity (2 Chron. 1–9).

Having demonstrated the historical pattern of Yahweh's interaction with Israel through material on Saul, David, and Solomon, Chronicles portrays the subsequent kings of Judah in quick succession (2 Chron. 10–36). Jehoshaphat, Ahaz, Hezekiah, and Josiah are explicitly compared to David and Solomon (17:3; 28:1; 29:2; 34:2–3). Other comparisons are implicit. If the king (usually with the people) engages in some form of seeking Yahweh, then Yahweh blesses him with military success, wealth, and the ability to execute building projects. If the king forsakes Yahweh, then he and the people meet with a reversal of fortune. This pattern continues down to the time of Zedekiah, when king, priests, and people forsake God, defiling the temple and rejecting all warnings of the prophets. As a result, the Babylonians, used by Yahweh, destroy the temple and carry the people off into exile (36:11–21). Chronicles closes with an allusion to the return from exile allowed under the rule of Cyrus (36:22–23).

Unlike Samuel–Kings, Chronicles does not record the accounts of the kings of the northern kingdom of Israel, the nation that was formed by the division of David's empire after the reign of Solomon. The north is mentioned only when its story overlaps with that of the south. The people of the north are still reckoned among the people of God, but are portrayed as having forsaken Yahweh by rejecting the institutions of the Davidic monarchy, the levitical priesthood, and the Jerusalem temple (see 2 Chron. 10:19; 11:13–15; and particularly Abijah's homiletical speech of 13:4–12). The south was not to attack the north, for they were still God's people (2 Chron. 11:1–4). But it was not to ally with the north (2 Chron. 18), for the northern kingdom was not legitimate (2 Chron. 19:2). When the northern kingdom fell to the Assyrians (722 B.C.), however, the south could welcome its people to return and worship Yahweh (2 Chron. 30:1, 6–9).

Chronicles' Key Subjects. *The Davidic Monarchy.* The "characters" in Chronicles are the Davidic monarchs. For the sake of the people of Israel, Yahweh established the rule of David (1 Chron. 14:2), a king who sought God and established the proper institutions of worship. God promised David that a dynastic successor would sit on the throne of Yahweh's kingdom forever (1 Chron. 17:11–14), although it was required that the king faithfully seek Yahweh (1 Chron. 28:6–7, 9). The Davidic monarchs held the primary responsibility for establishing and maintaining the proper worship of Yahweh. They could abandon the forms of Yahweh worship (Ahaz and Manasseh) or restore them (Hezekiah and Josiah). They sat on Yahweh's throne (1 Chron. 17:14; 28:5; 29:23). They represented the people in corporate petition before Yahweh (2 Chron. 6:18–42; 14:11; 20:5–12). Their positive or negative spiritual leadership influenced the response of the people of Israel (2 Chron. 14:4; 15:9–15; 19:4; 20:4, 20–21; 21:11; 28:19; 32:6–8; 33:9, 16; 34:33). When the people of the northern kingdom rejected this institution, they forsook Yahweh (2 Chron. 13:4–12). Chronicles, presenting this perspective of the Davidic monarchy at a time when Israel was under foreign dominion, projects hope for the return of a Davidic king to the throne of Yahweh.

The Worship of Yahweh and the Levitical Priesthood. Even though Chronicles is structured around the Davidic monarchs, the main subject and true core of the story is Israel's relationship to Yahweh. Chronicles focuses on how this relationship was expressed through the establishment and maintenance of the institutions that represented the presence of Yahweh: the ark of the covenant, Jerusalem, the temple, the sacrificial system, the officiating priests, their levitical assistants and musicians, and the Davidic king, who sat on Yahweh's throne. As these institutions fared, and, therefore, Israel's relationship with Yahweh, so fared the well-being of the nation.

The exile marked a historical turning point. Chronicles views Israel's failure to seek Yahweh humbly and in accord with the proper means of worship as the cause of the exile. Accordingly its attention is focused on Israel's religious institutions.

The levitical priesthood operated jointly with the Davidic monarchy in preserving the correct forms of seeking Yahweh, of maintaining the proper relationship with God. The king's civil power extended over these officials, but their domain represented a divinely given responsibility that the king could not usurp (2 Chron. 26:16–21). Moreover, when the Davidic lineage instituted by Yahweh was threatened, they stepped in to preserve it (2 Chron. 22:10–23:21). According to Chronicles, the northern kingdom forsook Yahweh by rejecting the institution of the levitical priesthood, as they rejected the Davidic monarchy (2 Chron. 11:13–15; 13:8–12).

"All Israel." A frequently occurring phrase in Chronicles is "all Israel." It may be used to refer to all of the Israelites (1 Chron. 11:1), to those of the south (2 Chron. 11:3), or to those of the north (2 Chron. 13:4, 15). To whichever group it refers, however, it generally identifies them as an entity responsible before Yahweh. The kings and religious leaders alone are not accountable for the destiny of the nation. The people as a unit are held accountable. The prophets address not only the kings but the people as well (2 Chron. 11:3–4; 20:14–15; 24:20). Sometimes the people are deemed guilty when the king is innocent (2 Chron. 27:2; 34:24–28). When the division between the north and south occurs, those who comprise all Israel must decide whether or not to seek Yahweh (2 Chron. 11:13–17). Therefore, each generation of the people, although tending to follow the model of their leaders, share in the responsibility for their state of affairs. All are accountable before Yahweh.

Chronicles' Worldview. Chronicles presents a worldview, a picture of reality. Even in the few narrative comments in the genealogical material of the first nine chapters a world in which Yahweh is the primary agent of history is evident. The existence of Yahweh and his supreme sovereignty are foregone conclusions. Chronicles does not seek to prove them, but to show how Yahweh acts in the life of Israel and why.

In Chronicles God is sovereign, but does not dictate the course people take. To be sure, Yahweh may choose to speak prophetically through a foreign king (2 Chron. 35:21; 36:22–23); he might even choose to manipulate nations such as Egypt or Babylon in order to achieve his ends. Still, all Israel, the kings, and the levitical priesthood are responsible for their actions, for maintaining a right relationship with God. They choose whether they will seek or forsake Yahweh. It is they who set in motion the divine principles that order the world.

Chronicles' view of the way the world operates is more positive than that of Samuel–Kings. Samuel–Kings represents a pessimistic and rather fatalistic attitude. At least from Manasseh on, the fate of Israel appears to be sealed; they are headed for disaster (2 Kings 21:10–15). The manner in which Chronicles portrays each king and his generation as self-contained units displays a different perspective. The course of history is not so determined. In Chronicles' representation of reality, reversals of negative or positive situations can take place within a given reign or generation, even more than once. The potential for change always exists. Access to the mercy of Yahweh and to restoration is always available to Israel, even if they should bring themselves to near extinction.

Chronicles' Message. Through the selection and arrangement of Israel's traditions, a stereotypical portrayal of characters, and the presentation of David and Solomon as model kings, Chronicles invites the reader to evaluate each generation of the past in order to understand why things happened as they did. The reader, however, is not to stop there, but must evaluate the current situation and respond appropriately. Relationship to Yahweh is still of ultimate importance. The divine "laws" of the past are still operative. The reader now knows what brings blessing and what brings ruin. One's situation may be reversed, depending on whether or not one seeks or forsakes

Yahweh. Through a re-presentation of their past, Chronicles calls the believing community to a proper relationship with Yahweh and offers them the hope of blessing. RODNEY K. DUKE

Bibliography. P. R. Ackroyd, *JSOT* 2 (1977): 2–32; idem, *Lexington Theological Quarterly* 8 (1973): 101–16; S. B. Berg, *The Divine Helmsman: Studies on God's Control of Human Events,* pp. 107–25; R. L. Braun, *Studies in the Historical Books of the Old Testament,* pp. 52–64; R. B. Dllard, *WTJ* 46/1 (1984): 164–72; R. K. Duke, *The Persuasive Appeal of the Chronicler: A Rhetorical Analysis;* S. Japhet, *The Ideology of the Book of Chronicles and Its Place in Biblical Thought;* W. Johnstone, *A Word in Season: Essays in Honour of William McKane,* pp. 113–38; J. M. Myers, *Int* 20 (1966): 259–73; R. North, *JBL* 82 (1963): 369–81; G. von Rad, *Old Testament Theology,* 1:347–54; G. E. Schaefer, "The Significance of Seeking God in the Purpose of the Chronicler" (Th.D. diss.); M. A. Throntveit, *When Kings Speak: Royal Speech and Royal Prayer in Chronicles;* H. G. M. Williamson, *Israel in the Book of Chronicles.*

Church, the. ***Definition of the Church.*** The New Testament word for "church" is *ekklēsia,* which means "the called out ones." In classical Greek, the term was used almost exclusively for political gatherings. In particular, in Athens the word signified the assembling of the citizens for the purpose of conducting the affairs of the *polis.* Moreover, *ekklēsia* referred only to the actual meeting, not to the citizens themselves. When the people were not assembled, they were not considered to be the *ekklēsia.* The New Testament records three instances of this secular usage of the term (Acts 19:32, 39, 41).

The most important background of the term *ekklēsia* is the Septuagint, which uses the word in a religious sense about one hundred times, almost always as a translation of the Hebrew word *qāhāl.* While the latter term does indicate a secular gathering (contrasted, say to *eda,* the typical Hebrew word for Israel's religious gathering, and translated by the Greek, *sunagōgē*), it also denotes Israel's sacred meetings. This is especially the case in Deuteronomy, where *qāhāl* is linked with the covenant.

When we come to the New Testament, we discover that *ekklēsia* is used of the community of God's people some 109 times (out of 114 occurrences of the term). Although the word only occurs in two Gospel passages (Matt. 16:18; 18:17), it is of special importance in Acts (23 times) and the Pauline writings (46 times). It is found twenty times in Revelation and only in isolated instances in James and Hebrews. We may broach the subject of the biblical teaching on the church by drawing three general conclusions from the data so far. First, predominantly *ekklēsia* (both in the singular and plural) applies to a local assembly of those who profess faith in and allegiance to Christ. Second, *ekklēsia* designates the universal church (Acts 8:3; 9:31; 1 Cor. 12:28; 15:9; especially in the later Pauline letters, Eph. 1:22–23; Col. 1:18). Third, the *ekklēsia* is *God's* congregation (1 Cor. 1:2; 2 Cor. 1:1; etc.).

The Nature of the Church. The nature of the church is too broad to be exhausted in the meaning of the one word, *ekklēsia.* To capture its significance the New Testament authors utilize a rich array of metaphorical descriptions. Nevertheless, there are those metaphors that seem to dominate the biblical picture of the church, five of which call for comment: the people of God, the kingdom of God, the temple of God, the bride of Christ, and the body of Christ.

The People of God. Essentially, the concept of the people of God can be summed up in the covenantal phrase: "I will be their God and they will be my people" (see Exod. 6:6–7; 19:5; Lev. 26:9–14; Jer. 7:23; 30:22; 32:37–40; Ezek. 11:19–20; 36:22–28; Acts 15:14; 2 Cor. 6:16; Heb. 8:10–12; Rev. 21:3; etc.).Thus, the people of God are those in both the Old and New Testament eras who responded to God by faith, and whose spiritual origin rests exclusively in God's grace.

To speak of the one people of God transcending the eras of the Old and New Testaments necessarily raises the question of the relationship between the church and Israel. Modern theologies prefer not to polarize the matter into an either/or issue. Rather, they talk about the church and Israel in terms of there being *both* continuity and discontinuity between them.

Continuity between the Church and Israel. Two ideas establish the fact that the church and Israel are portrayed in the Bible as being in a continuous relationship. First, the church was present in some sense in Israel in the Old Testament. Acts 7:38 makes this connection explicit when, alluding to Deuteronomy 9:10, it speaks of the church (*ekklēsia*) in the wilderness. The same idea is probably to be inferred from the intimate association noted earlier existing between the words *ekklēsia* and *qāhāl,* especially when the latter is qualified by the phrase, "of God." Furthermore, if the church is viewed in some New Testament passages as preexistent, then one finds therein the prototype for the creation of Israel (see Exod. 25:40; Acts 7:44; Gal. 4:26; Heb. 12:22; Rev. 21:11; cf. Eph. 1:3–14; etc.).

Second, Israel in some sense is present in the church in the New Testament. The many names for Israel applied to the church establish that fact. Some of those are: "Israel" (Gal. 6:15–16; Eph. 2:12; Heb. 8:8–10; Rev. 2:14; etc.); "a chosen people" (1 Peter 2:9); "the true circumcision" (Rom. 2:28–29; Phil. 3:3; Col. 2:11; etc.); "Abraham's seed" (Rom. 4:16; Gal. 3:29); "the remnant" (Rom. 9:27; 11:5–7); "the elect" (Rom. 11:28; Eph. 1:4); "the flock" (Acts 20:28; Heb. 13:20; 1 Peter 5:2); "priesthood" (1 Peter 2:9; Rev. 1:6; 5:10).

Discontinuity between the Church and Israel. The church, however, is not coterminous with Israel; discontinuity also characterizes the relationship. The church, according to the New Testament, is the eschatological Israel incorporated in

Jesus Messiah and, as such, is a progression beyond historical Israel (1 Cor. 10:11; 2 Cor. 5:14–21; etc.). What was promised to Israel has now been fulfilled in the church, in Christ, especially the Spirit and the new covenant (cf. Ezek. 36:25–27; Joel 2:28–29 with Acts 2; 2 Cor. 3; Rom. 8; etc.). However, a caveat must be issued at this point. Although the church is a progression beyond Israel, it is not the permanent replacement of Israel (see Rom. 9–11, esp. 11:25–27).

The Kingdom of God. Many scholars in this century have maintained that the life, death, and resurrection of Jesus inaugurated the kingdom of God, producing an overlapping of the two ages. The kingdom has "already" dawned, but is "not yet" complete. The first aspect pertains to Jesus' first coming and the second aspect relates to his second coming. In other words, the age to come has broken into this age and now the two exist simultaneously. This background is crucial in ascertaining the relationship between the church and the kingdom of God, because the church also exists in the tension that results from the overlapping of the two ages. Accordingly, one may define the church as the proleptic appearance of the kingdom. Two ideas flow from this definition: (1) the church is related to the kingdom of God; (2) but the church is not equal to the kingdom of God.

The Church and the Kingdom of God Are Related. The historical Jesus did not found or organize the church. Not until after his resurrection does the New Testament speak with regularity about the church. However, there are adumbrations of the church in the teaching and ministry of Jesus, in both general and specific ways. In general, Jesus anticipated the later official formation of the church in that he gathered to himself twelve disciples, who constituted the beginnings of eschatological Israel, in effect, the remnant. More specifically, Jesus explicitly referred to the church in two passages: Matthew 16:18–19 and 18:17. In the first passage, Jesus promised that he would build his church despite satanic opposition, thus assuring the ultimate success of his mission. The notion of the church overcoming the forces of evil coincides with the idea that the kingdom of God will prevail over its enemies, and bespeaks of the intimate association between church and kingdom. The second passage relates to the future organization of the church, particularly its method of discipline, not unlike the Jewish synagogue practices of Jesus' day.

The Church and the Kingdom of God Are Not Identified. As intimately related as the church and the kingdom of God are, the New Testament does not equate the two, as is evident in the fact that the early Christians preached the kingdom, not the church (Acts 8:12; 19:8; 20:25; 28:23, 31). The New Testament identifies the church as the people of the kingdom (Rev. 5:10; etc.), not the kingdom itself. Moreover, the church is the instrument of the kingdom. This is especially clear from Matthew 16:18–19, where the preaching of Peter and the church become the keys to opening up the kingdom of God to all who would enter.

The Eschatological Temple of God. Both the Old Testament and Judaism anticipated the rebuilding of the temple in the future kingdom of God (Ezek. 40–48; Hag. 2:1–9; 1 Enoch 90:29; 91:3; Jub. 1:17, 29; etc.). Jesus hinted that he was going to build such a construction (Matt. 16:18; Mark 14:58; John 2:19–22). Pentecost witnessed to the beginning of the fulfillment of that dream in that when the Spirit inhabited the church, the eschatological temple was formed (Acts 2:16–36). Other New Testament writers also perceived that the presence of the Spirit in the Christian community constituted the new temple of God (see 1 Cor. 3:16–17; 2 Cor. 6:14–7:1; Eph. 2:19–22; cf. also Gal. 4:21–31; 1 Peter 2:4–10). However, that the eschatological temple is not yet complete is evident in the preceding passages, especially with their emphasis on the need for the church to grow toward maturity in Christ, which will only be fully accomplished at the parousia. In the meantime, Christians, as priests of God, are to perform their sacrificial service to the glory of God (Rom. 12:1–2; Heb. 13:15; 1 Peter 2:4–10).

The Bride. The image of marriage is applied to God and Israel in the Old Testament (see Isa. 54:5–6; 62:5; Hos. 2:7; etc.). Similar imagery is applied to Christ and the church in the New Testament. Christ, the bridegroom, has sacrificially and lovingly chosen the church to be his bride (Eph. 5:25–27). Her responsibility during the betrothal period is to be faithful to him (2 Cor. 11:2; Eph. 5:24). At the parousia, the official wedding ceremony will take place and, with it, the eternal union of Christ and his wife will be actualized (Rev. 19:7–9; 21:1–2).

The Body of Christ. The body of Christ as a metaphor for the church is unique to the Pauline literature and constitutes one of the most significant concepts therein (Rom. 12:4–5; 1 Cor. 12:12–27; Eph. 4:7–16; Col. 1:18). The primary purpose of the metaphor is to demonstrate the interrelatedness of diversity and unity within the church, especially with reference to spiritual gifts. The body of Christ is the last Adam (1 Cor. 15:45), the new humanity of the endtime that has appeared in history. However, Paul's usage of the image, like the metaphor of the new temple, indicates that the church, as the body of Christ, still has a long way to go spiritually. It is "not yet" complete.

The Sacraments of the Church. At the heart of the expression of the church's faith are the sacraments of baptism and the Lord's Supper. The former symbolizes entrance into the church while the latter provides spiritual sustenance for the church.

Baptism. Baptism symbolizes the sinner's entrance into the church. Three observations emerge from the biblical treatment of this sacrament. First, the Old Testament intimated baptism, especially in its association of repentance of sin with ablutions (Num. 19:18–22; Ps. 51:7; Ezek. 36:25; cf. John 3:5). Second, the baptism of John anticipated Christian baptism. John administered a baptism of repentance in expectation of the baptism of the Spirit and fire that the Messiah would exercise (Matt. 3:11/Luke 3:16). Those who accept Jesus as Messiah experience the baptism of fire and judgment. Third, the early church practiced baptism, in imitation of the Lord Jesus (Matt. 3:13–17/Mark 1:9–11/Luke 3:21–22; see also John 1:32–34; cf. Matt. 28:19; Acts 2:38; 8:16; Rom. 6:3–6; 1 Cor. 1:13–15; Gal. 3:27; Titus 3:5; 1 Peter 3:21; etc.). These passages demonstrate some further truths about baptism: (1) baptism is intimately related to faith in God; (2) baptism identifies the person with the death and resurrection of Jesus; (3) baptism incorporates the person into the community of believers.

The Lord's Supper. The other biblical sacrament is the Lord's Supper, variously called "communion" (1 Cor. 10:16), "eucharist" (the prayer of thanks offered before partaking of the elements; Matt. 26:27; 1 Cor. 11:24), and the "breaking of the bread" (Acts 2:42; 20:7). This rite symbolizes Christ's spiritual nourishment of his church as it celebrates the sacred meal. Two basic points emerge from the biblical data concerning the Lord's Supper. First, it was instituted by Christ (Matt. 26:26–29; Mark 14:22–25; Luke 22:15–20; 1 Cor. 11:23–25). According to these passages, Jesus celebrated the Passover on the night before his betrayal. That commemorative meal would probably have included the following: the cup of wine, calling "blessing"; the four questions of the child concerning the nature of Passover; the second cup, called "deliverance"; the singing of the first part of the Hallel (Pss. 113–14); the Passover meal; the third cup, called "redemption"; the eating of the dessert; the fourth cup, called the "Elijah cup"; the singing of the second part of the Hallel (Pss. 115–18). Jesus introduced two changes into the Passover seder. He equated his body with the bread of affliction and his blood, which was to be shed on the cross, with the cup of redemption.

Second, the early church practiced the Lord's Supper (Acts 2:42, 46; 1 Cor. 11:23; etc.), probably weekly, in conjunction with the *agapē* feast (see 1 Cor. 11:18–22; cf. Jude 12). A twofold meaning is attached to the Lord's Supper by the New Testament authors. First, it involves participation in Christ's salvation—believers are to "do this in remembrance of me" (Luke 22:19; 1 Cor. 11:24–25). A couple aspects of this celebration call for comment. (1) Historically, the Lord's Supper was a rite commemorating Christ's redemptive death, even as the Passover was a remembrance of God's deliverance of Israel from Egyptian slavery (Exod. 12:14; 13:3, 9; Deut. 16:3). In remembering Christ's death, believers actualize its effects in the present. (2) Eschatologically, the Lord's Supper anticipates Christ's return (Matt. 26:29; Mark 14:25; Luke 22:16, 18; 1 Cor. 11:26) and, with it, the heavenly messianic banquet of the kingdom of God (Matt. 22:2–14; Luke 14:24; Rev. 19:9).

Second, the Lord's Supper involves identification with the body of Christ, the community of faith. Two aspects of this reality are touched upon in the New Testament, one positive, the other negative. Positively, the Lord's Supper symbolizes the unity and fellowship of Christians in the one body of Christ (1 Cor. 10:16–17). Negatively, to fail to recognize the church as the body of Christ by dividing it is to participate in the Lord's Supper unworthily and thereby to incur divine judgment (1 Cor. 11:27–33).

The Worship of the Church. The ultimate purpose of the church is to worship God through Christ. The early church certainly recognized this to be its reason for existence (Eph. 1:4–6; 1 Peter 2:5, 9; Rev. 21:1–22:5; etc.). Five aspects of the New Testament church's worship can be delineated: the meaning of worship; the time and place of worship; the nature of worship; the order of worship; the expressions of worship.

The Meaning of Worship. Although the Bible nowhere provides a definition of worship, one is left with the general impression therein that to worship God is to ascribe to him the supreme worth that he alone deserves.

The Time and Place of Worship. Although many Jewish Christians probably continued to worship God on the Sabbath, the established time for the church's worship came to be Sunday, the first day of the week (Acts 20:7), because Christ had risen from the dead on that day (Rev. 1:10). With regard to the locale, the early church began its worship in the Jerusalem temple (Acts 2:46; 3:1; 5:42), as well as in the synagogues (Acts 22:19; cf. John 9:22; James 2:2; etc.). At the same time, believers met in homes for worship (Acts 1:13; 2:46; 5:42). When Christianity and Judaism became more and more incompatible, the house-church became the established place of worship (Rom. 16:15; Col. 4:15; Philem. 2; 2 John 10; 3 John 1, 6; etc.). The use of a specific church building did not occur until the late second century.

The Nature of Worship. The biblical teaching on the worship of the church involves three components, which are rooted in the Trinity. First, worship is directed toward God; God the Father is the central object of worship, both as creator (Acts 17:28; James 1:17; Rev. 4:11; etc.) and redeemer (Eph. 1:3; Col. 1:12–13; 1 Peter 1:3; Rev. 5:9–14; etc.). Second, worship is mediated through Christ, the Son (Matt. 18:20; Rom. 5:2;

Eph. 1:6; 1 Tim. 2:5; Heb. 4:14–5:10; 10:20; etc.). Third, worship is actualized by the power of the Holy Spirit (Rom. 2:28–29; 8:26–27; Eph. 2:18; Phil. 3:3; Jude 20; etc.).

The Order of Worship. Both the language and the order of the early church's worship were rooted in Judaism. With regard to the former, the church utilized Old Testament terms like "high priest" (applied to Jesus, Heb. 4:12–16), "priests" (applied to Christians, 1 Peter 2:5–9), "sacrifice" (applied to Christ's death on the cross, Heb. 9:23–28; 10:11), and "temple" (applied to the church, 1 Cor. 3:16; 6:19). With regard to the order of worship, the early church incorporated into its worship the main elements of the synagogue service: praise in prayer (Acts 2:42, 47; 3:1; 1 Thess. 1:2; 5:17; 1 Tim. 2:1–2; etc.) and in song (1 Cor. 14:26; Phil. 2:6–11; Col. 1:15–20; 1 Tim. 3:16; Rev. 5:9–10; etc.); the expounding of the Scripture (Acts 2:42; 6:4; Col. 4:16; 1 Thess. 2:13; 1 Tim. 4:13; etc.); and almsgiving to the needy (Acts 2:44–45; 1 Cor. 16:1–2; 2 Cor. 8–9; James 2:15–17; etc.).

Expressions of Worship. The main ingredient of worship in the Bible is sacrifice. David put it well: "I will not sacrifice to the LORD my God burnt offerings that cost me nothing" (2 Sam. 24:24). In the New Testament, there are three main expressions connected with the worship of the early church, each of which is based on sacrifice: the sacrifice of one's body to God (Rom. 12:1–2; cf. Rom. 15:16; Phil. 1:20; 2:17; 2 Tim. 4:6); the sacrifice of one's possession for God (Matt. 6:2; Luke 6:38; 2 Cor. 8–9; 1 Tim. 6:10; etc.); and the sacrifice of one's praise to God (Acts 16:25; 1 Cor. 14:26; Eph. 5:19; Col. 3:16; Heb. 13:16; James 5:13; etc.).

The Service and Organization of the Church. We conclude the topic of the biblical teaching on the church by briefly calling attention to its service and organization. Five observations emerge from the relevant data. First, the ministry of the church centers on its usage of spiritual gifts (*charismata*), which are given to believers by God's grace and for his glory, as well as for the good of others (Rom. 12:3; Eph. 4:7–16; etc.). Second, every believer possesses a gift of the Spirit (1 Cor. 12:7; Eph. 4:7; etc.). Third, it is through the diversity of the gifts that the body of Christ matures and is unified (Rom. 12:4; 1 Cor. 12:12–31; Eph. 4:17–18). Fourth, although there was organized leadership in the New Testament church (elders, 1 Tim. 3:1–7 [also called pastors and shepherds, see Acts 20:17, 28; 1 Peter 5:1–4; etc.] and deacons, 1 Tim. 3:8–13), there does not seem to have been a gap between the "clergy" and "laity." Rather, those with the gift of leadership are called to equip all the saints for the work of the ministry (Eph. 4:7–16). Fifth, spiritual gifts are to be exercised in love (1 Cor. 13).

C. MARVIN PATE

Bibliography. J. C. Beker, *Paul the Apostle: The Triumph of God in Life and Thought;* H. Bietenhard, *NIDNTT,* 2:789–800; L. Coenen, *NIDNTT,* 3:291–305; W. D. Davies, *Paul and Rabbinic Judaism;* R. G. Hammerton-Kelly, *Pre-Existence, Wisdom and the Son of Man: A Study of the Idea of Pre-Existence in the New Testament;* H. Küng, *The Church;* G. E. Ladd, *A Theology of the New Testament;* P. S. Minear, *Images of the Church in the New Testament;* R. L. Saucy, *The Church in God's Program;* K. L. Schmidt, *TDNT,* 3:501–36; R. Schnackenburg, *The Church in the New Testament;* A. J. M. Wedderburn, *Baptism and Resurrection: Studies in Pauline Theology against Its Graeco-Roman Background.*

Circumcision. Removal of the foreskin or prepuce of the male genital organ, whether for religious reasons or as a purely hygienic measure. Circumcision was practiced in the ancient Near East by the western Semites, including the Ammonites, Moabites, Hebrews, and Edomites. The procedure was rejected by the east Semitic peoples of Mesopotamia, the Canaanites, and the Shechemites.

The Old Testament. The special meaning of circumcision for the people of Israel is found in Genesis 17 and occurs within the context of God's renewed covenant promise to Abraham, following the initial contractual relationship (Gen. 15). On the second occasion, God again promised lands and offspring to the still childless patriarch, and gave him the sign of circumcision, which was to be imposed upon Abraham and his descendants as a token of covenant membership (Gen. 17:10). For the Israelites circumcision was a religious rite and was intended to mark the beginning of covenant solidarity for Abraham's descendants rather than describing the historical origins of the procedure.

While Abraham and his household were circumcised forthwith, the Lord's command required that hereafter male infants were to be circumcised on the eighth day of life. This in itself was distinctively different from contemporary pagan practices, which seem to have associated the rite either with puberty or with approaching marriage.

From the beginning sharp knives made from chipped flints were used for the resection, since flint maintained a superior edge. For this reason the retention of flint instruments for purposes of circumcision endured for centuries after the beginning of the Iron Age (ca. 1200 B.C.). Traditionally the head of the household administered the rite in Israel, but on special occasions a woman might officiate (Exod. 4:24–26).

In the Mosaic law, a spiritual interpretation was imposed upon the procedure when the Israelites were instructed to circumcise their hearts (Deut. 10:16). This demand required them to recognize that, in addition to bearing the physical mark of covenant membership, they were also under obligation to manifest specific spiritual qualities of commitment and obedience to the Lord's will. Jeremiah (4:4) made precisely the same demands upon his contemporaries because of their evil deeds, which were the very opposite of what God required. For him, circumcision entailed consecration to the Lord and to the high moral ideals of the covenant, of which holiness was representative (Lev. 11:44). A true covenant member would be motivated by love of God (Deut. 6:5) and one's neighbor (Lev. 19:18).

The New Testament. When Greek paganism threatened to swamp Judaism some two centuries before Christ was born, circumcision became a distinctive indication of Jewish fidelity to the covenant. Thus John the Baptist was circumcised (Luke 1:59), as were both Jesus (Luke 2:21) and Saul of Tarsus (Phil. 3:5), on the eighth day of life, making them accredited members of the covenant people. But Jesus was already casting doubt on the preeminence of the rite when he stated that his healings made people completely whole (John 7:22–23). Stephen reinforced this by accusing contemporary Judaism of the very tendencies that Jeremiah had condemned (Acts 7:51). Although in the period of the primitive church the believers maintained Jewish religious traditions, problems began to arise when the gospel was preached among Gentiles. Christians who had come from a Jewish background felt that Gentiles should become Jews through circumcision before being able to experience Christ's saving work.

This attitude rested partly upon the contemporary notion that circumcision was a necessary part of salvation, as well as being its effective guarantee. Others repudiated this view of salvation by works, particularly when uncircumcised Gentiles received God's outpouring of the Holy Spirit (Acts 10:44–48). They saw that the prophecies of Ezekiel, in which the Lord promised a clean heart and an indwelling of his Holy Spirit (36:25–27), and the dramatic proclamation of Joel that God would pour out his Spirit upon all flesh (2:28; cf. Acts 2:17), were now being fulfilled. The spiritual significance of circumcision had been achieved by divine grace without the performance of the physical rite, thus making the latter obsolete.

Not all Jews rejoiced at their badge of pride and privilege being set aside (Phil. 3:4–6), and consequently a group of Pharisaic Jews known as the "circumcision party" proclaimed at Antioch (Acts 15:1–5) the necessity of circumcision for salvation. Peter opposed these Judaizers, affirming the saving efficacy of faith in Christ alone (Acts 15:8–11), and denying the necessity of circumcision for the Gentiles.

To resolve the issue Paul and Barnabas consulted with the elders in Jerusalem, where it was agreed that Gentiles should not be compelled to be circumcised (Acts 15:13–21). Paul was indifferent to the Judaizers' vaunted claims of "circumcision spirituality," and although he circumcised the partly Jewish Timothy (Acts 16:3) to facilitate his mission, he opposed circumcision for the Gentile Titus (Gal. 2:3). In Galatia, Paul resisted strenuously the Judaizers' doctrine of righteousness by works, which he stigmatized as a "different gospel" (Gal. 1:6–7), and reviled the proponents as "dogs" and "evil workers."

This controversy was to follow Paul throughout his ministry. To counter the Judaizers' position he conceded that, while circumcision was of great value for the old covenant, it carried no significance for the "covenants of promise" (Eph. 2:12). What was fundamentally important in God's sight was being a "new creation" (Gal. 6:15) and keeping God's commandments (1 Cor. 7:19), apart from which circumcision or uncircumcision are meaningless, and allowing faith to work through love (Gal. 5:6). Paul taught resolutely that, in the new covenant, salvation came by grace and faith, not works (Eph. 2:8). For the believer, circumcision or the lack of it was a matter of total indifference. What really counted was the faith and obedience that have always characterized covenants between God and humankind.

R. K. HARRISON

See also JUDAIZERS.

Bibliography. D. Jacobson, *The Social Background of the Old Testament;* R. Patai, *Sex and Family in the Bible;* R. de Vaux, *Ancient Israel: Its Life and Institutions.*

Citizenship. The concept of spiritual citizenship is most clearly expressed in Philippians 3:20, where Paul writes, "Our citizenship (*politeuma*) is in heaven." This is the only place in Scripture where the word is used, but the idea is found in both Jewish and Christian literature. In fact, the development of the idea may be traced from the record of Abraham's experience to the writings of the apostolic fathers.

Abraham viewed himself as a stranger (*gēr*) and a sojourner (*māgûr*) in the land of promise (Gen. 23:4). The same words are used consistently to describe the experience of the patriarchs (Gen. 17:8; 28:4; 47:9; Exod. 6:4). Even when Israel resided in Canaan, the people were to recognize that the land was God's and that they were merely aliens (*tôšābîm*) in it (Lev. 25:23; 1 Chron. 29:15; Pss. 39:12; 119:19). The Rechabites chose not to build houses, sow seed, or plant vineyards; they lived in tents as a reminder of their status as sojourners (Jer. 35:6–10).

Christ's teaching on the kingdom has a strong heavenly orientation. His followers are to seek the kingdom that the Father has chosen to give them (Matt. 6:33; Luke 12:32). The kingdom, however, is not of this world (John 18:36). Believers are to lay up treasure in heaven (Matt. 6:19–21). While Christ is absent, Christians are to take comfort in his promise that he is preparing a place for them in his Father's house (John

14:1–4). Ultimately, they will inherit the kingdom he has prepared for them (Matt. 25:34).

Paul reminds Christians that it is "the Jerusalem above" to which they are related (Gal. 4:21–31) and that they are seated with Christ in the heavenly places (Eph. 2:6; Col. 3:1–4). Peter describes Christians in the same language used to describe Abraham in the Septuagint. They are elect "refugees" (*parepidēmoi*) whose time on earth is a "temporary stay" (*paroikia*) in a foreign country (1 Peter 1:1, 17). Their status as "strangers" (*paroikoi*) and temporary residents provides an incentive for holy living (1 Peter 2:11).

The author of Hebrews brings these various themes together in the most comprehensive way. Abraham and the other patriarchs lived as strangers and exiles on earth, seeking the city designed, built, and prepared for them by God (11:8–16). Similarly, Christians do not have a lasting city; they seek the city that is to come (13:14). That city is the heavenly Jerusalem, the city of the living God and the capital of an unshakable kingdom (12:22–23, 28). JOHN D. HARVEY

Bibliography. P. E. Hughes, *A Commentary on the Epistle to the Hebrews.*

Clean, Unclean. ***The Old Testament.*** *How Uncleanness Was Contracted and Treated.* In Old Testament times the ordinary state of most things was "cleanness," but a person or thing could contract ritual "uncleanness" (or "impurity") in a variety of ways: by skin diseases, discharges of bodily fluids, touching something dead (Num. 5:2), or eating unclean foods (Lev. 11; Deut. 14).

An unclean person in general had to avoid that which was holy and take steps to return to a state of cleanness. Uncleanness placed a person in a "dangerous" condition under threat of divine retribution, even death (Lev. 15:31), if the person approached the sanctuary. Uncleanness could lead to expulsion of the land's inhabitants (Lev. 18:25) and its peril lingered upon those who did not undergo purification (Lev. 17:16; Num. 19:12–13).

Priests were to avoid becoming ritually defiled (Lev. 21:1–4, 11–12), and if defiled, had to abstain from sacred duties. An unclean layperson could neither eat nor tithe consecrated food (Lev. 7:20–21; Deut. 26:14), had to celebrate the Passover with a month's delay (Num. 9:6–13), and had to stay far away from God's tabernacle (Num. 5:3).

Purification varied with the severity of the uncleanness. The most serious to least serious cases in descending order were: skin disease (Lev. 13–14), childbirth (Lev. 12), genital discharges (Lev. 15:3–15, 28–30), the corpse-contaminated priest (Ezek. 44:26–27), the corpse-contaminated Nazirite (Num. 6:9–12), one whose impurity is prolonged (Lev. 5:1–13), the corpse-contaminated layperson (Num. 5:2–4; 19:1–20), the menstruating woman (Lev. 15:19–24), the handling of the ashes of the red cow or the Day of Atonement offerings (Lev. 16:26, 28; Num. 19:7–10), emission of semen (Lev. 15:16–18), contamination by a carcass (Lev. 11:24–40; 22:5), and secondary contamination (Lev. 15; 22:4–7; Num. 19:21–22).

Purification always involved waiting a period of time (until evening for minor cases, eighty days for the birth of a daughter), and could also involve ritual washings symbolizing cleansing, atoning sacrifices, and priestly rituals. "Unclean" objects required purification by water (wood, cloth, hide, sackcloth) or fire (metals), or were destroyed (clay pots, ovens), depending on the material (Lev. 11:32–35; Num. 31:21–23).

The Rationale of the Purity Laws. The central lesson conveyed by this system is that *God is holy but human beings are contaminated.* Everyone by biology inevitably contracted uncleanness from time to time; therefore, everyone in this fallen world must be purified to approach a holy God. Although "uncleanness" cannot be equated with "sin," since factors beyond human control could cause a person to be unclean, nonetheless, there is a strong analogy between "uncleanness" and "sin." The "sin offering" (better, "purification offering") served to cleanse both sin and ritual impurity (Lev. 5:1–5; 16:16–22). Moreover, the language of ritual impurity is used dozens of times metaphorically of various ethical sins. Human beings are "unclean" or "sinful" by nature and cannot approach a holy God. Just as uncleanness can come from within (natural bodily functions) or from without (contaminating things), so sin comes both from perverse human nature within and temptations without. The prohibition of eating the fat of sacrificial animals and the blood of any animal reminded Israel that blood sacrifice reconciles sinful/unclean people with a holy God (Lev. 7:22–27; 17:11).

The clean/unclean system divided animals, people, and land into three categories to teach separation from the Gentiles. Animals that could be sacrificed were "holy"; wild game and fish that could be eaten but not sacrificed were "clean"; and animals that could be neither eaten nor sacrificed were "unclean." This separation parallels that of people (cf. Lev. 21:18–21; 22:20–24, where the same defects disqualify both priests and animals): priests (holy), ordinary Israelites (clean), and Gentiles (unclean). With space, there is the tabernacle (holy), the land (clean), and the nations (unclean). Thus the food laws symbolically reinforced teaching elsewhere that Israel was a "holy nation" (Exod. 19:6) set apart from all others, and promoted practical holiness by discouraging table fellowship with the Canaanites whose diet would ordinarily include the pig and other "unclean" foods (Lev. 20:25–26), as modern kosher laws have helped maintain the Jewish race as a separate people. Other laws, by creating distinctive customs (even where such customs were without any inherent moral value, as in Lev.

18:19), nonetheless inculcated Israel with the concept of "holiness" and served as "object lessons," creating in Israel a sense of self-identity as a "separated" people.

Some laws of purity express ethical lessons. Even arbitrary rules cultivate the virtue of self-control, a step toward the attainment of holiness. Eating meat torn by wild beasts not only defiled ritually, but dehumanized, reducing people to the level of scavenger dogs (Exod. 22:31). Cooking a kid-goat in its mother's milk (Exod. 23:19; 34:26; Deut. 14:21) was a perverse act. Leaving a corpse of an executed man exposed on a tree overnight was barbaric (Deut. 21:23). That those involved in the slaughter of war (Num. 31:19–24) even at the command of God nonetheless became unclean hints at the moral impurity of war. Laws concerning sexual emissions encouraged restraint and sexual self-control (e.g., avoiding sex during menstruation) and would rightly stigmatize violators (such as prostitutes) as social outcasts.

The command not to eat the flesh with the blood inculcates respect for all animal life. Animal slaughter was limited: only for food, only certain species, only if certain procedures were followed. Moreover, ritual pouring of the blood back to God symbolically acknowledged that only by divine permission could any animal be killed (Gen. 9:2–5). If killing animals is not trivial, how much weightier it is to shed human blood.

The laws of purity prohibited connecting worship with sexuality. Since sexual acts made one unclean, Israel could not follow the practice of sacred prostitution where a god's giving of fertility was symbolized by sex acts in the cult. This further separated Israel from her pagan neighbors.

The purity system conveys in a symbolic way that Yahweh was the God of life and was separated from death. Most of the unclean animals were either predators/scavengers or lived in caves (e.g., rock badgers). The pig, moreover, was associated with the worship of Near Eastern chthonic deities. Leprosy made a person waste away like a corpse (Num. 12:12). Bodily discharges (blood for women, semen for men) represented a temporary loss of strength and life and movement toward death. Because decaying corpses discharged, so natural bodily discharges were reminders of sin and death. Physical imperfections representing a movement from "life" toward "death" moved a person ritually away from God who was associated with life. Purification rituals symbolized movement from death toward life and accordingly involved blood, the color red, and spring (lit. "living") water, all symbols of life. This symbolism excluded necromancy (Lev. 19:31).

Israel was not to cook a goat in its mother's milk not because it was a pagan practice, but because it was inappropriate to combine that which was a symbol of life (mother's milk) with the death of that for which it was meant to give life, especially in the context of the Festival of Tabernacles (so the context of Exod. 23:19) celebrating the life-giving power of Yahweh.

There is an incidental contribution made by the laws of purity/impurity to hygiene. Certainly the exclusion from the camp of those with possible symptoms of leprosy (Lev. 13–14) and gonorrhea (Lev. 15:2–15) in effect quarantined these dangerous diseases and contributed to public health. The avoidance of carcasses or contact with human sputum and discharges would do the same. The ritual baths associated with purification would also contribute to hygiene. Certain unclean animals are known to transfer diseases to humans: the pig bears trichinosis; the hare, tularemia; carrion-eating birds, various diseases. Eating animal suet is now known to lead to heart disease.

Hygiene, however, is at most a secondary explanation. Some excluded animals such as the camel, which have no association with disease when ingested. Most unhealthy foods (e.g., poisonous plants) and infectious diseases are not mentioned, surprisingly, if hygiene were the purpose. Moreover, why would Christ abolish the food laws meant for hygiene? Absolution took place after healing, whereas were hygiene the purpose it should have occurred before. Symbolism rather than hygiene must be the primary purpose of these laws.

The New Testament. The New Testament usually uses "unclean" in the moral rather than ritual sense, but it also testifies to the fact that the Jewish people practiced the biblical laws of ritual purity, as well as rabbinic elaborations thereupon. (The *Mishnah,* the Dead Sea Scrolls, and archeological remains of ritual baths, *miqvaot,* provide further evidence.) The New Testament refers to purification rites for birth (Luke 2:22–27), ritual washings (Mark 7:3–4; John 2:6), and disputes over ceremonial washings (John 3:25). Jesus allowed "unclean" or "evil" spirits (in the New Testament "unclean" is twenty-two times connected with demons) to enter swine, perhaps in part because it was fitting for one unclean thing to enter another (Matt. 8:28–34; Mark 5:1–16; Luke 8:29–33). Jews seeking Jesus' death refused to enter the palace of Pilate to avoid contracting ceremonial uncleanness during Passover (John 18:28).

Jesus condemned those who placed ritual above ethics. He rebuked those who, for ceremonial purity, cleanse the outside of the cup but do not practice inward moral purity or charity (Matt. 23:25–26; Luke 11:39–41). He implicitly condemned the priest and Levite who placed concern for ritual purity—they would be barred from temple service if they touched a corpse—over concern for human life (Luke 10:25–37).

Jesus did not allow the laws of purity to keep him from touching lepers (Matt. 8:1–4; Mark 1:40–45; Luke 17:11–17), and he deliberately touched rather than healed by his word to show compassion and to anticipate by his action the coming change in law under the new covenant. Nonetheless, in the age of transition he required cleansed lepers to show themselves to the priest in accord with Mosaic law (Luke 17:11–17). Jesus did not hesitate to touch the dead (Matt. 9:25; Mark 5:41; Luke 8:54), and allowed a sinful woman (e.g., a prostitute) to touch him (Luke 7:36–38), despite her ritual (as well as moral) uncleanness. In such cases, and that of a woman with a flow of blood (Matt. 9:20–22; Mark 5:27), Jesus is not defiled (he went through no ceremonial purification), but those are cleansed and healed. This speaks theologically of Christ's impeccable person.

Jesus turned water, in jars for ritual purification, into wine (John 2:6–9) to symbolize the replacement of ceremonial law with something better. He did not follow the ritual washing, going beyond Mosaic law practiced by rabbinic Judaism (Mark 7:3, 5), and implicitly declared all foods "clean" (Mark 7:19; cf. Rom. 14:14 "food is unclean in itself"). A new age had dawned with the coming of Christ and the ceremonial laws of purity were passing away. Typologically, the ashes of the red heifer (for corpse contamination), the sin offering, and the ritual baths foreshadowed the power of Jesus' blood to cleanse the conscience (Heb. 9:13–14; 10:22; 1 John 1:7; Rev. 7:14).

Although the apostolic council (Acts 15:29) encouraged Gentile Christians to avoid "unclean" foods ("food sacrificed to idols, from blood, from the meat of strangled animals [blood not drained]") to facilitate table fellowship with Jewish Christians, the matter is presented as advice rather than law. There was nothing morally wrong with Jewish Christians observing the old rituals, and, accordingly, Paul did (Acts 21:20–26, purification after a Nazirite vow), but Old Testament laws of purity, and all ceremonial laws, are optional, and even strangely out of place under the new covenant.

The abolition of the food laws conveys deep theological significance. The division of animals into clean and unclean symbolized the separation between Israelites and Gentiles. The abolition of the kosher laws then symbolizes a breaking down of the barrier between Jews and Gentiles. As is seen in God's lesson to Peter in Acts 10–11, God now declares the Gentiles "clean." In the new messianic age the principle that God's people are to be separate (holy) from the world remains, but the lines drawn are no longer ethnic in character.

JOE M. SPRINKLE

See also OFFERINGS AND SACRIFICES.

Bibliography. G. J. Botterweck and H. Ringgren, *TDOT,* 5:287–96, 330–42; H. C. Brichto, *HUCA* 47 (1976): 19–55; M. Douglas, *Purity and Danger;* J. E. Hartley, *ISBE,* 1:718–23; J. Milgrom, *Leviticus 1–16;* idem, *Religion and Law;* idem, *Semeia* 45 (1989): 103–9; J. M. Sprinkle, "A Literary Approach to Biblical Law: Exodus 20:22–23:19"; G. J. Wenham, *Numbers;* idem, *Christ the Lord;* S. Westerholm, *Dictionary of Jesus and the Gospels.*

Cloud, Cloud of the Lord. ***The Old Testament.*** *The Literal Cloud.* Natural phenomena involving clouds are depicted occasionally in the Old Testament, but far from being only "natural," these are invariably linked with the direct activity of God. Especially in the books of Job and Psalms, cloud-related phenomena are described as evidence of God's mighty, wondrous works and inscrutable ways (Job 22:14; 26:8–9; 35:5; 36:28–29; 37:11, 15–16, 18; 38:9, 34, 36–37; Pss. 77:17; 147:8). The rainbow in the clouds is a sign of the covenant (Gen. 9:13–14, 16), and clouds themselves are presented as witnesses to the surety of the covenant with David (Ps. 89:37). Withholding of rain from the clouds is seen as divine activity in fulfillment of the covenant curses (Isa. 5:6; Lev. 26:19; cf. Deut. 28:23–24), and the restoring of rain after drought is the sign of God's removing the covenant curse from Israel (1 Kings 18:44–45; cf. Zech. 10:1).

The Metaphorical Cloud. The biblical writers frequently employ phenomena of cloud formation and activity in order to metaphorically illustrate aspects of their theological message. In a positive sense, clouds represent unlimited extent (of God's faithfulness and truth, Pss. 36:5; 57:10; 108:4; of Babylon's judgment, Jer. 51:9); life-giving refreshment (of the king's favor, Prov. 16:15); a normal occurrence (cycle of nature, Eccles. 11:3); shade or shelter (from the "heat" of the ruthless, Isa. 25:5); calm (of the Lord in his heavenly sanctuary, Isa. 18:4); covering or concealment (of Israel's sins in forgiveness, Isa. 44:22); speed and mobility (of the Gentiles "flying" to Mount Zion, Isa. 60:8); and an abundant outpouring (of the "rain" of righteousness, Isa. 45:8, and of manna in the wilderness, Ps. 78:23).

In a negative sense, clouds are used to symbolize prideful self-exaltation (of the wicked, Job 20:6; of Satan, Isa. 14:14); misery or gloom (at the day of Job's birth, Job 3:5; at the day of the Lord, Isa. 60:2; Jer. 13:16; Ezek. 30:3; 34:12; Joel 2:2; Zeph. 1:15); pervasiveness (of enemy invasion, Ezek. 38:9, 16); transitoriness (of Job's prosperity and life, Job 7:9; 30:15; of Israel's love and life, Hos. 6:4; 13:3); futile, idle activity (Eccles. 11:4); dimness (of eyesight in old age, Eccles. 12:2; of a nation's splendor following divine judgment, Lam. 2:1; Ezek. 30:18); swiftness (of divine judgment, Jer. 4:13); and covering or concealing (of divine mercy in judgment, Lam. 3:44).

The Theophanic Cloud. The most common usage of the Hebrew terms for cloud comes in the context of divine theophany. By far the largest group (about fifty occurrences) of these refer to the visible manifestation of the divine presence during Israel's exodus from Egypt and wilderness wandering. This sign of God's presence is termed variously: pillar of cloud (Exod. 13:21–22, plus eleven times), pillar of fire and cloud (Exod. 14:24); a thick cloud (Exod. 19:9, 16), the cloud (Exod. 14:20, plus thirty-three times); and the cloud of the Lord (Exod. 40:38; Num. 10:34).

The pillar of cloud motif—set forth in the exodus account and expanded in the prophetic announcements of a new exodus after the Babylonian exile—encompasses a rich complex of theological meanings and functions: guidance/-leading (of Israel out of Egypt and through the wilderness to Canaan, Exod. 13:21; Num. 14:14; Neh. 9:12; Ps. 78:14); a signal for movement (breaking and setting up camp, Exod. 40:36–37; Num. 9:17–23); protection from danger (as a barrier of darkness between Israel and the Egyptians, Exod. 14:19–20); the sustained, immediate, personal presence of Yahweh/the angel of the Lord (Exod. 13:22; 14:19, 24; 40:38; Num. 9:15–16); an agency of summons (to battle, Num. 10:34–35; and to worship, Exod. 33:10); both a concealment and manifestation of divine glory (Exod. 16:10; 19:9, 16; 20:21; 24:15–18; 34:5; Deut. 4:11; 5:22); the place of propositional revelation (as an oracular cloud, Exod. 33:9; Ps. 99:7); the dwelling place/throne of divinity (over the tabernacle, Num. 9:18, 22; 10:11; and in particular, over the mercy seat, Lev. 16:2); the locus of cultic theophany (for the investiture of the seventy elders and Joshua, Num. 11:25; Deut. 31:15; for the inauguration of the tabernacle, Exod. 40:34–35); shade/protection from the sun or storm (Num. 10:34; Ps. 105:39; Isa. 4:5); illumination (as a pillar of fire by night, Exod. 14:20; Num. 9:15); and an agency of legal investigation and/or executive judgment (against Israel's enemies, Exod. 14:24; and against rebels within Israel, Num. 12:5, 10; 16:42).

Clouds are depicted in other Old Testament theophanies. At creation Yahweh makes the clouds his chariots (Ps. 104:3). The Song of Deborah describes the appearance of Yahweh in a thunderstorm (Judg. 5:4). Answering David's plea for help, Yahweh rides upon a cherub from his heavenly temple with thick clouds as his canopy (Ps. 18:11). Clouds are Yahweh's swift chariot as he executes judgment upon Egypt (Isa. 19:1). Nahum's theophanic vision portrays clouds as the dust of Yahweh's feet (1:3). In Ezekiel's inaugural vision, Yahweh emerges from a great cloud riding upon his celestial palanquin (1:4, 28), and the temple is filled with a cloud some fourteen months later when the covenant lawsuit is completed and executive judgment is about to be poured out (10:3–4).

The Eschatological/Apocalyptic Cloud. The eschatological day of the Lord is several times described as a day of cloud-mass and dark storm cloud for the nation(s) being judged (Ezek. 34:12; Joel 2:2; Zeph. 1:15; cf. Ezek. 30:2). On that day the anger of Yahweh will burn with "a thick rising (smoke-) cloud" (Isa. 30:27). Clouds of theophany are also associated with eschatological judgment/salvation (Isa. 4:5; Nah. 1:3).

The New Testament. *The Literal/Metaphorical Cloud.* The only New Testament reference to literal cloud phenomena is Jesus' graphic contrast between his hearers' ability to interpret the meaning of a cloud rising in the west—that a shower is coming—and their inability to interpret the present time (Luke 12:54). Metaphorical cloud references in the New Testament include Jude's depiction of the unstable, deceptive, false teachers as waterless clouds, carried along by winds (v. 12), and Hebrews' portrayal of the many worthy of faith as a great "cloud of witnesses" (12:1).

The Theophanic/Eschatological Cloud. The remaining twenty-two New Testament occurrences of the word "cloud" appear in the context of theophany, and encompass six theologically crucial, eschatologically related events or visionary scenes in salvation history: (1) the pillar of cloud at the exodus, viewed as a type of Christian baptism in the time of eschatological fulfillment (1 Cor. 10:1–2); (2) Jesus' transfiguration, as a foretaste of the kingdom of God, during which the Father appears and speaks in a cloud (Matt. 17:5; Mark 9:7; Luke 9:34); (3) Jesus' ascension, explained by the angels as a paradigm for his return (Acts 1:9); (4) the "mighty angel" descending from heaven wrapped in a cloud, announcing (against the eschatological backdrop of Dan. 12:7) that time should be no longer (Rev. 10:1); (5) the two resurrected witnesses ascending to heaven in a cloud, described in the context of the eschatological measuring of the temple of God (Rev. 11:12); and (6) Jesus' parousia, against the backdrop of Daniel 7:13, as the Son of Man coming with/on/in a cloud/the clouds/the clouds of heaven (Matt. 24:30; 26:64; Mark 13:26; 14:62; Luke 12:54; 21:27; 1 Thess. 4:17; Rev. 1:7; 14:14–16). RICHARD M. DAVIDSON

Bibliography. T. W. Mann, *JBL* 90 (1971): 15–30; A. Oepke, *TDNT,* 4:902–10; L. Sabourin, *BTB* 4 (1974): 290–311; R. B. Y. Scott, *NTS* 5 (1958–59): 127–32; idem, *ZAW* 64 (1952): 11–25; E. F. Sutcliffe, *VT* 3 (1953): 99–103.

Collection. Any organized gathering of funds or resources. In the Bible, collections are often taken for the benefit of others and not for oneself. The Hebrew term *tĕrûmâ,* refers to a contribution. The Greek terms are *logia* ("collection"), *koinōnian* ("participation"), and *diakonia* ("ministry").

The collection detailed in 2 Chronicles 31 was part of Hezekiah's reforms to make sure that God's ministers, the priests, received adequate provision as the law had commanded (Exod. 35:21, 24; Lev. 7:14, 32; Deut. 12:6, 17–19). When an excess came in, the remainder was stored for later use. The collection was administered with care.

The right of the New Testament minister to donated material support is affirmed by Jesus (Luke 10:7) and the early church (1 Cor. 9:1–14; 1 Tim. 5:18), but how this support is to be collected is not discussed anywhere in detail. Acts 4:32–37 discusses how believers voluntarily brought their gifts to help members to the apostles. Here the collection extends beyond ministers to any believer in need. A negative example of those who lie while making such a donation occurs in Acts 5:1–11.

The key New Testament passages on collection are Romans 15:25–26, 1 Corinthians 16:1–4, and 2 Corinthians 8–9. They all refer to Paul's aid from Gentiles for mostly Jewish believers in need in Jerusalem. Here believers in one locale help those of a different race in another locale. The gift expresses the sense of oneness in the body of Christ that comes through sharing and also reveals the church's sensitivity in meeting needs. First Corinthians 16:1–4 makes it clear that the gift is planned for and collected at a fixed time, and that much effort is made to insure the gift's integrity as it is delivered by trustworthy believers to those who are in need. In 2 Corinthians 8–9, the gift is of their own free will, according to means, is handled by trustworthy individuals, is planned for, is to be given with joy, is an expression of thanksgiving to God, and glorifies him because it is a mark of generosity. In this passage, the collection is called "ministry."

DARRELL L. BOCK

See also CONTRIBUTION; TITHE, TITHING.

Bibliography. S. McKnight, *DPL,* pp. 143–47; K. F. Nickle, *The Collection: A Study in Paul's Strategy.*

Color, Symbolic Meaning of. Although the Bible contains relatively few references to individual colors, their symbolic associations are theologically significant. Colors usually symbolize redemptive and eschatological themes. The Bible is, however, silent on whether the colors used in the tabernacle, temple, and priestly garments held symbolic meaning.

Black signifies gloom, mourning, evil, judgment, and death (Lam. 4:8; Mic. 3:6; Zech. 6:2, 6; Rev. 6:5, 12). Its image is often one of dense, impenetrable darkness (Job 3:5; Isa. 50:3). The terms "darkness" and "night" parallel this usage (Job 3:3–7; Joel 2:2; Zeph. 1:15). Hell is the place of "blackest darkness" reserved for the godless (2 Peter 2:17; Jude 13).

The pale horse of Revelation 6:8 resembles the color of the terror-stricken and corpses (cf. Jer. 30:6; Dan. 10:8). The horse's color matches the work of its rider. Its rider is called Death, who, with Hades, goes forth to kill a fourth of humankind.

An expensive dye, purple represents wealth and royalty (Judg. 8:26; Esther 8:15; Dan. 5:7, 16, 29; Luke 16:19); for this reason, idols were attired in purple (Jer. 10:9). The purple dress of the harlot symbolized Roman imperial rank (Rev. 17:4; 18:12, 16). Before his crucifixion, Jesus was robed in purple in mockery of him as "king of the Jews" (Mark 15:17, 20; John 19:2, 5; cf. Matt. 27:28, "scarlet robe"). Garments of purple suitably clothe a wife of noble character (Prov. 31:22).

Red symbolizes blood. Israel's sin as brilliant scarlet and deep-red crimson is analogous to the bloodstained hands of murderers (Isa. 1:15, 18). The images of red, blood-soaked garments of God as an avenging warrior (Isa. 63:1–6) and the fiery red horse bringing slaughter through warfare (Zech. 6:2; Rev. 6:4) describe divine retribution against evildoers (see also Joel 2:31; Rev. 6:12). The red color of the dragon (Rev. 12:3) and beast (17:3) symbolizes the shedding of innocent blood (cf. 11:7; 16:6). The red heifer (Num. 19:1–10) and scarlet wool (Heb. 9:19) symbolize the Old Testament means of purification through blood; the New Testament powerfully expresses the fullness of Christ's atoning work through a contradictory color image: believers' robes are washed pure white through the blood of the Lamb (Rev. 7:9, 13–14; 19:13–14).

White signifies purity and holiness. It depicts complete forgiveness of sin. David and Israel's bloodguilt would be fully removed, leaving them whiter than snow/wool (Ps. 51:7; Isa. 1:18). It represents the absolute moral purity of God (Dan. 7:9), Christ (Rev. 1:14; Mark 9:3 pars.), angels (Mark 16:5 pars.; Acts 1:10), and believers (Rev. 2:17; 3:4–5; 4:4), and thus of the divine judgment of God (20:11) and Christ (14:14). It indicates the certainty of God's conquest and victory over evil (Zech. 6:3, 6; Rev. 6:2; 19:11).

H. DOUGLAS BUCKWALTER

Bibliography. G. W. Thatcher, *Hasting's Dictionary of the Bible,* 1:456–58; P. L. Garber, *ISBE,* 1:729–32; A. Brenner, *Colour Terms in the Old Testament;* "Color," *BEB,* 1:494–96.

Colossians, Theology of. ***Introduction.*** Although short in length and written to a church Paul did not plant, Colossians stands tall in highlighting the centrality of Jesus Christ as the mediator of God's saving activity. It emphasizes that those who belong to Jesus need only draw on the resources God provides through Jesus in order to find blessing. This letter is known as one of the "Prison Epistles" (along with Ephesians, Philemon, and Philippians). Although some believe it was written by a student of Paul, it has traditionally been associated with Paul and his imprisonment at Rome, dating from around A.D. 61 to 62. Its major concern was to exhort the Colossians in the face of false teaching, which emphasized ascetic practice as a means of experiencing God's presence in a more meaningful way. Paul outlines the blessings of a God who acts through the Mediator-Enabler Jesus, who is the Lord. By doing so, he refutes the false teaching and lays the basis for articulating the call of the church. So we look at Paul's teaching about God, Jesus, the heresy, and the task of the church. These four themes are the center of Paul's teaching in this book, as the apostle seeks to carry out the ministry God has given him.

The Active God Who Saves. The letter begins with a note of thanksgiving for the Colossians, who reflect the faith and love that draw their vitality from the sure hope that God has provided in the gospel (1:3–8). This gift reflects God's gracious activity (1:6). Now Paul describes this activity in more detail after his note of thanksgiving. God directs the saving process. Paul uses the language of warfare, as he notes that God "rescued" believers out of Satan's dark domain and "transferred" them into the kingdom of his beloved Son (1:13–14). It was God's pleasure to work through the mediatorial effort of his Son, who is made in his image and in whom all the fullness of deity resides (1:15, 19; 2:9). In fact, God's desire was that the Son have preeminence in all things, as seen in the Son's work in creation and redemption (as evidenced especially by his own resurrection; 1:15–20).

God's work extends beyond rescue to transformation. He is also active in filling believers with the fullness of life that he graciously bestows to those in Christ (2:10). This transfer is pictured as a "circumcision" God performs as he buries us in baptism and raises us to new life through faith (2:11–12). This highly symbolic description of salvation really portrays the "new birth" and "new life" that God gives and effects. Thus, God "makes alive" by forgiving the sinner, cancelling out the debt of sin, and defeating those who stand opposed to humanity through Christ and the cross (2:13–15). As a result all growth comes through one's relationship to Christ and not through any series of rules or religious disciplinary practices (2:19).

Paul says it another way, when he stresses that the believer's life "is hidden" in God (3:3). This is why Paul can exhort the readers as "God's elect," since God is the active agent in their salvation from start to finish. This is also why God should be praised (1:3, 12; 3:16) and is the object of intercession for boldness (4:2–4). God's power, provision, and sovereignty are central for Paul.

Of course, God is active in another way. He is the one who directs Paul's ministry (1:1, 25). So Paul is called to reveal along with others, the riches God has made available to the saints, and especially to Gentiles (1:26–29). Paul calls these riches a mystery, the hope of glory, which is Christ in the believer (1:26–27). Christ is the center of God's work and it is through Christ that both maturity and glorification come (2:2; 3:3–4).

Jesus Christ—The Mediator-Enabler-Lord. The centrality of Jesus is also clear from the start of the letter. Paul is his apostle (1:1) and the brothers and sisters find their set-apart status in him (1:2). In fact, it is Christ Jesus who is the object of faith and the source of the concrete future hope that awaits them from heaven (1:4–5; 3:3–4). When God acted to rescue them, he took them out of the grip of Satan and placed them into relationship with Christ and his rule (1:13–14). The past tenses in 1:13–14 show that this transfer has already taken place, although its implications extend into the future toward things that have yet to occur (3:3–4). This discussion of the benefits that come from Christ is important to the letter, because before Paul even treats the problem that the Colossians face, he is exposing them to the rich benefits they already possess.

How great is the one into whose kingdom they have come? The answer to this question is the goal of the great hymnic section of 1:15–20. This passage has roots in the wisdom tradition of Judaism and its great confessions of the role of God in the creation (cf. Gen. 1:1; Job 28:23–28; Pss. 95:6–7; 100:3; Prov. 8:22; Wis. 7:22–27; Ecclus. 24). Wisdom is not found mainly in Torah, but in the one who is the image of the invisible God. He incarnates God's attributes and bears divine authority as one who participated in the creation itself. As the firstborn of all creation (Ps. 89:27), he is preeminent among all rulers. Everything in heaven and earth, visible and invisible, no matter what level of spiritual authority, was created by and is subject to him. He is the sustainer of creation and rules the kingdom to which the saints belong. Jesus serves as the sovereign mediator of creation, exercising divine prerogative.

Later in the letter Paul makes the same point by pointing out that Jesus is at God's right hand (3:1). To understand what God is doing and why, one needs only to look to Jesus (2:2–3).

The hymn not only considers Jesus' role in creation; it also considers his mediatorial role in redemption. This redemption involves not just human beings, but extends to the entire creation, both heaven and earth (1:18–20). Such authority starts in the church, where Christ functions as its head, its leader, the beginning, the first to rise from the dead. He is the first to manifest the characteristics of a new humanity, redeemed into newness of life. His preeminence extends into all areas, for not only did he create the cosmos and sustain it; he also is the means and example of its redemption. Such authority reflects God's desire that Jesus be the reflection of the presence of divine fullness (1:19). Such reconciliation begins at the cross.

When Paul considers such redemptive activity at a personal level, rather than a cosmic one, he recalls how estranged and hostile sinners were reconciled through Jesus' death in order that those who abide in faith might be set apart as special before God (1:21–23). Jesus is not only mediator, but enabler.

This is why Paul can speak of the church as so identified and united with Christ that it is called his body. He procured it with his very own death. In fact, for Paul to suffer on behalf of this church is for him to "fill up . . . Christ's afflictions" (1:24), because when the church suffers (as Christ's body), Christ suffers. Such a corporate identification reflects Christ indwelling the community, the great mystery of God (1:29).

To be in Christ means one should pursue the maturity that comes from him (1:28). Such theological reality enables the church to have unity and love. These truths about Christ mean that faith can have orderliness (2:2–4). When one turns aside from this focus of Christ, trouble follows (2:8). So one's walk should be with these realities directing the life, what Paul calls walking "according to Christ" (2:8). He is the one they received as Lord and in him they are to continue to walk, since he is the source of their enablement, wisdom, and knowledge (2:2–6). That is also why salvation can be described as "Christ's circumcision," since they are set apart for him (2:11). All throughout 2:9–15, Paul says again and again that what happens occurs "in," "with," or "through" Christ. It is also why Paul says that Christ is substantive life, while the practices others teach to be life bringing are merely shadows (2:17).

In fact, the believer's existence is so identified with Jesus that Paul speaks of dying with Christ to the elemental spirits of the world and being raised with him (2:20–3:11). This language repeats the imagery of 2:9–15. It reflects a change of identity and allegiance, so that one's life is defined not by the standards, methods, and created forces of the world, but by the desires of the God who rescued them in Christ. To be heavenly minded is not to escape or withdraw, but to reflect the divine attributes of the new life God makes available to the believer (3:1–17). In fact, one can speak of Jesus as the "new man" or new humanity in which people from various nations dwell and find renewal according to the image of God (3:10–11).

So Christ is mediator and enabler, the source of life. The response to that reality means that peace before God can reign in the heart (3:15), the Word of Christ can dwell richly in the life (3:16), and that all that is done occurs knowing that one is his (3:17). His lordship governs our relationships (3:18, 20, 24). Sharing in the gracious benefits of his rule means honoring his rule with one's life. This is the theological center of Colossians that enables believers to counteract the false teaching that approaches them (2:4). But what exactly was the problem that Paul deals with through this Christology?

The Colossian Heresy. The first hint of a problem appears in 2:4. Paul speaks of beguiling speech and the threat of delusion. The Colossian community is a healthy one (2:5), and Paul does not wish that anything distract it from being on course. But this false teaching is particularly subtle, because it draws on religious enthusiasm. It promises a deeper experience with God, one greater than even Jesus provides (2:16–23). But one must prepare for such an experience. It requires discipline and denial. On the surface, such an opportunity for a closer experience with God would be attractive to people who desire to know him. But Paul regards such a claim as a delusion, based on factors and standards of this world and the forces of this world, and not according to Christ (2:8).

There has been much discussion whether the heresy in view here is Hellenistic or Jewish. Those who see a Hellenistic influence appeal to Gnostic or mystery religion influence. It is probably best to see it as eclectic, combining features of both cultures. The reference to observing Sabbaths (2:16) indicates a Jewish flavor, while the emphasis on ascetic practice and heavenly mediaries, like the angels, has a Hellenistic character, although a connection to mystery influence is more likely than a Gnostic one. The key to understanding the heresy comes in the debated 2:18. Two readings are popular and the choice between them is difficult. The key phrase is "worship of angels."

One reading holds that this refers to the heresy's desire "to worship angelic beings." Taken in this sense, the heresy comes to have a strong Hellenistic background, for a Jewish monotheist would be unlikely to worship these mediatorial spirits. It is also this emphasis that makes the view unlikely. Would it be attractive to a church initially committed to Jesus?

The other reading takes the phrase as meaning "seeing the worship of angels." In the other words, the teaching emphasizes visions in which heavenly worship of the angels was observed. In order to have this experience and go into God's presence, one had to prepare for the experience through prayer, fasting, and rigorous disciplined worship. The offer of such a direct experience with God would be attractive to a church that desired to be close to him. Those who have criticized this view have argued that Jews would not be drawn to a teaching that elevated the angelic realm so highly as to challenge monotheism, but this misunderstands the view. The presence of angels merely reflects one's presence before God, not the worship of them. There is no demeaning of monotheism in the view; rather what is sought is a heightened experience of it! We take this second option as the most likely reading of 2:18.

There is precedent for this approach to spirituality in Judaism, in a movement that came to be known as "Merkabah mysticism." The Merkabah is a reference to Ezekiel 1 and the throne chariot of God that Ezekiel saw. This teaching spoke of days of fasting to prepare for a journey to the heavens to see God and have a vision of him and his angelic host in worship (Philo, *Som.* 1.33–37; *Mos.* 2.67–70; 1QH 6:13; 1 Enoch 14:8–25; 2 Bar. 21:7–10; *Apoc. Abr.* 9:1–10; 19:1–9; *Asc Isa.* 7:37; 8:17; 9:28, 31, 33). One could withdraw and eventually go directly into God's presence. Thus the emphasis in this false teaching falls on the humility of ascetic practice, visions, rigors of devotion, treating the body harshly, and rules about what should not be eaten or what days should be observed (2:16–23). All of this activity was aimed at preparing for the experience that took one beyond what Jesus had already provided.

Paul's attitude to such an invitation to superspirituality is condemnation. He says that this road really is a disqualification of what Christ gained (2:18). It is a shadow (2:17), not the substance of life. In fact, it fails to check the flesh and is of no value (2:23). It ignores Christ, who is the source of growth for the body (2:19). That is why Paul calls it a philosophy that comes from human tradition and the world, a philosophy that is really deceitful (2:8). It is important to observe that Paul's complaint about philosophy is not an attack on the syllogisms of atheism, but on a movement that had God and divine things in view, but in a way that distorted what Christ provided.

This desire "to experience heaven" also explains why Paul uses so much heavenly language in describing what Christ has done. The concept of being raised with Christ and setting one's mind on the things above means that the believer already has established a relationship with the divine forces of heaven, so that a trip into God's presence is unnecessary. God has not called his church to withdraw and await a great future experience of himself, but to engage the world with the kind of life that reflects the attributes that reflect the character and righteous morality of those who know God (3:1–17). They can do this boldly, because they know that one day God will complete what he has started and will take them to himself in glory. Asceticism is not the way to heaven: faith in Jesus is. Thus Paul comes to focus on the call of the church to know God's will and to reflect what it means to belong to the "new man."

The Nature and Task of the Church. Three texts are key to this area of theology. First, there is the description of the church as "the body of Christ" (1:18). This description reflects part of the Son's authority associated with his kingdom (1:12–20). The kingdom is more than the church, but the church is a part of its program. The church is the place where God's rule and attributes are reflected to the world, since it functions as light, a point made more explicitly in Ephesians than in this epistle (Eph. 1:19–23; 5:7–14).

A second description of the new community is that it is the "new man" or "new humanity," the incorporation of a new community before God in Christ, where there is no "Greek or Jew, circumcised or uncircumcised, barbarian, Scythian, slave or free, but Christ is all, and is in all" (3:10–11). The "new man" is not an internal attribute of the person (i.e., not the new nature), but a place where peoples reside. This means that the church was formed to be a community with values distinct from the world's, reflecting a distinct character. One is to identify with it and reflect its values. This explains the ethical exhortations and the new way of relating to others in 3:5–4:6. This community is to live differently, because God has transformed her members into a different kind of people, who know themselves to be chosen of God (3:12).

This background explains Paul's prayer at the beginning of the letter (1:9–14). He wants the Colossians to be filled with the knowledge of God's will. God's will is not facts about God, nor is it deciding where God would have one be or what one should do. In this text God's will is the kind of person one is, because they experience the benefits God makes available to the believer. This experience of God's will means that one not only completes the work God gives one to do but bears fruit while doing it (1:10). The bearing of fruit is not the completion of a task but *how* the task is done. What is the character manifested as it is accomplished? Such experience leads to an increase in one's knowledge of God (1:10). It takes enablement that goes through life with endurance, patience, and joy (1:11), since it understands that being God's child will mean being different than the way the world lives. Finally it is a life filled with gratitude to the Father for his rescuing work (1:12–14). Such is the life that Paul prays for believers to have and that he calls living worthy of the Lord, being fully pleasing to him, as one is filled with the knowledge of his will. So central is this goal in the letter that it is what Paul's coworker, Epaphras, prays for when he intercedes for the Colossians (4:12). There it is called maturity, and being fully assured in the will of God.

So ultimately Colossians is about the work of the Father in the Son on behalf of a people he calls to manifest his message and presence on earth. This new community is to realize that all the benefits God has already given are all that is needed to accomplish the task of living a life that is honoring to God. Any suggestion that someone needs anything more than to appropriate what Christ already makes available is a delusion. Blessing comes from God through the Lord Jesus Christ alone, and a life that pleases God draws on what the mediator and enabler provides.

DARRELL L. BOCK

See also CHURCH, THE; PAUL THE APOSTLE.

Bibliography. R. Argall, *CTJ* 22 (1987): 6–20; F. O. Francis, *Conflict in Colossae;* E. Lohse, *Colossians and Philemon;* P. T. O'Brien, *Colossians, Philemon.*

Comfort. The basic concept for comfort in both the Old and New Testaments is encouragement, whether by words or the presence of another to help in time of need. Synonymous words are console, help, give relief, cheer up, exhort, and fear not.

In the Old Testament *nāḥam* is most often translated "to comfort." God is the God of all comfort: "I, even I, am he who comforts you" (Isa. 51:12; see also 51:3, 19). God is not only the creator God who consoles, but he comes in time of calamity and gives help. The gospel is given in Isaiah 40:1, where he exhorts, "Comfort, comfort my people, says your God." The final twenty-six chapters of Isaiah are often called "the volume of comfort" with its promise of present comfort and the future promise of the suffering servant who comes to give hope, help, and release—"to comfort all who mourn" (61:3). The command of Moses to not be afraid (Exod. 14:13; 20:20) is a command intended to bring comfort to the people. Isaiah intends to bring comfort as he echoes God's presence among his people: "So do not fear, for I am with you" (41:10).

In the New Testament the words *parakaleō* and *paraklēsis* come from the verb *kaleō*, meaning "to call," and the preposition *para*, "alongside of." The meaning is to call or summon to one's aid, to call for help, to stand alongside of. Further meanings are to comfort, to encourage, to cheer up, to exhort. The second beatitude offers a blessing to those who mourn, "for they will be comforted" (Matt. 5:4). But the mothers whose children have been murdered by Herod refuse to be comforted (Matt. 2:18). In these instances the meaning is closely related to "console."

Paul's classic passages on comfort (2 Cor. 1:3–7; 7:2–16) suggest the dominant note of encouragement. The King James Version and the New International Version use the word "comfort." God is the author of comfort and "comforts us in all our troubles, so that we can comfort those in any trouble with the comfort we ourselves have received from God" (1:4). This is made possible through Christ, and makes patient endurance overflow to others. Paul was encouraged through the coming of Titus, who had received the comfort of the Corinthian church (7:4–7).

Jesus promised the disciples another Counselor (Comforter, KJV) who would be with them forever. He is the Spirit of truth; he will be sent in the name of Jesus; he will teach all things relating to what Jesus had taught them (John 14:15–27). He will be sent by Jesus after Jesus goes away. He appears in Christ's behalf as mediator, intercessor, helper, and comforter: "he will convict the world of guilt in regard to sin and righteousness and judgment. . . . He will guide you into all truth. He will not speak on his own; he will speak only what he hears, and he will tell you what is yet to come" (John 16:8, 13).

In both Testaments, God is the author of comfort (Isa. 51:12; 2 Cor. 1:3). Christ is comforter, intercessor, advocate. The Holy Spirit is the Counselor sent by Jesus to be our Comforter. The church and the Christian are to function as comforters (2 Cor. 1:4; 7:7). WILLIAM J. WOODRUFF

See also CONSOLATION.

Command, Commandment. The term "commandment" in the Bible (mainly Heb. *miṣwâ;* Gk. *entolē*) refers to orders or adjurations given by authorities. The plural predominantly refers to Mosaic laws.

The commandments were for Israel's good (Deut. 10:13) since God's covenant love was lasting for those who kept them (Exod. 20:6; Deut. 7:9). Obedience would result in prosperity, security, God's presence, longevity, the occupation of the land, a long dynasty, and blessings of all sorts (Lev. 26:3–13; Deut. 5:29–6:2, 17–18; 17:18–20; 28:1–14). Disobedience would result in terror, illness, oppression, infertility, exile, curses, and rebuke (Lev. 26:14–20; Deut. 28:15–68; Ps. 119:21). Because Israel disobeyed, these threats came to pass historically. Purification (sin) offerings were required to atone for "inadvertent" violations of commandments (Lev. 4; Num. 15:22–31).

God's commandments can be kept (Deut. 30:11–14). Abraham *in essence* kept God's "commands, decrees, and laws" (Gen. 26:5) even before these had been revealed through Moses, presumably via living by faith. The godly love, learn, and believe in God's commandments, for they contain precious, enlightening truth that makes one wise (Pss. 19:8; 119:47–48, 66, 73, 98, 151). The wise follow godly commands as a guiding light (Prov. 6:23), and keep God's commandments in view of impending judgment.

The observant wore as a reminder tassels symbolic of keeping God's commandments (Num. 15:38–40). Prosperity can cause one to forget them (Deut. 8:11–14), and adversity tests willingness to obey them (Deut. 8:2; Judg. 3:4; cf. Job's suffering, Job 23:12). One must not allow even a miracle-working prophet to lead one away from them (Deut. 13:4).

Those who hope in salvation keep God's commandments (Ps. 119:166), for keeping the commandments is essential for "righteousness," that is, a right personal relationship with God.

Jesus taught that all the commands could be reduced to two based on the single principle of love (Matt. 22:36–40; Mark 12:28–31). Jesus kept the Sabbath command (Luke 23:56), affirmed the keeping of others (Matt. 5:19; 19:17; Mark 10:19; Luke 18:20), and corrected misapplication of them based on rabbinic traditions (Matt. 15:3, 6; Mark 7:8–9; 10:5). All that Jesus did, including his death and resurrection, were at the Father's commandment and served to further eternal life (John 10:18; 12:49–50).

Old Testament commandments are not directly binding for Christians. Nonetheless, keeping the commandments remains imperative. Christian teaching viewed ethically can sometimes be described as "the sacred commandments" or "the command given by our Lord" (2 Peter 2:21; 3:2) and Christians are "those who obey God's commandments" (Rev. 12:17; 14:12), especially the command of faith in Christ and love of brother (John 13:34; 1 John 2:7–8; 3:23; 4:21; 2 John 4–6). Conversely, whoever does not keep God's commandments has not come to know God (1 John 2:3–4). Love of God is expressed by keeping his commandments (1 John 5:2–3). Those who keep them abide in God and he in them (1 John 3:24), and receive answers to prayer (1 John 3:22).

The commandments, although just and holy, are used by the sin nature to bring about spiritual death (Rom. 7:8–13). But through Jesus' atonement, humans are pardoned and the enmity between Jews and Gentiles created by the Old Testament commandments is removed (Eph. 2:15), perhaps by abrogating the ceremonial aspects of the law and by empowering Gentile Christians to obey the law of Christ.

Joe M. Sprinkle

See also Decrees; Law; Requirement; Statute; Ten Commandments.

Bibliography. C. E. Armerding, *ISBE,* 1:736; R. J. Bauckham, *Jude, 2 Peter;* D. A. Carson, *Matthew;* C. P. Craigie, *The Book of Deuteronomy.*

Command, New. *See* New Command.

Commission, The Great. *See* Great Commission, The.

Communion. *See* Fellowship; Lord's Supper, The.

Community. *See* Church, The; Israel.

Compassion. That (human) disposition that fuels acts of kindness and mercy. Compassion, a form of love, is aroused within us when we are confronted with those who suffer or are vulnerable. Compassion often produces action to alleviate the suffering, but sometimes geographical distances or lack of means prevent people from acting upon their compassionate feelings. Compassion is not a uniquely Christian response to suffering (cf. Exod. 2:6; Luke 10:33), even though Christians have unique reasons for nurturing their compassionate dispositions.

The Hebrew (*ḥāmal, rāḥam*) and Greek (*splanchnisomai*) words sometimes translated as "compassion" also bear a broader meaning such as "to show pity," "to love," and "to show mercy." Other near synonyms for compassion in English are "to be loved by," "to show concern for," "to be tenderhearted," and "to act kindly."

The Old Testament. God's compassion is freely (Exod. 33:19; Rom. 9:15) and tenderly given, like a mother's (Isa. 49:15) or father's (Hos. 11:8) compassion for a child. Yahweh boldly declares, "I will have compassion on whom I will have compassion" (Exod. 33:19). While his compassion can be thwarted by disobedience (Deut. 13:17; 30:3; 2 Chron. 30:9), there are times when his disobedient people's only hope is that his compassion overcomes his anger (Hos. 11:8). Yahweh's compassion is rooted in his covenant relationship with his people (2 Kings 13:23). Hope for the future (Isa. 49:13; Jer. 12:15) is also rooted in God's compassion. It is said that compassion follows wrath (Jer. 12:15; Lam. 3:32), is new each morning (Lam. 3:22–23), and overcomes sin (Ps. 51:1; Mic. 7:19) rather than ignoring it.

Since compassionate acts flow from compassionate persons, we are not surprised to learn that compassion is constitutive of God's very being (Exod. 34:6, "The Lord, the Lord, the compassionate and gracious God"). Echoes of this declaration are found throughout Scripture. God's compassion was essential for the maintenance of the covenant and his people praised him for it continually (Pss. 78:38; 86:15; 103:13; 145:8).

"Compassion" is not frequently used with a human subject. It is found, however, in a mother's attitude toward her son (1 Kings 3:26), a princess's reaction to an abandoned child (Exod. 2:6), and the Ziphites' treatment of Saul (1 Sam. 23:21).

The New Testament. The intertestamental literature and the New Testament continue to speak about God as the compassionate one. God's compassion is demonstrated in his Son's ministry for and among his people (Matt. 9:36; Mark 6:34). The messianic compassion is extended to the helpless crowds (Matt. 9:36), the sickly masses (Matt. 14:14), the hungry people (Mark 8:2), and the blind men (Matt. 20:34). The waiting father (Luke 15:20) is filled with compassion when he sees his wayward son returning—just as God has compassion on us and accepts us when we repent and return to him.

Believers learn about compassion through example and exhortation. Imitating God and/or Christ has led many to lives of exemplary compassion. The Scriptures also exhort believers to make compassion an integral aspect of their lives (Zech. 7:9; Col. 3:12). Compassion needs to be nurtured and practiced or even this basic love response can grow dull and cold.

David H. Engelhart

See also LOVE; MERCY.

Concubine. Female slave who functioned as a secondary wife and surrogate mother. The Hebrew word for concubine (*pîlegeš*) is a non-Semitic loanword borrowed to refer to a phenomenon not indigenous to Israel. Babylonian and Assyrian law codes regulate primary and secondary marriages more specifically than do the Old Testament laws. Exodus 21:7–10 has been appealed to as regulative of some aspects of concubinage, but that only implicitly.

Concubines are mentioned primarily in early Israelite history—during patriarchal times, the period of the judges, and the early monarchy—although some later kings also had concubines. While concubines did not have the same status as wives, they were not to be mistreated (Exod. 21:7–10) nor could they be violated by other males (Gen. 35:22) with impunity (Gen. 49:3–4). They seem to have received higher status if they bore sons, or at least they are remembered by name (Gen. 21:10; 22:24; 30:3; 36:12).

The sons of some concubines were treated as co-heirs with the sons of wives. Was this facilitated by the wife accepting and naming the child as her own, or was the father's act of "adopting" the son required? Paucity of information prevents us from answering this definitively. In at least one case the inheritance potential of the concubine's son seems to present a threat to the primary wife and her son (Gen. 21:10). Abraham eventually gives the full inheritance to Isaac, and only gives gifts to his concubines' sons (Gen. 25:6).

The story of Judges 19–20 suggests that the terminology used of relationships in a regular marriage are also used in a concubinage relationship. The man is called the concubine's "husband" (19:3; 20:4) and the woman's father is referred to as the man's "father-in-law" (19:9). Some evidence suggests that royal wives (concubines?) were inherited by succeeding kings (2 Sam. 12:8). Thus approaching the royal concubines (2 Sam. 16:21–22) or even requesting the king's female attendant for a wife (1 Kings 2:13–22) can be understood as the act of one attempting to take the throne away from its designated occupant (1 Kings 2:22).

The practice of taking concubines as "wife" was used to provide a male heir for a barren wife (cf. Gen. 16, 35, 36). In addition, the practice provided a social safety net for poor families who could sell their daughters in dire times (Exod. 21:7–10; Judg. 19:1). It seems plausible to suggest that the practice of taking concubines was perpetuated to meet the sexual desires of the males and/or to cement political alliances between nations. Nevertheless, the paucity of sufficient internal data requires dependence on comparative ancient Near Eastern evidence for these conclusions. Multiplying children through concubines would not normally complicate the inheritance lines, but would increase the available family workforce and the family wealth.

DAVID H. ENGELHART

See also MARRIAGE.

Condemnation. From the standpoint of semantics, condemnation is part of legal terminology. When it is discovered that a crime has been committed, that the law has been broken, the process of investigation may lead to formal charges being levied against a defendant. The process of litigation leads to the outcome, a verdict of acquittal or guilt. The verdict indicates that the defendant is either free from or accountable to the law's penalty for that crime. Thus the result is either vindication or condemnation. Condemnation can refer either to the legal status of liability to punishment or to the actual infliction of that punishment. At times the word is also used in a broader context to refer to negative evaluations of a person by peers or by one's own conscience. This legal process is to some extent the background for biblical language about judgment and condemnation.

In biblical theology, God as creator, redeemer, and lawgiver, is the judge of all humankind. He instituted the family, civil government, and the people of God as institutions governing human relationships. In the Old Testament theocracy God mediated his justice through judges, kings, priests, and prophets. In the New Testament the church's leaders are accountable for administering his justice to the people of God. All this is based on the fact that God has acted to redeem human beings and reveal his will to them. Those who refuse to believe and obey are guilty of breaking his law. Their punishment has already begun and their ultimate condemnation will occur at the final judgment if they do not repent before death.

In the Old Testament rebellion against God began in the garden of Eden (Gen. 3). Our first parents turned away from God's plan, leading to their death and alienation. Yet God patiently bore with his rebellious creatures, and chose Abraham and his descendants to be his special people and mediate his blessings to all nations (Gen. 12). He redeemed Israel from Egypt and gave them a land along with a covenant that set before them the conditions of his continued blessing (Exod. 19–20). God as creator, redeemer, and covenanter stood as judge over Israel and set before them life and prosperity, death and adversity (Exod. 34:5–7; Deut. 30:15–20). Through his prophets he continued to call Israel to obedience, yet his theocratic rulers frequently neglected his justice by condemning the innocent and vindicating the guilty. Eventually God condemned this miscarriage of justice by sending other nations to carry Israel into captivity. Thus the Old Testament generally stresses the justice of God in punishing sinners during the present life, not the afterlife (but see Dan. 12:2). To probe this theme further in the Old Testament, one should study the Hebrew words *šāpaṭ*, "to judge," and *mišpāṭ*, "judgment."

In New Testament theology the rebellion of the first Adam with its disastrous consequences of death and condemnation for all humankind is more than offset by the obedience of the second Adam, the Lord Messiah Jesus (Rom. 5:12–21; 1 Cor. 15:22). Jesus' sinless life and sacrificial death provide the basis for God's giving life and justification to all who believe in him. God remains just in justifying sinners because of the perfect redemption accomplished by Jesus, the sinners' substitute (Acts 13:38–39; Rom. 3:21–26). Those who have been made right with God by faith in Christ are not condemned (John 5:24; Rom. 8:1–4; Col. 2:14), but those who refuse to believe in Jesus are condemned already (John 3:16–18; Rom. 1:18–32; Gal. 1:8–9). Unless they repent they face the irrevocable finalization of this condemnation at the resurrection and judgment (Matt. 25:46; John 5:28–29; Acts 17:30–31; 24:15; Rom. 2:5–16; 2 Thess. 1:5–10; 2:9–12; 1 Peter 4:4–5, 17; 2 Peter 2:1–10; Jude 4–9; Rev. 20:7–14; 21:6–8; 22:12–17). In the meantime, expectation of this eschatological judgment motivates believers to scrutinize their lives so that they will not be condemned with the world (1 Cor. 11:31–32). The discipline of the church is also to be carried out with this eschatological perspective in mind (1 Cor. 5:1–13).

To summarize, the theme of condemnation is always seen in the Bible against the background of a just God who creates, redeems, and covenants with his people so that they may live out his justice on the earth. Sinners who come to this God in faith are not condemned, but are expected to live together in a community where justice prevails in the vindication of the oppressed and the condemnation of the oppressor.

David L. Turner

See also Hell; Judgment.

Bibliography. F. Büchsel et al., *TDNT,* 3:920–55; H. Buis, *The Doctrine of Eternal Punishment;* W. Eichrodt, *Theology of the Old Testament;* D. Guthrie, *New Testament Theology;* J. P. Louw and E. Nida, *A Greek-English Lexicon of the New Testament Based on Semantic Domains;* L. Morris, *The Biblical Doctrine of Judgment;* W. Schneider et al., *NIDNTT,* 2:361–71.

Confess, Confession. The biblical concepts expressed by the words "confess" and "confession" have in common the idea of an acknowledgment of something. This is the root idea of the two verbs that lie behind the great majority of occurrences of the words "confess" and "confession" in the English Bible: Hebrew *yādâ,* (in the hiphil root) and Greek *homologeō*. English versions such as the NIV therefore sometimes translate these verbs as "acknowledge." From this common root emerge two distinct theological senses: the acknowledging or confessing of faith (in God, Christ, or a particular doctrine), and the acknowledging or confessing of sins before God.

Confession of Faith. Those who are in relationship with God have the joy and responsibility of publicly acknowledging that relationship and the beliefs that are part of it. Solomon alludes to such public profession of commitment to God in his prayer at the dedication of the temple: "When your people Israel have been defeated by an enemy because they have sinned against you, and when they turn back to you and confess your name, . . . then hear from heaven and forgive the sin of your people Israel" (1 Kings 8:33–34; cf. v. 35; 2 Chron. 6:24, 26). But the reference to Israel's sins suggests that confessing God's name here involves also the acknowledgment of sin before him. The two biblical ideas of confession are here, therefore, united.

It is in the New Testament that confession in the sense of acknowledging allegiance to the faith becomes prominent. Confessing God's name (Heb. 13:15) or the "name of the Lord" (2 Tim. 2:19) is the mark of a believer. And, since God has revealed himself and his truth decisively in Jesus Christ, confessing Christ becomes the hallmark of genuine Christianity. Jesus taught that "Whoever acknowledges me before men, I will also acknowledge him before my Father in heaven" (Matt. 10:32; Luke 12:8; cf. Rev. 3:5). Reflected here is the secular Greek use of the word to denote solemn and binding public testimony in a court of law. Confession of Christ, then, is no private matter, but a public declaration of allegiance. Such claims can, however, be spurious, and are revealed by a lifestyle incompatible with a genuine relationship to Christ (Titus 1:16).

Confessing Christ, then, requires both a matching Christian lifestyle and a matching Christian theology. In what is perhaps the most characteristic New Testament use of the language, the writers stress that Christian confession includes adherence to certain truths about Christ. This doctrinal sense of the word can be seen generally in Luke's reminder that the Pharisees acknowledge the teachings about the resurrection and the spiritual realm (Acts 23:8). Central to New Testament doctrine, of course, is the truth about Jesus Christ, and this is the point continually stressed by the New Testament writers. Perhaps the earliest and most basic of Christian confessions was the simple assertion that "Jesus is Lord" (Rom. 10:9–10). Paul here makes "confessing with the mouth" parallel to "believing in the heart" as a means of salvation. He does not mean by this that public confession is a means of salvation in the way that faith is, for his choice of wording is dictated by the allusion to the heart and the mouth in his earlier quotation of Deuteronomy 30:14 (v. 8). But the text does highlight the fact that genuine faith has its natural result in a public confession of adherence to Christ.

A variation of the formula "Jesus is Lord" that is probably just as early is the confession "Jesus is the Christ, or the Messiah." John tells us that the Pharisees refused to confess that Jesus was the Messiah (12:42), and forced out of the synagogue all Jews who did make such a confession (9:22). Here also we see the way in which public confession of Christ could lead to persecution. It is perhaps because Timothy faces such persecution that Paul urges him to imitate his Lord's example before the Roman governor Pontius Pilate by making "your good confession in the presence of many witnesses" (1 Tim. 6:12; cf. v. 13).

As the church was exposed to more and more alien influences, Christian doctrinal confessions had to become more specific and detailed. Contesting heretics who denied the reality of Jesus' humanity, John insists that only those who confess that Jesus had come in the flesh could claim to know God (1 John 2:23; 4:2–3, 15; 2 John 7). Similarly, the author to the Hebrews exhorts his wayward readers to "hold fast our confession" (4:14, RSV; 10:23), a confession that is focused on the identity of Christ (see 3:1). This New Testament use of the language of confession led to the later church's use of the word "confession" to denote a summary of what Christians believe (e.g., "The Augsburg Confession," "The Westminster Confession of Faith"). From the beginning, the church found it necessary to define what it meant to be a Christian by formulating statements of Christian belief that could be recited publicly. First Timothy 3:16, introduced by the words "Great indeed, we confess, is the mystery of our religion" (RSV), may be just such an early confession; and scholars have suggested that other such early confessions or creeds may be found in texts such as Romans 1:3–4, Colossians 1:15–20, and Philippians 2:6–11.

Confession of Sins. If confession of faith is more prominent in the New Testament, confession of sins is found more often in the Old Testmaent. The word that is most often used in such contexts is the Hebrew verb *yādâ*, which can mean either to praise or give thanks to God or to confess sins before God. Indeed, in some verses (Josh. 7:19), it is not clear which is meant. Confession of sin in the Old Testament often comes in the context of the offering of sacrifices. Leviticus 5:5 makes confession of sin the intermediate step between awareness that a sin has been committed (vv. 3–4) and the offering of an atoning sacrifice (v. 6). Here we see the idea of confession as a conscious and public acknowledgement that God's holy law has been transgressed (see also Lev. 26:40; Num. 5:7). The Old Testament also stresses the way in which representative figures among the people of Israel can publicly confess sins on behalf of the people as a whole (the high priest on the Day of Atonement [Lev. 16:21]; Ezra [Ezra 10:1]; Nehemiah [Neh. 1:6; 9:2–3]; Daniel [Dan. 9:4, 20]). This acknowledging before God of the sins of the nation as a whole (an acknowledgment in which individual Israelites were to take part) was a necessary prerequisite for God's mercy and restoring grace in the midst of judgment. The confession needed, of course, to be sincere. Jeremiah's call on the people to acknowledge their guilt (3:13) leads only to an insincere confession (14:20) that the Lord does not heed. One way in which the sincerity of confession can be tested is by accompanying acts of repentance. In Ezra's day, for example, confession of sin in taking foreign wives was to be followed by a putting away of those wives (Ezra 10). But the Old Testament also recognizes the importance of individual confession of sins and in contexts not obviously tied to the sacrificial system. David reflects, "I acknowledged my sin to you and did not cover up my iniquity. I said, 'I will confess my transgressions to the LORD'—and you forgave the guilt of my sin" (Ps. 32:5). David experienced the principle stated in Proverbs 28:13: "He who conceals his sins does not prosper, but whoever confesses and renounces them finds mercy."

Confession of sins in the New Testament (usually expressed with the compound word *exomologeō*) is mentioned in only five passages. This is not, however, to minimize its importance, as confession is certainly included in the widespread call to "repent" from one's sins. Thus, John the Baptist's call for repentance is met by the people's confession of their sins (Matt. 3:6; Mark 1:5). Perhaps the most familiar text on confession is 1 John 1:9: "If we confess our sins, he is faithful and just and will forgive us our sins and purify us from all unrighteousness." Making forgiveness conditional on confession raises theological problems for some. For does not Christ's sacrifice wipe out for the believer the guilt of all sins—past, present, and *future?* Perhaps it is best to distinguish between the judicial basis for the forgiveness of sins—the once-for-all work of Christ—and the continuing appropriation of the benefits of that sacrifice—through repeated repentance and confession of sins. Secured for us eternally in our justification by faith, forgiveness is always provided, but we are to ask for it (Matt. 6:12, 14), as we confess our sins.

The setting of the confession of sins in the Old Testament is frequently public. This raises the question about whether confession should be private or public. James suggests the importance of public confession: "Confess your sins to each other" (James 5:16; cf. also Acts 19:18). This exhortation was a key scriptural basis for the early "methodist" lay gatherings, in which public confession of sin played a large role. Even in public confessions, of course, it is the Lord who is the primary "audience," for all sin is ultimately sin against him, and all confession must be directed ultimately to him. Moreover, public confession of sin does not seem to be a standard feature of New Testament church life. While its biblical basis is not completely clear, therefore, there is wisdom in the principle that sin should be confessed to those whom it has directly harmed. When the whole church has been affected, the whole church should hear the confession. When one other person has been harmed, we should confess to that person. But when the sin is a "private" one, we may well keep the confession between ourselves and God. Certainly there is no New Testament warrant for the later Roman Catholic insistence on auricular confession to a priest. Although "elders" are mentioned in James 5:14, the exhortation to confess sins to "one another" in verse 16 clearly has in view the entire Christian community. DOUGLAS J. MOO

See also FORGIVENESS; MOUTH.

Bibliography. O. Cullmann, *The Earliest Christian Confessions;* J. N. D. Kelly, *Early Christian Creeds;* O. Michel, *TDNT,* 5:199–220; V. H. Neufeld, *The Earliest Christian Confessions;* J. R. W. Stott, *Confess Your Sins: The Way of Reconciliation.*

Confidence. A multifaceted word that encompasses within Christian thought a range of aspects—faith in God, certainty and assurance of one's relationship with God, a sense of boldness that is dependent on a realization of one's acceptance by God, and a conviction that one's destiny is secure in God. To put one's ultimate trust or confidence either in human ability and power or in false gods and the things of this world is to discover with the men of Shechem the ultimate weakness of the mundane world (Judg. 9:26). But to place one's confidence in the Lord rather than in the power of a human army is to begin to confront the mysterious power of the true God, who engenders in his followers genuine, growing confidence (2 Kings 18:19–19:13; Isa. 36:4–37:20; cf. 1 Cor. 2:1–8).

This developing sense of confidence in the Lord provided the basis for a sense of assurance to Israel for living in this world as a people of God. In the New Testament era confidence in God was also foundational for the expectations of a wonderful future in the hereafter in heaven with Christ (2 Cor. 5:6–8; Phil. 1:6; 1 John 2:28; Rev. 21:1–8). Rooted in the confidence that came through the resurrection of Jesus, the early Christians were willing to follow their Lord's example of suffering and even death. Although Paul had once found his confidence in his Jewish heritage and his personal accomplishments, he discovered that true confidence was to be found only through the power of God in Christ. The result of his newfound confidence was that instead of being a persecutor he willingly accepted the role of becoming a persecuted one for Christ (cf. Phil. 3:4–16).

Jesus Christ is alive for Christians and he will return to claim his own, both those who have died and those who are still living (1 Thess. 4:13–18)! In this confidence the early Christians coined their Aramaic trademark prayer/greeting: *Maranatha,* "Come, our Lord!"/"Our Lord is coming!" (1 Cor. 16:22; Rev. 22:20). As Paul realized the end of his life was on the horizon (Phil. 1:21–23), he echoed separately that great expectation of the coming day of the Lord (Phil. 1:6; 2:16; 3:20; 4:5). Christians at their best have always been an eschatological community of hope.

This eschatological confidence is not a "do-nothing, pie-in-the-sky-by-and-by" philosophy but is wrapped in a summons to authentic, active, moral integrity based on the model life of Jesus, the servant Lord who gave his life for others. Christianity is not a mere religion humans practice; it is a confident way of living based on what God has done in Christ. But Christian confidence does not mean that Christians cease to be human or lack human characteristics. Even Paul went through periods of discouragement when his troubles were almost unbearable (2 Cor. 1:8). But the resurrection of Jesus provides the key throughout life that confidence is based not on ourselves or our activity but on God who can raise the dead and give us the capacity to face adversity (2 Cor. 1:9–10). GERALD L. BORCHERT

See also ASSURANCE.

Conscience. Conscience is a term that describes an aspect of a human being's self-awareness. It is part of a person's internal rational capacity and is not, as popular lore sometimes suggests, an audience room for the voice of God or of the devil. Conscience is a critical inner awareness that bears witness to the norms and values we recognize and apply. The complex of values with which conscience deals includes not only those we own, but the entire range of values to which we are exposed during life's journey. Consequently, there is always a sense of struggle in our reflective process. The witness of conscience makes its presence known by inducing mental anguish and feelings of guilt when we violate the values we recognize and apply. Conscience also provides a sense of pleasure when we reflect on conformity to our value system.

There is no Hebrew term in the Old Testament that is a linguistic equivalent for the classical Greek term *suneidēsis.* The Hebrew term for "heart," however, is a prominent term of self-awareness in the Old Testament. The lack of a developed concept of conscience in the Old Testament, as we see later in Paul, may be due to the worldview of the Hebrew person. Consciousness of life was of a relationship between God and a covenant community rather than an autonomous self-awareness between a person and his or her world. The only usage of *suneidēsis* in the canonical section of the Septuagint is in Ecclesiastes 10:20, "Do not revile the king even in your *thoughts,* or curse the rich in your bedroom," where it is clearly used as self-reflection in secret (cf. the only verbal variations in Job 27:6 and Lev. 5:1). Rabbinic Judaism and the Dead Sea Scrolls are consistent with the Old Testament in their lack of a vocabulary of conscience.

There are thirty occurrences of *suneidēsis* in the New Testament (one more possible usage in a variant on John 8:9). The verb form (*suneidon, sunoida*) occurs only four times. The thirty occurrences are almost exclusively Pauline (22, with an additional 5 in Hebrews and 3 in 1 Peter), and eleven of them are in the Corinthian correspondence. The classical use of this word-group for simple knowledge occurs in Acts 5:2, 12:12, and 14:6. The Pauline development of conscience as a monitor of actions and attitudes is particularly noted in the Pastoral Epistles, where adjectives like "good" (1 Tim. 1:5, 19; cf. Acts 23:1) and "clear" (1 Tim. 3:9; 2 Tim. 1:3; cf. Acts 24:16) are used to depict the conscience as affirming right action. This action, however, is not determined by conscience but by other criteria to which conscience bears witness. Paul's reference to the conscience being "seared" and "corrupted" (1 Tim. 4:2; Titus 1:15) indicates that the function of conscience as a capacity for sound inward critique has been thwarted by resistance to God's revealed values. The writer of Hebrews views conscience as bearing a witness of being "clear" or "guilty" (cf. 9:9, 14; 10:2, 22; 13:18). First Peter reflects both the classical use of "awareness" (2:19) and the Pauline "clear" (3:16) and "good" (3:21) pattern.

Why is there such a significant usage of this term by Paul when it seems almost nonexistent in the Old Testament? The idea has been proposed that Paul's usage of *suneidēsis* was prompted by his debate with the Corinthian church. The usages in the Corinthians correspondence are the first chronological occurrences of the term in the New Testament. They also present a unique critique of the role of conscience in relation to a knowledge base.

A thematic survey of the occurrences of *suneidēsis* in the New Testament yield at least three major ideas. First, conscience is a God-given capacity for human beings to exercise self-critique. First Corinthians 4:4 and Romans 2:14–15 illustrate this capacity. In 1 Corinthians 4:4 Paul reflects upon his ministry and motives and "knows nothing against himself" (*sunoida*; translated "My conscience is clear" by the NIV), but affirms that he is still subject to critique by God. Here Paul illustrates that conscience is not an end in itself, but is subject to critique. Romans 2:14–15 is used in its context as an illustration that the Gentiles are in one sense superior to the Jews. The Gentiles' "self-critique mechanism" (i.e., conscience) is more consistent in reference to their own law (i.e., values) than the Jews' is to theirs (i.e., the real law). The Jews resisted the law's role as convictor while the Gentiles' convictor (conscience) worked. The illustration serves to shame the Jews in their position of greater privilege. The point of Romans 2:14–15 is merely illustrative of how the two parties function. The Gentiles are demonstrating a more consistent "moral" consciousness, "the *work* of the law" (its function, not its content is in view), in regard to their values than the privileged Jew is in regard to the value of God's law.

Second, conscience is consistently imaged as a "witness" to something (cf. Rom. 2:15; 9:1; 2 Cor. 1:12; 4:2; 5:11; along with the implications of adjectives such as a "good," "clear" conscience). Conscience is not an independent authority that originates judgments. The idea of conscience as a judge or legislator in the sense of originating an opinion is a modern innovation. A witness does not create evidence but is bound to respond to evidence that exists. The conscience does not dictate the content of right or wrong; it merely witnesses to what the value system in a person has determined is right or wrong. In this regard, conscience is not a guide but needs to be guided by a thoroughly and critically developed value system.

Third, conscience is a servant of the value system. An analysis of 1 Corinthians 8 and 10 exposes this principle. In the context of 1 Corinthians, a weak conscience is one without an adequate knowledge base in regard to idols and meat (i.e., a wrong value system), and therefore suffers feelings of guilt. The strong have a proper knowledge and are therefore free of guilt (cf. how "knowledge" is used almost as a substitute for conscience in the Rom. 14 discussion). The issue is not resolved on the basis of conscience but on the basis of worldview. Conscience merely monitors the worldview that exists in our internal conversation. Paul's comments about "ask no questions on account of conscience" in 1 Corinthians 10 has often been used to mean "what you don't know won't hurt you." Paul would hardly promote such an idea! Rather, Paul's use of the fixed phrase "on account of conscience" actually means "ask no questions because it really isn't a matter of conscience and therefore is not open for debate."

Paul does protect the function of conscience in weak believers of 1 Corinthians, but not because they are correct or because their views should be forever tolerated. If the strong were to force the weak to conform against their values (albeit wrong), they would thereby destroy a process of conviction God created so society could police itself. The solution is to address the foundational values. As the value set is informed and changed, conscience will follow. Herein is a needful principle for the Christian community. While a person's judgment may be wrong in light of a biblically enlightened worldview, he or she must be given correct information and the opportunity to pursue maturity without oppressive external manipulation. This is the way of love (cf. 1 Cor. 8:1–3). On the other hand, the classic question, "How long do you put up with the weak?" is easily answered by contextual implication. You work with their weakness until they have had the opportunity to learn the correct way and it becomes a new conviction for them. If they refuse to learn and mature, then they have shifted from the category of weak to belligerent and thereby come under new rules of engagement.

Conclusion. Conscience is an aspect of self-awareness that produces the pain and/or pleasure we "feel" as we reflect on the norms and values we recognize and apply. Conscience is not an outside voice. It is a inward capacity humans possess to critique themselves because the Creator provided this process as a means of moral restraint for his creation. The critique conscience exercises related to the value system which a person develops. Romans 12:1–2 makes the point that God desires that his creation conform to divine values by a process of rational renewal. The Scriptures provide the content for this renewal.

Gary T. Meadors

Bibliography. P. W. Gooch, *NTS* 33 (1987); R. Jewett, *Paul's Anthropological Terms;* C. S. Lewis, *Studies in Words;* C. A. Pierce, *Conscience in the New Testament;* M. E. Thrall, *NTS* 14 (1964).

Consecrate. ***The Meanings of* qdš *in the Sinai Legislation.*** In the Sinai material (Exod. 19:1–Num. 10:10) *qdš*, which is translated "consecrate/sanctify/make holy," means separation with relationship to God. Of 263 occurrences the context implies separation in 260 instances and relationship to God in 252. Another meaning is perfection or excellence (70 times), whether ethical/behavioral (37), material (32), or both (1). Less frequent occurrences imply a mysterious/dangerous power (20 instances) or glory (5 instances).

Separation is particularly clear in the bounds set around Mount Sinai (Exod. 19:23; see also the wall around Ezekiel's temple, Ezek. 42:20) and in the veil setting off the Holy of Holies (Exod. 26:33). The function of the priests is to distinguish between the holy and the common (Lev. 10:10).

Both separation and relationship to God are explicit in the *qdš* cluster in Leviticus 20:23–26. God says, "You are to be holy to me because I, the Lord, am holy, and I have set you apart from the nations to be my own." Relationship to God is very clear also in the introductory command before the tabernacle instructions: "Then have them make a sanctuary for me, and I will dwell among them" (Exod. 25:8; cf. 29:43–46).

The clearest reference to ethical perfection in *qdš* is Exodus 19:5–6, where holiness is defined in terms of obedience to God's statutes: "If you obey me fully and keep my covenant, then out of all nations you will be my treasured possession. . . you will be for me a kingdom of priests and a holy nation" (cf. Lev. 20:7–8; 22:31–32).

Material perfection or excellence is most frequently involved in the use of *qdš* for the tabernacle materials. The requirements for perfect sacrifices and the exclusion of physically defective priests from service also include the idea of perfection in *qdš*.

Holy Persons, Objects, and Times in the Sinai Material. Persons, objects, and times are holy because they are set apart for God. Of persons, the priests most frequently receive the designation "holy." The firstborn are holy (Num. 3:13), as are the Levites who replace them (Num. 3:12–13), the Nazarites (Num. 6:8; cf. also those dedicated to Yahweh, Lev. 27:1–8), and all Israel (Exod. 19:6, 10, 14). The latter are sometimes described as sanctified by God (Lev. 20:8) and sometimes told to sanctify themselves (20:7). God sanctifies them by separating them from the nations and giving them his statutes; they sanctify themselves by obeying these laws (Exod. 19:5–6; Lev. 20:7–8; 22:31–32).

Of objects, the tabernacle and its appurtenances are commonly called holy. Whenever the text speaks of contagious holiness, the subject is the "most holy" things (*qōdeš qādāšîm* Exod. 29:37; 30:29; Lev. 6:10 [17], 18 [25], 22 [29]). Common things can be raised to the status of holy if the owner chooses to dedicate them to Yahweh (Lev. 27). This seems to have included even unclean animals (27:11, cf. vv. 26–27).

Of times, the Sabbath (Exod. 20:8; etc.), the feasts (Lev. 23:37), and the year of jubilee (Lev. 25:10, 12) are set apart as holy. The Sabbath is also a sign of holiness (Exod. 31:13—that Israel will realize it is Yahweh who is making them different for himself).

***Israel's Cultic Structure Was a Paradigm of* qdš.** The structure of Israel's cult pictures the predominant meanings of holiness: separation to God and perfection. This is to be seen in the organization of persons into priesthood and laity, in the layout of the sanctuary and the camp around it, and in the regulations for access of persons to holy territory. The nearer the relationship to Yahweh who is holy, the greater the separation from imperfection. For example, the Holy of Holies is the most separate spot and evidences the highest quality of materials and craftsmanship. The high priest only enters on one day of the year, and with no one else in the next room who might see in (Lev. 16:17). Spanning out from the sanctuary are concentric circles of decreasing holiness—

the Levites, the twelve tribes, the unclean and the heathen (Gentiles). The more serious the uncleanness, the greater the exclusion of that unclean person and the more elaborate the ritual required for him to regain access to the presence of the holy. Even the sacrifices and washings within the ritual themselves mirror the concept of holiness. That the offerer's sacrifice is killed serves as a metaphor for the separation of a holy God from imperfection. The washings, while serving generally as a hygienic measure to check or prevent disease, also have metaphoric value. The high priest bathes before entering and again upon exiting from the holiest place; contact with the most holy things is contact with contagious holiness, and contagion needs to be washed away to keep the most holy things set apart (Lev. 16:24; cf. 6:27). The sprinkling of the Levites at their induction is also a metaphoric cleansing (cf. also after leprosy the shaving of eyebrows, but not all body hair). As washing gets rid of dirt, so it seems on occasion to get rid of status with respect to purity of the cult. One step removed is to make washing a metaphor for riddance of sin—a step approached most nearly in the Sinai material in the ordeal for a wife suspected of adultery (Num. 5:17, 27–28).

The Development of* qdš *in Later Biblical Writers. Later writers in the Old Testament and also the New often emphasize holiness as an ethical and spiritual thing. The prophets during the time when there was no temple (586–516 B.C.) use the temple ritual as a metaphor for holiness (Lam. 1:8–9, 17; 4:13–15; Ezek. 36:17, 25; Hag. 2:10–19; Zech. 3). Ezekiel (chaps. 40–48) outlines the whole future temple and its ritual as a pattern of holiness (i.e., separation to God from uncleanness) so that Israel will become ashamed of her iniquities (43:10–12). Peter uses language from Exodus 19 to speak of the church as a holy priesthood/nation that offers up spiritual sacrifices (1 Peter 2:4).

As in the priestly legislation so in the New Testament God's people are sometimes described as sanctified by God (1 Thess. 5:23; cf. Eph. 1:4) and sometimes told to sanctify themselves (2 Cor. 7:1; 1 Thess. 3:13) so as to be blameless. The means whereby God sanctified his church was Jesus' sacrificial death (Col. 1:22). In response, believers are told to present their bodies as a living sacrifice, holy and acceptable to God (Rom. 12:1). Also they are disciplined by God in order to share his holiness (Heb. 12:10).

Paul calls believers the holy temple of God (1 Cor. 3:17). The direction is for all of one's life to be set apart to and blameless/perfect before God. Zechariah anticipated a day when the commonplace things of life would be raised to the status of holy (14:20–21). Isaiah looked forward to a "highway of holiness" upon which the unclean would not travel (Isa. 35:8). Whereas in the Sinai legislation uncleanness is more contagious than holiness, this appears to be reversed in 1 Corinthians 7:14—the unbelieving husband being sanctified by his wife. The encompassing goal in both Testaments is for God's people to be holy in all their behavior like the Holy One who called them (Lev. 11:45; 19:2; 20:26; 1 Peter 1:14–16).

DAVID HILDEBRAND

See also OFFERINGS AND SACRIFICES; PRIEST, PRIESTHOOD.

Bibliography. M. Haran, *Temples and Temple Service in Ancient Israel;* J. Milgrom, *Cult and Conscience;* idem, *Suppl. IDB,* 782-84; O. Procksch, *TDNT,* 1:88–115.

Consolation. Attempt to comfort someone who is in sorrow. The most frequently encountered Hebrew term is *niḥam; parakaleō, paramutheomai,* and other synonyms occur in Greek. In the English versions, "consolation" is practically interchangeable with "comfort."

Consolation for the Sorrowful. Consolation is the attendant to mourning (Job 29:25; Jer. 16:7), due perhaps to the loss of a close relative (2 Sam. 12:24; 1 Chron. 7:22; John 11:19). Such comfort goes out to people who are distressed and alone (Ps. 77:2–3), who weep bitterly (Isa. 22:4), or who are extremely anxious (Ps. 94:19). In extreme circumstances people may refuse to be comforted (Gen. 37:35; Jer. 31:15). When the ruined Jerusalem was figuratively in despair, she had "none to comfort her" (Lam. 1:2, 9; cf. Nah. 3:7).

Consolation normally requires a personal visit or perhaps a letter (2 Sam. 10:1–2). The thoughtful comforter does not forget to offer food and drink (Jer. 16:7) or financial help (Job 42:11). In postbiblical literature, the rabbis detail the correct procedures for consolation and underscore its worth.

Even though well-intended, consolation may at times do more harm than good. Job's friends agree to go and sympathize with him (Job 2:11), but Job calls them "miserable comforters": All they offer him are long-winded speeches (16:2–3; 21:34). Although the three imagine their wisdom is "God's consolations" (15:11), Job remains nearly disconsolate (but see 6:10).

Despite the value of human sympathy, it is God who ultimately eases our sorrows. The psalms overflow with prayer and thanksgiving for the comfort that comes from God (23:4; 42:11; 71:20–21; 86:16–17; 94:18–19; 103:13–14; 147:3) and his Word (119:49–50; cf. Rom. 15:4). God intervenes even if all human help fails (Ps. 69:20). But supernatural comfort must be sought from God alone, not from idols or fortune-tellers (Zech. 10:2).

The "Consolation of Israel." The return of the Jews from exile is the work of divine consolation (Jer. 31:10–14; Zech. 1:12–13; cf. Exod. 3:7–8). Isaiah in particular emphasizes both literal and spiritual restoration: "Comfort, comfort my people" (40:1–2; 51:3; 52:9; 66:13).

It is this prophetic language that underlies Luke 2:25. Simeon is waiting for the "consolation of Israel." This phrase is linked with "the redemption of Jerusalem" (Luke 2:38; cf. 24:21) and "the kingdom of God" (Luke 23:51). This consolation involves the coming of the Messiah (Luke 2:26) and the revealing of salvation for all nations (Luke 2:29–32).

Consolation and the Kingdom of God. The New Testament assumes that the righteous will go to a place of comfort when they die (Luke 16:22, 25). The Messiah announces the coming of the eschatological kingdom, where the afflicted will find consolation (Matt. 5:4; Rev. 7:15–17). Christians may comfort each other by reflecting on the future resurrection (1 Thess. 4:18).

Christians also experience the comfort of God presently. Jesus does not leave his disciples "orphans" when he returns to heaven. The Holy Spirit will give comfort by communicating the love and power of the Father to his children (John 14:16–18).

Consolation as a Christian Duty. The New Testament gives no precise formula for consolation; it does direct Christians to "mourn with those who mourn" (Rom. 12:15; cf. Job 30:25). Because God constantly reassures his children, they are enabled to comfort others (2 Cor. 1:3–7; 7:6–7, 13). When Christians experience and then share the consolations of Christ, they are able to live together in unity (Phil. 2:1–2). Consolation was part of the apostolic ministry (Col. 2:2; 1 Thess. 2:10–12). Barnabas, Paul's traveling companion, must have been exemplary in this respect, since he was nicknamed "the son of consolation" (Acts 4:36, KJV). GARY STEVEN SHOGREN

See also COMFORT.

Bibliography. G. Braumann, *NIDNTT,* 1:569–71; R. Martin, *2 Corinthians;* O. Schmitz and G. Stählin, *TDNT,* 5:773–814; G. Stählin, *TDNT,* 5:816–23; M. R. Wilson, *TWOT,* 2:570–71.

Contribution. Contributions come in various forms in the Bible. They were designed in the Old Testament to support the poor and, in the New Testament, the needy saints of the church. Some were organized collections, while others were the offering of alms as expressions of acts of mercy or "acts of righteousness." The poor often collected such benefits directly from those who gave.

The Old Testament. Deuteronomy 15:7–11 states the basic principle behind contributions. God's people are not to be tight-fisted but must offer aid to others with open hands. One should lend to a needy brother for a pledge and should not refuse such a loan simply because the year of remission, a sabbatical year, is near. The illustration of such giving is found in Esther 9:22, where it is associated with the feast of Purim.

The Torah also exhorted the people of God to leave some of their harvest to be collected by the poor and the foreigner (Lev. 19:9–10; 23:22). In fact, the Mishnah, the written collection of Jewish oral tradition codified in the late second century A.D., devotes an entire tractate to how this contribution is handled. The "performing of righteousness" has no fixed measure (1:1). In fact, after the poor have their turn, anyone can take grain from what remains of the harvest (8:1). The amount of harvest contributed to this cause should be no less than one-sixtieth of the whole. In determining what was to be left, consideration was to be given to the size of the field, the number of the poor, and the extent of the yield (1:2). When Jesus' disciples plucked grain on the Sabbath, it was probably from such harvest leftovers (Luke 6:1–5). A clear Old Testament example of such a collection for widows and the poor is the story of Naomi and Ruth (Ruth 2:2–8).

Psalm 37:21, 26 calls upon the righteous person to give with generosity. This idea is stated negatively in Isaiah 10:1–2. Yet another prophet issues a call for true justice and compassion (Zech. 7:9–10). The issuing of alms for the needy is a part of this call.

In Judaism. The Old Testament clearly made a great impact on Judaism, since many texts address this theme. It is clear that such contributions to the poor were a reflection of piety and occupied a major place in Jewish thinking. Such care is said to extend to older parents (Sir. 3:14). It is seen to preserve one's reward before God, as one is urged to give without a grudging eye (Tobit 4:9–10; 14:11; Sir. 28:12; 40:17). Such giving atones for sin (Sir. 3:30—"like water on a blazing fire"; Tobit 12:8–9). Like prayer, one should not be weary of it (Sir. 7:10). Yet such giving, at least according to some Jews, should not go to sinners (12:3), but to the penniless (29:8). Such giving is seen as a commendable means of aid, better than having family (40:24). A picture of such an honorable figure is the Jewish portrait of Tobit (Tobit 1:16–17). When one realizes that such giving came on top of money set aside for tithes to maintain the temple and priesthood, it is clear that such contributions represented a reaching out to those in need with unconditional mercy.

The New Testament. As one turns to the New Testament, the discussion of alms continues. Jesus exhorted that such giving should occur in secret (Matt. 6:2–4) and is a reflection of discipleship (Matt. 12:33). The examples of a candidate for alms is the lame man of Acts 3, while exemplary almsgivers include Cornelius (Acts 10:2, 4, 31) and Paul (24:17). The motive here seems similar to Judaism, although one was to take care not to draw attention to oneself in the midst of such giving.

Paul states the principle for giving in Romans 12:8: those who give are called to do so liberally.

Three other Pauline texts fill in the details. First Corinthians 16:1–3 speaks of a collection Paul was taking to aid the needy in the Jewish Christian church in Palestine. He advises that the amount to be given should be set aside and stored, that giving should be according to how one has prospered, and that the collection should come with a letter of commendation. The letter shows that one guards the integrity of the contribution with care and accountability.

Second Corinthians 8–9 discusses another collection Paul made for the same purpose. He exhorts that it should be according to means (8:3). Such giving allows one to share in a work of grace (vv. 1–2). However, it should be done voluntarily, even cheerfully (9:7). Still, such a contribution is a test of service (v. 13).

First Timothy 6:6–10, 17–19 places the rich under a special responsibility to be generous. God's kindness to them should be expressed in being kind to others, storing up treasure in heaven, not earth.

Summary. The contribution of funds or other means of sustenance for those in need reflects caring, mercy, and piety. Since God is generous to us, we should be kind to others. That is why alms and other such contributions are called acts of mercy. DARRELL L. BOCK

See also COLLECTION; TITHE, TITHING.

Convert, Conversion. Although the term "conversion" is common in theological and religious discussion today, it was a relatively rare term in the Bible. In its current popular usage it refers to someone who has come to Christ or become a Christian. The biblical roots of the concept involve the use of two terms that mean "to turn" (Heb. *ṣûb;* Gk. *epistrephō*). However, the New Testament usage is more like the common theological meaning. Examples of conversion, outside the New Testament, emerge when one looks at the term "proselyte," the convert from a Gentile way of life to Judaism. Such an example pictures in everyday Greek terminology what a convert looked like.

The Old Testament. The concept of conversion is actually very rare in the Old Testament. The key term for "turning" is used in a variety of ways that really do not describe conversion. (1) It can refer to nations turning to God in the future (Isa. 19:22). (2) It can describe an Israelite returning to God or, negatively, failing to do so (Isa. 6:10; 31:6; Jer. 3:10, 12, 14, 22; Amos 4:6, 8, 10; Zech. 1:2–4). A good illustration of this force is Jeremiah 4:1–2, where the call is to return to God by letting go of idols. (3) Sometimes God is said to return to his people (Isa. 63:17; Amos 9:14). In the Old Testament the passage that comes closest to meaning "convert" is Isaiah 55:7. Here the wicked are called upon to turn to God for mercy and pardon of sin. Those who thirst are to come.

In Judaism. Technical terminology for turning does not occur here, but the example of the proselyte coming to Yahweh from Gentile origins does. Tobit 1:8 and 13:11 recognize the presence of such proselytes in the synagogue. The term for proselyte is the Hebrew term for "alien" (*ger*). Such proselytes would be circumcised, picture their cleansing by engaging in a baptismal washing, offer sacrifices, and would be expected to live a life of moral virtue in contrast to their pagan past. The outstanding picture of such a conversion is the pseudepigraphical story of *Joseph and Aseneth.*

The New Testament. In the New Testament conversion seems to summarize the call of the church in response to Jesus' commission to preach repentance for the forgiveness of sins to all the nations, as the Old Testament called for (Luke 24:43–47). In sum, conversion is a turning to embrace God. So on a few key occasions the concepts of repentance and turning appear together in Acts (3:19; 26:20). Repentance reflects the attitude one brings into conversion, while turning pictures the change of orientation and direction that comes as a part of it (9:35—turned to the Lord; 11:21—alongside a reference to belief; 14:15—turn from worthless things; 15:19—turn to God; 26:18—turn from darkness to light). This is often Luke's way of describing what Paul refers to as faith, although Paul can speak of "turning to God from idols" as well (1 Thess. 1:9–10). First Peter 2:25 uses the picture of coming to the great shepherd to express this idea. As one can see, the term can describe what one has turned from or can indicate to whom one turns.

Examples of converts appear throughout the Book of Acts, although the technical terminology is not present. Among such examples are Paul's change of direction at the Damascus road, Cornelius, the instant response of the Philippian jailer, and the picture of Lydia. DARRELL L. BOCK

See also REPENTANCE.

Corinthians, First and Second, Theology of. Many modern interpreters believe that eschatology, the doctrine of the endtimes, is the center of the apostle Paul's thought, beginning with his presupposition of the two-age structure. According to early Judaism, time is divided into two consecutive periods: this age and the age to come. The former is characterized by sin and suffering, due to Adam's fall. The latter will be implemented when the Messiah comes and, with him, righteousness and peace. In effect, the age to come is synonymous with the kingdom of God. But according to early Christianity, the life, death, and resurrection of Jesus Christ marked a paradigmatic shift resulting in the overlapping of the two ages. The age to come of the kingdom of God was inaugurated within this present age. In other words, the two ages are now coterminous, and the Christian lives in the intersection of the two. This idea is commonly referred to as the "already/not yet" eschatological tension. That is, the age to come has already dawned because of the first coming of Christ but it is not yet complete; completion awaits the second coming of Christ.

The rather common occurrence of *aeon* (age) terminology in Paul's writings indicates that this teaching provided the foundation for his theology. It can be demonstrated that such an idea—the overlapping of the two ages—is the key to understanding 1 and 2 Corinthians as well. In short, eschatology is the overarching theme through which these letters should be interpreted.

In tandem with the aforementioned eschatological frame of reference is another matter that contributes to the theology of 1 and 2 Corinthians: the nature of Paul's opposition at Corinth. The Corinthian church, while loved by Paul, nevertheless provided a constant source of frustration to his ministry. The Corinthians' infatuation with themselves undoubtedly originated from some sort of overrealized eschatology. The Corinthians apparently believed that the kingdom of God had fully come and that they, as saints, were already reigning and judging in it (4:5, 8). Viewing their possession of the Spirit and his attendant charismatic gifts to them as proof of the arrival of the eschaton (chaps. 12–14), nothing remained for them to do but to enjoy the blessings of freedom (cf. their eating of meat offered to idols [chaps. 8, 10]) and liberation from the body (manifested in such diverse aberrant behavior as libertinism [chaps. 5–6] and asceticism [chap. 7]). They probably believed that baptism magically associated them with Christ and the Spirit, and that the Lord's Supper protected them from all physical harm (chaps. 10–11). In essence, the Corinthians thought they had attained the status of the angels (hence their claim to speak in angelic language [chap. 13]; their sexual abstinence in marriage [chap. 7; cf. Luke 20:34]; the egalitarian attitudes toward males and females [cf. chaps. 11, 14 and the equal role of women in the worship services]; etc.).

By the time Paul wrote 2 Corinthians, the plot had thickened in his relationship with the Corinthian congregation. Whereas in 1 Corinthians Paul was dealing with basically an in-house problem, he now had to respond to his audience's demands to supply proof of his apostolic call (no doubt fueled by outside intruders who denied Paul's ministerial credentials). The primary criticism that Paul felt constrained to ward off in that letter was his opponents' denial of his apostleship because he lacked outward power and glory (see 2 Cor. 3:1–7:16; 10:13). They judged that his afflictions disqualified him from being a true apostle. In essence, Paul's opponents mistakenly believed that the age to come, with its visible glory and power, had fully arrived, leaving no place in their theology for the harsh reality of this present age. Second Corinthians seeks to correct that imbalance by holding the concept of the two ages together in dynamic tension.

Therefore, it can be argued that the overlapping of the two ages colors the major theological categories that occur in the Corinthian correspondences: theology, Christology, soteriology, pneumatology, and ecclesiology. The ensuing remarks address these five areas relative to the Pauline eschatological tension.

Theology (Proper). With regard to theology proper (the study of God) in 1 and 2 Corinthians, one of the major themes developed therein is the kingdom of God. The term "kingdom" (*basileia*) occurs five times in 1 Corinthians (4:20; 6:9–10 [twice]; 15:24, 50). The concept was dear to Jewish apocalyptic writers, believing as they did that this age could be remedied only by the kingdom of God or the age to come (see Isa. 40–66; Dan. 2:44; 1 Enoch 6–36, 83–90; Sib. Oracles 3:652–56; 2 Baruch 39–40; 4 Ezra 7; etc.). For Paul, the kingdom of God has already been inaugurated (1 Cor. 4:20; 15:24) by virtue of the cross and resurrection of Jesus (1:18–2:5; 15:1–22), but it is not yet complete (1 Cor. 6:9–10; 15:50). The idea of the kingdom of God in 1 and 2 Corinthians transcends the terminology. Paul speaks of two basic results of the inbreaking of God's kingdom into this age: (1) the formation of God's people; (2) the defeat of the enemies of God. Both of these consequences are stamped by the already/not yet eschatology tension.

The Formation of God's People. One of the clearcut signs that the kingdom of God has come to earth is the formation of the church, the new people of God (1 Cor. 1:2; 2 Cor. 1:1). This group is identified by Paul, among other things, as the "saints" (1 Cor. 1:2; 2 Cor. 1:1). Both names, "church" and "saints," recall the nomenclature of the Old Testament people of God, the Jews, and signify that New Testament believers represented the reconstruction of spiritual Israel (cf. Rom. 2:28–29; Gal. 6:16; 1 Peter 2:9–10; etc.). Christians are indeed a kingdom of priests unto God. Furthermore, believers have been called into fellowship with God through his Son, Jesus (1 Cor. 1:9; 15:23–28; cf. Col. 1:12–13; etc.), undoubtedly a reference reflecting Paul's belief that Jesus' resurrection began the long-awaited messianic kingdom. In fact, Christians have already begun to reign in Christ's spiritual kingdom, and therefore should act accordingly (1 Cor. 6:2–3). Moreover, the formation of God's new covenant people in Christ (2 Cor. 3:1–18) is nothing less than a new creation (2 Cor. 5:17).

However, the new people of God are not yet complete; their perfection awaits the return of Christ. Their present struggle with sin attests to that stark reality (1 Cor. 6:9-10) as does the futurity of their resurrection bodies (1 Cor. 15:50).

The Defeat of God's Enemies. The second basic result of the inbreaking of God's kingdom into this age by the Christ-event is the defeat of the divine enemies. Jewish and Christian apocalyptic writers believed that the arrival of God's rule on earth would be marked by the defeat of the anti-God forces (see Ezek. 38–39; Dan. 7; 2 Thess. 2; Rev. 20; etc.). According to the Corinthian letters, that demise was initiated with the first advent of Christ. With his death on the cross and resurrection from the grave, the wisdom of this age, with its propensity to disobey God, has begun to pass away (1 Cor. 1:29; cf. 7:29–30). The same is the case for the rulers of this age (1 Cor. 2:6), however one may define those misinformed culprits (as demons, rulers, or, more likely, both; the former energizing the latter). As a result, Christ, through his servants like Paul, is leading the enemies of God as captives, parading their collapse (2 Cor. 2:14–18; cf. Col. 2:15) and destroying their spiritual stronghold by the word of his power (2 Cor. 10:3–6).

But it would be a tragic mistake to assume that the enemies of God are a banished foe. According to Paul, they are still alive and operative in the affairs of humans, blinding the minds of unbelievers (2 Cor. 4:3–4) and, if possible, even Christians (1 Cor. 10:20–21; 2 Cor. 6:14–18; 11:13–14). And still the greatest of God's enemies—death—remains at large (1 Cor. 15:25–27, 53–56). Nevertheless, the evil triumvirate (sin, the devil, death) is a conquered foe, whose fate is secure. The cross and resurrection of Christ spelled their defeat; the parousia (the second coming of Christ) will seal their doom. The former was like D-Day, the latter will be V-Day.

Christology. Perhaps the dominant christological perspective operative in 1 and 2 Corinthians is that Jesus the Messiah, by his death on the cross and resurrection from the grave, has effected the shift of the two ages. The first coming of Christ inaugurated the age to come. This is the "already" side of the Pauline eschatological tension. However, the age to come is "not yet" culminated; it exists within the context of this present age, which will be consummated only at the parousia. We delineate that twofold motif by taking note of the following pertinent passages.

According to 1 Corinthians 1:18–25, the cross was the turning point of the ages. Jesus' death, and subsequent resurrection, was the means by which God began the process of dismantling this present age (cf. 1 Cor. 2:6–8). Although the crucifixion of Jesus is nonsense and the epitome of weakness to the non-Christian, it is the wisdom and power of God to those who are being saved.

First Corinthians 10:11 continues the thought that Christ's death and resurrection inaugurated the age to come when it describes Christians as the ones "on whom the fulfillment of the ages has come." The catalyst for this inbreaking of the age to come was the sacrificial death of Christ (1 Cor. 10:16; cf. 5:7; 11:23–25; 2 Cor. 8:9). Paul expands on this theme in 1 Corinthians 15:3–4 which, in the context of the chapter, attests to the truth that Christ's death and resurrection have brought about several endtime blessings for Christians: (1) The general resurrection of the endtime has been projected back into the present period in the resurrection of Christ, the firstfruits of the dead (15:12–22). (2) The future messianic kingdom in which Jews expected to reign over their enemies on earth is now being actualized through Christ's heavenly session and shared by believers (vv. 23–28). (3) The hope for eschatological glory now resides in the Christian's heart which is proleptic of heavenly existence (vv. 41–57). (4) The promise of the bestowal of the Spirit on all God's people in the age to come (Ezek. 36:25–28; Joel 2:28–32; etc.) is currently being dispensed through Christ, the "life-giving Spirit," who is the "last" (*eschaton*) "Adam" (v. 45). The same basic point in made in 2 Corinthians 5:15–17, where Paul boldly announces that Jesus' death/resurrection has implemented a new creation, the controlling ethic of which is love for others. A similar statement occurs in 2 Corinthians 3:1–4:6. Using the metaphor of the new covenant, Paul asserts that the new dispensation that is based on Christ's death and resurrection has brought eternal glory to the hearts of Christians (cf. 1 Cor. 15:11–22, 42–49), who now must spread that message to others.

However, it will only be at the second coming of Christ that the age to come will be finalized. At that time the present, invisible glorious reign of Christ in heaven will be made visible on earth (1 Cor. 11:26; 16:22); such an event will cause the invisible glory within Christians to shine forth, transfiguring their earthly bodies (1 Cor. 15:50–57; 2 Cor. 4:16–5:10). Only at the parousia will that which is "perfect" arrive (1 Cor. 13:10). Thus, even Christ himself, according to the Corinthian letters, lives in the interfacing of the two ages, between his first and second advents.

Soteriology. We encounter in 1 and 2 Corinthians a certain amount of ambiguity concerning Paul's concept of salvation, which can be explained by the overlapping of the two ages. According to the apostle, the person who is in Christ is saved (the age to come is already present) but that salvation is not complete (the age to come is not yet consummated). Three terms, in particular, call for comment in this regard: salvation (*sōterios*), sanctification (*hagios*), and glory (*doxa*). These three words are salvific in import and impacted by the eschatological tension.

The first term, "salvation," is scattered throughout the Corinthian epistles. In a number of occurrences its setting is patently eschatological in import. In 1 Corinthians 1:18–31 Paul delineates the mixed reaction Christians receive. Because they have embraced the cross of Christ they have become members of the age to come and accordingly are experiencing the blessing of salvation (cf. 7:16; 9:22; 10:33; cf. Rom. 1:16). Since their faith is in Christ, they are divinely approved and participate in the wisdom and power of God. But, at the same time, Christians are still inhabitants of this age, and therefore their allegiance to the cross evokes the displeasure of non-Christians; to the latter the gospel is but foolishness and weakness.

The term "save" also occurs in 1 Corinthians 9:22 with reference to those who embrace Christ (cf. 2 Cor. 2:15). They are the ones upon whom the "fulfillment of the ages has come" (10:11) and yet their salvation is not finalized (1 Cor. 9:24–10:13). The downward pull of this age threatens to dilute their loyalty to God and thus tempt them to repeat ancient Israel's mistakes (10:1–10). Paul, too, feels threatened by the temptations of this world (9:24–27), which are the common lot of all believers (10:12–13). Nevertheless God is faithful to deliver all who rely on him (10:13).

The already/not yet tension is at work in two other key texts on salvation in the Corinthian letters. In 1 Corinthians 15:1–2 Paul reminds his audience that their salvation is based on the gospel, "the gospel . . . which you received. . . . By this gospel you are saved." However, that salvation is dependent on the Corinthians holding fast to the gospel. Otherwise their belief will be in vain. A similar statement is found in 2 Corinthians 6:2, where Paul announces that the day of salvation has arrived. Nevertheless the Christians at Corinth can forfeit that gift by failing to receive Paul as the apostle of grace (2 Cor. 6:1–7:2). On the positive side, their repentance toward God and acceptance of his servant Paul will sustain their salvation (cf. 7:10).

The second term in 1 and 2 Corinthians possessing salvific content is "sanctification," a word that means to set apart for holiness. On the one hand, the Corinthians (and all believers for that matter) are sanctified or set apart for God in Christ (1 Cor. 1:2, 30; 6:11 [cf. 3:16–17]). However, notwithstanding their exalted position as saints (1:2), the fact that the Corinthians still lived in this present age (1 Cor. 3:18) embroiled them in a deep-seated struggle with sin. The result was a long list of unsanctimonious behavior on their part, including division (1 Cor. 1:10–17); carnality (1 Cor. 3:1–15); the approval of immorality (1 Cor. 5:1–13), even to the point of engaging in it themselves (1 Cor. 6:16–18; cf. 7:2); litigation (1 Cor. 6:1–8); and the improper use of Christian liberty (1 Cor. 8:1–13). If the Corinthians persisted in these forbidden activities, they could jeopardize their salvation (1 Cor. 6:9–10; cf. 2 Cor. 13:5). The cure for their struggle was to glorify God in their bodies (1 Cor. 6:19–20), though sin will continue to wage spiritual holy war with them (and all Christians) until the age to come is fully realized.

The third related soteriological term in 1 and 2 Corinthians is "glory." For the apostle Paul, the death and glorious resurrection of Jesus Christ inaugurated the glory of the age to come (1 Cor. 15:42–49). This is clear from passages like 2 Corinthians 3:1–4:6 and 4:16 (cf. Rom. 8:17–30; Col. 3:4; etc.). However, this glory resides in the Christian's heart (2 Cor. 3:18; 4:6); it has not yet transformed the body. That event awaits the parousia (see 1 Cor. 15:50–56; 2 Cor. 5:1–5). In the meantime, because Christians continue to live in this evil age, they will share in the sufferings of this life (2 Cor. 1:1–22). Paul, too, suffers for righteousness' sake and in the service of his Lord in this present world (1 Cor. 4:9–13; 15:30–32; 2 Cor. 4:7–15; 6:3–10; 11:23–33; 12:7–10). Rather than negating Paul's credentials as an apostle, afflictions validate his call to the ministry. On the contrary, those who emphasize exterior glory and look upon suffering with chagrin, thinking that Christians are "divine men" displaying miraculous signs and wonders, are actually the false apostles (see 2 Cor. 5:12; 11:13–15). But according to the apostle Paul, because believers live at the juncture of the two ages, they possess the glory in their hearts while simultaneously suffering in their bodies.

Pneumatology. Paul's teaching on the Spirit is thoroughly eschatological in perspective. According to Paul and the early church, the Spirit is the sign par excellence that the age to come has arrived. The Corinthian correspondence associates three ideas with the Spirit: wisdom, the temple of God, and spiritual gifts.

Wisdom. First Corinthians 2:1–16 intimately associates wisdom and the Spirit. The wisdom of God was understood by Jewish apocalyptic writers to be the manifestation of the divine plan to holy men of God and, as such, was related to the idea of "mystery." That disclosure of truth was itself a proleptic experience of the age to come (Dan. 9:20–12:13; 1 Enoch 63:2, 32; 48:1, 49; 4 Ezra 14:25, 38–40; 2 Baruch 54:13; Rev. 4–22). Similarly for Paul, Christians, because they possess the Spirit, share in God's wisdom and understand the divine mystery of the ages (cf. 1 Cor. 2:1–16 with Rom. 11:25–36; Eph. 1:15–23; 3:14–21; Col. 2:9–29). However, the Corinthians, despite having the wisdom of the Spirit, nevertheless continue to live in this age. Consequently, they are enamored with its "wisdom," contrary to the will of God though it is (1 Cor. 1:20; 2:6; 3:18).

The Temple of God. Although God's dwelling with and among the people of Israel is a pervasive theme in the Old Testament, Israel is never identified with God's temple. Such an identification was relegated to the anticipated age to come (Isa. 28:16; Ezek. 40–48; Jub. 1:18; 4QFlor.; 1 Enoch 91:13; etc.). Therefore, for Paul to announce that the Christian and the church now constitute the temple of God's Spirit was nothing short of an eschatological pronouncement—the temple of the endtimes had arrived (see 1 Cor. 3:16; 6:19–20; 2 Cor. 6:16–18). A related concept to the temple of God is found in 2 Corinthians 1:22 and 5:5—the Spirit is the earnest of the resurrection body (cf. Rom. 8:23; Eph. 1:14).

Nevertheless, the Spirit is not the full payment but a reminder that the present bodies of believers, temples though they are, are frail and mortal, and therefore only the guarantee of the future, glorious resurrection. This point was one that the Corinthians needed to hear because, in their newfound enthusiasm over the Spirit, their tendency was to assume that the kingdom of God had fully arrived and that they had already received the resurrection body in this age (see 1 Cor. 4:8; 15:12–28). More than that, the Corinthians' mimicking of the "spirit" of this evil age tended to belie the truth that they were the temple of God's Holy Spirit: they divided, and thereby were destroying it (1 Cor. 3:12–17); they joined themselves to harlots, thereby defiling God's temple (1 Cor. 6:15–18); and, in general, they subjected it to idolatry (2 Cor. 6:14–18).

Spiritual Gifts. Spiritual gifts serve as visible proof that the Spirit indwells believers and, as such, are a sign that the age to come has dawned. Each of the gifts in 1 and 2 Corinthians can be understood eschatologically. Prophecy was expected to be renewed among God's people when the Spirit comes (cf. 1 Cor. 14 with Ps. 74:9; Lam. 2:9; Joel 2:28–32). We have already noted the apocalyptic flavor of wisdom (cf. also knowledge). The gifts of teaching and preaching were also eschatologically oriented by virtue of the content of their message, which was the kerygma, the basis of which was that the age to come has dawned (cf. 1 Cor. 12:28 with Acts 2–3). The gift of discernment of spirits served the purpose of distinguishing truth from error in the last days (cf. 1 Cor. 12:10, 29 with 1 Tim. 4:1; 2 Tim. 4:1–5). Tongues and interpretation of tongues were associated by Paul and the Corinthians with the proleptic restoration of paradise, especially in the worship setting of the church. The gifts of faith (1 Cor. 12:9; 13:2), miracles (1 Cor. 12:10, 28), and healings (1 Cor. 12:9, 28) continued the powerful ministry of Jesus through his church, and signaled the invasion of the earth by the messianic kingdom. Finally, the gifts of helps (1 Cor. 12:28) and administration (1 Cor. 12:28) provided the needed support and leadership of the people of God in the last days, respectively. However, for Paul the *charismata* are not an end in themselves. Gifts are only a means to the end, the end being love, the eternal ethic of the age to come.

Ecclesiology. The word used by Paul and the early Christians for the messianic community of believers is *ekklēsia*. The term probably corresponds to the Old Testament word, *qāhāl,* with reference to the Christian community as the continuation of Israel, the people of God. The Corinthian letters affirm this fundamental perception of Paul that the church is yet another sign that the age to come has already dawned, though it is not yet complete. Five aspects of the church illustrate this truth: the metaphor for the church (the body of Christ), the sacraments of the church, the worship of the church, the offering of the church, and the status of the members of the church.

The dominant metaphor for the church in 1 and 2 Corinthians is the body of Christ. Paul's primary usage of the metaphor is to demonstrate the interrelatedness of diversity and unity within the community of believers. If, as a number of scholars believe, the person of Adam in particular and the Hebrew concept of corporate personality in general inform the metaphor, then the eschatological nuance is thereby heightened. The body of Christ can be seen, then, to be the eschatological Adam (1 Cor. 15:45), the new humanity of the endtime that has appeared in history. Yet it is obvious from Paul's comments to the Corinthian church that it continues to exist in this age. Its inconsistent behavior and incomplete growth attest to that fact.

According to 1 and 2 Corinthians, the sacraments of the church are twofold: baptism and the Lord's Supper. The former marks the entrance into the kingdom of God and the age to come, but it does not magically prevent believers from being judged for their disobedience. The latter symbolizes the passion of Jesus and probably adumbrates the future messianic banquet. But neither does it ward off divine judgment for those whose lives disrupt the unity of the church.

The worship of the church in 1 and 2 Corinthians, as we noted earlier, centers around the community's usage of the gifts of the Spirit (1 Cor. 12–14), which is a foretaste of the restoration of paradise. But the Corinthians' confusion and misuse of the spectacular gifts like tongues is a stark reminder that the age to come is not complete; the perfect has not yet come (1 Cor. 13:9–13).

It may be that the church's giving also possesses eschatological significance for Paul. His collection of the Gentile offering for the purpose of ministering to the Jewish believers in Jerusalem (1 Cor. 16; 2 Cor. 8–9; cf. Rom. 15:16–33) may well have been intended by him to be the catalyst for initiating the nation's pilgrimage to Zion, predicted in the Old Testament and in Judaism, signaling the endtimes. Nevertheless Paul was also aware that that eventuality may be delayed (cf. 1 Cor. 15:50–58 with 1 Cor. 16:1–4).

Finally, the status of Christians as portrayed in 1 and 2 Corinthians is also stamped by the already/not yet eschatological tension. Because the age to come has dawned, and with it the passing away of the present age (1 Cor. 7:29–31), there is spiritual equality among Christians regarding gender (1 Cor. 11:11–12) and social freedom (1 Cor. 7:17–24). Nevertheless, because this age continues to exert its influence, there is still hierarchical structure and authority concerning male and female relationships (1 Cor. 11:1–11; 14:34–35) and the roles of master and slave (1 Cor. 7:20–24).

C. MARVIN PATE

See also PAUL THE APOSTLE.

Bibliography. F. L. Arrington, *Paul's Aeon Theology in 1 Corinthians;* J. C. Beker, *Paul the Apostle: The Triumph of God in Life and Thought;* R. E. Brown, *The Semitic Background of the Term "Mystery" in the New Testament;* W. D. Davies, *Paul and Rabbinic Judaism;* G. D. Fee, *The First Epistle to the Corinthians;* G. E. Ladd, *A Theology of the New Testament;* A. T. Lincoln, *Paradise Now and Not Yet: Studies in the Role of the Heavenly Dimension in Paul's Thought with Special Reference to His Eschatology;* C. M. Pate, *The Glory of Adam and the Afflictions of the Righteous. Pauline Suffering in Context;* H. Ridderbos, *Paul: An Outline of His Theology;* A. C. Thiselton, *NTS* 24 (1978): 510–26; A. J. M. Wedderburn, *Baptism and Resurrection. Studies in Pauline Theology Against Its Graeco-Roman Background.*

Cornerstone. Architectural term used twice in the New Testament (Eph. 2:20; 1 Peter 2:6) to speak of the exalted Jesus as the chief foundation stone of the church, the cornerstone on which all the building depends. The New Testament draws on two Old Testament passages about the coming Messiah (Isa. 28:16; Zech. 10:4). In Isaiah 28:16 the prophet speaks God's words directly to the rulers in Jerusalem who boasted that they were immune to the scourges of life because they were secure in themselves. God said their security was false because he would lay a stone in Zion, a precious cornerstone, which really was secure—and it was not those present rulers. Zechariah expands this promise by saying that the cornerstone will come from the tribe of Judah (10:4). Paul builds on this concept in Ephesians 2:20 by saying that Jesus Christ is the chief cornerstone, the apostles and prophets are foundation stones, and the whole building (the church) is a holy temple in the Lord. Peter's use of the idea is more complex, stringing three prophetic verses together (Ps. 118:22; Isa. 8:4; 28:16). The stone laid in Zion (Isa. 28:16) is precious to the believer, but as the stone placed at the "head of the corner" (*eis kephalēn gōnias*), that is, exalted (Ps. 118:22), he is a stone of offense and stumbling (Isa. 8:4) to those who refuse to believe. The metaphor seems obvious: the cornerstone is either a source of blessing or judgment, depending on a person's attitude toward it. Some modern interpreters, beginning with J. Jeremias in 1925, take a different tack, separating the two stones and making the cornerstone one thing and the stone at the "head of the corner" another, that is, a capstone or keystone. It is hard to visualize one stumbling over a capstone, but metaphors can be stretched. In any case, the point is that the very foundation of the church is Jesus Christ. This was prophesied by the prophets of old and fulfilled through the incarnation. Those who believe are blessed and those who stumble over that rock chosen by God are condemned.

WALTER A. ELWELL

See also CAPSTONE; CHURCH, THE.

Bibliography. J. Jeremias, *TDNT,* 1:791–93; H. Kramer, *Exegetical Dictionary of the New Testament,* pp. 267–69; R. J. McKelvey, *NTS* 8 (1961–62): 352–59.

Counselor. ***Old Testament Significance.*** The Old Testament counselor served to advise the king on such matters as national defense and plans for war (1 Kings 12:6–14; 2 Chron. 22:5). At times, however, this advisory capacity was granted to others (2 Chron. 22:3). David employed certain advisors or counselors in his court, including Ahithophel, Jehoida, and Jonathan (1 Chron. 27:32). That counselors occupied a strategic place in ancient governments is evident from Ezra 4:5; 7:14; 8:25; Isaiah 3:3; 19:11.

Metaphorically, God is identified as a counselor (Pss. 16:7; 32:8; 33:11; 73:24). God's Word serves as a counselor (Ps. 119:24). Isaiah presents a series of rhetorical questions that emphasize the fact that God needs no human counselors (40:13). The Creator God described his Messiah as "Wonderful Counselor" (Isa. 9:6).

Johannine Significance. In the Johannine writings the theological significance of the usage of "counselor" comes to the forefront. The ascended Christ is seen as a counselor or advocate in God's heavenly court (1 John 2:1). The resurrected and exalted Christ sent the Holy Spirit to his people (John 16:7) to actualize the presence of Jesus and reveal him to the disciples (John 14:16).

The term "counselor" is a translation of *paraklētos,* a favorite expression of John. It designates a function rather than the nature of something. The function of the *paraklētos* is to counsel, assist, advise, or support. The coming of the Spirit as counselor marks a new stage in redemptive history. The Spirit is called "another paraclete" because he comes to continue and universalize the ministry of Jesus (John 15:26). While being other than Jesus, the Spirit dwells in the followers of Jesus, like Jesus dwelt among and with believers (John 14:16–17).

The Counselor, the Spirit of truth, teaches and reminds believers regarding the things of Jesus Christ. This teaching and this reminding are done in close connection with Jesus, just as Jesus had carried out his mission in conjunction with the Father. The Paraclete leads believers into all truth and presents this truth in light of the resurrection. The Spirit, who defended the disciples in the Synoptics (see Mark 13:11), is the defender of the truth about Jesus in John.

Thus, the Holy Spirit, the Counselor and Comforter, does not leave the disciples desolate, but represents Jesus to them. To experience the Counselor is to experience Jesus (John 14:16–28). One cannot know Jesus unless enabled by the Paraclete. One cannot know the Counselor by any means other than belief in and submission to Jesus Christ. DAVID S. DOCKERY

See also HOLY SPIRIT.

Covenant. The word "covenant," infrequently heard in conversation, is quite commonly used in legal, social (marriage), and religious and theological contexts.

The Idea of Covenant. The term "covenant" is of Latin origin (*con venire*), meaning a coming together. It presupposes two or more parties who come together to make a contract, agreeing on promises, stipulations, privileges, and responsibilities. In religious and theological circles there has not been agreement on precisely what is to be understood by the biblical term. It is used variously in biblical contexts. In political situations, it can be translated treaty; in a social setting, it means a lifelong friendship agreement; or it can refer to a marriage.

The biblical words most often translated "covenant" are *berît* in the Old Testament (appearing about 280 times) and *diathēkē* in the New Testament (at least 33 times). The origin of the Old Testament word has been debated; some have said it comes from a custom of eating together (Gen. 26:30; 31:54); others have emphasized the idea of cutting an animal (an animal was cut in half [Gen. 15:18]); still others have seen the ideas of perceiving or determining as root concepts. The preferred meaning of this Old Testament word is bond; a covenant refers to two or more parties bound together. This idea of bond will be explicated more fully.

The New Testament word for covenant has usually been translated as covenant, but testimony and testament have also been used. This Greek word basically means to order or dispose for oneself or another. The though of the inequality of the parties is latent.

The generally accepted idea of binding or establishing a bond between two parties is supported by the use of the term *berît*. When Abimelech and Isaac decided to settle their land dispute, they made a binding agreement, league, or covenant to live in peace. An oath confirmed it (Gen. 26:26–31). Joshua and the Gibeonites bound themselves, by oath, to live in peace together (Josh. 9:15), although Yahweh commanded that Israel was not to bind themselves to the people living in the land of Canaan (Deut. 7:2; Judg. 2:2). Solomon and Hiram made a binding agreement to live and work in peace together (1 Kings 5:12). A friendship bond was sealed by oath between David and Jonathan (1 Sam. 20:3, 16–17). Marriage is a bond (covenant) for life.

The covenants referred to above were between two equal parties; this means that the covenant relationship was bilateral. The bond was sealed by both parties vowing, often by oath, that each, having equal privileges and responsibilities, would carry out their assigned roles. Because a covenant confirmed between two human parties was bilateral, some scholars have concluded that the covenant Yahweh established with human beings is also bilateral. This is not the case. God initiated, determined the elements, and confirmed his covenant with humanity. It is unilateral. Persons are recipients, not contributors; they are not expected to offer elements to the bond; they are called to accept it as offered, to keep it as demanded, and to receive the results that God, by oath, assures will not be withheld.

Scholars have learned by studying tablets found by archaeologists that legal treaties between kings (suzerains) and subjects (vassals) existed during the time of the biblical patriarchs, Moses, Joshua, the judges, and the first kings of Israel. These treaties were written on tablets for the purpose of establishing a continuing relationship as determined and authorized by the suzerain. Once written, the covenants were not to be altered or annulled although parts could be explicated or elaborated. Did biblical writers borrow the idea of the covenant and its integral elements from pagan sources when the Old Testament was written—elements such as a self-presentation of the suzerain and his activities, including those done on behalf of the vassals, statements of intent, stipulations, and assurances of well-being if obedient and of curses if disobedient? The legal covenants included provisions for continuity, with emphasis on the suzerain's claim to vassals' children, and were confirmed by an oath or a special ratification ceremony, like the cutting in half of an ox or cow or the sharing of a meal as the conclusion of the act of covenanting.

These nonbiblical covenants were intended to serve a number of purposes, two of which are especially important to understand. The suzerain stated that as victor and lord over the vassals he had spared them in battle, delivered them from extenuating circumstances, and placed them in situations of life and well-being. This was an undeserved favor. The suzerain's covenant was also intended to serve an administrative function. It informed the vassals how the king would govern them and what they were to do in obedient response to him. These two purposes, the reminder of deliverance and the information on administration of affairs in daily life, appear in Yahweh God's covenanting with his people but in radically different ways.

Covenants, neither suzerain-vassal nor biblical, were not made (nor did they function) in a vacuum. Covenants presupposed a king, a domain, a way of life, people, and often mediating servants. The covenant was an important administrative means within a kingdom.

Did biblical writers borrow from pagan sources when they wrote about Yahweh God's covenantal activities on behalf of and his relationships with his people? There is no reference of any kind in the Bible that this was done. There are marked similarities between biblical and the nonbiblical covenants. The most satisfactory and acceptable position is that Yahweh God is the source and originator of the entire covenant concept and phenomenon. He included the covenant relationship in his creation activity and handiwork. Covenant is germane to human life; it is God-implanted and -unfolded. Pagan kings gave concrete expression, in their proud and self-sufficient attitudes, to what Yahweh God had implanted and maintained within his created cosmos. This explanation calls for an answer to three important questions. When did Yahweh God first establish his covenant? What was the nature of that initial covenant? According to biblical revelation, did Yahweh God, after the initial one, establish any more covenants?

The Old Testament. The Hebrew word for covenant does not appear in Genesis 1–5. Some scholars say that this is evidence that there was no covenant in humankind's earliest history. Some say that the idea of covenant arose initially in the minds of the Israelites after they had been at Mount Sinai. To account for references to the covenant in the Noahic and patriarchal accounts, scholars have incorrectly said that later editors of Genesis inserted the idea of covenant to give historical evidence and credence to what Israel later believed. Other scholars, who accept Genesis as a record of Yahweh's revelation, also have difficulty accepting that God established his covenant when he created the cosmos mainly because of the lack of direct verbal reference to it.

Biblical testimony points to the fact that God covenanted when he created. Hosea (6:7) refers to Adam breaking the covenant. Jeremiah spoke of the covenant of the day and the night that no one can alter (33:19–20); this covenant is understood to have been initiated in creation when God separated light from darkness and gave the sun and moon their appointed place and role (Gen. 1:3–5, 14). When Yahweh God first spoke to Noah, he said he was going to wipe humankind from the face of the earth (Gen. 6:7). But he assured Noah he would uphold and cause his covenant to continue. Hence Noah did not have to fear that God's plan for and method of administering his cosmic kingdom would be different after the flood. But why, if God covenanted when he created, is the word "covenant" not in Genesis 1–2? Those who wish to speak of only the covenant of grace, referred to briefly and indirectly in the Noahic account (Gen. 6–9), believe that some of the basic elements of the covenant of grace were enunciated when Yahweh God promised victory through the woman's seed (Gen. 3:14–16). When Yahweh God covenanted with David, according to 2 Samuel 7, the term "covenant" does not appear but when David referred to what Yahweh had said and done, he said, "Has he not made with me an everlasting covenant?" (2 Sam. 23:5; cf. Ps. 89:3). As the elements included in covenant were present in the account of the covenanting with David (2 Sam. 7), so the elements constituting covenant are recorded in Genesis 1–2.

The basic elements of a covenant are imbedded in the Genesis account. God, in his revelation of creation, presented himself as the Creator. The historical record of what he has done was outlined. He created his image-bearers by means of which he placed and kept man and woman in a close relationship with himself and had them mirror (reflect) and represent him within the created cosmos. Humanity was given stipulations or mandates. As image-bearers they were to maintain an intimate and obedient fellowship with their Creator; the Sabbath was to enhance this. Humanity was to be fruitful, multiply, and fill the earth; this was to be done by establishing families; a man was to leave his parents and cleave to his wife (Gen. 2:24). Becoming one flesh, they would have children. As families increased, community would be formed. This social mandate thus was an integral aspect of covenant. So was the cultural mandate; man and woman were to cultivate (subdue NIV) and rule over the creation. When God saw all that he had done, he confirmed, not by expressing an oath or performing a ratifying ceremony, but by declaring all to be very good (Gen. 1:31). This he confirmed by ceasing from creating activity and establishing the seventh day as a day of rest, sanctity, and blessing (Gen. 2:1–3).

Yahweh God did more; he spoke of assured blessings. God blessed Adam and Eve; he thus gave them ability and authority to serve as his covenant agents. He provided for their sustenance (Gen. 1:28–30). He also spoke of the possibility of disobedience, if they ate of the forbidden tree of knowledge of good and evil (Gen. 2:17). The ideas of blessing (life) and curse (death) thus were also included. The forbidding of eating has been referred to as the probationary command but also as the integral aspect of "the covenant of works." An increasing number of biblical students and scholars have come to consider, on the basis of biblical testimony, that it is preferable to speak of the covenant of creation and that what was considered to constitute the "covenant of works" is but an integral part of the covenant of creation.

Yahweh's covenant agents were tempted by Satan. They doubted Yahweh's words; they accepted the lie. They fell. They broke the covenantal relationship between Yahweh and themselves. Creation was affected, for it too suffered the consequences of Adam and Eve's sin. It too began to groan (Rom. 8:22). But Yahweh did not break his covenant with creation and his vicegerents. He came to the fallen, shamed, and humiliated image-bearers and set about restoring humanity to fellowship with and service for him. Yahweh, graciously maintaining his mandates, revealed that Adam and Eve could still work under them. Spiritual fellowship was restored by Yahweh's assurance that the woman's seed would be victorious over Satan and his seed. The social mandate was maintained; Adam and Eve as one flesh would have offspring, but pain would be suffered. The cultural mandate was still to be obeyed, but it would cause labor and sweat. All the elements of the creation covenant remained. Then Yahweh added another dimension to this covenantal relationship. He pronounced in germinal form his plan for the full redemption and restoration of his image-bearers and their royal, priestly, and prophetic roles with their attendant privileges and responsibilities. Yahweh revealed how this was to be done by adding to his creation covenant the redemptive and restorative promises and implied stipulations of faith and obedience. He established what has been widely known as the covenant of grace.

Misunderstanding must be avoided. God has established an all-embracing binding relationship (covenant) with his creation, of which humanity is the central establishment of a second covenant within the context and framework of the creation covenant. As Yahweh God continued revealing himself, and how the redemptive/restorative "second covenant" was to be administered, it was always done with the context and framework of the creation covenant. Because the covenant of grace received direct and fuller "divine attention" as Yahweh God revealed his kingdom plan, goal, and certain consummation, many biblical students and scholars have concentrated their attention on it, failing to see, understand, or believe its position and role within the context and framework of the creation covenant that Yahweh certainly maintained and continues to maintain as he carries out and fulfills his plan and goal for his ever enduring kingdom.

Genesis 6–9 presents Noah as a faithful covenant man. In the midst of a very sinful, corrupt society, which God determined to wipe out, Noah lived obediently. Socially, he had one wife and three sons; he was blameless, so that others could not accuse him of wrongdoing. Spiritually he was in constant fellowship with God. He walked with God and was righteous; he lived according to God's will (6:9–10; 7:1). When commanded to build the ark, he proved to be a capable servant in the cultural dimension of life (6:14–16; 7:5). Yahweh assured Noah that his covenant of creation and its correlate, the covenant of gracious redemption and restoration, would be maintained with him and his family (6:18). After the flood had removed corrupt society and then receded, Noah the covenant man worshiped; he built an altar and sacrificed. Yahweh responded to Noah's worship and determined to continue his relationship with the cosmos (8:20–9:17). Parts of the creation covenant mandates were repeated; some were explicated. In confirming his creation covenant with humanity, God said every living creature was included (9:9–10); God included the death penalty for murder (9:5–6), and meat as legitimate food for humanity (9:2–3). This assurance concerning the continuity of the creation covenant certainly includes the implication that Yahweh would continue his gracious redemptive/restorative covenant. This continuity would be worked out particularly with Shem, blessed by Yahweh to serve as the builder of the tent that even Ham's offspring, Canaan, would enter. Japheth's offspring would benefit from it and enlarge it. Thus, Yahweh God maintained and explicated his covenant with Noah and his offspring.

After Yahweh God had given absolute assurance to Noah and his sons that the creation covenant would continue, there are not many direct references to it again. But its presence and role are constantly and consistently present.

Yahweh, revealing himself as the Sovereign One to Abram, gave him covenantal promises: spiritual well-being, making a great nation of him, making him famous, and using him as a channel of blessing to all peoples. Yahweh added to the assurances of blessings the certainty of the curse on despisers and rejectors of Abram and his sovereign God.

The process of God's covenanting with Abram was unfolded throughout the course of Abram's life. When Abram was afraid after his separation from and rescue of Lot (Gen. 13–14), Yahweh assured Abram of his abiding presence and protection for him (shield) and of the blessed spiritual future Yahweh had for him (great reward, Gen. 15:1). Abram realized his great future included children; he inquired about this. Yahweh assured him he would have many (Gen. 15:5). In this way the continuity of the covenant was assured. An added promise was given: that he would possess the land (15:7). A covenant ratification ceremony was performed in a vision to Abram in which the blessing of peace for Abram and a curse (punishment) was pronounced on those enslaving covenantal seed (15:12–21). Genesis 15 includes covenantal elements: (1) Yahweh's sovereign presence; (2) Abram's assured rich future; (3) continuity through much seed; (4) a place to live and serve in the midst of the nations; (5) a curse on opponents of the blessed; and (6) the response of faith and blessing of justification.

The covenanting process continued after Abram sinfully followed Sarai's suggestion to take Hagar the Egyptian maid as a concubine (Gen. 16). Yahweh came to Abram and gave further explication of the redemptive/restorative covenant within the context of the creational covenant.

Yahweh presented himself as the invincible, powerful, and exalted God. Yahweh emphasized the stipulations of the covenant: "walk before me" (remain in constant, everyday spiritual fellowship with me); "be blameless" (live uprightly according to my will among your fellowmen). Implied in these stipulations was Yahweh's awareness of Abram's lack of faith and obedience in his sovereign, exalted God and of his sin of adultery with Hagar. Abram had sinned spiritually and socially but Yahweh graciously confirmed his covenant(s) with Abram. The verb used in Hebrew is "give." The continuity of the covenant with Abram was a *gift of Yahweh's grace*. Abram responded in humility and worship (17:3). Covenantal elements were then repeated. Abram was promised many offspring; they would form nations and give rise to kings. This emphasized repetition of seed was strongly affirmed by the change of his name to Abraham and the assurance that the covenant with his offspring was for all time. The life-love bond between Yahweh and Abraham and his seed was strongly affirmed by the promise "to be your God and the God of your descendants" (17:8). Yahweh, by these words, assured Abraham of his abiding presence, his availability, his sure help, and his unfailing love, support, and comfort in all circumstances of life. Abram was also assured that he would possess the land (17:7–8). To the stipulations to walk and be blameless, Yahweh added the command to circumcise the male offspring who in turn would generate offspring. In the context of assuring Abraham of much seed, Yahweh gave the covenantal sign of circumcision (17:11), which sons were always to carry and by which he demonstrated that he claimed the seed as people in covenant with him. Circumcision was given such an emphatically important role in Yahweh's covenanting with Abraham and his offspring, that it was referred to as the "covenant of circumcision" (17:13). This was not a separate covenant, but was such an integral part of the redemptive/restorative covenant that it was referred to as representing the entire covenant (a part representing the whole). Also in the context of Yahweh's claim to Abraham's seed as his, the concept of divine election is included. Abraham pled that his son Ishmael be considered a covenant progenitor, but Yahweh emphatically stated Isaac, to be born of Sarah, was to be that one (17:15–21).

After God had tested Abraham's obedience, by oath (22:1–6) he repeated and confirmed elements of his covenant (22:17–18a). Of fundamental importance is Yahweh's statement "because you have obeyed me" (22:18b). This stress on obedience is strong evidence that the covenant with Abraham should not be considered basically as a covenant of promise with the response of faith. Important as promise and faith are, they should not be used to minimize the emphasis on stipulations: leave, go, fear not, walk before me, be blameless, circumcise, offer your son. Abraham was never given options that he could choose to accept or reject. As a "vassal" he was given commandments, laws, orders, regulations, requirements, and decrees (26:4). Yahweh's covenant with Abraham was characterized by promise and law. As these were not to be separated, so faith and obedience were not to be either.

As Yahweh had promised that his redemptive/restorative covenant in the broader context of the creation covenant was to be continued with Isaac (17:19–20), and because Abraham had obeyed Yahweh and kept his laws (26:5), Yahweh did accordingly confirm his covenant with Isaac (26:3–4, 24).

The gracious character of Yahweh's covenant with the patriarchs was highlighted in Yahweh's interactions with Jacob, who was chosen in spite of his covetousness (25:29–34), deception (27:19), and clever manipulations (30:31–43). Election to covenantal privileges and responsibilities was not on the basis of merit, but according to Yahweh's sovereign will and mercy (Rom. 9:10–18).

Yahweh God confirmed the covenant in all its aspects and ramifications with Jacob. When fleeing from Esau, Jacob was assured of these; the reassurance of Yahweh's presence was captured by the phrases "I am with you"; "I will watch over you"; "I will bring you back to the land"; "I will not leave you"; and "I will accomplish all I promise you." With these assurances Jacob could travel, live, work, and prosper anyplace in Yahweh's cosmic kingdom, for Yahweh had repeated his determination to uphold and carry out his creation covenant and its redemptive/restorative correlate. Jacob, having a home with his Uncle Laban, enjoyed the fulfillment of the covenant mandate to be fruitful and multiply, and the fulfillment of the covenant promise of seed (29:31–30:24). Jacob was blessed with prosperity (a creation covenantal cultural reality; 30:25–43; 35:23–26). When returning to the land of his fathers as Yahweh directed him (31:3) Jacob was assured of Yahweh's covenantal promise to be with him. When the time came to confront Esau, Jacob depended on Yahweh's covenantal relationship with his forbears and the promises made to them and him (32:9–12). After Jacob's wrestling with the Lord, he was named "Israel" because he overcame in his struggles (32:28; 35:10) and was blessed (32:29). Upon his return to Bethel, Yahweh God again confirmed the covenant with him, assuring Jacob he was El Shaddai and commanding him to be fruitful (35:11), confirming that nations and kings would come from him (35:11) and that he would receive land for himself and his children (35:12). When Jacob had been in the land for some time and was advised to go to Egypt, Yahweh assured him that he was not breaking covenant if he did (46:3–4). Rather, it was Yahweh's plan to fulfill his covenant word to Abraham that Israel was to spend 400 years in a foreign land (15:13–14) in which a son, Joseph, proved to serve as a type of Christ, the mediator of the covenant, and Judah was prophesied to become the ancestor of David, the covenant servant, and of Christ (49:8–12).

The Book of Exodus commences with covenantal statements. Patriarchal progeny increased as it was promised it would (1:2–5). The Israelites were obedient to the command to be fruitful, multiply, and become numerous (1:7). But the Israelites were under severe strain, because of oppressive slavery, to obey the cultural and spiritual mandates. The reality was that the Israelites as a whole seemed oblivious to the covenantal responses of faith and obedience demanded of them. In their misery, they groaned and cried out, and Yahweh heard them (2:23–24a). It is stated categorically that Yahweh God remembered his covenant with the patriarchs (2:24b). That he did is demonstrated by his call of Moses to be the covenant mediator who was to serve in the Israelites' deliverance and gaining of freedom. Yahweh identified himself as the covenant Lord of the patriarchs (3:6), as the ever faithful One (3:14) who would be with Moses (3:12a) as he served in the fulfillment of Yahweh's promise to Abraham to bring his descendants from a strange land (3:8). Moses was commanded to perform wonders before the doubting Israelites so that they would believe that their covenantal Lord had called Moses to be the "Old Testament redeemer" (4:1–7).

After Yahweh had humbled and broken powerful Egypt, he instituted a second covenantal sacrament, the Passover, a feast to commemorate Israel's deliverance and at which fathers were to instruct their children about Yahweh's faithful words and deeds (12:24–28).

The actual process of confirming the covenant with Israel took place at Mount Sinai. The first stage of the process included the following. First, Yahweh presented himself as the covenant-keeping, delivering, guiding, and protecting God of Israel who brought Israel to himself. He confirmed the life-love bond (19:3–4).

Second, he made an all-inclusive stipulation: obey my covenant. The stipulation was explicated later. This stipulation was not presented as a condition that Israel could choose to obey or reject. Rather, Yahweh revealed in what manner a rich, full-orbed, covenantal relationship would function. Israel, responding obediently to Yahweh's covenant demands, would realize the promises.

Third, the promises were in the form of four assurances that included responsibilities. (1) Israel would realize the life, love, and blessedness of being Yahweh's precious possession, chosen from all the nations. (2) Israel was to be a kingdom, a royal people, children in the family of the sovereign Lord of the cosmic kingdom. Implied was that all kingdom privileges, blessings, and responsibilities were to be theirs. (3) Israel was, as a kingdom, to be priestly in character and service. They were to see themselves as standing and serving in the presence of Yahweh as they ministered to and on behalf of the nations of the world. Thus the covenantal task of being a channel of blessing would be realized. (4) Israel was to be a sanctified, dedicated, and consecrated nation. As an organized people ruled by Yahweh, they were to avoid and fight against sin and corruption and reflect the purity, majesty, and grandeur of their holy Lord among the nations (19:5–6).

Fourth, Israel responded covenantally: "We will do everything Yahweh has said." They did not say, "We choose to" (they were not given an option) or "We will try"; they made a full commitment.

Fifth, Moses was reconfirmed as the mediator between Yahweh and the people. He was to be spokesman for Yahweh to the people and on behalf of the people to Yahweh. He was the representative of Yahweh whom the people were to trust; their trust would be motivated by their hearing of Yahweh promulgating his will (19:9).

Sixth, the Israelites had to consecrate themselves to Yahweh while keeping a distance from Mount Sinai (19:10–15).

The second stage in the process of covenant renewal and confirmation was the speaking by Yahweh, and hearing by the people, of the law. First the ten commandments were spoken; these were inclusive principles governing all aspects of kingdom living. The first four concerned the character of King Yahweh, how and when he was to be honored and worshiped. These explicated how life and worship would meet requirements of the creational covenant's spiritual mandate. The next three elaborated on fulfilling the social mandate and the last three on the cultural mandate. The interrelatedness of the commandments demonstrated how integrated faithful, obedient, covenant people would find kingdom life to be. For example, to steal would hurt a neighbor (social) while acting disobediently against Yahweh (spiritually) in the cultural area.

The speaking of the ten commandments was followed by explication and application. Instruction was given on how to worship (20:22–26), keep Sabbath laws, and when, and why, and how to celebrate the three major feasts (23:10–19). Concern for working people, slaves, and injured and violated individuals was explained (21:1–36;

22:16–23:9). Instruction concerning ownership of property, rights involved, punishment, and ways of making restitution was added.

After the laws were promulgated, the people were given assurances of Yahweh's guidance, protection, and bringing them into the promised land, where they were to remain covenantally faithful to Yahweh and not make a covenant with the people living in the land or with their gods (23:20–33). This was a strong reminder to trust Yahweh, believe in him, and love only him.

Moses told the people all that Yahweh had given as instructions and laws for them. The people made a second solemn response, saying they would do all that Yahweh had said. This response of trust and obedience came spontaneously (24:3).

Moses then wrote all the explications, applications, assurances, and responses (24:4). This writing of a covenant gave it permanence and authority. Once written, it was not to be altered; it would be explicated and more fully applied.

The third stage in the process of Yahweh's renewing and confirming of the covenant he had made previously with Adam, Noah, and the patriarchs was the actual ratification ceremony (24:4b–18). The ceremony consisted of the building of an altar to serve as the actual intimate meeting place of Yahweh and the people. Sacrifices were then offered. Blood had been collected and half of it was sprinkled on the altar. Then Moses read all of the covenant material he had written, to which Israel made a third spontaneous response, saying "We will do, we will obey." The climactic point of the ceremony followed; the people were sprinkled by the blood of the covenant. Thus, by the blood, in which is life, but which also speaks of the death of what is sacrificed, the people as a whole were signified and sealed as Yahweh God's precious possession. The holy marriage had taken place. Yahweh, the Husband, had taken the patriarch's progeny as his bride. The ratification of the covenant was finalized by Yahweh writing the ten commandments on tablets of stone and giving them to Moses. The whole ceremony ended with Yahweh displaying himself in his majesty, splendor, grandeur, and awesomeness as a consuming fire (24:17).

The Israelites did not remain faithful to their covenantal vow for long. While Moses was receiving instructions concerning worship (building of the tabernacle, its furnishings, ordaining Aaron and sons as priests) the Israelites made an idol and worshiped it (32:1–6). This breaking of the covenant aroused Yahweh's anger; he spoke of carrying out the curse of the covenant on them (32:9–10). Moses, however, served as a covenant mediator; the people were largely spared (32:28, 35).

The covenant was reconfirmed when Moses interceded further for the people and Yahweh declared that he was truly Yahweh, compassionate, gracious, patient, full of love, faithful, forgiving, righteous, and just (34:6–7). Promises of what he would do were repeated and stipulations, relevant to the immediate circumstances just experienced, were added. The call was repeated to worship only Yahweh, who as a jealous God would tolerate no rivals (34:14). Yahweh again enjoined the people to remember to celebrate the prescribed festivals (34:18–26). A forgiven people, with whom Yahweh reconfirmed his life-love bond with all its implications and ramifications for all aspects of life, were to be a joyous, feasting people.

In the context of Yahweh confirming his covenant with Israel, two other covenants are referred to. In Leviticus 2:13 the command was given not to leave "the salt of the covenant of your God out of your grain offerings." Then later the phrase "covenant of salt" is used when Yahweh assures the priests and Levites that their offspring would always be supplied with sustenance from offerings (Num. 18:19). The institution and purpose of this covenant of salt are not recorded. From the context it can be understood that when covenantally prescribed offerings were made, they had to be seasoned and given a means of preservation so that what was offered could be kept in good condition until eaten by the families of priests and Levites. In this way, one provision in covenantal life, work, and worship, namely, food for those not given a large portion of Canaan, was used to refer to the entire covenant. The permanency of the covenant was expressed by salt; for this reason the covenant with David was also referred to as a covenant of salt (2 Chron. 13:5).

Likewise, to not honor and keep the Sabbath was to break the entire covenant (Exod. 31:13, 16; see also Neh. 9:14; 10:31, 33; 13:15–22; Isa. 56:2–6; Jer. 17:19–29). Keeping the Sabbath was a definite requirement for faithful covenantal life and worship.

Within the scope of Yahweh's covenant with Israel as a nation, a "subcovenant" was made with the priesthood. This covenant is referred to as an everlasting covenant. Because one of Aaron's sons demonstrated great zeal for Yahweh's covenantal demand for holy living, assurance was given that the office of priest would remain with Aaron's progeny (Num. 25:10–13).

When the Israelites were prepared to enter the land promised to their patriarchal ancestors, Moses, Yahweh God's mediator for Israel, gave extended addresses that constitute the content of the Book of Deuteronomy.

The Hebrew term for covenant appears twenty-seven times. Once it should be translated "league" (7:2); it appears a number of times in the phrase "ark of the covenant." In some contexts the law is referred to as the covenant (4:13; 19:9, 11, 15; 29:1).

In his addresses, Moses reviewed a number of important events experienced during their desert travels (chaps. 1–3) in which the people's behavior was not commendable but Yahweh had remained faithful: He "blessed you. . . . He has watched over your journey" (2:7). Moses urged the people to remain faithful to Yahweh God's covenant (4:13) and to remember Yahweh as a jealous God demanding absolute loyalty (4:24). Moses stressed that Yahweh was merciful; he would not forget the covenant made with the forefathers that he had confirmed by an oath. Yahweh had covenanted with them because he loved them and chose their descendants (the people whom Moses was addressing) (4:37). Reminding the Israelites of the character and deeds of Yahweh (two essential aspects of Yahweh's covenant), Moses urged the people to follow Yahweh's commands (4:1) not add to but to keep them (4:2), to hold fast (4:4), to observe them faithfully (4:6), and to show their wisdom and understanding by so doing (4:6). They were to seek Yahweh their God with all their heart and soul (4:29). This call to loving obedience was followed by a repetition of the ten commandments (chap. 5) and the command to love Yahweh, to have his will in their hearts, and to teach their children (5:4–9).

Moses explicated and expanded on how the covenant of love Yahweh had made with the patriarchs (7:12) was to be known, obeyed, and followed in all of life. Reminders of Yahweh's love and his election of them and his calling them to be holy were repeated (see esp. chaps. 7–11). The place and manner of covenant worship and feasting were outlined again (chaps. 12–13, 16, 26). Instructions on social and legal matters as required by Yahweh's covenant were repeated (chaps. 14–15, 17, 19–24). Assurances that Yahweh would provide covenant leaders/mediators—kings, priests, and prophets—were explicated (17:14–18:22). Following this expansion on the law, with repeated references to the blessings that followed obedience (see esp. chap. 8), Moses reiterated the call to Yahweh's people to be holy, to obey and walk with Yahweh, and to be set in praise, fame, and high honor above all people (26:16–19).

Integral to a covenant, in addition to the Lord's self-presentation, review of deeds, stipulations and call to obedience, and assurance/promises were the blessings and curses. Moses emphatically presented these; first he stressed the curses (27:14–26), which were to be repeated by the Levites and to which the people were to respond with "Amen" (so it shall be). Moses summarized the blessings (28:1–14; 30:1–20) he had referred to before. In graphic detail he related what curses to expect if the people were disobedient (28:15–68).

Before Moses concluded his "covenant-reminding addresses," he ordained Joshua as his successor (31:1–8), wrote what he had preached and had it placed in the ark (31:9–29), wrote a song in which Yahweh's character and deeds were extolled and Israel's failures and the tragic consequences of these (32:1–43), and pronounced a blessing on the Israelites (chap. 33). He then told the Israelites that as they were standing before Yahweh, they were in covenant with Yahweh because Yahweh confirmed his covenant made first with the patriarchs.

Joshua reconfirmed this same covenant with Israel after they had taken possession of Canaan. He reviewed Yahweh God's work on their behalf (Josh. 24:1–13). He called on them to fear and serve Yahweh with all faithfulness (24:14–23). The people responded, "We will serve and obey" (24:24). Joshua wrote the decrees and laws, undoubtedly as these applied to the circumstances of settled life in "The Book of the Law of God." Joshua did not alter what Moses had written; he repeated, expanded, and made relevant to the new situation what Yahweh had given through Moses.

In the times of the judges, Yahweh assured Israel that he would never break his covenant made with the forefathers (Judg. 2:1). Israel repeatedly broke the covenant, yet Yahweh remained faithful. He provided deliverance when the people repented and called on him. There are no biblical references to ceremonies of covenant renewal, although some scholars consider Samuel to have led in a covenant renewal at Gilgal. This was when Saul was confirmed king and Samuel made his farewell address (1 Sam. 11:14–12:25). This renewal marked a definite progress in Yahweh God's revelation. As with each covenant-expanding, -renewing, and -confirming ceremony, additional revelation had been given by Yahweh, so significant added revelation was given in the time of Samuel and David. It pertained particularly to the role of a royal covenant mediator in the person of a king as promised through Moses. Samuel initiated the process of covenant expansion and renewal by the covenant renewal at Gilgal and the anointing of David as Yahweh's chosen king (1 Sam. 16:1–13).

The climax of added revelation and expansion of God's covenant came when Yahweh addressed David through Nathan the prophet (2 Sam. 7:1–17). The revelation to David commenced with a reference to how Yahweh had dwelt with his people since Mosaic times. Here there is a direct tie-in with the patriarchal covenant that was expanded and ratified at Sinai (7:5–8).

Essential features in the expansion of the covenant with David are as follows. David the shepherd was chosen to be king (7:8; cf. Ps. 78:70–72). The covenant formula "I have been with you" was repeated. Yahweh gave him victory. David's name was to be great. A place was to be given, and victory, rest, and peace were assured. Seed would continue after him. Sons would be kings. The throne of the kingdom of the son was to be established forever. Yahweh would be His father; he, David his son. Wickedness would be punished (curse of covenant). Yahweh's love would never leave (bond of love is assured). This covenant made with David was an initial fulfillment of Jacob's prophecy concerning Judah (Gen. 49:8–12) that a ruler would come forth from him. The fuller and complete fulfillment of Jacob's prophecy and Nathan's to David was realized in Jesus Christ, the mediator of the new covenant.

David's son Solomon expressed his awareness and loyalty to Yahweh and the covenant with the Davidic dynasty in the first years of his reign. He did this particularly when he dedicated the temple; the temple gave permanent expression to the covenant promise, "I am your God; I will be with you." Most of the kings succeeding Solomon, with exceptions such as Jehoshaphat, Hezekiah, and Josiah, were covenant breakers. They were not to be considered excusable or ignorant because the psalms, many written in the period of the kingdom, called attention to the covenant (at least 20 times). Even more so, the prophets called on the kings and the people to remember the one, all-embracing creation and redemptive/restorative covenant, with all its wonderful elements and serious warnings.

The kings of Judah, like Ahaz, ignored, disbelieved, and rejected the prophetic warnings, but Yahweh through his covenantal spokesman, the prophets, continued to hold his promises concerning his covenant and the promised mediator of the covenant before the people.

The prophets had repeatedly warned that Yahweh would uphold his covenant with persistent covenant breakers and despisers by executing the curse of the covenant on them. Jeremiah eloquently warned of impending doom by destruction and dispersion.

The New Covenant. Jeremiah, prophesying that the curse of the covenant would surely be executed by means of the exile, also prophesied concerning the sure continuity of the covenant (30:1–33:26). He gave absolute assurance that Israel and Judah would be brought back from captivity (30:3); Yahweh would restore blessings (30:18; fortunes NIV). He would love them with an everlasting love and continue to be Father to them (31:3–9). Yahweh would give cause for tears to dry and hope for the future (31:15–17) because Israel would be replanted (31:27–30). A renewed covenant would be confirmed (31:31–34). This covenant would be as sure and inviolable as Yahweh's covenant with David, the Levites (33:15–18), and creation (33:19–26). As he spoke of the renewed covenant he did so in the context of Yahweh's covenant with creation, the patriarchs (33:21), Israel at Sinai and in the desert (Levites taken as a part of the whole), and David (33:15, 26). Jeremiah does not speak of a discontinuity of past covenants. He makes it clear that Yahweh's covenant made, expanded, and administered in various situations, is one continuing covenant. A time is coming when the covenant would be renewed, expanded, and applied in a radically new way. Hence he spoke of what is translated as the "new covenant" with Israel and Judah (31:31) that would not be like the covenant made at Sinai (31:32). Some important points must be stressed: (1) The Hebrew term translated "new" basically refers to what was there before but appears in another (new, renewed) form like the moon, appearing as full, changes in appearance and is spoken of as the new moon. (2) A main aspect of the covenant with the patriarchs, Israel, and David will characterize the future covenant. "I will be their God, and they will be my people" (31:33b). (3) The law will continue to be an integral aspect (31:33a) but it will be internalized in the minds and hearts of the covenant people. (4) Yahweh remains the same; he is a forgiving and forgetting God (33:34).

The renewed covenant for the future will uphold the promises made throughout the Old Testament period. The greatest change will be in regard to the administrator of the covenant. No longer will this one be a Moses, a David, a high priest, or a great prophet like Isaiah. Jesus Christ, who had been typified by these Old Testament mediators, will be the Mediator of the covenant. He will inaugurate, fulfill, and permanently establish the renewed covenant. He did this by becoming the High Priest who offered himself as the Passover Lamb. He capsulized all this by his "I am" statements (John 4:26; 6:35; 8:12; 9:5; 10:7, 9, 11, 14; 11:25; 14:6; 15:1, 6) by which he identified himself with Yahweh, who, when he called Moses to be the mediator in the Old Testament era said, "I am who I am" (Exod. 3:14) and "this is my blood of the covenant" (Matt. 20:28). The Book of Hebrews expands on how Jesus and his blood are essential elements of the new covenant (9:11–10:18).

The renewed covenant Jeremiah prophesied was ushered in by Jesus Christ. It inaugurated the entire New Testament era, covers it entirely, and reaches into the eternal reign of Christ and the Father. The latter part of that renewed covenant that reaches into the future, the eternal state when heaven and a renewed earth are joined into regained and consummated Eden. This is inferred to be Ezekiel as the covenant of peace (34:25). This covenant is to be a complete consummation of the creation covenant. Fields will not longer have wild beasts; forests will be places of security; showers of blessing will fructify the orchards and fields (Isa. 11:6–9). This covenant of peace will be initiated, fulfilled, and consummated by the promised descendant of Judah referred to by Isaiah as the shoot and branch of David (11:1), and as the divinely provided One shepherd, David, Yahweh's servant's Son (Ezek. 34:24). The life-love bond established by God when he created the cosmos and placed Adam and Eve as his mediators in Eden, attacked by Satan and broken by humanity, ever maintained by Yahweh, will be fully restored, enriched in every respect, and fully realized under the mediatorial service of Yahweh's Son, Jesus Christ.

GERARD VAN GRONINGEN

See also CHURCH, THE; ISRAEL.

Bibliography. H. Buis, *The Encyclopedia of Christianity,* 4:219–29; W. J. Dumbrell, *Covenant and Creation;* W. Eichrodt, *Theology of the Old Testament,* vol. 1; M. J. Kline, *The Structure of Biblical Authority;* idem, *The Treaty of a Great King;* D. J. McCarthy, *Old Testament Covenant;* T. E. McComiskey, *The Covenants of Promise;* J. Murray, *The Covenant of Grace;* O. P. Robertson, *The Christ of the Covenants;* G. Van Groningen, *Messianic Revelation in the Old Testament;* G. Vos, *Biblical Theology;* J. Zinkand, *Covenants: God's Claims.*

Covenant, the New. *See* NEW COVENANT.

Covetousness. Strong desire to have that which belongs to another. It is considered to be a very grievous offense in Scripture. The tenth commandment forbids coveting anything that belongs to a neighbor, including his house, his wife, his servants, his ox or donkey, or anything that belongs to him (Exod. 20:17). Jesus listed covetousness or greed along with many of the sins from within, including adultery, theft, and murder, which make a person unclean (Mark 7:22). Paul reminded the Ephesians that greed or covetousness is equated with immorality and impurity, so that these must be put away (5:3). A covetous or greedy person is an idolator (5:5) and covetousness is idolatry (Col. 3:5). James warns that people kill and covet because they cannot have what they want (4:2).

Covetousness, therefore, is basic to the commandments against murder, adultery, stealing, and lying. Those who accept bribes are coveting, leading to murder (Ezek. 22:12). Coveting a neighbor's wife is a form of adultery (Exod. 20:17). Achan admitted to coveting a robe and silver and gold, so he stole them, which was a sin against the Lord (Josh. 7:20–22). Gehazi, the servant of Elisha, coveted the property of Naaman so much that he lied to get what he wanted from Naaman the leper (2 Kings 5:19–25) and was struck with leprosy. Proverbs warns that a covetous person brings trouble to his family (15:27). Thus covetousness is the root of all kinds of sins, so that Jesus gave the warning, "Be on your guard against all kinds of greed" (Luke 12:15).

WILLIAM J. WOODRUFF

See also ENVY.

Create, Creation. Who created and sustains the universe? Why was it created? What is the nature of the Creator-creature relationship? These are the sorts of questions that the Bible addresses when it treats the topic of creation. Such queries are essentially theological in nature. Therefore, the juxtaposition, by some modern interpreters, of scriptural assertions about creation with scientific evidence and theories regarding origins often results in fruitless comparisons of different, although equally relevant, bodies of knowledge. At the risk of oversimplifying the issue, one might say that Scripture deals with the who, why, and what questions posed above, whereas science investigates the problems of when and how the observable universe came into existence and continues to function.

In order to understand what the Bible teaches about creation, one must go beyond delineating the semantic range of relevant words to examine pertinent biblical passages in their historical, literary, and theological contexts. This sort of investigation reveals a degree of similarity between the Bible and antecedent Near Eastern literature. While it is unlikely that biblical authors consulted this corpus directly, they were presumably aware of the various creation traditions of the nations surrounding them. That would account for the similarities. There are also profound differences between the Bible's perspective on the cosmos and its origins and that of contemporaneous literature. The more one compares them, the more evident it becomes that scriptural authors were motivated both to make certain affirmations about creation and to contradict some conceptions about it that were current in their day.

The Eternal Creator Has No Peer. The assertion that the one, eternally existing God of the patriarchs and their descendants is the Creator must surely have been intended, at least in part, as a polemic against the pantheons of gods of other peoples—Mesopotamians, Egyptians, Canaanites—with whom the Israelites came in contact. The creation myths of these people often included accounts of the origins of the gods and conflicts between the gods. These divine rivalries frequently provided the context for the establishment of the universe and the rhythms of nature.

The Creator Has No Rival. The God of Israel's unchallenged hegemony over the various realms of the cosmos and the creatures that inhabit them further emphasizes his uniqueness in comparison to the gods of other nations. Whereas typically their domains are limited and they must contend with rivals, his rule is uncontested. The author of Genesis 1 takes great pains to demonstrate to his audience that the universe is not populated with deities or demons who need to be subdued or appeased, but that it is all controlled by one Creator. He does not need to struggle with nature in order to make it conform to his plan and purpose. Neither is his creative word the sort of magical incantation that is attributed to Ptah and Re in Egyptian mythology. It is the sovereign God's simple command which, when uttered, produces the desired result. Furthermore, the primeval ocean is not a divine behemoth, like Tiamat, to be butchered in order to fashion earth and sky, but an impersonal part of the universe over which God's potent wind/Spirit broods (v. 2). Indeed, the great sea monsters, which cavort with the myriads of other creatures in the watery depths, are his handiwork (v. 21; cf. Ps. 104:25–26). The seas, which are remnants of the original watery chaos, are assigned borders at earth's edges (vv. 9–10; cf. Job 38:8–11; Ps. 104:5–9; Prov. 8:29). The sun and moon are not afforded the dignity of their usual Hebrew names (*šemeš* and *yārēah*) because those designations might bring to mind the sun-god, Shamash, and the moon-god, Yarih. Instead they are referred to as the greater and lesser lights. These luminaries, along with the stars, are not depicted as deities controlling human destiny, but simply as components of God's creation that function in their assigned roles of providing light and the basis for calendrical calculations (vv. 14–18). Fertility is not something to be deified, as it is in Canaanite religion, for example, but a capacity created by God (vv. 11–12, 22, 28).

The Creator Brings Order. In Genesis 1, the drama of creation begins with the same opening scene as in other ancient traditions, the watery chaos (v. 2; cf. Ps. 24:1–2). The reference in 1:1 to the creation of the ordered cosmos (which is what the phrase "heavens and earth" connotes) is probably not to be construed as a description of the first act of creation, which is then followed by a chaotic state and then the return to order. Verse 1 may, instead, serve as a dependent, temporal clause (i.e., "In the beginning when God created" or "When God began to create"), with verse 2 then apparently functioning as a parenthetic comment inserted between verses 1 and 3, which would then be understood as the main clause (i.e., "[the earth being formless and empty]. . . God said"). Another possible interpretation is that verse 1 is an independent thematic statement that introduces the content that follows in chapter 1 and that corresponds to the summary statement in 2:1. Verse 2 would then constitute a circumstantial clause modifying verse 3 (i.e., "In the beginning God created the heavens and the earth. Now the earth being formless and empty . . . God said . . .").

In any case, the curtain that veils the primeval past rises at some point after the absolute beginning since watery chaos already exists. Creation in Genesis 1:1–2:3 has more to do with bringing order to that chaos and populating voids than with generating all matter. That does not mean that this passage is inimical to the idea of God creating all matter. It is just that the issue does not seem to be relevant to this biblical author and his contemporaries. The mystery of ultimate origins is addressed by subsequent revelation that acknowledges that absolutely everything, even the primeval deep, must have its origin in God (Neh. 9:6; Ps. 90:2; Prov. 8:22–31; 2 Macc. 7:28; Heb. 11:3). It is upon this fuller understanding of the limitless scope of God's sovereignty that the doctrine of *creatio ex nihilo,* creation out of nothing, may be based.

Creation Week. The portrayal of creation as work accomplished on successive days of the week raises a whole series of literary, chronological, and theological issues that are too involved to explore in any great depth here. Some essential considerations regarding this arrangement should be highlighted.

The first consideration is that the framework of the week of creation is an artistic one designed to convey primarily theological, rather than purely scientific, information. The evidence for this is abundant. First, the concept of the week coincides with the author's focus on the number seven—or a multiple thereof—in Genesis 1:1–2:3 (e.g., seven words in the original Hebrew version of the introductory verse [1:1]; seven paragraphs corresponding to the seven days following the introductory verse; fourteen words in v. 2; seven instances of the fulfillment formula signifying that what God called for did take place; seven examples of the approval formula stating that what God saw was good; seven occurrences altogether of the terms "light" and "day" in the first paragraph [1:2–5]; seven references to water in paragraphs 2 and 3 [1:6–13]; three consecutive sentences of seven words each in 2:2–3a that are part of the seventh paragraph [2:1–3] whose subject is the seventh day; thirty-five words in the seventh paragraph; thirty-five occurrences of the word "God" and twenty-one of the word "earth" throughout the narrative). In the Bible, seven and its multiples frequently connote completeness, totality, fulfillment, or perfection.

Second, compressed into six days of work there are eight creative acts, each introduced by the formula, *wayyōʾmer ʾĕlōhîm,* "And/Then God said." Analogous to this conforming of facts to a predetermined narrative structure is Matthew's arrangement of Jesus' lineage in three sets of fourteen generations. To achieve that sort of symmetry, however, the evangelist does not hesitate to omit names in a manner consistent with Jewish practice in the formation of genealogies (e.g., Ahaziah, Joash, and Amaziah between Joram/Jehoram and Uzziah/Azariah in 1:8–9 [cf. 1 Chron. 3:11–12] and Jehoiakim between Josiah and Jechoniah/Jehoiachin in 1:11 [cf. 1 Chron. 3:15–16]).

Third, there are differences with respect to both the sequence and duration of events when Genesis 1:1–2:3 is compared with 2:4–25. Whereas the first account depicts the creation of humans last, the second portrays man's creation first and woman's last. Furthermore, while in the first passage creation is described as a six-day task, in the second the only indication as to how long it takes is given in 2:4: "When the LORD God made the earth and the heavens. The juxtaposition of narratives with such obvious chronological differences makes it clear that an absolute chronology of creation events is not at issue here.

Fourth, the deliberate omission, in Genesis 2:1–3, of the refrain regarding the evening and morning for the seventh day would seem to suggest that the author intends to portray it as a day without an end. The fact that he does not explicitly call it the Sabbath may, in part, be his way of highlighting the sense in which it is distinct from the Mosaic Sabbath, although with the references in verses 2–3 to God resting from his work he certainly makes the connection implicitly. The author may also wish to prevent any connections between the Sabbath and *šabattu* or *šapattu,* which was what the Babylonians and Assyrians called the day of the full moon—the fifteenth of the month—a day dedicated to the worship of the moon-god.

The concept of the seventh day as an unending one is presumably part of the background to the discourse by the author of Hebrews on the eschatological Sabbath-rest for the faithful (4:1–11). Jesus, too, does not seem to regard the seventh day of creation week as a literal one, if his response in John 5:16–19 to charges that he has broken the law by healing a paralytic on the Sabbath is any indication. Jesus legitimizes his actions on the grounds that his Father is still working (v. 17) and that he does nothing but what he sees the Father doing (v. 19). His argument appears to be that his works on the Mosaic Sabbath are lawful because they correspond to the Father's activities on the continuing creation Sabbath. This Sabbath, which marks the end of the week of Genesis 1:1–2:3 but not the cessation of the Father's works, is apparently considered by Jesus to coincide with all of history after the six days of Genesis 1. That view is fully compatible with the understanding of creation week as a literary device.

If the creation week framework is artistic in nature, then what is its significance? The answer to that question is undoubtedly to be found in the linkage between creation and the Sabbath. The anthropomorphic figure of the week furnishes the context for a theology of the Sabbath. It is striking to note that ancient Assyrian calendars identify the seventh, fourteenth, twenty-first, and twenty-eighth days of the month (along with the nineteenth day, which occurs seven weeks after the beginning of the preceding month) as unlucky ones on which important tasks should not be attempted. In contrast, Israel's God designates every seventh day as a holy day, when regular tasks are to be laid aside and there can be pause for refreshment and a renewed focus on the relationship with the Creator (Gen. 2:3; Exod. 20:8–11; 31:12–17). The Sabbath thus symbolizes the fact that human worth and purpose are not to be derived from toil but from that relationship. This is not to denigrate human work, for God assigns responsibilities and duties even prior to the fall (Gen. 1:26–29; 2:15, 19–20). Nevertheless, it is particularly as humans set themselves apart to commune with their Creator, whether on the Sabbath or some other day (Rom. 14:5–6; 1 Cor. 16:1–2; Rev. 1:10), that they find fulfillment.

A second consideration pertaining to the creation week structure is that the events of Genesis 1:1–2:3 are arranged in a logical, although not necessarily chronological, order. The accomplishments of the first six days of that week, which are described in parallel triads, remedy the conditions of formlessness and emptiness described in verse 2. The key activity on days 1 to 3 is separation (i.e., light from darkness [vv. 4–5], waters above the firmament from those below it [vv. 6–8], waters under the sky from dry land [vv. 9–10]), and on days 4 to 6 it is population (i.e., luminaries [vv. 14–16], aquatic and winged creatures [vv. 20–21], animals and humans [vv. 24–27]). There are also connections between the triads due to the fact that the regions demarcated on the first three days are filled by creations fashioned on the next three. Thus luminaries (day 4) correspond to light and darkness (day 1), aquatic and winged creatures (day 5) to water and sky (day 2), and animals and humans (day 6) to dry land (day 3). Additional congruence is evident in that the vegetation created on day 3 is given for food to terrestrial and winged creatures on day 6. The author further distinguishes these two days by means of double usage of the creative utterance (vv. 9, 11, 24, 26), fulfillment (vv. 9, 11, 24, 30) and approval (vv. 10, 12, 25, 31) formulas. This kind of symmetrical arrangement shows that the goal of the inspired author is to compose a theological portrait of his subject in a manner reminiscent of the New Testament evangelists, not merely to chronicle events in the order of their occurrence.

The Creator's Crowning Achievement. A central theme of both Genesis creation accounts is that of humanity as the apex of God's creation. This motif stands in contrast to certain mythological depictions of the human species fashioned as an afterthought to relieve the gods of toil and provide them with sustenance. In Genesis 1, the primacy of humans is emphasized through their appearance as the last of God's creatures in the narrative sequence, the reference to their being created in God's image, the threefold use of the verb *bārā'*, in the description of their creation (v. 27), and their dominion over the earth and its creatures as God's vice-regents. In Genesis 2, human preeminence is highlighted by the male's creation before all other life, his being entrusted with custody of the garden, his being given the privilege of naming the other creatures, and the female's appearance as the last of God's creatures though, like the male, distinct from all other species.

The significance of references to humans created in God's image has long been debated by biblical scholars. The image of God, whatever it means, clearly distinguishes humanity from the rest of creation. Since it is linked in Genesis 1:26 to the mandate for humans to have dominion over the created order, some have equated it with the role of vice-regent. That role, however, seems to be a consequence or function of the divine image. As intimated earlier in comments about the Sabbath, the capacity for a unique and personal relationship with the Creator is apparently what is intrinsic to the concept of the image of God. This is perhaps signaled most clearly by the appearance in Genesis 2:4–7—where the central theme is human origins—of the name by which God typically identifies himself to those with whom he enters into covenant, Yahweh (rendered "LORD" in most English translations). Although the term "covenant" is not found in Genesis 1–2, it is implicit in the reciprocity of God's provisions for the original human couple and their conformity to his expectations of them. Their initial obedience to the command not to partake of the fruit of the tree of the knowledge of good and evil, which allows them to enjoy the benefits of covenant life, constitutes an acknowledgment of the fact that, as Creator, God alone has the prerogative to establish moral absolutes of right and wrong. Their subsequent disobedience, which results in the dissolution of the covenant and death, represents an attempt to usurp that divine prerogative. This whole sequence is typical of relationships between suzerains and their vassals in antiquity. Such relationships are codified in extant treaties whose format is reflected in Old Testament covenant formulations.

Creation Is Good. Another important theme in Genesis 1 is that God's creation is good. Various individual aspects of creation are so designated (vv. 4, 10, 12, 18, 21, 25) whereas the whole taken together is called "very good" (v. 31). These statements are intended to show not only that what God has fashioned and made to conform to the rule of law reflects his glory and his very nature (cf. Ps. 19:1–11 [12]; 97:6; Rom. 1:20), but also that the fall of humanity described in Genesis 3 cannot be attributed to any flaw in creation. Clearly Adam and Eve cannot excuse their transgression on the basis of a deficient environment because it is both perfect and provides bountifully for their every need (1:29; 2:8–16, 20–25). Neither can God be faulted, for, despite the fact that the serpent which becomes the agent of temptation in this episode is a creature that God has made (3:1), it is a subordinate creature over which humans are to exercise dominion (1:26–28; 2:19–20). Thus their transgression is a consequence of their failure to fulfill the creation mandate.

Community Is Good. Significantly, the prospect of the man being alone is the only thing in the prefall narrative that is explicitly called not good (2:18). This is indicative of the fact that humans are social creatures and that they have an innate need for community. The need is remedied when God creates woman—eventually named "Eve," the mother of all living (3:20)—because through her the rest of humanity comes into existence. The marriage relationship (2:24–25) symbolizes all other forms of human coexistence designed to satisfy the primal yearning for fellowship.

It should be pointed out that Genesis emphasizes the spiritual equality and interdependence of the original human couple (1:26–28; 2:18–23). This is epitomized by the expression, *kĕnegdô*, "corresponding to him" (2:18, 20), which is used of the partner whom God determines to provide for the man. The term, *ʿēzer*, "helper" (2:18, 20), does not inherently connote subordination because it is frequently used of God in relationship to man (e.g., Exod. 18:4; Deut. 33:7; Pss. 33:20; 70:5 [6]; 115:9, 10, 11; 146:5; see also 1 Sam. 7:12; Pss. 27:9; 40:17 [18]; 46:1 [2]; 63:7 [8]; 94:17). The reference to woman being created from man's rib highlights the kind of affinity between man and woman that is not possible between humans and other creatures. This is reinforced by man's joyful cry of recognition when God presents the woman to him: "This is now bone of my bones and flesh of my flesh" (2:23).

Although the preceding touches on the horizontal, human dimension of community, Scripture also emphasizes the vertical, Godward dimension. Both are represented already in Genesis 1:27 in the declaration that humankind is created male and female and in God's image. Indeed, the Bible is essentially a record of God's establishment of, and activity within, the community of faith. The community is expected to respond to him with worship and devotion and to function in an environment characterized by encouragement, instruction, and correction.

Creation and Redemption. A fundamental theme with which creation is combined, particularly in the Book of Isaiah, is redemption. In 43:1, Yahweh asserts that he has both created and redeemed Israel (cf. 44:2, 21, 24; 45:9–11; Mal. 2:10 and Isa. 41:14; 48:17; 49:7). The epitome of Yahweh's redemptive acts in the Old Testament is his deliverance of Israel from Egypt under Moses. It is not surprising, then, that exodus imagery should be used to describe subsequent instances of Yahweh's redeeming work. In Isaiah, the focus in this connection is on a second exodus, the return of the exiles from Babylonian captivity (43:14–21).

Through the prophet, Yahweh the Creator now declares his absolute sovereignty in the universe and in history. Furthermore, he assures his people that, contrary to what they assume, he is aware of their plight (40:12–28). Unlike the idols of Babylon, he announces in advance the overthrow of the Babylonian Empire by Cyrus the Persian and the subsequent emancipation of the Judean exiles. He will ransom them by supplying other nations for Persia to subdue. He will lead the erstwhile captives carefully through the wilderness between Babylon and Judah and provide for their every need along the way and in their restored land.

Re-creation. The theme of original creation also gives rise to another important theological concept: re-creation. It is featured in connection with both spiritual regeneration and eschatological renewal. In the former sense, we recall the plea of the psalmist who, burdened with his iniquity, earnestly entreats God to create a clean heart within him (51:10 [12]). In a similar vein, various passages in the New Testament speak of the Christian or the church as a new creation in Christ (2 Cor. 5:17; Gal. 6:15; Eph. 2:10, 15). Elsewhere the imagery is of the new self, fashioned according to the likeness or image of the creator (Eph. 4:24; Col. 3:10).

The idea of a new creation in an eschatological sense brings the original theme full circle. What is envisioned for the future is a return to the idyllic state of initial creation—nothing less than new heavens and a new earth. The consequences of the fall will be reversed and a renewal of the fruitfulness and vitality that first characterized the cosmos and the garden of Eden will take place (Isa. 65:17–25; 66:22; Ezek. 47:1–12; Joel 3:18; Amos 9:13; Rom. 8:18–23; 2 Peter 3:7, 10–13; Rev. 21:1–22:5). However, Scripture cautions that only those who have experienced spiritual re-creation may enjoy the eschatological Eden (Rev. 21:1–2, 6–8, 27; 22:14–15). ROBERT J. V. HIEBERT

See also ADAM; EVE; GENESIS, THEOLOGY OF; GOD; PERSON, PERSONHOOD; IMAGE OF GOD; SABBATH; WOMAN.

Bibliography. B. W. Anderson, *Creation in the Old Testament;* H. Blocher, *In the Beginning;* W. Brueggemann, *Genesis;* U. Cassuto, *A Commentary on the Book of Genesis;* H. H. Esser, *NIDNTT,* 1:378–87; T. Frymer-Kensky, *BA* 40 (1977): 147–55; J. H. Gronbaek, *JSOT* 33 (1985): 27–44; G. F. Hasel, *Andrews University Seminary Studies* 10 (1972): 1–20; idem, *EvQ* 46 (1974): 81–102; C. Hyers, *The Meaning of Creation;* D. Kidner, *Genesis;* J. B. Pritchard, *Ancient Near Eastern Texts Relating to the Old Testament;* A. P. Ross, *Creation and Blessing;* J. Skinner, *A Critical and Exegetical Commentary on Genesis;* E. A. Speiser, *Genesis;* H. J. Van Till, *The Fourth Day;* H. J. Van Till et al., *Portraits of Creation;* G. Von Rad, *Genesis;* B. K. Waltke, *BSac* 132 (1975): 25–36, 136–44, 216–28, 327–42; 133 (1976): 28–41; G. J. Wenham, *Genesis 1–15;* C. Westermann, *Genesis: A Practical Commentary.*

Creation, New. *See* NEW CREATION.

Cross, Crucifixion. The importance of the cross as a theological motif in the New Testament is impossible to overestimate. It stands as the center of the New Testament theology of salvation and is the starting point for not only soteriology, but all of Christian theology. It is the means by which we finally and fully understand the work of Christ on our behalf. The Gospel of Mark indicates that it is at the cross that we recognize Jesus as God's divinely appointed Savior of the world (10:45; 15:39). While the larger notion of the death of Christ may carry a broader and even deeper significance in New Testament theology, the cross as a symbol of God's action in Christ and a motivator for us to follow is worthy of discussion.

The cross of Christ is the center of the work that God did in Christ, "reconciling the world to himself" (2 Cor. 5:19). Paul emphasizes this work most notably in the early chapters of 1 Corinthians. The emphasis there is on power; the cross is held up as the power of God, which is seen as weakness by men. The statement of 1:17 belongs with the passage before, and introduces the thought Paul develops in 1:18–2:5. He is concerned "to preach the gospel—not with words of human wisdom, lest the cross of Christ be emptied of its power," and declares the message of the cross to be foolishness. However, this foolishness of God destroys the wisdom of the wise and is therefore central to the biblical notion of the salvation of God being a wise salvation because God is a wise God. The wise man, scholar, and philosopher of this age are dumbfounded by what appears to them to be foolishness.

The link of the cross with God's wisdom and power is intriguing, but perhaps most significant is the linking of the cross to Christ himself. Paul says that he preaches "Christ crucified: a stumbling block to Jews and foolishness to Gentiles, but to those whom God has called, both Jews and Greeks, Christ the power of God and the wisdom of God" (1 Cor. 1:23–24). The structure of this sentence equates the "Christ crucified" with "Christ the power of God and the wisdom of God." Hence the cross is seen as a defining revelation of who Christ is: the messianic wisdom of God and the dynamic power of God predicted in the Old Testament.

The cross is also seen as God's deliberate choice. He did not stumble onto it by accident but chose the weak and foolish things of the world in order deliberately to confound the wise and to shame the strong. Thus, a fourth element, and perhaps the most radical, of God's character is demonstrated in the cross: the love of God for the despised of the world. The cross is a symbol of shame in the Old Testament (Deut. 21:23; cf. Gal. 3:13–14) and thereby serves not only to state the radical nature of Christ's humiliation, but by implication to judge the world and all its inhabitants as being "the despised" who must identify with a crucified messiah in order to receive God's salvation. Thus, the statement in 1 Corinthians becomes not only a statement of theology but also a statement of anthropology.

Paul continues this theme in the statement about himself and his own weakness, which becomes a major theme of 1 Corinthians. He claims to have not come to them with eloquence or superior wisdom, but as one who resolves to know nothing except "Jesus Christ and him crucified. I came to you in weakness and fear and with much trembling. My message and my preaching were not with wise and persuasive words, but with a demonstration of the spirit's power, so that your faith might not rest on men's wisdom but on God's power" (2:2–5). Hence the passage comes full circle back to the wisdom and power of the cross, which seems to be foolishness and weakness to men. The central focus now, though, is not Christ but Paul himself who, as a minister of Christ, must come only in weakness and foolishness. So now a third theological category is defined by the cross, that of ministry in the world. It is to be characterized by foolishness and weakness. Of course the background of the passage is the contrast of Greek wisdom, which looked only for eloquence and style, not substance, and a power that was emotional, and for the moment, not lasting. Hence Paul comes with the power of substantial argument that can "demolish strongholds" (2 Cor. 10:4) and operates with a power that suffers and dies rather than victoriously triumphs.

While the cross is the means of the redemption of humankind and that fact is essential to any theology of the cross, the imagery used to discuss the cross has been highly disputed. The cross is displayed as a "sacrifice of atonement" in the well-known passage, Romans 3:24, which links it with the sacrificial death of the animals in the cultus of the Old Testament. The shedding of blood and the death of the sacrificed one are the two major links to this metaphor. The debate about this passage revolves around whether Christ's death merely obliterates the sin that caused the death to happen or assuages the wrath of God that is poured out upon humankind because of that sin. The link is clearly there with the wrath of God; the question seems to be how to understand that wrath. In any case, the wrath is not to be seen as the capricious anger of a malevolent God, but rather as the careful, considered fury of the Holy One of Israel against the evil that keeps man from his rightful place as God's highest and most prized possession.

Not only is the language of the cultus used in Romans 3, but also the language of justification (the law court) and redemption (the slave market). In this context the cross of Christ pays the penalty for the sins of humankind and therefore serves their sentence, freeing them from death, and pays the ransom needed to free the slaves from the power of sins and allow them to live.

Lastly, the cross of Christ speaks to the ongoing nature of the Christian life. In Galatians, Paul argues that those who have started so well need to come back to where they started, the cross of Christ. While crucifixion is not mentioned often in the book, two key places let us know that it is never far from Paul's mind. In 2:20 Paul speaks of being crucified with Christ, yet no longer living, but Christ lives in him, and the life he now lives in the body he lives by faith in the Son of God, who loved him and gave himself for him. This crucial verse describes the whole of Paul's attitude toward Christ, the Law, and grace in the book. The Galatians have gone back to observing the Law, when they started by being empowered by the Spirit through believing in the message of the cross (3:1). Thus, while Paul concentrates on faith versus observation of the Law as the mechanism for applying for the application of grace and the obtaining of righteousness, in the background is the means by which God has achieved this possibility for humankind: the cross.

The closing verses of the book show the centrality of the cross for Paul as well. Those who are compelling others to be circumcised are avoiding being persecuted "for the cross of Christ" (6:12), and Paul expressly declares that he will never boast in anything except "the cross of our Lord Jesus Christ, through which the world has been crucified to me, and I to the world" (v. 14). Thus the cross is as central to living the Christian life as it is to entering into it.

ANDREW H. TROTTER, JR.

See also DEATH OF CHRIST; JESUS CHRIST.

Bibliography. E. Brandenburger, *NIDNTT,* 1:389–405; C. B. Cousar, *A Theology of the Cross;* E. M. Embry, *NIDNTT,* 3:865–70; J. B. Green, *DJG,* pp. 146–63; idem, *DPL,* pp. 197–99, 201–9; M. Hengel, *The Atonement: The Origins of the Doctrine in the New Testament;* M. Hengel, *Crucifixion,* A. E. McGrath, *DPL,* pp. 192–97; L. Morris, *The Apostolic Preaching of the Cross;* idem, *The Cross in the New Testament.*

Crown. The concept of the crown originates from a cap, turban, or more formal metallic crown that was decorated with jewels. Its placement on one's head indicated that one was set apart (*nēzer*) for a particular task or calling. Such crowns were used for the high priest (Exod. 29:6; 39:30; Lev. 8:9) or for kings of Israel (2 Sam. 1:10; 2 Kings 11:12; Pss. 89:39; 132:18). The crown indicated the consecrated role of its wearer, since it could be profaned (Ps. 89:39). In the case of the king it also reflected his exalted position (Ps. 89:19–20).

Besides the concept of consecration and exaltation, a second term for crown in the Old Testament (*ʿaṭarâ*) indicated the presence of honor. In some cases it pictured the reception of honor because one entered into a special position. Wives were crowned with honor to show their new status, as is indicated in the metaphorical picture of Israel married to God (Ezek. 16:12). To remove the crown was an indication of shame (Ezek. 21:26).

In other cases, the crown indicated the presence of honor as a cause for glory and joy. These are more metaphorical uses. So a good wife is a crown to her husband (Prov. 12:4). So also are grandchildren (Prov. 17:6), living to old age (Prov. 16:31), riches (Prov. 14:24), or a good harvest (Ps. 65:11). God is also a crown in this sense. To experience the blessing of his character and activity on one's behalf is said to be a crown. So his lovingkindness and mercy can be a crown (Ps. 103:4), as can mere relationship with him (Isa. 28:5).

In the New Testament the image changes, since the major term for crown is *stephanos,* which referred in secular contexts either to the victory garland at a race of the sovereign crown that the Roman conqueror wore. This term is used eighteen times in the New Testament.

The image of the crown in Paul's writings is developed in detail in 1 Corinthians 9:24–27 with his image of the race and the perishable crown that the victor wins. In contrast to that crown stands the imperishable crown that goes to the Christian who completes the race. The crown is an honor received as a cause of joy. Its unfading character is highlighted in Peter's description of the "unfading crown of glory" (1 Peter 5:4). In cases where the crown bears a description, like "crown of righteousness," the characteristics described represent what is acknowledged as present by God. In other words, God does not hand out literal crowns, but offers the acknowledged honor of the presence of this characteristic in the believer for eternity. So we have the crown that is life (James 1:12; Rev. 2:10). There is also the crown that is glory in 1 Peter 5:4, the crown that is righteousness in 2 Timothy 4:8, and the crown that is rejoicing in 1 Thessalonians 2:19. In these uses the image is much like the Old Testament examples from Psalm 103:4 and Isaiah 28:5.

A second New Testament use looks back at the crown as honoring rule or sovereignty. Negative images exist alongside positive ones in Revelation. So the locusts wear crowns (Rev. 9:7), as does the woman of Revelation 12:1 and the beast and the dragon (12:3; 13:1). Here is negative, destructive sovereignty. Other images indicate honor and sovereignty of those who stand on the side of God or judgment, such as the elders of 4:4, 10 and the white horse of judgment in 6:2. But in contrast to all these images, both negative and positive, stands the one who is crowned with many crowns, Jesus (19:12). His superior authority is indicated by the multiplicity of crowns he wears. The honor and consecration he has, as well as his authority are unique.

The many crowns image also contrasts poignantly with the one crown image in the Gospels, where Jesus wears a crown of thorns. This image is designed to mock Jesus' claims to kingship. The biblical reply to that mocking image of the Passion is the decisive image of Revelation 19 and what it represents.

DARRELL L. BOCK

Cup. Throughout Scripture, as in the ancient Near East, the cup functions as a metaphor for an individual's fate. In Psalm 16, the psalmist credits the Lord with assigning his "portion and cup" in life. Psalm 23 equates an abundant life with an overflowing cup, a potent image in a semiarid world. The culmination of the positive image of the cup is in Psalm 116. Here the psalmist raises the cup of salvation as a thank offering to God, in effect offering the sum of his life to his lord.

The metaphor of the cup, like life itself, can also be negative. In numerous prophetic works, the cup retains its role as a representative of fate, but on a national level. The cup can function as a cup of wrath, a vessel pouring out God's judgment on the nations. The nations drinking from the "cup of his wrath" are often depicted as lost in drunkenness. Isaiah 51:17 personifies Jerusalem as a woman who drained the cup of wrath to its dregs. God takes pity on his city and intervenes. "See, I have taken out of your hand the cup that made you stagger . . . the goblet of my wrath" (v. 22). This cup is then given to the tormentors, indicating that they will suffer in their turn.

In a vision of destruction recorded by Jeremiah (25:15), God will force all the nations to drink from his cup and stagger to destruction. None are able to refuse it; all humanity will be judged and the wicked put to the sword. Ezekiel returns to the image of the cup of Jerusalem in a brutally explicit passage depicting Samaria and Jerusalem, representing the people of God, as two sisters who are prostitutes (chap. 23). The prophet calls the cup that Jerusalem drinks from the "cup of ruin and desolation, the cup of your sister Samaria" (v. 33). For Ezekiel, the cup stands for the destruction of the two kingdoms.

Zechariah uses the image of the cup of wrath to depict the fate of the enemies of Jerusalem. He adds a twist to the metaphor by making Jerusalem itself the cup (12:2). The author of revelation returns to the dark image of the cup of wrath, threatening all who follow the beast with the wine of God's judgment (14:10).

For the church, the cup has come to represent the central events of Christianity, the death and resurrection of Christ. In the Garden of Gethsemane, Christ returns to the fundamental meaning of the cup as a representative of fate. In his prayer, the cup symbolizes the pain, degradation, and death that will be required of him. He prays that the cup might pass undrunk, but it is Jesus' fate to drain it to its dregs. Christ becomes all the nations of the world, taking on their fate, and drains the cup of wrath. By drinking of the cup God placed before him, Christ transforms the cup of wrath into the cup of life. This transformation is foreshadowed at the last supper, where the cup of the new covenant, like the cup of wrath, is for all to partake of.

THOMAS W. DAVIS

Bibliography. A. A. Anderson, *Psalms;* W. S. LaSor, D. A. Hubbard, and F. W. Bush, *Old Testament Survey;* C. S. Mann, *Mark.*

Curse, Accursed. In the Old Testament being cursed includes loss of everything significant and a lowering to the most menial of positions. The serpent must crawl on his belly and eventually be crushed (Gen. 3:14–15). Cain can no longer farm and must become a vagabond (Gen. 4:11). Canaan becomes the lowest of slaves (Gen. 9:25).

Nowhere in the Bible is the state of being cursed portrayed in more graphic terms than in Deuteronomy 28:16–68. The curse follows its victims everywhere, extending to progeny and all means of livelihood. It includes incurable diseases, slow starvation, abuse by enemies, exile, panic, confusion, and eventual madness.

Curses are usually imposed by persons in authority for major breaches of the Torah that might threaten collapse of society. Thus in Deuteronomy 27:15–26 people who practice idolatry, incest, misleading the blind, ambush, disrespect for authority, and subversion of justice are cursed.

The curse is totally under Yahweh's control. It is his power, not magical forces, which brings about the curse. His sovereign decision alone decides who merits being cursed (1 Kings 8:31–32). He cannot be forced into action by proper wording or ritual. Thus a curse could not be used capriciously as a weapon against one's personal enemies.

A king might utter a curse against an innocent person but, like a nervous bird, it would not light (1 Sam. 14:24, 28; Prov. 26:2). A curse directed against the elect could be turned into a blessing or even come back against the one who sent it (Num. 24:9; Deut. 23:5–6). Curses could be removed by faithfulness. Levites were to be dispersed according to Jacob's curse (Gen. 49:7). Because of their faithfulness this scattering resulted in a widespread teaching ministry (Deut. 33:8–10).

The unusually severe imprecations hurled at enemies in psalms such as 109 and 137 may be understood as cries of agony. They accurately record a stage of human spiritual development in people longing for the deeper revelation of love that Christ brought into the world. In some cases these enemies appear more than human and may represent demonic forces of evil. In any case these psalms do not contain divine approbation of the curses.

In the New Testament Christ voluntarily assumed all the pain and agony reserved for those who do not keep the law (Deut. 27:26; Gal. 3:10, 13). He is publicly exposed in the same shameful manner as the rebellious son (Deut. 21:23; Gal. 3:13). Paul wished himself to be accursed for his brethren (Rom. 9:3).

A curse came to mean total removal of a person from the company of the redeemed where all blessings are localized. Thus *anathema* in the New Testament became equivalent to *ḥerem* in the Old Testament. This curse was imposed for apostasy (Gal. 1:8), not loving Christ (1 Cor. 16:22), and not extending loving care to the least of the brethren (Matt. 25:41).

First Corinthians 12:3 confesses the impossibility of an inspired curse against Christ. Revelation 22:3 looks forward to a day when the curse will be no more.

PAUL FERGUSON

See also DEVOTE, DEVOTED; WAR, HOLY WAR.

Bibliography. B. Anderson, *Out of the Depths;* H. C. Brichto, *The Problem of "Curse" in the Hebrew Bible;* D. R. Hillers, *Treaty Curses and the OT Prophets.*

Dd

Dagon. *See* GODS AND GODDESSES, PAGAN.

Daniel, Theology of. Daniel is one of the most controversial books of the Bible, yet its message is clear and unmistakable. While Bible scholars debate issues like when it was written and whether it is historically accurate, the Book of Daniel consistently calls God's people of every generation to faithfulness.

Daniel is the only Old Testament book written completely in apocalyptic language. As such, Daniel is similar to the Book of Revelation in the New Testament, which is the oldest document actually claiming the title "apocalypse" or "revelation." In this sense, Daniel forms an important bridge between the Testaments. Daniel, like other Old Testament prophets, is concerned with the Sinai covenant (9:11, 13, 15) and with the basic social message of the other prophets (4:27). At the same time, he deals with issues of the distant future in a manner that sets the pattern for New Testament prophecies.

Daniel's unique position in the Old Testament can also be seen in its purpose. Unlike other Old Testament prophecies, this book does not call its readers to repent and lead a new life. Daniel's concern is consistent faithfulness among believers, continued obedience among God's people during times of hardship.

The Book of Daniel has two discernible parts: the historical narratives of chapters 1–6 and the visions of chapters 7–12. The stories of the first half relate the events of Daniel and his ministry in the foreign courts of Babylonia and Persia. The visions of the second half are the personal accounts of Daniel dated to the later part of his life.

The narratives of chapters 1–6 have in common a single theme: Daniel and his three friends successfully bear witness to their faith before a hostile world. Though the circumstances are often unpleasant, these young men consistently stand up for righteousness against overwhelming odds. In the process they find that God is faithful. The historical section in general forms a theology of history in which God delivers those who faithfully represent him in the world and humiliates the proud who fail to acknowledge him.

Though the visions of chapters 7–12 are in general less well known than the beloved stories of the first half, they nonetheless contain individual passages that are noted for their theological importance. The vision of chapter 7 portrays God as "the Ancient of Days"; another figure is called "the Son of Man," a designation Jesus applied to himself (Matt. 16:27; 24:30; 26:64; Mark 8:38; 13:26, etc.). The interpretation of the vision of chapter 9 includes the hotly debated "seventy sevens" or "seventy weeks of years" passage (vv. 24–27). The concluding vision contains the only explicit Old Testament reference to the resurrection (12:1–3).

There are at least four themes that dominate this book: the sovereignty of God; the self-destructive pride of humankind; the ultimate victory of God's kingdom; and the coming of his servant, the Messiah.

The Sovereignty of God. Other Old Testament prophets knew that Yahweh, the god of Israel, was sovereign over the whole world, including the other nations. But Daniel illustrates this fact in graphic new ways. Through both the narratives and visions, Daniel demonstrates the lordship of God over the whole world, not just Jerusalem and the Israelites. This truth was meant to be a source of great comfort for exiled Israelites living in a foreign context.

This pervasive theme is apparent from the outset of chapter 1. The first verse of the book asserts that Nebuchadnezzar came to besiege Jerusalem. The reader of the book might assume the Babylonian king has come in his own awesome strength and at his own instigation. But the next verse makes it clear that Nebuchadnezzar was not acting in opposition to the will of God. In fact, whatever success [Nebuchadnezzar enjoyed was provided by God: "The Lord delivered Jehoiakim king of Judah into his Nebuchadnezzar's] hand" (v. 2, Heb. *nātan,* "give," is a key word in this chapter).

After Daniel steadfastly resisted the cultural pressure to compromise, God "gave" (*nātan*) him favor before Nebuchadnezzar's chief of staff (v. 9). Later, God "gave" (*nātan*) the four young Jews surpassing knowledge and discernment, particularly to Daniel, a gift for understanding visions and dreams (v. 17). So this chapter emphasizes God's sovereignty over the affairs of nations (Babylon and Israel, v. 2) as well as individuals (Daniel and this three companions, v. 17).

The sovereignty of God is played out in the rest of the book in the conflict between the proud and arrogant rules of the world and the kingdom of God. The stone cut by supernatural forces in chapter 2 demolished the statue of Nebuchadnezzar's dream symbolizing the human kingdoms of the earth. The God of Shadrach, Meshach, and Abednego controlled the forces of nature with startling effect on Nebuchadnezzar (chap. 3), as he also did for Daniel in the lions' den (chap. 6). Daniel is given the ability to interpret dreams and visions that are mysterious and impossible for the noblest and wisest of Babylon's wisemen to discern (chaps. 2, 4, and 5). The handwriting on the wall episode demonstrates God's sovereign control over nations and individual rulers (chap. 5).

The Book of Daniel adds a new twist to the prophetic view of the nations who might oppose God. Most of the other prophets have oracles against Israel's enemy nations, a prophetic form that is ancient in Israelite literature (see, e.g., Isa. 13–23; Jer. 46–51, etc.). But Daniel views the key empires in sequential order of four, followed by a fifth, eternal kingdom. Rather than present sermons against Israel's immediate neighbors, Daniel sees visions of future empires that oppose God worldwide and oppress his people everywhere. Both the historical narratives and the visions portray a struggle between these successive rulers of the world and God's kingdom. The stories relate how God's servants (Daniel and his friends) were able to overcome the strongest human forces of earth in their efforts to remain faithful to God.

The first of the visions (chap. 7) portrays three frightening beasts and a grotesque monster that threatens to exterminate God's people. But the Ancient of Days prevails and establishes an eternal kingdom for his saints. Even in persecution and death, the sovereign Lord of the kingdom will provide resurrection (12:1–3). God's sovereignty over the proud and arrogant rules of the world climaxes in Michael's final victory provided for all who are written in "the book" (12:1). In the historical narratives, God was sovereign over all his enemies of the past. The visions reveal how that sovereignty will play itself out in human history.

This emphasis on God's sovereignty leads naturally to the next two primary themes of the book: prideful and rebellious humankind is self-destructive because it fails to acknowledge the sovereign Lord of the universe; and God's people will ultimately succeed, because with him they cannot fail.

The Pride of Humankind. A further emphasis of the Book of Daniel is the pride and arrogance of humankind and God's total condemnation of egotism. In chapters 1–6 human pride is the subsurface issue behind the problem that introduces each chapter. In the visions of chapters 7–12, the arrogance of future world leaders is the enemy of God and his people. Ultimately, the each case, God has acted, or will act, to turn human pride and arrogance to shame and ridicule.

In the narratives of chapters 1–6, Nebuchadnezzar and Belshazzar are perfect examples of human leaders who rebel against God's authority. In both cases, their pride reduces them to pathetic states of helplessness and ridicule. After God has acted, they are hardly recognizable as kings of the great and mighty Babylon (4:33; 5:6).

The pride of the world empires is central to the ideas of chapters 7–12. The scheme of empires in chapters 7 and 8 is a succession of world leaders, which depicts the limits of imperial pride, reaching the climax at the little horn with the big mouth (7:8). But a new heavenly kingdom, led by the Ancient of Days and the Son of Man, replaces these proud earthly reigns. In chapters 10–12 the supernatural forces of heaven will move to crush the ultimate anti-Christian ruler of earth, who has arrogantly raised himself above every god (11:36).

The Book of Daniel is especially pertinent for every new generation of believers because it addresses the ultimate problem of the human condition. Sin and rebellion always find root in pride and self-absorption. So salvation must involve confession, rejection of prideful self-sufficiency, and dependence on God (Mark 8:34), all of which are so magnificently modeled by Daniel, his three companions, and later, by the saints of the Most High.

The Ultimate Victory of God's Saints. Daniel also reveals much about the kingdom of God. The fundamental message of Daniel is that through every possible circumstance of life, it is possible to live a life of faith and victory with God's help. God reigns supreme in heaven and earth, and those allied with him share in his triumph. No matter how severe the persecution, the enemies of God cannot bring an end to his community of believers. The unique apocalyptic nature of Daniel teaches that this has always been so (chaps. 1–6) and always will be (chaps. 7–12). Even in death, God's people are victorious (12:1–3).

Prevalent in this book is the idea of four great world kingdoms followed by a fifth (chaps. 2 and 7). Conservative authorities have traditionally taken these kingdoms to refer to Babylonia, Medo-Persia, Greece, and Rome, respectively. Though the precise details are in doubt, the message is clear and irrefutable. All earthly kingdoms are temporary, even fleeting, no matter how impressive they may look at the moment. Ultimately, the eternal kingdom of the Ancient of Days will be ushered in by the Son of Man (7:14).

Although this promise is certain and sure, the rest of the book describes a delay in the arrival of God's eternal kingdom. During the postponement, God's faithful people will endure severe testing and persecution at the hands of proud, irreligious leaders of the world. The seventy weeks of years (9:24–27) and the promise of the resurrection (12:1–3) presuppose that the faithful saints of God will have to endure hardship for a limited time. But those who faithfully endure and await his timing will participate in his final victory.

Daniel is the primary source in the Old Testament revealing events of the future. Together with the New Testament Book of Revelation, it provides data for the various theories about the end-times. Though Christians disagree on issues such as when Christ will return in relation to a millennial (thousand-year) reign, all are agreed that the most important question is whether the church is currently living a life worthy of his blessing and acceptance, whenever he comes again.

In other words, the details of eschatology are not as crucial as eschatological ethics: behaving Christ-like now in this world, and living in the expectation and anticipation of Christ's return. Daniel teaches that God's people can and should live holy, righteous lives while suffering the injustices of this life. They are encouraged to do so because, in the end, God will conclusively reward them with victory.

God's Messiah. The role of the "Son of David" is a central theme among Israel's prophets. Israel never forgot God's promise to provide seed from her ideal King to rule forever on the throne in Jerusalem (2 Sam. 7:16). Isaiah thought of God's commitment to David as a pattern for the everlasting covenant God wanted with Israel (55:3–4). Jeremiah asserted that the covenant with David was as unbreakable and secure as God's appointment of the sun to rule the day and the moon to rule the night (33:20–22).

The son of David figure was an "anointed one," since the kings of Israel were traditionally anointed with oil by a prophet. This anointed one ("Messiah" in Hebrew, "Christ" in Greek) was the principal figure for the prophets, who speak of a movement from chaos and defeat to victory and redemption for national Israel. But as an exilic prophet, Daniel was living and working after the actual loss of the monarchy. No ancient Near Eastern community could survive the absence of a king. But Israel had the capacity to preserve spiritually what she had lost materially.

In Daniel, the concept of the Messiah was reinterpreted toward the universal, rather than being limited to a single nation, Israel. Thus there is a Davidic substratum, or ideological undercurrent in Daniel 7:13–14. Daniel had envisioned evil incarnate in the form of the little horn, the symbol of a ruthless human dictator who stops at nothing to achieve his own selfish ambitions (7:8 and 8:9, though the two horns are not identical). Now Daniel sees the Messiah as the antithesis of personified evil. Eventually the Son of Man will lead his people ("the saints of the Most High") into triumph.

The political and military dimensions of the son of David, the king-Messiah, are broadened in Daniel. In chapter 7 the nationalistic interpretation of the Messiah is transcended. Instead of savior of national Israel, who leads his people to victory over enemy nations that are evil, the Messiah becomes victorious over evil in general.

William T. Arnold

See also Apocalyptic; Jesus Christ, Name and Titles of; Messiah; Revelation, Theology of.

Bibliography. J. G. Baldwin, *Daniel: An Introduction and Commentary;* J. E. Goldingay, *Daniel;* D. W. Heaton, *The Book of Daniel;* A. LaCocque, *Daniel in His Time;* D. S. Russell, *The Method and Message of Jewish Apocalyptic;* E. J. Young, *Daniel: An Introduction and Commentary;* idem, *The Prophecy of Daniel: A Commentary.*

Darkness. "Darkness" in both the Old Testament (Heb. *ḥāšak*) and New Testament (Gk. *skotos*) is an evocative word. If light symbolizes God, darkness connotes everything that is anti-God: the wicked (Prov. 2:13–14; 1 Thess. 5:4–7), judgment (Exod. 10:21; Matt. 25:30), and death (Ps. 88:12). Salvation brings light to those in darkness (Isa. 9:2). Although darkness is opaque to man, it is transparent to God (Ps. 139:12). Indeed, God can veil himself in darkness at moments of great revelation (Deut. 4:11; 5:23; Ps. 18:11).

God Rules the Darkness. The biblical view of darkness and light offers a unique contrast. There is no thought that darkness is equal in power to God's light. The absolute, sovereign God rules over the darkness and the powers of evil. This is evident in several ways. First, God knows the darkness. He knows where it is (Job 34:22) and what it contains (Dan. 2:22). Second, God rules over the darkness because he created it (Isa. 45:7; cf. Amos 4:13; 5:8). Third, God uses the darkness for his own purposes: to hide himself from the sight of men (Ps. 18:11; 1 Kings 8:12) and to bring his judgment on evildoers (Deut. 28:28–29; Matt. 8:12; 22:13), evil nations (Ezek. 30:18–19), and false prophets (Jer. 23:12; Mic. 3:6; Rev. 16:10). Finally, God rules over the darkness eschatologically. The time of God's ultimate judgment, the day of the Lord, is portrayed in both the Old Testament and New Testament as a day of darkness (Joel 2:2; Amos 5:18, 20; Zeph. 1:15; Matt. 24:29; Rev. 6:12–17).

Darkness and Crucifixion. It is against this background that the emphasis on darkness in the crucifixion scene may be understood. Luke records, "it was now about the sixth hour, and darkness came over the whole land until the ninth hour, for the sun stopped shining. And the curtain of the temple was torn in two" (23:44–45; cf. Matt. 27:45; Mark 15:33). While darkness often accompanies the conception of death in Scripture (cf. Job 10:21–22), darkness at the crucifixion scene displays God's displeasure on humankind for crucifying his son. It also indicates God's judgment on evil. But the torn curtain exhibits the opening of salvation to all through the death of God's Son.

Final Darkness. The Old Testament and New Testament describe the future of the ungodly in terms of eschatological darkness, symbolizing perdition (1 Sam. 2:9; Matt. 22:13; Jude 12–13). "Hell" and "pits of darkness" describe the fate of angels who sinned (2 Peter 2:4; Jude 6). But for believers darkness will be dispelled by the presence of the light of the glory of God (Rev. 21:23–24; 22:5). It is only through the light of God in Jesus Christ that darkness can be dispelled.

MICHAEL J. WILKINS

See also HELL.

Bibliography. E. R. Achtmeier, *Int* 17 (1963): 439–49; G. L. Borchert, *Dictionary of Paul and His Letters,* sv. "Light and Darkness"; F. G. Carver, *Wesleyan Theological Journal* 23 (1986): 7–32; H. Conzelmann, *TDNT,* 7:423–45; D. Guthrie, *New Testament Theology:* H.-C. Hahn, *NIDNTT,* 1:420–25; G. E. Ladd, *A Theology of the New Testament;* G. F. Shirbroun, *Dictionary of Jesus and the Gospels,* s.v. "Light"; G. Wenham, *Genesis 1–15.*

David. David was the founder of a dynasty that would rule in Jerusalem for over 350 years. His impact on the history of Israel is seen from the extensive interest in him and his successors as reflected in the Deuteronomic history, the prophets, the Chronicler's history, the psalms, and the New Testament.

David in the Deuteronomic History. The books from Joshua through Kings are often called the Deuteronomic history (DH) because the authors/compilers of these books used provisions and emphases unique to Deuteronomy in order to evaluate the history of Israel. Deuteronomy had authorized the nation to have a king (17:14–20), and the DH traces life in Israel both without a king (Joshua, Judges) and with a king (Samuel, Kings).

The majority of what we learn about David's life and times is contained in the accounts in Samuel. In Samuel the writer forges a contrast between Saul and David, "a man after his [God's] own heart" (1 Sam. 13:14). D. M. Gunn's analysis of the narratives about David focuses on two primary themes: David as king and David as a man. In his first role as king, David acquires the kingdom and assures his tenure in office (the accounts about David and Saul, the rebellions of Absalom and Sheba) and founds a dynasty (the birth of Solomon, the rebellion of Adonijah, the elimination of other contenders and factions). These narratives are intertwined with the theme of David as a man: a husband and father (Michal, Bathsheba, Amnon, Absalom, Solomon, Adonijah). The accounts are overlaid with themes of sexuality and political intrigue. Sexuality is a motif in the accounts of the sin with Bathsheba, the death of the child from an adulterous union, one son's rape of a daughter, the competition for the father's bedmate Abishag, Uriah's refusal to visit his wife, the seizure of David's concubines, and the childlessness of Saul's daughter Michal. Violence and political intrigue are interspersed in the accounts of David's wars, Saul's attempts on David's life, the violence of Joab and his brothers, the murder of Uriah, fratricide among David's sons, the slaughter of the helpless Absalom, and David's plans for the deaths of his enemies soon after his own death. The account of David's relationship with Bathsheba not only prepares for the eventual accession of Solomon, but it also sets in motion a curse that will dog the remainder of David's life: death and sexual outrage will follow, and "the sword will never depart from [his] house" (2 Sam. 12:10). The one word "sword" becomes a key term unifying aspects of the narrative from Samuel through Kings. The entire account of David is presented as the interplay of his public (kingship) and private (father, husband) roles as they impinge on the question of who will succeed him to the throne. Gunn also accents the themes of giving and grasping: whereas some accounts present David or other characters as somewhat passive in their roles, in others they seize or grasp at favor and power. For example, the king who will not seize the kingdom from Saul (2 Sam. 2–5) is nevertheless willing to seize a woman who is the object of his desire (Bathsheba); she who is seemingly passive in her seduction will later seize the kingdom for Solomon. Overall it is the story of how David gains the throne, loses it temporarily in the face of rebellions, only to regain it again, and then lose it in death. It is an intricate picture of human greatness and folly, of wisdom and sin, of faith and faithlessness, of contrasting perspectives and conflicting desires. The narratives about David also abound in irony. For example, the faithful Uriah unknowingly honors a king who has been unfaithful to him; Uriah retains his ritual purity during warfare by refraining from sexual intercourse during time of war, only to be sent to his death in battle by a king who enjoyed sexual congress with Uriah's wife instead of going to the battle (2 Sam. 11).

Within the larger DH, the writer is concerned to trace the faithfulness of God in his promise to David that he would never lack a descendant sitting on this throne (2 Sam. 7). This theme is played out in Kings: there were twenty kings in the southern kingdom, and twenty kings in the northern. But the northern kingdom lasted only two centuries while the southern kingdom endured for three and a half centuries. Why was life expectancy so much greater for a king in the South? In the North, there were nine different dynasties, most inaugurated by regicide or coup d'etat. In the South, by contrast, a single dynasty ruled until the Babylonian exile. God had indeed "maintained a lamp" for David (1 Kings 11:36; 15:4; 2 Kings 8:19).

David in the Psalms. The historical books recall David's skill as a musician and his concern with music in worship (1 Sam. 16:14–21; 1 Chron. 25; 2 Chron. 23:18; 29:25–30; 35:15). The many psalms assigned to David reflect this skill and interest. However, the psalms do not just record the compositions of David; they also celebrate the promises God made to him and his descendants (18:50; 78:70, 72; 89:3, 20, 35, 49). The royal psalms (2, 45, 72, 84, 89, 110) join with the prophets in giving voice to Israel's messianic hopes for another king like David. The royal psalms center on a king who meets universal opposition, is victorious, and establishes righteous rule from Zion over the nations. His kingdom is peaceful, prosperous, everlasting, and faithful to the Lord. He is the friend of the poor and the enemy of the oppressor. He is the heir of the promises to David. He is himself divine (Ps. 45:6); like the angel of the Lord, he is both God and distinct from God.

David in the Prophets. One of the recurring themes in the Book of Samuel is reference to the "Lord's anointed" (1 Sam. 16:3, 6, 12–13; 24:6; 26:9, 11, 16, 23; 2 Sam. 1:14, 16; 3:39; 19:21). The term "messiah" means "anointed one," and the idea of a messiah for Israel grows out of her ideology about a righteous king, one who would be like David. The messiah as a figure is integrally involved in Israel's unique understanding of her place in history: their awareness from the beginning that God had chosen them to bring blessing to the nations. God had raised up great leaders and deliverers for Israel during her history, and he would yet do so again in the person of a messiah. The failures of the kings who followed David set him in an increasingly favorable light, so that Israel's hopes crystallized around the coming of a future king like David (Isa. 16:5; 55:3–5; Jer. 23:5; 33:17–26; 36:30; Ezek. 34:23; Zech. 9:9; 12:8, 10). In the book of Immanuel (Isa. 7–12), the prophet speaks about the appearance of a wonder child who will be deliverer, world ruler, and righteous king.

David in the Chronicler's History. Chronicles is among the latest books of the Old Testament; it was written no earlier than the later decades of the fourth century B.C. When comparing the Chronicler's account of David and Solomon with that in Samuel/Kings, perhaps the most striking difference is the material that the Chronicler has chosen to omit. With the exception of the account of David's census (1 Chron. 21 // 2 Sam. 24), the Chronicler has not recorded incidents that would in any way tarnish the image of David or Solomon. The Chronicler does not report the rival kingdom in the hands of a descendant of Saul during David's seven years at Hebron or David's negotiations for rule over the northern tribes. He omits any account of the rebellion of Absalom and Adonijah and the actions of Amnon and Shimei; he makes no mention of David's sins in connection with Bathsheba and Uriah. The Chronicler deletes the narrative of Solomon's taking vengeance on David's enemies (1 Kings 2) and does not report the sins of Solomon which, according to Kings, were ultimately the reason for the break-up of the kingdom (1 Kings 11). Even the blame for the schism is shifted from Solomon to Jeroboam (2 Chron. 13:6–7).

In Chronicles David and Solomon are portrayed as glorious, obedient, all-conquering figures who enjoy not only divine blessing, but also the support of all the nation. Instead of an aged, bed-ridden David who only saves the kingdom for Solomon at the last minute due to the promptings of Bathsheba and Nathan (1 Kings 1), the Chronicler shows a smooth transition of power without a ripple of dissent (1 Chron. 21, 28–29). David himself publicly announces Solomon's appointment as his successor, an announcement greeted with enthusiastic and total support on the part of the people (1 Chron. 28:1–29:25), including the other sons of David, the officers of the army, and others who had supported Adnoijah's attempted coup (1 Chron. 29:24; 1 Kings 1:7–10). Whereas in Kings Solomon's sins are a reason for the schism and Solomon is contrasted to his father David (1 Kings 11), in Chronicles Rehoboam is commended for "walking in the ways of David and Solomon" (2 Chron. 11:17).

This idealization of the reigns of David and Solomon could be dismissed as a kind of glorification of the "good old days." Yet when coupled with the Chronicler's emphasis on God's promise to David of an enduring dynasty (1 Chron. 17:11–14; 2 Chron. 13:5, 8; 21:7; 23:3), the Chronicler's treatment of David and Solomon reflects a "messianic historiography." David and Solomon in Chronicles are not just the David and Solomon who were, but the David and Solomon of the Chronicler's eschatological hope. At a time when subject to the Persians the Chronicler still cherished hopes of a restoration of Davidic rule, and he describes the glorious rule of David and Solomon in the past in terms of his hopes for the future.

David in the New Testament. David's sins do not seem that much greater than Saul's. How is it that David can be described by the narrator as "a man after his [God's] own heart" (1 Sam. 13:14)? Israel had looked at Saul's height and build—there was no one like him among all the people (1 Sam. 10:24); although God had chosen Saul, he knew what was in his heart. Human beings might look at appearance and height, but God saw David's heart. David's heart was such that he would face Goliath virtually unarmed and would triumph through his faith, while Saul cowered in his tent (1 Sam. 17). The central demand of life in covenant with God, both from the mouth of Moses and Jesus, was to love him with the whole heart (Deut. 6:5; Mark 12:30).

Yet something happened to David along the way. When we first meet him in Samuel he has taken a club to kill a bear and a lion for the sake of sheep (1 Sam. 17:34–35), but by the end of the book, he has decided that the sheep should die for him, although this time the sheep were people (2 Sam. 24:14, 17). David will not be the good shepherd who will give his life for the sheep.

The writers of the New Testament see in Jesus the embodiment of a righteous king for Israel. They take pains to point to his descent from David (Matt. 1:1, 6, 17). The crowds and even the demons recognize him as the son of David, the Messiah of Israel (Matt. 12:23; 20:30–31; 21:9, 15). The title "Christ" is a Greek translation of the Hebrew anointed one or messiah. Jesus comes like David, as "the Lord's anointed."

Hannah's longing for a child and for a righteous king and anointed one (1 Sam. 2:10) is heard again in Mary's own magnificat as she anticipates the birth of Israel's king and Messiah (Luke 2:32–33, 46–55, 69). David had become the heir of God's promise to Abraham that he would give him a great name (Gen. 12:2; 2 Sam. 7:9). David's greater son receives a names above all others (Phil. 2:9–10). Just as David had once gone into singlehanded combat with the great enemy of Israel so Jesus would singlehandedly triumph over the enemy of our souls. He would establish an everlasting kingdom. RAYMOND B. DILLARD

See also JESUS CHRIST, NAME AND TITLES OF.

Bibliography. J. Flanagan, *David's Social Drama: A Hologram of Israel's Early Iron Age;* J. P. Fokkelman, *Narrative Art and Poetry in the Book of Samuel,* 3 vols.; K. R. R. Gros Louis, *Semeia* 8 (1977): 15–33; D. M. Gunn, *The Story of King David;* J. A. Wharton, *Int* 35 (1981): 341–54; R. N. Whybray, *The Succession Narrative: A Study of II Sam. 9–20 and I Kings 1 and 2.*

Day. Segment of time that includes the night (Gen. 1:8) as in a twenty-four hour day. "Day" also stands in contrast to "night" (Num. 11:32; Luke 18:7; Rev. 7:15). The term may refer to an era (Matt. 24:37) or to the span of human history (Gen. 8:22), or specify a memorable event (Isa. 9:4) or a significant time (Zeph. 1:14–16). The term often has a metaphorical meaning. A "day" is important largely for what fills it rather than for its chronological dimension.

The "Day" and Cosmic Order. The "days of creation" in Genesis 1, given the semipoetic nature of the composition, are quite possibly intended as literary devices, division markers as in a mosaic. The refrain, "And there was evening, and there was morning," speaks not only of sequence but of an order that is affirmed following the flood as a foundational element in creation and as an answer to chaos and destruction (Gen. 8:22). The succession of days is testimony to a God whose governance of the universe is not haphazard but marked by order and, especially, reliability. The regularity of day and night guarantees God's promises in history as trustworthy. So when God makes a new covenant and assures Israel of continuing as a nation indefinitely, God offers the constancy of the cosmic order ("he who appoints the sun to shine by day") as his credentials for following through on his intention (Jer. 31:35–37).

The "Day" and Redemption History. Certain days in Israel's history were clearly days of salvation, the most striking of which was the day of God's deliverance of Israel from Egypt at the exodus (Exod. 12:14; 13:3). In conjunction with Saul's conflict with the Philistines, it is said, "so the LORD rescued Israel that day" (1 Sam. 14:23).

Interest in "days to come" is a longstanding one (Gen. 49:1; Num. 24:14). The prophets speak of a coming day when God will intervene in history. In that day a root will emerge from the stem of Jesse. This remarkable person will be endowed with the sevenfold Spirit (Isa. 10:33–11:10). In coming days, God will be exalted in all of Israel and even over all the earth (Isa. 2:11). In that future day Israel will be saved from her enemies and will be safely secured in her land. God promises that "In the day of salvation I will help you" (Isa. 49:8). Evil will be decisively dealt with and righteousness will be established. That decisive action involving judgment and salvation is the day of the Lord.

At Pentecost Peter can speak of the fulfillment of Joel's prophecy of the day of the Lord (Acts 2:17–21; cf. Joel 2:28–32). Essentially this day is one in which God is fully on the scene; it is a day that he monopolizes. In the coming of Christ and in the Spirit's descent at Pentecost, Peter discerns a day of God. Because of God's grace and favor, the current day is the day of salvation (2 Cor. 6:2). The offer during this extended "day" remains: "and everyone who calls on the name of the Lord will be saved" (Acts 2:21). Such decision is urged because God has "set a day when he will judge the world with justice by the man he has appointed" (Acts 17:31). With regard to the history of redemption the word "day" is shorthand for a particular event (such as the exodus), but more often for an era as a singular stage in the progress of God's plan for salvation.

The "Day" and Calendars of Worship. Some days in Israel's calendar were set aside for special purposes (e.g., the Sabbath; Exod. 20:8–11; Deut. 5:12–15). In keeping with the purpose of the day, which was to bring wholeness (Heb. *šālôm*), Jesus healed individuals of their sicknesses. The writer to the Hebrews sees in the day a prefiguring of the greater "rest" that God envisions for his own (4:6–11).

Special days are holy days that belong to God (Neh. 8:9). In Israel's religious calendar the Day of Atonement, observed soon after the day of the New Year (Sept.–Oct), was a day when corporate and individual sins were confessed, appropriate sacrifices and rituals were performed, and divine forgiveness was extended (Lev. 16; 23:26–32). Other special days were the several festivals, such as the Passover, the Feast of the Firstfruits, and the Feast of Tabernacles (Lev. 23; Deut. 16:1–17). Taken together the days of festival indicated that Israel's religion was communal in character, that it came as an occasion for instruction, and that it was marked by joyfulness. Later in Israel's history the festival of Purim was added (Esther 9:18–32). In New Testament times, Christians worshiped on the first day of the week (1 Cor. 16:2), but Paul cautioned them not to overrate any festival (Col. 2:16).

The "Day" and Believer's Lifestyle. Life is lived a day at a time. Prayer is offered for daily bread (Matt. 6:9–13, 31–34). Like Paul, the Christian in one sense dies daily (1 Cor. 15:31), but in another sense is renewed day by day (2 Cor. 4:16). Since within the larger span of history, any one person's days are like a shadow (1 Chron. 29:15; Ps. 102:11), it is appropriate to pray for wisdom (Ps. 90:12). Believers recognize that days can be stressful (Gen. 35:3), but they do not share a pessimistic view about life as a series of meaningless days (Eccles. 6:12). Jesus urged his followers to work the works of God while it is day (John 9:4). Believers, children of the day as opposed to children of darkness, will do works of love and hope becoming to persons enlightened by the gospel (1 Thess. 5:5). ELMER A. MARTENS

See also DAY OF THE LORD, GOD, CHRIST, THE; LAST DAY(S), LATTER DAYS, LAST TIMES.

Bibliography. G. Delling, *TDNT,* 2:943–53; S. J. DeVries, *Yesterday, Today, and Tomorrow;* G. Hasel, *ISBE,* 1:877–78; M. Saebo, *TDOT,* 6:12–32.

Day of Atonement. *See* FEAST AND FESTIVALS.

Day of Christ. *See* DAY OF THE LORD, GOD, CHRIST, THE.

Day of Judgment. *See* JUDGMENT, DAY OF.

Day of the Lord, God, Christ, the. Expression, often in the context of future events, which refers to the time when God will intervene decisively for judgment and/or salvation. Variously formulated as the "day of the LORD" (Amos 5:18), the "day of our Lord Jesus Christ" (1 Cor. 1:8; cf. 2 Cor. 1:14), the "day of God" (2 Peter 3:12; Rev. 16:14), or "the last day(s)," the expression highlights the unmistakable appearance of God. God will make visible his rule of righteousness by calling for an accounting by the nations as well as individuals, dispensing punishment for some and ushering in salvation for others.

In the Old Testament the expression "day of the Lord" occurs eighteen times in prophetic literature, most often in the books of Joel and Zephaniah. It is not found in Daniel. A similar expression that stands close to it is "on that day," which occurs 208 times in the Old Testament; half the occurrences are in the prophets. In the New Testament, equivalent expressions, such as "day of Jesus Christ," are found in 1 Corinthians 1:8; 2 Corinthians 1:14; Philippians 1:6, 10; and 2 Peter 3:10, 12. "Day of the Lord" appears in 2 Thessalonians 2:2.

Origin of the Expression. The origin of the expression is in dispute. Some suggest that it is anchored in creation vocabulary (e.g., the seventh day as especially God's day). Others point to Israel's history, theologically interpreted. Scholars have suggested a cultic ritual, such as the day of a king's enthronement, as providing the setting for the expression. More likely, however, is the proposal that the wars of the Lord in Israel's history serve as the background, since battle images abound (Joel 3:9–10; Rev. 16:14) and issues of jurisdiction and authority are central to the day of the Lord.

The Quality of the Day. A cluster of various meanings belong to the expression, "day of the Lord." Its first occurrence (Amos 5:18), for example, does not refer to the end of the world; in the New Testament, however, such a meaning emerges.

In biblical thought the character or quality of a day (time period) was of greater importance than its date (the numerical quantity in a sequence). From the first mention of the expression by Amos (although some date Obadiah 15 and Joel earlier), the notion of *divine intervention,* of a "God who comes" is evident. Israel anticipated that for them God's coming would hold favorable prospects, that it would be a day of light. Amos announces that, given Israel's great evil, God's coming will signal for them disappointment and calamity, a day of darkness. Predominant in the divine intervention is the awesome presence of the Almighty. It is as though God not only comes on the scene, but fills the screen of all that is. His presence totally dominates. Human existence pales before this giant reality. On that day, "all hands will go limp, every man's heart will melt" (Isa. 13:7). At a later time the descriptions move beyond human experience. The cosmos will go into convulsions. In stereotyped language it is said that the sun will refuse to give its light, the moon and the stars will cease to shine (Isa. 13:10). Joel, preoccupied with the subject, cites wonders in heaven and on earth, including the moon turning to blood (Joel 2:30–31).

In the New Testament the appearance of God is more distinctly the coming of Christ, specifically the return of Christ, his second coming. Paul's mention of the "day of our Lord Jesus Christ" (1 Cor. 1:8) is likely the day of "the coming of our Lord Jesus Christ and our being gathered together to him" (2 Thess. 2:1). Whether the day is the parousia, or the climax of history and all things as in the "day of God" when the dissolution of the heavens occurs (2 Peter 3:12), the "day" will be characterized by the unquestioned and unmistakable presence of Almighty God.

As depicted by Joel, the day of the Lord means *decision:* "Multitudes, multitudes in the valley of decision! For the day of the LORD is near in the valley of decision" (3:14). A verdict will be rendered. God will adjudicate peoples. His decision for some nations, such as Tyre, Sidon, Moab, Philistia, and Assyria, will be punishment (Joel 3:4–13; cf. Zeph. 2:6–15). Divine judgment will be executed. On that day a decision will be rendered against everything proud (Isa. 2:12–18). God acts with dispatch as he judges nations in the Valley of Jehoshaphat (Joel 3:2, 12–13). The decision for others will have a saving dimension, for God's promise of blessing will be activated and realized (Joel 3:18–21).

The Calendaring of the Day. The "day of the Lord" is not a one-time occurrence. Days of the Lord, while often represented in the Bible as in the future, are not limited to the future. There have been days of the Lord in the past. The catastrophe of the fall of Jerusalem in 587 B.C. was described as a "day of the Lord" (Lam. 2:21). Isaiah says that the day of the Lord will involve the fall of Babylon. God's agency will be recognized, for he will "make the heavens tremble; and the earth will shake from its place" (Isa. 13:13). God's immediate agent will be the Medes whom he will stir up against Babylon; their action will be decisive. "Babylon, the jewel of kingdoms, the glory of the Babylonians' pride, will be overthrown by God like Sodom and Gomorrah" (13:19). Historically, that event is to be dated to 539 B.C. Joel, in turn, describes a grasshopper plague that for him represents the day of the Lord as imminent, even immediate. The day of Pentecost, now history, is described as the day of the Lord (Acts 2:16–21).

Still, for the prophets and for many of the New Testament writers, the day of the Lord points to the future. That future may be centuries distant, as in Isaiah's prophecy about Babylon (chap. 13) or Joel's prophecy about the Spirit (2:28–32), or it may be in the far distant future. Isaiah's language about the universal humiliation of the lofty and arrogant indicates a grand finale, possibly at the end of history (2:12–18). The New Testament, while speaking of the Christ event as a day of the Lord (Acts 2:16–21), also speaks of the anticipated day of Christ as his return (2 Thess. 2:1–2), which is yet, after almost two thousand years, still future. The surprise factor (it will come "like a thief in the night") is a marked feature of the day in the New Testament (1 Thess. 5:2, 4; 2 Peter 3:10). Eventually the day of the Lord (God) came to mean the termination of the world.

The Day of the Lord as a Day of Calamity. The day of the Lord means destruction of the godless. With metaphor the prophets excel in describing the calamitous aspect of day of the Lord. Amos speaks of it as a day of darkness (5:18). Joel depicts it as a day of clouds and thick darkness (2:2). Zephaniah's description (1:15–16a) is vivid as he mixes direct description and metaphor:

> That day will be a day of wrath,
> A day of distress and anguish
> A day of trouble and ruin,
> A day of darkness and gloom,
> A day of clouds and blackness
> A day of trumpet and battle cry.

Isaiah describes a massive leveling; whatever is lofty will be brought low (2:12–17). A frequent metaphor is war. Isaiah invokes the war model to characterize the day of the Lord—"The LORD Almighty is mustering an army for war" (13:4). With war comes fear and cruelty. The opponents are afraid; "pain and anguish will grip them. . . . They will look aghast at each other" (13:8). Joel describes the Lord's army: "They charge like warriors; they scale walls like soldiers. They all march in line" (2:7). Their effectiveness is telling: "Before them fire devours, behind them a flame blazes. Before them the land is like the garden of Eden, behind them, a desert waste" (2:3). The effect is awesome: "Before them the earth shakes, the sky trembles" (2:10). Zephaniah, emphasizing the destructive nature of that day, compares it to a sacrifice (1:8). In keeping with the motif of fire, the Septuagint renders Malachi 3:19: "For the day of the LORD is coming burning like an oven." The New Testament only confirms the destructive character of the "day" (1 Thess. 1:9–10). The author of 2 Peter reiterates the theme of fire and explains that by fire the earth and the elements themselves will be destroyed. The heavens will disappear, also by fire (2 Peter 3:10–11).

The elaborate description of the day of the Lord in Joel is about calamity for Israel. Drought has paralyzed the economy (1:4–12), brought the giving of gifts in worship to a halt (1:13), and jeopardized even the survival of animals (1:18). To forestall total disaster the prophet calls for a fast (1:14; 2:12). Amos depicts a day of darkness for Israel. The reason for such calamity lies in Israel's failure to do justice (5:7, 10–12) and her devotion to gods other than Yahweh (5:25–27). Zephaniah announces that great distress will come on the people, to the point that "their blood shall be poured out like dust." He explains that nothing—neither silver nor gold—will be able to save them (1:17–18). It is because the people have been violent and deceitful that such calamity will come (1:9, 17). The "day of the Lord" is focused, then, on Israel. Even though they expected their righteousness to be vindicated against their enemies, they were to discover that God's righteousness entailed his move against them.

Early descriptions of the day are found in the oracles against the nations. Joel graphically depicts a roll call of Tyre, Sidon, and Philistia. They will be judged on the basis of their treatment of Israel, the people of God. These nations are indicted for appropriating parts of the land of Israel (3:2), for inhumane treatment of young boys and young girls (3:3, 6), for traffic in slavery (3:6), and for expropriating temple articles (3:5). Obadiah announces that the deeds of the nations will return on their own heads (v. 15). Zephaniah's roll call is more extensive (Gaza, Moab, Ethiopia, Assyria) and the accusations include reproaching God's people (2:8, 10) and arrogance (2:15). Zechariah's announcement about the day of the Lord includes a battle with nations (14:3; cf. Rev. 16:14). More universally Isaiah lumps together all those who are proud, lofty, and arrogant: "The loftiness of man shall be bowed down and the haughtiness of men shall be brought low" (2:17). In the same vein, Paul associates the second coming of Christ with destructive power (1 Thess. 5:2–3).

The outcome, according to Isaiah, is the massive abolition of idols (2:18, 20). Threatened by God's fury, men and women will seek refuge in rocks (Isa. 2:21). One striking consequence of the day of the Lord for nations will be a recognition of Yahweh (Joel 3:17), but not without desolation (Zeph. 2:13–14) and death (Zeph. 2:12).

The day of the Lord also affects the natural order. The plague of locusts in Joel—whether a pointer to the day of the Lord or itself a "day of the Lord"—brings unproductive conditions for trees and vines and jeopardizes the survival of animals (1:12, 18). An upheaval of cosmic proportions means changes in the sun, moon, and stars (2:30). Some hold that these luminaries are symbolic, as often in the ancient Near East, of potentates and governmental powers. While there is no direct evidence that civil powers are intended, it must be understood that the authors were describing the indescribable, and that rigorous literalism need not always be required. Still, an overriding impression is that the day of the Lord will powerfully affect nature.

The Day as Salvation. While the judgment dimension is dominant in descriptions of the day of the Lord, the salvation dimension, although less emphasized, is nevertheless present. Some metaphors for the day are negative. Other metaphors are positive. It is a time of return to paradise (Isa. 35:1–10). The mountains will drip with new wine and the hills will flow with milk (Joel 3:18). The setting is as a day of abundant harvest (Joel 2:24).

The day of the Lord brings salvation for Israel. Drought and disaster drive Israel to their knees. They cry for God's mercy (Joel 2:17), and he answers. Salvation follows judgment. God forcibly and effectively removes the enemy (2:20). Salvation consists in abundance of grain, new wine, and oil, "enough to satisfy you fully" (2:19; cf. 2:24, 26). In the words of Zephaniah, God will "restore their [Judah's] fortunes" (2:7), an expression that implies the restoration of a desirable situation, a recovery of what has been lost. To God's saving activity will belong his pouring forth of his Spirit on all people (Joel 2:29). In the words of Zephaniah, "The LORD your God is with you, he is mighty to save. He will take great delight in you, he will quiet you with his love" (3:17). It will mean that "everyone who calls on the name of the LORD will be saved" (Joel 2:32).

In the New Testament the day of the Lord is more precisely the day of Jesus Christ and especially the manifestation of his glory. While this revelation of the person of Jesus spells calamity for unbelievers, for believers it means to be caught up to be with Christ their redeemer forever (1 Thess. 4:13–5:3). Such a prospect leads to joyous expectation and fervor. With this prospect and other promises in mind, Paul urges Christians to persevere (1 Cor. 1:8).

The day of the Lord portends salvation for the nations. Announcements about favorable prospects for Gentiles, while considerable, are not often found in conjunction with language about the day of the Lord. Still, pictures of Gentile response given elsewhere (such as Ps. 96) are reinforced by Zephaniah's classic description of the day of the Lord: "From beyond the rivers of Cush my worshipers, my scattered people, will bring me offerings" (3:10; cf. 3:9). The same prophet also portrays nations, each in their own place, bowing down to the Lord (2:11). Such a day is on the far side of the day of judgment, a situation true for peoples generally but also for the individual. Paul urges the church at Corinth to discipline the immoral person so that at the day of the Lord his spirit may be saved (1 Cor. 5:5).

The day of the Lord will transform nature. For God's people, Israel, the day of the Lord will mean physical abundance and spiritual blessing. Nature will be affected. Joel addresses an oracle to the earth, calling on it not to fear, and promises that it will be fertile and productive (2:22) so that threshing floors will be filled with grain and vats will overflow with new wine (2:24). Although the new heaven and earth are not in the Old Testament specifically connected to the day of the Lord (Isa. 65:17–25), that connection is made in 2 Peter 3:13. The old world has passed away to be replaced by a new heaven and a new earth. The table below sketches the nature of the day of the Lord as described by the preexilic prophets.

Text	Subject	Character	Effect	Figure of Speech
Amos 5:18–20	Israel	Judgment	Fear Surprise	Darkness/Light
Isa. 2:12–21	Proud and idolatrous people	Judgment	Terror	Massive leveling
Isa. 13	Babylon Nature (13:10–11)	Judgment	Terror Desolation Confusion	War
Isa. 34–35	Nations (34:1–17) Israel (35:1–10) Nature (34:4, 9) (35:1–2, 7)	Judgment Salvation	Desolation Renewal/Wholeness Disabled Transformed	Warfare Paradise
Zeph. 1:1–3:20	Judah (1:4)	Judgment	Distress Desolation	Sacrifice (1:8)
Zeph. 3:8–20	Nations (3:8) Israel (3:14)	Salvation	Worship Joy	Convocation (1:8, 18, 20)
Joel 1:1–3:21	Judah/Jerusalem Nations (3:2) God's People (2:18–20, 23–32) Nature (2:21–22)	Judgment Salvation Salvation	Destruction (1:15; 3:13) Renewal	War (2:2–11; 3:9–11) Fertility
Joel 3:18–20	Judah	Salavation	Joy Agricultural Prosperity	Paradise

Theological Significance. The theological significance of the day of the Lord may be summarized along three lines of thought. First, without question, the day of the Lord is a day of God's vindication. In the battle between evil and God, it is God who is victorious and vindicated. He is the ultimate power to whom is given the final word and against whom no force can stand (Isa. 2:17). God's summons of the nations for an accounting in Joel 3 and Zephaniah and the description of the cosmos being annihilated through fire (2 Peter 3:10–13) are two impressive ways of insisting on the truth that God is fully in charge. The preview of the day of the Lord, as in the destruction of Babylon or at the time of the Christ-event, including the day of Pentecost, already shows evidence of God's extraordinary work and power, so that the day of the Lord at the end of history is quite beyond human description.

Second, the day of Yahweh addresses the question of theodicy—not only the existence of evil, but especially undoing the havoc that it brings and making all things right. Ambiguities will be resolved. The message of the day of the Lord is that evil be trounced and evildoers will in the end receive their due. There is justice after all. God will settle his accounts with all that is godless and anti-God, arrogant and pridefully hostile against the Almighty. On the other hand, the scenes about God's blessing and the recovery of an Edenic paradise have and will continue to offer hope for those whose trust is in God (2 Peter 3:13).

Third, the certain coming of that day with its dark side of judgment and its bright side of a giant transformation encompassing human beings, human society, the world's physical environment, and the cosmos as such, calls on believers especially to live in its light. The purpose of discussions about the day of the Lord, past or future, is to illumine the present. Peter's question is rhetorical but pointed. In view of the coming day of the Lord, "What kind of people ought you to be?" (2 Peter 3:11).

Elmer A. Martens

See also Day; Judgment, Day of.

Bibliography. G. Brauman and C. Brown, *NIDNTT,* 2:887–88, 890–91; E. Delling, *TDNT,* 2:943–53; A. J. Everson, *JBL* 93 (1979): 329–37; E. Jenni, *IDB,* 1:784–85; W. C. Kaiser, Jr., *Toward an Old Testament Theology;* E. A. Martens, *God's Design;* R. L. Mayhue, *Grace Theological Journal* 6 (1985): 231–46; W. Van Gemeren, *Interpreting the Prophetic Word;* G. von Rad, *Old Testament Theology,* 2:119–25; B. Witherington, *Jesus, Paul and the End of the World: A Comparative Study in New Testament Eschatology.*

Deacon, Deaconess. The word "deacon" essentially means servant. The word group consists of *diakoneō* (occurring thirty-six times in the New Testament) meaning to serve or support; *diakonia* (occurring thirty-three times in the New Testament) meaning service, support, or ministry; and *diakonos* (occurring twenty-nine times in the New Testament), meaning server, servant, or deacon. The word group as a whole is scarce in the Septuagint, occurring approximately nine times. The word has both a general and technical sense in the New Testament. It may simply refer to any type of service or personal assistance performed for another. In the common usage of the day, the word meant to wait on tables or to assist or care for household needs. Eventually, the word came to mean "to serve" in any capacity.

The idea of serving others was not popular among the Greeks. Jews on the other hand found nothing inherently distasteful about service. Yet it was the Lord Jesus who raised service to a completely new level. He used the word as an expression of his humiliation in giving his life in suffering and death as a ransom (Matt. 20:28; Mark 10:45). Thus the word takes on the sense of loving action for others, especially in the community of faith, which is rooted in and founded upon divine love as seen in the atonement of Christ.

In this light, Paul could speak of being a servant of the new covenant (2 Cor. 3:6), of righteousness (2 Cor. 11:15), of Christ (2 Cor. 11:23; Col. 1:7; 1 Tim. 4:6), of God (2 Cor. 6:4), of the gospel (Eph. 3:7; Col. 1:23), and of the church (Col. 1:25).

The institution of the technical office seems to be found in Acts 6. Although the noun "deacon" (*diakonos*) does not occur, both *diakoneō* and *diakonia* are used, with emphasis resting more on the character of the men than any specific function. In this instance they cared for the needs of the Hellenistic widows and guaranteed fairness in the distribution of food. Their election was made jointly by the apostles and the congregation. It was determined that they must be men "full of the Spirit and wisdom" (v. 3). As one scans the Book of Acts, "fullness of the Spirit" almost always entails bold witnessing for the gospel of Christ (cf. Acts 1:8). That these men served in a manner transcending the traditional notion of deacon is clearly seen in the prophetic teaching activity of Stephen (Acts 6–7) and the evangelistic ministry of Philip (Acts 8).

First Timothy 3:8–13 is the most complete account in Scripture addressing the office of deacon. (In Phil. 1:1 it is only mentioned as being an office along with that of the bishops.) As in Acts 6, the emphasis is again on character qualifications rather than function. In fact, the qualities necessary for eligibility run in close parallel to those for bishops. Emphasis is placed upon the necessity of an exemplary life. Thus deacons must be worthy of respect, sincere (lit. "not double-tongued"), not indulging excessively in wine, not pursuing dishonest gain, holding the mystery (proved and approved), being found blameless, husband of one wife (a one-woman kind of man publicly and privately), and a good manager of children and household. The reward for such service found in verse 13 is having both an "excellent standing" and "great assurance" in the faith (before both God and people). Because teaching and leadership are not mentioned, the servant role of this office is made clear. These men are to be helpers in the practical areas of ministry, eligible to serve because of the unquestioned integrity of their lives.

It is possible, although not certain, that women served as deaconesses in the early church. In Romans 16:1 Phoebe of Cenchrea is commended as a sister of us, being also a *diakonon*. Whether the word is to be understood in a general or technical sense is open to debate. Of further significance for this issue is 1 Timothy 3:11; 5:3–16, and Titus 2:3–5. In 1 Timothy 3:11, there appears the phrase *gynaikas hosautos*, translated "likewise the women." "The women" has been variously interpreted to mean the wives of the deacons, female assistants to the deacons, deaconesses, or women in general. In favor of view 1 is the fact that *gunaikos* occurs also in verses 2 and 12, where it clearly means wife. Second, to return to qualifications for deacons in verses 12–13, and to address the children in verse 12, argues for wives being in view in verse 11.

In favor of views 2 and 3 is the use of the word "likewise." The same word also occurs in verse 8 and is used to introduce a distinct but related subject (deacons versus overseers). Second, the absence of the word "their" would seem to imply that the women in view are not the wives of deacons but rather women who serve in the same capacity as the men. Third, the list of qualifications for the women, although abbreviated (only one verse), is similar to those for the deacons. Fourth, the silence concerning any qualifications for the bishop's wife (3:1–7) argues against this being understood as referring to deacons' wives. When 1 Timothy 5:3–16 and Titus 2:3–5 are taken into consideration, it appears quite probably that there was a servant-oriented group of women in the early church. These women may have been wives of deacons. That such women would have ministered to other women, especially those in need of physical assistance and spiritual instruction, seems most likely. Practical considerations such as baptisms and intimate personal counseling and care would indeed have necessitated such a ministry of women to women.

DANIEL L. AKIN

See also CHURCH, THE; SERVANT, SERVICE; WOMAN.

Bibliography. H. W. Beyer, *TDNT,* 2:81–93; G. M. Burge, *EDT,* pp. 295–96; D. Guthrie, *New Testament Theology;* K. Hess, *NIDNTT,* 3:544–49; L. Morris, *BDT,* pp. 156–57.

Dead Sea Scrolls. Name given to over eight hundred ancient Jewish manuscripts recovered from eleven caves along the northwest shore of the Dead Sea.

The first cave, containing seven scrolls, was discovered accidentally in early 1947 by a young Bedouin shepherd. Between 1952 and 1956 ten more caves containing manuscripts and related material were found. Scholars have dated these manuscripts from the third century B.C. to the first century A.D. Most were not found intact; rather, scholars have had to piece together, and thereby attempt to understand, thousands of fragments. This process has been very tedious and slow; hence, many fragments remain unpublished.

Near the caves in which the scrolls were discovered lies an archaeological site known as Khirbet Qumran. Archaeologists excavated the ruins between 1951 and 1956 and determined that the site was inhabited by a community of Jews from the middle of the second century B.C. to A.D. 68. There were two main periods of occupation. The first period (c. 141–107 B.C.) consists of two phases: an initial phase involving modest, temporary buildings, and a second phase (107–31 B.C.) characterized by extensive building activity, which fixed the permanent lines of the settlement. Following an earthquake and fire in 31 B.C. the settlement was abandoned. The site lay deserted until 4 B.C., which marked the beginning of the second main period of occupation (4 B.C.–A.D. 68), during which the site was repaired and rebuilt along the same plan. Evidence of a great fire and the presence of Roman arrowheads and coins signal the destruction of the settlement by the Romans during the Jewish revolt in A.D. 68.

The Qumran complex included a large building and several smaller ones. In the large building was a tower, a kitchen, storage rooms, a large cistern, and several other rooms, one of which contained tables, benches, and inkwells, and seems to have been used for copying manuscripts. Just to the south of the main building was a large meeting hall with an adjoining pantry, from which over a thousand pieces of pottery were recovered. The settlement also included a pottery complex, a grain complex, a number of large cisterns and smaller pools, and an extensive aqueduct system. Outside the settlement are three cemeteries containing over a thousand graves. The main cemetery contains only men; two secondary cemeteries include women and children. At an oasis one mile to the south is a smaller settlement called Ain Feshka. This was apparently an agricultural and industrial center for Qumran. It included an irrigation system, an enclosure for animals, and what seems to have been a tannery.

Links between the ruins and the scrolls suggest that the scrolls belonged to this community. First, the caves are close to the ruins, most within five to ten minutes' walking distance. Cave 4, which contained more than five hundred of the eight hundred manuscripts, is literally a stone's throw from the site. Second, the manuscripts were copied during the same period of time that the settlement was occupied. Third, pottery found in the ruins matches pottery found in the caves. Fourth, writing found on pottery in the ruins matches that found on pottery in several of the caves. Finally, the character of the ruins provides the logical setting for the ritual washings, sacred meal, and manuscript copying reflected in the scrolls. The Qumran inhabitants probably hid the scrolls in the caves in anticipation of the advance of the Roman forces. Most scholars identify this community as a group of Essenes, a monastic sect of Jews described by the ancient writers Josephus, Philo, and Pliny the Elder.

The scrolls consist of four types of material. First, there are copies of Old Testament books. Only Esther is missing among the scrolls. Second, there are apocryphal books. Some, such as Tobit and Jubilees, were known prior to the discovery of the scrolls. Many others, such as the Genesis Apocryphon and the Testament of Amram, were not. Third, there are books that exhibit the distinctive doctrines and practices of the sect. These consist primarily of rules, poetical and liturgical books, and books of biblical interpretation. Finally, there are books that do not fit into any particular category, such as the Copper Scroll.

This article will focus on the sectarian documents. It will survey the main ideas found in these documents and, hence, give some insight into this community of Jews that, in its later stages, was contemporary with Jesus and the early church.

Although the origins of the sect are obscure, they seem to have centered around differences that the sect had with the temple leadership. The key figure in the early history of the sect was the Teacher of Righteousness, an otherwise unnamed individual who gave the sect direction and focus in its early stages. The sect believed that God had revealed to the Teacher of Righteousness the mysteries concerning the Law. Thus, he alone could properly interpret the Law; other Jews misunderstood it. Led by the Teacher of Righteousness, who was himself a priest, the sect rejected the temple cult in Jerusalem as it was currently practiced and probably even the ruling priesthood as being illegitimate. Guided by Isaiah 40:3 ("In the desert prepare the way for the LORD"; cf. Matt. 3:3), the sect removed itself to the desert area by the Dead Sea to await the final war, from which, with God's help, they as the true Israel would emerge victorious and after which they would restore the sacrificial cult and proper priesthood to Jerusalem.

The community was governed by stringent entrance procedures, a detailed code of conduct, and a strict organizational hierarchy under the leadership of the priests. The sectarians had a communal lifestyle, sharing property and work, studying the Torah, and meeting together for discussion of community matters and ceremonies. Worship was an important aspect of communal life; the sect understood itself as participating in the angelic worship of God. Especially significant was the sacred Meal. Ceremonial washings for purification were regular, and emphasis was placed on the use of the solar calendar rather than the lunar calendar of official Judaism. Unable to offer sacrifices in the defiled Jerusalem temple, the community viewed prayer and obedience as acceptable offerings. Other aspects of personal piety included a deep sense of human frailty and sinfulness and thanksgiving to God for his grace and election.

One of the foundational documents of the Qumran community is the *Manual of Discipline* (1QS) or the *Rule of the Community.* The *Manual* depicts its members as the Sons of Light; outsiders are the Sons of Darkness, from whom they have been called to separate. They have united together as the Community of God that has received his Covenant of Grace. They live a communal life, sharing property and work, studying the Law, and meeting together for discussion of community matters and ceremonies, such as the communal Meal. The community has a strict organizational hierarchy; virtually all matters, from the seating arrangement to the order of speaking, are determined by rank. At the top are the priests, the Sons of Zadok. Next come the Levites, or elders. Finally, there are the people, who are ranked in Thousands, Hundreds, Fifties, and Tens (cf. Exod. 18:25). Over the entire community stands the Master. Each individual is examined annually, at which time his rank may be adjusted upward or downward, depending on his understanding and behavior.

Entrance into the community is carefully regulated. The initiate first takes an oath, in the presence of the entire community, to obey the Law as it is interpreted in the community and to separate from the Men of Falsehood. He is examined by the Master and, if pronounced fit for the discipline, is admitted into the Covenant to begin receiving instruction in the rules of the community. During the first year he does not partake of the communal Meal, and he keeps his property separate from that of the community. At the end of the first year he undergoes a second examination. If he is allowed to continue, he embarks upon a second probationary year, during which he does not partake of the communal Drink and his property is held in trust by the community. At the end of the second year he undergoes a third examination. If he is found acceptable, he becomes a full-fledged member of the community and is given a rank, and his property is merged with that of the community.

The *Manual* also gives insight into some of the fundamental doctrines of the community. God has created for people Two Spirits in which to walk until the End: the Prince of Light/Angel of Truth/ Spirit of Truth and the Angel of Darkness/Spirit of Falsehood (cf. 1 John 4:6). Those who walk according to the Prince of Light will receive everlasting life; those who follow the Angel of Darkness, eternal torment. The spirit to which people belong is determined by God's choice, not theirs. The hymn that concludes the *Manual* expresses a deep sense of human sinfulness and dependence on the mercy of God. The *Manual* also reveals the messianic expectations of the sect. Three figures are anticipated: the Prophet and two Messiahs—the Messiah of Aaron, presumably a priestly Messiah, and the Messiah of Israel, presumably a royal Messiah.

A number of concepts in the *Manual* have striking New Testament parallels. The centrality of the sacred Meal (and Drink) calls to mind the importance of the Lord's Supper in the early church and reference to being sprinkled with purifying water has led some to think of baptism. Aspects of the organizational structure (elders, overseer) are reminiscent of that found in the Pastorals. The dependence on God's grace has been linked by some to justification by faith. In addition, there is list of attitudes that characterize those led by each of the Two Spirits (cf. Gal. 5:19–23), a call to love the sons of light (cf. John 13:34) and to hate the sons of darkness (cf. Matt. 5:43–44), and identification of the sect as the Way (cf. Acts 9:2), the use of Isaiah 40:3 to justify a movement in the wilderness (cf. Mark 1:2), the notion of prayer as sacrifice (cf. Heb. 13:15), and an interpretation of the cornerstone of Isaiah 28:16 (cf. 1 Peter 2:4–8).

A second important rule containing legal statutes and organizational regulations for the community is the *Damascus Rule* (CD). This document also provides important information about the origins of the community, praising the Teacher of Righteousness and castigating his chief adversary, the Scoffer, or the Man of Lies. The *Damascus Rule* seems to exhibit an expectation of one Messiah, the Messiah of Aaron and Israel, rather than two. In addition, it anticipates the coming of the Interpreter of the Law and the Prince of the whole congregation. In the meantime, the sect understands itself to be the community of the New Covenant.

The *Rule of the Congregation* (1QSa) is a short document setting forth regulations for ordering the Qumran community in the last days. It describes, among other things, the council meeting called by the priestly Messiah, to which the Messiah of Israel will come, and the ritual of the messianic meal. Significant is the preeminence of the priestly Messiah over the royal Messiah in this document. The *Rule of the Congregation* provides some noteworthy parallels to the New Testament. Its exclusion of those with physical defects from the council meetings (and, hence, from the messianic meal) forms a striking contrast to Jesus' teaching in Luke 14:12–24. To connect the rationale for this exclusion with the presence of angels is similar to one aspect of Paul's argument concerning a woman's head covering in 1 Corinthians 11:10. Its comments on the Meal, which are the most extensive in the scrolls, appear to link the regular communal meal with the eschatological messianic meal, much as Jesus does in Matthew 26:26–29.

The *Temple Scroll* (11QT) is a restatement of the Law given to Moses. It takes laws related by subject matter, but scattered throughout the Pentateuch, and brings them together to form a systematic code. It also rewrites some of the laws and adds new ones. In particular, it fills in the obvious gaps in the Pentateuch with detailed regulations concerning the temple and the king. It exhibits a special concern for the layout and purity of the temple, as well as of Jerusalem itself, and for the cycle of festivals and their sacrifices according to a solar calendar.

The *War Rule* (1QM) is a description of the eschatological war between the Sons of Light (i.e., the sect), and the Sons of Darkness, sometimes called the Kittim (cf. Dan. 11:30). The Sons of Light are under the dominion of the Prince of Light, apparently identified as the archangel Michael (cf. Dan. 12:1); the Sons of Darkness are ruled by Belial. The priests continue their preeminent role; they lead the troops into battle, although not as fighters themselves. The community's trust, however, lies not in its own military proficiency, but in the power of God. A large part of the *War Rule* is taken up with detailed descriptions of weapons, battle regalia, and strategy. On the surface, the *Rule* seems to have been written to provide a manual for how the final war was to be conducted. Its real purpose was probably to confirm the members of the community in their sectarian outlook by reassuring them their sojourn in the desert would not last forever; ultimately God would give them victory over their enemies and exalt them to their proper standing as his elect.

There are parallels between the *War Rule* and certain parts of Revelation. Certainly the idea of a final war depicted in cosmic terms is strong in both (cf. Rev. 12:7; 16:13–16; 19:11–21). They also share songs celebrating the defeat of the enemy (cf. Rev. 18). There is an interest in the role of trumpets (cf. Rev. 8–9) and in precise specifications and precious stones (cf. Rev. 21:12–21). Although overshadowed by Christ, the figure of Michael has a significant place at one point in Revelation (12:7); also, while the *War Rule* mentions the kingdom of Michael, Revelation speaks of the kingdom of Christ (11:15). The use of military imagery in the context of spiritual conflict is paralleled in Ephesians 6:13–17.

In addition to the rules, there are a number of poetical and liturgical documents among the scrolls. The longest is the *Thanksgiving Scroll* (1QH), a collection of psalms of thanksgiving and praise. Themes that permeate these hymns include a deep sense of human frailty and sinfulness, an affirmation of God's grace and election, a division of humanity into the righteous and the wicked, and God's revelation of this knowledge within the covenant community. One hymn speaks of the birth of a wonderful counselor, which some scholars have interpreted messianically; another depicts an eschatological war between God and Belial (i.e., Satan). Whether the collection was intended for private reading and meditation or had a liturgical role in communal worship is unclear.

The *Songs of the Sabbath Sacrifice* (4QShirShabb) is a collection of thirteen liturgical songs, one for each Sabbath during the first quarter of the year. The songs seem to follow a certain progression over the thirteen-week cycle: songs 1–5 focus on the earthly worshiping community; songs 6–8 shift the attention to the heavenly worship, highlighting the number seven, which is developed elaborately in song 7 in seven calls to praise directed to the seven angelic priesthoods; and songs 9–13 center on the features of the heavenly sanctuary and the participants in the heavenly worship. The songs may have been intended to lead the worshiper into an experience of angelic worship and thereby reinforce the community's understanding of itself as God's faithful and legitimate priesthood. Such mystical participation in the heavenly worship is paralleled in Revelation and may stand behind the problem addressed in Colossians.

The *Blessings* (1QSb) is a series of blessings pronounced by the Master over the members of the community, the high priest, the priests, the Sons of Zadok, and the Prince of the congregation, an eschatological figure who will establish, and rule, God's eternal kingdom. The *Berakoth* (11QBer) is a liturgical benediction petitioning God for natural blessings (e.g., rain, an abundant harvest) upon the community.

One of the most striking characteristics of the sect was its distinctive manner of interpreting the Old Testament. The members believed that the Old Testament books were full of mysteries that were fulfilled in the history of the community. The meaning of these mysteries was hidden until God revealed them to the Teacher of Righteousness and some of his followers; hence the need for interpretation. One approach to such interpretation was the production of continuous commentaries on the following Old Testament books: Habakkuk, Micah, Psalms, Isaiah, Hosea, Nahum, and Zephaniah. The commentaries are filled with enigmatic historical allusions to figures related to the history of the sect, such as the Teacher of Righteousness, the Man of Lies, the Wicked Priest, and the Lion of Wrath. Furthermore, they illustrate the sect's understanding of how the Old Testament has been fulfilled in it. One noteworthy example is the interpretation of Habakkuk 2:4 ("The righteous shall live by faith"), which was so important for Paul's understanding of justification by faith in Christ (Rom. 1:17; Gal. 3:11): the commentator views the righteous as those who are characterized by obedience to the Law and faithfulness to (the teachings of) the Teacher of Righteousness.

Another interpretive strategy of the sect was to collect and interpret Old Testament passages in accordance with a particular theme. *4QTestimonia* (4QTestim) seems to be an anthology of messianic texts; *4QFlorilegium* (4QFlor) is an amalgam of eschatological texts and interpretations. Together they anticipate a number of eschatological figures (the Prophet, the Star of Jacob, the Sceptre of Israel, the Branch of David, and the Interpreter of the Law), the precise relationship among which is not clear. By contrast, *Melchizedek* (11QMelch), a collection of Old Testament texts and interpretations centering around the mysterious Old Testament person of the same name (cf. Gen. 14:18–20; Heb. 5:10; 6:20–7:17), views Melchizedek as the key figure in the final jubilee who will restore and make atonement for the sons of light and will execute God's judgment against Belial and his lot.

Since their discovery the Dead Sea Scrolls have aroused intense controversy. Many have made sensationalistic claims about alleged connections between the scrolls and Christianity. The long delay in publishing all of the fragments has only fueled the controversy, leading to accusations of a scholarly and/or ecclesiastical conspiracy to suppress fragments that would be detrimental to Christianity and/or Judaism. Such allegations are surely false. Indeed, most conjectures of any direct link between the scrolls and early Christianity (e.g., that Jesus and/or John the Baptist were at one time a part of the Qumran community) have little support. On the other hand, the scrolls serve as important background material for the study of the New Testament and contain numerous verbal and conceptual parallels with New Testament books, especially the Gospel of John. Yet such parallels should not overshadow the differences between a monastic sect of Jews obeying the teachings of a dead Teacher and a missionary-minded movement of Jews and Gentiles proclaiming the death and resurrection of a living Lord.

Joseph L. Trafton

Bibliography. M. Black, *The Scrolls and Christian Origins;* idem, ed., *The Scrolls and Christianity;* J. H. Charlesworth, ed., *Jesus and the Dead Sea Scrolls;* idem, *John and the Dead Sea Scrolls;* idem, *Paul and the Dead Sea Scrolls;* idem, *The Dead Sea Scrolls;* E. M. Cook, *Solving the Mysteries of the Dead Sea Scrolls;* F. M. Cross, *The Ancient Library of Qumran and Modern Biblical Studies;* R. de Vaux, *Archaeology and the Dead Sea Scrolls;* W. S. LaSor, *The Dead Sea Scrolls and the New Testament;* H. Shanks, ed., *Understanding the Dead Sea Scrolls;* K. Stendahl, *The Scrolls and the New Testament;* G. Vermes, *The Dead Sea Scrolls: Qumran in Perspective;* idem, *The Dead Sea Scrolls in English;* J. C. Vander Kam *The Dead Sea Scrolls Today.*

Death, Mortality. Death is the absence or withdrawal of breath and the life force that makes movement, metabolism, and interrelation with others possible.

The Old Testament. *The Nature of Death.* Life and death are totally under Yahweh's sovereignty. God is the source of all life (Ps. 36:9). There are no organisms anywhere who have not received their life force from him: "In his hand is the life of every creature, and the breath of all mankind" (Job 12:10). The number of the days of our life is written in God's book before one of them comes to be (Job 14:5; Ps. 139:16).

The Hebrew verb *gāwaʿ*, which means "expire, breathe one's last," is used twenty-three times to describe death. Psalm 104:29b says, "when you take away their breath, they die and return to the dust." "If it were his intention and he withdrew his spirit and breath, all mankind would perish" (Job 34:14–15).

In the Bible, death is more than the cessation of all physiological processes. By divine command (Ps. 90:3), the body returns to dust and the spirit goes back to God who gave it (Gen. 2:7; Eccles. 12:7). Those who die are said to be gathered to their people (Gen. 25:8; 35:29; 49:33).

This gathering is often seen as a reference to the central repository of the family tomb where eventually everyone's bones were thrown. Abraham's people, however, were buried around Haran (Gen. 24:4, 10). Only he and Sarah were buried in Canaan (Gen. 23:19; 25:9). Jacob is gathered to his people at death, but not buried until at least seven weeks later (49:33; 50:3, 10).

When Jacob says he is "going down" to Joseph (Gen. 37:35), he cannot be referring to a common burial since no one knew where Joseph's body was. Deceased Samuel told Saul he and his sons would be with him the next day (1 Sam. 28:19). He could not have meant they would all be buried together the next day since Saul's headless body was buried in Jabesh Gilead some time after his death (1 Sam. 31:9–11). David said of his dead son, "I will go to him, but he will not return to me" (2 Sam. 12:23).

Samuel was buried in his house at Ramah (1 Sam. 25:1); but in 28:13, 15, he comes up from the earth to Saul at Endor protesting that he has been disturbed. The intense emotional reaction of Saul and the medium, as well as their remarks about Samuel, indicate that they believed they had actually seen his departed spirit. Had this been some sort of demonic delusion, the narrator would certainly have been obligated to call this to the attention of his audience.

It is difficult to avoid the fact that in the Old Testament people believed a person's physical remains were interred in one place, and that part of the person capable of consciousness and personality went to another location. The gathering to one's people was an event taking place before burial at the time of death.

The Origin of Death. Unlike the ancient Mesopotamian concept, death was not originally built into human constitution. People were created for life, not for death. They had access to both the tree of life and the tree of knowledge of good and evil. They were told they would certainly die if they ate from the latter (Gen. 2:17). Humankind was not tricked out of eternal life as in the Adapa myth, nor was it stolen from them as in the Gilgamesh epic. They partook of the forbidden tree with full awareness of the consequences. Apparently from close observation of the plant and animal kingdom they would have been able to know what death was.

Mortality. In the Old Testament death is an unavoidable reality. From a human point of view death was just as final as spilled water (2 Sam. 14:14) and a pot broken at the well (Eccles. 12:6). Death is so ominous and powerful it can be compared to a fortified city with gates and bars (Pss. 9:13; 107:18).

Our days are numbered (Gen. 6:3; Ps. 90:10). They pass swiftly like the life of a flower (Ps. 90:6; Isa. 40:6). Thus the psalmist prays that we might number our days so as to live our lives carefully and wisely (Ps. 90:12).

Life in the biblical world was very fragile. There was the constant fear that one might not survive until tomorrow. Death stalked on all sides (Ps. 91:5–7). Pestilence, malnutrition, an accidental fall, famine, war, ambush by enemies, being denounced by an enemy to a ruler, complications in childbirth, and even minor infections could all prove fatal. Death indeed, like fire, seemed never to be satisfied (Prov. 30:16). It seemed as though it had cords and snares that could pull a person down to the grave (Ps. 18:5).

Responses to Mortality. Israelites were not helpless pawns at the mercy of a capricious fate. They could respond to their own mortality with God-given resources. They knew God made the steps of a righteous man firm (Ps. 37:23). Unlike most of the ancient Near Eastern peoples, they did not have to worry that they might bring death down on themselves by unknowingly offending some minor deity. God had written a law telling clearly what pleased him. They knew if they meditated on this law day and night, they could be like a luxuriant tree (Ps. 1). Sages wrote inspired proverbs telling the people how to escape dangerous situations. They could even find emotional and spiritual release by writing laments to God.

Sometimes people seemed to respond rather pessimistically to death. Old Testament saints saw through a glass darkly. They could see mainly what happened to the physical body. Thus they could not see any productive activity beyond this life. The living know that they will die, but the dead do not know anything (Eccles. 9:5, 10). Men like Hezekiah could reason with God that they should go on living because no one worships God in death (Isa. 28:18–19).

The Preacher even extols the advantages of death (Eccles. 4:2; cf. Job 3:13–19). He is not, however, as negative in his stance as is commonly supposed. Since death is quick and inevitable, mortals should live life intensely to the fullest, enjoying every minute of everything they do (Eccles. 9:10). God has given them gifts of accepting their portion and finding satisfaction in their work (Eccles. 3:13; 5:17–18; 9:7). Since material things perish, we can best respond by orienting ourselves to the significant others God has given us (Eccles. 9:9).

Fatalism is never a response to mortality. A live dog is better than a dead lion (Eccles. 9:4). Taking one's life is never recommended. Even in the Book of Job it is never taken up as an option. The only victims of suicide in the Old Testament were men (Ahithophel and Saul) who were faced with imminent, unavoidable death anyway. These men believed they were choosing a better manner of death than their enemies would select for them (1 Sam. 31:1–6; 2 Sam. 17:23).

Victory over Death. The ancient Israelites knew they could find refuge in times of natural disaster under the wings of the Almighty (Ps. 91:1). They knew the valley of the shadow of death was unavoidable, but they also knew that in the end the Shepherd would walk it with them (Ps. 23:4). They knew that something about the day of death was better than the day of birth (Eccles. 7:1).

Even though God has set limits on human life, it is still valuable and sacred to him. "Precious in the sight of the LORD is the death of his saints" (Ps. 116:15). Murderers are to receive the sentence of capital punishment (Gen. 9:5–6) because we are made in the image of God. God takes no pleasure even in the death of the wicked (Ezek. 18:32).

There is evidence that in the Old Testament death is not as final as is sometimes supposed. True there was no price even a rich man could pay to avoid it (Ps. 49:7–8). Death comes like a shepherd to lead us into the grave. But the psalmist affirms in faith that God will himself pay the redemption price for release from the power of death (Ps. 49:15). In Psalm 73 the singer believes that though his frail flesh and heart may fail, God will be his portion forever and receive him to glory (Ps. 73:24, 26).

For God death is not an insurmountable obstacle. The death, indecision, barrenness, old age, and confusion of Genesis 11 actually becomes the stage on which God begins to play out his drama of redemption. Out of all this hopelessness and despair comes the life-giving blessing of Genesis 12:1–3.

Isaiah looks forward to a day when the death shroud will be removed, and death will be permanently swallowed up (25:7–8). A day will come when deadly forces that hurt and destroy will not exist in God's holy mountain (11:6–9).

The New Teastament. *Figurative Meanings.* The New Testament broadens the term "death" to include various figurative meanings. But the widow who lives for pleasure, says Paul, "is dead even while she lives" (1 Tim. 5:6). People who are alive physically may be dead in trespasses and sins (Eph. 2:1). Even weak Christians may be considered dead (Rev. 3:1).

In a positive sense believers may be said to be "dead to sin" (Rom. 6:1) and crucified with Christ (Gal. 2:20). Even becoming a disciple requires a new radical reorientation to death and a taking up of the cross daily (Matt. 16:24). In the New Testament way of thinking death is necessary for life and fruitfulness (John 12:24).

The Origin of Death. The New Testament enlarges our understanding of the origin of death. Death passed on all men because of one man's disobedience so that in Adam all die (Rom. 5:12–17; 1 Cor. 15:22). The wages of sin is death (Rom. 6:23). Even the mind set on the flesh is death (Rom. 8:6). The letter of the law kills by giving knowledge about sin (Rom. 7:7–12). Thus the law is considered the ministry of death (2 Cor. 3:6–7).

The Second Death. The New Testament delineates a deeper, more sombre meaning to death. Death is appointed to all men, but after that comes judgment (2 Cor. 5:10; Heb. 9:27). In death people do not live in a sort of nebulous twilight zone. The righteous are comforted, and the wicked are tormented (Luke 16:22–25). The final destiny of death and Hades is to be cast into the lake of fire. This lake of fire is the second death (Rev. 20:14–15). Jesus said that we are not to fear those who can kill the body but those who can kill both body and soul in hell (Matt. 10:28). The second death is a metaphorical term for eternal separation from the presence and glory of God (2 Thess. 1:7–10; Rev. 2:11; 20:6, 14–15).

Triumph over Death. While the New Testament makes the agony of death more intense and fearsome, it shows a greater triumph over it. It is not the second death but the death of Christ that occupies the center of attention. Through death he destroyed the devil, who had the power over death, and emptied death of its fear (Heb. 2:14–15). By dying Christ destroyed death and brought immortality to light (2 Tim. 1:10). In this event we are reconciled and brought to God (Rom. 5:10).

Even at the beginning of Christ's ministry light shone in the valley of the shadow of death (Matt. 4:16). Now being himself loosed from the pains of death (Acts 2:24) and crowned with glory and honor (Heb. 2:9), he has the keys of death and hell (Rev. 1:18).

Christians still die but their death is gain because they are now with Christ (2 Cor. 5:6; Phil. 1:20–21). Even death cannot separate us from the love of God in Christ Jesus (Rom. 8:38–39). In death Christians are given comfort, rest, and assurance (Luke 16:22–25; Rev. 6:9–11).

The dead are in Christ, asleep (1 Thess. 4:14), waiting for a day when death will be completely swallowed up by life (2 Cor. 5:4). Then mortality will put on immortality (1 Cor. 15:53). Death, the last enemy, will itself be destroyed (1 Cor. 15:26). There will be no more death or sorrow, and God will wipe all tears from all faces (Rev. 21:4).

For those who overcome and attain to the resurrection of Christ, the second death has no power (Rev. 2:11; 20:6). Those who believe in Christ will not see death (John 8:51–52).

PAUL FERGUSON

See also GRAVE; SECOND DEATH.

Bibliography. L. R. Bailey, Sr., *Biblical Perspectives on Death;* A. Heidel, *The Gilgamesh Epic and Old Testament Parallels;* O. Kaiser and E. Lohse, *Death and Life;* J. B. Payne, *Theology of the Older Testament;* K. Rahner, *On the Theology of Death;* E. F. Sutcliffe, *The Old Testament and Future Life;* N. J. Tromp, *Primitive Conceptions of Death and the Nether World in the Old Testament.*

Death of Christ. ***The Place in the Gospels.*** In the records of Jesus that the Gospels give us, it is clear that a place of supreme significance is given to the death—and the resurrection—of Christ. The story of the events of Jesus' last few days, culminating in the crucifixion, is given a considerable proportion of each Gospel (Matt. 21–27; Mark 11–15; Luke 19–23; John 12–19), and the record of the journey to Jerusalem and to the cross begins respectively in Matthew 20:17, Mark 10:32, Luke 9:51, and John 11:7.

In each of the Synoptic Gospels Jesus specifically predicts his suffering and death three times (Matt. 16:21; 17:22–23; 20:17–19; Mark 8:31; 9:31; 10:32–34; Luke 9:21–22; 9:44; 18:31–33). Intimations of his death are also given in his words about his anointing in Bethany being a preparation for his burial (Matt. 26:12; Mark 14:8; John 12:7), in the parable of the wicked tenants (Matt. 21:33–39; Mark 12:1–12; Luke 20:9–17), at the transfiguration when Moses and Elijah spoke with him "about his departure, which he was about to bring to fulfillment at Jerusalem" (Luke 9:31), in the words about the bridegroom being taken away (Matt. 9:15; Mark 2:20; Luke 5:35), and right back in the words of Simeon to Mary about the anguish that would come to her (Luke 2:35). In John there is reference to the destruction of the temple of Jesus' body (2:19–22), and frequent reference to the "hour" (8:20; 12:23, 27; 13:1; 16:32; 17:1) of his being "lifted up" (3:14; 8:28;

12:32, 34), the hour of his crucifixion to which the whole of Jesus' ministry inexorably moved.

The Reasons. When we consider the Gospels as written for the early church and related to its life and mission we can appreciate three supremely important reasons for this emphasis on the death of Christ:

- The centrality of the cross—and resurrection—in the *preaching* of the good news of Jesus.
- The centrality of the death—and resurrection—in the *worship* of the church, especially in relation to its ordinances of baptism and the Lord's Supper.
- The centrality of the suffering and death of Christ for the meaning of Christian *discipleship.*

The Preaching of the Early Church. The New Testament very clearly indicates that the death of Christ had central significance in Christian preaching. Paul could say to the Corinthian Christians, "I resolved to know nothing while I was with you except Jesus Christ and him crucified" (1 Cor. 2:2). The gospel for him was "the message of the cross," even though a "stumbling block to Jews and foolishness to Gentiles" (1 Cor. 1:18, 23). He sums up what he received and passed on to others "as of first importance: that Christ died for our sins according to the Scriptures, that he was buried, that he was raised on the third day according to the Scriptures" (1 Cor. 15:3–4). To the Galations he says, "before your very eyes Jesus Christ was clearly portrayed as crucified" (Gal. 3:1).

In the records that the Acts of the Apostles gives us of the preaching of apostles Peter and Paul, we find that the death of Christ always has a place of central importance (2:23; 3:13–15, 17–18; 4:10; 5:30; 7:52; 8:32–35; 10:39; 13:27–29; 17:2–3). In this preaching the human responsibility for the death of Christ is laid at the door of the Jews who handed him over to be crucified and of Pilate who condemned him to death, but it is also made clear that it was in fulfillment of the purpose of God expressed in the Scriptures (3:18). He was "handed over . . . by God's set purpose and foreknowledge" (2:23). His enemies did only what God's own "power and will had decided beforehand should happen" (4:28).

Opposition Described in the Gospels. When we turn back to the Gospels we find it made abundantly clear that the death of Jesus was, from the human standpoint, the culmination of opposition to him. In Mark a major section early in the Gospel (2:1–3:6) shows some of the reasons for such opposition, and that section concludes by saying, "the Pharisees went out and began to plot with the Herodians how they might kill Jesus." Luke (4:29) tells of an attempt on Jesus' life made in Nazareth in what appears to have been a very early stage in his ministry. Later Luke (13:31) tells how Herod wanted to kill him. In John's Gospel much is said about the constant opposition of "the Jews" to Jesus, because of his attitude to the Sabbath and because of the claims that he was making for himself (5:16, 18; 8:59; 10:31–32). John 7:1 speaks of his "purposely staying away from Judea because the Jews there were waiting to take his life." Then there was an occasion when "the chief priests and the Pharisees sent temple guards to arrest him" (John 7:32), but were not able to do so. All four Gospels tell of the plans ultimately made by the Jewish leaders, the part played by Judas, the arrest and the trials.

The Purpose of God Fulfilled. As in the preaching in the Acts of the Apostles, so much more in the Gospels, it is made clear that the reason for the death of Jesus was not just the opposition of his enemies. It was the purpose of God. The words spoken to Jesus at his baptism (Matt. 3:17; Mark 1:11; Luke 3:22), and his attitude in his temptations and often subsequently in his ministry make clear that Jesus was conscious of his messianic vocation, but that that vocation was to be fulfilled by him as Suffering Servant. So it was that as soon as Peter, in the presence of the other disciples, had confessed him as the Christ, Jesus "began to teach them that the Son of Man must suffer many things and be rejected by the elders, chief priests and teachers of the law, and that he must be killed" (Mark 8:31; cf. Matt. 16:21; Luke 9:22).

There is a repeated emphasis also on the fulfillment of the Scriptures. This is especially the case in the passion narratives themselves. In Matthew (26:52–56) there is the possibility at Jesus' arrest of force being used by his followers to prevent his being taken. Moreover, it could be said that "twelve legions of angels" were at his disposal, but Jesus' response to the thought of either human or angelic opposition was, "how then would the Scriptures be fulfilled that say it must happen in this way?" In fact he could say, "this has all taken place that the writings of the prophets might be fulfilled." In Luke (24:26–27, 44–47) the risen Christ said to the perplexed disciples, on the basis of the Scriptures, "Did not the Christ have to suffer these things and then enter his glory?" "Then he opened their minds so that they could understand the Scriptures. He told them, 'This is what is written: The Christ will suffer and rise from the dead on the third day, and repentance and forgiveness of sins will be preached in his name to all nations, beginning at Jerusalem.'" In the case of John's Gospel there is a constant emphasis on the fulfillment of Scripture, and that God is "glorified" in the "lifting up" of Jesus to die on the cross (12:23–24, 32–33; 13:31–32; 17:1–4). The prophecy of Caiaphas, in a way that that high priest could not himself realize, indicated the purpose of God that was to be fulfilled, "to have one man die for the people" (11:50–52; 18:13). When, immediately prior to his being handed over by Pilate to be crucified (19:11), Jesus said that Pilate would have no power to crucify him "if it were not given . . . from above," he was not just speaking of political power being delegated by God (in the sense of Rom. 13), but rather that Pilate was just doing what was being brought about according to the will and authority of God. (For the emphasis in Acts of the death of Christ being the fulfillment of Scripture, see 3:18; 8:32–35; 13:27; 17:2–3; 26:22–23).

The Death of Christ and the Forgiveness of Sins. When we follow what is said in the New Testament about the meaning and purpose of the death of Christ we find, in a number of different ways, that it is specifically related to the forgiveness of sins.

Most simply, and without any further amplification, it is said often that he "died for us," "for all," or "for others." The death of Christ is the supreme expression of the love of God and the love of Jesus himself (John 15:13; Rom. 5:8; Eph. 5:2, 25; 1 John 3:16; 4:10). In the language of John 10 Jesus is the Good Shepherd who gave his life for the sheep. He died in our place (Matt. 20:28; Mark 10:45), meaning that he died a sin-bearing death so that we might not have to. There are a number of places where it says simply that he "died for our sins" or for us as sinners (Rom. 4:25; 5:6–8; 1 Cor. 15:3; 2 Cor. 5:21; Gal. 1:4; 1 Peter 3:17–18).

Jesus' death as sin-bearing is explicitly referred to in Hebrews 9:28: "Christ was sacrificed once to take away the sins of many people." First Peter 2:24 puts it, "He himself bore our sins in his body on the tree"; implicit in the reference to the cross as a "tree" (cf. Acts 5:30; 10:39; 13:29) is what is made explicit in Galatians 3:10–13. We all in failing to keep the law of God are under a "curse," not in our own contemporary use of that term, but as stated in the Deuteronomic Law—"Cursed is everyone who does not continue to do every thing written in the Book of the Law." But "Christ redeemed us from the curse of the law by becoming a curse for us, for it is written: 'Cursed is everyone who is hung on a tree.'"

Thinking in these terms takes us back to the Gospels. In particular it is hard for us to begin to understand the agony of our Lord Jesus Christ in Gethsemane, and his words about the drinking of the "cup," other than through his consciousness of approaching, not just the physical pain and the shame of crucifixion, but the reality of what it meant for him to be the Suffering Servant, "pierced for our transgressions, . . . crushed for our iniquities," and "the iniquity of us all" "laid on him" (Isa. 53:5–6). The same must be said in relation to the cry from the cross, "My God, my God, why have you forsaken me?" (Matt. 27:46; Mark 15:34).

The benefits of the death of Christ for those who believe are thus spoken of in a number of ways. They are the *forgiveness* of sins (Acts 5:31; 13:38; 26:18; Rom. 4:7; Eph. 1:7; Col. 1:14; Heb. 9:22; 1 John 1:9; 2:12), our *cleansing* from sin (Eph. 5:26; Heb. 9:14; 10:22; 1 John 1:7, 9), our *healing* (1 Peter 2:24), our *salvation* (1 Cor. 1:18), our *life* (John 6:51–56; 12:24; 1 Thess. 5:10), our *justification* (Rom. 5:9; 8:33) or being granted God's righteousness as a gift of grace (2 Cor. 5:21), and our *sanctification* or being made holy (Heb. 13:12).

Reconciliation. The forgiveness of God means that rebel humanity is reconciled to God. Romans 5:1 puts it, "since we have been justified through faith, we have peace with God through our Lord Jesus Christ," which means that through him "we have now received reconciliation" (Rom. 5:11). Paul expresses this most powerfully in 2 Corinthians 5:18–20. More briefly Colossians 1:22 puts it, "now he has reconciled you by Christ's physical body through death." That reconciliation is a matter of his "making peace through his blood, shed on the cross" (Col. 1:20). This theme is developed in Ephesians 2:11–22, where it is made plain that peace with God and peace with one another through Christ belong together. "He himself is our peace," breaking down "the dividing wall of hostility" between Jew and Gentile, "making peace," and in one body reconciling both to God by the cross.

This in turn leads to the kindred thought that we "have *access* to the Father by one Spirit" (Eph. 2:18; cf. Rom. 5:2), or in terms of 1 Timothy 2:5–6, "There is one God and one mediator between God and men, the man Christ Jesus, who gave himself as a ransom for all." That openness of access to God is expressed symbolically in the tearing of the curtain in the temple at the very time Jesus died (Matt. 27:51; Mark 15:38). So 1 Peter 3:18 speaks of Christ dying for us "to bring [us] to God." In an essentially similar way the work of Christ's death is described in Hebrews 10:19–22: "we have confidence to enter the Most Holy Place by the blood of Jesus, by a new and living way opened for us. "Since we have a great priest over the house of God," the writer of that epistle continues, "let us draw near to God." This brings us to the language of priesthood, the dominant theme of Hebrews that is summed up in the words of 4:14–16: "Since we have a great high priest . . . let us then approach the throne of grace with confidence."

Sacrifice. Inevitably the concept of priesthood links with that of sacrifice. Sacrifices were offered in Old Testament ritual as sin-offerings, in the making of a covenant, and in relation to the celebration of the Passover. All of these have a place in the New Testament in the explanation given of the meaning of the death of Christ.

The work for which Jesus came into our human life was to "make atonement for the sins of the people" (Heb. 2:17) and this he did when "he sacrificed for their sins once for all when he offered himself" (7:27). Hebrews develops this theme in detail, showing the death of Christ to be the fulfillment and the replacement of the sacrifices of Old Testament times. When in the different strands of New Testament testimony we have reference to the "blood" of Christ, that word speaks of his sacrificial death (e.g., Rom. 5:9; Eph. 1:7; 2:13; Col. 1:20; 1 Peter 1:2; 1 John 1:7; 5:6; Rev. 1:5; 5:9). Paul penetrates more deeply into the meaning of that sacrificial death as he speaks of it "as a sacrifice of atonement" ("as a propitiation" KJV), since, because Christ bore our sins, there was no longer the "passing over of sins," but in what Christ did on the cross, God is shown to be "just and the one who justifies" those who have faith in Jesus. Human sins are not just swept aside as inconsequential; God's justice is shown in that they are borne by the sinless Son of God, and because they are borne, those who have faith in him are justified (Rom. 3:24–26). The same language of "propitiation" is used in 1 John 2:2 and 4:10.

We have noticed the place that Hebrews gives to the understanding of the sacrifice of Christ as making possible the making of a new covenant, a personal relationship with God based on forgiveness. This is an understanding that goes back to Jesus himself, in particular, to the way that he spoke at his institution of the Lord's Supper: "This is my blood of the covenant which is poured out for many for the forgiveness of sins" (Matt. 26:28; cf. Mark 14:24; Luke 22:20; 1 Cor. 11:25; Heb. 13:20).

When Jesus is spoken of as "the Lamb of God" (John 1:29, 35), it is not clear whether we should think of the daily sacrifice of lambs offered in the temple or the Passover lamb as background. It is abundantly clear, however, that the fulfillment of the Passover was prominent in the thought of Jesus himself as he approached his death (in all the Gospel records of the crucifixion this is evident: see Matt. 26:1–2, 17–19; Mark 14:1–2, 12–16; Luke 22:1–2, 7–16; John 11:55; 12:1; 13:1; 19:14), and so the early Christian understanding was expressed in these terms: "Christ, our Passover lamb, has been sacrificed" (1 Cor. 5:7).

This in turn links with the language of redemption, as the Passover stood for the redemption of the people from their slavery in Egypt and was celebrated with the hope of a new and greater redemption. "Redemption through his blood," Ephesians 1:7 puts it, and that "redemption" (Rom. 3:24; Gal. 3:14) means freedom from sin and evil and from the power of death (Gal. 1:4; Titus 2:14; Heb. 2:14–15; Rev. 1:5). For the death of Christ is a triumph over evil and over all the forces of evil (Col. 2:15). Alluding to his imminent death Jesus says in John 12:31, "Now is the time for judgment on this world; now the prince of this world will be driven out." Victory thus means redemption, but the New Testament also speaks of the costliness of our redemption (1 Peter 1:18–19). Jesus speaks of the Son of Man giving himself "as a ransom for many" (Matt. 20:28; Mark 10:45), and Paul can speak of our being "bought at a price" (1 Cor. 6:20; 7:23; cf. Acts 20:28; Rev. 5:9; 14:4), although the metaphor is never pressed to the point of to whom the price was paid.

The Death of Christ and Discipleship. In all the many ways listed, and more, the death of Christ is spoken of as the way of salvation, of our acceptance with God, of pardon and peace. It is also the indication of the way of discipleship. Thus Jesus spoke repeatedly to his disciples about taking up the cross and following him (Matt. 10:38; 16:24–25; Mark 8:34–35; Luke 9:23; 14:27). Baptism expresses the commitment of the believer to die (with Christ) to the old sinful way of life (Rom. 6:2–7). "I have been crucified with Christ" says Paul (Gal. 2:20); the things of the old life are put to death (Col. 3:5–8; cf. Gal. 5:24; 1 Peter 4:1). This also means a willingness to suffer as Christ suffered. The Acts of the Apostles indicates many parallels between the sufferings of the early Christians and the sufferings of Christ (Acts 7:56–60; 9:5; 12:1–4; 21:13). "I die every day," says Paul (1 Cor. 15:31; cf. 2 Cor. 1:5; 4:10–12). Paul can even speak of his sufferings as in some way filling up "what is still lacking in regard to Christ's afflictions, for the sake of his body, which is the church" (Col. 1:24). It is also a death to self: "he died for all, that those who live should no longer live for themselves but for him who died for them and was raised again" (2 Cor. 5:15); and it is a death to the world, as the apostle says, "May I never boast except in the cross of our Lord Jesus Christ, through which the world has been crucified to me, and I to the world" (Gal. 6:14).

In these ways the death of Christ is an example for the Christian. Yet in no place in the New Testament is the example of Christ's suffering and death presented without the emphasis also being on what was done in his death "for us." Thus the sacraments of the gospel indicate the lifestyle to which Christians are called, but also indicate and recall (requiring the response of repentance and faith) what Jesus Christ did once and for all for us by his death and resurrection. The Lord's Supper is nothing less than the constant proclaiming of the Lord's death until he comes (1 Cor. 11:26). Baptism is an identifying with Christ in his death and resurrection, speaking of the whole lifestyle of the Christian as (in Christ's name) a dying to self and living for him who has loved us and given himself for us (Gal. 2:20). Life, as long as it lasts on earth, is to be lived to the praise of the crucified and risen Lord, and the praise of heaven is of "the Lamb who was slain" as "worthy—to receive power and wealth and wisdom and strength and honour and glory and praise" (Rev. 5:12). FRANCIS FOULKES

See also ATONEMENT; CROSS, CRUCIFIXION; JESUS CHRIST; LAMB, LAMB OF GOD..

Bibliography. E. Brandenburger, *NIDNTT,* 1:389–403; J. Denney, *The Death of Christ;* M. Hengel, *The Cross of the Son of God;* L. Morris, *The Apostolic Preaching of the Cross;* idem, *The Cross in the New Testament;* J. Schneider, *TDNT,* 7:572–84; J. Stott, *The Cross of Christ;* R. S. Wallace, *The Atoning Death of Christ.*

Decrees. Decrees issued by rulers, written commands having the effect of law, and the metaphor of God as King of the world provide the imagery behind the Bible's references to God's "decrees."

Terms translated "decree" in Hebrew and/or Aramaic include *dāt* (a loanword from Persian) used in Daniel, Ezra, and Esther for decrees of God and human (especially Persian) monarchs, *ṭaᶜam* for the orders of high officials including kings, *ḥoq/ḥuqqâ,* used especially of God's laws, *ʾĕsar* (lit. "something binding"), and *gĕzērâ,* ("something decided"); and in Greek *dogma* ("a [public] decree, decision"). The idea of "decree" may be present even where a specific technical term for "decree" does not occur.

God and Human Decrees. Even in decrees by human monarchs God shows his own decrees or purposes to be sovereign.

In Exodus 7–14 God shows his decrees to be sovereign over Pharaoh's by "hardening" Pharaoh's heart. This "hardening" involves the creation of an irrational mind-set. Despite the miraculous plagues, Pharaoh refuses to do the reasonable thing (decreeing Israel's release from bondage), thereby bringing further disaster on himself and his land. In the early stages of the story Pharaoh appears to be a free agent, hardening his own heart (Exod. 8:15), but as the story develops God is increasingly portrayed as the direct cause of Pharaoh's stupidity. Pharaoh is ultimately reduced to a mere puppet of Yahweh (Exod. 14:4, 8).

The decrees of Cyrus (Ezra 5:13–15; 6:3–5; cf. 1:2–4) to allow the Jews to return from Babylonian exile and rebuild Jerusalem was prophesied beforehand (Isa. 44:26–45:4, 13) and providentially prompted by God, who "stirred up" Cyrus's spirit to issue it (2 Chron. 36:22; Ezra 1:1). Nonetheless, Ezra–Nehemiah sees a cooperation of heaven and earth in which human initiative (via Zerubbabel, Joshua, Ezra, and Nehemiah) and divine control are both prominent. Hence, the rebuilding of Jerusalem is said to be both "by the command of God" and "by the decrees" of several Persian monarchs (Ezra 7:13).

God delivers Daniel and his friends from various human decrees—one by Nebuchadnezzar to kill the sages of Babylon (Dan. 2:13), another to cremate anyone not worshiping the image of Nebuchadnezzar (Dan. 3:10–11), a third "immutable" decree to cast to lions anyone praying to a god or person besides Darius the Mede (Dan. 6:7–9). Providence reverses Ahasuerus/Xerxes' decree to exterminate the Jews (Esther 3:7–15) so that the enemies of the Jews are destroyed by royal decree instead (Esther 8:8–9:16). The decree of Caesar Augustus for a census (Luke 2:1) is providentially used to ensure the fulfillment of the prophecy that the Messiah would be born in Bethlehem (Mic. 5:2; cf. Matt. 2:4–6).

God's Decrees and the Law. The terms *ḥoq/ḥuqqâ,* ordinarily translated "statue," "prescription," or "ordinance" in reference to God's laws, are from the root (*hqq*), meaning to "engrave, carve; write; fix, determine." This root always involves an action of a superior that affects an inferior, and in some contexts refers to human decrees (Isa. 10:1—"Woe to those who decree iniquitous decrees"). Use of *ḥoq/ḥuqqâ,* seemingly conceptualizes God's "laws" as "decrees" (so NIV; cf. Deut. 4:1, 5–6, 8).

Colossians 2:14 (cf. Eph. 2:15) states that Christ by the cross canceled the certificate of debt consisting of "decrees" (NASB; Gk. *dogmata)* against us. Evidently this is in reference to God's laws that we have violated and which, apart from the cross, condemn us.

Prophetic Decrees. Predictive prophecies resemble decrees by God determining the course of history: "The Son of Man will go as it has been *decreed* (lit. *"written")"* in the prophets (Luke 22:22; cf. Matt. 26:53–54, 56). God decrees Ahab's doom (1 Kings 22:23) and destruction on Israel (Isa. 10:23); "Seventy 'sevens'" (often understood as "weeks of years") have been decreed for the history of Daniel's people (Dan. 9:24). The scroll sealed with seven seals in Revelation 5:1 perhaps represents a divine decree determining the destiny of the world.

Sometimes predictive "decrees" can be abrogated, repentance averting punishment and disobedience annulling blessing (Jer. 18:7–10; Jon. 3:10). Hence, despite the "decree" of the destruction, Zephaniah can call the people to seek God "before the *decree* takes effect. . . . Perhaps you will be hidden in the day of the LORD's anger" (2:1–3 NASB).

Political and Cosmic Order. Poetic texts describe God's decrees as having established political and cosmic order.

Psalm 2, an enthronement psalm, states that it was by the LORD's decree (*ḥoq*) that each Davidic king was adopted as a son of God at his coronation (cf. 2 Sam. 7:14). The language of this psalm was never literally fulfilled by any Davidic king during the monarchy, but rather finds its ultimate fulfillment in Christ. Romans 1:4, which says Jesus Christ was "declared [or possibly *decreed*] with power to be the Son of God by his resurrection from the dead," may well allude to the "decree" of Psalm 2:7.

The psalmist describes God's gift of the land as a decree (Ps. 105:10). Job felt his suffering was by divine decree (Job 23:14). Lamentations 3:37 states that all things, good or bad, have been decreed by God. God gave a lasting decree that fixed heavenly bodies in their places (Ps. 148:3–6).

God's Decrees and Election. Calvin understood God's choosing us in Christ before creation and predestinating us to adoption "in accord with his pleasure and will" (Eph. 1:3–5) as an immutable, divine decree.

Church Decrees. Paul and Timothy disseminated the Jerusalem church's decrees (the decision of Acts 15), presumably providentially guided, concerning relations between Jewish and Gentile Christians (Acts 16:4). Paul in his epistles never utilized this decree of Acts 15 as church "law," however, even where he could have. Ultimately in the postapostolic church this term for decree (*dogma*) comes to refer to authoritative teachings of church councils.

JOE M. SPRINKLE

See also COMMANDMENT; LAW; PREDESTINATION; REQUIREMENT.

Bibliography. M. Black, *Romans;* J. Calvin, *Institutes of the Christian Religion;* D. J. Clines, *Ezra, Nehemiah, Esther;* H. H. Esser, *NIDNTT,* 1:330–31; D. M. Gunn, *Art and Meaning: Rhetoric in Biblical Literature*, pp. 72–96; H. Ringgren, *TDOT,* 5:141–42; G. Schrenk, *TDNT,* 1:619.

Decalog. *See* TEN COMMANDMENTS.

Dedication, Feast of. *See* FEASTS AND FESTIVALS OF ISRAEL.

Defile. *See* CLEAN, UNCLEAN.

Delight. The idea of delight occurs approximately 110 times in Scripture in various forms. Less than fifteen occurrences are found in the New Testament. The related concept of "please" occurs about 350 times, about seventy-five of these occurrences in the New Testament.

The Old Testament. Two of the most common Hebrew terms for delight are *ḥēpeṣ*, "to bend towards, to be inclined towards [an object or person]," and *rāṣâ,* "to delight or take pleasure in."

God delights in the obedience of his children more than in sacrifices (1 Sam. 15:22). Obedience to his commands so pleases God that he will prosper his people as they walk in his way (Num. 14:8; Deut. 30:9). God delights in his people (Ps. 16:3).

God is also delighted with honesty in business (Prov. 20:23), a blameless life (11:20), truthfulness (12:22), and the prayers of the upright (15:8). God gives wisdom, knowledge, and happiness to those who please him (Eccles. 2:26), and he promises to deliver those in whom he delights (Ps. 18:19). God delights in showing mercy (Mic. 7:18), and kindness, justice, and righteousness bring him pleasure and cause him delight (Jer. 9:23).

God placed Solomon on the throne of Israel because he delighted in him (1 Kings 10:9; 2 Chron. 9:8). God had special delight in his Servant-Messiah, upon whom he put his Spirit (Isa. 42:1).

A man might delight in another man (1 Sam. 18:22; Esther 6:6–11), or a man might delight in a woman (Gen. 34:19). Well-behaved children bring delight to the heart of their parents (Prov. 29:17).

People are encouraged to delight in that which pleases God—his law (Pss. 1:2; 112:1–9). God's statutes are to be our continual delight (Ps. 119:24, 70, 77, 174). We are to delight in God's law because we love it (Ps. 119:41–48). We are to rejoice in the Lord and delight in his salvation (Ps. 35:9), for in so doing we will receive the desires of our hearts (Ps. 37:4).

It is possible for people to delight in or take pleasure in that which is foolish or evil. Some people "delight in doing wrong" (Prov. 2:14), in voicing their own opinions (18:2), in lying (Ps. 62:4), and in waging war (Ps. 68:30). It is clear that the object of our delight or pleasure is critical. It is possible to delight in those things that are good and proper; it is also possible to delight in that which is an abomination to the Lord (Isa. 66:3).

The New Testament. The Greek word most commonly used for "delight" is *eudokeō,* usually used when God's purpose, resolve, and choice are in view.

God points out his delight in his Son at both the baptism and transfiguration of Jesus (Matt. 3:17; 17:5). This pleasure points to a distinct anointing and blessing that rest upon Jesus. Indeed, "God was pleased to have all his fullness dwell in him" (Col. 1:19). God's peace rests upon those in whom he delights (Luke 2:14), and God works in those destined for salvation according to his good pleasure (Phil. 2:13). God is not pleased, however, with the disobedient and unbelieving (1 Cor. 10:5).

As our supreme example, Jesus took great pleasure in honoring and obeying his father (John 5:30; 8:29). That which delights Jesus should be our delight as well. We should make it our all-consuming desire to please him (2 Cor. 5:9; 1 Thess. 2:4; 4:1; 1 John 3:22).

We are to delight after God's law in the "inner man" (Rom. 7:22). We are to delight in our weakness, for this is when God's power is most clearly revealed in our lives (2 Cor. 12:10). We should not, on the other hand, delight in false humility or religion (Col. 2:18). Our desire should be directed toward the salvation of souls (Rom. 10:1). Faith is essential if we are to please God (Heb. 11:6), and God is especially delighted when we pray to those in authority (1 Tim. 2:3). In the essential relationships of life, God is pleased when wives submit to their husbands, husbands love their wives, children obey their parents, parents encourage their children, slaves obey their masters, and masters treat their slaves kindly (Col. 3:18–4:1). It is as living, holy sacrifices that we become pleasing to our Father in heaven (Rom. 12:1).

DANIEL L. AIKEN

Bibliography. M. Unger and W. White, *Nelson's Expository Dictionary of the Old Testament;* W. E. Vine, *Expository Dictionary of New Testament Words;* W. Wilson, *Old Testament Studies.*

Deliver. ***The Old Testament.*** The concept of deliverance occurs in the Old Testament with two meanings. The first is in a nontheological sense signifying "deliver over" or "give over into the possession or power of another." The Hebrew word, *nātan*, appears over 1,200 times in the Old Testament with this meaning. Sometimes the term refers to the giving of objects to another, such as books (2 Chron. 34:15), money (2 Kings 12:15), horses (2 Kings 18:23), and goods (Esther 6:9). More often the term refers to people delivered in the power of others, usually their enemies: "The LORD hates us; so he brought us out of Egypt to deliver us in the hands of the Amorites to destroy us" (Deut. 1:27).

The second usage of deliverance refers to the acts of God whereby he rescues his people from danger. The key words *nāsal* ("draw out, snatch away"), *pālaṭ* ("make an escape"), *mālaṭ* ("to cause to escape"), *hālaṣ* (to "draw out"), and *yāšaᶜ* ("to save") fall within the field of meaning describing God's redemptive activity on the part of his people. This usage of deliverance focuses on God's removal of those who are in the midst of trouble or danger.

In the Old Testament, God's deliverance is almost always from temporal dangers. He rescues his people from their enemies (1 Sam. 17:37; 2 Kings 20:6) and from the hand of the wicked (Pss. 7:2; 17:13; 18:16–19; 59:2; 69:14; 71:4). He preserves them from famine (Ps. 33:19), death (Ps. 22:19–21), and the grave (Pss. 56:13; 86:13; Hos. 13:14). The most striking deliverance, the exodus (Exod. 3:8; 6:6; 18:10), comprises the defining act of God as the deliverer of Israel. The promise that God delivers his people from sin and its consequences, although mentioned infrequently, completes the picture of God as the deliverer from all of humankind's fears (Pss. 39:8; 40:11–13; 51:14; 79:9).

The fact that God delivers as he does is a polemic against the pagan rulers who challenge his ability to rescue his people. Nebuchadnezzar (Dan. 3:15, 28), Pharaoh (Exod. 5:2), and Sennacherib (2 Chron. 32:10–15) railed against Israel for trusting in God's deliverance. The subsequent rescue serves as a demonstration of God's ability to deliver his people from the most powerful worldly forces.

While God is the great deliverer, there are no manipulative ploys by his people to effect his intervention. All acts of deliverance are totally his initiative and express his mercy and his love (Pss. 51:1; 71:2; 86:13). Therefore, there is no one to rescue the ungodly (Ps. 50:22). God's deliverance is for his people, those who trust and fear him: "To the faithful you show yourself faithful. . . . You save the humble but bring low those whose eyes are haughty" (Ps. 18:25, 27). Often, the people's fear of God and trust in him are seen as a part of the deliverance (Pss. 22:4; 33:18–19; 34:7; Ezek. 14:20). Their righteousness preserves them (Prov. 11:6; Ezek. 14:14, 20) but if they indulge in sin and rebellion, God may deliver them over to their enemies (1 Kings 8:46; Jer. 20:5; Ezek. 11:8–9).

The New Testament. As in the Old Testament, both meanings of deliverance are found in the New Testament. The Greek word *paradidomai* ("deliver over") is used to describe the deliverance of people (Matt. 5:25; 18:34; 20:19) and goods (Matt. 25:14) over to another. Jesus uses this word as a prophecy of his death at the hands of the chief priests and Gentiles (Matt. 20:18; Mark 10:33; Luke 9:44). Traditions and doctrine are also "delivered" to others (Mark 7:13; Acts 6:14; Rom. 6:17; 1 Cor. 11:2) with the idea that those who receive them will take possession of them as valuable commodities.

The second usage of deliverance is seen in the occurrences of the words *rhuomai* ("rescue") and *exaireō* ("take out of"), which are used most often in the New Testament to reflect the idea of deliverance from danger or distress. God is always the subject and his people are always the objects of the deliverance. The temporal deliverance so dominant in the Old Testament falls into the background in the New. However, the historical accounts in the Old Testament serve as proof that God is the great deliverer. For example, after recounting examples of God's deliverance, Peter concludes that "the Lord knows how to rescue godly men from trials and to hold the unrighteous for the day of judgment" (2 Peter 2:9). God still delivers his people from deadly peril (2 Cor. 1:10; 2 Tim. 4:17) and from wicked men (Acts 12:11; 2 Thess. 3:2).

The dominant idea in the New Testament is God's deliverance from humankind's greatest fears: sin, evil, death, and judgment. These more theological usages closely align with the biblical terms for salvation and redemption. Believers are to pray for deliverance from the threat of evil that dominates the world (Matt. 6:13; Luke 11:4). By God's power, believers are delivered from "this present evil age" (Gal. 1:4) and the power of Satan's reign (Col. 1:13).

The evil impulses that grip the human heart cause Paul's cry for deliverance: "What a wretched man I am! Who will rescue me from this body of death?" (Rom. 7:24). The answer to Paul's cry is "Jesus Christ our Lord" (v. 25). All pleas for deliverance are answered by the person and work of Jesus Christ. He was delivered up for us (Rom. 4:25) that he might deliver us from all that threatens us in this life and in the life to come.

The ultimate deliverance for humankind is from the coming wrath of God on the final day of judgment. Here again, the people of God have hope in the "The Deliverer" (Rom. 11:26) who will intervene and save them from the terrible fate reserved for the ungodly: "Jesus, who rescues us from the coming wrath" (1 Thess. 1:10).

WILLIAM E. BROWN

See also SALVATION.

Bibliography. J. Schneider and C. Brown, *NIDNTT,* 3:200–205.

Demon. Spirit being who is unclean and immoral in nature and activities. When demons were created, how they came to be demonic, and their organizational structure are not given significant attention in Scripture because the focus throughout the Bible is on God and his work in Christ rather than on the demonic attempts to demean that work.

The Old Testament. References to demons in the Old Testament are relatively scarce. Their existence is never proven; it is simply assumed. The Old Testament focus is not on demons and their schemes but on God and his sovereignty. Demons are not depicted as free, independent agents, but operate under God's direct control. Though they are not revealed as the malicious beings seen in the New Testament, there are still definitive commands for God's people to avoid them. The Old Testament word for demons (*šēd*) appears only twice. They are "gods they had not known, gods that recently appeared, gods your fathers did not fear" (Deut. 32:17), and Israel is condemned by God for sacrificing to them (Ps. 106:37). They are also called evil spirits sent from God. After Abimelech treacherously killed Gideon's sons, God sent an evil spirit that divided him from the citizens of Shechem (Judg. 9:23–24). God also sent an evil spirit to torment Saul. David's attempts to calm Saul by playing the harp (1 Sam. 16:15–16) are unsuccessful, as Saul, provoked by the spirit, tries to kill David (1 Sam. 16:14–23; 18:10–11; 19:9–10). A spirit from God's counsel volunteers to be a lying spirit in the mouths of Ahab's prophets (1 Kings 22:19–23; 2 Chron. 18:18–22). The medium from Endor sees "gods" or "spirits" coming up from the ground (1 Sam. 28:13). An angel is delayed twenty-one days in bringing an answer to Daniel's prayer by a prince of Persia, giving an indication of some organizational structure or ranking among demons (Dan. 10:13). This also gives us one of the few glimpses behind the curtains of history into engagements between demons and angels. Other possible Old Testament references to demons include goat idols (Lev. 17:7; 2 Chron. 11:15; Isa. 13:21; 34:14), night creatures (Isa. 34:14), and idols (LXX of Ps. 96:5).

Demons during the Life of Christ. There is more recorded demonic activity during Jesus' life than any other time in biblical history. Though demonic confrontations are mentioned throughout the Gospels, we find only eight case studies of actual encounters. These include Jesus' temptation (Matt. 4:1–11; Mark 1:12–13; Luke 4:1–13); the blind man (Matt. 9:32–33); the blind and mute man (Matt. 12:22–23; Luke 11:14); the Canaanite woman's daughter (Matt. 15:22–28; Mark 7:24–30); the man in the synagogue (Mark 1:23–27; Luke 4:31–37); the Gerasene demoniac (Matt. 8:28–34; Mark 5:1–20; Luke 8:26–37); the boy with seizures (Matt. 17:14–20; Mark 9:14–29; Luke 9:37–43); and the silencing of demons (Matt. 8:16; Mark 1:32–35; Luke 4:40–41). Other possible examples include the seven demons expelled from Mary Magdalene (Luke 8:1–2), Jesus' rebuke of Satan's suggestion through Peter (Matt. 16:23; Mark 8:33), and his command to Judas after Satan had entered him (John 13:27). Additionally, we are told that the disciples (Luke 10:17–20) and even someone they did not know (Mark 9:38–40) saw demons submit to them, but we are not given any other details. There are three main terms for demons in the New Testament: *daimonion* (demon; 60 times, 50 in the Gospels); *pneuma* (spirit; some 52 times) usually with a qualifying adjective such as *akatharton* (unclean; 21 times) or *pomēron* (evil; 8 times); and *angelos* (7 times of demonic agencies). *Daimōn* (demon), the term commonly used in classical Greek, appears only once (Mark 8:31).

Throughout Jesus' life we see his work against the devastating work of demons in the lives of people. The vocabulary of demonic activities against human beings is rich and varied, though it all shows movement toward the ultimate destruction of people. Demons troubled or annoyed people (Luke 6:18). They robbed a young boy of his speech (Mark 9:17, 25), rendered a man mute (Matt. 9:33; Luke 11:14), and froze the back of an elderly woman (Luke 13:11, 16). They seized the Gerasene demoniac (Luke 8:29) and a young boy (Luke 9:39) in order to destructively overcome him.

Throughout the Gospel accounts, spirits evidenced control over human hosts. Several terms are used to describe this. Jesus warned in a parable of the possibility of multiple demons living in or indwelling a person (Matt. 12:43–45; Luke 11:24–26). Evil spirits were *in* the demoniac in the synagogue (Mark 1:23); the Gerasene demoniac was a person who was *with* a spirit (Mark 5:2 "[in the power] of an unclean spirit," Amplified) that drove or impelled him (Luke 8:29). Many were described as *having* (*echō*) an evil or unclean spirit (Matt. 11:18; Mark 3:30; 7:25; 9:17; Luke 4:33; 7:33; 8:27; John 7:20; 8:48, 52; 10:20).

Such a spirit entered the young boy (Mark 9:25; Luke 8:30) and then mauled and convulsed him.

People who have demons are demonized (*daimonizomai*; Matt. 4:24; 8:16, 28, 33; 12:22; 15:22; Mark 1:32; 5:15, 16, 18; Luke 8:36; John 10:21). This term is generally translated as demon-possessed. However, *daimonizomai* does not convey the English concept of possession (either ownership or eternal destiny) as much as it does temporary control ("under the power of demons," Amplified). This idea is seen in the elderly woman who was bound by Satan for eighteen years before being set free by Jesus (Luke 13:16).

The New Testament describes physical, social, and spiritual symptoms of demonic control, though no exhaustive list is given. The physical symptoms include muteness (Matt. 9:32–33; Mark 9:17; Luke 11:14), blindness (Matt. 12:22), self-inflicted wounds (Mark 5:5; 9:22), crying (Mark 5:4), or screaming (Mark 1:26; 5:7; 9:26), convulsions (Mark 1:26), seizures (Matt. 17:15), falling to the ground, rolling around, foaming at the mouth, grinding of the teeth, and rigidity (Mark 9:18, 20), inhuman strength (Mark 5:3–4), and staying active day and night (Mark 5:5). The social symptoms include dwelling in unclean places (Mark 5:3; Luke 8:27) and going around naked (Luke 8:27). The spiritual symptoms include supernatural abilities such as recognition of the person of Christ and reaction against him (Mark 1:23–24; 5:7; Luke 4:40–41) and the ability to tell the future (divination; Acts 16:16). None of these symptoms by itself should be seen as proof of demonization. Rather, they are examples of the types of manifestations that come with demonic infestation.

Jesus came to set Satan's captives free (Matt. 12:22–29; Luke 4:18–21), and in all of his dealing with the demonized he demonstrated compassion for the people and authority over the spirits. He commanded the spirit in the Gerasene demoniac to come out (Luke 8:29) and ordered the demon out of the man in the synagogue (Mark 1:27) and the young boy (Mark 9:25). He did not have to be physically present to effect release, seen in the healing of the Canaanite woman's cruelly demonized daughter from a distance (Matt. 15:22–28). The people were amazed that he simply commanded the demons and they obeyed (Luke 4:36), as they were used to seeing elaborate exorcism rituals that were not always successful. The demons in the Gerasene demoniac needed Jesus' permission to enter the pigs (Mark 5:13; Luke 8:32) and he denied permission for demons to speak (Mark 1:34; Luke 4:41). He rebuked the demon in the young boy (Matt. 17:18; Mark 9:25; Luke 9:42) and the man in the synagogue (Mark 1:25; Luke 4:35).

The term most commonly used of the expulsion of demons in the New Testament is cast out (*ekballō*). In classical and Old Testament usage it had the sense of forcibly driving out an enemy. In the New Testament, it is typically used of a physical removal (John 9:34–35; see also Mark 1:12). Demons were cast out by the spirit of God (Matt. 12:28; cf. Luke 11:20, "by the finger of God"), and this was done by verbal command rather than the elaborate rituals of the exorcists. Jesus' authority to cast out demons was given to the Twelve (Matt. 10:1, 8) and others, who cast them out in Jesus' name (Mark 9:38–41; see also Acts 16:18). The disciples were successful in casting out demons, but needed a reminder to keep their priorities straight (Luke 10:17–20). With the young boy, however, they were unsuccessful because of lack of prayer (Mark 9:28–29).

There are several primary words employed in the Gospels to describe Jesus' healing ministry among the demonized. He released (*luō*) the woman bound by demons for eighteen years (Luke 13:16). He saved (*sōzō*) the Gerasene demoniac (Luke 8:36). He healed (*therapeuō*) many (Matt. 4:24; 10:22; 17:16; Luke 6:18; 7:21; 8:2; 13:14), a word used of healing the sick (lame, blind, mute, maimed, deaf) as well as the demonized and even of satanic healing. Its use implied that the restoration of demoniacs was on the same level of ministry as other types of healing, all of which showed Christ's mastery over Satan and sin. Jesus also healed (*iaomai*) many who had spirits (Luke 6:19; under the power of Satan), including the Canaanite woman's daughter (Matt. 15:28) and the young boy (Luke 9:42).

Demons in Acts and the Epistles. In comparison with the Gospels, demonic encounters are relatively rare. Spirits are mentioned in only five instances in Acts. Those tormented by evil spirits were brought before the apostles in Jerusalem and healed (5:15–16). Philip, not an apostle, exercised Christ's authority over demons in Samaria (8:6–7). Paul released a slave girl who had a fortune-telling spirit by simply commanding the spirit to leave (16:16–18). God performed extraordinary miracles through Paul in Ephesus, including the expulsion of demons (19:11–12). The final instance was between Jewish exorcists and a demoniac in which the exorcists were soundly beaten (19:13–17). When the church heard what happened, those who had not fully come out of their magical practices repented and publicly burned their expensive scrolls (19:17–20). The failure of the non-Christian exorcists shows that in power encounters authority is the underlying issue. Interestingly, the term "exorcism" is not used of Jesus' ministry. An exorcism implies a particular ritual, and Jesus, as well as the early church, relied on authority rather than ritual. It is not surprising, then, that nowhere in the New Testament is a Christian ritual for exorcism seen.

The relative paucity of overt examples of demonic confrontation is one indication of a shift from a form of direct power encounter with demons to a focus on knowing and correctly applying the truth to thwart demonic influence. This is also seen in the emphasis on deception as a tool of Satan and his demons. They pretend to be friendly spirits to deceive people (2 Cor. 11:15) and blind the minds of believers (2 Cor. 4:3–4). They lead people astray from truth (2 Tim. 3:13; 1 John 2:26; 3:7). They also lead people astray through the pursuit of pleasure or sensual gratification (Eph. 5:6; Col. 2:8; 2 Thess. 2:3).

The emphasis on truth in the Epistles does not mean that power encounters are unimportant or no longer viable today. Rather, the implication is that our day-to-day struggle with demonic forces will focus on truth issues without overlooking power issues. Appropriate truth encounter metaphors for spiritual conflict in the Epistles include walking in the light (1 John 1:5–7), the stripping off of the old and joyful putting on the new (Eph. 4:22–29), our participation in a kingdom transfer (Col. 1:13), which involves a transformation of our nature as people (2 Cor. 5:17), and our growth into the full measure of the stature of Christ (Eph. 4:14–16).

Believers are not immune from demonic attack. Demons seek to influence Christians through false doctrines and teachings (1 Tim. 4:1; 1 John 4:1–4) as well as false miracles and wonders (2 Thess. 2:7–11; Rev. 16:14). Paul was buffeted (2 Cor. 12:7; see Matt. 26:67; 1 Cor. 4:11; 1 Peter 2:20 for the physical aspect). Though there can be no certainty as to how this buffeting was manifested, we do know that an "angel of Satan" caused it and that Paul could not remove it through prayer. In the West evangelicals have been preoccupied with the question of whether a true Christian can be demon-possessed. Such a conclusion, however, can only be an inappropriate translation of *daimonizomai* because of the English connotations of possession with ownership, which is not in the original. Demons do not own or possess any Christians, who are God's sole possession (as are the demons themselves). Though Christians cannot be owned or have their eternal destiny controlled by a demon, this does not necessarily mean that they cannot be demonized or temporarily controlled by demons or have demons temporarily indwell them. The evidence pointing against demonization of the believer includes Jesus' defeat of Satan on the cross (John 12:31; Col. 2:14–15; Heb. 2:14–15), God's presence in (2 Cor. 6:16) and protection of the believer (1 John 5:18), and our status as being seated with Christ (Eph. 2:6). Evidence in favor of the demonization of believers includes the statements of our need to know Satan's schemes (2 Cor. 2:11) so that he will not gain a foothold on us (Eph. 4:26–27), the reality of demonic attack against believers (2 Cor. 11:3; 12:7; Eph. 6:10–12), and the commands to resist him (James 4:7; 1 Peter 5:8–9). No one should doubt that Satan and his demons are able to influence Christians; the question is whether that influence can result in demonization. Further evidence in favor of the possibility of believers being demonized are the instances of Saul's torment from an evil spirit (1 Sam. 16:14–23), the daughter of Abraham being bound by Satan for eighteen years (Luke 13:10–17), and Ananias and Sapphira having their hearts "filled by Satan" (Acts 5:3). None of these has been without dispute, but Scripture indicates that all were of the house of faith and all faced demonic attack. This parallels the experience of many people today. While experience is not the final arbiter of doctrinal formulation, our experience should be in accord with our doctrine. Thus, it is reasonable to conclude that Christians may be demonized and that the warnings to stand against Satan are not just to stop his attacks against the church or his control over those who do not believe.

Whatever our conclusion on demonization of believers, Christians clearly have the identity (being in Christ), the authority (being seated with Christ), and the mandate to resist Satan and his demons. We do so not on the basis of our own goodness, but on the basis of Christ's finished work on the cross. Because the One who is in us is greater than the one who is in the world (1 John 4:4), we can successfully stand against demonic schemes. Our weapons in this ongoing struggle include our authority as seated with Christ at the right hand of God, far above every power (Eph. 1:15–2:6), the name of Jesus (Phil. 2:10), our spiritual armor (Eph. 6:18), prayer (a must in some cases, Mark 9:29), simple resistance (James 4:7), forgiveness (Eph. 4:26–27), and exhibiting the fruit of the Spirit (Gal. 5:22–23; Eph. 4:22–29; 6:10–18).

Conclusion. The testimony of the Scriptures regarding demons is clear and cohesive. They are angelic entities who oppose God's sovereign control. They seek to work out their unholy rebellion through influencing people to live in a way contrary to God's expressed intentions. At the same time, they remain under his sovereignty and can be used of him to effect the divine plan. As Christians we are to submit ourselves to God and resist the attacks of Satan and his hosts. To do so, we must be aware of the basic truths presented in Scripture concerning not just the ontology of demons but their methods as they attempt to influence our lives. Once aware, we are to take our stand in Christ and oppose the working of demons, whether personally, corporately, or in the structures and systems of society.

A. Scott Moreau

Bibliography.: C. Arnold, *Powers of Darkness:* W. Carr, *Angels and Principalities* (1981); C. F. Dickason, *Angels: Elect and Evil:* idem, *Demon Possession and the Christian;* J. W. Montgomery, ed: *Demon Possession;* H. Schier, *Principalities and Powers in the New Testament* (1961); M. Unger, *Biblical Demonology;* idem, *What Demons Can Do to Saints*; M. Wink, *Naming the Powers;* idem, *Unmasking the Powers;* idem, *Engaging the Powers.*

Denial. To know what is true, yet confess a falsehood; the forsaking of self in wholehearted consecration to Christ and in service to his kingdom. The latter meaning of the term is related to the godly pursuit of true faith and piety. Christian spirituality is the fruit of the Spirit's sanctifying work in the life of every believer. This work of inner spiritual transformation stands in sharp contrast to mere outward conformity to the ethical and moral standards of biblical Christianity and those practices associated with so-called Christian asceticism (Rom. 12:1–2; Col. 2:20–23). Self-denial is the sum and substance of Christ's call to true discipleship, daily taking up his cross, and following him (Matt. 16:24).

The biblical terms for denial (Heb. *kāḥaš;* Gk. *arneomai, aparneomai*) more frequently employ the former meaning. Denial of godly faith or conduct is expressed in various degrees or intensities of conviction (compare, e.g., Peter's denial of our Lord and the denial of Hymenaeus and Alexander). Denial may take the form of deception, lying, or rejection of the truth on evidence to the contrary, as when the spies reported falsely about the land of Canaan (Num. 13) or when Sarah lied to conceal her lack of faith in the promise of God (Gen. 18:15). The ninth commandment prohibits false witness specifically against one's neighbor, although this commandment applies more broadly to one's duty to speak the truth in all circumstances (cf. Exod. 20:16; Lev. 6:2–7). Other examples of denial of Christian faith and practice include the Sadducees' rejection for the doctrine of the resurrection of the body (Luke 20:27), and the believer's failure to care for relatives, especially members of the immediate family (1 Tim. 5:8). Such false belief and conduct arise out of a willfull suppression of truth and denial of the power of godliness (Rom. 1:18; 2 Tim. 3:5; cf. Titus 2:12). Convenantal obligation requires that the servant of the Lord render faithful acknowledgment of God, the world, and oneself, knowing that God the Judge will render to us according to our words and deeds (Matt. 10:26–33; 12:37; Rom. 2:6–8). Denial as an act of covenant faithlessness contrasts with the abiding faithfulness of God as Savior (2 Tim. 2:12–13).

Israel's unfaithfulness—her denial and rejection of God and of his law—resulted in the breaking of the covenant relationship (2 Kings 17:15, 20; Jer. 9:6–9; 11:10; cf. Josh. 24:27). Israel serves as a warning and example to us of God's ultimate judgment against the denial of true faith and godliness (John 12:48; Heb. 12:25).

That Christ had to be rejected by humankind, including those who were of his own kindred and race, was in fulfillment of the Father's plan and purpose to achieve the redemption of God's elect seed in Christ (John 1:11–13; Luke 9:22; 20:17). Subsequent to the resurrection and ascension of Christ into heaven as our eternal high priest, unmitigating denial of Christ is identified as the sin of antichrist (1 John 2:22–23).

Mark W. Karlberg

See also Apostasy; Backsliding; Blasphemy Against the Holy Spirit.

Descent into Hell (Hades). Belief that between his crucifixion and resurrection Christ descended into the abode of the dead, as confessed in the Apostles' Creed. Since the New Testament declares that Christ really died, it is to be assumed that he went to Sheol (Gk. "Hades"), the abode of the dead. This is affirmed by the many declarations in the New Testament (over eighty times) that Christ was raised from (among) the dead, and by apostolic allusions to this event. But not all scholars accept this part of the Apostles' Creed, and some liturgical books either omit it or allow for its omission in the recitation of the creed.

The descent into Hades is a common motif in ancient religions. The heroes or the gods descend into Hades to perform a rescue, to triumph over death, or as part of the recurring seasons of the agricultural year. But in the Old Testament there is no instance of a human descent to, and return from, the underworld. There is only the one instance of consulting the dead, when Saul summoned the prophet Samuel through the witch of Endor (1 Sam. 28:3–25). This practice was condemned by the Law and the prophets.

Yet a descent into Sheol and return to the land of the living was the way in which the Old Testament described a near death experience (Ps. 107:18; Isa. 38:10). Only God was able to rescue them from death (Pss. 9:13; 30:3; 86:13; Isa. 38:17), since he is the one who "kills and makes alive" (Deut. 32:39; 1 Sam. 2:6; 2 Kings 5:7; cf. Rom. 4:17; 2 Cor. 1:9).

In the New Testament only Christ is said to have made such a descent into Hades and return to the land of the living. This corresponds with the uniqueness of his vicarious death and of his resurrection as an eschatological triumph.

Jesus himself used Jonah 2:6 to describe his death as three days and three nights in the heart (*en tē kardia*) of the earth. This corresponded with contemporary Jewish representations of Sheol as the belly of the fish, when speaking of death and the world of the dead.

So also the apostles understood the death and resurrection of Jesus "according to the scriptures," even as he instructed them (Luke 24:46; cf. Acts 17:2–3; 1 Cor. 15:4). Peter quoted Psalm 16:8–11 when he declared that God had released Jesus from the pangs of death by resurrecting him. God did not abandon him in Hades; that is, he raised him from the abode of the dead (Acts 2:24–27). Paul used Deuteronomy 30:12–13 and Psalm 71:20 in Romans 10:6–7 to explain the death of Christ as a descent into the abyss (*tis katabēsetai eis abusson*) and the resurrection as a going up from (among) the dead (*ek nekrōn anagagein*). And the author of Hebrews (2:14–16) declared that just as Jesus shared fully in the humanity of Abraham's seed, so also he shared the entire experience of death, by which he destroyed the power of Satan.

Yet the New Testament does not elaborate on this descent into Hades, unlike imaginative apocryphal writings. It assumes the reality of an intermediate abode of the dead to which Christ went after the parting of his soul from his body. Hades, then, is a reference to the general abode of the dead. Or it may reflect a developing understanding in contemporary Judaism that there was a distinction between the abode of the unrighteous dead (Hades) and the abode of the righteous dead (cf. the bosom of Abraham, Luke 16:22–23). The latter was also referred to as paradise (Luke 23:43), and was understood by some to be located in the heavens.

The significance of this is that the New Testament does not identify Hades as the place where Christ was punished for our sins. Rather, it is the crucifixion—which the disciples actually saw and experienced in all of its horror—that is developed in sacrificial language as the divine punishment and saving event. The use of the word "hell" to denote the place of punishment (Gehenna) is therefore inappropriate. The descent into Hades is rather a part of Christ's full identification with us, as well as the means by which he conquered death (Matt. 16:18; Rev. 1:18), and became the firstborn from among the dead (Col. 1:18; Rev. 1:5). NORMAN R. ERICSON

Bibliography. R. J. Bauckham, *ABD,* 2:145–59; G. W. Bromiley, *ISBE,* 1:926–27; W. Grudem, *JETS* 34/1 (1991): 103–13; J. R. McRay, *Dictionary of Bible and Religion,* pp. 624–25; J. M. Robinson, *IBD,* 1:826–28; D. P. Scaer, *JETS* 35/1 (1992): 91–99.

Desire. The word "desire" covers a wide range of human wants, emotions, and cravings. It can describe natural desires, which include hunger for food, sexual longings, and desire for God. It can also describe unnatural desires or cravings, which include such things as greed and lust. On a few occasions desires are ascribed to God. Most of the time they are ascribed to man, and these desires come under the scrutiny of God.

The Old Testament. There are twenty-seven Hebrew words translated "desire" (this includes root words and their derivatives).

Kāsap means to yearn for or to long after. *Hāpēṣ* has a basic meaning of feeling great favor toward something, and is found seventy-one times in the Old Testament, being translated "delight" or "pleasure" the majority of the time, and "desire" nine times. *Bāqaš* speaks of a person's earnest seeking of something or someone. It is usually translated "to seek," "require," or "desire."

The idea of "be attached to" and "love" comes from *hāšaq*. This root may denote the strong desire of a man toward a beautiful woman, as in Genesis 34:8. *Ḥāmad* is translated "delight in" and also "desire." The desire can be positive as in Exodus 34:24; Job 20:20; Psalm 68:16; and Isaiah 53:2. It can also be negative, in the form of "covet" or "lust after," as seen in Exodus 20:17; Deuteronomy 5:21; 7:25; Joshua 7:21; Proverbs 6:25; 12:12; and Micah 2:2. *Ḥāmad* describes both God's "pleasant" (desirable) trees in Eden (Gen. 2:9) and the tree forbidden to Adam, which became sinful when "desired" to make one wise (Gen. 3:6).

One of the most frequently used words in the Old Testament to indicate desire is *ʾāwâ* and its derivatives, which can be found almost fifty times. Often the subject of this verb is *nepheš,* meaning self, soul, or appetite. The term is translated as "desire," "lust," "will," "pleasant," "greed," "dainty," and "desirable."

One final word of importance is the root *shwq* and its derivative *těšûqâ*. It is translated as "desire" or "longing." This term is found only three times in the Old Testament: Genesis 3:16, 4:7, and Song of Solomon 7:10. In Genesis 3:16 the term is negative in nature, occurring in a context of sin and judgment. In Genesis 4:7 sin itself is described as desiring to have Cain. God describes sin "like a crouching beast," hungering and preying on Cain. In the Song of Solomon the term is positive in nature, in the context of joy and love, referring to the bridegroom's desire for his bride.

The New Testament. Matthew 9:13 (quoting Hos. 6:6) is the first instance of desire in the New Testament. The Greek term used is *thelō,* which can be translated will, be willing, want, or desire. This term is found 208 times in the New Testament. Most of the time it is translated as "willing," but it is translated as "desire" in the two Matthean passages, Luke 20:46, and Hebrews 10:5, 8.

The verb *epithymeō* and its derivatives are found scattered seventy-three times throughout the New Testament. *Epithymeō* is found sixteen times. Both it and the noun *epithymia* are derived from *thymos,* which means wrath, fierceness, indignation, and then passion, heat, or passionate desire. *Epithymeō* most often has an ambivalent sense, meaning simply desire, strive for, long to have/do/be something. Only in a few instances is the word used for (forbidden) desire. For example, 1 Corinthians 10:6 refers to godless desire.

The noun *epithymia* is used in a neutral or good sense in Luke 22:15; Philippians 1:23; 1 Thessalonians 2:17; and Revelation 18:14. All other uses of the noun are in the bad sense, usually with the translation of the word being "lust."

Zēloute, derived from *zēloō,* designates a passionate commitment to a person or cause. Five passages in the New Testament use this term (1 Cor. 12:31; 14:1, 39; Gal. 4:17, 4:7; James 4:2). *Zēloō* is found multiple times in the New Testament and is used in reference to Jewish "holy zeal," hostility occasioned by ill will, "jealousy," and the desire to attain goals or to be devoted to someone.

One of the stronger negative Greek words translated desire is *katastreniao*. It means to burn fiercely, to be covetous, to be sensually stimulated. Another word used in the negative sense is *orexis,* which indicates a lustful desire or longing.

Hēdonē is understood to mean desire, pleasure, or enjoyment. Originally *hēdonē* meant the feeling of desire perceived through the sense of taste. In the New Testament it represents desires that strive against the work of God and his Spirit. The word is found five times in the New Testament, and all five occurrences have a bad connotation. In Luke 8:14 it is the pleasures or desires of life that will choke out the Word. Titus 3:3 describes the lost sinner as being "enslaved by all kinds of passions and pleasures." James 4:1–3 says that fights and quarrels are the outward expressions of lusts or desires within the members, and the author warns against praying with wrong motives, intending to satisfy personal lusts or desires. Finally, 2 Peter 2:13 says that false teachers consider it desirous to riot or carouse in the daytime.

Conclusion. In the Old Testament human desires were viewed as something natural to humankind. But desire was to be subject in obedience to the will of Yahweh. The one who knew the true fulfillment of his or her desires relied on the Lord. Thus, the final object of desire was the Lord himself (Prov. 3:5–6).

Desire is treated in a similar manner in the New Testament. Human desire is viewed as being evil, lustful, covetous, and ungoverned, or as commensurate with the new life in Christ. Paul points out that the Christian is "to eagerly desire the greater gifts" (1 Cor. 12:31). He described how he "longed" to see his Thessalonian brothers in 2 Thessalonians 2:17. Christ "eagerly desired to eat the Passover" with his disciples (Luke 22:15). We see that Paul's greatest desire in Philippians 1:23 is the desire to "depart and be with Christ."

How do we know if a desire is good or bad? The answer lies in the object or reason for the desire. If the desire is self-centered then it is bad, because the essence of sin is the determination to have one's own way. It is an act of idolatry in that one has put self in the place of God. Good desire is simply the opposite. It is putting the desire for God's will first. When the Lord is our greatest desire, all other desires find their proper expression.

DANIEL L. AKIN

See also LUST.

Destroy, Destruction. "Destroy" in the Bible usually refers to violent action causing physical death (Num. 16:33; Ps. 2:12; Heb. *ʾābad*). But less intense meanings may be denoted. Exodus 10:7 describes economic ruin (cf. Matt. 9:17, Gk. *apollumi*). In 1 Samuel 9:3 *ʾābad* refers to lost animals (cf. Matt. 10:6). In the New Testament *katargeō* can mean "render powerless, ineffective" (Heb. 2:14).

The Amorites. Directions by God for extermination of the Canaanites have long been perplexing (Exod. 23:23–33; 34:12–17). Although life is sacred (Gen. 9:5–7), at times life has to be taken to preserve life. A man-eating lion must be destroyed (Ezek. 19:1–9). It was prophesied that these nations would be thorns in the eyes and snares (Josh. 23:12–13). Such objects sometimes cause infections necessitating surgical removal of an inflamed limb. In a vastly greater sphere no physical life could be more important than the redemption of the entire world.

The Baal and Aqht myths described the rampages of the goddess Anat. She offers to make blood run down her father's grey hair if Baal does not get a palace. She has Aqht's skull crushed to get his bow. She wades through blood of her own devotees whom she has killed for little or no reason.

With such models Jezebel had no problem killing Naboth for his vineyard (1 Kings 21). Abimelech killed his seventy half-brothers and roasted 1,000 people in his Canaanite mother's city (Judg. 9:4–5, 45–49). Adoni-Bezek mutilated seventy kings and kept them under his table (Judg. 1:7). The Baal-worshiping Athaliah almost ended David's line by slaughtering her husband's sons (2 Kings 11:1–3).

The result of sparing Canaanites was that Israel mingled with them and learned their practices. Sadly this caused shedding blood of children sacrificed to idols. They were to be removed so they would not teach them "to follow all the detestable things they do in worshiping their gods" (Deut. 20:18).

These gods were also sexually depraved. Before Baal's trip to Mot's domain he had intercourse eighty-eight times with a cow, who was really his sister. The story of El's adultery with two human wives is thought to have been worship liturgy. Leviticus 18 lists the Canaanites' abominations as incest, homosexuality, adultery, child sacrifice, and bestiality. Results of this immorality was that the land vomited them out. No country can long tolerate such destruction of family life. The coming of the Israelites simply hastened the inevitable demise of this society.

Altars. Sacred pillars, asherim (Exod. 34:13), altars, and cult centers were to be destroyed (2 Kings 21:3). According to the New Testament the altar is a symbol of fellowship with the deity behind the altar (1 Cor. 10:18–22). According to Jesus the altar represents both the sacrifice on it and the deity whose presence dwells there (Matt. 23:20–21). Paul refers to a pagan altar as "the table of demons" (1 Cor. 10:21).

In addition to child sacrifice Canaanite worship included many sexual immoralities. When the Israelites joined in these rites they yoked themselves to Baal (Num. 25:1–5). Paul reminds us that this immorality resulted in 23,000 deaths (1 Cor. 10:8; cf. Num. 25:9). With child sacrifices, self-mutilation, and other despicable acts being performed there, the altars became centers of demonic presence (Ps. 106:37–39). Destroying them would remove "the table of demons" from the people's midst.

When the Lord split apart the altar at Bethel it manifested the powerlessness of man-made religion (1 Kings 13:3–5). When Gideon destroyed the altar of Baal, his father pointed out to its defenders Baal's inability to stop the desecration of a structure sacred to him (Judg. 6:28–32). Apostate Israelites obviously wanted to make this demonstration about Yahweh by tearing down his altar (1 Kings 18:30; 19:10, 14). God, however, was able to validate his potency by sending fire down upon Mount Carmel (1 Kings 18:38; cf. Judg. 6:21). When Solomon dedicated Yahweh's altar, the priests were unable to approach because of the fiery glory (2 Chron. 7:1–3).

God himself will personally destroy apostate high places along with their altars (Lev. 26:30; Ezek. 6:4). Yahweh will reveal himself as the Most High God by actually standing next to the altar when he gives the command to destroy their worship center (Amos 9:1).

Israel. When golden calf worship broke the covenant, Israel fell under a sentence of destruction (Exod. 32:10). By intense intercession Moses "stood in the breach before him to keep his wrath from destroying them" (Ps. 106:23). "Then the LORD relented and did not bring on his people the disaster he had threatened" (Exod. 32:14). Thus in Exodus 32–34 the radical theological proposition was laid down that human responses might alter a divine pronouncement of doom. The mercy confession of Exodus 34:6 arose out of this context of judgment. It was reaffirmed on many different occasions throughout Israel's history (Num. 14:18; Deut. 4:31; Neh. 9:17; Pss. 86:15; 103:8; 145:8; Jon. 4:2).

Wicked Ahab could humble himself and be granted a postponement of his dynasty's destruction (1 Kings 21:27–29; 2 Kings 9:8). Even evil Ninevites by radical, plenary repentance could avert the prophecy of their doom (Jon. 3). From these specific examples of God's grace Jeremiah built a theology of repentance that gave hope to those facing exile (Jer. 18:7–10).

God, however, is not to be manipulated; and the altering of judgment is not a foregone conclusion. Thus Moses says, "*Perhaps* I can make atonement" (Exod. 32:30). As intense as the efforts of his people were, the king of Nineveh knew he could not force God. He qualified his expectations with a "perhaps" (Jon. 3:9).

Israel was told that continued disobedience would result in destruction and exile. They were warned they would be utterly destroyed from under heaven (Lev. 26:38; Deut. 4:26; 28:20). The sage had predicted that "a man who remains stiff-necked after many rebukes will suddenly be destroyed" (Prov. 29:1).

There will be no hiding from this destruction either in heaven, earth, the bottom of the sea, or sheol (Amos 9:2–3). Even if they are taken captive, the sword will follow them into distant lands (Amos 9:4, 8). Yahweh will stalk them like a bear and tear their hearts out (Hos. 5:14; 13:7–8).

Survival of Destruction. Israel, like the rebellious son in Deuteronomy 21:18–21, received the death sentence. God's people were bent on turning away, so the sword would whirl over them (Hos. 11:6–7). But when confronted with delivering the coup de grace, Yahweh experiences the most intense emotional trauma ever written about deity. His heart is overturned. His inner emotions come to a boil (Hos. 11:8). The lion cannot finish his kill. Instead he brings his trembling sons home (Hos. 5:14–15; 11:11).

"Not completely" is a motif of many destruction prophecies (Isa. 6:11–13; Jer. 5:10; 30:11; 31:35; Joel 2:32; Amos 9:8). Various synonyms denoting destruction are often paralleled with the words "build" and "plant" (Jer. 1:10; 18:7–10; 24:6; 42:10; Ezek. 36:35–36). Like Jonah, a person approaching the gates of sheol can suddenly be snatched back to the land of the living (Jon. 2:5–7). What the Babylonian sea monster has swallowed must come out of his mouth (Jer. 51:34, 44).

Thus the meaning "lost" becomes applicable to Israel (Jer. 50:6). Exiled Israelites are the Lord's lost sheep. Their shepherds have failed them, so the Lord himself will become their shepherd and lead them home (Isa. 40:10–11; Ezek. 34:1–16). Jesus himself claimed this shepherding ministry perhaps partially quoting the Septuagint of Ezekiel 34:4 (Matt. 10:6; 15:24; 18:11; Luke 19:10). The prophet Isaiah foresaw that lost exiles would return and worship on the holy mountain (27:13).

Paul was convinced that God had not rejected Israel whom he foreknew (Rom. 11:2). He had prepared them beforehand as vessels of mercy to show forth his glory (9:23). Even though some of the branches have been broken off, the root of Israel will be saved (11:17–18). Although individuals may perish, all Israel will be saved when the Deliverer appears and removes their ungodliness (Zech. 12:10; Rom. 11:26; Rev. 1:7–8). Unless the days of tribulation are cut short, no flesh will be saved. But for the sake of the elect those days will be shortened (Matt. 24:21–22).

The Devil's Works. According to Paul, God endured with patience vessels of wrath prepared for destruction. He raised them up and made them mighty for the purpose of revealing his power and glory (Rom. 9:17–22). The word translated "prepared" often refers to equipping someone for a task. Thus God merely makes pagan nations who have already chosen the road to destruction (Matt. 7:13) more powerful and hence more capable of expressing their rebellious tendencies.

These nations are depicted as ferocious animals (Dan. 7:1–4; Rev. 13:1–2). Their origin is the chaotic ocean. They are the devil's work. They are not made in God's image and are not of heavenly origin. They have allowed themselves to be shaped and molded by the devil's sinister artistry.

On the mountain of temptation Christ did not challenge the devil's temporary, partial sovereignty over these nations (Luke 4:6–8). But he knew one day the kingdoms of this world would become kingdoms of our Lord and of his Christ (Rev. 11:15, 17).

Nebuchadnezzar saw all these kingdoms in a dream as a mighty statue made of various metals. A stone hewn without hands (the work of God) came down and crushed the clay and iron (Satan's work). The devil's kingdom will be crushed and destroyed forever (Dan. 7:26). The armies of these nations are to be slain by the sword of the one sitting on the horse (Rev. 19:21).

Much of the devil's works is carried on by unseen, spiritual realities called "rulers, powers, and spiritual forces of evil" (Eph. 6:12). Their main works are accusation (Rev. 12:10), deception (2 Thess. 2:9; Rev. 12:9), and temptation (1 Thess. 3:5). The purpose of the appearance of Christ was to destroy these works (1 John 3:8). With the coming of Christ the prince of this world was thrown out (John 12:31).

The first demons to encounter Christ sensed that they would be destroyed by him (Mark 1:24). At the cross these powers were disarmed and openly defeated (Col. 2:15). The death of Christ destroyed the devil (Heb. 2:14). *Katargeō* (translated "destroy" in the AV) means to render powerless or ineffective. Thus in 1 Corinthians 2:6 the present participle of *katargeō* indicates that these powers are even now in the process of passing away.

The condemning work of Satan was destroyed by the cross (Col. 2:14). Satan's deception will be destroyed by bringing to light the hidden things of darkness (1 Cor. 4:5) and by the brightness of Christ's coming (2 Thess. 2:8). Satan's work will be ended when he is thrown into the lake of fire (Rev. 20:10).

Death. In Job 26:6 destruction is paralleled with sheol, the underworld. But this is not mere annihilation because the departed spirits there tremble (v. 5). Destruction is an actual place that is open before God (Prov. 15:11). In Revelation 9:1, 11, the king of this bottomless pit is called "Abaddon" (destruction). In Revelation 20:14 death itself and Hades will experience the second death by being cast into the lake of fire.

In the Baal myth Mot, the god of death, swallows his victims. In Isaiah 25:8, death will be engulfed for all time and tears will cease. At the cross Christ rendered death ineffective (2 Tim. 1:10; Heb. 2:14). According to Paul the last enemy to be destroyed at the second coming of Christ is death (1 Cor. 15:24–28).

Earthly Beauty. The present tense of the verb *paragō* in 1 John 2:17 indicates that the world is always in the process of passing away. Ecclesiastes 12:1–5 describes how the beauty of youth fades in old age. Assuming Solomonic authorship, the writer would have been able to observe his own father, the sweet singer of Israel, the slayer of ten thousands, becoming a weak, impotent, senile old man.

Solomon's own son saw the fading beauty of an entire kingdom. David's kingdom was divided and the treasury ransacked. In the end Solomon had to be content with shields of bronze rather than of gold (1 Kings 14:26–27). Many others would witness the impermanence of beautiful symbols of kingship (Isa. 28:1–4).

Jeremiah looked at Jehoiakim's palace on Ramat Rachel panelled with cedar and painted bright red. He asked, "Does it make you a king to have more and more cedar?" Prophetically he lamented, "Alas, his splendor" (Jer. 22:14–18). Some of the beautiful carvings are in the Israel Museum. The site is grown up with weeds and one cannot tell that it was once a palace. This is a silent witness to the fact that "man, despite his riches, will not endure" (Ps. 49:12).

The disciples of Christ, overawed at the beauty of the temple adorned with gifts, remarked at how wonderful the buildings were. Jesus told them that not one stone would be left upon another in the awesome destruction that would follow (Mark 13:1–2). He warned them that everything in heaven and earth would pass away except his words (Mark 13:31).

Eternal Destruction. The Bible seems to indicate that there is an unending destruction and that those who experience it will always be consciously aware of it. The words translated "destruction" do not always denote total extinction. Sometimes they denote a ruin that is beyond repair (Exod. 10:7; Matt. 9:17).

Thus when Revelation 17:8 says the beast is to go into destruction (*apōleia*), it does not mean termination of existence. Revelation 20:10 indicates that the beast will be tormented day and night forever and ever. The Old Testament also affirms that for the wicked there is no more expectation or future (Prov. 11:7; 24:20). They will be ashamed and dismayed forever and thus apparently always aware of their lost condition (Ps. 83:17). Job 26:5 indicates that the departed spirits realize their situation and tremble.

PAUL FERGUSON

See also ABADDON; DEATH, MORTALITY; DEVOTE, DEVOTED; HELL; JUDGMENT; WAR, HOLY WAR.

Bibliography. R. Adamiak, *Justice and History in the Old Testament;* P. Craigie, *Ugarit of the Old Testament;* Y. Kaufmann, *Biblical Account of Conquest of Palestine;* M. Kline, *A Tribute to Gleason Archer;* T. Longman and D. Reid, *Yahweh as Divine Warrior;* C. Pfeiffer, *Ras Shamra and the Bible.*

Deuteronomy, Theology of. The fifth book of the Pentateuch is not merely a recasting of the Sinai covenant text and all its derivative materials, but a new and fresh statement of Yahweh's covenant purposes to a new generation in a new place with new prospects. The nation with whom the Sinai covenant had been made had died in the wilderness and so was no longer on the scene (Num. 14:26–35). Deuteronomy was addressed to their offspring who were poised to enter the land of promise, and needed reassurance of Yahweh's covenant promises in light of the challenge of impending conquest and settlement.

Critical scholarship for nearly 200 years has uprooted Deuteronomy from its traditional Mosaic setting and has located it in the seventh century B.C., identifying it as the document that gave impetus for the reformation of Josiah of Judah (2 Kings 22:8–13). This view not only denies the book's authorship to Moses but has given rise to modern documentary hypotheses as a whole with their source-critical theories concerning the composition of the Pentateuch. It is now fashionable to speak of Deuteronomy—2 Kings as the "Deuteronomistic History," a massive theological work redacted in the sixth century. Deuteronomy itself is thought to have originated a little earlier, being a reflection of allegedly Mosaic teaching designed to provide a covenant standard by which to assess and judge Israel's actual history (cf. 2 Kings 17). The negative tone of the "Deuteronomistic" account is attributed to the antimonarchic traditionists who first had created Deuteronomy as an antimonarchical tractate and then wrote their history to show how the monarchy had, indeed, violated the book's covenant mandates.

More recently, comparisons have been made between the form and content of Deuteronomy and those of ancient Near Eastern treaty texts, especially from the Hittite Empire (ca. 1400–1200 B.C.) and Neo-Assyrian (ca. 700–600) periods. While the debate continues as to which parallels are more exact, the majority of scholars are persuaded of the Old Testament-Hittite analogies and therefore of the antiquity of the structure of Deuteronomy. This is not the place to argue the matter, nor is it important from a theological standpoint to settle the issue one way or the other. What is important is to recognize that Deuteronomy itself witnesses to its Mosaic authorship (1:1, 3, 5; 4:44; 31:1, 9, 22) and in its canonical form bears all the hallmarks of a covenant document, specifically that of a sovereign-vassal type. In fact, it is the genre of the book as a covenant text that is the key to its proper theological purpose and understanding.

Biblical scholarship has increasingly come to understand that one cannot separate the literary genre of a text from its intended message. The form of a composition, as well as its content, is critical to its meaning. If, then, Deuteronomy is cast in the literary mold of a sovereign-vassal treaty text, its message must be understood accordingly. Moreover, inasmuch as the theology of a text is dependent on the proper exegesis, analysis, and synthesis of that text, it is safe to say that a book's theology is a function of its form.

With this in mind, it is important that Deuteronomy be analyzed as a literary composition before any attempt be made to recover its theology. The following outline represents a fairly widely held consensus of the shape of the book as a covenant document:

The preamble, which provides the setting in which the Great King presents the covenant text to the vassal (1:1–5).

The historical prologue, which recounts the past relations between the two contracting parties (1:6–4:49).

The general stipulations, which present the basic principles of expectation of behavior that underlie the relationship (5:1–11:32).

The specific stipulations, which provide interpretation or amplification of the general stipulations, usually in terms of actual cases or precise requirements (12:1–26:15).

The blessings and curses, which spell out the results of faithful adherence to or disobedience of the terms of the covenant (27:1–28:68).

The witnesses, that is, persons or other entities to which appeal can be made as to the legality of the covenant instrument and to the commitments made by the contracting parties (30:19; 31:19; 32:1–43).

In light of the indisputable connection between form and function, it is safe to say that the concept of covenant lies at the center of the theology of Deuteronomy. Covenant, in turn, by its very definition demands at least three elements—the two contracting parties and the document that describes the purpose, nature, and requirements of the relationship. Thus the three major rubrics of the theology of Deuteronomy are Yahweh, the Great King and covenant initiator; Israel, the vassal and covenant recipient; and the book itself, the covenant vehicle, complete with the essentials of standard treaty documents. This means, moreover, that all the revelation of the book must be seen through the prism of covenant and not abstractly removed from the peculiar historical and ideological context in which it originated.

In Deuteronomy (and, indeed, in Scripture generally) God reveals himself in acts, theophany, and word. The acts of God, when viewed all together and as part of a pattern, constitute the essence of history. This obviously begins with

God as Creator (an aspect lacking in Deuteronomy) and continues, in its peculiar relationship to Israel, with God's self-disclosure as elector, redeemer, and benefactor of his people.

As the God who transcends history, Yahweh also reveals himself in the awe-inspiring splendor of theophany. In Deuteronomy this otherness of God finds expression typically in the brilliance of light, especially fire, and in its opposite, darkness. This polarity is suggestive of his immanence, his accessibility to his creation, but also of his transcendent remoteness. He is the Great King who desires to communicate with and to receive the homage of his people but who reminds them constantly that he is above and beyond them in unapproachable glory. It is precisely at the point of his making covenant with them that the theophanic disclosure is most emphatic.

The most intelligible and therefore least ambiguous mode of revelation is the prophetic word. That word of God in Deuteronomy is, of course, the book itself expressed in its uniquely covenant form. But Deuteronomy is a covenant text in a broader than normal sense inasmuch as it contains not only the sine qua non of standard documents of that genre but also itineraries, narratives, hymns, and homilies, all designed to provide both a covenant document as well as a historical, existential, and eschatological context in which to interpret it. Thus there are the solemn and formal pronouncements of covenant initiation (1:6b–8; 2:4b–7; 4:12–13; 5:4, 6–22) as well as constant enjoinders to be faithful to its stipulations.

The subject of divine self-disclosure, that is, the content of Yahweh's revelation about himself, must also be seen in terms of the covenant purposes of the Book of Deuteronomy. It is therefore not surprising that the covenant name "Yahweh" is by far the most commonly attested to, occurring about 221 times. By this name he encountered Moses at Sinai and it is in this name that he constantly commands his people to keep the covenant made there. The rare occurrences of Elohim (23 times) and other names and epithets (about 18 times) reinforce the covenant character of the book and its almost exclusive attention to Israel, for these names, especially Elohim and its byforms, occur most regularly in contexts describing God's more cosmic or universal interests in creation and history.

The revelation of God's person in Deuteronomy follows rather typical biblical patterns. In highly anthropomorphic terms he is said to possess hands (2:15; 3:24; 4:34), an arm (4:34; 5:15), a mouth (8:3), a face (5:4; 31:18; 34:10), a finger (9:10), and eyes (11:12; 12:28); he walks (23:14), writes (10:4), and rides (33:26). He is both immanent (4:7, 39; 31:8) and transcendent (4:12, 35–36; 5:4, 22–26), unique (3:24; 5:7; 6:4, 15) and without material form (4:12, 15).

In terms of his character and attributes Yahweh is gracious (5:10; 7:9, 12), loving (1:31; 7:7–8, 13), righteous or just (4:8; 10:17–18), merciful (4:31; 13:17), powerful (4:34, 37; 6:21–22), holy (5:11), glorious (5:24–26), faithful or loyal (7:9, 12), and upright (32:4). But he is also an angry God (1:37; 3:26; 9:18–20), and zealous for his own honor (4:24; 13:2–10; 29:20).

The second major theme of the theology of Deuteronomy—that pertaining to the recipient of the covenant initiated by Yahweh—consists primarily of references to the single nation or people Israel. Israel serves a functional role in Deuteronomy, one in line with the formal nature of the book, which portrays her as a servant of Yahweh whose mission is one of modeling the kingdom of God on earth and pressing its claims on the alienated nations so in need of God's salvation.

There is little concern with humankind apart from their constitution as nations, particularly the nation Israel. The typical terms *gôy* and *ʿam* are used, the latter with more of an ethnic rather than nationalistic sense. Both Israel and the pagan nations are called *gôy*, usually with the emphasis on Israel as a national unit called from among the others and charged with a specific mission as a nation (4:6–8, 34). That Israel is an ethnic entity as well, however, is clear from 27:9, where she is told that "you have now become the people [*ʿam*] of the LORD your God." There is more to Israel, then, than a national organization of tribes. Israel is an ethnic people, a kinfolk who can trace their origins back to a common ancestor whom God promised to make a great nation.

The third rubric of the theology of Deuteronomy is that of the covenant itself, both its form and its content. As has been noted, modern scholarship has drawn attention to the remarkable correspondence between Old Testament covenant form and pattern and that of Late Bronze Age Hittite vassal treaties. But of greater theological importance than the structure of the book is its content, one so inextricably linked to its covenant context that the theology of Deuteronomy should be viewed continually as a statement of relationship—that of Yahweh the Great King with his elect and commissioned people Israel.

More particularly, Deuteronomy is a covenant renewal document and not an initial statement of covenant establishment. This is clear from the frequent references to the original Sinai (or Horeb) covenant setting (1:6; 4:1–2, 5, 10, 15, 23, 33–40) and the change in language in Deuteronomy vis-à-vis Exodus due to the changed circumstances (5:12–15; cf. Exod. 20:8–11; 7:1–5; cf. Exod. 23:32–33; 12:5; cf. Exod. 20:24; 15:12–18; cf. Exod. 21:2–6). Moreover, Deuteronomy is a greatly expanded and more detailed rendition of the covenant text, for the complexities of life and expectation in the land of promise raise issues that were of little or no consequence in the wilderness of Sinai.

After tracing the course of events from Sinai (1:6–3:29) to the present site of covenant renewal in Moab, Moses urged the people to obedience as a precondition to blessing (4:1, 6, 40). He pointed out that the document of covenant was inviolable (4:2), that it must be taught to future generations (4:9–10, 40), and that its infraction would result in divine chastisement (4:26–28).

Moses next introduced the general stipulations of the covenant in a passage that clearly establishes the technical nature of the relationship (4:44–49). The "law" (or, better, "instruction"), he said, would consist of "stipulations," "decrees," "laws," terms associated with such treaties.

The form of the Decalogue here (5:6–21) is virtually identical to the one in Exodus although there are slight differences because of the new historical and environmental circumstances awaiting this new generation of Israel. Also like its model in Exodus, the Deuteronomic Decalogue provides a platform of principles upon which the remainder of the general stipulations must rest and, indeed, of which they are a detailed interpretation and elaboration (5:22–11:32).

These stipulations are described as commands, decrees, and laws (6:1; cf. 5:31). They are adumbrated in the Shema of 6:4–5, the confessional fulcrum of Old Testament faith that defines Yahweh as the unique Sovereign and reduces Israel's obligation to him to one of exclusive love, that is, obedience. The whole purpose of the collection of stipulations is, in fact, to set forth application of the principles of the Ten Words and the Shema (6:6; cf. 5:22) as an expression of the fundamental duty of the servant people.

The basic stipulations (7:1–11:32) require the dispossession of nonvassals who must be utterly destroyed because they will cause Israel to become disloyal. Moreover, the land belongs to Yahweh and since Israel is the vassal of Yahweh only she has legitimate claim to tenancy. They also insist that Israel recognize Yahweh as the only source of blessing and life in the land. He who supplied manna in the desert could and would provide all his people's needs in Canaan. The principles of the covenant stipulations go on, however, to emphasize that all blessings, past and future, are attributable to Yahweh's grace. Possession of the land is not just an accident of history but an outworking of Yahweh's irrefragable promises to the fathers and of his sovereign pleasure.

The specific stipulations (12:1–26:15), based squarely on the principles of the foregoing section, serve at least two major theological purposes. First, they further elucidate the fundamental covenant theme of Deuteronomy 4:40–11:32. That is, they function in a real sense as a case-by-case commentary on that section. Second, they define precisely the terms of the covenant relative to cultic, ethical, and societal/interpersonal/interethnic relationships. That is, they make practical application of what was more or less theoretical propositions. All the themes in this section find their center in Yahweh, his people, and the covenant that binds them together.

The exclusiveness of Yahweh is underscored by the insistence that worship be centralized in one place, the place where Yahweh would choose to "put his Name" (12:5, 11). There and only there could tribute offered to the Sovereign—especially that of the blood of sacrificed animals—be presented to him. This is in opposition to the notion of the multiplicity of pagan gods and their respective shrines, all of which must be eradicated, including the prophets who promote these competing (if nonexistent) deities (13:5, 9–10). Another mark of the distinction between the purity of Yahwistic faith and the corruption of paganism is the line of demarcation drawn between the clean and unclean animals (14:1–3). The arbitrary definition of a clean animal suggests the sovereign election by Yahweh of a people whom he alone declares to be holy. Finally, Yahweh's exclusiveness is celebrated by the tribute paid him by his vassal people Israel. This takes the form of the tithe (14:22–29); the release of bond-slaves who symbolize Israel as a liberated slave people; the dedication of the firstborn to Yahweh in recognition of his having spared the firstborn in the tenth plague; and annual pilgrimages to the central sanctuary, journeys whose purpose is to proclaim the lordship of Yahweh to whom his loyal subjects come in submissive presentation of tribute.

The chasm between the ineffable Lord and his theocratic citizens is bridged in part by officials appointed by him to represent him to them and them to him. Thus there are judges and "officials" (16:18), kings, levitical priests, and prophets, all of whom bear the awesome privilege and heavy responsibilities incumbent on those who would serve the King. For them to fail is to invite divine displeasure and judgment.

Israel's role as a theocratic community did not remove her from the ordinary definition of a nation. Therefore she had to know how to deal with all the exigencies of national life although, as the vassal people of Yahweh, in such a way as to draw attention to that unique role. This would influence the way the nation dealt with homicide, boundary disputes, due process, war, the just treatment of wives, children, and criminals, and moveable goods.

Purity laws, which deal directly or indirectly with forms of separation, testified to the need for Israel to maintain covenant purity and separation. They concerned such matters as clothing (22:5), mother birds (22:6–7), freedom from liability (22:8), mixed seed, animals, and cloth (22:9–11), and a variety of other cases whose significance with respect to the principle of purity is not always easy to determine. What binds them together theologically is the recognition of the fact that Yahweh himself is among his people and that his holiness demands their best efforts at holiness (23:14).

The theological importance of proper behavior of covenant members toward each other is reemphasized by another set of stipulations (23:20–25:19), similar in some respects to those already addressed (especially in 21:10–22:4), but with greater business and economic interests in view. Because all members of the theocratic community are equal before God, they must be absolutely evenhanded and scrupulously honest and fair in their dealings with one another. If the heart of covenant confession is the requirement of loving the Lord his God with all heart, soul, and strength (6:5), the corollary, loving neighbors as ourselves (Lev. 19:18), is equally obligatory.

The sixth area of concern in the specific stipulation section is that of regular and consistent recognition by vassals of their indebtedness to a beneficent God for all his redemptive and restorative acts of grace. This must find expression particularly at the time of harvest festival when worshipers, with offering in hand, recite the sacred history of their people, dedicate themselves anew to the task of covenant-keeping, and give evidence of that commitment by the presentation of a special tithe to God's dependent ministers (26:1–15). It is fitting that this pledge of covenant fidelity be made at precisely the place mentioned at the beginning of the special stipulation section, that is, at "the place the Lord your God will choose as a dwelling for his Name" (26:2; cf. 12:5).

The permanency of the covenant relationship is implied by the command that Israel, once in the land of promise, should undertake covenant renewal at Mount Ebal, a ceremony centered on the very words of the covenant text being composed by Moses (27:1–7). The solemnity of what they would do there would be apparent in the curses that would result from their disobedience to the aforementioned stipulations (27:11–26; 28:15–68) and the blessings that would ensue the pursuit of obedience (28:1–14). Such curses and blessings had already attended Israel's pilgrimage to that point, and were a guarantee that Yahweh's dealings with his people in the present and future would be no different. Therefore, Moses said, the present generation, as well as those to come, must commit and recommit themselves to covenant faithfulness (30:11–20).

Since the covenant was articulated in the Mosaic writings themselves, specifically in Deuteronomy (31:9), future commitment to its principles presupposed its preservation in a place that was both safe and accessible. The document was thus entrusted to the levitical priests and the elders of Israel who, upon stated occasions, would release it for public reading. As a reminder of the pledge the people had undertaken to keep covenant they would also regularly sing a song whose very content was a recitation of God's redemptive work on behalf of Israel (32:1–43). Finally, in affirmation of the steadfastness of Yahweh's commitment to the nation, Moses offered a promissory blessing in which the tribes are prophetically described as recipients of divine favor. EUGENE H. MERRILL

See also CLEAN, UNCLEAN; COVENANT; ISRAEL; LAW; MOSES.

Bibliography. R. E. Clements, *God's Chosen People: A Theological Interpretation of the Book of Deuteronomy;* J. G. McConville, *Law and Theology in Deuteronomy;* Eugene H. Merrill, *A Biblical Theology of the Old Testament;* Samuel J. Schultz, *Deuteronomy: The Gospel of Love.*

Devil. *See* SATAN.

Devote, Devoted. The Hebrew noun used to denote exclusive dedication of something to God is *ḥerem.* The root idea is separation and exclusion. This idea is also expressed in the Arabic word *ḥarem* (also in *Ḥarem el-Shariff,* "the noble enclosure," the temple mount). This property is exclusively Yahweh's and may be used constructively or be set apart for destruction. It is his to do with as he chooses.

Things that are devoted to the Lord are most holy and may not be sold or redeemed as might be done with ordinary donations and vows (Lev. 27:28–29). All devoted things belonged to Aaron and his sons as God's representatives (Num. 18:14). This same benefit was extended to the sons of Zadok (Ezek. 44:29).

The spoil of Jericho belonged solely to Yahweh. Metals went into the Lord's treasury (Josh. 6:19, 24); all living things were killed; everything else was burned (vv. 21, 24). Israel met with defeat at Ai because Achan kept some of this spoil (Josh. 7:1–5), and thirty-six men were killed. Joshua would later observe that wrath came on the whole community and that Achan "was not the only one who died for his sin" (Josh. 22:20). Later tradition called him the troubler of Israel and changed his name to Achar ("trouble"; 1 Chron. 2:7).

The Conquest. Over half the occurrences of the verb and noun for the root *ḥrm* concern the killing of nations associated with the conquest of Palestine. This does not mean that the Old Testament condones racial violence. At a time when the iniquity of the Amorites was not complete (Gen. 15:16), relationships with these people were normal and even cordial. The killing of Canaanites took place mainly during the conquest of the land.

Abraham was allied with Amorites (Gen. 14:13). Judah's best friend and wife were Canaanites (Gen. 1:5; 1 Chron. 2:3). Judah got Tamar, a local girl, as a wife for his son (Gen. 38:6–11). Killing of Canaanites at Shechem was rebuked by

Jacob using the same word for "trouble" Joshua did (Gen. 34:30). He later put a curse on his sons for this atrocity (Gen. 49:5–7). It is interesting to note that the first women mentioned in the New Testament were Canaanites (Matt. 1:3, 5).

When David conquered Jerusalem, he did not kill the Jebusites (2 Sam. 5:6–9). He did not confiscate Araunah's land but bartered with him as an equal (2 Sam. 24:21–24). Neither did Solomon kill the Canaanites when he finished subjugating them (1 Kings 9:21). No prophet rebuked him for sparing these people. In fact Hosea prophesied the fall of the house of Jehu for his wholesale shedding of blood in the Valley of Jezreel (1:4). Some of those killed by Jehu would probably have been Canaanites. (Some of the seventy sons of Ahab were half-Phoenician.)

It is important to understand that this killing was not racially motivated. In the Old Testament non-Israelites were not killed because of their race but because of the harm they might do. This killing was essential to the survival of pure Mosaic religion and hence crucial to the redemption of the world (Deut. 20:16–18; Ps. 106:34–39). When faith in Yahweh was sufficiently established to meet challenges of Baalism, the killing stopped.

It is also necessary to note that the Old Testament does not condone wartime atrocities. The Old Testament set rules for treatment of war prisoners (Deut. 21:10–14). Even trees were protected (Deut. 20:19–20). Severity beyond what is necessary to achieve normal military objectives was condemned (Amos 1–2). In 2 Kings 6:21–23 the king is forbidden to kill his prisoners but must feed them and let them return home. Even Ben-Hadad's advisors knew that the kings of Israel had a reputation for being merciful to enemies (1 Kings 20:31). That a military man was not God's ideal is seen in his refusal to allow David to build the temple because he had shed much blood (1 Chron. 22:8).

After the Conquest. The *ḥerem* was enjoined to enforce prohibition of idolatry (Exod. 22:19). Individuals or villages promoting paganism were to be destroyed (Deut. 7:26; 13:16–18). Loyalty to Yahweh was Israel's protection against the nations. Disloyalty would mean defeat and death (Deut. 28:25–26). Any attempt to break the covenant could cause the death of the nation and thus justly incurred the death penalty.

Amalekites fell under the ban because of atrocities committed during the wilderness wanderings (Deut. 25:17–19). Saul lost the kingship for his failure to carry out this command (1 Sam. 15:22–23). Samuel's rebuke seems to emphasize that the rules of holy war do not include sacrificing spoil to Yahweh.

Prophets applied the *ḥerem* ban to other enemies of Israel such as Ben-Hadad (1 Kings 20:41), Babylon (Jer. 50:21, 26; 51:3), Egypt (Isa. 11:15, unless the word should be translated "split" here), Edom (Isa. 34:2, 5), and other nations (Mic. 4:13). The context of some of these passages indicates that these nations may be symbolic for nations at the final battle against the forces of Satan. Much apocalyptic imagery is drawn from these sections.

The prophet Malachi closes with a promise that God will send Elijah to remedy family relationships so a *ḥerem* curse will not be necessary (4:6). Jesus understood this to refer to the ministry of John the Baptist (Mark 9:12). Christ rebuked James and John for suggesting that fire come down on a Samaritan city (Luke 9:54). Paul indicates that destruction of the flesh for the salvation of the soul was in Satan's domain (1 Cor. 5:5). Zechariah 14:11 looks forward to a day when there will be *ḥerem*. PAUL FERGUSON

See also CURSE, ACCURSED; DESTROY, DESTRUCTION; WAR, HOLY WAR.

Bibliography. N. Lohfink, *TDOT,* 5:180–203; A. Malamat, *Biblical Essays; Mari and the Early Israelite Experience;* E. Ullendorff, *Documents from Old Testament Times;* M. Unger, *Archaeology and the Old Testament.*

Disciple, Discipleship. During Jesus' earthly ministry, and during the days of the early church, the term that was used most frequently to designate one of Jesus' followers was "disciple" (*mathētēs,* 262 times). Hence, discipleship is a central theological theme of the Gospels and Acts. The situation is different in the Old Testament and in the rest of the New Testament. There is a curious scarcity of words for "disciple" in the Old Testament, and *mathētēs* does not occur at all in the Epistles and Revelation. However, other terms and expressions point to abundant theological concepts of discipleship everywhere in Scripture. Discipleship enjoys its most concrete expression in Scripture when Jesus walked with his disciples during his earthly ministry. Yet the Old Testament prepares for that relationship, and the Epistles and Revelation describe how that relationship was carried out after Jesus' ascension.

Called to a Relationship with God. The roots of biblical discipleship go deep into the fertile soil of God's calling. That calling is expressed in the pattern of divine initiative and human response that constitutes the heart of the biblical concept of covenant, manifested in the recurrent promise, "I will be your God, and you shall be my people." That call from Yahweh is reiterated in the call of Jesus, when he said, "Come to me, all you who are weary and burdened, and I will give you rest" (Matt. 11:28). God has called his people to represent him on the earth, to be with him in every circumstance of life, to be transformed in personal character to be like him. That calling is at the heart of biblical discipleship, both in the Old and New Testaments.

God and Israel. The ideal of discipleship in the Old Testament is the covenant relationship between Israel and God. Although the call came from God to individuals—Abraham, Isaac, and Jacob—it was directed toward their offspring (Gen. 13:15). God was creating a national community that would be his people. In turn, his people were to be a source of blessing to all peoples of the earth (Gen. 12:1–3). That calling was reiterated and confirmed in the exodus from Egypt and in the wilderness (Exod. 13:21–22). No other person or god was to take a place of preeminence and thus usurp God. While God placed men and women in leadership roles (e.g., Moses, Joshua, the judges, prophets), they were only intermediate leaders. God alone was to have the place of preeminence.

The ideal form of discipleship for Israel was the nation in covenantal relationship with God. That ideal is richly expressed in the prophets as they look ahead to the time when Israel would have the ultimate realization of that relationship. Isaiah expresses the personal nature of this relationship in the prophecies of the new covenant (Isa. 30:20–21; 31:31–34).

When giving the Law to Israel in the wilderness God stressed his covenant intent: "I will walk among you and be your God, and you will be my people" (Lev. 26:12). The nation was called to a relationship in which God was with his people.

Jesus and His Disciples. The Old Testament theme of God with his people finds explicit fulfillment in Jesus with his people. The promise of a coming Davidic Messiah is intertwined with the promise that God himself would be with his people. The significance of Matthew's interpretation of the meaning of Jesus' name, "Immanuel," therefore, cannot be overstated: "'The virgin will be with Child and will give birth to a Son, and they will call him Immanuel'—which means, 'God with us'" (Matt. 1:23). In Jesus, God has come to be with his people, to fulfill the deepest meaning of the covenant—God with his people as Master, Lord, and Savior.

Although discipleship was a voluntary initiative with other types of master-disciple relationships in the first century, with Jesus the initiative lay with his call (Matt. 4:19; 9:9; Mark 1:17; 2:14; cf. Luke 5:10-11, 27–28) and his choice (John 15:16) of those who would be his disciples. The response to the call involves recognition and belief in Jesus' identity (John 2:11; 6:68–69), obedience to his summons (Mark 1:18, 20), and counting the cost of full allegiance to him (Matt. 19:23–30; Luke 14:25–28). His call is the beginning of something new; it means losing one's old life (Matt. 10:34–37; Luke 9:23–25) and finding new life in the family of God through obeying the will of the Father (Matt. 12:46–50).

Following God. *Israel Walking in the Ways of God.* The relationship established between God and Israel was a divine-human relationship that anticipated the relationship to which Jesus would call his followers. To fulfill the covenantal relationship means simply that God must be God, giving him preeminence in all things. The abstract covenantal relationship with God finds concrete expression in "following God" and "walking in his ways." When the nation fulfills its commitment to the covenant it is said to be following God (e.g., Deut. 4:1–14; 1 Sam. 12:14) and walking in his ways (Deut. 10:12–13). When the nation violated the covenant, it is said to be following the gods of the heathen and walking in their ways (Deut. 6:14; Judg. 2:10–13; Isa. 65:2). Elijah calls to the people of Israel and says, "How long will you waver between two opinions? If the LORD is God, follow him; but if Baal is God, follow him" (1 Kings 18:21). Following God is understood in a metaphorical sense of walking in the ways of God.

Personal Commitment to Jesus. During Jesus' earthly ministry the disciple was to "follow" Jesus, an allegiance to his person regarded as *the* decisive act, whether a literal or figurative attachment. Jewish disciples would follow their master around, often literally imitating him. The goal of Jewish disciples was someday to become masters, or rabbis, themselves, and to have their own disciples who would follow them. But Jesus' disciples were to remain disciples of their Master and Teacher, Jesus, and to follow him only. Following Jesus means togetherness with him and service to him while traveling on the Way.

The call to be a disciple meant to count the cost of allegiance to Jesus, but this took various forms. The Twelve were called to leave all and follow Jesus around—including leaving family, profession, and property—as a training time for their future role in the church. Apparently others besides the Twelve were also called to such a following. But, while all disciples were called to count the cost of allegiance (Matt. 8:18–22; Luke 14:25–33), leaving everything and following Jesus around was not intended for all (Mark 5:18–19). Nicodemus and Joseph of Arimathea apparently became followers of Jesus sometime during his earthly ministry (John 3:1–14; 19:38–42), yet presumably remained with the religious establishment and retained their wealth. When demonstration of their faith and allegiance to Jesus was required, they came forward to claim the body of Jesus (Matt. 27:57–60).

Even as entrance to the Way of following Jesus required the would-be disciple to count the cost, so traveling on the Way requires disciples to count the cost (Mark 8:34). The disciple must *daily* deny self, take up the cross, and follow Jesus (Luke 9:23). It is possible for one not to be a true part of the Way while externally traveling with Jesus (e.g., Judas).

The Church Follows the Risen Christ. Peter exhorts those in the church to look at Jesus' example and to follow in his steps (1 Peter 2:21). One of Paul's favorite metaphors is "walking with God." The expression indicates how a person "lives" or conducts himself or herself in relationship to God and others. The summary of this theme is found in the statement, "But I say, walk by the Spirit, and you will not carry out the desire of the flesh" (Gal. 5:16 NASB). This defines Paul's concept of the Christian life.

The Goals of Discipleship. *Toward Self: Become Like Christ.* A primary goal of discipleship is becoming like Jesus (Luke 6:40). This is also understood by Paul to be the final goal of eternal election (Rom. 8:29). The process of becoming like Jesus brings the disciple into intimate relationship with the Lord Jesus Christ, and, as such, is the goal of individual discipleship.

Toward Others: Servanthood. But discipleship is not simply self-centered. In a classic interaction with two of his disciples who were seeking positions of prominence, Jesus declares that servanthood is to be the goal of disciples in relationship to one another (Mark 10:35–45). The reason that this kind of servanthood is possible is because of Jesus' work of servanthood in ransoming disciples. He paid the price of release from the penalty for sin and from the power of sin over pride and self-centered motivation. The motivation of self-serving greatness is broken through redemption, and disciples are thus enabled to focus upon others in servanthood. This is very similar to Paul's emphasis when he points to Jesus' emptying himself to become a servant: Jesus provides the example of the way the Philippian believers are to act toward one another (Phil. 2:1–8). Mark and Paul declare that even as Jesus was the redemptive servant, authentic discipleship entails selfless servanthood. This is the goal of disciples in relation to one another.

Toward the World: The Great Commission. Through his Great Commission Jesus focuses his followers on the ongoing importance of discipleship through the ages, and declares the responsibility of disciples toward the world: they are to make disciples of all the nations (Matt. 28:16–20). To "make disciples" is to proclaim the gospel message among those who have not yet received forgiveness of sins. The command finds verbal fulfillment in the activities of the early church, as they went from Jerusalem to Judea, to Samaria, to the ends of the earth proclaiming the message of Jesus and making disciples. In the early church, to believe in the gospel message was to become a disciple (cf. Acts 4:32 with 6:2). To "make disciples of all the nations" is to make more of what Jesus made of them.

Jesus concludes the commission with the crucial element of discipleship: the presence of the Master—"I am with you always, to the very end of the age" (Matt. 28:20). Both those obeying the command and those responding are comforted by the awareness that the risen Jesus will continue to fashion all his disciples. The Master is always present for his disciples to follow.

As disciples become salt and light in this world, walking the narrow path, loving and providing hope to the world, they become living examples for others to follow. Such is Paul's entreaty, "Follow my example, as I follow the example of Christ" (1 Cor. 11:1).

MICHAEL J. WILKINS

See also CHRISTIANS, NAMES OF; GREAT COMMISSION, THE; JESUS CHRIST.

Bibliography. E. Best, *Disciples and Discipleship: Studies in the Gospel According to Mark;* D. Bonhoeffer, *The Cost of Discipleship;* A. B. Bruce, *The Training of the Twelve;* D. G. Dunn, *Jesus' Call to Discipleship;* M. Hengel, *The Charismatic Leader and His Followers;* H. Kvalbein, *Themelios* 13 (1988): 48–53; D. Müller, *NIDNTT,* 1:483–90; K. H. Rengstorf, *TDNT,* 4:415–61; E. Schweizer, *Lordship and Discipleship;* F. F. Segovia, ed., *Discipleship in the New Testament;* G. Theissen, *Sociology of Early Palestinian Christianity;* M. J. Wilkins, *The Concept of Disciple in Matthew's Gospel: As Reflected in the Use of the Term Μαθητής;* idem, *Following the Master: A Biblical Theology of Discipleship.*

Discipline. ***The Old Testament Concept of Discipline.*** The notion of the discipline of God, and eventually the concept of the community and its leaders effecting God's discipline, derives from the notion of domestic discipline (Deut. 21:18–21; Prov. 22:15; 23:13). God is portrayed as a father who guides his child (i.e., the nation, more rarely an individual) to do right by the experience of physical suffering (Deut. 8:5; Prov. 3:11–12). Key ideas include "chasten/chastise" (Lev. 26:18; Ps. 94:12; Hos. 7:12), "discipline" (Lev. 26:23; Deut. 4:36; Prov. 12:1), and "reproof" (Job 5:17; Prov. 6:23). While God generally administers discipline to the nation, the community through its leaders is charged with the responsibility to administer the legal code for individuals. This code deals almost exclusively with severe offenses that require the "cutting off" (normally, education) of the offender and gives few details concerning lesser offenses and remedial disciplinary measures. Furthermore, because Israel does not yet perceive itself in the modern (or even New Testament) sense as a religious community within a larger society, it is difficult to detect religious discipline as distinct from the Old Testament legal code. The seeds of accountability among the faithful may be seen in several strands of the tradition: removal from the assembly for ritual impurity (Exod. 12:14–20; Lev. 17:3–9); standards for the evaluation of prophets (Deut. 13:1–5; 18:15–22); and admonitions to reprove other adults (Prov. 5:12–13; 9:7; 10:10; 19:25).

The New Testament and Personal Discipline. The notion of discipline as familial chastisement remains in the New Testament (Eph. 6:4; 2 Tim.

2:25; Heb. 12:5–11). In addition, the concept is derived from Hellenistic athletics of the Christian life as "training" for righteousness (1 Cor. 9:24–27; 1 Tim. 4:7–8; Heb. 5:14). Akin to these notions is the recurrent promise that instruction, submission to others, and experiences of pain will prepare the believer for greater righteousness and heavenly reward (Rom. 5:3–5; 2 Cor. 5:16–18; 2 Tim. 3:16; 1 Peter 2:18–21).

Community Discipline in Judaism and the Early Church. Community discipline was characteristic of Christian groups in the New Testament period. Paul, for example, probably borrowed some notions from Jewish groups like the Pharisees of whose disciplinary procedures he was himself a recipient. These systems of discipline developed during the intertestamental period as reform movements among the Jews, who developed ways to establish and regulate the boundaries between themselves and outsiders.

The Qumran sectaries developed an elaborate system of penalties intended to safeguard the purity and order of the community. This included a formal reproof procedure, short-term reduction of food allowance, exclusion from ritual meals, and permanent expulsion. Rabbinic traditions suggest that the Pharisees commonly imposed a "ban," a temporary state of social isolation imposed for deviation from ritual purity laws or for heretical views and designed to recall the offender to full participation in the community. The right to put someone under the ban was originally limited to the Sanhedrin, but some time before the destruction of the temple it was extended to groups of scribes acting together. Rabbinic sources are not clear with respect to complete expulsion from Pharisaic communities in the New Testament era, but it is reasonable to assume that unrepentant banned persons and heretics like Christians would incur more severe judgment. Paul himself five times received a severe form of punishment administered by the synagogue for heresy, the "forty lashes minus one" (2 Cor. 11:24). The number of lashes was reduced from the forty prescribed in Deuteronomy 25:2–3, presumably in order to safeguard against excessive punishment.

Luke 17:3–4 may represent the seed of an originally interpersonal "reproof, apology, forgiveness" formula that occurs in expanded form for community action in Matthew 18:15–17. The community becomes involved through its leaders when personal confrontation is ineffective; community action in the form of expulsion is a last resort. This deceptively simple formula combines redemptive purpose and caution with firm resolve in the process of community accountability, and it appears to be the basis of later New Testament practice.

Community Discipline in New Testament Churches. There is insufficient material to establish a "program" or "system" of community discipline for the New Testament period or even for the Pauline churches. It is possible, however, to gain some insights into disciplinary practice in the early Christian churches by examining key Pauline texts for evidence of procedural elements, culpable behaviors, and intended effects.

Galatians 6:1–5 suggests that the first step in correction of an erring believer is personal, private, and gentle (cf. 2 Cor. 2:5–11; Eph. 4:29–32; Col. 3:12–13; 1 Thess. 5:14–15). The stress on humility and readiness to forgive on the part of the person who admonishes recalls the teaching of Jesus (Matt. 7:1–5; 18:21–35). The notions of self-searching censure and eagerness to effect heartfelt reconciliation, practically nonexistent in Qumran and rabbinic sources, are pervasive in Paul's letters. Indeed, Paul's disciplinary practices are convincing as remedial rather than punitive measures only to the extent that they are infused from start to finish with a pure desire for the good of the offender.

Some offenses, or the stubbornness of some offenders, require that the wider community of believers and its leaders become involved. The command to "take special note of" (2 Thess. 3:14) those who are disobedient may be understood as a command to "keep written records concerning" such persons (cf. "watch out for" dissenters, Rom. 16:17). This formal element, employed at Qumran, may have been appropriate in the case of more serious offenses, especially if the accumulation of witnesses would have a bearing on further action. "Rebuke" or "refutation" is a common term in the Pastoral Epistles, which may pertain more to doctrinal correction by community leaders (1 Tim. 5:20; 2 Tim. 2:25–26; 4:2; Titus 1:9, 13; 2:15). Either "marking" or "rebuking" on the part of community leaders may constitute "witnesses" as required in the case of divisive persons in Titus 3:10–11 and in the case of elders in 1 Timothy 5:19. Paul equates warnings with witnesses when he writes of his impending third visit to the Corinthians (2 Cor. 13:1–2). It is not clear whether warnings could be construed as witnesses ex post facto, but this may have been an intentional flexibility designed to avoid the legal elaborations of the Qumran sectaries and Pharisees. It also allowed the apostle and his delegates to "troubleshoot" freely with the immature and often contentious local communities.

A survey of the key passages does not strongly support the view that disciplinary action becomes increasingly centralized and formalized through the New Testament period. Rather, it appears that a pattern exists wherein jurisdiction rises in the community hierarchy according to the severity of the offense. Thus we observe that commonly occurring misbehavior is handled by all believers individually (Gal. 6:1–5 and parallels); warnings are administered generally by the community (Rom. 16:17; 2 Thess. 3:6–15); the factious and elders are disciplined by apostolic delegates (1 Tim. 5:19–22; 2 Tim. 2:25–26; Titus 3:10–11); and the most serious cases are taken up by the apostle himself (2 Cor. 13:1–2; 1 Tim. 1:19–20; probably 1 Cor. 5:3–4; cf. Acts 5:1–11; 8:20–24). Admittedly, the evidence is too sparse to insist on a rigid structure. It is equally possible that, as in the case of Qumran, the group acted through its local community leaders when problems were brought to their attention, and higher authorities like Paul or his delegates acted when they deemed it appropriate. As in the case of the witness-warning sequence, a flexible adaptation of contemporary Jewish practice fit the dynamic spirit of the movement and the occasional aberrations of its local leadership.

When an individual did not respond to warning(s) or committed a serious offense, it became necessary to effect social isolation. The expressions used in the New Testament to convey this idea do not specify what is meant. Matthew 18:17 commands the community to treat the offender "as a pagan or a tax collector." Romans 16:17 tells believers to "watch out" for wrongdoers; 1 Corinthians 5:11 and 2 Thessalonians 3:14 enjoin, "do not associate" with offenders; 2 Thessalonians 3:6 commands, "keep away from" the disobedient. First Corinthians 5:11 is more specific in instructing believers not to eat with those under discipline (cf. 2 John 10–11). This recollects the Pharisaic ban, under which the offender was cut off socially from all but his immediate family. As in the case of the ban, the individual feels ashamed (2 Thess. 3:14) and, when proven repentant (it is not clear how), is welcomed back "as a brother" (2 Thess. 3:15; cf. 2 Cor. 2:5–11; Gal. 6:1).

In several instances, it appears that Paul goes beyond measures intended to recall erring individuals to a final expulsion from the community. The key text in this regard is 1 Corinthians 5:1–5, where Paul responds to a case of incest by commanding, "hand this man over to Satan," an expression employed similarly in 1 Timothy 1:20. It is clear that the early church understood the realm of Satan to be everywhere outside the fellowship of believers (2 Cor. 4:4; Gal. 1:4; Eph. 2:2) and that Paul's expression here denotes expulsion from the community. That the sentence is reformatory is confirmed by the fact that Paul ends the pronouncement in 1 Corinthians 5:5 with the express intent that the offender's spirit may be "saved in the day of the Lord"; similarly, 1 Timothy 1:20 notes that "Hymenaeus and Alexander were handed over to Satan to be taught not to blaspheme." The phrase in 1 Corinthians 5:5, "so the sinful nature may be destroyed," is ambiguous. It almost certainly denotes physical suffering, but it is unclear whether the sufferer's life will be spared by repentance.

Behaviors Subject to Discipline. Doctrinal deviations that create division in the community are a problem for Paul (1 Cor. 1:10–11; 11:18–19; cf. Heb. 12:15), and the disciplinary measures in Romans 16:17 and 2 Corinthians 13:1–2 appear to respond to division caused by heterodoxy (cf. Gal. 5:2–12). The Pastoral Epistles are dominated by this concern and 1 Timothy 1:20 is a clear case in point. The danger of heresy and resultant factions to the integrity of local communities and the movement as a whole is obvious. It is not clear, however, to what extent aberrant views that did not cause splits could be tolerated. Moral deviations are in view in the two most lengthy passages, 2 Thessalonians 3:6–15 and 1 Corinthians 5:1–13 (1 Tim. 5:19–22 is ambiguous; cf. James 5:19–20; 1 John 5:16–17). The charge that some were "idle" in Thessalonica is taken by many to denote inactivity in expectation of an imminent parousia, but it is more likely that Paul's instruction reflects a social situation typical of a large port city, where many laborers were inactive for periods of time and dependent on patrons. Within the community of believers, some appear to have begun to presume upon the Christian goodness of patrons, and the system was in danger of devolving into freeloading, resentment, and division (perhaps echoed in 1 Cor. 11:18–19). In 1 Corinthians 5, Paul is obviously concerned about *porneia,* sexual sin (vv. 1, 9, 11), but he also condemns any "so-called" brother (cf. simply "brother" in 2 Thess. 3:15) who is "greedy, or is an idolater, reviler, drunkard, or robber" (v. 11 NRSV). The fact that the list is expanded in 6:9–10 with special attention to sexual and property values suggests that it is not random, after the fashion of contemporary moralists, but is consciously directed at the sins of Corinth. These are of course not the only offenses subject to discipline (cf. Gal. 5:19–21), but they are particularly dangerous to the Corinthians. Although the list does not specify the extent of the sin, it does convey a very strict moral accountability. The reason for this ethical rigorism is implied in Paul's allusion to Deuteronomy 17:7 in 5:13, "Expel the wicked man from among you." The opposite of wickedness for Paul is not cultic purity but holiness in the sense of the Spirit-controlled life of each member of the unified community. Deviation from holiness will retard the growth of the entire body, or "leaven the lump."

Effective Community Discipline. For the individual offender, the New Testament practice is clearly intended to produce repentance in an atmosphere of support and forgiveness. For the community, to hold its members accountable through disciplinary measures will maintain the moral integrity of the group. All of these principles are present at least to some extent in the contemporary Jewish practices that were apparently adapted by the primitive church, albeit in a less systematized form. The unique and potentially potent aspect of the New Testament concept of discipline is the infusion of Christ-like love into disciplinary practice. Philippians 2:1–5, although it does not address discipline directly, expresses concisely the principle behind the scattered references on the subject. The incentive of love, the sharing of the Spirit, the humble attitude—that is, the mind of Christ—is that which makes it possible to hold another person accountable. Thus the key to effective discipline is its reflexive element. The one who holds another accountable is first accountable to be a loving person. When this is true of a community of believers, isolation of an offender will be a compelling remedial force; the community's power to persuade or to punish brings a person back into obedient fellowship. It is the community's ability to demonstrate love in its Spirit-transformed living that constitutes a compellingly attractive force.

THOMAS E. SCHMIDT

See also CHURCH, THE; ETHICS.

Bibliography. W. D. Davies and D. Allen, *Matthew 8–18;* G. Fee, *The First Epistle to the Corinthians;* G. Forkman, *The Limits of the Religious Community;* G. W. H. Lampe, *Christian History and Interpretation: Studies Presented to John Knox*, pp. 337–61; C. J. Roetzel, *Judgment in the Community;* C. A. Wanamaker, *The Epistles to the Thessalonians.*

Disease. To understand the biblical records concerning illness it is necessary to think oneself back into a world that knew nothing of germs, bacteria, viruses, antisepsis, anesthesia, the circulation of the blood, or the precise difference among catalepsy, "clinical death," coma, and "final death."

Something was known of anatomy from animal sacrifices; we read of heart, liver, kidneys, bowels, bones, sinews, flesh, and skin (with some hesitation over translation), but the function of each was not understood. Most references to human organs are metaphorical: The heart is the seat of the will, the bowels of compassion. Similarly, many of the terms used for diseases and infirmities are unknown, and translation is occasionally reduced to informed guessing.

It is helpful sometimes to suggest modern names for conditions whose description puzzles us. In Deuteronomy 28:22, "wasting disease" may well be tuberculosis; "fever" is likely to be the prevalent malaria; in the Greek version, the word chosen for "inflammation" means "ague," possibly another form of malaria; and "scorching heat" could be almost any skin infection. The most common "pestilence" in the Middle East over the centuries was the virulent "bubonic plague," its "tumors" being the swollen glands characteristic of the disease (2 Sam. 24:15; the Greek translation of 1 Sam. 5:6–12, and the Assyrian record of the story in 2 Kings 19:35, both mention rats, the usual carriers of this infection).

Psalms 31:10–11, 38:5–11, and Zechariah 14:12 are said to describe one disfiguring form of smallpox. Second Chronicles 21:19 probably refers to dysentery, and the RSV so translates at Acts 28:8. We would probably speak of Saul's manic-depressive insanity (1 Sam. 16:14–23; 18:10–16; 19:9–10); of Nebuchadnezzar's "paranoia with (ox?) delusions" (see Dan. 4:16, 25, 33); and of the "apoplexy" of Nabal (1 Sam. 25:37–38); and possibly also of Ananias and Sapphira (Acts 5:5, 10).

The Shunammite's child apparently collapsed because of sunstroke, a common danger (2 Kings 4:18–20; Ps. 121:6). "Crippled from birth" (Acts 3:2) suggests congenital club-foot; "she was bent over and could not straighten up at all" (Luke 13:11) recalls the widespread curvature of the spine (tubercular, or osteoarthritic?).

Among skin diseases we may hesitantly recognize boils, eczema, and skin cancer; the details in 2 Chronicles 16:12–14 suggest gangrene. Leprosy was prevalent, and variously described as "blotches," "scars," "eruptions," "whiteness," "bright patches," and "ulceration"; it had many forms, most of which can be only approximately identified in the Hebrew terms. Despite the ignorance about germs, the danger of contagion was realized and isolation enforced. Detailed religious rites of "purification" from leprosy's "uncleanness" were elaborated. Whether "true" (most virulent) leprosy is named in the Bible is much debated.

Nervous ailments are more difficult to recognize in the Bible's language. The paralysis of Mark 2:3 and the "shriveling" of Mark 3:1 were possibly of nervous origin, if not accidental. Much illness was attributed to "bile" ("gall," Job 16:13), and Timothy's trouble, in view of his timidity, could well have been nervous dyspepsia (1 Tim. 5:23).

Blindness was very common—both the highly contagious, lice-carried trachoma and optic atrophy in the aged (Gen. 27:1—Isaac; 1 Sam. 3:2—Eli). Sudden blindness (2 Kings 6:18; Acts 13:11) has been called "hypnotic." Based on Galatians 4:12–15, 6:11, it is often inferred that Paul's "thorn in the flesh" was eye disease (cf. Acts 9:3, 9, 18); others argue that the "thorn" was malaria.

Precision and certainty on the theme of disease are obviously rare, creating problems for translators. At Mark 9:17, 25, the RSV text speaks of spirit possession, the page-heading of "epilepsy"; at Matthew 17:15 the RSV uses "epileptic" for Matthew's "moonstruck"; at Matthew 4:24, epileptics are distinguished from demoniacs.

In general, neither climate, sanitation arrangements, water supply, nor prevailing ignorance, fostered good health in Bible lands. Infant mortality was high, and large families were in part compensated for it. Life expectancy is often asserted to have been short, despite the recorded ages of the patriarchs. But "sixty and ten" or "eighty" of Psalm 90:10 (even if amended to state life's "highest point") is not greatly different from our own life expectancy today. The gathering infirmities of old age are described in Ecclesiastes 12:1 with a sympathy and poetry rare in literature.

Lacking scientific explanations, Judaism had to seek other causes of the ubiquitous sickness. Disease had a religious dimension for all ancient peoples, partly from the natural recourse to superhuman help in danger or distress; idol shrines at Corinth, Ephesus, and Rome were as beset with sufferers as was the Jerusalem temple. Ill fortune of all kinds being inflicted by the gods, they alone could remove it.

For Jewish minds the underlying problem was especially acute. God created all things, and they were "very good." Whatever in human experience was not "good" was therefore alien to God's intention. Pain, sickness, and death must be due to self-willed interference by humankind with God's perfect plan. So Genesis 1–3 presents the most common Jewish theodicy: Sickness and distress are God's judgment on evil. Even the pains of childbirth are held to be a punishment for sin (Gen. 3:16; cf. Deut. 28:15–68; 32:39). The code of punishments prescribed by the law for particular sins rests upon this evaluation, that the sinner *should* suffer.

Job's friends thus argued that his disease and suffering proved his sinfulness; the Pharisees argued likewise, as did Jesus' disciples (John 9:2); and Paul so interprets the sickness prevalent at Corinth (1 Cor. 11:27–30). Job, however, resolutely affirmed his innocence, and the lesson of the book is that suffering may be permitted to test and vindicate devotion. Paul, too, looked upon his "thorn" as a spiritual discipline and education (1 Cor. 11:30).

Another modification of the assumed connection between sickness and sin accepted that others might be innocently involved. The sins of the fathers might be visited upon children unborn (Exod. 20:4), while social sins might bear most heavily upon one who bore the sins of others (Isa. 53). In this way, all are "bound securely in the bundle of the living" (1 Sam. 25:29), although against this Ezekiel and others protested (Ezek. 18; cf. Deut. 24:16; Jer. 31:29–30).

Jesus, too, very firmly rejected the theory that individual sickness and suffering were always due to individual sin, when the question was put to him concerning Pilate's cruelty to certain Galileans, and a falling tower that killed eighteen, and yet again in reply to his disciples (Luke 13:1–5; John 9:3). Jesus met sickness and affliction with unfailing sympathy, never with condemnation, even when some connection with sin might be assumed. He did pronounce forgiveness for a paralytic before healing him (Mark 2:5), possibly to remove from the sufferer's mind the obstacle, based on received doctrine, that healing could not begin until the sin that caused it was pardoned. Or he may have diagnosed that patient's spiritual condition as clearly as his physical need. So Jesus warned another healed man to "stop sinning," that nothing worse befall him (John 5:14).

The teachers of moral wisdom in Israel preferred to lay the blame for physical deterioration upon particular indulgences and excess. Overindulgence in wine is frequently condemned on health grounds; Proverbs 23:29–35 vividly describes the physical and mental effects of tarrying long over wine, especially mixed wines (cf. Isa. 28:7–8). Ben Sirach adds a strong warning, again on health grounds, against gluttony, and urges the therapeutic value of "industrious work" (margin: "moderate work"). He inculcates a wise self-understanding in diet, and avoidance of any mere habit of luxury and gluttony (Sirach 31:19–22; 37:27–31). Somewhat unexpectedly, Job blames unhealthy attitudes of mind for destroying those who know no better, "vexation" ("resentment" NIV), "jealousy" ("envy" NIV, Job 5:2; cf. cheerfulness, despondency, sorrow, Prov. 15:13; 17:22). A psalmist teaches those who desire long life and "many good days" to keep from speaking evil and falseness, to depart from evil and practice good, and diligently to pursue peace in all situations—a clean mind, unburdened conscience, and peaceable spirit, making for healthy living (Ps. 34:11–14, quoted in 1 Peter 3:10–12).

Later, another dimension of the cause of disease and affliction was added to those of theologians and moralists: the idea of a world infested with living spirits, some benign but most malignant. In Israelite thought, some spirits, although working to hinder and deceive humans, were nevertheless messengers of God (Judg. 9:23; 1 Sam. 16:14—note contrast with "the Spirit of the LORD"; 1 Kings 22:20–23). Such spirits, although evil, were under divine control.

New Testament belief in evil spirits ("demons") under the direction of a supreme devil was almost universal. To them were attributed disorders of all sorts, whether moral, mental, or physical. All were believed to be under the ultimate control of God, but he permitted their activity when sin gave them entrance, to punish sinfulness in humankind.

Evil spirits appear in the Gospels as causing dumbness (Matt. 9:32), deafness (Mark 9:25), blindness (Matt. 12:22), spinal malformation (Luke 13:11), epilepsy (Mark 1:26; 9:26), madness (schizophrenia? Mark 5:1–13). Often called "unclean" spirits (perhaps because of their association with Satan, degradation, and decay) the demons were recognized as powerful opponents of the divine will, in sharp contrast with the Holy Spirit, and everywhere the proximate cause of all humankind's misery and evil.

According to the Synoptic Gospels (John does not mention demons or exorcisms) Jesus dealt commandingly with sickness and affliction, firmly demanding the spirits be silent and leave the tormented. Luke, a physician, delights to show that Christ had overcome Satan, binding "the strong one" and spoiling his possessions. Jesus watched Satan fall from above, and by superior power delivered those whom demons had bound or afflicted (4:1–13, 36, 41; 6:18; 8:2, 26–35; 10:18; 11:15–26; 13:16).

The prevalence of disease and suffering in the ancient world inevitably influenced religious and ethical language. Isaiah describes the sad social and moral condition of Judah: "From the sole of your foot to the top of your head there is no soundness" (1:6). His terms hover between medical descriptions and metaphors for moral sickness, as do those of Psalm 38. And this use of medical metaphors for spiritual and moral "sickliness" or "infirmity" continues into the New Testament in phrases like "the body is weak" (Matt. 26:41), "weak in conscience" (1 Cor. 8:7–12), "weak in faith" (Rom. 14:1–2; 15:1) and (morally) "powerless" (Rom. 5:6).

A similar association of ideas shaped Jesus' defense of his friendship with sinners as *resembling* the concern of the physician with the sick (Matt. 9:11–12). Jesus does not say the sinner is "sick," which might imply that sinfulness is misfortune rather than fault. But the parallel he draws lends some authority to the compassion of those who see the sinful as victims of their own folly or viciousness, and i need of help and understanding.

There is a moral blindness, deafness, shortsightedness, madness, paralysis, weakness, "seizure," as deadly as the physical counterpart. It was easy to state the gospel of salvation in terms borrowed from unhappy experience of disease and affliction—as Jesus did at Nazareth (Luke 4:16–21)—and be sure of being understood. The thought is carried further in the "soundness," "healthiness" of true doctrine, teaching, words, faith, and speech, referred to nine times in the Pastoral Epistles, as appealing to, and promoting, sane, safe religion.

R. E. O. White

See also Heal, Health; Suffering.

Bibliography. A. W. F. Blunt and F. F. Bruce, *Hastings Dictionary of the Bible;* E. W. Heaton, *Everyday Life in Old Testament Times.*

Diversity and Unity of Scripture. *See* Unity and Diversity of Scripture.

Divination. Communication with a deity for the purpose of determining the deity's knowledge, resulting in clarification of a decision or discernment of the future. Two forms of divination developed in the ancient Near East, one using inductive manipulation of natural or human phenomena and the other taking intuitive forms of inner revelation.

The History of Divination. In Mesopotamia, Anatolia, Egypt, and Canaan, people communicated with their deities by means of divination, both on a personal and public level. From the Old Babylonian period (ca. 2000 B.C.) on in Mesopotamia, the reading of livers helped determine the actions of commoners and kings. A sheep was slaughtered, its liver removed, and the markings of the organ "read" for an answer. Other inductive types of divination included the analysis of stars, moon, entrails, lungs, weather, birds, and fetuses. Human-produced phenomena studied included casting lots, shooting arrows, dropping oil in water, drinking wine, calling the dead, and sprinkling water on an ox. Intuitive types of divination in the ancient Near East involved oracles, prophecies, and dreams.

In Israel, an official position on divination limited its uses to forms that did not reflect the practices of surrounding cultures. Most inductive forms were forbidden (Lev. 19:26; Deut. 18:11), although the use of Urim and Thummim and lots supposes some inductive approaches. Most ancient practices, however, were used by both the populace and the officials. The Bible alludes to the use of omens (Isa. 44:25), arrows (Hos. 4:12), animal actions (1 Sam. 6:7–12), the reading of livers (Ezek. 21:21–22), budding plants (Num. 17:1–11), necromancy (1 Sam. 28), and prophetic utterances, called false (Mic. 3:7, 11) or "lying divinations" (Isa. 44:25; Jer. 14:14; 27:9–10; Ezek. 12:24; Zech. 10:2). References to the "soothsayers' tree" (Judg. 9:37), the "sons of a sorcerer" (Isa. 57:3), and the girl with a spirit of divination (Acts 16:16–19) are evidence of widespread practice.

Theology of Divination. Divination presupposes that the divine communicates with the human. This communication takes both human and divine initiative. Inductive techniques depend on human initiation. The Bible supposes that a priority rests on revelatory forms (dream, vision, oracle) rather than on inductive ones (Urim/Thummim, ephod). Although natural phenomena may communicate God's will, their interpretation must be scrutinized and may be helped by the verbal. It seems clear that God is not limited to the use of any one means of revelation.

Why would the Bible record such strong negative injunctions against inductive divination? Deuteronomic law especially attacks everything connected with pagan religions. Foreign deities may have attached themselves to these methods. Even then, most of Israel's approved methods display parallels with the surrounding cultures. The question of veracity may be involved because they prove difficult to interpret. For this reason, verbal forms take precedence over inductive methods. Yet even prophecies need to stand the test of whether they come true (Deut. 18:21–22).

Human need requires discernment of divine desires. God chooses to communicate in a variety of ways, including divination techniques, but always in the clearest, most unambiguous way possible.

G. MICHAEL HAGAN

See also IDOL, IDOLATRY; REVELATION, IDEA OF.

Bibliography. M. deJong-Ellis, *Journal of Cuneiform Studies* 41 (1989): 127–86; H. A. Hoffner, *JETS* 30 (1987): 257–85; A. L. Oppenheim, *Ancient Mesopotamia.*

Divorce. Perversion of the marriage institution. Marriage was ordained by God as an intimate and complementing union between a man and a woman in which the two become one physically, in the whole of life, in its purpose to reflect the relationship of the Godhead, and to serve God. With the fall of humankind the divine purpose and function of marriage were damaged by sin, and the marriage relationship often destroyed.

Effect of the Fall on Marriage. The fall of humankind (Gen. 3) caused human hearts to become hard toward God and toward each other. The relational aspect of God's image, reflected in marriage, became marred. Satan tempted Eve to rebel against male leadership (Gen. 3:1–6, 17; contra. Eph. 5:33; 1 Peter 3:1). Men tended to become dominant and harsh in their leadership (cf. Col. 3:19; 1 Peter 3:7). Sin brought polygamy, concubinage, incest, adultery, rape, prostitution, and all kinds of immorality (cf. Lev. 18; 20; Rom. 1:26–32) that have damaged or destroyed the marriage relationship. Marriage covenants have been violated (cf. Mal. 2:14).

Termination of the marriage relationship is caused by sin that entered the world *after* Genesis 2:21–24. Death itself, which terminates marriage (Rom. 7:1–3), came by Adam's sin. Because of sin divorce arose, and Moses sought to regulate it (Deut. 24:1–4; Matt. 19:8). Divorce is not instituted or ordained by God; rather it is generated by sin and is contrary to God's ideal for marriage (cf. Mal. 2:14).

Divorce in the Old Testament. Divorce is first mentioned in the Mosaic covenant (cf. Lev. 21:14; Deut. 22:13–19, 28–29), but it was already occurring in Israel. Under the Mosaic covenant divorce was regulated in situations in which it might become common. It was not permitted (1) when false accusations were made about a bride's virginity; and (2) when marriage occurred because a man had forcibly violated a woman sexually. A high priest was not to marry a divorcee. Deuteronomy 24:1–4 prohibited remarriage of a woman to her first husband after the death or divorce of her second husband. These texts present legal policy whereby quick and frequent divorce is restrained and discouraged. Divorce is not commended, commanded, or approved by God in these passages, but failure to forbid divorce, especially in Deuteronomy 24, de facto means that God's law tolerated divorce to the extent that no civil or ecclesiastical penalty was imposed.

The basis for divorce in Deuteronomy 24:1 is "some indecency" (*ʿervat dābār*). The precise meaning of this phrase is uncertain. When the rest of the Old Testament and New Testament are examined, it appears that "some indecency" probably had sexual overtones—some lewd or immoral behavior including any sexual perversion, even adultery. The imagery of spiritual adultery, resulting in God's "divorcing" Israel (Isa. 50:1; Jer. 3:8), is based on a real referent. Divorce was socially permissible for adultery. Although adultery was punishable by death (Deut. 22:22–24), it could still be included in the broad concept of *ʿervat dābār.* It is likewise possible that Jesus employed the general term *porneia* (Matt. 5:32; 19:9) to refer to *ʿervat dābār* in Deuteronomy 24:1. However this phrase is understood, the text implies that this continued "indecency" was so vile that divorce was preferred by the husband. To protect the wife, however, he must provide her a certificate of divorce.

This text also recognizes and allows, without condemnation, the remarriage of the wife. In that culture remarriage would be expected since it was difficult for a woman to survive in life unless she was married or remained single in her father's house. This does not necessarily mean that God approves of the remarriage in this text. The text prohibits remarriage to the first husband since the woman has already been defiled. Defilement is best understood contextually as the "indecency" of verse 1, not "defilement" of adultery because of marrying the second husband. Adultery would have been punishable by death of the woman and the second husband, if such had been the case. The second marriage is not condemned, nor is a third marriage forbidden.

Deuteronomy 24:1–4, therefore, is a concession made by God to the fallen condition of humankind. It does not approve of or encourage divorce or remarriage, although it allows for both, except for remarriage of a woman to her first husband. These Deuteronomic texts, therefore, regulate divorce.

In Ezra 9–10 intermarriage with foreigners is viewed as a defilement of the holy race and as unfaithfulness to God (9:2; 10:2, 10). Shecaniah proposed sending away these foreign wives and children (10:3). Ezra concurred (10:11), so the people "divorced" the foreign wives and their children. The problem centers around Israelites marrying unbelieving foreigners. The "putting away" was to be "according to the law," but no specific command of this nature can be found in the Law. Although Deuteronomy 7:1–4 commands Israelites not to make covenants or to intermarry with the people in Canaan when they enter that land, this principle is not normative since the Old Testament permits marriage to believing foreigners (cf. Rahab, Ruth, and Christ's genealogy in Matt. 1:5). The principle of not marrying unbelievers pervades the Scriptures and appears to be the major concern of Ezra 9–10. It was feared that the holy seed would be defiled.

The dissolving of the marriages is problematic. This is de facto divinely approved divorce in order to preserve the holy people. We have already observed that God did not ordain divorce, and Malachi 2:14 clearly states that God hates divorce. We can only conclude that divorce is permitted in some situations. This particular situation related to Israel at that time and appears not to be normative.

Malachi rebukes Israel for profaning the Mosaic covenant (Mal. 2:10–16). One example is the breaking of the marriage covenant by divorcing ("breaking faith with") the wives "of their youth" (v. 14). God declares that he hates divorce! This is the most direct statement of God's feeling about divorce.

Therefore, although the Old Testament presents God's ideal for marriage as monogamous, permanent, and exclusive, the Old Testament likewise recognizes that divorce and remarriage are present because of sin and must be regulated.

Divorce in the New Testament. In Matthew 5 Jesus discusses the true intent of the Mosaic Law by emphasizing that righteousness issues from the heart, not from external compliance. Illustrating from the seventh commandment (vv. 27–32), Jesus argues that lust, as well as divorce, are the moral equivalents of adultery. Divorce is wrong because it produces adultery in the remarriage, except in the case of fornication (*porneia*). The exception clause (v. 32) most naturally implies that adultery is not caused by divorce when the sexual sin of fornication (*porneia*) has *already* been committed by one spouse. Rather, in this event divorce is permitted because of the fornication. The great question in Matthew 5:31 (and Matt. 19:9) is the meaning of "fornication" (*porneia*). *Porneia* is a broad term for many kinds of sexual impropriety. The early usages referred to prostitution, fornication, and extramarital intercourse. Greek translations of the Old Testament use this term to translate *zānâ*, "to prostitute." In later Judaism and New Testament times the word broadened to include adultery, incest, sodomy, unlawful marriage, sexual intercourse in general, and any sexual behavior that deviates from accepted social and religious norms. Usage in New Testament contexts does not change these options. The argument of Matthew 5 (and Matt. 19) does not provide sufficient data to limit the usage of *porneia* in this context to one specific meaning. *Porneia* is perhaps broad in its reference to illicit sexual intercourse in keeping with the breadth of the Hebrew phrase *ʿervat dābār* (cf. Deut. 24:1). Some form of illegitimate extramarital sexual intercourse is conveyed by the term. Therefore adultery in a real sense has already transpired, and Jesus states that this is a permissible ground for divorce. Divorce, however, is not required. Some argue that *porneia* cannot mean adultery since the Old Testament penalty for adultery was death, not divorce (cf. Lev. 20:10; Deut. 22:22–24). However, in New Testament times Jews were unable to impose the death penalty without Roman permission. Therefore, adultery severs the marriage relationship in the New Testament as did the adulterer's death in the Old Testament.

Therefore, Matthew 5:31–32 is stating that divorce is equivalent to adultery since the divorced person normally remarries. However, if illegitimate extramarital sexual intercourse is practiced by one spouse, adultery has already transpired, and this breaks the oneness of the marriage relationship. Divorce, therefore, is permissible, although never required.

In Matthew 19:1–12 and Mark 10:1–12 some Pharisees test Jesus by asking whether it is lawful for a man to divorce his wife for any reason. Jesus reminds them of God's original ideal for marriage in Genesis 2:24: a male and a female were created to become a permanent "one flesh" union. Humankind should not separate (divorce) what God has joined together. Unsatisfied with his answer, the Pharisees raise the issue of the divorce statement in Deuteronomy 24:1–4. Jesus states that Deuteronomy 24:1–4 permitted divorce solely because of man's hard (sinful) heart, but this was not God's original plan for marriage (Matt. 19:8). In Matthew 19:9 (cf. Mark 10:10–12) he reiterates the principle of Matthew 5:31–32: divorce generates adultery "except" in the case of fornication (*porneia*) where adultery has already transpired. The husband (or the wife in Mark 10:11–12) who initiates divorce for any reason other than spouse *porneia*, and marries another, commits adultery. Luke 16:18 looks at the situation from both directions: the one initiating divorce and the one marrying a divorced person have each committed adultery. For some reason in Mark's argument of the same event as in Matthew (and Luke's separate argument), the exception clause is omitted. The reason for this is uncertain. However, one must accept the exception clause as genuine, valid, and original in Matthew.

Jesus' teaching confirms and elaborates the Old Testament concepts of marriage and divorce. God's ideal for marriage is a monogamous, permanent, and exclusive union. Because of humankind's sin divorce arose, and Moses permitted a certificate of divorce to regulate it. Divorce, however, is equivalent to adultery because it generates adultery. So the one initiating divorce and the one marrying a divorced person commit adultery. The only exception to this rule is when one of the marriage partners has committed fornication (*porneia*), which itself is adultery. When this occurs, the other spouse may legitimately divorce the partner who has committed fornication. Such, however, is not required and should be a last alternative.

First Corinthians 7:1–16, 39 argues that married people should stay married. First, spouses should not leave/divorce (*chōrizō*) their marriage partners (v. 10). This is the ideal (v. 39). If a spouse should leave/divorce a marriage partner, he or she has only two options: (1) remain unmarried or (2) be reconciled. Remarriage is not an option. Second, a believer should not divorce an unbelieving spouse (vv. 12–13). However, if the unbeliever leaves, the believing partner is not bound to the principle about maintaining the marriage. The marriage is thereby dissolved. Paul says nothing about the issue of remarriage.

Conclusion. God-ordained marriage is a monogamous, permanent, and exclusive union. The entrance of sin into the world brought divorce. God hates divorce because it is contrary to his ideal. Understanding the sinfulness of humankind, he graciously tolerates divorce while establishing regulations to curb it. Jesus upheld the ideal of permanent marriage, making clear that divorce is equivalent to adultery in breaking the oneness of marriage. Initiating divorce and/or marrying a divorced person produces adultery. The only exception to this principle, and, therefore, the only legitimate ground for divorce is illegitimate extramarital sexual intercourse on the part of a spouse. Divorce is permitted for this reason, but not demanded. Reconciliation should always be sought when fornication or separation has occurred. It is also permissible to dissolve a marriage if an unbelieving spouse departs/deserts the believer. Believers should, however, always love and accept divorced people and seek to encourage them in reconciliation and godly ways.

RALPH H. ALEXANDER

See also FAMILY LIFE AND RELATIONS; MARRIAGE.

Bibliography. D. J. Atkinson, *To Have and to Hold;* H. W. House, ed., *Divorce and Remarriage: Four Christian Views;* W. F. Luck, *Divorce and Remarriage: Recovering the Biblical View;* J. Murray, *Divorce;* J. H. Olthhuis, *I Pledge You My Troth.*

Doctrine (Gk. *didaskalia*). Act of teaching or that which is taught. The use of the term in Scripture, however, is broader than a simple reference to information passed on from one person to another or from one generation to the next. Christianity is a religion founded on a message of good news rooted in the significance of the life of Jesus Christ. In Scripture, then, doctrine refers to the entire body of essential theological truths that define and describe that message (1 Tim. 1:10; 4:16; 6:3; Titus 1:9). The message includes historical facts, such as those regarding the events of the life of Jesus Christ (1 Cor. 11:23). But it is deeper than biographical facts alone. As J. Gresham Machen pointed out years ago, Jesus' death is an integral historical fact but it is not doctrine. Jesus' death for sins (1 Cor. 15:3) is doctrine. Doctrine, then, is scriptural teaching on theological truths.

Doctrine is indispensable to Christianity. Christianity does not exist without it. The New Testament repeatedly emphasizes the value and importance of sound doctrine, sound instruction (1 Tim. 6:3), and a pattern of sound teaching (2 Tim. 1:13–14). The apostles defended the faithful proclamation of the gospel (Gal. 1:8). They formulated Christian faith in doctrinal terms, then called for its preservation. They were adamant about the protection, appropriation, and propagation of doctrine because it contained the truth about Jesus Christ. Knowing the truth was and is the only way that a person can come to faith. So the apostles delivered a body of theological truth to the church (1 Cor. 15:3). They encouraged believers to be faithful to that body of information they had heard and received in the beginning (1 John 2:7, 24, 26; 3:11), that "faith that was once for all entrusted to the saints" (Jude 3). Believers, in general, were instructed to guard the faith, that is, to stand firm in sound doctrine (2 Tim. 1:13–14). Pastors in particular were admonished to cleave to sound doctrine so that they could be good ministers of the gospel (1 Tim. 4:6).

The use of the term "doctrine" in Scripture is important for at least three reasons. First, it affirms that the primitive church was confessional. The first generation of believers confessed apostolic teaching about the significance of the life of Christ. They delivered a body of information that included facts about Christ with interpretation of their importance. Second, the use of the term reflects development of thought in the primitive church. *Didaskalia* is used in the Pastorals with reference to the sum of teaching, especially of that which had come from the lips of the apostles. Doctrine plays a small role in Judaism and in the New Testament apart from the Pastoral Epistles, and yet is very important in the latter. By the time of the Pastorals the apostolic message had been transformed into traditional teaching. Third, it affirms the indispensable link between spirituality and doctrine. Christianity is a way of life founded on doctrine. Some disparage doctrine in favor of the spiritual life. Paul, however, taught that spiritual growth in Christ is dependent on faithfulness to sound doctrine, for its truth provides the means of growth (Col. 2:6). The apostle John developed three tests for discerning authentic spirituality: believing right doctrine (1 John 2:18–27), obedience to right doctrine (2:28–3:10), and giving expression to right doctrine with love (2:7–11). Faithful obedience and love, then, are not alternatives to sound doctrine. They are the fruit of right doctrine as it works itself out in the believer's character and relationships. SAM HAMSTRA, JR.

Bibliography. J. G. Machen, *Christianity and Liberalism;* D. F. Wells, *No Place For Truth: Or Whatever Happened to Evangelical Theology; TDNT,* 2:160–63.

Dominions. *See* POWERS.

Doubt. It is possible to have questions (or doubts) about persons, propositions, or objects. Philosophically and epistemologically doubt has been deemed a valuable element in honest, rational inquiry. It prevents us from reaching hasty conclusions or making commitments to unreliable and untrustworthy sources. A suspension of judgment until sufficient inquiry is made and adequate evidence is presented is judged to be admirable. In this light, doubt is not an enemy of faith. This seems to be the attitude of the Bereans in Acts 17:11. Questioning or doubting motivates us to search further and deeper in an understanding of faith.

With only rare exceptions, however, doubt in Scripture is seen as a negative attitude or action because it is directed toward God by man (or evil spiritual agents). The word connotes the idea of weakness in faith or unbelief.

If one accepts a typological understanding of Isaiah 14, doubt actually began in heaven in the heart of Lucifer. Here the object of doubt (and rejection) was the sovereignty and majesty of God (vv. 13–14). On earth doubt was conceived and given birth in the garden when the serpent cast doubt on God's character and goodness (Gen. 3:1–5). Tragically Eve and Adam bought into his deceptive plan and plunged humankind into the fall (vv. 6–19). In both instances doubt is clearly an aspect of sin; it is directed toward God and is characterized by rebellion and disobedience.

In the Gospels the word "doubt" consistently carries with it a negative aspect, and the object of doubt again is always the Lord in some sense. Peter doubted Christ's ability to keep him from drowning (Matt. 14:31). Here doubt is small or weak faith. Peter became doubtful as to the Lord's reliability and power to sustain him. The Pharisees doubted Christ's messiahship and asked for another sign (Matt. 12:38–42). If we have faith in God and do not doubt, we can move mountains and receive our request through prayer (Matt. 21:21; Mark 11:23). Here doubt is the antithesis of faith. In John 14:1 Jesus encourages the disciples to not have a troubled (doubting?) heart with regards to the future, but to believe in him, to trust him for their future needs. Some of the disciples, including Thomas, doubted the reality of the resurrected Lord (Luke 24:38; John 20:27). Here doubt is not outright denial or unbelief, but an attitude or feeling of uncertainty. Thomas is not severely rebuked, but nether is his skepticism commended. "Stop doubting and believe" is the word of the Lord to his disciple.

Abraham, as a positive example, is said not to have wavered" through unbelief [doubt] regarding the promise of God, but was strengthened in his faith" (Rom. 4:20). Doubt here is equivalent to unbelief.

James 1:6–8 tells us a doubting man is an unstable or divided man who lacks sufficient faith to lay hold of the promises of God. The doubting one sins against the Lord because he has questioned the character, goodness, and faithfulness of God. Unlike the God who does not change (v. 17), the doubting person is "like a wave of the sea, blown and tossed by the wind" (v. 6). Such an individual "should not think he will receive anything from the Lord" (v. 7).

A different use of the word "doubt" is found in both Romans 14:23 and Jude 22. In the Romans passage doubt is related to one's conscience. Doubt or uncertainty over a questionable action or a "gray area" of the Christian life (here it is eating idol-meat) is condemned because the action does not arise out of faith toward God. At this point the latter part of verse 23 is most instructive: "everything that does not come from faith is sin."

Jude 22 raises the issue of evangelistic apologetics toward the serious doubter who denies Jesus Christ as the only sovereign Lord (v. 4). Here doubt is a settled denial and rejection of both the person (Jesus Christ) and propositions affirmed about him (he is sovereign and Lord). Doubt of this nature is blatant unbelief involving the mind, will, and emotions.

Doubt in Scripture can be seen to be characteristic of both believers and unbelievers. In believers it is usually a weakness of faith, a wavering in the face of God's promises. In the unbeliever doubt is virtually synonymous with unbelief. Scripture, as would be expected, does not look at doubt philosophically or epistemologically. Doubt is viewed practically and spiritually as it relates to our trust in the Lord. For this reason, doubt is not deemed as valuable or commendable.

DANIEL L. AIKEN

Bibliography. A. K. Rule, NTCERK, pp. 272–73; B. Gartner, *NIDNTT,* 1:503–5; F. Buchsel, *TDNT,* 3:946–49; Os Guinness, *Doubt, Faith, and Two Minds.*

Dragon. *See* ANTICHRIST.

Drink. Palestine lacks fresh water rivers and lakes and its dependence upon rain after its yearly hot, dry period makes drought an ongoing possibility. In view of frequently occurring shortages of water, thirst and drinking are of particular significance in the Scriptures. The act of drinking as well as the object of drink became powerful metaphors in Scripture. Drink is used figuratively to symbolize participation in a number of acts or relationships, the reception (internalization) of a belief or teaching, or the sustenance needed to live.

Participation in and Sustenance of the Spiritual Life. Drink can be used metaphorically for that which sustains the spiritual life. Stemming from the fundamental fact that one needs to drink liquids in order to sustain life, drink used figuratively can speak of a consciousness that one does not live by physical elements alone but ultimately by spiritual nourishment from God. In Isaiah 55:1–5 the exiles are summoned to return and to be restored by satisfying their spiritual thirst. Against the physical background of Palestine, where drought was too often a reality and the need for drink to quench the thirst a necessity, the desire for God is spoken of as a "thirst" that God alone could satisfy (Pss. 42:1–2; 63:1; 143:6). Here "to drink" is to take the salvation offered by grace alone and to live by it. Amos 8:11 speaks figuratively of a famine or thirst for the Word of God that can be quenched only if God wills.

The phrases "drink from your river of delights" (Ps. 36:8) and "spring of living water" (Jer. 2:13) may well be sources of the title "river of the water of life" that flows from the temple of God, creating so many joys (Ezek. 47:1–12; Rev. 22:1–2). As well the metaphors of "cup" and "well of salvation" (Ps. 116:13; Isa. 12:3) are used to express the deliverance and goodness of the Lord. Spiritual participation with the true God brings not a mere existence but a life of joy and an experience of the goodness of God.

In the New Testament Christ invites people to drink the water that will "become in him a spring of water welling up to eternal life" (John 4:14). While the water here is designated as eternal life, in John 7:38–39 the drinking of "living water" is related to the Spirit who would be given after Christ was glorified. In the final chapter of the Bible the same invitation to participate in the eternal life of Christ and the Spirit is given. "The Spirit and the bride say, 'Come!' And let him who hears say, 'Come!' Whoever is thirsty, let him come; and whoever wishes, let him take the free gift of the water of life" (Rev. 22:17; cf. Rev. 21:6). This drinking of the water of life is parallel to eating the bread of life (John 6:27, 50–51). In another metaphor John records the words of Christ "unless you eat the flesh of the Son of Man and drink his blood, you have no life in you. Whoever eats my flesh and drinks my blood has eternal life, and I will raise him up at the last day" (John 6:53–54). Here Christ is again seen as the source of life; the appropriation of himself as God's appointed sacrifice is needed for eternal life.

Drinking Together as Denoting Fellowship. Drinking takes on a deeper significance when, often along with eating, it expresses the fellowship and unity that exist among those who share a meal. Because drinking together denotes fellowship and acceptance there will be those who will call upon the fact that they have eaten and drunk with Jesus to claim a place at his side in eternity (Luke 13:16). But Jesus will reply that he never knew them (Luke 13:27). Fellowship, while symbolized by drinking together, must be based on something greater.

Drink can in fact be a metaphor for consummation or initiation of a relationship. Israel eats and drinks before God at Sinai in a covenant meal celebrating the sealing of the Mosaic covenant (Exod. 24:11). This meal that includes the act of drinking may foreshadow the Lord's Supper, which celebrates the new covenant sealed by Christ's death (1 Cor. 11:25–26).

This symbolic meaning of fellowship also lies behind Luke 5:30; by eating with sinners the disciples, like Jesus, stand on their side. Luke brings an important qualification by inserting the words "to repentance," for true fellowship must be based on more than the mere physical act of drinking and eating together (Luke 5:32).

Drink as Sacrifice. Perhaps owing to its life-giving qualities and that it was seen as a blessing of God (Gen. 27:28), wine was designated as a form of daily sacrifice to the Lord called the drink offering (Exod. 29:38–41). Paul uses the drink offering to symbolize the possibility of his life being given ("poured out") as a sacrifice upon or accompanying the sacrificial service of the Philippians (Phil. 2:17). Though this may refer to his entire ministry it may be best to see it as referring to his death if he is killed as a martyr.

Even the water that David's mighty men had obtained from the well at Bethlehem at dire risk to their lives was viewed so dearly by David that he would not drink it but poured it out as an offering to God (2 Sam. 23:13–17). He regarded the drink as "the blood of men who went at the risk of their lives" (v. 17).

Drink as Symbolic of Acceptance of God's Will. Drink is used symbolically of Christ's acceptance of God's will. In John 18:11, when referring to his willingness to suffer God's judgment on man's behalf, Jesus asks Peter the question "Shall I not drink the cup the Father has given me?" Jesus was prepared to suffer the judgment of God as payment for humankind's sin as part of his acceptance of god's will (Matt. 26:42).

The suffering of the disciples, though not for God's judgment on humankind's sin but as a participation in Christ's suffering, is referred to by the figure of speech "drink the cup" (Matt. 20:22–23). To "drink the cup of suffering" is to experience and take to oneself the suffering sent by God (Mark 10:38). Their following Christ will necessitate an experiencing of suffering (v. 39).

Participation in Killing. Killing one's enemies is spoken of figuratively as a lion that "drinks the blood of his victims" (Num. 23:24). "To drink blood" is a figure for killing (Isa. 49:26; cf. Rev. 16:6; 17:6) taken from the actions of beast of prey (Num. 23:24; Ezek. 39:17–18). On the day of the Lord's vengeance the sword "will devour till it is satisfied, till it has quenched its thirst with blood" (Jer. 46:10). Battles often use the imagery of sacrifice including "drinking of blood" (Isa. 34:5–7; Ezek. 39:17–18).

Participation in Evil. Evildoing is spoken of as "drinking up evil" (Job 15:16). This is especially true of violence (Prov. 4:17; 26:6). This drinking seems to be symbolic of the sinner's habitual participation and internalization of all kinds of evil.

Reception of God's Judgment. Drink can stand for the way God's judgment comes to men as the "cup of God's wrath." The sinful will "drink" of this wrath, symbolic of their reception and suffering of God's judgment (Job 21:20; Isa. 51:17, 22). The image of drinking expresses the fact that those smitten by it execute the judgment on themselves by their own acts. This cup of wrath is often referred to also as a "cup of wine" and therefore experiencing God's judgment is compared to becoming drunk (Ps. 75:8; Rev. 14:10; 16:19). It is the fate of ungodly nations in particular (Pss. 60:3, 75:8; Isa. 29:9; 63:6; Jer. 25:15–16; Lam. 4:21; Ezek. 23:32–34; Hab. 2:16; Zech. 12:2). However in Jeremiah 8:14; 9:14, and 23:15, God is said to give poisoned water to his own people, referring to the bitter punishment they are being called to bear.

Drink Used to Refer to Sexual Relationships. "To drink water from one's own cistern" means to ensure that your wife is the source of your sexual pleasure, as water refreshes a thirsty man (Prov. 5:15). In this case drink is used symbolically to mean "appease desire." STEPHEN J. BRAMER

Drink Offering. *See* OFFERINGS AND SACRIFICES.

Duty. ***The Old Testament.*** The Old Testament concept of duty is largely related to the performance of the levirate marriage, where a brother undertakes the obligation to marry his widowed sister-in-law so that his deceased brother will have an heir.

The unusual instructions behind this duty appear in Deuteronomy 25:5–10. If a man dies without having a son, his brother is to marry the sister-in-law and "fulfill the duty of a brother-in-law to her. The first son she bears shall carry on the name of the dead brother so that his name will not be blotted out from Israel" (vv. 5–6). If the living brother chooses not to carry out his obligation, the widow then has the right to go to the elders at the town gate, where she can accuse her brother-in-law of his unwillingness to raise up seed for his dead brother. If he still refuses, the widow has the right to shame him, taking off one of his sandals and spitting in his face while saying, "This is what is done to the man who will not build up his brother's family line" (v. 10). Those who refused to carry out this duty caused family lines to die out.

A good illustration of the levirate marriage is that of Boaz, who sought to perform his duty for a deceased relative by marrying Ruth. Actually, a relative who was closer to Ruth's husband than Boaz was willing to redeem the land in restoring the family. When he discovered that he would also have to marry Ruth to raise up an heir to her husband, however, he refused (Ruth 4). Boaz then stepped in and was willing to take Ruth for his wife as well as to be her kinsman redeemer, redeeming the land for the family.

Another kind of duty in the Old Testament was related to the care of the God's dwelling-place. Those who served performed duties in the sanctuary (Num. 3:7) or were involved in its care (Num. 18:5). These responsibilities involved guarding the furniture in the tabernacle and temple and keeping it clean.

The New Testament. The concept of duty in the New Testament emphasizes service and piety. Jesus says that when a servant has done his best, serving his master, he is only performing his duty (Luke 17:10). The seven deacons who were chosen by the early church were to supervise the daily distribution of food; the apostles turned this responsibility over to them (Acts 6:3). Husbands are told to fulfill their marital duties to their wives (1 Cor. 7:3). Widows are exhorted to practice piety (1 Tim. 5:4), a duty that reflects pious care for the family. LOUIS GOLDBERG

Bibliography. D. K. McKim, *ISBE,* 1:998–99.

Ee

Ear. *See* HEAR, HEARING.

Earth, New. *See* NEW HEAVENS AND A NEW EARTH.

Ecclesiastes, Theology of. Debate surrounds the interpretation of Ecclesiastes. Some early Jewish interpreters even suspected the canonicity of the book. It sometimes gives apparently contradictory advice. The book's author, who goes by the name "Qohelet" (translated in modern versions as "the Preacher" or "the Teacher"), can, on the one hand, say that he "hated life" (2:17), but, on the other, assert that a "live dog is better off than a dead lion" (9:4). Not infrequently, Ecclesiastes clashes with the teaching of other biblical books. For instance, while the Book of Proverbs advocates a total commitment to the way of wisdom, Qohelet says, "Do not be overrighteous, neither be overwise" (7:16) and concludes that in the long run wisdom can get us no further than folly (2:12–16).

While, for these reasons, some Jewish interpreters turned away from Ecclesiastes, others justified its inclusion in the canon by straining its interpretation. The Targum to the book (Levine) is an instructive example. It, first of all, made explicit what the author skillfully and intentionally never stated, most notably the identification of Qohelet and Solomon. As all critical and many evangelical interpreters (notably Delitzsch and Young) have remarked, the two are not the same. Too many passages in the book could only be written by a nonroyal person (4:1–3; 3:8–9; 8:2–6). Nevertheless, the Targum makes the identification and this identification in part helped the religious communities accept the book. The same Targum stretched the interpretation of individual passages beyond all reason in order to turn Qohelet/Solomon into a teacher of pure orthodoxy. Thus, when Qohelet warns about the weariness of books, the Targum turns it into an exaltation of Torah study.

Early Christian interpretation took the same basic approach. It is noteworthy that the New Testament never directly quotes Ecclesiastes. The only mention of the book in the first centuries of the church is in the Shepherd of Hermas, and that book alluded to only the last two verses. It is in the third century that commentaries on Ecclesiastes are first attested.

These early Christian interpreters found theological meaning in the text through allegory. For instance, Qohelet's frequent refrain advocating his listeners to seek pleasure in eating and drinking is turned into an admonition to partake of the Lord's body and blood in communion. Ambrose finds a reference to the Trinity in the three-strand cord of 4:12.

The issue of the interpretation of Ecclesiastes continues to the present, with some commentaries arguing for an orthodox Teacher in the book who has a positive view of life. The theological contribution of the book, according to this approach, is its affirmation of the wisdom traditions of Proverbs and its encouragement of enjoying the little pleasures of the present life in the midst of a fallen world.

Such a view of the book, however, does not take into account the book's literary structure and treats certain, more negative aspects of the book, as secondary, or, if not, strains at the interpretation of individual words and passages to make it fit a preconceived idea of the function of the book.

On the contrary, the most natural reading of the book takes into account the presence of two speakers: Qohelet, who refers to himself in the first person in 1:12–12:7, and a second unnamed wise person, who describes Qohelet to his son (12:12) in the third person (1:1–11; 12:8–15). In effect, the speech of Qohelet is a quotation, which is framed by the words of the second speaker who is the narrator/author.

Qohelet's Theology (1:12–12:7). Qohelet is a wisdom teacher who struggles with the traditions of his people, including the normative traditions of a book like Proverbs. His most frequent refrain (and there are several of these) is "Meaningless, meaningless! All is meaningless!" He uses the term "meaningless" (*hebel*) in well over twenty passages. The second wise person, in fact, introduces and concludes Qohelet's teaching with the refrain, as if to say, "This is Qohelet's basic conclusion."

Qohelet is not satisfied merely to state that everything is meaningless, but specifies a number of areas and shows why they have no value. For one thing, toil is meaningless. He gives a number of reasons why toil cannot give ultimate satisfaction. Someone might work hard and succeed, but then die and have to leave it all to someone who has not worked for it (2:17–23). Further, the motivation to work hard itself is evil because it springs from envy (4:4). What does Qohelet advocate in terms of toil? It is hard to say. On the one hand, he quotes a proverb to the effect that to cease work leads to destruction (4:5), but quickly follows this with a second proverb that encourages a tranquil lifestyle (4:6).

Qohelet also pronounces the world meaningless in light of the oppression he sees wherever he turns (4:1–3). The government itself is responsible for much of the suffering of the people (5:8–9). He is obviously moved by what he sees, but he never sees ways to soften the suffering of the oppressed or even to become one of the comforters that they lack (4:1). He never considers action (doubly surprising if he is actually a king), but seems resigned to it all: "Consider what God has done: Who can straighten what he has made crooked?" (7:13).

Perhaps most surprising of all is his attitude toward wisdom. If there was anything that should have appealed to a wise person in Israel, it would have been the value of his wisdom. For Qohelet, however, wisdom has only a limited, relative significance in comparison to folly. An examination of 2:12–16 illustrates his attitude. In the initial phase of his comparison between wisdom and folly, he sounds very similar to the teaching of Proverbs and concludes that "wisdom is better than folly" (v. 13). Wisdom allows a person to "get on" in the world (v. 14a). But this advantage is short-lived as Qohelet then contemplates the long run. Both the fool and the wise die, rendering void the benefits of wisdom (vv. 14b–16).

Qohelet's search for meaning leads him to consider many different areas of life on earth. He not only explores wisdom and toil; he also considers political power (4:13–16), riches, large families, and long life (5:8–6:12). In each of these areas, he encounters "meaninglessness" and expresses his frustration that life is the way it is. As we read his reflections, we are struck by two inescapable facts of human existence that are the source of his anguish: death and the inability to control and know the appropriate time.

In terms of the latter, it must be remembered that it was of crucial importance for a wise teacher to know the right time. The Book of Proverbs does not give a list of truths that are always, everywhere appropriate, but a series of principles that are to be applied at the right time. The wise speak the right word at the right time. They know the conditions under which they should answer a fool (26:5) and when they should refrain (26:4). Qohelet, as a wise man, knows that there are right times for certain activities: "There is a time for everything and a season for every activity under heaven" (3:1). He also is fully aware that God "made everything beautiful in its time" (3:11). But he also understands that he cannot share God's knowledge. As a human being he can never be certain that this is the "right time," and this lack of knowledge, this lack of certainty, frustrates him to the point that he thinks that life "under the sun" is meaningless. Humans cannot know what will happen to them next, during or after life, "No one knows what is coming—who can tell him what will happen after him?" (10:14). "Since no man knows the future, who can tell him what is to come?" (8:7). This leaves humans at the mercy of "time and chance" (9:11). They cannot even know when they are going to die: "Moreover, no man knows when his hour will come: As fish are caught in a cruel net, or birds are taken in a snare, so men are trapped by evil times that fall unexpectedly upon them" (9:12).

But humans do know one thing for certain. They know that they will die. "For the living know that they will die" (9:5). And this knowledge frustrates Qohelet more than any other, so he reflected on it at great length.

We have already seen how death nullifies wisdom's advantage over folly (2:12–16). The same is true for hard work and the riches that come from work. Why bother working hard throughout life when at death it will go to some worthless person or even a person that you do not know (2:17–23)? Death renders every status and achievement of this present life "meaningless."

Further, as far as Qohelet knows for certain, death is the end of the story. He is not drawing his hearers/readers to the edge of despair just so he can tell them about the bliss of an afterlife. According to the Preacher, "the dead know nothing; they have no further reward, and even the memory of them is forgotten." In the long run there is no difference between humans and animals, for "all go to me same place; all come from dust, and to dust all return" (3:20). Indeed, Qohelet's last words in the book are a sad and moving reflection upon death, describing a person's end using three image clusters: growing old and dying is like watching the storm clouds move in and ruin a sunny day (12:1–2); it is also like an unmaintained house, slowly falling apart (12:3–5); it is like a severed rope, a broken bowl, a shattered pitcher, and a ruined wheel (12:6). Life is valuable on the short run; the rope is silver after all, but it is completely ruined at death, when the process of creation is undone and the body turns to dust and the spirit returns to God. The fundamental unity of a person as established at creation (Gen. 2:7) is thereby reversed and undone. Qohelet has no hope that things will be "put right" after death.

What is the theological message of Qohelet's speech? Life is full of trouble and then you die.

Some interpreters attempt to mitigate this hard message by appealing to six passages that they interpret as offering a positive view toward life (2:24–26; 3:12–14; 3:22; 5:17–19 [Eng. 18–20]; 8:15; 9:7–10). In the first place, however, Qohelet only suggests a limited type of joy in these passages. Only three areas are specified—eating, drinking, and work. Second, Qohelet's introduction to pleasure is hardly enthusiastic. For instance, in 2:24 he puts it this way: "A man can do nothing better than . . . " He believes that this joy comes only from the hand of God, a situation that brings him no ultimate satisfaction (see 2:26c where he pronounces it "meaningless"). Indeed, it is clear throughout the book that, although God grants enjoyment to some, Qohelet does not identify himself among the privileged few.

It is more in keeping with the book as a whole to understand these passages as they have been taken through much of the history of interpretation, that is, as a call to enjoy the day (*carpe diem*). In the darkness of a life that has no ultimate meaning, seize upon the temporal pleasures that lighten the burden.

The Theology of the Book as a Whole. Qohelet's pessimistic theology is not the concluding voice in the book. A second voice is heard in the book at the beginning (1:1–11) and at the end (12:8–15), placing a frame around Qohelet's speech and providing the perspective through which we should read his opinions. Many interpreters have acknowledged this function of the epilogue, although different explanations have been provided (for instance, 1:12–12:7 is the speech of Solomon as a young man and 12:8–15 contains his reflections late in life). When the structure of the book is taken into account, then we can understand how this rather unorthodox teacher can stand in the canon.

An analogy with the Book of Job further clarifies the situation. The Book of Job, in the main, is constructed of a dialogue between Job and his three friends, a conversation that is concluded with Elihu's monologue. While each of these speakers presents a perspective that in some respects conforms to normative biblical teaching, none of them offers the final perspective. This perspective comes only at the end when God speaks from the whirlwind. It is the Yahweh speeches that provide the prism through which the rest of the book must be understood—just as the second wise teacher's epilogue provides a hermeneutical grid for the Book of Ecclesiastes.

What does this normative voice tell the reader? In the first place, the second unnamed wise teacher gives a cautious approval to Qohelet's words (12:9–10), and indeed, as we think about what Qohelet says, we can see that he does accurately describe the situation on the earth apart from God ("under the sun"). To use language from elsewhere in the Bible, Qohelet aptly describes the frustrations of life in a postfall world, a world suffering under the curse of the covenant. As a matter of fact, the one allusion to Ecclesiastes in the New Testament confirms the truth of his insight. In Romans 8:18–22 Paul explains why the world seems so meaningless to us: "I consider that our present sufferings are not worth comparing with the glory that will be revealed in us. The creation waits in eager expectation for the sons of God to be revealed. For the creation was subjected to frustration, not by its own choice, but by the will of the one who subjected it, in hope that the creation itself will be liberated from its bondage to decay and brought into the glorious freedom of the children of God."

The world was subjected to *frustration*, the Greek word used in the Septuagint to translate "meaningless" (*hebel*) in Ecclesiastes. It is no wonder that Qohelet failed in his search for meaning under the sun. It simply is not there.

The epilogist, however, is not satisfied with Qohelet's conclusions. He registers criticism of Qohelet's conclusions in 12:11, 12 (obscured in the NIV by its debatable translation and capitalization of "shepherd," which is more probably a reference to human teachers). He tells his son that the words of the wise are like "goads" and "firmly implanted nails," both images of pain if nothing else. He warns him "of them" (not of "anything in addition to them"). And although the translation of verses 9–12 of the epilogue may be disputed, no one doubts the last two verses of the epilogue turn for the first time to a clear and ringing statement of the right way to go:

> Now all has been heard;
> here is the conclusion of the matter:
> Fear God and keep his commandments,
> for this is the whole duty of man.
> For God will bring every deed into
> judgment,
> including every hidden thing,
> whether it is good or evil.

In a short compass, the shaping voice of the Book of Ecclesiastes affirms the major tenets of Old Testament religion. It advocates a "right relationship" with God (*fear God*) that manifests itself in an obedient lifestyle (*keep his commandments*) and cites the coming judgment as a motive. In this way, Qohelet affirms the Pentateuch, Wisdom, and Prophets. Here we have the gospel in a nutshell in Old Testament language.

From a New Testament Perspective. The message of the book in its Old Testament context continues to have force today. We are to "fear God," obey his commandments, and look for the coming judgment. But from our New Testament perspective we can see how Jesus Christ allows us to transcend the meaningless of the postfall world.

Indeed, Jesus Christ subjected himself to the meaningless of the world under covenant curse so we might live meaningful lives. We may observe in the Gospel accounts how Jesus moved from one meaningless situation to another. When he was born, the inn had no room and he was born in the manger where the animals lived. John tells us that he, the Word of God, was born in the world, but the world "did not recognize him" (1:10).

Jesus felt the full effects of the covenant curse. This may be seen clearly toward the end of his earthly ministry. While enjoying brief popularity after the triumphal entry, he was rejected by humanity in stages. First the crowds abandoned him, then the broader circle of his disciples left him. The Gospel narratives pay special attention to Peter and Judas: one denied him and the other rejected him. But the climax of his experience of the postfall world comes when he is hanging on the cross and his Father abandons him,. so that he cries: "My God, my God, why have you forsaken me?" (Mark 15:34).

Christians read this and rejoice because they know that Jesus suffered the world under curse in order to release them from the meaninglessness of the fall. Thus, all the areas that Qohelet struggled with (work, riches, wisdom) may be properly enjoyed and are imbued with meaning. After all, Jesus Christ did away with the one thing that bothered Qohelet the most—death. Jesus Christ subjected himself to the curse of death (Gal. 3:13) that we might be released from that curse and find meaning in him.

TREMPER LONGMAN III

Bibliography. F. Delitzsch, *Commentary on the Old Testament*, vol. 6; M. V. Fox, *HUCA* 48 (1977): 83–106; idem, *Qohelet and His Contradictions;* J. Jarick, *Gregory Thaumaturgos' Paraphrase of Ecclesiastes;* E. Levine, *The Aramaic Version of Qohelet;* T. Longman III, *Ecclesiastes;* W. Kaiser, *Ecclesiastes: Total Life;* G. S. Ogden, *Qohelet;* R. N. Whybray, *Ecclesiastes;* S. Woudstra, *Koheleth's Reflections upon Life;* E. J. Young, *Introduction to the Old Testament.*

Education in Bible Times. Education is essential to the survival of any social group, since a community secures its continued existence and development only through the transmission of its accumulated knowledge, derived power, and ideological aims to the next generation. Education may be simply (and narrowly) defined as the process of teaching and learning, the imparting and acquisition of knowledge and skill(s).

The need for education was no less true for the Israelites than for any of the peoples of the ancient world. In fact, the Old Testament record indicates repeatedly that the success of the Hebrew community and the continuity of its culture were conditioned by the knowledge of and obedience to God's revealed law (Josh. 1:6–8). Thus, to ensure their prosperity, growth, and longevity as the people of Yahweh, Israel's mandate was one of education—diligently teaching their children to love God, and to know and obey his statues and ordinances (Deut. 6:1–9). Likewise, the New Testament record links the success of the church of Jesus Christ, as a worshiping community of "salt and light" reaching out to a dark world, to the teaching of sound doctrine (John 13:34–35; Eph. 4:14; 1 Tim. 1:10; Titus 2:1).

Education in the Ancient Near East. Since education is basic to the existence of any community or society it is only natural that certain foundational ideals, methods, and principles of education are shared properties among diverse people groups. The case is no different when we study the educational practices of the Israelites within the context of education in world of the ancient Near East.

Education in the ancient world was rooted in religious tradition and theological ideals. The goal of education was the transmission of that religious tradition, along with community mores and values, and vocational and technical skills. The by-product of this kind of education was a model citizen, loyal to family, gods, and king, upright in character, and productive in community life. More than liberally educated "free-thinkers," the important outcome of the educational system for the ancients was utilitarian—equipping people to be functional members of family and society.

For the most part the teaching method was based upon rote learning. This memorization of the curricular materials was accomplished by both oral and written recitation. Disciplined learning characterized educational instruction, with lessons taught at fixed times during the day and often for a set number of days in a month. In addition to being teachers and drill masters, parents (in the home) and tutors (in the formal schools) also functioned as mentors and role-models, teaching by example and lifestyle.

The primary agency of education in both ancient Egypt and Mesopotamia was the home. Parents and elders of the clan or extended family were responsible for the education of children. The invention of writing systems and the increasing shift toward urbanization gave rise to specialized schools associated with the major institutions of the ancient world—the temple and the palace. Whereas education in the home focused on vocational training and moral development, the temple and palace schools were designed to produce literate, informed, and capable religious and sociopolitical leaders and administrators.

However, more striking than these similarities are the difference between the educational ideals and practices of the Hebrews and those of their ancient counterparts. It is important to note that these educational distinctives of the Israelites are directly related to singular aspects of Hebrew religion. Five specific characteristics were not common to the religions of the ancient Near East.

First, the emphasis upon individual personality in Hebrew faith meant that education must respect the individual and seek to develop the whole person.

Second, the emphasis on the fatherhood of God in Israelite religion brought a sense of intimacy to the Creator-creature relationship and a sense of purpose and urgency to human history. Thus Hebrew education stressed the importance of recognizing and remembering acts and events of divine providence in history.

Third, the idea of indeterminism or personal freedom in Hebrew religion gave man and woman dignity as free moral agents in creation; likewise Hebrew education stressed the responsibility individuals have toward God and others, accountability of human behavior, and the need for disciplined training in making "right" choices.

Fourth, the notion of the Israelites as a divinely chosen people encouraged fierce nationalistic overtones in Hebrew religion and education; religiously the Israelites were obligated to the demands of God's holiness in order to remain his special possession, while educationally they were obligated to instruct all nations in divine holiness and redemption as Yahweh's instrument of light to the nations.

Fifth, the doctrine of human sin and sinfulness stamps both Hebrew religion and education; this introduced the concept of mediation in Israelite religion—a requirement for bridging the gap between a righteous God and his fallen creation; educationally this meant human knowledge and wisdom were flawed and limited and that divine illumination was necessary for grasping certain truths and divine enablement was necessary for doing right.

Education in Old Testament Times. Hebrew education was both objective (external and content oriented) and subjective (internal and personally oriented), cognitive (emphasis on the intellect) and affective (emphasis on the will and emotions), and both active (investigative and participatory) and passive (rote and reflective). Specifically the teaching-learning process involved disciplined repetition in observation, experiential learning (doing), listening, reciting, and imitating. On occasion special guidance (directed study) as well as correction and warning were a part of the educational experience. And finally, critical thinking skills were an important educational outcome because learning had application to daily living.

Aims. The aim or purpose of Old Testament education is encapsulated within the revelation given to Abraham concerning the destruction of Sodom and Gomorrah. Here God bids Abraham to direct his children in "the way of the LORD." This divine directive embodies the very essence of Hebrew education in the Old Testament, affirming the primacy of parental instruction. In addition, the verse identifies the desired goal or outcome of education: a lifestyle of doing justice and righteousness. There was also an attendant benefit attached to this "behavior modification in Yahwistic moral values"—the possession of the land of covenant promise for those Israelites who followed through on the charge to educate their children in the way of the Lord.

Content. Genesis 18:19 cryptically describes the content of Hebrew education as "the way of the LORD." What is meant by this phrase and how does it relate to the religious content of education in the Old Testament?

Generally speaking, "the way of the Lord" refers to knowledge of and obedience to the will of God as revealed through act and word in Old Testament history. The way or will of God for humanity reflects his personal character and attributes. As human beings love their neighbors as themselves (Lev. 19:18), practice righteousness and justice (Gen. 18:19), and pursue holiness (Lev. 11:44) they walk in the way of the Lord in that they mirror God's character.

More specifically, "the way of the Lord" denotes the particular content of the series of covenant agreements or treaties Yahweh made with his people Israel. These covenants formed the basis of Israel's relationship to Yahweh and were characterized by a stylized literary pattern that included legislation or stipulations necessary for maintaining that relationship. Often the covenant or treaty concluded with the promise of blessings or curses conditioned by Israel's obedience (or lack thereof) to the specific covenant stipulations.

Thus, Hebrew education was essentially instruction in covenant obedience or "keeping the way of the Lord" (Gen. 18:19). Moses summarized the basic components of this covenant obedience in his farewell address to the Israelites as loving God, walking in his ways, and keeping his commandments, statutes, and ordinances (Deut. 30:16). Later, the psalmist condensed this covenant content of Old Testament education into the phrase "the law of the LORD" (Ps. 119:1).

Naturally, the content of Hebrew education expanded as God continued to reveal himself and his redemptive plan to the Israelites through the centuries of Old Testament history. For example, the details of Yahweh's covenant with Abraham fills but three chapters in Genesis (12, 15, 17). By contrast, the details of the Mosaic covenant dominate the greater portions of the biblical literature found in Exodus, Leviticus, Numbers, and Deuteronomy.

Since the Israelites recognized Yahweh as the God of history, providentially active in the course of human events, history too became part of the content or curriculum of Hebrew education. The recitation and festal remembrance of divine acts in human history were instructive as to the nature of God and his purposes in creation. Of course, the primary example of this historical trajectory in Hebrew education is the Passover feast and exodus from Egypt (Exod. 12:24–27; 13:11–16).

In time, the Hebrew poetic and wisdom traditions and the prophetic tradition were included in the covenant content of Old Testament education. The wisdom tradition served as a practical commentary on the law or covenant legislation, while the prophetic tradition functioned as a theological commentary on Old Testament law. Like the legal tradition associated with the covenants, both wisdom and prophecy were rooted in the behavioral outcomes of loving God and doing righteousness and justice (Prov. 1:3, 2:9; Hos. 6:6; Mic. 6:8).

The Practice of Education. Until a child was about five years old informal education in the home was largely the responsibility of the mother, a nurse, or a male guardian. A youth between the ages of five and twenty usually worked with his father as an apprentice learning a vocation. No doubt parental instruction in the ways of the Lord continued through these years, reinforced by association with the extended family and involvement in the ritual of community worship. In later Judaism, male children between the ages of five and twenty usually attended synagogue schools and were trained in the Torah, the Mishnah, and the Talmud. At age twenty a young man was ready for marriage and independent full-time employment, and at age thirty he might assume an official position of responsibility.

Young women were educated in the way of the Lord and culturally acceptable domestic skills by their mothers or other women of some standing. Several professions were open to women, including those of nurse and midwife, cook, weaver, perfumer, singer, mourner, and servant. In certain cases women assumed prominent positions of leadership, like the prophet-judge Deborah (Judg. 4:4–5) and the prophetess-sage Huldah (2 Kings 22:14–15). It seems likely that women of royal standing in Jerusalem received some kind of formal schooling similar to that of their male counterparts since they were part of the official political system and queen rule was a possibility in the ancient Near Eastern world. Of course, common and cultic prostitution remained a source of employment for women in ancient society.

Outcomes. Theologically, the practice of education as outlined in Old Testament revelation resulted in God's covenant blessing for the Hebrew people. These divine blessings included political autonomy and security, and agricultural and economic prosperity (Lev. 26:1–8). Sociologically, the practice of education facilitated assimilation into the community of faith and ensured the stabilization of that community because the principle of "doing justice" permeated society (Lev. 19:15, 18). Religiously, the practice of education sustained covenant relationship with God through obedience and proper ritual, which prompted God's favor and presence with Israel (Lev. 26:9–12).

The Agencies of Education. There were basically three agencies or institutions responsible for the education of youth in Old Testament times: the home or family, the community, and formal centers of learning. Here it is important to remember that the process of education described in Scripture was predominantly informal (home and community), not the formal education of learned institutions.

The home was the primary agency for instruction in Hebrew society. While the Old Testament emphasizes the role of the father as teacher, both parents are given charge to train their children (Prov. 1:8, 6:20; 31:26). Since ancient Israel was largely a clan society, extended family members like grandparents, aunts and uncles, and even cousins might also participate in the educational process within the home. The "home school" curriculum was both religious and vocational, as parents and other family members tutored children in "the fear of the LORD" (Prov. 2:5) and a trade or professional skill—most often that of the father.

Since all Israelites were bonded together in covenant relationship as the people of God before Yahweh, the religious community also played an important role in the education of the Hebrew youth. Again, community instruction was essentially religious in nature and purpose and took the form of didactic and historical meditation, moral training, sign and symbol, memorization and catechism, festival and sacrificial liturgy, ritual enactment, and priestly role modeling. Specific examples of community education include: the three great pilgrimage festivals (Unleavened Bread, Weeks, and Tabernacles; Deut. 16:16; cf. Exod. 12:14–28), the public reading of the Mosaic law every seventh year (Deut. 31:12–13), the covenant renewal enactments (Deut. 29–30; Josh. 23–24), the annual national festivals/fasts, sabbath worship, historical teaching memorials, tabernacle/temple architecture and furnishings, the sacrificial system, and priestly dress and liturgical function.

Although the Old Testament lacks specific documentation, it is assumed by analogy to known practices in the rest of the ancient Near East that formal learning centers or schools existed in ancient Israel. Hints of these organized schools for particular training are scattered throughout the

Old Testament, especially in the company of the prophets associated with Elisha (2 Kings 2:3, 5; 6:1–2; cf. 1 Sam. 19:20), the wisdom tradition of the Book of Proverbs, the Jerusalem temple conservatory of music (cf. 1 Chron. 25:8), and the office of sage or counselor associated with Israelite kingship (cf. 1 Kings 4:5–6; 12:6, 10; Jer. 18:18).

In addition to formal learning centers, the Old Testament indicates specialized training took place in organized labor guilds of various sorts. This instruction for vocational, technical, and professional service to society (and especially palace and temple) included military training, arts and crafts (smiths, artisans, weavers, potters), music, royal officials (scribes, historians, overseers), temple personnel (priests, levites, gatekeepers, treasurers, judges), and domestic servants (midwives, cooks, bakers, perfumers).

Education in Later Judaism. Important developments in education during this period included the rise of the synagogue as both a religious and educational institution; the emergence of scribal schools for copying, studying, and interpreting the Hebrew Scriptures; and the establishment of "schools" or academies for the study of the Torah under the tutelage of well-known rabbis or teachers. However, three items deserve mention in the development of the educational process in Judaism because of their theological significance for the New Testament and Christianity.

First, the formative period of Judaism (roughly from the reforms of Ezra to the time of Maccabees) witnessed the expansion of the religious content or curriculum of Jewish education. This new material, known as the Mishnah, was accumulated oral tradition supplementing the Mosaic law. The Mishnah, along with analysis and commentary, was eventually codified in the Talmud, the final written form of this earlier oral tradition. The Talmud was accorded equal standing with the Old Testament Scriptures in the Jewish rabbinic schools. In part, this led to the rift between Jesus and his religious Jewish counterparts because he rejected the authority of the oral tradition, decrying a religion that neglected the law of God to cling to the traditions of men (Mark 7:1–9).

Second, the emphasis on law keeping or obedience to God's commands eventually led to a pharisaical legalism that tithed spice seeds with ruthless calculation (Matt. 23:23). Regrettably, devotion to the law of God displaced devotion to God himself so that certain circles of Judaism now ignored the very essence of Torah—faith, justice, and mercy. Ironically, this was the intended educational outcome of that original mandate for instruction in the way of the Lord given to Abraham (Gen. 18:19).

Third, the idea of biblical study (and study in general) as worship emerges during this time period. The precedent for understanding study as an act of worship stems from the Old Testament, where the psalmist remarked that all those who delight in the works of God study (or "worshipfully investigate") them (Ps. 111:2).

Education in New Testament Times. Much of the New Testament understanding of education is simply assumed from the practice of the Old Testament and Judaism. For example, the family remains the primary context for education, with prominence also given to the church as the extended family or community of faith. Likewise, the goal of educating the whole person, mind and character, carries over from Hebrew practice in the Old Testament. Even the methodology of both instilling information and drawing out or developing the innate talents and abilities of the student finds its antecedent in the Old Testament.

The New Testament focuses its attention on educating the whole person (intellect, emotions, and will), educating through personal relationship (i.e., the mentoring relationship of teacher and disciple), the process of both instilling knowledge and encouraging learning through discovery, and educating through experiential learning. Especially important theologically are the truths of educating the whole person (so that intellectual knowledge is applied to personal behavior; James 1:25; 1 John 2:2–6); and the work of God's Spirit in illuminating the learner as he or she is instructed in the faith (John 16:5–15; 1 John 2:26–27).

The Teacher Come from God. According to the Gospel records, much of Jesus' public ministry was spent teaching his disciples, as well as the crowds. Jesus was recognized and acknowledged as a teacher (or rabbi) by his disciples, the general public, and contemporary Jewish religious leaders, including Nicodemus who identified Jesus as "a teacher who has come from God" (John 3:2). Indeed, Jesus even referred to himself as teacher on several occasions (Mark 14:14; John 13:13).

The Gospels consistently report that people were astonished or amazed at the teaching of Jesus (Mark 1:22; 11:18; Luke 4:32). What made Jesus a "master teacher"? Granted he was God incarnate—a unique human being as the Son of Man. And yet, the approach, method, and content utilized by Jesus in his teaching continue to be paradigmatic for Christian education.

By way of approach, for instance, Jesus sometimes initiated the teaching moment (e.g., the Samaritan woman in John 4), but many times the learner(s) actually engaged Jesus in a teaching moment (Nicodemus in John 3). Jesus also had the ability to teach effectively informal educational settings (Mark 12:35), or more spontaneously as the need arose or circumstance dictated (Mark 9:33–37). Jesus was not afraid to hide the truth from some (those who were not seeking the truth or those who in their pride thought they already possessed it) so others find the truth (Matt. 13:10–17).

Perhaps the best word for describing the method of Jesus' teaching is "varied." Whether by object lesson or alternative speech forms (parable, rhetorical question, personal conversation, or public discourse), Jesus arrested and held the attention of the learner. His knowledge of human personality and behavior and his sensitivity to human need enabled him to meet the learner on his or her terms and turf.

Finally, Jesus amazed his audiences because he taught with authority. Not only was he forceful, persuasive, and dynamic in his presentation, but the content of his teaching was rooted in the message of the Old Testament Scriptures—the word of God. More important, he knew well the curriculum he taught and owned it personally—his life mirrored his teaching—much to the chagrin of the hypocrites who challenged him.

The Apostles' Teaching. Religious education or instruction in the Christian faith served another important purpose in the New Testament: exposing false teachers and their subversive doctrines. The teaching of sound biblical doctrine prevented the individual Christian and the Christian church(es) from being duped by "strange teachings" (Eph. 4:14; 2 Thess. 2:15; Heb. 13:9). Also, the teaching of apostolic doctrine both fostered Christian discernment of false teachers and their lies (1 Tim. 1:3–7) and authenticated the veracity of the Christian message (1 Tim. 6:1–5; 1 Peter 5:12). So much so that Paul reminded Titus that sound teaching shames the critics of Christianity because the doctrine of God is adorned by the lifestyle of "model citizens"—believers in Christ trained in godliness (2:6–10).

Catechism. Teaching, along with prophecy and revelation, are identified as those activities that will prove most beneficial for the building up of the church (1 Cor. 14:6, 12). Teaching was integral to the apostolic mission as Jesus charged his disciples to take the gospel of the kingdom of God to the nations (Matt. 28:20). Early on this teaching consisted of systematic instruction in the apostles' doctrine (informally?; cf. Acts 2:42), and the public reading and teaching of Scripture in corporate worship (1 Tim. 4:13). Later, catechism or oral instruction in Christian doctrine became a necessary prelude to baptism in early church practice. Only through sound teaching could people come to know the truth and escape the snare of the evil one (2 Tim. 2:24–26).

Since teaching was vital to Christian faith, life, and growth, Christ endowed his church with spiritual gifts including the office of pastor-teacher (Eph. 4:11) and the gift of teaching (Rom. 12:7; 1 Cor. 14:6, 26). Teachers were distinguished as leaders in the church, along with apostles and prophets, from the earliest days of church history (cf. Acts 13:1). In addition, one of the requirements for the office of bishop or elder in the church was the ability to teach (1 Tim. 3:2; 2 Tim. 2:24; Titus 2:9). The basic purpose of Christian teaching according to Paul was godliness—instruction leading to maturity in Christ (Col. 1:28).

The New Testament teaches us several important pedagogical and theological lessons appropriate for application in contemporary Christian education. First, education attends to the whole person—mind and body, emotions and will. Second, the New Testament understands education as a process of both instilling (imparting information to the pupil) and extracting (drawing out learning from the pupil or self-discovery). Third, effective education is rooted in a mentoring relationship (note Jesus with his disciples or the apostles training others to follow their lead). Fourth, the content of Jesus' and the apostles' teaching was essentially ethical; being or character and doing or practice are vitally connected with knowing.

Ultimately, biblical education is instruction in a lifestyle. For this reason, the apostle Paul reminded his pupil Timothy, "you . . . know all about my teaching, my way of life continue in what you learned" (2 Tim. 3:10, 14). Not only is biblical education a lifestyle—it is a lifetime!

ANDREW E. HILL

Bibliography. J. Adelson, ed., *Handbook of Adolescent Psychology;* W. Barclay, *Educational Ideals in the Ancient World;* S. Benko and J. J. O'Rourke, eds., *The Catacombs and the Colosseum;* S. F. Bonner, *Education in Ancient Rome from the Elder Cato to the Younger Pliny;* W. Brueggemann, *The Creative Word: Canon as Model for Biblical Education;* R. P. Chadwick, *Teaching and Learning;* M. L. Clarke, *Higher Education in the Ancient World;* N. Drazin, *History of Jewish Education from 515 B.C.E. to 220 C.E.;* J. Elias, ed., *Psychology and Religious Education;* T. H. Groome, *Christian Religious Education;* M. Haran, *VTSup* 40 (1988): 81–95; *ISBE,* 2:21–27; S. N. Kramer, *The Sumerians;* H. I. Marrou, *A History of Education in Antiquity;* F. Mayer, *A History of Educational Thought;* G. F. Moore, *Judaism;* I. A. Muirhead, *Education in the New Testament;* R. N. Whybray, *The Intellectual Tradition in the Old Testament;* M. Wilson, *Our Father Abraham;* R. Zuck, *Teaching as Jesus Taught.*

Egypt. One of the great powers of the ancient Near East, Egypt dominated the international stage during the prestate life of Israel. By the time of the united monarchy, Egypt had entered the long twilight of its power and influence. During its decline, the Nile kingdom remained a potential threat to the Hebrew state as exemplified, by the attack of Shishak in the fifth year of Rehoboam (1 Kings 14:25), but this threat diminished over time. To the independent states of Israel and Judah, international threats increasingly came from the north.

Despite its diminished historical role, Egypt remained a potent theological symbol. Throughout the Bible, Egypt fulfills a dual role both as a place of refuge and a place of oppression, a place to "come up out of" and a place to flee to. This role begins with Abraham. He seeks refuge in Egypt because "there was a famine in the land" (Gen. 12:10); yet he must leave when Pharaoh wants to place Sarah in the royal harem. This is also the first recorded encounter of the divine ruler of Egypt and Yahweh the God of Abraham.

The story of Joseph gives a much more detailed picture of Egypt and the ambiguity of its role. Egypt is a place of oppression, as Joseph is initially enslaved, eventually ending up in prison. Egypt is also a place of hope and refuge as Joseph is raised to be second in the land. From this position of great power he is able to provide a refuge from famine for his family. One of the themes of the Joseph story is that God is not restricted by national boundaries. He blesses the property of Potipher (and, by extension, Potipher himself) when Joseph is his overseer (Gen. 39:5). Egypt had a reputation as a place of wisdom, and Joseph appeals to this aura by calling on them to find a man "discerning and wise" (Gen. 41:33). Of course, Joseph is the man they need, one of the Wise, those who know the way the world works in both a divine and a human sense.

The place of wisdom, the land of refuge and hope, becomes the land of slavery when "a new king, who did not know about Joseph, came to power in Egypt" (Exod. 1:8). The harsh experience of the Israelites in Egypt colors all later references to the land. Throughout the course of the struggle between Pharaoh and Yahweh, Egypt comes to represent all that is opposed to God. The fabled wisdom of Egypt is revealed as false wisdom, powerless to help the Egyptians defeat the God of Israel. Even the divine Pharaoh is unmasked as a man subject to death like his people.

The equation of Egypt with oppression becomes foundational to the people of Israel, providing the setting for the fundamental religious ritual of Passover. For the Deuteronomist, the right of God to demand worship from his people is based partly on his historic role as liberator. "Do not forget the LORD; who brought you out of Egypt, out of the land of slavery" (Deut. 6:12). This was done because "the LORD loved you . . . and brought you out with a mighty hand and redeemed you from the land of slavery, from the power of Pharaoh king of Egypt" (7:8).

By the time of Solomon, Egypt is no longer an oppressor but a trading partner (1 Kings 10:28), diplomatic relation, and cultural influence. The writer of 1 Kings declares that Solomon's wisdom is "greater than all the wisdom of Egypt" (4:30). The Egyptian role as oppressor of the people of God soon shifts to Assyria and Babylonia.

In an ironic twist, Egypt becomes a place of refuge after the Babylonian capture of Jerusalem. Yet it is a false refuge, as the fleeing Hebrews place their trust in a dying nation rather than in the living God. Like the people lost in the wilderness, some of the survivors of the destruction of Judah would rather live in relative peace in Egypt than be available for God in Palestine. Jeremiah delivers the verdict of God: "I will punish those who live in Egypt with the sword, famine and plague, as I punished Jerusalem" (Jer. 44:13).

God speaks of his love for his people in an oracle of the prophet Hosea: "When Israel was a child, I loved him, and out of Egypt I called my son" (11:1). Yet the people reject God and he laments, "Will they not return to Egypt and will not Assyria rule over them because they refuse to repent?" (v. 5). In this oracle, Egypt functions again as a place of oppression, this time under Assyria.

In the Gospel of Matthew, Egypt is both a place of refuge and a place to come out of. One of Matthew's goals in writing his Gospel is to present Jesus as a new Moses. Matthew reports that Joseph was warned in a dream to take Jesus and his mother "and escape to Egypt" (Matt. 2:14). After the death of Herod, an angel tells Joseph to return to the land of Israel. Matthew applies the oracle of Hosea 11 to this situation, further linking Jesus with the historic suffering of the people of God (Matt. 2:15). Like Moses, Jesus comes out from Egypt, escaping the temptation of luxury, ease, and a peaceful life. Instead, he will fulfill the will of God and follow the lifelong road to Jerusalem. THOMAS W. DAVIS

See also EXODUS, THEOLOGY OF; MOSES.

Bibliography. D. Hill, *The Gospel of Matthew;* J. M. Miller and J. H. Hayes, *A History of Israel and Judah.*

El, Elohim. *See* GOD, NAMES OF.

Elder. In both the Old and New Testaments, the term "elder" indicates one of advanced age (Heb. *zāqēn;* Gk. *presbyteros*) who had a office of leadership within the people of God.

The Old Testament. We are not informed about the origin of this office, which was also known outside Israel (Gen. 50:7; Num. 22:7). It probably developed from the tribal structure, the elder being the head of a family or tribe. The basic criterion of age was significant, for it connoted both the experience and wisdom that comes with age (Deut. 32:7; cf. 1 Kings 12:6–8, 13; Ps. 37:25) and the respect owing the elder (Lam. 5:12). Growing older, however, did not necessarily mean growing wiser. Wisdom could be with the young rather than the old. Therefore elders had to be chosen carefully. Elders could serve locally as elders of a city (Judg. 8:14), regionally as elders of a tribe (Judg. 11:5), and nationally as elders of the nation (Exod. 3:16).

The key duties of the elders could be summarized as being the twofold task of judging and discipline generally, and of ruling and guiding the people in an orderly way. In this manner the elders were to be in God's serve and to be instrumental for the preservation of life with God in the covenant community.

With respect to the task of judging, elders were appointed in the wilderness wanderings by Moses, with the cooperation of Israel, in order to help him judge the people (Exod. 18:13–26; Deut. 1:13). In the promised land, elders were also to be appointed to maintain justice locally (Deut. 16:18; cf. 21:18–21; 22:15–19; Ruth 4:1–12), but a higher tribunal of priests and a judge existed for difficult cases (Deut. 17:8–9).

The ruling task of elders was theirs from earliest times. Their leadership position was evident from the fact that Moses had to go to the elders, he would have to go to Pharaoh (Exod. 3:16–18). The elders' position of authority was also clear from their asking Jephthah to lead them in the fight against the Ammonites (Judg. 11:4–11), from their seeking a king from Samuel (1 Sam. 8:4–5), and from their anointing David king over all Israel (2 Sam. 5:3; 1 Chron. 11:3; cf. 2 Sam. 3:17–18; cf. also the presence of the elders in 2 Sam. 17:1–4). The elders' leadership was evident in other ways as well. Along with the priests, they were responsible for seeing to it that Israel walked obediently in God's ways. They too received the law, which had to be read every seven years (Deut. 31:9–13). They had to make sure that the law functioned and that God's people remembered the mighty acts of God (Deut. 27:1; 31:28; 32:7; cf. 2 Kings 23:1–3). Faithful elders were of great importance to keep the nation faithful to their God (Josh. 24:31; Judg. 2:7). Indeed, the elders' first responsibility was to God. In this way they would serve the well-being of Israel.

To do their vital tasks of judging and ruling, elders were to be capable men who feared God and were upright (Exod. 18:21, 25); they were to be wise, understanding, and experienced (Deut. 1:13); and they were empowered by the Holy Spirit (Num. 11:16–17). Although bad counsel could be given (e.g., 1 Sam. 4:3), generally good advice was expected and that characteristic became associated with the elder.

The Intertestamental Period. The office of elder survived the Babylonian exile, but not without change. As previously, elders were in positions of leadership both in the homeland (Ezra 10:14) and Babylon (Jer. 29:1; Ezek. 8:1; 14:1; 20:1, 3). With the disintegration of the tribal unit, influential families came to fill the void of authority left by the breakdown of the clan. Whereas the elders' authority once derived from their position within the tribe, real authority now became based on the prominence of a particular family and an aristocratic ruling class emerged.

By the second century B.C., we read of a council comprised of aristocratic elders (cf. 1 Macc. 12:6 with 14:20; Josephus, *Antiquities*, 12.3.3), which by the first century was known as the Sanhedrin (Josephus, *Antiquities*, 14.9.3–5). Although elders were historically the oldest members, in later times they became less important compared to the priests and scribes and the term "elders" came to signify lay members. This is the situation encountered in the New Testament, where the triad of chief priests, scribes, and elders is often referred to as the Sanhedrin (Mark 11:27; 14:43; also cf. Matt. 16:21; Mark 15:1).

The New Testament. The office of elder in the New Testament church cannot be fully understood without the background of the Old Testament local elder, an office still functioning in New Testament Judaism with duties pertaining to discipline and leadership (cf. Luke 7:3 and the implications of Matt. 10:17 and John 9:22). The first Christians were Jewish and the office was familiar to them. Thus Luke did not need to explain his first reference to Christian elders in Acts 11:30.

New Testament elders (*presbyteroi*) are also called bishops (*episkopoi*) without implying any essential difference in the office referred to. In Acts 20:17, 28 and Titus 1:5, 7 the two names are used interchangeably. Also the requirements for the office of the elders and bishops are very similar (cf. Titus 1:5–9 and 1 Tim. 3:1–7). The term "elder" stresses the connection with the age of the office bearer, while the term "bishop" emphasizes the nature of the task that is to be done. A distinction is made (in 1 Tim. 5:17) between those elders who rule well, especially those who labor in the preaching and teaching (who are now called ministers), and others (who are now referred to as elders and whose full-time task is directing the affairs of the church).

With respect to the duties of an elder, there is a continuity with the basic tasks of the elder in the Old Testament. All elders have the task of oversight and discipline of the congregation (Acts 20:28) and all have the responsibility to rule and guide the people of God with the Word in a manner that is pleasing to God (Acts 20:29–31). Also elders in the new dispensation are to preserve and nurture life with God in the covenant community (1 Thess. 2:11–12). In executing this task they are in the service of their risen Lord (to whom they will have to give account; 1 Thess. 5:12; Heb. 13:17) and they are empowered by his Spirit (Acts 20:28; 1 Cor. 12:4–6).

The elders' task of oversight and discipline can be described in terms of keeping watch and shepherding on behalf of the great shepherd Jesus Christ. In Paul's farewell to the Ephesian elders he said: "Keep watch over yourselves and all the flock of which the Holy Spirit has made you overseers. Be shepherds of the church of God, which he bought with his own blood" (Acts 20:28). The pastoral character of this task of oversight is also indicated when Peter writes: "To the elders among you, I appeal as a fellow elder. . . . Be shepherds of God's flock that is under your care, serving as overseers—not because you must, but because you are willing, as God wants you to be; not greedy for money, but eager to serve; not lording it over those entrusted to you, but being examples to the flock. And when the Chief Shepherd appears, you will receive the crown of glory that will never fade away" (1 Peter 5:1–4).

With respect to the elder's task of ruling and guiding, he has been set over the congregation (1 Thess. 5:12; 1 Tim. 5:17). He is a steward of God (Titus 1:7), a manager of God's household who administers the spiritual treasures of the mysteries of God (1 Cor. 4:1; cf. Matt. 13:11, 52). Of prime importance, therefore, is to be the administration of the glad tidings. False doctrine must be opposed and the true safeguarded (Acts 20:28, 31; Titus 1:9–11). Like their Old Testament counterparts, the elders are to see to it that the gospel and the demands of the Lord are imprinted in the hearts and lives of God's people (1 Thess. 2:11–12; 2 Tim. 2:24–26).

In light of the awesome responsibilities, it is not surprising that the prerequisites of the office are high (1 Tim. 3:1–7; Titus 1:6–9). The elder must be a blameless and God-fearing man who shows the fruits of the Spirit in his walk of life. He must also be able to teach others the way of the Lord, and confute heretics (1 Tim. 3:2; 2 Tim. 3:14–17; Titus 1:9), but not be quarrelsome (1 Tim. 3:3) or enter into senseless controversies (1 Tim. 1:3; 6:4–5). A good knowledge of the Word of God is therefore essential.

The necessary qualifications for the office suggest that elders must be chosen very carefully. They are not to be recent converts (1 Tim. 3:6) and must have proven themselves (1 Tim. 3:7). Elders could be simply appointed (Titus 1:5) although congregational participation may very well have been involved in at least some instances.

In Revelation 4:4 the twenty-four elders sitting on twenty-four thrones surrounding the throne of God probably represent the entire church (twenty-four for the twelve patriarchs of the Old Testament and the twelve apostles of the New Testament; cf. Rev. 21:12–14). These heavenly elders wear white garments, have crowns of gold, and worship God (4:4, 10–11; 5:7–10; 11:16–18; 19:4).

CORNELIS VAN DAM

Bibliography. G. Berghoef and L. De Koster, *The Elders Handbook: A Practical Guide for Church Leaders;* W. Hendriksen, *Exposition of the Pastoral Epistles;* idem, *More Than Conquerors: An Interpretation of the Book of Revelation;* G. W. Knight, III, *The New Testament Teaching on the Role Relationship of Men and Women;* J. B. Lightfoot, *The Christian Ministry;* J. Piper and W. Grudem, *Recovering Biblical Manhood and Womanhood: A Response to Evangelical Feminism.*

Elect, Election. The term "elect" means essentially "to choose." It involves discriminatory evaluation of individuals, means, ends, or objects with a view to selecting one above the others, although not necessarily passing negative judgment on those others. It also involves the will, in that a determination is made, a preference expressed that one seeks to bring to reality. In that preference is expressed, the idea of bestowing favor or blessing is often present. After Judah had fallen because of her sin in 586 B.C., the prophet Zechariah proclaimed forgiveness, saying God would again "choose" (show favor to) Jerusalem (2:12), and he was told "Proclaim further: This is what the LORD Almighty says: 'My towns will again overflow with prosperity, and the LORD will again comfort Zion and choose Jerusalem'" (1:17).

In the Scriptures the term "choose" is used of both God and human beings. With respect to human beings, it covers all human decisions. We choose husbands or wives (Gen. 6:2), working companions (Acts 15:40), where to live (Gen. 13:11), and our way of life, whether good or bad (1 Peter 4:3). Sometimes the choice thrust on us is of the utmost consequence. We may choose life or death (Deut. 30:19; 2 Kings 18:32); we may choose to serve (or not to serve) God (Josh. 24:15). Our choices are seen to be consistent with what we are. A good tree bears good fruit, a brackish spring pours forth brackish water, and the pig returns to wallowing in the mire.

God also makes choices and by a large margin, the term "choose" is used in Scripture to refer to the choices of God rather than human choices. Indeed, we often do not know what to choose (Phil. 1:22) and often our choices are wrong and need to be overridden by God. David chose to build a temple for God, but was told by God, "Solomon your son is the one who will build my house and my courts, for I have chosen him" (1 Chron. 28:6). What human beings should ideally do is choose what is right and pleasing to God (Isa. 56:4). If we adjust our choices to God's choices (line our wills up with his will), we will have the fullest of God's blessings.

Since it is true that mere human choices are made according to what the person is, it goes without saying that God's choices are made in accordance with who God is. God's choices and decisions are fully consistent with his eternal wisdom, goodness, justice, fairness, and love. Nothing that God chooses to do is mean-spirited, vindictive, or wrong. God cannot act any other way than consistently with his eternal divine nature. For this reason, human beings may trust God to do what is right, and our highest good is to choose the will of God for ourselves.

This does not mean that we will always understand God's ways and the choices he makes. Often we will not. There are times when the ways of God are decidedly not our ways and his thoughts are past finding out. When Habakkuk was confronted by his own people's sin, he cried out for an answer as to why God seemingly chose to do nothing about it. "How long, O LORD, must I call for help? . . . Why do you tolerate wrong?" (1:2–3) was his question. But the answer was even more disturbing than the problem. God had chosen to use the Babylonians to punish sinful Judah (1:12–13). The Lord had determined that judgment would come upon Judah, but he also determined that Babylon would be held accountable for its sins, and in the end "the earth will be filled with the knowledge of the glory of the LORD, as the waters cover the sea" (2:13–14). God would triumph and Habakkuk was to live by faith in God, because God's choices, no matter how inexplicable they might be, in the end, produce what is best (2:4; 3:19).

God's choices not only arise from within his own eternal being and are consistent with what he is, but they are also based on his own divinely chosen plan. This renders them purposeful rather than arbitrary. They are not a randomly chosen collection of acts or decisions that have no inner coherence. Rather, according to an eternal plan, based on God's goodness, grace, and love, he weaves his will into the fabric of fallen human history and there triumphs (Eph. 1:9–12). Again, we might not always be able to see the ultimate intent of that plan but we may live in the assurance that it is operative in our lives and that it takes precedence over lesser plans and intents, no matter how urgent and all-encompassing they may seem at the moment. The ultimate explanation awaits its appointed time; it will certainly come and will not prove false (Hab. 2:2–3).

God's Election of Angels. There is only one reference to elect angels in the Scripture (1 Tim. 5:21). In this passage Paul is admonishing Timothy in the presence of God, Jesus Christ, and the elect angels to live a godly life. Here, the angels are described as elect, in all probability because of their confirmed goodness or perfection. Just as God and Jesus Christ are unalterably good, so are these angels of God, and we are to live in the presence of every form of ultimate goodness with that as a reference point.

God's Election of Israel. Both the Old and the New Testaments affirm the gracious election of Israel. It is clearly stated in terms such as these: "The LORD your God has chosen you out of all the peoples on the face of the earth to be his people, his treasured possession" (Deut. 7:6). There is an inexplicable mystery in this. Israel was not chosen because they were better, more faithful, more numerous, or more obedient than anyone else. The only reason given for Israel's election is the love of God—"Because he loved your forefathers and chose their descendants after them, he brought you out of Egypt by his presence and his great strength" (Deut. 4:37). The election of Israel was structured within the covenant that God made with his people. By accepting the terms of the covenant that signaled their election, Israel was privileged to experience a personal relationship with God. But it also brought with it a heavy responsibility. They were to be obedient to God and follow his commands implicitly. If they refused to do God's will they would experience the heavy hand of God's judgment to the same degree that they had experienced the grace and blessing of God. "You only have I chosen [known] of all the families of the earth; therefore I will punish you for all your sins" (Amos 3:2). But, as the apostle Paul saw it, the gifts and calling of God are irrevocable (Rom. 11:29) and Israel's disobedience did not cancel her out, but opened the way for everyone to enter in. This, to Paul, was perhaps the ultimate mystery: One man's fall (Adam) meant the redemption of many and one nation's sin (Israel) meant the inclusion of all. The grace of God was so vast and overwhelming that it broke apart every conventional limiting structure through that very limiting structure itself (election).

God's Election of the Place of Worship. God chose Israel to be his people and to reveal the truth about himself to them. This included the proper way to worship him, so he also chose the land they should dwell in (Deut. 10:11; 1 Kings 8:48), the mountain on which worship should take place (Ps. 68:16), the city where this worship should occur (1 Kings 8:48; 11:13; 14:21), and a temple for the people to worship in (1 Kings 9:3; 2 Kings 21:7). God also chose the priesthood (Num. 16:5, 7) as well as the way sacrifices should be offered.

God's Election of People to an Office. In order for Israel and later the church to function as God's people, specific functions of leadership needed to be exercised and God's choices needed to be honored. If the wrong people led, as was too often the case, disaster frequently followed. When God was consulted and his guidance was followed, blessing also ensued. The two areas where official leadership was exercised in the Old Testament were in the civil and the religious spheres. The civil leader was the king and Israel was told "be sure to appoint over you the King the lord your God chooses" (Deut. 17:15). That was the general rule. Specific kings were also pointed out, such as Saul (1 Sam. 9:15–17), David (1 Sam. 16:1–12), and Solomon (1 Chron. 28:5–7; 2 Chron. 1:8–10). God also made it known when he had not chosen someone (1 Sam. 16:5–10). In the religious sphere, the tribe of Levi was chosen as the priests (Deut. 21:5; 2 Chron. 29:5, 11) and Aaron to be the high priest (Num. 17:5, 8; 1 Sam. 2:27–28). In the New Testament, the apostles were originally chosen by Christ (Luke 6:13; Acts 1:2), but then after Christ's ascension, the church needed to fill the place of Judas. Two men were selected and then they prayed, "Lord, you know everyone's heart. Show us which of these two you have chosen to take over this apostolic ministry" (Acts 1:24–26).

God's Election of Individuals for Various Reasons. In addition to specific offices, God often chooses individuals for special tasks or for special reasons. There are many examples of this in both the Old and New Testaments. In the Old Testament, God chose Bezalel (Exod. 31:2; 35:30–33), Abraham (Gen. 18:19), Jacob (Ps. 135:4), Judah (1 Chron. 28:4; Ps. 78:68), Moses (Ps. 106:23), and Zerubbabel (Hag. 2:23). In the New Testament, God chose special individuals as witnesses to Christ's resurrection (Acts 10:41), Paul to be an apostle to the Gentiles (Acts 9:15; 22:13–14), Peter to be the first to minister to the Gentiles (Acts 15:7), and Barnabas to accompany Paul on his first missionary journey (Acts 13:2–3).

God's Election of the Messiah. The redemptive ministry of God's Anointed One, the Messiah, was carefully planned for by God. The Messiah, his own Son Jesus Christ, was the Chosen One, par excellance. Through prophetic utterances in the Old Testament there gradually accumulated a virtually complete picture of who the Messiah was to be, what he would do, and the consequences of his ministry. Isaiah 42:1 speaks of him as "My chosen one, in whom I delight." Jesus heard these very words on the Mount of Transfiguration (Luke 9:35) and his tormenters hurled these words at him while he was on the cross, fulfilling the prophecies spoken of old (Luke 23:35). Peter later reflects on Jesus' chosenness and speaks of it as eternal (1 Peter 1:20), as indeed it was, and emphasizes Jesus' divinely chosen task (2:4–5) and his chosen place as cornerstone of the church (2:6).

God's Election of Means to Accomplish Ends. In some instances the specific ways God chooses to accomplish his purposes are emphasized. This is usually to highlight that God's ways are not the ways human beings would have chosen. So Paul points out that God has chosen the foolish, weak, and lowly things, from the world's point of view as the instruments of mighty saving grace (1 Cor. 1:27–28). James says God chooses the poor to be rich in faith (James 2:5).

God's Election to Salvation of Believers and the Believing Community. In Scripture salvation is considered the work of God. People are lost and it is God alone who saves them; beside him there is no other savior (Isa. 43:11) and no other plan of salvation (Acts 4:12). Whatever it be, whether false gods, other human beings, angels or other supernatural beings, or even ourselves—they cannot save us. Because it is God alone who saves, those who are saved are seen to be the ones whom God has chosen (or elected) to be saved. This does not mean that they were not in some way involved in their salvation, but it does mean that God took the initiative, effected the plan, provided the grace, and deserves all the credit for the salvation of his people. None who is ultimately redeemed can boast that they saved themselves or that they added anything to the salvation that they received through Jesus Christ.

Those who are saved, the believers in Jesus Christ, are called "the elect (chosen)" (Matt. 24:22; Rom. 8:33; Col. 3:12; Titus 1:1; Rev. 17:14). This is based on Old Testament usage, where Israel is God's elect community. In the New Testament, the believers are God's elect. They are called the elect because God chose them to be saved (Matt. 22:14; John 6:37, 39; 15:16, 19; Acts 13:48; Rom. 11:5; 1 Thess. 1:4). This election is understood to be an eternal act in accordance with God's foreknowledge or predetermination (Eph. 1:4; 1 Peter 1:1–2). The term is applied to those who believe and also to potential believers—those whom God has yet to save are called the elect (2 Tim. 1:9).

Inasmuch as God has chosen some to be saved, he has also chosen how he will save them. Jesus the Messiah is God's Chosen One and believers are chosen in him (Eph. 1:4). God chooses to regenerate through the word of truth (James 1:18), the work of the Holy Spirit (1 Peter 1:1–2) and personal faith (2 Thess. 2:13).

God's elect are chosen specifically to show both God's praise (1 Peter 2:9) and to live in obedience to Christ (1 Peter 1:2). As God's chosen ones they are protected by him—God works everything together for their good (Rom. 8:28), none can bring any charge against them (Rom. 8:33), and nothing can separate them from the love of God in Jesus Christ the Lord (Rom. 8:39).

As with Israel in the Old Testament, so with the believers in the New Testament, the only reason given for why God chose someone to salvation is his love (Eph. 1:4–5).

Conclusion. Scripture presents God as a loving, personal being who created the universe and is intimately involved in its affairs, maintaining it and working out everything according to a benevolent, eternal plan. In order to accomplish this he elects (chooses) that certain things be done, that certain people do them, that it be done a certain way, and that, in the end, his redemptive purposes be accomplished. When human beings acknowledge God's choices by participating in them, they find life and blessing at its fullest. If they reject his choices, God will still accomplish his ultimate ends, but they suffer the consequences that attend the rejection of God's will.

WALTER A. ELWELL

See also ISRAEL; MESSIAH.

Bibliography. G. C. Berkouwer, *Divine Election;* D. A. Carson, *Divine Sovereignty and Human Responsibility;* L. Coenen, *NIDNTT,* 1:533–43; F. Davidson, *Pauline Predestination;* G. Quell, *TDNT,* 4:145–68; H. H. Rowley, *The Biblical Doctrine of Election;* G. Schrenk, *TDNT*, 4:172–92; H. Seebass, *TDOT,* 2:73–87; N. Turner, *Christian Words.*

Elijah. *Old Testament.* Elijah of Tishbe was a lone figure from the remote part of Gilead east of the Jordan. One of the better known characters in the Old Testament, he also made an impact on later Judaism and on the New Testament writers. A contemporary of the Israelite kings Ahab and Ahaziah (874–852 B.C.), Elijah represented a class of prophets who were normally not associated with any sanctuary or prophetic guild (but see 2 Kings 2:3–7). He challenged Ahab, whose policies were designed to replace the Israelite idea of kingship with the ancient Near Eastern concept of monarchy and royal law. Elijah defended Yahweh's sovereignty over history and justice, as well as over false gods (1 Kings 17–18).

The stories of Elijah (known as the Elijah cycle) dominate much of the latter half of 1 Kings (17–19, 21) and the early chapters of 2 Kings (1–2). The chronological order of the cycle is uncertain, making the course of Elijah's life obscure. The cycle was incorporated into the theological history of Israel and Judah, without which our knowledge for the reign of Ahab would be almost unknown. It contained six separate narratives that included several anecdotal stories about Elijah's life that may have circulated independently among his disciples in the northern kingdom. All but the last were concerned with the clash of Baal and Yahweh. Elijah appeared to vindicate the distinctive character of the people of God when their identification was threatened by Ahab's liberal policies. He also answered Jehoshaphat's question (2 Kings 3:11) and sent a letter to Jehoram (2 Chron. 21:12–15).

Elijah appeared on the scene without warning, introduction, or genealogy (1 Kings 17:1) to deliver an oracle to Ahab announcing a drought, presumably a punishment for defection to the Baal cult. Afterward, he returned to Zarephath where he was miraculously sustained (1 Kings 17:17–24). God then chose a Gentile believer (the Phoenician woman of Zarephath) to shame his people and to rebuke Jezebel, Ahab's Phoenician queen, showing that there was a Yahwistic believer in her own country. The unfailing water supply shows that God—not the king—was the dispenser of the water of life. Chrysostom said that Elijah learned compassion in the house of the widow so he could be sent to his own people. Yahweh did not just intervene at critical times in the affairs of people, but was now accessible to believers in the ordinary affairs of life (1 Kings 17:12).

Three years later there was a break in the drought and Elijah was successful in ending Baal worship at Carmel. The Baal priests were not completely destroyed; they actually continued on past the end of the Ahab dynasty, until the time of Athaliah of Judah (who was related to Ahab's royal house). Elijah helped Israel understand that Yahweh guided the fortunes of the nations; even the Baal cult was under his control. Yahweh, not Baal, had the power of life and death, and was the giver of rain and good things. The Carmel story showed a reminiscence of the change of political and religious sovereignty from Tyre to Israel. Israel was not truly synchretistic; Baal or Yahweh would be king, but not both (1 Kings 18:21). Ahab was not wholly Baalist; his family bore Yahwistic names, and he consulted with Yahweh after the encounter with Elijah (1 Kings 20:13–15, 22, 28). The Tyrian cult of Baal Melqart may have been a pseudo-monotheistic movement that precipitated this struggle. Israel now saw the mediation of God's will in history and the interpretation of his divine will.

Elijah's success was merely temporary; he fled to Mount Horeb (although this may not be in chronological order) to escape Jezebel's wrath (1 Kings 19). Here, the small voice of God was in direct opposition to the noisy and primitive sounds of the Canaanite deities, which pointed toward a more spiritual and transcendent concept of Yahweh. The theophany in 1 Kings 19 is similar to Exodus 33:19, and like the story of the widow, may show that God is to be found in the daily affairs of humans, rather than in supernatural phenomena.

Like Amos in a later period, Elijah showed an astute social concern, emerging as a leader with strong ethical ideals (1 Kings 21). The Naboth incident shows a social dimension in the clash between Israelite law and Canaanite kingship. By appropriating Naboth's land as crown property, Ahab was out of his jurisdiction. Inalienable land in Israel was in principle hereditary, although Yahweh was the true owner. In this position, God demanded the rule of law and justice, and watched over ethical and legal morals. Elijah, whom Ahab saw as a blood avenger (v. 20), is introduced with dramatic suddenness only at the end of this section, confronting Ahab for taking possession of the vineyard. The king was indicted for infringing on two of the ten commandments that were recognized as the basis for society: murder and forcible appropriation, both capital offenses. The curse concerning Ahab was not literally executed on him, however, but on his successor. This may have been because of his repentance, but probably was due to the Hebrew idea of the extended self, taking for granted the cohesion of life and liability between generations. Ahab's dynasty ended because of the Naboth incident, not because of the Baal struggle. Later, Elijah protested Ahaziah's appeal to Baal-Zebub, the local god of Ekron (2 Kings 1:9–15; Josephus called this god "the lord of the flies," as did the Ras Shamra texts). Elijah was here described as a hairy man with a shaggy cloak, evidently the insignia of a prophet (2 Kings 1:8).

The translation of Elijah into heaven occurs in an anecdotal section concerned mainly with Elisha (2 Kings 2:1–12). Elijah was associated with the prophetic guilds in Bethel, Gilgal, and Jericho. He did not bequeath his staff to Elisha, but his cloak, which had a spiritual not a magical power. Elisha desired a double portion of Elijah's spirit, a stipulation in Hebrew law whereby the eldest son received his share and was equipped as the true successor to his father. The whirlwind and sudden disappearance of Elijah, with the addition of a theophany, emphasize God's presence in the incident.

In later Old Testament prophetic tradition, Elijah was associated with the day of the Lord (Mal. 4:5–6), and was soon to be sent by God on the behalf of the people. He was described as similar to the messenger in Malachi 3:1 (which also may have been an allusion to Elijah, since both prepared the way for Yahweh). The purpose of Elijah's coming was either to pacify family quarrels (Mal. 2:10–16), culminating in a new social order, or to restore the covenant relationship.

Later Jewish Tradition. Elijah was prominently featured in popular legend and theological discussion of eschatological expectation during the intertestamental period. The reason for this may be his enigmatic rapture in 2 Kings 2:11 (the reward for his zeal for the law, according to 1 Macc. 2:58, which fostered the idea of his sinlessness), and the prophecy of his return in Malachi, which nurtured the idea of him becoming a messianic figure from the heavenly kingdom who came to purify the priesthood. He was said to be an intercessor for Israel in heaven, a heavenly scribe who recorded the acts of men, and who had an eternal existence (Ecclus. 48:1–14).

New Testament. The New Testament, which mentions the prophet nearly thirty times, shows the influence of the late Jewish tradition of Elijah being the forerunner of the Messiah. The expectation of Elijah's return occurs frequently in the Gospels (Matt. 17:10; Mark 9:11). Many were convinced that either Jesus (Matt. 16:14; Mark 6:15; 8:28; Luke 9:8, 19) or John the Baptist (John 1:21, 25) were the expected prophet. Although John denied that he was Elijah, he wore the prophet's style of clothing (a mantle of camel's hair and a leather girdle; Matt. 3:4; Mark 1:6). Moreover, Jesus said that John went forth as Elijah in spirit; he was thus the symbolic fulfillment of the prophet's mission (Matt. 11:14; Mark 8:28; Luke 1:17).

Although the tradition that Moses and Elijah would appear together in the last days was not to be found in rabbinic Judaism, both of these Old Testament characters were present and spoke at the transfiguration of Jesus, testifying to the importance of the impending events as eschatological (Matt. 17:3–4; Mark 9:4–5; Luke 9:30, 33). Some have seen the two as representing the Law and the Prophets, which were now both considered to be subservient to Christ.

Jesus' prayer on the cross with the opening words of Psalm 22:1, "Eli, Eli" (My God, My God) was either misunderstood or willfully misinterpreted as a petition for help to Elijah (Matt. 27:46–49; Mark 15:34–36). Jewish lore identified Elijah as a helper in time of need, and since Elijah did not come, Jesus' petition was considered a failure. The church, however, did not accept this figure of Elijah; only Christ himself would be called on in stressful times.

Various events of Elijah's life are alluded to in the New Testament. James uses Elijah as a powerful example of a supplicant (5:17), relying on Jewish tradition, which credited Elijah with a reputation for prayer (although this is not specifically mentioned in 1 Kings 17–18). He also describes the passage of time of the drought in 1 Kings 18:1 as three and a half years (cf. Luke 4:25; Rev. 11:6). James attempts to refute the Jewish tradition of the sinlessness and eternal nature of the prophet by stating that Elijah was a man "just like us." His prayers were effective because he was righteous.

Jesus used the story of God sending Elijah to the widow of Zarephath to show that the Gentiles were not to be excluded from salvation (Luke 4:25–26). Later church tradition takes the two witnesses of Revelation to be modeled after Moses and Elijah (Rev. 11:3–6). They were given the power to shut up the heavens and to bring the fire of judgment like Elijah in 1 Kings 17–18 (cf. Mal. 4:5; Ecclus. 48:1–14). In a similar vein, Jesus rebuked the sons of Zebedee for wondering whether they should call down fire from heaven on the Samaritan village (Luke 9:54).

Paul uses the rabbinic model of Elijah and the idea of the remnant of Israel in Romans 11:2–5 (see 1 Kings 19:10–18). Just as Elijah became aware that a remnant of true believers still existed in Israel, Paul understands that there was still a sacred remnant of Jews who were elected by grace.

MARK W. CHAVALAS

See also ISRAEL; KINGS, FIRST AND SECOND, THEOLOGY OF; PROPHET, PROPHETESS, PROPHECY.

Bibliography. F. Anderson, *JBL* 85 (1966): 46–57; H. Bietenhard, *NIDNTT,* 1:543–45; J. Gray, *I-II Kings;* J. Jeremias, *TDNT,* 2:928–41; H. H. Rowley, *BJRL* 43 (1960): 190–219; R. W. Wallace, *Elijah and Elisha.*

End, End Time. *See* DAY; DAY OF THE LORD, GOD, CHRIST.

Endurance Continuing Christian commitment in the face of difficulty. Born in a context of hostility, persecution, and the death of their Lord and his disciples, the endurance of Christians in the face of persecution and temptation underlies most the New Testament.

Pictorial athletic imagery was used to summon Christians to faithfulness as they prepared themselves for the race of life (cf. Rom. 12:11–12; 1 Cor. 9:24–27; Heb. 12:1–14). The repeated failures of Israel to maintain faithfulness to God in the exodus and at later times provided the New

Testament writers with forceful models of the nature of tragedy and unrealized hopes among God's people. These examples supplied the raw materials for Paul and others to formulate clear warnings to Christians about turning or retreating from the way of faithfulness and authenticity of life (e.g., 1 Cor. 10:1–12; Heb. 3:17–19).

While the warnings seem most severe in Hebrews (2:1–3; 5:11–6:8; 10:26–31)—a fact that has led many Christians to avoid reading the book—their point is rooted in the firm conviction of the writer that with the power of Christ believers will be able to endure no matter what the circumstance (6:9–19; 10:35–39) and persevere to the end (12:1–2).

The early Christians, however, were not superhuman. They failed their Lord in times of persecution and temptation, just as Peter did during the dark days of the crucifixion (John 18:10–11, 15–18, 25–27). But failure did not automatically mean their rejection in the manner of Israel's failure in the wilderness. Peter's restoration was for Christians a model of hope beyond painful denial (21:15–17). Yet restoration involved serious consequences. Reacceptance by Jesus and restoration for Peter meant he would have to endure to the point of death (21:18–19).

Because of the serious nature of renunciation in the early church, some Christians sought various means to ensure their endurance with God and their final acceptance into the kingdom of heaven. Some, viewing baptism as a cure-all for every sin, postponed their baptism until the point of death. Others developed a last rite that would sacramentally guarantee their acceptance from the time of their baptism or their final participation in a communion service.

Most evangelical theologians consider such views to be foreign to the New Testament perspective. They view endurance as a crucial aspect of a human's response in faithfulness to the gracious, loving God who in giving Christ provides acceptance and salvation (John 3:16). Endurance, then, is an inherent part of authentic "believing" that is expected of every Christian. Inadequate believing withdraws in times of confusion (John 6:66), but true commitment endures by looking to Christ for the resources of life (6:68).

Because Christians (like the authentic children of God in the Old Testament) take human weakness seriously, they realize the crucial necessity of divine support. Thus, prayer becomes a vital part of the Christian pilgrimage (Matt. 26:41; Acts 12:5; 14:23; Rom. 12:12; 2 Cor. 1:11; Phil. 4:6; 1 Thess. 3:10; 1 Peter 4:7). It is a key element in adequately arming the Christian for endurance in the battle against the forces of evil (Eph. 6:18). That battle is a lifelong one. To finish the race by keeping the faith offers to the one who endures the anticipation of a reward that is symbolized in a "crown of righteousness" (2 Tim. 4:1–8).

GERALD L. BORCHERT

See also APOSTASY; ASSURANCE; BACKSLIDING; DENIAL; PERSERVERANCE.

Bibliography. G. L. Borchert, *Assurance and Warning;* D. A. Carson, *Divine Sovereignty and Human Responsibility;* I. H. Marshall, *Kept by the Power.*

Enjoyment. *See* JOY.

Envy. Sin of jealousy over the blessings and achievements of others, especially the spiritual enjoyment and advance of the kingdom of Christ freely and graciously bestowed upon the people of God. Old Testament examples of the sin of jealousy include the rivalry of Joseph's brothers over the favor that Joseph received at the hand of God (Gen. 37:12–36; Acts 7:9), and Saul's animosity toward David for his physical and spiritual prowess (1 Sam. 18). Envy inevitably leads to personal harm and debilitation, affecting one's physical, spiritual, and emotional well-being (Job 5:2; Prov. 14:30). Unchecked, it gradually leads to a destructive and remorseful way of life (Prov. 27:4), and ultimately, to estrangement from God (Rom. 1:28–32).

Envy manifests the insidiousness of sin and human depravity apart from the intervention of God's redeeming grace. As a sin of the flesh, envy characterizes the lives of the unregenerate. Envy is one of the traits of the Christian's *former* way of life (Rom. 13:8–14; Titus 3:3). Those who practice envy and strife are barred from the kingdom of heaven (Gal. 5:19–26). Indeed, the unregenerate nature ever tends toward envy, manifesting the unbeliever's rejection of God, his truth, and his will for human conduct (James 3:14, 16).

The way of true wisdom counsels the faithful to avoid the company of such godless people (Prov. 24:1). Envy is listed among the sins of the flesh that must be conquered through the power of the Holy Spirit (1 Cor. 3:3; 2 Cor. 12:20; 1 Peter 2:1). "Do not let your heart envy sinners, but always be zealous for the fear of the LORD" (Prov. 23:17). Love is to have majesty over envy (1 Cor. 13:4).

As an example from former days, the righteous judgment of Yahweh against Edom was measured out in accordance with the measure of Edom's jealousy toward the people of God (Ezek. 35:11). But the mercy of God brought about the healing of animosity between Ephraim and Judah by means of God's righteous act of salvation (Isa. 11:13). In the time of Messiah's earthly ministry it was the envy of the Jews that led to the rejection and betrayal of Jesus into the hands of Pilate for crucifixion (Matt. 27:18). Nevertheless, in the providence and foreordination of God, what the wicked intended for evil was destined to be the instrument of God's redemption of his elect through the shed blood of Jesus Christ.

Paul points out how the good news of the gospel was preached at times out of envy and strife (Phil.

1:15). Yet in spite of the envious motives of the false apostles, Paul rejoiced that Christ was being proclaimed. Like Christ, the apostle in his ministry of the gospel experienced the hatred and jealousy of the Jews (Acts 13:45). This did not deter him from his divinely ordained mission. There were other times, however, that false teaching led to controversy and envy among the people of God (1 Tim. 6:4). Genuine, unfeigned love for God and his word prompts the disciples of Christ to proclaim and defend the full counsel of God's truth. Loving and consecrated devotion to Christ and his kingdom dissipates the sins of envy and jealousy.

MARK W. KARLBERG

See also COVETOUSNESS.

Ephesians, Theology of. Pauline authorship of Ephesians does not appear to have been doubted in the early church. It is listed among Paul's letters in the early manuscripts and cited as such by early Christian authors such as Irenaeus (*Against Heresies* 5.2.3), Clement of Alexandria (*Stromateis* 4.65), and Tertullian (*Against Marcion* 5.11.17; 5.17.1). It is included among Paul's letters as the Muratorian Canon, which is generally regarded as second century, and acknowledged as Paul's even by the heretic Marcion, who called it "Laodiceans."

Ephesians contains a carefully reasoned and precisely worded theology presented in a systematic way. There is no letter in the Pauline corpus that more precisely and succinctly presents the rudimentary elements of his understanding of salvation history than this one.

To grasp fully the theological core of this letter, it is important to remember the nature of Paul's conversion/call on the road to Damascus. He was told at that time by the divine voice: "get up and stand on your feet. I have appeared to you to appoint you as a servant and as a witness of what you have seen of me and what I will show you. I will rescue you from your own people and from the Gentiles. I am sending you to them to open their eyes and turn them from darkness to light, and from the power of Satan to God, so that they may receive forgiveness of sins and a place among those who are sanctified by faith in me'" (Acts 26:16–18).

Paul's entire life after this experience was guided by this commission he had received to take the gospel as a Jew to the Gentiles (Gal. 1:15–16). He functioned somewhat as a priestly servant sent "to be a minister of Christ Jesus to the Gentiles with the priestly duty of proclaiming the gospel of God, so that the Gentiles might become an offering acceptable to God, sanctified by the Holy Spirit" (Rom. 15:16).

The key to the theology of Ephesians is the second chapter, where Paul sets forth the implications of the equal union of Jews and Gentiles in the one body, the church. Both Gentiles (v. 1) and Jews (vv. 3–5) were once dead in their trespasses and sins. Nevertheless, the Jews had prepared the way for the Messiah and were the first to be called into the church. The Gentiles have since been included, largely by Paul's own work, in keeping with divine forethought and election. God had promised Abraham that his seed would be a blessing to all the nations, and they must now be accepted fully as equal partners in the kingdom.

It if foundational to the theology of Paul, in Acts and in his generally accepted letters as well as in Ephesians, that both Gentiles and Jews are made alive together with Christ, have been raised up together, and made to sit together with Christ in the heavenly places (vv. 5–6). Thus, the Gentile disciples are fellow citizens with the Jewish disciples and members together with them of the household of God (v. 19).

The church, Paul argues, was built upon the Jewish foundation of apostles and prophets, with Christ Jesus as the chief (Jewish) cornerstone (2:20; 3:5). The Gentiles have now been included and, being "joined together" with the Jewish foundation, they grow together into a holy temple in the Lord (2:20–21). Their daily moral and ethical conduct, which should be guided by this truth, is set forth in the last part of the letter (4:17–6:24).

A number of key theological terms and arguments in Ephesians revolve around these two concepts: (1) the historical and cosmological role of the Jews in God's redemptive history from the time of Abraham; and (2) Paul's own place in that process, that of bringing in the Gentiles as full participants in the kingdom, which evil forces in the cosmos conspired to prevent and thus to destroy the work of Christ.

There is a distinctive emphasis in Ephesians on Christ's exaltation above the heavens, his coronation at the right hand of God, and his subsequent cosmic lordship (1:3–4, 9–10, 20–23; 2:6; 4:8–10). The cosmological nature of the church being the central emphasis of the theological section of the letter (chap. 1–4), the author felt no need to argue here for the resurrection of the body of Jesus and his believers, which is of eschatological but not cosmological import. He makes no mention of an imminent return of Christ but rather speaks of the church's role in manifesting the glory of Christ Jesus to all generations. Aspects of the church's conduct until Christ's return are delineated in chapters 5–6, as they are is in Romans, Corinthians, Galatians, and Thessalonians.

Israel as God's Elect. It is in the context of the role of Israel as the elect, the chosen, descended from Abraham to propagate the Messiah, rather than in the context of individual predestination to salvation, that Paul speaks of election. The first chapter asserts that the Jews, God's saints or holy ones, were "chosen" to bring the blessing of redemption to all nations in fulfillment of the promise to Abraham. It was the Jews who were foreordained unto adoption for this purpose (v. 5), chosen in the beloved (Messiah) for God's glory, that is, to declare the sovereignty of monotheism, (v. 6), chosen before the foundation of the world to be "holy and blameless" (v. 4). They were the first to hope in the Messiah (v. 12).

The Specialized Application of Pronouns. Another key to understanding Ephesians is recognizing that in this book a Jewish author is writing to a Gentile audience. This is especially evident in Paul's discriminating use of first-person and second-person pronouns. Although most studies on Ephesians approach the letter by investigating its major theological terms and comparing their use in Paul's generally acknowledged letters, it is more likely that the thinking of an author (or redactor) will be found in those more commonly used parts of speech he employs at times almost subconsciously. These parts of speech may reflect the subconscious theological perspectives out of which an author or redactor formulates his doctrine and from which he expresses that doctrine. In this respect the pronouns in Ephesians provide a key to the theology of the book. If studied on the assumption of consistency in use, they reveal the thinking of the author in a way that allows us to draw important conclusions about the point of view from which he writes and therefore about his theology.

Paul consistently uses second-person pronouns in the letter in a specialized sense, that of addressing an exclusively Gentile Christian audience. The particularized use of the second-person pronoun in referring to Gentiles as the recipients of this letter is seen in 2:11, where he says: "remember that *you who are Gentiles by birth* and called uncircumcision." Again in 3:1 he writes: "I, Paul, the prisoner of Christ Jesus for the sake of *you Gentiles*." However, unlike Romans, where Paul addresses his dual audience on the one hand as Jews "who know the law" (7:1) and then on the other as Gentiles (11:13), Paul never addresses Jews directly in Ephesians using the second-person pronoun.

First-person pronouns, like those in the second person, are also used in a number of different ways, both traditional and specialized. Their customary epistolary use in personal communication may be seen in 6:12. They are also used in liturgical material and confessional formulas. For example, in the greeting "Grace to all who love *our* Lord Jesus Christ" (6:24) the pronoun is part of a standard expression and has no specialized reference.

Otherwise, the first-person plural pronouns, like the second-person pronouns, are used in a specialized way. In the first part of the letter, down to 2:3, they refer to Jews or Jewish Christians. At this point, following Paul's declaration of the inclusion of the Gentiles with the Jews, the first-person pronouns henceforth refer to Jews and Gentiles combined.

The significance of this pronoun use can be seen in the following example. After the epistolary greeting in 1:1–2, the Gentiles are not referred to until verse 13, where they are said to have been added to God's redemptive work among the Jews, who thus far have been designated by first-person plural pronouns. Paul then addresses the Gentile readers in verse 13 by saying "*you* heard the word of truth, the gospel of *your* salvation . . . marked in him with a seal, the promised Holy Spirit, who is a deposit guaranteeing *our* inheritance."

Thus, the Jew and Gentile are differentiated by these pronouns down to the second chapter. Then in 2:1–5 , after the declaration that the Gentiles now have been brought together with the Jews into the body of Christ, the first-person plural pronouns henceforth refer to Jews and Gentiles *together*. The transition point is verse 3, where Paul concludes that "*all of us* [Jew and Gentile] also lived among them [the sons of disobedience]."

Thus, the first ten verses of chapter 2 may be paraphrased as follows: "*You* Gentiles were dead in your trespasses and sins (v. 1) just as *we* Jews were (v. 5), so *we all* shared the same guilt of sin (v. 3). But God has now forgiven *us* (Jew and Gentile alike) by his grace (vv. 6, 8), made us alive *together* with Christ, raised us up *together* and made us sit *together* with Christ in the heavenly places" (vv. 5–8).

Therefore, from this point on (2:3) the first-person plural pronouns include the Gentiles as well, who have been grafted as wild olive branches into the Jewish tree (Rom. 11:17–24) and are henceforth, like the Jews, included among the descendants of Abraham, "in order that the blessing given to Abraham might come to the Gentiles through Jesus Christ, so that by faith *we* [Jew and Gentile] might receive the promise of the Spirit" (Gal. 3:14).

There are a number of significant occurrences of the first-person plural pronouns used in this inclusive way after 2:3, which further clarify the theology of the letter.

The first example and the most significant perhaps is in 2:5 where, following three compound verbs describing the uniting of Jews and Gentiles together in Christ ("made alive together, raised together, and made to sit together"—*sunezōopoiēsen, sunēgeiren*, and *sunekathisen*), Paul states (v. 7) that God's rich grace is manifested toward *us*, the first-person plural pronoun now meaning Jew and Gentile together, who are declared to be his workmanship (v. 10).

These compound verbs furnish a key point in the theology of Ephesians. Most commentators on the Greek text argue that chapter 1 deals with what God has done for Christ and chapter 2 with what God has subsequently done for all believers. These three compound verbs in 2:5 are thus taken to indicate the twofold union of Christ and his believers.

However, all of them express difficulty in dealing with the first five verses of chapter 2 and none of them deals with the passage in the context of the thematic consistency of pronoun use or sees the implausibility of his position due to the demands of the three compound verbs. The compounds themselves do not refer to any union including Christ—Christ and Jews, Christ and Gentiles, or Christ and Christians but to that of Jews and Gentiles. The Jews and Gentiles thus brought together, are then together, as an entity, united with Christ.

The use of compounds in this way occurs again in 3:6, where Paul says that the Gentiles are *fellow heirs* (*sunklēronoma*) *fellow members of the body* (*sussōma*) and *fellow partakers* (*summetocha*) of the promise in Christ Jesus through the gospel.

The second example of the special use of first-person plural pronouns is in 2:16–18 where Paul asserts that God has reconciled them *both* into one body and created of the *two* one new person. This statement of unification is then followed in verse 18 by a first-person plural construction referring to the result of that unity: "*we* both have access to the Father by one Spirit." The result is that the Gentiles are now "fellow citizens with God's people," the Jews.

A third example is in 3:8, where Paul calls himself the "less than the least of all God's people (Jewish Christians)" who was given the commission to "preach to the Gentiles the unsearchable riches of Christ." This statement of Gentile inclusion is then followed again (as in 2:16) by the first-person "we," (v. 12) signifying that *we* [both Jew and Gentile] can now approach God with freedom and confidence.

A fourth example may be found in 4:13, where it is stated that the work of God's people (Jewish Christians) in building up the body of Christ by including the Gentiles, will continue until *we all* attain unto the oneness of the faith. Then in verses 14 and 15, first-person plurals are used ("*we* will no longer be" and "*we* will . . . grow up") referring to the newly created union of Jews *and* Gentiles who should no longer be babes but grow up in every way into him who is the head, even Christ. That "growing up" or reaching "maturity" is done by including the Gentiles.

If this analysis is correct, 2:3 is the transition point in the letter, with all the first-person pronouns from this point on referring to the union of Jews and Gentiles. Prior to this they refer to the Jews as a people or to Jewish Christians. The third verse is the decisive point, indicated by the phrase "*we* all" which appears also in 4:13, in both instances expanding the first-person pronoun references to Jews to include the Gentiles as well.

The Special Use of "God's People." A third key element in the theology of Ephesians is the differentiation between Jewish and Gentile Christians by the consistent use of the words "God's people" in reference to Jewish Christians. This designation of Jewish Christians as God's people occasionally occurs in special contexts in other Pauline literature as well.

That the author of Ephesians considers himself among God's people and that they are Jewish Christians is clear from 3:1, 8. In verse 1 he says "I, Paul, the prisoner of Christ Jesus for the sake of *you* Gentiles" and in verse 8 he continues "I am less than the least of God's people." This distinction between Gentiles and saints is seen also in 3:18, where the text states: "in order that *you* (Gentiles) may have power together with all the *saints*" the greatness of God. It is significant that he does not say "with all the *other* saints." Further, the mystery in 1:9, which Paul says was made known to "us" (Jews), is identified in 3:3–5 as a revelation to God's people (Jews), that the *Gentiles* were to be fellow participants in God's eternal purpose.

The Role of Cosmic Powers. Another highly important element of the theology of Ephesians is the role of cosmic, demonic powers in the affairs of human activity. Paul emphatically asserts that "our struggle is not against flesh and blood, but against the rulers, against the authorities, against the powers of this dark world, and against the spiritual forces of evil in the heavenly realms" (6:12).

His perspective is that Satan, who dwells in the region around the earth (2:2), is actively trying to destroy the unity of the church. The Christian warfare is with him, not with flesh and blood. By fostering disunity in the body of Christ, as he did in the history of Israel, he destroys its witness to the oneness of God (4:4–6), which it constantly seeks to make known through its unity, even to these principalities and powers in the heavenly places (3:10).

The celestial world was highly structured in the Hellenistic Jewish thought of Paul's time, having multiple heavens, usually seven in number, and containing both angels and demons. The major dogmas of Jewish Christianity were developed along cosmological lines, although they were concerned with Christology rather than cosmology, and used cosmological data simply as a medium of expression.

Paul speaks in Ephesians of multiple heavens, saying that Christ ascended "higher than all the heavens" (4:10). These heavenly places are not synonymous with "heaven" because they include not only God and Christ, but also Jewish and Gentile Christians, *as well as* demonic powers (1:3, 10, 20; 2:2, 6; 3:10, 15; 4:10; 6:9, 12). Satan, the "ruler of the kingdom of the *air*" (2:2) dwells in a lower heaven around the earth known as the firmament in Jewish apocalyptic thought.

Concisely stated, the theology of Ephesians is that in the life, death, burial, resurrection, ascension, and enthronement of Jesus Christ, the church, which is his body, declares by its unity, the lordship of Jesus, not only over the church, but over the cosmos as well. JOHN MCRAY

See also PAUL THE APOSTLE.

Bibliography. F. F. Bruce, *The Epistle to the Ephesians;* idem, *The New International Commentary on the New Testament;* M. Barth, *The Broken Wall: A Study of the Epistle to the Ephesians;* F. Foulkes, *The Letter of Paul to the Ephesians: An Introduction and Commentary;* E. J. Goodspeed, *The Key to Ephesians;* idem, *The Meaning of Ephesians;* A. T. Lincoln, *Ephesians;* L. G. Mitton, *Ephesians;* B. F. Westcott, *St. Paul's Epistle to the Ephesians.*

Esther, Theology of. ***Understanding the Book.*** For many Christians, the Book of Esther is the basis for a Jewish festival that found no counterpart in the Christian calendar. The book is never alluded to in the New Testament or Dead Sea Scrolls, and even comments about it by the church fathers are rare. The book appears to be anthropocentric, and apart from fasting (4:16), there are no distinctly religious practices or concepts. God, prayer, the covenant, sacrifice, the temple, the promised land, as well as virtues such as love, kindness, mercy, and forgiveness are not mentioned. Because of the many omissions, the Greek version of Esther added personal prayers of the two main characters and reference to God. Moreover, a number of the moral and ethical practices of Esther have been considered questionable. Esther hid her identity from the king, was willing to marry a Gentile, did not feel out of place in a harem, had no mercy on Haman, did not observe dietary laws, was at first not willing to help her own people, and sanctioned the plundering of enemies. Furthermore, the author never explicitly condemns her shortcomings, but seems to describe her triumphs with approval. In spite of this, the Book of Esther was included in the canon and has significant theological value.

The Place of Haman. There is at least one aspect in Esther that is often overlooked: the association of Haman with the house of Agag, the king of Amalek (1 Sam. 15:30), the enemy of Israel. Long before Esther, God had ordained that there would be war with Amalek for generations (Exod. 17:16), and that his name would be blotted from heaven (Deut. 25:19; 1 Sam. 15:17–18). Although the Amalekite king Agag was captured, Saul spared him (he was ultimately slain by Samuel); thus his descendant Haman survived to contend with the Jews. (The Chronicler describes the destruction of the Amalekites later during the reign of Hezekiah [1 Chron. 4:43], but the writer of Esther believes that they did not come to a complete end.) Likewise, the mention of Kish (the father of Saul) at the end of Mordecai's genealogy (2:5) shows that he was descended from the mortal enemy of the Agagites. Mordecai would thus fulfill the command of God to Saul. The Jews did not take the spoils of Haman because of the dictum of not dividing the booty of Amalek (1 Sam. 15:21).

Although falling down before a superior in Israel was common, it is easier in this context to understand why Mordecai did not fall prostrate before Haman. Mordecai was not exhibiting pride in this case, but refused to bow down before a descendant of Agag. Josephus understands Mordecai as following the law of vendetta; his personal conflict was part of the providential plan. The author of Esther sees the destruction of Haman as salvation from God, who pursued his plan independent of human action. The Jews were saved, not so much for their sake, but for the fulfillment of the destruction of the Amalekites. Their deliverance became a part of a universal pattern of history.

Purim. Another purpose of the book is to provide the historical grounds and cultic significance for the celebration of Purim, a festival that is not mentioned in the Torah. The writer, however, spends little time on the subject (3:7; 9:20–32). It is not certain whether it was a pagan festival (either Babylonian, Persian, or indigenous) that was appropriated for Jewish purposes. Even the names of Mordecai and Esther betray a pagan background. Purim appears to be an Akkadian term for lot or chance; its etymology, however, does not help us retrieve the source of the festival. The lots were used in dice throwing, serving a purpose to those who had a widespread belief in a predestined fate with which people needed to cooperate if they were to succeed. The dice were thrown to establish auspicious dates for all known events. The Jews lived in such a culture in Persia; they needed to theologically comprehend a belief in the power of God to overrule the way the dice fell. God was able to annul the good or bad omen to deliver his people. This may explain why God is not overtly mentioned in Esther. The assurance provided by Purim was that no matter how severe the threat to God's people, he would help them. Human responsibility is prominent in Esther but not isolated from God's work; Esther and Mordecai were placed providentially to act in behalf of the people. Purim answered questions the Jews had about their future as scattered groups in alien cultures. Like the Passover, it celebrated deliverance from death.

The writer of Esther kept the original story, even with its questionable brutality, nationalism, intrigue, and secularism, but gave it a new theological interpretation within the worship and sacred tradition of Israel. The story of Esther was made relevant for future generations, while Purim was drawn into the orbit of Israel's religious heritage. Furthermore, the writer of Esther has stated the strongest case for the religious significance and survival of the Jewish people in the ethnic sense. In fact, the inclusion of Esther in the Christian canon has mitigated the attempt to spiritualize the concept of Israel. MARK W. CHAVALAS

See also FEASTS AND FESTIVALS OF ISRAEL.

Bibliography. J. Baldwin, *Esther: An Introduction and Commentary;* S. Berg, *The Book of Esther;* E. Bickerman, *Four Strange Books of the Bible: Jonah, Daniel, Koheleth, and Esther;* T. Gaster, *Purim and Hannakah in Custom and Tradition;* W. W. Hallo, *BA* (1983): 19–27; F. B. Huey, *Esther;* J. Lewy, *Revue Hittite et Asianique* 5 (1939): 117–24; C. A. Moore, *Esther;* S. Talmon, *VT* 13 (1963): 419–55.

Eternal Life, Eternality, Everlasting Life. The divinely bestowed gift of blessedness in God's presence that endures without end. This relates especially to the quality of life in this age, and to both the quality and duration of life in the age to come. Key to understanding the biblical meaning of these terms is the Bible's use of the word "eternal."

Old Testament Teaching. God is eternal (Deut. 33:27; Pss. 10:16; 48:14). Scripture does not provide philosophical reflection on this fact but assumes it. The Lord is the Rock eternal (Isa. 26:4) and the eternal King (Jer. 10:10). God's word, rooted in his being and will, is likewise eternal (Ps. 119:89), as are his righteous laws (119:60), his ways (Hab. 3:6), and his kingdom or dominion (Dan. 4:3, 34). Since God is eternal, so are his love (1 Kings 10:9), his blessings (Ps. 21:6), and all his other attributes and benefits. They endure without end; as long as God exists, so do they.

"His love endures forever" is repeated twenty-six times in Psalm 136 alone. Elsewhere in the psalms "forever" is used to describe God's reign (9:7), his protection (12:7), his plans (33:11), the inheritance of his people (37:18), his throne (55:19), his rule (66:7), his remembrance of his covenant (105:8), his righteousness (111:3), his faithfulness (117:2), his statutes (119:111, 152), and his name (135:13). Other Old Testament books offer abundant additional affirmation of these and other never-ending aspects of God or his saving provisions.

Some deny awareness of a personally significant eternity in most Old Testament Scripture and history. A prominent segment of modern biblical scholarship would concur that in Israel there was no belief in life after death. It is truth that many biblical characters, like some who study them, seem oblivious to their eschatological destiny. They show little awareness of a transcendent world order in which they will be personally involved, a divinely ordained future imposing imperatives on the present. It is likewise true that Old Testament awareness of eternal realities is less specific and complete than that of the New Testament. Yet the progressive nature of biblical revelation (as well as the necessarily restricted scope of each Old Testament book) should be borne in mind. Many central biblical doctrines (e.g., the Trinity, the incarnation, divine self-sacrifice for sin) are only adumbrated in earlier biblical history, to be fleshed out in the fullness of time. The numerous Old Testament references to the Lord's future and thus to the future of those who trust in him leave little room for insisting that the Old Testament contains no inkling of a life beyond the present world. Such insistence is understandable where Enlightenment or postmodern assumptions, methods, and conclusions are dogmatically embraced.

The Old Testament does not seem to conceive of eternity in purely abstract terms, as a static state of timelessness. The Greek word *aiōn* (age, era, lengthy time, eternity) in the Septuagint and New Testament corresponds to the Hebrew Old Testament's *ʾôlām* (a long time, eternity); neither word as used in Scripture answers to the notion of "eternity" that shows up in the ancient philosophies of Plato and Aristotle. For Plato, eternity is a timeless and transcendent state totally outside the dimension of time. For Aristotle, as for Thomas Aquinas who followed him at this point, eternity "becomes known from two characteristics: first, from the fact that whatever is in eternity is interminable, that is, lacking beginning and end . . . ; second, from the fact that eternity itself lacks successiveness, existing entirely at once [*tota simul*]" (Aquinas, *Summa,* I, 10, 1).

In this view eternity is a motionless, changeless state, remote and qualitatively distinct from time. Time and eternity are antithetical, and eternity is accessible to human thought only by logical speculation that views God not as the personal, living, historically self-revealing being described in Scripture but as the inscrutable "unmoved first mover" of Aristotelian reasoning. This understanding has had great influence on Western theology and on the way many Christians even today understand "eternity" and "eternal life" when they encounter them in the Bible.

The Old Testament, like the New, resists this time-eternity dualism. True, it speaks of a coming age from which evil will be banished and for which God's life and glory will be determinative for all that exists and takes place. This is quite different from the current world order. But that age has points of continuity with the present one because the God of that age is at the same time the God of the present age (allowing for the presence of Satan and evil in this "present evil age" [Gal. 1:4] until they meet their final end). His reign extends for all time and over all times.

This means that the temporal order has redemptive potential as the sphere in which God's Spirit, the Spirit of the incarnate and risen Jesus Christ, works out his will in human affairs. History, while it cannot fully contain the reality of the transcendent God, also is not incapable of receiving and responding to his presence. The incarnation offers abundant proof of this fact. And eternity, while it lies chronologically beyond temporal life in the here and now, is not in all respects qualitatively remote and aloof from it. We may thus look to biblical revelation as descriptive of God's presence in and intent for both the present world order and the coming one; we need not turn from Scripture to atemporal philosophical idealism for normative insight into the nature of eternity and its relation to present time.

The Old Testament, then, encourages us to define eternity in terms of the duration of the revealed God's dealings with his people in times past, now, and always. This God has ever been solicitous for his name and for the people with whom he has deigned to share it. This past state of affairs will continue for eternity, so long as God who lives and loves endures. To define eternity more closely, the Bible would seem to call for laying hold of personal relationship with God. To trust him is to begin to realize what "eternal" signifies. To live responsively before him means to gain understanding, indeed induction, into "eternal life."

Eternal Life. A dominant theme of the New Testament, though not without Old Testament grounding, is eternal (or everlasting) life. Eternal life is therefore one of the unifying themes of the New Testament. It is a term that describes the salvation that God bestows on those who trust and serve him. It denotes not only the *length of time* that God's favor extends to his people but also the *quality of existence* that they may enjoy as they worship and serve him.

John's Gospel is rich with references to eternal life. Nicodemus' questions about Jesus' ministry and teaching lead Jesus to speak of it (3:15–16). It is a gift to all those who believe in the Son but will be withheld from all those who reject him (3:36). Jesus likewise speaks of eternal life during his brief early ministry in Samaria. He assures the woman at the well that trust in him will slake the thirst of her soul; she will receive "a spring of water welling up" within her "to eternal life" (4:14; cf. 4:36). In response to charges of Sabbath breaking in Jerusalem Jesus urges listeners to heed his message and trust God; to do so is to have "eternal life." This means escape from condemnation on judgment day and in the age to come. In the present it means a crossing over "from death to life" (5:24). Eternal life is available through study of the Scriptures as they relate to Jesus Christ (5:39).

Jesus urges a crowd by Galilee's shores not to "work for food that spoils, but for food that endures to eternal life, which the Son of Man will give you (6:27). God wills that "everyone who looks to the Son and believes in him shall have eternal life." This will result in resurrection "at the last day" (6:40). Jesus' difficult statement that everyone "who eats my flesh and drinks my blood has eternal life" (6:54) is a summons for sinners to make the Father's will their meat and drink, by trusting in the Son, just as the Son made the Father's will his own daily fare (4:34).

The Christocentric nature of eternal life is underscored by Jesus' own words in prayer on the night he was betrayed. First, he reminds the heavenly Father that he gave the Son "authority over all people that he might give eternal life to all those you have given him" (17:2). Next he furnishes a succinct description of what eternal life involves: "Now this is eternal life: that they may know you, the only true God, and Jesus Christ, whom you have sent" (17:3).

Eternal life as presented in John's Gospel forms a solid core within apostolic preaching and teaching in the decades subsequent to Jesus' death and resurrection. Predictably, it receives repeated mention in John's own longest extant epistle (1 John 1:2; 2:25; 3:15; 5:11, 13, 20). Both Paul and Luke speak of it, too, in connection with Paul's first missionary journey (Acts 13:46, 48). In Paul's earliest extant epistle he avows that whoever "sows to please the Spirit" will also "reap eternal life from the Spirit" (Gal. 6:8). Paul refers, of course, to the Spirit of the living God, the Spirit of Jesus Christ (Rom. 8:9–11). The Epistle to the Romans reveals that God grants eternal life "to those who by persistence in doing good seek glory, honor, and immortality" (2:7). Yet eternal life is won not by human effort but by divine self-sacrifice as Christ undoes the woe that Adam's fall helped unleash on the human race (5:12–21). Through Christ grace reigns "through righteousness to bring eternal life through Jesus Christ our Lord" (5:21; cf. 6:22, 23).

Far from treating eternal life as a rudimentary or unimportant matter, in Paul's last extant letter he is still extolling its glories. "The hope of eternal life" is in fact foundational to faith in and knowledge of God (Titus 1:1–2). Here, as elsewhere in Paul, "hope" denotes a sure, if not yet fully realized, reality (Rom. 8:24). Paul, originally the arch-enemy of Christ, tells Timothy that his conversion serves "as an example for those who would believe on [Christ] and receive eternal life" (1 Tim. 1:16). He exhorts Timothy "to take hold of the eternal life" to which he was called (1 Tim. 6:12). It may have been in the same general span of time late in the apostolic era that Jude encouraged his readers, "Keep yourselves in God's love as you wait for the mercy of our Lord Jesus Christ to bring you to eternal life" (Jude 21).

If in Jude eternal life seems to be a future possession, many other references speak of it as a present reality. Which is it? The answer seems to be both. Eternal life has both an "already" and a "not yet" dimension. Interpreters have sometimes erred in stressing one to the exclusion of the other. Biblical statements taken in their entirety counsel careful regard for both aspects of a two-sided truth: eternal life is a present possession in terms of its reality, efficacy, and irrevocability (John 10:28). Yet its full realization awaits life with the Lord in the age to come.

"Eternal" Elsewhere in the New Testament. "Eternal" (Gk. *aiōnios*) occurs as an adjective in a number of noteworthy connections. In Luke 16:9 Jesus speaks of the "eternal dwellings" that await those whose use of mammon, or worldly wealth, is pleasing to God. This appears to be another way of referring to heaven using an earthly, spatial metaphor (John 14:2–3). Paul speaks of the "eternal house" that awaits humans after death (2 Cor. 5:1), but he has in mind the resurrection body rather than a heavenly dwelling place in terms of a building. Further, Paul uses this figure of speech to underline the temporary nature of life, not to speak of the Platonic release of the soul from captivity in the body. In the New Testament as in the Old, "eternal" carries a different connotation than it does in Greek philosophy.

God's "eternal power" is evident even to nonbelievers from the grandeur of the created order (Rom. 1:20). "Eternal" describes God himself, the King in his regal splendor who is at the same time "immortal, invisible," and unique (1 Tim. 1:17). Paul speaks of the "eternal God" whose command undergirded the apostolic proclamation to the nations (Rom. 16:26). God presides over an "eternal kingdom" (2 Peter 1:11), grants "eternal encouragement" (2 Thess. 2:16), works to effect his "eternal purpose" (Eph. 3:11), and offers "eternal glory" (2 Cor. 4:17; 2 Tim. 2:10; 1 Peter 5:10) to the elect who suffer for the sake of his kingdom and his Son. Enjoyment of "eternal glory" in the wake of suffering is explained elsewhere as one of the great privileges and assurances of union with Christ: Christians are "heirs of God and co-heirs with Christ, if indeed we share in his sufferings in order that we may also share in his glory" (Rom. 8:17).

The writer of Hebrews speaks of Jesus Christ as "the source of eternal salvation for all who obey him" (Heb. 5:9). "The resurrection of the dead and eternal judgment" are rudimentary truths that mature believers should long since have learned (6:2). Christ's blood, in contrast to that of Old Testament sacrifices, won "eternal redemption" (9:12), and it was by "the eternal Spirit" that Christ offered himself up to God (9:14). By faith in Christ "those who are called . . . receive the promised eternal inheritance" (9:15) by virtue of "the blood of the eternal covenant" (13:20).

In the same sense that "eternal" describes the boon that those who seek the Lord receive, now and forever, eternal condemnation threatens the rebellious and indifferent. Jesus speaks of the "eternal sin" of blaspheming the Holy Spirit; for this there can be no forgiveness (Mark 3:29), in part perhaps because the perpetrator of such a heinous act cannot muster the will to seek it (Heb. 12:17). The ultimate outcome of rejection of Jesus Christ is "eternal fire" (Matt. 18:8; 25:41; Jude 7), "eternal punishment" (Matt. 25:46) and "eternal [NIV: "everlasting"; the Greek word is *aiōn*] destruction." While such bleak pronouncements seem hard for some to square with the idea of a loving God, there is no linguistically convincing or theologically satisfactory way to avoid the conclusion that just as joy in the Lord's presence will endure for all time—for eternity—so will the experience of his hot displeasure.

Yet "the eternal gospel" (Rev. 14:6) offers hope, the entrée into an unending blessed future before the Lord rather than banishment from it. While the background assumption of both Old and New Testament is a coming judgment with eternal implications for every single soul, its prominent and urgent plea is for all people to heed the gospel, thereby being reconciled to God (cf. 2 Cor. 5:18–21).

Ethics and Worship. A major assumption of virtually all biblical writers is that the eternal has weighty and necessary implications for the temporal. They are aware that God is the "Everlasting Father" (Isa. 9:6) who gives good gifts to all, just and unjust alike. But they also insist that he will one day appear as eternal judge of all the earth (Gen. 18:25; 1 Sam. 2:10; 1 Chron. 16:33; Ps. 9:8; John 12:48; Rom. 2:16). What lies in the future—eschatological judgment—should be regarded as determinative for human thought and action in the present. "For God will bring every deed into judgment, including every hidden thing, whether it is good or evil" (Eccles. 12:14; cf. 1 Cor. 4:5; 2 Tim. 4:1). "But I tell you that men will have to give account on the day of judgment for every careless word they have spoken" (Matt. 12:36). If words will be so gravely assessed, how much more all human actions?

Eternality is, then, not a philosophical category serving sheerly speculative ends. It is rather a dimension of God's established order that calls people to seek God's pleasure here, making it their highest priority to further his interests and kingdom in every way, so they may enjoy his favor in the hereafter. In this sense reflection on eternality and eternal life is never complete without sober contemplation of ethical corollaries. The Lord who is "our king" and "our judge" is also "our lawgiver" (Isa. 33:22; cf. James 4:12). Unlocking the mysteries of eternity begins with careful attention and trusting response to the precepts and commands of the "righteous judge" (Ps. 7:11). Paul voices a fundamental if optimal Christian conviction regarding that day when God brings all things to light: "Now there is in store for me the crown of righteousness, which the Lord, the righteous Judge, will award to me on that day—and not only to me, but also to all who have longed for his appearing" (2 Tim. 4:8). Eternity—with the assurance of vindication before the eternal judge—rightly shaped Paul's present.

If ethical focus is one corollary of a biblical theology of eternity, another is worship. Eternity is the basis for doxology. Already in Moses' hymn of victory, God's eternal reign is the basis for praise: "The LORD will reign for ever and ever" (Exod. 15:18). David picks up and continues the strain: "The LORD is King for ever and ever" (Ps. 10:16). The place of God's dwelling is "secure forever" (Ps. 48:8); his "praise reaches to the ends of the earth . . . for this God is our God for ever and ever; he will be our guide even to the end" (vv. 10, 14).

Sinners receive access to God's everlasting throne (Ps. 45:6; Heb. 1:8), promised to David's descendants (2 Sam. 7) on behalf of Abraham's heirs (Luke 1:33, 55), through the priestly ministrations of Jesus Christ, "a priest forever" (Heb. 5:6; 6:20; 7:21). In keeping with the sober historical integrity of the four Gospels and Acts, the accounts of Jesus' life and ministry are not studded with lofty ascriptions of praise to Christ. His earthly rigors hid his eternal glory. But this alters perceptibly in the Epistles. Most of them well up in worshipful exclamation linked explicitly to God's, or Christ's eternality. He is praised "forever" or "for ever and ever." Other Epistles imply the same praise by extolling the Lord's eternal rewards: "a crown that will last forever" (1 Cor. 9:25); life "with the Lord forever" (1 Thess. 4:17; cf. Phil. 1:23). As John writes, the person "who does the will of God lives forever" (1 John 2:17) because of the gospel's "truth, which lives in us and will be with us forever" (2 John 2).

But it is Scripture's last book that most sweepingly links God's eternality to worship. John's vision begins with praise to God "for ever and ever" (1:6). The exalted Jesus Christ declares that he is "alive for ever and ever" (1:18). The Lord's power, reign, and glory in their ceaseless duration dot the literary landscape of subsequent chapters. Also never ending is the torment of God's enemies, the smoke of whose "torment rises for ever and ever" (14:11; cf. 19:3; 20:10). Yet happier prospects await all who have received the grace of the eternal God through his Son in this present life: in worshiping the eternal King "they will reign for ever and ever" (22:5).

ROBERT W. YARBROUGH

See also FAITH; GRACE; HEAVEN, HEAVENS, HEAVENLIES; SALVATION.

Bibliography. J. Auer and J. Ratzinger, *Eschatology: Death and Eternal Life;* O. Cullmann, *Salvation in History;* G. Habermas and J. P. Moreland, *Immortality: The Other Side of Death;* A. T. Lincoln, *Paradise Now and Not Yet;* O. O'Donovan, *Resurrection and Moral Order;* B. Witherington, *Jesus, Paul, and the End of the World.*

Eternal Punishment. Divinely instituted penalty of endless suffering, including banishment from God's blessed presence.

The Old Testament. A study of God's major judgments (e.g., the flood and the destruction of Sodom and Gomorrah) shows that the Old Testament focuses on premature death when dealing with the fate of the ungodly, not on life after death.

If the predominant evangelical view is correct, in the Old Testament sheol sometimes refers to a netherworld to which the wicked go at death. Sheol therefore, takes us beyond the primary judgment passages and speaks of life after death, although in vague terms.

Two passages paint a clearer picture of the final destiny of the wicked. Isaiah uses earthly images of corpses beset by an undying worm and inextinguishable fire to point to the final doom of the wicked—eternal punishment (66:24). Daniel teaches that whereas the godly will be raised to never-ending life, the wicked will be raised to never-ending disgrace (12:2).

The New Testament. *Jesus' Teaching.* The doctrine of hell ultimately derives from Jesus. He uses images of darkness and separation to communicate God's rejection of unbelievers and their exclusion from his blessed presence (Matt. 7:23; 8:12; 22:13; 25:30; Luke 13:27–28). Fire imagery signifies the horrible suffering of the unrighteous (Matt. 13:40–42, 49–50; 18:8–9; 25:41; Mark 9:44, 48; Luke 16:23–25, 28). It is significant that Jesus uses the "weeping and gnashing of teeth" image to qualify other images: "the fiery furnace" (Matt. 13:42, 50), darkness and separation (Matt. 8:12; 22:13; 25:30; Luke 13:28), and being cut into pieces (Matt. 24:51).

Jesus teaches that the suffering of the ungodly in hell is "eternal punishment" (Matt. 25:46; cf. John 5:28–29). Pictures of death and destruction speak of the ruin of all that is worthwhile in human existence (Matt. 10:28).

The Apostles' Teaching. The apostles reinforce Jesus' teaching, although they mention the topic less frequently. Paul combines pictures of punishment, destruction, and separation in 2 Thessalonians 1:5–9: God will "punish those who do not know God, and do not obey the gospel of our Lord Jesus. They will be punished with everlasting destruction and shut out from the presence of the Lord and from the majesty of his power."

Jude speaks of hell in terms of fire when he cites Sodom and Gomorrah as an earthly example of "those who suffer the punishment of eternal fire" (v. 7). He employs the image of darkness when he likens false teachers to "wandering stars, for whom the blackest darkness has been reserved forever" (v. 13).

Revelation combines the Old Testament picture of the wicked drinking the cup of God's wrath (e.g., Ps. 75:7–8; Jer. 25:15–29) with hellfire to depict the perpetual, conscious torment of the wicked (Rev. 14:10–11). In Revelation 20 the devil is cast into the lake of fire, where the beast and the false prophet had been thrown "one thousand years" earlier (19:20). They had not been annihilated; in fact, John says that all three "will be tormented day and night for ever and ever" (20:10). Lost human beings share the same fate (v. 15: cf. 21:8). The Apocalypse closes with the picture of the City of God representing God's comforting presence with his people (21:3–4). The wicked are not exterminated, but are outside the city, cut off from the blessings of God (22:15).

Purposes of the Doctrine of Hell. Why does God teach such a terrible doctrine in his Word? For two reasons: to provide believers with powerful motivation for evangelism, and to make us grateful to him who redeemed us by suffering the pains of hell for us, both negatively (*poena damni,* the deprivation of the Father's love, Matt. 27:45–46) and positively (*poena sensus,* the positive infliction of torments in body and soul, Matt. 26:38–39, 42, 44; John 18:11, against the Old Testament background of the cup of God's wrath).

ROBERT A. PETERSON

See also DESTROY, DESTRUCTION; FIRE; HELL; LAKE OF FIRE.

Bibliography. M. de S. Cameron, ed., *Universalism and the Doctrine of Hell;* W. V. Crockett, ed., *Four Views on Hell;* W. V. Crockett and J. G. Sigountos, eds., *Through No Fault of Their Own? The Fate of Those Who Have Never Heard;* L. Dixon, *The Other Side of the Good News;* D. L. Edwards and J. Stott, *Evangelical Essentials;* M. J. Erickson, *The Evangelical Mind and Heart;* E. Fudge, *The Fire That Consumes;* J. Hick, *Evil and the God of Love;* idem, *Death and Eternal Life;* R. A. Morey, *Death and the Afterlife;* C. Pinnock, *A Wideness in God's Mercy;* J. A. T. Robinson, *In the End God;* J. Sanders, *No Other Name: An Investigation into the Destiny of the Unevangelized.*

Eternal Sin. *See* BLASPHEMY AGAINST THE HOLY SPIRIT.

Ethics. The ancient world did not consider religion to be morally inspiring, creative, or corrective; the reputed behavior of gods and goddesses repelled cultivated minds. Even in Israel the Wisdom Literature (Proverbs, Ecclesiastes, Job, Wisdom of Solomon, Sirach), while never abandoning a religious outlook, made little of worship rituals or the traditional law. Their teaching is prudential: Since God made us, it is common sense to discover what he wants and then to do it (Prov. 9:10; Eccles. 12:1, 13–14). Job does emphasize responsibility to God, and his self-defense (chap. 31) forms a noble ethical creed, but of religious observances he says nothing.

Immoral Religion and Prophetic Protest. The prophets opposed the popular religion and even temple worship, resenting not only the use of images but the total divorce of such "worship" from morality. The Canaanite baals were fertility-spirits whose favor ensured increase of families, flocks, and herds as well as the fruitfulness of fields and vineyards. At their shrines they were "worshiped" with orgies of drunkenness and sexual license (male and female cult prostitution, incest). "A spirit of harlotry" thus gained religious sanction; greed and drunkenness degraded men and women; the people cast off discipline, defiled the land, and "knew not how to blush." Standing pillars (? female figures; "Asherah" = Ishtar, the mother-goddess) and the bull-calf represented deities, and infant sacrifice was frequent. Wizardry, sorcery, witchcraft, necromancy, and soothsaying flourished under the patronage of such religion, and eventually even the Jerusalem temple housed similar rights, together with sun-worship, astrology, and altars to foreign gods (1 Kings 12:28–32; 14:23–24; 2 Kings 17:7–18; 21:1–7; Isa. 8:19; Jer. 2:20–25; 3:1–13, 23; 5:1; 6:15; Hos. 2:5–8; 4:12, 18; 5:3–4; 8:4–6; 13:1–2; Amos 2:7–8; 6:4–6; Mic. 5:10–15; 6:6–7).

Orthodox worship could also be immoral when unrelated to behavior in society. The prophets called constantly for justice; they condemned perjury and bribery, the selfish luxury of women, the scarcity of upright men, the lack of trust between neighbors through lies, deceitfulness, and fraud, as people preferred lies to truth and nourished "the lie within the soul." Avaricious moneylenders exploiting hardship, wealthy landlords dispossessing small landowners, merchants who oppressed the poor by ruthless competition and unjust balances, those who sold debtors into slavery or prostitution or exacted forced labor—all are indicted. So is the prevalent theft, murder, violence, adultery, and constant neglect of widows, orphans, strangers. The ultimate condemnation was that God's people saw no contradiction between the state of their society and the crowded shrines. God hates the feasts, assemblies, offerings, and music. Micah says that only a prophet preaching drink will be welcomed! Isaiah calls Jerusalem "Sodom," and declares God's utter rejection of her worship. Jeremiah threatens that the temple will become ruinous as Shiloh of old. Malachi pleads for someone to slam the temple doors and let the sacred fire go out (Isa. 1:10-15; 29:13–14; Jer. 7:1–15; Amos 4:4; 5:21–24; Mic. 2:11; Mal. 1:10).

Thus both "religious perversion" and religion without ethical fruits are rejected by God. To watch each prophet elaborating this argument is to retrace the discipline that ultimately made Jewish ethics the envy of the ancient world. No prophet argued from psychological or social consequences, nor (until Jeremiah) did any cite divine law. They contended that such practices totally misapprehended Yahweh—Yahweh was not like that. Surrounding nations or primitive Canaanites might offer immoral "worship" to their vicious, characterless deities; to offer it to Yahweh was to insult him.

Appealing simply to his own moral insight Amos demands that Israel turn from her petty gods to seek him who made heaven and earth, day and night; who through repeated recent catastrophes has wrestled with Israel's waywardness, and will yet bring judgment upon all crimes against humanity, wherever committed. If Israel refuses, nothing can save her (1:2–3:2; 4:6–13; 5:6–9, 14–15).

Hosea declares repeatedly that Israel does not know her God. Yahweh is no sex-crazed drunkard! Israel's worship has numbed her moral sense, otherwise she would know that God loved her from the beginning as father, provider, and lover, and will not let her go. Sad domestic experience had taught Hosea that love outlasts unfaithfulness (2:8, 14–16, 19; 3:1; 4:1, 6; 5:4, 11; 6:3, 6; 11:1–4, 8–9).

Micah appeals briefly to nature and history to testify what God is like, but rests his argument chiefly on his own indignation at injustice, his inner sense of the kind of world God wants and will achieve if only people listen to their own hearts (6:1–5, 8). Isaiah repeats that Judah "does not understand" that God is "the Holy One of Israel" (eleven times in early chapters, twenty-four times in all). He learned that, unforgettably, at his call within the temple. "Holy" implies here perfect purity, freedom from fault, the absolute good. Only worship offered by those worthy to survive as nucleus of a holy nation could ever be acceptable to him (1:3; 5:16, 24; 9:2–7; 10:20; 11:1–11).

Jeremiah attained a daring familiarity with God, partly (as a poet-naturalist) from nature, partly (as a trained priest) from Israel's history, but mainly through forty years of struggle, protest, and disappointment, sometimes charging God with deceiving him, sometimes near despair, and so learning to know God (15:10–21; 20:7–18). Thereafter Jeremiah knew it was "not for man to direct his steps": he needed to know the Lord who practices and delights in kindness, justice, and righteousness. Such "knowledge of God," the essence of religion and life's highest good (9:23–24), included a knowledge of God's law, of the "homing instincts" within human nature, of God's "hand" in one's experience, what God can accomplish, and his true "name" or character. It demands "a heart to know," and a simple, contended, just, and generous mind. In coming days all will thus know God, without instruction. That will prove the panacea for all evils.

So the prophets argued: as Israel went after false idols and became false (2 Kings 17:15), so to know and worship the true God would ensure righteousness in individuals and society. They did not add ethics to religious piety; for them religion and morality matured together, under God's guidance, through experience. But it took the exile to make Judah listen.

A Changed Atmosphere. Turning to the Psalter, one finds nothing remotely resembling the indecencies, license, and infanticide of popular preexilic religion. Discussion of ethical problems would be out of place in a worship manual, but a much deeper sense of personal consecration and concern for social righteousness is evident in Judah's praise and prayer.

Many psalms celebrate the glory and majesty of the Creator, revealed in nature. All scenes, all living things exhibit his power and declare his glory. No one who joined in Psalms 8, 19, 29, 65, 89, 96, 104 could imagine that God would take pleasure in sexual promiscuity, drunkenness, infant sacrifice or emotional frenzy. He is high above all human imagination, clothed in majesty, light, and power; worship must be dignified, reverent, and exalted to be worthy of him.

In the psalms God is holy (seven times); so is his name (= character, six times), his temple, mountain, arm, city, heaven, throne, hill, and promise, and God swears by his holiness. Hence holiness alone is fitting for God's house (93:5); anyone who would stand in the holy place must have clean hands, a pure heart—the implications are fully analyzed in 24:3–6, 15:1–5. This clearly reflects the teaching of the "Holiness Code" (Lev. 17–26), with its theme "You shall be holy, for I the LORD your God am holy." The code expounded "holiness" in terms of love to God, the fellow Israelite, and the neighbor, shown in honesty, integrity, and charity. How seriously this demand was taken may be judged from the most searching confession ever penned (Ps. 51), and the moving testimonies to God's forgiveness (103:8–14, five times).

In the psalms cries for righteousness are heard repeatedly, sometimes impatiently, demanding that God will arise, wake up, stir himself to intervene within his world. Even when her prophets were silent, Judah's worship effectively kept alive the hope of a world governed by her righteous king.

With this conception arose a wholly new evaluation of the Divine King's law (mentioned thirty-four times, with varied synonyms almost two hundred times, in AV/KJV), as the rule of life and of society. This idea was to dominate Jewish thought for centuries. Though "the law" had come from Moses, from Joshua to the eve of the exile (Jeremiah, and the historian of 1–2 Kings) no prophet appealed to its authority. In the Psalter and afterwards the law becomes Judah's chief source of the knowledge of God.

The King's Law. The ground of the Ten Commandments (Exod. 20:1–17; Deut. 5:6–21) is what God has already done for Israel. The first commandment asserts God's supremacy, forbidding worship of other gods; the second, his spirituality. The third safeguards the oath in court and marketplace; the fourth asserts God's claim on human time, with humanitarian overtones. The fifth protects the order of primitive society; the sixth, seventh, and eighth, the sanctity of life, marriage, and property (on which life might depend). The ninth commandment protects an individual's good name, and the tenth forbids undisciplined desire.

The Book of the Covenant (Exod. 20:22–23:19) presupposes a simple agricultural background;

vengeful impulses of primitive society are here moderated by a sense of proportion and justice. The eye-for-eye rule was originally a limitation on unmeasured retribution. The book tolerates slavery but civilizes it; kidnapping slaves deserves death, and so do sorcery, idolatry, and bestiality. Compensation for neglected dangerous animals or buildings depends on circumstances, and restitution for theft is controlled. Seduction involves marriage and dowry. Oppression of widows, orphans, and foreigners and perversion of justice are strictly forbidden. Moderation, equity, and philanthropy, reinforced by religious reverence, are the Book's guiding principles: God defends justice—and is compassionate.

The Book of Deuteronomy stressed humanitarian concerns and an inward devotion to God. God is ever impartial, just, caring for the fatherless, the widow, and the alien: so must his people be. When slaves are freed, provision must be made for their immediate needs. Holiness, and lives worthy of sons of God, are required, from motives of gratitude and love toward God (6:5, 20–25). Prostitution, child sacrifice, and divination are suppressed; the right to glean, to receive wages before evening, regular provision for the poor, and reverence for the aged, are all enacted. Animals share in such consideration (22:1–4). All punishments must be strictly limited (25:3). Law and ethics have here coalesced.

Old Testament ethics are admittedly unsystematic, and largely unreflective. Developing in each generation from Israel's growing understanding of God, its insights possess a universality, and authority, conferred by long experience. The moral principles are the conditions of individual and social welfare, not an arbitrary prize for being virtuous but as the natural consequence of obeying the inner laws of well-being implanted by Him who made us.

Intertestamental Influence. In the years before Jesus, foreign occupation narrowed and hardened moral attitudes. God's kingship fed nationalistic hopes of deliverance through Messiah; delight in God's law sank into rigid legalism, fostering self-righteousness or despair. The law was "hedged" with innumerable minor rules, to express the whole duty of man; enthusiasts (Hasidim, later Pharisees) defended it, devoted scribes expounded it, synagogues inculcated it, exaggerated claims held it to be "superior to prophecy," "light and life of all," and "eternal." Essenes outdid Pharisees in strictness, discouraging marriage, sharing possessions, and rejecting the temple. Covenanters at Qumran sought "absolute" holiness through monastic discipline, based on moral dualism (light/darkness, truth/falsehood).

The standard was high, in sexual purity, piety, and charity; loyalty to the law did produce saints and martyrs. But legalism became self-serving, claiming merit before God; ethics became casuistry; for the weak, ignorant, poor, or sinful, legalism had no message and no mercy.

The Baptist's manner, his demand for repentance, and his regime of fasting and prayer appealed to the new ascetic tendency (Matt. 11:16–18; Mark 2:18; Luke 11:1), adding prophetic authority. Luke summarizes his practical ethical emphases (3:10–14). The priesthood meanwhile maintained the elaborate ritual of sacrifice and festivals; many common people worshiped at synagogues and sustained a simpler domestic piety—as at Nazareth. Into this confusion of ethical insights and tendencies Jesus stepped.

Jesus' Method. Jesus did not abate the divine law's ideals, but he severely criticized Judaism's legalism as academic (Luke 11:52), cruel (forbidding Sabbath cures, banishing the mentally ill and lepers from society), having wrong priorities, external in judgment, and burdensome (Matt. 23:23–28; Mark 7:14–23). It fostered self-righteousness and contempt for the weak and sinful (Luke 7:36–50; 15:25–32; 18:9–14; John 8:1–11). Jesus did not legislate.

Nor did Jesus cite authorities (Matt. 7:28–29). He appealed to the common moral judgment, very often by questions. Even his assertions often ended with "He that has ears . . . let him hear." Jesus assumes the capacity of the sincere to recognize truth when presented with it. Such consent of the enlightened conscience ensures that obedience is free, spontaneous, approving.

The Kingly Father. As in the Old Testament, so for Jesus ethics derives from a right relationship with God, rendering obedience filial. Yet not all live as sons; some are disobedient, wayward, lost. But God remains Father, and sonship remains available; the Father welcomes their return. In such a context legalism must wither, and the moral life gain new motivation, quality, and tone.

One implication of sonship is likeness: Resemblance proves relationship. The peacemakers, the merciful, those who love their enemies and persecutors, being as impartial and inclusive in their love as God is, those who do good, and lend, hoping for nothing again—all are, and are recognized as, children of the father (Matt. 5:9, 44–48; Luke 6:35–36). By this simple domestic simile Jesus initiates the supreme Christian ideal of Christlikeness, the imitation of God as beloved children, conformed to the image of his Son (Rom. 8:29; Eph. 5:1).

Second, the language of sonship is relentlessly plural. Such brotherliness forbids insult, and criticism, though brotherly rebuke may be necessary (Matt. 5:22; 7:1–3; Luke 17:3). It requires initiative toward reconciliation and understanding, and ready forgiveness (Matt. 5:23–24; 18:21, 35), and, in any need, service as for Christ (Matt. 25:40). At all times the duty of brethren is to strengthen each other (Luke 22:32).

The Fatherly King. In God's kingdom the supreme law must be to love the King with the whole personality (Matt. 22:36–38). The kingdom's second law commands love toward whoever is near enough to be loved, with a transferred self-love that makes our wants the criteria for our neighbors' (Matt. 7:12 = 22:39–40). Such love fulfills the whole law. Illustrations of its practical meaning are the cup of (scarce) water, visiting the sick, helping any mugged victim, clothing the naked, befriending the ill-deserving in prison, doing good, lending without interest. The nature of the King determines the law of the kingdom, a kingdom of love (Matt. 11:2–6; Luke 4:16–21).

Yet Christ's example of love includes sternness against evil enjoyed or inflicted; it sets high standards, warns of consequences, exposes hypocrisy, speaks of judgment. It is neither sentimental, soft, nor stupid, but a resolute moral attitude that seeks another's good, whether by gentle or ungentle means.

Jesus was a realist. To his mind, sinfulness was more, and more serious, than trespass against formal laws; it included sins of thought and desire, of neglect, of failure to love, and of sin against light (Matt. 5:27–28; 6:22–23; 12:35; 23:13–26; 25:41–46; Mark 3:22–30; Luke 10:31–32; 13:6–9). Life in God's kingdom, therefore, involves personal resistance, protest, conflict, and suffering, occasioned by loyalty to God in a godless world (Mark 8:34–38; Luke 22:35–36). But the citizen of the kingdom will seek peace with all where possible, never returning evil for evil (Matt. 5:9, 38–40).

In all situations the will of the King is to be the ultimate rule of life. And the King's will shall triumph in the end. Human beings may choose whether to live under God's reign or not, but he remains King. In parables (Matt. 21:33–43; 25:14–46; Luke 12:16–21; 13:6–9; 16:19–31) and numerous phrases the truth is made clear that people cannot trifle with God indefinitely. What is good news for the responsive is warning for the obdurate: The Father is King.

Even so cursory a review reveals how rich, varied, realistic, and practical is the ethical teaching of Jesus, and how directly it derives from the perceived character of God and from relationship with him. The good life is lived before God, by his help, in gratitude for his goodness; shorn of these religious roots, Christian values must die and Christian motivation fail. And all is illustrated, unforgettably, by the living example of Jesus, and therefore summed up in his "Follow me."

New Testament Moral Theology. Those who walk, live, and set their minds "according to the Spirit" find freedom, peace, acceptance with God, and constant renewal as sons of God (Rom. 8:5–17). This new, Spirit-ruled life is characterized by the absolute lordship of Christ over all attitudes and conduct (Rom. 1:3–4; 10:9–13; 14:7–9; 1 Cor. 6:13–20, etc.). Human personality being "open" Godward, as well as toward social forces that corrupt, the soul united to Christ becomes the vehicle of the divine Spirit, by whose guidance and enabling it is made capable of otherwise unattainable virtue (Rom. 8:9–14; 1 Cor. 6:17–20; 2 Cor. 4:7–18). Paul presents a perpetually progressive ideal, developing constantly in its scope of love, its depth of consecration, and in likeness to Christ. Paul does not claim to have attained the goal, only to be straining forward at the ever-upward call of God in Christ, toward the stature of Christ, being by degrees changed "into his likeness" and "conformed to his image" (Rom. 8:29; 2 Cor. 3:18; Eph. 4:13; Phil. 3:12–14).

Human ethics, based on philosophical, sociological or psychological premises, or intuitive responses to isolated "situations," attain only a consensus of good advice acceptable to people already virtuous in intention. Such moral counsel lacks permanence, authority, and motive power. Biblical ethics, deriving from knowledge and experience of God but forged always in historical real-life situations, problems and needs, reveals unchanging absolutes, inarguable authority, effective motivation, and redemptive power. The Old Testament emphasizes that God's requirements enshrine the secrets of total human welfare; the New Testament points to the man Jesus Christ and his intensely human story as embodiment of the ultimate ideal. Thus biblical ethics prove more truly human in the end, enshrining the Creator's intention for his highest creatures.

R. E. O. White

See also Deuteronomy, Theology of; Jesus Christ; Law; Salvation; Sanctification; Sermon on the Mount; Ten Commandments.

Bibliography. W. Barclay, *Ethics in a Permissive Society;* P. Carrington, *Primitive Christian Catechism;* C. F. H. Henry, *Christian Personal Ethics;* W. Lillie, *Studies in New Testament Ethics;* J. T. Sanders, *Ethics in the New Testament;* E. F. Scott, *Ethical Teaching of Jesus;* R. E. O. White, *Biblical Ethics.*

Eucharist. *See* Lord's Supper, the.

Evangelist, Evangelism, Gift of. *See* Holy Spirit, Gifts of.

Evangelize, Evangelism. ***Basic Definition.*** "To evangelize" is to proclaim the good news of the victory of God's salvation. "Evangelism" is the noun denoting that activity. This biblical concept is expressed through a Hebrew verb (*bāśar*) and a Greek verb and noun (*euangelizō* and *euangelion*). *Euangelion* is normally translated "gospel," denoting the content of the good news. But it can also be a noun of action, describing the activity of telling that news (e.g., 1 Cor. 9:14; 2 Cor. 2:12; Phil. 1:5).

The Old Testament. In family matters, one may "bring news" to a father that a male child is born (Jer. 20:15). In military matters, "to evangelize" is to bring news of the outcome of a military engagement, usually a victory (1 Sam. 31:9;

2 Sam. 18:31; 1 Kings 1:42; but cf. 1 Sam. 4:17). This secular usage serves as the background for the theological usage in Isaiah and the psalms.

Since Israel's national destiny is in God's sovereign hands, and he fights the nation's battles for her, any announcement of military victory necessarily has theological meaning. The victory over the Canaanite kings in the conquest of the land is so complete and certain that it is captured in a juxtaposition of its prelude—"The Lord announced the word"—and aftermath—"and great was the company of those who proclaimed it" (Ps. 68:11; cf. Exod. 15:20–21).

The initial act of bringing the news of military victory can be a religious act for pagan nations as well (1 Sam. 31:9; cf. 2 Sam. 1:20). But for Israel, the "good news" is that the Lord has freed (vindicated) the nation and its divinely anointed ruler from the hands of their enemies. When the lepers discover the abandoned camp of the Syrian siegemakers of Elisha's and Jehoram's day, they name it "a day of good news" (2 Kings 7:9). To withhold proclamation of this divinely accomplished victory is not right (7:9). Indeed, they must tell the beneficiaries of the victory immediately.

David appropriates "evangelism" terminology for the worship context as he describes his confession before the God of divine deliverance: "I proclaim righteousness in the great assembly" (Ps. 40:9). Again there is a protestation of moral constraint: "I do not seal my lips." The message proclaimed is that God has acted in accordance with his character, his righteousness. He explains God's actions further by referring to God's reliability: God's faithfulness, truth, covenant loyalty and love, and salvation (40:10). The audience is the people of God, "the great assembly" (40:9–10).

What is true on a personal level is true for the nation as the people return the ark of the covenant to its rightful place at the center of Israel's worship (1 Chron. 16:23–25/Ps. 96:2–4). In an act of worship the whole earth is exhorted to continually proclaim good tidings. The message is an announcement of the salvation, glory, and mighty deeds of the supreme God, who is great and greatly to be praised. The messenger, the message, and the audience all have a universal quality.

Isaiah makes the most extensive and significant contribution to understanding the proclamation of the victory of God's final salvation in its Old Testament promise form (40:9–11; 52:7; 60:6; 61:1). This prophet's teaching is not only foundational for seminal New Testament passages, but it is also the source for the New Testament use of the term "gospel."

Within the context of predicting comfort for Israel—the return to the land of those in exile in Babylon—Isaiah unfolds a scene of redemption that will only be fully realized at the end of time. The prophet relates the proclamation of the good news of the victory of God's salvation in progressive stages until the Gentiles are publishing it.

At God's initiative (41:27) a messenger arrives from Babylon bringing good news of happiness (good, 52:7). The "beautiful feet" figure, along with the joyful response, indicate the news' value and personal benefit. As in the military context, the basic message is one of complete victory: "Your God reigns!" God, with supreme sovereign power, has acted in covenant loyalty to Israel—to restore, comfort, redeem, save, and protect her (52:8–12). Israel will know peace, good, and salvation (52:7). To speak of restoration, redemption, and salvation in the sight of all the nations and all the ends of the earth points us beyond the return from exile to full salvation at the end of time (52:10). The prophet emphasizes a Spirit-empowered messenger divinely sent "to bring good news to the afflicted."

Isaiah 61:1–3 also unveils the physical/spiritual dynamic of this salvation along with the relationship between proclamation and accomplishment. It is possible to view the messenger's message and mission as dealing only with the external, physical, socioeconomic condition of the exile and the emotional trauma it has caused. Indeed many who practice a liberation theology hermeneutic see these verses and Jesus' appropriation of them as justifying a message and praxis of socioeconomic and political liberation. Is that not what it means to "preach good news to the afflicted (the oppressed poor)"? The term Isaiah uses (*ʿănāwîm*) refers to those who are poor because of the oppression of the rich and powerful.

One of Israel's sins was economic oppression of the weak and defenseless (10:1–2). For this their divine punishment was to experience oppression at the hands of the Babylonians. When God acts to save and restore Israel he will relieve physical oppression by release from exile and an establishment of justice in Messiah's reign (11:4; 29:18–19; 49:13). And he will get at the spiritual root of the problem by offering forgiveness to these former sinful oppressors (41:17; 55:1, 7). This they receive as they adopt a humble stance before the Lord as the oppressed in heart and spirit (57:15; 66:2). Any proclamation of good news to the oppressed poor, then, must present a holistic salvation with a spiritual center.

That the messenger's task is both to announce and to accomplish what is announced—"to bring good news to the afflicted . . . to bind up the brokenhearted"—has led some to conclude that Scripture views the proclamation itself as accomplishing the salvation. Such a view, although it takes cognizance of the Bible's claims for the saving power of the good news, fails to reckon with the distinction between Jesus, who both proclaims and accomplishes salvation, and those who come after him, who simply proclaim its accomplishment. In the sense that proclamation is the occasion for the appropriation of the salvation by the hearers, it can be said to effect it.

Although Isaiah 40:9 might be seen as another command to a messenger to Jerusalem, it is better, given grammatical considerations, to take it as an exhortation to the inhabitants of Jerusalem. They have received the good news of the victory of God's salvation and now are encouraged to become "bearers of good news" themselves. They are to carry the message to the surrounding towns of Judah. "Your God reigns!" becomes "Here is your God!" The salvation arrives with the coming of the powerful God who with a shepherd's gentleness brings his reward, but also exacts his judicial recompense.

The next step in the proclamation of God's victorious salvation is evidently to the Gentiles. They in turn will come to Jerusalem and "bear good news of the praises of the LORD" (60:6).

The New Testament. Other than 1 Thessalonians 3:6, all New Testament uses of the term have a theological meaning. Whether in predicting the forerunner's genesis (Luke 1:19) or announcing the Savior's birth (2:10), angels "evangelize" people. In the latter case, "great joy" is to be proclaimed as good news to all the people. The fulfillment of the promises through Isaiah have begun for a savior, Christ the Lord, is born.

John the Baptist's ministry is at the decisive boundary between promise and fulfillment in God's salvation history (Luke 16:16). Jesus characterizes it as a time from which "the kingdom (reign) of God is proclaimed as good news." Such preaching in John's case is termed "exhortation" (3:18). He announced both a preparatory repentance ethic, in the light of the approaching final judgment (3:3, 7–14), and a corrective to his audience's messianic expectations as he pointed to Jesus and the salvation blessings he offered (3:15–17).

Jesus' mission is to be the divinely sent proclaimer of the good news (Luke 4:43; Acts 10:36). This Jesus claims is in fulfillment of Isaiah 61:1–3 and establishes his messianic identity (Luke 4:18–21; 7:19, 22). Jesus' conduct of his earthly itinerant ministry of proclaiming the good news is accompanied by healing miracles and combined with teaching (4:43; 7:22; 8:1; 20:1). He sends out his disciples in Israel to follow the same pattern (9:2, 6).

The message Jesus proclaims is revelational (Acts 10:36) and points to the arrival of endtime salvation in terms of the coming of God's reign or of peace (Matt. 24:14; Mark 1:14–15; Luke 8:1; Acts 10:36; Eph. 2:17; cf. Isa. 52:7, 19). The response looked for is repentance and faith (Mark 1:15). Echoes of Isaiah and military victory imagery clearly underlie the expressions "proclaiming the good news of the reign of God" and "the good news of the kingdom." The "hiddenness" aspect of Jesus' precross earthly mission prevented him from making consistent and explicit reference to himself as the embodiment of the good news. Jesus makes clear the christological center of the gospel only after he has accomplished salvation, through his death and resurrection. Still, when Mark entitles his account of Jesus' life and ministry, he labels it "The beginning of the gospel about Jesus Christ, the Son of God" (Mark 1:1).

Jesus' teaching makes one point about evangelism. World evangelism is the one positive feature of the time between his return to heaven and his second coming (Matt. 24:14/Mark 13:10; Matt. 26:13/Mark 14:9): "And this gospel of the kingdom will be preached in the whole world as a testimony to all nations, and then the end will come." World evangelization is certain in its occurrence and universal in its scope. Jesus does not command it but predicts it and declares that its accomplishment is determinative of the end of human history. He says the whole inhabited world will be the arena for proclamation and that the witness will be addressed to every ethnic group. The last occurrence of *euangelizō* and *euangelion* in Scripture carries the same teaching (Rev. 14:6–7).

In the Book of Acts, whether as the activity to which God calls a person for lifelong service (20:24; cf. 1:8) or as the result of immediate divine guidance (15:7; 16:10), God is the source of evangelizing. The messengers may be apostles or evangelists (5:42; 8:12, 25, 35, 40; 15:7; 21:8), but not exclusively so. For the early church found the apostles evangelizing in company with nonapostles (13:32; 14:7, 21; 15:35). And in the same context where the work of Philip the evangelist is highlighted, believers dispersed by persecution following Stephen's death "preached the word wherever they went" (8:4). Anyone who has received, believed, and experienced the salvation blessings of the good news is qualified to proclaim it.

The message proclaimed is in continuity with Jesus' gospel in its eschatological/promise and fulfillment, soteriological, and ethical dimensions. Only now the revelational and christological aspects are central. To proclaim the good news is to proclaim Messiah Jesus or the Lord Jesus or simply Jesus. The response looked for is repentance (14:15) and faith (8:12; 15:7).

The early church also imitated her Lord in the way she evangelized. Teaching and making disciples were closely allied to it in an itinerant ministry that possessed a momentum moving the witnesses to the ends of the earth. Such evangelism evokes persecution, yet perseveres in the wake of it.

The good news concerns the fulfillment of promises made to the Jews (13:32), so it is right that the proclamation be made to them first (3:26; 13:46). But its Old Testament divine design and its very content—the universal offer of salvation to everyone who believes (Luke 24:47; Acts

13:39)—show that it is for the Gentiles as well. Almost every time a significant cultural threshold is crossed as the gospel reaches people who are farther and farther away from the light that God had given to Israel, *euangelizō* is used to describe what the church is doing.

Paul at the New Testament fulfillment stage as Isaiah at the Old Testament promise stage contributes the fullest exposition of "evangelize, evangelism." The divine source of this activity manifests itself both in the commissioning and the enabling of the apostle. He was "set apart for the gospel [proclaiming the good news] of God" (Rom. 1:1). This and this alone he was sent to do (1 Cor. 1:17). Taking the singular messenger of Isaiah 52:7 as a collective, Paul declares that all who evangelize are fulfilling Isaiah's prophetic pattern (Rom. 10:14–15). The divine enablement in proclaiming the good news is a grace given; a spiritual gifting from the risen and exalted Lord, so much the work of Christ that Paul can say that the risen One himself comes and preaches peace to those who are afar off and to those who are near (Eph. 2:17; 3:2, 8; 4:11; 6:19).

As modeled in the early church Paul teaches that the proper messengers of the good news are not only apostles and evangelists (Rom. 1:9; cf. 1 Cor. 9:18; Eph. 3:5) and full-time Christian workers (1 Cor. 9:14, 18; 2 Cor. 11:7), but all the church of Christ (Eph. 3:10; cf. Col. 1:7). Every member must have feet shod "with the readiness that comes from the gospel of peace" (Eph. 6:15).

Paul does give the content of the gospel in summary form several times (Rom. 10:8–10; 1 Cor. 15:3–4; 2 Tim. 2:8). The qualifying phrases he puts with the word "gospel" yield important insights. Yet, when it comes to presenting an object for *euangelizō,* which might give us clues as to Paul's understanding of the "good news" proclaimed, he seems to speak in tautologies. What is proclaimed as good news is the good news, *to euangelion* (1 Cor. 15:1; 2 Cor. 11:7; Gal. 1:11). Since there is only one good news, which Christians will recognize over against false gospels, this expression is in the end no meaningless tautology (Gal. 1:6–9). What Paul does bring out in his use of objects with *euangelizō* is the Christocentric and soteriological nature of the message. The messenger proclaims Christ, his unfathomable riches, and the faith (2 Cor. 4:5; Gal. 1:16, 23; Eph. 3:8). The response looked for is an understanding and believing of the good news that leads to a calling on the Lord for salvation and an active obedience to that same Lord Jesus in this new relationship (Rom. 1:5, 16–17; 10:14; Eph. 1:13; Col. 1:5–6).

Paul expounds the conduct of "evangelism" in terms of the motives for it, the spiritual transaction it is, and the imagery that may describe it. A person proclaims the good news moved both by the necessity of an entrusted stewardship (1 Cor. 9:12, 16–17, 23; 1 Thess. 2:4) and commitment to the audience (Rom. 1:15; Col. 1:7; 1 Thess. 1:5; 2:8–9).

Paul delights in highlighting the spiritual transaction that occurs during the proclamation of the good news. He may say power, the Holy Spirit, and deep conviction accompanied the preaching (1 Thess. 1:5). He may present the proclamation as the means by which God called persons to obtain salvation blessings (2 Thess. 2:14: cf. 1 Cor. 4:15). In fact, the proclamation may be personified as the power itself as what "all over the world . . . is bearing fruit and growing" (Col. 1:5–6; cf. Rom. 1:16–17).

Paul's imagery characterizes evangelizing as revelatory. It is making plain "the administration of this mystery, which for ages past was kept hidden in God" (Eph. 3:9; cf. 6:19; Rom. 16:26). By it the manifold wisdom of God is "made known to the rulers and authorities in the heavenly realms" (Eph. 3:10). Evangelism is also worship, for Paul says he ministers "with the priestly duty of proclaiming the gospel of God, so that the Gentiles might become an offering acceptable to God, sanctified by the Holy Spirit" (Rom. 15:16).

On the human plane evangelism is not only the proclamation of a commissioned witness (Rom. 10:15; Eph. 6:15; Col. 1:5). It is also a "traditioning" (1 Cor. 15:1–3) and a controversial activity for which one will suffer persecution and at the same time offer a defense (Phil. 1:7, 16; 2 Tim. 1:8, 12; 2:9).

For Paul the audience to be evangelized includes both unbelieving Jew and Gentile, although he notes Jewish rejection and Gentile receptivity. Paul also speaks of evangelizing Christians. For them such proclamation holds up a standard for their Christian conduct (2 Cor. 9:13; Gal. 2:14; Phil. 1:27) and strengthens them in their faith (Rom. 16:25; Col. 1:23; 2 Tim. 4:2, 5). Neither this use nor the fact that a local pastor, Timothy, is instructed to do the work of an evangelist should lead us to the false conclusion that the biblical understanding of evangelism in its full exposition by Paul is so broadened that in the end it does not retain its sharp focus of proclamation of the good news of salvation to the unsaved. Christians only rightly apply such evangelizing to themselves in their saved condition when they continue to receive it as the proclamation of the gospel.

Peter brings the biblical teaching on evangelism to an appropriate climax with an emphasis on the value and power of the message proclaimed. In continuity with the prophets, Jesus, and the other apostles, Peter recounts a gospel with the Messiah's suffering and glory at its center and salvation and grace as its benefit. The Holy Spirit not only revealed the message to the Old Testament prophets, but he, sent from heaven, empowered those who evangelized Peter's hearers (1 Peter

1:10–12). No wonder this gospel is things into which angels long to look (1:12).

Peter says that there is power in evangelism to make people be born again unto eternal life (1:23–25). Peter makes it clear that it is not the act of evangelizing but the good news communicated in that act, the Word of God that abides forever, which is the imperishable seed that by the Spirit (1:12) gives the new birth. It is no coincidence that Peter quotes verses that immediately precede Isaiah 40:9 when he describes the message that was proclaimed as good news to his hearers. This power Peter finally places in eschatological perspective when he notes the purpose for which those who had already died had been evangelized: "so that they might be judged according to men in regard to the body, but live according to God in regard to the spirit" (1 Peter 4:6).

William J. Larkin, Jr.

See also Mission; Testimony.

Bibliography. N. P. Bratsiotis, *TDOT,* 2:313–32; J. K. Chamblin, *BEB,* 1:892–97; G. Friedrich, *TDNT,* 2:707–21; M. Green, *Evangelism in the Early Church;* Y. Hattori, *Ev R Th* 12 (1988): 5–16.

Eve. All four passages in the Bible that contain the name "Eve" refer to the wife of the original man, Adam (Gen. 3:20; 4:1; 2 Cor. 11:3; 1 Tim. 2:13). Her creation takes place after God's assertion that "it is not good for the man to be alone" (Gen. 2:18), his announcement that he will make the man a helper who corresponds to him (*ʿēzer kĕnegdô*), his peer and complement, and the observation that no other creature yet formed is suitable (vv. 18–20). All this illustrates the innate human need for community. Indeed, the marriage relationship involving these first two humans (vv. 24–25) typifies all forms of human coexistence designed to satisfy the primal yearning for fellowship.

Subordination is not inherent in the use of the term, *ʿēzer*, "helper" (2:18, 20), as is clear from the fact that it is frequently used of God in relation to humans (e.g., Exod. 18:4; Deut. 33:7; Pss. 33:20; 70:5[6]; 115:9, 10, 11; 146:5). The description of the woman being created from the man's rib (Gen. 2:21–22) highlights the kind of affinity between man and woman that is not possible between humans and other creatures. That fact is emphasized in the man's joyful cry of recognition when God presents the woman to him: "This is now bone of my bones and flesh of my flesh" (v. 23). Some detect evidence of male headship in the prefall narrative (e.g., the man's prior creation, the woman's derivation from the man, his designation of her as woman, and the focus on a man's initiative in the establishment of a marriage relationship [2:7, 21–24]). Others suggest the idea of man's subjugation of woman is introduced only after the fall when God describes the various forms of humiliation, enmity, pain, and drudgery that result from human rebellion against him (3:14–19).

The woman's role in the narrative about the fall is significant, not least because it is she who has the exchange with the serpent, the agent of temptation. The focus on the conversation is the covenant that God initially establishes with the man (2:15–17). Although that covenant subsequently includes her (3:2–3), she is not an original party to it. Some commentators suggest that this makes her more vulnerable than the man to the serpent's intrigue in this regard, and that he addresses her specifically for this reason. In the course of the conversation she does, in fact, misrepresent the terms of the covenant by diminishing the generosity of the Creator's provision (3:2; "We may eat fruit from the trees in the garden"; cf. 2:16: "You are free to eat from any tree in the garden"), adding to the covenantal prohibition (3:3: "You must not eat fruit from the tree that is in the middle of the garden, and you must not touch it"; cf. 2:17: "but you must not eat from the tree of the knowledge of good and evil") and weakening the statement about the consequences of disobedience (3:3: "or you will die"; cf. 2:17: "you will surely die"). In the final analysis, however, both she and her husband challenge the Creator's prerogative to establish moral absolutes of right and wrong by eating the forbidden fruit (3:6; cf. 2:17) and both are held equally accountable (3:9–19).

The only positive prospect mentioned by God as he spells out the fall's consequences is that, in the context of the ongoing enmity between the woman and her offspring, on the one hand, and the serpent and his offspring, on the other, the woman's offspring will dominate the serpent's (3:15). In the immediate setting this statement is probably intended to represent humanity's continuing struggle with evil and to anticipate the eventual vanquishment of evil. From the perspective of the New Testament the ultimate realization of that hope is to be found in the triumph of God and his kingdom over evil and the evil one (Luke 10:17–19; Rom. 16:20; Heb. 2:14; Rev. 12).

Genesis 3:20 describes Adam assigning his wife the name, Eve, "because she would become the mother of all the living." The original Hebrew form of the name, *ḥawwâ*, is apparently a derivative of, or a paronomasia on, the verb *ḥāyâ*, which means "live." Adam's comment reinforces the idea that all of humanity constitutes a family, a family for which the unsavory consequences of human transgression and the possibility of human redemption are a common heritage.

When Eve is next mentioned by name it is in relation to her conception and delivery of Cain (*qayin*), after which she says that she has produced (*qānâ*) a man with Yahweh's help (4:1). Thus she who was derived from man now demonstrates her creative capacity in partnership with her Creator (cf. 1 Cor. 11:8–9, 11–12). Incidentally, she also has the distinction of being the first individual portrayed in the Genesis narrative as pronouncing that name by which God typically reveals himself to people with whom he binds himself in covenant.

In the New Testament, Eve is remembered for being created after Adam and for being deceived. Paul, in 2 Corinthians 11:3, expresses his fear that, as the serpent cunningly deceived Eve, the thoughts of the Corinthians "may somehow be led astray from your sincere and pure devotion to Christ." The theme of Eve's deception is also present in 1 Timothy 2:14 following the mention of her creation after Adam (v. 13) in the statement which, by means of analogy, provides the rationale for the prohibition against a woman teaching or having authority over a man (v. 12). This injunction must be seen against the backdrop of the situation in Ephesus, Timothy's location (1:3), where certain women in the church were creating problems (see 5:11–15). It cannot be used to support the idea that no woman may ever teach or exercise leadership in the church (see Acts 18:26; Rom. 16:1, 7). ROBERT J. V. HIEBERT

See also ADAM; FALL, THE; HEAD, HEADSHIP; WOMAN.

Bibliography. H. Blocher, *In the Beginning;* W. Brueggemann, *Genesis;* C. Brown, *NIDNTT, I*, pp. 87–88; U. Cassuto, *A Commentary on the Book of Genesis;* I. M. Kikawada, *JBL* 91 (1972): 33–37; W. E. Phipps, *Theology Today* 33 (1976): 263–73; M. L. Ronzenweig, *Judaism* 139 (1986): 227–80; A. P. Ross, *Creation and Blessing;* G. von Rad, *Genesis;* G. J. Wenham, *Genesis 1–15;* C. Westermann, Genesis: *A Practical Commentary.*

Evil. As a prerequisite for any discussion of evil, moral evil must be distinguished from physical or natural evil. This essay uses the term "moral evil" to include both social offenses (ethics—murder, theft) and cultic sins (those offenses aimed directly against the deity—blasphemy, idolatry). Moral evil, therefore, whether its setting be cultic or social, when carried out may be considered a sin. That cultic and ethical values were one and the same in the Hebraic mind may be illustrated by the similar penalties exacted for the severest offenses in either category (death, being cut off). Cultic values are addressed in the first four of the Ten Commandments (Exod. 20:3–11; Deut. 5:7–15) and by the first of Jesus' "Great Commandments" (Matt. 22:37–40; Mark 12:30; Luke 10:27; cf. Deut. 6:5); ethics are considered in the last six of the Ten Commandments (Exod. 20:12–17; Deut. 5:16–21) and by the second "Great Commandment" (Lev. 19:18).

Accordingly, what is morally good is not what human society decides is in its best interest, but what the revealed will of God declares. There can be no biblical ethics that stand apart from cult nor a biblical morality apart from theology. Instead, morality is defined by theology, which carries within it certain cultic affirmations and prohibitions together with the ethical. For example, the same Decalogue that declares that stealing and murder are wrong likewise forbids idolatry and blasphemy. What makes these things wrong is not some abstract quality called "the good" as sought by philosophers in time past. Instead, what constitutes social evil is what is so defined by God, and in that respect (i.e., as to why a given act is good or bad), differs little from cultic evil. There are, therefore, no grounds for the oft-repeated error wherein the "moral law" (the ethical) is in some way distinguished from the "ceremonial law" (the cultic) in Israel's values system. There can be no such distinction! That which is ethical is right because God has declared it so; the cultic portions of the Law likewise determine what is right for the same reason. Because of this, cult and ethics often appear fused in the Bible, as in Cain's admission of guilt for a faulty sacrifice and the murder of his brother (Gen. 4:13); a similar fusion of the cultic and the ethical occurs in Genesis 15:16 ("the sin of the Amorites"), where idolatry and unethical activity are considered as one.

If God is the definer of what is good (2 Sam. 10:12; Mark 10:18; Luke 18:19), right (Gen. 18:25), and just (Job 34:12), it is not surprising that the Bible never attributes moral or cultic evil to him (Job 34:10). Indeed, he hates evil (Ps. 5:6) and is the avenging judge who punishes those who practice it (Isa. 31:2; Mic. 2:1).

On the other hand, what ethicists term physical evil (or, natural evil) is often connected with the activities of God, and thus demonstrates the importance of defining these categories before discussing the subject further. An ethicist may distinguish these two types of evil thus: (1) moral evil, which is real if any intellectual being knowingly does anything he or she ought not to have done without being compelled to do it; and (2) physical evil, which is real if some beings have suffered in situations caused by nonrational beings, or through actions of rational beings acting nonrationally.

Moral Evil and Sin. Distinguishing moral evil from sin is no simple task, yet it must be attempted before any discussion may proceed further. First, it is important to differentiate *a* sin (an individual expression of sin) from *generic* sin, the condition that gives rise to its expression. An individual sin, as mentioned earlier, is an acting out of cultic or social evil. But generic sin) is the condition that gives rise to the evil expressed in the individual sin.

However sin and evil may be considered by a secularist, the theological perspective held by the Bible that presupposes an involvement by God in his creation and an active will of God governing that creation requires that evil assume a theological dimension. Accordingly, moral evil finds its roots in disobedience, whether deliberate or accidental, premeditated or unpremeditated, cultic or ethical, to the revealed will of God, and as such, becomes associated with generic sin and virtually synonymous with wickedness. The stress in the Old Testament lies not on the conceptual, but in the practical outworking of a state of disharmony with God and one's fellow humans. It may be expected, therefore, that there will be an extensive overlap between terms for sin and terms expressing moral evil, whether the expression of this sin/evil be cultic or social. The origins for sin and evil in both Old and New Testaments are traced to the activities of an evil creature, Satan (1 John 3:8: "the devil has been sinning from the beginning") and to human sin that led to a fall (Rom. 5:12–14) and banishment form Eden and the tree of life (Gen. 3).

Cultic and Social Evil. In biblical theology, natural revelation ties humanity in general to a responsibility before God which, when ignored, leads to human relationships that are immoral (Rom. 1:18–25). In both Testaments, proper worship and social ethics are subsumed in a common covenant that ties the people of God to him and to one another. Since what God ordains is good, what is ethical is not clearly differentiated from what is cultic. Both belong to that aspect of sin that sets itself against the divinely instituted order, whether social or cultic, and thus inexorable finds itself in incessant conflict with God. Like Gollum's ring in *The Hobbit* or the addict's first "fix," evil does not always seem immediately repulsive, but may even be seen as attractive on superficial examination (Gen. 3:6), while profoundly destructive at a deeper level (Isa. 59:7).

Because what is right was what was ordained by God, and what is wrong was what was proscribed by him, deviation from this paradigm constitutes what is evil. The most common term for cultic evil in the Old Testament (used over 200 times) is *ʿāwôn,* "perversion," possibly related to the verb *ʿāwāh,* "to be bent," "to twist." As such, it refers to what is theologically perverted in some way. Because of Israel's holistic modes of thought, the word may be used to describe: (1) the evil action itself (particularly when found in the plural, e.g., Neh. 9:2; Job 13:23, 26; Ps. 130:3; Jer. 5:25; 33:8; Ezek. 36:33; 43:10; Lam. 4:13; Dan. 9:16); (2) the ensuing guilt (often in formulations such as "bear their guilt" [NRSV; NIV, "held responsible"], Lev. 5:17; 17:16); and (3) the punishment for the act (e.g., Gen. 4:13; Job 19:29). It may be used to describe idolatry (Exod. 20:5; Josh. 22:17; cf. Jer. 11:10; Ezek. 7:19; 14:3, 4, 7), trivializing the deity (2 Sam. 3:13–14), apostasy (Jer. 13:22), breach of the covenant (Jer. 5:25), or other activities that would in some way demean God's character or name (1 Sam. 3:13–14). It may refer to doing away with the fear of God (Job 15:4–5) or a lack of steadfastness toward him (Ps. 78:37–38) and it functions to alienate the individual from God (Lev. 26:40; Isa. 59:4). Prohibitions sometimes list words for "sin" together with *ʿāwôn,* emphasizing its theological coloring (e.g., Deut. 19:15; Isa. 1:4).

A frequently used word to convey the wrongness of idolatry is *ʾāwen,* denoting what is empty of any redeeming value. It may, therefore, denote "trouble, sorrow" as when the dying Rachel names her son Ben-oni, "son of my sorrow" (Gen. 35:18). The word is often used along with "toil" or "labor," and in such cases may designate the sin that brings the trouble (Ps. 7:14; Isa. 10:1). It may also be used to emphasize the absence of any theological value to a religious exercise (Isa. 1:13). Taking on the nuance of power used in a harmful manner, in Psalm 36:4 *ʾāwen* may designate "deceit." When found in Job, Psalms, and Proverbs, the phrase "workers of *ʾāwen*" may indicate those skilled in the black arts (Job 31:3; Pss. 5:6; 6:9; Prov. 10:29; 21:15).

Other common words for evil include the nouns *ʿāwel, ʿāwlâ,* derived from a root meaning "to deviate." The two words have virtually no detectable difference in meaning and denote what is contrary to the character of God; thus they bring at their heels a divine response. They are used to describe what is not right (Lev. 19:15, 35) and dishonest business practices (Deut. 25:14–16). Although Ezekiel generally seems to stress a need for cultic correctness, he uses *ʾāwel* to denote moral lapse, dishonesty (3:20; 18:24, 26; 33:18) such as taking usury and showing partiality in judgment (18:8), dishonest trade that desecrates the sanctuaries (28:18), and taking pledges for loans, stealing, and so on (33:15). Moreover, *ʿāwel* is sometimes found in one's hand (18:8). Both words are clearly seen as denoting actions by their frequent use as objects of verbs of doing. They are frequently seen as antonyms for words denoting justice, faithfulness, honesty, proper (just) administration, and rightness. They are frequently paired with synonyms with other words denoting persecution, wickedness, rebellion, violence, and evil.

Many Hebrew words are used for both cultic and social evil. For example, *ʿāwôn* may also be used to describe social evil. In Genesis 44:16, the brothers use it to describe their abuse of Joseph. It is used frequently to describe unwholesome sexual activities (Lev. 18:20), adultery (Num. 5:15, 31), and other civil or social perversions (1 Sam. 20:1, 8; 2 Sam. 3:8; Neh. 4:5; Ps. 51:2). The words *rāšāʿ, rešāʿ* are the most important antonyms for "what is right, just."

The words *raʿ, rōaʿ, and rāʿâ,* "harmful, harm," may be used in indicating something *evil* as *bad,* with *raʿ* frequently appearing as the opposite of good. Sometimes its meaning is moral, sometimes cultic evil, but often both. Hosea's favorite word for evil is *ra*ʿ. The evil man in Proverbs 11:21 will be punished, will be ensnared by the transgression of his lips (12:13), and has no future (24:20). Job complains that the evil man is spared in the day of calamity (21:30). In Jeremiah 2:33, Israel, the unfaithful wife of Yahweh, has so departed from his ways that she is able to teach her ways even to evil women. The men in 1 Samuel 30:22 termed evil are those who had pursued the Amalekites with David but who had selfishly decided that those left to guard the baggage should not share in the Amalekite spoil. In Genesis 13:13 the word describes the men of Sodom. In Psalm 140:2, evil things are devised in the hearts of violent men. The Revised Standard Version interprets *ra*ʿ in Psalm 10:15 as the "evildoer."

In the New Testament the words *ponēros* and *kakos* and their compounds and derivatives along with *anomia,* "lawlessness," have been used to denote what is bad or evil, and may either denote violations of social or cultic norms. The word *kakos,* its compounds and derivatives, denoted what was "bad," the opposite of good. In the Septuagint *kakos* most often denoted an evil that objectively hurt one's existence, which may have come as a judgment of God (Deut. 31:17; Amos 3:6b). The word appears in the New Testament without the attendant problems of theodicy that appear in its Old Testament setting. As such the adjective *kakos* may characterize a morally bad slave (Matt. 24:48), what is harmful (e.g., the tongue, James 3:8; cf. Rom. 14:20), or, when used as a substantive, what is contrary to law (i.e., a sin, crime, John 18:23; Rom. 7:21). Most of its occurrences in the New Testament are found in Paul's writings, where it can depict the evil one does unwillingly (Rom. 7:15, 17–20) and which becomes a law that rules him (7:21, 23) and which can only be overcome by the grace of God through Christ (7:25).

The compounds and derivatives of the word *ponēros* are commonly used in the New Testament to express evil and personal guilt of a more profound sort, especially in the Gospels. For example, it is used to denote the general evil of humankind (Matt. 7:11), the hardened Pharisees (Matt. 12:34), and the Jews as the evil generation (Matt. 12:39). In Matthew 7:17–18, an "evil" tree bears "evil" fruit, whereas in 7:11 *ponēros* can designate the general evil nature of human beings. In Matthew 6:23/Luke 11:34 it designates an unseeing eye, whereas in 2 Timothy 4:18 it represents an action that is life-threatening. Used as a substantive, it can represent [an] evil person[s] (Matt. 22:10) who will be judged in the final judgment (Matt. 13:49–50). Anyone who decides against Jesus is evil (2 Thess. 3:2; 2 Tim. 3:13). Particularly when used with the definite article it may serve as a sobriquet for Satan (Matt. 13:19; Mark 4:15; Luke 8:12).

Although its literal meaning is "lawlessness," *anomia* was used in the Septuagint most frequently to translate *ʿāwôn* (sixty times) and renders *ʾāwen* and *rāšāʿ* ("wickedness, guilt") twenty-five times each. In the New Testament it generally indicates "wickedness," albeit often with an eschatological flavor (Matt. 7:23; 2 Thess. 2:7).

Physical Evil. The denominative Hebrew root *r*ʿʿ with its derivatives *ra*ʿ, *roa*ʿ, and *raʿâ,* is frequently used in the Old Testament to designate the physical aspect of the action, situation, or state as it appears to the one experiencing its effects.

What Is Harmful. This distinctive nuance of the root *r*ʿʿ may be clearly seen where one of the words listed above is used to designate something physically harmful and where no moral reference is clearly intended as primary. Examples of this are found in its use to describe poisonous herbs in Elisha's pot (2 Kings 4:41) and the bad water he heals (2 Kings 2:19). Closely allied to the latter are the "evil diseases" of Egypt (Deut. 7:15) and the "evil diseases" of Ecclesiastes 6:2. Similarly seen as harmful are the deadly sword of Psalm 144:10 and God's arrows in Ezekiel 5:16. Dangerous animals capable of destroying human life are called "evil" (Gen. 37:20, 33). God will remove them from Canaan (Lev. 26:6), but will send them again to destroy rebellious Jerusalem (Ezek. 5:17; cf. also 14:15), only to banish them again when Judah is restored from captivity (Ezek. 34:25). Edomites are chided for gloating over the disaster of the destruction of Jerusalem, called "his [Judah's] evil" (Obad. 13).

What Is Subjectively Perceived. Jacob's assertion that "my years have been few and difficult [evil]" (Gen. 47:9) may be interpreted as either subjective, wherein the "evil" indicates suffering, or objective, as a hyperbole of humility. However, in 1 Kings 22:8 and its parallel (2 Chron. 18:12) the king of Israel (Ahab) answers Jehoshaphat of Judah, declaring that there is indeed a prophet of Yahweh about, adding peevishly, "But I hate him because he never prophesies anything good about me, but always bad [evil]." That neither moral nor objective evil is intended is clear when the prophecy unfolds as a prediction of Ahab's death. The prophecy is evil to Ahab, for whom it bodes personal harm and by whom it must be subjectively received. Ahab recognizes this, and confirms this as what he intended when he had predicted an evil prophecy (22:18).

Almost as obvious as the preceding is the phrase an "evil name" found frequently throughout the Old Testament to designate an unsavory reputation. For example, the husband's charge of nonvirginity in his bride "gives her a bad [evil] name" (Deut. 22:14, 19). Nehemiah denounces the hireling of Tobiah and Sanballat as one who wished to intimidate him and thus "give me a bad [evil] name" (Neh. 6:13). The evil name does not indicate moral, objective evil (as, for instance, a blasphemous or lewd epithet or title), but a subjectively perceived harm. Similar is the "evil" report (NIV, "distressing words") of Exodus 33:4, in which Moses reports to the people God's displeasure at calf-worship. An objective moral evil would require a foul, malevolent report. Instead, it describes the evaluation of God's reaction to Israel's idolatry and his decision not to go with them any longer. Nor is Joseph's evil report of his brothers objective, moral evil (Gen. 37:2), but a tale of their behavior that cast them in an unfavorable light. In Jeremiah 49:23, Hamath and Arpad hear evil tidings about the fall of Damascus—evil to them because Damascus was their ally and her fall portends their own fates.

The Teacher in Ecclesiastes calls the disappointing pursuit of wisdom a "heavy burden" (1:13) and repeats the words in 4:8 to describe the unfruitfulness of materialism. In 5:13 he calls selfishness a "grievous evil" (RSV). Finally, discipline is called evil in Proverbs 15:10 because it brings pain. A net is evil to the fish it catches (Eccles. 9:12); misfortune is an evil to Solomon as its recipient (1 Kings 5:4; NIV "disaster").

To "be evil in someone's eyes," or "to displease someone" can describe a woman slave who does not please her master (Exod. 21:8) and Esau's Canaanite (Hittite) wives who displeased Isaac (Gen. 28:8). In 1 Samuel 29:7, Achish warns David against displeasing the lords of the Philistines. God's mercy to Nineveh displeased Jonah (Jon. 4:1) because it embarrassed him; he felt its effects in losing face.

Appearance is another way in which a subjective notion is expressed by the words in question. Ecclesiastes 7:3 speaks of an "evil of countenance" to indicate a sad expression, as the context demonstrates. The Persian king asks Nehemiah, "Why are your faces evil, when you are not sick?" (Neh. 2:2), or, "Why does your face look so sad when you are not ill?" (NIV). Evil appearance denotes the poor quality of the cattle in Pharaoh's dream (Gen. 41:3, 4, 19, 20, 21, 27); land (Num. 13:19); and a bargaining session (Prov. 20:14 [twice]). The figs in Jeremiah's vision were so "evil" they could not be eaten (24:2, 3, 8; 29:17; they were of such poor quality that they were already in a state of decomposition that rendered them inedible).

Prosperity and adversity are also seen in terms of good and evil. When the people say to Jeremiah, "Whether it is good or evil, we will obey the voice of the LORD our God" (42:6 RSV), they are really saying, "For success or failure, we will obey."

Evil as the Responsibility of God. While moral evil is never imputed to God, there is often a connection made between Yahweh and *ra*ʿ, *roa*ʿ, and *ra*ʿ*â*. The classical reference, Isaiah 45:7, wherein God is called creator of evil would then refer to physical destruction, rather than moral evil, as the parallel term "maker of peace" would seem to render conclusive. God's judgments are not moral evil, else they would hardly be called judgments, but are physical, and called evil because of the adverse effects.

When God is pictured as "bringing evil," it is nearly always an invasion of Judah by a foreign power as exemplified in Jeremiah 4:6, where the term clearly refers to the impending invasion of Judah by the Babylonians (similar are 1 Kings 9:9; 21:29; 2 Kings 21:12; 2 Chron. 7:22; Jer. 6:19; 19:3, 15; 36:31). Especially clear is Exodus 32:12a, which says, referring to the exodus from Egypt, "it was with evil intent that he [God] brought them [Israel] out." Isaiah 31:2 predicts the failure of the alliance between Judah and Egypt, proclaiming God as the one who is wise and "brings evil," that is, brings defeat to his enemies. Similarly, Amos 3:6 asks, assuming a negative answer, if evil befalls a city, unless the Lord has done it. The meaning is clear. If a city is captured by an enemy, God has ordained it. In each of the preceding cases, the context verifies the interpretation as physical evil, in these cases as experienced subjectively by the victim of the military action. Lamentations 3:38 declares that it is the decree of God that brings good and evil.

The "Evil Day" may likewise be resolved as a day on which something harmful occurs rather than a day evil in and of itself. For example, Jeremiah 17:16–18 indicates that the "day of evil" (RSV) is a day on which Yahweh judges those who are his enemies, in this case, those who persecute the prophet. The "evil day" of Amos 6:3 refers to the fall of Samaria and destruction of Israel as a judgment by God (for similar language for Judah, see Jer. 16:10). Similarly, the psalmist declares that God's chastening is designed to keep him from days of trouble (Ps. 94:13; cf. 27:5; 49:5). In Ecclesiastes 12:1, however, the phrase "evil days" alludes simply to old age, as the context shows.

For God to speak evil concerning someone (1 Kings 22:23) may mean passing sentence on him. Similar is Naomi's complaint that God has brought evil upon her (Ruth 1:21). Yahweh "brings evil" upon Absalom by defeating the counsel of Ahithophel (2 Sam. 17:14). The "evil" of which God repents in Jonah 3:9–10 is evil only to the Ninevites, for they would have felt its effects physically and subjectively. But objectively, the act would have been justice executed because of the immoral conduct of the Assyrians.

Saul's Evil Spirit. The evil spirit from Yahweh that plagued Saul (1 Sam. 16:14–16, 23; 18:10; 19:9) may be considered as a spirit (disposition) sent by God that eventually destroyed Saul. The spirit, then, was God's instrument of judgment on Saul because of his rebellious attitude. Morally, the issue is justice, not evil. Similar is the evil spirit sent between Abimelech and the inhabitants of Shechem, which turns the Shechemites against him (Judg. 9:23).

While the above cited evidence might lead one to conclude that all natural evil (disaster) is a judgment of God for some sort of evil committed by the afflicted party, the Bible will not bear this conclusion. Job and Ecclesiastes issue a sharp challenge to the doctrine of retribution in this life and John 9:1–3 repudiates it as a means of explaining all suffering.

Why Evil? The Bible does not answer the oft-posed problem of how a just, omnipotent, and loving God could permit evil to exist in a universe he had created. A detailed examination to this question lies outside the scope of this article. Some suggestions, however, that have been offered about moral evil are: (1) while God is perfect, creation is only pronounced "very good" (Gen. 1:31); it is impossible for a created universe to rival God in perfection and the existence of moral evil is one example of its imperfection; (2) to compel all beings to act morally is to override their free will; likewise, to grant them free moral agency is to concede the possibility that someone at some time will act in an evil manner; and (3) God in his infinite wisdom created the best of all possible worlds; one can only consider that, were the world created any other way it would have been less than the best of all possibilities. The latter consideration also holds true as a possible explanation for natural evil. WILLIAM C. WILLIAMS

See also DEMON; SIN.

Bibliography. E. Achilles, *NIDNTT,* 1:561–67; M. Barker, *Heythrop Journal* 19 (1978): 12–27; K. H. Bernhardt, *TDOT,* 1:140–47; R. H. Bube, *JASA* 27:4 (1975): 171–80; G. R. Castellino, *CBQ* 30 (1968): 15–28; W. M. Clark, *JBL* (1989): 266–78; M. Dahood, *Biblica* 53 (1972): 386–403; G. I. Davies, *VT* 27 (1977): 105–10; J. E. Davison, *JBL* 104 (1985): 617–35; M. Ferguson, *SWJTh* 5 (1963): 7–20; C. T. Francisco, *SWJTh* 5 (1963): 33–41; B. Gross-Antony, *Biblische Notizen* 53 (1990): 23–25; M. Greenberg, *Ezekiel 1–20;* R. Reuven, *Judaism* 39/3 (1990): 318–25; G. S. Kane, *Religious Studies* 11 (1975): 49–71; G. Krodel, *Currents in Theology and Mission* 17 (1990): 440–46; A. Lococque, *Biblical Research* 24–25 (1979–80): 7–19; W. F. Lofthouse, *ExpT* 60 (1949): 264–68; C. Morrison, *The Powers That Be: Earthly Rulers and Demonic Powers in Romans 13:1–7;* J. C. Moyer, *ISBE,* 2:825; G. S. Ogden, *Technical Papers for the Bible Translator* 38/3 (1987): 301–7; C. R. Priebenow, *Luth Th J* 15 (1981): 45–52; B. Ramm, *SWJTh* 5 (1963): 21–32; A. B. Randall, *Journal of Interdisciplinary Studies* 2 (1990): 39–55; J. F. Ross, *Introduction to the Philosophy of Religion;* D. S. Shapiro, *Judaism* 5 (1956): 46–52; J. A. Thompson, *The Book of Jeremiah;* W. Wink, *Naming the Powers: The Language of Power in the New Testament;* idem, *Unmasking the Powers;* A. D. Verhey, *ISBE,* 2:206–10; R. G. Wilburn, *Lexington Theological Quarterly* 16/1 (1981): 126–41; R. Yates, *EQ* 52 (1980): 97–111.

Evil Spirit. *See* DEMON.

Exaltation. In the Bible "exaltation" most often refers to the lofty position of God and of Jesus Christ, but sometimes the term is applied to human beings, especially to Israel and her king. The most common Hebrew terms for "lift up, exalt" are *rûm, nāśā̕,* and *gābah,* while *hupsoō* is the Greek equivalent.

The Exaltation of God and His Name. In the Old Testament the Lord alone is the One who deserves to be exalted (Isa. 2:11, 17). His power is beyond that of all others (Job 36:22) and he is exalted over all the nations and above the heavens (Pss. 46:10; 57:5; 113:4). Sometimes God's exaltation is demonstrated by his mighty acts on behalf of his people. When the Lord overthrew Pharaoh's chariots and soldiers in the Red Sea, his right hand "was majestic with power" (Exod. 15:1, 6). No king or god could stand before the God of Israel (Exod. 15:11). On such triumphal occasions the Lord's right hand is said to be lifted high (Ps. 118:16; Isa. 26:11) as he takes action against the enemy (Isa. 33:10). God's powerful help leads people to praise him and to exalt his name, for he alone deserves the glory (Ps. 148:13; Isa. 24:15; 25:1). Since the Lord is King, the psalmist calls on humankind to exalt him and worship at the sanctuary (Ps. 99:5, 9).

The Exaltation of God's People. In his sovereign rule, God has seen fit to bless and to elevate those he has chosen. Abraham and Isaac enjoyed God's spiritual and material blessing (Gen. 24:35; 26:13), and the miraculous crossing of the Jordan River served to "exalt" Joshua as a leader close to the stature of Moses (Josh. 3:7). Those who are righteous are lifted up and given honor (Pss. 75:10; 112:9); God takes special delight in raising up the poor and humble (1 Sam. 2:7–8). Those who exalt themselves will be humbled, and those who humble themselves will be exalted (Matt. 23:12; Luke 14:11).

Throughout the Old Testament the people of Israel in particular were exalted by God. As early as the time of Balaam, when Israel was about to conquer Canaan, God announced that their kingdom would be exalted (Num. 24:7). This prediction was fulfilled during the reign of David, when Israel's king was "the most exalted of the kings of the earth" (Ps. 89:27). David acknowledged that the Lord "had exalted his kingdom for the sake of his people Israel" (2 Sam. 5:12). David knew that his rise to the throne was part of God's redemptive program for Israel launched when the Abrahamic covenant was established (Gen. 12:1–3). After the death of David, the Lord highly exalted Solomon and gave him unparalleled splendor as the head of a powerful empire (1 Chron. 29:25). According to Proverbs 14:34 "righteousness exalts a nation"; the days of David and Solomon were characterized by just and wise decisions that contributed to the peace and prosperity of their realms.

Sinful Human Exaltation. Sin entered the world when Adam and Eve ate the forbidden fruit, hoping to become "like God" (Gen. 3:5). Often the proud and arrogant behavior of human beings constitutes an attempt to usurp God's position in direct rebellion against his word. Israel was cautioned not to be proud, but unfortunately the nation's rebellion against God brought his harsh judgment (Deut. 8:14). The arrogance of Israel's leaders and of other nations is directly contrasted to the splendor of God's majesty "when he rises to shake the earth" (Isa. 2:19, 21). The psalmist warns the arrogant not to utter threats against heaven, or God will judge them (Ps. 75:5–7).

In the Old Testament the best illustrations of arrogance come from the lives of Gentile rulers. Sennacherib of Assyria threatened Hezekiah and the God of Judah (2 Kings 19:22), but God humiliated Sennacherib by destroying most of his army. Nebuchadnezzar of Babylon did conquer Jerusalem and was overcome with pride, but after God struck him down with insanity, Nebuchadnezzar praised and exalted the King of heaven (Dan. 4:30, 37). In the second century B.C. Antiochus IV Epiphanes arrogantly tried to stamp out Jewish worship, foreshadowing a future ruler who would exalt and magnify himself against the Lord (Dan. 8:23–25; 11:36–37). This man of lawlessness will exalt himself to the point of claiming to be God, and then he will be destroyed (2 Thess. 2:3–4).

The Exaltation of Christ. As the God-man, Jesus Christ entered the world to redeem humankind from their sinful condition. Through his death and resurrection Christ was exalted to the right hand of the Father. Both Isaiah 52:13 and the Gospel of John (3:14; 8:28; 12:32, 34) speak of Christ's death in the double sense of being "lifted up" and being "highly exalted." By humbling himself and submitting to death by being "lifted" onto a Roman cross, Christ paid for the sin of humankind, and in so doing was exalted by the Father to the highest place and given "the name that is above every name" (Phil. 2:8–9). It was through the resurrection from the dead that Christ's death was demonstrated in a powerful way (Rom. 1:4). By the resurrection Christ's human nature entered the glorious state of the unending life, and the risen Lord swallowed up death in victory (1 Cor. 15:54).

Having finished his work on earth, Jesus was taken back to heaven and seated at the right hand of God. David had spoken of the Messiah's sitting at the Lord's right hand (Ps. 110:1). This most exalted and honored position confirmed Christ's glory and authority as the supreme ruler (Eph. 1:20–21). Christ's exaltation and lordship are evident in the titles "Prince" and "Savior," which are ascribed to him in his heavenly session (Acts 5:31). The "prince" or "author" of our salvation was made "perfect through suffering" and then "sat down at the right hand of the throne of God" (Heb. 2:10; 12:2). The son of David was now a king far above any earthly ruler.

At his second coming the King of kings and Lord of lords will return to earth to defeat the nations and to rule them with an iron scepter (Rev. 19:15–16). Christ's sovereign authority will be displayed; every knee will bow and every tongue will confess that he is Lord (Phil. 2:10–11).

HERBERT M. WOLF

See also ASCENSION OF JESUS CHRIST; PRIDE; WORSHIP.

Bibliography. G. Bertram, *TDNT,* 8:602–12; W. A. Grudem, *EDT,* 1053–54; R. Nicole, *ZPEB,* 2:421–22.

Exodus, Theology of. The disclosure of God in the Book of Exodus develops from a distant deity of an oppressed people in Egypt to one in intimate relationship with the people of Israel on their way to the promised land. A theological goldmine results, impacting the concepts and theological ideas of the rest of the Old Testament.

Perhaps the best way to approach the book's theology starts with its literary development, for the revelation of God unfolds in different ways as the book progresses. It begins with God delivering the Israelites from oppression in Egypt (chaps. 1–19). Deliverance leads to responsibility on the part of God's people (chaps. 20–40). Geographically, the first part takes place in Egypt, while the second part begins and ends at Mount Sinai in the wilderness. Themes include deliverance (chaps. 1–19), covenant (chaps. 20–24, 32–34), and presence (chaps. 25–31, 35–40).

Literary Development of the Theology. The book begins by tracing the growth of Jacob's family in Egypt. As a nation, Israel suffers oppression from Pharaoh (1:8–10). Despite the terrible conditions, the nation continues to grow (1:12), a hint that God is blessing them. New measures are taken to stop their population explosion, but the midwives become instruments of salvation rather than death because they "feared God" (1:17). The text states that God blesses them for their actions in preserving life (1:20–21).

Starting in 2:10, the narrator follows one child. He is named Moses, for Pharaoh's daughter "drew him out of the water." His name could also mean "deliverer," suitable to his role as a human agent to resolve the repression by Pharaoh. His zeal to alleviate oppression leads to misfortune and personal discouragement (2:11–15), but sets up the divine initiative leading to complete liberation. Chapter 2 ends with the cries of Israel to God and the message that God hears them (vv. 23–25).

A dramatic change takes place when God appears to Moses. The disclosure of God's will and plan revolves around the conversation with Moses. First, God appears in a burning bush (3:2), producing a sanctified space (3:5). Then God speaks directly with Moses. God reveals that he is the same deity that the patriarchs knew (3:6), is concerned with the deliverance of Israel (3:7–9), and wants to use Moses in the task (3:10).

In the process of the conversation, God also discloses a personal name, Yahweh (3:15). Based upon the enigmatic phrase in 3:14, "I AM WHO I AM," this name reveals that God exists as a deity who is active and will work in behalf of his people. Mere existence is not in mind, but the willingness to work for Israelite deliverance. The name acts as a word of assurance to Moses and to the Israelites. Additional confirmation of this deity's ability surfaces in the signs given to Moses to answer his objections to God's call (4:1–9).

Further clarification of the name "Yahweh" occurs in God's speech of reassurance to Moses in 6:2–9. After Moses' initial attempts at deliverance from Pharaoh fail, Yahweh puts the scene into theological perspective. The paragraph revolves on the self-identification formula, "I am Yahweh" (6:2, 6, 8). In the past, the patriarchs knew God as God Almighty. They did not understand the full capacity of the name "Yahweh." This limitation will now change. Continuity with the past rests in the covenant made with their forefathers (6:4–5), but full revelation of the name will involve liberation from the slavery of Egypt, redemption by God's own mighty deeds, election as his people, relational knowledge of Yahweh as their God, and the completion of the promises involving the inheritance of a land (6:6–8). Although the people are not impressed with this report, the book records the fulfillment of the speech and thus the revelation of the full capacity of this deity, Yahweh.

The ten plagues display the power of Yahweh. Nature bows under the will of this God. Each plague becomes more dangerous. They come in waves of three, the third one confirming the previous two. Although the Pharaoh's magicians imitate some of the plagues, human powers soon fade.

The conflict with Pharaoh, and probably with all that he stands for, is emphasized by the narrative. Almost every plague account notes the obstinate attitude of Pharaoh, an attitude that outwardly may give in to the danger of the moment, but resurfaces when the plague abates. God uses this hardness for his purposes (see 7:13, 22; 8:15, 19, 32; 9:7, 12, 35; 10:20, 27). What are those purposes? The narrative recounts one purpose with the words: "The Egyptians will know that I am Yahweh" (7:5; 8:22; 9:14, 16; 10:1–2). God's acts point to a reality who is able to work in powerful ways. Of course, Israel would also see this deity at work. A second purpose emerges in the direct contrast of Egypt's gods and Yahweh. Each plague addresses a deity of Egypt's pantheon (some five hundred to two thousand gods), including the tenth plague against the firstborn son (12:12). Yahweh is God of gods.

Liberation from oppression results from the contest. Israel leaves Egypt. A pillar of cloud by day and a pillar of fire by night, representing the presence of the Lord, lead them. The Egyptians follow and attempt to destroy them by the Sea of Reeds (chap. 14). Instead, deliverance comes from Yahweh through the parting of the sea. The Egyptian army drowns when they try to follow. Their words before destruction explain the intent of the events: "for Yahweh is fighting for them against Egypt" (14:25). The Lord "saves" Israel; he "is a warrior," fighting for the people of Israel (14:30; 15:3). As a result, the people believe in Yahweh and in his servant, Moses (14:31). Chapter 15 recounts in song the victory of the Lord.

God continues to provide for them as they march toward Mount Sinai. When they suffer from bitter water at Marah and no water at Rephidim, God provides (15:22–27; 17:1–7). When the Amalekites attack, the Lord again fights for them (17:8–13). At last, they arrive at Mount Sinai and experience the presence of the Lord in a theophany of lightning and storm (chap. 19). The people "fear" God as they prepare to meet him through the intermediary role of Moses. This deity is their God, and they are now to meet him.

As God's people, Israel must be responsible to the covenant stipulations given at the mountain. Israel agrees to obey (19:8). After the covenant commandments and ordinances are presented, the covenant is established with blood sprinkled on the people (24:8).

Relationship with Yahweh requires obedience. No other rationale is given except that the Lord requires it. A survey of the Ten Words or Commandments (20:1–17) and the "Book of the Covenant" (20:22–23:33) indicates that God's instructions cover both vertical and horizontal dimensions, involving both correct attitudes and actions toward God and toward humanity. Every area of life must yield to the relationship of covenant with the Lord, so family, social, individual, and corporate rights are presented.

While Moses and Joshua remain on the mountain to receive the tablets of Words, the people act in rebellion by making a golden calf for worship and leadership (32:1). The covenant is broken within forty days after it is initiated. After all the Lord has done for Israel, they turn away. As a result of their idolatry, God threatens to abandon Israel (32:7–10). Moses intercedes in behalf of his people (32:11–14; 33:12–16). He realizes that Israel is nothing without the Lord. In some inexplicable way, probably because of the covenant, God's character now is tied up with the destiny of Israel, God's people (33:13). God acts in graciousness and does not destroy Israel (33:19; 34:6–7). The covenant is renewed (34:10–28).

On this occasion, Moses receives a special revelation of Yahweh's character. He requests a look at God's glory (33:18). The audacity of the request is overlooked, and Yahweh promises to reveal all his "goodness" (33:19). Whether the "glory" and the "goodness" are the same is not explained. But when Yahweh passes Moses on the mountain, six words or phrases are proclaimed that provide one of the fullest descriptions of the Lord's character, no matter whether glory or goodness. Yahweh is compassionate, gracious, slow to anger, abounding in steadfast love, abounding in faithfulness, and forgiving (34:6–7).

Woven between the chapters on covenant and its breach stand the Lord's instructions on building a symbol of the presence of Yahweh in the midst of Israel—the tabernacle. Precise guidelines for the sanctuary's materials and the priest's garments are given. These instructions serve as the template for the actions of chapters 35–40 when it is erected.

The tabernacle fulfills the Lord's promise to dwell in the midst of Israel (cf. 6:8). It provides a place where worship and instruction take place. At Mount Sinai, the glory of the Lord came as smoke enveloped the mountain (24:16). But the mountain was not the permanent home for Israel; the sanctuary would move with Israel. The Lord would always be in the midst of his people by this dwelling.

When the tabernacle is dedicated, the glory of the Lord settles upon it (40:34). The book closes with the presence of Yahweh leading from the sanctuary. The God who met Moses at the burning bush (chap. 3) and the people on the mountain (chaps. 19–20) now resides in the midst of Israel.

Theological Reflections. The Book of Exodus is rich in theology. Its main significance lies in God's deliverance of Israel from Egyptian slavery. Confessions of faith and corporate worship in the Old Testament from this point on derive from the exodus events. Almost every part of the book yields reward to theological reflection. Some theological aspects stand out and must be noted.

"Name" Theology: Yahweh. In Israel, a name stood for character. The personal name of Israel's God is revealed in this book. Moses supposes that the people are going to ask God's name. What is he to say to them? His question assumes more than a name, for the name would answer what this deity could do for Israel. God answers, "I AM WHO I AM" (3:14), a sentence that continues to beg interpretation. In the context, the name signifies that this deity will act in behalf of Israel.

How will this God act? Yahweh's reassurance speech in Exodus 6 states that he exhibits continuity with his actions in the days of the patriarchs and will reveal himself more fully as a God who liberates from oppression, redeems, elects, establishes a relationship, and fulfills his promises (6:6–8).

Yahweh confirms his statements by action, evidenced by the events in the book. Pharaoh, the Egyptians, Moses, and the people of Israel witness the quality of the name. For this reason, the name is not to be used in an empty way, according to the third commandment (20:7). When God passes by Moses on the mountain, the proclamation begins with a twofold repetition, "Yahweh, Yahweh" (34:6), and is followed by theological terms that explain God's character of glory or goodness, all part of the content of who this deity is. Yahweh is the name of Israel's God with full meaning for them.

"Power of God" Theology. The Book of Exodus exudes the power of Yahweh. In the ten plagues, Yahweh pits his power against the power of Pharaoh. Each plague shows God's control of this world. Moses participates as the messenger because he has witnessed some miracles to affirm God's call (4:1–9).

Parting the Red Sea stands as a great example of God's power (chap. 14). The event not only saves Israel, but also destroys her enemies, the Egyptian army. Chapter 15 celebrates this power of God to bring victory (see 15:6; cf. "right arm" imagery in Isaiah). Salvation comes from the mighty acts of God, best seen in the parting of the sea.

In addition, God's provision for Israel shows his power. Water, manna, help in combat, and guidance display his abilities to provide for Israel's needs.

"Holiness" Theology. Exodus 15:11 asks, "Who is like you, majestic in holiness?" At the burning bush, Moses is warned to take off his sandals because the area is "holy ground" (3:5). Moral quality exemplifies this deity. The commandments assume God's holiness. In light of who God is, Israel is to be "a holy nation" (19:6), obeying the commandments and ordinances (see Leviticus and the word, "holy"). The Book of the Covenant (chaps. 21–23) outlines expectations for the extent of Israel's holiness: all of life must be lived in its light.

"Faithfulness" Theology. Exodus phrases God's faithfulness in terms of "remembrance." God remembered his covenant with the "fathers," Abraham, Isaac, and Jacob (2:24; 3:6; 6:3). To remember his promises means that he acts in light of his remembrance. In this case, he sends a deliverer (Moses) who will lead Israel to the land promised the patriarchs (6:8; 15:17).

God's promises to Moses and to the people of Israel also come true. The book records his faithfulness. In return, Israel is to be faithful to Yahweh. The first commandment states that they are to have "no other gods before" this deity (20:2). No idols or images are to replace this deity (20:4). After all, there are no other gods who can stand with this deity (15:11). Victory over the gods of Egypt confirms this viewpoint.

Israel's failure to be faithful to Yahweh leads to God's judgment (32:10, 28, 35). Israel knows that Yahweh is to be feared, for they witnessed his work in Egypt and experienced his presence on the mountain (20:19–20). However, their memory appears brief. God's anger may be averted by intercession (8:8; 32:30–34) and repentance holds the possibility of aversion of God's wrath, although Pharaoh does not do so in a meaningful way. Failure to obey may lead to a sin offering, an act that satisfies God (29:10–14). Atonement by blood cleanses the priests (29:35–37) and the people (24:6–8), satisfying God's wrath.

God holds Israel responsible for obeying his instructions. Psalms 78 and 106 recount what God did in the Book of Exodus and how Israel knew the commandments, but failed to obey. Relationship demands that both sides act faithfully.

"Salvation" Theology. God acts to save Israel from their plight. Ṣalvation has a tangible side, namely, deliverance from Egypt. God initiates his salvation by observing Israel's groanings (3:7). He then takes steps to realize change, first by choosing a deliverer (chap. 3) and then by bringing out the children of Israel from Egypt (15:13).

Redemption leads to a permanent relationship with the deity who worked for Israel. Although the redemption could be limited to political and economic conditions, as liberation theologians argue, the account in Exodus includes and goes beyond these areas. The relationship with their benefactor will impact their whole existence. "Covenant," the biblical word that indicates the relationship, demands total commitment from both parties, though God has already worked and will prove faithful in the future. Remembrance of the way God has worked takes place in the festivals (23:14–17), the Passover being the one that rehearses the exodus events (chap. 13). The festivals say to Israel that the God who worked in the past will continue to work in the present and in the future.

Israel has been chosen by God (6:7). They are his people, and he is their God. He has brought them out of Egypt, saving them, and now asks for their obedience to his instructions (20:2). This establishes the covenant upon the foundation of God's actions, actions based on his choice and grace.

"Presence" Theology. The revelation of God's presence develops from hiddenness to a permanent site of presence, the tabernacle. The narrator indicates that God lurks in the background in the first two chapters. In chapter 3 the Lord speaks with Moses, revealing himself and his plans. He even dialogues with Moses, showing that he speaks in ways humans understand.

As the book unfolds, God's presence takes tangible directions with specific instructions to Moses in Egypt and at the mountain. Israel witnesses God's presence in the storm at Mount Sinai. As the people draw nearer to the deity who has been working in their behalf, they fear for themselves and ask Moses to continue to intercede for them (20:18–21). It is as though they need distance from God; presence draws near, but the people cannot take it. God continues to speak through Moses, but Israel is held responsible for the words from their leader.

To more clearly demonstrate God's presence, the tabernacle is built. The presence of God rests in the midst of Israel in the tabernacle. It veils God's presence in a way that the people can handle. Yahweh meets with Moses there. The people understand the implications because of the specific symbolism of the sanctuary in the center of the camp.

With Yahweh at their core, Moses as intermediary, and the people in covenant relationship, Israel may advance beyond the Book of Exodus to experience the Lord's will. The book begins the great adventure of a nation in relationship with their deity, Yahweh. G. MICHAEL HAGAN

See also COVENANT; EGYPT; MOSES; TEN COMMANDMENTS.

Bibliography. B. S. Childs, *The Book of Exodus: A Critical, Theological Commentary;* R. Alan Cole, *Exodus: An Introduction and Commentary;* J. J. Davis, *Moses and the Gods of Egypt;* T. Fretheim, *Exodus.*

Exorcism. *See* DEMON.

Expiation. *See* ATONEMENT.

Ezekiel, Theology of. Ezekiel and his contemporaries confronted what for the Israelites was the most traumatic possible challenge to their faith: the destruction of Jerusalem and its temple. It is difficult for the contemporary Protestant to grasp the significance of this theological catastrophe. Perhaps the best we can do is imagine the impact it would have on Muslims if Mecca were to disappear under the mushroom cloud of an atomic warhead, or conceive how at a loss Roman Catholics would feel if the ground opened and swallowed the Vatican. Israel suffered at least as much confusion when they saw the temple of Yahweh go up in flames.

Ezekiel the priest, the son of Buzi, was probably born around 622 B.C. He was taken captive to Babylonia in 597 along with other prominent Jerusalemites. He settled near the "Kebar River" between Babylon and Nippur, and at age thirty was called to the prophetic office (so taking 1:1). From this vantage point, he watched the demise of Jerusalem around 586 B.C.

Israel, it seems, had come to feel that their status as the people of God and in particular that the presence of the house of God among them had made them invulnerable. Jeremiah 7:4 implies that the people trusted in the "temple of the LORD" for security. They could not imagine that God would allow his house to fall. Ezekiel's task was to demonstrate that this crutch was sure to fail even while he assured them that God himself had not failed.

Ezekiel 1 and Divine Transcendence. The Book of Ezekiel has a beginning few readers can forget. Standing by the Kebar River Ezekiel suddenly sees the vision of the chariot of Yahweh (1:2–28). The chariot comes in a storm, the sign of a theophany. In the chariot he sees the four creatures, each with four faces (of a human, an ox, an eagle, and a lion). He also views the strange "wheels within wheels" that were full of eyes. Above the creatures is a dome and above that, a throne. On the throne sits a fiery man-like figure. The chariot darts about without ever having to pivot.

While scholars have debated the details of the vision, it seems beyond question that it portrays God as the sovereign over the whole earth. The four faces of creatures represent four of the mightiest creatures (the ox, over domestic animals; the lion, over wild animals; the eagle, over birds; and the human, over all). The wheels within wheels represent the freedom to move in any of the four directions without having to pivot to the right or left, and thus symbolize God's omnipresence. The eyes imply sight in every direction, and thus indicate God's omniscience. The word "dome" is in Hebrew *raqîᶜa,* the same word used for the vault of heaven in Genesis 1. It symbolizes the physical universe as metaphorically under heaven, the throneroom of God. The human-like figure seated on the throne above the dome implied that Yahweh is sovereign over heaven and earth.

For the reader, the surprise is that Ezekiel begins his message of judgment not with the sinfulness of Judah but with the sovereignty of God. People in the ancient world connected their gods with local areas and specific domains (see 1 Kings 20:23–28). A god was supposed to protect his domain, and if one city conquered another, that meant that the god of the victor was greater than the god of the vanquished. Many Jews also embraced this thinking, and it led to two dangerous conclusions. First, they thought that Yahweh was bound to protect Jerusalem. Second, if the city should fall, it meant that Yahweh was weak and small.

Ezekiel's vision showed them that it was not that Yahweh was too small, but that he was too great. As the God who transcended the earth, he had no need of any temple. As Solomon had recognized, even heaven cannot contain him—"how much less this temple?" (1 Kings 8:27). Precisely because he was no local deity, he did not need to defend any earthly house. But as Lord over all, he was also judge of all, including Jerusalem. In short, the power and authority of God meant not that Jerusalem was impregnable, but that it was doomed.

The Radical Sin of Israel and the Radical Methods of Ezekiel. The opening vision is only the first of many strange messages in Ezekiel. While it may not quite be true to say that for Ezekiel the medium was the message, certainly the media he used carried within them a drama and force commensurate with the desperate nature of the situation.

More than any other prophet, Ezekiel acted out his message in parables. Among these actions was a pretend siege of Jerusalem, with a brick serving as the city (4:1–5:4). Like a child with toy soldiers, he built a siege ramp against his miniature Jerusalem and carried out the symbolic assault. But this was no game. Ezekiel was as much a prisoner as were the Jews trapped in Jerusalem. Day after day he lay on his side and was no more free to move about than they were free to escape the city. Like them, he ate food cooked over dung. At last, he cut off his hair and chopped, burned, and scattered it. Israel had been as near to God as Ezekiel's hair had been to the prophet, but they would be slaughtered and dispersed—save for a small remnant.

He even had to subordinate the death of his wife to his message (24:16–27). When she passed away, God told him not to enter into the customary period of mourning. He implied that the Jews were soon to have more than enough of dead wives, husbands, children, and parents. Times of sorrow for which no mourning could be adequate were about to descend upon them.

Ezekiel's language is the boldest, most graphic in the Bible. Chapter 16 describes the nation's history in a parable. She began life as an abandoned baby lying naked in blood and still attached to the placenta. Yahweh pitied her and protected her, and she grew to sexual maturity. Wealthy and beautiful, she turned to promiscuity and prostitution. If Ezekiel's language lacks delicacy, it is because he is trying to warn the people of the horrors soon to overtake them.

Ezekiel's language is not all emotional imagery, however. In chapter 14, using language that reflects the thoroughness of a trained priest, he describes in detail God's principles of judgment. He demonstrates first that God is not moved by outward acts of religion; even if people come to consult God, he will not receive them as long as they harbor apostasy (vv. 1–11). Second, he declares that no amount of pious intercession will save a people bent on rebellion (vv. 12–23).

The Duty of the Watchman. God routinely addresses Ezekiel as "son of man" (that is, "mortal"), and so reminds him that he and his people are small and fragile. Their only hope of survival is in God.

God commissions Ezekiel as the watchman over Jerusalem. If he carries out his responsibility and warns the people of the coming disaster, he will be innocent of their deaths when they refuse to listen. But if he shirks his duty, their blood will be on his head (3:16–21). God warned him that they would be both obstinate and vicious, and that he must not fear them (2:3–8).

More than that, Ezekiel in a vision ate a scroll that was the word of God (2:9–3:11). His only task was to receive and declare God's message. To emphasize this, Ezekiel fell dumb when not expressly preaching God's message (3:26–27; 24:27). In a time of crisis, no other words were worth speaking.

Individual and Corporate Responsibility. Many scholars assert, on the basis of chapter 18, that Ezekiel was a pioneer in developing the doctrine of individual responsibility. Following the lead of H. Wheeler Robinson, interpreters assert that earlier Israel was dominated by the idea of corporate responsibility and corporate guilt, whereby the guilt of the father could be transferred to the descendants. The classic example of this is said to be Joshua 7, where Achan's family shares in the guilt of his actions and are put to death.

In chapter 18 Ezekiel confronts the popular proverb of his time, "The fathers eat sour grapes, and the children's teeth are set on edge" (v. 2). The self-evident meaning is that the children suffer inevitably and unfairly for their father's actions. The implication is that God is unjust.

Ezekiel, speaking in God's name, responds first that every individual belongs to God and is responsible to him directly and not through his or her parents (v. 4). He then vies a hypothetical case involving three generations. If a man in the first generation lives a life of faithfulness, generosity, and integrity, that man will stand justified before God and suffer no retribution (vv. 5–9). If his son, the second generation, does not follow that path but lives a life of greed, apostasy, and selfishness, then that son will not be justified through the righteousness of his father. He will bear the full weight of his sin (vv. 10–13). If then this man's son, the third generation, reacts against his father's immoral ways and lives instead like his grandfather, this man will not suffer for his father's sin but will stand justified (vv. 14–18).

To this, Ezekiel adds the principle that if a sinful person repents, God will no longer hold that person's former sins against him. On the other hand, if a righteous person falls away and behaves corruptly, the former acts of righteousness will not protect that one from punishment (vv. 19–32). Ezekiel has laid out in clearest terms not only the idea of individual responsibility but also the possibility of repentance and the necessity of perseverance.

It is another question, however, whether Ezekiel's ideas represent a major break from previous Old Testament teachings. In the case of Achan's sin, it is not at all clear that the Israelites regarded either the entire nation or Achan's family as sharing in his guilt. While they knew that the whole people had suffered for what he had done (Josh. 7:4–5), the mere fact that they sought out the guilty individual (Josh. 7:13–19) indicates that they understood that the responsibility lay with one man. Also, the fact that they executed Achan's family along with him (Josh. 7:24–26), however that may strike us, does not mean that they thought that his guilt was somehow passed on to them. Rather, the point of Achan's punishment was that he lost his place in the inheritance of the land of Israel. Had his family survived and taken a share in the land, then in their eyes he would have through his descendants evaded the real point of the punishment. The guilt was his and the punishment was directed toward him.

In short, Ezekiel enunciated more clearly than before certain principles of divine judgment and human responsibility, and he corrected the misunderstandings of his contemporaries. It would not be accurate, however, to suppose that he repudiated earlier tenets of Israel's faith. Rather, he made the point that the Jews who saw their temple go up in flames had no one to blame but themselves.

Apostasy. More than any other prophet, Ezekiel graphically portrays the perversity and effrontery of apostasy. Here, too, the fall of the temple is before him, since it is the gravity of Israel's sin that explains how God could have allowed the temple to fall.

In chapter 23 using the most graphic sexual imagery found anywhere in the Bible, Ezekiel set out the parable of the sisters Oholah and Oholibah. Oholah, he tells us, represents Samaria just as Oholibah represents Jerusalem. Oholah first turned away from Yahweh, her true husband, and "lusted after" Assyria and Egypt. In response to her adultery, Yahweh turned her over to the viciousness of the Assyrians (23:5–10); in other words, God allowed Assyria to destroy Samaria.

Oholibah learned nothing from her sister's experience but instead behaved even worse. She committed adultery with the Assyrians, the Egyptians, and the Babylonians out of a lust for their glory and strength. As a result, she too was doomed (23:11–49).

The almost pornographic character of this parable serves several purposes. First, it vividly displays apostasy as an act as disgraceful and brazen as adultery. Second, it brings out the character of Israel's apostasy. When the Jews allowed themselves to be awestruck by the power of the great nations and sought alliances with them, they were in effect turning their back on God in the way a wayward wife might abandon her husband for a rich and handsome paramour. In addition, alliances with these nations inevitably drew Israel into the worship of their gods (23:30). Third, the parable illustrates the folly of Jerusalem, in that its people did not learn the lessons vividly acted out before them in the destruction of Samaria. Guilty of such outrageous behavior, the people hardly had a right to be surprised when they saw judgment bearing down on their city and temple.

In chapter 8, Ezekiel describes the apostasy that was being committed in the temple itself. He tells us that in the sixth month of the sixth year (about five years before the destruction of

Jerusalem), he was taken to the temple in a vision. There in the very house of God Ezekiel saw several examples of Jerusalem's apostasy.

First, he saw the "idol of jealousy" in the north gate (vv. 5–6). This may have been an image of Asherah (cf. 2 Kings 21:7). Its position in the north is significant since that is the direction from which Israel's enemies, as executioners of Yahweh's anger, generally came.

Next, he went into a secret room where the elders were worshiping images of animal gods (vv. 7–12). The zoomorphic nature of these gods would indicate that they were Egyptian; the secrecy of the cult reflected a desire to hide it not only from Yahweh but from the Babylonians, who would have regarded this as an act of rebellion against their empire. The Jews would soon learn that Egyptian help was empty.

Next, again at the north gate, he saw women "mourning for Tammuz" (v. 14). Tammuz was a dying and rising fertility god, and his adoration was meant to ensure success in agriculture. In this, the people had abandoned Yahweh as Lord of nature and turned to other gods for good crops and healthy cattle.

Finally, Ezekiel sees men on the east side of the temple bowing to the rising sun with their backs to the temple (vv. 16–17). The implication is that as they bow they turn their buttocks toward Yahweh. The phrase translated "putting a branch to their nose" should probably be translated, "they put a stench in my (God's) nose."

The outcome of apostasy is that God shows no pity (v. 18). For Ezekiel's readers, the reason for the destruction of the temple is obvious.

Oracles against the Nations. Like many other prophets, Ezekiel includes a series of oracles against the nations in his book (25:1–32:32). Here, however, these prophecies take on the added urgency of being set against the crisis of 586 B.C. Against Ammon, for example (25:1–7), Ezekiel makes the point that because they gloated over the fall of the Jerusalem sanctuary, God would hand them and all their possessions over to foreigners from the east.

Especially remarkable here are the lengthy laments over Tyre (26:1–28:19), a place of special significance because it was Tyre that built the Jerusalem temple (1 Kings 5:1–11). Using imagery that would have been meaningful for a priest, Ezekiel describes the king of Tyre as if he were a cherub statue standing in the holy of holies (28:13–14; cf. 2 Chron. 3:10–13). God would expel them from their seaside paradise and put an end to their wealth and trade.

For Ezekiel, the oracles against the nations meant that the same God who had condemned Jerusalem also stood in judgment over the nations. If the people of God had not escaped, neither would they.

Redemption and Transformation. For Ezekiel, the sovereignty of God, whereby he was free to judge Jerusalem and destroy its temple, was also the basis for Jerusalem's hope. The destruction of the temple did not mean that God had failed or that the promises were finished.

In chapter 37, Ezekiel lays out three aspects of the hope of restoration. He begins with the famous vision of the valley of dry bones (vv. 1–14). Israel, the vision implies, is a dead nation. Like many peoples before them, they have been swept off the historical map, and from the human viewpoint there is no reason to expect them ever to be a nation again. God, however, is not bound by human limitations, and this dead nation will live again.

Second, in a text that parallel's the promise in Jeremiah 31:31–37 of a new covenant with Israel and Judah, Ezekiel promises that God will draw together his people and give to them an obedient heart that they might never again wander from him (37:15–23).

Third, Ezekiel promises that "David" will be their faithful ruler forever. The term "David" is symbolic and messianic; it looks for the day when a king will arise who will love God with all his heart and who will stand in stark contrast to the kings and leaders who led Jerusalem into its disastrous apostasy and warfare.

Gog and Magog. In a surprising turn, Ezekiel interrupts his prophecies of future redemption and glory with the prophecy of the great war against Gog and Magog (chaps. 38–39). This is not a prediction of some specific war, least of all of a war against a modern nation such as Russia. The terms "Magog," "Meshech," and so forth refer to tribes in the Black Sea area (such as the Scythians), but the specific identity is not nearly so important as the fact that they were pagan, warlike peoples in the north. Biblical eschatology regularly speaks of the "enemies to the north" as the source of conflict and judgment, and the reference here is typological rather than literal.

The main point was that although Israel had already endured much at the hands of its enemies, more sorrows were yet to come before they entered the kingdom. The events of 586 B.C. were terrible, but they were not the last or even the worst of such calamities. Still, God would triumph over his enemies, and final victory for the people of God remained sure.

The Restored Temple. We have seen that the entire prophecy of Ezekiel focuses on the theological crisis occasioned by the destruction of the temple. That being the case, it is not surprising that Ezekiel the priest should crown his promise of restoration with a vision of a new temple (chaps. 40–48). The question that remains for us is whether we should take this prophecy as a portrait of a literal, future temple, or read it as an idealized, symbolic vision.

Careful analysis reveals that this prophecy cannot be taken literally. Apart from the fact that, for a Christian, the notion of a future temple with a levitical priesthood and animal sacrifices bluntly contradicts the New Testament (e.g., Heb. 8:1–10:17), the text of Ezekiel itself rules out such an interpretation.

Although the details of this chapter are perhaps exhausting to the modern reader, they are not really exhaustive. That is, they lack many specifications and dimensions, and omit such critical matters as the materials to be used (contrast Exod. 26 and 2 Chron. 3–4). Attempts to reconstruct a picture of this temple inevitably fail for lack of detail. Similarly, the portrayal of the division of the land among the twelve tribes (Ezek. 47:13–48:35) is highly idealized and resists any attempt to set down literal borders for the tribes (although this does not keep some imaginative interpreters from trying).

Most significant here is the portrayal of the river of life in 47:1–12. Taken literally, the details are impossible. A trickle of water comes out of the north gate of the temple, but in the short space of a few thousand meters, it is a mighty river too great and apparently too swift for any man to swim across. Where the text itself signals us that the literal meaning implies absurdities, it is folly to force such a meaning on the passage.

The vision is a prophet-priest's portrayal of the glories of the kingdom of God. The calamity of the exile has been reversed. Worship is orderly and beautiful. Leadership is subservient to God. There is a place for every one of God's people, and there is neither want nor need. Most important of all, the Lord is there (48:35). For the Christian, all the promises of God are Yes in Christ, and not one of them has failed.

DUANE A. GARRETT

See also PROPHET, PROPHETESS, PROPHECY.

Bibliography. W. Eichrodt, *Ezekiel;* H. W. Robinson, *Corporate Personality in Israel;* J. B. Taylor, *Ezekiel.*

Ezra, Theology of. ***The Sovereignty and the Works of God.*** God is "the God of heaven and earth" (5:11). He raises up kings and grants to them their authority (1:2). He is able to stir up their hearts so they will do his bidding (1:1). Mighty Artaxerxes, the king of kings, cannot refuse any request of a lowly scribe who has God's hand on him (7:6, 12). Satraps, nobles, governors, and sworn opponents are quietly turned into active assistants in Yahweh's program for the restoration of his people.

It is not enough that monarchs step aside to allow the plan of God to unfold; they themselves must become agents in bringing about the sovereign purpose of God. Cyrus the great, with world powers at his feet, first issues the great commission to return and build the temple (1:1–4). It is insufficient that the "king of kings" allow Yahweh's temple to be built. He must endow it with glory, subsidize its sacrifices, and put the entire resources of the province at its disposal (7:12–18). Artaxerxes must not only tolerate the Torah, but he also will command that whatever the Holy One commands must be done with zeal. He will authorize strict judgment on those who will not observe God's law (7:25–26).

There are no flamboyant, dramatic miracles in this book. Israel's God goes about quietly changing the hearts of all men, great and small. There is no mighty pharaoh to be humbled with great plagues. The great Creator silently steps to one side and allows his adversaries do the best they can to thwart his sovereign purpose (chaps. 4 and 5). When success seems hopeless, suddenly these enemies are not only commanded to leave the work alone; they must use their tax money to pay all the expenses (6:6–7). Ministers will be tax-exempt (7:24). Those who tried to stop the work must now be its patrons. Everything needed has to be provided without fail. Anyone who hinders the work will be impaled on a beam from his own house (6:11). From the least to the greatest the sovereign grace of God is irresistible.

No one sees him but God is at work. Golden vessels taken from his temple by Nebuchadnezzar are to be taken back. There is, however, no golden idol in this procession. The Cyrus cylinder informs us that various nationalities returned to their homeland and many idols were returned to their temples. The return of these lowly Judeans was unique in that they transported no graven image but only visible tokens of the sovereign power of their God.

The Immanence of God. God is not only God of heaven but is also "God of our fathers" (7:27). He not only stirs up the hearts of kings, but heads of Jewish families were stirred by the same Spirit to return and rebuild. In fact, God's hand is favorably disposed to all who seek him (8:22). His hand is over his people to deliver them from ambushes and hidden dangers. Thus they are able to refuse the king's armed escort (8:31). Ezra was strengthened to do his work and was brought to Jerusalem by the good hand of God (7:9; 8:17–18).

The Grace and Holiness of God. God is a righteous God before whom no impure person can stand (9:15). Israel's guilt has grown so large it reaches to the skies (9:6). In a brief moment of grace her dry bones came to life. Slaves in bondage were shown great favor in the presence of Persian royalty. A peg was given them in God's holy place. A nation without walls entered the fold of God's protection (9:8–9). In the midst of disobedience they were given hope in spite of it (10:2). Out of great guilt, they were given amazing, unmerited favor (9:13).

Scripture. God gave his Torah (instruction) to Israel by Moses, the man of God (3:2). Thus it may also be called Moses' Torah (7:6). It is not only spoken but written (3:2). Ezra not only sets his heart to study the Word; he also practices it (7:10). It is taught to others so that they may do the same. It must be obeyed or severe consequences ensue.

The People of God. The small group in the Book of Ezra are more than just a group of refugees. They are a holy remnant with a mission. Their great commission has been given by God through no less than the very king of the biblical world, Cyrus the great, God's anointed (Ezra 1:1–4; Isa. 45:1). His words are even introduced in the familiar style of prophetic communication ("thus saith").

As often in biblical commissions, this is followed by two imperatives. The Israelites are to go up and build the house of the Lord. Even though given by Cyrus, this was not a purely secular commission. The people who responded were everyone "whose heart God had moved . . . to go up and build the house of the LORD" (1:5). Those Jews who did not wish to return, with the authority of Cyrus, assisted them with their material goods (v. 6).

These were, perhaps, the "holy seed," the remnant, spoken of in Isaiah 6:12–13. The way they respond to the Torah and the words of their ordained, godly leaders will decide the shape of Judaism for centuries to come. In a sense, what they do will decide whether the biblical, Mosaic faith will survive into the New Testament era.

They are not an anonymous crowd. They are real, living people designated by name (Ezra 8:20). They have genealogical roots that connect them with all the people of God since the days of the exodus. The listing of the heads of households give not only numbers but identity (chap. 2; 8:1–14). Who they are is important. Family solidarity is crucial. They are a people with a destiny.

God has laid his hand on them (8:22). They have been ordained with a sacred mission. In a sense the future of God's redemptive purpose has been placed in their hands. This is why they must be a "separate" people. They are a holy race and cannot intermingle with foreign abominations. In 9:1 they are contrasted with the people who have filled the land with impurity from one end to another.

They have been promised the special favor of God if they seek him. They have been warned, however, that his power and his anger are against all those who forsake him (8:22). Unfaithfulness has brought the nation to the brink of destruction. Now a moment of God's saving grace has brought them from servitude and given them a second chance for survival.

All depends on their faithfulness. If they are true to their God, he will enable them to eat of the good of the land. He will also empower them to pass the land on to their ancestors (9:12). They are not only rooted in the past but grounded in the future. What they do will affect the well-being of their ancestors for generations to come.

Had they not held fast to the faith of their fathers, there would have been no Maccabbean patriots to oppose the Greek religion Antiochus IV tried to force on the nation. The disciples of Christ would have been born into a land overshadowed by the temple of Zeus.

The people of God in Ezra are a people of the covenant. They are those who tremble at the commandments of God (10:3). They are a nation that says to its leaders, "We will support you, so take courage and do it" (10:3). When confronted by their leaders with unpleasant decisions they say, "You are right! We must do as you say" (10:12). They are not like the people before Mount Sinai who made a great profession but sank immediately in worship of the golden calf (Exod. 24:3). Their response to their leaders is encapsulated in the terse notation, "the exiles did as was proposed" (Ezra 10:16).

The Means of Grace. The first recorded act of the pilgrims is that they gathered together "as one man" (3:1). They knew well the essentiality of unity and public worship. They repeat the same example of their father Abraham. The first thing they built in the land was an altar (3:2).

Even before the foundation of the temple was laid, they began celebrating the Festival of Booths (Tabernacles). God gave this feast to remind them of Israel's transient wilderness existence and the fragility of life (3:4). Their worship was accompanied by music, praise, and congregational singing (3:10–11). Their liturgy celebrated the timeless, eternal grace of God that had brought them out of servitude (3:11).

There was undoubtedly a bonding of this congregation at the special moment of laying the foundation of the temple. During this unique service they collectively shared their joy and sorrow (3:12–13). It would have been easy for them to have delayed worship until the temple was fully built. These pilgrims, however, knew that worship and piety come before public buildings.

Ezra's tiny flock was surrounded by powerful, predatory enemies. Therefore he would not allow them to start their journey without prayer and fasting (8:21). He had boasted to the king of the great providence of God. Together they sought the Lord for his protection. The text notes the efficacy of these resources by stating "[God] answered our prayer" (8:23). Ezra learned that not only does God stretch out his hand to his people, but they too are able, in times of need, to stretch forth their hand in prayer to him (9:5).

In addition to public worship the preaching of the Word proved itself invaluable to this new congregation. When their resolution to accomplish their mission faltered, the prophets Haggai and Zechariah arose. These men spoke in the name of the God of Israel who was over them (5:1). The people responded by rising up and resuming their divinely appointed task (5:2). The prophets stood by them and supported them with the anointed proclamation of the Word.

Leadership and Ministry. Ezra knew the importance of good leaders. He would not set out on his journey to the land until perceptive, sensible men had joined them (8:16–18). Knowledge and information were not the only qualifications for leadership. Ministers would have to submit themselves to a rigid system of accountability. Treasures of the congregation were carefully weighed out and then weighed and counted again upon arrival (8:25–34) in Jerusalem.

Leaders were expected to be examples to the flock. Ezra was totally devastated upon learning that the leaders had been foremost in taking foreign wives (9:2). Such leaders were not only removed from office but the book closes with a list of their names preserved as a warning for future generations (10:18–44).

The Jewish Talmud considers Ezra a second Moses. Biblically there is much to be said for this comparison. This man was not a mere legalist who gave excessive attention to the letter of the law. He was, in a sense, a second father to biblical Judaism, presiding over its rebirth and restoration. He gave to his people a solidarity and spiritual unity that kept the faith alive until the coming of Christ.

Like Moses, he was a skilled scribe who had set his heart to the study of God's law (7:6, 10). As with Moses he takes his people on a dangerous journey from a foreign land. He gathers up free will offerings for God's place of worship. He sets apart leaders to assist him in this task. His style of leadership is similar to Moses'. When confronted with a congregational crisis he falls down before the Lord (Num. 16:4; Ezra 9:5).

Ethics and Congregational Polity. At first glance the breaking up of foreign marriages in the last two chapters appears very cruel and extreme. It must be remembered that desperate times require desperate measures. Mingling with impurity had brought the congregation to the brink of destruction (9:14). The future of the biblical faith would hang on the way in which this problem was handled.

Divorce is a serious matter. It is not, however, more serious than the redemption of humankind. It should be pointed out that marital bliss could never grow out of such unions. When they had first come to the land, foreigners had come saying, "Let us help you build because we, like you, seek your God" (4:2). Everyone must have somehow heard of the reply of their leaders who said, "You have nothing in common with us." Marriage based on partners sharing no common interests, especially in sacred areas, are not likely to last in any case.

It should be noted that all marriages were not capriciously dissolved without any forethought. Leaders were appointed to judge each case separately (10:14). Doubtless there was room to decide whether a certain mate had been absorbed into the faith and could hence no longer be considered a foreigner.

Excommunication seems to be an extreme step. Nevertheless it must be remembered that the raison d' être of this congregation was to build God's house. People who could no longer be true to this central goal should not want to be involved in a group that based its entire existence on this foundation. PAUL FERGUSON

See also ISRAEL; NEHEMIAH, THEOLOGY OF.

Bibliography. J. Bright, *History of Israel*; B. Childs, *Introduction of the Old Testament as Scripture*; F. C. Fensham, *Ezra and Nehemiah*; D. Kidner, *Ezra and Nehemiah*; J. Myers, *Ezra–Nehemiah*; H. G. Williamson, *Ezra–Nehemiah.*

Ff

Faith. Belief, trust, and loyalty to a person or thing. Christians find their security and hope in God as revealed in Jesus Christ, and say "amen" to that unique relationship to God in the Holy Spirit through love and obedience as expressed in lives of discipleship and service.

The Old Testament. The Hebrew language has six terms that develop the fundamental ideas of belief, trust, and loyalty. The root *bṭḥ* expresses an individual's feeling of safety, and so means to feel secure. At times this confidence is self-centered (Ezek. 33:13) or related to warriors (Hos. 10:13) and riches (Jer. 49:4). But security that is a result of a trusting relationship with God is most important. It can be combined with the fear of the Lord and obedience to his Word so that the one who walks in the dark is encouraged to "trust in the name of the LORD and rely on his God" (Isa. 50:10). It can also be equated with acknowledging God in all our ways in contrast to relying on our own understanding (Prov. 3:5–6).

The term *ḥsh* describes the state of one in need of help who is dependent on another for protection. In Jotham's parable the thornbush challenges the trees who invite it to be their king: "If you really want to anoint me king over you, come and take refuge in my shade" (Judg. 9:15). While being pursued by an enemy, David asks the Lord to "save and deliver" him based on a similar assertion: "I take refuge in you" (Ps. 7:1). The idea of taking refuge can also be contrasted with trusting in people or princes (Ps. 118:8–9). It is not surprising then that "those who seek refuge" in God are the same as the godly who experience the love and salvation of God (Ps. 17:7). To acknowledge dependence on God for protection when in need of help is a unique mark of the godly.

The terms *qwh, yḥl,* and *ḥkh* express persistence, a simple hope, or a waiting for. Isaiah promises: "Those who hope in the LORD will renew their strength" (40:31). David prays: "May your unfailing love rest upon us, O LORD, even as we put our hope in you" (Ps. 33:22); he confesses: "We wait in hope for the LORD; he is our help and our shield" (33:20).These descriptions that express a hope in God that involves patience and persistence are expressions of faith. During the siege of Samaria, Ahab, who blamed his troubles on the Lord, showed a lack of faith when he asked, "Why should I wait for the LORD any longer?" (2 Kings 6:33).

The term *ʾmn* with its stress on firmness and stability emphasizes the varied activities of God and our responses to him. Deuteronomy 7:9 majestically calls us to an understanding of who God is: "Know therefore that the LORD your God is God; he is the faithful God, keeping his covenant of love to a thousand generations of those who love him and keep his commands." Because the person of God and his word are one, Solomon prays: "And now, O God of Israel, let your word that you promised your servant David my father come true" (1 Kings 8:26); and the prophet threatens, "I proclaim what is certain" when speaking of God's sure judgment (Hos. 5:9). The proper response of individuals to this firm and stable activity of God is modeled by Abraham, who is chosen by God. Because his heart is faithful, God enters into a covenant with him that involves a homeland (Neh. 9:7–8).

The recognition and acknowledgment of the relationship into which God enters with people is a declaratory saying of "amen" to God and a special religious attitude of the people of God. The commands of God demand a proper response. Individuals are to acknowledge his demands, regard him as trustworthy, and be obedient to him. Faith is a spiritual attitude involving activity. The children of Israel stood condemned because they rebelled at God's command to take possession of the land he had given them. Fundamental to this rebellion is the claim: "You did not trust him or obey him" (Deut. 9:23). On the other hand, Abram stood approved when he acknowledged the promise of God, and trusted God's power to perform what he had promised: "Abram believed the LORD, and he credited it to him as righteousness" (Gen. 15:6). The Lord indicated to Abram his plan for history, and Abram believed it to be something real and was filled with a firmness and security in the Lord. His subsequent exercise of patience and obedient actions are clear indications of the meaning of faith.

The setting and origin of the term "faith" as used in the Old Testament are intimately linked to the covenant between God and his people. The term sums up all the ways by which people express their relationship to God. Isaiah dares to equate existence and faith when he claims that the people of God have their particular manner of being, and are established through their faith (Isa. 7:9). This understanding is in sharp contrast with the picture of Ahaz, who rejects God's invitation to confirm the truth of his word, and then ironically is given the promise of Immanuel (Isa. 7:14). In the fulfillment of this promise lies the challenge of the New Testament to redefine faith.

The New Testament. The transition from the Old Testament to the New Testament understanding of faith involves an appreciation of the continuity between them and that which is unique in the New Testament. The concepts of covenant, people of God, revelation, and the activity of God in history continue from the Old Testament to the New Testament. The unique understanding in the New Testament is defined by a new covenant, and the people of God being identified by their response to God's Son, Jesus. In the language of the New Testament, the common Greek of Jesus' day, we are told how God enters history as the Christ in the person of his Son Jesus, and remains active in the world through his Holy Spirit and the church.

The Septuagint, as a transitional text between the Hebrew of the Old Testament and the Greek of the New Testament, fixes the theological vocabulary that the church uses to define what God has done, is doing, and will do. The meaning of faith in the New Testament is then both a reflection of its continuity with the Old Testament and an expression of its uniqueness in a different historical and cultural setting. In the representative selections from the Old Testament that we have examined, only one term, *ʾmn,* is consistently translated in the Septuagint by a single concept, *pisteuein/pistos.* It is this concept that the Synoptic Gospels, Acts, the Epistles, and the Johannine writings use to examine and illustrate the meaning of faith in the New Testament.

The Synoptic Gospels. As for the ancient Israelites so for the new people of God, faith means primarily confident trust based on God's promise as understood through his Word (Luke 1:20; 24:25). In Jesus Christ, the living Word of God, and the gospel, the true message of God, people are called to say "yes" to God and to recognize the messenger and the message as true (Mark 1:15).

For Jesus, God is Father and King. This claim involves a unique sense of presence and communion with God, as well as the call to his hearers to respond to his own claim of Sonship (Mark 12:1–12), and his interpretation of the kingdom of God as being near (Matt. 12:22–28). Mark opens his Gospel with the simple assertion that this is "the gospel about Jesus Christ, the Son of God" (1:1). It begins with the ministry of John the Baptist, which climaxes with the baptism of Jesus and the heavenly announcement of Jesus' Sonship (1:11; cf. Matt. 3:17; Luke 3:22). This announcement is repeated during Jesus' transfiguration and followed by the command, "Listen to him" (Mark 9:7; cf. Matt. 17:5; Luke 9:35). In the beginning of his ministry Jesus proclaims the gospel in terms of the nearness of the kingdom and the need to believe (Mark 1:14–15). Specifically, the parables of Jesus and the Sermon on the Mount call for a response. The parable of the sower calls the proper response to Jesus' word "believing" (Luke 8:12–13). The Sermon on the Mount (Matt. 5–7), as the ethics of those who are to live under the rule of God as Father, concludes with Jesus' admonition to be wise and to put these words into practice (7:24–27; cf. 5:19–20).

The results of faith are seen in the radical changes that people experience when they place their trust in Jesus. The Gospels make the faith response explicit in particular miracles. The centurion's servant (Matt. 8:13), a paralytic (Matt. 9:2), a woman who had been sick for twelve years (Mark 5:34), a twelve-year-old child who died (Mark 5:36), and a blind beggar (Luke 18:42) are all examples from the Synoptic Gospels of those who are told by Jesus: "Your faith has healed you."

In the Gospel of Mark the fearful and amazed responses of individuals to the person and work of Jesus are indicators of belief or unbelief. The amazement of the people in the Capernaum synagogue at Jesus' teaching and healing of a man possessed by an evil spirit leads to their recognition of his authority (Mark 1:21–27). When this same amazement is expressed by the people in the synagogue in Jesus' hometown, it leads to offense and Jesus' comment on their lack of faith (Mark 6:1–6). The side-by-side stories of the healing of the woman with a hemorrhage and the raising of Jairus's daughter from the dead have as a common theme the conquering of fear and the exercise of faith that results in new life (Mark 5:32–34, 36). In two incidents on the Sea of Galilee the disciples, when rescued by Jesus, respond with fear and amazement that are identified as a lack of faith (Mark 4:40–41) or a hardness of heart (Mark 6:50–52). These conditions prevent them from responding to Jesus when he reveals to them what it means to be the Messiah (Mark 8:31–32; 9:31–32; 10:32–34), or from hearing how believers can be true followers of this Messiah (8:34–38; 9:33–37; 10:41–45). Because Mark is intent on clarifying for the church the central truth that Jesus as the Son of Man is a suffering-servant Messiah whose example they must be willing to follow, a blind Bartimaeus, who is healed as he exercises faith, becomes the model disciple as he follows Jesus to Jerusalem and the way of the cross with his new sight.

Jesus asserts, in a discussion with skeptical disciples, that power is available to all who have faith (Mark 11:23), and that prayer is one means for expressing this faith (Mark 11:24). This paradoxical power of faith is seen not only in its "mountain-mover" quality, which is a kind of participation in God's creative activity, but also in its comparison with a minute grain of mustard seed (Luke 17:6). To place one's trust in Jesus is to open the door for radical change in the meaning of life itself.

The Book of Acts. In its record of the statements and activities of the early church, Acts emphasizes that Jesus Christ is the focus of faith. If faith in the Synoptic Gospels means confident trust based on God's promise as understood through his word and the person of his Son, then in Acts, which serves as a bridge between the Gospels and the Epistles, it is that and more. A single statement about faith in God is clarified as "belief in the Lord" (5:14; 9:42; 11:21; 14:23; 18:8) or "belief in Jesus" (3:16; 19:4), and made comprehensive when linked to the idea of salvation through the hearing of the word (4:4; 13:12). Gentiles (11:21; 13:12, 48; 15:7; 17:34; 21:25), Jews (6:7; 15:5; 16:1; 18:8; 21:20) and people of both genders (5:14) will be saved when they believe in the Lord Jesus Christ.

The church, in responding to the example and words of Jesus radicalized the Old Testament meaning of faith. By means of the ministries of Peter and Paul, Luke paints a vivid picture of the internal and external struggles of the Christian community as both the synagogue and the Jerusalem church resist breaking from the strict keeping of the law and the limitations of racial descent to acknowledge the claim that salvation is by faith in Jesus Christ alone (4:12; 15:14). All those who accept the gospel message and Christ's lordship are identified as "believing ones" (4:32; 11:21; 18:27; 19:18; 22:19), a synonym for "Christians."

In anticipation of the more formal analysis of the Epistles, faith in Acts is linked to baptism (8:12–13; 18:8; 19:2), confession (19:18), forgiveness (10:43), grace (15:11; 18:27), healing (3:16; 14:9), the Holy Spirit (19:2), justification (13:39), purification (15:9), and sanctification (26:18). Faith is also portrayed as something one can be full of (11:24), turned from (13:8), remain true to (14:22), and be strengthened in (16:5). Basic to all of these ideas is the understanding that the act of believing is also a commitment to a community of worship (5:12), the meeting of the needs of others (2:44–45), and the sharing of this faith with all as Jesus told them (1:7–8).

The Epistles. The fundamental Jewish position—that the law is God's love-gift to his people and that by fulfilling its requirements they could attain the righteousness of God—is countered in the Epistles by the claim that salvation is by faith in the crucified and risen Christ. Saul, a Jew whose persecution of the Christians was based on this premise (Acts 22:3–5), after meeting the risen Christ becomes a Paul who with opened eyes receives the Holy Spirit and preaches that Jesus is the Christ, the Son of God (Acts 9; Gal. 1:23). His letters to the churches validate the claim that faith in Christ is the only means of attaining the righteousness of God (Rom. 1:16–17; Phil. 3:7–9).

According to Paul in his letter to the church in Rome, the moral degradation of all people becomes the occasion for God's saving activity (1:18–3:20), with a resulting righteousness being received by faith (3:21–31). This salvation is variously described by Paul using the analogies of justification (Rom. 3:24; 4:25), redemption (Rom. 3:24; 1 Cor. 1:30), reconciliation (Rom. 5:10; 2 Cor. 5:18–20), and freedom (Gal. 4:1–7; 5:1). James' argument for the necessary outworking of this salvation in good works (2:14–24) is countered by Paul's insistence on the working of the grace of God in the act of faith for salvation (Rom. 3:24–31).

The effect of faith in the life of the believer can be generalized under the picture of a new creation (2 Cor. 5:17), but is also particularized in terms of sonship (Rom. 8:14–17; Gal. 4:4–7), unity (1 Cor. 1:10), love (1 Cor. 13; Gal. 5:6, 22), hope (Rom. 6:8; 1 Peter 1:21), and steadfastness (Heb. 11). Paul's letters to the churches, with their recitation of problems with unity, love, and hope, seem to deny these claims. If faith means being a new creation, why is there so little unity and love in the Corinthian church and so little hope in the Thessalonian church? Paul's answer is twofold. First, he acknowledges the tension between the power of God at work in the people of faith and their continuing mortality (2 Cor. 4:7–12). Second, he reminds the Corinthians that the presence of the Spirit empowers God's people in their mortality now and also serves as a deposit guaranteeing what is to come, so that they live now by faith and not by sight (2 Cor. 5:5–7; 2 Thess. 2:13–17). The writer to the Hebrews uses this same definition, plus the examples of Old Testament persons of faith and Jesus, as a basis for the exhortation to live the life of faith and Jesus, as a basis for the exhortation to live the life of faith in the face of its hindrances (Heb. 10:35–12:12).

The later letters in the New Testament to Timothy and Titus, in addition to their continuing use of these dynamic definitions of faith, distinguish true faith from false faith by making the content of faith confessional (2 Tim. 4:3; Titus 1:9). Sound doctrine becomes the basis for right teaching (Titus 2:1) and right living (2 Tim. 3:15). Paul's words to Timothy when faced with the prospect of death—"I have kept the faith" (2 Tim. 4:7)—can be a witness to both the dynamic quality of his life in Christ and the correctness of his understanding.

The Johannine Writings. The change to a specific vocabulary for speaking about faith is most evident in the Gospel and Epistles of John. The Greek verb "to believe" (*pisteuein*) is used in all instances except 1 John 5:4, which uses the noun to define "the victory that has overcome the world," although even it is followed by the verbal explanation that "he who believes that Jesus is the Son of God" overcomes the world (1 John 5:5). The Fourth Gospel's ninety-eight uses of the verb for believing contrast with only thirty uses in all of the Synoptic Gospels. All four Gospels refer to believing facts (*hoti* clause: Matt. 9:28; Mark 11:23–24; Luke 1:45; John 6:69), to believing people or Scripture (dative case: Matt. 21:25; Mark 11:31; Luke 1:20; John 2:22), and believing without a stated object (absolute use: Matt. 8:13; Mark 5:36; Luke 8:12–13; John 1:50). The Gospel of John alone stresses what it means to believe into (*eis*) Jesus Christ.

From the beginning of the Gospel, where we are told that John the Baptist's witness to Jesus as the light is "so that through him all men might believe" (1:7), until the Gospel's concluding statement of purpose—"That you may believe that Jesus is the Christ, the Son of God, and that by believing you may have life in his name" (20:31), the gospel is presented as a call to faith. Jesus Christ, as the object of faith, is first portrayed as the Word become flesh who comes into the world to make it possible for all to become children of God by believing/receiving him (1:10–14), and finally shown to be the risen Christ who in belief is acknowledged as Lord and God (20:28–29). In between these two brackets belief or unbelief is determined by people's responses to Jesus' signs in which he reveals his glory (2:11), his power to heal (4:53; 5:9), his willingness to meet the needs of the hungry (6:12–14), the helpless (6:21, 61–70), and the blind (9:38), and to raise the dead (11:25–26). To his disciples he explains how they too can "overcome the world" (16:33). Their confession of faith at the end of the discourse in the upper room affirms their willingness to let their relationship with Jesus define the essence of their life and faith (16:29–30; cf. 14:20–21; 15:1–17; 16:12–15).

The intensity of the relational in John's description of believing in Christ may be compared to Paul's use of the term "in Christ" to define what it means to be a Christian (Rom. 6:11, 23). The result of this relationship is a movement from darkness to light (John 12:46), from death to life (John 11:25–26), and a love that reciprocates the love of the Father for the Son and for the world (John 15:9–13; cf. 3:16) as the believer is involved in active, self-giving service (John 13:1, 12–17). The power for this is to be found after Jesus' resurrection in the continuing relationship between the Son and the believer through the Holy Spirit (John 14:15–27; 16:5–15; cf. 7:37–39).

The Book of Revelation, with its stress on that which is to come, sees faith almost entirely from the perspective of the end and the exalted role of the martyr as a faithful witness (2:10, 13, 19; 14:12) who is compared with Jesus Christ who is also designated as faithful (1:5; 3:14; 19:11). All whose names are written in the Lamb's book of life respond to the promise of this Faithful One, "I am coming soon," with the prayer, *"Marana tha."*

HERBERT L. SWARTZ

See also FAITHFULNESS; HEAL, HEALTH; UNION WITH CHRIST.

Bibliography. H. Berkhof, *Christian Faith;* R. M. Brown, *Is Faith Obsolete?;* G. Ebeling, *The Nature of Faith;* R. M. Hals, *Grace and Faith in the Old Testament;* D. B. Harbuch, *The Dynamics of Belief;* H.-J. Hermisson and E. Lahse, *Faith;* J. G. Machen, *What Is Faith?*

Faithfulness. In the Old Testament, God's faithfulness and covenant love are closely related (Deut. 7:9; Pss. 25:10; 85:10). The most profound example of his faithfulness is the bond between God and the people of the northern kingdom of Israel. In spite of their unfaithfulness, God reminds them that he is betrothed to them in faithfulness (Hos. 2:20).

The Israelites were expected to respond in faithfulness to God because he had acted faithfully to them through the covenant. David and other godly people chose to walk the faithful way—the way of truth (Ps. 119:30). Just as God is both faithful and loving, those who believe in God need to exhibit faithfulness and steadfast love in their lives (Prov. 3:3).

In the New Testament, God also acts in faithfulness: He provides for both good and evil people (Matt. 5:45); he rewards those who do his good will (Matt. 6:4, 6, 18); he provides a way out for believers in the midst of temptation (1 Cor. 10:13); he remains faithful as he fulfills his promises (2 Cor. 1:18–19). Paul reminds us that even when we are faithless God remains faithful because he cannot disown himself (2 Tim. 2:13). John declares that Jesus is the faithful and true witness (Rev. 3:14), the Faithful and True (Rev. 19:11). God remains faithful to New Testament believers, both fulfilling and promising to fulfill the promises of the Old Testament.

Christians, like the Israelites, are to respond to God in faithfulness. Trustworthy servants must prove themselves to be faithful (1 Cor. 4:2). Epaphrus and Tychicus are identified as faithful ministers of Christ (Col. 1:7; 4:7). Paul remains faithful to God in spite of tremendous pressures (1 Tim. 1:12). Timothy is to select teachers who will exhibit faithfulness, one of the outstanding characteristics of Christians. The Spirit of God enables Christians to remain faithful to both God and other believers (Gal. 5:22). Louis Goldberg

Bibliography. G. M. Burge, *EDT,* pp. 402–4; M. J. Erickson, *Christian Theology;* R. E. Nixon, *ZPEB,* 2:479–91; J. B. Payne, *The Theology of the Older Testament;* J. B. Scott, *TWOT,* 1:51–53.

Fall, the. The word "fall" is widely used to refer to what is recorded in Genesis 3, particularly to what is written of the temptation of Adam and Eve, their being overcome by it, and their immediate reactions after they became aware of the consequences (3:1–8).

Since the account includes the role of a speaking serpent in an environment of perfect peace, beauty, and well-being for Adam and Eve, critical scholars have proposed that the account is a myth. For them it does not portray a scene that really existed or an event that actually happened in the earliest history of humanity. The New Testament does not give any credence to that view. Passages such as Romans 5:12–19, 1 Corinthians 15:21–22, and 1 Timothy 2:12–13 definitely refer to the fall as having actually happened as recorded. Many biblical scholars have correctly pointed out that the entire biblical teaching of Jesus Christ's redeeming and restoring work is based on the veracity of the historical account. Christ came and actually undid what Adam and Eve had done.

Adam and Eve had been created as image-bearers of God. They were placed in the cosmic kingdom created by God in intimate relationship with him. They were to mirror and represent their Creator as they carried out the spiritual, social, and cultural mandates. They were called to serve as mediators of the creation covenant—specifically as royal representatives and as priests representing creation before God and God before creation. To so serve they were created as unblemished persons, having intellect, volition, emotions, physical potentialities, drives, and abilities. They were created as the crown of creation and given Eden, the garden palace, as their home in which they were to carry out their roles and mandates. This they could do for they were in a trusting, obeying, honoring relationship with God who, as the sovereignly present, good, truly reliable One, communicated with them daily.

In communicating with them God had given his command not to eat of one specific tree (2:17). He did not explain why they should not. He warned them of the consequences if they did: they would die. Adam and Eve did not question God; they accepted the prohibition.

Satan and evil were also present in the cosmos but neither had influence in it. Satan, having been a powerful and influential administrative archangel, had rebelled against God. He was cast out but not destroyed by God. Satan, undoubtedly very envious of Adam and Eve whom God had given the role of vicegerents in the cosmic kingdom, sought to become the sovereign ruler. To do this, he had to gain the submission and service of Adam and Eve.

Satan, with his wisdom and abilities, confronted Eve using a serpent whose cunning ways Satan was able to use to his advantage. Satan led Eve to doubt God's goodness, truthfulness, reliability, and honor. He had but to ask the question: Did God really say you must not eat from any tree in the garden? The question, as framed, led Eve to respond in such a way that she began to doubt God's goodness and reliability; she added, "you must not touch it." The added comment revealed Eve's uncertainty about herself—what would she do if she came near it and touched it?

Satan attacked God directly by contradicting him, saying Adam and Eve would not die and that God knew they would become as he was (3:4–5). Satan transformed human honor, desire, and dignity, all God-given qualities, into dishonor, greed, and pride. Eve led Adam to join her, acting with hearts deviated from God's stipulated way of life, service, and peace. It was a willfully chosen path. Sin, evil, and death became influential forces and realities throughout the cosmic kingdom.

The effects of Adam and Eve's unbelief, disobedience, and rejection of God's command not to eat is stated in a seeming euphemistic manner: "Their eyes were opened" and "they realized they were naked." The first phrase indicates that they were still persons who could know, understand, and evaluate themselves in relation to God. This is not to say they were perfect in exercising these human capacities. They were still image-bearers but their attitudes and dispositions were radically affected. They were no longer in fellowship with God; when he came to commune with them they hid. They turned from seeking him; they rejected his fellowship. The love-life bond was broken from their side. They had become and realized they were covenant breakers. The phrase regarding their nakedness revealed that they realized they stood guilty before God. They could not appear before him as they were; they were exposed as persons who needed covering, protection, and defense. They were now no longer at peace in a wholesome, well-functioning relationship with God, nor with each other, for they were quick to shift blame. The relationship of harmony and trust between God and them, between man and woman, between them and the cosmos, as represented by the serpent, was ruptured. Self-defense and accusation of others, motivated by pride arising from their perverted hearts, became a tragic reality, adding to the deepening and widening gulf separating them from God, intimate relationship with others, and the natural world. Shame and fear gripped them; they realized that a tragic separation had suddenly taken place. They experienced the horrible reality of death, which basically means to have torn apart what belongs together for the exercise and enjoyment of love, peace, goodness, contentment, and joy. With opened eyes they saw themselves dead to God, to each other, and to the created natural order. They saw and understood they were immobilized, incapable to stand and serve, ready, able productive, and blessed before their covenant God.

The consequences of Adam and Eve's disobedience, rejection, deviation, and transgression had far-reaching effects. God had ordained and placed them as progenitors of the human race and as mediatorial vicegerents in the cosmos. By God's ordinance human offspring would inherit a deceitful heart, inclined to all manner of evil and incurably corrupt (Jer. 17:9). All would be conceived in sin and be born with the guilt of sin (Ps. 51:5). No one would come into life with a pure heart and conscience. All would be, have been, and will be born with inherited sin and guilt. This sin has been properly referred to as original sin and it is the root, source, and motivating factor for all the actual sins committed in thought, word, and deed. Scripture teaches us that the human race increased in disobedience and wickedness since the initial fateful deviation. Cain, with envy and hatred in his heart, murdered his brother (Gen. 4:1–8). The wickedness of humanity became great and violence filled the earth; polygamy became a way of life (Gen. 4:19; 6:2, 5). Paul, under the Spirit's inspiration, wrote that through the one man's disobedience the many were made sinners (Rom. 5:19) and therefore all suffer the consequence of sin: all died in Adam (1 Cor. 15:22).

The natural world also was deeply affected. The harmony among forces in the cosmos was disturbed and disrupted. God informed Adam that creation would not respond to his efforts as before. Adam would labor and sweat; thorns would grow. The biblical references to droughts, famines, floods, earthquakes, and destructive burning are well known. These are all reasons for the frustrations and groanings of all creation which, by the ordinance of God and as a result of humanity's sin, will continue until the end of time (Rom. 8:18–22).

Adam, Eve, and all their posterity's disobedience, rejection, and deviation had a direct consequence on God also. His relation to humanity was altered. No longer did Adam and Eve hear only words of love and encouragement; they heard reproof, condemnation, and retribution. God himself did not change; humanity broke the covenant relationship and true to himself and his Word, God in righteousness and justice, dealt accordingly. By his decree death entered the world, and God had to deal with the cosmos in the throes of despair and death. But he demonstrated his love also.

God made six pronouncements, all of which revealed his mercy and grace. Mercy is love extended to those experiencing brokenness, pain, misery, and grief because of human depravity, corruption, sin, and guilt. Grace is love extended to those who do not deserve love; grace is love for the guilty.

First, God declared that enmity was to exist between Satan and the seed of the woman. This enmity would divide humanity into disobedient despisers and rejectors of God and his covenant and submitting, believing, and obedient recipients of mercy and love. This enmity would be expressed in an abiding antithesis between Satan's dominion and the cosmic kingdom of God.

Second, God pronounced victory, redemption, and restoration. The satanic dominion and its participants would be crushed. A mortal blow would be struck by the seed of the woman, who would suffer in delivering it. This was the first promise of what later became clearly enunciated as salvation wrought by Jesus Christ.

Third, while an absolute curse was pronounced upon Satan and his dominion, a mitigated curse was pronounced on Eve. She would have greatly increased pain in childbearing; pain would accompany her as she experienced motherhood; undoubtedly she had greatly increased pain when she lost Abel at her son Cain's hand.

Fourth, a mitigated curse was pronounced on Adam and the ground. Adam would experience painful toil and sweat as food was cultivated in a thorn- and thistle-infested ground.

Fifth, Adam and Eve were also informed that although they could be spiritually restored (delivered from spiritual death), they would experience physical death. They would be returned to the dust of the earth.

Sixth, while the mitigated curse was surely executed, an absolute curse on Adam and Eve and on the natural world would not be. God's covenant with creation would continue. Adam and Eve would continue as covenantal vicegerents—although in a weakened condition.

God revealed that although his wisdom, love, goodness, integrity, sovereignty, and majesty had been assaulted by Satan and violated by Adam and Eve, in his infinite compassion and with his unsurpassing power and authority he would destroy Satan and his dominion. He would undo the fall by providing full redemption and restoration through the mediatorial work of the seed of the woman, his incarnate Son, Jesus Christ, who would serve as the second Adam.

GERARD VAN GRONINGEN

See also ADAM; EVE; GENESIS, THEOLOGY OF.

Bibliography. H. Bavinck, *Our Reasonable Faith;* W. Broomall, *The Encyclopedia of Christianity,* 4:170–74; A. A. Hoekema, *Created in God's Image;* P. E. Hughes, *The True Image;* J. Murray, *ZPEB,* 2:492–94; N. Shepherd, *BEB,* 2:765–67; G. Vos, *Biblical Theology.*

False, Falsehood. *See* LIE, LYING.

False Prophet. Even though the Old Testament does not use the term "false prophet," it is clear that such "professional prophets" existed throughout much of Israel's history and that they were diametrically opposed to the canonical prophets. Scripture, however, regarded them as mere imitations of the genuinely appointed prophets of God.

Distinguishing Marks of False Prophecy and False Prophets. It was the Septuagint translators who introduced the term *pseudoprophētēs* ("false prophet") ten times where the Hebrew text simply used the generic term *nābîʾ* ("prophet") (Jer. 6:13; 26:7–8, 11, 16; 27:9; 28:1; 29:1, 8; Zech. 13:2). But the Hebrew text nevertheless still made the same point with the whole battery of negative descriptions.

False prophets prophesied lies (Jer. 6:13; 27:14; Zech. 13:3), deceived the people with their dreams (Jer. 29:8), prophesied by the alleged authority of Baal (Jer. 2:8; 23:13), threatened the lives of the true prophets (Jer. 26:7), and dared to speak when they had not stood in the council of Yahweh and received a word directly from the Lord (Jer. 23:18). Typically, their prophecies promised peace when there was no peace to be had (Jer. 6:14; 8:11; 14:3; 23:17; 28:2, 11; Ezek. 13:10; Mic. 3:5), for their visions were drawn out of their own hearts (Jer. 14:14; 23:16; Ezek. 13:2–3; 22:28). Some false prophets used magic (Ezek. 13:17–23), others appeared to use divination, soothsaying, witchcraft, necromancy, and sorcery, which were all forbidden arts and practices in the classical passage that set forth divine revelation in contrast to such practices (Deut. 18:9–13). The false prophets gave the people what they wanted to hear and thereby placed "whitewash" (Ezek. 13:10–12, 14–15; 22:28) over every situation, no matter how adverse it appeared.

The fullest discussion of charges that could be brought against false prophets can be found in Jeremiah 23:9–39. Jeremiah condemns the pseudoprophets on four grounds: (1) they are men of immoral character (v. 14—"they commit adultery and live a lie"); (2) they seek popular acclaim with their unconditional pledge of immunity from all imminent disasters (vv. 17–22); (3) they fail to distinguish their own dreams from a word from God (vv. 25–29); and (4) they are plagiarists who steal from one another words allegedly from the Lord (vv. 30–39). Rather than having a "burden" from the Lord, they themselves were another burden—both to the Lord and to the misled people!

The Theology of the False Prophets. The false prophets were zealous to maintain the inviolability and invincibility of Zion—for all times and for all occasions. They stressed the permanence of David's dynasty, the temple, and the covenant—as a guarantee that operated for every generation! They were overly dependent on promises made at Sinai that God would be Israel's God and Israel would be his people—thereby allowing more leeway than one would ordinarily think permissible. Any and all new revelations that would predict judgment, doom, and disaster were, from the false prophets' standpoint, contrary to their list of immutables; therefore, they preached that all such negative declarations were wrong, treasonous, and unnecessary.

Thus it was the false prophet Hananiah who predicted in the name of "the LORD Almighty, the God of Israel" (Jer. 28:2) that the exiles would be restored to their homeland and Jehoiachin and the temple vessels returned (vv. 3–4). At first, Jeremiah was startled by this apparent reversal in the revelation of God (v. 6), but he recovered sufficiently to add: "From early times the prophets who preceded you and me have prophesied war, disaster and plague against many countries and great kingdoms. But the prophet who prophesies peace will be recognized as one truly sent by the LORD only if his prediction comes true" (vv. 8–9).

This is what makes the discernment of what constitutes pseudoprophecy so difficult, for many of the false prophets also subscribed to some of the same theological traditions as did the canonical prophets.

The theology of the false prophets was characterized by the following: (1) a selective appeal to the Davidic/Zion and Sinaitic covenants as a type of fire insurance against any threatened calamity; (2) an exclusive teaching of hope/salvation with no attention given to any potential adversities for lack of obedience to God's Word; and (3) a constant appeal to what the masses wanted to hear as a basis for promoting their own power and the status quo. This list is very similar to the four charges that Jeremiah brought in 23:9–39.

The Criteria for Testing False Prophecy. The *loci classici* for determining true from false prophecy are Deuteronomy 13:1–5 and 18:15–22. These texts teach five tests for a true prophet: (1) he must be Jewish (Deut. 18:18); (2) he must speak in the name of the Lord (Deut. 18:19–20); (3) what he says must come to pass, the most proximate fulfillments being the validators of the more distant predictions (Deut. 18:21–22); (4) he must perform signs, wonders, or miracles that accompany his words (Deut. 13:1–2a); and (5) his message must conform to what God had revealed previously (Deut. 13:2b–5).

More often than not, the false prophets prophesied in the name of one or more false gods while they also syncretistically appealed to Yahweh's name (Jer. 23:13, 17, 25; 26:27). Such teachers easily exposed themselves as frauds. But there were also times when it was exceedingly difficult to determine if the prophecy were true or not. For example, the man of God from Judah was a true prophet, for what he said came to pass, both in his immediate and distant predictions (1 Kings 13). Nevertheless, when he disobeyed the command of God, he was deceived by a false prophecy. Remarkably that same false prophet who deceived him later delivered a true prediction (1 Kings 13:20–22). Thus, not everything a prophet said was divinely inspired. For example, the prophet Nathan told David to go ahead and build the temple to the Lord (2 Sam. 7:1–2), but that night God informed Nathan that this was not his plan. Thus Nathan had to reverse his advice to David the next morning! Accordingly, a prophet's words could be false if: (1) they were his own and not God's; (2) they were wrongly applied at a wrong time and to a wrong audience; and (3) they were not backed up by a life and character that one would expect from a servant of the Lord.

False Prophets in the New Testament. False prophets continued to make their presence felt well beyond the days of the Old Testament; indeed, Jesus warned his disciples, and through the apostles, he warned the early church about the character and teachings of such frauds.

As was characteristic of false prophets in the Old Testament, their New Testament counterparts were also motivated by greed (2 Peter 2:3, 13), exhibited arrogance (2 Peter 2:18), lived immoral lives (2 Peter 2:2, 10–13), and generally could be described as ungodly persons (Jude 4).

The classical encounter between true and false prophets of God in the New Testament is Paul and Barnabas's rebuke of the Jewish magician Bar-Jesus on the island Paphos (Acts 13:6–10). The Holy Spirit informed Paul that Bar-Jesus was full of deceit and a false prophet. Bar-Jesus belonged to the same line of pseudoprophets as the prophetess Jezebel from the church of Thyatira (Rev. 2:20).

Nor does the danger stop in the New Testament, for present-day believers are warned to test persons who make prophetic claims. For example, if anyone denies that Jesus has come in the flesh, that person is not a true prophet from God (1 John 4:1–3).

In the endtimes, false prophets will attempt to deceive the world's populace into following the false prophet, the beast, and Satan himself (Matt. 24:1, 24; Rev. 16:13–14; 19:20; 20:10)—even by performing miracles and signs. But this will be the last time false prophecy is seen, for Christ's return will destroy the whole institution of false prophecy along with its sponsors: Satan, the beast, and the false prophet.

WALTER C. KAISER, JR.

See also PROPHET, PROPHETESS, PROPHECY.

Bibliography. R. E. Manahan, *Grace Th J* 1 (1980): 77–96; T. W. Overholt, *The Threat of Falsehood: A Study in the Theology of the Book of Jeremiah;* J. T. E. Renner, *Rev Th R* 25 (1966): 95–104; H. W. Robinson, *Inspiration and Revelation in the Old Testament;* J. A. Sanders, *Essays in Old Testament Religion and Theology,* pp. 21–41; G. T. Sheppard, *Essays in Old Testament Religion and Theology,* pp. 262–82; G. V. Smith, *ISBE,* 3:984–86; A. S. Van der Woude, *VT* 19 (1969): 244–60; W. Van Gemeren, *Interpreting the Prophetic Word.*

Family Life and Relations. ***The Old Testament.*** In Western societies individuals are often considered the societal units, brought together by some commonly felt need (commerce, industry, mutual defense, etc.). In contrast, Israel's social structure was tribal and therefore corporate (solidary) in its internal relationships, generating tightly structured communities. Whatever their size, these communities perceived themselves as totalities, bound together through internal agencies that made their presence felt in each individual member. The individual was neither overlooked, nor was he considered the unit on which the society was built. Instead, the family was the unit, and the individual found his place in society through the family and its extensions. The subtribe was really a greatly extended family; a collection of related subtribes formed a tribe; and a federation of tribes yielded a people.

Nowhere is community stronger in Hebraic society than in that most foundational of the primary groups, the *bayit* (house) or *bêt ʾāb* (father's house), terms designating an extended family and variously rendered as family or household. It was not only the "life center" of the members, but also the nucleus about which was built the subtribe. The covenant between Yahweh and the people thus became his covenant with each family; should the security of any family be threatened, divine wrath was incurred (cf. Jer. 2:3–4). The household would embrace the mother and children, even after the latter had reached maturity (Judg. 6:15; 9:1; 1 Sam. 16:5). In its broadest definition, the household would also include its servants: Abraham had 318 who had been "born in his household" (Gen. 14:14).

Though every effort was expended to preserve the stability of the family, tensions existed, and the Bible makes no effort to conceal them (Abraham's quarrel with his nephew Lot, Gen. 13:5–8; Esau's hatred of Jacob, Gen. 27:41; and the favoritism shown Jacob by Rebekah, Gen. 25:28; 27:15–17). In a polygynous environment the only bond between siblings born to disparate mothers was the often remote father. At times bitterness developed between women such as Hannah and Penninah, both wives of Elkanah. The story of Joseph's sale into Egyptian bondage (Gen. 37:12–36) vividly portrays how competition between wives in childbearing (Gen. 30:1–7) could be transmitted to the children. An even more severe example may be seen in Amnon's rape of his half-sister Tamar and his subsequent murder by Absalom (2 Sam. 13:1–29). The bond of affection between Joseph and his only full brother Benjamin (Gen. 43:15–16) is also echoed in Absalom's concern over his sister's disgrace, contrasted to his cold hatred for his half-brother, Amnon.

In ancient Israel large families were deemed necessary to conduct the family business, to provide for the parents in their old age, and to carry on the family name. As a result, the large family was regarded as a blessing from God (Exod. 1:21; Ps. 128:3). Sons were especially valued (Ps. 127:3–5) to carry on the family name, yet it is against rebellious sons, not daughters, that legislation was directed and proverbs were coined (Prov. 20:20; cf. 30:11, 17).

Legally, children were regarded as the property, and therefore the responsibility, of the father. Accordingly, he is compensated for the loss of a fetus (Exod. 21:22), an unmarried daughter who is seduced (Exod. 22:16), and unfounded charges about his daughter's character lodged by his son-in-law (Deut. 22:13–19). The father may sell his daughter as a servant or concubine (Exod. 21:7–11), or even pledge his sons as a loan guaranty, although these practices seem to have arisen more out of cases of economic necessity than from established custom (cf. 2 Kings 4:1; Neh. 5:1–5). The distance between the father and his children in a polygynous household may be seen in Absalom's efforts to unseat his father David and kill him (2 Sam. 15:14; 17:2–4).

Government of the family was by its family head, usually the eldest male. The father and other aged males were shown respect and deference. It was the father's task to arrange marriages (Exod. 22:17) and to discipline his sons (1 Sam. 3:13). The age of the children determined their rank within the family, with the eldest having the position of privilege and with it, the responsibility of acting for his father in the father's absence. Joseph's brothers, for example, were seated in order of their birth, with the eldest presumably having the seat of honor (Gen. 43:33). The eldest daughter had an understood agreement with the family that she would be married before her younger sisters (Gen. 29:26).

Wives had much more power than they are often credited with. Sarah, for example, after urging Abraham to have sexual relations with Hagar to father a child, expels both the girl and her infant child over Abraham's protests (Gen. 21:9–13). The numerous stories of women who were heroes (Deborah, Jael, etc.) or villains (Jezebel, Athaliah) show that free women had a degree of self-determination that modern writers sometimes ignore. Likewise, the stories of the successes of Joseph and David and the failures of Reuben and Esau show that age was not inviolably superior to youth.

The functions of the extended family were to provide for its own perpetuation and to maintain an atmosphere of emotional warmth and stability for rearing children. The harmony of the home was necessary to provide a stable environment for its functions. Accordingly, in the Mosaic legislation a number of provisions were made to ensure this harmony and to circumvent rivalries that would endanger it and cause the home to break apart. A case in point may be seen in the command to honor one's father and mother (Exod. 20:12), with the death penalty prescribed for anyone who attacked or belittled his father or his mother (Exod. 21:15, 17; cf. Deut. 21:18–21).

Another effort to promote harmony in the family was the law forbidding marriage of sisters to the same husband (Lev. 18:18), an obvious effort to avoid the sort of strife that had infected Jacob's household. But not so obvious are the laws of incest. One's father's wife, mother-in-law, and sister (including one's half-sister) are forbidden degrees of sexual contact in Deuteronomy (22:30; 27:20, 22–23), to which the priestly formulation adds one's mother, granddaughter, aunt (including the wife of one's uncle), daughter-in-law, sister-in-law, wife's child or grandchild, as well as the sister of one's wife as mentioned already (Lev. 18:6–18). That the issue at stake is not genetic may be seen in the many forbidden relationships in which the female is not genetically related to the male (one's father's wife, mother-in-law, uncle's wife, daughter-in-law, sister-in-law, or wife's child, grandchild, or sister). The end, instead, is harmony in the home. Strife is to be avoided as destructive to the family's inner cohesiveness; any two males striving for the same woman would yield an incendiary situation (e.g., Reuben's liaison with Bilhah). The same obtains for adultery, a rebellion against the structure of the family: it is forbidden because of its destructive effects on the home, the fragmentation it yields, and the alienation that follows. Since the social structure was predicated on the family and its extensions, any violation of the integrity of the family could be perceived as a threat to the integrity of the entire group.

The social foundations for Israel's preoccupation with responsibility and motives may be traced to its understanding that an individual cannot act in such a way that his deeds have no effect on others, whether or not those effects are visible in the present. Rather than seeing infractions as isolated incidents, a violator endangered his group by bringing upon them guilt, whether it be upon an entire people (as the Gileadite altar, Josh. 22:19–20) or the succeeding generations (as in the sin of idolatry, Exod. 20:5; 34:7; Num. 14:18; Deut. 5:9). The woman convicted of adultery became a curse on the community to which she belonged (Num. 5:27). Oft-cited examples are Achan's sin that brought guilt on his family and through it, to the entire people of Israel (Josh. 7:24). The families of Dathan, Abiram, and Korah, and the latter's entire household, were destroyed because of the rebellion of their leaders (Num. 16:32–35).

Rooted in the promise given to Abraham, and through him to his seed (Gen. 12:1–3, 7), lay the assurance of an election, ever present and articulated in the covenant. Embracing the whole of the people of Israel (Gen. 15:5–21; 17:1–22), it was premised, not on the goodness of the people themselves, but on that of Abraham. Through him, all who claimed kinship to him were to receive blessing and to participate in the covenant (Gen. 26:3; 28:4; 35:12; Exod. 2:24; 6:8; Lev. 26:42; Num. 32:11; Deut. 1:8; 6:10; 9:5; 29:13; 30:20; 34:4; 2 Kings 13:23). In an earlier period, Noah was able to save his entire family from destruction (Gen. 7:1) because of his righteousness; Lot's entire family was spared because of him (Gen. 19:1–28). Rahab's favorable treatment of the Israelite spies brought her family mercy from human agencies (Josh. 2:12–14, 17–20; 6:22–25), and the house of Obed-Edom obtained blessing because he gave shelter to the ark (2 Sam. 6:11). While Exodus 20:5 is frequently cited as showing God's vengeance to the fourth generation, the following verse adds that his mercy embraces the myriads who love him.

The New Testament. Words used in the New Testament for family are *patria,* signifying a descent group similar to subtribe in the Old Testament, and *oikos,* signifying a household. Joseph is from the *oikos* and *patria* of David (Luke 1:27; 2:4). In Acts 3:25 *patria* is used to translate the word "peoples" from Genesis 12:3. The word *oikos* is much more common and represented a family as a household to the Greco-Roman world. The Jerusalem church was formed of groups of believers, worshiping in private homes (Acts 2:46; 5:42; 12:12). Paul frequently mentions households by name in his epistles (Rom. 16:10–11; 1 Cor. 1:11, 16; 16:15; 2 Tim. 1:16; 4:19) and recalls with great affection Priscilla and Aquilla and the church that met in their house (Rom. 16:5; 1 Cor. 16:19).

Perhaps because it assumes an understanding of the Old Testament or because it is less predicated on the social structure of a single people, the New Testament has much less to say about the family as a sociological unit. While not denying the value of strong internal ties in a traditional Jewish family (see Luke 1:17), Jesus would not permit such ties to stand in the way of one's decision to follow him (Matt. 10:35–36). Genesis 2:24 is cited with approbation twice in the Gospels (Matt. 19:5; Mark 10:8) and twice in the Pauline corpus (1 Cor. 6:16; Eph. 5:31) as indicating the close bonds between husband and wife and, therefore, of the family unit.

Paul and Silas seem to attribute a position of headship to the Philippian jailer not unlike the head of an Old Testament household (Acts 16:31): his belief will bring about the salvation of both himself and his entire family. Although certain women may have been the heads of their households (e.g., Lydia, Nympha; Priscilla is always mentioned *before* her husband), Paul's understanding of the family seems to have the husband generally as its head (1 Cor. 11:3; Eph. 5:23), yet involved in a loving (Eph. 5:25–33; Col. 3:19), caring relationship with his wife and with his children (Eph. 6:4; Col. 3:21).

Possibly because of the disruptive effect of Christian conversion on pagan homes, a considerable effort is made by the New Testament writers to articulate the familial nature of the kingdom of God. Paul stresses God as Father of believers (Rom. 1:7; 8:15; 1 Cor. 1:3; 2 Cor. 1:2; Gal. 1:3–4; 4:6; Eph. 1:2; Phil. 1:2; 4:20; Col. 1:2), while John emphasizes believers as God's children (John 1:12; 11:52; 1 John 3:1–2, 10; 5:2, 19). Believers, even Gentiles, are no longer "separate from Christ, excluded from citizenship in Israel and foreigners to the covenants of the promise, without hope and without God in the world" (Eph. 2:12), but have become members of God's own family (Gal. 6:10; Eph. 2:19; Heb. 3:2–6; 1 Peter 4:17) through the work of the Holy Spirit, the spirit of adoption (Rom. 8:15). God is their Father and Christ their elder brother (Rom. 8:29).

William C. Williams

See also Divorce; Marriage; Woman; Widow.

Bibliography. T. D. Alexander, *EQ* 61/1 (1989): 5–19; F. I. Andersen, *The Bible Translator* 20 (1969): 29–39; M. Burrows, *JBL* 59 (1940): 23–33; W. Eichrodt, *Theology of the Old Testament;* I. Ellis, *SJT* 38 (1985): 173–88; N. K. Gottwald, *The Tribes of Yahweh;* J. Hempel, *IDB,* 2:155; D. Jacobson, *The Social Background of the Old Testament;* H. van Oyen, *Ethik des Alten Testaments;* J. Pedersen, *Israel: Its Life and Culture;* C. S. Rodd, *The Bible Translator* 18 (1967): 19–26; J. Rogerson and P. Davies, *The Old Testament World;* M. J. Selman, *Tyn Bul* 27 (1976): 114–36; R. P. Shedd, *Man in Community;* W. R. Smith, *Lectures on the Religion of the Semites: The Fundamental Institutions;* F. Tönnies, *Community and Society;* R. de Vaux, *Israel: Its Life and Institutions;* W. C. Williams, *An Examination of the Relationship Between Solidarity and Adultery in Ancient Israel;* C. J. H. Wright, *ABD,* 2:761–69.

Fast, Fasting. Abstinence from food and/or drink as an element of private or public religious devotion. Fasting is nowhere commanded in the Torah and, in fact, is never attested earlier than the time of the judges of Israel (cf. Judg. 20:26). The fact that Jesus and the disciples sanctioned it by their own example (Matt. 4:2; Acts 13:2–3), however, is sufficient justification for its practice in biblical times and, in fact, in modern times as well.

The Hebrew verb *ṣûm* is the only one used to describe fasting as a religious exercise. It (and its cognate noun *ṣôm*) conveys the explicit meaning "to abstain from food" and thus occurs regularly as a technical religious term. The Greek verb *nēsteuo* and its companion noun *nēsteia* occur consistently in the Septuagint as translations of Hebrew *ṣûm* and *ṣôm* and as the usual terms for fasting in the New Testament.

By the ninth century B.C. fasting had become institutionalized or formalized to the extent that days or other periods of fasting were called as occasions for public worship. The usual way of describing such convocation is "to call for" or "proclaim" a fast. Thus, Jezebel, to provide an occasion whereby Naboth would be unjustly accused and condemned, proclaimed a fast (1 Kings 21:9, 12). Jehoshaphat later, and with much nobler motives, called for such an assembly in order to implore God's intercession on Judah's behalf (2 Chron. 20:3). The same formula appears in Ezra 8:21 and Jonah 3:5, in the last instance initiated by the people of Nineveh as an expression of their repentance at Jonah's preaching.

An informative description of the proclamation of a fast is in Jeremiah 36:9. There the people of Judah convened, apparently for the purpose of national repentance. This at least is what Jeremiah instructed Baruch to encourage them to do (vv. 7–8). Moreover, Jeremiah refers to the anticipated event as a "day of fasting" (v. 6), suggesting a common practice known to him and the people generally. In fact, Isaiah had spoken of such convocations a century earlier (58:3–6), gatherings on special days for special purposes. Regardless of Isaiah's feelings about the abuse of fasting, it is obvious that he recognized it as a legitimate form of worship and that he found no fault with it being carried out on specially called occasions.

Joel speaks twice of setting apart a fast and calling a sacred assembly (1:14; 2:15). The parallelism makes clear that the fast in view is a formal, community event, one involving all the people in an act of worship on a stated day and in a designated place.

As a whole, however, fasting appears to be a private matter in the Bible, an expression of personal devotion linked to three major kinds of crisis in life: lamentation/penitence, mourning, and petition. Without exception it has to do with a sense of need and dependence, of abject helplessness in the face of actual or anticipated calamity. It is in examining these situations that the theological meaning and value of fasting are to be discovered.

As an expression of lamentation and/or penitence, fasting nearly always is associated with weeping (Judg. 20:26; Esther 4:3; Ps. 69:10; Joel 2:12), confession (1 Sam. 7:6; Dan. 9:3), and the wearing of sackcloth (1 Kings 21:27; Neh. 9:1; Esther 4:3; Ps. 69:10; Dan. 9:3). In the New Testament Jesus chides the hypocritical Pharisees for disfiguring their faces when they fast (Matt. 6:16–18), a reference no doubt to the custom of smearing themselves with ashes. These objects and actions had no intrinsic penitential value but in a culture in which inner feelings were commonly displayed or even dramatized, when done sincerely they effectively communicated contrition. It became easy, however, for the outward exhibition of repentance to take the place of a genuine, inner attitude and thus become an act of hypocrisy.

Fasting also appears as a sign of mourning. Following Saul's death, the people of Jabesh-Gilead lamented his passing by fasting (1 Sam. 31:13) as did David and his companions when they heard the news (2 Sam. 1:12). David goes so far as to say that he commiserated with his enemies when they were sick, fasting and dressing himself in sackcloth (Ps. 35:13). Such behavior was a sign of his mourning over them (v. 14). Zechariah describes the commemoration of Israel's tragic days of past defeat and judgment as times of mourning attended by fasting (7:5). But these days of fasting in the fourth, fifth, seventh, and tenth months will one day be turned to times of joy (8:19). Jesus speaks of the time of his departure from his disciples as a time of mourning when it will be entirely appropriate to fast (Matt. 9:14–15; Mark 2:18–20; Luke 5:33–35).

Finally, fasting was frequently associated with supplicatory prayer. David prayed and fasted over his sick child (2 Sam. 12:16), weeping before the Lord in earnest intercession (vv. 21–22). Nehemiah, having heard of Jerusalem's desolation, wept, fasted, and prayed that God would give him favor with King Artaxerxes of Persia so that he might return to his homeland and repair its ruins (Neh. 1:4–11). Esther, under similar circumstances, urged Mordecai and the Jews to fast for her as she planned to appear before her husband the king (Esther 4:16). Clearly, fasting and petition are here one and the same (cf. Jer. 14:12).

Jesus equates supplication and fasting when he teaches that the removal of mountains comes about only by prayer and fasting (Matt. 17:21). The godly prophetess Anna looked for the redemption of Israel with supplicatory prayer and fasting (Luke 2:37). Before Paul and Barnabas appointed elders for the various churches, they committed them to the Lord with prayer and fasting (Acts 14:23). In all these instances there is the clear implication that fasting is an effective adjunct to petition.

The purpose of fasting is never explicitly stated in Scripture but its connection to penitence, mourning, and supplication suggests a self-denial that opens one to God and to the immaterial aspects of life. Inasmuch as food and drink typify life in the flesh and all its demands and satisfactions, their absence or rejection speaks to the reality of a higher dimension, one in which the things of the spirit predominate. The theology of fasting, then, is a theology of priorities in which believers are given the opportunity to express themselves in an undivided and intensive devotion to the Lord and to the concerns of the spiritual life.

EUGENE H. MERRILL

Bibliography. John E. Baird, *What the Bible Says About Fasting;* R. D. Chatham, *Fasting: A Biblical-Historical Study;*

Joseph F. Wimmer, *Fasting in the New Testament: A Study in Biblical Theology.*

Father. *See* FAMILY LIFE AND RELATIONS.

Fatherhood of God. Throughout the Bible we find God portrayed as a Father. This portrayal, however, is surprisingly rare in the Old Testament. There God is specifically called the Father of the nation of Israel (Deut. 32:6; Isa. 63:16 [twice]; 64:8; Jer. 3:4, 19; 31:9; Mal. 1:6; 2:10) or the Father of certain individuals (2 Sam. 7:14; 1 Chron. 17:13; 22:10; 28:6; Pss. 68:5; 89:26) only fifteen times. (At times the father imagery is present although the term "Father" is not used [Exod. 4:22–23; Deut. 1:31; 8:5; 14:1; Ps. 103:13; Jer. 3:22; 31:20; Hos. 11:1–4; Mal. 3:17]). This metaphor for God may have been avoided in the Old Testament due to its frequent use in the ancient Near East where it was used in various fertility religions and carried heavy sexual overtones. The avoidance of this description for God can still be found in the intertestamental literature. There its use is also rare: Apocrypha (Wis. 2:16; 14:3; Tob. 13:4; Sir. 23:1, 4; 51:10); Pseudepigrapha (Jub. 1:24, 28; 19:29; 3 Macc. 5:7; 6:4, 8; T. Levi 18:6; T. Judah 24:2); and Dead Sea Scrolls (1 QH 9:35f.).

The teaching of the Fatherhood of God takes a decided turn with Jesus, for "Father" was his favorite term for addressing God. It appears on his lips some sixty-five times in the Synoptic Gospels and over one hundred times in John. The exact term Jesus used is still found three times in the New Testament (Mark 14:36; Rom. 8:15–16; Gal. 4:6) but elsewhere the Aramaic term *Abba* is translated by the Greek *patēr.* The uniqueness of Jesus' teaching on this subject is evident for several reasons. For one, the rarity of this designation for God is striking. There is no evidence in pre-Christian Jewish literature that Jews addressed God as *"Abba."* A second unique feature about Jesus' use of *Abba* as a designation for God involves the intimacy of the term. *Abba* was a term little children used when they addressed their fathers. At one time it was thought that since children used this term to address their fathers the nearest equivalent would be the English term "Daddy." More recently, however, it has been pointed out that *Abba* was a term not only that small children used to address their fathers; it was also a term that older children and adults used. As a result it is best to understand *Abba* as the equivalent of "Father" rather than "Daddy."

A third unique feature of Jesus' teaching concerning the Fatherhood of God is that the frequency of this metaphor is out of all proportion to what we find elsewhere in the Old Testament and other Jewish literature. (Note 165+ times in the four Gospels compared to only 15 times in the entire Old Testament!) This was not just *a* way Jesus taught his disciples to address God; it was *the* way. They were to pray, "Father, hallowed by your name" (Luke 11:2). This is why the Greek-speaking Gentile churches in Galatia and Rome continued to address God as *Abba.* They used this foreign title for God because Jesus had used it and taught his followers to do so. It should be pointed out that although Jesus addressed God as "Father" and taught his disciples to do the same, he never referred to God as "our Father." (Matthew 6:9 is not an exception, for here Jesus is teaching his disciples how they [plural] should pray.) His "Sonship" was different from that of his followers. He was by nature the Son; they were "sons" through adoption. This is clearly seen in John 20:17 in the distinction between "my" God and "your" God. It is also seen in Matthew 5:16, 45, 48; 6:1, 4, 6; 7:21; 10:32–33, where Jesus refers to "your" (singular and plural) and "my" father but never "our" father.

Because of Jesus' use of this metaphor, it is not surprising that the rest of the New Testament also emphasizes the Fatherhood of God. In the Pauline letters God is described as "Father" over forty times. It occurs in blessings (Rom. 1:7; 1 Cor. 1:3), doxologies (Rom. 15:6), thanksgivings (2 Cor. 1:3; 1 Thess. 1:2–3), prayers (Col. 1:12), exhortations (Eph. 5:20), and creeds (1 Cor. 8:6; Eph. 4:6). For Paul this fatherhood is based not so much on God's role in creation but rather on the redemption and reconciliation he has made available in Jesus Christ. This is why Paul refers to "the God and Father of our Lord Jesus Christ" (Rom. 15:6; 2 Cor. 1:3; 11:31). It is through the work of Christ that God invites us to call him *"Abba,* Father." It is through Christ that grace and peace have resulted and we have become God's children (Rom. 8:12–16; 1 Peter 1:3–4; 1 John 3:1).

The description of God as "father" is under attack today in certain circles. It is charged by some that this leads to a false view that God is a male. This criticism should be taken seriously in that God is not a "man" (Num. 23:19). He is a Spirit (John 4:24) without sexual parts. When God is referred as a father, this is simply the use of a metaphor in which he is likened to a kind and loving father. Elsewhere God's love and care can be compared to that of a concerned and caring mother (Isa. 49:14–16; Luke 13:34). Yet to avoid the metaphor of father as a description and designation for God is to lose sight of the fact that Jesus chose this as his metaphor to address God and that he taught this as *the* metaphor by which his disciples should address God. It also loses sight of the continuity established by the use of this metaphor with those who have called God "Father" over the centuries. These include the disciples; the earliest congregations (Rom. 8:15; Gal. 4:6); the earliest church councils ("I believe in God the Father Almighty, Maker of heaven and earth . . ."); and Christian churches all over the globe who over the centuries have prayed together "Our Father who art in heaven, Hallowed by thy name." ROBERT H. STEIN

See also GOD; GOD, NAMES OF.

Bibliography. J. Barr, *JTS* 39 (1988): 28–47; R. Hamerton-Kelly, *God the Father;* J. Jeremias, *The Prayers of Jesus;* J. Scott Lidgett, *The Fatherhood of God;* W. Elwell, *TAB*, pp. 42–44.

Favor. Finding favor means gaining approval, acceptance, or special benefits or blessings. There is also a close association among favor, grace, and mercy, which are sometimes used to translate the same Hebrew and Greek words (such as *ḥēn* and *charis*). The favor that human beings receive from God depends on his good pleasure and is often extended in response to prayer or righteous living. Those whose walk is blameless, such as Noah or Moses (Gen. 6:8; Exod. 33:12–13), receive favor and honor from the Lord (Ps. 84:11). In Moses' blessing on the twelve tribes he speaks of Joseph's prosperity and fruitfulness as the one who enjoyed God's favor (Deut. 33:16). Gabriel told Mary (Luke 1:30) that she had "found favor with God" and would bear the Christ-child. When Christ was born the angelic host announced to the shepherds that God would send "peace to men on whom his favor rests" (Luke 2:14). At age twelve Jesus enjoyed the favor of God and men as he "grew in wisdom and stature" (Luke 2:52), a description similar to the one about the boy Samuel (1 Sam. 2:26).

Often the bestowal of God's favor comes in answer to prayer as people cry out for mercy. Moses pleaded that God would spare Israel in spite of their sinful worship of the golden calf (Exod. 32:11). Moses prayed that he might know God and learn his ways so that his favor might continue (Exod. 33:12–13). Sinful kings such as Manasseh humbled themselves and sought the Lord in their distress, and he graciously showed them favor (2 Kings 13:4; 2 Chron. 33:12). Sometimes, however, the Lord withheld his compassion and brought judgment on his people (cf. Isa. 27:11).

Still, when the full force of his judgment struck Israel, God did not abandon the nation but restored them from exile. He showed compassion to this people and saved them from their distress (Ps. 106:4; Isa. 60:10). Isaiah calls this deliverance the "time" or "the year of the LORD's favor" (49:8; 61:2), which is linked with the day of salvation in the New Testament (Luke 4:19; 2 Cor. 6:2). Those who believe the gospel receive the ultimate gift of God's favor: eternal life through Christ.

Human approval can be gained through faithful and effective service. Joseph enjoyed the favor of Potiphar as he wisely administered Potiphar's estate, though ultimately this recognition came through God's blessing (Gen. 39:4, 21). Ruth found favor in the eyes of the wealthy Boaz because of her kindness to her mother-in-law, Naomi (Ruth 2:2, 10, 13). Although David was badly out of favor with Saul, even the Philistines realized how quickly David could have regained that favor through his military skill (1 Sam. 29:4). A king's favor brought many benefits to the recipient (Prov. 16:15).

Because of sin God requires sacrifices to make atonement and restore his favor. In the Old Testament animal sacrifices were presented at the sanctuary with the hope that God would accept them and forgive the sins of the offerer (Lev. 1:3–4). Such acceptance was not automatic, however, for the offerer had to have an attitude of repentance and humility (cf. Gen. 4:4–5; Mic. 6:7–8). When Christ died on Calvary, the perfect sacrifice was presented, making it possible for all who believe to enjoy God's favor (2 Cor. 6:2).

HERBERT M. WOLF

See also GRACE.

Bibliography. G. Schrenk, *TDNT,* 2:743–51; W. Zimmerli and H. Conzelmann, *TDNT,* 9:376–81, 392–401.

Fear. Of some ten Hebrew nouns and eight verbs that are regularly translated "fear," "to fear," "to be afraid," and the like, only one of each is commonly used in the Old Testament and they both spring from the root *yrʾ* (the noun being *yirʾâ* or *môrāʾ* and the verb *yārēʾ*). The New Testament employs *phobos* and *phobeō* almost exclusively as noun and verb, respectively, and these are the terms consistently used by the Septuagint to translate Hebrew *yirʾâ*/*môrāʾ* and *yārēʾ*.

The fundamental and original idea expressed by these terms covers a semantic range from mild easiness to stark terror, depending on the object of the fear and the circumstances surrounding the experience. There is no separate Hebrew of Greek lexeme describing fear of God so presumably such fear was from earliest times, the same kind of reaction as could be elicited from any encounter with a surprising, unusual, or threatening entity. In time, however, fear of God or of manifestations of the divine became a subcategory of fear in general and thus developed a theological signification pervasively attested throughout the Bible. While the normal meaning of fear as dread or terror is retained in the theological use of the terms, a special nuance of reverential awe or worshipful respect becomes the dominant notion.

Fear of God or of his manifestations appears in the Bible either in the abstract, in which just the idea of God alone generates this response, or in particular situations such as theophany or miracle, the occurrence or performance of which produces fear. Examples of the latter are Israel's fear of the Lord following the exodus deliverance (Exod. 14:31) and the fear of Zechariah, father of John the Baptist, when he saw the angel of the

Lord (Luke 1:12). More common by far are the reactions of fear by God's people as they contemplate who he is and what he has done.

Fear as a response to God and his deeds is so important an aspect of biblical faith and life that Fear actually occurs as an epithet of God himself. Jacob describes the Lord as the "Fear of Isaac" his father (Gen. 31:42; cf. v. 53), suggesting that Isaac had such reverential submission to the Lord that the Lord, to him, was the embodiment of fear. Usually, however, the fear of the Lord is an inducement to obedience and service: to fear God is to do his will. This equation appears most prominently in covenant contexts, especially in Deuteronomy, where the appeal is to serve the Lord as evidence of proper recognition of his sovereignty. The Lord as King demands and deserves the awesome respect of his people, a respect that issues in obedient service.

Fear of God also lies at the heart of successful living in the world. Wisdom literature makes it clear that the fear of the Lord is the beginning of wisdom, a fear equated with the "knowledge of the Holy One" (Prov. 9:10; cf. 1:7; Ps. 111:10). To fear God is to know him and to know him is to fear him. Such healthy fear enables one to praise God (Ps. 22:23; Rev. 14:7); to enjoy benefits and blessings at his hand (Pss. 34:9; 103:11, 13, 17); to rest in peace and security (Ps. 112:7–8); and to experience length of days (Prov. 10:27; 19:23). But fear of God also produces fear of wrath and judgment in those who do not know him or who refuse to serve him. There are, thus, two sides of the fear of the Lord—that which produces awe, reverence, and obedience, and that which causes one to cower in dread and terror in anticipation of his displeasure.

EUGENE H. MERRILL

See also AWE, AWESOME.

Feasts and Festivals of Israel. The major festivals of Old Testament Israel were, in calendar order, Passover, Unleavened Bread, Firstfruits, the Feast of Weeks (Pentecost), the Feast of Trumpets, the Day of Atonement, and the Feast of Booths (Tabernacles or Ingathering). After the exile, the Jews added memorial days for the fall of Jerusalem (eventually fixed as the Ninth of Ab), Purim, and the Feast of Dedication (Hanukkah). In addition, the Israelites observed the Sabbath every week and the feast of the New Moon every lunar month.

Israel's festivals were communal and commemorative as well as theological and typological. They were communal in that they drew the nation together for celebration and worship as they recalled the common origin and experience of the people. They were commemorative in that they kept alive the story of what God had done in the exodus and during the sojourn. They were theological in that the observance of the festivals presented the participants with lessons on the reality of sin, judgment, and forgiveness, on the need for thanksgiving to God, and on the importance of trusting God rather than hoarding possessions. They were typological in that they anticipated a greater fulfillment of the symbolism of the feasts. It is not surprising that each of the major feasts is in some way alluded to in the New Testament. On the other hand, the festivals could become meaningless rituals and were subject to the criticism of the prophets (Isa. 1:13–14).

The Five Major Feasts. *The Passover.* The Bible traces the origin of Passover to the exodus. According to Exodus 12, on the evening of the 14th of the first month (Abib; later called Nisan), the Israelites gathered in family units to sacrifice a yearling sheep or goat. They used hyssop to apply blood from the lambs to the sides and tops of the door frames of their homes and roasted the lambs. They also prepared bitter herbs and bread without yeast. They ate the food hastily and with their sandals on their feet as a sign of their readiness for a quick departure. That night, the Lord killed Egypt's firstborn but spared Israel.

The subsequent festival was called *pesaḥ*, generally rendered "Passover" in reference to God's passing over or sparing of the Israelites, although the precise origin of the word is unknown. In Exodus 12:21, Moses tells the Israelites to "sacrifice the *pesaḥ*" without defining the term. This is evidence that some kind of Passover festival was already known and practiced by the Israelites prior to the exodus. Even if this is so, the events of the exodus redefined forever the significance of the festival. According to Exodus 12:26–27, when subsequent generations inquired about the meaning of the Passover, they were to be told that it commemorated the Lord's sparing (*pāsaḥ*) of the Israelites on the night he struck down the Egyptians.

Throughout Israelite history Passover continued to be a festival of supreme importance. Chronicles records in detail two great celebrations of Passover, one in Hezekiah's reign (2 Chron. 30), and one in Josiah's reign (2 Chron. 35:1–19).

Of all of Israel's festivals, Passover is of the greatest importance to the New Testament because the Lord's Supper was a Passover meal (Matt. 26:17–27; Mark 14:12–25; Luke 22:7–22; notwithstanding problems posed by the Johannine chronology, as in John 18:28; see the major commentaries on John). In passing the bread to the disciples and telling them that it was his body and that they should eat of it, Jesus was perhaps presenting himself as the Passover lamb. Christ is thus described as "our Passover lamb" in 1 Corinthians 5:7 and as "the Lamb who was slain" in Revelation 5:12. John's Gospel points out that none of Jesus' bones were broken in his crucifixion in allusion to the requirement that none of the Passover lamb's bones be broken (John 19:33–37; cf. Exod. 12:46).

The Feast of Unleavened Bread. The Feast of Unleavened Bread lasted for one week and followed immediately after Passover. For that week, the Israelites not only ate no bread with yeast, but they also removed all yeast from their homes. They held a sacred assembly on the first and seventh days of the week, and for the whole week they did no work except for the preparation of food.

In the context of the exodus, eating bread without yeast signified the haste of their preparation to depart. Because yeast was studiously avoided during this festival, however, it soon became a symbol for the pervasive influence of evil. Yeast was not used in most grain offerings to God (see, for example, Lev. 2:11).

In the New Testament, yeast is often associated with evil (1 Cor. 5:6–8; Gal. 5:9). The latter text explicitly draws a link between the Christian's relationship with Christ and the details of the Passover and Festival of Unleavened Bread. As the Passover lamb protected Israel from the plague on the firstborn, even so Christ's sacrifice saves his people from the wrath of God. Also, just as Israel was to remove all yeast from their homes during the subsequent Feast of Unleavened Bread, Christians should avoid contamination by expelling immoral members from their congregations. Paul thus sees the church as something of a new community of a new exodus, and is concerned that Christians maintain the purity of their community. He uses the analogy of the Passover and Feast of Weeks to encourage the Corinthians to expel an immoral member (1 Cor. 5). Jesus describes the hypocritical teaching of the Pharisees as "yeast" and warns his disciples to beware of it (Matt. 16:6–12).

Some biblical references to yeast, however, make no allusion to the Feast of Unleavened Bread and do not use yeast as a symbol of evil. In particular, Christ's parabolic reference to the kingdom of heaven being like yeast that a woman put in a lump of dough does not mean the kingdom of heaven is evil, but merely that it grows unobserved.

Firstfruits. The offering of firstfruits took place at the beginning of the harvest and signified Israel's gratitude to and dependence on God (Lev. 23:9–14). The word "firstfruits" translates both *reʾšît qāṣîr* ("beginning of harvest") and *bikkûrîm*. The word *rēʾšît* could mean "first" either in the sense of the first to appear or in the sense of "best," but *bikkûrîm* clarifies the issue; it means "firstfruit to appear" on the analogy of *bĕkôr,* "firstborn."

The offering of firstfruits described in Leviticus 23:9–14 occurred in conjunction with the Feast of Unleavened Bread and focused on the barley harvest, but there was also an offering of firstfruits associated with the Feast of Weeks (Num. 28:26–31) in celebration of the wheat harvest. It would seem that Israelites brought the firstfruits of their harvests before the Lord at various times in the course of the agricultural year, but that there was a special firstfruits festival every year in conjunction with Passover, seven weeks before Pentecost (Lev. 23:15).

According to Leviticus 23:9–14, an Israelite would bring a sheaf of the first grain of the harvest to the priest, who would wave it before the Lord as an offering on the day after the Sabbath. At that time the individual offered a yearling lamb and a grain offering as a sacrifice. The Israelites were not to eat of the new harvest until the firstfruits offering had been made. Leviticus 23 does not specifically link the offering of firstfruits with the exodus event, but Deuteronomy 26:1–11 states that when the Israelites brought the firstfruits of their harvest before the priest, they were to acknowledge that God had delivered them from Egypt and had given them the land just as he had promised.

The offering of the firstfruits to God was a statement of gratitude and a confession that the benefits of the harvest came by his grace. Also, in giving the very first of their produce to God, Israel learned not to hoard but to trust God for provision.

The concept of the firstfruits becomes a theological metaphor both in the Old Testament and the New Testament. Jeremiah 2:3 states that Israel was "holy to the Lord, the firstfruits (*reʾšît*) of his harvest." The image implies that Israel is unique among the nations as the special possession of God.

The New Testament uses the term "firstfruit" (*aparchē*) with a variety of referents but always following the same pattern. The household of Stephanus is called the *aparchē* of Achaia, that is, the first converts (1 Cor. 16:15; see also Rom. 16:5). In a more eschatological sense, James 1:18 speaks of Christians as the firstfruits of God's work since they have been given birth by the word of truth. The new birth experienced by the believer is the first appearing of the new order of creation in Christ. In a similar manner, Paul says that believers have the "firstfruits of the Spirit" and await the full eschatological adoption that will occur in the resurrection (Rom. 8:23). Christ himself is the firstfruit of the power of the resurrection, and his victory over death is the guarantee that believers too will experience resurrection (1 Cor. 15:20–23).

In the New Testament, therefore, *aparchē* is used to signify that the power of the resurrection and the new creation has broken into the present creation. Whether it be the first Gentile converts in a geographic area, the new birth and gift of the Spirit experienced by Christians, or the resurrection of Jesus himself, all are like the firstfruits of the harvest in that they are tokens of the new age in Christ and give the promise of greater things to come.

The Feast of Weeks (Pentecost). The Feast of Weeks occurred seven full weeks after the wave offering of the Firstfruits at Passover (Lev. 23:15; Deut. 16:9). It celebrated the end of the grain harvest. Because of the fifty-day interval (in the inclusive method of reckoning), it is also known by the Greek name "Pentecost." Like Firstfruits, it took place on the day after the Sabbath. Exodus 23:14–19 refers to the Feast of Weeks when it links the "Feast of the Harvest" to the Feast of Unleavened Bread and to the Feast of Ingathering (Booths) as the three major agricultural festivals of Israel (see Deut. 16:16; 2 Chron. 8:13).

Deuteronomy 16:10 simply stipulates that individuals were to make an offering in proportion to the size of the harvest they had taken in that year, but Leviticus 23:17–20 and Numbers 28:27–30 give much more detailed lists of what the priests were to offer on behalf of the nation. Following the stipulations in Leviticus (the two lists differ slightly), this included burnt offerings of seven male lambs, one bull, and two rams, followed by a sin offering of one goat and a fellowship offering of two lambs. It was a day of sacred assembly in which no work was allowed. The primary focus of the festival was gratitude to God for the harvest.

For Christians, Pentecost is of the highest significance; it is the day on which the Spirit was poured out on the church. A question here, however, concerns the significance of the Feast of Weeks for the giving of the Spirit. Why was the Spirit given to the church on an agricultural thanksgiving holiday? The solution is to be found in Joel 2:28–32 (Heb. 3:1–5), the text that Peter proclaimed to have been fulfilled by the events witnessed by the Jerusalem crowd that dramatic Sunday (Acts 2:16–21).

The catalyst for the Book of Joel was a terrible locust plague that left Israel destitute. Every type of crop, including grapes, olives, wheat, barley, figs, pomegranates, and apples had been ravaged (Joel 1:7–12). The cattle were left without pasture (1:18), and the severity of the catastrophe was compounded by a drought (1:19–20). Even so, Joel held out the prospect of healing if the people would come together in a sacred assembly and repent (2:12–17), and promised an agricultural restoration (2:21–27).

Then, having promised an agricultural healing, Joel abruptly proclaims that the Spirit will be poured out on all people regardless of gender, age, or social status (2:28–32). Joel links the concept of agricultural and economic abundance to spiritual restoration. His choice of the verb "pour out" (*šāpak*) in reference to the Spirit (2:28 [Heb. 3:1]) alludes to the healing rains God would send upon the land (2:23). Amos, similarly, speaks of a famine for the word of God (8:11–12), and describes a restoration in terms of an abundant harvest (9:13–15). For these prophets, therefore, a theological link existed between the material blessing of God seen in a rich harvest and the spiritual benefits obtained when God gives his Word and Spirit.

While the "sacred assembly" to which Joel called the people (2:15–16) may have been simply an ad hoc ceremony of mourning, it is in some ways reminiscent (albeit ironically) of the day of Pentecost. Instead of a thanksgiving harvest festival, in that year the Israelites held a special day of mourning and repentance because of the devastation of the crops. Just as Leviticus 23:21 commanded that all Israel should gather together and there should be no regular business conducted on Pentecost, Joel demanded that all the people, even the bride and bridegroom, assemble before Yahweh for the sacred assembly. It is appropriate, therefore, that the giving of the Spirit in fulfillment of Joel 2:28–32 should have come about on the harvest celebration day of Pentecost.

The sequence from Passover to Pentecost is meaningful from the New Testament perspective. The slaughter of the Passover lamb recalled the great deliverance of the exodus and marked the beginning of the harvest with the gift of firstfruits, and the Feast of Weeks was the great celebration in thanksgiving for the grain harvest. Jesus' crucifixion at Passover, similarly, was the sacrifice for the deliverance of his people, and the subsequent pouring out of the Spirit on Pentecost was the fulfillment of what his sacrifice had promised (John 14:16–20; 16:7).

The Feast of Trumpets. The law prescribes that the first day of the seventh month (Tishri) should be a holiday with a sacred assembly and special sacrifice (Lev. 23:23–25; Num. 29:1–6). Numbers 29:1 states that it is "a day of trumpet blast" (*yôm tĕrûʿâ*), hence the traditional name "Feast of Trumpets" even though that designation does not occur in the Bible. In fact, there is some question whether *tĕrûʿâ* means "trumpet blast" in this context, since it can also mean a "war-cry" (Josh. 6:5) or a "shout of joy" (1 Sam. 4:5). Numbers 10:1–10, however, establishes that *tĕrûʿâ* can mean both "trumpet blast" and that trumpets were sounded at the new moon; the traditional interpretation of this day as a day on which trumpets were sounded is thus reasonable and should be followed.

Insomuch as every new moon was a holiday in the Israelite calendar, the question naturally arises as to why the new moon of the seventh month is given special status. Since Tishri 1 became the New Year's Day (*Rosh Hashanah*) in postbiblical Judaism, many believe that the Feast of Trumpets was the ancient Israelite New Year's Day as well. Scholars who maintain that Israel observed the beginning of the New Year in autumn (in Tishri) put forth several lines of evidence. For example, Exodus 23:16 states that the Feast of Booths (Tishri 15) occurred "at the end of the year." The Year of Jubilee (and presumably also Sabbath years) began in Tishri (Lev. 25:9). Also, the Gezer Calendar (ca. 925 B.C.) begins with the olive harvest in autumn.

These and similar arguments are not compelling, however, and the calendar of festivals especially seems not to have followed an autumnal New Year cycle. Exodus 23:16 provides no real evidence that the early Israelite calendar commenced in autumn. The Feast of Booths is at the end of the agricultural year—that is, at the end of the harvests—but that does not mean that it was the end of the calendar year. For the same reason one would naturally expect the Sabbath year to begin at the close of the previous year's harvest. In modern society, analogously, one can speak of an agricultural year, a fiscal year, or an academic year, each of which may differ from the official calendar year. The Gezer Calendar is a schoolboy's exercise and not an official calendar. Postbiblical Jewish practice, similarly, is not decisive.

The very fact that Tishri is the seventh month should call into question whether it marked the beginning of the year. It is also difficult to see how the Feast of Booths on Tishri 15 could be called "the end of the year" if Tishri 1 was New Year's Day. Israel's calendar of festivals begins not in Tishri but in Abib (Nisan), the first month, with Passover. Exodus 12:2, in fact, explicitly calls the month of the Passover "the first of the months of your year." From the agricultural standpoint, the seventh month was the end of the year, but the beginning of the new year did not come until the following spring.

Ancient Israel did not have a single, uniform calendar throughout its history, and problems in Israelite chronology are well-known. For the purposes of the calendar of festivals, however, the Feast of Trumpets was not a New Year's festival. The two critical texts (Lev. 23:23–25; Num. 29:1–6) never imply that it had anything to do with the new year.

The Feast of Trumpets did, however, initiate the end of the agricultural and festival year. The seventh month was important for this and for having in it two major holy days, the Day of Atonement and the Feast of Booths. The blasting of trumpets on the first day was therefore in celebration of the commencement of this special month.

This is the natural conclusion from the text of Leviticus. Leviticus 23:23–25 simply and briefly states that trumpets are to sound the first day of the seventh month and that it is a sacred holiday; verse 27 follows with the statement that the tenth day of the month is the Day of Atonement and verse 34 with the statement that the fifteenth day is the Feast of Booths. The overall impression is that the seventh month is especially sacred.

The use of trumpets to mark the beginning of this month is noteworthy. Trumpets are associated with the theophany on Sinai (Exod. 19:16, 19). Priests sounded trumpets prior to the destruction of Jericho (Josh. 6:16), and trumpets were regularly used as a military signal (2 Sam. 2:28). Prophets regularly referred to trumpets as warnings of judgment and destruction to come (Jer. 4:5; 6:1; Ezek. 33:3). Trumpet blasts also signalled the inauguration of a new era, such as the installation of a new king (1 Kings 1:34).

The trumpet blasts on the first day of the seventh month were meant to signal to Israel that they were entering a sacred season. The agricultural year was coming to a close; there was to be a reckoning with the sins of the people (the Day of Atonement); and Israel was to reenact the time of sojourning prior to gaining the promised land (the Feast of Booths).

The New Testament associates trumpets with the end of the age. Revelation describes the apocalyptic judgments as occurring in a series of trumpet blasts (chaps. 8–9). Jesus stated that the last judgment would be inaugurated with a trumpet blast (Matt. 24:31), and Paul says that trumpets will sound on the day of the resurrection (1 Cor. 15; 1 Thess. 4:16). The point that trumpets initiate the end of one age in judgment and the beginning of another in resurrection should not be missed. Even if not a New Year's Day, the Feast of Trumpets heralded the close of the festival year, a time of reckoning with God, and a reenactment of the days of longing for the promised land.

The Day of Atonement (Yom Kippur). The Day of Atonement was Israel's most solemn holy day since it was exclusively concerned with atoning for the sin of the people. It is described in detail in Leviticus 16, and the solemnity of the day is underscored by the notation that the Lord spoke to Moses "after the death of the two sons of Aaron who died when they approached the LORD" (Lev. 16:1). This was not a ceremony to be taken lightly. The Day of Atonement is more briefly described in Leviticus 23:26–32 and Numbers 29:7–11. The Hebrew name *yôm hakkipûrîm* is popularized as "Yom Kippur."

The ceremony took place on the tenth day of the seventh month (Tishri 10) and is rich with symbolism. Briefly, the details of the ceremony are as follows. The high priest would first bathe and then put on white undergarments and a white tunic; he would not wear the ceremonial insignia of the high priest. He offered a bull for the sin of himself and his house, and then took a censer with burning coals and incense into the Most Holy Place and sprinkled some blood from the bull on the ark of the covenant. He cast lots over two goats; one would be sacrificed and the other became the "scapegoat" (the goat for *ʿăzāʾzēl*). He sacrificed the one goat for the sin of the people and sprinkled some of its blood on the ark. He then came out of the tent and cleansed the altar with the blood of the bull and the goat. He then put his hands on the head of the scapegoat and confessed the sins of the people over it. An appointed man then took the scapegoat out into the wilderness and released it; he had to wash his clothes and bathe before he could return to the camp. The high priest would leave his white clothing in the tent of meeting, bathe again, and then put on his regular priestly apparel. The bull and goat that had been sacrificed were to be burned entirely.

Aspects of the symbolism of the ceremony are fairly transparent in meaning. By bathing before entering the tent of meeting, the high priest avoided bringing any form of contamination into it. By bathing at the end of the ceremony, he removed the holiness from himself before returning to the community. In wearing linen garments rather than his regular priestly insignia, he showed himself to be a penitent sinner who had stripped himself of all dignity and presumption of rank. The clearest statement of the high priest's personal sinfulness was his sacrifice of a bull for the sin of himself and his family.

The real heart of the ceremony, however, and the real point of controversy, is in sacrifice of one goat and the release of the scapegoat. Two issues are at stake here. First, what is the meaning of the goat "for *ʿăzāʾ zēl*"? Second, what does this ceremony say about the Israelite concept of atonement?

Several interpretations of the goat for *ʿăzāʾ zēl* have been proposed. A common interpretation is that *ʿăzāʾ zēl* is a goat-demon of the desert. Verse 8 says there was one lot for Yahweh and one lot for *ʿăzāʾ zēl,* and this might imply that *ʿăzāʾ zēl,* like Yahweh, is the proper name of a supernatural being. Those who hold to this interpretation generally argue that the Israelites sent the goat to *ʿăzāʾ zēl* to placate the demon. This analysis is astonishing, however, in light of the prohibition against giving sacrifices to satyrs (*śāʿîr*) in a text as close as Leviticus 17:7. Some interpreters, however, take the more conservative line that this was merely a way of sending sin back to Satan. This interpretation is strained, however, since nowhere else does the Old Testament (or the New Testament) speak of returning sin to Satan as if it were his possession.

Another interpretation is that *ʿăzāʾ zēl* is a cliff from which the goat would be thrown. Others, similarly, take *ʿăzāʾ zēl* to mean "destruction" and thus understand the goat for *ʿăzāʾ zēl* to be a goat that will be destroyed. Either interpretation is possible, but if the goat was simply to be killed in the wilderness one might have expected the text to use more conventional language.

A traditional interpretation, however, that is still worthy of acceptance is *ʿăzāʾ zēl* is the "scapegoat," that is, a goat to be sent away. This interpretation is found in the Vulgate (*capro emissario*) and the Septuagint (*apopompaiō*), and is based on taking *ʿăzāʾ zēl* as a combination of *ʿēz* ("goat") and *ʾāzal* ("depart"). As such, *ʿăzāʾ zēl* is a technical term for a goat taken out and released in ritual fashion. Verse 8 thus speaks of one goat for (i.e., as a sacrifice to) Yahweh and one goat for (i.e., to serve as) the scapegoat. This interpretation is in accord with normal Hebrew grammar and *ʿăzāʾ zēl* need not be taken as the proper name of a demon. The meaning of the ritual of releasing the scapegoat can only be determined in the context of Israel's understanding of atonement.

For some time, theologians, especially New Testament scholars, have debated whether the biblical concept of atonement includes a notion of propitiation (that is, whether sacrifice in some sense appeases the wrath of God). Those who reject the idea of propitiation assert that it is a pagan notion that makes God appear vicious. Those who believe that atonement includes propitiation maintain that the justice of God must be reckoned with for the character of God to be consistent. Most of the debate focuses on various New Testament passages such as Romans 3:25–26 and the precise meaning of Greek words such as *hilasmos* ("atonement" or "propitiation").

Apart from any New Testament considerations, however, it is certain that the Old Testament includes the idea of propitiation in its presentation of atonement. As mentioned already, the very beginning of Leviticus 16 alludes to the episode of Leviticus 10, in which Nadab and Abihu put "strange fire" to God in their censers and offered it before God, but were consumed by fire from God's presence. The stated lesson behind this episode is that God is "most holy" and that those who approach him must do so in fear of him and his wrath. To speak of propitiating the wrath of God is entirely consistent with this outlook.

Throughout the Old Testament, the holiness of God is an object of dread. When an ancient Israelite expressed terror at being in the presence of God (e.g., Judg. 6:22–23; Isa. 6:5), that attitude was no aberration. It arose from a universal conviction that no one could stand before the holiness of God. The only escape was for propitiation to be made.

In the modern world, we have little conception of what animal sacrifice involved. It was at best a bloody and difficult affair. It is all but inconceivable that ancient Israelites could watch the painful slaughter of animals as their sin offerings to Yahweh and not come away with a profound sense of the wrath of God that had to be propitiated.

In addition, the noun *kōpher* ("to atone") and related words frequently refer to a "ransom" or a gift meant to appease someone. Texts that illustrate this usage include Exodus 21:30, Numbers 35:31–33, and 2 Samuel 21:3–6 (using the verb *kipper*). In the latter text, David asks how he might appease the anger of the Gibeonites for the massacre they had suffered at the hands of Saul. The concept is that God (or a person) will avenge some wrong unless his anger is turned aside.

The foundational command for the entire ritual of the Day of Atonement, moreover, is that the high priest must not come into the Most Holy Place whenever he chooses or else he will die (Lev. 16:2). The ceremony allows the high priest to propitiate God in order that he may enter Yahweh's presence and not be destroyed.

If one acknowledges the reality of propitiation in Old Testament theology, one may see more clearly the two great aspects of atonement that are portrayed in the ritual of the Day of Atonement. The first is propitiation, as illustrated by the sacrifice of the one goat chosen by lot to be a sin offering. The slaughter of this goat and the sprinkling of its blood on the mercy seat of the ark ritually appeased the wrath of God. The second is expiation, the removal of sin so that it was forgotten and no longer clung to the people. This was ritually carried out by the scapegoat, who was released far out in the desert to carry sin away. It is significant that the scapegoat was not sacrificed. The scapegoat did not pay the penalty for sin or appease the wrath of God; it carried sin away and was a living parable of the promise that, "As far as east is from west, so far has he removed our transgressions from us" (Ps. 103:12). The two goats symbolized both propitiation and expiation and together illustrate what atonement means.

The Book of Hebrews draws on the ritual of the Day of Atonement to demonstrate the supremacy of Christ's priesthood. In Hebrews 9:7–10 the author points out that the high priest could enter the Most Holy Place only once a year and needed to make sacrifice for himself with the blood of animals, but that Christ entered once for all and offered his own blood as a sacrifice for his people. The ritual of the Day of Atonement was a shadow of things to come; now that Christ has come, it is obsolete. The Gospels, similarly, teach that the curtain between the Holy Place and the Most Holy Place split open at the moment of Christ's death in proof that the final and perfect atonement for sin had been made (Matt. 27:51; Mark 15:38; Luke 23:45).

Feast of Booths (Tabernacles or Ingathering). The Feast of Booths took place on Tishri 15, five days after the Day of Atonement, in what is now mid-October. The festival is described in Leviticus 23:33–43 and Deuteronomy 16:13–15, but the most elaborate presentation of the details of this week is found in Numbers 29:12–40. For seven days the Israelites presented offerings to the Lord, during which time they lived in huts made from palm fronds and leafy tree branches. The stated purpose for living in the booths was to recall the sojourn of the Israelites prior to their taking of the land of Canaan (Lev. 23:43). The offering of the first day was thirteen bulls, two rams, and fourteen male lambs as burnt offerings, with one goat as a sin offering. Each day thereafter the number of bulls offered was decreased by one. The eighth day was exceptional: one bull, one ram, seven lambs, and one goat were offered (Num. 29:12–38). These were all in addition to the grain offerings and freewill offerings (Num. 29:39). The week was to be a time of joy as a final celebration and thanksgiving for that year's harvest (Deut. 16:14–15).

The series of offerings for this week constituted an extraordinary expense (71 bulls, 15 rams, 105 lambs, and 8 goats). A burnt offering was entirely consumed by fire; even the priests could not eat it. That expense, coupled with the requirement that the Israelites abandon the comfort of their homes for a week and live in flimsy huts, implies that a principal lesson behind this week was that all the good things of the promised land are gifts from God. They cannot be hoarded or taken for granted. At the same time, returning to a period of living as aliens in huts helped to recall the sense of national community experienced in the period of the exodus.

Zechariah 14:16–19 looks for an eschatological celebration of the Feast of Booths. The time will come when all the Gentiles will join Israel in participating in this festival and worship the Lord; any nations that do not will suffer drought. Zechariah's point is that the Gentiles must identify with Israel in its deliverance and sojourn.

John 7 describes a visit of Jesus to Jerusalem during the Feast of Booths (vv. 2–10). On the last day of the feast Jesus promised that any who came to him would experience streams of living water flowing from within (i.e., the Holy Spirit; vv. 37–39). By New Testament times, the tradition had developed that during the feast a priest would draw water from the pool of Siloam and carry it in a sacred procession to the altar. This apparently was behind Jesus' metaphor. The New Testament also reflects the theology and symbolism of the Feast of Booths in its use of the term "tent" as a metaphor for the mortal body awaiting the glory of the resurrection (2 Cor. 5:1–4; 2 Peter 1:13–14).

The Postexilic Feasts. *The Ninth of Ab.* Ab is the fifth month of the Jewish calendar. Zechariah 7:3–5 alludes to ritual fasting and mourning carried out in the fifth and seventh months in commemoration of the destruction of the temple. Eventually, the Jews settled on the Ninth of Ab as a day to commemorate both the first destruction of the temple by Nebuchadnezzar and the subsequent destruction of Herod's temple by the Romans in A.D. 70.

Purim. Purim was established to celebrate the failure of Haman's plot against the Jews as described in the Book of Esther. The festival originally took place on the fourteenth and fifteenth of Adar, the twelfth month. The word "Purim" means "lots" and refers to the lots Haman cast in order to find an auspicious day for the destruction of the Jewish race (Esther 9:18–28).

Feast of Dedication (Hanukkah or Lights). Hanukkah was established to commemorate the recapture and cleansing of the temple by Judas Maccabeus from the Greek forces of Antiochus IV in about 164 B.C. The ceremony took place on the twenty-fifth of the ninth month (Chislev). First Maccabbees 4:52–59 describes the initiation of the festival; John 10:22–23 mentions the holiday as an occasion on which Jesus was in Jerusalem.

The Regular Holidays. *The Sabbath.* The Sabbath was observed every seventh day to commemorate both the creation (Exod. 20:11) and the exodus (Deut. 5:15). The day was not to be neglected or violated (Num. 15:32–36). It would eventually become the object of controversy between Jesus and the Jewish leaders (see Matt. 12:1–14; John 9:16). On the other hand, the Sabbath was the basis for major theological developments in the New Testament (John 5:16–30; Heb. 3:7–4:11).

The Feast of the New Moon. The first day of every lunar month was observed with the blowing of trumpets and a special sacrifice (Num. 10:10; 28:11–15). As a regular, periodic worship day, it is sometimes mentioned in parallel with the Sabbath (2 Kings 4:23; Amos 8:5).

DUANE A. GARRETT

Bibliography. D. I. Block, *ISBE,* 3:529–32; P. J. Budd, *Numbers;* J. I. Durham, *Exodus;* L. L. Morris, *The Gospel According to John;* G. J. Wenham, *The Book of Leviticus.*

Fellowship. To appreciate the full meaning of the word-group in the New Testament that conveys the nature and reality of Christian fellowship (i.e., the noun *koinōnia,* the verb, *koinōnein,* and the noun *koinōnos*) as used in the New Testament, it is necessary to be aware of two fundamental points.

First, the fact and experience of Christian fellowship only exists because God the Father through Jesus Christ, the Son, and by/in the Spirit has established in grace a relation (a "new covenant") with humankind. Those who believe the gospel of the resurrection are united in the Spirit through the Son to the Father. The relation leads to the reality of relatedness and thus to an experienced relationship (a "communion") between man and God. And those who are thus "in Christ" (as the apostle Paul often states) are in communion not only with Jesus Christ (and the Father) in the Spirit but also with one another. This relatedness, relationship, and communion is fellowship.

By his sacrificial death and glorious resurrection/exaltation, Jesus Christ brought into being a new creation, a new order, and a new epoch. Though this new situation will only be present in fullness at the end of this evil age, it is a reality now on this earth. Christ exercises his relation in this new creation in and through the controlling and liberating Holy Spirit, whom the Father sends in the name of Christ. Thus to be "in the Spirit" is also to be "in Christ." And this is another way of saying that Christians who are baptized into Christ and given the gift of the Spirit are dynamically related to the Father through the incarnate Son in and by the Spirit of the Father and the Son. On the basis of this relation there is fellowship for Christians both with God and with each other.

In the second place, it is probably best not to use the word "community" as a synonym for "fellowship." The reason for this is that in modern English "community" presupposes "individualism" and thus carries a meaning that is necessarily foreign to biblical presuppositions since individualism (i.e., the thinking of a human being as an "individual" and as the basic unity of society) is, technically speaking, a modern phenomenon. So "community" seemingly inevitably today usually refers to a group, body, or society that is formed by the coming together of "individuals" in a contractual way. The emphasis is on the initiative of the "individuals" and on the voluntary nature of the group thus formed. In contrast, *koinōnia* has its origin in a movement out of the internal, eternal relation, relatedness, and communion of the Godhead of the Father and the Son and the Holy Spirit. *Koinōnia* for baptized believers is thus a participation within human experience of the communion of the living God himself.

General Background. In the colloquial Greek of the New Testament period, *koinōnia* was used in several ways. It was used of a business partnership, where two or more persons share the same business and are thus closely connected in work. Also it was used of marriage, of the shared life of two persons, a man and a woman, together. Further, it was sometimes used of a perceived relatedness to a god, such as Zeus. Finally, it was used to refer to the spirit of generous sharing in contrast to the spirit of selfish acquiring.

Much of the use of the word group—*koinōnia, koinōnein,* and *koinōnos*—in the New Testament corresponds to general Greek usage. Thus the fellowship and sharing are religious or specifically Christian only if the context requires this meaning. For example, in Acts 2:42 we encounter the word *Koinōnia* and read that the new converts continued in "the apostles' teaching and *to the fellowship.*" Here it is a normal meaning adapted to Christian usage. Then the verb, *koinōnein,* is found in Hebrews 2:14 with an ordinary, general meaning: "children *share* flesh and blood." Likewise, *koinōnos* occurs with the meaning of "partner" in Luke 5:10—"[James and John] . . . Simon's *partners.*"

However, it is especially, but not solely, in the writings of the apostle Paul that the theological dimension of *koinōnia,* "fellowship/sharing/participation" is developed and clearly presented. Here the normal meanings of the words are transformed in service of the kingdom of God and as they identify a sharing in the communion of the blessed and Holy Trinity. That is, they point specifically to the supernatural life of God given to and shared with humankind through Jesus Christ in the Holy Spirit. The emphasis of the New Testament is also on participation in something that is an objective reality rather than on an association with someone.

Theological Use. Perhaps the clearest theological use of *koinōnia* is in 1 John 1:3–6, where we read that when we walk in the light truly our fellowship is with the Father and with his Son, Jesus Christ and that this relation of grace has profound implications for daily living. For if we say that we have fellowship with God and walk in darkness, we lie! Here the basic meaning of "fellowship" is a real and practical sharing in eternal life with the Father and the Son.

In Paul's letters we find that the apostle emphasizes the faithfulness of the call of God the Father in the gospel "into fellowship with his Son Jesus Christ our Lord" (1 Cor. 1:9). In other places Paul makes it clear that Christians were buried with Christ in baptism and raised up with him into newness of life (Rom. 6:4, 6, 11; Gal. 2:20; Eph. 2:4–6; Col. 2:20; 3:3). So the fellowship is based on the great saving acts of God the Father through his Son. The character of this fellowship is made clear in the celebration of the Lord's Supper, the Holy Communion, where there is intimate fellowship or communion with Jesus Christ, the exalted Lord, and with those who are "in Christ," for those who faithfully participate (1 Cor. 10:16–17). Here is not a mere act of historical memory and imagination but a real and vital union and communion with Jesus Christ, the exalted Head of the Body.

Fellowship with Jesus Christ also entails fellowship in his sufferings (Phil. 3:10; cf. 1 Peter 4:13). Paul is convinced that the churches are partakers in the sufferings of Christ (2 Cor. 1:5–7).

Paul also points to a fellowship in the Spirit (2 Cor. 13:14; Phil. 2:1), a dynamic experience that is inextricably related to receiving the love of the Father and the grace of the Lord Jesus Christ, the Son. In fact, to be "in the Spirit" is possible because of the fundamental truth of Christ's establishment of the new order, age, and epoch by his death and resurrection. "Therefore, if anyone is in Christ, he is a new creation; the old has gone, the new has come" (2 Cor. 5:17). It is important to note that Paul wrote in the indicative mood. It was not his purpose to urge Christians to become new creatures; also it was not his aim to tell them what they could or would become if they stayed Christian.

The present position of Christians is that "in Christ"—united to him in the Spirit—they are a part of the new order and creation. So Paul elsewhere writes of congregations being "in Christ" (Phil. 1:1; 1 Thess. 1:1), of members of such being "the faithful in Christ Jesus" (Eph. 1:1; Col. 1:2), and of the churches of God (in Judea) in Christ Jesus (1 Thess. 2:14). Further, he insists that as such Christians are sealed in the Spirit (Eph. 4:30), consecrated in the Spirit (Rom. 15:16), righteousness in the Spirit (Rom. 14:17), and have life through the Spirit (1 Cor. 6:11). Therefore, the richness of the experience of fellowship in the Holy Spirit is because of the reality of the new creation and of being "in Christ."

Christian fellowship is also a practical reality. So Paul was clear that the relatedness of Gentile and Jewish believers "in Christ" leads to mutual obligation. "For if the Gentiles have shared (verb, *koinōnein*) in the Jews' spiritual blessings, they owe it to the Jews to share with them their material blessings" (Rom. 15:27). In *koinōnia* the Jewish Christians have given the message of Jesus the Christ to the world, and in *koinōnia* the Gentile Christian are to give material assistance to the Jewish Christians. The leaders of the church in Jerusalem gave the right hand of fellowship to Paul and Barnabas, who had been given the mission to the Gentiles. In response Paul called for the collection to be made from the Gentile world for the poor in Jerusalem and Judea. Fellowship as practical sharing within the wider church is highlighted in Romans 15:25–31 and 2 Corinthians 8–9 (see also Heb. 13:16 and Phil. 1:5; 4:15). Such fellowship is a practical "fellowship of the mystery" (Eph. 3:9), a mystery now revealed—that Jews and Gentiles are one body in Christ Jesus through the gospel.

Practical sharing by Christians because of their relatedness in Christ is sometimes communicated by the verb *koinōnein,* which has already been noticed (see Rom. 12:13; 15:27; Gal. 6:6; 1 Tim. 5:22). Further, to suffer for the gospel is to share the suffering of Christ (1 Peter 4:13).

Apart from its general use as a companion and fellow worker (e.g., 2 Cor. 8:23) *koinōnos* is used in the plural of the recipients of the grace of deification in 2 Peter 1:4, where Christians are said to be partakers of the divine nature.

PETER TOON

Bibliography. J. Y. Campbell, *Three New Testament Studies;* G. Panikulam, *Koinonia in the New Testament.*

Fellowship Offering. *See* OFFERINGS AND SACRIFICES.

Female. *See* SEXUALITY, HUMAN.

Fire. One of the most arresting and suggestive metaphors in the Bible is that of fire, a phenomenon common to all cultures ancient and modern and one that lends itself to a variety of imagery. The most prevalent term for fire in the Hebrew Bible is *ʾēš*. The Greek word *phōs*, also normally rendered "light," occurs a couple times in the New Testament as "fire" (Mark 14:54; Luke 22:56). The usual word for fire in the New Testament is *pur*, the regular Greek translation of Hebrew *ʾēš* in the Septuagint.

As a commonplace in ancient Israel, fire obviously is to be taken literally in most of the several hundred references to it in the Bible. Its figurative or theological attestations are also numerous, however, generally relating to some manifestation of God's being or action.

Fire, as theophany of existence, communicates, first of all, the very presence of God. This is especially evident in the burning bush from which God spoke to Moses (Exod. 3:2–6). Here fire is a manifestation of God himself, for Moses turned away from the sight "because he was afraid to look at God" (v. 6). Similar to this is Yahweh's descent upon Mount Sinai "in fire" (Exod. 19:18; cf. Deut. 4:11–12, 15, 33, 36). In the New Testament Paul describes the second coming of Christ as "in blazing fire" (2 Thess. 1:7), an appearance that carries overtones of judgment as well as mere presence. Also akin to Old Testament imagery is John's vision of Jesus with eyes "like blazing fire" (Rev. 1:14; cf. 2:18; 19:12), again in judgment contexts.

It is not always possible to distinguish the presence of God from his glory for, indeed, glory is frequently a figure itself for divine presence. However, a number of passages focus on fire as synonymous with or in association with God's glory. For example, to the Israelites at Sinai "the glory of the Lord looked like a consuming fire" (Exod. 24:17; cf. Lev. 9:23, 24; Deut. 5:24). In visions of God in his glory in both Old and New Testaments, fire is a regular phenomenon.

A special use of fire imagery in the New Testament is that connected with baptism with fire. John the Baptist predicted that Jesus would baptize "with the Holy Spirit and with fire" (Matt. 3:11; cf. Luke 3:16), a promise that was fulfilled on the day of Pentecost. Then "tongues of fire" rested upon those gathered in the upper room with the result that they "were filled with the Holy Spirit" (Acts 2:3–4). The fire here is a manifestation of God, in the case of the Third Person of the Godhead, a theological conception unknown to the Old Testament.

Fire as theophany of action reveals God at work in a number of ways. One of the earliest and clearest of these ways is his appearance in a pillar of fire that led the people of Israel out of Egypt and through the Sinai deserts. Another instance of God's use of fire as an active manifestation of his presence is his sending fire from heaven to consume sacrifices offered up to him on special and unusual occasions. The first of these inaugurated Aaron's ministry as priest. Having blessed the people, Moses and Aaron witnessed the appearance of the glory of the Lord, a striking manifestation of which was fire that "came out from the presence of the Lord" to consume the sacrifices already placed on the altar (Lev. 9:23–24). Other examples of fire as the expression of God's acceptance of offerings are those of Gideon (Judg. 6:19–24) and of the father and mother of Samson (Judg. 13:15–20). In both cases Yahweh is present in the person of the angel who touches the altar, causing the sacrifices to erupt in flame.

Because of fire's heat and destructive capacity, it frequently appears in the Bible as a symbol of God's anger and of the judgment and destruction that sometimes are extensions of that anger. The psalmist employs fire as a simile for divine displeasure when he asks the Lord, "How long will your wrath burn like fire?" (Ps. 89:46) Isaiah, referring to God's coming in judgment, sees him "coming with fire" and bringing down his rebuke "with flames of fire" (66:15). Jeremiah says in reference to the destruction of Jerusalem that Yahweh "poured out his wrath like fire" (Lam. 2:4). Ezekiel uses the term "fiery anger" to speak of God's outpoured judgment, especially when speaking of the impending Babylonian conquest (21:31; 22:31). This is also the language by which he describes the overthrow of Gog in the end times. In his "zeal and fiery wrath" he will bring about massive calamity (38:19).

In other passages, the anger of God is not only metaphorically represented by fire, but fire becomes a literal vehicle of his wrath. At Taberah in the Sinai desert Yahweh's "anger was aroused" and "fire from the Lord burned among" the people (Num. 11:1). And the rebellion of Korah and his followers also resulted in many of them perishing by fire, a manifestation of God's hot anger (Num. 16:35; cf. 26:10; Lev. 10:2). A most impressive display of fire as an instrument of judgment is the destruction of the messengers of Ahaziah of Israel who attempted to seize Elijah the prophet only to be struck with fire "from heaven" (2 Kings 1:10, 12, 14). This is probably an example of lightning, which otherwise is clearly a means of inflicting divine judgment and destruction (cf. Exod. 9:23–24; Job 1:16; Ps. 18:13–14).

The same imagery of fire as a sign of God's anger and judgment continues in the New Testament. James and John asked Jesus whether or not they should invoke fire from heaven in order to destroy the Samaritans (Luke 9:54). Paul speaks of fire as a purifying agent capable of testing the quality of one's life and works (1 Cor. 3:13). Most commonly, fire is associated with the judgment of hell (Matt. 3:12; 5:22; 18:8–9; Mark 9:43, 48; Luke 3:17; 16:24; James 3:6; Jude 7; Rev. 20:14–15), or with the destruction of the old heavens and earth in preparation for the new (2 Peter 3:10, 12). Eugene H. Merrill

See also Hell; Judgment; Judgment, Day of; Lake of Fire; Theophany.

Bibliography. E. M. Good, *IDB,* 2:268–69; J. Patrick, *Dictionary of the Bible,* 2:9–10; J. C. Slayton, 5:372–73; H. Van Broekhoven, Jr., *ISBE,* 2:305–6.

Firstborn. Frequently employed in the Bible in the literal sense of offspring, "firstborn" acquired metaphorical applications over time. Two such New Testament uses, as a term for the church and as a title for Christ, are theologically significant.

The firstborn son in patriarchal society was regarded as special (Gen. 49:3; Exod. 13:2). He became the head of the family upon his father's death, having received his father's blessing (Gen. 27) and a double portion of the inheritance (Deut. 21:17).

After the Passover event in Egypt, every firstborn male belonged to God. This implied priestly duties, an obligation later transferred to the Levites (Num. 8:14–19).

Of special significance is the divine claim that Israel was God's firstborn (Exod. 4:22–23). This signified Israel's favored status among the nations to be in covenant relationship with God. But it also meant Israel had a priestly function to perform as God's saving light to Gentile peoples.

In the Book of Hebrews the author appears to call Christians "firstborn ones" (*prōtotokōn*) in virtue of their relationship to Christ, whom he has already called the "firstborn" (*prōtotokon*) in 1:6. Through him they have been "enrolled in heaven."

The context of Hebrews 12:18–29 gives substance to this expression as a term for Christians. The spiritual nature of the church is underscored. "Mount Zion" is a "heavenly Jerusalem," a "city of the living God" (v. 22) contrasted both to Mount Sinai where the Law was given (vv. 18–21) and to the earthly Jerusalem and its temple worship.

Christian life and worship occur in a spiritual community that includes God, angels, and human beings (vv. 22–24). The hosts of angels are in festal array, reminiscent of their task of worshiping the Son brought into the world for human redemption (1:6), rather than as the mediators of the Law during the awesome display at Mount Sinai. The church is composed not only of present earthly believers but also of the "spirits of just persons who have been made perfect." This latter expression likely refers to the Old Testament faithful who could not reach completion until the Christian dispensation (11:40); these now comprise the cloud of witnesses who applaud the race of the earthly Christians (12:1). The "church of the firstborn" does not displace faithful Israel, but joins with them in perfect worship to God through the mediation of Christ.

The "church of the firstborn" lives in humility, gratitude, and awe (vv. 26–29), for in Christ they have received a kingdom that will endure the judgment of the eschaton. Christ has given them both the gift of his salvation and the obligation to be his priestly community among unbelieving peoples (Heb. 13).

Christ is called God's "firstborn" in Hebrews 1:6. This is a metaphorical use of the term and does not imply that Christ merely was created prior to other beings or the world in general. Rather it connotes his special status as the unique Son of God. Luke L. Keefer, Jr.

See also Jesus Christ, Name and Titles of.

Bibliography. F. F. Bruce, *The Epistle to the Hebrews.*

Firstfruits (Heb. *rēʾšît;* Gk. *aparchē*). The concept of firstfruits derives from God's creation work. Because God created everything that exists, all of creation belongs to him (Ps. 24:1). Consequently, that which is first and best belongs to him and is to be given to him.

Because of God's creative power and ownership of all, the Bible instructs believers to give God the best of the animal sacrifices (see Lev. 1–5). The land is also viewed as a gift from God and the best of it, its "firstfruits," is to be given to him—crops (Exod. 23:16, 19), the wheat harvest (Exod. 34:22; Lev. 2:14; 23:20), olive oil (Num. 18:12; Deut. 18:4), the finest new wine (Num. 18:12; Deut. 18:4), honey (2 Chron. 31:5), sheep wool (Deut. 18:4), and fruit (Neh. 10:35). The Old Testament makes it clear that everything that God's people have is to be viewed as from God and gained through his providence (Ps. 50:10).

Believers are the "firstfruits" of God—"a kind of firstfruits of all he created" (James 1:18). Spiritual "firstfruits" may be the first converts in an area (Rom. 16:5). As "firstfruits" believers are a testimony to God's power in salvation. They are his first born, redeemed by Christ's blood. In their holy standing, believers are God's firstfruits—"holy to the Lord, the firstfruits of his harvest" (Jer. 2:3). God's people are therefore to present themselves as holy firstfruits to God, as "living sacrifices, holy and pleasing to God" (Rom. 12:1). In having the "firstfruits of the Spirit," the work of the Spirit in effecting the present redemption of their souls, believers are given the guarantee that they will have the future redemption of their bodies at the second coming of Christ (Rom. 8:23).

In 1 Corinthians 15:20, 23, Paul teaches that Christ in his bodily resurrection is the "firstfruits of those who have fallen asleep." As such, he is the guarantee that all those who belong to him will be raised from the dead at his second coming. In the natural world, the first sheaf of the crop was to be brought to God (Lev. 23:10, 11, 17) as a guarantee that the rest of the harvest was coming. So it is in God's redemption harvest.

First, Christ the "firstfruits" has triumphed in his resurrection; then, the rest of his "crop," the redeemed, will be raised triumphantly at his second coming (1 Cor. 15:23).

In light of this, God's people, as his "firstfruits," are to have a sanctifying effect on others (1 Cor. 5:6–7), just as Abraham and the patriarchs had a sanctifying effect on disobedient Israel (Rom. 11:14–16). Believers are to be true followers of the Lamb, just as the saints in the second coming, who are described as holy in life, "purchased from among men and offered as firstfruits to God and to the Lamb" (Rev. 14:4).

W. Harold Mare

Bibliography. P. Levertoff, *ISBE,* 2:307–8; J. P. Lewis, *ZPED,* 2:541.

Firstfruits, Feast of. *See* Feasts and Festivals of Israel.

Flesh. The range of meanings borne by this term in the Bible starts from the literal use denoting the material of which the human body is chiefly constructed, but quickly takes on other senses derived from the writers' understanding of the created order and its relation to God. Careful attention to context is needed to catch the precise nuance in any given case.

The Old Testament. *Fundamental Data.* The Old Testament employs two terms to denote flesh: *bāśār,* which occurs 266 times; and *šĕʾēr* which occurs 17 times. The two terms are identical in meaning. Their basic reference is to the material substance of which earthly creatures are made. This is true of humans (Gen. 2:21; Lev. 13:10–11; Ezek. 37:6; Dan. 1:15; Mic. 3:3) and animals alike (Exod. 21:28), including animal flesh used for food (Gen. 9:2–4) and in sacrifice (1 Sam. 2:13; Isa. 65:4; Hos. 8:13).

Extended Senses. What one individual is all kindred individuals will be. Flesh thus comes to denote blood-relationship (Gen. 2:23–24; Lev. 18:6), and beyond that, kinship to all humans, "all flesh" (Ps. 65:2; Isa. 40:5; 49:26). Yet another extension of significance is the use of flesh in reference to the human body as a whole (Lev. 13:13; 16:4; 2 Kings 6:30). While in such uses it can denote a corpse (1 Sam. 17:44; 2 Kings 9:36), it more commonly denotes the whole life of the individual viewed from an external perspective so that safety of the flesh is life (Pss. 16:9; Prov. 4:20–22) and its endangerment a threat to life (Job 13:14; Prov. 5:11).

Transferred Senses. It is an easy step from flesh as denoting life viewed externally to life viewed more comprehensively. "Flesh" is thus used interchangeably with "soul" and "body," and credited with the emotions and responses of the whole person (Pss. 63:1; 84:2). In some instances it carries the sense of self (Lev. 13:8). In short, the human creature is flesh in essence. Implicit in this is the idea that humans do not *have* flesh, but *are* flesh. If at times the outer being ("flesh") is distinguished from the inner ("heart" or "soul"), this is not because one is seen as more important than the other, but because both are indispensable for the existence of a whole person. In the Hebrew understanding of a human being there is nothing that is merely physical. As constituted essentially of flesh the human creature stands over against God. By virtue of being God's creation flesh is good, like all other parts of God's creation (Job 10:8–12; Ps. 119:73; Isa. 45:12). At the same time, flesh as dependent on God, and in particular God's spirit (Gen. 2:7; 6:3; Isa. 31:3), is frail and transitory (Ps. 78:39; Isa. 40:6). While at no time is flesh said to be sinful, it is implied that, by virtue of its frailty, flesh is exposed to the onslaught of sin (Gen. 6:3, 5, 13). It is safe to say that all of the New Testament uses of flesh are made from these Old Testament building blocks.

The New Testament. *Terms.* The Greek word used most commonly in the New Testament to render the Hebrew word for flesh (*bāśār*) is *sarx,* which occurs 147 times. Of this total, 91 are found in the Pauline writings, mostly in Romans and Galatians. While the New Testament appropriates the Old Testament foundation, it also builds on it, some writers giving the term their own distinctive twist. From this perspective it is possible to group the New Testament writings into three categories.

Writings Employing Chiefly the Old Testament Usages. In the Synoptic Gospels "flesh" is used only four times (aside from Old Testament quotations in Mark 10:8 and Luke 3:6). In Matthew 16:17 "flesh and blood" stands for human beings in their wholeness, but especially in their mental and religious aspect. At the same time they stand over against God, the true revealer. Mark 13:20 is a typical use of the Old Testament expression "all flesh." Mark 14:38 has a dualistic ring, but need not do more than contrast the human and the divine as in Isaiah 31:3. In Luke 24:39 the "flesh and bones" of the risen Jesus contrast with the immateriality of ghosts, implying a positive estimate of materiality that again harmonizes with the Old Testament. In Acts there are 3 instances of "flesh" (2:17, 26, 31). The first two are Old Testament quotations. In 2:31 "flesh" clearly refers to Jesus in his wholeness, but with the important idea added that in his wholeness he survived death. The Epistle to the Hebrews likewise reflects Old Testament usage. Of its six examples, three are literal in meaning (2:14; 5:7; 12:9). The first two, however, use the term to make the significant point that it was "flesh"—true human nature—that Christ assumed in his incarnation. In 9:10, 13 the rituals of the old order affect only external purification, leaving the conscience untouched. Jesus, through the spilling of his blood, opened the way into God's presence through the veil, which is interpreted as his flesh (10:20). Just as it was only when the curtain was torn open that access to the Most Holy Place was possible, so it was only by the tearing of Jesus' flesh in death that access to God's presence was made permanently available. Here, then, flesh stands for Jesus' life in its wholeness: incarnate and surrendered in death. The remaining concentration of instances of flesh in this grouping is found in the First Epistle of Peter, where there are examples (aside from the Old Testament quotation in 1:24). First Peter 3:21 echoes the same contrast found in Hebrews 9 between the cleansing of the flesh and the conscience. The remaining examples (3:18; 4:1, 2, 6) contrast death in the flesh with life in the Spirit in reference both to Christ and the believer. They are best taken to refer to the death and resurrection of Christ, which is reproduced in the life of the believer, bringing death to sin and resurrection to new life. The contrast throughout, then, is between "flesh" understood as earthly existence and "spirit" as life in the Spirit. The adjectival form *sarkikos*, "fleshly," occurs at 2:11 and is probably best understood within the same frame of reference as the examples of the noun.

The Johannine Writings. In the Gospel of John the term occurs thirteen times, seven in 6:51–63. The strictly literal sense is not found, but the extended sense, "all flesh," occurs at 17:2. In other examples the idea present is that of limitation, in which the flesh or the sphere of the flesh is contrasted with the divine sphere (1:13; 3:6). The flesh is not evil; it simply is not the sphere of salvation, which rather is that of the Spirit. Both of these uses are in line with Old Testament thought. Cognate with these uses, though advancing beyond them, are passages in which flesh denotes mere appearance rather than inner reality. To measure Jesus thus, rather than by the insight of faith, is to be blind to his identity (6:63; 8:15). The obverse of this is that flesh may indeed be the medium of the revelation of God himself. It is against the background of the affirmation of the incarnation that the six examples in 6:51–58 are to be read. The Incarnate One is he who has come from above from whence alone life can come. Therefore to feed on his flesh and blood is to share in his life (6:57–58). In the Epistles of John the accent falls on confession of Christ's coming in the flesh as decisive for salvation (1 John 4:2; 2 John 7). "The desire of the flesh" (1 John 2:16) is condemned not because it refers to the material realm, but because it refers to what is earthly and therefore transitory (v. 17).

The Pauline Writings. The uniqueness of these in this regard is sufficiently indicated in that approximately two-thirds of the New Testament occurrences of flesh are found in them, almost half of these in Romans and Galatians. They may be considered in two broad categories.

Uses Akin to the Old Testament. Most of the uses found in the Old Testament are also present in the Pauline literature. There flesh can denote the physical flesh (1 Cor. 15:39; 2 Cor. 12:7) and, by extension, the human body (Gal. 4:13–14), humanity as a whole (Rom. 3:20; Gal. 2:16), human descent (Rom. 1:3; 9:3), and human relationships (Rom. 4:1; 9:3–5). By this point the term acquires the transferred sense of that which is frail and provisional (1 Cor. 1:26; Gal. 1:16; Phil. 3:3). As transient, it is not the sphere of salvation, which is rather the sphere of the Spirit. This does not imply that flesh is evil per se: life "in the flesh" is normal human existence (Gal. 2:20), but it is still merely human. This picture accords generally with that of the Old Testament.

Distinctive Pauline Uses. The uniquely Pauline understanding begins from the idea that flesh, as weak, becomes the gateway to sin (Rom. 8:3; 2 Cor. 12:7; Gal. 4:14). Still more, as the arena in which sin entrenches itself it becomes the instrument of sin (Rom. 6:12–14) to the extent that it becomes sinful itself (Rom. 8:3), and so an occupying alien power (Rom. 7:17–20). The accompanying war Paul describes as a struggle between flesh and Spirit (Rom. 8:5–17; Gal. 5:16–24). The seriousness of the struggle is indicated by the fact that the mind-set of the flesh leads to death (Rom. 8:6), and that those living in the flesh cannot please God (Rom. 8:8). Accounts of this conflict are most vivid in contexts where Paul is describing the demands of the law on the one hand (Rom. 7:4, 7–11; Gal. 5:2–5), and its impotence to enable the believer to meet them on the other (Rom. 8:3; Gal. 3:10–12). Flesh, however, is not intrinsically sinful, and may therefore be the scene of sin's defeat. This it became through Christ's coming and crucifixion in the flesh (Rom. 8:3). Those who identify themselves with him by faith likewise crucify the flesh (Gal. 2:20; 5:24) so being emancipated from the power of sin in the flesh (Rom. 6:14; 8:9). This reading appears to be confirmed by the Pauline use of the largely parallel term "body." The "body of sin" was done away with at the cross (Rom. 6:6). The "body of our humiliation" (Phil. 3:21), which is weak and still subject to the attack of sin, is the body of the interim. The "body of glory" (Phil. 3:21), transformed and imperishable (1 Cor. 15:42–44, 50–53), is the body of the age to come.

A. R. G. Deasley

See also Body; Sin.

Bibliography. J. Christiaan Beker, *Paul the Apostle: The Triumph of God in Life and Thought;* R. Bultmann, *Theology of the New Testament;* R. Jewett, *Paul's Anthropological Terms;* A. Sand, *EDNT*, 3:230–33; H. Seebass and A. C. Thiselton, *NIDNTT*, 1:671–82; C. Ryder Smith: *The Bible Doctrine of Man.*

Flock. Two Hebrew words, *ʿēder* and *ṣōʾn*, are regularly translated "flock" in the Old Testament and both are rendered by Greek *poimnē* (or its diminutive *poimnion*) in the Septuagint and New Testament. The word *ʿēder* connotes a more collective sense than *ṣō'n*, which can also be translated "sheep." Both occur figuratively (as do the Greek terms), almost always with Israel (or Judah) and the church in view as the "flock" or people of God.

The designation "flock" is used a number of times simply as an epithet of the people, one that inherently communicates their helplessness, naiveté, simplicity, and dependence (Pss. 74:1; 77:20; 78:52; 79:13; 80:1; 100:3; Isa. 40:11; Zech. 9:16; 10:3; 11:7, 17; John 10:16). More particularly, it speaks of Israel as subjects of earthly kings (Jer. 13:20; 25:34–36; Ezek. 34:2–3) or of the elders of the church (Acts 20:28; 1 Peter 5:3), who are held accountable for their leadership. Failing that leadership, or perhaps in rebellion to it, Israel is seen as a people without a shepherd (Num. 27:17; 1 Kings 22:17), helpless ones (2 Sam. 24:17) who wander and go astray (Isa. 53:6; Zech. 10:2). Isaiah makes it clear that such behavior is sinful, willful departure from the shepherd.

Although the flock is sometimes scattered in judgment (Ezek. 34:12) it is never without the hope of regathering (Jer. 23:1–3). The reason for this hope is that Israel is under the care of Yahweh, the Good Shepherd (Ps. 95:7; Ezek. 34:31; cf. John 10:11–18), who has made his people the objects of his saving grace and heirs of all the covenant promises (Mic. 7:14).

EUGENE H. MERRILL

Bibliography. P. L. Garber, *ISBE*, 4:463–65; B. D. Napier, *ISBE*, 4:315–16; G. E. Post, *Dictionary of the Bible*, 4:486–87.

Flood, the. *Terminology.* The Genesis flood is denoted in the Old Testament by the technical Hebrew term *mabbûl* (etymology uncertain; perhaps from the root *ybl*, "to flow, to stream"). All thirteen Old Testament instances of this word refer to the Genesis flood; all of them are found in the Book of Genesis except Psalm 29:10. Occurrences in the flood narrative are usually associated with *mayim*, "waters." The Septuagint and the New Testament consistently employ the Greek term *kataklysmos* ("flood, deluge") for this event (four times in the New Testament, plus once using the related verb *kataklyzō* ["flood, inundate"], 2 Peter 3:6).

Extrabiblical Parallels. Ancient flood stories are almost universal (up to 230 different stories are known). Floods are by far the most frequently given cause for past world calamities in the folk literature of antiquity. The stories nearest to the area of the dispersion at Babel are the closest in detail to the biblical account.

Four main flood stories are found in Mesopotamian sources: the Sumerian Eridu Genesis (ca. 1600 B.C.), the Old Babylonian Atrahasis Epic (ca. 1600 B.C.), the Gilgamesh Epic (Neo-Assyrian version, ca. eighth to the seventh centuries B.C.), and Berossus' account (Babylon, third century B.C.).

The Unity of the Genesis Flood Account. The detailed chiastic literary structure of Genesis 6–9 argues for the unity of the flood narrative instead of small textual units (J and P) as suggested by the Documentary Hypothesis. A close reading of the flood narrative as a coherent literary whole, with particular attention to the chiastic structure, resolves apparent discrepancies in the Genesis account.

Theology of the Flood. *Theology as History: The Historical Nature of the Flood.* In the literary structure of the flood narrative the genealogical frame or envelope construction (Gen. 5:32 and 9:28–29) plus the secondary genealogies (Gen. 6:9–10 and 9:18–19) are indicators that the account is intended to be factual history. The use of the genealogical term *tôledôt* ("generations," "account") in the flood account (6:9) as throughout Genesis (13 times, structuring the whole book), indicates that the author intended this narrative to be as historically veracious as the rest of Genesis. A number of references in the Book of Job may allude to the then-relatively-recent flood (9:5–8; 12:14–15; 14:11–12; 22:15–17; 26:10–14; 27:20–22; 28:9; 38:8–11). The occurrence of the flood is an integral part of the saving/judging acts of God in redemptive history, and its historicity is assumed and essential to the theological arguments of later biblical writers employing flood typology.

The Motive or Theological Cause of the Flood. In contrast with the ancient Near Eastern flood stories, in which no cause of the flood is given (Gilgamesh Epic) or in which the gods decide to wipe out their human slaves because they are making too much noise (Atrahasis Epic and Eridu Genesis), the biblical account provides a profound theological motivation for the flood: humankind's moral depravity and sinfulness, the all-pervading corruption and violence of all living beings ("all flesh") on earth (Gen. 6:1–8, 11–12), which demands divine punishment.

The God of the Flood (Theodicy). The theological motivation provides a divine justification (theodicy) for the flood. In contrast to the other ancient Near Eastern stories, in which the gods are arbitrary, acting out of unreasoning anger, selfishness, and caprice, seeking to deceive the people and not inform them of the impending flood, the biblical picture of the God of the flood is far different. God extends a probationary period during which his Spirit is striving with humanity to repent (Gen. 6:3). God warned the antediluvian world through Noah, the "preacher of righteousness" (2 Peter 2:5; cf. 1 Peter 3:19–20).

God himself makes provision for the saving of humankind (Gen. 6:14–16). He "repents"—he is sorry, moved to pity, having compassion, suffering grief (Gen. 6:6). God takes up humanity's pain and anguish (Gen. 6:6; cf. 3:16–17). The divine act of destruction is not arbitrary. God "destroys" what humanity had already ruined or corrupted; he mercifully brings to completion the ruin already wrought by humankind.

The God of the biblical flood is not only just and merciful; he is also free to act according to his divine will, and he possesses sovereign power and full control over the forces of nature (in contrast to the weakness and fright of the gods during the flood, according to ancient Near Eastern stories). Yahweh's omnipotent sovereignty seems to be the theological thrust of Psalm 29:10, the only biblical reference outside Genesis employing the term *mabbûl:* "Yahweh sat enthroned at the flood."

The choice of divine names throughout the flood narrative, instead of indicating separate sources, seems to highlight different aspects of God's character: the generic *Elohim* when his universal, transcendent sovereignty or judicial authority is emphasized; and the covenant name *Yahweh* when his personal, ethical dealings with Noah and humankind are in view.

Human Moral Responsibility. The portrayal of humanity's moral depravity as the cause of the flood highlights human responsibility for sin. Noah's response of faith/faithfulness (Heb. 11:7) underscores that accountability to God is not only corporate but individual: Noah found "favor" in God's sight, he was "righteous," "blameless," and "walked together" in personal relationship with God (Gen. 6:8–9); he responded in implicit obedience to God's commands (Gen. 6:22; 7:5, 9; cf. Ezek. 14:14, 20).

Eschatological Judgment. When God announced the coming of the flood to Noah he said, "I have determined to make an end of all flesh" (Gen. 6:13). The "eschatological" term *qēṣ* (end), later became a technical term for the eschaton. The divine judgment involved a period of probation (Gen. 6:3), followed by a judicial investigation ("The LORD saw . . ." Gen. 6:5; "I have determined," Gen. 6:13 RSV), the sentence (Gen. 6:7), and its execution (the bringing of the flood, Gen. 7:11–24). The New Testament recognizes the divine judgment of the Genesis flood as a typological foreshadowing of the final eschatological judgment.

The Noahic Covenant. The word *bĕrît,* "covenant," first appears in Scripture in connection with the flood (Gen. 6:18; 9:8–17), and the covenant motif is an integral part of the flood narrative. The Noahic covenant comes at God's initiative, and demonstrates his concern, faithfulness, and dependability. He covenants never again to send a flood to destroy the earth. This covenant promise flows from the propitiatory animal sacrifice offered by Noah (Gen. 8:20–22).

Unlike the other biblical covenants, the Noahic covenant is made not only with humankind but with the whole earth (Gen. 9:13) including every living creature (Gen. 9:10, 12, 15, 16), and is thus completely unilateral and unconditional upon the response of the earth and its inhabitants. The sign of this everlasting covenant is the rainbow, which is not primarily for humankind, but for God to see and "remember" the covenant he has made with the earth (Gen. 9:16).

The Flood Remnant. The flood narrative contains the first mention in the biblical canon of the motif and terminology of remnant: "Only Noah and those who were with him in the ark remained [*šāʾar*]" (Gen. 7:23). The remnant who survived the cosmic catastrophe of the flood were constituted thus because of their right relationship of faith and obedience to God, not because of caprice or the favoritism of the gods, as in the extrabiblical ancient Near Eastern flood stories.

Salvific Grace. God's grace is revealed already before the flood in his directions for the building of the ark to save those faithful to him (Gen. 6:14–21); and again after the flood in his covenant/promise never again to destroy the earth with a flood, even though human nature remained evil (Gen. 8:20–22; 9:8–17).

But the theological (and literary, chiastic) heart of the flood account is found in the phrase "God remembered Noah" (Gen. 8:1). The memory theology of Scripture does not imply that God has literally forgotten; for God to "remember" is to act in deliverance (see Exod. 6:5). The structural positioning of God's "remembering" at the center of the narrative indicates that the apex of flood theology is not punitive judgment but divine salvific grace.

Numerous thematic and verbal parallels between the accounts of Noah's salvation and Israel's exodus deliverance reveal the author's intent to emphasize their similarity. Various references in the psalms to God's gracious deliverance of the righteous from the "great waters" of tribulation, may contain allusions to the Genesis flood (Pss. 18:16; 32:6; 65:5–8; 69:2; 89:9; 93:3; 124:4).

Flood Typology. The typological nature of the flood account is already implicit in Genesis. Isaiah provides an explicit verbal indicator that the flood is a type of covenantal eschatology (54:9), along with several possible allusions to the flood in his descriptions of the eschatological salvation of Israel (24:18; 28:2; 43:2; 54:8). The prophets Nahum (1:8) and Daniel (9:26) depict the eschatological judgment in language probably alluding to the Genesis flood.

The New Testament writers recognize the typological connection between flood and eschatology. The salvation of Noah and his family in the ark through the waters of the flood finds its antitypical counterpart in New Testament eschatological salvation connected with water baptism (1 Peter 3:18–22). The flood is also a type of the final eschatological judgment at the end of the world, and the conditions of pre-flood morality provide signs of the endtimes (Matt. 24:37–39; Luke 17:26–27; 2 Peter 2:5, 9; 3:5–7).

Universality of the Flood. One of the most controversial aspects of flood theology concerns the extent of the flood. Three major positions are taken: (1) the traditional, which asserts the universal, worldwide, nature of the deluge; (2) limited flood theories, which narrow the scope of the flood story to a particular geographical location in Mesopotamia; and (3) nonliteral (symbolic) interpretation, which suggests that the flood story is a nonhistorical account written to teach theological truth. Against the third interpretation, we have already discussed the historical nature of the flood. Of the two first positions, the limited flood theories rest primarily on scientific arguments that set forth seemingly difficult physical problems for a universal flood. These problems are not insurmountable given the supernatural nature of the flood; numerous recent scientific studies also provide a growing body of evidence for diluvial catastrophism instead of uniformitarianism. Only the traditional universalist understanding does full justice to all the biblical data, and this interpretation is crucial for flood theology in Genesis and for the theological implications drawn by later biblical writers.

Many lines of biblical evidence converge in affirming the universal extent of the flood and also reveal the theological significance of this conclusion: (1) the trajectory of major themes in Genesis 1–11—creation, fall, plan of redemption, spread of sin—is universal in scope and calls for a matching universal judgment; (2) the genealogical lines from both Adam (Gen. 4:17–26; 5:1–31) and Noah (Gen. 10:1–32; 11:1–9) are exclusive in nature, indicating that as Adam was father of all preflood humanity, so Noah was father of all postflood humanity; (3) the same inclusive divine blessing to be fruitful and multiply is given to both Adam and Noah (Gen. 1:28; 9:1); (4) the covenant (Gen. 9:9–10) and its rainbow sign (Gen. 9:12–17) are clearly linked with the extent of the flood (Gen. 9:16, 18); if there was only a local flood, then the covenant would be only a limited covenant; (5) the viability of God's promise (Gen. 9:15; cf. Isa. 54:9) is wrapped up in the universality of the flood; if only a local flood occurred, then God has broken his promise every time another local flood has happened; (6) the universality of the flood is underscored by the enormous size of the ark (Gen. 6:14–15) and the stated necessity for saving all the species of animals and plants in the ark (Gen. 6:16–21; 7:2–3); a massive ark filled with representatives of all nonaquatic animal/plant species would be unnecessary if this were only a local flood; (7) the covering of "all the high mountains" by at least twenty feet of water (Gen. 7:19–20) could not involve simply a local flood, since water seeks its own level across the surface of the globe; (8) the duration of the flood (Noah in the ark over a year, Gen. 7:11–8:14) makes sense only with a universal flood; (9) the New Testament passages concerning the flood all employ universal language ("took them *all* away" [Matt. 24:39]; "destroyed them *all*" [Luke 17:27]; Noah "condemned the *world*" [Heb. 11:7]); and (10) the New Testament flood typology assumes and depends upon the universality of the flood to theologically argue for an imminent worldwide judgment by fire (2 Peter 3:6–7).

The theology of the flood is the pivot of a connected but multifaceted universal theme running through Genesis 1–11 and the whole rest of Scripture: creation, and the character of the Creator, in his original purpose for creation; uncreation, in humankind's turning from the Creator, the universal spread of sin, ending in universal eschatological judgment; and re-creation, in the eschatological salvation of the faithful remnant and the universal renewal of the earth.

RICHARD M. DAVIDSON

See also GENESIS, THEOLOGY OF.

Bibliography. D. J. A. Clines, *CBQ* 38 (1976): 483–507; idem, *Faith and Thought* 100/2 (1972–73): 128–42; W. A. Gage, *The Gospel of Genesis: Studies in Protology and Eschatology;* G. F. Hasel, *Origins 1* (1974): 67–72; idem, *Origins 2* (1975): 77–95; idem, *Origins 5* (1978): 83–98; W. C. Kaiser, Jr., *New Perspectives on the Old Testament;* J. P. Lewis, *A Study of the Interpretation of Noah and the Flood in Jewish and Christian Literature;* B. C. Nelson, The *Deluge in Stone: A History of the Flood Theology of Genesis;* A. A. Roth, *Ministry* 59 (July 1986): 24–26; idem, *Origins* 12 (1985): 48–56; idem, *Origins* 15 (1988): 75–85; W. H. Shea, *Origins* 6 (1979): 8–29; G. J. Wenham, *Genesis;* idem, VT 28 (1978): 21–35; J. C. Whitcomb and H. M. Morris, *The Genesis Flood: The Biblical Record and Its Scientific Implications;* R. Youngblood, *The Genesis Debate: Persistent Questions About Creation and the Flood.*

Follow, Follower. The noun "follower" is seldom used in Scripture for the people of God, possibly due to its frequent references to idol worshipers (Deut. 18:9; 1 Kings 18:18) or those following evil desires (Eph. 2:2–3; Jude 16–18). Words meaning "to follow" are used in both Testaments to highlight various aspects of discipleship.

For the Israelites, people of the promises and the covenant, to follow God was a matter of both trust and obedience (Num. 14:24; Josh. 14:8). It meant keeping the commandments (Deut. 33:3–4; 1 Kings 14:8) and obeying the prophetic word (Dan. 9:10).

New Testament believers were exhorted to follow the Lord's commandments (2 John 6) and sound doctrine (1 Tim. 4:6; 2 Tim. 1:13), much like the Israelites were told to observe the Law. The chief development of the concept came in the literal following of the incarnate Son of God and the new meaning this gave to discipleship.

Discipleship was initiated by the explicit command, "Follow me" (Matt. 4:19). All who wished to follow Christ were confronted by the narrow door of his absolute authority. To follow meant to submit to his personal lordship.

Following also meant complete identification with the life of Jesus. Forsaking family, home, and means of income (Luke 5:11; 18:28–29), the disciples were to share Christ's life and ministry (Luke 10:1–16).Ultimately Jesus required them to participate in the act of cross-bearing (Mark 8:34–38).

The Johannine accounts depict the relational aspect of following Jesus. The disciples experienced his shepherding care (John 10). Reversing the teacher-pupil relationship, Jesus washed their feet (John 13:1–17), called them his friends (15:13–15), and commissioned them to do his work (20:21–23). Following not only meant submission and identification; it also meant intimacy.

Christ's ascension could have resulted in a loss of intimacy and concreteness in the experience of following him. The sense of intimacy was maintained, however, in the Holy Spirit, who is to believers everything Christ was for the disciples (John 14:15–26).

Concreteness in discipleship was realized in a new note of imitation. Christians can imitate God's mercy in practicing forgiveness (Eph. 4:31–5:1; cf. Matt. 18:23–35) or copy Christ's example of suffering wrong rather than inflicting it (1 Peter 2:20–23).

Furthermore, the church helped by models of mature discipleship (Phil. 3:17). Frequently Christian leaders provide this example for their people (Heb. 13:17). Sometimes a group of believers furnish the pattern for the larger church (1 Thess. 1:7; 2:14). Paul's invitation to his converts to follow him as he followed Christ (1 Cor. 11:1; 1 Thess. 1:6) expresses the ultimate challenge of Christian discipleship.

"To follow" in the Gospels and "to imitate" in the Epistles capture the essence of discipleship as submission to Christ's authority as Lord, as identification with the way of his cross, and as intimate sharing in his kingdom work and its final reward: eternal life (Luke 18:30).

LUKE L. KEEFER, JR.

See also DISCIPLE, DISCIPLESHIP.

Bibliography. G. Kittel, *TDNT,* 1:210–16; W. Michaelis, *TDNT,* 4:659–74.

Fool, Foolishness, Folly. ***The Old Testament.*** Several Hebrew words are rendered "fool," with nuances ranging all the way from the naive but teachable person (Prov. 14:15—*petî,* derived from the Hebrew root meaning "open," hence impressionable) to the hopelessly incorrigible person who deserves no corrective efforts since such will be in vain (Prov. 26:3—*kĕsîl).* In most cases the context will help the reader determine which of the many meanings is to be preferred.

The heaviest concentration of the Hebrew words referring to foolishness is in the Wisdom literature, where the fool is constantly contrasted with the wise. The fool is not so much stupid (except when the context demands such a meaning) as immoral and pernicious. The fool's problem is not so much intellectual as practical and spiritual. In fact, the terms "wise" and "fool" are used by the sages to designate respectively the faithful and the sinners. This characterization is well depicted in the competition between Wisdom and Folly for the attention and loyalty of the young man. Folly is a seductress who seeks to allure the young man away from the wife of his youth (Prov. 5:18). She personifies more than stupidity. She is immorality and adultery (Prov. 6:23–35; 7:6–27; 9:13–18). The fool is the naive person who succumbs to her amorous overtures.

A further insight into the nature of the fool is provided by the Hebrew word *nābāl.* This is the word used in Psalm 14:1, where the fool declares, "There is no God." Not only is the fool immoral, he is also godless. His mind is closed to God (as Nabal's mind was closed to reason—1 Sam. 25:25). He conducts his life without any recognition of God and thus is corrupt and perverse (Ps. 14:1, 3). He does not fear the Lord and hence knows nothing of wisdom (Prov. 1:29). The same Hebrew term is also applied to the nations. Wisdom is seen as the gift of God, expressed in the Torah. To be without it—as the Gentile nations were (Deut. 32:21)—or to ignore it—as Israel did (Deut. 32:6)—is to be foolish.

The New Testament. There are fewer Greek terms employed for the fool and these are essentially negative, indicating that the fool is lacking in sense and intelligence. The gravity of the condition of the fool can be seen in the warning of Jesus that to call a person such is to be in danger of "the fire of hell" (Matt. 5:22). The designation "fool" is considerably more derogatory than other terms of abuse. Clearly, to be a fool in this biblical sense is a serious matter.

Paul makes frequent ironic reference to foolishness, particularly in 1 and 2 Corinthians. He deprecates the wisdom of the world, which characterizes God's action in Jesus as nonsensical and scandalous. Human understanding erroneously takes God's wisdom to be foolishness and God's strength to be weakness since God's actions do not fit human reason or expectation. Indeed, from a worldly perspective God uses the foolish thing and calls the foolish person (1 Cor. 1:27–28).

Paul characterizes his self-defense in 2 Corinthians as foolish. He is forced by circumstances to employ worldly methods of refutation of charges arraigned against him (2 Cor. 11:1–6). He is forced to fight fire with fire. Further he recognizes that he is considered a fool by the world because of his suffering for the gospel (1 Cor. 4:10).

Elsewhere in the New Testament foolish has a more conventional sense. Believers are urged not to be foolish (Eph. 5:15–16) and to distinguish carefully between heavenly and earthly wisdom (James 3:13–18).

This negative attitude toward foolishness is understandable when its practices are observed. Among these practices are: relying on earthly wealth (Luke 12:20); failing to recognize that the ministry of Jesus is God's visitation to claim his own bride (Matt. 25:1–13); turning away from the gospel of grace to legalism (Gal. 3:1–3); worshiping the creature rather than the Creator (Rom. 1:18–23); and abrogating the demands of God with meaningless distinctions (Matt. 23:16–22). Perhaps even more significant than the above characteristics is a failure to act on the words of Jesus by building a house without an adequate foundation (Matt. 7:26–27), and a failure to believe the good news of Jesus' resurrection (Luke 24:25—here the foolish are described as "slow of heart"; the Old Testament expression is "without heart," without understanding, as in Prov. 9:16). The believer is not to be foolish, but to "understand what the Lord's will is" (Eph. 5:17).

CARL SCHULTZ

Bibliography. R. L. Harris, et al., *TWOT;* D. Kidner, *Proverbs;* A. Richardson, *A Theological Word Book of the Bible.*

Foreigner. Person from a different racial, ethnic, and linguistic group as in contrast to a "native." Circumstances during biblical times often forced people to emigrate to another country, where they would become "resident aliens" (see Gen. 19:9; Ruth 1:1). A less permanent settler was known as a "stranger" or "temporary resident." Sometimes the term "foreigner" is used to translate a Hebrew word that generally means an "outsider" from a different race, tribe, or family.

The Old Testament. The creation account records the first human residence in the garden of Eden. With the fall, humanity is exiled from God's immediate presence into a "foreign" land. This is the background to the important Old Testament theme of the promise of land.

After the judgment of the flood, the Book of Genesis records the Table of Nations (chap. 10), portraying the remarkable growth of the human community with its variety of racial, linguistic, and political divisions. The tower of Babel incident (11:1–9) is the reason for these divisions, as God confuses the language and disperses the human race. A divided humanity, alienated from God and from itself, is in desperate need of a home.

If the early history of the Bible ends with curse—the disintegration of humanity into many nations—the beginning of Israel's national history (chap. 12) commences with blessing as a family receives a divine pledge of land and a promise of progeny that will bless the alienated nations. Abram and his family, the founders of the Israelite nation, obeyed the call of God to emigrate to this land, leaving Mesopotamia to become resident aliens in Canaan (12:10; 20:1; 23:4). The patriarchs' lives were marked by a rootlessness, as the only land they actually received was a grave for Sarah, Abraham's wife (chap. 23). This pilgrim existence characterized early Israel (Exod. 6:4), as the embryonic nation was shaped in Egypt, another foreign country (Exod. 22:20; 23:9).

When Israel was constituted as a nation at Sinai (Exod. 19–24), a concern for resident aliens was etched into the legal system. The alien peoples received special protection under the law (Exod. 22:21; 23:9), and were even to be loved as native Israelites (Lev. 19:34). Such protection was particularly necessary as immigrants would not have the social network of kinship relations for support during exigencies. Yet, although ancient Near Eastern law codes stressed protection for the widow and orphan, only Israel's contained legislation for the resident alien. This was probably due to the peculiar circumstances of her origin.

After Sinai and the wilderness wanderings, Israel received the gift of the promised land. In order to occupy it, however, she had to purge the land of its foreign population. Foreigners in this context represented hostile agents that would contaminate Israel and render her unholy before God. For the same reason, covenants and marriages with foreigners were forbidden. Paradoxically, only if her religion was pure could Israel be of help to foreigners (cf. Rahab, Ruth, Naaman, the widow of Zarepath). If Israel became sinful in the holy land, she would lose God's permanent presence, as he would become like a temporary resident (Jer. 14:8).

And yet Israel's entire existence was bound up with being a blessing to foreigners (Gen. 12:3). Some psalms envisioned the time when all nations would become subject to an Israelite king who would rule the world with justice. Solomon's prayer at the inauguration of the temple implied that it was to be a house of prayer for all peoples, as Israelite and foreigner could both pray to its Lord (1 Kings 8:41–43; cf. Isa. 56:3–8). The prophets predicted that all nations would go up to Jerusalem to learn the Torah and depart changed people, no longer alienated from each other (Isa. 2:1–4; Mic. 4:1–5). There would be one humanity (Isa. 19:23–25), speaking a purified language (Zeph. 3:9).

Although Israel received a residence in the promised land, she was reminded that the land was God's and that he allowed her to settle on it as a resident alien (Lev. 25:23; cf. 1 Chron. 29:15; Pss. 39:12; 119:19). Israel must wait for a true home.

The New Testament. By the time of the New Testament, Israel had become extremely exclusive, largely forgetting her mission to the nations. When the Messiah arrived, however, foreigners were present (Matt. 2:1–12). During his ministry, he constantly interacted with them, indicating that God's love embraced the world (Luke 17:18; John 4). A Roman soldier pronounced a eulogy at his death (Luke 23:47). Death broke the hostile powers that caused human divisions (Eph. 2:14–18). In Christ there was no longer any important racial, linguistic, or ethnic difference (Gal. 3:26–29). Pentecost (Acts 2) reversed the judgment of the tower of Babel (Gen. 11:1–9).

At the same time, there was the realization that while members of the church had their citizenship in heaven, they were resident aliens on earth (1 Peter 1:17; 2:11). Before the coming of the kingdom, they had to live a nomadic existence as strangers and pilgrims, much like the patriarchs of the Old Testament (Heb. 11:9–16). They must live in hope and faith, praying for the invasion of the kingdom and waiting patiently for the gift of a new Canaan, a new Eden, where they can reside with their God (Rev. 21–22). Meanwhile the church must act by helping literal strangers and foreigners, remembering her own identity and God's love for the powerless (Matt. 25:35, 38, 43, 44). Hospitality (*philoxenos,* lit. love for the stranger) is to be a characteristic of the follower of Christ (1 Peter 4:9; cf. Rom. 12:13; Heb. 13:2).

STEPHEN G. DEMPSTER

See also NATIONS, THE.

Bibliography. G. Ahlström, *TDOT,* 4:52–58; F. C. Fensham, *JNES* 21 (1962): 129–39; D. E. Gowan, *Int* 41 (1987): 341–53; D. Kellerman, *TDOT,* 2:439–49; B. J. Malina, *Int* 41 (1987): 354–67; G. C. Moucarry, *Themelios* 14 (1988): 17–20; R. Patterson, *BSac* 130 (1973): 223–34; H. E. von Waldrow, *CBQ* 32 (1970): 182–204.

Foreknowledge. In his omniscience God knows what the future holds both for individuals and for nations. He knows and sees everything in advance and his will is carried out in accord with his plans and purposes. In the Old Testament God's foreknowledge is usually represented by the verb *yādāʿ*, which is the normal verb for "know." In the New Testament the main verbs are *proginōskō,* "to know in advance," and *prooraō,* "to see what is ahead." Foreknowledge is closely connected to election and predestination and to God's sovereign rule of his universe.

As the all-knowing One, God knows everything about us, including "all the days ordained for me . . . before one of them came to be" (Ps. 139:16). He knows our thoughts and words even before they are expressed (Ps. 139:4; Matt. 26:34), and he can determine our life's work before we are born. Jeremiah was set apart in the womb to be a prophet, chosen to minister to the nations (Jer. 1:5). The idea of choice is also evident in the call of Abraham to be the founder of God's covenant nation. When Genesis 18:19 says "I have chosen him," the verb is literally "I knew him." The same is true of Amos's description of Israel, "You only have I chosen of all the families of the earth" (3:2a). Compare Paul's statement in Romans 11:2: "God did not reject his people, whom he foreknew." God's sovereign choice of Israel established a unique relationship with a particular people.

Through the ministry of the Old Testament prophets, God often revealed specific information about the future. Micaiah accurately predicted that Ahab would die in an upcoming battle (1 Kings 22:17). Elisha knew that the Syrian siege of Samaria would be lifted the next day (2 Kings 7:1), and Isaiah anticipated the coming of the Persian king Cyrus, who would rescue Israel from exile (41:2; 44:28; 45:1). Isaiah also spoke of the advent of the Servant of the Lord who would come to Zion to be the Redeemer of the world (42:1; 59:20; 61:1). And Isaiah's contemporary, Micah, prophesied that the Messiah would be born in Bethlehem (5:2).

In accomplishing his purposes, God is able to work through the evil actions of those who have no desire to do his will. When Joseph's brothers sold him as a slave, God was in reality sending Joseph to devise a plan that would save the whole family from starvation (Gen. 45:5–7). The brothers intended to harm him, but God knew that many lives would be saved through Joseph's wise planning (50:20). By storing food in Egypt, Joseph partially fulfilled the promise to Abraham that "all peoples on earth will be blessed through you" (Gen. 12:3).

In the New Testament God's foreknowledge is clearly linked to the death of Christ and to the salvation of the elect. "Before the creation of the world" Christ was "chosen" or "foreknown" to be the Redeemer (1 Peter 1:20), a clear indication that God knew from the beginning that humankind would fall into sin. On the day of Pentecost the apostle Peter denounced the wicked men who put Christ to death, but he acknowledged that they had acted in accord with "God's set purpose and foreknowledge" (Acts 2:23). Evil rulers conspired to kill the Son of God, but yet his death was something that God "had decided beforehand should happen" (Acts 4:28).

The same juxtaposition of foreknowledge, election, and predestination also applies to individual salvation. We, too, were chosen "before the creation of the world," in accord with the foreknowledge of God (Eph. 1:4; 1 Peter 1:2). And the apostle Paul tells us that "those God foreknew" were also predestined and called to be justified by faith (Rom. 8:29–30). In each case foreknowledge precedes election and is intricately linked with God's will and purpose. Yet we should not think of this as some kind of fatalism or determinism. God does not force anyone to become a believer but works in a person's heart so that the individual freely chooses to receive Christ as Savior. When Pharaoh refused to let the Israelites leave Egypt, it appeared that he had no choice, because God would harden his heart (Exod. 4:21). But not until the sixth plague does the text say that the Lord hardened Pharaoh's heart (Exod. 9:12). During the first five plagues Pharaoh hardened his own heart, refusing to listen to Moses and Aaron; after that the Lord confirmed him in his hardened condition (Exod. 7:13-14; 8:15, 19, 32). In accord with his sovereign purposes, God brings some to salvation and others to perdition.

HERBERT M. WOLF

See also ELECT, ELECTION; GOD; PREDESTINATION.

Bibliography. G. W. Bromiley, *EDT,* pp. 419–21; J. Murray, *ZPED,* 2:590–93.

Forgiveness. ***Terminology.*** There are several Hebrew terms equivalent to the English "to forgive," as defined below. The three most common are verbs (used transitively): *sālaḥ, kāpar,* and *nāśā'*. The New Testament most commonly expresses the act of forgiving by *aphiēmi* (noun form: *aphesis*). The verbs *charizomai* (e.g., 2 Cor. 2:7) and *apoluō* (e.g., Luke 6:37) express the same idea.

Divine Forgiveness. God's restoration of relationship that entails the removal of objective guilt. Thus, to forgive the offense against God's holiness or the perpetrator of the offense are synonymous. Forgiveness can be extended both to nations (especially Israel) and to individuals.

The Old Testament. God is depicted in the Old Testament as merciful. He is described as "slow to anger" and "abounding in love/mercy," "compassionate and gracious" (Exod. 34:6; Num. 14:18; Neh. 9:17; Pss. 86:15; 103:8; 145:8; Joel 2:13; John 4:2). God is lenient toward his people, not treating them as their sin deserves (Ezra 9:13–15; Pss. 78:35–38; 103:8–10), and willing to forgive wickedness, rebellion, and sin (Exod. 34:7; Num. 14:18).

There is, however, a tension in the character of God as depicted in the Old Testament, because juxtaposed to the characterization of God as merciful is the warning that God as righteous will not forgive sin or at least not leave sin unpunished (Exod. 34:7; Num. 14:18; Nahum 1:3). Although he is predisposed to be merciful, nonetheless he is a jealous God (Exod. 20:5; 34:14; Deut. 4:23–24; 5:9; 6:15; Josh. 24:19–20; Nahum 1:2). Amos 7:1–9 illustrates God's character as both merciful and righteous: God forgives and repents of punishing Israel twice but after that, when Israel does not return, he can no longer spare the nation. This tension in God's nature manifests itself in God's dealings with nations—especially Israel—and individuals.

National Forgiveness. In one case God forgave a nation other than Israel and did not bring the punishment on it that he had planned. God as righteous was compelled to bring judgment on Nineveh, but God as merciful sent Jonah to warn the city of the impending judgment. The Ninevites, including the king, believed and repented of their evil ways and their violence (Jon. 3:8). As a result God as merciful relented from the evil that he had planned to bring on them. This is an illustration of the general principle by which God deals with nations (Jer. 18:7–8).

Israel is distinguished from other nations as being chosen by God out of all the nations of the earth as his special possession (cf. Exod. 19:15; Deut. 7:6; 14:2; 26:18; 1 Kings 3:8; 1 Chron. 16:13; Pss. 33:12; 105:6; 106:4–5; 135:4; Isa. 41:8; 43:10; 44:1–2). Israel's election has its roots in God's covenant with Abraham, renewed with Isaac and Jacob, thus giving God's relationship with the nation an unconditional basis (Gen. 12:1–3; 15:18; 17:8, 21; 22:17; 26:3–5; 28:13–15; 35:11–12; Exod. 2:24; 6:4; 13:5, 11; 32:13; 33:1; Deut. 1:8; 4:37; 7:8; 10:11; 26:15; 34:4; Josh. 1:6; 21:43–44; 1 Kings 8:40; 1 Chron. 16:16–18; 2 Chron. 20:7; Neh. 9:7–8; Ps. 105:8–11). So, in spite of Israel's disobedience, after he has punished the nation, God is committed to dealing mercifully with it because of the covenant made with the fathers and his love for them (Lev. 26:42; Deut. 4:31; 9:26–27; 2 Kings 13:23; Ps. 106:40–46; Jer. 33:25–26; Mic. 7:20).

Although God made a covenant with the fathers, the generation of the exodus was required to enter into a covenant with him as well. At Mount Sinai the people agreed to do everything that was written in the Book of the Covenant (Exod. 24:1–8). About forty years later the children of the generation of the exodus renewed this covenant (Deut. 27–30). The covenant entered into by these two generations of Israelites, unlike the covenant made with the fathers, was to be conditional on their obedience. God would bless them with prosperity in the land promised to the fathers, so long as they kept the law revealed through Moses; otherwise they would come under the curses of the covenant. It is significant that Exodus 19:5 makes Israel's status as God's special possession conditional on obedience. Unfortunately, rebellion in the wilderness made the fulfillment of the promises given to the fathers impossible for the generation of the exodus (Num. 14:23, 30; 32:11; Deut. 1:35); not surprisingly, in Deuteronomy the next generation is advised as to the conditionality of its standing (6:18; 11:8–9; 30:19–20; cf. Jer. 11:1–5). The covenant made with Moses, in other words, was to be perpetually renewed by Israel.

A tension was thereby created between the indicative and imperative of Israel's life before God: God unconditionally promised the land and prosperity in the land to the fathers and their descendants (Abrahamic covenant). Their descendants, however, would possess the promises only on the condition of their obedience to the Law (Mosaic covenant), and, after they had sinned, would be restored to a state of prosperity and security in the land only on the condition of national repentance (Deut. 30:1–10; 31:14–32:47; Book of

Judges; 1 Kings 8:33–40, 46–51; 2 Chron. 6:24–31, 36–39; 7:13–16). God as merciful made unconditional promises to Abraham and his descendants, but God as righteous demanded obedience to the Torah as the condition for the realization of these promises for each generation.

Individual Forgiveness. God as righteous required obedience from individual Israelites; by observance of all that God commanded each would live (Lev. 18:5; Neh. 9:29). Only some violations of the Torah were forgivable, and these through the cult.

In the Torah the intention of the agent is irrelevant to a determination of whether an act needs expiation; any violation of the Torah renders the agent culpable. The expressed purpose of the sin offering, in fact, is to provide expiation for those who sin unintentionally (Lev. 4:2). The stress is on the objective status of the person or community before God. Even unavoidable things like childbirth (12:1–8) and skin disease (14:1–32) render a person in need of expiation. In some cases nonmoral entities, such as the altar (8:15) or houses, must be expiated (14:53).

There is nonetheless the recognition that there is a difference in kind between intentional and unintentional violations of the Torah. With the exception of theft or fraud against one's neighbor (Lev. 6:1–7; Num. 5:5–8), taking careless oaths (Lev. 5:4–5), and a lesser sexual offense (Lev. 19:20–22), intentional violations of the Torah were not forgivable; the perpetrator was to be killed or cut off. Numbers 15:22–31 explicitly distinguishes between one who disobeys unintentionally, for whom a priest can atone, and one who disobeys intentionally, for whom the penalty is extirpation. The one who sins in a defiant manner despises the word of the Lord.

The cult provided the means of expiation for those violations of the Torah that were forgivable. Three types of sacrifice that could be brought by an individual were expiatory (Lev. 1–7): the burnt offering, the sin offering, and the guilt offering. Commonly in Leviticus and Numbers, a priest expiates for the offerer by means of a sacrifice and the offerer is pardoned. One of these sacrifices could also be offered for communal guilt (cf. Num. 15:22–26; 2 Chron. 29:24).

These expiatory sacrifices that could be brought by individuals also formed part of daily, weekly, and monthly sacrifices, as well as special offerings during the festivals. In three instances expiation is said to be effected for all individuals within the community by a public offering comprised of one of these expiatory sacrifices (Num. 28:22, 30; 29:5). This raises the possibility that all such public sacrifices not explicitly said to expiate do so also.

The Day of Atonement was another means by which individual sins could be forgiven. In Leviticus 16 Aaron (or his descendants) is instructed first to expiate himself and his house annually . Then, taking two goats, Aaron is to offer one—chosen by lot—as a sin offering for the expiation of the sanctuary (v. 16), while over the other he is to confess all the wickedness of the sons of Israel and all their rebellion—their sin—and release this second goat into the wilderness. The released goat removes all wickedness. This was a national ritual designed to remove individual offenses against God's holiness.

In his dealing with individual Israelites, God as merciful stands in tension with God as righteous. He does not deal with individual sin as it deserves, but forgives and mitigates punishment.

The Day of Atonement seems designed to atone for all the sins of an individual—even those that should result in extirpation. Consistency should demand that the violations of the Torah to be expiated on the Day of Atonement be those unknown and forgivable violations committed by individuals during the past year. But Leviticus 16:21 stipulates that Aaron will confess over the goat "all the wickedness and rebellion of the Israelites—all their sins"; the fact that these three terms are used in tandem to denote sin in its totality implies that otherwise unforgivable violations of the Torah were forgiven on that day. To the objection that what is forgiven must be that which the Torah allows to be forgiven, it can be countered that God is described as one who forgives wickedness, rebellion, and sin (Exod. 34:6).

In addition, God forgives people who should not be forgivable; for the sake of mercy God violates the conditions of his own covenant and often acts more leniently than the Torah would allow. David murdered Uriah and committed adultery with Bathsheba (2 Sam. 11); both actions were punishable by death so that both David and Bathsheba should have been killed. Instead, God forgave David (and presumably Bathsheba), although he was punished for his deeds (2 Sam. 12). In Psalm 51, said to have been occasioned by Nathan's rebuke, David asks God to forgive him (vv. 1–2) and expresses confidence that his sacrifice of a broken spirit and contrite heart are acceptable to God (vv. 16–17). Solomon went so far as to worship other gods, including the detestable god Molech (1 Kings 11). Although God removed the kingdom from his son as punishment, Solomon was not judged according to the Torah, which required death for those who turned away from worshiping and serving God (Deut. 17:2–7). God's dealings with the subsequent kings of Israel and Judah also reflect a much greater leniency than was allowed in the Torah. In spite of all the evil Ahab had done, God did not kill Ahab, which was the required penalty for his sin of complicity in the murder of Naboth. Because Ahab repented God did not even bring punishment on Ahab's house (1 Kings 21:27–29), as he had originally planned.

Repentance is a factor causing God to depart from the standards of the Torah. The individual is understood on analogy to the nation, so that, just as the nation is restored to favor after repentance, so is the individual. Although the prophets mostly spoke to Israel as a nation, in Ezekiel 18:21–23, 27 the individual Israelite is addressed and offered God's unconditional forgiveness. Repentance after committing a violation of the Torah punishable by death has the effect of bringing about God's mercy.

The Eschatological Resolution of the Tension. The tension between God as merciful and God as righteous manifesting itself on both national and individual levels was to be resolved by God at the time of Israel's eschatological renewal. The prophets often spoke of a time when the nation would be restored to the land and forgiven. At this time God would also give to individual Israelites the means by which to meet the conditions of the Mosaic covenant, so that the tension between God's unconditional and conditional promises (the Abrahamic and Mosaic covenants) would become irrelevant: since individual Israelites would have a heart to obey God, the nation would be obedient. This restoration is often spoken of as the establishment of another (eschatological) covenant, which will issue in both forgiveness and the spiritual transformation of the people, and is often associated with the giving of the Spirit (Jer. 31:31–34; 32:27–41; 50:5, 20; Ezek. 16:59–63; 36:24–32). Related to the eschatological resolution of the tension is the Isaian servant, who is said to be the servant of the covenant (Isa. 42:6) and whose death is expiatory (Isa. 53).

The New Testament. The tension between God's dealings with human beings in terms of his mercy and righteousness finds resolution in the New Testament. That the eschatological promises of forgiveness and spiritual transformation have become realities through the appearance, death, resurrection, and exaltation of Jesus Christ is assumed throughout the New Testament. This eschatological resolution pertains to the nation, individuals within the nation, and individual Gentiles.

John the Baptist offered eschatological forgiveness to the nation on the condition of repentance (Mark 1:4; Luke 3:3). His offer exemplified the tension between God as merciful and God as righteous, as shown by the fact John rejected some who had not first produced the fruit of repentance before seeking the baptism of repentance for the forgiveness of sin. He evidently assumed that Israel was the totality of Jews who were faithful to the covenant. John the Baptist pointed to the resolution of this tension, however, when he said that the one who would come after him would baptize with the Holy Spirit (Matt. 3:11; Mark 1:8; Luke 3:16).

Jesus proclaimed the kingdom of God, and offered his hearers the possibility of entrance into this kingdom on the condition of repentance. He was the mediator of eschatological salvation, which included the extension of forgiveness (Matt. 9:3–6; Mark 2:7–12; Luke 5:21–25; 7:36–50). Like John the Baptist, Jesus required that the offer of eschatological salvation be appropriated by individuals; the process of entering the kingdom was that of becoming a child, by passively receiving God's eschatological forgiveness. It is for this reason that Jesus said to his opponents that "the tax collectors and the prostitutes are entering the kingdom of God ahead of you" (Matt. 21:31b).

Jesus' offer of the kingdom to all on the condition of repentance led to the charge that he associated with tax-collectors and sinners, which his opponents considered offensive to God's righteousness (Matt. 9:10–13; 11:19; Mark 2:15–17; Luke 5:30–32; 7:34; 15:2). The offense probably lay not in the fact that Jesus taught that God would forgive the repentant, but that Jesus actively sought out sinners and offered them the possibility of eschatological forgiveness. In Jesus' opponents' view, sinners ought to take the initiative.

One must remember that for a Jew repentance meant more than simple remorse; it included moral reformation. This explains why some of Jesus' sayings emphasize the need for righteousness in order to be included in the kingdom of God. The same stress on God as both merciful and righteous found in the Old Testament period is found in Jesus' teaching about the kingdom. The mere fact that Jesus required repentance as a condition of entrance into the kingdom is sufficient to make the point. These two aspects of Jesus' teaching, however, are not in tension, because he saw his time as that of eschatological salvation, the time of the resolution of the tension between God as merciful and God as righteous in his dealings with human beings. Jesus proclaimed the kingdom of God and later taught that his death would be the means by which the new covenant would be realized. He also taught that the Spirit would be given after his return to the Father (John 7:39; 14–16). Understood against the background of the eschatological promises of the Old Testament, Jesus was saying that the time of Israel's eschatological forgiveness and spiritual transformation had come.

Jesus' preaching of the kingdom of God led to his arrest and execution. This had two consequences. First, in response to the crisis in his ministry that this produced, Jesus incorporated his rejection and impending death into his message. He interpreted his death as vicarious and expiatory, as the means by which eschatological forgiveness and renewal would come to Israel and the nations in spite of Israel's rejection of the messenger of the kingdom. Jesus understood his death in light of the destiny of the Servant as a guilt offering for many (Matt. 20:28; Mark 10:45; Luke 22:37). He also interpreted his impending death at the Last Supper as that of the eschatological Passover lamb whose sacrifice would bring about the possibility of forgiveness and the realization of the new covenant (Matt. 26:26–28; Mark 14:22–24; Luke 22:19–20). Second, Jesus' rejection would bring into being a messianic community, the church (*ekklēsia*). Since Jesus required personal repentance as a condition for entrance into the kingdom of God, the potential existed for distinguishing a faithful remnant from those who were unrepentant and disobedient. Judgment would come to those who rejected him, while those who accepted Jesus' message would receive the Spirit and be constituted as the messianic community, for whom some of the eschatological promises would be realized (Acts 1:8; 2:1–13). Also Gentiles would become part of this community and receive the Holy Spirit (Matt. 28:18–19; Acts 10). Jesus still foresaw, however, a future for the nation (Luke 21:24; Acts 1:6–7), when God would bring about eschatological salvation on a national basis.

Paul writes that Jesus' death is the means by which eschatological forgiveness comes not only to the Jew but also to the Gentile (Gal. 3:7–9; cf. Acts 3:25). Like Jesus, he sees the tension between God as merciful and God as righteous resolved in the realization of the eschatological promises of forgiveness and spiritual transformation.

There are some passages in the New Testament that suggest baptism is a necessary condition for acquiring eschatological forgiveness (Acts 2:38; Rom. 6:3–4; Col. 2:12; 1 Peter 3:21). This is a controversial subject; suffice it to say that at the very least baptism is intricately bound up with the reception of eschatological forgiveness.

First John speaks of forgiveness after having received eschatological forgiveness. The author says that the one who is in him (Christ)/born of God does not sin habitually (3:6, 9); this person has the Spirit (3:24). But John recognizes that nonhabitual sin is an inevitability and requires a means of expiation (1:7–2:2). Expiation comes by confession, after which the sinner will be cleansed from all unrighteousness by Jesus' expiatory sacrifice.

In the New Testament there are references to sins that are unforgivable. Jesus spoke about blasphemy against the Spirit for which there could be no forgiveness (Matt. 12:31–32; Mark 3:28–29; Luke 12:10). The author of Hebrews also allows for the possibility of sins committed by "believers" that are not forgivable (6:4–8; 10:26–31), and 1 John refers to a sin that leads to death (5:16–17). These are difficult passages to interpret, but probably should be understood as denoting apostasy issuing in sins for which there is no repentance. The apostate, moreover, never had a genuine experience of God's eschatological salvation.

Human Forgiveness. In the Lord's Prayer, receiving forgiveness from God is joined to forgiving others (Matt. 6:12; Luke 11:4). Jesus' parable of the unmerciful servant makes the point that human beings are obliged to forgive because God has forgiven them (Matt. 18:23–35). God's forgiveness is actually said to be conditional upon forgiving others (Matt. 6:14; 18:35; Mark 11:25–26; Luke 6:37). Jesus says that there ought to be no limit on the number of times that one should forgive another so long as the offender repents and asks for forgiveness (Matt. 18:21–22; Luke 17:3–4).

BARRY D. SMITH

See also ATONEMENT; BLASPHEMY AGAINST THE HOLY SPIRIT; DEATH OF CHRIST; FAITH; REPENTANCE.

Bibliography. A. Büchler, *Studies in Sin and Atonement;* P. Garnet, *Salvation and Atonement in the Qumran Scrolls;* M. Hengel, *The Atonement;* G. E. Ladd, *A Theology of the New Testament;* E. A. Martens, *God's Design: A Focus on Old Testament Theology;* J. Milgrom, *Cult and Conscience: The Asham and the Priestly Doctrine of Repentance;* G. F. Moore, *Judaism in the First Centuries of the Christian Era;* G. F. Oehler, *Theology of the Old Testament;* E. P. Sanders, *Paul and Palestinian Judaism;* B. D. Smith, *Jesus' Last Passover Meal;* V. Taylor, *Jesus and His Sacrifice.*

Fornication. *See* IMMORALITY, SEXUAL.

Foreordination. *See* PREDESTINATION.

Free Will. *See* WILL.

Freedom. The theme of freedom rings loudly in one of the most crucial sections of Scripture, namely the narrative of the exodus. Already when establishing his covenant with Abraham, God had predicted the bondage and suffering of the Hebrews in a foreign land (Gen. 15:13). That long period of Egyptian slavery became a powerful symbol of oppression, and so the deliverance of the Israelites through Moses spoke to them of freedom in a more profound sense—indeed, of spiritual redemption. It should be noted, moreover, that this liberation had as its purpose *serving* God and obeying his Law (Exod. 19:4–5; cf. also 20:2 as the introduction to the Ten Commandments). In other words, from the very beginning God's people were taught that the alternative to servitude was not freedom in some abstract sense, but rather *freedom to serve the Lord.*

It is not surprising that built into the very fabric of Israelite society was a constant reminder of God's deliverance and its significance. The fourth commandment, for example, had reference not only to God's resting on the seventh day of creation (Exod. 20:8–11), but also to the liberation of Israel from the hands of Egypt (Deut. 5:12–15). Israelites who sold themselves because of poverty were to be freed after six years and to be given a generous supply of food. "Remember that you were slaves in Egypt and the LORD your God redeemed you. That is why I give you this command today" (Deut. 15:15; cf. Lev. 25:42). Every seventh year the debts of all Israelites were to be canceled (Deut. 15:1–2). Clearly, God was showing his people the greatness of his forgiveness and the implications of that forgiveness for their own behavior. In addition, the fiftieth year (i.e., after seven sets of seven years) was consecrated as a year of jubilee, in which the Israelites were to "proclaim liberty throughout the land to all its inhabitants" (Lev. 25:10).

The ensuing history of the Israelites was one of repeated disobedience to their God. By their actions they indicated that they had forgotten his liberating work. Not surprisingly, they were given over to destruction and captivity. Now their exile in Babylon, as well as their subsequent submission to various powers, including Rome, became a reminder of their sin and fueled their longing for God's final deliverance. For many of them, however, freedom came to be seen more and more as a political hope. The very concept of Messiah was widely understood against the background of earthly kingship.

It was into this setting that Jesus' proclamation came. Although the Synoptic Gospels do not treat the theme of freedom in an explicit way, Jesus' message as a whole must be understood as a response to Jewish aspirations for deliverance. The Gospel of Luke in particular grounds the coming of Christ in the promises of divine liberation. Mary's Magnificat stresses God's power and justice in bringing down the proud and mighty from their thrones while exalting the humble and oppressed (Luke 1:51–53). Then, in celebration of the birth of John the Baptist, his father Zechariah sees the promises of God beginning to be fulfilled. Remembering the covenant to Abraham, the Lord is accomplishing "salvation from our enemies and from the hand of all who hate us" (Luke 1:71). Moreover, Luke introduces Jesus' public ministry by relating the visit to the synagogue in Nazareth. There Jesus announced the fulfillment of the Old Testament promises, proclaiming "good news to the poor" and "freedom for the prisoners" (Luke 4:18, citing Isa. 61:1).

In the Gospel of John there is only one passage that makes an explicit reference to freedom, but this passage is of special significance, because it contrasts the political or external concept of freedom with the "spiritual" or theological work of salvation. According to John 8, Jesus made the claim that truth was to be found in his teaching; then he assured his hearers that his truth could make them free (vv. 31–32). This claim drew a sharp response from the audience, who appealed to their kinship with Abraham and deduced that they had never been slaves (v. 33). In view of their long history of subservience to other powers, this response was probably an appeal to a sense of spiritual freedom that transcended the political situation. Their notion that physical descendance guaranteed their place as the people of God was a fundamental mistake, and Jesus proceeded to disabuse them of their pride: "Everyone who sins is a slave to sin. Now a slave has no permanent place in the family [because his descendants have no claim to the household], but a son belongs to it forever. So if the Son sets you free, you will be free indeed" (vv. 34–36). One can hardly imagine a more powerful critique of misconceived ideas about freedom.

The notion of slavery to sin is especially prominent in Paul, who writes to Gentile audiences against the background of Greco-Roman thought. Undoubtedly, Paul's writing parallels some ideas current in his day, such as the emphasis on internal freedom even in the midst of social slavery (cf. the long discussion of freedom in Epictetus, *Discourses* 4.1). It is just as clear, however, that the apostle develops his teaching in distinction from—even in opposition to—contemporary thought. Hellenistic philosophers, for example, tended to place considerable emphasis on the concept of *natural* human freedom, but Paul appears to reject any such idea. Writing to the Roman Christians, he reflects Old Testament teaching when he argues that freedom and slavery are simply relative to whatever it is that has our allegiance (Rom. 6:15–23). If I render obedience to sin, I am a slave to sin and lawlessness but I am "free" with respect to righteousness (cf. 2 Peter 2:19). If, on the other hand, I render myself as a "slave" to righteousness, I become free with respect to sin.

This conception explains why Paul characteristically refers to himself as a *servant* (Gk. *doulos*, "slave") of Christ and is even willing to make himself a slave to everyone (1 Cor. 9:19). Moreover, when addressing the controversial problem whether Christian slaves in Corinthian society should seek to become free, he appeals to the higher principle of spiritual freedom: anyone who is in Christ and bears the label of "slave" is in fact the Lord's freeman, while the one who bears the label of "freeman" is truly Christ's slave (1 Cor. 7:22; cf. Gal. 3:28; Col. 3:11). It appears then that Paul was not comfortable with the popular notion of freedom as "being able to do whatever one desires" (there are various references to this view, such as Aristotle's objection to it in *Politics* 5:7.1310a and Epictetus's nuancing of it in *Discourses* 4.1.1–5).

Among Paul's writings—indeed, among all the books of the Bible—none addresses the topic of freedom more forcefully than Galatians, a letter sometimes described as the Magna Charta of Christian Liberty. Interestingly, the central concern of this letter parallels the issue reflected in John 8: What is the relationship between freedom and being a descendant of Abraham? The Gentile Christians of Galatia were being persuaded by some Judaizing groups to adopt circumcision and other distinctive Jewish ceremonies. Apparently, these Judaizers argued that such conversion to Judaism was necessary to participate fully in the blessings God promised to Abraham. In other words, if the Galatians wanted to be truly part of God's people (and thus spiritually free?), they must become descendants of Abraham by submitting to the Mosaic law.

Paul had little patience with this type of thinking. In his view it was "another gospel" that did not really deserve the name "gospel": those who proclaimed such a message were perverting the true gospel and deserved God's curse (1:6–9)—indeed, they were false brothers whose real purpose was to undermine the freedom that believers have in Christ (2:4–5). In developing his theological argument against these Judaizers, Paul points out that the function of the Mosaic law was that of a temporary guardian (the Greek word used in 3:24–25 is *paidagōgos,* which ironically was itself used of slaves who had the responsibility to look after children and discipline them). In 3:22–23 the language of "imprisonment" and "confining under sin" is used to describe that function.

The apostle's negative remarks about the Mosaic Law raise a difficult question. After all, God had given that law precisely in the context of liberation from bondage. In a very profound sense, the Law was both a symbol of freedom and even the means of enjoying that freedom in the service of God. James goes so far as to speak of "the law of freedom" (1:25; 2:12). The problem is that, because of sin, the law was impotent to grant life and freedom; instead, it cursed and killed (Rom. 7:9–11; 8:3; Gal. 3:10). Christ, however, came specifically to *redeem,* that is, to liberate those who were under the law by delivering them from its curse (Gal. 3:13–14; 4:4–5). Through faith and the power of the Holy Spirit we are freed from the law of sin and death (Rom. 8:2); we are no longer slaves, but children—and not merely children of Abraham (Gal. 3:29) but children of God (Rom. 8:15; Gal. 3:26; 4:6–7). Truly where the Spirit of the Lord is, there is freedom (2 Cor. 3:17; cf. Gal. 4:28–5:1)!

Paul, however, makes clear that this freedom is not license to do whatever we want. On the contrary, it leads to moral transformation (2 Cor. 3:18) and even to the fulfillment of the law, which tells us to be slaves to one another in love (Gal. 5:13–14). Paradoxically, the life that comes from the Spirit and frees us from the enslaving power of the law (Gal. 5:18) produces in the believer the very conduct that the law calls for (Gal. 5:22–23).

Finally, we should note that the believers' experience of the Holy Spirit is only a down payment, a foretaste, of their inheritance (cf. Eph. 1:13–14). Our final liberation is yet to come, when we receive the full adoption of sons, when even our bodies are redeemed, and when the whole creation will be freed from its bondage and decay and brought into the glorious freedom of the children of God (Rom. 8:18–23).

MOISÉS SILVA

See also REDEEM, REDEMPTION; SALVATION.

Bibliography. E. M. B. Green, *Jesus Spells Freedom;* P. Richardson, *Paul's Ethic of Freedom;* E. Käsemann, *Jesus Means Freedom.*

Friend, Friendship. Most of the Old Testament words translated "friend," "friendship," or "be friendly" come from two Hebrew roots, *rʿh* and *ʾhb.* The most common terms for friend are *rēʿeh,* "friend," and *ʾōhēb,* a participial form meaning "one who loves." In the New Testament several words appear, including *philos,* "friend," *hetairos,* "companion, comrade," and *plēsion,* "neighbor," along with a variety of kinship terms such as "brother," "mother," or "child," extended to refer to people outside one's family for whom one feels special affection. The terms used most include *philos,* "friend," and *adelphos/adelphē,* "brother/sister," the last of which becomes a technical term for a fellow believer.

In both Testaments the ideas of friend and friendship involve three components: association, loyalty, and affection. There are also three levels of meaning: friendship as association only; friendship as association plus loyalty; and friendship as association plus loyalty plus affection.

At the lowest level a friend is simply an associate or "the other fellow" (Judg. 7:13; Rom. 15:2; James 4:12). In Jesus' parables the vineyard owner addresses a laborer (Matt. 20:13) and the host speaks to a wedding guest he does not know (Matt. 22:12) using the term "comrade." Jesus addresses Judas in this way in the garden: "Friend, do what you came for" (Matt. 26:50).

At a higher and theologically more interesting level the idea of friendship contains not only the component of association but also that of loyalty. The "king's friend" (2 Sam. 15:37; 16:16; 1 Kings 4:5; 1 Chron. 27:33) serves as a royal advisor or, in the Maccabean period, as a member of a favored class of nobles (1 Macc. 2:18; 3:38; 6:10; 10:65). Hiram of Tyre's "friendship" with David (1 Kings 5:1) is actually a political alliance that may have little to do with affection but everything to do with treaty obligations. The "friend who sticks closer than a brother" (Prov. 18:24) shows loyalty. When the Jews accuse Pilate of not being "a friend of Caesar" (John 19:12), they are questioning his loyalty to the emperor.

The highest level of friendship contains the components of association and loyalty along with affection. The friendship of David and Jonathan (1 Sam. 18:1–4; 20:14–17) has all three components, as does the friendship between Paul and the Philippian church (see, e.g., Phil. 4:1, 15–20).

According to Scripture there are three possible objects of friendship: another person, God or his Son, or someone else who follows Jesus.

The first involves human friendship based simply on common humanity with all the joys and dangers associated with it. Human friendship brings help in time of trouble (Prov. 17:17; 27:10; Luke 11:5–8) and advice in perplexing situations (Prov. 27:9). A friend may provide consolation in trouble, as when Barzillai the Gileadite consoles the hunted David (2 Sam. 19:31–39), or when the friends of Jephthah's daughter help her mourn her early death (Judg. 11:37–38). A friend may offer help at the risk of death, as Hushai the Arkite does when he spies for David in the court of Absalom the usurper (2 Sam. 15:32–37; 16:16–19; 17:5–16). A friend may rebuke in love, proving more faithful than a flatterer (Prov. 27:6). Ecclesiastes develops the theme of friendship in the "two are better than one" passage (4:9–12).

One of the greatest biblical examples of the "friend who sticks closer than a brother" is the relationship between David and Jonathan. Jonathan's loyalty to David runs deeper than his loyalty to his father Saul or his own ambitions (1 Sam. 18:1–4; 20:14–17). The dirge David sings when he hears of Jonathan's death marks their relationship as a high point of human friendship (2 Sam. 1:17–27). Ruth's stubborn loyalty to her mother-in-law Naomi stands as another display of human friendship at its highest.

In the New Testament Paul shows a talent for gaining friends. In his letters he names many people as his special friends in Christ. In the Book of Acts Paul's friends include even the pagan officials of Asia known as Asiarchs (Acts 19:31).

While friendship on the human level has its joys and consolations, it also has its dangers. Sometimes a friend can fail to dissuade one from an evil action, as Judah's friend Hirah the Adullamite does when he helps Judah make arrangements with a supposed prostitute (Gen. 38:12–23). A friend can lead one into sin, as when Jonadab son of Shimeah persuades his cousin Amnon to rape his half sister Tamar (2 Sam. 13:1–6). A friend can even lead one to worship other gods (Deut. 13:6–11). Proverbs contains warnings about the dangers of bad company (1:10–19; 4:14–19).

Even if a friend does not lead one astray, the friend may cause grief through misunderstanding. Job's three comforters, although they try to be his friends, only make his suffering worse (2:11–13; 6:14–27; 19:21–22; 42:7–9).

Friends may prove false, pretending affection and loyalty from ulterior motives (Ps. 55:12–14; Prov. 14:20; 19:4, 6–7). A friend may put one into debt by asking security for a loan (Prov. 6:1–5; 11:15; 17:18; 22:26–27). Friendship can break down through gossip (Prov. 16:28) or holding grudges (Prov. 17:9). Friends may abandon one in trouble (Ps. 38:11; cf. Ecclus. 9:10). The disappearance of true loyalty to friends is one of the symptoms of social and moral breakdown addressed by the prophet Micah in eighth-century Judah (Mic. 7:5–6).

As one can be a friend to another person, so one can be a friend of God or of God's Son. Abraham gains the title "friend of God" by his faith and obedience (2 Chron. 20:7; Isa. 41:8; James 2:23). Those who keep God's covenant are called his friends (Ps. 25:14). By contrast, one can be a friend of the world, which excludes the possibility of friendship with God (James 4:4; 1 John 2:15).

Many show they are friends of God by becoming friends of Jesus. His open acceptance during his ministry of all kinds of people displays not simply a tendency toward human friendship but portrays the possibility of divine-human loyalty and affection. The "disciple Jesus loved" (John 19:26; 20:2; 21:7) enjoys more than a human relationship with Jesus. Their friendship is more spiritual than social, as no doubt Jesus' friendship with Lazarus was (John 11:3, 5, 36). Jesus shows this kind of divine-human friendship by addressing his disciples as friends (Luke 12:4), by letting them know the inner meaning of his life and ministry (John 15:15), and, most clearly, by dying on the cross as the sacrifice for sin (John 15:13). When Jesus tells his disciples, "You are my friends if you do what I command" (John 15:14), the components of association, loyalty, and affection all appear.

If one can be a friend of God or of God's Son, this friendship can extend as well to others who are also friends of God. Christian friendship finds its basis in the friendship between each believer and God. When John refers to fellow believers simply as "the friends" (3 John 15), he implies the loyalty and affection for one another that spring from loyalty and love for God. Seven times in 1 John the writer addresses his readers as "dear children," using the language of family to express this deep affection (1 John 2:1, 12, 28; 3:7, 18; 4:4; 5:21).

Paul expresses this loyal and affectionate relationship when he refers to or addresses several individuals with the language of family love. He speaks to Timothy and Titus as his true children (1 Tim. 1:2; Titus 1:4), and to Timothy as his "dear son" (2 Tim. 1:2). Onesimus is not only Paul's "son" but his "very heart" (Philem. 10, 12). An unnamed woman in the Roman church is mother literally to a Christian named Rufus and figuratively to Paul (Rom. 16:13).

The New Testament shows a certain "in-group" mentality by making a distinction between members of the household of faith and outsiders (Gal. 6:10). But the writers never press this distinction, and they often make the point that Christian friendship should not appear only within Christian circles. While Paul, for example, encourages special concern for believers, he does so in connection with encouragement to "do good to all" (Gal. 6:10). Jesus encourages his followers to invite needy strangers, not friends, to their tables (Luke 14:12–14), and in the parable of the Good Samaritan he extends the concept of neighbor to include anyone in need (Luke 10:25–37).

CARL B. BRIDGES, JR.

Bibliography. D. A. Carson, *NIDNTT,* 1:259–60; U. Falkenroth, *NIDNTT,* 1:258–59; W. Günther, *NIDNTT,* 1:254–58; G. A. Lee, *ISBE,* 2:361–62; C. S. Lewis, *The Four Loves;* N. J. Opperwall and G. A. Lee, *ISBE,* 2:363.

Fruit. ***Terms and Meaning.*** Among the number of Hebrew words for fruit, fruit-producing, is *pĕrî,* to bear fruit, be fruitful. The basic Greek word for fruit is *karpos,* used literally of fruit, offspring, and figuratively of the consequence of physical, mental, or spiritual action; *karpophoreō,* means to bear fruit or crops, and figuratively, bear fruit in the heart (Luke 8:15); and *akarpos,* means fruitless, as of unproductive, unregenerate lives (Matt. 13:22).

Physical Fruits and Their Spiritual Application. In his original creation God commanded the land to produce "vegetation: seed-bearing plants and trees on the land that bear fruit with seed in it, according to their various kinds" (Gen. 1:11). Scripture refers to a number of the Near East plants, trees/bushes, and spices to teach or enhance a spiritual lesson (e.g., the grain seeds sown, Matt. 13:1–9; the fig tree cursed, Matt. 21:18–22; the grape vine likened to God's people, Jer. 2:21; John 15:1–7). To make the spiritual point that God's disobedient people needed his mercy and saving power to heal them, Jeremiah effectively refers to the healing effect of the balm or gum oil of a well-known bush/small tree growing in Gilead.

Spices and unguents, the fruit of exotic plants, trees, and small bushes in the Middle East, frequently played an important role in enhancing one's social position or indicating one's respect, adoration, and devotion, particularly to God. Examples include myrrh (aromatic gum of the tree/bush of Arabia, Ethiopia, and Somalia), cinnamon (of the cinnamon tree), and olive oil for the sacred oil for the tabernacle (Exod. 30:22–33); the fragrant spices of gum resin (the aromatic myrrh gum), onycha (made from mollusk shells), galbanum (resin from plant roots), and frankincense (resin from a small tree/bush from Ubar, Oman) for the sacred fragrant tabernacle incense (Exod. 30:34–38); frankincense and myrrh given by the magi in their worship of Jesus (Matt. 2:11); the nard (perfume made from a Middle East plant) Mary poured out in worship on the feet of Jesus (John 12:3); the seventy-five-pound mixture of myrrh and aloes (aromatic resin of a Near Eastern tree) Joseph of Arimathea and Nicodemus used in wrapping up the body of Jesus (John 19:39–40) and the spices and perfumes the women took to the tomb to anoint the body of Jesus (Mark 16:1; Luke 23:56–24:1).

Man, the Special Fruit of God's Creation. When God created man and woman (Gen. 1:26), endowing them with moral, intellectual, and spiritual power (cf. Eph. 4:24; Col. 3:10), he said to them, "Be fruitful and increase in number; fill the earth and subdue it" (Gen. 1:28). This implies that Adam and Eve's progeny were not only to be the physical fruit of the pair but also to be endowed with moral, intellectual, and spiritual power, since they too, as descendants of the God-created pair, were made in "the image of God" (Gen. 1:27; cf. Gen. 9:6; 2 Cor. 4:4). The offspring of the human pair is called, from the woman's viewpoint, "the fruit of the womb" (Deut. 7:13; 28:4, 11, 18, 53; 30:9; Luke 1:42), and from the husband's standpoint, "fruit of his loins" (Ps. 131:11, LXX; Acts 2:30, Greek text; cf. "the fruit of my body," Mic. 6:7).

A Figurative Meaning. Scripture speaks of eating "the fruit of your labor" (Ps. 128:2), and defines the activities of the godly as "the fruit of the righteous" (Prov. 11:30). Those who reject God's wisdom are described as eating "the fruit of their ways . . filled with the fruit of their schemes" (Prov. 1:31; cf. Jer. 6:19). "The fruit of the lips," the blessing of one's speech, adds blessing to one's daily life (Prov. 12:14; 13:2; 18:20–21). John the Baptist and Jesus teach that the disciple is to produce fruit (good works) as evidence of true repentance (Matt. 3:8; Luke 3:8), and they explain that a good tree (the repentant individual) cannot produce bad fruit, that is, a life filled with wicked acts, and a bad tree (an unrepentant person) cannot produce good fruit, that is, a life of godly works (Matt. 3:10; 7:16–20; Luke 3:9; 6:43).

To aid Christians in their walk before the Lord, God-given wisdom is made available to them, wisdom whose "fruit is better than fine gold" (Prov. 8:19), and the Holy Spirit develops within Christians the fruit of "love, joy, peace, patience, kindness, goodness, faithfulness, gentleness and self control" (Gal. 5:22–23). Thus, with the enablement of the Holy Spirit, the Christian can flourish "like a tree planted by streams of water, which yields its fruit in season" (Ps. 1:3).

W. HAROLD MARE

Bibliography. D. J. Burke, *ISBE,* 2:364–66; W. E. Shewell-Cooper, *ZPED,* 2:614–16.

Fruit of the Spirit. The fruit of the Spirit is the result of the Holy Spirit's presence and working in the lives of maturing believers and is itemized in Galatians 5:22–23. In the context of these verses, the singular fruit of the Spirit is contrasted with the plural works of the flesh (5:19–21). Neither listing is exhaustive, as is clear from Paul's ending of his list of the works of the flesh with the phrase, "and things like these," and his statement at the close of his itemizing of the fruit of the Spirit that "against such things there is no law."

Several attempts have been made to explain the reason why "works" is plural and "fruit" is singular. Some have suggested that the singular stresses the truth that the fruit is one cluster with many individual parts, as one diamond has many facets. Others have suggested that the singular refers to one harvest and the unity of the characteristics that the Spirit produces within the individual. Another possibility is that the fruit of the Spirit is actually one, love, with the other virtues being different manifestations of love in operation. A support of such a view may be 1 Corinthians 13:4–7, where several of the things itemized as fruit in Galatians are included as identifying features of *agapē* love. It is notable that the fruit of the Spirit, as listed, is in direct opposition to the works stemming from the flesh.

An Identification of the Fruit. The fruit of the Holy Spirit's work in the life of the individual Christian, which is enumerated in Galatians 5:22–23, can be described as follows: an active love for God and one's fellowman; a rejoicing in all kinds of circumstances; peacefulness and serenity of character and peacemaking among people; patience and longsuffering with persons, some of whom may not be easy to get along with; kindness toward others; goodness that seeks to aid others; faithfulness and dependability in one's relationships with God and other people; gentleness and meekness in accepting God's will and in dealing with others; and the ability to keep oneself in check and under control in all kinds of circumstances. Paul concludes by observing the obvious: "Against such things as these virtues no law has been enacted."

A Contrast of the Fruit with the Gifts of the Spirit. This fruit is the evidence of the Spirit-filled, sanctified life. The evidence is not, as some claim, the gifts of the Spirit called *charismata*. The fruit is one but the gifts are various. The fruit is shared by and expected from all Christians alike, while the gifts are parcelled out to various members of the body of Christ as the Holy Spirit wills (1 Cor. 12:8–11). In addition, love, which seemingly is the chief element in the fruit, being named first in Galatians 5:22 and being declared the greatest of Christian virtues in 1 Corinthians 13, is never said to be a gift but rather "the most excellent way" in which the spiritual gifts are to be used (1 Cor. 12:31). In other words, the fruit of the Spirit sets forth the manner in which those who have the gifts of prophesying, teaching, administering, helping, speaking in tongues, and the others are to utilize their gifts. For example, as Paul writes, if I speak in the tongues of men or of angels and do not have love, the fruit of the Spirit, I am just noise (1 Cor. 13:1). The Christian should use whatever gift or gifts he or she may have been given lovingly, joyfully, peacefully, patiently, kindly, and in keeping with the other fruit of the Spirit. The problem in the Corinthian church with which Paul had to deal was not their lack of the gifts of the Spirit but their lack of the graces or the fruit. In 1 Corinthians 1:4–7 Paul thanks God, among other things, for the fact that the Corinthian congregation was not lacking any spiritual gift; yet at the same time he rebukes them for their being carnal and obviously lacking the fruit of the Spirit in their lives (1 Cor. 3:1–3).

The Requirement of Human Cooperation with the Spirit. Finally, it is important to note that, as with all analogies, the comparison of natural fruit with the metaphorical fruit of the Spirit's work in individual Christians breaks down. Naturally good fruit is produced without any effort by a good tree; however, the fruit of the Spirit does not come into being that automatically. Regularly it requires effort on the Christian's part. It demands a heeding of the commands of Scripture and a cooperation with the Holy Spirit in his work in the believer's life. The declaration of the Bible, that this fruit is the production of the Holy Spirit, must be balanced with the demands found in the Bible. The declarations of the indicative mood are to be balanced with all of the exhortations of the imperative mood. All of the fruit of the Spirit are, in other biblical references, expected from and commanded of the believer. For example, the fruit of the Spirit is love and yet Christians are commanded to love God with all their heart and to love their neighbor as themselves (Matt. 22:37–39; Gal. 5:13–14). Another fruit of the Spirit is declared to be joy, and yet the individual believer is commanded to continue rejoicing always in all circumstances (Phil. 4:4; 1 Thess. 5:16). The peace of God is something the Christian is expected to enjoy (Phil. 4:7). The believer is commanded to continue living at peace with all people (Rom. 12:18) and to seek to be reconciled with those who consider themselves enemies (Matt. 5:23–24). Another facet of the fruit is goodness and yet Paul commands us to overcome evil done to us by doing good in return (Rom. 12:20–21).

Either by direct commands or by divinely approved examples, such as the self-control Paul declared was his practice as a Christian (1 Cor. 9:25–27), it is the responsibility of each Christian to yield to the Holy Spirit. In other words, one is not passive but very active in the development of the fruit of the Spirit. In fact, in Colossians 3:10–15 Paul commands Christians to put on many of these same virtues. Peter in 2 Peter 1:5–8 commands his readers to add to their faith some of the same characteristics that are called the fruit of the Spirit in Galatians 5.

Consequently it is important not only to know what the fruit of the Spirit is but diligently to attempt to make it an integral part of one's own Christian life. No one ever drifts into spiritual maturity or excellence. It demands a yielding of life to the Spirit's leading by means of the Bible (Rom. 8:14; Gal. 5:18) and this can involve, at times, a real battle. The Christian life for Paul is always a combination of the work of the Spirit of God in originating fruit and the cooperation of the will of the individual. WESLEY L. GERIG

See also FAITH; GOOD, GOODNESS; JOY; LOVE; MEEKNESS.

Bibliography. F. F. Bruce, *The Epistle to the Galatians: A Commentary on the Greek Text;* E. De Witt Burton, *A Critical and Exegetical Commentary on the Epistle to the Galatians;* R. Y. K. Fung, *The Epistle to the Galatians.*

Fulfillment. State, process, or act by which a situation comes to a complete end, whether ultimately good or bad. While fulfillment may be extended over an indefinite period of time, there are several occasions in Scripture in which a specific situation is being described, such as gestation and birth (Gen. 25:25; Job 39:1–2; Luke 1:57; 2:6), or the forty-day period of time announced by Jonah for the destruction of Nineveh (3:3), which was averted when the Ninevites repented.

The Old Testament. The concept of fulfillment is expressed chiefly by the Hebrew words *mālāᶜ*, "fulfill, accomplish, terminate," and *kālâ*, "be finished, completed." The word *qûm*, which has a wide range of meanings, also carries the sense of accomplishment in the causative form, "made to stand." The first of these terms is often used of God bringing to fruition something that he has promised, and is thus important in the context of prophetic utterances. Predictions of this kind could be fulfilled within a short period of time, as occurred when a godly man prophesied the end of the house of Eli the priest (1 Sam. 2:27–36). This dire prediction was fulfilled when Solomon removed Abiathar from the high priesthood (1 Kings 2:27), a circumstance that did not escape the notice of the author of Kings.

By contrast, a longer interval of time elapsed between Jeremiah's prophecy that Judah would be enslaved by Babylon for seventy years (25:11) and the accomplishing of that act (52:12–15). Again, the fulfillment of the process was duly recorded, this time by the Chronicler (2 Chron. 36:21). The prayer of Daniel for the restoration of the devastated Jerusalem temple was answered by the startling revelation of seventy weeks that would involve the Messiah (9:1–27).

The New Testament. The Greek vocabulary for fulfillment consists of the terms *plēroō*, "to fill," which reflects the sense of the Hebrew *mālāʾ*, and *teleō*, "to complete, bring to an end," along with their cognate forms. Because of the development of a messianic expectation over the centuries, the Jews of Jesus Christ's day were filled with the thought that the Messiah might appear at any moment to overthrow the oppressive Rome and lead the Jews to supremacy in the world. Peter, for example, espoused initially the belief that the Messiah was to be a national leader, bringing victory in battle for his enslaved people (Mark 8:32–33). Only after the resurrection did Peter gain lasting insight into the true character of Christ's messiahship.

It was the custom in the early Christian church to interpret many Old Testament passages in a typological manner. This meant that some early events, personages, and religious traditions were understood to have been foreshadowings, predictions, or "types," the significance of which would become clear when they were fulfilled in the larger context of the Christian gospel. The "type" was then contrasted with an "antitype" or counterpart, which constituted the reality of what had been prefigured. Thus the Passover lamb was the "type" or figure of Christ, our Passover sacrificed for us (1 Cor. 5:7). Similarly the Hebrew holy places of human construction, such as the wilderness tabernacle, were the types and shadows of that true abode of spirituality into which Christ, our High Priest, entered with his own blood (Heb. 8:5–6; 9:11–12).

Jesus himself gave sanction to this form of interpreting Old Testament events by describing the elevation of the serpent in the wilderness (Num. 21:8–9) as a type of symbol of his own saving work on Calvary (John 3:14–15). In the same manner Melchizedek, king of Salem, was a type of the eternal priesthood of Christ (Heb. 7:1–10). In his teachings, Jesus employed the typological approach to contrast the temporality of the wilderness manna with the permanent quality of the sustenance that he, as the living bread, could offer (John 6:32–35).

Again, the manna (Exod. 16:14–16) and the water that gushed from the rock in the wilderness (Exod. 17:6; Num. 20:11) were interpreted by Paul as depicting the sustaining Christ who was with the Lord's ancient people in their journey (1 Cor. 10:3–4). John the Baptist was the one who fulfilled Malachi's prediction of a forerunner for the Messiah (Mal. 4:5) in his preaching and his life, while Jesus in his atoning death brought to fulfillment the new covenant promised by Jeremiah (31:31–34; cf. Heb. 8:8–12; 10:16–17). In this connection it is important to notice that typology considers the various types in their historical framework and stresses their reliability accordingly.

Enough had been said to demonstrate the way in which early believers perceived a deeper level of spirituality in what could have been taken simply as ordinary historical occurrences in the Old Testament period. That they were able to do this satisfactorily, encouraged by the approach of the Master himself to typology, contrasted sharply with the attitude of most contemporary Jews toward Christ's teaching. The reason for this was that the Jews were looking for the fulfillment of messianic prophecies in terms of nationalistic and materialistic considerations. For them, the Messiah would appear as God's champion to expel the hated Roman occupation army and introduce the age when powerful nations would do homage to the Lord in Jerusalem (Zech. 8:20–23). But when Christians began to appreciate Christ's teaching that his kingdom was not of this world (John 18:36), they also perceived that the fulfillment of the predictions concerning the coming of a new covenant relationship between the believer and God constituted the beginning of a new phase of spirituality in which some messianic promises were yet to be fulfilled.

In the light of this situation it appears necessary to look more closely at the dynamics of fulfillment. Unfortunately, no matter how or when it occurs, whether as the result of prediction or of naturally occurring cycles, a process is involved that in most instances is inscrutable or at best poorly understood. This process simply could not come to completion unless it was fostered and sustained by specific forces. Even if it is plain that God was acting as the causative agent, as in creation, for example, all that can be said with certainty is that there was a consistently high quality of power and planning that guided the process in all of its phases, and that quality controls ("and God saw that it was good") were being exercised at certain intervals. As the project became more complex the creative powers were able to sustain the growth schedule required so that the various phases came into interrelated operation on time ("third day," "fourth day," etc.). When the entire process had been assessed and the final stage had been completed satisfactorily, the fulfillment received God's seal of approval—"very good" (Gen. 1:31).

To our embarrassment we know nothing about the mechanics of the creative process as such, and in any event it defies scientific definition since it is impossible to replicate it. What is apparent even to the casual observer, however, is that it was characterized by enormous power that functioned under strict control in fulfilling the purposes of God. By the time that the earth had been made ready for human habitation, God was ready to prepare *Homo sapiens* for the earth (Gen. 2:18–25). It is significant that human beings took absolutely no part whatever in this creative activity, and in the end were only passive participants in what had been fulfilled. Clearly God does not need human beings to fulfill his major creative plans, but has included them so that they will glorify him as Creator and Lord by their way of life and their personal commitment in obedience, faith, and holiness.

This relationship, however, not only draws human beings into the privileged position of participating in God's will for earth's inhabitants, but also in a more narrowly defined sense establishes them as individual messengers of God's purposes for his creation. Accordingly God chose a certain group to be his representatives, and entered into a covenant relationship with them in the expectation that they would be a priestly kingdom and a holy nation (Exod. 19:6). This group, the Israelites, was to glorify God at the level of local community living as well as in the area of international relationships.

Because they were the visible presence on earth of an invisible deity and a guarantee of his existence in human society, they functioned as his messengers, individually and corporately, to the ancient Near Eastern world. Those of God's servants who observed the covenant stipulations rigorously and obeyed God's leading were endued with his creative and sustaining power. Some of them, in fact, have gone down in history for their messages of weal or woe. In the main they were prophetic personages, although not necessarily of a major order.

The character of their activities has been much misrepresented by attempts to explain the nature and function of the title "prophet." This is actually a Greek term comprising the preposition *pro,* meaning "before" in space or time, and a noun derived from the verb *phēmi,* "to speak." An enormous amount of fruitless debate has arisen over the question of whether the prophet was a "foreteller," involving prediction, or a "forthteller," that is, the proclaimer of a message to his contemporaries without any necessarily futuristic content. What debaters should have done was to ignore the Greek term and concentrate on the meaning of the most commonly used Hebrew term, *nabîʾ*.

This word, related to the Mesopotamian *nabu* ("announce"), actually means "one called." Having established that the prophet had in fact been called to his vocation by God, a simple perusal of prophetic messages would demonstrate that those who proclaimed them normally spoke not only to their own times but also to the future as they proclaimed God's tidings. The true prophetic call placed the recipient firmly within the stream of the Holy Spirit's power (Num. 11:17, 25), which used him to point in various ways to the fulfillment of God's purposes in society.

Visions, dreams, and direct communications were the principal means by which God conveyed his will (Num. 12:5–8) to his prophetic servants. As a result, their messages carried a special dynamism which, interestingly enough, makes their ethical and spiritual pronouncements relevant for modern times. That prophecies were no idle proclamations is evidenced by the number that were fulfilled. They included unheeded warnings about the impending destruction of Near Eastern peoples who disobeyed God's laws for society. Their outworking is now merely a matter of historical record.

The most dynamic of these utterances was one that linked the old and new covenants. Proclaimed at the fall of humanity (Gen. 3:15), the promise of deliverance from evil was continued in the Abrahamic covenant (Gen. 22:18), confirmed in David's succession (2 Sam. 7:12–13), and announced as a messianic figure by Isaiah (7:14; 53:1–12), Jeremiah (23:5–6), and Malachi (3:1), among others. On the purely social level the messianic line was very nearly severed in the time of Athaliah, who usurped the throne of Judah and killed all the royal family except the young Joash (2 Kings 11:1–12). God's messianic plan was not to be thwarted, however, and in the fullness of time (Gal. 4:4) Christ, the Lord's Anointed One, was born, thus fulfilling the pledge made to Abraham. In the New Testament the fulfillment of prophecy by Christ validated the long-cherished messianic expectation, leading Paul to state that Jesus was the person in whom every one of God's promises was fulfilled with an emphatic "yes" (2 Cor. 1:20).

Some Old Testament predictions are still firmly enshrined within the stream of human history and await future fulfillment. Prominent among these are the apocalyptic pronouncements of Zechariah (14:1–9) that describe the second coming of Christ. This situation is also true of the New Testament, where the atoning work of Jesus, while bringing one era to fulfillment, has actually opened a new and wider vision of God's power working through the fellowship of believers. With the coming of the Holy Spirit (Acts 2:1–4) an unprecedented burst of divine power was unleashed upon the world, sustaining those who proclaimed the gospel initially (Acts 1:8), and assuring their successors of grace and strength to bring the mission to its proper fruition. Christians are thus part of a dynamic prophetic process which, in the Lord's good time, will culminate in the return of Jesus in glory and all that such a fulfillment of divine promise implies. Sincere discipleship demands that believers should not merely expect this event but should work actively toward its realization.

R. K. Harrison

See also Promise; Prophet, Prophetess, Prophecy.

Bibliography. F. F. Bruce, *This Is That;* C. H. Dodd, *According to the Scriptures;* P. Fairbairn, *Typology of Scripture;* W. G. Scroggie, *Prophecy and History.*

Fullness. While the word "fullness" occurs several times in the Old Testament, only one occurrence—Deuteronomy 33:16—seems to have theological significance. In Deuteronomy 33:16–17, Moses blesses the tribe of Joseph. As he describes the various facets of God's blessing on Joseph, he moves from material blessing to the favor of God. Moses' reference to the "best gifts of the earth and its fullness" may anticipate spiritual blessings such as peace and joy, which come from God himself.

The New Testament uses the word "fullness" (*plerōma*) seventeen times. The four occurrences in Matthew and Mark (Matt. 9:16; Mark 2:21; 6:43; 8:20) are not theologically significant. The use of the term in John 1:16, however, is. There John the Baptist speaks of the One who comes after him as blessing "from the fullness of his grace."

The remaining twelve uses of the term all occur in Paul's writings (in 1 Corinthians, Romans, Colossians, and Ephesians). The statement in 1 Corinthians 10:26 is actually a quotation of Psalm 24:1. Like many Old Testament references, it remains on the material level. The four occurrences in Romans, however, are highly theological.

In Romans 11, Paul discusses the fate of the nation of Israel, which has rejected its Messiah. Beginning in verse 11, Paul explains God's purpose in Israel's unbelief. He says that God's plan is to use Israel's unbelief to bring about the salvation of the Gentiles, which in turn will provoke Israel to faith in their own Messiah. Then in verse 12, he contrasts the results of Israel's transgression/defeat for the world with the results of their "fullness" for the world. Paul does not spell out the results here, but verse 15 speaks of "life from the dead." This phrase has been interpreted to mean either an extensive turning to faith in Christ by the Gentiles or the actual resurrection in conjunction with the return of Christ. But it seems clear that in this context, "fullness" refers to an extensive acceptance of Jesus as the Messiah by the nation of Israel. The illustration of the olive tree in verses 17–24 makes the point that God is able to regraft the natural branches (unbelieving Israelites) back into their own olive tree (salvation brought about through Israel's Messiah).

The conclusion of Paul's treatment of Israel's unbelief is presented in 11:25–32. In verse 26 he clearly states that through God's plan the nation of Israel will be saved, brought to faith in Jesus. Israel's temporary unbelief will last only until the "fullness" of the Gentiles comes about (v. 25). Although the meaning of this entire passage is intensely debated, this verse seems to refer to the complete number of the elect among the Gentiles who must be saved before the conversion of Israel and the coming of Christ.

In Romans 13:10, Paul asserts that the "fullness" or complete purpose of the law is love. He speaks of himself in 15:29 as coming to the church at Rome in the "fullness of the blessing of Christ." Both are straightforward statements about the completeness of abundance that the word "fullness" implies.

To the church at Colossae, which was struggling against heretical teachings that detracted from the person of Christ, Paul stresses that all the fullness of God dwells in Christ (1:19; 2:9).

This usage is also highly theological and intends to assert the deity of Christ.

In Ephesians, Paul speaks of the times reaching their fulfillment (lit. the "fullness of the times"). This eschatological statement affirms that human history will be brought to its God-ordained purpose in Christ the head. Ephesians 1:23 has been understood in two different ways. "Fullness" may be viewed as going with Christ's body, in which case it would speak of the importance of the church to Christ. It is his completeness, and in some way manifests Christ's presence on earth. "Fullness" might also be viewed as referring back to Christ. In this case it would affirm that Christ is the fullness or completeness of God who fills everything.

In Ephesians 3:19 Paul expresses his prayer for the Ephesian believers, that they may be strengthened and come to understand Christ's love for them. He then states that this love of Christ is to be filled with the "fullness" of God. Although Paul does not spell out his intent here, it seems that as the believer is controlled by Christ's love, that person is indwelt by God's presence or "fullness." Later in the letter, Paul describes the practical qualities that God desires in the body of Christ: unity and maturity. Christ causes the body to be built up until each believer attains to the "fullness" of the perfection that is found in Christ (4:13). HOBERT K. FARRELL

Bibliography. F. Foulkes, *Ephesians;* L. Morris, *The Epistle to the Romans;* N. T. Wright, *Colossians and Philemon.*

Fullness of Time. Well-known phrase from Galatians 4:4 that conveys Paul's understanding of salvation.

The churches of Galatia were the fruit of Paul's first missionary journey (Acts 13–14). But they were almost immediately troubled by people (the Judaizers) who distorted the gospel that Paul had proclaimed.

In his letter to the churches of Galatia, Paul defends the gospel and his ministry. He first asserts the divine origin of the gospel, and backs up that origin from his own life and experience (Gal. 1–2). In Galatians 3–4, he then goes on to explain the faith-nature of the gospel.

Galatians 3:8 serves as the framework for 4:4. Paul notes that Scripture foresaw God's justification of the Gentiles based on the Old Testament promise to bless the nations through Abraham (Gen. 18:18). Paul develops this line of thought, concluding that we receive the promise of the Spirit through faith (3:14). The Galatians' reception of the Spirit, then, is the fulfillment of God's promise to Abraham.

The climax of the letter is in 3:23–4:7. Before faith, we were under the law awaiting the coming of faith (3:23). It is the justification of faith (3:24) that was promised to Abraham and anticipated throughout history that has now come in the fullness of time. The result is that we are all children of God through faith, the actual seed of Abraham and heirs of the promise (3:26–27). After an illustrative analogy about a minor son come of age (4:1–2), Paul boldly declares that we too were once "minors," but that in the "fullness of time" God sent his Son to redeem us and to make us his sons (4:3–5). By talking about a "time that had fully come," Paul focuses on the coming of Christ and his bestowal of the Spirit in contrast to the former period of the law, which only pointed forward to Christ.

God planned the redemption of humankind. At just the right time, God sent his Son into the world. The time of the incarnation, crucifixion, and resurrection is the time of completeness—a time when God fulfilled the promises of the Old Testament. This redemption will, of course, be ultimately completed at the second coming of Christ. The salvation that Jesus inaugurated in the church at his first coming will then be consummated for all the world to see.

HOBERT K. FARRELL

See also AGE, AGES; DAY OF THE LORD, GOD, CHRIST; GALATIANS, THEOLOGY OF.

Bibliography. R. A. Cole, *Galatians;* R. Y. K. Fung, *Galatians.*

Funeral. In ancient Israel burial occurred soon after death. In a hot climate, internment took place as quickly as possible after a person had expired (Deut. 21:23). For this reason rules about dealing with corpses arose limiting what could take place (Num. 19:11–22; 21:1–4). The short period of time between death and burial also placed limitations on ancient Israelite funerals.

Some customs were forbidden, such as self-mutilation (Lev. 19:28; 21:5; Deut. 14:1). In the Baal epic, El cuts deep gashes in his chest because Baal is in death's domain (cf. 1 Kings 18:28). In the Bible the body is part of the image of God (Gen. 9:6). No disfigured person could approach God because this was inconsistent with his holiness (Lev. 21:17–23).

Cremation was considered an outrage reserved for criminals (Gen. 38:24; Lev. 20:14; 21:9). In Amos 2:1 the cremation of the king of Edom is classed as a heinous war crime. The burning of the bodies of Saul and Jonathan may have been an unusual local custom (1 Sam. 31:12).

Rites observed at the death of Abner (2 Sam. 3:31–36) included public mourning, tearing of clothes, and donning of sackcloth. There was a solemn procession followed by the king himself. At the grave there was a great deal of weeping and the king chanted a lament. On the same day all the people came "to console David with food" (v. 35, NEB). David's refusal of this food is impressive.

In the Old Testament a funeral meal may have been served after burial, designed to console family members (Jer. 16:5–9; Amos 6:4–7). Amos denounces the lavish excesses of such feasting and the fact that the national demise has been ignored (6:6). Jeremiah is told by God that no consolation will be given to Judah (Jer. 16:5–9). Perhaps the inappropriateness of such funerary gaiety is hinted at when the preacher states that it is better to go to the house of mourning than to the house of feasting (Eccles. 7:2).

In biblical days mourning was a fine art. One needed a teacher to learn such a profession (Jer. 9:20). Funeral songs were frequently composed and published in collections (2 Sam. 1:19–27; 3:33–34; 2 Chron. 35:25). Curiously, the only two dirges written for individuals are secular in content (2 Sam. 1:19–27; 3:33–34).

Biblical prophets borrowed this lament genre to add realism to their predictions of doom. They were so certain about them that they sang funeral songs in advance (Jer. 9:9–11, 16–21; Ezek. 19:1–14; Amos 5:1–2). Amos predicted that in the ensuing judgment so much mourning would need to be done that laypeople would have to be enlisted to help the professionals (Amos 5:16–17). At times the prophet reversed his style by forbidding mourning rites. Ezekiel was forbidden to carry out such practices for his own wife (24:16–19). This was done to show that God would have no compassion when Jerusalem fell.

The announcement that people would not have a proper burial served to emphasize the serious nature of their sins. For his opulence and lack of sensitivity to poor workers, Jehoiakim's body was to be thrown outside the gates like a donkey's (Jer. 22:19). The seven months needed for burying of Gog and Magog (Ezek. 39:12) was a strong contrast to the usual speedy burial. In mocking parody to the funeral meal, vultures will feed on their corpses (Ezek. 39:4). In the New Testament an angel even appears to invite these creatures to this "funeral banquet" (Rev. 19:17–18).

Jesus compared some in his audience to uncooperative, unresponsive children who will not join in a funeral game (Matt. 11:17). He stopped the funeral procession at Nain by touching the bier. Thereby he showed that the uncleanness of death could not taint him. By restoring the son to his mother, he showed that the kingdom of God had broken through into human history (Luke 7:11–16). In ejecting the mourners and musicians at the death of Jarius's daughter he prefigured a day when grief would be no more (Matt. 9:23–25).

PAUL FERGUSON

See also BURIAL; DEATH.

Bibliography. W. Coleman, *Today's Handbook of Bible Times and Customs;* R. de Vaux, *Ancient Israel,* vol. 1; P. King, *Amos, Hosea, Micah—An Archaeological Commentary;* M. Pope, *Ugarit in Retrospect.*

Furnace of Fire. *See* FIRE.

Gg

Galatians, Theology of. More than any other book in the New Testament, including perhaps even Romans, Paul's letter to the Galatians has been the source of theological teaching for the church in the midst of its deepest crises. Already in the original context of the letter, the Judaizing heresy threatened to undermine the work of the gospel among the Gentile churches and thus destroy the unity of God's people. In the second century, as the Christian church struggled with the Marcionite heresy, Galatians played a central role in the controversy. Much later, at the time of the Reformation in the sixteenth century, the Protestant leaders identified in this letter the key to the fundamental theological problems facing them. Just what is the teaching of Paul's letter to the Galatians?

If we wish to answer that question accurately, we must not dissociate the theology of the letter from the historical setting in which it was written. All of Paul's letters were written to deal with specific problems, but in the case of Galatians the situation was especially urgent. The crisis was so great that Paul begins the letter, not with the kind of thanksgiving he normally used, but with an expression of amazement that the churches of Galatia had been persuaded by certain teachers to follow a false gospel (1:6). These teachers argued that Gentile Christians, if they wanted to share in Abraham's blessing, must be circumcised and submit themselves to the Old Testament Law. Because this requirement contradicted the message Paul preached, the false teachers also claimed that Paul did not have proper authority.

Traditionally, interpreters have divided the letter into three sections. The first section (chaps. 1–2), in which Paul defends his authority, is historical in character; the second is theological (chap. 3–4); and the final two chapters are practical or hortatory. While this division is useful, it may give the wrong impression, as though chapters 1–2 and 5–6 were not theological (or as though the first four chapters were not practical!). In fact this epistle is forcefully theological from beginning to end. Already in the salutation, which is longer than usual, Paul addresses the major issues, such as the divine origin of his apostleship and the redeeming character of Christ's work. The rest of chapters 1 and 2, true, are written in the form of a narrative, but even this section is fundamentally concerened with "the truth of the gospel" (2:5): the reason Paul must defend his apostleship is that the integrity of the Christian message is at stake. Moreover, the practical or ethical thrust of chapters 5–6 cannot be dissociated from the theological questions in view. In the past, scholars have tended to view Paul's exhortations in this letter as more or less "tacked on," but recent studies have demonstrated that such a perspective is inadequate.

The thesis of chapters 1–2—but in a general sense also of the letter as a whole—is stated in 1:11–12: the message the Galatians heard from Paul has a divine, not a human, origin. This point is set forth very emphatically in verses 15–16. Just as God had chosen Jeremiah even before his birth (Jer. 1:5), so Paul's ministry and message were the result of divine initiative and grace. Neither Paul's pre-Christian experience (vv. 13–14) nor his first years as a Christian (vv. 17–24) can explain the origin of his gospel. Moreover, it was not true—as his opponents probably claimed—that the integrity of his preaching had been compromised on two specific occasions—his consultation with the leaders of the Jerusalem church (2:1–10) and his confrontation with Peter in Antioch (2:11–14).

This last incident is of special significance, because it leads Paul to address the theological issue in a very explicit way (2:15–21). The moment Peter decided to stop having meal-fellowship with the Gentile Christians, he was in fact suggesting that they could not be fully accepted into God's people without first becoming Jewish. But such a view would contradict the very faith that Peter himself proclaimed. When Peter put his faith in Christ, he was acknowledging that even Jewish people (who were not considered "sinners" in the same way the Gentiles were) could not expect to be justified by fulfilling the requirements of the Mosaic Law. In other words, by seeking salvation in Christ, Peter was recognizing that he was as needy a sinner as the Gentiles were. Therfore, it was quite proper to break down the barriers of Jewish ceremonies and to eat with the Gentiles.

But now, afraid of what some Jews might think, Peter had decided to go back to his earlier and stricter Jewish conduct (2:12). By breaking meal-fellowship with the Gentiles, Paul charged, Peter was in effect building up what he had already torn down, and that made him a transgressor of the law (2:18; Paul says "I" perhaps to be polite, but Peter clearly is in view). How can Paul make such a claim? Because the Law itself, he says, leads people to die to the Law (2:19)—a remarkable and powerful statement that he develops in 3:19–24. This death, however, results in true life through Jesus Christ. The concluding statement (2:21) reveals Paul's true motivation: if our actions indicate that justification can be reached by the observance of the Law, then Christ's death must have been unnecessary and the doctrine of grace is subverted.

We get a new insight into the nature of the Galatian problem in the first few verses of chapter 3. There Paul describes the change in behavior among the Christians of Galatia by suggesting that, although they had begun in the power of the Spirit are now seeking to complete their salvation by means of the flesh. This contrast between Spirit and flesh is very important for Paul, especially in this letter. The word "flesh" is appropriate because of the Judaizers' emphasis on circumcision (cf. 6:12–13), but it also suggests the weakness of human nature and thus our inability to please God (cf. Rom. 8:7). At the end of chapter 4 Paul uses the same two terms to contrast the birth of Ishmael (by natural human abilities) with that of Isaac (by the supernatural power of the spirit in fulfillment of the promise). Accordingly, the term "flesh" becomes shorthand to describe the character of the present evil world (a phrase used in 1:4), that is, everything that is opposite the world to come, which in turn is represented by the Spirit.

The world of the Spirit, however, is a world of faith, not of works of the law. If the Galatians really want to share in the Abrahamic inheritance—if they really want to be regarded as Abraham's children—they must live by faith as Abraham did (3:6–7, 29). Perhaps the Judaizers claimed that Paul created a contradition between the Abrahamic promise and the Mosic Law. In fact, says the apostle, it is the Judaizers who oppose these two principles. When God gave the Law four centuries after Abraham, he could not have intended that Law to alter the promise. But if the Judiazers were right, that is, if the inheritance could be received by the works of the Law, then the Law would be against the promise, which can only be had by faith (3:12–21).

No, the real purpose of the Law was temporary: to function as a guardian or jailor, condemning the sin of the Israelites, and thus preparing the way for Christ. Once Christ comes, the new age of faith breaks in and we do not need a guardian. It is union with Christ by faith that makes us not merely children of Abraham, but also children of God. All of this means that, so far as our standing with God is concerened, there are no differences among God's children: we are all one in Christ (3:22–28; 4:4–7).

In the course of his argument, Paul sets up a sharp distinction between two modes of existence, represented by various concepts. Reflecting on these contrasts provides significant insights into Paul's theology.

flesh	Spirit
works of the law	faith, promise
curse	blessing, inheritance
slavery	freedom, sonship
sin and death	justification and life
Hagar the slave woman	[Sarah] the free woman
Sinai and present Jerusalem	Jerusalem from above
Ishmael	Isaac
persecutor	persecuted
cast away	heir
being under law	being led by the Spirit
works of the flesh	fruit of the Spirit

The last two sets of items occur in the hortatory section, particularly in 5:13–26. As already suggested, the practical concerns of the epistle are woven into its theological message. Paul's concern with the behavior of the Galatian Christians, that is, must not be viewed as an ethical question more or less unrelated to the doctrinal conflict they were facing. It may be that the emphasis on Law-keeping, which focused on ceremonial regulations, ironically made them insensitive to serious moral issues. Or perhaps they were simply confused about proper guidelines for godly conduct and the means to sanctification.

Whatever the precise circumstances behind the Galatians' problem, Paul's answer suggests that the Law does indeed represent accurately God's will for them (5:14); however, the Law gives no power to fulfill the divine will (as suggested by 5:18; cf. 3:21 and Rom. 8:3; elsewhere Paul points out that the Law actually abets sin, Rom. 7:7–13; 1 Cor. 15:56). The only way to conquer the impulses of the flesh is to "walk" in the Spirit, to be led by the Spirit, to bear the fruit of the Spirit, to "keep in step" with the Spirit (5:16, 18, 22, 25). This emphasis on the power of the Spirit for sanctification raises the possibility that back in 3:3 Paul was already thinking about the ethical conduct of the Galatians. Their moral lives as much as their submission to ceremonial rules indicated a serious lapse in their relationship with God.

Central in this discussion is 5:6, one of the most important statements in all of Paul's letters: "For in Christ Jesus neither circumcision nor uncircumcision has any value. The only thing that counts is faith expressing itself through love." The phrase "expressing itself" translates the Greek verb *energeō,* "to work, be effective." It is evident that in opposing faith to the works of the law, the apostle does not view faith as a passive idea. On the contrary, true faith *is at work* through love. A comparison of this verse with 6:15 and 1 Cor. 7:19 suggests that, in Paul's theology, the principle of a working faith corresponds to the concept of the "new creation" and to the responsibility of "keeping the commadments of God." Because the leading of the Spirit produces conduct that the Law does not condemn (5:23), by implication those who live by the Spirit are the ones who truly fulfill the Law (cf. also 6:2 and Rom. 8:4).

For some scholars, such an emphasis in this part of Galatians does not cohere with Paul's negative statements about the Law in the earlier sections of the letter. What needs to be recognized, however, is that the discussion in chapter 3 was not intended to provide a comprehensive essay on "the Pauline theology of the Law" (several aspects of that theology, not covered at all in Galatians, do surface in some of the other letters). The controversy that motivated Paul to write Galatians focused specifically on the relationship between the Law and justification. While Paul affirms that the believer *is justified apart from the Law*, he nowhere suggests that we are therefore free to break that Law. If anything, the gospel confirms the Law (cf. Gal. 3:21 with Rom. 3:31).

An additional question has been raised by recent scholarship. During the second half of the twentieth century, researchers have gained a fresh understanding of the positive qualities in Jewish theology at the time of the New Testament. It is clear, for example, that much rabbinic teaching appreciated the biblical emphasis on divine grace and that the Pharisees did not necessarily have a crass view of "works righteousness." On that basis, some theologians have argued that Protestant theology was misguided by Luther's own conversion experience. The medieval doctrine of human merit, we are told, was read into ancient Judaism and that affected our interpretation of Paul. According to this new approach, Paul did not really oppose the concepts of faith and Law-obedience. What he argued against in Galatians and elsewhere was the tendency to take the distinguishing marks of Judaism (circumcision, food laws, etc.) and use them to exclude Gentiles from God's purposes.

Undoubtedly, the Jewish-Gentile question was the fundamental issue facing early Christianity, and it may well be that the sixteenth-century Reformers did not sufficiently appreciate that factor as they sought to interpret Galatians. On the other hand, it would be a grave mistake to assume that the insights of the Protestant Reformation are incompatible with a recognition of such a factor. To say that Paul was concerened with nationalistic pride and not with personal self-righteousness is to fall into a false dichotomy (as Phil. 3:3–9 plainly indicates). The Judaizers who were troubling the Galatian churches indeed focused on Jewish ethnic-religious identity as the means of enjoying the divine blessings. But because such an identity is something that can be achieved by personal effort (the "flesh"), the attempt to gain it reflects not confidence in God (faith) but confidence in one's own righteousness.

Today, no less than in the first century, Paul's letter to the Galatians reminds believers about the inseparability of theology and life. By setting forth in clearest terms what is "the truth of the gospel," the apostle was able, under divine direction, to preserve the glorious doctrine of salvation by grace. MOISÉS SILVA

Bibliography. F. F. Bruce, *Commentary on Galations;* J.D.G. Dunn, *Jesus, Paul and the Law;* D. Guthrie, *Galatians;* W. Neil, *The Letter of Paul to the Galatians;* J. R. W. Stott, *The Message of Galatians.*

Gehenna. *See* HELL

Genesis, Theology of. The theology of Genesis can be studied on three levels. The first level of study focuses on its message in and of itself. This is the attempt to determine what the meaning of the book is apart from its place in the larger canon of Scripture, and particularly relates to the question of what it might have meant to its original readers. The second level of study concerns the theology of Genesis within the Old Testament canon. This relates to how the rest of the Old Testament looks back to Genesis and draws upon its theology. The third level of study looks at the theology of Genesis from the New Testament perspective. This relates to how Genesis feeds into the Christian faith.

The first level involves one's critical outlook more than the other two. Scholars who in some fashion accept the documentary hypothesis of Julius Wellhausen are less concerned with the theology of Genesis as a whole than the respective theologies of J, E, D, and P. Other scholars, such as those who follow the tradition criticism of Martin Noth, believe that Genesis is the result of legends and traditions that grew and underwent transformation throughout the centuries of Israel's history. These scholars, too, tend to find diverse messages in the various streams of tradition they claim to uncover and rarely concern themselves with the book as a whole. Some critics have attempted to bridge the gap between critical theory and biblical theology with "canon criticism" (following especially Brevard Childs) and thus have a theology of the whole book of Genesis without abandoning the reigning critical theories. Even so, it is fair to say that those who hold to the view that Genesis is a late work (ca. 450 B.C.) and is the result of competing traditions or schools either have great difficulty describing a theology of Genesis or simply do not consider the concept meaningful.

Scholars who essentially hold to Mosaic authorship contend for a unified message for the book since they believe that it has a unified background and purpose. It is not enough, however, simply to say that Moses wrote Genesis to be in a position to grasp its message. Since the stories in Genesis presumably circulated among the Israelites in Egypt log before Moses, one must ask what significance the stories would have had to them. Another question is how these stories were put together into a coherent package as the Book of Genesis. Assuming that Moses did receive these stories and gave them coherent form, much as Luke did with the stories of Jesus (Luke 1:1–4), one can work through the structure of Genesis to its message for the earliest Israelite community.

The structure of Genesis parallels an ancient Near Eastern model in which there is a prologue, three threats to an ancestor or community of ancestors, and a concluding resolution. A story in this pattern describes how the community has come through a series of dangers in the persons of the ancestors. On the one hand, it is a story of triumph but, on the other hand, it can be rather bleak since the "concluding resolution" tends to be semitragic in this pattern. The main purpose of this kind of story is to tell the community of descendants how they came to be in the situation in which they now find themselves. Genesis has the following structure:

Prologue	Primeval History	1:1–11:26
Transition	Genealogy	11:27–32
Threat	The Abraham Cycle	12:1–25:11
Transition	Genealogy	24:12–18
Threat	The Jacob Cycle	25:19–35:22b
Transition	Genealogy	35:22c–36:40
Threat	The Joseph Cycle	37:1–46:7
Transition	Genealogy	46:8–27
Resolution	Settlement in Egypt	46:28–50:26

The "Primeval History" (Gen. 1:1–11:26) sets the stage for the whole of the book. It tells how humanity began in paradise and yet lost its hold on the tree of life through disobedience. It explains how the world we live in came to be. This concerns not only the creation of the physical universe and living things, but also the origin of both human evil and of the diverse, competing nations of the present world order. This sets the stage for the emergence of Israel among the nations.

Beginning in Genesis 12, the text focuses on the ancestors of Israel. Although the ancestors are Abraham, Isaac, Jacob, and the twelve, the literary narrative concentrates on Abraham, Jacob, and Joseph. This is because each of these men must leave his home to face diverse dangers in an alien, hostile world, whereas Isaac stays in the relative security of his family and the land of his birth throughout his life. Each of the three major characters wanders among strange and sometimes hostile peoples. We can well imagine how the earliest Israelite audience may have heard this story with rapt attention as the ancestor (and by extension his descendants) is placed in mortal danger. The tension is resolved with the welcome of Jacob into Egypt. The young nation comes into a place of nurture and refuge. Even though Egypt is a haven, however, it is still alien, and the Israelites are in a land not their own. Hence the story ends on a bleak note with Joseph, their sponsor and protector, placed in a coffin.

If one wishes to determine the theology of Genesis, one must take into account this narrative framework. And theology, particularly the theology of divine guidance and providence, is at the heart of the narrative. It is a divine call that first takes Abraham away from his homes in Ur and Haran to Canaan (12:1–5). By divine intervention Abraham is repeatedly delivered and even prospers, as in his sojourn to Egypt (12:10–20). Jacob is tricked into marrying Leah, sister of his beloved Rachel, and Rachel is for some time barren. Out of this situation comes the twelve sons who become twelve tribes (29:15–30:23). Joseph is first cruelly sold into slavery by his brothers and then wrongly accused of rape by his master's wife, but through this series of cruel circumstances, he rises to the summit of power in the Egyptian empire (chaps. 37–41). Joseph aptly describes the providential nature of his story: "Even though you intended to harm me, God intended it for good, in order to preserve a numerous people, as he is doing today" (50:20 NRSV). For the earliest audience, the story of Genesis would have been the story of how they, by the providence of God, came to find themselves in the land of Egypt. It would also tell them that although Egypt was not their land they were there legitimately since they had been welcomed by Pharaoh himself (47:7–12).

Genesis also contains a statement of hope for Israel in Egypt so profound that it may almost be called gospel. This "gospel" is built around Abraham. The relevant texts here are 12:1–9; 15:1–21; 17:1–27; and 22:1–19. In the first text (12:1–9), Abraham receives the command to abandon his homeland with the promise that his offspring will be a great nation. He obeys, goes to Canaan, and there builds altars to Yahweh his God. In the second text (15:1–21), God makes a covenant with Abraham. God identifies himself, then rejects the suggestion that Eliezer of Damascus might be Abraham's heir, and promises Abraham many descendants and the land of Canaan. Abraham believes, offers a sacrifice, and hears a prophecy concerning his offspring of dark days of slavery followed by the possession of the promised land. The third text (17:1–27) introduces circumcision as the sign of the covenant. God again identifies himself to Abraham and again promises many offspring and the possession of Canaan. He rejects the suggestion that Ishmael may be the heir, and demands that Abraham and all his male descendants undergo circumcision as the sign of the covenant. Abraham obeys. The fourth text (22:1–19), like the first, begins with God commanding Abraham to leave his home, only this time it is to take his son up a mountain and sacrifice him to God. Abraham obeys, only he is prevented from carrying out the sacrifice by the angel of the Lord and sacrifices a ram instead. Having passed this greatest of tests, he is again promised the land and many offspring.

The theological importance of these narratives to early Israel, particularly Israel in Egypt, can hardly be missed. They owed their very existence to the divine promise of the birth of a son, a promise that was fulfilled by miracle long after any natural hope for a son was dead. Through these stories the Israelites learned that they were heirs of a covenant between Yahweh and Abraham. They also learned of the origin and meaning of the covenant sign of circumcision, a sign that for Israel had the same importance as does baptism and communion for the church. They also saw, vividly portrayed in the life of Abraham, the importance of faith and obedience to Yahweh. Finally, for Israel in Egypt, this story had a kind of eschatology in the promise that they would one day inherit the land of Canaan.

When one investigates how the rest of the Old Testament uses Genesis, one is struck by how little direct reflection on that book exists. Most of these are brief references to the promises given "to Abraham, to Isaac, and to Jacob" (e.g., Exod. 3:15–16; 4:5; 6:8; Lev. 26:42; Deut. 6:10; 30:20; Josh. 24:2; 2 Kings 13:23; 2 Chron. 20:7; Neh. 9:7–8). Sodom is sometimes cited as a paradigm of evil and divine judgment (e.g., Deut. 29:23; Isa. 1:9–10; Jer. 23:14; 49:18; Ezek. 16:46–56; Amos 4:11; Zeph. 2:9). Psalm 105:9–23 briefly recounts the story of Genesis with emphasis on the Joseph narrative. Theological reflection on Genesis occurs in the Book of Ecclesiastes, which includes meditations on the human condition after the fall. Allusions to Genesis tend to be rather veiled here, however, as in the refrain that everything is "meaningless" (*hebel*, 1:2, which is also "Abel," the name of Adam and Eve's murdered son). Poetic and wisdom texts also reflect on the doctrine of creation.

The limited nature of theological reflection on Genesis in the rest of the Old Testament is meaningful, however, as it points again to the fact that the message of Genesis was originally a message for Israel in Egypt. It told that community who they were, why they were there, and what future God had promised to them. After the conquest of Canaan it is not Genesis but the exodus event that stands at the center of Israelite theology.

The New Testament and subsequent Christian theology deals with Genesis more directly. First and foremost, Christ is regarded as descended from Abraham and as the fulfillment of all the promises (Matt. 1:1–2; cf. Luke 24:27). Although the New Testament itself is not explicit in tracing Christ through all the related passages in Genesis, Christian interpreters have regarded Christ as the true "seed of the woman" who would fight against the serpent (Gen. 3:15). The line of the promise was narrowed to the line of Seth (Gen. 5), Shem (9:26–27), Abraham (12:1–3), Isaac (26:2–5), Jacob (28:10–17), and Judah (49:10). Genesis tells of the fall into sin but also immediately begins the story of redemption through the promised son.

Stephen, in his Acts 7 speech, briefly recounts the story of Genesis (vv. 2–16) with emphasis on how God overruled the jealousy of Joseph's brothers in order to fulfill the promises. He implies that God in the same way used the sin of the Jews to bring about redemption through Jesus' crucifixion.

Paul draws upon Genesis at several points. His case for justification by grace through faith to a great degree rests upon the story of Abraham and in particular on Genesis 15:6, which records that Abraham believed God and that God reckoned his faith as righteousness. In Romans 4:1–12, Paul argues that this can only be an act of grace on God's part and is not a matter of works or merit. He further observes that since this act of justification occurred prior to circumcision, it demonstrates that Gentiles do not need to receive circumcision in order to enter the company of the redeemed. Similarly, in Galatians 3:6–18, he cites Genesis 15:6 to establish that justification is not by works, and further argues that the promise is not nullified by the law that came 430 years later.

Paul also sees the miraculous birth of Isaac as a type of grace through faith. In Romans 4:18–25 he compares the faith of Abraham in the promised son to the faith of Christians in Jesus and the resurrection. In Galatians 4:21–31, the miraculous birth of Isaac contrasts with the natural birth of Ishmael, and the two are types respectively of justification by grace and by the law. James, by contrast, emphasizes the obedience of Abraham in offering up his son Isaac for sacrifice (2:21).

Paul also extracts theological lessons from the story of the fall. In Romans 5:12–21, he observes that through the sin of one man, Adam, death and sin spread to all humanity, and that in the same way the obedience of one man, Jesus, provided justification and life for all. In the same fashion, he develops the concept of the first and second Adam in 1 Corinthians 15. As the first brought death to humanity, the second opened the way to eternal life (vv. 21–22, 45). Taking Genesis 3 in a completely different direction, he also uses it to help define the role and duty of Christian women in 1 Timothy 2:9–15.

Hebrews uses Genesis 14:17–20 to demonstrate the supremacy of Christ's priesthood (the order of Melchizedek) to that of the Levites, since Levi was in effect in the loins of Abraham when he gave the tithe to Melchizedek (7:1–10). On a less complex level, Hebrews also refers to Abel, Enoch, Noah, Abraham, Isaac, Jacob, and Joseph as examples of persevering faith (11:4–22). Finally, Revelation closes the canon by looking back to the early chapters of Genesis. It proclaims the victory of Christ over the serpent (20:2) and free access to the tree of life for the redeemed (22:2).

Duane A. Garrett

See also Abraham; Adam; Create, Creation; Eve; Fall, the; Flood, the.

Bibliography. W. Brueggemann and H. W. Wolff, *The Vitality of Old Testament Traditions;* B. Childs, *Introduction to the Old Testament as Scripture;* D. A. Garrett, *Rethinking Genesis;* D. Kidner, *Genesis;* G. Wenham, *Genesis 1–15;* C. Westermann, *Genesis 1–11.*

Gentiles. *See* Nations, the.

Gentleness. Sensitivity of disposition and kindness of behavior, founded on strength and prompted by love.

The Old Testament. Gentleness is suggested by the waters of a stream (Isa. 8:6) or by wine flowing over lips and teeth (Song of Sol. 7:9). It stands in contrast to baseness (Deut. 28:54, 56), harshness (2 Sam. 18:5), and wildness (Job 41:3). Gentle words wield great power (Prov. 15:1; 25:15). Job's counsels were well received, because he spoke them gently (Job 29:22). Gentleness evidences itself in a willingness to yield, reminiscent of a lamb being led to slaughter (Jer. 11:19; cf. Isa. 53:7). The supreme exemplar of gentleness is Israel's God. He cares tenderly for the flock under his care, and "gently leads those that have young" (Isa. 40:11). He discloses himself not just in wind and earthquake and fire, but in "a gentle whisper" (1 Kings 19:11–13). His consolations are spoken gently (Job 15:11). As Yahweh's representative, the messianic king comes in humility and gentleness (Zech. 9:9).

The New Testament. That king, now come in the flesh, is "gentle and humble in heart" (Matt. 11:29). In accord with the prophecy, he enters Jerusalem in gentleness and lowliness (Matt. 21:5). Paul appeals to believers "by the meekness and gentleness of Christ" (2 Cor. 10:1). By his Spirit, Christ cultivates the same quality in his people (Gal. 5:23). Following Jesus' example, Paul treats his people gently, "like a mother caring for her little children" (1 Thess. 2:7). He comes to them not "with a whip [but] in love and with a gentle spirit" (1 Cor. 4:21). Church leaders are admonished to be "not violent but gentle" toward persons under their care (1 Tim. 3:3); it is a quality they are avidly to pursue (1 Tim. 6:11). Knowing themselves to be subject to weakness, they can more readily deal gently with the ignorant and the erring. Believers ensnared by sin must be restored gently (Gal. 6:1). A witness to Christian truth is the more effective for being made "with gentleness and respect," especially toward a hostile or an unbelieving listener (2 Tim. 2:25; 1 Peter 3:15). The qualities to which gentleness is joined elucidate its setting and character. Wives should seek "the unfading beauty of a gentle and quiet spirit" (1 Peter 3:4). "Be completely humble and gentle; be patient, bearing with one another in love," exhorts Paul (Eph. 4:2). Let believers clothe themselves "with compassion, kindness, humility, gentleness and patience" (Col. 3:12). "The fruit of the Spirit is love, joy, peace, patience, kindness, goodness, faithfulness, gentleness and self-control" (Gal. 5:22–23), a cluster of qualities each of which reinforces and finds expression in the others.

J. Knox Chamblin

See also Fruit of the Spirit.

Bibliography. W. Barclay, *New Testament Words,* pp. 94–96, 240–42; W. Bauder, *NIDNTT,* 2:256–64; H. Preisker, *TDNT,* 2:588–90; F. Hauck and S. Schulz, *TDNT,* 6:645–51.

Gift. In Old Testament times a gift was customarily given for the price of a bride (Gen. 34:12). The gifts of all the wave offerings of the Israelites were given by God to the priests and their families (Num. 18:11). Fathers gave gifts to sons before sending them away (Gen. 25:6); sons would receive inheritances from their fathers (2 Chron. 21:3). Gifts were often given to the poor. Gifts were sometimes spiritual in orientation: gifts would be given to God (Exod. 28:38) or for service by the Levites and priests (Num. 18:6, 9).

Gifts can be used to gain friends (Prov. 19:6) or influence (Prov. 18:16). God gives gifts to people so that they can enjoy life (Eccles. 3:13). Some people boast of gifts, and then never give them (Prov. 25:14).

In the New Testament a gift was given by the priest as an offering to God (Heb. 5:1). The magi presented gifts to the infant Jesus (Matt. 2:11). God gave the gift of redemption to humankind (Eph. 2:8).

God's righteousness is a gift (Rom. 5:17); God has provided for us an "indescribable" gift (2 Cor. 9:15). Paul talks about the gifts of the Spirit (1 Cor. 12). Those who have tasted the heavenly gift have been enlightened (Heb. 6:4). Paul is a servant of the gospel by the gift of God's grace (Eph. 3:7).

In general, in Scripture the word "gift" has three senses: gifts men give to men; sacrificial offerings presented to God; and gifts God gives to men, especially in connection with salvation, righteousness, and his grace.

LOUIS GOLDBERG

See also OFFERINGS AND SACRIFICES.

Bibliography. F. F. Bruce, *ISBE,* 2:395–96; F. Buchsel, *TDNT,* 2:860–66; D. G. Burke, *ISBE,* 2:465–67; W. Kaiser, *TWOT,* 2:600–602; G. Thompson and W. A. Elwell, *EDT,* pp. 1042–46; W. White, Jr., *ZPEB,* 2:721.

Gifts of the Holy Spirit. *See* HOLY SPIRIT, GIFTS OF.

Giving. *See* CONTRIBUTION.

Glorification. In the Scripture the idea of glorification deals with the ultimate perfection of believers. The word "glorification" is not used in the Hebrew Old Testament or the Greek New Testament, but the idea of glorification is conveyed by the Greek verb *doxazō* ("glorify") and the noun *doxa* ("glory") as well as in passages that do not use any word from this root. Although the Old Testament may anticipate the theme to some extent (Ps. 73:24; Dan. 12:3), the New Testament is considerably fuller and richer in its development, making it explicit that believers will be glorified (Rom. 8:17, 30; 2 Thess. 1:12).

Despite the fact that one of the key verses (Rom. 8:30) appears to place glorification in the past, it is in all other passages seen as future, to be hoped for (Rom. 5:2; Col. 1:27), to be revealed (Rom. 8:18; 1 Peter 5:1), and to be obtained (2 Thess. 2:14; 2 Tim. 2:10). Specifically, glorification arrives with the second coming of Christ (Eph. 5:27; Phil. 3:20–21; Col. 3:4; 2 Thess. 1:10), accompanied by the resurrection of believers (1 Cor. 15:43) and the day of judgment (Rom. 2:5–10). Its duration is eternal (2 Cor. 4:17; 2 Tim. 2:10; 1 Peter 5:10).

Like other facets of salvation, glorification is the work of God (Rom. 8:30). To it believers are called (1 Thess. 2:12; 1 Peter 5:10), brought (Heb. 2:10), and foreordained (1 Cor. 2:7). God both prepares us for glory (Rom. 9:23) and prepares glory for us (1 Cor. 2:9). It is ours by inheritance (Rom. 8:17). At the same time, however, we have our part to play: glorification should be sought (Rom. 2:7), and it will be wrought in us through our affliction and suffering (Rom. 8:17; 2 Cor. 4:17; 2 Tim. 2:10–11).

Glorification involves first of all the believer's sanctification or moral perfection (2 Thess. 2:13–14; Heb. 2:10–11), in which the believer will be made glorious, holy, and blameless (Eph. 5:27). The process of sanctification is at work in us now (2 Cor. 3:18) but moves from one degree of glory to another until it reaches final glory.

Second, the body participates in glorification (Rom. 8:23; 1 Cor. 15:43; Phil. 3:21), which is the believer's deliverance and liberty (Rom. 8:21). As a result, the glorified body is immortal (Rom. 2:7), imperishable, powerful, and spiritual (1 Cor. 15:43–44). Moreover, creation itself participates in this aspect of glorification (Rom. 8:21).

In the third place, glorification brings participation in the kingdom of God (1 Thess. 2:12), even to the point of our reigning with Christ (2 Tim. 2:10–12).

Finally, glorification is in some sense a partaking of God's own glory (Rom. 5:2; 1 Thess. 2:12; 2 Thess. 2:14; 1 Peter 5:10).

DAVID K. HUTTAR

See also SALVATION.

Bibliography. S. Aalen, *NIDNTT,* 2:44–52; R. B. Dillard, *BEB,* 2:869–70; M. R. Gordon, *ZPEB,* 2:730–35; E. F. Harrison, *EDT,* pp. 443–44; idem, *ISBE,* 2:477–83; B. L. Ramm, *BEB,* 1:869–70.

Glory. ***Natural Objects.*** When used in reference to natural objects "glory" may refer to the brightness of heavenly bodies (Acts 22:11; 1 Cor. 15:41), the fruitfulness of a forest (Isa. 35:2; 60:13), the awesomeness of a horse's snorting (Job 39:20), or the ornateness of expensive clothing (Luke 7:25).

Human Beings. The glory of human beings is spoken of in reference to a number of external manifestations and conditions, aspects of internal character, and the inherent condition of human nature. As applied to external manifestations and conditions of human beings, glory may refer to position, possessions, strength, or length of life.

Joseph's glory (Gen. 45:13) is his position in Egypt, David's (Ps. 21:5) and Jehoiakim's (Jer. 22:18) their royal position in Judah, and Joshua's (Num. 27:20) his position of authority over the people of God.

In the sense of possessions, Jacob's glory (Gen. 31:1) is his servants and animals (Gen. 30:43). Glory is the wealth of the wicked rich (Ps. 49:17) as well as of the industrious, ideal wife (Prov.

31:24–25). And the wealth of the nations is the glory of restored Jerusalem (Isa. 66:11–12).

"The glory of young men is their strength" (Prov. 20:29), and glory as strength is illustrated in the righteous Job (Job 29:20), the arrogant king of Assyria (Isa. 8:7), and the long life of the elderly (Prov. 16:31).

At a somewhat deeper level, glory can be seen in various aspects of human character such as willingness to overlook the faults of others (Prov. 19:11) or avoiding strife (Prov. 20:3).

Further, Psalm 8:5 ("You . . . crowned him with glory and honor") may point to an even more essential glory in humans, an inherent glory resulting from their being created in God's image (cf. 1 Cor. 11:7). While humans may not have entirely lost this God-given glory through their fall into sin, their pursuit of folly shows that they do not live up to their glorious calling (Prov. 26:1). Moreover, this human glory, which can often be viewed as a positive good or at least neutrally, can also get out of hand and become an expression of independence from God (Isa. 10:12) and pride (Prov. 25:27).

God. The most significant use of the ideas of glory and majesty is their application to God. In this regard, it is sometimes stated that God's glory is the external manifestation of his being. God's glory is something that appears (Exod. 16:10), is revealed (Isa. 40:5), or can be seen (Num. 14:22). There is also a more fundamental sense in which God has glory prior to any external manifestation of it. An important passage in this regard is Exodus 33:18–23, which shows that, while there are aspects of God's nature that are revealed to Moses (his name, "back"), there are other aspects that are not manifested (his glory, "face"). Thus, God's glory exists prior to and apart from any manifestation of it.

The same teaching is implied in John 17:5, when Christ refers to the glory that he had with the Father before the world was. And in Proverbs 25:2, the glory of God is in concealing, rather than in manifesting. Moreover, the titles of God as the Glorious One (Ps. 3:3) and the Majesty on High (Heb. 1:3; 8:1) point to the same conclusion, that God's glory is fundamentally independent of external manifestation.

In keeping with this thought, glory is spoken of as attaching to God's kingly rule (Ps. 145:11–12) and his presence (Ps. 96:6), and as being his clothing (Job 40:10; Pss. 93:1; 104:1) and above the heavens (Pss. 8:1; 113:4; 148:13).

Yet it is true that God's glory is also manifest. It is in the thunderstorm (Job 37:22; Ps. 29:4) and more commonly in the events and institutions surrounding the exodus from Egypt. Thus, God's glory is seen in the plagues and other miracles (Num. 14:22), in the cloudy pillar (Exod. 16:10), in the theophany at Mount Sinai (Exod. 24:17; Deut. 5:24), in the tabernacle (Exod. 29:43; 40:34–35; Num. 14:10; 16:19, 42; 20:6), in the fire initiating the sacrificial system (Lev. 9:23), and in the ark of the covenant (1 Sam. 4:21–22) and the temple of Solomon (1 Kings 8:11; 2 Chron. 7:1–3). Its presence is anticipated in the restored Zion (Ps. 102:15–16; Isa. 60:19; Zech. 2:5), is actualized at the birth of Christ (Luke 2:9), and will be further accomplished in the heavenly Jerusalem (Rev. 21:11, 23).

In addition to referring to the actual glory of God, the words sometimes refer to the recognition of his glory. This is of course true whenever we read of giving glory to God or of glorifying him. We do not add to his glory; we merely recognize and acknowledge it. In a number of passages it is difficult to know whether God's glory refers to his actual glory or to human recognition of it. This is true, for example, when Scripture speaks of the earth being full of the glory of the Lord (Isa. 6:3). DAVID K. HUTTAR

See also GOD.

Bibliography. S. Aalen, *NIDNTT,* 2:44–52; R. B. Dillard, *BEB,* 2:869–70; M. R. Gordon, *ZPEB,* 2:730–35; E. F. Harrison, *EDT,* pp. 443–44; idem, *ISBE,* 2:477–83; B. L. Ramm, *BEB,* 1:869–70.

Glossolalia. *See* HOLY SPIRIT, GIFTS OF.

God. ***The Old Testament.*** In the Old Testament the plural form *ʾĕlōhîm* became the favored generic term for God. This development is lost in obscurity, but the evidence from ancient literature contemporary with the Old Testament attests to the use of the plural form in other cultures around Israel as the designation of a single deity that embodies the entirety of divine life. Some have taken the plural form as a plural of intensity, representing the indescribable, or as an abstract plural, corresponding to our words "Godhead" or "divinity," and there is justification for both views.

Precisely when and why the Israelites took this title for their God, rather than the singular *ʾēl* or *ʾĕlôah,* is not known. However, based on the Book of Genesis and the story of the revelation of the divine name in Exodus 3:14, we suspect that *ʾĕlōhîm,* along with other terms, was widely used by the Israelites from the earliest times as a designation for God.

In the course of time, however, God revealed his distinctive divine name, *Yahweh,* by which Israel should know him. This name, according to Genesis 4:26, was known in the prepatriarchal era, but Exodus 3:14 leads us to the conclusion that it assumed a new and more distinctive meaning in the Mosaic era.

As a general rule, the literary context has a great deal to do with which of the terms (*Elohim* or *Yahweh*) the text used to designate Israel's God. *Elohim* seems more appropriate for contexts that require a universal view of the deity, or contexts that connote his power and omnipotence, while *Yahweh* may be more appropriate for those contexts that deal with Israel and Israel's historical experience, or the deity's personal presence and involvement in Israel and the world. For example, the creation narrative of Genesis 1 employs *Elohim*, since the creation of the universe is in view and God is acting in his sovereign role, but the parallel narrative of Genesis 2 introduces the dual name *Yahweh God* (LORD God), in view of Yahweh's personal involvement in the creation of man and woman.

God as Creator. It is significant that the first impression of God the Bible gives is God as Creator of the heavens and earth (Gen. 1:1). The phrase "heavens and earth" is a merismus, which means that everything in the universe as we know it was created by God.

The Bible makes no attempt to prove that God exists. Rather, the universe is the affidavit of his existence. Moreover, the fact that he is the Creator means that the world belongs to him. So when God offers Abraham the land of Canaan, it is his right to give it because he created the world.

The gods of Canaan represented natural forces; there was no clear dividing line between nature and the divine. On the other hand, the creation narratives of Genesis 1–2, which are best understood as depicting twenty-four-hour days, establish the theological premise that God is distinct from nature, that he brought nature into existence, and that he controls nature. In addition to being God's supreme witnesses in the world, human beings are also his representatives to bring the natural world into the service of God ("Rule over the fish of the sea and the birds of the air and over every living creature that moves on the ground," Gen. 1:28). Thus the God of the Old Testament is from the beginning the God who stands apart from nature and rules over it. As the story of the Old Testament unfolds, it is appropriate to describe him as the God of history.

The creation narrative puts forward what is perhaps, along with the doctrine of the incarnation in the New Testament, the most remarkable concept for making God known in all of Scripture, the image of God (Gen. 1:26–27; 9:6). This distinctive of creation meant that God related to humankind personally and imparted something of his own nature to his creation. While the history of interpretation has offered no unanimity on the meaning of this phrase, the most satisfactory explanation is a comprehensive one. The image of God implies all that is distinctive to human nature: the spiritual, psychological, sociological, and physical aspects, all of which are reflections of God's nature. The spiritual implies that human beings are made to relate to their Creator; the psychological, that they are reasoning and emotional creatures; the sociological, that they are created to relate to one another; and the physical, that man's corporal form reflects an essential aspect of God's—not in the sense that he has a body, but in the sense that his being is multifaceted and multifunctional. He speaks, sees, hears, and walks, for example, without requiring the physical organs that human beings must have to enable these activities. The ultimate expression of this attribute of God's being is his incarnation in human flesh. So the image of God is not limited to one aspect of human nature, like the mind or the spirit, but is comprehensive. Therefore, when God created man in his image, he left the indelible stamp of his nature on human beings. They were not divine, but reflected the nature of the deity.

The view of God as personal is grounded in the image of God. He is a self-conscious being, who has will and purpose. The parallel creation narrative of Genesis 2:4b–25 further communicates this view of God as personal in anthromorphic terms as he forms man from the dust of the ground, breathes the breath of life into his nostrils, makes the birds and beasts of the field, fashions woman from the man, and finally plants a garden for their habitat in Eden. This initial portrait of God, therefore, invests the biblical story with a view of God who is personal. Regardless of whether the creation narrative is early or late in its composition, its canonical position in the Old Testament gives it anterior advantage, and the biblical reader proceeds through the Old Testament with this view of the Creator God who was personally involved in the world he created. So one is not surprised to find him walking in the garden, addressing Adam and Eve, laying out plans to save a morally debased world, covenanting with Abraham, intervening on Moriah to spare Isaac's life, speaking to Jacob in a dream, and preserving Joseph in a foreign and hostile environment in order to procure his will for the people he had chosen to bear his name in the world.

God of the Fathers. With the introduction of the patriarchs of Israel (Abraham, Isaac, and Jacob), God became known as the "God Almighty," *El Shaddai* (Gen. 17:1; 28:3; 35:11; 48:3; 49:25; Exod. 6:3; Ezek. 10:5), and less frequently "God everlasting" (*El Olam*), "God of seeing" (*El Roi*), and "God most high," *El Elyon* (Gen. 21:33; 16:13). The latter two terms arise out of specific historical situations and suggest something about God's involvement in the lives of his people.

The name of God is personalized in the general title "God of your fathers," referring to the patriarchs (Exod. 3:13–16; Deut. 1:11, 21; 4:1; 6:3; 12:1; 27:3; Josh. 18:3, etc.). He is also called the "Shield of Abraham" (Gen. 15:1), the "Kinsman of Isaac" (Gen. 31:42, 53), and the "Mighty One of Jacob" (Gen. 49:24). As a rule, the Canaanite deities were named by the place where they were worshiped, but in this personal form, the God of the patriarchs is revealed as an omnipresent God who is involved in history and the lives of those whom he chooses.

God of Israel's National Events. *The Exodus.* Perhaps the single most important era for the shaping of Israel's God-concept, despite the opinions of the historical critics, was the Mosaic era, and no text is more important in this regard than Exodus 3:14, where God identifies himself to Moses as *I am who I am.* This text stands alongside Genesis 1:27 in theological importance. Its complementary text is Exodus 6:2–9. Numerous explanations have been offered for this enigmatic statement. The key word is the verb "to be" (*hāyâ*), occurring here in the imperfect form (lit. I will be who I will be), but the Hebrew imperfect verb can bear both the future and the present senses ("I am who I am"). The shortened form of the name occurs at the end of the sentence, "I AM has sent me to you." And Exodus 3:15 equates I AM with the God of the fathers: "The LORD . . .—the God of Abraham, the God of Isaac and the God of Jacob—has sent me to you."

The most satisfactory explanation of this name is one that grows out of the context. Recognizing this, Walter Eichrodt suggested that its significance lies in the promise of God's presence. When Moses objected to Yahweh's plan that he should go to Pharaoh, Yahweh said, "I will be with you" (Exod. 3:12). This meaning not only takes seriously the immediate context, but the larger context of the Old Testament as well. Yahweh (the vocalization of the name is the contribution of modern scholars) will be with the Israelites. This promise of God's presence became a crucial factor during the Mosaic era and was the point of contention in Exodus 33, when Yahweh responded to the golden calf episode by first declaring that his presence would not accompany Israel into Canaan. Moses thereupon pleaded with God to go personally with them, or otherwise not take them into Canaan at all. God acceded to this request and promised his personal presence. This promise of divine presence with Israel reaches its summit in the Old Testament text of Isaiah 7:14, when God promises that a child would be born and that his name would be Immanuel, which means "God is with us."

The sum of the matter is that God or Yahweh is a God who is present with his people, present in the world he made, present in peace and war, present in crisis and serenity, especially present in the soon-occurring exodus from Egypt toward which Exodus 3:14 is pointing.

God as the saving God can be seen on a universal scale in the story of the flood (Gen. 6–9), and on a personal scale in the stories of the patriarchs (Gen. 12–50). This notion of God is raised to a national level in the exodus from Egypt, a narrative for which the Joseph story serves as an appropriate transition from the view of God as personal Savior to national Savior. God's saving Israel from Egypt becomes the paradigm of saving in the Old Testament, so that when Israel faces the national crisis of exile to Babylonia, the imagery of God's saving Israel from Egypt is the standard with which the return to Judea is compared. In the historical books, God as the saving God delivers his people from national oppression and humiliation, and in the psalms, delivers Israel and individuals from personal danger, sickness, and other threatening circumstances. While God's saving action in the Old Testament is largely set in time and space, it is the foundation on which the New Testament builds the doctrine of eternal salvation that transcends time and space. Further, already in the Fourth Servant Song of Isaiah (Isa. 52:13–53:12), God's saving action becomes passive suffering and thus forms a link between the Old Testament view of God and the New Testament view of the suffering Messiah.

Sinai. What God had done on behalf of the patriarchs, he had done on Israel's behalf. Sinai was a summing up of his work that preceded it and that aimed to make Israel Yahweh's special people and shape them into a community loyal to him. God began this work when he created the world, and continued it in his work of grace executed in the lives of the heroes and heroines of faith, like Enoch who walked with God (Gen. 5:22, 24), Noah who found favor in the eyes of the Lord (Gen. 6:8), Abraham whose faith God counted as righteousness (Gen. 15:6), and Joseph whom God sustained in Egypt through adversity and success (Gen. 39:23). Sinai was the place where God revealed himself to Israel. This revelation took the form of Torah (law). The reconciling work God had engaged in since the fall (Gen. 3) assumed institutional status in the Torah. God instituted an agent (priesthood) to serve as an intermediary of reconciliation between himself and Israel, a place (tabernacle) where he and Israel should meet each other in worship, and a means (sacrificial system) that provided the formal expression of Israel's and the individual's desire to do God's will and to live in obedience to his commandments.

While the Torah was the broad revelation of God's will and Israel's responsibility toward God, God put his signature on the Torah in a more formal arrangement called a covenant (*bĕrît*). The covenant he made with Abraham was activated on a national level at Sinai and designed with particulars that formalized the relationship between Israel and Yahweh. Not only did God commit himself to Israel, but he called Israel to a binding commitment to him.

In this covenant, God established the theological premise of his oneness: "The LORD our God, the LORD is one" (Deut. 6:4). While this premise distinguishes him from the pluralistic notion of deity so common in the ancient Near East, it also makes a statement about his inner unity, involving his unity of both person and purpose. Although the Old Testament can speak of God in plural terms (e.g., "let us make man in our image," Gen. 1:26), his plurality of inner being, perhaps indicative of the interactive and complex nature of his person, functions with a unity of purpose. He should not be conceived of, therefore, like the ancient pantheon of gods and goddesses who sometimes worked against one another's purposes. Rather, he is one in person and purpose. Thus, Israel was called to worship God with a singleness of devotion, giving their loyalty to him and to no other gods (Exod. 20:3–6). The prophets later helped Israel understand that this undivided loyalty was in fact directed to the only God who existed (e.g., Isa. 45:5). The other gods were mere figments of the imagination.

The Sinai covenant had a dual purpose, stipulating how God would relate to Israel and how Israel should relate to God and the world. The same vocabulary that describes God in the Old Testament is used to call Israel to covenant loyalty.

For example, God calls Israel to be holy premised on *his* being holy: "Be holy, for I am holy" (Lev. 11:44–45; 19:2; 20:26; 21:8). The Sinai legislation provides no more distinctive concept of God than God as holy. This character of God by extension applies to the high priestly garments, the tabernacle, the Sabbath, and Israel. The Book of Leviticus is so devoted to the concept of holiness that chapters 17–20 have been called the Holiness Code. Basically the word "holy" connotes separation from the profane and appointment to Yahweh's service. Yahweh's holiness involves his power (1 Sam. 6:20), transcendence, and moral perfection (Isa. 6:3; 35:8). His commandment to be holy does not imply the assumption of his incommunicable attributes by human beings such as transcendence and omnipotence, but requires one to fear him and to seek moral perfection. Isaiah, deeply moved by his encounter with the holy God (Isa. 6:3), sensed his own uncleanness (v. 5). His recognition of God's holiness is confirmed by his frequent reference to God as the Holy One of Israel.

The moral core of the covenant, however, was described by another word, *ḥesed,* a rich concept requiring multiple terms in translation, such as "steadfast love," "lovingkindness," "mercy," "faithfulness," "trustworthiness," and "loyalty." This "trustworthiness" or "loyalty" that characterized God is set down in the ethical centerpiece of the law, the Ten Commandments, where God declares that he will show *ḥesed* "to a thousand generations of those who love me and keep my commandments" (Exod. 20:6). In some instances, it also carries the idea of compassion (Jer. 16:5).

Whereas God related to Israel with a steadfastness of love and compassion, Israel should also relate to him with the same kind of loving loyalty. The prophet Micah (6:8) articulated it most clearly: "He has showed you, O man, what is good. And what does the LORD require of you? To act justly and to love mercy (*ḥesed*), and to walk humbly with your God."

Thus, at Sinai God spells out his holy and loving character toward Israel and calls Israel to the same kind of holy living and loving loyalty toward him and toward their neighbors.

Wilderness Wanderings and Conquest. The Old Testament God as a God of war becomes prominent in the era between the exodus and the monarchy. Already at the exodus from Egypt the Israelites proclaimed him as "warrior" (Exod. 15:3), and the writer of Samuel speaks of Israel's battles belonging to the Lord (1 Sam. 18:17; 25:28).

The Book of Judges operates on the thesis that Joshua tried to carry out the commandment to destroy the Canaanites, but the period of the judges operated by a new principle, allowing the Canaanites to remain in the land in order to test Israel's resolve to follow the Lord (Judg. 2:20–23). In Judges, God intervenes in history at critical moments and manifests his sovereignty over nations.

Yet we must admit that the command to wage war against the Canaanites and God's involvement in such wars pose a challenge to Old Testament theology. At the same time, we also have to remember that the Old Testament speaks out of an ancient context in which survival was most often the survival of the fittest. War was part of life. When human beings reject God's kindness, he resorts to methods that characterize sinful human nature—not to redeem the methods, but to redeem Israel and the world. Paul articulated this principle clearly in Romans 2:4–5. Another dimension of the command to exterminate the Canaanites is that they posed a threat to Israel's faith (Exod. 23:23–33; Num. 33:50–56; Deut. 7:1–6; Judg. 2:2). Even in the time of Abraham, the Lord noted that the iniquity of the Amorites (Canaanites) was not yet full (Gen. 15:16).

Thus, God's presence was critical to the success of the conquest of Canaan. He involved himself personally (Josh. 6:8; 10:11, 12–14) and the writer of Joshua took account of this in his statement, "the LORD, the God of Israel, fought for Israel" (10:42).

Exile and Restoration. Israel's history concludes with the fall of Samaria in 722 B.C., and Judah's history dips into a hiatus called the exile with the fall of Jerusalem in 586 B.C. In these national crises, God is seen as a God of judgment and wrath, but in the return from exile and the restoration, the Old Testament presents him as the God of compassion and salvation.

From the time of Moses to Malachi, God sent his servants the prophets, as his messengers. Whereas he had spoken to the patriarchs in dreams and visions, and to Moses directly, he spoke to Israel through the prophets. Elijah was the exemplary prophet, calling Israel to return to Yahweh's covenant and worship only him. Through these intermediaries God again took the initiative in revelation and action as he had done in Israel's past, choosing the time and place where he would speak to his people. Just as he had entrusted his word to Moses, he also gave his word to the prophets and equipped them to speak it boldly (Isa. 6:6–13; Jer. 1:9–10).

Their message was basically twofold. First, *God is Judge.* The sins of Israel had earned God's just punishment, which came ultimately in the form of conquest and the exile of Israel (722 B.C.) and Judah (586 B.C.), a series of events that the prophets were inclined to call the *day of the Lord* (Amos 5:18–20). Yahweh was not a despot whose actions were irrational, but he acted according to the principles of justice that he had set forth in the Torah, and he required that Israel operate by the same standard of justice. At the heart of that system was the demand for undeviating loyalty to God and his will. This meant, as the Torah had commanded, that the Israelites should have no other gods besides Yahweh. Thus, the disloyalty for which the prophets indicted Israel was best summed up in their blatant idolatry. The Book of Lamentations stands as an assessment of Judah's fall and a witness to Yahweh's mercy, which is renewed every morning (Lam. 3:22–24). The writer attributes the disaster to the failure of the prophets and priests, who were more interested in personal gain than the souls for whom they were responsible (Lam. 4:13–16). The restoration, originating in God's mercy, would be hastened by the people's despairing of their sin and hoping in the Lord. With a prayer for restoration the book closes (5:19–22).

Second, *God is compassionate.* The final word in prophetic theology is grace. No prophet knew that better than Isaiah, who announced the era of restoration as a time when Yahweh would comfort his people and proclaimed Yahweh's forgiveness of Judah's sins (40:1–2). God's actions to restore Judah after the exile to Babylonia would be as mighty and compassionate as his deliverance of their ancestors from Egypt; that is, he would perform a second exodus (Isa. 35; 45). This miraculous era would manifest Yahweh's greatness in ways that would summon the nations to turn to him for salvation (Isa. 45:22). So deep was God's compassion for Israel and the world that he would assume the form of a servant and take on himself Israel's suffering and sin (Isa. 53:4–6).

The God of Israel's Sages and Singers. *God of Israel's Sages (Wisdom).* God is known in the Old Testament as the God of wisdom in the Torah and Prophets, but this attribute never receives the kind of emphasis it does among the wise men (sages) and in the Wisdom Literature they produced (Job, Proverbs, Ecclesiastes). The idea of God's wisdom implies his understanding of the universe and its operation, both on the broad scale and the personal level. Thus, the wisdom of God includes his knowledge and administration of the created order (Job 38–39). It further implies that God implanted a certain orderliness and regularity in the universe, and that same design should be reflected in human life. It is this latter dimension of wisdom that contributes to the personal and practical expressions of wisdom in the Book of Proverbs. Thus, one must live an orderly (moral) life in society so that society might become a reflection of the orderly universe, which in turn reflects something important about the nature of God.

Rather than emphasizing the precepts of the Torah or the oracles of the prophets, wisdom stresses the design of nature as a means of divine revelation. Since God, then, speaks more indirectly through nature than the Torah and prophets, it is not surprising that the Book of Ecclesiastes describes him as sometimes elusive, particularly in revealing to men and women the meaning of life. Yet to the persistent, a modicum of meaning can be found in the routine and work of life (Eccles. 2:24–26).

The God of wisdom operates on the principle of just rewards and punishment. That is, he rewards the righteous and punishes the wicked—a principle promoted by Job's friends and espoused by the Book of Proverbs. Yet the view of Wisdom Literature is broad enough to consider those cases when the innocent suffer and the wicked prosper. This is the problem of Job; even though the principle of retribution is basic to an orderly universe, Job insists that God does not always honor that principle. When Yahweh finally speaks to Job out of the whirlwind (Job 38:1–42:6), he does not defend the principle or explain the breath of it, but proclaims his majestic knowledge and expert operation of the universe he made, and expounds the finite understanding of man. While human beings would argue the issue on the level of justice, God would prefer to argue it on the level of grace. So in the epilogue of Job (42:7–17), he not only restores Job's possessions but doubles them.

God of Israel's Singers (Psalms). To sum up the view of God in psalms poses the same difficulty as the Torah and the Prophets. In the psalms God is so multifaceted and multifunctional that any summary is inadequate. Yet the psalms are a microcosm of Old Testament religion. They contain some law, some prophecy, and some wisdom. Whatever portrait of God one finds in these genres of the Old Testament can generally also be identified somewhere in the psalms. God is Creator and Sustainer (Ps. 104), Redeemer and Savior (Ps. 25:22), Vindicator of the Innocent (Ps. 26), and Giver of mercy to the guilty (Ps. 51). Although they portray God as the God of Israel who acts on their behalf in history, the psalms are the basic Old Testament witness to personal religion. They are indeed Israel's hymnbook of worship, but they also document God's responsiveness to the devout worshiper who comes to him for mercy and help.

The New Testament. From the Christian point of view, the God of the Old Testament is the same God as in the New, except he manifests himself in different ways, most importantly in the incarnation. Yet the basic attributes of God are the same as those of the Old Testament. In one sense, the study of God in the New Testament is a study of Christology, even though that is not the focus of this article.

The generic term for God in the New Testament is *theos,* but *kurios*, the Greek rendering of the Hebrew YHWH, is frequently used instead of the generic term. Long before the Christian era, the Jews had stopped pronouncing the divine name so as not to disrespect or defame it. Instead, they gave to this four-consonant name (YHWH) the vowels of another Hebrew word, *ʾAdonai,* which means "my Master" or "my Lord." Rather than pronouncing it, they pronounced the loan word, *ʾAdonai.* When the Old Testament was translated into Greek, the name YHWH or Adonai was rendered by the Greek word *kurios,* which means "Lord." So the God of the New Testament is frequently called *kurios* or *Lord,* as is Jesus.

The New Testament, like the Old, does not try to prove God's existence. Rather it declares, also like the Old Testament, that he exists and manifests himself in various ways, but finally he speaks through his Son Jesus Christ (Heb. 1:1–4), who is superior to angels, priests, and all other manifestations of the divine Word.

God in the Synoptic Gospels. The Synoptic Gospels present the story of the birth, life, death, and resurrection of Jesus Christ. Yet behind that story is God. Matthew relates the birth of Jesus as a fulfillment of Isaiah's prophecy of the coming of Immanuel, "God with us" (Matt. 1:23). The God of the Old Testament makes himself present in the world in the form of human flesh.

The Kingdom of God. The Synoptics focus on the God who sends Jesus and empowers him by stressing the kingdom of God, the salvation of God, and Christ as the son of God. They present the message of Jesus in terms of the imminent approach of the kingdom of God (Matthew prefers kingdom of heaven), a phrase that has both material and spiritual connotations. In the Old Testament Yahweh's kingdom refers to his sovereign reign over the world (Pss. 103:10; 145:13). The principles of this kingdom derive from its King, God himself, and they are laid down in the Sermon on the Mount (Matt. 5–7). The citizens of the kingdom are known as "children of God" (Matt. 5:9), and the standard of righteousness demanded of them originates in God himself (Matt. 5:48), in much the same way as God demanded Israel to be holy because he was holy. The kingdom of God is a concept that links to the original command that humankind as his agents should subdue and take dominion of the earth (Gen. 1:28). This long process with its successes and failures laid out in Old Testament history, finally arrives at a new level of accomplishment in the appearance of the Messiah, Jesus Christ, of whose divinity the Synoptics are convinced. On behalf of humankind, he personally took dominion over the world as he cast out demons, healed diseases, commanded nature (Mark 11:20; Luke 8:24–26), and forgave sinners. In Christ God was taking dominion of the world he had made. The kingdom of God was realized in Jesus Christ as the reign of God in much the same way as a modern monarch reigns (but does not rule), anticipating the rule of God in the eschatological age. Yet the reign of God can become the rule of God in the hearts of those individuals who submit to the power of Christ as they await the historical reality of the kingdom when the kingdom of the world becomes "the kingdom of our Lord and of his Christ" (Rev. 11:15).

The Salvation of God. In the Old Testament God's saving action appears in the form of deliverance from war, personal distress, illness, and political oppression. While these dimensions of salvation are not all laid aside in the New Testament, the concept has assumed a spiritual dimension that becomes the controlling idea. In sending Jesus, declared Luke, God has "raised up a horn of salvation" for Israel in the house of David (Luke 1:69), which includes the forgiveness of sins (Luke 1:77). When Simeon saw the infant Christ, he declared "My eyes have seen your salvation" (Luke 2:30). Luke interprets the ministry of John the Baptist in the wilderness as the fulfillment of Isaiah's prophecy (40:3–5) that the salvation of God would illuminate the wilderness (Luke 3:4–6). This is the sense of salvation in Luke 19:9, where Jesus declares that as a consequence of Zacchaeus's repentant spirit, salvation had come to his house.

The Son of God. This phrase can refer to human beings (Luke 3:38), but the meaning that concerns us here is its reference to Jesus because he is God and partakes of the divine nature. The title could simply designate the Messiah (Mark 1:1; Matt. 16:16), but in Matthew 11:25–27 Jesus' sonship involves a unique and exclusive relationship between the Father and the Son. His knowledge of the Father is in the same degree as the Father's knowledge of him.

God in the Fourth Gospel. If the Synoptics leave a slight margin of uncertainty about the divinity of Jesus, the Gospel of John declares it unequivocally, calling Jesus the Word (*logos*) and declaring that "the Word was God" (1:1). John accents the theological doctrine that Isaiah had expressed so clearly (43:1–7, 14–16; 45:1–7), that the Creator and the Redeemer are one (1:10–13; see also 1 Cor. 8:6; Col. 1:16). Further, the Gospel subtly identifies Jesus with Yahweh of the Old Testament, who revealed himself as I AM to Moses (Exod. 3:14; see John 6:35, 48; 8:12; 10:7, 9; 10:11, 14; 11:25; 14:6; 15:1, 5).

God as Father. The concept of God as Father of Israel (Deut. 32:6) and the individual (Deut. 8:5) originates in the Old Testament. While the Synoptics use the term also, John's Gospel capitalizes on this title for God, emphasizing Jesus' intimate relationship to God as Son: "I and the Father are one" (10:30). Jesus' enemies heard in the description of his relationship to the Father a claim to equality with God (5:18). Yet Jesus' reference to God as his Father is only one side of the picture. The other is that God acknowledges Jesus as his Son, a point made more directly by Matthew and Luke than by John. At the baptism of Jesus the voice from heaven declared, "This is my beloved Son, with whom I am well please" (Matt. 3:17; Luke 3:22).

God as Spirit. The Old Testament witnesses insist that God is a spiritual Being, even though they often speak of him in anthropomorphic terms. Indeed, they urge an absolute difference between God and man (Num. 23:19; Hos. 11:9). Jesus puts the idea of God as Spirit in the context of worship in the new age that he inaugurated: "God is spirit, and his worshipers must worship in spirit and in truth" (John 4:24). The spiritual nature of God demands a spiritual response from human beings that is not tied to localities as was worship in the temple, whether on Mount Gerizim or in Jerusalem, but is centered on Christ the Truth.

John goes beyond this idea and lays out the doctrine of the Holy Spirit, who proceeds from the Father (15:26) and is sent by the Son (16:7). In the Old Testament the term "holy Spirit" refers to the manifestation of God's presence in the world (Ps. 51:11). In the Fourth Gospel the Holy Spirit is a Person as are the Father and Son. Yet the unity of God is still maintained by Jesus and by Paul (Mark 12:29; Rom. 3:30). The trinitarian view of God is already implied in the baptismal formula of Matthew 28:19 and the Pauline benediction of 2 Corinthians 13:14.

God in the Acts of the Apostles. The Book of Acts represents God's action in history after the resurrection and ascension of Christ. God sent the Holy Spirit to empower his people for the task of proclaiming the good news of Jesus. Peter announced at Pentecost that God had raised Jesus from the dead (Acts 2:24). The reality of the resurrection, so shattering to the kingdom of sin and death, is the dominating theme of this new age. While Acts is a witness to the risen Christ, it was the God of the fathers who raised him from the dead (Acts 5:30) and empowered the disciples to carry on his mission to the world.

God in the Pauline Letters. The apostle Paul plumbs the depths of the meaning of the cross and the resurrection. In these events, God has revealed his wisdom and power. In the cross God took on himself the weakness of human flesh and showed that his weakness is insurpassably greater than the power of men and that his wisdom is unimaginably wiser than human understanding (1 Cor. 1:22–25). The blessings that God has prepared for those who love him are summed up in the cross and resurrection (1 Cor. 2:9–10). In fact, the salvation that God had bestowed upon Old Testament Israel only in part became a historical reality in Christ (1 Cor. 15:15). God has elected believers, not merely in Abraham, but before the foundation of the world (Eph. 1:4). Paul understands the mystery of the gospel that the Old Testament witnesses had not comprehended—that God has united in one body both Jews and Gentiles through the cross (Eph. 2:15–16; 3:4–5), and through Christ has reconciled the world to himself (2 Cor. 5:19). Indeed, in Christ God has not merely repaired the broken human creature, but has re-created him (2 Cor. 5:17) and conformed him to the image of his Son (Rom. 8:29).

God in the General Epistles. God, who spoke so clearly and in various ways in the Old Testament, ultimately and decisively has spoken in the new age through his Son Jesus Christ (Heb. 1:1–3). The old ways of speaking through angels, Moses, Joshua, and the levitical priests were inadequate, so God has spoken through Christ with decisive finality. When Christ's suffering on the cross was finished, he sat down in his place of honor and authority at the right hand of God in heaven (Heb. 10:12; 12:2). The entire historical process of faith, represented by Old Testament worthies known and unknown, reached its climax in Jesus Christ, who has become the focus of faith. The rallying cry of the weak and heartless is now, "Consider him who endured from sinners such opposition from sinful men" (Heb. 12:1–3).

How one should live during the interim between the resurrection and the second coming of Christ was a major topic of discussion in the New Testament church. That concern preoccupied James. Although God, the Father of lights, has redeemed his people (1:17–18) and planted his Word in their hearts (1:21), there are yet temptations and trials to deal with before they inherit the kingdom of God (2:5). James offers admonitions for this interim period.

Peter's understanding of God contains the basics of the doctrine of the Trinity. He mentions the Father, Spirit, and Jesus Christ in 1 Peter 1:2, and the three Persons of the Trinity figure prominently in the work of redemption as Peter outlines it. This marvelous light into which God, sovereign and transcendent, has called his people, was planned by God before the world came into existence (1 Peter 1:20). And not only had he preordained this work of grace, but he had reconstituted the nation as a "chosen people, a royal priesthood, a holy nation, a people belonging to God," that they might declare his praises (1 Peter 2:9).

John's teaching in this three epistles also provides instruction for living during this interim period. When one sins, Christ is the Advocate with the Father (1 John 2:1), who forgives and cleanses us from unrighteousness (1 John 1:9). In addition to portraying God as a loving Father, John provides two other descriptive themes: God is light and God is love. Both originate in the Old Testament. The concept of God as light, in whom is no darkness, links John's thought to Genesis 1:3, where God created light and separated it from darkness, thus separating himself from darkness and associating himself with light. This light has shone finally and resplendently in Jesus Christ, and it is in that light that the new life becomes reality (1 John 1:5–7). The second theme, so reminiscent of Old Testament theological language to describe God's relationship to Israel (cf. Deut. 7), declares God is love (1 John 4:8). Only in that truth can one fulfill the commandment to love one's neighbor as oneself, a commandment based in the nature of Yahweh (Lev. 19:18). This commandment, so contrary to human nature, has found in Christ a new orientation (1 John 3:16) and a new enablement by a rebirth into God through Christ (1 John 3:9; 4:7).

God in the Revelation of John. In the canonical order of the Bible there is a wonderful symmetry between the first book (Genesis) and the final book (Revelation). The sovereign, omnipotent God, who created the universe by his Word, recreates the heavens and earth and takes his abode among his people, destroying death and all its emotional accouterments (Rev. 21:1–4). By his omnipotent power God brings his kingdom, outlined in Israel's history and anticipated by the prophets, to reality, transforming the kingdom of the world into his kingdom, and thus achieving the subjection of the world to his sovereign will and purpose, a task encumbent upon the first man (Gen. 1:28) and accomplished by the Second Man Jesus Christ (Rev. 11:15).

C. Hassell Bullock

See also God, Name of; God, Names of; Fatherhood of God; Holy Spirit; Jesus Christ, Name and Titles of; Presence of God.

Bibliography. C. Barth, *God with Us;* W. Eichrodt, *Theology of the Old Testament;* G. W. Bromiley, *ISBE,* 2:493–503; C. H. Bullock, *An Introduction to Old Testament Prophets;* J. S. Chesnut, *The Old Testament Understanding of God;* P. C. Craigie, *The Problem of War in the Old Testament;* R. W. Gleason, *Yahweh, the God of the Old Testament;* G. E. Ladd, *A Theology of the New Testament;* W. H. Schmidt, *The Faith of the Old Testament: A History;* M. C. Tenney, *New Testament Survey;* C. Westermann, *What Does the Old Testament Say about God?* W. Elwell, *TAB* pp. 44–66.

God, Name of. The God of Israel was known by many different names, titles, and epithets. God's particular names derive both from his revealing his attributes and character to Israel and from Israel's response to him. However, alongside this wealth of names and epithets in the Bible, the concept of God's "Name" itself plays an important role. In the Bible God reveals his Name, puts his Name in a place, causes places to bear his Name, protects by the power of his Name, and acts for the sake of his Name. People call on, pronounce blessings, minister, preach, speak, pray, believe, take oaths, and wage war in his Name. They may revere, fear, suffer for, blaspheme, misuse, be called by, be kept by, or build a temple for the Name.

As God's image-bearer Adam imitated God's creative speech by naming the creation (Gen. 2:19–20): this naming gave expression to the order in the universe and showed Adam's understanding of the character, place, and function of the animals. Adam may well have been able to name other creatures, but only God can assign his own name; only he can fully understand himself and reveal his character and nature (Exod. 3:13–14; 6:2–3). God's "Name" becomes a summary statement of his own nature and of how he has revealed himself to the world; it becomes virtually synonymous with the word "God" itself.

God's "Name" and God's "Glory." In studies of the Old Testament it has become commonplace to distinguish rather sharply between the "glory theology" of the cultic/priestly literature and the "name theology" of Deuteronomy and the Deuteronomistic history (Joshua through Kings). This distinction is ordinarily portrayed as emphasizing either God's transcendence or his immanence. Biblical literature oriented to the activities of the priests and Levites in their duties at the sanctuary is said to emphasize God's immanence, his real presence in the world. The pillar of fire and cloud—the theophany of the divine presence, the Shekinah glory—appears physically and materially with Israel in the wilderness and at her sanctuaries. The tabernacle and temple were viewed as God's dwelling-place (Exod. 15:13, 17; Lev. 15:31; 26:11; 2 Sam. 7:6; 15:25; 1 Chron. 9:19; Pss. 84:1; 132:5, 7). The ark was God's throne and footstool (1 Sam. 4:4; 2 Sam. 6:2; 1 Chron. 28:2; Ezek. 43:7). Wherever the ark went, God went. Israel served "in the presence of the Lord" at the tabernacle and temple. Some have argued that the development of a "name theology" in ancient Israel was given impetus by the loss of the ark itself.

Deuteronomy and the Deuteronomistic history are then widely viewed as a corrective to this earlier "cruder" concept that God dwelled in a building. Deuteronomy seeks to preserve the transcendence of God with an idea theologically more sublime and subtle. It is not God himself—materially and physically—who dwells at the sanctuary, but rather God's "Name" dwells there. Deuteronomy is quite clear. Heaven is the dwelling-place of God (26:15). When Solomon dedicates the temple, he says, "But will God really dwell on earth? The heavens, even the highest heaven, cannot contain you. How much less this temple that I have built!" (1 Kings 8:27). Solomon goes on to pray that when the Israelites direct their prayers toward the temple, God would "hear from heaven, your dwelling place" (vv. 30, 39, 43, 49). Rather than God's "Glory"—the pillar of fire and cloud—coming to the city (Ezek. 10:1–5, 18; 43:3–7), Deuteronomy prefers to speak of God as "choosing a place as a dwelling for his Name" (12:11; 14:23; 16:2, 6, 11; 26:2) or "putting his Name in a place" (12:5, 21; 14:24). The "Name" became a hypostasis for God, an alternative realization of his presence, but freed from the corporeal and physical notions associated with "glory theology"; this substitute way of speaking thus preserved the transcendence of God above and beyond the creation.

In spite of the fact that this contrast between "glory theology/immanence" and "name theology/transcendence" has been widely adopted among Old Testament scholars, it needs rather to be set in a different context, one that does not pit crude against sublime or early against later. A number of passages show the complete compatibility of the two concepts and suggest a different way of relating them. Most important in this regard is Exodus 33:12–23. Here four different "manifestations" of God are described in juxtaposition: his presence, his glory, his name, and his goodness. In response to God's assurance that his presence would go with Israel, Moses requests to see God's glory (vv. 14, 18). The Lord, however, declines this request and says instead, "I will cause all my goodness to pass in front of you, and I will proclaim my name, the Lord, in your presence. I will have mercy on whom I will have mercy, and compassion on whom I will have compassion. But no one can see my face [= "presence"] and live" (vv. 19–20). This incident follows the account of Israel's worshiping the golden calf, a moment in her history that prompted deep concern that a holy God would not continue with this nation but would erupt in judgment against it. How can a holy God be in the presence of a sinful nation? In God's own answer to this issue, a careful distinction is made between God's presence/glory and his name/goodness. God's presence and glory were holy, awesome, and unapproachable, and sinners must be shielded from exposure (v. 22). But Moses could experience the name and goodness of God, both of which express the disposition of the divine nature to show mercy (v. 19). Those who worship the Lord become familiar with his name (Exod. 3:14; 6:2–3).

The distinction suggested here is borne out in the remainder of the Old Testament as well. God's glory remains an awesome, holy, unapproachable, and dangerous manifestation. When his glory appears before the nation, it is the cloud-encased pillar of fire—the cloud shielding and protecting from exposure to the consuming fire of divine glory (Exod. 16:10; 24:16; 40:34; 1 Kings 8:11; 2 Chron. 7:2). God's name, by contrast, is that which Israel can know, approach, and experience—it suggests his goodness and mercy. The psalmists do not trust in or call upon God's glory, but rather on his name. God's majestic self-manifestation in the form of his glory is common in dramatic and occasional theophanies attended by fire, noise, and earthquake, but his name is the mode by which he is known in the context of ordinary, ongoing worship. "Glory" is the form of the divine appearance in the dramatic events of redemptive history—at the exodus, at Sinai, at the dedication of the tabernacle and temple. But "Name" portrays God's approachability and mercy, and it is the mode of worship as Israel approaches the sanctuary, the "place where he has chosen to put his name."

But even with this more nuanced approach in view, God's glory and his name are both divine self-revelations and must be closely related. Isaiah most clearly takes this step: "See, the Name of the Lord comes from afar, with burning anger and dense clouds of smoke" (Isa. 30:27). Here it is the Name that becomes the cloud-encased pillar of fire. Though name and glory are distinguishable for their own respective nuances, they are ultimately revelation of one and the same Lord, the God who is judge and yet who is disposed to show mercy.

Extrabiblical texts may also enhance appreciation for what it means that the Lord "set his name" in a place. A similar expression is found twice in the Amarna letters from the second half of the second millennium B.C. King Abdu-Heba "set his name in the land of Jerusalem." This expression suggests both ownership and conquest. For God to place his name on a place or nation is also to imply his ownership—of the world, of Israel, and of her land. In Deuteronomy where the emphasis is on possessing the land and on Israel's covenant with God, expressing God's presence through his "name" reminds the nation of his ownership and dominion. Rather than diminish or correct the notion of God's immanent presence, God's name in Deuteronomy affirms the very real presence of God in the fullness of his character and covenantal commitment to those on whom he had set that name.

God's Name in the New Testament. The New Testament draws on the Old and continues to use the wide range of idioms associated with God's name. God's name is the theme and basis for worship, prayer, and actions just as it was in the Old Testament.

Of particular interest in the New Testament, however, is the way in which the writers treat the theme "the name of Jesus." This is especially true in the writings of John. People are to believe on Jesus' name (John 1:12; 2:23) and to pray in his name (14:13–14). The power of God's name is in the name that God gave to Jesus (17:11–12). Jesus associates himself with God's mighty self-disclosure as "I AM" (8:58). John reports Jesus' promise to the one who overcomes, "I will write on him the name of my God and the name of the city of my God, the new Jerusalem, which is coming down out of heaven from my God; and I will also write on him my new name" (Rev. 3:12; cf. 22:4). Just as God had put his name on the place Jerusalem in the Old Testament, now Jesus puts his new name—the name he won for himself in his warfare at the cross—on individuals; he proclaims his ownership and dominion, that they belong to him through his conquest on the cross.

Paul also reports that God has given to Jesus a name that is above all other names, so that at the mention of his name every knee in heaven, on earth, and under the earth should bow (Phil. 2:9–10). The writer of Hebrews describes Jesus as the exact representation of the glory of God, one who has a name superior to that of the angels (1:4).

RAYMOND B. DILLARD

See also GOD; GOD, NAMES OF; JESUS CHRIST, NAME AND TITLES OF.

Bibliography. J. Barr, *Congress Volume, Oxford,* pp. 31–38; R. de Vaux, *Das Ferne und Nahe Wort,* pp. 219–28; L. Laberge, *Estudios Biblicos* 43 (1985): 209–36; J. G. McConville, *Tyn Bul* 30 (1979): 149–64; G. von Rad, *Studies in Deuteronomy,* pp. 37–44; J. G. Wenham, *Tyn Bul* 22 (1971): 103–18, W. Elwell, *TAB* pp. 5–10.

God, Names of. Names are more than labels. In Old Testament times a name expressed identification, but also identity. Significant meaning often attached to a name. Names had an explanatory function (cf. Abigail's explanation about her husband, "He is just like his name—his name is Fool" [1 Sam. 25:25]). Name changes were important, since a message attached to the name. Abram (great father) became Abraham (father of a multitude) (Gen. 17:5; cf. 32:28). In some sense a name was the expression of an inmost reality.

Scripture makes much of the name for deity because in the name lies a theology. "I am the LORD, that is my name!" (Isa. 42:8; cf. Exod. 15:3). The name of God is a surrogate for God himself (Ps. 54:1; Prov. 18:10; Jer. 23:27). To give attention to the name (i.e., to God himself) is to put oneself in the place of blessing (Mal. 3:16).

God (*ʾElohim, ʾEloah, ʾEl*). The subject of the Bible's first sentence is God (Gen. 1:1). *ʾElohim, ʾEl,* and *ʾEloah* are from related roots. *ʾEl* (God) is a generic Semitic designation for deity. Judged by Canaanite usage at Ras Shamra/Ugarit, the term signified a god of the highest rank who was something of a father god figure. The term means a god in the widest sense. Etymologically *ʾel* appears to mean "power" as in "I have the power (*ʾel*) to harm you" (Gen. 31:29; cf. Neh. 5:5). Job and Psalms have most of the 238 occurrences of *ʾEl*. *ʾEl* is associated with other qualities such as integrity (not lying) (Num. 23:19; Deut. 32:4), jealousy (Deut. 5:9), and compassion (Neh. 9:31; Ps. 86:15), but the root idea of "might" remains.

The word *ʾEloah* (60 times), occurring most often in Job, etymologically underscores the idea of "power." The term is also generic for "god," and while it refers most often to the true God, it can refer in instances to any god.

ʾElohim (God), a plural of *ʾEloah*, occurs more than 2,250 times, sometimes with an addition such as "God of Abraham/Israel," but mostly it is free standing. Next to Lord (Yahweh), *ʾElohim* is the major designation for God. *ʾElohim* is generic, (as are *ʾEl* and *ʾEloah*) and refers to "deity" but comes virtually to be a name for the true God. All three are represented in the Septuagint as *theos* ("God"), which is also the New Testament term for God. *ʾElohim* sums up what is intended by "god" or the divine.

The plural form (although used with verbs in the singular form) is likely a plural of majesty or perhaps of intensity, either of deity or of power to signify "highly or intensely powerful." The plural form is accommodating of the doctrine of the Trinity. From the Bible's first sentence the superlative nature of God's power is evident as God (*ʾElohim*) speaks a world into existence (Gen. 1:3, 6, 9). His actions also bespeak his power, enabling barren women such as Sarah and Rebecca to conceive (Gen. 18:10, 14; 25:21), bringing an oppressed people out of Egypt (Exod. 20:2), and with power raising Jesus Christ from the dead (Rom. 1:1–4). Believers, Peter writes, are "shielded by God's power" (1 Peter 1:5). In the name *ʾElohim* is fullness of divine power.

Compounds with ʾEl. *ʾEl ʾElyon*. A pervasive compound is *ʾEl 'Elyon* (lit. God, most high). derives from the root "go up," "ascend," so that *ʾEl ʿElyon* may be thought of spatially as the highest. Abraham mentions *ʾEl ʿElyon* when addressing Melchizedek (Gen. 14:18, 19, 20, 22). Closely linked to temple services, twenty of its forty-five occurrences are in the Psalter. Sometimes the compound is construed as a name: "It is good . . . to make music to your name, O Most High" (Ps. 9:1). *ʾEl ʿElyon* denotes exaltation and prerogative and belongs to "monarchical theology" for it speaks of absolute right to lordship. In the same vein may be found the question, "Who is like you?" (Ps. 35:10). Yet this pointer to hierarchy is not about a God of arbitrariness, but about power in the service of life.

ʾEl Shaddai. To Abraham God appears as God Almighty, *ʾEl Shaddai* (Gen. 17:1). The designation "Shaddai," which some think is the oldest of the divine names in the Bible, occurs forty-eight times, thirty-one of which are in Job. The traditional rendering "God Almighty" is debated. A consensus of sorts holds that "shaddai" is to be traced, not to the Hebrew, but to an Accadian word that means "mountain" so that the expression produces a meaning like, "ʾEl, the One of the mountains." If so, *ʾEl Shaddai* highlights God's invincible power. Or, the name may point to his symbolic dwelling. The juxtaposition of *ʾEl Shaddai* and *ʾEl 'Elyon* (Num. 24:16; Ps. 91:1) may suggest that *ʾEl Shaddai* is a God who is chief in the heavenly council, whose residence was sometimes broadly associated with mountains (Hab. 3:3).

Other Compounds with ʾEl. Some compounds with ʾEl register a significant encounter with ʾElohim or may be loosely associated with certain geographical sites. The list would include *ʾEl Ro'* ("God of seeing," Gen. 16:13), ʾEl Bethel ("God of Bethel," house of God, Gen. 35:7), *ʾEl 'Olam*, ("Everlasting God," Gen. 21:33), and *ʾEl* Berith ("God of Covenant," Judg. 9:46).

Yahweh/Yah. YHWH, the tetragrammaton because of its four letters, is, strictly speaking, the only proper name for God. It is also the most frequent name, occurring in the Old Testament 6,828 times (almost 700 times in the Psalms alone). Yah is a shortened form that appears fifty times in the Old Testament, including forty-three occurrences in the Psalms, often in the admonition "hallelu-jah" (lit. praise Jah). English Bibles represent the name YHWH by the title "Lord" (written in capitals to distinguish it from "lord" [ʾadonai]). The Septuagint rendered YHWH as *kyrios* (Lord). The line from YHWH to *'adonai* to *kyrios* is significant for the Pauline statement: "And every tongue confess that Jesus Christ is Lord" (Phil. 2:11).

In the postexilic period the Jews, for reverence reasons, did not pronounce the name but substituted for it the word *ʾadonai* (lord), and in written form attached these vowels to the tetragrammaton. The resulting misguided pronunciation of the name YHWH as a three-syllable word, Y[J]ehovah, continued in English Bible translations until early in the twentieth century. Evidence from Greek usage in the Christian era points to the two-syllable pronunciation, "Yahweh."

The meaning of the name YHWH may best be summarized as "present to act (usually, but not only) in salvation." The revelation of the name is given to Moses, "I AM WHO I AM" (Exod. 3:14), and later in a self-presentation, "I am the LORD" (Exod. 6:2–8). The name YHWH specifies an immediacy, a presence. Central to the word is the verb form of "to be," which points in the Mosaic context to a "being present," and may in Israel's later history, as some suggest, have come to mean "I (and no other [god]) Am" (Isa. 41:4; 43:10). Such was Paul's understanding (1 Cor. 8:4, 6; 1 Tim. 2:5). Quite possibly we need to hear the Old Testament meaning for Yahweh behind the words of Jesus when he speaks of himself as "I am" ("It is I," Matt. 14:27; "I am the one," John 8:24, 28, 58). For Moses and for Israel the question was not whether the Deity existed, but how that Deity was to be understood.

The name YHWH was probably given to Moses as a new revelation; the "faith" that came to be associated with the name YHWH, although in continuity with that of the patriarchs, was different from theirs. Mosaic Yahwism differed from patriarchal religion in that Mosaic Yahwism stressed, among other matters, divine intervention in oppressive situations and holiness—features not central to patriarchal religion.

The theological significance that attaches to the name YHWH is multiple. Judging from the etymology, but more particularly from the context in which the name is disclosed (Exod. 3:12, 14; 6:2–8), the name signifies "presence." God is "with," he is near and among his people. This overtone of presence is reiterated in the naming of the wilderness structure as "tabernacle" (lit. dwelling), and in the promised name Immanuel ("God with us," Isa. 7:14; Matt. 1:23). Yahweh is present, accessible, near to those who call on him (Ps. 145:18) for deliverance (107:13), forgiveness (25:11), and guidance (31:3). Yahweh is dynamically near, but as God (*ʾElohim*) he is also paradoxically transcendent.

The name YHWH defines him as involved in human struggle. Yahweh's name is forever tied, through the exodus event, with salvation and liberation (Exod. 15:1–13; 20:2–3). The salvation promise given in Exodus 6:6–8 is an expansive one, including intimacy with God and blessings of abundance, but is decidedly bracketed first and last with "I am Yahweh." The name YHWH is prominent in salvation oracles (Zeph. 3:14–17) and in petitions (Pss. 79:5, 9; 86:1). The salvation dimension of the name recurs in the announcement of the incarnation: the one born is to be called "Jesus" for (as an echo of the name YHWH) "he will save his people from their sins" (Matt. 1:21). In the name YHWH God's character as the savior of a people is revealed.

Theologically the name of Yahweh resonates with covenant, partly because in the explication of the name in Exodus 6:6–8 the covenant formula is invoked ("I will be your God and you will be my people"). The name YHWH is a name to which Israel can lay particular claim. In covenant, matters such as justice (Isa. 61:8) and holiness (Lev. 19:2) have an extremely high profile.

The name YHWH is anything but empty. The name carries overtones of presence, salvation defined as deliverance and blessing, covenantal bondedness, and integrity.

Compounds with Yahweh. *Yahweh of Hosts.* The most pervasive compound with Yahweh is "Lord of hosts," which occurs 285 times in the Bible and is concentrated in prophetic books (251 times) especially in Jeremiah and Zechariah. The hyphenation has a double-edged meaning. As a military term it signifies that Yahweh is, so to speak, "Commander-in-chief" (1 Sam. 17:45). The "hosts" or "armies" may be heavenly beings, part of the "heavenly government" (1 Kings 22:19), the astral bodies of sun, moon, and stars (Deut. 4:19), or Israel's armies (1 Sam. 17:45). As a military title, it signifies that God is equal to any adversary and well able to achieve victory. The Septuagint sometimes translates the compound as *kyrios pantokratōr* (Lord Almighty); this designation appears also in the New Testament.

A second "edge" to the compound is more royal than military, since it is monarchs who in the ancient Near East and Scripture are said to be "enthroned upon the cherubim" (1 Sam. 4:4; 2 Kings 19:15; Ps. 80:1). The expression "Lord of hosts," frequent in worship-type psalms (especially those that mention Mount Zion), emphasizes God's royal majesty. It designates God as the regnant God (Ps. 103:19–21), the enthroned God whose royal decrees will carry the day (Isa. 14:24; Jer. 25:27).

The title addresses religious pluralism, both past and present. God retains exclusive prerogative as deity. Any competing ideology is idolatry, whether that be the ancient worship of Baal or the modern preoccupation with technique, nationalism, or militarism. The title underscores God's presence, but also the force behind divine decisions affecting political history (Isa. 19:12, 17; Jer. 50:31).

Less Frequent Compounds with Yahweh. Several hyphenations or compounds are attached, for the most part, to some notable experience, as with Yahweh-Nissi ("The-LORD-is-my-Banner") where "banner" is understood as a rallying place. This name commemorated the desert victory of Israel against the Amalekites (Exod. 17:15). From the wilderness experience of bitter waters at Marah emerges another such "name": Yahweh *Rophe* ("The LORD who heals," Exod. 15:26; cf. Ps. 103:3). Abraham memorialized God's provision of a sacrifice in the name Yahweh-jireh ("The LORD will provide," Gen. 22:14). Jeremiah identifies the name of the "Righteous Branch" as "The LORD our Righteousness" (Jer. 23:5–6). Names for structures in which hyphenated Yahweh names occur include Gideon's altar, named *Yahweh-shalom* ("The LORD is peace," Judg. 6:24) and the temple *Yahweh-samma* ("The LORD is There," Ezek. 48:35).

Yahweh and ʾElohim. The combination, "Yahweh *ʾElohim*" (Lord God), is found in Genesis 2 and 3 (nineteen times; twenty-one times elsewhere). A double name was not strange for deities in the ancient Near East. The double name in Genesis 2:4b–3:24, may be to emphasize that the majesty of God that attaches to the name *ʾElohim* in Genesis 1 is not to be separated from the immediacy of a Yahweh in the garden. (English Bibles commonly also employ "lord God" to translate *ʾadonai Yahweh* [lit. lord LORD]).

The Deity named Yahweh (Lord) is identical with *ʾElohim* (God). The shema—"Hear, O Israel: The LORD our God, the Lord is one" (Deut. 6:4) underscores that identity, as do expressions like "Yahweh your/our God." Yahweh as God is exclusively God: "This is what the LORD says—Israel's King and Redeemer, the LORD Almighty: I am the first and I am the last; apart from me there is no God" (Isa. 44:6).

Titles, Epithets, Figurative Language. There are over one hundred descriptive "names" for God. The subject is large and the adjectives are overpowering.

Holy One. Of the fifty-six lexical attestations to God's holiness in the Old Testament, many include the name/title of "The Holy One" or "Holy One of Israel," which occurs thirty-one times in the Old Testament, twenty-five occurrences being in Isaiah. The demand for human holiness is rooted in divine holiness or cleanness (Lev. 19:2; 21:6). The "entrance liturgies" stress the importance of moral and ritual cleanness (Pss. 15; 24:3–6). Holiness speaks of God as supraworldly, as "Other," and as one virtually unapproachable in majesty (1 Sam. 6:20; Isa. 6:3; 33:14–16).

Ruler. A highly significant epithet for God, which is strikingly metaphorical, is "Ruler." The term occurs forty-three times. It is clustered in poetic passages in the prophets and the Psalter. The idea of rule is expressly asserted in the enthronement psalms (93, 96–99), but is already found in Psalm 2. This suggests that the entire Book of Psalms should be read with an emphasis on God's rulership. The origin of the epithet precedes the Israelite monarchy. It signals rulership and sovereignty, and so reinforces the names for God such as *ʾEl ʾElyon* and Lord of hosts (Ps. 84:3). Kingly rule, however, also called for defense of the poor and needy (72:4) and deliverance of those victimized by wickedness (98:9). Around it cluster other epithets/metaphors, such as Judge (Isa. 33:22; cf. Ps. 99:4).

Father. The Old Testament designation of God as Father (Deut. 32:6; Isa. 63:16; 64:8; Jer. 3:4, 19; 31:9; Mal. 2:10) is employed often in the New Testament: by Paul (Eph. 1:3; 3:14–19; 4:6; 5:20; 6:23; cf. Rom. 1:7; 8:15; 15:6; 1 Cor. 8:6); by Jesus (Mark 8:38; 11:25; 13:32; cf. "*Abba*, Father," Mark

14:36). It is the word for God in the Lord's prayer (Luke 11:2). The epithet is strikingly frequent in John (108 times) and also in Matthew (forty times). The range of meanings include those of authority and discipline, but also those of compassion, care, protection, and provision.

Other Titles, Epithets, Figurative Language. "God of the ancestors (fathers)" is a title associated with the patriarchs, and especially with God's promises to them (Exod. 3:13). Other titles are "God of Abraham" (Gen. 28:13; 31:53; 1 Chron. 29:18), "Fear of Isaac" (Gen. 31:42, 53), "Mighty One of Jacob" (Gen. 49:24), and especially (more frequent than the foregoing three) "God of Israel" (Num. 16:9; 1 Sam. 5:8; Ps. 41:13).

Rich symbolism is also found in role descriptions that include language pictures like judge (Isa. 33:22), warrior (Exod. 15:3), and shepherd (Ps. 23). God is also pictured as a mother who gives birth, nurtures, and trains (Deut. 32:18; Isa. 49:15; Hos. 11:1–4). God is spoken of in metaphors such as Rock (Deut. 32:4, 15, 18, 31), the stability of which is proverbial.

Honoring the Name of God/Lord. That God discloses his name means that his name can be invoked, but it should not be invoked "in vain," carelessly or glibly as in an oath (Lev. 19:12), or misused in other ways (Exod. 20:7). Jesus instructed us to pray, "Hallowed be your name" (Luke 11:2). In stressful times one calls on the name of the Lord (Pss. 79:5; 99:6; Zeph. 3:9). Foremost among the ways God's name is to be invoked is honorifically. His name is to be praised (Pss. 7:17; 9:2). Other admonitions call for blessing the name (103:1), offering thanks to the name (106:47), or ascribing glory or blessedness to the name (96:8; 113:2). ELMER A. MARTENS

See also FATHERHOOD OF GOD; GOD; GOD, NAME OF; PRESENCE OF GOD.

Bibliography. S. Dempster, *Revue Biblique* 98 (1991): 170–89; W. Eichrodt, *Theology of the Old Testament;* D. N. Freedman, *Magnalia Dei: The Mighty Acts of God,* pp. 5–107; J. Goldingay, *Tyn Bul* 23 (1972): 58–93; C. D. Isbell, *HUCA 2* (1978): 101–18; J. G. Janzen, *Int* 33 (1979): 227–39; G. A. F. Knight, *I AM: This Is My Name;* L. Koehler, *Old Testament Theology;* H. J. Kraus, *Theology of the Psalms;* H. Kleinknecht, et al., *TDNT,* 3:65–123; G. T. Manley and F. F. Bruce, *IBD,* 1:571–73; E. A. Martens, *Reflections and Projection: Missiology at the Threshold of 2001,* pp. 83–97; T. N. D. Mettinger, *In Search of God: The Meeting and Message of the Everlasting Names;* R. W. L. Moberley, *The Old Testament of the Old Testament;* J. A. Motyer, *The Revelation of the Divine Name;* G. H. Parke-Taylor, *Yahweh: The Divine Name in the Bible;* M. Riesel, *The Mysterious Name of YHWH;* H. Rosin, *The Lord Is God: The Translation of the Divine Names and the Missionary Calling of the Church;* J. Schneider, et al., *NIDNTT,* 2:66–90; H. T. Stevenson, *Titles of the Triune God: Studies in Divine Self-Revelation;* N. J. Stone, *Names of God;* W. A. Van Gemeren, *JETS* 31 (1988): 385–98; R. de Vaux, *Proclamation and Presence,* pp. 48–75; W. Zimmerli, *Old Testament Theology in Outline;* W. Elwell, *TAB,* pp. 10–34.

God, Presence of. *See* PRESENCE OF GOD.

Godly, Godliness. Reverence for God and a life of holiness in the world.

The Old Testament. "The LORD has set apart the godly for himself" (Ps. 4:3); they are, and are to become, his holy people (Lev. 11:44–45). Communion with God is to be zealously cultivated: "Let everyone who is godly pray to you while you may be found" (Ps. 32:6). To neglect God is to invite catastrophe: "Such is the destiny of all who forget God; so perishes the hope of the godless" (Job 8:13; cf. Isa. 10:6). It is especially tragic when persons appointed to be spiritual leaders abandon God's way: "Both prophet and priest are godless; even in my temple I find their wickedness" (Jer. 23:11). Ungodly behavior is by nature destructive: "With his mouth the godless destroys his neighbor" (Prov. 11:9). So it is disastrous when a nation loses the leavening influence of persons who know God: "Help, LORD, for the godly are no more; the faithful have vanished from among men" (Ps. 12:1); "The godly have been swept from the land; not one upright man remains" (Mic. 7:2). It is therefore vital that God's people be obedient to the mandate of Genesis 1:28. "Has not the LORD made them [husband and wife] one? . . . And why one? Because he was seeking godly offspring" (Mal. 2:15).

The New Testament. Godliness is the reverent awareness of God's sovereignty over every aspect of life, and the attendant determination to honor him in all one's conduct. "Godliness" and "holiness" denote one reality (the terms are joined in 1 Tim. 2:2 and 2 Peter 3:11).

Godliness depends on knowing God's revealed truth. Paul speaks of "the knowledge of the truth that leads to godliness" (Titus 1:1), and of "godly sorrow . . . that leads to salvation" (2 Cor. 7:10). Peter declares that God's "divine power has given us everything we need for life and godliness through our knowledge of him" (2 Peter 1:3). God imparts knowledge of himself by revealing his Son.

The godly person is committed to obeying God in the world: "We know that God does not listen to sinners. He listens to the godly man who does his will" (John 9:31). The shape of obedience is clarified by the terms to which "godliness" is joined. "But you, man of God, . . . pursue righteousness, godliness, faith, love, endurance and gentleness" (1 Tim. 6:11). "Make every effort to add to your faith goodness; and to goodness, knowledge; and to knowledge, self-control; and to self-control, perseverance; and to perseverance, godliness; and to godliness, brotherly kindness; and to brotherly kindness, love" (2 Peter 1:5–7)—qualities which, in turn, deepen one's "knowledge of our Lord Jesus Christ" (1:8). Christ, moreover, furnishes power for the godly life: "Why do you stare at us as if by our own power or godliness we had made this man walk?" asks Peter (Acts 3:12). Without divine power, godliness becomes an empty form (2 Tim. 3:5).

Godliness in both respects (knowledge of God and holiness of life) is jeopardized by the propagation of falsehood: "If anyone teaches false doctrines and does not agree to the sound instruction of our Lord Jesus Christ and to godly teaching, he is conceited and understands nothing. He has an unhealthy interest in controversies and quarrels about words that result in envy, strife, malicious talk, evil suspicions, and constant friction between men of corrupt mind, who have been robbed of the truth and who think that godliness is a means to financial gain" (1 Tim. 6:3–5). Accordingly, "the wrath of God is being revealed from heaven against all the godlessness and wickedness of men who suppress the truth by their wickedness" (Rom. 1:18).

Godliness is costly: "everyone who wants to live a godly life in Christ Jesus will be persecuted" (2 Tim. 3:12). Hope of eternal life enables them to endure. "The Lord knows how to rescue godly men from trials and to hold the unrighteous for the day of judgment" (2 Peter 2:9; cf. 3:11–12). "Train yourself to be godly. For physical training is of some value, but godliness has value for all things, holding promise for both the present life and the life to come" (1 Tim. 4:7–8). Grace teaches us "to say 'No' to ungodliness and worldly passions, and to live self-controlled, upright and godly lives in this present age, while we wait for the blessed hope—the glorious appearing of our great God and Savior, Jesus Christ" (Titus 2:12–13). Seeing this life in light of the next encourages "godliness with contentment" (1 Tim. 6:6–7). J. Knox Chamblin

Bibliography. W. Barclay, *New Testament Words*, pp. 106–16; J. Bridges, *The Practice of Godliness;* W. Foerster, *TDNT,* 7:168–96; W. Mundle and W. Günther, *NIDNTT,* 2:90–95.

Gods and Goddesses, Pagan. God early and clearly commanded the descendants of Abraham not to have any other gods besides him (Exod. 20:3). This strict, undivided loyalty was the basis of the covenant relationship God established between himself and the people of Israel.

Sadly, the whole of biblical history is punctuated by the numerous times the people of God turned away from him to engage in the worship of a strange god or goddess. People in the lands surrounding Israel had deities that continually tempted the Israelites to turn from their own God.

Artemis. Greek goddess (K. J. V. Diana) of fertility worshiped at Ephesus and elsewhere during the New Testament era. Her worship combined Greek, Roman, and Anatolian elements and dates back to ca. 1000 B.C. In Ephesus a temple was built in the third century B.C. to replace an earlier one that burned down and became known as one of the seven wonders of the ancient world. A well-known statue of Artemis emphasizes fertility. Paul's preaching directly challenged her worship and precipitated a riot that only official interaction could quell (Acts 19:23–41). In the end the worship of Christ prevailed and the cult of Artemis disappeared from history.

Asherah. The people of Israel had been settled in the promised land for only a brief time before their attention turned to the deities of the Canaanites. The Book of Judges chronicles this apostasy. The people forsook the Lord God to serve Asherah and her husband Baal (Ashteroth is an alternative name for Asherah; Judg. 2:13, 3:7).

The name "Asherah" and its variant spellings occur thirty-nine times in the Old Testament. In a number of these instances, Baal is mentioned along with Asherah. Evidence from Ugaritic mythologies and other texts suggests that the term refers to both the Canaanite goddess and cultic objects facilitating her worship.

That Baal and Asherah are mentioned together in several Old Testament passages suggests that the Canaanites and other peoples considered Asherah to be an important "high deity" along with Baal. The most explicit passage disclosing the close relationship between the two comes from the narrative about Ahab and Jezebel's confrontation with Elijah (1 Kings 18:1–19:18). Their endorsement of and participation in the worship of these Canaanite deities is the most extreme of any incidents related in Scripture concerning Israelite rulers who adopted the worship of these gods. In fact, Jezebel went so far as to insist that Ahab provide for the worship of her Phoenician deities.

Asherah was one of the three chief consort-goddesses within the Canaanite pantheon, along with Astarte (or Ashtaroth) and Anath. These three goddesses were jealous rivals. In the mythology, Asherah is portrayed as the consort of both El and Baal. In the Ugaritic myths she clearly emerges as the consort of El, the chief high god of the west Semitic pantheon. The Canaanite myths associated El with the source of fresh water, located in the distant west or north. On this basis El's consort was identified mainly as a sea-goddess. During the kingdom period of Israel's history she was the goddess at the side of Baal. On some occasions, however, she comes across as a fierce opponent of Baal—particularly when she thought she would lose her authority or influence among other members of the pantheon or when Baal preferred Anath instead of Asherah as his sexual intimate. The conflict and enmity between Baal and Asherah provided an explanation for the alternating two-climate season each year in the Mediterranean region.

The most shocking endorsement of Israel's buying into Canaanite religion was the construction of a temple for the worship of Baal at Samaria. This, as mentioned above, was promoted by Ahab (869–850 B.C.) and Jezebel, his wife, who was the daughter of the Tyrian king Ethbaal (1 Kings 16:29–34). This temple was constructed with the help of Tyrian artisans, along with an altar on which to offer sacrifices and a "sacred pole" (NRSV) or "wooden image" (NKJV). Because of this apostasy, judgment was poured out on Ahab and Jezebel. Jehu later destroyed this temple (2 Kings 10:18–31).

During the reign of Manasseh (687–642 B.C.) Canaanite religion was appropriated by the people of Judah from Geba to Beer-sheba (2 Kings 16:4–14). Manasseh added various aspects of Canaanite (a carved image of Asherah, 2 Kings 21:7) and other religions to the city of Jerusalem. He even offered his own son as burnt offering (2 Kings 21:6). Josiah later cleansed Jerusalem of the excesses of Canaanite worship (2 Kings 23).

The Israelites had been warned before settling the land of Canaan about established religious worship sites, particularly the "high places" taken over intact during the conquest. These sites were often furnished with basic cultic objects and resident sacred personnel. Cultic features included the following: small clay figurines (Judg. 3:7; Mic. 5:13); "sacred pillars" (1 Kings 14:23); an "incense altar" (2 Chron. 30:14); an altar for offering the whole burnt offering (2 Kings 21:5) and "priests" and "priestesses."

Several Canaanite high places were appropriated by Israel's religious leaders early in the settlement, including Bethel (Judg. 1:22–26), Shiloh (1 Sam. 1:1–18), and Gibeah (1 Sam. 13:1–4). Both Solomon (1 Kings 11:1–4) and Manasseh (2 Kings 21:1–17) encouraged worship at high places. Asherah and Baal worship caused the downfall of the northern and southern kingdoms of Israel.

Ashtoreth. Ashtoreth was a popular goddess in several cultures. Her worship attracted the Israelites shortly after their settlement in Canaan. At the heart of this pagan religion was the worship of the fertility or fecundity "forces/features" that characterized the animate aspects of the created world. Ashtoreth's popularity among the Phoenicians and other northwest Semitic peoples was long-standing.

The major confrontation between Ashtoreth and Yahweh took place during the days of Eli, Samuel, and Saul. Particularly after the defeat on Mount Gilboa, the people of Israel faced an almost imponderable theological dilemma. Instructions were sent throughout the land of the Philistines to proclaim victory over Israel and their God Yahweh. The proclamation was to be made in the temples of their idols and among the people (1 Sam. 31:6–10): the Baals and Ashtoreths were mightier than the Lord!

Ashtoreth's influence was finally discredited by Josiah, who "cleaned house" by destroying the shrines erected by Solomon. He made clear that Yahweh was the only—and true—God for the people of Israel

Baal. Baal—the most significant male deity of the Canaanites—and his consort Asherah were the most alluring deities confronting Israel in the promised land following the conquest. The numerous references to Baal in the Old Testament indicate his attractiveness and influence on the Israelites. The Book of Judges chronicles the numerous times the people fell to the temptation to worship Baal. During the time of Ahab and Jezebel Baal was declared the official national deity. A temple and hundreds of officiants were established for Baal's worship in Samaria (1 Kings 16:29–34). A final chapter concerning Baal worship was written during the reigns of Jehu and Josiah, when the southern kingdom and its capital were purged of the worship of Baal (2 Kings 10; 23:1–30).

Baal's name derives from the Semitic word *ba'lu*, meaning "lord." He was assumed to fulfill several significant roles by the peoples who worshiped him. As god of the storm the roar of his voice in the heavens was the thunder of the sky. He was the god who both created and granted fertility. He was the deity slain by enemies who thus fell into the hands of Death. During the time that Baal was under the control of Death, the vegetation wilted or ceased and procreation stopped. He was the god of justice, feared by evildoers.

The Book of Kings recounts that Jezebel used the plan of the Baal temple in Sidon for the construction of a similar temple in Samaria. Ahab agreed with her to make Baal worship the royal religion of the northern kingdom (1 Kings 16:29–31). Baal, like Asherah, was also worshiped at high places.

The cult of Baal involved the offering of many animal sacrifices. Priests would officiate on behalf of the persons presenting sacrificial animals to the god. Some of the northern kingdom rulers even "made their sons pass through fire"—offering their own sons as sacrifices to Baal. "Holy prostitutes"—both male and female—were available to worshipers, encouraging the fertility of both land and people.

Baal-zebub, Beel-zebul. Phoenician god worshiped at Ekron in Old Testament times (2 Kings 1:2–16). Original meaning of the name is unknown but the Old Testament form, Baal-zebub, means "Lord of the flies"; in Jesus' day this god is derisively called Beel-zebul (NIV Beelzebub), "lord of dung," and identified with Satan, the ruler of demons (Matt. 12:24). Jesus' enemies accused him of casting out demons by invoking Beel-zebul (Mark 3:22) and even of being his embodiment (Matt. 10:25). Jesus, rejecting this calumny, pointed out that the expulsion of demons was Satan's defeat, heralding the arrival of God's kingdom (Luke 11:20–22).

Chemosh. Chemosh was the primary national god of the Moabites and Ammonites. The Moabites are called the "people of Chemosh" in the passage of Scripture that details the travels of the Israelites through Edom, Moab, and Ammon, (Num. 21:21–32). During the reign of Solomon worship of Chemosh, along with that of other pagan gods, was established and promoted in the city of Jerusalem. Jeremiah specifically condemns the worship of Chemosh (chap. 38). The prophet focuses on the god's impotence by showing him going into captivity with his priests and people.

Dagon. Dagon was the highly venerated national deity of the Philistines. Each city of the Philistine pentapolis had its temple for the worship of this god. The temple statuary portraying Dagon was characterized by an upper human torso, with the lower torso of a fish. The major cultic rite in Dagon's worship was human sacrifice.

When the Philistines captured and overcame Samson, the five Philistine cities planned a great celebration. Dagon had delivered their enemy into their hands (Judg. 16:23–24)! The Philistines called for a sacrifice to their god. Presumably they intended to offer Samson as a human holocaust/offering. Dagon was, however, defeated by Yahweh.

Dagon haunted the reigns of both Saul and David. The Israelites relied on their theological understanding that Yahweh was mightier than Dagon—but, unfortunately, with an inexcusable naivete. When they brought the ark of the covenant from Shiloh and took it into battle against the Philistines, it did not result in their victory. However, the presence of the ark in Philistine hands led to the challenge to their god, Dagon, and the return of the ark to the Israelites.

Throughout the narratives relating the encounters between the people of Israel and the Philistines, there persists an underlying theological dilemma. Which deity is greater—and therefore the one to worship and serve: the Lord God or Dagon?

Hadad. Hadad was a prominent god among the Arameans, Syrians, and other west Semitic peoples. The name appears especially in the Edomite genealogy of Genesis 36 and in the history of the two Israelite kingdoms to the downfall of the northern kingdom in 722 B.C.

Hadad was the deification of natural forces and war. He was viewed as the god of the storm, who displayed his power in thunder, lightning, and rain. He was credited with both the good (desirable) and bad (undesirable) sides of storms. He was regarded as the origin and regulator of the beneficial rains, making him the principle of life and fertility. The Assyrians saw him as a mighty warrior-god. He was portrayed as standing on the back of a bull, wearing the horns of the bull on his helmet and wielding a mace and thunderbolt.

The name "Hadad" was used in reference to a human individual to indicate the essence or being of the patron deity, the power bestowed on that person, and bestowal of favor or help against an enemy or opponent. The name is used of a number of important persons in the scriptural record. Several rulers of the Edomites contemporary with David and Solomon had the name "Hadad."

Leviathan. Leviathan can be identified with Lotan, sea-monster of the Ugaritic Texts mythology. The Ugaritic myth recounts how Lotan and Baal were locked in mortal combat, until Baal killed the sea-monster. Leviathan is also mentioned in the Epic of Gilgamesh. The references to Leviathan in Scripture occur almost exclusively in poetic or semipoetic passages, emphasizing the might and control of the Lord God over the forces of nature.

Marduk. Marduk was the chief deity of Babylon. He became the supreme god among the older Sumerian gods as creator and ruler. Enlil was the original chief god until the Code of Hammurabi and the Creation Epic focused on Marduk instead. Jeremiah prophesied that Marduk would be put to shame (Jer. 50:2).

Milcom. Milcom, called the "abomination" of the Ammonites, was apparently the chief deity of the Ammonites or Moabites. The "abomination" label seems to convey both the detestable aspect of origin and of the worship of Lot's descendants. Solomon built a worship facility for this foreign deity (see 1 Kings 11:5, 7, 33). Milcom is sometimes identified with Molech, but this is incorrect since the two gods were worshiped individually.

Molech. Molech or Moloch was another "abomination" of the Ammonites. Solomon also built a high place for this god in Jerusalem. The worship of this god was particularly odious, as it required human sacrifice.

Queen of Heaven. Jeremiah was directed by God to speak out the Lord's disapproval of Israel's worship of the "Queen of Heaven" (7:18; 44:17–19). This female astral deity was particularly worshiped by the women in Judah and Egypt during the time of Jeremiah. Children were gathering firewood; women were busily kneading dough for cakes to be offered to this queen. The details and activity suggest that the Canaanite goddess Astarte was the deity motivating the people in Jerusalem to such frenzied worship activity.

Tammuz. Tammuz was a Syrian and Phoenician god of fertility, venerated in the worship of idols and elaborate, extreme rituals. The Greeks adopted Tammuz as one of their prominent deities, changing his name to Adonis. Ezekiel lists the worship of Tammuz as one of the abominations in God's sight (8:1–18) that was being practiced in the temple precincts in Jerusalem. The chanting of a litany of woes (or, singing a song, of lamentation—see Ezek. 8:14) shows that the cult of Tammuz was active in Jerusalem.

HARVEY E. FINLEY

See also IDOL, IDOLATRY.

Bibliography. W. F. Albright, *Archaeology and the Religion of Israel;* idem, *From the Stone Age to Christianity;* idem, *History, Archaeology and Christian Humanism;* idem, *Yahweh and the Gods of Canaan;* W. Dever, *Recent Archaeological Discoveries and Biblical Research;* M. Eliade, ed., *Encyclopedia of Religion;* J. Finegan, *Myth and Mystery;* A. Lamaire, *BAR* (1984): 43–51; J. B. Pritchard, ed., *Ancient Near Eastern Texts Relating to the Old Testament;* M. S. Smith, *The Early History of God;* G. E. Wright, *Biblical Archaeology.*

Golden Rule. ***The Old Testament.*** The term "Golden Rule" is not found in Scripture, but is the popular way of referring to the words of Jesus in Matthew 7:12 and Luke 6:31. Jesus states, "Do to others as you would have them do to you." With regard to the Old Testament, two main points prevail. Matthew's citation presents the Golden Rule as encapsulating the teachings of the law and the prophets. Matthew 7:12 reads, "So in everything, do to others what you would have them do to you, for this sums up the Law and the Prophets." Second, even though the Golden Rule addresses human interpersonal relationships, its message is essentially *theo*-logical. That is, the very character of God prescribes how we should relate to one another (Matt. 5:45; Luke 6:35–36).

Matthew 22:37–40 may serve as the "hermeneutical bridge" that joins the Golden Rule with the message of the Old Testament. For these two points, the sum of the law and the theocentric nature of the Golden Rule, are both found here. When asked what was the greatest commandment, Jesus claimed that to love God totally and to love one's neighbor as oneself was the sum of the Law and the Prophets (cf. also Mark 12:30–33; Luke 10:25–28). So adherence to the Shema (Deut. 6:4–5) and obeying the mandate to love one's neighbor (Lev. 19:18) essentially conveys the Golden Rule.

The immediate context of Leviticus 19:18 is restricted to the covenant community. Impartiality in judgment and forbidding vengeance is applicable to a "brother" (Lev. 19:17). From a Jewish perspective the words "fellow covenant member," "brother," and "neighbor" were synonymous. Yet within the same chapter the injunction to love one's neighbor as oneself is directed toward noncovenant members. Leviticus 19:34 requires that the "alien" in Israel is not to be mistreated, but is to be regarded as a native-born Israeli. So Jews must love noncovenant members just as themselves. This is the Golden Rule, if only in embryonic form.

Such themes are present throughout the Old Testament. In the Exodus motif the covenant mercies of God came to Israel not because of her righteousness, but because they were "aliens" in Egypt. God loves the alien, the fatherless, and the widow (Deut. 9:5–6; 10:18), and the Israelites are to love the alien as well (Deut. 10:19). Impoverished aliens are to receive aid so that they might remain in the land (Lev. 25:35; Deut. 15:7–8). Even the livestock of one's enemy is to be cared for and relieved of undue suffering (Exod. 23:4–5). Impartial judgment is to be meted out to both Israel and alien alike. There is to be no respecting of persons (Deut. 1:15–17). Likewise Exodus 34:6 represents an oft repeated theme in the Old Testament. God's love, mercy, and grace far exceed his desire to punish the wicked (cf. also Exod. 20:6). The classic example of God's love for the alien can be found in the Book of Jonah. Jonah laments the extraordinary grace and love shown to the Godless Ninevites (4:2). Similarly, God's unfailing love is clearly evident throughout Hosea.

God's benevolence to Israel is paradigmatic of his goodwill toward all humans. His compassion for people is seen in his love for the aliens among Israel, pagan nations such as Nineveh, and sinful persons such as Gomer in Hosea.

Yet the Old Testament is replete with exhortations to hate the wicked. Jehu inquires, "Should you help the wicked and love those who hate the LORD? Because of this the wrath of the LORD is upon you" (2 Chron. 19:2; cf. also Pss. 5:5; 26:5; 119:113–15; 139:19–22). The rabbis debated whether "neighbor" could ever be construed as "enemy." So the question of "Who is my neighbor?" was hotly debated in Jesus' day.

The New Testament. It is important to note that for both Matthew and Luke the broader context of the Golden Rule is the Sermon on the Mount (Matt. 5–7), or in Luke's case, the Sermon on the Plain (6:20–49). And just as the Golden Rule is the sum of the law and prophets, it can be argued that it also summarizes Jesus' teachings here. In these passages the longstanding ambiguity surrounding the meaning of "neighbor" is resolved with force and clarity. Matthew speaks of the Father giving good gifts to those who are "evil" (7:7–11). Luke expands upon this principle by associating the Golden Rule with loving one's enemies, blessing those who curse you, turning the other cheek, and being gracious to those who borrow, expecting nothing in return (cf. also Matt. 5:38–48). And with regard to the burning question, "Who is my neighbor?" Jesus responds with the parable of the good Samaritan (Luke 10:25–36).

From these passages the following principles arise:

1. The character of God serves as the paradigm for interpersonal relationships. The "Most High" is perfect, being kind and merciful to the ungrateful and wicked (Matt. 5:48; Luke 6:35–36).
2. Since the standard for conduct is the benevolent heart of God, the moral condition or evil behavior of the neighbor is irrelevant (Matt. 5:44).
3. Vengeance and retaliation are prohibited (Matt. 5:38–41; Luke 6:27–29).

Therefore the "Golden Rule" presents God as having unconditional positive regard for all human beings. In order to be perfect as he is perfect, and to be "sons of the Most High," we are to emulate the purest altruism and uncompromising impartiality of the Father, who seeks only the good of his creatures. WILLIAM A. SIMMONS

Bibliography. W. D. Davies and D. C. Allison, *The Gospel According to Saint Matthew,* vol. 1; J. D. M. Derrett, *NTS* 11 (1964–65): 22–37; N. Geldenhuys, *Commentary on the Gospel of*

Luke; R. K. Harrison, *Leviticus;* I. H. Marshall, *Commentary on Luke;* R. H. Mounce, *Matthew;* M. Noth, *Leviticus;* O. J. F. Seitz, *NTS* 16 (1969): 39–54; G. J. Wenham, *The Book of Leviticus.*

Good, Goodness. The main Old Testament words for good/goodness come from the Hebrew word *ṭôb* while the most common New Testament words are *kalos, agathos, chrēstos,* and their cognates. These words often appear in a nonmoral sense; a "good" or "good-of-appearance" woman is beautiful (Gen. 6:2; 24:16; 26:7; 2 Sam. 11:2; Esther 1:11; 2:2–3, 7) and a "good" man is handsome (1 Sam. 9:2). A land may be good (Deut. 1:25, 35) and so may gold (2 Chron. 3:5, 8), soil (Luke 8:8), a tree (Matt. 7:17), wine (John 2:10), or all of creation (seven times in Gen. 1). But the most theologically important uses of these words have to do with moral qualities.

God's goodness is a bedrock truth of Scripture. His goodness is praised in the psalms (25:8; 34:8; 86:5; 100:5; 118:1; 136:1; 145:9). Jesus affirms the Father's goodness when speaking to the rich young ruler (Matt. 19:17; Mark 10:18; Luke 18:19). In 1 Peter 2:3 Peter echoes the language of Psalm 34:8: "Taste and see that the LORD is good!"'

Although we might discuss God's goodness in some abstract philosophical sense, in Scripture his goodness appears most clearly in his dealings with people. He is not only good in general, but he is good *to us* (Ps. 23:6; 68:10; 73:1; 119:65; 145:9; Lam. 3:25; Luke 6:35; Rom. 2:4; 11:22; Eph. 2:7; Titus 3:4). Human goodness is modeled on divine goodness (Matt. 5:48). For human beings goodness involves right behavior, expresses itself in kindness and other praiseworthy qualities, includes avoiding evil, and springs from the inner person.

It is nearly impossible to think about goodness in the abstract. In Scripture goodness always involves particular ways of behaving. Because God is good, he is good to his people; when people are good they behave decently toward each other, based on God's goodness to them. Moses' invitation to Hobab expresses this emphasis: "Come with us and we will treat you well, for the LORD has promised good things to Israel" (Num. 10:29). The general biblical words for "good/goodness" include this idea of right behavior, although the idea is often expressed by means of a more specific term like "upright/uprightness" or "righteous/righteousness."

The goodness God's people exhibit shows itself in various moral qualities, notably kindness; *ḥesed,* translated "goodness" or "kindness," serves as one of the major synonyms of *ṭôb,* "good," in the Old Testament. In the New Testament many words describe the specific characteristics and behaviors of good people, including "just/justice," "righteous/righteousness," "holy/holiness," "pure/ purity," "gentle/gentleness," and "kind/kindness." If "goodness" is the general term, these other specific terms show what goodness means in daily living.

Goodness involves not only right behavior but also avoiding its opposite, evil. The choice between good and evil has lain before people since the garden of Eden when Adam and Eve ate fruit from the "tree of the knowledge of good and evil" (Gen. 2:9). Since then God's curse has fallen on "those who call evil good and good evil, who put darkness for light and light for darkness, who put bitter for sweet and sweet for bitter" (Isa. 5:20). A wise ruler like Solomon, or indeed anyone who wants to obey God, needs the wisdom to tell good from evil (1 Kings 3:9; Heb. 5:14). Those who serve God will "seek good, not evil, . . . hate evil, love good" (Amos 5:14–15).

For the Christian or the faithful Israelite, goodness has never been a matter of outward behavior alone; it comes from within. An evil person is evil within (Gen. 6:5; Mark 7:14–23 and parallels). In the same way a good person's good behavior shows a good heart (Matt. 12:33–35).

In the Old Testament God's goodness to his people and their goodness in response is based on the covenant between them. God's appeal to his people to return to the covenant relationship finds expression in a call to simple goodness (Mic. 6:6–8). In the New Testament goodness is a fruit of the Spirit (Gal. 5:22), while moral excellence is one of the steps on the "ladder of virtue" (2 Peter 1:5). CARL B. BRIDGES, JR.

See also FRUIT OF THE SPIRIT.

Gospel. "Glad tidings" or "good news," from Anglo-Saxon *godspell.*

The Old Testament. Good news is proclaimed *widely* (1 Sam. 31:9; Ps. 96:2–3; Isa. 40:9; 52:7), spread *rapidly* (2 Sam. 18:19–31; 2 Kings 7:9; Ps. 68:11), and declared and received *joyfully* (2 Sam. 1:20; Ps. 96:11–12; Isa. 52:7–9; Jer. 20:15).

Where the message is gospel for Israelites and based on fact, the news is in every case but one (Jer. 20:15) related to God the Savior. Psalm 40:9–10 celebrates his saving help. Kings and armies are scattered by the Almighty (Ps. 68:11, 14). It is he who delivers David from his enemies (2 Sam. 18:19–31). A direct act of God puts the Syrians to flight (2 Kings 7:1–9); he breaks the Assyrian yoke (Nah. 1:13, 15). Having conquered Babylon by the hand of Cyrus (Isa. 41:25, 27), the mighty God returns to Zion (40:9–10). The peace and salvation announced in Isaiah 52:7 are won by his sovereign power ("Your God reigns!"). "The year of the LORD's favor" brings glad tidings to the afflicted (61:1–2).

The explanation for God's saving action lies nowhere but in God himself. In whatever measure Israel has paid for her past sins (Isa. 40:2), she remains a sinful people (42:25; 46:12–13). She is saved by divine grace alone (55:1–7). There being no righteousness to reward, Yahweh acts to create righteousness in Israel (45:8; 61:3, 10–11). The penalty for sin is exacted not from Israel but from the Servant appointed to stand in her place (53:4–12). Through the Servant's work, many will be justified (53:11); those who possess no righteousness (43:25–28) will be acquitted.

The joy that attends the gospel finds ultimate expression in the praise of God. "Praise be to the LORD your God!" exclaims Ahimaaz in reporting victory to David (2 Sam. 18:28). The glad tidings of Psalm 68:11–14 are recollected during a festal procession celebrating God's enthronement (cf. Ps. 40:9–10). The watchmen of Isaiah 52:7–8 shout for joy over Yahweh's return to Zion. Psalm 96:1–3 summons the whole earth to tell of Yahweh's salvation, to "bless his name" and "declare his glory."

With the return of the exiles from Babylon, the salvation announced in Isaiah is but partly realized. The foreign nations, far from becoming her fellow worshipers, remain Israel's oppressors. Israel's own unrighteousness was to persist; the Servant appointed to bear her iniquities has not yet appeared. As Isaiah makes clear, the full realization of salvation awaits the dawn of a new age—an age created by the saving God. At the close of the Old Testament, the inauguration of this new age is still awaited.

The New Testament: Stage One. Except for Galatians 3:8 and Hebrews 4:2, 6, the New Testament restricts gospel terminology to proclamations made during the time of fulfillment, when the salvation promised in the Old Testament is *actually accomplished*. According to Mark 1:1–4 the gospel "begins" not in the Old Testament but with John the Baptist, in whom Old Testament prophecy is fulfilled. The promised birth of John, Messiah's forerunner, is good news (Luke 1:19). John's own preaching is gospel, too (Luke 3:18): it warns sinners of impending doom and urges them to repent before the axe falls (3:7–9); it assures the repentant of forgiveness (3:3) and membership in Messiah's community (3:17). Messiah's own birth is announced as "good news of great joy" (2:10–11). According to Romans 1:1–5 the gospel promised in the Old Testament is actually given when Jesus comes (see also Acts 13:32–33).

Jesus' gospel declares: "The time has come. The kingdom of God is near" (Mark 1:14–15). God reigns eternally over all that he has made. Yet his will is not done on earth as it is in heaven; wrong, not right, prevails. But these conditions are not final. With the *coming* of the kingdom, God's rule will be complete; wrong will be judged and right established. That kingdom is now being inaugurated: "The time has come" (Mark 1:15a) for Old Testament promises to be fulfilled. The consummation of the kingdom is no longer a distant prospect; the full realization of God's rule is "near" (Mark 1:15b).

In the synagogue at Nazareth, Jesus reads from Isaiah 61: "the Spirit of the Lord is on me, because he has anointed me to preach good news to the poor. He has sent me to proclaim freedom for the prisoners and recovery of sight for the blind, to release the oppressed, to proclaim the year of the Lord's favor" (Luke 4:18–19). the prophecy is fulfilled in Jesus' own ministry (4:21). He has come to free the physically infirm, such as the blind (4:18) and the leprous (4:27; cf. 7:21; 9:6). He helps the materially poor, like the widow in Elijah's day (4:25–26; cf. 6:20–25, 30–38). Yet the spiritually poor are primarily in view—people broken and grieved by misery and poverty, oppression and injustice, suffering and death, national apostasy and personal sin, who in their extremity cry out to God to bring forth justice, bestow his mercy, and establish his kingdom (Matt. 5:3–10). Jesus has come to usher in the kingdom, to rescue the lost, to liberate the enslaved, to cure the afflicted, and to forgive the guilty (Mark 2:5, 10, 17; 10:45; Luke 7:48–49; 19:10).

The coming of the kingdom is not the effect or the reward of human effort, but God's answer to the human predicament—the gift of his favor (Luke 12:32). The explanation for the salvation of the poor lies nowhere but in the gracious God. As the prodigal son recognizes, he is not worthy to be called his father's son; nothing he has done, not even his repentance, accounts for the father's love (Luke 15:11–32). In the parable of Matthew 20:1–16, it is owing to the goodness of the employer that the last workers hired receive a full day's wages. The first debtor in Matthew 18:23–35 has earned nothing but the right to be sold into slavery; instead the king cancels his enormous debt. The publican with nothing to offer God but a confession of sin and a plea for mercy is justified (Luke 18:13–14). The same holds true for the more virtuous among the poor, such as those described in Matthew 5:7–10. Their virtue is real, not imagined. Yet in keeping God's commands, they do not put him in their debt; they are simply doing their duty (Luke 17:7–10). Even the most merciful need divine mercy (Matt. 5:7); for even those most zealous to obey God's law are unable to fulfill all its requirements (Matt. 11:28–30). Grace depends for its exercise upon the inability of its objects (Luke 14:12–14).

As the Israelites are a sinful people (Matt. 1:21; Luke 1:77), Jesus proclaims his gospel to the whole nation (Matt. 4:23; 9:35; 15:24). From the most respectable to the least, all are summoned to submit to God's rule, to come to the banquet he has spread (Luke 14:16–24). Salvation must be received to be experienced (Mark 10:15). While it is a gift that costs nothing, it is also a priceless treasure for which a wise person will sacrifice all else (Matt. 13:44–46). "Repent and believe the good news!" commands Jesus (Mark 1:15). The self-righteous and the self-sufficient must be jolted out of their false security and recognize their need of God (Luke 6:24–26). An announcement of liberation (Luke 4:18–19) is good news only to people who are enslaved and know they are. Even the destitute and the afflicted must learn that it is being personally related to God as subject to sovereign and as child to father, which makes one "blessed" (Matt. 5:3–10). Even those who are already "poor in spirit" in the sense defined above, are not really "blessed" until they acknowledge the truth of Jesus' claims (Matt. 11:6) and commit themselves to a life of obedience on his terms (Matt. 7:21–27).

Throughout Jesus' ministry, the theme of his gospel remains the dawning kingdom of God (Matt. 4:23; 24:14; Luke 4:43; 16:16), a message preached almost exclusively to Jews (Matt. 10:5–6; 15:24). Yet Jesus provides glimpses into what the gospel is to become. He speaks of persons who make sacrifices "for me and for the gospel" (Mark 8:35; 10:29). Jesus and the gospel are here associated in the closest way. We are moving toward the time when the Proclaimer of the gospel will become the Proclaimed. Mark 13:10 and Matthew 24:14 foretell the preaching of the gospel of the kingdom to the Gentiles. Mark 14:8–9 indicates that Jesus and his death will be prominent themes in the worldwide gospel. Here we have an indication of the cruciality of Jesus' death both for the provision of salvation announced in his gospel and for the launching of the mission to the Gentiles.

The New Testament: Stage Two: For the gospel declared after Jesus' resurrection, our main sources are Acts and the letters of Paul.

God authors the gospel and authorizes its proclamation (Acts 15:7; 16:10; Rom. 1:1–5; Gal. 1:11–16; 2:7–9; 1 Thess. 2:2–9). God himself is an Evangelist, personally calling persons to salvation through his human agents (Acts 10:36; 2 Cor. 4:4–6; Gal. 1:6; 2 Thess. 2:13–14; Rev. 10:7). Paul's gospel is both a witness to an expression of God's grace (Acts 20:24; Col. 1:5–6), power (Rom. 1:16; 1 Cor. 1:17–25), and glory (2 Cor. 4:4–6; 1 Tim. 1:11). To accept the gospel is to turn to God (Acts 14:15; 1 Thess. 1:5–9). To disobey the gospel is to be deprived of the knowledge of God (2 Thess. 1:8). To trade the true gospel for a false one is to turn away from God (Gal. 1:6).

Risen from the dead, Christ again evangelizes (Eph. 2:16–17) through his representatives (Rom. 15:16–18; 1 Cor. 1:17; 9:12–18; 2 Tim. 1:9–11). Moreover, Christ has become the gospel's major theme. This is repeatedly affirmed in Acts and in Paul's writings. Mark describes his whole book as "the gospel about Jesus Christ" (1:1). Galatians 2:7–9 speaks not of two gospels but of two mission fields; Paul (apostle to the uncircumcised) and Peter (apostle to the circumcised) are both entrusted with the "gospel of Christ" (Gal. 1:7), the message ordained for the salvation of Jews and Gentiles alike (Rom. 1:16). The "different gospel" of Galatians 1:6–9 and 2 Corinthians 11:4 is not another gospel about Jesus, but a message about "another Jesus"—not the real Jesus, but one who exists only in the minds and the message of its advocates. On the other hand, to preach the true Christ is to preach the true gospel, however questionable one's motives (Phil. 1:15–18); to respond rightly to the gospel is to turn to Christ (Acts 11:20–21; Rom. 10:8–17; Gal. 2:14–16).

The gospel bears witness to every aspect of Christ's saving work, from his birth and public ministry to his second coming and the last judgment. But Christ's death and resurrection, the crucial saving events, are the gospel's most prominent themes. Mark's whole Gospel prepares for Passion Week. In Paul's gospel Jesus' death and resurrection are central (1 Cor. 15:1–4), with the cross at the very center (1 Cor. 1:17–2:5; Rom. 3:21–26; 2 Cor. 5:14–21). Acts proclaims Jesus' death (8:35; 20:24, 28) and preeminently his resurrection, the event by which he conquered death and was exalted as Lord and coming Judge (10:36–43; 13:32–33; 17:31). According to 1 Peter the bearers of the gospel focused, as had the Old Testament prophets, upon "the sufferings of Christ and the glories that would follow" (1:11–12).

Paul declares (Rom. 1:16; 1 Cor. 1:17–18) the gospel to be "the power of God"—not merely a witness to, but an expression of his power. The gospel is no bare word but is laden with the power of the Holy Spirit (1 Cor. 2:1–5; 1 Thess. 1:5–6). Thus it cannot be fettered (2 Tim. 2:8–9). The gospel effects the salvation it announces and imparts the life it promises.

The gospel offers salvation "through the grace of our Lord Jesus" (Acts 15:11). Paul testifies "to the gospel of God's grace" (Acts 20:24). The gospel is a *witness* to God's grace. In offering his Son as a sacrifice for sins (Rom. 3:25a), God demonstrates his righteousness (3:25b, 26). In Jesus' death sins formerly "passed over" (3:25c) become the object of divine wrath (1:18). Yet in the place where God deals justly with sins, he shows grace to sinners. For the judgment is focused not upon the sinners themselves but upon the One who stands in their place (4:25; 5:6–11; 2 Cor. 5:21; Gal. 3:13). Sinners are therefore freely pardoned (Rom. 3:24). The gospel is a *channel* of God's grace. "A righteousness from God is revealed" in the gospel (Rom. 1:17)—not merely expounded but unleashed, so that the gospel becomes "the power of God for salvation" (1:16). God activates his righteousness by bestowing it freely upon sinners (5:17). They are acquitted, justified, "declared righteous," by God the Judge by virtue of their union with Christ, who is himself their righteousness (1 Cor. 1:30; 2 Cor. 5:21; Phil. 3:9).

The gospel calls for a threefold response. (1) *Believing*. The gospel is "the power of God for the salvation of everyone who believes" (Rom. 1:16). Faith abandons all reliance on "works of law" for justification (Rom. 3:28) and trusts in God's grace imparted in Christ (Rom. 3:22, 26; Gal. 2:16, 20). One must believe the gospel for here God's salvation is mediated. (2) *Growing*. The gospel is both a message to be received and a place in which to stand (1 Cor. 15:1–2); it both gives and sustains life. The Spirit imparts wisdom by taking persons ever more deeply into the gospel of the cross (1 Cor. 1:18–2:16). Paul is eager to declare the gospel to the Christians in Rome (Rom. 1:15), by both his letter and his visit. (3) *Hoping*. "The hope held out in the gospel" (Col. 1:23) includes Christ's return and the heavenly glory (Col. 1:5; 2 Thess. 2:14–16), as well as the final judgment (Rom. 2:16). For those who embrace the gospel the judgment holds no terrors, because the Judge has rescued them from the wrath to come (Rom. 8:1; 1 Thess. 1:10); the last judgment marks their final vindication (1 Cor. 4:5; Gal. 5:5). Those who died after believing the gospel (1 Peter 4:6) have not suffered the fate of the lawless; their response to the gospel assures them of approval by the coming Lord (4:5–6; 5:4) and of a share in the imperishable inheritance of heaven (1:4).

J. KNOX CHAMBLIN

See also DEATH OF CHRIST; FAITH; GRACE; JESUS CHRIST; *KERYGMA*; SALVATION.

Bibliography. W. Barclay, *New Testament Words*, pp. 101–6; U. Becker, *NIDNTT*, 2:107–15; K. Chamblin, *Gospel according to Paul;* G. Friedrich, *TDNT*, 2:707–37; P. Stuhlmacher, ed., *The Gospel and the Gospels*.

Government. Administration of life in an organized society as well as the body of officials that presides over the process. Human beings discovered at an early stage in their history that a social situation in which "everyone did as he saw fit" (Judg. 21:25) proved to be an unstable, disorganized, and frequently even a dangerous one, in which unenlightened self-interest took precedence over the concerns of other citizens.

Consequently, what has been called a "theory of social contract" came into being. This meant that people agreed to live together as free citizens, and behave in such a manner that the interests of others were not harmed in the process. As a result, the various behavioral rules that were developed over a period of time came to be recognized as mechanisms designed for the common good. Some of these ancient social regulations have been unearthed in Mesopotamia by archeologists, and contain statements governing property rights, damage, reparations, and so on.

The earliest observable city-states are those occurring in Mesopotamia, some of which go back to at least 4500 B.C. One of these, Eridu, is the earliest example of settled occupation discovered so far in Iraq, dating back to 4000 B.C. A millennium later the Sumerians, a highly cultured group of uncertain origin, stated that history began when "kingship was lowered from heaven" to the city of Eridu. When the Sumerians came to Iraq they discovered that the land was already organized loosely into groups of villages and small towns, a system that they further developed. These aggressive, superstitious Sumerians set about devising patterns for civic life, and went on to lay the foundations of modern knowledge. In addition to the office of king, they believed that the gods had sent down to earth a collection of civic regulations that were intended to cover all sorts of social situations.

Under the Sumerians, communities such as Eridu, Ur, and Lagash became city-states, which were independent of each other and comprised the settlement itself and adjoining grazing and agricultural land. Sometimes these city-states cooperated socially, but more frequently tried to subjugate each other, and it was this threat of invasion that established the tradition of the king (*lugal*) as leader of the city's armed forces. Although his office became hereditary in time, his main concern was with the defense of the city-state rather than with its administration. After a time the city-state became a model for settlements in other parts of the ancient Near East.

The state's most prominent building was the main temple, which served as a center for worship and also as a depot for the priests to store agricultural supplies and goods intended for use in the temple workshop. Despite the widespread influence of the priests over the community, secular government was under the control of the governor (*ensi*), who not surprisingly came into conflict periodically with the temple priesthood. As a standard administrative procedure the *ensi* divided the free citizens into two groups for purposes of making important decisions. The first consisted of community elders who formed an "upper chamber," while the second or "lower chamber" comprised the young men who would rally to the defense of the city when threatened by a neighboring state, or pursue aggressive action themselves against a potential enemy. This bicameral, or "two-chamber," system proved to embody the checks and balances needed for good government and has survived the millennia to flourish in modern democracies.

Law and justice in society were fundamental concerns for the Sumerians, as well as for the later Mesopotamians, since they believed that upon such principles the survival of the state depended. The law was administered by the civil governor and his deputy, and numerous tablets recovered from levels dating from about 2500 B.C. on have illustrated the scope of their concerns. Court cases were heard by a tribunal of three judges, usually priests, who allowed both written and oral evidence, the latter being given under oath.

Their decisions were binding, but a case could be reopened if fresh evidence warranting it came to light. Where matters of minor importance were involved, the judges could order the plaintiff and defendant to settle the matter by engaging in a wrestling bout. The winner of the contest was the one who removed his opponent's belt first. The moral qualities of God's champion wrestler are stated in Isaiah 11:5, where he is girded with righteousness and faithfulness.

While the Sumerians were organizing their city-states, a single large counterpart was flourishing at Ebla in Syria. At its height, around 2300 B.C., it was a bustling commercial center that manufactured metal objects, textiles, semiprecious stones, and pottery, as well as bred cattle and grew grain. The state was engaged in trade with the Mesopotamians, Egyptians, Syrians, and Palestinians, and at its height it was one of the most powerful communities in the Near East.

Excavations at the site (Tell Mardikh) have shown that Ebla and its holdings were governed by the king and members of his family. In the upper area of the city were four administrative centers: the royal palace, which no doubt coordinated the functions of all the other offices; the city palace, which evidently handled civic affairs; the stables, the administrators of which would have dealt with imported and exported goods; and the palace of service, in which workers were apparently hired and their tasks regulated.

In the first two palaces ten officials directed the duties of about six deputies, while in the second and third palaces eighty leaders were in charge of about one hundred workers of lesser rank. In the lower part of Ebla were four areas of buildings, supervised by a chief inspector, with between ten and twenty leaders who supervised from thirty to one hundred assistants, depending upon the nature of Ebla's economy. From surviving tablets it appears that an estimated population of 250,000 persons was governed by a bureaucracy of about 6,000 people. For a third millennium B.C. empire this is an impressive achievement, matched only in complexity by modern civil services.

The ruler of Ebla was deemed to be the owner of the large city, as well as all the lands and vineyards that surrounded it, these being worked by tenant-farmers. Interestingly enough, the king was known by the Sumerian title *en* or the Syrian *malik,* the latter being similar to the Hebrew *melek,* ("king"). The royal sons assisted in governing this large city-state, some tablets indicating that a senior prince dealt with home affairs, while another was in charge of foreign concerns. Administrative officials below the level of royalty were styled either *lugal* or *diku,* the latter meaning "judge." Not very much is known about other facets of civic life because of the enormous difficulty experienced in attempting to translate a highly sophisticated language.

A more complete picture comes from the ruins of nineteenth-century B.C. Mari on the Euphrates. Over 20,000 tablets have been recovered dealing with religious, administrative, legal, economic, and other matters. As with Ebla, the government of this large Amorite city-state was complex and well organized, and included women functioning in prominent positions. The Mari population was probably less homogeneous than that at Ebla, consisting of seminomadic peoples and the settled Akkadians.

To make government even more difficult, the nomads had links with a group known as the Yaminites or "sons of the south." They were actually dispersed widely throughout Mesopotamia and parts of Syria, and raised flocks and cattle as well as being involved in some agricultural work. To raise their animals properly it would be necessary for the tribes to search for pasture in the steppe lands, and to withdraw later to their winter homes. They tended to resist government from the capital, preferring instead the nomadic system of rule by tribal chiefs. These heads of families would decide about matters such as local feuds, alliances, and some trading, but when summoned for consultation by the central authorities they acted as spokesmen for the tribe. It was usually difficult to keep abreast of their movements, and even more difficult to impose taxes on them. They apparently had their own "king" or "kings," but those persons were probably military commanders of the Sumerian variety, and not city-state rulers as such.

The formulating of covenant agreements was prominent at Mari, but unlike Hittite covenants they were largely exercises in symbolic ritual rather than being written contractual statements. The Mari Empire had its own class of judges, whose status was actually more that of provincial rulers than persons who simply made judicial decisions based upon evidence. The judge was probably an individual of great prestige among his fellow-tribesman, and as such would be able to negotiate with the central government on behalf of his people.

Contracts dealing with adoption occur in the Mari archives, and these are of interest because they are connected with the transfer of property. The law forbade the sale of inheritances, stipulating that they could only be transferred legally upon the death of the owner. It was possible, however, for a nonfamily member to be "adopted" on the payment of an appropriate fee, and this practice circumvented the law. Some adoption contracts stipulated that the firstborn was to receive double the amount allotted to other family members (cf. Gen. 15:2; Deut. 21:15–17). In other legal matters, the terminology of the royal census relating to enrollment procedures, the forms of ritual purification, and questions of discipline exhibit parallels with Exodus 30:13–14.

Prominent Sumerian rulers had identified themselves with law and justice in an attempt to reduce the amount of administrative corruption in their city-states. Early proponents of civic reform were Urukagina (ca. 2350 B.C.) and Ur-Nammu (ca. 2070 B.C.), both of whom produced lists of regulations that have survived in fragmentary form. But the most famous royal legislator of antiquity was Hammurabi of Babylon (ca. 1792–1750 B.C.). This man was an outstanding administrator, military strategist, and lawgiver. He manifested a pronounced sense of concern for his subjects' welfare, often attending personally to complaints about corruption in his kingdom. While there were government officials responsible for administration, they are seldom mentioned in surviving diplomatic correspondence. His major contribution to society was to formulate the so-called Code of Hammurabi, a collection of enactments covering civil, criminal, administrative, and other issues. It was based in part upon earlier Sumerian sources, but it is by far the most comprehensive statement of its kind in antiquity. It survived in the form of a broken black diorite monument with a base of just over six feet and tapered to a height of over seven feet. It was recovered from Susa in 1902, and was a codification of the laws of Hammurabi's day. Whether the contents were meant to be imposed upon his kingdom, or served merely as a guide when he made judicial decisions, is uncertain.

The Hebrews of Abraham's day were mostly semisedentary, living in constructed dwellings during the winter and in spring setting out with their flocks to find new pasture, a tradition they followed for some centuries (see Gen. 37:13–17). The fundamental unit of patriarchal society was the family, and this was augmented by various family groups to become a tribe. The heads of families became rulers in the tribe, and these persons, known as elders, administered customary law, made treaties, and occasionally allied with other tribes in battle.

Abraham and his descendants could be described as theocratic groups insofar as they considered themselves bound by obedience to God. This concept took dramatic shape when, under Moses, the twelve tribes pledged allegiance to God at Mount Sinai, and among other privileges received a gift of land, from which they were instructed to drive out the inhabitants. The pledge to God (Exod. 24:7) made a theocratic society out of tribes who had normally followed a casual and unregulated life, and the constitution given to them in the Sinai covenant contained specific laws that they were required to obey if they were to become a holy nation (Exod. 19:6). For nomadic people to be compelled to live according to strict and detailed regulations, some of which were similar to Hammurabi's enactments, was a severe discipline in itself that proved to be a sore burden, even in later sedentary times.

God's rule over Israel was that of a king who mediated his will on specific occasions through elders, military leaders such as Moses and Joshua, and the priestly hierarchy, which was responsible for maintaining the strict purity of religious rituals. When Canaan was conquered, the various tribes settled in the territories that God had allotted to them through Moses (Num. 34:2–15), and built small settlements. The transition to a theocratic commonwealth occurred at a covenant-renewal ceremony (Josh. 8:30–35), in which an expanded form of the covenant, including stipulations from Deuteronomy, was accepted.

With the passing of strong leadership at the death of Joshua and the increasing influence of pagan Canaanite customs on Israelite life, the covenant fell into disrepute and the elders lost control of their communities. The old nomadic ideal of people following their own individual ways of life overtook the covenant concept of communal and spiritual solidarity and led to the demand for a king to maintain order (1 Sam. 8:5). This pagan model was contrary to theocratic concepts and met with God's disapproval. Nevertheless, he allowed Samuel to anoint Saul as Israel's first "king" (Saul was really a charismatic leader rather than a pagan type of king). Such persons were supposed to govern under God's guidance, but from the end of the Solomonic period, kings in northern Israel became absolute monarchs. This meant that their behavior was unhampered by exceptions or restrictions, giving them complete ownership of their subjects and property alike. David had established an administrative pattern for kingship in a theocracy by delegating many duties to persons known officially as "servants." The role of elders and nobles was recognized (1 Kings 21:8, 11), the former discharging their duties as judges at the city gate and the latter acting as advisors to the royal court.

David instituted a number of bureaucrats such as the recorder (1 Chron. 18:15), a powerful archivist who also controlled much of court life; the scribe (1 Chron. 18:6), who with his assistants maintained official records; the priest (1 Chron. 18:17), who evidently served the king in an advisory capacity; the supervisor of labor (2 Sam. 20:24), who recruited captives and others for forced labor in the kingdom; the palace steward (1 Kings 18:3, 6), who was a highly placed royal official; and the bureaucrat, who was chiefly responsible for collecting taxes.

Solomon adopted an Egyptian administrative procedure when he divided the kingdom into twelve districts controlled by deputies, who were responsible for providing food successively each month for the king and his officials. For military protection David enlisted skilled fighters to command units of various sizes (2 Kings 1:9–14), and these were supplemented by specially trained groups (2 Sam. 10:7, 9; 11:17) and foreign mercenaries (2 Sam. 8:18; 15:18). Archers were part of Israel's armed forces but chariots were not used in battle until Solomon's reign (1 Kings 10:28).

During this period the Israelites became involved increasingly in treaty relationships with foreign nations. Sometimes the encounter took the form of an alliance, as with Asa of Judah and Ben-hadad (1 Kings 15:18–20), but also occurred as a peace treaty or as a coalition against a common enemy (2 Kings 3:6–9). When Solomon ventured into international politics, he amassed a large number of foreign princesses as wives and these marriages seem to have been integral to the validation procedures of the various treaties (1 Kings 3:1; 11:1–3). At a later period in the monarchy it became the tradition to appoint special court officials to serve as ambassadors (cf. Isa. 18:2; Jer. 49:14) and representatives of the monarch. These sophisticated procedures were maintained in varying degrees until Judah's captivity in 581 B.C.

The return from exile in Babylonia furnished an opportunity for the restoration of a true theocracy. The population of Judea was organized in terms of temple worship under the leadership of a high priest and his priestly subordinates. Since Palestine was part of the Persian Empire, it fell under the jurisdiction of the provincial governor who oversaw "Beyond the River" (Ezra 5:6). Zerubbabel was one of these persons (Hag. 1:1, 14), and ruled in Jerusalem (Ezra 5:9; 6:7) with the Jewish elders who had reconstructed the second temple. When Nehemiah came to Jerusalem in 446 B.C. he did so as the governor and established the city as the capital of Judah. For administrative purposes the area was divided into districts (Neh. 3:9–18), which were under the control of a prince (*sar*).

The Persians were lenient rulers and consequently the Judeans enjoyed a significant measure of autonomy, due to the official policy of encouraging local culture and religion. Ezra's great contribution to true theocracy came with his insistence upon the Mosaic law as the basis of all spiritual life. The high priest became an important religious and political figure, while the emphasis on the law brought the scribes into new prominence as interpreters of the words of Moses. This powerful religious combination was augmented subsequently by the rise of the Sadducees and Pharisees, who exercised an important influence over Jewish life when Palestine was occupied by the Romans.

Theocratic principles were reinforced by the institution of the synagogue, which had its roots in exilic worship in Babylonia. Each small town had its own synagogue, where the men met to worship on the Sabbath and to hear the law explained. The gathering was presided over by a "ruler," who also supervised the work of three governing "elders."

In addition to its purely religious functions, the synagogue was a place where meetings could be held to discuss community concerns. But the most important governing body in postexilic Judaism was the Sanhedrin (Matt. 26:59; Acts 5:21). Its origins are obscure, but it may have developed during the Greek period that followed Persian rule. At that time the Jews established a council of elders, which was accepted as the legal representative of Judaism. Under Roman rule the Sanhedrin was responsible for governing Judea, and in Christ's time it was respected as the supreme court of justice (Matt. 26:59; John 11:47). There were a few subsidiary sanhedrins in Judea that were directed by elders, but the final authority lay with the Jerusalem Sanhedrin.

The concept of a Sanhedrin or "council" may have been Sadducean originally, since the Sadducees were a priestly aristocracy. But by the Roman period the Pharisees and scribes had been included in the Jerusalem Sanhedrin. In the Jewish commonwealth the office of high priest had come into increasing importance. By the Greek period (331–65 B.C.) he had acquired prominence as the person empowered to levy taxes in Judea and to ensure that they were collected. It was not long before the high priesthood became a political appointment, which was unfortunate for Jews and Romans alike when the Maccabeans revolted after 167 B.C. against attempts to secularize Jewish culture.

In New Testament times these conditions were still being maintained. Thus Jesus was familiar with the established bureaucracy, which he criticized in various ways. He recognized the status of the occupying Roman power and taught the rebellious Jews to pay appropriate tribute (Matt. 22:16–21). While acknowledging the supremacy of God, he submitted himself to the power of the Jewish authorities (Matt. 26:57–66) in order to fulfill God's plan for human salvation. The Sanhedrin did not have the power to execute Jesus, however, since that was the prerogative of the Romans.

Submission to authority was characteristic of the Lord's behavior, since the state was understood to be God's provision for human safety and well-being. While the ideal state was theocratic, it could not be realized until the kingdom of God was consummated. Meanwhile the governing authorities had to be accepted as a divine surrogate, and consequently, disobeying them was the same as disobeying God (Rom. 13:2). Peaceful behavior as a citizen would be rewarded in due time, but evildoing would be punished, because that was one of the important responsibilities of the state (Rom. 13:4).

Paul taught his hearers that, regardless of the character of the state's leaders, its authority was still to be recognized because that authority proceeded ultimately from God. Paul set an example for all believers by submitting to the laws of the Roman Empire, which in any event was a matter of moral obligation since he was a Roman citizen. By following established procedures he enjoyed the protection of the state at times when fanatical Jews would have killed him (Acts 23:12–13), and was actually treated reasonably well by Roman authorities such as Felix, Festus, and even Agrippa, who was of the family of Herod and owed his title of "king" (Acts 25:24) to the Romans.

The remarkable period of peace and prosperity (Pax Romana) which the emperor Augustus instituted established the authority of the emperor, but also placed considerable emphasis upon the emperor's subjects, one-half of whom were slaves. It was thus entirely proper for Christian leaders such as Peter to require believers to submit to "every authority instituted among men," whether to a supreme king or state officials appointed by him (1 Peter 2:13–14). While the official worship of the emperor was incompatible with acknowledging Jesus as Lord, the king was to be given the honor due to his position as an authority figure under the hand of God (1 Peter 2:17).

The New Testament does not forbid Christians to serve as government officials, which is proper inasmuch as it permits the leaven of the gospel to work in secular society. Whatever Christians may think about the nature and objectives of civil government they are encouraged to work toward such changes as will benefit society and honor Christ. But civil disobedience, whatever the intentions of the participants, will bring down upon them the wrath of the state, and may well thwart movements toward the same objectives that are being done legally, if covertly. Anything that disintegrates the state inevitably brings social chaos and this is contrary to the Lord's decree that everything should be done decently and in order. R. K. HARRISON

See also ISRAEL.

Bibliography. R. D. Culver, *Towards a Biblical View of Civil Government;* C. F. H. Henry, ed., *Aspects of Christian Social Ethics;* K. A. Kitchen, *The Bible in Its World;* A. N. Sherwin-White, *Roman Society and Roman Law in the New Testament;* W. Temple, *Citizen and Churchman.*

Grace. The word "grace" in biblical parlance can, like forgiveness, repentance, regeneration, and salvation, mean something as broad as describing the whole of God's activity toward man or as narrow as describing one segment of that activity. An accurate, common definition describes grace as the unmerited favor of God toward man. In the Old Testament, the term that most often is translated "grace," is *ḥēn;* in the New Testament, it is *charis.*

The Old Testament. The word *ḥēn* occurs around sixty times in the Old Testament. There are examples of man's favor to man, but the theological concept of importance to us is the grace of God demonstrated toward man. The term occurs most often in the phrase favor "in your (i.e., God's) sight" or "in the eyes of the Lord." This assumes the notion of God as a watchful master or king, with the one who is finding favor, a servant, an employee, or perhaps a soldier.

The concept first occurs in Genesis 6:8. Noah finds "favor in the eyes of the LORD." The context is that the Lord was grieved at "how great man's wickedness on the earth had become" (Gen. 6:5). This statement about the Lord's antipathy toward man is followed by his promise that he will wipe humankind from the face of the earth, that is, completely destroy him, because of his anger at their condition. Noah is then described as having found favor in the eyes of the Lord. The themes of judgment and salvation, in which the vast majority of humankind are condemned to destruction, while God finds favor on a few (Noah and his family), reoccurs often in connection with the idea of grace. Hence, concepts of election, salvation, mercy, and forgiveness are all linked in this first illustration of grace in the Old Testament. Interestingly, the rest of the references to favor in Genesis all describe favor in the eyes of man (e.g., Jacob begging Esau's favor, 32:5; 33:8, 10, 15).

Crucial among the Old Testament passages on the unmerited favor of God is the conversation between Moses and God recorded in Exodus 33. There, in the space of six verses, Moses is said to have found favor with God five times, *ḥēn* being translated either "find favor" or "be pleased with." At the beginning of the chapter, Moses goes into the tent of meeting, while the pillar of cloud stands at the entrance to the tent, and the people of Israel stay outside, worshiping (v. 10). The Lord speaks to Moses "face to face, s a man speaks with his friend." In the passage, the conversation between Moses and the Lord has to do specifically with the favor that God shows to Moses, and Moses requests that God demonstrate that favor toward him. Moses begins by reminding God that he has called Moses to lead these people, but that God has not let him know whom he will send with Moses. The statement echoes the original conversation between Moses and God at the burning bush in chapter 3, where God promises to send Aaron with Moses to help him get the people out of Egypt. Here, the Lord promises only that his "Presence" will go with Moses, and that he will give him rest (v. 14). Moses has just stated that he knows God's name (another echo of chap. 3), and that he has found favor with God; he requests that God teach him his ways, so that he may "know you and continue to find favor with you" (v. 13). Moses demonstrates his humble dependence upon the grace of God by affirming that if God's Presence does not go up with them, he does not want to be sent, because he knows they will fail (v. 15). But he asks the reasonable question, "How will anyone know that you are pleased with me and with your people unless you go with us?" (v. 16). God promises to go with him in the next verse because "I am pleased with you and I know you by name" (v. 17).

Moses then makes one of the most remarkable requests of God ever made in Scripture, asking God to "show me your glory." Just as remarkable is that God answers his request positively. He promised to "cause all my goodness to pass in front of you" and that he will proclaim his name "Yahweh" in Moses' presence. He then makes a statement that is connected with grace throughout Scripture, one that Paul will quote in the context of election in Romans 9: "I will have mercy on whom I will have mercy, and I will have compassion on whom I will have compassion." This is a remarkable example of the unconditional and full character of the grace of God. God holds very little back, only telling Moses that he "cannot see my face, for no one may see me and live." Even this is an act of unconditional and full grace in that God has withheld from Moses what would destroy him. The passage closes with the strange instruction that God will cause his "glory" to pass by, Moses being hid in a cleft in a rock and covered with the hand of God until the glory has passed by. Then God will remove his hand and allow Moses to see the back of his glory, but not his face. Again, this protective, gracious act of God emphasizes the extent to which God is willing to go with his faithful servant to show his favor toward him.

Moses again speaks of finding favor with the Lord in Numbers 11:4–17. When the people of Israel complain at having only manna and not any meat, Moses cries out to the Lord in an apparently sincere state of vexation at the burden of judging this entire people by himself: "I cannot carry all these people by myself; the burden is too heavy for me. If this is how you are going to treat me, put me to death right now—if I have found favor in your eyes—and do not let me face my own ruin" (vv. 14–15). Without questioning his integrity or his strength of character, God immediately gives Moses a solution to his problem by appointing seventy of the elders of Israel to help him carry the burden of the people, "so that you will not have to carry it alone" (v. 17).

At the same time, God even answers the question that Moses has not asked: What about meat for the complaining people? God instructs Moses that he will give them meat for the month, though he will give them more meat than they want, as the story makes clear. The fact that the Lord brings judgment upon the people, however, does not vitiate the point of God's favor toward Moses in this passage. He still acts as a sovereign who gives complete, unmerited favor to his servant.

God's favor sometimes extends to the fact that he will wait upon man as if he were his servant. Gideon, when called by God to lead Israel against Midian, asks God to wait while he goes to get his offering to set before him (Judg. 6:17). As with Moses, the statement is in the context of the promise of the Lord to be "with you, and you will strike down all the Midianites together" (Judg. 6:16). When Gideon actually brings the offering that he has prepared, God shows his grace beyond what Gideon has asked by giving him instructions on where to place it and how to arrange it, then creating a supernatural fire that consumes the meat and the bread. After he disappears, Gideon realizes that he has seen the "angel of the Lord" and, interestingly, makes reference to the fact that he has seen him "face to face," recalling the passage in Exodus. God shows his grace one more time by assuring Gideon that although he is afraid since he has seen the angel of the Lord face to face, he is not going to die (Judg. 6:23).

Samuel, too, finds favor in the eyes of the Lord (1 Sam. 2:26). Here, the boy Samuel is described as growing in stature and in favor, not only with the Lord, but also with men. This verse is quoted, of course, in the New Testament, using the heavily theologically weighted term *charis* in relation to Jesus (Luke 2:52). It is significant because it is a description of the growth of a child in the favor of God. The child cannot earn that favor since he is merely a child. Thus, God's grace toward those whom he loves grows in its extensiveness, as the child grows. This is perhaps no less important because of Samuel's unique relationship to salvation history. He is the last of the judges and is the transitional figure between the period of the judges and the period of the kings in Israel's history, as John the Baptist is in the New Testament between the Old Testament prophets and the New Testament evangelists.

Remarkably, the life of David is devoid of references to finding favor in the eyes of the Lord, though often he finds favor in the eyes of men, or requests such favor (1 Sam. 16:22; 20:3, 29, etc.). One reference, however, is striking, especially in light of the dearth of references elsewhere. As David flees the city of Jerusalem after hearing that Absalom has been crowned king in Hebron, he takes the ark with him. A particularly faithful servant named Ittai, the Gittite, has declared his faithfulness to David, even though David has given him leave to go back and spare himself potential death by association with David. The procession continues into the desert, where it stops so that they can offer sacrifices with the ark in their midst. Then the king tells Zadok the priest to take the ark back into the city because he knows it belongs in the temple of the Lord. In a remarkable display of trust in God and in his sovereignty, David says that if he finds favor in the Lord's eyes, then God will bring him back.

But if he does not, then David is ready; as he puts it, "Let him do to me whatever seems good to him" (2 Sam. 15:26). David recognizes that the unmerited favor of God has to do with God's choice, not his. Grace in the Old Testament is just as much an act of the sovereign will of God as is grace in the New Testament.

The last prominent example of grace in the Old Testament is found in the Book of Esther. Of course, the book does not speak of *God's* favor at all, but Esther's humility in seeking the favor of the king has always been understood as a pointer toward human responsibility to humbly accept the grace of God. Esther finds favor in the eyes of the king and is rewarded with the freedom of her people (5:1–8; 7:3; 8:5–8).

Only a few references close out the notion of grace in the Old Testament, but they are significant. Ezra in his notable prayer to God when he finds that the people have intermarried with foreigners against God's will (Ezra 9), states that God has been gracious to the people of Israel "for a brief moment," in doing two things. The first is that he has left the people of Israel a remnant. The remnant is a sign that God's gracious favor bestowed upon Israel in the covenant continues on even in times of great disobedience and/or destruction among the Israelites, though this is the only reference to the remnant in the context in which *ḥēn* is used in the Old Testament.

God has also given them "a firm place in his sanctuary, and so our God gives light to our eyes and a little relief in our bondage" (Ezra 9:8). Here is a reference to the grace that is shown the people in the giving of the temple and the light that it brings to Israel. But in the context of the Book of Ezra, this may also be a reference to the grace shown by God in giving Israel the Law, since the reading of the Law and the confession of the sin of the people on the basis of that reading is so important to this book.

Another crucial reference is found in Jeremiah 31. The famous passage about the new covenant (vv. 31–34) is enough of a statement about the grace of God on its own, but it is linked to the *ḥēn* of God by the occurrence of that word in 31:2. Introducing the same passage with the phrase "at that time," an echo of the beginning of the covenant passage in 31:31, God says that "the people who survive the sword will find grace in the desert; I will come to give rest to Israel." Here is a promise of the grace of God given to the people when they are given the new covenant. The new covenant, of course, is a promise that God will be their God, and they will be his people, with the Law written upon their hearts and present in their minds, and the gracious promise that all God's people will know him. From the least of them to the greatest, they will be forgiven their wickedness, and God will remember their sins no more.

The New Testament. Grace in the New Testament is largely encompassed by the use of the word *charis.* While the idea of unmerited favor is found in some other places, the concept may be fairly restricted within the bounds of this article to the use of that term. It is worth noting that, though Jesus is never quoted as using the word *charis,* his teaching is full of the unmerited favor of God. Perhaps the parable of the prodigal son is the most obvious example. In that parable grace is extended to one who has no basis upon which to be shown that grace, other than the fact that he has asked in humility and repentance to be shown it. Other parables demonstrate grace in the teaching of Jesus, perhaps most notably the parable of the laborers in he vineyard (Matt. 20:1–16) and the parable of the great supper (Luke 14:16–24).

While the idea of grace can be said to be largely a Pauline one, there are references to it in John and Luke as well. John describes Jesus as "full of grace and truth" and speaks of his people receiving grace upon grace from the fullness of his grace (John 1:16). In one of the most important theological statements about grace in Scripture, John says that the Law, a good thing, was given through Moses; the better things of grace and truth came through Jesus Christ (John 1:17).

When we turn to the writings of Luke, we find that Jesus is described as having the grace of God upon him (Luke 2:40) and as growing in grace with God and man (Luke 2:52). Many more references to grace are found in the Book of Acts. Luke makes a strong association between grace and power, especially in the early chapters (4:33; 6:8; 11:23). Grace is found without qualifier (18:27) and in the phrases "message of his grace" (14:3), "grace of God" (14:26), "grace of our Lord Jesus" (15:11), "grace of the Lord" (15:40). The distinction between these phrases does not seem acute, and therefore the basic synonymity between them points to an intention on Luke's part to make a statement about the deity of Christ. Again, these phrases often seemed to be linked with the power of God to create spiritual life and to sustain Christians. This grace is, as in the Old Testament passages, an unmerited favor, but now a new aspect of power in the Spirit has been added to it.

The concept of grace is most prominently found in the New Testament in the epistles of Paul. The standard greeting in the Greek ancient world generally involved the verb *charein.* Paul's greeting, however, was unique, combining the Hebrew greeting, *shalom* (*eirene* in Greek) with the word *charis.* This in itself is enough to note that Paul is thinking and not simply reacting as he writes his greeting.

The fact that he sometimes uses grace in his benedictions as well, which clearly are intentional, indicates that his greetings are to be taken with some seriousness. For instance, the benediction in 1 Corinthians 16:23, coming just after his dramatic plea to the Lord to come, demonstrates a strong belief in the grace of God. In the salutation of the letter (1:3), one gets a greeting that follows on from a strongly worded theological statement about sanctification and calling (1:2) and that leads into a statement about grace in 1:4 demonstrating the theological import Paul intends. A similar seriousness could be argued about the other salutations in Paul's letters.

Overwhelmingly in the letters of Paul God is the subject of grace. He gives it freely and without merit. Hence the many different phrases connected with grace: the grace of God (Rom. 5:15), the grace of our Lord Jesus Christ (2 Cor. 13:14), and the like. Sometimes this is explicitly stated, as in Ephesians 4:7: "to each one of us grace has been given as Christ apportioned it."

Interestingly, Paul sometimes mentions the gift of grace from God using alongside it language that speaks of human responsibility. So in Romans 15:16, Paul speaks of "the grace God gave me to be a minister of Christ Jesus to the Gentiles, with the priestly duty of proclaiming the gospel of God." Grace, then, is the power with which the human being then performs his or her gifted task. This is even more clearly seen in Paul's self-defense in Galatians. In one of the most truly dialectic passages in Scripture, Paul proclaims that he has died, yet lives, yet not he but Christ lives, yet he lives in the body by faith. He then argues that in living "by faith in the Son of God, who loved me and gave himself for me," that he is not "setting aside the grace of God" (2:20–21). Only an argument that Paul was too dependent upon works in his life would create the argument that he was not setting aside the grace of God in his understanding of the sanctified Christian life.

Grace can be such a forceful thought for Paul that he sometimes anthropomorphizes it. Hence, in 1 Corinthians 15:10, in the midst of an emotional defense of his apostleship despite the fact that he had persecuted the church of God, Paul says that he is what he is by the grace of God. He then goes on to compare himself to others who had worked among the community, the other apostles, and declares that he worked harder than all of them. In order that this statement might not seem boastful, Paul follows it up by saying "yet not I, but the grace of God that was with me." Though this grace is said to be God's grace, it nevertheless is said to be "with him," and working harder than the other apostles, and is tantamount to equating the grace of God with the Holy Spirit.

In Ephesians 1:6 Paul speaks of the "glorious grace" of God, which should garner our praise. Of course, once again, Paul is not expecting us to praise an abstract comment, but he is thinking of the grace of God working so mightily in his life that it becomes a metonymy for God. The highly rhetorical character of the passage in which this verse is found (1:3–14) helps explain the power of this statement. The point is that Paul was so saturated with the notion of grace in his writing that he thought of it as an essential, if not *the* essential attribute of God.

Grace is most often associated in Paul with other terms having to do with salvation. We see it related to election (Eph. 1:3–6), to the gospel (2 Cor. 4:15; Col. 1:5–6), explicitly to justification (Romans *passim*, esp 3:23–26; Eph. 2:8–9), and most often to sanctification (Rom. 5:2, 21; 6:1, 14, 15; 2 Cor. 12:9; Eph. 2:10; Titus 2:11–14). It is even used with the human subject in speaking of the collection for Jerusalem as a work of grace.

In connecting grace to election Paul sees God as electing us before the creation of the world for the purpose of holiness and blamelessness (Eph. 1:4). He predestined us to be adopted as sons into the family of God (Eph. 1:5). All of this elective work is so that we might "praise his glorious grace." In other words, election and grace go hand in hand because of their free character. We can do nothing to deserve them.

This is the essential connection also with the gospel. In one of Paul's passages about the suffering that a minister of Christ undergoes, he speaks of faith and continuing in ministry "because we know that the one who raised the Lord Jesus from the dead will also raise us with Jesus and present us with you in his presence" (2 Cor. 4:14). Paul sees this as the benefit of not only the Corinthians but also all who receive his ministry, so that "the grace that is reaching more and more people may cause thanksgiving to overflow to the glory of God. Therefore we do not lose heart" (vv. 15–16). Grace thus renews Paul's inward spirit and assures him of glory in the afterlife (vv. 16–17). Hence, Paul's ministry is not one that he always does joyfully or motivated by his own power, but rather motivated by faith that God is working in the present and will reward him in the eschaton.

In the same way, he links the grace of God with the gospel in Colossians 1:5–6. The word of truth, the gospel, is bearing fruit and growing at the present time "just as it has been doing among you since the day you heard it and understood God's grace in all its truth" (v. 6). The parallel descriptions of "gospel" and "grace" as "truth" link the two as synonyms in the passage. This grace is therefore the "hope that is stored up for [them] in heaven" (v. 5), presumably something God is doing in heaven for them, and hence free from merit.

Perhaps the most dominant metaphor with which grace is associated is the legal metaphor of justification. We see the two linked in two very important passages in which grace is used in Paul. Romans 3:23–24 states quite clearly that all have fallen short of the glory of God and are "justified freely by his grace through the redemption that came by Christ Jesus." Here, while the language of the slave market may be implied in the use of the word "redemption," and that of the cultus in the use of the phrase "sacrifice of atonement" in the next verse, the strongest linking with grace in this passage is with the word "justified" in verse 24. Hence the unmerited favor of God buys us legal freedom from our sin and cancels the sentence of guilt the judge has had to declare in order "to be just and the one who justified those who have faith in Jesus" (v. 26). It is interesting to note that the next thought of Paul is: "where, then, is boasting? It is excluded" (v. 27), again emphasizing that grace is free and not the work of man.

In Ephesians 2:8–9 Paul states the free character of grace perhaps even more explicitly, now not using the language of justification but simply of salvation. We are told that we have been saved "by grace" but "through faith." Grace is seen here as the means by which we are saved, a free gift; faith is seen as the mechanism by which that salvation or grace is appropriated. Paul must then go on to argue that even faith is "not by works so that no one can boast" (v. 9).

This does not mean that Paul keeps grace separate from works in sanctification, for he goes right on to speak of us being God's workmanship created in Christ Jesus to do good works (v. 10). Similarly, grace is seen as being in the midst of our present Christian life. In Romans 5:2 Paul speaks of gaining "access by faith into this grace in which we now stand" and in 5:21 of grace reigning "through righteousness to bring eternal life through Jesus Christ our Lord." While all of this is in the context of the grace of God as a gift versus the Law of God as a work, nevertheless grace is viewed as reigning even as we live the life we are supposed to live in Christ. Hence the argument of Romans 6 that we are not to go on sinning so that grace may increase, but we are to "count [ourselves] dead to sin but alive to God in Christ Jesus . . . for sin shall not be [our] master, because [we] are not under law, but under grace" (vv. 11–14). The key metaphor used in this chapter to describe this "work" of sanctification is "offer." Hence we are not to "offer the parts of [our] body to sin as instruments of wickedness," but rather offer ourselves to God, "as those who have been brought from death to life" (v. 13). This is done as slaves, offering ourselves in obedience to him (v. 16).

Even the suffering of the present Christian life is linked to the grace that God gives us. In Paul's famous statement about the thorn in his flesh (2 Cor. 12:7–10), he speaks of asking three times that this thorn be taken from him, only to receive the answer "my grace is sufficient for you, for my power is made perfect in weakness." Here grace is equated with the power to live the Christian life and to do ministry in the name of Christ. So Paul delights even in the hardships of that ministry. In a similar way, the whole of the Christian life is linked to grace in Titus 2:11–14. This grace "teaches us to say 'No' to ungodliness and worldly passions, and to live self-controlled, upright and godly lives in this present age, while we wait for the blessed hope." Here we see both the ethic of the Christian life (saying no and living uprightly) and the thought of the Christian life (the blessed hope) combined under the reign of grace.

Finally, grace is associated strongly with the gifts of the Spirit. This is true of the list of gifts in Ephesians 4:3–11 corporately to the church and the gifts given to individuals within the church for its edification (Rom. 12:4–8; 1 Cor. 12). In all of the work of grace about which Paul speaks, the Spirit has been implicit if not directly explicit. Hence, even though grace is not specifically mentioned in 1 Corinthians 12, we find that the Spirit gives to each one a gift "as he determines" (v. 11). The simple mention of these attributes as "gifts" throughout the chapter implies that they are a work of grace as well, but the connection with grace is explicit in the parallel passage of Romans 12:3–8. Here Paul states we have different gifts "according to the grace given us" (v. 6), and he has opened the passage by proclaiming that the source of his statement about thinking of others more than you think of yourself by saying that it comes through grace (v. 3). The somewhat different list in Ephesians 4 is similarly controlled by the notion of grace. Paul states in verse 7 "to each one of us grace has been given as Christ apportioned it." As he then describes this grace that has been given, it comes in the form of apostles, evangelists, and pastors/teachers in order "to prepare God's people for works of service, so that the body of Christ may be built up" (v. 11).

The notion of grace as connected to the Spirit of God is continued by the author of Hebrews in such a way that even mentions "the Spirit of grace" (10:29). Hebrews also emphasizes the connection of grace to salvation (2:9), sanctification (4:16; 12:15; 13:9), and the final blessing of God (13:25).

The other literature in the New Testament also emphasizes the free character of grace. The one reference in James links it to God's gift (4:6). Peter, who also includes it in his greeting, quotes the same Old Testament verse as James (1 Peter 5:5) and speaks of us as stewards of the grace of God (4:10). Peter also closes his second epistle with a benediction in joining us to "grow in the grace and knowledge of our Lord and Savior Jesus Christ." The Book of Revelation also begins with a salutation and closes with a benediction that includes grace (1:4; 22:21), the only two references to grace in the entire book.

ANDREW H. TROTTER, JR.

See also FAVOR; PAUL THE APOSTLE.

Bibliography. H. Conzelman, *TDNT,* 9:359–415; H.-H. Esser, *NIDNTT,* 2:115–24; A. B. Luter, Jr., *DPL,* pp. 372–74; J. Moffatt, *Grace in the New Testament;* C. R. Smith, *The Bible Doctrine of Grace;* J. H. Stringer, *NBD,* pp. 442–44.

Grain Offering. *See* OFFERINGS AND SACRIFICES.

Gratitude. *See* THANKFULNESS, THANKSGIVING.

Grave. Place where the physical remains of a deceased person are interred. It is "the place appointed for all living" (Job 30:23). It is where all go, even animals (Eccles. 3:19–20). It is a place with no class distinctions (Job 3:14–19).

In Old Testament times, a person who touched a grave was unclean (Num. 19:16–18). Thus almost all burials took place outside the city except for certain kings. Ezekiel prophesies that Judah will never again defile God's name with the corpses of their kings. The grave became a metaphor for human depravity. Paul quotes Psalm 5:9 ("their throat is an open grave") as part of his scriptural basis that all people are under sin (Rom. 3:9, 13). Jesus compares some people in his day to whitewashed tombs that are beautiful on the outside but "full of dead men's bones and everything unclean" on the inside (Matt. 23:27). They are only outwardly righteous.

A grave could be a symbol of pride. Absalom followed the practice of ancient Near Eastern kings when he built himself a monument (2 Sam. 18:18). Isaiah proclaimed that no one had the right to build such arrogant structures. Shebna, the royal steward, was told that he would be hurled out of the country for chiseling out a resting place for himself on the high rock (Isa. 22:15–19).

A grave might be a symbol of respect. Nehemiah remembered Jerusalem as the place of his father's grave (Neh. 2:5). Jacob set up a pillar to mark Rachel's tomb (Gen. 35:20). Not being interred in the family tomb was considered unthinkable. The anonymous prophet was punished in this way (1 Kings 13:22). Josiah did not desecrate this tomb out of respect for him (2 Kings 23:15–18). Jeroboam's baby was the only one good enough to deserve a burial (1 Kings 14:13).

To show disrespect for idolaters the dust of broken cult symbols was scattered over their graves (2 Chron. 34:4). Josiah broke into the tombs at Bethel and burned the bones of the idolatrous priests upon the altar there to defile it (2 Kings 23:15–17). In Revelation 11:9 men do not bury the two witnesses to show contempt for them.

Graves at times symbolized hopelessness. The Gadarene demoniac made his home among the tombs (Mark 5:2). It is a place of no return, where there is gloom, deep shadow, and disorder (Job 10:21–22). There is no activity there (Ps. 88:5, 16; Eccles. 9:10). But it is not necessarily a final resting place. Human beings will lie there until the heavens are no more (Job 14:12). The tomb is not an "eternal home" but a "dark house" (Eccles. 12:5).

A grave is also a symbol of hope, however. With the resurrection of Christ tombs in Jerusalem were opened and the dead came out (Matt. 27:52). When people threw a body into Elisha's grave, it came back to life (2 Kings 13:21). David's tomb reminded Peter of his prophecy that says, "You will not abandon me to the grave" (Acts 2:27–29). Jesus said that "all who are in their graves will hear his voice and come out" (John 5:28–29). Christianity is still best represented by the empty grave (John 20:1–9). PAUL FERGUSON

See also BURIAL; DEATH; FUNERAL; HELL.

Bibliography. W. Coleman, *Today's Handbook of Bible Times and Customs;* R. de Vaux, *Ancient Israel,* vol. 1; N. J. Tromp, *Primitive Conceptions of Death and the Nether World;* H. W. Wolff, *Anthropology of the Old Testament;* R. Youngblood, *A Tribute to Gleason Archer.*

Great Commission, the. Mandate to "make disciples of all nations" given by Christ to his disciples following his death and resurrection (Matt. 28:16–20; Mark 16:15–18; Luke 24:46–49; John 20:21–23; Acts 1:8). Because Christ has been given all authority in heaven and on earth (Matt. 28:19), the Great Commission is to be taken with the utmost seriousness by all of his disciples, "to the very end of the age" (Matt. 28:20).

The impetus for the Great Commission springs from the heart of God. He loved us and gave his Son or us (John 3:16). The disciples are sent out to accomplish what God had started in the sending of his Son (John 20:21). The Great Commission is thus linked to God's words to Abraham: that "all peoples on earth will be blessed through you" (Gen. 12:3).

The Great Commission is accomplished through witnessing (Acts 1:8), preaching (Mark 16:15), baptizing, and teaching (Matt. 28:20). Jesus' disciples are to replicate themselves in the lives of those who respond to the Good News. The Holy Spirit is the empowering agent for those who witness (Acts 1:8), as well as the one who convicts sinners of their need for Jesus (John 16:8–11). The disciples will have success because Jesus, the Lord of heaven and earth, will be with them as they undertake their assignment (Matt. 28:20).

The Great Commission necessitates taking the gospel message to "the ends of the earth" (Acts 1:8), to "all nations" (Matt. 28:19). The Good News is to be shared with all peoples, for all are sinners, Jews and Gentile alike, and in need of deliverance from sin (Rom. 3). All peoples, by faith, can receive God's provision and are baptized into Christ. In Christ, all distinctions between Jew and Gentile disappear (Rom. 10:12–13; Gal. 3:28). GLENN E. SCHAEFER

Greatness. Something or someone that is larger in size, quality, or quantity may be called "great." It is a term used for something beyond the ordinary. In the Bible, God, humans, and Christ receive this designation with theological significance.

God. The Bible describes God as the greatest of gods (Deut. 10:17); his greatness is unsearchable (Ps. 145:3). In discussing this theological characteristic of God, how do we understand an attribute that is not understandable? Its very abundance makes our task difficult (Ps. 150:2).

God by nature is great. The Bible affirms the greatness of his power (Job 23:6; Ps. 66:3, Eph. 1:19). Strength and might describe him (Isa. 40:26; 63:1). The "greatness of majesty" becomes the worshiper's cry for who God is (Exod. 15:7; Deut. 5:24).

Of course, the clearest view of God's greatness comes from his actions toward creation, especially toward his people. Creation records his greatness and leads to our praise (Ps. 145:6). God's care of the children of Israel in the wilderness demonstrated his greatness (Deut. 3:24; 11:2). When Jesus healed a boy suffering from demon possession, the people affirmed the greatness of God in the act (Luke 9:43).

God also exhibits greatness in love toward humanity by forgiving (Num. 14:19) and by redeeming (Deut. 9:26). Nehemiah asks God to remember him for his attempt to preserve the holiness of Israel. The basis for his request revolves around the greatness of God's lovingkindness (Neh. 13:22).

As an attribute, the greatness of God describes the extent and magnitude of his qualities.

Humans. Humans also may be considered "great." After the plagues of Egypt, Moses was "great" in importance both in Egypt and among the people of Israel. The queen of Sheba attested to the great wisdom of Solomon (2 Chron. 9:6). Nebuchadnezzar's greatness returned to him after he humbled himself before the Lord (Dan. 4:36). Mordecai achieved greatness in his position in the Persian government (Esther 10:2).

Human greatness depends on the quality of a person's life. It is something that may be taken away, as in the case of Nebuchadnezzar, or may be lost, as in the case of the greatness of the nation of Egypt (Ezek. 31). "Great folly" takes away any semblance of greatness (Prov. 5:23).

Psalm 71 explains that the actions of some enemies, perhaps due to old age, may lead to lost prestige. The psalmist's prayer attests to a trust in God to restore the former "greatness" (v. 21). Right standing in the community will be restored in the same way that God worked before the difficulties that took them away.

Christ. Christ turned the definition of human greatness in a profound direction. Jesus modeled greatness by humbling himself in coming to earth and dying on the cross (Phil. 2:5–11). Jesus made this perspective clear in his teachings. When the disciples asked who is the greatest in the kingdom, Jesus answered by bringing a child into their midst and declaring that even admission into the kingdom depended on a similar attitude of humility (Matt. 18:1–4).

The mother of James and John asked if her boys could sit on the right and left hands of Jesus in the kingdom. The other disciples became upset with the brothers. Jesus used the occasion to say that the one who wanted to be great among them had to be their servant (Matt. 20:26; cf. 23:11). Jesus noted that his life would exemplify this attitude by his service, including the gift of his life (Matt. 20:28).

The greatness of a person is measured by service to others. Christ set the example.

G. Michael Hagan

See also God.

Greeks. *See* Nations, the.

Grief, Grieving. Scripture often speaks of God as being grieved or experiencing grief. This holds true for each member of the Trinity. In Genesis 6:6–8 the Father is grieved because of the sinfulness of the human race. The disobedience of Israel and the church grieves the Holy Spirit (Isa. 63:10; Eph. 4:30). The Son of God is a man of sorrows, acquainted with grief (Isa. 53:3–10; Matt. 23:37–39; Luke 13:34–35; John 11:35).

The Bible often expresses the things of God in human form or with human feelings in order to accommodate our limited understanding. Yet with regard to grief and grieving, the Scriptures are not simply explaining a divine action in human terms. Rather, the subject of divine grief addresses the very essence of God as a person and the image of God in all persons. The grief of God testifies to that dynamic, living relationship that exists between God and humankind. Right as Aristotle was in many ways, God is not an "Unmoved Mover."

God is grieved when his covenantal love is rebuffed by human disobedience and sin. His anguished response to sin is evidenced in two main ways: divine judgment and compassion for the sinner. Although antithetical in nature, these aspects of God's grief work together for salvation. Genesis 6:5–8 serves as a paradigm in this regard. The Hebrew root for "grieve," *nḥm,* communicates a mixture of divine indignation against sin and a heartfelt anguish concerning the plight of his creation. Thus, in grief, God responds in judgment against sin, yet bestows saving grace and mercy on Noah and his family (Gen. 6:7–8). The end of the ordeal is marked by a reaffirmation of God's covenantal faithfulness to his entire creation (Gen. 8:21–22). So in grief God punishes, identifies with the moral plight of his creatures, and accomplishes his redemptive purposes.

This pattern occurs repeatedly in God's dealing with Israel. God was grieved when Israel rebelled and forgot his special covenantal favors (Pss. 78:40–55; 95:10). They grieved his Holy Spirit, which led God to become the very opposite of what he wished to be. He ceased to be their loving Father and became their enemy (Isa. 63:10). Yet his chastening hand relents and ultimately brings restoration (Ps. 106:45–46; Jer. 26:19; Amos 7:3–6; Jon. 3:10).

The punitive and salvific aspects of God's grief coalesced in the person and work of Jesus Christ. Sin grieved the goodness of God and assailed his holiness. In judgment he condemned the creation of his own hands. Yet in grief and through grief he redeemed the world by his Son (John 3:16). Isaiah's messianic prophecy describes God's Anointed as a man of sorrows, acquainted with grief (Isa. 53:3). Jesus wept at the death of Lazarus, pleaded with Jerusalem, and agonized in the garden (John 11:33; Matt. 23:37–39; Luke 13:34–35; Matt. 26:38; Mark 14:34; Luke 22:44). He learned obedience through suffering so that in all things he might be touched by the suffering of all people (Heb. 4:15; 5:7–8).

WILLIAM A. SIMMONS

Bibliography. E. Brunner, *The Christian Doctrine of God;* V. P. Hamilton, *The Book of Genesis: Chapters 1–17;* K. Kitamori, *Theology of the Pain of God;* L. J. Kuyper, *SJT* 22 (1969): 257–77; J. K. Mozley, *The Impassibility of God;* J. N. Oswalt, *The Book of Isaiah: Chapters 1–39;* J. Ridderbos, *Isaiah;* G. J. Wenham, *Genesis 1–15;* C. Westermann, *Isaiah 40–66.*

Guilt. ***Definition.*** The meaning usually given to the word "guilt" in Christian circles today bears little relation to the biblical meaning. Recent Christian interest in the subject focuses on its psychological dimension, analyzing the causes (and cures) of the sense of guilt, which is deep-seated in all of us and paralyzes the lives of some. It would seem to be easy to distinguish between this subjective sense of debt, which may be fed by groundless fears, and the objective guilt of sinners before God, with which the Bible is concerned.

The distinction is valid but there is more overlap than first appears. The Bible is alive to the psychological effects of guilt, as can be seen, for instance, in characters like Jephthah and David: Jephthah in his horrifying violence against fellow Israelites after his daughter's death, and David in his supine attitude toward the sins of his sons. A deep feeling of guilt, even if caused by oppressive parenting, can yet have a positive effect in deepening our appreciation of our failures before God and the debt of obedience that we owe.

The Old Testament has a semitechnical term foundational for the biblical concept of guilt, and which teaches us that guilt is fundamentally a relational idea.

Guilt and Guilt Offering in the Old Testament. The Hebrew noun *ʾāšām* means both "guilt" (e.g., Jer. 51:5) and "guilt offering" (the term used in Lev. 5:14–19; 7:1–10, etc.). The difference between "guilt" and "sin" is important here. Whereas the words for "sin" focus on its quality as an act or as personal failure, *ʾāšām* points to the breach in relationships that sin causes, and in particular to the indebtedness that results. When Isaac tries to pass off Rebekah as his sister, Abimelech accuses him of nearly bringing *ʾāšām* upon him (Gen. 26:10)—the kind of *ʾāšām* he had already incurred with Abraham, when he had to make expensive amends for taking Sarah into his household (Gen. 20:14–16), even though God prevented him from actually committing sin (Gen. 20:6).

The legislation in Leviticus 5:14–6:7 and Numbers 5:5–10 makes this special quality of *ʾāšām* clear. When someone incurs "guilt" toward a neighbor, full restitution must be made, plus an extra fifth. And then, in addition, a "guilt offering" must be made to the Lord, because when we sin against others and incur "indebtedness" to them, we violate the order that God prescribes for his world and his people, and have thus incurred a debt toward him also.

So an *ʾāšām* is a debt for which we must make amends. The Old Testament points to a coming figure whose life will be an *ʾāšām* for others (Isa. 53:10).

Liability and Forgiveness in the New Testament. The New Testament has no word equivalent to *ʾāšām*, but this idea of indebtedness is clearly still crucial. Sins are called "debts" in the Matthean version of the Lord's Prayer (6:12, 14). But the idea of making restitution has vanished: the debts that others owe us must simply be written off. And this is modeled on God's action toward us: we must forgive, as he forgives us. The lost son returns to his father with an *ʾāšām* in his hands—his readiness to make amends by being a servant rather than a son (Luke 15:18–19). But he is accepted unconditionally. In the parable of the unmerciful servant Jesus shows that we owe God an enormous debt, far greater than we could possibly repay (Matt. 18:21–35). By the smallest words of hostility we make ourselves "liable for" the fires of hell (Matt. 5:21–22), a debt we can never pay and remain alive (cf. Matt. 5:26; James 2:10).

The New Testament has no need for a word equivalent to *ʾāšām* because we do not need to pay. The Son of Man gives his life as a "ransom for many" (Mark 10:45), paying our indebtedness for us.

STEPHEN MOTYER

See also FORGIVENESS; SIN.

Bibliography. L. Aden and D. Benner, eds., *Counseling and the Human Predicament: A Study of Sin, Guilt, and Forgiveness;* M. France, *The Paradox of Guilt: A Christian Study of the Relief of Self-Hatred;* P. Tournier, *Guilt and Grace.*

Guilt Offering. *See* OFFERINGS AND SACRIFICES.

Hh

Habakkuk, Theology of. The prophet Habakkuk faced the violence and injustice of King Jehoiakim (609–597; see Jer. 22:13–18) as well as the cruel onslaught of Babylonia. Interestingly the book that bears his name begins with an extended description of the coming of the Chaldeans. This has an unsettling effect on Habakkuk (1:6–11), causing him to focus on the problems around him even more. The book ends with a revelation of the coming of the awesome God (3:3–15). This causes Habakkuk to focus on God, resulting in joyous peace (3:17–19).

The book begins with a lament asking "why" and "how long," but ends with a song of victory. The triumph of faith in the life of Habakkuk illustrates that our greatest struggles come not in our relationship with other people but in our relationship with God.

God. God's works are incomprehensible, stupefying, and sometimes horrifying (1:5; 3:2, 16). He has sovereign control over human history. The seemingly invincible Chaldean army becomes totally subservient to his every wish (1:6). His decrees seem slow but they are infallible and sure (2:3). He is enthroned in his holy temple and all the earth must keep silent before him (2:20).

God is eternal and immortal (1:12). He is holy and unable to look on evil (1:13). His glory and brilliance eclipse all the forces of nature. The sun and the moon are overwhelmed by his brilliance (3:3, 11). All the dreadful phenomena of the storm attend his coming, yet he is separate from all this. All nature is a passive creation that must do his bidding. He is exalted in his temple (2:20), yet he is a personal God who can be called "my God" (1:12). He possesses such unchangeable stability that he can be called "Rock" (1:12).

God is not affected by age. He can act today with just as much power as he ever did. Habakkuk finds upon his watch tower a theology sufficient even for a nation confronted with its demise. The psalm in chapter 3 reflects Habakkuk's thoughts about God's saving acts of the past (v. 2). Perhaps he regularly heard singing about God's redemptive acts for Moses (Deut. 33:2–5, 26–29), for Deborah and Barak (Judg. 5), and for David (Ps. 18). His psalm has almost direct quotes from them (cf. Ps. 18:33 with Hab. 3:19).

The most striking difference is that the old traditions the prophet draws on for strength regularly portray the coming of the Divine Warrior in the perfect tense of the Hebrew verb, denoting completed action. Habakkuk, however, consistently uses the imperfect tense to emphasize progressive action, vividly showing that he sees those fortune events happening before his very eyes in a vision of faith.

Habakkuk sees God coming, not to defeat the sea god as in Canaanite mythology, but on behalf of his scattered, downtrodden people. Through eyes of faith Habakkuk can see God's awesome power unleashed in his very own day against the arrogant nations who would destroy God's chosen ones (3:13, 16).

All the forces of death and destruction are under God's command. All manner of invincible weaponry are at his disposal. Chariots do not belong to Pharaoh but to God. His brilliant lance and his dazzling arrows frighten even the sun and moon into stunned silence (3:11). He tramples the ancient sea in his fury (3:8, 15). The most permanent and immovable objects are shaken violently at his coming (3:6, 10). Geography itself is radically altered before him (3:9). Spectators along the route of his march are shaken (3:7). Baal's palace crumbles into dust when Yahweh, the Divine Warrior, passes by on his way to battle elsewhere.

Humankind. People are apt to be violent, impulsive, destructive, and unjust. Human nature is such that if justice is delayed, they will be swift to do evil. Humans are prone to gather up what does not belong to them with insatiable greed (1:5–6, 9; 2:5–8). They worship might, or whatever they perceive to be necessary for an elegant lifestyle (1:11, 16).

But while people can be fierce, they are also frail, undependable, and prone to self-destruction

(1:14–15). They can be as helpless as fish caught in a net (1:14). They can be as erratic as creatures creeping upon the earth. Only a direct act of God can save us from ourselves. True life is not to be found in an arrogant, self-assured attitude, but through faith in God (2:4).

Salvation. Habakkuk searches feverishly for theoretical answers, but instead he is given a practical way of relating to his life. He is challenged to a life of faith that will take him through the period between prophecy and fulfillment: "The righteous will live by his faith" (2:4).

Faithfulness is an inner feeling of total dependence, an inner attitude as well as the conduct it produces, rather than an outer behavior. Those of faith will look back to God's known saving acts and be able to face the unknown future unafraid. Habakkuk's faith is so vivid that through the eyes of his soul he can already see the salvation of God.

Habakkuk's faith comes by hearing the word. He fills his heart with God's words. They become so real to him that he is able to speak forth, to add his own testament to faith as one of the greatest affirmations of trust in the entire Bible. He senses that in his lifetime he might see deprivation and famine, but his faith, grounded in the old traditions and alive in his heart in the present, gives him joy (3:18). His faith provides relief and ecstasy. He is as free as a deer on the mountains (3:17–19).

The person who lives by faith is contrasted with the arrogant, puffed up person whose soul is not right with God. The writer of the Book of Hebrews follows the Septuagint, which renders the first part of the verse as "if he shrinks back, I will not be pleased with him" (Heb. 10:38), and then goes on to say that "we are not of those who shrink back and are destroyed, but of those who believe and are saved."

Ethics. Insatiable greediness leads only to frustration (2:5). Such people will become the victims of stinging proverbs (2:6). Personal property is inviolable in God's sight (1:6). Those who live only for things and try to enslave or use their neighbors for their benefit will meet the same fate (2:6–7). God is especially sensitive to the plight of the weak and defenseless, pronouncing a woe on those who prey on them (2:10–12). Building is not wrong in itself but doing it at the expense of others makes even the rafters cry out (2:11–12). God is equally concerned about the exploitation of natural resources such as cedars of Lebanon used in Nebuchadnezzar's building program and the animals that he ruthlessly hunted down (2:17).

People who are arrogantly trying to set their nest in the heavens at the expense of others are really sinning against themselves (2:9–10). It is not clear whether the woe pronounced against drink is literal or figurative, but the cup will eventually pass back to the one who first offered it (2:15–16). Idolatry carries its own judgment by leaving the worshiper without hope (2:18–19).

The various woes pronounced by God indicate that he sees everything, certainly more than the prophet does. In his own good time he will take action. But he will not be driven by emotions. He will not act until the fullness of time comes.

Eschatology. There will be a day when the earth will be filled with the knowledge of the glory of God as the waters cover the sea (2:14). This is the final goal of all God's work. History is not cyclical, a never-ending recurrence of one bad thing after another. It is linear, moving toward the goal of the kingdom of God. The prophet knows that there is no power in the world of nature or any human ruler that can subvert God's plan for the world.

God is still working in the arena of human history. He has not yet abandoned the prophetic for the apocalyptic. We need Habakkuk's keen sense of faith. What is happening in our world is the work of God, although we do not always understand that work.

PAUL FERGUSON

See also ISRAEL; PROPHET, PROPHETESS, PROPHECY.

Bibliography. D. Baker, *Nahum, Habakkuk, Zephaniah;* R. D. Haak, *Habakkuk;* A. Jepsen, *TDOT,* 1:316–20; R. D. Patterson, *Nahum, Habakkuk, Zephaniah;* J. J. M. Roberts, *Nahum, Habakkuk, and Zephaniah;* R. L. Smith, *Micah-Malachi;* M. E. Szeles, *Habakkuk and Zephaniah;* J. D. Watts, *The Books of Joel, Obadiah, Jonah, Nahum, Habakkuk and Zephaniah.*

Hadad. *See* GODS AND GODDESSES, PAGAN.

Hades. Greek term widely used to denote the deity of the underworld and the abode of the dead. The New Testament use of Hades (*hadēs*) builds on its Hebrew parallel, Sheol (*šĕʼôl*),which was the preferred translation in the Septuagint.

The Old Testament. Sheol refers primarily to death and the abode of the dead, both godly and ungodly (Gen. 37:25; Pss. 16:10; 88:10–12; Isa. 14:9). These conscious souls face a lethargic existence, apparently without reward or retribution (Job 10:21; Eccl. 9:10; Isa. 14:10). Since death is not a natural occurrence but invaded creation through the fall and Satan's destructive work (Gen. 2–3), the Old Testament personifies Sheol as the power of Satan and his demonic hosts (Job 18:14; Ps. 18:4–5; Isa. 28:15; Jer. 9:21). While an antagonist, Sheol ultimately exists at Yahweh's service (1 Sam. 2:6; Pss. 55:23; 139:8). The Old Testament confidently awaits God's victory over Sheol (Ps. 98; Isa. 25:8; Hos. 13:14). But the precise expectation of a bodily resurrection for the wicked and the related conception of Sheol as an intermediate state is late (Dan. 12:2).

The New Testament. This indeterminate picture of Sheol and its Greek translation, Hades, allowed varying interpretations by intertestamental Jews.

In the New Testament Christ's revelation and salvific work decisively shape this term. For Christ has established authority over all powers (Eph. 1:20–23), even the one who "holds the power of death" (Heb. 2:14; 2 Tim. 1:10). He is the "Lord of both the dead and the living" (Rom. 14:9).

Hades is the state in which all the dead exist. In the New Testament a descent to Hades may simply refer to someone's death and disembodied existence. In this sense even Jesus enters Hades. Following David's prophecy in Psalm 16:10, Peter interprets the resurrection as God delivering Jesus from Hades (Acts 2:27, 31). Similarly, Jesus prophesies that the Son of Man will be delivered from the heart of the earth, just as God delivered Jonah from Hades (Matt. 12:40). In both instances, Hades refers to a disembodied existence.

The New Testament does not explore Jesus' precise residence or activity while in Hades, unlike the later church traditions of the "harrowing of hell" or a "Hades Gospel." It is widely accepted that the proclamation in 1 Peter 3:19 occurs after rather than before his resurrection (v. 18, "made alive by the Spirit"), and that the dead in 1 Peter 4:6 are deceased believers who heard the gospel while alive. However, Jesus' descent to Hades is theologically important. This is the path of the Old Testament righteous (Isa. 53). Furthermore, this descent confirms that God assumed human nature and even our sinful destiny, death (2 Cor. 5:14, 21; Heb. 2:14). Finally, Jesus' deliverance from Hades establishes the new life for humanity (1 Cor. 15).

Jesus' parable of the rich man and Lazarus portrays additional features of this state (Luke 16:19–31). An unbridgeable chasm separates the wicked and the righteous dead. Death has fixed the human's destiny without further opportunity for repentance. The rich man recalls his fate and that of his family, and cries out in distress for Abraham to send them a sign and relieve his punishment, but to no avail. Usually the details of parables should not be pressed to teach doctrine. In this case Jesus' vivid description of the basic conditions of the godly and ungodly dead is indispensable to the parable's point. Other Scriptures also portray the requests of the dead and the fixity of their future (2 Cor. 5:10; Heb. 9:27; Rev. 6:9–10).

Hades is the place where the wicked dead reside and are punished. In the parable of the rich man and Lazarus, the rich man experiences torment in Hades. This is the intermediate state, for the bodily resurrection and the final judgment are still future. Jesus' point is that Hades foreshadows the rich man's final judgment. Similarly, Lazarus rests at Abraham's side, connoting the joyous abode of the righteous dead (Luke 16:23).

This differentiation between the wicked and the righteous dead continues throughout the New Testament. The righteous dead are "at home with the Lord" (2 Cor. 5:8), "in paradise" (Luke 23:43), or in the presence of God (Rev. 6:9; 7:9; 14:3). The unrighteous are held in punishment and wicked angels are imprisoned in Tartarus, a Greek term designating the lowest part of Hades (1 Peter 3:19; 2 Peter 2:4, 9; Jude 6). Jesus' woe to unrepentant Capernaum that it will be brought down to Hades is not simply a prophecy of its earthly demise, but its judgment (Luke 10:15).

For some commentators these references to Hades and the dead are problematic and contradict the Old Testament. G. Vos resolves these problems by distinguishing between Hades as a disembodied state for all the dead and the specific abode of the ungodly. As he astutely notes, only the ungodly reside in a punitive place called Hades. The godly dead are with Jesus in a disembodied state also called Hades. The New Testament does significantly modify the Old Testament concept of Hades as a shadowy abode of all the dead. This further development, however, concurs with Jesus' lordship over the living and the dead.

Hades' power is conquered. Like the Old Testament, the New Testament personifies Hades and associated terms, such as death, abyss, and Abaddon, as the demonic forces behind sin and ruin (Acts 2:24; Rom. 5:14, 17; 1 Cor. 15:25–26; Rev. 6:8; 9:1–11; 20:14). When Jesus promises that the "gates of Hades" will never overcome the church (Matt. 16:18), this phrase parallels Old Testament expressions tied to evil's power and persecution (Pss. 9:13; 107:17–20). Jesus' reference to the future in Matthew 16:18 concurs with Revelation's vision of Satan's final attack on God's people (19:19; 20:7–9). Jesus has promised that he will conquer Hades so that it will not defeat the church. Indeed, his resurrection establishes that this evil empire is already broken. Christ now holds the keys, the authority over death and Hades (Rev. 1:18)!

The end of Hades. Jesus is the conqueror of all powers, the exalted One, and as such he has graced his church (Eph. 4:7–10). With Hades vanquished (Rev. 1:18) believers know that nothing, not even death, cannot separate them from Christ (Rom. 8:39). They still await the next act in the history of salvation, when Jesus consummates his kingdom. Then Hades will release its dead for the final resurrection and judgment (Rev. 20:13). Thereafter Hades, Satan, and the reprobate will be thrown into Gehenna, the place of God's final retributive punishment. (Hades has only a limited existence; Gehenna or hell is the final place of judgment for the wicked. Many English versions foster confusion by translating both terms as "hell.")

In summary, the New Testament affirms that Christ has conquered Hades. While dead believers exist in this state, they are also "with the Lord." Hades also denotes the vanquished stronghold of Satan's forces whose end is certain and the intermediate place of punishment for the wicked dead until the final judgment.

TIMOTHY R. PHILLIPS

See also ABRAHAM'S BOSOM; DEATH; GRAVE; HELL; SHEOL.

Bibliography. J. W. Cooper, *Body, Soul, and Life Everlasting;* W. J. Dalton, *Christ's Proclamation to the Spirits: A Study of I Peter 3:18–4:6;* M. J. Harris, *Themelios* 11 (1986): 47–52; R. L. Harris, *TWOT,* 2:892–93; A. A. Hoekema, *The Bible and the Future;* J. Jeremias, *TDNT,* 1:146–49, 657–58; 6:924–28; T. J. Lewis, *ABD,* 2:101–5; G. Vos, *ISBE,* 2:1314–15.

Haggai, Theology of. The prophets Haggai and Zechariah joined forces in 520 B.C. to encourage the rebuilding of the temple following the Babylonian exile. After the Persian king Cyrus had allowed the Jews to return to Jerusalem in 538 B.C., work on the foundation of the temple was completed by 536 B.C. But opposition arose and no further progress was made until Haggai and Zechariah burst upon the scene. Through their effective preaching, Zerubbabel the governor and Joshua the high priest were able to complete the "'second temple" by 515 B.C., and once again the Jewish nation had a worship center that bound them together as a people.

The Book of Haggai consists of four short messages delivered from August through December of 520 B.C., the second year of Darius Hystaspes. Each of the messages is clearly dated and the style is similar enough to insure the unity of the book. Brief but hard-hitting, Haggai's messages reached the hearts of the Jewish remnant, and the people obediently responded to his call to finish the temple.

Punishment and Blessing. Although the returnees had been back home in Israel for only eighteen years, the disobedience of the people had brought on them a series of problems characteristic of a nation about to go into exile. God had sent drought and meager harvests, making economic conditions deplorable. Moses had warned that a failure to keep the covenant would bring about calamities like this and eventually captivity (Deut. 28:38–40). The blight and mildew mentioned in Haggai 2:17 are specifically cited as covenant curses in Deuteronomy 28:22. Rather than working to finish the temple, the Israelites were beautifying their own homes and letting the Lord's work lag far behind (Hag. 1:4).

Stung by the truth of Haggai's words, the people repented of their lethargy and resumed work on the temple in September 520 B.C. Just as the Lord had stirred the hearts of the people to return home in 538 B.C. (Ezra 1:5), so the hearts of Zerubbabel and Joshua were stirred to lead the people in obedience once more (Hag. 1:14). And even though there were very few grapes, figs, or olives growing in the land, God promised that "from this day on I will bless you" (2:19). Obedience always brings blessing, and the people's willingness to put God first in their lives would bring material as well as spiritual blessing. Harvests would once again be plentiful as the drought and famine would come to an end.

God's Presence with His People. As the people responded favorably to Haggai's challenge, the Lord graciously promised that he would be with them (1:13). God had been with Joshua when he led Israel into the promised land (Josh. 1:1), and now another Joshua is told to "be strong . . . and work. For I am with you" (Hag. 2:4). When Solomon was given the heavy responsibility of building the first temple he, too, was told to take courage and do the work (1 Chron. 28:10, 20).

The reference to the Holy Spirit and the Sinai covenant in 2:5 serve as a reminder that Moses and the seventy elders were empowered by the Spirit as they led Israel out of Egypt and through the wilderness (Num. 11:16–17, 25). Rebuilding the temple would not be easy, but divine enablement would be assured.

God's presence with his people may also be implied in the reference to the "glory of this present house" in 2:9. In the Old Testament the glory of the Lord referred to the pillar of cloud that filled the tabernacle and then the temple. Such occasions were among the most significant in Israel's experience (see Exod. 40:34–35; 1 Kings 8:10–11), so Haggai is anticipating a future for the remnant even more glorious than the nation's illustrious past.

The Coming Messiah. One way that the glory of the second temple surpassed the glory of Solomon's temple was the presence of the Son of God in Zerubbabel's temple. When Jesus was brought to the temple as a child the aged Simeon identified him as a light to the Gentiles and glory for Israel (Luke 2:32). A messianic connection with "glory" would be strengthened if "the desired (or "desire") of all nations" in 2:7 also refers to Christ. From the context it is clear that "desired" can refer to valuable articles such as silver and gold (2:8), but from other passages it seems equally clear that "desired" can also refer to individuals. Three times Daniel is called "highly esteemed" or "highly desired" (Dan. 9:23; 10:11, 19). Possibly the term was chosen to refer both to valuable possessions and to a highly valued individual in order to approximate the breadth of the term "glory."

Another messianic foreshadowing is found in the last verse of the book, where Zerubbabel is called "my servant" and "my signet ring, for I have chosen you" (2:23). "Servant" is applied to Christ mainly in Isaiah's songs (42:1; 49:3; 50:10; 52:13), where the servant is also called "my chosen one" (42:1). The obscure reference to the signet ring is illuminated by Jeremiah 22:24, where Zerubbabel's ancestor, Jehoiachin, is pulled off like a signet ring and handed over to Nebuchadnezzar. By making Zerubbabel "like my signet ring" the Lord may be reversing the curse against Jehoiachin, reinstating his family so that a descendant of his could again sit on the throne of Israel. Zerubbabel was not destined to be a king, but Christ was his descendant and eligible for the throne. Both Jeconiah—another name for Jehoiachin—and Zerubbabel are included in Christ's genealogy in Matthew 1:12.

The Shaking of the Nations. Twice in chapter two Haggai states that the Lord will shake the heavens and the earth (vv. 6, 21). Verse 7 then predicts that God "will shake all nations" and verse 22 speaks of overthrowing thrones and kingdoms. Just as the Lord brought judgment on Pharaoh and his chariots at the Red Sea, so he will once again display his awesome power over the nations in the endtimes. Hebrews 12:26 quotes Haggai 2:6 as it looks ahead to the second coming of Christ and the defeat of the kingdoms of this world. Since Haggai says that God will shake the nations "in a little while" perhaps the near fulfillment includes the fall of the Persian Empire and the rise of Greece and Rome.

HERBERT M. WOLF

See also ZECHARIAH, THEOLOGY OF.

Bibliography. R. Alden, *Haggai;* J. G. Baldwin, *Haggai, Zechariah, Malachi;* R. J. Coggins, *Haggai, Zechariah, Malachi;* C. L. Meyers and E. M. *Haggai, Zechariah 1–8;* R. L. Smith, *Micah–Malachi;* H. M. Wolf, *Haggai and Malachi.*

Hand, Right Hand. "Hand" most frequently represents the ownership, power, or control that its possessor (either an individual or a people) exercises. This can be seen in the story of the exodus from Egypt. God's hand, described as mighty (Exod. 3:19–20), overcomes the hand of the Egyptians (3:8) through miraculous plagues and the parting of the Red Sea. These are performed by the hand of Moses and of Aaron who act as instruments of divine power, taking the staff of God in their hands (4:2; 14:16). As a symbol of divine power and salvation the hand is remembered at the Passover celebration in which a staff is to be held in the hand and the event described as a "sign on your hand" (12:11; 13:9, 16).

The hand can represent the whole person, symbolizing the achievement of what is promised with the mouth (1 Kings 8:15, 24). The hand's raised position can be used in blessing (pl. in Lev. 9:22), in making an oath before God (Gen. 14:22), or in God's making an oath (Num. 14:30; right hand in Isa. 62:8). Placing the hand under the patriarch's thigh forms part of the oath that his servant makes to Abraham (Gen. 24:2, 9). The hand of the person seeking atonement for sins is placed on the animal when it is sacrificed (Lev. 1:4). More specifically, the thumb of the right hand receives the sacrificial blood or the oil when the whole person is ritually cleansed (Lev. 8:23; 14:14–28). This symbolism is carried into the New Testament, when Jesus and the apostles heal and deliver through the touch of the hand (Matt. 8:3; Acts 3:7).

The hand has a variety of other associations. The hand of the Lord comes upon Elisha through the playing of a harp and leads him to prophesy (2 Kings 3:15). Naaman expects Elisha to cure him through the waving of his hand (2 Kings 5:11). Writing on the hand can signify allegiance or ownership (Isa. 44:5; Rev. 13:16). Mourning can involve the slashing of the hand (Jer. 48:37). If the lover's "hand" in Song of Solomon 5:4 is a sexual metaphor, it avoids altogether the additional ritual associations of this phallic image in Ugaritic (and presumably Canaanite) religion. God's hand is normally understood as a metaphor but in the prophetic books something like a hand is felt (Dan. 10:10) and is seen lifting Ezekiel (Ezek. 8:3), writing on a wall (Dan. 5:5), holding a plumb line (Amos 7:7), and emanating rays (Hab. 3:4; cf. Rev. 1:20 and 2:1, where Christ holds seven stars).

The right hand can be used interchangeably with the hand in poetic texts (Judg. 5:26; Ps. 74:11). The hand of God, and especially the right hand, is also understood as a place of salvation, refuge, and protection (16:8). It is the favored position for the firstborn of Joseph to receive Jacob's blessing (Gen. 48:13–18), for the bride of the king (Ps. 45:9), and for the chosen one who sits at God's right hand while judgment is rendered upon the earth (110:1; Jer. 22:24). This is applied to Jesus (Mark 14:62; 16:19). He sits at God's right hand, where he intercedes as a priest for believers (Rom. 8:34; Heb. 8:1) and exercises authority over all powers (1 Peter 3:22). The apostles extend the right hand of fellowship to Paul (Gal. 2:9), perhaps reflecting an ancient practice of greeting (2 Sam. 20:9). In other cases the position at the right hand has no apparent advantage over the left (1 Chron. 6:39, 44; Jon. 4:11). In Hebrew, the direction "south" is designated by the word for "right hand" (*yāmîn*).

RICHARD S. HESS

Bibliography. J. Bergman, W. von Soden, and P. R. Ackroyd, *TDOT,* 5:393–426; J. A. Soggin and H.-J. Fabry, *TDOT,* 6:87–98; W. Grundmann, *TDNT,* 2:37–40; E. Lohse, *TDNT,* 9:424–37; J. C. de Moor, *An Anthology of Religious Texts from Ugarit.*

Happiness. *See* JOY.

Hardening, Hardness of Heart. In the Scriptures various aspects of human anatomy are used to define the whole person, but the most frequently used is heart. The heart is the seat of emotion (Ps. 25:1; Prov. 14:10; Isa. 66:14; John 14:1; Rom. 9:2), intelligence (Prov. 16:1; Luke 9:47), morality (Ps. 58:2; Rom. 1:24), human choice (Deut. 8:2; Luke 21:34; Acts 11:23), and one's religious life (Deut. 6:5; Jer. 31:33; Rom. 10:9–10; Gal. 4:6). The heart, in effect, is the whole person in all of his or her distinctive human activity as a thinking, planning, willing, feeling, worshiping, socially interacting being. And, of course, when the person is not living according to God's will, it is the heart that is described as darkened, rebellious, callous, unfeeling, or idolatrous. It is within the heart that God works; hence the human heart may be tender and soft or as hard as stone (Ezek. 11:19). It is in this context that hardening or hardness of the heart must be understood. The heart represents the total response of a person to life around him or her and to the religious and moral demands of God. Hardness of heart thus describes a negative condition in which the person ignores, spurns, or rejects the gracious offer of God to be a part of his or her life.

Jesus speaks of a general condition of human hardness (*sklērokardian*) that God takes into consideration when dealing with us (Matt. 19:7–8; Mark 10:4–5). The heart is deceitful above all things and beyond cure (Jer. 17:9); it is hard, but not necessarily hardened. Hardening of the heart goes beyond the tragic obtuseness of our inherited condition. So, working upon the fertile ground of our innately hard hearts, sin may harden them further (Dan. 5:20; Eph. 4:18; Heb. 3:12). People may harden their own hearts, in sinful rebellion, in bitterness over circumstances, or in sheer self-will (Exod. 9:34–35; 2 Chron. 36:13; Zech. 7:12; Heb. 3:15). In a few instances, such as Pharaoh and the Egyptians (Exod. 7:3; 9:12), Sihon, king of Heshbon (Deut. 2:30), and the Hivites living in Gibeon (Josh. 11:19–20), it is said that God hardened their hearts. There is something of a mystery here, but apparently these people were so irremediable in their rebellion against God that God entered into the hardening process so that he could accomplish his purposes in spite of, and yet in and through, that hardness. It is God's prerogative, as God, to do this (Rom. 9:18–21). That they were morally responsible for their condition is a theological given, and we are warned not to harden our hearts as they did, a command that would make no sense if hardening were simply God's act (1 Sam. 6:6).

Israel's hardening as a nation represents a special set of circumstances. In the psalms, the wicked are described as having a calloused heart (17:10; 73:7; 119:70). God tells Isaiah that Israel, with its calloused heart, will reject him as God's messenger when he goes to them (Isa. 6:9–10). This event was taken as prophetic by Jesus (Matt. 13:14–15) and Paul (Acts 28:25–27) as referring to Israel's rejection of Jesus as God's Messiah. For Paul, Israel's hardening paved the way to a ministry to the Gentiles (Acts 28:28) and was not intended by God to be final, but only until the full number of the Gentiles had come in; then all Israel will be saved (Rom. 11:25–27).

For the believers of both the Old Testament (Ps. 95:8) and the New Testament (Heb. 3:8, 15; 4:7) the hardness of Israel's heart served as a warning and a challenge not to react in the same way. Jesus, at one point, alludes to this by rebuking his disciples for the hardness of their hearts (Mark 8:17–21).

Ultimately the hardness of the human heart can only be repaired by the grace of God. It is he who can restore us, by taking away our heart of stone and giving us a heart of flesh (Ezek. 11:18–21).

WALTER A. ELWELL

See also HEART.

Bibliography. B. S. Childs, *Exodus*, pp. 170–75; L. J. Kuyper, *SJT* (1974): 459–74; H. Räisänen, *The Idea of Divorce Hardening;* K. L. Schmidt, *TDNT* 5:1028–31.

Harvest. The gathering of things planted, a natural time of reaping in joy what has been produced during the year in an agricultral community. Jesus reflects the Bible's theological viewpoint on harvest when he enjoins believers to ask the "Lord of the harvest" for laborers (Matt. 9:38). God stands in control of the harvest time; it is part of his work (Jer. 5:24; Amos 4:7).

Human Response. In an agrarian society such as that reflected in the Bible, a human response to God came with planting and reaping. Offerings came from the fullness of one's harvest (Exod. 22:29). At least two festivals focused on harvest. The Festival of Harvest or firstfruits came in the spring, fifty days after Passover (Exod. 23:16). The Festival of Booths fell at the end of harvest in the fall.

Farmers needed to do their part in planting to be able to reap (Prov. 6:8). But the focus in harvest revolved around the product and the work of the Lord in bringing it to completion. Even during harvest, the Sabbath rest was to be kept so that the focus would remain on the Lord (Exod. 34:21–22). Of course, great joy accompanied the harvest (Isa. 9:3).

The firstfruits came to the priest, who would offer them to the Lord. If a person brought them, then the Lord might accept them (Lev. 23:10–11), an acceptance perhaps reflected in the successful completion of the harvest in the fall, a "blessing" (Deut. 24:19; Ps. 107:37–38). Some of the harvest remained in the fields for the poor (Lev. 19:9; 23:22).

Acknowedgment of the Lord's part in the harvest was important, perhaps best seen when crops failed, usually attributed to the Lord for the failure of Israel to recognize God's part (Isa. 17:11; Amos 4:7; Hag. 1:6). Metaphorical uses of the word stem from this viewpoint.

Metaphorical Usage. Metaphorical usage of harvest takes on a positive sense when Jeremiah refers to Israel as God's fruitfruits of harvest (2:3). In the New Testament, believers may sow and reap a spiritual harvest of righteousness (2 Cor. 9:10).

However, most usages allude to judgment. The prophets indicate that the Lord destroyed the harvest in judgment (Isa. 18:4–6; Jer. 12:13). As God of the harvest, the Lord speaks and takes it away (Hos. 2:9). In fact, Israel herself becomes a harvest (Hos. 6:11). The nation of Babylon comes to "harvest" her (Jer. 51:33). The judgment of God uses a familiar image in the life of Israel, but it does not carry the joy experienced at the seasonal gathering. Israel turned away from the Lord and suffered a punishment like a harvest.

Jesus described the last judgment in a parable about harvest (Matt. 13:30, 39). The Jews of his day understood the connection of harvest and judgment. Judgment is the focus again in the words of the angel in Revelation 14:15.

G. Michael Hagan

Hate, Hatred. Hate derives from a strong dislike or ill will toward persons or things. As an emotional attitude, a person may oppose, detest, or despise contact with a thing or a person. Love and hatred often stand opposed. Wisdom says, there is "a time to love and a time to hate" (Eccles. 3:8). In the biblical record, every being may express or experience hate.

The Bible says that God hates religiosity (Isa. 1:14; Amos 5:21), hypocrisy and lies (Zech. 8:17), wrongdoing (Isa. 61:8); divorce (Mal. 2:16), violence (Mal. 2:16), idolatrous practices (Hos. 9:15), and the way the prophets are treated (Jer. 44:4). The theology underlying God's hatred rests upon two essential qualities of God: holiness and justice. As a divine being with standards, God hates anything that despises, detests, or disregards those standards. In return, people hate God (Ps. 139:21–22). Humanity may choose to follow in God's path in hating anything that hates the Lord or his standards (Ps. 139:22).

The Bible notes that people can hate discipline (Ps. 50:17), peace (Ps. 120:6), and knowledge (Prov. 1:22). This sense of "hatred" carries the meaning of "loathing." A person so characterized is viewed in a negative sense, often labeled as a "fool." Some people hate anything that is good (Mic. 3:2). They are viewed as "evil." They may hate God's people as well. The psalmist tells us, "I suffer from those who hate me" (9:13). A strong dislike surfaces for a variety of reasons, all encompassed by the term "hatred." Jesus accepted that believers would be hated, pronouncing a blessing on those so hated (Luke 6:22). In fact, one mark of a disciple derives from being hated (Luke 14:26). Of course, the world hated Jesus first (John 7:7). True disciples hold an attitude of love toward those who hate them (Luke 6:27). This hatred of God's people appears to be an inevitable fact of life (Pss. 25:19; 35:19; 41:7; 83:2; Prov. 9:8). God may be involved on occasion in turning people to hate his people (Ps. 105:25). This idea attests how everything fits into God's plan in some way.

The response by God's people needs to mirror God's attitude toward evil. We are to hate evildoers (Ps. 26:5), idolaters (Ps. 31:6), the false way (Ps. 119:104), falsehood (Ps. 119:163), and anything that is evil (Ps. 97:10; Prov. 8:13; Amos 5:15).

Normal relationships may produce hatred between people. A husband may hate his wife (Gen. 29:31, 33). Joseph's brothers hated him (Gen. 37:4). Amnon's lust turned to hate after he raped his sister, Tamar (2 Sam. 13:15). A parent may hate a son (Prov. 13:24). Neighbors, nations, and classes of people, such as the poor may be hated (Deut. 19:11; Prov. 19:7; Isa. 66:5). Hatred proves to be a tangible measurement of evil in the world. Its ugliness may extend in any direction. Any aversion of humans to others expresses hatred.

G. Michael Hagan

Bibliography. G. Van Groningen, *TWOT,* 2:880.

Head, Headship. The head is the topmost part of the body, where symbols of power, authority, and honor were displayed. Kings and priests were anointed on their heads, and this is where their crowns were placed (1 Sam. 10:1; 2 Sam. 1:10; 2 Kings 9:3; Ps. 21:3).

Adam was crowned with glory and honor (Ps. 8:5). Prudent men wear knowledge there (Prov. 14:18). Gray hair is a symbol of glory (Prov. 16:31) that younger people must respect (Lev. 19:32). Lifting up of the head was symbolic of promotion (Gen. 40:13; Ps. 3:3). Saul was head and shoulders above everyone else (1 Sam. 9:2).

The head is a site where beauty is displayed (Song of Sol. 5:11; 7:5). It is a place where much time and effort is spent on techniques of beautification (2 Kings 9:30; Isa. 3:24; Jer. 4:30; Ezek. 23:40). It is where the power of one's personality shines forth.

It is a center of communication. Blushing, tears, paleness, and flushing may show fear, anger, or mourning. Tossing, shaking, or wagging of the head may convey wonder, mockery, or rejection (Isa. 37:22). The eyes, mouth, and facial features may show favor, boldness, sadness, impudence, or scorn (Gen. 4:6; Neh. 2:2; Prov. 7:13; Isa. 3:16).

From the king's head comes his words, which may have power of life or death (Eccles. 8:4). Hence in the Septuagint Greek Old Testament translation *kephalē* may be used of an older, prominent person, a chieftan, or a king.

Covering the Head as a Social Custom. While Greek women sometimes covered their heads, there was no social compulsion for them to wear a veil in public. Greek statues show bare-headed Greek women displaying extravagant hairstyles. Jews regarded this as typical of Gentiles.

Required head coverings for women are an Eastern custom. A Middle Assyrian law required that all women except prostitutes and slaves be veiled. Jewish communities of the New Testament period were strict about this. The Mishnah (A.D. 250) held that failure to comply was grounds for divorce (Ketubin 7:6).

A moral, unmarried woman even wore a veil in front of her parents. Removal of the veil was a sign of disgrace (3 Macc. 4:6). Philo of Alexandria indicated that this regularly worn covering was a symbol of modesty (Special Laws 3.56; Josephus *Ant.* 3.270). Women charged with adultery had this veil removed.

Jewish men often refused to cover their heads because it represented subjection to foreigners. Men covered their heads in times of despair, mourning, and defeat (2 Sam. 15:30; Esther 6:12; Jer. 14:3).

"Paul of Tarsus" (Acts 9:11) was accustomed to seeing women veiled in public. Dion Chrysostom, an orator (A.D. 110), commended ladies there because they never appeared unveiled in public.

William Ramsey saw the woman's head covering as her power. It authorized her to go anywhere in public with respect and protection. Women who failed to wear veils would be objects of contempt and abuse. This might explain why Paul says "a woman ought to have a sign of authority on her head" (1 Cor. 11:10). Interestingly Aramaic words for "authority" and "veil" are similar.

First Corinthians 11:2–16. Corinth was a port city and a commercial crossroad. Many customs and styles were present. The church there grew out of the synagogue (Acts 18:4, 7, 8). New Testament churches were often located in houses of wealthy converts. Rich Greek women would appear uncovered with elaborate hairstyles.

Poorer Jewish women might feel such customs were done to attract men. This would eventually become a source of disunity. It is not surprising Paul introduces this passage by an exhortation not to offend Jew or Greek. He offers himself as an example of one who tried to please everybody for the sake of their salvation (1 Cor. 10:31–11:1). He closes the passage by stating the churches of God repudiate practices that might cause contention (11:16).

In 11:2 Paul praises the Corinthians for always following his directions. Evidently he had previously taught use of veils by women there. As the church grew many wanted to know the reason for this custom.

Paul begins by presenting a hierarchy of headship: God, Christ, man, and woman. Paul regularly uses the idea of headship in a context of submission to authority (Eph. 5:21–25; Col. 1:18; 2:10, 19). A man may pray to God in public but not dressed so that he shows allegiance to another, namely, with head covered. A woman may pray and prophesy in public if her dress shows submission to her husband's authority (1 Cor. 11:5–6).

If people do not treat each other with respect, their prayers may be hindered (1 Peter 3:7). If a woman's outward appearance reflects gentleness and submission to her husband, it may win him to Christ (1 Peter 3:1–6). The appearance of women who take part in the service should show respect to required social customs. Use of head coverings enhanced the acceptance of a woman's contribution to the service.

Paul based his view about the woman's place in the authority continuum on Genesis 2:18–24. Here the woman is formed from man's side in response to a need for companionship and help. She is not formed from dust but was taken from Adam. As a suitable helper she makes man complete.

Woman reflects the glory of God in man so that both bear the image of God (Gen. 1:26–27). As a suitable complement to the man, a noble wife is his crown (Prov. 12:4). Genesis Rabbah, an ancient Jewish commentary, stated her husband is adorned by her. Her pleasures, beauties, and charms are for her husband alone (Prov. 5:17). She is covered as a sign that she is accessible to none but him.

Headship of Husbands. Headship does not mean that man is an unlimited monarch. He is to cherish and nurture his wife as his own body (Eph. 5:28). He may not deprive her of what she needs for her happiness and well-being (1 Cor. 7:3). He must be understanding, considerate, and respectful of her as a joint heir of life (1 Peter 3:7). His love for her is more than physical. It must be the same kind of sacrificial love Christ has for the church.

Sarah is presented as an example of the submissive wife (1 Peter 3:5–6). She assented to his decisions even when he was wrong (Gen. 12:11–13). Yet Abraham also listened to her (Gen. 16:2). In Genesis 21:12 God tells Abraham to "listen to whatever Sarah tells you" (about Ishmael). Sarah's orders about Ishmael were used by Paul as binding Scripture in his teaching about law and grace (Gal. 4:30). Even though Sarah is obedient, her thoughts and her feelings may not be disregarded and trampled upon. There is a place for mutual submission one to another (Eph. 5:21).

Christ as Head of His Church. The church must submit to Christ. We are not our own but are bought with a price (1 Cor. 3:23; 6:19–20; Eph. 5:23–33). He has all authority in heaven and earth (Matt. 28:18). He is the head of all principality and power (Col. 2:10). People who wander from Christ are like those who have lost their heads (Col. 2:18–19). Without the head no nourishment or growth is possible (Eph. 4:15; Col. 2:19). Paul was not dealing in philosophical speculation in his headship analogies. Even the simplest person knew that food, water, and air were taken in by head. He would know that the eyes and ears gave guidance to the whole body.

PAUL FERGUSON

See also ADAM; CHURCH, THE; EVE; MARRIAGE.

Bibliography. G. Bilezikian, *Beyond Sex Roles;* J. A. Fitzmyer, *NTS* 35 (1989): 503–11; W. Grudem, ed., *Manhood and Womanhood: A Biblical Perspective;* idem, *Trinity J* NS (1985): 1438–59; G. Hawthorne, et al, *Dictionary of Paul and His Letters;* W. Neuer, *Man and Woman in Christian Perspective;* W. Ramsey, *The Cities of St. Paul;* C. L. Thompson, *BA* (1988): 101–15.

Heal, Health. With characteristic realism the Bible accepts the prevalence in God's world of ill-health and affliction, although originally it had no place in God's plan, and declares that God who made us is our only healer. The fact the Lord is our healer echoes through patriarchs, law history, psalms, and prophecy. Psalm 103:1–5 traces among God's "benefits" the separate stages of convalescence.

That God alone heals remains true even though human and traditional means are used. "Physicians" embalmed Isaac (Gen. 50:2), and apparently practiced in early Israel (Exod. 21:19); later both doctors and healing balm were associated with Gilead (Jer. 8:22; cf. Luke 4:23, and probably Mark 2:17, for familiar proverbs). Sirach 38:1–15 praises highly, if defensively, the physician's skill and prayerfulness when making diagnosis (contrast 2 Chron. 16:12). Priests, too, as God's representatives bore medical responsibilities (Lev. 13:2–45), while prophets were consulted for medical advice and action (1 Kings 14:1–3; 17:17–24; 2 Kings 4:18–37; note 5:1–3; 20:1–11). Naaman the Syrian vividly describes how a prophet was popularly expected to proceed (2 Kings 5:11). In New Testament times, Jewish exorcists practiced, evidently with some success (Luke 11:19; Acts 19:13), and Luke became Paul's "beloved physician" (Col. 4:14).

Ordinary means of healing were of most diverse kinds. Balm (Gen. 37:25) is thought to have been an aromatic resin (or juice) with healing properties; oil was the universal emollient (Isa. 1:6), and was sometimes used for wounds with cleansing wine (Luke 10:34). Isaiah recommended a fig poultice for a boil (38:21); healing springs and saliva were thought effectual (Mark 8:23; John 5; 9:6–7). Medicine is mentioned (Prov. 17:22) and defended as "sensible" (Sirach 38:4). Wine mixed with myrrh was considered sedative (Mark 15:23); mint, dill, and cummin assisted digestion (Matt. 23:23); other herbs were recommended for particular disorders. Most food rules had both ritual and dietary purposes, while raisins, pomegranates, milk, and honey were believed to assist restoration.

One extraordinary means of healing is recorded in 2 Kings 4:25–37: Elisha first ordered that his staff be laid on the inert body of a child, and when that failed, he lay face to face upon the child until warmth and life returned. Nevertheless, ordinary or exceptional, agent and method were but channels of divine healing, which could operate efficiently without either (2 Kings 5:10–14).

The Healing Messiah. With this background, the prevalence of sickness in the ancient world, it was natural that hearts should hope for a better future, when sorrow and sighing would flee away (Isa. 29:17–19; 35:10). There is rabbinic evidence that some were looking for a Messiah who would heal the world's sickness. The Talmud later preserves among "signs of the Messiah" the portrait of "one in the midst of the suffering poor . . . tending their wounds." This may look back for scriptural warrant to Isaiah's picture of the Servant of the Lord who would bear our griefs and carry our sorrows. That such a hope was current much earlier is shown by Matthew's quoting these words (in a variant version, 8:17) to "explain" the healing mission of Jesus. For Matthew understands "he took up our infirmities and carried our diseases" to mean, not that Jesus was sick, but that he was concerned about the sick.

Luke shows Jesus announcing in similar terms the arrival of God's kingdom—"freedom for the prisoners and recovery of sight for the blind, to release the oppressed" (the healing of society, Luke 4:18). And when the Baptist, hearing in prison of Jesus' ministry, sent someone to ask Jesus if he was indeed the Messiah, Jesus sent back the message, "The blind receive sight, the lame walk, those who have leprosy are cured, the deaf hear, the dead are raised. . . . Blessed is the man who does not fall away on account of me" (Matt. 11:4–6). Christ's healing ministry was sufficient evidence that the king had come, and that the kingdom of God was gracious and kind, not as John had foretold, a realm of axe and flail, of fire and judgment, but of healing and liberation.

So concern for suffering and the impulse to heal became vital elements in Christianity. On the disciples' first mission they were charged to "heal the sick, raise the dead, cleanse those who have leprosy, drive out demons" (Matt. 10:8); visitation of the sick (always an obligation in Jewish piety, Sirach 7:35) was made an issue in the last judgment in Christ's last parable (Matt. 25:36, 44).

Luke, especially, emphasizes that Christ's healing ministry was far wider than the few miracles described (4:40; 5:15; 6:17–19; 9:11; cf. Matt. 15:30–31; Mark 1:38). Among Jesus' motives, simple compassion is mentioned nine times—an attitude rare when most sickness was ascribed to sin. Jesus never recoiled from disease or mental illness, but touched lepers, allowed the "unclean" to touch him, conversed with the deranged, spoke gently to those in distress who challenged him, and sprang to the defense of the maimed or diseased who intruded into synagogues or wealthy houses. He took great pains with a deaf-mute to establish communication; for a blind man, whose wild excitement at cure could cause ridicule, he provided privacy; a young girl was raised from death without knowing it (Mark 7:32–35; 8:22–26; 5:35–43). To Jesus' mind, the cure of suffering took precedence, repeatedly, over the Sabbath rules (Luke 13:14–17; 14:1–6).

Besides demonstrating the nature of God's kingdom as health-giving, down-to-earth, and relevant to the daily problems of the whole person, and the compassion of Jesus toward ordinary, undervalued individuals, the healing miracles left no doubt that a new power was at work in the world, and available through Christ (Luke 4:36; 5:17; 6:19). To those who watched, the miracles declared that "God was with him" (Luke 7:16; Acts 2:22; 10:38). Jesus' presence proclaimed and achieved victory already over all demonic forces that degraded and tormented humankind; the frontiers of God's kingdom were being advanced, and God's will was being done.

The forms of Christ's healing, moreover, illustrated his redemptive mission, as bringing light to the blind soul, a kindling word to the deaf mind, sanity to the deranged personality, a lighter step to the lame spirit, a song to the dumb heart, calmness to the fevered life, and use again to the paralyzed will.

There is no doubt that the healings were miraculous. The resurrection of Jesus makes all lesser miracles credible—but not every Christian credulous: quality, motive, evidence, still demand consideration. The Gospel writers would assume that the God who made the world is not fettered by it, but free to act in any way consistent with his character and purpose.

Yet Jesus continually "played down" his spectacular deeds. No theatrical flourish, no fixed pattern of action or words added drama to the healing (except, for special reasons, in John 9). A simple touch, a quiet word, a command (to an evil spirit), a "morning call" to a "sleeping" girl, a touch from behind himself, even an assurance from a distance was enough. All is done naturally, informally, simply.

And Jesus set limits to his miracle-ministry. He did not allow it to distract him from the preaching of the kingdom. Sometimes he withdrew to other places (Luke 4:42–43; 5:16), or checked enthusiasm with warning of approaching death (Luke 9:43–45). Power over spirits is no true basis of Christian joy (Luke 10:20). God's kingdom cannot be built on signs and wonders (Luke 4:3–4, 9–12); a generation that demanded "signs" was "evil"—incapable of discerning God wherever and however he spoke and acted. The need was not for visual evidence to gape at, but for inward light (Luke 11:29–30, 32–36; 20:1–8). Nothing resembling a campaign inviting all comers to attend and be healed is recorded of Jesus. Even with Jesus himself visibly present, no healing was possible except "according to your faith" (Matt. 9:29); without faith, even Jesus "could not do any miracles" (Mark 6:5–6). To discourage the wonder-seeking excitement in Galilee, he often warned the cured to be silent, and to maintain reserve. Yet, in spite of all Jesus' avoidance of display, "the healing Messiah" left everywhere a deep and lasting impression, still plainly visible in the Gospel records, kindling new hope for the afflicted and a strong motive of active compassion in the church.

The Healing Church. For, as the disciples shared the healing work in the earlier years, so the church continued to do so through the apostolic age. Although our information is confined to Acts and a few allusions in the Epistles, we know of the healing of a lame man at the temple, of the sick in the streets (Acts 5:12–16), of the spirit-possessed in Samaria (8:7), of Aneas' paralysis (9:33–35); of the raising of Dorcas, the healing of a cripple at Lystra, and the slave girl at Philippi. We read of "extraordinary miracles" at Ephesus (19:11), the restoration of Eutychus at Troas (20:9–12), and the healing of Publius's father on Malta.

Indirectly we learn of signs and wonders during Paul's missions (Rom. 15:18–19; cf. 2 Cor. 12:12; Gal. 3:5). It is evident that the gift of healing was by no means limited to apostles, but bestowed "as the Spirit wills" (1 Cor. 12:9, 11). Although the picture so presented is incomplete and unsystematic, it is clear that the power to heal was neither universal nor constant, but spasmodic and occasional. An impression of surprise and wonder, of something "extraordinary" indeed, shows that healing never became commonplace or automatic.

Dorcas died. Epaphroditus was close to death for some time. Timothy, for years Paul's constant attendant, was troubled with "frequent illnesses" (1 Tim. 5:23). Trophimus had to be left at Miletus, sick (2 Tim. 4:20). There was repeated and serious illness in the churches at Corinth and Thessalonica (1 Cor. 11:30; 1 Thess. 4:13–18). Paul himself prayed, repeatedly and "unsuccessfully," for release from his physical affliction (2 Cor. 12:7–9; Gal. 4:13–15). The apostolic church had its invalids, gifts of healing notwithstanding.

Luke's constant care of Paul reminds us that nonmiraculous means of healing were not neglected in that apostolic circle. Wine is recommended for Timothy's weak stomach, eye-salve for the Thyatiran church's blindness (metaphorical, but significant). James offers pastoral counsel for the sick: Send for elders of the church, who will encourage, advise, and intercede for the patient; if sin truly underlies the sickness, let the sick confess and receive forgiveness; let soothing oil, the universal panacea for all discomforts, be applied. (No brother gifted with healing is here mentioned: James 5:14–16.)

Paul offers his own example. Of course he prayed concerning his affliction, but like all truly Christian prayer, that petition was subject to God's will. When the trouble was not removed, he sought instead the meaning of his "thorn"—and discovered it. In his case it was to keep him, despite his great privileges, humble and usable in God's hands. Thereafter he accepted the experience, although "a messenger of Satan" in some respects, as permitted for a purpose. And he accepted with it the grace God promised to be "sufficient" for endurance without resentment or self-pity, and the divine strength most plainly manifest through human weakness (2 Cor. 12:1–10).

Behind that courageous attitude lay the profound conviction that God makes all things work together to make us Christ-like; and therefore nothing, nothing at all, neither tribulation, nor distress, nor peril, nor things present or to come, will separate us from God's love (Rom. 8:28–29, 35–39).

Between them James and Paul describe what has become (for whatever reason) the "normal" Christian attitude toward sickness, and it obviously finds justification in the New Testament. But so does the expectation that, when God so wills, miracles will sometimes occur.

R. E. O. WHITE

See also DISEASE.

Bibliography. V. Edmunds and C. G. Scorer, *Some Thoughts on Faith Healing;* A. G. Ikin, *The Background of Spiritual Healing;* E. H. Robertson, *Biblical Bases of Healing;* C. G. Scorer, *Healing—Biblical, Medical, and Pastoral.*

Healing, Gift of. *See* HOLY SPIRIT, GIFTS OF.

Hear, Hearing. Most Old Testament words for hear(ing) come from the root *šmʿ*, "hear," or *ʾzn*, "(give) ear," although *qšb*, "pay attention," sometimes appears. The New Testament words are *akouō*, "hear," along with its several compounds and cognates, and *ous*, "ear" with its diminutives *otion* and *otarion*.

Scripture often refers to the physical ear (Gen. 35:4; Exod. 29:20; Deut. 15:17; Mark 7:33; Luke 22:50; 1 Cor. 12:16) or the physical faculty of hearing (Deut. 31:11; 1 Sam. 15:14; Mark 7:35), but relies more heavily on the figurative meanings of the words. In Scripture God hears; he pays attention to his people. His people should, but do not always, listen to him. Hearing is the mode by which the Son of God and his followers receive God's word.

In the Old Testament God hears both his people's groaning in trouble (Gen. 16:11; Exod. 2:24; 3:7; 6:5; Pss. 69:33; 102:20) and their grumbling against him (Exod. 16:7–9; Num. 14:27). Throughout Scripture God hears his people's prayers (1 Kings 8:31–53; Ps. 34:15, quoted in 1 Peter 3:12; more than fifty times in the Psalms; Isa. 59:1; Matt. 6:7–8; Luke 1:13; 1 John 5:14). In contrast, idols have physical ears but cannot hear their worshipers (Pss. 115:6; 135:17).

Since God hears his people, his people should also hear him. The prophets frequently call Israel to "hear the word of the Lord." Even pagans may hear about God's wonderful actions and be impressed (Josh. 2:10–11; 2 Chron. 9:1–8). Often in Deuteronomy, Moses calls on Israel to hear, especially in the Shema (literally the "Hear": 6:4–5; cf. 4:1; 5:1; 9:1; 20:3; 27:9).

Although Job refers to his indirect and partial understanding of God's character as hearing of God by the hearing of the ear (42:5), more often hearing refers to a deeper understanding. God's people are to "hear" (take heed of) the Prophet like Moses who will appear (Deut. 18:15–20; cf. Acts 3:22). In the "third heaven" Paul hears "inexpressible things" (2 Cor. 12:2–4), revealing matters that may not be passed on to others. The recovery of hearing by deaf people serves as a sign of the messianic kingdom (Isa. 29:18; 35:5–6; cf. Matt. 11:5; Mark 7:37). Hearing the voice of God's Son will cause the dead to rise (John 5:25–29).

Some among God's people have "ears to hear" his voice, while others do not. God accuses his people when they refuse to use their ears and listen to him (Isa. 6:9–10, quoted in Matt. 13:14–15 and parallels, also in Acts 28:26–27). Both before (Matt. 11:15; 13:9, 43 and parallels) and after (Rev. 2:7, 11, 17, 29; 3:6, 13, 22) his resurrection, Jesus calls on those who have spiritual ears to use them.

The Old Testament image of an "inclined" ear suggests a person leaning over to listen closely. Those whose ears and hearts are inclined toward God (Isa. 55:3; cf. Prov. 5:1) want God's ears to be inclined toward them (Pss. 31:2; 71:2; Dan. 9:18).

Because of his unique identity, the Son of God hears the Father's word and passes it on (John 3:32; 8:40; 15:15), and the Father in turn hears the Son's prayers (John 11:41–42; Heb. 5:7). Jesus' immediate followers testify to what they have seen and heard both during his ministry and after his resurrection (Acts 4:20; 22:15; 1 John 1:3, 5).

As hearing is the mode by which the Son receives the Father's word, and the Son's immediate followers receive it from him, so hearing is the means by which each believer receives the word. "Faith," says Paul, "comes from hearing the message, and the message is heard through the word of Christ" (Rom. 10:17; cf. Acts 4:4, and often in Acts). The Holy Spirit comes through the "hearing of faith" (Gal. 3:2, 5; cf. Acts 2:37–41). Those who become believers should go on to maturity, not being "dull in hearing" (Heb. 5:11) or remaining only hearers of the truth (James 1:22–25; cf. Rom. 2:13; Matt. 7:24–27 and parallel; Matt. 13:19 and parallels). Believers should especially avoid turning from hearing the truth, listening to false teachers who will scratch their "itching ears" (lit. "itching hearing"; 2 Tim. 4:3–4).

In following Jesus, believers should "consider carefully how they listen" (Luke 8:18), making sure the truth they already have will not be "taken away." In their interpersonal relations, they should be "quick to listen" (James 1:19), always ready to hear what the other person has to say. CARL B. BRIDGES, JR.

See also OBEDIENCE.

Bibliography. J. Horst, *TDNT,* 5:543–59; G. Kittel, *TDNT,* 1:216–25.

Heart. "Heart" (Hebrew *lēbāb/lēb;* Gk. *kardia*) occurs over one thousand times in the Bible, making it the most common anthropological term in the Scripture. It denotes a person's center for both physical and emotional-intellectual-moral activities; sometimes it is used figuratively for any inaccessible thing.

The Heart as Center of Physical Activity. "Heart" denotes to both ancient and modern peoples the beating chest organ protected by the rib cage. Ancient people, however, understood the heart's physical function differently than moderns. From their viewpoint the heart was the central organ that moved the rest of the body. Ancients ate to strengthen the heart and so revive the body. Abraham offers his weary guests food so that they might "sustain their hearts" and then go on their way (Gen. 18:5). Since moderns understand the anatomy differently than the ancients, the English versions gloss the Hebrew to accommodate it to a more scientific viewpoint.

A Figure of Inaccessibility. The hiddenness and inaccessibility of the physical heart give rise to its figurative sense for anything that is remote and inaccessible. The "heart of the seas" (Jon. 2:3) refers to the sea's fathomless, unapproachable depths and the "heart of the heavens" is its most unreachable height.

The Heart as Center of Hidden Emotional-Intellectual-Moral Activity. "Man looks at the outward appearance," says Samuel, "but the LORD looks at the heart" (1 Sam. 16:7). The king's heart is unsearchable to humankind (Prov. 25:3), but the Lord searches all hearts to reward all according to their conduct (Jer. 17:10). In the time of judgment God will expose the hidden counsels of the heart (1 Cor. 4:5).

Jesus says that the heart's secrets are betrayed by the mouth, even as a tree's fruit discloses its nature (Matt. 12:33–34). "A wise man's heart guides his mouth," says Solomon (Prov. 16:23). Most important, the mouth confesses what the heart trusts (Rom. 10:9; cf. Deut. 30:14).

Moderns connect some of the heart's emotional-intellectual-moral functions with the brain and glands, but its functions are not precisely equivalent for three reasons.

First, moderns do not normally associate the brain/mind with both rational and nonrational activities, yet the ancients did not divorce them (Ps. 20:4).

Second, the heart's reasoning, as well as its feeling, depends on its moral condition. Jesus said that "from within, out of men's hearts, come evil thoughts" (Mark 7:21). Because the human heart is deceitful above all things (Jer. 17:9) and folly is found up in the heart of a child (Prov. 22:15), the Spirit of God must give humans a new heart (Jer. 31:33; Ezek. 36:26) through faith that purifies it (Acts 15:9; cf. Eph. 3:17).

Third, moderns distinguish between the brain's thoughts and a person's actions, but the distinction between thought and action is inappropriate for heart. "The word is very near you," says Moses to a regenerated Israel, "in your mouth and in your heart" (Deut. 30:14).

The Heart's Emotional Functions. The Lord, who knows our hearts (Luke 16:15), experiences its full range of emotions: for example, its joy (Deut. 28:47; 1 Sam. 2:1; Prov. 15:15) and its sorrow (1 Sam. 1:8); its raging (2 Kings 6:11) and its peace (Col. 3:15); its feeling troubled (John 14:1) and its rejoicing (1 Sam. 2:1; Ps. 104:15); its love (Rom. 5:5; 1 Peter 1:22) and its selfish ambition (James 3:14); its modes of doubts (Mark 11:23) and of fear (Gen. 42:28) and its mode of trusting (Prov. 3:5); when it rises up in repulsive pride (Deut. 8:14) or, as in the case of Jesus, is lowly and humble (Matt. 11:29); and when one loses heart (Heb. 12:3) or takes heart (John 16:33).

The emotional state of the heart affects the rest of a person: "A happy heart makes the face cheerful, but heartache crushes the spirit" (Prov. 15:13); "a cheerful heart is good medicine, but a crushed spirit dries up the bones" (17:22).

The heart also wishes, desires. The father warns his son against coveting the adulteress's beauty (Prov. 6:25) and against envying sinners in his heart (Prov. 23:17). Above all else the heart of a saint seeks God (Ps. 119:2, 10). Believers set it on things above (Col. 3:1). This is effected, says Jesus, by putting your treasures in heaven, for "where your treasure is, there your heart will be also" (Matt. 6:21). If we look for God with all our heart, Moses promises we will find him (Deut. 4:28–29).

The Heart's Intellectual-Spiritual Functions. The heart thinks (Matt. 9:4; Mark 2:8), remembers, reflects, and meditates (Ps. 77:5–6; Luke 2:19). Solomon's comprehensive knowledge of flora and fauna is described as his breadth of heart (1 Kings 4:29).

More specifically, as the eyes were meant to see and the ears to hear, the heart is meant to understand, to discern, to give insight. The Alexandrian Jewish scribes translated into Greek about 200 B.C. the Hebrew text of Proverbs 2:10, "wisdom will enter your heart" by "wisdom will come into your understanding (*dianoian*)" because to them it meant the same thing. When a person lacks insight the Hebrew speaks of a "lack of heart."

Understanding cannot be separated from morals. Isaiah was commissioned: "Make the heart of this people calloused; . . . otherwise they might . . . understand with their hearts" (Isa. 6:10). Pharaoh hardened his heart lest he hear Moses and gain insight about the Lord (Exod. 8:15), and the Lord hardened it irrevocably (7:13; 9:12). Paul says of the perverse, their foolish hearts were darkened (Rom. 1:21); they could not see the light of moral truth. The hearts of saints, however, are enlightened (2 Cor. 4:6; Eph. 1:18).

Moderns speak of learning by heart, by which they mean rote memory. In the Bible, however, learning by heart is not like memorizing the multiplication tables; it must be mixed with spiritual affections. The Lord complains of apostate Israel that their worship "is made up only of rules taught by men" but "their hearts are far from me" (Isa. 29:13).

As the mouth reveals what is the heart, the ear determines what goes into it. The father tells his son to "store up my commands within you"; he then adds: by "turning your ear to wisdom, and you will incline your heart to understanding" (Prov. 2:2). When Moses says, "these commandments . . . are to be upon your hearts" (Deut. 6:6), he commands his hearers to remain conscious of them. This idea is expressed by the metaphor of writing on the tablet of the heart (Prov. 3:3; Jer. 17:1). In short, the heart needs to be educated by filling it with God's word (Prov. 22:17–18). In that way a person will grow in favor and good name (3:3–4) and be safeguarded against sin (Ps. 119:11).

The heart functions as the conscience. After David showed insubordination against the anointed king by cutting off the corner of his robe, his heart smote him (1 Sam. 24:5), and after Peter's sermon the audience was "cut to the heart" (Acts 2:37). The heart may condemn us, but God is greater than our hearts (1 John 3:20). David prays that God would create for him a pure heart to replace his defiled conscience (Ps. 51:10).

Finally, the heart plans, makes commitments, and decides. It is the inner forum where decisions are made after deliberation; here a person engages in self-talk. "In his heart a man plans his course, but the LORD determines his steps" (Prov. 16:9). Because of this critical function, the father instructs the son: "Above all else, guard your heart, for it is the wellspring of life (4:23). The Lord detests "a heart that devises wicked schemes" (6:18).

The greatest commandment according to Jesus is "Love the Lord your God with all your heart" (Matt. 22:37). Love here is more than emotion; it is a conscious commitment to the Lord.

One speaks to the heart of another to move that person to a decision (Isa. 40:2; Hos. 2:14). The father asks the son for his heart (Prov. 23:26), by which he means that the son make a conscious decision to follow his instructions. The impenitent, however, have hearts that are insensitive, obstinate (Mark 3:5; 6:52), and hard (Matt. 19:8); they cannot be moved in a new direction.

BRUCE K. WALTKE

See also HARDENING, HARDNESS OF HEART.

Bibliography. F. Baumgärtel et al., *TDNT,* 3:605–14; R. Bultnamn, *Theology of the New Testament,* 1:220–22; R. Jewett, *Paul's Anthropological Terms;* T. Song, *NIDNITT,* 2:80–84; H. W. Wolff, *Anthropology of the Old Testament,* pp. 40–58.

Heathen. *See* NATIONS, THE.

Heave Offering. *See* OFFERINGS AND SACRIFICES.

Heaven, Heavens, Heavenlies. "Heaven" is the created reality beyond earth. "The heavens and the earth" (Gen. 1:1) circumscribe the entire creation, or what we call the universe. God does not need heaven in which to exist. He is self-existent and infinite. Place is an accommodation of God to his finite creatures. God transcends not only earth, but heaven as well.

"Heaven" designates two interrelated and broad concepts—the physical reality beyond the earth and the spiritual reality in which God dwells. Frequently, the word "heaven" appears in the plural. The nearly exclusive word for heaven in the Old Testament, *šāmayîm,* is an intensive plural more literally translated "heights" or "high places." Jehovah is, therefore, "God most High" (Gen. 14:18–20; Ps. 18:13). Of the 284 occurrences of its New Testament counterpart, *ouranos* (lit. "that which is raised up"), about one-third are plural.

The Physical Heavens. The ancient distinguished between two domains of the physical heaven perceivable by the senses. The immediate heaven is the surrounding atmosphere in which the "birds of heaven" fly (1 Kings 21:24). The phenomena of weather occur in the atmospheric heaven, including rain (Deut. 11:11; Acts 14:17), snow (Isa. 55:10), dew (Dan. 4:23), frost (Job 38:29), wind (Ps. 135:7), clouds (Ps. 147:8), thunder (1 Sam. 2:10), and hail (Job 38:22). Beyond the atmospheric heaven is the celestial heaven, also called the "expanse" or "firmament" (Gen. 1:8). It includes the heavenly lights—stars having "fixed patterns" (Jer. 33:25; Nah. 3:16), and the sun and moon (Gen. 1:14–16). The fixed character of the celestial heaven has evoked figures of speech to describe it. For example, it has windows (2 Kings 7:2), a foundation (2 Sam. 22:8), a gate (Gen. 28:17), ends (Deut. 3:43), a remote part (Neh. 1:9), and is like a curtain (Isa. 40:22).

God employs the atmospheric and celestial heavens in his self-revelation to human beings. First, the heavens witness that a glorious God exists. "The heavens declare the glory of God; the skies proclaim the work of his hands" (Ps. 19:1; Rom. 1:19–20). Moreover, the pattern of seasons, yielding life-sustaining food, witness to God before believers.

Second, heaven contains signs establishing God's promises. The rainbow signifies that God will never destroy the world by a flood again (Gen. 9:12–16). The innumerable stars are an object lesson of the abundant way God will fulfill his covenant with Abraham (Gen. 22:17; Exod. 32:13; Deut. 1:10; 1 Chron. 27:23; Neh. 9:23).

Third, God displays miraculous signs in the heavens. Fire comes down from heaven, both to judge (Gen. 19:24; 1 Kings 18:38–39) and to indicate acceptance of a sacrifice (1 Chron. 21:26). God provided the Israelites with "bread from heaven" during their wilderness trek (Exod. 16:4). God stopped the sun's movement (Josh. 10:12–13) and used a star to pinpoint the Messiah's coming (Luke 2:9). He also spoke audibly from heaven on occasion (Gen. 21:17; 22:11, 15; Acts 11:9). Believers look for the return of Christ in the clouds of heaven (Mark 14:62; Acts 1:11; 1 Thess. 4:16–17).

Fourth, the vastness and inaccessibility of heaven are visual reminders of God's transcendence, God's otherworldliness, however, is a spiritual, not a spacial, fact. When Solomon prayed at the dedication of the temple, he acknowledged, "the heavens, even the highest heaven, cannot contain you" (1 Kings 8:27).

The Dwelling Place of God. Heaven most commonly refers to the dwelling-place of God. Heaven is where the glory of God is expressed in pristine clarity. The term "glory," therefore, has popularly been used as a synonym for heaven (Rom. 8:18). Actually, God's glory is above the heavens (Pss. 113:4; 148:13) because it is the sum total of his attributes that are expressed wherever he is present (Exod. 13:21–22; Ps. 108:5; 2 Cor. 3:7–18). In heaven there is a continual acknowledgment of God's glory (Ps. 29:9). Various figurative expressions identify God's heavenly abode such as "the highest heaven" (1 Kings 8:27), "the heavens" (Amos 9:6), and "his lofty palace in the heavens" (Amos 9:6). Paul speaks of being taken up into "the third heaven" (2 Cor. 12:2). Although he does not identify the first two, possible references to the atmospheric and celestial heavens are suggestive.

The Heavenly Perspective. God invites human beings to adopt his heavenly perspective. All blessings, whether natural or supernatural, are from God (James 1:17; see John 3:27), who is Creator and Sustainer of the universe (Rom. 11:36). Israel rightly regarded rain as a heavenly gift from God (Deut. 28:12). Likewise, drought was a sign of God's displeasure (Deut. 28:23–24).

The extent to which earthly blessings evidence heavenly approval needs to be conditioned. Job, for example, suffered many things unrelated to his faith and obedience. In Job's suffering, however, God was orchestrating his sovereign and just purposes from heaven (Job 41:11). Jesus taught that the span of life on earth is severely limited when considering heavenly blessing. When the godly suffer at the hands of the unrighteous, for example, rejoicing is commanded knowing that a great reward *in heaven* awaits (Matt. 5:12). Nevertheless, "Our Father who is in heaven" gives daily bread (Matt. 6:11) and "good gifts to those who ask him" (Matt. 7:11).

What of those who do not adopt a heavenly perspective? Ecclesiastes, with its theme the meaninglessness of life lived "under heaven" (i.e., from a purely earthly perspective), asks readers to consider that "God is in heaven and you are on the earth" (5:2). Jesus solemnly warned, "Not everyone who says to me, Lord, Lord, will enter the kingdom of heaven" (Matt. 7:21). (The phrase "kingdom of heaven," found only in Matthew's Gospel, is a circumlocution for the "kingdom of God" [see 19:23–24, where they are used interchangeably], owing to the Jews' reticence to utter the holy name of God.) Also, Paul warns that partiality is forbidden even in the case of a master-to-slave relationship, because "both their Master and yours is in heaven, and there is no favoritism with him" (Eph. 6:9).

Those claiming a heavenly inheritance are required to bring the earthly and the heavenly into alignment. Jesus linked entrance into the kingdom of heaven to repentance (Matt. 4:17), humility (5:3; 18:1–4), witness (5:10, 16; 10:32; 16:19), obedience (5:19), righteousness (5:20), compassion (18:10, 14; 23:13) and stewardship (19:23). Proactively, believers store up treasures (6:20) by being prudent managers of the little and perishable on earth in order to insure the abundant and enduring in heaven (Luke 16:1–13). Either the earthly or heavenly value system will prevail. So, those who pray, "Your will be done on earth as it is in heaven" (Matt. 6:10) are obliged to live from a heavenly vantage point.

Christ and Heaven. The greatest witness on earth to heavenly glory is Jesus Christ (John 1:14, 18). As the temple was the dwelling-place of God in the midst of Israel, so in a greater way the Incarnate is the dwelling-place of God. The Son uniquely preexisted with the Father in glory (17:5), "come down from heaven" (6:38), was "the bread from heaven" (6:32; see 6:41, 50, 51, 58) entered into heaven (1 Peter 3:22), and ascended far above all the heavens (Eph. 4:10). Christ's essential oneness with the Father is established in that the Old Testament notion that Jehovah "fills heaven and earth" (Jer. 23:24) is ascribed to Christ (Eph. 1:23; 4:10; Col. 1:16, 20).

The writer to the Hebrews details the person and work of Christ from a heavenly perspective. Although Creator of heavens and earth (1:10), the Son is now seated at the right hand of God's throne in heaven (1:4), mediating for believers (4:14–16). Christ is to be worshiped because God exalted him "above the heavens" (7:26; see Phil. 2:9–11). His redemptive work is completely efficacious because, unlike the priests of the old economy who ministered in a copy of the heavenly temple, Christ alone was qualified to enter the presence of God in heaven (9:23–24). Believers now "have confidence to enter the Most Holy Place by the blood of Jesus" (10:19).

The second coming is the *terminus ad quem* of Christ's intercessory work in heaven (Acts 3:21). Believers await anxiously for Christ's coming "from heaven" (1 Thess. 1:10; 4:16) at which time unbelievers will be judged (2 Thess. 1:7–8). John, looking forward to "that day," said it was "heaven standing open" (Rev. 19:11). The figure of an opening heaven is employed at the revelation given to Ezekiel (1:1), the phenomena surrounding the Lord's baptism (Mark 1:10), Stephen's vision of Christ (Acts 7:56), and John's vision of the apocalypse (Rev. 4:1). But it is on account of Christ (John 1:51) and his work (Rev. 11:19; 15:5) that the opening of heaven is complete. It is fitting that all manner of celestial phenomena will accompany the opening of heaven. It was a frightful thing for Israel to have the heavens shut and the blessing of God's physical provision withheld (Deut. 11:17; 2 Chron. 7:13; Luke 4:25). How much more terrible is it to be shut out of the kingdom of heaven where there is living water (Matt. 23:13; 25:10)?

The Spirit and Heaven. The giving of the Holy Spirit is directly tied to Jesus' entrance into heaven (Acts 2:33). The Spirit was sent from heaven (1 Peter 1:12). He is the heavenly gift (Acts 2:38), a foretaste of the blessings of heaven (John 7:37–39). He is also a guarantee of believers' future inheritance (Eph. 1:13–14). The writer of Hebrews indicates a relationship between "the heavenly gift," the Holy Spirit, and the powers of the age to come (6:3–4). When Peter linked the Spirit's coming with Joel 2:28–32 (Acts 2:17–21), he was saying that the eschatological hope of heaven was near. The "last days" had begun.

Believers and Heaven. Believers have a present and future heavenly status. Presently believers are citizens of heaven (Phil. 3:20–21) with a heavenly calling (Heb. 3:1); their names are written in heaven (Luke 10:20). They groan to be clothed with a resurrection body, "a building from God, an eternal house in heaven, not built by human hands" (2 Cor. 5:1). It will be a body like Christ's. The restoration of the image of God in human beings—from earthly to heavenly—will be complete (1 Cor. 15:45–49). The eternal inheritance of future blessings promised by God is secure because it is "kept in heaven" (1 Peter 1:4), and because believers are joint-heirs with Christ who has already been glorified (Rom. 8:17).

The heavenly future all believers anticipate is the fulfillment of God's purpose in creating the universe. It will include worship of the type revealed in the Book of Revelation (7:10; 11:16–18; 15:2–4). Worship will involve rehearsing God's glorious acts (19:1–2). In addition to ascription of worth, worship will involve service—unspecified works done in obedience to God and for God (22:6). Believers are to offer this kind of service to God now (Rom. 12:1). In contrast to present suffering, God promises believers that they will reign with Christ in heavenly glory (2 Tim. 2:12; see Matt. 19:28; Rev. 20:4, 6). In heaven believers will have fellowship with God and with each other in a perfect environment (Heb. 12:22–23).

In the Heavenlies. Paul stresses the believer's solidarity with Christ. Since a believer is "in Christ" and since Christ is in heaven, the believer is "in the heavenlies" (*en tois epouraniois*). Accordingly, God has blessed the believer "in the heavenly realms with every spiritual blessing in Christ" (Eph. 1:3). This precise phrase occurs only five times in the New Testament, and only in Ephesians (1:3; 1:20; 2:6; 3:10; 6:12). The believer's heavenly blessings depend on Christ's heavenly session (Eph. 1:20) and the spiritual union each believer shares "with Christ" (Eph. 2:6). God does not merely apply the ministry of Christ to believers. He sees believers with Christ wherever he is—and he is now in heaven. Believers are commanded to adopt an earthly lifestyle of dying to sin and living to righteousness (Rom. 6:4), and to set their minds on the heavenly reality that will soon be revealed in Christ (Col. 4:1–4). In other words, believers should live consistently with who, and where, they really are.

Paul indicates, however, that "the heavenlies" are also the realm of spiritual powers. Paul likely is referring to Satan and his demonic host, calling them "rulers," "authorities," and "spiritual forces" (Eph. 3:10; 6:12). Although their final defeat is sure (Eph. 1:19–23), believers are called upon to practice an eschatological lifestyle, equipped with heavenly weaponry wielded by those who are "strong in the Lord" (Eph. 6:10). The battles of life are won on earth with heavenly weapons, not earthly ones.

The Consummation. At the final consummation, God will make "new heavens and a new earth" (Isa. 65:17; 66:22; Rev. 22:1). It is "new" (*kainos*) in kind, not merely in time. One may wonder why a new heaven is necessary. One possibility is that the heavens (the plural is employed in Hag. 2:6; Heb. 12:6; see also Heb. 1:10; 2 Peter 3:7, 10, 12) have been affected by sin inasmuch as they are the place of the activity of evil angels and forces (Matt. 24:29; Eph. 6:12). The "new heavens and earth" follow the judgment of Satan (Rev. 20:7–10) and the Great White Throne judgment (20:11–15), both of which take place in heaven and will never be repeated. Also, the "new Jerusalem" that John saw "coming down out of heaven from God" (21:2, 10) is a new characteristic of heaven, perfectly suited to extend God's glory (21:11).

The sharp distinction between heaven and earth will be removed when God makes all things new. The essential feature of the New Jerusalem is the intimate presence of God among his people (21:3; 22:4). Interestingly, there will be no temple, "for the Lord God Almighty and the Lamb are its temple" (21:22). Its magnificence is only hinted at in figurative terms (21:11–22:5). Everything that is not consistent now with this picture of heaven will be done away with (21:4).

The Angels, Satan, and Heaven. "The host of heaven" can refer to the stars (Neh. 9:6; Isa. 24:21; 34:4; Matt. 24:29), but more frequently in Scripture it denotes angels (1 Kings 22:19; Luke 2:13). God warns against worshiping the celestial host (2 Kings 23:5; Jer. 19:13; Acts 7:42) as well as the angelic host (Col. 2:18). When referring to the angels the term carries a military connotation (Josh. 5:14–15; Dan. 4:35). God at times employs angels from heaven to do his bidding. They will be particularly active at Christ's return (Matt. 24:31; 2 Thess. 1:7–8; Rev. 8:2–10:11). Who can say to what extent angels are active today on earth? The truth might be found in Jacob's vision of a ladder extending from earth to heaven on which the angels of God ascended and descended (Gen. 28:12). Nevertheless, the dwelling-place of angels is heaven (Mark 12:25; 13:32; Luke 2:15), where they worship God (Matt. 8:10). The heavenly host rejoice when human beings repent (Luke 15:10; cf. 15:7).

Satan is a fallen angel who apparently had access to the presence of God in heavenly places (Job 1:6–7). If Revelation 12:7–12 looks back to the ministry of Christ, the "casting out" of Satan and his evil angels from heaven occurred when Christ entered heavenly glory (see Luke 10:17–20). Now Satan's sphere is more limited. He is "the prince of the power of the air" (Eph. 2:2) in the process of moving downward in successive stages until he is thrown into the lake of fire (Rev. 20:10). Bradford A. Mullen

See also Eternal Life, Eternality, Everlasting Life; Glorification.

Bibliography. J. Gilmore, *Probing Heaven: Key Questions in the Hereafter;* K. Schilder, *Heaven, What Is It?;* C. R. Schoonhoven, *The Wrath of Heaven;* U. E. Simon, *Heaven in the Christian Tradition;* W. M. Smith, *The Biblical Doctrine of Heaven;* P. Toon, *Heaven and Hell: A Biblical and Theological Overview;* A. E. Travis, *Where on Earth Is Heaven?*

Heaven, New. *See* New Heavens and A New Earth.

Hebrews, Theology of. The theological epicenter of the Epistle to the Hebrews may be summed up in one word: Christology. No biblical document outside of the four Gospels focuses as totally and forcefully on the person and redemptive achievement of Jesus. Likely this factor more than any other secured its prominent place in the early church's canon of Scripture in spite of doubts concerning its apostolic origin in the West (Carthage and Rome) prior to the fourth century. Eastern Christendom appears to have regarded it as Pauline from the beginning.

The preface (1:1–3) sets the stage with a magnificent vignette of the divine Son exercising his universal headship. Amidst a variety of allusions to his deity, Jesus is declared to have fulfilled the three divinely ordained Old Testament offices of prophet, king, and priest. The prophetic element appears in verses 1–2, where he is declared to be the Son through whom God has spoken his ultimate redemptive word. Next, his universal kingly enthronement is depicted in the first part of verse 3: "he sat down at the right hand of the Majesty in heaven." This exalted position is the direct outcome of his priestly achievement: "After he had provided purification for sins." It is this priestly aspect of Jesus' person and ministry that takes center stage as the message of Hebrews unfolds.

For purposes of analysis the epistle may be divided into two major sections. In 1:1–10:18, the primary theme is the superiority of Christ as eternal high priest. He is declared ultimately superior to the most cherished institutions of the ancient Hebrew faith. He is superior to the word of God spoken through the prophets since he himself is God's ultimate redemptive word. He is superior to the angelic hosts because no angel can boast of being the Son of God, fully divine (1:4–14), and yet fully human (2:5–18). These two factors qualify him uniquely to be the faithful and perpetual sin-bearer of his people. On the basis of that same uniqueness of being, he is as superior to Moses the great lawgiver of Israel (3:1–6), as Creator is to the created. The spiritual rest from dead works offered by Jesus is superior to that temporal one represented in Moses and Joshua through the occupation of the promised land (4:1–11; esp. vv. 9–10). Beginning with chapter 5 the central theological concern of the epistle emerges: the eternal spiritual priesthood assumed by Jesus through offering up himself as the once-for-all sacrifice for sins. It is infinitely superior to the temporal earthly ministry exercised by Aaron and his descendants (4:14–5:11; 7:1–10:18).

Here the Christology of Hebrews reaches its loftiest peak as Jesus, the eternal high priest, enters the inner sanctum of the universe where he offers up his own body and blood in voluntary submission to God as a sacrifice for sins once, forever, in behalf of all humanity. He is both priest and victim, offerer and offering!

In 10:19–13:25 the christological emphasis shifts from formal argument to practical application. The theme now takes the form of an urgent call for the readers to place their trust unswervingly in the sufficiency of Jesus as eternal high priest (10:19–39), motivated by the supreme example of faith and endurance he demonstrated during the days of his flesh (12:1–4). He appears as the last, and by far the greatest of all, in the long line of heroes and heroines of faith summoned to the witness stand in the famous eleventh chapter. It is he, and he alone, upon whom the readers are summoned to focus their concentrated attention if they are to be successful in running the race of life. Four "warning" sections (2:1–4; 3:7–19; 4:11–13; 5:11–6:20) highlight the intense pastoral concern sustained throughout the entire epistle.

A second significant feature in the theology of Hebrews is its bibliology, reflected both in the Old Testament foundation that permeates its overall message and in the distinctive way the author applies it. First, the priestly and sacrificial cultus of Israel, as recorded in Exodus 24–40 and in the entire Book of Leviticus, provides the message with its primary background.

Second, the author's method of introducing quotations from Scripture demonstrates a high view of biblical authority. With only two exceptions (4:7 and 7:14, where the human author is named) passages are cited in terms of their divine, otherwordly source:

"God says" (1:5; 4:3; 5:5–6; 7:21; 8:8; 12:26; 13:5)
"Someone has testified" (2:6)
"Jesus says" (2:12; 10:5)
"The Holy Spirit says" (3:7; 10:15, 17)
"It is declared" (7:17)
Direct citation—no source cited (10:37)
"Word of encouragement" (12:5)
"We may say with confidence" (13:6)

Third, the message of Hebrews is structured around certain proof-texts that may be considered primary because of the pivotal function each appears to have in the unfolding argument of the epistle. To be sure, these represent numerically only a small fraction of its total saturation in Old Testament citations and allusions, but the other appear more or less incidental and may be subsumed under the rubric of the primary text under consideration. Ten in all, the substance of each may be summarized as follows:

Theme	OT Source	Hebrews Ref.
1. The divinenature and appointment of the Son	Ps. 2:7	1:5; 5:5
2. The human nature and identification of the Son	Ps. 8:4–6	2:6–8
3. Warning against spiritual regression ("Today . . . enter his rest")	Ps. 95:7–11	3:7–11
4. The eternal nature and office of the son	Ps. 110:4	5:6; 7:17, 21
5. A new covenant providing the sanction for Jesus' priesthood and sacrifice	Jer. 31:31–34	8:7–12; 10:15–17
6. A willing self-offering marking the ultimate superiority of Jesus' redemptive achievement	Ps. 40:6–8	10:5–7
7. Exhortation to persevere by remaining faithful	Hab. 2:3–4	10:37–38
8. Exhortation to persevere under spiritual discipline	Prov. 3:11–12	12:5–6
9. The final shaking of all things	Hag. 2:6	12:26
10. Exhortation to be content	Deut. 31:6; Ps. 118:6–7	13:5–6

These texts provide a basis for consideration of the remaining theological features of Hebrews.

The Divine Nature and Appointment of the Son. In establishing Jesus' superiority to the angelic hosts his deity is clearly affirmed (1:1–4). Beginning with 1:5 and running like a thread through the rest of the chapter a whole string of direct Old Testament citations is marshaled as evidence. This is the most obvious demonstration of the author's commitment to proof-texting anywhere in the epistle.

The Human Nature and Identification of the Son. Jesus' superiority to angels also provides the ground for affirming the completeness of his humanity (2:5–18). "But we see Jesus" (v. 9) is the pivotal clause. Jesus, the "son of man," has become the messianic representative of humankind as a whole. As the sinless son of God, his total involvement in the human predicament, especially in suffering and death, has destroyed the devil and his morbid agenda for our race. This involvement, moreover, identifies him unashamedly with us as "brothers," and qualifies him to be our "merciful and faithful high priest" (v. 17).

Warning Against Spiritual Regression. The author of Hebrews is critically concerned for the spiritual survival of his readers and offers a poignant glimpse into the epistle's teaching on the Christian life, which may be summed up in the word "perseverance."

The call to enter into rest is not referring to heaven, but to the spiritual rest of one who is walking by faith, in full fellowship with Jesus. Faith in

Hebrews is viewed primarily in terms of pilgrimage—a long trek over the path of life with the distant shore in view (11:13–16, 39–40). Perseverance, of which Jesus presents the supreme example, (5:7–9; 12:1–4), is demonstrated through "holding on" to our assurance firm to the end (3:6, 14).

The words of the psalmist make it clear that the rest is available yet today (4:7–11). Entry into the promised land under Joshua cannot have exhausted its application. Securing it is worthy of the most concentrated effort (v. 11).

The Eternal Nature and Office of the Son. In 5:5–6, the author transacts a subtle shift in proof-texting from Psalm 2:7, on Jesus' divine sonship to Psalm 110:4 in order to highlight the central theme of the epistle: the eternal nature of Jesus' priesthood. Like the Aaronic priests he holds his office by divine decree (5:4–5a), but in contrast to them his appointment derives from an entirely different covenant basis (7:11–14), which declares him to be a priest *forever* (7:15–22). Hence the superiority of his office: he *always* lives to intercede in behalf of his people (v. 25). But this can only occur through his ministry of reconciling holy God and sinful humanity. Jesus is both priest and victim (v. 27). The stage is now set for another distinctive motif in Hebrews: its theology of atonement (8:1–10:18).

A New Covenant. The author's penchant for proof-texting is magnified in chapter 8, where five of the thirteen verses encompass a direct citation of the new covenant passage from Jeremiah 31:31–34. Verse 6 contains the interpretive key by summarizing the earlier argument of 7:11–14. Jesus' ministry as eternal high priest includes a mediatorial role that guarantees a better covenant based on better promises (cf. 7:22, where this thought is first introduced).

This new covenant involves a direct heart relationship between God and his people. Under its conditions the badge of identity for each person is the very relationship itself: all shall know me from the least of them to the greatest. Its guarantee is the superior sacrifice made by Jesus himself, the eternal high priest, not by the offering up of the blood of animals (9:11–15; 10:1–4). Instead of a temporary covering for sin it provides for each believer "a purifying of the conscience to serve the living God," from a heart motivated totally by confidence in the unconditional nature of his redemptive love.

A Willing Self-Offering. Jesus too was motivated by a heart totally committed to accomplishing the will of his Father. This is the essence of the proof-text from Psalm 40:6–8. The Old Testament clearly recognizes the potential detachment with which sacrifices might be made (1 Sam. 15:22–23; Ps. 51:16–17; Hos. 6:6). It has always been the case that the heart attitude validates any offering in the sight of God. Jesus as God's appointed high priest offers the ideal sacrifice as he surrenders his will to the will of his Father in offering up himself. This ultimate level of self-giving by a perfect, once-for-all sacrifice underscores Jesus as the guarantee of a better covenant. Repetition of the Jeremiah covenant passage in 10:16–18 is of great significance here. The believer is provided with optimum assurance of salvation: a conscience purified from the tyranny of dead works, released to serve the living God.

Exhortation to Persevere by Remaining Faithful. Biblical faith is more than a cognitive abstraction; it has the notion of concrete action most accurately conveyed by the adverbial idea of "faithfulness." This sense is reinforced in Hebrews probably more than anywhere else in the New Testament. In the second half of chapter 10 the exhortations "let us draw near" (v. 22), "let us hold unswervingly" (v. 23), and "let us consider" (v. 24), followed by such key words as "confidence" (v. 35) and "persevere" (v. 36) serve as poignant illustrations. The author, in applying the Habakkuk proof-text (vv. 37–38) views faith in terms of persevering to salvation (v. 39). Finally, from the broader perspective, God's gallery of heroes and heroines in chapter 11, culminating with Jesus as the supreme example of faith and endurance (12:1–4) is followed by a call to be disciplined by grace in the remainder of the epistle. This reaffirms that faith in Hebrews is viewed primarily in terms of pilgrimage.

Exhortation to Persevere under Spiritual Discipline. It is Jesus, more than the Old Testament heroes of chapter 11, to whom we are to fix our eyes on for our example of what it means to persevere (12:1–4). As he submitted to the discipline of his Father's will, which was ultimately the cross, so must we.

The appeal to scriptural authority is cited from Proverbs 3:11–12. The pain of applying physical exercise and therapy to impaired limbs provides a striking analogy to the spiritual impairment handicapping the readers (vv. 11–13). Focus on the possibility of their coming up short on grace (v. 16) highlights the sad but all too common tragedy in the spiritual realm of a dull, complacent spirit. Apparently the readers were being forced out of their perceived comfort zone in Judaism. They, like we, must risk all to experience the total sufficiency of Jesus, their eternal high priest for this life and the next.

The Final Shaking of All Things. Chapter 12 concludes on a somber eschatological note (vv. 18–29), with the reminder that God has spoken his ultimate word in Jesus, through the sprinkling of the blood he offered up as the mediator of the new covenant (v. 24). There is a strong affirmation here of the words of Jesus (Matt. 24:35), that though heaven and earth pass away, "my words will never pass away."

It was on this very theme that the epistle opened. God, who first spoke to his people through various ways and means in former times, has in these last days spoken to us in a Son (1:1–2). Here the contrast is between the fiery blackness of earthly Mount Sinai on the one hand, and the radiant glory of the heavenly Jerusalem on the other. As his voice shook the earth in the former setting, his final word will shake all things (Hag. 2:6). The dissolution of the physical universe will make way for the eternal order to appear in all of its glorious permanence.

The exhortation "let us be thankful" (v. 28) occurs again as a reminder that there is no way for mortals to render God acceptable service except through grace (Rom. 12:1). Only through grace can we lay hold of his eternal kingdom.

Exhortation to Be Content. Hebrews 13 conveys the image of a practical postscript. That a group of people under the particular pressures suggested by this letter should be challenged to be content is understandable. They were apparently of some affluence (10:32–34) and their earthly way of life was clearly in jeopardy. To be coveteous of more favorable, secure circumstances would have been only too natural.

As earlier in the letter, so here the call is to focus on the sufficiency of Jesus our eternal high priest (vv. 8–15). True contentment comes from being anchored to the promises of God. If we have the assurance that he, the eternal One, will never leave or forsake us, we are insulated against the fear of man.

Such a posture can only result from a heart that is established by grace rather than on external ritual. God's unconditional acceptance of us by virtue of the priestly achievement of Jesus has been the primary point of contact for the author throughout the epistle in seeking to motivate the readers to accept their high privilege and responsibility of persevering to the end.

LEONARD S. WALMARK

Bibliography. G. L. Archer, Jr., *The Epistle to the Hebrews: A Study Manual;* F. F. Bruce, *The Epistle to the Hebrews;* T. Hewitt, *The Epistle to the Hebrews: An Introduction and Commentary;* W. L. Lane, *Call to Commitment: Responding to the Message of Hebrews;* B. F. Westcott, *The Epistle to the Hebrews: The Greek Text with Notes and Essays.*

Heir. *See* INHERITANCE.

Hell. Place of God's final retributive punishment. Scripture progressively develops this destiny of the wicked: the Old Testament outlines the framework, while the New Testament elaborates on it. Jesus, however, is most responsible for defining hell.

The Old Testament. In the Old Testament Sheol denotes the abode of the dead; conscious souls face a shadowy existence in this "land of oblivion" (Job 10:21; Ps. 88:12; Eccl. 9:10; Isa. 14:10). Since death is not a natural occurrence but issues from the fall, the Old Testament confidently awaits God's demonstration of his lordship over Sheol by raising the righteous to life (Gen. 2–3; Pss. 16:10; 49:15; Isa. 25:8; Hos. 13:14). While God's kingship also has implications for the wicked, here the Old Testament is more reserved. The Old Testament infrequently suggests a bodily resurrection for the wicked (Dan. 12:2), a final judgment and retribution for evil deeds (Pss. 21:10; 140:10; Mal. 4:1–2). Nevertheless, the contemptible and horrible destiny of the wicked, irretrievably isolated from the righteous, is clear (Pss. 9:17; 34:15–16).

The Intertestamental Period. The intertestamental literature constructed divergent scenarios for the wicked dead, including annihilation (4 Ezra 7:61; 2 Apoc. Bar. 82:3ff.; 1 Enoch 48:9; 99:12; 1QS iv. 11–14) and endless torment (Jub. 36:11; 1 Enoch 27:1–3; 103:8; T. Gad. 7:5). Sheol frequently became an interim location for the dead, distinguished from the place of final punishment (1 Enoch 18:9–16; 51:1). This final punishment was usually located in a valley south of Jerusalem, known in Hebrew as *Ge Hinnom* or the Valley of Hinnom (2 Apoc. Bar. 59:10; 4 Ezra 7:36), and in Greek as *gehenna* (2 Esdr. 2:29). This valley had a long history as a place of infamy. Notorious for the child sacrifices offered to Molech during the reigns of Ahaz and Manasseh (2 Kings 16:3; 2 Chron. 28:3; 33:6; Jer. 7:31–34; 19:6), this valley was further desecrated when Josiah used it as Jerusalem's refuse dump (2 Kings 23:10) and it was prophesied as the place of God's future fiery judgment (Isa. 30:33; 66:24; Jer. 7:31–32). While some intertestamental writings equate hell with the "lake of fire" in this "accursed valley" of Hinnom (1 Enoch 90:26, 27; 54:1, 2), others use it to denote a place in the underworld (Sib. Or. 4:1184–86).

In addition, the respective scenarios for the wicked, whether annihilation or eternal torment, shaped images of God's judgment. For instance, at times fire consumes the wicked (1 Enoch 99:12); in other texts fire and worms torment their victim to a useless existence (Judith 16:17).

The New Testament. In the New Testament hell is where the reprobate exist after the resurrection from Hades and the final judgment. In this lake of fire God punishes the wicked, along with Satan and his henchmen (Matt. 25:41), bringing an end to evil's free ways.

Gehenna is the standard term for hell in the New Testament. Related phrases include "punishment of eternal fire" (Jude 7), "lake of fire" (Rev. 19:29; 20:14–15), and "judgment." English versions occasionally translate *hades* (esp. Luke 16:23) and *tartaroō* (2 Peter 2:4) as hell. However, these terms appear to denote the intermediate state, not the final destiny of the wicked.

Jesus says more about hell than any other biblical figure. His warnings of the eschatological judgment are liberally colored with the imagery of hell (Matt. 5:22; 7:19; 8:12 par. Luke 13:28–30;

Matt. 10:15, 28; 11:22, 24; 18:8–9 par. Mark 9:43–49; Luke 17:26–29; John 15:6). He portrays this future judgment through pictures of Sodom's destruction (Luke 17:29–30): fire, burning sulfur, and a fiery furnace (Gen. 19:24–25). These images of God's judgment were well established in the Old Testament and intertestamental literature. Important portrayals of hell are also present in Jesus' parables, including the tares (Matt. 13:40–42), the net (Matt. 13:50); the great supper (Matt. 22:13), the good servant and the wicked servant (Matt. 24:51 par. Luke 12:46–47), the talents (Matt. 25:30), and the last judgment (Matt. 25:46). Here "weeping and gnashing of teeth" (Matt. 13:50; 24:51; 25:30) and "darkness" (Matt. 22:13; 25:30) are key descriptive phrases.

The New Testament conception of hell does not exceed Jesus' description. The following headings outline its essential features.

1. *Sinners will occupy hell.* While God created us for a loving relation with himself, at the fall humankind rebelled. God's judgment falls on all sinners, unless they have faith in Jesus. After the provisional state of Hades and the final judgment, God's wrath culminates in hell. According to the New Testament, the objects of God's wrath range from the pious hypocrites (Matt. 23:33) and those failing to help the poor (Matt. 25:31–46; Luke 16:19–31) to the vile and murderers (Rev. 21:8).

Some argue that only an explicit repudiation of Jesus attracts God's eternal wrath, referencing Luke 12:8–9. However, Jesus says "the Son of Man came to seek and to save what was lost" (Luke 19:10). In other words, he came offering grace to a world that was "condemned already" (John 3:17–18).

Since hell is not a natural fixture of creation but results from the fall and is destiny of the wicked, the New Testament occasionally personifies hell as the demonic forces behind sin. The sinful tongue is itself aroused and "set on fire by hell" (James 3:6). Similarly, Jesus labels the Pharisees "sons of hell," identifying the root of their hypocrisy (Matt. 23:15).

2. *Hell exists for the requital and retribution of evil deeds.* Hell is the place of God's final judgment. Here God, our King and Supreme Judge, finally rectifies wrongs through his retributive wrath. Here the damned will be paid back for the harm they have done (Matt. 16:27; Luke 12:47–48; 2 Peter 2:13; Jude 15; Rev. 14:9–11). Wrath is not the natural consequence of evil choices in a moral universe or the sinner's misconstrual of God's love. Rather, as Paul's use of *orgē* shows, wrath is an emotion or feeling in the Godhead, and thus God's personal action (Rom. 1:18–32). By extrinsically imposing penal conditions on the sinner, God rectifies wrongs and reestablishes his righteous rule (Matt. 25:31–46; Rom. 12:19; 1 Cor. 15:24–25; 2 Cor. 5:10).

3. *Hell is a final place of bondage and isolation from the righteous.* After the resurrection and the final judgment, the wicked and even Hades are thrown into hell. The New Testament describes hell as a place: a furnace (Matt. 13:42, 50), a lake of fire (Rev. 19:20; 20:14–15; 21:8), and a prison (Rev. 20:7). The wicked are imprisoned here so they cannot harm God's people (Matt. 5:25–26; 13:42, 50; 18:34; Jude 6; Rev. 20:14–15).

While the parable of Lazarus and the rich man occurs in Hades, the intermediate state, and not Gehenna, it does foreshadow the latter. Jesus says an unbridgeable spatial chasm separates these two so no one can "cross over from there" (Luke 16:26). John's vision in Revelation 21 of the new city on a high mountain confirms this separation between the blessed and the damned after the day of judgment. Consequently, Scripture provides no warrant for those speculative images of the righteous rejoicing in the torture of the damned. The prophecy in Isaiah 66:24, which has been so used, does not refer to this eschatological event, for the resurrection of the body has not occurred.

4. *Sinners suffer penalties in hell.* Jesus repeatedly accentuates hell's dreadfulness and horror: "if your eye causes you to sin, gouge it out. . . . It is better . . . to enter life with one eye than to . . . be thrown into the fire of hell" (Matt. 18:9). While Scripture remains reticent on the specific torments for the impenitent, certain dimensions are clear.

At the final judgment, God will declare, "I don't know you. . . . Depart from me, you who are cursed, into the eternal fire" (Matt. 25:12, 41). The wicked in hell are excluded from God's loving presence and the "life" for which humans were originally created (John 5:29). The damned are "thrown outside, into the darkness" (Matt. 8:12; 22:13). Consequently this "second death" (Rev. 21:8) is a useless and ruined existence (Matt. 25:30; Luke 9:25; John 3:16–18; 2 Thess. 1:9; 2 Peter 2:12; Jude 12; Rev. 21:8). Sin has thoroughly effaced every virtue. The reprobate have become obstinate in their rebellion against God, like "unreasoning animals" (Jude 10, 13; 2 Peter 2:12–22). Consequently, the doors of hell can be locked from the inside, as C. S. Lewis observes.

In hell, the damned receive their due for "things done while in the body" (2 Cor. 5:10; 2 Peter 2:13; Jude 15; Rev. 14:9–11). The "undying worm" has often been interpreted as the soul's internal torment, coveting and grieving what has been lost (Mark 9:48). This regret is compounded since the reprobate are not penitent but locked into their rebellion. But the grave's worms and darkness are also common images of a contemptible fate. Scripture suggests that there are degrees of punishment in hell. The one "who does not know and does things deserving punishment will be beaten with few blows." More severe is the punishment due to the disobedient who were "entrusted with much" (Mark 12:40; Luke 12:48).

Annihiliationsim and the Extent of Hell. The extent of hell has occasioned much debate in recent scholarship. There are three major points of contention.

Some annihilationists have argued that the biblical imagery of a consuming fire, destruction, and perishing implies the cessation of life (Stott). However, Jesus' pictures of hell are not literal descriptions but metaphors. They are mutually exclusive, if taken literally, for the fires of hell conflict with its "utter darkness." In the intertestamental literature the metaphorical image of a fire could suggest annihilation or everlasting punishment, showing the inconclusiveness of this argument.

Some annihilationists have argued that when the Greek adjective for eternal, *aiōnios,* is used with nouns of action, it refers to an occurrence with eternal results, not an eternal process (Fudge). "Eternal punishment," it is argued, denotes a punishment that occurs once with eternal results. However, counterfactuals dispute this argument. The eternal sin (Mark 3:29), for example, is not just one sin, but an action that irretrievably debilitates so one only sins. Similarly, everlasting salvation (*aiōnios sōtēria*) does not refer solely to Christ's work long ago, and thus preclude his sustaining and preserving presence. For Scripture describes believers, even in the age to come, as existing "in Christ" (Rom. 8:1; Eph. 1:13; Col. 2:6–7; 2 Tim. 2:10). So *aiōnios sōtēria* refers to Christ's eternal (*aiōnios*) salvation of the blessed, an action that is everlasting as well as final.

In Matthew 25:46 Jesus differentiates the two futures of eternal life and eternal punishment, using the same adjective for each, *aiōnios.* In Jesus' mind, it appears, the extent of each future is identical. If the existence of the righteous is endless, so also is the existence of the wicked. Other statements suggest the same conclusion. Jesus teaches that "whoever rejects the Son will not see life, for God's wrath remains on him" (John 3:36). As long as God's wrath abides on them, the damned must exist. Jesus' picture of hell as a place where "their worm *does not die,* and the fire is not quenched" (Mark 9:48) indicates that this manifestation of God's wrath is unending. Other passages in the New Testament reiterate Jesus' dreadful warning, by describing hell as "everlasting torment." Even annihilationists admit the difficulty of such texts for their position.

Objections to Hell. Hell is a dreadful reality. Just as Christ wept over Jerusalem, believers are similarly troubled and anguished by this destiny of the lost. Some have raised serious challenges to the reality of hell.

One perennial difficulty concerns the relationship between God's love and holiness: How could a loving God reject *forever* the creature he loves? This question assumes that the creature is the highest intrinsic good, even for God. But the highest good for the God of Scripture is not humanity. Humanity was created for God, and cannot be defined in terms of itself; we exist to glorify God (Ps. 73:24–26; Rom. 11:36; 1 Cor. 10:31; Col. 1:16). That is why Jesus insists it is idolatrous to enlist God as humanity's servant (Luke 17:7–10). Certainly God loves the creature; creation itself reflects God's free love. But since God's love is complete in himself, even before creation, the creature cannot be presumed as his one and only end. Nor can the character of God's love be decided a priori, but only by revelation. Consequently, Jesus' warning of the wrath to come (Matt. 25:31, 41, 46) must be accepted as an inherent possibility of God's love.

Some acknowledge retribution, but question why the wicked are eternally kept in existence to suffer. At issue is the punishment due sin. Since pride conceals the sinner's true debt to God the Judge, again this question should be answered by examining Christ's priestly work of propitiation. At the cross God in Christ became our substitute to bear the punishment for our sins, so as "to be just and the one who justifies the man who has faith in Jesus" (Rom. 3:26; cf. 2 Cor. 5:21; 1 Peter 2:24). The God-man propitiated our sin. This fact, that God the Judge, the "Lord of glory" himself (1 Cor. 2:8), accepted the punishment due us, suggests that the penalty for sin against the Infinite is infinite.

Questions will remain. But believers personally know God's love in Jesus Christ. And their response to a lost world will parallel that of their Lord, who humbled himself to our condition, suffered, and died for the wicked.

TIMOTHY R. PHILLIPS

See also DEATH, MORTALITY; ETERNAL PUNISHMENT; GRAVE; HADES; JUDGMENT; JUDGMENT, DAY OF; SHEOL.

Bibliography. D. L. Edwards and J. Stott, *Evangelical Essentials;* E. Fudge, *The Fire that Consumes;* A. A. Hoekema, *The Bible and the Future;* C. S. Lewis, *The Problem of Pain;* S. McKnight, *Through No Fault of Their Own: The Fate of Those Who Have Never Heard,* pp. 147–57; T. R. Phillips, *Through No Fault of Their Own: The Fate of Those Who Have Never Heard,* pp. 47–59; W. G. T. Shedd, *The Doctrine of Endless Punishment;* D. F. Watson, *ABD,* 2:926–28.

Hell, Descent into. *See* DESCENT INTO HELL (HADES).

Helps, Gift of. *See* HOLY SPIRIT, GIFTS OF.

High, God Most. *See* GOD, NAMES OF.

High Priest. *See* PRIEST, PRIESTHOOD; PRIEST, CHRIST AS.

Holy, Holiness. One does not define God. Similarly, the idea of holiness is at once understandable and elusive. Nevertheless, there is not term equal to the fullness inherent in holiness. All of heaven's hosts, Israel, and the church ascribe praise to a holy God because that idea sets him apart from everything else (Exod. 15:11; Isa. 6:3; Rev. 4:8). Holiness is what God is. Holiness also comprises his plan for his people.

In Genesis we read that the seventh day is "holy" (Gen. 2:3). In the same book Tamar is referred to by the Hebrew term, *qadešâ* (Gen. 38:15, 21). The latter is highly instructive at this point. In Old Testament times what was holy belonged to the gods in an absolute way. Judah's misperception of Tamar was based on awareness of how people viewed the holy. If the gods were sexed and needed sex, then it is no shock that those who served in the temple should be set apart for similar activity.

In the first clear biblical usage of the term that introduces a human to the character of God as holy, there are both similarities to and differences from pagan attempts to define holiness. It is intriguing to ponder the possible theological and religious categories that may have prepared Moses to hear Yahweh's command to remove his shoes because the ground on which he stood was "holy" (Exod. 3:5). The universal description of the holy is that which is separated from the normal in a conceptual way. Yet through revelatory instruction Moses taught Israel that their conception of the holy affirmed an essential difference between themselves and deity. Pagan worshipers in that region could not have reflected on the nature of the holy with that sort of clarity. What was "other" than the normal for them was distinct in Israel as a personal "Other."

Moses recognized, as others would have, a difference that meant that the one addressing him had special rights to determine the sanctity of the place where he was present. It was the content of the term to come that was to set Israel apart. These ideas, apparent in the pagan religions, were incorporated and then transformed by the Israelites in light of the Holy One who revealed his nature by word and action. The concepts that replaced the typical understanding of the holy were to revolutionize the history of Israel and, consequently, the world.

Holiness in the Ancient Near East: Fear and Manipulation. Although the terms from the root *qdš*, holy or holiness, used in the cultures surrounding Israel do not appear in the extant texts as often as one might expect, there remains enough textual evidence to conclude basic agreement on meaning. Recent scholarship in a variety of disciplines has confirmed that holiness pertains primarily to that which is recognized as divine. Rudolf Otto's ground-breaking work on this issue set a trajectory for much of the discussion of the phenomenon of the holy in this century. Apparently, when it comes to ancient Near Eastern views of holiness, similarities in general emphases are profound enough to outweigh the differences in deity names and the cultic practices instituted in relation to them.

Without the concept of a personal God to discern the meaning of existence, the pagan mind formulated a variety of interpretive tools to express reality. Awe, dread, unapproachability, vitality, and mystery are the most common atttributes indicated in texts that reveal how the ancients perceived the holy. The aspect of separation between the sacred and the profane can be seen in each of these. The inherent presupposition was that the holy elicited the irrational responses of humans. People knew their place in relation to the holy. When confronted with something other than themselves, the immediate response was fear mixed, as Otto indicates, with fascination.

Several notes of contrast with Israel's faith highlight what continually occurred in the absence of biblical revelation in minds that were confronted with the unknown. It is evident that the religions that intersected Israel's history found their predominant motivation in existence to be servile fear. Fear of the fickle actions of nature and spirit was projected onto the gods they made and worshiped as holy. Human worth was exhausted in the sole purpose of serving the basic need of the gods, in order to escape impending judgment. That dread of the holy was dealt with by a complex system of cultic appeasement that was, in essence, the attempt to manipulate the "gods," which were personified spiritual and natural forces. Response to the "holy" resulted in the complex system of polytheistic pantheons of ancient cultures. They were similar in one regard: what was holy could never be trusted, only feared.

Though religion was recognized as the central issue of life, its connection to the holy reveals rigorous attempts to bring what was feared (e.g., dead crops, dry riverbeds, rainless clouds) into alignment with the wishes of the worshiper. Morality was connected to a notion of the holy only in the slightest of ways. At best, contractual social agreements were made and kept for the sole purpose of insuring personal safety and success. Both gods and humans had to be viewed with mistrust.

The holy was nothing more than, as Kaufmann expresses it, a metadivine, or a nontranscendent realm of "gods" vying for power. Therefore, culture could be nothing more than an expression of these realities. The holy, often perceived as "above," was never completely distinct from the profane "below." It just bore more prowess and shrewdness. The powers, drives, and desires that ruled below were projected onto the above and labeled holy. The ethical implications resulting from this worldview were based solely on power and the attempt to coerce the holy ones to agree with one's agenda. Sacrifices were offered in hopes that a malevolent force could be outwitted by the satisfied power to whom the offerings were made. Consequently, those without status in those cultures suffered immeasurably. The weak, the young, women, the old, and outsiders were at the mercy of those able to enforce their will.

In an explanation of how holiness might be revealed to persons, a Mesopotamian understanding of the burning bush would focus on both the power behind the bush and the power inherent in the bush. Since each god had only a local habitation, the next step would be to see how Moses would be able to turn that awesome power to his own good. What one notes immediately, however, is that Moses does nothing but obey and tremble. He offers no offering or incantation. Even if one allows the similar idea of an essential difference between deity and humanity, this occurrence indicates both a contradictory conception of holiness from the typical and a radical transformation of the categories. At the same time this God issues a personal call to one he would talk with as a friend (Exod. 33:10–11). This denotes a crucial distinction for the Hebraic concept of holiness. Personal relationship based on faithfulness was a ludicrous idea outside Israel.

Holiness in the Old Testament: Relationship with the Transcendent. No one can explain the phenomena of Israel and the Holy One of Israel adequately without realizing the fundamental distinctive of Yahweh's transcendence. The pagan format of a "below-above" interpretation of reality, which scholars have called a "continuous" worldview, was challenged by the audacious claim of Israel to be created by and related to the only Holy One. Separation of the holy from the profane then had as its base the creatorial majesty of God, who creates out of no necessity other than a perfect, holy will (Isa. 41:20). That Being was self-sufficient in every respect (1 Sam. 2:2). It is apparent that Moses understood this division of reality. He bowed in awe, because an Other had confronted him—One who is not to be manipulated and who desires a relationship prior to any service. Israel's existence was marked indelibly by the nature of its deity, "I am holy" was the basis for their worldview, history, spirituality, and purpose (Lev. 11:44).

In the incident of the burning bush holiness as brilliance is evident symbolically in the fire, which is a recurrent theme throughout the history of Israel. Various manifestations of the brightness of the glory of God were constant reminders that the Holy One was in the midst of his people (Exod. 13:21; 15:11; 40:34; 1 Kings 8:10–11). More than simply a show of searing brilliance, however, the God of Israel appears in ways that indicate his desire to communicate his very nature to his own. It is here that Moses may have already had some intimation from prior history beyond that of surrounding cultures.

Though the word "holy" does not appear as often in Genesis, the outlines of desired relationship between a holy God and his chosen people are laid down there. The Holy One is the transcendent Creator, whose "is-ness" provides the sole source of all that exists. In light of his unapproachable majesty there is a corresponding dispositional fear. But it does not appear in destructive ways (15:12; 28:17). Rather, there is always a corresponding rational awareness of God's personal presence and purpose (28:15, 20). There are no laws or standards. Instead, God is looking for total trust and commitment to covenant that he binds his own existence to (15:17–18; 17:19). The rudiments of God's moral nature are revealed early on by his decision to delineate what pleases him as "good," perhaps best interpreted as "the way it should be because Yahweh made it so" (used fifteen times in Gen. 1–3). Though the law is not present, internal standards of purity and righteousness surround the covenants Yahweh makes with his people (Gen. 6:5, 9; 15:6; 17:1). Probably most instructive of all, as well as being a radical polemic of the irrational motivations behind pagan notions of holiness, is the fact that Yahweh is looking for those who are willing to "walk" with him rather than cower in fear alone (5:22, 24; 6:9; 24:40; 48:15).

It is illuminating to note that once Yahweh communicates his fundamental nature to Moses, and consequently to a redeemed nation, that the usage of the terms related to holiness explodes. Of over 830 instances of term in all its forms in the Old Testament, nearly 350 occur in the Pentateuch after Genesis. We thus begin to see that the ultimate purpose of God is the production of a people who bear his holy name or character (Exod. 19:6; Lev. 11:44).

When Yahweh appears to his own there is the requisite reminder of the essential difference between Creator and created. This discontinuity results in awesome wonder at his majesty and power (Exod. 19:18, 19, 21; Isa. 6:1). God's glorious nature, though radically distinct from creation, is nonetheless manifested (Exod. 19:18; Isa. 1, 4). The mystery that fascinates is present everywhere (Exod. 19:9, 24; Isa. 6:1, 4). In order to relate to him, Israel must be clean, revealing the inherent purity Yahweh alone can impart (Exod. 19:10; Isa. 6:5). This purity far exceeds mere cultic interpretation. It is the indication of the moral cleanness from which is to issue a lifestyle pleasing to Yahweh and that has at its base an other-orientation (Exod. 19:6; Isa. 6:5–8). Every possible abuse of power finds its condemnation in what is holy. Those who live in fear because of weakness or uselessness are to experience thorough protection and provision based on the standards of righteousness that issue from God's holy reign (Exod. 20:12–17; Lev. 19; Ps. 68:5).

The One who is Other in nature and character provides the means by which Israel can live in the full reality of his nature, and in turn can come to share his aversion to all that is fundamentally unreal. This is shown most graphically in the distinction between the clean and the unclean, the sacred and the profane, the holy and the common throughout Israel's practical worship. Yahweh, who has sanctified a day and a bush, moves in deliberate steps to reveal actualized holiness in everyday life. Gammie illustrates this in a "mapping" of the sacred in which the demarcations of reality for the Israelites center on God's holiness. All of life is seen as having the option of moving from the natural to the spiritual, from the relatively secular to the totally Holy. Sinai, the tabernacle, Israel's two camps, (one for the clean and one for the unclean), and ultimately the temple, each with their accompanying physical elements and human ministers, point to one goal: the possibility of dwelling with the Holy One (cf. Zech. 2:13–8:23; 14:20–21).

Though it is difficult to distinguish clear shifts in the progress of revelation in the Old Testament, it is quite apparent that holiness remains the central theme by which Israel understands its God and its relationship to him. There are discernible shifts in the usage of terminology—from holiness as seen in things (all the cultic elements, e.g., 1 Chron. 22:19), to its transmission to persons in relation to God (Exod. 19:2, 6). And, finally, holiness carries strong moral and ethical implications. While awe of the Holy One remains (Isa. 6:5) there is a complementary seeking of God because he invites his people to relationship (Hos. 11:8–9). Yahweh's personal presence affects every area of life. Thus, it is arguable that holiness is the primary way of describing God and his ultimate means of revealing who he is. Both grammatically and essentially, the word "holy" is synonymous with the God who confronted Israel. The attributes of sovereignty, purity, righteousness, steadfast love, and mercy are all defined by his holy name. They are qualified, measured, and defined by the essential nature of Yahweh, the Holy One (Isa. 6:3; Ezek. 36:22–29).

Holiness in the New Testament: Transforming Triune Presence. The terms *hagios* (holy) and other derivatives (holiness, sanctifying, sanctification) are unique terms that are not used in the extant Greek literature in the same way they appear in the New Testament. The holy takes on profound personal and spiritual realities in the New Testament text through its 230 instances.

Everything in the Old Testament begins and ends with the holiness of God. That emphasis is not lost but expanded in the New Testament. One inadequately interprets the New Testament if the Holy One of Israel is not presupposed in everything that is written. Holiness as the moral excellence of Yahweh is the same principle and standard for the life and ministry of Jesus. The radical discontinuity of Israel's monotheistic God is deepened in the appearance of the Holy One in incarnate flesh. Jesus is holy as his Father is (John 6:69). Apart from angelic proclamation (Luke 1:35), the only ones who recognize his unique essence at first are demons (Luke 4:34). Where the Holy One is, all that realize his presence are altered. Holiness as glory, power, and majesty are revealed in real ways tinged with mystery (John 18:6). Jesus' miracles attest his nature (Mark 4:35–5:43). Various uncleannesses are confronted and removed. The awareness of his purity brings immediate conviction (Luke 5:8; Rev. 1:17). Every element of holiness in the Old Testament is rehearsed and particularized in the person and work of Jesus.

Jesus shares the Holy Name of Yahweh, and therefore the title "Holy Father" is an acclamation of his nature as well (John 17:11; cf. Matt. 28:19). The Holy Spirit, that is, the Spirit who both is and makes holy, is the specific title given for the third person of the Trinity in the New Testament (93 usages, cf. to 133 times of Spirit without "holy"). It is clearly discernible that the Triune God is holy in essence and in character. The expectation of the Holy One has not been altered either. His character unalterably demands a likeness in those who bear his Name. He consistently requires and supplies the means by which to produce a holy people (1 Peter 1:15–16).

The outward associations of the holy in Old Testament, postexilic, and rabbinic literature are radically internalized in the New Testament believer. Priestly rituals, prophetic descriptions of a holy social order, and the individual appropriation of holiness in the wisdom literature pointed to the people God was calling to himself. Jesus verifies this in the only usage of holiness attributed to him that is not a reference to divinity in John 17:17: "Sanctify them by the truth." This statement may be seen as the summation and purpose of the atoning work of Christ. He is not speaking about the endtimes but of a desire for the church to take on the likeness of the essential nature of God (Heb. 12:10). It is no surprise, then, that the common description for those who believe on the Triune God and relate to that God is "holy ones" (*hagioi*—over sixty times in the New Testament). They are to be separated unto God as living sacrifices. (Rom. 12:1) evidencing purity (1 Cor. 6:9–20; 2 Cor. 7:1), righteousness (Eph. 4:24), and love (1 Thess. 4:7; 1 John 2:5–6, 20; 4:13–21). What was foretold and experienced by only a few in the Old Testament becomes the very nature of what it means to be a Christian through the plan of the Father, the work of Christ, and the indwelling presence of the Holy Spirit.

The moral and ethical results of this new realization of the consecrated will are radical indeed. Sexual purity within and without marriage, real and submissive lifestyle commitments that cause unbelievers to reflect on the nature of the Christian God, blamelessness of heart, good works, contentment, and constant praise are but a few of the results of the new nature God both imputes and imparts to the New Testament believer. There is no area left untouched by the holiness of God, not as an external standard alone but as the impartation of the divine nature in all of its fullness (2 Cor. 5:21; Heb. 12:10; 2 Peter 1:4). There is an inheritance for the people of God that includes not just eternal glories but the possibility of living a life that is good, one that is what God intended. Sobering is the thought that the final distinction recorded in Scripture in the judgment at the end of human history will be whether one is holy or not (Rev. 22:11–15).

It is important to note that no one is ever called to be or can become holy alone. The saints comprise the church as a holy community. It is in the middle of normal life that the central factors of holiness are worked out. In ways similar to the transmission of the covenant in the Old Testament, there is a mutual accountability and encouragement inherent in the call to reflect the character of God (cf. 1 Thess. 2:10–12; Heb. 10:25; 13:7, 17).

The God who revealed himself to Israel and the church does so in an instructive manner. Progressive revelation is evident in the methodical way in which God shows himself to be both Holy and Love. Those ideas, though never exhausted by the human mind, become the essential terms for biblical faith. All else about God is comprised in and issues from his holiness. The believer is invited to live in his holy presence but only if that includes living with others who desire nothing less than God's holiness (Heb. 10:19–26). Once a person begins to comprehend the heart of holy love, then there is no response other than an outward orientation, in worship and service (Heb. 12:10, 14). Both Testaments attest that nothing less than holiness will fully satisfy the nature of God. Thus, redemption is not complete in deliverance alone. The believer is set free in order to become like the One who redeems. It is his will that his own would be like him in every respect.

M. William Ury

See also God; Priest, Priesthood; Saint(s).

Bibliography. J. Gammie, *Holiness in Israel;* O. R. Jones, *The Concept of Holiness;* Y. Kaufmann, *The Religion of Israel;* D. Kinlaw, *Beacon Dictionary of the Bible,* s.v. "Holy, Holiness"; R. Otto, *The Idea of the Holy;* O. Procksch, *TDNT,* 1:88–110.

Holy of Holies. *See* Tabernacle; Temple.

Holy One. *See* God, Names of.

Holy One of God. *See* Jesus Christ, Name and Titles of.

Holy Place. *See* Tabernacle; Temple.

Holy Spirit. Third person of the Trinity.

Old Testament. Some have argued that Old Testament believers were saved and sanctified by the Spirit just as New Testament believers. But such teaching appears nowhere in the Old Testament. However people were made right with God, the focus of the Old Testament roles of the Spirit lies elsewhere.

In the earliest Scriptures, the Spirit does not clearly emerge as a distinct personality. The Hebrew word for "spirit" (*rûaḥ*) can also mean wind, breath, or life-force. Most commonly designated as "of God" or "of the Lord," the Spirit appears as God's agent of creation (Gen. 1:2; Job 33:4; 34:14–15), a mode of his interacting with humans (Gen. 6:3), his agent of revelation (Gen. 41:38; Num. 24:2), and a mode of empowering select leaders of God's people (Moses and the Seventy—Num. 11:17–29; possibly Joshua—Num. 27:18; Deut. 34:9). All of these uses recur throughout the Old Testament, but one other remains unique to these earliest days—equipping Bezalel and Oholiab with the skills of craftsmanship for constructing the tabernacle (Exod. 31:3; 35:31), although the provision of gifts of the Spirit in the New Testament will become a close analogue.

In the books of Judges, Samuel, and Kings, certain characteristic activities of the Spirit begin to emerge. He comes upon significant individuals, almost as an energizing power, temporarily equipping leaders for physical prowess and military victory. Four judges are so characterized (Othniel—Judg. 3:10; Gideon—6:34; Jephthah—11:29; Samson—14:19; cf. Amasai—1 Chron. 12:18). This supernatural power combines with inspiration for verbal utterances in the earliest form of prophecy, usually assumed to have been somewhat uncontrollable or "ecstatic" (cf. Saul's "ravings" in 1 Sam. 19:20–23 with 10:6, 10; 11:6; for David, see 2 Sam. 23:2). With the advent of the monarchy, the presence of the Spirit functions as divine authentication of the legitimate king. When Saul no longer remains God's choice for the throne, the Spirit leaves him and comes upon David instead (1 Sam. 16:13–14). First Samuel 16:13 further suggests that David retained the Spirit as a permanent possession, apparently unlike others in the Old Testament. In 1 Chronicles 28:12, the Spirit reveals to David the blueprint for the temple. By the time of the divided kingdom, the Spirit is beginning to inspire and empower prophets, guiding individuals to specific places where they proclaim messages of salvation or judgment from God to appointed audiences (Elijah—1 Kings 18:12; 2 Kings 2:16; Micaiah—1 Kings 22:24; Azariah—2 Chron. 15:1; Jahaziel—2 Chron. 20:14; Zechariah son of Jehoiada—2 Chron. 24:20).

Of all the canonical Wisdom literature, the Spirit appears unambiguously only in the psalms. In addition to uses already noted, the Spirit is now for the first time called "Holy" (Ps. 51:11) and "good" (143:10). The first of these texts demonstrates a characteristic fear in Old Testament times; even David in his unique situation did not have the assurance of God's abiding presence that would later characterize the New Testament age. The second text reflects the development of a belief in the Spirit's role in personal and moral guidance. Psalm 139:7 ("Where can I go from your Spirit?") is embedded in a key passage on the omnipresence of God.

The writing prophets preserve many of the older insights about the Spirit but for the first time begin to disclose the coming of a new era in the Spirit's ministry. God's people can look forward to restoration from exile and to a new covenant in which the Spirit will empower *all* his followers in the creation of a new spiritual community.

Isaiah develops this theme in several texts. God will bring a new spirit of judgment and of fire (4:4)—perhaps the inspiration for John the Baptist in Matthew 3:11. The Spirit will rest on the messianic "branch" with wisdom, power, knowledge, and holiness (11:2; cf. 42:1 and 61:1, in which the Spirit similarly anoints the Suffering Servant). He will be poured out corporately on all of God's people to bring about justice, righteousness, and peace (32:15; 34:16), including their descendants forever (44:3; 59:21). Isaiah 63:10–11 contains the only other Old Testament use of "Holy Spirit," harking back to God's guidance of Moses and the wilderness wanderers. Isaiah also recognizes the Spirit as the inspiration for his own prophecy (48:16; 59:21).

For Ezekiel, the most characteristic activity of the Spirit is "lifting" him up, sometimes literally from prostration (2:2; 3:24), many times transporting him to new locations (3:12–14; 11:1; 37:1; 43:5), including those seen only in visions (8:3; 11:24). In 11:5, he is explicitly said to be the source of Ezekiel's prophecy. In 36:27, the future eschatological restoration again appears. God will give Israel a new spirit: He will put his spirit in them and move them to obey the law and receive the fulfillment of all of his promises. Again we see a corporate presence of the Spirit not previously encountered (cf. also 37:14; 39:29).

Perhaps the most important prophetic text on the Spirit is Joel 2:28–32, which Peter quotes at Pentecost (Acts 2:17–21). Here the prophet envisages a day in which God will pour out his Spirit on individuals irrespective of gender, age, social status, or ethnicity, particularly bestowing the gift of prophecy on many of his choice. Other themes recur too. Micah 3:8 affirms the prophecy's origination in the Spirit. Haggai 2:5 and Zechariah 4:6 connect the Spirit's presence with the empowerment for rebuilding the temple. In Zechariah 6:8 the execution of God's will brings his Spirit rest.

The Old Testament thus concludes self-consciously open-ended, anticipating a new era in which the Spirit will work among a greater number of individuals and different kinds of people to create a more faithful community of men and women serving God. Apparently they will also be more mightily empowered. The fulfillment of these promises in the New Testament conforms to the prophecy of the Old Testament.

New Testament. Although relatively infrequent in his Old Testament appearances, the Spirit now emerges to dominate the theology and experience of the major New Testament witnesses. The term "Holy Spirit" (*pneuma hagion*) becomes common, although the absolute use remains frequent and "Spirit of God/the Lord" and even "Spirit of Christ" appear too. A distinct personality emerges and, ultimately, explicit trinitarian teaching.

The Spirit is the agent of Mary's virginal conception of Jesus (Matt. 1:18, 20; Luke 1:35). Christian theology has frequently perceived here God's chosen manner of enabling his Son to be fully divine as well as fully human. John the Baptist, the prophet who will herald Jesus as Messiah, "will be filled with the Holy Spirit even from birth" (Luke 1:15). This prophecy alerts his parents to his unique nature; no one in Old Testament times was filled so early. John announces Jesus as the one who will baptize with the Holy Spirit and fire (Matt. 3:11), purifying and judging his people, to be classically fulfilled at Pentecost and finally consummated at the final judgment. The Spirit himself descends and anoints Jesus at his baptism to prepare him for ministry. All four evangelists use simile in describing the descent like a dove (Matt. 3:16; Mark 1:10; Luke 3:22; John 1:32); what was literally seen remains unknown. Symbolically, the dove may represent peace, re-creation, or love. The Spirit's arrival should not be taken to imply that Jesus had no previous experience of the Spirit but, in characteristically Lucan fashion, reflects empowerment for bold proclamation of the gospel.

First, however, the Spirit must lead Jesus to the place of temptation by the devil (Luke 4:1). Will Christ succumb to the lure to use his power for self-aggrandizement or will he follow the road to the cross? The Spirit's role here teaches two important truths: God remains sovereign over the devil but God himself tempts no one (cf. James 1:13). When Jesus resists the tempter's wiles, the Spirit again empowers him for service (Luke 4:14), which John makes clear is a gift without its previously characteristic limits (John 3:34). Jesus' whole ministry is therefore Spirit-led, but particularly significant manifestations include the fulfillment of prophecy (Matt. 12:18, citing Isa. 42:1; Luke 4:18, citing Isa. 61:1), exorcisms (Matt. 12:28), and miracles more generally

(Acts 10:38; Rom. 15:19). Because Jesus' signs and wonders most directly reveal God's spirit at work, attribution of them to Satan puts one in jeopardy of committing an unforgivable sin (the "blasphemy against the Spirit" [Matt. 12:31]—probably equivalent to persistent and unrepentant rejection of Christ).

Jesus agrees with the Old Testament prophets that Scripture is Spirit-inspired (Matt. 22:43, citing Ps. 110:1). The Holy Spirit gives him joy (Luke 10:21). Christ gives as part of the Great Commission a trinitarian baptismal formula (Matt. 28:19), which even if it reflects the liturgical language of the later church (contrast Acts 2:38), gathers together Jesus' authentic self-understanding as uniquely one with God and the Spirit (cf. Matt. 11:26–27; 12:28–32).

As the Spirit has empowered Jesus, so Jesus promises that he will similarly empower the disciples. John 7:39 and 14:17 make plain that the full future outpouring of the Spirit is not yet present even with Jesus but awaits his glorification. Then his followers will be emboldened to testify even under hostile circumstances (Matt. 10:19–20). The Spirit will be the preeminent good gift for which they can pray (Luke 11:13; cf. Matt. 7:11). He will make possible the new birth, over which Nicodemus so marvels (John 3:5–8), and will create new spiritual lives (6:63).

Jesus' most extensive and distinctive teaching about the Spirit emerges in the five "Paraclete" passages found only in John's Gospel. *Paraklētos* can be translated variously as "advocate," "exhorter," "encourager," or "counselor." He is Jesus' personal representative and substitute, enabling the disciples to carry on ministry without Christ's physical presence on earth (John 14:16). Five distinct functions can be discerned in these passages: The Spirit will *help* Jesus' followers, remaining with them forever (14:15–21); he will enable them to *interpret* Jesus' words (14:15–17); he will *testify* to the world who Jesus is (15:26–16:4); he will *prosecute* sinners, convicting them of their offenses (16:5–11); and he will *reveal* further truth (16:12–15), doubtless including though not explicitly specified as the New Testament canon. A week after his resurrection, Jesus begins to fulfill these promises as he breathes the Spirit on the eleven (20:22); fuller fulfillment will come a month and a half later at Pentecost.

Luke develops several distinctive themes of the Spirit's work. Most characteristic are his references to people whom the Spirit "fills." Consistently such individuals quickly proceed to speak inspired words or otherwise boldly proclaim God's Word. With Elizabeth (Luke 1:41), Zechariah (1:67), and Simeon (2:25–27), the Spirit comes with temporary power as in the Old Testament. From Pentecost on, however, the Spirit becomes a permanent possession of God's people, yet believers may still be repeatedly "filled" in order to speak courageously for Christ (the 120—Acts 2:4; Peter—4:8; all Jerusalem believers—4:31; Saul—9:17, 13:9). On the other hand, Luke reserves the expression "full of the Spirit" to refer to a mature, godly character (the first "deacons"—Acts 6:3, 5; Barnabas—11:24).

The testimony of Acts agrees with the Gospels that the Old Testament writers were inspired by the Spirit (Acts 1:16: 4:25; 28:25), as was Jesus himself (1:2). The Spirit and God in certain contexts are interchangeable (5:3–4). The Spirit is clearly a person who can be resisted (7:51) and lied to (5:3). He supplies personal guidance and instruction (for obliterating social taboos—10:19; 11:12; for choosing church leaders—13:1–4; 20:28; for making difficult theological decisions—15:28; for making travel/ministry plans (16:6–7). He inspires predictive prophecy (11:28; 21:11), even if it remains subject to potential misinterpretation by the prophets in ways not found in the Old Testament.

Three passages in Acts are particularly controversial. At Pentecost (2:1–41) the Holy Spirit "comes on" the disciples (1:8), but also fills them (2:4), leading them to speak in foreign languages that they did not previously know. But this phenomenon (vv. 5–13) was not required to facilitate communication because Peter subsequently explains what has happened in normal speech (vv. 14–36). Rather, it must be a sign to *authenticate* the message and ministry of the disciples. Here is the fulfillment and end of the old covenant and the beginning of the new. The Spirit who has spoken in past prophecy (2:17–18), including through Jesus (2:33), now makes himself available as a "gift" along with the forgiveness of sins to all who repent (2:38) and obey (5:32). Although baptism is closely linked as a testimony to this repentance, Peter does not likely see it as essential for reception of forgiveness or the Holy Spirit, since his next closely parallel sermon concludes only with the call for repentance (3:19). The four elements of this "Pentecostal package" (repentance, baptism, the coming of the Spirit, and forgiveness) nevertheless provide a paradigm for much subsequent New Testament theology (cf. Peter's own repeated references back to this event in passages that mention the Spirit—10:44; 11:15–16; 15:8).

In two places in Acts, however, the "package" seems to be broken up. In 19:1–7 Paul encounters in Ephesus followers of John the Baptist whom Luke calls "disciples" (v. 1). But upon subsequent conversation, he discovers they have never heard of the Holy Spirit (v. 2). This suggests that they were not Jews and that they had a very truncated understanding even of John's message. So it is inconceivable that Paul could have viewed them as truly regenerate believers in Christ. They do respond to his preaching about faith in Jesus, though, and are thereafter baptized, upon which they receive the Holy Spirit and speak in tongues and prophesy. The Pentecostal package, in fact, remains intact.

Acts 8:1–7 proves more complex. Samaritans "believed Philip as he preached" (v. 12a) and are baptized (v. 12b); yet they do not receive the Holy Spirit until Peter and John come from Jerusalem to see what has happened (vv. 14–17). At least three interpretations are defensible and it is impossible to choose definitively among them. First, the belief of verse 12 may have been more intellectual than volitional and hence not salvific. The baptism then, though well-intentioned, would have been premature. Second, because of the unusual hostility between Jews and Samaritans, God may have chosen to act differently on this occasion at the beginning of the church's mission outside Jewish boundaries. The Jewish apostles' arrival then enables them to confirm the salvation of the Samaritans and to begin to dissipate the previous hatred that had divided them. Third, the Spirit may not have come in a consistently predictable fashion among the first believers; he has the sovereign freedom to act however he wants (John 3:8)! Whichever explanation is given, however, the passage remains an anomaly, even in Acts, and therefore cannot be made paradigmatic for subsequent Christian experience.

Paul's theology of the Spirit is the richest of all of the biblical witnesses and least amenable to short summary. He echoes previous themes, seeing his own writing as Spirit-inspired (1 Cor. 7:40), as with the ministry of apostles and prophets more generally (Eph. 3:5). Incipient trinitarianism emerges in the benediction of 2 Corinthians 13:14 (cf. also Eph. 2:18). The word of God contains dynamic, Spirit-induced power to overwhelm the forces of evil (Eph. 6:17), and the Spirit may bring physical deliverance (Phil. 1:19).

Paul develops several relatively new themes as well. The constituting characteristic of a Christian is the presence of the Spirit (Rom. 8:9). Paul commands all believers to be continually or repeatedly "filled" with the Spirit (Eph. 5:18), defined as including musical praise of God, thanksgiving, and mutual submission (vv. 19–21). The Spirit is the person who raised Jesus from the dead and exalted him to heaven, thereby vindicating his message and ministry (1 Tim. 3:16), and powerfully confirming his Sonship (Rom. 1:4). Christ's resurrection guarantees that all believers will be raised by the Spirit as well (Rom. 8:11). One of Paul's most distinctive contributions is his concept of the Spirit as "deposit" (2 Cor. 1:22) and "seal" (Eph. 1:13–14). The Spirit's presence in a believer's life is a promise of more to come, a partial installment of future blessings, and a divine guarantee of preservation by God.

The Spirit is God's agent for bringing people to himself and helping them to mature spiritually. Only through his power can individuals first receive God's Word as divine (1 Thess. 1:5–6). Those who convert are "saved . . . through the washing of rebirth and renewal by the Holy Spirit" (Titus 3:5). The Spirit "justifies" them, acquitting them of sin (1 Cor. 6:11). He then initiates the lifelong process of sanctification (Rom. 15:16; 2 Thess. 2:13), producing attributes such as love, righteousness, peace, joy, and hope. These are well-epitomized as the "fruit of the Spirit" (Gal. 5:22–23).

In sharp contrast stand the works of the flesh (vv. 19–21), reflecting a characteristic Pauline opposition between a Spirit-controlled life and attempts to live under one's own power, variously attributed to the flesh, body, sin, or law (Rom. 2:29; 7:6; 8:1–14; 2 Cor. 3:1–18; Gal. 3:1–5; 5:16–26). In short, Paul is closing the door on a past reliance on one's own accomplishments (and, arguably, for Jews, on their national identity) which is incompatible with the new covenant and the endowment of the Spirit. But believers should want to "walk by the Spirit" (Gal. 5:25), in this new sphere of existence, because he alone provides true freedom, glory (2 Cor. 3:17–18), and mastery over sin (Rom. 6:1–14). The distinctive and characteristic form of ministry for each believer is then described in terms of the diverse "gifts" of the Spirit (Rom. 12:1–8; 1 Cor. 12–14; Eph. 4:7–14).

The Spirit also makes unique spiritual insight available to believers (1 Cor. 2:10–16). In light of the consistent scriptural use, this likely involves more volition (obedience to God) than cognition (the mere ability to state truths about God accurately, which many unbelievers can in fact do!). Corporately, the Spirit indwells his church to make her holy, like the temple of old (1 Cor. 3:16; cf. 6:19), and to build her up like a dwelling (Eph. 5:23), creating unity and fellowship out of former enemies (Eph. 2:18; 4:3–4; Phil. 2:1). Individually, he aids in believers' prayers, bringing a newfound intimacy with God (Rom. 8:15–16; Gal. 4:6).

No other New Testament writer gives the Spirit nearly so prominent a role. He is the author of Scripture (Heb. 3:7; 10:15), the one who empowers Christ (9:14) and believers (6:4), sovereignly bestows gifts (2:4), and can be insulted through apostasy (10:29). He sanctifies (1 Peter 1:2), inspires prophets (1 Peter 1:11–12; 2 Peter 1:21), vindicates Christ (1 Peter 3:18), and brings blessing to believers (1 Peter 4:14). He provides assurance of salvation (1 John 3:24; 4:13), testifies to who Jesus is (5:6–8), and produces orthodox Christology (4:1–3). He is the characteristic mark of Christians (Jude 19) who pray in him (v. 20). The Spirit creates the states in which John receives his visions (Rev. 1:10; 4:2; 17:3; 21:10), is the source for the messages to the seven churches (chaps. 2–3), and one of the heavenly speakers John overhears (14:13; 22:17).

A biblical theology of the Spirit is difficult to epitomize. He sovereignly acts as he chooses! Most Christian traditions stress the data of certain portions of Scripture (most notably Acts or

Paul) at the expense of others. But an essential summary ought to include at least that the Spirit is the transcendent, omnipresent spiritual and localizable presence of God's personality and power, living in and divinely empowering all of God's true people in diverse and incomplete ways that foreshadow their complete, future renewal at the end of the age. CRAIG L. BLOMBERG

See also BLASPHEMY AGAINST THE HOLY SPIRIT; GOD; HOLY SPIRIT, GIFTS OF.

Bibliography. D. I. Block, *JETS* 32 (1989): 27–49; G. W. Bromiley, *ISBE,* 2:730–46; G. M. Burge, *The Anointed Community;* J. D. G. Dunn, *Jesus and the Spirit;* D. Ewert, *The Holy Spirit in the New Testament;* M. Green, *Believe in the Holy Spirit;* D. Guthrie, *New Testament Theology;* G. F. Hawthorne, *The Presence and the Power;* W. E. Mills, *The Holy Spirit: A Bibliography;* G. T. Montague, *The Holy Spirit;* C. F. D. Moule, *The Holy Spirit;* H. Müller, *NIDNTT,* 3:689–709; L. Neve, *The Spirit of God in the Old Testament;* J. I. Packer, *Keep in Step with the Spirit;* W. Russell, *Trinity J* 7 (1986): 47–63; E. Schweizer, *The Holy Spirit;* idem, *TDNT,* 6:332–455; R. J. Sklba, *CBQ* 46 (1984): 1–17; R. Stronstad, *The Charismatic Theology of St. Luke;* L. J. Wood, *The Holy Spirit in the Old Testament.*

Holy Spirit, Gifts of. Four New Testament passages delineate specific gifts that God's Spirit gives to his people (Rom. 12:3–8; 1 Cor. 12–14; Eph. 4:7–13; 1 Peter 4:10–11). The terminology varies from ordinary words for gift (*dōrea, dōma*—Eph. 4:7–8) to a cognate of grace (*charisma*—Rom. 12:6; 1 Cor. 12:4, 9, 28, 30–31; 1 Peter 4:10), to a substantive formed from the adjective "spiritual" (*pneumatika*—1 Cor. 12:1; 14:1, 37). But the concept remains the same: distinctive, divinely originated endowments to serve the Triune God for the common benefit of his people, the church (Rom. 12:4–5; 1 Cor. 12:7; Eph. 4:12–13; 1 Peter 4:10). No text enables us to determine the relation of spiritual gifts to "natural" talents or abilities; scriptural examples suggest that some are given entirely de novo (e.g., the prophets and tongues-speakers in Acts 19:6), while others build on a lifetime of divinely superintended preparation (as with Paul's apostleship, prepared for by his unique blend of Jewish, Greek, and Roman backgrounds). The Spirit must be given freedom to give his gifts any way he desires.

The four lists of spiritual gifts demonstrate significant overlap as well as important variations. This suggests that none of the lists, taken either individually or together, is intended to be comprehensive. Rather each is suggestive of the diversity of ways God endows Christians for spiritual service. Broader classifications may therefore suggest other gifts not specifically listed. One may distinguish between gifts that require miraculous intervention or divine revelation (e.g., prophecy, healings, miracles, tongues and their interpretation) from other less "supernatural" gifts, although one suspects that first-century Christians may have considered all of them supernatural to some extent. One may separate gifts of leadership (apostles, administrators, teachers, pastors, and evangelists) from the rest, although one must be careful not to confuse gifts with offices (humanly appointed positions of ecclesial authority). One may identify a number of gifts that apparently involve an extra measure of virtue or responsibility commanded of all Christians (e.g., faith, service, giving, mercy, or evangelizing) as over or against those for which some believers have no ability or responsibility (e.g., miracles, tongues, or administration). First Peter 4:11 suggests perhaps the simplest division (gifts of speech and gifts of serving). But a biblical theologian will wish to proceed differently, considering each of the three major Pauline passages in turn, interpreting each list in light of the larger historical and literary contexts of each epistle.

Theological Principles. In 1 Corinthians 12, Paul enumerates nine key principles. (1) A basic criterion for distinguishing Spirit-gifted people from impostors is whether they confess Jesus as Lord (vv. 1–3). (2) All the gifts originate from the Triune God (vv. 4–6). (3) All Christians have at least one gift (v. 7a). This implies that no one need wait for some postconversion experience to be empowered for service, although it does not preclude God bestowing *additional* gifts on an individual subsequent to conversion. (4) Gifts are for the common upbuilding of the church (v. 7b). (5) There is diversity within unity (vv. 8–10). Christians ought not to expect others to have the identical gifts they do. (6) The gifts are given as the Spirit determines (v. 11). One may seek and pray for certain gifts (12:31a; 14:1, 12), but God makes no guarantees that he will give any one particular gift as requested. (7) All the gifts are necessary for the maturity of the church; none may be jettisoned as nonessential (vv. 14–26). Indeed, those God honors most may be the least visible (vv. 22–25). (8) There is a ranking of gifts (vv. 27–28) but the sequence is more one of chronology than of priority. Apostles and prophets are foundational in the life of any church (cf. Eph. 2:20); teachers then nurture young believers and newly planted congregations; finally, all of the rest of the gifts can come into play. (9) No one gift is available to all Christians (vv. 29–30; 14:31 is best taken as referring to "all prophets" not "all believers"); hence no specific gift may be made a criterion of salvation, sanctification, or spiritual status.

First Corinthians 13 stresses that without love spiritual gifts are worthless. Verses 1–3 illustrate this point with four representative examples: tongues, prophecy, faith, and giving. This suggests that verses 8–9 offer similar examples, making a point that could have been illustrated with any of the gifts—that, compared with love, all are temporary. The verbs "cease," "stilled," and "pass away" appear in synonymous parallelism in the

Greek, with merely stylistic variation. There is no lexical or grammatical justification for translating "tongues will be stilled [or will cease] *by themselves.*" Thirteen of the other fourteen New Testament uses of *pauō* are middle/passive, in contexts where the middle force is never clearly demonstrable, and there is evidence that *pauō* was becoming a deponent verb in koine Greek. Tongues, like wisdom and knowledge (or any other gift), will cease "when perfection comes" (13:10). But no text betrays any awareness that New Testament writers suspected the close of an age with the death of the apostles or the completion of the canon. Instead, the *telos* word group (from which *teleiōn,* "perfection," here comes) consistently refers to the end of the age when Christ returns (in 1 Cor. the most relevant passage is one that makes clear that spiritual gifts are given to the church until the parousia—1:7).

Paul's second treatment of spiritual gifts appears at the beginning of the hortatory section (Rom. 12–16) of that epistle which contains the most systematic presentation of Paul's gospel (chaps. 1–11). The most fundamental Christian obligation is complete dedication of body and mind to God (Rom. 12:1–2). Second, believers must faithfully exercise their unique spiritual gifts (vv. 3–8). Crucial to success here is an accurate self-estimation (vv. 3–5). Echoing the identical sequence of 1 Corinthians 12–13, Paul then moves on to exhortations concerning love (12:9–13:10).

In Ephesians 4 Paul focuses more on gifted persons than on the gifts themselves, but the broader theological issues remain similar. The gifts come from Christ, who distributes them to all believers as he determines (v. 7) as the result of his incarnation and exaltation (vv. 8–10). Here the specific examples focus solely on gifts for leadership (v. 11), but leaders' responsibilities center on mobilizing the laity for "every member ministry" in unity (vv. 12–13a). Only then may the church be said to be mature (v. 13b).

The Individual Gifts. The two most controversial gifts in Corinth were tongues and prophecy, so Paul devotes an entire chapter to their regulation (1 Cor. 14). These two gifts still merit the greatest attention today.

In the Old Testament, prophecy involved the foretelling or forthtelling of God's Word based on a revelation from Yahweh himself. In the Hellenistic world of the first century, prophecy took many forms, but its unifying feature was the belief that a message had come directly from God or the gods. This message was usually intended for a specific audience in view of concrete needs. This sense of reception of a revelation neither requires nor precludes previous preparation or meditation. In the New Testament, Agabus exemplifies a prophet who can predict the future (Acts 11:27–30; 21:10–11; cf. John as a seer in Rev. 1:1–4). Other individuals called prophets include Paul and Barnabas (Acts 13:1). Barnabas perhaps best illustrates the spirit of prophecy with his nickname "Son of Encouragement" (4:36). Quoting Joel's prediction (2:28–32) as fulfilled at Pentecost, Peter points out that prophecy will characterize "the last days," the entire New Testament age. God will bestow this gift on many of his people irrespective of gender, age, or social class (Acts 2:17–21; for additional examples, see Acts 19:6; 21:9).

In 1 Corinthians 14, Paul enjoins the Corinthians to prefer prophecy to tongues because it is more immediately intelligible (vv. 1–19). He also requires prophets to regulate their behavior (vv. 29–33a), presupposing that their speech is not ecstatic but subject to their control (vv. 30–32). "Two or three prophets should speak, and the others [i.e., the congregation] should weigh carefully what is said" (v. 29). First Thessalonians 5:20–21 and 1 John 4:1 also stress this need for assessment. Criteria for evaluating purported prophecies would have included seeing if predictions came true (Deut. 18:21–22) and, presumably, testing the content of forthtelling against already accepted (i.e., scriptural) revelation. Whether or not a message edified the church was doubtless equally crucial. Although all believers must "test the spirits," each church's leadership must ultimately render a verdict on the legitimacy of any alleged prophecy. Herein lies the most probable explanation of the restriction on women speaking in 1 Corinthians 14:33b–38.

Unlike the Old Testament, in which divinely accredited prophets were not subject to constant reassessment, New Testament prophecy seems less immediate or infallible (apart from the exceptional instances that created the New Testament canon). Acts 21:4 refers to an apparently prophetic message "through the Spirit" (cf. the language of 11:28) and yet 21:11, 13–14 suggests that it contained both a divine and a human (errant) component. Probably the message from God was limited to the prediction that Paul would be imprisoned if he went to Jerusalem, but the Christians in Tyre wrongly concluded that it was the Lord's will for him not to go there. Contemporary prophecy, which may range from carefully prepared messages that God has powerfully applied to a Christian's own heart (although not necessarily equivalent to many sermons) to more instantaneous revelations of God's will in particular circumstances, may similarly mix together genuinely divine words with potentially fallible human interpretations. Precisely because such prophecy is not on a par with Scripture and does not in any way supplement the canon, the argument that prophecy must have ceased with the apostolic age becomes fallacious. But this does not excuse churches from failing to take action against individuals who have uttered demonstrably false prophecies. Capital punishment may no longer be appropriate (Deut. 18:20), but surely no one need fear (or heed!) such individuals (v. 22).

As a spiritual gift given only to those whom God chooses, discernment of spirits (1 Cor. 12:10) cannot be the same as the responsibility of evaluating prophecy incumbent on all believers. Presumably, therefore, it refers to a special ability to judge the source of an allegedly inspired utterance, readily distinguishing true from false *messengers* of God, rather than evaluating the legitimacy of any particular *message*.

The nature of the gifts of tongues and their interpretation must be determined by Paul's own teaching, rather than presupposing that the three instances of tongues-speaking in Acts (2:1–13; 10:46; 19:6) must determine the form of glossolalia in Corinth. That the spiritual gift of tongues requires a subsequent interpretation at once sets it off from the experience of Pentecost. The reference to angelic language in 1 Corinthians 13:1 makes it even more likely that Corinthian tongues were not merely foreign languages; parallel phenomena in the surrounding cultures strongly confirms this. *Glōssa* in Greek can refer to virtually any kind of vocal utterance, with or without discernible linguistic structure. The gift of tongues then refers to a divinely given utterance, unintelligible to its speaker or to most in that speaker's audience, but which will subsequently be "translated" into an understandable language, either by the original speaker or by another with the gift of interpretation. If such an interpretation does not emerge, and as long as there is no reason to believe that someone with the gift of interpretation has appeared, the original speaker should remain silent (14:27–28).

Glossolalia may be practiced as a private, prayer language (vv. 18–19); it is not clear if Paul would consider this the same gift as public speaking in tongues, but he clearly tries to temper the Corinthians' enthusiasm for this gift in church (v. 19). In fact Paul calls it a sign for unbelievers (v. 22), which, given the quotation from Isaiah 28:11–12 (v. 21), must mean a sign of judgment. Unbelievers find glossolalia unintelligible, even repulsive, and so are driven away from the gospel (v. 23). There is a place for tongues in a fully Christian assembly, but as with prophecy, it must remain within strict boundaries: no more than three exercising their gift at any given time and always with an interpretation (v. 28), which presumably would be subject to the same kind of evaluation as prophecy.

Healings and miracles are the other two more "supernatural" charisms. The plural nouns (1 Cor. 12:10, 28) in each instance suggest that there may be different kinds of miraculous gifts or that these gifts are not the permanent possession of an individual but repeatedly given for the specific occasions in which they are to be used. The terminology (*iamata* and *dunameis*, respectively) harks back to the various miracles worked by Jesus in the four Gospels and by his followers in Acts, miracles that were by no means limited to the apostles (cf. esp. Stephen and Philip—Acts 6–8). "Healings" would involve the restoration of physical health to the sick or injured while "miracles" would embrace a wider variety of supernatural phenomena. A spiritual gift of healing should be distinguished from both a miraculous healing that God works in answer to prayer (as in James 5:13–18) and the ordinary therapeutic work of physicians. Rather, gifts of healing will be exercised in the ministry of a particular person possessing those charisms. Such a person need not expect a 100 percent success rate any more than do teachers or evangelists or those with various other gifts. On the other hand, ministries that only rarely experience the miraculous phenomena that they advertise prove more suspect.

Wisdom and knowledge manifest themselves in wise and knowledgeable speech (1 Cor. 12:8). Wisdom in Scripture consistently refers to applied knowledge or practical insight and is fundamentally moral in character. Knowledge refers especially to the acquisition and impartation of spiritual truth. The Corinthians had boasted of their wisdom and knowledge (1 Cor. 4:10; 8:1), perhaps in the tradition of the pagan Sophists, but Paul recognized their boasts as hollow and unfounded. For him truth centered on the "foolishness" of the cross, while true godly wisdom brings spiritual maturity (chap. 2). In 13:2 possessing knowledge parallels fathoming mysteries, understanding previously secret information that God reveals to his people.

Faith is the clearest example of a gift that amplifies an attribute required of all Christians (1 Cor. 12:9). In view of 13:2, the gift of faith presumably involves a distinctive ability to trust God to work in unusual ways or in particularly difficult situations.

Service, giving, mercy, and helps also magnify character traits that all believers should exemplify. "Serving" in Romans 12:7 comes from the same root as "deacon" and may involve the kind of practical aid rendered in Acts 6:1–6. Giving could also be translated "contributing to the needs of others" (Rom. 12:8a) and probably focuses on material assistance to the poor. "Showing mercy" (v. 8b) may highlight other forms of compassionate care for the needy, sick, aged, or disabled. "Those able to help others" (1 Cor. 12:28) may be the Corinthian equivalent to three of the above gifts.

Although Luke usually reserves "apostle" for one of the Twelve (Acts 1:21–22; but cf. 14:14), Paul uses the term less technically as a spiritual gift (1 Cor. 12:29; Eph. 4:11). Not only does he refer to himself as an apostle (Rom. 1:1) but he also includes Titus and Epaphroditus (2 Cor. 8:23; Phil. 2:25), Andronicus and Junia (Rom. 16:7), and James, the Lord's brother (Gal. 1:19), none of whom could have satisfied Luke's criteria. Clearly he is using the word in its more common Greek sense of one sent out on a mission. In a Christian context this will be a divinely sent mission; contemporary synonyms include "missionary" and "church planter."

Like apostles, evangelists (1 Cor. 12:28; Eph. 4:11) preach the gospel to unsaved people. Unlike apostles, evangelists do not necessarily organize their converts into local churches. All Christians must evangelize (Matt. 28:18–20), but those with this gift are particularly capable of leading people to faith in Christ.

Teachers in the biblical cultures played a more limited role than they do today. Their task primarily involved the communication of a fixed body of information to their students, often solely by rote memory work. In the New Testament a distinction is often made between evangelistic preaching (proclamation or *kerygma*) and subsequent doctrinal instruction (teaching or *didachē*). Acts 2:42 refers to the "apostles' teaching" as part of the daily ministry of the fledgling church in Jerusalem. Teaching may overlap with prophecy (Acts 13:1), because both can expound God's Word, but teaching focuses more on the mastery of content. The lack of a second demonstrative adjective in the expression "some to be pastors and teachers" (Eph. 4:11) suggests another overlap: Christian teachers ought always to exercise a pastoral role; shepherds should always communicate accurate content.

The expression *poimēn* (Eph. 4:11) refers to a shepherd. This gift does not necessarily correspond to the entire role of the modern-day pastor but to that component of pastoral care and nurture. Acts 20:28–31 and 1 Peter 5:1–4 spell out the servant leadership required of these overseers.

Kybernēsis (1 Cor. 12:28), generally translated as "administration," may also be rendered "oversight" or "guidance," and encompasses the ruling or governing aspect of church leadership.

The verb *proistēmi* (Rom. 12:8) can refer to leadership or to giving practical aid. It may be the Romans equivalent to all of the gifts of leadership of Ephesians 4, though the immediate context (contributing, showing mercy) favors the latter. The cognate noun *prostatis* refers to a patron, so perhaps the best option explains this gift as the use of one's wealth to sponsor or support needy people within the body of Christ.

Contemporary Applications. There is no exegetical warrant for claiming that any of the gifts have ceased. They are God's characteristic endowments for Christian service in the New Testament age, arguably the most fundamental way ministry occurs (Acts 2:17–21; 1 Cor. 1:7). Against the view that maintains, from the lack of the more supernatural gifts throughout much of church history, that these charisms were limited to the apostolic age, three points must be noted: (1) these gifts did not end at the close of the first century, but continued well into the third; (2) their subsequent diminution can best be attributed to a growing, unscriptural institutionalization of the church and an overreaction to the abuse of the gifts in heretical (most notably Montanist) circles; (3) even then, no era of church history was completely without examples of all the gifts. The twentieth century resurgence of the gifts cannot be attributed to the arrival of the last days, since for the New Testament "the last days" refers to the entire church age. They may, however, reflect a recovery of more biblical, spontaneous, and all-inclusive worship and ministry.

In short, attempts to attribute all current charismatic phenomena to the devil or mere human fabrication are misguided. Still, there is no guarantee that any alleged manifestation of the Spirit is genuine; each must be tested. First Corinthians 14:39–40 concludes Paul's treatment of the topic with remarkably clear commands, which, if obeyed, could go a long way toward eliminating divisiveness in the church over the gifts. On the one hand, none of the gifts should be forbidden, even tongues (v. 39). On the other hand, "everything should be done in a fitting and orderly way" (v. 40), as illustrated by the regulations for prophecy and tongues in verses 26–38. A growing number of charismatics and noncharismatics alike are beginning to heed these twin commands, but many still do not, to the detriment of the unity of the church and the success of her mission. CRAIG L. BLOMBERG

See also HOLY SPIRIT.

Bibliography. D. Aune, *Prophecy in Early Christianity and the Ancient Mediterranean World;* D. Bridge and D. Phypers, *Spiritual Gifts and the Church;* F. F. Bruce, *The Epistles to the Colossians, to Philemon, and to the Ephesians;* D. A. Carson, *Showing the Spirit;* C. E. B. Cranfield, *The Epistles to the Romans,* vol. 2; J. D. G. Dunn, *Romans,* vol. 2; E. E. Ellis, *Pauline Theology;* G. D. Fee, *The First Epistle to the Corinthians;* C. Forbes, *NovT* 26 (1968): 257–70; R. Y. K. Fung, *EvQ* 56 (1984): 3–20; M. Green, *I Believe in the Holy Spirit;* W. A. Grudem, *The Gift of Prophecy in 1 Corinthians;* K. S. Hemphill, *Spiritual Gifts;* D. Hill, *New Testament Prophecy;* R. P. Martin, *The Spirit and the Congregation;* W. E. Mills, *A Theological/Exegetical Approach to Glossolalia; Speaking in Tongues;* S. Schatzmann, *A Pauline Theology of Charismata;* M. Turner, *VoxEv* 15 (1985): 7–64.

Homosexuality. It is significant that the word "homosexuality" did not enter the English vocabulary until the early twentieth century. The word, and with it the concept of lifelong primary sexual orientation toward members of one's own gender, was unacknowledged and probably unknown in the biblical world. Some today will therefore argue that what the Bible appears to condemn can be distinguished from homosexuality. They maintain that the homosexual orientation, to the extent that it develops in early childhood or even before birth, is not consciously chosen and is therefore not sinful. As long as this form of sexuality is expressed monogamously, it is argued, homosexual relations merely constitute an expansion of the biblical view of marriage. In order to assess the legitimacy of this approach, it is important to begin with an understanding of the view of same-gender sex in the ancient world.

The Ancient World. Because there is so little evidence of same-gender sex before the New Testament period, our view of "the ancient world" must focus more narrowly on the Greco-Roman period. Writings during this period demonstrate familiarity with sexual acts between members of the same gender, but these were not understood to result from an "orientation." Sexuality was important in the ancient world only in terms of male progeniture. It appears that the rape of other males and the use of boys for sexual pleasure (pederasty) were performed as acts of dominance, violence, or experimentation by otherwise heterosexual men. As a phase or as an occasional act, sex between males did not detract from male progeniture. In some circles, most notably those of the intellectual elite philosophers and poets, relationships between men and boys were lauded as the highest expression of romantic love. These relationships were not reciprocal, however. Males who were (willing or not) the receiving partners in these acts, especially on a repeated basis, were socially outcast. Boys were bought as slaves and discarded when they reached puberty. Lesbians, who were by definition reducing the possibility of male progeniture, were scarcely mentioned but consistently condemned. Thus the modern supposition of a tolerant pagan society subsequently oppressed by Judeo-Christian taboos is a complete myth. It was, rather, a culture almost empty of regard for the sexual rights or desires of anyone but the small ruling class of men, who commonly exercised their almost limitless privilege at the expense of those young women and men in their power.

The Old Testament. Into this world of ruthless sexuality came the biblical message of restraint, justice, and sexual complementarity, which was revolutionary in its implications. From the beginning it is acknowledged that humankind is created in two genders that together bear God's image (Gen. 1:27) and together constitute a unity of flesh (Gen. 2:24). The reaffirmation of these two notions in key New Testament passages on sexuality (Matt. 19:1–12; 1 Cor. 7:12–20) demonstrates the continuity and importance of sexual differentiation in the construction of a normative biblical sexuality. More simply put, humankind is created to find human completion only in the (marital) union of two sexes. While there may be legitimate conditions under which this union will *not* occur (e.g., celibacy), there are no conceivable conditions in which the union *can* occur fully without sexual differentiation. More specifically in terms of homosexuality, then, same-gender partners can at best *pretend* to effect a differentiation that is physiologically (and perhaps psychologically) impossible.

Some theologians have suggested that to be created in the image of God according to Genesis means to be in social fellowship with other persons. Others deduce that homosexual relations are merely an expansion of the category of marriage under this rubric of fellowship; that is, intimacy and not biology is the appropriate measure of conformity to the Genesis marriage model. But apart from the debatability of this notion of the image of God in Genesis (*dominion* is the probable focus of the term), the definition of marriage cannot be limited to the meaning of the image of God. However important the social and spiritual aspects of marriage may be, the physical aspect is no less fundamental to its definition. Sexual differentiation (1:27) intends physical union, the becoming of one flesh (2:24). Because a homosexual relationship cannot produce a unity of sexually differentiated beings, there cannot be a marriage.

Condemnations of sexual sin in the Old Testament focus on heterosexual acts, but it is important to note that all sexual sin, including homosexuality, is prohibited in relation to the positive model of marriage presented in Genesis. Thus, while the Old Testament describes homosexual activity as intrinsically unjust or impure, these condemnations do not differ qualitatively from condemnations of heterosexual deviations from the marriage model.

The first and most familiar Old Testament passage is the account of intended male rape at Sodom (Gen. 19). References to the city later become common extrabiblical Jewish euphemisms for sexual perversion in general and homosexual practices in particular (in the New Testament, see 2 Peter 2:6–7 and Jude 7). Some modern revisionists point to the subsequent Jewish tradition condemning Sodom for inhospitality and argue that the passage does not have homosexual rape in view. In this view, when the Sodomites demand to "know" Lot's visitors, they want to interrogate them, and Lot considers this breach of hospitality as so objectionable that he offers to distract the men with sex, offering his own daughters. The major obstacle to this interpretation is the Hebrew verb "to know" (*yādaʿ*), which, while not often used in a sexual sense, is used in just that sense in verse 8—only two verses after its occurrence expressing the desire of the men of Sodom. Clearly the Sodomites desired sexual relations with Lot's guests. The later references to inhospitality in relation to Sodom are not due to a misunderstanding of the sin of Sodom on the part of the Jews, but to their habit of speaking indirectly of sexual matters out of modesty.

A parallel account of sexual violence occurs in Judges 19–20, where the men of Gibeah rape a man's concubine to the point of death in substitution for the man himself. There can be no doubt that this is fundamentally an act of violence, but the initial desire for the man coupled with the sacrifice of the concubine to avoid "such a disgraceful thing" (19:24) suggests that same-gender sex, and not only inhospitality, is seen in a very negative light.

More obscure reference to same-gender sex may be found in Genesis 9:20–27, where the statement that Ham "saw his father's nakedness" may be a euphemism for rape. There may be a connection here to two additional references to sexual sins involving one's father (Lev. 18:7; Deut. 23:1), since Ham is the father of Canaan, the nation traditionally associated with same-gender sex and whose impure practices are condemned in detail in the context of these references.

Explicit condemnation of same-gender sexual relations occurs in two Old Testament passages. Leviticus 18:22 reads, "Do not lie with a man as one lies with a woman; that is detestable." Leviticus 20:13 reads, "If a man lies with a man as one lies with a woman, both of them have done what is detestable. They must be put to death; their blood will be on their own heads." The wording here is ambiguous with regard to rape or manipulation versus mutual consent; instead, the focus is on the act itself as a mutual defilement. Modern revisionists often dismiss these strong passages on the grounds that they are part of the Old Testament purity code and therefore irrelevant to a gospel that frees believers from the constraints of Jewish cultural taboos. But the surrounding verses, which involve such concerns as care for the poor and respect of property show that it is impossible to make a simplistic distinction between purity laws and permanent moral principles. The reaffirmation of sexually differentiated marriage in the New Testament, as noted above, suggests that this levitical condemnation of the violation of differentiation retains its force throughout the entire biblical period.

The New Testament Message of Liberation. Some revisionists maintain that the message of Jesus is fundamentally a message concerning the liberation of captives (Luke 4:18–19). These captives, it is argued, are to be understood not in individual terms as sinners, but in corporate terms as those who are forgotten or oppressed by the proud and powerful. In this view, the place to begin a truly Christian consideration of sexual ethics is not with Genesis and the legal code but with Exodus and freedom from law proclaimed by Jesus. The homosexual community, with its long history of persecution, naturally sees itself described in the Beatitudes and other offers of hope to the downtrodden. It sees analogies to modern "heterosexism" in the historic subjugation of women and of blacks. There are, however, many problems with an approach that so simply makes biblical material a vehicle for experience. One objection is that the choice of one kind of sexual proclivity as "oppressed" is arbitrary: there is no definitive reason to exclude pederasty or sadomasochism or adultery. Furthermore, the analogies to other modern liberation movements are dubious. In the case of slavery, for example, the biblical message is ambiguous; in the case of homosexual acts, on the other hand, what little material we have is all decidedly negative. Finally, it is impossible to evaluate a behavior by means of its perception, as if disapproval by the majority automatically constitutes legitimacy on the part of a persecuted minority. At some point the behavior itself must be held up to a light other than the fire of its own passion. The light of revelation in the New Testament message offers liberation, but explicit in this offer is the provision of power to conform individuals to full humanity as God created it. In order to exercise responsibility in relation to such an offer it is essential for believers to take seriously both the construction of full humanity as the Scriptures describe it, and deviations from that full humanity as the Scriptures warn against them.

The Gospels. There is no explicit reference to same-gender sex in the Gospels, but there may be an echo of a reference in Mark 9:42–10:12 (cf. Matt. 5:27–32). A passage in the Talmud (*b. Niddah* 13b) links masturbation and pederasty together as violations of marriage, and in so doing makes reference to harming children, offending with the hand or the foot, and cutting off offending limbs rather than going down to the pit of destruction. These similarities of wording to the Gospel passages may suggest a common understanding in the first century that "putting a stumbling block before one of these little ones" involved sexual sin against them.

Paul's Epistles. Two brief references in Paul's letters, where same-gender sex is mentioned in lists of prohibited activities, are important especially for their link to the Old Testament. In 1 Corinthians 6:9 and 1 Timothy 1:10 *arsenokoitai* are condemned. The word, a compound of "male" and "coitus" or "intercourse," does not occur prior to the New Testament. Some modern writers have attempted to narrow its meaning from homosexual acts in general to male prostitution, solicitation of male prostitutes, or (coupled in 1 Cor. 6:9 with *malakoi,* another obscure word possibly meaning "the effeminate") the active partners in homosexual relationships. These suggestions, however, ignore the Greek Old Testament (LXX) versions of Leviticus 18:22 and 20:13, which use both *arsenos* and *koiten,* the latter passage placing them side-by-side; literally, "whoever lies with a *male, having intercourse* (as with) a female." This is the obvious source of the compound word. Perhaps Paul himself, who knew and used the Septuagint extensively, or some other Hellenistic Jew not long before Paul's time, derived from the passages in Leviticus a compound word that described homosexual acts in general. This drawing in of Leviticus to Paul's letters is also significant in that it provides further demonstration that he perceived a moral and not merely purity-based prohibition of homosexual acts in the Old Testament.

Romans 1:26–27. The remaining passage appears to be an unequivocal condemnation of homosexuality. While many modern revisionists simply disagree with Paul or discount his proscription as applying only to prostitution or pederasty, some have attempted to reinterpret the passage as tacit approval of homosexuality. The argument is that Paul portrays homosexual acts as impure but carefully avoids the language of sin; he intends merely to distinguish a Gentile practice considered by Jews to be "unclean" in order to draw Jews (or "weaker brethren") into his subsequent explanation of the gospel. Careful investigation of the passage, however, shows this explanation to be untenable.

Paul's general purpose in the context (Rom. 1:18–32) is to show the need for the gospel in the Gentile world. As a result of idolatry, God "gave them over" to all kinds of sinful behavior. The trifold structure of the passage is a rhetorical device to drive home the point: a general complaint (vv. 24–25), consideration of a specific vice (vv. 26–27), and a culminating list of various vices (vv. 28–32). The distinction between the second and third sections may follow another Greek-styled distinction of sins of passion and sins of the unfit mind.

Paul is accused of everything from extreme prejudice to repressed homosexual urges for choosing same-gender sex as his focus in verses 26–27. But the scarcity of other references and the use of impersonal, rhetorical language here suggests, on the contrary, considerable detachment. The choice of homosexuality in particular is due to Paul's need to find a visible sign of humankind's fundamental rejection of God's creation at the very core of personhood. The numerous allusions to the creation account in the passage suggest that creation theology was foremost in Paul's mind in forming the passage.

Paul's terminology in the passage clearly denotes sin and not mere ritual impurity. The context is introduced by the threat of wrath against "godlessness and wickedness" (v. 18). Those in view in verses 26–27 have been given over to "passions," a word group that elsewhere in Romans and consistently in Paul's writings connotes sin. Words like "impurity" (v. 24) and "indecent" (v. 27; cf. "degrading," v. 24) had in Paul's time extended their meaning beyond ritual purity to moral and especially sexual wrongdoing. To do that which is "unnatural" (vv. 26–27) or "contrary to nature" was common parlance in contemporary literature for sexual perversion and especially homosexual acts. Paul uses several expressions here that are more typical of Gentile moral writers not because he is attempting to soften his condemnation but because he wishes to find words peculiarly suited to expose the sinfulness of the Gentile world in its own terms.

The substance of Paul's proscription of homosexuality is significant in several respects. First, he mentions lesbian relations first and links lesbianism to male homosexuality. This is unusual if not unique in the ancient world, and it demonstrates that Paul's concern is less with progeniture than with rebellion against sexual differentiation or full created personhood. Second, Paul speaks in terms of mutual consent (e.g., "inflamed with lust *for one another,*" v. 27), effectively including acts other than rape and pederasty in the prohibition. Third, the passage describes corporate as well as individual rebellion, a fact that may have implications for modern discussions of "orientation." In other words, although Paul does not address the question here directly, it is reasonable to suppose that he would consign the orientation toward homosexual acts to the same category as heterosexual orientation toward adultery or fornication. The "natural" or "fleshly" proclivity is a specific byproduct of the corporate human rebellion and in no way justifies itself or the activity following from that proclivity. On the basis of any of these three implications, it is legitimate to use the word "homosexuality" as it is conceived in the modern world when speaking of Romans 1 and, by cautious extension, when speaking of the related biblical passages.

Responses to Paul's Proscription. The discussion does not end with the conclusion that Paul condemns homosexuality. Some argue that a modern understanding of "natural" differs from Paul's and requires that we absolve those who discover rather than choose a homosexual orientation. These, it is argued, should be seen as victims, or simply different, and our definition of allowable sexual activity expanded accordingly. The major problem with this response is that it shifts the meaning of "natural" from Paul's notion of "that which is in accord with creation" to the popular notion of "that which one has a desire to do." But deeply ingrained anger does not justify murder, nor does deeply ingrained greed justify theft or materialism, nor does the deeply ingrained desire of many heterosexuals for multiple partners justify promiscuity. Desire in all of these areas, chosen or not, must come under the reign of Christ. The action in question must be considered not in terms of its source in the person but in light of the relevant biblical principles. These principles often involve denial of deeply ingrained desires, for the heterosexual who desires multiple partners no less than for the homosexual who laments the option of celibacy.

There is considerable evidence that a homosexual orientation, and certainly the occasional homosexual experience, does not indicate a permanent state but an immature stage of sexuality that may be "fixed" at some point by physiological, psychological, or social factors, and by the individual will, all acting in combination. This has theological significance because it implies that movement toward completion or maturity will involve movement toward obedience to the biblical model. One need not conclude, then, that the homosexual orientation is an indication either of God's approval of the orientation or that the orientation is God's "curse" of the individual. It is, rather, a challenge to growth in discipleship, more or less difficult depending on individual circumstances, but accompanied by the promise of grace equal to those circumstances (Rom. 5:19–21; 1 Cor. 10:13; 2 Cor. 12:9).

THOMAS E. SCHMIDT

See also ETHICS; IMMORALITY, SEXUAL.

Bibliography. J. Boswell, *Christianity, Social Tolerance, and Homosexuality;* L. W. Countryman, *Dirt, Greed, and Sex;* J. B. De Young, *JETS* 31 (1988): 429–47; idem, *BSac* 147 (1990): 437–54; G. W. Edward, *Gay/Lesbian Liberation: A Biblical Perspective;* S. Grenz, *Sexual Ethics: A Biblical Perspective;* R. B. Hays, *Sojourners* (July 1991): 17–21; idem, *JRE* 14 (1986): 184–215; R. Scroggs, *The New Testament and Homosexuality;* D. F. Wright, *EvQ* 61 (1989): 291–300; J. I. Yamamoto, *The Crisis of Homosexuality.*

Honor. Social term describing how people within a society evaluate one another. Most occurrences of honor in the Old Testament are translations of some form of *kabod,* while in the New Testament they are derivatives of *timaō.* These terms are generally used with reference to the honor granted fellow human beings, though in some cases they are used to describe the honor a person grants God.

The root of *kabod* literally means heavy or weighty. The figurative meaning, however, is far more common: "to give weight to someone." To honor someone, then, is to give weight or to grant a person a position of respect and even authority in one's life. A person grants honor most frequently on the basis of position, status, or wealth, but it can and should also be granted on the basis of character.

While honor is an internal attitude of respect, courtesy, and reverence, it should be accompanied by appropriate attention or even obedience. Honor without such action is incomplete; it is lip service (Isa. 29:13). God the Father, for example, is honored when people do the things that please him (1 Cor. 6:20). Parents are honored through the obedience of their children.

The source of all honor is God on the basis of his position as sovereign Creator and of his character as a loving Father. God the Father has bestowed honor on his Son, Jesus Christ (John 5:23). He bestowed honor on humanity by creating man a little lower than the angels (Ps. 8:5–6). He has also created spheres of authority within human government, the church, and the home. The positions of authority in those spheres are to receive honor implicitly.

The granting of honor to others is an essential experience in the believer's life. Christians are to bestow honor on those for whom honor is due. The believer is to honor God, for he is the sovereign head of the universe and his character is unsurpassed. The believer is to honor those in positions of earthly authority, such as governing authorities (Rom. 13:1–7), masters (1 Tim. 6:1), and parents (Exod. 20:12). As a participant in the church, the believer is also called to honor Jesus Christ, the head of the church (John 5:23), fellow believers (Rom. 12:10), and widows (1 Tim. 5:3).

While the reception of honor is a positive experience, it is not to be sought (Luke 14:7–8). When honor comes from others by reason of position or status, it is not to be taken for granted. The recipients should seek to merit honor through godly character. Honor can be lost through disobedience or disrepute, though in exceptional cases, dishonor is a mark of discipleship (2 Cor. 6:8).

SAM HAMSTRA, JR.

Hope. To trust in, wait for, look for, or desire something or someone; or to expect something beneficial in the future.

The Old Testament. There are several Hebrew verbs that may in certain contexts be translated "to hope" in English. One of them, *qāwâ,* may denote "hope" in the sense of "trust," as when Jeremiah addresses God, "Our hope is in you" (Jer. 14:22). He also uses a noun formed from the root *qwh* to teach that the Lord is the hope of Israel (14:8; 17:13; 50:7), which means that Israel's God is worthy of trust. Another noun from the same root, *tiqwâ,* is often also translated "hope" meaning "trust." Similarly, the verb *qāwâ* is parallel to *bāṭaḥ,* "to trust," in Psalm 25:2–3.

In the Old Testament believers are encouraged to wait for God hopefully, expectantly. In times of trouble one should wait for the Lord, who will turn things around (Pss. 25:21; 27:14; 40:1; 130:5). Sometimes expressions of hope are accompanied by the prayer that the supplicant will not be ashamed, that is, disappointed. "May those who hope in you not be disgraced" (Ps. 69:6; cf. Pss. 22:5; 25:2–3, 20). God promises that those who wait for him will not be disappointed (Isa. 49:23). God is able to bring about the realization of one's hopes. Looking with expectation is akin to hoping (Job 6:19; Jer. 8:15). From "looking for" or "expecting" it is a small semantic shift to desiring (Isa. 26:8).

Twenty-seven times *qāwâ* comes into the Greek Old Testament as *hupomenō,* "to wait," "to be patient," "to endure." Where suffering is present, the term may indicate that the individual is bearing affliction patiently while hopefully waiting for the Lord's deliverance. Psalm 40 is a psalm of thanksgiving that recounts the suffering of an individual whose hope was realized. "I waited patiently for the LORD" (Ps. 40:1; 130:5–6).

Because of the close connection between hope and trust and because of the requirement to trust in God alone, a number of passages warn against trust in other things. We should not trust in riches (Job 31:24–28; Ps. 52:1–7; Prov. 11:28), idols (Ps. 115:3–11; Hab. 2:18–19), foreign powers (Isa. 20:5), military might (Isa. 30:15–16; 31:1–3; Hos. 10:13), princes (Ps. 146:3–7), or other humans (Jer. 17:5–8). God is the true object of hope, but occasionally there are others. One may put one's hope in his steadfast love (Ps. 33:18), in his ordinances (Ps. 119:43), and in his word (Ps. 119:49, 74, 81, 114, 147). Besides waiting in eager expectation for God, one may wait or hope for his teaching (Isa. 42:4) and for his salvation (Ps. 119:166).

For much of the Old Testament period hope was centered on this world. The beleaguered hoped to be delivered from their enemies (Ps. 25); the sick hoped to recover from illness (Isa. 38:10–20). Israelites trusted God to provide land, peace, and prosperity. In early passages there are few expressions of hope for the next world. Those who descend to the grave have no hope (Isa. 38:18–19). Only those still living could hope (Eccles. 9:4–6, 10), as salvation was for this life. Toward the end of the Old Testament God made known his plan to bring his everlasting kingdom to earth (Dan. 2:44; 7:13–14) and to raise the dead (12:2). At that point hope became more focused on the next world, especially on the resurrection. God will "swallow up death forever" (Isa. 25:7), and the dead will rise again (26:19); this is the salvation for which the faithful wait (25:9).

The New Testament. The New Testament consistently uses the verb *elpizō* and the noun *elpis* for hope. Just as the Old Testament emphasizes hope as trust, Paul writes about setting our hope on God (1 Tim. 4:10) and on Christ (Eph. 1:12). As Jeremiah proclaims that God is the hope of Israel, Paul announces that Jesus Christ is our hope (1 Tim. 1:1).

Parallel to those passages in the Old Testament where those who hope are not put to shame, Paul says hope does not disappoint us (Rom. 5:5). The reason is that we already have a taste of the future glory because of the love with which the Holy Spirit fills our hearts. In other words, the gifts of love and of the Spirit are downpayments of future glory for which we hope (Rom. 5:2; cf. Eph. 1:13–14).

In the Old Testament hope has to do with waiting for, looking for, desiring. This is paralleled in the Gospels, where the word "hope" is not very frequent but the idea of looking expectantly is. Simeon looked for Israel's consolation at the advent of the Messiah (Luke 2:25–26). Likewise, Anna, the prophetess, upon recognizing who Jesus was, proclaimed him to all those who were anticipating redemption (Luke 2:36–38).

In connection with hope in Romans 8:18–25 Paul speaks of waiting with eager expectation for the revelation of the children of God (v. 19), waiting for the adoption as sons (v. 23). We are waiting "for the righteousness for which we hope" (Gal. 5:5) and for "the blessed hope," namely, the glorious appearing of our Lord (Titus 2:13). Paul has both an eager expectation and a hope for God to be glorified in him, whether in life or death (Phil. 1:20). He goes on to express his desire to leave this world to be present with Christ (1:23).

As hope is connected with patient endurance in the Old Testament, so in the New Testament trials lead to hope (Rom. 5:3–4) and hope is steadfast (1 Thess. 1:3). When we hope for something we wait for it through patience (Rom. 8:25; cf. 15:4).

In the Old Testament hope is linked with "putting confidence in" or "taking refuge in." Paul also parallels hope with trust. He hopes to send Timothy and trusts in the Lord that he himself will come (Phil. 2:23). Hebrews talks about courage and hope (3:6). Likewise, Paul links hope and boldness (2 Cor. 3:12). In a passage about the confidence we can have in God's promises, Hebrews 6:18–19 mentions taking refuge by seizing the sure anchor of hope that is set before us.

Reminiscent of the Old Testament false objects of hope, Paul counsels the wealthy not "to set their hope in wealth" (1 Tim. 6:17). In addition to putting hope in God and Christ, we hope for salvation (1 Thess. 5:8); God's glory (Rom. 5:2; Col. 1:27); resurrection (Acts 23:6; 24:15; 1 Thess. 4:13); the redemption of our bodies (Rom. 8:23); righteousness (Gal. 5:5); eternal life (Titus 1:2; 3:7); the glorious appearing of Jesus (Titus 2:13); and that we shall become like him when he does appear (1 John 3:2–3).

From the above list it is apparent that, in contrast to the Old Testament, New Testament hope is primarily eschatological. After being introduced late in Old Testament times, hope in the resurrection of the dead grew in the intertestamental period in such proportion that Paul could speak of the resurrection as the "hope of Israel" (Acts 28:20; cf. 24:15; 26:6–8). If our hope is only for our present existence, it is most pitiable (1 Cor. 15:19). When our believing friends and relatives die we grieve in hope of the Lord's return, unlike unbelievers who have no hope. The only sure hope is Jesus: when he returns, believers who have died and those still living will both be given imperishable bodies like that of the risen Lord (1 Cor. 15:20–23, 51–52; 1 Thess. 4:13–18).

Hope is the proper response to the promises of God. Abraham serves as a prime example here. Even though he was very old, he had confidence that God would fulfill his promises. "Against all hope, Abraham in hope believed" (Rom. 4:18).

Like Abraham, we can trust in God's promises and "seize the hope set before us" (Heb. 6:18). More generally, we are told that the Scriptures engender hope (Rom. 15:4). The Holy Spirit is also a source of hope, for his power causes hope to abound (Rom. 15:13). Finally, hope comes as a gift from God through grace (2 Thess. 2:16).

Hope leads to joy (Rom. 12:12) boldness (2 Cor. 3:12), and faith and love (Col. 1:4–5). Hope also leads to comfort; we are to encourage one another with the knowledge of the resurrection (1 Thess. 4:18). Though boasting in our works is disallowed, we may boast or exult in hope of sharing God's glory (Rom. 5:2; cf. Heb. 3:6).

Hope has a sanctifying effect. We who look expectantly for the return of Christ, knowing that when we see him we shall become like him, purify ourselves "as he is pure" (1 John 3:3). Hope also stimulates good works. Following his teaching on resurrection of the dead, Paul exhorts his readers to do the Lord's work abundantly since such "labor is not in vain" (1 Cor. 15:51–58).

William B. Nelson, Jr.

Bibliography. E. Hoffman, *Dictionary of New Testament Theology,* 2:238–46; P. S. Minear, *IDB,* 2:640–43; C. F. D. Moule, *The Meaning of Hope;* W. Zimmerli, *Man and His Hope in the Old Testament.*

Horns of Altar. *See* Altar.

Hosanna. Joyful Aramaic exclamation of praise, apparently specific to the major Jewish religious festivals (especially Passover and Tabernacles) in which the Egyptian Hallel (Pss. 113–118) was recited. Originally an appeal for deliverance (Heb. *hôšîʿâ nāʾ,* Please save; Ps. 118:25), it came in liturgical usage to serve as an expression of joy and praise for deliverance granted or anticipated. When Jesus came to Jerusalem for his final presentation of himself to Israel, the expression came readily to the lips of the Passover crowds.

In the Bible the expression occurs only in accounts of that event. Matthew, Mark, and John all transliterate it (Luke does not, but appears to paraphrase it with the Greek word for "glory": see his "glory in the highest," 19:38). According to Matthew, the crowd that accompanied Jesus that day shouted "Hosanna to the Son of David!" (21:9), as did the children later in the temple (v. 15). Mark (11:9) and John (12:13) do not have "to the Son of David," but all three follow the opening cry with, "Blessed is he who comes in the name of the Lord!" (from Ps. 118:26). Matthew and Mark conclude the people's cries with "Hosanna in the highest" (apparently an echo of Ps. 148:1), which John omits. But Mark inserts "Blessed is the coming kingdom of our father David" (11:10), and John adds, "Blessed is the King of Israel" (12:13). These appear to be interpretations of "he who comes in the name of the Lord." And they agree essentially with Luke's formulation of the people's words taken from Psalm 118:26, "Blessed is the king who comes in the name of the Lord" (19:38).

Those from whose lips "Hosanna" rose that day seem to have looked on Jesus as God's anointed one from the house of David of whom the prophets had spoken and through whom they hoped that all their messianic expectations would be fulfilled. However misguided their particular expectations may have been, their actions underscore the theme of the Gospels that Jesus is indeed the promised son of David through whom the redemption announced by God's prophets has come. In him the age-old cry, "Lord, save us," has become the glad doxology, "Hosanna," which equals: "Praise God and his Messiah, we are saved."

Most likely the authors of the Gospels transliterated "Hosanna" rather than translating it because it served on the people's lips as a joyful exclamation which, if translated, would have sounded like a prayer. In similar fashion, John transliterated "Hallelujah" in Revelation 19:1, 3, 4, 6 because it had become an exclamation of praise whereas originally it was a call to praise ("Praise the Lord").

John H. Stek

Bibliography. R. E. Brown, *The Gospel According to John I–XII;* G. F. Hawthorne, *ISBE,* 2:761.

Hosea, Theology of. Foundational to Hosea's message and teaching about God are his marriage to Gomer and her departure after the birth of three children. The opening surprise of the book is that God initiated Hosea's marriage to this harlot (1:2); but the greater, unexpected surprise is that he tells Hosea to find his adulterous wife, bring her back, and love her again (3:1–2). Hosea's personal tragedy speaks to readers at the deepest level, moving them emotionally, intellectually, and spiritually.

Hosea's theology brings together an awareness of God as holy (11:9, 12) and sovereign (12:5) with an appreciation for his actions as husband (2:16) and parent (11:1–4) toward his people. Hosea's theology is not remotely theoretical but grows out of a grassroots understanding of his people as illustrated by frequent allusions to historical events and places and his personal involvement.

The details of Hosea's marriage begin the book but are quickly dropped as the focus shifts away from the personal life of Hosea to the relationship between God and Israel. Immortalized in this event that transcends culture are the message and emotions of God. The love, care, and feelings of God for his people as he calls for their return in the face of imminent judgment are a major part of Hosea's theology.

Fueling the symbolism of Hosea's marriage was the covenant, which provided a legal form for the expression and governance of the relationship God desired with his people. For Israel it provided a blueprint for the historical foundation of their faith and gave tangible evidence for God's requirements. At the same time it provided God with an acceptable witness to their loyalty and love. The Book of Hosea is a commentary on that relationship. It moves from the heights of an intimate knowledge, symbolized by marriage and paternal love, to the depths of anguish and despair over Israel's apostasy and idolatry as pictured by the adultery of Gomer.

The love of God for his people is more graphically portrayed by Hosea than any other Old Testament prophet. Refusing to give up on Israel, God continued to seek their return even in their apostate condition. Judgment and exile would come but restoration and future hope were always in sight. Israel would not be annihilated like the cities around Sodom but preserved (11:8–9).

God's continual provision for his people was further evidence of his love. Hosea likens God's care for Israel to that of a parent who daily provides for a child. In one of the most moving images in the book God depicts his paternal care for Israel when he says, "I . . . bent down to feed them" (11:4). Through Hosea's life and message we see the strength of God's feeling for Israel—his compassion (11:8), his love (11:4), and his longing to be with them (7:13).

Yet, while glimmers of hope permeate the prophet's oracles God's judgment is given a more prominent place in his theology. After years of waywardness God was going to scatter the Israelites among the nations whose gods they served. In keeping with previous revelation the Lord would not allow his people to continue to violate their relationship with him. Just as an adulteress was stripped naked and expelled from her house (2:3, 10) so too the land would be denuded of God's blessings (2:9–12; 9:2) and its people sent into exile (5:14; 9:15–17). The graciousness and mercy of God did not include ignoring sin!

Hosea's understanding of sin and its effects upon people is vividly presented through his own marriage and the list of crimes levied against his people. Enumerated are social, moral, political, and religious evils (4:2; 6:9; 7:1; 12:1). Attention is called to Israel's pride (5:5; 7:10), false trust (5:13; 8:14; 10:13), and violent actions (4:2; 6:9; 12:1). Paramount, however, was their neglected and broken relationship with God.

Impending judgment was a result of their breaking the covenant. Punishment was outlined in the covenant stipulations, which they had violated at every turn. Just as Jacob of old (12:2) they would reap the disaster of their ways (4:9; 8:7; 10:13). God sent his prophets to warn the people (6:5; 12:10), but eventually he allowed an enemy to conquer them and devastate the land (10:14; 13:16) with none to deliver them (13:10). Even future generations would be affected by their sin (4:14; 9:11–12, 16).

Hosea focuses on Israel's accountability with specific reference to the covenant requirements. The covenant blessings and curses (Deut. 28) as well as the required reading of the law (Deut. 31:10–13) were constant reminders of the people's obligation to the Lord. Despite God's warnings to the contrary Israel forgot God (2:13; 4:6). Turning away from God they took the fruits of the land and offered them to pagan idols, eventually attributing the source of these blessings to the gods of Canaan (2:8; 11:1). In contrast to Israel's unfaithfulness Hosea presents God as one who remembers and provides for Israel.

A major theological theme developed by the prophet is the concept of the knowledge of God. Hosea uses this concept to show the extent of God's relationship with his people and its reciprocal nature. The verb "to know" reflects both the intimacy of a relationship and mutual recognition on the part of suzerain and vassal. God's legal case against Israel was that there was "no faithfulness, no love, no acknowledgment of God in the land" (4:1). But this was not a passive situation. Israel had willfully rejected the knowledge of God and would be judged accordingly (4:6). The key to the knowledge of God was obedience that came from the heart. God's reminder "For I desire mercy, not sacrifice, and acknowledgment of God rather than burnt offerings" (6:6) confirmed that their religious practices were without proper motivation and therefore worthless.

While God knew Israel (5:3) in the closeness of a relationship that could be imaged by marriage, Israel no longer knew God (2:8; 11:3). Their actions led them farther away from God (4:6; 5:4) and although they thought they still knew him (8:2) their actions proved otherwise. God announced his judgment so that Israel would realize the consequences (9:7–9). In the end, however, God's love would triumph by bringing back Israel to himself as Hosea did Gomer, by paying a price. Israel would once again know the Lord (2:20).

Undoubtedly the most blatant rejection of God was Israel's idolatry. It distorted their thinking and ultimately replaced God with another (4:11–12). Gomer's adulterous affairs provided penetrating images of Israel's apostasy and revealed the hurt and disaster associated with idolatry—hurt suffered by God and disaster suffered by the people since the eventual outcome led to exile and destruction.

Fueled by a fertility cult religion Israel's neighbors linked productivity of the land, animals, and people with their gods. Caught up in the rituals of this fertility cult Israel attributed the gifts of God to pagan gods (2:8). Years of participation led them so far from the Lord that they could not return. They had developed a spirit of prostitution in their hearts (5:4; cf. 4:12). Altars and idols were proliferated (8:4, 11), with special emphasis on the bull (8:5–6; 10:5; 13:2). Hosea understands idolatry's grip upon the people. Their pride and arrogance caused them to pursue it more vehemently. They multiplied altars and alliances, which drove them farther from God (5:4–5). In an inescapable spiral this path led them even farther away from God (11:2) until they completely corrupted themselves (9:10). God, however, would not force them to return (4:17), but sadly watched as they withdrew from him (4:17; 11:8).

By emphasizing Israel's idolatry Hosea underscores both the waywardness of Israel and the jealousy of God. Having chosen, cared for, and entered into a special relationship with his people, God would accept no rival, especially the emptiness of idolatry. In the end God would destroy their idols (10:2).

Predating the parable of the prodigal son Hosea portrays Israel as realizing that the best days were those spent close to God (2:7, 15). Israel had been taught the way back and the mercy of God (6:1–3), but they were blinded by arrogance and adultery (7:10, 16; 11:7). Instead of moving back to God they went to their idols and formed alliances with Egypt and Assyria (7:11; 11:5).

For the most part God's endeavors to reach them went unheeded. Israel's half-hearted attempts to return were met by his absence (4:17; 5:6). True repentance was to be evidenced by internal (7:14) and external change (14:2–3). God wanted action—covenant loyalty that evidenced kindness in action, justice at all levels, and a knowledge that portrayed the Lord's righteousness (6:6; 10:12; 12:6)—but Israel offered insincerity and rejected God (6:4; 8:2–3).

Hosea never waivers from his understanding of the Lord as sovereign. God was in control of the situation rather than Israel and certainly not their impotent idols. Hosea effectively brings out the tension God felt as he agonized over the demands of his holiness and his love for his people. This is portrayed by Hosea with surprising force when the Lord says: "My heart is changed within me; all my compassion is aroused" (11:8). God's justice meant that he would bring judgment upon them; his holiness meant that it was inescapable. But judgment, applied by a gracious Lord, is also discipline and effective discipline seeks restoration rather than alienation so God worked to restore his people to himself (2:12). In language reminiscent of a lover Hosea presents God as alluring and speaking tenderly to Israel to affect her return (2:14).

Hosea's eschatology is built upon the covenant relationship as administered by a sovereign Lord. The oscillation between hope and the certain judgment parallels the tension God feels between loving and judging his people. God's love, so powerfully illustrated by Hosea, reached beyond the people's stubborn rebellion and offered a future hope. But Hosea does not play God against himself. He presents restoration as God's planned goal in light of Israel's repentance, a repentance nurtured and won by God (2:14–16).

Restoration, however, depended upon genuine confession (5:15) and repentance (6:1–3). In its full form restoration would bring both physical and spiritual blessings. Hosea envisioned a new betrothal (2:19) and a new relationship (1:10; 2:16) that would produce the true covenant fruit of righteousness, justice, love, compassion, and knowledge (2:19–20). Material blessings of peace (2:18), unity (1:10–11), and productivity of the land (2:21–22) would also characterize this new relationship. Although judgment was inevitable God desired restoration reaching even to the grave (13:14).

Attempts to sever from the prophet's words the message of hope and the invitation to return that concludes the book have not effectively dealt with the continuity of its perspective. The allusions to a new, restored relationship so strongly portrayed in Hosea's marriage and by the names of his children are effectively balanced at the end of the book, which encloses the judgment of God within the parameters of his love and mercy. The people were challenged to understand that their salvation was only in God (13:4), anticipating the full scope of God's redemption through Christ.

Robert D. Spender

See also Israel; Prophet, Prophetess, Prophecy.

Bibliography. F. Anderson and D. N. Freedman, *Hosea;* H. L. Ellison, *The Prophets of Israel;* D. A. Hubbard, *Hosea;* H. B. Huffmon, *BASOR* 181 (1966): 31–37; D. Kidner, *Love to the Loveless;* J. L. Mays, *Hosea;* N. H. Snaith, *Mercy and Sacrifice;* J. O. Strange, *Rev Exp* 82 (1967): 437–48; D. Stuart, *Hosea–Jonah.*

Hospitality. Hospitality plays no small role in the realm of biblical ethics. Biblical admonitions exhorted the Israelites and the early Christians to practice this virtue. Its practice characterized Abraham (Gen. 18:2–8) and the church leaders (1 Tim. 3:2; Titus 1:8). And, as hospitality is an attribute of God, one finds its images in the biblical proclamation of the relationship between God and the covenant people.

Hospitality in the ancient world focused on the alien or stranger in need. The plight of aliens was desperate. They lacked membership in the community, be it tribe, city-state, or nation. As an alienated person, the traveler often needed immediate food and lodging. Widows, orphans, the poor, or sojourners from other lands lacked the familial or community status that provided a landed inheritance, the means of making a living, and protection. In the ancient world the practice of hospitality meant graciously receiving an alienated person into one's land, home, or community and providing directly for that person's needs.

Some forms of hospitality toward nonforeign strangers appear to have been commonly practiced among the nations of the biblical world. There appears to have been some decline in hospitality from the period of the Old Testament to that of the New Testament, since hospitality is omitted from later Greco-Roman virtue lists. In its literature, Israel alone seems to have included the foreign sojourner along with those other alienated persons who were to receive care: the widow, the orphan, and the poor. Although the narratives of the patriarchal period advocate receiving the foreigner/stranger at least on a temporary basis (Gen. 18–19), landed Israel showed some ambivalence toward foreign strangers by favorably distinguishing the sojourner, who made some allegiance to the Israelite community of faith, from the foreigner, who might represent some threat to cultic purity. For the early church, hospitality remained an important expression of lovingkindness, one that received support in the teaching of Jesus (Matt. 25:31–46; Luke 10:30–37; 14:16–24; 16:19–31).

Hospitality took several forms. Acts of hospitality included the humble and gracious reception of travelers into one's home for food, lodging, and protection (Gen. 18:2–8; 19:1–8; Job 31:16–23, 31–32), permitting the alienated person to harvest the corners of one's fields (Lev. 19:9–10; Deut. 24:19–22; Ruth 2:2–17), clothing the naked (Isa. 58:7; Ezek. 18:7, 16), tithing food for the needy (Deut. 14:28–29; 26:1–11), and including the alien in religious celebrations (Exod. 12:48–49; Deut. 16:10–14).

The hospitable act of the communal meal possesses great symbolic significance. In the ancient world, to share food with someone was to share life. Such a gesture of intimacy created a bond of fellowship. Hence, God's meal with the elders of Israel (Exod. 24:1–11), Jesus' meals with tax collectors and sinners (Luke 11:37; 15:1; 19:5–6), the Lord's Supper (Mark 14:17–26), Jesus' postresurrection meals (Luke 24:30–31, 40–43; John 21:12–13; cf. Acts 1:4; cf. 10:41), Peter's meal with Gentiles (Acts 10:48–11:3), and the common meal of the early Christians (Acts 2:42–47) communicated a powerful message of intimacy and unity.

The Old Testament. *Israel as Guest, God as Host.* Old Testament teaching identifies the Israelites as alienated people who are dependent on God's hospitality (Ps. 39:12; see also Heb. 11:13). God graciously received the alienated Israelites and met their needs, redeeming them from Egypt and feeding and clothing them in the wilderness (Exod. 16; Deut. 8:2–5), bringing them as sojourners into God's own land (Lev. 25:23), where God offered them health, long life, peace, and fertility (Deut. 11). In a figurative sense, table fellowship is offered during meals of peace offerings and religious feasts where part of the sacrifice is offered to God and the rest is eaten by the sacrificer or community (Lev. 7:11–18; 23; Ps. 23:5; Prov. 9:1–6; Isa. 25:6). Indeed, God serves as host to humanity as the one who provides food and clothing for all (Gen. 1:29–30; 2:9; 3:21; Pss. 104:10–15; 136:25). God particularly cares for the alienated person (Exod. 22:22–24; Deut. 10:17–18; Pss. 145:14–16; 146:9).

Israel as Host. Old Testament teaching also expected the Israelites to practice hospitality and serve as hosts, treating human life with respect and dignity. Hospitality is an act of righteous, godly behavior. When the angels journeyed to Sodom and Gomorrah in search of a righteous man, only Lot and his family were set apart to be saved. Lot was deemed righteous by the fact that he alone imitated Abraham's behavior of hospitality (Gen. 19:1–8; cf. 18:2–8). Besides presenting the model of Abraham, the Old Testament specifically commanded hospitality. As Israel received the loving care of Yahweh, so Israel was to love and care for the alienated person (Exod. 23:9; Lev. 19:33–34; Deut. 10:19; Isa. 58:6–10).

God as Guest. Another theme possibly provided an incentive for hospitality: God might be the guest. God or the angel of the Lord at times unexpectedly appeared in the person of the stranger (Gen. 18:1, 10; 19:1; Judg. 6:11–24; 13:2–23).

The New Testament. *Jesus as Guest.* Symbolically Jesus came as an alien figure to "tabernacle" in a world that did not recognize or receive him (John 1:10–14). He continues after his resurrection to offer himself as guest (Rev. 3:20). On a literal level, Jesus' itinerant ministry placed him in dependence on the hospitality of others (Luke 9:58; 10:38). In his capacity as guest, Jesus bound himself to the lost, sharing table fellowship with tax collector, "sinner," and Pharisee alike (Mark 2:15; Luke 14:1; 19:1–10). Jesus equates himself with the needy alienated person (Matt. 25:31–46).

Jesus as Host. Jesus, the guest, also becomes the host who receives an alienated world. The Old Testament allusions in the feeding of the 5,000 (Mark 6:30–44) reveal the identity of Jesus. Taking the role of host to the multitude, Jesus is portrayed as one like Yahweh, who fed the people in the wilderness (Exod. 16); as one like the prophets of Yahweh, who fed his disciples and had food left over (2 Kings 4:42–44); as one like the coming Davidic shepherd, who would care for his flock in the wilderness (Ezek. 34:11–31). In the institution of the Lord's Supper, Jesus not only serves as host, washing the disciples' feet (John 13:3–5) and directing the meal, but becomes the spiritually sustaining "meal" itself (Mark 14:12–26; see also John 6:30–40; 1 Cor. 10:16–17). Identifying himself with the symbolic elements of the Passover meal, Jesus associated his body with the bread of affliction that was offered to all who were hungry and needy, and he associated his blood with the third cup of wine, the cup of redemption. Moreover, by halting the meal before the traditional fourth cup, Jesus anticipates his role as eschatological host, when he will drink again at the messianic banquet celebrating the consummation of the kingdom of God (Isa. 25:6; Matt. 8:11; Luke 14:15; Rev. 19:9). In postresurrection appearances the disciples perceive the identity of Jesus when he takes the role of host (Luke 24:13–35; John 21:1–14).

Christians as Guests. As persons originally alienated from God, Christians are invited to respond to Jesus as host in the celebration of the Eucharist and in anticipation of the eschatological messianic feast. Those who confess Jesus as Christ become aliens and strangers in the world (John 15:18–19; 1 Peter 1:1; 2:11). The audience of 1 Peter apparently suffered social ostracism because of their Christian confession (4:12–16), but in turn they received divine hospitality as members of the "household of God" (4:17; 2:9–10; Eph. 2:19; Phil. 3:20). Itinerant Christian ministers and refugees often found themselves in need of sympathetic hosts (Rom. 16:1–2, 23; 1 Cor. 16:10–11; Titus 3:13–14; Philem. 22; 3 John 5–8).

Christians as Hosts. As in the Old Testament, righteous behavior in the New Testament includes the practice of hospitality. One finds the commands to act hospitably in the context of other expressions of love (Rom. 12:9–21, esp. vv. 13, 20; Heb. 13:1–3; 1 Peter 4:8–11; 3 John 5–8). In a general sense, Christians now serve as cohosts with Christ to a world consisting of those who are "excluded from the citizenship in Israel and foreigners to the covenants of the promise" (Eph. 2:12). Certainly, held up before the Christian is the model of Jesus, who serves as host to an alienated world, who commended hospitality in his teaching, and who himself is encountered as one receives the alienated person (Matt. 10:40; 25:31–46). RODNEY K. DUKE

See also ETHICS.

Bibliography. G. Downey, *ATR* 47 (1965): 3–15; R. K. Duke, "Toward an Understanding of Hospitality in the Old Testament"; J. H. Elliot, *A Home for the Homeless: A Sociological Exegesis of 1 Peter, Its Situation and Strategy;* K. L. Gibble, *Brethren Life and Thought* 26 (1981): 184–88; R. B. Herron, *Word and World* 6 (1986): 76–84; R. Jewett, *Letter to Pilgrims: A Commentary on the Epistle to the Hebrews;* D. Kellermann, *TDOT,* 2:439–49; J. Koenig, *New Testament Hospitality: Partnership with Strangers as Promise and Mission;* A. J. Malherbe, *Social Aspects of Early Christianity;* B. J. Malina, *Social-Scientific Criticism of the New Testament and Its Social World,* pp. 171–94; J. B. Mathews, "Hospitality and the New Testament Church: An Historical and Exegetical Study"; P. Parker, *The Company of Strangers: Christians and the Renewal of America's Public Life;* F. A. Spina, *The Word of the Lord Shall Go Forth: Essays in Honor of David Noel Freedman in Celebration of His Sixtieth Birthday,* pp. 321–25; G. Staehlin, *TDNT,* 5:1–36; R. A. Wright, "Establishing Hospitality in the Old Testament: Testing the Tool of Linguistic Pragmatics."

Hosts, Lord of. *See* GOD, NAMES OF.

Hour, the Last. *See* LAST DAY(S), LATTER DAYS, LAST TIMES.

Humanity, Human Person. *See* PERSON, PERSONHOOD; SOUL; SPIRIT; WILL.

Humility. Biblical humility is grounded in the character of God. The Father stoops down to help the poor and needy (Ps. 113:4–9; cf. 138:6–7); the incarnate Son exhibits humility from the manger to the cross (Matt. 11:29; Acts 8:32–33; Phil. 2:5–8). The dual usage of "meek" (Gk. *praus*) and "humble (*tapeinos* "low") in heart" in Matthew 11:29 emphasizes Christ's humility before humankind, whom he came to serve (Matt. 20:28; Mark 10:45; Luke 22:27) and his submission before God. Humility and meekness are often inseparable (2 Cor. 10:1; Eph. 4:2; Col. 3:12).

As a sign of genuine religion (Mic. 6:8) humility is necessary to enter God's kingdom (Matt. 5:3; 18:1–4) or to be great in it (Matt. 20:26–27; Mark 10:43–44). As the absence of self (Matt. 10:38–39; Luke 9:23–25), it is a bankruptcy of spirit (Matt. 5:3) that accrues no merit but depends solely on God's righteousness for salvation (Luke 18:9–14, 15–17). It may involve praying (2 Chron. 7:14; Dan. 6:10; 9:3–20), fasting (Lev. 16:29–32; 23:27–32; Ezra 8:21, 23; Ps. 35:13; Dan. 10:1–3, 12), and falling prostrate (Ezek. 1:28; Dan. 6:10; Rev. 1:12–17) before the Lord. Since the Lord denounces hypocritical worship (Isa. 58:3–7; Matt. 6:5–8, 16–18) and false humility (Col. 2:18, 23), a person's heart must match his or her posture (Isa. 57:15; Luke 18:9–14; cf. Isa. 6:5; Matt. 11:29).

Humility is the prerequisite for honor (Prov. 15:33; 18:12; 22:4; 29:23) and physical blessing (Ps. 37:11; Matt. 5:5). Intimately associated with the fear of the Lord (Ps. 25:9, 12–14; Prov. 15:33), it may provide the key to wealth and life (Prov. 22:4); but even when blessings are postponed, a humble spirit is necessary (Prov. 16:18–19; cf. Rom. 12:14, 16–17). It is the gateway to eternal life (Matt. 5:3; 18:1–4), not necessarily physical reward (5:10–12).

God gives grace to the humble (or afflicted) but resists the proud (Prov. 3:34; James 4:6; 1 Peter 5:5). Regardless of social or moral position (Luke 1:48, 52–54; cf. Ps. 51:16–17), God often delivers people who humble themselves before him—whether righteous kings (2 Chron. 32:24–26; 34:26–28), wicked rulers (1 Kings 21:27–29; 2 Chron. 33:12–13), or commoners (2 Chron. 30:8–11).

The Lord exalts the humble (Matt. 23:12; Luke 1:52; 14:11; 18:14; James 4:10) in his proper timing (1 Peter 5:6). A person must not claim honor for self (Prov. 25:6–7; Luke 14:7–11) but have an unassuming attitude (Rom. 12:3). Jesus' teaching and life illustrate this perfectly. He humbled himself as a servant (John 13:1–16), even unto death (Isa. 53:7–8; Acts 8:32–33) in obedience to the Father (Phil. 2:5–8), who highly exalted him (vv. 9–11).

The Lord rewards the humble with wisdom (Prov. 11:2). He does not ignore the plight of the humble and contrite (Isa. 66:2, 5) but encourages the lowly and afflicted of heart (Isa. 57:15; 2 Cor. 7:6).

The Christian ought to emulate Christ's example (Matt. 11:28–30; 2 Cor. 10:1) of meekness and humility. Humility is the foremost test of a truly great person or leader (Luke 22:24–27). Paul's teachings and life (Acts 20:18–21) emphasize and elucidate Christian humility. Recognizing he was the chief sinner (1 Tim. 1:15) and the least saint and apostle (1 Cor. 15:9; Eph. 3:8) he gloried in the grace of God (1 Cor. 15:10; cf. 2 Cor. 12:9–10) and in the cross of Christ (Gal. 6:14; cf. 1 Cor. 1:18–2:5) rather than self-righteousness (Phil. 3:3–9).

GREG W. PARSONS

Bibliography. J. Knox Chamblin, *Paul and the Self: Apostolic Teaching for Personal Wholeness;* H.-H. Esser, *NIDNTT,* 2:256–64; F. S. Fitzsimmons, *New Bible Dictionary,* p. 500; R. E. O. White, EDT, p. 537.

Husband. *See* MARRIAGE.

Hypocrisy. Although no distinct Hebrew word for hypocrisy occurs in the Old Testament, the concept does—primarily in terms of insincere worship. The Lord rejects sacrificial offerings and temple attendance (Jer. 7:4–11) when worshipers have no intimate knowledge of him or genuine love (Isa. 1:11–17; Hos. 6:4–6; Amos 4:4–5; 5:21–24). Hypocrisy manifests itself in an inconsistency between external religious activity and religious profession (Isa. 1:10–17).

The root idea in the Old Testament may be that the hypocrite has a godless heart (Job 36:13—LXX *hypocritēs* for Heb. *ḥānēp,* "godless, profane") that rebels against God's laws (Jer. 7:21–24; Hos. 7:13–16; 8:1–2; cf. Jer. 6:19–20) and generates wrongful acts, including injustice and oppression (Isa. 1:10-17; 58:2–7; 59:2–4, 13–15; Jer. 7:5). In contrast, the true worshiper must come before the Lord with a pure heart (Pss. 15:2; 24:4). The hypocrite is also an ungodly rebel who flatters and deceives with his or her tongue (Pss. 5:9–10; 12:2–4; 78:36–37; Dan. 11:21, 27; cf. Ps. 55:20–21) to promote godlessness (Dan. 11:32, 34).

The New Testament seems to combine the Old Testament concept of the godless rebel and the Attic Greek *hypokrisis,* "stage-playing or acting." The Greek idea of "play-acting" seems para mount in Matthew 6:2, 5, 16, where Jesus warns against religious performance to impress men (vv. 5, 16, 18; cf. Matt. 23:5). Hypocrites make an outward show of religion, whether in giving alms, praying, or fasting. The English concept of hypocrisy as failing to practice what one preaches is rarely found (Matt. 23:3).

The hypocrite is self-deluded by his or her own pretension, which fools no one else (Matt. 7:5; Luke 6:42). Hypocrisy may involve a failure to discern spiritual truth (Luke 12:54–56; 13:15; cf. Matt. 12:7; 23:23) or even a willful blindness to spiritual matters (Matt. 23:17, 19, 23–24, 26).

The hypocrite pretends goodness, but beneath a religious veneer is a malicious or deceitful heart (Matt. 22:15–18; cf. 1 Peter 2:1). Though hypocrites justify their religious activity, their hearts are not true to God (Matt. 15:7–9, 18–19; cf. Isa. 29:13–14). As in the Old Testament a discrepancy exists between outward conformity to religious ritual and the true state of their hearts (Matt. 23:25–30; contrast 5:8). Thus, the term "hypocrite" (Matt. 24:51) can occur as a synonym for "unfaithful/unbeliever." Such "hypocrites" hinder others from coming to Christ and even make converts to their godless lifestyle (Matt. 23:13, 15; cf. Dan. 11:32, 34). Or they deceive others into doctrinal error (1 Tim. 4:1–2). Thus hypocrisy is implied as one of the evidences of earthly or demonic wisdom (James 3:13–17).

The absence of hypocrisy (genuine faith and sincere love from a pure heart) is a mark of godly character (1 Tim. 1:5; 2:5, 7; cf. Pss. 15:2–5; 24:3–5; 2 Cor. 6:6–7).

GREG W. PARSONS

Bibliography. U. Becker and H.-G. Link, *NIDNTT,* 2:467–74; H. L. Ellison, *New Bible Dictionary,* p. 502; D. A. Hubbard, *EDT,* p. 539.

Ii

Idol, Idolatry. The most prevalent form of idolatry in biblical times was the worship of images or idols that represented or were thought to embody various pagan deities.

The Old Testament. From the beginning the threat of idolatry was in the midst of Israel. The forefathers were idolaters and, while Abraham was called out of a polytheistic background (Josh. 24:2), some persons brought their gods with them (Gen. 35:2–4). Israel's sojourn in Egypt placed them under the influence of the Egyptian religion, but God's sovereignty was manifest by his judgment upon the gods of Egypt (Exod. 12:12; Num. 33:4). Israel, however, quickly succumbed to idolatry by worshiping a golden calf at Mount Sinai (Exod. 32).

In Canaan Israel was influenced to worship Baal and other deities. Perhaps it was the fact that the Canaanites, who controlled all of the fertile valleys, offered their fertility cult religion as an explanation for greater productivity to the Hebrews, who had to settle for the less productive hills, or it may have been the emphasis upon sexuality that eventually seduced Israel to the worship of idols. Other reasons included materialism (Deut. 31:20), intermarriage (1 Kings 11:2–4), political persuasion (1 Kings 12:28), environmental factors (1 Kings 20:23), the conquest of other nations (2 Chron. 25:14), and power (2 Chron. 28:23).

The erection of two golden calves at northern cult centers by Jeroboam testifies to the syncretistic worship of Yahweh and idols that marked the remainder of the Old Testament period as Israel increasingly came under the influence of the Assyrian and Babylonian religions. Toward the end of the divided monarchy idolatry became so rampant that Jeremiah remarked that every town (2:28; 11:13) and all members of the family (7:18) were tainted.

Israel's calling was to the worship of the one true God. God's election separated the people from unholiness and to himself as his special possession. The covenant provided legal parameters for this unique relationship, and the limitation of exclusive worship was a significant part of the covenant. God had chosen Israel and they were to worship and serve him only. They were not to forget God—a process evidenced by disobedience and progressive apostasy to idols (Deut. 8:19; 11:16). This relationship with God and subsequent legislation by him made idolatry anathema for Israel.

The first commandment is to have no gods before God (Exod. 20:3; Deut. 5:7). In addition, the construction of any images (Exod. 20:23) or even the mention of the names of gods (Exod. 23:13) was forbidden. Invoking the name of a god was an acknowledgment of its existence and gave credence to its power. By swearing in the name of another god (1 Kings 19:2; 20:10), the people would be binding themselves to an allegiance other than God (Josh. 23:7).

Since idolatry substituted another for God it violated the people's holiness and was parallel to adultery; hence the frequent use of negative sexual imagery for idolatry, especially by the prophets. Both intermarriage and formal treaties were prohibited because of necessary affiliation with pagan gods (Exod. 23:32–33), leading to eventual fellowship (Exod. 34:15) and worship of idols (Num. 25:2–3).

Among the most severe commands were the instructions to destroy the inhabitants of Canaan because they served idols (Deut. 7:16). Included was the destruction and desecration of their idols (Deut. 7:25) and all cultic paraphernalia (Deut. 12:2). Insightful are the verbs employed for the destruction of idols. Eradication included cutting and pulling down, smashing, grinding, breaking, burning, and similar physical actions—all reminders of the inability of idols to protect themselves.

Beyond destruction, desecration by scattering the corpses and bones of slain idol worshipers upon centers of idolatry, underlined the degree of impurity idolatry caused (Lev. 26:30). Destruction was to be so extensive that their names (memory) would be eliminated from the cult site (Deut. 12:3).

The testimony of Scripture is that God alone is worthy of worship. Active acknowledgment of idols by prostration, sacrifice, or other means of exaltation is not only a misdirection of allegiance; it robs God of the glory and honor that is rightfully his (Isa. 42:8). God even placed limits of philosophical inquiry upon his people, indicating that they were not to seek the method of pagan worship because of associated evil practices (Deut. 12:30–31). The sense of Scripture was to destroy idolatry or be destroyed by it.

Since idolatry presented an alternative worldview the pressure to worship idols was felt in all aspects of life. Socially idolatry became a family affair, involving cities, towns, clans, and tribes. Both external documents and the Bible itself testify to pagan theophoric elements in the naming of children. Economically it took the produce of the land and many hours of labor from the worker who brought the fruit of his labor to the priest who officiated over the pagan rituals. The harshest economic contribution were children themselves. Politically the leaders were deeply involved—from the elder who sat at the city gate (Ezek. 8:11) to the king as final authority. Neither priest, prophet, nor prince were exempt from the corruption of idolatry (Jer. 32:32–35). Leadership was harshly condemned for leading the people astray.

Moral degradation was most pronounced in the act of child sacrifice, but included all of the immorality of the Canaanite fertility cult like the male and female prostitutes at cult sanctuaries. Religious corruption pervaded every area of Israel's life, especially since little distinction was made between spiritual or religious spheres and other areas of life. Priests offered sacrifices to Baal and Yahweh and idols were erected in the temple itself (2 Chron. 15:16; Jer. 32:34; Ezek. 8:5–11). Places of historic value that testified to the power and presence of God, like Bethel, were turned into cultic shrines (Amos 4:4). As time progressed the people even began to explain their past actions in terms of idols.

In contrast to such a bleak picture it is interesting to note that some of the highest accolades of Scripture are reserved for those individuals who shunned idolatry: Abraham, the friend of God; Moses, to whom God spoke face to face; and David, a man after God's own heart, are three examples.

Theologically the reason given for prohibiting idols is that God is unique and unrepresentable. Deuteronomy 4:15–19 states that Israel saw no form of God at Sinai; therefore they were not to make any images of him or any other object of creation. Failure to acknowledge God as sovereign Creator opens the door to idolatry and spiritual blindness (Isa. 42:5–9). Making images of foreign gods and attempting to represent the Lord were both forbidden as contradictions of the monotheistic revelation of God.

Scripture views idols as impotent. They are powerless to save (Isa. 45:20). When Israel called upon idols there was no response. Israel was even told, with the voice of irony, to call upon idols for help (Deut. 32:28; Judg. 10:14; Jer. 11:12) but the gods could not even save their own people (2 Chron. 25:15). Idols are nothing (Jer. 51:17–18) and lifeless (Ps. 106:28).

Reference to the construction of idols in Scripture is more prevalent than might be expected. From the selection of materials to the final embellishment of eye paint the process is most effectively portrayed in the great prophetic parodies of Isaiah 44:6–20 and Jeremiah 10:1–16. This attraction for many to worship an idol—its tangible nature—is also its greatest weakness. Fabricated by human hands, idols cannot see, hear, smell, walk, or talk (Deut. 4:28; Ps. 115:5–7; Hab. 2:18–19). Idols are not to be feared since they can do neither harm nor good (Jer. 10:5). What makes the polemic against idols so significant is that other religions condoned the making of images—the Lord did not!

Recorded in Scripture are the results of idolatry for both humankind and God. Those who venerate images are said to be deceived (Isa. 44:20), shamed (Isa. 44:11), and foolish (Jer. 10:8), eventually imitating the worthless idols they worship (2 Kings 17:15; Hos. 9:10). The inevitable outcome is destruction, death, and the judgment of God (Jon. 2:8).

God's first and foremost reaction to idolatry is anger. Because idolatry challenges his person and his love for his people it is viewed in terms of God being jealous (a consuming zeal for what was rightfully his) and impugns his very name (Exod. 34:14). That God did not destroy Israel because of their idolatry is clear evidence of his mercy and faithfulness. In the end God promises to destroy all the gods of the nations (Zeph. 2:11) and looks forward to the day when the people will throw away their idols and return to him (Isa. 30:22).

The New Testament. Following the exile and subsequent intertestamental struggles, the Jews no longer fell prey to physical idolatry. This is why idolatry is rarely mentioned in the Gospels. As the gospel message spread it encountered various forms of idolatry in the pagan world as attested in Acts, especially Paul's encounters at Athens (17:16–31) and Ephesus (19:23–34).

The pressure of idolatry on Gentile believers explains the numerous references to idolatry in Paul's Epistles. Teaching about foods offered to idols is an excellent example of the struggle of maturing Christians with idolatry. The fact that idolatry would continue to be a threat to the church is underscored by the many references to the worship of the image of the beast in Revelation.

The New Testament stresses the exceeding sinfulness of idolatry. Frequent listing of sins includes idolatry (1 Cor. 6:9–10; Gal. 5:20; Eph. 5:5; Col. 3:5; 1 Peter 4:3; Rev. 21:8) and Paul instructs believers not to associate with idolaters (1 Cor. 5:11; 10:14). Distortion brought about by idolatry is emphatically set forth in Romans 1:18–32, where image worship is seen as a downward spiral away from the true God.

The Bible understands that idolatry extends beyond the worship of images and false gods. It is a matter of the heart, associated with pride, self-centeredness, greed, gluttony (Phil. 3:19), and a love for possessions (Matt. 6:24).

Idolatry is a major theme of the Bible. It challenges God's sovereignty and attempts to offer an alternate explanation to the issues of life. But Scripture not only records people's failures; it also records the hope of repentance. In his mercy God raised up men and women who challenged the faulty theology of the community. Admonitions are laced with appeals for repentance, reform, and restoration, one indication being the elimination of idolatry. To serve other gods is to forsake God; to eliminate idolatry is a sign of return. Paul's commendation to the Thessalonian believers emphasized their turning from the service of idols "to serve the living and true God" (1 Thess. 1:9). ROBERT D. SPENDER

See also DIVINATION; GODS AND GODDESSES, PAGAN.

Bibliography. F. Büchsel, *TDNT,* 2:375–80; F. M. Cross, *Canaanite Myth and Hebrew Epic;* D. N. Freedman, *Int* 21 (1967): 32–49; J. A. Gileadi, ed., *Israel's Apostasy and Restoration: Essays in Honor of Roland K. Harrison;* R. L. Harris, *TWOT,* 1:353–54; Y. Kaufmann, *The Religion of Israel from Its Beginning to the Babylonian Exile;* W. Mundle, *NIDNTT,* 2:284–86; T. Overholt, *JTS* 16 (1965): 1–12; H. D. Preuss, *TDOT,* 2:1–5.

Ignorant, Ignorance. ***The Old Testament.*** While the concept of ignorance is found often in various equivalents, the word itself rarely appears (only twice in the RSV: Ps. 73:22; Ezek. 45:20). The latter passage, which contains the expression "sinned through ignorance," is likely grounded in Leviticus 4–5 and Numbers 15, where a distinction is made between unintentional and deliberate (high-handed) sin. The context here makes it clear that unintentional sins are not only attributable to ignorance, but also to negligence and human frailty. Ignorance does not so much characterize the sin as it does the circumstances under which the sin was committed. While ignorance did not eliminate guilt it did attenuate it, for in contrast to high-handed sins a purification offering was available for sins done through ignorance (Num. 15:27–31).

The New Testament. Here also the word appears a limited number of times (thirteen in the RSV) but its concept is a significant and pervasive one. As in the Old Testament, lack of knowledge mitigates sin. Peter, while not exonerating those who crucified Jesus, does seem to attenuate the guilt somewhat, noting that they "acted in ignorance" (Acts 3:17). So Paul observes that he received mercy because in persecuting the church he "acted in ignorance" (1 Tim. 1:13). Jesus extended forgiveness to his tormentors, noting they did not know what they were doing (Luke 23:34). Characterized as a great high priest in Hebrews 5:2, Jesus is said to deal gently with the ignorant.

Other passages, however, indicate that ignorance can be culpable without any palliation. Intentional ignorance associated with deliberate blindness (Rom. 1:18–23) and with hardness of heart (Eph. 4:18) is not lightly dismissed by Paul.

Ignorance requiring mercy and forgiveness is not then so much a quality of the uneducated as it is the quality of a sinner; it is not so much an intellectual issue as it is a moral one. Even as biblical wisdom is not intellectual fullness, so ignorance is not an intellectual privation, but rather a spiritual one. It is through such ignorance (an unwillingness to forgive) that a person can be outwitted by the designing Satan (2 Cor. 2:11).

Ignorance is used to characterize the pagan world that had not received the special revelation of God (Acts 17:23, 30; 1 Peter 1:14—cf. Wisd. of Sol. 14:22, "Err about the knowledge of God . . . live in great strife due to ignorance"). Thus education is not so much needed as is the proclamation of the gospel (Rom. 1:16–17). Likewise, needing the kerygma are the legalists who through ignorance believe that they can effect their own righteousness (Rom. 10:3). But even the revealed and received word can be twisted by the ignorant (2 Peter 3:16).

In a few passages ignorance simply indicates the lack of knowledge (2 Cor. 1:8; 1 Thess. 4:13) or special training (Acts 4:13). CARL SCHULTZ

Bibliography. R. Bultmann, *TDNT,* 1:116–19; J. Daane, *ZPEB,* 3:251–52; D. K. McKim, *ISBE,* 2:801; A. Richardson, *A Theological Word Book of the Bible.*

Illness. *See* DISEASE; HEAL, HEALTH; SUFFERING.

Image of God. It would be difficult to overstate the centrality of the image of God as a crucial theme in biblical theology. From the beginning of the end in Genesis (protology) to the end of the beginning in Revelation (eschatology), the image of God is crucial for understanding the flow of redemptive history. God creates humans in his image, justly punishes them for rebellion, yet graciously provides redemption from that rebellion, and then finally consummates redemptive history by transforming the whole creation into new heavens and a new earth.

Genesis 1:26–27 indicates that God created humankind as male and female in his image (*ṣelem*) and likeness (*dĕmût*). It is doubtful that distinctions between the meanings of these two words are to be pressed. Rather, the pair of words conveys one idea through a literary device known as hendiadys. Later, in Genesis 5:1–3, after God's image-bearers had sinned against him, the language of Genesis 1:26–27 is repeated as a prelude to a list of Adam's posterity. Significantly, this passage links God's original creation of humans in his likeness with the subsequent human procreation of children in Adam's image and likeness. Following the Genesis narrative further, after the flood of Noah, Genesis 9:6 indicates that due to the image of God capital punishment is required in cases of murder. To murder a creature who images God is tantamount to an attempt to murder the God who created the image-bearer, and the heinous nature of this offense warrants the forfeiture of the murderer's life as well.

But what is meant by the terms "image" and "likeness"? Three approaches to this question are commonly found, and no doubt all three have some merit. Many have concluded that humans are image-bearers due to their superior intellectual structure. Others have stressed that God mandates that humans function as rulers and managers of the creation as they image him (Gen. 1:26–28; Ps. 8:5–8). Yet another approach stresses the created relationships of humans; they image God as they relate to him, to each other, and to nature. Just as the Creator is a being in relationship, so are his creatures. Putting these views together, humans are like God in that they are uniquely gifted intellectually (and in many other ways) so that they may relate to God and to each other as they live as stewards of the world God has given them to manage. While an image is a physical representation of a person or thing (Exod. 20:4; Matt. 22:20), the human body does not mechanically image God, as if God had a body. Rather, the whole human being, including the body, images God's attributes by ethical living in concrete settings.

Sadly, the pristine beauty and harmony of this original created order were shattered by the rebellion of Adam and Eve, and the record in Genesis 3 as well as the history of human cultures show how alienation between humans and God, humans and other humans, and humans and nature quickly became the normal state of affairs. Yet even in this sorry state of alienation and disharmony, humans can still image God, although in an inconsistent and perverted fashion (Gen. 5:1–3; 9:6; Ps. 8; cf. 1 Cor. 11:7; James 3:9). God calls his redeemed covenant people to the highest ethical standard. They are to be like him; their ethical obedience images God.

In the New Testament the teaching of Jesus indicates the value of human beings implicit in their being God's image-bearers (Matt. 6:26; 12:12). More important, Jesus himself perfectly images God in his life and ministry as he relates sinlessly to God, people, and nature. As the first Adam failed the satanic test, the second Adam passed with flying colors (Matt. 4:1–11). Jesus did not forsake God as did Adam, but as the sin-bearer Jesus was forsaken by God (Matt. 27:46) so that he might restore his people to harmonious relationships to God, neighbor, and nature.

It is primarily Paul who develops the New Testament teaching on the image of God. Paul sees Jesus as the one who preexisted in God's form (*morphē;* Phil. 2:6) and whose incarnation supremely imaged God (2 Cor. 4:4; Col. 1:15; cf. John 1:1, 14, 18; 14:9; Heb. 1:3). Jesus' work of redemption is both compared and contrasted to Adam's work of rebellion (Rom. 5:12–21; 1 Cor. 15:22). Those who believe in Jesus are renewed in the image (*eikōn*) of God and are expected to live as renewed people (2 Cor. 3:18; Eph. 4:22–24; Col. 3:9–10). Their destiny is ultimately to be made like Jesus, to image him perfectly as he perfectly images God (1 Cor. 15:49; Eph. 4:13; Phil. 3:21). In this respect Christians are like children who look up to their big brother and want to be like him (Rom. 8:29). For the Christian, then, godliness in a world is Christ-likeness.

For Paul salvation from start to finish, encompassing regeneration, sanctification, and glorification, is nothing less than new creation (Rom. 8:18–30; 2 Cor. 4:6; 5:17; Gal. 2:20; 6:15; Eph. 2:10; cf. John 3:5; 5:24). This new creation is not merely individual but corporate and cosmic as well. The salvation of individual believers places them into community with other believers whose destiny augurs that of the physical universe itself (Rom. 8:19–21; 1 Cor. 15:24–28; Col. 1:16; cf. Matt. 19:28; Heb. 2:5–8). The community of believers in Jesus has already experienced image renewal and with perseverance they hope for the consummation of that renewal. In the meantime their ethical obedience is not merely to be like God but to be like Christ, who has provided not only an incarnate model for godliness but also a dynamic for attaining godliness through the Spirit (John 13:14; 1 Cor. 11:1; Eph. 4:32–5:2; Phil. 2:5; Col. 3:13; 1 Thess. 1:6; 1 John 3:3).

Any discussion of the image of God would be incomplete without some elucidation of the glorious future that awaits those who have been renewed in the image of God. This is the prospect of new heavens and new earth where righteousness dwells. God's plan of redemption in Christ would be severely truncated if it involved only the "spiritual" salvation of individuals who believe in Jesus. The original created order encompassed not only a "spiritual" relationship to God but also a social relationship to other humans and a material relationship to the world. Thus biblical eschatology envisions the restoration of all three of these relationships in a world where God's people may experience unhindered fellowship with him (Rev. 21:3–5) because the Edenic curse has been removed (Rev. 22:3). Ever since

Abraham, the prototypical person of God, God's people have longed for this time when life in all its facets may be lived fully to God's glory. This glorious biblical vision of a time when creatures will fully reflect the Creator's splendor ought to provide strong encouragement to Christians who presently reflect God's likeness in an imperfect yet improving manner. DAVID L. TURNER

See also ADAM; EVE; FALL, THE; PERSON, PERSONHOOD; SALVATION; SIN.

Bibliography. W. J. Dumbrell, *The End of the Beginning;* D. J. Hall, *Imaging God: Dominion as Stewardship;* A. A. Hoekema, *Created in God's Image;* P. E. Hughes, *The True Image: The Origin and Destiny of Man in Christ;* M. G. Kline, *Images of the Spirit;* A. M. Wolters, *Creation Regained: Biblical Basics for a Reformational Worldview.*

Images. *See* IDOL, IDOLATRY.

Immanuel. When the angel appeared to Joseph in a dream, he learned that his fiancée Mary was "with child through the Holy Spirit" and would give birth to a son named "Immanuel" (Matt. 1:18, 23). "Immanuel" is a Hebrew word meaning "God with us" and expresses the wonder of the incarnation, that God "became flesh and made his dwelling among us" (John 1:14). In the Old Testament God's presence with his people Israel was particularly evident in the tabernacle (Exod. 25:8), but the glory that filled the tabernacle was surpassed by the personal presence of God the Son as he revealed the Father during his ministry on earth. Christ's glory was revealed through the miracles he performed (John 2:11).

The birth of Immanuel to the virgin Mary fulfilled the prophecy of Isaiah 7:14, the sign given to Ahaz about seven hundred years earlier. At that time the wicked Ahaz ignored Isaiah's advice and appealed to the king of Assyria for help in a political crisis. Both the context of Isaiah 7 and the use of "Immanuel" two more times in chapter 8 (vv. 8, 10) raise the distinct possibility that the sign had a near fulfillment that affected Ahaz directly. Such a possibility is supported by the two verses immediately after 7:14 that tell us that the boy will still be young when Ahaz's enemies—the kings of Samaria and Damascus—will lose their power (a prediction fulfilled in 732 B.C.). The birth of a boy who would serve as a sign to Ahaz appears to be closely linked to the birth of Isaiah's son Maher-Shalal-Hash-Baz in 8:1–4. Both Immanuel in 7:15–16 and Maher-Shalal-Hash-Baz in 8:4 are young children when Damascus and Samaria collapse. And in 8:8 the two boys may be identified as Isaiah addresses Immanuel as if he were already present in Jerusalem. Verse 10 contains another occurrence of "Immanuel" in the words "God is with us." The prophet was challenging Ahaz to trust God, who was "with" his people just as he had promised to be with them constantly. In Numbers 14:9 Joshua and Caleb had urged the Israelites to acknowledge that the Lord was with them and to begin the conquest of Canaan, but just like Ahaz the people chose the path of unbelief with its tragic consequences. An earlier king of Judah, Abijah, believed that God was with his people as they faced the numerically superior army of Jeroboam. Abijah's faith was honored as the Lord gave him a resounding victory (2 Chron. 13:12–15).

If "Immanuel" was another name for Isaiah's son, the use of "virgin" for Isaiah's wife refers to the time when she was his fiancée. The sign of Isaiah 7:14 constitutes a blessing on an upcoming marriage, predicting that a virgin who was engaged to be married would be able to have a child early in the marriage. Unlike Mary she was not a virgin after she became pregnant. It is likely that Isaiah's marriage to a prophetess is in fact briefly described in 8:1–3. Matthew's use of this verse was extraordinarily appropriate in light of Mary's unique virginity and the incarnation of Jesus, who was God in the flesh. Matthew ends his Gospel with Jesus' own assurance to his disciples that he was Immanuel: "And surely I am with you always, to the very end of the age" (28:20).

HERBERT M. WOLF

See also VIRGIN BIRTH.

Bibliography. J. Lindblom, *A Study of the Immanuel Section in Isaiah;* J. Oswalt, *Isaiah 1–39;* H. M. Wolf, *Interpreting Isaiah.*

Immorality, Sexual. Interpersonal activity involving sex organs that does not conform to God's revealed laws governing sexuality. The account of creation (Gen. 1:1–28) includes reproductive activity as an essential part of the developmental scheme. This important function is given special prominence in the narrative describing the creation of woman (Gen. 2:21–24). In a process cloaked in mystery, God takes an aspect (Heb. *ṣēlāᶜ*, improperly translated "rib" in many versions) of Adam and fashions it into a genetic counterpart that is specifically female, and which matches Adam's maleness for purposes of reproducing the species. Adam and Eve are thus equal and complementary to one another, of the same physical and genetic composition apart from the slight difference that governs the characteristic nature of male and female fetuses. God tells them to "Be fruitful and increase in number; fill all the earth and subdue it" (Gen. 1:28).

In normal males the sex drive is a powerful biological and emotional force that is often difficult to control satisfactorily, particularly when it expresses itself in aggressive terms. But in the early narratives dealing with human family life there are no specific regulations for sexual behavior apart from the statement that Eve's husband will be the object of her carnal desires (Gen. 3:16). As the world's population grows, so do the human misdemeanors (Gen. 6:5–6), which seem to include mixed marriages (Gen. 6:2) and possible sexual perversions, although the latter are not mentioned explicitly. At the same time there are certain situations of a sexual nature that are to be avoided by followers of the Lord. The shame associated with the exposure of male genitalia and the penalties that might accrue to observers (Gen. 19:22–25) illustrates one form of prohibited sex-related activity. This represents the beginning of later Jewish traditions that held that nakedness was shameful.

In the patriarchal age, homosexuality was a prominent part of Canaanite culture, as the incident involving Lot in Sodom illustrates (Gen. 19:1–9). So rampant was sexual perversion in that place that in later times the name of the city became synonymous with homosexual behavior. God's judgment upon such a perversion of sexuality was to destroy the city and its corrupt inhabitants.

When God entered into a covenant relationship with the Israelites on Mount Sinai (Exod. 24:1–11), his intent was to assemble and foster a select group of human beings who would be obedient to him, worship him as their one and only true God, and live under his direction in community as a priestly kingdom and a holy nation (Exod. 19:6). Holiness demands adherence to certain stringent rules regarding worship and general conduct, but also requires a complete commitment of will and motive to the Lord's commandments.

Because of the gross promiscuity of surrounding nations, whose behavior the Israelites are warned periodically to avoid, the covenant Lord reveals through Moses a collection of strict regulations that are to govern Israelite sexuality and morality. If these directives are followed, the individual and the community alike can expect blessing. But if the Israelites lapse into the immoral ways of nations such as Egypt and Canaan, they will be punished. God's keen interest in the sexuality of his chosen people has two objectives: to exhibit Israel to the world as a people fulfilling his standards of holiness, and to ensure that, in the process, they enjoy physical, mental, and moral health.

The pronouncements on sexuality given to Moses while the Israelites are encamped at Mount Sinai occur in two separate places in Leviticus (18:6–23; 20:10–21). It should be remembered that Leviticus (the "Levite" book) comprises a technical priestly manual dealing with regulations governing Israelite worship and the holiness of the covenant community. God had chosen the covenant nation to be an illustration to pagan society of how individuals can become as holy as God through implicit faith in him and continuous obedience to his commandments. By setting out guidelines for the priests to teach to the Israelites, God promulgates explicitly a catalog of what is, and is not, acceptable social, moral, and spiritual behavior. In the distinctions between clean and unclean that occur in various parts of the priestly handbook, the emphasis is on that purity of life that should characterize God's people. Enactments of this kind are unique in the ancient world, and only serve to demonstrate the seriousness of God's intent to foster a people that can indeed have spiritual fellowship with their Lord because they reflect his holy and pure nature as they walk in the way of his commandments.

A closer look must now be taken at the regulations governing sexuality. In Leviticus 18:6–23, the matter is approached by the use of denunciations to describe immoral behavior. These fall into two groups, one dealing with carnal associations among people closely related by blood (consanguinity), and the other governing the sexual behavior of persons related through marriage (affinity). Accordingly a man is prohibited from copulating with his mother or any other wife belonging to his father; a sister or half-sister, a daughter-in-law or a granddaughter, an aunt on either side of the family, a woman and her daughter or her son's daughter or daughter's daughter, a wife's sister as a rival wife, a neighbor's wife, and a woman during the menses. Homosexuality is castigated as reprehensible morally, and bestiality is condemned summarily. Everything forbidden had already led to the moral defilement of the nations surrounding Israel, and for these perversions they are to fall under divine judgment (v. 24).

Homosexuality is described in the Mosaic legislation in terms of a man lying with a man "as one lies with a woman" (Lev. 18:22; 20:13), that is, for purposes of sexual intercourse. The practice originated in humanity's remote past, and appears to have formed part of Babylonian religious activities. The Canaanites regarded their male and female cultic prostitutes as "holy persons," meaning that they were dedicated specifically to the service of a god or goddess, not that they were exemplars of moral purity in society. While general condemnations of homosexuality occur in Leviticus, none of the pagan Near Eastern religions thought it either necessary or desirable to enact comparable legislation, since for them such activities were all part of normal religious life in temples or other places of cultic worship.

In general, homosexuality in Mesopotamia is not documented to any extent in surviving tablets, but that it was a widespread problem in the Middle Assyrian period (1300–900 B.C.) is indicated by the fact that legislation from that time stipulates that an offender, when caught, should be castrated. This judicial sentence, when compared with the Hebrew prescription of death (Lev. 20:13), shows that in Mesopotamian society the offense was regarded as a secondary civic infraction. While homosexuality seems to have been a recognized part of Hittite life, their laws nevertheless prescribe execution for a man who sodomizes his son.

Hebrew tradition, in contrast, is emphatic in condemning homosexuality, even though some Israelites succumbed to it. In Deuteronomy 23:18, male cultic prostitutes, and perhaps homosexuals also, are castigated as "dogs," which is most probably the significance of the term in Revelation 22:15. Since the dog was generally despised by the Hebrews as an unclean animal, serving much the same scavenging purpose as the vulture (1 Kings 22:38), the disparaging nature of the allusion is evident.

Bestiality, defined in terms of a man or woman having sexual relations with an animal (Lev. 18:23; 20:15–16), is stigmatized in the Mosaic enactments as a defilement for a man and a sexual perversion for a woman. It appears to have been fairly common in antiquity (Lev. 18:24), being indulged in by the Mesopotamians, Egyptians, and Hittites.

The shorter list of prohibited relationships in Leviticus 20:10–21 deals with many of the same offenses, but also prescribes punishments for such violations of Israel's moral code. Thus a man who commits adultery with his neighbor's wife is to be executed, along with his sexual partner. This is also the penalty for a man who defiles his father's wife or his daughter-in-law, because such activity constitutes sexual perversion as defined by God's laws. Homosexuality is once again condemned, and the sexual perverts sentenced to death. The marriage of a man, a woman, and her mother is deemed wicked, and the offenders sentenced to be burned with fire so as to expunge completely the wickedness of the act from the holy community. Bestiality, condemned already as a perversion, is regarded as a capital offense, which includes the animal also.

The marriage of a man with his sister from either side of the family is declared a highly immoral union, and the participants are to be put to death. The same is true of a man and a woman engaging in sexual activity during the woman's menstrual period. Such blood is considered highly defiling, and a gross violation of the purity that God desires as the norm for Israel's social behavior. The seriousness with which God assesses his holiness is reflected in the severe penalties prescribed for the infractions listed above. The phrase "their blood will be on their own heads" is a euphemism for capital punishment. Sexual relations between a man and his aunt, or between a man and his brother's wife, are regarded as dishonoring the legal spouses, and are accorded the lesser sentence of childlessness. In some cases, however, this is tantamount to causing the death of the family, a prospect that few Hebrews could contemplate with equanimity. In Deuteronomy 25:5–10, the law allows a man to marry his deceased brother's childless wife so as to rear a son for his brother's family, but this is very different from a man marrying his brother's wife while her legal husband is still alive.

There are important reasons why these enactments were part of ancient Hebrew law. Moral purity and spiritual dedication were fundamental requisites if the chosen people were to maintain their distinctive witness to God's power and holiness in society. The prohibitions reinforced the traditional emphasis on family honor, since the family was the building block of society. It had to be maintained at all costs if society was to survive. Any marriage relationship that was too close would have exerted a devastating effect on community solidarity by provoking family feuds that could last for centuries.

Serious problems would also have arisen through intermarriage when the result of such unions was the concentration of lands and riches in the hands of a few Hebrew families. For modern observers, however, the greatest danger by far would have resulted from the pollution of the genetic pool because of inbreeding. The bulk of the relationships prohibited by the legislation involved first and second degrees of consanguinity, that is, parent-child and grandparent-grandchild incest. Coition within the forbidden degrees of family relationships generally results in genetic complications when offspring are produced. Recessive genes often become dominant and endow the fetus with various kinds of diseases or congenital malformations. This seems to have been the force of the Hebrew *tebel,* a word that occurs only in Leviticus 18:23 and 20:12. It comes from *bālal,* meaning "to confuse," and conveys aptly the genetic upheaval that occurs in many cases of inbreeding, since God's rules for procreation have been upset. Only in a few instances does close inbreeding produce beneficial effects by removing recessive lethal genes from the genetic pool. (This may have happened in the case of ancient Egyptian royalty.) Nevertheless, even in such instances, inbreeding diminishes the energy and vigor of species that are normally outbred, and reinforces the wisdom and authority of the Mosaic legislation.

When God entered into a covenant relationship with the Israelites he furnished them with certain fundamental regulations engraved in stone to symbolize their permanence. These "Ten Commandments," as they are styled, contain certain injunctions of a moral character dealing with adultery, theft, false witness, and covetous behavior (Exod. 20:14–19). The last three offenses are social in character, involving the community of God to a greater or lesser degree. But the commandment prohibiting adultery deals with an act of a highly personal nature, occurring between normally consenting adults, which violates the "one flesh" character of marriage.

The fact that a commandment deals specifically with this form of behavior seems to indicate that adultery was common among the ancient Hebrews. At all events, adultery was understood as sexual intercourse between a man and another man's wife or betrothed woman. Similarly, any act of coition between a married woman and a man who was not her husband was also regarded as adultery. Certain exceptions to these stringent rules were tolerated in Old Testament times, however. A man was not considered an adulterer if he engaged in sexual relations with a female slave (Gen. 16:1–4), a prostitute (Gen. 38:15–18), or his wife's handmaid with the spouse's permission (Gen. 16:4). Nor was a man deemed to be in an adulterous relationship if he happened to be married to two wives.

The traditions banning adultery, made specific in the Decalog, were enshrined deeply in Israel's national life. The prophets warn that divine judgment will descend upon those who practice it (Jer. 23:11–14; Ezek. 22:11; Mal. 3:5). The Book of Proverbs, however, takes more of a social than a specifically moral view of adultery, ridiculing it as a stupid pattern of behavior that leads a man to self-destruction (6:25–35). The prophets use the term figuratively to describe the covenant people's lack of fidelity to the high ideals of Mount Sinai. The prophets view the covenant as equivalent to a marriage relationship between God and Israel (Isa. 54:5–8). Any breach of the covenant, therefore, is an act of spiritual adultery (Jer. 5:7–8; Ezek. 23:37).

In his teachings Jesus stands firmly in the traditions of the Mosaic law and prophecy by regarding adultery as sin. But he extends the definition to include any man who lusts in his mind after another woman, whether she is married or not. It is thus unnecessary for any physical contact to take place, since the intent is already present (Matt. 5:28). By this teaching Jesus demonstrates that, under the new covenant, motivation is to be considered just as seriously as the mechanical act of breaking or keeping a particular law. The motivation of a believer should always be of the purest kind, enabling obedience to God's will freely from the heart, and not just because the law makes certain demands.

Whereas the female is cast in an inferior, passive role in the Old Testament sexual legislation, Jesus considers the woman as equal to the man in his teachings about divorce and remarriage. In consequence the woman has to bear equal responsibility for adultery. Much discussion has taken place about Christ's return to the strict marriage ideals of Genesis 2:24 (Mark 10:6) and the explanatory clause "except for marital unfaithfulness" (Matt. 5:32; 19:9), which allows for remarriage after divorce and which does not occur in either Mark 10:11 or Luke 16:18.

Before New Testament technical terms are discussed, it is important to realize that Christ was directing his teaching at the new age of grace, which in his death was to render Old Testament legal traditions ineffective. The Mosaic law was specific about the conditions under which divorce could occur. The wife had fallen into disfavor because her husband had found something unclean or indecent about her, and therefore he was entitled to divorce her. Jesus teaches that this procedure was allowed by God as a concession to human obduracy (Matt. 19:8), even though the Creator hated divorce.

In New Testament times, only the man was able to institute divorce proceedings. It was in reality, however, a rare occurrence, and at that mostly the prerogative of the rich, since poor men could not afford another dowry or "bride price" for a subsequent marriage. The accused woman was protected under the law to the extent that her husband's accusations had to be proved. Thus some scholars have seen the Matthean explanatory clause as indicating immorality as the sole ground for divorce, following the contemporary rabbinical school of Shammai, and not for some purely frivolous cause, as the school of Hillel taught. If this explanation is correct, Jesus was addressing a Jewish controversy that had no bearing on God's marriage ideals in the age of grace, and which Mark and Luke consequently ignored because the exception did not apply to their audiences of Christian believers.

The most common term in the New Testament for sexual immorality is *porneia,* and its related forms *pornos* and *porneuō*. An emphatic form of the verb, *ekporneuō*, "indulging in sexual immorality," occurs in Jude 7. These words have been translated variously into English, some renderings for an immoral person being "whoremonger," "fornicator," "loose liver," and "sexually immoral." The term *pornos* refers to a man who engages in coition with a *pornē,* or female prostitute. The extended description of wanton immorality in Romans 1:24–32 discusses women spurning natural sexual relationships for unnatural ones, that is, indulging in lesbian activities of the kind practiced at Lesbos in pagan Greek religious ceremonies. The males are described as inflamed with lust for one another, and this leads to indecent and immoral behavior. In 1 Corinthians 6:9 the sexually immoral are classified as adulterers, male prostitutes, and homosexual offenders. In 1 Timothy 1:10, sexually immoral people are described comprehensively as adulterers and perverts.

The New Testament contains far less teaching about sexual immorality than the Old Testament, on which Christian morals and ethics are based. The Mosaic law condemned adultery, but placed less emphasis on prohibiting some other sexual offenses. In the end, disregard for the

Mosaic enactments brought Israel to ruin, and this made it important for the Christian church to distinguish carefully, among other matters, between adultery as a sin and *porneia,* which was a fatal perversion.

The New Testament requires believers to deny physical and spiritual lusting after people and false gods, and to conduct their behavior at a high moral and spiritual level. Sexual activity is to be confined to the marriage relationship, and if a married man or woman has sexual intercourse with someone other than the spouse, that person has committed adultery. To be most satisfying for the Christian, sexual activity must reflect the values of self-sacrificing love and the unity of personality to which the Christian's reconciliation to God by the atoning work of Jesus brings the believing couple. R. K. HARRISON

See also ETHICS; HOMOSEXUALITY.

Bibliography. D. S. Bailey, *Sexual Ethics;* H. P. Bell and M. S. Weinberg, *Homosexualities: A Study of Diversity among Men and Women;* H. Thielicke, *The Ethics of Sex;* H. L. Twiss, ed., *Homosexuality and the Christian Faith.*

Immortality. A state or condition free from both death and decay. The Bible affirms that only God by nature has immortality (1 Tim. 6:16; cf. Deut. 32:40; Rom. 1:23; 1 Tim. 1:17). It also implies that it is a potential state for human beings. Humankind failed to obtain this state because of sin (Gen. 2:17; 3:19), but it is given by God to righteous persons (Rom. 2:6–7; 1 Cor. 15:23–56).

The concept of immortality is present in the Old Testament, but there is no Hebrew word for it. In Proverbs 12:28 (NASB)—"In the way of righteousness is life, and in its pathway there is no death"—immortality (as the word is translated in the NIV) is, literally, the Hebrew phrase "no-death" (*ʾal-māwet*). "Sheol" occurs sixty-five times throughout the Old Testament; it is an obscure, shadowy, gloomy place of existence, but also of forgetfulness. The hope is for deliverance from it after death (Pss. 49:15; 86:13). Job 10:20–22 anticipates only a sheol-like state after death, but 19:25–26 seems to look for something more. Isaiah's prophecy ends with a vague expectation of continued existence for good and evil (66:22–24; cf. 26:16; Ps. 23:6); such is made clear in Daniel 12:2.

The New Testament writers present the idea of immortality with (1) the nouns *aphtharsia,* "not-perishable," "incorruptibility," or "immortality" (Rom. 2:7; 1 Cor. 15:42, 50, 53–54; Eph. 6:24; 2 Tim. 1:10); and *athanasia,* "no-death," "deathlessness," or "immortality" (1 Cor. 15:53–54; 1 Tim. 6:16); (2) the adjective *aphthartos,* "imperishable," "incorruptible," "immortal" (Rom. 1:23; 1 Cor. 9:25; 15:52; 1 Tim. 1:17; 1 Peter 1:4); and (3) the phrase "eternal life" (lit., "life of the ages," *zōēn aiōnion*). All these terms, except the latter (which Paul uses elsewhere), occur in 1 Corinthians 15. "Eternal life" is a favorite expression of John (3:15, 16, 36; 10:28; 17:2–3; 1 John 1:2; 2:25; 5:11, 13, 20) and is frequently used by Paul (e.g., Rom. 2:7; 5:21; 6:22–23; Gal. 6:8; 1 Tim. 1:16; 6:12; 2 Tim. 2:10; Titus 1:2; 3:7). Passages such as 2 Corinthians 5:1–10 refer or allude to the concept with metaphors. Immortality is a corollary to references to existence after death or to the resurrection in general.

Jesus assumes a continuing existence after death throughout his teachings. Certainly the future aspects of the kingdom of God imply as much. He speaks of it directly in the parable of the rich man and Lazarus (Luke 16:19–31) and in the judgment scene of Matthew 25:31–46. To make "everlasting life" available is at the heart of Jesus' mission: "I have come that they may have life, and have it to the full" (10:10; cf. 5:40; 20:31). John 14:1–3 assumes not only a continuing existence but also that for believers it will be with Jesus.

Peter says Christians have been given "new birth into a living hope through the resurrection of Jesus Christ from the dead, and into an inheritance that can never perish, spoil or fade" (1 Peter 1:3–4). Later he states that this new birth is "not of perishable seed, but of imperishable" (v. 23). The judgment scenes of Revelation 20–22 display eternal life of bliss for believers and punishment for the rest.

It is Paul who gives the clearest explanations of immortality. It is a gift made available through the work of Christ (Rom. 2:7; 2 Tim. 1:10), the lasting reward of the believer in contrast to the perishable wreath won by the athlete (1 Cor. 9:25). At the same time Paul asserts that the wicked face continuing, conscious alienation from God and positive punishment (2 Thess. 1:9).

First Corinthians 15:35–57 contains the most lengthy discussion of immortality, but is actually only a corollary to Paul's affirmation of the resurrection. Here Paul clearly sets forth the fact of an incorruptible, permanent existence in contrast to our present condition. However, as the planted seed and the stalk that grows from it are both the same yet different, so the future spiritual-immortal body will be both a continuation of and different from the physical-mortal one.

Second Corinthians 5:1–10 affirms that the future, eternal, heavenly "house" is the present possession of believers ("we have," v. 1). In spite of the present undesirable state, a mortal one in which "we groan" (vv. 2–4), the Spirit is "the guarantee" of the better one that awaits the believer (v. 5). Furthermore, Paul maintains that to be "away from the body" is to be "at home with the Lord" (v. 8). Similarly, Philippians 1:20–21 asserts that through the believer's union with Christ the future (immortal) life is a present possession. Philippians 2:10–21 has the same expectation of a changed or transformed body, by implication an immortal one, as the Corinthians correspondence. Indeed, Paul assumes that immortality as a permanent, incorruptible, never-ending state and life not only await the Christian after death but is actually the present possession of the believer.

Differing views about nature of life beyond the grave are tied to differing views about the nature of humankind. Traditional Christianity has held a dualist or tripartite view of persons (soul-spirit and body or soul, spirit, and body) and that between death and the resurrection there is some sort of an intermediate state in which the immaterial part of the individual continues a conscious existence apart from the physical. Some who emphasize a holistic view of persons assume that at death there is an immediate resurrection of a new spiritual body and union with God. Others with a similar anthropology propound a form of re-creationism, a temporary extinction at death that ends at the resurrection in a new creation. An associated issue, "soul sleep" (psychopannychy), could be a corollary to either the traditional view or that of re-creation.

In summary, the Bible clearly teaches a continuing existence after death for all. For believers this will be deathless and imperishable, marked by that glory and honor that come from union with Christ. Because immortality is now obscured in corruptible bodies, changes will occur. Believers will have appropriately different bodies; their immortality will be evident. This fact, along with the bodily resurrection, Paul sees as assured because of the Spirit's guarantee, the defeat of death, and the ultimate victory of God through Jesus Christ (1 Cor. 15:54–57).

J. JULIUS SCOTT, JR.

See also DEATH, MORTALITY; ETERNAL LIFE, ETERNALITY, EVERLASTING LIFE; RESURRECTION.

Bibliography. F. F. Bruce, *Scottish Journal of Theology* 24 (1971): 457–72; J. W. Cooper, *Body, Soul, and Life Everlasting;* O. Cullmann, *HDSB* (1955): 7–36; G. R. Habermas and J. B. Moreland, *Immortality: The Other Side of Death;* M. J. Harris, *Raised Immortal: Resurrection and Immortality in the New Testament;* idem, *From Grave to Glory;* G. E. Ladd, *A Theology of the New Testament;* A. Lincoln, *Paradise Now and Not Yet;* G. W. E. Nickelsburg, Jr., *Resurrection, Immortality and Eternal Life in Intertestamental Judaism.*

Incest. Illicit marital relations between a man and woman who belong to the same kinship group. Biblical Hebrew has no term for incest, but the Old Testament spells out marital relations that were forbidden. In the New Testament, the Greek term *porneia* refers to unlawful sexual intercourse in general, which included incest, and which might be the intended meaning of the term in Matthew 5:32; 19:9; Acts 15:20, 29; 21:25. The issue of incest receives particular attention in the New Testament in two passages: Mark 6:17–29 and 1 Corinthians 5:1–5. In general, a member of the community of faith who violated the biblical incest prohibitions endangered the community's relationship with God and would receive judgment carried out by the community and/or by God.

The biblical prohibitions against incest are found in the Old Testament in three main groups of texts: Leviticus 18:6–18; 20:11, 12, 14, 17, 19, 20, 21; Deuteronomy 27:20–23. Marital relations with the following persons are forbidden: one's mother, father's wife, sister and half-sister, son's daughter, daughter's daughter, step-sister (a possible meaning of Lev. 18:11), father's sister, mother's sister, father's brother's wife, daughter-in-law, brother's wife, wife's mother, and the joint marriage of a woman and her daughter, a woman and her son's or daughter's daughter, a woman and her sister (while the former is still alive, Lev. 18:18), a woman and her mother. Hebrew and Jewish practice as found in the biblical narratives does not always accord with the above prohibitions (cf. Gen. 20:12; 29; Exod. 6:16, 18, 20; Num. 26:59; 2 Sam. 13:12–13; Mark 6:17–29). Such practices may be accounted for individually on the basis that they occurred: prior to the origin of the prohibitions, in ignorance, or possibly in defiance of them. Also, in contrast to Leviticus 20:21 stands the legislation and practice of levirate marriage, a special case in which a brother or close kin is expected to marry the childless widow of a brother and father a child who would carry on the family lineage in the dead brother's name.

The guidelines that defined the kinship limits of Hebrew marriage practice are not stated in the biblical texts. One can note, however, how the prohibitions corresponded with the ancient Hebrew social structures. Hebrew marriage practices were exogamous on the level of the household, the extended patrilineal family that was the foundational social unit of ancient Hebrew society. However, Hebrew marriage practice was also basically endogamous on the level of clan and tribe, so that one married within one's clan to create lineage solidarity and to preserve the clan's landed inheritance. This practice explains the absence of cousins from the incest prohibitions. Parallel patrilineal cousins, who could be living one's household, were allowed, even preferred, in marriage.

An examination of the Old Testament incest prohibition lists reveals the nature of the transgression and the judgment it received. Each of the lists of prohibitions is distinct in character and function. Deuteronomy 27:20–23 is included in a list of the curses of the covenant ratification ritual in which the Israelites recognized that violation of the covenant should justly incur divine curse. Those items mentioned in the list apparently represented a larger body of known laws, probably such as found in Leviticus 18 and 20.

Leviticus 18:6–18 states its prohibitions in absolute form (apodictic), as in the Decalog, without identifying case-by-case consequences. The force of these prohibitions rests on divine authority, "I am the LORD" (18:5, 30). The material bracketing these laws (18:15, 24–30) reveals a theological reason for the prohibitions. The banned behavior was associated with the Egyptians, whose land the Israelites had left, and the Canaanites, whose land the Israelites came to possess. The morally corrupt practices of the Canaanites had so defiled the land that they were to be eradicated from it. So, too, if Israelites allowed such behavior, God's land, in which they were sojourners (Lev. 25:23), would be defiled and they too would be "vomited out." Incestuous practice, then, was a crime against God which, through its polluting influence, would contaminate Israel's relationship with God and result in divine punishment of the community in general.

Leviticus 18:29 states the consequence for individuals who violate any of the bracketed laws: they will be "cut off." This penalty has often been interpreted to be excommunication (a punishment for incest found in Hittite laws and an interpretation held by the Qumran community) or even the death penalty. However, all of the crimes that result in this penalty are religious sins against God. In the levitical laws, sins against God are punishable by God. Therefore, two other interpretations fit the evidence better. The penalty might refer (1) to the offender's family lineage being cut off by God, or (2) to the offender being cut off from his kin in the afterlife existence of Sheol, or possibly to both consequences together.

The incest laws of Leviticus 20 provide more information about the consequences of incest violations. These texts share a form common to ancient Near Eastern legal texts. Such texts identify specific violations and consequences in the form of case law (also called casuistic law: "If one commits A, then the consequence is B."). They presented individual cases, which served as representatives of the larger body of commonly known law, for the purpose of identifying the relevant principles of justice. Lists of such laws were not intended to be inclusive of all possible cases, nor was each case intended to present all the criteria employed for making a judgment and assessing the consequences. These lists were scholarly texts employed by the experts. Perhaps this characteristic common to ancient Near Eastern law explains why there is not a one-to-one correspondence among the three biblical lists of prohibitions and why no biblical text forbids marital relations with one's daughter. Since one's daughter was one of the "flesh" relatives (see Lev. 21:2–3), and since one's daughter's daughter was forbidden (Lev. 18:10), one must assume union with one's daughter was forbidden in Israelite practice as well.

Furthermore, a difficulty in understanding the consequences prescribed in Leviticus 20 for incest may be resolved. In this chapter three cases of incestuous relations receive the death penalty (vv. 11, 12, 14), which was carried out by the community; and three receive a form of divine punishment (vv. 17, 19, 20). If degrees of incest are being distinguished here, the exact principles used and how such principles would be applied to other unmentioned cases are unclear. Since such laws in the ancient Near East assume an audience skilled in legal matters, they do not always mention various options regarding the consequences. It is possible that total body of violations of 20:1–21 came under two understood conditions: when such violations occurred unknown to the community (as several of these violations could), the violator would receive divine punishment; but when the violator was known to the community, that person would receive the death penalty as well. This conclusion is supported by the fact that Leviticus 18:6–18 places all of its more inclusive list of incest violations under the consequence of divine punishment.

The theological principle behind Leviticus 18 and 20 involves the understanding that incest crimes could not be tolerated in the Israelite community, which was to remain holy before God. No purification ritual for the individual is provided for such violations. One who would pollute Israel's relationship with God, if caught, was to be eradicated from the community in order that the community's relationship with God might remain unimpeded.

Recognition of the above Old Testament theological principle sheds light on a difficult passage in 1 Corinthians 5:1–5 involving incest, a passage that has received various interpretations. In a case where a man has committed incest (apparently marrying the former wife of his father) without the objection of the Christian community, Paul banishes the man and hands him over to Satan for the destruction of the flesh and the preservation of the Spirit (v. 5). (The usual translation, "*his* spirit," is not supported by the Greek text.) Paul's concern in this text is focused on the community, who, like dough, can be totally corrupted by a little yeast (vv. 6–13). The Christian community collectively is the temple of God in which the Spirit dwells (6:19–20). Immoral practice within the community must be eradicated to preserve the presence of the Spirit. Therefore, Paul banishes the man and hands him over to Satan, the agent of destruction. In essence Paul leaves the penalty to God. The opportunity for the brother to repent, although not mentioned, is no doubt assumed, for, in the end, he did repent. Paul's focus is on preserving the holiness of the community and presence of the Spirit from the pollution of incest.

RODNEY K. DUKE

See also IMMORALITY, SEXUAL.

Bibliography. A. Y. Colins, *HTR* 73 (1980): 251–63; T. Frymer-Kensky, *The Word of the Lord Shall Go Forth: Essays in*

Honor of David Noel Freedman, pp. 399–414; H. A. Hoffner, Jr., *Orient and Occident*, pp. 81–90; B. A. Levine, *Leviticus;* J. Milgrom, *Leviticus 1–16;* G. J. Wenham, *The Book of Leviticus;* R. Westbrook, *Studies in Biblical and Cuneiform Law;* idem, *ABD*, 5:546–56; B. Witherington, *NTS* 31 (1985): 571–76; D. Wold, *SBLSP*, 1:1–45; C. J. H. Wright, *ABD*, 2:761–69.

In Christ. *See* UNION WITH CHRIST.

Inheritance. Legal inheritance refers to actual property or goods received after a family member's death. While Jewish inheritance customs were linked to family blood lines, Greek and Roman laws also provided for the disposition of family possessions through the adoption of an heir. The Scriptures transform the concept of inheritance to include the acquisition of spiritual blessings and promises from God.

The Old Testament. The Old Testament is rich in its usage of the inheritance metaphor. The terms for inheritance occur over two hundred times, most frequently in Numbers, Deuteronomy, Joshua, and Psalms. While Jewish inheritance laws were specific and complete (Num. 27:8–11), almost all references to inheritance in the Old Testament are theological, not legal.

In the theological sense, to inherit means to "receive an irrevocable gift" with an emphasis on the special relationship between the benefactor and the recipients. Unlike legal inheritance, the benefactor, God, does not die, yet he provides material and spiritual blessings for his people.

The focus of the inheritance concept in the Old Testament is God's promise to Abraham. The land of Canaan was bequeathed to him and his descendants as an eternal possession (Gen. 12:7). Each family in Israel was apportioned its own inheritance as an inalienable possession (Josh. 13–31) and given the task to occupy the land (Judg. 1:3). As the biblical history of Israel unfolds, the promised inheritance specifies a righteous remnant who will inherit the world as an everlasting possession (Ps. 2:8; Isa. 54:3; Dan. 7:14).

From the promise of Canaan as Israel's inheritance came other aspects of the concept. The nation is described as God's inheritance (1 Kings 8:51, 53; Ps. 78:71; Isa. 19:25; Zech. 2:12) whom the Lord will never forsake (Ps. 94:14). The Lord is conversely described as the inheritance of the nation (Ps. 16:5). The privileged position of Israel as God's chosen people placed them at the center of God's plans for blessing.

Between the Testaments. In the intertestamental period the actual appropriation of this promise seemed remote due to the domination of Persian, Greek, and Roman powers. The reality of the inheritance of the land was deferred to the future and intertestamental literature emphasized the inheritance of eternal life and the world to come. The focus of the promised inheritance was less on national prominence in the present and more on personal participation in the future life with God. This idea was broadened in the rabbinic literature where having an inheritance or share in the world to come was a primary aspiration of the Jews. A notable dichotomy existed between those who would inherit the future world (the redeemed) and those who would not (the condemned). By the time of the New Testament, it was common for a person to ask a rabbi, "What must I do to inherit eternal life?" (Matt. 19:16).

The New Testament. The legal-historical milieu of the first century provided an array of inheritance traditions. Jewish, Greco-Hellenistic, and Roman inheritance laws differed greatly in the meaning and implementation of their traditions. However, as in the Old Testament, almost all occurrences of the terms for inheritance in the New Testament are theological (Luke 12:13 is the lone exception).

Who Are the Heirs? Three major characters dominate the inheritance usage in the New Testament: Abraham, Christ, and the believer. The New Testament continues the focus on Abraham as a central figure of the inheritance metaphor. The initial promise to Abraham of the land of Canaan (Heb. 11:8) is broadened to include "the world" (Rom. 4:13). While the fact of Abraham's inheritance is significant, the New Testament concentrates on the means by which he received the inheritance: God's promise and Abraham's faith, not by works of the law (Rom. 4:14; Gal. 3:18).

The second major character is Jesus Christ. His prominent position as the Son of God uniquely qualifies him as God's heir. He is presented as the heir of all things (Heb. 1:2, 4) and the promises of God's kingdom are focused in him (Matt. 21:38).

Finally, for the believer in Christ, heirship is a natural result of justification: "He saved us, . . . so that, having been justified by his grace, we might become heirs having the hope of eternal life" (Titus 3:5–7). Since all believers are children of God they are necessarily heirs of God (Rom. 8:17; Gal. 4:7). It follows naturally that Christians are also heirs along with Abraham and Christ (Gal. 3:29). They receive their inheritance by faith as did Abraham (Rom. 4:13–14) and share in the inheritance with Christ as sons (Rom. 8:17).

What Is the Inheritance? Throughout the New Testament, a striking promise for believers is simply "the inheritance" (Acts 20:32; 26:18; Eph. 1:14, 18; Col. 3:24). Generally, the promise refers to the possession of salvation (Heb. 1:14). The believer's inheritance is described more specifically as eternal and joyful existence with God. Believers are promised "an inheritance that can never perish, spoil or fade—kept in heaven for you" (1 Peter 1:4). Inheriting the "world to come" is a guarantee for all those who belong to God's family.

The apostle Paul employs the inheritance metaphor more than any other New Testament writer. For him, the object of the inheritance is the kingdom of God. He never states exactly what constitutes the believer's inheritance of the kingdom, but asserts emphatically that unbelievers will not inherit the kingdom (1 Cor. 6:9–10; Gal. 5:21; Eph. 5:5).

The Bible is clear that inheriting eternal life is synonymous with entering the kingdom. At the judgment, the righteous will inherit the kingdom (Matt. 25:34) but the wicked will be eternally tormented (Matt. 25:46). The finality of the separation of those outside of the family of God is clearly seen in their lack of a share in God's inheritance.

The concept of the believer's inheritance highlights the dignity of the family relationship of the believer in Christ. No higher position or greater wealth can an individual acquire than to become an heir of God through faith in Christ.

William E. Brown

See also Eternal Life, Eternality, Everlasting Life; Reward.

Bibliography. E. P. Sanders, *Paul, the Law and the Jewish People;* A. N. Sherwin-White, *Roman Society and Roman Law in the New Testament.*

Iniquity. *See* Evil; Sin.

Inspiration of Scripture. *See* Bible, Inspiration of the.

Intercession. *See* Prayer.

Intermediate State. Christianity postulates that there will be a resurrection of the body at the end of the age. Because many people physically die before that time, in what state of being do they exist until that time? That state of being is called an "intermediate state" because it stands between our state of being while alive on earth and our final state of being that will include a resurrected body.

In the Old Testament little was revealed by God concerning the specifics of the afterlife. Believers died in hope of what God in his mercy would yet do for them. Their trust was in God who would ultimately redeem them, and if the specifics of what would transpire after death were not clear, their faith in God was and from this arose an assurance that God would not abandon them in the darkness. In some instances their faith took concrete shape, as in Psalm 49:15, "God will redeem my life from the grave; he will surely take me to himself," or in Job 19:25–27, "I know that my Redeemer lives . . . and after my skin has been destroyed, yet in my flesh I will see God. I myself will see him with my own eyes—I, and not another." The future resurrection is spoken of in Daniel 12:2. But what the precise state of those who die will be was not disclosed in any detail.

In the New Testament, Jesus affirms the certainty of the coming resurrection (Matt. 22:23–30; Luke 14:14; John 5:28–29) which, of course, requires the existence of an intermediate state. These passages shed light on it. In Matthew 22:31–32, Jesus affirms the coming resurrection of the dead, but then says no one is really *dead*, that is, snuffed out of existence. Because God says, "I am the God of Abraham, Israel and Jacob," they are not dead, but living. Luke 16:19–31 tells us of two who retain consciousness after their demise and the thief is told in Luke 23:43, "You will be with me in Paradise today." None of this tells us what the interim body is like, but it does tell us that a conscious existence, morally continuous with this life awaits us—Paradise or Abraham's bosom for the righteous, torment for those who reject God's offer of mercy.

The apostle Paul looks forward to being with Christ upon death (Phil. 1:20–24) and believed that Christ would bring with him those who had previously died (1 Thess. 4:14). Paul also says that at the second coming the dead in Christ will rise first (1 Thess. 4:17). These are not contradictory ideas. To Paul, those who die in Christ go immediately into Christ's presence in a noncomplete (unresurrected) form, there to await his second coming when their soul will be reunited with a resurrected body. Those who are alive at that moment will be instantly transformed (1 Cor. 15:50–53; 1 Thess. 4:17).

When reflecting on what it will be like to be in that interim state between death and resurrection, Paul likens it to being unclothed. The soul has shed its body and is naked (2 Cor. 5:3–4). Paul appears to have somewhat ambivalent feelings about entering this state. On the one hand, he does not look forward to being bodiless—Greeks thought positively about leaving the body behind at death, but Jews did not. On the other hand, to be away from the body is to be at home with the Lord, and that is a highly desirable state (2 Cor. 5:6–8). Paul does not attempt to describe what the disembodied soul is like; he only knows it is a temporary state. At the resurrection of the dead we will be made complete again, like Christ in his resurrected body.

Walter A. Elwell

See also Abraham's Bosom; Paradise; Resurrection; Sheol.

Bibliography. P. Cotterell, *What the Bible Teaches about Death;* K. Hahnhart, *The Intermediate State in the New Testament;* A. A. Hoekema, *The Bible and the Future*; X. León-Dufour, *Life and Death in the New Testament;* H. R. Mackintosh, *Immorality and the Future.*

Isaiah, Theology of. Isaiah, the son of Amoz, was an eighth-century prophet who appeared at a critical time in Judah's history, proclaiming a message of judgment. However, Isaiah apparently always entertained the hope that the nation would turn back to God and be spared from severe punishment. As Isaiah was beginning his ministry, the Assyrians were in the process of building an empire that threatened to swallow up Israel unless Yahweh would deliver his people. This is why the decision Ahaz was forced to make in Isaiah 7 was so crucial. He had to choose between placing his trust in human wisdom and power or in Yahweh to deliver the nation from war. God even graciously offered to give Ahaz a sign to enhance his faith, but Ahaz would not commit himself to trust in Yahweh. The outcome was the Syro-Ephraimite War (734–732 B.C.) and Judah's loss of political independence (they became vassals successively to Assyria, Babylonia, Medo-Persia, Greece, and Rome). In spite of this, Yahweh promised to one day restore his people—not the entire nation, as he had done in the past, but a remnant. Isaiah was one of the first to prophesy that Yahweh was not limited by the people's unbelief, but that he could raise up and deliver a believing remnant. This remnant would be comprised of those righteous people of Judah who would turn to Yahweh and thereby be brought through the crisis.

The basis for this deliverance, even though rarely mentioned (54:10; 55:3–5; 56:4–5; 59:21; 61:8), is grounded upon the covenant that Yahweh originally made with Abraham. On several occasions in the Book of Isaiah, Yahweh steps in to deliver a remnant of the nation so that the covenant would continue. One such occasion was when Assyria, led by Sennacherib in 701 B.C., marched into Judah with the chief aim of annihilating it (10:7). They had destroyed all of Judah except for Jerusalem; the night before Sennacherib was to begin siege of the city, the text says that "the angel of the LORD" descended and killed 185,000 Assyrian soldiers. The Assyrians subsequently returned to Nineveh without capturing the city. On another occasion Yahweh used Cyrus as his servant to deliver the nation from Babylonian captivity and allow them to return to Jerusalem (44:28–45:13).

Early in his ministry Isaiah was warned that his message would go unheeded by the vast majority of the nation (6:9–13); however, his call in the year of King Uzziah's death (6:1–8; approximately 740 B.C.) encouraged him to continue proclaiming his unpopular message. He was given a vision of the holiness of God that colored the rest of his ministry. Thus it is no wonder that the key title for Yahweh, "The Holy One of Israel," is used twelve times in the first thirty-nine chapters and fourteen times thereafter. Unfortunately Isaiah was one of the few people in Judah who comprehended the extent of his unholiness (6:5); if more of the nation had had a similar perspective, they may have lived differently. God gave the nation extended opportunities to repent and turn back to him so that divine punishment could be averted, but the message never seemed to penetrate the people's hardened hearts.

Introduction. The first chapter of the book contains important theology regarding both Yahweh and man. Yahweh is long-suffering and merciful, but he must also punish sin. In fact, punishment appears to be administered by Yahweh to encourage the nation to repent (vv. 5–6). Sacrifices and empty prayers do not satisfy or impress Yahweh (vv. 11–15); a change of behavior accompanied by a proper heart attitude is what he demands (vv. 16–17). The nation needed to turn from their evil deeds and demonstrate practical good deeds, such as seeking after justice, punishing evildoers, and helping those in society who have no one else to come to their aid, such as orphans and widows. Yahweh graciously says that if the nation will turn back to him, he will remove their sins and bestow a blessing (i.e., eating the best of the land, vv. 18–19), but they will be punished if they rebel (v. 20), which is similar to the blessings and cursings found in Deuteronomy 27–28. In this section man is seen as more rebellious than dumb animals (i.e., donkeys and oxen) since even these animals know enough not to bite the hand that feeds them. By contrast, Yahweh's people rebel against him without considering the consequences (v. 3). They have the form of religion (offering sacrifices and prayers), but their hearts are far from Yahweh and therefore he refuses to listen to their prayers. Verse 15 says that the people's hands are full of bloodshed, either from their sacrifices or, more likely, in the literal sense, by allowing orphans, widows, and other poor people to be treated unjustly. In spite of their reprehensible behavior, some of Yahweh's people will be delivered and become righteous. The names for God, the Lord God of Hosts and the Mighty One of Israel, reinforce the certainty that these things will be accomplished.

Judgment. Chapters 2–4 are in the form of an inclusio: The beginning (2:1–4) and end (4:2–6) deal with the future prospects of Judah and Jerusalem, whereas the middle section (2:5–4:1) concerns the present, disgraceful condition of Jerusalem. The land is filled with influences from the East (v. 6); there are soothsayers (v. 6) and idol worshipers (v. 8). God will bring destruction and punishment so that the people will finally turn to him. The key verse in this section on restoration is 4:4, which states that Yahweh will purge Jerusalem of filth and bloodshed by the spirit of judgment and burning.

Chapters 5–12 contain a message very similar to the preceding one, but describe in more detail the series of purgings and deliverances that will result in the final restoration of the nation. These chapters form a palistrophe (a literary structure in which the features in the first half of the story correspond to features in the second half), arranged as follows:

- a) The Song of the Vineyard [essentially destruction] (5:1–7)
  - b) Six "woe" oracles pronounced upon the wicked (5:8–24)
    - c) "The raised hand of God" oracles culminating in destruction by Assyria (5:25–30)
      - d) The Isaianic Memoir (6:1–9:6)
    - c′) Four "the raised hand of God" oracles culminating in destruction by Assyria (9:7–10:4)
  - b′) "Woe" oracles pronounced upon Assyria, which give rise to the restoration of Judah (10:5–11:16)

The structure of this section emphasizes the central portion of the polystrophe, which contains Isaiah's call and commissioning (chap. 6). God used Isaiah as his spokesman to the nation. His message contains both judgment and subsequent restoration if the nation will trust in Yahweh. In actuality, however, only a remnant will turn back to Yahweh. The key verses of the Isaianic Memoir are 6:12–13, which mention two different purgings (namely, the Syro-Ephraimite War in 734–732 B.C. and the destruction by Sennacherib in 701 B.C.), from which will emerge a remnant called, in verse 13, the "holy seed." This remnant will be led by a future deliverer who, in the course of history, turns out to be the Messiah, the one of whom Christ claims to be the fulfillment. It would appear, according to the Isaianic Memoir, that restoration will immediately follow Assyria's defeat, but in actual fact the entire program, to be concluded by the rule of a future deliverer from the line of David, is still futuristic, even from our perspective.

The theme of judgment is continued in chapters 13–27, which contain oracles against the foreign nations. Isaiah 11:10 mentions that nations will rally to the Root of Jesse, but before this can happen they need to undergo a cleansing process similar to that of Judah. Chapters 13–27 specify that a cleansing will occur among the foreign nations so that they will turn to Yahweh. This section concludes with what is generally known as "The Little Apocalypse" (chaps. 24–27), in which Yahweh is pictured as pouring out judgment upon the whole earth, following which he prepares a banquet for those who are left (25:6) and establishes a kingdom of peace and safety for the righteous ones.

Chapters 28–35 contain a mixture of oracles of judgment and deliverance, warning listeners that even though Yahweh's people (both Israel and Judah) enjoy special consideration as a result of his covenant with them, they nevertheless will be purged through punishment, just like the other nations. The message of punishment and restoration is repeated again and again, emphasizing that only a remnant will be delivered (28:5, 16, 23–29; 35:10). The idea of a remnant had to have been a new theological concept for the nation of Israel. In the past Yahweh had worked with the people as a national unity, but now each person was required to maintain a proper inward attitude in order to be pleasing to Yahweh. Mere nationality could not guarantee favor with God; a new heart was necessary, one whose trust and belief in Yahweh would result in changed behavior. This is why Yahweh repeatedly directs them to look after the poor orphans and widows, for this would demonstrate a genuinely changed life.

Though there have been many suggestions as to why chapters 36–39 were added here, it seems most reasonable, in accordance with the theology of the book, that it provides a suitable illustration of dependence upon Yahweh that would be required of the remnant mentioned so often by Isaiah. Hezekiah both positively and negatively exemplifies this dependence upon Yahweh. As a positive example, Hezekiah trusts in Yahweh to deliver Jerusalem from the armies of Sennacherib (chaps. 36–37). This is almost certainly why the author carefully omits Hezekiah's attempts to pay off Sennacherib (2 Kings 18:13–16) and, instead, emphasizes Hezekiah's prayer and Yahweh's answer of deliverance for Jerusalem. The second illustration of dependence upon Yahweh is seen in chapter 38, when Hezekiah prays for deliverance from his illness and God graciously does so. As a negative example, however, Hezekiah demonstrates a lack of dependence upon Yahweh when he became proud and sought to impress the emissaries from Babylon. Hezekiah's punishment appears particularly harsh, except when we realize that it is representative of the severe consequences for all those who do not place their trust in Yahweh. If the nation of Israel at first thought that Hezekiah was their future deliverer, in retrospect they must have realized that he would not bring in this kingdom of peace, prosperity, and righteousness, and that they must look for another.

Comfort. There has been much disagreement as to whether the Book of Isaiah was written by two or more authors, primarily because of the mention of Cyrus about 150 years before his birth. To further support dual authorship, it has been argued that the basic nature of prophetic material is to call for repentance or to warn against judgment in the immediate future, since calling for action in the present against some distant judgment would be of little value. It is a mistake, however, to define prophecy so narrowly, for unless the prophet is able to pronounce the ultimate consequences of the people's actions, his message is of little value. In any case, there is no question that the final form of the book was intended to be understood as a unity. In fact, the strongest theological point supporting unity can be found in 41:21–29, where Yahweh argues that the real test of divinity is whether he is able to control and predict the future. Yahweh claims that he is the only true God because he is the one who planned history from the beginning and is thereby able to tell the Israelites what will transpire in the future. Yahweh forces the issue even further: If he is not able to announce future events, he is no different than the other false gods.

It seems best to divide chapters 40–66 into three units of eight chapters (40–48, 49–57, 58–66), according to the recurring refrain at the end of each, "There is no peace, says the LORD, for the wicked" (48:22, and cf. 57:21; this refrain is greatly expanded at the end of the book, 66:24).

Chapters 40–48 offer promise of deliverance. Beyond the statement in 39:6 that Israel would be taken captive to Babylon, there is little information given. Instead the author emphasizes that Yahweh will bring them back to their land through his servant Cyrus (44:28–45:7). During the Babylonian captivity, the Israelites no doubt felt abandoned by Yahweh and fearful that the covenant with him had been annulled because of their wickedness. Isaiah 40–48 therefore begins with Yahweh's assurance that Israel had been punished sufficiently for her sins (40:2) and that he is willing (41:8–16) and able (40:12–31) to bring his people back to the promised land. Yahweh draws a very strong contrast between the "former things" (punishment and exile) and the "latter things" (deliverance from exile). He claims that he alone directed history to prepare the way for Israel's emergence from captivity, in a manner that no one would have ever imagined (48:7)—by guiding a Persian king named Cyrus to do Yahweh's will (41:2–4, 25; 44:28–45:7; 45:13; 46:11; 48:14–15). It is plausible that Yahweh's servant described in the first servant song (42:1–9) is Cyrus but, once again, he is only Yahweh's tool, not the future deliverer whom the people should continue to expect. According to 48:4–11, Yahweh foretold events far in advance and directed history in such a way that the hard-hearted Israelites could not claim to have been delivered by their idols; the people were instead to serve as his witnesses (43:10, 12; 44:8). One of the major theological concepts Yahweh wished to convey to the Israelites is that he will not share his glory with another, for Yahweh, and no one else, had delivered his people (43:11, 13; 44:8; 45:5; 47:10).

Chapters 49–57 make it clear that Zion will be restored through Yahweh's servant. Three of the four "servant songs" are recorded here (49:1–7; 50:4–9; 52:13–53:12). The key to understanding the flow of thought in this passage, 51:18, states that Yahweh looked among all the sons of Israel and could find no one to lead the nation, to take her by the hand and lead her to victory. To accomplish this, Yahweh must raise up his own servant, before whom will appear a forerunner to announce the coming deliverance. This servant, a suffering servant, will apparently have a part in their purification. He will be the long awaited future deliverer described in chapters 9, 11, and 32 and ultimately fulfilled in Christ, the Messiah. Israel was intended to be a light to the nations but had failed miserably. Yahweh will use this servant to bring light to the nations (49:6, 26; 52:10); through Israel's deliverance Yahweh will be glorified and the nations will finally learn how truly awesome and powerful he is. After the final "servant song," there is a significant change in the flow of the passage; the emphasis hereafter is on the restoration and glorification of the nation of Israel. The author continues to emphasize that the promised deliverance is only for those who have a personal belief and trust in Yahweh (49:23; 50:10; 51:7–11; 55:1–11; 56:1–8). Isaiah 54:7–8 stresses the fact that Yahweh turned away from Israel only for a brief moment and then, with great compassion, delivered her and brought her back to himself. The section closes with a plea to accept Yahweh's salvation and come to him while he may be found. This invitation is open to anyone who is willing to trust in Yahweh and live righteously, but for those who are not willing to live righteously there will be no peace.

Chapters 58–66 begin with a description of the proper way to come to Yahweh. For him to heed prayers and fastings and move into action, the people's hearts must be open and obedient to him, and their lives must demonstrate true righteousness, without which, ritual fastings will accomplish nothing. Yahweh makes it clear that it is sin that separates the people from him, and that he is in no way lacking in power (59:1–2). The flow of thought changes abruptly in 59:15, when Yahweh sees the desperate conditions of his people and decides it is time to intervene. However, Yahweh will not deliver everyone; according to verse 20, only those who turn from their transgressions will be delivered. Yahweh is pictured as the divine warrior coming powerfully to the aid of his people. The next several chapters look forward to Zion's restoration, during which time the prosperity and glory of Jerusalem will be evident to all. The inhabitants of Jerusalem will no longer remember their former rejection, but will rejoice in their new status. Yahweh will protect his servants (65:13–16) and create new heavens and a new earth (65:17–20), in which there will be peace and safety. Yahweh's original intention of letting Israel serve as a light to the nations will now finally be fulfilled; nations will come to learn about Yahweh's glory and will declare it to yet other nations. It is interesting to note that the book ends almost as it began: The commencement announces judgment upon those who rebel against Yahweh and the conclusion pictures the punishment of transgressors against Yahweh.

The New Testament's Use of the Book of Isaiah. The Book of Isaiah is quoted or alluded to approximately 419 times in the New Testament, which is more than any other book (the psalms are next closest, about 414 times). It appears that most of the New Testament authors use either the Septuagint's translation of Isaiah, or some form or slight modification of it. Two New Testament authors who are noteworthy for either not using the Septuagint's translation or modifying it significantly are Matthew (1:23; 8:17; 11:5; 12:18–21; 15:8–9; 24:29) and John (1:23; 6:45; 12:40). The passage from the Book of Isaiah that is quoted most often in the New Testament, in full or in part, is Isaiah 6:9–10 (Matt. 13:14–15; Mark 4:12; Luke 8:10; John 12:40; Acts 28:26–27). It refers to the hard hearts of the people of Israel, a condition apparently little changed in the seven hundred years until the time of Jesus, who was able to quote this passage from Isaiah with equal relevance. The next most quoted passages from Isaiah are 40:3 (Matt. 3:3; Mark 1:3; John 1:23) and 56:7 (Matt. 21:13; Mark 11:17; Luke 19:46). The former is used by the Gospel writers to refer to John the Baptist, who preceded Jesus and prepared the way for him. In the Old Testament this verse specifically proclaims God's deliverance of the exiles from Babylon, but it was easily applied to the spiritual deliverance Jesus was to accomplish. Isaiah 56:7 foresees a time when people from all nations will come and worship the one true God, and their worship will be acceptable to Yahweh. The New Testament authors announce that salvation is open to every one, no matter their nationality or background, which is a decisive fulfillment of this promise. In general these three examples (6:9–10; 40:3; 56:7) indicate the various ways New Testament writers employ an Old Testament passage: (1) it speaks to a situation that has remained unchanged through history and thus is still applicable to the New Testament audience (6:9–10); (2) it speaks to significantly different circumstances, but the New Testament writer sees connections between the two occasions and reapplies the Old Testament passage to the present (40:3); (3) it is not fulfilled in the historical context of the author but is expected to have a future fulfillment (56:7).

PAUL D. WEGNER

See also ISRAEL; PROPHET, PROPHETESS, PROPHECY.

Bibliography. R. E. Clements, *Int* 36 (1982): 117–29; idem, *Isaiah 1–39;* idem, *JSOT* 31 (1985): 95–113; W. J. Dumbrell, *Tyn Bul* 36 (1985): 111–28; W. S. LaSor, et al., *Old Testament Survey: The Message, Form, and Background of the Old Testament;* J. N. Oswalt, *The Book of Isaiah Chapters 1–39;* J. J. M. Roberts, *Int* 36 (1982): 130–43; N. Whybray, *Isaiah 40–66;* H. Wildberger, *Isaiah 1–12;* J. T. Willis, *Isaiah.*

Israel. ***The Name and People.*** Jacob, grandson of Abraham, was named Israel after he had wrestled with God (Gen. 32:28). This name is a combination of the Hebrew words for "wrestle" and "God" (because *sārêtā* [you have wrestled] with God [*'el*] and men you will be called *yiśrā'ēl*). When Jacob had returned to Canaan, God commanded him to settle in Bethel; there God appeared to Jacob again and repeated that his name was no longer Jacob but Israel. This confirmation of the naming was followed by God confirming his covenant with Jacob (Gen. 35:9–12), emphasizing specific elements of the covenant he had made with Abraham (Gen. 17:1–8). The name, expressing the concept of wrestling, clinging firmly to God, and overcoming, and God's confirming of his covenant with Jacob, indicates that Israel is to be understood as Jacob's covenant name. The name spoke of his being bound with a bond of life and love to God. His descendants were at times referred to as Hebrews (Gen. 39:14, 17; 40:15; 41:12), and when they were slaves in Egypt (Exod. 1:15; 2:13), and occasionally in other contexts (e.g., Deut. 15:12; 1 Sam. 4:6; Isa. 36:11; Jer. 34:9, 14). Eventually they were known as Jews (first mentioned in Jer. 32:12). The use of these references, "Hebrew" and "Jew," indicated that among the nations, Abraham and Jacob's descendants were thus known nationally and/or ethnically. The name "Israel," however, referred to Jacob's descendants' spiritual, covenantal, and religious heritage. The name "Israel" spoke of the ethnic or national Hebrews' and Jews' unique relationship with God. There was a time when the name was not used to refer to all of Jacob's descendants because after the division of the tribes, the northern ten tribes were known as Israel and the southern tribes as Judah. After the exile it was used again to refer to the entire community.

The Old Testament is often considered to be specifically a record of Israel's national history, of its unique religion, and of its hopes for the future. The Scriptures are also used as a source for understanding God's redemptive activities on behalf of and goals for Israel. While it is true that these are aspects of the Old Testament record, the more inclusive message is to reveal how God sovereignly chose to prepare and use Israel as his unique mediatorial agent. He unfolded his kingdom plan on behalf of all races, nations, peoples, and ethnic groups.

God's Purposes. God's purpose for electing Israel can be divided into five interrelated and correlated themes.

First, Israel was to, and did, bring the Messiah to Israel and to the nations of the world. God had assured Adam and Eve that the seed of the woman would crush Satan's head and thereby undo the disobedience, sinfulness, and corruption resulting from their deviation from God and their breaking of the covenant. Of Noah's progeny, Shem was identified as the seed-bearing progenitor (Gen. 9:24–27). Then Abram/Abraham was called and told by God that through him all nations were to be blessed (Gen. 12:3). It was to be through Abraham's seed (Gen. 15:5; 17:1–8) that God would bring in the Messiah and the sure redemptive victory over Satan, sin, and its effects. This seed line was narrowed to Isaac, Jacob/Israel, Judah, and David. Meanwhile all of Abraham's seed was to serve as light to the peoples of the world (Isa. 9:2–7; 42:6; 49:6).

Second, inseparably related to this first and all-inclusive purpose, was Israel's divinely determined role to give, uphold, and preserve the Scriptures, both the Old and New Testaments. This written Word is the sure, infallible record of how God created the cosmos, and how he purposed to bring redemption and restoration to the cosmos and its inhabitants. Without this written word there would be no record of what God had done, promised, and carried out. Once Israel was formed as a people under Moses' mediatorial leadership, this first part of the word was written by him; and it was added to by other Israelite writers, historians, poets, sages, and prophets. Thus, Israel's divinely determined purpose was to bring the eternal living Word, Jesus Christ (John 1:1–3), and the inspired, inerrant, and infallible written word to all the nations of the world—including themselves.

Third, Israel, by God's determinate counsel, was given the unique role of being a mediatorial people. God called Abraham from a "corner" of the then known world to place him in the center among the nations. There, with smaller nations as near neighbors, Syria, Ammon, Moab, Edom, Philistia, Tyre, Sidon, and larger ones beyond, the Arabians, Egyptian, Hittite, Assyrian, and Babylonian, Israel was made to be a peculiar treasure, to be a kingdom, a priestly people, and a holy nation (Exod. 19:4–6). This multifaceted role was not just simply for Israel's sake. Israel was elected, empowered, qualified, and given the opportunity in centrally located Canaan to mediate between God and the nations. This mediatorial work was to be carried out through living according to the word God had given so that nations would take note of and desire to join in the blessing, wonder, and glory of life with and under his beneficient reign (Isa. 2:1–5; Mic. 4:1–5). Israel's initial purpose was not to witness verbally, but to exhibit the rich blessedness of covenantal life. The non-Israelite, drawn to Israel in this way, was expected to learn and submit to God's revealed demands. Such was the case with Rahab (Josh. 2:9–13), Ruth (Ruth 1:16–18), and Uriah (2 Sam. 11:6, 11). They were neither Hebrew nor Jew but became true citizens of Israel, God's covenant people.

Fourth, God called, elected, and declared that Israel as a people were to be a kingdom (Exod. 19:6). Moses emphatically declared they were chosen because of no merit of their own. God chose Israel to be his covenant/kingdom people because he loved them with a gracious love (Deut. 7:7). Israel, however, had its responsibilities placed before it. The people had to acknowledge and exhibit in the totality of their lives that God was their one and only King. No other gods were to be recognized as their sovereign ruler or as their source of life and its inclusive blessings. Israel was to know itself as a theocracy under the reign of God. As such they were called to be royal, loving, obedient, serving people.

Israel had the duty, according to God's purposes, to demonstrate to itself, its children, its non-Israelite neighbors living within Canaan's borders, and surrounding nations, how, as a redeemed, covenantal serving people, they should live as a theocratic kingdom. This could only be done by faithfully carrying out the three creation covenant mandates: the spiritual, the social, and the cultural.

The spiritual mandate called for loving fellowship with God and an adoring worship that would glorify the sovereign covenant Lord. Fellowship and worship were to be carried out in families (e.g., Passover, Exod. 12) but particularly in the courts of the tabernacle and temple. The people, old and young, were to be called together, and as an assembly were to pay homage to their Lord. Means for the assembly's worship were prescribed. The tabernacle and later the temple, giving symbolic and typological expression to the the covenant promise, "I am your God, I am with you," was to be the central place of worship (Deut. 12:1–14). Moses later told the people they could assemble for worship around local altars at which priests officiated (Deut. 12:15–19). Yahweh provided the priesthood and the prescribed sacrifices to enable the assembly to worship as a devout kingdom people. Some sacrifices were to be offered daily (Lev. 6:1–8), others at appropriate times (feasts or for specific situations); the Sabbath was to be the day of no work but to be the time of worship for the entire assembly. God repeatedly reminded his people that they were not to assemble around and worship other gods because he was a jealous Lord (Deut. 4:15–24; 13:1–18). Nor were the people to worship as they saw fit (Deut. 12:8); they were to keep the basic principles for obeying and carrying out the spiritual mandate as these were stated in the first four commandments.

God called Israel as a covenant community to live and exhibit kingdom life to the world. Israel was to obey and carry out the creation covenant social mandate. Commandments 5–7 provided basic guidelines. Within the community, family life was to be fundamental; parents were to teach, train, and discipline their children (Deut. 6:4–9; Ps. 78:1–8). Children were to respond to parents with honor and dignity. Marriage with noncovenant people was strictly forbidden (Deut. 7:1–6). However, those who were not biological descendants of Abraham could be taken as mates if they became members of the Israelite community. Procreation was to be considered a divine ordinance for thus seed would come forth to continue covenantal service within the theocracy. Abuse of sexual potential was strictly forbidden as was adultery.

Israel as a holy nation was to exhibit the kingdom of God to the world by heeding and carrying out the creation covenant cultural mandate. Prerequisites were their activities as a worshiping assembly and their communal life expressed by their mutual love and joy in marriage, family, clan, and entire covenant community. God's purpose for Israel as a holy nation was that they be totally separated from heathen practices spiritually, socially, and culturally and be consecrated to their sovereign Lord who had commanded "Be holy because I, the LORD your God, am holy" (Lev. 19:2). Israel, the holy nation, was to be organized politically. Yahweh was their sovereign King. Elders and judges had to carry out administrative and judicial duties; priests had to assist particularly in regard to health laws.

Israel, to meet the challenge of being a holy, politically organized, governed, and law-abiding nation, was called to live separately among the nations. God gave them Canaan as their land, not first of all for their own advancement and enjoyment but to enable Israel to serve as the mediatorial nation in the midst of the nations. Each tribe and clan was given an inheritance from which they were to remove all Canaanite inhabitants so that they could live without unholy pressures and truly be free to live up to God's purposes for them. Israel was promised prosperity but these material blessings were to be received as means to serve. Thus, as good stewards, they could develop and beautify their natural surroundings and with skill produce materials that would enhance the beauty of their environment. The tabernacle and temple were examples of highly developed cultural craftsmanship.

Fifth, to work out his purposes for the world under sin, God chose Israel to be his covenantal servants who were to live by faith and demonstrate it to the nations. Noah and Abraham exercised faith as did many others (Heb. 11). This faith included knowing the Lord, trusting in him, and living a life of courage and hope. This faith was inseparable from obedience to all of God's revealed will. Through obedience Israel would exhibit to its offspring and neighbors what service to God entailed. Indeed, the life of faith, obedience, and service would fulfill the purposes God had in mind and revealed to them. In this way, Israel would serve mediatorially as a messianic people and in time bring forth the Messiah himself, receive and give to the world God's inscripturated word, and show that the kingdom of God included all of life's activities and relationships.

Israel's Privileges. In the economy of God's kingdom, privileges involve responsibilities. Israel, called and enabled to carry out God's purposes, was given privileges commensurate and in correlation with the responsibilities given them. These privileges were many.

First, it was Israel's privilege to represent and mirror the Sovereign of the cosmos to the nations. Israel's privilege was to serve! Self-serving and self-aggrandizement were entirely contrary to the responsibilities and privileges given to the descendants of Jacob. The people, as an assembly, as a community, and as a nation, were never to consider themselves *only* as objects of God's election, love, and providential goodness; they were to consider themselves basically as subjects called for the purpose of serving. In service according to God's purposes, Israel would be honored by the privileges made available to them.

Second, it was Israel's privilege to be in a unique covenantal relationship with God. God, referring to himself as the Husband (Jer. 31:33) and Israel as his precious possession whom he had brought to himself, implied Israel was his bride (Exod. 19:4–6). This covenantal/spiritual marriage relationship was a bond of life and love God would not break. He would not divorce her though he would send her away for a time (Isa. 50:1). Israel had assured security in the love, goodness, and faithfulness of God.

Third, Israel had unique access to God. God dwelt in the midst of his people. First by Moses and then via the priests, the people could come into the presence of God. He communed with them, receiving their sacrifices, praises, and prayers. He spoke to them directly, through his written Word read to the people, and by the prophets. In this intimate relationship, Israel could know the character of their God. He was sovereign and all-powerful; he declared and showed himself to be compassionate, gracious, patient, full of love, faithful, forgiving, righteous, and just (Exod. 34:6–7; Num. 14:17–18; Ps. 103:8–13; Jon. 4:2–3).

Fourth, it was Israel's privilege to have a land and cultural blessings that God had prepared for them by Canaanite endeavors. It was a land with flourishing cities, houses filled with good things, wells providing water, productive vineyards, and fruitful orchards (Deut. 6:10–12). This promised land was their inheritance to be possessed for service and not to be occupied for self-satisfaction and feelings of superiority. The land was never to be seen as a prize or as a possession without regard for the reasons that it was given: to be central among the nations so that the messianic light of God's kingdom would shine out to all nations. In this land, then, Israel had the privilege of carrying out its spiritual, social, and cultural mandates. It was to be a place of rest, prosperity, security, and peace; Israel thus had the privilege of portraying to all nations what the redeemed and restored cosmos would be like. By its serene, serving life Israel could portray hope for a blessed future for peoples of all nations who joined them in faith, obedience, and service to God, thus bringing glory to the cosmic King.

Fifth, within their promised land and to the nations beyond, Israel had the privilege of proclaiming, as no other could, that God reigned. This message was one of assurance for present and future times. The Sovereign God was in control and directed all the affairs of the cosmos, of the nations, and of individuals. Moses sang, "The LORD will reign forever and ever" (Exod. 15:18). The psalmists sang it (Pss. 93:1–2; 97:1; 99:1–5). The prophets proclaimed it to Israel (Isa. 52:8) and to the nations (Obad. 1, 21).

Sixth, Israel was given promises concerning its continuation as a people. This privilege had the potential of breeding a false security that irrespective of circumstances, Israel as a nation could expect to endure throughout all ages. Inseparably involved, however, with this tremendous privilege was the demand that the people live by faith, obediently and in the service of God and his purposes concerning his enduring kingdom.

Israel's Response. Biblical revelation records how Israel responded to its call to believe, obey, and serve God's purposes for Jacob's descendant's and to the privileges given so that God's purposes could be fulfilled. The account is a revelation of faithfulness, obedience, and service on the part of varying numbers of the people in various ways, and unfaithfulness, disobedience, and lack of service, often on the part of most of the people. God, however, remained faithful and steadfast in working out his kingdom, covenantal, and mediatorial plan. He did so by blessing, by withholding blessings, and by executing, in a mitigated way, the curse of the covenant. Israel was never completely destroyed as a community although it suffered severely when the warnings Moses had enunciated (Deut. 28–29) went unheeded. God humiliated Israel by bringing famines, hardships, military defeats, foreign oppressions, and eventually exile.

The tensions between covenantal living and violations of it were starkly present among Jacob's twelve sons. Ten brothers sold Joseph into slavery and lied about his disappearance. Judah had sex with a woman he considered a prostitute (Gen. 38) while Joseph refused the sexual temptations in Egypt. In spite of his humiliations he remained faithful and served his covenant Lord. Jacob referred to various other sins of his sons (Gen. 49:4, 5, 17, 27). Yet in spite of Judah's failings he was prophesied to be a forbear of the Messiah Israel was to bring into the world (Gen. 49:8–12). It was Joseph, richly blessed (Gen. 49:22–26), who acknowledged God's faithfulness and sovereign providential guidance (Gen. 50:19–20).

Israel as a growing community in Egypt suffered as slaves; there is little evidence of conscious obedience and service to Yahweh once Joseph had died, except for the midwives who spared Moses (Exod. 1). Ready to be freed as slaves under Moses' leadership and spontaneous in vows to obey and serve Yahweh as a covenant community and nation (Exod. 19:8; 24:3, 7), Israel's sons and daughters soon exhibited their fickleness and hankering for life in Egypt (Exod. 32:2–8). Moses' intercession was heard and Israel was made to know that God was a faithful, covenant-keeping God whose jealously preserved his character and his people (Exod. 34:5–14).

Once Israel had received the tabernacle, the Aaronic priesthood, and the prescriptions for sacrifices and feasts, the people had every opportunity to be a believing, obeying, worshiping, serving community and theocratic nation. But there were murmurings and rebellions (Num. 11:1; 12:1–2; 14:1–4; 16:1–3; 21:4–5); two of the twelve spies trusted in and honored God (Num. 13); ten did not. Nor did the nation as a whole. When under Moses and Joshua's leadership the Transjordan was conquered, God had Moses reveal to the people that he, the covenant Sovereign of earth and heaven, called upon and demanded the people to love, obey, worship, and serve as a devout covenant people. Joshua, divinely ordained, was an effective military leader. Israel as a nation was given the promised land, cultivated, built up, and productive.

After Joshua's death, the people repeatedly broke covenant with God. They were humiliated by military defeats and economic hardships. Ever faithful, God moved his people to acknowledge him by means of these hardships and provided leaders so that the people had freedom and prosperity again. Throughout the turbulent times of the judges, from Othniel to Samuel, God continued to work out his messianic purposes. The judges, Boaz and Ruth, and Samuel, the judge/prophet, stand out.

God's faithfulness in regard to his messianic purposes and goals was dramatically revealed in the time of David and Solomon. David, a descendant of Judah, of the seedline of Abraham and Shem, was anointed and enthroned. David, the poet and prophet, in spite of his sins, was a man after God's heart. He conquered and reigned over the entire territory God had promised to Abraham (2 Sam. 8:1–14). His reign is described as just and right (2 Sam. 8:15). The covenant was confirmed and expanded with specifics concerning covenant seed and an eternal dynasty (2 Sam.

7:1–28). His son Solomon carried out the plans David made for the temple and worship. Solomon exhibited wisdom (1 Kings 10:1–13) and the splendor of the theocratic monarchy was unsurpassed (1 Kings 10:14–29). Psalm 72 expresses the glory of the messianic kingdom, as initially realized under David and Solomon and to be fully and finally realized under Jesus Christ.

The prophetic office served Yahweh's purposes. Moses had been a prophet par excellence; Samuel fulfilled a key role in anointing David (1 Sam. 16:13) and Nathan pronounced one of the most significant prophecies when he addressed David, assuring him that a descendant would reign, that David's throne and kingdom would last forever. In this prophecy no reference is made to the nation of Israel itself but rather to the central person, David, and to his seed. Israel would provide the context but the central thrust was on the house of David, his throne, and the kingdom God was to bring to ever fuller manifestation.

The high points, as exhibited in the covenant with David, his victories, his just and righteous reign, the wisdom of Solomon and grandeur of his throne and kingdom, were not maintained. God's purposes did not diminish; the privileges given to the royal house of David were initially expanded. But Solomon in his later years and the majority of the Davidic dynasty did not remain faithful covenant and kingdom believers and obedient servants. A major part of the theocratic nation seceded and took the name "Israel." The tribes of Judah, Simeon, and Benjamin constituted the ongoing environment in which God continued to work out his purposes. The low point came after Israel was deported into exile in 722 B.C. (2 Kings 17:21–23). A small remnant from Judah fled to Egypt (Jer. 41:16–18; 44:26).

The prophets continued to speak God's words of both warning and promise. Judah particularly was repeatedly reminded that God's kingdom and covenant would continue; the promise of the messianic mediator was repeated before (Isaiah and Micah) and during (Ezekiel and Daniel) the exile. The descendants of Jacob, the Israelite covenant community, whether in homeland or in exile, would continue so that God's covenant promises concerning the conquering seed, as represented by the Davidic dynasty, and concerning his all-encompassing kingdom would in time be realized. Thus the nation of Israel was not the central focus; God's purposes to be realized through Israel were. Israel, as a people, would bring in the Messiah.

After the exile, the descendants of Jacob, often referred to as Jews rather than Israelites, formed a social and religious community. The efforts to be a worshiping, called-out people were diminished by legalistic scribal and priestly activities and by various fanatic attempts that failed to transform the people living in Palestine into a nation again. Thus, while Israel as a nation no longer functioned, it did as a social and religious community. In that setting the ultimate purpose for Israel's call and existence was fully realized in Jesus, even as God had purposed. Forty years, the same period of time Israel wandered in the desert, after Jesus ascended to reign over the kingdom, the Israelite community, temple, and sacrificial system were removed. The promise God made to Adam and Eve, repeated to Abraham, Judah, and David concerning the conquering, reigning Seed of the woman was fully kept. Israel, in spite of its repeated acts of unbelief, disobedience, and rebellion, fulfilled the purposes for which God had called and prepared it.

Contemporary Issues Regarding Israel. The relationship of Israel to the Scriptures is definite. Both the Old and New Testaments were written by people who were known to be of Israelite nativity. The entire Bible is God's gift to the world via the people of Israel—whether one wishes to refer to the Bible as Hebrew (Old Testament) and Jewish (New Testament). The fact remains, the entire Bible was given by God through the believing, obeying, and serving covenant community. Moses and the historical, poetic, wisdom, and prophetic writers were covenant servants; equally so were the New Testament evangelists, historical epistolary, and apocalyptic writers. Serious differences of views pertain, however, concerning the nature of the entire Bible. Is it a record of Israel's origins, existence, and development as a nation? In other words, is the Bible a strictly human book or is it a divinely inspired book that has the message of divine creation, humanity's fall, God's redemptive and restorative program, and his enduring kingdom to and initially carried out largely by Israel? The biblical account is clear and definite: Israel was God's instrument by which the Bible was given to the entire world.

The biblical record concerning Israel's origin is clear. Scholars, working in the areas of Near Eastern archaeology and historical criticism have offered variant views. That Israel as a body of approximately two million people lived and served as slaves in Egypt is not accepted by many such scholars. That there is some evidence that a group of Semitic people lived and were enslaved in Egypt is generally accepted. But the manner and time of the dramatic exodus event are not accepted as historically or archaeologically verifiable. Likewise, the Sinai experience, the forty-year wandering in the wilderness, and the military conquest of Canaan have been seriously doubted. Alternate views are projected, such as a small group that escaped from slavery in Egypt, joining other groups, gradually infiltrated Canaan and took on many of its ways of life. The development of Israel as a nation has been seen as a gradual formation of a league of tribes of various origins. The evidence presented by archaeologists and historical critics has not bee accepted by many scholars, particularly evangelical, conservative scholars. These scholars, however, have shown that archaeological and scientific historical studies do not contradict the biblical record but illumine it.

A third debated issue in relation to Israel, and closely related to the two already mentioned, is the origin and nature of Israel's religion. Reference is made particularly to Israel's beliefs, worship patterns, and practices. The Scriptures testify to Israel's faith as revealed by God and its worship activities directed by him. With the aid of scholars who have studied Israel's social structures and psychological attitudes, students of Israel's surrounding nations and their religions have attempted to demonstrate that much of what Israel practiced religiously was adopted from those of the peoples around them. Israel did not live in isolation from its neighbors; it had various religious practices that were outwardly similar, such as portable shrines, systems of sacrifice, and religious objects such as altars. Israel's religion was unique, however, in origin and practice. God revealed himself directly to Abraham, as he had done to Adam and Noah. He especially revealed himself as a covenant Lord to them and this covenantal relationship with all its ramifications and implications was explicated in detail by God through his appointed mediatorial agents. Israel's faith and religious life and activities had their origin in revelation, not in borrowing or in religious perceptions. It must be added, however, that Israel was not always faithful to their sovereign covenant Lord. There was much vacillation in its loyalty to him and there is much evidence of disobedience as exhibited in Israel's following of their neighbors' detestable idolatrous practices.

Much discussion is involved in the issue of Israel and the land. That God promised Abraham and his progeny a land as their possession cannot be doubted. But did God unconditionally promise that it would be an eternal possession? Many evangelical Christians believe this is the case; they speak of the Palestinian covenant on the basis of their interpretation of Deuteronomy 28. Other equally sincere evangelical biblical students point to five important qualifying factors. First, Moses emphatically stated that obedience was a basic requirement to inherit the land and to remain blessed possessors (Deut. 4:25–31; 28:15–68). Second, the term translated "everlasting" is often translated correctly "for a long time," "for ages." The term cannot mean eternal, in the sense of never-ending, for at the Lord's return at the end of time, the order of the renewed heavens and earth will be ushered in. Third, God fulfilled his promises regarding the land and its extent at the time of David and Solomon (2 Sam. 8:1–4; 1 Chron. 18:1–13; 1 Kings 4:20–21; Ps. 72:8). Fourth, the prophetic promise of a return to the land after the exile was fulfilled when a remnant returned (Ezra 2). Fifth, the New Testament does not refer to Israel as a nation possessing the land forever; rather, it speaks of Abraham's believing covenant offspring inheriting the world (Rom. 4:13).

Another issue concerns the interpretation of prophecies concerning Israel. This issue is closely related to Israel's relationship to the land, the church, and the millennium (Rev. 20). The following factors must be kept in mind. The prophets spoke of a future for Israel. They did not, however, always refer to Israel as a political entity, an organized nation. The concept of the remnant is dominant, particularly of Israel as a believing covenant community. Furthermore, when the prophets spoke to their contemporaries they did so in terms the people at that time understood. Hence, when prophets spoke of the wonderful future of Yahweh's covenant people, they did so in simple urban, pastoral, agricultural, and natural (nature) terms (Isa. 35). Strict literal interpretation, often controlled by certain presuppositions regarding Israel as a political, national entity, must be used very discretely if not completely avoided.

Another specific issue concerns the relationship of Israel and the New Testament church. On the basis of a too literal interpretation of Old Testament prophecies concerning Israel and maintaining the view that New Testament writers referred to a politically organized national entity rather than to the believing covenant community, a strict separation is posited between Israel as a nation and the non-Jewish New Testament covenant community of believers, the church. It is believed that God has two distinct people in mind with a distinctly separate program for each. Many biblical scholars have difficulties with this separation. Some of the points stated in preceding paragraphs should be kept in mind. Moreover, Jesus never spoke of Israel's continuation as a politically separate religiously oriented nation; rather, he spoke of God's all-encompassing kingdom. And while it is true Paul spoke of his ethnic people as "the people of Israel" (Rom. 9:3–5), he spoke of all true believers in Jesus Christ as Abraham's seed, heirs according to the promise made to Abraham's descendants (Gal. 3:28). He also wrote of all believers, Gentiles as well as ethnic Jewish people who believed in Jesus Christ, as Israel (Gal. 6:16). It is therefore believed that Paul, when speaking of his own ethnic people, many of whom did not accept Jesus as the promised Messiah, and of many Gentiles coming to faith, includes all believers, whether they be Jews or Gentiles, to constitute the "all Israel," that is, the unified body, the covenant community of believers (Rom. 11:25–32).

The last issue to be referred to, although others could be included, is Israel's national existence as a millennial kingdom. This issue has many ramifications that cannot be included in this essay. Suffice it to state that John did not write that Israel as a distinct religious national entity would be a separate kingdom for a thousand years. Nor did Jesus say he would return to earth to reign over the Jewish kingdom. In addition, various scholars have pointed out in times past and present that the Israelite kingdom, first as a theocracy and then under the reign of David's dynasty as a monarchy, was a type of the eternal kingdom Jesus is perfecting and will return to the Father (1 Cor. 15:24–28). GERARD VAN GRONINGEN

Bibliography. F. F. Bruce, *Israel and the Nation;* L. A. DeCaro, *Israel Today: Fulfillment of Prophecy?;* A. Gileadi, ed., *Israel's Apostasy and Restoration;* W. Hendrikson, *Israel in Prophecy;* A. W. Kac, *The Rebirth of the State of Israel;* M. Karlberg, *JETS* 31/3 (1988): 257–69; G. E. Ladd, *The Last Things;* H. K. LaRondelle, *The Israel of God in Prophecy;* J. B. Payne, *Encyclopedia of Biblical Prophecy;* P. Richardson, *Israel in the Apostolic Church;* J. F. Walvoord, *Israel in Prophecy;* M. J. Wyngaarden, *The Future of the Kingdom.*

Jj

Jacob. *See* ISRAEL.

James, Theology of. The Letter of James is a practical exhortation, assuming more theology than it teaches. Some claim that the letter has no theology. The validity of this assertion depends on what is meant by "theology." On the one hand, James has little to say about most Christian doctrines, nor does he consistently relate his exhortations to the person of Christ. In fact he mentions Jesus Christ only twice (1:1; 2:2), and only once as the object of belief (2:1). If, then, by theology we mean a system of belief that consistently refers to the person and work of Christ as a major focal point, then the Letter of James does indeed lack a theology.

This is, however, too narrow a definition of "theology." Understood as the set of beliefs that are explicitly stated and implicitly assumed as the basis for its exhortations, theology is very much present in the letter. James, after all, is writing to Christians who already know the basics of the Christian faith; his purpose is to bring their conduct in line with those beliefs. Moreover, we must not overlook the specific theological teaching that is found in James. His letter makes an important contribution to our understanding of issues such as the relationship of faith and works, prayer, the nature of God, and materialism. All these are set in a practical context, but it will be a sad day for the church when such "practical divinity" is not considered theology.

Therefore, while the occasional and homiletical nature of the letter prevents us from sketching a theology of James, we can survey his contribution to several important areas of theology.

God. If we use the word "theology" in its strictest sense, as the doctrine of God, then James certainly has a considerable amount of theology. For James consistently bases the kind of conduct he expects of his readers on his understanding of the nature of God. Christians are to live, James argues, in full consciousness of the character of the God they serve. Thus, it is because God gives "generously without finding fault" that Christians should not hesitate to ask him for wisdom (1:5). The goodness of God's gifts is emphasized in 1:17, where James also stresses the invariability of God's character. God gives everything that is perfect, James asserts, and is incapable of being enticed by evil. Because of this, people are foolish to think that God would ever be the author of their temptation (1:13).

Theology proper is also at the heart of one of the key texts in the letter, 4:4–10. James here indicts his readers for their worldliness and summons them to repentance. Both the indictment and the summons are based on God's character. Because God "jealously longs" for the spirits of those he has redeemed (NIV marg.; cf. also NASB), his people must give themselves wholly to their God; to give our affections to the world is to commit spiritual adultery (v. 4). But because God is also gracious (v. 6), he willingly accepts back those who turn to him in sincere repentance (vv. 7–10).

James, of course, believes that there is only one God (2:19)—"one Lawgiver and Judge" (4:12). Striking, therefore, is James' application of the appellation "Judge" to Jesus Christ (5:7–9). Moreover, while James uses "Lord" to denote Jesus (2:1; 5:7, 8), he uses it also to denote God the Father (3:9; 4:10; 15; 5:4, 10, 11, 15). By speaking this way, James implies that Jesus is God.

Eschatology. Many of James' ethical exhortations find parallels in Jewish and even pagan Greek literature. What makes James' teaching Christian is the eschatological context in which it is set. James warns about the coming judgment (1:10–11; 2:12–13; 3:1; 5:1–6, 9, 12) but also draws attention to the reward that will be given those who have proved faithful in service (1:12; 2:5; 4:10; 5:20). James teaches that this time of judgment and salvation is imminent: "the Lord's coming is near"; "the Judge is standing at the door" (5:8–9). These statements need not be taken to mean that James was sure the Lord would return within his own lifetime. He is teaching, rather, that the time of the coming of the Lord is unknown and that it could, therefore, take place within a very short period of time. As do other New Testament writers, James views the uncertain time of our Lord's return as reason for holy living.

James also refers clearly to the "present" eschatological dimension. Christian existence (1:18; 2:5; 5:3 [probably]). James holds to the same kind of "inaugurated eschatology" typical of the New Testament perspective: the days of the fulfillment of God's promises have begun, but a climax to those days is yet expected. It is the eschatological tension of that "already but not yet" that is the basis for James' ethics.

Faith, Works, and Justification. James' most controversial theological contribution is his teaching about the relationship of faith, works, and justification in chapter 2. He stresses that right belief must be followed by right action (vv. 17, 20, 26). He is worried about people who were confining faith to a verbal profession (v. 19) or to empty, insincere good wishes (vv. 15–16). This faith is dead (vv. 17, 26) and barren (v. 20) and will be of no avail the day of judgment (v. 14). This faith of which James speaks, a faith that people are claiming to have (v. 14), does not correspond to James' own teaching about faith. He views faith as a firm, unwavering commitment to God and Christ (see 2:1) that is tested and refined in trials (1:2, 4) and which grasps the blessings of god in prayer (1:5–8; 5:14–18). These texts show that it is wrong to accuse James of having a "Sub-Christian" or "sub-Pauline" conception of faith. Rather, James and Paul are in complete agreement on this point. As Paul himself says in Galatians 5:6, it is "faith expressing itself through love" that counts before God; so James notes that faith without works is dead.

However, on another point, it is claimed that James and Paul are in disagreement: the place of works in justification. Paul stressed the complete sufficiency of faith for justification: "we maintain that a man is justified by faith apart from observing the law" (Rom. 3:28). James, on the other hand, claims that "a person is justified by what he does and not by faith alone" (2:24). Some see these two perspectives as contradictory, and as representing two different approaches to the question of salvation in the early church. But we are not forced to this radical conclusion. Understood in their own contexts, and with careful attention to the way each is using certain key words, James and Paul can be brought into harmony on this issue. First, Paul and James are combating different problems. Paul is contesting a Jewish tendency to rely on obedience to the law for salvation. James is fighting against an underemphasis on works, an attitude that turned faith into mere doctrinal orthodoxy. Naturally, then, what they say on this matter will be coming from different perspectives.

Second, Paul's claim that a person cannot be justified on the basis of works of the law is speaking about works that precede conversion. James, however, is talking about works that stem from and are produced by faith: works that follow conversion. The works done before a person has faith in Christ and works done as a result of faith in Christ are obviously going to have different roles in salvation.

Third, and most important, the justification that James and Paul are speaking about are different things. Paul uses the Greek verb *dikaioō* ("justify") to depict the dynamic activity of God graciously giving the sinner a new status. The new status is based on the sinner's union with Christ through faith. Thus, for Paul, *dikaioō* is a term that denotes the transfer of a person from the realm of sin and death into the realm of holiness and life. James, however, uses *dikaioō* with a meaning well attested in the Old Testament, in Jewish sources, and in the Gospel of Matthew (cf., e.g., 12:37). James is referring to a verdict that is based on the actual facts of the case: God declaring a person to be righteous on the basis of works as the fruit of faith. While Paul, then, is looking at the beginning of the Christian life, James is looking at its end. Paul makes clear that it is by faith alone that we can enter into a relationship with God. James is teaching that once that relationship is established there must be works flowing from it that will be used by God at the last judgment as evidence of our genuine union with Christ.

The Law. While conflict between James and Paul is usually seen on the matter of justification, the place of the Mosaic law in the Christian life is also an area of difficulty. Paul tends to suggest that Christians are no longer directly under the Mosaic law (Rom. 6:14–15; 7:4; Gal. 5:18). James, on the other hand, calls on Christians to be doers of the law (4:11) and insists that the "whole law" will be the standard of judgment (2:9-12). Quite apart from whether this understanding of Paul's teaching is correct, we must recognize that James does not as clearly uphold the law as these texts might suggest. In this regard, his qualifications of the word "law" are significant. He calls it "the law that gives freedom" (2:12), "the perfect law that gives freedom" (1:25), and the "royal law" (2:8). While Jews sometimes used this language about the law of Moses, the context of James suggests that he intends something different. The law in 1:25, for instance, is related to the "word of truth" by which Christians are born again (1:18) and to "the word planted in you" that brings salvation (1:21). This shows that James aligns his law very closely with the gospel. Similarly, James' designation of the law as "royal" probably alludes to the love command as the "law of the kingdom" that Jesus has inaugurated.

James, then, does not seem to be alluding directly and simply to the Old Testament law in these passages. Reference to the law of Moses may be included, but the primary reference is to the law as Jesus has fulfilled it and taught it. This is confirmed by the frequency with which James alludes to the teaching of Jesus in his letter. Thus, James' "law" is the standard of conduct taught by Jesus that is to be applied to those who belong to the kingdom of God.

The Christian Life. James makes his most important contribution to this area of theology. As we stressed earlier, James' ethics are firmly rooted in his eschatology. His advice, while sometimes having the quality of timeless, "wisdom" teaching, is always oriented to the "saved but not yet glorified" situation of his readers. He realizes that his readers will not be able to escape entirely from the impulse to sin (3:2) but he wants them to work strenuously toward the goal of "perfection" or "completeness" (1:4). James is particularly upset about his readers' tendency toward "doubleness": the condition of being divided in loyalty between God and the world. Thus, he condemns his readers as "double-souled people" (*dipsychos*, 1:6; 4:8). Such a "divided" condition reveals itself in speech (3:9–10) and in the failure to live out one's faith in practice (1:19–2:26). James' desire is that Christians leave this unstable and inconsistent "halfway faith" and move toward a wholehearted, unvarying commitment to God.

James' insistence that Christians practice, and not just listen to, the word of God (1:22) is part of the same emphasis. Obedience to "the law of liberty" must be heartfelt and consistent. Central to this "law" is Jesus' own demand that we love one another (2:8): a demand that he scolds his readers for violating when they show favoritism toward the rich (2:1–7). Following Christ's law also has social implications. Loving our neighbors as ourselves means having a pure and undefiled religion that will show concern for the underprivileged and disadvantaged (1:27) and in a meek and unselfish attitude toward others (3:13–18).

Materialism. James' social concern surfaces particularly in his denunciations of the rich and commendations of the poor (1:9–11; 2:5–7; 5:1–6). Liberation theologians have seized on this language to support their own radical political agenda, but an understanding of the background of James' language shows how unwarranted this use is. Old Testament writers often use the word "poor" to characterize people who are righteous and the word "rich" to denote people who are wicked. This "religious" significance of the terms is found elsewhere in the New Testament (e.g., Matt. 5:3) and has influenced James. Thus, James' strong condemnation of the "rich" in 5:1–6 is directed simply to people who are wealthy but to people who have abused their wealth, as the basis for his denunciation in verses 2–6 makes clear. In fact, it is likely that in 1:9–10 James recognizes the presence of rich people among his congregation. Similarly, James' assertion that God has chosen the poor (2:5) means not that all poor people are chosen by God to be his people, but rather that God has in fact chosen many poor people precisely because their attitude of humility and openness to the Lord enables them to have the kind of faith that God rewards. DOUGLAS J. MOO

See also FAITH; JUDAIZERS; JUSTIFICATION; LAW; PAUL THE APOSTLE; WORKS OF THE LAW.

Bibliography. P. H. Davids, *Commentary on James*; M. Dibelius, *James;* S. Laws, *A Commentary on the Epistle of James;* R. P. Martin, *James;* P. U. Maynard-Reid, *Poverty and Wealth in James;* D. J. Moo, *The Letter of James;* J. H. Ropes, *A Critical and Exegetical Commentary on the Epistle of James.*

Jealousy. Jealousy is used in the Scriptures in both a positive and a negative sense. When jealousy is used as an attribute of God, it is obviously used in a positive sense. Probably the most striking example of the anthropomorphic portrayal of God is in those passages where he is said to be jealous. The language is based upon the relationship of husband and wife and is frequently associated with Israel's unfaithfulness to God.

The Hebrew word *qānāʾ* and its cognates are the most extensively used words for jealousy in the Old Testament. In Exodus 34:14 we learn that "the LORD, whose name is Jealous, is a jealous God." In Deuteronomy 4:24, God is described as "a consuming fire, a jealous God," giving the idea that he will judge because of his jealousy. In Joshua 24:19, Joshua challenges the people to serve the Lord but reminds them that serving God will be difficult because "He is a holy God; he is a jealous God." In Zechariah 1:14, when the Lord is asked why he allows Jerusalem to be down-trodden by the nations, he replies, "I am very jealous for Jerusalem and Zion." In verse 15, he continues to explain that while he intended to punish Israel for her sin, the nations have "added to the calamity." Because of his jealousy, God will restore Jerusalem to its rightful people and will build his temple there (v. 16). This concept is also brought out in context of the last days in Joel 2:18: "the LORD will be jealous for his land and take pity on his people." The Hebrew noun is also used to describe a man's jealousy for his wife (Num. 5:14–30) and God's passionate anger against sin (1 Kings 14:22; Ps. 78:58). It is used in a negative sense in Proverbs 6:34, where a man is in a rage because of his jealousy. In Song of Solomon 8:6 jealousy is described as being as "unyielding as the grave." Ezekiel 8:3 describes an idol that was set up in the temple mount "that provokes to jealousy." This image, along with other idols, caused God to remove his shekinah glory from the temple.

The Greek word *zēlos* and its verb form *zēloō* are only used five times in the New Testament. In Romans 10:19, Israel is said to be provoked to jealousy by Gentile nations that receive divine blessings. The same use of the word is recorded in Romans 11:11 because "salvation has come to the Gentiles." In 2 Corinthians 11:2, Paul declares his deep concern for the Corinthians when he says, "I am jealous for you with a godly jealousy."

The Corinthian Christians are said to be provoking God to jealousy because of the worship of idols (1 Cor. 10:22). This is followed by the question, "Are we stronger than he?" meaning "Can we afford to defy his power?" Therefore, to arouse the jealousy of God is a very dangerous action on our part. On the other hand, God's jealousy is based on his love and concern for us.

ALAN N. WINKLER

Jehovah. *See* GOD, NAMES OF.

Jeremiah, Theology of. To state the theology of a book is to offer a synthesis of the material from a theological rather than historical angle of vision. A theology of Jeremiah is derived by observing the structure of the book, its genres (e.g., judgment oracles, laments), the traditions on which it draws (e.g., covenant), its vocabulary (e.g., turn, *šub*), its "characters" (God, Israel, nations, the prophet), and the religious/social agenda of the time (i.e., a threat on Judah from the northern foe and subsequent siege). To determine a theology of the book one asks in essence, "What convictions drive this book?"

The structure of the Book of Jeremiah, much debated, may be sketched in envelope fashion by chapters as follows:

A. God's Personal Message to Jeremiah (1)
B. Speeches Warning of Disaster (2–10)
C. Stories of Prophet Wrestling with People and God (11–20)
D. Disputation with Kings and Prophets (21–29)
E. The Book of Comfort (30–33)
D1. Disputation with Kings (34–38)
C1. Stories of a Sacked City and the Aftermath (39–45)
B1. Oracles against Nations (46–51)
A1. Appendix: Historical Documentation (52)

A fresh approach to the theology of Jeremiah is by means of a two-directional grid: (1) the book's chiastic structure and (2) the "characters" within the book. Our discussion proceeds via the chiastic couplets.

The Dynamic of a History of Salvation (chaps. 2–10 = B; 46–51 = B1). The first major section, leaving aside chapter 1, contains speeches and is matched by the oracles against nations. The theological rubric in which the sermons and the oracles are cast is the history of both salvation and judgment. The section begins in a review mode: "I remember . . . [how] you loved me and followed me through the desert" (2:2). The recital, alternately of God's actions and Israel's response, is capsulized in 2:21: "I had planted you like a choice vine. . . . How then did you turn against me into a corrupt, wild vine?" God's salvific actions include the "exodus" (2:6; 7:22) and Israel's "entry into a fertile land" (2:7; 3:19; 7:7). God's judgment on the "corrupt, wild vine" will include disintegration and dislocation.

The indisputable lordship of God over history is poignantly made through the repeated designation (more than eighty times) of God as "the LORD of hosts" (NIV "God Almighty"). This title, associated closely with verdicts of judgment (thirty times), is liberally sprinkled in the oracles against the nations. World history, as well as redemptive history, proceeds under the eye of the cosmic commander-in-chief.

God: Benevolent, Angry, and Pained. Yahweh, the God of Israel is magnanimous but just. God is solicitous. "How gladly would I treat you like sons and give you a desirable land" (3:19). Despite Judah's gross evils, the Holy One of Israel will not forsake his people (51:5). A succinct characterization of God is given in 9:24: God delights in steadfast love, justice, and righteousness.

Because of the people's sin, however, and the departure from the "ancient paths" (6:16), God is about to act with anger and fury (7:20). Warnings and exhortations are cast in graphic pictures of coming devastation of Judah by enemy forces, primarily the foe from the north (5:15–17; 6:22–26; 7:32–8:3; 8:13–14, 17; 9:20–22; 10:18) and also in scenarios of cosmic catyclism not unlike the prospects of atomic destruction (4:23–26). God is also angry with nations (50:21; 51:25). These scenes of judgment are driven by God's anger, which "burns like a fire" (4:4, 8). One of several terms for anger, *'ap*, is found twenty-four times in Jeremiah—more often than in any other biblical book. Forty-two different passages in Jeremiah speak of God's anger. The tradition of God's anger against evil reaches far back (cf. Exod. 32:10). This anger is not wrath on a rampage but a holy anger, for the nexus between sin and punishment is unambiguous (4:18; 51:6).

It would be totally wrong, however, to conclude that Jeremiah's God is nothing but harsh. It is especially in chapters 2–3 that the pain of God surfaces, and in the context of rejection, as of a spouse in a marriage: "Does a maiden forget her jewelry, a bride her wedding ornaments? Yet my people have forgotten me, days without number" (2:32). The tradition of God's pain over a people's sin reaches back to the flood, if not earlier (Gen. 6:6). Expressive of his own pain and God's, the prophet sobs over the waywardness of the people (8:21–9:2). The pathos is echoed by Jeremiah: "O my anguish, my anguish! I writhe in pain" (4:19).

The People of God: Violating the First Commandment and More! The Temple Sermon pinpoints Judah's sin. Other speeches cite her ungrateful response to a gracious God. She has rebelled (2:8, 29). Most repugnant of all is her sin of idolatry (7:9), the exchange of other "gods" for the true God (2:11). This monstrous evil, described classically in chapter 10, is contrary to the first commandment. Descriptions of God as great, "the true God," "the living God, the eternal King," "the Maker of all things," "the Portion of Jacob," and the "LORD of hosts" ("Lord Almighty" NIV; vv. 6–7, 10, 12–13, 16) alternate with the sarcastic description of senseless, worthless, perishable idols (vv. 8–9, 11, 14–15). Further, God charges his people with deceit and insensitivity to injustice (5:23–29). A poll of the citizenry shows that there is no one with integrity (5:1–9; cf. 9:3–6). Back of the indictments of adultery (lusty stallions, each neighing for another man's wife, 5:8; 3:2–3; 7:9), stealing, and murder (7:9), lie the Ten Commandments. A sinful people is characterized as two sisters, "ever-turning" Israel and apostate Judah ("faithless Israel" and "unfaithful Judah," 3:11). Urgings toward repentance, a concept that is deepened, are many. *Šub* ("turn" or "return" in the sense of repent) is a verbal trademark of the book.

Nations Destined for Judgment and Salvation. The oracles against the nations do not so much present the case for punishment as they do the certainty and nature of God's judgment. Significantly, Egypt, with a history of oppression, heads this roll call of nations. She will flee like a hissing serpent (46:22), and Moab, because of pride (48:29), will be emptied like jars (48:12). A sword will come against Babylon (50:35–38) for her wrongdoing to Israel (51:24). Surprisingly, there are also bald, unconditional announcements of restoration for Egypt (46:26b), Moab (48:47), Ammon (49:6), and Elam (49:39).

The Dynamic of Covenant (chaps. 11–20 = C; 39–45 = C1). The next block of material, together with its complementary section in the latter half of the book, moves to stories about Jeremiah personally, especially his "inner life" (chaps. 11–20 = C) and national events (chaps. 39–45 = C1). The theological matrix for this block is primarily covenant, a subject introduced at the outset: "Cursed is the man who does not obey the terms of this covenant" (11:3).

A fundamental understanding beginning with Moses and continuing in Jeremiah was that covenant differed from contract. Covenant was a matter of divine initiative, not mutual negotiation. In covenant, loyalty to a person was the critical factor; in a contract performance of set stipulations was central. Failure in a covenant relationship was a failure in interpersonal relationships, and not alone failure in adhering to a set of requirements. Moses warned against breaking the covenant (Deut. 28:15–68). For Jeremiah a broken covenant was a reality; covenant curses such as loss of land were imminent. The nexus between wrongdoing and retribution was clear: "I am going to bring . . . disaster . . . because they were stiff-necked and would not listen to my words" (19:15; cf. 15:4; 40:3).

The Prophetic Ministry: Pathos and Conflict. Jeremiah, in contrast to Moses, an earlier covenant mediator, was involved more in the dissolution of the covenant than in its institution (1:10; but cf. 24:6). A perspective on the pain of this task is given in the seven laments (1:18–23; 12:1–6[13]; 15:10–12, 15–21; 17:14–18; 18:18–23; 20:7–13). Like prophets before him, Jeremiah's personal life was far from untouched by his role. He was not to marry (16:1). An intercessory role in behalf of his people was forbidden him (11:14; 14:11). The task of uprooting and tearing down institutions and misguided theologies (1:10; 7:1–15) brought tears, misery, and depression (9:1–2a; 15:15–18). Like Elijah (1 Kings 19:4), Jeremiah would rather die than continue (20:14–18).

Jeremiah, like other servants of God, was divinely called (1:4–10; cf. Moses, Exod. 3:1–14; Isa. 6). Like others, his call put in him conflict-filled situations. In Jeremiah's self-disclosing laments, quite unparalleled in prophetic literature, one glimpses the discomfort that prophetic role brought him. Confused, he asks about justice (12:1c). Pained, beset with hostility, he blurts, "Remember me and care for me" (15:15; cf. Baruch, 45:3). Angry and frustrated, he protests, "O LORD, you deceived me," for his role set him in tension even with God (20:7–13).

Israel and Judah: Disloyal Covenant Partners. Loyalty in covenant is demonstrated in obedience. God's people have been disobedient. "Obey" (*šāmaᶜ*) is a key word in these sections and throughout the book. More than thirty times, especially in chapters 7, 11, 26, 35, and 42, the word is found in the charge, "You (they) have not obeyed (listened)." Worse than disobedience is a deliberate commitment to waywardness: "We will continue with our own plans; each of us will follow the stubbornness of his evil heart" (18:12; cf. 44:16; 17:9, 23). In brief, Israel and Judah have "broken the covenant" (11:10). Consequences will follow. A trio of disasters—sword, famine, and plague—to which is added exile, surfaces frequently, in whole or in part (14:12, 16, 18; 15:2; 16:4; 44:12–13, 27).

A God of Persistence, Integrity, and Freedom. God is depicted not as an umpire who upon determining that the covenant is broken heartlessly announces the punishment. On the contrary, God coaxes his fickle covenant partner to keep the covenant intact. Symbolic actions are a marked feature in chapters 11–20. Two of these, one about a belt and another about a jar, symbolize an evil portent of ruin (13:9; 19:11; cf. 43:8–13). God employs every means—verbal appeals (11:4), warnings (15:7), and sign-acts—to mend a covenant that is breaking.

These two narrative sections (chaps. 11–20, 39–45) underscore a fundamental conviction: that which God announces, he fulfills. The frequent threats in chapters 10–20 are reported as fulfilled in the narrative of Babylon's siege of Jerusalem and deportation of her citizenry (esp. 39:1–9). Nebuzaradan, a Babylonian commander, articulates the theology of God's integrity succinctly: "The LORD your God decreed this disaster for this place. And now the LORD has brought it about; he has done just as he said he would" (40:2–3; cf. 44:29).

Yet God was not bound, as another sign-act makes clear, even with a covenant virtually shattered, to proceed with implementing the covenant consequences (18:1–12). Prophecy about the future is conditional; it is not the announcement of a fated destiny. The declaration in Section E is that God is free to initiate a new covenant (31:31–34). God is and remains free.

The Dynamics of an Agenda for Justice (chaps. 21–29 = D; 34–38 = D1). The overriding theological concern in the disputations of Sections D and D1 is justice: "Administer justice every morning" (21:11). The biblical concept of justice involves much more than fairness. It includes compassion for those marginalized and powerless, such as victims of oppression, aliens, widows, and orphans (21:12; 22:3). Justice, the fundamental requirement for political life, is a topic that surfaces sharply in the royal roll call (22:10–23:6). In building an ostentatious palace at the expense of the poor and needy, Jehoiakim failed to do justice (22:13–17). In the section's counterpart (chaps. 34–38 = D1), the same concern for justice appears in the story of Zedekiah's freeing and then reenslaving the slaves (34:1–22). A fundamental conviction is that God is tenacious about justice.

Integrity, part of the justice agenda, is the forefront issue in the indictment against another leadership group, the prophets. A key word in this section is *šeqer*, "deceit." It occurs thirty-seven times in the book, more often than in any other biblical book. The prophets are charged with telling lies and living a lie (23:14). Hananiah is a case in point (chap. 28; cf. 23:16, 25–40; 27:16). Prophets lack integrity; they commit adultery. Ahab and Zedekiah are examples (29:23; cf. 23:14). Any misuse of power, whether by kings or prophets, is altogether counter to "justice," a matter of "doing the right."

The Prophetic Role: Confrontation. The episodes in these sections are mostly about encounters of confrontation and disputation with leaders. Already clear in the exchanges of Samuel and Saul centuries earlier is the understanding that the call to be a prophet includes confronting public leaders. Standing over the king, given Israel's hierarchy, is the prophet who in the name of God calls the king to account (1:10). In the two sections, evil has faces: Jehoiachim (22:13–19; 36:1–33), Zedekiah (34:8–22), Hananiah (28:1–17), Ahab and Zedekiah (29:20–23), Shemaiah (29:24–32). The prophet names the evil in the lives of these "dignitaries," and calls down the consequent punishment. One of the functions of prophets is to identify the shape of evil in a society irrespective of consequences (26:11, 20–23; 37:16; 38:4, 6–9).

People: Free to Choose, but Responsible. An anthropology that holds to the individual's freedom of moral choice is basic to the book, but is highlighted in this section. Early in the section Zedekiah is presented with options: "See, I am setting before you the way of life and the way of death" (21:8). This theme of choice for both Israel and other nations is made visual in the symbolic action of Jeremiah's wearing the yoke (27:1–15). The theme of choice, accompanied by persuasion (even threats) to choose the good (22:4–5; 25:5–6), surfaces climactically in the final meeting of Jeremiah with Zedekiah (38:20–21). As always, the nexus between choice and destiny is forthrightly stated: to choose the way of disobedience is to be doomed to destruction (21:8–9; 25:8–9; 27:4–6; 38:17–18); to obey is to live (26:13; 35:15).

God: Not Infinitely Patient but Nevertheless Gracious. God pleads for the people not to listen to counterfeit messages (27:16; 29:8–9). Patiently God has dispatched prophets "again and again" (25:4). But God's patience has a limit, which is reached when people and especially leaders reject his communication. Jehoiakim burns the written word (chap. 36). Zedekiah silences the oral word by incarcerating Jeremiah (37:16–38:9). God's patience is exhausted (36:31). A key word, "burn," in chapters 37–38 recurs in the historical record (39:8).

Beyond judgment lies hope. God's intention is not destruction. His plans for his people are to give them "a hope and a future" (29:11). God remains accessible (29:13). He will watch over the exiles, give them a heart to know him (24:7), and return them from exile to their land (24:6; cf. 23:5–6).

The Dynamics of Hope (chaps. 30–33 = E). The Book of Comfort (chaps. 30–33) occupies a strategic place in the larger book in two ways. The book's chiastic structure puts these four chapters in a pivotal position. Seen as introductory to the second half of the book, these chapters may be compared with the speeches that introduce the first half of the book. The pivotal section takes up, as might be expected, all the threads of the book, but one—hope—dominates.

The motivation for words of hope, unlike the judgment speeches, is without rationale other than God's willing: "I have loved you with an everlasting love" (31:3; 33:11; cf. Deut. 7:7–8).

The Saving God. Saving history (cf. Jer. 2–10) meets us here. Echoes of the judgment, even allusion to God's anger, have not disappeared (30:23–24; 31:2; 32:28–29), but the promised salvation lies beyond the exile. God will create a new thing on the earth: his people will be enamored of God (31:22, a likely interpretation of a difficult text). The theme of the little "book," announced in the opening verses, is restoration: a people spiritually restored to God, a people physically restored to the land (30:3, 3a is better rendered "bring about the restoration of my people Israel"). A spiritually restored people will be intent on the worship of Yahweh instead of idols (30:9, 17; 31:6). Geographically a deported people will be returned from exile to their own land (30:10; 31:8–9, 16). The message is exhilarating: "There is hope for your future" (31:17).

Israel: A Covenant People. Just as other sections (chaps. 11–20, 39–51) turned on covenant, especially covenant curses, so that theme is featured here. Echoes of sin and the fracturing of the earlier covenant remain (30:14; cf. 32:30–35). The concentration of the covenant formula, variously worded, points to a new reality: "I will be your God; you shall be my people" (30:22; 31:1, 33; 32:38). The remarkable announcement of a new covenant moves beyond the broken covenant (31:31–34). By his initiative God sets in place a covenant both like and unlike the earlier Sinai covenant. The goal of bondedness remains; the means for achieving that bondedness between people and God is forgiveness and the placing of God's law in people's hearts. It is as though with renewed energy God commits himself to covenant (31:35–37; 33:19–21).

Justice for All. The subject of justice, highlighted in surrounding chapters (21–29, 34–38), also brackets the enlarged Book of Comfort (30:11; 33:15). God will do right by his people (30:11). God's intention is unchanged: he will "rejoice in doing them [Israel] good, and will assuredly plant them in this land" (32:41). If doing justice means to pay attention to the oppressed, then God, fully committed to justice, has swung into action because Israel had become known as "an outcast . . . for whom no one cares" (30:17). God will do right by Israel's enemies, too. Those who oppress and plunder will be exiled (30:16, 20). In the future time God will establish the righteous Branch (Messiah) who will do "what is just and right in the land"; so the banner over the land will read, "The LORD Our Righteousness" (33:15–16).

The central chapters (30–33) gather up the theology of the book. They offer a synoptic view of God, of Israel (past and future), of nations, and of the prophet, who, caught in the mystification of purchasing land when Jerusalem is besieged, is given and then gives a word of ultimate hope.

ELMER A. MARTENS

See also ISRAEL; PROPHET, PROPHETESS, PROPHECY.

Bibliography. A. R. Diamond, *The Confessions of Jeremiah in Context: Scenes of Prophetic Drama;* R. B. Chisholm, Jr., *A Biblical Theology of the Old Testament,* pp. 341–59; J. P. Hyatt, *IB,* pp. 784–87; G. McConville, *Judgment and Promise: The Message of Jeremiah;* R. E. Manahan, *Grace ThJ,* 1 (1980): 77–96; E. A. Martens, *Reflection and Projection,* pp. 83–97; T. W. Overholt, *The Threat of Falsehood: A Study in the Theology of the Book of Jeremiah;* T. M. Raitt, *A Theology of Exile: Judgment and Deliverance in Jeremiah and Ezekiel;* C. R. Seitz, *Theology in Conflict: Reactions to the Exile in the Book of Jeremiah;* J. A. Thompson, *The Book of Jeremiah;* J. Unterman, *From Repentance to Redemption: Jeremiah's Thought in Transition;* W. A. VanGemeren, *Interpreting the Prophetic Word;* G. von Rad, *Old Testament Theology.*

Jerusalem. ***The Name.*** The name "Jerusalem" occurs 806 times in the Bible, 660 times in the Old Testament and 146 times in the New Testament; additional references to the city occur as synonyms.

Jerusalem was established as a Canaanite city by the Chalcolithic period (ca. 4000–3100 B.C.), occupying the southeast hill that currently bears the name "City of David." Steep slopes on each side of the hill provided a defensible site, and a spring at the foot of the hill provided necessary water. The earliest probable occurrence of the name appears in the Execration Texts of Egypt (nineteenth to eighteenth centuries B.C.) as *Rušalimum.* The Amarna Letters from Late Bronze Age Egypt (fourteenth century B.C.), written in the Akkadian language, include the name *Urušalim.* In Assyrian and Babylonian texts relating to the kingdom of Judah, *Ursalimmu* or a similar form appears.

The archaeological investigation of Jerusalem is hampered by continued occupation; thus, even though no evidence exists for the sanctity of the site in Canaanite thought, human nature supports the assumption that the city had a religious center. The name consists of two elements: *yrw* and *šalem. yrw* may signify "foundation" or "city," while *šalem* is the name of a deity. The name means either "the foundation of (the god) Shalem," the patron-god of the city, or "the city of Shalem." Thus, a certain sanctity adhered to the city long before David acquired it.

Jerusalem in the Old Testament. *Salem.* The first occurrence of Jerusalem is in Joshua 10:1, but an allusion to Jerusalem appears in Genesis 14:18 with the reference to Melchizedek, king of Salem. Poetic parallel construction in Psalm 76:2 (Heb. 76:3) equates Salem with Zion. Theologically, the Canaanite city of Shalem has become the biblical city of Shalom, Peace. Prophetically, Isaiah spoke of the Prince of Peace (Shalom) who would reign on David's throne (in Jerusalem), a reference full of messianic portent (Isa. 9:6).

Jebus. At the time of the Israelite occupation of Canaan, Jerusalem was known as Jebus, a shortened expression for "City of the Jebusites." References in Joshua, Judges, and 1 Chronicles note that Jebus is another name for Jerusalem. The Romans also renamed the city Aelia Capitolina, but in both cases the older name revived.

City of David. Second Samuel recounts David's conquest of Jebus, exploiting the secret watershaft from the spring Gihon outside the city wall to its exit within the city. From that time on David "took up residence in the fortress, and called it the City of David" (5:9). His subsequent construction of a palace made Jerusalem a royal city. His decision to rule from Jerusalem elevated a city, poorly situated for either trade or military activity, to capital status. The politically neutral city, belonging to neither the northern nor southern tribes, also became his personal property.

David transformed Jerusalem into the religious center of his kingdom by bringing into it the ark of the covenant (2 Sam. 6:1–19). Although David was not allowed to construct a temple, the arrival of the ark forever linked Jerusalem with the cult of Yahweh. Solomon, David's son, enhanced the religious dimension of the city by constructing the temple of the Lord, symbolizing the presence of Yahweh in Jerusalem and Israel. David began the process of establishing the royal and religious nature of Jerusalem, but it was Solomon who transformed the former Jebusite stronghold into a truly capital and national cultic center. The royal and covenantal functions of Jerusalem are linked in Psalm 2:6, where God announces that "I have installed my King on Zion, my holy hill."

Jerusalem is imbued with an eternal nature in several passages in the Old Testament. As Yahweh's spokesman, Nathan promised David a dynasty that would rule in perpetuity (2 Sam. 7:15). This promise was extended to Jerusalem because of its function as the royal city. In addition, Solomon described the temple as the place for God to "dwell forever" (1 Kings 8:13). While both kingship and covenant were to be centered in Jerusalem forever (cf. Ps. 132), the promise was conditional (1 Kings 9:6–9).

The Bible is full of references to the tension confronting the prophets and people of Jerusalem over the "eternal" nature of the city and the conditions. Isaiah, for example, understood that the Lord would shield Jerusalem (31:5), but he was also aware that certain conditions did apply (1:19–20; 7:9b). Although painfully aware of the transgressions of the city (1:21–23), he nevertheless retained a hopeful vision for its future (2:3). Micah, Isaiah's contemporary, held similar views (3:12; 5:1–4). The prophets knew that the destruction of the city was imminent, for the cult had become corrupt and Jerusalem, the home of the covenant, would have to pay the price. The people's belief in the mere presence of the cult as a talisman against harm was not enough to save them from the discipline of destruction.

The idea that Jerusalem was inviolable persisted, however, no doubt strengthened in part by the deliverance of the city from the siege of Sennacherib (2 Kings 19:20–36). Nearly a century later, following the apostasy of Manasseh and the reforms of Josiah, Jehoiakim ascended the throne of David in Jerusalem. The prophet Jeremiah, his contemporary, early on dismissed Jehoiakim as a despot worthy of the "burial of a donkey" (Jer. 22:19). Jeremiah had supported the reforms of Josiah, but in the end the people were too hardened to change. They were convinced that the indestructible city and temple of the Lord would protect them in spite of their depravity (Jer. 7:4). When Jeremiah denied this and predicted the destruction of the temple, a century-old echo of Micah, it nearly cost him his life. Jerusalem did not change and the doom of exile was the result.

The Babylonian exile provided the environment for the transformation of Jerusalem, which lay desolate in ruins, into a spiritual symbol for the Jews. As important as Jerusalem had been as a royal center for the kingdom of Israel and, after Solomon's death, for the kingdom of Judah, through the ages its importance has been as "the city of the Great King," the Lord (Ps. 48:2; Matt. 5:35). The demise of the kingdom of Judah brought the political rule of the Davidic dynasty to a close; thereafter the rule of the Davidic house was perceived in messianic and eschatological terms. Upon the return of the Jews from the exile to the ruins of Jerusalem, they rebuilt the temple but not the palace. The true sovereignty of God was spiritual rather than political.

Zion. "Zion" is likely derived from a Semitic root related to a fortified tower atop a mountain. Its earliest appearance in the Bible equates the stronghold of Zion with the City of David (2 Sam. 5:7). Zion, then, was the fortified hill of Jebus conquered by David.

Zion was originally a geographic term for the City of David, but with the extension of the city northward to incorporate the Temple Mount, Zion came also to signify the dwelling place of Yahweh (Ps. 9:11 [Heb. 9:12]). The move of the ark of the covenant from the tent in the city to the temple proper may have prompted the shift of name.

The name "Zion" is seldom used in historical passages, but it occurs frequently in poetic and prophetic compositions as a synonym for all Jerusalem. In time Zion took on figurative as well as geographical connotations. Jerusalem is called the "Daughter of Zion (Isa. 1:8) and the "Virgin Daughter of Zion" (2 Kings 19:21). Jerusalem's inhabitants are called "sons of Zion" (Lam. 4:2), the "women of Zion" (Isa. 3:16), and the "elders of the Daughter of Zion" (Lam. 2:10). In these expressions the city has been personified. The extension of a place name to refer to its inhabitants recognizes that the character of a city is determined more by the traits of its population than by its buildings.

A visitor to modern Jerusalem will be shown the western hill rather than the City of David as Mount Zion. Through changing usage over the centuries the name has migrated to the west, but archaeology has shown that the original site was identical with the City of David. No matter where the name rests geographically, Zion's true significance is in the heavens where God's dwelling will be with his people (Rev. 21:3–4).

Moriah. Moriah occurs only twice in the Bible (Gen. 22:2; 2 Chron. 3:1). The rare use of the name, however, belies its theological significance. Abraham was instructed by God to take his son to the land of Moriah and there to offer him as a sacrifice. The place was three days' journey from Beersheba. The Chronicler, writing in the postexilic period, has connected the place of the offering of Isaac with not only Jerusalem but specifically with the Temple Mount. This is the earliest evidence for this connection which is also attested in Josephus (*Ant.* 1.13.1f [222–27]; 7.13.4 [329–34]), Bk. Jub. 18:13, rabbinic literature, and Islamic thought (although with Ishmael as Abraham's son). This connection enhanced the sanctity of Jerusalem and the Temple Mount and contributed to the basis for the Islamic name for the city, El-Quds, "The Holy (City)."

After Abraham was prevented from slaying Isaac, and the ram was provided as a substitutionary sacrificial victim, Abraham called the name of the place *Yahweh-jireh*, "The Lord sees." Even so, the name never attained common usage.

The connection of Jerusalem with the sacred mountain of Yahweh is implicit in many of the references to mountain (Heb. *har*) in the Old Testament. The concept of a sacred mountain as the abode of deities was common in the ancient Near East. At Ugarit on the North Syrian coast, Mount Zaphon to the north was the sacred mountain. The most active of the gods of Ugarit was called Baal-Zaphon. Psalm 48:3 (Heb. 48:2), refers to Jerusalem as "the utmost heights of Zaphon is Mount Zion, the city of the Great King." The poet has drawn on Canaanite imagery to enhance praise of the Lord.

Isaiah saw that ultimately the mountain of the Lord would be the goal of nations. In the last days "Many peoples will come and say, 'Come, let us go up to the mountain of the LORD'" (2:3). The word of the Lord will go out from Jerusalem; nations will convert weapons into agricultural implements and men will not learn war anymore. Then Jerusalem shall become the city of peace indeed.

Ariel. "Ariel" occurs five times as the name of David's city only in Isaiah 29. The meaning of the name is obscure. Perhaps it means "the hearth of God," compared to Ezekiel 43:15, or the "lion of God," or, by a slight emendation, "the city of God." Another emendation would yield "the mountain of God," congruent with similar references noted above.

Postexilic Jerusalem. The restoration of the Jewish people to Jerusalem was decreed by the Persian ruler Cyrus following his conquest of Babylon in 539 B.C. Sheshbazzar, a prince of Davidic descent, led the first group of exiles back in 538 B.C., but there is no hint of the renewal of the monarchy. Persian political policy dominated the returnees. During this time a meager attempt at rebuilding the temple was undertaken. A second group of returnees arrived with Zerubbabel around 520 B.C. and work on the temple was accelerated through the prodding of the prophets Haggai and Zechariah; the structure was completed and dedicated in 516 B.C. The city's walls were rebuilt under Nehemiah's leadership (ca. 445 B.C.). Ezra instituted religious reforms based on the "Book of the Law of Moses," probably the Pentateuch, which he brought back with him from Babylon (Neh. 8:1). With this, the cult of Yahweh was fully reestablished in Jerusalem.

Jerusalem in the New Testament. New Testament Jerusalem is Herodian Jerusalem, a city four centuries beyond the time of Ezra-Nehemiah. In those four hundred years, Jerusalem witnessed the demise of the Persian Empire and the domination of the Greeks. Under the Ptolemaic dynasty of Egypt, the attractive influence of Greek culture affected Jerusalem and its people, weakening religious devotion and practices particularly among the priestly ruling elite (cf. 1 Macc. 1:14). The Syrian Seleucid dynasty wrested control of Jerusalem from the Egyptians in 198 B.C. Finally, after Antiochus IV desecrated the temple by sacrificing a hog on the altar, devout Jews led by the Hasmonean family (Maccabees) rose in rebellion to reclaim Jerusalem in 164 B.C. The Hasmoneans attained political independence and became a dynasty of priest-kings who ruled until Herod the Great became king of Judea.

The Romans ended independent Jewish rule in 63 B.C. They place Herod on the throne in 37 B.C., and he began the greatest building program Jerusalem had known. He constructed a new city wall, a theater and amphitheater, athletic fields, and a new palace. His reconstruction of the temple and the expansion of its platform made it the crown jewel of Jerusalem. At the same time, the Dead Sea Scroll community who deemed the Jerusalem temple despised by God, contemplated a New Jerusalem, completely rebuilt as a Holy City and with a new temple as its centerpiece (Temple Scroll). Herodian Jerusalem survived until the war with Rome in 66–70 A.D.; the city then suffered siege and destruction. It is in the context of Jerusalem before the destruction occurred that New Testament references are set.

Jesus and Jerusalem. In the Synoptic Gospels Jerusalem is first mentioned in connection with the birth stories of Jesus: Zechariah's vision in the temple (Luke 1:5–23), the visit of the Magi (Matt. 2:1–12), and the presentation of the infant Jesus (Luke 2:22–38). Luke records the visit of Jesus to the temple at age twelve (2:41–50), and in fact New Testament references to Jerusalem are predominantly in Luke–Acts. Jesus is tempted by Satan at the highest point of the temple just prior to the start of his ministry in Galilee (4:9–13). Further, Luke records the "travel account" (9:51–19:27) in which Jesus sets his face toward Jerusalem and the inevitable events that were to take place there for, as Jesus observed, "surely no prophet can die outside Jerusalem!" (13:33). Jerusalem and the temple symbolized the covenant between God and his people, but the covenant relationship was askew. Luke records Jesus' tears and sorrow over Jerusalem and his prophecy of its destruction (19:41–44).

Jewish messianism had long anticipated the return of a Davidic king to the city. The arrival of Jesus in Jerusalem on Palm Sunday, described in Luke 19, was perceived as a royal procession by followers and adversaries alike. Jesus saw that the temple had become a commercial establishment rather than a center of spirituality. By "cleansing" the temple he reaffirmed its place of honor.

Jesus' role was to put humanity back in line with the will of God. Although the fulfillment of this role through his death upon the cross was to take place outside the city, Jerusalem provided the backdrop for his Passion. Luke records many of the activities of that last week: the Last Supper, the arraignment before the high priest, Peter's denial, the trial before Pilate all took place within Jerusalem. And some postresurrection appearances of Jesus took place in Jerusalem (24:33–49) where his disciples were to await the coming of the Holy Spirit (24:49). Luke's Gospel closes with the call of Jesus to preach in his name to all nations "beginning at Jerusalem" (24:49).

Matthew recalls the sanctity of Jerusalem as the "holy city" (4:5), and Jesus refers to it as "the city of the Great King" (5:35). The name "Zion" in Matthew refers to fulfilled prophecy (21:5; cf. Rom. 11:26). New Testament references to Zion mainly recall Old Testament passages; however, the heavenly Jerusalem is identified as Zion in Hebrews 12:22 and Revelation 14:1.

Mark's references to Jerusalem are set mainly in the Passion narrative; however, he notes the "massive stones" of the temple (13:1). All three Synoptic Gospels record the splitting of the curtain in the Jerusalem temple during the crucifixion. The Holy of Holies, the former center of covenant, was opened by this event to the new covenant with Christ.

The Synoptics are largely silent concerning any visits by Jesus to Jerusalem between childhood and his last week, but the Gospel of John supplements the record in this respect. According to John, Jesus cleansed the temple early in his ministry, following the "first sign" at Cana (John 2:13–16). Jesus also attended the Feast of Tabernacles and taught in the temple (7:14). And he healed the blind man at the pool of Siloam (chap. 9). The healing of the lame man at the pool of Bethsaida is also recorded in John (chap. 5).

Paul and Jerusalem. Acts 1:4 notes that the apostles were to wait for the promised gift of the Father in Jerusalem, and the gospel began to be preached there (chap. 2). In Jerusalem Stephen delineated the differences between Christianity and mainstream Judaism. The city was central to the early Christian community, and its leaders frequented the temple as a place of prayer. In Jerusalem Paul received his commission to preach to the Gentiles (22:17–21). Paul remained in contact with the temple, praying (22:17) and seeking purification there (24:18). Paul expected Gentile Christians to identify with Jerusalem and to develop a sense of kinship with the Jerusalem church. He actively encouraged outlying churches to send support to the "poor among the saints at Jerusalem" (Rom. 15:26).

The Heavenly Jerusalem. New Testament Christians held the view that there was a city with foundations whose architect and builder was God (Heb. 11:10). Further, this was a heavenly Jerusalem "Mount Zion, . . . the city of the living God" (12:22). The population would consist of those whose names are written in heaven. The eschatological view of Jerusalem that developed among Christians, aside from that of Judaism (cf. Isa. 60:14), looked forward to the fulfillment of the promise of the kingdom in the establishment of a New Jerusalem that would come "down out of heaven from God" (Rev. 21:2). This city is described in contrast to the city allegorically called Sodom and Egypt, that is, the earthly Jerusalem, "where also their Lord was crucified" (Rev. 11:8).

The Bible begins with a bucolic setting in the Garden of Eden; it closes on an urban scene, and that city is the New Jerusalem. For Christians, the identification of earthly Jerusalem as the dwelling place of God, which figures so frequently in the Old Testament, has been transformed into a heavenly Jerusalem, the true sanctuary of the Lord (cf. Gal. 4:26; Heb. 12:22–29). Nevertheless, Christians have always been drawn to the earthly Jerusalem, as have Jews and Muslims, for it has retained through the centuries its role as the center of the three monotheistic religions.

KEITH N. SCHOVILLE

See also NEW JERUSALEM.

Bibliography. M. Barker, *The Gate of Heaven: The History and Symbolism of the Temple in Jerusalem;* G. A. Barrois, *IDB,* 4:959–60; M. Burrows, *IDB,* 2:843–66; R. E. Clements, *Isaiah and the Deliverance of Jerusalem;* P. J. King, *ABD,* 4:747–66; W. H. Mare, *ABD,* 6:1096–97; idem, *The Archaeology of the Jerusalem Area;* B. C. Ollenburger, *Zion the City of the Great King;* J. Simons, *Jerusalem in the Old Testament;* P. W. L. Walker, *Jerusalem: Past and Present in the Purposes of God.*

Jesus Christ. By anyone's account, Jesus of Nazareth is the most significant person who has ever lived. He has influenced more lives and had more written about him than any other person in history. He is the only one who ever made a credible claim to being more than just another human being and to this day almost a billion people revere him as the supreme revelation of God. The purpose of this article is to provide a summary of Jesus' life and his basic teachings, with each topic being introduced by a short account of the modern discussion that surrounds it. Introducing the whole is a brief discussion of the nature of the sources from which Jesus' life and teachings are derived and concluding it is a discussion of who Jesus understood himself to be.

The Nature of the Sources. The primary sources for the life of Jesus are and will probably always be the four Gospels of the New Testament. New discoveries are made periodically, such as the Dead Sea Scrolls and the Gnostic Scriptures at Nag Hammadi, but immensely valuable as they are, they tell us nothing new about Jesus. They are either too late in time, too tangential, too geographically distant, or too obviously a distortion of more traditional Christian thought to be of much value. Some of this material has been available for a long time and has been made available in such works as R. McL. Wilson's *New Testament Apochrypha* (2 vols.), but no one was inclined to rewrite the story of Jesus on the basis of that. Other fragmentary material from Jewish and pagan sources is also well known and has a certain corroborative value that is quite helpful. We learn that Jesus lived during the reign of Tiberius Caesar (A.D. 14–37) somewhere in Palestine; that he was a religious leader who worked miracles and exorcised demons and was later regarded as a deity by his followers; that he was executed by crucifixion by the Jewish and Roman authorities during a Passover season; that reports circulated about his resurrection from the dead. All of this is very helpful, even if the Christian faith is sometimes described by these very sources as an unfounded superstition, because in its own way it reflects what Christians believes. It does not add anything new to what we know about Jesus, however. For that, one must turn to the four Gospels.

Because the Gospels are basically the only sources we possess for the life of Jesus, the question inevitably arises concerning reliability. Regarding this, four things can be said. First, there is no agreed definition of reliability. Everyone approaches sources from a point of view that either includes, excludes, or leaves open the possibility of what is recorded. Given Christian presuppositions, the story makes perfect sense; given non-Christian presuppositions, the rejection of the sources as unreliable is understandable. It is not really a question of the sources, but a question of the interpreter of the sources. Second, the Gospel writers and their subject matter argue in favor of their truthfulness. They were attempting to present a true account of the One who claimed to be the Truth, did so on the basis of careful research (Luke 1:1–4), and were willing to die for the results of their efforts. That does not necessarily make it true, but it does mean they were not inventing things they knew to be false. Third, the church from the beginning believed that God had a hand in the writing of the material and that guaranteed its trustworthiness. This does not make it so, but that belief did arise from contact with those who knew Jesus and contact with the risen Jesus who confirmed in their own experience what the sources said about him as incarnate. If they were right in this, it confirms the reliability of the sources. Fourth, the Gospels are all we have. If they are allowed to speak for themselves, they present a consistent picture that gave rise to the Christian faith and has been confirmed in the lives of believers from that day to this. The simple fact is, there is no other Jesus available than the one presented in the Gospels. Either that is accepted or one creates his or her own Jesus on the basis of what is thought to be possible or likely. It might be a Jesus acceptable to the modern or postmodern mind, but it will not be the Jesus of the Gospels.

The Gospels as sources are what they are, shot through with supernatural occurrences from beginning to end and they present a Jesus who is both powerful and puzzling to our modern mind. They ought to be examined with the utmost care, but allowed to speak for themselves and appreciated for what they are, documents written from within the faith, honestly depicting what they believed Jesus said and did, to the best of their recollection.

The Life of Jesus. *The Search for the Real Jesus.* From the time when Jesus lived until the eighteenth century it would never have occurred to anyone to search for a real Jesus. The Gospels were considered to be divinely inspired, accurate accounts of Jesus' life; hence, the real Jesus was found by reading them. A change occurred with the coming of the Enlightenment that no longer saw the truth of the Gospels as guaranteed by God. They were to be read as any other book; the supernatural elements were to be discounted entirely or taken as myths or symbols of some higher truth. This meant that the real Jesus, a Jesus fully explainable in human terms, had to be disentangled from the pious, but historically inaccurate elements that smothered him.

During the nineteenth century an enormous number of lives of Jesus were written that attempted to reconstruct who Jesus really was, some of them showing real insight but most straying so far from the Gospels as to make Jesus virtually unrecognizable. A few achieved immense popularity because of their radical originality, like D. F. Strauss's *The Life of Jesus Critically Examined* (1835) and E. Renan's *Life of Jesus* (1863), but most came and went and in fact are almost unknown today. In 1903 Albert Schweitzer surveyed over two hundred such lives and convincingly showed that none of them had found the real Jesus.

This earliest attempt to find the real Jesus, which came to be known as "the Old Quest," was set aside in the early twentieth century by a group of theologians led by Rudolph Bultmann, who felt that the "historical" Jesus was essentially irrelevant to Christian faith. Christians were to put their faith in the risen Christ, not a reconstructed historical Jesus. They also believed that none of the supernatural elements of the Gospels, such as the virgin birth, the miracles of Jesus, or his bodily resurrection was true, anyway, but only an ancient way of describing an existential experience of the present day.

The extreme skepticism of this movement brought about a strong reaction in the 1950s, called the "New Quest of the Historical Jesus," led by some of Bultmann's students, notably E. Käsemann and G. Bornkamm. Bornkamm's *Jesus of Nazareth* (1956) and J. M. Robinson's *A New Quest of the Historical Jesus* (1959) were the high points, but this quest also faded away, itself being too problematic and inconclusive to help much.

Following this, numerous renewed attempts to find the real Jesus were made, which are together called the "Third Quest." They include everything from depicting Jesus as a magician (M. Smith, *Jesus the Magician,* 1979), a Marxist (M. Machorec, *A Marxist Looks at Jesus,* 1976), to an outright fraud (B. Thiering, *Jesus the Man,* 1992). Others wrote of Jesus along more traditional lines (D. Guthrie, *Jesus the Messiah,* 1972; B. F. Meyer, *The Aims of Jesus,* 1979) and yet others wrote scholarly attempts to understand what could be known purely as history about Jesus, such as E. P. Sanders (*The Historical Figure of Jesus,* 1995) and J. P. Meier (*A Marginal Jew,* 2 vols., 1991, 1995). John Reumann has attempted to classify all of this (taking it back to 1900) into twenty different categories as "Types of Lives . . . Some Key Examples" (*The New Testament and its Modern Interpreters,* eds. E. J. Epp and G. W. MacRae, pp. 520–24).

This confusing welter of lives raises the question whether there is a "real" Jesus. The answer to that, in the end, must go back to the only real sources that we have, namely, the four Gospels of the New Testament. Any reconstruction that differs fundamentally from what is depicted there will not qualify, nor strengthen the church, nor stand the test of time. Jesus will always elude us if we look for him only in history and any attempt to depict him as simply another part of history will inevitably be unconvincing.

The Life of Jesus. *Jesus' Birth and Youth.* Two of our four canonical gospels (Matthew and Luke) contain material dealing with Jesus' earthly life prior to the beginning of his public ministry. Matthew's basic emphasis is on Jesus as descendant of David; hence he focuses on Joseph's line, Jesus being the legal heir of Joseph. Luke presents information gathered from Mary's side, either from Mary herself or from those who knew her. There is very little overlap between the accounts.

The events that precede Jesus' birth concern primarily two miraculous conceptions, that of John the Baptist and, of course, Jesus. John's father, the priest Zechariah, was told by the angel Gabriel that his aged wife Elizabeth would bear a son in her old age. Mary was told by the same angel, Gabriel, that she would bear a son, though a virgin. Zechariah's response was incredulity, where Mary's was respectful joy and acceptance (Luke 1:18, 38).

A census decreed by Caesar Augustus sent Mary and Joseph to Bethlehem where, during the last years of Herod the Great, Jesus was born to the acclaim of angels and shepherds. The exact date of Jesus' birth is debated by any time from late 7 to 5 B.C. is possible. Jesus was circumcised on the eighth day (Luke 2:21) and on the fortieth day taken to the temple in Jerusalem, where he was presented to the Lord and his parents were ceremonially purified according to levitical custom (Luke 2:22–38; Lev. 12:1–8). They returned to Bethlehem were, apparently, they intended to stay. Magi came from the east, following a miraculous star. They found Jesus after making inquiries in Jerusalem, upsetting the rulers there. This visit could have been up to two years after Jesus' birth. Herod's desire to kill the child Jesus was thwarted by God and the family escaped to Egypt. After Herod the Great's death in 4 B.C., the family decided to return to Nazareth after hearing that Archelaus was ruling over Judea (where Bethlehem was) in place of his father. Only one episode is recorded of Jesus' early years. When he was twelve years old, on the eve of adulthood according to Jewish custom (Luke 2:41–50), he showed his profound identification with the temple and the things of God.

These events are characterized by the miraculous and the extraordinary. Modern attempts to make them pious fiction or mythological are only required if one is unable to accept God's direct intervention in human affairs. They are wholly consistent with the rest of Jesus' extraordinary career and, indeed, make an appropriate introduction to it.

The Year of Obscurity. James Stalker described the three-year public ministry of Jesus as the year of obscurity, the year of public favor, and the year of opposition. Although not wholly accurate, this does serve as a handy guide to those years.

The year of obscurity began sometime in A.D. 26. John the Baptist appeared in the wilderness near the Dead Sea preaching a message of baptism and repentance for the forgiveness of sins. Some scholars have connected John with the Qumran community. Although this is possible, the message of John is altogether different from theirs. He was an exceptional figure, recalling the days of Elijah. He spoke out against false trust in one's Jewishness, demanded conversion in the light of the coming judgment, required a changed life as evidence of conversion, and spoke of the coming Messiah, of whom he was the forerunner. John's denunciation of Herod Antipas's illegal marriage to his brother's wife provoked her ire, his imprisonment, and ultimately his death. Jesus spoke in the highest possible terms of John and his ministry, in spite of John's troubled questionings while in prison at Machaerus.

Jesus went from Nazareth to be baptized by John in order "to fulfill all righteousness" (Matt. 3:15). Jesus showed his sense of mission by identifying with the sins of the world at the very beginning of his ministry. Divine confirmation came from heaven with the voice of God and the descent of the Holy Spirit in the form of a dove (Matt. 3:16–17). This affirmation of the Trinity will later by repeated at the end of Matthew's Gospel (28:19).

A time of severe testing in the wilderness followed Jesus' baptism, in which Jesus' commitment to his task and understanding of his mission were resolved.

After a short trip to Cana in Galilee where the water was turned into wine Jesus returned to Jerusalem for the Passover of A.D. 27. His expulsion of the moneychangers from the temple was more than just a rejection of corrupt practices. He was rejecting the temple itself by offering himself as a new temple for a new people of God (John 2:18–21).

Sometime in the fall of A.D. 27 John the Baptist was arrested. Jesus took this as a sign to return to Galilee to begin his own ministry. As long as John was preaching, he held back. Now that John was gone, the time of fulfillment had arrived. On the trip back to Galilee, Jesus rather openly declared to the woman at Jacob's well in Samaria some of his challenging, new ideas. The time has arrived when true worship of God will not concern where it takes place, whether in Samaria or Jerusalem, but how it takes place. God seeks the right attitude, spirituality, and truth, not the right location (John 4:21–24).

Jesus was warmly received upon his arrival in Galilee (John 4:45) and everyone praised him as he began to preach the gospel of the kingdom of God (Mark 1:15; Luke 4:14–15).

The Year of Public Favor. Jesus' ministry in Galilee and the regions to the north of it are described in some detail by the Gospel writers and, although, in general, it was a time of public acclaim by the people, the clouds of opposition were arising from official quarters in Jerusalem.

After an initial rebuff in his hometown of Nazareth, Jesus settled in at Capernaum by the Sea of Galilee, using it as a base of operations for his ministry in Galilee. Large crowds began to follow Jesus because of the miraculous events and healing that were taking place, but also because of the gracious words that he spoke. Rather than focusing on the minute regulations that had grown up along with biblical tradition, Jesus stressed the love and nearness of God to everyone personally. Rules were made for people, not people for the rules. The Good News of the kingdom is that the power of God is available for all who put their trust in God and are poor in spirit, pure in heart, loving, merciful, and followers of peace. Jesus saw himself as the embodiment and establisher of that kingdom and offered himself to the people as the one who was bringing that kingdom to pass (Matt. 11:25–30). Matthew summarizes this by saying "Jesus went throughout Galilee, teaching in their synagogues, preaching the good news of the kingdom, and healing every disease and sickness among the people" (4:23).

Jesus made at least three major preaching tours through Galilee at this time, as well as two that took him into Gentile territory to the north and east. In one instance, he felt it necessary to send out his recently appointed leaders, the apostles, to engage in ministry in his name, because the task was too large to be done single-handedly (Mark 9:1–2).

It would be hard to say which of the many episodes that are recounted in the Gospels are the most important, because what we have are a selection of those deemed most important to begin with. However, four stand out as particularly instructive. First, Jesus chose twelve of his followers to become a nucleus of leadership (Mark 3:13–19). This was to establish a new Israel that would in time replace the old Israel as the people of God. Second, when John the Baptist asked Jesus from prison if he was the Messiah, Jesus replied with a definition of messiahship that was one of service and suffering rather than of immediate triumph (Matt. 11:2–19). Here, again, Jesus pointed out that the old age was drawing to a close and that the new age was dawning. Third, at the miraculous feeding of the five thousand and the subsequent sermon in Capernaum reflecting on that event, Jesus offers himself as the essence of the kingdom, as the bread come down from heaven and a new manna in a new wilderness (Matt. 14:13–21; John 6:1–69). Fourth, during Jesus' second trip outside of Galilee, he disclosed at Caesarea Philippi and at his transfiguration who he really was and what his ultimate task was to be (Mark 8:27–38; 9:2). He was the eternal Son of God who had come to die for the sins of the world.

The Year of Opposition. As Jesus' ministry in Galilee was drawing to a close, he was preparing to move south to continue his work in the regions of Perea and Judea. He knew that he was moving into dangerous territory. Even while he was in Galilee spies and representatives were being sent from Jerusalem to observe his actions and, perhaps, to find some grounds for legal action against him. In three areas they were dissatisfied with what he was doing: he was violating the Sabbath rules (Matt. 12:1–8; Mark 3:1–6); his miraculous healings were attributed to demonic activity, rather than to divine intervention (Mark 3:22–30); and he set aside traditional rules regarding hand washing, and, adding insult to injury, accused the leadership of being hypocritical (Mark 7:1–13). While he was in Galilee, he was more or less out of their jurisdiction, but traveling to Jerusalem would provoke open conflict.

Jesus arrived in time for the feast of Tabernacles (September–October) in A.D. 29. Conflict immediately broke out, some saying he was the Messiah or a Prophet, others denying it (John 7:11–13, 40–43). Jesus proclaimed himself to be the water of life, the light of the world, the special representative of the Father, the dispenser of eternal life, and timeless in his existence (John 7:16, 37–38; 8:12, 16, 28, 51, 56–58). Further controversy arose after Jesus healed a man who had been born blind. This could not be denied by the rulers and only deepened their hostility toward him.

Jesus traveled throughout Judea and Perea, teaching, preaching, and healing, as he had done in Galilee. At one point he sent out a group of seventy-two disciples, by twos, to preach and heal in his name, knowing that his time was growing short. He spent some time in Bethany, where another notable miracle took place (the raising of Lazarus from the dead). After a short trip back north, taking him to the border of Galilee once more, Jesus returned by way of Jericho to Jerusalem for the last time.

During this time Jesus was preparing his disciples for what was coming, although they had a difficult time accepting the fact that he was going to Jerusalem to die and rise again. Their thoughts were full of coming glory and the power that Jesus so manifestly displayed. For Jesus triumph in Jerusalem meant death and resurrection; for the disciples it meant a special and obvious place in God's kingdom. Jesus tried to explain what the cost of discipleship would be, but his disciples seemed incapable of hearing it (Luke 14:25–35).

The Trial and Death of Jesus. Jesus arrived in Jerusalem on the Sunday before Passover (March–April) of A.D. 30, entering the city to the acclaim of the people and in triumphal glory. He repeated his actions of three years earlier, again demonstrating his authority over the temple. This created a great stir among the people and a murderous hatred in the hearts of the leaders.

During that week there was public and unresolved conflict with the authorities and they made plans to do away with Jesus, penetrating the group by way of Judas, one of the twelve apostles.

On Thursday night Jesus ate a Passover meal with his followers and established a communal ceremony for them that consisted of a participation in his coming death, concretized in the partaking of bread and wine. This was the establishment of the New Covenant that had been prophesied by Jeremiah (Luke 22:17–20; see Jer. 31:31–34).

Jesus' agony began in the garden of Gethsemane where he was arrested after going there to pray. He was taken to the high priest's compound where he was interviewed, first by Annas, then by Caiphas, then when it had fully gathered, by the whole Sanhedrin, the ruling body of the Jews. It was difficult to get the witnesses to agree, but a charge of blasphemy was settled on, because Jesus had claimed to be equal to God (Matt. 26:63–68). By now it was near morning and Peter had disgraced himself by denying publicly that he even knew Jesus.

The Jewish authorities took Jesus to Pontius Pilate, the Roman procurator, for him to ratify their sentence of death (they did not have the authority to execute it). The grounds of their condemnation of Jesus had expanded considerably on their way to Pilate. They charged that Jesus had actively misled the people, opposed payment of taxes to Caesar, and claimed to be the Messiah, a king (Luke 23:2). They later added a fourth charge—Jesus was a revolutionary, inciting people to riot (Luke 23:5). Pilate made a series of attempts to release Jesus, including the offer to release a prisoner (they chose Barabbas instead) and the flogging of Jesus as punishment, but death by crucifixion was their ultimate demand. With mingled contempt and fear, Pilate granted them their wish when they accused him of being unfaithful to Caesar, by allowing one who claimed to be a king to live.

Jesus was crucified at 9 A.M. on Friday morning, the actual day of Passover, and died at 3 P.M. that afternoon. He prayed forgiveness for his tormentors, went through a sense of abandonment by God, and expired with "It is finished; Father, into your hands, I commit my spirit." Jesus had finished the work he had come to do—to die for the sins of the world.

Jesus' body was hastily placed in a tomb by Joseph of Arimathea and Nicodemus, because the day ended at 6 P.M. according to Jewish reckoning and everything must be finished before the Sabbath. A seal was set on the tomb and the women were waiting for the Sabbath to end so they could prepare the body properly for permanent burial.

Jesus' Resurrection and Ascension. Early on Sunday morning, when the women went to visit the tomb, they were startled to see that the tomb was empty and an angel announced the good news: "He has risen! He is not here" (Mark 16:6). There followed that day a confusing set of actions that included other visits to the tomb, visits to the apostles, and appearances of Jesus. Three of these appearances are especially noteworthy. First, Jesus appeared to two disciples as they were on their way out of town in utter dejection and nearing Emmaus. Jesus explained the Scriptures to them, especially the necessity of his suffering, in order to enter his glory (Luke 24:35). Jesus fellowshiped together with them and their eyes were opened to see the truth. Second, a special appearance was granted to the apostle Peter (Luke 24:34; cf. John 21:15–23) in order to strengthen him after his ignominious failure. Third, Jesus appeared to the eleven (minus Judas) in Jerusalem to show that the reports were true; he had, indeed, risen and was the same Jesus, now glorified. He was not a ghost or spirit, but risen in a body capable of being seen, touched, and participating in events related to this life (Luke 24:36–43).

Other appearances followed over a period of forty days, both in Jerusalem and in Galilee. There were appearances to individuals, groups of individuals, and in one case to over five hundred people at one time (1 Cor. 15:6). They occurred in various places and at various times of day. All of this was to remove any doubt whatsoever about the reality of what had taken place. Jesus had risen and the once fearful flock was now emboldened and empowered to preach the message of the risen Christ as the salvation of the world. In the end neither rejection, nor persecution, nor death could shake their conviction that Jesus had conquered death. He had risen, indeed.

After forty days Jesus left this earth as miraculously as he had come. During the forty days Jesus had confirmed the fact of his resurrection, instructed his disciples about his new relationship to them, and promised them a new work by the Holy Spirit in their lives. His ascension was the return to his Father that he had spoken about (John 20:17) and the inauguration of his reign that would be consummated on this earth with his second coming (Acts 1:9–11). Thus began a new phase of Jesus' dealings with his followers. His physical presence was replaced by a spiritual presence (Matt. 28:20) as they set out to fulfill his last commission to them, to be witnesses unto the ends of the earth (Acts 1:8).

The Teaching of Jesus. *The Search for the Real Words of Jesus.* The search for the real words of Jesus arose at the same time that the search for the real Jesus began, with the Enlightenment of the eighteenth century. With the collapse of confidence in the Gospels as infallible sources of information about Jesus came skepticism about what Jesus said as well. However, that did not come to the same degree or at the same time as skepticism about his life, the reason being it was easier to reinterpret what Jesus said in modern terms than many of the things he was recorded to have done. His walking on water or raising the dead could only be understood as ancient superstitions or myth. His statements about the kingdom of God or messiahship could rather easily be turned into modern ethical statements and made consistent with other religious teachings.

The teaching of Jesus as understood by the "Old Quest" concerned individual piety, personal relations, and the social betterment of the world. The kingdom of God that Jesus proclaimed was understood to be the gradual improvement of society by permeating it with the lofty moral ideals of Jesus. This conception reached its classic statement in Adolf von Harnack's *What Is Christianity?* (1901) with his epitomizing Jesus' teachings as the Fatherhood of God, the brotherhood of all human beings, and the infinite value of the human soul.

It was Johannes Weiss (*Jesus' Teaching on the Kingdom of God,* 1892) and Albert Schweitzer (*The Quest of the Historical Jesus,* 1903) who helped bring an end to this understanding of Jesus' words by pointing out that just as Jesus as a person did not fit into modern categories, neither did his message. Jesus was not a Kantian ethicist, but rather an ancient apocalyptic prophet, proclaiming the end of the age with the coming of an enigmatic figure called the "Son of Man."

The existentialist underpinnings of both the Bultmannian rejection of the Old Quest and the subsequent New Quest of the Historical Jesus made the search for Jesus' real words theologically secondary. The primary importance of Jesus' words—what we may know of them—is to challenge us to new life or a new self-understanding. Taken in their historical context Jesus' words were nothing more than what historical research could show them to be, whether rabbinic, apocalyptic, esoteric, or basically indeterminate. But as used by God, they become an existential challenge to our smug self-satisfaction and a call to encounter the living God.

The need to know what Jesus really said did not go away, however, and many in the New Quest and the subsequent "Third Quest" went back to the task of seeking Jesus' real words. There was a problem, however. The problem was now, in the light of developed Gospel studies, how to sift the material so that later additions and changes made by the church communities, the redactors, the legend-making propensities of the time, the oral transmitters of the tradition and the final "author" of the finished gospel can be set aside, leaving us only what Jesus really said. So the search for criteria to distinguish the authentic from the inauthentic began. To date, no fewer than twenty-five such criteria have been suggested, some of them mutually exclusive, such as multiple source attestation, dissimilarity, consensus of scholars, multiple forms of a statement, and Palestinian environment. Interestingly, rather than create more confidence in the gospel materials, in general, this has brought about a greater skepticism.

The recent "Jesus Seminar" has also taken a skeptical line on this. After working six years trying to answer the question "What did Jesus really say?" these seventy scholars published their results in *The Five Gospels: The Search for the Authentic Words of Jesus* (1993)—the fifth gospel being the apocryphal "Gospel of Thomas." They concluded "Eighty-two percent of the words ascribed to Jesus in the gospels were not actually spoken by him" (*The Five Gospels,* p. 5).

Responses to this excessive skepticism are now arising in such works as C. Blomberg's *The Historical Reliability of the Gospels* (1987), *Jesus Under Fire* (1995), eds. M. J. Wilkins and J. P. Moreland, and *Is the New Testament Reliable?* by Paul Barnett. No doubt, the pendulum will swing back toward a more sensible position in the future.

The Teaching of Jesus. *Jesus' Teaching Method.* Jesus was in every respect a master communicator. He employed methods that were sufficiently familiar to his hearers to make them comfortable but sufficiently different to arrest their attention. What struck them most forcefully of all, however, was the person himself—Jesus taught them as one having authority. It is hard to define, even inhuman terms, what authority really is, but in Jesus' case it is even more difficult, because his authority made claims that went beyond the merely human, causing those who heard him to exclaim "Who is this man?" At least three things combined to make Jesus' very presence an unsettling challenge, a call to decision. First and foremost, he embodied what he taught, and what he taught seemed clearly beyond human capacities. Yet he embodied those principles to the highest degree without any embarrassment or arrogance. Was he *more* than merely human?—that was the implied question on everyone's mind. Second, his teaching was derived solely from the Old Testament, which was, of course, God's Word, and it was mediated directly through himself; he identified directly with it. The rabbis found it necessary to bolster their interpretations by extensive references to one another. Jesus never quoted another rabbi. "You have heard it said, but I say unto you" is how Jesus taught. God's word and his own words merged into one. Third, Jesus' words were backed up by demonstrations of power. Anyone can claim anything, but only one with more than human authority can say to the waves "Be still" and have those waves obey him.

Jesus' very presence caused the crowds to gather, but what he said caused them to gather as well. His teaching method was very much like the parables that he taught. It was designed to reveal enough of the truth to draw people it, but to conceal enough to cause people to stop and reflect. These people had heard biblical truth on many occasions; Jesus' task was to cause them to hear it afresh, perhaps even to hear it as a reality for the first time. To accomplish this Jesus would sometimes bury his meaning somewhere below the surface, so that people would have to dig for it. On other occasions, Jesus would use highly graphic language to make a point. It certainly caught their attention when he told them to take the plank out of their eye in order to see the speck in another's (Matt. 7:3–5) and called their religious leaders snakes (Matt. 23:33). Sometimes Jesus' words were seemingly self-contradictory ("The first will be last, and the last will be first"—Mark 10:31) and at times even shocking ("Cut off your hand; cut off your foot"—Mark 9:42–48). In all of this, Jesus' creative use of language was designed to force his hearers to a decision. He knew that giving them information was not enough. They must be challenged to embody and act on that information in order for it to change them. When attempting to do that they would be forced to confront their own inabilities and cast themselves on God, which was Jesus' ultimate intention. So Jesus and his message and his method of delivery all blended together to challenge the people. They either believed or they were offended and left.

Jesus' View of God. The foundation of everything that Jesus said and did was his conviction that God existed, knew what he was doing, and was involved in human affairs. From the very earliest time of Jesus' life of which we have record, he was in the house of God busy about his Father's affairs (Luke 2:46–49). Jesus lived in unbroken and immediate fellowship with God, virtually a life of prayer. He spent long periods of time in intimate communion with God and at critical junctures during his public career, such as his baptism, his transfiguration, his agony in the garden, and his death, God's presence was a vivid reality, more real than even the seemingly substantial reality around him. It was out of this profound personal experience that what Jesus had to say about God arose. He never doubted that God existed nor did it occur to him to attempt to prove that there was a God. All of Jesus' reassuring began with the fact of God and moved downward toward human affairs. He never started with an undefined human situation and argued his way to the conclusion that somehow God must be there. For him that God existed was a given.

For Jesus, that God could be known personally, directly, and intimately was also a given. This meant that religious ritual and complicated ceremonial activity should not be inserted between a person and God. Too often these things become primary and the vision of God is obscured. The term that Jesus used most frequently to define what kind of person God is was heavenly Father. This term is found in the Old Testament, as, indeed, virtually everything Jesus says about God's nature and actions is, but it had become so vague by Jesus' time as to be almost meaningless. Consequently, Jesus emphasized this in order to make it alive for us once more. Jesus' chief concern was to renew in the people of his day a sense of the divine reality—the presence of a personal, loving God, who is our heavenly Father. It is for this reason that Jesus never mentioned what might be called the harder aspects of God's being, calling God King or Judge. He knew very well that God was both King and Judge, but he wanted people to know that a heavenly Father ruled and judged.

The attributes, or qualities, that God possesses are all derived from God's self-revelation in the Old Testament and can be verified anew in the life of the believer. God is good, glorious, true, loving, giving, righteous, perfect, all-powerful, all-knowing, wise, and sovereign, to mention just a few. Sometimes these are stated as abstract theological truth or fact (e.g., "All things are possible with God"—Mark 10:27) but most often they are related to concrete human situations. God, in the totality of his being, is vitally concerned with human beings in every aspect of their lives, from the number of hairs on their head, to the need for daily bread, to their eternal salvation.

It was Jesus' supreme desire that people know God as he really is once more. He set out to accomplish this by offering himself as the unique embodiment of that reality and introducing them to the one true God, their heavenly Father.

The Kingdom of God. That God existed was the essence of Jesus' teaching; that God ruled over the world he had created was the way in which what might have been simply an abstract idea (God is) was concretely related to everyday human life. The term Jesus chose to express this understanding was the "kingdom of God." This was no new idea, but drawn directly from the Old Testament (1 Chron. 16:31; Pss. 9:7–8; 97:1). What Jesus wanted the people to see was that the reign of God had been brought down from heaven to earth in the work that he was doing and in the gospel of salvation that he was preaching.

What was this kingdom that Jesus was proclaiming? Primarily, it was a spiritual realm or reality where God's will was being accomplished and people were invited to enter it. It was not restricted to one small nation or geographical place, but included everything. God exercised his sovereignty everywhere. But Jesus was proclaiming more than just the generalized providence of God. Jesus was preaching the kingdom as the realm where God's saving will was being done. In this sense the kingdom of God was nothing less than eternal salvation. To be in the kingdom was to be saved; to refuse entrance into the kingdom was to be lost.

Another important aspect of the kingdom as Jesus proclaimed it was that it is both a present and a future reality. In Jewish theology the kingdom was commonly understood to be arriving at the end of this sinful age. When this world ends, the kingdom of God will begin. For Jesus the kingdom is both present and future. We may enter into God's eternal salvation now and begin to experience its benefits at this present time, while still living in this fallen age. From now until the end of this age we will be in the world but not of it. But the kingdom is also future, in that, when this age ends only the kingdom will remain. So we look forward to that day when God will be all in all and pray "Your kingdom come."

Many things are said by Jesus about entering into the kingdom. The simplest way to say it was repent and believe the gospel (Mark 1:14–15). In another instance Jesus said we must be converted and become like little children (Matt. 18:3). To Nicodemus he says "you must be born again" (John 3:3). Jesus likens this to entering through a narrow gate (Matt. 7:13–14) and building a house upon a rock (Matt. 7:24–27). It is of such immense value that we should be willing to sacrifice anything for it (Matt. 18:8–9), hard as that might be, as it was for the rich young man (Matt. 19:23–24). When Jesus' disciples asked how then anyone could be saved, his answer was, "With man this is impossible, but with God all things are possible" (Matt. 19:26), which is the whole point. To enter the kingdom by our own effort is impossible; it takes the renewing power of God to make us new people and establish us in God's kingdom.

Salvation as New Life in God's Kingdom. When, by the renewing grace of God, one enters the kingdom, that person is converted, born again, made new, and a whole new life begins. The newness of life is not an option, but a fact. Being in the kingdom means being new. If there is no newness of life, regardless of what one says—even, "Lord, Lord" (Matt. 7:21)—that person is not truly known by God. Jesus likens this to a bush or a tree. Good trees produce good fruit, bad trees produce bad fruit (Matt. 7:16–20).

Jesus' mission was that we might have life at its fullest (John 10:10) and that is to be found in the kingdom. Life outside the kingdom is not really life at all. Throughout his teaching Jesus contrasted true life in the kingdom and false life on the outside. Those outside the kingdom imagine that the true purpose of life is to amass possessions, or gain status, or appear pious, or see the fruits of our human endeavors, or achieve some inner self-realization. None of these things embody the essence of true life. Life does not consist of the abundance of our possessions (Luke 12:15–21) and we are not to store up for ourselves treasures on earth (Matt. 6:19–20). Nor does life consist of our privileged position or status no matter how exalted that might be (Matt. 21:43; Luke 11:27–28). Even outward piety and religious correctness are of no value in defining what life is (Matt. 6:16). As for human endeavor, what profit would there be if we gained the whole world and lost our soul in the process (Mark 8:36–37)? And the one who seeks to fulfill life by saving it, will in fact lose it (Mark 8:35). All of the values that are operative in the world are to be left behind when one enters the kingdom. There is an entirely different set of values operating that in fact reverse the values of the world.

The new life that Jesus offers when we enter the kingdom is like an inexhaustible well of water within us that refreshes us in this life and springs up into life eternal (John 4:13–14; 7:37–38). The most characteristic feature of the new being that we have become is love. We are to love God with all of our being as or highest priority (Mark 12:30). The second requirement of living in the kingdom is to love our neighbor as well (Mark 12:31). The transformed heart is able to do what humanly cannot be done. We are enabled to dethrone ourselves and our own ambitions and give God his proper place in our lives and see him reflected in those around us (Matt. 25:44–45). A new set of positive spiritual qualities replaces the destructive, self-defeating characteristics of the old life. Jesus summarizes these in the Beatitudes as poverty of spirit, meekness, desire for righteousness, mercy, purity of heart, the ability to bring peace, and the ability to love and forgive those who revile us (Matt. 5:1–12). All of these spiritual qualities will express themselves in concrete action toward those around us, even our enemies, and in doing this we will be showing that we are true children of our heavenly Father, who also loves in this way (Matt. 5:43–48).

Humanity and Sin. In Jesus' teaching there is no finely developed doctrine of the human person and of sin. He was too busy dealing with the practical consequences of humanity's weaknesses and sinfulness to spend much time speculating about it. He had compassion on the crowds, seeing them as sheep without a shepherd (Mark 6:34). It is possible, however, to draw together what Jesus did say and get a rather clear picture of what he taught.

The most fundamental thing to be said about human beings is that they are created by God. When this is understood, everything else falls into its proper place. As creatures of God, we are not answerable to ourselves or to anyone else, but to God. We do not own ourselves, or define ourselves, or live for ourselves, but rather for God. By the same token, we cannot own someone else or define them either. We are all alike in our creaturely status, made in God's image and responsible for one another to God. Being made by God, we must find out what God intended us to be, if we are to fulfill our true destiny. It is only when we live up to what he intended that we find out who we really are. For Jesus, the finding of our true selves will take place only in the kingdom of God, which is our true home.

Jesus taught that all human beings are valuable (Matt. 10:31; 12:11–12), we are not to be anxious about our lives and the necessities of life. We have a heavenly Father who knows our needs and has made provision for them (Matt. 6:25–33). Even the hairs of our head are numbered (Matt. 10:30). God does not discriminate, but sends his blessings, rain and sun, upon the just and the unjust alike (Matt. 5:45). Because we are valued by God, we can value ourselves and others, and relax in the knowledge that God cares infinitely for us and has our best interest at heart.

That we are sinful was also taught by Jesus. He made no special point of emphasizing this. It was simply taken for granted (Matt. 7:11). What is extraordinary about Jesus' attitude is that he did not see this as an ultimate barrier between us and God but as a platform from which to rise. Indeed, we must start with the frank recognition of our helplessness if we are to make any progress at all. "I have not come to call the righteous, but sinners to repentance," is how Jesus put it (Luke 5:32). Jesus saw the tragic consequences of sin everywhere, rebuked the self-righteous who would not acknowledge their own sinfulness, and severely criticized those who caused other people to sin (Luke 17:1–2). But Jesus looked beyond sin to the ultimate intention of God for us. Our sinfulness is not the essence of what we are but rather a distortion of that essence. Salvation in God's kingdom restores us to what God intended us to be.

Eschatology. Eschatology is the doctrine of the last things and deals with the ultimate fate of both the individual and the universe. Jesus had much to say on both aspects of this subject, but never as an attempt to satisfy mere curiosity. He always spoke in terms of the subject's profound significance and of the effect it should have on our life as we live it now. What awaits the individual is death, the intermediate state, the resurrection of the body, the last judgment, and the eternal state in heaven or hell. What awaits the universe, in particular the world in which we live, is the events leading up to the end of the age, the second coming of the Messiah, the millennial age, the renovation of this world order, and the final state of the cosmos. Personal and cosmic eschatology intersect at the point of the messiah's second coming when the resurrection of the just and the last judgment occur. There will be one generation of people, the very last, who experience both personal and cosmic eschatology at the same time. Many theologians, from the earliest days of the church until now, do not believe Jesus taught a millennial age for this earth, so they would telescope the return of Christ, the resurrection of the just and the unjust, the last judgment, the renovation of the universe, and entrance into the eternal state into one momentous event.

Individuals, whether redeemed or unredeemed, will live out their lives in this age and pass through death to the intermediate state, there to await the end of the age, either in blessedness or in self-chosen separation from God (Luke 16:19–31). We will take with us into the afterlife what we are, either our redemption or our condemnation. Jesus speaks of no second chance after death or of any reincarnation to provide an opportunity for salvation in a second or third lifetime. Jesus speaks of the believer's death as in fact not being death at all, but a shift from a more limited interaction with God to a fulfillment of that, hence "whoever lives and believes in me will never die" (John 11:25–26). To the thief on the cross he says, "Today you will be with me in paradise" (Luke 23:43). The unbelievers, however, will die in their sins and cannot go where Jesus is (heaven) because they have refused the salvation of God (John 3:18, 36; 8:21–24).

This age continues on until it is brought to a close with the second coming of Christ. Jesus was asked by his disciples to explain all of this and much of what he said is found in the so-called Olivet Discourse (Matt. 24–25). There he outlines the conditions that will prevail until this age ends and some of the events that must take place before that occurs, such as apostasy (Matt. 24:10), false christs (Matt. 24:11, 24), increase of evil (Matt. 24:12), wars and rumors of wars (Matt. 24:8) and the worldwide proclamation of the gospel (Matt. 24:14). The exact time of Jesus' second coming is unknown to us (Matt. 24:42; 25:13); it will be sudden (Mark 13:33–36) and unexpected (Matt. 24:44), like a thief in the night (Matt. 24:42–44).

When Jesus returns at the end of the age, it will be from heaven in great glory, accompanied by angels, to gather his saints together for the new age that is arriving (Matt. 24:29–31). It is at this point that the resurrection takes place (Mark 12:26–27; Luke 20:37–38; John 5:21–29; 6:39–40). Some theologians make this a general resurrection, in which both the saved and the lost are raised. At this point also the last judgment takes place that Jesus frequently spoke of in general terms to emphasize the contrast between the saved and the lost, such as the parables of the net (Matt. 13:47–50), the sheep and the goats (Matt. 25:31–46), and the wheat and the weeds (Matt. 13:24–43). The judgment will be based upon the use of our opportunities on earth (Matt. 11:20–24; 16:27; Luke 12:42–48).

After the millennial reign on earth (Matt. 5:5; 19:27–28; 25:34; Luke 22:29–30), the redeemed inherit eternal life in heaven (Matt. 6:19–21; Luke 10:20). Jesus calls this his father's house (John 14:2) and the place where he is (John 12:26; 14:4; 17:24). Those who have rejected the salvation that God offered to them will enter into a place of condemnation (John 5:29), anguish (Matt. 25:29–30), and destruction (Matt. 7:13). Jesus likens it to a burning furnace (Matt. 13:42) of eternal fire (Matt. 25:41), and calls it hell, where both body and soul are destroyed (Matt. 10:28).

The heavens and earth all pass away in accordance with Jesus' word (Matt. 5:18; 24:35) and the final state begins. The Gospels do not record exactly what Jesus said about the new heavens and the new earth that is to come but no doubt his two apostles, Peter (2 Peter 3:10–13) and John (Rev. 21:1–22:6), reflect this when they speak of the glories to come.

Jesus' Understanding of Himself. The Jesus who is presented to us by the four Gospels is a figure who defies purely human characterization. The only conclusion the rest of the New Testament can draw with respect to him is that he was in fact Immanuel, God with us (Matt. 1:23; John 1:1, 18; 20:28; Rom. 9:5; Col. 1:19; Titus 2:13; Rev. 19:16). Jesus was a human being, fully human in every way, but was vastly more than that, and that "moreness" could only be understood as essential deity. Jesus was nothing less than an incarnation of the eternal God himself. But the question arises, What did Jesus claim about this? Did he see himself as in some way an incarnation of God? If the Gospels are taken at face value, the answer must be yes. Modern critical scholarship denies this by asserting that the early church, convinced by its "Easter faith" that Jesus was something exceptional, altered his historical utterances and made up yet others reflecting this and then read them back into the life of this historical Jesus, a Jesus who never made such claims. This theory is based on the presupposition that Jesus could not be more than human and that God could not have become incarnate in Jesus of Nazareth. If, however, one does not categorically reject that possibility, then Jesus' claims, the teaching of the Gospels, and the rest of the New Testament paint a consistent picture that challenges the confronted person to the utmost. Is Jesus or is Jesus not the ultimate revelation and embodiment of the eternal God? The challenge was no different two thousand years ago than it is today.

The evidence for the uniqueness of Jesus as presented in the Gospels falls into two categories: those things that Jesus did not say and do and those things that he did in fact say and do. Both sets point to Jesus as unique among us.

What Jesus did not say and do. Simply put, Jesus never put himself in the same category as other human beings. What he was with respect to God was something he was alone; he never invited anyone to share his relationship with God. Consequently, Jesus never said to his disciples, Let us worship God together; Let us put our faith in God; Let us pray together; Let us trust or hope in God. Jesus never asked forgiveness from God, nor showed any awareness of sin in his life. He never called God his savior, as though he needed saving. Jesus never even called God Father or God and included his followers. It is always "your heavenly Father; your God" and "my Father; my God." He never used an expression that includes them, such as our Father, our God, our faith, our trust. The one time he did use an expression like that was to accentuate the difference that existed between him and his followers. When asked by his disciples to teach them to pray, he said to them, "This is how you should pray, our Father . . ." (Matt. 6:9–13), but he himself never prayed that with them. When he did pray, it was as one wholly apart, as at the transfiguration (Luke 9:28–36). Jesus knew that he was not simply one of us and never invited us to become what he was, nor did he put himself in the same category that he put us.

What Jesus claimed for himself. When asked about his origin, Jesus said "I am from above. . . . I am not of this world. . . . I came from God and now am here. . . . You are from below. . . . You are of this world" (John 8:21–23, 42); "I have come down from heaven. . . . I am the bread that came down from heaven" (John 6:32–42). He who has come down from heaven is the only one who has ever known God (John 6:46) and those who have seen him, have seen the Father (John 14:8–11) because he and the Father are one (John 10:30–33). At another point Jesus startles his hearers by claiming to be the "I Am" who antedated Abraham and spoke to Moses in the desert (John 8:54–59). The Gospel of John also provides a series of supernatural claims by Jesus based on the "I Am" formula—I am the bread of life (6:35), the light of the world (8:12), the gate for the sheep (10:7), the good shepherd (10:11), the resurrection and the life (11:25), the true vine (15:1), and the way, the truth, and the life (14:6). All of these claims are deeply rooted in God's revelation of himself in the Old Testament and are claims by Jesus to represent deity.

In other instances Jesus exercised God's authority in forgiving sins (Mark 2:1–12; Luke 7:44–49) and accepted honors that are due to God alone, such as prayer, praise, and worship (Matt. 14:33; 15:25; 21:15–16; 28:9, 17).

The Scriptures were understood by Jesus and the Jews of his day to be the Word of God. Jesus claimed that the Scriptures spoke directly about him (John 5:39) and he was the fulfillment of its prophecies (Luke 4:16–21), indeed of the whole of Scripture (Matt. 5:17).

The temple and the Sabbath represented the highest expressions of God's presence to the Jewish mind, yet Jesus claimed to be greater than the temple (Matt. 12:6), in his own person being a new temple (Matt. 26:59–61; John 2:19–21), and also the Lord of the Sabbath (Matt. 12:8).

Jesus believed that his words had special, indeed, eternal significance: "Heaven and earth will pass away, but my words will never pass away" (Matt. 24:35). Those who keep Jesus' words will live forever (John 8:51; 11:26) and those who reject his words will personally be rejected by him (Mark 8:38). Over seventy times Jesus uses a special formula to introduce his words—"Amen, I say unto you." Ordinarily "Amen" follows a statement or prayer, affirming its truth. In Jesus' case it comes first, asserting that whatever he said was true, simply because he said it. No one else spoke that way in his time.

Jesus claimed to be the answer to humanity's deepest needs (Matt. 10:28–30; John 10:10) and that our eternal destiny depends on him (Matt. 7:21–23; Mark 8:34–38). He claims to have power over space (Matt. 18:20) and time (Matt. 28:20) and to possess cosmic significance; bringing about the end of the age (Matt. 24:30–31). He had power over the supernatural forces, both angels (Matt. 26:53) and demons (Mark 5:6–8), and he sent his disciples out with his authority to cast out demons and to heal (Luke 9:1–2).

Jesus offered himself to his generation as the Messiah, God's special representative (Matt. 11:2–6; 26:62–68; Luke 19:37–40; John 4:25–26). The Book of Daniel (7:13–14) had prophesied a coming supernatural "Son of Man," whose kingdom would never end and who would be worshiped by all the nations of the world, and Jesus claimed to be that Son of Man (Matt. 16:13–16).

Conclusion. Christianity centers around Jesus Christ; indeed, some have said Christianity *is* Christ. To attempt to abstract from Jesus a "religion" that can operate independently of who he is, what he did, and what he taught would not be Christianity at all. Some attempts have been made to formulate a "universal" religion, that is, one that seeks a commonality in the major religious points of view in the world. Such attempts have invariably failed. Although it is true that the religious ideas of some of the other major religions can be separated from their founders to be pulled together into a collective "religion," the same cannot be said of Christianity. It stands or falls with its founder. He is inextricably a part of what he preached; his message is essentially who he was and what he did; his actions presuppose what he said about himself and his mission; the ultimate validation of the salvation (if that be called "religion") that he offered is found in his present ministry as crucified and risen again.

Walter A. Elwell

See also Ascension of Jesus Christ; Beatitudes; Christ, Christology; Cross, Crufixion; Death of Christ; God; Immanuel; Jesus Christ; Kingdom of God; Lamb, Lamb of God; Lord's Prayer, the; Messiah; Resurrection; Second Coming of Christ; Sermon of the Mount; Virgin Birth.

Bibliography. C. Blomberg, *The Historical Reliability of the Gospels;* G. A. Boyd, *Cynic Sage or Son of God?;* F. F. Bruce, *The Hard Sayings of Jesus;* B. Chilton and C. A. Evans, eds., *Studying the Historical Jesus: Evaluations of the State of Current Research;* W. L. Craig, *The Son Arises;* idem, *The Historical Argument for the Resurrection of Jesus;* C. A. Evans, *Life of Jesus Research: An Annotated Bibliography;* idem, *Noncanonical Writings and New Testament Interpretation;* L. Goppelt, *Theology of the New Testament: The Ministry of Jesus in Its Theological Significance;* J. B. Green, S. McKnight, and I. H. Marshall, *Dictionary of Jesus and the Gospels;* M. Green, *The Empty Cross of Jesus;* A. E. Harvey, *Jesus and the Constraints of History;* J. Jeremias, *New Testament Theology: The Proclamation of Jesus;* T. W. Manson, *The Teaching of Jesus;* J. P. Meier, *A Marginal Jew: Rethinking the Historical Jesus;* B. F. Meyer, *The Aims of Jesus;* L. Morris, *New Testament Theology;* J. Pelikan, *Jesus Through the Centuries;* R. H. Stein, *The Method and Message of Jesus' Teaching;* D. Wenham, ed., *Gospel Perspectives V: The Jesus Tradition Outside the Gospels;* J. Wenham, *Easter Enigma;* M. J. Wilkins and J. P. Moreland, *Jesus under Fire: Modern Scholarship Reinvents the Historical Jesus;* B. Witherington III, *The Christology of Jesus;* N. T. Wright, *Jesus and the Victory of God;* idem, *Who Was Jesus?*

Jesus Christ, Name and Titles of. In our culture names serve primarily to distinguish one person from another. In Bible times names had other significant functions. In the New Testament, names that were applied to Jesus often had special meanings that went back into Old Testament and intertestamental times.

"Name" in the Ancient Near East. Outside Israel knowledge of the name of a god or goddess was important in the performance of magical rites, by which a person could get control of the deity. Benevolent deities would reveal their names and protect or aid their human contacts; unwilling or malevolent deities would be reluctant to reveal their names and thereby come under the control of the magician.

Though it is anachronistic to speak of "secular" Greek, non-Christian Greek literature used "name" in a number of different ways. For example, if a stranger expected hospitality, he first had to indicate to his host what his name was. Philosophers such as Plato attacked the widespread idea that the root meaning of the names of gods or humans revealed their character. Though Stoicism argued that there was really only one god, it also held that the deity was known by many different names. At the other extreme, the seventeen tractates of the Greco-Egyptian god Hermes Trismegistos argue that he is so lofty that no name is appropriate for him and that, as in rabbinic Judaism, human beings should not attempt to utter his name at all.

The Old Testament uses the word, *shēm*, "name," no less than 854 times, with "in the name of" occurring over 130 times. The idea of Name often revealed a basic characteristic of an individual. Similarly, names could be changed to reflect changes in circumstances (e.g., Jacob becomes Israel—Gen. 32:28).

Of special importance is *shēm Yahweh*, "the name of the Lord" (or similar expressions such as "in the name of [our] God"). Though some scholars suggest that the "name" is somehow a being separate from the Lord who is present in the angel of the Lord (Exod. 23:20–21) or in the temple (1 Kings 8:14–30), such a conclusion was contradicted by the monotheistic history of Israel.

The name of God was significant to the ancient Hebrews because it comprehended in itself all that God is. In fact, "the name" was a synonym for God; hence believers are not to take the name of the Lord in vain (Exod. 20:7). The name of God is holy and awesome (Pss. 99:3; 111:9) and signifies his personal presence (2 Chron. 7:16; Ps. 75:1). God's people are to reverence (Ps. 86:11), love (Ps. 5:11), praise (Ps. 97:12), trust (Isa. 50:10), call upon (Isa. 12:4), and hope in the divine name (Ps. 52:9). In God's divine name is the ultimate salvation of his people.

In the pseudepigraphical and rabbinic writings of later Judaism, two significant developments centering on the "name" of God occur, though in general the tendency is to repeat the practices of the Old Testament. The apocalyptic literature of the period tends to focus on the meaning of the names of saints and angels, not God. Seven divine names are mentioned in 4 Esdras 7:132–39. The rabbinic writings mention the healing of a rabbi "in the name of" another person. The most important development was the substitution of "Adonai" (Lord) for "Yahweh" in synagogue usage and the use of *hashēm*, "the name," for both "Yahweh," "Elohim" (God), and even "Adonai" in the rabbinic schools, at least when quoting the Tanach, so the rabbis forgot how YHWH was orginally pronounced.

The "Name" of Jesus. The expression the "Name" of Jesus is frequent and highly significant in New Testament usage in that it parallels the use of the name of God in the Old Testament. The early Christians had no difficulty substituting the name of Jesus for the name of God. Indeed, for them the divine name, YHWH, was given to Jesus, that every knee should bow to him and every tongue confess that he is Lord (Phil. 2:9–11; cf. Isa. 45:20–23). New Testament believers are to live their lives in Jesus' name just as the Old Testament believers were to live in the name of God the Lord.

People who hear the gospel and respond positively, call upon Jesus' name for salvation (Acts 2:21), put their faith in Jesus' name (John 1:12; 1 John 5:13), are then justified (1 Cor. 6:11) and forgiven in Jesus' name (Acts 10:43; 1 John 2:12), and are then baptized into Jesus' name (Acts 2:38; 10:48; 19:5). Having then, life in his name (John 20:31), believers are to glorify the name of Jesus (2 Thess. 1:12) and give thanks for and do everything in the name of Jesus (Eph. 5:20; Col. 3:17). Just as in the Old Testament where the name of God represents the person of God and all that he is, so in the New Testament "the Name" represents all who Jesus is as Lord and Savior. LESLIE R. KEYLOCK

The Titles of Jesus. In addition to the comprehensive idea that is found in the idea of Jesus' name there are also a number of significant titles that are ascribed to Jesus in the New Testament. Each one has something special to say about who Jesus is and together they constitute a definition of his person and work, and become as it were his "name."

Author-Prince. Jesus is called "Author" in Acts 3:15 and Hebrews 2:10; 12:2 and "Prince" in Acts 5:31 (NIV). In each case the Greek word is the same: *archēgos.* Uses of the term in the Greek Old Testament (LXX) and nonbiblical Greek suggest it carries a threefold connotation: (1) pathbreaker (pioneer) who opens the way for others, hence, "guide" or "hero"; (2) the source or founder, hence "author," "initiator," "beginning"; and (3) the leader-ruler, hence, "captain," "prince," "king." The ideas may well overlap or be combined. In its fullest sense the Greek word denotes someone who explores new territory, opens a trail, and leads others to it. The *archēgos* builds a city or fortress for those who follow and leads them in defense against attackers. When the peace has been won he remains as their ruler and the city or community bears his name. He is thereafter honored as the founding hero.

In Acts 3:15 Peter accuses the Jews of killing the "author (*archēgos*) of life," suggesting that Jesus is not only the orgin of biological life, but also of "new life" and the provider-proctor of those identified with him. Later Peter speaks of Jesus as the "Prince (*archēgos*) and Savior" who gives repentance to Israel (5:31). The word "Savior" was associated with the Judges of old. Jesus is the one who meets the emergency situation caused by the sin of God's people and he comes to bring not only deliverence but also the continuing service of Author (*archēgos).* The writer to the Hebrews speaks of the suffering "Author (*archēgos*) . . . of salvation" (2:10) and the "author (*archēgos*) and perfecter of our faith" (12:2). In each case Jesus not only initiates and provides the new life for his people but remains with them through it; they bear his name, he is their king.

J. JULIUS SCOTT, JR.

The Chosen One. Jesus is referred to as God's chosen in Luke's account of the transfiguration (9:35) and by Matthew (12:18) as he applies Isaiah 42:1 to Jesus. In 1 Peter he is designated as the one "chosen before the creation of the world . . . revealed in these last times" (1:20) and as the "living stone—rejected by men but chosen by God" (2:4).

In the Old Testament Israel's leaders—Abraham (Gen. 18:19), Moses and Aaron (Pss. 105:26; 106:23), priests and Levites (Deut. 2:5), Saul (1 Sam. 10:24), David (1 Kings 8:16; 2 Chron. 6:6; Ps. 89:3), and the Servant of the Lord (Isa. 42:1; 43:10)—are said to be chosen by God. Israel as a whole is frequently designated as God's chosen (Deut. 7:6; Isa. 41:8; 44:1; Amos 3:2). All of these were earthly persons or groups through whom God carried on his work of revelation and redemption.

Jesus is "The Chosen One" par excellence and been appointed by God to accomplish his task on earth. He embodies all that Old Testament chosen ones were to have been. He is the special object of God's love and the perfect divine messenger-redeemer.

Jesus refers to his apostles as those whom he has chosen (John 6:70; 13:18; 15:19), and church is also called God's "chosen" (Eph. 1:11; Col. 3:12; James 2:5; 1 Peter 1:2; 2:9), by virtue of being Christ's body. As the church abides "in Christ" she shares that special designation of being "chosen." The church is the object of Christ's love and redemption, called to have fellowship with him and to continue his work on work.

J. JULIUS SCOTT, JR.

Christ, Messiah, Anointed One. The title "Christ" or "Anointed One" (Heb. *māšîaḥ;* Gk. *Christos*), which occurs about 350 times in the New Testament, is derived from verbs that have the general meaning of "to rub (something)" or, more specifically, "to anoint someone." The Old Testament records the anointing with oil of priests (Exod. 29:1–9), kings (1 Sam. 10:1; 2 Sam. 2:4; 1 Kings 1:34), and sometimes prophets (1 Kings 19:16b) as a sign of their special function in the Jewish community. The prophet Isaiah recognizes his own anointing (to preach good news to the poor, 61:1) and that of Cyrus, king of Persia (to "subdue nations," 45:1), apparently as coming directly from the Lord without the usual ceremony of initiation. As a noun, the Lord's "Anointed" usually refers to a king (1 Sam. 12:3, 5), while designation of a priest (Lev. 4:5) or the partriarchs (Ps. 105:15) is less common.

The word "anointed," however, is not used directly in the Hebrew Bible as a title for a future messianic person, who would save Israel. The word "Messiah," therefore, does not appear in major English translations of the Hebrew Bible such as the Revised Standard Version or the New International Version. "Messiah" appears only twice in the New Testament (John 1:41; 4:25) as an explanation of the Greek word "Christ."

By the time Jesus was born, however, a number of passages in the Hebrew Bible were understood to refer to a specific anointed person who would bring about the redemption of Israel, and that person was called "the Christ" (Acts 2:27, 31). The Samaritans were looking for him (John 4:24). The Jews looked for him and expected him to perform great miracles (John 7:31). He was to be the son of David (Matt. 22:42) and, like David, come from Bethlehem (John 7:41–42). Even criminals condemned to death on a cross knew about a Christ and asked Jesus if he was that person (Luke 23:39).

The word "Christ" is used to identify Jesus of Nazareth as that person whom God anointed to be the redeemer of humanity. It thus often appears as a title in the phrase "Jesus the Christ" (Acts 5:42; 9:22; 17:3) or "the Christ was Jesus" (Acts 18:28). Peter referred to him as "both Lord and Christ" (Acts 2:36). Very frequently the word is coupled with the name of Jesus and appears to be virtually a second name "Jesus Christ" (Acts 2:38; 3:6; 9:34; 10:36; Rom. 1:6–8; 1 Cor. 1:6–10), through not a surname, because "Christ Jesus" is also commonly used (1 Cor. 1:1–30; Gal. 2:4). In close proximity in the same chapter, Jesus can be called "Jesus Christ" (Gal. 3:22), "Christ" (3:24), and "Christ Jesus" (3:26).

In Paul's writings "Christ" is used both with and without the definite article (1 Cor. 6:15; Gal. 2:17), in combination with the title Lord (*kyrios*, Rom. 10:9), as well as combined with such ideas as gospel (Rom. 1:16) or faith (Gal. 2:16).

Elsewhere in the New Testament, the author of the Epistle to the Hebrews picks up on the Old Testament anoiting of priests and applies the same in relation to Jesus (1:9; 5:8–10; 7:1–28). The name occurs also in the Petrine Epistles (1 Peter 1:13; 3:15; 2 Peter 1:1–2, 16; 3:18), as well as those of James (1:1; 2:1) and Jude (1, 17, 21, 25). The Apocalypse of John describes Jesus as the Anointed One when looking forward to the end when the kingdom and salvation of the Lord and his Messiah will enjoy an eternal and full dominion (11:15; 12:10; 20:4, 6).

The significance of the name "Christ" lies in the fact that it was a title granted to Jesus by virtue of his fulfillment of Old Testament prophecy and by his resurrection from the dead. The name "Jesus" was a common Hebrew name (the Greek form of Joshua, cf. Luke 3:29; Heb. 4:8, where Jesus in the Greek text is translated Joshua) and is borne by other people in the New Testament including Barabbas (Matt. 27:17) and Justus (Col. 4:11). But no one else bears the name Christ. It is significant that early disciples of Jesus were not called "Jesusites" but "Christians," followers of Christ (Acts 11:26; 26:28; 1 Peter 4:16). James A. Kelhoffer and John McRay

Firstborn. Jesus is referred to by the singular form of the word "firstborn" (*prōtotokos*) in six passages in the New Testament. He is called the physical firstborn of Mary in Luke 2:7, because he subsequently had brothers and sisters (Matt. 13:55). In a spiritual sense, he is called firstborn to differentiate him from the angels (Heb. 1:6). He is the firstborn of all creation (Col. 1:15), and to those who believe in him he is the "firstborn among many brothers" (Rom. 8:29). He is unique among human beings, among other reasons, because of his resurrection from the dead. He was the first one resurrected to die no more, and thus he has the preeminence (Col. 1:18; Rev. 1:5).

John McRay

God. The New Testament rarely calls Jesus "God" as such (Gk. *theos*). "Lord," stressing his co-regency with the Father as Son, or "Christ," hallowing the kingly function he fulfilled, is preferred. Still, references to Jesus as God are not absent. John 1:1 clearly equates "the word" with God; in 1:14 it becomes clear that "the word" is Jesus. Arguments by Jehovah's Witnesses and others proposing different renderings of John 1:1 are untenable. In John 1:18 some translations call Jesus "God the One and Only" (NIV). The King James and other translations, however, follow a manuscript tradition that calls him "Son" here, not God.

Other passages, too, explicitly name Jesus as God. Romans 9:5 speaks of "Christ, who is God over all, forever praised!" Grammatical rules permit rending 2 Thessalonians 1:12 as " the grace of our God and Lord, Jesus Christ." The same holds true of Titus 2:13 ("our great God and Savior, Jesus Christ") and 2 Peter 1:1 ("our God and Savior Jesus Christ"). Hebrews 1:8 calls the Son God; 1 John 5:20 says of Jesus,"He is the true God and eternal life." Such texts confirm the impression given indirectly in other places that Jesus merits the name "God" by virtue of his mastery over wind and sea (Mark 4:41), personification of God's kingdom (Luke 11:20), ability to forgive sins (Mark 2:7), and intimacy with the invisible Father by which, enemies charged, he presumed to be "equal with God" (John 5:18). They could not accept that this was not effrontery but his due and possession (Phil. 2:6) from all eternity (John 17:24). It can be concluded that belief in Jesus' essential divinity (along with his obvious full humanity) extends to all levels of early Christian confession.

At the same time New Testament writers are not indiscriminate in speaking of Jesus as "God." They realized that despite the Father's virtual presence through his Son, "no one has ever seen God" in terms of mortals on earth beholding the unmediated fullness of God in heaven (John 1:18). They intuited, if they did not spell out and reflect on, the subtle offsetting truths of later Trinitarian affirmations. Their restraint in predicating full deity of Jesus is due, among other thing, to his humanity (which the good news of the incarnation [Luke 2:10] was bound to emphasize) and to their theological sophistication: Jews imbued with the sacred truth of God's oneness—Deuteronomy 6:4, "the Lord is one," rang out daily in worship—were not so callow as to label fellow humans "God."

Their own Scriptures, in fact, forbade this (Deut. 4:15–16), violation of which was blasphemy. Those same Scriptures sternly denounced any man "hung on a tree" (Deut. 21:23). Yet the crucified Jesus must be hailed as redeemer, not censured as a crimal (Gal. 3:13–14). By the same logic he must be granted his apparent divine parity. Thus was the man Jesus hailed rightly as God. ROBERT W. YARBROUGH

Holy One of God. In the Old Testament, "the Holy One of God" is a divine epithet common in the prophets and poetic literature used to communicate the separateness of the Lord. The New Testament applies this name to Jesus on two occasions in the Gospels (Mark 1:24 = Luke 4:34; John 6:69), once in Acts (3:14) and possibly on two other occasions (1 John 2:20; Rev. 3:7).

In the Gospel of Mark, Jesus begins his public ministry teaching in a Capernaum synagogue (1:21–22). Someone possed with an evil spirit then cries out, "What do you want with us, Jesus of Nazareth? Have you come to destroy us? I know who you are—the Holy One of God!" (1:23–24). The event is probably best understood in light of the secrecy motif of Mark's Gospel, whereby human beings rarely comprehend the true identity of Jesus. Instead, it is usually God (1:11; 9:7) or, as in this passage, demons (5:7) who know who Christ is before the crucifixion. In addition, knowing someone's "name" can communicate that an individual possesses power over that person. In spite of the demon's knowledge of his potential exorcist as "the Holy One of God," Jesus casts him out with a short command and amazes the crowd by his teaching and authority (Mark 1:25).

John contrasts the turning away of "many" disciples with the faith of the Twelve (John 6:66–69). Peter responds to Jesus, "Lord, to whom shall we go? You have the words of eternal life. We believe and know that you are the Holy One of God." First John 2:20 can refer to either God or Jesus when writing, "But you have an anointing from the Holy One. "The above reference to the Gospel of John makes it possible that Jesus is the giver of this anointing, but the author may intentionally leave this designation unclear.

In the Book of Acts Peter addresses the curious crowd on the role they played in the crucifixion of Jesus. Nothing could be worse than denying "the Holy and Righteous One" and asking for the release of a murderer instead (3:14). Finally, in the letter to the angel presiding over the church at Philadelphia, Jesus is him who is holy and true, who holds the key of David" (Rev. 3:7). This verse, like Acts 3:14, illustrates how the full epithet ("the Holy One of God") could be abbreviated and combined with other descriptions of Jesus to enhance the main thrust of the passage. In Acts Peter aims to convict his audience, while the apocalyptic writer offers multiple images of Jesus to encourage the congregation in a time of intense persecution. JAMES A. KELHOFFER

Lord. Scripture ascribes glory to Jesus Christ in numerous ways, but in naming him "Lord" (Gk. *kyrios*) it makes an ultimate statement. In the Septuagint the word appears over nine-thousand times; in over six-thousand of those passages *kyrios* replaces YHWH (Yahweh, Jehovah), the so-called sacred tetragrammaton. This was the name revealed by God to his covenant people through Moses affirmation (Exod. 3:14), a name held in such high esteem that by New Testament times it was rarely spoken out loud.

The truth of God's holy oneness, a nonnegotiable Old Testament affirmation (Exod. 20:3, Deut. 6:4; Isa. 43:10–11), would seem to rule out, at least among Jews, any application of *kyrios* to mere flesh and blood. Yet this is precisely what Paul does in testifying that God the Father bestowed on the Son "the name that is above every man" in order that all creation might acknowledge Jesus Christ as "Lord [*kyrios*], to the glory of God the Father" (Phil. 2:9–11). "Lord" thus serves as the name par excellence for Jesus Christ.

But Paul was by no means the first to apply this sacred title to Jesus. The Old Testament had predicted that a deliverer would come in the name of Lord. He would somehow be the Lord himself. Jesus invites reflection on this logically difficult truth in asking what David meant by affirming, "The LORD [Heb. YHWH] says to my Lord (LXX *kyrios*) . . ."(Ps. 110:1). In modern and postmodern thought Jesus' essential oneness with God the Father, his full divinity as second person of the Trinity, has been widely rejected as Hellenistic embellishment of earliest Christian belief. Yet ascription of full deity to Jesus seems necessitated by Old Testament prophecies as interpreted by Jesus himself. Jesus' disciples, taught by him from the Old Testament and witnesses to his numerous and varied mighty acts, came to understand and proclaim the truth of Thomas' outburst of recognition: "My Lord [*kyrios*] and my God!" (John 20:28).

Writing in the middle of the A.D. 50s Paul could already draw on an older tradition hailing Jesus as Lord: "Come, O Lord!" (1 Cor. 16:22) is not Greek (the language of Paul's Corinthian readers) but the Aramaic *maranatha* (one of the languages of Jesus' Palestinian surroundings). The confession is therefore rooted in the earliest days of church life where the prevailing linguistic milieu was Semitic. This rules out an older but still popular theory that the name "Lord" was projected back onto Jesus only long after his death by Gentile Christians whose pagan religious background caused them to have no scruples about applying the title *kyrios* to a mere human being.

While *kyrios* was common as a polite, even honorific title for "sir" or "master," calling Jesus "Lord" to imply divine associations or idenity was by no means a convention readily adopted from the Roman world. In Jesus' more Eastern but militantly monotheistic Jewish milieu, where the title's application to humans to connote divinity was not only absent but anathema, the title is an eloquent tribute to the astoning impression he made. It also points to the prerogatives he holds.

Since Jesus is Lord, he shares with the Father qualities like deity (Rom. 9:5), preexistence (John 8:58), holiness (Heb. 4:15), and compassion (1 John 4:9), to name just a few. He is co-creator (Col. 1:16) and co-regent, presiding in power at the Father's right hand (Acts 2:33; Eph. 1:20; Heb. 1:3), where he intercedes for God's people (Rom. 8:34) and from whence, as the Creed states, he will return to judge the living and dead (2 Thess. 1:7–8). Just as it is impossible to overstate the power, grandeur, and goodness of the *kyrios* the Father, so there is hardly limit to the glory ascribed in Scripture to the *kyrios* the Son. Therefore Isaiah's counsel, and Peter's, is to be heeded: "Sanctify the Lord [LXX *kyrios'* Heb. *'adonai sabbaōth*] himself" (Isa. 8:13 LXX), which Peter tellingly restates as "sanctify Christ as Lord" (1 Peter 3:15 NASB). ROBERT W. YARBROUGH

One and Only, Only Begotten. Jesus is called *monogenēs* (KJV "only begotten") in five New Testament passages (John 1:14, 18; 3:16, 18; 1 John 4:9). Modern translations tend to render the word "only" (RSV) or "one and only" (NIV). In any case, emphasis falls on Jesus' singular status: He is uniquely related to the Father, so close to him as to be one with him (John 5:18; 10:30), yet as distinct from him as was neccessary to allow for full identification with humanity through the incarnation (John 1:14).

Monogenēs is used in Luke 7:12, 8:42, and 9:38 to refer to the only child of the widow's son at Nain, to Jairus' daughter, and to an epileptic son, respectively. This shows that in conventional usage the word connoted being the solitary child. The one other New Testament occurrence of the word is Hebrews 11:17, speaking of Abraham's near-sacrifice of "his one and only son" Isaac. It has been suggested that for John as for the writer of Hebrews this incident (Gen. 22:1–18) serves as primary background for early Christian understanding of Jesus' sonship and sacrificial death.

Recent translations correctly reflect that Jesus' status as "only begotten" underscores his uniqueness rather than his place or mode of origin—it does not directly refer to his virgin birth. Both as unrivaled expression of the Father's glory and as distinct from any created human, he holds preeminemce (Col. 1:18). He is *monogenēs,* utterly unique, in his person and saving role. The church father Jerome (ca. A.D. 400) supplied the Vulgate's *unigenitus* ("only begotten") to help counter the Arian view that Jesus was a created being; *unigenitus* permitted Jesus to be "begotten" of the Father in the sense implied in certain Bible passages (e.g., Ps. 2:7; Acts 13:33), while "only" left room for affirmation of his divine nature. Through the Vulgate's influence on early English versions of the Bible, the traditional translation "only begotten" still rings true for many today.

ROBERT W. YARBROUGH

Son of David. We can trace two lines of interpretation regarding the Son of David (Gk. *hyios Dauid*) in the Old Testament, one that draws attention to a direct successor during the united monarchy (2 Sam. 7:12–16), and the other that applies the earlier promises to the coming of a future individual (Isa. 9:6–7). Both are crucial to understanding the title for Jesus in the New Testament.

Mention of the Son of David begins in the Old Testament with the oracle the prophet Nathan delivers to David (2 Sam. 7:12–16). God promises David offspring to succeed him. God "will be his father," and David's house and kingdom will be established forever. Numerous psalms highlight the same excitement over the continuation of the Davidic line (89:3–4; 110; 132). Even after the collapse of the united monarchy, the line of David remained significant for describing a future leader for the covenant people. Isaiah, for example, looks to the future for a child to be born who will reign on David's throne (9:6–7; cf. 55:3–4; Jer. 23:5; Ezek. 34:23).

In the century before Christ, moreover, both the Psalms of Solomon and the Qumran literature look to the same "Son" or "shoot" of David either as an ideal Hasmonean king or a ruler for the expectant Dead Sea community (Ps. Sol. 17–18; 4Qpatr 1–4). These last references would be of concern to New Testament authors since at least two (most probably opposing) Jewish groups had expectations for the Davidic line that were at odds with the historical Jesus. The former author, who portrays a triumphant and politically successful king, would never be satisfied with Jesus, who neither purged Jerusalem nor placed the Gentiles "under his yoke" (Ps. Sol. 17:30–32), but instead came "to seek and save that which was lost" and "to give his life as a ransom for many" (Mark 10:45).

The New Testament addresses this issue by affirming that Jesus is both a direct descendent of David and yet more than another human successor. The two most significant passages using this title are Mark 12:35–37a and Romans 1:1–4. In the Synoptic text Jesus questions the assumption that the son of David is merly a descendant of David since David himself in Psalm 110:1 refers to him as "Lord." In Romans 1:1–4 an ancient Christian creed to which Paul refers clarifies this same problem from the above Synoptic passage. Jesus was *both* "born through the seed of David according to the flesh (*kata sarka*)" and "foreseen as the Son of God in power by the Spirit of sanctification (*kata pneuma hagiōsunēs*) through the resurrection of the dead." In 2 Timothy 2:8 we also find the resurrection and Christ's having "descended from David" in a creedal context.

The Evangelist Matthew takes special interest in this title for Jesus, emphasizing that both Jesus (1:4) and Joseph (1:20) are direct descendants of the great Israelite king. Elsewhere Jesus is referred to as the "Son of David" in connection with healing (Matt. 12:23; 15:22; Mark 10:47–48), and the triumphal entry into Jerusalem (Matt. 21:9, 15). JAMES A. KELHOFFER

Son of God. Mark begins his Gospel with the statement: "The beginning of the gospel of Jesus Christ, the Son of God" (Mark 1:1). The phrase "Son of God" (*huios theou*) is a title used of Jesus to indicate that he is divine in nature, just as the title "Son of Man," among other things, indicates that he is human. Although the title is not used in a trinitarian context in the New Testament, the word Son is so used in Matthew 28:18–20, where Jesus commanded baptism to be performed in the name of the Father, Son, and Holy Spirit.

The title "Son of God" is used twenty-six times in the Gospels referring to Jesus. He is called Son of God by Satan (Matt. 4:3, 6; Luke 4:3, 9), by demons (Matt. 8:29; Mark 3:11; Luke 4:41), by John the Baptist (John 1:34), by his followers (Matt. 14:23; John 1:49; 11:27; 20:31), by angels (Luke 1:35), and by a Roman centurion (Matt. 27:54; Mark 15:39).

Those who passed by while he was on the cross derided him, asking for proof that he was the Son of God by coming down from the cross (Matt. 27:40). They were joined in their taunts by the most eminent of Jewish religious leaders: chief priests, scribes, and elders (Matt. 27:43; cf. 26:63). Jews considered the title to be an assumption of equality with Jehovah the God of Israel (John 10:36; 19:7); most were unprepared to allow a human being to occupy that position.

Jesus on occasion referred to himself with this title (John 3:18; 5:25; 10:36; 11:4) and on other occasions acknowledged its validity (Luke 22:70).

After his conversion and call to apostleship, Paul immediately began to declare in the synagogues that Jesus was indeed the Son of God (Acts 9:22). In his letters Paul used the phrase in reference to Jesus, saying he was "designated Son of God in power according to the Spirit of holiness by his resurrection from the dead" (Rom. 1:4; cf. 2 Cor. 1:19; Gal. 2:20). The only other letter in the Pauline corpus to use this title is Ephesians (4:13). It is used in Hebrews (4:14; 6:6; 10:29), in the letters of John (1 John 3:8; 4:15; 5:5, 10–13, 20), and once in the Book of Revelation (2:18). JOHN MCRAY

Son of Man. The term "Son of Man" occurs sixty-nine times in the Synoptic Gospels, thirteen times in John, and once in Acts. All but three occurences come from the lips of Jesus. In John 12:34, the crowd, equating the Son of Man with eternal Messiah, was puzzled at Jesus' prediction that he would be "lifted up" and inquired about the idenity of the Son of Man. The dying martyr Stephen said he saw "the Son of Man standing at the right hand of God" (Acts 7:56). Jesus frequently refers to the Son of Man in the third person, causing some to assume he was not speaking of himself. Nevertheless the term seems to be not only a self-designation, but Jesus' favorite one.

In the Synoptics references to the Son of Man may be loosely grouped into three categories: those which speak of him as: (1) present with authority and power (Mark 2:10, 27); (2) suffering rejection and death by crucifixion at the hands of humans as a ransom for many (Mark 8:31; 9:12, 31; 10:45; 14:41); and (3) returning at some future time in glory to judge, and bring the consummation of all things (Mark 8:38; 13:26; 14:62). Son of Man references in John fall roughly into the same categories but with some special emphases. John 3:13 and 6:27, 62 allude to the eternal existence of the Son of Man; 1:51 and 8:28 imply an invisible continuing relation with God not found in the Synoptics; 12:23 and 13:31 speak of his glorification during his earthly life; and 3:13–16 and 6:53 make plain that the Son of Man's work brings eternal life.

Elsewhere in the New Testament the phrase "Son of Man" occurs in Hebrews 2:6, a quotation from Psalm 8:4 which is clearly applied to Jesus. In Revelation 1:13 the Son of Man is in the midst of the lampstands (the churches); in 14:14 he sits on a cloud, wearing a golden crown and holding a sharp sickle.

Ninety-three of the 106 occurences of the term in the Old Testament are in the Book of Ezekiel where it is God's standard way of addressing the prophet. Elsewhere it is also a reference to either humanity as a whole or to a particular human person except in Psalms 8:4; 80:17; and Daniel 7:13. As already noted, the writer to the Hebrews interprets Psalm 8:4 messianically and probably 80:17 should be as well. Daniel 7:13–14 introduces a different perspective. Here one like a Son of Man is an apocalyptic figure from heaven who receives an all-inclusive kingdom, unlimited by space or time.

Intertestamental references to Son of Man are in the same vein as that of Daniel's vision. In that section of 1 Enoch called the Similitudes or Parables (37–71) the Son of Man is a heavenly person, eternal, righteous, and holy, who rules and judges. Second Esdras (4 Ezra) 13 relates a vision of "something like the figure of a man come up out of the heart of the sea . . . this man flew with the clouds of heaven" (v. 3). He defeats the hostile (cosmic) powers and delivers captives through a series of actions that precede the confirmation of his reign.

Controversies abound about the origin, use, meaning, and implications of "Son of Man" in biblical literature and particularly its use by Jesus. The term could be a synonym for "I" or "a human person." Some scholars have thought it to be a corporate term including Israel (n.b., Dan. 7:18) or the church (e.g., T. W. Manson), an office Jesus expected to receive (e.g., A. Schweutzer), or a figure imported into Judaism from a foreign source.

Jesus was in constant danger of being forced into limited or illegitimate messianic role (John 6:15). In response to Peter's confession (Mark 8:29–31) he accepted the title "Messiah," equated it with Son of Man, and linked his work with that of the Suffering Servant. In the Judaism of Jesus' day "Messiah" was frequently understood as a political-military leader whose primary concern was for the welfare of Israel. Jesus' usage seems to be an extension of the portrayal of the Son of Man in Daniel and the intertestamental literature. With the term Jesus dissociated his nature and mission from purely earthly, nationalistic notions. He is a transcendent, preexistent person whose mission is primarily a spiritual one that orginates in heaven and whose concern is with all peoples, nations, and languages.

J. JULIUS SCOTT, JR.

See also GOD; JESUS CHRIST; MESSIAH.

Bibliography. O. Cullmann, *The Christology of the New Testament;* W. Elwell, *TAB*, pp. 117–34; L. Goppelt, *Theology of the New Testament;* D. Guthrie, *New Theology;* F. Hahn, *The Titles of Jesus in Christology;* M. J. Harris, *Jesus as God: The New Testament Use of THEOS in Reference to Jesus;* S. Kim, *The Son of Man as the Son of God;* B. Lindars, *Jesus Son of Man;* I. H. Marshall, *The Origins of New Testament Christology;* C. F. D. Moule, *The Origin of Christology;* A. E. J. Rawlinson, *The New Testament Doctrine of the Christ;* L. Sabourin, *The Names and Titles of Jesus;* V. Taylor, *The Person of Christ in New Testament Teaching;* B. B. Warfield, *The Lord of Glory;* B. Witherington, *The Christology of Jesus.*

Jews, Judaism. ***The Old Testament.*** *Judah the Patriarch.* Judah initially referred to the fourth son of Jacob (Israel) by his wife, Leah. Direct references to the patriarch Judah are limited to the Book of Genesis. He was born in Paddan Aram before Jacob returned to Canaan (Gen. 35:23). In the brotherly conspiracy to eliminate Joseph, Judah recommended selling Joseph to a passing caravan of Ishmaelites rather than killing him, and his brothers agreed (Gen. 37:26–28).

Later, Judah moves west to Adullam, away from the Jacob clan, where he married a Canaanite woman. She bore him three sons—Er, Onan, and Shelah. The two oldest sons died young, but not before the eldest had married Tamar. According to custom, she should have become wife of Judah's youngest son; however, Judah feared that Shelah might also die, so through a ploy Judah denied Tamar her due. Subsequently, Tamar became pregnant by Judah by means of deception, bearing him twin sons, Perez and Zerah (Gen. 38). David was a Judahite through Perez. The one notable descendant of Judah through Zerah was Achan, who brought calamity on the Israelites when he took booty from Jericho at the time of the conquest (Josh. 7:1, 18, 24).

Judah went to Egypt with his brothers for food in both expeditions (Gen. 42:3; 43:3–5). He appears to have been the leader on the second trip, for it is he who pleads with Joseph for Benjamin's release. When the extended family of Jacob immigrated to Egypt, Judah's family was in the retinue while he was in the advance party (Gen. 46:12, 28).

The blessing of Jacob suggests the significant future role Judah's descendants were destined to play. They are to be ferocious warriors and powerful rulers in a fertile and productive land (Gen. 49:8–12). Judah died and was buried in Egypt (Exod. 1:6).

The Tribal Name. The name appears frequently in the Old Testament to identify the tribe of Judah. Bezalel, the chief artisan in beautifying the tabernacle, was of the tribe of Judah (Exod. 31:2). The third tribe mentioned in the census of Numbers is Judah (Num. 1:7), and they possessed the largest group of fighting men (Num. 1:26). The tribal contingent led by Judah was first in the line of march through the wilderness (Num. 2:3–9), and Caleb of Judah joined Joshua, of the tribe of Ephraim, in bringing back a good report about the trip of the twelve spies into Canaan. In the second census, Judah was still the predominant tribe (Num. 26:22).

The Territorial Name. The division of the land takes the size of the tribe into account, allotting a large region to Judah. The Negeb in the south and the wilderness to the east, however, were marginal areas, not capable of sustaining agriculture. The northern boundary extended from the point where the Jordan River enters the Dead Sea westward (to the north of Jerusalem) along the Wadi Sorek to the Mediterranean Sea. Smaller tribal groups and clans within the tribal boundaries were in time absorbed into Judah—Kenites (Judg. 1:16), Kenazzites (1:11–15), Simeonites (1:17), Jerahmeelites, and Othnielites.

The State Name. The tribal elements of Judah were united under the rule of David at Hebron (2

Sam. 2:4, 11), and he subsequently united the kingdoms of Judah and Israel (2 Sam. 5:3). David was addressed as "king of Israel" by Michal (2 Sam. 6:20), but after the division of the kingdom upon the death of Solomon, Rehoboam bore the title "king of Judah" (1 Kings 14:21). The rulers of the southern kingdom continued to bear that title; the last to be called king of Judah was the captive Jehoiachin (2 Kings 25:27).

Israel and Judah. The title "king of Israel" was comparable to "king of Judah" during the period of the two kingdoms; however, the name "Israel" also could connote the whole people of God, including Judah. Early texts identify Israel as the people of Yahweh, the God of Israel (Exod. 5:1). The concept is clearly that of a religiously identifiable group.

The political distinction between Judah and Israel apparently developed early in the period of David, but following the demise of the northern kingdom, prophets and poets continued to speak of Israel, obviously including the people of Judah (Ps. 76:1; Isa. 1:3–4; 5:7; Jer. 2:1–4). Isaiah referred to "both houses of Israel" (8:14), and Jeremiah, in prophetic speech intended for those in exile, referred to Judah as the "Virgin Israel" (31:21). Ezekiel also refers to the exiled community in Babylonia as "the house of Israel" (3:1) and as the "people of Israel" (4:13). Other postexilic writers also employed the expression "Israel" in reference to the nonpolitical, cultic community of the exiled people of Judah (Ezra 2:70; Neh. 7:73). In Babylonia, those exiled from the kingdom of Judah adapted the Israelite religion, which had been bound to territory and temple, transforming Yahwehism into a universalistic early Judaism.

The Development of Judaism. *Nascent Judaism.* The Judahites became the Jews in Babylon. Even Mordecai of the tribe of Benjamin is identified as a Jew (Esther 2:5), although the designation "Israel" also continued in use to identify the whole of the ethnic and cultic community (Ezra 2:70). The first Jews to return from the Babylonian exile to Jerusalem rebuilt the temple; however, the religious practices of the next generation did not conform to the vision of Judaism that the Babylonian Jewish community held. The reforms of Ezra, based on the Torah, which he brought to Jerusalem and read publically to its inhabitants, revived and redirected Palestinian Judaism (Neh. 8–10).

The reforms of Ezra resulted in a number of practices. There was a strict prohibition against mixed marriages. All who were of foreign descent were excluded from Israel (Neh. 13:3), including wives and children (Ezra 10). Thus, a Jew was one born of a Jewish mother. Adherents pledged to observe the Torah. Thereafter the Jews were identified as the people of the Book, a people committed to keeping the law of Moses. There was also strict observance of the Sabbath.

Jewish tradition holds that the *shekinah*, the Spirit of Divine Inspiration, departed Israel after Ezra, who was himself ranked second to Moses. With Ezra, the law of Moses was a given; there was no need for further revelation. What was needed was the transmission of the text by careful scribes and the interpretation of the text by competent scholar-teachers. These circumstances led to the ongoing interpretive expansion of the traditions into the oral law.

Despite the departure of the prophetic spirit, certain devout Jews were inspired to write religious works during the intertestamental period. These survive as the Apocrypha, works found in the Greek translation of the Hebrew Bible, the Septuagint, but later denied a place in the Hebrew Bible by Jewish leaders. However, in the Roman Empire outside Palestine, the Septaugint was the Bible of Jewish communities and the early church until the end of the first century A.D. Other works similar to the Apocrypha written in the same period were never considered for inclusion in the canon. These include the pseudepigrapha and the sectarian documents of the Dead Sea Scroll community.

The noncanonical writings of the intertestamental period attest to the development of Jewish religious thought. The transcendence of God was stressed; he was remote from humankind and the world. Angels, as intermediaries between God and man, were emphasized, as well as their demonic counterparts. Jews thought much about the cause and manifestation of human sin and conflict between good and evil. Related to this problem was the development of ideas latent in Hebrew Scripture on resurrection of the body, immortality of the soul, and the concept of the afterlife. During this period the biblical concept of the Messiah took on new importance. He was to be the eschatological figure chosen by God to lead in the last great conflict between good and evil and to institute the kingdom of God that would last forever.

Ezra and Nehemiah acted under the authority of the Persian monarch. They imposed ethnic cleansing on the population within the small province named *Yehud* (Judea), a province that included Jerusalem and its hinterland in a radius of ten to fifteen miles. At first under Persian authority, then under the Greeks, the province was governed by high priests who were descendants of Aaron. The Maccabean revolt established an independent commonwealth under priest-kings of the Hasmonean house rather than the line of Aaron. Herod the Great married into the Hasmonean family, and he and his successors were kings under Roman authority. High priests continued to control the temple until its destruction in the first revolt of the Jews against the Romans in A.D. 70.

Early Jewish Sects. The Samaritans became the earliest Jewish sect. The ethnic division may be traced back to the eighth century B.C. (2 Kings 17:24–41), but the religious separation apparently became permanent due to the reforms of Ezra (Neh. 13:28). The Samaritan sect believed only in the Five Books of Moses.

Following the conquests of Alexander the Great, Greek culture predominated. Jewish leaders in Jerusalem tended to assimilate Hellenistic culture, subtly undermining the strict religious practices of the Judaism Ezra had mandated. Those opposed to Hellenization tended to stand apart from the Jerusalem hierarchy, forming a pious group of Hassideans who opposed foreign rule and culture. The Maccabean revolt against Syrian sovereignty broke out, and an extremely religious fanatical sect of Zealots supported the revolt and high priesthood of the Hasmoneans. Controversy over the high priesthood and other issues led to the fragmentation of Judaism. The Pharisees were strictly orthodox, holding to the authority of both the Torah and the oral tradition, and believing in resurrection and immortality. They conflicted with the Sadducees who believed in the Torah only, rejecting the interpre tation of the rabbis of the Pharisees. The Essenes separated themselves from much of Jewish society. The Qumran community opposed the loss of the Aaronide priesthood; they may have been associated with the Essenes. Others opposed the alliance between political power and religious authority, advocating instead lay leadership. The Qumran community apparently believed in the revealing presence of the Shekinah; the Temple Scroll is written as inspired scripture.

Christianity also began as a Jewish sect. Jesus insisted on a moral and ethical life based on love for God and love for one's neighbor, rather than the observance of a multitude of rules as advocated by the rabbis of the Pharisees. The first revolt of the Jews against the Romans deeply affected both Judaism and Christianity. The Jewish-Christian sect in Palestine was superseded by Gentile Christianity due to the missionary efforts of Paul, the destruction of the Jerusalem temple, and the defensive efforts of rabbinical Judaism to separate the church and the synagogue.

The New Testament. The word "Jew" (Gk. *Ioudaios*) and its derivatives occur many times in the New Testament, with the largest number of occurrences in the Gospel of John and the next largest number occurring in Acts. Judah occurs eleven times, four times in reference to the patriarch (Matt. 1:2–3; Luke 3:30, 33; Heb. 7:14), twice to the territory (Matt. 2:6; Luke 1:39), and three times to the tribe (Heb. 8:8; Rev. 5:5; 7:5). References to Judah are contained in quotations from or references to the Old Testament, frequently related to Jesus as the fulfillment of ideas or statements in the Hebrew Bible.

References to Jews and Judaism, however, bear a range of negative, neutral, and positive connotations. For example, John's Gospel contains sixty-three references to the Jews, of which approximately 60 percent are negative in nature, with another 20 percent neutral and a group of 20 percent that reflect a positive image. When Luke refers to Jews in Acts, the references tend toward anti-Judaism. Overall, when Jews are mentioned in the New Testament, the connotation usually is negative, reflecting the developing rift between the church and the synagogue. Unfortunately, this became the seed that in time would mature into modern, ungodly, anti-Semitism.

Theology. Genesis provides hardly a hint that Judah, the fourth son of Jacob, would providentially become the conduit through which God would fulfill his promises to Abraham. The biblical biography of Judah is not pleasant reading. He helped pillage the Shechemites after his brothers, Simon and Levi, had slain the men of the city (Gen. 34:27). He moved away from his kindred into Canaanite territory and married a Canaanite woman (Gen. 38:2). He failed to bring his sons up in the way of the Lord (Gen. 38:7, 10), and he failed to do right by his daughter-in-law, Tamar (Gen. 38:11–26). Yet it was through Perez, one of the twin sons born to Tamar and fathered by Judah, that David's lineage is traced, and ultimately that of Jesus, the Messiah (Matt. 1:3–6). Only the Blessing of Jacob hints at not only the dynasty of David but the enigmatic "Shiloh," which has traditionally been interpreted as a prophetic reference to Christ (Gen. 49:10). The story of Jacob illustrates how unsearchable are God's judgments (Rom. 11:33).

The dynasty of David and the kingdom of Judah survived intact for over four centuries before it succumbed to the destructive power of Nebuchadnezzar's army. The history of that kingdom was marred and largely inglorious, despite the reforms of devout kings such as Hezekiah and Josiah. The demise of the kingdom and the deportation into exile of its leaders and much of its population was the direct result of ill-conceived international politics, domestic inequities and injustice, and religious deviation (2 Chron. 36:13–20). Yet among the deportees was the remnant of the faithful who saved the precious scrolls that comprise the bulk of Bible and carried them into exile with them. And in exile the people of Judah became the Jews, the people of the Book, transforming the territorial temple-centered religion of their forefathers into a universal religion devoted to the worship of the one true God. Prophetic promises and messianic hope based on the study of God's Word among those in exile made possible the remnant that returned to rebuild temple and town, as God had promised through the prophet Jeremiah (25:11; 29:10–14). The establishment of nascent Judaism and the return and rebuilding of Jerusalem testify to the graciousness of God and his faithfulness in all generations.

The intertestamental period established the Jewish matrix into which Jesus of Nazareth was born at the turn of the era. In that period various currents of thought in Judaism resulted in the development of the oral law, the writing of the Apocrypha, and the fragmentation into factions such as the Sadducees, Pharisees, and the Dead Sea Scroll sect. This environment stimulated Jews to develop ideas that would be important in the rise of Christianity. These ideas included messianic stirring, interest in the eschaton (the end of days), the resurrection from the dead, and the rule of God. The Jewish soil in which the church sprouted and grew reflects the fullness of time (Gal. 4:4). R. David Rightmire

See also Apocrypha; Dead Sea Scrolls; Israel; Pharisees; Sadducees.

Bibliography. J. Collins, *The Apocalyptic Imagination; Encyclopedia Judaica,* 10:21–25, 383–97; J. Gager, *The Origins of Anti-Semitism: Attitudes Toward Judaism in Pagan and Christian Antiquity;* H. R. Greenstein, *Judaism—An Eternal Covenant;* N. P. Lemche, *Early Israel;* M. Mansoor, *Jewish History and Thought: An Introduction;* E. M. Meyers and J. Strange, *Archaeology, the Rabbis, and Early Christianity: The Social and Historical Setting of Palestinian Judaism and Christianity;* H. A. Oberman, *The Roots of Anti-Semitism in the Age of Renaissance and Reformation;* M. Shermis, *Jewish-Christian Relations: An Annotated Bibliography and Resource Guide;* M. H. Tanenbaum, M. R. Wilson, and A. J. Rudin, eds., *Evangelicals and Jews in Conversation;* R. de Vaux, *Translating and Understanding the Old Testament.*

Job, Theology of. ***Introduction.*** The reader who desires to unlock the rich theological treasures contained in the Book of Job should assume its literary unity. Also he or she must interpret each part in light of its whole.

Although the Book of Job is a complex work composed of many different speeches, its almost architectonic symmetry argues for a literary unity. The prose framework (prologue [chap. 1–2] and epilogue [42:7–17]) encloses the intricate poetic body (3:1–42:6). After Job's initial monologue (chap. 3) a dialogue of three cycles occurs between Job and his three friends, Eliphaz, Bildad, and Zophar (chaps. 4:27). Since Job's response to each friend is always longer than the corresponding speech, the short speech by Bildad (chap. 25) and the absence of Zophar's speech in the final cycle may indicate Job's verbal victory over his friends, who fail to refute him (see Elihu's remarks in 32:3, 5). Chapter 28, a wisdom interlude between the three cycles of dialogue and the three monologues by Job, Elihu, and the Lord, marks the futility of dialogue as long as Job and his friends rely on human reasoning (see vv. 12–13, 20–22). Job's closing monologues (chaps. 29–31) ignore the friends and appeal to God for legal vindication (see 31:35–37). Elihu's speeches (chap. 32–37) foreshadow theological concepts in and prepare the way for the Lord's speeches (chap. 38–41).

Critics interpret the inconsistency between the "patient Job" who never complains (see 1:21–22) and the "impatient Job" of the poetic body who curses the day of his birth (chap. 3) and considers God an enemy (6:4; 16:10–14) as indicating "sloppy editing" by the final author. It is better to view these two contrasting portraits of Job as intentionally displaying that Job was no "plaster saint" who suffered stoically. Rather, he was a real person struggling with emotions and feelings believers still have today.

Since most of the Book of Job contains human reasoning, one must interpret each individual unit within the contest of the book as a whole and of the main purpose of the book. The reader must pay special attention to the prologue (chap. 1–2) and the Lord's speeches (38:1–42:6) to avoid erroneous conclusions. The former notifies the reader (like the narrator in a dramatic production) that Job is innocent and that Satan is the instigator of Job's sufferings. The latter is the most determinative part, since God himself addresses Job.

Though many suppose that the main purpose of the Book of Job is to explain the mystery of the suffering of the righteous, it does *not* provide a definitive answer to this matter (and neither do the Lord's speeches address it directly); therefore, it must *not* be the main issue. Rather, the problem of innocent suffering serves as a catalyst for the question of the proper motive for man to relate to God (see 1:9). Thus the main purpose of the book seems to be to show that the proper relationship between God and humankind (in all circumstances) is based solely on God's sovereign grace and the human response of faith and submissive trust.

The Doctrine of God (in the human speeches). *The Friends' Doctrine of God.* Though the three friends basically have an orthodox view of God, they often misapply the doctrine to Job's situation. Eliphaz acknowledges that God does great and inscrutable deeds in governing the world (5:9). God utilizes his power and wisdom to bring about social justice, whether delivering the lowly or thwarting the schemes of crafty criminals (5:10–16). Sometimes he disciplines humans through suffering (5:17). Eliphaz accuses Job of possessing a distorted view of God's transcendence (22:12–14)—that he is so lofty in heaven that he cannot see what is happening on earth.

Bildad emphasizes that God is just because he never rejects an innocent man (8:3, 20–22) but punishes the wicked (18:5–21). He lauds God's sovereign power and awe-inspiring rule over the cosmos (25:2–3).

Zophar agrees with Eliphaz that God is wise and inscrutable to man (11:6–9), and states that he is omnipotent (11:10).

Wrongly assuming that Job's condition indicates some secret sin, all three friends urge him to repent so God can deliver him (5:8, 18–20; 8:5; 11:13–14; 22:21–24).

Job's View of God. Job possesses an ambivalent view of his Maker. Having carefully constructed him and infused him with life, the Almighty used to watch over him and his family (29:2–5). Now he believes that God has turned against him (10:8, 17; 30:11) and treats him as an enemy (6:4; 13:24–28; 16:9–14; 19:8–12). This belief affects Job's understanding of God's attributes and actions.

Although Job acknowledges that God is wise and so mighty in strength (9:4–6; 12:13) that he is omnipotent (9:12; 23:13; 42:2), he seems to abuse his power in an arbitrary way (9:13–24; 12:14–25; cf. 30:18–20). The Almighty uses his power indiscriminately to mistreat innocent Job (6:4; 27:2) or to punish the wicked who deserve it (21:15, 30; 27:10, 11, 15). Also Job portrays God as unjust Judge (9:22–24) who is cruel (30:21–22) and unfair to him (19:6–22) and to many innocent victims of social injustice (24:1–12). Job depicts the Lord as an angry God who punishes him harshly (9:13–24; 10:17; 16:9–14; 19:11–22). On the other hand, he perceives God as a hidden and invisible Judge (9:11, 15; 23:7–9) who would listen fairly to his case *if* he could be found (23:3–7; cf. 13:3, 15–24).

On a positive note, Job agrees with his friends that God is sovereign Creator and Ruler who has done unsearchable things (9:10) in the creation and control of the cosmos (9:5–9; 26:7–14). He realizes that all things are in God's hand (12:9), including Job's persecution (30:21) and his disease (19:21). Job has believed from the outset that God is responsible for his circumstances (see 1:21). Yet the prologue reveals that this was only God's permissive will since he had given limited authority over Job into Satan's hand (1:12; 2:6). Since the life and breath of all humankind are in God's hand (12:10) he is ultimately responsible for all things, including calamities (12:16–25) and the prosperity of the wicked (whose circumstances are not in their own hand(s) [21:16]). Thus, Job trusts that god's hand controls the elements of chaos in creation such as the sea, the storm cloud, and the cosmic sea monster Rahab (26:12–13).

Elihu's View of God. Preparing the way for the Lord's appearance, Elihu presents a more balanced view of God and his relationship to humankind. He corrects Job's view of God's hiddenness by arguing that God reveals himself in mysterious ways (including dreams, pain and illness, and angels) (33:13–23). Supplementing Eliphaz's teaching about pain and suffering, he mentions a preventive purpose (to help keep a person from sinning and destroying himself—33:17–18, 30a) as well as a disciplinary and educational objective (33:16, 19–22, 30b; cf. 36:10). Elihu calls God the sovereign Teacher (36:22) who will instruct Job (chaps. 38–41) with dozens of rhetorical questions. God uses affliction to get man's attention concerning pride (33:17; 36:8–10). Although Elihu errs in assuming Job has had pride from the beginning of his suffering, the speeches of Job and of the Lord reveal the subsequent pride of Job.

Elihu states that the Almighty does not pervert justice (34:12) but is a sovereign (v. 13), immanent (vv. 14–15), just (vv. 17–18), and impartial Ruler (vv. 19–20) who does not reward on man's terms (v. 33). As omniscient Judge who sees all the ways of humankind, he often brings judgment (34:21–28) but must not be questioned when he does not decree speedy retribution (34:29–30). One reason God seems cruel in ignoring cries of the afflicted is that he does not hear the insincere cries of the proud (35:9–13). God's transcendence means that he is not affected by a man's righteousness or sin (35:5–6). However, this does not mean that he is impersonal (36:7). Anticipating the Lord's teaching of 41:11, Elihu states that a person (no matter how righteous) cannot put God under obligation (35:7; cf. 34:33).

Elihu corrects Job's theology by arguing that God is mighty but not arbitrary in his power (36:5–6). He is the exalted and sovereign Teacher whom Job should not try to correct; rather Job should magnify his strength and power through song (36:21–24) and meditate reverently on his awesome majesty and wonderful works in nature (37:1–2, 14–18, 22–24). God is great beyond understanding in the mighty thunderstorm and snowstorm (36:26–37:13). He is the great and sovereign Warrior who commands the thunderstorm as he dispenses lightning (like arrows) from his hands (36:32). He lifts up his majestic voice in thunder (37:2–5). This metaphorical description of God counteracts the pagan myths, which depicted the Canaanite storm-god Baal-Hadad and the Mesopotamian counterpart Adad holding a flash of lightning as a weapon. The clouds and lightning obey the sovereign command of the true God (37:11–12).

The Lord reinforces this teaching (38:22–30, 34–38) by demonstrating his unique sovereignty over the weather. Only the Lord (not any so-called god, much less any human) can lift up his voice to command the thunderclouds and to dispatch the lightning (38:34–38).

Elihu emphasizes the divine attributes of omnipotence. Three times he states that God is "mighty" or "great" (34:17; 36:5 [twice]). A half-dozen times he utilizes the divine title "Almighty"

(32:8; 33:4; 34:10, 12; 35:13; 37:23). This epithet is used in the Book of Job by all the characters in the poetic body for a total of thirty-one times in contrast to seventeen times in the rest of the Old Testament. Though its etymology is disputed, the Septuagint translation (*pantokratōr,* "all-powerful") and its usage in parallelism with the divine name *ʾĒl* "God, the strong one" (see 27:2, 13; 33:4; 34:10, 12; 35:13) support the traditional translation "Almighty."

Lord's View of Himself and His Relationship to Humankind. Because of his omnipotent work of creating and sustaining the order of the universe, Yahweh alone is its sovereign and benevolent Lord who relates to finite humankind only on the basis of his own sovereign grace and man's joyous trust in him.

Ignoring Job's cries for a verdict of innocent or an indictment of specific charges, the Lord confronts Job with his ignorance of Yahweh's ways in governing the universe (38:2). Utilizing dozens of rhetorical questions, he documents human ignorance of and impotence in controlling each domain of inanimate (38:4–38) and animate (38:39–39:30) creation, which are under the sovereign care of the all-knowing Lord. Almost all the rhetorical questions beginning with "who?" (Heb. *mî,* 38:5, 6, 25, 28, 29, 36, 37, 41; 39:5—which expect the answer "none but Yahweh") emphasize the incomparable sovereignty of Yahweh as ruler of the universe. No human or any so-called god can usurp his role. Questions beginning with "where?" (38:4, 19, 24), "on what?" (38:6), and sentence questions including the pronoun "you" or "your" (38:12, 16, 17, 18, 22, 31, 32, 33, 34, 35, 39; 39:1, 2, 9, 10, 11, 12, 19, 20, 26, 27; 40:8, 9) expose Job's impotence and finiteness in light of God's sovereignty and infinite greatness. Since God is nobody's equal, Job's audacious attempt to subpoena God (31:35) and to wage a "lawsuit" to enforce his rights (40:2) is absurd.

The Lord demonstrates his wise and sovereign control over things humankind has considered chaotic or evil. He has restricted the chaotic sea with its proud waves (38:8–11) yet provides the precise amount of rain to inhibit the encroachment of the desert (38:26–27, 37–38). By daily commanding the sun to rise (38:12–15), he limits darkness and the wicked who operate at night. Thus he has assigned places for both light and darkness (38:19–20) and sovereignly controls the dark underworld (38:16–17). He is master of the wild animals, which man can seldom tame and often fears (38:39–39:30). He benevolently provides food for the mightiest carnivore (the lion) to the weakest carrion-eating raven (38:39–41). The Lord's dominion allows room for chaotic forces (cf. 4:7–11, where Eliphaz employs the lion as a symbol of the wicked). But the Lord also protects the weak and vulnerable deer and mountain goat (the prey of the lion—39:1–4). He has created vultures with the instinct to feed on the wounded (including humans slain in battle—39:30) to help prevent the spread of disease. Since Yahweh wisely supervises the balance of nature, which includes chaotic forces, humankind should trust him to restrict properly the chaotic and evil forces in society.

Yahweh confronts Job's prideful questioning of his justness as ruler of the universe (see 40:8–14). He ironically challenges him to clothe himself in the divine attributes of kingship (vv. 10–12) in order to subdue Behemoth and Leviathan (40:15–41:34), which represent the proud and wicked elements in the cosmos (see 40:11–13; 41:34). Since Job does not dare rouse Leviathan (41:1–10a), how much more absurd that he has challenged the authority of Yahweh, the maker and ruler of Leviathan (41:10b–11).

Fundamental Issues Concerning God's Relationship to Humankind. *Theology of Retribution.* One common denominator between the theology of Job and his friends is a belief in the retribution dogma, a simplistic understanding of the principle of divine retribution: God (without exception) punishes the wicked and rewards the righteous. Since the righteous are always blessed and the wicked always receive God's judgment, Job must be a sinner since God has removed his physical blessings. Because God never punishes the godly man or preserves the evildoer, all three friends contend that Job's suffering is a sign of hidden sin (4:7–11; 5:8–16; 8:11–22; 11:4–6, 14–20, 18:5–21). Eliphaz implies (4:11—see the context of vv. 7–10) and Bildad (8:4) states that Job's children were killed as punishment for their sins. In the second cycle of speeches, all three friends emphasize God's certain punishment of the wicked. Both Eliphaz (15:17–35) and Zophar (20:4–29) explain Job's initial prosperity by the prevailing idea that the wicked many enjoy temporary prosperity before God metes out retributive judgment.

Job denies the accusations of his three friends that he is being punished for sin and openly questions the validity of the retribution dogma by citing counterexamples of the prosperity of the wicked (21:7–16, 31). Furthermore, he properly challenges the corollary that God punishes children for the sins of their parents (21:19–21; see also Deut. 24:16). Yet, when Job accuses God of unjustly punishing him for sin (in order to maintain his own innocence—9:20–23; 40:8), he unconsciously retains the dogma of divine retribution.

Even Elihu argues that God operates according to retribution so that he ought not be accused of perverting justice (34:11–12).

The purpose of the Book of Job (negatively stated) involves the refutation of this retribution dogma, which assumes an automatic connection between one's material and physical prosperity and one's spirituality. Both Job and his friends unknowingly restrict God's sovereignty by their assumption that he must always act according to their preconceived dogma. Because of this dogma, Job impugns God's justice in order to justify himself (see 40:8). Though divine retribution is a valid principle (see Deut. 28) the error is making it an unconditional dogma by which one can predetermine God's actions and judge a person's condition before him. God is not bound by this man-made dogma but normally will bless the righteous and punish the wicked.

The Book of Job also refutes the corollary that God is obligated to bless man if he obeys. This issue surfaces in the prologue, when Satan claims that Job serves God only for profit (1:9–11). After Job's numerous possessions are removed, Job demands that God give him a fair trial in court (10:2). Because God does not answer his plea to specify charges against him, Job dares to challenge the sovereign power of the Almighty by trying (as it were) to subpoena him for testimony (31:35). He accuses God of oppressive tactics (10:3), including apparently the forcible removal of what rightfully belongs to him. When Job assumes that God owes him physical blessing since he has been obedient to Him, he was imbibing a concept that undergirded ancient Near Eastern religions—that the human relationship to the gods was like a business contract of mutual claims that was binding in court. The Book of Job shows the absurdity of demanding that God operate in this manner since he is obligated to no one: "Who has a claim against me that I must pay? Everything under heaven belongs to me" (41:11). Thus, God's free sovereignty is independent of all human rules, including those imposed by any religion.

Need of a Mediator. Since Job perceives of God as unjust and inaccessible, he expresses a desire for an impartial mediator (9:33—Heb. *môkîaḥ,* the probable term for the ancient Near Eastern judge who functioned like a modern arbitrator) between God and himself.

The identity of Job's "witness" or "legal advocate" (16:19) in heaven is disputed. Job's appeal to God (17:3) to act as his advocate by laying down a pledge (i.e., to provide the bail or surety needed in his desired court case) may support that Job refers to God in 16:19. However, Job's wish for an impartial "mediator" between God and himself (9:33) and the context of 16:21 suggest that Job is using a legal metaphor for an advocate who would plead for him with God. Since he believes strongly in his innocence, there must be someone pleading his case in the heavenly court just as in an earthly court. This anticipates the role Christ now plays as intercessor (see Heb. 7:25) and advocate (1 John 2:1).

In 19:25 Job expresses his confidence in his living redeemer. Although he may be referring to God (see mention of "God" in v. 26 and the prior context of 17:3), the context of 9:33 (his desire for a neutral party) and of 16:19–21 implies that Job more likely refers to someone other than God. By again using the legal metaphor, Job expresses his conviction that he would be vindicated as innocent (which in an earthly lawsuit would require a vindicator or legal advocate). Job believes that surely there is a legal advocate in his "lawsuit" against God. Though Job probably uses a legal metaphor for someone other than God, his longing for a "vindicator" is eventually fulfilled in God (see 42:7, where God says his servant Job spoke what was right about him). One must not assume that Job had any knowledge of Christ as his Redeemer (a truth revealed only in the New Testament); nonetheless the paramount fulfillment of Job's need for a mediator and legal advocate has now been found in the person of Jesus Christ.

Concepts of Death and the Grave. Job longs for death as an escape from God and the unrelenting trouble that God has caused him (3:10–13, 20–22; 7:15, 19–21). At first Job perceives of the grave as a place of rest and quiet (3:11–13, 17) in contrast to life (3:26) and as freedom from bondage (3:18–19) and as separation from God (7:21). He compares death to sleep (14:12) and wishes that the grave could hide him from God's wrath (14:13). Yet Job stresses that it is dark, gloomy, and without order (10:18–22).

Sheol is a land of no return (10:21) and a place without hope (17:15–16). The dead person is oblivious to life on earth (14:21), and those on earth quickly forget him (18:27). Job portrays Sheol as a house (or home—17:13) and a meeting house appointed for all the living (30:23). He realizes that in the grave the pit and the worm (17:13–14) would become deadly relatives, consuming both the righteous and the sinner (17:13–14; 24:19). Bildad portrays disease as the "firstborn of death" (18:13) and death as "the king of terrors" (18:14).

Though Sheol is very deep and far away (11:8), dark (10:21–22), and sealed up (7:9–10), Job believes that Sheol is not concealed from God's purview (26:5–6). Though he has wished that he could hide from God there, he acknowledges the reality that even the dead are not immune from God's all-pervasive sovereignty. The Lord confirms this truth (38:16–20).

Thus, Job expresses confidence of seeing God after death (19:26). Interpretation of the difficult phrase (Heb. *mibbĕśarî*) "from [or apart from] my flesh" determines whether Job conceives of bodily resurrection or merely conscious awareness of God after death.

***Conclusion. Practical Theology*.** The Book of Job presents a lofty view of God as One worthy of our worship and trust no matter how enigmatic our circumstances. A person ought to trust God even when his ways are inscrutable (42:2–3; cf. 5:9; 9:10–12; 11:6–9). Yet the book also teaches that we may ask honest questions of God when we do not understand "why?" (see 3:11–20;

10:18; 13:24; 24:1–12) or even express strong emotions such as bitterness (7:11; 10:1) or anger. The Lord does not give a direct answer to Job's question "why?", but communicates that when things seem chaotic and senseless he himself is still in charge. The book as a whole teaches that God is ultimately the author of pain and suffering (5:18), which he may use for various purposes (see 5:17; 23:10; 33:16–30). Since Satan cannot inflict suffering without God's express permission (1:12; 2:6), believers can find strength from the assurance that God sovereignly limits Satan's evil activities.

The heated debate between the impatient Job and his dogmatic "friends" must not overshadow Job's overall example of practical holiness and ethical purity. Job's model of a blameless servant fearing God (1:1, 8; 2:3; 42:2–6, 7–8) and the message of the book demonstrate that reverential submission is always the proper response for believers—whether in prosperity or tragedy. Job's blameless record as a neighbor and city official (29:12–17; 31:16–23), including pure inward motivations (31:1–2, 24–25, 33–34) and attitudes (see 31:1, 7, 9, 26–27, 29–30) toward God and neighbor, are lofty ethical standards to emulate. This example is unique and unparalleled until the Sermon on the Mount (Matt. 5–7).

GREG W. PARSONS

See also ISRAEL; SUFFERING.

Bibliography. G. L. Archer, Jr., *The Book of Job: God's Answer to the Problem of Undeserved Suffering;* E. Dhorme, *A Commentary on the Book of Job*; J. E. Hartley, *The Book of Job*; G. W. Parsons, *BibSac* 138 (1981): 139–57; R. B. Zuck, *A Biblical Theology of the Old Testament*, pp. 207–55.

Joel, Theology of. The Book of Joel has been dated by conservative scholars from the ninth to the fifth centuries B.C.: more recent scholars tend to date the book to the latter end of the spectrum. Particularly important in supporting this later date are Joel's apparent quotations from earlier Old Testament literature. Because of the relative uncertainty regarding the date, this article discusses the book's theology without heavy dependence on the question of its date.

Nothing more is known concerning Joel than what is given in the book: that he was the son of Pethuel and that he lived in or near Jerusalem. There is not reason to connect him with any of the other Joels mentioned in the Old Testament.

Like that of other prophets, Joel's theology is not set forth systematically. Nevertheless, it will be convenient and appropriate to trace a selection of his themes, giving particular prominence to his most distinctive theological contribution: the expected outpouring of God's Spirit on all flesh.

God. God is both the Lord God of Israel and the Judge of all nations. As the Almighty, Shaddai (1:15), he controls the invading, destructive locusts, which are his army obeying his command (2:11). Likewise, he takes them away (2:20), doing great things (2:21) and wonders (2:26). He moves the powers of the heavens to do his will (2:31; 3:15) and brings the nations into judgment (3:2, 12). There is no one like God (2:27).

The People of God. For Joel, as for the Old Testament generally, the Lord has a special relationship with the people of Jerusalem and Judah. They are his people (2:17–19, 26–27; 3:2–3, 16), and he is their God (1:16; 2:13–14; 3:17). They are his inheritance (2:17; 3:2), and their possessions are his (3:5). Their land is his land (1:6; 2:18; 3:2), and its crops belong to him (1:7).

It is true that Joel does not dwell on specific great acts of God in the past associated with the patriarchs, the bondage in Egypt, the exodus, the theophany at Mount Sinai, and the conquest of Canaan. Nor does he mention the law, animal sacrifice, the king, the sages of the wisdom tradition, or other well-known aspects of Old Testament religion. This silence, however, should not be overly stressed, as if he did not hold to the realities involved, or as if such elements either did not yet exist or no longer existed in his day. Joel does draw on the teaching of his sacred literature, particularly the books of Deuteronomy and Obadiah, and he clearly embraces the traditions surrounding God's dwelling in Zion, his holy mountain (2:1; 3:16–17, 21) and in its temple (1:9, 13–16). Moreover, the Zion–Jerusalem tradition is seen in the context of the larger and older Israel tradition (2:27; 3:2, 16).

Joel exhibits a striking understanding of solidarity within his community and between his people and the natural environment in which they live. The locust plague affects human beings (1:5), the ground (1:10), and the beasts (1:18–20). Correspondingly, the restoration comes to them all (2:21–22; 3:18). The call for repentance encompasses the whole population (2:16), just as the locusts had affected all (1:2).

The Day of the Lord. The fact that the first mention of this theme in the book calls it simply "the day" (1:15) probably indicates that it was an established concept, that Joel was drawing on earlier prophetic voices such as Amos (5:18–20), Obadiah (15), or Zephaniah (1:7, 14) in his depiction of the crisis present to his people. Moreover, it is perhaps debatable whether Joel, in the final analysis, viewed the devastating locust plague as actually the day of the Lord or as merely its harbinger. At least the plague did not exhaust the day of the Lord concept. For beyond the present calamity, however terrible it was, would be yet another, more awesome manifestation of God's judgment, this time affecting not merely Judah, but all the nations (3:14), the Lord's people being spared (2:32; 3:16).

In spite of this difference in time, the present calamity and the future day of the Lord are described in strikingly similar terms, including irregular cosmic phenomena (2:10, 30–31; 3:16) and temporal imminence (2:1; 3:14). The apparent nearness of the future day of the Lord is probably to be explained as a foreshortening of time from the prophet's perspective. The cosmic phenomena theme comes to expression again in the New Testament, as, for example, in the Lord's prediction of future events (Mark 13:24; Luke 21:26) and in the Apocalypse (Rev. 6:12).

Sin and Repentance. Joel does not appear to castigate his people for their sinfulness, as do other prophets. But this is only appearance. Joel clearly recognizes the sins of the nations (3:2–7, 19). His failure to be explicit about the sins of Judah is probably due to his being thrust into the crisis situation of the plague, in which causal explanations were assumed rather than stated. Furthermore, some would argue that the three groups addressed in chapter 1 are selected because of sins they were committing: drunkards (1:5), farmers (1:11, perhaps involved in fertility rites), and priests (1:13, who fail to lead the nation faithfully). And, of course, the appeal to repentance makes no sense apart from presupposing national sin. Perhaps it is chiefly the sin of mere formality in religion, since Joel urges an inward repentance of the heart and not merely an outward rending of garments (2:13).

True repentance, then, must come from a sincere heart, must consist in a return to the Lord and presumably to his standards for living (2:13), and is based on the possibility that God will respond to such turning to him. That he would respond to repentance is consonant with his nature as a gracious and merciful God (2:13), but it is not a necessity that he do so ("Who knows?" 2:14). Ultimately God is sovereign in his response to even sincere human repentance. Moreover, Joel's emphasis on repentance of the heart should not be understood to render the more formal aspects of religion unnecessary or wrong. The repentance he urges flows from the heart but is to be expressed in the religious forms of weeping (2:12), fasting (2:12, 15), assembling at the temple (2:15), and communal prayers led by officiants (2:17).

Salvation. In this case God responded to the people's repentance and restored their material losses (2:23–26). It is noteworthy, however, that the prophet still holds to God himself as the ultimate good for his people, not their material possessions. It is in the Lord that they are to rejoice (2:23) and it is his name they are to praise (2:26).

Joel's further statement (2:32) that all who call on the Lord will be saved probably refers initially to a deliverance from the physical terrors of the day of the Lord. Yet in light of the foregoing appreciation of the need for a deep experience of repentance, one cannot exclude the possibility that a deliverance from the Lord's judgment on sin may also be involved. This certainly appears to be the way the passage is understood and applied in Acts 2:21 and Romans 10:13.

God's Spirit. Joel's announcement of God pouring out his Spirit (2:28–29) can be analyzed under three aspects.

Its Degree. It is probable that the word "pour out" draws attention to God's generosity and graciousness. Throughout its usage in the Old Testament it tends to speak of a pouring out that is complete, or at least abundant or extravagant because it is unnecessary.

Its Recipients. These are indicated not only by the words "all flesh" but also by the word "your." It is, therefore, not possible that expressions like "your sons and daughters" could refer to all humankind indiscriminately. Rather, this refers initially to Judah, whether all Israelites, all kinds or classes or Israelites, or primarily Israelites but extending to some Gentiles as well. Of these three alternatives, the last depends on the assumption that the servants mentioned in verse 29 would be non-Israelite. But this may be assuming too much. Non-Israelite slaves would normally be assimilated into the nation and so become virtually Israelite. Moreover, at some points in history, Israelites may themselves have been enslaved to fellow Israelites. This may in fact have been the case in the postexilic period (Neh. 5:5, 8), and this would be especially relevant if the commonly adopted postexilic date for the Book of Joel is correct. If the third alternative seems weak, the other two remain grammatically possible.

Its Results. The recipients of the Spirit are said to prophesy and have dreams or visions, words capable of a wide variety of interpretation, largely due to the fact that Joel's announcement comes rather abruptly, having no apparent conceptual connection with earlier material in the book. Therefore, the explanation of Joel is often sought in other passages, such as Numbers 11:29, Jeremiah 31:31–34, Ezekiel 36:26–27, or Acts 2. But since this method risks importing extraneous elements into Joel's thinking, the present approach will be to probe the actual statements before relating them to other passages.

On the assumption that dreams and visions represent merely poetic variation, there are two phenomena said to result from the Spirit's outpouring: prophecy and dreams/visions, the former referring to the proclamation of God's message, the latter to its reception. It is doubtful that the reception is to be emphasized, since prophesying would presumably not be listed first if it were a subordinate element. Moreover, in the Old Testament the exact mode of receiving the message was not as important as the fact that it was from the Lord and that it was faithfully proclaimed. Joel was announcing, then, that the people of God would faithfully proclaim God's Word.

This bare description is not elaborated in terms of who are addressed by the proclamation. Presumably it could be either the people of God or the nations or both. Some support for the idea of a proclamation to the nations may be found in the reference to those who find security through the Lord's call (2:32) and the fact that sometimes God is said to extend his call through the work of prophets (Jer. 35:15–17). On the other hand, it must be admitted that, since many interpreters do not see 2:32 as referring to the nations, such a reference is at best tentative, although supported by the application of the verse in the New Testament. Furthermore, any interpretation of 2:32 has to struggle with the roughness of its syntax. Still, a reference to proclaiming God's Word to the nations is possible.

The content of prophetic proclamation in the Old Testament varies according to context. Quite exceptionally, prophesying may be thanksgiving and praise to the Lord (1 Chron. 25:3). Typically, however, it refers to delivering words of threat and warning (Jer. 26:9; 28:8; 32:3), or of encouragement and hope (Jer. 37:19; Ezek. 13:16; 37:4). Its meaning in Joel should be sought along these lines. On the basis, therefore, of 2:28–32 alone, the Spirit's outpouring can be said to produce the faithful proclamation of God's word of warning and encouragement.

A great many interpreters, making a connection with Numbers 11:29, see Joel as announcing the realization of a wish of Moses that all of the Lord's people be prophets having God's Spirit. The value of this appeal, however, may be questioned. First, the nature of the elders' prophesying may be atypical, there being nothing in Numbers to indicate that their prophecy was proclamation: furthermore, it is not clear that interpreters are correct in holding that this is in fact a real wish or hope on the part of Moses. It may be simply Moses' attempt to renounce any heavy-handed means of defending his authority, as Joshua appears to have asked him to do.

A connection with Ezekiel 36:26–27 is often affirmed. However, in Ezekiel the effect of the Spirit's presence is obedience to God's Word, whereas in Joel it is proclamation of God's Word. True, the two are not mutually exclusive; but neither are they identical.

The same difficulty exists in attempting to define Joel's prophecy in terms of Jeremiah 31:31–34, in addition to the fact that Jeremiah's prophecy does not explicitly concern the Spirit. Nor do other Old Testament passages (Isa. 44:3; Ezek. 39:29; Zech. 12:10) offer sufficient help in interpreting Joel, being themselves quite general and not specific in terms of the results of the Spirit's outpouring.

Joel and the New Testament. Joel's prophecy is quite widely quoted or alluded to in the New Testament, occasionally being transformed in its application. The primary passage, of course, is Acts 2:16–39, where the words of Joel are seen to be at least partially fulfilled in the proclamation of the mighty works of God (v. 11) by the band of 120 (Acts 1:5; 2:1), which presumably included women (Acts 1:14), the young, and the humble poor. But now it is the risen and exalted Jesus who pours out the gift (2:33). The echo of Joel 2:32 in Acts 2:39 brings together the gift of the Spirit and the calling of God, although the call is not yet seen here as extended to Gentiles (Acts 2:5). Things are different, however, in Acts 10:45, where the Holy Spirit is "poured out" on Gentile converts. Their speaking in tongues and praising God (v. 46) may be a transmuted form of Joel's "they shall prophesy." The words of Joel are again applied to Gentiles in Romans 5:5, which, though somewhat wordy, means that God, out of his love, has poured his Spirit into all believers' hearts. And the same general thought is present in Titus 3:6. In Romans 10:13 a different aspect of Joel's passage has likewise been extended to Gentile believers; the promise that "every one who calls on the name of the Lord will be saved" applies equally to Jews and Greeks (v. 12). Finally, Galatians 3:28 generally echoes Joel's thought in saying that possession of God's Spirit is not restricted by considerations such as one's religious or ethnic background, social position, or sex. DAVID K. HUTTAR

See also DAY; HOLY SPIRIT; ISRAEL; PROPHET, PROPHETESS, PROPHECY.

Bibliography. L. C. Allen, *Joel, Obadiah, Jonah and Micah;* T. J. Finley, *Joel, Amos, Obadiah;* D. A. Hubbard, *Joel and Amos;* D. Stuart, *Hosea–Jonah;* H. G. M. Williamson, *ISBE*, 2:1076–80.

John the Baptist. Apart from Jesus Christ, John the Baptist is probably the most theologically significant figure in the Gospels. As was the case with Jesus, his birth was meticulously recorded (Luke 1:5–25). His entrance into the world was marked by angelic proclamation and divine intervention (Luke 1:57–80). John's birth not only parallels that of Jesus, but echoes the momentous occasion of the birth of Isaac to Abraham and Sarah (Gen. 17:15–22; 21:1–7). John is clearly a pivotal figure in the salvation history of God.

Although his formative years were lived in obscurity in the desert (Luke 1:80), his public ministry ended nearly four hundred years of prophetic silence. John was that voice crying in the wilderness preparing the way for the coming Messiah (Isa. 40:3; Matt. 3:3; Mark 1:2–3; Luke 3:3–6). In this sense his message and ministry marked the culmination of the law and the prophets, but heralded the inbreaking of the kingdom of God (Matt. 11:12; Luke 16:16). So John was truly a transitional figure, forming the link between the Old and New Testaments. He spans the ages with one foot firmly planted in the Old Testament and the other squarely placed in the New.

The central theme of his ministry was, "Repent, for the kingdom of heaven is near" (Matt. 3:2). He was called "The Baptist" because his practice was to baptize those who responded to the message he proclaimed and sincerely repented of their sins (Matt. 3:1; Mark 6:14; Luke 7:20).

John was an end-times prophet. He conducted his ministry with an eschatological authority that demanded immediate action. He taught that judgment is at hand. The axe is laid to the roots and God will thoroughly purge his threshing floor (Matt. 3:10–12; Luke 3:9, 17). And the authenticity of repentance was evidenced in very practical terms: share with those in need, eliminate graft, and prohibit extortion (Luke 3:11–14).

John's lifestyle was as austere as his message. He was an ascetic living in the wilderness, clothed in camel hair and subsisting on locusts and wild honey (Matt. 3:4; Mark 1:6). Unlike Jesus, he expected people to come to him, rather than he going to them (Matt. 3:5).

John was no "crowd pleaser." He willingly confronted the hypocrisy of the religious establishment (Matt. 3:7; Luke 3:7). He did not hesitate to expose the immorality of Herod and chose to die a martyr's death rather than compromise his convictions (Matt. 14:3–12; Mark 6:17–29).

All of these characteristics portray John as a fiery prophet proclaiming the apocalyptic message of God. Indeed, Luke says that John came "in the spirit and power of Elijah" (Luke 1:17). He goes on to allude to Malachi 4:5, which states that Elijah will return "before that great and dreadful day of the Lord." In fact, some contemporaries of John inquired if he were Elijah (John 1:21).

The belief that Elijah would return and prepare the way of the Lord can be traced to Malachi 3:1 and 4:5. Such belief is also found in the extrabiblical accounts of Sirah 48:10 and 2 Esdras 6:2f. The Gospels also indicate that many believed that Elijah would come first, and then the Christ (Matt. 11:14; 17:10; Mark 6:15; 9:11; Luke 9:8).

John flatly denied that he was Elijah reincarnated (John 1:21, 25). Nevertheless Jesus affirmed that Elijah must come first and that he had come in the person of John the Baptist (Matt. 17:11–13; Mark 9:12–13). John fulfilled Malachi's prophecy in a spiritual sense, rather than in a literal way.

In this way Jesus acknowledges the central role that John played in God's plan of salvation. He was the greatest born among women because he had the privilege of pointing to the Lamb of God (John 1:29–34). Yet as the last great prophet of the pre-Christian era, he was the least in the kingdom of God (Matt. 11:11; Luke 7:28).

John fully accepted his subordinate role to Christ. He denied that he was the Christ and repeatedly emphasized that he was simply a witness to the Light (John 1:19–23; cf. also 1:6–9; 3:27–30). John stated that Jesus was greater than he, and that Jesus had a more powerful ministry and baptism (Mark 1:7–8; Luke 3:16; John 1:26–27). He did not want to baptize Jesus, but rather desired to be baptized by Jesus (Matt. 3:13–14). John allowed his disciples to leave his own leadership and follow after Jesus (John 1:35–39).

But for all of his greatness, John was merely human. In this sense he too joined in the popular speculations about the identity of Christ. It may be that John's vision of the Messiah varied so much from what he heard and saw in Jesus, that he came to question if Jesus were really the Christ (Matt. 11:1–2; Luke 7:18). The fact that Jesus was not an ascetic, and that he actively sought the fellowship of publicans and sinners may have been an offense to John and his disciples (Matt. (9:9–17; 11:18–19; Luke 7:33–34). Jesus may have rebuked John in this regard when he said, "Blessed is the man who does not fall away on account of me" (Matt. 11:6; Luke 7:23).

Finally, even though John was merely a witness serving as a transitional figure, the impact of his life and ministry should not be underestimated. During his lifetime he had a following of disciples who shared common practices such as fasting and prayers (Matt. 9:14; John 1:35–37; 4:1–2). John's disciples survived his death and spread throughout the Mediterranean world. Apollos was from Alexandria in North Africa and at one point knew only of the baptism of John (Acts 18:24–25). Similarly, upon arriving in Ephesus, Paul encountered about a dozen disciples of John. They too had only experienced the baptism of John (Acts 19:1–7). These instances indicate that the Baptist's movement may have had more influence than what we are able to glean from the New Testament.

In recent scholarship, the historical relationship between Jesus and John has been the subject of study. How did Jesus view John and what did John make of Jesus' ministry? In this type of study, John often serves as a paradigm for interpreting the life and ministry of Jesus. For example, the inclusion of the suffering and death of John may foreshadow the pain and death of Jesus on the cross. Also, to what extent did John influence the life and ministry of Jesus? Indeed, the ill treatment of John by Herod Antipas may have had a significant impact upon Jesus' early ministry in Galilee and in his final days in Jerusalem.

The early Christian traditions that form the Gospel material on John are also the focus of modern research. For example, the scathing accusations and warnings of John are associated with the ministry of Jesus (Luke 3:7–18), but in the end are not typical of his message. Also there appears to have been an early tradition that John had been raised from the dead (Mark 6:14–16). What possible sources may have given rise to these traditions?

Even the topographical setting of John's ministry may be of theological significance. The desert setting may underscore the stark nature of John's message or may be symbolic of Israel's struggle in the desert.

And finally, the psychological and sociological analysis of John is of interest here. In accordance with the criteria of the sociology of deviance, John's behavior and message could be classified as "deviant." In this light, Matthew's use of Isaiah 40:2–3 in 3:7–10 may seek to justify John and endorse the legitimacy of his ministry.

In conclusion, John the Baptist is of great theological importance in the New Testament. He ended nearly four hundred years of prophetic silence and paved the way for the Messiah. In the spirit of Elijah, he preached a message of repentance and baptism. In his darkest hour he questioned if Jesus was the One who was to come, or whether there would be another. He inaugurated a spiritual movement that had influence long after his death and extended throughout the Mediterranean world. WILLIAM A. SIMMONS

See also ELIJAH; JESUS CHRIST.

Bibliography. R. E. Brown, *New Testament Essays;* M. Cleary, *ITQ* 54 (1988): 211–27; M. Faierstein, *JBL* 100 (1981): 75–86; R. C. Kazmierski, *Bib* 68 (1987): 22–40; J. Lambrecht, *NTS* 38 (1992): 357–84; P. J. Meier, *JBL* 99/3 (1980): 383–405; J. R. Miller, *NTS* 34 (1988): 611–22; S. J. Nortje, *Neotestamentica* 23 (1989): 349–58; P. Parker, *Perspectives in Religious Studies* 8 (1981): 4–11; J. A. T. Robinson, *NTS* 4 (1958): 263–81; idem, *Twelve New Testament Studies;* C. Scobie, *John the Baptist;* W. Wink, *John the Baptist in the Gospel Tradition.*

John, Theology of. Johannine theology organizes the unifying theological subjects belonging to the New Testament literature traditionally attributed to John. While some critics would say that a comprehensive, coherent theology may not be within reach, still we can outline those unifying themes that undergird these writings. The Johannine literature includes the Fourth Gospel, three letters, and the Book of Revelation. While they no doubt share a common background, the Book of Revelation is quite different in terms of genre and purpose and should be left to another discussion. This leaves the Gospel and three letters (two of which are very short and of limited theological importance). Johannine theology, therefore, has been anchored in the Fourth Gospel and the First Epistle of John.

The Structure of the Gospel. The Fourth Gospel is organized into two principle sections and these are framed by a prologue (1:1–18) and an epilogue (21:1–25), each of which were likely added at some later date either by the Gospel's author or one of his followers. The prologue introduces the incarnation of the preexistent Word and poetically sets the stage for all that is to follow: God discloses his Son in the world of darkness; he is popularly rejected; a select group of followers discover life; and even though the darkness tries, it cannot defeat this Son.

The first section is commonly called the Book of Signs (1:19–12:50) in order to describe how Jesus appears within Judaism replacing its institutions (the temple, sacred wells, teachers) and festivals (Passover, Tabernacles). He offers overwhelming messianic gifts that exploit images intrinsic in the Jewish setting in the narrative (wine, wisdom, water, healing, bread, light, life). The final event is the raising of Lazarus—which utterly discloses Jesus' identity—as well as seals his fate. But even though Jesus experiences hostility among the Jewish leaders in Jerusalem, still he discovers receptivity in Galilee (2:11; 4:45; 7:1; etc.) and at the end of this section, Greeks from Galilee eagerly line up to follow him (12:20–26).

The second section is called the Book of Glory (13:1–20:31) because now Jesus takes aside his followers, washes their feet at his final Passover meal (13:1–20), and exhaustively explains to them who he is and what will happen (13:31–17:26). But hinted throughout the Gospel is the notion that the impending cross of Christ will be no tragedy, but a time when his glory will become visible to all (3:13–15; 13:31; 17:1–5). The cross is one more sign given to disclose that Jesus has been sent by the Father and is now returning to him. For John, this cross is voluntary (10:11, 17, 18). Christ is departing, having completed the work he set out to do. But before he goes, he distributes gifts to all among his followers (20:19–29), blessing them one more time.

Most scholars think that the earliest ending of the gospel is in 20:30–31 and that chapter 21 is a later addition no doubt from the same Johannine sources that supplied the original Gospel. If it is secondary, it nevertheless has the ring of historicity and the echo of Johannine language. Jesus makes a resurrection appearance and commissions his followers in anticipation of his permanent absence.

Theology. *Christology.* Both the Fourth Gospel and First John begin with a prologue that establishes the importance of incarnational Christology for salvation. When a reader completes the Gospel, he or she has had a compelling, informed exposure to the person of Jesus Christ in the context of first-century Jewish messianism. Jesus figures prominently in every scene as one sent directly from God for our benefit.

Jesus as the Revelation of God. Jesus is able to disclose the identity of God because he alone originates from God (1:18), has been sent by God (17:3), and has shared God's glory (17:5, 24). Therefore, on earth he is capable of revealing the glory of God unlike any other (1:14). This *revela-*

tion of glory is a key to the Gospel. In the Book of Signs (chaps. 1–12) Jesus' miracles are aimed to show glimpses of God's glory (2:11) and those who believed could see it (11:40). In the Book of Glory this revelation comes on the cross. But at no time did Jesus glorify himself (7:18; 8:50, 54). In a similar manner, the Johannine Christology concerns the *revelation of truth.* Jesus brought "grace and truth" from the Father (1:14, 17) alongside God's glory. In a world of falsehood and error, Jesus cuts a path, a way, to God that is true and life-giving (14:6). Indeed he is the incarnation of truth and thereby confronts those who promote lies (8:31–32). Hence right knowledge about Jesus is essential. The Johannine portrait of Christ outlines various titles to make this knowledge clear. Even at the Gospel's first call to discipleship (1:35–51) reads like a catalog of christological titles picked up later in the story.

The Identity of Jesus. John's first christological title comes in the introduction, where Jesus is described as *the Word* (*logos*) of God (1:1). This is unparalleled in the other Gospels. Debate continues whether this is a Jewish or Greek idea, but the evidence points to a meaningful link for both. Judaism had already personified God's Word (and wisdom) as distinguishable from God. Hellenism (especially Stoic philosophy) saw the Logos as an eternal principle of order in the universe. Philo, in some respects, even allegorizes God's Word in the Old Testament to wed his Jewish faith with pagan ideas. But what John says is shocking to both. The Word eternally existed with God in eternity and was God's agent in creating this world. But most shocking is that this very Word became flesh and spoke directly for the first time (1:14). The high divinity implied in this concept is wed to genuine humanity in Johannine Christology and is never compromised. This is a Word "that we have seen with our eyes, what we have looked at and touched with our hands" (1 John 1:1; 5:6).

When John describes Jesus as *the messiah* we are firmly in a traditional Jewish framework. Christ (which translates "messiah" in Greek, 1:41) is almost always used as a title of identity, not a proper name (1:17 and 17:3 are the only exceptions of eighteen uses). For the Jewish authorities, Jesus' identity as the messianic king (1:49; 6:15; 12:13, 15) is a major concern (7:26–27; 10:24). He is the one who fulfills the Old Testament expectation (1:45) and belief in his messiahship is inherent in discipleship (4:29; 9:22; 11:27; 20:31).

The *Son of Man* is Jesus' favorite self-description in the Synoptics. However the usual synoptic theological meanings (suffering and humiliation, hiddenness, apocalyptic judgment) seem absent in John. Perplexity shows up in 9:35 and 12:34 as inquirers wonder what Jesus means. John's use (13 times) emphasizes the "lifting up" of Jesus, his glorification and return to the Father (3:14–15; 8:28; 12:23, 34; 13:31). It also signals the ultimate authority the Father has given to Jesus (5:27; 9:38). John's portrait here avoids futurist eschatology but this does not mean necessarily that he is at odds with the synoptic tradition.

No doubt *Son of God* is central to John's theology. It reflects John's primary christological assertion that Jesus, once preexistent with the Father, has been sent by him to us. Unlike in the Synoptics, in John Jesus speaks of God as his Father frequently (106 times) and sonship language is commonplace (over 25 times). This is a relationship that is exclusively reserved for Jesus and cannot be shared by others. As God's Son, Jesus enjoys God's love (5:20; 10:17) and shares it with his followers (15:9). As God's Son, he can do God's works (5:17–19) because all his deeds come from the Father (10:32; 14:10). In the same way, his words are God's words: he listens to the Father (8:26) and utters what he hears (8:28). Thus, Jesus' words are not his own. They belong to his Father who sent him (14:24).

Sonship expresses the ultimate authority of Jesus. He is not a prophet representing God, but in fact bears divine authority itself. As Son, he has an exclusive knowledge of God (6:47; 10:15; 17:25) and therefore enjoys equal glory with God among people (5:23). Jesus can even say that he and the Father are one (10:30), not in purpose, but in being (10:38; 14:20). And yet this oneness does not negate Jesus' utter dependence on the Father at every turn (4:34; 5:19, 30; 17:2).

John's suggestion of oneness leads to a final thought. The Fourth Gospel describes Jesus with terms reserved for God. In passages such as the Sabbath debate of John 5, Jesus assumes divine prerogatives in his argument ("if my Father is working, so may I"). But the Gospel text goes further, making him not just the son but God. This happens at the opening of the Gospel (1:1) and at the Gospel's closing frame when Thomas names Jesus "my Lord and my God" (20:28).

Jesus' Self-Disclosure. As Jesus moves through Israel his identity is gradually unveiled throughout the Gospel story. First, this is done with *signs and works* (John does not use the synoptic word, "miracle"). Seven signs not merely display the miraculous power of Jesus, but reveal his role as the Son of God and savior of the world. Lengthy discourses accompany these signs to expand on their meaning and lead observers to faith. Among these discourses are seven separate "I am" sayings (6:35; 8:12; 10:7–11; 11:25; 14:6; 15:1), which function like spoken signs to describe Jesus more fully or to give a concealed reference to his deity (10:30–39).

Second, *witnesses* step forward to identify him and validate his claims as if Jesus were on trial. John the Baptist, the Samaritan woman, the disciples, witnesses at the cross, and even the evangelist bear testimony. In chapter 5 Jesus' signs, the Father, and God's Word are likewise witnesses in his defense. This accumulation of "evidence" for Jesus has led many interpreters to think that John's Gospel is using a trial motif. Jesus is on trial in Judaism. Those who read the Gospel—like those who appear in the story—are forced to make a judgment of the truth of Jesus' claims.

Third, Jesus appears in the Book of Signs at prominent Jewish *institutions and festivals,* using their symbols to identify his person or mission. The religious value of ceremonial water (2:9–11), the temple (2:20–22), rabbinic teaching (3:1–15), and Jacob's well (4:13–15) are all replaced by Christ. Likewise Jesus appears at the festivals of Sabbath (chap. 5), Passover (chap. 6), Tabernacles (chaps. 7–8), and Hanukkah (chap. 10), displacing the blessings they offer.

The Gifts of Christ. Those who truly know Jesus and embrace him by faith are offered divine gifts. And no doubt, we are to see these things as constituent parts of the Christian life. These are gifts possessed exclusively by those who belong to Jesus' flock (10:1–10) and which remain mysterious to those in the world, whose domain is darkness. One function of literary irony in the Gospel is to illustrate the utter misunderstanding of unbelievers: they cannot comprehend Jesus, his mission, or what he can give (3:4; 4:11; 6:52; 7:15, 35; 8:22; 9:39; 11:50). If the Samaritan woman had known "the gift of God" (4:10) she would have seen that Jesus possessed the superior supply of water.

Eternal Life. The premier gift in Johannine thought is undoubtedly *eternal life.* The world is dead (5:24), but Jesus offers life to those who believe (1:4; 3:15–16, 36; 4:14; 5:24; 6:35, 47; 8:12; 10:10). Jesus' emphasis on eternal life (mentioned over twenty times) is without parallel in the Synoptics and almost replaces the synoptic "kingdom of God." Jesus even calls himself "life" (11:25; 14:6). Sometimes this gift is placed in metaphor, such as "living water" (4:14) or "living bread" (6:33); in each instance it means a faithful consumption of who Jesus is and what he offers. To eat and drink of Christ (6:33—which may be an allusion to the Lord's Supper) is to gain life. In the case of Nicodemus the metaphor is rebirth, a powerful engagement with God that again is life-giving (3:15–17).

Light. A similar idea is found in the metaphor of *light.* In 8:12 light and life are juxtaposed: "I am the light of the world. Whoever follows me will never walk in darkness, but will have the light of life." As the world is in death (and needs life), so, too, it exists in darkness and needs light (1:5; 11:10; 12:35–36, 46; 1 John 2:8, 11). Jesus is even called the light (1:9; 3:19–21; 12:46; 1 John 1:7).

Salvation. Jesus is also the giver of *salvation.* This is implied in the offer of life. Christ presents an opportunity accept him and to pass from death to life or to continue in sin until judgment (12:46–48). Life is not simply knowledge or enlightenment; it is the result of Jesus' sacrificial death. Jesus came to take away sins (1 John 3:5; cf. 1 John 2:2; 4:10). John the Baptist sounds this note when Jesus is introduced (1:29): "Look, the Lamb of God who takes away the sin of the world." Even the short parable of 12:24 makes this clear: "unless a kernel of wheat falls to the ground and dies, it remains only a single seed. But if it dies, it produces many seeds." Thus in 6:51b Jesus says, "This bread is my flesh, which I will give for the life of the world." Jesus understands that his mission is also sacrificial, costing him his life.

Again and again, Jesus refers to his "lifting up," which is a symbolic reference to his cross and departure. It is "the hour" that he anticipates (2:4; 12:23, 27; 13:1; 17:1). Most graphically, the shepherd discourse of John 10 describes this voluntary death that will save the life of the sheep.

The Holy Spirit. Unlike the Synoptic Gospels, the Johannine Jesus speaks frequently about the gift of the Spirit. The Spirit permanently alights on Jesus at his baptism (1:32–33) and continues as an important presence throughout his life (3:34; 6:27). Even Jesus' words are "spirit and life" (6:63). Jesus is described as a vessel in whom the Spirit is welling up (7:37; the living water metaphor of 4:10 may be another reference), but we are consistently told that the full distribution of the Holy Spirit must await Jesus' glorification at the cross (7:39). When Jesus dies hints appear that in his death, when his life is poured out, the Spirit is released (19:30, 34). And on Easter, Jesus seems to give his Spirit to his followers (20:22). John's conceptual framework is that the Spirit is the Spirit of Jesus, forever continuing his presence with his followers (14:15–31; 1 John 4:13).

In Jesus' farewell discourse in the upper room, he speaks at length about the coming Spirit whom his followers would enjoy. It is sometimes called "the Spirit of truth" (14:17; 15:26; 16:13), no doubt because Jesus himself is the Truth. Jesus also gives the Spirit a new name, the Paraclete (14:16, 26; 15:26; 16:7). This describes the Spirit as an advocate, a defender who will stand with the disciples, strengthening them before the world (15:18–27; 16:8–10). The Paraclete will recall to mind what Jesus has said (14:26) as well as lead them prophetically into new truths (16:12–13). This dynamic presence of the Spirit was well known among the followers of John (1 John 2:20–21) and became a hallmark of Johannine discipleship (1 John 3:24; 4:13).

The New Community. Those who believe in Christ and follow him are recipients of the gifts listed above. Moreover, they belong to a community that has stepped out of the world and its darkness and built a refuge for others who seek community. This is Jesus' flock and he is the shepherd (chap. 10). Jesus is the vine and these are his branches (chap. 15). This community is a place of love, obedience, faithfulness, and worship. And, to no one's surprise, it experiences conflict with the world.

The Command to Love. John understands that the love shared among disciples should have the same quality as that between the Father and the Son (3:35; 14:31). This command is repeated frequently (13:34–35; 15:12, 17). First John emphasizes this command repeatedly ("love" occurs thirty times) and implies that love is the foremost feature of being a believer. First John 4:12 seems characteristic of the Johannine imperative: "No one has ever seen God; but if we love one another, God lives in us and his love is made complete in us."

Obedience and Discipleship. In the Johannine ethic, love is meaningless if it is not expressed in tangible form. In John's thought, love *is* obedience. Jesus says if we love him we will keep his commands (14:15, 21–24). In fact, his commands become opportunities to exhibit love (15:17). Thus, in Jesus' discussion with Peter (21:15–19) the question of Peter's love is tested against the call to nurture and love Christ's followers. Such obedience becomes proof of discipleship: "We know that we have come to know him if we obey his commands" (1 John 2:3).

John anticipates a life of spiritual and moral dedication that is completely devoted to God (10:36) and conscious of its separation from the world (1 John 2:15–17). Believers are not removed from the world; they live in it (17:15–19) and therefore are subject to temptation and evil. They must not neglect confession as a means of renewing their dedication to God (1 John 1:8–10).

Faith and Perseverance. The Johannine literature only uses the noun "faith" once (1 John 5:4) but employs the verb "to believe" many times (107 times). Faith is a relationship, not an initial act of intellectual consent. It is a personal investment in the personhood of Christ. This intimate union of ongoing trust is expressed in a variety of ways. John stresses how the believer must *abide* in Christ as a branch abides in the vine (15:1–11). This means that discipleship is an intimate union or fellowship with God. First John describes how the believer should abide in him (2:24, 28; 3:6). But this does not leave us on our own. Jesus abides in us (15:4) so that there is a mutual coming together, a mutual embracing. The language of indwelling moves easily between Jesus and the Father. The Father also abides in us and we in him (1 John 2:24; 3:24) as well as the Holy Spirit (John 14:17). In fact, the Johannine language of indwelling is expressed in categories that anticipate the Trinity.

Worship. The worship of the church gains little attention in the Johannine literature although certain passages are often viewed as windows into community worship. The exhortation in 4:23–24 anticipates an hour when true worship will be localized neither in Samaria nor in Jerusalem. It will be worship in Spirit and truth. The Johannine church lived within this hour and likely pursued such worship.

Debate has also centered on the Johannine interest in sacraments. For some scholars, sacramental language is found in abundance. Others see limited interest. In particular, the Nicodemus dialogue in chapter 3 and the Passover discourse of chapter 6 betray hints of baptism and the Lord's Supper respectively. In each case, an allusion is made to the rite (rebirth in water/consuming Christ's flesh and blood) but then a critique is given in terms of the Holy Spirit. The description of Nicodemus's rebirth focuses exclusively on spirit, leaving water behind. Likewise 6:63 says that it is the Spirit that gives life and the flesh to be consumed is of no avail.

Together these themes suggest a Johannine interest in pneumatic worship driven not by a rigid sacramentalism, but a cautious critique of ritual. If the experience of worship no longer brings the immediacy of the Holy Spirit, such worship is no better than that at Samaria.

Conflict in the World. The worldview of the Johannine literature is consistently dualistic. Believers are reminded that they no longer belong to the world (15:19) because the world is openly hostile to Jesus and his followers. The experience of Jesus becomes the paradigm for discipleship: "If the world hates you, keep in mind that it hated me first" (15:18).

That this outlook continued in the Johannine community is evident when we look at John's letters. The hatred of the world is everywhere (1 John 3:13) because it is under the power of the evil one (1 John 5:19). The world brings theological falsehood through its religious corruption and false teachers (1 John 4:3–5; 2 John 1:7). It also brings moral conflict with its temptations (1 John 2:15–17). But the Christian who is diligent and faithful will conquer the world (1 John 5:4).

Eschatology. Eschatology concerns the "last things" and usually in the Gospels refers to the events surrounding the second coming of Christ. However, serious debate surrounds Johannine eschatology because the futurist categories well-known in the Synoptics appear absent. Few verses describe the second coming as the final climactic end to history that inaugurates the judgment. Johannine eschatology is thus described as *realized eschatology.* Among severe critics of John, the Gospel has reinterpreted futurist categories so that everything anticipated in the eschaton is available now. In particular, Christ's second coming has been spiritualized in the coming of the Holy Spirit. When Jesus says the hour is coming and now is (4:23; 5:25; 16:32), he implies a sort of fulfillment absent elsewhere in the New Testament.

However, the Johannine literature still expresses a futurist orientation. Not only does Jesus predict a time of suffering and persecution (15:18–25) but 1 John 2:18–19 predicts the coming of an antichrist. Further, John anticipates the resurrection on the last day (6:39, 44, 54; 11:24) as well as the final judgment (5:25–29; 12:48). Jesus promises us that he is going before us to make a dwelling place with him (14:3). At the end of the Gospel, the resurrected Christ dismisses a query about the Beloved Disciple's remaining until the parousia (21:22).

While futurist eschatology can be demonstrated in John, still, Johannine theology has a decided emphasis on the present. John emphasizes the blessed presence of Jesus in Spirit and his gifts in the Christian community now. The church need not live troubled by Jesus' absence while it yearns for the future. Jesus promised, "I will not leave you as orphans; I will come to you" (14:18). The Holy Spirit that gives the church life today is Christ's Spirit, present until he returns.

GARY M. BURGE

See also JESUS CHRIST; JESUS CHRIST, NAME AND TITLES OF; MESSIAH.

Bibliography. J. Ashton, *Understanding the Fourth Gospel;* C. K. Barrett, *Essays on John* (1982):1–18; idem, *The Gospel According to St. John;* G. R. Beasley-Murray, *Gospel of Life: Theology in the Fourth Gospel*; J. M. Boice, *Witness and Revelation in the Gospel of John;* R. E. Brown, *The Gospel According to St. John,* pp. cv-cxxviii; idem, *The Community of the Beloved Disciple;* idem, *The Epistles of John*; idem, *The Gospel According to John;* G. M. Burge, *The Anointed Community. The Holy Spirit in the Johannine Tradition* (1987); R. A. Culpepper, *Rev and Exp* 85 (1988): 417–32; C. H. Dodd, *The Interpretation of the Fourth Gospel;* J. D. G. Dunn, *The Gospel and the Gospels,* pp. 293–322; R. Kysar, *The Fourth Evangelist and His Gospel;* G. E. Ladd, *A Theology of the New Testament;* I. H. Marshall, *ISBE,* 2:1081–91; idem, *The Epistles of John;* W. A. Meeks, *The Prophet-King;* C. F. D. Moule, *The Origin of Christology;* J. Painter, *Reading John's Gospel Today;* S. Pancaro, *The Law in the Fourth Gospel: The Torah and the Gospel, Moses and Jesus, Judaism and Christianity according to John;* T. E. Pollard, *Johannine Christology in the Early Church;* J. A. T. Robinson, *The Priority of John;* R. Schnackenburg, *The Gospel according to St. John;* E. M. Sidebottom, *The Christ of the Fourth Gospel;* S. Smalley, *1,2,3 John;* idem, *John: Evangelist and Interpreter;* J. R. W. Stott, *The Epistles of John.*

Jonah, Theology of. Jonah is a book that probes the perplexing question of why God's mercy is sometimes dispensed to people who do not seem to deserve it. Nationalities seem to be subdued. Jonah is a Hebrew, not an Israelite (1:9). He ignores a series of questions seeking to ascertain his nationality (1:8–9). The racial origin of the sailors is not mentioned. Jonah's audience is called "the men of Nineveh," not "Assyrians." There is no direct reference in the book to Israel's election or to their special salvation history.

Neither is there any mention of the historical sins of the Assyrian military machine that were so well known in the ancient Near East. The king of Nineveh is nameless, as is the captain of the ship. Identities or nationalities are not important. Rather, the stress is on the relationship of people to God. The Book of Jonah is not a story about Jew and Gentile but about how God relates to total repentance by those who are least expected to exhibit it.

God. God is in total control of the forces of nature but is not part of them. The sea is not a person but a part of creation. Yahweh can make it rage or be still (1:4, 13, 15). He can send the wind and cause a storm (1:4). He can remove the clouds and make the sun bear down with all its force (4:8). He can use the fierce desert wind to carry out his plan (4:8).

He can appoint huge denizens of the deep (2:1) or commission a tiny worm (4:7) to do his will. If he wishes, he can make a special plant come up from the earth to fulfill his purpose (4:6). He can also control people—even those who have not previously known him. In 1:15 the sailors throw Jonah into the ocean, but in 2:4 the action is attributed to Yahweh. He is the God of heaven but also Creator of the sea and dry land (1:9).

The corollary of the doctrine of creation is that the Creator's prime desire is to preserve life and not to take it. He has pity on the teeming masses of people and animals who may be in danger of destruction because he is both their Creator and Sustainer (4:10–11).

There is no escaping this sovereign Creator. One cannot even go out on the sea to the farthest reaches of the earth where the Word of God has never been spoken (1:4; cf. Isa. 66:19). Jonah cannot even hide in the lowest deck of the ship (1:5). Here the captain meets Jonah and unknowingly repeats some of the wording of Jonah's original commission ("Rise, call"; 1:2, 6).

The sovereign Lord even controls the casting of the lots so that they identify Jonah as the source of the calamity (1:7–10). The sailors know that God is sovereign and that he does whatever he wants (1:14). He cannot be resisted even by the most stubborn individuals. His will cannot be countered by professional expertise or by the most intense will power (1:5, 13). He cannot be manipulated into action by incantation or ritual.

God is "gracious and compassionate, . . . slow to anger and abounding in love, a God who relents from sending calamity" (4:2). He is not willing that any should perish but that all should come to salvation. In Nineveh God saw their deeds not their nationality (4:10).

Humankind. All people are first and foremost the creatures of God. Israel has no corner on piety. Gentiles in life-threatening situations somehow instinctively act with the same fervent piety as the greatest of the Old Testament saints. When they experience salvation, they make vows and thank offerings. When faced with death, they may even outstrip any form of piety ever recorded. When they believe in God, the same vocabulary is used of them that is employed to describe the faith of the patriarch Abraham (3:5; cf. Gen. 15:6). The message of the book is that God's choice transcends nationality or race. His people may be found in the least likely of places (3:4–5).

Religious people want to usurp God's sacred prerogative to choose those who are his. Jonah believes that those who worship idols automatically forfeit saving grace (2:9–10). He believes that because he performs certain rituals he is therefore entitled to it. He is of course unaware that the sailors, apparently under the guidance of the Holy Spirit, have also offered sacrifices and made vows (1:16).

It seems to be human nature to attempt to achieve salvation by works. Sailors pray but also throw out cargo, cast lots, row, and interrogate (1:5–13). But in the end they learn that God is sovereign and people must be saved by simple submission to his will (1:15).

Ethics. The Gentiles in the Book of Jonah are not reproved in any way for their idolatry. The sin is identified as evil conduct and violence in their hands (3:8). According to Isaiah 59:6–8 this might include the shedding of innocent blood and various types of injustice. Whatever it would include the Ninevites already know what it is, and what they are to do about it. They are given no instruction by the prophet about piety.

The sanctity of life is a central theme of the book. Even though the sailors know they must throw Jonah overboard, they are afraid of shedding innocent blood (1:14). In other lot-casting scenes that identify a person allegedly threatening the life of the community, the judge after ascertaining what was done seeks to pass the death sentence forthwith. But in Jonah one sees these "judges" doing everything they possibly can to avoid carrying out the death penalty. In the Book of Jonah not only is the taking of life a last resort, but every possible step must be taken to preserve life.

Jonah's anger and displeasure at the sparing of the great city (4:1–2) are described with the same vocabulary used to portray Cain's murderous wrath (Gen. 4:5–6). Like Cain Jonah is questioned about his attitude (4:3, 9; Gen. 4:6). Like Cain Jonah leaves the presence of God (1:3; Gen. 4:16). They both go to the east and build something (4:5; Gen. 4:16–17). Jonah is extremely happy as he watches to see what will happen in Nineveh (4:6). In using the language and style in which Cain is pictured the author clearly labels Jonah's callous attitude about human life as murderous.

Salvation. Salvation is Yahweh's exclusive possession (2:10). God is sovereign and can have mercy on whomsoever he chooses (Exod. 33:19; Rom. 9:15). Other prophets were confronted with death for deviating from details of their calling (Num. 22:33; 1 Kings 13:24). Jonah refuses the entire commission, afterwards rebukes God (1:3; 4:2–3), and almost dares God to kill him. Yet he escapes unscathed at the end of the book.

God seems ever willing to accept sincere repentance even if it comes from people who have had a death pronouncement spoken over them (3:4–10). Thus the book might be thought of as a midrash on Jeremiah 18:7–10. These verses lay down the general rule that any nation under the ban that repents will find life. The Book of Jonah is a specific, concrete example of that ruling.

At the beginning of the book Jonah appears as the opposite. Here we have an accredited prophet who has been the servant of the Lord. He brings himself to the gates of death by his disobedience. His defection shows how easy it is to become alienated from God. In 1:3 five short actions follow each other in rapid sequence. Everything seems to go like clockwork to get the prophet started toward the city of Tarsus.

While life still remains, it is never too late to pray for salvation. As Jonah is at the point of losing consciousness, he remembers, and his prayer leads to his deliverance (2:1, 6, 8). Jonah and the Ninevites appear as paradigms illustrating the least likely candidates for salvation.

One who is truly penitent must, like the king of Nineveh, remove all symbols of personal sovereignty and abdicate the throne to acknowledge the total lordship of God (3:6). Interestingly, salvation by faith is not emphasized. In 3:10 God sees the deeds of the Ninevites that are an outgrowth of their belief in God (3:5).

PAUL FERGUSON

See also PROPHET, PROPHETESS, PROPHECY.

Bibliography. L. Allen, *The Books of Joel, Obadiah, Jonah and Micah;* J. Bewer, *Jonah;* E. Bickerman, *Four Strange Books of the Bible;* T. Fretheim, *The Message of Jonah;* A. Lacocque and P. Lacocque, *The Jonah Complex;* J. Magonet, *Form and Meaning;* D. Stuart, *Hosea-Jonah;* H. W. Wolff, *Obadiah and Jonah.*

Joshua, Theology of. ***Joshua the Faithful Warrior and Leader.*** Moses gave Joshua his name, meaning, "the LORD has delivered." The change from his former name, Hoshea ("he has delivered," Num. 13:16; Deut. 32:44), reflects a confession of the God of Israel as Savior. Joshua first appears in Israel's war with the Amalekites (Exod. 17:8–13). He fights on behalf of Moses and leads Israel to victory. He thus personifies Israel at war. When he reappears in Exodus 24:13, Joshua climbs Mount Sinai alongside Moses. Later (32:17), Joshua warns Moses of the noise that comes from the camp below where Israel engages in idolatry. He joins Moses in the covenant-making process and in watching over its preservation. With Caleb, Joshua spies out the land and returns a positive evaluation of the possibilities of Israelite occupation (Num. 14). He appreciates and bears witness to the promised land as God's gift to Israel. Finally, Joshua is designated as Moses' successor and is commissioned to succeed him.

Four theological themes appear in the descriptions of Joshua in the Pentateuch: Joshua's divine commission as leader of Israel, his military leadership, his allocation of the land, and his role in Israel's covenant with God. In each case, God's word and power lie behind Joshua. These same four themes reappear in the Book of Joshua.

The Commission of a New Leader. The first chapter of the Book of Joshua establishes Joshua's leadership as divinely appointed successor to Moses. With Moses' death, God addresses Joshua directly, promising both the land which he promised to Moses (Deut. 34:4) and his divine presence, just as he had given it to Moses (Josh. 1:3–5). The commands to be strong and courageous (vv. 6, 7, 9) define the mission of Joshua. Their context of God's promised presence suggests that it is the divine choice and enablement of Joshua that precedes his leadership and gives it success. It only remains for Joshua to be recognized as leader by the Israelites, something he achieves through completion of the divinely appointed tasks involved in crossing the Jordan River. This miraculous crossing is God's means for exalting Joshua in the eyes of all Israel (Josh. 4:14).

Holy War and the Extermination of the Canaanites. Joshua's military leadership recurs throughout the first twelve chapters. Its theological dimensions incorporate questions of holy war and the extermination of all people from the land. How could a loving God allow such a slaughter, not only of the idolatrous Canaanites but also of their innocent children? Appeals to the sovereignty of God and his wrathful judgment may be made but the question persists as to the apparent wantonness of the destruction. An alternative, or perhaps complementary, explanation focuses on the exceptions of Rahab's family and of the Gibeonites, who escaped divine wrath through confession of faith in Israel's God (2:8–13; 9:9–10, 24–25). Does this imply that such an option was always open to those who would renounce idolatry and submit themselves to Israel and to Israel's God? Although the Israelites seem reluctant to allow any who live in Canaan to survive (9:7) and the Gibeonites are saved only by deceit, it remains true that we are never told of any Canaanites who confessed the lordship of Israel's God and who subsequently were put to death. As to the slaughter of innocents, there is no specific mention of the killing of children. The accounts of Jericho's defeat and of the massacre at Ai mention men and women, as well as young and old, but they do not specify children (as opposed to "youth, young man"; cf. 6:21; 8:22–24). This may be due to the nature of these places as fortresses rather than as population centers. Hazor's destruction mentions the extermination of everything that breathed (8:11–14). Even here, however, it is not certain that any others than the army remained in the city by the time the Israelites reached it. This is not intended to suggest that no innocents were killed, but rather to point out how little the Bible informs us about such matters. The concept of the ban, in which divine judgment required Israel to render back to God through killing and destruction all who rejected Israel's God, was common throughout the ancient Near East. What is unique in the theology of Joshua is the record of exceptions to this rule, lives spared through the confession of belief in the God of Israel and in his mission for his people.

The Land as an Inheritance. Joshua's allocation of the land in chapters 13–21 continues the process already begun by Moses in Transjordan. Although the land west of the Jordan had the unique role of divine promise to the patriarchs and to Moses, the allotments of Reuben, Gad, and part of Manasseh also formed part of what was to become the land of Israel. Insofar as God is giving this land to his people as an inheritance, the tribal allotments, as well as the Levitical cities and the cities of refuge, take on a covenantal character. This land inheritance formed the material wealth of the families of Israel. It could be passed on from generation to generation as a means of preserving the wealth of the family and as a means of integrating the life, livelihood, and faith of each new generation with those preceding it. For this reason many of the towns mentioned in the town lists and boundary descriptions of these chapters are identical to the names of families found in the extended genealogies of 1 Chronicles 1–9. The idealistic nature of these allotments is suggested from Joshua 13:1–7 and throughout the allotments. The witness of the Canaanite presence and occupation of parts of the land is not negated by the affirmation that all of God's promises were fulfilled (21:43–45). Instead, this promise looks forward to the completion of the settlement process and the full occupation of the land by Israel such as would be confirmed by the Bible during the reigns of David and Solomon. The whole account bears witness to God's gracious provision for the lives of his people and to the faithfulness of their response in laying claim to their inheritance.

The Covenant between God and Israel. The covenant making over which Joshua presides dominates the book. It is explicitly detailed in 8:30–35 and in the whole of chapter 24. In both of these sections Joshua's leadership establishes Israel in close relationship with God. God's grace enables the nation to occupy its land and to worship God alone. Yet the covenantal aspect of the text is not found only here. Indeed, the circumcision and Passover celebration in chapter 5, as well as the theological role of the tribal allotments as part of Israel's covenantal inheritance from God, suggest that fulfillment of the covenant remains an integral part of the whole book.

The text that confirms God's covenant with his people includes a divine rehearsal of the words of the Lord through Moses (24:2). There follows a review of God's work among the patriarchs, as well as Moses and Aaron, in promising and bringing the people into the land. This is supplemented by God's continual leadership and provision for the present generation in bringing them through the kingdoms east of the Jordan River, in enabling them to cross the Jordan, and in waging war on their behalf so that they can occupy the land. All these activities are interpreted as part of God's gift to the people. In return, his covenant requires exclusive loyalty to the Lord as the only God worshiped in Israel. The people agree to this and bear witness against themselves if they forsake God and serve foreign deities.

God as Holy and as Deliverer. The character of God is evident throughout the book, especially in terms of his holiness and his saving acts. The divine holiness is found in the ceremonies that are commanded and observed. These include the memorial stones set up at Gilgal to commemorate the crossing of the Jordan River (4:19–24) with a special role for the priesthood and the ark of the covenant (chaps. 3–4); the Israelite circumcision (5:1–3); the Passover celebration (5:10); Joshua's confrontation with the commander of the Lord's army (5:13–15); the special instructions for crossing the Jordan with the ark (chaps. 3–4) and for marching around Jericho for seven days (chap. 6); the identification of the sin of Achan, his capital punishment, and the marking of the site of his burial (chap. 7); the erection of an altar east of the Jordan in order to remember the lordship of Israel's God (22:26–27); and the establishment of a memorial stone at Shechem after the ceremony of covenant renewal (24:26–27). These acts and memorials point to God's special selection of his people. God's holiness could only be challenged at the peril of those who did so, whether in the case of Achan or of the many peoples who opposed the Israelites and thereby rejected God's will for his people. All faced death for their sins.

The saving acts of God are clearly represented in the military victories of the people against their enemies, especially in the miraculous collapse of Jericho's walls (6:20) and the divine control of the sun and the hailstones in such a manner as to aid Israel (10:11–14). They are found in the content of the confessions of Rahab, of the Gibeonites, and of Joshua as already mentioned. In addition, they occur in notes of how the enemies of Israel hear of the Israelite victories and how their courage melts (5:1); how God's presence with Joshua leads to his fame spreading throughout the land (6:27); and how the armies of Canaan learn of God's acts but still refuse to accept God's sovereignty and signify this by perpetrating war against Israel (9:1–2; 10:1–5; 11:1–5).

The Inheritance of the People. In addition to the obedience of the people in taking possession of the land according to God's will, there is a significant theological theme of rest before God. After the wars the whole land has rest (11:23). The people as well find rest as they enter into their inheritance. This is generally true of the division of the land. Specific references are also found, as in the cases of Caleb whose conquest of Hebron results in the land being given rest (14:15) and of Joshua who settled in Timnath Serah (19:50). The records of the deaths and burials of Joshua, Joseph, and Eleazar, which conclude the book (24:29–33) reflect a final resting place for them in three sites located throughout the central hill country of Palestine, the region where Israel first settled.

Joshua in the Context of Israel's History. As a book that provides a transition from the Pentateuch and the lawgiving of Moses to the settled society and rule of the judges and the kings of Israel, this work presents a past ideal in which a leader like Moses brought the people into the promised land and proceeded on faith to lay claim to it. God's gracious gift of the land and his provision for the people as their leader and guide bear witness to later generations of divinely willed leadership for Israel and of how the faithful fulfillment of the covenant could bring upon God's people all the blessings involved in their occupation of the land. The later failures of Israel's leadership and of the people brought divine judgment, which revoked these blessings by uprooting the people from that land and sending them into exile. Even so, the prophetic promises looked forward to a return to the promised land and to a full claim of these blessings under a messianic leader who would rule the people in perfect fulfillment of the covenant and in a renewal of the rich blessings of the land to which Joshua had led the people so long ago.

RICHARD S. HESS

See also ISRAEL.

Bibliography. T. C. Butler, *Joshua;* L. G. Lawson, *CBQ* 53:25–36; M. H. Woudstra, *The Book of Joshua;* K. L. Younger, Jr., *Ancient Conquest Accounts: A Study in Ancient Near Eastern and Biblical History Writing.*

Joy. Happiness over an unanticipated or present good. In the Old Testament joy (Heb. *śāmâ*) covers a wide range of human experiences—from sexual love (Song of Sol. 1:4), to marriage (Prov. 5:18), the birth of children (Ps. 113:9), the gathering of the harvest, military victory (Isa. 9:3), and drinking wine (Ps. 104:15). On the spiritual level it refers to the extreme happiness with which the believer contemplates salvation and the bliss of the afterlife. Unexpected benefits from God are expressed in terms of common experiences. The psalms express the joyous mood of believers as they encounter God. Believers rejoice because God has surrounded them with his steadfast love (32:11) and brought them to salvation (40:16; 64:10). David rejoices that God has delivered him from the hand of his enemies (63:11). Joy is a response to God's word (Ps. 119:14) and his reward to believers (Isa. 65:14) and their strength (Neh. 8:10).

Fundamental to the Old Testament understanding of joy are God's acts in history, the most important of which is Israel's deliverance from Egypt (Exod. 18:9–11). Israel's return from the Babylonian exile (Jer. 31:1–19) to Jerusalem is above the highest joy (Ps. 137:6). The restoration of Israel will be an occasion for joy (Ps. 14:7) in which nature shares (Ps. 98:4–6). Joy characterizes Israel's corporate worship life (Deut. 16:13–15; 2 Chron. 30:21–22) in which the individual participates: "I rejoiced with those who said to me, 'Let us go the house of the LORD'" (Ps. 122:1). Whereas for the believer the secular joys common to human existence are distinguished from spiritual ones, they are not separated. Spiritual joys are expressed by the metaphors of feasting, marriage, victory in military endeavors, and successful financial undertakings. The joy of the harvest is used to describe the believer's final victory over his adversaries (Ps. 126:5–6). Christ's coming is described by the joy of the harvest and dividing up captured military booty (Isa. 9:2–7). In turn, spiritual joys elevate the secular happiness of believers. Secular successes are regarded as unexpected benefits from God.

Old Testament imagery for joy is carried over into the New. Jesus joins the joys of marriage and spiritual ones by describing John the Baptist's reaction to his coming as the joy (*chara*) of the friend of the bridegroom (John 3:29–30). This is accentuated by this pericope's proximity to the Cana wedding miracle where the water changed to a superior wine relieves an embarrassed host (John 2:1–11). Wine, a source of joy, anticipates eschatological joy of which Christ is an endless source (Ps. 104:15). Joy is associated with the nativity. The birth of John the Baptist as the forerunner of the Messiah is an occasion of joy for his father and others (Luke 1:14). The angel's greeting (*chaire*) to Mary followed by "highly favored," a word of the same family in Greek, may be taken as a command to rejoice as the Redeemer's mother (Luke 1:28). Shepherds hear that news of the birth of Christ is an occasion for great joy for all people (Luke 2:10). Luke's cycle is completed with the disciples returning with great joy after Jesus' ascension (24:52). The Magi, upon finding the infant Jesus, are "overjoyed" (Matt. 2:10).

Joy belongs also to the realm of the supernatural. Angels rejoice at an unbeliever's conversion (Luke 10:20). Luke places three parables together in which God, in two instances with the angels, rejoices at the redemption. Upon finding the lost sheep, the shepherd rejoices (15:3–7). The woman rejoices upon finding the lost coin (15:8–10). The prodigal son's return brings rejoicing (15:11–32). The parable of the man who liquifies his assets to purchase the treasure hidden in the field teaches us that God has joy in bringing about the atonement (Matt. 13:44). This parallels Jesus who with joy "endured the cross, scorning its shame" (Heb. 12:2). Also for believers, trials and persecution are occasions for joy (James 1:2). Peter and John found their scourging an occasion for "rejoicing because they had been counted worthy of suffering disgrace for the Name" (Acts 5:41). Suffering brings joy as believers are united with Christ in his suffering (1 Peter 4:13–14). Paul speaks of his joy in the midst of affliction (2 Cor. 7:4–16). It is a part of faith (Phil. 1:25). Joy expresses the relationship between the apostle and his congregations and an opportunity for thanksgiving (Rom. 15:32; Phil. 2:28), with each rejoicing in the other. God's kingdom is described as "righteousness, peace and joy" (Rom. 14:17). Certainty of salvation is a cause for joy, as the disciples are commanded to "rejoice that your names are written in heaven" (Luke 10:20). Fellowship with Jesus brings continuous joy (John 15–17).

DAVID P. SCAER

See also BLESSEDNESS; HOLY SPIRIT; HOLY SPIRIT, GIFTS OF.

Bibliography. J. Moltmann, *Theology and Joy;* W. G. Morrice, *Joy in the New Testament*.

Jubilee, Year of. Year beginning on the Day of Atonement every fiftieth year and proclaiming a nationwide release for Hebrew society. The word "jubilee" comes from the Hebrew word *yôbēl,* ("ram's horn") for the sounding of the ram's horn signalled the Jubilee's beginning. Another related Hebrew word is *dĕrôr* ("release, liberty").

The key text, Leviticus 25:8–55, describes the festival's three basic features. First, as in the sabbath year (Lev. 25:2–7), the land was to be fallow. The people were not to farm the land, but were to eat what grew naturally. Both people and land should enjoy their release.

Second, all Hebrew slaves were to go free. The law allowed poor people to become slaves to pay their debts. Owners were to treat their Hebrew slaves kindly. All slaves were to be freed in the Year of Jubilee.

Third, the land reverted to its original owner. This practice ensured that no citizen would remain poor or a slave forever. A person who sold land to another was really selling a certain number of crops, so the number of years before the Jubilee, determined the sale price. Property within walled cities did not revert in the Year of Jubilee except for the property of the Levites, which was always redeemable. A few other modifications of the normal procedure also existed. Daughters who inherited land had to marry within their own tribes in order to keep the land (Num. 36:4). The law also prevented individuals from abusing the reversion principle. People who vowed a portion of their fields to the Lord and then sold them to escape their vows could never get their land back; rather, the ownership transferred to the priests (Lev. 27:21).

The Year of Jubilee contained two important theological implications. First, the land belonged to the Lord, who determined its proper use. The people were to avoid selfish accumulation of land (Isa. 5:8), for it did not really belong to them. Second, God's people were to be free. Even when one was in slavery, redemption was possible. In any case, the Year of Jubilee freed all. Freedom was always the ultimate goal.

Unfortunately, evidence from the Old Testament seems to indicate that Israel hardly ever celebrated the sabbath year or the Year of Jubilee. Christ's quoting of Isaiah 61:1 and the word *dĕrôr* may suggest that Christ's ministry provided the ultimate fulfillment of the jubilee concept (Luke 4:16–21). BRYAN E. BEYER

See also FEASTS AND FESTIVALS OF ISRAEL.

Judaizers. Those who adopted Jewish religious practices or sought to influence others to do so. The Greek verb *ioudaizō* ("to judaize") appears only once in the Septuagint (Esther 8:17) and once in the New Testament (Gal. 2:14). In the Septuagint this verb is used in relation to the Gentiles in Persia who adopted Jewish practices in order to avoid the consequences of Esther's decree (Esther 8:13), which permitted Jews to avenge the wrongs committed against them. The Septuagint not only uses *ioudaizō* to translate the Hebrew *mityahădîm* ("to become a Jew"), but adds that these Gentiles were circumcised.

In Galatians 2:14 it means to "live like Jews" (RSV, NEB, NASB, Phillips), "follow Jewish customs" (NIV), or "live by the Jewish law" (Barclay). The context for this reference is the episode in Antioch when Paul condemns Peter's withdrawal from table fellowship with Gentile Christians. Peter's actions are viewed by Paul as a serious compromise of the gospel of salvation by grace through faith alone, lending support to the position that sought to impose Jewish ceremonial law on the Gentiles. Thus, Paul interprets Peter's withdrawal in terms of its effect in compelling Gentile Christians to live like Jews.

The term "Judaizer" has come to be used in theological parlance to describe the opponents of Paul and Barnabas at the Jerusalem Council (Acts 15) and those who sought to preach "another gospel" in the churches of Galatia (Gal. 2:4, 12; 6:12; cf. Phil. 3:2). In this sense, "Judaizers" refers to Jewish Christians who sought to induce Gentiles to observe Jewish religious customs: to "judaize." It appears that these individuals agreed with much of the apostolic kerygma but sought to regulate the admission of Gentiles into the covenant people of God through circumcision and the keeping of the ceremonial law. Insisting that "Unless you are circumcised . . . you cannot be saved" (Acts 15:1), these "believers who belonged to the party of the Pharisees" (Acts 15:5) posed a serious threat to the gospel of grace and the universality of the Christian mission.

Paul's Galatian epistle portrays the Judaizers as having come from the Jerusalem church to his churches in Galatia, stressing the need for Gentiles to be circumcised and keep the law, both for full acceptance by God (legalism) and as the basis for Christian living (nomism). They understood keeping the law not only as the means by which the blessings of the Abrahamic covenant could be appropriated, but also as the regulative guide for Christian life within that covenant relationship. Although the Judaizers appear to be concerned with bringing the Galatian Christians to perfection through the observance of the law, Paul charges them with being motivated by a desire to avoid persecution (Gal. 6:12–13). Amidst the rising pressures of Jewish nationalism in Palestine during the mid-first century, and increased Zealot animosity against any Jew who had Gentile sympathies, it would appear that these Jewish Christians embarked on a judaizing mission among Paul's converts in order to prevent Zealot persecution of the Palestinian church. R. DAVID RIGHTMIRE

See also GALATIANS, THEOLOGY OF; JAMES, THEOLOGY OF; PAUL THE APOSTLE; PHARISEES.

Bibliography. F. F. Bruce, *Galatians;* J. Dunn, *Unity and Diversity in the New Testament;* R. Fung, *Galatians;* W. Gutbrod, *TDNT,* 3:383; R. Jewett, *New Testament Studies;* R. Longenecker, *Galatians.*

Jude, Theology of. Jude wrote this urgent letter to counter ungodly persons who turned the grace of God into lawlessness, and by their audacious blasphemy denied the Lord Jesus Christ. These false teachers claimed the authority to teach on the basis of their so-called visions and were causing division within the churches.

Jude exhorts the churches to defend the apostolic faith and to recognize that God will judge these false teachers. Therefore they continue to engage in spiritual discipline and anticipate the coming of Jesus Christ, at which time God will present the faithful to himself as a holy and rejoicing people.

Jude's method is to remind the readers of what they already know and to reinforce that message. By appealing to the Old Testament, to contemporary writings, and to the teaching of the apostles, he affirms the certainty of divine judgment. By a denunciatory description of the false teachers and their fate, he renders them unattractive to the readers. And by an exhortation to spiritual discipline he assures them of their stability in the faith. Finally, in the doxology he gives ultimate assurance that God is able to preserve the faithful and to present them to himself holy and blameless.

Jude (or Judah) identifies himself as "the brother of James," implying that he is also the step brother of Jesus (Matt. 13:55; Mark 6:3) and that he has the authority to address these churches and condemn the false teachers. Some have suggested that the author was not a contemporary of the apostles (v. 17) and that the book was written later by another Jude or some unknown person. But the brother of our Lord was the only man in the early church who could be called simply "James" without ambiguity. And there is no evidence that the early church would accept letters written falsely in the name of an important person. The date of this letter then must fall within Jude's lifetime, that is, in the middle or latter half of the first century.

The recipients of the letter are not specified but they are familiar with the Old Testament, contemporary Jewish literature, and methods of interpretation. This is appropriate to Jewish Christians in Palestine or Syria, though Christian Gentiles would likely be included. These may be churches Jude had visited on his itinerant ministries.

Eschatology. The overarching theological perspective in Jude is eschatology. This appears in three primary ways: (1) the eschatological fulfillment of the types and prophecies in the Old Testament and apocryphal literature; (2) the certainty of divine judgment upon ungodly sinners; (3) the anticipation of salvation by spiritual discipline and divine protection.

The dominant eschatological motif in Jude is the certainty of divine judgment. God judges sin, rebellion, and apostasy whenever and wherever it occurs—before creation in the heavenly court (v. 6), in the evil cities at the time of the patriarchs (v. 7), and among God's people in the wilderness (vv. 5, 11). Jude's emphasis is upon the eschatological judgment of the great Day (v. 6). Yet judgment continues in the present, as indicated by the angels who are currently being kept under judgment (v. 6) and the process of corruption in the lives of the ungodly (v. 10).

These judgments are presented in Jude as types or prophecies that were being fulfilled by the false teachers (v. 7). They were long ago prescribed to the same condemnation (vv. 4, 14–15). The punishment of the ungodly will be the "eternal fire of judgment" (vv. 6–7) in contrast to eternal life for the faithful (vv. 21, 24). Yet some persons who had been victimized by the false teachers could be rescued from eternal judgment prior. So Jude exhorted his readers to persuade some and to rescue others.

Soteriology. Salvation in Jude is a call to eternal life (vv. 1, 21), which culminates in a royal presentation before Almighty God (v. 24). It is motivated by the love of God, implemented by the Spirit, and completed by the mercy of Jesus Christ. This salvation is shared equally by all with no elitism, or any advantage of time, place, or nationality.

The called are required to be faithful by adhering to the apostolic faith, living under the authority of the Lord Jesus Christ (vv. 17, 25), and engaging in the disciplines of the church to keep themselves in the love of God (vv. 20–21). In this way the faithful enjoy the increasing mercy, peace, and love of God (v. 2). In contrast, the unfaithful—like Israel in the wilderness—place themselves under the judgment of God by presuming on his grace, neglecting spiritual discipline, and repudiating Jesus Christ in word and deed (v. 4).

But the Almighty God who delivered Israel from Egypt is the one who will bring salvation to completion for his eternal glory. He keeps the faithful for Jesus Christ (v. 1) and guards them lest they fall (v. 24). And he will cause them to stand honorably in his royal, glorious presence.

Ecclesiology. Even though the word is not used, the church is the central concern of Jude's letter. The church is the "called" people of God (v. 1) who assemble for worship (and to hear this letter) and to keep the love feast, including the Lord's Supper. This letter seems to reflect an early Christian sermon with its statement of purpose, appeal to Scripture, exhortation, and benediction.

Jesus Christ is the sovereign Lord over the church. This authority is extended through his apostles and their teaching. It is evidenced by Jude, who addresses these churches as a servant of Jesus Christ and as a brother of James, the renowned leader of the church in Jerusalem (Acts 15:13; 21:18). Jude describes the ministry of local leaders as "sheperding" (v. 12). He himself models this by his concern (v. 3) and emulation of God's love for them (vv. 3, 20). His gentle attitude is expressed in his "wish" to "remind" them, rather than to scold or rebuke them.

Jude also appeals to Scripture as having authority for the church. These writings are the authoritative record of God's working in history, and they provide a prophetic perspective for interpreting the current experiences of the church. In addition, Jude makes use of materials from the apocryphal writings of 1 Enoch (v. 14) and the Assumption of Moses (v. 9) as affirmation of his message to the churches.

The mission of the church is expressed in three exhortations: to defend the faith (v. 3), to keep themselves in the love of God (v. 21), and to rescue some while maintaining her own purity.

Theology Proper. The theology of Jude is explicitly monotheistic and implicitly Trinitarian. God is our Father (v. 1) and Savior (v. 25). He is the eternal one to whom glory, majesty, might, and authority belong for ever and ever (v. 24). He is also the Lord—an allusion to the divine name in the Old Testament (vv. 5, 9, 14)—who saves his people, and the Judge who condemns the world, sinners, and evil angels (vv. 5, 9, 14). And he is the King who will summon his people to appear before him for a royal audience (v. 24).

The second person of the Trinity is "our Lord Jesus Christ" (vv. 4, 17, 21, 25). His messianic office is assumed, and the primary emphasis is on his lordship (vv. 4, 17, 21). Jude emphasizes this by the use of two nouns, both "Master" (*despotēs*) and "Lord" (*kurios*). In three instances (vv. 5, 9, and especially 14), Jude's use of "Lord" may imply a reference to Jesus Christ as the fulfillment of the typological message of the texts, and the unity of Father and Son.

Jesus Christ is the Lord of the Church, and the mediator between God and the faithful. Through him praise is offered to God (v. 25), and by him God will grant the final expression of mercy in the gift of eternal life (v. 21). It is for Jesus Christ and his day that God is keeping the faithful (v. 1).

The Holy Spirit is mentioned twice in Jude. Unlike the false teachers, those who are faithful have the Spirit (v. 19). And it is in the Spirit that the church conducts her worship and Christian discipline (vv. 20, 21). NORMAN R. ERICSON

Bibliography. R. J. Bauckham, *2 Peter, Jude;* D. Guthrie, *New Testament Theology: A Thematic Study;* G. E. Ladd, *A Theology of the New Testament.*

Judges, Theology of. The Book of Judges is ordinarily spoken of as part of the Deuteronomic history, that single narration from Joshua through Kings, covering the period from Israel's entry into the land through the time that the land was lost in the Babylonian exile. This group of books is called "Deuteronomic history" because the authors/compilers viewed the history uniquely through the eyes of Deuteronomy. The theology of Deuteronomy, laws unique to that book, or perspectives emphasized there, became the spectacles through which these subsequent writers viewed the history of Israel. Two prominent themes from Deuteronomy capture much of the Book of Judges.

Conditionality versus Unconditionality; Grace versus Law. Throughout the Deuteronomic history, the narrator probes the nature of God's relationship with Israel. Will God's holiness, his demand for obedience to his commands, override his promises to Israel? Or will his irrevocable commitment to the nation, his gracious promises to the patriarchs, mean that he will somehow overlook their sin? As much as theologians may seek to establish the priority of law over grace or grace over law, the Book of Judges will not settle this question. What Judges gives the reader is not a systematic theology, but rather the history of a relationship. Judges leaves us with a paradox: God's relationship with Israel is at once both conditional and unconditional. He will not remove his favor, but Israel must live in obedience and faith to inherit the promise. It is this very tension that more than anything else propels the narrative of the entire Deuteronomic history. The Book of Deuteronomy emphasizes both God's gracious commitment to the patriarchs, his promise to give them the land (1:7–8, 21, 25, 31; 3:18–20; 6:3), and the fact that staying in the land is conditioned by obedience (1:35; 4:1, 10, 21, 26, 40; 5:33; 6:15, 18). Moses foresees that Israel will not succeed in light of God's commands and that the story will end in disaster (31:27–29).

It is the dialogue between God's promises and his law that underlies the cyclical stories of the individual judges. Any reader who has even a cursory acquaintance with the Book of Judges is familiar with the series of stories that make up the core of the book (2:6–16:31). The accounts of the major judges (Othniel, Ehud, Deborah, Gideon, Jephthah, and Samson) are among the most familiar stories in the Bible. These stories are introduced by a brief "philosophy of history" (2:6–3:6) that summarizes the material to follow. The accounts of the individual judges follow a fairly stable framework.

1. The children of Israel do evil in the eyes of the Lord (2:11; 3:7, 12; 4:1; 6:1; 10:6; 13:1).
2. Although the nature of this evil is rarely spelled out, their sin prompts the anger of God and results in oppression at the hands of some foreign nation (2:14; 3:8; 4:2; 10:9). Because of their sin the Israelites are not only unable to expel the Canaanites, but they themselves fall before foreign powers.
3. During their oppression, the Israelites cry out to the Lord (3:9, 15; 6:6–7; 10:10).
4. The Lord hears their cry and raises up a deliverer, one of the judges (2:16; 3:9, 15; 10:1, 12). The deliverer is chosen and empowered by the Spirit of the Lord (3:10; 6:34; 11:29; 13:25; 14:6, 19).
5. It is often reported that this deliverance was followed by the submission of the enemy and a period of peace during which the deliverer judged Israel, followed by the death and burial of the judge (3:10–11; 8:28–32; 10:2–5; 12:9–15).

God's irrevocable commitment to Israel is seen in his providing them with a deliverer/champion; but his holiness requires that he not ignore their sin, and so he brings oppressors to chasten the nation and turn them back to himself.

Deuteronomy looked forward to a day when Israel would have rest from her enemies in the land God had promised, but it would not come during the days of the judges.

God's Rule over His People. The Book of Deuteronomy is the farewell address of Moses. Moses had been Israel's judge, leader, lawgiver, ruler, and religious authority. How will Israel be governed when Moses is dead? This question is the focus of Deuteronomy 16:18–18:22; here God provides through Moses the basic guidelines for governing Israel when Moses is gone. Israel will have judges (16:18–20), a system of courts (17:2–13), a king (17:14–20), priests and Levites (18:1–8), and a succession of prophets (18:9–22).

Although it may not appear so at first glance, it is the provisions for a king (17:14–20) that particularly concern the author of Judges. For that matter, one way an individual could divide the Deuteronomic history is into two parts: life without a king (Joshua, Judges) and life with a king (Samuel, Kings). The writer of Judges makes it quite clear that this is a concern by the constant refrain at the end of the book, that "in those days Israel had no king; everyone did as he saw fit" (17:6; 21:25; cf. 18:1; 19:1). During the period of the judges, Israel had devolved into anarchy. Would kingship solve her national problems? Would kings help the nation hold the land and have rest from their enemies? Would kings rule as faithful representatives of the Lord? The writer prepares us for the remainder of the story in Samuel and Kings.

The collection of accounts about the individual judges is often described as "cyclical." This designation is acceptable insofar as it catches the repeated elements that make up the characteristic framework of the individual stories. However, it is misleading if taken to imply that the story lacks forward movement and direction. A better way to describe it would be as a "downward spiral": it is not that each cycle is more or less a repeat of the earlier ones, but rather that there is a deterioration in the quality of the judges and the effect of their leadership. A survey of the major judges will demonstrate this.

Othniel (3:7–11) appears first as the model of what a judge should be. He is raised up by God and invested with his Spirit; he was an able warrior when Joshua lived (Josh. 15:13–19), and he leads Israel in successful warfare as Joshua had done. He provides the model from which all subsequent judges depart to varying degrees.

In the case of Ehud (3:12–30) several important items are missing. The author does not tell us that God raised him up as he had done with Othniel; Ehud does not enjoy investiture with the Spirit of God, nor does he "judge" Israel. Ehud delivers Israel by deceit and treachery, and the text is silent about Yahweh's will and relationship to him.

Deborah (4:1–5:31) was a prophetess as she judged Israel. But in spite of her accomplishments and those of Jael, her judgeship raises questions about the failure of male leadership in Israel. Both Barak and Sisera lose the glory that should have been theirs to a woman (4:9). Is Israel unable to produce worthy male champions to lead in her wars for the land? Victory once again is less a feat of arms than a product of treachery. Jael, who finally destroys Sisera, is neither a judge nor a prophetess, and only half-Israelite (4:11, 17; 5:24). Rather than a nation acting in concert and in faith, Deborah's song includes curses against other tribes that did not join the battle (5:15b–18, 23). The account anticipates the factionalism and intertribal disunity that will ultimately culminate in the final episodes of the book.

Gideon the farmer (6:1–8:35) is slow to recognize and respond to God's call for him to lead Israel; three miracles are required to convince this reluctant champion. And his obedience, when it does come, is not exactly courageous: he does tear down the Baal altar and the Asherah pole in his community as God commanded—but still a bit the coward and skeptic, he does it at night (6:25–27). Although Gideon earns the sobriquet "Jerub-baal" ("Let Baal contend [with him]"—6:32), he himself eventually succumbs to false worship that leads Israel astray (8:22–27). After the great battle when Gideon's three hundred prevail over a far greater number through faithful obedience, Gideon seems to forget the whole point of the exercise (7:2) and calls up his reserves, an army of 32,000 (7:3, 24). A great victory once again erupts in factional rivalry and quarreling among the tribes and clans (8:1–9). Beyond the victory God had promised and given, Gideon pursues a personal vendetta (8:10–21).

After Gideon's death, Israel again does wrong (8:33–35), and one anticipates the appearance of another judge/deliverer. But not so! Instead, Abimelek, Gideon's son by a concubine, attempts to seize power. God does not raise him up or call him to office. The intertribal rivalry (8:1–9) during Gideon's time now becomes intrafamily strife and murder. In spite of the good that Gideon had done for Israel, his son becomes not a deliverer but an oppressor, not a servant to the nation but a murderer of Israelites and of his own family. Gideon serves the Deuteronomic historian as an example of abortive kingship.

Jephthah is the next major figure in the book. Full of self-interest Jephthah negotiates his way to power from his position as an outcast (11:1–11). Although God's Spirit had already come upon him for the battle with Ammon (11:29), as if more were needed to secure the victory Jephthah makes a rash vow (11:30). The one who had been so calculating in his self-interest ends up destroying that which he counted most dear, his only child (11:34–40). Once again a victory erupts into intertribal squabbling and regional rivalry (12:1–6).

Samson is the last of the major judges, but he is a shadow of what a judge was supposed to be.

He is full of self-indulgence and cannot control his sexual appetite. Samson's proclivity for foreign women has become metaphorical for Israel itself, unable to resist going whoring after the enticement of foreign gods (2:17; 8:27, 33). Although like Israel he had been set apart to God from birth (13:5), Samson would not fulfill his potential. Intermarriage with the Canaanites violated the command to drive them from the land (3:5–6). How could Samson succeed as the leader of Israel? He was more successful in death than in life (16:30).

Leadership like that of these judges would not secure the land for Israel. The legacy of a unified Israel left by Joshua had disintegrated into factional and regional rivalries. Conditions promoting religious and political chaos called for a different kind of leadership if Israel were to secure the land. Would having kings make the difference? The last two stories prepare the way for Israel's experiment with kingship.

The account of Micah's idols and the migration of the tribe of Dan (chaps. 17–18) suggests that the author was making a point about idolatry in the northern tribes. Micah's shrine and idols were initially located in the hill country of Ephraim (presumably near Bethel—17:1; 18:2) and were then purloined and installed in Dan. The author may be making the point that the northern tribes were always involved in idolatry. From a point in time after the schism and the erection of golden calves at Dan and Bethel by Jeroboam, the author could in effect be saying, "Look, this is no surprise—those tribes were always prone to false worship and idolatry." These chapters both describe the idolatry in Israel during the period of the judges, and also make a political point against the northern tribes in favor of the temple-centered religion in Judah described in Samuel and Kings.

The account of the Levite and his concubine (chap. 19) and the subsequent war against Benjamin (chaps. 20–21) also makes a few political points that contribute to the larger concerns of the Deuteronomic history. In the earlier story a Levite from the hill country of Ephraim travels to Bethlehem to retrieve his concubine from her father's house. In Bethlehem he is treated royally and shown every courtesy. As he sets out with his concubine and servant for the return trip, the Levite is unwilling to stop in a city Israel had not conquered (Jebus or Jerusalem) and travels on to Gibeah in Benjamin before turning aside for the night. In Gibeah (the hometown of Saul) his party is not shown any hospitality by the native citizens of the town; rather a man from Ephraim finally comes to his aid. The Levite and his party are then confronted by great evil, evil reminiscent of Sodom and Gomorrah (19:22–26; cf. Gen. 19:1–11). After the death of the concubine the Levite rallies the tribes to war against Benjamin. Underlying the details of the story is a political allegory addressed to those from Ephraim and the northern tribes: Who will treat you well? [someone from Bethlehem] Who will treat you poorly? [someone from Gibeah] Who will remove the aliens from Jebus and make it safe? Everyone reading the story knows that David and his lineage were from Bethlehem, and that David had made Jebus/Jerusalem a safe city. The story appears to advocate loyalty from the northern tribes to a family from Bethlehem, rather than to a family from the corrupt Gibeah (Saul and his descendants). This historical account is strongly pro-David and anti-Saul, anticipating the stance of the Book of Samuel and the overall concern of the Deuteronomic historian with God's faithfulness to his promise to David.

Judges in the New Testament. The concern in the Book of Judges with the relationship of law and grace and with the character of God's rule over his people is prominent in many passages in the New Testament.

Readers today cannot but identify with these ancient champions in their own struggles and failures with godly living. Strange heros they were—a reluctant farmer, a prophetess, a left-handed assassin, a bastard bandit, a sex-addicted Nazirite. It is easy at a distance to point out the foibles and failures of the leading characters in this downwardly spiraling story. But lest we get too proud, Paul reminds us "that is what some of you were" (1 Cor. 6:11). With similar mixtures of ignorance, rebellion, frail obedience, and tangled motives, we with them were "washed, sanctified, and justified" by the grace of God. For all of their flaws, we can learn from their faith. For it was in faith that Gideon, Barak, Jephthah, and Samson "conquered kingdoms, administered justice, and gained what was promised" (Heb. 11:32–33).

In spite of their failures, their faith was not misplaced. They are part of that great cloud of witnesses calling for us to persevere and to fix our eyes on Jesus (Heb. 12:1–2). We too need a champion to fight our battles for us, one raised up by God and invested with his Spirit in full measure; we too need a leader to secure for us the inheritance that God has promised, one who will perfect our faith.

RAYMOND B. DILLARD

See also ISRAEL.

Bibliography. D. R. Davis, *Such a Great Salvation;* K. R. R. Gros Louis, *Literary Interpretations of Biblical Narratives;* L. R. Klein, *The Triumph of Irony in the Book of Judges;* J. P. U. Lilley, *Tyn Bul* 18 (1967): 94–102; B. G. Webb, *The Book of the Judges: An Integrated Reading.*

Judgment. The Hebrew term *mišpāt* is an important Old Testament concept and one closely linked with God. It may denote the process whereby a verdict is reached or the verdict itself; it is bound up with the notions of justice (modern translations often have "justice" for *mišpāt*) and righteousness and it is of fundamental importance for biblical religion. Thus Abraham could ask, "Will not the Judge of all the earth do *mišpāt?*" (Gen. 18:25); it is fundamental that God engages in judgment. Indeed, God is the God of *mišpāt*. Judgment is essentially his own activity. Nobody taught him (Isa. 40:14), and "all his ways are just" (Deut. 32:4). Judgment is linked with righteousness as the foundation of his throne (Ps. 97:2). Judgment is as natural to God as the movements of the birds are to them (Jer. 8:7).

We should be clear that judgment is of great importance for biblical religion. The gods of the heathen were capricious and unpredictable; their worshipers could never know what they would do next, nor whether what they themselves did would be pleasing to their deities or not. The Hebrews knew that God is righteous and that he demands righteousness of his people.

Sometimes God's judgments are seen in the present life, but often it is the future judgment that is in mind. "For he comes, he comes to judge the earth. He will judge the world in righteousness and the peoples in his truth" (Ps. 96:13). This tells us something important about God. All people, and not only Israel, will answer to him. And it tells us something important about the way people live. Somewhere among the many gods he acknowledged the polytheist would come across a deity who was not too demanding and he could live his life accordingly. But the pious Hebrew knew that in the end every human work would be judged by the all-holy and all-powerful God. There was no escape. And while he had opportunity it was important that the Hebrew should right wrongs, overthrow the oppressor, and deliver the oppressed.

In the New Testament the Old Testament thoughts about judgment, both present and future, are continued. But there is a striking new thought, namely, that judgment is connected with the cross of Christ. As he drew near to his death Jesus said, "Now is the time for judgment on this world, now the prince of this world will be driven out" (John 12:31). And in the upper room as he spoke of the coming of the Holy Spirit, he said that the Spirit would convict the world of judgment, "because the prince of this world now stands condemned (lit. is judged)" (John 16:11). The use of the judgment terminology in connection with the defeat of Satan is important, for it shows that this was no arbitrary happening. Nor did it mean simply that God is stronger than Satan. That is true, but the manner in which Satan was defeated was righteous.

God's present judgment of people is forcefully brought out in Romans 1 with its threefold "God gave them over" (vv. 24, 26, 28). God is hostile to every evil and this is made manifest in his judgments here and now. An interesting aspect of present judgment is brought out in the words of Jesus: "This is the verdict (*krisis*): Light has come into the world, but men loved darkness instead of light because their deeds were evil" (John 3:19). The love of darkness is itself judgment (cf. the words of a poet, "For thirty pieces Judas sold himself, not Christ"). Paul sees a present judgment in the punishment of the Corinthian church (1 Cor. 11:29–32).

That there will be a final judgment is regarded as axiomatic (Rom. 3:5–6). "Eternal judgment" is one of the "elementary teachings about Christ" (Heb. 6:1–2), and all face it (Heb. 12:23). It is as inescapable as death (Heb. 9:27). Even "the family of God" is included and indeed judgment begins with them (1 Peter 4:17). Sinners may not trust that somehow their worst failings may be hid for God will judge our secrets (Rom. 2:16). All evil will be reckoned with for on the day of judgment "every careless word" will be called to account (Matt. 12:36). Judgment will be on the basis of works (Matt. 16:27). An important passage is that in which Paul makes it clear that salvation is on the basis of Christ's saving work and that alone, but what we build on that foundation will be tested "with fire" (1 Cor. 3:10–15). Believers will be saved by Christ, but their work will be judged on judgment day. LEON MORRIS

See also JUDGMENT, DAY OF; JUDGMENT SEAT OF CHRIST.

Bibliography. H. Butterfield, *Christianity and History;* L. Morris, *The Biblical Doctrine of Judgment.*

Judgment, Day of. Throughout the Bible it is accepted that people are accountable to God. Good deeds are commended and evil deeds are blamed. The day of judgment is the culmination of the whole process. At the end of this world order God will judge all people and all deeds. Nothing will be excepted; every secret thing, good or bad, will be brought into judgment (Eccles. 12:14). Sometimes, of course, judgment is seen as a present activity (Ezek. 7:7–8), but there is also strong emphasis on final judgment, the judgment at the end of this world system as we know it, a judgment that ushers in the final state of affairs. This will be a judgment of all the nations and all the people, for the Lord "comes, he comes to judge the earth. He will judge the world in righteousness, and the peoples in his truth" (Ps. 96:13). There will be judgment on Israel (Ps. 50:4) and there will also be judgment on the whole Gentile world (Ps. 9:8; Rom. 14:10; cf. the magnificent picture of the final judgment in Rev. 20:11–15).

Judgment day may be referred to in any one of a number of ways. It may be spoken of strictly as "the day of judgment" (Matt. 10:15; 1 John 4:17), or with reference to its chronological place as "the last day" (John 6:39). Mostly John's references to this day refer to Jesus' raising of people but he also tells us that Jesus said that the word that he spoke would on the last day judge anyone who despised him and refused to hear his words (John 12:48). The most common way of referring to it appears to be simply "that day" (Luke 21:34); the day of judgment was so outstanding that nothing more was needed to draw attention to it. Indeed, it may be called "the great Day" (Jude 6), or simply "the Day" (Heb. 10:25; 2 Peter 1:19).

Sometimes the day is characterized by the outcome of it all. Thus it is "the day of redemption" (Eph. 4:30). In one sense redemption is accomplished here and now when the sinner comes to trust Christ, but in another sense the Day of Judgment seals it all. And, of course, for the finally impenitent sinner it is "the great day of his wrath" (Rev. 6:17), "the day of God's wrath, when his righteous judgment will be revealed" (Rom. 2:5).

There are other ways of putting it; this list is not exhaustive. The point of it all is that the day in question is the decisive day. What happens then is the culmination of the history of the world. A judgment will take place from which there is no appeal.

The Teaching of Jesus. Jesus emphasized the importance of final judgment. He told the Twelve that they were to warn their hearers that it would be "more bearable for Sodom and Gomorrah" on the day of judgment than for them (Matt. 10:15). He himself had a similar message for the people of Chorazin and Bethsaida: It will be more tolerable for Tyre and Sidon on judgment day than for them (Matt. 11:22; Luke 10:14). On both occasions he warned that the people of Capernaum should not think of heaven as their final destination; that would rather be Hades. "The men of Nineveh" and "The Queen of the South" will stand up and condemn Jesus' hearers at the day of judgment because they responded to the wisdom of Solomon and the preaching of Jonah and those hearers did not (Matt. 12:41–42). We should be clear that Jesus unhesitatingly spoke of judgment day and of what would happen on it.

Jesus also related the words uttered by his hearers to what will happen at the day of judgment. It is what goes on in our hearts that determines what we say and thus our words are important; our words reveal what we are. On the day of judgment we will be called on to give account of "every careless word" we have spoken and it is this that will determine our acquittal or our condemnation (Matt. 12:34–37).

Faith and Works. When we think of the reality and the seriousness of judgment day we must be on our guard against holding that our final salvation is to be decided on the basis of merit. The New Testament makes it abundantly clear that salvation is not the reward of the good deeds that people do. It is emphasized as strongly as it could possibly be that Christ came to this world to save sinners and that he saved them by laying down his perfect life on Calvary's cross. Salvation comes through what Christ has done and it is applied to the individual by his or her faith. It is not any merit we may have but our faith that is the channel whereby Christ's salvation reaches us. That must be given the strongest emphasis. And that has its consequences. There is "no condemnation for those that are in Christ Jesus" (Rom. 8:1). To put our trust in Christ is to pass from death to life and among other things to know that we will receive a favorable verdict on judgment day.

But to trust in Christ is to undergo a transformation. Justification leads to sanctification as believers are transformed by the power of God. While believers can look forward to the day of judgment with calm rather than fear they do so because of what God has done in them and not on account of any merit of their own.

The believer and the nonbeliever are both accountable and judgment day is the occasion when that account is rendered. It is not then a question of whether we are saved or not. It is the issuing of a verdict on what we have done; it is the answer to the question of what believers have done with their salvation and what unbelievers have done with their unbelieving lives. All will be required to give account of themselves to God.

There are those who see judgment day as pointing to salvation by works. The verdicts on the sheep and the goats on the basis of what they have done or failed to do to "the least" of Christ's brothers (Matt. 25:31–46) are said to mean that the verdict is given for those who have done good works. But this overlooks a number of facts. First whether they are "sheep" or "goats" has already been determined. Then we should notice that the good deeds are done to Christ's "brothers." We are saved not by acts of kindness but only by Christ (Acts 4:12). Good deeds may be done by unbelievers, but this is due to "common grace" at work in our fallen society, not a reason for salvation.

Salvation is by grace alone, but judgment day registers the verdict on what we have done or failed to do with God's grace. Jesus is not saying that there are some people whose good deeds merit salvation, but that there are some whose good deeds are evidence of their salvation. Scripture sees the whole race as under condemnation (Rom. 3:22–23). Unbelievers are under condemnation even before they hear the gospel for their lives do not measure up; they are sinners. We are not to think that it is only when they explicitly reject the gospel that they are condemned.

Judgment Day Is More than Present Judgment. That there will be a "judgment day" is significant for an understanding of a good deal of Scripture. In these days there are many who are ready to accept the thought of accountability but who reject the idea of judgment day. They see this as no more than a needless piece of imagery and hold that what the Bible really means is that God is constantly at work judging his people.

There is, of course, a truth here. God does watch over his people and in the happenings of every day he disciplines them. This is scriptural, but it is not the whole of the teaching of the Bible. In addition to any earlier judgments Scripture looks forward to God's judgment at the end of time.

Paul tells the Romans that what the law says is written on the hearts of the Gentiles and that their response to this will determine what will happen to them on judgment day (Rom. 2:15–16). It is what God has done in them and not what they have decided for themselves that forms the standard. For an understanding of judgment day it is important to bear in mind that God knows what goes on in the hearts of all people and he knows accordingly whether they are responding as they should to the leading he has given them.

The Judge. Very often the day is related to God or to Christ. Thus it is "the great day of God Almighty" (Rev. 16:14); it is "the day of God" (2 Peter 3:12). The earliest use of this imagery is when Amos pronounces a woe on "you who long for the day of the LORD" (5:18). Clearly the Israelites expected that day to be a day of deliverance and blessing, but Amos goes on to assure them that "That day will be darkness, not light." "The day he (God visits us" (1 Peter 2:12) means of course "the day when God visits" so it belongs here. It reminds us that God's "visitation" on judgment day will be a serious affair. So is it when we read of "the great and glorious day of the Lord" (Acts 2:20). This occurs in a quotation from Joel, so "the Lord" is clearly Yahweh.

In other places however "Lord" may refer to the Lord Jesus Christ (e.g., 1 Thess. 5:2; 2 Peter 3:10), and this is beyond doubt when we read of "the day of our Lord Jesus Christ" (1 Cor. 1:8; 5:5). Judgment day is the day of Christ (Phil. 1:10) or the day of the Son of Man (Luke 17:24). Jesus taught that the Father does not judge people, but that "he has entrusted all judgment to the Son" (John 5:22; cf. v. 27). This is distinctively Christian teaching, for the Jews do not seem to have thought of the Messiah as the Judge. He would bring deliverance to the people, but it was God the Father who would be the judge.

The point of all such references is that in the end it will be a great divine act, whether we emphasize the Father or the Son, that distinguishes the day of judgment. Paul tells us that on judgment day the Father will judge all people through Christ Jesus (Rom. 2:16) and this perhaps clears up the references which link either of the two with final judgment.

For many modern theologians the doctrine of final judgment is a relic of the past and they put no emphasis on it. This is curious in view of the facts that in modern times there has been a great upsurge of interest in eschatology and that the final judgment is at the very heart of biblical eschatology. The witness of Scripture in both Old and New Testaments is clear: We are all accountable and at the end of time we will be called on to give account of ourselves before God. LEON MORRIS

See also JUDGMENT; JUDGMENT SEAT OF CHRIST.

Bibliography. O. Cullmann, *Christ and Time;* H. E. Guillebaud, *The Righteous Judge;* J. P. Martin, *The Last Judgment;* L. Morris, *The Biblical Doctrine of Judgment;* idem, *The Wages of Sin;* J. A. Motyer, *After Death;* J. O. Sanders, *What of the Unevangelized?;* C. V. Pilcher, *The Hereafter in Jewish and Christian Thought.*

Judgment Seat of Christ. The word we translate "judgment seat" (*bema*) basically means "step" from which it comes to be used as a unit of measure (Acts 7:5). It is used of a raised platform on which the judge sat during judicial proceedings (and from which he pronounced his verdict) or of the seat itself. Most of the examples of the use of the term in the New Testament refer to human tribunals, but we have one explicit reference to the judgment seat of Christ (2 Cor. 5:10; there are also references to Christ's activity in final judgment as 1 Cor. 4:5; 1 Thess. 2:19). We also read of God's judgment seat in a passage where several manuscripts have "Christ's judgment seat" (Rom. 14:10). These passages clearly refer to the judgment at the end of the world.

"We must all" appear before Christ's judgment seat, where "must" points to a compelling divine necessity: There is no escaping it. And "all" from another point of view makes it clear that everyone must face this prospect. Paul is writing to Christians, so that "we . . . all" signifies all believers; they have all built on the one foundation though what they have built differs (1 Cor. 3:12–15). Other passages make it clear that there is a judgment for nonbelievers also, but that is not the apostle's concern at this point.

"Appear" renders a verb that the lexicon defines as meaning "reveal, make known, show." Calvin held that the word means more than "appear"; people will then come into the light whereas now many are hidden as in darkness. People will not be able to hide anything or disguise themselves at Christ's judgment seat; they will be made known for what they really are and have done.

The judgment seat is, of course, more than a place where people are known for what they have done. There is a purpose involved; they will be there "in order that" judgment be passed on them for what they have done or failed to do. "Each" (the word is important as showing the universality of the judgment) "will receive what is due," which makes it clear that justice will be done; there will be nothing capricious or half-hearted at that tribunal. That "each" will receive what is due makes it clear that Christ's judgment is to be an individual matter. It is not a question of what will happen to classes.

The judgment given will concern the things done while in the body or perhaps by means of the body (the Greek could mean either). There is probably no great difference and in the end we must say that Paul is making it clear that we all, believers and nonbelievers alike, will one day be held responsible for what we have done in this bodily life. "Whether good or bad" makes it clear that deeds of all kinds will be taken into consideration. For some reason Paul uses the singular here, so that the good or the bad is taken as a whole. This may also be the point of his use of the aorist tense, "what he did," rather than the imperfect, which would draw attention to the succession of acts. Paul is looking at the life of the believer as a whole.

We should be clear that the apostle is not speaking here of the way we are saved. Throughout his letters it is clear that salvation is brought about by the atoning work of Christ. He is here referring to the heavenly reward (or otherwise) of the redeemed. Elsewhere he has made it clear that the works believers do can be likened to gold or silver or precious stones, or on the other hand to wood or hay or stubble. The day of judgment is like a fire that will purify the first group and consume the second (1 Cor. 3:10–15). Poor works will be destroyed, but that does not mean that the builder is also destroyed.

The passage where some manuscripts refer to "the judgment seat of Christ" but most to that of God (Rom. 14:10) forbids us to judge one another and tells us that God or Christ will judge us all. Probably we should understand this to mean that the Father will judge us all through the Son (cf. John 5:22).

That we are all to stand before Christ's judgment seat is a reminder that we are accountable and that in the end we must render account of our stewardship to none less than Christ.

LEON MORRIS

See also JUDGMENT; JUDGMENT, DAY OF; REWARD.

Bibliography. J. Baillie, *And the Life Everlasting;* R. Bultmann, *Theology of the New Testament;* J. P. Martin, *The Last Judgment;* B. Van Elderen III, *ISBE,* 2:1163–64.

Justice (Heb. *ṣedeq, mišpāṭ;* Gk. *dikaiōsynē*). ***God, the Righteous Judge.*** Justice is rooted in the very nature of God (Isa. 40:14). He evenhandedly rewards good, and he does not ignore the sins of any (Pss. 33:5; 37:6, 28; 97:2; 99:4). Human judges do well to remember God in their courts. God does not take bribes (Deut. 10:17) or pervert justice in any way (Gen. 18:25; 2 Chron. 19:7).

At the same time, God rarely delivers instant justice. The world does not seem fair while evil still abounds, and so the oppressed petition God to intervene on their behalf (Ps. 7:9; Prov. 29:26). Their prayers may even take the form of a complaint (Hab. 1:2–4), although people must not challenge God's essential justice (Job 40:8; Mal. 2:17). That God will decisively intervene in the future is the biblical hope.

This philosophical issue of theodicy underlies the story of Job. On the one hand is his friends' false assumption that Job's trouble must fit his crimes (8:3–7), whereas on his part, Job claims to be the victim of an injustice, and demands that God remedy the situation (19:7; 27:2; 29:14; 34:5–6).

The justice of God is reaffirmed in the New Testament (Rom. 3:5–6; 9:14; 1 John 1:9; Rev. 16:5–7; 19:11). Because he is just, God never shows partiality or favoritism (Matt. 5:45; Acts 10:34–35; Rom. 2:6, 11; Eph. 6:9; 1 Peter 1:17).

Human Justice Based on God's Law. Just law is law that reflects God's standards (Gen. 9:5–6; Deut. 1:17), and not mere human reasoning (Hab. 1:7). According to the Sinai covenant, judges are to uphold the Mosaic law by acquitting the innocent and condemning the guilty. A breach of justice consists of a verdict that runs contrary to the law or that does not accord with the known facts (Exod. 23:1–9; Deut. 25:1–3).

In a culture where judges, not juries, render a verdict, false accusations, bribery, and influence peddling are the favored devices of injustice (Deut. 16:18–20; 1 Sam. 8:3; Prov. 17:23; 19:28; Isa. 5:23; Jer. 5:28; Ezek. 22:29; Amos 2:6–7; Zech. 7:9–10). The victims are disproportionately from the poor, among whom are the fatherless, the widow, and the resident alien (Deut. 27:19; Ps. 82). The righteous judge must never show partiality to the rich (Deut. 24:17), nor for that matter to the poor (Lev. 19:15); he must render true judgment at all times.

Under the monarchy, the king is the final arbiter of justice (2 Sam. 8:15; 15:3–4; 1 Kings 10:9; Prov. 20:8). Kings are warned about injustice (Prov. 16:10; Jer. 21:12; 22:2–3; Mic. 3:1–3, 9–11). Solomon's wisdom makes him a just king (1 Kings 3:11–12, 28; 2 Chron. 9:8).

At the same time, justice is not a virtue for judges and kings alone; all Israel is to follow in the "paths of justice" (Gen. 18:19; Ps. 106:3; Prov. 21:15; Isa. 1:17, 59). Pursuing justice in life is of greater worth than religious ritual (Prov. 21:3; Mic. 6:8; cf. Matt. 23:23). Justice must lead to honesty, even in mundane business transactions (Lev. 19:35–36; Hos. 12:7).

In the New Testament, the love of justice is a virtue (2 Cor. 7:11; Phil. 4:8), yet Christians may not take justice into their own hands (1 Thess. 4:6). At times it is better to suffer injustice than to bring the gospel into disrepute by taking a brother to court (1 Cor. 6:7–8).

Divine Justice and the Justification of the Wicked. The gospel promises escape from God's just wrath against sin (Rom. 1:32). Before human judges the Savior was unjustly tried and executed

(Isa. 53:8; John 7:24; Acts 3:14). From the divine perspective, however, Jesus' death satisfied God's justice (Rom. 3:26). Thus God remains a righteous judge even as he justifies those sinners who believe in Christ (Luke 18:14; Gal. 3:11–13).

Justice and the Kingdom of God. The Old Testament looks forward to the time when God will exercise absolute justice over all creation (Ps. 98:9; Eccles. 3:16; Isa. 28:5–6; 29:19–21). The New Testament emphasizes the approach of final judgment, when all people will be evaluated according to their works (Rom. 2:5; 3:5–6; Rev. 20:13).

Psalm 72 is a prayer for a king who would protect the poor, a psalm that looks beyond Solomon to an ideal just king. The Old Testament goes on to predict that the Messiah will execute justice on God's behalf (Isa. 9:7; 11:3–4; 16:4b–5; 28:17). In the New Testament, Jesus already begins to carry out the Father's justice while on earth (Matt. 12:18–21; John 5:28–30), but it is in the future that he will execute God's will over all (Acts 17:31; Rev. 19:11). GARY STEVEN SHOGREN

See also JUSTIFICATION; RIGHTEOUSNESS.

Bibliography. F. Büschel and V. Herntrich, *TDNT,* 3:921–54; R. D. Culver, *TWOT,* 2:948–49; C. Hodge, *Systematic Theology,* 1:416–27; G. Quell and G. Schrenk, *TDNT,* 2:174–225.

Justification. Justification is the declaring of a person to be just or righteous. It is a legal term signifying acquittal, a fact that makes it unpalatable to many in our day. We tend to distrust legalism and thus we dismiss anything that savors of a legalistic approach. We should be clear that our hesitation was not shared by the biblical writers. In their day it was axiomatic that a wealthy and important citizen would not be treated in a law court in the same way as an insignificant person. Indeed this was sometimes written into the statutes and, for example, in the ancient Code of Hammurabi it is laid down that if a citizen knocked out the tooth of another citizen his own tooth should be knocked out. But if the victim was a vassal it sufficed to pay a small fine. Nobody expected strict justice in human tribunals but the biblical writers were sure that God is a God of justice. Throughout the Bible justice is a category of fundamental importance.

It mattered to the biblical writers that God is a God is a God of perfect justice, a truth expressed in Abraham's question, "Will not the Judge of all the earth do right?" (Gen. 18:25). God can be relied on to act in perfect justice and without giving preference to the wealthy and the highly placed in our human societies. "The LORD takes his place in court; he rises to judge the people. The LORD enters into judgment against the elders and leaders of his people" (Isa. 3:13–14). Over and over the punishment of evil is put in legal terms (Exod. 6:6; 7:4) and specifically Israel's sin is brought out with the use of legal imagery (Mic. 6:1–2).

Accordingly it is not surprising that salvation is often viewed in legal terms. The basic question in all religion is, "How can sinful people be just (i.e., be justified) before the holy God?" Justification is a legal term with a meaning like "acquittal"; in religion it points to the process whereby a person is declared to be right before God. That person should be an upright and good person, but justification does not point to qualities like these. That is rather the content of sanctification. Justification points to the acquittal of one who is tried before God. In both the Old Testament and the New the question receives a good deal of attention and in both it is clear that people cannot bring about their justification by their own efforts. The legal force of the terminology is clear when Job exclaims, "Now that I have prepared my case, I know I will be vindicated" (Job 13:18).

Justification (*dikaiosis*) is connected linguistically with righteousness (*dikaiosune*); in the first century it is clear that all the words with this root were concerned with conformity to a standard of right. And in Scripture it is not too much to say that righteousness is basically a legal term. The law that mattered was, of course, the law of God, so that righteousness signified conformity to the law of God.

The Old Testament. We do not find the full New Testament doctrine of justification by faith in the Old Testament, but we do find teachings that agree with it and that in due course were taken up into that doctrine. Thus it is made clear that sin is universal, but that God provides forgiveness. For the first point, "All have turned aside, they have together become corrupt; there is no one who does good, not even one" (Ps. 14:3). And when God looks down from heaven he sees that "they have together become corrupt; there is no one who does good, not even one" (Ps. 53:2–3). Many such passages could be cited. And for the second point, "If you, O LORD, kept a record of sins, O LORD, who could stand? But with you there is forgiveness" (Ps. 130:3–4). The end of Micah's prophecy emphasizes that God is a God "who pardons sin and forgives the transgression of the remnant of his inheritance" and that he "delights to show mercy" (7:18–20).

Sometimes we find the thought that God imputes righteousness to people. He did this to Abraham, who believed God "and he credited it to him as righteousness" (Gen. 15:6). Again Phinehas took decisive action so that the plague was checked and "This was credited to him as righteousness" (Ps. 106:31; Phinehas is described in the words, "as zealous as I am for my honor among them," Num. 25:11). And the prophet can say, "He who vindicates (or justifies) me is near" (Isa. 50:8).

The New Testament. When we turn to the New Testament we must be clear that the righteousness and justification terminology is to be understood in the light of its Hebrew background, not in terms of contemporary Greek ideas. We see this, for example, in the words of Jesus who speaks of people giving account on the day of judgment: "by your words you will be acquitted, and by your words you will be condemned" (Matt. 12:37; the word NIV translates "acquitted" is the one Paul normally uses for "justified"). Those acquitted on the day of judgment are spoken of as "the righteous" (Matt. 25:37; they go into "eternal life," v. 46).

The verb translated "to justify" clearly means "to declare righteous." It is used of God in a quotation, which the New International Version renders "So that you may be proved right when you speak" (Rom. 3:4; the NRSV has more exactly, "So that you may be justified in your words"). Now God cannot be "made righteous"; the expression obviously means "shown to be righteous" and this helps us see that when the word is applied to believers it does not mean "made righteous"; it signifies "declared righteous," "shown to be in the right," or the like.

Paul is fond of the concept of justification; indeed for him it is the characteristic way of referring to the central truth of the gospel. He makes much more use of the concept than do the other writers of the New Testament. This does not mean that he has a different understanding of the gospel; it is the same gospel that he proclaims, the gospel that the death of Christ on the cross has opened a way of salvation for sinners. But he uses the concept of justification to express it whereas the other writers prefer other terms. He says, "Just as through the disobedience of the one man the many were made sinners, so also through the obedience of the one man the many will be made righteous" (Rom. 5:19). We should not understand "were made sinners" in any such sense as "were compelled to be sinners." It signifies "were constituted sinners," "were reckoned as sinners." Paul is saying that the whole human race is caught up in the effect of Adam's sin; now all are sinners. Paul speaks of God "who justifies the wicked" (Rom. 4:5): it is not people who have merited their salvation of whom he writes, but people who had no claim on salvation. It was "while we were still sinners" that Christ died for us (Rom. 5:8). But the effect of Christ's saving work is that now all believers are "made righteous," "accepted by God as righteous."

Paul insists that people are not justified by what they themselves do. Justification is not the result of the infusion of new life into people, but comes about when they believe. The apostle points to the important example of Abraham, the great forbear of the Jewish race, as one who was not justified by works (Rom. 4:2–3). And, of course, if Abraham was not justified by works, then who could possibly be? Specifically Paul says, "a man is not justified by observing the law"; indeed, "by observing the law no one will be justified" (Gal. 2:16; cf. also Gal. 3:11).

There is something of a problem in that, whereas Paul says quite plainly that justification is by faith and not by works, James holds that "a person is justified by what he does and not by faith alone" (2:24). James chooses Abraham and Rahab as examples of people who were justified by works (2:21, 25). He points out that Abraham "offered his son Isaac on the altar" and that Rahab lodged the spies and sent them away.

But we should notice that both these Old Testament worthies are elsewhere singled out as examples of faith. Paul cited Abraham to establish the truth that we are justified by faith rather than by works. Indeed, he quotes Scripture, "Abraham believed God, and it was credited to him as righteousness" (Rom. 4:3, citing Gen. 15:6; he cites it again in v. 22). In Romans 4 Paul has a strong argument that it was not works that commended the patriarch to God, but faith: Abraham is, for Paul, the classic example of a man who believed and who was accepted by God because of his faith. And the writer to the Hebrews says plainly that it was "by faith" that Rahab welcomed the spies (Heb. 11:31).

If we look more closely at what James says we see that he is not arguing for works in the absence of faith, but rather for works as the evidence of faith. "Show me your faith without deeds," he writes, "and I will show you my faith by what I do" (2:18) and goes on to cite the demons who believe that there is one God as examples of the kind of faith he deprecates. James is sure that saving faith transforms the believer so that good works necessarily follow; and he complains about people who say they have faith, but whose lives show quite plainly that they have not been saved. When people have saving faith God transforms their lives and James' point is that in the absence of this transformation we have no reason for thinking that those who profess to be believers really have saving faith. We should not overlook the fact that James as well as Paul quotes Genesis 15:6 to make it clear that Abraham was justified by faith. And we should bear in mind that this was many years before he offered Isaac on the altar; indeed it was before Isaac was born. While the offering of Isaac showed that Abraham was justified, his justification, even on James' premises, took place long before the act that showed its presence.

And we must say much the same about Paul. He certainly calls vigorously for faith, but he calls equally vigorously for lives of Christian service. And when he writes, "The only thing that counts is faith expressing itself through love" (Gal. 5:6), he is saying something with which James would surely agree. For James says, "I will show you my faith by what I do" (2:18).

Paul continually emphasizes the importance of justification by faith. In his sermon at Antioch in Pisidia he points out that "through Jesus the forgiveness of sins is proclaimed to you" and immediately adds, "Through him everyone who believes is justified from everything you could not be justified from by the law of Moses" (Acts 13:38–39). More than once he quotes the words from Habbakuk 2:4, "the righteous will live by faith" (Rom. 1:17; Gal. 3:11; cf. also Gal. 2:16; Heb. 10:38). He says explicitly that justification is by faith and not by observing the law (Rom. 3:28), or simply that "we have been justified through faith" (Rom. 5:1).

Paul does not, of course, argue that faith is a meritorious act that of itself brings about justification. He is not saying that if we believe strongly enough we somehow get rid of our sins. But real faith means trust in God and when we trust God we are open to the divine power that works in us to make us the sort of people we ought to be and to accomplish the divine purpose. When we insist on our own moral performance we cut ourselves off from the good that God works in believers.

At the center of Paul's religion is the cross of Jesus, and faith means trusting the crucified Lord. Thus Paul says that Jesus "was delivered over to death for our sins and was raised to life for our justification" (Rom. 4:25). We should not, of course, put too strong a distinction between the effects of Jesus' death and the effects of his resurrection. Paul is saying that Jesus' death and resurrection meant a complete dealing with sins and a perfectly accomplished justification. We are "justified freely by his grace through the redemption that came by Christ Jesus" (Rom. 3:24), which means that Jesus' atoning death is critically important in our justification. Similarly we are justified "by his grace" (Rom. 3:24), "by his blood" (Rom. 5:9), "in the name of the Lord Jesus Christ" (1 Cor. 6:11), and "in Christ" (Gal. 2:17), which are all ways of saying that it is the saving work of Jesus that brings about the justification of sinners.

Salvation by the way of the cross was so that God would be "just and the one who justifies the man who has faith in Jesus" (Rom. 3:26). This will be in mind also in the reference to God as presenting Christ "as a sacrifice of atonement (better, "a propitiation") through faith in his blood" (Rom. 3:25). That we are "justified by his blood" (Rom. 5:9) points to the same truth: It is the death of Jesus that makes us right with God. This is the meaning also when we read that we are "justified by his grace" (Titus 3:7). It was God's good gift that brought justification, his "one act of righteousness" in Christ that effected it (Rom. 5:16, 18). Another way of putting it is that the saved are saved not because of their own righteousness (they are sinners), but because of the righteousness that is from God and which they receive by faith (Phil. 3:9; cf. 2 Cor. 5:21).

It is plain from the New Testament teaching throughout that justification comes to the sinner by the atoning work of Jesus and that this is applied to the individual sinner by faith. That God pardons and accepts believing sinners is the truth that is enshrined in the doctrine of justification by faith.

LEON MORRIS

See also ATONEMENT; CROSS, CRUCIFIXION; DEATH OF CHRIST; FAITH; PAUL THE APOSTLE; WORKS OF THE LAW.

Bibliography. M. Barth, *Justification;* G. C. Berkouwer, *Faith and Justification;* J. Buchanan, *The Doctrine of Justification;* F. Colquhoun, *The Meaning of Justification;* L. Morris, *The Apostolic Preaching of the Cross;* idem, *The Cross in the New Testament;* P. Toon, *Justification and Sanctification;* F. B. Westcott, *The Biblical Doctrine of Justification.*

Kk

Kairos. *See* TIME.

Kerygma. Transliteration of the Greek word that means proclamation or preaching. Depending on the context, it may refer to either the content proclaimed or the act of proclaiming. The word is used once in Matthew (12:41), once in Luke (11:32), and six times in Paul's letters (Rom. 16:25; 1 Cor. 1:21; 2:4; 15:14; 2 Tim. 4:17; Titus 1:3). All of these New Testament occurrences appear to refer to what is being proclaimed.

Both Matthew and Luke apparently refer to Jonah's message as the content proclaimed. The parallel statement in Matthew 12:42 speaking of the wisdom of Solomon also points toward content as the intended meaning of kerygma. Thus the statement in both Matthew and Luke would mean that the men of Nineveh repented at the message of Jonah.

There are two occurrences (1:21; 2:4) of the term "kerygma" in the first major unit of 1 Corinthians (1:18–2:5). In this large passage Paul is explaining his gospel in contrast to the influence of the Jews who are concerned about signs and of the Greeks who are concerned about wisdom. This Greek influence seems to have come from the Sophists (the wisdom teachers). The believers in Corinth seem to view the gospel through Sophist eyes as "wisdom" and the evangelists as "wisdom teachers." Paul is correcting this kind of misunderstanding of the gospel. His opening reference to "the message of the cross" (1:18) clearly indicates that he has a definite content in mind. His reference to "the wisdom of the world" (1:20) shows what the kerygma has rendered untenable. Then comes the crucial assertion in 1:21 that God is saving those who believe through the kerygma—the message about Jesus' death and resurrection, which from the viewpoint of the world is foolishness. Verse 23 combines the cognate verb (*kērysso*) with the primary content of the kerygma by saying, "We preach Christ crucified." Paul goes on to declare that this message is the power and wisdom of God that, in fact, the Jews and Greeks are seeking; yet they fail to perceive these qualities in the gospel and reject it as an offense or foolishness. God's purpose in allowing this failure and rejection is explained in verses 26–31. The twofold purpose is stated negatively as preventing people from boasting and positively as allowing them to boast only in the Lord. For Paul kerygma is the gospel or the proclamation of the death of Christ to bring about the salvation of all those who believe. Verses 1–5 of chapter 2 explain that belief in the message comes about not by human wisdom or eloquence, but by means of the demonstration and power of the Spirit. Verse 4 refers to Paul's word or proclamation (*kerygma*), and verse 5 asserts that faith in this proclamation results in trust in the power of God. That is, the believer in this message is brought into a relationship with God: salvation or redemption.

At the end of 1 Corinthians, in the last major unit on the resurrection (15:1–58), Paul returns to the theme of kerygma. Interestingly, at the beginning of this section Paul uses the word "gospel" (*euangelion*) and spells out the four crucial elements of the gospel: Christ's death, burial, resurrection, and appearances (vv. 1–8). Then, in the process of asserting the absolute necessity of the resurrection, Paul refers to "our preaching [kerygma]" (v. 14). Clearly Paul understands "our preaching" as the gospel he has just defined in the opening verses of the chapter. The interchangeability of kerygma and gospel in this passage brings out unmistakably that the kerygma is the gospel message about Christ's death and resurrection. These two large units (1 Cor. 1:18–2:5; 15:1–58) are the definitive passages in the New Testament on kerygma.

There are three other references to kerygma in Paul's letters. In the closing doxology of Romans, Paul parallels gospel (*euangelion*) and proclamation (*kērygma*) (16:25). Probably the conjunction "and" (*kai*) would be better translated "that is," which would show that by proclamation Paul means the gospel or message about Christ. As it is here paralleled with gospel, kerygma is certainly intended to mean the content or message Paul proclaims. Because the entire Letter to the Romans is an elaborate and systematic development of the gospel, it might be suggested that Romans is at the same time the most extensive statement of Paul's kerygma. Thus, even though the word "kerygma" occurs only in the closing doxology, Romans in fact is Paul's own masterful development of his earlier definition of kerygma in 1 Corinthians, which was written about two years before Romans.

Paul includes in the opening salutation of his Letter to Titus a reference to the proclamation. The context might possibly be understood with either meaning here. The immediately preceding reference to "his Word" (*ton logon autou*) could be viewed as the message Paul declares in proclaiming (*en kērygmati*). But it seems more natural to understand "his word" to refer back to God's promise (v. 2) which is then embodied in "the proclamation" that has been entrusted to Paul. Thus, throughout the salutation "truth," "knowledge," "promise," "word," and "preaching" (*kērygmati*) all refer to the message or the gospel Paul proclaims. Thus it may be said that the context indicates that he is referring to the content of the gospel he proclaims, which is the message that has been entrusted to him from God.

In the closing instructions of his final letter (2 Tim. 4:17) Paul makes his last reference to the *kērygma*. The context indicates that he means the gospel or the message he has proclaimed throughout his ministry. His statement is that "through me the *kērgyma* might be fully proclaimed." The use of "words" (*logois*) at the end of verse 15 further strengthens the understanding that *kērygma* in verse 17 does refer to the gospel or message about Jesus' death and resurrection.

The meaning of *kērygma* all six times that Paul uses this term is consistently the message about Jesus, the content of the gospel Paul so courageously proclaimed throughout his ministry.

HOBERT K. FARRELL

See also PAUL THE APOSTLE; PREACH, PROCLAIM.

Bibliography. F. F. Bruce, *Romans;* C. H. Dodd, *The Apostolic Preaching and Its Development;* G. D. Fee, *The First Epistle of the Corinthians;* D. Guthrie, *The Pastoral Epistle;* L. Morris, *1 Corinthians.*

Kidney. *See* PERSON, PERSONHOOD.

Kill, Killing. ***The Old Testament.*** The Old Testament uses many terms to refer to the act of killing, some of which can be used interchangeably (see 2 Sam. 14:7, where three terms for killing are used). The most common of these is *hārag,* a neutral term found over 160 times. It is used to convey the concept of the violent death of persons at the hands of other persons (individuals, Israelites, or foreigners), whether justified or unjustified; it also includes the idea of murder or judicial execution (the offender was to be killed in agreement with the command in Gen. 9:6).

Killing Enemies in Battle. The Hebrew term *hārag* can mean killing enemies in battle. In a holy war, the Israelites would undertake the ritual mass destruction of enemies in obedience to the command of God (Num. 31:7, 17; Deut. 2:34; 3:6; 7:22–26; 13:16; 20:10–14; Josh. 8:26–28; 1 Sam. 15:3). Even Pharaoh participated in the mass destruction of enemies (1 Kings 9:16).

Killing Opponents. The killing of political opponents occurred during periods of revolution, in disputes with prophets, or in the battle for succession to the throne. Gideon destroyed Peniel and its people when they refused his aid (Judg. 8:17); Saul thought about killing Samuel (1 Sam. 16:2), and was successful in having the priests of Nob slain (1 Sam. 22:17); Jezebel killed the prophets of Yahweh (1 Kings 18:13; cf. 1 Kings 19:10); Zechariah was stoned during the reign of Joash (2 Chron. 24:21); Abimelech killed his seventy brothers (Judg. 9:5); Athaliah killed her family and was herself killed (2 Kings 11:16; 2 Chron. 23:15); and Jehu destroyed the line of Ahab (2 Chron. 22:8). The festival of Purim was associated with the slaying of political enemies (Esther 3:13; 7:4; 8:11; 9:2). Pharaoh intended to kill the Hebrew sons (Heb. causitive of *mût,* Exod. 1:16; also see 1 Sam. 17:50; 2 Sam. 3:30). *Hārag* is also used for the killing of personal enemies and rivals (by Lamech [Gen. 4:23–24]; for the intended killing of Joseph [Gen. 37:20; *mût* was used in Gen. 37:18; also see 1 Sam. 19:1; 1 Kings 11:40]; Jacob versus Esau [Gen. 27:41]; and Cain versus Abel [Gen. 4:1–6]).

Killing as a Crime. There were at least four types of criminal homicide: murder, accidental homicide, the goring ox, and justifiable homicide. Murder was a premeditated act (Exod. 21:13; Num. 35:20–22) punishable by death (Num. 35:31–33; Deut. 19:13). Moses' killing of an Egyptian was considered a crime by Pharaoh (Exod. 2:14–15), as was Joab's blood vengeance against Abner (2 Sam. 3:30; cf. 1 Kings 2:5) and David's plotting the death of Uriah (2 Sam. 12:9, 14). Judicial murder was also condemned (Exod. 23:7; Pss. 10:8; 94:5–6).

A distinction was made between homicide and premeditated murder (Exod. 21:13–14), although the blood avenger was required to act against both, primarily as a safeguard against the killing of relatives. The one who committed accidental manslaughter was able to receive asylum (Exod. 21:13; Num. 35:9–30 [Heb. *nākâ,* a mortal blow]; Deut. 19:1–10). Accidental manslaughter could result from a sudden shove or unintentional throwing of an object (Num. 35:22), the dropping of a stone or random missile (Num. 35:22–23), a fall from a roof with no rail (Deut. 22:8), or assault by a killer who was not lying in wait (Exod. 21:12–13). An ox who killed a man was stoned (Exod. 21:28–32). A property owner was justified in killing a thief in the act of stealing (Exod. 22:2; in daylight hours).

Killing as Punishment for a Crime. Israel's death penalty showed moral sensitivity and placed a high value on human life. Punishment was often regarded as God's vengeance on the crime. Capital punishment was employed for the following criminal cases: intentional homicide (Exod. 21:12; Lev. 24:17; Num. 35:16–21), kidnapping (Exod. 21:16; Deut. 24:7), prostitution by the priest's daughter (Lev. 21:9), persistent disobedience against parents (Lev. 20:9; Deut. 27:16), apostasy from the Lord (Num. 25:5; Deut. 13:10), killing the king (2 Sam. 4:10–12), fratricide (Gen. 4:14; Exod. 21:14; Judg. 9:56; 2 Sam. 14:7), child sacrifice (Lev. 20:4; Heb. *mût*), and false prophecy (Deut. 13:1–5). It was also enforced for sexual abuses such as adultery (Lev. 20:10; Deut. 22:22), incest (Lev. 20:11–17), sodomy (Lev. 20:13), and bestiality (Exod. 22:19; Lev. 20:15–16), and for cultic abuses including idolatry (Lev. 20:1–5; Num. 25:1–5; Deut. 13:6–18; 17:2–7), blasphemy (Lev. 24:15–16), profanation of the Sabbath (Exod. 31:14–15; Num. 15:32–36), and sorcery (Exod. 22:17; Lev. 20:27). One aspect in criminal law was the idea of corporate personality; Achan's death penalty was extended to his entire family (Josh. 7).

Killing as Sacrifice. The term *shāḥat* was used for the slaughter of animals, either for sacrifice or for food (Exod. 29:11, 16, 20; Lev. 1:5), for child sacrifices (Ezek. 16:21; 23:39), and for Jehu's mass killing (2 Kings 10:7, 14). Other terms (e.g., *zābaḥ*) were used for butchering (Lev. 17:3–9).

Yahweh as the Subject. Yahweh punished misdeeds, was a military hero (Yahweh of hosts), and killed personal opponents (Num. 22:21–35). He killed Pharaoh's firstborn (Exod. 4:23; 13:15), the Philistines (Isa. 14:28–32), Babylonians (Isa. 14:4–21), and even his own people (Jer. 5:14; 23:29; Hos. 6:5; Amos 9:1–4). Yahweh was also described as killing his enemies in prophetic visions of judgment (Ezek. 23:9–10; Amos 4:10; 9:1).

The New Testament. The New Testament also uses a variety of words for the concept of killing. The most common is *apokteinō*, a term used nearly seventy-five times. The writers of the Septuagint employed this word on over 150 occasions (normally for the Hebrew term *hārag*). Its generic meaning appeared to signify the ending of someone else's life in a violent way, and could signify murder, execution, or killing. It was found most often in the Gospels and Revelation, while rarely in the Pauline Epistles. The objects of the term were most often those who speak for God (Matt. 14:5; 23:30; Mark 6:19; John 16:2; for the killing of God's messengers) and were condemned to death. The disciples were threatened with death (Acts 21:31; 23:12–14), as were martyrs (Rev. 6:11; 11:7). It could also be used figuratively (2 Cor. 3:6; Eph. 2:16; sin forces one into a conflict that ends in death), in parables (Matt. 23:37; Mark 12:5–12), or in prophetic narratives (with reference to the disciples in Matthew's apocalypse [24:9]). It was used concerning Christ in the passion predictions (Mark 8:31; 9:31; 10:34). Killing was used to execute God's judgment (Rev. 6:8; 9:15–18; 19:21); hostility was behind the killing of Christ (Eph. 2:15–16).

Other terms for killing are also used, but on a less frequent basis. Luke often uses a term (*anaireō*) that means to do away with, usually in a violent way (Luke 22:2; Acts 9:24; 16:27; 23:15; 26:10). The New Testament term for committing murder (*phoneuō*) is used by Matthew to signify the sixth commandment (5:21; 19:18), and by Paul in summarizing the law (Rom. 13:9; see James 2:11). Other terms include "handle violently" (in the extended sense to mean "kill": *diacheirizō;* the killing of Jesus on the cross; Acts 5:30; 26:21), "deliver up to death" (*thanatoō;* Rom. 7:4; 8:36; 2 Cor. 6:9; also, "put to death"; Matt. 27:1; Mark 13:12; 14:55; 1 Peter 3:18), "to slaughter" (*sphazō;* Rom. 5:6, 8, 12; 6:9; 1 John 3:12). The New Testament term for immolation (*thuō*) has a ritual character (Luke 15:23, 27, 30). It could be used of oxen (Matt. 22:4), flocks (John 10:10), by Peter in Acts (10:13; 11:7), for the Passover (Luke 22:7), of Christ as the Passover lamb (1 Cor. 5:7), and by Paul in comparing pagan and Hebrew sacrifice (1 Cor. 8:4–13; 10:25–30).

MARK W. CHAVALAS

See also MURDER; WAR, HOLY WAR.

Bibliography. L. Conene, *NIDNTT,* 1:429–30; M. Greenberg, *JBL* 78 (1959): 125–32; J. J. Finkelstein, *TAPS* 71 (1981): 1–89; H. Fuhs, *TDOT,* 3:447–57; H. McKeating, *VT* 25 (1975): 46–68; R. de Vaux, *Ancient Israel.*

Kindness. An attribute of God and quality desirable but not consistently found in humans.

The main problem in understanding kindness is the fact that it is one of a series of terms that are overlapping and not clearly or consistently distinguishable in meaning. This is true not only in English (kindness, goodness, mercy, pity, love, grace, favor, compassion, gentleness, tenderness, etc.) but also in Greek (*chrēstos, eleēmōn, oiktirmōn, charis, agapē, splanchnon, epieikeia,* etc.) and in Hebrew (*ḥesed, ṭōb, raḥămim, ḥemlah, ḥēn,* etc.). Consider, for example, the relationship of love, goodness, kindness, and mercy in Luke 6:35–36. Nevertheless, although distinctions are not consistent, kindness (like goodness, love) tends to cover a broad range of meaning, with mercy and grace being progressively narrower.

Divine Kindness. God's kindness is presupposed or taught throughout Scripture.

It is manifest in what is called "common grace." God is kind to all he has made (Ps. 145:9), even when his creatures are ungrateful and wicked (Luke 6:35; cf. Matt. 5:45). His kindness is intended to lead to repentance, not to rejection of him (Rom. 2:4).

In the second place, it is the believer who can truly celebrate God's kindness, even in areas of experience not directly related to salvation from the guilt and punishment of sin. God's kindness is seen in his deliverance of the believer from affliction, fear, and trouble.

Third, God's kindness is manifest in the full salvation that comes through Christ (1 Peter 2:3). Indeed, our salvation derives from the kindness of God (Eph. 2:7–8), and it is through continuing in his kindness that we are saved (Rom. 11:22).

What is true of God in general is also specifically attributed to Christ, who is gentle (Matt. 11:29–30). In this connection, Jesus' kind yoke might better be understood to speak of the fact that it is gently and considerately laid upon his disciple rather than that it is easy to accomplish.

Human Kindness. The Scriptures also teach that divine kindness is to be reflected in the human experience. Indeed, expressing kindness to other human beings is more important than performing ritual sacrifice to God (Hos. 6:6; Matt. 9:13; 12:7). Thus, we are to love kindness (Mic. 6:8) and to be children of the Most High, exhibiting his kindness and mercy (Luke 6:35–36). Even more direct is the simple injunction to be kind (Eph. 4:32). Kindness often finds a place in the lists of Christian virtues (1 Cor. 13:4; Col. 3:12). Paul can take the injunction a step further and claim to exemplify kindness in his own life to a degree that commends his ministry as authentic (2 Cor. 6:6).

Yet human imitation of God's kindness does not come naturally. In fact, ultimately no one is kind (Ps. 14:3; Rom. 3:12). It is only as the fruit of God's Spirit that kindness can be a consistent part of the believer's experience (Gal. 5:22).

David K. Huttar

Bibliography. E. Beyreuther, *NIDNTT,* 2:105–6; D. N. Freedman, *TDOT,* 5:22–36; R. L. Harris, *TWOT,* 1:305–7; D. K. McKim, *ISBE,* 3:19–20; K. Weiss, *TDNT,* 9:483–92; H.-J. Zobel, *TDOT,* 5:44–64.

King. *See* God, Names of.

King, Christ as. ***The Old Testament.*** Beginning with Genesis 1:1, the Bible portrays God as the Lord and Sovereign over all creation, God Most High (Gen. 14:18; cf. Pss. 24:1; 93:1; 95:3–7). The central theme of the covenant God made with Abraham was the promise that the land of Canaan would be "an everlasting possession" to him and his descendants (Gen. 17:8). The land is the gift of God (Exod. 32:13; 33:1; Deut. 1:8, 25). Yet it "must not be sold permanently, because the land is mine and you are but aliens and my tenants" (Lev. 25:23). God owns the land and lives among his people in a covenant relationship (Lev. 26:11–12; Deut. 4:1; 6:5–15). He is the ideal King, the Lord Almighty, over the kingdoms of mortals (Isa. 6:5; Jer. 46:18; Dan. 4:25).

In Deuteronomy 17:14–20 Moses prophesied that a time would come, following the settlement of the land, in which the nation would want a king like all the nations around them. He warned them to "be sure to appoint . . . the king the Lord your God chooses" (v. 15). From the conquest, all of Israel's neighbors had kings. When the Priest-Judge Samuel grew old, the elders of Israel determined that the time had come for a change (1 Sam. 8:4–22). Samuel acquiesced to their request, and anointed Saul as their king (1 Sam. 10:1, 24–25; 11:14–15). From the anointing of Saul on, the monarchy developed as a secondary institution alongside the priesthood and temple cult. One can discern two views of the anointed monarchy in the Old Testament: it was either the gift and servant of God, or it was God's rival and a symbol of Israel's rejection of the reign of God.

In David the Lord found a person after his own heart (1 Sam. 13:14), one to whom he made a solemn and everlasting promise: "The Lord . . . will establish a house for you: When your days are over and you rest with your fathers, I will raise up your offspring to succeed you, who will come from your own body, and I will establish his kingdom. . . . Your house and your kingdom will endure forever before me; your throne will be established forever" (2 Sam. 7:11–13, 16). When Jerusalem fell in 586 B.C., this promise seemed to end in failure.

After the united kingdom of Israel was divided in 931 B.C., the prophets of the Old Testament increasingly interpreted the promise made to David in spiritual terms, rather than in political, terrestrial ones. Isaiah prophesied in the eighth century B.C.: "The Lord himself will give you a sign: The virgin . . . will give birth to a son, and will call him Immanuel" (7:14). His reign would be supranational and everlasting, possessing divine characteristics, restoring peace and justice (9:2–7; 11:1–10). Isaiah's contemporary, Micah, likewise prophesied that he would be born in Bethlehem, but his origins were "from of old, from ancient times" (5:2–5). Jeremiah and other later prophets continued to cultivate the hope of a future anointed deliverer who would be the righteous Branch of Jesse (Jer. 23:5–6; 33:15).

The fall of Jerusalem in 586 B.C. intensified the hope of witnessing the kingdom of God, but in apocalyptic terms—the anticipation of a divine warrior, a messianic king who would appear as God's deliverer (Zech. 9:9–17; 12:8–10; 14:3–9). In Daniel one finds a new distinction. "God is God of gods and the Lord of kings" (2:47), who is "sovereign over the kingdoms of men and gives them to anyone he wishes" (4:25). Sometime in the future, however, God will set up a kingdom that will crush all the kingdoms of the earth and bring them to an end, but will itself endure forever (2:44). In Daniel's apocalyptic vision, he sees a future divine king—"one like a son of man, coming with the clouds of heaven. He approached the Ancient of Days and was led into his presence. He was given authority, glory and sovereign power; all peoples, nations and men of every language worshiped him. His dominion is an everlasting dominion that will not pass away, and his kingdom is one that will never be destroyed" (7:13–14). David served as the definitive authority for Jesus, for he interpreted the promise in other than human terms, "The LORD says to my Lord: 'Sit at my right hand until I make your enemies a footstool for your feet'" (Ps. 110:1). Jesus understood David to have called the Christ "his Lord" (Mark 12:36; cf. Acts 2:34–35; Heb. 1:13).

The New Testament. In the time of Herod king of Judea (Matt. 2:1; Luke 1:5) and Caesar Augustus who reigned over the Roman world (Luke 2:1), Jesus was born. Magi came to Jerusalem looking for "the one who has been born king of the Jews" (Matt. 2:2; cf. Luke 2:11). The genealogies of Matthew 1:1–17 and Luke 3:23–38 confirm Jesus' human descent from David, a prominent motif in Matthew. After Jesus fed the 5,000, the crowd wanted to force him to become king (John 6:15). Blind Bartimaeus saw what others had missed, as he shouted, "Jesus, Son of David, have mercy on me!" (Mark 10:46–52). Jesus entered Jerusalem like a king, riding on the colt of a donkey (Matt. 21:5; Luke 19:38; John 12:13, 15; cf. Zech. 9:9). When Jesus was on trial, the high priest questioned him, asking, "Are you the Christ, the Son of the Blessed One?" Jesus responded prophetically, "I am. And you will see the Son of Man sitting at the right hand of the Mighty One and coming on the clouds of heaven" (Mark 14:61–62; cf. Dan. 7:13; Zech. 12:10). Similarly, the governor Pilate asked, "Are you the king of the Jews?" To which Jesus answered, "Yes, it is as you say" (Mark 15:2). Throughout the balance of the New Testament Jesus is described as the Son of David, a king.

The Kingdom of God (Heaven). The devil tempted Jesus by taking him to a high mountain and showing him all the kingdoms of the world and their splendor. He promised to transfer his usurped authority to Jesus, if Jesus would bow down and worship him. Jesus corrected the devil's theology, reaffirming that the Lord alone has power over the kingdoms of the world and he alone is worthy of worship (Matt. 4:8–10; Luke 4:5–8). God Almighty is the Great King (Matt. 5:35; cf. 1 Tim. 1:17). Consistently in the parables of the kingdom, God is understood as the master and owner or the King.

After receiving the divine anointing at his baptism (Mark 1:9–11), Jesus begins to proclaim the inauguration of the kingdom in Galilee: "The time has come. The kingdom of God is near. Repent and believe the good news!" (Mark 1:15). This becomes the central theme in all that Jesus preaches, and he seeks to define its nature in the expanded response to Pilate: "My kingdom is not of this world. If it were, my servants would fight to prevent my arrest by the Jews. But now my kingdom is from another place" (John 18:36). The disciples, however, persistently misunderstood the nature of the kingdom to the very end. For this reason, Peter rebuked Jesus when he spoke of going to Jerusalem to die (Mark 8:32), and then drew his sword in an attempt to fend off the arresting crowd in Gethsemane (Mark 14:47). The kingdom remained a mystery, hidden from the understanding of the disciples.

The kingdom is present in the person, ministry, and miracles of Jesus (Matt. 12:28; Luke 11:20). Jesus likens himself to the narrow gate (Matt. 7:13–14; Luke 13:24; John 10:7, 9), the one who has the key to open the way for people to enter the kingdom. When he is present, the kingdom of God is present (Luke 11:20; 17:21; 1 Tim. 4:1), but it is not a visible, political, or temporal kingdom (Luke 17:20–25). As in the Old Testament, the kingdom is the gift of God (Luke 12:32), but now the emphasis is on the universal opportunity open to all who believe (Matt. 16:19; 21:43; Luke 12:32; John 3:3–8, 15–16).

The kingdom, on the other hand, is also described by Jesus as eschatological, and will be consummated at a future time. Frequently, Jesus says, "Repent, for the kingdom of God (heaven) is near" (Matt. 4:17; 10:7; Mark 1:15; Luke 10:9, 11). This reference to time is debated among scholars, as the perfect tense of the Greek verb (*ēngiken*) can be interpreted to mean that the kingdom has come at some point in the past and is now present, or it is imminently near and will be realized sometime in the future. There are, however, other statements that are less ambiguous. The disciple is told to pray, "Your kingdom come" (Matt. 6:10; Luke 11:2), implying that the kingdom is not fully realized. In the parables of the judgment, the kingdom will be a future, eternal inheritance prepared for those who have done the will of God, a reward for those who have worked in God's vineyard (Matt. 20:1–16) and for those to whom God chooses to show his mercy. This inheritance is associated with the second coming of the Son of Man and the eschatological invasion of his kingdom "with power" (Mark 9:1).

The motif of Christ as King and the kingdom is less common outside the Gospels in the New Testament, except in Revelation. As the church grew beyond Palestine and the synagogues of the Jews, the Gentiles preferred other metaphors to refer to their relationship and the supremacy of Christ, such as bridegroom and bride and Christ the head of the body.

"Jesus is King" became the confession of the early Christian community. Nathanael declares, "Rabbi, you are the Son of God; you are the King of Israel" (John 1:49). With the same profound meaning, the early church adopted the baptismal confession, "Jesus is Lord!" (Rom. 10:9; 1 Cor. 12:3). This emphasis upon Jesus Christ the King brought persecution to the church, for Jesus was viewed as a rival to Caesar and the laws of the Roman Empire. But the church persisted in her belief that Jesus was the "King of the ages!" (Rev. 15:3), "King of kings and Lord of lords!" (Rev. 17:14; 19:16; cf. 1 Tim. 6:15).

MELVIN H. SHOEMAKER

See also CHRIST, CHRISTOLOGY; JESUS CHRIST.

Bibliography. G. R. Beasley-Murray, *Jesus and the Kingdom of God;* W. Bousset, *Kyrios Christos;* G. W. Buchanan, *Jesus the King and His Kingdom;* R. Bultmann, *Theology of the New Testament;* C. C. Caragounis, *Dictionary of Jesus and the Gospels,* pp. 417–30; O. Cullmann, *The Christology of the New Testament;* idem, *The Early Church: Studies in Early Christian History and Theology;* R. H. Fuller, *The Foundations of New Testament Christology;* F. Hahn, *The Titles of Jesus in Christology: Their History in Early Christianity;* J. Knox, *Jesus, Lord and Christ: A Trilogy;* C. N. Kraus, *Jesus Christ Our Lord: Christology from a Disciple's Perspective;* G. E. Ladd, *The Presence of the Future: The Eschatology of Biblical Realism;* I. H. Marshall, *Jesus the Saviour: Studies in the New Testament Theology;* N. Perrin, *Jesus and the Language of the Kingdom: Symbol and Metaphor in New Testament Interpretation;* R. Schnackenburg, *God's Rule and Kingdom.*

King, Kingship. The terms "king" and "kingship" are common biblical words, occurring over 2,500 times in the Old Testament and 275 times in the New Testament. The terms are applied not only to human rulers but also to God. The concept of the kingship of God is regarded by many scholars as so basic to biblical revelation that it is viewed as an organizing theme for all of Scripture.

In general, the words *melek* (Heb. king) and *basileus* (Gk. king) designate the person who holds supreme authority over a nation or city. In the Old Testament the most numerous references to "king" and "kingship" occur in the narratives dealing with the periods of the united and divided kingdoms of ancient Israel. Saul, David, and Solomon were kings who ruled over a united Israelite kingdom. After Solomon's death the kingdom divided into northern (Israel) and southern (Judah) segments. Then a long succession of kings in both Israel (nineteen kings) and Judah (nineteen kings, one queen) ran from 931 B.C. until 721 B.C. in the north and 586 B.C. in the south.

Much of 1–2 Samuel, 1–2 Kings, and 1–2 Chronicles describes matters pertaining to the lives and reigns of these kings. This, however, does not mean that reference to kingship is limited to narrative sections of the Old Testament. In fact, significant sections of the writings of the prophets and poets also involve the actions of the various kings of Israel and Judah.

The use of "king" and "kingship" however, is not limited to the occupants of the thrones in Samaria and Jerusalem. Reference is also found to numerous foreign kings whose activities affected Israel in some way. But more important, there is a strong and conspicuous emphasis on the kingship of God, the "Great King" who rules over his people (Exod. 15:18; Deut. 33:5; 1 Sam. 8:7; 12:12; 1 Chron. 17:14; 28:5; Ps. 114:2). God's kingship, however, contrasts with that of Israel's rulers in that God's rule is not limited to the nation of Israel. While he *is* king over his people in a special sense, by virtue of his covenantal relationship to them, his kingship is at the same time universal, extending to all nations and peoples and even the natural environment.

This juxtaposition of divine and human kingship in the Old Testament period presented ancient Israel with a duality of sovereigns. God was the great King who ruled the universe as well as his people, Israel. He had not only delivered Israel from bondage in Egypt and taken them to himself to be a "kingdom of priests" (Exod. 19:6), but he was sovereign beyond Israel's borders as the ruler over all of nature and history. Yet in the course of time Israel also had her own human kings, the rulers in Jerusalem or Samaria who exercised their royal power to govern the nation. This duality of sovereigns was the source of one of the major theological problems in the Old Testament period. How was Israel to understand the relationship between their obligation to Yahweh, the divine King, on the one hand, and their obligation to the human king on the other? What was the role of the human king in ancient Israel, and to what extent was this role realized? What conditions gave rise to the idea of the coming of a future messianic king who would someday establish peace and justice in all the earth?

It is important to understand the way in which the Old Testament presents the relationship between divine and human kingship. Contrary to the idea of certain scholars (e.g., Vatke, Gressmann, von Rad), the Old Testament does not suggest that the idea of the kingship of Yahweh was a projection derived from the human institution. It is not warranted to assert, as some have, that the title of king was not ascribed to Yahweh prior to the time of the Israelite monarchy. To do this requires the late dating of explicit statements of Yahweh's kingship in texts such as Exodus 15:18; Numbers 23:21; Deuteronomy 33:5; Judges 8:23; and 1 Samuel 8:7; 10:19; 12:12. To do this also denies the close relationship that exists between the establishment of the Sinai covenant and the acknowledgment of Yahweh's kingship over Israel. Parallels in literary structure between the Sinai covenant and certain international treaties drawn up by the kings of the Hittite Empire in the fourteenth century B.C. show that in the Sinai covenant Yahweh assumes the role of the Great King, and Israel, that of his vassal. All of this suggests, very clearly, that Israel recognized Yahweh as her Great King long before kingship was established in Jerusalem.

This recognition has caused other contemporary scholars (Mendenhall, McKenzie) to suggest that the establishment of human kingship in Israel was a rebellion against divine rule and represented an alien paganizing development in the social structure of ancient Israel. For these scholars the establishment of the monarchy represented a return to the social model of the old Bronze Age paganism of the Canaanites, and a rejection of religious foundations derived from the Mosaic formulations of the Sinai covenant.

This approach, however, does violence to the many positive biblical statements concerning God's design for the institution of kingship in the context of this sovereign plan for the redemption of his people, and ultimately for the universal triumph of peace and justice on the earth. Kingship in Israel was not unanticipated. God had even provided for it in antecedent revelation. Abraham was told that "kings" would arise among his descendants (Gen. 17:6). Jacob said that royalty would arise from the tribe of Judah (Gen. 49:10). Moses provided for the eventual rise of kingship in Israel when he gave the "law of the king" (Deut. 17:14–20) as part of the renewal of the covenant in the Plains of Moab just before Israel's entrance in the promised land. So it is clear that in God's purpose it was right and proper for Israel to have a king. To question this erodes the institutional basis of the messianic hope that arose in connection with the failure of Israel's kings to function as God had instructed.

The question of the Old Testament's apparently ambivalent attitude toward the institution of the monarchy is rooted in the description of the rise of kingship in Israel (1 Sam. 8–12). The tension in these chapters is evident. On the one hand Samuel said that Israel had sinned in asking for a king (1 Sam. 12:17–20). On the other hand the Lord told Samuel to give the people a king (1 Sam. 8:7, 2, 22). Later, after Saul was chosen by lot, Samuel said, "Do you see the man the LORD has chosen?" The issue here is not whether kingship in itself was right or wrong for Israel. At issue was the kind of kingship Israel desired, and her reasons for wanting a king. The elders of Israel asked Samuel to give them a "king like the nations" around them (1 Sam. 8:20a). They wanted a king to fight their battles and give them a symbol of national unity. This request betrayed their rejection of the kingship of Yahweh (1 Sam. 8:7; 10:19; 12:12) and denial of the covenant. The Lord, however, told Samuel to give them a different sort of king. After warning them about what it would be like to have a king like the nations (1 Sam. 8:11–18) Samuel defined how kingship was to function in Israel (1 Sam. 10:25). This description was a supplement to the "law of the king" given by Moses (Deut. 17:14–20). Samuel then inaugurated the reign of Saul, Israel's first king, in the context of a renewal of the covenant with Yahweh (1 Sam. 11:14–12:25). This had enormous significance. Kingship was subordinated to covenant. Israel's king was to be a covenantal king. He was not autonomous. He was always obligated to submit to the law of Israel's (and his) Great King, Yahweh (Deut. 17:18–20; 1 Sam. 12:14) as well as to the word of the prophet (1 Sam. 12:23; 13:13; 15:11, 23; 2 Sam. 12:7–13).

Unfortunately Saul fell far short of living up to the requirements of his office. He disobeyed the word of the Lord and rebelled against the Lord (1 Sam. 13, 15). Because of this the Lord rejected him from being king (1 Sam. 15:23), and sent Samuel to annoint David in his place (1 Sam. 16). David was an imperfect but true representative of the ideal of the covenantal king. David grievously sinned in the matter of Bathsheba (2 Sam. 11, 12), but in contrast to Saul when Nathan, the prophet, confronted him, he repented and sought the Lord's forgiveness (2 Sam. 12:13; Ps. 51). Late in his reign he sinned again in taking the census of his fighting men, but again he sought the Lord's forgiveness (2 Sam. 24). David is thus termed a "man after God's own heart" (1 Sam. 13:14; Acts 13:22), and the writer of Kings makes his reign the standard by which to assess the reigns of subsequent kings.

For the most part the history of the kings of Israel and Judah is a history of failure to live up to the covenantal ideal. All of the kings of the north are said to have "done evil in the eyes of the LORD" because they continued the worship of the golden calves in Bethel and Dan that had been begun by the northern kingdom's first king, Jeroboam 1 (1 Kings 12:26–33). Even among the kings of Judah, only Hezekiah and Josiah receive unqualified approval (2 Kings 18:3–7; 22:2).

This failure of the kings of both Israel and Judah to live up to the covenantal ideal provided the backdrop as Israel's prophets began to speak of a future king who would be a worthy occupant of the throne of David. As the profile of this king slowly develops it is clear that he will come as the fulfillment of the promise of an eternal dynasty to David (2 Sam. 7; 23:1–7; Pss. 89; 132:11–12; Isa. 55:3–5). He will not only be a descendant of David, but is also identified with deity (Isa. 7:14; 9:6–7; Jer. 23:5–6; Ezek. 36:24–28). During his reign wars will cease and peace and justice will be established in the earth (Isa. 2:1–5; 11:1–10; Amos 9:11–15). This future king came to be known as the "Messiah" (in Hebrew, "the anointed one") and longing for his appearance came to be known as messianic expectation.

In the New Testament the kingship theme is carried forward and its ambiguities resolved. Jesus is the one who fulfilled the royal messianic promises of the Old Testament. The Greek word translated "Christ" in our English versions of the Bible is a translation of the Hebrew term for Messiah (the anointed one). In the words of the angel who spoke to Mary: "He will be great and will be called the Son of the Most High. The Lord God will give him the throne of his father David, and he will reign over the house of Jacob forever; his kingdom will never end" (Luke 1:32–33). Jesus laid claim to fulfillment of the messianic prophecies of the Old Testament when at his trial before the Sanhedrin he was asked by the high priest whether he was the Messiah. Jesus replied, "I am, and you will see the Son of Man sitting at the rights hand of the Mighty One and coming with the clouds of heaven" (Mark 14:62). In Jesus Christ, the God-man, human and divine kingship are united in one person. In Jesus the duality of sovereigns present in the Old Testament period is eliminated.

J. ROBERT VANNOY

See also ISRAEL; LEADERSHIP.

Bibliography. F. F. Bruce, *New Testament Development of Old Testament Themes;* G. Van Groningen, *Messianic Revelation in the Old Testament;* D. M. Howard, Jr., *TrinityJ* 9 NS (1988): 19–35; idem, *WTJ 52* (1990):101–15; G. E. Mendenhall, *Int* 29/2 (1975):155–70; J. J. M. Roberts, *Ancient Israelite Religion: Essays in Honor of Frank Moor Cross,* pp. 377–96.

Kingdom of God. The heart of Jesus' teachings centers around the theme of the kingdom of God. This expression is found in sixty-one separate sayings in the Synoptic Gospels. Counting parallels to these passages, the expression occurs over eighty-five times. It also occurs twice in John (3:3, 5). It is found in such key places as the preaching of John the Baptist, "Repent, for the kingdom of heaven is near" (Matt. 3:2); Jesus' earliest announcement, "The time has come. . . . The kingdom of God is near. Repent and believe the good news!" (Mark 1:15; cf. Matt. 4:17; Luke 4:42–43); the prayer Jesus taught his disciples, "your kingdom come" (Matt. 6:10); in the Beatitudes, "for theirs is the kingdom of heaven" (Matt. 5:3, 10); at the Last Supper, "I will not drink again of the fruit of the vine until that day when I drink it anew in the kingdom of God" (Mark 14:25); and in many of Jesus' parables (Matt. 13:24, 44, 45, 47; Mark 4:26, 30; Luke 19:11).

It was once popular in certain circles to argue that the expressions "kingdom of God" and "kingdom of heaven" referred to two different realities. It is now clear, however, that they are synonyms. This is evident for several reasons. For one, the two expressions are used in the same sayings of Jesus, but where Matthew uses "kingdom of heaven," Mark or Luke or both use "kingdom of God." Second, Matthew himself uses these two expressions interchangeably in 19:23–24, "it is hard for a rich man to enter the kingdom of heaven . . . for a rich man to enter the kingdom of God." Finally, we know that "heaven" was frequently used as a circumlocution for "God" by devout Jews. Due to respect for the third commandment ("You shall not misuse the name of the LORD your God" [Exod. 20:7]), pious Jews used various circumlocutions for the sacred name of God (YHWH) in order to avoid the danger of breaking this commandment. One such circumlocution was the term "heaven." This is seen in the expression "kingdom of heaven" but also in such passages as Luke 15:18, 21 ("Father, I have sinned against heaven and against you") and Mark 11:30.

Various Interpretations. Despite the centrality of this expression in Jesus' teachings, there has been a great deal of debate over the years as to exactly what Jesus meant by it. One reason for this is that neither Jesus nor the Evangelists ever defined exactly what they meant by this expression. They simply assumed that their hearers/readers would understand.

The Political Kingdom. According to this view Jesus sought to establish a Davidic-like kingdom in Jerusalem. This kingdom was political in nature and sought to free Israel from the Romans. Jesus was in essence a political revolutionary who sought to arm his disciples (Luke 22:35–38), entered Jerusalem on Palm Sunday as a king (Mark 11:11), challenged the political establishment by cleansing the temple (Mark 11:15–18), urged people to rebel by not paying their taxes (Mark 12:13–17 is reread to teach the opposite of its present meaning), enlisted zealots as disciples (Mark 3:18), used the taking up of the cross (which was a symbol of zealot sacrifice for enlisting disciples; Mark 8:34), and was crucified as a political rebel (Mark 15:26) between two other rebels (Mark 15:27).

This interpretation has found few supporters over the years, but it is continually raised. It is an impossible view, however, for the evidence against it is overwhelming. The presence of a tax collector among the disciples is impossible to explain if Jesus were a revolutionary, for tax collectors were seen as collaborators with the Romans and hated by zealots. Such teachings as Matthew 5:9 ("Blessed are the peacemakers"); 38–42 ("If someone [a Roman soldier] forces you to go one mile, go with him two miles"); 43–47 ("Love your enemies"); Matthew 26:52 ("all who draw the sword will die by the sword"); Mark 12:13–17 ("Give to Caesar what is Caesar's") simply do not permit such an interpretation. To claim that all such sayings in the Gospels are inauthentic or to reconstruct their supposed original form in a radical way is to manipulate the evidence to sustain a thesis, rather than to allow the evidence to determine the thesis.

The "Liberal" or Spiritual Kingdom. During the height of theological liberalism the kingdom of God was understood as God's rule in the human heart. One of the favorite passages used to support this was Luke 17:20–21, "the kingdom of God is within you." Any eschatological thoughts associated with this expression were seen as unrefined, primitive, Jewish apocalyptic thinking that Jesus never outgrew and that was only the "husk" and not the "kernel" of his teachings. Or they were interpreted as symbols of the inner rule of God in the heart. The kingdom of God was God's spiritual reign in the life of the believer that resulted in an inner moral ethic. This ethic focused on Jesus' teachings concerning the universal Fatherhood of God, the infinite value of the human soul, and the love commandment.

Liberal theology, which was built upon a belief in continual evolutionary progress and the ultimate goodness of humanity, was dealt a mortal blow with the coming of World War I, and the subsequent years have done nothing to revive its naive optimism in humanity. This, along with the rediscovery of the eschatological element in the teachings of Jesus, brought about the demise of this interpretation. Like the liberal interpretation of the nineteenth century, modern attempts to eliminate the eschatological dimensions of Jesus' teachings by seeing them as symbols to which the present reader gives his or her own meaning, are also impossible to accept. One simply cannot eliminate the eschatological dimension of Jesus' teachings. The biblical evidence will not permit it.

The "Consistent" or Future Kingdom. At the turn of the nineteenth century the eschatological dimension of Jesus' teachings was rediscovered. It became evident that Jesus was not a nineteenth-century liberal but a first-century Jew. As a result it was clear that Jesus must have thought to a great extent like a first-century Jew. Since the kingdom of God was seen by most Jews in Jesus' day as a future, supernatural kingdom that would bring history to a close, it was logical to think that Jesus thought similarly. Jesus' sayings concerning the kingdom of God would have been understood by his audience as referring to such a kingdom, and since Jesus made no radical attempt to correct such thinking, we must understand his teachings on the kingdom of God as eschatological.

According to this view Jesus taught that the kingdom of God, which would bring history to its end, was future. Yet this event lay not in the far distant future. On the contrary, it was very near. It had not yet arrived, but it was to appear momentarily. Signs and powers of the kingdom were already at work, and prefigurements of its glory were already present. As a result Jesus taught along with announcement of the kingdom of God's nearness an "interim ethic" for this brief in-between period of history. Soon the Son of Man would come, the final judgment would take place, and world history as we know it would cease. During this in-between period believers were to live a heroic ethic. They were to avoid divorce, refrain from marriage, love their enemies, turn the other cheek, not retaliate, give to whoever had a need.

It is clear that this interpretation takes seriously the future dimension of Jesus' sayings concerning the kingdom of God. On the other hand, it ignored another kind of saying found in the Gospels, which involves the announcement that the kingdom has already in some way come. These sayings involving the arrival of the kingdom of God were usually seen as inauthentic and later creations of the church by advocates of this view.

The "Realized" or Present Kingdom. In response to the former view, which arose in Germany, there arose in England an opposing view. According to this view Jesus did announce the coming of the awaited kingdom. However, he did not announce that it was coming in the near future. On the contrary, he announced that it had already arrived. Now in Jesus' ministry the kingdom of God had already come. There was therefore no need to look for something in the future. The Son of Man had already come, and he had brought with him the kingdom. Nothing is still awaited. In its entirety the kingdom of God was realized in the coming of Jesus.

This view, like the "consistent" view, has the benefit of taking seriously certain biblical data. There is no doubt, as we shall see, that there are in the Gospels sayings of Jesus that announce that the kingdom has come. They do not announce simply that it is near. They announce that it is *here.* It is evident that these last two views, unless modified in some way, contradict one another. Yet both offer convincing biblical evidence in support of their views. (This cannot be said of the first two views.) Like the "consistent" view, this view also tends to see the biblical data that contradicted it as being inauthentic. Only in this instance it was the sayings that spoke of the kingdom of God being future that were inauthentic.

The Biblical Evidence. It is evident that there is biblical evidence to support both the "consistent" and "realized" views. In certain passages, for example, it is clear that the kingdom of God is future. In the Lord's prayer we pray "Your kingdom come" (Luke 11:2), and the kingdom must as a result be future. Jesus' saying that "Not everyone who says to me 'Lord, Lord,' will enter the kingdom of God" must also refer to a future event, for he continues "Many will say to me *on that day*" (Matt. 7:21–23). Jesus' institution of the Last Supper also looks forward to "that day when I [Jesus] drink it anew in the kingdom of God" (Mark 14:25). Other passages associate the coming of the kingdom of God with the final judgment (Matt. 5:19–20; 8:11–12; 25:31–46; Luke

13:22–30). It cannot be denied therefore that there are numerous passages in the Gospels that indicate that Jesus understood the kingdom of God to be still future.

In other passages, however, it is equally clear that the kingdom of God is already present. Jesus told his hearers "if I drive out demons by the finger of God, then the kingdom of God has come to you" (Luke 11:20; cf. Matt. 12:28). In four of the other instances where the same verb "has come" (*ephthasen*) is used in the New Testament it clearly means "has arrived," is "now present" (Rom. 9:31; 2 Cor. 10:14; Phil. 3:16; 1 Thess. 2:16). In the other instance where it is future, however, the tense is future (*phthasōmen,* 1 Thess. 4:15). Elsewhere Jesus declared that his coming marked the end of the old era when he said "The Law and the Prophets were proclaimed until John. Since that time, the good news of the kingdom of God is being preached" (Luke 16:16). Here two distinct periods of history are distinguished. The former is referred to as the period of the Law and the prophets. The second is the period of the kingdom of God. John the Baptist is seen as a bridge who both brings the "old" to its conclusion and announces the breaking in of the "new." This "new" thing, which cannot be mixed with the old (Mark 2:21–22), which gathers the outcasts (Matt. 11:4–6) and the lost tribes of Israel (Mark 3:13–19; Matt. 19:28), which manifests signs and marvels (Matt. 13:16–17), which inaugurates a new covenant (1 Cor. 11:25), is nothing other than the arrival of the kingdom of God. Jesus also announced that now already the long-awaited messianic banquet had begun (Luke 14:15–24). The kingdom of God was now in their presence (Luke 17:20–21—"among" is a better translation than "within").

How should one deal with this apparently contradictory data? Should we decide the issue by majority vote? If so, the "future" interpretation would win over the "present" one, because there are more examples in its support in the Gospels. Yet rather than claim that one group of these sayings is "authentic" whereas the other is not, we should first analyze carefully exactly what the word "kingdom" means. Perhaps this will provide the key for understanding what Jesus meant by the "kingdom of God." How is the term "kingdom" to be understood? Should it be understood statically as denoting a realm or place? If this is correct and "kingdom" refers to a territory or piece of real estate, then it is evident that the kingdom of God cannot have arrived. There has been no geographical or cosmic changes that have taken place in the coming of Jesus. The planet remains today essentially as it was in the time of Christ. No new territory exists. No place on this planet can be designated "the kingdom of God." On the other hand, should we understand the term dynamically as referring to the rule or reign of a king?

Both in the Old Testament and in the New Testament the term "kingdom" (*malkut* and *basileia*) is understood as dynamic in nature and refers primarily to the rule or reign of a king. It is seldom used in a static sense to refer to a territory. As a result, in the vast majority of instances it would be better to translate the expression "kingdom of God" as the "rule of God." That Jesus understood it this way is evident from such passages as Luke 19:12 ("A man of noble birth went to a distant country to have himself appointed king," literally "to receive a kingdom [*basileia*]"; cf. also v. 15); Matthew 6:33 ("seek first his kingdom"); and Mark 10:15 ("receive the kingdom of God like a little child").

Understood as the "reign of God" it is possible for Jesus to announce that in fulfillment of the Old Testament promises the reign of God has arrived. In Jesus' coming Satan has been defeated (Luke 10:18; 11:20–22), the outcasts of Israel are being gathered as predicted (Mark 2:15–16; Luke 14:15–24), the Old Testament promises are fulfilled (Luke 10:23–24), the resurrection of the dead has begun (1 Cor. 15:20), a new covenant has been inaugurated (1 Cor. 11:25), the promised Spirit has come as the prophets foretold (Mark 1:8). Indeed the kingdom is "already now" realized in history.

However, the consummation of the "already now" still lies in the future. The coming of the Son of Man, the final resurrection, faith turning to sight, are "not yet." The kingdom of God is both now and not yet. Thus the kingdom of God is "realized" and present in one sense, and yet "consistent" and future in another. This is not a contradiction, but simply the nature of the kingdom. The kingdom has come in fulfillment of the Old Testament promises. A new covenant has been established. But its final manifestation and consummation lie in the future. Until then we are to be good and faithful servants (Luke 19:11–27).

Implications. If the kingdom is both already now and not yet, the believer must be on guard against the danger of emphasizing one aspect of the kingdom at the expense of the other. A one-sided emphasis on the "already now," which emphasizes miracles, healing, victory over sin, and gifts God has given his church, and ignores the "not yet" may lead to an optimistic triumphalism that will result in disillusionment. Jesus' teachings concerning the tribulation(s) that lay ahead (Mark 13; Matt. 24–25; Luke 21) warn against such optimism. The symbol of discipleship Jesus gave to his disciples is that of bearing a cross! The crown awaits the consummation. The enjoyment of the firstfruits of the kingdom must be tempered by the fact that we still live by faith and not sight. We still long for the perishable to become clothed with the imperishable, the mortal with immortality (1 Cor. 15:53). In the meantime we are called to endure to the end.

On the other hand, a one-sided emphasis on the not yet may lead to defeatism and despair in this life and a neglect of the joy and victory over sin and death in the Spirit's having already come. The "gates of Hades" (Matt. 16:18) shall not overcome the church! Even in this life because the kingdom has come, we can be "transformed into his likeness with ever-increasing glory" (2 Cor. 3:18). The now and the not yet must be held in tension. Believers can rejoice in having passed from death into life and in the abiding presence of the Spirit of God. But the victories in the present life, are also accompanied with all too many defeats.

Believers are thus encouraged both by the victories of the already now and the defeats of the not yet. The former having provided a taste of the glory which is to be revealed (1 Peter 5:1) causes us to long all the more for the not yet. Similarly, because of the experience of defeat, sorrow, and in seeing the corruption of the world around us, we also long all the more for the not yet that awaits. Thus Christians continue to look longingly toward the blessed hope (Titus 2:13), when the Son of Man will return and bring the kingdom to its consummation. Having tasted of the firstfruits that are already realized, the believer prays all the more earnestly "your kingdom come" (Matt. 6:10) and *"Marana tha"* (1 Cor. 16:22; cf. Rev. 22:20). ROBERT H. STEIN

See also JESUS CHRIST.

Bibliography. D. C. Allison, Jr., *The End of the Ages Has Come;* G. R. Beasley-Murray, *Jesus and the Kingdom of God;* B. Chilton and J. I. H. McDonald, *Jesus and the Ethics of the Kingdom;* O. Cullman, *Christ and Time;* R. H. Hiers, *The Kingdom of God in the Synoptic Tradition;* W. G. Kümmel, *Promise and Fulfillment;* G. E. Ladd, *Jesus and the Kingdom;* G. Lundström, *The Kingdom of God in the Teaching of Jesus;* N. Perrin, *The Kingdom of God in the Teaching of Jesus;* R. Schnackenburg, *God's Rule and Kingdom;* R. H. Stein, *The Method and Message of Jesus' Teachings;* W. Willis, ed., *The Kingdom of God in 20th-Century Interpretation.*

Kings, First and Second, Theology of. Since the books of 1 and 2 Kings possess an inner unity and ideology, it is appropriate to view them as a single work; both the Talmud and Josephus saw them as one book. In fact, the division of the two is completely artificial. Furthermore, Kings shares a thematic unity and overlap in subject matter with the books of Samuel, and these two major works were apparently part of an even greater work that included Joshua and Judges.

Theological Emphasis. The structure of Kings is somewhat similar to that of Judges in that it discusses the cyclical rise and fall of states and leaders (from the accession of Solomon to the exile). It was probably written in the mid-sixth century B.C., since there is no evidence of the rebuilding of the temple or Persian occupation. The text is usually silent about the political significance of the rulers, but is more interested in their religious import; thus the author relays only those events that are pertinent to his message. These themes often dictate the length of and the detail in which certain elements are treated (e.g., details in Josiah's reign are discussed only after the discovery of the Book of the Law). Important contemporary events in the ancient Near East are mentioned only when relevant to the interests of the author. Thus, this work is not an exhaustive history of the divided kingdom. Although the author does not write a complete history of Israel, he does provide a theological commentary on Israel's history. Even social and humanitarian concerns found in concurrent prophetic writings are not found here. Often, leaders who had relatively little political importance are featured as main characters (e.g., Ahaziah, Athaliah), while a struggle that did not effectively alter the international scene (e.g., Moab versus Israel, 1 Kings 3) is featured as of great importance. Judgments abound in standard statements, signifying that the author sees a pattern in the events, but not that he manufactures the events discussed in his work.

The Judgment of God. One of the immediate purposes of Kings is to explain how the exile came about and to express the idea that God had compelling reasons for judgment. With the destruction of Jerusalem, dissolution of the monarchy, and subsequent deportation, it appeared that God had proved incapable of dealing with the nations surrounding Israel. However, using a lawsuit motif following the breach of covenant law (see 2 Kings 17:20–23), the writer of Kings presents an explanation of history that shows that their tragedy was a product of God's judgment, not his weakness. God's intentions can be deduced from the course of events (e.g., 1 Kings 9:6–9). This is an apparently unique explanation for a national tragedy, at least in comparison with that of the surrounding nations, which normally concluded that their god(s) had abandoned them in times of national crisis.

The Davidic Succession. The Book of Kings opens with the account of David's last days and the succession of his son Solomon by the agency of the prophet Nathan and the priest Zadok. The dynastic succession was a crucial issue for the nation, since most apparently still held to the tradition of the popularly acclaimed charismatic leadership of an individual chosen by a prophet in God's name. Thus, the first two chapters are in effect a theological justification of the accession of Solomon, which was authenticated by his dream at Gibeon (1 Kings 3:4–15).

In the Solomonic succession account, the writer emphasizes human agents. Actions are not strictly determined by a deus ex machina through the medium of miracles or charismatic leaders as before, but by human designs. Although there is less emphasis on direct divine intervention, the author still shows a deep faith in providence. In fact, one of the great theological contributions of Kings is to emphasize the working of God in the Solomonic succession, not through direct divine intervention, miracles, prophets, or sacred institutions, but through ordinary personalities and individuals working in the secular sphere.

The Temple and Jerusalem. One of the dominant themes in the early chapters of Kings is the preparation for the Solomonic temple (1 Kings 5–8), a theme treated with relatively disproportionate length in the work. Other matters in Solomon's reign are dealt with sporadically and comparatively briefly. For example, Solomon's relations with Hiram of Tyre are important only because of the mention of the construction of the temple. The author of Kings is also concerned about recording the occasions when the temple treasury was appropriated for war indemnity, whether by foreigners (Shishak, 1 Kings 14:25–28; and Nebuchadnezzar, 2 Kings 24:13; 25:13–17) or Judeans (Asa, 1 Kings 15:18; Joash, 2 Kings 12:18; Jehoash, 2 Kings 14:14; and Hezekiah, 2 Kings 18:16). Some have postulated that the writer was basing his sources on a nonextant temple history.

Before the existence of the temple, Yahweh was worshiped wherever he appeared. The biblical writers spoke of the revelatory presence of God without compromising his transcendence. However, Solomon adopted the idea of the temple as God's divine residence. Thus, the writer of Kings condemns heathen shrines (1 Kings 11:7–8), high places (1 Kings 3:3–4; 12:28–33), and cult objects in Dan and Bethel (1 Kings 12:28–32) from an ideological standpoint. Fearing that the multiplicity of shrines would ultimately lead to polytheism, he insists on the sole legitimacy of the Jerusalem temple as opposed to any local high place (2 Kings 23; cf. Deut. 12:10–14). He presents Jerusalem as the holy place of God's choice (1 Kings 11:13, 32, 36).

Prophecy and Fulfillment. The ministry of prophecy attained a prominent position during the period of the kings. The spoken word of the prophets was considered equal in authority to the Torah (2 Kings 22:13–20), to which the prophets continually alluded. There are numerous cases of prophecy being fulfilled according to the word of Yahweh (e.g., 1 Kings 8:20; 12:15; 2 Kings 23:16–18). The course of Israelite history had an integral connection with and was shaped and led to a fulfillment by the prophetic word of judgment, which was often delayed (2 Kings 2:19–22; 13:14–19; 20:8–11). The writer of Kings clearly identifies his interpretation of Israel's history with that of the prophets. God is not to be blamed for the failure of the nation since he had sent numerous prophets. Of significance is the lack of any mention of Jeremiah, who figured so prominently at the end of Judah's political history.

The lengthy treatment of Jeroboam I shows an interest in the fulfillment of prophecy (1 Kings 11:29–40; cf. 12:1–20). Great prominence is also given to the defection to the Baal cult. Jehu's revolt is sanctioned by the prophets Elijah and Elisha (2 Kings 9:7–10, 26, 30–37). The prophet Isaiah is the most important character behind the scenes in the tense struggle with the Assyrians during Hezekiah's reign. When Hezekiah falters in the face of crisis, it is Isaiah who stands firm (2 Kings 19).

Criteria for Monarchical Judgment. The loyalty of the monarchy (an institution accepted without discussion in Kings) to the God of Israel as worshiped in Jerusalem determined the course of the nation's history. The king was a representative of the people before God. The writer of Kings uses a somewhat mechanical norm of cultic purity found in Deuteronomy (chaps. 27–28) as a criterion to evaluate the rulers of Israel and Judah. In turn, this becomes one of the theological themes for the author's philosophy of history (i.e., opposition to any continuing Canaanite high places). The author occasionally refers to the Book of the Law, or Book of the Law of Moses (e.g., 2 Kings 14:6; 22:8, 11; 23:2), showing that he is not a theological innovator but a faithful representative of a cultic perspective found in Deuteronomy. The writer elevates the opposition to the Canaanite cults to a central position in the Yahwistic faith. In fact, he pursues history writing from the standpoint of obedience or lack thereof to this issue, either pronouncing a curse or a blessing. Furthermore, the writer emphasizes the long-suffering mercy of God who continued to postpone the execution of judgment that disobedience to the covenant rightly entailed.

Virtually all of the kings of Israel are criticized for "walking in the ways of Jeroboam" (the first king of divided Israel). The "sin" of Jeroboam (ordaining priests for high places outside of Jerusalem, 1 Kings 13:34) was the crucial event in the history of the northern kingdom of Israel. Jeroboam's sin and his consecration of non-Levitical clergy sealed the doom of his royal house (1 Kings 12:28–31; 13:33; 14:9). His misdeeds became the prototype for the entire nation's history. Jeroboam and Ahab sinfully influenced Israel so that the people copied attributes of supplanted peoples (2 Kings 17:8, 11), served other gods (2 Kings 17:12), and seduced surrounding peoples (2 Kings 17:15). However, even Jehu, who had cleansed the nation of Baal, failed to eradicate the high places (2 Kings 10:31).

The criterion the author uses in evaluating the southern kingdom is slightly different. Although the nation of Judah was expected to learn from its northern neighbor's disaster, the high places,

Asherim, and male prostitutes continued to exist (1 Kings 14:22–24), and Hezekiah had to replace them (2 Kings 18:22). The fate of each king was conditioned on his behavior. For example, Solomon was rewarded with the continuation of his dynasty and a lengthy reign (1 Kings 3:14). However, he sowed the seeds of schism with his religious infidelity stemming from foreign influences, which would accelerate the nation's destruction. His son Rehoboam was thus deprived of the undivided throne of Israel (1 Kings 12:15). The kingdom of Judah would be spared only for David's sake (1 Kings 11:13). The writer of Kings provides a theological explanation for the division of the kingdom, which does not contradict the secular reasons for the division.

In Judah, only five kings are approved as righteous, based upon their behavior in relation to David (two others are unqualified). The datum point of Judah's history was the great reform of Josiah, while the great villain was Manasseh, who was considered to be immediately responsible for the downfall of the kingdom. Manasseh's cultic deviations are discussed in great detail (2 Kings 21:2–9). However, the writer does not mention Manasseh's involvement in Assyrian politics, which is not relevant to his theme. On the other hand, Solomon's international relations are often discussed because of his own cultic violations (1 Kings 11:14–40). The writer of Kings recognizes that God's justice does not always work out in every way the same; Manasseh lived a long time (2 Kings 21; 24:3–4), while Josiah died in battle, a fateful omen for the nation (2 Kings 23:29). Much space, however, is given to Josiah's reform, which, although being an immediate failure, set the stage for the restoration (2 Kings 23:29–30).

The Davidic Promise. The writer of Kings not only condemns the sins of the rulers of Israel and Judah, but is concerned about giving a word of hope and promise to the house of David and its continuation in spite of the destruction of the Judean kingdom. Judah ultimately would not suffer the same fate as Israel because of the righteousness of David, who kept the statutes of Yahweh (1 Kings 11:33, 38). Thus, the writer infers that the well-being of the people was tied to the king's behavior. Yahweh's election and covenant with Israel were bound with David, although the continuation of the Davidic dynasty was conditioned upon the proper cultic observances and the acceptance of the Mosaic covenant. The belief in the Davidic covenant was a guarantee of stability and a perseverance of hope that his line would continue (2 Kings 25:27–30). The release of the Davidide Jehoiachin at the end of Kings serves as a subtle reminder that the covenant was still in effect; the people could be assured of their continuing election by God. Moreover, the theme of repentance is essential to the author, forming a design of faith for later Israel. Thus, the Book of Kings is an important link in the religious change that led to the postexilic restoration of Israel.

A Theology of History. One may get the superficial impression that the author had primary interests in cultic purity, the centralization of the cult, and the mechanical judging of each monarch. But the theology of history in Kings is much deeper. The author is not writing a history of Israel, but primarily a theological and somewhat didactic interpretation of Israel's history, with the religious struggle of Israel and Canaan as a central focus. He discerns his work in the context of Israel's salvation history, presented as a continuing history of the confederate tribes, who realized their covenant relationship with Yahweh. His goal is to see the operation of the word of God in history. In fact, it is not the actors on the historical stage who command the primary attention, but God's manipulation of the events. The sufferings of Israel and Judah are seen as operations of the curse upon a broken agreement. The desire to employ local shrines was only a symptom of the problem.

Kings is a purposeful and positive work at the nadir of Israel's fortunes. Not only does it mirror God's judgment; it also reflects the theme of forgiveness and grace, which fosters the hope of revival. Israel's distress was not accidental or haphazard, but evidence of God's character consistent with his self-revelation in the covenant. The key is his renewed grace. The past sins created the consequence of an immediate future without monarchy, government, or structured religious center. However, the nation would now be identified by their fidelity to the Mosaic religion and the demands of the covenant.

MARK W. CHAVALAS

See also ISRAEL.

Bibliography. P. Ackroyd, *Exile and Restoration: A Survey of Hebrew Thought of the Sixth Century B.C.;* B. Childs, *Introduction to the Old Testament as Scripture;* M. Coogan and H. Tadmor, *II Kings: A New Translation with Introduction and Commentary;* F. M. Cross, *Canaanite Myth and Hebrew Epic;* S. De Vries, *I Kings;* J. Gray, *I–II Kings;* B. Halpern, *The First Historians: The Hebrew Bible and History;* T. R. Hobbes, *II Kings;* J. Montgomery and H. Gehman, *A Critical and Exegetical Commentary on the Book of Kings;* G. von Rad, *Studies in Deuteronomy,* pp. 74–79; J. van Seters, *In Search of History: Historiography in the Ancient World and the Origins of Biblical History.*

Kinsman-Redeemer. Male relative who, according to various laws found in the Pentateuch, had the privilege or responsibility to act for a relative who was in trouble, danger, or need of vindication.

Although the term "kinsman-redeemer" is used only seven times in the NIV (all in the Book of Ruth) and "avenger of blood" is used twelve times, the Hebrew verb *ga'al,* from which both of these terms are translated, is used over 100 times and rendered by such additional terms as "redeemer" or "near relative." The Hebrew term designates a male relative who delivers or rescues (Gen. 48:16; Exod. 6:6); redeems property (Lev. 27:9–25) or person (Lev. 25:47–55); avenges the murder of a relative as a guiltless executioner (Num. 35:9–34); and receives restitution for wrong done to a relative who has since died (Num. 5:8). The unique emphasis of the redemption/salvation/vindication associated with the kinsman-redeemer is the fact that this action is carried out by a kinsman on behalf of a near relative in need. This idea is most clearly illustrated in the Book of Ruth.

God is Israel's Redeemer, the one who will defend and vindicate them. The idea that God is a kinsman to Israel can be defended by those passages of Scripture that identify him as Israel's Creator and Father (Exod. 4:22–23; Deut. 32:6), Deliverer (Exod. 20:2), owner of the land (Lev. 25:23), the one who hears innocent blood crying out for vengeance (Deut. 19:10; 21:6–9), and the King who has made his covenant with the people (Exod. 6:2–8). David, in his use of the term (Pss. 19:14; 103:4), doubtless has in mind the actions of his great-grandfather Boaz (Ruth 4:9–10).

In the psalms God often redeems in the sense of rescuing from danger. In Job 19:25 the term "redeemer" in context refers to God who, as friend and kinsman of Job, through faith will ultimately defend and vindicate him. The same idea of vindication (this time with the term translated "Defender") is used in Proverbs 23:11.

Although the doctrine of redemption from sin is taught extensively in the New Testament, it is not connected closely with the Old Testament concept of kinsman-redeemer. Christ can, however, be regarded as an example of a kinsman-redeemer since he identified himself with us and redeemed us because of our need. Hebrews 2:11 states that "Both the one who makes men holy and those who are made holy are of the same family. So Jesus is not ashamed to call them brothers." Jesus is not only our redeemer from sin, but as Hebrews 2:16–18 and 4:14–16 point out, he is a kinsman to us and understands our struggles. Thus he is able to help us in our times of need. STEPHEN J. BRAMER

See also REDEEM, REDEMPTION.

Bibliography. R. L. Harris, *TWOT,* 1:144–45; D. A. Leggett, *The Levirate Goel Institutions in the Old Testament;* H. Ringgren, *TDOT,* 2:350–55.

Know, Knowledge. ***The Old Testament.*** The Hebrew root *yādaʿ*, translated "know"/"knowledge," appears almost 950 times in the Hebrew Bible. It has a wider sweep than our English word "know," including perceiving, learning, understanding, willing, performing, and experiencing. To know is not to be intellectually informed about some abstract principle, but to apprehend and experience reality. Knowledge is not the possession of information, but rather its exercise or actualization.

Thus, biblically to know God is not to know about him in an abstract and impersonal manner, but rather to enter into his saving actions (Mic. 6:5). To know God is not to struggle philosophically with his eternal essence, but rather to recognize and accept his claims. It is not some mystical contemplation, but dutiful obedience.

In the doing of justice and righteousness, Josiah is said to have known God (Jer. 22:15–16). True knowledge of God involves obeying the stipulations of his covenant. It is expressed in living conformity to his will. The opposite of knowledge is not ignorance, but rebellion (Jer. 22:11–14).

To know is to realize the loss of children (Isa. 47:8), grief (Isa. 53:3), guilt (Jer. 3:13), expediency (Eccles. 8:5), conversion (Jer. 16:19–21), and judgment (Ezek. 25:14).

The word "know" reflects a variety of skills and professional abilities such as hunting (Gen. 25:27), sailing (1 Kings 9:27), playing the harp (1 Sam. 16:16), professional mourning (Amos 5:16), and reading (Isa. 29:11). It also is used to indicate the ability to distinguish between good and evil (Gen. 3:5; Isa. 7:15), the left and right hand (Jon. 4:11), the wise and the foolish (Eccles. 2:19), the desirable and the undesirable (2 Sam. 19:35), and life and death (2 Sam. 12:22).

The word "know" is used as a euphemism for sex and intercourse: Adam knew his wife Eve and she became pregnant (Gen. 4:1). Women who have "known" a man are no longer virgins (Num. 31:17, 35). In his declining days David had an attractive attendant who served him but did not have sexual relationships with him (1 Kings 1:4). Even sexual perversions such as sodomy (Gen. 19:5; Judg. 19:22) and rape (Judg. 19:25) are designated by the word "know."

The word "know" is used also to express acquaintance with a person. Jacob questioned the shepherds of Haran, "Do you know Laban?" (Gen. 29:5). The pual participle of the Hebrew word indicates a close friend (Job 19:14; Ps. 55:13), a neighbor (Ps. 31:11), a companion (Ps. 88:8, 18), and a relative (Ruth 2:1).

Divine-human relationships are also expressed by this term. The Lord knew Moses very well—"by name" (Exod. 33:11, 12, 17). Moses sought a reciprocal acquaintance with God (Exod. 33:13). The psalmist is amazed at God's intimate knowledge (Ps. 139:6) of his personal life, his daily activities (139:1–2), even his unuttered and unformed thoughts (139:4).

The fact that God knows often indicates divine choice. He knew Jeremiah before his birth, singling him out to be a prophet (Jer. 1:5). He chose Abraham to be the father of a great nation (Gen. 18:19). The statement of Amos 3:2, "You (Israel)

only have I chosen of all the families of the earth," indicates divine selection. It is the way of the righteous that the Lord knows, endorses, and cherishes (Ps. 1:6).

"Know" also is used as a treaty term. To know is to acknowledge. Thus when the new king of Egypt did not know Joseph (Exod. 1:8) he did not recognize the agreement that had been developed between Joseph and Pharaoh at the time his family came to Egypt. While the ox and donkey know their owner, Israel does not know (Isa. 1:3). More than instinct is intended here. Loyalty to the covenant is clearly in mind since the witnesses of that covenant are invoked (Isa. 1:2). Moses demands that those who had stood at Mount Sinai and entered into covenant with the Lord acknowledge that agreement and live by it (Deut. 11:1–25).

The New Testament. The Greek words commonly translated know are *oida* and *ginōskō*. These words have the various nuances of meaning of the English word "know." They have been influenced by the Hebrew word *yādaʿ*, such influence having been mediated through the Septuagint, but they also reflect an adaptation demanded by a pagan world ignorant of God's existence.

The New Testament emphasizes that knowing God is not simply an intellectual apprehension, but a response of faith and an acceptance of Christ. It is he who has made God known (John 1:18). To know Christ is to know God (John 14:7). Eternal life is to know the true God and Jesus Christ (John 17:3). Paul desires to know Christ in his death and resurrection (Phil. 3:10). Failure to know Jesus as Lord and Messiah (Acts 2:36) resulted in his rejection and crucifixion (1 Cor. 2:8).

To know Christ is to know truth (John 8:32). While this is personal, it is also propositional. Knowledge of the truth (1 Tim. 2:4; 2 Tim. 2:25; 3:7; Titus 1:1) is both enlightenment and acceptance of the cognitive aspects of faith.

Paul uses the rhetorical question, "Don't you know?" several times in 1 Corinthians (3:16; 5:6; 6:2, 3, 9, 15; 9:13, 24). This may be an appeal to common knowledge, or a reference to a corpus of teaching that the apostle had communicated.

Affirmations about God's knowledge are more limited in the New Testament than in the Old Testament. He knows the human heart (Luke 16:15). He knows his children's needs such as clothing and food (Matt. 6:32). He even anticipates our petitions (Matt. 6:8). In fact, he knows everything (1 John 3:20).

Jesus uniquely knows God (John 8:55—here knowledge and obedience are equated). He knows the hidden designs of his questioners (Luke 11:17). He is also perceptive of humankind. Nowhere is his penetrating knowledge noted more than it is in the Fourth Gospel (2:25; 5:42; 6:64; 10:14; 13:1, 11; 18:4; 19:28).

The limits of human knowledge are recognized in the New Testament. It is not through wisdom that the world knows God, but rather through the divine initiative (Gal. 4:8–9). It is through the kerygma that humans can know God (1 Cor. 1:20–25). Spiritual discernment is not the result of profane reasoning (1 Tim. 6:20). God's revelation in Christ has made knowledge of him possible. But at best, this knowledge is partial. Perfection in the area of knowledge is reserved for the age to come (1 Cor. 13:12). Carl Schultz

See also Elect, Election; God; Knowledge of God.

Bibliography. R. Bultmann, *TDNT,* 1:689–719; P. R. Gilchrist, *TWOT,* 1:366–67; C. F. H. Henry and R. K. Harrison, *ISBE,* 3:48–50; A. Richardson, *A Theological Word Book of the Bible,* pp. 121–22; H. Ringgren, *TDOT,* 6:448–81.

Knowledge of God. The key biblical terms for knowledge assume a personal familiarity, even an intimate involvement, with the known object. Similarly, knowing God entails acknowledging him as Lord in obedience and praise. As a result, human knowledge of God is decisively shaped by the fall and God's salvation.

Adam and Eve knew God. They acknowledged him as their Lord and obediently carried out their responsibilities as his stewards in creation. However, eating from the forbidden tree of the knowledge of good and evil decisively shaped humanity's future (Gen. 2:9, 17). The knowledge derived from eating this fruit is called godlike (Gen. 3:5, 22), denoting a rebellious attempt to decide good and evil independently of the Creator.

The fall, however, did not destroy the availability of God's knowledge. General revelation, God's universal revelation, still exists. However, Scripture treats general revelation as ineffective in guiding humanity to God. Just as "the ox knows his master" (Isa. 1:3), humanity ought to recognize the Creator, but does not. Sin is the obstacle. Nothing in general revelation hints that God is gracious to the sinner. The sinner distorts the realities of general revelation, fabricating a suitable idea of God (Rom. 8:7–8; Phil. 3:19). This failure to know God issues in all other sin. Consequently, Scripture indicts humans who do not know the one and only God as morally perverse (Isa. 1:2–4; Hos. 4:1–2), rebellious sinners (1 Sam. 2:12; Jer. 2:8), apostates (Jer. 9:1–6; Hos. 4:6), idolaters (Ps. 79:6; Hos. 2:13), and deceivers engrossed in an delusion (John 1:5, 10; 1 Cor. 1:18–2:16). After explicating these dynamics in Romans 1:18–2:1, Paul concludes that after the fall, general revelation only renders sinners inexcusable before God.

After the fall, saving knowledge of God is grounded solely in God's decision to reveal himself to sinners (Gen. 18:18–19; Exod. 33:17; Ps. 139; Jer. 1:5; Eph. 3:35). In these acts of special revelation, God chooses a people for his purposes and guides them back to himself (Amos 3:2). For sinners can come into fellowship with God only through God's prior act, which objectively makes known his mercy, and subjectively makes us rightly related to Him.

Seeking God is dependent on the proper perspective. God has revealed himself through his prior acts, and this revelation forms the proper historical context for understanding God in the present (Deut. 4:29–39; 1 Chron. 16:11–12). Consequently, knowledge of God frequently depends on the witness of others to whom God has revealed himself (Ps. 44:1–4; Isa. 51:1–2). Only those who know God may seek him. In the New Testament, for example, the first step toward knowledge consists of receiving Jesus' message (John 7:16–17; 12:37–46; 20:30–31). Only those willing to believe that Jesus is doing the will of the Father receive the light enabling them to discern that he is the Son of God. On this path, followers are led to the full truth. Sinners, on the other hand, come to a knowledge of God through judgment and repentance. In repentance one recognizes the holy God who demands righteousness: the fear of the Lord is the beginning of wisdom (Pss. 25:14; 111:10; Prov. 1:7; 2:5; 9:10).

Unlike other types of knowing, God engages and draws us to himself (John 6:44). When we surrender to him and acknowledge him as Lord, God "shows us the way we should go" (Ps. 143:8; John 14:6). The biblical terms associated with knowing God, like trusting, acknowledging, and believing in God as Lord (1 Chron. 28:9; Pss. 36:10; 79:6; Isa. 43:10; Hos. 6:3), have a covenantal context. As a result, knowledge of God involves not simply propositions about God, but encountering and embracing God as Lord (Pss. 25:4, 12; 119:104), so that God becomes the center of our desires, affections, and knowledge.

Paul reinforces these connections by linking the love, knowledge, and glory of Jesus Christ: Christians know this love, are established in love (Eph. 3:16–19), and perceive the glory of God in his face (2 Cor. 4:6). Knowing Christ is a living relationship (John 7:29; 10:14; 11:25) in which he abides in and transforms the believer into his life (John 14:17; 17:3; 1 John 3:2).

If knowledge of God is the "path of our life," this must manifest itself in godly relationships to others (Matt. 7:17–20; John 10:27; 1 Cor. 12:31–13:2; Phil. 4:9; Col. 1:23). "We know that we have come to know him if we obey his commands" (1 John 2:3). Those who know God willingly practice his will and thus manifest his character by defending the cause of the poor (Jer. 22:16; Hos. 6:6). In addition, the one following God's path becomes a co-worker for God's kingdom (Isa. 43:10–12).

Reflecting the messianic promise of knowledge (Jer. 24:7; 31:33–34), there is a finality to the Christian's knowledge of God (Matt. 11:27; Rom. 16:25–27; Eph. 1:9–10; Col. 1:26–28). In Christ "are hidden all the treasures of wisdom and knowledge" (Col. 2:3). Moreover, in contrast to ordinary historical knowledge, this knowledge of God is self-authenticating. God himself personally confronts each individual in the Word (2 Cor. 4:6; 1 John 2:27), foreshadowing the future when teaching is no longer necessary (Jer. 31:34).

On the other hand, the believer's knowledge of God in Jesus Christ is only provisional. It is sufficient for recognizing and trusting the object of faith (John 17:3; Rom. 10:9): "I know my sheep and my sheep know me. . . . My sheep listen to my voice" (John 10:14, 27). Without answering all our questions, it provides an adequate light for the journeyer in this darkened world (2 Peter 1:19). But this knowledge is only a foretaste of knowing God "face to face" in the hereafter (1 Cor. 13:12), when "the day dawns and the morning star arises in your hearts" (2 Peter 1:19).

Timothy R. Phillips

See also God.

Bibliography. J. Bergman and G. J. Botterweck, *TDOT,* 5:448–81; R. Bultmann, *TDNT,* 1:689–719; C. H. Dodd, *The Interpretation of the Fourth Gospel;* E. A. Martens, *God's Design: A Focus on Old Testament Theology;* W. Elwell, *TAB,* pp. 39–41, 564–67.

Ll

Lake of Fire. God's final retributive punishment. After Armageddon the beast and false prophet will be tossed into this "lake of burning sulfur," joined by Satan at the millennium's end, and "tormented day and night for ever and ever" (Rev. 19:20; 20:10). After the final judgment, Hades (the personification of God's adversaries) and the wicked are cast here (Rev. 20:14–15). Jesus calls this "fiery furnace" *gehenna* or hell (Matt. 13:42; 18:8–9; 25:41).

The Old Testament explicitly portrays God's fiery judgment at history's consummation, but not hell (Isa. 66:15–16, 24; Ezek. 38:22). This concept is developed during the intertestamental period (1 Enoch 90:24–6; 103:8; 4 Macc. 12:12; 4 Ezra 7:38). Jesus extensively uses the imagery of "hell-fire" (Matt. 5:22; 7:19; 13:40–42, 50; 18:8–9; 25:41; Mark 9:43, 48–49; Luke 16:24; John 15:6), derived from the Old Testament descriptions of God's retributive judgment, particularly Sodom's ruin (Gen. 19:24; Lev. 10:2; Num. 16:35; Isa. 34:10; Luke 17:29; Jude 7).

This lake of fire and associated imagery convey three important ideas. First, thrown into this lake, the wicked are permanently separated from God's love and good creation, and thus experience the "second death" (Rev. 20:14; 21:8). Second, fire denotes God's searing holiness exacting retribution for evil deeds (Heb. 10:30; Rev. 14:9–11). Third, this "unquenchable fire" portrays hell as everlasting (Mark 9:43, 48; Rev. 20:10). TIMOTHY R. PHILLIPS

See also HELL.

Lamb, Lamb of God. ***Definitions.*** In the pastoral setting of the Bible, there were numerous words for a lamb or a sheep. The Hebrew words were *kebeś*, lamb (Exod. 29:38–39); *keśeb*, lamb (Lev. 3:7); *ṣō'n*, small cattle, sheep and goats, flock, flocks (1 Sam. 25:2); *ʾayil*, ram (Gen. 15:9); *kar*, he-lamb, battering-ram (Isa. 16:1); *śeh*, one of a flock, a sheep (or goat) (Isa. 43:23); *ṭāleh*, lamb, a sucking lamb (1 Sam. 7:9). The Aramaic *ʾimmĕrîn* refers to lambs as sacrificial victims (Ezra 6:9).

The Greek words were *amnos*, lamb (John 1:29, 36; Acts 8:32); *arēn*, lamb as an animal for slaughter (Luke 10:3); *arnion*, sheep, lamb, a diminutive of *arēn* but less so in the New Testament, in Revelation a designation of Christ (Rev. 5:6; 6:1); *probaton*, sheep, small cattle (Matt. 12:11; 18:12; Mark 6:34; 14:27; John 2:14; 10:1–16, 26; Rom. 8:36).

The Old Testament. *Pastoral Economy.* Lambs graze Isa. 5:17; Hos. 4:16), provide wool (Job 31:20; Prov. 27:26) and meat (2 Sam. 12:1–4), and are offered as sacrifices (Lev. 9:3). Within the culture, the metaphor of the Lord being the shepherd of his people was quite vivid (Ps. 23:1; Isa. 40:11; Ezek. 34:12–16); thus, people without leaders are like sheep without a shepherd (Num. 27:17; 1 Kings 22:17; Ezek. 34:5).

The Passover Lamb. The Passover Feast marked the crucial tenth plague, which resulted in the deliverance of Israel from Egypt and slavery. Each family took a year-old male lamb without defect from their flock, and on the fourteenth day of the month it was slaughtered at twilight (Exod. 12:1–30). Some of the blood was put on the sides and top of the doorframe of the house. The lamb was then roasted and eaten. This became a very significant holy day in Jewish tradition and is prominent throughout the Old Testament.

The Sacrificial Lamb. Two-year-old lambs (*kebeś*) were offered on the altar of the tabernacle and temple each day, one in the morning and the other at twilight (Exod. 29:38–41; Num. 38:3–8). A lamb was offered as a sin offering (Lev. 4:32–35), and as a burnt offering for the purification of the priests (Lev. 9:3), a new mother (Lev. 12:6–7), the temple and nation (2 Chron. 29:21), and the returning exiles (Ezra 8:35). In addition to the central place of the sacrificial lamb at the Passover meal, seven to fourteen lambs were offered as burnt offerings during the Feast of Trumpets (Num. 29:2), the Day of Atonement (Num. 29:8), and the Feast of Tabernacles (Num. 29:13).

The Suffering Servant/Lamb. The disfigured, suffering Servant of Isaiah 52:13–53:12 is commonly interpreted as a messianic prophecy. The Servant would arise from humble origins, be despised and rejected, suffer physical wounds, and be treated like a leper, while taking upon himself our infirmities, diseases, transgressions, iniquities, and deserved punishment for sin. The climax of the Servant's vicarious suffering is analogous to a lamb that is led to the slaughter, and is silent (Isa. 53:7).

The New Testament. *The Gospels.* The Fourth Gospel seems to give a composite of the Old Testament typology. John the Baptist testifies and introduces his disciples to Jesus, "Look, the Lamb of God, who takes away the sin of the world!" (1:29, 36). To this title the Evangelist adds other titles: "Son of God" (1:34, 49), "Messiah" (1:41), "King of Israel" (1:49), and "Son of Man" (1:51). Jesus, the Lamb of God, entered the temple courts at the time for the Passover (2:13, 23), made a whip out of cords, drove out the sheep and cattle, scattered the coins of the money changers, and announced, "Destroy this temple, and I will raise it again in three days" (2:19). The temple of which he had spoken was his body (2:21), but this was not understood until after his resurrection (2:22). The Passover is a prominent motif in John (2:13, 23; 6:4; 11:55; 12:1; 13:1; 18:28, 39; 19:14, 31, 42), as are also the many references to the glorification of Jesus in his death upon the cross (3:14–15, 16–17; 8:28; 12:23, 32; 13:31; 17:1, 5). The suffering Servant-Lamb collage of Isaiah 53:7 is completed in Jesus' washing of the disciples' feet (13:1–17). In both Mark 14:12 and Luke 22:7, the arrest, trial, and crucifixion of Jesus are associated with the customary sacrifice of the Passover lamb.

Acts and the Epistles. Luke provides the interpretation of Isaiah 53:7–8 in the early church, through the preaching of Philip to the Ethiopian official (Acts 8:26–40). The "lamb led to the slaughter" was at the theological center of the good news about Jesus (v. 35). This metaphor seems to have less meaning to Paul's urban, Gentile listeners, as "Christ, our Passover lamb" is only mentioned in 1 Corinthians 5:7. Christ, the crucified Son of God, however, remains at the heart of Paul's gospel. Although the term "lamb" does not appear, Hebrews affirms that Jesus Christ was God's promised sacrifice, destined to die once, to take away sins (7:27; 9:26–28; 10:1–18). Those who believe are redeemed through "the precious blood of Christ, a lamb without blemish or defect" (1 Peter 1:19; cf. Mark 10:45).

Revelation. The christology of the Lamb of God rises to its zenith in the last canonical book, where *arnion* appears in the Greek text twenty-nine times. In the heavenly vision of chapter 4, the choir of twenty-four elders and four living creatures worship the "Lord God," who sits on the throne, for he is worthy (v. 11). He holds a sealed scroll—Holy Scripture containing his will and testament—in his right hand. For the promised inheritance to become reality, the one who made the covenant must die. Through the ages people like John had been expecting a militant, divine warrior—"the Lion of the tribe of Judah" (5:5)—to appear in a magnificent display of power against evil. The triumph of God, however, came through his Son, a Son of David, who appeared like a Lamb (5:6). The Lamb, looking as if it had been slain (5:6, 9, 12; 13:8), stood in the center of the throne. He alone was worthy to open the scroll. When he took the scroll, the prayers of the saints were fulfilled (5:8) and all heaven erupted in praise: "Worthy is the Lamb, who was slain, to receive power and wealth and wisdom and strength and honor and glory and praise!" (5:12). Therefore, Jesus, the Lamb of God, is "Lord of lords and King of kings!" (17:14).

MELVIN H. SHOEMAKER

See also ATONEMENT; ISAIAH, THEOLOGY OF; JESUS CHRIST; OFFERINGS AND SACRIFICES.

Bibliography. C. K. Barrett, *NTS* (1955): 210–18; G. R. Beasley-Murray, *John;* R. E. Brown, *The Gospel According to John (1–12);* G. L. Carey, *Tyn Bul* 32 (1981): 97–122; J. D. Charles, *JETS* 34/4 (1991): 461–73; G. Florovsky, *SJT* 4 (1951): 13–28; N. Hllyer, *EvQ* 39 (1967): 228–36; J. Jeremias, *TDNT,* 1:185–86, 338–41; 5:896–904; I. H. Marshall, *Dictionary of Jesus and the Gospels,* pp. 432–34; H. Preisker and S. Schulz, *TDNT,* 6:689–92; M. G. Reddish, *JSNT* 33 (1988): 85–95; D. B. Sandy, *JETS* 34/4 (1991): 447–60; W. C. van Unnik, *Melanges Biblicques en Hommage,* pp. 445–61; S. Virgulin, *Scr* 13 (1961): 74–80.

Lamentations, Theology of. Lamentations is a soliloquy. There is no word from God, although there are words about God. The structure of the book, apart from the final chapter, is a set of acrostics (not obvious in English translations). Its genre is lament. Several traditions, such as the sin-punishment nexus, inform the book. The setting is the historical crisis of a destroyed city, Jerusalem. The speaker is both a spectator and victim of the tragedy. A dominant personality within the monologue is God; human agents such as Babylon (unnamed) and Edom also come into view. The language is laced with metaphor. It is with an eye to the form, genre, traditions, situation, and characters that a theology of the book can best be laid bare.

The Pathos of Suffering. The perspective in the book is initially this-wordly. The tragedy of Jerusalem, now devastated by the Babylonians (587 B.C.), and of a people in exile, is faced head on (1:3; 2:8–9). The citizenry is humiliated and in desperate straits (1:1–21a; 5:1–18). The calamity and pathos of suffering is a central theme (cf. 3:1–20). Poetry, rather than prose, is the vehicle of pathos. The funeral dirges set the tone (chaps. 1, 2, 4). Four of the five chapters are in acrostic form utilizing the Hebrew alphabet, perhaps as a way of reaching for a total expression of grief. The vocabulary and metaphors describing the suffering are graphic and earthy. The once proud city is now like a widow, a queen become a slave (1:1). Zion theology, which stressed the indestructability of the city and the temple (Pss. 48; 132:13; Jer. 7:4), has been shown to be bankrupt. The good life of joy, feasting, treasures, and prosperity is gone (1:7; 3:17). Once elegant and bedecked with finery, the leaders are now blacker than soot, with their skin shriveled (4:8; cf. 1:6). Women have been ravished (5:11). Children cry for food (2:12). There is no one to comfort Zion (1:17). The harsh reality is described, not denied. The grief is not muted or misrepresented even though it raises large questions about God. Grief, for therapeutic reasons, as for Job, must be brought to speech.

Out of such pain God is addressed on the understanding that he attends to suffering people. A first step, then, is to face him with the grief. The devastation of property, the stress of losing virtually everything, and the deep despondency are vividly pictured—so that God will take notice! Famine is the focus (2:20; 4:10), perhaps because of the tradition of God working his purposes through famine (Gen. 12:10; Ruth; Jer. 14). Arising out of the suffering is the cry for rehabilitation and restoration (5:21–22).

An Interventionist God. The series of poems represents description but also an analysis on which past tradition is brought to bear. That tradition includes a belief about the nexus between sin and suffering. Job, likely written earlier than Lamentations, makes clear that the theory that all suffering is inevitably the result of wrongdoing is reductionistic. Still, that sin results in punitive measures is an understanding dating from the transgression in Eden.

In Lamentations that connection between sin and suffering is at once made explicit: "The LORD has brought her grief because of her many sins" (1:5). Sin is a breach in the relationship. Israel, to resort to metaphor, has been under a heavy yoke, and so her strength has been sapped (1:14). God, so says the sufferer, has dragged him "from the path and mangled [him] and left [him] without help" (3:11). Israel explains her circumstances in light of the tradition: "We have sinned and rebelled . . . we have suffered . . . ruin and destruction" (3:42, 47). Each of the five poems identifies sin as the reason for the disaster (1:8; 2:14; 3:42; 4:13; 5:7).

Her sin, while not to be excused, can be better understood in the light of another tradition: the ministry expected from prophets. Leaders are to blame (4:12–13). Israel's wound, now deep as the sea, came because the prophets failed to expose her sin and so failed to ward off her captivity (2:14). Back of this charge is the conviction that one of the functions of the prophets was to identify the shape of evil in the society (cf. Jer. 7:1–15). The reference in 2:14 to prophets whose oracles were false may well be to those who announced peace to a sinning people, and with whom Jeremiah so vigorously debated (23:16–18).

Another tradition transparent in Lamentations is that of God fighting against his people. Isaiah states succinctly: "So he [God] turned and became their enemy and he himself fought against them" (63:10; cf. Num. 14:39–45). That statement, echoed in "The LORD is like an enemy" (2:5), now explains the tragedy of 587 B.C. but at another level. The devastation is ultimately attributed to God's action (3:38). "He [God] has laid waste his dwelling like a garden; he has destroyed his place of meeting" (2:6, 17; cf. 1:12; 2:1; 3:1).

God is ruler (5:19). He is also Savior, and so the hope for redemption, grounded in God's faithfulness, remains alive. The imprecations against the enemies (1:21–22; 3:59–66; 4:21–22), and a litany of repentance (3:40–41) are two facets of that hope.

God: Righteous, Angry, Compassionate. The character of God is assumed to be both daunting and appealing. The righteousness of God is affirmed (1:18). Given the evil of his people, however, more is said in Lamentations about God's anger than about his righteousness. Wrath, idiomatically described as "hot of nose," is expressive of God's righteousness. Each acrostic, but especially the second, includes mention of his anger (1:12; 2:1, 2, 3, 4, 21, 22; 3:43; 4:11). God's anger, speaking metaphorically, is poured out like fire (2:4; cf. 4:11) with the result that the strongholds of Judah have been torn down (2:2), king and priest have been spurned (2:6), and young and old have been slain (2:21). Jeremiah and other prophets before him warned Israel of the severity of God's anger should it be unleashed (30:23–24; Amos 1:3–5, 6, 10, 11).

No attempt is made to reconcile God's anger and God's compassion, but compassion is no less characteristic of God than is anger. The tradition of God as resolutely compassionate and gentle, yet just in retribution, persists. The main section of the third acrostic, roughly the central section of the book, describes God's faithfulness as great and resilient (3:23). The flood of emotion, building in the two previous acrostics, is reined in by sound theology. God's compassion and love do not fail (3:22, 32). God is fundamentally unwilling to bring about grief (3:33). The belief in God as compassionate gives an intimation of hope to this suffering city, its inhabitants, and its exiles (3:21).

God: Experienced as Distant. The lament genre—both individual lament (chap. 3) and communal lament (chap. 5)—colors the book. Central to the lament is the complaint, which can take various shapes (cf. Pss. 6, 13). Basic to the complaint in Lamentations is God's perceived absence, inaccessibility, and even abandonment. Again, metaphors come into play. God has barred the petitioner's way as "with blocks of stone"

(3:9). God has covered himself with a cloud so "no prayer can get through" (3:44).

Yet prayer continues. As Moses not only stated petitions but urged reasons for God to respond (Exod. 32:11–14), so here the poet "motivates" God by noting the taunt and mockery of the enemies (3:61–63). Another incentive is the sheer helplessness and distress of the victim (1:20; cf. Amos 7:2). Still another is God's former intervention: God was once near and reassuring (3:55–57). The complaint builds on the understanding that God is a God who, even if experienced as absent, is a God whose concern is for victims, and whose actions are initiated, as at the exodus, by cries for help. Hence the persistent cry, "Look, O LORD" (1:9, 11; 3:63; 5:19–21). In the end God will hear. ELMER A. MARTENS

See also ISRAEL; JEREMIAH, THEOLOGY OF.

Bibliography. B. Albrektson, *Studies in the Text and Theology of the Book of Lamentations;* R. B. Chisholm, Jr., *A Biblical Theology of the Old Testament,* pp. 359–63; N. K. Gottwald, *Studies in the Book of Lamentations;* B. Johnson, *ZAW* 97/1(1985):58–73.

Land (of Israel). ***The Abrahamic Covenant and the Land.*** The Lord "cut" an unconditional covenant with Abraham in which he stated, "To your descendants I give this land, from the river of Egypt to the great river, the Euphrates" (Gen. 15:18). The Lord periodically reconfirmed the aspect of the land to Abraham (Gen. 12:7; 13:14–17; 17:8; 24:7). The reason the Lord gave this land to the children of Israel was because he was faithful to his covenant to Abraham (Deut. 9:4–5), his love for Abraham (Deut. 4:37), and his love for Israel (Deut. 7:8).

The Mosaic Law and the Land. Just before the children of Israel entered the land of Canaan, Moses reiterated the Law as recorded in the Book of Deuteronomy. He commanded the people to obey the Law "in the land" (4:5, 14; 5:31; 6:1; 11:31; 12:1; 17:14; 18:9; 19:1; 21:1; 26:1). A number of laws in the Book of Deuteronomy are rooted in the land: the year of release from debt (15:1–11), appointing just judges (16:18–20), selection of a king (17:14–20), abominations of the nations (18:9–14), the cities of refuge (19:1–13), removing landmarks (19:14), unknown murder (21:1–9), leaving a hanged man on a tree (21:22–23), divorce (24:1–4), and just weights and measurements (25:13–16).

The Borders of the Land. Abraham, by faith, left Ur of the Chaldees to go to the "land I [the Lord] will show you." When he arrived in Shechem, the Lord appeared to him and said, "To your offspring I will give this land" (Gen. 12:7). However, the borders of this land were not set. It was only after the Lord "cut the covenant" with Abraham that he gave a general delineation of the land. He said, "To your descendants I give this land, from the river of Egypt to the great river, the Euphrates" (Gen. 15:18).

A detailed description of the land's borders was given to the children of Israel as they were about to enter the land after four hundred years in Egypt. Numbers 34:1–5 sets forth the southern borders of the land of Canaan. The general line of the southern border is from the Dead Sea, through the Wilderness of Zin to Kadesh Barnea. It then turns north to the "Wadi of Egypt" and the Mediterranean Sea. Joshua gives a similar description (15:1–4). The identification of the "Wadi of Egypt" is the only point in question in this passage. Some have suggested it is the Nile River or one of its tributaries. Most Bible atlases place it at Wadi el-Arish. Recently, N. Na'aman of Tel Aviv University suggested that the Brook of Egypt was the Nahal Basor, just south of Gaza. The territory south of the Wilderness of Zin (called the Central Negev Highlands today) belonged to Edom. The Aravah and the mountains to the east of the Aravah were also Edomite territory. Eilat, the seaport on the Red Sea, belonged to Edom (1 Kings 9:26).

The western border of the land of Israel is the "Great Sea," the Mediterranean Sea (Num. 34:6).

The northern border goes from the "Great Sea" (the Mediterranean) to Mount Hor and continues on to the entrance to Hamath; then the border goes to Zedad, proceeds to Ziphron, and ends at Hazar Enan (Num. 34:7–9).

The eastern border is marked out from Hazan Enan to Shepham, and then goes down from Shapham to Riblah on the east side of Ain; it goes down and reaches to the eastern side of the Sea of Chinnereth; the border goes down along the Jordan, and ends at the Salt Sea (Num. 34:10–12; Deut. 3:17).

Ezekiel gives a similar description of the borders of the Land of Israel as revised in terms of the geographical concepts of his day (47:15–20; 48:1, 28).

Gad, Reuben, and the half tribe of Manasseh settled on the east side of the Jordan River (Num. 32:1–5; 34:13–15). Moses and Joshua allowed them to settle there even though it was not part of the promised land (Deut. 3:12–17, 20; Josh. 12:6; 13:8–33; 22:4, 19, 27). It is important to note that this land was given to them by Moses, not the Lord. The reason it was given to them was because it was uninhabited after the Israelites defeated Sihon, king of the Amorites, at Heshbon and Og, king of Bashan (Num. 32:29, 33). The territory of Bashan (the Golan Heights today), however, was settled by part of the half tribe of Manasseh and it was part of the promised land.

Three cities of refuge—Kedesh in Galilee, Shechem, and Kirjath Arba (Hebron)—were located "in the land" (Deut. 19:1–3), but provision was made for three more, two of which were outside the land when the territory was enlarged (Josh. 20:1–9). Bezer and Ramoth Gilead were in Transjordan and Golan was in Bashan.

Description of the Land. The Bible describes the land of Israel at least nineteen times as "a land flowing with milk and honey" (Lev. 26:3–12; Num. 13:23, 28; 14:7; 24:3; Deut. 6:3; 11:9; 26:9, 15; 27:3; 28:2–7, 11–12; 31:20). The image can denote a lush green land that produces an abundant and fruitful harvest. But this word picture may not be an accurate representation of the term. Isaiah used the phrase "milk and honey" to describe the devastation of the land after the Assyrians conquered it (Isa. 7:21–25). This seeming paradox is resolved by considering the perspective of the audience being addressed.

The idea of plenty and abundance is partially true. When God described the land of Canaan to Moses, he used the term "milk and honey" to imply the bountifulness of the land (Exod. 3:8, 17; 13:5; 33:3; Lev. 20:24). When the twelve spies returned from the land of Canaan, they recounted their adventures and characterized the land as "flowing with milk and honey" (Num. 13:27; 14:8). The spies observed that cattle and goats produced more milk in areas abundant with forage. Thus, an area abundant with vegetation would be considered a land "flowing with milk." Honey, in the biblical period, was not a cultivated product. It was associated with nonagricultural areas that were covered with wild vegetation. This is demonstrated by the account of Saul swearing his men to an oath when they fought the Philistines (1 Sam. 14:25–26).

When Israel entered the land of Canaan, the hill country was uninhabited and covered with natural forests and thickets. Joshua commanded the tribe of Joseph to go up to the forest country and clear a place. When they took the wooded area, cut it down, terraced it, and planted trees on the terracing, the Israelites passed from a pastoral society to an agricultural/farming society.

The entire land was not uninhabited and forested. The Canaanites lived in the valleys and cultivated them (Josh. 17:16). The twelve spies returning from their trip into the land of Canaan carried the bounty of the summer harvest—-grapes, pomegranates, and figs—from the cultivated Valley of Eshkol (Num. 13:23).

The Purpose of the Land. Why is this land called the promised land? After all, life was easier in Egypt (barring the oppression of Pharaoh, of course). Every year the Nile River overflowed its banks with rich alluvial soil. The farmers also had a constant supply of water with which to irrigate their fields. Just before the children of Israel entered the land, Moses contrasted the land of Canaan with Egypt. He said, "The land you are entering to take over is not like the land of Egypt, from which you have come, where you planted your seed and irrigated it by foot as in a vegetable garden. But the land you are crossing over to take possession of is a land of mountains and valleys that drinks water rain from heaven" (Deut. 11:10–11). The Israelite farmer, living in the land of Israel, had to plow the soil after the early rains loosened the hard soil in the fall and had to depend on the rains throughout the winter months. If it did not rain, drought and famine resulted.

Monson observes that the purpose of the land was to serve as God's testing ground of faith! The Lord wanted to see if his people, redeemed by his matchless grace and mighty power out of slavery in Egypt, and brought through the wilderness and into the promised land, would worship him and him alone. The tenor of the Hebrew Scriptures seems to indicate that the people of Israel were to be an agrarian society, living in dependence upon the Lord. They were not to be an international mercantile society like the Phoenicians.

After contrasting Egypt with the land of Israel, Moses continued to describe the land as a land for which the Lord cared. Nonetheless, the people were reminded to diligently obey God's commandments and to love the Lord (Deut. 11:12–15). The expression of faith for the Israelite believer living in the land of Israel was to be obedient to the Law. Moses also warned the people to be careful not to be deceived to serve other gods and to worship them.

The borders of the land of Israel demonstrate an important principle in the life of faith. Israel was supposed to live within the borders God gave them, and not engage in foreign trade or adopt expansionist policies beyond its borders. The southern border of Israel went only as far as the wilderness of Zin, not down to Eilat. In the course of Israel's history, three kings expanded their kingdom to Eilat and the Red Sea; Solomon, Jehoshaphat, and Uzziah. Their purpose was to engage in the lucrative trade in spices and the gold of Ophir that went through this port. This would enhance their wealth, and in so doing, violate a commandment the Lord had laid down for the king: "Nor shall he greatly multiply silver and gold for himself" (Deut. 17:17). The life of Uzziah, recounted in 2 Chronicles 26, illustrates this principle. GORDON FRANZ

See also ISRAEL.

Bibliography. Y. Aharoni, *The Land of the Bible;* W. Brueggeman, *The Land;* N. Hareuveni, *Nature in Our Biblical Heritage;* P. Miller, *Int* 23 (1964): 451–65; J. Monson, *Geographical Basics in the Land of the Bible;* N. Na'aman, *Tel Aviv* 6/1–2 (1979): 68–90; 7/1–2 (1970): 95–109; H. Orlinsky, *Eretz Israel* 18: 43–55; A. Rainey, *Tel Aviv* 9/2 (1982): 130–36; G. von Rad, *The Problem of the Hexateuch.*

Last Day(s), Latter Days, Last Times. There are problems with the terminology of "the latter days" in that, for example, the King James Version quite often refers to "the latter days," an expression not found in modern translations. Further, it is not always clear whether "the latter days" means a somewhat later period than that of the writer or the latest times of all, the end of the world. There are also expressions that locate the day being discussed in the time of the speaker. Care is needed as we approach the passages that use these terms.

There is another problem in that in modern times we find it difficult to think that the New Testament writers were living in "the last times." Centuries have gone by; how could their times be the last times? We should be clear that the scriptural writers did not always use the terms in the same way as we would naturally do. For them the supremely great event had taken place in the coming of Jesus Christ into the world to effect the salvation of all believers. This was not just an event in history; it was *the* event. Because of what Christ had done everything was altered. From then on, however long it would be until God intervened and set up the new heaven and the new earth, people were living in "the last times." The days in which it is possible for people to put their trust in Jesus Christ and to enter into the fullness of the salvation he has brought about differ from all the days that went before. They are days of opportunity, days when people can put their trust in the crucified, risen, and ascended Lord and enter into the salvation he won for sinners.

Present Happenings. The writer to the Hebrews tells his readers that "in these last days he (God) has spoken to us by his Son" (Heb. 1:2), and Peter says that Christ "was revealed in these last times for your sake" (1 Peter 1:20). In such passages the meaning clearly is that something has happened in recent times that is in sharp contrast to what occurred in earlier ages. Or in similar expression may look to the future of the recipients of the message, as when we read, "in later days you will return to the LORD your God and obey him" (Deut. 4:30), or in the reminder to the hearers that God gave them manna in the wilderness "to humble and to test you so that in the end it might go well with you" (Deut. 8:16).

The point of such passages is to make it clear that God is at work in the passage of time here and now. His people are to bear in mind that in what happens in their lives and in the world around them God is working out his purposes. In this spirit the psalmist prays, "Show me, O LORD, my life's end and the number of my days; let me know how fleeting is my life" (Ps. 39:4), and in Proverbs we find that receiving instruction is the path to being wise in "the latter end" (19:20). Contrariwise Babylon is blamed for not remembering "the latter end" (Isa. 47:7). By taking heed of what God is doing, his people will be strengthened in their faith and better able to appreciate the significance of the times in which they live. It is important that God's people are never alone and that they will discern the outworking of the divine purposes if only they have eyes to see.

Future Happenings. Quite often "last" or "latter" is used of times other than the end of all things. The prophets could speak of a "day" when the Lord would act, sometimes in punishment of evil, sometimes in bringing blessing. Especially important are passages that speak of "the last day(s)," which point to the future but without being specific. In such passages it may mean "later in the present scheme of things," that is, later in the life of a person or, more often, later in the history of the world. For the former use we might notice the warning in Proverbs that a misspent life means that you will groan "at your latter end" (Prov. 5:11). For the other use Jacob summoned his sons to tell them what would happen to them "in the latter days" (Gen. 49:1). This clearly refers to the distant future, but not to the end of the world. So with Moses' prophecy that after his death Israel would turn away from the right with the result that evil would befall them "in the latter days" (Deut. 31:29). We might say something similar about Daniel's prophecy of things that would happen "in the latter time of wrath" (Dan. 8:19; the references to the kings of Media, Persia, and Greece show that there is a reference to what we would call antiquity, not the end of the world). Hosea looks forward to the Israelites coming trembling to the Lord "in the latter days" (3:5).

So also Jeremiah looks forward to people understanding the working of the divine wrath "in the latter days" (Jer. 23:20; 30:24). He also looks for blessing in those days, for the Lord will restore Moab (48:47) and Elam (49:39). We usually look for blessing on Israel, and it is interesting that Jeremiah sees the divine blessing as coming also on these Gentile nations. Similarly Daniel says that God has shown Nebuchadnezzar what is to happen in "the latter days" (2:28; for other examples of his use of the expression, see 8:23; 10:14; 11:29).

In the New Testament it is not so much a question of what will happen to nations, as of the way God will work out his purpose in the affairs of the church and of individual believers. Peter says that the coming of the Holy Spirit on the infant church fulfilled a prophecy of what would happen "in the last days" (Acts 2:17). In the same spirit we notice a statement in Hebrews: Christ "has appeared once for all at the end of the ages to do away with sin by the sacrifice of himself" (9:26). The great events concerning the coming of the Savior and the establishment of salvation are linked with "the last days." So also is the opposition of evil to all that is good. In those days "The Spirit clearly says that . . . some will abandon the faith and follow deceiving spirits and things taught by demons" (1 Tim. 4:1). There is a sense in which the church has always lived in "the last days."

The Final Situation. The major topic in Jesus' teaching was "the kingdom of God." Sometimes this appeared as a present reality, sometimes as a future happening. The most significant feature is that it is intimately connected with Jesus himself; he could tell his hearers that the kingdom was there, among them, in his coming (Luke 17:21). In one sense the kingdom awaited the distant future; in another the coming of Jesus meant that it was already there. The appearance of Jesus was the decisive happening; it changed everything.

The New Testament makes it clear that the coming of Jesus Christ was the critical event. His atoning death was God's final answer to the problem of human sin and once that had been accomplished nothing could be the same again. For our present purpose the important thing is that Jesus ushered in a new state of affairs. He wrought the atonement that made it possible for sinners to be forgiven and to enter God's kingdom and to be fitted to take their part in God's final kingdom. That gives a different quality to all time after the coming of Jesus, and the scriptural writers bring this out by referring to all that is subsequent to the coming of Jesus as "the last times" or the like.

Sometimes the New Testament speaks of the end of all things as though it were very near and sometimes there seems to be a long interval. We must bear in mind that "with the Lord a day is like a thousand years, and a thousand years are like a day" (2 Peter 3:8). It is not always easy to be sure whether a passage is speaking of the end of this world and its affairs or of something that will happen prior to that. We should exercise due caution as we approach difficult passages. But what is abundantly clear is that God is working his purpose out and that this involves a final state of affairs in which his will will be perfectly done.

Sometimes the scriptural writers look beyond the present system to the final state of affairs when they use the "latter days" terminology. This happens in a wonderful passage in both Isaiah and Micah in which these prophets look forward to the Lord's house as being established above the hills and of many nations as coming to it to find God's teaching so that they may walk in his ways (Isa. 2:2–4; Mic. 4:1–5). A very different picture is given in Ezekiel's prophecy that in "the latter days" Gog, the chief prince of the forces of evil, will come against Israel and be defeated (chaps. 38–39). This is not to be thought of as a contradiction of the former passages. There are other references both to final bliss and to the final rebellion of the forces of evil. It means that in the end all evil will be decisively overthrown and God's kingdom established forever.

That there will be an upsurge of evil in the last days is made clear by a number of passages. Sometimes this relates to the daily life of the believer, as when Jesus says, "All men will hate you because of me, but he who stands firm to the end will be saved" (Matt. 10:22). But evil will be more widespread than that, for "There will be terrible times in the last days. People will be lovers of themselves, lovers of money, boastful, proud" (2 Tim. 3:1). "In the last days scoffers will come, scoffing and following their own evil desires" (2 Peter 3:3). In the Olivet discourse there is difficulty in being sure whether some of the items refer to the life of the believer set in the midst of the ungodly or whether they refer to the endtime, but there is surely a reference to the end when Jesus says, "All men will hate you because of me, but he who stands firm to the end will be saved" (Mark 13:13). This will be the point also of his explanation of a parable, "The harvest is the end of the age" (Matt. 13:39). Similarly Peter speaks of salvation as "ready to be revealed in the last time" (1 Peter 1:5). We should notice here the references to "the seven last plagues" (Rev. 15:1; 21:9) which point to troubles in the last times.

In John's Gospel there is also the thought that God will take care of his own in those troubled times. Jesus repeatedly said concerning those the Father "has given" him that he will "raise them up at the last day" (John 6:39, 40, 43, 54). John is the only New Testament writer to use the expression "the last day," an expression that points to Jesus' activity right to the end of time. It also makes it clear that Jesus' care for his own extends right through time to the ushering in of the final state of affairs. On the negative side, the person who rejects Jesus and his teaching will find that that teaching "will condemn him at the last day" (John 12:48).

That evil will continue to the end is clear, as many passages testify. There are problems, such as the difficulty of being sure what parts of Jesus' discourse on the Mount of Olives toward the end of his earthly life refer to the destruction of Jerusalem and what to the end of the world. But he makes it clear that, while his followers will hear of "wars and revolutions" which must happen, "the end will not come right away" (Luke 21:9). Believers will encounter troubles throughout this world's history and this will persist right to the very end. Peter can speak of "the end of all things" as "near" (1 Peter 4:7). The coming of Christ means that salvation is now made available and this transforms all things. But the New Testament writers were clear that this was but the prelude to God's final state of affairs and that, in the perspective of eternity, that final state was not far off. Then believers will enter into the fullness of "eternal life" (Rom. 6:22–23).

Very important is the fact that the final, great day will see the triumph of God. This is foreshadowed in the Old Testament, for example, in the great passage in which Job says, "I know that my Redeemer lives, and that in the end he will stand upon the earth. And after my skin has been destroyed, yet in my flesh I will see God" (Job

19:25–26). There are problems in this passage but plainly there is the clear expectation of God's final triumph. Before Jesus was born the angel told Mary that the child she was to bear "will reign over the house of Jacob forever; his kingdom will never end" (Luke 1:33). And in his great passage on the resurrection Paul says that Christ will come with "those who belong to him. Then the end will come, when he hands over the kingdom to God the Father after he has destroyed all dominion, authority and power" (1 Cor. 15:24). The apostle goes on to speak of the raising of the dead in a different form, one in which they will be "imperishable" (v. 52). Again and again the New Testament brings out the truth that when Jesus returns all evil will be defeated and the redeemed will know the fullness of everlasting life.

For the New Testament writers the coming of Jesus Christ into the world to bring about our salvation was the decisive happening in the entire history of the world. That set in motion the train of events that would bring about the salvation of sinners and eventually see the setting up of God's kingdom, as Revelation makes so clear. This did not mean that all evil would immediately disappear; both the New Testament writings and Christian experience make it plain that evil continues. But the important thing from the Christian point of view is that the saving work of Christ has altered everything. Sin has been decisively defeated and believers have already entered into salvation. However long or short a time it will be before the end of this world as we measure time, we are living in the last times as the New Testament writers understand it.

LEON MORRIS

See also DAY; DAY OF THE LORD, GOD, CHRIST; SECOND COMING OF CHRIST.

Bibliography. O. Cullmann, *Christ and Time.*

Last Judgment. *See* JUDGMENT, DAY OF.

Last Supper. *See* LORD'S SUPPER, THE.

Last Things. *See* DAY OF THE LORD, GOD, CHRIST; LAST DAY(S), LATTER DAYS, LAST TIMES.

Law. ***The Nature of Biblical Law.*** The usual Hebrew term translated as "law" is *tora. Tora,* used 220 times in the Old Testament, more specifically means "instruction." Our English term "law" usually brings to mind the norms of society as enforced by the state. The Old Testament, however, often presents moral admonitions that are hardly amenable to state enforcement (e.g., Exod. 20:17; 23:4–5); is silent about state enforcement (Exod. 21:2–6); or specifies God rather than the state as the enforcer (Exod. 22:21–27). In addition, the label "law" seems inappropriate for certain ceremonial instructions.

Biblical civil laws differ from the "positive law" of modern jurisprudence, which tries to legislate in exhaustive detail. Biblical laws are insufficiently comprehensive to be considered a "law-code," but served as paradigmatic illustrations (not rigid rules) of justice that a judge could apply or modify according to circumstances. For example, whereas capital offenses state the maximum penalty for certain crimes, extenuating factors could lead a judge, legitimately, not to execute the offender. This is stated explicitly in the case of murder (Exod. 21:12–14), and is implicit elsewhere. Thus, although Exodus 21:15 states "Whoever strikes his father or his mother shall surely be put to death" (NASB), it would be absurd to apply this rule to an angry toddler.

Many biblical precepts are expressed as broad principles without legalistic detail. For example, "work" is prohibited on the sabbath yet is never defined legally. This ambiguity, which allowed for some flexibility, was considered a liability by Pharisaic Judaism. In an attempt to make sure the command proper was never violated, the rabbis created secondary, rigid rules which, if followed, would theoretically prevent a person from ever violating the biblical command itself. This was known as "putting a fence around the law." Such nonbiblical rules (e.g., the sabbath day's journey) are prescribed exhaustively in the Talmud, but this burdensome "tradition" is contrary to the spirit of biblical law (Matt. 15:3; 23:4).

An important law is the lex talionis, "life for life, eye for eye, tooth for tooth" (Exod. 21:22–25; Lev. 24:19–20; Deut. 19:15–21), which is sometimes misunderstood as a barbaric justification of personal vengeance and maiming. On the contrary, it expresses the just principle that judicial punishments should fit the crime, thereby limiting permissible punishment. One who is responsible for the loss of another's eye deserves, in principle, to give up his own eye. In practice, however, the offender ordinarily would placate the aggrieved party by paying an amount proportional to the degree of the maiming to substitute for the infliction of literal *talion*. Note how such "ransoming" operates in Exodus 21:29–30, and how literal *talion* fails to occur in 21:18–19 and 21:26–27 where it might be expected. The availability of ransom seems to be so prevalent that it must be explicitly prohibited to exclude it (Num. 35:31). Jesus, in accord with Leviticus 19:18, teaches patient suffering instead of the misapplication of lex talionis for personal revenge (Matt. 5:38–42).

Legal Corpora in the Old Testament. The laws (traditionally 613 in number) are concentrated in certain passages in the Pentateuch. Some of these are given special names.

The Decalog was given at Mount Sinai (Exod. 20:1–17) and repeated in Moses' sermon over forty years later (Deut. 5:6–21). The formulation in the Decalogue (the traditional "thou shalt/shalt not") is apodictic, that is, unqualified; God as King imposes demands upon his subjects. These commandments represent the minimum moral and religious requirements for those in covenant relationship with God.

The Book of the Covenant (Exod. 20:22–23:33, partially repeated in 34:10–26) consists of cultic, humanitarian, and civil regulations. Most of its civil regulations follow the casuistic formulation of cuneiform laws: "If X happens (protasis), then Y will be the legal consequences (apodosis)."

Deuteronomy has many regulations. Chapters 5–11 emphasize the general requirement to obey God; chapters 12–25 offer specifics in various areas of life (worship, festivals, officials of the theocratic state, manslaughter, warfare, sexuality, etc.). The structure of Deuteronomy follows that of second-millennium covenant treaties in which the laws correspond to stipulations within the covenant. The topical units of chapters 12–25 are arranged according to the order of the Ten Commandments.

Cultic laws concerning the tabernacle, sacrifices, priests, ritual purity, festivals, and ethical and ritual holiness (especially in sexual and social matters; cf. Lev. 18–26, the so-called Holiness Code) are scattered throughout Genesis through Numbers, Leviticus consisting almost entirely of this kind of material. Some call these laws the Priestly Code on the dubious assumption that they once existed as an independent collection.

Biblical and Cuneiform Laws. Scholars commonly compare biblical civil laws with contemporary laws found by archaeologists in the ancient Near East. Extrabiblical laws include those by Ur-Nammu of Ur (ca. 2112–2095 B.C.), Lipit-Ishtar of Isin (ca. 1925 B.C.), some ten Sumerian Laws (ca. 1800 B.C.) of unknown provenance, the Laws of Eshnunna (ca. 1800 B.C.), the Laws of Hammurapi (ca. 1750 B.C.), the Edict of Ammisaduqa (ca. 1650 B.C.), Middle Assyrian Laws (ca. 1100 B.C.), Hittite Laws (before ca. 1200 B.C.), and Neo-Babylonian Laws (seventh century B.C.).

Biblical civil laws resemble extrabiblical laws in topics covered and formulation. For example, cases of striking pregnant women resulting in miscarriage (presumably an unusual circumstance) occur in HL §17, Sumerian Laws §§1–2, LH §§209–214, MAL §§A 21, 50–52 as well as Exodus 21:22–25. There are general parallels with laws on slaves and goring oxen, and in one (but only one) case, a cuneiform law's reading is identical with a biblical one: LE §53 and Exodus 21:35. The parallels are insufficient to suppose biblical laws were simply borrowed from ancient Near Eastern ones. On the other hand, the parallels seem too close for chance. It is best to say that the Bible shows awareness of extrabiblical laws and often deliberately chooses type cases from such laws on which to make moral comment. Where an existing law is just, the Bible can happily adopt it (e.g., Exod. 21:35). Accordingly, comparison with cuneiform law is useful; nonetheless, the contrasts with cuneiform laws are usually more telling than the similarities.

These contrasts reflect differences in ideology between Israel and Mesopotamia. Cuneiform laws are overwhelmingly secular whereas the Bible freely mixes moral, civil, and cultic laws, and more often includes religious motivations for compliance. It is true that Hammurapi receives authority to rule from the god Shamash, but Shamash is custodian of impersonal cosmic truth that Hammurapi uses to make his own laws that are only indirectly attributable to deity. In the Bible, however, the laws are directly from God; Moses is only a mediator. Biblical law is designed to educate the public, to mold the national character, and to glorify Yahweh as a just lawgiver; cuneiform laws are meant to glorify the kings who created them and lack pedagogic application, being placed in a temple outside public view in a script (cuneiform) only academics could read.

Contrasting ideology is reflected in biblical law's setting limits on the authority of kings (Deut. 17:14–20), cuneiform laws reflect the unlimited authority of the king. Biblical laws elevate human life over property to a greater degree than do cuneiform laws. Hence, cuneiform laws required up to thirtyfold restitution for theft and the execution of the thief who could not pay (LH §§8, 265; HL §§57–59, 63, 67, 69); biblical law limits restitution to no more than fivefold and prohibits the execution of a thief (Exod. 22:1–4). Similarly, cuneiform laws make no sharp distinction between cases involving an ox goring a slave, and that of an ox goring an ox, both being property (LE §§53–55); biblical law deliberately separates these cases (Exod. 21:28–31, 35–36), expressing by its structure the ideology that cases involving humans are of an entirely different category than those involving animals.

Cuneiform law agrees with biblical law in condemning murder, adultery, and incest (LH §1, 129, 157); however, biblical law differs by making many religious sins, so-called victimless crimes, and crimes against family capital offenses.

"Law" and "Covenant." All biblical laws are placed in the context of God's covenant with Israel. Covenant, not law-keeping, establishes a relationship, just as signing a contract, rather than doing the specified job, establishes an employment relationship. The covenant in Genesis 15 was not established by "law" but by God's gracious offer accompanied by Abram's faith (although he later in some sense kept "the law," Gen. 26:5). Nor did Israel establish a relationship with God by keeping "law." The commandments are given to a people who are already "saved" (Exod. 20:2) through a covenant relationship based on God's gracious love and despite Israel's lack of merit (Deut. 7:7–9; 9:4–6). "Legalism" that makes "law-keeping" a means of salvation is not taught in the Old Testament.

The role of law is to administrate the covenant. Laws prohibit things destructive to a relationship with God (e.g., worshiping other gods). The law gives direction to what a loving response to God should be, and tells how to reap the full benefits of the relationship. Viewed from one perspective, the promises formalized by covenant were unconditional; but from an individual's perspective, benefits could be forfeited by disobedience. Disobedience does not automatically invalidate a covenant, any more than a husband's rudeness to a wife he vowed to cherish invalidates his marriage covenant. Yet disobedience mars the relationship, and may reduce its benefits. In the desert a whole generation of Israelites forfeited their covenant benefits (the promised land) through disobedience, yet the covenant continued.

The Law under the New Covenant. The New Testament's statements about Old Testament law are difficult to harmonize. On the one hand, some New Testament statements indicate that under the new covenant the whole law is in some sense abrogated (Rom. 6:14, "you are not under law"; Rom. 10:4, "Christ is the end of the law"). Direct application of cultic laws is clearly excluded in the New Testament. Food laws, circumcision, sacrifices, temple, and priesthood have been superseded (Mark 7:19; 1 Cor. 7:19; Heb. 7:11–19, 28; 8:13; 10:1–9). Christ has abolished in his flesh the commandments and regulations that separated Jew from Gentile (Eph. 2:15). Dispensationalism concludes from these statements that Christians are under no Mosaic laws, not even the Decalogue, but are instead under the law of Christ (Gal. 6:2; 1 Cor. 9:21).

On the other hand, the law cannot be altogether invalid since the New Testament affirms its abiding applicability. "All Scripture is . . . useful" (2 Tim. 3:16–17), including Old Testament laws. Jesus came not to abolish the law, but to fulfill it (Matt. 5:17–20). The law is the embodiment of truth that instructs (Rom. 2:18–19). It is "holy" and "spiritual," making sin known to us by defining it; therefore, Paul delights in it (Rom. 7:7–14, 22). The law is good if used properly (1 Tim. 1:8), and is not opposed to the promises of God (Gal. 3:21). Faith does not make the law void, but the Christian establishes the law (Rom. 3:31), fulfilling its requirements by walking according to the Spirit (8:4) through love (13:10). When Paul states that women are to be in submission "as the Law says" (1 Cor. 14:34) or quotes parts of the Decalogue (Rom. 13:9), and when James quotes the law of love (2:8 from Lev. 19:18) or condemns partiality, adultery, murder, and slander as contrary to the law (2:9, 11; 4:11), and when Peter quotes Leviticus, "Be holy, because I am holy" (1 Peter 1:16 from Lev. 19:2), the implication is that the law, or at least part of it, remains authoritative.

Part of the problem is that not all the "laws" are of the same order. Jesus designates justice, mercy, and faithfulness as "more important" matters in the law (Matt. 23:23). A similar distinction was made by the prophets who indicate that cultic observance was less important than treating people decently, and ritual without repentance was ineffective. That these cultic regulations were, even in the Old Testament, considered of secondary value, prepares the way for their elimination in Christ.

Covenant theologians have traditionally divided laws into three categories: moral, civil, and ceremonial. Moral laws (e.g., the Decalogue), based on the unchanging character of God, are eternally binding. Civil laws (e.g., Exod. 21–23), although they may illustrate moral law, were limited historically to the theocratic state of Israel and are not binding on the church. Ceremonial laws (e.g., sacrifices) were intended to prefigure Christ, and ceased to be applicable upon his first advent. A problem with this approach is that the categories "moral, civil, and ceremonial" are artificial. There is often a mixture of these categories: the ceremonial sabbath among "moral" laws (Exod. 20:8), ceremonial food regulations among "civil" laws (Exod. 21:28; 22:31), "moral" motivations in civil laws (Exod. 22:21, 26–27) and in cultic laws (Exod. 20:26). There is considerable subjectivity in labeling laws as "moral," "civil," or "ceremonial."

Another approach is that of theonomy or Christian reconstructionism. Theonomists wish to work toward a theocratic state where Mosaic civil laws can again be instituted into modern society. However, this approach takes insufficient account of the new theological and cultural setting of the new covenant. Some laws became impractical and unenforceable if applied literally even in Old Testament times. The Year of Jubilee regulations, requiring the return of property to original families every forty-nine years, seem *never* to have been enforced as law because (among other reasons) by the time Israel controlled the land, there were no records of the original owners. Moreover, although Jubilee was a practical solution for a tribal, agricultural society, this model would already be somewhat antiquated under Israel's urbanization during the monarchy, and is certainly impractical in modern, mobile, urban societies. Some laws assume the existence of conditions such as debt slavery (Exod. 21:2–11), specific species of animals (Exod. 29:22–fat tail sheep), or the climate of Palestine (feast held at end of harvest season, Lev. 23:33–39), which make these laws inapplicable in other cultural environments. Some laws seem tied to the specific theological context of the Old Testament. The death penalty for cultic offenses was based on the special holiness of Israel with the tabernacle of God among them. Violation could bring immediate wrath upon the people. However, the church is not a nation, and does not camp around the tabernacle.

Usage of Old Testament laws suggests that biblical authors sought out and applied the inherent religious and moral principles in the laws even when changed historical, cultural, and theological settings made literal application inappropriate. Ezra applied a law prohibiting marriage to Canaanites, who had ceased to exist historically, broadly to marriage with non-Canaanite foreigners, because *in that situation* the same principle (marriage to foreigners leads to religious assimilation) applied, even though the letter of the law could not (Ezra 9:1–2; cf. Deut. 7:1–5).

The New Testament writers also apply the principles in the law. From Deuteronomy 25:4 ("Do not muzzle an ox while it is treading out grain"), Paul derives a principle that workers ought to be rewarded for their labors and applies that principle in the case of Christian workers (1 Cor. 9:9–14). In 1 Timothy 5:18, Paul again quotes Deuteronomy 25:4, this time in parallel with a saying of Jesus (Matt. 10:10) as if both are equally authoritative. Likewise, the principle of establishing truth by two or three witnesses (Deut. 19:15), originally limited to courts, is applied more broadly to a church conference (2 Cor. 13:1). The principle that believers are not to be unequally yoked together with unbelievers is derived from a law concerning the yoking animals (2 Cor. 6:14; cf. Deut. 22:10).

In 1 Corinthians 5:1–5, 13, Paul affirms on the basis of Leviticus 18:29 that incest, a capital offense in the Old Testament, is immoral and deserves punishment. A person practicing incest in the church must be excommunicated to maintain the church's practical holiness. Paul maintains the law's moral principle, yet in view of the changed redemptive setting, makes no attempt to apply the law's original sanction.

The Law and the Christian Today. Mosaic law is of value for the Christian in several ways.

The Law Prepares Sinners for the Gospel. No one can receive eternal salvation by works of the law (Gal. 2:16) because none perfectly keeps the law (Rom. 3:23), and violation of any part of it makes one guilty of the whole (James 2:10; cf. Rom. 2:25; Gal. 3:10). Instead, salvation is a gift obtained by faith, not works (Rom. 4:4–5; Eph. 2:8–10; Phil. 3:9). Nonetheless, the law was meant to lead us to Christ (Gal. 3:24). It makes the sinner conscious of sin (Rom. 3:20; 7:7; 1 John 3:4). It provokes and incites rebellion (Rom. 5:20; 7:13), thereby making one fully accountable before God for violation of God's moral requirements (Rom. 3:19; 4:15; 5:13; 7:8–10). By this means, the law shows sinners their need for a mediator to redeem them from the law's condemnation (Gal. 3:13). Hence, the law is an essential prerequisite in preparing sinners for the gospel.

The Law Is a Guide for Christian Living. The believer, through the Spirit, keeps the righteousness requirements of the law (Rom. 8:3–4), following the principle of love which is the fulfillment of the law (Rom. 13:8–10; Gal. 5:14; Mark 12:31, cf. Lev. 19:18). As the New Testament use of Old Testament laws shows, the moral aspect of the law continues to define proper and improper behavior for Christians. Old Testament laws supplement New Testament morality by addressing some issues not directly treated in the New Testament. God's commandments were intended to bring life (Rom. 7:10), and the promises of life associated with the law remain applicable (Eph. 6:2–3; cf. Exod. 20:12).

The Law Is of Value for Jurisprudence. Law, when enforced by the state, serves to restrain evildoers (1 Tim. 1:9–10). Biblical civil laws, although not directly applicable under the new covenant, are at least suggestive for improving modern jurisprudence. The Bible treats theft and manslaughter as torts against the victim (or the victim's family) rather than crimes against the state, and requires monetary restitution to the victim's family rather than imprisonment or fines to the state. This is arguably superior to the modern system where victims often get nothing, and where incarceration is ineffective for rehabilitation and extraordinarily expensive. The capital offenses in the Bible are suggestive for what crimes might legitimately be permitted as capital offenses for today (e.g., intentional murder), and crimes that should never be capital offenses (e.g., crimes of property).

The Law Points Typologically to Christ. The laws foreshadow Christ typologically in many ways. Moral and civil laws reflect the righteousness of Christ and his kingdom, while the cultic laws emphasize his holiness. The tabernacle prefigures the presence of Christ among his people; the sacrifices foreshadow the sacrifice of Christ on the cross. The priesthood anticipates Jesus' priestly function. The whole cultic system with tabernacle, sacrifices, and priests prefigures union with Christ through the atonement. The penalties in the law anticipate Christ's judgments; the annihilation of the Canaanites anticipates the judgment of hell. Commands concerning occupying the promised land anticipate the future kingdom of God, heaven and the blessings in Christ himself.

JOE M. SPRINKLE

See also COMMAND, COMMANDMENT; DECREES; ORDINANCE; REQUIREMENT; STATUTE; TEN COMMANDMENTS.

Bibliography. G. Bahnsen, *Theonomy in Christian Ethics;* W. S. Barker and W. R. Godfrey, eds., *Theonomy: A Reformed Critique;* H. J. Boecker, *Law and the Administration of Justice in the Old Testament and the Ancient Near East;* U. Cassuto, *A Commentary on the Book of Exodus;* D. A. Dorsey, *JETS* 34/3 (Sept. 1991): 321–34; H.-H. Esser, *NIDNTT* 2:438–51; M. Greenberg, *Yehezkel Kaufmann Jubilee Volume,* pp. 3–28; idem, *Studies in Bible: 1986,* pp. 3–28; idem, *Religion and Law,* pp. 101–12,

120–25; H. W. House and T. Ice, *Dominion Theology: A Blessing or a Curse?;* W. C. Kaiser, Jr., *Toward Old Testament Ethics;* idem, *JETS* 33/3 (Sept. 1990): 289–302; G. E. Mendenhall, *Religion and Law,* pp. 85–100; Dale Patrick, *Old Testament Law;* V. Poythress, *The Shadow of Christ in the Law of Moses;* R. J. Rushdooney, *The Institutes of Biblical Law;* R. Sonsino, *Judaism* 33 (1984): 202–9; J. Sprinkle, *A Literary Approach to Biblical Law: Exodus* 20:22–23:19.

Law of Christ. The phrase "the law of Christ" appears only in Galatians 6:2, although it is implied by the wording of 1 Corinthians 9:21 as well. In both places, its precise meaning is difficult to fix. In Galatians, Paul argues vigorously that the law given at Sinai makes no claim on those who believe in Christ, whether Gentile or Jew (2:15–21; 3:10–14, 23–26; 4:4–5; 4:21–5:6). He then appeals to the Galatians to engage in ethical behavior by walking in the Spirit (5:16), being lead by the Spirit (5:18), and fulfilling "the law of Christ" (*ho nomos tou Christou*) through bearing one another's burdens (6:2). In 1 Corinthians 9 Paul demonstrates how Christians should, out of love for the weaker brother or sister, refrain from demanding their rights. By way of illustration Paul says in verses 19–23 that he adopts certain Jewish customs when among Jews, although he is not under the Jewish law, and that he adopts some Gentile customs when among Gentiles, although he is not without the law of God but rather "in the law of Christ" (*ennomos Christou*).

It seems fairly clear from these two texts that Paul uses the phrase to mean something other than the law given to Israel at Sinai and considered by most Jews to be their special possession.

Help is found in the prophets. In Isaiah 42:1–4 we read that God's chosen servant will one day establish justice throughout the earth and that "the coastlands will wait expectantly for His law" (NASB). If we take this passage to refer to the Messiah, then we could paraphrase it by saying that the Christ, when he comes, will teach God's law to the Gentiles ("the coastlands"). Jeremiah 31:31–34 similarly predicts the coming of a time in which disobedient Israel will receive a new covenant, consisting of a law written on the heart and therefore obeyed (cf. Ezek. 36:26–27).

Jesus' teaching, although standing in continuity with the law given at Sinai, nevertheless sovereignly fashions a new law. In some instances Jesus sharpens commandments (Matt. 5:17–48) and in others considers them obsolete (Mark 7:17–19). On one occasion, having been asked to identify the greatest commandment, Jesus concurs with the Jewish wisdom of his time (Mark 12:32–33) that the greatest commandments are to love God supremely and to love one's neighbor as oneself (Mark 12:28–31). He breaks with tradition, however, by defining the term "neighbor" to mean even the despised Samaritan (Luke 10:29–37).

Paul believed that the life, death, and resurrection of Jesus Christ marked the beginning point of God's new covenant (2 Cor. 3:1–18; Gal. 4:21–31; cf. Rom. 8:2). Like Isaiah, he believed that this covenant included the Gentiles (Gal. 3:7–20), and like Jeremiah he believed that it offered Israel a remedy for the curse that the old Sinaitic covenant pronounced on Israel's disobedience (Gal. 3:10–13). In light of this, Paul may have understood the teaching of Christ as a new law. If so, then the correspondence between the ethical teaching of Jesus and Paul on many points (e.g., 1 Cor. 7:10–11/Mark 10:2–9; 1 Cor. 9:14/Luke 10:7; Rom. 14:1–23/Mark 7:18–19) is a matter of Paul's intention rather than happy accident. Paul's own admonition to fulfill the law of Christ by bearing one another's burdens provides both a pithy restatement of Jesus' summary of the law and an indication that Jesus' teaching fulfills prophetic expectations. FRANK THIELMAN

See also GALATIANS, THEOLOGY OF; PAUL THE APOSTLE.

Bibliography. C. H. Dodd, *More New Testament Studies;* R. N. Longenecker, *Paul, Apostle of Liberty;* W. D. Davies, *Paul and Rabbinic Judaism;* S. Westerholm, *Israel's Law and the Church's Faith.*

Lawlessness. ***The Old Testament.*** The concept of lawlessness comes to expression frequently in the Old Testament through more than twenty Hebrew terms (all of which the Septuagint translates with *anomia*). Although the Greek term *anomia,* which translates all of these terms in the Septuagint, might lead one to suspect that breaking of the Mosaic Law (*ho nomos*) is primarily in view, the more general idea of iniquity or of acts that reflect rebellion against God is the basic one. The law as such may be the criterion or standard for determining what constitutes lawlessness (as with sin in general), but at its root lawlessness is rebellion against God, whether viewed as the condition of one's life or as specific acts that demonstrate a determined refusal to acknowledge God.

The New Testament. These same ideas are in view in the New Testament's development of lawlessness (*anomia*). The unique circumstances that these writings address, however, called forth additional reflection that both confirms and enlarges on the picture drawn from the Old Testament evidence.

The Relation of Lawlessness to Sin. First John 3:4 is perhaps the classic statement of the relation of lawlessness and sin. In asserting that "Everyone who sins breaks the law; in fact, sin is lawlessness" the author was probably correcting a misconception about sin that had crept into the community through false teaching. Sin was being disregarded or trivialized, and 3:4 counters by defining it in terms of lawlessness. Sin is thus an act of rebellion against God, and cannot be thought of as harmless, neutral, or imaginary. Through the category of lawlessness, John clarifies that one cannot sin without declaring oneself to be in direct opposition to God. Romans 4:7 (quoting Ps. 32:1; see also Num. 14:18) makes the same connection between sin and acts of lawlessness. Together with passages such as Titus 2:14 and Hebrews 10:17, Romans 4:7 indicates that acts of lawlessness and the rebellious condition of fallen humankind that issues in these acts stand in need of God's forgiveness. Receiving the righteousness of God depends on being forgiven.

Lawlessness and Righteousness. In Romans 6:19, 2 Corinthians 6:14, and Hebrews 1:9, "lawlessness" as a state or condition is contrasted with righteousness. Righteousness is the condition characteristic of faith, while lawlessness is the condition characteristic of unbelief. As the contrast continues, it becomes clear that the two categories have nothing in common; they are as different as light and darkness. Moreover, as Hebrews 1:9 (quoting Ps. 45:7) reveals, the Son distinguishes himself in manifesting the attitude of God toward these two states: he hates lawlessness but loves righteousness. Lawlessness is the state defined by sin and sinning; righteousness, both declared and bestowed by God on believers, creates the possibilities of obedience and holiness. Finally, Romans 6:19 makes it clear that the Christian has a conscious choice to make: to live in the condition of lawlessness and do its deeds, or to serve righteousness and do its deeds.

Lawlessness as Acts of Sin. By means of the concept of "doing lawlessness" (Matt. 7:23; 13:41; cf. 1 John 3:4), lawlessness takes the meaning of deeds of lawlessness (cf. Matt. 24:12; Titus 2:14). They are deeds that manifest rebellion against God. To be "full of lawlessness" (Matt. 23:28) is to lead a life characterized by wrongdoing.

Lawlessness and the Eschatological Rebellion against God. What is perhaps the most striking development in the biblical concept of lawlessness comes through a series of New Testament passages that view rebellion against God as an eschatological characteristic. The preparation for this application of the concept might be descriptions of the rebellious posture of God's enemies in the final battle in some of the extracanonical writings of Judaism (see Testament of Dan. 5:4–5; Testament of Naphtali 4:1; 1QS 1:23–24; 3:18–21; 4:19–20). On the one hand, the occurrences in Matthew are particularly related to the persistent refusal to accept the Messiah on God's terms and to harassment of God's people by those in opposition. The setting is either the final judgment (7:23; 13:41; 23:28) or the last stage of history when lawlessness is to reach an unprecedented height (24:12). Thus, lawlessness comes to be seen in direct connection with opposition to the Messiah and his message. This connection is completed in the description in 2 Thess. 2:3, 7 of the eschatological "man of lawlessness," who will lead the final rebellion against God that will precede Christ's second coming. In this figure the rebellion that has exerted itself against God's will in every age reaches its height in the last day.

By bringing Johannine and Pauline teaching on lawlessness together, we can see how the concept serves to underline the seriousness of sin for the individual. Any sin, no matter how inconsequential it might seem, is the acting out of rebellion against God. This rebellion apparently draws its strength from spiritual forces opposed to God—John's antichrists—which, John tells us, are already active and whose opposition, Paul tells us, will reach a crescendo in the end, just before Christ's return. People always have the possibility to opt out of this rebellion, but it requires receiving forgiveness from God. The choice to decide between righteousness and lawlessness is one that believers continually face. Understanding lawlessness as rebellion and as the opposite of righteousness allows us to see that at the practical level it is ultimately a question of taking sides. Moreover, the decision taken is one that has eternal consequences: salvation or judgment. PHILIP H. TOWNER

See also SIN.

Bibliography. H.-H. Esser, *NIDNTT,* 2:436–50; H. Kleinknecht and W. Gutbrod, *TDNT,* 4:1022–91; L. Morris, *The Epistles of Paul to the Thessalonians;* I. de la Potterie and S. Lyonnet, *The Christian Lives by the Spirit;* A. Wanamaker, *Commentary on 1 & 2 Thessalonians.*

Laying on of Hands. The Bible frequently invests this simple gesture with weighty symbolism. Its significance can be fruitfully evaluated in connection with four concepts: blessing, miraculous power, separation, and the coming of the Holy Spirit.

Although the imposition of hands accompanies the pronouncement of blessing relatively infrequently in Scripture, the association occurs with remarkable consistency. Just as Jacob blesses Joseph's children by the imposition of hands (Gen. 48:14), so Jesus takes little children in his arms, places his hands on them, and blesses them (Mark 10:13–15; cf. Matt. 19:13–15). Related to these passages are those that speak of the high priest raising his hands over the people in order to bless them (Lev. 9:22), a pattern Jesus follows when he, perhaps acting as the great high priest, blesses his followers immediately before his ascension (Luke 24:50).

Jesus and his followers also frequently placed their hands on those whom they intended to heal by miraculous power. Although the term "blessing" does not appear in these contexts, certainly those who experienced these healings understood in an especially powerful way the benediction of

God's favor (Mark 5:23; 7:32; 8:23–25; Luke 4:40; 13:13; Acts 9:12, 17; 28:8; cf. 5:12).

Often the imposition of hands is associated not with blessing but with separation from the larger group. Thus in the Old Testament hands are imposed on sacrificial animals in order to set them apart for a special purpose (Exod. 29:10, 15, 19, 33; Lev. 1:4; 4:4, 15, 24; 8:14, 18, 22; 16:21; Num. 8:5–15; 2 Chron. 29:3). The notion of separation for an uncommon purpose probably also lies behind the imposition of hands on the Levites during their ceremony of consecration (Num. 8:5–15) and behind Moses' imposition of hands on Joshua during the ritual in which he was designated as Moses' successor (Num. 27:18–23; cf. Deut. 34:9).

The concept of separation may explain references to the laying on of hands in Acts and the Epistles as well. The gesture was included in the ceremony that separated seven gifted men from the rest of the early Jerusalem church for the task of overseeing the distribution of food to those in need (Acts 6:3–6). Similarly the prophets and teachers of the church at Antioch laid their hands on Saul and Barnabas in order to "separate" them for their ground-breaking mission work (Acts 13:3). In view of the critical nature of the tasks for which the imposition of hands set people apart, Paul naturally wanted Timothy to avoid laying hands on people too quickly as a precaution against putting people in charge of tasks for which they were not qualified (1 Tim. 5:22; cf. Heb. 6:2).

The concept of separation may also explain why the imposition of hands occurs so frequently (although not invariably) in connection with the coming of the Holy Spirit or with the giving of the gifts that the Spirit distributes (Acts 8:17–19; 19:6; cf. 1 Tim. 4:14; 2 Tim. 1:6). Since God's Spirit is the Spirit that sanctifies or sets apart (hence the term "*Holy* Spirit"), it inevitably separates those on whom it falls from the world around them. Moreover, by the gifts it distributes, God's Spirit separates some from others within the church for special tasks.

There is a sense in which the idea of separation for a special purpose, so clearly visible in many instances, binds together all the occurrences of the phrase. Even in the context of formal blessings and astonishing miracles, the imposition of hands signifies the separation of a person, a people, or even a bodily part (Mark 8:25) as the recipient of an unusual manifestation of God's grace.

FRANK THIELMAN

Bibliography. E. Lohse, *TDNT,* 9:428–29, 431–34; M. H. Shepherd, *IDB*, 2:521–22; M. Warkentin, *Ordination: A Biblical-Historical View.*

Leadership. ***The Old Testament.*** In the earliest days of the Old Testament, leadership of the people of God was by the family head or patriarch, to whom God spoke his messages.

Civil Leaders. By the time of the exodus, tribal elders were on the scene. We're not told how they were appointed. They served as representatives for the whole nation (Exod. 3:16; 4:29; 12:21), but without any apparent initiative or governing power. On occasion Moses was told by God to assemble them to impart to them, and through them to the people, God's message (Exod. 3:16; 4:29; 12:21; 19:7; Josh. 24:1). They accompanied Moses and Joshua following the sins of Dathan and Abiram (Num. 16:25) and Achan (Josh. 7:6). Moses selected seventy of them to be specially endued with God's Spirit to help share the burden of the people (Num. 11:16–17). By the time of the judges and the monarchy there were elders of Israel who met for common decisions, such as the appointment of a king. There were elders in the individual towns (Judg. 11:3–11; 1 Sam. 16:4; 30:26–31; 1 Kings 21:8, 11). First Samuel 30:26–31 indicates that the elders of Judah were comprised of the elders of the individual towns, though later Ezekiel speaks of "seventy elders of Israel" (8:11–12). The local elders were responsible for legal action at the city gate (Deut. 22:15; 25:7; Ruth 4:1–11) in cases of murder (Deut. 19:11–13; 21:1–9) and in cases dealing with family matters (21:18–21; 22:13–21; 25:5–10).

During the exile there were still elders in Judah (Ezek. 8:11–12). They opposed Jehoiakim, and pled with the people on Jeremiah's behalf (Jer. 26:17). In exile also there were elders heading up the community (Jer. 29:1; Ezek. 8:1; 14:1; 20:1, 3). The elders stood at the head of the people in the rebuilding of the temple and even in dealings with the Persian government (Ezra 5:9; 6:7, 8, 14). The system of city elders is evidenced with Ezra resolved to excommunicate those who had married foreign wives (Ezra 10:8, 14). By Nehemiah's time the elders are referred to as the nobility (Neh. 2:16; 4:14, 19; 5:7; 7:5).

The call for a king came from the people toward the end of Samuel's judgeship. The people were no longer satisfied to have God as their King, and God viewed their request as a rejection of himself (1 Sam. 8:7; 12:12). In the end God told Samuel to listen to the people. He anointed Saul and told him that he was anointed by the Lord (10:1; cf. 12:13). Three subsequent errors on Saul's part (chaps. 13, 14, 15) showed that his heart had become proud (15:17) and he no longer fully obeyed the Lord. The Lord regretted having made him king, and Saul's kingdom was not established forever as it might otherwise have been (13:13).

In Saul's place God had Samuel anoint David, a man whose perspective was in line with God's (13:14). With him God made a covenant forever that forecast that any well-being would be by his appointment, and that any necessary correction he would accomplish through their enemies (2 Sam. 7:9–16). Care had been taken already in

Deuteronomy to warn future kings against self-indulgence, against lifting themselves up above their fellow countrymen. Pride spelled ruin. On the positive side faith, along with obedience, was determinative for success (Deut. 17:14–20). These were the terms of the theocracy. David's son, Solomon, began to rule following his father's footsteps, but in the course of his reign he multiplied for himself horses, wives, and silver and gold—all three areas against which Deuteronomy had sounded a warning. His foreign wives turned him away from trusting in God, and for this the Lord said he would tear from him the kingdom and give it to his servant, leaving him but one tribe for his father's sake (1 Kings 11:1–13; cf. chap. 12).

The chronicler is especially careful to point out how the successors in David's line failed to meet the terms of the theocracy. For example, through a prophet Asa was told that if he sought the Lord, he would let him find him; but if he forsook God, God would forsake him (2 Chron. 15:2). Hezekiah sought the Lord with all his heart and prospered (31:21)—until he became proud (32:25). Subsequent humbling postponed God's wrath during Hezekiah's time (32:26), as it did again near the end of Manasseh's wicked reign (33:9–19). In summary, God warned the kings again and again for their unfaithfulness, sending them his messengers, the prophets, but they did not listen until finally God moved in wrath to judge them at the hands of the Babylonians (36:12–16).

When the ten northern tribes seceded from Judah the Davidic covenant did not apply to their kings, but the issue of obedience as outlined in Deuteronomy still obtained. Jeroboam, their first king, set up the calf cult at Dan and Bethel. For this his own family line was blotted off the face of the earth (1 Kings 13:33–34), and for this eventually the whole kingdom went into captivity (2 Kings 17:16–18). The kings who followed Jeroboam persisted in his ungodly direction.

After Jerusalem fell to the Babylonians, Judah was ruled by governors chosen by Babylon and then Persia, some at least from Judean royal blood (Gedaliah, 2 Kings 25:22; Zerubbabel, 1 Chron. 3:10–19). Not that this was so different from the situation just prior to Jerusalem's fall—the kings then, too, sere set up and removed at the will of foreign powers, Jehoiakim favored over his brother by Egypt and Zedekiah over his nephew by Babylon (2 Chron. 36:3, 10). Nehemiah's lineage is not recorded. He was recognized by the Persian king for his faithful service as his cupbearer and for his concern for his own people back in Jerusalem. Faith and obedience were still integral to God's blessing on leadership.

Charismatic Leaders. The Old Testament leader par excellence was Moses. Unlike others, God spoke mouth to mouth to him (Num. 12:6–8). At the age of forty he expected that his people would recognize him as God's appointed leader to bring their deliverance, but this first initiative was prematurely aborted and he fled the country (Acts 7:23–29). Forty years later he was clearly called of God, and this time he returned to Egypt and first gained the support of the elders of Israel (Exod. 4:29–31). Through signs and wonders his own people and also the people of Egypt came to recognize him as God's man. At Sinai the Law and the tabernacle instructions were given to Moses to pass along to the people. He acted on behalf of God at the installation of Aaron and his sons to the priesthood. On occasion God needed to vindicate Moses' leadership before the people (Exod. 16; Num. 12–13). God viewed their grumbling against Moses as grumbling against himself (Exod. 16:7–8). Conversely, Moses was held accountable when he broke faith and did not represent God as holy in the sight of the people (Num. 20:12). For this he was disallowed entrance into the promised land. He did actively prepare a successor, Joshua, and the people to accept him as their leader under God (Deut. 31:2–8).

Joshua began his term of leadership with a challenge from God to take courage. If he obeyed carefully God would grant him success in taking over the land of the Canaanites (Josh. 1:2–9). Having accomplished that goal by the end of his life, he apparently did not see a need to prepare a successor.

The judges were charismatic leaders raised up by God (Judg. 2:16) to deliver his people. Their work was both military and supervisory in kind, and though not all were involved in the military, this is the aspect that comprises much of the biblical record and therefore for which they are best known. Likely their supervisory activities normally resulted from their military success (Deborah is an exception). The judges seem to have been engaged in supervisory activity; no military involvement is mentioned for four of them. Their area of jurisdiction was local, sometimes extending to several tribes, and their judgeships apparently overlapped (e.g., Jephthah and Samson, Judg. 10:7). Though the law did not prescribe the office of judge, it was approved by God for Scripture regularly states that he raised up the judge (Judg. 3:9, 15, etc.), and at least four were specially enabled by the Holy Spirit (3:10; 6:34; 11:29; 13:25; 14:6, 19; 15:14). None of them appointed successors to carry on their work. In the two instances where sons attempted to carry on in their father's footsteps, they did not succeed (Gideon's son, Abimelech; Samuel's sons).

Jeremiah 18:18 speaks of the priests, the prophets, and the counselors. At David's court there were permanent counselors (1 Chron. 27:32–33). These men were recognized and chosen for their wisdom. It was said of Ahithophel that his advice was as if one inquired of the word of God.

The prophets/prophetesses were God's mouth to the people similarly as Aaron was Moses' mouth (Exod. 4:16). They spoke out to kings, princes, priests, false prophets, and people, and even to the nations. Elisha took God's message to Syria (2 Kings 8), Jonah to Nineveh, and Ezekiel preached among the exiles in Babylon. But most of their attention was focused on Israel. God sent prophets to sound a warning before the northern kingdom fell to Assyria (Amos, Hosea, Isaiah, Micah) and before Babylon took Judah (Zephaniah, Habakkuk, Jeremiah, Ezekiel). Since these recorded their messages future generations had to take notice that they had been warned.

How the prophets were received was in direct proportion to the Godward bent of their audience, the rulers in particular. Samuel's influence with the people was strong enough that Saul didn't think of harming him. David bowed to Nathan's condemnation. Isaiah and Hezekiah worked well together, Jeremiah mourned Josiah's death, and Haggai and Zechariah collaborated with Zerubbabel to get the temple rebuilt. But others fared worse, for example, Elijah with Ahab and Jezebel, Amos with Jeroboam and Amaziah, priest of the Bethel calf cult, and Jeremiah with Josiah's three reigning sons and grandson. It's difficult to be a leader if the people are unwilling to follow.

Religious Leaders. The official leaders in Israel were the priests, headed by the high priest. Their office was hereditary, with the eldest living son of the high priest continuing his father's position. While God charged all Israel to be a people that functioned in a priestly ministry to the world (Exod. 19:6), it was Aaron and his family who were consecrated to do the service at the tabernacle (Lev. 8). Their ordination ceremony was repeated on seven successive days—surely an indication to all that they were specially set apart for their priestly ministry.

The functions of the priests were several. Primarily they were to mediate between God and man. By officiating in the offerings God had prescribed, they led the people in acquiring atonement for their sin. Second, in their person and in their dress they were to represent the holiness of God to the people. Their garments were "for glory and for beauty," the high priest's especially, and on his mitre was a gold band engraved "holiness to Yahweh" (Exod. 28:2, 36). Conversely when he represented the people to God on the Day of Atonement, he donned plain white garments. Physical wholeness and exemplary conduct were requisites for the priesthood (Lev. 21–22:9). Third, the priests were to render the will of God by means of the Urim and Thummim worn by the high priest in his breastplate (Num. 27:21). Finally, it was their responsibility to instruct the laity in the distinction between holy and profane, clean and unclean (Lev. 10:10–11).

From the day of the first Passover in Egypt the firstborn of every household specially belonged to God. After the golden calf incident it was the tribe of Levi who stood out to count themselves on the Lord's side (Exod. 32:26), and thereafter they took the place of the firstborn (Num. 8:14–19). At their induction they were sprinkled and offered as a wave offering—a kind of living sacrifice.

Their function was twofold. They were to assist their brothers, the priests, in the service of the tabernacle from age thirty to fifty (4:3). Second, they were to keep watch over the tabernacle—that is, in effect, to do guard duty from the age of one month old and upward by living around the tabernacle. Their dwellings thus formed the buffer zone to prevent others from incurring God's wrath by approaching too nearly to this holy spot (1:53; 3:28; 8:19).

The New Testament. In New Testament times there were no longer the civil leaders of the Old Testament theocracy. There were official religious leaders, but their office was no longer hereditary. And there were charismatic religious leaders, though none of these bore the prominence of the prophet-statesmen of the Old Testament. This may be explained by the fact that the official leaders were to be chosen on recognition of their godliness and gifts, quite a different system than the Old Testament priesthood. The Jewish priesthood continued in New Testament times, but the church and its government evolved outside the purview of Judaism. In fact, the New Testament seems to have resisted using clerical words for their ministers.

Religious Leaders. The twelve apostles were chosen not in recognition of special spiritual endowment but solely on Jesus' initiative. Their purpose was to be with him and then to go out to preach (Mark 3:14) and to do miracles (Matt. 10:7). After the ascension those Twelve who had been closest to Jesus during his life now became his representatives, assuming an authoritative position in the company of Christians. New converts early came under their teaching ministry (Acts 2:42). They continued to do miracles of healing and exorcism of demons (Acts 5:12; 2 Cor. 12:12). Administratively they oversaw the common fund (Acts 4:37—until the job was too big and was transferred to others [6:1–6]). They exercised discipline on occasion (5:1–11) and likely led in the celebration of the Lord's Supper. When problems arose they took the lead in their resolution, including the elders in the process. With the church expanding to other areas their attention involved the oversight of those groups also (8:14; 9:32). Galatians 1:19 assumes that most of them are out of town (Jerusalem), presumably on missionary endeavors. Their commitment was to the congregation of believers, not to Peter.

The substitute for Judas was chosen by lot under the direction of the Holy Spirit and also with the qualification of being an eyewitness from John's baptism till the ascension (Acts

1:21–22). After this no effort was made to select successors for those who died (12:2).

As the apostles and missionary prophets and teachers died off or moved on, there was left a need for someone or some persons to be the focal point for the community life of the local group of believers. These leaders were referred to as *presbuteroi* (elders) and *episkopoi* (overseers/bishops). Paul spoke to the Ephesian elders to shepherd the flock over which God's Spirit had made them overseers (Acts 20:28), yet in verse 17 they are called elders. Their status was "elder" and their job was to oversee.

The elders are first mentioned in Acts 11:30. In the narrative concerning the Council in Jerusalem they are always named in conjunction with the apostles as the decision makers (15:2, 4, 6, 22–23). They functioned as a supreme court for the entire church. Out beyond Jerusalem elders were appointed in the churches founded by Paul and Barnabas already on their first missionary journey (14:23; cf. Titus 1:5–9).

The episcopate was a distinct office that one might seek (1 Tim. 3:1) and that was to be done voluntarily and eagerly, not for gain. The qualifications were listed, though not the duties. Moral reliability came first—the overseer needed to live an honorable and exemplary life, avoiding excesses. Then there must be proof in his own home of his ability to lead the life of the congregation—high value was placed on a well-ordered and hospitable home. The overseer should be an apt teacher. He must be mature and not susceptible to pride, which comes all too naturally to those who do well. Finally, he must be without reproach according to the standards of the non-Christian world so as to be kept away from scandal.

In the first mention of persons called deacons (Phil. 1:1), we find them linked with the overseers and mentioned after them. Their qualifications are listed in 1 Timothy 3 after those of the overseer. The second listing is evidence that the two are distinct offices. While many qualifications are the same for both, the deacons need not be apt to teach, but are not to be double-tongued or greedy—qualities very apt for those who visit in many homes and who have the administration of funds. Their capacity to serve as deacons was a gift from God (1 Cor. 12:28). Their function seems to carry through the original meaning of their name (*didaskein,* "to wait at table") as it is used in Acts 6:2. There the Twelve led the congregation to select seven men for that job (though Stephen and Philip at least were also known as preachers and teachers of the Word). The church seems to use this term to express generally the same love and care of others. In the early Jerusalem church the apostles yet carried out the functions that would be taken up by the overseers/elders, and accordingly the need for deacons became the first obvious vacancy in church community leadership.

Along with the deacons there were also deaconesses—the first mentioned is Phoebe (Rom. 16:1). The question is open whether she served in the office of deaconess or whether her service to the church community is simply being referred to. Likewise it is not clear whether 1 Timothy 3:11 refers to deaconesses or to the wives of deacons.

Charismatic Leaders. In the New Testament there is not a clear delineation between official leaders and charismatic leaders for the office was by the very nature of it intended for persons who were recognized for, among other qualifications, their spiritual gifts.

Though prophets ranked in importance second only to the apostles (1 Cor. 12:28–31; Eph. 4:11), none carried the role of statesmen as did Samuel, Elijah, Isaiah, and Jeremiah. The prophets' ministry included revelation (1 Cor. 14:29–32), prediction, identifying individuals for specific ministry (Acts 13:1–3), and bestowing on them the spiritual gifts that would enable them to carry out these tasks (1 Tim. 4:14). Prophecy was intended for the edification, exhortation, and consolation of the church community (1 Cor. 14:3; cf. Acts 15:32).

Theological Dimensions of Leadership in the Bible. The Scriptures indicate that there is no authority except what has been established by God (Rom. 13:1). He sets over the realm of humankind whomever he wishes (Dan. 4:32; 5:21) to be his minister to us for good. Moses and Joshua were assigned their leadership by God (Exod. 4; Josh. 1); Aaron and his sons were singled out for the priesthood (Exod. 28:1); the judges were raised up by God (Judg. 2:16). Saul was anointed by the Lord (1 Sam. 10:1); David and his line were chosen by God (13:14; 2 Sam. 7); the prophets were called of God, like the apostles. The capacity to serve in the church is described as a gift from God (1 Cor. 12:28). Promotion, and by inference the absence of it, comes neither from the east nor from the west but from the Lord (Ps. 75:6–7).

The role of leadership was not intended for self-advantage but for service (Luke 22:26). Accordingly Israel's kings were not to lift themselves up above their countrymen (Deut. 17:20). Paul saw his apostleship as a call to sacrificial labor rather than an occasion for glorying in the office (1 Cor. 15:9–10). The elders were to shepherd the flock—to care self-sacrificially for the souls of the faithful, giving account to God (Heb. 13:17; 1 Peter 5:2–3). Gifts were to be used in serving one another as good stewards of God's grace (4:10). When Korah was not content to serve in the secondary role of leadership appointed him, he was rebuked and judged (Num. 16:9–33). James and John likewise needed to learn the humility of serving (Mark 10:35–45).

Leaders are accountable to God (Heb. 13:17). The maxim "to whom much has been given will much be required" (Luke 12:48) is nowhere more evident than in Moses' disobedience at Meribah (Num. 20:12). The same maxim was applied to teachers in the New Testament (James 3:1). David Hildebrand

See also Apostle; Church, the; Deacon, Deaconess; Elder; Israel; King, Kingship; Overseer.

Bibliography. H. W. Beyer, *TDNT,* 2:81–93, 599–622; K. O. Gangel, *Chr Ed Jour* 12 (1991): 13–31; E. F. Harrison, *EDT,* pp. 70–72; G. W. Knight, *Cov Sem Rev.* 1 (1975): 111–16; A. Lamorte and G. F. Hawthorne, *EDT,* 2:86–87; W. H. Mare, *JETS* 13(1970): 229–39.

Leaven. In the New Testament the noun for "leaven" is *zumē* and the verb for "to leaven" is *zumoō*. The noun occurs eleven times, and the verb four times. There are, however, really only three distinct uses of "leaven" in the New Testament.

The first occurrence is in the parable of the leaven (Matt. 13:33; Luke 13:20–21). This parable teaches that the reign of God is like what happens when leaven permeates a batch of dough. Jesus' point is that the small, insignificant beginnings of God's reign in himself will one day be great. Although the parable does not describe how this will happen, it alludes to Jesus' future reign as the Son of Man.

The second occurrence of "leaven" is Jesus' warning to his disciples (Matt. 16:5–12; Mark 8:15; Luke 12:1–12). Mark (8:11–15) presents Jesus' warning following the Pharisees' questioning of Jesus about a sign from heaven. After Jesus' curt statement that no sign will be given to this generation, he and his disciples sail across the Sea of Galilee. In the boat Jesus warns them about leaven, really meaning the attitude or perspective of the Pharisees and Herod. In the ensuing discussion (8:16–21) it is apparent that the attitude that Jesus is warning about is that of blindness toward his identity as the Messiah. He repeatedly asks them, "Do you still not understand?" (8:21). And significantly, after Jesus performs a second remarkable process miracle of Jesus' healing the blind man (vv. 22–26—the first was 7:31–37), Peter "finally" confesses that Jesus is the Messiah (8:27–30). For Mark, then, leaven stands for the obdurate refusal to perceive that Jesus is the Messiah.

Matthew (16:1–6) presents Jesus' warning in the same context as Mark, but brings out some distinctive nuances. Matthew records that Jesus' response to the questioning of the Pharisees and Sadducees included some symbolic discussion about weather and a reference to "the sign of Jonah" (v. 4). Then, in the following discussion with his disciples after they have reached the other side, Jesus warns against the leaven of the Pharisees and Sadducees. Matthew clarifies with Jesus' statement (v. 12) that the disciples finally understood that Jesus was referring to the teaching (*didachē*) of the Pharisees and Sadducees. Matthew does not record either process miracle, but immediately narrates the confession of Peter that Jesus is the Messiah. The way Matthew presents the whole scene, with the explicit use of teaching in verse 12, seems to focus the meaning of leaven in his Gospel on the attitude of the rejection of Jesus by the Pharisees and Sadducees. The meaning is essentially the same as in Mark, but Mark's sensitivity to the struggle of the disciples to perceive Jesus' identity as symbolized in the two process miracles is not present in Matthew.

Luke (12:1–12) presents Jesus' warning about leaven in the context of his large central section on Jesus' teaching journey to Jerusalem (9:51–19:44). He has just narrated Jesus' woes on the Pharisees and Scribes (11:37–53) and now describes the gathering of a large crowd. Jesus warns his disciples against the leaven of the Pharisees, which Luke notes is hypocrisy (v. 1). Thus, Luke brings out that Pharisaical hypocrisy is the point of Jesus' warning. Luke then illustrates this with Jesus' words about everything being finally revealed (vv. 2–3). And, significantly, he continues with Jesus' further discussion about the proper fear of God, rather than fearing human persecutors (vv. 4–5). Following this Luke includes Jesus' words about acknowledging him before men (vv. 8–10) and his encouragement that the Holy Spirit will assist them in times of persecution (vv. 11–12). Thus, Jesus' warning about the leaven of the Pharisees in Luke seems to stress preparation for times of persecution.

The third occurrence of "leaven" in the New Testament is found in Paul's letters. In what is probably his earliest letter, Paul cites the proverbial statement, "A little yeast works through the whole batch of dough" (Gal. 5:9). This proverb is intended by Paul to cause the Galatians to expel the dangerous Judaizers from their churches. Leaven here symbolizes wrong teaching that destroys true Christianity.

The same proverbial citation and symbolism occur in 1 Corinthians 5. Here Paul is strongly urging the Corinthians to expel the incestuous offender from the church. In the development of his argument Paul includes the statement, "Don't you know that a little yeast works through the whole batch of dough?" (v. 6). He then explains that "Christ, our Passover lamb, has been sacrificed" (v. 7). He refers to "the old yeast of malice and wickedness" (v. 8). Paul makes his point that just as at the Passover ancient Israel was instructed to remove any leaven from their homes, so now the church, believing Israel, must remove all sin and evil in order to worship God in the observance of the new Passover of the Lord's Supper. Here, leaven symbolizes sin that defiles the believer and disrupts the church's worship of God. First Corinthians 5:1–8 also reminds us that the Old Testament background (leaven or leavened is used twenty-two times in the Old Testament) and foundational meaning of leaven goes back to the Passover of Exodus 12–13 and the instruction given in Leviticus and Deuteronomy. Throughout the Old Testament, and into the first century A.D., leaven symbolized corruption, defilement, and sin.

Hobert K. Farrell

Bibliography. R. A. Cole, *Galatians;* F. E. Gaebelein, *The Expositor's Bible Commentary,* vol. 8; L. Morris, *1 Corinthians;* R. Young, *Analytical Concordance to the Bible.*

Legalism. The term "legalism" commonly denotes preoccupation with form at the expense of substance. While it is now used metaphorically in all areas of human life, it appears to have had a theological origin in the seventeenth century, when Edward Fisher used it to designate "one who bringeth the Law into the case of Justification" (*The Marrow of Modern Divinity,* 1645). No equivalent term existed in the biblical languages. However, the idea is found in both Testaments.

The Old Testament. In Judaism the entire Old Testament could be called the Law—a usage reflected in the New Testament (John 10:34; 1 Cor. 14:21; Gal. 4:21–22). From this perspective the strictly legal parts of the Old Testament stand in a narrative setting whose design is to recount God's dealings with his people so as to give them Torah or instruction in the way of life he desires for them. The narrative setting of the law is essentially an account of God's choosing of Israel to be his people (Gen. 12:1–3; Deut. 1:1–4:49), while the law itself is both a prescriptive statement of the life God expects his people to lead as well as a picture of the kind of life that leads to joy and fulfillment. In short, the law is part of the covenant, and constitutes both God's gracious gift to his people and the vehicle of their grateful response to him (Exod. 19:3–6; Deut. 7:1–16; 26:1–19). This explains the positive picture of the law in the Old Testament. It is made equally clear that the law could be abused and subverted. Such subversion (which differs from blank rejection) consists in the observance of its literal dictates while overlooking or evading its underlying intent. The prophets in particular denounce preoccupation with the niceties of sacrificial ritual while inward obedience expressed in justice, compassion, and humility is lacking (1 Sam. 15:22–23; Isa. 1:10–20; Amos 2:6–8; 4:4–5; 5:21–24; Mic. 6:6–8). In the postexilic era this danger becomes, if anything, greater. For with the disappearance of the kingdom, the law became the focal point of national life, and conformity to it the mark of belonging to the people of God. The grounding of the law in the covenant grace of God was never wholly forgotten (Ezra 9:5–7), any more than was the sense of authentic piety (Ps. 119, *passim*) or the awareness that mere performance apart from genuine piety was worthless (Prov. 15:8–9; 21:3). However, it was easy for the law to assume independent significance and its observance to be viewed as the condition of God's grace rather than the response to it. Jeremiah had seen earlier that the corruption of the human heart apart from inward renewal made compliance with the law impossible in any case (Jer. 31:31–34). The increased focus on the law during the postexilic era intensified the danger confronted by the earlier prophets: concentration on the latter at the expense of the spirit. This persisted in the Judasim of the first Christian century even though it was recognized that mere conformity to the law was not enough (M.Ber. 2.1), and that repentance was a continual necessity.

The New Testament. No more than Hebrew does the Greek language have a word denoting legalism. Yet it seems clear that criticism of attitudes to the law describable as legalistic constitutes a significant element in New Testament teaching. Three representative areas may be examined.

Legalism and the Teaching of Jesus. The center of Jesus' message was that, in an important measure, the kingdom of God and its power had come in himself (Matt. 12:28; Mark 1:14–15). This posed a challenge to the most distinctive features of Jewish religion: the identity of the chosen people, the temple, and the life of piety, all of which found their focus in the law. Jesus both affirmed and critiqued the law. While attending the synagogue regularly (Luke 4:16) he did not hesitate to break the purity laws (Mark 3:13–17) or rigid interpretations of Sabbath law (Mark 3:1–6). Refusal to do so he denounced as nullification of God's will in the interests of external conformity (Mark 7:1–23). His interpretation of the law exhibited an incisiveness that pierced to the law's intent beyond its surface meaning (Matt. 5:21–48). Still more, he implied that this intent was both revealed and fulfilled in himself, so that legalistic conformity stood exposed and condemned.

Legalism and the Earliest Church. The problem of legalism arose in sharp form when the gospel crossed the boundaries of Judaism and penetrated the Gentile world. The forms were much the same as in Jesus' day: association with sinners, observance of the ceremonial law, and, above all, acceptance of the ritual mark of the people of God—circumcision. However, the issue was more acute: Was salvation possible for Gentiles apart from law observance (Acts 11:3; 15:1)? The Jerusalem Council affirmed that it was (Acts 15:11, 13–14) and sought to resolve the practical difficulties arising from this decision (Acts 15:28–29), though with what success is not clear.

Legalism and the Teaching of Paul. While Paul can speak positively of the law (Rom. 7:7, 12, 14), including circumcision (Rom. 3:1–2; 4:10–12), he also speaks of it negatively. It is powerless to deliver from sin (Rom. 8:3; Gal. 3:21b–22) and was a temporary measure until the coming of Christ (Gal. 3:19). Moreover, continued attachment to it is not only fruitless, but dangerous since the law demands total obedience of which none is capable (Gal. 3:10–12). Law observance is thus both futile and fatal. As a substitute for or supplement to faith in Christ it ministers to legalism. Acceptance by God is possible only through faith in

Christ crucified (Rom. 8:3; Gal. 2:16; 3:13–14). This picture of the law as occasioning legalism has been hotly contested. However, there is evidence of a vein of Judaism in which "the works of the law" were seen as a pathway to righteousness (e.g., the Qumran text 4QMMT). There is likewise evidence in the literature of the Second Temple period that sin was defined in terms of the law, and divine intervention in the eschaton was seen as the only cure. While Paul's use of the term "works" exhibits a wide range of meaning from good to bad (see the double use in Eph. 2:8–10), the significant phrase "the works of the law" often stands in explicit contrast with faith in Christ as the means of salvation (Rom. 3:20–22, 28; Gal. 2:16; 3:2, 5, 10). It is noteworthy that in several of these contexts the idea of boasting is also present (Rom. 3:27; Gal. 2:20a; cf. 6:13). These examples seem best taken to mean legal works, that is, works done to commend the doer to God. As holding out the hope of salvation on the basis of human effort, such works are the antithesis of God's saving grace set forth in Christ crucified. Confidence in him alone, who, by his death fulfilled the law, is the sole means of deliverance from the law's demands, and so of avoiding legalism. A. R. G. Deasley

See also James, Theology of; Justification; Works of the Law.

Bibliography. D. J. Moo, *WTJ* 45 (1983): 73–100; T. R. Schreiner, *The Law and Its Fulfillment: A Pauline Theology of Law;* F. Thielman, *From Plight to Solution: A Jewish Framework for Understanding Paul's View of the Law in Romans and Galatians;* idem, *Paul and the Law, A Contextual Approach;* J. A. Fitzmyer, *According to Paul.*

Leviathan. *See* Gods and Goddesses, Pagan.

Levite. *Pentateuch.* The Hebrew word for Levite (*lēwî*) indicates a descendant of Levi, the son of Jacob and Leah (Gen. 29:34). There were three family clans within the tribe of Levi—Gershon, Kohath, and Merari—but it was only Kohath who supplied the Aaronic priests. Subsequent to the induction of Aaron and his sons into the priesthood, the entire tribe of Levi was "set apart" following the golden calf incident (Exod. 32:26–29). They were blessed and chosen because their actions signified their loyalty to the covenant. Thus, the prophecy of Jacob that Levi's descendants would be scattered throughout Israel (Gen. 49:5–7) was fulfilled, not as a curse but as a blessing (Exod. 32:29; Deut. 33:8–9). Their zeal for the Lord caused the male Levites (except for Aaron's family, who were already designated as priests) to be set apart as caretakers of the tabernacle and as aides to the priests (Num. 1:47–53). Each clan in the tribe now had specific duties related to the tabernacle (Num. 3:14–18). Because this appointment came about due to their actions and was not based on their relationship with Aaron or his family, it was "providentially coincidental" that it was the tribe that contained the priests. Because of this a progression can be demonstrated in terms of separation and responsibilities from nation to tribe (Levi) to priesthood.

The Levites' "set apart" status is demonstrated by their taking the place of the firstborn, who by right belonged to God (Num. 3:41). Another indication of Levi's distinction is found in Numbers 1:47–54, where God instructs Moses not to number the Levites with the other tribes. The Levites were set apart but their status must still be seen as significantly different from that of the priests (even though all priests were Levites too). As aides, not officiating priests, theirs is an intermediate status between the people in general and that of the priesthood (i.e., the priests were made holy, the Levites were made clean; the priests were anointed and washed, the Levites were sprinkled; the priests were given new garments, the Levites washed theirs; blood was applied to the priests, but was waved over the Levites). The Levites were explicitly permitted to go near the Tent of Meeting, and this special privilege more than any other duty distinguished them from ordinary Israelites (Num. 8:19; 16:9–10).

Part of the support of the Levites was to come from the tithe they were to be allotted of the income of the other tribes (Num. 18:20–25). Since the reception of this tithe was dependent on the faithfulness of all the people, the financial position of the Levite was unpredictable. The Levites are therefore included in the legislation, along with the aliens, fatherless, and widows, as those whom the people must remember to care for (Deut. 12:19; 14:27–29).

In Deuteronomy, with a view to entering the land, the Levites were given an additional duty since their tabernacle transport obligations would be diminished. It was now the important duty of the Levites and the levitical priests, who would live throughout the land, to instruct the people in the law (Deut. 33:10).

Preexilic Historical Books. At the conquest the Levites received no tribal inheritance but were given forty-eight cities with their pastures (Josh. 21:1–42). This along with the tithe was to be their means of support as they pursued their work as aides to the priests and helpers at the sanctuary. This lack of land inheritance is to be understood by the statement that "the priestly service of the Lord is their inheritance" (Josh. 18:7).

During the temple period, with the ark permanently in Jerusalem and in view of their numbers, the Levites were given additional responsibilities as officials, judges, gatekeepers, and musicians, all of which assisted the priests (1 Chron. 23:4–5). They also continued to serve as teachers and administrators of the law. That function was not always carried out well; hence the need for specific times of teaching (2 Chron. 17:7–9; 35:3).

Postexilic Historical Books. While 4,289 priests (approximately one-tenth of the entire returning number of exiles) returned from captivity with Zerubbabel, only 341 Levites, singers, and gatekeepers are recorded as returning (Ezra 2:36–58). Ezra succeeded in persuading only thirty-eight Levites to return with him (Ezra 8:15–19). The fact that many of the menial tasks of temple service were the responsibility of the Levites and that the temple first had to be rebuilt and when it was, it was not as glorious as Solomon's temple (Ezra 3:12), may have affected the willingness of the Levites to return. Some of the Levites became involved, however, in the interpretation and teaching of the law (Neh. 8:7–8) and in the leading of the people in worship (Neh. 9:4–5; 12:8–9, 27–47).

Prophets. Though rarely referred to in the prophets, and even then usually in the context of priests who are Levites, the Levites as distinct from the Zadokite priests are mentioned in Ezekiel 44:11. The future acquisition and redistribution of the land would include a specific area in which the Levites could live (Ezek. 45:5).

The New Testament. The term "Levite(s)" is only used three times in the New Testament. They were still a distinct class connected to the temple in Jerusalem along with the priests (John 1:19). As teachers of the law, the Levites, together with the priests, were probably sent with this role in mind, to question John the Baptist. It is possible that many scribes were Levites. In the parable of the good Samaritan both a priest and Levite are mentioned, though not in a commendable manner (Luke 10:31–32). Barnabas is referred to as a Levite (Acts 4:36).

In summary, though the conclusions of the majority of modern critical scholars concerning the identity and purpose of the Levites (and priests) are in sharp contrast to the view presented here, the Scriptures clearly indicate that the Levites should be seen as a tribe that was below the priestly group of Aaronic priests but still distinct from other Israelites. They were "set apart," handled the sacred articles of the tabernacle, served as substitutes for the firstborn who belonged to God, taught the law of God, served as judges, enhanced the worship at the temple in music, and guarded the treasures and moneys associated with the temple, but did not serve as mediators of the covenant. Their significant contribution was that they made it possible for the people to worship and fulfill their obligations to God. Along with the honor that the Levites had in their unique appointment, there was the need for their total dedication to the work of the Lord, not that of pursuing material gain, and the necessity to look to him to supply some of their needs through the people. It was a life of sacrifice and service with their service to the Lord being their valuable inheritance that they could pass on to the next generation. They did not always value their function and inheritance, as evidenced after the exile. STEPHEN J. BRAMER

See also OFFERINGS AND SACRIFICES; PRIEST, PRIESTHOOD.

Bibliography. O. T. Allis, *Baker's Dictionary of Theology,* pp. 321–22; W. C. Kaiser, *TWOT,* 1:1093–94; G. Smith, *Holman Bible Dictionary,* s.v. "Levites."

Leviticus, Theology of. Leviticus is one of the most intensely theological books of the Old Testament. It contains the core of the priestly ritual material of the Pentateuch and, in fact, the entire Old Testament. The regulations are often quite specific and detailed, being tied to the very fabric of personal and communal life in ancient Israel, but always from a markedly priestly point of view. The laws in this book carry deep theological impact for the Old Testament as well for the New Testament (e.g., holiness, purity, sacrificial atonement, forgiveness, etc.), but the most important theological issue from the point of view of the historical situation is the "presence" of God in the midst of Israel.

In the final chapter of Exodus, Moses sets up and prepares the tabernacle for the Lord (40:1–33), leading directly to his habitation there in the form of the "cloud" of his "glory" that had fire in it by night. A second and somewhat expanded description of the cloud and its function in leading Israel through the wilderness appears in Numbers 9:15–23. These two descriptions of the glory cloud and fire form an envelope around the tabernacle-related legislation in Leviticus 1:1–Numbers 9:14.

The literary and theological significance of this structure is threefold. First, the only mention of the appearance of the "glory" of the Lord to the people between Exodus 40 and Numbers 9 is Leviticus 9:23 (cf. v. 6). In that context, "the glory of the LORD appeared to all the people," and "fire came out from the presence of the LORD and consumed the burnt offering and the fat portions on the altar" (Lev. 9:23–24). Second, the only place where the "cloud" of the glory of the Lord appears between Exodus 40 and Numbers 9 is in Leviticus 16:2, where the Lord explains, "I appear in the cloud over the atonement cover." Third, the death of Nadab and Abihu in Leviticus 10:1–2 occurred sometime *during* the same day when the Lord manifested his glory to all the people as recorded in Leviticus 9 (see esp. vv. 1, 23–24), but *before* the expected eating of the sacrificial meat of the sin offering by the priests on that same day (cf. 10:16–19 with 9:15). Just as fire had come out from the "presence" of the Lord and consumed the altar offerings in 9:23–24, a few verses later "fire came out from the presence of the LORD and consumed them, and they died before the LORD" (10:2). Moreover, 16:1–2 refers back to 10:1–2 as the context and basis for the careful regulation of the Day of Atonement.

Thus, the deaths of Nadab and Abihu provided an opportunity for the Lord to state the basic principles underlying priestly theology and, therefore, summarize the primary theological concerns of the Book of Leviticus. All of these concerns reflect primarily on the fact that the Lord was dwelling in the midst of Israel. He was "present" there in the tabernacle, manifesting his glory in cloud and fire.

The Threefold Theological Core of Leviticus. In 10:3 Moses explains the Lord's action against Nadab and Abihu: "This is what the LORD spoke of when he said: 'Among those who approach me I will show myself holy; in the sight of all the people I will be honored.'" There are two categories of people referred to here: "those who approach" the Lord (i.e., the priests) and "all the people." In one way or another, the Lord will show his glory so that he is honored as holy among the people. In this instance, he accomplished that goal by striking out against Aaron's two sons who had not paid due attention to the requirements of holiness as they approached and "offered [lit. 'brought near'] unauthorized fire before the LORD" (10:1).

The Lord emphasized the important lesson to be learned from this incident when he spoke directly to Aaron (not Moses) in 10:9–11 and instructed him and his sons to: (1) avoid "strong drink" when approaching the Lord lest they die in his presence (v. 9; the point seems to be that this might cloud their minds and cause a similar disaster); (2) "distinguish between the holy and the common, between the unclean and the clean" (v. 10); and (3) "teach the Israelites all the decrees the LORD has given them through Moses" (v. 11). To understand the theology of the Book of Leviticus requires a clear grasp of two polarities (i.e., holy versus common and unclean versus clean) plus the concept of atonement, which Moses highlighted when he spoke to Aaron: "Why didn't you eat the sin offering in the sanctuary area? It is most holy; it was given to you to take away the guilt of the community by *making atonement* for them before the LORD" (v. 17).

First, "holy" versus "common" (v. 10a) is concerned with the status of a person, place, or thing. Second, "clean" versus "unclean" (v. 10b) is a matter of their condition, whatever their status might be. Third, "atonement" (v. 17) is the primary focus of many of the sacrificial procedures for dealing with violations of boundaries or with transitions between the categories of holy and common or clean and unclean. With regard to "clean" versus "unclean," the making of atonement was required for "cleansing" irregular or severe uncleanness (e.g., 12:6–8 [the woman after childbirth], 14:18–20 [the leper], and 15:13–15, 25–30 [irregular discharges from male and female genitalia]). With regard to "holy" versus "common," atonement was required in "consecration" procedures for sanctifying persons, places, or things to make them "holy" (e.g., 8:15, 34, the tabernacle and the priests).

The Internal Theological Structure of Leviticus. Leviticus divides naturally into two major sections, chapters 1–16 and 17–27. On the one hand, chapters 1–16 deal primarily with consecrating and cleansing the tabernacle itself. On the other hand, while chapters 17–27 continue to show concern for the holiness and purity of the tabernacle, the focus broadens to encompass the whole land and the people at large. One might say that the shift is from *tabernacle* holiness and purity to *national* holiness and purity.

This distinction between the world of the tabernacle and the everyday national life of common Israelites should not, however, lead one to conclude that the two were not connected. On the contrary, when the Israelites first arrived at Sinai one of the main features of the Lord's proposal of covenant in Exodus 19:3–6 was that Israel would become "a kingdom of priests" (v. 6). They were consecrated as such in the ritual of Exodus 24:3–8. In relation to the Book of Leviticus, the national priesthood of all the people corresponds to the need for national holiness and purity as emphasized in chapters 17–27. The family of Aaronic priests, however, had charge of the tabernacle and, therefore, the responsibility to make sure that neither they nor the people (individually or as a whole) violated the holiness and purity of the tabernacle emphasized in chapters 1–16.

A careful theological analysis of the Book of Leviticus will relate the categories of holiness and purity (i.e., holy and common versus unclean and clean) to both the tabernacle itself and the nation as a whole. Atonement applies to both and, in fact, is especially emphasized at the point of transition in the book (i.e., chap. 16, the Day of Atonement), thus once again focusing on the primary concern for the presence of God in the tabernacle. The internal theological structure of the book, therefore, features these three main topics: atonement, tabernacle holiness and purity, and national holiness and purity.

Atonement. Although structurally chapter 16 is the conclusion to the first major section of the book, it also functions as the theological center of the book and binds the two halves together. On the Day of Atonement the holiness and purity of both the tabernacle and the nation were in view. There were actually five offerings on that day: the two blood atonement sin offerings for the priests and the people (vv. 3, 5, and esp. vv. 11–19), the single scapegoat sin offering for the whole congregation (including the priests and the people, vv. 20–22), and the two burnt offerings for the priests and the people (vv. 23–24). All of these offerings are specifically said to have "made atonement."

The "sin offering" blood atonement rituals for the priests and for the people cleansed and (re)consecrated the tabernacle from their impurities (vv. 11–19). The "scapegoat" ritual, which was a different kind of "sin offering" (vv. 5, 7–10, 20–22), also made a kind of atonement (v. 10). But in this case the atonement facilitated the removal of all the iniquities of all the people of the nation by sending them away from the tabernacle and the nation on the head of the goat into the wilderness (vv. 20–22).

Therefore, the sin offering rituals on the Day of Atonement cleansed not only the tabernacle (vv. 32–33, referring to the blood rituals in vv. 11–19) but also all the people (vv. 29–31, referring to the scapegoat ritual in vv. 20–22). The "burnt offering" blood atonement rituals that followed after the sin offerings on the Day of Atonement apparently functioned on a different level (vv. 23–24). It will be recalled that according to verse 19 the sin offering blood both "cleansed" the altar and "consecrated" it. Apparently, it was the scapegoat ritual that "cleansed" the people, but it was the subsequent burnt offerings that "consecrated" them. The focus shifts from the tabernacle to the people. This shift corresponds to the distinction between tabernacle (chaps. 1–16) and national (chaps. 17–27) holiness and purification discussed above. The sin offering blood atonement procedures purified and consecrated (i.e., made holy) the tabernacle altar. The combined scapegoat and burnt offering atonement procedures purified and consecrated the people.

Tabernacle Holiness and Purity. The tabernacle holiness and purity regulations in Leviticus 1–16 fall into two main subsections, chapters 1–7 and 8–16. The first gives detailed regulations for the basic sacrificial procedures. In light of the reference to the "ordination offering" in 7:37 it seems that these descriptive ritual texts were placed at the beginning of the book as background to the narratives of "ordination" and "inauguration" of the tabernacle and priesthood in chapters 8 and 9.

The second main subsection is chapters 8–16. It begins in 8:1–2 with the Lord's command to Moses that he consecrate the tabernacle and priesthood. Chapter 9 is the inauguration of the tabernacle, which ends with the fire from the Lord consuming the sacrifices (vv. 22–24) as well as Nadab and Abihu (10:1–2). Chapter 16 returns to the Nadab and Abihu incident (vv. 1–2) as the basis for the annual Day of Atonement, the purpose of which was to purify, consecrate, and inaugurate the tabernacle, priesthood, and congregation for the next year.

We cannot deal with the details here, but chapters 11–15 represent a hiatus in the progress of the narrative. It is a coherent unit of regulations focusing almost exclusively on the problem of purity (i.e., "unclean and clean"; cf. 10:10b) and its importance for the community, especially the tabernacle presence of God (15:31, "You must keep the Israelites separate from things that make them unclean, so they will not die in their uncleanness for defiling my dwelling place, which is among them").

In the ancient Near Eastern world it was common for people to struggle with the fear of unseen supernatural malefic forces (e.g., witchcraft, demons, vitriolic gods, etc.) that might break out against them in the form of disease or other misfortunes in life, especially if a person should violate some sort of taboo. The Old Testament gives no credence to such fears. Instead, the only real danger is that the people of Israel might defile the sanctuary of God so that he himself might break out against them (e.g., 10:1–2) or abandon the sanctuary altogether. Leviticus 15:31 emphasizes this point.

The emphasis on physical purity and impurity has troubled many readers of the Old Testament. It helps to recognize that, in the Old Testament, God made himself actually, personally, physically "present" with Israel by inhabiting the tabernacle. This place of physical presence was precisely the focus of the priestly worldview and theology with which the Book of Leviticus is so closely identified. The physical purity laws correspond to the physical "presence" of the Lord in the tabernacle.

National Holiness and Purity. The structure and thematic development of chapters 17–27 (the second major section of the book) is more difficult to discern than that of chapters 1–16. The relationship between these two sections of the book is likewise complicated. In general, it is not so much a matter of a change in topic as it is a shift in perspective. Chapters 17–27 offer another look at everything from the larger perspective of the community and nation as a whole. For example, although these chapters still make reference to the holy offerings, here they are viewed from the perspective of how the priests, their families, and the rest of the people of Israel should handle the offerings at communal feasts (chap. 22), or the relationship between that which has been consecrated as holy and the community at large (chap. 27).

From the perspective of purity, the clean and unclean animal laws that upheld the "wall of partition" between Jews and Gentiles in New Testament days actually provide one of the primary links between these two major sections of Leviticus and their theological emphases. According to 20:25–26, "You must therefore make a distinction between *clean and unclean* animals and between *unclean and clean* birds . . . Those which I have set apart as *unclean* for you. You are to be holy to me because I, the Lord, am holy, and I have *set you apart from the nations* to be my own." There are absolutely *no* clean and unclean animal laws in chapters 17–20. Instead, 20:25–26 assumes chapter 11 and, therefore, uses the clean and unclean animal laws to link 1–16 and 17–27 together in spite of the obvious separation and differences between them.

From the perspective of holiness, both chapters 11 and 20 connect the clean and unclean animal laws with the "holiness formula" (e.g., "be holy because I am holy," 11:45), but they make the connection in two different ways. Chapter 11 focuses simply on the matter of physical contact with unclean animals (vv. 44–45). But in the context of chapter 20 the expression "You are to be holy to me because I, the LORD, am holy" refers to the intended effect clean and unclean animal laws should have on setting Israel "apart from the nations" roundabout them. It should be recalled that this setting apart of Israel from the other nations was God's intention from the very start of their national existence as "a kingdom of priests, a holy nation."

There is an obvious linguistic connection between the "holiness formula" just mentioned and the "I am the LORD (your God)" formula, which occurs frequently in chapters 18–26. Both formulas begin with "I am" and 20:7 mixes the two together: "Consecrate yourselves and *be holy, because I am the LORD your God.*" In its various contexts this "I am the LORD (your God)" formula emphasizes the importance of exclusive worship and obedience to Yahweh because he is truly the Lord.

Israel was to have no other gods: The Lord *alone* was their God. This, in fact, would also have the effect of distinguishing Israel from the other nations, who worshiped and served other gods. One legitimate way of looking at the "Holiness Code" is, therefore, to view it from the perspective of the summary in 26:1–2, "Do not make idols or set up an image or a sacred stone for yourselves, and do not place a carved stone in your land to bow down before it. I am the LORD your God. Observe my Sabbaths and have reverence for my sanctuary. I am the LORD." There are three categories of concern here: (1) national fidelity to the Lord (i.e., no idolatry and distinctively pure and holy community life), (2) national sanctuary and sancta reverence, and (3) national Sabbath observance. Overall, therefore, the theology of the Book of Leviticus focuses on the presence of God in the tabernacle, but that presence was to effect everyone and everything in ancient Israel. RICHARD E. AVERBECK

See also ATONEMENT; OFFERINGS AND SACRIFICES; PRIEST, PRIESTHOOD; TABERNACLE; TEMPLE.

Bibliography. P. J. Budd, *The World of Ancient Israel*, pp. 275–98; W. W. Hallo, *The Book of the People;* J. E. Hartley, *Leviticus;* P. P. Jenson, *Graded Holiness: A Key to the Priestly Conception of the World;* I. Knohl, *The Sanctuary of Silence: The Priestly Torah and the Holiness School;* B. A. Levine, *Leviticus;* J. Milgrom, *Leviticus 1–16;* idem, *Numbers;* H. T. C. Sun, *ABD*, 3:254–57; G. J. Wenham, *The Book of Leviticus;* D. P. Wright, *The Disposal of Impurity.*

Liberty. *See* FREEDOM.

Lie, Lying. To practice deceit, falsehood, and treachery either by word or action. It is the exact opposite of truth. The sanctity of truth is fundamental in biblical teaching since it is based on the nature and character of God (Num. 23:19; 1 Sam. 15:29; Rom. 3:4; Titus 1:2; Heb. 6:18). Therefore, to despise truth is to despise God, and the Scriptures treat this topic with profound seriousness.

In the garden of Eden the serpent denied the truth of God's pronouncement and encouraged the woman to act in defiance of divine truth (Gen. 3:4). The results of this action (3:7–24) demonstrate clearly that it is God and his word that are true. The Mosaic Law, summarized in the Ten Commandments, presents the bearing of false witness as a malicious sin against one's fellow man (Exod. 20:16; Deut. 5:20; 19:18–19; cf. Exod. 23:1–2, 7; Deut. 22:13–21). Lying undermines moral standards and is, therefore, often associated with even more glaring sins (e.g., 2 Sam. 11:6–27; 1 Kings 21:10).

The Wisdom Literature, too, prohibits all false witness and lying (Prov. 6:16–19; 12:22). It particularly points out how lying destroys community and interpersonal relations (Prov. 25:18; 26:18–19, 28). A God-honoring community is built on truth and trust, the opposite of lying and deceit. Judgment for lying will be incurred from God, who cannot lie (Prov. 19:5, 9; 25:18). The psalmists repeatedly warn against all falsehood and commend truth-telling (24:4–5; 27:12), for a liar disqualifies himself from worship (15:2).

The Old Testament prophets emphatically forbid lying and all deceit and show that this standard is fundamental to those who are in covenant relationship with the Lord (Isa. 59:4, 14–15; Jer. 7:28; Ezek. 13:9; Hos. 4:1–2; Zech. 8:16–17). One reason that the nation suffers the discipline of the Lord is her insistence on lying. False prophets (i.e., those who prophesy false visions, divinations, and delusions of their own minds) are frequently condemned (Isa. 9:15; Jer. 14:14; 23:25–26; 28:15; Ezek. 13:6–7; 21:29; 22:28; Mic. 2:11; Zech. 10:2; 13:3).

In the New Testament, Christ as the Son of God is spoken of as absolutely true (John 1:17; 14:6). The New Testament uses a number of Greek words to deal with the concept of lying, though the primary words used are *hypokrinō* and *pseudomai*. These are translated by words such as falsehood, craftiness, error, deceive, mislead, and cheat.

As expected, there is no change of standards in the New Testament in regard to lying. Simple honesty is a fundamental virtue of the follower of Christ (Matt. 5:37); lying is the basic sin denoting the opposite. The seriousness of lying in relation to the Holy Spirit of Truth (John 16:13) is indicated in Scripture by the fate of Ananias and Sapphira (Acts 5:1–11). Lying characterizes the unregenerated person (Eph. 4:22–24; Col. 3:9) and is part of the old life that is to be put off by the believer (Eph. 4:25). John points out that to lie is to engage in the surrender of personal integrity, of one's standing with his brother, and of one's standing with God (1 John 2:4; 4:20). The paramount lie in the New Testament is the denial that Jesus is the Christ (1 John 2:22). An ever-present danger of sin lies in exchanging "the truth of God for a lie" and in subsequently reaping impaired moral standards (Rom. 1:25). Since "no lie comes from the truth" (1 John 2:21) and because lying is obviously hateful to the God of truth and is in fact attributed to the devil ("for there is no truth in him," John 8:44), there will be no place for any form of deception, pretense, or hypocrisy in the New Jerusalem (Rev. 21:27; 22:15). The one characterized by lies forfeits any hope of eternal salvation, for he does not truly know the God of truth (Rev. 21:27; 22:15).

The Scriptures bear universal, consistent, and clear testimony to the absolute sin of lying. It can never be right to lie because it is contrary to the nature of God. However, there are difficulties to be reckoned with in Scripture such as the lack of condemnation of untruths in certain circumstances, the use made of lies in the fulfilling of God's purposes, the approval of the use of partial truth, and the appearance of God as being the sponsor of falsehood in connection with inspiring false prophets with erroneous messages.

Concerning the lack of condemnation, at times, of untruth in Scripture (e.g., Rahab, Josh. 2:4–6), it must be understood that lack of condemnation is not approval nor is commendation of an individual by God a commendation of every element or action of that person. Nowhere is lying approved. Rather, lying that is not denounced must be seen as that which is assumed as wrong in keeping with the universal teaching of Scripture on truth. In the case of the commendation of Rahab it is her faith that welcomed the spies that is sanctioned (Heb. 11:31) and so the lie must be seen as an unnecessary addition. Commendable biblical characters who become entangled in a lie or lies (i.e., Abraham, Gen. 20:2; the midwives in Egypt, Exod. 1:17–21; David, 1 Sam. 21:2; Peter, Matt. 26:72) should have this period or incident seen as the exception (though still inexcusable) rather than the pattern.

Similar to the difficulty above is the apparent use made of lies in the fulfilling of God's purpose (e.g., Jacob's deception to obtain the blessing promised to him by God, Gen. 25:23; 27:35). It must be explicitly stated that God does not approve or need methods that are alien to the integrity of his character to fulfill his purposes. However, God by his sovereignty in his work with sinful humankind, is able to accommodate such lapses and still fulfill his purposes. Never, however, is lying a prerequisite to fulfilling the divine plan.

Concerning the approval of the use of partial truth (e.g., God's instructions to Samuel, 1 Sam. 16:2–3) a careful distinction must be maintained between partial truth and untruth. Some, like Saul, have forfeited their right to know all the truth as demonstrated by past actions and the willingness, as Saul had, to commit murder if all the truth be known. Therefore, God demonstrates the right to conceal certain facts from such a person. God's people have no right to speak an untruth, but there are times when the right to know all truth has been forfeited by someone.

The appearance of God as being the sponsor of falsehood in connection with inspiring false prophets with erroneous messages (e.g., 1 Kings 22:21–22; Jer. 4:10; Ezek. 14:9) must be taken in context. It is true that God's role is expressed in an imperative form but it is in the context of those who have already committed themselves to such a role in life. God himself cannot do or will evil. He can, however, in his sovereignty, use committed false prophets to accomplish his divine purpose. Although God does not lie, he does allow others to use lies and at times applies this to further his own plans (i.e., 1 Kings 22:23; 2 Thess. 2:11).

STEPHEN J. BRAMER

See also SIN.

Bibliography. U. Becker and H.-G. Link, *NIDNTT,* 2:467–74; D. W. Gill, *EDT,* pp. 639–40; W. Kelly, *Baker's Dictionary of Theology,* p. 323; W. C. Kaiser, Jr., *Toward Old Testament Ethics.*

Life. ***God (Yahweh) as the Source and Sustainer of Life.*** According to Genesis 2:7, "the LORD God formed the man from the dust of the ground and breathed into his nostrils the breath of life, and the man became a living being." This "breath of life" does not distinguish human beings from other animals, nor perhaps even plant life, as can be seen in Genesis 1:29–30. When God declared his judgment against Noah's generation, all creation in which there was the "breath of life" would suffer the destruction of the flood (Gen. 6:17; 7:15, 21–23). The breath of life distinguishes the living from the dead, not human beings from animals (Eccles. 3:18–19). Consistently throughout Scripture God is portrayed as the giver of life, which distinguishes living organisms from inanimate things (Rom. 4:17).

Life is contingent upon the continuing, sustaining "breath" of God. When God ceases to breathe, life is no more, "How many are your works, O LORD! In wisdom you made them all; the earth is full of your creatures. . . . When you take away their breath, they die and return to the dust" (Ps. 104:24, 29). Death is frequently described as the cessation of this divine activity (Gen. 25:8; Mark 15:37). It is for this reason that the psalmist concludes, "Let everything that has breath praise the LORD" (Ps. 150:6; cf. Rom. 1:20–21).

The Quality and Duration of Life. Between birth and death, creation and cessation of life, the living experience varying qualities of life and length of days. On the one hand, the Creator is the sovereign Lord of the days of one's life. He sends poverty and wealth, humility, and exaltation, makes paupers to be princes and princes to be paupers (1 Sam. 2:6–9). For this reason, those who live by faith are not to worry, for they rest in the assurance that God cares about their life (Matt. 6:25–34; Luke 12:22–31). One cannot add a single hour to the span of life by worrying (Matt. 6:27). "The length of our days is seventy years—or eighty, if we have the strength; yet their span is but trouble and sorrow, for they quickly pass, and we fly away" (Ps. 90:10). Long life is viewed as the evidence of divine favor (Exod. 20:12; Deut. 5:16; Pss. 21:4; 91:16; Prov. 10:27; Isa. 65:20), so to die in the midst of one's years was a calamity (Isa. 38:10–14; Jer. 11:22; Lam. 2:21). On the other hand, the situation and quality of life may be diminished and even destroyed by chance, circumstances, and the conduct of unrighteous or negligent persons. In such circumstances, the lowly pray for divine mercy and help. Worries, riches, and pleasures (Mark 4:19; Luke 12:15), as well as hunger, sickness, sorrow, and sin can choke and even destroy life.

Life as a Choice. In Moses' third address to Israel (Deut. 29:1–30:20), he calls them to reaffirm their covenant with God. A choice, not a difficult one, must be made (Deut. 30:11), for God had set before them "life and prosperity, death and destruction . . . blessings and curses. Now choose life" (Deut. 30:15, 19). In a similar manner. Joshua appeals to the next generation after the settlement in the promised land (Josh. 24:14–15).

The choice is not always one of obedience and disobedience, but rather one of wisdom that results in health, prosperity, honor, and a better quality of life (Exod. 15:26; Prov. 3:22; 4:13, 22; 6:23; 8:35; 10:17, 28; 19:23; 21:21; 22:4; Eccl. 9:9–10). Such a Person experiences the *shalom* and peace of God (Prov. 14:30; Gal. 1:3). This choice is inherent in the psalms and the Beatitudes of Jesus. The promised blessed life is contingent upon the community and/or individual response of obedience to the will of God (Matt. 7:24–27).

The Sanctity of Life. In a physical sense, life is associated with the blood of an animal (Lev. 17:11–14; Deut. 12:23). As long as there is blood, there is life. When the blood is drained from the body, so is life. The connection is so strong that the law forbade the consumption of blood or meat with blood in it (Gen. 9:4; Lev. 17:12, 14; Deut. 12:23; Acts 15:20, 29). Also, the blood of an animal could make atonement for the transgressions and sins of the people of God (Lev. 16:14–19). The lifeblood of the sacrifice was substituted for the lifeblood of the worshiper, although inadequate and creating a longing for the perfect sacrifice of Christ (Ps. 49:7–9; Heb. 10:1–4).

God demands a reverence for human life (Ps. 139:13–14), and forbids murder (Exod. 20:13; Deut. 5:17; Matt. 5:21). Where violence has shed blood, there must be an accounting and a just penalty (Gen. 4:10–11; 9:5–6; Exod. 21:23; Lev. 24:17–22; Deut. 19:21; Matt. 5:38). Jesus enlarges this understanding of life to include more than physical life, proscribing angry words, insults, and name calling (Matt. 5:22), for these wound and kill the spirit, self-esteem, and well-being of another. The perpetrator becomes subject to judgment. The gospel of God extends a special invitation to the poor, the disabled, the weak, the oppressed, and the children, offering hope and new life.

Sin and Spiritual Death. Mortal humanity was created in the image of God (Gen. 1:26–27), and given the opportunity of eternal life in relationship with the Creator (Gen. 2–3). Central and vital to life in paradise was access to the tree of life in the midst of the garden of Eden (Gen. 2:9). There was one commandment, "You are free to eat from any tree in the garden; but you must not eat from the tree of the knowledge of good and evil, for when you eat of it you will surely die." When Eve and Adam listened to the tempter and disobeyed the commandment, eating the fruit of the forbidden tree, they brought a curse upon themselves (Gen. 3:16–19), their descendants (Rom. 5:12–14; 1 Cor. 15:21–22), and upon all creation (Gen. 3:17; Rom. 8:19–22). The human race lost innocence, knowing right from wrong, and, even more, the disobedience abolished a continuing privileged access to the tree of life (Rev. 2:7; 22:2, 14, 19), and thus eternal life. Spiritual death, separation from the tree of life, and a broken relationship with God resulted. The human race was destined to die, as were all living creatures, but now without hope beyond the grave. Spiritual death reigned from Adam to Christ (Rom. 5:14, 21; 1 Cor. 15:20–26).

The Good News of the Gospel. Life is a central motif of the four Gospels. John summarizes his purpose in writing the Fourth Gospel: "These are written that you may believe that Jesus is the Christ, the Son of God, and that by believing you may have life in his name" (20:31).

Jesus announced that he alone is the narrow gate or entrance into the way that leads to life (Matt. 7:13–14; John 10:7, 9; 14:6). As the Son of God, he had been active in creation (John 1:1–4), and came to give new life or birth (3:3, 5, 7; 6:33, 51) to all who believe in him (3:16). Those who experience the new birth are described as having been formerly dead (Luke 15:32; John 5:21). Thus, Jesus stands alone at the center of history as "the Author of Life" (John 5:40; Acts 3:15). This life is nearly synonymous with entering into the kingdom of God and experiencing the restoration of the divine-human relationship intended in creation. When Jesus healed the sick, exorcised demons, and cleansed lepers, he was restoring life to its intended, physical wholeness (Luke 4:18–19; 6:9). When he proclaimed the good news of God, he was seeking to save and restore the spiritual life lost in Adam's sin.

Eternal Life. There is only an embryonic understanding of eternal life in the Old Testament. The psalms frequently reveal a deep longing to be permitted entrance into the presence of God, which goes beyond earthly, temporal worship in the sanctuary or temple. In Psalm 71:9 the psalmist prays in his old age, not that he might escape death, but rather that the Lord would not forsake him as his strength fades and death approaches. It is pious Job who becomes the champion of eternal hope (Job 19:25–27). This hope, which seems to burst through the boundaries of death, is expressed in more apocalyptic terms in Isaiah 65:17–19. Daniel envisions a resurrection and judgment assigning those raised to everlasting life or everlasting shame and contempt (Dan. 12:1–3). To die, however, generally meant that one entered the mysterious underworld beyond of Sheol or Hades.

Life in the New Testament, beginning with Jesus, predominantly has a metaphysical and spiritual meaning, an indestructible quality, which supersedes physical death and the grave. This life is more important than eating, drinking, and clothes (Matt. 6:25; Luke 12:22–33), and more valuable than physical wholeness and health. The distinction becomes clearer when Jesus commands disciples to deny themselves, take up the cross daily, and follow him (Mark 8:34 par.). There is a tension, even a conflict, between the present physical existence with its passions, and the spiritual life that will continue beyond physical death. Whoever loses or denies the present life for the sake of Christ, finds eternal life, life in the age to come (Mark 8:35–37 par.; 10:30 par.; John 12:25). The rich young ruler desired to inherit eternal life, but to him the cost of denying his present life by selling all that he had and giving to the poor in order to gain the eternal was too great (Mark 10:17–31 par.).

"Eternal life (*zōēn aiōnion*)" becomes a common phrase in the Johannine writings. Jesus is life (1:4; 5:26; 11:25; 14:6; 1 John 1:2) and the giver of life (John 5:40; 6:33, 35, 48, 51, 63; 10:10; 17:2; 1 John 5:11–12) to all who believe in him (John 1:7; 3:15, 16, 36; 6:40; 11:26; 12:46). The beginning of life as a child of God is likened to a new birth (John 3:3–8; 1 John 2:29; 3:9; 4:7; 5:1, 4, 18), which is not of human decision, but the result of the divine, spiritual action of God (John 1:13; 3:5–8; 6:63). It is a transformation from death to life, becoming a present reality. This life is available to "all who believe" in Jesus, the Son of God.

According to Paul, the death of Jesus on the cross opens the way to reconciliation with God, and it is the resurrection of the Lord Jesus Christ that gives life to those who believe (Rom. 5:10; 6:3–4; Gal. 2:20). Those who have experienced the free gift of life from God (Rom. 5:15; 6:23) are led in triumphal procession spreading the knowledge of the gospel of Christ everywhere (2 Cor. 2:14). They walk in newness of life (Rom. 6:4; 7:6), and the righteousness of God reigns in their mortal bodies to eternal life through Jesus Christ (Rom. 5:21; 6:13, 22). The Spirit of God at work in them gives life, peace, and freedom (Rom. 8:6, 11; 2 Cor. 3:6), which is witnessed by the present world in their love for one another.

MELVIN H. SHOEMAKER

See also ETERNAL LIFE, ETERNALITY, EVERLASTING LIFE; NEW LIFE.

Bibliography. G. R. Beasley-Murray, *SJT* 27 (1974): 76–93; G. Bornkamm, *Early Christian Experience;* F. F. Bruce, *SJT* 24 (1971): 457–72; R. Bultmann, G. von Rad, and G. Bertram, *TDNT,* 2:832–75; J. C. Coetzee, *Neot* 6 (1972): 48–66; C. H. Dodd, *The Interpretation of the Fourth Gospel;* A. J. Feldman, *The Concept of Immortality in Judaism Historically Considered;* G. E. Ladd, *A Theology of the New Testament;* J. Pedersen, *Israel: Its Life and Culture;* H. H. Rowley, *The Faith of Israel;* R. Schnackenburg, *Christian Existence in the New Testament;* V. Taylor, *ExpT* 76 (1964–65): 76–79; H. W. Wolff, *Anthropology of the Old Testament.*

Life, New. *See* NEW LIFE.

Light. Light always involves the removal of darkness in the unfolding of biblical history and theology. The contrast of light and darkness is common to all of the words for "light" in both Old and New Testaments (esp. Heb. *ʾôr*; Gk. *phōs*). The literal contrast between metaphysical good and evil, God and evil forces, believers and unbelievers. The Bible entertains no thought that darkness is equal in power to God's light. God is the absolute Sovereign who rules over the darkness and the powers of evil.

Light Is Good. The importance of light and darkness is dramatically presented in the opening sentences of the biblical record. In response to the darkness that was over the surface of the deep (Gen. 1:2), God spoke and light came into being. Darkness and light are evocative words in Hebrew. Darkness evokes everything that is anti-God: the wicked (Prov. 2:13), judgment (Exod. 10:21), death (Ps. 88:12). Light is the first of the Creator's works, manifesting the divine operation in a world that is darkness and chaos without it. While light is not itself divine, it is often used metaphorically for life (Ps. 56:13), salvation (Isa. 9:2), the commandments (Prov. 6:23), and the divine presence of God (Exod. 10:23). In the first creative act, "God saw that the light was good" (Gen. 1:3).

God Is Light. If light represents goodness in antithesis to the evil associated with darkness, it is a natural step for the biblical authors to understand God, the ultimate good, as light. Light symbolizes the holy God. Light signifies God's presence and favor (Ps. 27:1; Isa. 9:2; 2 Cor. 4:6) in contrast to God's judgment (Amos 5:18). Throughout the Old Testament light is regularly associated with God and his word, with salvation, with goodness, with truth, with life. The New Testament resonates with these themes, so that the holiness of God is presented in such a way that it is said that God "lives in unapproachable light" (1 Tim. 6:16). God is light (1 John 1:5) and the Father of lights (James 1:17) who dispels darkness.

The Johannine writings gather up the Old Testament understanding of light and show its summation in Jesus Christ (thirty-three of the seventy-two occurrences of *phōs* in the New Testament are found in the Johannine literature). Light is the revelation of God's love in Jesus Christ and the penetration of that love into lives darkened by sin (1 John 1:5–7). Jesus declares that he is "the light of the world" (John 8:12; 9:5). Jesus is the incarnate Word of God, who has come as the light that enlightens all people (John 1:4–14), so that those believing in him will no longer be in darkness (12:46).

Paul concurs as he harks back to the creation account: "For God, who said, 'Let light shine out of darkness,' make his light shine in our hearts to give us the light of the knowledge of the glory of God in the face of Christ" (2 Cor. 4:6). Through the Word of God light came into existence (Gen. 1:1–3), and through the revelation of God in Jesus Christ the Word brought light to humanity.

The Light of Salvation and Life for Believers. Those responding to the light are ushered into the sphere of life in which darkness is dispelled. Salvation brings light to those in darkness (Job 22:28; Ps. 27:1; Isa. 9:2; Matt. 4:15–16). Jesus Christ is life-giving light, in whom is life (John 1:4), and those who follow him "will never walk in darkness, but will have the light of life" (John 8:12). Believers are "sons of light" (John 12:36; Eph. 5:8; 1 Thess. 5:5).

Light possesses powers essential to true life. Hence "to be in the light" means simply "to live"—both life eternal and life temporal. The one who has come into the light of Jesus Christ is brought into the ethical life characterized by light (cf. Luke 16:8; John 3:19–21; 12:36; 2 Cor. 6:14; Col. 1:12–14; 1 Thess. 5:5; 1 Peter 2:9). The godly person enjoys the light of life in the present age (1 John 2:10). Paul intentionally contrasts the old life in darkness with new life in the light in Christ Jesus (Eph. 4:17–24). Although Satan can disguise himself as "an angel of light," Christians live in the true light of salvation, laying aside the deeds of darkness and putting on the protective "armor of light" (Rom. 13:12). The revealed will of God provides light to the heart, soul, and mind of humanity, providing guidance in a dark world (Pss. 19:7–10; 119:105, 130). A stark contrast will characterize the old life and the new: "For once you were darkness, but now in the Lord you are light. Live as children of light—for the fruit of the light is found in all that is good and right and true" (Eph. 5:8–9). The truly Christian life is a life of light.

A Light to the World. God is light, who dispels the darkness of this world. Jesus came as the light of the world, breaking through the darkness of sin by his work on the cross. It follows that believers are a light to the world as well. Jesus describes his disciples as light and light-bearers (Matt. 5:14–16). Paul indicates to believers in Asia Minor and Macedonia that their lives are a shining light of witness to the world around them (Eph. 5:8; Phil. 2:15). It is the task of all believers to pass on the divine light they have received. What they have received in the secret intimacy of the community of believers they are to proclaim fearlessly "in the light" of public (Matt. 10:27; Luke 12:3). All those who have entered into the light now bear responsibility as missionaries of Christ, shining out as "lights in a dark world" with the light of God himself (Phil. 2:15).

The Light Yet to Come. While both the Old Testament and New Testament describe the future of the ungodly in terms of eschatological darkness, symbolizing perdition, they equally describe the future glory for believers in terms of light. In the New Jerusalem there will be no more night (Rev. 22:5), and the city will not need the sun, moon, or created light to shine on it, "for the glory of God gives it light, and the Lamb is its lamp. The nations will walk by its light" (Rev. 21:23–24). The prophetic word of God is what brings hope of the light yet to come, and Peter provides an appropriate admonition: "You will do well to pay attention to it, as to a light shining in a dark place, until the day dawns and the morning star rises in you hearts" (2 Peter 1:19). At the future appearing of the Lord Jesus Christ all darkness will be dispelled, and believers will walk in purity, peace, and joy in the light of the living God.

MICHAEL J. WILKINS

Bibliography. E. R. Achtemeier, *Int* 17 (1963): 439–49; F. G. Carver, *Wesleyan Theological Journal* 23 (1986): 7–32; H. Conzelmann, *TDNT*, 9:310–58; D. Guthrie, *New Testament Theology;* H.-C. Hahn et al., *NIDNTT*, 2:484-96; G. Hawthorne, R. P. Martin, and D. G. Reid, *Dictionary of Paul and His Letters;* G. E. Ladd, *A Theology of the New Testament;* G. Wenham, *Genesis 1–15.*

Likeness of God. *See* IMAGE OF GOD.

Lion. Although most Hebrew and Greek words for lion are used in a figurative sense, nevertheless we can draw a number of inferences regarding the perceived characteristics and behavior of literal lions. They are, among other things, strong (Prov. 30:30), especially in their teeth (Job 4:10) and paws (1 Sam. 17:37), fearless (Prov. 28:1; 30:30), stealthy (Ps. 17:12), frightening (Ezra 19:7; Hos.

11:10; Amos 3:8), destructive (1 Sam. 17:34; Mic. 5:8), and territorially protective (Isa. 31:4). Yet for all its seeming autonomy, the lion is ultimately dependent on God (Job 38:39–40; Ps. 104:21), answerable to him (Job 4:10), and subdued in the millennial age (Isa. 11:6–7).

The many notable qualities of the lion are often applied figuratively in a variety of ways to individuals and nations. The king is frightening in his anger (Prov. 19:12; 20:2), the soldier courageous (2 Sam. 17:10), national leaders vicious (Ezek. 22:25; Zeph. 3:3), enemy nations destructive (Isa. 5:29; Jer. 2:15) and protective of their conquests (Isa. 5:29), and personal enemies stealthy in their pursuit to harm (Pss. 10:9; 17:12).

God is described with a number of leonine features. He is strong (Isa. 38:13), fearless in protecting his own (Isa. 31:4), stealthy in coming upon his prey (Jer. 49:19; Hos. 13:7), frightening (Hos. 11:10; Amos 3:8), and destructive (Jer. 25:38; Lam. 3:10; Hos. 5:14; 13:8). In Amos 3:8 "The Lion" even appears as a title for God.

The idea of a Lion of the Tribe of Judah is problematic because the fundamental passage (Rev. 5:5) is grammatically ambiguous and because there is no exact antecedent parallel. First, it is unclear whether in Revelation 5:5 we have one title of Christ (Lion of the Tribe of Judah) or two titles standing in apposition (The Lion; The One of the Tribe of Judah). Second, the alleged parallels are only approximate parallels. In Genesis 49:9 there is no lion of Judah; rather, Judah is a lion. In 2 (4) Esdras 11:37; 12:1, 31 the Messiah is pictured as a lion, but not specifically of Judah. In the Testament of Judah 24:5 the Messiah is from Judah but not specifically as a lion. Given the imprecision in the alleged parallels, the cautious interpreter would not make much of the tradition that combines "lion" and "of the Tribe of Judah" into one idea, but rather would understand Jesus the Lamb to be called Messiah under two images derived from separate traditions.

Finally, the lion figure is expansive enough in its manifold facets to suggest its application to Satan. Such meaning is possible in 2 Timothy 4:17, but 1 Peter 5:8 is its classic occurrence. Here Satan is portrayed as both frightening his prey and silently stalking it to devour it. This devouring is best seen as potentially successful and as consisting of physical death. Therefore, professing believers should not lose faith, even in the face of the devil's most relentless pressures to give up.

DAVID K. HUTTAR

See also GOD; MESSIAH; SATAN.

Bibliography. G. J. Botterweck, *TDOT,* 1:374–88; R. K. Harrison, *ISBE,* 3:141–42; W. Michaelis, *TDNT,* 4:251–53; J. R. Michaels, *I Peter.*

Lips. *See* MOUTH.

Listen. *See* HEAR, HEARING.

Lord. *See* JESUS CHRIST, NAME AND TITLES OF.

Lord's Day, the. The expression "the Lord's day" is found only once in the Bible. In Revelation 1:10 John relates the beginning of his visionary experience to being in the Spirit "on the Lord's Day." The phrase seems to have become more common in the second century A.D., where it is found in such early Christian writings as Ignatius's *Epistle to the Magnesians* 9:1 (c. A.D. 108), the Didache 14:1 (c. A.D. 100–125), and the Gospel of Peter 9:35; 12:50 (c. A.D. 125–50).

The presence of the adjective *kuriakos* makes the expression grammatically different from the common biblical phrase "the Day of the Lord," which uses the genitive form of the noun *kurios.* The adjective is found only one other time in the New Testament, in 1 Corinthians 11:20, where Paul speaks of "the Lord's Supper." Non-Christian parallels suggest that the adjective was used with reference to that which belonged to the Roman emperor; early Christians seem to have used it, perhaps in conscious protest, to refer to that which belonged to Jesus.

The particular "day" that belonged to Jesus seems to have been Sunday, or, by Jewish reckoning, Saturday sundown until Sunday sundown. According to the Gospels, Jesus was raised from the dead on "the first day of the week" (Matt. 28:1; Mark 16:2; Luke 24:1; John 20:1), that is, Sunday. New Testament evidence suggests that by the 50s, if not earlier, Christians were attaching special significance to Sunday. In 1 Corinthians 16:1–3 Paul exhorts the church at Corinth to set aside a sum of money "on the first day of every week" for the church at Jerusalem, as the Galatian churches were already doing. Similarly, Luke notes that when Paul arrived at Troas near the end of his third missionary journey, the church gathered together to break bread "on the first day of the week" (Acts 20:6–7). Although the identification is not made explicit, there is therefore good reason to believe that John has Sunday in mind when he mentions "the Lord's Day" in Revelation 1:10. Certainly the second-century Gospel of Peter, which twice speaks of the day of Jesus' resurrection as "the Lord's Day" (9:35; 12:50), makes the connection. Similarly, the *Epistle of Barnabas* (c. A.D. 130) notes that Christians celebrate Jesus' resurrection of "the eighth day" (15:9; cf. John 20:26), or Sunday, which is the day after the seventh day—that is, the Jewish Sabbath (Saturday). Justin Martyr affirms that Jesus was raised on "the day of the Sun" (*Apology* 67).

How quickly the Lord's Day emerged as a specific day of worship for the early church is not clear. Luke observes that in the period immediately following the outpouring of the Holy Spirit at Pentecost the earliest Christians met "every day" in the temple courts. Whether their breaking of bread in their homes was a daily or weekly occurrence he does not specify, but the former seems more likely (Acts 2:46). Alternately, Paul's comments to the Corinthians concerning the laying aside of money on the first day of the week do not indicate whether this action was connected with a formal gathering of the church (1 Cor. 16:13). Luke's description of the meeting of believers at Troas is the first clear indication of a special gathering as taking place in the evening, by which he probably means Sunday, using Roman reckoning from midnight to midnight, rather than the Jewish system. By the second century the Lord's Day was clearly set apart as a special day for worship. In a letter to the emperor Trajan (c. A.D. 112), the Roman governor Pliny the Younger notes that Christians assembled before daylight "on an appointed day" (*Epistle* 10:96), undoubtedly Sunday. The Didache specifically exhorts believers to come together on the Lord's Day (14:1), and the *Epistle of Barnabas* sees it as a special day of celebration (15:9). Indeed, Justin Martyr (c. A.D. 150) gives a detailed account of typical Sunday worship (*Apology* 67).

A clear picture of how the early Christians celebrated the Lord's Day emerges only gradually. Luke records that the Christians at Troas came together to break bread, which may well denote a meal that included the Lord's Supper (cf. Acts 2:42; 1 Cor. 11:20–22). That Paul spoke (at great length!) to the assembled believers (Acts 20:7–11) implies nothing about their typical practice, since Paul was a special guest and intended to leave the next day. The Didache makes explicit the connection between the breaking of bread and the Lord's Supper on the Lord's Day but says little else concerning the meeting, apart from mentioning the practice of confession of sin (14:1). Pliny mentions two meetings on the "appointed day": the Christians first meet before dawn to sing a hymn to Christ "as to a god" and to affirm certain ethical commitments; then they depart and reassemble for a meal. Not being a Christian himself, Pliny would not have understood the significance of the meal as a setting for the Lord's Supper; for him it was enough that the meal consisted "of ordinary, innocent food" (*Epistle* 10:96).

The most extensive account of an early Christian Sunday worship service is provided by Justin Martyr (*Apology* 67, cf. 65). According to Justin, the gathering begins with readings from "the memoirs of the apostles" —the Gospels—or the writings of the prophets for "as long as time permits." The "president" then delivers a sermon consisting of instruction and exhortation. Next, the congregation rises for prayer, following which the bread and wine are brought in for the Lord's Supper. After prayers and thanksgivings by the president and a congregational "Amen," the deacons distribute the bread and wine to those who are present (and then carry some to those who are absent). There follows a collection of "what each thinks fit" for the needy, and, apparently, the end of the service.

Noteworthy in these early texts is the lack of identification of Sunday with the Jewish Sabbath. Luke has little to say about early Christian observance of the Sabbath, apart from recording Paul's preaching on the Sabbath in Jewish synagogues (Acts 13:14, 42, 44; 17:2; 18:4; cf. 16:13), which perhaps says less about Paul's commitment to Sabbath observance than about his missionary strategy. Indeed, Paul has little interest in observing special days as sacred (Rom. 14:5–6; Gal. 4:9–11; Col. 2:16). Ignatius contrasts observance of the Sabbath with living for the Lord's Day (*Magnesians* 9:1). The *Epistle of Barnabas* views the significance of the biblical Sabbath as being a symbol of the future rest established at the return of Jesus (15:1–8; cf. Heb. 4:3–11). Justin Martyr speaks of the Sabbath in terms of a perpetual turning from sin (*Dialogue with Trypho* 12). In 321 Constantine proclaimed Sunday to be official day of rest in the Roman Empire (*Codex Justinianus* 3.12.3), but this does not seem to have been related to any concern with the Jewish Sabbath. By the end of the fourth century, church leaders such as Ambrose and John Chrysostom were making such a connection, defending relaxation from work on Sunday on the basis of the Fourth Commandment and paving the way for later Catholic and Protestant elaboration on Sunday as the Sabbath.

In the early church, then, the Christians began to give a special place to Sunday as the day on which Jesus was raised from the dead. It soon became a fixed day for worship, a celebration of the resurrection centered around the Lord's Supper. As Christianity distanced itself from Judaism, it is not surprising that eventually the church would see its special day in terms of the special day of the Jews, the Sabbath, and would transfer the provisions of the Fourth Commandment to Sunday.

JOSEPH L. TRAFTON

See also WORSHIP.

Bibliography. P. K. Jewett, *The Lord's Day;* W. Rordorf, *Sunday.*

Lord's Prayer, the. Jesus teaches this prayer to his disciples as a paradigm of proper prayer as he trains them for the missionary task of the messianic age that he is inaugurating in his own person as the incarnate Son of God and Son of man. The prayer needs to be seen in the larger contexts of the Sermon on the Mount and the Gospel of Matthew. The shorter version in Luke 11:2–4 appears in a different setting; during Jesus' itinerant ministry he paraphrased important teachings in training his followers for prayer and mission.

Both versions of the Lord's Prayer imply the importance of a vertical dimension of personal purity in worship of the Father as a prerequisite of valid missionary activity on the Lord's behalf.

A second requirement of successful mission is the horizontal bearing of fruit, as evidenced in Jesus' teaching that his true followers will be known by their fruits (Matt. 7:15–20). Both vertical and horizontal dimensions are emphasized as a unit in the Sermon on the Mount, which summarizes the purpose of the Gospel of Matthew as a whole. The Gospel was likely written to serve as a manual for mission in the early church and was based on eyewitness accounts of Jesus' work and teaching. Matthew then would have been written within the nascent Jewish Christian mission originating in and emanating from Jerusalem, reflecting Jesus' exemplary training of the first line of missioners with a view to serving as model for all his subsequent followers.

A study of the four Gospels affirms a recurrent pattern: Jesus as incarnate Son of God and Son of man models in action for his disciples what he teaches, since he embodies the ideal image of God in humanity. Where Adam failed he succeeds in his redemptive and exemplary work. Since God is the relational Trinity in everlasting and inexhaustible fellowship as Father, Son, and Holy Spirit, the divine design and nature of created humanity are to reflect relatedness and fellowship both vertically and horizontally as the Old Testament Decalogue indicates, and this Jesus does to perfection. While his relation to the Father and the spirit is unique in view of his oneness and equality within the Triune Family, as incarnate Son he also exemplifies direct address, passionate intent and purity, unostentatious setting in prayer, and concern with the two dimensions of proper prayer—honoring the Father vertically and asking for help in realizing the Father's will in the present mission horizontally. These two dimensions constitute the heart of the Sermon on the Mount and the Lord's Prayer.

The immediate context of the Lord's Prayer in Matthew 6 is the triple teaching of Jesus on alms (vv. 1–4), prayer (vv. 5–15), and fasting (vv. 16–18). In each Jesus warns against ostentatious hypocrisy and requires worship *en tō kryptō* ("in secret"). This has to do not so much with privacy and isolation ("*Our* Father" indicates a communal prayer), but praying with pure intent for the honor and pleasure of the Father, not for selfish and transient approval from the world. When this proper attitude is fulfilled God rewards the worshiper, but "in secret," on his own terms (vv. 4, 6, 18).

With the crucial matter of proper intent established at the outset, Jesus instructs his disciples as to the priority and content of the ideal prayer. The prayer is not necessarily given for strict liturgical use, for Jesus says, "This, then, is how you should pray." If used as a set prayer, the conditions of the teaching unit are to be observed, especially the warning not to "keep on babbling like pagans" (6:7). The significance of the Lord's Prayer lies in the fact that every prayer directed to God should function in two spheres. The basic format of the prayer is accordingly divided into two sections. The first is directed vertically in glorification of the Father and in petition that his name be hallowed, his reign realized, and his will accomplished on earth as in heaven. Where the first section (vv. 9–10) focuses on the Father, the second (vv. 11–13) focuses on us: give us, forgive us, lead us. The priority is important, for according to Jesus' own formula the second set will not function without the first in place. Glorification of God must be given pride of place in prayer and takes precedence over "us" petitions.

Examining the opening vertical unit of the prayer we notice its poetic arrangement in the following sentence flow of verse 9–10:

Pater hēmōn ho en tois ouranois,
(Our Father who art in heaven),
hagiasthētō to onoma sou.
(Let thy name be hallowed).
elthetō hē basileia sou,
(Let thy kingdom come),
genēthētō to thelēma sou,
(Let thy will be done),
hōs en ouranō kai epi gēs.
(As in heaven so upon earth).

The opening line of the prayer is a declarative statement; it affirms that God is (implied), that he is in heaven (distant and sovereign), and that he is also our Father (near, familial, and personal). The three petitions follow with imperatives up front, emphasizing all three aspects of the Greek aorist tense: let the action begin (inceptive), let it continue (durative), let it be completed (terminal). The triplet indicates not so much the power of the petitioner to bring about what is petitioned, but agreement with the fact that God is already sovereignly bringing to pass all three petitions. In the person of Jesus the Son his name is being hallowed, his kingdom is now coming, his will is in process of being done on earth as it is in heaven.

All three petitions are to be understood in light of inaugurated eschatology that Jesus embodies in his own words and work and will bring to completion at his second coming. The three petitions accordingly are "joining" petitions in the sense that Jesus is asking his followers to join him in what already are the sovereign realities and doings of the Father through the Son. In praying the disciples are in effect serving notice that they want to be part of this great, ongoing, glorifying ministry, desiring that all humankind will come to honor God as he deserves to be honored. Hence the petitions acknowledge the already and not yet aspects of Jesus' ministry and the disciples' desire to participate in the mission of realizing on earth what is enjoyed in heaven.

The second unit in the prayer comprises three parallel "us" petitions that request divine help in the mission to which Jesus' followers are being called: "give us"; "forgive us"; "deliver us." These correspond on the human side to the three petitions in the first unit, which focus on God. As the Father's name is to be hallowed, so the disciples ask to be honored with spiritual and material sustenance because they bear the image of God and reflect his glory, especially now that they are experiencing the redeeming work of Jesus the Son of God in their lives and are engaged in sharing the good news of salvation in the mission of fruitbearing.

The key here is "not too much, not too little, but just enough," as with God's supply of manna in the morning and quail in the evening for Israel during the wilderness mission—just enough for the day, no more (Exod. 16:4, 12–21). Hence *epiousion* is best translated "what is sufficient"—"Give us food sufficient for the day," remembering that the setting of the Gospel of Matthew, the Sermon on the Mount, and the Lord's Prayer (in Luke as well) is one of eschatological urgency and preparation for mission in the new exodus inaugurated by Jesus, and of traveling light; it is not a general prayer for common grace. There was no ordinariness for Israel in the wilderness, nor is there for God's people in the new mission. As with Israel, Jesus' disciples are to acknowledge the honor of being called to represent God's image in the world, to conquer enemy-held territory in his name, and to exhibit faith in the Lord that he will provide daily sustenance for their extraordinary eschatological journey.

The second petition in the "us" section parallels the second petition in the "Father" section. How does "your kingdom come"? It comes by the Father's bringing forgiveness through the redemptive work of Jesus the Son, who personifies the redeeming reign of God. Accordingly, the kingdom comes as sinners ask forgiveness of the Lord by acknowledging moral and spiritual obligations, receive saving grace by faith, and then pass along the good news of Jesus to others with a forgiving heart. The petition is not conditional; sinners are not forgiven because they forgive others. They are saved by grace through the redeeming work of Jesus alone. But they have no right to claim forgiveness for themselves if they are unwilling to forgive others, for that would undermine the purpose of the disciples' mission: as they have been forgiven by God's grace in Jesus the Son, so they are to share the message of forgiveness with the world.

The mission of proclamation to which the disciples of Jesus are called leads to the third "us" petition, which corresponds to the third "Father" petition. How shall "your will be done on earth as it is in heaven"? It is done by proclaiming the work of reconciliation Jesus came to accomplish and so binding the devil and plundering his goods (Matt. 12:28–30; Luke 11:20–23). Jesus defeated the tempter by successfully passing the probation of testing (Matt. 4:1–11), and hence proved worthy as his disciples' savior and exemplar. Thus the third petition is best understood if it focuses on the prayer "deliver us from the evil one," taking the clause "and lead us not into temptation" as explanatory of what is involved in the petition: protection from the adversary who would keep us from salvation and from sharing it with others. This is essentially the prayer Jesus prays in Gethsemane (Matt. 26:39; cf. 4:7) as he resists the temptation not to drink the cup of redemptive suffering, thus again foiling the devil who is seeking to divert the image-keeper from his redemptive role.

With the exception of the petition for forgiveness of sins (Jesus is the sinbearer who provides forgiveness), the eschatological themes of the Lord's Prayer would have been prayed by Jesus throughout his ministry; they are thus fitting for his followers, who are given the honor and responsibility of sharing in his mission by proclaiming the coming of the kingdom and doing the will of God, to his glory. ROYCE GORDON GRUENLER

See also JESUS CHRIST; PRAYER.

Bibliography. W. Barclay, *The Beatitudes and the Lord's Prayer for Everyman;* A. W. Pink, *The Beatitudes and the Lord's Prayer.*

Lord's Supper, the. The richness and importance of the Lord's Supper in Christianity are conveyed by the various names given to it. It has been called both a sacrament and an ordinance of Christ. In terms of its origin in history, it is called "the Last Supper"; as an act of thanksgiving by the church, it is called the Eucharist (from Gk. eucharistein/eulogein) and the Eucharistic Assembly (synaxis); from its Jewish-Christian origins, it is the Breaking of Bread and the Memorial of the Lord's passion and resurrection; in patristic development, it is the Holy Sacrifice because it mysteriously makes present the one, unique sacrifice of Christ and includes the church's offering; also it is the Holy and Divine Liturgy because the whole worship of the church finds its center in the celebration of this Sacred Mystery. Within the liturgy it is called the bread of angels and bread from heaven and the medicine of immortality. It is also Holy Communion since it is union with Christ. Finally, since the liturgy ends with the sending forth (missio) of the faithful to fulfill God's will in their lives, it is called "the Mass."

The New Testament both describes its institution by the Lord Jesus and refers to its actual implementation and celebration by the church. Further, the New Testament sets the context for the institution of the Last Supper by an emphasis on table fellowship. Jesus was both the guest at (Luke 5:29–32; 7:36–50) and the host at meals during his ministry (Mark 2:15). Further, the feeding miracles of Jesus (Mark 6:31–44; 8:1–11) point not only to shared fellowship but also to the future "messianic banquet" (see Isa. 25:6–12). Jesus spoke of meals and joyous banquets in his parables (e.g., Matt. 22:1–14; Luke 14:15–24). Further, according to Luke, the disciples "ate and drank with him after he rose from the dead" (Acts 10:41; cf. Luke 14:30).

Institution. Before looking at the actual records of the institution of the Lord's Supper, it is necessary to note the debate as to whether the institution occurred within the Passover celebration. The majority opinion has been and remains that the Lord Jesus ate the Passover meal with his disciples on Thursday evening (the beginning of Nisan 15) and when doing so instituted the Lord's Supper. Then he was crucified on Friday. This is clearly what the Synoptic Gospels teach. However, it has been argued that since John's Gospel affirms that Jesus was crucified on the afternoon of Nisan 14, when the paschal lambs were being sacrificed in the temple (18:28), the Last Supper was a pre-Passover meal the night before—at the beginning of Nisan 14.

Here, it is assumed that the Lord's Supper originated in the context of the Passover; the actual texts of the institution point to this fact and so does the whole theology of the meaning of the Lord's Supper in terms of the sacrificial death of Jesus, the Lamb of God, who inaugurates the new exodus. Further, we assume that the words of institution were said by Jesus within the Passover, when the head of the family prayed over the unleavened bread before the main meal and over the third cup of wine after the main meal.

The Meaning of Jesus' Sayings. The two sayings, "This is my body" and "This is my blood," were interpolations into the Passover ritual at two important points—before and after the main meal. The central content of the meal is the flesh of the slain lamb.

Jesus transcends the original meaning of this feast, for he is the fulfillment of the Passover Lamb/Victim. The unleavened bread now stands as a symbol of his body and the wine of "the cup of blessing" as a symbol of his blood.

The disciples did not eat the flesh of Christ by taking the bread and they did not drink his blood in taking the wine. In the Passover the slain lamb represented the efficacious death of the lambs in Egypt. In the Lord's Supper, which emerges from the Passover, the bread and wine represent the atoning sacrifice of Christ Jesus as the true paschal lamb. Neither the slain lamb nor the bread and wine contain in and of themselves any efficacy. So both at the Passover and at the Lord's Supper the sacrificial death is presupposed and is no part of the actual meal. So the Lord's Supper is both a proclamation and a remembrance (memorial) of what God the Father has done in his Son, Jesus Christ, just as the Passover is a proclamation and a remembrance of what Yahweh did for Israel through the slaughter of the lambs in Egypt.

Further, since the bread and wine symbolize the sacrifice of Christ on the cross, to be invited to partake of them is a great privilege. It is the grace of being one with him in his sacrifice and also of sharing by anticipation in the fruit of his atonement—partaking of the messianic banquet in the kingdom of God. After his resurrection from the dead and before his ascension into heaven, the disciples ate with Jesus on various occasions (e.g., Luke 24:30–31; John 21). After Pentecost (Acts 2) they celebrated the Lord's Supper on each Lord's Day. In their breaking of bread they knew the presence of the same Lord who had dined with them during the forty days. However, the slaughtered lamb no longer had any part in the meal for its central position had now been taken by the bread and the wine. So the Lord's Supper is a remembrance of the sacrificial death of Jesus Christ and an expection of the joy of being with him in his kingdom. It is also the fellowship of and in the new covenant, that is, of a relation with the Father through the Son and by the Spirit.

The Teaching of Paul. The apostle's teaching on the Lord's Supper is found not only in 1 Corinthians 11:23–26, but also in other parts of the epistle. We need, therefore, to examine 5:6–8, 10:1–22, and 11:18–34.

In 5:6–8 Paul refers to Christ, "our Passover lamb" who has been sacrificed, and writes: "Therefore let us keep the Festival . . . with the bread of sincerity and truth." It is probable that here we have an allusion to the Lord's Supper.

In 10:1–22 Paul presents the important analogy for the Lord's Supper from the Old Testament (Exod. 16:4, 14–18; 17:6). The supernatural food was the manna that came down from heaven and the supernatural drink was the water that gushed from the rock. However, despite their reception of supernatural sustenance, most Israelites perished because of their idolatry. Let this be a warning to believers, says Paul. To eat at the table of pagan gods is to fellowship with demons and to make a mockery of the Lord's Supper, for in the Eucharist there is fellowship with God in Christ and with fellow believers in the body of Christ. Also evident in this passage is a particular emphasis on the actual bread and wine: they are the actual means of sharing in the body and blood of Christ, but they are not equated with that body and blood.

In 11:18–34 we find that the Lord's Supper is the whole of the common meal that concluded with the Eucharist. Paul writes to admonish the church for its abuse of the common meal and in so doing he probably contributed toward the separation of the Eucharist from the common meal. His words in verses 27–30 are very strong. He says that "anyone who eats and drinks without recognizing the body of the Lord eats and drinks judgment on himself." Paul could mean that to treat the sacramental bread and wine like any other food is sinful; or he could mean that the abuses at the common meal by the Corinthians reveals that they do not appreciate the true nature of the body of Christ (as the communion and fellowship of believers in Christ).

The Teaching in John's Gospels. There is no account of the institution of the Lord's Supper in the Gospel of John. This may mean that (as Rudolf Bultmann maintained) John is antisacramental. Or it may mean that John presupposes the institution and brings out its full meaning in various places. This second possibility is adopted here and can be illustrated as follows.

At the wedding of Cana (2:1–11) the changing of water into wine is a sign. The wine represents the wine of the Eucharist and is the blood of Christ that cleanses from all sin. It replaces the purifications and washings in water in Judaism.

After the feeding of the multitude (6:1–15), Jesus spoke of himself as the "bread of life" or "the bread of God" that comes down from heaven to give life to the world (vv. 22–51). Then he identified this bread with his flesh, which is eaten (lit. munched), and also spoke of his blood, which is drunk and which gives eternal life (vv. 52–59). (Some scholars see the latter as an addition by a redactor, but the passage can also be seen as a natural climax to the teaching on the bread of life.) The use of the term "flesh" belongs to the antidocetic emphasis of the Gospel and thus the element of the Eucharist is here flesh (not body) and blood. For the Evangelist the presence of Jesus Christ in the Lord's Supper/Eucharist is more real than was his physical presence to the disciples in Palestine. This is because partakers of the Eucharist enjoy a communion with him in the eating of his living flesh (vivified by the Spirit) and the drinking of his blood, which was not possible before his glorification to the Father's right hand. Yet this eating and drinking of flesh and blood are not physical but spiritual ("the words I have spoken to you are spirit and they are life," v. 63).

It is generally agreed that the foot-washing in John's Gospel (13:1–20) replaces the institution. The words of Jesus to Peter point to the necessity of feeding on Christ in his appointed way: "Unless I wash you, you have no part with me." The "person who had had a bath" points to baptism, which cannot be repeated. The foot washing is an allegory of the Lord's Supper—"I have set you an example, that you also should do as I have done for you." The Eucharist is one (or *the*) way appointed by Christ for the washing away of postbaptismal sins. It is also the inspiration for the life of love in following the example of Jesus himself.

In the farewell discourses of Jesus (chaps. 14–17) there are various indications of the reality of the Eucharist and its being made life-giving through the gift and presence of the Paraclete, the Spirit sent from the Father in the name of the Son. The Vine with its wine (15:1–8) points to Christ and his blood. Then, in the high priestly prayer of Jesus we hear him consecrating himself as the source of the flesh and blood, which are to be the heavenly food of the future Eucharist (17:19).

Finally, the piercing of the side of Jesus and the coming forth of blood and water (19:34) graphically state that the two sacraments, baptism and Eucharist, flowed from the atoning and liberating death of Jesus Christ (see also 1 John 5:6–8).

Summary. Whatever name is given to that which Jesus instituted, it would seem that it has the following characteristics.

First, the *ekklēsia* and its holy meal belong to the new covenant in much the same way that Israel and its Passover belong to the old covenant. Second, Christians are to rejoice in the living presence of the Lord Jesus in their midst as they remember his atoning, sacrificial death. Third, the early church encountered the vital presence of Jesus Christ not in the bread and wine as such but in his presence in their midst and in their hearts. The purpose of the elements (which are truly holy and indispensable for they replace the Passover lamb) is to symbolize and recall the once-for-all and unrepeatable death of Jesus Christ. Finally, the joy of knowing Christ in the holy meal is a foretaste of the fuller communion and friendship in the life of the future kingdom of God.

The key theological elements of the Lord's Supper as it was celebrated in the early church are: (1) the proclamation of the death of Jesus through "memorial" and "remembrance" and a sacrifice of praise and thanksgiving; (2) the inauguration of the new covenant in the sacrificial blood of Jesus; (3) the participation and fellowship in Christ unto the Father, and with one another in Christ; (4) the experiencing the firstfruit of the joy of the eschatological kingdom of God; (5) the presence of the Spirit of the Father to vivify; and (6) the presence of faith, which is faithful and obedient, in the hearts of believers.

Immediately after the period of the apostles there was a speedy development of eucharistic practice and theology in the ante-Nicene and then post-Nicene church. The results of this often appear to have moved far away from the New Testament foundations, because of the emphasis on sacrifice in terms of the Eucharist itself.

Peter Toon

See also CHURCH, THE; DEATH OF CHRIST; JESUS CHRIST; LOVE FEAST.

Bibliography. J.-J. Allmen, *The Lord's Supper;* I. C. Heron, *Table and Tradition;* A. J. B. Higgins, *The Lord's Supper in the New Testament;* J. Jeremias, *The Eucharistic Words of Jesus;* J. Reumann, *The Supper of the Lord.*

Love. God is love and has demonstrated that love in everything that he does. Paul compares faith, hope, and love, and concludes that "the greatest of these is love" (1 Cor. 13:13).

"God Is Love." *Agapē,* the love theme of the Bible, can only be defined by the nature of God. John affirms that "God is love" (1 John 4:8). God does not merely love; he *is* love. Everything that God does flows from his love.

John emphasizes repeatedly that God the Father loves the Son (John 5:20; 17:23, 26) and that the Son loves the Father (John 14:31). Because the Father loves the Son, he made his will known to him. Jesus in turn demonstrated his love to the Father through his submission and obedience.

The theme of the entire Bible is the self-revelation of the God of love. In the garden of Eden, God commanded that "you must not eat from the tree of the knowledge of good and evil, for when you eat of it you will surely die" (Gen. 2:17). We are not prepared, then, when God looks for Adam after his sin, calling out "Where are you?" God seeks Adam, not to put him to death, but to reestablish a relationship with him. God, the Lover, will not allow sin to stand between him and his creature. He personally bridges the gap.

That seeking and bridging reaches its pinnacle when God sends his Son into the world to rescue sinners and to provide them with eternal life (John 3:16; Rom. 5:7–8; Eph. 2:1–5). John declares, "This is how we know what love is: Jesus Christ laid down his life for us" (1 John 3:16). God's love is not based on the merit of the recipient (Deut. 7:7–8; Rom. 5:7–8). Because he is love, God is not willing that any person should perish, but wills that everyone repent and live (Ezek. 18:32; 2 Peter 3:9).

"Love the Lord Your God." We are totally incapable of loving either God or others—a condition that must be corrected by God before we can love. The Bible's ways of describing this process of correction are numerous: "circumcision of the heart" (Deut. 30:6); God's "writing his laws" on our hearts (Jer. 31:33); God's substituting a "heart of flesh" for a "heart of stone" (Ezek. 11:19); being "born again" by the Spirit (John 3:3; 1 John 5:1–2); removing old clothing and replacing it with new (Col. 3:12–14); dying to a sinful life and resurrecting to a new one (Col. 3:1–4); moving out of darkness into light (1 John 2:9). Until that happens, we cannot love.

God alone is the source of love (1 John 4:7–8); he "poured out his love into our hearts by the Holy Spirit, whom he has given us" (Rom. 5:5). God's love then awakens a response in those who accept it. God loves through believers, who act as channels for his love; they are branches who must abide in the vine if they are to have that love (John 15:1–11). We have the assurance that we have passed from death to life because we love others (1 John 3:14).

Once we have received God's love as his children, he expects us to love. In fact, "Whoever does not love does not know God, because God is love" (1 John 4:8). Jude urges his readers to keep themselves in God's love (v.21).

"Love the Lord Your God with All Your Heart." Love of God is a response of the whole of the believer—heart, soul, mind, and strength (Deut. 6:5; Matt. 22:34–40; Mark 12:28–34)—to the whole of God. Jesus serves as the believer's model (John 14:21; Phil. 2:5–8). Obedience to God (Deut. 6:7; 7:9) and renunciation of the world-system (1 John 2:16) are critical elements of our love of God.

Our love, however, is easily misdirected. Its object tends to become the creation rather than the Creator; it loses sight of the eternal for the temporal; it focuses on the self, often to the exclusion of God and others. We become idolaters, focusing a part or all of our love elsewhere. We are "love breakers" more than "law breakers."

Genesis 22 presents a classic struggle: the conflicting pulls of love. Abraham loves Isaac, the son of his old age, the child of God's promise. But God tests his love. For the sake of the love of God, Abraham is willing to sacrifice the son he loves. His response is to a greater love. Jesus describes this conflict as hating father and mother in order to love and follow God (Luke 14:26).

"Love Your Neighbor as Yourself." Love for neighbor is a decision that we make to treat others with respect and concern, to put the interests and safety of our neighbors on a level with our own. It demands a practical outworking in everyday life—placing a retaining wall around the roof to keep people from falling (Deut. 22:8); not taking millstones in pledge, thus denying someone the ability to grind grain into flour (Deut. 24:6); allowing the poor to glean leftovers from the orchards and fields (Lev. 19:9–12). Our actions illustrate our love. Love for neighbor is "love in action," doing something specific and tangible for others.

The New Testament concept closely parallels that of the Old Testament. John writes: "Dear children, let us not love with words or tongue but with actions and in truth." Believers need to share with those in need, whether that need is for food, water, lodging, clothing, healing, or friendship (Matt. 25:34–40; Rom. 12:13). The love demonstrated in the parable of the good Samaritan shows that *agapē* love is not emotional love, but a response to someone who is in need.

The command to love others is based on how God has loved us. Since believers have been the recipients of love, they must love. Since Christ has laid down his life for us, we must be willing to lay down our lives for our brothers (1 John 3:16).

Many people in Jesus' day believed that a neighbor was a fellow Israelite. When asked to define "neighbor," however, Jesus cited the parable of the good Samaritan—a person who knowingly crossed traditional boundaries to help a wounded Jew (Luke 10:29–37). A neighbor is anyone who is in need. Jesus also told his disciples that a "neighbor" might even be someone who hates them, curses them, or mistreats them. Yet they must love even enemies (Luke 6:27–36) as a witness and a testimony.

The Old Testament charge was to "love your neighbor as yourself" (Lev. 19:18). But Jesus gave his disciples a new command with a radically different motive: "Love each other as I have loved you" (John 15:12). Paul affirms that "the entire law is summed up in a single command: 'Love your neighbor as yourself'" (Gal. 5:14). James sees the command to love one another as a "royal law" (2:8).

Love is the motivation for evangelism. Christ's love compels us to become ambassadors for Christ, with a ministry of reconciliation (2 Cor. 5:14). GLENN E. SCHAEFER

See also FRUIT OF THE SPIRIT; NEW COMMAND.

Bibliography. H. Bergman, *TDOT,* 1:99–118; E. Brunner, *Faith, Hope, and Love;* E. J. Carnell, *BDT,* pp. 332–33; C. E. B. Cranfield, *A Theological Word Book of the Bible,* pp. 131–36; V. P. Furnish, *The Love Command in the New Testament;* N. Glueck, *Hesed in the Bible;* W. Gunther et al., *NIDNTT,* 2:538–51; H. W. Hoehner, *EDT,* pp. 656–59; C. S. Lewis, *The Four Loves;* J. Moffatt, *Love in the New Testament;* L. Morris, *Testaments of Love: A Study of Love in the Bible;* G. Outka, *Agape: An Ethical Analysis;* P. Perkins, *Love Commands in the New Testament;* G. Quell and E. Stauffer, *TDNT,* 1:21–55; F. F. Segovia, *Love Relationships in the Johannine Tradition;* G. A. Turner, *ISBE,* 3:173–76.

Love Feast. The only certain biblical reference to the love feast comes in Jude 12, where the plural form of the word "love" with the definite article (*hai agapai*) probably denotes a communal celebration in the church (there is another possible reference in 2 Peter 2:13, but it is probably not genuine). But there is some uncertainty as to whether the reference is to that church's observance of the Lord's Supper (which elsewhere Paul can describe with terms like "coming together to eat," 1 Cor. 11:17–22), or to a fellowship meal that may have preceded or followed observance of the Lord's Supper.

The record of the early church's development preserved in Acts makes it clear that at least in the beginning communal meals, characterized by the sharing of food and worship, were commonplace (2:44–47; 6:1–2). There were also excesses and oversights connected with these fellowship meals (6:1–2; 1 Cor. 11:17–22). But there is no reason to think that the practice of a communal fellowship meal, conceived of as a normal aspect of church life or worship, could not have developed in the church addressed by Jude. The importance of eating together in Jewish culture is well known, and in Greco-Roman culture communal meals often played an important role in the life of organizations.

Whether Jude 12 alludes to a fellowship meal or to the Lord's Supper, the term chosen to describe it reveals that it was to be an event in which love was expressed and fellowship confirmed. In the Greco-Roman or Jewish household of that day sharing in a meal signified acceptance and fellowship, and the love feast in the church was to be a living example of unity. That this unity was a very serious matter can be seen in that the love feast is mentioned in the context of a denunciation of false teachers and admonishment of the congregation. The significance of the event was such that the unhindered participation of false believers in the love feasts, which signified their acceptance into the fellowship, was a "blemish" or taint on the event and also a danger for the church.

But it is really evidence from the second-century church that suggests the meaning of love feast. Yet in the later church, too, there is nothing like complete consistency in its practice or relation to the Lord's Supper. The church order of Hippolytus (*Apostolic Tradition* 26.5), which is much later than the New Testament, gives the fullest description of what had come to be called the *agapē*. It consisted of a meal that was taken by believers at someone's house or in the church and was presided over by a church officer (normally the bishop). Ignatius, in his letter to the *Smyrneans* (8), may give evidence that the love feast and communion were closely connected: "It is not lawful apart from the bishop either to baptize or to hold a love-feast [*agapē*]" (see Ignatius, *To the Romans* 7). However, Tertullian's description is of a communal meal, which begins with prayer, followed by people eating and drinking, the singing of hymns, and a closing prayer (*Apology* 39). He does not connect this event with the bread and wine of the Eucharist. A note from Chrysostom suggests that the *agapē* feast of his day developed from the practice of the early church in Acts. Then, there was a radical sharing of all things in common (Acts 2:44). This practice ended, but the *agapē* meal, in which the rich provided food for the poor and all shared it together, became the "contemporary" expression of the earlier communal sharing (*Homilies* 12; 27).

Whether these developments are relevant to an understanding of the love feast as it occurs in Jude cannot be determined. What can be said is that the event (whether originally observance of the Lord's Supper, a fellowship meal, or some combination of the two is meant) was to be a visible expression of love and unity. It is quite possible that the elements that only come to light in the later descriptions played some part in the earlier practice. PHILIP H. TOWNER

See also LORD'S SUPPER, THE.

Bibliography. R. J. Bauckham, *Jude, 2 Peter;* J. F. Keating, *The Agape and the Eucharist in the Early Church;* H. Lietzmann, *Mass and Lord's Supper: A Study in the History of the Liturgy;* J. W. C. Wand, *The General Epistles of St. Peter and Jude.*

Lucifer. *See* SATAN.

Luke–Acts, Theology of. The initial verses of both the Gospel of Luke and the Book of Acts indicate they were written to an otherwise unknown person named Theophilus. Acts 1:1–3 refers to the "former book" in which Luke has described the life and teachings of Jesus, an obvious reference to a writing like the Gospel. The author considers Acts as the second of a two-part work. A second-century document, the Muratorian Canon, states that the third Gospel and the Book of Acts were written by "Luke." Luke is mentioned in Colossians 4:14, Philemon 24, and 2 Timothy 4:11 as a companion of Paul, "the beloved physician." In Acts 16:10–17; 20:5-16; 21:1–18; 27–28 (the "we" sections), the pronoun changes from the third to the first person, indicting the writer was a participant in the events described. Otherwise, little is known of Luke save that he was probably a Gentile, possibly from Syria. Although much contemporary scholarship has raised objections to the conclusion that Luke–Acts was written by Luke, an occasional travel companion of Paul, there is no solid reason for concluding otherwise. At the same time it should be noted that Luke drew information from a variety of sources, a fact he himself acknowledges in the first three verses of the Gospel.

Dates of the events recorded in Luke–Acts can be fairly easily established. The birth of Jesus, according to Matthew 2, took place before the death of Herod the Great in 4 B.C. The data of Luke 3:1–2 locate the ministry of John the Baptist and the beginning of that of Jesus about A.D. 27–28. Acts 24:27 refers to the change of Roman governors, about A.D. 59, as Felix succeeded Festus. Paul's trip to Rome (Acts 27) took about a year. Paul then lived in Rome for two years (28:30), which places the end of the book about A.D. 62.

The theology of Luke consists of two parts: (1) that which he shares in common with the other Gospel writers, especially Matthew and Mark; and (2) his own distinctive material, emphases, organization, and contributions, both in the Gospel and in Acts. With the other Synoptic writers Luke shares the basic outline of the ministry of Jesus and includes much the same content as they do. Luke also portrays Peter's confession (9:18–19) as an important turning point, and, both by the amount of space devoted to it and the content included, depicts the arrest, trial, death, and resurrection of Jesus as the focal point and climax of his Gospel. He shares the Synoptic evaluation of the person of Jesus as the messianic son of David, the kingly Messiah, the Suffering Servant of the Lord, and the heavenly Son of Man who was predicted "in the Law of Moses, the Prophets and the Psalms" (24:44).

The differences between Luke and Mark are found in: (1) the distinctive ways in which Luke presents and emphasizes the material found in both Gospels; (2) the inclusion of primary "sayings" (teaching) material also found in Matthew but not in Mark ("Q"), primarily located in Luke 6:20–8:3 and 9:51–18:14; and (3) in the material Luke includes but which is not found in any other Gospel. Luke's special material ("L") may be grouped into the following categories:

1. John the Baptist and Jesus: the mission of John (3:1–6, 10–14, 18–20) and the genealogy of Jesus (3:23–38)
2. The rejection at Nazareth (4:16–30)
3. Certain mighty works/miracles, including the wonderful catch of fish (5:1–11); the raising of the son of the widow of Nain (7:11–17)
4. Special lessons and teachings: to the disciples in Samaria (9:51–56); to the seventy (10:1, 17–20); to Martha (10:38–42); about the master and the servant (17:7–10); to the ten lepers (17:11–21); to Zaccheus (19:1–10)
5. Parables found only in Luke: the good Samaritan (10:25–37); the friend coming at midnight (11:5–8); the rich fool (12:13–21); the barren fig tree (13:1–9); on seeking the honored place and hospitality (14:7–14); of the lost sheep, coin, and son (chap. 15); the unjust steward (16:1–12); the rich man and Lazarus (16:19–31); the importunate widow (18:1–8); the Pharisee and the publican (18:9–14); the parable of the pounds (19:11–27)
6. Warnings and controversies: opposition from Pharisees (11:53–14:4); warning about Sabbath observance—the hunchback woman (13:10–17) and the man with dropsy (14:1–6); about Herod Antipas (13:31–33); on counting the cost (14:28–33)
7. Jesus' final visit to Jerusalem: approach to the city (19:37–44); apocalyptic sayings (21:11b, 18, 25b, 26a, 28, 34–36); the passion and the resurrection (22:14–24)

Luke's distinctive emphases are numerous. Some include his special concerns for time, geography, and history. Even a cursory survey of Luke's two-part work shows his deep concern and interest in history. He dates events by references to rulers and relates some events in his account to those of the greater society and world.

Before presenting the ministry of Jesus, he establishes its setting. Luke details Jesus' birth, experience at age twelve (chaps. 1–2), and a genealogy (3:23–38). He appears to associate certain themes with geographical locations at which they were prominent. Although his is not a complete history of either Jesus or the early church, it is an account in which history—reliable history—is a significant element.

As a Gentile Luke stresses the universal scope of Jesus' ministry as Savior of all humankind, not just the Jews; he frequently points out the ethnic-national background of persons. He focuses on the church as both an institution and an organization and its relation with the state. Luke stresses the role of the Holy Spirit in both the ministry of Jesus and the church. Commentators frequently note Luke's concern for the underprivileged: the poor, the downcast, women, children, publicans, the sick, the Gentiles, the Samaritans. Similarly he shows a special interest in "social concerns," and responses to human need by Jesus and the church. Both by relating Jesus' words and recounting the experience of early Christians, Luke emphasizes the importance of prayer and teaches that discipleship is costly. He stresses the return of Christ (the parousia) and such concepts as praise, forgiveness, glory, joy, weeping, peace, love.

Of course, the most obvious unique fact about Luke's writing is that, unlike other Gospel writers, he includes a second volume. Acts portrays the establishment of the church and its early activities in Jerusalem (chaps. 1–7), as well as the scattering of its members as a result of persecution, and their subsequent proclamation of the gospel in other areas (chaps. 8–11). Of particular concern is the inclusion among the believers of persons and groups other than Jerusalem Jews—Samaritans, an Ethiopian, inhabitants along the coastal plain of the land of Israel, a Gentile (Cornelius), and unnamed Jews and Hellenists in the Syrian Antioch; this section also notes the conversion of a Jewish persecutor, Saul, later called Paul (9:1–31). Chapter 12 marks shifts in leadership away from the original Twelve to James and Paul and of the geographical center from Jerusalem to Antioch. The final fifteen chapters (13–28) show evangelistic activity, under Paul, moving into the larger world, as far as Rome; it shows how significant numbers of Gentiles came to be included in the church. The Council of Jerusalem (chap. 15) depicts the church, under the guidance of the Holy Spirit, clarifying its understanding that Christian salvation comes by grace through faith.

The History of Salvation. The history of salvation in Luke–Acts must be understood in two parts. First is the basic assumption that God works out salvation within a special history that is also a part of general world history. Micah calls his readers to remember certain events of the history of the nation Israel, "that you may know the righteous [saving] acts of the LORD" (6:5). This history begins with creation and the fall of humans into sin and ends with the return of Christ and the end of the world as now known; its time is virtually synonymous with human history. The events Luke surveys are a part of this larger stream of God's history of revelation and redemption; they depict God at work in the time and space of this world.

Second, Luke is intent to present the Jesus-event as not just another event in God's special saving history, but as *the* event in that history. His birth was through the miracle of the virgin birth, which was predicted and heralded by angels. Even as a babe righteous persons recognized him as God's "salvation" (2:30) and associated him with "the redemption of Jerusalem" (2:38). As a boy of twelve Jesus was aware of a special relation with God and a special mission (2:41–51). Throughout his Gospel Luke intimates that "more than meets the eye" is involved in such things as Jesus' baptism and temptation (3:21–22; 4:1–13), parables and miracles, his awareness of the presence of the kingdom of God (17:20–21) and of the overthrow of Satan as his disciples preached (10:17–18), the transfiguration (9:28–36), arrival at Jerusalem (13:34–35; 19:41–44), appearance before Herod (Antipas) as well as Pilate at his trial (23:6–16), and even his journey to the cross, which was marked by the lament of the daughters of Jerusalem (23:27–31).

Although Luke's direct quotations from the Old Testament are proportionately fewer than those in Matthew and Mark, he firmly establishes its relationship with the events he relates. He makes numerous allusions to Old Testament events and concepts. At a crucial point, the post-resurrection appearances, he shows that Jesus himself saw his life and ministry within the larger context of the Old Testament (24:12–49). This is also the practice of the apostolic preachers, who make constant reference to the Old Testament as the setting within which the Jesus-event must be understood. Jesus is the climax of God's saving work; therefore, "salvation is found in no one else, for there is no other name under heaven given to men by which we must be saved" (Acts 4:12).

The Day of Salvation. Throughout the Old Testament the "Day" refers to critical points at which God moves decisively in judgment and salvation. A common Jewish view of history divided it into two "ages." The first was a time of proclamation and preparation in which God often worked indirectly and figuratively. The second age was the "age of fulfillment," when God would work personally and directly to deal with human sin and resultant problems; at that time he would reestablish his sovereign control (the kingdom of God). This second period would last until the "world (or age) to come," the consummation of

God's work and of world history. The point of passage from the former to the latter age was expected to be marked by the direct intervention of God, either personally or through his agent (the Messiah). At that point the kingdom of God, the age of fulfillment, the messianic age, the age of salvation, would become a present reality.

Luke opens his account of Jesus' mission proper with the scene in the synagogue of Nazareth (4:16–30). Jesus read from Isaiah 61:1–2a, which poetically predicts the coming time ("the acceptable year of the Lord") of deliverance and salvation. Jesus then dramatically announced the arrival of that age with his own appearance: "Today this scripture is fulfilled in your hearing" (v. 21). Jesus pointedly stopped in the middle of Isaiah 61:2, omitting the prediction of a time of judgment—that, in Jesus' view, would come at the end, not the beginning, of the period just inaugurated. The rejection by his fellow townsmen came not because of his claim to be the Messiah (and that is the essence of his statement) but because he challenged the assumption that God's work and favor would be extended beyond the limits of the Jewish people.

Acts begins with a similar announcement of the arrival of the age of fulfillment. Peter, explaining the ecstatic behavior of the disciples at Pentecost, quotes Joel's (2:28–32) prediction of a coming time at which God would break into history in a unique way. What Joel spoke of as future ("it shall come . . . I will pour out . . .," 2:28) Peter declares as present ("this is what was spoken," 2:16). The intent of the two passages is inescapable; Jesus is the crisis point in time; he and his ministry are not the middle period (as Conzelmann asserts), but the central, decisive moment, the "Day" in God's saving history. The teachings of Jesus, the preaching and actions of the apostles, assume that what was future to Old Testament writers is now present; Jesus had harsh words for those who failed to recognize it (Luke 12:56). God's work had entered a new phase; things would never be the same again. It was for this reason that old patterns, law, practices, and the rest could and must be reevaluated. Life between the arrival and the consummation of this new age of salvation is the theme of Luke–Acts and the rest of the New Testament.

The Messengers of Salvation. The messengers of salvation are Jesus, his associates, and all those who proclaim his person, work, and their significance. Jesus is the messenger of salvation; he is the self-revelation of the God who saves, the one who proclaims the presence, kingdom, and will of God, and the one in whom God's will and work are carried out. Here the whole of Luke's Christology, a part of the message of salvation, is relevant.

In the Gospel other messengers include the Twelve and the seventy whom Jesus sent out (9:1–6, 10; 10:1–12, 17–20). Just before Jesus' ascension he commissioned others as "witnesses" (24:48). The Twelve and a growing number of converts become the "witnesses" in Acts. The Twelve, the apostles, were especially chosen persons who had been with Jesus from "John's baptism to the time when Jesus was taken up" (Acts 1:21). This special group seems to have been expanded to include such persons as Barnabas, James (the brother of Jesus), and Paul. Their task was both to proclaim and to give the significance of Jesus and his work.

The Message of Salvation. For Luke Jesus was not only the messenger of salvation but also its message. The message of salvation involves first, the person and then the work of Jesus. Information about the person and nature of Jesus is weaved throughout the Gospel. He, the supernaturally born babe, "will be called the Son of God" (1:35); angels proclaim him as "a Savior . . . Christ [= Messiah] the Lord" (2:11). At his baptism God acknowledges Jesus as "my Son . . . with you I am well pleased" (3:22). Jesus, "full of the Holy Spirit" (4:1), meets and rebuffs the tempter and takes up his ministry (4:1–14). He teaches and acts with authority; a demon recognizes him as "the Holy One of God" (4:32–34). With Matthew Luke relates that Jesus, in speaking to the messengers of John the Baptist, demands that he be evaluated in view of his words and deeds (7:18–23; note that Jesus alludes to the words and works prophesied of the Messiah in Isa. 29:18–19; 35:5–6; 61:1–2)—he acts and says what he does because of who he is. Peter acknowledged him as "The Christ of God" (9:20); the account of the transfiguration (9:28–36), which follows almost immediately, seems to give credence, commentary, and expansion of the meaning of the statement. As Messiah, Jesus has a ministry to perform, "a baptism to undergo" (12:50); he is the bearer, definer, and implementer of the kingdom of God. Jesus is aware of a unique relation with God, his Father (10:21–22; 22:29–30, 42; 23:34, 46; 24:49).

With the other Synoptic writers Luke records the phrase "Son of man" as Jesus' favorite self-designation. In Luke it appears more often. The origin and meaning of the term are hotly debated. The phrase occurs in Daniel 7:13–14, designating one who comes "with the clouds of heaven" and who approaches "the Ancient of Days." He receives a kingdom unlimited by race or nationality, time or space. It appears that Jesus used the phrase to clarify his mission as a spiritual one to counter the political-nationalistic overtones of the contemporary use of "Messiah." The final evaluation of the person of Jesus is Luke's joining with other writers to report his resurrection. Then, with far more emphasis than others, Luke also describes the ascension.

For Jesus the message of his work was synonymous with "the good news of the kingdom of

God" (Luke 4:43) and he, as its representative and spearhead, was at war with the kingdom of Satan and he is winning (11:14–22). Because of who Jesus was and because of the in-breaking of the new order, past traditions, practices, and expectations need to be reevaluated. Membership in the kingdom requires radical self-denial and identification with Jesus (5:10–11; 9:23–26, 59–62; 12:8; 14:25–33). The message in the Gospel is largely an announcement and clarification of these facts. Jesus' message always has the cross in view. With the other Synoptics Luke relates that from Peter's confession on Jesus spoke openly of the fact and necessity of his coming rejection, suffering, death, and resurrection (9:21–22).

The early chapters of Acts record a number of titles used of Jesus by the early Christians: Christ = Messiah, Lord, Servant (of the Lord), the Holy One, the Righteous (or Just) One, the Leader-Captain-Ruler-Author-Founder-Pioneer (all these are included in the Greek *archēgos,* 3:15; 5:31), Savior, Prophet (like Moses), the Stone, Judge, and Son of Man. Each of these have their roots in the Old Testament, were modified by intertestamental Judaism, and were further adapted by the early Christians to speak of different aspects of the person and work of Jesus. Even more, Jesus is the subject of the message of the early church. It is only through him that God can be known, sins forgiven, and salvation obtained; he is also the Lord, the head, of the church whom believers gladly obey.

Furthermore, the content of apostolic preaching in Acts centers on Jesus and his work of providing salvation. Since C. H. Dodd's *The Apostolic Preaching and Its Development,* it has become common to summarize the preaching designed to win converts, the *kerygma,* under a number of points that recur in the sermons of Acts. One of the several possible reconstructions is as follows:

1. The age of fulfillment predicted in the Old Testament has dawned, the promises have been fulfilled, the Messiah has come.
2. This has taken place in Jesus of Nazareth. He
    a. was descended from the seed of David
    b. went about teaching, doing good, and executing mighty works by the power of God through which God indicated his approval of him
    c. was crucified in accordance with the purpose of God
    d. was raised by the power of God
3. The church is witness to these things.
4. Jesus has been exalted into heaven at the right hand of God, where he reigns as the messianic head of the New Israel with the title "Lord."
5. The Holy Spirit in the church is now the seal of Christ's present power and glory.
6. Jesus will come again for judgment and the restoration of all things.
7. Therefore, all who hear should repent and be baptized for the remission of sins.

The apostolic message can also be summarized in Paul's words, "Believe in the Lord Jesus, and you will be saved" (16:31).

The Universality of Salvation. The message of salvation also contains the affirmation of its unlimited character. There are at least three features. First, although many Jews of Jesus' day assumed that God was concerned only with their people and race, frequently only pious Jews, Jesus asserted this is not the case. He associated with the common people, with publicans, prostitutes, and sinners (5:30–32; 7:34; 15:1). He pointedly noted that even in the Old Testament God at times showed favor to Gentiles over Hebrews who had the same needs (4:23–27). He made a hated Samaritan the hero of a parable that cast Jewish religious leaders in a bad light (10:25–37). Joy comes over the repentance of the lost, not those who are already part of the favored group (15:1–32; note that the elder son in the parable of the prodigal son probably represents the Pharisaic attitude of earning acceptance with God—"All these years I've been slaving for you, and never disobeyed your orders," (v. 28). The universality of salvation is a major theme of Acts. Jesus' last words before his ascension declared that his associates are to be witnesses "to the end of the earth" (1:8). The rest of the book depicts the initial, labored steps in carrying out that directive.

The second feature of the message of the universality of salvation is that salvation is not limited to a particular culture and is not to be earned by observing ethno-cultural religious rights and laws, even Jewish ones. This was a difficult truth for the early church to grasp; thus the expansion of Christianity beyond the Jewish people and territory required the clarification of its message. The Council of Jerusalem (Acts 15), under the guidance of the Holy Spirit (v. 28), recognized that God makes no distinction (v. 9) and that salvation is by grace through faith (vv. 9–11). This means that in addition to Jews, God accepts "the remnant of men . . . all the Gentiles who bear [his] name" (v. 17). Restrictions of place, ritual cleanness, race, and commandments such as circumcision are not required by God for salvation.

At the same time, the law-free gospel carries responsibilities. The conduct of believers must be pleasing to and in harmony with the nature of the God with whom they are in relationship; they are not to associate with anything pertaining to idolatry, are to observe basic moral behavioral standards, and are to be sensitive to the concerns of their fellow Christians (vv. 19–21, 29—this is another way of stating the requirement of Luke 10:27, to love God and neighbor).

The third factor of the universality of salvation is the responsibility to make it known throughout the world. It is no happenstance that following Stephen's vision of Jesus, the glorified Son of Man (Acts 7:56), the church began to claim for Christ the territory over which Daniel (7:14) said he would reign—"all peoples, nations, and men of every language . . . his dominion is an everlasting dominion that will not pass away, and his kingdom is one that will never be destroyed." The universality of salvation carried with it the mandate for both evangelism and missions. Luke–Acts ends as Paul, in Rome, proclaims "the kingdom of God and . . . about Jesus . . . that God's salvation has been sent to the Gentiles" (Acts 28:23, 28). Thus, the good news, the gospel, of salvation reaches the very capital of the human kingdoms of the then-known world.

J. Julius Scott, Jr.

Bibliography. C. K. Barrett, *Luke the Historian in Recent Study;* F. F. Bruce, *Bulletin of the John Rylands Library* 65/1 (1982): 36–56; H. Conzelmann, *The Theology of St. Luke;* M. Dibelius, *Studies in the Acts of the Apostles;* J. A. Fitzmyer, *Luke the Theologian: Aspects of His Teachings;* H. Flender, *St. Luke, Theologian of Redemptive History;* E. Franklin, *Christ the Lord: A Study in the Purpose and Theology of Luke–Acts;* W. W. Gasque, *A History of the Criticism of the Acts of the Apostles;* E. Haechen, *The Acts of the Apostles, A Commentary;* C. J. Hemer, *The Book of Acts in the Setting of Hellenistic History;* M. Hengel, *Acts and the History of Earliest Christianity;* J. Jervell, *Luke and the People of God: A New look at Luke–Acts;* L. Keck and L. J. Martyn, eds, *Studies in Luke–Acts: Essays Presented in Honor of Paul Schubert;* I. H. Marshall, *Luke: Historian and Theologian;* J. C. O'Neil, *The Theology of Acts in Its Historical Setting;* J. J. Scott, Jr., *JETS* 21/2 (1978): 131–41; C. H. Talbert, ed., *Luke–Acts: New Perspectives from the Society of Biblical Literature Seminar.*

Lust. A strong craving or desire, often of a sexual nature. Though used relatively infrequently (twenty-nine times) in Scripture, a common theme can be seen running through its occurrences. The word is never used in a positive context; rather, it is always seen in a negative light, relating primarily either to a strong desire for sexual immorality or idolatrous worship. In secular literature, the word indicates only a strong desire and can carry either good or bad connotations. The Greek word *epithymia* and the Hebrew words *ʿawâh* and *hāmad* can themselves be used in a neutral or good sense (i.e., Matt. 13:17). In these instances the New International Version does not translate the word as "lust." Rather, it is translated as "desire," "longing," and the like. The context surrounding the word lends to this translation in such instances. However, in Scripture, as translated in the New International Version, the word is used for a strong desire that is negative and forbidden. Indeed, the unregenerate are governed and controlled by deceitful lusts or desires (Eph. 2:3; 4:22; Col. 3:5; Titus 2:12).

In the Old Testament, the word is primarily used to describe idolatrous activities, although it does have sexual concerns in at least two instances (Job 31:1; Prov. 6:25). In both, the context is negative in meaning and is accompanied by a strong warning of God's impending punishment on those with such a strong, all-encompassing desire for inordinate affections. The lust involved in the realm of idolatry involves Israel's strong desire to be like other nations, who worship their gods of wood and metal. The language of Job is especially potent in regard to sexual immorality. Job is kept from looking "lustfully at a girl" because he knows that God's plan is "ruin for the wicked, disaster for those who do wrong." In the other Old Testament instances, the meaning clearly displays an idolatrous relationship, primarily Israel's desire to be like her surrounding neighbors (cf. Isa. 57:5; Jer. 13:27; Ezek. 6:9; 16:26; 20:24, 30; Nah. 3:4).

In Numbers 15:39 Moses is told by God to command that the Israelites wear tassels on the corners of their garments to remind them of the commands of the Lord. This reminder is seen in contradistinction to the outcome of not wearing the tassels, namely, "going after the lusts of your own hearts and eyes."

Almost half the occurrences of the word and its derivatives are in the Book of Ezekiel. In every instance, it refers to Israel's idolatrous worship. An interesting display of this attitude is seen in chapter 23, where God's prophet uses the parable of two adulterous sisters, Oholah (representing Samaria) and Oholibah (representing Jerusalem). The imagery involves sexual lust but is descriptive of Israel's spiritual idolatry. Just as Oholah's and Oholibah's love was misdirected toward the officers of enemy armies, so Jerusalem's desire was for the things of her enemies. Throughout the parable, God warns of the judgment that awaits Oholah and Oholibah for their idolatrous lust. Indeed, such judgment occurred for Oholah (Samaria) in 722 B.C., when Assyria conquered her. Oholibah (Jerusalem) fell in 586 B.C.

In the New Testament, the word moves from referring primarily to idolatry to referring instead almost exclusively to sexual immorality. While the idea of idolatry is not completely absent, the primary intention is as a strong, inordinate desire for sexual relations. This sexual immorality, however, is not intended to represent actions alone since lust occurs first as a thought in the mind. The warning is to stop the lust before it moves into the realm of action. For instance, Jesus commands that a man is not to even look at a woman lustfully (i.e., with a desire to have sexual relations with her) because that is the same as committing the physical act of adultery (Matt. 5:27–30); both are sin.

In each of the texts where Paul uses the word, it clearly is condemnatory of sexual immorality, both homosexual (Rom. 1:26–27) and heterosexual. The command from Paul is to utterly destroy those inordinate desires that most often manifest themselves in the area of sexuality (cf. Col. 3:5). Paul continues to warn that we must learn to control our bodies and be sanctified rather than giving in to our base desires, which is characteristic of those who do not know God (cf. 1 Thess. 4:3–5).

Paul is not alone in pointing out that the lustful lifestyle is characteristic of lost humanity. Peter concurs, and exhorts his readers to quit living as they did before they received Christ. He points out that lust is evidence of a pagan lifestyle (1 Peter 4:3). Also, according to Peter, lustful desires (not necessarily just sexual desires, but desiring anything more than one desires God) are a basic motivation inherent in human sinful nature (2 Peter 2:18).

It is obvious from John's writings that our lusts do not come from God but from the world. However, we are reminded by John that the world and its desires (lusts) pass away, whereas "the man who does the will of God lives forever" (1 John 2:16–17). Here we see that our lusts are in direct violation of God's perfect will, because they usually are misdirected, moving and leading us away from God to our own selfish desires.

Our lusts have a very powerful influence on our actions if they are not caught and corrected immediately. We must remember that lust occurs in the mind and is not a physical action in and of itself. It does, however, have great potential of becoming an action—indeed a very damaging action. That is why we must heed the admonition of Paul in 2 Corinthians 10:5: "We demolish arguments and every pretension that sets itself up against the knowledge of God, and we take captive every thought to make it obedient to Christ."

DANIEL L. AKIN

See also IMMORALITY, SEXUAL; SIN.

Mm

Magic. ***The Old Testament.*** Magic—the attempt to exploit supernatural powers by formulaic recitations to achieve goals that were otherwise unrealizable—was seen in a negative light in the Old Testament (Lev. 19:26, 31; 20:6; 1 Sam. 28:9; Isa. 8:19; 44:25; 57:3; Jer. 27:9; Ezek. 22:28; Mic. 5:12; Nah. 3:4; Mal. 3:5) and was banned under penalty of death (Exod. 22:18; Lev. 20:27; Deut. 18:10–11). However, many Canaanite magical practices were later widespread in the divided monarchy: Jezebel practiced sorcery (2 Kings 9:22); Manasseh encouraged divination (2 Kings 21:6; 2 Chron. 33:6); Hebrew seers and diviners practiced the magic arts (Mic. 3:7); and Isaiah condemned women who wore charms (Isa. 3:18–23). The multiplicity of terminology used in the bans testifies that magic was a pervasive problem in the Israelite world. However, many of the banned terms (primarily in Deut. 18:10–11) have defied easy explanation, including child sacrifice (possibly used for divinatory purposes; Deut. 18:10; 2 Kings 21:6), types of divination (Num. 23:23; Deut. 18:10–11; 1 Sam. 15:23; 2 Kings 17:17; Mic. 3:6), sorceries (Exod. 22:18; Deut. 18:11; Jer. 27:9; Mic. 5:12; Mal. 3:5), and necromancy (1 Sam. 28).

Magic was considered an aspect of pagan wisdom; magicians were counted as wise men (Ps. 58:5; Dan. 1:20; 2:13) and officials of foreign governments (Gen. 41:6; Exod. 7:11; Dan. 2:2). Different from pagan sources, the Old Testament writers did not see a connection between magic and the gods. Foreign magicians in Scripture did not invoke help of their gods for magical formulas, but often called upon self-operating forces that were independent of the gods (Isa. 47:13; the monotheistic Israelites did not accept the existence of the foreign gods). Moreover, the biblical writers seemed to attribute a reality to magical power that it did not ascribe to the gods. Magic was considered human rebellion that unlocked divine secrets, making humanity equal with God.

Although there was a formal ban on magic, Israelite religion appeared on the surface to have adopted some Canaanite magical practices. There are many references scattered throughout the Old Testament to various imitative magical practices, including the use of clothing (2 Kings 2:13–14), magic staffs (Exod. 7:9), hands (2 Kings 5:11), mandrakes (Gen. 30:14–18), instruments (2 Kings 6:7), hair (Judg. 16:17), whispering (2 Sam. 12:19), spells (Josh. 10:12), belomancy (1 Sam. 20:20–22), hydromancy (Exod. 15:25), and various blessings, curses, and dreams. Old Testament ceremonial regulations appear to have had a magical flavor to them. Animals for sacrifice had to be the proper age, sex, and color; many were probably not used because they were utilized in the magic arts of the Canaanites (Deut. 14:21).

However, foreign materials and technical terms of magic were simply used as vehicles of expression in Israelite religion. The magical features preserved ancient elements whose original meaning had been radically altered. The writers stripped the magical actions of their autonomous power and made them serve as vehicles of God's will. Yahweh's name was invoked by the miracle worker (Exod. 7:8–9; 15:25; 1 Kings 17:21; 2 Kings 2:14). Miracles were merely signs validating the mission of the prophet, who did not work by his skill but by the power of Yahweh (Exod. 3:14–17; Deut. 13:2–3; Judg. 6:17, 36; 1 Kings 18:36; Isa. 7:10–11). The writers took great pains to show that Moses was helpless without God (Exod. 4:10; 6:12, 30). Even Balaam, both a magician and prophet, could only do God's will (Num. 23:12). God could overturn a curse and make it a blessing (Ps. 109:28). The man of God healed the sick, revealed hidden things, performed wonders, and pronounced curses and blessings, just like a pagan magician. However, it was not done with any technical skill, nor were these people praised for any wisdom (2 Kings 5:11). All procedures were commonplace and untraditional.

The Israelites viewed divination as a subsidiary of magic. The biblical writers banned all of the foreign techniques employed for divinatory oracles (Lev. 20:6, 27; Deut. 18:10; 1 Sam. 28:3; 2 Kings 23:24; Isa. 2:6; 8:19; 57:3; Ezek. 13:17), including hydromancy (Gen. 44:5, 15) and astrology (Isa. 47:13; Jer. 10:2). They were distinguished from inquiries of Yahweh (Urim and Thummin, Num. 27:21; ephod, 1 Sam. 23:9; lots, Num. 26:55; dreams, 1 Sam. 28:6) on the grounds that divination was a custom of the nations. However, the Israelites believed in its power (1 Sam. 28:8–20). As with magic, the biblical writers did not view divination as connected with the gods, but instead considered it a magic or wisdom art that revealed secrets of God in a wrong way (Isa. 19:3; Ezek. 21:26; Hos. 4:12). Thus, the divinatory technician trusted in omens and in human wisdom, rather than in God. Inquiry was acceptable, as long as it was only to God and confirmed by him (Judg. 6:36; 7:4; 2 Sam. 5:23). The Israelites preferred the simple technique of lot inquiry, addressing God and relying on his decision instead of going through an elaborate system of ritual. In sum, they did not reject divination in the strictest sense, but approved of the technique of inquiring of God to learn of his decisions.

The New Testament. Magical practices were also prevalent in the New Testament world. Although the New Testament writers did not explicitly condemn magic, none who practiced magic arts were described in a flattering way. There were numerous warnings against sorcery (Gk. *pharmakos,* one who dealt with drugs and potions; Gal. 5:20; Rev. 9:21; 18:23; 21:8; 22:15).

New Testament Christians viewed magical practices like their Old Testament counterparts. Although Simon the magician (Gk. *magos;* originally a term for an Iranian priestly group, it came to have a technical meaning; cf. Herodotus, *The Histories* 1.101, 132; Matt. 2:1–16; Acts 13:6–8) was severely criticized by Peter (Acts 8:9–24), the efficacy of his power was not denied, and he was considered dangerous. The story of Bar-Jesus (who attempted to resist Paul and Barnabas; Acts 13:4–12) was used by the writer to exhibit the differences between Christ and magic. The only other magicians mentioned by name were Jannes and Jambres, the Egyptian priests of Moses' time (2 Tim. 3:6–8); these names were noted in later Jewish writings and even by Pliny the Elder, who thought Moses was one of the Egyptian magicians (*Natural History* 30, 1 11). These two were looked upon by Paul as examples of those who opposed the truth. The one who had a spirit of divination (Gk. *pneuma python;* normally a spirit connected with the Delphic oracle; Acts 16:16) was forced to acknowledge Jesus, but the apostles did not accept this testimony because of the ungodly source. The burning of books on magic arts (Acts 19:19–20) was seen as a sign that the word of the Lord was growing. Seducers (a term that probably signified a spell-binding magician; 2 Tim. 3:13) were thought by Paul to be deceived, and Paul claimed figuratively that the Galatians had been bewitched (Gal. 3:1). He likely alluded to magical practices in his treatment of heresy in Colossians 2:8–23.

Many of the accepted practices in the New Testament (exorcisms, faith healing, and the use of lots; Acts 1:26) could have been construed by the Gentiles as similar to their own rituals. In fact, there were some linguistic similarities between words used for exorcism and healing in the New Testament and pagan magical rites. The Gentiles saw miracles as magical in nature, and thus confused those of the apostles with their own magic (Acts 8:9–11). The exorcisms of Jesus appeared to some as magical (Matt. 12:25–37; Mark 3:23–30; Luke 11:17–20), as well as his use of saliva to heal the blind (Mark 7:33). In fact, some rabbinical references claimed that Jesus was a magician. But the New Testament writers regarded Jesus and the apostles' miraculous acts as of divine origin. The healing of the woman with the issue of blood was done because of her faith (Matt. 9:20–22; Mark 5:25–34; Luke 9:34–38), not by magic.

MARK W. CHAVALAS

See also DIVINATION; IDOLS, IDOLATRY.

Bibliography. H. C. Brichto, *The Problem of "Curse" in the Hebrew Bible;* A. Guillaume, *Prophecy and Divination Among the Hebrews and Other Semites;* H. Huggman, *The Word of the Lord Shall Go Forth: Essays in Honor of David Noel Freedman in Celebration of His Sixtieth Birthday,* pp. 355–59; S. Iwry, *JAOS* 81 (1961): 27–34; J. Lindbloom, *VT* 12 (1962): 164–78; M. Unger, *Biblical Demonology;* R. B. Zuck, *Bibliotheca Sacra* 128 (1971): 362–60.

Majesty. *See* GLORY.

Malachi, Theology of. After the return from the Babylonian exile in 538 B.C., the Jewish remnant led by Zerubbabel the governor was able to complete the rebuilding of the temple by 515 B.C. With their beloved worship center restored, the Jews hoped to avoid the sins of the past and to serve the Lord faithfully. During the next century, however, we learn from the books of Ezra and Nehemiah that serious problems arose in Jerusalem. Commitment to the law of Moses weakened, and some of the people intermarried with non-Jews. When Nehemiah came to Judah as governor in 445 B.C., he discovered that the Sabbath was not being observed properly and that tithes and offerings were being neglected (Neh. 10:30–31, 37–39). Even the priests were prone to corruption (Neh. 13:7, 28–30). Since several of these sins are mentioned in Malachi, the book may have been written while Nehemiah was governor or after he returned to Persia in 433 B.C. Making use of linguistic analysis, other scholars prefer to date Malachi from 500 to 475 B.C., during the decline that preceded Ezra's return to Judah.

The name "Malachi" (Heb. *malʾākî*) means "my messenger" (see 3:1) and could be interpreted as a title rather than a proper name. Since all the other prophetic books are named after a particular individual, however, it is likely that Malachi was indeed the author's name.

God's Love for Israel. In a passage made famous by its quotation in Romans 9:13, the Book of Malachi begins with the statement, "I have loved Jacob, but Esau I have hated" (1:2–3). In Romans Paul was dealing with election, and this helps us understand that to "love" Jacob was to choose Israel as his special people. Esau, though Jacob's twin brother, was the founder of Edom, a nation that God turned into a wasteland as he poured his wrath upon it (1:3–4). According to Obadiah the Edomites rejoiced over the fall of Jerusalem and did not assist their "brother" Israel (Obad. 10–12). At Mount Sinai the nation of Israel became God's "treasured possession" (Exod. 19:5), a term used in Malachi 3:17 also. In spite of the fact that many Jews questioned God's love for them (1:2), the Lord promised that those who feared him would indeed be his special people. God would never forget his covenant with Abraham by abandoning his people (3:6). In fulfillment of the Abrahamic covenant, the day would come when all the nations would call Israel blessed (3:12).

The Character of God. Although some of the Jews were dishonoring the Lord by their sinful attitudes and actions, the greatness of Israel's God was evident among the nations. God had brought destruction on Edom and earlier on Assyria and Babylon, showing that he was superior to the gods of these nations (1:5). Yahweh was "a great king" and his name was "to be feared among the nations" (1:14). Ultimately, offerings and praise will be brought to the Lord from all over the world (1:11), a prediction that especially looks forward to the inclusion of Gentiles in the New Testament church. How ironic that Israel, God's chosen nation, failed to acknowledge the greatness of her God while pagan Gentiles became believers in him (see Rom. 9:26–33).

The Israelites were a fickle people, but the Lord was unchangeable. His love for Israel continued in spite of their sin, and he would never forget that they were his covenant people (3:6). Yet God was a holy God who demanded obedience, so if Israel refused to repent she would have to be judged (4:6).

Throughout the Scriptures the Lord is portrayed again and again as a God of justice and righteousness, but strangely, here at the end of the Old Testament his justice is questioned (2:17). Perhaps the Jews were struggling with their relative insignificance within the Persian Empire or with the delay in the fulfillment of the messianic age. From 3:13–15 it appears that some people were frustrated by the prosperity of the wicked. Whatever the reasons for their doubt, the Lord assured them that the wicked will receive just punishment and those who serve the Lord will be marvelously blessed (see 4:1–3).

The Sinfulness of the Priests and the People. The rebuilding of the temple should have been a strong incentive to holy living, but both priests and people failed to honor the Lord. According to 1:6–14 the priests set a poor example by showing contempt for the sacrificial system by offering crippled or diseased animals. Their careless attitude made a mockery out of worship, and the Lord asked them to shut the temple doors and put an end to their hypocrisy. Religious activity without a heart committed to the Lord is useless (see Isa. 1:11–17).

Led astray by the priests, the people in general were guilty of oppression and immorality, and divorce became widespread. Ezra and Nehemiah had condemned intermarriage with foreigners, a practice that may have gone hand in hand with divorce. Men were breaking their marriage covenants and wedding pagans, a sure way to get entangled with idolatry (2:11–14). In response to their actions the Lord stated clearly "I hate divorce," because the disintegration of the family would affect society adversely and would make it difficult to teach spiritual values to children (2:16).

The Rewards of Faith and Fearing the Lord. Six times in the book the people are urged to fear (revere, respect) the Lord and serve him wholeheartedly (see 1:6, 14; 2:5; 3:5, 16; 4:2). If the priests and the people continued in their sin they would be under a curse (2:2; 3:9), including the threat of total destruction, the "ban" to which the Canaanites and Edomites were subjected (4:6; see Josh. 6:17; Isa. 34:5). Those who truly feared the Lord would have their names recorded in a "scroll of remembrance" and would be duly rewarded (3:16).

One practical way to serve the Lord was to bring him tithes and offerings. Instead of "robbing" God, the people were to bring their gifts to the Levites, and the Lord would "throw open the floodgates of heaven" and provide crops in such abundance that they would "not have room enough for it" (3:9–10).

The Messenger of the Lord. Three times in the New Testament John the Baptist is identified as the messenger "who will prepare the way" before Jesus (Matt. 11:10; Mark 1:2; Luke 7:27; cf. Mal. 3:1). Normally a prophet or a priest was called a messenger. Luke also connected Malachi 4:5–6 with John the Baptist, noting that John ministered "in the spirit and power of Elijah" and called the nation to repentance (Luke 1:17).

The Coming Messiah. A second "messenger" is mentioned in 3:1, this time "the messenger of the covenant," who is also identified with "the Lord you are seeking." Since "messenger" (*malʾāk*) can also be translated "angel," the reference to "covenant" could be to the angel of the Lord and his involvement in the Mosaic covenant. Christ came to fulfill the law of Moses, but he also came to establish the New Covenant by giving his life to redeem humankind. Most of the Messiah's judging work is associated with his second coming, but Christ did cleanse the temple and denounce the hypocrisy of the teachers of the law and the Pharisees.

Another messianic reference may be found in the phrase "sun of righteousness" included in 4:2. Zechariah, the father of John the Baptist, called Jesus "the rising sun" who would bring the light of life to those living in darkness (Luke 1:78–79).

The Day of the Lord. In the prophetic books the day of the Lord signifies the time when God intervenes in the affairs of nations to judge the wicked and rescue the righteous. In Malachi the judgmental aspect is emphasized, in that the day of the Lord is a "dreadful day" in which evildoers will be set on fire (4:1, 5). Much of the judgment connected with the Messiah will take place at Christ's second coming, but in 3:2–4 it is the priests and Levites who are refined and purified. Perhaps Christ's severe criticism of religious leaders followed by the destruction of the temple in A.D. 70 shows how judgment can be tied in with his first coming also. For those who revered his name and received him as Savior, Christ's coming brought spiritual and even physical healing (4:2–3; see Acts 3:8). HERBERT M. WOLF

See also ISRAEL; MESSIAH; PROPHET, PROPHETESS, PROPHECY.

Bibliography. R. Alden, *Malachi;* J. G. Baldwin, *Haggai, Zechariah, Malachi;* R. B. Chisholm, Jr., *A Biblical Theology of the Old Testament,* pp. 397–433; R. J. Coggins, *Haggai, Zechariah, Malachi;* R. L. Smith, *Micah–Malachi;* P. A. Verhoef, *The Books of Haggai and Malachi;* H. M. Wolf, *Haggai and Malachi.*

Male. *See* SEXUALITY, HUMAN.

Man, Mankind. *See* PERSON, PERSONHOOD.

Man from Heaven. English translation of several Greek phrases with which both John and Paul describe Jesus (*ho ek tou ouranou katabas,* John 3:13; *ho ek tou ouranou erchomenos,* John 3:31; *ho epouranios,* 1 Cor. 15:48–49). Although John and Paul each use the phrase for different purposes, the theological meanings they attach to it are strikingly similar.

A major point of debate among those with whom Jesus comes into contact in John's Gospel concerns Jesus' origin. The people of Jerusalem and some Pharisees know that he is from Galilee but are puzzled by his messianic actions and teachings since the Messiah (they believe) will not come from there (7:26, 52). Other Pharisees declare that they can trust Moses, but that they "don't even know where he [Jesus] comes from" (9:29). In response to this debate Jesus says time and again that he is "from above" or "from heaven" (3:13; 6:33, 41–42, 50; 8:23), something John the Baptist confirms (3:31). When John the evangelist uses the phrase "man from heaven" in 3:12 and 3:31, therefore, he means to set Jesus apart from all other claimants to the privilege of direct communication with God (3:13), and especially from Moses whom many may have viewed as just such a direct link (6:32, 58). The phrase also places Jesus firmly on the side of God rather than on the side of humanity either in its limited, "earthly" capacity (3:31) or in its sinful rebellion against God (8:23).

The phrase is not only linked with Jesus, however, but also implies something about those who want to follow him. Jesus tells Nicodemus, for example, not only that he is from heaven but that those who wish to see the "kingdom of God" must be born from above by water and Spirit (3:5) because "flesh gives birth to flesh, but the Spirit gives birth to spirit" (v. 6). Those who wish to side with Jesus, therefore, must experience a transformation of their nature so that it is in some measure consistent with Jesus' own heavenly origins.

In one of only seven references to the kingdom of God in Paul's letters, Paul makes the same point. He tells the Corinthians that the resurrection of both Christ and believers is critical to a proper understanding of the gospel (1 Cor. 15:42–50). He explains that eternal existence is qualitatively different from mortal existence and that eternal existence therefore demands a special body that all who are in Christ will obtain at the resurrection. Whereas the first man, Adam, was a man of dust, the last man, Jesus, is "from heaven" (v. 47); whereas believers now inhabit a body inherited from the man of dust, the resurrection will provide them with a heavenly body patterned after that of the resurrected Christ (v. 49). The reason that this is necessary, says Paul, is that "flesh and blood cannot inherit the kingdom of God" (v. 50). Understanding this important teaching should cause believers to begin to bear the image of the man from heaven now (v. 49, margin) by engaging in behavior that is consistent with their eternal destiny (v. 58).

The phrase "man from heaven," therefore, tells us something about both Christ and Christians. It reminds us that Jesus' relationship with the Father is unique and that he stands with the Father over against the rebellious world. It also reminds us, however, that those who believe in Jesus have experienced a transformation in their spiritual natures that will one day be matched by a transformation in their physical natures, and which should lead them to "stand firm. Let nothing move you. Always give yourselves fully to the work of the Lord" (1 Cor. 15:58).

FRANK THIELMAN

See also Christ, Christology; Corinthians, First and Second, Theology of; Jesus Christ; John, Theology of.

Bibliography. G. Fee, *The First Epistle to the Corinthians;* M. J. Harris, *Raised Immortal.*

Man, New. *See* New Man.

Man of Lawlessness. *See* Antichrist.

Manna. The miraculous "bread of heaven" (Ps. 78:24) that God provided for the Israelites while he led them through the Red Sea on dry ground and into the Wilderness of Sin (Exod. 16). The "small round substance" (v. 14) may have been produced by insects that punctured the fruit of the tamarisk tree, through it was consistently regarded in the Bible as a miraculous gift from God rather than as a product of nature. It was certainly miraculous in terms of its timing and quanity.

Manna looked like coriander seed and tasted like wafers made with honey (v. 31). When the Israelites saw it, they asked each other, "What is it?" (Heb. *mān hû*ʾ). This led to the name "manna," "what?" It came each morning, except on the Sabbath day. It could be collected each day for that day alone, and only as much as could be eaten in one day. If a person tried to collect more than needed or to store the manna for future needs, it would grow wormy and foul (v. 20). In this way it was impossible for the Israelites to evade total dependence on God or to use the manna greedily for personal gain. Miraculously, the manna could be preserved on the sixth day and eaten on the Sabbath, and it was not to be found on the Sabbath morning (vv. 22–29).

Eventually, the rebellious Israelites grew tired of the manna and regretted the day they were delivered from their bondage (Num. 11:6). They came to detest the manna and longed instead for the rich foods of Egypt (v. 5). But God continued to give the Israelites a steady supply of manna during their forty years of desert wanderings. When Joshua and the children of Israel crossed the Jordan River and entered the promised land at Gilgal, they celebrated the Passover and ate the produce of the land. On that day, the manna ceased, again illustrating its miraculous provision (Josh. 5:12).

The purpose of the manna was to test Israel's faith, to humble them, and to teach them that one "does not live on bread alone but on every word that comes from the mouth of the Lord" (Deut. 8:3, 16). A hungry Jesus used this quote to refuse Satan's suggestion that he turn stones into bread (Matt. 4:4). Like the Israelites in the desert, Jesus was totally dependent on the provisions of his heavenly Father while in the wilderness of temptation (Matt. 4:11).

The people in Jesus' day misunderstood the significance of the manna. They longed for a physical miracle, like the manna, which would prove to them that Jesus' words were true (John 6:31). But Jesus wanted his disciples to seek for the bread of heaven that gives life to the world, instead of physical bread to satisfy their appetites. When they asked, "From now on give us this bread," he answered, "I am the bread of life" (vv. 32–35). To the church in Pergamos, Jesus encouraged faithfulness by promising that true believers would receive "hidden manna" to eat (Rev. 2:17). Just as Moses' manna brought with it physical blessing, so this heavenly reward will bring eternal life.

William T. Arnold

See also Jesus Christ; John, Theology of.

Bibliography. F. S. Bodenheimer, *BA* 10 (1947):1–6; J. C. Slayton, *ABD,* 4:511; E. M. Yamauchi, *WTJ* 28 (1966):145–56.

Marduk. *See* Gods and Goddesses, Pagan.

Mark of the Beast. Revelation 16:2 and 19:20 cite the "mark of the beast" as a sign that identifies those who worship the beast out of the sea (Rev. 13:1). This beast is usually identified as the antichrist. This mark is first mentioned in 13:16–17, where it is imposed on humanity by the beast out of the earth (13:11). This second beast is the false prophet (19:20), who forces the worship of the antichrist and brands those who do so with the mark. This mark is equivalent to the beast's name or number (13:17; cf. 14:11). This enigmatic number is announced in 13:18 as 666.

The term "mark" has no special biblical usage apart from its association with the beast. The Greek term *charagma* was most commonly used for imprints on documents or coins. *Charagma* is well attested to have been an imperial seal of the Roman Empire used on official documents during the first and second centuries. This term does not occur in the Septuagint, and its use in the church fathers is insignificant. The only other reference to *charagma* in the New Testament besides those in Revelation, is Acts 17:29, where it stands for an image formed by art. A more common term for "mark" or "brand" is *stigma* in its noun and verb forms. Branding was practiced in the ancient world, and even in relation to religious concerns. Religious tattooing was observed (cf. Lucian, *Syr. Dea* 59; Herodotus 2.113). Third Maccabees 2:29 records an incident in which Jews were branded by Ptolemy Philopator I (217 B.C.) with the Greek religious Dionysian ivy-leaf symbol. The "mark" on Cain in Genesis 4:15 is rendered by *sēmeion* in the Septuagint, the term for "sign." Paul's reference to his bearing in his body the "marks" of Jesus (Gal. 6:17) utilizes *stigma,* not *charagma.*

The contextual significance of marking those who worship the beast may be accounted for by noting how this motif answers to the seal on the foreheads of those who worship the Lamb (Rev. 7:3; 14:1). This contrast is particularly noted in 20:4, where those who are martyred for the Lamb are resurrected to reign with Christ. The mark and seal well image the two earthly groups who dominate the narrative.

The interpretive difficulty in understanding the mark of the beast resides in identifying what response John expected by his challenge in Revelation 13:18 to calculate the number of the beast. The process of working from a number to a name was an ancient process called *gematria* in Hebrew and *isopsēphia* in Greek. Many ancient languages utilized the letters of the alphabet for their numerical systems. The letter and number ratio was known by all. This existing process was used in enigmatic statements to conceal the identity of the person under consideration. An oft-quoted graffito from Pompeii (about A.D. 79) reads "I love her whose number is 545." Only those who knew the name or the pool of candidates could work out the riddle. The apocalyptic *Sibylline Oracles* used "888," the numerical equivalent of *Iēsous* (Greek letters for Jesus), as an indirect reference to Jesus as the incarnate God. Therefore, John could have expected his audience to solve the riddle, but only if there was a shared pool of understanding concerning the enigmatic nature of the reference.

The history of interpretation concerning the correlation of a person with the number 666 has only resulted in endless speculations. One of the most prominent candidates has been the first-century Roman emperor Nero. A rare rendering of his name into Neron Caesar, transliterated into Hebrew as *nrwn qsr,* renders the number 666 (nun/50, resh/200, waw/6, nun/50, qof/100, samech/60, and resh/200 = 666). This rare form of Nero's name was actually found in an Aramaic document from Qumran (cf. John's play on Hebrew words in the Book of Revelation at 9:11 and 16:16). It is also noteworthy that a variant reading in Greek New Testament manuscripts exits that cites the number as "616" rather than "666." The transliteration of the normal Nero Caesar into the Hebrew *nrw qsr,* renders the number 616. There was also a belief in a revived Nero as the antichrist from the first century (cf. book 5 of the *Sibylline Oracles*) to the time of Augustine, who cites this idea in *The City of God.*

Irenaeus, however, wrote within a century of the apostle John and did not mention Nero. He proposed a number of options, including *lateinos,* meaning a Latin (30 + 1 + 300 + 5 + 10 + 50 + 70 + 200 = 666), and thus a Roman ruler, and *teitan,* a Roman name with which he was enamored (*Contra Haereses* 5.29–30). A few modern scholars have noted that the numbers can also argue for a connection with Babylon and Nimrod. The list is expanded with the creative use of numbers during times of modern crises (e.g., Hitler was a major candidate during World War II).

It is possible that John merely intended the number to be symbolic of what the beast and his followers represent: humankind in their ultimate rebellion against God, his Lamb, and the followers of the Lamb. John explains in 13:18 that the number 666 is the number of man. The number 7 is well established as a number of completeness or perfection. The number 6, being one less than 7, may symbolize humankind, which falls short of perfection. Irenaeus notes that the image set up by Nebuchadnezzar was 60 cubits high by 6 cubits wide. The number 666 could well personify the imperfection of man, even implying in the triple number the unholy trinity of the dragon, antichrist, and the false prophet. The identity of those who follow the Lamb or the beast is self-evident to the observer, whether it is the first century or the eschatological future. The vision calls John and his audience to discern the spirit of sinful humanity that accompanies the antichrist rather than to decode his identity.

GARY T. MEADORS

See also NUMBERS, SYMBOLIC MEANING OF; REVELATION, THEOLOGY OF.

Bibliography. R. Bauckham, *The Climax of Prophecy;* I. T. Beckwith, *The Apocalypse of John;* M. E. Boring, *Revelation;* G. A. Deissmann, *Bible Studies;* G. E. Ladd, *A Commentary on the Revelation of John;* J. Massyngberde Ford, *Revelation;* R. H. Mounce, *The Book of Revelation;* H. B. Swete, *Commentary on Revelation;* J. Swete, *Revelation.*

Mark, Theology of. The Gospel of Mark teaches about the person and acts of God as revealed in the words and works of his Son, Jesus Christ. Mark's theology is a record of history written in narrative style.

Structure. Jesus' ministry is introduced in the actions of John the Baptist who, as God's promised messenger, is to "prepare the way for the Lord" (1:2–3). In this ministry, defined as good news (gospel), Jesus as the Christ fulfills the promises of the Old Testament concerning the Davidic Messiah-King in a unique way as the Son of God (1:1, 11).

Mark presents Jesus as the one God empowers with his Spirit (1:8–10), and as the proclaimer of God's good news (1:14). Jesus announces the special action of God in relation to the coming of the kingdom of God and calls for responses of repentance and belief in that good news (1:15).

The messianic ministry of Jesus is focused first in Galilee (1:16–8:26), where Jesus calls disciples, teaches with authority, heals, and casts out unclean spirits, while identifying himself as the Son of Man. The focus then shifts to Jerusalem (8:27–16:8), where he suffers, dies, and is raised by God from the dead, as "a ransom for many" (10:45).

Old Testament Promises. When compared with the Gospel of Matthew where the person and ministry of Jesus, from his birth until his death, are presented as a fulfillment of Old Testament prophecies, the Gospel of Mark interprets the relationship between Jesus and the Old Testament more broadly.

The coming of John the Baptist and his prophetic role are linked directly in Mark 1:2–3 to the eschatological promises of Malachi 3:1 and Isaiah 40:3. Similarly, the scattering of the sheep in Mark 14:27, as a result of the arrest, trial, and death of Jesus, is traced to the eschatological promise of Zechariah 13:7.

Jesus' use of the title "Son of Man" is the clearest indication in Mark of a radical reinterpretation of the Old Testament eschatological promises. In the "little apocalypse" of Mark 13 the figure of the Son of Man of Daniel 7:13 appears after great suffering (13:19; cf. Dan. 12:1) and the destruction of the created order (13:24; cf. Isa. 13:9–10; Joel 2:10, 31). In the biblical history of salvation the time of the gospel is the time of fulfillment. Jesus reveals himself as the Son of Man to counter the false messianic interpretations of the Pharisees, to prepare his disciples for how he will ransom many, and to show the faithful how they can rightly follow him.

The basic theology is clear. The Sonship of Jesus and the coming of the Spirit in Mark 1:9–11 (cf. 12:35–37) are allusions to the promise of God's in-breaking kingdom in Psalm 2:7, 110:1, and Isaiah 42:1. As a rabbi Jesus boldly reinterprets and applies the law in relation to this in-breaking kingdom (10:1–12; 12:13–17, 28–34), and on the basis of Old Testament authority declares that his hearers are either insiders or outsiders (4:10–12; cf. Isa. 6:9–10) according to how they respond to his teachings.

The meaning of the many miracles of Jesus is summarized in Mark 7:37, which reflects the hopes of the redeemed in Isaiah 35:5–6 when God is present. While the crowds who welcome Jesus as he entered Jerusalem rightly proclaim him as the Davidic Messiah-King (11:9–10; cf. Ps. 118:25–26), Jesus' redefinition of the role of the Son of Man of Daniel 7:13 as God's suffering servant is the most essential part of the disciples' learning experience (8:31; 9:31; 10:33–34). It is also his final word to the high priest who asks him if he is "the Christ, the Son of the Blessed One" (14:61).

Christology. By beginning the story of Jesus with his baptism, divine empowerment, and temptation by Satan, Mark emphasizes that Jesus is a divine being who is the Son of God. However, a paradox develops in the continuing story when Jesus is shown to be a person who has emotions, hopes, and responses similar to our own. The third element in the christological puzzle arises from Jesus' insistence on secrecy about his messianic indentity along with his persistent use of the title "Son of Man."

The narrative interpretation of what it means to be the Son of God is contained in those stories where the authority of Jesus as a teacher evokes the amazement of the crowd or the anger and unbelief of the religious authorities. These stories are often linked to his power to heal and to forgive sins (1:21–28; 2:1–12; 5:21–43; 6:1–6). Jesus' assertion of power over the unclean spirits in the healing process calls forth the preventative counterclaim from them that he is the Son of God. As they heed his call for silence they validate his claim to be the Son of God (1:24–26; 3:11; 5:7–13).

The association of the title "Son of God" with the messianic idea seems to suggest a purely functional use (1:1; 14:61); however, the qualifying adjective "beloved" with Jesus' Sonship describes the divinely certified relationship between Jesus and his Father (1:11; 9:7; cf. 13:32; 14:36). That this relationship is also humanly recognized at the time of seeming defeat, when the centurion sees the dying Jesus and confesses him as the Son of God (15:39; cf. 12:6), focuses on the meaning of the cross for persons of faith as a revelation of the power and wisdom of God.

The later Jewish objection that Jesus' death indicated defeat and a denial of his earlier claims is countered in Mark's Christology. Jesus, the Son of God, is also a person from Nazareth (1:9, 24; 10:47; 14:67; 16:6) who reacts with anger (3:5; 8:33; 10:14; 11:15–16), is disappointed (6:5–6; 9:19; 11:12–14), and not only dies (15:45) but is deeply disturbed at the inevitability of death (14:33–34) and its meaning (15:34). In the face of this paradox only the eye of faith can recognize that as the Son of God Jesus obeyed and suffered freely (10:45) and rose from the dead as he promised (8:31; 9:31; 10:34; 14:28; 16:6).

The words and works of Jesus during his public ministry in and around Galilee prompt persons to wonder who he is. The failure to conclude that he is the Messiah is shared by the crowds (1:27), the religious leaders (2:7), the disciples (4:41), and his acquaintances (6:3). Could it be that the secret of his true identity can only be resolved when it is clear what it means for Jesus to be the Messiah? Jesus' order to his disciples not to tell others about his Messiahship (8:29–30) supports this conclusion.

If Jesus' Messiahship is minimally identified by the usual title, it is clear that the kingdom of God is one of the major topics of Jesus' teaching, and that his Davidic ancestry and subsequent claim to kingship are stated by friend and foe alike. Whatever else miracles mean in the Gospel of Mark they too are proof of Jesus' Messiahship. Jesus performs "deeds of power" by the Spirit

(6:1–6; cf. 1:32–34; 3:7–12; 6:53–56, 7:37) in contrast to the false messiahs who perform signs and miracles (13:22).

The frequent use of the title "Son of Man" with its narrative interpretations indicates its singular significance for Mark's Christology. As a public title, in contrast to the use of Messiah as a confessional title, it is related to three key aspects of Jesus' ministry. First, his earthly ministry is characterized by divine authority (2:10, 28). Second, it is as a suffering servant who rises from the dead that Jesus is obedient to God and redeems us (8:31; 9:9, 12, 31; 10:33, 45; 14:21, 41). Third, he promises to return at the end as one exalted to universal rule for judgment (8:38; 13:26; 14:62). If Jesus' other titles are interpreted in different ways by his audience, the title "Son of Man" uniquely defines Jesus' ministry in terms of both majesty and humility.

Salvation. The story of Jesus in Mark is bracketed between the beginning of his ministry in Galilee where he calls for people to "repent and believe the good news" (1:15), and the end of his ministry in Jerusalem where the centurion at the cross confesses that he is "the Son of God" (15:39). Salvation is defined by the responses of Jesus' audiences to his miracles, sayings, and parables within a variety of settings between these two events, and Jesus' interpretation of his actions.

The faith responses in Mark come from those who are catalysts for the exercise of Jesus' mighty power (2:5; 5:34, 36; 9:23–24; 10:52; cf. 7:29). The spectacular character of Jesus' deeds makes it clear that a new age is dawning, and their responses assert that God in Jesus can supply all human need.

The crowds that are amazed at Jesus' teachings and mighty works (1:22, 27; 2:12; 5:20, 42; 6:2; 7:37; 9:15; 10:32; 11:18; 12:17) are located almost entirely in Galilee and symbolize the universal character of salvation. On the other hand, Jesus' enemies in Jerusalem exhibit a fear of the approving crowds as they seek to kill him (11:18–32; 12:12), and so reject the change that Jesus' offer of salvation entails, while unwittingly making it possible through his death on the cross.

The disciples' mixed fear and amazement responses indicate the struggle to bring together Jesus' claims to meet all human need and his outspoken acceptance of the way of suffering and death as the way to life. So when the stormy seas and the disciples' fears are stilled on two occasions their lack of faith is duly noted (4:40–41; 6:50–52); and when Jesus speaks plainly about his passion the disciples' fear and lack of understanding prompt them first to rebuke Jesus (8:32), then to remain quiet (9:32), and finally to follow him in fear to Jerusalem (10:32). The fear and amazement of the women who visit Jesus' tomb, with their subsequent silence about Jesus' promise to meet his disciples in Galilee (16:5–8, cf. 14:28), serve to warn disciples how these responses can hinder a faith response to the offer of salvation in Jesus Christ, the Son of God.

Discipleship. The disciples' role in the ministry of Jesus is a starting point for an understanding of discipleship in Mark. As a revelatory record of events the disciples' story reflects a historical reality and speaks to the needs of Mark's time and our own. It also gives evidence of the same tension present in the christological paradox (Jesus is both the Son of God and man), and in the interpretation of salvation as life coming from death. The disciples willingly follow Jesus but lack understanding and are afraid.

The development of the meaning of discipleship follows the structure of the Gospel of Mark with its division between Jesus' ministry in Galilee (1:16–8:26), Jerusalem (8:27–13:37), and his passion and resurrection (14:1–16:8). The Galilean ministry begins with the disciples heeding the call of Jesus, and leaving all to follow him and to be trained by him (1:16–20; 2:13–14; cf. 10:28).

For the extended ministry in Galilee Jesus commissions twelve as apostles who are to be with him, to be sent out to proclaim the good news, and to have the same authority Jesus has over demons (3:13–19). To do the will of God as realized in Jesus is to be a member of his family (3:35), but seemingly does not guarantee understanding of Jesus' teaching (4:10–12) or his actions (4:35–41).

As a preparation for the extension of Jesus' ministry beyond Galilee into the Gentile world the twelve are sent out as before, except this time they are to go in pairs and to live dependently among the people (6:7–12). Their immediate success (6:13, 30) stands in contrast to their later failure to understand how to meet need (6:35–37; cf. 8:4) or to recognize Jesus when he comes to them in their hour of need (6:49–52).

The three explicit teaching sections on discipleship following Peter's confession of Jesus as the Messiah (8:29) occur as Jesus is on the way to Jerusalem and the cross. The model for discipleship is Jesus' life of obedience and service, even unto death (10:45). First, he rejects the desire to rule by power (8:34–9:1), then the compulsion to grasp for prestige (9:33–37), and finally the need to occupy a position (10:35–45). He calls his followers to learn the meaning of life by the way of the cross, to set aside status as a means for achieving rights, and to accept the role of the servant by being humble, willing to suffer and even die for others.

Eschatology. The abruptness of the ending of Mark at 16:8 was solved by the early church with shorter or longer (16:9–20) textual additions. This means that there is no clear statement after Jesus' resurrection of his intention to return as in Matthew 28:18–20 or Luke 24:50–53 (cf. Acts 1:11). The references in Mark to a return and its results, outside of an explicit eschatological context, may be taken as either an interpretation of events related to Jesus' resurrection, or the end of the age.

The transfiguration story (9:2–13), with its emphasis on the presence of Elijah and Moses and the uniqueness of Jesus as God's beloved Son, also stresses the passion and resurrection of the Son of Man. The story makes it clear that Jesus is not just another great figure like Elijah and Moses who will not die. Jesus is to suffer the same fate as John the Baptist, the new Elijah, but will rise from the dead. With the disciples we ask, "What does 'rising from the dead' mean"? (9:10).

The Olivet Discourse or "little apocalypse" in Mark 13 provides the answer. Jesus relates Jewish apocalyptic descriptions of events that are to precede the end of history, including false messiahs (vv. 6, 21–23), wars, earthquakes, famines (vv. 7–8), persecution (vv. 9–13), and the abomination of desolation (v. 14), to the impending destruction of the temple (vv. 2–4). Jesus also urges his disciples to see this time as an opportunity to be active and faithful in preaching the gospel to all nations (v. 10), as well as patient and faithful whatever the circumstances (vv. 11–13, 35–37).

Finally, Jesus warns that the destruction of the temple will be followed by the end of the age. The cosmic signs predicted by the prophets (vv. 24–25) will announce the return of the Son of Man whose power and glory will be seen by all as he gathers his chosen ones (vv. 26–27). It is these chosen ones who are warned about the certainty of Jesus' return and the need to be ready (vv. 28–31), even though the timing of the event is known only to the Father (v. 32).

In this way Mark presents Jesus as the Lord of history who knows the future and promises to be with his disciples as they follow him in the way of the cross and spread the good news of what God has done and is doing in Jesus Christ.

HERBERT L. SWARTZ

Bibliography. J. D. Kingsbury, *The Christology of Mark's Gospel;* W. J. Lane, *The Gospel According to Mark;* R. P. Martin, *Mark: Evangelist and Theologian;* R. P. Meye, *Jesus and the Twelve;* W. M. Swartley, *Mark: The Way for All Nations.*

Marriage. An intimate and complementing union between a man and a woman in which the two become one physically, in the whole of life. The purpose of marriage is to reflect the relationship of the Godhead and to serve him. Although the fall has marred the divine purpose and function of marriage, this definition reflects the God-ordained ideal for marriage from the beginning.

The Image of God. Genesis 1:26–27 declares that mankind (*ʾadam*) was created in God's image with a plural composition of male and female, each separately in God's image (cf. Gen. 5:1–3; 9:6; 1 Cor. 11:7; Col. 3:10; James 3:9). Although the image of God is never defined in Scripture, contexts in which God's image are discussed must define the concept (cf. 2 Cor. 3:18 and Col. 3:10). God's image in Genesis 1 includes ruling, creativity (procreation), reasoning power, decision-making, and relationship.

The relational aspect of God's image is reflected in the bringing together of male and female in "one flesh" (Gen. 1:27; 2:21–24). This oneness with sexual differences portrays various aspects of God's image: same nature and essence, equal members, intimate relationship, common purpose, and distinct personalities with different roles, including authority and submission. In the Trinity the Father leads, the Son submits to the Father, and the Holy Spirit submits to both the Father and the Son. However, all three are fully and equally deity. Likewise, male and female in the marriage relationship are of the same nature and essence, equal as persons (cf. Gal. 3:28), intimate in relationship, common in purpose, but distinct personalities with different roles: the husband leads and the wife submits to his leadership (cf. Eph. 5:31). Marriage appears designed to reflect the same relational unity-in-plurality as the Godhead. Marriage, the most intimate human relationship, was appropriately chosen to reflect this relational aspect of the divine image. Each sex alone incompletely exhibits this part of the divine image. This open intimate relational aspect of God's image, reflected in marriage, was marred by the fall (cf. Gen. 3:7, 10), causing each mate to hide (cover oneself) from each other and from God.

Marriage is the most basic and significant social relationship to humankind. This relationship must be nurtured and maintained for the welfare of all. Without marriage, society will fail.

God's design for marital relationship is heterosexual, not homosexual, and monogamous, not polygamous. This relational aspect of God's image in marriage has analogues portrayed in Yahweh's relation with Israel (Isa. 54:5; Jer. 31:32; Ezek. 16:8–14; Hos. 2:14–20) as well as in Christ's relation with the church (Eph. 5:21–33; cf. 1 Cor. 11:1–3; 2 Cor. 11:2; Rev. 19:7–9). Israel is portrayed as Yahweh's wife (Isa. 54:5; Jer. 31:32; Ezek. 16:8–14; Hos. 2:14–20). Her idolatrous unfaithfulness and disobedience to Yahweh are frequently depicted as spiritual "adultery" (Num. 25:1–4; Judg. 2:17; Jer. 3:20; Ezek. 16:15–59; 23:1–48; Hos. 1:2; 2:2–13; 3:3) for which she was punished by captivity. Yahweh "divorced" his "unfaithful wife" (Isa. 50:1; Jer. 3:8; Hos. 2:2), but ultimately will have compassion and delightfully restore her to faithfulness and holiness (Isa. 54; 62:4–5; Ezek. 16:53–63; Hos. 2:14–3:1).

New Testament marriage imagery describes the relationship between Christ and his church (cf. 2 Cor. 11:2; Eph. 5:21–33; Rev. 19:7–9). The church, Christ's bride, is sacrificially loved by Christ, just as a husband should love his wife (Eph. 5:25, 28–30, 33). The husband's responsibility is leadership, even as Christ is the head of the church, his body (Eph. 5:23). The wife responds submissively to her husband's sacrificial love like the church submits to Christ's (Eph. 5:22, 24, 33). The husband's love assists her in becoming holy and blameless before God, even as Christ presents the church without blemish to the Father (Eph. 5:26–28). Christ's relationship with the church becomes the functional model for a marriage relationship.

God commanded the male and female to perform two specific functions: procreation ("fruitful and multiply") and ruling over the earth ("subdue" and "rule") (Gen. 1:28). These are functions that reflect God's image. Humankind (male and female) receive God-ordained authority to rule over the rest of creation, but not over each other.

Human reproduction comes through intimate sexual union designed only for the marriage relationship. Cohabitation abuses the procreative nature of the marriage relationship. While reproduction is a divine purpose of marriage, some couples are unable to have children for various physical reasons. This does not make their marriage second-rate or inferior. However, a married couple should desire to obey the divine injunction of procreation if possible. Children are one manifestation of the "one flesh" of marriage. The procreative injunction obviously precludes homosexual "marriages."

The Marriage Union as God's Work. God brings a man and a woman together in marriage (Matt. 19:6; cf. Eve to Adam, Rebecca to Isaac). It is not humankind's prerogative to separate what God has chosen to put together (Matt. 19:6).

As creator of the marriage relationship, God becomes the essential supporting party to a marriage, giving wisdom, discretion, understanding, and love to protect the union and to enable it to honor God (Prov. 2:6–16; 1 Cor. 13). A marriage can glorify God and function properly only when both partners are believers in the Messiah, Jesus. Then the Holy Spirit guides and enables them in their roles and functions. Continued reliance upon God is imperative for believing spouses.

Marriage as God's Norm for Humankind. God made man a relational being in his own image. Therefore, there is the need for intimate relationship within humankind (Gen. 2:18). Such a relationship is also necessary for the reproduction and multiplication of humankind. Without the fall, probably no one would have ever been single. Perfect people would have yielded perfect marriages. Sin brought flaws in humans that sometimes make it difficult to find or sustain a suitable marriage relationship. Being single for life is an exception and, therefore, is declared to be a gift from God (1 Cor. 7:7). The single person is normally less encumbered in God's work. So, although marriage appears to be God's norm, singleness is neither more nor less spiritual than marriage (1 Cor. 7:32–36).

The Nature of Marriage. *Complementarity.* The woman was created as "a helper suitable" for the man (*ezer kenegdo*) (Gen. 2:18). The English "complement" best conveys the meaning of *neged.* A wife is a "helper" who "complements" her husband in every way. A helper always subordinates self-interests when helping another, just as Paul reminds us in Philippians 2:1–11. A helping role is a worthy one, not implying inferiority. The wife, therefore, helps the husband to lead their family to serve and glorify God. The husband also complements his wife so that together they become a new balanced entity that God uses in an enhanced way.

A new permanent union (Gen. 2:24). "Cleaving" in Genesis 2:24 pictures a strong bond between the members of this union. The marriage bond was to be permanent. Separation or termination of the marriage union was not an option before sin entered the world and death with it (Gen. 3). All later revelation shows that separation/divorce was because of sin (Deut. 24:1–4; Ezra 9–10; Mal. 2:14; Matt. 5:31–32; 19:1–12; Mark 10:1–12; Luke 16:18; 1 Cor. 7:1–16, 39). God's ideal was for marriage to be permanent and exclusive.

One flesh (Gen. 2:24). "One flesh" involves the unity of the whole person: purpose, physical, and life—a unity whereby the two become a new, God-designed, balanced life. They counterbalance each other's strengths and weaknesses. Sexually the two become "one flesh" physically as reflected in their offspring. God's ideal exclusiveness of the "one flesh" relationship disallows any other relationship: homosexuality, polygamy, adultery, premarital sex, concubinage, incest, bestiality, cultic prostitution. These and other sexual perversions violate the "oneness" of the marriage relationship and were often punishable by death (Lev. 20:1–19; Deut. 22:13–27; cf. Rom. 1:26–32). Becoming "one flesh" is used in Scripture for the consummating sexual act of marriage.

These aspects of "one flesh" argue against premarital sex, promiscuity, and perversion of the sexual act. The body is the temple of the Holy Spirit (1 Cor. 6:19), so believers should be holy in their sexual conduct (Lev. 19:2; 1 Thess. 4:3–6; 1 Peter 1:15–16), keeping marriage pure.

Intimacy. Commitment to exclusive sexual intimacy is treated with dignity, considered honorable and undefiled (Heb. 13:4). Mutual consent is required for any temporal abstinence from sexual relations (1 Cor. 7:1–5). Neither spouse is to exploit the other sexually nor use sex to gratify passionate lust (1 Thess. 4:3–7). One is to delight always in the wife of his youth (cf. Prov. 5:15–19; Eccles. 9:9). This intimate relationship is encouraged by God's portrayal of its beauty and dignity in the Song of Songs.

Covenant commitment. The covenant analogy attests the commitment between two married partners (Prov. 2:17; Mal. 2:14). Emphasis is upon an agreement, a commitment, not upon an analogy of conditionality and unconditionality of some biblical covenants that would extend the marriage covenant analogy beyond its expected scope. This marriage commitment, and faithfulness to it, preclude sexual relations with anyone except one's spouse (Exod. 20:14; Lev. 18, 20; Rom. 1:24–27). Although kings frequently employed marriages to seal foreign treaties in the ancient Near East, such commitments were spiritual as well as physical adultery.

Roles. Although male and female are equal in relationship to Christ, the Scriptures give specific roles to each in marriage. Paul, in continually emphasizing the terms "head" and "submit," summarizes the basic role of husbands and wives respectively.

The husband is to assume headship/leadership (1 Cor. 11:3; Eph. 5:23). The normal meaning of biblical headship is leadership with authority, as exemplified in Christ (cf. 1 Cor. 11:1–10; Eph. 1:22; 4:15; 5:23). Headship is a benevolent responsibility without disdaining condescension and patronizing of the woman (cf. Matt. 7:12; Luke 22:26; 1 Peter 3:7). Although the husband leads as Christ leads the church, the husband does not have all the rights and authority of Christ. He leads his wife toward dependence upon Christ, not upon himself, for all human leaders are fallible. The husband leads like Christ, being considerate of his wife with respect and knowledge. He considers the ideas of those he leads, because they may be better than his own. Leadership's goal is not to show the leader's superiority, but to elicit all the strengths of people for the desired objective. Headship is not male domination, harshness, oppression, and reactionary negativism (cf. 2 Cor. 1:24; Eph. 5:29; Col. 3:19), for "no one ever hated his own body."

Leadership assumes the responsibility to initiate and implement spiritual and moral planning for a family. Others, however, should also think, plan, initiate, and give input. The husband, however, must accept the burden of making the final choice in times of disagreement, although seldom should this be needed.

The husband's leadership and its authority is a God-given responsibility to be carried out in humility. Inappropriate use of leadership should be curbed by the unique intimacy and union implied in the phrases "one flesh," "no one ever hated his own body, but he feeds and cares for it," and "joint heirs of the grace of life" (Eph. 5:29–31; 1 Peter 3:7).

The husband leads with an attitude of love. Christ's love for the church provides the model (Eph. 5:25–33; Col. 3:19). The husband loves his wife as he would his own body (Eph. 5:25), nourishing and cherishing her (v. 29). He gives himself sacrificially for *her* benefit as Christ sacrificially loved the church. Such love rules out treating his wife like a child or servant; rather he assists her to be a "fellow-heir."

Biblical love thinks first of the other person (cf. 1 Cor. 13). It is a mental decision and commitment. God also gave emotions of love that should follow the mental act of love else the emotional aspect becomes infatuation or lust. Love protects, cares, trusts, and delights in the best for the other. The husband initiates love (Eph. 5:25; 1 Peter 3:7). He who loves his wife surely loves himself.

The husband is to treat his wife with respect and considerateness (1 Peter 3:7). The husband bestows honor upon his wife. He always shows respect for her privately and in public.

The husband appropriately provides for and protects his wife. This does not mean that the wife cannot assist in supporting the family, for Proverbs 31 demonstrates that a godly wife may surely do so. The husband should always be willing to suffer for her safety.

The wife submits to her husband's headship (Eph. 5:21–24; Col. 3:18; 1 Peter 3:1–6). Submission's basic meaning is "to submit or subordinate to a higher authority." It is a predisposition to yield to the husband's leadership and a willingness to follow his authority. The husband does not command the wife to do this. The verb implies that she does this voluntarily. Submission does not imply that the wife is inferior, less intelligent, or less competent. Christ submitted to the Father but was not inferior or less God than the Father (1 Cor. 11:3; 15:28). Submission does not indicate that the wife puts her husband in the place of Christ. Christ is supreme in all things! The submissive wife does not give up independent thought. Believing wives with unbelieving husbands think independently, while still submitting to their husbands (1 Cor. 7:13–14). She might seek to influence her husband for right and to guide him in righteousness (1 Peter 3:1–2). Submission never signifies that a wife gives in to her husband's every demand. If demands are unrighteous, she submits to her higher authority, Jesus.

A wife submits to her own husband. Relationships with other men are different in areas of submission and leadership.

Some feel that Ephesians 5:21 argues that the husband and wife are equally submissive. In its context the best understanding sees this verse as an introduction to three particular areas where people are submissive to one another: wives to husbands (vv. 22–33); children to parents (6:1–4); and servants to masters (6:5–9). Mutual submissiveness does not fit the latter two categories.

A wife should submit with an attitude of honor, reverence, and respect (Ps. 45:11; Eph. 5:33). A wife affirms and nurtures her husband's leadership. She submits in the same *manner* that she and the church submit to Christ (1 Peter 3:6). This analogy provides a good gauge. The wife demonstrates a gentle and quiet spirit (1 Peter 3:4), not demanding her own way or insisting on her rights. A wife's respect is primarily for the role of leadership that her husband occupies, not necessarily for his merits, though that would be the ideal. She recognizes the God-given leadership with regard and deference.

Effect of the Fall on Marriage. The fall made human hearts hard toward God and toward each other. The relational aspect of God's image became marred. Rebellion against submission to male leadership was Satan's initial temptation (Gen. 3:1–6, 17; contra. Eph. 5:33; 1 Peter 3:1). Male domination and harshness crept into leadership (cf. Col. 3:19; 1 Peter 3:7). Sin caused polygamy, concubinage, incest, adultery, rape, prostitution, and all kinds of immorality (cf. Lev. 18; 20; Rom. 1:26–32) to damage or destroy the marriage relationship. Marriage commitments are violated. Divorce, premarital sex, and couples living together out of wedlock would never have occurred had not sin entered the world. The fall severely damaged the marriage relationship.

For marriage to function now according to God's ideal, believers in Christ need to marry only believers. Whenever God directly brought a man and woman together in marriage, both were believers. Although pagan customs encouraged marriage with anyone (cf. Gen. 16), Israel was given explicit commands not to marry foreigners who would lead them to worship foreign deities (Deut. 7:1–4; cf. 13:6–11; 17:1–7; 20:17; 23:2). New Testament believers are also not to be "unequally yoked" with unbelievers (2 Cor. 6:14), meaning any action causing the union of believer with nonbeliever, or nonbelieving ways, must be avoided.

RALPH H. ALEXANDER

See also DIVORCE; FAMILY LIFE AND RELATIONS; SEXUALITY, HUMAN.

Bibliography. G. W. Bromily, *God and Marriage;* L. J. Crabb, *The Marriage Builder: A Blueprint for Couples and Counselors;* J. Piper and W. Grudem, eds., *Recovering Biblical Manhood and Womanhood: A Response to Evangelical Feminism;* E. Wheat and G. Perkins, *Love Life for Every Married Couple.*

Mary. Mary, the mother of Jesus, is called *theotokos* by the church because her Son is the one and only Son of God, *homoousios* (consubstantial) with the Father. In the New Testament Mary is presented as the true Israelite, the model disciple, the woman of faith/faithfulness, and a type of the church.

Mark presents only a rapid sketch or silhouette of the Jewish woman who is the mother of Jesus. In 3:31–35 Jesus acknowledges his mother, brothers, and sisters, but then states that whoever does the will of God is a member of his family. In 6:1–6a Jesus is identified as "the son of Mary, a brother [*adelphos*] of James, Joseph, Judas and Simon," and he is said to have "sisters." The meaning of *adelphos* here is disputed. It may mean a blood-brother, a half-brother, or, within the extended family, a male cousin. Likewise the word "sister" (*adelphē*) has been interpreted as a blood-sister, a half-sister, and a female cousin. Since the early church maintained the perpetual virginity of Mary, it could not accept that Jesus had full blood brothers or sisters.

Matthew fills out the silhouette of Mary provided by Mark, but only in terms of the birth and infancy of her Son.

In the genealogy of 1:1–17 there are no less than four women (Tamar, Rahab, Ruth, and Bathsheba), all of whom have irregular marital unions. Nevertheless all served God's messianic plan; so does Mary, whose son was not begotten by Joseph (v. 16).

In 1:18–25 Joseph acknowledges Jesus as his son by claiming him and naming him, so that he is truly "a son of David." Further, Joseph is told and recognizes that Mary conceived her Son in a miraculous way through the direct and unique action of the Holy Spirit. Thus, we have the doctrine of the virginal conception/birth of Jesus.

Luke presents Mary as the perfect disciple of her Son, who is also her Lord.

In the annunciation (1:26–38) Mary is called to unique discipleship. As a virgin she will conceive and bear a son who is "the Son of God."

In 1:39–56 we read of Mary's visit to Elizabeth, of Elizabeth's hymn to Mary, and then of Mary's "Magnificat." Mary is both "the handmaid of the Lord" and "the mother of my Lord," for her Son is the Son of God, the Messiah of Israel and Savior of the world.

Mary is also very much present in chapter 2 as the "mother of my Lord." We read of the birth of Jesus (vv. 6–7), the visit of the shepherds (vv. 8–20), the naming of Jesus and the purification of Mary (vv. 21–40), and (much later) the finding of the boy Jesus in the temple (vv. 41–52).

Luke 8:19–21 is similar to Mark 3:31–35 but Luke 11:27–28 is only found in Luke's Gospel. Here the mother of Jesus is presented as worthy of beatitude, not only because of giving birth to her Son but also because of her faith, obedience, and discipleship.

From the hand of Luke we also learn in Acts 1:14 that Mary was present with others waiting for the arrival of the Holy Spirit. Thus, she is always the faithful disciple.

At the wedding in John 2:1–12 Jesus appears to reject his mother's request and then immediately does what she asks! However, she is there as his first disciple to behold his first miraculous sign. Further, she is there also "with his brothers" (v. 12), who (as noted above) may be her sons, Joseph's sons by a previous marriage, or the cousins of Jesus.

John 19:25–27 presents Mary at the foot of the cross, where Jesus entrusts Mary to John and John to Mary. Here, it may be said, the new fellowship, the new *ekklēsia,* is born and Mary has a central place within this communion of love. She who gave birth to her Son is there to see him die.

Paul states (Gal. 4:4) that Jesus was born of a woman (who is not named) and because she was a Jewish woman he was circumcised and submitted to the Law. Paul's words here or elsewhere tell us nothing about the nature of his conception.

In Revelation 12:1–6 we see into heaven and there behold the woman, the dragon, and the woman's child. In verses 7–12 we read of the archangel Michael and the dragon who move from heaven to earth, and then in verses 13–17 of the dragon, the woman, and her child, all of whom are on earth. It would appear that the woman has a primary reference to the people of God, Israel, and the church, with a secondary reference to Mary, mother of the Messiah: she is a "type" of the church.

Mary is a unique woman because she is the mother of the Son of God and also the first Christian disciple. The Catholic Church of East and West has developed its teaching concerning her not only by speaking of her as *theotokos* but also by speaking of her virginity before birth (virginal conception), at birth (miraculous delivery), and after birth (perpetual virginity). Liberal theology tends to deny all three. Classical Protestantism (Luther, Calvin) accepted all three, but modern biblically based Protestants tend only to accept the first. PETER TOON

Bibliography. R. E. Brown et al., *Mary in the New Testament;* J. McHugh, *The Mother of Jesus in the New Testament;* A. J. Tambasco, *What Are They Saying about Mary?*

Matthew, Theology of. In writing his work, the author of the first Gospel sought to make the life, teachings, and work of Jesus relevant to his own Christian community. Because his portrayal of Jesus is so complete, we are able to speak of the "theology of Matthew," meaning "the teachings of Jesus as presented in the first Gospel." But, in light of his purpose, that of setting out the ministry of Jesus, we are not able to speak with a great deal of certainty about the "theology" of Matthew in the finest sense of the "theology." We would like to know a lot more about what Matthew (the author) believed, but we have no access to such ideas apart from the contours Matthew leaves as he presents the ministry of Jesus.

General Overview. According to Wright, Matthew is a revision of the story of Israel as understood in contemporary Judaism. The story of Israel is well known: God, the Creator of heaven and earth, chose Abraham, formed a covenant with him, and promised to remain faithful to his covenantal relationship with both Abraham and his descendants for all time (Gen. 12:1–3; 13:14–17; 15:1–6, etc.). To clarify this covenantal relationship, the Creator-God gave to Moses and his generation the Law, with its specific details for obedience, sacrifice, and regulations for social life (Exod. 20–40). Israel, the descendants of Abraham, however, did not always live in covenantal faithfulness; thus, God developed a system of punishment or reward, depending on Israel's faithfulness (cf. Lev. 26). Over centuries of this pattern of sin and obedience, it became known in Israel that a greater Day was coming, a Day that would begin with a potent judgment on sin and that would climax in a glorious reign of Israel's God in Jerusalem. Attached to this expectation of God's intervention was the hope of a personal Messiah who would lead Israel (e.g., Isa. 9:1–6; 11:1–9; Jer. 23:1–4; Ezek. 34; Mic. 5:1–3; Zech. 9:9–10). The hope of restoration for Israel, of vindication of Israel, and of salvation for Israel were all intertwined in second temple Judaism and out of this hope grew Matthew's conviction that the story of Israel acquired its conclusive chapter in the birth, life, death, and resurrection of Jesus, son of Mary and Joseph. Such is the implication of Matthew's genealogy (Matt. 1:1–17).

In short, Matthew presents the story of Israel from a radically new angle: from the beginning (cf. the citations of the Old Testament in Matt. 1:18–2:23) it was God's purpose to bring the Messiah to Israel for the deliverance of Israel (1:21). This Messiah is Jesus, son of Mary and Joseph (1:18–25). The story is now different: those who follow Jesus are the true descendants of Abraham and they alone will enjoy the covenantal faithfulness of Israel's God. This covenant with Abraham, however, has been renewed in the new covenantal arrangement established by Jesus (26:26–30).

Thus, the theology of Matthew is salvation-historical and christological in orientation. Who is this Jesus, according to Matthew? Jesus is the one who, as Messiah (1:1), fulfills the messianic expectations of the Old Testament, and who, as Son of God, brings the salvation of God (cf. 3:17; 11:27; 17:5; 27:54). As the Son of God, Jesus teaches the will of God (5:17–20) and inaugurates the kingdom by obeying God's will (cf. 3:15; 4:17; 8:16–17; 20:28). In Matthew's Gospel the kingdom of heaven (a Jewish expression for kingdom of God) is understood as the rule of God, through Jesus, in power and righteousness, in love and forgiveness.

Matthew's Theology. There are at least four questions that Matthew's theology answers. Who are we? Where are we in history and location? What is the problem we face? What is the solution of God to our problem?

Who Are We? Matthew's Gospel presents the answer to this complex question in the simplest of terms: we, the readers of Matthew and the followers of Jesus (4:18–22; 28:16–20), are the church (16:18; 18:17), the true and New Israel. We are the true successors of Abraham's physical descendants (3:7–10) who are now bringing forth the fruits God wants from his people (21:33–44).

The presupposition of this answer is that Israel has persisted too long in sin but God, in his grace, has brought the Messiah to his people to reveal his grace and truth. This Messiah, through his life, teachings, death, and resurrection, has inaugurated the kingdom of heaven. All those who respond to Jesus in faith and covenantal faithfulness enjoy that kingdom (4:17; 8:14–17; 16:21; 20:28; 26:29).

Where Are We? Matthew presents the new people of God as a people inhabiting a world that is the preliminary life to a fuller, more glorious life that will come when the Son of Man appears in his glory (16:28; 25:1–46). Thus, the church is the people of God, participating in Israel's long story, and is living just beyond the fork in the road that separated physical Israel from eschatological Israel (the church). Put differently, the exile of Israel ends its awful time in the birth of the Messiah (cf. 1:11–12 and 1:16–17). Thus, the church is in the world, living in the era of the Messiah who inaugurates the restoration of Israel, but still awaiting (with the rest of Israel's history) the final age that comes when the Son of Man appears to bring God's promises to Israel to their consummation.

What Is Our Problem? The problem of Israel, and therefore of the new people of God, is the disobedience of Israel, which is related to the rule of Rome as God's punishment for disobedience, and, for the church especially, the presence of "weeds" among the wheat (i.e., the dawn of the kingdom of God but the remaining presence of unbelievers and sin; 13:24–30, 36–43). Matthew's Gospel, it must be inferred, also addresses the moral lethargy that seems to be facing the church—hence, Matthew's extreme emphasis on righteous living and the final judgment (5–7; 23; 25:31–46). Thus, the Gospel addresses the problem of an Israel still led by the Pharisees even though it is clear that God's Messiah, Jesus, has appointed the apostles as the new shepherds for the new Israel (9:35–11:1; 23).

What Is the Solution? The words of Jesus, quoted early in Matthew's Gospel, spell out the solution: "Repent, for the Kingdom of heaven has come near" (4:17, NRSV). All of Israel must now turn to Jesus, the Messiah, at this crucial juncture in history, and in so doing must turn from sin to follow Jesus, the way the disciples of Jesus did (4:18–22). The implications of repentance and following Jesus are explicated in the Sermon on the Mount (chaps. 5–7), a sermon that is designed by Matthew to present to the church the covenantal demand of God for the new people of God. Furthermore, the church is to live patiently in a suffering world and wait for God's judgment on the unfaithful leaders of Israel and those who follow them (23:1–24:36). At that time, the apostles of Jesus will reign (19:28). Once again, however, this solution presupposes the life and ministry of Jesus: through Jesus God's salvation, the kingdom of God, has come to the people of God (1:21).

Symbols of Matthew. Every religious movement has its own symbols, whether liturgical or ideological. Matthew's symbols include the Messiah, the Torah (as understood by Jesus), the church as the new people of God, baptism, and the Lord's Supper.

Symbols function to mark off one's community and, through use and remembrance, to reinforce one's perception of the world and the story one writes to understand that world. Those out of whom the church grew were Jews, and Jews had a rich heritage of symbols. Those symbols were the temple, the land of Israel, the physical heritage from Abraham, and the Torah, God's covenantal arrangement with Israel. Any reading of Matthew highlights the tension the followers of Jesus encountered with these symbols. The temple, according to Jesus, was defiled and needed to be cleansed (21:12–17). Physical heritage from Abraham no longer mattered because what mattered was following Jesus (3:7–10; 8:5–13; 15:21–28; 21:33–44; 28:16–20). While the Torah may well have had continuing guiding force in the church of Matthew, it is abundantly clear that the Torah of Moses was now fulfilled in Jesus' teaching and life (5:17–20, 21–48). Thus, apart from the symbol of the land, Matthew's theology is at odds with the standard symbols of Judaism. Such tension over symbols leads to, and probably already reflects, the formation of a new people, the church.

In the place of temple, Israel, and Torah, the church seems to have developed new symbols. Replacing Torah as the central symbol of the church was Jesus, the fulfillment of God's revelation to Israel. Furthermore, Jesus also taught a new ethic; this ethic, what Paul called the "law of Christ" (Gal. 6:2), formed a replacement of the Torah symbol in Judaism. The foundation of Israel's faith was the covenant God made with Abraham to multiply the descendants of Abraham, forming a massive nation for God (Gen. 12:1–3). The faithfulness of Israel's God to the nation of Israel was the bedrock of Israel's confidence in God. What Matthew's Gospel presents is the formation of the church, the New Israel, which is the replacement of Israel in the age of the kingdom of heaven (21:33–44). This new people, then, forms a new symbol: the followers of Jesus, while they may have seen themselves as true Jews, saw themselves as the church, the new Israel of God. Just as important is the consciousness that this new Israel of God is transnational in its essence; the new people of God is not just comprised of those who are physical descendants of Abraham but of all who follow Jesus (2:1–12; 8:5–13; 15:21–28; 27:54; 28:16–20). It was this conviction, the denationalization of the people of God, which created a great deal of social disturbance in the mission of Paul in the diaspora; we can only assume that Matthew's bold convictions led to as much, if not more, disturbance.

As for the land symbol, we have almost no evidence in Matthew, apart from the possibility that the third beatitude may have been understood as promising the inheritance of the "land" (the Greek word is *gē* and could be understood as "land") for those who are meek followers of Jesus (5:5). If this is the case (and it is far from clear), it would suggest that Matthew believed that the land would be inherited by the meek followers of Jesus, not by Israel per se. On the other hand, the depictions of the future in Matthew are not tied into promises of the land. Thus, the grand visions of Matthew 24:37–25:46 are more otherworldly and less this-worldly. If these formed the essence of the hope for the community of Matthew, then we are bound to conclude that land simply did not figure in Matthew's theology of the future. This would again form a distinct tension with the land symbol of Judaism.

Symbols that did seem to function sociologically and theologically in Matthew are baptism and the Lord's Supper. Jesus was baptized (3:13–17) and so were his followers; he commands his apostles to baptize those who commit themselves to Jesus (28:16–20). In fact, this baptism is in the name of the Father, Son, and Holy Spirit, demonstrating the theological convictions inherent to such a commitment. And this baptism was the prelude to a life of obedience to all the commandments of Jesus (28:20), surely an allusion in part to the Sermon on the Mount.

The Lord's Supper, as we have become accustomed to naming it, was the last Passover meal Jesus shared with his disciples. As such, it was a reenactment of the story of Israel's deliverance from the bondage of Egypt; the reformation of this meal into Jesus' last supper as a meal of remembrance, not of Egypt but of his death, demonstrates that Jesus saw his role in Israel's history as the antitype of the deliverance of Israel from slavery. In the same way, the death of Jesus is a ransom price paid for the salvation of the new people of God (cf. 20:28). Jesus, then, by swallowing up the Passover meal into a remembrance-of-him meal, forms the covenantal basis of the new covenant (26:28) that brings the forgiveness of sins.

Praxis. If orthopraxy was more central to Israel's perception of its faith than orthodoxy, then (with little adjustment) the same can apparently be said of Matthew. Matthew's Gospel is synonymous with the demand of God for righteousness. To become a Christian, or more particular a part of Matthew's church, meant to follow Jesus and following Jesus involved a whole-hearted commitment to a life of righteousness and love.

Righteousness. This term was used in Judaism for a life of obedience to the will of God, expressed most clearly and finally in the Law of Moses. Matthew's Gospel uses the same term as the crucial term for those who are pleasing to God but it now has an added dimension that shifts the meaning dramatically. Whereas righteousness in Judaism described those who lived according to the Law faithfully (Matt. 1:19, of Joseph), now it describes those who live faithfully according to the teachings of Jesus, who brought the fulfillment of the Law (5:17). Thus, Jesus expects his followers to live in a way that is superior ("exceeds") to the way of the scribes and Pharisees (5:20). Thus, those who are righteous are blessed by Jesus (5:6, 10); however, the "piety" (in Greek the word is "righteous acts") of those who follow Jesus is not to be done in such a way that it attracts attention to the doer of such deeds (6:1). The whole of life is to be directed by a pursuit of righteousness (6:33). In fact, the entirety of the Sermon on the Mount can be understood as the exposition of Jesus of the "way of righteousness."

Love. If Jesus demanded that his followers obey him, and those who were obedient to his will would be called "righteous," it is also the case that he called his followers to a life of love: for God and for others. As Jesus showed his compassion for others by healing them and helping them (9:32–34), so the followers of Jesus were to do the same (10:5–8). As Jesus was willing to reach out to help people of all nations (15:21–28), so the disciples were charged to make their love transnational (5:44–45; 28:16–20). Thus, the foundation of the tension the church had with Israel over the symbolic value of the nation of Israel may have been rooted in Jesus' teaching to love and minister to all nations. This universal love will be a fundamental factor in the final judgment of God (25:31–46). Thus, according to Jesus, love of God and others is the greatest commandment (22:37–40).

Mission. While righteousness and love may have been the key ingredients to a life that is pleasing to God, another feature of praxis in Matthew's Gospel is mission. As Jesus was "sent to the lost sheep of the house of Israel" (10:5–6; 15:24), so Jesus sends the disciples out to carry on and extend this very mission of saving the people of God (1:21; 10:5–8). Thus, the disciples' efforts are rooted in prayer (9:37–38); they go as a result of the choice of Jesus (10:2–4); they are to extend Jesus' mission (vv. 5–8); they are to expect opposition (vv. 17–25); and they are to remain faithful and fearless in their proclamation (vv. 26–39). One could speculate that this short discourse quickly became a manual for Christian missionary work. In fact, the structure of the Gospel itself is the constant interchange Jesus has with others as he continually evangelizes Israel with the message and ministry of the kingdom of heaven. The climax of the Gospel itself is the sending out of the apostles to bring the message of Jesus to "all nations" (28:16–20). Typifying the movement from a national Israel to a transnational church, we can compare the coming of the Gentile magi to Jerusalem (2:1–12) to the departure of the apostles from Jerusalem to Galilee of the Gentiles to carry out the mission of Jesus to "all nations" (28:16–20).

Summary. What we find in Matthew's Gospel is a retelling of the story of Israel in such a way that the story itself is both new and old. Clearly, the author of Matthew saw the fulfillment of God's promises to Israel in Jesus and in the new people of God he formed, the church. In retelling the story, Matthew picks up the central themes of Israel's message and recasts them in light of an overall christological orientation. God is one, but now is flanked by the Son and the Spirit. Israel is the people of God, elected by God and chosen to be his faithful heritage; however, this people of God is now fulfilled in the church, the body of those who trust and obey Jesus, the Messiah. Put differently, it might be said that the church is the true remnant. And this new people of God is united by a new covenant, in fulfillment of Jeremiah 31, the remembrance meal that recalls for the church the saving death of Jesus. The eschatological hopes of Israel, looked forward to throughout the history of Israel, are now presented by Matthew as having been partially fulfilled in Jesus and the church. What remains from that hope is the glorious climax, when the Son of Man will return with his holy angels to reward each person according to that person's life (16:28).

Scot McKnight

Bibliography. J. D. G. Dunn, *The Partings of the Ways;* R. T. France, *Matthew: Evangelist and Teacher;* J. D. Kingsbury, *Matthew: Structure, Christology, Kingdom;* S. McKnight, *Dictionary of Jesus and the Gospels,* pp. 411–16, 526–41; B. Przybylski, *Righteousness in Matthew and His World of Thought;* N. T. Wright, *The New Testament and the People of God.*

Mediator, Mediation. On the human plane, mediation takes place in the Bible, as it has in many cultures throughout history, both in innocent circumstances and when people are at odds with one another. People use interpreters to mediate the metaphorical distance between them created by a foreign language (Gen. 42:23) and envoys to mediate the real distance created by the geography of the region (2 Chron. 32:31). They also use mediators to argue a case or to negotiate terms of peace with a hostile party, as Moses did with Pharaoh on behalf of Israel (Exod. 6:28–12:32) and Joab did with David on behalf of Absalom (2 Sam. 14:1–24). Both kinds of mediation are sometimes intertwined in the Bible, as when Moses used Aaron to mediate between himself and Pharaoh (Exod. 7:1–2) and Joab used the wise woman of Tekoa to mediate his message about Absalom to David (2 Sam. 14:2–20).

God's dealings with his people throughout Scripture also incorporate these two kinds of mediation. Some kind of mediation between God and humanity is necessary simply because God is separate from all he has created and, yet, graciously extends his fellowship to his creatures. Mediation takes on a particularly important role, however, in light of humanity's rebellion against the Creator. The situation of hostility that resulted from Adam's fall could only be remedied through the mediation of a third party.

Innocent mediation, with no connotation that the mediation is necessary because of sin, takes place between God and his people in Scripture through angels, through "Wisdom," and through ordinary people whom God uses for the purpose. The angel of the Lord frequently appears in Scripture as God's messenger and spokesperson, one who graciously extends God's help to those in need and delivers important instructions for the execution of God's saving purposes in history. In Proverbs 8, Wisdom takes on a personal role and announces that God created her so that people might obtain "favor from the Lord" by finding her (v. 35).

People, too, serve as God's mediators. Priests served as mediators between God and his people not only when sin was at issue but also when the people of God wanted simply to make offerings of gratitude (Lev. 2:1–16). Similarly, the king often functioned as the channel through which God mediated his blessings to his people (2 Sam. 7:5–17; Ps. 72:1–4), a role the Messiah especially was expected to perform (Isa. 9:2–7; 11:1–9). Likewise, God graciously provided for the communication of his will to his people in special circumstances through the prophets. God used Nathan's prophetic word to tell David of his desire for a temple (2 Sam. 7:2–17) and Isaiah to calm the fears of Hezekiah about Sennacherib's threatened invasion (2 Kings 19:1–37; Isa. 37:1–38).

Just as broken human relations often require the reconciling services of a mediator, however, the Bible often speaks of mediation when God and his people are at odds. Abraham mediated between Sodom and God when he pled with the Lord to spare the city for the sake of even ten righteous people who might have lived there (Gen. 18:23–33). In a similar way, Job wished for an "umpire" who would lay his hand on both Job and God to end their wrestling match long enough for Job to speak with his apparent adversary (9:32–35).

The greatest of all mediators in the Old Testament, however, is Moses. Moses not only served as a mediator in the innocent sense when, at

God's gracious initiative, he communicated the terms of the Sinaitic covenant with Israel (Exod. 19:9; 20:19; 24:1–2; 34:27–28; Lev. 26:46; Deut. 5:5); but he served as Israel's intercessor after they had broken the covenant and stood in danger of God's righteous wrath according to the covenant's terms (Exod. 32:7–14; 33:12–23; Num. 14:13–19). After Moses' death, and in the face of continued violation of the covenant, other figures arose to urge Israel's compliance with the law and to intercede for Israel during times of disobedience. Samuel pled with God for the people generally and for the king in particular (1 Sam. 12:17–18; 13:13–14; 15:10–33); the true prophets attempted to stand between God and his disobedient people to avert disaster; and the priests, when they were faithful to their appointed tasks, offered sacrifices to atone for the people's sins (Lev. 4:1–5:19).

The prophets recognized, however, that Israel's sin was too deeply etched into their hearts for these measures to effect a lasting reconciliation between God and his people (Jer. 13:23; 17:1; 18:12). Jeremiah and Ezekiel, therefore, spoke of a time when God would give his people a new heart and a new, everlasting covenant whose terms a fresh outpouring of his Spirit would enable them to keep (Jer. 24:7; 31:31–34; 32:40; 50:5; Ezek. 11:19; 18:31; 34:25; 37:26; 39:29). According to the New Testament, the coming of Jesus ushered in the era of this new covenant, and Jesus himself is its mediator.

Paul echoes the new covenant language of the Old Testament when he tells us that believers have peace with God (Rom. 5:1), have experienced the outpouring of God's love in their hearts through the Holy Spirit (Rom. 5:5), and have been reconciled to God (Rom. 5:10–11; cf. 2 Cor. 5:11–20). All of this, he says, has happened through faith in Christ, whose death served as the ultimate atoning sacrifice for sin (Rom. 3:21–26; 5:1, 6–9). The covenant mediated through Moses was glorious, he says, but the new covenant is far more so, for unlike the old covenant that punished sin and therefore brought death, the new covenant brings life (2 Cor. 3:4–18; John 1:17; cf. Gal. 3:19–22). Paul ties these concepts neatly together in 1 Timothy 2:4–6 when he declares that God's desire to save all people is expressed in the "one mediator," Christ Jesus, who gave himself as a ransom for all.

The most sustained theological treatment of the concept of the mediator in the Bible, however, comes from the author of the letter to the Hebrews. The author writes to a church that has endured persecution (10:32–34) for its faith and, becoming weary in its trial, is tempted to convert to Judaism (13:9–13), a widely known and well-respected religion within the Roman Empire at the time. His response to this church is a carefully argued reminder of Christ's superiority to every aspect of Israel's Old Covenant, and a crucial step in this argument is that Christ is the mediator of a new covenant (8:6; 9:15; 12:24).

The author observes that Moses' mediatory role not only involved communicating the terms of the covenant from God to Israel but also serving a priestly function in light of Israel's sinfulness. Moses both gave directions for building the earthly tabernacle (8:5) and sprinkled the people, the scroll, the tent, and the vessels with blood since "without the shedding of blood there is no forgiveness" (9:22). Jesus, too, performed all these functions; but his work and what it effected were superior in every way to the mediatorial role of Moses, for he was the mediator of a better covenant (8:6; 9:15). The author gives two reasons for his contention that the covenant Jesus mediated was better than the Mosaic covenant. First, he says, the prediction in Jeremiah 31:31–34 of a new covenant proves that the first one was not blameless (8:7)—the very use of the word "new" in that passage implies the obsolescence of the old (8:13). Second, Christ's service as high priest involved the shedding of his own blood rather than the mere shedding of animal blood (9:11–15). As a result of this superior sacrifice, all the transgressions condemned by the old covenant have been forgiven (9:15), and blood sacrifice of any type need never be offered again (9:18–26; cf. 7:27). This does not mean, however, that Christ's work as mediator in other capacities has ended. Just as Moses, the priests, and the prophets continued to mediate between God and Israel after the covenant was established, so Jesus "always lives to intercede" on our behalf and therefore to bring complete salvation to us (7:25; cf. John 15:26–16:11; 17:1–25; Rom. 8:26–34).

The author's purpose for mounting this extensive and complex argument is to call the church to obedience. He does this most clearly in 12:18–29, where he reminds his readers of the magnificent display of God's power and holiness that accompanied Moses' mediation of the first covenant. In a way similar to Paul (2 Cor. 3:9), the author argues that Moses' mediation of the old covenant was a magnificent event, accompanied by splendid displays of God's power which, appropriately, struck terror into the hearts of God's people (vv. 18–21). From this the author concludes that since Jesus is the mediator of a new covenant of forgiveness (v. 24), our fear of the future judgment should be even more intense than that of ancient Israel if we turn our backs on him (vv. 25–29).

For Paul and the author of Hebrews, therefore, Christ's role as mediator received a covenantal interpretation that echoes the Old Testament at every step. Whereas Moses mediated a temporary covenant whose primary purpose was to pronounce the just penalty of death over those who sinned, they argue, Jesus mediated the new covenant predicted by the prophets. Since this covenant was accompanied by Christ's superior high priestly role with its superior sacrifice, it is the answer to the plight of sin that the first covenant made so clear. Understanding this should encourage believers to persevere in hardship, looking toward the time when they will receive "a kingdom that cannot be shaken," and give thanks to God "with reverence and awe" (vv. 25–28).

The idea of mediation in the Bible, then, is important both on the level of human relationships and on the level of humanity's relationship with God. It provides an excellent example of how God has stooped to our weakness and used language readily intelligible in any culture to describe his holiness, our sin, and his gracious provision of Christ as the "one mediator" of our salvation. FRANK THIELMAN

See also HEBREWS, THEOLOGY OF; JESUS CHRIST; PRIEST, PRIESTHOOD.

Bibliography. G. A. Lee and R. S. Wallace, *ISBE*, 3:299–305; E. Brunner, *The Mediator;* T. F. Torrance, *The Mediation of Christ.*

Medium. *See* DIVINATION; IDOL, IDOLATRY; NECROMANCY.

Meekness. Late twentieth-century Western culture does not hold meekness to be a virtue, in contrast to the ancient Near East and the Greco-Roman world, which placed a high premium on it. This dramatic shift in values is problematic for contemporary biblical translation. Most modern versions replace the noun "meekness" by "gentleness" or "humility," largely as a result of the pejorative overtones of weakness and effeminacy now associated with meekness. These connotations were not always predominant in the word, for ancient Near Eastern kings were not reluctant to describe themselves as meek in the same context in which they described themselves as mighty kings (Babylonian *ašru* and *sanāqu;* Aramaic *ʿnh*). What has prompted the discrepancy between the biblical and contemporary attitudes toward this virtue?

There are two essential components for this quality to come into play in the Bible: a conflict in which an individual is unable to control or influence circumstances. Typical human responses in such circumstances include frustration, bitterness, or anger, but the one who is guided by God's spirit accepts God's ability to direct events (Gal. 5:23; Eph. 4:2; Col. 3:12; 1 Tim. 6:11; Titus 3:2; James 1:21; 3:13). Meekness is therefore an active and deliberate acceptance of undesirable circumstances that are wisely seen by the individual as only part of a larger picture. Meekness is not a resignation to fate, a passive and reluctant submission to events, for there is little virtue in such a response. Nevertheless, since the two responses—resignation and meekness—are externally often indistinguishable, it is easy to see how what was once perceived as a virtue has become a defect in contemporary society. The patient and hopeful endurance of undesirable circumstances identifies the person as externally vulnerable and weak but inwardly resilient and strong. Meekness does not identify the weak but more precisely the strong who have been placed in a position of weakness where they persevere without giving up. The use of the Greek word when applied to animals makes this clear, for it means "tame" when applied to wild animals. In other words, such animals have not lost their strength but have learned to control the destructive instincts that prevent them from living in harmony with others.

Therefore, it is quite appropriate for all people, from the poor to ancient Near Eastern kings, to describe their submission to God by the term "meek" (Moses in Num. 12:3). On the other hand, this quality by definition cannot be predicated of God, and therefore constitutes one of the attributes of creatures that they do not share with their Creator. Nevertheless, in the incarnation Jesus is freely described as meek, a concomitant of his submission to suffering and to the will of the Father (Matt. 11:29; 21:5; 2 Cor. 10:1). The single most frequently attested context in which the meek are mentioned in the Bible is one in which they are vindicated and rewarded for their patient endurance (Pss. 22:26; 25:9; 37:11; 76:9; 147:6; 149:4; Isa. 11:4; 29:19; 61:1; Zeph. 2:3; Matt. 5:5). SAMUEL A. MEIER

See also HOLY SPIRIT, GIFTS OF.

Melchizedek. Priest of "God Most High" who appeared in patriarchal times, but whose significance was remembered throughout Old Testament times and eventually explained in the Book of Hebrews.

Melchizedek and Abraham. Melchizedek of Salem came out to pronounce a blessing on Abraham who was on his way back to Hebron after rescuing Lot from Kedorlaomer, king of the East (Gen. 14:18–24). Melchizedek provided food and wine for a sacral meal. As they ate, Melchizedek pronounced a blessing on Abraham in the name of God Most High.

The willingness with which Abraham acceded to Melchizedek as a priest of God Most High is a most interesting aspect of this narrative. This name apparently connoted the same meaningful theology to Abraham as the name "God Almighty" (Exod. 6:3). Abraham also equated God with "Creator of heaven and earth" (Gen. 14:22; cf. v. 19) in his ascription-confessional to the king of Sodom.

A Priest Forever. Psalm 110:4 reads: "The LORD has sworn and will not change his mind: 'You are a priest forever, in the order of

Melchizedek.'" This is a royal psalm. Two significant points are made about the One who is to sit at God's right hand. First, the order of Melchizedek is declared to be an eternal order. Second, this announcement is sealed with God's oath. Neither of these affirmations applied to the Aaronic order of priesthood.

Jesus Christ as the Great High Priest after the Order of Melchizedek. The Book of Hebrews presents Jesus Christ, Lord and Savior, as a priest after the order of Melchizedek (4:14–7:28, esp. 5:5–11; 6:13–7:28). The author draws directly from Psalm 110:4 several crucial points to explain that the high priesthood of Christ has superseded and is superior to the priesthood of Aaron.

First, the priesthood of Melchizedek is an "order forever" (5:10). In contrast, the priesthood of Aaron had a history of disruptions and termination.

Second, the references to being "without father or mother" (7:3) and to being an "order forever" (7:3, 16, 17, 24) are to be understood as referring to the *kind of priestly order* rather than to the longevity of a particular priest of Abraham's time. Jesus even carries the longevity of his priesthood back to the Godhead (7:15, 26; cf. 1 Peter 1:20).

Third, the divine guarantee for the priesthood of Melchizedek rests on God's oath.

For the writer of Hebrews to look at these Old Testament passages about Melchizedek along christological lines is in keeping with the practice of other New Testament writers. Early Christians were convinced that it was they upon whom the end of the ages had come and hence felt that the Old Testament was written in some divinely intended way to point to them. HARVEY E. FINLEY

See also HEBREWS, THEOLOGY OF; PRIEST, PRIESTHOOD.

Bibliography. G. W. Buchanan, *To the Hebrews;* M. Dahood, *Psalms III: 101–150;* E. A. Speiser, *Genesis;* R. S. Taylor, *Hebrews–Revelation.*

Memorial. The concept of "remembering" recurs prominently in the Bible, particularly in the Old Testament. God remembers his covenant with his people, whereupon God's people are enjoined to remember him. Remembering, frequently placed in opposition to "forgetting," focuses not only upon the past, but upon the present and future as well (Eccles. 11:8).

God Remembering. In the Old Testament God may remember to have mercy or to judge. God's covenant with his people lies behind each occasion of God's memory, whether for grace or retribution. God's remembrance often yields forgiveness (Jer. 31:34). Calling on God to remember his people (or an individual) is the essence of prayer. When God recalls iniquity, remembering is synonymous with pronouncing judgment (Ps. 109:14; Hos. 7:2). Not remembering the memory of the wicked is one of God's ultimate expressions of judgment (Ps. 34:16) in contrast to the memory of the upright, which is a blessing (Prov. 10:7).

Human Remembrance of God. The most prevalent use of remembrance in the Bible is the command to remember the Lord and his mighty deeds. No biblical book utilizes this motif more fully than Deuteronomy, where God exhorted the people to remember him, the exodus, and the wilderness experience in order to prepare themselves for the conquest of Canaan. Even the Shema (6:4–12) stresses remembering the Lord as the fundamental element in the Israelites' theological education.

Psalm 105 is entirely devoted to rehearsing God's wondrous deeds. Ezekiel provides another notable example, but he often uses memory to chastise Israel for her sins (16:60–63).

Perhaps the single most significant expression of remembering God rests with God's self-disclosure through his name (Exod. 3:14–15). Israel must remember their God as the "God of Abraham, Isaac, and Jacob," the "I am," forever.

The "memorial" is equivalent to a "sign" in the Bible. Numerous items and institutions serve as a reminder of Yahweh. The rainbow, which portended God's promise, symbolized the Noahic covenant; phylacteries recalled the Law (Exod. 13:16); and the Sabbath commemorated God's rest from his creative activity (Exod. 20:8–11).

Finally, even the gospel represents the recollection of God's mightiest act of salvation. This memory is epitomized in the Lord's Supper (1 Cor. 11:24–25) whose purpose is to lead believers to recall the atoning work of Christ.

GEORGE L. KLEIN

See also LORD'S SUPPER, THE.

Memorial Offering. *See* OFFERINGS AND SACRIFICES.

Mercy. Mercy is a concept integral to an understanding of God's dealings with humankind. In English translations of the Bible, it comes to expression in phrases such as "to be merciful," "to have mercy on," or "to show mercy toward." The corresponding term, "merciful," describes a quality of God and one that God requires of his people. The noun denotes compassion and love, not just feelings or emotions, as expressed in tangible ways.

Several Hebrew and Greek terms lie behind the English term "mercy." The chief Hebrew term is *ḥesed,* God's covenant "lovingkindness." In both the Greek translation of the Old Testament (the LXX) and the New Testament, the term behind "mercy" is most often *eleos* in one form or another, but *oiktirmos/oiktirō* (compassion, pity, to show mercy) and *splanchna/splanchnizomai* (to show mercy, to feel sympathy for) also play roles.

The Old Testament. *Mercy: A Part of God's Nature.* Although people have the capacity for showing mercy, especially toward those with whom they already have a special relationship (1 Kings 20:31; Isa. 49:15; Jer. 31:20; cf. 1 Macc. 2:57), a lack of mercy is more natural to the human condition (Prov. 5:9; 12:10; Isa. 13:18; 47:6; Jer. 6:23; 50:42; cf. Wisd. of Sol. 12:5). Mercy is, however, a quality intrinsic to the nature of God. It is for this reason that in some situations "merciful" was a sufficient description of God (Ps. 116:5; cf. Tobit 6:17). Sometimes it appears alongside other qualities as one expression of his nature that God's children particularly observe and recount (Exod. 34:6; Deut. 4:31; 2 Chron. 30:9; Ps. 86:15; Dan. 9:9; Jon. 4:2). The experience of God's people is that God's mercy, unlike human mercy, cannot be exhausted (2 Sam. 24:14; Lam. 3:22). Yet divine mercy is not blind or dumb; although God tolerated Israel's rebellion with mercy for a very long time (Neh. 9:17, 19, 31; Jer. 3:12), ultimately ungodliness in Israel was met by a withdrawal of God's mercy, leading to judgment (Lam. 2:2, 21; Zech. 1:12). But even in judgment and discipline God's mercy can be seen and hoped for (2 Sam. 24:14; Ps. 57:1; Isa. 55:7; 60:10; Jer. 31:20; Hab. 3:2; cf. Tobit 6:17), for it is part of the basic disposition of love toward his people, and it directs his actions ultimately in ways that benefit his people.

Mercy as the Foundation of God's Covenant. Mercy and *ḥesed,* God's covenant love, are integrally related. So close is the relationship that *ḥesed* sometimes is to be viewed in terms of mercy. In this relationship, mercy then comes to be seen as the quality in God that directs him to forge a relationship with people who absolutely do not deserve to be in relationship with him. Mercy is manifested in God's activity on behalf of his people to free them from slavery; it is neither theory nor principle. As the passages taken up with the establishment of the covenant with Israel show, God's mercy is a driving force in leading him to create a relationship with Israel (Exod. 34:6; Deut. 4:31; 13:17; Hos. 2:19); its meaning through *ḥesed* extends to that of loyalty based on merciful love, a loyalty that maintains the covenant despite Israel's own resistance (Pss. 25:6; 40:11; 69:17; Isa. 63:7; Jer. 16:5; 42:12; Hos. 2:19; Joel 2:13; Zech. 7:9). God's mercy is mediated through the covenant, by which he becomes the God of a people promising protection, provision, guidance, and his constant presence (Ps. 23:6). Because God is the initiator, the mercy he gives is gracious, unmerited, undeserved (Gen. 19:16; Exod. 33:19; Jer. 42:12). Within the relationship, God's mercy is thus closely linked to forgiveness (Exod. 34:9; Num. 14:19; Jer. 3:12; Dan. 9:9), a more basic disposition of compassion (Deut. 13:17) leading to forgiveness, and to the steadfast love by which God sustains the covenant and repeatedly forgives his people (Pss. 25:6; 40:11; 51:1; 69:16; 103:4; 119:77; Jer. 3:12; 16:5).

Salvation, membership in the covenant, and the promises of God all derive logically from the constellation of divine qualities that includes mercy. God's ability to provide, protect, and sustain a people finds its channel and direction through his gracious mercy acted out in historical contexts.

Mercy in the New Testament. The pattern of God's dealings with people in the Old Testament, at the core of which is mercy, also provides the shape for understanding his dealings in the New Testament. God desires a relationship with humankind, but must show mercy to them in order for this relationship to be built. Of course, the New Testament expounds the theme of God's mercy in the light of Christ, the supreme expression of love, mercy, and grace.

The Continuance of God's Covenant Mercy. Although the redemptive ministry of Christ comes to be thought of as the clearest expression of God's mercy, the Old Testament theme continues to be sounded as the basis for a people of God. In the "Magnificat" Mary recalls the mercy of God, God's *ḥesed*-love, expressed in his continuing faithfulness to Israel (Luke 1:50, 54, 58, 72, 78). Paul links this same divine commitment of mercy to undeserving people in the Old Testament with God's stubborn pursuit of Israel in and through Christ in the New Testament era and its extension to the Gentiles (Rom. 9:15–16, 23; 11:31–32; cf. 15:9). This latter thought is taken up in 1 Peter 2:10: "Once you were not a people; but now you are God's people; once you had not received mercy, but now you have received mercy" (NRSV). Applied with special emphasis to the Gentile believers to remind them of their undeserved blessings, the fact is equally true of Gentiles *and* Jews: people come into relationship with God only because God shows mercy to them.

Similarly, the New Testament writers echo the Old Testament belief that mercy belongs to God (2 Cor. 1:3; James 5:11) and that this resource of mercy is inexhaustible (Eph. 2:4). For this reason, people can confidently cry out to God for mercy in time of need (Luke 18:13; 2 Tim. 1:16, 18; cf. Matt. 15:22; 17:15).

God's Mercy Displayed in the Ministry of Christ. The great acts of mercy shown by God to the people of Israel found intimate expression in the ministry of Christ. The pattern he set, however, was not a new one, for he simply worked out the mercy of God at the human level. This is seen most clearly in his acts of healing. Cleansed of the legion of demons, the healed man is told to return home and declare the mercy that God has shown to him (Mark 5:19). The man had received from God without even asking. Others who beseeched Jesus to heal them or people with various afflictions knew that what they requested was for God to "be merciful" (Matt. 15:22; 17:15; Mark 10:47–48 [par]; Luke 17:13). And invariably he was. Mercy was manifested in practical help, not simply in a consoling message that God was sympathetic with their plight.

Mercy as the Foundation of Salvation. Ultimately the mercy of God that Jesus demonstrated in individual salvific acts becomes for the New Testament writers the illustration of the release from sin and death that God offers to the whole world through the sacrificial death and resurrection of Christ. The counterpart to the theme of the establishment of God's covenant with Israel in the Old Testament is the New Testament theme of God's gracious provision of salvation through the work of Christ. Each redemptive act of God—the exodus from Egypt and Jesus' crucifixion/resurrection—is interrelated. The one grounds and shapes the other, which receives clarity and development through the concept of salvation in the New Testament. What God did for Israel in rescuing them from slavery in Egypt—he "saved" them—was a part of the relationship he made with this people. Now in Christ the new exodus—salvation from sin—forms the basis for the relationship God desires with humankind. But the fundamental factor in each act of God is mercy: God's compassionate love for his creation that leads him to do for it what it cannot do for itself. Mercy thus forgives and liberates those who have no right to such blessings.

Salvation thus rests on God's mercy as executed in and through the Christ-event. This is perhaps seen most clearly in Paul's discussion with the Roman Christians about the Gentiles' place in God's family in Romans 9:15–18 (cf. 11:30–32). The point is made that salvation depends utterly on God's mercy and that the salvation of the Gentiles is but another display of this mercy: "For he [God] says to Moses, 'I will have mercy on whom I have mercy, and I will have compassion on whom I have compassion'" (9:15; quoting Exod. 33:19). Mercy is such a dominant concept within salvation that the heirs of salvation are called "vessels of mercy" (9:23) in contrast to those who fail to receive it and are called "vessels of wrath" (9:22).

This theme is echoed elsewhere in the New Testament. Peter (1 Peter 1:3) reached back to the Old Testament records of God's establishment of a covenant with Israel and connected them with the new life in Christ to describe the salvation of Christians: "By his great mercy he has given us a new birth through the resurrection of Jesus Christ from the dead" (NRSV). Titus 3:5 declares: "he saved us not because of any works of righteousness that we had done, but according to his mercy" (NRSV). Ephesians 2:4–5 links the salvation of the Gentiles with God's richness of mercy. Throughout the New Testament it is clear that God's mercy is displayed to the world in Christ.

Mercy as the Response of Those to Whom Mercy Has Been Shown. Beyond viewing salvation as God's great act of mercy, the profound effect on the early church that God's mercy had can be seen in several other ways. Paul was conscious that his own rescue from a life as the church's and God's enemy came about because of God's mercy (1 Tim. 1:13, 16). His behavior deserved judgment, but God in his mercy bestowed salvation instead. Paul also regarded the right to participate in ministry as a decision of God grounded on his mercy (2 Cor. 4:1). He saw with great sensitivity that even seemingly mundane events were actually manifestations of God's helping mercy (Phil. 2:27). It is this kind of imprint on the heart that made mercy a common wish and blessing of one believer to another (2 Tim. 1:16, 18), and in some cases the opening greetings of letters included the wish for mercy (1 Tim. 1:2; 2 Tim. 1:2; 2 John 3; Jude 2; cf. Gal. 6:16). In view of these examples, it is not exaggerating to say that life in Christ gives birth in believers' hearts to a consciousness not only of being recipients of God's mercy in one gift of salvation, but also of being daily recipients of fresh "mercies" of God, emblems of his ownership of us and care for us (Rom. 12:1; 2 Cor. 1:3; all of the greetings; cf. Lam. 3:22–23).

In this awareness of God's past, present, and future (Jude 21) mercy toward us, an element of our response to God takes on a new force in the New Testament. Christians are to be channels of God's mercy in the church and in the world.

The awareness in Judaism and early Christianity of the responsibility to show mercy is evident in the practice of almsgiving (*eleēmosynē*), a term developed from *eleos*. This expression of mercy in the form of charitable giving might be driven by wrong motives (Matt. 6:2–4), but in Luke's writings especially it is cited as an example of true spirituality. Thus in Luke 11:41 the value of giving alms is placed high above religious rules about purity, which the Pharisees guarded so carefully. In 12:33 mercy expressed in charitable giving is made a characteristic of discipleship. This specific way of showing mercy is praised in the early church (Acts 9:36; 10:2) and clearly regarded as an aspect of the normal Christian life (cf. Acts 24:17). In this way Christians become living signs of God's perfect mercy introduced in Christ and one day to be fully realized (cf. Acts 3:3, 6).

In more general terms, to show mercy is a characteristic of life in God's kingdom, a demonstration of kingdom power. The beatitude (an announcement of blessing) in Matthew 5:7 indicates that showing mercy is one of the marks of righteousness, the gift of God associated with the inbreaking of God's kingdom. God has made it possible; therefore his people must do it. In so doing, they mirror the God who has saved them (Luke 6:36; cf. the opposite picture in Matt. 18:33; James 2:13). To illustrate fulfillment of the half of God's law given to direct human relationships, Jesus told the parable of the good Samaritan. Thus, showing mercy to our "neighbors" is part of the basic response of God's people to his covenant (Luke 10:25–37; cf. Lev. 19:17–18; Deut. 6:4–5). Compassion and merciful action in behalf of those around us are the essence of spiritual living. The absence of mercy is a sign of unbelief and rejection of God (Rom. 1:28, 31). The Jews were reprimanded for emphasizing cultic acts and ignoring mercy toward one another (Hos. 6:6). Jesus took up this reprimand to denounce the legalistic practices of the Pharisees (Matt. 9:13). True Christian faith produces genuine compassion and fruit in the form of acts of mercy toward those in need. It was this characteristic of mercy that caused Christ to go among all kinds of people to help. Believers are to respond to the mercy shown them in the same way.

PHILIP H. TOWNER

Bibliography. R. Bultmann, *TDNT,* 2:477–87; 5:159–61; J. D. M. Derrett, *Law in the New Testament;* H.-H. Esser, *NIDNTT* 2:593–601; N. Glueck, *Hesed in the Bible;* R. A. Guelich, *The Sermon on the Mount: A Foundation for Understanding;* E. Käsemann, *New Testament Questions of Today;* N. H. Snaith, *The Distinctive Ideas of the Old Testament.*

Messiah. The term "messiah" is the translation of the Hebrew term *māšîaḥ,* which is derived from the verb *māšaḥ,* meaning to smear or anoint. When objects such as wafers and shields were smeared with grease or oil they were said to be anointed; hence the commonly used term was "anoint" when grease or oil was applied to objects by Israelites and non-Israelites. The term "messiah" is not used to refer to "anointed" objects that were designated and consecrated for specific cultic purposes but to persons only. Persons who were anointed had been elected, designated, appointed, given authority, qualified, and equipped for specific offices and tasks related to these.

When the concept of messiah is considered from a specifically biblical-theological perspective, various questions come to the fore. The first concerns the origin of the concept. Various critically inclined scholars have searched Near Eastern documents for possible references or incipient thoughts that biblical writers borrowed and developed. A careful study of Egyptian, Mesopotamian, Hittite, and Canaanite texts reveals various factors that could be related indirectly to the biblical concept. The Egyptian texts, for example, speak of a divine king who would bring deliverance and prosperity but this god-king and his work were totally different from the biblical concept of the messiah. The Mesopotamian, Hittite, and Canaanite texts also exhibit a common literary and historical background with the Scriptures, but the views concerning kingship and priesthood, the interrelationships between these, and their relationship to gods are radically different from the biblical explanations. Thus, while some formal similarities are present the messianic concept presented in the Bible is radically different. There is no possibility of considering the Near Eastern views to be the sources from which the biblical concept is lineally developed.

The biblical idea of the messiah and his work is divinely revealed. It did not originate in human thought. While the act of anointing was not foreign to non-Israelites, the intent and consequences of the act are not found in nonbiblical documents. God made his intent and the consequences of the anointing act progressively known in the course of his self-revelation to humanity.

A second question concerns the specific objects that were anointed and therefore had messianic significance. Not all anointing acts had direct messianic significance. For example, anointing a shield (smearing it with oil) (2 Sam. 1:21; Isa. 21:5), while preparing and qualifying it for effective service, did not have messianic intentions; nor did men and women who anointed themselves for cleansing, beautifying, or preparing for participation in worship have messianic significance. Nor did the smearing or pouring of oil on wafers and cultic objects indicate a specific messianic purpose. What must be kept in mind, however, is that this anointing of shields, cultic objects, and men and women did convey ideas, such as qualification, beautification, and consecration, which are inherent in the anointing acts and purposes that do have messianic significance. A further qualification to be kept in mind is that not all objects that had a messianic significance, for example, types of Jesus Christ the Messiah, his person and work, were anointed. Classic examples of this are the tabernacle, temple, and sacrifices.

A third question concerns the messianic concept as it is expressed most adequately and fully in an anointed person. The anointed person was chosen, designated, qualified, and consecrated to a position with correlated tasks. Some scholars have insisted that only an actual reigning king could be considered as the messiah. This view, however, is not consistent with the biblical revelation concerning the messiah. True, the messiah was to be considered as a royal person. This personal aspect has been referred to as the narrower view of the messianic idea. But the personal is not to be limited to royalty because the biblical messianic idea includes the priestly and the prophetic offices also.

The messianic concept also has a wider dimension than the royal, priestly, and/or prophetic person. Included in this wider view are the characteristics, tasks, goals, means, and consequences of the messianic person. Thus, a passage in Scripture should be considered to be referring to the messiah when reference is made, for example, to the character, task, and influences of the messiah even though there is no direct mention of the personal messiah himself.

The fourth question concerns the actual position and task of the messiah. The Near Eastern texts presented a divine-royal personage who would fight, kill, and plunder; this was especially true of the gods represented by the divine kings to gain advantage and thus set up their political organization, be it thought of in terms of a kingdom or empire. The biblical messiah, who was symbolized and typified, as explained below, was a divine-human being, ordained by God the Father to be the mediator of the covenant and as such to be the administrator of the kingdom of God.

What is the biblical portrait of the messiah?

Adam and Eve, created in God's image, were placed in a living, loving, lasting relationship, a covenant bond, with the Creator God. These human beings were given authority, ability, and responsibility to mirror, represent, and serve the sovereign Creator and King of the entire created cosmos. Adam and Eve were to believe, obey, and serve God in the living, loving, covenantal relationship. The account of Adam and Eve's deviation, under Satan's influence, from the will, purposes, and goals of God is well known.

God immediately intervened. He cursed the serpent/Satan and all his followers. He promised that the covenantal relationship would be restored through the victory that the seed of the woman would have over Satan. Yet, God did not remove or permit Adam and Eve to abdicate their creational covenantal position and responsibilities. Rather, God assured Adam and Eve that redemption and restoration would become realities in the lives and history of their seed (Gen. 3:14–20). The seed of the woman would restore, continue, and bring to full fruition God's kingdom plans and goals.

Satanic efforts to render the redemptive/restorative covenant ineffective are recorded throughout the Scriptures. The murder of Abel (Gen. 4:8) and the violence that saturated society before and during the first part of Noah's life, bear testimony to Satan's efforts (Gen. 4–5; 6:1–8). But God kept covenant with righteous, blameless, obedient, believing, and serving Noah. Noah stands as a prefigurement of the promised Messiah who, in the midst of judgment, would effect a complete and final redemption. Noah, late in life, prophesied that Shem would be the messianic seedline bearer (Gen. 9:25–27).

Abraham, descendant of Shem, was called and appointed to be the covenant agent. He was to leave country, clan, and family to become the channel of messianic blessings to all nations (Gen. 12:1–3). God covenanted in a special manner with Abraham, assuring him that via his seed God would carry out his redemptive/restorative work. That Abraham and his seed would be able to do this was confirmed by God's assuring covenantal affirmation: "I am God Almighty . . . I will make you very fruitful . . . be your God . . . and of your descendants" (Gen. 17:1–7). Two important messianic factors stand out: (1) the covenant Lord would continue the seedline; and (2) Abraham was called to believe, obey, and serve as the father of all believers who would receive the benefits of the Messiah.

The messianic seedline continued through Isaac and Jacob; Jacob prophesied that that line would continue through Judah (Gen. 49:8–12); the line continued through Boaz and Ruth (Ruth 4:16–22); and David was told that his son's throne would be established forever (2 Sam. 7:11b–16). The royal descendants of David were not all believing, obeying, serving covenant messianic forbears of Jesus the Messiah/Christ. God, however, maintained the seedline from Abraham, through David, through Zerubbabel, through Mary and Joseph. This seedline referred especially to the royal dimension of the messianic office and task. Other dimensions were also included to reveal the inclusive position, tasks, and influence of the Messiah. The royal aspect was central, pervasive, and supportive of all the other dimensions. This dominating royal aspect led many in Old Testament, intertestamentary, and New Testament times to think of the Messiah strictly in terms of his kingship and his setting up and ruling an earthly political entity in which Hebrew/Jewish people would be the kingdom people.

Whereas the narrower view of the messianic idea is central, the wider dimension was clearly present at all times also. Adam and Eve had a wider task to perform than strictly royal. Noah, an ancestor of the Messiah personally, while not a royal person, performed a redemptive messianic function. The redemptive task pertained not only to the saving of eight people but also included the animal world.

The wider dimension of the messianic concept is evident in Abraham's life of faith, intercession on behalf of Sodom and Gomorrah (Gen. 18), and offering of the ram substituted for his son Isaac (Gen. 22). Abraham's grandson Joseph, serving as a type of the Messiah, performed in a royal capacity but before he was lifted to that capacity he suffered humiliation. Once in a royal position, he became the savior of the seedline by functioning in the creational covenantal setting, collecting, preserving, and distributing food during years of famine.

Moses, another type of the Messiah, functioned in a royal capacity as lawgiver but he also served as a prophet. He was the greatest of the Old Testament prophets and the model of all faithful prophets who spoke God's word. In addition, through Moses, God ordained the priesthood, ordered the building of the tabernacle, and prescribed the sacrifices. These were symbols and types of the messianic task, giving expression to the priestly mediatorial office, the God with you (Immanuel) principle, and the substitutionary death on behalf of sinners. Another messianic representation in the days of the patriarchs and Moses was the angel of the Lord, who appeared in theophanic form as the preincarnate Christ. The angel of the Lord phenomenon particularly gave emphasis to the divine character of the Messiah. Still more expressions of the messianic task were given in the time of Moses; consider the pillar of fire (Christ is the light), manna (Christ is the living bread), the water from the rock (Christ is living water and the rock), and the lifted-up bronze serpent (Christ is the lifted-up One who gives life).

The psalmists and prophets gave further explication of the Penteteuchal presentations of the Messiah. The psalms gave expression to the royal character of the Messiah. The suffering, priestly dimension is spoken of as well. This dimension includes references to death and resurrection. According to the psalmists, it is the royal One (the narrower view) who also carries out the priestly and prophetic tasks, that is, bringing in salvation and giving instruction in the truth.

The prophets especially brought together the wider and narrower views concerning the Messiah. Consider Isaiah's proclamation of the birth by a virgin (7:14), the wise, all-knowing ruling son of David (9:1–6), the fruitful branch who would bring redemption, restoration, and blessings in life (chap. 11). It was Isaiah who proclaimed that the Messiah was to be the light to the Gentiles (49:6), the suffering, exalted One (52:13–53:12). The Messiah was to be the great comforting preacher of freedom, the healer and bringer of joy (61:1–3). Micah prophesied that the Messiah was to come through the royal Davidic seedline to shepherd his people and bring them security (5:1–4). Amos likewise proclaimed that the Messiah of Davidic lineage would fulfill Yahweh's covenant promises to the nations (9:11–15). Jeremiah prophesied of the Messiah, the one of Davidic lineage who was to be the king of righteousness (23:5–6). Ezekiel called the exiles' attention to the Son of Man, the covenant mediator who would restore and shepherd his people (chaps. 34; 36). Postexilic prophets spoke of the Messiah as the royal, redeeming, restoring One to come (Hag. 2:20–22; Zech. 4:1–14; 6:9–15; 9:9–10), Malachi spoke of the Messiah as a cleansing agent who, as messenger of the covenant, would bring healing in his wings (3:1–4; 4:1–3).

The New Testament writers, evangelists, and apostles give no reason to doubt that Jesus is the Messiah, or in New Testament language, the Christ. He came, born of Abrahamic and Davidic lineage (Matt. 1:2–16; Luke 2:4–15). John the Baptist identified Jesus as the Messiah by referring to the wider dimension: "Look, the Lamb of God, who takes away the sin of the world!" (John 1:29). Jesus was the One who would bring judgment as well as life by the Spirit of God (Matt. 3:1–12). The evangelists record that Jesus was anointed by the Spirit when he was baptized. Jesus proclaimed himself as the Messiah in Nazareth (Luke 4:16–22) and at Jacob's well to the Samaritan woman (John 4:24–25).

GERARD VAN GRONINGEN

See also JESUS CHRIST, NAME AND TITLES OF.

Bibliography. C. A. Briggs, *The Messiah of the Gospels;* N. L. Geisler, *To Understand the Bible—Look for Jesus;* E. Hengstenberg, *Christology of the Old Testament and a Commentary on the Messianic Predictions;* J. Jocz, *The Jewish People and Jesus Christ;* H. Lockyer, *All the Messianic Prophecies of the Bible;* W. Manson, *Jesus the Messiah;* S. Mowinckel, *He That Cometh;* E. Riehm, *Messianic Prophecy: Its Origin, Historical Growth, and Relation to New Testament Fulfillment;* G. A. Riggan, *Messianic Theology and Christian Faith;* O. P. Robertson, *The Christ of the Covenants;* G. Stibitz, *Messianic Prophecy;* G. Van Groningen, *Messianic Revelation in the Old Testament;* M. Wyngaarden, *The Future of the Kingdom in Prophecy and Fulfillment.*

Micah, Theology of. Although unlike Isaiah (6:1–9), Jeremiah (1:4–10), and Ezekiel (2:1–3:27) Micah gives his audience no autobiographical account of his call to prophetic ministry, the superscription to his book (1:1), "the word of the LORD that came to Micah," affirms that the invisible God becomes audible in it. In 6:1b–8 Micah is pictured as the Lord's plenipotentiary from the heavenly court, who has come to Jerusalem to accuse Israel of having broken the Mosaic covenant. Unlike the false prophets, for whom money speaks louder than God (3:5, 11), Micah, filled with the power of the Lord's Spirit, preaches justice (3:8).

Micah's theology represents both aspects of the Lord's covenant with Israel: the Lord will sentence his covenant people to exile out of the land of blessing if they fail to keep his righteous law, but he will always preserve from them a righteous remnant to whom he will give his sworn land after the exile (2:5) and through whom he will bless the nations (4:1–5).

Micah organizes the approximately twenty prophecies that comprise his book into three cycles—chapters 1–2, 3–5, and 6–7—each beginning with the command to either "Hear" (1:2) or "Listen" (3:1; 6:1). Each cycle begins with judgment-oracles against the nation for having failed to keep the Mosaic covenant, followed by salvation-oracles based on God's promises to Abraham and the patriarchs to be their god forever—so reflecting both aspects of the Lord's covenant with Israel. In the first two prophecies of the first cycle, Samaria (1:3–7) and Judah (1:8–16) are sentenced to destruction and exile because of their idolatry (vv. 5, 7). In the third prophecy

(2:1–5), Micah accuses rich land barons of exploiting Israel's middle class by taking their lands away from them in corrupt courts (vv. 1–3). It is often said that Micah is the champion of the poor; in truth, he champions the cause of Israel's middle class—stalwart farmers whose wives live in luxurious homes and whose children enjoy the Lord's blessing (2:9). The Lord will take the lands away from the venal land barons and send them into exile (2:4–5). Israel possessed the promised land as a usufruct from the Lord. While he gave it to them to enjoy to its full measure, he reserved the right to take it away from them if they abused it (Lev. 25:33).

Micah's fourth prophecy is against the false prophets who abet the rapacious racketeers with their half-baked theology. Their identifying badge is that they preach only God's love, never his wrath and judgment. Their half-truth distorted the covenant by emphasizing only Exodus 34:6 ("The Lord . . . the compassionate and gracious God, slow to anger, abounding in love and faithfulness") and omitting Exodus 34:7 ("yet he does not leave the guilty unpunished"). Their false doctrine of eternal security helped lead the nation to its death (2:6–11). In these four oracles Micah predicts Israel's exile, but looking beyond the judgment, he concludes the first cycle with a prophecy that the Lord will preserve a remnant with him as their triumphant King (2:12–13).

In the second cycle (3:1–5:16), Micah delivers three oracles of judgment against Jerusalem's corrupt leaders: the avaricious magistrates, who cannibalize their subjects (3:1–4); the greedy prophets, who should be the nation's watchdogs but only wag their tails if fed a bone (3:5–7); and all the leaders, rulers, prophets, and priests (3:8–11), who are in cahoots to plunder their subjects. Micah concludes these oracles with the climactic prediction that Jerusalem will fall (3:12; cf. Jer. 26:18).

In a breathtaking turn, he shifts from these judicial sentences reducing Jerusalem to a heap of rubble and its temple to a forested height to seven visions pertaining to Israel's "last days" (4:1, 6; 5:10), a future that paradoxically reverses the present situation—the "now" of distress (4:9, 11; 5:1, not translated in NIV)—and at the same time brings to a fitting outcome that toward which it is striving. In his first sermon Peter goes out of his way to identify the coming of the Spirit at Pentecost with the epoch labeled by Micah and his contemporary, Isaiah, as "in the last days" (Acts 2:17). Peter's primary text is Joel 2:28–32. The inspired apostle, however, curiously and interpretively transforms Joel's text. Joel's prophecy begins, "and afterward . . . "' (Joel 2:28), but instead of this introduction Peter substitutes the words of Micah 4:1 and the parallel passage in Isaiah 2:2. Since that wording is found in no text or version of Joel, Peter seems deliberately to link Pentecost and the ensuing age until the return of Jesus Christ with Isaiah's and Michah's prophecies about Israel's golden age "in the last days." The author of the Letter to the Hebrews likewise speaks of the church as now living "in these last days" (1:2). However, the phrase has a temporal thickness embracing many events over an extended period of time. In Micah it embraces the remnant's restoration from Babylon (4:9–10), the birth of the Messiah (5:2), and his universal and everlasting peace (5:5–6). Moreover, while the church today fulfills these prophecies it awaits the new heaven and new earth when they will be consummated.

In the first of these visions with regard to the last days Micah sees Mount Zion established as the true religion over all false, pagan religions (4:1). He overhears the regenerate nations exhorting one another to come to Mount Zion to learn God's law, to hear God's word and to carry it back with them (v. 2). Reflecting upon what he saw and heard he predicts for these people a kingdom of peace: "they will beat their swords into plowshares" (v. 3); "every man will sit under his own fig tree" (v. 4). Until that happens, however, Micah and the remnant "will walk in the name of the Lord our God for ever and ever" (v. 5).

In the second vision of these last days, Micah sees the lame remnant regathered as a strong nation (4:6–7); and in the third, the kingdom's former glory is again restored to Jerusalem (4:8). It should be borne in mind that earthly Jerusalem was always a replica of the heavenly, that the church today has come to the reality (i.e., the heavenly Jerusalem [Heb. 12:22]), and that the old earthly symbols of the kingdom, including the temple on Mount Zion, have been done away forever (Heb. 8:13).

In the fourth vision, Micah transforms the cry of the exiles going into Babylon into the cry of a woman in labor. The remnant that survives the Babylonian exile will ultimately give birth to the new age (4:9–11); those who appeared defeated will become victorious (4:11–13).

In the fifth vision and at the center of these glorious prophecies (5:1–6), Micah now predicts that the remnant will give birth to the Messiah, who will be born in lowly Bethlehem, David's cradle (v. 2; cf. Matt. 2:1–6). He will shepherd his flock in the strength of the Lord (v. 4; cf. John 10:11; Heb. 13:20; 1 Peter 2:25; 5:4), and they will live securely (cf. Matt. 16:18). He will be their peace, protecting them from all their enemies, including Assyria, the very symbol of oppression (vv. 5–6; cf. Luke 2:14; 24:36; Rom. 5:1; 8:31–39; Eph. 2:14).

In the sixth vision, Micah foresees that the restored remnant will become a savor of life and death among the nations (5:7–9) (cf. 2 Cor. 2:14–15).

Finally, "in that day," Micah says, the Lord will purge his people of all their former false confidences: military hardware, witchcraft, and idolatry (5:10–15). Having purged his imperium within, thereby protecting it from the divine anger against unholiness, the Lord promises to guard it from enemies without (v. 15).

In the third cycle (6:1–7:20), Micah begins with a covenant law suit (6:1–8). Here the Lord clearly profiles the covenant relationship. He dealt with his people in sovereign grace, saving them from Egypt and bringing them safely into the promised land (vv. 1–5). However, instead of responding to his grace with a total commitment of trust in him that leads to covenant fidelity and obedience, they reduced the covenant to a bargaining contract (vv. 6–7). Micah shows the reader how absurd it is to try to establish a relationship with God in this way. The false worshiper begins bargaining with holocausts; he then offers one-year calves (already more costly) (v. 6), then thousands of rams, then ten thousand torrents of oil. Finally, he even offers the cruel sacrifice of his own child (v. 7). "Ten thousand rivers of oil" suggests that this approach to God has no limit and establishes neither a covenant relationship with God nor assurance of salvation. Oil is measured by the pint or quart (Exod. 30:24; Num. 15:9; 28:5). False worshipers think God's favor, like theirs, can be bought! Comparative religionists refer to Micah 6:8 as the quintessential expression of true religion. What the Lord actually requires is that the believer practice justice and faithful love, walking wisely with him. False worshipers offer the Lord everything but what he asks for: their loving and obedient hearts. Only those who comprehend his grace can and will offer him that.

The prophet follows this law suit with yet another oracle of judgment (6:9–16). For Judah's corrupt and deceptive commercial practices (vv. 9–12), the Lord will bring on it all the curses of the covenant: sickness, sword, and exile (vv. 13–16). In the final judgment oracle (7:1–7) the ship of state breaks apart. Not an upright official is left (vv. 1–4), and so the nation falls into anarchy (vv. 5–6). Micah, however, confident of God's covenant faithfulness to the patriarchs, hopes in his saving God (v. 7). He will not be disappointed. His final prophecy concludes with a victory song (vv. 8–20). Micah's name means, "Who is like Yah," and in this concluding prophecy he asks, "Who is a God like you, who pardons sin and forgives the transgression of the remnant of his inheritance?" (v. 18). As at the beginning of Israel's history the Lord hurled Pharaoh into the sea, now at the end of their history he will hurl all their sins into the sea (v. 19). Although Israel has been unfaithful, the Lord will remain faithful to his covenant promises to Abraham and the fathers (v. 20); he cannot deny himself (2 Tim. 2:13).

As God's justice informs Micah's judgment-oracles and his righteousness the salvation-oracles, so God's other sublime attributes inform both. The omniscient God even knows what the greedy land barons are plotting on their beds (2:1). He predicts the Babylonian exile and the survival of the remnant, and the birth of his Messiah in Bethlehem and the triumph of his rule, and brings them to pass.

In his first prophecy, Micah pictures Israel's Ruler as a victorious conqueror. He rises from his heavenly throne, marches forth from his holy sanctuary, and strides upon the earth's heights (1:3). Under the heat of the Lord's glowing wrath and under his heavy tread, the eternal and majestic mountains melt and flow like hot wax, and the arable plains where humankind finds its immediate source of life split apart like waterfalls roaring down a rocky gorge (v. 4). When this majestic God suddenly erupts with awesome power, puny human walls and fortifications crumble and fall into ravines (vv. 6–7). Humans feel secure as long as the long-suffering God remains in heaven; but when he marches forth in judgment, they are gripped by the stark reality that they must meet the holy God in person. BRUCE K. WALTKE

See also ISRAEL; PROPHET, PROPHETESS, PROPHECY.

Bibliography. D. W. Baker, T. D. Alexander, and B. K. Waltke, *Obadiah, Jonah and Micah;* R. E. Clements, *Canon and Authority;* E. Clowney, *Dreams, Visions and Oracles;* K. H. Cuffey, "The Coherence of Micah: A Review of the Proposals and a New Interpretation"; G. Hasel, *The History and Theology of the Remnant Idea from Genesis to Isaiah;* A. J. Heschel, *The Prophets;* D. Hillers, *Covenant: The History of a Biblical Idea;* idem, *Micah;* B. K. Waltke, *Continuity and Discontinuity,* pp. 263–88; idem, *Commentary on Micah.*

Might. *See* POWER.

Milcom. *See* GODS AND GODDESSES, PAGAN.

Mind/Reason. That part of the human being in which thought takes place and perception and decisions to do good, evil, and the like come to expression. A number of terms in the Hebrew Old Testament and Greek New Testament are used for mind/reason, some of which overlap in meaning and others that view the internal person from differing perspectives. The importance of this dimension of human existence can be seen especially in its relation to God and his revelation.

The Old Testament. *Basic Difference Between Hebrew and Greek Thought.* The Old Testament terms that serve as references to the mind or reason most often (especially "heart," "spirit," "soul") are not limited to these meanings, but cover a wide range of ideas as they seek to describe the inward or invisible dimensions of the human being in a holistic manner (characteristic of "Oriental" thought). Thus, a rather limited vocabulary serves different purposes in different contexts, and can refer alternately to the seat of a person's thought and emotional life, the emotions, and more broadly, to the inner person.

The array of terms that figure in the development of the concept of the mind and reason in the Greek-speaking world include a number related to the basic term *nous* (meaning mind, reason, intellect, understanding, and even perhaps in its broadest sense something like our modern term "worldview"). The *phren* (mind, understanding) word-group also comes into play.

Developments in the Hebrew Old Testament are not, for lack of such specialized vocabulary, to be thought of as less sophisticated, but rather as closely related to the Hebrew culture, which considered the intellectual and emotional dimensions of human life from the perspective of the whole person: heart, soul, and spirit are not separate parts of the inner person, but each is a reference to the whole inner person and is to be viewed in relation to the body. As a result, the inner thought and knowledge dimension is regarded in close relation to right conduct.

The Heart as the Mind. The Hebrew term "heart" (*lēb, lēbāb*), in its figurative usage, is the most important term for the inner person. It views the inner person from a number of angles, of which the concern here is its reference to the thought or will of human beings or to the organ of understanding. Thus, "heart" or "to set the heart" means to make up the mind or decide (2 Chron. 12:14; Neh. 4:6). "Calling to mind" is meant in Deuteronomy 30:1; Isaiah 46:8; 65:17; Jeremiah 3:16; "recalling" is similar (Deut. 30:1; Jer. 51:50: Ezek. 38:10). Wisdom and understanding are located in the heart (1 Kings 3:12; Prov. 16:23) and perceived with the heart (Prov. 18:15; 22:17; Eccles. 8:16). Moreover, it is the heart that plans or purposes to act (Prov. 16:1, 9). God's "mind" is sometimes described this way (Jer. 19:5; 32:35; 44:21). Decisions of a moral nature take place in the heart (Gen. 20:5; Job 11:13). This being the case, evil will also be manifested in the heart, where decisions to disobey and rebel take place (Jer. 17:9). A heart/mind can be perverse and therefore incapable of apprehending truth and wisdom (Prov. 10:20; 11:20; 12:8; 17:16, 20). The heart is also the place where deception occurs (Isa. 44:20). "Heart" thus serves as a reference to the person as a thinking, perceiving, and willing being, bringing together the ideas of knowledge, understanding, and will.

The Spirit as the Mind. The Hebrew term for spirit (*rûaḥ*) depicts the inner person from the perspectives of the mind, understanding, and reason on a number of occasions (with various Greek equivalents). Exodus 28:3 and 1 Chronicles 28:12 view the human mind in relation to skills and planning. Ezekiel 11:5 and 20:32 have spirit as a reference to the conscious thoughts of a man. Daniel 5:20 has the mind-set or determination of the will in view in this description of Nebuchadnezzar: "his heart [spirit] became arrogant and hardened with pride." In this case, it is a mind set against God in rebellion.

The Soul as the Mind and Reason. Another term for the inner person that can refer to the intellectual or mental dimension of life is "soul" (*nepeš*). In the well-known command of Deuteronomy 6:5, the soul, along with the heart, contributes to a description of the whole inner person as a thinking, knowing, and willing force, which must decide to serve God (cf. 1 Chron. 22:19; 28:9). "Soul" describes a man from the perspective of the choices he makes in Deuteronomy 18:6, and as a thinking, inquiring being (Eccles. 7:28). The thought, counsel, or mind of God is also described with the Hebrew term "soul" in 1 Samuel 2:35. The same term can stand for one's wish or determination (2 Kings 9:15).

The New Testament. In the New Testament the *nous* word-group tends to be concentrated in the Pauline writings. Paul seems to have been the main pioneer in exploring this Greek region of thought for viable expressions with which to carry on his dialogue. We will concentrate our attention on terms that speak specifically of the mind and reasons (*nous, phronesis,* and related terms). While this line of description was of special interest to Paul and he develops it beyond the stage reached in the Old Testament, his thought corresponds closely with the Old Testament.

Primarily through the *nous* word-group, the New Testament employs a broad concept of the mind. It includes one's "worldview" or outlook and the way in which it influences perception. But the particular perspective can vary; it extends to ideas such as disposition and inner orientation or moral inclination (Rom. 1:28; Eph. 4:17; Col. 2:18; 1 Tim. 6:5; Titus 1:15), or an organ that determines a course of action (Rom. 7:23) or the state (or act) of understanding (Luke 24:45; 1 Cor. 14:14–15, 19; Phil. 4:7; 2 Thess. 2:2; Rev. 13:18; 17:9). The related verb (*noeō*) and noun (*noēma*) describe the mind in action (thinking and discerning) and the result (thoughts).

The Mind of Unbelief. One dominant usage of "mind" (in certain contexts or with appropriate modifiers) is to describe a way of thinking or entire understanding that stands in opposition to God. Romans 1:28 and Ephesians 4:17–18 have the unbeliever in view. The "mind" of the one who does not know God is in a state of futility and debasement, and by implication this state, though reversible, exists because of refusal to acknowledge God or at a time prior to coming to that knowledge that brings renewal. This set of the mind is hostile to God (see Rom. 8:7 with *phronēma*; and Col. 1:21 with *dianoia*). Paul indicates that this condition is the result of "the god of this age," who has blinded the minds of unbelievers (2 Cor. 4:4; the mind here [with *noēmata*] conceived of as a framework resulting from the thought process). Similarly, the false teacher's mind is described variously as "fleshly" (Col. 2:18), depraved (1 Tim. 6:5), and corrupt (2 Tim. 3:8; Titus 1:15). In this case, the condition of the mind is determined by decisions about the orthodox apostolic doctrine; rejection of God's Word renders the mind or the complete worldview (perception of reality or of God's will) ineffective.

This same unbelieving mind is also described with the negatives, *anoia*, meaning the absence of understanding, and *anoētos*, meaning foolish. In the New Testament these conditions are not innocent but culpable. Thus the failure to understand Jesus' ministry on the Sabbath and the mistakes of false teachers each stem from a basic ignorance related to rebellion against God (Luke 6:11; 2 Tim. 3:9). The foolish lack spiritual understanding (Luke 24:25; Gal. 3:1, 3; cf. Rom. 1:14).

Renewal of the Mind. Two passages indicate that the mind must be renewed in order to conform to or apprehend the will of God. Romans 12:2 is the classic statement: "Do not conform any longer to the pattern of the world, but be transformed by the renewing of your mind. Then you will be able to test and approve what God's will is." Ephesians 4:23 ("be made new in the attitude of your minds") is similar in thrust. In each case, the issue is the discernment of God's will over and against an opposing and imposing mind-set. Renewal, which is related to conversion and regeneration by the Holy Spirit (Rom. 8:9–11; Col. 3:10), is the prerequisite for reaching an understanding of God's will.

The Mind of Belief. There is, then, a "renewed" or Christian mind: "But we have the mind of Christ" (1 Cor. 2:16). Here the regenerate mind or mind of the Christian is described in terms of a correct understanding of the things and plans of God. It is a worldview in synchronization with God's will. Second Thessalonians 2:2 may have something like a correct Christian understanding in view as well: Paul encourages the Thessalonian believers not to allow their understanding to be shaken by false reports that the day of the Lord is already here. Revelation 13:18 uses mind in the sense of "having the mind of a believer," that is, able to discern the times (cf. 17:9).

The Mind as the Faculty of Understanding and Perceiving. Underlying the notion of a Christian "mind" is the more basic tenet that understanding takes place through the faculty or operation of the mind. This in turn leads to another corollary: it is with the mind that God can and must be apprehended (cf. Philo, *Virt.* 57). The mind as one's organ of spiritual consciousness is meant to be pure (2 Peter 3:1; cf. Test. Benj. 6:5), but the opposite possibility exists (Col. 1:21). Scripture is understood through the mind, though it requires "opening" for this to take place (Luke 24:45). Similarly, Paul contrasts a message or prayer given through tongues, which pertains to the spirit, and the engagement of the mind, which suggests that the mind pertains to consciousness and a way of thinking that corresponds to human language (1 Cor. 14:14–15, 19).

The human mind and volition play a dominant role in responding to God. Thus Jesus affirms the relevance of Deuteronomy 6:5: "love the Lord your God with all your heart and with all your soul and with all your mind" (Matt. 22:37). If understanding occurs in the mind, it is not surprising that Paul implies that it is with the mind, not the flesh, that God is served (Rom. 7:23, 25). He means that the relationship to God and service or worship involve a complete commitment and act of human volition. The entire mind/way of thinking must be inclined toward God and in harmony with him (2 Cor. 10:5), and this requires knowing that, left to itself, it tends in another direction.

In another context, and with another Greek term (*phroneō, phronēma*), Paul relates the Christian understanding/mind to the Holy Spirit. Within the argument of Romans, chapter 8 takes up the contrast between the law/flesh/death and Spirit/life. Here, the "mind controlled by the Spirit" refers to the renewed way of thinking or renewed worldview. It inclines toward God. But the "mind controlled by the sinful nature" is that same determined rejection of God's revelation mentioned in Romans 1:28.

From the human perspective, the spiritual life must be sustained by the conscious decision to maintain communication with and commitment to God. Thus, in a very real sense willing to act, thinking, and deciding all come under the category of the human power of the mind. People must make a decision about God, and volition is clearly involved. And though renewal or enlightenment is required for this power to be used effectively, and the other possibility clearly exists, it remains the human responsibility to make the godly decision.

Summary. Throughout both the Old and New Testaments, the mind/reason is alternatively the thought system and the faculty of conscious reflection and perception. It is with the mind that decisions are made, whether moral or amoral in nature. It is with the mind that one chooses to accept God and obey his commandments, or to reject him and rebel against him. The New Testament sheds additional light on the concept of the mind by relating its condition directly to conversion. Renewal (resulting from the Spirit's work in conversion) makes apprehension and acceptance of God's will possible. Before renewal occurs, futility and blindness characterize the human mind (faculty of perception) and the broader description is "ignorance" or "folly." Especially in the Pastoral Epistles, the relation between the condition of the mind and the apprehension of and/or commitment to correct doctrine is emphasized.

What is at stake in Christian living and mission is, then, very much the human mind.

What must not be missed in the biblical development of the mind concept is the role of human volition that is implied in the relationship between God and human beings. While it is true that renewal is necessary, nowhere does this remove the responsibility from the human being to decide at each point to believe, and keep believing God. Through the mind concept, the delicate (though mysterious) balance between divine sovereignty and human responsibility is maintained. God may make apprehension of his revelation possible, but the human must decide to employ the mind to so apprehend it. PHILIP H. TOWNER

See also HEART; PERSON, PERSONHOOD; SOUL; SPIRIT.

Bibliography. J. Behm and E. Würthwein, *TDNT*, 4:948–1022; G. Bornkamm, *NTS* 4 (1957–58): 93–100; R. Bultmann, *Theology of the New Testament;* W. Eichrodt, *Theology of the Old Testament;* G. Harder and J. Goetzmann, *NIDNTT*, 3:122–34; R. Jewett, *Paul's Anthropological Terms*.

Ministry, Minister. It is reasonably clear in Scripture that (1) ministry means the service of God and his creatures; (2) the one essential ministry is that of Jesus Christ; (3) the whole membership of the old and the new Israel is called to share in ministerial service, of which there are many forms; and (4) certain persons in both the old new Israel are set apart for special ministry, within the total ministry.

The Old Testament. There are three distinct ministries in the Old Testament: the prophetic, the priestly, and the kingly. All three are essential within the covenantal relation between Yahweh and Israel. However, more basic than these three is that the whole people, Israel, is the minister of God. The election and call of Israel is the foundation of the service of Israel to God. Nowhere is this mode more clear than in Isaiah 40–66, where the missionary calling of the people of God is made explicitly clear. Much earlier the people had been told that they were "a kingdom of priests and a holy nation" (Exod. 19:6). Thus, in a basic sense every person, male and female, insofar as he or she is a member of Israel is a minister/servant of Yahweh; so the whole of life has a Godward dimension (as the Law makes very clear).

The service rendered by prophet, priest, and king was that of maintaining the personal relation between Israel (the bride) and Yahweh (the Bridegroom) required by the covenant. Within this relation of grace there was need of a minister of God who would speak for him to the people (thus the prophet; Isa. 6:8; 50:4); of a minister to stand before God to teach the people, lead in worship, and offer sacrifice on their behalf (on many occasions priests and Levites are called ministers—e.g., Exod. 30:20); and of a king to express the sovereignty and kingship of Yahweh unto and within Israel and to show that the sacred and secular realms belong together.

The New Testament. Each of these ministries comes to fulfillment in Jesus Christ, who is himself the Prophet, Priest, and King. At the same time, the corporate ministry of Israel as a people finds fulfillment first in Jesus Christ as the new Israel and then in his body, the church.

Christ in His Church. Jesus Christ came not to be ministered to but to minister (Matt. 20:28). In his life and particularly in his death, Jesus fulfilled the prophecy of the Messiah as the Suffering Servant of Yahweh (Isa. 52:13–53:12). By washing the feet of his disciples he gave an example (John 13:15) of true service; and in the Upper Room he declared, "I am among you as one who serves" (Luke 22:27). The unique, ministerial servant example of Jesus is beautifully commended by Paul (Phil. 2:5–8) and Peter (1 Peter 2:21–25).

The Word Incarnate ministered to people in their deepest need. He entered fully into the pitiful and perverse condition of the human race as it exists before God, sharing its pain and estrangement. He did this in order, by meek and gracious service in doing good and bringing healing and liberation, to bring peace and reconciliation between man and God. The climax of his diaconal, servant ministry was to offer himself as an atonement for sin on the cross of Calvary.

This diaconal ministry of Jesus Christ continued after his exaltation into heaven. As the Head of the church, which is his body, he continually ministers to and through his members as their King, Priest, and Prophet. He rules and guides, prays and intercedes, proclaims and teaches, loves and rejoices for, in, and through them. The whole church is a holy priesthood and a chosen race, a royal priesthood, God's own people (1 Peter 2:5, 9). In union with Christ, his body shares in his priestly, kingly, and prophetic work. The whole point of Paul's argument in both Romans 12 and 1 Corinthians 12 is that each and every member of the church has a part to play in the service of God.

By three basic words—*doulos, leitourgos, diakonos*—the call to serve God in Christ is made clear. Christians are to be slaves and servants of Jesus Christ. They were bought from slavery to Satan, sin, and death by a great price (1 Cor. 6:19–20; 1 Peter 1:18–19) and now they are slaves of Jesus Christ (Rev. 1:1; 1 Peter 2:16) who are to serve righteousness in Christ (Rom. 6:15–16). The Christian ministers by being a bondservant (*doulos*) of Jesus Christ.

There exists within the church, by God's will, a universal duty and right of service; however, with this there also exists the greatest possible differentiation of forms and functions of service.

Ministries in the Church. The ways of serving the Lord in his church are many and varied. These types overlap and members of the body will partake of more than one type. There is ministry of the Word in evangelism, founding and guiding churches (apostles, prophets, evangelists, teachers, etc.); ministry of healing (workers of miracles, gifts of healing, etc.); ministry of leadership/administration (helpers, administrators, etc.); and ministry to the congregation (tongues, interpretation of tongues, etc.).

Apostles. While it is important to recognize the whole ministry of the whole body, the place of the original apostles is unique (Rev. 21:14). The Twelve were chosen, appointed, ordained, and sent by Jesus Christ himself. Matthias replaced Judas among the Twelve (Acts 1), and Paul became the apostle to the Gentiles through a gift of the Spirit given by the exalted Lord (Acts 9). So in a vital sense their ministry is that ministry which is necessary for the full ministry of the whole body. They are eyewitnesses of the resurrection and/or exaltion of Christ and they are the living foundations on which the church is built. It is their testimony that is the basis of the books of the New Testament. They were the gift of God to the church in its infancy and are irreplaceable.

Local Leadership. Apart from the apostles, prophets, and evangelists, we read of elders/presbyters, bishops, and deacons, who were settled in local congregations. They facilitated the ministry of the whole church by being servants of Jesus Christ.

Elder/presbyter (*presbuteros*) was the equivalent in the Christian congregation of the elder in the synagogue, with duties of oversight, supervision, and leadership (Acts 15:2; 20:17; 21:18; 1 Tim. 3:1–7; 5:17; Titus 1:5–9; Heb. 13:17). Therefore, in terms of what he did the elder was sometimes called the bishop or overseer (*episcopos*). That the elder is the bishop seems to be the natural meaning of Acts 20:17, 28; Philippians 1:1; 1 Timothy 3:4–5; 5:17–19; Titus 1:5–7; 1 Peter 5:2 (KJV). Apparently the elder was set in office by an act of ordination, but there are only minimal details of this in the New Testament (e.g., 1 Tim. 4:14; 5:22; 2 Tim. 1:6).

Within a short time of the apostolic age, when the church was separated from the synagogue, the distinction between the bishop and the presbyter (priest) developed. In the New Testament period the real distinction was among the itinerant apostles, evangelists, and prophets and the settled presbyters and deacons.

Diakonia simply means "ministry" and "service" and so has reference to Christ and to all his servants. The noun *diakonos* is often applied to the seven men who were set apart by prayer and the laying on of hands and appointed to serve tables by the apostles (Acts 6:1–6). Yet they are not called deacons. However, deacons are mentioned in Philippians 1:1 and in 1 Timothy 3:8–13. Phoebe is called a deacon in Romans 16:1.

While the presbyterate may be said to originate within the synagogue, this cannot be said of the diaconate. There is no parallel to it in Judaism. The main tasks of deacons, who were to be of sound character and with a firm hold on the faith, were administrative and financial.

Summary. Whether in the Old or New Testaments, ministry finds its meaning and expression in Jesus Christ. He is the Minister par excellence and the only source of ministry. The Old Testament looks forward to him while the New Testament looks both back, up, and forward to him. In relation to Christ every member of Israel or the church has a ministry of serving the Lord by proclaiming the Word of God by word and deed both inside and outside the people of God. In this sense all are royal priests. Further, in relation to Christ there are specific or particular forms of ministry within and for the sake of the church in its mission for God in his world. These are given only to a few and they include the callings of prophet, priest, and king in the Old Covenant and apostle, evangelist, presbyter, and deacon in the New Covenant. Though not a strictly biblical expression "ordained ministry" refers to persons who have received a gift of the Spirit and have been appointed by the church, through prayer and the laying on of hands, to specific offices within the church.

PETER TOON

Bibliography. R. E. Brown, *The Churches the Apostles Left Behind;* J. D. G. Dunn, *Unity and Diversity in the New Testament;* R. P. McBrien, *Ministry;* L. Morris, *Ministers of God;* E. Schweizer, *Church Order in the New Testament.*

Miracle. Although English speakers regularly use "miracle" to refer to a broad range of wondrous events, the biblical concept is limited to those not explainable solely by natural processes but which require the direct causal agency of a supernatural being, usually God. These occur throughout all major eras of history but do appear with greater frequency at key periods of God's self-revelation.

Genesis. The Bible begins with one of God's greatest miracles—the creation of the universe out of nothing. However literally the various details are taken, Genesis 1–2 primarily describes not the "how" but the "who" of creation. Against somewhat similar stories in polytheistic religions, Genesis affirms the complete, cosmic sovereignty of the Lord God. All else is subordinate and never to be worshiped. Humanity is categorically distinct from the rest of creation by virtue of being created in the image of God (Gen. 1:26–28). The fall, followed by an increase in evil, begins to thwart God's creative purposes. The next major miracle, the flood, thus affirms both God's judgment on extreme wickedness and his grace in promising never again to destroy humanity so completely (6:3; 9:15–16). The promise does not preclude judgments of a lesser nature, though, such as Babel (11:1–9) or Sodom and Gomorrah (19:1–29). Miracles throughout the rest of Genesis deal primarily with God's preservation of his chosen line, when his promises to Abraham (Gen. 12:1–3) seem about to be broken, most notably Sarah's conception of Isaac at an advanced age (21:1–7). A seemingly miraculous provision of water in the desert preserves Hagar and Ishmael (21:14–21), reminding us of God's care for other peoples as well.

Exodus–Deuteronomy. The first major cluster of biblical miracles surrounds the central Old Testament act of redemption—the exodus of the Israelites from Egypt. Here too appear thirteen of the eighteen Old Testament uses of "signs and wonders," an expression that focuses on the miracles' redemptive significance. In the burning bush, God reveals his name (Yahweh) to Moses as the eternally existing one and promises his presence with his servant who is terrified of what God is asking him to do (Exod. 3). Further signs are promised to encourage him that he can overcome Pharaoh and the Egyptians (4:1–17). Ten plagues ensue, from which the Israelites are miraculously protected (7:14–11:10). None of the plagues itself is necessarily supernatural; in fact, their sequence is often scientifically logical. But their timing and geographical limitations point to God's sovereign intervention on Israel's behalf. The climactic plague of the death of firstborn sons finally motivates Pharaoh to let Moses and his people go.

Pharaoh quickly changes his mind, though, and it seems that his armies will obliterate Israel. The miraculous crossing of the Sea of Reeds (14:21–31), therefore, becomes the prototypical Old Testament miracle of the deliverance of God's people and the destruction of his enemies (15:1–2). It also discloses God's merciful initiatives prior to his giving of the law (20:1–2); in the Old Testament as in the New Testament, salvation by grace precedes God's demands for good works. The Israelites' wandering in the wilderness is punctuated by various miracles of preservation and judgment—rescue when it seems they will perish (by the ongoing provision of manna and quail—chap. 16; and special provisions at key moments, most notably water from the rock—17:1–7; Num. 10:1–13) and destruction of those who disobey God and challenge his appointed leaders (most notably the sudden deaths of Nadab and Abihu—Lev. 10:1–7; and the earthquake that swallows Korah and his fellow rebels—Num. 16). Plagues, too, require divine intervention to be stopped and Aaron's rod buds to authenticate him as the legitimate priest (chap. 17). In short, God's mighty acts intend to foster dependence of his people on him, that they might not trust in themselves or any other gods. And, as with Hagar, he occasionally reminds them that he can work to and through people outside the chosen line, even in humorous ways (Balaam's donkey—22:21–35).

Joshua–2 Samuel. With Moses' death, Joshua becomes his appointed successor to lead the Israelites into the promised land. A water crossing (of the Jordan) similar to the exodus initiates this period and authenticates Joshua's privileged role (Josh. 3:7). Subsequent battles are often won or lost despite the relative strengths of the armies, to remind God's people that he alone is in charge (cf. esp. the conquest of Jericho versus the defeat at Ai—chaps. 6–7). Although no miracle, per se, occurs as Gideon fights the Midianites, the confusion that causes his enemies to slay each other, despite the small number of opposing forces, is equally attributed to the Lord's direct intervention (Judg. 7). The report of sun and moon standing still while Joshua fights the Amorites comes in a poetic passage and is perhaps not meant to be taken as literal cosmic upheaval (Josh. 10:12–13). But it continues the theme of God's sovereign agency as the cause of victory. Subsequent miracles are also "borderline"—Samson's superhuman strength when he is "filled with the Spirit" (Judg. 13–16) and the ark's "power" over Dagon (1 Sam. 5) and the cattle that return it to Beth Shemesh (chap. 6). These and many other passages highlight how the biblical world's divisions between natural and supernatural were far more fluid than today and how most momentous events were attributed to various divinities.

First Kings–Nehemiah. The next major cluster of miracles involves the prophets Elijah and Elisha. The faithful remnant of Israel is locked in a mortal, spiritual battle with idolatry, especially Baal worship. The predominant purpose behind the miracles of these two prophets is to demonstrate Yahweh's superiority over Baal and to call God's people back to worship him. The classic expression of this combat comes at Carmel, as fire from heaven consumes Elijah's sacrifice and the prophets of Baal are destroyed (1 Kings 18:16–40). But other mighty deeds also demonstrate the Lord's supremacy over the pagan god of water, fertility, and life: Elijah alone can predict drought and rain (chaps. 17–18), and God will nourish his people (17:1–6) and others (vv. 7–16) during the former. Elisha purifies poisoned water and causes an axhead sunk in the river to float (2 Kings 2:19–22; 6:1–7). Both prophets, too, work Scripture's first miraculous resuscitations (1 Kings 17:17–24; 2 Kings 4:8–37). Elijah appropriately becomes the second person in history never to die but to be taken directly to heaven (2 Kings 2:1–18; cf. Enoch in Gen. 5:24).

Elijah's successor certifies his prophetic role with closely parallel miracles. In addition to those already noted, Elisha provides unfailing oil for a needy widow (2 Kings 4:1–7), purifies a pot of food, feeds a hundred men with twenty small loaves, and again demonstrates God's concern for foreigners in healing Naaman's leprosy (4:38–5:27). The latter two miracles closely resemble

Jesus' later feeding of the multitudes, cures of lepers, and concern for Gentiles. Indeed Jesus himself will liken parts of his ministry to God's choice in the days of Elijah and Elisha to favor those outside Israel (Luke 4:25–27). Although Elisha dies a normal death, even his bones cause a corpse thrown into his grave to be resuscitated (2 Kings 13:20–21). The two other major miracles that occur in the Old Testament historical books involve the leprosy with which faithless Uzziah is afflicted and the sundial shadow's retreat as a sign to portend Hezekiah's recovery from illness (2 Kings 15:1–8; 20:1–11).

Job–Malachi. Two books whose genre is disputed contain major miracles: Job with his remarkable collection of afflictions and subsequent recovery and Jonah with his preservation by and expulsion from the great fish. Both teach of God's judgment and salvation, and of how even affliction is under his sovereign control for ultimately good purposes. The psalms frequently recount and reflect on God's past signs and wonders. The prophets speak of present and future signs, some more supernatural than others, to corroborate their message. Most famous is the prophecy of the virginal conception in Isaiah 7:14. The only other major cluster of Old Testament miracles centers on the life of Daniel and his friends in exile in Babylon. Once again Yahweh proves his supremacy over foreign gods and rulers. Thrown into the fiery furnace for refusing to worship Nebuchadnezzar's image, Shadrach, Meshach, and Abednego are miraculously spared, while the great heat burns up their captors (Dan. 3). Thrown into the lion's den for praying to the Lord, Daniel too escapes harm (chap. 6). Other miracles give Daniel the ability to interpret Nebuchadnezzar's dream (chap. 2), and the miraculous writing on Belshazzar's wall (chap. 5).

Matthew–John. The greatest of all biblical miracles is the incarnation—God becoming human (John 1:1–18). Foreshadowed by the birth of John the Baptist to the previously barren Elizabeth (Luke 1:5–25), the virginal conception of Jesus, the God-man, fulfills prophecy (Matt. 1–2) and demonstrates the Spirit's parentage (Luke 1:26–38). Jesus' adult ministry regularly features miracles for a variety of purposes. Sometimes they respond to individuals' faith in Christ (e.g., Jairus—Matt. 9:18; and the hemorrhaging woman—9:22) or are hindered by their lack thereof (the disbelief in Nazareth—Mark 6:4–6a). On other occasions they seem more designed to instill faith where it has been lacking (e.g., the stilling of the storm—Mark 4:40; or the healing of the nobleman's son—John 4:48).

Other important motifs include Jesus' compassion for the needy (e.g., in feeding the five thousand—Mark 6:34; or in restoring the two blind men's sight—Matt. 20:34) and breaking down social barriers in preparation for the universal offer of the gospel (e.g., in cleansing the ritually impure lepers—Mark 1:40–45; Luke 17:11–19 [where the thankful one is explicitly a Samaritan]; healing the Syrophoenician woman's daughter—Mark 7:24–30; or feeding the four thousand in Gentile territory—Matt. 15:29–39). Frequently Jesus challenges the prevailing sabbath traditions (e.g., the man with the withered hand—Mark 3:1–6; or the closely parallel healings of cripples in Luke 13:10–17; 14:1–6) and exposes Israel's predominant faithlessness (e.g., in praising the great faith of the centurion whose servant was sick—Matt. 8:5–13), including the periodic lack of faith of his own disciples (e.g., with the epileptic they could not cure—Matt. 17:14–21). In still other instances, Jesus wants to teach a lesson about sin. Sickness may be the result of one's own wickedness; its healing, therefore, an incentive to repent (John 5:1–15). In other cases, though, it is wrong to blame anyone; God's greater glory is what is involved (John 9:1–5).

But none of these themes proves as prominent as the most central one: Jesus works miracles to demonstrate that the kingdom of God has been inaugurated, the messianic age has arrived, and he is the Christ who will fulfill all of God's previous Scriptures. In explaining the significance of his exorcisms, Jesus makes this claim explicit (Matt. 12:28). In replying to John the Baptist about his identity, the claim is more implicit but equally clear (Matt. 11:4–5). Once he heals a paralytic to demonstrate his authority to forgive sins (Mark 2:9–10). His transfiguration is introduced as God's kingly reign come in power (Mark 9:1). Lazarus' revivification grounds Jesus' subsequent claim to be the resurrection and the life (John 11:25). And the evangelists' summaries regularly link his mighty deeds with his teachings so that the former legitimate the latter.

These direct statements give clues how to interpret some of the more unusual of Jesus' miracles that often have parabolic or symbolic elements. Turning water into wine probably demonstrates the joy attached to the arrival of the new age (John 2:1–11). Cursing the fig tree symbolizes the impending destruction of Israel just as much as the temple cleansing it sandwiches (Mark 11:12–25). Feeding the five thousand recalls the manna in the wilderness and sets up Jesus' bread of life discourse (John 6:1–15, 25–59). Walking on the water is a theophany; Jesus' words of self-revelation echo Exodus 3:14—literally, "I am" (Mark 6:50). Healing the deaf-mute effects a rare miracle predicted to herald the messianic age (Mark 7:31–37; cf. Isa. 35:6). Raising the son of the Nain widow closely resembles the reanimations by Elijah and Elisha (Luke 7:11–17) and occurs on virtually the identical site as one of them (Old Testament Shunem). The two great fish catches point to the disciples' call to be spiritual fishers of people and to Peter's reinstatement after his denial for this continued ministry (Luke 5:1–11; John 21:1–14).

The greatest miracle of Jesus' life, of course, is his resurrection. Immediately following his death, nature heralds its unusual significance with an earthquake, the rending of the temple veil, and the opening of tombs of certain Old Testament saints, who would then be raised following Jesus' resurrection (Matt. 27:51–54). God's resurrection of Jesus vindicates his claims, gives atoning meaning to his death, serves as a prelude to his ascension and exaltation, and makes eternal life and bodily resurrection available to all who trust in him. The best theological commentary on this event is 1 Corinthians 15.

Each evangelist has his own thematic emphases concerning Jesus' miracles. Mark sharply contrasts the glory of Jesus' public ministry and its preponderance of wonders with the road to the cross and his teaching on suffering (1:1–8:30; 8:31–16:8). Mark, too, introduces the so-called messianic secret motif following several miracles (e.g., 1:34; 3:12; 5:43). Matthew's miracle-stories fit his overall narrative progression from Jesus' particularism to universalism (with chap. 13 as the hinge) and his stress on the fulfillment of Scripture (8:17; 11:4–5). Luke highlights Jesus' compassion for the outcasts of society (4:18; 17:11–19) and his role as a new Moses (9:28–36) and Elijah/Elisha (7:1–28). John's views prove the most distinctive. Whereas the Synoptics use "signs" in a negative sense as that which unbelieving skeptics demand but do not receive save for the resurrection as the "sign of Jonah" (Matt. 12:38–42), John consistently speaks of Jesus' miracles as "signs" meant to lead people to faith in Christ (2:11; 4:54; cf. 20:31). But he encourages a maturity that does not require dependence on miraculous proofs (4:48; 20:29). John also pairs seven signs with seven discourses to form the first major half of his Gospel (1:19–11:57). The signs require interpretive teaching even as they legitimate Jesus' claims.

Acts. Jesus' ascension ends his resurrection appearances, marks his return to the Father, and enables him to bestow the Spirit permanently on all believers (1:1–11). The Spirit comes with miraculous confirmation at Pentecost (2:1–3). Apostolic preaching picks up the Old Testament phrase "signs and wonders" to stress the redemptive significance of Christ's ministry (2:22) and to describe how the first Christians continued that work (4:30; 5:12), as commissioned earlier by Jesus himself. Many different believers perform miracles, not just the twelve (Stephen and Philip in 6:8 and 8:13), and they continue with about the same frequency throughout the book. Peter and Paul, as the two protagonists of the two halves of Acts (chaps. 1–12, 13–28), each work a specially large number, several pairs of which are remarkably parallel (earthquakes to get out of jail—12:5–10; 16:22–34; healings of the lame—3:1–10; 14:8–10; raising the dead—9:36–43; 20:7–12). The apostolic miracles often closely parallel Jesus' mighty works, too (cf. 9:32–35 and Mark 2:1–12; 9:36–42 and Mark 5:35–42). Luke thus stresses that the disciples are the authorized successors of Jesus, and that Peter's Jewish-oriented ministry and Paul's Gentile-centered work equally fulfill Christ's commission. As in other periods, occasional miracles also reflect God's judgment on his enemies (13:6–12) or his rebellious children (5:1–11).

Romans–Revelation. For Paul, healings and miracles are spiritual gifts (1 Cor. 12:9–10) God gives to those whom he chooses (vv. 29–30) throughout the entire period of history until Christ's return (1:7; 13:10–12). But he often withholds miraculous healing because of the remedial value of suffering (2 Cor. 12:8–9). Miracles further certify apostolic credentials (12:12), characterize Paul's ministry (Rom. 15:19), and attest the truth of Christian life in the Spirit (Gal. 3:5). Counterfeit miracles will proliferate in the end times (2 Thess. 2:9), as Jesus himself had prophesied (Matt. 24:24), and as Revelation will describe in greater detail (e.g., 13:13–14a). James attributes a ministry of anointing with oil and prayer for healing to the eldership of the local church (5:14–16).

Conclusion. Throughout the Bible, miracles consistently serve to point people to the one true God, ultimately revealed in Jesus Christ. Their primary purpose is not to meet human need, although that is an important spinoff blessing. But they are first of all theocentric and Christocentric, demonstrating the God of Israel and of Jesus to be supreme over all rivals. Contemporary experience suggests that this pattern continues; miracles today seem most frequent in regions where Satan has long held sway and where people require "power evangelism" to be converted. But God's sovereignty warns against trying to predict when they may occur and refutes the "name it and claim it" heresy that tries to force God to work miracles upon demand, if only one exercises adequate faith.

Craig L. Blomberg

Bibliography. B. Blackburn, *Theios Aner and the Markan Miracle Traditions;* L. Bronner, *The Stories of Elijah and Elisha;* C. Brown, *Miracles and the Critical Mind;* R. T. Fortna, *The Fourth Gospel and Its Predecessor;* B. Gerhardsson, *The Mighty Acts of Jesus according to Matthew;* J. Green, S. McKnight, and I. H. Marshall, eds., *Dictionary of Jesus and the Gospels,* pp. 299–307, 549–60; M. J. Harris, *From Grave to Glory;* C. Hyers, *The Meaning of Creation;* R. Latourelle, *The Miracles of Jesus and the Theology of Miracles; ISBE,* 3:371–81; 4:505–8, 1100–1101; H. Lockyer, *All the Miracles of the Bible;* L. O'Reilly, *Word and Sign in the Acts iof the Apostles;* L. Sabourin, *The Divine Miracles Discussed and Defended;* G. Theissen, *Miracle Stories of the Early Christian Tradition;* H. van der Loos, *The Miracles of Jesus;* D. Wenham and C. Blomberg, eds., *Gospel Perspectives,* vol. 6.

Mission. ***Basic Definition.*** Mission is the divine activity of sending intermediaries, whether supernatural or human, to speak or do God's will so that his purposes for judgment or redemption are furthered. The biblical concept is expressed by the use of verbs meaning "to send," normally with God as the expressed subject. The Hebrew verb is *šālaḥ* and the Greek is *apostellō*. These terms emphasize the authoritative, commissioning relationship involved. The Scriptures also employ the cognates *apostolos* ("apostle," the one sent) and *apostolē* ("apostleship," the function of being sent), referring to the one sent and his function.

The biblical concept of "mission" comprehends the authority of the one who sends; the obedience of the one sent; a task to be accomplished; the power to accomplish the task; and a purpose within the moral framework of God's covenantal working of judgment or redemption.

Mission in the Old Testament. The first records in biblical history of God's sending is his banishment of Adam and Even from the garden and the angelic mission to destroy Sodom and Gomorrah (Gen. 3:23; 19:13). The redemption from Egypt and the conquest of the land has its dark side: judgment on the idolatrous nations Israel escapes from or displaces. The emphasis, however, in the Pentateuchal accounts on mission centers on God's positive action. In securing a bride for Isaac and thus keeping the hope of the covenant promise alive for another generation, God sends his angel before Abraham's chief household servant to give him success on his journey (Gen. 24:7, 40). And in the fourth generation it is Joseph, as he says to his brothers, whom "God . . . sent ahead of you to preserve for you a remnant on earth and to save your lives by a great deliverance" (45:7; cf. vv. 5, 8; Ps. 105:17). In Joseph's case, aside from prescient dreams in his youth (Gen. 37:5–11), there was no specific call to mission. But he could look back on harmful circumstances and discern God's sending of him to Egypt to preserve the nation.

Moses does receive a call from God, who sends him to Pharaoh to bring his people out of Egypt (Exod. 3:10). God has heard their cry under Egyptian oppression, and sends Moses as leader and redeemer (Acts 7:35). So closely are Moses' and God's work identified that in some passages it is Moses who brings the people out (1 Sam. 12:8) while in other places it is God (Josh. 24:5; Ps. 105:43, cf. v. 26; Mic. 6:4).

At other points redemption from Egypt is a commissioned angel's work (Num. 20:16). And an angel, which could well be a Christophany, is sent by God to protect the people in their wilderness wanderings and powerfully fight on their behalf in the conquest of Canaan (Exod. 23:20–33; 33:2).

Signs and wonders are what God sent Moses to do in Egypt and in the sight of Israel (Deut. 34:11–12), as a means of liberation (Ps. 105:27) and validation of his divinely given authority (Num. 16:28–29). Moses is the quintessential divinely commissioned redeemer in the Old Testament.

During the time of the judges, God's intervention to deliver Israel after a cycle of apostasy, punishment, oppression at the hands of her enemies, and a cry for deliverance involved various missions. Prophets were sent to interpret to Israel the moral and spiritual dimension of her suffering (Judg. 6:8). God sent angels to announce to the parents or to the judge himself his role as divinely sent deliverer and to commission him to that task (Judg. 6:11–12, 14; 13:8).

The line of prophets from Moses to Samuel was sent by God to provide deliverance for Israel (1 Sam. 12:11). Samuel was sent by God to anoint kings (15:1; 16:1). Samuel communicated to Saul his positive mission of deliverance, which took the form of punishment of the Amalekites (15:18, 20). All other missions by the prophets to kings and to Israel involved confronting sin using God's law, calling for repentance, and warning of judgment if the monarch or the nation did not turn back to God (2 Sam. 12:1; 1 Kings 14:6; 2 Chron. 25:15). In fact, summaries of the northern kingdom's rebellion leading to Assyrian subjugation and exile and Judah's similar end at the hands of Babylon stress that again and again God in his pity sent prophets to the people (2 Kings 17:13; 2 Chron. 24:19; 36:15; Jer. 29:19; 35:15; 44:4).

Of the Old Testament prophets, Isaiah and Jeremiah have the clearest articulation of God's personal call to mission (Isa. 6:8; Jer. 1:7). Their immediate mission was to announce judgment to a rebellious people who, they were told, would reject their message (Isa. 6:9–12; Jer. 26:12, 15; 42:5–6; 43:1–2; cf. Ezek. 2:3–4; contrast Hag. 1:12). Though their mission would be a failure in terms of a positive response to their message, their commission charged them to be totally obedient (Isa. 6:8; Jer. 1:7).

When the prophets did speak of a hope for future deliverance "in the last days," they refer to a mission for God's messenger or Elijah whom God sends to prepare his way (Mal. 3:1); of the Servant-Messiah, anointed to preach good news to the oppressed, whom the Lord sends to bring deliverance (Isa. 61:1); and of a remnant of survivors who are sent to evangelize the nations: "They will proclaim my glory among the nations" (Isa. 66:19).

Mission in the Ministry of Jesus. So significant is the redemptive mission of the Messiah, the Son of God, that God sends an angel not only to announce his birth (Luke 1:26), but to announce the birth of John the Baptist, the messenger who will be sent to prepare his way and introduce him (1:19; Matt. 11:10; cf. Mark 1:2; Luke 7:27; John 1:6, 33).

Jesus had much to say about his own understanding of his mission. He saw his purpose as being sent by God his Father to proclaim and accomplish spiritual deliverance for humankind (Luke 4:43; John 3:34; 8:42; 10:36). He consciously appropriates Isaiah 61:1–2 as the Old Testament passage his ministry fulfills (Luke 4:18–19).

Jesus characterizes his mission as authenticated and sustained by the Father who sent him (John 5:37; 6:57; 8:18, 29). More than that—Jesus comes with the full authorization of God, so that he fully, even interchangeably, represents him (John 12:44–45). So he can say to his disciples when he sends them on mission: "He who receives you receives me, and he who receives me receives the one who sent me" (Matt. 10:40; cf. Mark 9:37). At the same time, Jesus carries out his mission in full obedience to the will of the one who sent him (John 4:34; 5:30; 6:38–39; 7:18). He speaks his words and does his works (7:16; 8:26; 9:4; 12:49; 14:24).

To believe that God has sent his Son Jesus on this saving mission is critically decisive for an individual's eternal destiny. "Now this is eternal life: that they may know you the only true God, and Jesus Christ, whom you have sent" (17:3; cf. 5:24; 6:29; 11:42; 17:21). To reject divinely sent messengers and their message will mean, even for the sons of Israel, receiving the retributive justice and forfeiting kingdom blessings at the last judgment (Matt. 22:1–14; Luke 14:17).

Jesus recognized his place in the midst of a long train of divinely sent, yet humanly rejected, messengers—both past and future. There were the prophets, wise men, scribes, and apostles, whom Israel had and would reject, even kill (Matt. 23:33–36; Luke 11:47–51; 13:34; cf. Matt. 22:3–4; Luke 14:17). Through parable Jesus let them know that he, the Son, was among that number (Matt. 21:34–37; Mark 12:2–6; Luke 20:10–13).

Unlike any previous human sent on a mission by God, Jesus proceeded to send his followers on a mission with the same authority and the same tasks. During his earthly ministry Jesus designated the Twelve as "apostles" (Matt. 10:2; Luke 6:13; Acts 1:2). He is the source of the title and the instructions he gives the apostles enables us to fill out the picture of what Jesus meant by being one sent on a mission. The authorization is complete. Apostles are fully representative of their Lord (Matt. 10:40). This is seen from their tasks. Not only do they preach the same message as Jesus—"The kingdom of heaven is near" (10:7)—but they are given authority by him to do the same miraculous works: casting out demons and healing the sick (10:1; Mark 6:7; Luke 9:1). Interestingly, the focus of their mission was the same: "the lost sheep of the house of Israel" (Matt. 10:6; 15:24). Jesus sent them on their mission as innocents, unprotected and unprovisioned (10:9, 16; Mark 6:8–11; Luke 9:3–5). They go to complete the work begun by others, to harvest what they have not labored for (John 4:38). Though they are not labeled apostles, the Seventy, sent out two by two, go on the same basic mission (Luke 10:1–12). They also have full authorization from Jesus, so that those who are listening to them are listening to him (10:16).

The pattern of mission set by Jesus' sending of his followers during his earthly ministry was repeated and extended during his post-resurrection appearances. At that time he clearly defined the mission for each generation until he returns (Matt. 28:18–20). Their message's perspective and the scope of the audience, however, would now be different. The risen Lord commissioned his followers to proclaim a salvation fully accomplished in his atoning death and victorious resurrection and freely offered to those who repent and receive it (Luke 24:44–48). He sent them to "all the nations . . . to the end of the earth" (Matt. 28:19; Luke 24:47; Acts 1:8; 22:21; 26:17). The manner of the mission must now be carried out with due regard to protection and provision (Luke 22:35–38).

This commissioning is not limited to the twelve apostles. The Gospel of John presents Jesus as commissioning all disciples with the same mission. He prays in the high priestly prayer, "As you sent me into the world, I have sent them into the world" (17:18). In a post-resurrection appearance to the disciples he says, "As the Father has sent me, I am sending you" (20:21). In his further instructions he indicates that this comparative formula means a full authorization in mission. As they go about preaching the gospel of salvation, God the Holy Spirit empowers them (20:22).

Jesus also sends the Holy Spirit on a mission. He will empower Christian believers for witness to the good news of salvation (Luke 24:49; cf. vv. 46–48; Acts 1:8). He will bring not only full knowledge of the saving truth in Jesus' teaching (John 14:26; 15:26; this is promised particularly to the twelve apostles), but he will bring to the unbelieving world convincing conviction of sin, righteousness, and judgment to come (16:7–11).

Finally, Jesus speaks of sending angels on mission. Not only does the exalted Lord Jesus send his angel to reveal to John what shall occur at the end (Rev. 22:16), but, as the glorious, returning Son of Man, he will send angels both to gather the elect to himself (Matt. 24:31; Mark 13:27) and to gather out of his kingdom "everything that causes sin and all who do evil" and cast them into eternal punishment (Matt. 13:41–42).

Mission in the Early Church. *God Sends Salvation.* As the apostles reflected on the Savior God sent they highlighted the motive, context, task, and result of his mission. God's self-initiating love sent Jesus (1 John 4:9–10). As with Moses and the judges, Jesus is sent into a situation of bondage, this time spiritual, to fulfill God's saving purposes (Gal. 4:3–5). The comparison and contrast with Moses, God's first "apostle-redeemer," reveals not only Jesus' comparable faithfulness but his superiority (Heb. 3:1–6). He has greater glory as the creator of the household of faith and as a Son who rules over it. In these two ways his role as fully authorized, indeed interchangeable, representative of God is brought out.

Jesus' task is to be savior of the world (1 John 4:14); redeemer of those under law (Gal. 4:4); sacrifice for sin and condemnation of sin (Rom. 8:3); and propitiation (1 John 4:9–10). The result of this rescue mission is not only redemption from the penalty of sin, but an introduction into eternal life, that is, "living through him" and receiving an inheritance: "full rights as sons" (Rom. 8:1–4; Gal. 4:4–5; 1 John 4:9).

The apostles were also very much aware of God's sending of the Spirit in these last days. He comes to empower the witness to the gospel (1 Peter 1:12) and to be a salvation blessing, bearing witness to the intimate union believers have with the Father (Gal. 4:6). He is the means by which the Godhead is omniscient and omnipresent in the world (Rev. 5:6).

Angels, too, are sent. They minister to believers, even to the extent of the miraculous intervention so that the mission may go forward (Acts 12:11; Heb. 1:14). They provide revelation of events of the end of history (Rev. 1:1; 22:6).

The work of all these messengers comes to nothing if the word, the message of salvation, is not sent and heeded (Acts 10:36; 13:26; cf. 28:28, salvation sent to those who will listen). It must go to Israel and the Gentiles. So intent is the Godhead that the mission go forward and so essential is the human messenger, that through a vision spiritually needy Gentiles are sent to summon a Jewish Christian apostle to preach to them under their roof (10:3–6, 20). The proclaimers of this message are divinely sent (Rom. 10:15).

Apostle. Originating in Jesus' choice and commissioning of the Twelve, the concept of apostle as divinely commissioned messenger of the good news of salvation plays a major role in the church's thinking about mission. The term can apply uniquely to the foundational apostles of the church's first generation, the Twelve. Outside traditions in which ecclesiastical authority involves apostolic succession, any continuing presence of apostolicity is usually thought of in terms of "apostolic function," namely, pioneer church planting missionary endeavor. Though this is certainly at the core of the biblical teaching, there is much else the term can teach us about mission.

There a number of categories of individuals who are called "apostles" in the New Testament: the Twelve (Luke 6:13); the 120 to 500 who saw the risen Christ (1 Cor. 15:7); Paul (15:8–9); missionaries (Acts 14:4; Rom. 16:7; 1 Cor. 9:5); and church envoys (2 Cor. 8:23; Phil. 2:25). The qualifications for fitting one of these categories involves the call of the risen Christ who sends. If one has been personally commissioned by the risen Lord in a post-resurrection pre-ascension appearance, he fits into the category of "the Twelve" or the 120 to 500. Of course, the Twelve met the added qualification of having been chosen by Jesus during his earthly ministry (cf. the criteria and method of choice for Judas's replacement, Acts 1:21–26). Paul realized that he did not meet the criteria for being part of the Twelve or even the 120 to 500. Comparing himself to "one abnormally born," he claims the title "apostle" because of a personal call from the risen Lord in an appearance from heaven after the ascension (1 Cor. 15:8–10). Though the evidenced is less clear, it seems that there is biblical precedent for labeling as "apostles" missionary messengers of the saving gospel in each generation of the church, who receive an inward, subjective call to fulfill an apostolic function of pioneer church planting cross-culturally, a calling that in turn is confirmed by the "outward commissioning" of the church (Acts 14:4, 14; Rom 16:7; 1 Cor. 9:5; cf. Acts 9:17; 13:3; Rom. 10:15). Church envoys, who are termed "apostles," are qualified to serve because of the church's call. Those sent as church envoys engage in spiritual ministry: validating the advance of the gospel (Acts 8:14; 11:22); communicating decisions about doctrine and behavior (15:27, 30, 33; 21:25); providing physical aid that promotes unity (11:29–30; 1 Cor. 16:3); and serving as apostolic agents to give guidance and encouragement (Acts 19:22; 1 Cor. 4:17; 2 Cor. 12:17; 2 Tim. 4:12). Since, however, they are not presented as being sent directly by the Father or the Son, their work is beyond the bound of our definition of mission.

The tasks of the apostle varies to some extent according to category. Apostles are first and foremost missionaries, sent out to bear witness to the good news of salvation (Acts 2:37–39; 20:24; Rom. 1:1; Eph. 3:2–6; 1 Tim. 2:7; 2 Tim. 1:11; 4:7). When they are numbered among the Twelve or the 120 to 150, they give their eyewitness testimony to the central saving event that makes gospel proclamation possible: the resurrection (Acts 1:21–22; 5:29; 1 Cor. 9:1; 15:7).

The Twelve have the unique function of providing the revelational and organizational foundation for the church (Luke 22:14, 28–30; Eph. 2:20; Rev. 18:20; 21:14). They guarantee the church's doctrine and its mission (Acts 2:42; 8:14, 18; 15:2, 22; Eph. 2:20; 1 Tim. 2:7; 2 Peter 3:2; Jude 17). They are its early chief administrators (4:35–37; 5:2; 6:6; 9:27). Paul, though of "abnormal birth," also participates in the unique revelatory function.

The empowerment the apostle knows is a gracing, a gifting of effective missionary witness (Rom. 1:5; 1 Cor. 12:28–29; Gal. 2:8; Eph. 4:11). This, as well as signs and wonders (Acts 2:43; 4:33; 5:12;

2 Cor. 11:5; 12:11–12), appears to rest uniquely on apostles with foundational revelatory and organizational functions: the Twelve and Paul. Still, any missionary exercising the "apostolic function" knows the empowerment of God in witness, for the fruit is always God's doing (1 Cor. 3:7–9; 9:2).

The manner of the apostle's ministry is a paradoxical mixture of honor and dishonor. He is a chosen representative of Jesus Christ according to God's will and decree (1 Cor. 1:1; 2 Cor. 1:1; Gal. 1:1; Col. 1:1; 1 Tim. 1:1; 2 Tim. 1:1; Titus 1:1; 1 Peter 1:1). At the same time, he is "a spectacle to the whole universe, to angels as well as to men," the object of disdain and persecution (1 Cor. 4:9; cf. Acts 5:18, 40; Rev. 18:20). Humankind's sinful rebellion, expressed as rejection of the message and the messenger, creates this paradox. It places the messenger at the vortex of the battle for the souls of people. How individuals respond to the mission and message is critically decisive. It will mean either final redemption or judgment (2 Cor. 2:14–17).

William J. Larkin, Jr.

See also Evangelize, Evangelism; Testimony.

Bibliography. J.-A. Bühner, *Exegetical Dictionary of the New Testament,* 1:141–42, 142–46; F. Hahn, *Mission in the New Testament;* R. E. Hedlund, *The Mission of the Church in the World: A Biblical Theology;* L. Legrand, *Unity and Plurality: Mission in the Bible;* K. H. Rengstorf, *TDNT,* 1:398–406; M. R. Spindler and P. R. Middlekoop, *Bible and Mission: A Partially Annotated Bibliography 1960–1980;* P. M. Steyne, *In Step with the God of the Nations: A Biblical Theology of Missions.*

Molech, Moloch. *See* Gods and Goddesses, Pagan.

Money. A variety of monetary systems are represented in the Bible, corresponding to the political powers that dominated the cultures represented there, from the darics named after the Persian monarch Darius (these are the first actual coins mentioned in the Bible; see 1 Chron. 29:7; Ezra 8:27; Neh. 7:70–72) to the coins of the Roman Empire that bore Caesar's image (Matt. 22:20–21). Unlike the coinage of the United States, which by law cannot bear the image of a living person, the coins of the ancient world were more explicitly political, bearing the representation of the living monarch who sponsored the mint that produced the coins. As Jesus affirms in Matthew 22, coins really belong to the person whose likeness appears on them, in contrast to God, who imprints his likeness (and hence his mark of ownership) on a living humanity (Gen. 1:27).

Although the word "money" appears frequently throughout some translations of the Old Testament, the first coins were not produced in the ancient Near East until the seventh century B.C. Consequently, when one finds the word "money" in Bible versions used to translate the Hebrew term *kesep* (lit. "silver"), one must recognize that it is usually not coins that are to be understood but refined, unminted silver. When one exchanged this silver for a commodity, the silver was weighed (*šāqal*) in balances to determine the proper quantity of silver appropriate to the bargain. It was the term for the calibration of this weighing that gave the name of *shekel* to the first Judean coins whose size corresponded to a shekel weight (a little less than half an ounce).

The genius of money is that it simplifies and facilitates the exchange of goods and services between humans. Greek Christians would not have been able to assist Christians in Judea had it not been for the existence of money, which functioned as a substitute for their labor and was easily transported (Rom. 15:26–27). The Old Testament acknowledged that there could be times when it was difficult for God's people to bring the actual firstfruits of their harvests and flocks over the great distances separating them from the temple in Jerusalem. In such cases, the people were to sell the products in question for silver and bring the silver to Jerusalem, where one could purchase the appropriate products necessary for the cultic celebration (Deut. 14:24–26; cf. Ezra 7:17).

This perception of a convenient exchange reappears when substitutions are required for other aspects of the cult. Since all firstborn Israelites originally belonged to God as a result of his saving their lives in the exodus (Exod. 13:11–16), firstborn Israelites had to find human substitutes if they wished to be released from God's full-time service (Num. 3:40–45). The Levites fulfilled this function as substitutes, but since there were not enough Levites to take the place of all firstborn Israelites when this was first enacted, God also accepted a monetary substitution of five shekels for those firstborn who could find no Levite to substitute for them (Num. 3:46–51). Ever after, any firstborn human (or unclean animal) that reached the age of one month had to be redeemed at the price of five shekels (Num. 18:15–16).

This monetary evaluation of humans is not a simple matter, and a variety of standards appear in the Bible. In addition to the cultic redemption of five shekels for the firstborn, there was also a monetary redemption of a half-shekel "atonement" or "ransom" applied to all male Israelites over twenty years of age (Exod. 30:11–16; 38:25–26). Such evaluations were independent of other factors, for "the rich are not to give more . . . and the poor are not to give less" (Exod. 30:15).

There was also a monetary substitution that could be applied to those who vowed themselves into God's service contingent on God's fulfillment of a request they asked of him. Instead of personally fulfilling the vow, the individual could pay a monetary substitute, determined in accord with the person's sex, age, and economic class (Lev.

27:1–8). Another monetary substitution was found in the legal sphere, where the general principle of lex talionis mandated that when one human takes another human's life, the offender must compensate by surrendering a human life in turn, usually his or her own. However, collections of laws in the ancient Near East allowed payment of money as a fine in cases of murder where the victim was from a lower social class. Sectors of the Old Testament echo the notion that money might serve to ransom one's life when one was legally liable to be put to death as a punishment (Exod. 21:29–30; 2 Sam. 21:4; 1 Kings 20:39), but Numbers 35:31 clarifies Israel's distinctiveness: "Do not accept a ransom for the life of a murderer." God did not permit monetary fines in such cases, but insisted on the death penalty for all murders. The single clear exception where monetary compensation covered a lost human life was in the case of the slave killed by a negligent owner's goring ox: thirty shekels (the general price of a slave) was to be paid to the dead slave's owner so that he could replace his lost property (Exod. 21:32).

The ease with which money could substitute for goods and services allowed it to be a ready means of replacing items lost or damaged in civil conflicts. Money appears not as a punitive measure in biblical legislation but as a compensation for commodities such as dead cattle (Exod. 21:33–36) and lost virginity (the price determined by the general dowry expected for a virgin; Exod. 22:16–17; Deut. 22:28–29). Money could function as a punishment when damages were less tangible (e.g., one hundred shekels for slander in Deut. 22:19; a variable amount for a miscarriage in Exod. 21:22), but these are infrequent in biblical law. Should money become a substitute for other punishments such as lex talionis or beatings, the law would become less fair in allowing the wealthy to be less affected by their misdeeds than the poor.

Although money had beneficial results in simplifying the exchange of goods and services, these advantages could be turned to evil purposes. In the same way that money facilitated the rewarding of work done well, it became equally easy to motivate individuals to do reprehensible crimes with bribes (Judg. 16:5, 18; Esther 3:9; 4:7; Matt. 28:12; Mark 14:11).

Money also could be used to affirm one's status as a subordinate who owed allegiance to another: it was humiliating for the kings of Israel and Judah to pay tribute to foreign monarchs (2 Kings 15:19–20; 18:14; 23:33, 35), but it was a sign of Israel's high standing when other nations paid annual tribute to her (2 Chron. 27:5). Of course, rulers could pay such money only if they had taxed their own people (2 Kings 15:20), and hence taxes were (and still are) a sign of the individual's submission to the government.

Expressing allegiance to a human authority in this fashion raises a dilemma for the one whose first allegiance is to God, a dilemma that Jesus resolves by insisting that one should return to any sovereign whatever has the sovereign's mark of ownership on it: "Whose portrait is this? . . . Give to Caesar what is Caesar's, and to God what is God's" (Matt. 22:20–21). Jesus provides a different perspective when asked to pay the temple tax, affirming that although he and his disciples are the sons of the divine King and need not pay the tax for God's temple, it should nevertheless still be paid so as not to offend fellow Jews (Matt. 17:24–27). There is a larger irony in this latter account, where the requisite amount for the tax is found in a fish's mouth. Unlike the righteous' gift to God, which must be personally costly (2 Sam. 24:24), it does not matter from what source one finds the tax or tribute to surrender to a human sovereign.

Money is one of the least trustworthy and most deceptive elements of human existence. It is an unpredictable and wildly vacillating guide to value. Large quantities of silver and gold, such as when one finds "silver as common . . . as stones" (1 Kings 10:27; cf. v. 14), generate inflation, which devalues the currency and its buying power. A shortage of certain commodities may drive up prices exorbitantly (2 Kings 6:25; Lam. 5:4; Rev. 6:6), while the sudden availability of products may cause the value of money to plunge (2 Kings 7:1, 16, 18). In response, one finds in the ancient Near East and the Bible attempts to stabilize currency and exchange rates (Ezek. 45:12). But even the currency itself is subject to loss (Luke 15:8), theft (Matt. 6:19), destruction (James 5:3; 1 Peter 1:18), and misuse (Luke 15:13–14). Hordes of coins found in archaeological excavations echo the frequency with which money is described as buried in the Bible, for money is so vulnerable that there is little else one can do to protect it. It is ironic that money loses its ability to protect its owner (Luke 12:20–21), who on the contrary is soon consumed with protecting the money instead (Eccl. 5:13). This is one reason why Jesus insists that his followers not accumulate money (Matt. 10:9) and why members of the earliest Jerusalem church did not claim that anything belonging to them was their own (Acts 4:32).

It is a repeated theme in the Bible that the monetary value of items does not reflect the value that God places on them. Jesus notes that although one can purchase a pair of sparrows in the market for a single copper coin comparable to a penny, this market value does not reflect the great attention that a single one of these birds receives from God (Matt. 10:29). So persistent is this theme of skewed values that it becomes predictable for items of low market value to figure high on God's list of valuables, and vice versa. Joseph was sold for less than the price of a slave (twenty shekels, Gen. 37:28), but he became the savior of Egypt who ironically purchased its entire population into slavery (Gen. 47:13–25). Jesus' betrayal price of thirty silver pieces is a tragic miscalculation of his true status (Zech. 11:13; Mark 14:11; Luke 22:5). Others may look with disdain upon a donation of a few copper coins to the temple treasury, but it is not the market value of the widow's gift that Jesus finds important: "She . . . put in everything—all she had to live on" (Mark 12:41–44). It is this confusion of market value with spiritual value that irritates Peter when Simon Magus offers to pay money in return for the power of the Holy Spirit (Acts 8:18–24). One should not even consider any amount of money in exchange for the most intense suffering for the sake of Jesus (1 Peter 1:7). It is for this reason that those who lead the church must have no fondness for money (Acts 20:33; 1 Tim. 3:3, 8; Titus 1:7, 11; 1 Peter 5:2 contrast the Pharisees in Luke 16:14). There is no greater demonstrations of the contrary value system represented by money than Paul's observation that the love of money is the root of all evil (1 Tim. 6:10).

Money is also unreliable because people falsify the standards of measurement for personal gain, or, in the words of Amos 8:5, "make the shekel bigger" (cf. the ideal of just balances and weights in Lev. 19:36; Job 31:6; Ezek. 45:10). The arbitrary and flexible nature of monetary standards, permitting easy manipulation, is evident in the variety of calibrations that are mentioned in the Bible: the royal standard (2 Sam. 14:26), the merchant's standard (Gen. 23:16), and the "sanctuary shekel" (Exod. 30:13; 38:24–26). Mesopotamia attested simultaneous usage of a "heavy" and "light" shekel in both a royal and a common standard; ancient Near Eastern standards not only varied within one geographical locale but fluctuated from place to place and over time. Such practices prompted legislation in Israel: "Do not have differing weights in your bag—one heavy, one light" (Deut. 25:13).

People tend to cling to money, addicted to its false security. Because money behaves like a spiritual narcotic, deadening one's sensitivity to real value, Jesus insists that one cannot be committed simultaneously to both God's values and "mammon" (an Aramaic word meaning money, wealth, or property; Matt. 6:24). Ananias and Sapphira tried to pursue both and proved the veracity of Jesus' words as well as the spiritual corruption that money serves to catalyze (Acts 5:1–10). Money is therefore quite dangerous, prompting Jesus to advise his followers not to take any money with them on their preaching tours (Mark 6:8; Luke 9:3) and to give away any money that came from the sale of their estates (Luke 18:22; cf. Acts 4:34–37).

A further problem with money surfaces when one uses it to earn more money at the expense of others in need, specifically in the charging of interest for monetary loans. Jesus' parables portray the phenomenon of interest in order to underscore the point that God expects his people to use his gifts productively (Matt. 25:27). Extraordinarily high interest rates could make loans a lucrative enterprise, when, for example, annual interest rates on silver in Mesopotamia were attested as high as 80 percent. There was a stage when the interest on monetary loans was legally distinguished from the interest on loans of food (a distinction attested elsewhere in the ancient Near East). It was a general perception that one who borrowed was in a state of curse, while the one who lended was in a position of being blessed by God (Deut. 28:12, 44; Ps. 37:26; Prov. 22:7). Nevertheless, lending freely to those in need was a sign of the godly person, and loans, even to the poor, were an accepted part of life governed by ideals that would prevent humiliation (Deut. 24:10–13). However, it was legally prohibited to use money to make money specifically at the expense of a poor Israelite (Exod. 22:25; Lev. 25:35–37). This would seem to imply that interest on loans to those who were well-off was acceptable, but other passages clarify that although non-Israelites could be charged interest, one could not take interest from any Israelite, whether poor or not (Deut. 23:19–20). The righteous person does not use his money to make money at anyone's expense (Ps. 15:5), for it is the wicked person who becomes wealthy by taking interest (Prov. 28:8). In spite of such guidelines, the postexilic Jewish community monetarily enslaved poor Jews by loaning money at interest so that they could pay their taxes, a travesty that angered Nehemiah and prompted a reform so that such loans became interest-free (Neh. 5:4–12).

The power of money is no more dramatically confronted than when one uses money to purchase another human being. When one paid money for a human in the Old Testament, that purchase brought the slave into the sphere of the owner's household comparable to the status of one born in the house, eradicating the slave's former ethnic and social ties as far as cultic matters were concerned. A slaveowner could mistreat a slave with impunity short of actually killing him or her for, in the words of Exodus 21:21, "the slave is his property." The reality of purchasing humans becomes one of the more powerful images for depicting God's "redemption" (an economic term) of his people: this image conveys God's ownership of his people and their resulting obligation to obey him (cf. Gen. 47:13–26). As Peter stresses, however, money is inadequate for this transaction, for we were not redeemed with perishable things like silver or gold, but with the precious blood of Christ (1 Peter 1:18–19).

There is no record of money or precious metals being treated as unfit for sacred purposes in the Old Testament. Quite the contrary—even the wages of a harlot could be used for the support of the temple (Isa. 23:18). Nevertheless, the priests in the New Testament were reluctant to incorporate into the temple treasury money that was used to betray a man to death (Judas's "blood money" for handing over Jesus; Matt. 27:6)—a curious irony since the men who participated in the transaction continued to serve in the temple with no sense of impropriety. SAMUEL A. MEIER

See also WAGES; WEALTH.

Bibliography. O. Borowski, *BAR* 19/5 (1993): 68–70; A. Kindler and A. Stein, *A Bibliography of the City Coinage of Palestine from the 2nd Century B.C. to the 3rd Century A.D.;* S. E. Loewenstamm, *JBL* 88 (1968): 78–80.

Moon, New, Festival of. *See* FEASTS AND FESTIVALS OF ISRAEL.

Mortality. *See* DEATH, MORTALITY.

Moses. This godly man towers above all other persons in the Old Testament period because he was God's instrument for the introduction of covenant law in Israel. In his long life he also acted on behalf of God to bring into being an enduring nation, while functioning as a prophet, judge, recorder of God's pronouncements, intercessor, military leader, worker of miracles, and tireless shepherd of the unruly Israelite tribes. By the time of his death he had welded his people into a highly efficient military force that would occupy the land promised by God to Abraham (Gen. 12:7).

All that is known about Moses is found in the Bible. There are no surviving monuments to him, although some may have existed prior to his abrupt departure from Egypt (Exod. 2:15). It is therefore impossible to prove that he ever lived, as far as evidence from statues and inscriptions is concerned. But his existence cannot be disproved, either, since other prominent Old Testament figures have neither names nor monuments, as, for example, the Pharaoh with whom Moses contended, and the Egyptian princess who rescued the infant Moses from the Nile.

Moses is so strongly interwoven with the religious tradition involving God's plan for human salvation through Abraham, Isaac, Jacob, and ultimately the Davidic Messiah, and attested to as an authoritative figure for Hebrew culture even in the New Testament period, that he could not possibly have been an invention or a fictional character used as an object of religious or social propaganda. Unquestionably he stood head and shoulders above all other Hebrews, and was for the Old Testament period what Paul was for the New.

Perhaps out of deference to his stature there was nobody else in the Old Testament named Moses. There has been some debate about the meaning of his name, with some scholars relating it to a root "to bear," and found in such Egyptian names as Ahmose and Thutmose. In Exodus 2:10, the name given to him by the princess is connected with a Hebrew verb meaning "to draw out" (cf. 2 Sam. 22:17), but it could also have come from an Egyptian term meaning "son."

The Book of Exodus divides Moses' life into three periods of forty years each. The first of these deals with his birth in Egypt and his education as a prince of the royal harem (cf. Acts 7:21–22). The second phase occurs in Midian, where he fled for refuge after murdering an Egyptian (Exod. 2:15). The final stage involves him liberating the enslaved Hebrews, establishing God's covenant with them in the Sinai desert and leading them to the borders of the promised land. The Scriptures indicate that two-thirds of Moses' life served as a preparation for the crucial final third, which was so important for the divine plan of salvation. Accordingly we will focus on Moses' ministry as a mediator and teacher of God's revealed Word, since theology was henceforth to be the basis of Israelite life (Exod. 19:6).

While Moses may have learned about his ancestral God from Jethro, his father-in-law, the "priest of Midian" (Exod. 3:1), his first encounter with the Lord is at Mount Horeb, where he observes a bush burning with fire, and hears God's announcement that he is the God of Moses' ancestors. Moses is given a commission to return to Egypt and lead out the captive Hebrew people. God reveals to him the new name by which God will become known: "I am who I am." Moses is to say to the Hebrews that "I am" had sent him, and this name is to empower all subsequent pronouncements. Not surprisingly it has also been a matter of debate, and many explanations of its meaning have been advanced. It certainly points to God's eternal existence, self-sufficiency, and continued activity in human history. Intensely dynamic in nature, it transcends and fulfills all other forms of being.

This description of the divine name is supplemented by an additional revelation of his name as Yahweh (Exod. 6:3). So sacred is this designation that its pronunciation has not survived; the Hebrew consonants have been vocalized from another word, "lord," to produce the classic "Jehovah." Modern attempts to vocalize the original consonants are uncertain at best. Nevertheless, this mysterious Name and its power sustain Moses as he struggles with Pharaoh for the liberation of the Hebrew slaves. The conflict ends with the first Passover celebration, which coincides with the death of Egypt's firstborn (Exod. 12:29).

Dramatic though the crossing of the Re(e)d Sea is for the destiny of the Hebrews, the peak of Moses' career is attained on Mount Sinai, when God appears to him and delivers the celebrated Ten Commandments as the basis of Israel's covenant law. In conjunction with this revelation, God enters into a binding agreement with the twelve tribes that in effect welds them into one nation. God promises to provide for all their needs and give them the land promised long ago to Abraham if they, for their part, worship him as their one and only true God.

God's purpose for his newly created nation is that the Israelites should be visible among their contemporaries as a priestly kingdom and a holy people (Exod. 19:6; Lev. 11:44). Every man in Israel is to live as though he has been consecrated to the high and sacred office of a priest in God's service, and be holy and pure in all his doings. He is to abstain from the iniquitous ways of pagan neighboring nations, and be to them an example of what God himself is by nature (Exod. 34:6–7). Moses acts on behalf of God at the covenant ratification ceremony (Exod. 24:6–8) and thereafter is the recipient of instructions concerning the building of a sacred national shrine known as the tabernacle.

Of high theological significance for the Israelites, this structure was rectangular in shape and contained a tent where the cultic structure known as the covenant ark was housed. God's presence rested upon the ark, which was so sacred that the Israelites were prohibited from even seeing it. When the Israelite tribes were camped in order around the tabernacle, God's presence was indeed in their midst.

During the wilderness period Moses receives from God other laws dealing with sacrifices and offerings, rules governing social behavior, prohibitions against idolatry and immorality, and positive promises of God's blessings upon the Israelites, provided always that they keep the covenant obligations that they had assumed under oath.

From what has been said already it will be clear that Israelite life under Moses and his successors was grounded upon divine revelation and its accompanying theology. Distinctiveness in society as God's people, strictness of living in obedience to his laws, and unswerving trust in his power to save and keep were to be the hallmarks of Hebrew life. God's people were to be holy as he is holy (Lev. 11:44), and any deviations from these requirements would result in severe punishment. In mediating this theology and setting an example of it in his own life of dedication to God and fellowship with him, Moses serves as the exemplar of spirituality for all Israel to observe.

In dealing with the chosen people, Moses periodically acts as an intercessor with God, so as to avert divine displeasure with Israel (Exod. 33:12–16; Num. 12:13). The call that he had received from God involves his acting in the capacity of prophet to the nation, wherein he serves as God's spokesperson to Israel. So effective is he in this function that God promises to raise up other prophets after his death who will also serve as spokespersons (Deut. 18:15–18), thus indicating that God regards Moses as the standard by which his successors will be judged.

Yet despite his deeply spiritual life and his sense of commitment to covenantal ideals, Moses is still a human being. The task of organizing community living among people of a seminomadic disposition is formidable. In the wilderness he bears the brunt of complaints (Num. 11:1–25) and feels the crushing weight of his responsibilities (Num. 11:14). When he is overwhelmed by the numbers of people coming to him for legal decisions (Exod. 18:13), he willingly follows the advice of Jethro as to how he should conduct his judicial responsibilities (Exod. 18:24–26). Under obvious stress he goes beyond God's instructions in dealing with the complaining Israelites (Num. 20:10–12), and is forbidden to lead the conquering Israelites into the promised land. Yet he is recognized as being "a very humble man, more humble than anyone else on the face of the earth" (Num. 12:3), which has been urged commonly as a testimony to his humility in the service of Israel's most holy God. It is probable, however, that the term rendered "meek" actually means "more long-suffering than," "more tolerant than," which places a rather different construction upon the explanatory phrase.

In New Testament times the law of Moses constituted the standard of faith and conduct for the Christian church, which was commanded to observe Old Testament obligations of holiness (1 Peter 1:16). At the transfiguration of Christ, Moses appears with Elijah and converses with Jesus, signifying the harmony of law, prophecy, and the gospel (Mark 9:4). The sermon of Stephen before the Sanhedrin quotes Moses several times (Acts 7:20–44). Moses is referred to authoritatively in the Epistles, and is celebrated as a man who lived by faith (Heb. 11:23–29). In Revelation, the victorious saints chant the song of Moses (Exod. 15:1–19). R. K. Harrison

See also Exodus, Theology of; Israel.

Bibliography. O. T. Allis, *God Spake by Moses;* M. Buber, *Moses;* R. A. Cole, *Exodus;* R. K. Harrison, *Numbers;* F. B. Meyer, *Moses the Servant of God.*

Most High. *See* God, Names of.

Mother. *See* Family Life and Relations; Marriage; Woman.

Motives. Motives pose at least a twofold dilemma: (1) the status of a good deed done for the wrong reason or an evil deed done with good (or even without) intent; and (2) the effect of a motive (good or bad) that never has opportunity to find fulfillment. The fundamental issue prompting the dilemma is that there is not a one-to-one correspondence between a given action and the motive of its agent: the same action may be either censured or defended depending upon one's motive. For example, a difference between first- and second-degree murder resides in whether or not the homicide was intentional: the former is punishable by death, while the latter allows for clemency (Exod. 21:12–14; Num. 35:9–25; Deut. 19:4–13; Josh. 20:1–9). Offenses against God can become less heinous if they are accidental, as the sacrifices for accidental sins make clear (Lev. 4:1–5:19; Num. 15:22–31). An individual whose actions are, or result in, evil becomes less reprehensible when it is discovered that the person did not intend that consequence. This principle is apparent when Jesus does not want his executors condemned because their motives are not commensurate with the great crime they are committing: "Father, forgive them, for they do not know what they are doing" (Luke 23:34; cf. Acts 3:17). Good motives can prompt people to actions that have unfortunate results (Matt. 13:28–30), a legal principle that has become the basis of much Western law: *actus non facit reum nisi mens sit rea* ("The act itself does not make one a criminal unless done with criminal intent").

In the same way, otherwise acceptable deeds become less attractive, even repulsive, when base motives are behind them. Prayer, giving to the poor, and fasting are activities encouraged throughout the Bible, but Jesus underscores that God will not reward those who do them for selfish reasons (Matt. 6:1–18). The ritual associated with the temple (sacrifices, prayer, holy days) was a legitimate expression of piety for the ancient Israelites, yet the prophets insisted that God was disgusted with the whole enterprise when the people did it without humility and repentance (Isa. 1:11–15; 29:13; 58:3–7; Amos 4:4–5; 5:21–24). The most powerful symbols of spiritual identification (circumcision, baptism) can be undermined by one who submits to them but is not inwardly changed (Jer. 9:25–26; Matt. 3:7–8; Rom. 2:25–29; 1 Peter 3:21).

Since there is no one-to-one correspondence between deeds and motives, one must be extremely cautious in deducing others' motives merely from observing their actions. Jesus rebukes the disciples for jumping to inappropriate conclusions about people and their deeds after observing only their actions (Matt. 26:6–13). After all, a little given sacrificially is more commendable than giving much where no sacrifice is involved (Mark 12:41–44). It is this difficulty in discerning motives that lies behind the extensive warnings against judging others (Matt. 7:1; Luke 6:37; Rom. 14:1–15:14; 1 Cor. 4:5; James 4:12). Good motives may result in conflicting actions: some early Christians did not, while others did, eat a special diet; some believers did not, while others did, observe certain days as sacred. In each case, it is the motive that makes these otherwise neutral actions acceptable: if one is seeking to please God (i.e., not other people or oneself), then the individual is exonerated (Rom. 14:1–14; 1 Cor. 10:31; Col. 3:17). Sometimes Paul would recommend circumcision and sometimes he would be adamantly opposed, positions that he took for different reasons that varied with circumstances (Acts 16:3; 1 Cor. 7:18–20; Gal. 2:3; 5:6; 6:15), ultimately seeking to please God by his faithfulness in spreading the gospel (1 Cor. 9:20–23; 10:31–33). Since individuals cannot reliably judge others' motives, we have no recourse in human affairs but to "know a tree by its fruit" (Matt. 7:15–20; 12:33; Luke 6:43–45) even while recognizing the limitations of not being able to see another's heart. Therefore, one should be concerned about one's own actions in order not to give others wrong impressions that might mislead (Matt. 17:24–27; 1 Cor. 10:23–33; 2 Cor. 8:21).

Since there is not a one-to-one correspondence between motives and deeds among humans, it becomes even more precarious to try to deduce God's motives based upon God's actions: "My thoughts are not your thoughts. . . . As the heavens are higher than the earth, so are . . . my thoughts than your thoughts" (Isa. 55:8–9). Ignoring this distinction is the mistake Job's friends made in supposing that God afflicted Job because Job must be a sinner, or the error the disciples made in assuming a blind man was afflicted because of sin. In each case, the text underscores that humans typically underestimate God's options and motives (Job 42:7–9; John 9:1–3).

Unlike humans, God clearly sees both the actions and the intents of human beings, a fact that means God has a considerably different evaluation of our deeds, one that is based upon our motives: "God knows your hearts. What is highly valued among men is detestable in God's sight" (Luke 16:15; cf. 1 Sam. 16:7; Ps. 7:9; Jer. 11:20). At times the Bible seems to speak of God responding to people primarily or only on the basis of their motives, but in other places the Bible seems to depict God judging on the basis of their deeds alone. It is by a careful balancing of both deeds and motives that God judges humans and consequently rewards or punishes them (1 Kings 8:39; Jer. 17:10; Rom. 2:2–16; 1 Cor. 3:8–4:4; Eph. 6:5–8; Col. 3:22–25; Rev. 2:23). How God sorts out motives and deeds is not discussed and is by definition beyond human scrutiny. The matter is further complicated by the fact that what individuals intend by their actions is not always achieved, and, conversely, every action results in unintended consequences (both good and evil). God's habit of transforming the evil motives of humans into good results suggests that God is mercifully sympathetic with the human condition: "You intended to harm me, but God intended it for good in order to accomplish what is now being done, the saving of many lives" (Gen. 50:20; cf. Acts 2:23–24).

God's careful scrutiny of motives ("searching the heart") indicates that motives and intentions never resulting in action are still judged by God. Jesus notes that it is the "pure in heart" who will be rewarded (Matt. 5:8; 22:37–38; Mark 7:20–21), even as he equates anger with murder and lust with adultery (Matt. 5:21–22, 28). This corresponds to the climax of the Ten Commandments, which, unlike the preceding forbidden actions, prohibits an attitude: "You shall not covet" (Exod. 20:17). A sin of omission becomes reprehensible for "anyone . . . who knows the good he ought to do and doesn't do it" (James 4:17).

Although prosperity and success are mentioned in the Bible in order to motivate behavior (e.g., Prov. 10:4; 12:7; 13:21, 25; 21:20–22), eudaemonism is not an accurate synthesis of the Bible's stance on motives, for suffering is everywhere depicted as an appropriate consequence of ethical behavior. The utilitarian perspective that one should be motivated by the good or bad effects that result from an action, not the intrinsic good or evil of an action, finds little support in the Bible, since performing a deed for what one perceives to be a good result presumes upon the future: one cannot know for sure that the deed will have the desired effect that the motive seeks, and none can calculate all the consequences of any deed. SAMUEL A. MEIER

See also ETHICS; HEART; TEN COMMANDMENTS.

Bibliography. W. C. Kaiser, Jr., *Toward Old Testament Ethics;* B. Gemser, *Adhuc loquitur: Collected Essays by Dr. B. Gemser;* W. Eichrodt, *Theology of the Old Testament.*

Mouth. In the Old Testament, "mouth" (Heb. *peh*) often refers to inanimate openings: the entrance of a cave (Josh. 10:18, 22), a well (Gen. 29:2, 8, 10; 2 Sam. 17:19), a sack (Gen. 42:27), or a lion's den (Dan. 6:17). "Mouth" also refers to the biological organ, whether human (Exod. 4:11–12) or animal (Num. 22:28). It is used for the necessities of human life, eating and drinking (Ps. 78:30; Dan. 10:3), or for intimate contact, kissing (Job 31:27; 1 Kings 19:18). The idiomatic phrase "mouth to mouth" means to speak personally and in a straightforward fashion with another (Jer. 32:4). Unity is expressed by the phrase "one mouth" (1 Kings 22:13; cf. Rom. 15:6).

The anthropomorphic phrase "mouth of God" refers to God's revelation and sustenance for humankind (Deut. 8:3; Jer. 9:12). Jesus quotes Deuteronomy 8:3 when Satan tempts him and reveals that life is more than what one puts in his or her mouth. Rather, true existence originates from "every word that comes from the mouth of God" (Matt. 4:4). Whether one acknowledges it or not, God's immanence is necessary for existence.

The mouth is the means for expressing what is in one's heart. The association of the Law and the mouth is often made because it is with the mouth that one expresses the essence of his or her religious belief.

In the New Testament, "mouth" (Gk. *stoma*) is used much as it is in the Old Testament. The mouth reveals what is in one's heart. In James 3:3–12 the point is made that if people can control the speech of their mouth, they can control their actions. What people speak is consistent with what is in their hearts. Therefore, slanderous speech reveals an evil heart (cf. Rom. 3:14).

The concept that the mouth reveals the true nature of the heart is consistent with what Jesus taught: "Out of the abundance of the heart the mouth speaks" (Matt. 12:34 NRSV). Jesus points out that it is not the food that goes into the mouth that defiles, but the words that come out of the mouth because they come "from the heart" (Matt. 15:17–18).

In Colossians 3:8 Paul tells the Colossians to get rid of filthy speech from their mouths. He also says that the confession of the mouth, "Jesus is Lord" (Rom. 10:7–10), reveals the belief in one's heart. It is not the confession that redeems a person, but the belief of the heart, where the confession originates.

Revelation sometimes uses "mouth" in a literal sense (e.g., 14:5) but most references are used in an apocalyptic, symbolic way. In this apocalyptic framework, fire (9:17–18; 11:5) and a two-edged sword (1:16) come out of the mouth. Additionally, other apocalyptic imagery is found (13:2, 5, 6; 16:13; 19:21). ERIC W. ADAMS

See also ANTHROPOMORPHISM; CONFESS, CONFESSION; PERSON, PERSONHOOD.

Murder. ***The Old Testament.*** Although the Israelites did not have a term that precisely fits our present-day idea of murder, they differentiated among killing, manslaughter, and murder in their legal terminology.

The Term for Murder in the Sixth Commandment. The sixth commandment ("you shall not murder"; Exod. 20:13; Deut. 5:17) has been misunderstood because of an ambiguity in terminology. The Hebrew word that was used in this case for "kill" (or murder) was the somewhat rare term *rāṣah* (derivatives can be found with the meaning of shatter [Ps. 42:11] or slaughter [Ezek. 21:27]). Although its exact meaning has defied explanation, in other contexts it could refer to killing that was inherently evil (Judg. 20:4; Job 24:14; Ps. 94:6; Isa. 1:21; Hos. 6:9). It was also listed in abuses of the covenant community (Jer. 7:9; Hos. 4:2) and in lists of curses (Deut. 27:24–25). Jezebel committed murder (*rāṣah*) against the prophets (1 Kings 18:13), as did Ahab against Naboth (1 Kings 21:19) and Simeon and

Levi against the Shechemites (Gen. 34:26). However, the same term could also have applied to unintentional manslaughter (Deut. 4:41; 19:3–6; Josh. 20:3), blood vengeance (Num. 35:27, 30), the legal execution of a criminal (Num. 35:30), attempted assassination (2 Kings 6:32), and on one occasion it was used for the figurative killing of humans by animals (Prov. 22:13).

Discernment in Homicide Cases. The death penalty was posed for one who killed with premeditation, but not for accidental manslaughter (Exod. 21:12–13; Lev. 24:17; Deut. 27:24). In fact, premeditated murder did not require a trial (Exod. 21:14; Num. 35:19; Deut. 19:11–13). Thus, the Old Testament saw a fundamental difference between the two types of homicide (Deut. 19:1–13; Josh. 20:1–7), providing two levels of meaning for *rāṣah.* One who killed out of enmity was not allowed sanctuary in the city of refuge. The victim's clan could demand that the killer be delivered up to the blood avenger (2 Sam. 14:7–11), who presented the evidence against the individual. Guilt was determined either by the intention of the killer or by the type of object used in the apparent manslaughter (Num. 35:16–21; some iron, stone, or wooden objects were considered likely to cause death). However, there had to be at least two witnesses to convict a murderer (Num. 35:30; Deut. 17:6; 19:15; 1 Sam. 21:4). The blood avenger, who was responsible for the execution, was not allowed to pity the murderer or else the land would be defiled (Num. 35:34; David put himself in the hands of God because of this—2 Sam. 12:13). No ransom was allowed since this would have signified consent with the crime, undermining the value of human life and breaking the covenant with God. There was also no substitutionary punishment (Deut. 24:16; although Saul's sons were demanded as ransom after his own death because he had murdered the Gibeonites—2 Sam. 21:1–9).

The Meaning of Rāṣah. *Rāṣah* probably had a specialized meaning, possibly in connection with the killing (whether premeditated or accidental) of anyone in the covenant community, especially that which brought illegal violence. The sixth commandment therefore protected the individual Israelite within the community from any danger. Only God had the right to terminate life; murder was an abrogation of his power that ignored humanity's created nature and value in the sight of God. God had to be propitiated since the covenant relationship had been broken (Num. 35:33). Murder deprived God of his property (the blood of the victim; Lev. 17:11, 14), which apparently passed to the control of the murderer (2 Sam. 4:11). Thus, the murderer's life was ransomed. Underlying this was the dictum in Genesis 9:6 concerning the sanctity of life. The murderer had to receive a penalty consistent with this law (lex talionis) to purge the evil from their midst (Gen. 4:10–11; Deut. 21:8) and to deter others (Deut. 13:11; 17:13; 19:20; 21:21). *Rāṣah* did not cover the subject of killing in war or capital punishment, which were done only at the command of God; thus, they were not in the same category as murder.

Other Terms for Murder. The most common Hebrew word for killing (*hārag*) could also be used for murder. Pharaoh viewed Moses' killing of an Egyptian as a crime (Exod. 2:14–15). Joab's spilling of the blood of Abner was condemned (2 Sam. 3:30; 1 Kings 2:5). David was responsible for the death of Uriah, although he did not physically kill him (2 Sam. 12:9). Judicial murder was also condemned (Exod. 23:7; Pss. 10:8; 94:6). *Hārag* was the term used for Cain's crime against Abel (Gen. 4:8), and for the murderers of Ishbosheth (2 Sam. 4:11–12). Striking a parent (possibly with the intent to murder; Exod. 21:15), inducing death by miscarriage (Exod. 21:22–23), and sacrificing children to a foreign god (Lev. 20:2–3) were apparently considered murder and were capital crimes. If a man beat a slave to death, he was probably punished (or better avenged) by being put to death by the covenant community (Exod. 21:20). There was no legislation outlawing suicide, as it must have been very rare. Those who committed suicide in Scripture had been placed in a situation of certain death (Judg. 9:54; 16:30; 1 Sam. 31:4; 2 Sam. 17:23; 1 Kings 16:18).

Unsolved Murder. A strange ceremony was performed when the murderer (or manslayer) was not known (Deut. 21:1–9). Since there were religious implications (murder was a crime against God), the matter could not be left alone; the guilt had to be atoned for. The elders of the closest city were obliged to take responsibility for the act and instigated a procedure to remove the guilt. They took a heifer and broke its neck. They then washed their hands over the dead creature, symbolizing their accepting the burden for it, but not the guilt. They then declared that they were not eyewitnesses, and prayed for the innocence of the entire community. There was no compensation for the family of the victim.

The New Testament. Although the New Testament writers lived in a different legal environment, they were consistent in their view of murder with their Old Testament counterparts. Jesus interpreted the sixth commandment differently than the contemporary Jewish scholars (who had a narrowly literal view), and agreed with the spirit of the Old Testament law on homicide (Matt. 5:21–22). He pointed out a spiritual cause for murder; its root was internal anger. One was not righteous by simply refraining from homicide; an angry person was also subject to judgment. He thus contended that hating one's brother was in the sphere of the command against murder, as it was part of a process leading to a potential murderous act (cf. Lev. 19:17–18). Jesus' words were in effect a full summary of the murder law (cf. Exod. 21:12; Deut. 17:8). The intention as well as the act came under God's judgment. He condemned the evil disposition of the heart that lay at the root of the transgression. The beginning of the outward act of murder was sinful anger or hatred, an attitude that was a sin against the sixth commandment. James added that the cause of murder was a consequence of frustrated desire (4:2; cf. 1 Kings 21).

Humans were given the right to exact the death penalty for murder (John 19:10–11; Rom. 13:1–4). The murderer's children were not guilty unless they had willingly participated in the crime (Matt. 23:34–36; 27:25). A whole nation could be guilty of murder (Matt. 27:25; Acts 2:23, 36; 3:15; 5:28; 7:52). Satan was considered the original murderer (John 8:44). Murderers had no place in God's kingdom (Gal. 5:20; Rev. 21:8).

The death of Christ was the supreme example of murder in the Scriptures (Matt. 27:20; Mark 13:12; 14:55). His murder was predicted in the Passion narratives (Mark 8:31; 9:31; 10:34). The Jews sought to murder him (John 7:1, 19; 11:53). His violent death was recounted by Peter (Acts 5:30) and Paul (Acts 26:21; Eph. 2:16—Christ was murdered in hostility). Christ was symbolized as the slaughtered Lamb, signifying his humble obedience and innocence (Rev. 5:6–12; 13:8). Slain martyrs were likewise labeled (Rev. 6:9).

MARK W. CHAVALAS

See also KILL, KILLING; TEN COMMANDMENTS; WAR, HOLY WAR.

Bibliography. H. Boecker, *Law and the Administration of Justice in the Old Testament;* E. Nielsen, *The Ten Commandments in New Perspective;* A Phillips, *Ancient Israel's Criminal Law: A New Approach to the Decalogue;* idem, *Journal of Jewish Studies* 28 (1977): 105–26; J. Stamm and M. Andrew, *The Ten Commandments in Recent Research;* R. Westbrook, *Studies in Biblical and Cuneiform Law.*

Mystery. Scripture frequently describes God as one who knows all things, even that which the human mind could never know or finds incomprehensible. Thus he sees the secret intentions of human hearts (Ps. 139:1–4, 23; Matt. 6:4–6; Rom. 2:16; 1 Cor. 4:5; 14:25; Heb. 4:13), comprehends the seemingly unfathomable mysteries of the universe (Job 38:1–39:30), and, most important, understands the meaning of human history. God understands human history because the events that comprise it correspond with his own intentions: he wills all that happens, and does so to accomplish his own purpose (Dan. 2:37; 5:21; Rom. 11:25–36). People, on the other hand, both because of their sin and because of their human limitations, remain ignorant of God's purpose when left to their own reckoning (Dan. 2:27, 30; Mark 4:10–12; Luke 19:41–44). God graciously responds to this human inadequacy by revealing his purpose to his people. When God's purpose is revealed in this way, the Bible frequently refers to it as a "mystery."

The content of the divine mystery is painted in broad strokes in the Old Testament, takes on greater detail in the Gospels, and receives its finishing touches in Paul's letters. In Daniel, where the term first appears (*rāz* in Aramaic, always translated with *mysteriōn* in the LXX), it refers to God's understanding of the symbols in Nebuchadnezzar's dream, symbols that stand for the rise and fall of human empires and to the eventual establishment of God's own, eternal kingdom (2:44; cf. Rev. 1:20; 17:5, 7). The details of these events, however, and the nature of God's kingdom, once established, remain sketchy in Daniel. The mystery of God's purposes gains greater specificity in the Gospels, where Jesus, particularly in his parables, reveals the "mystery of the kingdom of God" (Mark 4:11; cf. Matt. 13:11; Luke 8:10). Paul also identifies the divine mystery with the revelation of God in Christ (Col. 2:2; 4:3) but gives the concept even greater clarity in three ways. First, he equates the divine mystery with the gospel of Christ's atoning death on the cross (1 Cor. 2:1); second, he describes it as God's plan, through Christ's atoning death (Eph. 2:13–16), to include the Gentiles among his chosen people; and third, he defines it as the reconciliation of all things to God (Eph. 1:9–10). Thus, Daniel described the divine mystery in general terms as the eventual establishment of God's eternal kingdom; Jesus defined it more specifically as his proclamation of God's kingdom; and Paul described it more specifically still as the constitution of a new people, from among both Jews and Gentiles, through the atoning death of Christ on the cross.

This understanding of divine mystery illustrates three aspects of God's character. First, it emphasizes God's *omniscience.* After God revealed the "mystery" of the interpretation of Nebuchadnezzar's dream to Daniel, Daniel thanked God in prayer for his wisdom and power (2:23; cf. 2:20) and described him as a God who "knows what lies in darkness" (2:22). Paul, similarly, after revealing the mystery of God's plan to include the Gentiles among his chosen people breaks into praise of the "depth of the riches of the wisdom and knowledge of God" (Rom. 11:33).

Second, the biblical concept of divine mystery emphasizes God's *sovereignty.* The mystery revealed to Daniel and communicated to the king demonstrates not only that God knows the beginning of history from its end but that the rise and fall of human empires and the establishment of God's own kingdom happen according to his decree (2:36). Similarly, Paul says that the mystery of God's intention to unite both Jews and Gentiles in the body of Christ has been in place from ages past (Eph. 3:9–11; Col. 1:26–27; cf. Eph. 1:9–10; 3:5).

Third, and most important, the biblical understanding of divine mystery emphasizes God's *grace.* This can be seen immediately in the stark contrast between the biblical use of the term "mystery" and its use as a technical term in ancient Hellenistic mystery religions. In these cults the term was used to signify the esoteric knowledge that initiates were instructed, with threats of severe punishment, not to reveal to the uninitiated. The Bible, however, emphasizes God's gracious willingness to reveal the mystery of his purposes to his servants the prophets and through them to other people (Rev. 10:7; cf. Amos 3:7). The biblical emphasis is well illustrated in Daniel. There God graciously reveals his mysteries to Daniel to save him from the king's cruel sentence of death upon the royal wise men for their inability to interpret the king's dream (2:16-19). Because Daniel recognizes the graciousness of God's response, he is quick to acknowledge before the king that the dream's interpretation has come from God, not from Daniel's abilities as a counselor (2:27, 30). Similarly, Jesus graciously explains the parable of the sower to his disciples with the comment that, although the parables baffle those on the outside, the mystery of the kingdom of God has been given to them (Matt. 11:25–26).

In Paul's letters this aspect of the mystery of God comes to a climax. Paul points his readers again and again to the unique position they occupy as those who have experienced the fulfillment of the mystery of God's purposes. Although predicted in the Scriptures, the mystery was kept silent for long ages (Rom. 16:25–26), hidden for generations past (Col. 1:26; cf. Eph. 3:5, 9, 11) that it might be revealed to apostles and prophets such as Paul himself and through them to believers (Eph. 3:1–12; cf. 1 Peter 1:10–12). Paul describes his calling to reveal the mystery of God to the Gentiles as "the grace of God given to me for you" (Eph. 3:2), and a few verses later, in a magnificent piling up of the language of grace, he identifies it as "the gift of the grace which God gave to me according to his effective power" (v. 7).

The biblical idea of mystery, then, reminds Christians that God holds the course of human events in his hands and has so shaped them that they work for the salvation of his people. It also demonstrates the graciousness of God in revealing his redemptive purposes to prophets and apostles and, through them, to all who are willing to hear.

FRANK THIELMAN

See also PAUL THE APOSTLE.

Bibliography. G. Bornkamm, *TDNT,* 4:802–28; R. E. Brown, *The Semitic Background of the Term "Mystery" in the New Testament;* A. E. Harvey, *JTS* 31 (1980):320–36; J. A. Robinson, *St. Paul's Epistle to the Ephesians.*

Myth. The word "myth" (Gk. *muthos*) only appears five times in the Bible, all in the New Testament, and all but one in the pastoral epistles (1 Tim. 1:4; 4:7; 2 Tim. 4:4; Titus 1:14; 2 Peter 1:16). All of these were translated in the King James Version as "fable." More recent versions (such as RSV, NASB, NEB, and NIV) have almost uniformly used the word "myth."

In all of these occurrences, the context makes it plain that Paul and Peter are using the term in its common sense of something false. Thus, it is what is contrary to sound doctrine (1 Tim. 1:4), particularly in relation to asceticism and spirit-worship (1 Tim. 4:7). Those who leave the Word of God and its sound teachings will choose myths and not truth (2 Tim. 4:4). If people are to have a sound faith, they must not listen to myths taught by those who reject the truth (Titus 1:14). Finally, the gospel narratives are not fictional tales, but actual eyewitness reports (2 Peter 1:16). In each case, *muthos* is used to describe something that is contrary to the truth, whether that truth be the doctrines relating to Christian behavior or the accounts of Christ's life, death, and resurrection.

What is not clear is whether any of these references have in mind the ancient legends of the gods that we commonly think of in reference to the term "myth." With regard to the references in the Pastoral Epistles, the answer seems to be no. In fact, in one case (Titus 1:14), they are specifically labeled "Jewish myths," which certainly did not include any legends of the gods. While it is possible that 2 Timothy 4:4 may speak of Christians who will abandon the truth of their religion and turn to the pagan religions, the two references in 1 Timothy (1:4 and 4:7), along with the one in Titus, seem to be referring to the kind of Jewish mysticism described in Colossians 2:16–23. This was an elitist kind of piety that emphasized secret religious knowledge and rigorous self-denial. Part of the secret knowledge involved knowing the secret names of a whole hierarchy of angels (Col. 2:18; 1 Tim. 1:4, "genealogies"). This concept of a hierarchy of angels was almost certainly the result of the contamination of Jewish thought by pagan thought, but there is little reason to think that Paul was thinking of that derivation when he called these ideas "myths." It appears that he is only describing them as falsehoods. So, in Goodspeed's version of the New Testament the translation used is "fictions."

It is somewhat more likely that Peter does have in mind the classical myths when he says that the Gospel accounts are not myths, but eyewitness reports. On this reading, he would be saying that the gospel narrative is not like the pagan myths. The myths are merely fictional and fantastic tales, but the gospel, while it incorporates the miraculous, actually took place. At this place the New International Version has "stories" and the New English Bible has "tales." But even here where there may be some connotation of the pagan stories of the gods, the chief emphasis is upon falsehood versus truth.

This unrelenting use of "myth" by the Bible as a synonym for lies and falsehood is ironic, given the present positive valuation put on the term. While the common person still uses the word as the Greeks did, to describe something that is untrue, this is not the way sociologists of religion use it. With the rediscovery of the ancient world, especially in the nineteenth century, there arose a certain fascination with the stories of the gods and with the power of those stories to convey a meaningful vision of reality to those who accepted them. A number of studies of myth were undertaken, one of the most famous being Frazier's *The Golden Bough*. These studies suggested that myth should be understood as a vehicle by which extrascientific truth may be expressed. Of course, this represents an almost complete reversal in the understanding of myth. Instead of being false because of its failure to conform to a scientifically derived view of reality, it is true precisely because it does not!

According to this view, whenever a people express their views of reality in other than mechanistic and naturalistic terms, they are speaking mythically. Thus, to speak of God as a person who causes the rain to fall is to speak in mythical terms. While the statement may be "true" in some sense, it is false, scientifically speaking, because it cannot be verified. Used in this way, "The resurrection of Jesus Christ is a myth" would say that while the body of Jesus remained in the tomb and was not seen by the disciples, the narrative serves to express the Christian conviction that the human spirit perseveres after the death of the body. This point of view would argue that ultimate truth has no connection with historical facts.

As this way of defining myth has become more popular, it has become increasingly common, even among some Christians, to refer to the Bible as part of the world's great mythic literature. The reasons for this are not hard to find. First, there are the questions about the historical reliability of the Bible. If it can be granted that historical reliability is really of no consequence to the meaning or value of the Bible, those questions are no longer troublesome. A second reason is the growing distaste for exclusivism of all sorts. If the Bible can be defined as one more of the world's religious tales, then its embarrassing particularity can be disposed of. Finally, although the death of the enlightenment is frequently announced, the idea that there is a personal deity who transcends all our means of containing him, and to whom we are accountable, is still unacceptable to many. If the language can be reduced to a merely figurative expression for a generalized life force that inhabits the universe, it is more palatable.

The response of Paul or Peter—or Isaiah—to the idea that the Bible is myth is unmistakable. They insist that their theology is true precisely because it has been validated in the world of time and space, the world of facts. They would vigorously resist any attempt to make their assertion about what God has done in this world merely figurative. But beyond this, the Bible is at odds with the ancient stories of the gods at every point. This is not an enclosed, cyclical existence where the forces of nature have been turned into deities. It is not a shadowy stage where timeless, placeless stories of the gods must be acted out in order to appropriate divine power for an otherwise meaningless existence. Rather, God has broken into the world of time and space in unique, nonrepeateable events that have revealed his character and his grace. Real human persons have seen the evidence, have received divine interpretations of that evidence, and have recorded it all under supernatural guidance. As Peter would tell us, these are not myths; they are the reports of people who have been visited by the holy God. Whatever the Bible is, it is not a myth.

John N. Oswalt

Bibliography. B. Childs, *Myth and Reality in the Old Testament;* T. H. Gaster, *Myth, Legend and Custom in the Old Testament;* G. Stahlin, *TDNT,* 4:762–95.

Nn

Nahum, Theology of. Nahum is a biblical book that Christians find easy to avoid. In the first place, it is among the shortest of the Minor Prophets and is overshadowed by Micah, which precedes it and contains some well-known messianic prophecies. The Book of Nahum can be off-putting and even revolting to Christians who know Jesus' teaching about turning the other cheek (Matt. 5:39) and putting a sword back in its place (Matt. 26:52). After all, the prophet exults in the violent downfall of the city of Nineveh and the death of its inhabitants. The book's structure works hand-in-hand, however, with its content to present a theological message of lasting value that can stir the Christian to deeper faith and obedience today.

In Its Old Testament Setting. Nahum must have been written after 663 B.C. because it mentions the fall of Thebes (3:8), which took place at that time. If taken seriously as a prophecy, the book's message must have been presented to the people before 612 B.C., the year Nineveh fell to the invading army made up of Babylonians and Medes. Perhaps it is significant for dating that Assyria is called "intact" in 1:12. This description may point to a date before 626 B.C. when Assyria's vulnerable position became public.

Thus, the historical context of the book may be described at least in broad outline. By the mid-seventh century B.C., Assyria had been the dominant power in the Near East for centuries. Nahum's obvious anger may be understood against the background of the cruel Assyrian oppression that God's people, as well as other nations, had suffered.

The book begins with a hymn of praise to God the divine warrior. This hymn is similar in several ways to the hymns of victory identified in the Psalter (Pss. 24, 68, 96, 98). It praises the Lord, who brings judgment against his enemies (1:2–6) and salvation to h is people (1:7–8). At this point in the book God's enemies and people are not specifically named, but are only generally described.

The themes of salvation and judgment continue into the next major section of the prophecy (1:9–2:2), where the writer magnificently interweaves oracles of judgment and salvation. The objects of salvation and judgment are still not named (with the exception of Judah in 1:15); rather, the second-person pronoun occurs throughout the section. This delay of precise identification causes the reader to be more attentive and also produces a dramatic sense of suspense. Salvation-oracles occur in 1:12–13, 15, and 2:2; judgment-oracles are found in 1:9–11, 14, and 2:1. The interweaving judgment- and salvation-oracles are followed by a prophetic vision in which Nahum describes the future downfall of the city as if he were there. He sees the invading chariots (2:4), the advancing troops (v. 5), the collapse of the gates and palace (v. 6), and the plundering of the city (v. 9).

This representation of the fall of the city evokes a series of taunts and woes directed toward Nineveh. The once proud lion of city is now without prey (2:11–13). It is likened to a whore who has been caught and now faces public ridicule (3:4–6). Between these two metaphorical taunts stands a woe-oracle (3:1–3). This oracle finds its origin in a funeral ritual, but here no sympathy or sense of loss is expressed. The only intention is to threaten and curse. Nineveh is as "good as dead."

The metaphorical taunts are followed by a historical taunt. Nineveh feels invulnerable, but then so did Thebes and look what happened to that bastion of Egyptian strength (3:8–10).

Insult follows insult in the next section (3:11–15c). Nineveh's fortresses are "ripe figs" about to be eaten and her troops are like women. Nahum closes the long series of taunts by comparing Assyria to a locust horde (3:15d–17). In the Bible, locusts are agents of destruction and are used to depict a devastating army (see Joel 1:2–12; 2:1–11). Here another characteristic of locusts is highlighted: their tendency to fly away.

Appropriately, the book closes with a dirge (3:18–19). The frenzy of staccato visions, of war and sharp insults gives way to calm, mournful expression. As with the woe-oracle, the dirge has its origin in funerary mourning. It is relief and joy, however, not sadness and compassion that are felt at this funeral.

Nahum brought his generation a message from God about his relationship with his people: God is a warrior who is coming to free his people from the oppressive dominance of wicked Assyria. At another time, God had shown compassion toward that city, but now is the time for the judgment of God's enemies and the salvation of his people.

From a New Testament Perspective. The theological value of this book for the Christian church has often been overlooked. The prophecy seems narrow. Nahum speaks an oracle of doom against Assyria, a nation that existed in the distant past. The book's relevance for today is difficult to grasp.

Close attention to the literary structure of the book will draw our attention back to its beginning. Before specific application is made to Judah and Assyria, Nahum presents us with a hymn that focuses on God as the saving and judging divine warrior (1:2–8). This picture of God is applicable for all times—he is the warrior who judges evil.

The Book of Nahum thus fits into an unfolding drama of God's warring activity as it is described from Exodus to Revelation. By the time of Nahum, the Israelites were well aware of God as the divine warrior. He had rescued their forefathers from bondage and judged the Egyptians at the Red Sea. He had also turned against his people in righteous judgment at the time of Samuel's youth and the exile of the northern kingdom.

The divine warrior theme in the New Testament grows out of the motif as we have seen it in the Old. At the end of the Old Testament period the prophets looked forward to the coming of a mighty warlike deliverer (Zech. 14) who would deliver the people of Israel out of their oppression. John the Baptist expected the imminent arrival of such a Messiah: "You brood of vipers! Who warned you to flee from the coming wrath? Produce fruit in keeping with repentance. And do not think you can say to yourselves, 'We have Abraham as our father.' I tell you that out of these stones God can raise up children for Abraham. The ax is already at the root of the trees, and every tree that does not produce good fruit will be cut down and thrown into the fire" (Matt. 3:7–10). When Jesus appeared, however, he did not match John's expectations. Instead of bringing an immediate and violent judgment, Jesus healed the sick and exorcised demons. Later, when John was in prison, he began to doubt Jesus' identity; so John sent two of his followers to question Jesus (Matt. 11:1–19). Jesus responded with more healings and exorcisms. By his actions, Jesus was letting John know that he was the divine warrior whom John expected. The warfare, however, was more intense than John had imagined. Jesus waged holy war, not against the flesh-and-blood enemies of Israel, but against Satan himself. This warfare culminated in the crucifixion, resurrection, and ascension (Eph. 4:7–13; Col. 2:13–16), at which time Jesus defeated Satan.

While the victory was won on the cross, the warfare will not be complete until the end of time. Thus, the church struggles even today against Satan and evil. As the Old Testament people were commanded to wage war against the Canaanites, so our mandate is to resist the devil (Eph. 6:10–20).

Nahum reveals God as a warrior who fights for his people. As New Testament Christians, we recognize that Jesus Christ empowers the church to fight evil today. When we read the Book of Nahum in conjunction with the Book of Revelation, we are reminded that Jesus Christ is coming again at the end of time to put an end to all evil, whether spiritual or human (Rev. 19:11–21).

TREMPER LONGMAN III

See also ISRAEL; PROPHET, PROPHETESS, PROPHECY.

Bibliography. D. W. Baker, *Nahum, Habakkuk, and Zephaniah: An Introduction and Commentary;* K. J. Cathcart, *Biblical Studies in Contemporary Thought: The Tenth Anniversary Commemorative Volume of the Trinity College Bible Institute 1966–1975,* pp. 68–76; idem, *CBQ* 35 (1973): 179–87; T. H. Glasson, *ExpT* 81 (1969–70): 54–55; W. C. Graham, *AJSL* 44 (1927–28): 37–48; D. R. Hillers, *Treaty-Curses and the Old Testament Prophets;* W. Janzen, *Mourning Cry and Woe Oracle;* B. O. Long, *JBL* 95 (1976): 230–54; T. Longman III, *WTJ* 44 (1982): 290–307; idem, *JETS* 27 (1984): 267–74; idem, *Reformed Theological Journal* 1 (1985): 13–24; idem, *The Minor Prophets,* vol. 2; J. M. P. Smith, *A Critical and Exegetical Commentary on the Books of Micah, Zephaniah, and Nahum.*

Name. In contemporary Western culture a name rarely possesses significance beyond that of a highly sentimental, perhaps aesthetically conditioned response on the part of proud, doting parents to the intoxicating joy of a new arrival. Not so in the Bible. There a human name typically reflects character and mission anticipated in life, which may turn out for either good or ill. It may embody the spiritual vision of parents for their child's future. In other instances, it is prophetic of future outcomes or events. On the negative side, it may typify a life come to ruin.

The name "Samuel," for example, may be translated "asked of God" (1 Sam. 1:20—or possibly, "Name of El"). When accompanied by the like-sounding Hebrew term *šāʾal,* "to ask/dedicate," a play on words occurs that highlights both the fervent intercession that characterized Hannah's intense travail over her barren condition and her subsequent consecration of her child back to God (1 Sam. 1:27–28).

Isaiah's son's name, *Shear-Yashub,* translates "a remnant will return." It was to be a prophetic indicator to beleaguered Hezekiah that God would turn the seemingly impossible plight of Judah into deliverance (Isa. 7:3–4; 10:21–22). This was also the local setting for the well-known prophecy that "A virgin shall be with child and will give birth to a son, and will call him *Immanu El*" ("God with us," Isa. 7:14). The name of Isaiah's second son, *Maher-Shalal-Hash-Baz,* was a prophecy of coming doom—the fall of the northern kingdom at the hands of the Assyrian armies, as the name graphically portrays ("quick to the plunder, swift to the spoil" Isa. 8:1–3). Whether the Immanuel prophecy had any local fulfillment in relation to this second son is a debated subject (cf. Isa. 8:8–10). That it has ultimate messianic significance in connection with Jesus of Nazareth is clear from Matthew 1:22–23.

On the negative side, *Ichabod,* "Where is the glory?" (1 Sam. 4:21), recalls a gripping personal tragedy for the high priestly family at a time of national trauma for the entire people of God. The name *Nabal* embodies a poignant description of a man whose life of "folly" had degenerated to the sordid level of a "fool" (1 Sam. 25:25).

Finally, the name *Adam* carries the collective meaning of "humankind." Thus God's call "Where are you?" to the first Adam (Gen. 3:9), becomes universalized in Jesus, the second Adam, through whom his redemptive pursuit of the entire race is consummated (Heb. 1:1–2; cf. Rom. 5:12–19; 1 Cor. 15:21–22, 45–50). That salvific mission is also revealed in the name *Yeshua*/Joshua/Jesus—"Jehovah is salvation" (Matt. 1:21). LEONARD S. WALLMARK

See also GOD, NAME OF; JESUS CHRIST, NAME AND TITLES OF.

Name, New. *See* NEW NAME.

Nations, the. ***The Old Testament.*** The English word "nations" is used in the New International Version to translate several Hebrew terms. Most often it refers to *gôyim,* a word thought to derive from *gēw,* which means "body" of a person and thus by extension, the corporate body of a people.

The writers of the Hebrew Bible applied the term "nations" to various peoples, but at times the term is used quite specifically. In Genesis 10 Israel is included among the list of more than seventy nations. Seven nations larger and stronger than Israel appear in three passages (Deut. 7:1; Josh. 3:10; 24:11): the Hittites, Girgashites, Amorites, Canaanites, Perizzites, Hivites, and Jebusites.

The Noahic laws found in Genesis 9:1–17 were understood as the minimum requirements binding on all people, Hebrew and non-Hebrew alike. The exhortation to "be fruitful and multiply" (vv. 1, 7), the allowance to eat any meat, although without the lifeblood in it (vv. 3–5), and the declaration that "whoever sheds the blood of man, by man shall his blood be shed" (v. 6) were applicable to all people in all times. But it is clear that the Old Testament writers generally viewed the nations as failing to fulfill even these broad parameters. Approximately half of the references to the nations in the Old Testament refer to them in a negative fashion. The nations are described as "vomit" (Lev. 18:28), a "drop in a bucket" and "dust on the scales" (Isa. 40:15), and the source of slaves (Lev. 25:44). Negative references are often made to the nations in comparison to Israel.

The actions of the nations are depicted as evil, but the almost formulaic comparison between the wicked nations and the chosen people of Israel takes an ironic turn in 2 Chronicles 33:9. There the evil perpetrated by the people of Jerusalem, having been led astray by Manassah, was more grievous than that of the nations the Lord had destroyed before the Israelites. The evil ways of the nations are depicted as a source of temptation to the true faith of Israel. God used the attraction of evil to test the faith of his chosen people (Deut. 12:30; 29:18).

The nations are found in synonymous poetic parallelism with wickedness (Ps. 9:17) and enemy (Isa. 64:2), a further indication of the low esteem in which the biblical writers held their neighbors. Still, the nations were often used by God. In Judges 2:21–23 the Lord, angry with Israel, allows the nations that had not been driven out by Joshua to remain to test Israel, to see "whether they will keep the way of the LORD and walk in it as their forefathers did."

For the prophets, the failure of Israel and Judah to stand against the opposing nations served as a sign of God's judgment against his people rather than the superiority of the nations themselves. God's use of the nations in the Old Testament underscores the fact that, for the biblical writers, both the nations and Israel were under the sovereignty of God.

The Old Testament is usually negative and seldom positive toward other ethnic groups, but the nations can stand as neutral observers of God's glory (1 Chron. 16; Ps. 45:17; Mal. 1:11), of God's wrath (Isa. 12:4), and of the Suffering Servant (Isa. 52:15). Still, several texts hold out for the ultimate conversion of all peoples (see Jer. 16:19).

The intertestamental period, as indicated by the books of the Apocrypha, exhibits a continued distinction between the Jews and the "nations." Maccabees reflects the deepest point of this division. The defilement of the temple by Antiochus IV and the Jewish response dramatizes the struggle between Judaism and the forces of Hellenization.

The New Testament. The New Testament Greek *ethnos* is rendered "nation(s)" (36 times), "pagan(s)" (8 times), "Gentiles" (84 times), and "heathen" (one time) in the New International Version. The Greek term tends to represent a positive image nearly half of the time; one-quarter of the occurrences are negative and the other quarter present a neutral impression. *Ethnos* is translated as "nations" when it takes on a more negative aspect. Forty-one percent of the occurrences of *ethnos* as "nations" are negative; only 28 percent are positive; 31 percent are neutral. When referring to the nations, *ethnos* continues the negative attitude embodied in its use in the Old Testament.

Other related terms are *hellēn* and *akrobustia* (uncircumcised), both of which the New International Version translates as "Gentile." *Hellēn* literally means Hellenes or Greeks and is so translated twenty-two times. The New International Version translates *telesphoreō* and *ethnikos* as "pagan." *Hellēn* can refer to non-Jews in both the cultural and religious sense (see Rom. 1:14 and 1 Cor. 1:22). All these terms reflect the distinction between Jew and non-Jew in first-century Palestine.

Jesus understood this distinction. Early in his ministry he directed his efforts toward his fellow Jews. Still, even after referring to non-Jews with the image of "dogs" (Mark 7:27), Jesus drove the demon from the Greek woman's daughter. The final words of his ministry, the Great Commission of Matthew 28:16–20, indicate how his ministry had expanded to "make disciples of all nations."

The work of the apostle Paul reflects the conflict between Jew and non-Jew in early Christian communities. Acts 15:29 delimits the minimum legal requirements to be applied to Gentile Christians: to abstain from (1) food sacrificed to idols, (2) (consuming) blood, (3) the meat of strangled animals, and (4) sexual immorality. It has been suggested that these rules are simply an expression of the Noahic laws found in Genesis 9. The requirements for Jewish and non-Jewish Christians were problematic for the early church. Among these the incident between Paul and Peter concerning the necessity of circumcision for the non-Jewish Christian (Gal. 2) highlights this problem. But in the final analysis, there is "neither Jew nor Greek, slave nor free, male nor female, for you are all one in Christ Jesus. If you belong to Christ, then you are Abraham's seed, and heirs according to the promise" (Gal. 3:28–29).

Theologically, the Bible reflects a symbiotic relationship between God's people and others. Other peoples posed both threat and promise. The nations always outnumbered the people called of God. The lifestyle of the nations, often involving illicit ritual sex, threatened God's people by appealing to their inherently base nature. The promise of the nations was that they might be redeemed for the purposes of their Creator. The intent of the Lord from the beginning was that all the nations would be blessed. Thus the call of Abraham looked toward the time when all peoples would become the children of Abraham by faith. For the nations as for the ethnic descendants of Abraham, the person and ministry of Jesus were indeed good news, providing the means of reconciliation to God and with one another. Thus the church was destined to move out of Palestine and into all the world to further that end. KEITH N. SCHOVILLE

See also FOREIGNER; NEIGHBOR.

Bibliography. D. L. Christensen, *ABD*, pp. 1037–49; K. R. Joines, *Mercer Dictionary of the Bible*, pp. 666–67; H. C. Kee, *Understanding the New Testament;* D. A. Smith, *Mercer Dictionary of the Bible*, p. 325; F. Stagg, *Mercer Dictionary of the Bible*, pp. 324–25.

Nature, Natural. The Hebrew language has no word for "nature" equivalent to the Greek word *physis*. Hebrew thought and language were essentially concrete. Old Testament writers described the world around them, but spent little time in abstract reflection on it. Their basic interest in nature focused on God as Creator and on heaven and earth as his creation.

Genesis makes it clear that there is a creation order established by God. Plants bear fruit according to their "kind" (Gen. 1:11–12). God created fish (1:21), birds (1:21), and the other animals (1:24–25) which multiply according to their "kind." It is clear from these verses that various plants and animals have inherent characteristics that make them distinct from one another. It is also clear that God views these distinctions as "good."

There is a close bond between humankind and the rest of creation (Gen. 3:17–18; Ps. 96:10–13). There are physiological similarities between humankind and the rest of creation (Gen. 18:27; Job 10:8–9; Ps. 103:14). Humankind shares in creation's dependence on God's goodness for its continuance (Pss. 103:15; 104; Isa. 40:6–7). Nevertheless, creation order distinctiveness is particularly apparent as it pertains to humankind. Only people were created in the image of God (Gen. 1:26–27). Only people were the result of God's direct creative activity (2:7). Only into humankind did God breathe the breath of life (2:7). Only to people did God give dominion over the earth and the other creatures in it (1:28–30). Only to people did God give the responsibility to cultivate the earth (2:15). Only to humankind did God give special instructions regarding the tree of the knowledge of good and evil (2:16–17). When a helper for Adam was sought, none of the other creatures was suitable (2:18–20); only God's special creative act could provide that helper (2:21–23). Humankind's creation order distinctiveness is also described as "very good" (1:31).

The fall disrupted God's intended order for creation and for humankind (Gen. 3:16–19). Although it is cursed because of sin (3:17–18), creation is still viewed positively (Pss. 33:5; 119:64). God still sustains it (Ps. 104), uses it to fulfill his purposes (Job 37:1–13; Pss. 29; 148:8), and declares his glory through it (Pss. 19:1–6; 50:6; 97:1–6). Humankind, however, is regarded less positively. Men and women are viewed as conceived and brought forth in iniquity (Pss. 51:5; 58:3). They are rebellious (Isa. 48:8), incapable of purity (Job 14:4; 15:14), and completely wicked (Ps. 14:1–3). Every intent and thought of their hearts is unremittingly evil (Gen. 6:5–6; 8:21). They have been corrupted at the very core of their being (Jer. 17:9). As a result of the fall, humankind has become absolutely sinful.

The noun *physis* and its cognates occur seventeen times in the New Testament. James uses the noun with the sense of "species" or "kind" (3:7). Jude uses the adverb (*physikōs*) with the sense of "by instinct" (Jude 10) to refer to those things men and women know without conscious reflection. Peter uses two different forms of the word. He uses the adjective (*physikos*) similarly to Jude (2 Peter 2:12) in comparing the unrighteous to "creatures of instinct." He uses the noun to refer to the innate character of God when he comments that God's promises have been granted to believers in order that they might become partakers of the "the divine nature" (1:4).

The other occurrences of *physis* (or *physikos*) are in Paul's writings. The basic concept underlying all thirteen uses is that of correspondence to the post-fall creation order. There is a distinction between olive trees that are wild "by nature" and those that are cultivated (Rom. 11:24). Each type of tree grows certain branches "by nature" (11:21, 24), and any grafting of branches from one type to the other is "contrary to nature" (11:24). Similarly, there is an ethnic distinction between those men and women who are Jews "by birth" (Gal. 2:15) and those who are "physically" circumcised (Rom. 2:27).

Men and women are "by nature" objects of wrath (Eph. 2:3), but some dimly reflect the goodness of God's creation order in that they do "by nature" the things of the law (Rom. 2:14). "Nature" also makes a distinction between men and women (1 Cor. 11:14). This distinction is respected in "natural" sexual relations between heterosexual partners (Rom. 1:26–27), but is contravened by sexual relations between homosexual partners who are described as acting contrary to nature (1:26).

The fact that Paul can describe idols as those that are "by nature" not gods (Gal. 4:8) suggests that there is One who has a divine "nature." As in the Old Testament, some of the attributes of this divine nature can be seen in the visible world of creation (Rom. 1:18–20).

God's original creation order established certain distinctions that he declared to be good. That creation order was disrupted by the fall, but it was not destroyed. The visible world of creation still displays, but remains distinct from, God's divine nature. Certain innate qualities remain that distinguish plants from animals. Distinctions among species (kinds) separate various plants from one another; the same is true of animals. Humankind retains its creation order distinctiveness, and within the unity of humankind certain ethnic and sexual distinctions are evident. Although the fall corrupted human nature and predisposed people to turn away from God, Christ's work on the cross has made it possible for redeemed humankind to turn toward God and partake of his divine nature once again. Similarly, although creation suffers under the curse of the fall, it too looks forward to the restoration of the original creation order. JOHN D. HARVEY

Bibliography. F. H. Colson and G. H. Whitaker, *Philo in Ten Volumes;* C. E. B. Cranfield, *A Critical and Exegetical Commentary on the Epistle to the Romans;* P. Evdokimov, *SJT* 18 (1965): 1–22; G. Harder, *NIDNTT,* 2:656–11; H. D. McDonald, *EDT,* pp. 676–80.

Necromancy. Form of divination in which a person calls upon the dead to receive communication that clarifies knowledge. Ugaritic texts from the middle second millennium B.C. attest to a belief in calling ancestors, even demonstrating that a deceased ancestor could be referred to as a god. Archaeological evidence from tombs at Ugarit support the possibility that libations or drinks were poured out to the deceased. Although the evidence is sparse, it seems to indicate that necromancy made up a part of the ancient Near Eastern world.

Necromancy received an absolute ban in the Old Testament. Israel was not to consult "mediums" (Lev. 19:31) or they would risk being cut off from the covenant community (Lev. 20:6). Necromancers themselves should be put to death (Lev. 20:27). Included under these statements were those who consulted ghosts or spirits or who sought oracles from the dead (Deut. 18:11).

Although it is clear that these abhorrent practices came from their neighbors (Deut. 18:9; Isa. 19:3), it is less clear whether Israel ever embraced them in any way (see Ps. 106:28). Biblical evidence suggests that it was never eradicated. Why would the prophets mock such behavior if it did not exist (Isa. 8:19–20)? The list of idolatrous practices and divinatory rites condemned by the prophets certainly included necromancy (Isa. 56:9–57:13, esp. 57:6). Cutting the flesh when a person died (Jer. 16:5) or certain burial practices (Ezek. 43:7–9), acts condemned by the prophets, may allude to acts associated with necromancy.

Of course, one clear example of necromancy occurs in the biblical narrative: the story of Saul and the medium of Endor (1 Sam. 28). Saul sought the Lord when the Philistines threatened at Shunem. He received no communication from Urim and Thummim, dreams, or prophets (v. 6). As a result, he turned to a woman known to Saul's court as a "medium." He disguised himself and went to her at Endor by night. Saul asked her to "bring up" Samuel, presumably from Sheol. When an "old man" comes up, she realizes that the disguised person is the king, Saul. Her description of the being from the dead as a "god" (*ʾĕlōhîm*) gives an insight into her theology of the dead. The details about the visit give some insights into necromancy. It takes place at night, after fasting (v. 20), and through a medium, who seeks help from the dead. Samuel, the old man who came forth, gives the Lord's answer to Saul's dilemma, an answer proclaimed already in the prophecy to Saul in 1 Samuel 15. Within the borders of Israel, necromancy takes place. In fact, it is used to confirm God's will for Saul.

Vestiges of necromancy may be seen in other narrative passages. The "keeping" of a name for Absalom suggests association with the dead (2 Sam. 18:18). Elisha's bones brought a man back to life (2 Kings 13:20–21). Manasseh's evil included consultation with mediums (2 Kings 21:6). Josiah's reform targeted all forms of abomination, including mediums (2 Kings 23:24).

In the New Testament, necromancy may be in mind when the populus believed that Jesus ministered in the power of John the Baptist (Mark 6:14–16). Allusions to the descent of Jesus to the dead after crucifixion could be understood in this way, but probably should be interpreted otherwise (Eph. 4:9–10; 1 Peter 3:18–19).

The prohibition against seeking mediums who would call upon the dead attempts to clarify the channels that God approves when communicating with humanity. No other source should take the place of God when a person seeks guidance. Mistaken allegiance could result. The first commandment is clear: you shall have no other gods before me. G. MICHAEL HAGAN

See also DIVINATION; IDOLS, IDOLATRY; GODS AND GODDESSES, PAGAN.

Bibliography. T. J. Lewis, *Cults of the Dead in Ancient Israel and Ugarit;* R. de Vaux, *Ancient Israel.*

Needy, the. *See* POOR AND POVERTY, THEOLOGY OF.

Nehemiah, Theology of. ***Doctrine of God.*** God is introduced as the God of heaven (1:4–5). He is great, mighty, powerful, and awesome (1:5; 6:16; 9:32). The one whose name is Yahweh is the only being worthy to be called God (9:6). Multitudes of heaven bow down before their Creator, who made all their host and gave life to all (9:6). This great Lord is exalted above all blessing (9:5).

God also enters into covenant with men. He brought Abram out of Ur and changed his name to Abraham (9:7). He was able to look into the man's heart and know that he was faithful. He himself makes his promises and fulfills them (9:8). Yahweh is reliable and can be counted on to do what he says (9:32). He preserves his covenant and lovingkindness for those who love him and keep his word (1:5). He fulfills his promises because he is righteous (9:8).

Yahweh is the redeemer who brought his people out of Egypt by his great power and strong hand (1:10). He first saw their affliction and then delivered them with wondrous signs (9:9). He is their lawgiver from Mount Sinai and their preserver and sustainer in the wilderness.

He is not only the God of redemptive history; he is also the God who was favorable to Nehemiah (2:18). Nehemiah recognized that all of his thoughts prompting him to rebuild were put into his heart by God (2:12). The carrying out of these thoughts was done by the help of his God (4:14).

The greatest emphasis on the nature of God in this book concerns his lovingkindness, grace, and mercy. The remnant based their hopes for survival on the ancient "mercy confession" of Exodus 34:6. The Lord is a God of forgiveness, grace, and compassion, slow to anger and abounding in lovingkindness (9:17). Therefore he did not forsake Israel because of the golden calf episode (Exod. 32). He had great compassion on Israel in the wilderness, providing for all their needs (9:27–31).

For the small group of refugees God's mercy was not only a historical event but also a present reality. They base their ability to survive as a nation on it. Although God is compassionate, however, he is also just and righteous. Everything he brought upon the rebellious people was fair and just (9:33).

The People of God. To their enemies they are "feeble Jews" (4:2). They are in dire straights, having become slaves on their own land (9:36). Persian kings rule over their own bodies (9:37). Even their own brethren threaten to plunge them into serfdom (5:1–5). Yet, at the same time, they are the people whom Yahweh redeemed by his great power and strong hand (1:10).

In the midst of weakness and distress they "worked with all their heart" (4:6). Almost as one person they put their hand to the good work (2:18). Though there are some nobles who disdained to work on the wall, daughters are said to have worked alongside their father (3:5, 12). With swords in one hand and tools in the other they worked from dawn until the stars came out (4:17, 21).

In the past their fathers acted arrogantly, would not listen, and failed to remember God's wondrous deeds (9:16). They cast the law behind them and killed the prophets (9:25). Their sons are mourning and confessing their sins. They stand as one person shivering in the rain to listen to the Torah in chapters 8 and 9.

Over a hundred names are recorded on a written, sealed covenant (10:1–27). With knowledge and understanding they pledged themselves to walk in God's law. They renounce foreign marriages and working on the Sabbath. In the midst of poverty they pledge to renounce crops the seventh year and to remit slaves and debts in the year of jubilee. They promise in writing to honor their financial obligations to the house of God and to its ministers. Though they have meager means of existence, they will not neglect the house of God (10:32–39).

Scripture. On Mount Sinai Yahweh gave commands, decrees, and laws (9:14). He also gave his good spirit to instruct them (9:20). Their rule of faith and practice includes more than the law of Moses. Their manner of praise and worship goes back to the commandments of David and Solomon. David, like Moses, was a man of God. His prescriptions are considered binding (12:24, 46). Information recorded in the historical books is also considered binding in moral situations (13:26).

Early in the book it is recognized that the law foretold their scattering and also their return (1:7). It is more than a historical record. It is something the people separate themselves to and a way of life in which they walk (10:29–30). The book of the law is not something restricted to temple worship.

The reading of the law was done in the city square at the Water Gate. This entrance led to the spring of Gihon, the source of the city's water supply. The reading was commenced on the first day of the seventh month. This would begin the civil new year. Thus it was emphasized that the Torah must overshadow secular as well as religious life (8:1–2).

A wooden tower was built large enough for fifteen people to stand on. The purpose of this tower was for the reading of the Word (8:4–5). It reminded the people that the Torah stood above everything in their lives.

It was the people themselves who requested this reading. They all stood when the scroll was opened. Scripture was read from early morning until noon before men, women, and children who could understand (8:3–5). Thirteen Levites went through the crowd assisting people in understanding the law (8:7).

The law was reverenced. People bowed low and worshiped when it was read (8:7). It was not, however, worshiped. Yahweh himself is the only one granted this service. Leaders reminded the people that gloom and holiness do not go together. When all the people are weeping and mourning, they are exhorted to rejoice and send gifts to each other (8:9–10). They are made to realize that the joy of the Lord is their strength. They celebrate a great festival because "they understood the words that had been made known to them" (8:12). This practice probably lies behind the "Simchat Torah" ("Joy of the Torah"), a special day observed in modern synagogues around this time of the year.

Prayer. The Book of Nehemiah probably contains the shortest prayer in the Bible and one of the longest. The shortest prayer occurs in 2:4 between the king's question about what Nehemiah wants from him and this man's reply. The longest prayer takes up most of chapter 9.

This prayer came after the festivals of Yom Kippur and Sukkoth. The fact that it was not on one of the prescribed holy days indicated that consecration is not to be restricted to certain special days in the year. The people separated themselves to the Lord. They read the law for a fourth of a day and confessed sins for another fourth (9:1–2).

In the Greek text of the Septuagint this is said to be Ezra's prayer but the Hebrew text is indefinite about the speaker in 9:6. The entire prayer is a national confession of sin and a plea for mercy in the midst of oppression and disgrace. It forms a centerpiece of the book.

There are thirteen instances of prayer in Nehemiah. The book opens with a prayer and closes with one (1:4–11; 13:31). The recorded prayer of the first chapter is the culmination of many days of praying and fasting for the ruined city of Jerusalem. Nehemiah has been praying night and day for this city. This man of God identifies himself with the sin of his people that he is confessing. He, himself, and his father's house have acted corruptly (1:7). He calls God's attention to Leviticus 26:33, which promises a regathering of the nation in response to their repentance. He closes his prayer by requesting success and compassion before the king. This is truly one of the great intercessory prayers of the Bible.

At many points of crisis Nehemiah's short prayers are recorded. When news of conspiracy is heard, they pray and set up a guard (5:19). After five attempts to ambush him he breathes a brief prayer that is only three words in the Hebrew text: "Now strengthen my hands" (6:9). He continually requests that God remember his faithful acts during his governorship. This man is possibly one of the most prayerful persons in the Bible outside of Christ. He realized there were times for long, sustained prayer and times for hard work and quick, whispered prayer.

Ethics. Before the wall was even finished a crisis concerning ethics must be dealt with. Wealthy Jewish landowners are forcing their brethren into serfdom by high-interest loans. Courageously the governor faces them with the wrongs they have done. To their lasting credit, they responded by remitting the debts (5:1–12).

Nehemiah is not a heartless legalist who slavishly follows the letter of the law. He is constantly sacrificing for the welfare of the people. He realizes that the law is built on both the love of God and love for one's neighbor. He disdains to take his legal right as governor to require a subsidy from the people for his official expenses. He did not domineer the people but rather paid for the expenses of his table from his own money (5:15–18). He did not consider common labor beneath his dignity as a governor, but diligently applied himself to the work on the wall (5:16).

When he discovers Levites and singers have had to leave their duties because tithes are not being paid, he quickly reorganized the country's financial policies. He placed reliable people in charge of storing the tithes (13:10–14). For sake of accountability the high priest was to be present when Levites gathered tithes (10:38).

Upon discovering Tobiah had commandeered a storeroom in the temple for his personal use, Nehemiah personally threw his household goods out into the street (13:4–9). The room was quickly cleansed and rededicated to temple use. Corruption and self-aggrandizement were not tolerated in any area.

People who were breaking the Sabbath were first admonished (13:15), then reprimanded (v. 17). After this, gates were locked and force was threatened (vv. 18–21). When the survival of the biblical Mosaic faith was concerned Nehemiah was not always gentle. At times he resorted to physical force (13:25). When foreign marriage laws were disregarded he struck the offenders and even pulled their hair out. The book simply reports these extreme methods without passing judgment on them.

These marriages were threatening to undermine the very core of Israel's national identity. They even resulted in offspring who could not speak the language of Judah and hence could not understand the laws that guaranteed their survival (13:24). Nehemiah realized from his own knowledge of Scripture that this had caused Solomon to sin and had brought the nation to disaster (13:26). His style of leadership differed from Ezra's, who pulled his own hair out over this situation (Ezra 9:3). One must remember Nehemiah was fighting for the spiritual and temporal survival of his nation.

The City of Jerusalem. Jerusalem is an important city. It is the place of the tombs of Nehemiah's fathers. It was also the place where God chose to have his Name dwell (1:9). It is to be a holy city. The first ones to start the building are the priests. As they build they consecrate the walls and gates (3:1). Guards were appointed to watch the gates. It was important who lived there and who entered the city. Lots were cast to insure there would be people residing there. The people who inhabited the city were blessed by the others (11:1–19). Their names and numbers were carefully recorded.

Dedication of the walls was a religious service accompanied with a great deal of gladness and celebration. Two great choirs lead a procession in two different directions up from the south end of the city to the temple on the north (12:31–43). The march was consummated with a great deal of sacrifice and rejoicing. Celebration was so loud that it was heard from afar (12:43).

This consecration of the city reminds us of dedication of the altar in Ezra 3:8–13. Piety is not to be restricted to the altar site, but encompasses everything within the walls of the city. Building these walls was a great work commissioned by God himself.

Kings and Human Government. The book recognizes that their kings and leaders were given by God (9:34) and that he reserves the right to withdraw the blessing of the kingdom he gave them. The nation is to be a holy commonwealth. Foreign leaders have no portion, right, or memorial in it (2:20).Try as they might, they cannot stop the work because God himself frustrated their plans (4:15). They completely lost their confidence when the work was accomplished with God's help (6:16). PAUL FERGUSON

See also ISRAEL; JERUSALEM.

Bibliography. J. Bright, *History of Israel;* B. Childs, *Introduction of the Old Testament as Scripture;* F. C. Fensham, *Ezra and Nehemiah;* D. Kidner, *Ezra and Nehemiah;* J. Myers, *Ezra–Nehemiah;* H. G. Williamson, *Ezra–Nehemiah.*

Neighbor. Once a lawyer, in an attempt to rationalize his own racial prejudice, asked Jesus, "And who is my neighbor?" (Luke 10:29). This lawyer-scribe unknowingly expresses a fundamental issue in all of ethics: For whom are we responsible in issues of justice and mercy? Jesus' answer was the parable of the Good Samaritan and the fundamental ideas of the parable find their roots in both Old Testament and Jewish soil.

The problem of "neighborliness" was acute in Judaism because of the people's self-consciousness of being the chosen people (Gen. 12:1–3; 15:1–6; 17:1–8), sealed in the rite of circumcision (17:9–14). Election set Israel apart, made the people particularly loyal to their own kind (cf. Matt. 5:43–48) and, at the same time, permitted the tendency to neglect, even condemn, those who were not Israelites. With such tendencies, it is not surprising that legislation had to be given to Israel to encourage compassion and justice for the non-Jew. Thus, Moses prescribes rites of conversion for the foreigner who wants to eat Passover with Israel (Exod. 12:43–49) and, even more, prohibits the reaping of the crops entirely; instead, some crops were to be left "for the poor and the alien" (Lev. 19:9–10; cf. Deut. 24:19–22) and every third year a tithe was to be shared with the sojourners (Deut. 14:29; 26:12–13). The fundamental basis for this is that at one time Israel was also a sojourner while in Egypt; therefore, Israel is to treat its sojourners with compassion and justice (Lev. 19:33–34; Deut. 10:19;

24:22). Essentially, then, the Mosaic laws demand both compassion and justice to be guaranteed for the foreigner because God loves the sojourner (Deut. 10:18). It is impossible for us to know just how Israel treated the foreigner who decided to live with, or near, them. The records show both slave labor (1 Chron. 22:2; 2 Chron. 2:17–18) and inclusion among the people (2 Chron. 30:25).

In spite of this insistence of the law that Israel was to be kind to foreigners and treat them with compassion and justice, the preponderance of emphasis is on the "neighborliness" to be shown to fellow members of the covenant with Israel. We ought to see this as special benevolence among Israelites; it did, however, develop at times into racial favoritism and discrimination. In fact, to be a "neighbor" was to be a "brother" (cf. Jer. 31:34): at the end of seven years release was granted from debts owed to a "neighbor-brother" but this same privilege of release was not granted to foreigners (Deut. 15:2–3). Thus, when the Old Testament prescribes treating one's neighbor as oneself (Lev. 19:18b), we are to envisage how Israel was to treat fellow Israelites (Lev. 19:17–18a) and, only by extension, Gentiles. There developed then an entire network of legal prescriptions and prohibitions about dealings with one's neighbors, including attitudes and actions like adultery and business relations. The vision of Zechariah for the final days included the refreshing fellowship of neighborliness (3:10).

Thus, when we enter into the New Testament period we are to understand the biblical laws of the Old Testament that speak of neighborliness as injunctions for special treatment of fellow Jews. Jews showed special love for fellow Jews because they were covenantally and racially bound together. The social realities of Jewish history, with the constant battering of the people of Israel by other nations, also inclined the Jewish people to favor their own. Social realities also reveal that Jews were kind to Gentiles in general and for those Jews who lived in the diaspora there was also a general social friendliness to be observed. Early Christianity showed a similar kind of "prejudiced love" (Gal. 6:10) and it would be wrong to vilify either Jews or Christians for their "prejudiced love" unless that love becomes neglect, or even contempt, of outsiders in need.

Jesus sought to expand the concept of "neighbor" to include non-Jews; while this is not contrary to Jewish law or to Jewish practice, it clearly was challenging to many in Judaism. Jewish practice had come to the general conviction that a "neighbor," in purely legal terms, was a Jew or proselyte to Judaism. For Jesus, a neighbor was anyone with whom you came into contact—whether Jew, Samaritan, or Gentile (Luke 10:25–37). In fact, this focus on an expanding definition led to the breaking down of Jewish barriers that were constructed around the traditional interpretations of cleanness and uncleanness. At the time of Jesus, various restricting movements, like the Pharisees and Essenes at Qumran, naturally tended to show favoritism to members of their own social groups. While the War Scroll at Qumran may be from one extreme end of the evidence, its emphasis on hating all those who were sons of darkness (non-Essenes) illustrates the point being made. Thus, we are to understand the parable of the good Samaritan as addressing the issue of the "limits" of one's responsibility and we are to see Jesus saying that there are no limits; one cannot exclusively exercise compassion or justice for one's own kind.

This profound parable of Jesus, with its teaching on the importance of showing love for anyone within one's reach, along with Jesus' command to love one's enemies (Matt. 5:43–48) and his overt friendliness to Gentiles become foundational for the early church's missionary efforts and for interpersonal relationships within the largely Gentile churches of Paul. Paul urges the Galatians to love their neighbors as themselves and here the implication is that it involved both Jewish and Gentile Christians (Gal. 5:14) and we find in Matthew an emphasis on loving one's enemy (=Gentile; Matt. 5:43–48). Once again, while this idea is not new to Judaism, the emphasis of seeing neighbors as Gentiles as well clearly expanded the Jewish horizons.

It is also clear that the early churches found a special love for one another and addressed themselves as neighbors. Paul can say that one is to do good especially to other believers (Gal. 6:10) and James can see the principle of Leviticus 19:18 applying to what was probably Jewish Christians (2:1–14). Furthermore, Paul urges his congregations to be neighborly, and we are probably justified in seeing such exhortations applying primarily to Christian fellowship (Rom. 13:8–10; 1 Cor. 10:24; Eph. 4:25). SCOT MCKNIGHT

See also FOREIGNER; NATIONS, THE.

Bibliography. J. D. G. Dunn, *Jesus' Call to Discipleship;* H. Greeven and J. Fichtner, *TDNT,* 6:311–15; W. Günther, U. Falkenroth, and D. A. Carson, *NIDNTT,* 1:254–60; J. J. Hughes and N. J. Opperwall, *ISBE,* 3:517–18; S. McKnight, *Dictionary of Jesus and the Gospels,* pp. 259–65; idem, *A Light among the Gentiles: Jewish Missionary Activity in the Second Temple Period;* E. P. Sanders, *Judaism: Practice and Belief.*

New. Word used in the New Testament to contrast and compare both the quantitative concept of the recent with the former and the qualitative idea of the better with the inferior. The theological connotation of the word is used with both these meanings in phrases such as "new covenant" (Luke 22:20; 2 Cor. 3:6; Heb. 8:8, 13; 9:15), "new creation" (2 Cor. 5:17), "new commandment" (John 13:34), and "new self" (Eph. 2:15; 4:24; Col. 3:10).

Two words are employed in the Greek New Testament to convey these ideas. The word *kainos* appears more than forty times and the word *neos* is used more than twenty times. Efforts have been made to differentiate these by ascribing to the former a qualitative meaning such as "fresh" and to the latter a quantitative or temporal meaning such as "new" or "recent." According to this distinction Jesus introduced a new covenant (*kainē*, Luke 22:20) in the sense of its being a fresh understanding of the former covenant rather than a different and supplanting one.

However, there are places where the two words seem to be used synonymously. For example, Hebrews 8:8, 13 refers to the new covenant with the word *kainē* while 12:24 calls it a *neos* covenant. Mark 2:21–22 speaks of sewing a new (*kainon*) patch on an old garment and putting new *neos* wine in old wineskins. Thus, it is probable that the words are virtually synonymous in the New Testament unless contextually differentiated.

Generally the word "new" is used to draw a contrast with the old. Jesus' teaching was contrasted with that of the scribes by some who heard him, calling it "new" (Mark 1:21–27). The new aspect was that Jesus taught with authority. Paul wrote that "if anyone is in Christ, he is a new creation; the old has gone, the new has come!" (2 Cor. 5:17). John looked for new heavens and a new earth, because the first ones had passed away (Rev. 21:1).

Most of what Jesus taught was rooted in the Hebrew Scriptures and was new only in point of emphasis or application. He reaffirmed the teaching of Hebrew Scripture that centralized the Shema as the heart of Jewish religion: "Hear, O Israel: The Lord our God, the Lord is one. Love the Lord your God with all your heart and with all your soul and with all your strength" (Deut. 6:5–6). To this Jesus added the corollary: "Love your neighbor as yourself" (Matt. 22:39). He said these two commandments fulfilled the Law and the Prophets.

Jesus made love for one another the mark of discipleship: "A new command I give you: Love one another. As I have loved you, so you must love one another. By this all men will know that you are my disciples, if you love one another" (John 13:34–35). His command to love one's enemies seems to be an innovation (Matt. 5:44).

John McRay

New Birth. Cleansing from sin that God gives to all who believe on his Son through the Holy Spirit.

It is absolutely necessary for a person to be born again in order to enter the kingdom of God. In the central passage in the New Testament about the new birth (John 3), Jesus tells Nicodemus, a member of the Jewish ruling council, that he will not enter the kingdom of God unless he is born anew. The alternation between singular and plural Greek pronouns in the passage shows that Jesus is speaking to Nicodemus both personally and representatively. The need for the new birth is not only true of Nicodemus, but of the entire Sanhedrin, all Jews, and, by extension, all people.

Some have considered the new birth to be a process a person experiences, even over a period of years. Such an interpretation is not congruent with the tense of the Greek verb in this passage. The aorist tense suggests that the new birth is an event rather than a process. Prior to a certain point in time, a person is not-born-again or regenerated; after that point, the person is.

Probably the most difficult interpretative issue in John 3 is found in verse 5. The best view appears to be that "being born of water and the Spirit" presents a unified thought for the supernatural cleansing from sin that God through the Spirit effects on all who believe on his Son. This water-Spirit combination is a reflection of Ezekiel 11, 36, and Jeremiah 31. In these Old Testament passages God's Spirit is viewed as doing a revolutionary work in the lives of God's people in the new covenant age. There are a number of reasons that this interpretation is preferable.

The use of one Greek preposition (*ek*) before the two nouns indicates a close relationship between them. Water and Spirit are complementary rather than antithetical to each other. It does not see water as a reference to Christian baptism at a time in Jesus' ministry when such baptism was not yet a historical reality. It fits well contextually in terms of Nicodemus' familiarity with the Old Testament and the need for some intelligibility on his part. It interprets "born of water and the Spirit" as equivalent to "born of God," a common Johannine term (John 1:13; 1 John 2:29; 3:7–10; 4:7; 5:4). It comports well with the emphasis on Spirit and truth in the Johannine literature. Finally, it coheres with the use of water in the Old Testament to symbolize renewal and cleansing.

Whether Old Testament believers possessed the new birth is a difficult question. No Old Testament text explicitly states that Old Testament believers were born again or regenerated. There is a relative absence of a developed theology of the Spirit in the Old Testament. But, given the universality of the need for the new birth, it can be argued that Jesus' teaching on the absolute necessity of the new birth for entrance into the kingdom of God analogically demands that Old Testament believers also had to have the divine life imparted to them through God's Spirit.

Many commentators argue that Titus 3:5 argues for water baptism as the referent of the word "washing." Based on the Greek grammar, however, the translation should be rendered "the washing [produced by] regeneration and the renewal [produced by] the Holy Spirit." This interpretation also coheres with the translation of John 3.

First Peter 1:23 adds a more explicit dimension to the means whereby the new birth is produced: the preached message of the truth of Jesus Christ. The key words in 1 Peter 1:22–25 expand upon and reinforce words referring to the new birth.

The new birth is, then, a sovereign act of God by his Spirit in which the believer is cleansed from sin and given spiritual birth into God's household. It renews the believer's intellect, sensibility, and will to enable that person to enter the kingdom of God and to do good works. The Old Testament saints were born again when they responded in faith to God's revealed message; New Testament saints, when they respond in faith to Jesus Christ. Carl B. Hoch, Jr.

Bibliography. L. L. Belleville, *Trinity* 1 (1980): 125–41; F. Büchsel, *TDNT,* 1:665–75, 686–89; S. Charnock, *The Works of Stephen Charnock,* vol. 3; J. Dey, *Encyclopedia of Biblical Theology,* pp. 725–30; N. R. Gulley, *ABD,* 5:659–60; Z. C. Hodges, *BSac* 135 (1978): 206–20; A. Kretzer, *Exegetical Dictionary of the New Testament,* 1:243–44; W. L. Kynes, *Dictionary of Jesus and the Gospels,* pp. 574–76; J. I. Packer, *EDT,* pp. 924–26; A. Ringwald, *NIDNTT,* 1:176–80; P. Toon, *Born Again: A Biblical and Theological Study of Regeneration.*

New Command. On the night before his death, Jesus gave a new command to his disciples: "Love each other as I have loved you."

The fact that Jesus called this commandment "new" is perplexing in light of Leviticus 19:18, which is part of the Torah of Moses. That passage states: "Love your neighbor as yourself. I am the Lord." Jesus had previously appealed to this command in conjunction with Deuteronomy 6:4–5 as constituting the basis for all the divine directives in the Law and the Prophets (Matt. 22:34–37 and par.). In other words, how could Jesus designate something as "new" that had been in existence for centuries and was in a true sense very "old"?

While the Greek adjective *kainos* does not have to mean something brand new or totally new, there are at least five factors that explain why Jesus called this a "new" commandment and legitimize his use of this adjective to describe something he was inaugurating.

First, Jesus provided a new model for love. The directive to the disciples followed one of the most humiliating acts Jesus performed during his lifetime—he had washed his disciples' feet. This act of servanthood was to serve as a model or example to the disciples of their relationship with another: "I have set you an example that you should do as I have done for you" (John 13:15). The disciples were to love one another as Jesus had loved them (John 13:34). The disciples' love on the horizontal plane would reflect their relationship with the Son and with the Father on the vertical plane: "As the Father has loved me, so have I loved you. Now remain in my love. If you obey my commands you will remain in my love, just as I have obeyed my Father's commands and remain in his love" (John 15:9–10).

Second, Jesus provided a new motive for love. The disciples were to be motivated to love one another because Jesus demonstrated love by giving his life as an atoning sacrifice for sins. John emphasizes this motivational act in his First Epistle: "This is love: not that we loved God, but that he loved us and sent his Son as an atoning sacrifice for our sins. Dear friends, since God so loved us, we also ought to love one another" (1 John 4:10–11).

Third, Jesus provided a new motivator for love. The great gift of Jesus to the church was the Holy Spirit, the Paraclete. The great command of Jesus is to believe in the name of the Son, Jesus Christ, and to love one another (1 John 3:23). Those who obey his commands reveal an intimate knowledge of the Holy Spirit (1 John 3:24). This Spirit produces his fruit of love in Jesus' disciples (Rom. 5:5; Gal. 5:22).

Fourth, the disciples are to practice the love command because of a new mission. All men will know Jesus' disciples by their love for one another (John 13:34). Just as Jesus has revealed the Father to men (John 1:18), his disciples reveal him to men by loving one another: "No one has ever seen God; but if we love each other, God lives in us and his love is made complete in us" (1 John 4:12). Love as the voluntary sacrifice of oneself for the benefit of someone else so that God's will might be perfected in that person is the vital force in mission to a world in darkness that needs the light of life.

Fifth, the new commandment is new because of a new milieu. The coming of the Son has introduced newness. This fact is proven by the centrality of the concept of newness for New Testament theology: new teaching (Mark 1:27; Acts 17:19); new wine and new wineskins (Luke 5:37–39); new commandment (John 13:34; 1 John 2:7–8; 2 John 5); new covenant (Luke 22:20; 1 Cor. 11:25; 2 Cor. 3:6; Heb. 8:8, 13; 9:15; 12:24); new creation (2 Cor. 5:17; Gal. 6:15); new self (Eph. 2:15; 4:24; Col. 3:10); new heaven and new earth (2 Pet. 3:13; Rev. 21:1); new name (Rev. 2:17; 3:12); new Jerusalem (Rev. 3:12; 21:2); new song (Rev. 5:9; 14:3); and all things new (Rev. 21:5).

The new command is an eschatological command. It is the central command for the new age and the basic ethic for the final times. As such it is the decisive command because it fulfills the will of God for his people and displays God's gift of love in the Lord Jesus Christ. Carl B. Hoch, Jr.

See also Love.

Bibliography. R. Brown, *The Community of the Beloved Disciple;* R. E. Collins, *Christian Morality;* idem, *These Things Have Been Written;* idem, *ABD,* 4:1088; V. P. Furnish, *The Love Command in the New Testament;* N. Geisler, *The Christian Ethic of Love;* R. Harrisville, *The Concept of Newness in the New Testament;* C. B. Hoch, *All Things New: The Central Importance of*

Newness for New Testament Theology; E. Lee, *The Religious Thought of St. John;* R. Michaels, *Dictionary of Jesus and the Gospels,* pp. 132–36; L. Morris, *Testaments of Love;* P. Perkins, *Love Commands in the New Testament;* R. Schnackenburg, *The Moral Teaching of the New Testament;* S. Schneiders, *CBQ* 43 (1981): 76–92; F. Segovia, *Love Relationships in the Johannine Tradition;* C. Spicq, *Agape in the New Testament;* W. Swartley, ed., *The Love of Enemy and Nonretaliation in the New Testament.*

New Covenant. Eschatological stage of salvation history in which God, through the work of the Messiah and the Spirit, would unconditionally bring about Israel's full salvation.

The Old Testament. The only explicit reference to the new covenant in the Old Testament is found in Jeremiah 31:31–34. The prophet contrasts the existing covenant made with the fathers when he brought them out of Egypt (cf. Exod. 24:8) with a covenant that God will make with the house of Israel and Judah in the latter days. The new covenant is distinguished from the older covenant in four ways: (1) God will write the law in the minds and on the hearts of those in the new covenant; (2) God will be the God of those in the new covenant and they will be his people; (3) those in the new covenant will know God; (4) God will forgive the iniquities and the sins of those in the new covenant. The new covenant, therefore, has two basic characteristics: an internal spiritual transformation resulting in a new relationship with God and a new possibility of obedience and forgiveness of sins. Jeremiah 31:31–34 falls into the context of the promise of the future regathering of Israel and its restoration to the land, which Jeremiah 29:10 says will take place after seventy years of exile.

Synonyms for the new covenant appear in other Old Testament texts. In Jeremiah what is denoted as the new covenant in 31:31–33—with the exception of the explicit promise of the forgiveness of sins—is also called an everlasting covenant (32:37–41; 50:5). Ezekiel 16 contrasts Jerusalem's (a metonymy for all Israel) present state of unfaithfulness with its beginnings and its future. Like an exposed child Israel was helpless until Yahweh adopted her. But she grew up to be a prostitute, unfaithful to her original benefactor. Nonetheless, Yahweh will both remember the covenant made with Israel in her youth and establish an everlasting covenant with the nation, making expiation for all that it has done. God speaks through Isaiah, saying that he will make an everlasting covenant with his restored people (61:8).

In Ezekiel 34:25, God promises that he will gather his sheep Israel and place his servant David over them as their shepherd; then he will make a covenant of peace with them, so that Israel will live in the land in safety and prosperity. In Ezekiel 37:24–28, God promises that he will make a covenant of peace with a restored Israel under a Davidic king. The people will obey God; he will be their God and they will be his people. This covenant of peace is also called an everlasting covenant. In Isaiah 54:8–10, Yahweh promises that when he restores Zion he will never again become angry, but will have compassion on his people. His covenant of peace will not be removed.

In the prophets the promises of restoration, the new possibility of obedience, and national forgiveness of sin occur frequently without being connected to the concepts of the new covenant, eternal covenant, or covenant of peace. It should be noted also that in Ezekiel 36:26–27 the new possibility of obedience given at the restoration is associated with the giving of the Spirit (cf. also Isa. 32:15; 44:3; Ezek. 37:12–13; 39:29; Joel 2:28).

Isaiah's Servant of the Lord plays a role in the realization of the (new) covenant. Yahweh says of his Servant in 42:6 that he will make the Servant a covenant for the people and a light for the nations. Similarly in 49:6–8 the Servant is said to be appointed to restore the tribes of Jacob, be a light to the nations, and become a covenant for the people. The "people" likely denotes Israel as opposed to the nations, which denotes the rest of humanity. Gentiles will benefit from God's eschatological saving act.

The Second-Temple Period. Insofar as it denotes Israel's eschatological salvation, the concept of the new covenant permeates Jewish literature of the second temple period. The restoration under Ezra and Nehemiah was seen as only the precursor to the salvation promised by God through the prophets and did not exhaust these promises. There are, however, only a few instances where Jeremiah 31:31–34 and related passages have had direct influence on the conceptualities of the extant literature of the second temple period. Jubilees 1:22–25 speaks of the new possibility of obedience to be given at the restoration. Baruch 2:30–35 says that God will make an everlasting covenant with his people at the restoration, so that he will be their God and they will be his people. In the same work (3:5–7) it is implied that this new possibility of obedience was given to the exiles even before the restoration. In two places in the Damascus Document (text A) it is said explicitly that those who belong to the community have actually entered the new covenant (6:19; 8:21; cf. also 20:12 text B). Because of their disobedience, the members of the covenant of the forefathers came under the wrath of God, which culminated in the exile; in contrast God made a covenant forever with the remnant who held fast to the commandments, revealing to them the hidden things in which Israel went astray (3:10–14). It is not so much that there exists in God's purposes two different covenants, but rather one covenant with two different phases: a preliminary phase ending in failure and an eschatological phase ending in God's final victory over all wickedness, beginning at some point after the exile. In 1QH 4:10–12, the author speaks of the Torah engraved upon his heart, possibly implying that the promise of internal spiritual transformation in Jeremiah 31:31–34 and related passages has been realized; there is also a probable reference to the new covenant in 1QHab 2:3.

Although the Feast of Weeks was understood by some Jews of the second temple period as the time when God made covenants with human beings and became, therefore, the occasion of the annual renewal of the covenant (cf. Jub. 6:17; 1QS), the new covenant by implication came to be associated with Passover, since Passover was seen as the day of eschatological salvation.

The New Testament. At his last Passover meal Jesus said of the cup of blessing that it was the blood of the covenant poured out for many (Mark 14:24); the blood of the covenant poured out for many for the forgiveness of sins (Matt. 26:28); the new covenant in my blood (1 Cor. 11:25); the new covenant in my blood poured out for you (Luke 22:20). In so doing he was affirming that his death was the means by which the new covenant—the kingdom of God—would come about. That Jesus did this on Passover is also significant, since Passover and eschatological salvation were salvation-historically related concepts. Jesus likely conceived himself as the eschatological Passover sacrifice bringing about the eschatological salvation of all Israel, typologically parallel to the original exodus. In addition, Jesus probably understood his death and its salvation-historical significance in light of the Servant of the Lord passages. As the servant, Jesus would be a covenant for the people and a light for the nations, but only by means of his vicarious and expiatory death.

Apart from its occurrence in the words of institution quoted by Paul in 1 Corinthians 11, the concept of the new covenant is found only twice in Paul's writings. Paul understood the new covenant as having been realized through the death and resurrection of Christ and the giving of the Spirit, and contrasted this salvation-historical phase with that of the law. In Galatians 4:21–31 he contrasted two covenants represented by Hagar and Sarah and their sons Ishmael and Isaac. The former produced slavery to the law (represented by Mount Sinai/present Jerusalem), whereas the latter produced freedom from the law and correlatively life in the Spirit (represented by Jerusalem above). In 2 Corinthians 3:3–18 Paul similarly contrasted the old covenant that condemned (identified with the law or letter) with the new covenant that brought righteousness (identified with the Spirit). Paul's statement in 2 Corinthians 3:3 that the Corinthians were a letter of Christ written with the Spirit on the fleshy tablets of the heart evokes the Old Testament promise that God would write the law upon the hearts of his people.

The author of Hebrews explicitly asserted that Jeremiah 31:31–34 was fulfilled by means of the death of Jesus, who was both the greater high priest and better sacrifice. Jesus as mediator of the new covenant was superior to the Aaronic high priests, the mediators of the first covenant; likewise, as the better sacrifice, Jesus truly expiated guilt unlike the blood of animals. The focus of the letter is on the forgiveness of sins promised in the new covenant; the author's purpose is to prove that the levitical sacrificial system, the means of obtaining forgiveness in the first covenant, has been rendered obsolete and will soon disappear. Jesus' blood is said to be the blood of the covenant parallel to the blood of the first covenant in Exodus 24:8.

Two questions arise from the New Testament's statements about the new covenant: How does the new possibility of obedience said to consist in conformity to the law relate to Paul's and other New Testament authors' claim that at least parts of the Torah are obsolete? Why when speaking about the realization of the new covenant is the New Testament silent about the promise of Israel's restoration to the land? Dispensational theology distinguishes two fulfillments of the promise of the new covenant, one relating to the church as a present reality and the other relating to a restored Israel as a still future reality. The benefits of the new covenant received by the church are forgiveness and the Spirit (the means of the internal spiritual transformation) whereas restored Israel will receive in addition the promised land under the Messiah's kingship and will be subject to the law (written on the heart) as the governing code of the messianic kingdom. (In the church age believers are not under the law.) Paul's citation of Isaiah 59:20–21 in reference to the future salvation and forgiveness of empirical Israel can be interpreted as meaning that Paul believed that the new covenant had yet another future fulfillment. Covenant theology, on the other hand, has been willing to spiritualize the new covenant promises and to see their nonliteral fulfillment in the church. The law written on the heart is the moral law—to which Christians are subject—and the promises of Israel's future restoration and prosperity relate symbolically to the church. The historical premillennial view offers something of a compromise between these two positions, allowing for the possibility of both the transmutation of the Old Testament promises and their literal fulfillment. BARRY D. SMITH

See also COVENANT; JEREMIAH, THEOLOGY OF; LORD'S SUPPER, THE.

Bibliography. J. Fischer, *Ev R Th* (1989): 175–87; J. Hughes, *NovT* 21 (1979): 27–96; J. A. Huntjens, *Revue de Qumran* 8 (1972–75): 361–80; S. Lehne, *The New Covenant in Hebrews;* W. E. Lemke, *Int* 37 (1983): 183–87.

New Creation. The specific term "new creation" (*kainē ktisis*) occurs only twice in the New Testament (2 Cor. 5:17; Gal. 6:15). It is, however, the anthropological and individual side of the broad concept of the renewal of creation that is developed more widely in the New Testament. It is the broader idea, which goes back to passages in the latter part of Isaiah, developments in apocalyptic Jewish thought, and Qumran, which probably gave rise to Paul's specific application. Consequently, it will be helpful to consider this background before attempting to explain the concept in its final form.

Renewal in Isaiah. In the latter half of Isaiah (42:9; 43:18–19; 48:6; 65:17–25; 66:22) two strands of teaching begin to emerge that seem to have played a part in Paul's thinking about salvation. On the one hand, the prophet declares that God is about to do something new (42:9; 43:18–19; 48:6). Salvation is described along the lines of a new exodus ("I am making a way in the desert and streams in a wasteland," 43:19), and what God is about to do will completely surpass old categories ("new things, . . . hidden things unknown to you. They are created now, and not long ago; you have not heard of them before today," 48:6b–7). These passages together declare the promise of God's intervention to deliver his people by doing a new thing.

Then, repeating and enlarging on the themes of newness and renewal, chapters 65 and 66 declare God's intention to "create new heavens and a new earth" (65:17). This act of God involves a complete reorganization of life; the hazards of life are removed (65:19–20, 23, 25). The God who has seemed far off will now be near (65:24), and the existence of his people will no longer be precarious and uncertain but perpetual and safe (66:22).

Both strands of teaching brought hope to the nation, whose sin threatened to destroy its hope in God. The punishment of the exile was replaced by the promise of renewal of the covenant and the establishment of God's kingdom on earth. It is clear that a drastic change was necessary. God himself would carry out this new thing, and it would affect the life of his people.

The Renewal of Creation in Apocalyptic and Sectarian Judaism. During a period of time when Jewish communities felt increasingly the pressure of dominion under foreign powers, religious literature emerged to encourage hope in an imminent, final intervention of God. These extracanonical writings picked up on the theme introduced in the last chapters of Isaiah of the creation of a new heavens and new earth. First Enoch 91:16 speaks of the passing away of the old order and the appearance of the new ("And in it [the great judgment] the first heaven shall pass away, and a new heaven shall appear"). First Enoch 72:1 classifies this as a "new work" of God ("until the creation will be made anew to last forever"; cf. Isa. 43:19). Similarly, Jubilee 1:29, which casts this message of hope in the form of a revelation from God to Moses on Mount Sinai, speaks of "the day of the new creation, when heaven and earth will be renewed." In 4:26 the term "new creation" appears to have become a technical term within the vocabulary of this stream of Jewish eschatology ("the Garden of Eden, and the Mount of the East, . . . Mount Sinai, and Mount Zion . . . will be sanctified in the new creation"); connected with the concept are the ideas of the purification of the earth and God's people from sin. In what is probably the latest phase of Jewish apocalyptic literature (4 Esdras 7:75; Syr. Bar. 32:6; 57:2; Apoc. to Abraham 17:14) the hope in a final eschatological renewal of the world is repeated without much variation. The literature of Qumran also registers the firm belief in the new creation of the world by God on the final day (1QH 13:11–12: "For Thou has caused them to see what they had not known, by bringing to an end the former things and by creating things that are new" = Isa. 65:17; 1QS 4:25: "For God has allotted these [spirits] in equal parts until the final end, the time of renewal" = Isa. 43:19). 11QTemple 29:9 shows evidence that "creation" in the sense of the day of the new creation has become a technical term ("for I shall cause my glory to dwell upon it until the day of blessing on which I shall create [anew] my sanctuary"). But while the apocalyptic literature of Judaism and Qumran reflect a growing belief in God's final solution, it is limited to a future, eschatological event (however imminent) and never "individualized" or applied as a description of a new condition of life as in Paul (though these developments may have influenced the apostle's thought).

The Renewal of Creation in the New Testament. That the early church also believed in the ultimate renovation or re-creation of the heavens and the earth at the close of history is clear from 2 Peter 3:13 and Revelation 21:1–5. Both passages draw on Isaiah 65 and 66, but 2 Peter 3:13 is unique in its emphasis on the destruction of the heavens on the day of God. In this vein, Paul writes of the creation's longing to be set free from the futility and bondage to decay, to which is linked the promise of the completion of redemption (Rom. 8:19–22). When creation is viewed in these general terms, the focus continues to be on God's intervention on the last day.

The New Creation. With this background in mind, we can now consider the two passages in which "new creation" (*kainē ktisis*) actually occurs, along with three others in Paul's writings that seem to reflect the concept.

Paul's earliest recorded use of the term occurs in Galatians 6:15. The question is, To what does the term refer? The passage shows that the issue was the proper grounds for boasting. To base one's boast on one's confidence in the rite of circumcision or one's refusal to be circumcised amounted to reliance on "the flesh," or in this case on a ceremony or ritual. Paul's point is that these things provide no grounds for confidence; only Christ's death in our behalf is sufficient (5:12–14). Verse 15 then restates this in principle form: "For neither circumcision nor uncircumcision is anything; but a new creation is everything" (NRSV). Verse 16 reveals that this has indeed the force of a principle or rule: "As for those who will follow this rule (*kanon*)." In Paul's logic, the death of Christ stands parallel with the "new creation." But the return to the personal perspective suggests that the new creation is the status of the genuine Christian that Paul has been seeking to elucidate for the misguided Galatians in the letter. The old creation would be represented by life in the flesh (1:1, 10–12; 2:16; 6:1). The new creation, which stands in need of some clarification here (though presumably the Galatians knew the concept already), is characterized by all that participation in Christ's death (5:24; 6:14) affords: new life from death (2:19–20) "in Christ" (3:26–28); "belonging" to Christ (3:29; 5:24); possession of the Spirit (3:3; 4:6); life lived in dependence on and submission to the Spirit (5:16–18, 25; 6:8). These are the images that combine to define new creation. According to Paul's theology, salvation, an eschatological promise, has begun now in the present age; the renewal, which is to affect the entire universe, has begun in the hearts and lives of those who respond to the gospel. This means for the Christian the possibility of experiencing life in the Spirit, marked by the fruit of the Spirit (5:22–23) in the present situations of life.

The same connections are evident in 2 Corinthians 5:17. In response to a situation in which some so-called superapostles were putting confidence in what Paul calls "outward appearance" (whether he means the way one carries oneself, or one's speaking ability, dress, etc.), that is, things that have no eternal significance (v. 12), he drives home again the basic fact of Christ's death for us (vv. 14–15), which should force people to view life in a different way. Again, new creation describes the condition of the one now "in Christ," for whom "everything is new." The imagery depicts the experience of renovation which, though future in final completion, has already begun in the believer. This participation in "the world to come," while yet living in the present age, brings a radical reorganizing of priorities (described as living for Christ; v. 15) and a "new" way of looking at life and the people around (v. 16).

Several passages in Ephesians (2:10, 15; 4:24) employ the verb "create" (*ktizō*) to describe aspects of the new existence in Christ. The first two are again concerned with grounds for boasting (see 2:9): salvation from God (2:8) is defined in anthropological terms as being "created in Christ" (2:10), all of which implies that there is no human ground for boasting. Then, with the Jew/Gentile debate in view—circumcision versus uncircumcision—Christ's work of "creating" a "new" humanity is introduced to demonstrate how the old distinctions and privileges have been rendered obsolete. Finally, in 4:24 Paul says that God has solved the dilemma of the old way of life (sin leading to death) by "creating" a "new" human, whose life is characterized instead by righteousness and holiness. New creation, then, is a Pauline concept in the New Testament. It is clearly related to Paul's belief that the new age (salvation, life in the Spirit) has broken into the old age. The idea of a new heavens and earth or of a renewal of the universe may be behind Paul's concept. If there is a direct relationship, what we have is Paul's anthropological and soteriological application of the broader future promise to the life of individuals in the present age. New creation status implies newness of life and a new manner of life that accords with God's will. The two thoughts are inseparable. PHILIP H. TOWNER

See also AGE, AGES; NEW HEAVENS AND A NEW EARTH; RENEWAL, RESTORATION; UNION WITH CHRIST.

Bibliography. J. Baumgarten, *EDNT,* 2:230; H. D. Betz, *Galatians*; R. Bultmann, *Theology of the New Testament;* W. D. Davies, *Paul and Rabbinic Judaism;* W. Foerster, *TDNT,* 3:1033–35; V. P. Furnish, *2 Corinthians.*

New Heavens and a New Earth. The idea of new heavens and a new earth is explicitly noted in Isaiah 65:17; 66:22; 2 Peter 3:13; and Revelation 21:1. The Old Testament has no term that directly translates as "universe"; the phrase "heavens and earth" was the Hebrew way of referring to the universe they knew. This imagery is set in prophetic-apocalyptic texts that hold forth future hope for a redeemed world that transcends the sinful world we know. It is especially noteworthy to observe how the closing chapters of Revelation reflect the motifs of Genesis 1–3. The world God originally created suffered the catastrophe of sin and all of its consequences but the future new world will be a perfect world in which the effects of sin are no longer present. The phrase in Revelation 21:1, "and there was no longer any sea," illustrates this imagery of a new perfect environment. The sea is used in apocalyptic literature as a symbol of chaos and may symbolize evil. The beast came from the sea (Rev. 13:1). The great harlot sits on many waters (Rev. 17:1). The absence of the sea in the restored universe symbolizes that the deliverance for which the creation groans has been realized (cf. Rom. 8:18–22; Rev. 21:27).

The concept of new things is a major motif in redemptive history, especially in eschatological passages. The new heavens and earth in Revelation 21 is the consummation of many new things. The crescendo for redemptive history is stated in verse 5, "everything new"! The journey toward this climax includes a new covenant (Jer. 31:31), a new name (Isa. 62:2; cf. Rev. 2:17; 3:12), a new song (Isa. 42:10; Rev. 5:9; 14:3), a new spirit/heart (Ezek. 11:19; 18:31; 36:26), new wine (Matt. 9:17; Mark 2:22; Luke 5:37–38), and the new Jerusalem (Rev. 3:12; 21:2). The concept of newness and renewal is prominent in extrabiblical apocalyptic literature as well.

The primary new heavens and new earth texts yield a variety of contexts while still focusing upon the future restoration. Isaiah 65–66 provides comfort that the devastation Israel has observed in their history is not Yahweh's ultimate intention for his people. The use of *bara*ʾ (to create) in 65:17 probably calls to mind the creation account of Genesis 1. The old and new creation thus become the terminal points of redemptive history. Second Peter 3:13, while in a context that addresses eschatological issues, is actually focused on ethics. The ethical dimension of Christian living is intensified by the prospect of the future renovation of heaven and earth. Second Peter 3:1, 11, 14, and 17 exhort godly living in light of the future. The final clause of 3:13 also highlights this nuance by noting that it will be an earth in which righteousness dwells. The call to ethics is a prominent theme in New Testament prophetic passages. The last reference is Revelation 21:1. Revelation 21–22 provides the crescendo to prophetic-apocalyptic biblical revelation. It is interesting that the imaging of eternity has humankind on a restored earth, not in God's heavenly realm. This is certainly the eternal state and not a millennial scene. The sea is gone from Revelation 21 but not from other millennial images. Human history climaxes where it all began: on the earth.

The manner in which the new heavens and earth come into existence is a matter of debate among biblical scholars. Are these descriptions purely apocalyptic genre, and thereby merely mythical symbols of an eschatological salvation without historical continuity? Or are these prophetic statements that utilize certain characteristics of apocalyptic imagery to describe the historical future? It seems wiser to speak in terms of the latter and call it prophetic-apocalyptic. Therefore, the question of the nature of bringing the new heavens and earth into existence is in regard to whether the new creation comes into existence by means of renewal (a renovation of the old) or replacement (a totally new act of creation). Such a question may be more influenced by our modern scientific curiosity than by textual indicators. The apostle John was more impressed with the fact and nature of the new order than by how it will come about. Yet part of exegesis and theology is to theorize these questions.

The replacement view claims 2 Peter 3:12b–13 as its key text. It is claimed that this tradition is reflected in Matthew 5:18 (cf. Mark 13:31; Luke 16:17) and 1 John 2:17. References in the *Didache* (10:6), 2 Clement (16:3), and 1 Enoch (72:1; 83:3–5; 91:15–16) are cited as reflecting a replacement view. Some would note that Isaiah 65:17 uses the same term as Genesis 1:1 (*bārā*ʾ, as ex nihilo is contextually dependent and does not always apply as in Genesis 1 (cf. Ps. 51:10).

The renewal (also called renovation) view is more widely represented in the literature on this subject. Second Peter 3:12b–13 is viewed as a purging of the old heaven and earth and forming it into the new. The catastrophe is comparable to Noah's flood, which was only a temporary fix. This provides a continuity and fulfillment of the purposes God began in the original creation and has now been brought to completion. There is a continuity of substance now given new form. Christ's incarnation and the believer's resurrection body provide analogies although in different realms. The term *palingenesia*, "renewal," in Matthew 19:28, argues for renovation rather than replacement. The term *kainos*, "new," in contrast to *palaios*, "old," may mean new in character rather than substance (cf. 2 Cor. 5:17; Heb. 8:13).

GARY T. MEADORS

See also NEW CREATION; RENEWAL, RESTORATION.

Bibliography. G. R. Beasley-Murray, *Revelation;* J. M. Ford, *Revelation*; W. J. Harrington, *Revelation;* P. E. Hughes, *The Book of the Revelation;* A. J. McClain, *The Greatness of the Kingdom;* J. A. Motyer, *The Prophecy of Isaiah: An Introduction and Commentary;* R. H. Mounce, *The Book of Revelation;* H. B. Swete, *Commentary on Revelation;* C. Westermann, *Isaiah 40–66.*

New Jerusalem. The eternal climax of redemptive history is previewed in John's description of the new Jerusalem in Revelation 21–22. The new Jerusalem is the focus for activity on the new earth. The new Jerusalem motif provides an elaboration of the nature of the new heavens and new earth introduced in Revelation 21:1. The first explicit reference to the new Jerusalem is in the message to the Philadelphia church in Revelation 3:12, where it is promised as a reward to those who overcome (a synonym for believers, cf. 1 John 5:4–5). Jerusalem provides an image of continuity that brings together earth and eschatological history in regard to where God and his people dwell together. The general image of a future Jerusalem symbolizes the fulfillment of many of God's promises to his people (cf. Isa. 2:1–5; 49:14–18; 52; 54; 60–62; 65:17–25; Jer. 31:38–40; Mic. 4:1–4; Zech. 14). The idea of an idealized and/or eschatological Jerusalem is referred to in other ways than the phrase "new Jerusalem." Although the Old Testament contains no explicit reference to a new Jerusalem, Isaiah includes Jerusalem in his new heavens and new earth statements (65:17–19; 66:22). Paul's allegory of the "above Jerusalem" in Galatians 4:25–26, provides an idealized imagery for Jerusalem. Hebrews 12:22 speaks of the "heavenly Jerusalem." Revelation 21:2, 10 refer to the new Jerusalem as the

"Holy City" (cf. Matt. 4:5; 27:53). Revelation 2:7, "paradise of God," may anticipate the new Jerusalem of Revelation 21–22.

The concentration on a restored Jerusalem as a symbol of the fulfillment of God's promises to the Jewish people is also present in noncanonical literature. These occurrences highlight the Jewish hope for a new world where their ideals would be fulfilled. First Enoch 90:28–29 relates a vision of a transformation of the "old house" into a new one, representing a transformed Jerusalem. Sibylline Oracles 5:414–29 record God's provision of a new city (a temple is included in contrast to Rev. 21–22, which may reflect a more earth-oriented perspective). Second Baruch 32:1–4 speaks of the new city that will be rebuilt after the old is shaken and uprooted as being "perfected into eternity" (cf. 2 Esdr. 7:26; 10:25–28; 13:36; Tob. 13:8–18; T Dan 5:12–13). Second Baruch 4 compares the new city to the original "paradise," an interesting comparison in light of Revelation 2:7. God's creative work begins and ends with paradise.

The contextual setting of the new Jerusalem in Revelation 21–22 is closely related to the evil city, Babylon, of the Great Harlot in Revelation 17–19. The linguistic comparisons of the possible terminal points of each vision are most striking (cf. 17:1–3 with 21:9–10; 19:9b–10 with 22:6–9). Both cities are also viewed as women, the harlot and the bride. God's answer to the evil structures of this world is the paradise regained in the new Jerusalem.

The meaning of the imagery of Revelation 21:9–22:5 is reasonably well established in biblical and extrabiblical patterns. The use of the bride metaphor (21:2) does not restrict the reference to the church of the new Testament, but should be viewed in its wider biblical usage as a reference to the people of God who are married to the Lord (cf. Isa. 61:10; Hos. 1–3; John 3:29; Eph. 5:25–33). Revelation 21:9 equates the images of bride and wife. The inclusion of both Israel and the church is required by the description of the city (cf. Heb. 11:10, 16). Israel's twelve tribes and the church's twelve apostles are both included. The stones (21:19–21) solicit remembrance of the high priest's breastplate (Exod. 28:17–21; 39:10–14) and Ezekiel's garden of God (28:13), although the lists are not the same and John applies the stones to the twelve apostles. The fountain of life (Rev. 21:6) and the river (22:1–2) remind one of Ezekiel 47, but in Ezekiel the river proceeds from the temple and in Revelation 22 from the throne. The new city, however, is essentially a new temple since it is God's dwelling place and the center of religious activity. The new Jerusalem is a cube of enormous proportions (12,000 furlongs is about 1,500 miles), although the use of the number 12 could be symbolic. The Holy of Holies in the temple of the Old Testament was also a cube (cf. 1 Kings 6:20). The tree of life (Rev. 22:2) hearkens back to the prefall Eden. It is noteworthy that the new Jerusalem has no sun or moon but is illuminated by the effulgence of God's glory.

How is the reality of the new Jerusalem on the new earth of Revelation 21–22 to be understood? Is it merely an allegorical description of the final state of the church with no real future new earth locality in view? Is it a literal city that may hover over the millennial earth and house the glorified church-age saints during that period and then be transferred for expanded purposes into the eternal state after the renovation of the earth (some dispensationalists; but, some nondispensationalists also apply it to the millennial period)? Is it a literal city distinctly designed as a center focus for all the redeemed in the eternal state? Is the vision of John, given in apocalyptic motifs, merely a statement in sophisticated symbolism that God will be victor in the climax of history? These and other proposals appear in the literature that addresses this interpretive aspect of the new Jerusalem. Many commentaries prefer to focus on an explanation of the larger meaning of the symbolism without addressing this question. Apocalyptic genre neither demands nor excludes a literal future city. It does, however, expect the interpreter to concentrate on the message of the symbolic motifs rather than endeavor to draw a blueprint of the structure. GARY T. MEADORS

See also NEW HEAVENS AND A NEW EARTH.

Bibliography. R. Bauckham, *The Climax of Prophecy;* G. R. Beasley-Murray, *Revelation;* M. E. Boring, *Revelation;* J. M. Ford, *Revelation;* W. J. Harrington, *Revelation;* G. E. Ladd, *A Commentary on the Revelation of John;* J. Walvoord, *The Revelation of Jesus Christ.*

New Life. God has brought his people salvation in Jesus Christ, a gift that is described throughout the Scriptures as new life. Two words are used in the New Testament to describe newness. The first, *neos,* describes that which is new in time. It is used infrequently to describe new life in Christ (Col. 3:10). The more popular and definitive term is *kainos.* It, and its derivatives, describe that which is new in nature, different from usual, better than the old, and superior in significance. Used in conjunction with *zōē, kainos* describes the essence of what God has done through Jesus Christ: he has given his children new life.

Believers begin a new life when they are born again by the Spirit (1 Peter 1:3). Regeneration places believers on the road of faith whereby they become new creations (2 Cor. 5:17) and enjoy a new life in Christ (Rom. 6:4). In spite of that reality, believers wrestle with the old nature and old self. They must seek to put on the new self (Eph. 4:24) and to follow the new commandment of Christ (1 John 2:8).

The gift of new life was foretold by the prophets in the Old Testament. Ezekiel prophesied the gift of a new heart and a new spirit (Ezek. 36:26). Jeremiah told of a new covenant (Jer. 31:31). Isaiah spoke of a new name (Isa. 62:2). The new age promised by the prophets came in Jesus Christ, the new Adam. Yet that which is presently realized by believers is only a foretaste of that which is yet to come in fullness. The apocalyptic Book of Revelation tells us that God will make everything new (21:5). He will create a new heaven and new earth (21:1), a new Jerusalem (3:12), where the saints enjoy a new name (2:17) and sing a new song (5:9).

SAM HAMSTRA, JR.

See also ETERNAL LIFE, ETERNALITY, EVERLASTING LIFE; LIFE.

New Man. Older translations use the expression "new man" to render the Greek words *neos anthrōpos*, which actually convey the idea of new self or new human with no reference to gender. Later, politically correct translations reflect this fact with greater accuracy. For example, the New Revised Standard Version and the New International Version translate the words as "new self" in Ephesians 4:24 and Colossians 3:10.

The appellation "new man" is not used in the New Revised Standard Version and appears only once in the New International Version where the expression is used in Ephesians 2:15 to refer collectively to the church, the body of Christ, which is an amalgamation of the many diverse and often discordant elements of society. Converts to Christ, whether Jew, Greek, male, female, slave, or free, have become part of one new person, the body of Jesus.

Speaking of Jews and Gentiles as disparate entities, Paul declares that Christ's "purpose was to create in himself one new man ("humanity" NRSV) out of the two, thus making peace, and in this one body to reconcile both of them to God through the cross, by which he put to death their hostility."

JOHN MCRAY

See also CHURCH, THE; NEW SELF; PAUL THE APOSTLE; UNION WITH CHRIST.

New Moon. *See* FEASTS AND FESTIVALS OF ISRAEL.

New Order. Expression found in Hebrews 9:10 that refers to the greatness of salvation provided in Jesus Christ. This meaning is clearly furnished by the context, though "new order" is a loose (NIV) translation of the Greek expression *kairou diorthōseōs* (lit. a time of setting straight).

The key to understanding the expression is to see what is meant by the "old order." Hebrews 8 announces the new covenant that made the old obsolete. Chapter 9 pursues this in regard to worship. The old order required an earthly tabernacle and priests to offer animal sacrifices. Christ, however, entered a heavenly tabernacle (vv. 11, 23–28) and offered the sacrifice of his own blood. His atonement is able to "cleanse our consciences from acts that lead to death, so that we may serve the living God" (v. 14). The old sacrificial system was defective precisely because it was not "able to clear the conscience of the worshiper" (v. 9). Therefore, access to God, symbolized by the tabernacle's Holy of Holies, is not a matter of priestly privilege but of a purified heart (v. 8; 10:15–23).

Hebrews compares Christ to four key elements of the "old order": the law (1:1–2:4), Moses' leadership (3:1–4:11), the Aaronic priesthood (4:12–8:5), and the sacrificial system (8:6–10:25). In each case Christ's superiority turns the comparison into a contrast. The "new order" is unique.

There is, then, a dialectical relationship between the "old order" and the "new order." On the one hand, the old was a necessary preparation for the new. Hebrews 9:10 acknowledges that the sacrificial regulations had a function until Christ arrived. On the other hand, the "new order" makes the old one obsolete because it completes what was incomplete, perfects what was inadequate, and makes actual what was only symbolic (10:1).

Thus, the warnings of Hebrews (2:1–4; 3:7–19; 6:1–12; 10:26–31; 12:25–29) indicate the folly of turning from the security of the "new order" to the inadequacies of the provisional order. Only in Christ is the substance of salvation to be found: the reality of sins forgiven, the confidence of spiritual access to God, and the firm hope of participating in the eternal kingdom (10:12–25; 12:26–29).

LUKE L. KEEFER, JR.

Bibliography. F. F. Bruce, *The Epistle to the Hebrews.*

New Self. Paul refers to the transformation that occurs at conversion as the creation of a new self. "Do not lie to each other, since you have taken off your old self with its practices and have put on the new self, which is being renewed in knowledge in the image of its Creator" (Col. 3:9–11). The Greek term for "new self," *neos anthrōpos*, depicts an individual, male or female, who possesses a "new nature" or "new humanity." It characterizes a metamorphosis in conduct from a life of sin to one of righteousness and is equivalent in meaning to being born again. A parallel expression occurs in 2 Corinthians 5:17 where the individual is described as a "new creation."

The process of transformation into a new self is described by Paul in Ephesians 4:22–24 as involving three stages: (1) putting off the old self, which belongs to the former way of life; (2) being made new in the attitude of one's mind; and (3) putting on the new self. The words translated "put off" and "put on" in (1) and (3) are past tense in Greek, indicating a completed action (perhaps baptism). The word "made new" in (2) is present tense, indicating a continuing development of spiritual attitude.

In this process, the former self, which was given to the gratification of human desires, is put away (Col. 3:8), stripped off like filthy clothes (v. 9). Baptism, unlike circumcision, which was the putting away of a mere piece of flesh, represented rather the stripping off of the whole body of flesh (v. 11). It s the entire former self that dies. Paul states in Romans that "our old self was crucified with him so that the body of sin might be done away with, that we should no longer be slaves to sin" (6:6).

Becoming a new person in Christ begins with the transformation of the mind. "Do not conform any longer to the pattern of this world, but be transformed by the renewing of your mind" (Rom. 12:2). However, although the decision to become a Christian may be instantaneously made, the transformation of a sinful human body into one that exemplifies the conduct appropriate to the mind of the new self (righteousness and holiness, Eph. 4:24) requires a lifetime of determination and discipline (Eph. 4:22–5:21).

Peter writes: "Like newborn babies, crave pure spiritual milk, so that by it you may grow up in your salvation" (1 Peter 2:2). For Paul, the creation of the new self is the antithesis of the decay and death of the old self, the human body: "Though outwardly we are wasting away, yet inwardly we are being renewed day by day" (2 Cor. 4:16).

This renewal is possible because the Spirit of God "helps us in our weakness" (Rom. 8:26). "If the Spirit of him who raised Jesus from the dead is living in you, he who raised Christ from the dead will also give life to your mortal bodies through his Spirit, who lives in you" (Rom. 8:11).

JOHN MCRAY

See also NEW CREATION; NEW MAN; SANCTIFICATION; SPIRITUALITY; UNION WITH CHRIST.

New Song. The newness theme is reflected throughout Scripture. Isaiah prophesied of a new order that would bring new blessings to the people of God. This new order with its attendant blessings is expressed by the climax of the newness theme in the New Testament Book of Revelation: a new name (2:17; 3:12); the new Jerusalem (3:12; 21:2); a new heaven and a new earth (21:1); and "all things new" (21:5).

The death of Jesus is a cosmic turning point, introducing the new creation (2 Cor. 5:17; Gal. 6:15). It is he who focuses and culminates newness. The new song of Revelation 5 praises the Lamb for his worthiness to carry out God's redemptive plan, employing motifs from the exodus of Israel. This redemptive work includes four qualitative aspects: (1) it is for God; (2) it is accomplished through Christ's blood; (3) it is universal (every tribe, tongue, people, and nation); and (4) it establishes God's kingdom or rule. The new song therefore encapsulates the theology of Revelation: the redemptive work of Christ is the sine qua non for the establishment of God's kingdom.

The new song of Revelation 14:3 is sung by the 144,000 who have been redeemed from the earth. Despite the intense debate over the identity of these 144,000, the emphasis is the same: praise for God's (Christ's) redemption. The controversy over the singers should not obscure the importance of the song! The debate has been complicated by a textual problem in 5:9–10 and the symbolism of 144,000 (a multiple of seven, a highly symbolic number in Scripture). In spite of our ignorance of specifics, of utmost importance is the praise God's creatures bring to him for his mighty redemptive acts. These redemptive acts are rehearsed and celebrated in the hymnic portions of Revelation (4:8, 11; 5:9–10, 12–13; 7:10, 12; 11:15, 17–18; 15:3–4; 19:1–2, 3, 5, 6–8; 22:20). One could say that there is one new song but this song has many stanzas. All of God's redeemed will add stanzas to that song throughout eternity as they praise him progressively and continually for his mercy, love, and grace to the children of men in both the exodus from Egypt and the cross of Calvary.

CARL B. HOCH, JR.

Numbers, Symbolic Meaning of. ***The Old Testament.*** The ancient Babylonians and Egyptians had a developed numerology based on astrological divination, which is forbidden in the Hebrew Scriptures. The ancient Chaldeans sectioned the stars into twelve regions. Numerology is also consequential in Hinduism, Buddhism, Magic texts, and other occultic, pagan religions.

In contrast to the numerical speculation of Gentile religions, the Hebrew Scriptures use numbers in their conspicuous, literal sense, although occasionally numbers may have a representative meaning (cf. the more symbolic numerical use in Gen. 4:24 and the literal use in 14:14). For example, the large numbers of the ages of the progenitors in Genesis 5 is to be taken literally, not figuratively. The symbolic use of numbers in the Hebrew Scriptures is quite different from the speculation of pagan religions. The symbolic, even poetic use of numbers in the Bible is not inordinate speculation concerning the universe. Even in the later, more apocalyptic texts of Daniel and Isaiah, prophetic symbolism is rooted in historical data. The association of numbers and polytheism in pagan religions is absent in the monotheism of Israel.

The creation of the world was completed in six days. The earliest use of "seven" (the Hebrew word is spelled out, as are all numbers in the Bible) is likely less symbolic than the later, more symbolic use. In fact, the world's completion in six days and the subsequent day of rest to complete the week is a key reason why "seven" symbolized completion and goodness in later apocalyptic texts. The Sabbath was implemented in terms of set days, weeks, and years (e.g., Dan. 9:24).

"Ten" was the number of the Decalogue. Its significance is to be taken literally and there does not seem to be any further meaning intended. "Twelve" is the number of the tribes of Israel, and it, too, should be regarded as literal. Even though there are twelve months in the year, this symbology is unsatisfactory, and there is probably no connection. The lack of chimerical uses of numbers attests to the functional and responsible nature of the Hebrew Scriptures, especially when compared to other religious texts in the ancient world.

Second Temple Jewish Literature. Second temple Jewish literature should be discussed briefly, as it influenced the New Testament use of numbers greatly, especially the Book of Revelation. One can see a trend in late Old Testament apocalyptic literature toward a cryptic use of numbers. For example, in Daniel 4:16 it is predicted in a vision that Nebuchadnezzar will have the mind of an animal until "seven times pass over him." Daniel 8:8 mentions the "four winds of heaven." This tendency toward a clandestine use of numbers is developed in Jewish pseudepigraphical texts.

The New Testament. "Number" comes from the Greek noun *arithmos* or the Greek verb *arithmeō*, which means "to reckon," "to number," or "to count." As in the Old Testament, numbers almost always carry a literal connotation (e.g., Matt. 16:21; Mark 9:2; Acts 11:10; 1 Cor. 15:5; 2 Peter 2:5; Rev. 1:4). Sometimes numbers are rounded off (e.g., John 6:10, 19); at other times hyperbole is used (e.g., Matt. 18:12, 22) to heighten a specific point.

Paul, borrowing from commonplace Jewish apocalyptic beliefs, says that he was "caught up to the third heaven" (2 Cor. 12:2). The third heaven was the place of revelation in the sevenfold schema of second temple apocalyptic literature. It is unclear whether Paul actually believed in multiple heavens, although he probably did as evidenced by his plural use of "heavens" in Colossians regarding the resurrection of Christ.

The most enigmatic use of numbers in the New Testament is found in Revelation. It should not be surprising that many idiosyncratic theories have developed concerning the meaning of the use of numbers in Revelation, most notably, the designation of "666" (spelled out in the Greek text) in 13:18. No other verse in the New Testament designates, in a cryptogrammatic fashion, the hidden nature of the number.

Some ancient manuscripts designate the number as "616," but "666" has the incontrovertible support of all the oldest and best manuscripts. Irenaeus points out that scribes changed the number to "616" to align with the Roman emperor Caligula.

The designation of a modern "antichrist" presumes a futuristic interpretation that has been widely criticized. Gematria, the practice of assigning numerical values to the letters in a word or phrase, is found in classical and Hellenistic Greek, early Hebrew, and rabbinic literature. The practice of gematria was used as early as the second century A.D. in an attempt to discover the identity of the person intended in 13:18, which reveals that there was no set tradition concerning the number's identification.

Even though it is impossible to know for certain the identity of "666," a conspicuous designation is "Caesar Nero" because the title/name equaled 666 in Hebrew numerical value. Irenaeus suggested Titus or the Roman Empire, both of which point to a nonfuturistic interpretation.

Regardless of the meaning of the number, the passage makes it clear that the number is being used as a symbolic reference to a person. The text reads "a number of a human" (Greek *anthropos,* not *andros,* the Greek word for "man"). The language presumes that the readers understood the number's designation. In keeping with the historical nature of Daniel's symbolic use of numbers, it is likely that Revelation, which borrows heavily from the imagery of Daniel, roots the symbolism of "666" in historical data, not the imaginative guesswork of later rabbinics.

The biblical method of using numbers is not common to the haphazard conjecture of some modern interpreters, who claim that a sort of allegory lies behind the true meaning of the numbers of Revelation. Apocalyptic numerology should not be confused with eccentric interpretation. Apocalyptic literature is highly developed in its symbolism. When one is familiar with this genre of literature, a more historical, less arbitrary interpretation prevails.

"Seven" figures prominently in Revelation. The seven plagues represent judgment in its completion. The "seven churches in Asia" are to be taken literally, not figuratively, although the number may have been rounded out to fit the number seven. The meaning of "seven golden lampstands," and "seven stars" in 1:12, 16 are given in 1:20. The seven-branched menorah is apparently used as a symbol of the seven churches of Asia Minor, possibly as the representative light of Torah as incarnated through Jesus Christ.

It is debated what the meaning of the "twenty-four thrones" and "twenty-four elders" in 4:4 signifies besides the manifest description given concerning a scene in heaven. The "four living creatures" are four angels in the celestial scene. "Seven flaming torches" are said to refer to the "seven spirits of God." The "seven spirits" is probably a reference to the Holy Spirit. In Isaiah 11:2

the Spirit functions in seven ways. Revelation 1:4 may have Isaiah 11:2 in mind.

Twelve thousand people from each of the twelve tribes of Israel equal 144,000 people from Israel (7:4–8), all with God's seal on their forehead. The meaning of this number has been debated and it is difficult to ascertain its meaning, but one thing is clear: Israel, as God's remnant, is marked out in God's program through the apocalyptic tumult.

The "four corners of the earth" and the "four winds of the earth" is keeping with second temple use of the numeral four as representing the earth.

The meaning of the beast with seven heads, ten horns, and seven diadems (12:3) is given in 17:9, 12: "The seven heads are seven mountains on which the woman is seated. Also they are seven kings"; "The ten horns that you saw are ten kings." It may be that Rome, the "city of seven hills," was thought of as the amalgamation of the Gentile nations. In any case, the number seven here represents Gentile, pagan nations perhaps in their consummation. The numbers are representative with a historical undercurrent with literal significance, not simply allegorical and capricious in nature.

There are many other numbers in Revelation that cannot be deciphered. But in general, Revelation is more panoramic than allowed by some, and deals with Jews and Gentiles in a sweeping fashion. Attempts to immoderately particularize events and numbers trivializes the nature of this Jewish apocalypse. ERIC W. ADAMS

Bibliography. J. J. Davis, *Biblical Numerology;* L. E. Dickson, *History of the Theory of Numbers;* W. M. W. Roth, *Numerical Sayings in the Old Testament: A Form Critical Study;* E. D. Schmitz, C. J. Hemer, M. J. Harris, and C. Brown, *NIDNTT,* 2:683–704.

Numbers, Theology of. Integral to a discussion of the theology of Numbers is an understanding of the book's structure and its relationship to the rest of the Pentateuch. Chronologically Numbers covers Israel's thirty-eight-year wilderness period from the second year after the exodus (10:11–12) until the arrival at the border of the promised land (33:38) while geographically it moves from Mount Sinai to the plains of Moab. Yet neither of these aspects appears to supply the primary motivation for the book's structure. The earlier dates of 7:1 and 9:1 suggest that strict chronological arrangement was not the primary concern and the great visibility given to the beginning and end of the wilderness period while most of the thirty-eight years pass in silence suggests a reason other than geographical locations for its arrangement. The best position seems to be with those scholars who hold that the book was arranged primarily with theological concerns in mind.

Numbers is a book of practical theology and emphasizes the interaction between the sovereign God and his people as recent recipients of the covenant stipulations. Marked by direct address Numbers shows the people's dependence upon God for daily guidance and provisions. This fourth book of the Pentateuch continues many of the themes of the previous three books and anticipates the promised land that becomes so prevalent in the fifth. Therefore, any discussion of a theology of Numbers must be done in relationship to the rest of the Pentateuch.

Numbers portrays God as a God of order. Israel's quick release from Egyptian bondage into an unknown land necessitated a certain amount of structure for the tribes and their families. This book depicts the growth of order in Israel's society as a direct result of God's blessing. In Numbers the distinction between the priests and Levites is presented as the work of God (8:19; 18:1–20) as is the selection of seventy elders to lead the people (11:25). Furthermore, the people witness the transition of leadership from Aaron to Eleazer (20:25–28) and from Moses to Joshua (27:16–23) under God's direction. The theme of God's orderliness, apparent from the days of creation in Genesis, is also reflected in the census lists, camp arrangement, and the order of march.

At God's initiation, a census was taken before and after the wilderness wanderings. For the families and tribes these enumerations provided increased individual significance but for the reader they accentuate the fact that evil and rebellion will not ultimately deter the plan of God (11:23). The camp arrangement, also specified by God, provided order in the midst of a great number of people. It allowed for orderly assemblies that were called by trumpets, clear delineation of duties like those assigned to the levitical families, and military protection since the bulk of the men of arms encircled the Levites and tabernacle. The tabernacle in the midst of the camp and the ark in the tabernacle underscored the centrality of God.

Emphasis on covenant promises along with the blessings and curses of the covenant give further testimony to the continuity of Numbers with the rest of the Pentateuch. The multiplication of Israel, portrayed by the numbering of the people, along with the anticipation of the land remind the reader of the promises given by the Lord to Abraham (Gen. 12:1–3; 17:4–8). Consistent with the covenant blessings and curses the Lord provided a way for the priests to bless the people (6:24–27) yet he cursed those who would disobey; whether unbelieving Israel in rebellion (14:29–35) or the nations who opposed his blessing of Israel (21:1–3). So indelible was this promise that the words of Balaam's mouth were guided to produce blessings rather than imprecations against Israel (24:8–9).

The covenant is also an expression of God's faithfulness to his own word. The first census provides an enumeration of those who left Egypt and Sinai but becomes a roster of unbelief

(14:29) while the second census provides graphic testimony to the faithfulness of God in bringing his people through the wilderness despite their sin, for even with a shift of numbers among the tribes the total number of the new generation remains essentially the same (1:46; 26:51). God's sovereignty insured covenant stability (23:19).

Grumbling and rebellion are not new themes for Numbers. What is new is the accompanying discipline or judgment by God. God works with his people and holds them accountable for their actions. Instances of the people's rebellious actions permeate the text of Numbers, beginning with their departure from Sinai (11:1) and continuing to the border of Edom (21:4–9). This creates the desired effect that rebellion along with God's judgment was characteristic of the wilderness period. Both groups and individuals took part. Dissatisfaction arose from the people in general (14:1), the Levites (16:1), and even the leaders (12:1) underscoring the pervasiveness of disbelief.

God's reaction to Israel's rebellion was anger (11:1, 10, 33; 12:9) or the manifestation of his glory (14:10; 16:19, 42; 20:6). Results of the rebellions appear to be progressive in their severity beginning with some who were consumed at the edge of camp (11:1–3) and moving to increasing numbers who die (250 in 16:35 to 14,700 in 16:49). The final rebellion, however, is answered by God's merciful provision of a bronze snake lifted in their midst and accompanied by the instruction to look and live (21:4–9).

These tests by God were met by the people's continued failure whereas Moses responded with intercession for his people and an increasing awareness of God's work in their midst. Yet even Moses, distressed by the continued rebellion of his people, transgressed the limits of the Lord and was disciplined for it. For this violation of God's holiness Moses lost the privilege of leading Israel into the promised land (20:10–12).

One of the key theological themes of Numbers, continued from Exodus–Leviticus, is the holiness of God. It is this aspect of God's character, considered by some to be the central theme of the book, which provides the reason for many of the requirements and commands found in Numbers.

Holiness, directly associated with the presence of God (5:3; 35:34), necessitated that unclean persons (5:1; 19:11–20), events (5:6–7), or objects (31:22–23) be cleansed or be removed from the camp. In addition, priests and Levites, the divine caretakers and mediators of God's holiness, had to be purified before they could serve (8:21) and they alone were charged with the oversight of the holy things (4:4), which they could not touch (4:15) or even look at (4:20)! Violation of the holiness of God or his commands brought plague (8:19), exile (5:3; 12:14), or death (9:13; 15:35).

The grace of God, also evident in Numbers, should be understood in relationship to his holiness. His willingness to forgive Israel was seen as a manifestation of his grace but not in opposition to his holiness (14:18–19). The people were held responsible for their actions (14:22–23, 40–41) and Moses' challenge—"be sure that your sin will find you out" (32:23)—was a reminder of their continued responsibility as they anticipated entering the land.

The Lord's presence, symbolized by the ark, was manifested by the cloud and fire that led Israel from place to place (9:17–18; 33:1–49). His desire for his people was for them to be holy but at least one group attempted to turn this holy calling against God's choice of Moses and Aaron in order to provoke a rebellion (16:3). God, however, provided the distinctions of holiness in choosing the priests to serve him (16:5) and in distinguishing between the clean and the unclean (18:15–17). God's people were called to echo that holiness in attitude and action (19:20; 25:11–13). Their desire to return to Egypt was an evidence of unbelief (14:3, 11), a violation of their holy calling (32:11), and a rejection of the grace of his presence and provision (11:20).

Failure to obey and failure to evidence his holiness was sin, another key theme of Numbers. The sinfulness of God's people is emphasized in the book by the many rebellions and the ensuing judgment from God. The well-known thirty-eight years of wandering, a direct result of God's judgment upon their unbelief, is only one of many such lapses.

The major theological theme developed in the New Testament from Numbers is that sin and unbelief, especially rebellion, reap the judgment of God. First Corinthians specifically says (and Heb. 3:7–4:13 strongly implies) that these events were written as examples for the believer to observe and avoid (1 Cor. 10:6, 11).

Numbers, however, affirms that sin and rebellion will not thwart the purposes of God. A generation is lost but the plan of God moves forward. God's intercessor speaks for the people and God forgives (14:19–20). The people rebel, repent, and rebel again but God continues to move them toward the promised land. Eventually the land comes in sight and they continue to witness the gracious provision of God.

Anticipation of the promised land is on the horizon throughout the Book of Numbers but it increasingly comes into focus as God's gift and the fulfillment of his promise toward the end of the wilderness journeys. The diversity of topics found in chapter 21 (after the deaths of Aaron and Miriam) conclude the rebellion narratives, announce movement toward the promised land, and anticipate the Balaam oracles where Israel's success over its enemies and the neighboring nations are prophetically stated. The main emphasis on the land is found in chapters 26–36. Here, matters of inheritance, land boundaries, and future regulations look forward to possession of the long-awaited gift from God.

Among the most intriguing passages in Numbers are the Balaam oracles. These chapters (22–24), which do not mention Moses, offer powerful testimony to the sovereignty of God. God controls the mouth of the donkey and the mouth of Balaam. Emphasizing the covenant of Abraham, the curse becomes a blessing (23:8, 20, 25–26; 24:9), a fact which Balaam recognizes and a major theme of the oracles. In addition, the size, beauty, prosperity, strength, and victory of Israel, all alluded to by Balaam, attest to God's continued work with his people and the blessings which lie ahead. Balaam's oracles include a striking statement about the nature of God as being not human but truthful (23:19) and a promise linking the Messiah with the tribe of Judah (24:17). Such positive messages on the heels of the wilderness period bear witness to God's elective grace toward Israel.

In the canon, Numbers relates most directly to material from the Pentateuch but both the Old Testament and New Testament make frequent reference to the wilderness period and events from that time. Jesus himself uses the lifting of the serpent in the wilderness as a type of his crucifixion (John 3:14). The Old Testament assesses the wilderness wanderings from a dual perspective, understanding it both as a time of rebellion and sin and as a time of God's grace and provision. Both perspectives are true and are not to be set against each other but, instead, reveal God's relationship and work with his people as preparatory—a perspective reflected by Moses' statement that "the LORD has promised good things to Israel" (10:29).

ROBERT D. SPENDER

See also ISRAEL; MOSES.

Bibliography. P. J. Budd, *Numbers;* B. Childs, *Introduction to the Old Testament as Scripture;* G. W. Coats, *Rebellion in the Wilderness;* V. P. Hamilton, *Handbook of the Pentateuch;* R. K. Harrison, *Numbers;* J. Milgrom, *Numbers;* J. Oswalt, *ZPEB,* 4:462–68; G. J. Wenham, *Numbers.*

Obadiah, Theology of. Obadiah, the shortest Old Testament book with only twenty-one verses, was probably written shortly after the fall of Judah and Jerusalem to the Babylonians in 587 B.C. (see 2 Kings 25). The author, unknown apart from his name heading this message from God, brings hope to God's people who have been devastated by the recent events.

Hope envelops the book even in identifying the source of the message as "the LORD" in the first and last verses (see also vv. 4, 8, 15, 18). This is the usual English rendering of the personal, covenant name of Yahweh/Jehovah, Israel's God. Yahweh had promised Abram a special relationship with himself (Gen. 12:1–3). This intimacy was expanded through the covenant that Yahweh made through Moses with Abram's descendants at Mount Sinai (Exod. 19–24). God renewed and expanded his unique covenant relationship with David (2 Sam. 7), with special places reserved for Zion as his capital and his sons as kings.

Judah, facing a destroyed capital and deposed king, feared that God was either dead or had forgotten or abandoned them because of their sins. Imagine their relief when he addressed them in this oracle not only with words of encouragement, but even using his special, intimate, covenant name. He is still their God, and they are still his people in spite of their sin.

Obadiah also provided the people concrete hope in that he declared the defeat of a perennial enemy, Edom. These people are portrayed in the Bible as related to the Israelites, being descendants of Esau (Gen. 36, especially vv. 1, 9), though they did not get along well with each other during most of their history. Edom troubled Israel during the exodus wanderings (Num. 20:14–21; 24:18), and often during the monarchy (1 Sam. 14:47; 2 Sam. 8:13–14; 1 Kings 9:26–28; 11:15–16; 2 Chron. 20:1–2; 25:11–12). While not confirmed by any other historical sources, Edom, which became a vassal first of Assyria and later of Babylonia, is credited with burning the temple in Jerusalem when Jerusalem fell to Babylon in 587 B.C. (1 Esdras 4:45).

Edom is the subject of the first part of Obadiah. Though considering itself impregnable due to its geographical setting in the inaccessible mountain crags of Transjordan (v. 3), it is not able to escape the wrath of its most powerful enemy. God, who has a special place in his heart and his promises for his people Israel, looms even higher than Edomite strongholds. He will repay their pride in thinking that they are so secure that they can blatantly oppose his people without reprisal (v. 4). It seems from the prophecy itself that Edom had not only stood by while Judah was under attack, but had gloated over its plight, even entering the capital, possibly to plunder, and also had turned over refugees to the conquerors in cold-blooded disregard for kinship loyalty (vv. 11–14).

God promised not to leave Judah unavenged, but swiftly acted in judgment. Within the century, Edom's fortunes started to slide, finally losing its land to the Arabs, though its ethnic presence is still evident in southern Transjordan and Palestine (see Neh. 2:19; 4:7; 6:1), even in the later name of the Negev region in southern Palestine as Idumaea (1 Macc. 4:29).

This response of judgment shows that opposition to God, whether direct or indirect, as here with the Edomites acting against his chosen people, will not go unnoticed. God, who is just and holy, takes appropriate action in his time. This punishment of its enemies brought some measure of comfort and vindication to Israel.

The second part of the book (from v. 15) shifts from a focus on Edom to the whole world. Edom is an example of God ultimately calling all nations to account for their deeds. As a day of judgment comes for Edom (v. 8), a wider-scale day of the lord (v. 15) will bring judgment for all.

Punishment is closely related to the wrongdoing that caused it. The proud (v. 2) face humiliation (v. 3) and those who watched the looting of their neighbor (vv. 11–14) will suffer the same fate themselves (vv. 5–9). Those who endanger survivors of destruction (v. 14) will have no survivors themselves (v. 18); those who drive their kin from home and land (v. 14) will themselves be driven out (vv. 7, 19). This theological principle of lex talionis, or a crime resulting in a related and appropriate punishment, is specifically stated in verse 15. Common in the Old Testament, it shows that judgment is not capricious, brought simply by the whom of a fickle God. It follows the breach of a known law. This punishment, oddly enough, provides security for the followers of a God who reveals himself. Either in Israel or today, one does not have to second guess a deity who can change his mind and expectations at any time. Yahweh's person and desires are known, as are his rewards for those who respect them. David W. Baker

See also Israel; Prophet, Prophetess, Prophecy.

Bibliography. L. C. Allen, *The Books of Joel, Obadiah, Jonah and Micah;* D. W. Baker, *Obadiah.*

Obedience. To obey or not to obey the Lord God—this has been and is the crucial question for every human being. Obedience as opposed to disobedience is a life-and-death issue. God has given humankind the innate power of choice: the choice of obedience leads to God's promised blessing of life; the choice of disobedience leads to curse, judgment, and death.

God's clear instructions to the very first human beings in the garden of Eden was to refrain from eating the fruit of the tree of knowledge of good and evil (Gen. 2:16). He expected their obedience. They disobeyed, thereby losing initial favor with God. Nonetheless, they were restored to favor when God granted them the privileged role of being the first parents of all subsequent generations of humankind.

The obedience of Abraham is perhaps most exemplary in the Old Testament. On two occasions, he demonstrated total submission to God's will. First, he obeyed God's command to go to a new land (Gen. 12). This response meant leaving Ur of the Chaldees, a highly developed city, to go to the unknown, unfamiliar land that God would show to him—the land of Canaan. Abraham's obedience results in his being elected a chosen one for a special role in God's salvation-plan for humankind. Second, he obeyed God's command to offer his son as a sacrifice (Gen. 22:1–19).

Obedience was a main concern during the time of the encampment of the people of Israel at the base of Mount Sinai, to which God directed Moses to lead them after their deliverance from the Egyptians. There God, with Moses as mediator, provided the people with general and specific stipulations for conforming to his will. At Mount Sinai God established a special covenant relationship between himself and the people of Israel. He also gave them the Decalogue or "Ten Words" (Exod. 20:1–17), which constituted a list of basic moral and religious guidelines for those who were in this special relationship with God.

The call to be obedient underlies two or more key verses of the Pentateuch. One is Leviticus 19:2: "Be holy because I, the Lord your God, am holy." Obedience should emanate from a commitment to live a holy life before God and others in the covenant community. A second key passage is Deuteronomy 6:4–5: "Hear, O Israel: The Lord our God, the Lord is one. Love the Lord your God with all your heart and with all your soul and with all your strength." This is a divine call, urging a total love for God that results in unhesitating obedience to his will.

Unfortunately, obedience on the part of Israel was preempted by disobedience as the predominant characteristic of the nation's history. Only a small segment of God's chosen people chose to follow his word. During most of the two-kingdom times, gross apostasy and disobedience were widespread. During the course of Israel's history, Deuteronomic theology (see Deut. 28:15–68)—if obedient, blessing; if disobedient, then curse/judgment—remained operative. The massive turning away from God and the refusal to heed the prophets' warnings left God no alternative but to exercise his judgment and to destroy both kingdoms.

The prophets called for a new covenant, which would resolve the problem of failure to remain obedient to God. Jeremiah, after denouncing the unfaithfulness of God's people, made the pronouncement of this covenant (31:31–34). This covenant would be placed in the people's minds and in the people's hearts. Jeremiah provides details of how in "new covenant" times obedience will have first and only place. The law of God in hearts and minds will preclude any sinful acts against God and fellow humankind.

The reality of this new covenant was portrayed in Jesus' supreme example of obedience to the heavenly Father, when he gave himself as the ultimate sacrifice for atonement of sin.

Jesus' emphasis on being born again underscores the need of atonement for effecting forgiveness of sins. Jesus talks to Nicodemus about being born again or "from above" as the requirement for entering the kingdom of God (John 3:3–6). The way of death would be thus changed to the way of life.

Jesus prayed that his disciples would be sanctified, be made inwardly holy, and thereby be enabled to live a holy life outwardly (John 17:6–19). Provision for this inner holiness and cleansing—requisite for true obedience—was effected by his atoning sacrifice on the cross.

The Holy Spirit is provided to all who believe in Jesus. The Spirit's abiding presence enables all

God's people to carry out God's will and to live obediently before him. HARVEY E. FINLEY

Bibliography. W. Brueggeman, *Interpretation and Obedience;* P. C. Craigie, *The Book of Deuteronomy;* W. E. McCumber, *Holy God, Holy People: Holiness in Matthew, Mark, and Luke;* R. S. Taylor, *Exploring Christian Holiness.*

Offense. Two Greek words are translated "offense": *scandalon* and *proskomma.* Both carry the connotation of "sinfulness" or "stumbling block."

The key Old Testament verse that is quoted several times in the New Testament and formulates the significant function of Christ as the "rock of offense" is Isaiah 8:14: "He will become a sanctuary, a stone one strikes against; for both houses of Israel he will become a rock one stumbles over—a trap and a snare for the inhabitants of Jerusalem" (NRSV). Paul applies the concept to coming to Christ by faith in Romans 9:32. Christ, as the cornerstone of the analogical temple, is stumbled over by those who approach him by works. The offense of the cross is the idea that equality of Jews and Gentiles is established through faith.

Isaiah 28:16 is used in conjunction with the concept of stumbling over Christ in 1 Peter 2:5–8. The emphasis of 1 Peter is holiness of one's life before God and the subsequent rejection of the pagan nations. It is interesting that Paul, the apostle to the Gentiles, applies the notion of stumbling to the Jews as those who stumbled; in 1 Peter, the "apostle to the Jews" applies the concept to disobedient ones who were "destined" for stumbling. The reference may be to Gentiles.

In 1 Peter 2:12 the admonition is to "conduct yourselves honorably among the Gentiles"—a reference to Jews living holy and separate in terms of moral purity, which was always the design for Jews. Therefore, the "scandal" of the cross was that both Jews and Gentiles stumbled over the rock because they did not approach him by faith. Some Jews were prideful in their nationalistic heritage, which Paul addresses in Romans 9–11, and some Gentiles were disobedient as they had always been, which may be what is addressed in 1 Peter 2. Because faith equalized both Jews and Gentiles, the offense of the cross was that one could not approach Christ pridefully or in terms of nationalistic superiority.

Paul points out by asking a rhetorical question in Galatians 5:11 that the Jewish nationalistic requirement of circumcision has been removed for Gentiles, which is the "offense of the cross." In other words, the offense to the Jews is that there is no favoritism of Jews over Gentiles; they are equal. Paul says in 1 Corinthians 1:23: "We preach Christ crucified, a stumbling block (*scandalon*) to the Jews and foolishness to Gentiles" (NRSV).

The concept of "offense" is used elsewhere in the New Testament as well. In general, the idea is used to donate a person who seeks to trip up the innocent. In Matthew 16:23 Jesus calls Peter a "stumbling block" because he had his mind on human things and was unable to see the divine design of the cross. ERIC W. ADAMS

See also SIN.

Offerings and Sacrifices. The Old Testament regulations for offerings and sacrifices are renowned for their many and complicated details, and the overall sacrificial system is quite foreign to our Western culture. Yet one could hardly overestimate the significance of the Old Testament sacrificial system for the theology of the Bible. Even before the revelation to Moses at Sinai, offerings and sacrifices were a key part of the practice of relationship with God from Cain and Abel, to Noah, to the patriarchs, to Jethro the priest of Median, to the ratification of the Mosaic covenant by sacrifice before the tabernacle was built. They remained central to the ritual systems of the tabernacle and the first and second temples and, therefore, to the Old Testament theology of God's "presence" and his relationship to ancient Israel as his "kingdom of priests." When God became present with us by means of the incarnation of Jesus Christ the Old Testament offerings and sacrifices continued to yield much in terms of Jesus as our sacrifice, Jesus as our High Priest, and our Christian commitment and ministry as a sacrifice to God of ourselves and our kingdom labors.

The Old Testament. The Hebrew expression "to present an offering" is a combination of the verb "to present, bring near, offer" (*hiqrîb*) and its cognate noun "offering" (*qorbān*). The Hebrew word normally translated "sacrifice" (*zebaḥ*) does not occur in Leviticus 1–3 until 3:1 in the introduction to the "peace offering" section (see also vv. 3, 6, 9). The term for "offering" continues to be used there (vv. 1, 2, 6, 7, 8, 12, 14). Thus, one can say that the peace offering was a particular kind of "offering" that was also a "sacrifice"—it involved an animal that was killed and then eaten as part of a communal meal.

In this article the word "offering" will be used as a comprehensive term including both grain and animal offerings. "Sacrifice" will refer only to animal offerings.

Offerings and Sacrifices outside *the Sanctuary.* According to the earthen altar law in Exodus 20:24–26 and the many references to such altars in the early history of Israel as a nation in the land of Canaan, the Lord clearly intended that the Israelites perpetuate the practice of building solitary altars and worshiping at them even after the tabernacle altar existed. These altars and the practice of worship at them were relatively simple compared to that called for in the "sanctuary" (i.e., the tabernacle and later the temple). The sanctuary included a corresponding burnt offering altar but it was also an actual residence of God. The sanctuary system of offerings and sacrifices included the major features of the previously existing external system (i.e., the burnt, grain, drink, and peace offerings at the solitary altars), but the solitary altar system did not include sin and guilt offerings.

Even as early as Genesis 4:3–5 Cain brought an offering to the Lord from the fruit of the ground and Abel brought one from his flock. The Hebrew term for both offerings in this context is *minḥâ*, which can be either a general term for "offering, gift, present, tribute" or a specialized term from "grain offering." Some have argued that Cain's offering was rejected precisely because, not being an animal offering, it did not include blood atonement. A better explanation is that the lack of descriptive terms such as "firstfruits" for Cain's offering is conspicuous for its absence in light of the description of Abel's offering as "fat portions" and "firstborn" (Gen. 4:3b–4a). Cain's response only made matters progressively worse and may indicate that there was a preexisting problem in Cain's relationship with both God and Abel.

The first reference to "burnt offerings" is Genesis 8:20, where it is said that "Noah built an altar to the LORD, and, taking some off all the clean animals and clean birds, he sacrificed *burnt offerings* on it." The word for "sacrifice" (*zebaḥ*) first occurs in Genesis 31:54 in the covenant-making ceremony between Jacob and Laban: "He [Jacob] offered a *sacrifice* there in the hill country and invited his relatives to a meal" (cf. Gen. 46:1). These two terms occur together in Exodus 10:25, where Moses explained to Pharaoh, "You must allow us to have *sacrifices* and *burnt offerings* to present to the LORD our God."

The first occurrence of the term "peace offering" (*šĕblāmîm*, NIV "fellowship offering") is in Exodus 20:24, where the Lord refers to it along with "burnt offerings" as part of the altar law: "Make an altar of earth for me and sacrifice on it your *burnt offerings* and *fellowship offerings*, your sheep and goats and your cattle. Wherever I cause my name to be honored, I will come to you and bless you." Finally, all three terms appear together in Exodus 24:4–5 in the ritual for the ratification of the covenant at Mount Sinai: "He [Moses] got up early the next morning and built an [earthen] altar at the foot of the mountain. . . . Then he sent young Israelite men, and they offered *burnt offerings* and sacrificed young bulls as *fellowship offerings* to the Lord" (here the NIV translates the apposition "sacrifices, fellowship offerings" simply as "fellowship offerings"; both terms are there in Hebrew).

After the tabernacle had been established the nation continued to offer burnt, grain, drink, and peace offerings on solitary earthen altars as well as on the altar in the tabernacle. In fact, the Lord himself commanded that they build such an altar at Shechem (i.e., Mount Ebal) and offer burnt and peace offerings there as part of the initial covenant ceremony in the land (Deut. 27:5–7). At least part of the purpose of this ceremony appears to have been to lay claim to the land that the Lord had promised Abram long before when he first entered the land and built an altar in the same general location, near Shechem (Gen. 12:6–7). In some cases such altars and the burnt and/or peace offerings presented on them were a means of calling on the name of the Lord in specific situations (see, e.g., Gideon in Judg. 6:24–27, the Benjamites in Judg. 21:3–4, Samuel in 1 Sam. 7:8–10, David in 2 Sam. 24:25, and Elijah in 1 Kings 18:23–24, 30, 36–39). In other instances altars on high places were used for communal sacrificial meals before the Lord.

Offerings and Sacrifices inside *the Sanctuary.* From a literary point of view, the rules for burnt, grain, and peace offerings in Leviticus 1–3 is a unified whole. The repetition of the introductory formula and address to "the sons of Israel" in Leviticus 4:1–2 separates the rules for sin and guilt offerings in Leviticus 4:1–6:7 from those in Leviticus 1–3. This seems to be a literary reflection of the historical reality that before and even after the construction of the tabernacle the burnt offerings (Heb. *ʿōlâ*) and peace offerings (Heb. *šĕblāmîm* or *zebaḥ*, "sacrifice," or some combination of the two; see below), and the grain offerings that often came with them (Heb. *minḥâ*; see Lev. 2 and Num. 15:1–16), constituted a system of offerings used by the faithful at solitary Yahwistic altars outside the tabernacle (see above).

The burnt offering. The burnt offering could be from the cattle (Lev. 1:3–9), the sheep and goats (vv. 10–13), or the birds (vv. 14–17; usually limited to the poor, e.g., Lev. 12:8; 14:22). Amid the diversity of different kinds of animal offerings and the many distinctive ways they were offered to the Lord it appears that there was one constant in the presentation of sacrificial animals: the laying on of the hand (or pl. hands if more than one person was involved). The purpose of this act was to identify the offerer with his or her offering and possibly also to designate or consecrate the offering for the purposes of the offering: "He is to lay his hand on the head of the burnt offering, and it will be accepted on his behalf to make atonement for him" (Lev. 1:4). The laying on of the hand did not transfer anything to the offering animal, least of all sin. Only holy things could have contact with the altar. In the scapegoat ritual the high priest was to lay *both* hands on the animal and confess the sins of the whole congregation in order to expressly transfer the sins to the goat. But in that case the animal was not offered upon the altar but instead sent as far away from the altar as possible (e.g., Lev. 16:21–22).

The normal form of blood manipulation for the burnt offering was relatively simple: the priest would "splash it around on the altar" (Lev. 1:5). This was not just a way of disposing of the blood, but a way of offering it on the altar. It corresponded to arranging the pieces of the animal's carcass on the altar (Lev. 1:8–9).

The offerer normally slaughtered the animal, but the priests placed its various parts on the altar fire (Lev. 1:7–9a) "to burn all of it on the altar" as a "burnt offering, an offering made by fire, an aroma pleasing to the LORD" (v. 9b). The basic principle behind the burnt offering was that the whole animal was offered on the altar, that is, with the exception of the hide of the larger animals that had been skinned as part of the slaughtering process (Lev. 1:6; 7:8) and "the crop" of the birds "with its contents" (Lev. 1:16).

It was the burning of the offering that made it a pleasing aroma to the Lord which, in turn, caused it to arouse a certain kind of response from the Lord. According to Genesis 8:20–22 it was the pleasing aroma of the burning meat that led the Lord to promise that he would never again destroy the earth and mankind as he had done in the flood. The burnt offering was a way of calling on the Lord to pay attention to the needs, requests, and entreaties of his worshipers either independently or in association with the peace offering. It was also a means of expressing worshipful responses to the Lord (Lev. 22:18–20) and, along with its accompanying grain offerings, was the staple of the daily, weekly, monthly, and annual festival cycle in the sanctuary (Exod. 29:38–45; Num. 28–29).

The grain and drink offering. The Hebrew term for "grain offering" is *minḥâ*, which, as noted above, can also mean generally "gift, present, tribute." In Leviticus (and other sanctuary contexts) it always means "grain offering." The grain offering pericope in Leviticus 2 stands between the burnt and peace offering chapters (Lev. 1 and 3, respectively). This is as it should be since the grain offering was a regular part of a burnt or peace offering along with a prescribed libation (Num. 15:1–15).

Like the grain offering, the practice of offering drink offerings (i.e., libations) predates the tabernacle system and continued at other altars even after the tabernacle and temple were available (see above). However, within the sanctuary system they constituted a significant part of the ritual procedures even on a regular daily basis. It was specifically legislated that libations along with grain offerings should normally accompany any burnt or peace offering (Num. 15:1–5).

The priest was to offer a part of the grain offering on the burnt offering altar as a "memorial (portion)" to the Lord along with the salt of the covenant (v. 13). If the grain was offered raw then incense was to be added to the memorial portion to lend it an especially pleasing aroma as it burned on the altar (vv. 1–2, 15–16). According to the law of the test of adultery in Numbers 5:11–31 the purpose of the "memorial (portion)" (see v. 26 there) seems to have been to call to mind the reason for the offering in the presence of the Lord. The term itself is directly related to the Hebrew verb meaning "to remember" and in this passage the whole of the grain offering was viewed as literally "an offering of memorial causing remembrance of iniquity" (5:15b; cf. v. 18). The grain offering of jealousy did not include oil or frankincense because it called to mind the accusation of iniquity. The grain offering used as a sin offering was similar (vv. 11–13).

Since the memorial portion was burned on the altar, the whole of the grain offering was to be unleavened with no honey added (Lev. 2:11), and the priests were to consume the remainder as unleavened cakes (Lev. 6:16–17). The prohibition against leaven and honey is probably best explained by their association with decay through fermentation. The "bread of presence" placed on the table before the Lord in the Holy Place every Sabbath was also conceived of as a "grain offering" (Lev. 24:5–9).

Leviticus 2:13 refers to the importance of adding "the salt of the covenant of your God" to every grain offering. This expression occurs in only two other places in the Old Testament: once in reference to the covenant commitment of the Lord to provide for the Aaronic priests (Num. 18:19) and once in reference to the covenant commitment to the dynasty of David and his descendants (2 Chron. 13:5). The preserving character of salt suggests the enduring nature of the covenant bond between the Lord and his people. The commitment was permanent.

The peace (or fellowship) offering. The peace offering emphasizes the fact that the people of ancient Israel had the opportunity for close communion with the Lord. They could eat the flesh of an animal that had been presented, identified, and consecrated as an offering to the Lord (Lev. 3:1–2; 7:11–21). This signified that all was well (i.e., peaceful) in the relationship between the Lord and his people and therefore always came last when offered in a series with other kinds of offerings.

The blood manipulation for a peace offering was normally the same as that for a burnt offering (Lev. 3:2b; cf. vv. 8, 13). However, only the fat parts of the carcass were offered on the altar to be burned "as an offering made by fire, an aroma pleasing to the Lord" (vv. 5, 11, 16). Thus, the fat parts of the carcass became like the whole carcass of the burnt offering and accomplished the same purpose. It is likely that the fat was not to be eaten because it was viewed as a delicacy. For example, according to Deuteronomy 32:13–14 the Lord fed the people the best of the land including, among other things, the "fat" of lambs, rams, goats, and even wheat as well as the "blood" of grapes. The "fat of the kidneys of the wheat" (v. 14) is clearly a play on words for the best of the wheat.

Leviticus 7:11–34 is important to a fuller understanding of the peace offering. Aside from the prohibition against eating blood or fat in verses 22–27, there are two major sections here. The first deals with the various kinds of worship rationale associated with the peace offering (thanksgiving, votive, or freewill) and rules for eating the meat that went to the offerers (vv. 11–21). The second section is about the portions that went to the priests from every peace offering (vv. 28–34): the breast of the "wave offering" (vv. 29–31; the noun derives from the Hebrew verb, "to wave") and the right thigh of the "contribution" to the particular priest who officiated at the offering of the particular peace offering (vv. 32–33). The latter derives from the Hebrew verb "to raise up" and for that reason is called a "heave offering" in some English versions (cf. English "to heave," meaning to lift, raise up). However, in ritual contexts this verb actually means "to remove" something in order to present it to the Lord (i.e., to set it aside as a special contribution).

These were the standard prebend for the priests (Lev. 7:34) and they could be eaten in any clean place (Lev. 10:14; i.e., they were "holy," not "most holy," contrast the grain offering prebend in vv. 12–13). Therefore, not only the priests themselves, but also all who lived in their households and were clean could eat of these portions of the peace offerings, but no common persons of a non-priestly household (Lev. 22:10–16). For a common person to eat of these portions would be to violate the sancta, the holy things of the Lord (see the "guilt offering" below).

The sin (or purification) offering. The sin offering was the primary blood atonement offering in the sanctuary system of offerings through which worshipers could receive forgiveness for their sin and deal with the degree to which they might have contaminated the tabernacle. Very detailed rules of blood manipulation were the focal point of this ritual procedure.

Leviticus 4:1–2a sets the sin offering pericope off from Leviticus 1–3. Unlike the previous sections virtually every paragraph in Leviticus 4:1–5:13 either begins or ends with a statement of sin committed and its associated guilt. Leviticus 4:2 states: "Say to the Israelites: 'When anyone sins unintentionally and does what is forbidden in any of the LORD's commands. . . .'" Leviticus 4:3 then begins the first of the four major divisions: the sin offering of the priest (4:3–12), the whole congregation (4:13–21), the leader (4:22–26), and the common person (4:27–5:13).

Sin offerings were used on several unique occasions (see, e.g., the consecration of the priests, Exod. 29:14, 36; Lev. 8:2, 14; the inauguration of altar worship, Lev. 9:2–7, 8–11, 15–17). They were also called for on regular occasions monthly (Num. 28:15), at various annual festivals, and especially on the annual Day of Atonement (Exod. 30:10; Lev. 16; Num. 29:11). Other specific situations that occurred throughout the year would also require a sin offering (e.g., the cleansing of the woman after childbirth, Lev. 12:6–8; the cleansing of irregular unclean discharges, Lev. 15:15, 30; in our age the term "sin offering" could be construed to mean that this offering focused on the problem of moral and social sin. In the Old Testament such sins were included as part of the purpose for sin offerings, but the sin offering could also be brought for physical impurities that had nothing to do with moral failure).

The focal point of the sin offering ritual was blood manipulation and the way it was done was different when it was brought for the priest and whole congregation as opposed to the leader and the common people. For the priests and the whole congregation the priest sprinkled the blood with his finger seven times in front of the veil of the sanctuary (i.e., the tent of meeting inside the tabernacle complex), put some of the blood on the horns of the incense altar inside the Holy Place, and simply poured out the remainder of the blood at the base of the burnt offering altar near the gate of the tabernacle complex (Lev. 4:6–7, 17–18). In other words, the blood penetrated the tabernacle complex as far as the contamination did (i.e., the "priest" could enter the Holy Place, and the "congregation" included the priests). The blood of the leader and the common Israelite was applied only to the horns of the burnt offering altar (Lev. 4:30, 34; 5:9), which was the boundary of penetration for the non-priestly Israelite into the tabernacle. The principle is that the blood went as far as the particular person or collective group of persons could go and, therefore, decontaminated the tabernacle to that point.

Leviticus 16:29–34 is a summary of the intended effect of the three sin offerings on the Day of Atonement: the scapegoat sin offering cleansed the *people* from their sins (vv. 29–31), and the slaughtered sin offerings for the priests and the people cleansed the *tabernacle* from the impurity of their sins (vv. 32–33). Some scholars have argued that the cultic regulations dealt with only cultic infringements, and that the cultic system and the larger everyday community life of the nation were disconnected. However, the scapegoat ritual suggests that this was not the case. On the contrary, the Day of Atonement cleansed both the cultic impurities and the various kinds of iniquities of the people that could defile the tabernacle. The tabernacle holiness and purity emphasized in Leviticus 1–16 and the national holiness and purity which is the primary concern of Leviticus 17–27 were viewed in close relationship to each other—so close that both were dealt with on the Day of Atonement.

The guilt (or reparation) offering. The purpose of the guilt offering was to make atonement for "desecration" of "sancta," that is, the mishandling of holy (sacred) things by treating them as if they were common rather than holy. For example, according to Leviticus 22:10–16 the holy food gifts were to be eaten by the priests and those in their household, not the common people. To do so would be to "profane" the "holy" gifts (v. 15). However, if a common person ate holy meat mistakenly, then he had to give the same amount back to the priests plus one-fifth as reparation for what he had done. This passage is an instructive parallel to the major guilt offering pericope (i.e., Lev. 5:14–6:7).

The guilt offering law begins as follows: "When a person commits a violation and sins unintentionally in regard to any of the Lord's holy things" (Lev. 5:15a). The word "unintentionally" is the same one used in reference to the sin offering. It refers to "straying" or "erring" from the commands of the Lord, in this case, specifically the commands about "the Lord's holy things" (i.e., the things dedicated to the Lord for the tabernacle or priesthood).

The basic idea behind the expression "commits a violation" is that the person has acted unfaithfully against God by violating the boundary between the common and the holy. In this context, therefore, it means "to commit a sacrilege." However, the guilt offering was also brought in cases of violations against the property of other people, not only the Lord's "sancta" (Lev. 6:1–7; 19:20–22; Num. 5:5–10). Therefore, whether the property belonged to the Lord or to other people, a guilt offering was presented to the Lord to make atonement and the violated property was restored plus one-fifth to the one whose property had been violated (Lev. 5:14–16, the Lord's property; Lev. 6:1–7; Num. 5:5–10, other people's property). Therefore some scholars refer to this as the "reparation offering." The violator not only brought the offering to the Lord but also made reparation for the property he had violated. In both cases the final result for the one who committed the violation was that it would "be forgiven him" (Lev. 5:16, 18; 6:7). Once the reparation had been made it was possible for the offender to make atonement and receive forgiveness from the Lord (vv. 15b and 16b).

The violation in Lev. 5:15 was done "in error" and "known" by the violator. The violation in verses 17–18 was also done "in error" but it was "not known" by the violator. The assumption is that he might come to know his error either through remembering after the fact or being informed by another person that, for example, the meat he had eaten was from the "holy" portion that belonged to a priest and his family. Even though it was done in ignorance (vv. 17–18), if he did indeed come to know about it he was still responsible for bringing a guilt offering to make atonement and obtain forgiveness (vv. 18–19).

A good example of the use of the guilt offering is the ritual procedure for the cleansing of the "leper" (Lev. 14:1–20; the term "leper" probably includes any person whose skin showed any kind of infectious blemishes). After the initial cleansing by special water and the "scapebird" (vv. 1–9), the first standard blood atonement ritual was the guilt offering (vv. 10–18). The point of the guilt offering at the beginning of this series of offerings was to reconsecrate the leper so that he could once again become part of the "kingdom of priests, a *holy* nation" (Exod. 19:6) from which he had been expelled and therefore, in a sense, "desecrated" because of his diseased condition (Lev. 13:45–46).

The word for guilt offering also occurs in Isaiah 53:10, where it is said of the suffering servant "though the LORD makes his life a *guilt offering,* he will see his offspring and prolong his days, and the will of the Lord will prosper in his hand." How was the suffering servant a guilt offering? The answer is that he was estranged and "desecrated" from the nation as a leper was estranged and desecrated. He suffered this at the hands of and yet also on behalf of the nation in order to make atonement for them before the Lord. In the days of Isaiah the ultimate suffering servant was yet to come, the Lord Jesus Christ. That brings us to the New Testament.

The New Testament. The verb *thuō,* "to slaughter, sacrifice" an animal, is used fourteen times in the New Testament referring to (1) nonsacrificial animals killed (John 10:10; Acts 10:13; 11:7) and prepared for a wedding feast (Matt. 22:4) or other kind of celebration (Luke 15:23, 27, 30); (2) the slaughter of the Passover lamb (Mark 14:12; Luke 22:7; 1 Cor. 5:7); and (3) offerings to pagan gods (Acts 14:13, 18; 1 Cor. 10:20).

The noun *thusia,* "sacrifice, offering, act of offering" (cf. the verb above), occurs twenty-nine times referring, for example, to specific Old Testament passages (e.g., Matt. 9:13; 12:7), fulfillment of Old Testament sacrificial regulations (Luke 2:24) or festival celebrations (1 Cor. 10:18), and the sacrifice of Christ on the cross (Eph. 5:2). *Prosphora,* "offering, sacrifice, gift; act of offering; grain offering" (9 occurrences; cf. the verb *prospherō,* "to offer, present"), refers to Christ's presentation of himself to God as an offering (Eph. 5:2, Heb. 10:10, 14) and the Old Testament offerings (Heb. 10:5, 8). The term *dōron,* "gift," occurs nineteen times in the New Testament; sixteen of those times it refers to sacrificial gifts or offerings to God.

Jesus Christ and the Old Testament Sacrificial System. During his incarnation Jesus explicitly honored the Mosaic sacrificial system (Matt. 8:4; Mark 1:44; Luke 5:14; 17:14). He lived as a Jew and encouraged others to also keep every "smallest letter" and "least stroke of a pen" (Matt. 5:18). However, he was also in continuity with the Old Testament prophetic critique of the cult. For example, in the Sermon on the Mount Jesus suggested that the relationship with one's brother needed to be resolved before presenting offerings in the temple (Matt. 5:23–24). He also expressed frustration with loopholes in the present priestly system whereby one could violate other Old Testament laws (e.g., the requirement to honor one's parents by taking care of them) by substituting the cultic piety of making offerings to the Lord (Matt. 15:5; Mark 7:11, the well-known "corban" passage).

Another dimension of the relationship between Jesus and the Old Testament sacrificial system is his own personal identification with different aspects of the system. There are two aspects of this: Jesus as our High Priest and Jesus as the sacrificial victim offered to God on the altar. It is important to remember that the New Testament offers a *metaphorical* application of the categories of the Old Testament system of offerings and sacrifices to Jesus in order to explain and illustrate the various ways in which his death on the cross was beneficial to us. Jesus was not literally slaughtered at the burnt offering altar, his blood was not applied there, and his body was not burned there. Nevertheless, the different kinds of offerings and sacrifices serve as metaphors to illustrate the various purposes and complete efficacy of Jesus' death on the cross.

Jesus as our "Passover sacrifice." There are many possible references to Jesus as a Passover sacrifice in the New Testament. However, the most certain of them all is in the exhortation to purity in 1 Corinthians 5:7, "Get rid of the old yeast that you may be a new batch without yeast—as you really are. For Christ, our Passover lamb, has been sacrificed." In the context Paul uses this to rebuke the Corinthians for not removing an evil man from their church fellowship. The Passover sacrifice was associated with the removal of leaven from every Jewish household (see Exod. 12:15–20 and cf. Mishnah Pesahim 1–3). Therefore, the leaven image could be used to refer to the polluting effect of one evil person in the midst of the congregation. Since Christ has already been sacrificed it was certainly time now to get rid of the leaven.

Jesus as our suffering servant "guilt offering." When John the Baptist said "Look, the Lamb of God, who takes away the sin of the world" (John 1:29), it is not certain whether he was referring to Jesus as the Passover lamb or as the suffering servant of the Lord mentioned in Isaiah 53:7b, "he was led like a lamb to the slaughter, and as a sheep before her shearers is silent, so he did not open his mouth." The Passover lamb option has been favored by some but the general consensus is that it refers to Isaiah 53:7.

Jesus as our new covenant ratification "peace offering." According to Luke 22:1–23, the "last supper" of Jesus was a Passover meal. Toward the end of that meal Jesus created a new ritual on the foundation of the Passover ritual. The new ritual is the basis of the ordinance that we have now come to call "Communion," the "Eucharist," the "Last Supper," or the "Lord's Supper." As is well known it includes Jesus words over the *bread* (Luke 22:19) and the *cup* (Luke 22:20). Both elements were part of the underlying Passover ritual, but Jesus referred to the bread as his own "body" and the cup as his own "blood."

Jesus referred to the cup as "the *new* covenant in my blood." The similarity to Moses' statement in Exodus 24:8 that "this is the blood of the covenant" makes it inconceivable that the apostles would have failed to connect Jesus' words with the covenant ratification ritual back in Exodus 24. In this case, however, the blood was for the ratification of the *new* covenant, which of course recalls Jeremiah 31:31–37 (see esp. v. 31).

Jesus as our "sin offering." The Old Testament word for "sin offering" can also mean "sin." According to the NIV translation of Romans 8:3, God sent his Son "in the likeness of sinful man to be a sin offering" but marginal option is "in likeness of sinful man, for sin," which reflects the fact that the Greek text has only the word "sin." This translation problem appears again in 2 Corinthians 5:21, where Paul writes, "God made him who had no sin to be sin for us." In this case the NIV translation decision is reversed from that in Romans 8:3 because here the marginal option is "to be a sin offering for us." The important question is, did Christ become "sin" or did he become a "sin offering" for us? From an Old Testament cultic perspective the translation "sin offering" might make more sense in these passages.

It is the sin offering rationale that is at the foundation of atonement, redemption, forgiveness, and purification terminology and concepts in the New Testament. For example, according to Romans 3:24b–25a, we are justified before God "through the *redemption* that came by Christ Jesus. God presented him as a *sacrifice of atonement,* through faith in his blood." It will be recalled that the offering with which atonement was most associated was the sin offering. Moreover, the sin offering blood atonement was foundational to Old Testament forgiveness.

In the New Testament the connection between redemption or atonement and forgiveness of sins is also explicit. For example, in its context the reference to Jesus as "the atoning sacrifice for our sins, and not only for ours but also for the sins of the whole world" (1 John 2:2) is a continuation of the argument that "if we confess our sins, he is faithful and just and will *forgive* us our sins and purify us from all unrighteousness" (1 John 1:9).

The sacrifice of Jesus and the whole Old Testament sacrificial system. Hebrews 9–10 opens with a summary of the Old Testament sanctuary system, beginning with a description of the sanctuary itself and ending with the distinction between the sacrifices that were offered throughout the year versus the Day of Atonement. The background is the quotation of the new covenant passage from Jeremiah 31:31–34 in Hebrews 8, to which the writer will return in Hebrews 10:16–17. In the meantime Hebrews 9:1–10:15 is devoted to a comparison between: (1) the Old Testament sacrificial system in general versus the sacrifice of Christ (Heb. 9:8–14), (2) the Old Testament covenant ratification sacrifice (Exod. 24:5–8) versus the new covenant sacrifice of Christ (Heb. 9:15–20; see above), (3) the cleansing of the Old Testament tabernacle with blood (Exod. 29:10–14; Lev. 8:15; Num. 7:1) versus the blood of Christ cleansing the heavenly tabernacle (Heb. 9:21–24), and (4) the Old Testament Day of Atonement (Lev. 16) versus the sacrifice of Christ (Heb. 9:25–10:14).

With regard to the sacrificial system in general, the writer begins by saying that, since even the high priest could only enter the most holy place once a year (9:7), therefore, "The Holy Spirit was showing by this that the way into the most holy place had not yet been disclosed as long as the first tabernacle was still standing" (9:8). The first reason for this is that the Old Testament gifts and sacrifices "were not able to clear the conscience of the worshiper" (9:9b). This stands in contrast to the sacrifice of Christ our High Priest. The Old Testament sacrifices accomplished only the "cleansing of the flesh" (v. 13, NASB) whereas the blood of Christ cleansed the "conscience" (v. 14).

With regard to covenant ratification, since Christ's sacrifice was better than the sacrifices that ratified the covenant at Sinai (vv. 18–20), the covenant ratified by his sacrifice was a better covenant (i.e., the new covenant, v. 15). Moreover, regarding the use of blood to cleanse the tabernacle (Heb. 9:21–24), it is well known that this was the essential purpose of the sin offering in the Old Testament sacrificial system. However, there is no mention of sprinkling the whole "tabernacle and everything used in its ceremonies" (Heb. 9:21) with blood on that day.

The final section of the writer's excursus on the Old Testament sacrificial system is the most extended of the four (Heb. 9:25–10:15). In it he recalls that the Old Testament sacrifices could not remove the "conscience of sins" (10:2). Instead, those sacrifices were "an annual reminder of sins" (10:3). Thus, he brings his earlier argument with regard to the *level of cleansing* accomplished by the Old Testament sacrifices (i.e., they only worked on the level of the flesh) into his discussion of the *temporal limitations* of the cleansing accomplished by the Old Testament sacrifices. Even the annual Day of Atonement sacrifices only accomplished cleansing for one year (9:25–10:4), much less the regular offerings, which were even more limited since they had to be offered time after time throughout the year (10:10–11).

It is important to recognize that the difference in sacrificial efficacy corresponds to the difference between the two covenants to which the sacrifices were relate. In the old covenant the law was written on tablets of stone, but in the new covenant it was written on the tablets of human hearts (2 Cor. 3:3). No law, not even God's law, can change the heart (i.e., cleanse the conscience) of a person unless it is somehow written on the heart of the person. The new covenant functions on this very level by the power of the Holy Spirit who works in the human heart. He applies the law, including the sacrificial law, to the heart (conscience) of the person who trusts in Christ by faith. He thereby transforms their heart and with it their life.

The Christian and the Old Testament sacrificial system. The fact that the Old Testament sacrifices and the New Testament sacrifice of Christ functioned on altogether different levels is reflected also in the fact that Paul was willing to continue to offer temple sacrifices long after he had become a Christian. In fact, he even paid for other Jewish Christians to do the same thing and thereby encouraged the practice (Acts 21:23–26). This suggests that, although he did not see himself or any other Jewish or Gentile Christian as being under the law, nevertheless, the apostle Paul did indeed view the Old Testament sacrificial system as a legitimate means of expressing piety and worship for first-century Jewish believers. This, of course, ended with the destruction of the temple in A.D. 70, but by that time Paul was also off the scene.

In the meantime, Paul also used the Old Testament sacrificial laws as a metaphorical foundation for teaching Christian life principles and practices. The foundation for this metaphorical shift was already laid in the Old Testament, where we find such statements as, "The sacrifices of God are a broken spirit; a broken and contrite heart, O God, you will not despise" (Ps. 51:17). Therefore, in view of the multitude of mercies that God has shown to us, the apostle Paul urges Christians to "present your bodies a living and holy sacrifice, acceptable to God, *which is* your spiritual service of worship" (Rom. 12:1, NASB). To live as a sacrifice involves several things. For Paul it meant that he was willing to be "poured out as a drink offering upon the sacrifice and service" of those whom he led to the Lord (Phil. 2:17). Sometimes this required suffering. Paul was no stranger to it and the apostle Peter used the example of Jesus as the suffering servant to encourage Christians to be willing to suffer patiently for Christ (1 Peter 2:18–25).

Other New Testament metaphorical applications of sacrificial law to the Christian life focus on the service and worship we can offer to God. For example, Paul viewed the fruit of his ministry to the Gentiles as "an offering acceptable to God, sanctified by the Holy Spirit" (Rom. 15:16b). Finally, the writer of Hebrews exhorts us to "continually offer to God a sacrifice of praise—the fruit of lips that confess his name" and "to do good and to share with others, for with such sacrifices God is pleased" (13:15–16). In a sense, therefore, just as Jesus fulfilled the Old Testament sacrificial laws, in a similar way we can fulfill them by living like Jesus lived.

RICHARD E. AVERBECK

See also ALTAR; ATONEMENT; DEATH OF CHRIST; LAMB, LAMB OF GOD; LEVITICUS, THEOLOGY OF; LORD'S SUPPER, THE; PRIEST, PRIESTHOOD; SPIRITUALITY; TABERNACLE; TEMPLE.

Bibliography. G. A. Anderson, *ABD,* 5:870–86; C. Brown, *NIDNTT,* 3:415–38; P. J. Budd, *The World of Ancient Israel;* W. W. Hallo, *The Book of the People;* M. Haran, *Temples and Temple-Service in Ancient Israel;* J. Henninger, *The Encyclopedia of Religion,* 12:544–57; P. P. Jenson, *Graded Holiness: A Key to the Priestly Conception of the World;* H. J. Klauck, *ABD,* 5:886–91; I. Knohl, *The Sanctuary of Silence: The Priestly Torah and the Holiness School;* J. Gordon McConville, *Law and Theology in Deuteronomy;* J. Milgrom, *Leviticus 1–16;* idem, *Numbers;* R. de Vaux, *Ancient Israel,* 2:415–56; G. J. Wenham, *The Book of Leviticus;* D. P. Wright, *The Disposal of Impurity.*

Oil. The most common word for "oil" in the Old Testament is the Hebrew word *šemen.* It occurs 192 times, and in the large majority of those cases it refers to "olive oil," so much so that the expression "tree(s)/wood of oil" (1 Kings 6:23, 31–33; Isa. 41:19) is a natural way to refer to "olive wood." In one place it refers to the "oil of myrrh" (i.e., an aromatic gum resin that comes from a shrub-like tree) used in the beautification process of Esther and other women in the Persian royal harem (Esther 2:12). The New Testament Greek word that corresponds to Hebrew *šemen,* "oil," is *elaion.* It occurs eleven times and refers exclusively to "olive oil." The Mount of Olives was named for its numerous olive groves and the olive oil presses located at its base. Jesus spent his last evening there ("Gethsemane" = Heb. *gat šemen,* lit. "press of oil"; see Matt. 26:36; Mark 14:32). The corresponding Aramaic word is *měšaḥ,* "(anointing) oil," (2 occurrences, Ezra 6:9; 7:22), which refers to the oil needed for the temple cult and is directly related to the Hebrew verb *māšaḥ,* "to anoint."

The term *yiṣhār,* "fresh oil," occurs twenty-one times, most frequently in parallel with "new wine," referring to the fresh olive oil produce of the land, the stores of which were a sign of the Lord's blessing of prosperity (2 Chron. 32:28; Jer. 31:12; Hos. 2:8, 22; Joel 2:19, 24) while the loss or lack of it was a sign of his judgment (Deut. 28:51; Joel 1:10; Hag. 1:11). The firstfruits or tithe of "fresh oil" went to the priests and Levites. Zechariah 4:14 uses this word to refer to Joshua the high priest and Zerubbabel the governor as "the two who are anointed (lit. 'the sons of oil') to serve the Lord of all the earth." The image of two olive trees supplying one lampstand with oil suggests that these two men together were the means through which the Lord would bless Israel.

Olive trees took a long time to grow and mature, but they also lasted for hundreds of years. Therefore, a good oil supply was a sign of stability and prosperity (e.g., Deut. 8:8; 33:24; 2 Kings 20:13; Ps. 92:10; Prov. 21:20; Isa. 39:2; Joel 2:19, 24). The lack of oil was a sign of the curse of God and agricultural disaster (e.g., Deut. 28:40; Joel 1:10). As a sign of judgment Micah predicted that the nation of Israel "will press olives" but not have the opportunity to "use the oil" (6:15).

Oil was used as a commodity of trade or personal income, for various kinds of common daily consumption (as part of the bread diet in tabernacle grain offerings, as fuel for lamps in the tabernacle, or homes, as a lubricant for one's hair and skin, sometimes with a special sense of honor, as an aromatic substance, as a medication, or in healing contexts, for royal and religious ritual procedures (see below), and in figurative expressions (e.g., for fertility and prosperity [Deut. 33:24; Job 29:6]; "oil of joy" [Ps. 45:7; Isa. 61:3; Heb. 1:9]).

Jacob anointed his memorial pillar at Bethel with oil and thus sanctified it as "the house of God" (Gen. 28:18; 35:14). The practice of anointing kings with oil is well known in Israel. In this case it appears to have the effect of consecrating them to their office. The same idea is present in the consecration of the tabernacle and especially the priesthood. Even though the Old Testament records the anointing of the priests in the days of Moses, some critical scholars have argued that, historically, priests were not anointed in Israel or generally in the ancient Near East until the postexilic period. A recent text from Emar (ca. 1300 B.C.), however, refers to the anointing of a priestess there.

According to Exodus 30:22–33 Moses was to mix a special "sacred anointing oil" (vv. 25, 31). This recipe was not to be used by anyone else and none of it was to be poured on any common person. It was limited to particular uses in the tabernacle (vv. 31–33). First, Moses was to use this oil to anoint the whole tabernacle, all its furniture (even the ark of the covenant), and all the vessels used therein (vv. 26–28). By this means Moses would "consecrate them so they will be *most holy,* and whatever touches them will be (or 'must be') *holy*" (v. 29; cf. Exod. 29:37). The "will be" translation would mean that any person or thing that touched the altar (or other anointed parts of the tabernacle) would contract holiness therefrom as if "holiness" were contagious. A person who contracted such holiness would be liable to death (see, e.g., the warning to the Kohathites in Num. 4:15). The "must be" translation would only suggest that it was forbidden for anything or anyone that was not "holy" to come into direct contact with the altar (etc.). The contrast between these two terms in this verse suggests the latter translation.

Second, Moses was to use this oil to anoint the priests and thereby consecrate them to minister in the consecrated tabernacle (v. 30; cf. Exod. 29:7; 40:12–15; Lev. 8:12). In this way they would become "holy" (Lev. 21:6, 8) and could therefore come in direct contact with the "most holy" tabernacle, its furniture, and its vessels (see above). This created a grading effect so that the tabernacle, its furniture, and its vessels were "most holy" and could be touched only by the "holy" priests. The priests therefore became the mediators that stood between the "common" people and the immediate presence and holiness of God in the tabernacle. The people could come in contact with the priests (i.e., the "holy" men) but they could not come in contact with the "most holy" parts of the tabernacle that had been anointed with the "sacred anointing oil."

RICHARD E. AVERBECK

See also ANOINT; HOLY, HOLINESS; OFFERINGS AND SACRIFICES; PRIEST, PRIESTHOOD.

Bibliography. J. A. Balchin, *ISBE*, 3:585–86; D. E. Fleming, *The Installation of Baal's High Priestess at Emar;* R. J. Forbes, *Studies in Ancient Technology;* R. T. France, *NIDNTT*, 2:710–13; H. N. Moldenke and A. L. Moldenke, *Plants of the Bible;* J. F. Ross, *IDB*, 3:592–93; H. Schlier, *TDNT*, 2:470–73; J. A. Thompson, *IDB*, 3:593–95; J. C. Trever, *IDB*, 3:593; R. de Vaux, *Ancient Israel;* M. Zohary, *Plants of the Bible.*

Old Testament in the New Testament, the. The New Testament proclaims its indebtedness to the Old Testament on the very first page. Matthew begins with an Old Testament genealogy that makes sense only to those who are familiar with the people and events to which it refers (1:1–17). Thus the New Testament signals at the start an engagement with the Old Testament that touches every page and makes great demands on its readers.

Statistics and Styles of Quotations. The New Testament does not simply express its dependence on the Old Testament by quoting it. The fourth edition of the United Bible Societies' Greek Testament (1993) lists 343 Old Testament quotations in the New Testament, as well as no fewer than 2,309 allusions and verbal parallels. The books most used are Psalms (79 quotations, 333 allusions), and Isaiah (66 quotations, 348 allusions). In the Book of Revelation, there are no formal quotations at all, but no fewer than 620 allusions.

As far as the styles of quotation, sometimes the New Testament authors employed techniques current among first-century Jewish teachers. These include midrash, a style of expanded narrative with interpretive comments inserted (e.g., Stephen's speech in Acts 7:2–53); pesher, a style found particularly in the Dead Sea Scrolls, in which Old Testament texts are connected with specific contemporary events (e.g., Acts 2:16; Rom. 10:8); and gezerah shawa, a style in which two or more verses that use the same word in different parts of the Bible are interpreted in the light of each other (e.g., Heb. 4:3–7). But generally the New Testament authors show considerable independence in forging wholly new ways of reading the Scriptures, based on their revolutionary experience of Jesus the Christ. For instance, Paul's conversion experience revolutionized his attitude toward the Law. After all, obedience to the Law had led him to persecute the Messiah! Following this, he could not continue to read and interpret the Scriptures as before. "Through the law I died to the law," he exclaims (Gal. 2:19). New styles of exegesis resulted, as we shall see below.

New Testament Interpretation of the Old Testament: Legitimate? *New Testament "Awareness" of the Old Testament.* Many New Testament scholars maintain that the New Testament use of the Old Testament works within a closed logical circle: it depends on Christian presuppositions and reads the Old Testament in a distinctly Christian way (even if employing Jewish methods of exegesis), often doing violence to the true meaning of the Old Testament texts employed. Thus, New Testament arguments based on the Old Testament, it is held, would generally be convincing to Christians but hardly to Jews. If this is true, it will be hard to vindicate the New Testament authors from the charge of misusing the Scriptures.

This approach, however, ignores several crucial features of the use of the Old Testament by the New Testament authors. As numerous studies have now shown, these authors generally assumed knowledge of the Old Testament context from which quotations were drawn. They were concerned to communicate with and convince their fellow Jews, not just to nurture a private faith. They did not want simply to jettison their Jewish heritage, but sought genuinely to understand how the "word" spoken through the prophets related to the new "word" now revealed in Christ (this applies even to Paul, whose "not under law, but under grace" [Rom. 6:15] looks at first sight like wholesale rejection of the Old Testament). Finally, they sensitively explored the Old Testament for points at which *its very inconsistencies or incompleteness pointed ahead to Jesus as the answer.* It is worth giving some examples of this latter point.

Matthew has a special fondness for the messianic prophecies in Isaiah (1:23; 2:23; 4:15–16; 8:17; 12:17–21) and other prophets (2:6, 17; 21:5;

26:31). He clearly regarded these as incomplete without Jesus.

John focuses his presentation of Jesus around the figure of Moses. One of the arguments he deploys is that even the mighty Moses was unable to deliver Israel from her most powerful enemies: death (6:49; 8:51–53) and sin (8:12, 31–34). But Jesus does!

Stephen's powerful speech (Acts 7:2–53) turns on the thought that the promise given to Abraham in Genesis 15:13–14—paraphrased by Stephen as "you will worship me in this place" (v. 7)—has never yet been fulfilled. Stephen traces a history in which all the significant encounters with God occurred away from "this place," and then points to the ambivalent Old Testament traditions concerning the temple, the "place" above all where God was meant to be worshiped yet a "place" where by definition he cannot dwell (vv. 48–50)!

Paul is naturally drawn to the Old Testament prophecies concerning the blessing of the Gentiles. In connection with these he discerns a tension at the heart of Old Testament theology, between the exclusivism of the covenant and the central covenant confession, the Shema: "Hear, O Israel: The LORD our God, the LORD is one" (Deut. 6:4). But if God is one, reflects Paul, then he cannot be just the God of Israel, but must treat all his creatures equally. Is he not the God of Gentiles too? (Rom. 3:29–30). And in 2 Corinthians 3:7–11 Paul employs an argument about Moses similar to that in John 6: for all his glorious status, the effect of Moses' ministry was condemnation and death.

The author of Hebrews employs this kind of argument frequently. The string of quotations from the psalms in 1:5–13 are applied to Christ because they say things about the human Davidic king that actually could be true of no mere human being. Similarly, Psalm 8:4–6 (Heb. 2:6–8) says things about "man" that are not true of any man—except one. The author also discerns tensions within the Old Testament theology of priesthood. How can priests save people from things to which they themselves are prey (5:2–3; 7:23)? But Jesus makes up this deficiency (7:25–28). And alongside the levitical priesthood another priesthood inexplicably appears in the Old Testament, that of Melchizedek. Similarly, the tabernacle itself harbors contradictions: it was meant to be "the tent of meeting," and yet it was structured to keep God separate! "The Holy Spirit was showing by this that the way into the Most Holy Place had not yet been disclosed" (9:8). And, above all perhaps, the sacrificial system of the Old Testament proclaims its own inadequacy by the requirement of constant repetition (10:1–4). In passages like Jeremiah 31:31–34 (8:8–12; 10:15–17) and Psalm 40:6–8 (10:5–7), the author finds, within the Old Testament itself, the expectation of something better.

Do such arguments distort and wrench the Old Testament? Many argue that, even though they arise from Christian faith, they nonetheless show true sensitivity to its inner dynamic. Rabbinic Judaism in the post-New Testament period sought to "complete" the Scriptures by filling out the body of its case law, reinterpreting the sacrificial legislation ethically, and gently downplaying the significance of the messiah (in the main). The New Testament authors, by contrast, focus the whole "story" of the Old Testament onto Jesus, as summarized below, using even its tensions prophetically, to point toward the Christ who is Jesus. Undoubtedly, the New Testament authors believed that their Christian faith enabled them to make better sense of the Old Testament than they ever could as Jews.

Patterns of Use. The New Testament authors both use the Old Testament to explain Jesus and use Jesus to explain the Old Testament—a circular process in which each is illuminated by the other. This circular relationship may be helpfully summarized under the following five headings.

Old Testament Theology Confirmed. The authority of the Old Testament is nowhere questioned in the New Testament, even at the points where—dramatically—the authority of Jesus is set alongside or even over it (e.g., Matt. 5:17–18, 27–30; Mark 7:19; Heb. 1:1–3). Thus, all the great themes of the Old Testament are confirmed, even when they are also developed in various ways: God as the one creator and ruler of the nations, the election of Israel to be the light of salvation for the world, the presence of God with his people, the possibility (and actuality) of revelation through appointed instruments, history as moving toward God's purposed goal for the world.

But the New Testament is no mere restatement of Old Testament themes, because of its vital focus on Jesus. So, for instance, the "wisdom" theme of Proverbs and Job, which had already been considerably developed in the intertestamental period, is used by both John and Paul to help explain Jesus, who is both God and separate from God (John 1:1–14; Phil. 2:5–11).

Old Testament Prophecy Fulfilled. All the New Testament authors (except James) pick up messianic and other prophecies from the Old Testament and locate their fulfillment in Jesus and in the church. Some prophecies are quoted frequently—especially those relating to the Davidic Messiah, the Son of Man, the prophet like Moses, and the "Servant" of Isaiah (see examples below). But it is possible to discern particular interests:

- Matthew finds prophecy fulfilled in several individual features of Jesus' ministry (e.g., 2:6, 17, 23; 4:15–16; 8:17; 10:35–36; 12:18–21; 13:35; 21:5).

- Mark focuses particularly on the prophecy of the suffering "servant" in Isaiah 53 (10:45), which he links to the "Son of Man" prophecy of Daniel 7:13–14.
- Luke adds an interest in the prophecies concerning Israel (e.g., Luke 1:68–73; Acts 2:17–21; 15:16–18; 26:22f).
- John finds special importance in the prophecy of Deuteronomy 15:15–18, that God will raise up a figure like Moses to speak his word to his people (1:45; 5:46; 6:14; 7:40; 8:28; 12:48–50).
- Paul draws especially on the prophecies of the blessing of the Gentiles (e.g., Rom. 10:19; 15:9–12; Gal. 3:8–9).
- Hebrews makes prominent use of the "new covenant" prophecy of Jeremiah 31:31–34 (8:7–13; 9:15; 10:15–18).
- The climax of Revelation draws on the climax of Isaiah: both conclude with the vision of a "new heaven and a new earth." Revelation also draws on Ezekiel's concluding prophecy of the rebuilding of the temple (Ezek. 40–48).

Old Testament History Reread. Claiming the fulfillment of specific, future-oriented prophecies is only a small element in the prophetic treatment of the Old Testament. Some basic features of the Old Testament "story" *become* prophetic in the light of Christ—that is, they are discovered to have a forward-looking, predictive function because their provisionality is revealed by the appearance of something (some*one*) much greater and better. The word often used to describe this treatment of the Old Testament is "typology." This technique may be illustrated by the use made of the Exodus, which receives frequent typological treatment.

- Matthew suggestively applies Hosea 11:1 to Jesus' return from Egypt (2:15), highlighting the parallel between Israel, who failed the temptations in the wilderness, and Jesus, who came through them victoriously to form the heart of a renewed people of God.
- John 6 presents the feeding of the five thousand as a glorious repetition of the manna miracle, signaling a greater exodus from sin and death.
- Paul applies the exodus themes of "slavery" and "redemption" spiritually to the work of the cross (e.g., Rom. 3:24; 8:23; Eph. 1:7, 14), and finds in the wilderness wanderings several typological foreshadowings of Christ and the church (1 Cor. 10:1–13).
- Hebrews develops the theme of the political "rest" enjoyed by Israel in the promised land and applies it typologically to that spiritual sharing of the life of God himself, which is the fruit of the work of Christ for all believers (3:1–4:13).
- First Peter 2:9–10 uses Exodus 19:5–6, a central statement of exodus theology, to make Israel a type of the church.
- Revelation uses the Egyptian plagues typologically (8:7–12), and applies the numbering of the exodus tribes to the church (7:4–8).

These examples do scant justice to the extent to which the exodus is used as a "type" of the salvation now to be experienced in Christ. Other Old Testament features treated typologically include the temple, Jerusalem (and the associated ideas of worship, security, and the presence of God), the annual festivals, and kingship. This treatment is symptomatic of a fundamental "rereading" of the history of Israel.

Old Testament People Expanded. One of the most surprising features of the New Testament use of the Old Testament is the way in which the exclusivism of the Old Testament covenant (Israel as the elect) gives way to a new understanding of the people of God in which racial identity plays no role, and Jews and Gentiles have equal membership based just on faith and common possession of the Spirit. The movement from one to the other is a special interest of Luke (see especially Acts 10–11) and of Paul (see especially Romans 9–11), one of the most sustained New Testament engagements with Old Testament texts).

Many Jewish Christians did not want to "reread" the Old Testament understanding of "people" in this way. Paul had to labor hard to defend his conviction that Abraham was the father of *all who believe in Christ*, not just the father of the Jewish nation (Rom. 4:9–17; Gal. 3:6–9). Certain Old Testament texts were especially important for him, but more important than particular texts was the conviction that the *spiritual experience* described by texts like Genesis 15:6, Psalm 32:1–2, and Habakkuk 2:4 was exactly that now being enjoyed by his Gentile converts: by believing in Jesus, they were being "justified by faith" just like Abraham and David (Rom. 4:22–25).

Old Testament Religion Renewed. The New Testament understanding of the Spirit builds on that of the Old Testament, but is surprising nonetheless. Only prophets and other leaders were anointed with the Spirit in the Old Testament. Hence the shocking nature of Jesus' encouragement actually to ask God for the Holy Spirit (Luke 11:13)! So now, possessing the Spirit in common, *the whole church* occupies a prophetic status, admitted like the prophets of the old covenant into the presence of God himself and is now enabled to share the worship of heaven by the Spirit, and to "worship in spirit and in truth" (John 4:24), rather than through a program of ritual.

The worship of the Old Testament is focused on a physical temple on earth. New Testament worship focuses on its heavenly counterpart by the Spirit—the heavenly temple where God truly dwells and Christ has gone before.

STEPHEN MOTYER

Bibliography. G. L. Archer and G. C. Chirichigno, *Old Testament Quotations in the New Testament: A Complete Survey;* D. L. Baker, *Two Testaments, One Bible: A Study of the Theological Relationship between the Old and New Testaments;* D. A. Carson and H. G. M. Williamson, *It Is Written: Scripture Citing Scripture;* B. S. Childs, *Biblical Theology of the Old and New Testaments: Theological Reflection on the Christian Bible;* E. E. Ellis, *Paul's Use of the Old Testament;* R. T. France, *Jesus and the Old Testament;* R. B. Hayes, *Echoes of Scripture in the Letters of Paul;* K. Stendahl, *IDB*, 1:418–32; P. Stuhlmacher, *Reconciliation, Law and Righteousness.*

One and Only, Only Begotten. *See* JESUS CHRIST, NAME AND TITLES OF.

Ordain. *See* APPOINT.

Order, New. *See* NEW ORDER.

Ordinance. With the defeat of Og of Bashan and Sihon of Heshbon, Israel was poised on the east bank of the Jordan to enter Canaan. Moses led a covenant renewal ceremony in which he explained the commandments, ordinances, and statutes of the Law. This included ordinances given at Mount Sinai and those given during the forty years that Israel wandered in the wilderness. These ordinances and statutes are the crown jewels of Israel. Israel's careful observance of them will reveal to the surrounding nations the chosen people's wisdom and understanding. No other nation has statutes and ordinances so righteous as those given by Yahweh to Israel (Deut. 4:5–8). These are words of life.

But life is not found in outward adherence to sacrificial, dietary, or social ordinances and statutes. Thus Yahweh demands of Israel, "Who asked you for this multitude of sacrifices, new moon, and Sabbath ceremonies" (Isa. 1:11–15). The answer, of course, is Yahweh himself. But God cannot tolerate iniquity and religious ritual. God is not fooled when the wicked recite the statutes of the covenant (Ps. 50:16). When the wicked perform the required sacrificial ordinances of the Law they might as well be offering swine's blood or committing murder (Isa. 66:3–4). The apostle Paul states that the work of Christ has abolished the law of commandments and ordinances (Eph. 2:15). The author of Hebrews explains how the levitical priesthood and its ordinances were temporary and have been superseded by the work of Jesus. He also reveals that all of God's saints have been saved by faith. God repudiates any attempt to use the ordinances to manipulate Him (chaps. 9–11).

Yet the ordinances and statutes are still words of life. Isaiah and James give the same solution to the faithless observance of outward forms: cease to do evil, learn to do good, seek justice, correct oppression, defend the fatherless, plead for the widow (Isa. 1:16–17; James 1:27). The ordinances and statutes reveal God's will and his understanding of what it means to do good, seek justice, and correct oppression. Psalm 119 beautifully illustrates the wisdom and joy of meditating on ordinances, statutes, commands, and judgments. They are a part of the canon and not to be neglected.

The Israelites made no distinction between ritual or procedural ordinances and legal or moral statutes. They are equally a part of Israel's covenant with God. To neglect one or the other was to court disaster. To observe them carefully was to court God's blessings on the individual and the community (Deut. 28). God's desire for his ordinances and statutes remains unchanged as is made clear in the quote of Jeremiah 31:33–34 in Hebrews 10:16–17: "I will put my laws in their hearts, and I will write them on their minds."

MARK D. MCLEAN

See also COMMAND, COMMANDMENT; DECREES; LAW.

Orphan. Person who has been deprived of parents. The meaning is clearly demonstrated in Lamentations 5:3: "We have become orphans and fatherless, our mothers like widows." Since the father was the main means of economic support for the family unit in the ancient Near East, his absence left his wife and children in a particularly vulnerable condition (2 Kings 4:1–7). Consequently in the Bible, and in the ancient Near East, orphans and widows are usually mentioned together as the epitome of the poor and deprived of society, the *personae miserabiles.*

The Old Testament. The first reference to orphans in the Bible is found in the earliest law code of ancient Israel, the Covenant Code (Exod. 21–24). In this text, given to a group of recently liberated slaves, the Lord passionately desired the protection of the orphan: "Do not take advantage of a widow or an orphan. If you do and they cry out to me, I will certainly hear their cry. My anger will be aroused, and I will kill you with the sword; your wives will become widows and your children fatherless" (22:22). To have compassion on the powerless, represented by the orphan, is to have the same zeal as God, who is known especially as "the helper of the fatherless" (Ps. 10:14), the helper of the helpless (Job 29:12).

Consequently the yardstick by which Israelite society is measured in the prophetic critique is its concern to protect and provide for the totally dependent, a prime example of which was the orphan (Isa. 1:23; 10:2; Jer. 5:28; Ezek. 22:7; Mal. 3:5). True repentance meant justice for the orphan (Isa. 1:17; Jer. 7:6; 22:3; Zech. 7:10).

Israel used the metaphor of an orphan to describe its own origins. A fatherless Israel was adopted by Yahweh and became his firstborn son (Exod. 4:22). Ezekiel described Israel as an infant abandoned to die by its parents; Yahweh, however, had mercy and adopted her into his family (chap. 16). If Yahweh judged the people, it was as if they had become orphans without a father (Lam. 5:3). But they could at the same time hope for salvation, for in Yahweh "the fatherless find compassion" (Hos. 14:4).

The New Testament. There are only two certain references to orphans. James 1:27 emphasizes the Old Testament teaching. The essence of true religion is "to look after orphans and widows in their distress." Helping the helpless is at the core of what it means to be religious, as it was in the Old Testament.

A metaphorical usage also occurs. Christ stated at the last supper that he would not leave his disciples as orphans but come to them in the presence of his Spirit (John 14:18). It is this Spirit that allows Christians to call out, "*Abba,* Father" (Rom. 8:15). They are no longer spiritual orphans but can begin to pray, "Our Father" (Matt. 6:9).

STEPHEN G. DEMPSTER

Bibliography. F. C. Fensham, *JNES* 21 (1962): 129–39; D. E. Gowan, *Int* 41 (1987): 341–53; R. Patterson, *BSac* 130 (1973): 223–34; H. Ringgren, *TDOT,* 6:477–81; H. E. von Waldow, *CBQ* 32 (1970): 182–204.

Overcome. *See* VICTORY.

Overseer. The word "overseer" (Gk. *episkopos*) is used a limited number of times in the New Testament, but it has significant implications for a proper understanding of leadership in the church.

The noun *episkopos* appears five times in the New Testament and means overseer, guardian, bishop. It is used in reference to Jesus Christ in 1 Peter 2:25 and in other places of individuals who have a function of leadership in the church (Acts 20:28; Phil. 1:1; 1 Tim. 3:2; Titus 1:7). The verb *episkopeō* appears in 1 Peter 5:2 and means to take care of, to oversee, or to care for. *Episkopē* appears in 1 Timothy 3:1 and refers to the position or office of overseer or bishop. It seems clear that a plurality of overseers (elders) was the New Testament model, though flexibility apparently existed as to structure. It is quite likely that one overseer or elder would have primary leadership as the pastor among the other elders in the local church, such as James in the church at Jerusalem (cf. Acts 15:13–21). The office itself is restricted to men. As men are called to be the spiritual leaders in the home, so they are to be the spiritual leaders in the church (cf. 1 Cor. 11:2–16; Eph. 5:21–33; 1 Tim. 2:9–3:7).

The first responsibility God has given the overseer is to watch over the flock. Acts 20:28a states, "Keep watch over yourselves and all the flock of which the Holy Spirit has made you overseers"; and Hebrews 13:17b says, "They keep watch over you." The idea is one of spiritual alertness, being on watch, being ready. Overseers watch for the souls of those entrusted to them in the Lord. They know that to protect them, constant attention is necessary.

A second responsibility of the overseer is to shepherd the flock of God as instructed in 1 Peter 5:2. To shepherd carries the idea of tending, caring for, feeding, protecting, and leading. All these tasks are involved in the overseer's service of ministry to the spiritual flock of God. Responsibility is not a compulsion but something that the overseer has entered into willingly.

In Acts 20:27–30 overseers are told to shepherd the flock of God, by declaring the whole counsel of the Word of God (v. 27). The reason is because there will arise false teachers who will seek to lead many astray (vv. 29–30). The importance of shepherding is revealed by Paul in 1 Thessalonians 5:14–15, when he instructs leaders to confront personally those who are idle, timid, or weak.

First Peter 5:2d–3 also addresses the issue of attitude and motivation of the overseer when it commands spiritual leaders to be "eager to serve; not lording it over those entrusted to you, but being examples to the flock." "Eager" carries the idea of ready and willing. The point is that the overseer should be quick to serve but careful to curb the desire to rule in an autocratic or dictatorial manner. There is always the temptation to abuse authority. The key is to maintain balance in this area of the ministry. The overseer clearly is to direct, lead, guide, even rule (Heb. 13:7, 17). However, his model is the Lord Jesus; therefore he is a shepherd leader, a servant leader who sets a humble example for the flock to follow. If the people are to see the pastor as a ruler (or leader), the pastor is to view himself as a servant. Trouble begins when one or both reverse those role assignments. A pastor who exalts himself as ruler is an unbearable tyrant; a flock that views its shepherd as its slave is destined for spiritual disaster.

It is important to consider the relationship among the overseer or bishop (*episkopos*), the pastor (*poimen*), and the elder (*presbuteros*). Scholars are virtually unanimous that in the early church the *presbuteros* and the *episkopos* were one and the same. Indeed, there is no clear evidence for a monarchical episcopate being firmly established until the early decades of the second century.

There are solid biblical reasons to justify the assertion that overseer and elder refer to the same person. In Acts 20:17, 28 Paul addresses the same group of men in the same speech as both elders and bishops or overseers as he reminds them of their work of shepherding. In 1 Peter 5:1–2 Peter calls himself an elder and instructs the elders to oversee the flock. In Titus 1:6–7 the same group is called both elders and overseers.

In writing to a local congregation, the church at Philippi, Paul addresses himself to the bishops or overseers (1:1). It is inconceivable that Paul would have sent no greetings at all to the elders, who were in every church. The bishops and the elders must be one and the same body of individuals.

Finally, the qualifications for the overseers in 1 Timothy 3:1–7 and the elder in Titus 1:5–9 are basically identical. *Episkopos* and *poimen* clearly refer to the function of the office, while *presbuteros* emphasizes the character of spiritually mature men of God. It was a term of respect and esteem the early church employed to describe its pastoral leaders, even though they were, on occasion, very young.

The qualifications the Bible gives for the overseer strongly emphasize character in all aspects of life, both personal and public. Most of the qualifications are self-explanatory, and they are listed in 1 Timothy 3:2–7 and Titus 1:6–9. That the overseer must be above reproach appears to be an overriding qualification, expressing the idea that the overseer should demonstrate integrity in every area Paul mentions. His life and reputation are of such a nature that he is not open to attack or censure. No fault can be found in him that would disqualify him from office or open him to discipline by the body (cf. 1 Tim. 5:19–20).

The overseer is to be above reproach in his personal life. He must be temperate, self-controlled, respectable, hospitable, upright, holy, disciplined, loves what is good, not given to drunkenness, not violent but gentle, not quarrelsome, not overbearing, not quick-tempered, and not a lover of money.

He must also be above reproach in his family life. He is to be the husband of but one wife (lit. "a one woman kind of man"), manage his own family well, and see that his children obey him with proper respect. Being the husband of but one wife is widely debated, but the idea of fidelity to one's wife is certainly the underlying principle.

The overseer must be above reproach in his public life. He must not be a recent convert, and for good reason: he may become conceited and fall under the same judgment as the devil. Also, he must have a good reputation with outsiders, so that he will not fall into disgrace and into the devil's trap.

Finally, the overseer must be above reproach in his professional life. He must be able to teach and hold firm to the message so that he can encourage others by sound doctrine and refute those who oppose it.

The authority of accountability of the overseer is summarized in Hebrews 13:17. The duty of the congregation is twofold: they must obey and submit. Three motivations are given for obedience and submission to the leadership. First, they watch over the people. The imagery is possibly that of the leaders keeping awake at nights in their concern for God's people. Second, they will give an account to God for their oversight of the flock (his flock; cf. 1 Peter 5:2). God has placed them in this position and therefore they will answer to him. The final motivation is that they may serve with joy and not grief. If there is a lack of obedience, it is of no advantage to the church. Hebrews 13:17 is a somber reminder that the welfare of the community is intimately related to the quality of the people's response to their leaders.

The office of the bishop or overseer is both a great privilege and an awesome responsibility. The pastor/elder/overseer is to shepherd, direct, teach, and protect the flock of God entrusted to him with integrity and humility, looking to the Lord Jesus as the model for ministry.

DANIEL L. AKIN

See alo CHURCH, THE; ELDER; LEADERSHIP.

Bibliography. H. W. Beyer, *TDNT,* 2:608–22; L. Coenen, *NIDNTT,* 1:188–201; D. Deer, *Biblical Translator* 30 (1979): 438–41; G. Knight, *Presbyterion* 11 (1985): 1–12; G. E. Ladd, *A Theology of the New Testament;* T. Rohde, *Exegetical Dictionary of the New Testament,* 2:35; P. Toon, *EDT,* pp. 157–58; R. S. Wallace, *EDT,* pp. 346–48.

Pp

Pagan. *See* NATIONS, THE.

Pain. *See* SUFFERING.

Parable. The range of meaning of the term "parable" (Gk. *parabolē*) in the New Testament closely parallels that of the Hebrew *māšāl* in the Old Testament and related Hebrew literature. As well as referring to narrative parables, the term identifies similitudes (Matt. 13:33; B. Pes. 49a), allegories (Ezek. 17:2; 24:3; Matt. 13:18, 24, 36), proverbs (Prov. 1:1, 6; Mark 3:23), riddles (Ps. 78:2; Mark 7:17), and symbols or types (Heb. 9:9; B. Sanh. 92b). "Parable" is a general term for a figurative saying.

The conceptual background for the concept of parable in the New Testament was Semitic, not Aristotelian Greek. This single insight could have saved the history of interpretation of the parables of Jesus from several key misconceptions. From Jülicher on, based on the Aristotelian Greek idea of parable as "pure comparison" conveying only a single point, there has been a significant school of interpretation that has regarded all allegorical traits as foreign to the parables of Jesus and has insisted that each parable has only one point. This narrow definition of parable has led interpreters to regard the allegorical interpretations of parables in the Gospels (e.g., Mark 4:14–20) as later misinterpretations, even though the earliest written gospels have the highest percentage of allegorical elements, and the latest, the Gospel of Thomas, has the least. It has also led to a seemingly endless series of variations of exactly just what was the "one point" of each parable. A study of the many interpretations shows a wide range of views of just what that one point must have been. For many parables, such as the prodigal son, limiting the interpretation to "one point" has proved to be a procrustean bed.

Nathan's parable of the ewe lamb in 2 Samuel 12:1–4 foreshadows in several respects many of Jesus' parables. The story of the rich man who slew a poor man's beloved pet lamb caused David to judge the rich man worthy of death. Nathan's "You are the man!" struck David to the quick precisely because he recognized the parallels between his actions and the rich man's, between Uriah and the poor man, and between Uriah's wife and the ewe lamb. This is reinforced with specific imagery ("It shared his food, drank from his cup, and even slept in his arms") that could be applied just as well to Uriah's wife. Similarly, many of Jesus' parables elicit a judgment that invites repentance, such as the good Samaritan. His parables lead us to a new way of seeing life and invite us to adopt a whole new perspective that changes how we live.

The parable of the vineyard in Isaiah 5:1–6 is immediately interpreted in verse 7 with explicit allegorical identifications: "The vineyard of the LORD Almighty is the house of Israel, and the men of Judah are the garden of his delight." Thus, the allegorical interpretations of Jesus' parables in the Gospels follow the pattern in the Old Testament, a pattern that is abundantly exemplified in rabbinic literature as well.

Jesus' narrative parables are probably best understood as extended metaphors. The story (the image) is a window through which a larger reality (the referent) is depicted. Understanding the message of a parable is more than identifying its "point," though many parables do have a focal point that is reinforced by the parable as a whole. Thus, it is crucial both to understand the story as it would have been understood by Jesus' original hearers, and to understand the referent, the wider reality about which it gives insight. Typically the referent is some aspect of the kingdom of God, the reign of God in people's hearts, or the realm of God's sovereignty. In order to let the parable have its full impact, we need to see the referent in a new way through the parable story.

To understand a parable we first need to listen to the story. We need to appreciate how its various details support the focus of the whole. For instance, the words describing the fate of each of the seeds that did not bear fruit—devoured, scorched, choked—have terrifying overtones. This is a story about the reception of seed in various soils. The three examples of multiplied fruitfulness balance the former three examples of fruitlessness. By their concluding position the multiplied fruitfulness of the good soil offers hope in contrast to the devastation where the Word does not take root. The interpretation in each of the Synoptics fits the story perfectly: a person's destiny depends on his or her response to the Word. It both offers hope and warns of devastation to those who will not accept the message. Such a combination of cursing and blessing seems to have been typical of Jesus' contrast parables: eschatological blessing for those who respond properly to God's invitation, but cursing for those who do not.

Of Jesus' fifty-two recorded narrative parables, twenty seem to depict him in imagery that in the Old Testament metaphorical use typically referred to God. The frequency with which this occurs indicates that Jesus regularly depicted himself in images that were particularly appropriate for depicting God. Such self-portrayal appears to be unique to Jesus. In the vast corpus of rabbinic parables there seems to be none in which a rabbi depicted himself. This distinctiveness, like the distinctive artistry of Jesus' parables, is further evidence that the parables recorded in the Gospels are authentic to Jesus.

The imagery that Jesus used to depict himself is an integral and often necessary part of the parables in which they occur. For instance, take the "father" out of the prodigal son, the "bridegroom" out of the bridegroom, the "shepherd" out of the lost sheep, or the "rock" out of the two houses and the parable disintegrates. Furthermore, these symbols for God applied by Jesus to himself in the parables are not interpreted in the Gospels as divine claims. In light of these factors, we can be confident that they were not later, theologically motivated insertions.

The argument implicit in many of these parables depends on the hearer's making an association that equates Jesus' act with God's act. Jesus implicitly claimed to be performing the work of God: as the sower, sowing the kingdom and implanting his word in people; as the director of the harvest, assuming God's role as judge in the endtimes; as the rock, providing the only secure foundation; as the shepherd, seeking out his lost sheep and leading his own; as the bridegroom in the wedding feast of the kingdom, where fasting is unthinkable; as the father, welcoming repentant sinners into the kingdom and calling his children into his service; as the giver of forgiveness, even to grievous sinners; as the vineyard owner, graciously giving undeserved favor; as the lord, who has final authority over his servants, who calls them into responsible participation in the kingdom, and who will ultimately determine the destiny of each of them, depending on their response to his lordship; and as the king, who has authority to allow or refuse entry into the kingdom, and to increase the responsibility of people who develop his resources, or to take away those resources from people who fail to develop them.

Not only do these parables depict Jesus as performing the work of God; they implicitly apply various titles of God to Jesus: the Sower, the Rock, the Shepherd, the Bridegroom, the Father, the Lord, and the King. Each of these parables adds to the overall impression that Jesus implicitly claimed to be God. Most parable studies that deal with the sort of implicit claim Jesus was making through the parables assume that it is a messianic claim, but most of this imagery was not used in the Old Testament to depict the Messiah. Even those symbols that were occasionally also used of the Messiah in the Old Testament (shepherd, king, stone) in Jesus' parables refer more naturally to God.

However, could Jesus' use of these symbols for God mean simply that he saw himself, as all of the prophets did, as doing God's work and speaking God's word? A few of these parables, like the two houses and the two sons, with their particular focus on obedience to Jesus' word, could be interpreted in this way. But three points support the view that Jesus was in fact presenting himself *as* God:

1. None of the prophets applied symbols for God to himself in the way that Jesus did so consistently in his parables.
2. None of the prophets claimed that they were doing or would do what the Scriptures specifically say that God will do. Yet it is precisely these things that Jesus so often depicted himself as doing in the parables: forgiving sin, sowing the kingdom, sowing his word in men's hearts, graciously welcoming undeserving sinners into the kingdom, seeking out and rescuing his lost sheep, directing the harvest of the great judgment, and dividing between those who will and those who will not enter the kingdom.
3. Many of the images through which Jesus refers to himself focus not so much on his activity as on who he is: the bridegroom of the kingdom, the good shepherd, the one who will return as king, the one with authority as vineyard owner and lord to do what he wishes with what is his, the one with authority to forgive sins, and the lord with authority to give or refuse entry into the kingdom and to reward the faithful.

This is of vital relevance to the current debate on the deity of Jesus. Did he really understand himself to be deity? Here in the parables, the most assuredly authentic of all the traditions about Jesus, is a clear, implicit affirmation of Jesus' self-understanding as deity. His sense of identification with God was so deep that to depict himself he consistently gravitated to imagery and symbols that in the Old Testament depicted God.

Jesus' parables depict many aspects of the kingdom of God. God's reign requires total devotion to him and a life exemplifying repentance, trust, love, and obedience. The forgiving quality of God's love and his merciful invitation to the kingdom inspire trust, the rejection of prejudice, and love for our neighbors. PHILIP BARTON PAYNE

See also ALLEGORY; JESUS CHRIST; KINGDOM OF GOD.

Bibliography. K. Bailey, *Poet and Peasant;* idem, *Through Peasant Eyes;* C. Blomberg, *Interpreting the Parables;* C. H. Dodd, *The Parables of the Kingdom;* J. Jeremias, *The Parables of Jesus;* P. B. Payne, *Trinity J* 2 ns (1981):3–23; R. H. Stein, *An Introduction to the Parables of Jesus;* D. Wenham, *The Parables of Jesus.*

Paraclete. *See* HOLY SPIRIT.

Paradise. Persian loanword for "an area enclosed by a wall" or "garden." Its three uses in the Hebrew Bible (Neh. 2:8; Eccles. 2:5; Song of Sol. 4:13) retain this meaning. The Septuagint uses the Greek *paradeisos* for the garden of Eden in Genesis (called the "garden of God" in Isa. 51:3 and Ezek. 28:13).

The intertestamental literature completes the transition of the word to a religious term. Human history will culminate in a divine paradise. Since Israel had no immediate access to the garden at history's origin or conclusion, paradise, sometimes called Abraham's Bosom, was associated with the realm of the righteous dead awaiting the resurrection of the body.

The New Testament understands paradise in terms of its Jewish heritage. In Luke 23:43 Jesus promises the penitent thief: "Today you will be with me in paradise." The intermediate state was transformed by Jesus' emphasis on being with him "today." No longer is paradise just an anticipatory condition awaiting the messianic presence at the end of the age. Those who die in faith will "be with Christ" (Phil. 1:23). The dead in Christ will not experience life diminished, but life enhanced, as Jesus' words to Martha in John 11:23–26 imply.

According to Revelation 2:7, the overcoming church will eat from the tree of life in the eschatological garden. Sin and death through redemption are now cast out of human experience. The way is open for the faithful to return to the garden of God. Paradise is the Christian's final home.

Paul's glimpse of paradise (2 Cor. 12:4) likely refers to the intermediate state. If so, it is one source of Paul's confidence that Christ is present among the righteous dead, even though he does not relish the unnatural state of death (2 Cor. 5:1–10). Yet it is quite possible that the dead in Christ more clearly see the paradise at history's conclusion than do earth-bound believers. Thus, Paul tells the Thessalonians that it is a matter of small consequence if one dies in the Lord or is still alive at the second coming (1 Thess. 4:13–18). Christ's presence pervades both the intermediate state and the final kingdom.

LUKE L. KEEFER, JR.

See also ABRAHAM'S BOSOM; INTERMEDIATE STATE.

Bibliography. V. R. Gordon, *ISBE,* 3:660–61; J. Jeremias, *TDNT,* 5:765–73.

Pardon. *See* FORGIVENESS.

Parousia. *See* SECOND COMING OF CHRIST.

Passion of Christ. *See* DEATH OF CHRIST.

Passover. *See* FEASTS AND FESTIVALS OF ISRAEL.

Pastor. *See* HOLY SPIRIT, GIFTS OF.

Paul the Apostle. ***Life.*** Paul's exact date of birth is unknown. It is reasonable to surmise that he was born within a decade of Jesus' birth. He died, probably as a martyr in Rome, in the mid- to late A.D. 60s.

Paul's birthplace was not the land Christ walked but the Hellenistic city of Tarsus, chief city of the Roman province of Cilicia. Tarsus, modern-day Tersous in southeastern Turkey, has never been systematically excavated to first-century levels, so extensive archaeological data are lacking. Literary sources confirm that Paul's native city was a hotbed of Roman imperial activity and Hellenistic culture. Yet his writings show no conscious imitation, and scarcely any significant influence, of the pagan leading lights of the era. Instead, as Paul himself suggests, he was a Jew in terms of his circumcision, Benjaminite lineage, Hebrew ancestry, and Pharisaic training (Phil. 3:5).

Paul, in the New Testament known by his Hebrew name Saul until Acts 13:9, was apparently educated from boyhood in Jerusalem, not Tarsus (Acts 22:3). It is not clear whether his family moved to Jerusalem (where both Greek and Jewish schooling was offered) while he was young, or whether Paul was simply sent there for his education. He studied under the ranking rabbi of the era, Gamaliel. His exegesis of the Old Testament bears testimony to his rabbinic training. Paul was at least trilingual. His letters attest to an excellent command of Greek, while life and studies in Palestine presuppose knowledge of Hebrew and Aramaic. Facility in Latin cannot be ruled out. His writings show intimate knowledge of the Greek Old Testament, though there is no reason to suppose that he was ignorant of or unskilled in Hebrew.

Some (e.g., William Ramsey, Adolf Schlatter) insist that Paul had personal knowledge of Jesus during his earthly ministry. Hengel goes so far as to assert that it is almost probable that the young Saul even witnessed Jesus' death. In any case, only a couple of years after Jesus' crucifixion (ca. A.D. 30), Paul's hostile attitude toward the latest and most virulent messianic movement of the time underwent radical change. As he traveled the 150 miles from Jerusalem to Damascus armed with legal authority to hunt down Jewish Christians (Acts 9:1–2), bright light and a heavenly voice stopped him dead in his tracks. It was Jesus—to Paul's chagrin not a dead troublemaker but the risen Lord. Paul's conversion was never the focal point of his preaching—he preached Christ, not his personal experience (2 Cor. 4:5)—but it does not fail to influence him in later years (Acts 22:2–12; 26:2–18).

We can only sketch the rough outlines of Paul's life from his conversion to his first missionary journey in the late A.D. 40s. He spent various lengths of time in Arabia, Damascus, and Jerusalem, eventually spending a lengthier stint far to the north in Syria and his native Cilicia (Gal. 1:15–21). From there Barnabas enlisted his services for teaching duties in the church at Syrian Antioch (Acts 11:25). Ironically, this multiracial church had been founded by Christians driven out of Palestine by persecutions instigated by Saul of Tarsus (Acts 11:19–21). It is from this period that our sources permit us to speak in some detail about the biblical theology of the apostle Paul.

Missionary Journeys. Paul's writings all arise from the crucible of missionary activity and the theological effort required to educate and sustain those who found Christ through his preaching. Galatians was probably written following Paul and Barnabas's tour of the Roman province of Asia around A.D. 47–49. This is the so-called first missionary journey (Acts 13–14). A second foray, this time with Silas and Timothy, lasted almost three years (ca. A.D. 50–53) and resulted in churches founded in Philippi, Berea, Thessalonica, and Corinth. The Thessalonian letters were written during this period.

Paul's third missionary journey (Acts 18–21) lasted from about A.D. 53 to 57 and centered on a long stay in Ephesus, from where he wrote 1 Corinthians. During a sweep through Macedonia he wrote 2 Corinthians. At the end of this time, awaiting departure for Jerusalem, he wrote Romans from Corinth (ca. A.D. 57).

Paul's arrival in Jerusalem was followed quickly by arrest and a two-year imprisonment in Caesarea Maritima. Thereafter he was shipped to Rome on appeal to the imperial court of Nero. There (see Acts 28) he apparently wrote his so-called prison letters: Ephesians, Philippians, Colossians, and Philemon. From this point reconstructions of Paul's movements are tentative. Assuming release from imprisonment Paul may have managed a fourth journey, perhaps as far west as Spain and then back into the Aegean area. One or more of the Pastoral Epistles may date from this period. Second Timothy concludes with Paul once more in chains. Reports of uncertain reliability place Paul's death at about A.D. 67 under the deranged oversight of Nero.

Sources. The exact shape of Paul's theology depends to a considerable degree on which writings are used to reconstruct his thought. Since the Enlightenment most critics have agreed that Romans, 1 and 2 Corinthians, Galatians, Philippians, 1 Thessalonians, and Philemon are definitely from Paul's hand. Some deny Paul's authorship of Ephesians, Colossians, and 2 Thessalonians, but others demur, and there is ample scholarly justification for drawing on them in outlining Paul's theology. Most modern critics deny that Paul wrote the so-called Pastoral Epistles (1 and 2 Timothy, Titus). Yet scholars like D. Guthrie and E. Ellis urge that Pauline authorship is entirely feasible—the documents do state that Paul wrote them. Even M. Prior's recent study critical of Pauline authorship argues that the basis on which the Pastorals are excluded from the Pauline corpus is not secure. S. Fowl finds a significant line of continuity among Philippians, Colossians, and 1 Timothy. It is not irresponsible to draw from the entire thirteen-letter New Testament collection in summarizing Paul's theology.

An equally pressing question is whether data from Acts can be merged with material in Paul's letters. This complex issue hinges on Acts' historicity. Those who see Acts as probably well-meaning, perhaps literarily skillful, but ultimately fanciful storytelling will naturally reject it as a source for reliable information about Paul and his message. A sizeable and growing body of research, however, spearheaded by the late W. Ramsey, F. F. Bruce, and C. Hemer and continued by I. H. Marshall, M. Hengel, B. Winter, and others is more optimistic that Luke was as careful about his reports as he claimed to be (see Luke 1:1–4). Paul's own writings remain the primary source for his theology, but mounting evidence suggests that Acts is a reliable guide for the historical framework of Paul's life and travels. It is also a dependable third-person (and sometimes first-person) account of the kinds of things Paul was wont to urge on his listeners in the various situations he faced.

Paul and Jesus. Since the Enlightenment the claim recurs that Jesus taught a simple ethical spirituality, or called for political or social revolution; then Paul came along and transmuted the gentle or revolutionary Jesus into an idealized divine man. Classic creedal Christianity, in this view, was never Jesus' intention but purely the brainchild of Paul.

Clearly there are differences between Jesus' proclamation of the kingdom of God and Paul's proclamation of the risen Jesus. But the differences are incidental to the overarching truth that God was manifesting himself definitively, in the threat of judgment and the offer of free pardon, in the ministry of Jesus Christ. Jesus announced, explained in advance, and finally carried out the atoning ministry God laid on him; Paul acknowledged Jesus' saving death and resurrection, became his follower, and spread the word of his glory across the Roman world. Paul and Jesus are not identical in either their words or their work; but they are wonderfully complementary. Paul's theology is Christ's own authorized extension of the gospel of salvation for Jew and Gentile alike (Acts 9:15).

Paul's Theology. *God.* The New Testament uses the word "God" over 1,300 times. Over 500 of these occurrences are in Paul's writings. At the center of Paul's theology is God. Several doxological statements capture Paul's majestic vision. God's wisdom and knowledge transcend human ken; he is infinitely wise and all-knowing; all things are "from him and through him and to him" (Rom. 11:36). "To him be the glory forever" (Rom. 16:27; Gal. 1:5; Eph. 3:21; Phil. 4:20; 1 Tim. 1:17; 2 Tim. 4:18) might well be the best summary of Paul's theology yet suggested.

"By the command of the eternal God" the gospel of Jesus Christ is made known "so that all nations might believe and obey him" (Rom. 16:26). God comforts the afflicted and raises the dead (2 Cor. 1:3, 9). He is faithful (2 Cor. 1:18); his "solid foundation stands firm" (2 Tim. 2:19). He grants believers his own Spirit as a downpayment of greater glory in the coming age (2 Cor. 1:21–22). The "living God who made heaven and earth and sea and all that is in them" (Acts 14:15) is, quite simply, "the King, eternal, immortal, invisible, the only God" (1 Tim. 1:17). Or again, he is "the blessed and only Ruler, the King of kings and Lord of Lords, who alone is immortal and who lives in unapproachable light, whom no one has seen or can see" (1 Tim. 6:15–16). No wonder Paul, like his master Jesus before him, lays such great stresses on hearing, obeying, and proclaiming the Lord God.

Against polytheism Paul insisted that God is one. Against stoicism Paul preached a God that was personal and accessible rather than impersonal and inscrutable. Against most pagan religions Paul presented a God concerned with social morality and personal ethics; God is not a cipher for a spirit experienced through rites of worship, ascetic denial, or mystical sensuality. Both Paul's example and his teaching affirm that God is to be feared, love, and served.

Evil and the Human Dilemma. Paul was not a pure dualist, positing one all-embracing eternal reality that was part good and part evil. God, all of whose ways are perfect, is solely sovereign over all. All reality will one day reflect his perfect justice and glory, even if the human eye cannot yet see or the human mind imagine this. Paul was rather a modified, or hierarchical, dualist. There is God, perfectly just (Rom. 3:5–6). And under his ultimate sway there is evil, somehow orchestrated by Satan (10 times in Paul) or the devil (5 times). Paul does not speculate on evil's origin. But his belief in a personal, powerful, malevolent being (and subservient underlings, human and angelic: 2 Cor. 11:12–15; Eph. 6:11–12) is an important feature of his outlook. It is also one that links him readily to Jesus, whose dramatic encounters with Satan form a major motif in the Gospels.

Evil is real and influential (Eph. 2:2) but fleeting. In the end it will not triumph. "The God of peace will soon crush Satan under your feet" (Rom. 16:20). But until that day, sinners (every single person: see Rom. 3:23) languish in "the trap of the devil, who has taken them captive to do his will" (2 Tim. 2:26). They need someone to save them. The reality of evil, as intrinsic to Paul's theology as the reality of God, sets up the need for the deliverance Paul preaches. This need is delineated most emphatically in his teaching about the law.

Paul and the Law. Paul believes that the Old Testament, as expressive of the God of all, is binding on all. A central tenet of the Old Testament is the radical lostness of humankind. "There is no one righteous, not even one; there is no one who understands, no one who seeks God" (Rom. 3:10–11, quoting Ps. 14:1–3). The litany continues for many verses. Paul, like Jesus, takes the Old Testament as authoritative and avows that "all have sinned and fall short of the glory of God" (Rom. 3:23). The law stops every self-justifying mouth and underscores humankind's universal bondage to a pattern of rebellion against God, estrangement from God, and, worst of all, legalism (the view that salvation is attained by the merit of one's good works) in the name of God. It points to the radical need of all for pardon and liberation lest they face eternal perdition for their willful error (2 Thess. 1:8–10). It thereby points to Christ (Rom. 3:21; Gal. 3:24).

Both Romans and Galatians warn against the snare of self-salvation by law keeping. "We maintain that a man is justified by faith apart from observing the law" (Rom. 3:28). The Galatian letter was occasioned by a move within a number of churches to establish circumcision and other traditional Jewish observances as necessary—and sufficient—for salvation. In response Paul speaks disparagingly of the "law," by which he often means his opponents' legalistic misrepresentation of the Old Testament in the light of then-current oral tradition. "A man is not justified by observing the law, but by faith in Jesus Christ" (Gal. 2:16). Such criticism of legalism is not a Pauline innovation; it was already a prominent feature of the Old Testament itself (1 Sam. 15:22; Pss. 40:6–8; 51:16–17; Isa. 1:11–15; Mic. 6:6–8) and figures prominently in Jesus' teaching (Matt. 23; Mark 7:1–13; Luke 11:37–54).

Yet on other occasions, even in Romans and Galatians where faith's virtues are extolled, Paul speaks positively of the law (Rom. 3:31; 7:12, 14; Gal. 5:14; 6:2). His dozens of Old Testament quotations, many from the books of Moses, challenge the theory that Paul rejected out of hand the Mosaic Law for Christians. The mixed nature of Paul's assessments of the law result from the contrasting situations he addresses. If legalists threaten to replace the gospel of free grace with a message of salvation by works, Paul responds that the law, understood in that way, leads only to death and destruction. But if Spirit-filled followers of Christ seek the historical background of their faith or moral and theological instruction, then the Old Testament corpus, including the legal portions, may have a beneficial function.

In recent decades Paul's view of the law has been the most disputed aspect of his theology. Building on groundwork laid by W. Wrede and A. Schweitzer, E. P. Sanders rejects justification by faith as the center of Paul's theology. In order to call in question this basic Reformation (and many would say Pauline) emphasis, Sanders and others (H. Räisänen, L. Gaston, J. Gager) have mounted a radical reinterpretation of Paul's various statements about the law, the human dilemma, and the nature of salvation in Christ as understood in Augustinian or Reformation terms. Studies such as T. Schreiner's *The Law and Its Fulfillment* respond to the challenge of what J. Dunn has called the "new perspective" on Paul.

Children of Abraham, Children of God. Paul's preaching in Acts 13:17 and his numerous references to Abraham in Romans and Galatians (9 references in each epistle; see also 2 Cor. 11:22) confirm that Paul did not see himself as founder of a new religion. (Stephen in Acts 7:1–8 [cf. Peter in Acts 3:25] likewise traces the gospel message back to God's promise to Abraham; is Paul Luke's source for what Stephen said on that occasion? Did Stephen have a hand in instructing Paul?) The foundation of the gospel Paul preached was the covenant God made with Abraham (see Gen. 12:1–3; 15:1–21). As Paul writes, "The Scripture . . . announced the gospel in advance to Abraham. . . . So those who have faith are blessed along with Abraham, the man of faith" (Gal. 3:8–9).

This is not to deny the importance of other dimensions of the Old Testament, the bounties of Israel that are the taproot of the church (Rom. 11). These include "the very words of God" that God entrusted to Old Testament sages and seers (Rom. 3:2). They also include "the adoption as sons, . . . the divine glory, the covenants, the receiving of the law, the temple worship and the promises," as well as "the patriarchs [Abraham, Isaac, and Jacob] and . . . Christ" (Rom. 9:4–5).

Nor is it to deny that Jesus Christ, as the fulfillment of God's prior promises, transcends all that went before. It is, however, to underscore that Paul's gospel was, in his view, in continuity with God's saving work over past millennia. Paul's references to *tekna theou* ("children of God"; Rom. 8:16, 21; 9:8; Phil. 2:15; cf. Eph. 5:1, 8) or "children of promise" or "heirs" of salvation (Rom. 8:17; 9:8; Gal. 3:28, 31) hark back in every case to God's saving work in Old Testament times. In this sense Paul was not the originator of Christianity but merely its faithful witness and divinely guided interpreter (1 Cor. 7:40)—granted, with the advantage of hindsight available after "the time had fully come" when "God sent his Son . . . to redeem those under law, that we might receive the full rights of sons" (Gal. 4:4–5).

But the mention of hindsight raises the question of Paul's source of insight. How did he come into possession of the startling and controversial body of lore and counsel found in his epistles?

Revelation and Scripture. Paul saw himself claimed by the God of the ages, who had chosen him—of all people, for he had persecuted Christ by persecuting the church (Acts 9:4; cf. 22:4; 26:11; 1 Cor. 15:9; Gal. 1:13, 23; Phil. 3:6)—to make plain secrets that were previously hidden (Eph. 3:4–9). The heart of this *mustērion* (divinely divulged verity) was, first, the very word of salvation in Christ itself (on which, more below). But additionally and significantly, at the center of the gospel of Christ was the good news that believing Gentiles are co-heirs with believing Israel of God's covenant favor. Peter had anticipated Paul in announcing this (Acts 10–11), just as Jesus foresaw that the gospel would open God's saving grace to the Gentiles in unprecedented ways (Matt. 8:11–12; 28:19–20; John 12:20–24; Acts 1:8). But Paul bore the brunt of the responsibility of announcing the new wrinkle in the work God was bringing to pass. He was the primary founder of many assemblies of worship and mission that would take the word yet farther. God granted him special cognitive grace, an authoritative didactic vision, commensurate with his task (see Paul's references to "the grace given me" in Rom. 12:3; 15:5; 1 Cor. 3:10; Gal. 2:9; Eph. 3:7–8).

Yet it would be misleading to overemphasize the uniqueness of what was revealed to Paul. His views were seconded by other apostles (Gal. 2:6–9). His teachings further and apply that which Jesus himself inaugurated and accomplished. Most of all, the revelation of which Paul speaks was corroborated by Scripture: his gospel and "the revelation of the mystery hidden for long ages past" is now "revealed and made known," not only by Paul's divinely given wisdom, but "through the prophetic writings" of the Old Testament (Rom. 16:25–26; cf. 1:2). Paul testified before Felix: "I believe everything that agrees with the Law and that is written in the Prophets" (Acts 24:14). Old Testament writings and the revelation Paul received—much of which became New Testament writings—combined to form an authoritative deposition, God's own sworn testimony as it were, grounding God's saving work in centuries past and confirming it in the days of Jesus. Those same writings, combined with others of earliest New Testament times, were destined to serve as a primary source and standard for all Christian theology in the centuries since Paul's earthly course was run.

Messiah. Old Testament writings promised a God-sent savior figure who would establish an everlasting kingdom, bringing eternal honor to the Lord by exalting God's people and punishing his enemies. By the first century messianic expectations were many and varied. Under the pressures of Roman rule in Palestine literally dozens of figures rose to lay claim to the role. It is hazardous to guess just what Saul the Pharisee believed about the messiah. But first-century writings, especially the New Testament, confirm that Jesus was rejected by the Jewish hierarchy as a messianic candidate. Clearly Saul shared this conviction.

It is therefore all the more striking that Paul later produced writings in which messianic honor is so ubiquitously ascribed to Jesus. By rough count of the Greek text, Paul uses the word "Christ" (an early Christian neologism, translating the Hebrew word *māšîaḥ*) close to four hundred times. He often uses the combination "Jesus Christ," other times writes "Christ Jesus," and most often uses the name "Christ" alone, as in the phrase "in Christ" (see below).

This frequency of use is probably best explained by analogy with Paul's even more frequent mention of "God." God, not a concept or idea but the living, divine person who creates and redeems, is the sole ordering factor over all of life. He is the basis and goal of all Paul does. But Paul was convinced that this same God had come to earth in human form, died for the forgiveness of human sin, and ascended to heaven to blaze a path for all that love him to follow. "Jesus" (over 200 occurrences in Paul's letters) was the human locus of God's incarnate self-revelation. "Christ," "Christ Jesus," and "Christ" are simply synonyms for the divine-human person in whom God brought his gracious saving will to pass.

A trio of texts encapsulates Paul's teaching on Christ's excellencies. First, Philippians 2:6–11 underscores Christ's essential oneness with God, yet his willingness to humble himself by taking on human form and enduring the shameful cross. God shares his very "name" (biblical shorthand for "personal identity" or "self") with him; he is the king-designate before whom every knee will bow, "in heaven and on earth and under the earth" (vv. 9–10). Second, Colossians 1:15–20 (cf. Eph. 1:20–23) expands on this soteriological vision to emphasize the cosmic dimensions of Christ Jesus' work. He was integral in creation and even now somehow upholds the created order (vv. 16-17). The fullness of the unseen God dwelt in him as he undertook his redemptive work (vv. 19–20). Third, in compressed confessional form Paul summarizes his teaching about Jesus Christ in 1 Timothy 6:16. His sixfold affirmation mentions incarnation, vindication by the Holy Spirit, angelic attestation, proclamation among the nations, appropriation by believers in the world, and ascension to heavenly glory.

In theory Paul's high view of Jesus Christ (Paul knows no dichotomy between a "Christ of faith" and the "Jesus of history" in the modern sense, nor is "Christ" a spiritual being or symbol somehow discontinuous with Jesus of Nazareth) could be justified simply by virtue of his divine identity. Who would be so rash as to quibble with God (Rom. 9:20)? Praise and honor befit whatever God deigns to do. But Paul's praise of Jesus Christ is not born of sheer necessity. It springs from the joyful awareness that God in Christ has regard for sinners in their lowly estate. God has expressed fierce, transforming love for his people through Christ's gracious work of redemption.

Redemption. Arguing from everyday experience Paul points out that only in a rare case would someone lay down his own life for the sake of another (Rom. 5:7). But God has shown the depth of his love for the lost in that Christ died on their behalf while they were yet in their woeful state (Rom. 5:8). Through Christ there is "redemption" from sin. "Redemption" refers to the paying of a price for the release of prisoners from captivity and occupies a central place in Paul's understanding of Christ's ministry. It has a rich Old Testament background in the liberation of God's people from Egyptian bondage.

Jesus spoke of redemption (*apolutrōsis*) in connection with events surrounding the return of the Son of Man (Luke 21:28). Paul uses the same word to describe the process by which sinners are justified (reckoned righteous in God's sight) through Jesus' death (Rom. 3:24–25; cf. 1 Cor. 1:30). But redemption is not only a past event. It is a future hope, as believers eagerly await the redemption of their bodies (Rom. 8:23), their resurrection at the end of this age. Paul speaks of redemption most often in Ephesians, where he associates it with forgiveness of sins through Christ's death (1:7), the future heavenly inheritance of believers (1:14), and the coming day of vindication for Christ's followers.

The logic of redemption requires that a price, or "ransom" (*antilutron*), be paid for prisoners' release. That price was the life of Jesus, "who gave himself as a ransom for all men" (1 Tim. 2:6). In Paul's theology the cross is the means and central symbol of Christ's redeeming death.

The Cross. Paul can summarize the message he preaches as "the message of the cross" (1 Cor. 1:18; cf. 1:23; 2:2). In itself the cross, reserved by Roman overlords for the most despicable crimes and criminals, had no connotation but agony and shame. Jews in Jesus' day interpreted Deuteronomy 21:23 ("anyone who is hung on a tree is under God's curse") to apply to crucified persons, and this helps explain why Jewish leaders pressed for a Roman death sentence for Jesus. This would mean crucifixion, and crucifixion would be proof that Jesus was not God's messianic deliverer.

The strategy succeeded—but then backfired. Yes, Jesus was cursed by God. The Gospels imply this in recording Jesus' cry of dereliction, the prolonged midday darkness, and an earthquake at his death. But Paul points out that he became "a curse for us" so that "the blessing given to Abraham might come to the Gentiles through Christ Jesus" and so that "by faith we might receive the promise of the Spirit" (Gal. 3:13–14). Christianity's elevation of the cross is directly related to the fixation on it in Paul's writings.

Paul uses the noun "cross" ten times and the verb "crucify" eight times. In addition, his numerous references to Jesus' "death" and "blood" likewise cast a spotlight on the cross. Yet it is not only a symbol for the means by which God in Christ atoned for sins; it is also the means by which believers walk in the footsteps of the one who calls them. As the cross is the source of strength in Christ's ministry, it is the source of strength for Paul (2 Cor. 13:4; cf. Gal. 6:14). For all believers the cross serves as inspiration and effective agent in mortifying "the sinful nature" with "its passions and desires" (Gal. 5:24). A key link between Jesus and Paul is their shared emphasis on death to sin and self as requisite for life to righteousness and God. For both, the cross functions as Moses' bronze serpent—a most unlikely symbol mediating eternal life to all who gaze on it with trust.

The cross, however, does not stand alone in Paul's theology. His gospel is not a call to cruciform masochism. The Pauline cross stands firmly planted in the rich soil of the resurrection.

Resurrection. The Christian message stands or falls with the truth or falsity of the claim that following his death for sin Jesus Christ rose from the dead (1 Cor. 15:14). Paul's preaching on the first missionary journey keyed on the resurrection (Acts 13:34, 37). Several years later at Athens Paul's stress was the same (Acts 17:31): God "has given proof . . . to all men" of coming judgment through Jesus Christ "by raising him from the dead" (cf. Rom. 1:4). While it is generally true to say that Paul's witness in Acts is Christ-centered, it can also be said to be resurrection-centered. Scarcely a major message or testimony passes without mention of Christ's resurrection or the assurance of future resurrected blessedness that Christ's resurrection guarantees those who trust him (Acts 17:18, 32; 23:6; 24:15, 21; 26:23).

Paul refers to the resurrection over five dozen times in his letters. Only 2 Thessalonians, Titus, and Philemon lack such mention. Like "cross" and "crucify," "resurrection" and "raised" refer to both an event in Christ's life and a reality for believers. Cross and resurrection serve together to make the benefits of Christ's righteousness available: "He was delivered over to death for our sins and was raised to life for our justification" (Rom. 4:25).

The resurrection is a key truth for daily Christian living. Jesus' resurrection from the dead means victory over sin (the ultimate cause of death, Rom. 5:12), and believers are urged to appropriate this victory in their own lives: "offer yourselves to God, as those who have been brought from death to life" (Rom. 6:13). The logic of growing in Christ-likeness, or sanctification, is based on Jesus' resurrection: "If the Spirit of him who raised Jesus from the dead is living in you, he who raised Christ from the dead will also give life to your mortal bodies" (Rom. 8:11).

Paul's final extant letter urges Timothy to "remember Jesus Christ, raised from the dead" (2 Tim. 2:9). This core Christian claim, still disputed yet defended today, remains the fundamental hope of all true believers, for it defines the promise and power of the salvation that the gospel has granted them.

The Church. In Paul's theology it is not believers as autonomous, self-sufficient units to whom God directs his saving efforts. Yes, God views persons as individuals. But the horizon of his saving acts extends to the entirety of the "all peoples on earth" cited in God's promise to Abraham (Gen. 12:3; cf. Eph. 2:11–13). Christ died and rose to rescue a corporate body, the company of the redeemed, the elect, the people of God as a whole stretching from earliest Old Testament times to the present. In Paul's writings the term that denotes this entity is "church," a word that occurs some sixty times and is found in every Pauline epistle except 2 Timothy and Titus. Perhaps most distinctive to his usage is the claim that Christ's very purpose was to have created "one new man out of the two" of Jew and Gentile, "thus making peace, and in this one body to reconcile both . . . to God through the cross" (Eph. 2:15–16). For this reason the church is not a side issue or subpoint for Paul but a first-level corollary of his Christology.

The trademark Pauline phrase "in Christ (Jesus)" requires mention in connection with his stress on the church. Paul uses the phrase (or "in the Lord") some 150 times. Contrary to older theories it does not denote a quasi-physical essence like air "in" which believers exist. While its uses are varied, M. Seifrid finds that more than one-third relate to God's saving work through Christ (e.g., Rom. 3:24) and one-third to the manner in which Christians should behave (Phil. 4:4) or the redeemed state they enjoy (Rom. 16:3). Perhaps most fundamentally, "in Christ" (virtually absent from non-Pauline New Testament writings) bespeaks believers' unity and interdependence. It refers to their organic relatedness to the heavenly Father, and to each other as his redeemed children because of what Christ has accomplished on their behalf.

The social reality denoted by "church" is often expressed using the metaphor of "body." Believers are responsible for living humbly and exercising their gifts for the sake of others in the body of Christ (Rom. 12:3–5; cf. 1 Cor. 12–14). Their organic connection to Christ, their being "members of Christ himself" (1 Cor. 6:15), is the basis for many a Pauline imperative—for example that the Corinthians defy their social norms and practice marital fidelity (or celibacy) rather than engage in casual or ritual sex (1 Cor. 6:12–20). Ephesians is especially notable for its preponderance of references to "church" (nine times) and "body" (six times) in the sense of God's people in Christ. Under God's all-encompassing purpose the church is the direct recipient of Christ's fullness (Eph. 1:22–23). Ephesians 4 stresses the unity of the Triune God's work in Christ and the effects of this in the church, of which Christ is head (v. 15; cf. 1:22; Col. 1:18; 2:10, 19). Ephesians 5:22–33 spells out the glories of Christ's love for the church, and the church's high calling of attending to its Lord, in a didactic discussion of Christian marriage.

In the individualistic climate of the West it is difficult to overstate the importance of the corporate solidarity of God's people in Christ. Paul's frequent use of "church," "body" (along with other metaphors), and "in Christ" assure that careful readers will not facilely impose modern or postmodern theories of selfhood and politics on Paul's radically Christocentric affirmations.

Ethics. Paul's letters go beyond theological teaching and religious directives. Principles and precepts regulating practical behavior, both individual and social, permeate his writings. It would be reductionist error to reduce Paul's ethic to a solitary basis; he seems to make use of a multiplex rationale (quite apart from the imponderables of divine guidance). Drawing on Old Testament precedent he charges believers with ethical imperatives based on the theological indicative of God's character, as when he calls on them to be imitators of God (Eph. 5:1; cf. Lev. 11:44: "I am the LORD your God; consecrate yourselves and be holy, because I am holy"). Their conduct should be regulated by God's presence in their midst (1 Cor. 3:17) and his holy purpose in their election and calling (Eph. 1:4; 4:1; cf. 2 Tim. 1:9). Old Testament commands have a prominent place in Paul's ethic, but so does Christ's powerful example of humility and self-sacrifice (Phil. 2:5–11). Put slightly differently, believers' lives should be regulated by what God has accomplished for them through Christ (1 Cor. 5:7; Eph. 5:8). Love is the crowning virtue (1 Cor. 13:13), in Paul's ethic as in Jesus' (Mark 12:29–31). In the end, "the only thing that counts is faith expressing itself through love" (Gal. 5:6; cf. 1 Tim. 1:5).

Pauline ethics is a subject too vast to be treated as a subpoint of his theology, but it is important to note that Paul's doctrine is not rightly comprehended when it does not translate into transformation of behavior at both personal and corporate levels. Paul's theology is important, but it does not stand alone. The epistle to Titus commends good works to God's people repeatedly (2:7, 14; 3:1, 8, 14) and excoriates pseudo-Christians who confess God but live ethically indifferent lives (1:16).

Last Things. Paul's eschatology is if anything even more vast and complex a subject than his ethics. The two areas are in fact related. Jesus' preaching of God's at-hand kingdom, vindicated by his resurrection from the dead, means that the end of the age has already dawned (Rom. 13:12). As they live out their daily lives on earth, believers' "citizenship is in heaven," from which they "eagerly await a Savior . . . the Lord Jesus Christ" (Phil. 3:20; cf. Col. 3:3). Paul's view of things to come has profound implications for the way life is to be lived now.

Pauline eschatology, like all of his teaching, grows out of his convictions about God generally and Jesus Christ in particular. Since Jesus was the Messiah, his victorious ministry signaled the arrival of the final stages of God's redemptive work prior to the consummation. This will include final judgment at the parousia (second coming; see Rom. 2:1–11; 14:10–12; 1 Cor. 3:12–15; Phil. 2:16; 1 Thess. 3:13; 2 Thess. 1:5–10). Evildoers who have not obeyed the gospel will face God's wrath (Rom. 1:18; Eph. 5:6; Col. 3:6). It is incumbent on believers, following in Paul's train, to proclaim the gospel to the nations (also to unrepentant Israel; Rom. 9–11) as a faithful witness to the unfolding of God's eschatological aims.

Eschatological boon is already available in the present. Believers enjoy the Holy Spirit, a sure sign of the end of the age. He is "the firstfruits" of their coming redemption (Rom. 8:23), the "guarantee" or "down payment" of greater things to come (2 Cor. 1:22; 5:5; Eph. 1:14), a seal of the inheritance and adoption that enables them to call Almighty God "Abba" (Rom. 8:15–17).

In the contemporary setting, when coming divine judgment is merely tolerated as private delusion if not belittled as rank superstition, Paul's dramatic emphasis on an imminent future order that calls for immediate, radical personal reorientation is readily written off as quaint mythology or overwrought apocalyptic imagery. It even becomes the stuff of Hollywood parody. Such dismissal is perilous if Paul—in this area once again echoing many a dominical declaration—speaks with the authority he claims. Endorsing wholeheartedly the Pauline vision with its cosmic implications means true life, life "in Christ," in this age and unspeakable enjoyment of God in the coming one (Rom. 8:18; 1 Cor. 2:9). Equally urgent is Paul's insistence that rejecting his gospel will in due course bring God's eternal displeasure. This is not to mention the tragedy of a life that squanders the opportunity to worship and share the resurrected Lord.

ROBERT W. YARBROUGH

See also CHURCH, THE; DEATH OF CHRIST; MESSIAH; SECOND COMING OF CHRIST; UNION WITH CHRIST.

Bibliography. C. Arnold, *Ephesians: Power and Magic;* D. Brewer, *Techniques and Assumptions in Jewish Exegesis before 70 CE;* F. F. Bruce, *Paul;* D. Carson, *The Cross and Christian Ministry;* K. Donfried, ed., *The Romans Debate;* E. Ellis, *Paul and His Recent Interpreters; Paul's Use of the Old Testament;* S. Fowl, *The Story of Christ in the Ethics of Paul;* G. Habermas and A. Flew, *Did Jesus Rise from the Dead?;* M. Hengel, *The Pre-Christian Paul;* S. Kim, *The Origins of Paul's Gospel;* A. Lincoln, *Paradise Now and Not Yet;* R. Longenecker, *Biblical Exegesis in the Apostolic Period;* idem, *Paul, Apostle of Liberty;* A. McGrath, *The Mystery of the Cross;* J. G. Machen, *The Origin of Paul's Religion;* I. H. Marshall, *Jesus the Saviour;* idem, *Luke: Historian and Theologian;* A. D. Nock, *St. Paul;* J. O'Grady, *Pillars of Paul's Gospel;* J. Plevnik, *What Are They Saying about Paul?;* M. Prior, *Paul the Letter-Writer;* W. Ramsey, *Pauline and Other Studies;* H. Ridderbos, *Paul;* E. P. Sanders, *Paul and Palestinian Judaism;* idem, *Paul, the Law, and the Jewish People;* T. Schreiner, *The Law and Its Fulfillment;* A. Scheweitzer, *Paul and His Interpreters;* M. Seifrid, *Dictionary of Paul and His Letters;* W. C. van Unnik, *Tarsus or Jerusalem;* S. Westerholm, *Israel's Law and the Church's Faith;* B. Winter and A. Clark, *The Book of Acts in Its First Century Setting.*

Peace. ***The Meaning of Peace.*** In English, the word "peace" conjures up a passive picture, one showing an absence of civil disturbance or hostilities, or a personality free from internal and external strife. The biblical concept of peace is larger than that and rests heavily on the Hebrew root *slm*, which means "to be complete" or "to be sound." The verb conveys both a dynamic and a static meaning—"to be complete or whole" or "to live well." The noun had many nuances, but can be grouped into four categories: (1) *šālôm* as wholeness of life or body (i.e., health); (2) *šālôm* as right relationship or harmony between two parties or people, often established by a covenant (see "covenant of peace" in Num. 25:12–13; Isa. 54:10; Ezek. 34:25–26) and, when related to Yahweh, the covenant was renewed or maintained with a "peace offering"; (3) *šālôm* as prosperity, success, or fulfillment (see Lev. 26:3–9); and (4) *šālôm* as victory over one's enemies or absence of war. *Šālôm* was used in both greetings and farewells. It was meant to act as a blessing on the one to whom it was spoken: "May your life be filled with health, prosperity, and victory." As an adjective, it expressed completeness and safety. In the New Testament, the Greek word *eirēnē* is the word most often translated by the word "peace." Although there is some overlap in their meanings, the Hebrew word *šālôm* is broader in its usage, and, in fact, has greatly influenced the New Testament's use of *eirēnē*.

God as the Source of Peace. God alone is the source of peace, for he is "Yahweh Shalom" (see Judg. 6:24). The Lord came to sinful humankind, historically first to the Jews and then to the Gentiles, desiring to enter into a relationship with them. He established with them a covenant of peace, which was sealed with his presence (see Num. 6:24–26). Participants were given perfect peace (*šālôm šālôm*) so long as they maintained a right relationship with the Lord (see Isa. 26:3; 2 Thess. 3:16).

The Old Testament anticipated, and the New Testament confirmed, that God's peace would be mediated through a messiah (see Isa. 9:6–7; Mic. 5:4–5). Peace with God came through the death and resurrection of Jesus Christ (Rom. 5:1; Eph. 2:14–17; Col. 1:19–20; see Heb. 13:20). Peter declared to Cornelius: "You now the message God sent to the people of Israel, telling the good news of peace through Jesus Christ, who is Lord of all" (Acts 10:36).

The Relationship of Righteousness to Peace. The Lord established a covenant, which resulted in the participants receiving his *šālôm* in abundance, "like a river" (see Isa. 48:18). However, peace could be disturbed if one did not live before the Lord and others in righteousness; in fact, peace is one of the fruits of righteousness (Isa. 32:17–18). The psalmist poetically describes the relationship between the two as righteousness and peace kissing each other (Ps. 85:10). The God of peace and the peace of God sanctify the child of God (see 1 Thess. 5:23). On the other hand, Scripture specifically states that there can be no peace for the wicked (Isa. 48:22; 57:21). Paul described the difference as follows: "There will be trouble and distress for every human being who does evil: first for the Jew, then for the Gentile; but glory, honor and peace for everyone who does good: first for the Jew, then for the Gentile" (Rom. 2:9–10).

One of the key issues among the prophets was the doctrine of "peace." The false prophets proclaimed "peace, peace" and in that announcement hoped to create peace for their constituency. The true prophets argued that peace could never be achieved apart from righteousness and justice. In this light, one can better understand what Jesus meant when he declared, "Do not suppose that I have come to bring peace to the earth. I did not come to bring peace, but a sword" (Matt. 10:34). And Paul wrote, "The God of peace will soon crush Satan under your feet" (Rom. 16:20). Judgment on sin, historically and eschatologically, must come prior to peace.

Peace in the Age to Come. In the age to come the animal kingdom will be restored to its paradisiacal tranquility. The image in Isaiah 11:6–11 is among the most picturesque in Scripture. Animals are paired off in a strange and wonderful way: the wolf and the lamb, the leopard with the kid, the calf with the lion, the cow with the bear, the lion with the ox. They shall be led by a little child. The emphasis is on the harmony, the *šālôm* between the animals and the animal kingdom with man. Children shall, in that day, be able to play with snakes and they will not be hurt.

In addition, the curse of the ground will be removed and the land will again be characterized by *šālôm*, which includes both harmony and productivity (see Amos 9:13–15). The desert will become a fertile field (Isa. 32:15), while the cultivated lands will drip with "new wine" and the "ravines of Judah will run with water" (Joel 3:18).

The nations of the world will come under the dominion of the "Prince of Peace" and in so doing, "will beat their swords into plowshares and their spears into pruning hooks" (Isa. 2:4; Mic. 4:3). Isaiah poetically characterizes it as a time when "You shall go out with joy and be led forth in peace; the mountains and hills will burst into song before you, and all the trees of the field will clap their hands" (Isa. 55:12).

One cannot overlook the fact that this harmony will never happen until man has a right relationship (*šālôm*) with Yahweh; it will be the result of the righteous rule of the "shoot from the stump of Jesse" who has upon him the Spirit of Yahweh; he is the "Prince of Peace" (Isa. 9:6; see Jer. 33:8–9).

GLENN E. SCHAEFER

See also FRUIT OF THE SPIRIT.

Bibliography. H. Beck and C. Brown, *DNTT,* 2:776–83; J. I. Durham, *Proclamation and Presence: Old Testament Essays in Honor of Gwynne Henton Davies;* W. Eichrodt, *Theology of the Old Testament;* W. Foerster, *TDNT,* 2:400–420; D. J. Harris, *Shalom!: The Biblical Concept of Peace;* P. B. Yoder, *Shalom: The Bible's Word for Salvation, Justice, and Peace.*

Peace Offering. *See* OFFERINGS AND SACRIFICIES.

Pentecost. *See* FEASTS AND FESTIVALS OF ISRAEL.

Perfect, Perfection. Two word-groups in the Hebrew Old Testament are translated "perfect" or "perfection": *tāmam* and *cālal.* The former connotes wholeness, soundness, integrity, and often takes on ethical significance; the latter connotes completeness, perfection, and can carry the aesthetic sense of comeliness or beauty. Nearly all New Testament occurrences translate Greek words sharing the *tel*-stem, from which some half-dozen words are formed that bear the sense of completion or wholeness.

Divine. In Scripture essential perfection belongs to God alone. Jesus assumes that the "heavenly Father is perfect" (Matt. 5:48). Paul speaks of God's will as perfect (Rom. 12:2). This view is solidly based in a wide range of Old Testament passages that use words from the *tāmam* group with its ethical connotations. Of foundational importance here is Moses' statement that the Lord's "works are perfect" (Deut. 32:4). Light is shed on this claim by four other clauses in the same verse that parallel and thereby explain it: (1) "[God] is the Rock"; (2) "all his ways are just"; (3) "[he is] a faithful God who does no wrong"; (4) "upright and just is he." God's perfection is an attribute of who he is as a person, not an idea or theoretical postulate, and it involves ethical qualities like justice and uprightness rather than properties that would indulge selfish human desire and pleasure (as in "a perfect meal" or "a perfect day"). Elsewhere the Old Testament asserts that God's "way is perfect; the word of the LORD is flawless" (2 Sam. 22:31; Ps. 18:30). God "is perfect in knowledge" (Job 37:16). God's "law is perfect, reviving the soul" (Ps. 19:7). In the New Testament James speaks similarly of "the perfect law that gives freedom" (1:25).

Old Testament references to perfection using the *cālal* root speak often of a passing perfection, a beauty granted by God but squandered, whether by God's own people (Lam. 2:15; Ezek. 16:14) or by a city-state like Tyre (Ezek. 27:3, 4, 11; 28:12). The same word is used positively of Zion (Ps. 50:2). Elsewhere the psalmist contrasts the Lord's commands with what seems perfect from a human point of view: "To all perfection there is a limit; but your commands are boundless" (119:96).

Christ. The New Testament is aware that Jesus Christ was sinless (John 8:46; Heb. 4:15; 7:26). It speaks of him being "perfect," however, only in the Book of Hebrews. God made Christ "perfect through suffering" so that he could bring "many sons to glory" (2:10). "Once made perfect, he became the source of eternal salvation for all who obey him" (5:9). Paul surely refers in part to Christ when he says that "when perfection comes, the imperfect [lit. that which is partial] disappears" (1 Cor. 13:10). The New Testament does not belabor the perfection of the Son of God, perhaps because the divine nature (and therefore perfection) of someone who forgave sins, raised the dead, and ascended to the right hand of God seemed to make the point obvious enough.

God's People. Less obvious perhaps is the biblical insistence that God's people are called to be perfect: "Be perfect . . . as your heavenly Father is perfect" (Matt. 5:48). In Scripture nothing is clearer than the unique holiness of God, so this cannot be a command for sinners to become God's ethical equals. It is rather the call to "be imitators of God . . . as dearly beloved children" (Eph. 5:1). Children who treasure their parents typically mimic them. Christians should mimic their Lord, who is perfect, thus reflecting his perfection in their lives. For some this will involve voluntary impoverishment for the sake of gaining true riches: "If you want to be perfect, go, sell your possessions and give to the poor, and you will have treasure in heaven. Then come, follow me" (Matt. 19:21). For others it is not the pride of possessions but the pride of self-expression that must go: "If anyone is never at fault in what he says, he is a perfect man, able to keep his whole body in check" (James 3:2).

While Paul calls on readers, not only to imitate God (Eph. 5:1), but also to imitate him (1 Cor. 4:16; 11:1; 2 Thess. 3:7), Paul denies that he is perfect (Phil. 3:12). Yet he calls believers to share in the derivative excellence that life in Christ bestows (Col. 1:28; 3:14). Hebrews likewise speaks of the perfection of God's children, stressing that it is the result of Christ's death on their behalf: "by one sacrifice he has made perfect forever those who are being made holy" (10:14; cf. 11:40; 12:23).

A key New Testament verse for understanding perfection in the Christian life is 2 Corinthians 12:9: "But he said to me, 'My grace is sufficient for you, for my power is made perfect in weakness.'" Believers are perfect to the extent that they participate in the cruciform grace that God offers in Christ. Christ was perfected through the travail of righteous living amid the bruising realities of an unjust world. The means and abiding symbol of the perfection he won is the cross. His followers know perfection as they abide in the bright shadow of this same sign.

ROBERT W. YARBROUGH

See also SANCTIFICATION; SPIRITUALITY.

Persecution. Just as the Bible graphically describes the introduction and spread of sin in the world, it also depicts the presence and reality of oppression and persecution in the world and presents many examples of people persecuting God, people persecuting people, nations persecuting nations, the wicked persecuting the righteous, and even, in some cases, the righteous persecuting the wicked or other righteous persons.

The Meaning of Persecution. The primary Hebrew word for persecution, *rādap,* and the Greek words, *diōkō/diōgmos,* both emphasize the concept of pursue (Gen. 44:4; Luke 17:23), press on (Prov. 11:19; Phil. 3:12); their meanings can be extended to include pursuing or pressing on, to oppress, harass (Deut. 30:7; Job 19:22; Acts 8:1), and also to bring to judgment or punishment (Jer. 29:18; Lam. 3:43; Matt. 5:11–12; Luke 11:49). Two other Greek words, also sometimes used to mean "oppress," "persecute," are *thlipsis* (oppression, affliction) and *thlibō* (press on, oppress; in the passive, to be oppressed, persecuted).

The Nature of Persecution. Both the Old Testament and New Testament give examples of physical, social, mental, and spiritual persecution. Physical persecution includes taking another's life (Gen. 4, Cain murdering Abel) or maiming the body (Exod. 22, 23). Social persecution (sometimes called discrimination) consists of making individuals or a group outcasts. An example of extreme mental and spiritual persecution is seen when Peter and John were threatened not to preach the gospel (Acts 5:28, 40).

The Objects of the Persecution. The Bible teaches that those who follow Christ and God's Word and who practice his commandments will be persecuted. Examples in the Old Testament include Abel, who offered a better sacrifice than Cain (Gen. 4:4–10; Heb. 11:4); Lot, also a "righteous man who was distressed by the filthy lives of lawless men" (2 Peter 2:7) who rejected him and who "kept bringing pressure on [him] and moved forward to break down the door" of his house in Sodom (Gen. 19:9); Elijah, who spoke against the prophets of Baal (1 Kings 18:25–40) and against the idolatry of Israel (1 Kings 18:16–21), and was persecuted by Jezebel for his godly stand (1 Kings 19:1–3); David, who conducted himself in a godly manner despite the machinations and pursuit of Saul (1 Sam. 19–27:1); Jeremiah, who spoke God's message of condemnation against Judah for her sins and the coming judgment against her to be brought by the Babylonians (Jer. 9:11, 13–16; 21:3–7; 25:1–14), had his message rejected (Jer. 36–37), was beaten (Jer. 37:15), and finally dropped into a muddy cistern (Jer. 38:6–13). Examples in the New Testament include John the Baptist, who spoke out against the adultery of Herod Antipas and was beheaded (Mark 6:21–29); Stephen, the deacon, who, preaching the gospel before the Sanhedrin and proclaiming God's judgment because of the sins of the people, was rejected and stoned (Acts 6:5; 7:1–60); Paul, who was persecuted, beaten, and imprisoned as he preached from place to place, and was finally killed in Rome (2 Tim. 4:6–8); and climactically, Jesus himself who preached God's grace and judgment (Matt. 4:17; 11:28–29), was persecuted by his hearers (Luke 4:28–30), plotted against by his adversaries (Mark 3:6), rejected (Luke 13:34; John 6:66), tried (John 18:12–40), and finally crucified (John 19:16–37; Phil. 2:9). His was a perfect and God-honoring life and message, reflected in part by the Old Testament prophets whom, as Jesus reminds them, they had also persecuted and killed (Matt. 23:29–36). All of this persecution of the godly came as the result of the sin and the animosity of sinners who rejected these who lived godly lives and also rejected their message that sinners must repent (Acts 2:38) and turn in faith to Jesus Christ for salvation (1 Thess. 1:9–10).

The Lord, too, in his righteous indignation, raised up adversaries against his backsliding people, against Abimelech for his murder of his seventy brothers, sons of Gideon (Judg. 9:22–25); against Solomon for his sin (1 Kings 11:14, 23); against rebellious Israel (2 Kings 17:7–20); and against Judah (Jer. 20:4) and Babylon for their wicked, ungodly acts (Jer. 25:12–14). Also the Lord, through natural elements and his own direct power, brings persecution and calamity on the whole world (Gen. 6–7; Matt. 24:21, 29; Mark 13:19).

Reasons for Persecution. The Bible gives examples of good people pursuing and persecuting others (Judg. 8:16, Gideon against the men of Succoth, to teach them a lesson; Mark 9:38–41, the disciples, in prejudice, opposing a brother witnessing to God's power). However, in contrast, the Scriptures teach that we are to love our enemies, "because he [God] is kind to the ungrateful and wicked" (Matt. 5:44; Luke 6:35), and to exercise forbearance and mercy, because "'It is mine to avenge; I will repay,' says the Lord" (Rom. 12:19; Deut. 32:35). The Scriptures are also full of examples of evil persons persecuting the good and righteous persons for various reasons, such as jealousy for a godly sacrifice (Gen. 4:2–10); revenge for a godly humanitarian deed done (1 Sam. 21:1–19); vengeance for action against heathen worship (1 Kings 19:2, Jezebel against Elijah); vengeance for warnings against idolatry and ungodly living, as exemplified by opposition to the messages of Jeremiah and John the Baptist (Jer. 37; Matt. 4:1–12); vengeance against preaching the gospel and condemnation of rebellion against God (Acts 7:54–60); opposition to the Jerusalem church for its stand for Jesus (Acts 8:1; 11:19), to the Thessalonian Christians for their stand for Christ (1 Thess. 3:3–4) to Paul for his faithfulness to the Lord Jesus (2 Cor. 11:16–33; cf. Gal. 6:17), etc.

A godly testimony will often result in ridicule, scorn, deprivation, physical harm, and even death. Jesus and his disciples were, are, and will be, subject to ridicule/insult: Jesus, "despised and rejected of men" (Isa. 53:3; Matt. 27:39; 1 Peter 2:23) and finally crucified (John 19:16–18); his disciples, insulted (Matt. 5:11), jeered (Heb. 11:36), mistreated (v. 25), deprived (clothed in sheepskins and goatskins), destitute, persecuted, wandering in deserts and mountains, "in caves and holes in the ground" (vv. 37–38), tortured (v. 35), sawed in two (v. 37), jailed (Acts 5:18; 16:23), flogged (Heb. 11:36), chained (v. 36), "shut the mouths of lions" (v. 33), "put to death by the sword" (v. 37), "quenched the fury of the flames" (v. 34), and stone (v. 37; Acts 7:59).

The underlying biblical reasons given for persecution consist of an antipathy of evil toward the good (Rom. 8:6–8); of wicked men opposing God and rejecting his divine precepts (Rom. 3:10–18). Jesus indicated that since the world hated him, it will hate his disciples (John 15:18–19), and declared that if they persecuted him, they will also persecute his disciples (v. 20). The Bible's climactic teaching about the believer and persecution: "Everyone who wants to live a godly life in Christ Jesus will be persecuted" (2 Tim. 3:12).

Reaction to Persecution. Forbearance: Turn the other cheek (Matt. 5:38–42). Mercy: "If your enemy is hungry, feed him; if he is thirsty, give him something to drink. In doing this you will heap burning coals on his head" (Rom. 12:20). Love: "Love your enemies and pray for those who persecute you" (Matt. 5:44). Confidence: "'It is mine to avenge; I will repay,' says the Lord" (Rom. 12:19). Realization: "If they persecuted me, they will persecute you also" (John 15:20). Concentration on Jesus: "Let us fix our eyes on Jesus, the author and perfecter of our faith" (Heb. 12:2). A firm stand with Paul and other saints: "I have fought the good fight, I have finished the race, I have kept the faith. Now there is in store for me the crown of righteousness which the Lord, the righteous Judge, will award to me on that day—and not only to me, but also to all who have longed for his appearing" (2 Tim. 4:7–8). Challenge: "You should follow in his steps. 'He committed no sin, and no deceit was found in his mouth.' When they hurled their insults at him, he did not retaliate; when he suffered, he made no threats. Instead, he entrusted himself to him who judges justly" (1 Peter 2:21–23).

W. Harold Mare

Bibliography. G. W. Bromiley, *ISBE,* 3:771–74; W. H. C. Frend, *Martyrdom and Persecution in the Early Church;* W. S. Reid, *ZPEB,* 4:704–7; H. Schlier, *TDNT,* 3:139–48; W. B. Workman, *Persecution in the Early Church.*

Perseverance. In the NIV the term "perseverance" occurs thirteen times, all in the New Testament. Verbal forms appear a total of eight times. The noun always translates the Greek word *hypomonē;* the verbs translate several Greek verbs *(hypomenō, epimenō,* and *kartereō).*

The root of *hypomonē,* the verb *menō,* is often used of God's permanence in contrast to the mutability of human beings and the world. In *hypomonē* there is the idea of energetic resistance, steadfastness under pressure, and endurance in the face of trials.

In the Septuagint the word refers to either confidence in or tense expectation of ("waiting on") the power or the faithfulness of God, who delivers his people (Ps. 37:9; Isa. 51:5; Mic. 7:7; Zeph. 3:8). It is closely linked with the idea of hope (Pss. 5:11; 7:1; 15:1; 16:7).

Passing into Judaism, *hypomonē* appears as an inward work, of great profit to the righteous in Hebrew life. Abraham persevered in ten temptations (Jub. 17–18); Isaac, Noah, and the prophets stood fast (4 Macc. 13:12; 15:31; 16:21); the mother and her seven sons withstood the cruelty of the tyrant (16:1; 17:7) and conquered him (1:11). Such behavior was done "for the sake of God" (16:19).

In the New Testament, the main sense of *hypomonē* is perseverance or endurance. Faith and hope are emphasized, and there is little of the Old Testament sense of "waiting for" or "expecting." One needs to persevere to attain personally to the ultimate salvation of God. Some texts emphasize perseverance in good works (2 Cor. 12:12); others, more passive, show perseverance under suffering (2 Thess. 1:4). Such a stance—Paul boasting of the believers because of their steadfastness—stands in contrast to the ethics of the Greek world, which regarded this as demeaning behavior.

There are two main strands of teaching about perseverance in the New Testament: (1) the indicative or doctrinal-type statements, which basically describe the nature and the presence of this virtue in the lives of believers; and (2) the imperative or hortatory statements, stressing the need for or the results of perseverance. The only exception to this general pattern is one text in which Paul makes reference to "Christ's perseverance" (2 Thess. 3:5). Many scholars regard the genitive case here as subjective, denoting Christ as the model of perseverance for believers. Such understanding accords well with the frequent New Testament references to Christ as the example for his followers (1 Peter 2:21; 1 John 2:6).

The indicative or descriptive texts occur in the letters of Paul and James, in Hebrews, and in the Apocalypse. They refer to perseverance on the part of Paul (2 Cor. 12:12), his converts (2 Thess. 1:4), Job (James 5:11), Moses (Heb. 11:27), and the believers in Ephesus and Thyatira (Rev. 2:2–3, 19).

Paul's life consisted of many sufferings and hardships (see 2 Cor. 11:23–33), circumstances associated with his ministry as an apostle. The word of the Lord to the newly converted Paul through Ananias was, "I will show him how much he must suffer for my name" (Acts 9:16). As apostle, in both the synagogues and to Gentile audiences, he persisted, God working through him signs, wonders, and miracles.

Paul's converts in Thessalonica had endured persecutions and trials, their lives marked by perseverance and faith. They had suffered from their own countrymen (1 Thess. 2:14); they had undergone trials (3:3). Paul was concerned that the tempter might have tempted them (3:5). Yet they had persevered in faith (3:7) and would be counted worthy of the kingdom of God for which they suffered (2 Thess. 1:5).

James appeals to Job as an example of those who had persevered. While the prophets were examples of patience (*makrothymia*, 5:10, a term meaning "longsuffering" or "forbearance"), Job's experience mirrored perseverance. He remained steadfast under very difficult situations. The conclusion James draws is that "the Lord is full of compassion and mercy" (5:11), probably basing his statement on the conclusion of the story of Job (42:10, 12), where the blessing of the Lord on Job is described.

According to the Epistle to the Hebrews, Moses persevered in the face of the Egyptian king's anger "because he saw him who is invisible" (Heb. 11:27). One "sees" the "invisible" by faith, an expression used three times to describe Moses' response (11:24, 27, 28).

Finally, in two of the letters addressed to the churches of Asia, the risen Lord assures believers that he knows of their perseverance (Rev. 2:2–3, 19). In the face of threats against orthodox teaching and against hardships they stood fast. The former were pressures from without; the latter inward endurance of trial, whatever the source.

The imperative or hortatory sorts of statements occur once in the Gospels (Luke 8:15), and in the letters of Paul (Rom. 5:3–4; 1 Tim. 4:16), James (1:3–4, 12), Peter (2 Peter 1:6), and the epistle to the Hebrews (10:36; 12:1).

In the parable of the sower, those who hear and produce a crop stand in contrast to the second and third types in the parable who fall away in time of trial, for they do not remain constant in adversity and they apostasize, or do not grow into maturity (Luke 8:13–14). Thus, Jesus' parable is meant to encourage believers to produce "for the long haul."

In Paul's only use of the noun *hypomonē* (Rom. 5:3–4) he shows the crucial importance of growth between justification (5:1) and the anticipated glory (5:2). In the interim there will be suffering, but that produces steadfastness, which in turn produces (approved) character. But, one may ask, how does this occur? Do not many rebel at suffering, and even curse God? Here the end of the process is in view, what suffering finally achieves.

Timothy is called to persevere (*epimenō*) with respect to his duties as a leader in the church (1 Tim. 4:16). His persevering will result in his personal reputation being saved (cf. 1 Cor. 9:27), and the people to whom he ministers attaining salvation.

Similar to Paul's words in Romans is the text in James 1:3–4. Testing leading to approval or showing genuineness, "develops perseverance. Perseverance must finish its work so that you may be mature and complete." But an important addition by James is the promise of "the crown of life" to those who, by their perseverance, show their love for God (1:12). Those who do persevere show their confidence in God's goodness and care, their sense that God loves them. That is an important motivation for withstanding the trial.

The list in which perseverance occurs in 2 Peter 1:5–7 is more extensive. This literary form, sometimes called *climax* or *gradatio,* was common in Stoicism and Greek popular philosophy, and occurs also in early Christian writings, although it is found otherwise only in Romans 5:3–5 among the New Testament lists of virtues. This example of perseverance is set between God's gift of life (1:3–4) and the anticipation of being welcomed into the eternal kingdom of Christ (1:11). It is because of what God has bestowed that believers are exhorted to employ faith in producing virtue. Each of those listed is the means whereby the next is produced.

The writer of Hebrews stresses the need to persevere in order to "receive what he [God] had promised" (10:36). The expression "you need to persevere" underlines the moral effort involved in doing the will of God, and thus being eligible to receive the salvation God has promised (see 11:39). In 12:1 the writer calls on readers to divest themselves of everything that would hinder running the race, and persevere, while fixing their eyes on Jesus. He is the supreme model of perseverance, and the one who gives ultimate motivation.

Because God has bestowed the gift of life by grace through faith, continuance is urged upon believers. Growth into maturity is of the nature of salvation (1 Peter 2:2b). God's grace continues to uphold and enable. Faith must be nurtured and strengthened. Hope points forward to the eschatological climax of salvation. That which God has prepared as an inheritance of believers can be attained. To those who persist he will give eternal life (Rom. 2:7). WALTER M. DUNNETT

See also ASSURANCE; ENDURANCE.

Bibliography. F. Hauck, *TDNT,* 4:581–87; A. S. Martin, *DAC,* 2:186–90; J. M. Gundry Volf, *Paul and Perseverance.*

Person, Personhood. The biblical view of humanity is critical to our understanding of the Scriptures and God. Anthropology is an essential element of theology. Man-talk and God-talk are closely related and only possible as they are related one to the other. Themes such as sin, grace, faith, redemption, and the church must not only be viewed from the God-side, but also from the human side. While God is absolute in the Old Testament, he revealed his Godness through his contact with humans in words and deeds. In the incarnation in the New Testament he is completely defined.

Now this is not to suggest that the human being is the measure of all things. Anthropocentric concerns must not so dominate theology that its focus is the nature of the human being, rather than the character of God. But there is real danger when the consideration of anthropology is pursued in isolation quite apart from theology. It is critical that anthropology be considered from a biblical perspective. Human preoccupation results in narcissism. The question of what human beings are must be answered biblically.

The creation account of Genesis 1 portrays human beings as part of the material world created by God. As such they have solidarity with the natural order and a creature relationship to God. This is the emphasis of Psalm 8, in which the human being is seen as a little lower than God, but crowned with glory and honor.

The boundary lines between humans and God on the one hand, and that between humans and nature on the other hand are never violated. Humans can only have a proper understanding of themselves as they have a proper understanding of God. This results in self-awareness, in a creature consciousness—but not in a debasing sense. As uniquely created in God's image, humans are his agents ruling over and caring for the earth.

Commonality with all other creation gives humans their earthiness. They are embedded in creation, but they are not only in nature, they are also over nature. While they are *a part* of nature they are *apart* from nature. They not only have solidarity with nature, but transcendence over it. Not only do they have a special relationship to God, they also have one with other humans.

It is exceedingly difficult to systematize biblical anthropology since the Bible does not set out to present an encyclopedic treatment of it. At best, reference to it seems to be incidental and informal.

This effort to understand humankind biblically is further complicated by the multiplicity of terms such as heart, soul, spirit, and body, which, while having distinct meaning, are frequently used interchangeably in Scripture. Stereotyped translation of Hebrew words is not wise or possible.

The development of a biblical anthropology is also complicated by the movement of the Hebrew Scriptures into the Greek world and language. The Septuagint translations of the Hebrew terms has led in the false direction of a dichotomic or even an trichotomic anthropology, in which body, soul, and spirit stand in contrast and conflict. The "wholeness" of the human being in Semitic thought gives way to a more fractionalized consideration of the person.

Terminology. While the word *ʾādām* can indicate the first man, it is most generally generic, designating humankind. The etymology of this word is uncertain. It should be distinguished from Hebrew words of gender. It is this word that is associated with the image of God (Gen. 1:26), depicting human dominion over the nonhuman world. Even after the fall, *ʾādām* is used of humankind. The image of God is still the distinctive.

Another Hebrew word used for humankind is *ʾĕnôš*. This represents the weakness or mortality of humanity, although such an understanding may be more attributable to theology rather than etymology.

The Greek counterpart of the Hebrew *ʾādām* is *anthrōpos*. This too is a generic term, used without sex distinction. It depicts humanity in contrast to animals and provides us with the English word "anthropology." Implicit in this term is an acknowledgment of humanity's finiteness and creatureliness.

The Nature of Humankind. A careful study of biblical words and expressions used for the person need to be made to facilitate our understanding of humankind.

Soul. This is the traditional English translation of the Hebrew word *nepeš*, but most generally it refers to the person as a needy/longing creature rather than to some indestructible spiritual substance. Such is observable in Genesis 1:20, 21, 24, where the qualified (living) *nepeš* refers to animals and is rendered "living creatures." Thus this term is not reserved for human beings and when used of a person it does not so much suggest what a person *has* as what a person *is*. This term is even used where *nepeš* is detached from the concept of life and simply designates a corpse.

Nepeš is often used to express physical needs such as hunger (Deut. 12:20; 1 Sam. 2:16) and thirst (Prov. 25:25). It can be used of excessive desires (gluttony—Prov. 23:2) and of unfulfilled desires (barrenness—1 Sam. 1:15). Volitional/spiritual yearning is also assigned to the *nepeš* such as the desire for God (Ps. 42:1–2) and justice (Isa. 26:8–9), but also for evil (Prov. 21:10) and political power (2 Sam. 3:21).

The counterpart to *nepeš* in the New Testament is *psychē*. It is difficult to draw hard and fast lines between the various meanings of this many-sided Greek word. It can mean "life" of a particular person or animal (Matt. 2:20; Mark 10:45; John 10:11; Rom. 11:3) or person (Acts 27:37) or be reflexive, designating the self (Luke 12:19). There are passages where *psychē* stands in contrast to body (*sōma*) and there it seems to refer to an immortal part of man (Matt. 10:28). Nevertheless, on the whole, in the New Testament soul retains its basic Hebrew meaning.

Flesh. The Hebrew word *bāśār* so rendered, represents that which humans share in common with the animal world. While *bāśār* stands primarily for the visible part of the body, it is also used to designate the body as a whole. Hebrew has no word for body, but the frequency with which *bāśār* is so translated suggested that this term often served in that capacity. That these uses refer to a body can be seen in the treatment that *bāśār* received: anointed, washed, clothed, cut, pained, and in particular in its capacity to thirst, tremble, faint, and grow weary. These latter qualities show that *bāśār* can also indicate the whole person.

Thus, common Old Testament anthropological thought holds that a human being is a body, rather than having a body. The distinctions between soul and body are minimized. A human being is an animated body rather than an incarnated soul. The body is none other than the soul in its outward form, allowing the various parts of the body to think and act as representations of the soul.

While weakness is associated with *bāśār* in the Old Testament, there is no indication that it is a source of evil. This is in contrast to the New Testament where flesh is the locus of sin and the term "fleshly" becomes virtually synonymous with "sinful."

The Greek word for body is *sōma*. While it can designate the physical entity, it is often used as a comprehensive term for the whole person. Such a holistic definition of *sōma* is widely accepted today. This view minimizes dualism where the body and soul oppose each other and it advocates unity. This unity is not to be seen as monadic, denying either the corporeal or the incorporeal side of the person.

Spirit. The Hebrew word so rendered is *rûaḥ*. Its basic meaning is "wind" or "breath" and by extension comes to mean "strength"—the vital power necessary to sustain life. The spirit that animates man comes from God. It can be crushed (Ps. 34:18), necessitating the Lord to save, or it can be taken back, causing the person to return to dust (Job 34:14–15; Ps. 104:29). These latter verses suggest that the person's spirit and God's are virtually inseparable.

If the concept of "body" associates human beings with the animals and suggests weakness, the concept of "spirit" stresses the affinity we have for God and stresses power. While *nepeš* pertains to God in a few instances and *bāśār* never applies to God, *rûaḥ* is used more often of God than humans. Thus, the human spirit calls out for its divine complement, while God desires worshipers who will worship in spirit and truth. It is the spirit that provides the energy and capacity to worship.

This term is also used to indicate the dominant impulse or disposition of a person so that the text can speak of bitterness of spirit (Gen. 26:35), spirit of jealousy (Num. 5:14, 30), broken spirit (Exod. 6:9), right spirit (Ps. 51:10), and a "generous spirit" (Ps. 51:12). In Numbers 14:24 Caleb is distinguished from the others by his attitude—"different spirit."

Spirit can also refer to the life center of the body. This is seen in Ecclesiastes 3:18–21 where a comparison is made between the spirit of a person and the spirit of a beast. When the *rûaḥ* departs mortals return to the earth. The *rûah* returns to God who gave it.

Heart. The Hebrew word *lēb* is the most common Old Testament term for the person. Its traditional translation "heart" has hidden its meaning, since our present understanding of the term has but little of its biblical meaning.

The Old Testament has little interest in anatomy. No connection is made in the Old Testament between the heart and the beating of the pulse.

Upon learning of his wife's approach to David, Nabal's heart dies and became like stone, but he continued to live for ten more days (1 Sam. 25:37–38). Obviously this refers to his emotions not to his physical heart. The whole spectrum of emotions is attributed to the heart—positive emotions like love, loyalty, joy, comfort and negative ones like grief, envy, anger.

Thought functions are also attributed to the heart where *lēb* is better translated "mind." Wisdom and understanding are located in the heart. The heart is the seat of the will, so that a decision can be described as "setting" the heart (2 Chron. 12:14).

Thus, *lēb* in its more abstract meaning refers to the inner or immaterial part of the human being, being, in fact, the most frequently used word and the richest.

The Greek word *kardia* in the New Testament also includes the mental, moral, rational, and emotional elements of human nature. While "soul" and "spirit" deal with the essence of a human being, "heart" reflects the qualitative—the matter of character.

Other Functions. A survey of the above four terms reveals the absence of a variety of English terms and functions we associate with personhood. Rational functions are frequently assigned to the heart (*lēb*) that we would ascribe to the head, and more precisely to the brain, the mind. Lack of heart in the Old Testament does not mean coldness of feeling, but lack of thought (Prov. 10:13). The "wise heart" (Ps. 90:12) indicates intelligence.

The conscience is also associated with the heart. This is clearly seen in the statement: "Afterward David was conscience-stricken for having cut off a corner of his [Saul's] robe" (1 Sam. 24:5). The cry for a "clean heart" in Psalm 51:10 is a plea for a pure conscience.

Another function of personhood—will—is related to both the heart (*lēb*) and spirit (*rûaḥ*). In "planning the heart" (Prov. 16:19) the emphasis is not only upon understanding, but execution, an activity of the will. Sometimes spirit indicates will, such as in Ezra 1:5, where reference is made to the exiles whose spirit God had stirred up to go up to rebuild the temple.

Relationship among Persons. That human relations are critical to a person's wholeness is seen in the creation account of Genesis, when God created persons male and female, and in Genesis 2 where the divine assessment is that "it is not good" for the man to be alone—a partner is necessary. Singularity is not good. Even as there is diversity (trinity) within unity in the Godhead so there is unity within diversity in humanity. Maleness and femaleness are basic to humanity.

Human relationship in the Old Testament goes beyond marriage. The life of the individual Israelite was always integrated in the bonds of the family. The elimination process in Joshua 7:16–18 that finally isolated Achan reflects this solidarity.

This solidarity is referred to as corporate personality. While individual value, worth, and responsibility are recognized in the Old Testament, there is no tendency to the rugged individualism of Western culture. Rather in the Old Testament the individual was able to implicate the entire nation either in blessing or judgment and a single person such as the king could represent the whole nation as if it were an individual.

While to stand alone was viewed negatively as an affliction (Ps. 25:16–17) and an occasion for taunting (Ps. 102:6–8), there are individuals who are singled out, who stand alone, but not for their own benefit, but for that of the group such as Abraham and Moses.

The concept of solidarity is continued in the New Testament. Individual distinctions are lost since "you are all one in Christ Jesus" (Gal. 3:28). The representation of the church under the metaphor of the body also stresses unity: "The body is a unit, though it is made up of many parts; and though its parts are many, they form one body. So it is with Christ. For we were all baptized by one Spirit into one body" (1 Cor. 12:12–13).

Conclusion. In this consideration of the person two tensions stand out.

First, should the person be viewed as a unity or a duality? Scriptural evidence can be advanced for both of these positions. This would call for caution. The individual, on the one hand, must not be fragmented or disassembled. On the other hand, the material and the immaterial must not be so homogenized that there is a denial of either materiality or spirituality.

The second tension is individualism versus corporate solidarity. Again scriptural evidence can be presented for both realities. The oscillation of Scripture, the ready movement between the *I* and the *we*, demands a careful balance between them.

CARL SCHULTZ

See also SOUL; SPIRIT; WILL.

Bibliography. W. Dryness, *Themes in Old Testament Theology;* R. H. Gundry, *Sōma in Biblical Theology;* R. Jewett, *Paul's Anthropological Terms;* N. Snaith, *The Distinctive Ideas of the Old Testament;* H. W. Wolff, *Anthropology of the Old Testament.*

Peter, First, Theology of. First Peter was written as a circular letter to churches in five provinces of northwestern Asia Minor. Because of their conversion to Christ these people had been alienated from their culture and their former friends (1:14, 18; 2:9; 4:3–4), and the letter encourages them in the midst of slander, personal abuse, and ostracism (1:6; 2:12; 3:15-16; 4:4). Peter instructs them to understand their sufferings as an emulation of the passion of Christ (2:21; 4:13), to anticipate the glory they will enjoy when Christ is revealed to the whole world (1:13; 4:13), and to recognize that the church has become their primary social group (2:1–10; 3:8–12; 4:7–11). The message of this letter is the genuine grace of God (5:12) to be realized in their disciplined response to persecution.

The author calls himself Peter, an apostle of Jesus Christ (1:1), a fellow elder, a witness of the sufferings of Christ, and a participant in the eschatological glory (5:1). He has written by means of Silvanus (5:12, or Silas; cf. Acts 15:22, 27, 32), with greetings from his "son," Mark (Acts 12:12; 15:37; Col. 4:10) as well as from the elect church in "Babylon"—a symbolic name for Rome (5:13; cf. Rev. 17:5, 18; 18:2, 10).

Some scholars have questioned apostolic authorship on the basis of the quality of Greek, the absence of personal references to the life of Jesus, and the absence of persecution by the state during the lifetime of Peter. Yet Peter was to some degree bilingual with thirty years of preaching experience, and the skills of Silvanus would have been significant. The purpose of the letter is exhortation, not a rehearsal of the gospel or personal experiences. And finally, the internal description of persecution is that it was spontaneous, local, and sporadic (3:13–15), not official persecution by the state (2:13–17). This would suggest that the letter was written prior to Nero's attack on Christians in A.D. 64. Peter's authorship is also supported by the early use of the letter, the consistent affirmation in Christian tradition that he was its author, and its early acceptance in the developing canon.

The dominant theological emphasis of 1 Peter is an ecclesiology that provides believers a self-understanding for the outworking of their salvation in a hostile society. The importance of ecclesiology is indicated by the appearance of ecclesiological emphases at the end of each major section in the letter (2:1–10; 3:8–12; 4:7–11; 5:1–7), even though the word "church" is not used in the letter.

The church is comprised of the elect (1:1), regenerate persons (1:3) who have been baptized (3:21) and are being built into the temple of God (2:5) as a royal priesthood; they thus actualize the titles and purposes of Israel (2:9–10). The church's members engage in the disciplines of eschatological hope, reverent fear of God, love for each other, and worship of Christ (1:13–2:10).

The church lives in the world as an alternate society. Her members have been marginalized by their conversion and departure from the ignorance and evils of the traditions of their former culture, and have thereby become aliens and sojourners in the world (1:1; 2:11). Their purpose is to live in the fear of God as his slaves (2:16) and still fulfill the obligations placed on each of them by their position in society. By this submission to their societal counterparts—the unconverted governors, masters, and husbands—believers maintain an honorable lifestyle that will repudiate false accusations and prepare those "Gentiles" for divine visitation (2:12). Even husbands must reject the shameful way that society treats women and give honor to their wives as equals (3:7), who of necessity converted with them. The secret to a good and happy life comes from living with other members of the church in harmony, love, and humility, not from societal recognition or personal achievement (3:8–12). Peter thus recognizes the affirmative nature of a societal organization and emphasizes that while these Christians were in no position to modify social structures, yet they were able to live within them and have a dynamic effect on the non-Christian members of society.

The church must understand the accusations, abuse, and ostracism she experiences from hostile neighbors. This is her opportunity to articulate her faith (3:15–17), to enjoy a fresh release from sin (4:1–6), and to express, with eschatological expectation, the gifts of the Spirit in the life of the church (4:7–11).

Persecution is to be accepted as a blessed partnership in the messianic sufferings. Like Christ, believers must commit their lives to God, who is the faithful Creator (4:19), and realize that if judgment begins with God's people in this life, then the final judgment of the unrepentant is incomprehensible (4:17–18). In contrast the church will share in the glory that belongs to Jesus Christ when he is revealed to the entire world (5:1, 10). That is why she must resist the devil, who, as the ultimate source of all persecution, seeks to destroy the church.

The church lives under the authority of Jesus Christ through his apostle (1:1) and the elders (5:1–4). The elders are responsible for the particular implementation of this letter, which they must do in an exemplary and honorable fashion. Younger men must submit to these elders, and all Christians must live in humility toward each other (5:5–7), especially before God, who gives honor at the appropriate time, when they will inherit the fullness of their salvation (1:4–5).

Christology is central to the church's understanding of salvation and persecution. By Christ's sacrificial death she has been redeemed from her vain and futile life, and by his resurrection she has been regenerated to a living hope and an imperishable inheritance (1:3, 18–20; 3:18). According to God's eternal plan Christ has already been presented to the church (1:11; 20, 25), and his revelation to the entire world will be the completion of her salvation when she will share in his glory (1:11; 4:13; 5:4, 10).

Jesus Christ is the cornerstone (or capstone) of the church, and the priest through whom she offers spiritual sacrifices to God (2:5–7). He is also the model for understanding and enduring abuse and persecution (1:11; 4:1, 13–15). His demeanor in crucifixion is exemplary for slaves with cruel masters (2:21–25). His resurrection and ascension affirm the church's ultimate triumph over her enemies, just as Jesus announced his triumph to the spirits in prison on his journey through the heavens (3:18–22). Jesus Christ is the Son of God (1:3), seated at his right hand; he shares with God the title of Lord (1:25; 2:3; 3:12, 15).

The Holy Spirit is the Spirit of Christ who spoke through the prophets (1:11), has been given to the church through the preaching of the gospel (1:12), and is engaged in the sanctification of the church (1:2). This unity of the Godhead is made explicit in salvation by the election of the Father, the sanctifying of the Spirit, and the sacrificial death of Christ (1:2).

God is also the caring Father of believers by regeneration (1:2, 17, 23). The church has placed her faith in him who is the Creator (1:21; 4:19) and who provides the gifts of the Spirit (4:10–11). She humbly fears God as her impartial judge (1:17; 4:17) in order to live according to his will and holiness (1:15; 2:16, 19; 4:2) and to be honored by him (5:5). The ultimate purpose of the church is to glorify God (1:3; 2:12; 4:11, 16; 5:11).

Norman R. Ericson

See also Capstone; Cornerstone; Persecution; Peter, Second, Theology of; Spirits in Prison.

Bibliography. R. J. Bauckham, *Jude, 2 Peter;* P. Davids, *The Book of 1 Peter;* D. Guthrie, *New Testament Theology;* S. J. Kistemaker, *Peter and Jude;* G. E. Ladd, *A Theology of the New Testament;* J. R. Michaels, *1 Peter;* L. Morris, *New Testament Theology.*

Peter, Second, Theology of. Second Peter was written to believers who were being influenced by false teachers who advocated an indulgent, libertine lifestyle and denied the second coming of the Lord. In conformity to the evil influences of their pagan culture, they distorted the apostolic teachings about freedom from the law (1:20–21; 2:21; 3:15–16; cf. Rom. 6:1, 15) and claimed a superior spirituality that freed them from regulation and judgment.

The author identifies himself as "Simon Peter," a combination of names that occurs only here in the New Testament and early Christian literature. Due to the internal features such as the mention of Peter's death (1:14), the difference in the style of the Greek, and the relatively slow recognition of the letter, some scholars argue that this letter was not written by the apostle, but by a disciple soon after Peter's death or by a second-century pseudepigrapher. Yet early Christian evidence affirms the apostolicity of the letter, and, unlike some more popular writing, it was actually accepted into the canon. In addition, critical issues can be explained, such as the difference in style being due to the use of a different amanuensis than Silvanus (1 Peter 5:12).

Peter wrote this letter to announce the certainty of divine judgment on the false teachers (chap. 2) and to declare that God is able to preserve all who engage in the spiritual disciplines of grace and knowledge (3:18). Jesus Christ will certainly appear, and those who have fallen from the faith will be judged along with this evil world. Peter's second letter is presumably addressed, like 1 Peter, from Rome to the churches in northern Asia Minor about A.D. 65.

Eschatology is the dominant theological focus in 2 Peter, with an emphasis on the certainty of divine judgment on ungodliness and apostasy. This judgment has happened in the past, continues in the present, and will find ultimate expression on the day of the Lord (3:10). This is proven by the destruction of the ancient world in its ungodliness, the continuing detention of insubordinate angels, and the catastrophic destruction of Sodom and Gomorrah for their evil and immorality (2:4–10).

These models of judgment correspond directly to the sins of the false teachers, including audacity, insurrection, blasphemy, immorality, indulgence, and deception (2:10b–19). They have compounded their guilt and punishment by turning against Jesus Christ and by luring recent converts back into their original corruption (2:20–22). Additional images of sin include idleness, fruitlessness, blindness (1:8–9); falling (1:10); returning to filth (2:22); defilement (2:20); a lustful journey (3:3).

The final judgment of ungodly persons will occur at the second coming of Christ (1:16; 3:4). It will be so severe and comprehensive that it will include the destruction of the heavens, the earth, and everything in them. All evil will be brought under the scrutiny of God and will be punished by him (3:5–7, 10–12).

Salvation is God's ability to protect the righteous and deliver them from their evil environment, like Noah and Lot (2:5, 7–8), which will be completed at the appearing of Jesus Christ. Because of the divine provision (1:3–4), which must be complemented by their own spiritual discipline (1:5–11), the righteous will not fall away under the testings that arise from their evil surroundings or from the false teachers (3:17).

This spiritual discipline requires the development of Christian character (1:5–7), adhering to the faith and true teaching of the apostles (1:12–21; 3:15–16), anticipating the day of the

Lord (3:11–12), and keeping oneself blameless and unspotted by the world (1:4; 3:14).

Such is the essence of participating in the divine nature (1:4). It is the means by which the faithful increase in godly grace and in the true knowledge of Jesus Christ (3:17). Traveling on this righteous road (2:21) is the way to confirm their calling and election (1:10–11), and to enjoy the new heaven and earth (3:13). All three persons of the Trinity are mentioned in 2 Peter, with strong expressions of the unity of the Father and the Son, and evidence of the unity of the Godhead in divine revelation.

God the Father is glorious and virtuous, and by these virtues he called a people to himself. By his divine power he provides for them all that is necessary for life and holiness (1:3). He is patient and wishes for all people to be saved. Even when people are most sinful, he delays judgment so that more people will respond to his call (3:9). Since he is unaffected by time, he can be patient without contradicting his promises (3:9). And because he is just, he imposes judgment on all unrighteousness (2:4–10; 3:12), and he will provide a new heaven and a new earth as the abode of the righteous (3:13).

Jesus Christ is the beloved Son of the Father (1:17), the Lord over the apostles (1:10), the Lord and Savior of the church (1:8, 11; 2:20), and the Lord of the eternal kingdom (1:11).

The unity of the Father and Son is shown by the grammatical constructions that declare that they have a common righteousness (1:1) and that as one they are the object and essence of Christian knowing (1:2). The Father displayed his glory and honor on the Son at the transfiguration (1:17), and they share the title "Lord" (1:2, 11, 14, 16; 2:9, 11; 3:8). They are interchangeably identified with eschatological events (1:16; 2:4, 9–10; 3:4, 12), and the Son receives the final doxology in words commonly addressed to the Father (3:18).

Divine revelation is foundational to the message of 2 Peter. It not only describes the inspiration of Scripture (1:21–22), but also presents the unity of the Godhead in revelation. It is the Spirit who spoke through the prophets (1:21; 3:2), the Father who spoke to the disciples (1:17), and Jesus who delivered his commandment(s) to the churches through the apostles (3:2).

The ecclesiology of 2 Peter is implicit, yet of great importance since the preservation of holiness in the church is the intended outcome of the letter. The church is equated with Israel by their common experience of false prophets or teachers within the community (2:1), by their common possession of divine revelation in the prophetic word (1:19; 3:2), and by their common claim to the patriarchs who have long since fallen asleep (3:4).

The church is governed by the authority of Jesus Christ mediated through the apostles (1:1; 3:2). Their primary task is to remind the churches of the apostolic teaching received from Jesus Christ (3:2) and to transmit it in a manner that will be effective even after their death (1:15). This apostolic teaching, like the writings of Paul (3:15–16), has a divine authority (1:18–19) equal to that of the prophets of Israel and the Hebrew Scriptures. NORMAN R. ERICSON

See also PETER, FIRST, THEOLOGY OF.

Bibliography. R. Bauckham, *Jude, 2 Peter;* D. Guthrie, *New Testament Theology: A Thematic Study;* G. E. Ladd, *A Theology of the New Testament;* L. Morris, *New Testament Theology.*

Pharisees. Jewish group mentioned, either collectively or as individuals, ninety-eight times in the New Testament, all but ten times in the Gospels.

The root meaning of the word "Pharisee" is uncertain. It is probably related to the Hebrew root *prš*, meaning "separate" or "detach." From whom did the Pharisees separate? From those, especially priests or clerics, who interpreted the Law differently than they? From the common people of the land (John 7:49)? From Gentiles or Jews who embraced the Hellenistic culture? From certain political groups? All these groups of people the Pharisees would have been determined to avoid in their resolution to separate themselves from any type of impurity proscribed by the levitical law—or, more specifically, their strict interpretation of it.

Josephus's references to the Pharisees are selective, probably because he was adapting them to a cultured Gentile audience. His information comes in two forms: direct descriptions and the role the Pharisees play in the history that he depicts.

Josephus says the Pharisees maintained a simple lifestyle (*Ant* 18.1.3 [12]), were affectionate and harmonious in their dealings with others (*War* 2.8.14 [166]), especially respectful to their elders (*Ant* 18.13 [12]), and quite influential throughout the land of Israel (*Ant* 13.10.5 [288]; 17.2.4 [41–45]; 18.1.3 [15])—although at the time of Herod they numbered only about six thousand (*Ant* 17.2.4 [42]). Josephus mentions their belief in both fate (divine sovereignty) and the human will (*War* 2.8.14 [163], *Ant* 18.1.3 [13]) and in immortality of both good and evil persons (*War* 2.8.14 [16]; *Ant* 17.1.3 [14]). Some Pharisees refused to take oaths (*Ant* 17.2.4 [42]). Of particular importance are Josephus's statements that the Pharisees adhered to "the laws of which the Deity approves" (*Ant* 17.2.4 [41]) and that they "are considered the most accurate interpreters of the laws" (*War* 2.8.14 [162]). Pharisees "follow the guidance of that which their doctrine has selected and transmitted as good, attaching the chief importance to the observance of those commandments which it has seen fit to dictate to them" (*Ant* 18.1.3 [12]) and they "passed on to the people certain regulations handed down by former generations and not recorded in the Laws of Moses" (*Ant* 17.2.4 [41]; 13.10.6 [297]). Although the phrase "Oral Law" is not used, it appears Josephus understood that the Pharisees affirmed a body of traditional interpretations, applications, and expansions of the Old Testament law communicated orally.

The Pharisees first appear in Josephus's account of intertestamental history as he describes the reign of John Hyrcanus (134–104). He assumes they had been in existence for some time. This raises the much discussed question of their origin. Some see the Pharisees' roots in the biblical Ezra (Ezra 7:10 shows his concern for exact keeping of the Law, especially ceremonial purity), others in the Hasidim (the Holy/Pure/Righteous) who supported the Maccabean revolt as long as its motives were religious but withdrew when it became primarily political (1 Macc. 2:42; 7:13; cf. 2 Macc. 14:6). Recent studies suggest the Pharisees were part of a general revolutionary spirit of the pre-Maccabean times and that they emerged as a scholarly class dedicated to the teaching of both the written and oral Law and stressing the internal side of Judaism. In any case, they were certainly one of the groups that sought to adapt Judaism for the postexilic situation.

John Hyrcanus was at first "a disciple" of the Pharisees but became their enemy (*Ant* 13.10.5 [288–98]). The Pharisees were opponents of the Hasmonean rulers from then on. The hostility was especially great during the reign of Alexander Jannaeus (103–76), and they seem to have taken a leading part in opposition to him; it is usually assumed that Pharisees composed either all or a large part of the eight hundred Jews he later crucified (*Ant* 13.14.2 [380]). The one exception to Pharisaic opposition to the Hasmoneans was Salome Alexandria (76–67), under whom they virtually dominated the government.

Josephus's information about the Pharisees under the Romans is spotty. Under Herod (37 B.C.–4 B.C.) the Pharisees were influential, but carefully controlled by the king. Some individual Pharisees did oppose Herod on occasion. Josephus gives almost no information about the Pharisees from the death of Herod until the outset of the revolt against Rome (about A.D. 66). At first they attempted to persuade the Jews against militant actions (*War* 2.17.3 [411]). Later Pharisees appear as part of the leadership of the people during the revolt, some individuals playing a leading role in it.

The New Testament depicts the Pharisees as opponents of Jesus or the early Christians. On the other hand, they warn Jesus that his life is in danger from Herod (Luke 13:31), invite him for meals (Luke 7:36–50; 14:1), are attracted to or believe in Jesus (John 3:1; 7:45–53; 9:13–38), and protect early Christians (Acts 5:34; 23:6–9). Paul asserts he was a Pharisee before his conversion (Phil. 3:5).

The clearest New Testament statement of Pharisaic distinctives is Acts 23:8: "The Sadducees say that there is no resurrection, and that there are neither angels, nor spirits, but the Pharisees acknowledge them all." This would give the impression that doctrine was the basic concern of the group. However, Mark 7:3–4 says that "The Pharisees . . . do not eat unless they give their hands a ceremonial washing holding to the tradition of the elders. When they come from the marketplace they do not eat unless they wash. And they observe many other traditions, such as the washing of cups, pitchers and kettles." Thus, we are also told of the Pharisees' concern for washing (ceremonial cleansing) and observance of "the traditions of the elders," a description of the Oral Law. Matthew 23 calls attention to their (1) positions of religious authority in the community, (2) concern for outward recognition and honor, (3) enthusiasm for making converts, and (4) emphasis on observing the legalistic minutia of the law. In verse 23 Jesus condemns them, not for what they did, but for neglecting "the more important matters of the law—justice, mercy and faithfulness."

There is general recognition that Josephus's description of the Pharisees as a "sect" (*hairesis*) should not be understood in the modern sense. Instead, it seems to denote something like a "religious party," "community," or "denomination" within mainstream Judaism. Pharisaic zeal for the Law is obvious, but what is meant by Law? The sanctity of the written Law was never questioned, but intertestamental Jewish groups differed on how it was to be interpreted and applied. The Pharisees developed their own body of interpretations, expansions, and applications of the Law that they came to regard as of divine origin (Mishnah, *Aboth,* 1:1). This was to assist in understanding and keeping the Law, often added regulations ("fences" or "hedges") were designed to prevent even coming close to breaking the Law. Most of these traditions, the Oral Law, dealt with matters of levitical purity. Some contained other additions that had come into prominence in the intertestamental situation. These included belief in immortality, angels and demons, spirits, and divine sovereignty. Expansions of such doctrines led to others. For example, belief in immortality resulted in expanded messianic and eschatological views. Their social and political views were based on their premise that all of life must be lived under the control of God's Law. The Pharisees opposed Hasmoneans who, contrary to the Law, sought to combine the monarchy and priesthood. Likewise, they rejected Roman authority when it appeared to conflict with the Law of God.

Some modern scholars have objected to the assumption that intertestamental Judaism, including Pharisaism, believed in a "wage price-theory of righteousness," that eternal life is granted on the basis of faithfulness in keeping the Law. Rather, they insist, Israel's religion was a "covenantal nominism" in which Law-keeping was a response to God's grace offered in his covenant with Israel. These studies provide a helpful corrective to traditional views of intertestamental Judaism, including Pharisaism, as merely a blatant legalism. Yet the New Testament assumes that Jesus and his disciples were at times in conflict with just such legalism (e.g., Mark 10:17; Luke 15:29 [note that "the older brother" most likely represents the Pharisaic point of view]); John 6:28; and Paul's constant fight against earning salvation by works of the law (note: Rom. 9:30–32, Israel "pursued it [righteousness] not by faith but as if it were by works"). Of particular relevance here are the contrasting prayers of the Pharisee and the Publican, the results of which the latter "went home justified" (Luke 18:9–14). Intertestamental Judaism was far from a monolithic whole; many, if not most, of the common people, who were influenced by the Pharisees, seem to have held a legalistic view of their religion. Jesus and the early Christians strongly opposed views that externalized religion and/or sought God's favor on the basis of human effort. J. JULIUS SCOTT, JR.

See also JESUS CHRIST; LEGALISM; PAUL THE APOSTLE.

Bibliography. J. W. Bowker, *Jesus and the Pharisees;* L. Findelstein, *The Pharisees: The Sociological Background of Their Faith;* L. L. Grabbe, *Judaism from Cyrus to Hadrian;* J. Neusner, *Formative Judaism: Torah, Pharisees and Rabbis;* idem, *The Rabbinic Traditions about the Pharisees before 70;* E. Rivkin, *A Hidden Revolution: The Pharisees Search for the Kingdom Within;* E. P. Sanders, *Judaism: Practice and Belief, 63 BCE-66 CE;* idem, *Paul and Palestinian Judaism;* Emil Schürer, *The History of Their Jewish People in the Age of Jesus Christ;* Moisés Silva, *WTJ* 42 (1979–80): 395–405; M. Simon, *The Jewish Sects at the Time of Jesus.*

Philemon, Theology of. The letter to Philemon is also addressed to Apphia and Archippus (v. 2). That Philemon is the intended primary recipient, however, is clear from the fact that, apart from the conclusion of the letter (vv. 22, 25), which uses the second-person plural pronoun (referring to all three addressees), the rest of the letter employs the second-person singular pronoun (Gk. *su*) in addressing the primary recipient, who is surely Philemon.

Paul's reference to the "church in *your* (sing.) home" (v. 2) clearly indicates that a single household is intended. Therefore, these three individuals were probably related. Perhaps Apphia was the wife of Philemon and Archippus was his son.

The letter of Philemon is little more than a note in length, consisting of only 335 words in Greek, and hardly more than a memo in nature. Although the letter contains no theological arguments, it is written from a definite theological presupposition centering on Onesimus's new postconversion relationship (v. 10) in the flesh and in the Lord (v. 16). The theological premise is that upon conversion even a slave becomes an equally important part of the body of Christ, the Christian family; the premise is that, in Christ, there is no longer slave nor free (cf. Gal. 3:28). Paul had earlier written to the Corinthian believers that whoever was called in the Lord as a slave is a freed person belonging to the Lord, just as whoever was free when called is a slave of Christ (1 Cor. 7:22). In Philemon, as in the beginning of every letter in the Pauline corpus except Titus, the readers are reminded that every Christian is a slave of the Lord Jesus Christ.

This reality applied with equal validity to both Philemon and Onesimus, to master as well as slave. Paul's ultimate desire was that a new sociological relationship would emerge based on this reciprocal spiritual reality. JOHN MCRAY

See also PAUL THE APOSTLE.

Philippians, Theology of. Paul's letter to the Philippians is not a treatise on theology. Rather, it is a personal letter dealing primarily with personal matters that concern the Christians in Philippi for whom Paul has the greatest affection (1:7). And yet Paul, whose mind is filled with thoughts of God, Christ, the Spirit, salvation, resurrection, and the new world to come, cannot write even the briefest of letters without thinking and writing theologically. Hence, when he discusses any aspect of life in its many and varied dimensions he views it always in light of God and what God has done and is doing in the world.

God. The noun "God" appears twenty-four times in this short letter—a fact that makes it clear that for Paul, God is at the very center of things! The word he uses for God, *theos,* the Greek translation of the Hebrew *ʾĕlōhîm,* reveals that Paul sees in this one appellation all the wide-ranging ideas of the Old Testament. God for him is the Almighty, the Creator of heaven and earth, the Master of the universe, transcendent above his creation, himself life and the author and sustainer of life, Father, the one set apart from all other beings, sole, supreme, and sovereign. He is God, *theos,* the One before whom all people should reverently bow in awe. Glory and praise belong to God (1:11; 2:11); worship is to be given to God (3:3); sacrifice is to be made to God (4:18; cf. Rom. 12:1–2); doxologies are to be sung to God (4:20); prayer is to be directed to God (1:3, 9). God, for Paul, is distinct from every other person or thing, unique.

And yet God is not so distinct, so wholly other, that he has absented himself from his world, possessing no interest in it or in the lives of those whom he has created in his own image. On the contrary, Paul understands that God is so close and so intimate that those who believe in him are free to speak of him as "*my* God" (1:3; 4:19). He is aware, too, that God is continuously breaking into human history, constantly at work in the lives of his people to create within them both the desire for and the power to achieve the good (2:13).

Epaphroditus's sickness is to Paul still further evidence of the immediate presence of God and of his willingness to act in individual human histories. When this special friend is restored to wholeness Paul notes that "God had mercy on him; and not on him only but also on me" (2:27). He is convinced that God stepped in and put an end to this near-fatal illness. It is Paul's overwhelming conviction that God is transcendent and thus not at all entangled in the web of human problems. Yet he is also immanent and thus free and able to extricate humans from these problems. This realization gives Paul great incentive to pray for his friends (1:9) and strong confidence to encourage his friends to do the same—to worry about nothing but to pray about everything (4:6). God, for Paul, is present and mindful of the needs of his people, ready and able to fill up what they lack from the boundless richness of his resources in Christ Jesus (4:19) if that should be his will.

Paul also knows that God broke into human history in order to undo the damage that had been done as the consequence of sin by reconciling the disobedient to himself and by acting to provide salvation for all sinners. God is holy, God most high, but not so high and holy that he will not step down to involve himself in human affairs. Most profoundly God stooped down in the person of his incarnate Son to save his people from destruction and to provide for them the very righteousness he demanded from them. Thus God for Paul is not only Sovereign but Savior of sinful humanity (1:28).

Christ. The preeminence of Christ pervades Philippians, not in any structured, formal way but in almost every comment the apostle makes, even in the most mundane of them. Seemingly the whole of Paul's thought is affected by the power and presence of the Christ who had changed his own life so radically (see 1:21; 3:4b–10), and thus everything he writes, every bit of advice he gives, every word of encouragement he offers he does in the name of Christ and in the reality of his living presence.

Although "Jesus" was the name given to this special person by an angel (Matt. 1:21), and used so frequently in the Gospels, Paul is not inclined to use it, at least by itself. And never does he do so in his letter to the Philippians except once, and that in a hymn he may be quoting (2:6–11; see esp. v. 10).

"Christ" is the designation Paul prefers to use when speaking or writing about this most significant person in his life. Perhaps it is because this word, "Christ" (Gk. *christos;* Heb. *māšîaḥ*), meaning "the Anointed One," held in it the hopes and dreams of those generations before him—hopes and dreams that now at last had come to realization.

The word "christ" was an ancient designation for almost any person chosen and equipped by God to do God's special work in the world (1 Sam. 16:1–3; 1 Chron. 16:22; Isa. 45:1). David, a man "after God's own heart," was God's "christ" in this sense, as were the kingly descendants who succeeded him (2 Sam. 22:51; Ps. 89:35–36). But when the Davidic monarchy eventually was overthrown and Israel was in disarray, a promise came of a future king, a greater descendant of David, the Christ par excellence whose rule would be surpassingly righteous (Isa. 9:6–7; 42:1–4; Ezek. 34:23–24). The darker Israel's history became, the brighter burned this hope for such a deliverer, a mighty king, son of David, anointed of the Spirit, a king whose kingdom would be great, an eternal kingdom of goodness and justice (Isa. 11:1–5).

What was different in the writings of the New Testament from those of the Old Testament and the literature between the Testaments is that the Messiah, the Anointed of the Lord who was to come, had come and could be identified. He was Jesus (Luke 1:31–33). But contrary to expectations he was not a warrior-king, establishing his rule by force of arms, bringing political deliverance to Israel from the oppressive power of foreign invaders. And for this reason his coming was either overlooked or rejected by many. Rather, Jesus was God's humble servant, the Anointed of the Lord, sent not only to Israel but to the world, to show them his strength by his weakness; his power to save people, not from Rome, but from death by his own death upon a cross; his ability to reverse the destructive forces not of the emperor but of the Evil One by his resurrection from the dead. He was God's Anointed, God's "Christ" par excellence!

Paul came to understand all this as a result of having encountered the living, resurrected Christ on the road to Damascus, who, in a moment, had transferred him out of the kingdom of darkness, freed him from the power of evil, saved him from his sin, and gave him life instead of death. It was this message, then, that he preached to the Philippians: God's action to save the world through Christ, the long-expected Messiah (1:15–18, 27; 3:9, 18). Paul is so overwhelmed by the majesty, love, goodness, and mercy of Christ that he sees no reason for his existence except "to be for Christ" (1:21).

Although Paul is reluctant to use the name "Jesus" by itself, he nevertheless frequently links it with the title "Christ" (1:1, 6, 8, 11, 26; 2:5, 21;

3:3, 12, 14; 4:7, 19, 21). In this combined name he makes it clear to his friends at Philippi that the longed-for deliverer, the long-awaited Savior, the hope of ancient Israel and of the world, the Messiah, was Jesus of Nazareth.

And this "Jesus Christ" whom he preaches is also Lord (1:2; 3:8; 4:23), declared to be so by God himself (2:11). Because of the willingness of Jesus Christ to humble himself, to pour himself out for others, to obey the will of his Father even to the point of accepting death—because of this attitude and action on his part, God highly exalted him and gave him the name that is above every name, "Lord," so that at this name every knee should bow in reverence and awe (2:6–11). "Lord," then, is the title that for Paul best puts into perspective who Jesus Christ is. It is the title that the earliest church settled upon (Acts 2:32, 36) and which Paul also chooses to use (Phil. 1:2, 14; 2:11, 24, 29; 3:1, 8; 4:1, 2, 4, 10, 23). By it he is able to say that Jesus is divine, that he shares the very nature of God (2:6–11: "Lord" in the Old Testament was the Greek word that translated the Hebrew, "Yahweh," "Jehovah"). "Jesus Christ is Lord" becomes Paul's creed, the creed he lives by. As Lord, Jesus Christ is to be served. As Lord he is to be obeyed. Paul sets the whole course of his life to fulfill this freeing obligation, and he encourages his friends at Philippi to do the same. For he knows that the one who is the "slave" of Christ is the one who is truly free (Rom. 6:17–23).

Salvation. The need for salvation is made very clear in the pages of the Bible, for here it is spelled out that people, made in the likeness of God, formed to worship and enjoy God, made to live in harmony with God and with one another, created to corule with God, and like God to be crowned with glory and honor, find themselves sadly alienated from God and from each other, enemies of God, hostile toward one another, dethroned, adrift in the world they were intended to rule, afraid, desperate, traveling away from the light toward the darkness, headed for destruction. It is against this backdrop that Paul's remarks to the Philippians about salvation are to be understood, especially as they are articulated in chapter 3. To be sure, he does not use the word "salvation" in this chapter. Nevertheless the idea of salvation is present in his thinking all the way through as he shares his own life's history, describing by means of it the beguiling nature of sin and its devastating consequences. Put simply, Paul says in essence that all people, himself included, are sinful and cannot possibly extricate themselves from this ultimate human predicament of sin by their own personal pedigree or moral endeavor. But what is humanly impossible is possible with God. God himself has acted to save. And he has done it all through Christ!

Instead of the word "salvation" Paul prefers in Philippians 3 to use a word that certainly includes the idea of salvation but exceeds it in meaning. The word he chooses is "righteousness," a word borrowed from the Old Testament and expanded upon by him. "Righteousness" for Paul is God giving back to people that which sin took away from them and more (Rom. 5:15–18), the ultimate goodness he demands. It is his raising human beings again to that high standard of their humanness that he had originally designed for them. It is the full restoration of humans to their right relationship with himself. It is reconciliation.

But this righteousness, Paul makes clear, is not attainable by personal endeavor. It is the "righteousness of God" (3:9), by which Paul in effect states that this is a righteousness that has its origin with God, a righteousness that God has taken the initiative to provide out of his own great love even for those hostile to him (Rom. 5:10), a righteousness that people cannot possibly buy, earn, or merit. It is a righteousness that comes from God freely and without charge through the faithfulness of Jesus Christ and through faith in Jesus Christ (3:9).

The person of Christ, then, is central to this righteousness. For by Christ and only by him God has worked in a truly indescribable way to save human beings, to reconcile them to himself, to bring them out of slavery to sin, out of desperation and despair into hope, out of death into life. All that people could not do for themselves because of their weakness and sinfulness God did for them through the life and death and resurrection of Christ (Phil. 3:4b–9; cf. 2:6–11; Rom. 1:17; 3:21–28).

Faith. The proper response to God's good news is faith (3:9). But when Paul speaks of faith as the proper response he does not mean that faith is some new kind of "work" that people have to do, or some new kind of action they must undertake to earn God's favor. For Paul faith is a glad and open admission that we cannot earn God's approval by meritorious effort but rather a simple reaching out of empty hands to receive God's free offer of forgiveness, grace, and love in Jesus Christ. Faith is the "Yes" of our whole personality to the personal address of God in Christ.

Sanctification. Righteousness (salvation) was God's action in Christ to recreate people in his image and likeness, an image that had been savagely marred by sin (Col. 3:10). Righteousness for Paul is both an accomplished fact and a continuing process. He makes it clear that the Philippians are "saints" (1:1) and that God looks upon them as such—not only "as if" they were righteous but as indeed righteous by virtue of their being "in Christ." And yet he also makes it clear that this being righteous, good, noble, and true not only involves the intervening action of God, but also a moral striving on the part of Christians, a movement toward moral goodness that they themselves are responsible for. True, God is at work in their lives through the Holy Spirit. But Christians must also work (2:12–13). Such a process of growth in the Christian life, in theological terms, is called sanctification.

This dynamic aspect of sanctification is so very important to Paul that he cannot imagine leaving it to chance or intuition. Hence, running throughout this brief letter are numerous uses of the imperative mood, where he appeals directly to the will of every Christian reader. Among other things he urges his friends to forget the past with all of its successes and failures and live full out, stretching forward to what is ahead, straining toward the goal of the high calling of God in Christ Jesus (3:13–14).

He urges the Philippians to pray with thanksgiving so that they might keep their equilibrium and direction in a world heaving with anxiety-creating situations (4:6).

He urges them to discipline their minds because he knows that how people think determines how they act, that thought governs conduct. And so he tells them to think about things that are true, to focus their minds on things that merit respect, to ponder things that are just, to reflect on things that are pure, to dwell on all those things that are lovely, amiable, attractive, winsome, to think long and hard about those things that are likely to draw people to the faith and help them grow in the faith (4:8).

He urges the Philippians to act (4:9). It is not enough for Christians to think lofty thoughts. They must put these good thoughts into practice. Thought and action, mind and body working together must be inseparably linked (4:8–9). But Paul wants them to act in a certain way, in accord with what they have learned from him, in harmony with the traditions he has passed on to them, in keeping with the gospel of Christ (4:9; cf. 1:27).

And finally he urges them to keep focused on Christ and continually to adopt for themselves the attitude that was in Christ Jesus. For this one who was in the form of God did not consider the equality he shared with God something to be exploited for his own advantage. On the contrary, he poured himself out to benefit others; he became a human being and set himself to serve; he humbled himself and did not put himself at the center, but he determined wholly to obey God. Hence, God honored and exalted him. It is Paul's passionate desire for his friends that this same attitude of mind that controlled Christ's actions controls their actions also. As Christ had set his own interests aside and had given first place to the interests of God and people, so those who follow Christ must put the interests of God and people first. For Paul, steady, constant reflection on the course that Christ took results in the "ought to be" becoming a reality in the Christian pilgrim's progress, in the movement toward sanctification.

Joy. No person can read Paul's letter to the Philippians and miss the note of "joy" that runs like a refrain throughout it (1:4, 18, 25; 2:2, 17, 18, 28, 29; 3:1; 4:1, 4, 10). And yet joy is no shallow word. It carries deep theological meaning. Joy is not mere happiness. Nor is it the absence of pain or emotional distress (2:27). When one carefully examines the contexts of this recurring word, one begins to see that when Paul talks of joy he is in reality describing a settled state of mind characterized by peace—an attitude that views the world and all of its ups and downs with equanimity, a confident way of looking at life that is rooted in faith, in a keen awareness of a trust in the living Lord of the church (3:1; 4:4, 10; cf. 1:25–26). In other words, joy for Paul is an understanding of existence that can include both elation and depression, delight and dismay, affliction and ease, prosperity and poverty, because joy is that which enables the Christian to see beyond the circumstances of life to the sovereign Lord who stands above all circumstances and has ultimate control over them.

GERALD F. HAWTHORNE

See also COLOSSIANS, THEOLOGY OF; EPHESIANS, THEOLOGY OF; PAUL THE APOSTLE; PHILEMON, THEOLOGY OF.

Bibliography. L. Cerfaux, *Christ in the Theology of Saint Paul;* J. D. G. Dunn, *Christology in the Making;* G. F. Hawthorne, *Philippians;* idem, *Word Biblical Themes: Philippians;* R. P. Martin, *Carmen Christi: Philippians 2:5–11 in Recent Interpretation and in the Setting of Early Christian Worship;* C. F. D. Moule, *The Origin of Christology;* P. T. O'Brien, *The Epistle to the Philippians;* J. Ziesler, *Pauline Christianity.*

Philosophy. ***The Old Testament.*** Biblical philosophy is not an abstract monologue but a dialogue with God. The Bible never attempts to prove the existence of God, bur starts from the premise that God exists (i.e., Gen. 1:1); philosophy, in contrast, takes up questions concerning the nature of the universe and existence that do not necessarily presume the verity of God. Therefore, philosophy can be an effective tool if properly used as a means of understanding pretheological questions, but not as a method of supplanting the revelation already made available by faith through God's Scriptures. The limitations of human reason, especially in light of the moral degeneracy in humans, requires God's help in resolving philosophical questions.

The sacrificial structure of the Hebrew Scriptures reveals a simple, nonesoteric approach to the questions concerning solidarity with God and oneself. Faith was a prerequisite for abiding in the covenant. There is rarely a philosophical concern, although in the psalms occasionally deeper questions concerning the afterlife are considered in the light of theodicy.

The New Testament. It is not surprising that Paul, "the apostle to the Gentiles," is more philosophical and deals with the problem of onerous philosophy more than any other writer in the New Testament because of the pragmatic issues of polytheism and atheism he confronted. The only time the world "philosophy" is used in the Bible is in Colossians 2:8. The problem addressed by Paul is probably an incipient form of gnosticism. One fascinating aspect of this passage is the idea that one can be taken "captive" through philosophy. Paul is not anti-intellectual, as is evidenced by the fact that he quotes Greek poets in Acts 17:28; also, in Acts 17 he directs his teachings toward Epicurean and Stoic philosophers, which shows that he was knowledgeable of their philosophy. He even agreed with it where he could. But, when the apocalyptic element is understood, it becomes clearer the philosophical deficiency that Paul was pointing out. The recipients of the second-person plural pronoun in Colossians 2:8 are Gentiles (cf. 1:27). The philosophy is more clearly spelled out in 2:16: "Therefore do not let anyone condemn you in matters of food and drink or of observing festivals, new moons, or sabbaths" (NRSV). Food laws and calendar observance were not required for the Gentiles' newfound faith. The observance of these nationalistic requirements was synonymous with being under the influence of "elemental spirits of the universe," that is, the evil spirits that swarmed the cosmos. To be under this demonic influence was not necessary because Christ "disarmed the rulers and authorities and made a public example of them, triumphing over them in it" (Col. 2:15).

Another aspect of the philosophy was esoteric speculation. Two examples are given: "worship of angels" and "dwelling on visions." Hebrews 1 also addresses the problem of the worship of angels (Christ was erroneously thought to be an angel). In Colossians, Paul contrasts arrogant, earthly, speculative philosophy with humble, transcendental, and righteous philosophy derived from God.

The problem of exploitative philosophy in Colossians 2:8 is not simply an aversion toward a theory of analysis underlying deportment, thought, knowledge, and the constitution of the universe. Rather, it is unwarranted speculation that encroaches on the freedom of another. The regulations "do not handle, do not taste, do not touch" (v. 21) reveal that a personal, introspective analysis concerning one's desire for meaning is not in view, but a philosophy that requires a change in behavior in another. It is the type of conjecture that places cultural, not moral demands on one and begins with the supposition of ethnic and religious superiority. This predicament was precisely the quandary of gnosticism. The elitism that proliferated gnosticism was largely based on the philosophical premise that gnostics were superior and held a secret knowledge.

The term "philosopher" (literally "lover of wisdom") appears in Acts 17:18. It is clear that the first time Christianity was taught in Athens, an intellectual hub of the ancient world, the message of monotheism was equated with obtuseness. Ironically, much of their philosophy was derived from superstition.

Epicurean philosophy originated from its founder Epicurus, who died in 270 B.C. Epicureans did not believe in an afterlife; therefore, one should neither fear death nor believe in supernatural beings. There was no jurisdiction over the state of affairs of humans. That which brought the most felicity now was the highest aim in life. Unlike the Stoics, the Epicureans rejected fate because there were no governing principles or beings that controlled one's destiny. The body was an indispensable part of human nature. Eventually, against the concept envisaged by Epicurus, this philosophy became associated with hedonistic practices because there was no infinite reference point to dictate morality.

Stoic philosophy was founded by Zeno around 300 B.C. In contrast to Epicurean philosophy, individuals achieve well-being and peace through their consonance with nature (which was in a constant state of change) by having the qualities of bravery, justice, self-control, and a competent intellect. All people have the divine spark of godhood (i.e., the logos) within them. Stoicism was monistic or even pantheistic because of the belief that divinity was so immanent that nature itself was part of the divine spark.

Therefore, providence governed the affairs of humans. The form of Stoic philosophy found in the New Testament was amalgamated with Roman polytheism. Paul was "deeply distressed" because the city was "full of idols." Undoubtedly, some of these idols were worshiped by the Stoics (not the Epicurean atheists).

Paul's sermon is directed toward Stoic and Epicurean philosophy. Addressing Stoic fatalism, he points out that God created the world and does not dwell in idols (17:24). Unlike Stoic pantheism, God "gives to all mortals life and breath and all things" (v. 25). God is not so immanent that he is the creation itself.

Unlike the Epicureans, Paul announces that God requires repentance by all (v. 30) "because he has fixed a day on which he will have the world judged in righteousness" (v. 31). The resurrection of Christ is the "assurance" that all will raise from the dead and stand before God (v. 31). The resurrection of Christ, with the subsequent philosophical and logical argument that Paul makes in 1 Corinthians 15, stands in sharp contrast to hedonistic Epicureanism. Like Colossians 2, Acts 17 demonstrates how philosophy, erroneously applied, can lead to "captivity" (e.g., Epicurean hedonism) and the control of "elemental spirits of the universe" (e.g., Stoic idolatry).

Even though Paul's philosophy in Acts 17 is logical, it is not acrimonious. Paul practices the principle he sets forth in 1 Corinthians 9:22: "I have become all things to all people, that I might by all means save some." The fact that Paul quotes some of their poets (17:28) corroborates the notion that he was not anti-intellectual; instead, he gives a reasonable, philosophical deposition when challenging the intellectuals of Athens.

Another example of Paul's cultural sensitivity can be found in Acts 19:9. Paul argued in the Hall of Tyrannus in Ephesus for two years. Tyrannus was probably a school named after a Greek philosopher. The Jewish apostle to the Gentiles was undoubtedly skilled in Greek rhetoric and philosophy.

In Romans 1:18–23 Paul's philosophical logic is essential a "teleological" argument, that is, a testimony of the existence of God based on the order and purpose of the universe. Paul uses philosophical reasoning to discredit pagan superstition.

Eric W. Adams

Bibliography. J. Guttmann, *Philosophies of Judaism: The History of Jewish Philosophy from Biblical Times to Franz Rosenzweig;* J. Hick, ed., *Classical and Contemporary Readings in the Philosophy of Religion;* C. S. Lewis, *The Problem of Pain;* G. Vesey, ed., *The Philosophy in Christianity;* H. A. Wolfson, *The Philosophy of the Church Fathers.*

Pit. ***The Old Testament.*** "Pit" denotes a large hole in the ground. Pits were used to catch wild animals (Ezek. 19:1–8) or to collect water for drinking ("cisterns," Deut. 6:11). Sometimes they were used as dungeons or prisons (Gen. 37:24; Exod. 12:29; Jer. 38:6).

Very often, however, "pit" is used figuratively. For example, enemies seek to harm the psalmist by "digging a pit" for his life (Ps. 35:7). Commonly it is a metaphor for Sheol ("the grave," Ps. 16:10) or death (Ps. 30:9). Since God did not reveal the hope of resurrection and the glories of heaven until late in Old Testament times, many expressions are quite negative. Everyone dies, so no one can avoid the pit (Ps. 49:9). It is a place of destruction (Isa. 38:17), a dark and deep place where the dead are without strength, forsaken by the living, and forgotten by God (Ps. 88:3–6). There is no thanksgiving, praise, or hope there (Ps. 38:1–8).

The New Testament. In the New Testament "pit" is used literally of a place into which an animal (Matt. 12:11; Luke 14:5) or the blind (Matt. 15:14; Luke 6:39) might fall (the latter is also a figure for the spiritually blind Pharisees). In addition, it is used metaphorically for an underworld dungeon: a gloomy prison for the fallen angels (2 Peter 2:4) or a bottomless abyss for Satan during the millennium (Rev. 20:1–3).

William B. Nelson, Jr.

See also Death, Mortality; Hell.

Poetry. ***Introduction.*** The significance of studying biblical poetry lies largely in the amount of the Bible that is penned in poetic style. No doubt many readers will conjure images of the so-called poetic books in the Old Testament (Job, Psalms, Proverbs, Ecclesiastes, and Song of Solomon) upon hearing the term "biblical poetry." Unfortunately, this preconception is not wholly accurate for at least two reasons.

First, the books deemed "poetic" do not always yield solid examples of biblical poetry. For instance, Ecclesiastes does not consistently exhibit examples of verse. Major sections of the book are prosaic. The Book of Job manifests prosaic sections that frame the book (cf. chaps. 1, 42).

Second, the term "poetic books" implies that the other Old Testament material is not poetic. This simply is not the case. Some of the most sublime poetry in the Bible lies in such diverse texts as Exodus 15 and Deuteronomy 32–33 in the Pentateuch, to Judges 5 and 2 Samuel 1 in the historical books, to the majority of the Book of Isaiah in the prophets, to name only a few. Indeed, one should note that most of the prophetic books are poetic. Although there is some difference of opinion among scholars about certain texts between one-third and one-half of the Old Testament is written in a poetic style. Clearly, when such a large portion of Sacred Writ occurs in poetic shape, one should note carefully the distinguishing characteristics.

Another reason for studying poetry rests with the unique effect it produces on the reader. Although we will develop this point later, poetry is particularly appropriate for numerous types of passages because of its powerful ability to communicate an emotional message. Thus, for emotions as diverse as laments, oracles of judgment, and paeans of praise, poetry is perfectly suited.

Definition. There are basically two schools of literary thought on how to define the basic nature of poetry. One approach attempts to make the matter purely subjective, arguing that if a text "feels" poetic and impresses itself upon the mind of the reader as such, then the text is indeed poetic. The other school analyzes texts for diagnostic features that could delimit a passage as poetry.

A genuinely poetic text should impress itself upon the reader as poetry on an emotive level. However, there are characteristics of poetry that can be objectively described.

The Old Testament. When many think of poetry, common characteristics of English poetry such as rhyme, alliteration, and assonance come to mind. However, Old Testament poetry does not rhyme, and examples of alliteration and assonance are rare.

Hebrew poetry does possess some form of meter, but there is no agreement about how to analyze it with precision. For instance, some would try to count larger stressed units such as words, while others seek to count syllables. The former method is much more widely utilized, although all recognize great uncertainty regarding their analyses. Despite the uncertainties, enough texts exhibit clear metrical patterns that meter cannot be dismissed outright (for example, Gen. 49 generally manifests a 3:3 pattern).

Perhaps one of the two most distinguishing features of Old Testament poetry is the presence of figurative language. Of course, both formal prose and casual conversation are well sprinkled with figurative language. However, in poetry, the frequency and sophistication of the figures rise dramatically.

When one encounters a text where figurative language might be present, two issues arise. The first relates to knowing how to determine whether an expression is a figure of speech. In other words, should the expression be taken "literally" (many interpreters prefer either the word "normal" or "plain") or "figuratively"? The second matter concerns the proper interpretation of the figure once it is identified as such.

It would be misleading to imply that one can always know without the slightest uncertainty if an expression is a figure. Despite this qualification, however, one can be confident about the author's intent the overwhelming majority of the time. The basic question the reader should ask when looking for a figure is, "does this text make sense in its *normal* sense?"

When presented with a figure, the reader must then attempt to understand it precisely. One of the biggest misunderstandings at this point is the notion that figurative language cannot be interpreted as accurately as can nonfigurative expressions. This is a common misapprehension. Figures can be interpreted with as much accuracy as can nonfigurative language. The difference lies in the figure's ability to communicate on an emotive level in addition to the cognitive.

Finally, how does one begin to analyze a figure of speech in a biblical text? Some figures are relatively simple and easy to analyze. For instance, most metaphors and similes offer few difficulties. Other types, such as metonymy, are significantly more challenging. Unfortunately, the diversity of figures makes it impossible to study the different types of figures here.

The second characteristic of Old Testament poetry, one that is unique to poetry in the ancient Near East, is parallelism. In the mid-nineteenth century Robert Lowth formulated the understanding of parallelism that still prevails today in modified form. Parallelism is an analogy drawn from geometry that assumes that two (or sometimes more) lines are paired in such a fashion that the meaning of one line relates to the meaning of the other line(s) in one of several predictable ways.

The basic unit in the parallel lines is the word pair, that is, two or more words that naturally pair together as synonyms, antonyms. or amplifications of one other. "Day" and "night," "sun" and "moon," and "earth" and "world" serve to illustrate this phenomenon. Much of the poet's ingenuity lies in the ability to use well-known stock pairs in surprising and innovative ways.

Although word pairs are the building block of parallelism, the basic unit is the poetic line. Usually biblical poetry utilizes pairs of lines called couplets. Less frequently, three lines (or triplets) occur. Four paired lines are called a quatrain. Old Testament poetry only rarely utilizes strophes, unlike much English poetry.

In the Old Testament one encounters several different types, or aspects, of parallelism, each demonstrating a different semantic relationship between the lines. Although not one of the most common aspects, "synonymous" parallelism is one of the simplest. In synonymous parallelism the second line of the pair essentially restates the meaning of the first.

It is misleading to describe the two lines as being synonymous in the strict sense since the meaning of the two lines is not precisely equivalent. The second line gives a subtly different view in comparison to the first, contributing more than a simple restatement or paraphrase of the first. To illustrate, consider the perspective on an object seen with binocular vision. If while viewing that object, one closes one eye and then opens it and closes the other eye, the perspective from either eye singly will be quite similar to that of the other. However, the differences will be perceptible. The perspective given by both eyes together, like that of the pair of synonymous lines, yields a unique perspective and a depth of perception available only in tandem.

Consider the following example:

> Surely he took up our infirmities
> and carried our sorrows. (Isa. 53:4a)

The lines emphasize the same message by creative restatement. In the following case,

> The heavens declare the glory of God;
> the skies proclaim the work of his hands. (Ps. 19:1)

we also see synonymy. However, the context of the couplet helps us understand "glory of God" as basically equivalent to "work of his hands." Without the context the reader might not make such a connection, but the poet guides his readers to this conclusion with a skillful use of parallelism.

A second expression of parallelism has been named "antithetical" parallelism. Antithetical parallelism sets the paired lines in opposition to one another. One line restates the other, but negatively. Most examples of antithetical parallelism occur in the Wisdom Literature, where the two paths, the way of wisdom and that of folly, are contrasted for the one who would be wise. The following couplet illustrates this type of parallelism:

Whoever loves discipline loves knowledge,
but he who hates correction is stupid. (Prov. 12:1)

The third aspect of parallelism, called "synthetic" (or "formal") parallelism is the largest grouping, and also the most controversial. With synthetic parallelism, the second line presupposes the thought of the first and advances the thought of the initial line. Before we proceed with the discussion, it might prove helpful to examine examples:

Before a word is on my tongue
you know it completely, O LORD (Ps. 139:4)

I will sing to the LORD,
for he is highly exalted.
The horse and its rider
he has hurled into the sea. (Exod. 15:1)

Some have argued that this type of parallelism is no parallelism at all because the second line typically differs so significantly from the first that the meaning of the pair seems to be more akin to prose than poetry. However, the symmetry of paired lines, figurative expressions, and occasionally meter argue convincingly that synthetic parallelism is a legitimate understanding.

Although synonymous, antithetical, and synthetic parallelism comprise the major types of parallelism, several additional types of parallelism occur. We will mention only two. In emblematic parallelism, one line states a poetic proposition while the other illustrates with a simile. A well-known example is:

As the deer pants for streams of water,
so my soul pants for you, O God. (Ps. 42:1)

Another kind of parallelism is chiastic parallelism, where the second line restates the first in reversed order. Note the following example:

Ephraim will not be jealous of Judah,
nor Judah hostile toward Ephraim. (Isa. 11:13b)

The New Testament. The New Testament does not include extended sections that could be designated as poetic in the same sense as in the Old Testament. However, there are several brief passages that are generally regarded as poetic. The kenosis passage in Philippians 2:6–11 offers an excellent example. Another is 1 Timothy 3:16. A cursory comparison of several modern translations of the New Testament reveal disagreement over which passages are rightly considered poetic. In a slightly different vein, Paul quoted "some of your (Greek) poets when he stated, "In him we live and move and have our being" (Acts 17:28).

Conclusion. Finally, we should ask, "Why was the Bible written in poetic style?" Although no specific biblical answer is given to this query, a reasonable reply can be offered. Of paramount importance is the emotional quality inherent in poetry. Although one must recognize that prose is not devoid of emotional content, poetry conveys feelings with singular effect. In the prophetic oracle of judgment, the reader senses the fury of God's wrath, effectively communicating nuances of God's emotions ranging from cajolery to sarcasm. With love poetry such as the Song of Solomon, lovers express much of the deep emotions they hold for each other. Poetry serves the psalmist with equal dexterity as he expresses lament, praise, or thanksgiving. From complaints concerning the tardiness of God's salvation to hymns extolling the Lord's great acts of salvation, poetry conveys the deepest emotions of the author.

A second reason for poetry is the memorable quality of verse. Poetry impresses itself more effectively upon the hearer's memory, allowing far easier recall than with a comparable prosaic text. It is no coincidence that the effectiveness of a great deal of poetic literature is contingent upon the audience's ability to remember specifically what the text said. For instance, the wisdom writer's message demanded that the proverb would be precisely recalled. The prophets' sermons also had to be remembered (and applied to life) by the recipients in order for the intended effect to occur.

Finally, one should note that poetry is inherently esthetic, particularly with its extensive utilization of figurative language. Again, this is not to say that prose is not esthetic. Indeed, current studies in narrative strategies, for example, well illustrate a concern with style. The convergence of manifold, sophisticated figures of speech, including parallelism, reveal that poetry was very concerned not only with what was communicated, but also how the message was disclosed.

The esthetic quality of poetry is particularly appropriate in God's Word, for the Lord is a God who is both creative and places great value upon beauty. The creation itself manifests God's creativity and esthetic nature. How appropriate that his word reveals the same qualities.

GEORGE L. KLEIN

Bibliography. R. Alter, *The Art of Biblical Poetry;* E. W. Bullinger, *Figures of Speech Used in the Bible;* G. B. Caird, *The Language and Imagery of the Bible;* G. L. Klein, ed., *Reclaiming the Prophetic Mantle;* N. W. Lund, *Chiasmus in the New Testament;* L. Ryken, *Words of Delight: A Literary Introduction to the Bible;* L. Ryken and T. Longman III, *A Complete Literary Guide to the Bible.*

Poor and Poverty, Theology of. Poverty in Scripture can be both social and spiritual. The words "poor" and "poverty" cover a wide range of meaning, overlapping with terms like "widow" or "orphan," which underscores the expansive nature of the topic. In addition, because not all poor people are destitute the meaning of these terms is heavily dependent upon context.

The Old Testament. The Pentateuch emphasizes equitable treatment for the poor. Justice was neither to be withheld from the poor (Exod. 23:6) nor distorted because a person was poor (23:3; Lev. 19:15). Such equity is illustrated by the collection of ransom money from rich and poor alike (Exod. 30:15). As part of the covenant community the poor person was to be treated with respect (Deut. 24:10–11) and supported, even economically, by other Israelites, since they were not to charge interest to the poor of their people (Exod. 22:25; Lev. 25:35–38).

Beyond direct legislation a number of institutions contained special provisions for the poor. Gleaning laws focused on the widow, fatherless, stranger, and poor (Lev. 19:9–10; 23:22; Deut. 24:19–22). During the Sabbatical year debts were to be canceled (Deut. 15:1–9) and Jubilee provided release for Hebrews who had become servants through poverty (Lev. 25:39–41, 54). During these festivals the poor could eat freely of the produce of all of the fields (Exod. 23:11; Lev. 25:6–7, 12).

Further stipulations to aid the poor included the right of redemption from slavery by a blood relative (Lev. 25:47–49), support from the third-year tithe (Deut. 14:28–29), and special provisions regarding the guilt offerings. This latter law illustrates the relative nature of the concept of poverty. If someone cannot afford the normal atonement lamb he or she can bring two pigeons (Lev. 5:7) but further consideration, (substituting one-tenth ephah of flour), is made for one who cannot afford even two pigeons (5:11). Clearly, the Law emphasized that poverty was no reason for exclusion from atonement and worship!

Motivation for such legislation was God's concern for the poor. God listened to the cry of the needy (Exod. 22:27), blessed those who considered them (Deut. 24:13, 19), and held accountable those who oppressed them (Deut. 24:15). The Lord based this position on his relationship with his people; he was their God (Lev. 23:22) and had redeemed them from slavery (Deut. 24:18).

Poverty is not a frequent subject of the Old Testament historical books but striking instances are recorded. Hannah's prayer reveals the plight of the poor along with their dependence upon the Lord (1 Sam. 2:5–8), while Nathan's parable to David shows the nature of oppression, the relativity of poverty (this poor man was not destitute), and the concern of the king to provide justice for the poor (2 Sam. 12:1–4). As the monarchy developed the economic policies of Solomon eventually strained the resources of Israel and increased the level of poverty (1 Kings 12:4). This situation was further accentuated with the influx of idolatry and increase of injustice during the divided monarchy. A striking example from the northern kingdom shows the predicament of an indebted woman who, having lost her husband, was about to lose her sons to a creditor. God's provisions through Elisha is but one example of his "listening" to the cry of the poor in the Bible (2 Kings 4:1–7).

The highest concentration of terms for the poor in the Old Testament is found in the poetic books. The psalms dramatically portray the difficulties of physical poverty. Helping the poor is identified with righteousness (112:9) while oppression of the afflicted is one of the crimes of the wicked (109:16). The psalms also move beyond the sphere of social poverty to speak of spiritual humility (25:9). The poor are paralleled to the godly (12:1, 5), the upright (37:14), and those who love the Lord's salvation (40:17; 70:5) and are contrasted to evil men (140:1, 12), the wicked (37:14; 109:2, 22), and fools (14:1, 6; 74:21–22).

Frequently in the psalms, especially lament psalms, the poor called to the Lord for help (34:6; 70:5; 86:1; 109:21–22) knowing that he heard their cry (69:33). The psalmist understood that God was the just judge of the poor. The Lord was seen as their refuge (14:6), deliverer (40:17), and provider (68:10). He rescued (35:10), raised (113:7), and satisfied them (132:15); it was the Lord who secured justice for the poor and the needy (140:12).

More than any other book Proverbs gives visibility to the causes of poverty. Because of the book's didactic nature the emphasis is upon controllable circumstances but other reasons are included. Poverty is a result of laziness (6:10–11; 10:4; 20:13; 24:33–34), lack of discipline (13:18), idleness (14:23; 28:19), haste (21:5), excess (21:17; 23:20–21), and injustice (13:23).

The Wisdom Literature paints a realistic picture of poverty in the ancient world. The poor are vulnerable (Prov. 18:23), shunned by friends (14:20; 19:4, 7), and become servants to the rich (22:7). Poverty brings sorrow (31:7) and can lead to crime (30:8–9). Poverty is quite realistically presented in Job 24, where the poor are portrayed as hungry, thirsty, naked, and suffering from various kinds of injustice and oppression including the loss of poverty, family, and life. Yet obedience to the Lord is more important than riches. This priority is evidenced in the comparison of poverty with other areas of life. It is better than foolishness (Prov. 19:1; Eccl. 4:13), lying (Prov. 19:22) or a rich liar (28:6), and rich pride (28:11).

The Wisdom Literature is emphatic in its encouragement to help those who are poor. Giving to the poor is encouraged (Prov. 11:24; 28:8, 22, 27) while oppression of the poor is against one's Maker (14:31; 17:5). Rulers are taught not to oppress the poor (28:3; 29:14; 31:9). Those who help the poor are the righteous (Job 29:12–17; Prov. 29:7; 31:20) while the wicked do not (Job 20:19; Prov. 29:7; 30:14).

Certainly the most grievous examples of poverty and severest rebukes come from the prophets. It should be noted, however, that the prophets were not primarily spokespersons for the poor or the oppressed peoples; they were spokespersons for God. The key terms for "poor" are used almost exclusively by Isaiah, Amos, Jeremiah, Ezekiel, and Zechariah while Hosea and Micah, who also showed great sensitivity to the needs of their people, do not use the terms at all. Prophets clearly called attention to the misuse of riches and the abuse of the poor but they were primarily messengers of the Lord. Attempts to narrow the agenda of the prophet to one interest group or another have not understood the largess of God and his concern for all persons.

Amos is quite graphic in his portrayal of the oppression of the poor. The poor are bought and sold, trampled, crushed, oppressed, forced, and denied justice by those who are in a position to do otherwise. Their treatment is a striking example of the waywardness of God's people from the covenant obligations and their unique relationship with the Lord. Amos underscores this situation: "They sell the righteous for silver, and the needy for a pair of sandals. They trample on the heads of the poor as upon the dust of the ground and deny justice to the oppressed" (2:6–7).

The emphasis of the prophetic invective fell upon the leaders. Instead of defending the poor and upholding the Law of God they took bribes and gifts to pervert justice (Isa. 1:23). Neglecting the clear call of Scripture to provide for the poor, they passed unjust laws and deprived the poor of their rights (10:1–2; Jer. 5:27–28), taking their goods and their land (Isa. 3:13–15; 5:8). Isaiah accents their abuse: "What do you mean by crushing my people and grinding the faces of the poor?" (3:15). Yet the people were held accountable for their actions as well. Ezekiel, for example, reminded the people that they had joined with the leaders in such oppression (22:26–29) and pointed out the primary responsibility of the individual was to obey God (18:16–17).

The New Testament. Most of the teaching about the poor in the New Testament occurs in the Gospels. Jesus understood the reality of poverty in society (Matt. 26:9–11) and the difficulties of the poor (Mark 12:42–44). He stressed the need to give to the poor (Matt. 19:21; Luke 12:33) and to provide for them (Luke 14:13, 21). Jesus himself identified with poor people and, like many poor persons, did not have a home (Luke 9:58). He taught how difficult it was to be rich (Matt. 19:23–24) and the necessity of spiritual poverty for a relationship with God (Matt. 5:3).

Paul's sensitivity to the poor is consistent with the teaching of Jesus and the agenda of the early church. He understood that the word of Christ cut across sociological boundaries and that the church was made up of poor and rich alike (Gal. 3:28; Col. 3:11; cf. 1 Cor. 1:27–29). His stress on the collection for the Jerusalem church exhibits this concern in a practical way (Rom. 15:26; 1 Cor. 16:3; 2 Cor. 8–9; Gal. 2:10).

The equality of persons before God is an important principle of the New Testament with the most powerful statement of the equality of rich and poor coming from James, who emphasizes God's sensitivity to the poor and their faith (2:5). He notes that discriminating between the rich and the poor is both a sin against God (2:9) and an insult to the poor (2:6).

Scriptural terminology includes those who are "meek" and "poor in spirit" (Matt. 5:3), yet the biblical stress is that both the individual and the church are to be engaged in helping the poor of society. The believer's model for this action is the life of Jesus and the Word of God, which grounds such sensitivity in the very nature of God himself.

ROBERT D. SPENDER

See also BEATITUDES; MEEKNESS.

Bibliography. G. J. Botterweck, *TDOT,* 1:27–41; L. Coenen, C. Brown, and H.-H. Esser, *NIDNTT,* 2:820–29; R. J. Coggins, *ExpT* 99 (1987): 11–14; H-J. Fabry, *TDOT,* 3:208–30; S. Gillingham, *ExpT* 100 (1988): 15–19; D. E. Gowan, "Wealth and Poverty in the OT," *Int* 41 (1987): 341–53; D. E. Holwerda, *ISBE,* 3:905–8; W. C. Kaiser, Jr., *Trinity J* 9 (1988): 151–70; B. J. Malina, *Int* 41 (1987): 354–67; C. U. Wolf, *IDB,* 3:843–44.

Possessions. *See* WEALTH.

Power. Power is an English logical construct referring to a variety of ideas relating to ability, capacity, authority, and might/strength. In human relationships, power is the authority one person holds over another. Terms such as boss, president, sheriff, and sexual harassment bring the picture of power to mind. The images that exist among Christians concerning "power" often depend upon the English translation with which they are familiar. The Bible uses a variety of Hebrew and Greek terms that represent the semantic domain of power although they may be translated in different ways. For example, the King James Version uses "power" for a large number of Hebrew and Greek terms. The Greek term *exousia* is most often translated "power" in the King James Version but it is almost always translated "authority" in modern versions. The contextual nuance of each occurrence of a Hebrew or Greek word must be considered in translation.

Power (*dunamis*) in the ancient Greek world was portrayed as a major cosmic principle. Some philosophers viewed it as second only to mind (*nous*). They viewed God and cosmic principle as equivalent. It was rare for them to speak of "the power of God" since these ideas were nearly equivalent. In the Bible, however, God is a person not merely power. Therefore, a phrase like "the power of God" takes on new meaning because a person who possesses the characteristic of power is the prime mover of the universe. Furthermore, the biblical deity is a God of history, not just nature. Therefore, this God brings the world into existence (Jer. 27:5; 32:17) and distributes power to people to fulfill his historical purposes (cf. Exod. 15:6, 13; Deut. 3:24; Pss. 46:1; 86:16).

The biblical description of power relates primarily to God and people. Power is an inherent characteristic of God (Rom. 1:20). It is the result of his nature. God's kind of power is seen in his creation (Ps. 19; 150:1; Jer. 10:12). His inexplicable power is the only explanation for the virgin birth of Jesus (Luke 1:35). Power is always a derived characteristic for people, who receive power from God (Deut. 8:18; Isa. 40:29; Mic. 3:8; Matt. 22:29; 1 Cor. 2:4; Eph. 3:7), from political position (Esther 1:3; Luke 20:20), from armies (1 Chron. 20:1), and from other structures that provide advantage over others. When humans perceive that their power is intrinsic to themselves, they are self-deceived (Lev. 26:19; Deut. 8:17–18; Hos. 2:7–9; John 19:10–11).

Jesus as the God-Man demonstrated both the intrinsic and derived aspects of power. He proclaimed his power and authority as derived from the Father (John 5:27; 17:2; cf. 5:16–23). He also demonstrated that his power was derived from his authority as the Son of Man and that the two were an inseparable testimony to his divine nature (Matt. 9:6–7; Luke 4:36; 9:1).

Power in the New Testament is used to describe the unseen world. The angelic realm is described as "powers" or "authorities" (Rom. 8:38; Eph. 3:10; 6:12; Col. 1:16; 2:10, 16). Jesus exercised power over the unseen world through his exorcism of demons (Mark 6:7; Luke 9:1).

Paul especially images the living of the Christian life as an empowerment from God. The believer's union with Christ delivers him or her from the power of sin (cf. Rom. 6–8) and introduces him or her to the "power of [Christ's] resurrection" (Phil. 3:10). Salvation and holy living provide the Christian with a "spirit of power" for witness (2 Tim. 1:7–8). Paul's view of the gospel itself is imaged as power (Rom. 1:16). "Power" in Romans 1:16 renders the Greek word *dunamis*. It is often noted that the gospel is the "dynamite of God" because the English word "dynamite" is derived from *dunamis*. Such an observation, however, is not a valid use of etymology. Dynamite was not in existence during Paul's time. He had no such image in his mind. For Paul, the gospel *dunamis* was the dynamic of God's power conveyed through God's message. When presented to the world, the gospel dynamically works salvation in those who believe. Paul develops the motif of divine power as the key to Christian living by noting that unless the believer is empowered, it is impossible to please God (Rom. 6–8; 1 Cor. 15:56–57).

Peter also utilizes the concept of power to image the Christian life as an empowerment from God. Second Peter 1:3 states that "His divine power has given us everything we need for life and godliness." The context views this power as channeled through knowledge and virtue. Peter does not view this power as passive, but as the foundation and motivation to pursue a circle of virtues (1:5–9) that produce and evidence productive Christian living. GARY T. MEADORS

See also GOSPEL; POWERS.

Powers. The uses of this biblical term fall into two major divisions: referring to "miraculous powers" and to angelic beings belonging to the hierarchy of heaven. "Powers" translates a number of biblical words. The background of the key Greek word (*dynamis*) is found in the Old Testament. It translates the Hebrew word *hayil* (over 150 times), often used as "host" or "power of a host." *Dynamis* is first found in Jewish writings referring to angels, and indicates the power of angelic and demonic forces. There are frequent references in the intertestamental writings, most notably in 1 Enoch (61:10; 82:8) and Jubilee (2:2).

The New Testament references to miraculous works occur in relation to Jesus' miracles and the presence of such works in the life of the early church. The New International Version translates *dynamis* as "miraculous powers" in the Gospels (Matt. 13:54; 14:2; Mark 6:14) and in Paul's writings (1 Cor. 12:10), where it relates to spiritual gifts. In Hebrews 6:5, the reference to "the powers of the coming age" may allude to similar phenomena (cf. Acts 8:13). Rather than relating to magic or magical formulas, common in the ancient world, Jesus' powerful Word overcame demonic forces, and demonstrates "the invading dominion of God," expelling Satan and the demons.

There are more frequent references to angels and demons, members of the hierarchy of heaven, including such titles as authorities, powers, dominions, principalities, and thrones. These supernatural beings are the *dynameis* ("powers"), linked with angels and demons (Rom. 8:38) and authorities (1 Pet. 3:22). These forces are not able to defeat believers, or to separate them from the love of Christ, for Christ has subordinated them through the cross and his resurrection.

Paul also describes the rulers (*archas*), the authorities (*exousias*), the powers (*kosmokratoras*) of this dark world, the spiritual forces (*pneumatika*) of evil in the heavenly realms (Eph. 6:12). The term *kosmokratoras* does not appear in the Old Testament (LXX), but does occur in the

Jewish work *T. Solomon,* joined with the expression "the heavenly bodies" (*stoicheia*) (8:2; 18:2). Once these "rulers of this world of darkness" are made up of seven spirits; again, of thirty-six spirits. When queried by King Solomon the former reply, "Our stars in heaven look small, but we are named like gods" (8:4). Yet each of the seven are opposed and thwarted by one of God's chief angels. All of these creatures bring about certain types of maladies within human life, but are ultimately subject to God's judgment. *Archas* is variously translated as "powers" (Col. 2:15) or "rulers" (Eph. 3:10; Col. 1:16). It denotes primacy, sometimes temporal and sometimes in rank, yet these beings are subject to Christ as the head (Col. 2:10), and they were created by him (Col. 1:16). In his death Christ triumphed over them, and made a spectacle of them. They are described as a train of captives behind a victorious general (Col. 2:15). Finally, "powers" translates *kyriotētes* (Col. 1:16), also rendered "dominion" (sing., Eph. 1:21). This word emphasizes the power or rule of a lord. In turn, these angelic beings are subordinated to the rule of Christ, for he is the ultimate *kyrios* or Lord, both in virtue of his role as Creator and as the risen Lord (cf. 1 Cor. 15:23–24; Eph. 1:21; Phil. 2:10).

The related word "authorities" is also used in two basic ways in the New Testament: of earthly rulers (Luke 12:11; John 7:26; Acts 16:19; Rom. 13:1; Titus 3:1); and of supernatural or supraterrestrial beings (Eph. 3:10; 6:12; Col. 1:16; 2:15; 1 Peter 3:22). The singular, "authority," is used in 1 Corinthians 15:24; Ephesians 1:21; and Colossians 2:10. While John and Acts use the word *archōn,* all the other texts have the word *exousia.*

In the Pauline writings the context is frequently apologetic in nature; Paul is countering various heresies. With the possible exception of Ephesians 3:10, the "authorities" appear to be beings of an evil nature, opposing the rule of God, the supremacy of the Lord Christ, and the life of the church.

Finally, the word "thrones" means the royal seat, or the symbol of rule, first of human rulers, then of heavenly beings. It appears ten times in the Old Testament (NIV), most commonly as a translation of the Hebrew *kissē.* An unusual use, and the only one in the New Testament, occurs in the listing "thrones or powers or rulers or authorities" (Col. 1:16). While no real distinction is possible among these terms, the references taken together may well be to the highest classes of angelic/demonic beings. And all, being created in, through, and for Christ, are subject to him.

WALTER M. DUNNETT

Bibliography. W. Foerster, *TDNT,* 2:562–73; W. Grundman, *TDNT,* 2:284–317; R. C. Trench, *Synonyms of the New Testament.*

Poverty. *See* POOR AND POVERTY, THEOLOGY OF.

Praise. Praise, mostly of God, is a frequent theme in the psalms, the Hebrew title of which is "Praises." Yet praise is a theme that pervades the whole of Scripture. Genesis 1 is indirect praise; direct praise is found in hymns scattered throughout the books of Exodus, 2 Samuel, Isaiah, Daniel, Ephesians, and Revelation. Words that are often used as synonyms or in parallel with "praise," and so help point to its meaning, are "bless," "exalt," "extol," "glorify," "magnify," "thank," and "confess." To praise God is to call attention to his glory.

A Vocation of Praise. Praising God is a God-appointed calling. Indeed, God has formed for himself a people "that they may proclaim my [God's] praise" (Isa. 43:21; cf. Jer. 13:11). God's actions, such as Israel's restoration from the exile, are to result in God's "righteousness and praise spring[ing] up before all nations" (Isa. 61:11). God has also predestined the church "to the praise of his [God's] glorious grace" (Eph. 1:6; cf. Matt. 5:16; Eph. 1:14; Phil. 1:11; 1 Peter 2:9). The future vocation of the redeemed in glory is to sing praise to God and the Lamb (Rev. 4:11; 5:12–14; 7:12). Doxologies are fitting because they capture what God intends for people (Pss. 33:1; 147:1).

In the light of this calling to praise God, the oft-declared intention, "I will praise you, O God," and the exhortations for others to praise God take on additional meaning. In giving oneself to praise the worshiper declares his or her total alignment with God's purposes. The environment of those gathering for worship, judged by such admonitions, was one of lavish praise to God. Since God is holy and fully good, God is not to be faulted, as some do, for requiring praise of himself. Praise is fitting for what is the highest good, God himself. Praise is both a duty and a delight (Ps. 63:3–8).

Reasons for Praising God. In addition to being the fulfillment of a calling, praise is prompted by other considerations, chief of which is the unique nature of God (1 Chron. 29:10–13). One genre of the psalms, the hymns, is characterized by an initial summons, such as "Praise the Lord," which is followed by a declaration of praise, introduced by the word "for," which lists the grounds for offering praise, often God's majesty and mercy. The shortest psalm (117), a hymn, offers a double reason for praise: God's merciful kindness (loyal love) is great, and his truth endures forever. Other hymns point out that God is good (Ezra 3:10–11; Pss. 100:5; 135:3), or that his ordinances are just (Ps. 119:164), that he remembers his covenant (Ps. 105:7–8), that his love is enduring (Ps. 136), or that he is incomparable (Ps. 71:19). A basic understanding in the hymns, if not in all the psalms, is captured in the theme "The Lord reigns." God's kingship is pronounced both in his majestic power displayed through the creation of the world (Pss. 29, 104) and in his royal rule, often as deliverer, over his people (Pss. 47, 68, 98, 114). As king, God is judge, warrior, and shepherd. Often too, praise is to the name of God (Pss. 138:2; 145:2; Isa. 25:1). That name, Yahweh, conveys the notion that God is present to act in salvation (Exod. 6:1–8).

The biblical examples of praise to God, apart from citing his attributes and role, point to God's favors, usually those on a large scale in behalf of Israel. A hymn in the Isaiah collection exhorts, "Sing praise to the LORD for his glorious achievement" (Isa. 12:5 NAB). Exhortations to praise are sometimes followed by a catalogue of God's actions in Israel's behalf (Neh. 9:5; Ps. 68:4–14). God's most spectacular action involves the incarnation of Jesus, an event heralded in praises by angels in the heavens and shepherds returning to their fields: "Glory to God in the highest" (Luke 2:14, 20). Praise is the legitimate response to God's self-revelation. Personal experiences of God's deliverance and favor also elicit praise (Pss. 34; 102:18; 107; cf. Dan. 2:20–23; Rom. 7:25; the healed paralytic, Luke 5:25; Zechariah, Luke 1:68; the response at Nain, Luke 7:16; and Jesus himself, Matt. 11:25).

An intimate relationship of a person or a people with God is sufficient reason for praise. A psalmist, captivated by the reality of God's choice of Jacob, exhorts, "Sing praise" (Ps. 135; cf. Rev. 19:5).

Expressions of Praise. The believing community is both a fitting and frequently mentioned context for praise. The author of Hebrews quotes the psalter: "In the midst of the assembly I will praise you" (Heb. 2:12). The audience is enlarged beyond the worshiping community when the worshiper announces, "I will praise you [in the sense of confessing], O Lord, among the nations" (Ps. 57:9), and more enlarged still, "In the presence of angels ["gods" NIV] I will sing my praise" (Ps. 138:1 NAB). While privately spoken praise to God is fitting and right, it is virtually intrinsic to the notion of praise that it be publicly expressed. Indeed, David appointed Levites to ensure the public praise of Israel (1 Chron. 16:4; 23:4, 30).

The Scriptures offer a language of praise and so are instructive on how expressions of praise might be formulated. Nehemiah leads in praise by saying, "Blessed be your glorious name, and may it be exalted above all blessing and praise. You alone are the LORD" (Neh. 9:5–6a). The chorister Asaph followed David's cue: "Sing praise to him; tell of his wonderful acts" (1 Chron. 16:9). Persons intent on cultivating spirituality are often helped, at least initially, by repeating and personalizing such lyrics of praise.

Praise to God in Israel took the form of artfully composed lyrics. A significant number of psalms are identified in their headings as "A Psalm," a technical term meaning "a song of praise." Israel's expressions of praise to God could include shouts (Ps. 98:4), the plying of musical instruments (1 Chron. 25:3; 2 Chron. 7:6; Ps. 144:9; cf. 150:1–5), making melody (Ps. 146:2), and dancing (Ps. 149:3). A public expression at Jesus' entry into Jerusalem took the form of devotees waving palm branches (Matt. 21:1–11). Praise for Israel consisted, in part, of the spoken word, "Open my lips, and my mouth will declare your praise" (Ps. 51:15) behind which, however, was a total person committed to praise: "I will praise you, O LORD, with my whole heart" (Ps. 9:1). Such praise is not tainted with bitterness or in other ways qualified but is from someone who is thoroughly thankful.

The Bible speaks also of persons praising or commending others (Gen. 12:15; 49:8; Prov. 31:28, 30; 2 Cor. 8:18). However, it counsels, even warns, about the giving and receiving of praise lest it be for the wrong reasons or be misconstrued (Ps. 49:18; Prov. 12:8; 27:2, 21; John 5:44).

Unquestionably the Book of the Psalms is centerpiece for any discussion about praise. In it the believer's vocation to praise is wonderfully modeled, so that even laments (one-third of all the psalms) contain elements of praise. As a book of praises, the psalms build to a remarkable crescendo of praise (Pss. 145–150), in which all creatures are summoned to incessant praise of God, as are the stars and planets in the heavens, and even the angels.

Very appropriately, then, does the Christian community repeatedly resort in its worship to the Gloria Patri, "Glory be to the Father" and in clusters large and small sing, "Praise God from whom all blessings flow." ELMER A. MARTENS

See also WORSHIP.

Bibliography. W. Brueggemann, *Israel's Praise: Doxology Against Idolatry;* L. J. Coppes, *TWOT,* 2:217–18; J. C. Lambert and B. L. Martin, *ISBE,* 3:929–31; C. S. Lewis, *Reflections on the Psalms;* P. Miller, Jr., *Interpreting the Psalms;* H. Schultz and H.-H. Esser, *NIDNTT,* 3:816–20; G. von Rad, *Old Testament Theology;* R. S. Wallace, *IBD,* 3:1256–57; C. Westermann, *The Praise of God in the Psalms.*

Prayer. An examination of the Old and New Testaments and of the early Church Fathers reveals certain "minimal" beliefs or assumptions that underlie the practice of Christian praying. This is not to deny that there was a development in the conception of prayer, though this development is more pronounced in the Old Testament than it is in the New Testament and early church. The consistency in the latter case is seen in the close correspondence between Jesus' prayer life and the prayer life of the New Testament church. This consistency extended into the patristic period, for the early Father's understanding of prayer was thoroughly shaped and limited by the Lord's Prayer, particularly through mutually influencing exegetical literature on it, devotional and liturgical use of it, and the catechetical tradition that employed it.

Petition. Though prayer also includes adoration (e.g., Pss. 144–150; Luke 1:46–55), confession (e.g., Ps. 51; Luke 18:13), and thanksgiving (e.g., Ps. 75; 1 Thess. 1:2), Christian prayer has always been essentially petitionary. Indeed, the simple and almost naive petitioning that marks New Testament prayer is reflected in all its humanness in the psalms—the liturgical inheritance of the early Christians—as well as in the rest of the early church's Scriptures. Petitions are made for rain and fire, relief from famine and plague, resurrections from the dead, and so forth (e.g., see 1 Kings 8:35–40; 17:20–22; 18:26–39). In fact, most Hebrew terms used in the Old Testament for prayer refer in some sense to petition; prayer in the Old Testament more frequently expressed supplication than anything else.

Christian prayer, then, shared a simple belief that God could be petitioned to intervene and effect changes in nature and in the course of world events. The immediate source of this confidence came from the teachings and examples of Jesus himself, such as the model prayer he offered (Matt. 6:9–13; Luke 11:2–4) and his assurance that one had only to ask the Father in order to receive what was needed (Matt. 7:7; Luke 11:9). We can readily document that Jesus' instructions were taken to heart by his early followers: there were prayers for the selection of leaders, for deliverances from prisons, for the spread of the gospel, for healings, and so on (e.g., see Acts 1:24; 12:5; 13:3). Indeed, Paul's teaching in Philippians 4:6 echoes Jesus' own. Thus, prayer was unquestioningly believed to be an effective cause of God's actions such that a difference resulted in human events.

Such petitions were, in part, motivated by the need of the moment. In fact, a notable characteristic of New Testament prayer (and its predecessor) was its spontaneity. Prayer was to be placed in the midst of everyday life, not just reserved for liturgical contexts. Accordingly, petitions were to cover the entire gamut of one's life, including material and spiritual needs, though by the time we reach the New Testament period the former has been subordinated to the latter, as the pattern of the Lord's Prayer suggested. The pray-er should feel free to make requests of God, which, according to biblical material is equivalent to letting God know the desires of one's heart (see Job 6:8; Ps. 21:2; Phil. 4:6).

At this point we must guard against equating Christian belief in the efficacy of prayer and magic. Magic attempts to *control* or *manipulate* the divine will in order to induce it to grant one's wishes, especially through the use of techniques such as charms, spells, rituals, or ceremonies. Christian prayer involves a struggle of wills in which the pray-er attempts to *persuade* God, all the time seeing prayer as a divinely given means whereby the pray-er can participate in *God's* agenda.

God. One's understanding of prayer varies in accordance with one's conception of the two parties involved—namely, the divine and the human—and their relation to each other. We turn then to the biblical conception of the first party—God. The view of prayer found in the Old Testament, the soil for that in the New Testament, was founded on the Hebraic conception of God as both immanent and transcendent.

The prayers of Israel reveal their fundamental belief that they were talking to a God who, though mysterious, was immediately and actively present.

This immanent God of Israel was addressed as "you who hear prayer" (Ps. 65:2). That is to say, from the beginning of the Old Testament traditions, God and humans engaged in dialogue—in conversation made possible by the ascription of personhood to God. Thus, Elohim was a God who listened and answered (Gen. 21:16–18; 22:11–12). The Divine shares his intentions (Gen. 18:17; Exod. 3). The human questions (Gen. 15:2, 8), requests guidance (Exod. 5:22–23; 32:11–13), complains (Num. 11:1–15), reasons (Gen. 18:23), and bargains (Gen. 28:20–22). This personal relationship established in prayer recurs in almost every book of the Old Testament (especially in Jeremiah). This understanding of prayer as personal confrontation with a responsive objective referent continues into the New Testament and makes Christian prayer distinctive from merely reverencing an impersonal sacred object that can never be prayed to, petitioned, or thanked. Personhood includes mutuality, rapprochement, and reciprocity—addressing and being addressed. Christian prayer is possible only if it is an event between two persons in an essential reciprocal relationship. This sense of reciprocity, which is found in the Judeo-Christian concept but is lost in a monistic understanding of prayer, allows us to speak of prayer as talking to God.

The essence of Judeo-Christian prayer conceives of this fellowship between God and humans as a communion reflecting the forms of the social relations of humanity (friendship, master–servant, groom–bride, father–child). (One implication is that anyone capable of conventional interhuman discourse is capable of praying.) It is the last relationship that is most important as we move from the Old Testament's conception of God to the New Testament's. In fact, it has been suggested that the outstanding idea of Christ's teaching was the fatherhood of God.

The notion of God as father is not absent from the Old Testament, though it appears only fifteen times. Still, nothing in all the extant literature of ancient Palestinian Judaism indicates that "my Father" was used as a personal address to God. The *community* did pray to God as Father, and the individual occasionally spoke *of* God as his heavenly Father; but this was rare before the diaspora, and other titles for God were far more frequent in Jewish prayers. Instead, "my Father" is characteristic of the *ipsissima vox Jesu.* (Jesus *always* addresses God in prayer as "Father" except for the "cry of dereliction" on the cross.) With the word "abba" Jesus introduced a new way of praying—talking to God as naturally, intimately, and sincerely as a child talks to his or her father. "Abba" reveals the heart of Jesus' relationship with God, marking his complete obedient surrender to the Father (Mark 14:36) and his authority as the one to whom God reveals his thoughts (Matt. 11:27). The early church used this same address and thereby appropriated the central element of Jesus' understanding of God (see Rom. 8:15; Gal. 4:6). Indeed, by giving the disciples the paradigm prayer with the address "Our Father," Jesus invited his followers to share in the same relationship with God he had, for it was customary in the Judaism of that time for individual religious groups to be united and characterized by a particular prayer (hence the disciples' request in Luke 11:1).

The Christian tradition also conceives of God as susceptible to human influence by means of prayer. The conception of a real influence of humans on God lies at the root of the prophetic belief that God hears or answers prayer. God can let himself be determined by the pray-er and grant what is asked for or, because God is Person, he can refuse the petitioner and deny the request. (The very notion of "petition" or "request" implies this.) Certainly this is true of the Old Testament. For example, one thinks of Abraham's intercession for Sodom (Gen. 18:22–23), Moses' intercession for his people (Num. 14:12–20), or Israel's desire to have a king against God's wishes (1 Sam. 8:19–22). But while this belief is presupposed by those who pray and teach about prayer in the Gospels and the New Testament church, in two prominent cases God's will is precisely *not* changed by human petitioning: in Jesus' Gethsemane prayer and in Paul's thrice-prayed request to have his "thorn in the flesh" removed. (Again, though, even in these cases pray-ers must have presupposed that God's will *could* be influenced in order to pray such prayers.) In fact, the New Testament emphasis seems not to be on changing *God's* will through prayer, but on changing the *human's* will. Nonetheless, in Christian prayer the human response to the Word of God has an effect on God. These words constitute part of the history between God and humans, and thus become part of God's history as well.

While the immanence of God formed much of the basis for prayer in the Judeo-Christian tradition, God's transcendence is important as well. We have already implied it by noting that God maintains the prerogative of denying the pray-er's request. God's hand cannot be forced. In fact, even the intimacy of the "abba" in the Lord's Prayer is mitigated by the following phrase, "who are in heaven," to insure that petitioners remember that they and the addressee are not on a par with each other. God is the Supreme Being or reality, both omnipresent and omnipotent. He *can* perform what is asked, but he stands over against the prayer and, as such, he is sovereign over the petitioner, in providential control of the universe, and the source and bestower of all that we receive.

Humans. If God is the sovereign Lord of the universe from whom we should seek and receive the provision of spiritual and physical necessities, then we are reminded of our utter creaturely dependence on God. The divine-human relationship is understood to have its origin and the determination of its character entirely from the divine side, so that prayer is but a trusting response in a relationship that has been initiated by God. Prayer's form, content, and efficacy belong to the divine economy of human salvation.

Christian prayer has traditionally also expressed the human's freedom to play its essential role in prayer. Prayer in the Old Testament often pictures the pray-er as an active cooperator. Such prayer is a dynamic dialogue that expresses the history Immanuel wills to have *with* humans. Prayer thus becomes one of the ways in which the creature cooperates with God in order to bring about God's plan. This is evident in God's history of salvation when many significant events include the prayers of mediators such as Abraham, Moses, Samuel, David, and others. In fact, it sometimes even seems in the Old Testament that God so desires obedience and cooperation that he is unwilling to carry out his purposes until men and women have recognized the divine summons and answered it (e.g., see Exod. 4:10–17).

This Old Testament emphasis is not as clearly set forth in the New Testament, which may account, for example, for some disagreements about the intention of the first three petitions in the Lord's Prayer—whether they are a call for God to act alone (Lohmeyer, for example) or a call to God for help (Augustine, Luther). If the latter is the case (as the majority think), then why ask God to do for us what should be our duty? It is certainly not to escape our responsibility for action, but to enter into this human–divine partnership in which we offer ourselves at God's disposal, expecting and seeking him to be at work to make our efforts effective. This raises two important Judeo-Christian themes regarding prayer.

First, while prayer is a kind of work, the corollary is not necessarily (nor even usually) true. We must guard against the reductionistic motto "To work is to pray." It should be obvious that work cannot be a substitute for prayer, for no matter how faithful one has been in planning and toil, the harvest ultimately depends on factors outside of human control. The reduction of work to prayer may even be a manifestation of the human proclivity toward self-justification.

Second, both Testaments insist that while prayer and service are not to be equated with each other, they are also not to be separated from each other. With this insistence goes the belief that only the prayer of the righteous is efficacious (Prov. 15:29). This set of convictions is particularly a prophetic emphasis in the Old Testament, beginning as early as Samuel's intercession for Saul, which leads to the conclusion that prayer must result in obedience (1 Sam. 7:12, 15; 15:22–23). It was especially the eighth-century prophets who emphasized the necessity for moral goodness of the one who prayed. Prayer was not to be substituted for righteousness. Jahweh wanted more than mere ritual and ceremony, notwithstanding Israel's elected status. There can only be true prayer if one is simultaneously actively seeking good; insincere prayer cannot be a substitute for justice and responsible action.

These twin virtues of service and prayer were also inseparably linked in the New Testament. Prayer in the early church is depicted as producing encouragement (Acts 18:9–10; 23:11), guidance (Acts 8:26–40; 10–11; 13:1–3), and power (Acts 16:25–26) in one's work. And again, effective prayer in such cases is not to be disassociated from righteousness (e.g., see James 5:15–16).

The Basis of Prayer. The true basis of prayer in the Judeo-Christian tradition is the recollection of God's acts in history. Such remembrances establish the ground on which a request can be made and guide the petitioner to make appropriate requests. This is especially seen in Deuteronomy where appropriate prayer is prompted by the recollection of God's mighty deeds (4:9, 32–39; 9:25–29; 32:1–43). The memory of God's lovingkindness often becomes the preamble and ground for the petition (Gen. 32:10–13; 1 Kings 3:3–14). In fact, failure to recall God's past acts might prevent a favorable response to prayer (Jer. 2:5–13). Thus, prayer in the Old Testament must be discussed in the light of God's covenantal relationship with Israel. This is quite noticeable in the psalms, which recapitulate the great events of salvation history. The grounding of prayer in the recollection of God's nature and deeds contains the seeds of New Testament liturgical practice and teaching (e.g., see 2 Kings 19:14–19; Matt. 6:5–8).

"Christian" Prayer. If prayer is based on God's acts, then prayer is ultimately a response to the prior activity of God. In *Christian* prayer, the primary divine act is God's new revelation in Jesus Christ, in whom all the promises of God find their "yes." Christian prayer is, thus, a sequel in a relationship that begins before the idea of praying even occurs to us. One is summoned to continue the dialogue by the God who offers the *gift* of prayer, who guarantees its reality, and who calls on men and women to pray through the instrumentality of human speech. Thus, Christian prayer is not conceived of as the natural human's own achievement. Though our own endeavors are not precluded, ultimately the believer is impelled to pray by the indwelling God at work in the deepest places of his or her soul. In the New Testament, this understanding of prayer as God's work focuses on the roles of Christ and the Holy Spirit.

First, Christian prayer is to be prayed "in the name of Christ" (John 14:13–14; 16:23–28). This is not some magical formula. It signifies that the suppliant takes the posture and attitude of Christ toward God and toward the world. To pray "in his name" is therefore to pray in a manner consistent with our new identity effected by the reconciliation of God and humans in Jesus Christ. That is to say, the use of Jesus' name in prayer is effective not as some sort of password that can be used indiscriminately by every petitioner. It is only effective to pray "in Jesus' name" if we are truly *living* in the name of Jesus. This phrase, then, has more to do with the identification of the person who prays than it does with right methods or conditions of prayer (e.g., see Acts 19:13–16). Such prayer guards against a misreading of God's nature and will, and saves prayer from human selfishness and presumption.

Prayer "in Christ's name" is usually associated with prayer that is in keeping with God's will. Indeed, the patristic exegesis of the third petition of the Lord's Prayer insisted that God's will is expressed by the divine economy in Christ. In the third petition we ask not only for *God's* will to be done; we pray that it may be done among and through us—that we may become obedient participants in its accomplishments. By so praying, we also guard against the self-centered request for personal gain, away from which biblical prayer seems to move, at least in the New Testament.

Second, Christian prayer is mediated by Christ, a theme that is particularly found in John's Gospel and the letter to the Hebrews. This role of Christ began with his ascension to the Father and is made possible, in part, by his experiences whereby he empathizes with our condition (Heb. 4:14–16). The role of mediator in prayer was prevalent in the Old Testament (as in Abraham, Moses, David, Samuel, Amos, Solomon, Hezekiah, Elijah, Elisha, Jeremiah, Ezekiel, and Israel). But Christ is pictured in the New Testament as the ultimate intercessor, and, because of this, *all* Christian prayer becomes intercession since it is presented through and by Christ to God. In fact, Calvin insisted that without Christ's intercession we are cut off from the benefits of prayer, for the only hope that our prayers are heard lies in the fact that Christ causes them to be heard in his mediatorial role.

Third, Christian prayer is prompted and guided by the Holy Spirit. In the New Testament the Spirit is that which makes possible even the address of God as "abba" (Rom. 8:15–16; Gal. 4:6). The precise meaning of the Spirit's role in Romans 8:26–27 is variously interpreted, though it is usually associated with the regulation and purification of our requests as the interpreter of the mind of God. Thus, the Holy Spirit is the arbiter, director, and interpreter of all our wishes. Accordingly, God may answer our petitions in his own way (see 2 Cor. 12:7–9).

Wrestling in Prayer. We have established that prayer is a dialogue between two distinct partners. In fact, prayer in the Judeo-Christian tradition is often a *struggle* between two wills—between two covenant partners. And though the two partners are not equal, the human agent is not precluded from the complaining, questioning, and passionate vehemence that characterize true dialogues.

The psalms offer some of the best examples of this. We must not overlook or censor the humanness of the psalmist just so that our modern "piety" will not be disturbed.

The prototype of this wrestling or conflict with God is the story of Jacob in Genesis 32:22–32. Jacob engages God with a perseverance that refuses to let go until Jacob's desire is met. In this case, the struggle results in a character change and marks the petitioner for life. Other outstanding Old Testament examples of contention with God in prayer include the prophets Jeremiah (see Jer. 12:1) and Habakkuk (see Hab. 1:2–4). In these cases, the arguments result in assurances that all is in God's control and a deepened understanding of God's purposes; however, while Habakkuk finally takes delight in God's providence, Jeremiah never seems to be sure whether he should delight in or despair over such divine government (compare Hab. 3:17–19 with Jer. 20:7–18). Somewhat paralleling these prophets, especially with regard to the subsequent submission of the suppliant, the exemplary New Testament models of the engagement of two wills in prayer are Jesus' Gethsemane prayer (Matt. 26:36–46, par.) and Paul's "thorn-in-the-flesh" prayer (2 Cor. 12:7–10).

The New Testament passages that are more difficult to explain include those that seem to teach importunity in prayer (e.g., Luke 11:5–13; 18:1–8). Some argue that these parables teach perseverance in a request until either our wills or the circumstances of our lives are altered. Others argue that the original design of these stories may not have been to teach importunity. In Luke 11 and 18, for instance, Jesus is telling his hearers that if humans are like this, how much more readily will God respond to petitions. In Luke 11, then, Jesus was concerned to teach that the needy may always resort to God without hesitation. Luke added his application in verse 8 ("I tell you . . ."). In Luke 18 the parable is placed in an eschatological setting regarding the vindication of sufferers, and verse 1 does not specify persistence with respect to the *same* request. Even if this latter interpretation is correct regarding the *original* intention of these parables, one must still deal with the way they were understood and applied by the early church. And we are still left with the examples of persistent storming of heaven in the Old Testament—examples in which the petitioners sometimes get their way (e.g., refer to Israel's request for a king in 1 Sam. 8).

In the Bible there seem to be what C. S. Lewis calls two "patterns" of petitionary prayer. On the one hand, there is the wrestling that strives with God to change God's will and/or the circumstances. On the other hand, there is the resignation to God's will and to the circumstances.

God's Response. If God is to be thought of in the Judeo-Christian tradition as a personal being with whom one wrestles in prayer, it is not surprising to find that within this tradition God is sometimes conceived of as *not* "hearing" or "answering" prayer. In fact, if petitionary prayer is request, it follows that it may or may not be granted, since that is the nature of requests over against compulsion. Just as God cannot be bound by human wishes nor induced to carry out the petitioner's will just because the prayer is long or eloquent or the pray-er is pious, so there are no automatic guarantees that God will hear our prayers.

There is certainly an expressed confidence that God will answer prayer (Pss. 3:4; 6:9; 17:6; 138:3; Matt. 7:7–11). But God sometimes seems far off or silent (see Pss. 10:1; 13:1–2; 77:5–9; 89:46). In fact, there are times when God does *not* answer or hear prayer. There is no formal treatment of this phenomenon in the Bible, though recurrent episodes suggest reasons why God does not hear some prayers. Such reasons include broken taboos (1 Sam. 14:36–42), divine displeasure with a people's behavior (Deut. 3:23–27), sins of various sorts (Ps. 66:18; Isa. 1:15; 59:1–3), selfish ends (James 4:3), and so forth. At times, the silence of God is simply inexplicable (as in Job).

But to be fair to the Judeo-Christian tradition more needs to be said. First, it is assumed that prayers that will be answered in due time (that is, in God's time) are prayers prayed in accord with God's will, particularly as that is expressed in Christ. This is especially the New Testament answer to the "problem of unanswered prayer." Thus, such silences are only temporary; for example, the silence of God experienced and expressed by the psalmist is not typically isolated in the biblical accounts but is set in the context of God's answering (e.g., see Pss. 22 and 28). Second, prayers that are answered in a way that we do not expect give us the *appearance* of God's silence only because we do not hear the response we want to hear; such "unanswered" prayer may really uncover a moral problem on the petitioner's part. Third, in refusing the specific answer requested, God may truly be hearing and answering our prayers if our intention is to seek God's will, because God sometimes wrathfully gives exactly what the wicked seek to their own damnation (see Rom. 1).

A caution is in order here. The suggestion is often made that prayer is "unanswered" because one does not pray "in Christ's name" nor "according to God's will." Not only does such a way out of the problem raise some interesting questions regarding Jesus' Gethsemane prayer, but it ignores the times when one *seems* to pray in Christ's name or according to God's will and does not receive an answer. Any solution must being with the reminder that answers to prayer are grounded in God's graciousness and faithfulness to his promises, not in the petitioner's rights.

DENNIS L. OKHOLM

Bibliography. K. Barth, *The Christian Life;* D. G. Bloesch, *The Struggle of Prayer;* G. A. Buttrick, *Prayer;* J. Calvin, *Institutes of the Christian Religion;* A. Cunningham, *Prayer: Personal and Liturgical;* G. Ebeling, *On Prayer: Nine Sermons;* J. Ellul, *Prayer and Modern Man;* F. L. Fischer, *Prayer in the New Testament;* R. J. Foster, *Prayer: Finding the Heart's True Home;* M. Greenberg, *Biblical Prose Prayer: A Window to the Popular Religion of Ancient Israel;* F. Heiler, *Prayer: A Study in the History and Psychology of Religion;* H. T. Hughes, *Prophetic Prayer: A History of the Christian Doctrine of Prayer to the Reformation;* J. Jeremias, *The Prayers of Jesus;* P. LeFevre, *Understandings of Prayer;* C. S. Lewis, *Letters to Malcolm: Chiefly on Prayer;* R. L. Simpson, *The Interpretation of Prayer in the Early Church; Tertullian's Tract on the Prayer;* H. Thielicke, *Our Heavenly Father: Sermons on the Lord's Prayer;* E. D. Willis, *Daring Prayer.*

Preach, Proclaim. The word for "preach," "proclaim" in the Greek New Testament is *kēryssō*. It is used thirty-two times in the Gospels, but about half of these are parallel occurrences within the Synoptic Gospels. "Proclaim" is complementary to the more specific term "evangelize" (*euangelizomai*) or the phrase "announce the good news," which contains within its meaning the object that is announced or proclaimed—the good news. However, usually when "proclaim" (*kērysso*) is used the context includes its object, which in the majority of instances is the gospel or Jesus. The noun proclaimer, herald (*kēryx*), refers to one who proclaims news publicly.

The Gospels. The usage of the term is very similar in the Synoptic Gospels. It is not used in John's Gospel. All three Synoptic Gospels include the use of the term to describe John the Baptist's activity and message (Matt. 3:1; Mark 1:4; Luke 3:3). It is obvious that the intent is to speak of John's activity as a proclaimer, but the message is also included. Matthew 3:2 describes the message most extensively as repentance because the reign of God is near.

Mark 1:7 also uses the word "proclaim" to describe John's proclaiming of the Coming One who will baptize with the Holy Spirit. Matthew and Luke use different words to speak of this proclamation.

After speaking of the introductory ministry of John the Baptist, the Synoptics turn to the ministry of Jesus. Both Matthew (4:17) and Mark (1:14) use "proclaim" to describe Jesus' activity of announcing the reign of God. Matthew gives a concise summary of Jesus' message. Mark designates the content of Jesus' proclamation as "the gospel of God" and goes on to give a summary (1:15). At this point Luke speaks of Jesus teaching (*didaskō*) in the synagogues (4:15). However, in his distinctive account of Jesus' sermon at Nazareth (4:16–30), Luke records Jesus' own quotation of Isaiah 61:1–2a, which contains the statement of his (the Servant's) task as "to proclaim freedom to the prisoners" (4:18) and "to proclaim the year of the Lord's favor" (4:19). Here it is evident that the New Testament understanding of "proclaim" goes back to the Old Testament, especially to Isaiah, and includes the object of God's saving activity. Mark (1:38) uses the term to express the purpose of Jesus' departure from Capernaum. Luke (4:43) uses the synonym "proclaim the good news" (*euangelizomai*). All three Synoptics go on to describe Jesus' first preaching tour in Galilee using "proclaim" (Matt. 4:23; Mark 1:39; Luke 4:44). Only Matthew (4:23) includes the content ("the good news of the kingdom") and makes this proclamation part of his distinctive threefold summary of teaching, preaching, and healing.

Mark uses "proclaim" to describe the leper's telling of how Jesus healed him (1:45). Neither Matthew nor Luke use the term here. However, Luke's expression of "news" (*logos*) spreading (5:15) enhances the understanding of "proclaim" as viewed by the inspired writer Luke.

Only Mark (3:14) relates that when Jesus chose the twelve that he commissioned them to proclaim. And certainly the content of "the kingdom of God" is implicit in this commission. Luke does not use the term here (6:13), and Matthew's structure is unique.

Matthew (9:35) and Luke (8:1) tell of Jesus proclaiming the gospel throughout cities and villages. This gives a clear picture of the meaning of the term. Further, Luke here distinctively combines "proclaim" (*kērysso*) and "proclaim the good news" (*euangelizomai*), showing that the two terms complement each other, with the latter making the content more explicit. But it must be noted that Luke does include the separate, explicit phrase describing the content—the kingdom of God (*tēn basileian tou theou*).

All three Synoptics use the term to describe Jesus' commissioning of the twelve. Mark says that "they went out and preached" (6:12). At this point Luke (9:6) uses "proclaim the gospel" (*euangelizomai*), but in 9:2 Luke uses "proclaim" (*kērysso*) to describe their commissioning by Jesus. Matthew distinctively brings together the choosing and commissioning in his Gospel and uses proclaim (*kērysso*) at the point of commission (10:7), as Luke does.

Matthew (10:27) and Luke (12:3) also use "proclaim" in the special exhortation to the disciples to courageously confess Jesus. Jesus says that in the future, secret things will be proclaimed publicly. This instruction makes clear the meaning of proclaim—to publicly declare a matter.

Mark (5:20) and Luke (8:39) use "proclaim" to describe the actions of the Gerasene demoniac after Jesus casts out the demons. The healed man goes out to proclaim what Jesus had done for him. Matthew does not record this action in his distinctive account in 8:28–34.

Matthew's distinctive description (11:1) of Jesus' journey throughout the cities teaching and proclaiming uses this term (*kērysso*), showing the public nature of Jesus' proclamation.

The account of Jesus' healing of a deaf and mute man in Mark 7:31–37 uses "proclaim" to describe the action of the crowds following Jesus' healing of the dumb man in verse 36. Luke does not record this incident, and Matthew does not record this statement (15:30).

As they record Jesus' eschatological discourse, Matthew (24:14) and Mark (13:10) both use "proclaim" to speak of Jesus' assertion that the gospel must first be proclaimed to all nations before the coming of the end. This statement, perhaps, pictures the broadest public proclamation mentioned in the Gospels.

Matthew (26:13) and Mark (14:9) also use the term to relate Jesus' defense of the woman who anointed his body for burial. In response, Jesus here speaks of the gospel being proclaimed in the whole world. The content of gospel is explicit in both Matthew and Mark, and both express clearly Jesus' worldwide public proclamation. This echoes the similar statement in the eschatological discourse.

The distinctive conclusion of Luke's Gospel records Jesus' final instructions. The resurrected Lord opens the minds of the disciples to the Scriptures and gives the Great Commission. Jesus points out that the Messiah had to suffer and rise, and that forgiveness of sins must be proclaimed (*kērysso*) to all the nations. Although the unit is not in the oldest manuscripts, the longer ending of Mark (16:9–20) contains a use of "proclaim" similar to that of Luke 24:47. Mark 16:15 gives Jesus' Great Commission to his disciples to go into all the world and proclaim the gospel. Verse 20 reports that they did go out and proclaimed everywhere. Thus, in the Gospels "proclaim" is used to describe the public heralding of the reign of God by Jesus and his disciples.

Acts. The word "proclaim" (*kērysso*) is used eight times in Acts. Acts 8:5 states that Philip began to proclaim the Christ in Samaria. The mention of crowds and the reference to great joy in the city would point to a public proclamation of Jesus as the Messiah to the whole city.

The usage is quite similar in Acts 9:20. Here it is the converted Saul who proclaims Jesus as the Son of God in the synagogues of Damascus. Again the great response and the plot against Saul's life by the Jews point to the public nature of the proclamation. Also here the content of the proclamation is very specific and similar to Paul's own letters.

In Acts 10:37 reference is made to the proclamation by John the Baptist. In Acts 10:42 Peter states that Jesus had commanded the disciples/witnesses to proclaim to the people that Jesus had been appointed by God as the final Judge. Acts 15:21 is an explanatory note given by James to support the conclusions of the Jerusalem Council. It speaks of Moses as having been proclaimed in every city from the earliest times.

Acts 19:13 is a brief reference to the practice of Jewish exorcists who used the command, "In the name of Jesus whom Paul preaches (*kērysso*), I command you to come out." Acts 20:25 records the words of Paul's farewell address to the Ephesian elders. He declares that he has gone about proclaiming the kingdom.

Finally, in the last verse of Acts (28:31), Luke summarizes Paul's prison ministry in Rome. He states that Paul proclaimed the kingdom of God and taught about Jesus for two whole years. It should be noted that in this verse the kingdom and Jesus are spoken of together. The teaching of the Gospels would support the conclusion that it was Jesus who inaugurated the kingdom of God.

It is impressive that these passages of Acts all describe a public proclamation; usually the content is the kingdom or Jesus.

Paul's Letters. "Proclaim" is used twice in Galatians. The first occurrence (2:2) is Paul's mention of the gospel that he proclaims. The second (5:11) is a hypothetical argument with the intended conclusion that Paul no longer proclaims circumcision. The single reference in 1 Thessalonians describes Paul's ministry as proclaiming the gospel of God (2:9). First Corinthians contains four occurrences of "proclaim." In 1:23 Paul declares that he proclaims Christ crucified. First Corinthians 9:27 is a brief reference to Paul's having proclaimed to others—the gospel is understood. Then 15:11 and 12 both refer to proclaiming Christ in defending the reality of the resurrection. Second Corinthians 1:19 affirms that Jesus Christ was proclaimed to the Corinthians by Paul. Second Corinthians 4:5 asserts that Paul proclaims Jesus

Christ as Lord. Second Corinthians 11:4, as part of Paul's defense of his apostolic authority at Corinth, contains two mentions of "proclaim." The same statement mentions his opponents' proclamations and also that he had proclaimed the true gospel to the Corinthians.

Romans contains four occurrences of "proclaim." Romans 2:21 refers simply to Jewish proclamation not to steal. However, chapter 10 focuses on faith. Here (v. 8) Paul refers to the word of faith that he has proclaimed. Then in verses 14 and 15 Paul argues that proclamation is necessary for hearing, and that proclaimers must be sent by God. Here it is clear that proclaiming the gospel is a crucial part of God's work of salvation.

Two of Paul's letters from prison use the term "proclaim." Colossians 1:23 gives Paul's statement that the gospel has been proclaimed to every creature and that he is a servant of that gospel. In Philippians 1:15 Paul discusses the different motives that lead to the proclamation of Christ. Paul's later pastoral letters contain two occurrences of "proclaim." In 1 Timothy 3:16 Paul seems to give a concise summary of the gospel, speaking of Jesus as having been proclaimed among the nations. In 2 Timothy 4:2 Paul charges young Timothy to proclaim the Word.

These uses, like those in the Gospels and Acts, set forth the public nature of the Christian proclamation. They also show that the content of this proclamation is the gospel or Christ—his death and resurrection for the salvation of humankind.

General Letters and Revelation. Finally, two occurrences of "proclaim" in the general letters and Revelation are to be noted. In 1 Peter 3:19 reference is made to the exalted Jesus' own proclamation of victory over the evil spirits to encourage the persecuted recipients of that letter. And in Revelation 5:2 John describes the awesome scene of the scroll in the hand of the One on the throne. He tells of a mighty angel asking the urgent question about who is worthy to open the scroll. Certainly both of these uses confirm the public nature of the proclamation being given.

HOBERT K. FARRELL

See also EVANGELIZE, EVANGELISM; GOSPEL; *KERYGMA.*

Bibliography. K. Aland, ed., *Synopsis of the Four Gospels;* C. H. Dodd, *The Apostolic Preaching and Its Development.*

Predestination. *The Concept.* Divine predestination means that God has a purpose that is determined long before it is brought to pass. It implies that God is infinitely capable of planning and then bringing about what he has planned, and Scripture speaks of him as doing this (Isa. 14:24–27; 22:11; 37:26; 44:7–8; 46:8–10). Prophecy in its predictive mode is to be understood accordingly. God plans and makes his plans known, as he chooses, to his servants the prophets (Amos 3:7). God's purpose is one of love and grace (Deut. 7:6–8; Isa. 41:8–9), above all because in love he predestined what should come to pass in his plan to save and to restore sinful humanity through Christ (Eph. 1:5). Colossians 1:26 speaks of this purpose as "the mystery that has been kept hidden for ages and generations, but now is disclosed." This implies that all that is in God's good purpose for us, individually or as part of the people of God, is by God's initiative and thus is a work of grace, something that we could never instigate or deserve (Deut. 9:4–6; 2 Tim. 1:9).

God's Predestining Purpose. From the call of Abraham (Gen. 12:3) his descendants, in particular the progeny of Jacob/Israel, are predestined to fulfill the purpose that God has for them (Ps. 105:5–10). They are to be seen in the world as his people (Deut. 7:6; Ps. 33:11–12), holy and obedient to him, living to his praise (Isa. 43:21), a priestly nation bringing the knowledge of God to other nations (Exod. 19:5–6). The New Testament bears witness also to this purpose and foreknowledge of God concerning Israel (Rom. 11:2).

It is also made clear in the Old Testament in a number of ways that the purpose of God embraces all nations. He has foreordained it when a nation is used to chasten Israel and then when a Gentile ruler sets them free (Isa. 10:5–6; 44:28–45:1). Yet irrespective of Israel Yahweh has a plan determined for the whole world as his hand is stretched out over all nations (Isa. 14:27). God "determined the times set" for the different nations "and the exact places where they should live" (Acts 17:26). In relation to the nations the word of the Lord in Isaiah 46:10 is, "I make known the end from the beginning, from ancient times, what is still to come. I say: My purpose will stand, and I will do all that I please."

Predetermined also, and thus mentioned variously in the prophets, is the purpose of God to be fulfilled in a Messiah of the house of David (Isa. 9:6–7; 11:1–9; Jer. 23:5–6; Ezek. 34:23–24; 37:24–28). It is also planned and foreordained that through Israel the knowledge of God should go out to the nations that they might be drawn to the worship of the Lord, a purpose to which the New Testament in turn bears witness (Gal. 3:8; Col. 1:27). In the New Testament it is stressed repeatedly that the divine plan to be fulfilled in Christ was predestined. Paul speaks of the purpose in him as "God's secret wisdom, a wisdom that has been hidden and that God destined for our glory before time began" (1 Cor. 2:7). "God's eternal purpose" it is called in Ephesians 3:11. Although there was a human responsibility for the death of Jesus, all that happened was by "God's set purpose and foreknowledge" (Acts 2:23). So also was the resurrection of Jesus (Acts 2:31), and furthermore he is "appointed as judge of the living and the dead" (Acts 10:42).

The people of God in the New Testament, like Israel in the Old Testament, have a destiny to fulfill. They are appointed to have an inheritance (Matt. 25:34), to receive God's kingdom (Luke 12:32), to have "the hope of glory" (Col. 1:27), which is "eternal life" (Acts 13:48). This appointed destiny for God's people can also be spoken of as their being chosen to be born anew (James 1:18), to gain salvation (2 Thess. 2:13), and to be adopted as children of God through Christ (Eph. 1:5). In terms similar to those applied to Israel, the people of God in the New Testament are chosen to be holy, to be obedient, to live to God's praise (Eph. 1:6, 11, 12, 14; 2 Tim. 1:9; 1 Peter 1:2), and, going beyond anything in the Old Testament, "predestined to be conformed to the likeness" of God's Son (Rom. 8:29). In practical terms Ephesians 2:10 says that "we are . . . created in Christ Jesus to do good works, which God prepared in advance for us to do."

Both Old and New Testaments also speak of individuals being predestined to fulfill a divine purpose. Jeremiah (1:5) is spoken of as being set apart before he was born to be a prophet to the nations. The servant of Yahweh in Isaiah 49:5 is conscious of being "formed in the womb to be his servant." In Genesis 25:23 a statement is made concerning the destinies of Jacob and Esau before they were born. In the New Testament Paul speaks of himself as set apart from birth to know God's Son and to make him known (Gal. 1:15–16).

A final question that has concerned—and divided—Christian people down through the ages is whether some are predestined to life and salvation and others predestined to condemnation ("double predestination"). On certain things Scripture is clear: (1) we all, because of our sinfulness, deserve only God's condemnation; (2) our salvation is entirely because of God's grace and God's initiative; (3) the dominant emphasis is not on the fact that some are chosen by God and some are not, but on what is the purpose of God for those chosen: "to be conformed to the likeness of his Son" (Rom. 8:29), or, "adoption as his children through Jesus Christ . . . to the praise of his glorious grace" (Eph. 1:5–6 NRSV). What, then, should be said of Paul's argument in Romans 9–11? In those chapters much is said in positive terms of God's purpose, grace offered in turn to Jews and to Gentiles. Much also is said of human responsibility in the rejection of God's grace on the part of many in Israel and thus their failure to obtain God's salvation. The only verse that can be and is often taken to speak of predestination to condemnation is in the form of a hypothetical question (and one capable of very diverse interpretations, as the commentaries indicate): "What if God, choosing to show his wrath and make his power known, bore with great patience the objects of his wrath—prepared for destruction?" (Rom. 9:22). It would be hard to fit together a predestination to judgment and the operation of human free will and our responsibility. The failure to find the salvation offered to humankind by a gracious and loving God seems more wisely assigned to the way men and women "reject God's purpose for themselves" (Luke 12:30) rather than to a prior, unalterable rejection by God.

FRANCIS FOULKES

See also ELECT, ELECTION; FOREKNOWLEDGE.

Bibliography. G. C. Berkouwer, *Divine Election;* P. Jacobs and H. Krienke, *NIDNTT,* 1:692–97; J. I. Packer, *NBD,* 1:435–38; 3:1262–64; H. H. Rowley, *The Biblical Doctrine of Election.*

Presence of God. The Scriptures often speak of God's presence in human history. The most common Hebrew term for "presence" is *pānîm,* which is also translated "face," implying a close and personal encounter with the Lord. The Greek word *prosōpon* has the same semantic range. The Greek preposition *enōpion* also commonly appears; several other Hebrew and Greek words occur only a few times.

God's presence carries a wide range of meaning. It may be something people fear. Adam and Eve's sinfulness drove them to hide from the Lord in the garden of Eden (Gen. 3:8). God's holiness cast light on Isaiah's sinfulness (Isa. 6:5). Many people who encountered God or his angel feared for their lives (Judg. 13:22; Luke 1:11–12; 2:9). Others tried unsuccessfully to escape his presence (Jonah 1:3). As God displays his presence through his great power, the whole earth trembles (Judg. 5:5; Ps. 68:8). False gods also become powerless before him (Isa. 19:1). Fear and trembling are proper responses before the One who controls all creation (Jer. 5:22).

God's presence provides comfort in times of trouble or anxiety (Josh. 1:5). The downcast seek him and find encouragement and strength to praise him (Ps. 42:5).

Knowing God is present should keep our behavior respectful and humble, for God hears our every word and holds us accountable (Eccles. 5:2, 6). He will not tolerate pride, and will bring our speech under his judgment (Ezek. 28:9). However, he will exalt those who humble themselves before him (James 4:10).

God also displayed his presence at a place of worship. The Israelites brought their sacrifices to the tabernacle—and later the temple—because God chose to establish his name there (Deut. 14:23, 26). Worshipers thus experienced a special closeness to the Lord in such a place. Inside the place of worship, the bread of the Presence reminded Israel of God's nearness (2 Chron. 4:19). When Solomon dedicated the temple, the manifestation of God's glorious presence prevented priests from fulfilling their usual duties (1 Kings 8:10–11). Reverent and proper behavior was important, for disastrous consequences might result if people did not follow God's pattern for worship (Lev. 10:1–2).

God's presence also accompanied times of covenant renewal and other solemn occasions. Before Isaac died, he determined to bless his son "in the presence of the LORD" (Gen. 27:7). Aaron was confirmed as high priest in God's presence (Num. 16:7; 17:9). As the Israelites prepared to enter Canaan, Moses told them they stood in God's presence (Deut. 29:15). God would guide them as they undertook the enormous task of conquering the land (Num. 32:29, 32), and would provide Israel's leaders the strength they needed (Josh. 1:9). The apostle Paul charged Timothy to remain faithful to the Lord, reminding his son in the faith of God's watchful presence as Timothy performed his ministry (1 Tim. 5:21; 2 Tim. 4:1).

The Bible describes heaven as a place filled with God's presence. Angels stand in God's presence and act on his authority as he directs them (Luke 1:19). Satan came before the Lord when he sought permission to attack Job (1:6, 12). The heavenly host rejoice before God when one sinner repents (Luke 15:10). Christ completed his earthly ministry by entering "heaven itself, now to appear for us in God's presence" (Heb. 9:24). Since heaven is the highest, most exalted place of all, it is fitting that God display his presence there.

God's presence is a place where prayer is heard. David sought the Lord's presence when Israel faced a three-year famine (2 Sam. 21:1). God's spokesman called the nation to cry out to the Lord in the face of Jerusalem's destruction (Lam. 2:19). Paul constantly interceded for the Thessalonian church, bringing their name before the Father's presence (1 Thess. 1:3). Christians may approach the Lord with confidence because of Christ's finished work on our behalf (Heb. 4:15–16). Furthermore, God promises to hear and forgive those who come into his presence with humble repentance (2 Chron. 7:14).

God's presence is also a place of judgment. The Lord cast his people from his presence (Jer. 15:1; 52:3). The Scriptures describe this action as God hiding his face (Isa. 59:2; Ezek. 39:29). But God's presence for judgment also carries an eschatological dimension. The Lord will one day summon all nations before him; heaven and earth will flee his holy presence (Rev. 20:11). Those who see this judgment coming will beg for deliverance, but to no avail (Rev. 6:16). The most awful aspect of God's judgment is eternal separation from his presence (2 Thess. 1:9).

But God's presence is also a place of blessing. David counted it a joy to experience the Lord's presence (Acts 2:25, 28), and Peter described it as the source of blessing for all who place their faith in Christ (Acts 3:19). To experience God's presence is to experience the shining of God's face (Ps. 67:1). Believers always live in God's presence, and he notes all their deeds (Mal. 3:16). He has promised to be with us until he comes again (Matt. 28:20).

In the age to come, God's presence will be the ultimate blessing, for believers will see him face to face (1 John 3:2). His immediate presence will render a temple unnecessary (Rev. 21:22). It is the anticipation of this presence that should motivate Christians to faithful service in this present age (1 Thess. 2:19; 2 Peter 3:10–11). BRYAN E. BEYER

See also ARK; CLOUD, CLOUD OF THE LORD; GLORY; GOD; TABERNACLE; TEMPLE.

Pride. ***The Old Testament.*** While pride is sometimes used in the Old Testament in a positive sense (i.e., the "pride" of the land of Israel [Ps. 47:4; Ezek. 24:21]; or, God's "pride/majesty/excellency" [Exod. 15:7; Job 37:4; Isa. 2:10]), its negative sense predominates, occurring in sixty-one texts. "Pride" is found mainly in the prophets and the books of poetry.

The main Hebrew root is *gʾh;* the most common term is *gāʾôn,* which occurs a total of twenty-three times. Included are the ideas of arrogance, cynical insensitivity to the needs of others, and presumption. Pride is both a disposition/attitude and a type of conduct.

A synonym *gābâ* means "to be high." While used in a variety of senses, the normal meaning is pride or arrogance, in particular "an inner attitude of pride," often linked with parts of the human body (Isa. 2:11, 17). There is pride of the eyes (Ps. 101:5; Isa. 5:15); of the heart (Ezek. 28:2, 5, 17); of the spirit (Prov. 16:18; Eccles. 7:8); and of one's mouth/speech (1 Sam. 2:3). A classic text includes the words "pride," "conceit," "arrogance," and "haughtiness" (Jer. 48:29).

Fifteen Old Testament texts (NIV) contain the word "arrogance," nearly half of them (7) in the prophets (Isa. 2:17; 9:9; 13:11; Jer. 13:15; 48:29; Ezek. 7:10; Hos. 5:5; 7:10). Five references are in poetical texts (Job 35:12; Pss. 10:2; 17:10; 73:8; Prov. 8:13), and three others are found in Deuteronomy 1:43; 1 Samuel 2:3; 15:23.

What constitutes a "proud" person? The negative sense points to a sinful individual who shifts ultimate confidence from God to self. In the Wisdom literature, "the proud" are distinct from "the righteous" and "the humble." Here the term is applied to non-Israelites, rather than to Israel. The Septuagint uses *hyperēphanos,* meaning one who is insolent, presumptuous, or arrogant, a scoffer or a mocker (Ps. 119:21, 51; Prov. 3:34). When the prophets accuse Israel of pride (Jer. 13:9; Ezek. 7:10, 20; 16:56; Hos. 5:5; 7:10; Amos 6:8; 8:7; Zeph. 2:10), the word *hybristēs* connotes a wanton, insolent person. Thus, in the Old Testament books, the prideful are generally associated with the wicked, the arrogant, the presumptuous, and those who are insolent toward God.

Most of the adjectives joined with "pride" in the Old Testament are negative in connotation, including words such as "stubborn" (Lev. 26:19), "overweening" (Isa. 16:6), "willful" (Isa. 10:12), and "great" (Jer. 13:9). In one instance the positive phrase "everlasting pride" describes the status of a restored Zion (Isa. 60:15). Most of the synonyms give a negative sense: contempt (Ps. 31:18); wrongdoing (Job 33:17); trust (Ps. 62:10); arrogance (Prov. 8:13; Isa. 2:11, 17; 9:9); insolence (Isa. 16:6); and conceit (Jer. 48:29). An exception is "glory" (Isa. 4:2).

Finally, in the Old Testament, what are some of the results of pride? It led to Uzziah's downfall (2 Chron. 26:16); it hardened the heart of Nebuchadnezzar (Dan. 5:20); it goes before destruction (Prov. 16:18); it does not seek God (Ps. 10:4); it brings disgrace (Prov. 11:2); it breeds quarrels (Prov. 13:10); it deceives (Jer. 49:16; Obad. 3); it brings low (Prov. 29:23; Isa. 2:11; 23:9); it humbles (Isa. 2:17; Dan. 4:37).

The New Testament. In the New Testament, the abstract use of *hybris* (pride) is completely absent. Rather, it refers to ill-treatment, hardship, disaster, or a violent or insolent person (Acts 27:10, 21; 2 Cor. 12:10; 1 Tim. 1:13). The word *hyperēphanos* and its derivatives occur six times; twice in the Gospels (Mark 7:22; Luke 1:51) and four times in the Epistles (Rom. 1:30; 2 Tim. 3:2; James 4:6; 1 Peter 5:5). In its Greek background, the word meant overweening, arrogant, haughty.

Mark 7:22 includes arrogance in a list of vices, the only such example in the Gospel texts. (Two other lists are found in Paul's letters [Rom. 1:29–31; Gal. 5:19–23].)

God opposes the proud (Prov. 3:34). Both James (4:6) and Peter (1 Peter 5:5) cite this Old Testament text, including the word *hyperephanos,* the "proud/arrogant" person. It stands in contrast to the word "humble," a quality that God honors. Paul's list (Rom. 1:30) includes *hybristēs,* one who behaves arrogantly toward those who are too weak to retaliate.

Finally, a remarkable example of *hyperēphanos* occurs in the Magnificat (Luke 1:51). Using language largely from the Old Testament, Mary tells how God will scatter the proud—possibly a reference to a specific group in society and political life. They are characterized by suppressing the masses, the poor and humble in Israel. God will overthrow them and exalt the lowly. While his wrath is upon the proud, he will visit the humble in grace.

Walter M. Dunnett

Bibliography. G. Betram, *TDNT,* 8:295–307, 525–29; V. P. Hamilton, *TWOT,* 1:143.

Priest, Christ as. ***The Old Testament.*** The priestly activity of drawing near to God in sacrifice and prayer is introduced in the Old Testament through Abel the head of a family (Gen. 4:4), Melchizedek the king of Salem and priest of God Most High (Gen. 14:18), Jethro the priest of Midian (Exod. 18:1), Aaron (Exod. 28:1), and the Levites (Exod. 32:28–29; Num. 1:47–53). The law of Moses established a closed, hereditary, vocational priesthood in Israel (Exod. 28:1; 29:9; 40:12–15). It was their assignment to serve the Lord with dignity and honor in the tabernacle and later in the temple, representing the people in the presence of God (Exod. 28:29; Num. 3:5–10). Through the casting of lots, they possessed the oracular power of pronouncing divine decisions (Exod. 28:30; 33:7–11; Lev. 13–16; Deut. 17:8–12; 1 Sam. 28:6). They were the guardians of the sanctuary and the spiritual piety of the nation (Num. 18:1–7). The extensive cultic instructions concerning sacrificial and ceremonial duties in the tabernacle and temple overshadow their responsibility to teach the truth of God (Exod. 7:1; Lev. 10:11; Deut. 17:11; 27:9–10; 33:10; Ezra 7:10–12, 21), and soon this role is assumed by the prophets of Israel.

Although the Levites served in the tabernacle and temple, caring for its furnishings and maintenance, and assisting the priests (1 Chron. 23:28–32), the responsibility of presenting offerings and leading ceremonial rituals was restricted to the levitical family of Aaron and his descendants (Num. 3:5–10; 16:8–11; 2 Chron. 13:9). A physical deformity or disability disqualified them from approaching the altar of God (Lev. 21:16–23; cf. Luke 22:50), and those who qualified to serve had to be thirty to fifty years of age (Num. 4:47; 8:23–26). They were to avoid uncleanness by contact with the dead (Lev. 21:1–4, 11), remain unshaven (Lev. 21:5–6, 10), and marry a virgin (Lev. 21:7–8, 13–15). Only the high priest could enter the Most Holy Place on the Day of Atonement (Lev. 16). Through the appointment of David and later exilic developments, the office of high priest became restricted further to Zadok and his descendants (2 Sam. 15:24–29; 1 Kings 2:35; 4:2; Ezek. 40:46).

The ritual of ordination consecrating Aaron to the office of high priest lasted seven days (Exod. 29:35). At the entrance to the Tent of Meeting (Exod. 29:4; Lev. 8:1–3), he was washed with water and dressed in priestly garments; anointing oil was poured on his head (Exod. 29:4–7; 40:12–16; Lev. 8:12, 30; Ps. 133:2). Aaron and his sons laid their hands on a bull and one of two rams without defect, which were sacrificed as offerings (Exod. 29:10–28). A feast followed on that first day, during which Aaron and his sons ate the meat of the ram with unleavened bread (Exod. 29:32). The consecration continued with the daily sacrifice of two lambs a year old, and when completed, "the glory of the Lord filled the tabernacle" (Exod. 40:35).

The Gospels. There were several ways in which Jesus fulfilled the function of the messianic priest, although he neither refers to himself nor to his disciples as priests. He justifies his Sabbath activity on the basis of the priestly exemption in

Matthew 12:3–8. When he healed lepers, he sent them to the priest for the determination of cleanness in accordance with the law (Mark 1:44; Luke 17:14). Luke reports a scathing criticism of priests and Levites who would pass by a dying man, while a heretical Samaritan models divine love for his neighbor (Luke 10:30–35).

During the week of his passion, Jesus wept over the city of Jerusalem and prophesied her future destruction (Luke 19:41–44; cf. Deut. 17:8–11). Entering the temple he cleansed it of the merchants and money changers (Matt. 21:12–13; Luke 19:45–46; cf. Mark 11:15–17; John 2:13–16), affirming the temple as "a house of prayer" (cf. Num. 18:1; Acts 2:46; 3:1; 5:12). This was clearly interpreted as an affront to the authority of the chief priests and teachers of the law, for they began plotting to kill him (Mark 11:18; Luke 19:47; cf. Matt. 21:15). Observing the rich putting their gifts into the temple treasury, he praised the poor widow who put in two small coins (Luke 21:1–4). Jesus left the temple and went out of the city to Bethany, the village of Simon the Leper (Mark 14:3) and the resurrected Lazarus (John 11:1; 12:2). While at a dinner given in his honor, Mary took an alabaster jar of very expensive perfume and anointed Jesus' head (Matt. 26:6–13; Mark 14:3–9; John 12:2–8), which echoed the anointing of Aaron to the office of high priest (cf. Exod. 40:13). Jesus warned Simon Peter of his approaching trial by Satan, and comforted him with the assurance of his priestly intercession on his behalf (Luke 22:31–32). Perhaps the ultimate priestly action of Jesus is recorded in John 17. He prayed for himself, his disciples, and then for those who would believe through the disciples' message. Each of these acts had priestly implications.

The Epistle to the Hebrews. In Hebrews the motif of Jesus Christ as High Priest is most prominent, and serves as an early church, theological commentary on the life, suffering, and exaltation of Jesus. Jesus experienced human nature, being "made like his brothers in every way, in order that he might become merciful and faithful high priest in service to God, and that he might make atonement for the sins of the people" (2:17; cf. 4:15; 7:26; 9:14).

The basis for the priestly Christology of Hebrews is found in the familiar words of Psalm 110, where a connection is made between the anticipated messianic King and Priest. The Messiah is told to sit at Yahweh's right hand, assuming the ceremony of royal enthronement to kingly power, but in the very presence of God (v. 1). This apparently was the consensus of rabbinic interpretation at the time of Jesus, for this Old Testament verse is the most frequently quoted in the New Testament (Matt. 22:44; Mark 12:36; Luke 20:42–43; Acts 2:34–35; Heb. 1:13). The psalm of David continues with a reference to the mysterious king-priest Melchizedek: "The LORD has sworn and will not change his mind: 'You are a priest forever, in the order of Melchizedek'" (Ps. 110:4). Abraham recognized the greatness of Melchizedek, who served in the dual offices of king of Salem and priest of God Most High, offered his tithe, and received a blessing (Gen. 14:18–20; cf. Heb. 7:6–10). As with Melchizedek, Jesus was without the ancestral, genealogical credentials necessary for the Aaronic priesthood (7:3, 13, 16), he was also before Aaron and the transitory, imperfect law and levitical priesthood (7:11–12, 17–18; 8:7). Melchizedek, Aaron, and his descendants all died, preventing them from continuing in office (7:23). Jesus Christ has been exalted to a permanent priesthood by his resurrection and enthronement at the right hand of God in the heaven (8:1).

The new covenant, which Jesus inaugurates and serves as mediator of, supersedes the old (7:22; 8:6–13; 9:15; 12:24; cf. Jer. 31:31–34; 1 Tim. 2:5). Jesus has become the High Priest in the true tabernacle (8:2), which is not of this world (9:11). He is qualified to enter the Most Holy Place, not by the blood of a bull and a ram, but by his own blood (9:12). Whereas the blood of Aaronic sacrifices could make the people outwardly clean but had to be repeated (9:13; 10:1–4, 11), Jesus continues in the presence of God (9:25) as the perfect High Priest (9:25–26), offering his own blood as the perfect sacrifice to take away sins and cleansing the consciences of many people (9:28; cf. Isa. 53:12). The people of Christ now have confidence that they also may enter the very presence of God by the blood of Jesus (10:19), and participate in "a holy priesthood" (Exod. 19:6; 1 Peter 2:5, 9).

Christ the Priest will appear a second time, not to bear sin, but to bring salvation to those who are waiting for him (9:28). MELVIN H. SHOEMAKER

See also CHRIST, CHRISTOLOGY; PRIEST, PRIESTHOOD; TABERNACLE; TEMPLE.

Bibliography. J. Baehr, *NIDNTT,* 3:32–44; B. S. Childs, *Old Testament Theology in a Canonical Context;* G. L. Cockerill, *The Melchizedek Christology in Heb. 7:1–28;* A. A. Cody, *A History of the Old Testament Priesthood;* O. Cullmann, *The Christology of the New Testament;* R. H. Culpepper, *Theological Educator* 32 (1985): 46–62; W. Horbury, *JSNT* 19 (1983): 43–71; W. L. Lane, *Hebrews 1–8;* M. C. Parsons, *EvQ* 60 (1988): 195–215; G. Schrenk, *TDNT,* 3:221–83; H. S. Songer, *RevExp* 82 (1985): 345–59.

Priest, Priesthood. *Old Testament Priesthood.*

The primary word for "priest" in the Old Testament is the Hebrew masculine noun *kōhēn,* for which we have no certain etymology. It occurs approximately 750 times and can refer to priests of the one true God or of other supposed gods that other nations and sometimes also the ancient Israelites themselves worshiped (for the latter, see, e.g., Gen. 41:45, 50; 2 Kings 10:11, 19). Related terms are the verb *kāhan,* "to act as (or become) a priest" (23 occurrences), the feminine abstract noun *kĕhunnâ,* "priesthood" (14 occurrences; see Exod. 29:9; 40:15; Num. 3:10; 18:1, 7; 1 Sam. 2:36; Ezra 2:62; Neh. 7:64; 13:29, referring to the exclusivity, perpetuity, and responsibility of the Aaronic office of "priesthood"; cf. Num. 16:10 for Korah's rebellion against the Aaronic exclusivity, and Josh. 18:7 for the "priesthood" of the tribe of Levi as a whole), and the Aramaic masculine noun *kāhēn* "priest" (8 occurrences, all in Ezra 6–7). Another Hebrew word, *kōmer,* "(idolatrous) priest," occurs only three times in the Old Testament (2 Kings 23:5; Hos. 10:5; Zeph. 1:4) referring exclusively to priests of foreign gods.

The first occurrence of "priest" in the Old Testament is the reference to the pre-Israelite "Melchizedek king of Salem . . . priest of God Most High" (Gen. 14:18). Jethro, Moses' father-in-law and the priest of Midian, was also recognized as non-Israelite priest of the true God of Sinai by Moses, Aaron, and the elders of Israel (Exod. 2:16; 3:1; 18:1, 10–12).

Priests of foreign gods in foreign lands referred to in the Old Testament are Potiphera, Joseph's father-in-law, who was a "priest of On" in Egypt (Gen. 41:45, 50; 46:20), the whole priestly organization in Egypt (Gen. 47:22, 26), the "priests of Dagon" in Philistia (1 Sam. 5:5; 6:2), the "priests of Chemosh" in Moab (Jer. 48:7), and the "priests of Malcam" in Ammon (Jer. 49:3). Unfortunately, there were also priests of foreign gods who practiced their priesthood within the boundaries of Israel, sometimes even under the auspices of certain unfaithful Israelite rulers (see, e.g., 2 Kings 10:11, 19, 23; 23:5).

Second Kings 23:4–20 lists five categories of priests that existed in ancient Israel before Josiah's reformation, and arranges them according to their proximity to the Jerusalem temple: (1) the high priest (v. 4), (2) the second-order priests (v. 4), (3) the idolatrous priests in the cities of Judah and in the area surrounding Jerusalem (v. 5); (4) the priests of the high places in the cities of Judah from Geba to Beersheba (vv. 8–9); and (5) the priests of the high places in Samaria (i.e., the remnants of the priests of the former northern kingdom, v. 20). According to this passage, a significant feature of Josiah's religious reformation was his eradication of all priests (and their cultic accouterments) except those who functioned legitimately within Jerusalem temple. Therefore, only the first two categories of priests in 2 Kings 23 retained their office: the "high priest" (v. 4, here Hilkiah) and "the priests of the second order" (v. 4; i.e., other descendants of Aaron).

A Kingdom of Priests. One of the foundational principles of the Israelite covenant with God at Sinai was that the nation as a whole would become "a kingdom of priests" (Exod. 19:6a). There have been many proposed interpretations of this expression. Some say that it refers to Israel as a kingdom ruled by priests or a nation whose kings are also priests. In the immediate context as well as in the theology of the Old Testament overall, however, this expression seems to support two main ideas corresponding to the surrounding statements that covenant Israel would become the Lord's "special treasure" and "holy nation" (Exod. 19:5b, 6b).

First, the closest Old Testament parallel is Isaiah 61:6 (cf. 66:21), which designates the nation of Israel as the priestly mediators for all the nations of the world when they come to worship the Lord on Mount Zion in the eschatological future. This seems to be part of the intended meaning in Exodus 19:5b–6a as well, since Israel was to become the Lord's special treasure among all the peoples. "Although the whole earth is mine, you will be for me a kingdom of priests" (in Hebrew the "you" is emphatic, contrasting Israel with the other nations).

Second, the covenant ratification ritual in Exodus 24:3–8 actually inaugurated Israel as a "kingdom of priests," that is, a nation that had direct access to God through his presence in the tabernacle and to which they would come and worship. The ritual procedure itself involved splashing the blood of the burnt and peace offerings (v. 5) both on the altar (v. 6) and on the people (v. 8). There is a striking similarity between this ritual in Exodus 24 and the consecration of the Aaronic priests by putting some of the blood of the ordination peace offering on the right ear, thumb, and big toe of Aaron and his sons, and afterwards splashing some of it around on the altar (Exod. 29:20; Lev. 8:23–24).

That differences between Exodus 24:5–8 and Exodus 29:20 are due primarily to one or both of the following factors: (1) the consecration in Exodus 24 was for the priesthood of the whole nation so that the corporate general splashing of blood was appropriate to the meaning of the ritual; and (2) in the instance of Exodus 24 specific touching of each person's body by Moses was precluded by the large number of people involved. Moreover, the connection between Exodus 24 and 29 is confirmed by the blood manipulation for the guilt offering used to cleanse the leper in Leviticus 14 (presumably the same for all lepers whether or not they were priests). The procedure there is virtually identical to that performed for the consecration of the priests.

The rationale seems to have been that since the leper had been expelled (i.e., desecrated) from the "holy"' community (Lev. 13:46), therefore, it was necessary to resanctify him (i.e., make him holy once again) and thereby readmit him to the national community that had originally been established as a consecrated community by the ritual in Exodus 24. The manipulation of oil in the case of the leper (Lev. 14:15–18) also corresponds to priestly consecration procedures (cf. Exod. 29:21 and Lev. 8:30) and further substantiates this suggestion that, from the start (i.e., from Exod. 24 forward), the whole nation was a "kingdom of priests"—they were "a holy people" (Exod. 19:6, immediately following "a kingdom of priests").

Finally, the cult granted the entire nation the privilege of eating at the Lord's table on regular occasions in accordance with the peace offering regulations in Leviticus 3 and 7:11–34. Therefore, Israel was to be a "kingdom of priests" in terms of its corporate participation in the service of worship to the Lord in the sanctuary (Exod. 24:3–8) as well as in its position and ministry toward the nations roundabout them (Isa. 61:6).

The Aaronic Priesthood. Moses functioned as the original priest of Israel by initially consecrating (1) the whole kingdom of priests (Exod. 24:3–8), (2) the perpetual priesthood of Aaron and his descendants, who would in turn mediate for that kingdom of priests (Exod. 29; Lev. 8), and (3) the tabernacle (Num. 7:1). However, there are several passages that seem to indicate that Aaron and his sons functioned as priests in Israel even before the official consecration of the Aaronic priesthood (Exod. 19:24; 24:1; 32:3–6). Of course, as brothers and sons of Amram and Jochebed (Exod. 6:20) Moses and Aaron were both from the tribe of Levi through Kohath. Therefore, it was natural that the Lord should then choose the whole tribe of Levi to assist the clan of Aaron with all their priestly duties in place of the firstborn of all Israel (Num. 8:14–19).

So, although the entire nation constituted "a kingdom of priests," the Lord established Aaron's descendants as the perpetual priestly clan in Israel. Together they were responsible for maintaining the proper relationship of the people to Lord in regard to the two major foci of the Mosaic covenant: (1) the administration and ministry of the sanctuary and (2) the custody and administration of the law of Moses.

The Administration and Ministry of the Sanctuary. The ministry of priesthood focused especially on administering and ministering at the place of the Lord's "Presence" (see esp. Exod. 33:14–15; Lev. 10:2) according to the basic principles of holy versus profane (Lev. 10:10a), clean versus unclean (v. 10b), and atonement (v. 17). Following these rules and procedures was a matter of survival for the nation in general (Lev. 15:31b, "so they will not die in their uncleanness for defiling my dwelling place, which is among them"; cf. Exod. 32:35; 33:2–3, 14–15) as well as for the priests in particular (see the death of Nadab and Abihu in Lev. 10).

It was not just the sons of Aaron but the whole tribe of Levi who were responsible for maintaining proper levels of sanctity and purity in regard to the sanctuary presence of the Lord as a whole (Num. 18:1a "You [Aaron], your sons and your father's family [i.e., the Levites] are to bear the responsibility for offenses against the sanctuary"; note the clarification regarding the Levites in Num. 18:2–6 and cf. Deut. 18:5–8).

Initially, the duties of the Levites in assisting the priests focused on such tasks as the transportation of the tabernacle (see, e.g., Num. 3–4; 1 Chron. 15:2) and guarding the doorway to the tabernacle (see, e.g., 1 Chron. 9:19, 22–27). David assigned them other tasks in assisting the priests within the sanctuary (e.g., purification procedures, preparing the showbread and other grain offerings, leading in the praising of the Lord through song, special responsibilities for festival burnt offerings, etc., 1 Chron. 23:27–32; 25:1–8). The importance of the Levites in the priestly functions of the sanctuary are well illustrated by their involvement in the reforms of Hezekiah (2 Chron. 29–31) and Josiah (2 Chron. 34:9; 35:10–15).

On the other hand, although the Levites assisted the priests, it was the priests alone, Aaron and his descendants (no other Levites), who were responsible for dealing directly with the burnt offering altar or anything inside the Holy Place or Holy of Holies (Num. 18:1b).

First, they had the oversight of the various offerings and sacrifices in the tabernacle, certain specific responsibilities regarding the actual handling of the blood, fat, flesh, and special portions, and the benefit of certain parts of the offerings as their payment for performing the requisite rituals. The priestly responsibilities and prerogatives for each of the major ritual procedures is prescribed in detail in Leviticus 6:8–7:36.

There were also daily, weekly, monthly, and periodic festival offerings that the priests were responsible to offer as part of the regular pattern of tabernacle worship (Num. 28–29). Regular daily responsibilities included keeping the lamps burning continually in the tent of meeting by attending to them each evening and morning (Lev. 24:3–4; cf. Exod. 27:20–21), and keeping the fire continually burning on the burnt offering altar as part of the regular morning and evening burnt offering rituals (Lev. 6:12–13; cf. Num. 28:3–8). Weekly responsibilities included replacing the twelve cakes of the "bread of presence" on the table in the tent of meeting each sabbath (Lev. 24:5–9; cf. Exod. 25:30), and the regular additional Sabbath burnt offerings (Num. 28:9–10).

At the special festival times the priests had specific responsibilities in handling the offerings brought by the people (Lev. 23:9–21, 25, 36–38). In addition to the normal regulations for offering sacrifices and offerings the priests were in charge of the valuation for the redemption of vows and things consecrated to the Lord (Lev. 27), the oversight of the sin offering for jealousy (Num. 5:11–31), and the regulations for the Nazirite vow (Num. 6:1–21). They also blew the trumpets in Israel for summoning and directing the congregation and its leaders in their travels (Num. 10:2–6), convening the congregation (10:7–8), blowing the alarm in battle (10:9), or on worship and festival occasions (10:10).

Second, the Aaronic priests were responsible to maintain the sanctity and purity of the sanctuary (Lev. 10:10). Since the Lord was physically present within the physical tabernacle structure in their midst, therefore, the physical purity of Israel was essential to the habitation of the Lord among them (note the contrast between cleansing the "flesh" by the Old Testament sacrifices as opposed to the cleansing of the "conscience" by the sacrifice of Christ in Heb. 9:8–10, 13–14). They were to accomplish this by teaching the people the laws of purity (Lev. 11:46; 12:7; 13:59; 14:57; 15:32) and by functioning as the regulators of certain aspects of the society based on those rules.

Sometimes this involved presiding over certain specified sacrificial cleansing procedures on irregular occasions: for example, the burnt and sin offering rituals for the woman after childbirth (Lev. 12:6–8), the combination of two bird, guilt, sin, and burnt offering rituals for the cleansing of the leper (Lev. 14:4–20), the sin and burnt offering rituals for the man or woman with an irregular discharge (Lev. 15:13–15, 25–30), and the preparation of the ashes of the red heifer for purification for touching a dead corpse (Num. 19:1–10). In addition, they diagnosed and regulated the expulsion and readmission of people with infectious skin diseases (Lev. 13; cf. the cleansing procedures in Lev. 14 referred to above), and were responsible to preside over the removal of bloodguiltiness for an unsolved homicide in the land (Deut. 21:1–9, esp. v. 5).

The Custody and Administration of the Mosaic Law. Leviticus 10:10 relates primarily to issues of "the holy and the common" and "the unclean and the clean." The next verse introduces the matter of administration of the Mosaic law: "you must teach the Israelites all the decrees the LORD has given them through Moses" (10:11). Deuteronomy 21:5 is particularly instructive regarding these responsibilities of the priests: "The priests, the sons of Levi" were charged to "pronounce blessings in the name of the LORD and to decide all cases of dispute and assault." The standard priestly blessing formula found in Numbers 6:24–26 was given as a means of invoking the name of the Lord upon the nation so that he might bless them in their various endeavors (Num. 6:27). This may have been particularly important in situations where there was a need to clear the nation of guilt, in this case bloodguiltiness for an unsolved homicide (Deut. 21:1–9).

The last clause of Deuteronomy 21:5 especially highlights the judicial side of the priestly office. The resolution of disputes was not always achieveable in the local courts. Since the levitical priests were the custodians and teachers of the Mosaic Law (Deut. 17:18; 24:8; 31:9–13, 24–26; cf. 2 Chron. 15:3; 31:4; 35:3; Ezra 7:24–26), those who staffed the central sanctuary were naturally the final court of appeal in Israel (Deut. 18:8–13; 19:17).

The Levites shared not only in the sanctuary duties of the Aaronic priests (see above) but also in their judicial duties (see esp. 2 Chron. 17:8–9; 35:3; Ezra 7:5–10; Neh. 8:1–2, 9–11, etc.). Samuel is a good example of a Levite who legitimately did both (cf. 1 Sam. 1:1; 8:2, with 1 Chron. 6:28, 33–38). In his early days he was levitical assistant to Eli the Aaronic high priest in the service of the tabernacle (1 Sam. 2–3). Later he became a "judge" of Israel (1 Sam. 7:15–17).

The High Priesthood. *Special Obligations.* There were special obligations for which the high priest alone was responsible. On any normal day any priest might perform atoning sacrificial procedures, but not on the Day of Atonement (Lev. 16). On this day, and only on this day, the high priest would enter alone into the Most Holy Place to purge it from the impurities of the priests (vv. 11–14) and the people (v. 15) by sprinkling sin offering blood on the mercy seat. After this he also purged the other parts of the sanctuary with blood (vv. 16–19), performed the scapegoat ritual (vv. 20–22), and offered his burnt offering, the burnt offering of the people, and the fat of the sin offerings on the burnt offering altar (vv. 23–27). Thus, the high priest would yearly cleanse (i.e., "purify") himself, the other priests, and all the people of the assembly (vv. 30, 33b) by purging (i.e., "atoning") the Most Holy Place, everything in the tent of meeting, and the burnt offering altar (v. 33a) on their behalf (vv. 30, 33b).

Furthermore, all the priests were under strict restrictions to avoid defilement by contact with a corpse (except for their immediate family), or by marriage to a divorced woman or former harlot (Lev. 21:1–4, 7). The high priest, however, could not defile himself even by attending to his dead father or mother, and marriage was restricted to a virgin (i.e., he could not marry a widow, much less a divorced woman or former harlot; Lev. 21:10–14). Moreover, he was responsible to function as the head of the priestly system at the festivals and was in charge of everything that happened in the tabernacle (see, e.g., Eli's supervision in 1 Sam. 1:9, 12–17), including the actions of the other priests (see, e.g., the problem of Eli's rebellious priestly sons in 1 Sam. 2:29). Finally, another well-known and exclusive function of the high priest was to possess and manipulate the Urim and Thummim housed in the "breastpiece of judgment," which was attached to the high priest's ephod (Exod. 28:28–30). He used them to obtain oracular answers from the Lord regarding specific situations in Israel.

History. The history of the Old Testament high priesthood is complex. After the death of Nadab and Abihu, Eleazar seems to have been the oldest remaining son and it is he who became the next high priest (Num. 20:22–29; 26:1–4; 27:21; Josh. 19:51), his brother Ithamar being second to him. Certain passages suggest that Phinehas followed Eleazar his father (Num. 31:6; Josh. 22:13, 30–32; Judg. 20:28). The high priestly line evidently shifted from the descendants of Eleazar to Ithamar during the period of the judges. Eli, the high priest and Judge of Israel at Shiloh (1 Sam. 1:9), was from the line of Ithamar. The line of Eli continued in the high priesthood for a time (see 1 Sam. 14:3, 18; 21:1; 22:19–20). However, the judgment of the Lord against Eli in 1 Samuel 2:22–36 would eventually bring the office back to the line of Eleazar when Solomon dismissed Abiathar (1 Kings 2:27) and appointed Zadok to be the high priest (1 Kings 2:35). Thus, the Lord's "covenant of a perpetual priesthood" with Phinehas was fulfilled (Num. 25:13).

New Testament Priesthood. The primary New Testament Greek word for "priest" is *hiereus* (32 occurrences). Six other terms derive from it: the verb *hierateuō* for Zacharias "serving as priest" (Luke 1:8), the verb *hierourgeō* referring to Paul "serving as a priest" by offering the Gentiles up as a holy offering to God (Rom. 15:16), and the nouns *hierateia* for the "priestly office" of Zacharias (Luke 1:9) and the sons of Levi (Heb. 7:5), *hierateuma* in reference to the "priesthood" of the church (1 Peter 2:5, 9), *archieratikos* referring to those of "high priestly" descent (Acts 4:6), and especially *archiereus* ("high or chief priest(s)," 123 occurrences). With only one exception (Acts 14:13, the priest of Zeus), all the New Testament references to priests or priesthood are in some kind of continuity with the Old Testament.

High Priests, Chief Priests, and Priests. The Old Testament Aaronic and specifically Zadokite line of high priests continued down into the intertestamental period until about 172 B.C., when the Syrian (i.e., Seleucid) ruler of Palestine, Antiochus IV (Epiphanes), began to assign the office to whomever was in political and financial favor with him at any particular time (2 Macc. 4). Although they were not Zadokites, the Maccabeans (i.e., Hasmoneans) were a priestly family that successfully led a revolt against the Syrian rulers and eventually became not only the political leaders of the Jews but also assumed the role of high priest (i.e., beginning with Jonathan, ca. 152 B.C., 1 Macc. 10:18–21). During this time the Qumran community prided itself on being the enclave of the legitimate Zadokite high priesthood over against the Hasmonean high priesthood in Jerusalem.

In 37 B.C. the rule of the Hasmoneans came to an end and the family of Herod the Great began the practice of appointing high priests from various priestly families (again, not necessarily Zadokites) from time to time, sometimes year by year (note John 18:13, "Caiaphas, the high priest *that year*"). This led to an oligarchy of a few privileged high priestly families who obtained their position through bribery. The New Testament refers often to the "chief priests," apparently referring to a group of priests who had the oversight of the cultus, many of whom belonged to these privileged families. This group seems to have included the current high priest (John 18:13), all those still alive who had previously held the position (Luke 3:2; John 18:19, 24), and those of high priestly descent (see esp. Acts 4:6, 23). Three New Testament high priests are specifically named: Annas (Luke 3:2; John 18:19, 24), Caiaphas (Luke 3:2; John 18:13b, 24), and Ananias (Acts 23:2; 24:1).

Of course, the priests (i.e., the high priests, chief priests, and regular priests) were the source of much opposition to Jesus and the apostolic spread of the gospel. Nevertheless, Paul confirmed his respect for the office of Ananias after unintentionally insulting him (Acts 23:2–5). Jesus refused the same to Annas (John 18:19–24), but during his ministry he sometimes affirmed the priests (see, e.g., Matt. 8:4 the cleansing of the leper). Zecharias, the father of John the Baptist, was a priest (Luke 1:8). Interestingly, the high priest Caiaphas unwittingly prophesied the substitutionary death of Jesus for Israel and for all believers even among the gentiles (John 11:47–53; 18:14). Moreover, it was not long before "a large number of priests became obedient to the faith" (Acts 6:7).

Jesus as Priest and High Priest. Although the high priesthood of Jesus is often described solely in terms of his status according to the order of Melchizedek, Hebrews 2–4 devotes a great deal of attention to the matter of the high priesthood of Jesus before introducing Melchizedek in 5:6. In 2:17 the writer of Hebrews describes Jesus as the one who has come to our aid as our high priest by making "atonement for the sins of the people." The emphasis is on the fact that, because he himself suffered the same sorts of temptations that we face, he is a "merciful and faithful" high priest (2:17–18) and, as such, he is "the apostle and high priest whom we confess" (3:1). After a lengthy digression about the faithfulness of Jesus and the importance of a corresponding faithful commitment to him on our part (3:7–4:13), the writer returns to the same issue and exhorts us to "hold firmly" to our sympathetic high priest (4:14–16) because it is in him that "we may receive mercy and find grace to help us in our time of need" (4:16).

This argument regarding the gentle and sympathetic nature of our high priestly mediator continues into 5:1–10. Old Testament high priests could sympathize with the people for whom they mediated because they had to offer sacrifices for their own sins before they could offer for the people (5:2–3; 7:27; and cf. Lev. 16:11–14 with Lev. 16:15–19). Jesus as our New Testament high priest is sympathetic because, even though he was the son of God, he suffered agony in the face of death (Heb. 5:7–8). This is where Melchizedek comes into the picture.

The first occurrence of the term "priest" in the Old Testament is in reference to the pre-Israelite "Melchizedek king of Salem . . . priest of God Most High" (Gen. 14:18), to whom Abram paid a tithe. Melchizedek reappears in Psalm 110:4, referring to the royal Davidic "priest forever, in the order of Melchizedek" (v. 4). This, in turn, became the pattern for the thematic development of the Melchizedekian priesthood of Jesus Christ in Hebrews 5–7 since, not being a descendant of Aaron, he could not be a priest according to the order of Aaron (Heb. 7:11–14). Nevertheless, just as Aaron was divinely appointed to this office so was Jesus (vv. 4–5), but the high priesthood of Jesus was "in the order of Melchizedek" (vv. 6, 9–10).

This makes the high priesthood of Jesus distinct and superior from that of Aaron and his successors on several counts. First, Jesus "has become a high priest forever" (6:20). Aaronic priests died and therefore had only a temporary priesthood (7:23). But Jesus abides forever as a priest according to the order of Melchizedek and therefore has a permanent priesthood through which he can save us completely and eternally (7:24–25).

Second, since the Old Testament levitical priests paid a tithe to Melchizedek while they were still in the loins of Abraham, their order of priesthood is inferior to the order of Melchizedek (7:4–10). Third, if the Aaronic priesthood had brought perfection there would have been no need for another priest to arise according to another order (i.e., the order of Melchizedek, 7:11). Moreover, in this connection, there was a necessary and corresponding shift from the old and obsolete covenant mediated by the old priesthood (i.e., the Mosaic covenant with its relatively weak and useless law, 7:11, 18–19; 8:13) to a new and better covenant mediated by the better priesthood (i.e., the New Covenant with its better promises, 7:22; 8:1–13).

Direct references to Melchizedek and to Jesus as a priest according to the order of Melchizedek as opposed to the order of Aaron are limited to Hebrews 5–7. Therefore, just as the discussion of the high priesthood of Jesus in the Book of Hebrews begins without direct reference to Melchizedek (see above), so it ends without it. In fact, the references to the (high) priesthood of Christ in Hebrews 9:7–11 and 9:24–10:25 focus more on the offering of his own blood as a sacrifice than on his priestly office.

However, in Hebrews 10:13 the writer once again alludes to Psalm 110:1 when he refers to Jesus as the priest who has offered himself up as our sacrifice and since that time "waits for his enemies to be made his footstool." This is, of course, a royal motif. This suggests that Jesus, like Melchizedek, is a king who is also a priest. In fact, in some sense David, who is likely to have been the initial referent in Psalm 110, also legitimately exercized priestly prerogatives on some occasions (see esp. 2 Sam. 6). According to some scholars, even if David wrote Psalm 110 (as the title of the psalm seems to suggest), still "my lord" in verse 1 may be a formulaic way of saying "me" (thus yielding the translation, "The Lord says to me"; but see Matt. 22:41–46).

The Priesthood of Believers. This (royal) high priesthood of Jesus Christ connects to the "royal priesthood" of believers: "you are . . . a royal priesthood, a holy nation" (1 Peter 2:9a). The obvious reference to Exodus 19:6 suggests that the church functions in this present age as God's New Testament kingdom of priests much like the nation of Israel did in the Old Testament. As such we are responsible to carry out the ministry of proclaiming to the world "the praises of him who called you out of darkness into his wonderful light" (1 Peter 2:9b).

A closely related idea (but without the "royal" connections) is Peter's earlier description of the church as a group of believers who are being (NIV), or should allow themselves to be (NRSV), "built into a spiritual house [Jesus himself being the living and choice cornerstone, 1 Peter 2:4, 6–8] to be a holy priesthood, offering spiritual sacrifices acceptable to God through Jesus Christ" (1 Peter 2:5). Thus, as fellow priests with Jesus we offer up to God our sacrifices of praise (Heb. 13:15), our doing good and sharing (Heb. 13:16), and ultimately our present physical bodies in the interest of conforming to his standards (Rom. 12:1–2). It is important to observe that here the corporate priesthood of the church shades into the priesthood of the individual believer. Moreover, our ministry in the gospel can be described as an offering of our very life in priestly service to the church (Phil. 2:17), by which we can produce a harvest of sanctified people whom we present to God as an acceptable offering.

Finally, corporate Israel in the Old Testament functioned as a kingdom of priests in both its mediation between God and the other nations and in its service of worship to the Lord in the sanctuary (Exod. 19:5–6). Similarly, the priesthood of the church has mediatorial features as well as aspects that correspond to the sanctuary worship of the Old Testament, sometimes expressed separately and sometimes jointly in the various New Testament passages related to the priesthood of believers. RICHARD E. AVERBECK

See also ALTAR; ANOINT; ATONEMENT; LEVITICUS, THEOLOGY OF; MELCHIZEDEK; OFFERINGS AND SACRIFICES; OIL; PRIEST, CHRIST AS; TABERNACLE; TEMPLE.

Bibliography. J. Baehr, *NIDNTT,* 3:32–44; A. Cody, *A History of Old Testament Priesthood;* D. Guthrie, *New Testament Theol-*

ogy, pp. 483–86; M. Haran, *Temples and Temple-Service in Ancient Israel;* R. A. Henshaw, *Female and Male, The Cultic Personnel: The Bible and the Rest of the Ancient Near East;* K. Koch, *"Sha'arei Talmon': Studies in the Bible, Qumran, and the Ancient Near East Presented to Shemaryahu Talmon,* pp. 105–10; J. Gordon McConville, *Law and Theology in Deuteronomy;* W. O. McCready, *ISBE,* 3:960–63; E. Merrill, *Bib Sac* 150 (1993):50–61; W. J. Moulder, *ISBE,* 3:963–65; *ABD,* 4:297–310; J. R. Spencer, *ABD,* 1:1–6; R. de Vaux, *Ancient Israel,* 2:345–405.

Principalities. *See* POWERS.

Prison, Spirits in. *See* SPIRITS IN PRISON.

Proclamation. *See* PREACH, PROCLAIM.

Promise. Undertaking or assurance given to indulge in or refrain from some specific form of activity. Such commitments are made commonly between individuals, and can embrace a wide range of human activity. Simple promises can be both written and oral. They can be temporary in nature or made binding for the indefinite future.

In secular situations the declaration may be sealed by some gesture, such as a simple handshake or a solemn oath; more complicated undertakings may need ratification by witnesses, whether legal officers or not. Specific forms of promise such as the mutual plighting of troth in marriage ceremonies often form part of a religious ritual.

Promises may also be made between groups of people, and because of their greater complexity they frequently necessitate the presence of witnesses. Where important bodies such as governments are involved, such promises generally assume the form of treaties, the provisions of which are accepted as binding on all those participating. Among honest individuals a promise carries with it the expectation that the promisor is both willing and able to fulfill the commitment to the promisee, with the undertaking being accepted by the latter on the basis of good faith.

Should circumstances arise in human society where it becomes evident that the promisor is no longer able to bring the promise to fruition, or that the promise was not made in good faith at the beginning, the promisee has the option of writing off the entire situation and becoming reconciled to whatever loss has been sustained. If this course is not deemed satisfactory, it may be possible for him or her to renegotiate the matter so that at least some portion of the undertaking may be salvaged. A more drastic way of seeking redress would be to apply to the courts for damages because of breach of promise. In interpersonal undertakings, however, such a procedure might be undesirable on a number of grounds, one of which would be the expense involved were the negotiations to be unduly protracted.

Where groups of people are involved, litigation is often resorted to in order to resolve the damage occasioned by the failure of the promisor to fulfill the stated obligations. Where fiscal default is involved, it may be impossible for the promises to be fulfilled, no matter how protracted the litigation may become. In the case of broken international treaties, appeal may be made to an international judicial body for recompense. Under some circumstances, military action might even be undertaken by the aggrieved party, regardless of future consequences. Such intervention could well be pursued in any event if there was evidence of deliberate fraud or bad faith when the commitment was made.

From the foregoing it will appear that promises are to be treated as serious undertakings made between people of good will and solemn intent, in the expectation that the promise will come to fruition as intended by the participants. When the third millennium B.C. Sumerian kings promised the inhabitants of their Mesopotamian city-states that current fiscal and social abuses would be rectified, they furnished evidence of good intent by enacting legislation to resolve the various problems that had arisen. But if the reforming intent was ultimately sabotaged accidentally or deliberately by inefficient or dishonest priestly or civil bureaucrats, the promises remained unfulfilled, even if they had been made under oath to a god. Consequently the credibility of the promisor was impaired, sometimes irreparably, even when he himself was blameless. A situation of this sort would be equally damaging to those persons whose expectations remained unfulfilled.

Agreements between individuals have been recorded in second millennium B.C. Mesopotamia, a classic example being the one between Laban and Jacob (Gen. 31:43–55), when the latter was seeking his independence. What amounted to a covenant was established between them, in which the participants promised not to act aggressively toward one another. Each man swore an oath by his god, and erected a stone marker to solemnize the occasion.

Promises of a prophetic order were also prominent in ancient Mesopotamia, especially where last wills and testaments were concerned. Thus Jacob on his deathbed promised his twelve sons that the future would hold certain prospects for them, and according to contemporary custom this statutory declaration to each one of them gave the pronouncements legal force (Gen. 49:1–33). Subsequent events were to demonstrate how accurately these promises were fulfilled.

Archeological discoveries have revealed the existence of international treaties made between Hittite kings and vassal states. In these documents the great king declares his power and beneficence to former subject states, and promises to protect the current participants in a covenant relationship provided that they keep the terms that are agreed upon under oath. In these contracts mechanisms existed for the punishment of disobedient vassals, who by breaking their promises had in effect nullified the oath of the great Hittite king. But if the covenant conditions were observed by the subject state, the king would fulfill his promises and heap blessings upon the people.

A promise that was to bring great blessing to humanity was made by God to Abraham (Gen. 12:2–3), in which the latter, although childless, was to become the progenitor of a great nation. Later this promise was repeated (Gen. 15:5), and to his credit Abraham believed God's utterances. The promise was given added credibility by means of a sacrificial ritual (Gen. 15:9–17), following which God listed the territories that Abraham's offspring would inhabit. On yet another occasion (Gen. 17:1–27) God brought his promise even closer to fulfillment by stating that Sarah would have a son (Gen. 18:10), because nothing was too hard for God to accomplish. Thereafter Abraham rested his confidence in this divine power, and lived to see the Lord's assurances implemented in what Paul, millennia later, was to call the "covenants of the promise" (Eph. 2:12; cf. Gal. 3:6–17).

God's promises to Abraham's descendants took definite shape in the Sinai covenant (Exod. 19–20, 24), which resembled a Hittite vassal treaty in form. God, the Great King, promised land and rich blessings to the Israelites if they for their part, would worship him alone as their one true God and live in pagan society as a holy nation, thereby witnessing to God's reality and power. This proposition was ratified in a formal ceremony at Sinai (Exod. 24:3–8), and thereafter the sons of Jacob became the chosen people of God.

Coexisting with the promise to Abraham was a more general declaration made by God at the time of the fall (Gen. 3:15), and continued in a promise to David (2 Sam. 7:12–13) that his seed would continue forever. This messianic utterance still prevailed when, over the centuries, the Israelites became disobedient to God's covenant and ultimately were punished by exile. So desperate was the nation's spiritual condition that Jeremiah promised that God would implement a new, spiritual covenant based upon individual response to him in faith (Jer. 31:31–37). In the postexilic period the expectation of a Messiah was quickened by prophecy (Mal. 4:5–6), and when Jesus began his ministry he was expected by some to behave like a conquering king, liberating his people from Roman oppression and fulfilling ancient expectations.

Christ's kingship, however, was not of this world, as he pointed out to his accusers (John 18:36). At his coming he fulfilled the divine promises made to Abraham and David (Luke 1:68; Acts 13:23). Events occurred just as God had promised, because it was impossible for him to lie (Titus 1:2). Although there was an interval of time between the promise and its fulfillment, the delay did not thereby invalidate the promise, any more than it would for a human promise that was fulfilled eventually.

When the new covenant was initiated in the coming of Jesus Christ, it not merely represented the completion of one phase of promise, but in fact commenced a new dispensation, that of grace, which contained its own promises to be fulfilled by God in future times. The rites and ceremonies inherent in the Mosaic covenant had become obsolete with the appearance of our great High Priest, who is the mediator of a new testament (Heb. 9:11–15). Instead, while sharing in all the benefits of Abraham's covenant (Eph. 3:6), the Christian looks forward to a time when the kingdom of God, which was ushered in with the age of grace, will be realized when Christ returns to complete the kingdom of believers and establish it for all eternity before God in heaven.

One important difference between Israel of old and the body of Christ is that the Christian is inspired by the working of the Holy Spirit as a normative part of experience. Before his death, Jesus promised that the Holy Spirit would be given to believers and would guide them along true ways and instruct them in the deep realities of God. The dramatic bestowal of the Spirit upon the Christians at Pentecost (Acts 2:1–4) fulfilled the Lord's promise, and so possessed the early Christians that they accomplished many deeds of grace by his power.

Paul gave great prominence to the work of the Holy Spirit, teaching that believers were sealed with the promised third person of the Trinity (Eph. 1:13), thus culminating an ancient Hebrew promise (Isa. 32:15; Ezek. 36:27). For the Holy Spirit to be present in a believer guarantees that person's inheritance (2 Cor. 1:22), and points to future glorification when the hope of our salvation becomes a reality (Rom. 8:23). Peter stressed the final promise to Christians, that Jesus will return one day in glory to establish new heavens and a new earth (2 Peter 3:4–13). The promises of God find an emphatic "yes" in Christ (2 Cor. 1:19), thus guaranteeing the certainty of the Christian's hope. R. K. Harrison

See also Fulfillment; Prophet, Prophetess, Prophecy.

Bibliography. D. Baker, *Two Testaments: One Bible;* W. D. Davis, *The Gospel and the Land;* W. Kaiser, *Towards an Old Testament Theology;* W. Vischer, *The Witness of the Old Testament to Christ.*

Prophet, Christ as. The largest Old Testament passage on the coming Messiah in the role of a prophet is Deuteronomy 18:15–19. There God promised, through Moses, that he would raise up a prophet from among the Jewish people who would be like Moses. This declaration led many to inquire who this prophet like Moses would be. Many Jewish commentators answered that it was Joshua, the son of Nun. Joshua was indeed a man full of wisdom, but Deuteronomy 34:9–12, almost as if it had anticipated this identification of Joshua with that prophet who was to arise and be like Moses, effectively closed the door on that equation by saying, "Now Joshua son of Nun was filled with the spirit of wisdom, because Moses had laid his hands on him. . . . But no prophet arose in Israel like unto Moses, whom the LORD knew face to face. . . . For no one had ever known the mighty power or performed the awesome deeds that Moses did in the sight of all Israel" (author's translation).

When Jesus began to perform his miracles, the crowds of that first Christian century exclaimed, "Surely this is the Prophet who is to come into the world" (John 6:14). The Samaritan woman recognized Jesus as the Messiah and the Prophet who would come (John 4:19, 25). This identification is also in accord with what Jesus told the Pharisees in John 5:46–47: "If you believed Moses, you would believe me, for he wrote about me. But since you do not believe what he wrote, how are you going to believe what I say?" Of all the places that Jesus could have been referring to in Moses' writings, none would be a more obvious candidate for a messianic reference than Deuteronomy 18:15–19, where the Messiah would function as the prophetic teacher. Other New Testament passages where Jesus is recognized as a "Prophet" include Mark 6:15; Luke 7:16; 24:19 [parallel to Matt. 21:11]; John 7:40; 9:17.

The characteristics of the prophet that Moses announced in Deuteronomy 18:15–19 are: (1) that he would be an Israelite; (2) that he would be like Moses; and (3) that he would be authorized to declare the word of God with authority. The key interpretive crux, however, is whether the term *nabîʾ*, "prophet," is a collective singular or a simple singular. Does it refer to the institution of the prophetic order, or to an individual prophet? Jewish and most recent commentators regard the term "prophet" in Deuteronomy 18:15–19 as a collective and generic term. This, of course, must be admitted, for the context of Deuteronomy 17–18 speaks of classes or groups of leaders such as the priests and Levites. However, most of the previous Old Testament messianic prophecies are generic and collective in nature. And the context definitely favors an individual prophet in that the prophet is not only represented as coming out of Israel, but is compared to the individual Moses. Presumably, therefore, he too will be an individual. Therefore, this passage at once provides for a whole order, or institution of prophets, while it incorporates within that same seminal thought the provision for one who would be the representative of all of prophets par excellence. However, unlike the institution of the priesthood, which was transmitted to each successor through the Aaronic family within the tribe of Levi, the prophetic office of Moses was not transmitted to its successors. That prophet would need to be directly summoned by Yahweh. Thus, in accordance with the general prophetic principle, the divine instruction given to Moses was left incomplete by him until it could be completed by a prophet greater than himself in the messianic era.

Within the term "prophet," three different functions are embraced, all of which were exercised by Moses. The first is *teacher* (Deut. 4:5; 31:22; 2 Kings 4:22–23). A prophet was charged with more than merely delivering the oracles of God to the people; he was to teach them how to live and how to bring their lives into conformity with that revelation. He taught the people in "parables" and uttered "hidden things, things from of old" (Ps. 78:2). Matthew concluded that this prediction was fulfilled after he recorded that long chapter of the parables of Jesus (Matt. 13:35). On Jesus rested "The Spirit of the LORD, . . . the Spirit of wisdom and of understanding, the Spirit of counsel and of power, the Spirit of knowledge and of the fear of the LORD" (Isa. 11:1–2). Thus he would "teach us [God's] ways, so that we may walk in his paths" (Isa. 2:3b). Even Jesus' enemies complimented him, even if it might have been somewhat sarcastic (Mark 12:14): "Teacher, we know you are a man of integrity. You aren't swayed by men, because you pay no attention to who they are; but you teach the way of God in accordance with the truth." Jesus, like Moses, gave the law once again as he proclaimed the Sermon on the Mount (Matt. 5–7). The words Jesus spoke were spirit and life (John 6:63), to instruct all in the way that everyone should go.

The second function of a prophet was that of *foretelling the future*. Christ's predictions bear a striking similarity to Moses' predictions, for both spoke of Israel's dispersion, her spiritual apostasy, and the dreadful calamities that were to come on her during the time that she became subservient to the Gentiles (cf. Deut. 28–29 and 31:19–21 with Matt. 21:28–45; 23:37–39; 24:4–31).

We need only look at one prediction to illustrate the credibility of Jesus as a prophet whose word came to pass: the destruction of the temple. In Matthew 24:2, Jesus predicted that the temple would be destroyed. And the Jews knew that it was vain to look for the Messiah while there was no temple, for Haggai 2:1–9 and Malachi 3:1 had told them that Messiah would come to his temple when he came. Thus it had happened several items in history that the Jewish people have attempted in vain, during the reigns of Adrian, Constantine, and especially under Julian, to restore the temple. The ruins continue to stand as a mute testimony to the predictive abilities and the veracity of Jesus as a Prophet.

Jesus not only made predictions concerning individuals (John 1:42), but also concerning the kingdom of God (Matt. 11:12; Luke 17:21) and the material world (Matt. 5:5; 19:28); regarding himself (Matt. 16:21; Mark 8:31; 9:31; 10:33); regarding the destruction of Jerusalem (Luke 19:41–44; 21:24); and regarding his parousia (Matt. 26:64; Mark 14:62; Luke 22:69). Just as Moses not only spoke of Israel's scattering, but their future blessing as well, so did Christ when he spoke of a time when the fig tree would blossom again (Matt. 24:32–33). Christ's predictive utterances were greater than all other prophetic announcements, for his revelation was not intermittent, but constant; his revelation was not partial, but complete; his revelation was final in that everything previously announced led up to this one grand disclosure.

The third function of a prophet was to be a *judge*. Just as Moses judged Israel so Christ fulfills the same function in his prophetic role. "Moreover, the Father judges no one, but has entrusted all judgment to the Son" (John 5:22). While Christ is currently judge and arbitrator of everything in the body of Christ, yet one day he will assume this task when he comes again and sits on the judgment seat to judge everything and everyone (Dan. 12; Matt. 25; 2 Cor. 5:10; Rev. 22:12).

The prophetic office of Christ did not cease when he ascended into heaven, for the role of prophet continues to belong to his essential activities even now. He continues his prophetic work through his church (Mark 16:20). And the Spirit of Jesus continues to work with his messengers.

WALTER C. KAISER, JR.

See also PROPHET, PROPHETESS, PROPHECY; TEACH, TEACHER.

Bibliography. D. E. Aune, *The Messiah: Developments in Early Judaism and Christianity*, pp. 404–22; D. Baron, *Rays of Messiah's Glory: Christ in the Old Testament;* C. A. Briggs, *Messianic Prophecy: The Prediction of the Fulfillment of Redemption Through the Messiah;* C. T. P. Grierson, *A Dictionary of Christ and Gospels*, pp. 431–44; H. M. Teeple, *The Mosaic Eschatological Prophet.*

Prophet, Prophetess, Prophecy. A prophet was an individual who received a call from God to be God's spokesperson, often connected with some crisis that was about to occur, and then announced God's message of judgment and/or deliverance to Israel and the nations. The importance of this office can be seen in the fact that the word "prophet" occurs over 300 times in the Old Testament and almost 125 times in the New Testament. The term "prophetess" appears 6 times in the Old Testament and 2 times in the New Testament.

The Derivation and Meaning of "Prophet." The derivation and meaning of the word "prophet" has been a matter of controversy for several centuries now with no prospect of closure on this debate. Since most of the solutions to this enigma have been based on etymologies or terms in cognate languages, it is small wonder that no resolution has been forthcoming. Linguists are especially agreed that the most that etymologies can yield are only various suggestions. The only safe course in resolving the meaning of a word is to depend ultimately on usages in contexts.

Early attempts to explain the meaning of prophet were based on trying to derive the noun from a verbal root. The older Gesenius Lexicon edited by Tregelles hypothecated that the noun "prophet" came from the verb *nābaᶜ*, in which the original final letter, *ayin*, was softened into an *aleph* (*nābāᵓ*); this verb meant "to bubble up" or "boil forth." Hence the prophet was one who entered an ecstatic state of utterance, pouring forth words automatically under divine inspiration. Almost all scholars now reject such a suggestion because it remains unattested and cannot be demonstrated from known rules of philology.

More recent suggestions have shifted to viewing the word as being denominative in form, as coming from a noun rather than a verb. If the noun *nābîᵓ*, "prophet," is the original form, then the suggestion of W. F. Albright that the Akkadian verb *nabû*, "to call," is helpful in suggesting that the passive meaning may well be "one who is called [by God]." If the verb is taken in its active form, the prophet is "an announcer [for God]," the meaning favored by König, Lindblom, and Westermann. However, there still exists the possibility that an unknown Semitic root exists that perhaps gives the real source from which the noun "prophet" is derived.

However, in spite of the absence of any definitive consensus on the real meaning of the word "prophet" there are at least two classical texts that demonstrate the usage of this term and its meaning in the biblical texts. The first is Exodus 7:1–2 (cf. Exod. 4:15–16): "Then the LORD said to Moses, 'See, I have made you like God to Pharaoh, and your brother Aaron will be your prophet. You are to say everything I command you, and your brother Aaron is to tell Pharaoh." What could be clearer? A prophet (*nabîᵓ*) is one who receives a word from God, just as Moses acted in the place of God in passing on the divine revelations he received from the Lord to his brother Aaron, now functioning as a prophet. Moreover, a prophet is authorized to communicate this divine message to another. Thus Aaron was to function as Moses' mouthpiece.

The second classical text is Numbers 12:6–8: "When a prophet of the LORD is among you, I reveal myself to him in visions, I speak to him in dreams. But this is not true of my servant Moses; he is faithful in all my house. With him I speak face to face, clearly and not in riddles; he sees the form of the LORD." In the case of Moses, vis-à-vis all other prophets, God would speak in direct conversation—"face to face." Other prophets would receive no less a revelation from God, but in their case the means God would use to communicate his word would be the less direct, somewhat enigmatic form of dreams and visions.

Clearly, then, a prophet is an authorized spokesperson for God with a message that originated with God and was communicated through a number of means. When God spoke to these spokespersons, they had no choice but to deliver that word to those to whom God directed it.

The Call of the Prophet. It is impossible to demonstrate from the text of Scripture that each person called to be a prophet received a specific call from God; however, that fact may be explained by the brevity of our records and by the fact that it was not the purpose of Scripture to record all such details. It is enough for us to know that in many cases there was such a definite call from God, as the testimonies of Elisha, Isaiah, Amos, Hosea, Jeremiah, and Ezekiel demonstrate.

It is true, nevertheless, that there were many who "prophesied" who were not called to be prophets, but were called to be judges, leaders, or priests. Thus, Gideon delivered Israel from the hand of the Midianites, acting on rather detailed instructions from the Lord as to how he was to effect such a deliverance, much as a true prophet would receive revelation from God (Judg. 7:2–8). David is specifically said to be a prophet in Acts 2:30, yet his primary call in life was to be king over Israel. And few prophets could rank or rate as high in esteem as Moses, but his call was primarily not to the office of prophet but to being a leader of God's people in the exodus (Exod. 3:10). Therefore, we conclude that many more individuals "prophesied" than those who were specifically called to the office of prophet.

It is true that Acts 3:24 speaks of "all the prophets from Samuel on," making Samuel appear to be the first to prophesy. Samuel was not the first person to prophesy, however, for "Enoch, the seventh from Adam, prophesied" (Jude 14). Enoch was well before Abraham's day, much less Samuel's. Psalm 105:14–15, in referring to the patriarchs Abraham, Isaac, and Jacob, urged, "do my prophets no harm." Many others could be included in this list of those who exercised this gift prior to the days of Samuel, including Moses, Aaron, Miriam (Exod. 15:20), Eldad, Medad, the seventy elders (Num. 11:24–29), Balaam (Num. 21–24), Deborah (Judg. 4:4), and Minoah and his wife (Judg. 13:3, 10, 21).

The official institution of the office of prophet took place in Moses' day (Deut. 18:15–22): After God had warned Israel about attempting to get supernatural information from bogus pagan sources (Deut. 18:9–14), he announced that he would "raise up for [them] a prophet like [Moses] from among [their] own brothers" (v. 15). God would "put [his] words in [the prophet's] mouth and [the prophet] will tell [the people] everything [God] commanded him" (v. 18).

In Deuteronomy 18:15–22 and Deuteronomy 13:1–5 God listed five certifying signs by which a true prophet of God could be recognized: (1) a prophet must be an Israelite, "from among [his] own brothers" (Deut. 18:15) (Balaam is the exception that proves this rule); (2) he must speak in the name of the Lord ("If anyone does not listen to my words that the prophet speaks in my name" [Deut. 18:19]); (3) he must be able to predict the near as well as the distant future ("If what a prophet proclaims in the name of the LORD does not take place or come true, that is a message the LORD has not spoken" [Deut. 18:22]); (4) he must be able to predict signs and wonders (Deut. 13:2); and (5) his words must conform to the previous revelation that God has given (Deut. 13:2–3).

Elisha is one of the earliest individuals in Scripture to receive a specific call from God to be a prophet. Even though the call was mediated through Elijah, it was nonetheless divine in origin. In 1 Kings 19:15–16, God directed the disheartened Elijah to "Go back the way you came . . . and anoint Elisha the son of Shaphat from Abel Meholah to succeed you as prophet." While the text does not indicate whether the oil of anointing was poured over the head of Elisha, it does note that Elijah found Elisha plowing in the field, whereupon Elijah "threw his cloak [the prophetic mantle] around [Elisha]" (v. 19) and as a result Elisha immediately left his oxen and ran after Elijah. Indeed, as Elisha later requested, a double portion of the Spirit that rested on Elijah fell on him (2 Kings 2:9–14). The miracle of the parting of the waters of the Jordan River, with the use of the mantle that had dropped from the ascending Elijah, was God's further attestation to both the validity and reality of that call of God.

Isaiah describes how he felt when he saw the Lord on a throne in his temple (Isa. 6:1–5). It was such an overwhelming experience that he was filled with the impropriety of his being in the presence of a holy God, much less being called to serve such a high and exalted Lord. However, the seraphim took a live coal from the altar and touched Isaiah's lips, thereby purging his sins and iniquities (vv. 6–7). This was followed by a voice that inquired, "Whom shall I send? And who will go for us?" Isaiah's answer was immediate: "Here am I. Send me!" (v. 8). Even though this call does not come until we are six chapters into the book, it is not to be concluded, as some interpreters have complained, that this was not Isaiah's original call, for part of the call of God was in the desperate spiritual vacuum that had grown up in Israel. Isaiah 1–5 sets the backdrop against which the call of God to Isaiah was issued. Isaiah's call in chapter 6 involved the four significant elements: a theophany, the purification of the prophet's lips and heart, the commission to "Go!" and the content of the message he was to proclaim.

Amos had not been unemployed, with no other option but to become a prophet. On the contrary, he was a most successful shepherd in Tekoa and a grower of sycamore-fig fruit (1:1; 7:14). It was the Lord who "took" him from tending the flock and the orchards and commanded him, "Go, prophesy to my people Israel" (7:15). In fact, Amos protested that he was neither a prophet nor the son of a prophet (7:14); therefore, no one was to think that he merely fell into this occupation, or that he sought it as a career goal. He did not! It was the compelling call of God that forced him to leave what he was doing—and apparently doing with no small degree of success—and directed him to prophesy in the name of the Lord to a culture that had become sensate and sin-sick.

No less direct was God's call on Hosea. The first three chapters of his book reveal how his own personal story mirrored the desperate state of affairs that northern Israel found herself in and how deeply offended God, Israel's spiritual husband, was at all that had happened. Just as resolute as God was in his call of Hosea, so too was Hosea in his resolve to love his wife Gomer even after she had forsaken him for other lovers. After bearing three children to Hosea, whose very names were as symbolic as the message and love of this man for his estranged wife, Hosea wooed back his wife again as God would ultimately his people Israel.

Jeremiah's call came even before he was formed in the womb (1:5a)! In that prenatal period, God set Jeremiah apart and "appointed [him] as a prophet to the nations." The Lord himself would "put [his] words in [Jeremiah's] mouth" (1:9) and make him like a "fortified city, an iron pillar and a bronze wall to stand against the whole land" (1:18). In retrospect, Jeremiah felt overpowered and powerfully constrained by the Lord. This divine constraint is one of the most characteristic elements in God's calling of his prophets.

Ezekial, like Isaiah, was given a vision of the greatness of God and his glory. The whole scene of the throne, with the spectacular radiance of the glory of God, was to assure Ezekiel that nothing less than the personal presence of God could be expected to go with him wherever he went. The throne of God was situated on wheels that were solid and thus able to go in any direction his servant Ezekiel went.

Even though the prophets professed strong feelings of inadequacy and unworthiness (Isa. 6:5; Jer. 1:6), they nevertheless could not resist the strong divine compulsion they were under (Jer. 15:20; Ezek. 1:3; 3:14; 8:1). Their "accreditation" came from God (1 Sam. 3:20—"all Israel . . . recognized that Samuel *was attested* [or better still: *was accredited*] as a prophet of the LORD").

The Terminology of Prophecy. The most common term for prophet (occurring over three hundred times in the Old Testament) is *nābîʾ*. The feminine form of this noun, *nābîʾâ(h)*, is used six times of women who performed the same task of receiving and proclaiming the message given by God. These women include Miriam, Aaron and Moses' sister (Exod. 15:20); Deborah (Judg. 4:4); the prophet Isaiah's wife (Isa. 8:3); and Huldah, the one who interpreted the Book of the Law discovered in the temple during the days of Josiah (2 Kings 22:14; 2 Chron. 34:22). There were false prophetesses just as there were false prophets. The prophetess Noadiah was among those who tried to intimidate Nehemiah (Neh. 6:14).

Another general designation for these servants of God is "man of God," appearing over seventy-six times. Nearly half of these references (36) are used of Elisha, fifteen of the unnamed prophet in 1 Kings 13, and the other twenty-five are scattered: five refer to Moses, four to Samuel, seven to Elijah, three to David, two to Shemaiah, and five to unnamed individuals. Another general name for the prophets in Scripture is "My servants." This title is first used of Moses in Joshua 1:1, but it appears with a fair degree of frequency in Kings, Ezra, and Nehemiah.

The prophets are also given figurative names. Haggai is uniquely called the "LORD's messenger" (1:13), while Ezekiel is called a "Shepherd" (chap. 34) and a "Watchman" (chap. 33).

The oldest term, however, is the participial form of the verb "to see," *rō'eh*. Apparently this was the older name for a prophet, for 1 Samuel 9:9 notes in an aside, "(Formerly in Israel, if a man went to inquire of God, he would say, 'Come, let us go to the seer,' because the prophet of today used to be called a seer.)" The term is used in six out of a total of thirteen times in the Old Testament to refer to Samuel, with the only occurrence in the prophetic books proper coming in Isaiah 30:10—"They say to the seers, 'See no more visions!'" In 2 Kings 17:13 seer is used in parallelism with prophet, thus also showing the equation of the two terms.

Another participial form of the verb "to have a vision" or "to see a vision" is *hōzeh*. This word can also be translated "seer" or "visionary." It appears sixteen times in the Old Testament. The priest Amaziah called Amos a *hōzeh*, "seer" (Amos 7:12). The name is also applied to David's seer, Gad (2 Sam. 24:11), and to Hanani and his son Jehu (2 Chron. 16:7; 19:2). Only in 1 Chronicles 29:29 are the three terms, *rōeh*, *nābî'*, and *hōeh* used together while referring to Samuel, Nathan, and Gad respectively.

A *rōeh*, then, was one who was given divine insight into the past, present, and future so that he could see everything from lost items to the great events of the last days. A *nābî'* was one who was called of God to announce the divine message, while a *hōzeh* was given messages mainly in visions.

The Prophetic Activity. It is of more than just passing interest to learn how the prophets received their messages from God and how they delivered them to their intended recipients.

The prophets were neither especially precocious savants who could render wise counsel at will nor were they mere automatons through whom God spoke as they remained in a zombielike trance. They were mere mortals with differing abilities and with the human capacity to make mistakes. Thus, when the prophet Nathan was asked for his own human opinion as to whether David should build the temple for God, he enthusiastically urged the King to do so. But Nathan spoke as a mere mortal; God had to instruct him to return and give a divine answer to the question prefaced with the prophetic formula of divine authority: "This is what the Lord says!"

Oftentimes a prophet knew only a portion of the divine will. For example, Samuel knew that he was to anoint one of Jesse's sons, but he did not know which one (1 Sam. 16). His guess was that it would be one of the older sons, but it was only after David, Jesse's youngest son, stood before him that he knew that he had been looking at external appearances while God looked on the heart of the one who was to be anointed as king.

How did God communicate his word to his prophets? In rare cases, God spoke in an audible voice that could be heard by anyone who might have been in the vicinity. Such was Samuel's experience when he heard his name being called out in the middle of the night (1 Sam. 3:3–9). Moses spoke directly with God on Mount Sinai (Exod. 19:3–24). Elijah would later come to this same cave, where God would converse with his thoroughly disheartened servant (1 Kings 19:9–18).

More frequently, the prophet received a direct message from God with no audible voice. Instead, there must have been an internal voice by which the consciousness of the prophet suddenly was so heightened that he knew beyond a shadow of a doubt that what he said or what he was to do was exactly what God wanted done in that situation. In 1 Kings 13:20–22, a prophet suddenly rebuked the man of God from Judah with a word that he said an angel had given to him. The fact that what he said came to pass validated his claim that it was from God, even though that same prophet had previously lied to the man he now rebuked in the name of the Lord.

So accurate was this type of communication by a man of God that "Time and again Elisha warned the [Israelite] king so that he was on his guard in such places" (2 Kings 6:10). When the enraged Syrian king demanded to know where the leak was in his organization, the answer was, "None of us [is on the side of the king of Israel] . . . , but Elisha, the prophet who is in Israel, tells the king of Israel the very words you speak in your bedroom" (v. 12).

God also communicated with his prophets in a third way: by opening the prophet's eyes so that he could see realities that ordinarily would be hidden. Thus, just as the Lord opened the eyes of Balaam's donkey so that she saw what Balaam at first could not see (Num. 22:31), so God opened the eyes of the prophet Elisha's servant so that he could see the angelic armies of the Lord that surrounded Samaria were indeed greater in number than the Syrian armies (2 Kings 6:15–17).

The fourth way that God communicated with his prophets was the extensive use of visions, dreams, and elaborate imagery. God's word was sometimes clothed in symbolic imagery that left a firm imprint on the mind of the prophet and his listeners. Some of the images were explained in the very same context. For example, the head of gold on Daniel's image was the nation Babylon with its king Nebuchadnezzar while the stone that grew to fill the whole earth was the kingdom of God (Dan. 2:37–39). In other instances, the imagery was drawn from revelation that had already been given to God's people. Thus the Book of Revelation makes extensive use of such Old Testament symbols as the tree of life (Rev. 2:7; 22:2; cf. Gen. 2:9; 3:24); the key of David (Rev. 3:7; cf. Isa. 22:22); and the four horseman (Rev. 6:1–8; cf. Zech. 1:8–11). Some symbols, however, are deliberately left unexplained; hence the partial enigmatic quality of prophecy.

The visions God gave did not come at any special time. Some came while the prophet was awake; others came while the prophet was awakened from his sleep or was sleeping. In some cases the prophet was transported in a vision to places far distant from the locale where he was (Ezek. 8:1–3; 11:24). Yet the prophet always retained the ability to distinguish between his own dreams and those that were given by God.

The fifth and final way that God revealed his message to his prophet was through the use of symbolic actions. Scripture is replete with examples of such activity, which can best be described as outdoor theater, pantomimes, or parables in action. The prophet Micah went about naked as a sign that Samaria would go into captivity (Mic. 1:8). Jeremiah wore a yoke in a downtown area to warn Judah that they would shortly be going into exile to Babylon (Jer. 27:2–13). Ezekiel was the strangest of them all. He set up a sandbox siege of Jerusalem to portray the city's pending plight (Ezek. 4:1–3), then laid on his left side for 390 days and on his right side 40 days with meager siege rations to warn the people what was ahead of them for not repenting of their sin (vv. 4–17).

In all these ways, God wanted his prophets to receive his message and the people to remember what he had said. In delivering these messages, often the prophet would deliver a brief word of rebuke or encouragement, or present a specific order that was to be carried out.

At other times, the prophets were available to answer direct questions, such as the time when the kings of Israel, Judah, and Edom came to Elisha as an embarrassed delegation to ask how they could extricate themselves out of the military mess that they had managed to get themselves into (2 Kings 3:11–19). Often such answers were followed by longer rejoinders that called for some type of believing or confessing response; more often than not, however, the response was one of unbelief. One outstanding case of unbelief was the instance of the ungodly aide to the king who refused to believe God's miraculous provision of grain in the midst of a frightening siege (2 Kings 7:1–20). He lived only long enough to see the prophecy fulfilled as he died in the stampede for the miraculously provided food.

The Interpretation of Prophecy. Biblical prophecy is more than "fore-telling": two-thirds of its inscripturated form involves "forth-telling," that is, setting the truth, justice, mercy, and righteousness of God against the backdrop of every form of denial of the same. Thus, to speak prophetically was to speak boldly against every form of moral, ethical, political, economic, and religious disenfranchisement observed in a culture that was intent on building its own pyramid of values vis-à-vis God's established system of truth and ethics.

However, prediction was by no means absent from the prophetic message. The prophets were conscious of contributing to the ongoing plan of God's ancient, but constantly renewed promise. They announced God's coming kingdom and the awful day of the Lord when God's wrath would be poured out on all ungodliness. In the meantime, before that eschatological moment, there would be a number of divine in-breakings on the historical scene in which the fall of cities such as Samaria, Damascus, Nineveh, Jerusalem, and Babylon would serve as harbingers or foreshadowings of God's final intrusion into the historical scene at the end of history. Thus each minijudgment on the nations or empires of past and present history were earnests and downpayments on God's final day of coming onto the historic scene to end it in one severe judgment and blast of victory. So said all the prophets. And in so saying they exhibited the fact that all their messages were organically related to each other; they were progressively building on one another. And, being focused distinctly on God, they were preeminently theocentric in their organization.

Therefore, the predictive sections of biblical prophecy exhibit certain key characteristics: (1) they are not isolated sayings, but are organically related to the whole of prophecy; (2) they plainly foretell things to come rather than being clothed in such abstruse terminology that they could be proven true even if the opposite of what they appear to say happens; (3) they are designed to be predictions and are not accidental or unwitting predictions; (4) they are written and published before the event, so that it could not be said that it was a matter of human sagacity that determined this would take place; (5) they are fulfilled in accordance with the original utterance, unless expressly attached to a condition; and (6) they do not work out their own fulfillment, but stand as a verbal witness until the event takes place.

History, then, is the final interpreter of prophecy, as Jesus said, "I have told you now before it happens, so that when it does happen you will believe" (John 14:29). Moreover, in addition to leaving the details of fulfillment to be disclosed when the historical process uncovers them, it is to be noted as well that it is not the interpreter who is to receive the plaudits of humans, but Jesus; prophecy points to him. Jesus taught: "I am telling you now before it happens, that when it does happen you will believe that I am He" (John 13:19).

Prophecies may be placed in several categories, based on their fulfillment: unconditional prophecies, conditional prophecies, and sequentially fulfilled prophecies. The first category is the simplest and most straightforward. Included in this category are the divine promises relating to God's covenant with his people Israel and our salvation. Examples are the covenants made with Abraham and David and the new covenant. However, God's covenant with the seasons (Gen. 8:21–22) and his promise of a new heaven and a new earth are also unconditional prophecies. They are unconditional because they rely upon God's faithfulness for their implementation and not on our obedience or response.

The best way to demonstrate this one-sided obligation is to point to Genesis 15:12–19, where God told Abraham to cut animals in half and form an aisle down the middle so that the person obligating himself could walk down the aisle outlined by the pieces. In this case, however, only the Lord, here depicted as a smoking fire pot with a blazing torch, moved between the pieces; Abraham did not go between the cut animals. Therefore, God would perform what he promised regardless of what Abraham did or did not do.

Most of the prophecies in the Bible fall into the conditional category in that they pose alternative prospects, depending on whether Israel, the individual, or the nation to whom they were addressed, obeyed and responded to the conditions set forth in them. Two controlling passages that governed much of Old Testament predictions were Leviticus 26 and Deuteronomy 28. There God promised blessing if Israel obeyed, but punishment if they disobeyed.

Alternative outcomes were predicted for individuals, depending on whether they responded in belief or not. For example, Jeremiah laid before King Zedekiah two possible scenarios (Jer. 38:17–19), and he did the same for the people of Judah (Jer. 42:10–16).

The clearest statement of this principle of conditional fulfillment can be found in Jeremiah 18:7–10. Here it is announced as a principle that relates to any nation or political entity. It read: "If at any time I announce that a nation or a kingdom is to be uprooted, torn down and destroyed, and if that nation I warned repents of its evil, then I will relent and not inflict on it the disaster I had planned. And if at another time I announce that a nation or kingdom is to be built up and planted, and if it does evil in my sight and does not obey me, then I will reconsider the good I had intended to do for it." It is this principle that explains why the prophet Jonah was so reluctant to announce God's imminent judgment on Nineveh. He feared that the message of the threatened judgment might be heeded by the Ninevites, resulting in their repentance, in which case the threatened judgment would be rescinded by God to the great dismay of the aggrieved prophet. It must be carefully noted, however, that not all conditional prophecies have an expressed condition attached to them, just as was the case in the prophecy of Jonah. The conditions are known from the context or from the progress of revelation. The fact that the prophecies were not given with the obligation only resting on God is another sign that such prophecies fell in the conditional category rather than the unconditional one.

One other rather limited number of prophecies must be noted here. In actuality, they are a subcategory of the conditional type: the sequentially fulfilled type. Ezekiel 26:7–14 is an excellent example of this third category. This prophecy warned that many nations would come up against Tyre; however, the focus of the prophecy was on Nebuchadnezzar's destruction of the mainland city of Tyre on the coast of the Mediterranean Sea. Suddenly, in the midst of the prediction, there is a sudden switch from the third-person masculine pronoun "he" and "his" to the third-person masculine plural "they." Some have contended that since Nebuchadnezzar was frustrated because he was unable to capture the people of Tyre, who merely moved from the mainland city of Tyre to an island one-half mile off-shore, that this was an indication that the prophecy was unfulfilled. But it is not an example of an unfulfilled prophecy, for it was fulfilled sequentially. After the Babylonian nation worked its destruction of the mainland city in the 580s B.C., Alexander the Great came along in the 330s B.C. and finished the rest of the prophecy by throwing the "stones, timber, and rubble" of the city that Nebuchadnezzar had destroyed "into the sea" in order to build a causeway from the mainland out into the Mediterranean Sea to the island city and capture the city. The prophecy was fulfilled, but it was fulfilled sequentially.

New Testament Prophecy. Old Testament prophecy came to an end with Malachi, approximately four hundred years before the time of Christ. No formal declaration was made that prophecy had ceased; it was only as time went on that the people began to realize that divine revelation had been absent for a period more protracted than ever before. Three times in the book of 1 Maccabees, written during the events of the revolt against the Syrian Antiochus Epiphanes in days following 168 B.C., the fact that there was no prophet in Israel was noted with sadness (4:46; 9:27; 14:41).

Suddenly, Jesus Christ, the greatest of all the prophets, and the one anticipated in Deuteronomy 18:15–19, appeared on the scene. The title "prophet" is applied to him about a dozen times in the Gospels. His forerunner, John the Baptist, was considered by Jesus to be the last of the prophets who prepared the way for the coming of the Messiah. In fact, John the Baptist formed the natural dividing point between the Old Testament prophets and those who were to come in the New Testament, as Matthew quoted Jesus as saying of John, "For all the Prophets and the Law prophesied *until John*" (Matt. 11:13).

What was the nature of prophecy in the New Testament? Were the New Testament prophets as absolutely authoritative as their predecessors?

Many interpreters divide the New Testament prophetic phenomena into two classes: (1) the authoritative prophecies demonstrated by the apostles and their associates who functioned much as the Old Testament prophets did; and (2) a type of prophetic activity that made no claims to being the very word of God, but which was for the "strengthening, encouragement and comfort" of believers (1 Cor. 14:3). It is this second type of prophetic activity in the New Testament that has drawn so much current interest, especially if the argument also holds that this gift of prophecy is still operative in the church today.

Usually the case for sustaining the argument that the New Testament apostles are linked with the Old Testament prophets as authoritative recipients of the word of God is made by noting that the Book of Hebrews avoids applying the word "prophet" to Jesus, but uses instead the word "apostle" (3:1—"fix your thoughts on Jesus, the apostle and high priest whom we confess").

What about this other type of Christian prophecy where believers, who prophesy, do not regard themselves as the bearers of the very words of God? Did not the apostle Paul teach in 1 Corinthians 13:8–9 that "where there are prophecies, they will cease. . . . For we know in part and we prophesy in part, but when perfection comes, the imperfect disappears." When would that cessation of prophecy take place? After the early church had matured? Or after the completion of the canon of Scripture? Probably neither of these suggested termination points answers the completion of the perfection process. Perfection cannot be expected before Christ's second coming. Thus, the believer's present, fragmentary knowledge, based as it is on the modes of knowledge now available to us, will come to an end.

How long, then, will prophecy last? The argument at this point now shifts to Ephesians 2:20—the church is "built on the foundation of the apostles and prophets" (also see Eph. 3:5). If the apostle Paul refers here to two different functions or gifts—the apostles and the prophets of the New Testament era—then the gift of prophecy was so foundational in building the Christian church that it does not continue to our day; its foundational work has been completed. But if, as others contend, the expression "apostles and prophets" refers to one and the same group in a type of figure of speech called a hendiadys, where two distinct words connected by a conjunction are used to express one complex notion ("apostles-who-are-also-prophets"), then the gift may still be operative today. However, no Greek examples of two *plural* nouns in this type of construction have yet been attested even though the construction is known in other combinations of words.

Two answers are given, therefore, to the question of the termination of New Testament prophecy by modern interpreters. All agree that classical Old Testament prophecy and apostolic prophecy that delivered to us God's authoritative Scriptures have ceased. Others feel, however, that a secondary type of Christian prophecy continues today in the tradition of the New Testament prophet Agabus (Acts 11:28; 21:10) and the prophets of 1 Corinthians 12–14. This second group is subordinate to the teaching of the apostles and subject to the criticism and judgment of the body as two or three individuals prophesy in the regular meetings of the church.

WALTER C. KAISER, JR.

See also FALSE PROPHET; ISRAEL; PROPHET, CHRIST AS.

Bibliography. W. F. Albright, *Interpreting the Prophetic Tradition,* pp. 151–76; R. L. Alden, *New Perspectives on the Old Testament,* pp. 131–45; F. D. Farnell, *The Master's Seminary Journal* 2 (1991): 157–79; H. E. Freeman, *An Introduction to the Old Testament Prophets;* R. B. Gaffin, Jr., *Perspectives on Pentecost: New Testament Teaching on the Gifts of the Holy Spirit;* K. L. Gentry, Jr., *The Charismatic Gift of Prophecy: A Reformed Response to Wayne Grudem;* W. A. Grudem, *The Gift of Prophecy in the New Testament Today;* A. J. Heschel, *The Prophets,* 2 vols.; G. Houston, *Prophecy;* W. C. Kaiser, Jr., *Back Toward the Future: Hints for Interpreting Biblical Prophecy;* J. L. Mays and P. J. Achtemeier, eds., *Interpreting the Prophets;* R. L. Thomas, *BSac* 149 (1992): 83–96; W. A. Van Gemeren, *Interpreting the Prophetic Word;* R. F. White, *WTJ* 54 (1992): 303–20.

Prophet, False. *See* FALSE PROPHET.

Propitiation. *See* ATONEMENT.

Prosperity. *See* WEALTH.

Prostitution. ***The Old Testament.*** *Common Prostitution.* While the law forbids parents from forcing daughters into prostitution, there is no penalty attached (Lev. 19:29). In one case there is a penalty: If a woman has been betrothed to a man and he discovers that she is not a virgin, she may be stoned to death for prostituting herself (Deut. 22:13–21). These two passages lead some scholars to conclude that when two adults, neither of which was betrothed or married, consented to have sex, it was not considered a very serious crime, because no sanctions were expressed. However, before the Mosaic Law, burning was the penalty in one instance (Gen. 38:24). Perhaps Israelite society, like modern ones, tolerated a certain amount of prostitution, but it was clearly immoral and the sages sternly warned against it (Prov. 23:27; 29:3). Priests were held to a higher standard than non-priests for they could not marry harlots, although again, there was no specified punishment for doing so (Lev. 21:7, 14). A priest's daughter, on the other hand, could be burned for harlotry (Lev. 21:9); the intent of this was to keep the priestly line pure.

Apparently, prostitutes in ancient times dressed in recognizable ways (Prov. 7:10). In the patriarchal period, a face covering might be a distinguishing feature (Gen. 38:14–15). Some well-known biblical passages mention prostitution. Rahab, who helped the Israelite spies at Jericho, was a harlot (Josh. 2:1; 6:17, 22, 25); she figures in the genealogy of David and Jesus (Matt. 1:5). Jephthah was the son of a harlot (Judg. 11:1). Samson slept with one (Judg. 16:1). Two prostitutes asked Solomon to adjudicate between them over a child (1 Kings 3:16). For resisting the word of the Lord, the priest Amaziah would be taken into exile, forcing his wife into prostitution to survive (Amos 7:17).

Sacral Prostitution. The fertility cult was a central part of Canaanite religion. It is thought that sacral prostitution was a form of sympathetic magic. As people performed sex acts with the temple harlots, this stimulated sexual activity among the gods, ensuring the fertility of the soil. The terms *qādēš* and *qĕdēšâ* (Deut. 23:17) designate male and female sacral prostitutes. The words come from the root *qdš,* meaning "set apart," "holy," "consecrated." These men and women considered themselves consecrated to their gods for the purpose of religious prostitution.

The practice was known by the patriarchs, for Tamar was taken for a cult harlot (Gen. 38:21).

The law of Moses forbids the practice of sacral prostitution (Deut. 23:17), but Israelites were led astray by the fertility rites of Baalism in Moab before they even entered the promised land (Num. 25:1–5). Although sacral prostitution is not specifically mentioned, it is likely, since they were priests, that when Hophni and Phineas slept with the women who ministered at the entrance to the tabernacle, that they were borrowing the Canaanite practice (1 Sam. 2:22). The fertility cult was established in Judah early in the monarchy (1 Kings 14:24) and periodically purged (1 Kings 15:46). When Josiah carried out his reform, he had to remove the male cult prostitutes from the temple itself (2 Kings 23:7).

Spiritual Prostitution. The relationship between Yahweh and Israel was that of husband and wife. Therefore, when the Israelites went astray by worshiping other deities, they were prostituting themselves to other gods (Exod. 34:15). Ezekiel gave female names to Samaria and Jerusalem (symbolizing Israel and Judah), calling them Oholah and Oholibah. He described their harlotry and pronounced judgment on them (Ezek. 23). Hosea entered into an elaborate sign act in order to preach to the northern kingdom about its sin of spiritual harlotry. God told him to marry Gomer (Hos. 1:2–3). When she was unfaithful, he took her back in love (3:1–3). In the same way, God had taken Israel as his bride (2:15), but she had prostituted herself to the Canaanite deities (2:2–13). The divine husband was going to punish his "wife" for a time so that Israel would repent and return (2:3, 8–13). Although divorce was invoked (2:2) the ultimate goal was reconciliation (2:16–20).

The New Testament. Jesus pointed out that harlots and tax collectors were quicker to repent, believe, and enter the kingdom of God than the proud religious leaders (Matt. 21:28–32). The prodigal son, who apparently wasted his inheritance on harlots (Luke 15:13, 30), was welcomed home when he repented (vv. 20–24). Paul warns against immorality, because he who sleeps with a prostitute becomes one with her, which is not fitting for the believer, who belongs to Christ (1 Cor. 6:15–20). The Apocalypse refers to Rome (= Babylon) as "the great harlot," which will be punished forever for persecuting the Lord's servants (17:1–18; 19:1–3). WILLIAM B. NELSON, JR.

See also GODS AND GODDESSES, PAGAN; IDOL, IDOLATRY; IMMORALITY, SEXUAL.

Proverbs, Theology of. Proverb's theology consists of five aspects: (1) God has immutably structured both the cosmos and society; (2) God has revealed the social structure through this book; (3) the social structure consists of a nexus uniting deed and destiny; (4) adherence to the Lord's ordained structure is a matter of the heart; and (5) words are powerfully effective in shaping young hearts.

A Structured Society. Woman Wisdom, a personification of Solomon's teachings, was both present when the Lord created the cosmos with its vast seas, its high heavens, and its good earth (8:22–26), and celebrated daily the way in which he fixed the limits of these vast cosmic entities, enabling humanity to live within them (vv. 27–31). She delighted when he set for the random, chaotic sea its limit (v. 29). Wisdom's celebration of the Lord's beneficent cosmic order whereby he restrained chaos in primordial time corresponds to her role in carving out social order, restraining evil within historical time. By following these teachings pertaining, among other things, to the acquisition of enduring wealth (10:2–5), performing righteous acts of charity toward the needy (vv. 6–7), and speaking to form loving relationships (vv. 10–14), the faithful carve out for themselves an eternal kingdom (8:15–21). The wise live securely within the limits of these teachings, but fools, who without discipline wantonly crave what lies outside these prescribed boundaries (10:3b), die by transgressing the Lord's fixed social order (4:10–19).

These social structures do not exist autonomously, independent from the Lord who ordained them. Rather, the Lord upholds them: "He holds victory in store for the upright, he is a shield to those whose walk is blameless, for he guards the course of the just and protects the way of his faithful ones" (2:8–9; cf. 3:26; 5:21–23; 16:1–5). The proverbs are true only if God upholds them. One's faith is not in the proverbs themselves, but in the LORD who stands behind them (3:5; 22:19). Indeed, the teachings of this book are equated with knowing God himself: "My son, if you accept my words . . . then you will . . . find the knowledge of God" (2:1, 5).

A Revealed Structure. Solomon explains why accepting his teachings pertaining to fixed social structures is equivalent to knowing God: "For the LORD gives wisdom, and from his mouth come knowledge and understanding" (2:6). Solomon's mouth has become God's mouth.

God spoke in various ways in times past to the fathers (Heb. 1:1). Unlike Moses, who spoke to God face to face, and the prophets, to whom he gave visions and dreams (Num. 12:6–8), the Lord "spoke" to Solomon and other inspired sages such as Agur (Prov. 30:1) and King Lemuel (31:1) through their observations of creation and humanity. The sage's laboratory is the world. "I went past the field of the sluggard," he writes, "[where] thorns had come up everywhere . . . and the stone wall was in ruins. I applied my heart to what I observed" (24:30–32). Whereupon he coins his proverb: "A little sleep, a little slumber . . . and poverty will come on you like a bandit" (vv. 33–34). In other words, the inspired sage observes that within the fallen creation there is a principle of entropy that destroys life, but with discipline one can overcome the threatening chaos. Of course, the sage is a moral teacher, not a natural scientist. His exemplar drawn from the cosmic order functions to instruct the faithful that discipline can overcome social chaos.

The book's theology is not a natural theology. Woman Wisdom is not the cosmic order per se, as many claim. Rather, Solomon speaks as the king of Israel (1:1), and as such has himself been carefully schooled in the Mosaic Law. In this book Solomon consistently uses God's name, "the Lord," which signifies his covenantal relationship with Israel (Exod. 3:13–15; 6:2–8). Through the lens of the Mosaic covenant, the inspired king coined his proverbs (Prov. 29:18).

Although the sage does not speak with the prophetic thunder of heaven—"thus saith the Lord"—he does speak with divine authority, using the same vocabulary that Moses used for his revelation: *tôrâ*, "law/teaching," and *miṣwâ*, "commandment" (3:1).

The Conduct-Consequence Nexus. The social structure ordained and upheld by God and revealed in this book entails an inseparable connection between deed and destiny. This nexus is represented by the metaphor "way," which occurs about seventy-five times in the entire Book of Proverbs and thirty times in chapters 1–9, a collection of admonitions to embrace the book's teaching and the hermeneutical key to the book. The metaphor denotes a traversable road, or movement on a road, leading to a destination and connotes at one and the same time "course of life" (i.e., the character and context of life), "conduct of life" (i.e., specific choices and behavior), and "consequences of that conduct" (i.e., the inevitable destiny of such a lifestyle). The wise are on the way of life (2:20–21); fools are on the way to death (1:15–19). Whereas Christianity thinks of itself as a "faith," the Book of Proverbs, like most of the Bible, thinks of the faithful as following a *way*, a *halakah*, a life-path.

Life in this book refers to the abundant life in fellowship with the eternal and living God. According to Genesis 2:17, disruption of the proper relationship with the One who is the source of life means death. Wisdom is concerned with establishing and maintaining that proper relationship and so life (see 2:5–8). The first pericope (1:8–19) assumes that the wicked might send innocent blood to a premature death, even as Cain prematurely dispatched the righteous Abel (Gen. 4:1–9). The promise of life in this book (2:19; 3:2), as in the Bible as a whole, must entail a reality that transcends clinical existence and outlasts clinical death. If not, the murder of Abel in Genesis 4, of the innocent blood in Proverbs 1:8–19, and of the Son of God deconstructs both the Bible and this book, for the wicked will have triumphed over the righteous.

Solomon likens his teachings to a tree of life (3:18). The religious literature of the ancient Near East, particularly Egypt, and Genesis 2–3 suggest that the tree of life symbolizes eternal life in the full sense of that term. The seduced fool in Proverbs 5 rues after his body is spent that he wasted his life (vv. 7–14). Without specifying how, the received Hebrew text promises the righteous "immortality" (12:28) and a secure refuge even in clinical death (14:32). Yet unlike apocalyptic literature, which draws a sharp distinction between this world and the one to come, Wisdom Literature regards life as both already and yet to come. The sage emphasizes embracing life now.

The book also focuses on the end. "Though a righteous man falls seven times, he rises again, but the wicked are brought down by calamity" (24:16). Job and Ecclesiastes, in contrast, focus on the present reality "under the son," when the righteous seem "knocked out for the count of ten." Even as Proverbs 24:16 almost dismisses the fall of the righteous in a concessive clause, other proverbs also, while affirming the moral order, also assert or imply that the righteous suffer while the wicked prosper. It qualifies the conduct-consequence nexus by the "better than" proverbs (e.g., 15:16–17; 16:16, 19; 17:1; 19:22b; 21:3; 22:1; 28:6). These proverbs link poverty with righteousness and wealth with wickedness and so make it perfectly plain that piety and morality do not lead immediately to a joyous end.

Because of the epigrammatic nature of the proverbs, each expresses a truth with the greatest concentration on its subject matter. To get the full truth, however, one must read them as a collection. For example, after the wonderful promises in 3:1–10, Solomon adds: "My son, do not despise the LORD's discipline" (vv. 11–12). Prosperity and adversity are the wise and necessary mixture of the son's formation. Solomon's explanation, "because the LORD disciplines those he loves, as a father the son he delights in," shows that the father's tutelage passes into the heavenly Father's. The sage qualifies wisdom's palpable rewards catalogued in 3:13–20 with the admonition "do not withhold good from those who deserve it" (v. 27), an admonition that implies good people may be in need of help. His teachings about wealth in 10:2–5 are not to be read in isolation but together: verse 2 pertains to wealth and ethics, verse 3 to wealth and religion, and verses 4–5 to wealth and prudence. Read in this fashion the book does not teach a wealth and prosperity gospel, but promises that the Lord will reward the faithful.

The Heart. Adherence to the God-ordained social structure(s) is a matter of the heart, a person's emotional-intellectual-moral center (2:2; 4:23). Solomon does not deliver his teachings in cold, rational propositions calling for an equally rational, dispassionate response. Rather, in a fine piece of literary fiction, "Wisdom calls aloud in the street, she raises her voice in the public squares" (1:20). "She raises her voice" refers to a fervent and emotional situation. Solomon calls on the son in turn to "raise your voice" ("call out," NIV) to wisdom (2:3). When Solomon's wisdom is accepted with the whole heart, then wisdom that was in God's heart enters the believer's heart: "For wisdom," which originated in God's mouth (v. 6), now "will enter your heart, and knowledge [of God and of his teachings] will be pleasant to your soul" (v. 10).

Wisdom promises life to those who love her (8:17, 21) and asks her lovers to watch daily at her doors as for a bride (v. 34). To have this bride, one must be willing to sell all as her dowry (4:7). She must be held in awe and reverence: the fear of the LORD is the first principle of wisdom (1:7; 9:10).

By contrast, malformed simpletons, who pass into adulthood without having made a commitment to wisdom, love their openness; fools hate knowledge; and mockers covet the ability to mock (1:22). The choice or rejection of Solomon's teachings is affective, not merely cognitive. The formative simpleton, to whom the book is addressed (1:4), needs to make a decision for religious and ethical prudence before entering the city and engaging in its commerce and politics (8:3). Such a decision is also necessary to prepare them to resist the wicked men and women within it.

The Power of Words. Solomon so ordered this book that covenantal parents could teach it within the home, the place of education in ancient Israel. It is addressed to the covenantal child about to enter maturity. The seam between the generations is most vulnerable to being rent by outsiders at this juncture when pride and passion run at full tide. The voices of both parents (1:8; 31:26) compete with the voices of apostate men and unfaithful wives. Parents are armed by Solomon with all his rhetorical skill in robust man-to-man talk to outduel the temptation to easy money, offered by apostate men (1:10–19; 2:12–15), and to easy sex, offered by unfaithful women (2:16–19; 5:1–23; 6:20–35; 7:1–27; 9:13–18).

The mention of the mother as a teacher is unique within ancient Near Eastern Wisdom Literature. In the Old Testament both parents are put on equal footing before the child (Lev. 19:3). For "faithful instruction" to be on the mother's tongue, she herself must first have been taught. Although the book is addressed to "sons" who would take responsibility for the home, daughters are not excluded.

Throughout Solomon assumes the power of speech: indeed, it has the power of life and death (18:21). Although children are accountable for their own decisions (Ezek. 18:20), parental training will have its effect (Prov. 22:6, 15). Children who make it into the rank of the wise bring their parents joy, but those who fail to embrace the inherited wisdom bring them pain (10:1).

BRUCE K. WALTKE

See also HEART; WISDOM.

Bibliography. L. Bostrom, *The God of the Sages: The Portrayal of God in the Book of Proverbs;* B. S. Childs, *Old Testament Theology in a Canonical Context;* W. Cosser, *Glasgow University Oriental Society Transactions* 15 (1955): 48–53; G. Goldsworthy, *Gospel and Wisdom;* L. Kalugila, *The Wise King: Studies in Royal Wisdom as Divine Revelation in the Old Testament and Its Environment;* D. Kidner, *The Wisdom of Proverbs, Job and Ecclesiastes;* K. A. Kitchen, *TB* 28 (1977): 69–114; W. McKane, *Proverbs: A New Approach;* C. A. Newsom, *Gender and Difference in Ancient Israel,* pp. 142–60; R. C. Van Leeuwen, *Semeia* 50 (1990): 111–44; idem, *Hebrew Studies* 28 (1992): 25–36; G. von Rad, *Wisdom in Israel;* B. K. Waltke, *Presbyterion* 14/1 (1988): 1–15; idem, *Presbyterion* 13/2 (1987): 65–78; idem, *Alive to God: Studies in Spirituality Presented to James Houston,* pp. 17–33; R. N. Whybray, *The Intellectual Tradition in the Old Testament.*

Providence of God. The word "providence" comes from the Latin *providentia* (Gk. *pronoia*) and means essentially foresight or making provision beforehand. On the human plane it may be used positively, as when Tertullus praised Felix by saying, "Your foresight has brought about reforms in this nation" (Acts 24:2), or negatively, as when Paul admonishes us to "make no provision for the flesh, to gratify its desires" (Rom. 13:14, RSV). When applied to God the idea takes on a vastly larger dimension because God not only looks ahead and attempts to make provision for his goals, but infallibly accomplishes what he sets out to do. And because it is God's governance that is in view, it encompasses everything in the universe, from the creation of the world to its consummation, inclusive of every aspect of human existence and destiny. Providence, then, is the sovereign, divine superintendence of all things, guiding them toward their divinely predetermined end in a way that is consistent with their created nature, all to the glory and praise of God. This divine, sovereign, and benevolent control of all things by God is the underlying premise of everything that is taught in the Scriptures.

A doctrine of providence appears in intertestamental Jewish and Greek thought, as well as in the Scriptures. Much of Jewish thought closely paralleled that of the Old Testament and emphasized the freedom of God to accomplish his purposes (1 Macc. 3:60) and even used the term "providence." The Wisdom of Solomon identifies the providence of God with his will and wisdom, assuring us that one can embark on even the most perilous journey with assurance because God is in control (14:3–5). It also speaks of the inscrutability of God's providence and the vain attempts of the wicked to hide from the all-seeing control of God, calling them "exiles from eternal providence" (17:1–3). At the time of Jesus, one finds varying views on this subject. Josephus describes it this way: "The Pharisees say that some actions, but not all, are the work of fate, and some of them are in our power, and that they are subject to fate, but not caused by it. The Essenes affirm that fate governs all things and that nothing befalls us but what is according to its determination. The Sadducees take away fate, denying there is such a thing, affirming that the events of human life are not subject to it. All our actions are in our own power, so that we are the cause of what is good and we receive what is evil from our own folly" (*Antiq.* 13.5.9; see also *War* 2.8.14).

In Greek thought the most highly developed form of the doctrine was found in stoicism, an essentially pantheistic system. God was understood to be the immanent principle of Reason (Logos) within the universe that is ordering all things according to rational principles. The stoic system was essentially a determinism, even if defined as basically benevolent and rational.

The fundamental difference between Jewish (and biblical) understanding of providence and the stoic view lies in the emphasis of Greek thought upon the impersonal, though rational, nature of the divine immanent principle that could be approached by human minds and the personalistic approach of Jewish thought that sees God as a Person calling us to faith, not speculation. Jesus' profound contribution to this is his revelation that God is our heavenly Father, who cares infinitely for his helpless creation. We are to love and trust God, not necessarily to understand all that he does.

Foundational Ideas. Providence is a pervasive idea in the Scriptures, which makes it difficult to summarize. However, there are some general statements that can be made, before a specific look is taken at the various aspects of providence. Underlying any discussion of providence are these fundamental principles. First, God is sovereign in this universe and in complete control of all things (1 Chron. 29:11–12; Pss. 24:1; 115:3; 135:6). Nothing is able to stand up to him, defy him, or do that which will defeat him in the end. Not only is this true on earth; this is true among the so-called gods. In fact, there are no other gods, only idols; God alone is God in all the universe (Deut. 4:35, 39; Isa. 45:5–6; 1 Cor. 8:4–6; 1 Tim. 1:17) and nothing is impossible for him (Jer. 32:27; Luke 1:37). Second, the one and only God created the world; hence, it is his and subject to him (Deut. 10:14; Job 9:5–10; Pss. 89:11; 95:3–5; 1 Cor. 10:26). It is impossible that anything or anyone, whether in heaven or on earth, whether supernatural being, king, or simple peasant, should imagine that they are self-sufficient or answerable only to themselves (Isa. 45:11–12; Jer. 37:17–23; Dan. 4:35; Rev. 20:11–13). Third, the God who alone is God and who made and governs this world has an eternal plan for it. This plan is not just what he desires will be done but is in fact the very essence of this world's existence and the explanation of it (Ps. 33:11; Prov. 19:21; Eccles. 3:14; Isa. 14:24–27; 46:8–11). Fourth, God's will and purpose are realized in and through Jesus Christ (Eph. 1:9–10; 3:11). God's will is not the outworking of some impersonal abstract principle, as with Greek thought, but the personal, saving will of a heavenly Father. God is involved directly in our affairs and we have learned through revelation (reason alone could never have guessed this) that he became one with us through the incarnation of his Son for our redemption. This was part of an eternal purpose that existed before the world began and was effectuated in time at the moment of God's own choosing. He decided when the time had arrived and brought it all to pass. On the basis of this God has spread his beneficence throughout all the ages and will someday draw all things together in Christ, for "from him and through him and to him are all things" (Rom. 11:36). Finally, although the plan of God has been partially revealed to us, in its totality it remains an ultimate mystery. We are not capable of grasping what it ultimately means because God himself is ultimately beyond us (Job 11:7–9; 26:14; 36:26; Eccles. 3:11; 11:5; Isa. 40:28; 55:8). This limitation on our part is not designed by God to humiliate us, but to humble us, to help us realize our creaturely status and find our appropriate place in his scheme of things. We are not God. We will never understand the depths of God. This should call us to faith and trust in him and teach us to obey him, whether we discern what God intends or not. Our deepest prayer should be, as Jesus taught us, "your will be done on earth" (Matt. 6:10).

In summing up the general points that form the groundwork for the scriptural doctrine of providence, we find that the eternal God, who made and governs this universe, has a personal investment in it in the person of his Son Jesus Christ. Through Christ he deals redemptively with the world through all its ages, from creation to consummation. In the depth of the mystery of God's being he has formulated a benevolent, all-encompassing plan that is being worked out. This should evoke from us, not curiosity and speculation, but faith, praise, and submission. We may someday understand some of these things; we may not. But whatever the case, "God is his own interpreter, and he will make it plain," as Cowper said.

The Extent of Providence. Simply put, providence encompasses every aspect of the created order. From beginning to end, from heaven to earth, from animate to inanimate, from individuals to nations, from hours to ages, from weeds to wheat, from birth to death, from catastrophe to calm—everything is within the loving presence and involvement of the heavenly father. In his wisdom, power, righteousness, and love he is hastening slowly to work out his own eternal purposes for his own glory and for our eternal good. Because this is such an all-pervasive theme throughout the Scriptures it is possible only to give a selective, though representative account of what is taught there.

God's Involvement in the Natural World Order. It has already been pointed out that God is the originator of the entire created order. Nothing exists (other than himself) that he did not create. In the supernatural created order, often simply called "heaven," it is taken for granted that God's will is done (Matt. 6:10). In John's breath-taking vision of God upon his throne (Rev. 4–5) the picture is of ceaseless adoration and service of God by all that inhabit heaven. Day and night, thunderously and unendingly, all the heavenly beings cry out "Holy, Holy, Holy is the Lord God Almighty." God is also accomplishing his will in the material world order. Sun, moon and stars (Ps. 104:2, 19; Isa. 40:26; Jer. 31:35; Matt. 5:45), celestial activity (Job 9:7; Ezek. 32:7–8; Amos 8:9), clouds (Job 37:15–16; Ps. 135:7), dew (Gen. 27:28), frost (Ps. 147:16), hail (Job 38:22; Ps. 147:17), lightning (2 Sam. 22:13–15; Job 36:30, 32), rain (Deut. 28:12; 1 Kings 18:1; Job 5:10), snow (Job 37:6), thunder (Exod. 9:23; Jer. 10:13), and wind (Ps. 147:18; Ezek. 13:13) are all subject to God's command. They do his bidding under both ordinary and extraordinary circumstances, whether supporting earth functions for the sustenance of life or crashing down judgment upon evil. The earth itself is also included. God works his will through earthquakes (Job 9:6; Isa. 13:13), famine (Lev. 26:18–20; Amos 4:6), drought (Ps. 107:33–34; Amos 4:7–8), fire (Ezek. 20:45–48; Amos 7:4), plagues and calamities (Exod. 9:1–4; Ezek. 38:22), floods (Gen. 6:17), and normal supply of water (Pss. 104:10–13; 107:35). All the forces of nature are subject to the sovereign word of God, who works his will through them.

God also has control over the plant and animal world. Plants, trees, grass, flowers, and crops are all under God's benevolent care (Pss. 65:9–13; 104:14–16; Isa. 41:19; Matt. 6:28–30). Birds (Matt. 6:26; 10:29), fish (Jon. 1:17; Matt. 17:27), animals (Ps. 147:9; Hos. 2:18; Joel 2:21–22), indeed, every living thing is God's (Job 12:10; Ps. 145:13–16) and in their own way they are all praising God (Ps. 148:3, 4, 7–10).

God's Involvement in Israel and the Nations. God rules the destiny of all the peoples of the earth and of his people Israel in particular. This is in accordance with his own benevolent purposes in order to bring them all to a saving knowledge of himself (Acts 17:24–28). Israel, as the nation through which the redeemer would come, was guided by God in a specific way. It included the call of Abraham (Gen. 12:1–3), the lives of the patriarchs (Gen. 17:3–8; 28:20–21; 49:22–25), bondage in Egypt (Gen. 15:13), redemption from Egypt (Deut. 5:15), guidance and sustenance in the wilderness (Exod. 13:21–22; Neh. 9:19; Pss. 105:39–41; 136:16), entrance into the land (Exod. 15:13–18; Deut. 4:37–38; Amos 2:10), and the whole of their history (1 Chron. 29:10–13; 2 Chron. 32:22; Isa. 43:1, 15), including the judgments that fell upon them (Deut. 32:15–26; Jer. 52:3; Mal. 3:5). God also guides the destinies of all the nations of the earth. He is their king and ruler (Job 12:23; Pss. 22:27–28; 47:7–9; Isa. 14:24–26; Ezek. 29:19–20). He has foreseen all that will take place in the course of time (Isa. 22:11; 44:7), guides the national destinies of the peoples of the earth (Amos 9:7), uses them in his service (Job 12:23; Isa. 10:5–14; Jer. 27:3–7), and makes the choice as to who will do what in the accomplishment of his purposes (Isa. 49:1–7; 54:16; Dan. 2:21; 4:34–35).

God's Involvement in Human Life. Every aspect of human life is included in God's providential orderings. Just as with the formation, growth, existence, fortunes, and destiny of the world as a whole, the nations of the earth, and Israel in particular, so is it with the individual. God formed us in the womb (Job 10:8–12; Ps. 139:13–14; Jer. 1:5), ordained what all lives should be (Ps. 139:15–16), guides us in our life's circumstances (Job 5:18; Prov. 3:5–6; Acts 18:21; James 4:13–15), meets our temporal needs (Lev. 26:4–5; Job 36:31; Matt. 5:45; Acts 14:16–17), sends prosperity and adversity (Job 36:11; Isa. 45:7; Lam. 4:5, 11), and ultimately takes us off this earth in death at his own appointed time (1 Sam. 2:6, 25; Job 14:5; 2 Peter 1:13–14). None of this should cause anxiety. In fact, we are told all of this to encourage and strengthen us in the uncertainties of life. We must remember that it is God our heavenly Father who is ordering our lives. He knows and loves us infinitely; even the hairs of our head are numbered (Matt. 10:30). He who clothes the grass and flowers of the field in striking beauty will also take care of us (Matt. 6:25–32) and nothing is left to chance. A heavenly Father guides our lives.

Nor should any of this be looked at fatalistically or deterministically. God is not a blind, arbitrary force, crushing the human will into submission, but rather in some mysterious way is a caring, sovereign Father who works his will in and through our wills. This includes even the evil that people intend to do (Gen. 50:20); indeed, it includes everything (Rom. 8:28). In some instances, God works along with and through human intentions (1 Chron. 5:26; 2 Chron. 36:22–23; Phil. 2:13), sometimes he overrules them (Gen. 45:5–8; 2 Sam. 17:14; Ps. 33:10; Isa. 10:5–7), but in all cases the intention of God takes precedence and his purposes are ultimately accomplished (1 Sam. 2:4–8; Prov. 16:1, 9; 19:21; Isa. 14:26; Jer. 10:23).

There is a special providence for those who put their entire trust in God. Our times are in his hands (Ps. 31:15) and he is directing our steps (Pss. 40:5; 73:23–24). Throughout all of our lives there is a special deliverance from evil and calamity (Job 5:17, 19–21; Pss. 32:7; 33:18–19; 56:13; 91:9–10; 2 Tim. 4:18), healing and help in time of need (Pss. 30:2; 37:40; 54:4; 103:2–5; Heb. 4:16), preservation and protection (Pss. 37:28; 138:7; Prov. 3:25; 14:26; 18:10; Isa. 43:1–2), blessing and strength (Pss. 65:4; 84:11; Rom. 10:12; 2 Cor. 4:7; 2 Tim. 4:17).

The eternal destiny of all human beings is in the hands of God. The redeemed know that in some inexplicable way it is God who has planned and effectuated their salvation (Eph. 1:3–8, 11–12). To God is due all the praise for the salvation of those who are redeemed. The status of the lost is more problematic, but no one, not even the unredeemed, are ultimately outside the will of God (Prov. 16:4; Rom. 9:14–18; 1 Peter 2:7–8). They are not forced to be lost, but choosing to reject God's offer of mercy does not somehow free them from the control of God. Even their rejection has been included in the eternal plan of God. This is perhaps the worst part of it for them. In their attempt to be free from God by rejecting him, even if at the cost of their own souls, they find that there is no such thing. The net of God's providence includes even the vain attempt to be outside the net.

God's Intention in Evil and Suffering. Nowhere is it taught in the Scriptures that God causes people to sin or that evil can be somehow turned into good or dialectically merged with good in such a way that it is neutralized or made necessary. Evil is always evil and, as such, can never be traceable to God. However, God is able to take the evil that human beings do and incorporate that into his plan in such a way that at no compromise to himself he is able to use it for his own good ends. The supreme example of this is the death of Jesus Christ for the salvation of the world. He was the lamb slain from the creation of the world (Rev. 13:8) according to the set purpose and foreknowledge of God (Acts 2:23), fulfilling the prophecies given by God of old (Isa. 53:4–10). Yet those who crucified Jesus were responsible for the evil that they had done, as indeed, is everyone who does evil (James 1:13–17). The God who can take the worst that human beings can do and bring out of it the best that he can do is the God who works across the whole spectrum of human action, from good to neutral to unqualified evil, accomplishing his own good ends. God works his purposes sometimes by allowing evil to work itself out (Hos. 4:17; Acts 14:16; Rom. 1:24, 26, 28), sometimes by directing evil (Gen. 45:8; Isa. 10:5; Acts 4:27–28), yet at other times by limiting (Job 2:6; Ps. 124:1–3; 1 Cor. 10:13) or preventing evil from coming to full fruition (Gen. 20:6; Hos. 2:6–7). There is unquestionably a great mystery here as to how a holy God who cannot even look upon evil (Heb. 1:13) can work his will through evil, but that he does it is the clear teaching of Scripture. If something could get outside the ultimate will of God, it would become a god unto itself and a rival to God. Such can never be the case. God alone is God; there is no other.

God also works his will through human suffering. Sometimes there is a correlation between sin and suffering (Pss. 55:19; 119:75), sometimes not (Luke 13:1–5; John 9:1–3), but in all cases God is able to use suffering to discipline (Deut. 8:5), correct (Job 5:17), instruct (Isa. 26:8–9), teach (Ps. 119:67, 71), draw us to himself (Isa. 26:16; Hos. 5:14–15), refine (Isa. 48:10), and encourage us (Heb. 12:4–11). In all of our afflictions God comforts and sustains us (Isa. 66:13; Lam. 3:19–28; 2 Cor. 1:3–7) so that we will not be crushed beyond measure. Nothing in all creation can separate us from the love of God which is in Christ Jesus our Lord (Rom. 8:37–39).

WALTER A. ELWELL

See also ELECT, ELECTION; FATHERHOOD OF GOD; GOD; PREDESTINATION; SUFFERING.

Bibliography. G. C. Berkouwer, *The Providence of God;* A. B. Davidson, *The Theology of the Old Testament;* W. Eichrodt, *Theology of the Old Testament,* 2:167–85; W. Elwell, *TAB*, pp. 189–221; B. W. Farley, T*he Providence of God;* P. Helm, *The Providence of God.*

Psalms, Theology of. The Book of Psalms is a sizable collection of musical poems and prayers of diverse authorship and form. Psalms are independent literary units that have grown out of, and speak to, a wide range of individual and communal human experience. They differ from prophetic oracles, moral imperatives, or propositional statements of doctrine that presuppose a revelatory flow from God to humans. Psalms, on the other hand, serve to articulate the hope and despair, the faith and fear, the praise and invective of those who express themselves to God in the vicissitudes of life.

Although the canonical psalms are poetic and musical compositions authored by humans as vehicles of expression to and about God, they are nevertheless regarded by believers as inspired by God for use in the community of faith in worship and meditation. This realization highlights the validity and importance of such expression in the life of individual believers as well as the spiritual community of which they are a part. The biblical Psalter has been called the hymnbook of the second temple, but the faithful in every subsequent period of history have found something in its hymns and prayers that resonates with their experience of life lived in relation to God.

The continuing appeal of the canonical psalms bears witness to a feature of their composition that contributes to their ongoing usefulness in public and private worship. Ever since the groundbreaking work by Hermann Gunkel and Sigmund Mowinckel on the literary analysis of the Psalter, most biblical scholars have recognized that psalms may be grouped into definite literary types based both on their distinctive structure and content and on the religious settings in which they would have been employed in ancient Israel. It seems clear that psalms were composed mainly for use on typical, cultic occasions, not as reflections of particular, historical ones. Thus the psalmists crafted their poems in such a way as to ensure their continuing relevance for people in covenant with God.

The understanding that the canonical psalms were composed as generalized expressions suitable for cultic use runs counter to the impression given by certain psalm titles that associate the accompanying psalms with events in the life of King David (3; 7; 18; 34; 51–52; 54; 56–57; 59–60; 63; 142). Most biblical scholars concede that psalm titles in general, and these links with the Davidic narratives in 1 and 2 Samuel in particular, are not to be attributed to the original authors but probably to postexilic Jewish editors and interpreters. Evidence for the secondary nature of these titles may be deduced from the fact that some of the psalms assigned to David presuppose later historical realities such as the existence of a temple (e.g., 5:7; 27:4; 65:4; 68:29; 138:2) or the Babylonian exile (e.g., 51:18–19; 69:33–36). As a matter of fact, the expression *lĕdāwīd* is ambiguous and does not necessarily have anything to do with authorship. It could legitimately be translated "to/for/of/by/in regard to/belonging to David" and be intended to associate a given psalm with this son of Jesse, any Davidic king, or a Davidic collection of psalms. Furthermore, an analysis of the original Hebrew and subsequent daughter versions of Psalms reveals that the titles were subject to variation and expansion during the course of their transmission in postexilic times and beyond, in contrast to the poems themselves whose text remained relatively constant. Clearly, those in antiquity whose task it was to preserve holy writ did not regard these titles to have the same stature as the psalmists' own words. The preceding evidence does nothing to undermine David's reputation as a psalmist nor does it disprove that he composed some of the psalms contained in the canonical Psalter. There is no compelling reason not to take seriously biblical portrayals of him as an accomplished musician and poet (1 Sam. 16:14–23; 2 Sam. 1:17–27; 3:33–34; 23:1–7; 2 Chron. 29:30; Amos 6:5). This evidence does, however, highlight the fact that psalm titles cannot be relied upon to elucidate the original context and meaning of biblical psalms.

Psalm Types and the Theology of Psalms. There is evidence that the division of the Psalter into five books (1–41; 42–72; 73–89; 90–106; 107–150) represents a final stage in the process of compiling the Book of Psalms, and that earlier collections were gathered together to produce the Psalter as it now exists. These collections would have included psalms associated in the Hebrew Bible with the likes of David (3–9; 11–32; 34–41; 51–65; 68–70; 86; 101; 103; 108–110; 122; 124; 131; 133; 138–145), Solomon (72; 127), the Korahites (42; 44–49; 84–85; 87–88), and Asaph (50; 73–83); psalms of the so-called Elohistic Psalter (42–83) in which the generic term for Israel's deity, *ʾelōhîm*, translated "God," came to be substituted for his personal name, "Yahweh," which Jews were increasingly disinclined to pronounce; the Hallelujah Psalms (105–106; 111–118; 135–136; 146–150) which usually begin and/or end with that expression of praise; and the Songs of Ascent (120–134), ostensibly sung by pilgrims on their way to celebrate the great festivals at the temple in Jerusalem.

But more relevant to the task of working out the theology of the Psalter than these observations is an understanding of the functionality of biblical psalms. The inspired authors composed them to help connect Israelites with their God in worship. Various aspects of worship called for different types of psalms, each of which is represented throughout the Psalter.

Complaint Psalms. There are more complaint psalms in the biblical Psalter than there are of any other type. Exhibiting either the singular or plural number, they provide the individual or the community with the vehicle to speak to God in situations of distress. They are characterized by some or all of the following components arranged in varying sequences.

Complaint psalms usually begin with an invocation of Israel's God. In the Hebrew Bible he is normally (except in the Elohistic Psalter) addressed by the name, "Yahweh," which is rendered LORD in the English versions. The pronunciation of Yahweh's name implies that complainants are in covenant relationship with the God who has revealed himself to Israel. Attention is thus focused on the only one who can remedy their situation.

The invocation is followed by the complaint in which worshipers, often with great pathos and highly figurative language, communicate honestly the reasons for their distress. Typically, the individual speaks of being falsely accused (4:2; 5:6, 8–9; 7:1–5, 8, 14–16; 17:1–5, 8–12; 22:6–8; 26:1–12; 27:12; 35:11–12, 19–26; 38:11–12, 19–20; 52:1–4; 59:12–13; 69:4; 71:10–11; 109:2–4; 120:2–3; 140:9–11), of being threatened or attacked by foes of various sorts including sorcerers who employ curses and black magic (10:2–11; 28:3; 55:2–5, 9–15, 20–21; 58:1–5; 59:1–7; 69:9–12, 19–21; 109:2–20, 28–29; 140:1–5), of having committed sin (25:7; 38:18; 39:8; 51:1–9; 69:5; 130:3; 143:2), or of suffering due to some sort of illness or incapacity (6:2; 22:14–15, 17–18; 38:3–10, 17; 71:9; 88:3–9, 15–18; 102:3–11). In communal laments the causes of distress include the threat of attack by foreigners (83:2–8, 12), the experience of military defeat, invasion, and humiliation (44:9–16; 60:1–3, 9–11; 74:3–11; 79:1–4; 80:4–6, 8–16), and natural disasters such as drought, famine, or plague (126:4–6).

Supplicants also normally express trust in Yahweh, based on such realities as his steadfastness and dependability, his presence with worshipers, and his concern for justice and the vindication of the righteous (7:10–11; 13:5; 28:7–8; 31:14; 52:8; 56:3–4; 130:4–6; 140:7, 12). Some biblical scholars isolate a whole other psalm type, called the song of trust/confidence, to categorize a group of psalms in which this sort of expression is expanded to become the main theme (11; 16; 23; 27:1–6; 62; 91; 125; 131).

It is this trust that leads complainants to petition Yahweh for deliverance from their difficulty. The use of the imperative mood, which contributes to the sense of urgency, is usually the formal indicator of this component of the psalm (3:7; 22:19–21; 35:17, 22–24; 69:14–18; 143:7–9).

A feature at times associated with the petition is imprecation—the invocation of curses or the call for divine judgment upon enemies. Vivid examples may be found in 12:3–4; 35:1–8; 58:6–10; 59:10–13; 69:22–28; 83:9–17; 109:6–20; 137:7–9; 140:9–11. This feature serves two purposes. The first is cathartic in that it allows complainants to verbalize honestly to God the anger they feel toward those who have proven themselves to be foes. The second is judicial in the sense that supplicants, rather than acting vindictively, ask God to see to it that covenantal judgment is executed on perpetrators of wickedness. What is called for is just retribution, often envisioned as judgment in kind in which enemies will experience the harm that they had intended to inflict on complainants (5:10; 7:15–16; 10:2; 28:4; 35:7–8; 26; 79:12; 109:2–20, 29).

Another common feature associated with either the complaint or the petition is the additional argument. It serves to justify the appropriateness of Yahweh's intervention on behalf of petitioners and to provide motivation for him to act in response to prayer. In this connection, supplicants may protest their innocence with regard to false charges (7:3–5; 35:11; 44:17–21; 59:3–4), confess their sin (25:7, 11, 18; 38:18; 51:3–5; 79:9), provide extravagant descriptions of their distress in order to move Yahweh to pity (6:6–7; 22:12–18; 31:9–12; 38:3–10; 88:15–18; 102:3–11; 109:22–25) or appeal to Yahweh's honor and reputation (6:5; 58:11; 59:13; 74:10, 18, 22–23; 88:10–12; 109:21; 143:11–12).

In complaint psalms petitioners typically express the assurance that Yahweh will do what they have asked (6:8–10; 7:10; 13:5–6; 22:24; 28:6–8; 54:7; 56:13; 71:20–21; 109:31; 140:12). This is somewhat parallel to the articulation of trust discussed earlier. Scholars have struggled to account for the often dramatic shift in mood from despair to optimism that is evident in these psalms. Various hypotheses are put forward. One is that such expressions were uttered after deliverance had been experienced but that they were joined to the original complaint when these psalms were compiled in their present form. If that were the case, however, one might expect a thanksgiving psalm rather than a complaint. Another conjecture is that petitioners may have received a favorable oracle, presumably mediated by a priest or other cult official, in response to their supplication. Unfortunately, no example of such an oracle exists in the canonical psalms. A third proposition is that complaint psalms were formulated in such a way as to bring supplicants to the point of assurance. This was accomplished by causing worshipers to focus on and invoke the powerful name of the God with whom they were in relationship and who could be relied upon to deliver honest petitioners.

Finally, in conjunction with this assurance concerning Yahweh's favorable response to suppliant requests, there is normally a proclamation of praise or a vow that praise will be forthcoming once deliverance has been experienced (7:17; 13:5–6; 22:22–31; 28:6–7; 35:9–10, 18, 28; 43:4; 51:13–15; 54:6; 56:12; 69:30–31; 79:13; 109:30; 140:13). Praise is surely the appropriate expression of trusting petitioners who have left their complaints with the Lord.

The complaint psalms teach several significant things to worshipers who suffer affliction. First, servants of God should focus on him rather than despair over their difficulties. Second, God accepts—indeed encourages—honest and forthright expressions of distress from his servants. He does not require sugar-coating or euphemisms. Third, God expects that his servants will trust him to help, a faith to which they are expected to testify in their declarations of confidence and praise even as they articulate their complaints and petitions. Fourth, God does take pity on those who trust him and intervenes on their behalf. He thereby demonstrates his covenantal faithfulness, establishes his justice, and maintains his honor and reputation. Fifth, God is a formidable opponent to those who cause his servants to experience anguish since he vindicates pious complainants and exacts just retribution on their foes. Furthermore, petitioners whose distress is due to personal sin would be advised to confess it and to ask for forgiveness since God's judgments on members of the covenant community can be grievous as well.

Thanksgiving Psalms. Thanksgiving psalms were composed to celebrate Yahweh's answering of complaints and his deliverance of petitioners. The canonical Psalter contains both individual and communal psalms of this type. They exhibit some or all of the following structural components.

Typically, thanksgiving psalms begin with an expression of praise or thanksgiving to Yahweh and a short reference to what it is that he has accomplished (18:1–3; 30:1–3; 65:1–2; 107:1–3; 116:1–2; 118:1–4; 138:1–2).

A more detailed statement—though often couched in metaphorical imagery—as to the circumstances that preceded Yahweh's saving action is usually to be found in the erstwhile supplicants' recollection of their previous distress (18:4–5; 30:6–7; 32:3–4; 65:3a; 107:4–5, 10–12, 17–18, 23–27; 116:3; 118:10–13; 124:1–5). The situations that are recounted are of the sort described in the complaint psalms discussed above. Worshipers will then normally recall the petitions they uttered while in trouble and their ensuing deliverance by Yahweh (18:6–19, 31–45; 30:8–12a; 32:5; 40:1–2; 65:3b–5; 107:6–7, 13–14, 19–20, 28–30; 116:4–11; 118:5–18; 124:6b–8; 138:3).

What usually follows is an utterance of praise and thanksgiving to Yahweh and/or a call for others to join in worship of him (18:46–50; 30:12b; 32:11; 40:3–5, 9–10; 107:8–9, 15–16, 21–22, 31–32; 116:12–19; 118:19–29; 124:6a; 138:4–6). This expression may be associated with the fulfillment of a vow made in anticipation of his intervention (40:9–10; 116:14, 18; cf. 22:22–25).

Thanksgiving psalms serve to emphasize the fact that it is only right for worshipers to give thanks to God (7:17; 54:6; 92:1; 106:1; 107:1; 118:1, 29; 136:1). Indeed, thanksgiving is expected of the faithful (30:4; 97:12). They enter God's presence with it on their lips (95:2; 100:4; 118:19). They proclaim it in the presence of others to give public witness to his goodness and thereby honor him (9:1; 26:7; 50:23; 57:9; 75:1; 108:3; 109:30; 111:1).

Hymns. The hymnic psalms focus on the praise of Yahweh for his majesty and his sovereignty and beneficence in the realms of creation, history, and human affairs. What distinguishes hymns from thanksgiving psalms is that they make no particular reference to a worshiper's earlier distress or to recent divine intervention. They tend, therefore, to be broader in scope or perspective than thanksgiving psalms.

The formal structure of hymns normally includes three elements. The introduction typically contains a summons to sing Yahweh's praise or an expression of praise to him. The body provides the motivation for praise in the recitation of Yahweh's attributes and actions. The conclusion frequently recapitulates sentiments expressed in the introduction that means a renewed outpouring of praise.

Various themes are addressed in the hymns. Yahweh is glorified as the creator who governs and sustains nature (8; 19:1–6; 29:3–9; 33:6–9; 104:2–30; 135:6–7; 136:4–9; 146:6; 147:4–5, 8–9, 15–18; 148:1–10), the omnipotent one in contrast to impotent pagan deities (135:5, 15–18; 136:2), the controller of the destinies of people and nations (33:10–19; 100:3; 114:1–2; 136:3; 147:6; 149:2–9), the lawgiver (19:7–11), and the one who manifests his goodness through his enduring covenantal love, faithfulness and benefactions toward his people (100:5; 111:5–9; 113:7–9; 136:1 *passim*; 145:4–20; 146:5–9; 147:2–3, 13–14, 19–20; 148:14).

Other psalm groupings that may be included in the hymnic type are the redemptive history, Zion, processional, and enthronement songs. Generally speaking, they exhibit the formal structure of the hymns but are marked by the distinctives in content these designations suggest.

Redemptive history psalms (78; 105; 106; 135:8–12; 136:10–22) focus on Yahweh's dealings with the Israelites, whether in acts of deliverance and providential care or in judgment because of their covenantal unfaithfulness. Traditions associated with the patriarchs, the exodus, the wilderness wanderings, the conquest, the period of the judges, the career of David, and the construction of the temple are recalled. These psalms were composed to drive home the lessons of Israel's history—lessons that were to be passed on from generation to generation—and to inspire the people to trust and worship their sovereign God.

The songs of Zion (46; 48; 76; 84; 87; 122) celebrate the holy city, Jerusalem. From the time of David and Solomon onward the city is associated with Yahweh's name and habitation among his people because of the sanctuary's location there (Deut. 12:1–28; 2 Sam. 6:12–17; 1 Kings 8:1–30). The reality of Yahweh's majestic presence, the beauty and impressiveness of the city and its temple, and the prospect of participation in the festal gatherings inspire the poets to produce hymns that exude anticipation and joy. Because of Yahweh's choice of this city as his earthly dwelling, Zion songs speak confidently of its inviolability. But Psalms 46, 48, and 76 in particular seem to point the worshiper in the direction of an eschatological realization of this ideal when the everlasting kingdom that the prophets envision will finally be established.

Psalms like 15 and 24, which seem to have been composed as liturgies for entrance into the sacred precincts, have Zion's sanctuary as their focus. They are called processional songs. In question-and-answer antiphons they spell out the qualifications for admission into Yahweh's courts. As in the oracles of the prophets, the emphasis in these psalms is on integrity and moral purity as defined by the Sinai covenant rather than merely on ritual purity and sacrifices. Psalm 24:7–10 describes another kind of procession into the temple—this one involving Yahweh himself whose presence is presumably symbolized by the ark of the covenant. Psalms 68:24–27 and 132:8–9, 13–16 may provide glimpses of this sort of temple ritual.

The enthronement psalms (47; 93; 96–99) celebrate the kingship of Yahweh. They frequently exhibit the formula *yhwh mālak,* "Yahweh is king" or some similar sentiment. The psalmists emphasize Yahweh's all-encompassing rule by extolling his work as creator (93:1b; 96:5b), his evident glory and majesty (47:1–2; 93:1–4; 96:1–3, 6–9; 97:1–6; 99:1–3), his sovereignty and victorious exploits among the nations (47:3–9; 98:1–3), his omnipotence in comparison to the impotence of pagan deities (96:4–5; 97:7–9), and his establishment of universal justice and righteousness (96:10–13; 98:4–9; 99:4). Thus worshipers are encouraged to look back on Yahweh's great accomplishments in history and ahead to the emergence of his everlasting kingdom in all its fullness.

Royal Psalms. Another group of psalms deals with the theme of kingship—in this case the kingship of Israel's monarchs. The so-called royal psalms (2; 18; 20–21; 45; 72; 89; 101; 110; 132; 144) do not, technically speaking, constitute a distinctive psalm type since they can be associated with one of the three main categories already discussed (complaint, thanksgiving and hymn). They do, however, merit special consideration because of their contribution to our understanding of Israel's worship and the theological significance of the king.

Five of the preceding psalms (2; 21; 72; 101; 110) seem to have been created for use during the king's coronation and/or to mark the anniversary of his accession. The time of transition from the reign of one king to that of his successor was often a dangerous time politically when rivals vied for the throne and subject peoples attempted revolt. But the Israelite king, the heir to the Davidic covenant, was adopted by Yahweh as his son when he ascended the throne (Ps. 2:7; cf. 2 Sam. 7:14; Ps. 89:26–27). Yahweh, who both installed him as king and sustained him in the face of such opposition, granted him the right to rule not only his compatriots but also the nations (2:4–12; 72:1–2, 8–11; 110:1–3, 5–6). The king was expected, indeed he undertook, to rule with justice and integrity (72:1–7, 12–14; 101).

Another entitlement affirmed in the royal psalms is the king's role as a priest of the Melchizedekian order (110:4). This connection with the Canaanite priest-king of Salem = Jerusalem in Abram's day (Gen. 14:17–24; Ps. 76:2) highlights the sacral nature and privileges of Israelite kingship, privileges that were seldom exercised by Israel's monarchs. It also points to the link between the throne and the sanctuary that was forged for the Judean monarchy by David when he established Jerusalem as the political and religious capital (2 Sam. 5:6–10; 6:12–17; Ps. 132). The psalmists looked for the king's reign to be an enduring one marked by righteousness, peace, prosperity, and blessing of every sort (21:1–7; 72:5–7, 15–17).

One of the royal psalms, Psalm 45, was apparently intended for the celebration of a royal wedding. The poet has woven the themes touched on in the preceding paragraphs into a song of praise for the king (vv. 2–9, 16–17). He even calls the king God (v. 6), though his subordination to *the* God is made clear (v. 7). There is also a description of the beautiful bride, arrayed in rich finery, being led with her attendants in the wedding procession into the palace (vv. 10–15).

Several other royal psalms were likely composed to be recited either before or after the king went into battle. In Psalms 20, 89, and 144 Yahweh is entreated to grant victory of the king's foes. Yahweh's unrivaled sovereignty and power (89:5–18) and his promise of an enduring Davidic dynasty (89:3–4, 28–37) are recalled. The insufficiency of human resources and the need for Yahweh's intervention and enablement are also acknowledged (20; 89:46–51; 144:1–11). In Psalm 18 Yahweh is thanked for having responded to the kind of request contained in the preceding prayers. His dramatic intervention on behalf of the upright supplicant is recounted (vv. 6–24, 31–45).

Royal psalms give evidence of the Israelite king's special relationship with Yahweh, Israel's ultimate King. The human king, Yahweh's adopted son, serves as vice-regent over the covenant people and, ideally, the nations.

Wisdom Psalms. A final category of psalms to be considered here is that of wisdom (1; 34; 37; 49; 73; 112; 119; 127–128; 133). Psalms of this type exhibit stylistic forms and techniques commonly employed in wisdom literature. There are proverbial sayings (127; 133), acrostics (34; 37; 112; 119), "better . . . than" comparisons (37:16; 119:72, 103, 127), rhetorical questions (119:9), "beatitudes" (1:1; 112:1; 119:1–2; 128:1), personalized reflections on life (37:25–26; 35–36), comparisons with the realm of nature (1:3–4; 37:1–2, 20; 128:3).

These psalms champion the cause of life lived in accordance with the tenets of wisdom through their descriptions of exemplary conduct and its benefits and their delineation of the contrasts between those who embrace, and those who spurn, the path of righteousness. The celebration in wisdom psalms of Torah, which embodies Yahweh's expectations of his covenant partners, highlights the clear connection between wisdom and God's law (1:1–2; 37:30–31; 112:1; 119). Wisdom is essentially living in compliance with that law.

Wisdom psalms also lead the worshiper to consider some of the themes and problems commonly taken up in wisdom literature. In view of the fact that the faithful servant of Yahweh is often promised rich blessing, considerable attention is paid to the dilemma which that servant faces when confronted with the prospect of the prosperity of the wicked and the suffering and hardships of the righteous (37; 49; 73). Although it may initially seem as though there is no advantage to living uprightly (73:13–14), the psalmists assert that Yahweh's ultimate vindication and blessing of the righteous (37; 49:15; 112:1–3, 6–9) and his judgment and destruction of the unrighteous (1:5; 34:16, 21; 37; 49:13–14, 16–20; 73:16–20, 27; 112:10) will prove that the way of wisdom—covenantal faithfulness—is the one to follow. Armed with this knowledge, the worshiper is encouraged to trust Yahweh and wait patiently for him to act (37:3–7, 34).

The Psalms and Christology. Exerpts from, or allusions to, the canonical Psalter in the New Testament are often associated, either explicitly or implicitly, with the person, life, and mission of Jesus. This fact raises hermeneutical queries with regard to both the intentions of the original Hebrew poets and the uses to which the New Testament puts the passages in question. This is certainly not the place for an exhaustive examin ation of that issue. But suffice it to say that those in the New Testament who quote or otherwise employ the psalms in this fashion often overlay the psalmists' intentions with additional significance in view of the Christ event. This is readily observable when one compares the same passages in their original and secondary contexts.

For example, Psalm 41, either a lament/liturgy for someone enduring sickness, the slander of enemies and the perfidy of a close friend or a thanksgiving song sung after the experience of deliverance, is cited in connection with Judas's betrayal of Jesus (John 13:18). It is clear that the psalmist does not regard his subject to be the divine Son of God because he depicts the speaker readily acknowledging personal sin (v. 4). The same can be said of Psalm 69, a lament calling on Yahweh to rescue the supplicant from enemies, which is used in narratives concerning Jesus' cleansing of the temple (John 2:13–17), his experience of unjustified hatred by others (John 15:24–25), his being offered wine mixed with gall and wine vinegar/sour wine to drink at his crucifixion (Matt. 27:34, 48), as well as in Peter's recollection of Judas's sorry end (Acts 1:15–20). In this psalm, too, there is a confession of personal folly and wrongdoing (v. 5). Psalm 22, a lament for someone suffering great distress because of serious illness and the taunts of those who regard sickness as a sign of divine disapproval, is employed in the description of various aspects of Jesus' passion (Matt. 27:39–46; John 19:23–24). Psalm 2, a royal psalm celebrating Yahweh's adoption and installation of the Israelite king as his vice-regent in the face of incipient rebellion by Israel's subject peoples, is excerpted by the fledgling Christian community to characterize the opposition experienced by both Jesus and that community (Acts 4:23–30) and by Paul to demonstrate that Jesus' resurrection was accomplished by God in fulfillment of his word (Acts 13:32–33). Psalm 16, a song of confidence/trust in which the psalmist rejoices because of his assurance that Yahweh will not allow him to succumb to the ordeal in which he finds himself, becomes another testimony to Jesus' resurrection (Acts 2:22–32). Psalm 118, a thanksgiving psalm in which gratitude is expressed to Yahweh for his intervention on behalf of the supplicant resulting in victory over enemies, is also applied to God's raising Jesus from the dead (Acts 4:8–11). Psalm 45, a psalm composed for the occasion of a royal wedding in which the Israelite king is greatly revered, is employed to celebrate the divine Son of God's eternal kingship (Heb. 1:8–9). From Psalm 102, a lament for one experiencing illness and the derision of adversaries, Hebrews 1:10–12 quotes a hymnic fragment extolling the eternality of the creator to describe Jesus. Psalm 110, a royal psalm that depicts the Israelite king as Yahweh's victorious vice-regent and enduring priest, is transformed into an affirmation of Jesus' messiahship (Matt. 22:41–45), post-resurrection exaltation (Acts 2:32–36), and superior priesthood (Heb. 4:14–5:10; 7:11–28).

Several observations may be made concerning these links between the psalms and Jesus. First, they reinforce the idea that Jesus in his incarnation identified with, and in some ways epitomized, the individual worshiper and the community of faith. The New Testament gives ample evidence that Jesus experienced the pain and joy, the despair and hope of the human condition which is so vividly depicted in the canonical Psalter. Second, such links are not surprising given the psalmists' vision of the establishment of Yahweh's universal and everlasting kingdom of righteousness, justice, and peace and its temporal, historical embodiment in the rule of the Israelite king. The often exalted and hyperbolic language of the psalms in which these themes are expressed coupled with the inability of Israelite kings to live up to this ideal fueled anticipation about an anointed one who would fulfill all such expectations and paved the way for Christians to identify Jesus, the divine Son of God, with that messiah. Third, the connections between the psalms and Jesus are, for the most part, typological, not intentionally predictive. That is to say, the inspired Hebrew poets would have been unaware that portions of the hymns and prayers which they composed for use by Israelite worshipers foreshadowed specific aspects of Jesus' life and ministry. The New Testament does, however, testify to a divine purpose and intentionality in this regard so that it can be said that the meaning of the divine author of the canonical psalms exceeds that of the human authors. Psalms then are messianic insofar as they reflect the ideal of Yahweh's universal rule through the agency of his anointed designate and/or are employed in the New Kingdom to chronicle and explicate Jesus' role in bringing God's kingdom to light.

ROBERT J. V. HIEBERT

Bibliography. P. R. Ackroyd, *Doors of Perception: A Guide to Reading the Psalms;* L. C. Allen, *Psalms 101–150;* A. A. Anderson, *The Book of Psalms;* B. W. Anderson, *Out of the Depths: The Psalms Speak for Us Today;* C. F. Barth, *Introduction to the Psalms;* C. A. and E. G. Briggs, *A Critical and Exegetical Commentary on the Book of Psalms;* P C. Craigie, *Psalms 1–50;* F. Delitzsch, *Biblical Commentary on the Psalms;* J. H. Eaton, *Kingship and the Psalms;* idem, *Psalms: Introduction and Commentary;* G. D. Fee and D. Stuart, *How to Read the Bible for All Its Worth;* H. Gunkel, *The Psalms: A Form-Critical Introduction;* J. H. Hayes, *Understanding the Psalms;* D. Kidner, *Psalms 1–72;* idem, *Psalms 73–150;* H.-J. Kraus, *Worship in Israel: A Cultic History of the Old Testament;* C. S. Lewis, *Reflections on the Psalms;* W. S. LaSor, D. A. Hubbard, and F. W. Bush, *Old Testament Survey;* S. Mowinckel, *The Psalms in Israel's Worship;* H. Ringgren, *The Faith of the Psalmists;* L. Sabourin, *The Psalms: Their Origin and Meaning;* E. Sellin and G. Forhrer, *Introduction to the Old Testament;* M. H. Shepherd, *The Psalms in Christian Worship: A Practical Guide;* L. E. Stradling, *Praying the Psalms;* M. E. Tate, *Psalms 51–100;* T. H. Troeger, *Rage! Reflect! Rejoice! Praying with the Psalmists;* A. Weiser, *The Psalms;* C. Westermann, *The Praise of God in the Psalms;* J. W. Wever, *VT* 6 (1956): 80–96.

Punishment. ***Earthly Punishment.*** *The Old Testament.* Early in Israel's history, guilt and punishment were understood to be communal. When Achan broke the law by taking some of the spoil from Jericho, the whole Israelite army was defeated at Ai (Josh. 7:1–5). Once it was discovered what Achan had done, his whole family was stoned along with him (Josh. 7:22–26). The sins of parents could be punished to the third and fourth generation (Exod. 20:5; 34:7; Deut. 5:9–10). However, the Lord later revealed that individuals would bear their own guilt (Deut. 24:16; 2 Kings 14:6; Jer. 31:29–30; Ezek. 18:1–4, 20).

Sometimes punishment was meted out by God directly, as when fire and brimstone destroyed Sodom and Gomorrah (Gen. 19:24–25) or when the ground opened up to swallow those who rebelled in the wilderness (Num. 16:31–33). On a national level, God punished his people using the instrumentality of foreign nations. For example, Assyria was seen as the Lord's rod of wrath (Isa. 10:5). Most crimes and punishments, however, were dealt with through Israel's judicial system, which is found in the Pentateuch.

The Decalogue is in apodictic or absolute form, giving the most important requirements of the law in general terms without listing punishments. One has to examine the casuistic or case law to discover specific violations and their penalties. In the following paragraphs, both are reviewed.

The first and second commands concern foreign deities (Exod. 20:3–6). Worshiping gods other than Yahweh was a capital crime (Exod. 22:20) for which the punishment was stoning (Deut. 13:6–10). Molech worship, involving infant sacrifice, was specifically forbidden, also requiring death by stoning (Lev. 20:1–5). Likewise, those who prophesied in the name of other gods, or who led the people into idolatry were to be executed (Deut. 13:1–5; 18:20). Other pagan religious practices such as witchcraft, consulting of spirits, necromancy, divination, sorcery, augury, and soothsaying were proscribed (Lev. 19:26; 20:6; Deut. 18:10–11). Death is indicted for a sorceress (Exod. 22:18); stoning is designated for a medium (Lev. 20:27).

The third command prohibited taking Yahweh's name in vain (Exod. 20:7; Lev. 19:12; cf. Exod. 22:28, "revile God"). Offenders were stoned (Lev. 24:10–23; falsely accused, in Naboth's case, 1 Kings 21:8–14).

The fourth command, breaking the Sabbath (Exod. 20:8), was also a capital offense (Exod. 31:14–15; 35:2). An example of its enforcement is found in Numbers 15:32–36, where the penalty was stoning.

The fifth command entails respect for parents (Exod. 20:12). According to the case law, death was the punishment for the one who struck (Exod. 21:15) or even cursed a parent (Exod. 21:17; Lev. 20:9).

The sixth command prohibits murder (Exod. 20:13). Those who intended to kill were to be executed while those who slew accidentally could flee to a city of refuge (Exod. 21:12–14; Num. 35:9–28; Deut. 19:4–13). However, if two men were fighting and one of them accidentally hit a pregnant woman so that she both miscarried and died, he would suffer death also (Exod. 21:22–25). If the owner of a dangerous ox did not keep it fenced in and the ox gored someone to death, both the ox and the owner were to be put to death (Exod. 21:28–32). Killing a burglar at night incurred no guilt (Exod. 22:2). Obviously, the taking of human life was allowed in war and when punishing capital offenses. If someone caused bodily harm to another rather than death, lex talionis, or the law of retaliation was invoked: "an eye for an eye and a tooth for a tooth" (Exod. 21:23; Lev. 24:19; Deut. 19:21; Matt. 5:38). The intention was to make the law more equitable by making the punishment fit the crime.

The seventh command forbids adultery (Exod. 20:14). Stoning is stipulated in Leviticus 20:10 and Deuteronomy 22:22–24. Prostitution was outlawed but no punishment is listed (Lev. 19:29; Deut. 23:17). In the case of a man raping a single woman, he could be forced to marry her (relinquishing the right to divorce) and pay her father the marriage present, but no punishment was required (Deut. 22:28–29). In the case of seduction, the result was the same except that no mention is made of divorce and the father could still be paid the marriage present though he disallowed the wedding (Exod. 22:16–17). Incest was proscribed (Lev. 20:11, 12, 14, 17, 19–21; Deut. 27:20, 22–23) for which the penalty in certain cases was death by burning (Lev. 20:11, 14). Sexual relations between two men or between humans and animals were punishable by death (Exod. 22:19; Lev. 18:22–23; 20:13, 15–16).

The eighth command concerns stealing (Exod. 20:15). The law requires restitution with interest (Exod. 22:1–4, 7; Lev. 6:4–5). If the thief could not pay, he could be sold as a slave to pay the debt (Exod. 22:1). Kidnappers, who stole humans, were to be put to death (Exod. 21:16; Deut. 24:7).

The ninth command prohibits bearing false witness (Exod. 20:16). Whatever the false witness intended to do to the innocent party would be done to him (Deut. 19:15–19).

The tenth command deals with coveting (Exod. 20:17). No penalty is recorded.

The New Testament. As in the Old Testament, so in the New Testament. God occasionally punished people directly, as when Ananias and Sapphira were struck dead (Acts 5:1–11), but this was rare. Unlike Israel, the church is not a nation. Therefore, it does not have a set of laws with crimes and punishments. That is left to the secular authorities, which are instituted by God (Rom. 13:1–7). However, Jesus did provide for church discipline. If one believer sinned against another, the offended party was to confront the guilty party. If the offender refused to repent, the one wronged should go back to him, bringing one or two others with him. If that failed, he was to bring the accusation to the church, which may then excommunicate the sinner (Matt. 18:15–17). The church has the power of "binding and loosing," which is the power to determine what is forbidden and what is allowed (Matt. 16:18–19; 18:18).One illustration of church discipline in a case of gross immorality is found in 1 Corinthians 5:1–5. Paul instructs the assembly to hand the transgressor over to Satan for the destruction of the body in order that the spirit might be saved. This may refer to excommunication (if cast out of the church one is under the domain of Satan) or to a mortal illness invading the sinner's body. Either way, the goal is redemption more than punishment. The hope is that after being handed over to Satan, he will repent and return to the fold, or at the very least, that his spirit will go to heaven in spite of his body's death. Another illustration may be Ananias and Sapphira. Although God seems to have struck them dead, it was while Peter was presiding and executing judgment as God's representative (Acts 5:1–11).

Eternal Punishment. The Old Testament introduced the notion of eternal punishment in Daniel 12:2, indicating that the lost will also be resurrected, but for the purpose of eternal shame and contempt. While the worst punishment that earthly courts can inflict is death, Jesus taught his disciples not to fear those who can kill the body, but rather God, who can also cast people into hell (Luke 12:4–5). Isaiah 66:24 speaks of an undying worm and unquenchable fire—the same imagery Jesus uses to warn about hell (Mark 9:42–43, 47–48). Jesus also described it as "outer darkness," where people "weep and gnash their teeth" (Matt. 8:12). The Lord described eternal punishment for the wicked as well as eternal life for the righteous, showing that both are without end (Matt. 25:46). The rest of the New Testament is in agreement (2 Thess. 1:9; Rev. 20:10–15). Just as that Bible utilizes earthly things to symbolize heavenly bliss, so the description of hell as fire may be metaphorical for torment. However, the torment of hell is as real as the joy of heaven, even if our pictures of the two are less than perfect.

WILLIAM B. NELSON, JR.

See also ETERNAL PUNISHMENT; JUDGMENT; TEN COMMANDMENTS.

Bibliography. W. Eichrodt, *Theology of the Old Testament;* G. E. Ladd, *A Theology of the New Testament.*

Purchase. *See* REDEEM, REDEMPTION.

Purification. *See* CLEAN, UNCLEAN.

Purity (Heb. *niqqāyōn*; Gk. *hagneia*). ***The Old Testament.*** In the Old Testament, the basic sense of the Hebrew word for purity is probably an emptying out or being clean. The verb appears about forty times, most occurrences with an ethical, moral, or forensic sense. Purity is opposed to being guilty. It stands over against such conduct or attitudes as unfaithfulness to God's covenant (Hos. 8:1), rebellion against God's law (v. 1), and idolatry (vv. 4–6, 11). Purity consists of "clean hands" (Gen. 20:5), innocence (Pss. 26:6; 73:13), and an "empty stomach" (Amos 4:6).

Purity is related to guiltless, blameless, or innocent behavior. In Exodus 23:7, an innocent person is portrayed as someone who is righteous as measured by the demands of the law. Purity is not a cultic term; in fact, it does not appear in the rules for holiness detailed in Leviticus. Yet the idea of purity does surface in a number of instances. Before they can engage in any cultic or ceremonial activity, God's people must be consecrated or had to sanctify themselves (Exod. 19:10, 14; Josh. 7:13; 1 Sam. 16:5; Job 1:5).

The New Testament. In the New Testament, there is little emphasis on ritual purity. Rather, the focus is on moral purity or purification: chastity (2 Cor. 11:2; Titus 2:5); innocence in one's attitude toward members of the church (2 Cor. 7:11); and moral purity or uprightness (Phil. 4:8; 1 Tim. 5:22; 1 Peter 3:2; 1 John 1:3). Purity is associated with understanding, patience and kindness (2 Cor. 6:6); speech, life, love, and faith (1 Tim. 4:12); and reverence (1 Peter 3:2).

Paul as God's servant commended himself through his sufferings and his moral and spiritual qualities. His ministry was enhanced and accredited because of the kind of person he had shown himself to be. Paul encouraged Timothy to set an example in his lifestyle and his purity (1 Tim. 4:12), as well as in his relationships with other believers (5:2).

WALTER M. DUNNETT

Bibliography. H. Baltensweiler, *NIDNTT,* 3:100–102; H. Balz, *EDNT,* 1:22–23; F. Hauck, *TDNT,* 1:122; F. Danker, *II Corinthians.*

Purpose. (Heb. *yāʿaṣ*; Gk. *boulē*). ***The Old Testament.*** The verbal root of the Hebrew word for purpose means to give counsel, deliberate, purpose, or determine. In five passages where the noun appears, four refer to God's purpose and one to the purpose of a person's heart (Prov. 19:21; 20:5; Isa. 46:10–11; Jer. 32:19). God's plans stand firm forever (Ps. 33:11); his purpose will stand (Isa. 46:10). What God intends, what he has in mind, what he purposes and plans, what he pleases—these together give the basis for a theology of history. God stands in the center of history as One who acts. He has a goal in what he does. Nothing can thwart his plan. His purpose is consistently related to what he does in the world.

Two key passages in Isaiah reveal how God will carry out his purpose to deliver his people from darkness and oppression. Isaiah 9:6 refers to the "Wonderful Counselor" who will reign on David's throne and administer justice and righteousness forever. Isaiah 11:2 refers to the stump of Jesse who will be given "the Spirit of counsel and of power."

The New Testament. While David served God's purpose as ruler over Israel (Acts 13:36), the Pharisees and legal experts reject God's purpose for them and refuse to submit to John's baptism (Luke 7:30).

It was by God's set purpose and foreknowledge that Jesus was handed over to death at the hands of wicked people (Acts 2:23). His power and will decided that critical, necessary salvific event beforehand (4:28).

A key passage is Epheisans 1:9–11. Paul explains that God works out everything—brings all things under Christ—in conformity with the purpose of his will. The whole economy of God is linked with his purpose.

Paul understands that the believer's part in the people of God is not an accident or random phenomenon, but part of the divine purpose from the very beginning of time (Rom. 8:28–29). God's purpose is specifically characterized by the words "foreknew" and "predestined."

The good pleasure that God purposed in Christ has now been put into effect and will be seen in its completion when he sums up all things in Christ. In the meantime, however, God has called his people to live a holy life because of his own purpose and grace—a grace given before the beginning of time in Christ Jesus, but now revealed in the Savior's appearing.

WALTER M. DUNNETT

See also FOREKNOWLEDGE; PREDESTINATION.

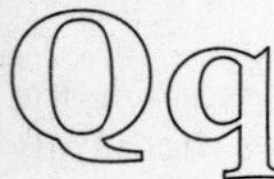

Queen of Heaven. *See* GODS AND GODDESSES, PAGAN.

Rr

Ransom. *See* REDEEM, REDEMPTION.

Reason. *See* MIND/REASON.

Rebirth. *See* NEW BIRTH.

Reconciliation. Reconciliation comes from the Greek family of words that has its roots in *allassō*. The meaning common to this word group is "change" or "exchange." Reconciliation involves a change in the relationship between God and man or man and man. It assumes there has been a breakdown in the relationship, but now there has been a change from a state of enmity and fragmentation to one of harmony and fellowship. In Romans 5:6–11, Paul says that before reconciliation we were powerless, ungodly, sinners, and enemies; we were under God's wrath (v. 9). Because of change or reconciliation we become new creatures. "Therefore, if anyone is in Christ, he is a new creation; the old has gone, the new has come!" (2 Cor. 5:17).

Reconciliation has to do with the relationships between God and man or man and man. God reconciles the world to himself (2 Cor. 5:18). Reconciliation takes place through the cross of Christ or the death of Christ. Second Corinthians 5:18 says that "God . . . reconciled us to himself through Christ." God reconciles us to himself through the death of his Son (Rom. 5:1). Thus, we are no longer enemies, ungodly, sinners, or powerless. Instead, the love of God has been poured out in our hearts through the Holy Spirit whom he has given to us (Rom. 5:5). It is a change in the total state of our lives.

Reconciliation is the *objective* work of God through Christ (2 Cor. 5:19). But it is also a *subjective* relationship: "Be reconciled to God" (2 Cor. 5:20). Thus, it is Christ through the cross who has made reconciliation possible, for "God made him . . . to be sin for us" (2 Cor. 5:21).

Reconciliation is also related to justification. God has reconciled the world, not counting people's sins against them. It is related to justification in Romans 5. We have been justified through faith (v. 1) by his blood (v. 9).

Reconciliation is also subjective in that the sinner is spoken of as being reconciled. It is a relationship that comes between man and wife as well as Jew and Gentile. If a person is about to offer a gift at the altar and remembers that he has something against his brother he should leave his gift and be reconciled first to his brother and then come and offer his gift. Reconciliation is something done by the one who offers it; it is not just something that happens to the estranged people. It is the cross of Christ that reconciles both Jew and Gentile. They are brought near by the blood of Christ. Because of this, Jew and Gentile have access to the Father by one spirit. They are no longer foreigners and aliens but fellow citizens with God and members of the same household (Eph. 2:11–22). Gentile and Jewish believers are reconciled to God and the middle wall of partition is broken down; both are brought near by the blood of Christ. They are all built on the foundation of the apostles and prophets with Christ as the Chief Cornerstone. This is made possible by the cross of Christ, but only appropriated when we make the cross and the death of Christ applicable to our life or our relationships.

This message of reconciliation or salvation that has come from God through Christ has been passed on to us. "God . . . gave us the ministry of reconciliation" (2 Cor. 5:18); "he has committed to us the message of reconciliation" (v. 19). The ultimate aim is that we are not only justified, but that we might become the righteousness of God (v. 21).

The whole message of reconciliation is centered around the love of God and the death of Christ. Paul reminds us that "God demonstrates his own love for us in this: While we were still sinners, Christ died for us" (Rom. 5:8). This brings peace with God, access to God through Christ, rejoicing in the hope of the glory of God, making us rejoice in suffering, and having the love of God poured out in our hearts through the

Holy Spirit (Rom. 5:1–5). We rejoice in God through our Lord Jesus Christ, through whom we have now received reconciliation (Rom. 5:11).

WILLIAM J. WOODRUFF

See also FAITH; JUSTIFICATION; REDEEM, REDEMPTION; SALVATION.

Bibliography. D. M. Baillie, *God Was in Christ;* J. Denney, *The Christian Doctrine of Reconciliation;* R. Martin, *Reconciliation;* L. Morris, *The Apostolic Preaching of the Cross;* V. Taylor, *The Atonement in New Testament Teaching.*

Redeem, Redemption. Finding its context in the social, legal, and religious customs of the ancient world, the metaphor of redemption includes the ideas of loosing from a bond, setting free from captivity or slavery, buying back something lost or sold, exchanging something in one's possession for something possessed by another, and ransoming.

The Old Testament. In the Old Testament, redemption involves deliverance from bondage based on the payment of a price by a redeemer. The Hebrew root words used most often for the concept of redemption are *pādâ, gāʾal,* and *kāpar.*

The verb *pādâ* is a legal term concerning the substitution required for the person or animal delivered. *Pādâ* is also used in relation to legislation with regard to the firstborn. Every firstborn male, whether human or animal, belonged to Yahweh, and hence was to be offered to Yahweh. The firstborn males of ritually clean animals were sacrificed, while firstborn unclean animals were redeemed (Exod. 13:13; 34:20; Num. 18:15–16). Human firstborn were also redeemed, either by the substitution of an animal or by the payment of a fixed sum (Num. 18:16). The Levites are also said to be a ransom for the firstborn of Israel (Num. 3:44–45). Money was sometimes paid to deliver a person from death (Exod. 21:30; Num. 3:46–51; 18:16; cf. Ps. 49:7–9).

The verb *gāʾal* is a legal term for the deliverance of some person, property, or right to which one had a previous claim through family relation or possession. *Gôʾēl,* the participle of *gāʾal,* is the term for the person who performed the duties of "redeemer." This term is found eighteen times in the Old Testament (13 times in Isaiah). It was the duty of a man's redeemer, usually his next of kin, to buy back the freedom that he had lost (e.g., through debt). An example of such "redemption" is found in Leviticus 25:47–49, where an Israelite who has had to sell himself into slavery because of poverty may be redeemed by a kinsman or by himself. Property sold under similar conditions could likewise be redeemed, thus keeping it within the family (Lev. 25:24–25; Ruth 4:1–6; Jer. 32:6–9).

The meaning of the third verb, *kāpar,* is to cover. To cover sin, atone, or make expiation are associated meanings. The substantive *kōper* (ransom) is of interest in that it signifies a price paid for a life that has become forfeit (Exod. 21:30; 30:11–16).

As one who delivers his people, Yahweh is called Israel's "Redeemer," especially in Isaiah where "redemption" is a key metaphor (41:14; 43:1; 44:6; 47:4). The paradigm of Yahweh's redemptive activity in the Old Testament is the historical deliverance of Israel from Egyptian bondage, but the metaphor of redemption was also utilized by the prophets in relation to the Babylonian captivity.

Although most often found in relation to the redemption of God's people, the concept of redemption was also applied to individuals in distress (Gen. 48:16; 2 Sam. 4:9; Job 19:25; Pss. 26:11; 49:15; 69:18; 103:4). The redemptive activity of God is most often described in terms of physical deliverance, but these redemptive acts are not devoid of spiritual significance. There is only one explicit Old Testament reference to redemption from sin (Ps. 130:8), the emphasis falling in the majority of references on God's deliverance from the results of sin.

The New Testament. By the first century A.D. the concept of redemption had become eschatological. Redemption of Israel from Egypt was but the foreshadowing in history of the great act of deliverance by which history would be brought to an end. In rabbinic expectation the Messiah would be the Redeemer of Israel, and the great Day of the Lord would be the day of redemption. It is possibly due to the nationalistic expectation that became attached to the concept of the coming Messiah-Redeemer that Jesus is never called "redeemer" (*lytrōtēs*) in the New Testament.

Fundamental to the message of the New Testament is the announcement that Jesus of Nazareth is the fulfillment of Israel's messianic hope and that, in him, the long-awaited redemption has arrived. Deliverance of humankind from its state of alienation from God has been accomplished through the death and resurrection of Christ (Rom. 4:25; 2 Cor. 5:18–19). In the New Testament, redemption requires the payment of a price, but the plight that requires such a ransom is moral not material. Humankind is held in the captivity of sin from which only the atoning death of Jesus Christ can liberate.

Although the concept of redemption is central to the New Testament, the occurrence of redemption terminology is relatively limited. When reflecting on the work of Jesus Christ, New Testament writers more frequently utilize different images (e.g., atonement, sacrifice, justification). The concept of redemption is nevertheless conveyed in the New Testament by the *agorazō* and *lyō* word groups. These terms have in mind the context of a marketplace transaction with reference to the purchase of goods or the releasing of slaves. In using these words, New Testament writers sought to represent Jesus' saving activity in terms that convey deliverance from bondage. Most of these words infer deliverance from captivity by means of a ransom price paid. The noun "ransom" (*lytron*), however, only appears in three locations in the New Testament (Matt. 20:28; Mark 10:45; 1 Tim. 2:6). Redemption language is merged with substitutionary language in these verses and applied to Jesus' death. Pauline usage of the noun "redemption" (*apolytrōsis*) is limited and generally conveys the meaning of deliverance (Rom. 3:24; 8:23; 1 Cor. 1:30; Eph. 1:14; 4:30), although substitutionary meaning is evident in Ephesians 1:7, where Christ's blood is depicted as the means of redemption.

Jesus conceived his mission to be that of the Son of Man, who came to offer himself in obedience to God's redemptive plan. He applied to himself the things said in the Old Testament of the Servant of the Lord concerning his rejection, humiliation, death, and resurrection (Mark 8:31; 9:31; 10:33–34). Likewise, New Testament writers apply to him the Servant texts and terminology from the Old Testament (e.g., Matt. 8:17; 12:18; Acts 4:27, 30; 8:32–33; Rom. 15:21; 1 Peter 2:22–25). An important text with regard to Jesus' understanding of his redemptive work is Mark 10:45, in which Jesus declares that his mission not only includes self-sacrificial service, but also involves giving his life as a "ransom" for many. Thus, Christ's death is portrayed as the payment price for the deliverance of those held captive by Satan (the ransom metaphor must be understood in the light of Jesus' offering of himself in obedience to the Father, however, and not interpreted as a payment to Satan). As the means of redemption, the death of Jesus provides a deliverance that involves not only forgiveness of sin (Eph. 1:7; Col. 1:14), but also newness of life (Rom. 6:4). Even though Christ's redemptive work is perfect (Heb. 9:25–28), the redemption of the believer will not be complete until the return of Christ (Luke 21:28; Rom. 8:23; Eph. 4:30).

The central theme of redemption in Scripture is that God has taken the initiative to act compassionately on behalf of those who are powerless to help themselves. The New Testament makes clear that divine redemption includes God's identification with humanity in its plight, and the securing of liberation of humankind through the obedience, suffering, death, and resurrection of the incarnate Son. R. DAVID RIGHTMIRE

See also DEATH OF CHRIST; REVELATION, IDEA OF; SALVATION.

Bibliography. C. Brown, et al., *NIDNTT,* 3:177–223; F. Büchsel, *TDNT,* 4:328–56; I. H. Marshall, *Reconciliation and Hope,* pp. 153–69; L. Morris, *The Apostolic Preaching of the Cross;* J. Murray, *Redemption: Accomplished and Applied;* H. E. W. Turner, *The Patristic Doctrine of Redemption;* V. Taylor, *The Atonement in New Testament Preaching;* W. Pannenberg, *Basic Questions in Theology,* 1:15–80; B. B. Warfield, *The Person and Work of Christ.*

Refreshing, Times of. The stunned amazement of the people at the temple who saw a crippled beggar healed in the name of Jesus Christ of Nazareth (Acts 3:10–11) prompted Peter to deliver a two-part sermon in which he traced the source of the miracle to the power of Jesus (vv. 12–16) and acknowledged that the people had acted in ignorance when they killed God's Messiah (vv. 17–26). Included in the second part of the sermon is the invitation to repent/turn to God so that their sins might be wiped out and times of refreshing might come from the presence of the Lord.

The link between repentance and the forgiveness of sins is also included in Peter's first sermon (Acts 2:38a), but there the gift of the Holy Spirit is the promised result (v. 38b). That the plural times of refreshing (*kairoi anapsyxeōs*) includes the gift of the Holy Spirit and is also a broader eschatological term, is suggested by Peter's additional assertion that the Messiah will only return after these times of refreshing have come (3:20). But that this is different from events following the second advent is made clear by Peter's followup reference to it as a time of universal restoration (*chronoi apokatastaseōs,* 3:21).

While the phrase "times of refreshing" occurs only here in the New Testament, the noun "times" (*kairoi*) is used by Jesus with periods/dates (*chronoi*) in Acts 1:7 to refer to special areas of his Father's authority in relation to restoring the kingdom to Israel and the responsibility of the disciples to witness in the power of the Holy Spirit to all peoples. The root meaning of refreshing (i.e., cool by blowing), when linked to the derived meaning of strengthening, can then be interpreted as a definitive age of salvation that comes as a result of repentance and the forgiveness of sins. This age, with its potential for change and renewal, is thus seen as a fulfillment of the promises of the prophets as to what will happen when people experience the presence of God, and a precursor of the final event when God makes all things new. HERBERT L. SWARTZ

See also AGE, AGES; KINGDOM OF GOD; RESTORE, RENEW; SECOND COMING OF CHRIST.

Regeneration. *See* NEW BIRTH.

Rejoice. *See* JOY.

Religion. Due to the wide range of its usage, the English word "religion" (from Lat. *religio*) is not easily defined. Most commonly, however, it refers to ways in which humans relate to the divine (a presence [or plurality of such] or force [sometimes construed as plural] behind, beyond, or pervading sensible reality that conditions but is not conditioned by that reality). All such "ways" include a system of beliefs about the divine and how it is related to the world. Most also involve an attitude of awe toward the divine, and a pattern of actions (rituals and an ethical code). By extension, "religion" is often used to refer to systems of belief and related practices that play an analogous role in people's lives (e.g., Buddhism, Confucianism, and even humanism). The word is, thus, an abstract term adaptable to a great variety of referents.

Neither the Hebrew nor the Aramaic languages of the Old Testament have a word with a corresponding semantic field. For that reason, one does not find "religion" or "religious" in most English versions of these Scriptures. English translators of the New Testament do use these words at times to render various forms of three Greek terms: *deisidaimonia, thrēskeia,* and *eusebeia.* Yet all three words also fail to fully capture the import of the more abstract English "religion."

Both Old and New Testaments speak pervasively about matters "religious." Every word in these writings is in one way or another focused on the Creator-creature relationship. Every line revolves around that thematic center of gravity: how the Creator relates to his creation, especially humanity, and how humanity does and/or ought to relate to the Creator. In fact, every line of Scripture seeks to evoke from the reader right ways of relating to the Creator. In that sense, "religion" is pervasively the theme of Scripture.

To be sure, the Bible speaks of all creatures, resounding to God: they do his bidding (angels, Ps. 103:20; Heb. 1:14; storm winds, Pss. 104:4; 148:8) and they rejoice before him with songs of joy and praise (Job 38:7; Pss. 89:12; 96:11–13; 98:7–9; Isa. 44:23; 49:13; 55:12; see especially Pss. 103:22; 145:10; 148). But the concern of the biblical texts is to promote among humankind right beliefs about God, right attitudes toward God, and right conduct before the face of God. Biblically, religion has to do with *human* responses to the Creator.

That religion has a place in human life springs from two fundamental realities: (1) humans have been created in the image of God (Gen. 1:26–27; 9:6; Ps. 8:5; 1 Cor. 11:7; Col. 3:10; James 3:9), and so are both addressable by God and capable of responses appropriate to persons (beliefs, attitudes, and conduct that is consciously chosen); and (2) the Creator has disclosed himself to humankind and continues to address them. The whole visible world proclaims that its Creator has been and still is at work. It reflects his power, wisdom, righteousness, glory, and goodness (Pss. 19:1–4; 29:3–9; 97:6; Isa. 40:12–14, 21–22, 26, 28; Acts 14:17; 17:24–29; Rom. 1:19–20). What Psalm 104 makes its central theme is elsewhere many times assumed or hinted: that the secure order of creation, sustaining as it does a profusion of life, is the visible glory-robe of the invisible Creator (see esp. vv. 1–2). So the creation itself is theophanous—and not just here and there in special "holy" places. The visible creation is itself the primal temple of God not built by human hands, where his "power and glory" are ever on display (Pss. 29:3–9; 63:2).

Nor are the effects of the Creator's actions in and on the creation discernible only in what is commonly referred to as "nature." God is equally engaged in the arena of human affairs. So, for example, he knows both the external acts of all human beings and the secrets of every human heart. And he deals with persons accordingly. He even intersects the flow of human affairs at their fountainhead, as the teachers of Yahwistic wisdom summed it up for ancient Israel: "In his heart a man plans his course, but the Lord determines his steps" (Prov. 16:9); "The king's heart is in the hand of the Lord; he directs it like a watercourse wherever he pleases" (Prov. 21:1); "Many are the plans in a man's heart, but it is the Lord's purpose that prevails" (Prov. 19:21; cf. Isa. 10:6–7).

The arenas of such divine intersection extend from individual lives to the rise and fall of empires. God appoints nations their place and establishes their boundaries (Deut. 32:8; Amos 9:7). He makes them great, and destroys them (Job 12:23). He summons international armies to be "the weapons of his wrath" against an arrogant empire (Isa. 13:4–5; Jer. 50–51; Ezek. 30:25). To serve his historical purposes, God calls Assyria "the rod of my anger . . . , the club of my wrath" (Isa. 10:5), Nebuchadnezzar "my servant" (Jer. 25:9), and Cyrus "my shepherd" to "accomplish all that I plan" (Isa. 44:28).

Ancient peoples believed that the gods intersected human affairs, determining the outcome of battles and the fortunes of kingdoms. Hence, in the rise and fall of kingdoms and empires the peoples of ancient Israel's world assumed that they experienced the workings of the gods. In that environment, Yahweh's sovereign control over the fortunes of nations, kings, and peoples (especially their downfall) humbled human arrogance (Gen. 11:1–9; Ps. 9:20; Isa. 31:3; Ezek. 28:2), exposed the powerlessness of the gods that humans made to fill the void left by their "forgetting" the Creator (Pss. 96:5; 115:4–7; 135:15–18; Isa. 44:9–20; 46:1–7), and testified to the sole rule of Yahweh (Exod. 9:16; 14:17–18; Ps. 106:8; Ezek. 25:11, 17; 26:6; 28:22–24; 29:6, 9, 21; 30:8, 19, 25–26; 32:15; 35:15). Paul pointed to this divine disclosure in history when he said to the Greek intelligentsia, "From one man he made every nation of men, that they should inhabit the whole earth; and he determined the times set for them and the exact places where they should live. God did this so that men would seek him and perhaps reach out for him and find him, though he is not far from each one of us. For in him we live and move and have our being" (Acts 17:26–28).

So, according to the Bible, humankind is addressed by God through every component, process, and event in so-called nature and through every event, big and small, that makes up human history. Human beings live and move and have their being within the arena of God's creation. And through God's pervasive engagement with his creation as he sustains and governs it, they are always and everywhere confronted with the display of his power and glory. Wherever humans turn and by whatever means they experience the creation, the Creator calls to them for recognition and response. From this perspective, *all* human life is inherently "religious."

In two other ways "religion" (humankind's ways of relating to the divine) encompasses the whole of human life. First, humans are created in God's image to be his stewards of the creation—as vocation, not avocation (Gen. 1:26–27; 2:15; Ps. 8:6-8). In *whatever ways* they act on the creation they do so as faithful or unfaithful stewards of God's handiwork. Second, humans live and prosper in all they undertake only by God's gifts and blessings (Gen. 1:28–29; 9:1–3; Deut. 7:13; Pss. 34:8–10; 127; Hos. 2:8–9). Thus in *everything* humans have to do with God.

But a breach has brought alienation between the Creator and humankind. Humanity has claimed autonomy as the implication of human freedom to make moral choices (Gen. 3:5–6) and self-sufficiency as the implication of humankind's power to "rule" and "subdue" God's earthly creatures (Gen. 4:19–24; 11:3–4). As Job said of the "wicked": "They say to God, 'Leave us alone! We have no desire to know your ways. Who is the Almighty, that we should serve him? What would we gain by praying to him?'" (21:14–15). They lean on their own understanding (Prov. 3:5), being wise in their own eyes (Prov. 3:7; 26:5, 12; Isa. 5:21). In a very real sense, as Habakkuk (1:11) wrote of the Babylonians, they have become people whose own strength is their god.

Still, this alienation from the Creator has left a void at the center—and there are obviously powers in the world not subject to human control that impinge on human existence and radically relativize humanity's self-sufficiency. So people have conceived of many gods, composed mythologies expressing what is believed about them, and devised ways to worship and appeal to them. Religion has broken up into many religions. Yet these have all been responses to the inescapable manifestations of the Creator's glory in the creation and the pervasive experience of humanity's existence being conditioned by a power or powers other than its own (Rom. 1:21–23).

This radical breach and its massive consequences have occasioned a second work of God, a work that rivals the first in its disclosure of the Creator's glory. Not willing to let the alienation stand or to yield his glory to other gods (Isa. 42:8; 48:11), the Creator has undertaken to effect reconciliation. It is with this mission of God to his world that the Bible is centrally concerned. It bears witness to God's "mighty acts" of redemption in the history of Israel, and to the culmination of those acts in the earthly ministry and heavenly reign of Jesus Christ. By this invasion of the alienated world with its many gods (2 Kings 17:29–33; Jer. 2:28; 1 Cor. 8:5), the Creator calls all peoples of the world to turn from the sham gods they have made and return to him. Only as people rightly relate to him, "the true God" (Jer. 10:10; cf. 1 John 5:20), can their religion be "true."

What, then, constitutes the religion that God accepts as pure and faultless?

First, it believes the testimony of the spirit of God contained in the Scriptures of the Old and New Testaments that arose in conjunction with God's saving acts in Israel's history and culminated in Jesus Christ.

Second, it is filled with reverent awe before the majesty of the One who discloses himself in creation, history, and redemption. It bows in humble repentance before the Holy One for the alienation that turned to other gods and corrupted the "heart" from which springs every belief, attitude, and action. It receives in faith the grace of God offered in Jesus Christ. And in gratitude it dedicates the whole of self to the service of the Creator-Redeemer.

Third, certain activities or life expressions fall within its sphere: worship, prayer, and praise, both private and communal, and proclamation—telling the story of what the one true God has done (Isa. 43:10, 12; 44:8; Matt. 28:18–20; Acts 1:8). But to Israel God gave directives for more than cultic worship. *All* of Israel's life was to be brought into accordance with the will of the Creator, whose concern about his whole creation remained undiminished. And because no listing of do's and don'ts could be adequate in themselves, an all-encompassing commandment had to be appended: "Hear, O Israel, the Lord our God, the Lord is one. Love the Lord your God with all your heart and with all your soul and with all your mind and with all your strength [power and resources] . . . [and] love your neighbor as yourself" (Mark 12:29–31 and parallels; cf. Lev. 19:18, 34; Deut. 6:4–5; John 13:34; Rom. 13:9; Gal. 5:14; James 2:8).

In biblical perspective, no human activity is any less "religious" (how humans relate to God) than worship, prayer, and praise. For that reason the apostle Paul instructed the church at Corinth, "So whether you eat or drink or whatever you do, do it all for the glory of God" (1 Cor. 10:31). And for that reason James wrote, "Religion that God our Father accepts as pure and faultless is this: to look after orphans and widows in their distress and to keep oneself from being polluted by the world" (1:27). JOHN H. STEK

See also GOD; PROVIDENCE OF GOD; WORSHIP.

Bibliography. R. A. Clouse, *The Myth of Religious Neutrality: An Essay on the Hidden Role of Religious Belief in Theories*; R. Otto, *The Idea of the Holy*; J. Wach, *The Comparative Study of Religion.*

Remember, Remembrance. To remember is a normal part of the activity of the human mind. When, however, God is the One who is remembered in prayer and ritual, or, when it is believed by the faithful that God himself is actually remembering his own relation to his people, then "to remember" with its appropriate nouns becomes a special verb in the religious vocabulary of Israel and the church of God.

The Old Testament. Yahweh is bound to his elect people, Israel, by his covenant and thus there is a unique relation between the two covenant partners. Not only does Israel remember Yahweh, but Yahweh actually remembers his relation to his people. The primary verb is *zākar.*

God remembers. On at least ten occasions, Yahweh is said to remember his covenantal relation with Israel (Lev. 26:45; Pss. 105:8; 106:45; 111:5). He also remembers his covenant with Noah (Gen. 9:15). God also rememers the actual occasion of the making of his covenant(s) (Exod. 32:13; Deut. 9:27; 2 Chron. 6:42). "I will remember my covenant with Jacob . . . and my covenant with Abraham" (Lev. 26:42). The call for God to remember his unique relation to Israel does not mean that God always remembers to bless, for in his justice he will also punish (Jer. 14:10; Hos. 7:2; 8:13; 9:9). For God not to remember human sin is for God to forgive (Ps. 25:7; Jer. 31:34).

Israel remembers. The Book of Deuteronomy is rich in its call to remember the words and deeds of God. The exodus or deliverance of Israel by Yahweh from Egypt is central to this remembering (see 5:15; 15:15; 16:3, 12; 24:18, 22; and cf. 7:18; 8:2, 18; 9:7). The prophet Ezekiel also speaks of God's deeds in the past in order to bring right thinking and behavior into the present life of Judah (6:9; 16:22, 43, 60–63; 20:43; 36:31). Further, Isaiah recalls and portrays God remembering how he delivered his people in earlier times, in the days of old, of Moses his servant (63:11–14). Within the Psalter the call to remember is a central motif. Yet Israel, when they were in Egypt, did not consider God's wonderful works or remember the abundance of is steadfast love (106:7). Finally, there is the actual remembering of God as God, that is God according to his character (Pss. 42:6–7; 119:55; Isa. 46:8; Jer. 20:9).

Memory. The noun *zēkher* is used of God, who has his own memory or remembrance because of the way he reveals his name YHWH. Thus, s the name of God is praised, so is his memory (Pss. 30:4–5; 97:12; 111:4; 145:7).

Memorial. The noun *zikkārôn* is used of a sign that causes or evokes remembrance; such a memorial can cause either God or man to remember (see Exod. 12:1–20; 13:9; Num. 17:3, 5). For example, after the crossing of the Jordan twelve stones were set up by Joshua in obedience to God as a memorial (Josh. 4:3, 7). The festival on the first day of the seventh month is a memorial, proclaimed with trumpets (Lev. 23:24; cf. Num. 10:9). And the breastplate of the high priest likewise is a memorial (Exod. 28:12, 29; 39:7).

The question arises, When believers remember the deeds of God and when God remembers his relation to Israel what kind of remembering is in view? Is it merely recollection of information about the past? Or is it remembering the past in such a way that the facts remembered have some impact on the present? As a minimum, this remembering within the Old Covenant would seem to imply that the God who performed the past mighty deeds, which are remembered, is the God who is present with his people as he or they remember those deeds. And he is present as the same, living God, bound to them in election and covenant as he was to their ancestors in days past, for he is Yahweh, "I am who I am."

The New Testament. The verb "to remember" (*mnēmoneuō*) is used on several occasions in its ordinary secular meaning to instill or teach moral or theological lessons. For example, Jesus asked the disciples if they remembered the five loaves for the five thousand in order to encourage faith (Matt. 16:9; Mark 8:18). And Peter remembered Jesus' prediction and was suitably ashamed of himself (Matt. 26:75). Further, in the parable of the rich man and Lazarus, Abraham says to the rich man "Remember that in your lifetime you received your good things" (Luke 16:25). The thief on the cross asked Jesus to remember him unto salvation (Luke 23:42). Paul urged the Gentile churches to remember the poor Christians in Jerusalem by making an appropriate collection for them (Gal. 2:10).

The act of remembering persons from the history of Israel has a positive use in strengthening faith or issuing a timely warning (Luke 17:32). Remembering the courage and blamelessness of the apostles (Acts 20:31; 1 Thess. 2:9) or the good works within a congregation (1 Thess. 1:3) also functions as encouragement in the Christian life. In contrast, remembering in terms of keeping someone in mind to pray and to care for them is also present (e.g., Gal. 2:10; Col. 4:18).

Old Testament themes are obvious in Mary's Magnificat and Zechariah's Benedictus. Mary said, "[God] has helped his servant Israel, remembering to be merciful" (Luke 1:54); and Zechariah blessed God and recalled how God would perform the mercy promised to our fathers, remembering his holy covenant (Luke 1:72). Such themes are also prominent in the exhortation to remember the predictions of the holy prophets and the commandment of the Lord (2 Peter 3:2; cf. 1:12–15).

In fact, the theological meaning of remembrance that builds on the Old Testament is clear in about one-third of the occurrences in the New Testament. For example, there is a remembering in prayer before God. This can be in the form of effectual intercession (1 Thess. 1:2–3) or as a specific, effective memorial (Acts 10:4). The Holy Spirit, the Paraclete, assists in recalling the message of Jesus (John 14:26; 15:20, 26; 16:4).

The most discussed, and possibly the most important use of the theme of memory, is related to the Last Supper. Both in the account of Luke (22:19) and of Paul (1 Cor. 11:24) we read, "Do this in remembrance of me . . ." The Greek noun is *anamnēsis.* Luke connects the command with the word over the bread and Paul with both the word over the bread and the word over the cup. What is intended by this word? Obviously any explanation must be sensitive to the meaning of *zkr* in the Old Testament and in Judaism, which points to making present the past, so that it can be effective in the present.

Not a few modern liturgists insist that the eucharistic memorial or remembrance is an objective act in and by which the person and event commemorated is made present or brought into the here and the now. So for the early Fathers it is the recalling before the Father of the one and once for all, as well as utterly complete, sacrifice of his Son, Jesus Christ, in order that its power and efficacy will be known and operative within the Eucharist and thus received by those present.

In contrast to this it has been argued that the meaning is "that God may remember me"—Jesus asks the disciples to petition the Father to remember Jesus and come to his rescue. Also, it has been suggested that to remember is to proclaim and so in the celebration of the Supper the church proclaims Jesus who died for us. The further suggestion that the remembering is merely to meditate on the past death and future coming of Jesus, the Lord, seems to be inadequate because it does not emphasize that he who is remembered is very much present at the memorial/remembrance.

The word *anamnēsis* also occurs in Hebrews 10:3, "those sacrifices [of the temple] are an annual reminder of sin." that is, the sacrifices of the law do not produce a full purification from sin but only serve to be a reminder of the reality of sin.

The word *mnēmosunon,* meaning memory or memorial, occurs in the significant story of the woman who anointed Jesus (Mark 14:3–9). Of her Jesus said, "Wherever the gospel is preached throughout the world, what she has done will also be told, in memory of her" (v. 9). We know that the dead body of Jesus was never anointed. Thus this anointing with expensive ointment some two days before his death points forward not only to his death but also to his resurrection. The woman anointed not his feet but his head and in so doing did what the high priest should have done when Jesus was before him on trial—anoint him as the King! PETER TOON

See also LORD'S SUPPER, THE.

Bibliography. B. S. Childs, *Memory and Tradition in Israel;* J. Jeremias, *The Eucharistic Words of Jesus.*

Remnant. Leftovers or remainders, whether of daily food (Ruth 2:14, 18), food at the Passover (Lev. 7:16, 18), anointing oil (Lev. 14:17), or even and especially people who survive a major disaster. A remnant of people is what is left of a community following a catastrophe (e.g., Noah's family after the flood, Gen. 6:5–8:22; Lot's family after the burning of Sodom and Gomorrah, Gen. 19; those who remained in the land after the deportations of 597 B.C., Ezra 9:8; Jer. 24:8; 52:15; those left behind under Gedaliah, Jer. 40:6, 11, 15; or the Jews who came out of exile Ezra 9:8, 13; Zech. 8:6, 11–12). Terms for remnant in the Old Testament derive from six roots and occur some 540 times (forms of Heb. *šʾr, ytr, plt, śrd*; Gk., *leimma, hypoleimma, loipos, kataloipos*). Remnant, frequently in the sense of residue or refugee, takes on theological hues when it becomes the object of God's address and/or action.

Sociologically the remnant could be described variously as refugees, a community subgroup, or a sect. Canonically one may find language of remnant in the Pentateuch, in historical books (e.g., of groups subjugated or not yet subjugated), in the prophets, and in the New Testament. Historically, an illustration of remnant are the seven thousand in Israel who in times of apostasy of the Ahab/Jezebel era had not defected from the Lord (1 Kings 19:9–18). Theologically, remnant language clusters in several Old Testament books, the authors of which lived at some hinge point in history: Isaiah (37:31–32) and Micah (4:7; 7:18) near the time of Israel's collapse; Jeremiah (11:23; 50:20) and Zephaniah (2:7–9) near the time of Judah's fall; and Paul near the time of the emergence of the church (Rom. 11:5). Remnant language is associated with both judgment and salvation.

Remnant and the Oracle of Judgment. The language of remnant in announcements of judgment was used to emphasize the totality of the judgment—whether of non-Israelites or Israelites—so that no trace, no remnant would in the end remain. Obadiah, whose book targets Edom, asserts, "There will be no survivors from the house of Esau" (v. 18). Damascus will become a ruinous heap, and the remnant of Syria will cease (Isa. 17:3). Most conclusive is the statement against Babylon, which combines the ideas of reputation (name) and remnant, perhaps as an idiom for total destruction: "I will cut off from Babylon her name and survivors (*sa'ar*)" (Isa. 14:22; cf. 2 Sam. 14:7). For Israel especially language of remnant was also invoked to disabuse any who might consider themselves exceptions to the predicted casualties. Should there be temporary survivors of a catastrophe, such as Nebuchadnezzar's siege, they would ultimately not be spared (Jer. 21:7). Such news of total destruction was evidence of God's determination to proceed in judgment, but the news was intended to persuade vacillating persons to spare their lives by defecting to the Babylonians (Jer. 21:8–9).

The name Shear-Jashub ("a remnant will return," Isa. 7:3), often thought to be seminal to the prophets' thought on remnant, is, even in context, ambiguous in meaning. Did the expression portend misfortune, or did it convey that all was not lost? The expression, "a remnant will return," when applied later to Israel, became, even if marginally, a message of hope (Isa. 10:20–23; cf. 37:31–32 = 2 Kings 19:30–31).

Remnant and Oracles of Salvation. Oracles of salvation may follow immediately on the heels of announcements of judgment, and paradoxically, both entail a remnant. In Amos 9 the destruction is said to be total (vv. 1–4, 10b); still there is a glimmer of hope: "I will not totally destroy the house of Jacob" (v. 8b). One frequent proposal at reconciling these opposites is to resort to the theory of editorial splicing, which softens the severity of the message but does not deal with the theological dissonance. A more acceptable answer takes God's justice into account. God will destroy the sinful kingdom—not a territory, but the aggregate of wicked leaders. All these shall perish. But not all the populace is equally guilty, and while the pious do not escape the effects of the destruction, God in his justice spares them; they become the remnant. Paradigms for wholesale destruction in which some are nevertheless spared exist in the story of Noah's family in the flood and Lot's escape from Sodom.

Since acceptance with God is not based on merit, one dimension of remnant theology is its message of God's grace (Isa. 1:9; Amos 5:15). Judgment, whereby all is destroyed, is not the last word. Beyond judgment is God's readiness, because of his loyal love, to continue with his people. It is too mechanical to think of wrath and grace within God vying with each other for the upper hand, but given that hypothetical scenario, the message is that God's grace triumphs in the end.

The remnant is future-oriented. What prospects has the remnant that becomes, as in the exile, the carrier of God's promise? The prospect was for the exiles to be gathered together and to return to the homeland (Jer. 23:3; 31:7–9; Mic. 2:12–13; 4:6–7). The exodus from the exile, like the exodus from Egypt, was accompanied with miracles (Isa. 11:11–16). The solution to the tension between God's earlier unchangeable promise and Israel's sad history lies in the remnant. Those returning with Zerubbabel (Hag. 1:12, 14; Zech. 8:6, 11, 12) and those returning at the time of Ezra (Ezra 9:13–15) regarded themselves as that remnant. Isaiah had graphically depicted the Assyrian takeover with the image of God cutting down the tall trees and lopping off boughs with "terrifying power" (Isa. 10:28–34 NRSV). Equally graphic was to be the recovery as "the outcasts of Israel" and the "dispersed of Judah" would be gathered together. Also, there would emerge a shoot (remnant?) from the stump of Jesse (Isa. 11:1). Upon this shoot, customarily interpreted as the Messiah, rests the sevenfold spirit (vv. 2–3a) with the promise that he would rule in righteousness (v. 5). The eschatological picture of the cessation of all hostilities among humans and among animal leans on the existence of a remnant. In the prophet's mouth, remnant language for Israel is hope-engendering.

The remnant was the recipient of other promises: granting of pardon (Mic. 7:18–20); God's everlasting love (Jer. 31:2); taking root (2 Kings 19:30; cf. Isa. 37:31–32); removal of enemies and becoming established like a lion in the forest (Mic. 4:7–9); the Lord's promise to be a garland of glory for the remnant (Isa. 28:5–6); and a grant by God for the people to possess all things (Zech. 8:6).

The texts announcing salvation for the remnant raise the question of the relation of the remnant to its base group. Jeremiah addresses this question for his situation: God's future lay with those who had been taken to Babylon (the good figs), not with those who stayed in the land (the bad figs, Jer. 24). The Qumran community saw itself as the "remnant of thy people [Israel]" (1QM14.8–9; cf. CD 2.11). Paul clarified the relationship between the remnant, those who accepted the gospel, and the larger body of unbelieving Jews, by noting: (1) that the remnant represented the ongoing activity of God with the chosen people, "a remnant chosen by grace" (Rom. 11:5) since it is the spiritual Israel; (2) that the function of the Jewish remnant, to which are not attached the Gentile believers, is to serve as a vehicle of retrieval or recovery for the larger Jewish community; and (3) that the exclusion of the larger is for a limited time (Rom. 11:11–32).

One might ask, of course, how it is that God holds with the remnant, which is usually the small rather than the large body, the minority rather than the majority. Where is God's ultimate triumph? One answer is to examine the larger sweep of salvation history. The story of the primeval history was discontinued in favor of the election of Abram, a remnant, so to speak, from the larger group. Similarly the New Testament story discontinued the story of mainstream Israel and related the story of the faithful remnant. This remnant, however, received from Jesus a mission that was world-embracing (Matt. 28:18–20). The remnant was called to redemptive activity. The

Book of Revelation depicts, as does the primeval history, a great diversity of people, people now in God's presence. The remnant has accomplished God's purpose. Questions on the order of majority/minority may be misplaced. By God's measure, more on the order of righteousness, his triumph is not in doubt (Zeph. 3:11–13). The doctrine of the remnant is in part that failure of a larger body will not impair God's purposes.

Because the criterion is not ethnicity but righteousness, the Scripture applies "remnant" language to peoples other than Israel. In a pivotal text Amos speaks of a remnant of Edom, interpreted by James as referring to all humankind, which will come under the saving umbrella of David (Amos 9:12). Philistines, like Judah, are envisioned as a "remnant for our God."

ELMER A. MARTENS

See also CHURCH, THE; ISRAEL.

Bibliography. J. C. Campbell, *Scottish Journal of Theology* 3 (1950): 78–85; R. E. Clements, *Pauline Studies,* pp. 106–21; W. Guenther and H. Krienke, *NIDNTT,* 3:247–54; G. F. Hasel, *ISBE,* 4:130–34; E. W. Heaton, *JTS* 3 (1952): 27–39; V. Herntrich and G. Schrenk, *TDNT,* 4:194–214; B. F. Meyer, *JBL* 84 (1965): 123–30; J. Watts, *Perspectives in Religious Studies* 15 (1988): 109–29.

Repentance. The most common term in the Old Testament for repentance is *šûb*; the verbal forms appear well over 1,050 times, although translated "repent" only 13 times, and the substantive "repentance" occurs only once in the New International Version. More commonly the translation is "turn" or "return." A related term is *nāḥam,* which is translated three times as "repent" in the New International Version. In the New Testament, the most common verb is *metanoeō* (33 times) and the noun *metanoia* (20 times). A synonym *metamelomai* is once translated "repent" (Matt. 21:32).

Two requisites of repentance included in *šûb* are "to turn from evil, and to turn to the good." Most critical theologically is the idea of returning to God, or turning away from evil. If one turns away from God, apostasy is indicated. Three times Ezekiel included God's call to the people of Israel: "Repent! Turn from your idols and renounce all your detestable practices!" (14:6); "Repent! Turn away from all your offenses" (18:30); "Turn! Turn from your evil ways" (33:11). Such a call was characteristic of the prophets (see, e.g., Isa. 45:22; 55:7; Joel 2:12–13). The Septuagint underlines this idea by usually translating *šûb* by *epi(apo-)strephō* (to turn about, or to turn away from). To be abandoned are both evil intentions and evil deeds, and both motive and conduct are to be radically changed. A striking example is found in Isaiah 1:16–17: "Take your evil deeds out of my sight! Stop doing wrong, learn to do right! Seek justice, encourage the oppressed. Defend the cause of the fatherless, plead the case of the widow."

One may detect two sides to this turning/converting. There is the free sovereign act of God's mercy, and a conscious decision to turn to God (a turning that goes beyond sorrow and contrition).

Confession of sins is both commanded and frequently illustrated (e.g., in the penitential prayers, as Pss. 25 and 51). When one is guilty of various sins, "he must confess in what way he has sinned" in order to receive atonement and forgiveness (Lev. 5:5; 26:40–42). Thus, confession belongs to repentance, and is needed for divine forgiveness (cf. 1 John 1:9). A great prophecy/promise is given in the Book of Isaiah: "The Redeemer will come to Zion, to those in Jacob who repent of their sins" (59:20).

The two chief forms of repentance in the Old Testament were cultic and ritual (e.g., expressed in public ceremonies, fasting, various displays of sorrow, liturgies, or days of repentance), and the prophetic concept (e.g., people are to "return to the Lord"). The latter stresses a change in relation to God.

To repent and to convert involved obedience to God's revealed will, placing trust in him, turning away from all evil and ungodliness. Each person was to "turn from his wicked evil way" (Jer. 26:3; 36:3). Amos gave God's lament, that despite all he had done for or to the people, "yet you have not returned to me" (4:4, 8–11). Hosea anticipated the day when Israel "will return and seek the LORD their God and David their king" (3:5). Thus he pled with them to return to the Lord their God and to say, "Forgive all our sins and receive us graciously" (14:2b).

Included also in the Old Testament is the idea of "regretting" something. The Septuagint used *metamelomai* of the indecision of the people coming out of Egypt, that "they might change their minds and return to Egypt" (Exod. 13:17). Lady Wisdom warned against immorality by saying, "At the end of your life you will groan" (Prov. 5:11).

The use of the Hebrew word *nāḥam* often refers to God "repenting," along with human beings doing the same. The basic sense is "being sorry, or grieved" for something that has been done. Frequently God "relents" or "changes his dealings" with humans. God was "grieved" at human evil in the earth, resulting in the flood (Gen. 6:6–7); the Lord "relented" and turned away his threat of disaster (Exod. 32:14); he was "grieved" at having made Saul king, and deposed him (1 Sam. 15:11, 26). These descriptions may be regarded as anthropopathic, in which God exhibited emotional responses known to be present in humans also. Not infrequently God relented and withheld predicted judgment on Israel. An especially vivid illustration of this reversal is found in Hosea 11:8–9: "How can I give you up, Ephraim? . . . My heart is changed within me. . . .

I will not carry out my fierce anger." God's true love for Israel would triumph, and he would keep covenant with his people.

In the New Testament, the key term for repentance is *metanoia*. It has two usual senses: a "change of mind" and "regret/remorse."

In the Synoptic Gospels *metanoia* indicated "turning away from sin" (Mark 1:4), made imperative by the nearness of judgment (see Matt. 3:10, "already"), despite having Abraham as ancestor. John the Baptist called for a break with the old and a turning to God.

According to Matthew 3, John was not specific about "the fruits of repentance," except in his call for baptism with water. But the Lukan narrative includes the question of people, "What should we do then?" To the crowds, the tax collectors, and the soldiers, John spelled out specific ways in which the validity of their repentance should be demonstrated (Luke 3:10–14). Thus, *metanoia* was to be concretized by the baptism of repentance (Mark 1:4; Luke 3:3), and was to be evidenced by the changed attitudes and deeds of the respondents.

In both Mark (1:15) and Matthew (4:17) Jesus began his public proclamation with the call "Repent." Mark connects it with believing the good news; Matthew, with the nearness of the kingdom of heaven. While Luke does not include this initial call, he notes several strong calls for repentance in Jesus' teachings (see esp. 10:13; 11:32; 13:3, 5; 17:3–4). The Book of Acts often connects *metanoia* with remission of sins (see 2:38; 3:19; 5:31; 8:22; 26:18, 20). There are strong reminiscences here of John's proclamations, but one striking difference is in the audiences. While John addressed Jewish hearers only, those in Acts were comprised of Jews, Samaritans, and Gentiles. The first four incidents feature Peter as speaker; the last text refers to Paul's statement about his mission. In addition, Paul is said to have preached to both Jews and Gentiles/Greeks to "turn to God in repentance and have faith in our Lord Jesus" (20:21). These two elements are also found in the Markan account, where Jesus called people to "repent and believe [in the good news about himself]" (Mark 1:15). Further, *metanoia* is joined with *epistrephō* in Acts 3:19 (Peter) and 26:20 (Paul). Thus, repentance leads to conversion, and "deeds consistent with repentance" are to follow.

In Paul's letters the verb *metanoeō* occurs once only (2 Cor. 12:21) and the noun *metanoia* four times (Rom. 2:4; 2 Cor. 7:9, 10; 2 Tim. 2:25). The negative word "unrepentant" appears in Romans 2:5. Many conclude that for Paul the more comprehensive term "faith" (*pistis*) and "to believe" (*pisteuō*) include the idea of repentance. As noted, Luke joined them in his report of Paul's preaching in Ephesus (Acts 20:21).

A knotty problem arises in Hebrews 6:4–6 in the text, "It is impossible for those . . . to be brought back to repentance, because . . ." For persons described as "fallen away" is repentance repeatable in any sense? Much depends on the context and syntax of the text, and the reader is referred to commentaries for detailed discussion. Probably the statement of the text is a pastoral rather than a dogmatic theological assertion, but nonetheless the warning is to be taken seriously. The final epistolary occurrence is 2 Peter 3:9, describing the Lord's patience in waiting for all who will repent.

Finally, *metanoia* is frequent in Revelation, often as part of formulaic exhortations (2:5, 16, 21–22; 3:3, 19). Believers are called to repent of various malpractices, and to exercise their former faithfulness. Those outside the church, despite various warnings, did not repent of their deeds (9:20–21; 16:9, 11).

The other Greek word for repenting (*metamelomai*) occurs six times in the New Testament, but is translated "repent" in the New International Version only once (Matt. 21:32). There the temple authorities are confronted by Jesus with their failure to repent at the preaching of John. In Greek usage, this term referred to changing one's mind or one's feelings; according to Aristotle it showed inner inconsistency.

The sense of "regret" is common to New Testament uses. A son "changed his mind" about doing his father's bidding (Matt. 21:29). Judas Iscariot was "seized with remorse" after betraying Jesus (Matt. 27:3). Paul did not "regret" the sorrow caused by his severe letter to Corinth (2 Cor. 7:8); instead, the pain brought "repentance" (*metanoia*) that leads to salvation, and leaves no "regret" (vv. 9–10). WALTER M. DUNNETT

Bibliography. J. Behm, *TDNT,* 4:975–1006; V. P. Hamilton, *TWOT,* 2:2340; H. Merklein, *EDNT,* 2:415–19; O. Michel, *TDNT,* 4:626–28; G. F. Moore, *Judaism,* 1:507ff.; M. R. Wilson, *TWOT,* 2:571.

Request. *See* PRAYER.

Requirement. By right and authority, our Creator makes certain demands or claims upon us his creatures. God requires us to give up our life to him by dying (Luke 12:20, "this very night your soul is required of you," NASB). God's general requirement for his people is to fear and love him, to walk in all his ways, to serve him wholeheartedly, and to keep his instructions (Deut. 10:12–13).

Mosaic ceremonial law required such things as Aaronic priests, offerings for supporting priests and Levites (Neh. 12:44; Ezek. 20:40), and burnt offerings to be placed on the altar (Ezra 3:4).

For those who ignore God's morality, God will "require it," that is, will call into account and punish. The wicked mistakenly suppose that God will not require such an accounting (Ps. 10:13). God requires the lifeblood of a murderer (Gen. 9:5), often via civil authorities (cf. 2 Sam. 4:11). God will require an accounting from those who do not heed his prophet (Deut. 18:19), or who violate their vows (Deut. 23:21). God even requires punishment of a prophet who fails to warn sinners (Ezek. 3:18, 20; 33:6, 8). Asking that God "require it" is sometimes part of curse formulas for violation of oaths (Josh. 22:23; cf. 1 Sam. 20:16).

What the LORD requires for reconciliation with wayward people is not exorbitantly expensive offerings, but repentance leading to decent behavior toward others, love of "mercy" (*ḥesed,* "[acts of] covenant-loyalty/love"), and a walk with God that affects behavior toward others (Mic. 6:6–8). It is not "burnt offering and sin offering" that God "requires" so much as an ear open to hear and obey God's instructions from his Book (Ps. 40:6–8).

Abraham by faith fulfilled God's requirements (Gen. 26:5), Zecharias and Elizabeth were righteous, keeping all the Lord's commandments and requirements (Luke 1:6). This does not mean sinless perfection, but godly, obedient character.

Even Gentiles without the Law do some of its moral requirements (Rom. 2:14–15, 26), although this is insufficient for salvation. Apart from regeneration, we all stand condemned by the Law as sinners (Rom. 3:23; 7:9), and in the "flesh" are in bondage to sin, unable to obey God's Law (Rom. 7:17). However, God through Christ's atoning death "condemned sin in the flesh," that is, set us free from the Law's condemnation by Christ's taking upon his own flesh the death penalty that the Law required for us sinners, in order that the "requirement (*dikaioma*) of the law," that is, the ethical obligations of the Law as a whole, might be "fulfilled" not only vicariously (our sin being properly punished in Christ) but also in actual practice (the moral law being obeyed) by those regenerated and empowered by the Holy Spirit (Rom. 8:2–4). Thus, ironically, we are freed from the Law so that we might fulfill its requirement.

JOE M. SPRINKLE

Responsibility. God has entrusted humankind—both individually and collectively—with responsibility. Humankind is, therefore, answerable to God. Initially, God gave humans the responsibility of multiplying, subduing the earth, and having dominion over creation (Gen. 1:28). As God revealed more of himself to man, man was given greater responsibility and thus became more accountable.

Jesus told several parables in which responsibility and accountability are at the center. Illustrative is the parable of the talents. Before a man went on a journey, he entrusted money to his servants. When he returned, each servant had to give an answer for what he had done with the money assigned to him. To those who doubled their money, the master exclaimed, "Well done!" However, the one who hid the money in the ground was severely judged for his irresponsibility (Matt. 25:14–30; see also Luke 19:11–27).

The Bible continually emphasizes the fact that the greater the privilege the greater the responsibility or accountability. Jesus concluded the teaching of a parable with the statement, "From everyone who has been given much, much will be demanded; and from the one who has been entrusted with much, much more will be asked" (Luke 12:48). Peter noted that judgment begins with the family of God (1 Peter 4:17). The Lord revealed to Ezekiel what he expected of his people and the dangers of disobedience. The prophet is a watchman who is accountable to warn the people when danger comes (3:18, 20; 33:6, 8). On another occasion, the Lord spoke to Israel, "You only have I chosen of all the families of the earth; therefore I will punish you for all your sins" (Amos 3:2). This verse has been dubbed the greatest "therefore" in Scripture.

The sin-nature in man seeks to shirk responsibility and to blame others for failures. There are a number of illustrations in Scripture in which a person attempted to shift responsibility for an action onto others. Adam pointed to Eve, and ultimately to the Lord, for the sin in which he found himself. Likewise, Eve sought to lay the blame on the serpent (Gen. 3). Sarah became upset with Abraham when Hagar bore him a child, even though Abraham was following Sarah's advice (Gen. 16:1–5). Esau complained that Jacob "deceived" him and got the birthright, when in fact he had sold it to his brother (compare Gen. 27:36 with Gen. 25:27–34). Aaron would not own up to the fact that he had formed the golden calf (Exod. 32:21–24). Pilate wanted to wash his hands of Jesus' death (Matt. 27:24).

The Bible teaches both corporate and individual accountability. Solidarity in accountability is seen early in Scripture. For example, at Sinai, the Lord commanded the people not to make an idol to worship. If they did, he would punish the children for the idolatry of the fathers "to the third and fourth generation of those who hate me," but he would show "love to a thousand generations of those who love me and keep my commandments" (Exod. 20:5; Deut. 5:9). Likewise, in the wilderness, Moses affirmed that although the Lord is slow to anger, "he does not leave the guilty unpunished; he punishes the children for the sin of the fathers to the third and fourth generation" (Num. 14:18). One sees how this principle worked its way out in a historical setting at Jericho. Not only was Achan held accountable for his misdeeds; so were the other family members (Josh. 7:24–25). On the other hand, Moses specifically commands that parents should not be held accountable for their children's sins nor should children suffer the consequences of their parents' sin; "each is to die for his own sin" (Deut. 24:16). During the Babylonian exile, Ezekiel amplified the ramifications of this latter verse, arguing that it was not the sins of the fathers but the sin of his generation that was being judged. He quoted a proverb: "The fathers eat sour grapes, and the children's teeth are set on edge" (Ezek. 18:2; see also Jer. 31:29). Ezekiel commanded them to quit hiding behind the proverb; they were also accountable. Instead, he had them focus on the truth that "The soul who sins is the one who will die" (v. 4) and "The righteousness of the righteous man will be credited to him, and wickedness of the wicked will be charged against him" (v. 20).

Of all of the writers of Scripture, Paul addressed the issue of accountability most extensively in the Book of Romans. He affirmed that God is righteous and his judgment is based on truth (2:2). Each person individually will give an account to God (14:12). Humankind rejected truth, choosing instead to follow a lie and worship created things rather than the Creator (1:25). To the Israelites, God gave the Law; it brought privilege but also greater responsibility (2:9). In various ways, the Israelites demonstrated that they were opposed to God. Paul affirmed that no one was righteous; all had sinned and fell short of the glory of God (3:10, 23). The whole world is accountable to God (3:19). However, God has revealed a righteousness that comes through faith to all who believe in Jesus Christ (3:22). Jews as well as Gentiles must acknowledge their sinfulness and repent, trusting in Christ's finished work on the cross (5:9).

GLENN E. SCHAEFER

Rest. Most uses of the noun and verb in the Bible are nontheological. However, the verb and noun take on theological and/or spiritual meaning in relation to God, to the people of both the old and new covenants, and to individual believers under both covenants. The most significant theological use in the Bible is found in Hebrews 3:7–4:11.

The Old Testament. Yahweh, the Creator of the universe, rested from the act of creating on the seventh day. "God blessed the seventh day and made it holy because on it he rested from all the work of creation he had done" (Gen. 2:2). God contemplated his own work, knowing that it was good.

The people of Yahweh were also given the blessing of rest—a whole day out of each week in which to rejoice in and contemplate God's works and words. The seventh day was the day of complete rest, the Sabbath, and sacred to the Lord (Exod. 16; 23; 25). It was a day on which everyone, whatever his or her status, had to rest from daily labors; it was a festival for al to keep in honor of the Lord God, who himself rested (Exod. 20:10; 23:12; 31:15).

The tribes of Israel also enjoyed God's gift of rest when they settled in the promised land, which flowed with milk and honey (see Josh. 1:13–15; 23:1). Canaan is actually called "the resting place [Heb. *mĕnûḥâ*] . . . the LORD your God is giving you" (Deut. 12:9). They also knew such rest when they were delivered from their enemies (Josh. 14:15; 21:44; Judg. 3:11, 30). This rest of peaceful living was granted by God as the people looked to him alone and sought to keep his covenant.

With respect to the covenant relation of Yahweh to his people, we read that his fury rested on them in judgment (Ezek. 5:13; 16:42; 21:7) and that his hand and Spirit rested on them in blessing (Isa. 11:2; 25:10; Jer. 6:16).

The New Testament. The primary Greek words are the nouns *anapausis* and *katapausis,* and the verbs *anapauō* and *katapauō*.

In the Gospels the theology of rest is most clearly articulated in the words of Jesus: "come to me . . . and I will give you rest. . . . and you will find rest for your souls" (Matt. 11:28–30). The rest he promises is certainly for the world to come, but it is also for this world. It is the sense of security and peace that flows from a right relation with God, the Father, through obedience to his Son, the Messiah, and membership in his kingdom.

In Hebrews 3–4 the verb *katapauo* occurs three times and the noun, *katapausis,* eight times. Also, the Greek text of Psalm 95:11 ("they shall never enter my rest") is cited eight times. Joshua was given the task by Yahweh of leading the tribes of Israel into the promised land, into the rest promised them by their God. This task was fulfilled in an earthly sense by Joshua, as the Book of Joshua describes. However, the fuller meaning of the everlasting rest of God promised to his people and related to the gift of rest of the seventh day was not achieved by Joshua and the tribes under the old covenant. Jesus the Christ, the greater Joshua, was sent by the Father to bring into being the true nature and fullness of the gift of rest for the people of God.

The rest is rightly called a "sabbath rest" because it is a participation in God's own rest. When God completed his work of creation, he rested; likewise when his people complete their service to him on earth, they will enter into God's prepared rest. Now, in this age, the rest is before them as their heritage and by faith they live in the light of it in this world. How this is done is wonderfully illustrated with the wealth of biographical detail in Hebrews 11. Here the rest is also portrayed as a city prepared for God's faithful people—a city whose builder is God himself. Whatever this rest consists of it is not a state of complete inactivity, such as the rest of the wicked (Job 3:17–19).

In Revelation 14:13–14 the heavenly voice speaks of the blessedness of those who die in the

Lord and the Spirit replies: "They will rest from their labor for their deeds will follow them." Here a different dimension of the meaning of rest is being pointed to—a rest that is not inactivity but is certainly free of the burdens of the flesh and of the present, evil age.

Finally, we note that as the Spirit of the Lord rests on the Messiah (Isa. 11:2), so in the new covenant, "If you [Christian believers] are insulted for the name of Christ, you are blessed, for the Spirit of glory and of God rests on you" (1 Peter 4:14). PETER TOON

Restore, Renew. The Old and New Testaments use terms such as "restore" and "renew" to image God's control of history and the believer's spiritual life. Both terms, represented by a variety of Hebrew and Greek words, are used in literal and figurative contexts. It is the extension of the literal meaning into a figure for explaining God's program or the nature of spiritual living that presents challenges for interpretation.

The literal meaning of these terms is clear and needs little comment. The usage pattern for the words translated "restore" is mostly a literal meaning. Life, land, property, health, and other tangible items are the subject of restoration (Gen. 42:25; 1 Kings 20:34; Job 20:10; Ezek. 18:7; Mark 3:5; Luke 19:8). On the other hand, the "renew" pattern is predominantly figurative. Passages on literal renewal (to take something up again), such as kingdom renewal at Gilgal (1 Sam. 11:14), are rare (cf. 2 Chron. 15:8; Job 10:17; 29:20; Ps. 103:5). The New Testament usage is exclusively figurative.

The figurative usage of "restore" falls into three areas with only about six passages to consider. First, there is personal spiritual restoration. In Psalm 23:3 the psalmist pleads for strength in trials. In Psalm 51:12 David is seeking a sense of restoration in light of grievous sin against God. Second, Galatians 6:1 calls for mature believers to identify their areas of strength and to mentor back to spiritual health another ailing believer. Third, there are references (Matt. 17:11 = Mark 9:12; Matt. 19:28; Acts 1:6; 3:21) to an eschatological restoration. This latter category is the focus of much theological discussion and will be examined below.

The figurative usage of "renew" occurs in over two-thirds of the passages. There is a renewal that is the regaining of inner strength and resolve in our pursuit of God (Isa. 40:31; 41:1; Lam. 5:21; 2 Cor. 4:16). Some contexts stress the acquisition of knowledge as a means of providing mental renewal (Rom. 12:2; Eph. 4:23; Col. 3:10). This mental alignment to God's truth is the foundation of the value clarification the believer begins to pursue at conversion (Rom. 12:2). Two references view renewal from the perspective of repentance (Ps. 51:10; Heb. 6:6). The use of *palingenesia* and *anakainōsis* in Titus 3:5 provides metaphors for rebirth (NIV; "regeneration" KJV) and renewal. Paul finishes the sentence of 3:5 in 3:7 with the crescendo of justification.

Passages on renewal and restoration illustrate two important issues for the Bible student: (1) no theological concept can be treated by merely looking up a key word or two (i.e., theological concepts are often conveyed by a variety of terms); (2) the reader of English versions should beware. The King James Version translated *palingenesia* as "regeneration" while more recent versions translate this term as "renewal" (Matt. 19:28 NIV). But compare the New International Version on Titus 3:5, where the same Greek term is translated "rebirth," a translational necessity since a more direct term for "renew" follows in this verse. The older popular concordances (e.g., Strong's, Young's) use the King James Version as a database and the important Matthew passage for the subject of renewal would be missed. The Bible student now needs several concordances for careful study due to the proliferation of English versions (e.g., NASB, NIV).

The eschatological concept of renewal and restoration occurs in a few key passages (Matt. 19:28; Matt. 17:11 par. Mark 9:12; Acts 1:6; 3:21; cf. Eph. 1:10). Two Greek words highlight restoration in these texts, *palingenesia* and *apokathistēmi* (verb and noun forms). *Palingenesia* is used only two times in the New Testament (Matt. 19:28; Titus 3:5 for personal salvific regeneration). It literally means "rebirth" and was used in both Greek (there is a reference in the Greek mystery religions to being "born again/anew") and Jewish literature for the beginning of something new, especially renewal after some catastrophe. Philo used it to describe the renewal of the world after the flood (*On the Life of Moses* 2.12; 2.65) and of the restoration of the world after a judgment of fire (*On the Creation*). Josephus talks about the rebirth of the nation of Israel after the exile (*Antiq*. 11.66). There was a widespread belief among the Jews that the messianic era would be accompanied by a new age (e.g., new heaven and new earth; Isa. 65:17; 66:22; Rev. 21:1–5; 2 Baruch 32:6; 44:12). Jesus identifies the time of Matthew 19:28 with Daniel 7:13–14 when he refers to the throne of his glory, an event that ushers in the eternal kingdom of God. Some interpreters view 19:28 as a reference to the millennial kingdom, based upon the reference to the apostles judging Israel. Most, however, view 19:28 in reference to the ultimate consummation of the world and understand Jesus' reference to judgment either as part of the transition that ushers in the new era or as a statement that demonstrates the importance of the disciples among the Jewish people (cf. 19:27).

Apokathistēmi is the term that forms the rest of the passages that refer to the consummation as a restoration (Matt. 17:11 with Mark 9:12; Acts 1:6; 3:21). The parallel references in Matthew and Mark focus on the disciples' question about the coming of Elijah before the day of the Lord and the scribal tradition on this subject. Some view Jesus as correcting the scribal tradition by observing that John the Baptist, who came in the spirit and power of Elijah (cf. Luke 1:17), fulfilled Malachi's prediction and that no future coming was in view. Others contend that John fulfilled the spirit of Malachi's statement about Elijah for the first advent. Yet John was not the final Elijah of Malachi (cf. John 1:21). Malachi's Elijah is related to the second advent (cf. Rev. 11:1–13) and is yet to come. Jesus has a point to score in these texts that goes beyond the historical nature of Elijah's coming. The greater contexts of Matthew and Mark place some of the disciples with Jesus on the Mount of Transfiguration where Elijah appears and discusses the exodus (death) of the Messiah. The disciples were probably struggling to understand the seeming incompatibility of kingdom restoration and messianic death. When they raised this issue to Jesus, he notes that the rejection of John was equivalent to rejecting the spirit of Malachi's Elijah and thus implies an analogy for Jesus' own rejection and death. Therefore, while the spirit and power of Elijah in John were rejected, there remains a still future restoration. This is the very point of Acts 1:6 and 3:21. In 1:6 the disciples are still confused about the issue of restoration and hope that now is the time. But in 3:21 Peter has progressed to understand that the restoration belongs to the eschaton.

Gary T. Meadors

See also Age, Ages; Refreshing, Times of; Second Coming of Christ.

Bibliography. W. C. Allen, *The Gospel According to S. Matthew;* F. F. Bruce, *The Acts of the Apostles;* D. A. Carson, "Matthew," in *Expositor's Bible Commentary;* W. D. Davies and D. C. Allison, *The Gospel According to Saint Matthew;* G. D. Fee, *1 and 2 Timothy, Titus;* D. J. Harrington, *The Gospel of Matthew;* E. F. Harrison, *Interpreting Acts;* L. T. Johnson, *The Acts of the Apostles;* H. G. Liddell and R. Scott, *A Greek-English Lexicon;* L. Morris, *The Gospel According to Matthew;* R. V. G. Tasker, *The Gospel According to St. Matthew;* S. Toussaint, *Behold the King;* J. Walvoord, *Matthew: Thy Kingdom Come.*

Resurrection. ***The Old Testament.*** In the Old Testament, the idea of bodily resurrection evolves from a vague concept into a developed expectation. Beginning with the judgment of death in Genesis 3:6, the divine plan of God unfolds in history. The patriarchal period is more concerned with the first stages of the design. Community function is central because of the "promise" concerning the "seed." The extension of existence is passed through progeny (Gen. 12:1–3; 15:1–6) and individual resurrection is not the central concern.

Nonetheless, in the Old Testament concern is expressed for the individual soul. Job's despairing vacillation over death and decay is answered by the radiant expectation of preservation: "For I know my Redeemer lives, and that at the last he will stand upon the earth; and after my skin has been thus destroyed, then in my flesh I shall see God" (Job 19:25–26 NRSV; cf also Ps. 16:10; Isa. 26:19).

One of the principal factors in the development of a fixed notion of an individual resurrection is in response to the problem of theodicy. Because it could easily be seen that corrupt people sometimes were not punished for every wrong and that God's people were at times unjustly treated, individual resurrection was a natural philosophical resolution to this quandary. The resurrection of the just to reward and the unjust to punishment resolved the otherwise meaningless existence for those who followed Yahweh during times of persecution. There must be incentive to faithfulness toward God when there is no prosperity and no immediate compensation for belief. A further affront was the prosperous nonbeliever who endured no immediate, perceivable effects of sin and selfishness. Therefore, reward for one's earthly actions is integral to individual resurrection and is its initial catalyst.

Psalm 49 points out that all die, the "wise" and the "fool" alike. Fools are appointed to Sheol (which is used as a synonym for death or the grave) and "their forms will decay in the grave" (v. 14). Fools cannot continue in their resplendence of material possessions; therefore, the psalmist says, "Do not be overawed when a man grows rich . . . for he will take nothing with him when he dies" (vv. 16–17). Even though theodicy is not directly in view, at the core of the psalm is a proclamation of God's justice, which is dispensed to the fool and the wise person after death. The wise follower of Yahweh is triumphant: "But God will redeem my life from the grave, for he will surely take me to himself" (v. 15).

In Psalm 88 the psalmist's existence is about to cease. This is evidenced by the words used to denote death: "the pit" (vv. 4, 6); "the dead" (vv. 5, 10); "the grave" (vv. 5, 11); "the darkest depths" (v. 6); "the lowest pit" (v. 6); "Abaddon" (v. 11); "the place of darkness" (v. 12); "the land of oblivion" (v. 12); and "darkness" (v. 18). The psalmist says, "my life draws near to *Sheol*" (v. 3), the penumbral expanse of the netherworld. The psalmist then asks the rhetorical questions: "Do you work wonders for the dead? Do the shades rise up to praise you? Is your steadfast love declared in the grace, or your faithfulness in Abaddon? Are your wonders known in the darkness, or your saving help in the land of forgetfulness?" (vv. 10–12 NRSV). As with Psalm 6:4–6 the point is that one must be alive in order to praise God. The reference reveals a cognizance of the concept of an individual's resurrection even though the questions are unanswered (cf. Pss. 7:15; 49:15).

Psalm 6:5 says, "For in death there is no remembrance of you; in Sheol who can give your praise?" (NRSV). The psalm reveals God's justice being demonstrated in theodicy: "Deliver me; save me because of your unfailing love." Psalm 73 is enlightening in regards to the development of the concept of individual resurrection. The psalm begins, "Truly God is good to the upright, to those who are pure in heart" (NRSV). The problem is stated clearly: "I saw the prosperity of the wicked" (v. 3 NRSV). These wicked people mock, do violence, oppress, are prideful, and speak evil (vv. 6–9). Yet they are at ease and their wealth has increased (v. 12). The psalmist then makes the rhetorical statement, "Surely in vain have I kept my heart pure" (v. 13). Seeking to understand this seeming incongruity was troublesome to the psalmist (v. 16) until he perceived the end of the unfaithful (v. 17). They will be destroyed in a moment (vv. 19, 27), but the righteous Yahwist will receive a different recompense. Even though his flesh and heart may fail, God is his "portion forever" and "afterward . . . will take [him] into glory" (v. 24b).

Isaiah 26:10 says, "If favor is shown to the wicked, they do not learn righteousness; in the land of uprightness they deal perversely" (NRSV). Yet God's justice is revealed in the afterlife, as indicated in verse 19: "Your dead will live; their bodies will rise. You who dwell in the dust, wake up and shout for joy!" But the wicked have a different end: "The LORD is coming out of his dwelling to punish the people of the earth for their sins; the earth will disclose the blood shed upon her; she will conceal her slain no longer" (v. 21).

Just prior to the exile, an eschatological emphasis instilled by prophetic preaching imparted a growing concern for individuals. The result was a heightened awareness of the afterlife. For example, Jeremiah 31:30 says, "But everyone will die for his own iniquity" (NASB). The concern was no longer just for the nation of Israel or for Abraham's descendants, as it tended to be in the pre-Mosaic period, but for individuals as well.

The most conspicuous references to a resurrection are to be found in later apocalyptic literature, as the salvation leitmotif moves closer to the comprehensive perception that is later spelled out in Christ's resurrection. A resurrection of the just and the unjust is affirmed in Daniel 12:2–3: "Multitudes who sleep in the dust of the earth will awake: some to everlasting life, others to shame and everlasting contempt. Those who are wise will shine like the brightness of the heavens, and those who lead many to righteousness, like the stars for ever and ever." Unlike the "resurrections" of 1 Kings 17:17–24, 2 Kings 4:31–37, and 2 Kings 13:20–21, which are resuscitations to the conditions of earthly life, Daniel 12:2–3 apportions a future allotment by the use of the future tense (both in the Hebrew text and LXX).

Second Temple Judaism. With the prophetic voice being silent in the second temple period, and a feeling of the remoteness of God, harmonization with the justice of God took the form of requital after death. The question of why bad things happen to righteous people continued to fuel the concept of the resurrection, especially in light of the failure to establish Israel as the powerful nation it had once been. Apocalyptic literature was more commonplace, and the afterlife and the concern for individual salvation were prominent. It is in the context of persecuted saints in the second temple period that resurrection from the dead was developed into the form that is found in the New Testament. It is during this period that the concept of bodily resurrection takes shape.

The Maccabean revolt in 167 B.C. incited the earlier belief in the resurrection of the just and polarized it to new heights. The second of seven tortured brothers responds to his persecutors "in his last breath of consciousness" by saying, "You like a frenzy take us out of this present existence but the King of the universe shall raise us up to eternal life, because we have died on behalf of his laws" (2 Macc. 7:9, translation mine). The third brother, after putting forth his hands to the fire, says, "I received these [hands] from heaven . . . and from him I hope to receive them again" (2 Macc. 7:11). After the seven brothers are slain, their mother says, "The Creator of the universe . . . will give you breath and life again" (2 Macc. 7:23).

Other Jewish sources reveal a belief in a resurrection. The early second-century Syriac (translated from Greek) text 2 Baruch is an example. Baruch ask God the questions, "In which shape will the living live in your day? Or how will remain their splendor which will be after that? Will they, perhaps, take again this present form, and will they put on the chained members which are in evil and by which evils are accomplished?" (2 Bar. 49:2–3). The answer that is given in 2 Baruch 50–51 is that initially the "earth will surely give back the dead . . . not changing anything in their form" (2 Bar. 50:2). After this event, "the shape of those who are found to be guilty as also the glory of those who have proved to be righteous will be changed" (2 Bar. 51:1–2). The evil will take a more evil "shape" and the righteous will take a more righteous "shape."

By the time of Christ, the Pharisees (the most influential Jewish sect just prior to the Christian period who dated back to at least the second century B.C.) believed in a resurrection (Acts 23:8) whereas, the Sadducees did not (Matt. 22:23; Acts 23:8).

The New Testament. The resurrection of Jesus is the principal tenet of the New Testament. Baptism is centered in Jesus' resurrection. Even though Jewish illustrations were present for at least a hundred years before Christ, Paul applies the act symbolically to death, burial, and resurrection. He says, "When you were buried with him in baptism, you were also raised with him through faith in the power of God, who raised him from the dead" (Col. 2:12 NRSV; see also Rom. 6:3–5; 1 Peter 3:21–22).

The Lord's Supper is less connected in its symbolism than baptism, but the early correlation that it was celebrated on the Lord's day, that is, on the day that Jesus raised from the dead, reveals an early association.

The retelling of the empty tomb of Jesus is found in all four Gospels (Mark 16:1–8; Matt. 28:11–15; Luke 24:1–12; John 20:11–18). The empty tomb of Christ stands in sharp contrast to other world religions whose prophets and their adherents never make such a claim.

The appearances of Jesus after his resurrection to chosen individuals play an important role in the proclamation of the gospel message (e.g., Matt. 28:9–10, 16–17; Luke 24:34; John 20:11–17; 21:1–2; Acts 2:32; 3:15; 4:20; 10:40–41; 13:30–31; 1 Cor. 15:5–7).

The resurrection of Jesus is a testimony to the general resurrection of all humans, which will be followed by the dispensing of God's justice; to the righteous there will be a "resurrection of life" and to the unrighteous a "resurrection of condemnation" (John 5:28–29; cf. Rev. 20:4–6). Regardless of the complex time sequence involved in the various resurrections recorded in the New Testament, Jesus' bodily resurrection is the basis for the future resurrection of humans (1 Cor. 15:42–50). The Spirit, which was given after his resurrection, is the "guarantee" (or "first installment") that God will raise the righteous from the dead, and that they will not be found "naked," that is, incorporeal (2 Cor. 5:1–5; cf. Eph. 1:13–14), but will have a corporeal existence with God. Even though believers "groan" while in their bodies (2 Cor. 5:2), they will be "further clothed" after their resurrection (v. 4). There will be recompense for what was done in the body; therefore, one must seek to please God (vv. 6–10).

First Corinthians 15. The earliest teaching in the New Testament concerning the resurrection is undoubtedly 1 Corinthians 15. Paul "passes on" that which he has received (presumably by oral tradition), which is of "first importance." Paul says that the resurrection was in accordance with the Scriptures—a perception that was an important one considering the magnitude of the teaching. The seemingly insignificant detail of the time sequence ("the third day") is not an inconsequential component; rather, it reveals the historical nature of the event, which was not a private, subjective experience but one that occurred in actual time and was attested by Cephas, the Twelve, and five hundred people.

Paul, using simple logic, concludes several things "if the dead are not raised." The specific problem that he is addressing is that some of the Corinthians were saying that there was no resurrection of the dead. If there is no general resurrection, then the conspicuous conclusion that "Christ has not been raised" can be deduced. If "Christ has not been raised," then several philosophical conclusions can be outlined.

First, the missionary proclamation concerning Christ "is useless" (v. 14). This perception was undoubtedly an important one for Paul considering that his commission to the Gentiles was rooted in the idea that Jesus was "first to rise from the dead" (Acts 26:23). Therefore, Paul's mission to the Gentiles unfolds in light of the resurrection of Christ and the corollary futility of his own life ensues if there is no resurrection. Paul corresponds with the Corinthians with much passion in these verses. The collapse of the resurrection was commensurate to Christianity being fallacious for Paul.

Second, if there is no resurrection the faith of the believer is "vain" and "futile" (vv. 14, 17). The eschatological aspect of faith is rooted in the notion of resurrection. The resurrection of Jesus guarantees the resurrection of the believer. Future salvation is based on the resurrection of Jesus. Therefore, faith in God's justice in resolving the problem of theodicy is "vain" (cf. 1 Peter 3:21; Rom. 4:25) if there is no resurrection.

Jesus' resurrection is a prototypical event. As "the firstfruits" (1 Cor. 15:23) he gives the Spirit as the firstfruits to the believer (Rom. 8:23). This Spirit indwelling is the "first installment" (2 Cor. 1:22; 5:5; Eph. 1:14) and the basis for the hope of the "redemption of our bodies" (Rom. 8:23).

Third, the early missionaries were "misrepresenting God" if there is no resurrection (1 Cor. 15:15). Paul's logic allows no room for a "spiritual" approach that discounts the resurrection. The belief in bodily resurrection is commensurate with belief in God. If God exists and if he created the universe and has power over it, he has power to raise the dead. Attempts to explain the resurrection as a mere sociological phenomenon without the supernatural element minimizes the magnitude of the event and the role that it played in the formation of Christianity.

For example, the fourth of Paul's conclusions—"you are still in your sins" (v. 17)—shows the magnitude for Paul of the resurrection. The resurrection of Jesus showed that Christ's oblation as the sacrificial lamb was accepted by God, which is the basis for the giving of the Spirit to believers and the forgiveness of their sins.

Fifth, if there is no resurrection "those who have fallen asleep in Christ are lost" (v. 18). In other words, they have returned to dust with no future cognizance of any existence. This statement gets at the core of the basis for hoping and not fearing death. It also affects morality. God's future judgment modifies earthly behavior. Paul's conclusion that "If the dead are not raised, 'Let us eat and drink, for tomorrow we die'" (v. 32) reveals the tenable resolution of materialistic hedonism, when the resurrection of Christ as the firstfruit and the ensuing general resurrection are dismissed. As in the Old Testament, theodicy, especially in times of persecution, was perceived as futile if there was no future vindication.

Finally, the result of such logic led Paul to declare that "If for this life only we have hoped in Christ, we are of all people most to be pitied" (v. 19 NRSV). Paul articulates the persecution he received at Ephesus in verse 32, which only has meaning if the dead are raised. The persecution and even death of many of the early Christians led to Paul's conclusion that theodicy is resolved by bodily resurrection.

The rhetorical question is asked in verse 35, "With what kind of body will they come?" Paul's answer is to stress continuity of identity. Even though individuals will be "changed," they will remain in essence who they are. He illustrates this by using a grain of wheat that will, after it is planted, be changed, but will remain wheat. In the Gospels, the appearances of Jesus stress the continuity of his identity even though he changed. His pierced hands and side attest to the continuity of his identity.

Paul's discussion on the "first Adam" who is born of "dust" and the "second Adam" who is Christ and is a "life-giving spirit" has as its goal the statement "flesh and blood cannot inherit the kingdom of God." In other words, spiritual rebirth is necessary to enter the eternal kingdom of God.

Not only does the resurrection of Jesus have implications for the individual, according to Paul, but Christ's passage through the cosmos unharmed by evil spirits has placed the universe itself in his subjection (vv. 24–28). This early perception, the so-called classic view of the atonement, is common in the New Testament (cf. Acts 2:32–35; Eph. 1:20–23; Heb. 1:13). In second temple Judaism, ascension into the cosmos by a saint who confronted evil spirits (e.g., Eth Enoch) was commonplace, but none were permitted passage to "the right hand of God." Jesus' resurrection and subsequent ascension (which are often treated together as one event) is unique in that sense.

ERIC W. ADAMS

See also SECOND COMING OF CHRIST.

Bibliography. J. E. M. Dewart, *Message of the Fathers of the Church;* R. B. Gaffin, Jr., *The Centrality of the Resurrection: A Study in Paul's Soteriology;* G. R. Habermas, *The Resurrection of Jesus: An Apologetic;* M. J. Harris, *Raised Immortal: Resurrection and Immortality in the New Testament;* G. E. Ladd, *I Believe in the Resurrection.*

Retribution. *See* JUDGMENT.

Return of Christ. *See* SECOND COMING OF CHRIST.

Revelation, Idea of. The central question of religion is that of revelation. May God be known? Has he revealed himself? If he may, if he has, where? In the Christian faith this question is asked side by side with that of salvation: If this God may be known, how may I come to him? What may be known of him? translates into How may I come to know him—for myself? To put these questions alongside each other is to show how central is the question of the knowledge of God.

The Idea of Revelation. The claim of the Bible, from beginning to end, is that God has spoken. The repeated refrain, "And God said" tells how he called the universe into being and instructed his creatures to live. In Genesis 1 we read his mandate to the first humans, then in chapter 2 his specific instructions for life in Eden, and in chapter 3 his discovery of and response to the sin—in all of which we read of this characteristic divine activity in *speech.* And the pattern established in the opening chapters of Scripture is repeated, with a dramatic range of variation, right through to the Book of Revelation. In law, prophets, and history we read the speech of God; the most common of all the acts of God in history is the use of quotation marks. Small wonder that Christians have relished the apostle's use of the term "the oracles of God" for his Bible. Certainly, the prevalence of quoted divine speech, which peppers the canon, suggests a presumption in favor of speech as *the* category within which to understand God's communication with his creatures. That is why the Bible's own statements about the speaking God are in sharp focus when we address the question of the authority of "the books." For its religion is the religion of the speaking God, and a concern to maintain the continuity of contemporary Christianity with the religion of the biblical communities suggests a like understanding of God as the speaking God, and a like use of the texts that are held to record the divine speech. Such a reflection helps anchor our understanding and use of Scripture in the religious veneration and doctrinal authority of the Bible books in their original communities, which reaches its remarkable climax in the use made of the Old Testament Scriptures by Jesus himself, which set the pattern for the Christian understanding of both Old and New Testaments. And in the New Testament we witness a double focus, on Jesus as the incarnate Word of God, and as, himself, God who speaks and whose speaking is recorded at length. These factors together provide an anchor for the use of Scripture as a source for a doctrine of Scripture, in just the way in which Scripture is universally employed in the church as the source of every other doctrine. And they fill out a pattern of understanding of the God of biblical and Christian religion as a God who speaks.

Yet not only *does* he speak, he surely *must.* For how else would we know of God? Across the double barrier of our creatureliness and our sin, he has chosen to reveal himself and his saving purposes. To recognize Holy Scripture as the chief locus of that revelation is not to deny that there is also revelation elsewhere. Christians have customarily seen general revelation in creation and in conscience, distinguished from special, saving revelation in word (Holy Scripture), history (the "acts of God"), and the Person of Jesus Christ (incarnation). Much of the theological debate of the nineteenth and twentieth centuries has been taken up with the relative significance of these loci of revelation. Evangelicals have sought to maintain a balance, tied firmly to the teaching of Scripture itself. Most have accepted general revelation, while resisting the suggestion that it might provide an adequate ground for salvation. They have welcomed the fresh stress on the revelatory significance of the acts of God recorded in Scripture, though recoiled from the suggestion that such a historical focus to revelation should somehow be accessed in any other way than through Holy Scripture—in which the revelatory speech of God himself records and interprets these events. And they have professed themselves uncomprehending of the accusation that their high view of Holy Scripture somehow demeans or undermines the personal revelation of God himself in the incarnate Jesus Christ—not least because that historical person is mediated to us in Holy Scripture and presented as one who himself believes in the revelatory character of the Old Testament Scriptures. It is in the fact of his teaching that we find the analogical connection between incarnation and inscripturation—the Word made flesh, and the word of Scripture. The whole of Scripture testifies to Jesus himself, in prospect, in record, and in retrospect.

Part of the reason why evangelicals have resisted moves to emphasize other loci of revelation at the expense of Scripture is a recognition of the role of Scripture as *the* control on our theological formulation, as the definitive source for our knowledge of God, as the record and interpreter of the biblical history, and as the depository of the teaching of the living Jesus Christ. The need for such a control is evident from a consideration of the logic of divine revelation. For since God is not part of the world that we directly experience, we are unable to study him in the manner in which we study other objects of human research. There are parallels between our study of God and the scientific study of his world, but there is also radical dissimilarity. As we have noted, this means that unless he reveals himself he remains hidden. In so far as he does reveal himself he becomes accessible to us, whether in the shadowy and outline form of general revelation—"his eternal power and deity" (Ps. 19; Rom. 1)—or in the particularity and detail of the special revelation in history, in Scripture, in Jesus Christ. Yet by virtue of the same fact we can study him *only* under the impress of revelation; we do not have other data by which to assess or interpret that revelation. Of the sources of revelation we have discussed, it is Scripture that offers us the opportunity for sustained study of its subject; its author. And we should note this also. It has become fashionable to stress the acts of God in history as over against his speech. That stress may be welcomed as redressing what has sometimes been an imbalance. Yet it has led to an imbalance of another kind, in which mute acts are severed from their spoken interpretation. From such a perspective we must say that the Bible is not simply the record and interpretation of the acts of God in history, but itself—compiled as it was over more than a thousand years of history—not least among those mighty acts in its faithful recording of that most frequent of all those acts, the speech of God. And as the book which, supremely, testifies of Jesus and records his teachings, which was written under the impress of his Spirit, "who spoke by the prophets," and which is today illumined by that same Spirit as it is read, preached, made the subject of theological formulation—it serves most appropriately as the "supreme rule of faith and practice" of his own church.

Moreover, those who seek to claim the authority of Scripture in some lesser fashion undermine their own position. For every appeal to Holy Scripture as a source of theological authority entails the general authority of the whole; that this massive collection of texts is in fact one single, highly complex text, the work of the one Holy Spirit of God.

A Biblical Theology of the Speaking God. Divine speech plays a central role in Scripture, both in the texts themselves and in the history to which they witness. The sheer abundance of the speech of God in the canonical texts may actually help explain the lack of attention that has been paid to this very remarkable fact, which is surely the most evident of all phenomena in the canon. The variety of forms divine speech takes (from the writing on the wall in Balshazaar's palace to the familiar prophetic formula "Thus says the Lord" and the supernatural speech of Balaam's ass) should not obscure its common character. It offers a highly specific context to the general biblical claim to offer an account of a *revealed* religion.

Though Scripture itself testifies that there are other forms employed to accomplish the revelation of God, the direct divine speech is both chief among them and paradigm for them all. Two straightforward examples can be offered from the psalms. In the first part of Psalm 19 we learn that "The heavens declare the glory of God. . . . Day after day they *pour forth speech.*" And throughout Psalm 29 we read that the *voice of the Lord* is heard in the great events of nature. In both cases

God's revelation in nature is presented as his speech. These are striking illustrations both of the ready Old Testament acceptance of general revelation and of the overarching significance of revelation by the divine speech. They suggest that we should be wary of setting nonverbal models of revelation over against revelation by word and statement, since there is no such antithesis. And they encourage us to examine Scripture for the wealth of evidence of God's speaking, where several kinds of divine speech become evident.

1. The creative speech of Genesis 1 is immediately evident. It is in only the second verse of the Bible that we first read "And God said," the phrase that initiates every stage of the creative process. Here is the first instance of revelation, as it is by speech that the Creator orders his time-space universe from the beginning of its creaturely existence; "Praise the Lord, for he has spoken," as the hymn notes, and in response to these first statements by Creator to creation, "Worlds his mighty voice obeyed." If we pause to ask how we are to imagine the circumstances thus described, and conclude that they are beyond our understanding when conceived as speech, we nevertheless note that here, once again, the fundamental category of divine revelation is taken to be speech—even in address to the subpersonal creation. If in Psalms 19 and 29 speech is the paradigm of nonverbal witness in the created order, here it is the model of divine address to creation itself. And as in creation, so in sustaining providence, he upholds all things by his powerful word.

2. Hard on the heels of these words uttered into an obedient and yet impersonal universe, in Genesis 1:28 we read the first words of revelation addressed to God's human creatures: "Be fruitful and increase in number." And then, as the cosmogony resolves into the narrower dimensions of Eden, we read that the Lord God commanded Adam concerning the trees of the garden—which to eat, and which not to eat (2:16–17). A chapter later, the next divine words—"Where are you?" (3:9)—represent the opening salvo in the sustained interchange that exposes sin and announces its penalty for Adam, Eve, the serpent, and the world. The pattern continues, with recorded exchanges between God and Cain, and then at much length the sustained conversation with Noah; and then with Abraham, and others in the patriarchal period.

3. Then comes Moses. His lengthy interviews with God are followed by the giving of the law, the most sustained and formal example of the divine speech in Holy Scripture which offers us—in the Ten Commandments, but also in the whole of the extensive Mosaic legislation—the paradigm of divine speech issuing in divine writing—of, precisely, inscripturation.

4. As with the law, so with the prophets: The form changes, but the extensive first-person accounts given as from the mouth of God serve as the chief content of the prophetic books.

5. In the New Testament several different situations are found, but at their heart lie the four Gospels, whose major content is the teaching of Jesus. Since we are introduced to him as God incarnate, his teaching brings to a climax the biblical witness to the speaking God as the divine speech incarnated, God who "spoke by the prophets" speaking now by himself. Indeed, we could go further: Our understanding of the inspiration of Holy Scripture is signally illumined by the phenomenon of the speaking God taking flesh and, therefore, actual vocal cords. Here we find the key to the incarnational analogy of the Word made flesh and the word made Scripture. The twin foci of law and gospel—in the giving of the Mosaic legislative corpus and in the human speech of the incarnate Jesus Christ—offer dynamic illustrations and also controls of the method of inspiration and the character of revelation, as the very words of God are issued as the words also of writing and speaking human beings.

One question this raises is the relation between the text we possess (a text about which there are many, if generally minor, uncertainties, in the light of its long history) and that text to which our bibliological formulations apply. The conventional and reasonable response has been to focus on the "original" text, the autograph of the human author. This matter is more complex in the case of multiauthor or multiedition documents, whether deriving from one writer who made different use of his material (as may be the case with some of the prophets) or several writers whose work was collected (as with the psalms). The discussion is anchored in a concern to recover specifically *canonical* authority, and inevitably we must engage in complex historical and theoretical discussion about the process of canonical recognition. Here again our identification with the ancient believing communities in common canonical obedience is both a goal and a means of resolving our own uncertainties.

Needless to say, such observations do not absolve the theologian of the need to address the range of interpretive questions posed by any ancient texts, and therefore by the texts contained in the canon. On the contrary, they underline the need for such an address to be energetic since it is required in order that the text should properly be heard. But they help explain the centrality of the tradition of the Christian God as the speaking God, and that understanding of Holy Scripture as the deposit of his spoken revelation. And they underline the role of Holy Scripture, above all, in the theological formulation of the church, offering explicit and coherent resolution to the (still) widespread though haphazard use of Scripture to authorize theological proposals in many streams of contemporary theology. If it is the task of evangelical theology to understand God in accordance with his own nature, as he has revealed himself—just as it was the duty of the ancient Hebrews to order their worship of God in accordance with his revelation through Moses—then evangelical theology will be done "according to the Scriptures." NIGEL M. DE S. CAMERON

See also BIBLE, INSPIRATION OF THE.

Bibliography. D. McDonald, *Ideas of Revelation;* P. Helm, *The Divine Revelation;* C. F. H. Henry, *God, Revelation and Authority;* L. Morris, *I Believe in Revelation;* B. B. Warfield, *The Inspiration and Authority of the Bible.*

Revelation, Theology of. The theology of Revelation stands in the mainstream of first-century Christian thought, for it presupposes, with other New Testament books, the message of the crucified and risen Christ (1:18; 2:8; 11:8); a two-stage eschatology in which Christ is presently enthroned in heaven (3:21; chap. 5; 12:5, 10) and will return to extend God's rule over the earth (2:27; 11:15); and a church in which Gentiles share the covenantal prerogatives of Israel (5:9–10; cf. Exod. 19:6). The book's distinctive accents arise from the crisis to which it was addressed.

A Theology for Churches under Pressure. Revelation was written from exile by John (1:1) as a circular letter to the churches of Asia Minor (1:4) during the reign of Domitian, when growing persecution had already led to at least one martyrdom, at Pergamum (2:12–13), portending a worse crisis. Pergamum had been the regional pioneering city for the imperial cult. When a temple was dedicated to Domitian on the western side of the marketplace in Ephesus, the leading city of Asia Minor and the first to be mentioned in John's letters to the churches, other cities of the province followed suit in a wave of popular fervor. Christians, informed against by their Jewish enemies (2:9; 3:9), who were exempt from the requirement to participate, were pressed to join in honoring the Roman emperor *divus;* refusal could be a capital offense. The choice was between Caesar and Christ. From beginning to end revelation presents itself as an exhortation to endurance. Its large predictive element supports this thrust, a point that is important for its balanced interpretation.

Literary Craft as a Vehicle of Theology. Any synthesis of the theology of Revelation will depend on assumptions about its literary structure. Apart from the epistolary elements (chap. 1; 22:6–21), the most obvious division is that between the letters (chaps. 2–3) and the visions (4:1–22:5), each introduced by a voice "like a trumpet" (1:10; 4:1). The gist of the book comes in relatively plain language in the letters.

A bifurcation of the visions is indicated by thematic differences between chapters 6–11 and 12–22, as well as by the formal device of two scrolls (5:1–9; 10:2–11). That 11:15–19 marks a terminus, so that what follows is a second prophecy, is stated in the passage introducing the second scroll (10:7, 11). Further subdivisions are shown by a complex system of refrains (e.g., 8:5b; 11:19b; 16:18, ending the enumerated seals, trumpets, and bowls, respectively; or 19:9b; 21:5b; 22:6a, ending Babylon material, dragon-beast material, and Jerusalem material, respectively), and antitheses of form and substance (e.g., 17:1–3 versus 21:9–10 to contrast Babylon and Jerusalem). The parts are unified by an intricate fabric of foreshadowing and backflashes (e.g., many phrases in chaps. 2–3 recur in chaps. 21–22; motifs in 11:1–13 anticipate chaps. 12–20; the bowls in chap. 16 recall the seals and trumpets in chaps. 6–11). Reiteration is built into the macrostructure of the book, probably to emphasize the certainty and urgency of the message (cf. Gen. 41:32).

Near the beginning of each major section stands an affirmation of Christ's authority as the one who has conquered death (1:13–18; 5:6–14; 12:1–11). This literary fact indicates the main purpose of the book: to set the sufferings of the church in the perspective of the Lamb's triumph.

The Mutual Relation of Present and Future. We must reckon with florid symbolism in this book. The preface speaks of "showing" and "signifying" (*deiknynai, semainein,* 1:1). Elsewhere we find the term "mystery" to designate symbols (1:20; 17:5, 7), use of allegory (*pneumatikōs,* 11:8), invitations to the reader to apply "wisdom" (13:18; 17:9), and specific, interpretative comments, all of which bring out figurative meanings (1:20; 4:5; 5:6, 8; 7:13–14; 11:3–4; 14:3–4; 16:13–14; 17:9, 10, 11, 12, 15, 18; 19:8; 20:4–5, 14). But the dreamlike character of the language, in places bordering on the bizarre, is on the book's face. Typology, allegory, and myth are tools of biblical prophecy and its offspring, Jewish apocalyptic; in this whole tradition John consciously stands (1:3; 10:11; 22:7, 9–10, 18–19).

Figures can have multiple levels of meaning. The key verse (1:19) suggests that symbols in this book may refer to people and events of John's day (e.g., chaps. 1–3 in the main) or to the time of the end (e.g., the trumpets and bowls; the final events in 20:7–22:5), or, possibly, to both at once.

Even the predictions are not straightforward. It is hard to know to what extent the descriptions of the trumpets (8:6–9:21; 11:15–19) and bowls (15:5–16:21) look back to the Egyptian plagues as prototypes of whatever signs God will send before the last exodus (cf. Luke 21:25–26). Cubical new Jerusalem (21:16), obviously not a literal city, is an antitype of the inner sanctuary in the temple (1 Kings 6:20), the place of God's very presence.

Typology of the sort just mentioned talks about future realities in terms projected from the past. John also uses a reversed typology that talks about people and events of his time using pictures retrojected from antitypes in the future. Christ's imminent warning to some at Pergamum, for example, borrows the image of his coming to make war with the sword of his mouth, from eschatology (2:12, 16; cf. 19:15, 21; Isa. 49:2). John explicitly identifies the great harlot as the Rome of his day, which was famous for its "seven hills" (17:9, 18), and the beast as the succession of emperors (17:10), while later he paints the fate of both the harlot and the beast in cosmic size, with apocalyptic colors (19:1–8, 11–21). He thus caricatures the emperor as though he were the antichrist who will come. Of course, the emperor was no more the final antichrist than the Lord's "war" against the Nicolaitan element in the church at Pergamum was the second coming. But if the very spiritual forces that will become manifest in that future moment are operative already (cf. 2 Thess. 2:7; 1 John 2:18), both metaphors are intelligible. For reversed typology there are ample precedents in the Old Testament (for example, compare the exaggerated details of David's sufferings in Ps. 22:14–18 with Jesus' crucifixion, or note Isaiah's use of the term "day of the Lord" for the downfall of the Babylonian empire: Isa. 13:6 with 13:1). If we recognize this phenomenon in blocks of visionary material where the beast is a major character (11:1–13; chaps 12–14; 17:1–20:6), our interpretation will follow the author's own clues and maintain the book's relevance for its original hearers. Only in this way can we do full justice to both its eschatological tenor and its imminent fulfillment (1:3; 2:16; 3:11; 22:7, 10, 12, 20).

The Sovereign God, Christ, and Spirit. Reassurance for persecuted Christians is offered in the picture of God as the one who sits on the throne (4:2–6, 9–10; 6:16; 12:5; 20:11–12; 22:1, 3), whose rule is eternal (1:4, 8; 4:8–10; 21:6) and universal (*pantokratōr,* "almighty one," nine times in Revelation, only once elsewhere in New Testament). Nowhere is God a direct participant in the conflicts that rage below. A cosmic dualism in which good and evil oppose each other as equals is not contemplated. God's plan, written on the two scrolls, includes, and is not put in question by, the troubles of the church.

Jesus Christ sits with God on God's single throne (3:21; 12:5; 22:1, 3), shares God's predicates of eternity (1:17; 2:8; 22:13), and receives worship (5:8–14; 7:9–10), which is due to God alone (15:4). The Christian minority in Asia, surrounded by pagans who adored the emperor among other divinities, would have seen in the many worship scenes dotted throughout Revelation a forceful reminder of the true state of affairs in heaven. The most characteristic image for Christ is that of the lamb once slain (chap. 5; 7:14; 12:11; 13:8), now capped with seven horns representing a plenitude of power (5:6). He is sovereign over earthly kings (1:5; 17:14; 19:16). Revelation stands out among the books of the New Testament for its unique visions of Christ in his present state of glory (1:13–16; chap. 5; 19:11–16).

The Spirit (the author does not use the term "Holy Spirit") is not mentioned in many passages that speak of God and Christ side by side (5:13; 6:16; 7:10; 11:15; 12:10; 14:4; 20:6; 21:22, 23; 22:1, 3), but appears as seven spirits who wait before God's throne (1:4; 4:5) and serve as the Lamb's intelligence in the world (3:1; 5:6). Most often he is associated with prophetic revelation.

The Opposition. Over against God, his truly divine king, and his prophetic spirit, stands a trio made up of a dragon, a beast, and a false prophet (16:13). Most fully described is the beast. In contrast to the gentle Lamb, it is a composite of terrifying wild animals (13:2; cf. Dan. 7:4–6). It too has been healed of a mortal wound, mimicking the crucified one (13:3, 12, 14; 17:8, 11). Instead of the Lamb's seven horns it has a monstrous seven heads and ten horns, with diadems on the horns to rival the Lamb (13:1; 17:3, 7). It aspires to universal dominion (13:7b–8; 17:8) and receives worship (13:4, 12). So the emperor is a parody of Christ. The policy of beheading any who refuse to worship Caesar (20:4) is depicted as a war against Christ and the saints (11:7; 13:7; 16:14, 16; 17:14; 19:19).

The dragon has the same attributes as the beast, including diadems on its multiple heads, which lend it a political air (12:3 with 13:1), and it works through and with the beast (12:17–13:2; 13:4; 16:13–14). It represents Satan (12:9; 20:2, 7), but not simply. It is the satanic inspiration behind the hubris of the emperor, even as God is the supreme authority who accomplishes his will through Christ as his plenipotentiary. The dragon, like the beast, is violent (12:4) and makes war on the saints (12:17; 20:7–9).

The false prophet (13:11–18) almost certainly represents the officers of the state cult. In the provinces, they performed religio-political rites on the emperor's behalf, honoring his effigies, which stood in temples or squares in most cities. From the time of the emperor Gaius they had the technology to produce convincing fire and speech miracles of the sort described in 13:13–15. Their whole enterprise, for John, is deceptive.

The Church in a Hostile World. Revelation, like the Fourth Gospel, splits the human race into those who are for Christ and those who are not. The people of the new Jerusalem keep themselves pure to become the bride of the Lamb (14:1–5; 19:7–9; 21:9–22:5). In contrast, Rome, under the cipher of Babylon, goes whoring after the emperor and prostitutes herself to his wishes, beckoning the nations of the world to join (14:8; 17:1–7, 9, 15–18; chap. 18). The latter figure draws on the Old Testament prophetic metaphor of marital unfaithfulness to denote idolatry. Each group has its identifying mark on the forehead: the mark of the beast (13:16–17) or that of the Lamb (14:1).

Lax churches are due for a purge if they do not repent (chaps. 2–3, except Smyrna and Philadelphia). General exhortations to purity are concentrated in the letters, but are found in other parts of the book too (7:13–14; 16:15; 18:4–5; 19:8; 22:11, 14–15). Specific among the temptations mentioned in the letters are eating food that has been sacrificed to idols, and practicing immorality (2:14, 20). Elsewhere hearers are warned against, among other things, idolatry (9:20; 21:8) and telling lies (14:5; 21:8, 27), reminders that were apropos when Christians were induced to honor images of Caesar.

Life and Martyrdom. As in the Fourth Gospel, the dominant soteriological term is "life." The book gives relatively scant space to its free offer (21:6; 22:17), perhaps because John's audience needed encouragement, not to gain spiritual life, but to persevere in it. The verb "believe" (*pisteuō*), frequent in the Fourth Gospel, is absent here; the adjective "faithful" (*pistos*), wanting (in this sense) in the Gospel, occurs eight times in Revelation. Accordingly, stress falls on having works (e.g., 2:23; 14:13; 20:13; 22:12). Various salvific benefits are held out to those who "conquer" in the moral and spiritual conflict (2:7, 11, 17, 26; 3:5, 12, 21; 21:7, reflecting a usage characteristic of 1 John). There is no assurance of life except for those who resist the beast (20:4–6); those who worship the beast will receive everlasting torment (14:9–11).

A unique contribution of Revelation is its rich martyrology. Jesus was the first martyr (1:5; 3:14), and because of his death and resurrection he can promise life to those who, like him, are faithful to death at Roman hands (2:8, 10; 11:7–13). God has ordained martyrdom for some (6:11; 13:9–10). The trumpets are in part God's answer to their cry for vengeance (6:9–10; 8:1–6), as are the string of judgments that round off the book: of humanity (16:5–7), of Babylon (17:6; 18:24–19:2), and of the evil trio (19:19–21; 20:9–10). Far from expressing a sub-Christian vindictiveness, as some have supposed, these passages guarantee to victims of the ultimate injustice that God will right their wrong. Promises of comfort for martyrs abound: They will enjoy the sundry blessings of the age to come (7:9–17); they will live (11:11–12); they will rest; and God will remember their deeds (14:12–13).

However one may interpret the millennial passage (20:1–6), it surely belongs under this rubric and crowns the martyrology of the book. Flanked by portrayals of God's final judgment of the persecutors (19:19–21; 20:7–10), it holds before the eyes of those threatened with martyrdom (20:4) a vista of life and glory with the reigning Christ, drawing together graphic images from promises elsewhere (2:11; 3:21; 5:10; 7:15; 11:11–12). Its object is to steel them for their ordeal.

A Theology of History. The triumph of the church is assured by the dual fact that the Lamb "has conquered" (past aorist, 5:5; cf. 3:21) and "will conquer" his foes (future, 17:14).

A spiral of evil turns over more than once before the end. The beast came (probably in Nero, who was the first Roman emperor to persecute Christians), went to the abyss (a lull in persecution for several decades) and will soon come out again (probably in Domitian as *Nero redivivus:* 11:7; 17:8, 11). This pattern recurs on a grander scale: Satan's activity through the Roman emperor (the dragon symbol) will be curtailed, but he will eventually return from the abyss, last of all with Gog (20:1–3, 7–10). Persecution of the church must break out, die off, and raise its head again—perhaps many times—before the very end. Nevertheless, God preserves the church corporate (11:1; 12:1–6, 13–15; 20:9).

Similarly, the final events are doubled. In 19:17–20:6, we see Christ lead a celestial army to eradicate the beasts and the dragon from the earth, raise the martyrs, and (apparently) give the martyrs thrones and authority to judge with him. After the thousand years there is a second worldwide conflict, another resurrection, and another throne scene for judgment (20:7–15). Indeed, virtually everything that happens after the millennium finds some counterpart beforehand. Even Ezekiel's prophecy of Gog is alluded to, not only in its natural place afterwards (20:8–9), but also before (19:17–18; cf. Ezek. 39:17–20). John seems to have looked for two complexes of the last things, with a long interval between them. Either he expected a literal fulfillment of both—which would amount to a form of chiliasm—or the first complex, in which the objects of Christ's conquest are the beasts and dragon whom John has identified as Roman imperial personnel of his day, is, like the related war metaphor in earlier visions, yet one more bold retrojection of eschatological pictures to events that took place shortly after the book was written.

Eschatology. If we take into account the book's intricate literary structure, and extract from its apocalyptic antitypes the information they yield about John's assumed scheme of strict eschatology, we can, with guidance from more systematic New Testament statements of eschatology (e.g., Mark 13; 2 Thess. 2), tease a simple pattern of events from Revelation. After an increase in natural calamities (6:1–11), there will be a short period (2:10; 11:2–3; 12:6, 12, 14; 13:5; 17:10; 20:3) when the antichrist will hold sway and trouble God's people (11:7; 12:13–14:5; the term "antichrist," however, does not occur in Revelation). Signs of God's wrath (6:12–17; trumpets; bowls) will precede the return of Christ to dispose of God's enemies (2:27; 14:14–20; 19:17–21), followed by a general resurrection and judgment (11:18; 20:11–15), and the eternal kingdom of God and Christ (11:15; chaps. 21–22). Most of these elements are found in sequence in the futuristic passage (20:7–21:8).

Other points, such as the length of the tribulation period, the time at which Christ will return relative to that period, and the nature of the millennial reign of the martyrs, are still debated in some schools of thought.

Revelation adds little of substance to what other New Testament writings say about eschatology. John probably shares the common schema, but uses it as a reservoir of images to illumine the current situation, scattering them in a literary web that highlights his primary concern: to encourage the church. PAUL ANDREW RAINBOW

See also APOCALYPTIC; PERSECUTION; SECOND COMING OF CHRIST.

Bibliography. P. Barnett, *JSNT* 35 (1989): 111–20; G. Caird, *The Language and Imagery of the Bible;* A. Collins, *The Combat Myth in the Book of Revelation;* E. Fiorenza, *The New Testament and Its Modern Interpreters,* pp. 407–27; D. Guthrie, *The Relevance of John's Apocalypse;* C. J. Hemer, *The Letters to the Seven Churches of Asia in Their Local Setting;* R. H. Mounce, *The Book of Revelation;* S. R. F. Price, *Rituals and Power: The Roman Imperial Cult in Asia Minor;* S. J. Scherrer, *JBL* 103 (1984): 599–610; L. L. Thompson, *The Book of Revelation: Apocalypse and Empire.*

Reward. ***A Definition of Reward.*** The word "reward" has both a favorable and an unfavorable meaning in English. In its favorable sense, it is something given in return for a good thing done, a service rendered, or some merit earned. For example, in Matthew 5:11–12, Jesus says, "Blessed are you when people insult you, persecute you and falsely say all kinds of evil against you because of me. Rejoice and be glad, because great is your reward in heaven." In its opposite sense, the word "reward" can refer to punishment for a wrong or wrongs committed, although it is rarely used this way in the Bible. In Revelation 22:12 the Greek word for "reward" is probably used with both favorable and unfavorable meanings in mind: "Behold, I am coming soon! My reward is with me, and I will give to everyone according to what he has done." In this article, the word is limited to the more favorable meaning of recompense for good done rather than punishment for evil committed.

The Location of the Giving of Rewards. The rewards Christians will receive for faithful service to the Lord will be given out at the judgment seat of Christ or the *bema* judgment. The Greek word *bēma* appears in 2 Corinthians 5:10 and Romans 14:10 and refers to the place where the works of believers will be evaluated by Christ for purposes of reward. In 2 Corinthians, a context in which Paul has stated several other incentives for faithful Christian service, Paul adds this additional encouragement: "For we must all appear before the judgment seat of Christ, that each one may receive what is due him for the things done while in the body, whether good or bad." In Romans 14:10, where Paul is speaking about exercising love for fellow Christians, be they weak or strong in the faith, he again uses the *bēma* judgment as a motive for doing it, only here he calls it "God's judgment seat." "You, then, why do you judge your brother? Or why do you look down on your brother? For we will all stand before God's judgment seat (*bēma*)."

It is clear that this is not a judgment resulting in salvation or damnation. Nevertheless, it is an important judgment for it will determine what responsibilities Christians will have in the coming kingdom (Matt. 25:21). According to Paul, some will come through with very little to show for their Christian lives, saved as though "through the flames" (1 Cor. 3:15). What he means is that some Christians will be saved but with little, if anything, to show for their years on earth. Whether because of wrong motives or laziness or misplaced priorities, they will conclude their lives with very little of any eternal worth to show. While the whole salvation process is a gift (Rom. 6:23; Eph. 2:8–10), rewards are the result of human effort and are earned (1 Cor. 3:14).

Depending on one's view of the temporal location of the rapture of the church, the *bēma* judgment will take place either in heaven, while the great tribulation is transpiring here on the earth, or on earth at the beginning of Christ's reign after his second coming. In either case, it is preparatory to the Christians' reigning together with Christ on earth following his return.

An Identification of the Rewards. The rewards to be given out for faithful service at the *bēma* judgment are dealt with in various ways. Those spoken of in terms of "crowns" are nonmaterial, thus doing away with their being materialistic motives for divine service. The "crowns" that are biblically identified as being given on that day include: a crown that will last forever for those who have kept their sinful nature in check (1 Cor. 9:25–27); a crown of righteousness for those who have longed for Christ's appearance (2 Tim. 4:8); a crown of life for those who have endured testing successfully, even to the point of death (James 1:12; Rev. 2:10); a crown of rejoicing for those who have seen souls saved (1 Thess. 2:19); and a crown of glory for those who have faithfully served God's people (1 Peter 5:4). In other places, the rewards are spoken of as "treasures in heaven" (Matt. 6:20), a share in Christ's future role (Rev. 2:26–27), and additional responsibilities and words of praise ("Well done, good and faithful servant"; Matt. 25:21, 23; Luke 19:17, 19). It is worth noting again how intangible and immaterial these rewards are. Even the gift of eternal life is set forth as a prize to be gained. Eternal life is something to be laid hold of by the individual (1 Tim. 6:17–19).

While emphasizing the future rewards, it is also well to remember that there are many good results that come to the faithful believer in this life, things that can be called "rewards." Jesus said that he had come that his own might have life and have it to the full (John 10:10). He also said that if his own would continue to seek first his Father's kingdom and his righteousness, all the temporal things they needed would be given to them as well (Matt. 6:33).

The Standards for Reward. One clearly stated standard for rewards at the *bēma* judgment will be whether the works done by the Christian have been good or bad (2 Cor. 5:10). It is significant that Paul uses the Greek word "foolish" or "worthless" and not one of the Greek words for "evil." His point is that there are some things that are good for the advancement of the kingdom and righteousness and others that are not, even though one would not call them evil. For example, some may spend a great deal of time and money on personal hobbies that have no eternal worth. They are not evil, unless undue amounts of time and money are spent on them; but they may not be of any eternal profit either. In that sense, they can be said to be foolish, although not sinful.

Another point to be stressed regarding standards is that rewards will not be given necessarily for successful service as the world so often evaluates it. Paul notes that "it is required that those who have been given a trust must prove faithful" (1 Cor. 4:2). Note that he does not say "successful" as one might consider success here on earth. What is rewarded is not primarily the visible accomplishments of the individual, but the faithful labor expended (1 Cor. 15:58). On this basis, some who have been very faithful in a more private ministry may come in alongside of and even ahead of some others who have had more public ministries, but who have not been as faithful or as purely motivated. It is also significant to note that the five-talented and the two-talented servants (Matt. 25:21, 23) were given the same reward because both were equally faithful with what had been entrusted to them.

The Variation in Reward. Salvation and eternal life are the same for all Christians but the rewards given to each varies, dependent upon the faithful labor expended. It is clear from the parable of the talents in Matthew 25 that the lord of the servants expected more from the five-talented man than he did from the two-talented or the one-talented individuals. Note that the talents were dispensed according to personal ability to handle them (v. 15). The ones with lesser amounts had lesser responsibility. Paul says that at the judgment of the believer's works, each will receive a reward according to his or her labor. Matthew 5:12 speaks of great reward in heaven and 2 John 8 speaks of a full reward, both references indicating that the rewards will not all be the same.

The Forfeiture of Reward. Several passages warn against the forfeiture or loss of reward. It is clear that this does not mean a repossession of the reward by the Lord, for the rewards being spoken of here have not yet been given. According to Paul, it is possible to "build" on the foundation, which is Christ, but to be building with "wood, hay or straw," which cannot stand the test of fire; the builder will be saved but "only as one escaping through the flames" (1 Cor. 3:11–15). In other words, people can be busy with the Lord's work and still receive no reward. They may be taking advantage of opportunities to labor for the Lord and yet not be engaged in endeavors that meet with God's approval because they have the wrong motives. For example, if they seek the praise of others, they can have that praise but receive no reward from God later (Matt. 6:1–18). Along with this forfeiture of reward will go a severe sense of shame and remorse (1 John 2:28) and a possible divine reprimand for wasted living as a Christian (Matt. 25:26–28). It is to be underscored, however, that this loss of reward does not mean a loss of salvation.

The Motivation of Reward for Christian Service. It is true that the reward motive for Christian service is not the *highest* biblical motive but it *is* a biblical one. As the highest, we are told to do all we do for God's glory (1 Cor. 10:31; Col. 3:23–24). We are to do all we can to be accepted by Christ, for the good of others, and out of gratitude and love for all God has done for us. Even the fear of the Lord that is going to fall on the unsaved is a legitimate incentive for service in seeing the lost saved (2 Cor. 5:11).

Down the line, but certainly in the line of biblical motivations for ministry, is the reward motive. Jesus, knowing our human nature, spoke much about the rewards to come for Christian labor for the Christian cause. It must also be remembered, however, that Jesus encouraged humble, unselfish service for God's kingdom and his church, even without reward. He taught that, even if we could do everything commanded of us, we are still unprofitable servants since we have just done our duty (Luke 17:7–10). In Matthew 20:1–16, all the servants receive a denarius for a day's work in the field, even though some had worked only a small fraction of the day. In fact, the righteous in Matthew 25:37–39 were so unimpressed by the reward motive for doing good that they could not remember when they did the good things cited by the Lord. Apparently the promise of reward does not spoil the conduct coming from it or Jesus would not have used it; nor does it contradict the doctrine of salvation by grace through faith alone. We cannot demand recompense from the Lord, but he can sovereignly give rewards if he so wills.

Finally, two things should be pointed out. According to Romans 8:8 and Hebrews 11:6, it is impossible for unbelievers to do anything that fundamentally meets with God's approval or that will receive a reward from God, no matter how impressive their deeds may be. However, once one is a believer, even as small a service as a cup of cold water given in the Lord's name (Mark 9:41) will not go without divine notice and reward. Second, even the rewards earned are totally a result of God's grace since all successful labor for Christ is accomplished by Christ working in and through us. In Romans 15:18, Paul says he will not dare to speak of any accomplishment except those Christ has done through him.

WESLEY L. GERIG

Bibliography. H. Z. Cleveland, *EDT*, pp. 951–52; W. M. Knoll, *It Will Be Worth It All: A Study In Believer's Rewards.*

Riches. *See* WEALTH.

Right Hand. *See* HAND, RIGHT HAND.

Righteousness. God the Father is righteous (just); Jesus Christ his Son is the Righteous (Just) One; the Father through the Son and in the Spirit gives the gift of righteousness (justice) to repentant sinners for salvation; such believing sinners are declared righteous (just) by the Father through the Son, are made righteous (just) by the Holy Spirit working in them, and will be wholly righteous (just) in the age to come. They are and will be righteous because they are in a covenant relation with the living God, who is the God of all grace and mercy and who will bring to completion what he has begun in them by declaring them righteous for Christ's sake.

The noun righteousness/justice (Gk. *dikaiosunē*) bears meanings in the New Testament related to two sources. The major one is the Hebrew thought-world of the Old Testament and particularly the *sdq* word group, which locates the meaning in the sphere of God's gracious, covenantal relation to his people and the appropriate behavior of the covenant partners (Yahweh and Israel) toward each other. The other is the regular use of the words in everyday Greek as spoken in New Testament times, which fixes the meaning in the sphere of a life in conformity to a known standard or law—thus honesty, legality, and so on. This latter meaning in terms of doing God's will is of course also found in the Old Testament.

When we translate the Greek words based on the stem *dikai-* into English we make use of two sets of words based on the stems, just and right. So we have just, justice, justify and right, righteous, righteousness, rightwise (old English). The use of two sets of English words for the one set of Greek words sometimes causes difficulties for students of the Bible. This is especially so when the verb "to justify," describing God's word and action, is used with the noun "righteousness," pointing to the result of that action.

The Gospels. The appropriate background to bear in mind for understanding the teaching of both John the Baptist and Jesus the Christ on righteousness/justice are two of the dominant ideas of the Old Testament. First, Yahweh-Elohim, the Lord God, is righteous in that he speaks and acts in accordance with the purity of his own holy nature; further, what he says and does for Israel is in accordance with his establishment of the covenant with this people (see Pss. 22:31; 40:10; 51:14; 71:15–24; Amos 5:21–24). Micah declared the righteousness of God as his faithfulness to keep and act within the covenant and thus to save Israel from her enemies, as well as to vindicate the penitent.

Second, the covenant people of God are called to live righteously, that is, in conformity to the demands of the covenant and according to God's will (see Pss. 1:4–6; 11:7; 72:1; Isa. 1:16–17). Having within the covenantal relation with God the gift of salvation, they are to behave as the people of the holy Lord. Hosea, the prophet of divine love, ties righteousness with mercy, loving kindness, and justice (2:19; 10:12).

John the Baptist called for repentance and righteous behavior such as is pleasing to God (Luke 3:7–9). Further, it was because of the demands of such righteousness—fulfilling the will of God—that he actually was willing to baptize Jesus (Matt. 3:15). Likewise Jesus presents righteousness as conformity to the will of God expressed in the Mosaic law (Matt. 13:17; 23:29; 27:4, 19, 24) and also conformity to his own teachings concerning the requirements of the kingdom of heaven (Matt. 5:17–20). However, conformity to his own teachings presupposes that he is the Messiah, that he fulfills the Law and the Prophets, and that what he declares is the morality of the kingdom of God relating to the totality of life, inward and outward, seen by God. Further, Jesus does allow that conformity to the norms of the scribes and Pharisees is a certain kind of (inferior) righteous living, but he contrasts it with the proper righteousness he exhibits, proclaims, and looks for (Luke 5:30–32; 15:7; 18:9) in the disciples of the kingdom. So in a fundamental sense, in the four Gospels righteousness as a quality of living is intimately related to the arrival and membership in the kingdom of God and is only possible because God has come to his people as their Redeemer.

The Gospel of Matthew makes clear that from the beginning Jesus' mission is to fulfill God's righteousness (3:15). This is brought to realization in his words and ministry so that the kingdom and salvation of God are in him and come through him. Alongside this is the righteousness in the new covenant, which is right thinking, feeling, speaking, and behavior on the part of disciples of the kingdom, who do what God approves and commands. This moral substance is very clear from the detailed contents of the Sermon on the Mount (chaps. 5–7), where the will of God is set forth by Jesus and is contrasted with a mere legalism. Yet what Jesus proclaims and outlines is certainly not a self-righteousness, for it is portrayed as the outflowing of a life that is centered on submitting to, worshiping, and seeking after God and confessing Jesus as the Messiah (see especially 5:17–42).

In the Gospel of Luke, we read of Zechariah and Elizabeth, Simeon and Joseph of Arimathea being called righteous (1:6; 2:25; 23:50) because they embody genuine religion according to the norms of the Old Covenant. They trust in and obey God. Further, Jesus himself as the Servant of Yahweh is the righteous or innocent one (23:47), even as the centurion confessed at the cross. The righteousness of the kingdom of God is practical and reverses the standards of the regular social order (3:11, 14; 6:20–26). At the last day it will be those who have been genuinely righteous in terms of doing the will of God who will be declared just (14:14).

In the Gospel of John, God is righteous (17:25) and the Holy Spirit, the Paraclete, has a specific role with respect to righteousness (16:8, 10). It is the unique work of the Spirit, who comes into the world in the name of Jesus the Messiah, to convince/convict the world of righteousness. The Spirit both vindicates Jesus as the Righteous One, whom the Father has raised from the dead and exalted into heaven, and also makes clear what kind of righteous life is required by, and, in grace, provided by God.

The Letters of Paul. The uses the noun *dikaiosunē* (righteousness), the adjective *dikaios* (righteous), and the verb *dikaiō* (to justify or to declare and treat as righteous) over one hundred times and his usage reflects a particular development from the use of *sdq* in the Old Testament. God is righteous when he acts according to the terms of the covenant he has established. Righteousness is God's faithfulness as the Lord of the covenant. God acts righteously when he performs saving deeds for his people and thereby in delivering them places them in a right relation to himself (see especially Isa. 51 and 61). The interchangeability of righteousness and salvation is seen in this verse: "I am bringing my righteousness near, it is not far away; and my salvation will not be delayed. I will grant salvation to Zion, my splendor to Israel" (Isa. 46:13).

Thus God's people are righteous when they are in a right relation with him, when they enjoy his salvation; they are considered by God as the Judge of the world as righteous when they are being and doing what he requires in his covenant. So it may be said that the concept of righteousness in Paul belongs more to soteriology than to moral theology, even though it has distinct moral implications.

God's righteousness is, for Paul, God's saving activity in and through the life, death, and resurrection of Jesus Christ, his Son. It is activity that is directly in line with the saving activity of God in the Old Testament. The acceptance of the unique saving deed of God at Calvary by faith in the person of Jesus Christ is that which God has ordained to be the means for sinners (the unrighteous and the disobedient ones) to enter into the right with God, the Father, and receive the forgiveness of sins. God as the Judge justifies believing sinners by declaring them righteous in and through Jesus Christ; then he expects and enables these sinners to become righteous in word and deed. Faith works by love.

The righteousness of which Paul speaks, especially in the letters to Galatia and Rome, stands in contrast to the righteousness that is based on the fulfillment of the law by man as the covenant partner of God. It is "the righteousness of faith" and "the righteousness of God" (Rom. 10:6; Phil. 3:9), and is most certainly the gift of God. From the human standpoint what God looks for in those who receive the gospel is "faith in the Son of God, who loved me and gave himself for me" (Gal. 2:20). God's gift to those who believe is a righteousness that exists and can be given only because of the sacrificial death of Jesus for sinners and his resurrection from the dead as the vindicated Lord of all.

So God as the righteous Judge justifies—places in a right relation with himself within the new covenant of grace—those who believe the gospel of the Father concerning his Son, the Lord Jesus Christ. And he justifies Jew and Greek alike on precisely the same basis, by faith alone without works, and he makes no distinction whatsoever between the people of the Old Covenant and the Gentiles. Abraham, says Paul, was himself justified by faith alone (Gen. 12:3; 15:6; 18:18; Rom. 4:3; Gal. 3:8). In fact, Paul confessed that the power of the gospel to be the word of salvation to both Jew and Greek was based on the revelation of the righteousness of God therein—of God the Father acting justly for the sake of his Son (Rom. 1:16–17).

The gift of a right relation with the Father through the Son in the Spirit, which is justification, creates a relationship for believers both with God and fellow believers that they are to dedicate to righteousness in the sense of obeying Christ (Rom. 6:12–14; cf. 2 Cor. 6:7, 14; 9:10; Eph. 4:24; Phil. 1:11). Though they could never become righteous before God by their efforts to conform their lives to his will, out of gratitude and love they are to serve him because he has given them the gift of salvation through the grace of the Lord Jesus Christ. He has pronounced them righteous, he has reconciled them to himself and removed their alienation, and he has transformed their relation to him into that of friendship. Therefore, since God has made them his own and given to them his righteousness, their duty and privilege is to be righteous in conduct. And he promises that on the last day and for the life of the age to come he will actually make them to be truly and effectually righteous in all that they are, become, and do.

The word "eschatological" is often used with reference to this gift of righteousness. The reason is this. It is in anticipation of what God will do for the sake of his Son Jesus Christ at the last day that he pronounces guilty sinners righteous now in this evil age. At the last day, God the Father will be vindicated and all will confess that Jesus Christ is Lord. Those who believe will become and remain righteous in their resurrection bodies of glory. Now and before the new age arrives, by the proclamation of the gospel and by the presence of the Spirit, that which is not yet (the fullness of righteousness of the age to come) is actually made available by the will and declaration of the Father, through the mediation of Jesus Christ the Lord and by the presence and operation of the Holy Spirit. Already there is the provision of a right relation with God through the preaching of the gospel, but there is not yet the experience of the fullness of righteousness as an imparted gift. Now believers merely have the firstfruits of that which awaits them in the age to come.

It would be a mistake, however, to think that Paul does not use the word "righteousness" in its more familiar meaning as a virtue. In fact he does so particularly in 1 and 2 Timothy. He commends striving for righteousness (1 Tim. 6:11) as the right motivation of a person of God; and he sees the use of the inspired Scriptures as being to train Christians in righteousness (2 Tim. 3:16). Further, as a reward for his efforts for the kingdom of God he looks for "the crown of righteousness" (2 Tim. 4:8).

Other New Testament Books. Righteousness in terms of the actual doing and completing the will of God is found outside the Gospels in various places. It is found in Acts 10:35 in terms of fearing God and doing righteousness. In Hebrews 12:11 we read of the peaceful fruit of righteousness. In 1 Peter Christians are to die to sin and live to righteousness (2:24) and be prepared to suffer for righteousness' sake (3:14). In 1 John the doing of righteousness in terms of following Jesus Christ, the righteous One, who came in flesh and will come again in glory, is what vital Christianity is all about. Believers who act righteously in word and deed proclaim their righteous Lord and show the error of the false teachers (2:29; 3:7–10).

The most discussed passage outside the Pauline corpus with respect to righteousness and justification is James 2:14–26. Here, at least on the surface, it appears that James is disagreeing with Paul. In fact the truth is that they have different starting points and are facing different missionary and pastoral situations.

A faith without works is said by James to be a dead faith, and Abraham is presented as being justified by his works because he was prepared to sacrifice his beloved son. For James, faith comes to completion in practical works and it was this completed faith of Abraham, says James, which was reckoned to him for righteousness (Gen. 15:6; James 2:23). Thus for James a person is placed in a right relation with God by a faith expressed in works. It is possible to reconcile Paul's approach and that of James if it is remembered that Paul himself spoke of "faith expressing itself through love" (Gal. 5:6; cf. James 2:1, 8).

PETER TOON

See also ETHICS; GOD; JUSTICE.

Bibliography. B. Przybylski, *Righteousness in Matthew and His World of Thought;* J. Reumann, et al., *Righteousness in the New Testament;* P. Stulmacher, *Reconciliation, Law and Righteousness;* J. A. Zeisler, *The Meaning of Righteousness in Paul.*

Romans, Theology of. While a study of Paul's theology in Romans may be undertaken without regard to the setting of the letter, it is more profitable to consider the probable reason for his writing and what he sought to accomplish by highlighting his specific theological agenda. Briefly, the church at Rome, which originally had strong Jewish Christian leadership (its founders may have been Roman Jewish pilgrims to Jerusalem at Pentecost who carried the gospel back to Rome), defaulted to Gentile leadership at the expulsion of Jews from Rome by edict of Emperor Claudius in the 40s. Following his death Jewish Christians returned with the result that there was bad feeling between the two groups in the church, the Gentiles with their larger numbers and leadership assuming superiority, the returning Jews claiming their own priority because they had been there first and had a more noble heritage. The resulting contention was of concern to Paul the missionary because it weakened the formerly strong outgoing mission of the Roman church by dissipating energy with internal strife. The major thrust of Paul's theology in the letter, therefore, is to bring them back to their earlier enthusiasm for evangelism and missionary activity by leveling their pride and leading them forward to a new commitment to Christ and his sovereign plan of salvation. Chapter 15 is a critical key in understanding Paul's major theological mission thrust in the letter.

Typical of all his theological writings Paul in Romans uses the technique of gentle persuasion, not heavy-handed fiat (even in Galatians, after a righteously indignant introduction, he settles into the rhetorical technique of persuading the Galatian Gentiles of the logic of his case). While the Lord anoints apostles, prophets, evangelists, pastors, and teachers for the formation and nurture of the churches, he does so "to prepare God's people for works of service, so that the body of Christ may be built up" (Eph. 4:11–12). Individual churches and their members accordingly are expected to react intelligently and responsibly to reasoned propositional theological appeals, thus "owning" Paul's agendas as congregations and individuals. Since Paul's theological agendas usually deal with recurring problems in churches then and now, his letters, originally addressed to specific occasions, providentially take on the nature of general pastoral epistles that are relevant to every age. While fine commentaries on Romans can bracket the question of historical setting (Cranfield's commentary is an example; he deals with the setting only at the end of his study), subtle nuances of Paul's theology appear only when the reader has the original occasion in mind. The theology of Romans has as its central focus the mission theme of evangelism. Paul's missionary agenda affects the presentation of his theological rhetoric as he attempts to persuade the Roman readers to forsake a bad course of interfamily strife that is draining their energy, for a good course of outward-looking evangelistic action.

Introduction: A Theology of Servant (1:1–18). Paul's basic theology centers on the generous nature of the Triune God as preeminent Servant, from whom all genuine human generosity is derived. Paul quickly moves off his own role as servant in verse 1 to honor the archetypal source of all generous servanthood in Christ, who is designated Son of God by his resurrection from the dead (v. 4). A trinitarian theology is immediately invoked that focuses on the resurrection of Christ as the culminating event "in power" of divine generosity, which is spelled out in verse 5 and establishes the theme of the entire letter.

The societal nature of the enterprise of bearing the gospel to the nations is heightened by Paul's sense of the interrelation of his apostleship with the Romans, that they be mutually encouraged by his visit and that he reap a harvest in Rome as he has elsewhere (vv. 8–15). The social nature of Paul's theology reflects the social nature of the Triune God and God's societal mission of redeeming creation. This introductory societal and mission theme is summarized in Paul's digest of the mission theology (vv. 16–18): On the positive side, the gospel is powerful to save everyone who has faith, Jew and Gentile alike; but it also has a negative cut like the sword of Hebrews 4:12, for those who suppress the truth in unrighteousness receive the gospel as the wrath of God against their ungodliness. Accordingly, the theology of Romans is seen to cut both ways in realistic exposition of God's holy nature: God is the God of grace to those who accept the gift of the Son in faith, and the holy God of wrath to sinners who reject the gift of the Son; to those who join the family, life; to those who reject the family, judgment. The mission of proclaiming the gospel will for Paul always articulate the theology of up and down, life and death, and these vectors will be seen to be connected to preaching, hearing, receiving, or rejecting, all under the sovereign election of God (v. 18 should be taken with v. 17, both being explanatory of v. 16).

Diagnosis: The Knowledge of God and the Sinful Fall of Humanity (1:19–3:20). Paul's theology of the double effect of the gospel creates the first half (a b) of a chiasm (a b b′ a′), the second half of which (b′a′) he proceeds to develop. As righteousness by faith is represented by letter a, and divine wrath against ungodliness by letter b, Paul now expands on the wrath of God against wickedness as b′ (1:19–3:20), followed by a lengthy exposition of righteousness by faith in Christ in 3:21–8:17 (a′). Paul's doctrine of the wrath of God (1:18) is slighted in modern liberal and process theology, but is crucial in his overall view of the nature of God, for God is holy and perforce must deal with wickedness. Paul takes ungodliness and wickedness and the wrath of God seriously, and this affects his theology of atonement in a′. The exchange of the truth about God for a lie by sinful humanity and the worshiping of creation rather than the Creator (1:23) brings about a giving up of human beings to divine wrath (three times: 1:24, 26, 28), even though deep within they knew of God's eternal power and deity and are without excuse (1:19–21, 28). There are no grounds for a natural theology in 1:19–20 in light of the larger context of the passage, for while men and women know better they go on sinning and are under the condemnation of death (1:32). In 1:18–32 Paul succeeds in leveling all humanity in general as guilty before God.

So serious is God's giving up humans to their own folly that Paul now details their fall, all the way to 3:20. In 2:1–16 he reveals the indefensible position of the moral person, whether Gentile or Jew, who criticizes others yet is equally guilty and is therefore also liable to divine wrath. Paul is not teaching a general works theology in this section, which would be antithetical to his justification by faith in Christ alone theology in the letter as a whole, but is addressing his Gentile and Jewish readers who have been guilty of hypocritical judgment. Christians need to be exhorted to persevere in belief and behavior appropriate to their confession, else they may not prove to be elect. Believers cannot presume upon God's grace and act like the devil; hence Paul can warn his readers like the writer to the Hebrews (6:4–12; 10:19–39) that better things are expected of them than to act inappropriately as followers of Christ. Only doers of the Law will be justified before God, whether Jew or Gentile; hence prideful superiority among Christians is unacceptable. Paul is consistently addressing a practical theological theme of the letter, that performative discipleship begins at home. Paul addresses Jewish believers more directly in 2:14–16 and again in 2:17–3:8 for their pride and ineffectiveness as witnesses, and then makes the notable observation that being a Jew in the true sense is a matter of inner not outer circumcision (2:28–29), thus establishing an inclusive category of Jew-Gentile that Jesus had already intimated in his teaching on inward intention (Matt. 6:4, 6, 18). Jew and Gentile believers are on the same footing within the church and are brought to the level of humility. (In chaps. 9–11 Paul will level the Gentile believers specifically for discounting the fact that ethnic Jews still are being welcomed to faith.) Yet in spite of the special advantage of the Jews in being entrusted with the oracles of God (3:2), they are now no better off under the leveling justice of God (3:9). This point gives Paul the opportunity to return again to the theme of the larger picture and the universal leveling guilt of humanity (3:9–20). The entire somber section on God's wrath against universal sin that began at 1:18 concludes with a string of quotations from the Old Testament, attesting the historical continuity of the nature of God's holiness against human sin. Paul's theological argument is now complete on the negative side and his boasting and strife-ridden Roman audience of Jewish and Gentile Christians are properly brought down from pride to humility.

At this point, the lowest in the letter, Paul now introduces the major positive thesis of his argument and the only one that can provide the foundation for the restoration of the Roman believers and their mission responsibility. They must get back to the all-sufficient work of Christ and have done with any kind of boasting other than in him. This leads to Paul's third principal theological point.

First Fundamental Prognosis: Justified by Faith in Jesus Christ (3:21–8:17). This is the first prognosis of hope (in 8:20 Paul says that God subjected the creation to futility because of human sin, but "in hope") and is signaled by the "but now" of 3:21. This hope is spelled out in view of the believer's personal relationship to Christ. Later, in 8:18–11:36, hope is described in cosmic dimensions, for individual believers are part of the cosmic plan of salvation, and Paul's theology is characterized by a theme of the one and the many. In our present unit, Christ is the one who performs a vicarious and redemptive work for the many. In the first section Paul asserts that the righteousness of God through faith in Jesus Christ excludes boasting (3:21–31). It is in faith in Christ and in his faithful work that salvation for Jew and Gentile resides (but note that objective faith in Jesus rests on Jesus' subjective faithfulness). In him the Law is perfectly kept through his active obedience; in his passive obedience on the cross divine wrath is propitiated, turned into grace. The believer is accordingly saved by the twofold work of Christ: in his life of faithful perfection, which is imputed to the Christian, and in his death and resurrection, which remove the penalty of eternal separation from God. Boasting is therefore excluded (3:27), for both Jew and Gentile are justified on the ground of the faith in Christ, who has kept the Law for us.

Paul now proceeds to show the continuity between the old and the new by citing Abraham as a primary example of the person of faith and humility (4:1–25), making the point that the faith principle was operating before Abraham became technically a Jew by circumcision. The Abraham of faith is therefore to be seen as the father of both Gentile and Jew—of the Jew because David personifies the grace and faith principle operative in the Mosaic period (vv. 6–8), and of the Gentile because Abraham was a Gentile before he was circumcised (vv. 9–25). Though different typologies were operative during the Abrahamic and Mosaic periods, and though Christ is the superior typology in this age because he embodies the old in himself as the new, the nature of God and salvation remain essentially the same. God is always the God of grace and of holiness, and faith is always "faith that works," that evinces behavior appropriate to faith (hence, there is no conflict between Paul's emphasis on faith and James 2:18–26, since each emphasizes one pole of the equation).

The Old Testament example of Abraham is complemented in 5:1–21 with a fuller comparison of two principial personalities, Adam I and Adam II. While Abraham functions as a secondary figure as patriarch of righteousness by faith for Gentile and Jewish believers, Adam and Christ represent archetypal progenitors of the human race where works are the primary focus. In this chapter Paul presents a theology of representative behavior that affects the entirety of human history. The first Adam forsook the image of God for which he was responsible, and by his work of sin spread death and sin to all (vv. 12–14). The far greater work of Christ the second Adam is a righteous work of grace and life (v. 17). The "much more" is qualitative, not quantitative, for only those who believe reign with Christ (the second "the many," is to be understood in this sense). Since the Roman believers are showing signs of weakness, and since salvation is integrally tied to eschatology in process of realization, Paul appeals to his readers at the beginning of the chapter (vv. 1–11) to lay hold in practice (existentially) of what they have in principle (essentially). It is necessary for them to walk out their faith and demonstrate in fact the peace they have in principle; so verse 1 should likely be rendered, "Therefore, since we have been justified by faith, let us have peace with God through our Lord Jesus Christ." This is supported by the emphasis on hope in verses 2–5 and the processive tenor of verses 9–10. Paul's theological challenge is to put into action a faith that works and endures to the end.

The existential appeal to proper behavior continues on a more personal level in chapter 6. Here the already and not yet aspects of Christian living and salvation are illustrated by the foundational work of Christ in his death and resurrection. Christians cannot continue in sin that grace may abound (v. 1) because participation in Christ's death and resurrection through the baptism of faith enjoins the believer to walk in newness of life (vv. 2–11). This appeal continues to the end of chapter 6 and through 7. "You have it, so *have* it!" Paul's theology of salvation is thoroughly eschatological and hortatory; redemption in the believer's life has been inaugurated, and if one truly has it, he or she will walk it out and faithfully persevere.

The exhortation of 6:15–23 is for the Romans to live no longer as slaves of sin but as slaves of God; in 7:1–6, to live as those freed from a former marriage by death of the previous partner so that one may marry again (in this case, Christ). One is no longer under the condemnation of the Law, though the Law is holy, just, and good; but since the vestigial remains of sin still hang over the Christian there must be a concerted exercise of the will to claim the victory that is realized in Jesus Christ our Lord (7:7–25). The Christian struggles between the times of Christ's first and second comings; hence inner conflict is inevitable, as is the need for continual exhortation. Paul continues his appeal in 8:1–17, reminding his readers that the whole Godhead of Father, Son, and Holy Spirit has been engaged to give the believer victory over sin. Paul seems to mix the types of conditional "ifs" in this section, the first three (8:9, 10, 11) being of the first class that indicates certainty, while the last two (8:13, 17) function as third class and connote likely possibility but not certainty. It is a delicate point Paul is making, but it is the same as Jesus' insistence on not only hearing but doing his words and bearing fruit (Matt. 7:15–20), and like the warning in Hebrews that faith must be faith that works in faithful mission (10:19–39). The Romans must start showing evidence of evangelistic zeal.

Further grounds for their revival of this responsibility are now spelled out by Paul in the next large theological section of the letter, which describes the cosmic scope of what God has done in Christ.

Second Prognosis: The Cosmic Plan of Redemption (8:18–11:36). Theological confidence is the compelling thrust of this unit, which is designed to overcome even Paul's questions about God's plan of salvation. In the prologue (8:18–39) the apostle comes to terms with present suffering and coming glory and the tension that arises between them. The latter overwhelms the former, 8:20 being the centerpiece: although God has subjected the creation to futility because of human sin, he has also subjected it in hope. Since the groaning of creation and the groaning of believers is undergirded by the divine groaning of the Spirit in intercession for the saints, there is reason for hope and victory, for nothing in creation "will be able to separate us from the love of God that is in Christ Jesus our Lord" (8:39).

But Paul confesses he still has a problem, and he proposes to work this out before the eyes of the Romans to demonstrate how theological reflection on the sovereignty and goodness of God can sustain the confidence of 8:31–39 and lead to the doxology of 11:33–36. Paul's personal difficulty lies with the failure of his kinsmen by race to rally around the gospel message and follow after Christ, who is the culmination of their covenant promises (9:1–5; again in 10:1–4 and 11:1a). His first theological answer to the why of 9:1–5 is to reassert that not all who are descended from Israel belong to Israel (9:6–13), a point made earlier in 2:28–29. His second reply invokes the sovereignty of God, God's freedom to decree what he wills, to choose whom he wills, and affirms the goodness of all God does, since there is none higher than he (9:14–33). Whether it is Jacob over Esau, Moses over Pharaoh, or now the Gentiles over Paul's own kind, it is by God's sovereign grace that even a remnant is saved.

Yet there is an added ingredient in the formula of election, for God does not choose capriciously but through valid secondary agents, and in each case the nonelect are seen to be lacking in faith: Esau, Pharaoh, and now Israel who have not pursued righteousness through faith, but as it were based on works (9:30–33). This emphasis on human choices leads into chapter 10, where Paul lays great stress on personal responsibility. Paul and the early church have been faithful in proclamation but, as in the Old Testament with Moses and Isaiah, Israel has rejected the good news. That is Paul's second answer to his earlier cry.

The third answer, found in chapter 11, returns to the hope that overcomes futility (cf. 8:20). God has not totally rejected Israel; Paul himself is evidence to the contrary, as were the seven thousand who did not bow the knee to Baal in the Old Testament, which attests the graciousness of God; and even now "there is a remnant chosen by grace" (11:5). If Israel's present default means grace for the Gentiles, "how much greater riches will their fullness bring" (11:12). A warning to the Gentiles now ensues (vv. 13–32), again attesting that Paul is addressing prideful factions in Rome and leveling them before the awesome sovereignty and freedom of God. Paul does not specify how many from ethnic Israel will return, or the time of their return, but what is clear is that just as a complement (11:25–26). The exact meaning of "all" in verse 26 is in question. Since "all" in 5:18–21 and in 11:32 does not imply every single member of a group, so here "all Israel" in context most likely means the whole (unspecified) remnant of Israel will be saved, the point being, against Gentile arrogance, that God still has a place in his sovereign plan for Paul's ethnic people. The gospel is for Jews and Gentiles (1:16). So moved is Paul by his own theological argument against his earlier doubts and misgivings, that he breaks into a doxology that sings the praises of the inscrutable God of grace, who is sovereign and from whom, through whom, and to whom are all things.

Concluding, then, the formal theological section of his letter, Paul is seen to have been mixing theology and exhortation to his factional Roman readers in order to bring them around to proper thought and action. So far Paul has dealt with the intellectual ground of theology in the work of Christ, though not without appeals to application; now he turns to exhortations to actual performance in detail.

The Practical Theological Remedy: Servants Who Are Faithful in Mission (12:1–15:13). As the previous eleven chapters deal with the vertical question of humility before the all-sufficient work of Christ, Paul's final appeal focuses on faith that works horizontally both within the body of believers and beyond in the wider world of mission. Practical theology begins with the believer's embodying servanthood in living and humble self-sacrifice (12:1–2), in loving and creative relation of the one to the many, not seeking to please oneself but one's neighbor, as Christ did not seek to please himself (12:3–21; 14:1–23; 15:1–13). At the same time Paul exhorts the Roman believers to live within the civil structure of common grace as agents of light in a world of darkness (13:1–14).

Paul's Mission Theology and Purpose for Writing Boldly (15:14–16:27). Finally, Paul discloses the real purpose of his writing such a carefully drawn out and persuasive argument: to enlist his Roman readers in supporting a mission to unreached Gentiles in Spain and the delivery of a love gift to suffering Jewish Christians in Jerusalem (15:14–33). Seeing to it that everyone hears of the power of the gospel is the heart of Paul's theology (1:16). As an example of the kinds of people he has in mind to carry out this honorable task, Paul lists twenty-nine people of various ethnic and social backgrounds and gender who are exemplary and well-known to the Romans (16:1–16). By contrast, his readers are to avoid contentious and unorthodox persons and to be wise and discerning (16:17–20), for in the end what matters is that theology bring about obedience of faith among the nations, to the glory of God (16:25–27; the opening theme of 1:5).

ROYCE GORDON GRUENLER

Bibliography. K. Barth, *The Epistle to the Romans;* F. F. Bruce, *The Letter of Paul to the Romans;* C. E. B. Cranfield, *A Critical and Exegetical Commentary on the Epistle to the Romans;* F. Godet, *Commentary on St. Paul's Epistle to the Romans;* H. Hendricksen, *Romans* (2 vols.); E. Käsemann, *Commentary on Romans;* H. C. G. Monle, *The Epistle to the Romans;* L. Morris, *The Epistle to the Romans;* J. Stott, *Romans.*

Rome. The church in Rome, to which Paul wrote the Roman letter from Corinth, was not founded by Paul. He had not yet been to Rome, but hoped to visit the city soon and with that church's help go on to preach in Spain (Rom. 15:22–24).

The church in Rome was probably founded by early converts, "visitors from Rome," who had been converted on the Day of Pentecost (Acts 2:10). It seems to have been composed of both Jews (Rom. 7:1, 4) and Gentiles (11:13) when Paul wrote his letter. The letter addresses problems between the two groups.

Rome was typical of the urban metropolises of the day, filled with arches, streets, and aqueducts, crowded with buildings, and, unlike some others, punctuated with imported Egyptian obelisks. Its population is estimated to have been between six hundred thousand and one million in the first century. Rome was built on seven hills along the east bank of the Tiber River, twenty-two miles from its mouth. The heart of the city was the area between the Palatine and Esquiline Hills, occupied by the Roman Forum and the Imperial Fora. Adjacent to this area on the south was the Colosseum and to the west, between the Palatine and Aventine Hills, stood the Circus Maximus. Not a few ancient Christians lost their lives in this circus. Many impressive buildings, such as temples and bathhouses, were built surrounding this central area. These included the still beautifully preserved Pantheon.

During the period of the Republic, prior to first century B.C., many ancient buildings were restored or rebuilt and the Appian Way, the major road from Rome to points south culminating in Brindisium, was lined with tombs. Paul traveled a part of this road from Capua to Rome as he passed through Three Taverns and the Forum of Appius (Acts 28:15). At the close of this period,

Julius Caesar reconstructed the Roman Forum. It has been suggested that Paul probably heard his death sentence in the Basilica Julia at the western end of this forum.

In the period of the empire, the city was greatly expanded, beginning with the work of Augustus, in whose reign Christ was born. The Mausoleum of Augustus was erected in the Campus Martius on the east bank of the Tiber River as was the Pantheon, which was a temple dedicated to all the gods by Augustus's architect Agrippa, between 27 and 25 B.C.

After the fire of Rome in A.D. 64, which the first-century Roman historian Tacitus insisted was caused by Nero, this depraved emperor rebuilt a considerable portion of the city, including his two hundred-acre imperial palace, the Golden House, which contained a 120 feet high gilded bronze statue of himself as the Sun.

Vespasian began work in 72 on the Colosseum, which his son Titus completed as emperor in 80. It still stands as a landmark in Rome. The beautifully preserved Arch of Titus, giving access to the Forum Romanum from the south, was erected by Domitian and the Senate in honor of Titus in A.D. 81, just after his death. Faced with Pentelic marble, it contained one arch with depictions on the inside. Among other things these include the spoils of Jerusalem's temple being carried away—the minora, the table of showbread, the sacred trumpets, and tablets fastened on sticks.

Paul spent two years under house arrest in Rome (Acts 28:16–30) and years later was imprisoned again, awaiting execution (2 Tim. 4:6–8). It is possible that Paul was incarcerated in the Mammertine Prison, located at the foot of the Capitoline Hill. Since the sixteenth century it has been called *San Pietro in Carcere,* preserving a tradition that Peter was imprisoned here as well.

Four churches in Rome were possibly directly connected with the New Testament. The Church of St. Peter in the Vatican, on the west side of the Tiber River, has marked the spot where tradition dating to the second century places the burial of Simon Peter. Excavations have produced no conclusive evidence of the bones of Peter as some have claimed.

The Church of St. Clement located in the district of the Caelian Hill, east of the Colosseum, is built over a first-century house that is thought to have belonged to Clement of Rome, who was the probable author of a letter (1 Clement) around A.D. 90 from the church in Rome to the church in Corinth.

This may be the person who is referred to by Paul in his letter from Rome to the Philippians (4:3). Irenaeus, in the late second century, wrote that Peter and Paul founded the church in Rome and were succeeded by Linus, Anacletus, and *Clement.* Jerome seems to have known this church.

The Church of Santa Pudenziana, located on the Via Urbana, between the Viminal and the Esquiline hills, may stand over the site of the house of Pudens, a person referred to by Paul in his last letter, written from Rome (2 Tim. 4:21). He was a Roman Christian who sent greetings to Timothy via Paul's letter. A tradition suggests that he may have been a senator in whose home Christians met and that the church may preserve the name of his daughter.

The largest church in Rome after St. Peter's is the Church of St. Paul Outside the Walls, located about a mile from the Gate of St. Paul, on the Via Ostiense. No real excavation has been done here, but the site is thought to be the location of the church built by Constantine to replace an oratory that had been built over the place where Lucina, a Roman matron, had buried Paul in her vineyard.

JOHN MCRAY

Bibliography. M. Cary, *A History of Rome Down to the Reign of Constantine;* S. A. Cook, et al., eds., *The Cambridge Ancient History,* Vol. 10, *The Augustan Empire 44 B.C.–A.D. 70;* J. Finegan, *The Archaeology of the New Testament: The Mediterranean World of the Early Christian Apostles;* J. McRay, *Archaeology and the New Testament.*

Ruler. *See* GOD, NAMES OF.

Ruth, Theology of. The Book of Ruth furnishes a panorama of God's sovereignty in everyday life, especially in the three most important needs of ancient Near Eastern people: food, marriage, and children. Famine drove Elimelech's family from the land of Judah; the likelihood of starvation appears to have compelled Naomi to return to her native land after the death of her husband and sons. The need for the protection of marriage induced Ruth to implement the bold plan of requesting Boaz to act as her kinsman redeemer. Barrenness in ancient times was a cause of embarrassment and concern; without an heir, the family name and lineage could not be carried on, and estates were forfeited. God blessed Ruth with both a child and an important lineage, the lineage of David.

Another major theme in the Book of Ruth is that of "loving-kindness" (Heb. *ḥesed*), first mentioned by Naomi in her claim that both Ruth and Orpah had displayed *ḥesed* to the "living and the dead" (1:8) and deserved to be shown *ḥesed* by Yahweh. Naomi later praised Boaz for showing Ruth *ḥesed* in exceeding what was required by the gleaning laws and making special provisions for her (2:20). Boaz said that Ruth had outdone her former *ḥesed* by desiring to marry him and rear a family for Naomi (3:10). In each case, the human agents manifested considerable self-giving love, which was ultimately rewarded even more graciously by Yahweh; they were not able to outgive their God.

Hardships in Moab. The events of this story are said to have occurred during the period of the judges (1:1), which was a difficult time for Israel, as underscored by the repeated phrase, "In those days Israel had no king; everyone did as he saw fit" (Judg. 17:6; 18:1; 19:1; 21:25). Much of what befell Elimelech and his family was to happen to the people of Israel if they disobeyed Yahweh after entering the promised land: drought (Deut. 28:23–24); crop failure (Deut. 28:18); cursing the fruit of their womb (Deut. 28:18); and removal from the land (Deut. 28:36). However, in the midst of these punishments, God displays grace to Naomi and Ruth.

Naomi, upon learning that God had once again provided food for the people of Judah, desires to return to her homeland, presumably in hopes of finding family members willing to care for her. However, she is keenly aware of her inability to provide for her daughters-in-law and therefore attempts to send them away. Orpah returns to her family, but Ruth chooses to stay with Naomi, sealing her decision with an oath. Ruth's decision was far-reaching: she would have to leave her people and journey to a foreign land; there was little chance that Naomi would be able to remarry and thereby provide for Ruth; and, perhaps of even more consequence, she would have to renounce her god and embrace Yahweh. The latter would require great faith since, thus far, she had only seen his judgment; even Naomi attributed her distressing circumstances to Yahweh (1:20). It appears that Ruth's great love for Naomi causes her to determine to serve this God.

Gleaning in Boaz's Field. Naomi and Ruth arrived in Bethlehem at the beginning of barley harvest (late April/early May; the eighth month according to the Gezer Calendar), shortly after which would follow the wheat harvest (2:23). This was perfect timing for two widows in need of food, as gleaning laws required landowners to leave corners of fields and all fallen shafts of grain for the poor. We learn of God's sovereignty over life's details when the text says that Ruth happened to come to the portion of the field belonging to Boaz (v. 3); it is this seemingly incidental circumstance that effectually opens the door for the blessing Yahweh had in store for Ruth and Naomi. When Ruth asks Boaz why he has shown such kindness (apparently unexpected) to her, a foreigner, he responds that her reputation of kindness had preceded her (v. 11). Boaz then invokes a blessing that he ultimately would help to fulfill: "May the LORD repay you for what you have done. May you be richly rewarded by the LORD, the God of Israel, under whose wings you have come to take refuge" (v. 12). Because Boaz treated Ruth kindly and with great generosity, Ruth learns about the gracious provision of Yahweh. Ruth returned home with a bountiful measure of barley (about two-thirds of a bushel). Later that evening, Naomi explains that Boaz is one of her nearest relatives, one who might be prevailed upon as a *go'el* ("kinsman-redeemer"; see Lev. 25:25–55). Marriage is not mentioned as a responsibility of a *go'el*, but this seems to be her purpose in revealing this kinship. Verse 23 indicates that Naomi did not act at that point, waiting instead several weeks until the barley and wheat harvests were finished (between late April and early June).

A Request for Redemption. Naomi determines to gain the security of marriage for Ruth by appealing to the right of *go'el*, but apparently Boaz was not required to accept this responsibility. This may be why Naomi waited until after the harvests, allowing greater time for him to observe Ruth. Naomi's plan of a secret meeting involved great risks of both physical danger and social ostracism should Ruth be discovered, yet Ruth bravely followed through in every detail. Ruth's entreaty for Boaz to spread his covering over her must be understood as a marriage request, which Boaz appears happy to fulfill, for several reasons: (1) Ruth has chosen to fulfill the familial obligations of her new country; (2) she chose Boaz over younger men; (3) she was generally recognized in the city as a "woman of excellence." Boaz was favorably impressed by Ruth's dedication and willingness to set aside her own passions and desires. In effect, Boaz would be the means of answering his prayer of 2:12, except that the protective wing of Yahweh is seen tangibly in Boaz's garment corner. However, Boaz knew of a nearer kinsman who would have the right of first choice of redemption. In the morning, Ruth is sent back to her mother-in-law with a generous gift (probably six seahs [about fifty-eight to ninety-five pounds] of barley) and a promise to see to her request. God had dealt favorably with Ruth, and Naomi was certain that Boaz would do his best to fulfill the request.

Boaz went to the city gate and shrewdly began the process of acquiring Elimelech's inheritance and Ruth. The other near relative was happy to acquire more land, but not at the costs associated with Ruth. Apparently the inheritance rights also required the kinsman to raise up a child for the deceased if there were any possibility of doing so. Naomi was probably too old to bear a child for Elimelech, but not so Ruth. The near relative would need to spend assets from his own inheritance to gain Elimelech's land, but the child, when of age, could claim back the purchased land. Thus he determines it is not profitable for him to acquire the land; Boaz, whose circumstances are substantially different, willingly offers to redeem the land and raise up a child to Elimelech. Boaz and his near relative, in the presence of witnesses at the gate, sealed their transaction by the accepted custom of trading sandals. Once again, the sovereignty of God is seen to extend over all the practical details of everyday life, including strategic legal transactions.

The witnesses at the gate then bless the transaction, requesting Yahweh to make Ruth like Rachel and Leah, who built the house of Israel, and to provide Boaz with a house like Perez, whom Tamar bore to Judah (Gen. 38). Even though Perez was born under scandalous circumstances, his offspring became one of the most important clans in Judah. Ruth later bore a son, named Obed, who carried on the family lines of both Boaz and Naomi. The name "Obed," meaning "the one who works or serves," suggests in this context that Obed served Naomi by ensuring her family's survival.

The Genealogy of Obed. This genealogy furnishes the important link between Obed (Ruth's offspring) and David (the future royal line). God not only gave Naomi and Ruth offspring and a family, but incorporated them into one of the most important lines of Judah. This genealogy is crucial for the Book of Ruth since it indicates that Yahweh providentially preserved righteous families through these times of great apostacy, among them, the line of David. PAUL D. WEGNER

Bibliography. A. A. Anderson, *JSS* 23 (1979): 171–83; D. Atkinson, *The Wings of Refuge: The Message of Ruth;* E. F. Campbell, *Ruth;* H. Fisch, *VT* 32 (1982): 425–37; M. Gow, *BT* 35 (1984): 309–20; R. Grant, *Biblica Sacra* 148 (1991): 424–41; R. M. Hals, *The Theology of the Book of Ruth;* R. L. Hubbard, *The Book of Ruth;* O. Loretz, *CBQ* 22 (1960): 391–99; E. Merrill, *Biblica Sacra* 142 (1985): 130–41; W. S. Prinsloo, *VT* 30 (1980): 330–41; E. Robertson, *BJRL* 32 (1950): 207–28; B. Vellas, *Theologia* 25 (1954): 201–10.

Ss

Sabbath. The origin of the Hebrew *šabbāt* is uncertain, but it seems to have derived from the verb *šābat,* meaning to stop, to cease, or to keep. Its theological meaning is rooted in God's rest following the six days of creation (Gen. 2:2–3). The Greek noun *sabbaton* translates the Hebrew noun *šabbāt*. The noun form is used primarily to denote the seventh day of the week, though it may occasionally refer to the Sabbath week (Lev. 23:15–16) at the end of every seven Sabbaths or fifty days, or the Sabbath year (Lev. 25:1–7) in which the land was to be at complete rest.

The Old Testament. The observance of the Sabbath is central to Jewish life. Of the eight holy days (Shabbat, the first and seventh days of Pesach, Shavout, Rosh Hashanah, Yom Kippur, and the first and eighth days of Succot) proscribed in the Torah, only the Sabbath is included in the Decalogue. Though not holier than other holy days like Yom Kippur or Rosh Hashanah, the Sabbath is given special attention because of its frequency. Yet despite any significance that accrues on the basis of its frequency or inclusion in the Decalogue, its importance rests ultimately on its symbolic representation of the order of creation. For, according to the Genesis narrative, God himself rested on the seventh day, thus making it sacred (Gen. 2:1–2). For the pious Jew, keeping the Sabbath holy is a *mitzvah,* or duty, before God. Indeed, The Old Testament takes Sabbath observance so seriously that profaning it results in the death penalty (Exod. 31:14; 35:2; Num. 15:32).

The meaning of the Sabbath institution comes to light against the background of several key facts. First, Exodus 20:8–11 makes a clear connection between the Sabbath day and the seventh day on which God the Creator rested. Sabbath observance therefore involves the affirmation that God is Creator and Sustainer of the world. To "remember the Sabbath" meant that the Jew identified the seven-day-a-week rhythm of life as belonging to the Creator. This connection is particularly important in light of the Jewish doctrine that human beings are co-partners with God. They receive the world in an unfinished state so that they may share with God the purposes he seeks by continuing to fashion and subdue the creation. If the Creator stopped his creative activity on the seventh day, then those who share in his creative work must do the same. Sabbath contravenes any pride that may accompany human mastery and manipulation of God's creation. In ceasing from labor one is reminded of one's true status as a dependent being, of the God who cares for and sustains all his creatures, and of the world as a reality belonging ultimately to God.

Second, the Sabbath is an affirmation of Israel's identity. The words of Moses to the people in Deuteronomy 5:12–15 demonstrate that, however much its rhythm reflects the order of God-created life in general, the Sabbath functions also to remind Israel of her specific origins. "Remember that you were slaves in Egypt and that the Lord your God brought you out of there with a mighty hand and an outstretched arm. Therefore the Lord your God has commanded you to observe the Sabbath day." Here the acknowledgment that God is the Creator of life is intensified by the acknowledgment that he is also the saving presence in the history of the Jewish people, and by that means of the entire creation. Israel's keeping of the Sabbath was a reminder of her very identity as a people liberated from slavery to the Egyptians and for a special role in the cosmic drama of human salvation. As such it was a cherished gift of God, "a sign between me and you for generations to come" (Exod. 31:12–17), testifying of God's faithfulness to his covenant throughout the generations. The covenant relationship demands Israel's sanctification, and by keeping the Sabbath holy Israel is reminded continually that the God who sanctified the seventh day also sanctifies her.

Third, the Sabbath is a day of rest and worship given as a gift from the restless condition of slavery. The prohibition of work extended to all those living within Israel, including slaves and animals

(Exod. 20:10), even during the plowing season (Exod. 34:21). This necessitated additional work on the sixth day (Exod. 16:5, 23). What constitutes rest and work? In the Torah there are only two explicit prohibitions concerning work on the Sabbath. No fires were to be kindled in Jewish dwellings (Exod. 35:3), and no one was to leave their place (Exod. 16:29). However, more can be inferred from other texts. For example, Moses instructed the people to bake and boil the manna and put it aside until morning (Exod. 16:23–24), hinting that cooking was not fitting for the Sabbath. A man found gathering sticks on the Sabbath was stoned to death (Num. 15:32–36). The carrying of a burden or bringing it by Jerusalem's gates was prohibited (Jer. 17:22). Nehemiah closed the city gates to the merchants who were said to profane the Sabbath by carrying their goods and selling them (Neh. 13:15–22). Most important is the Torah's placement of the laws concerning the Sabbath directly adjacent to the instructions for building the tabernacle (Exod. 31), implying that each of the many varieties of work associated with tabernacle construction was prohibited on the Sabbath.

Just as joy is more than the absence of sorrow, the Sabbath is more than cessation of labor. Resting in bed all day does not amount to a keeping of the Sabbath. The Sabbath is to be a delight and joy (Isa. 58:13). Noteworthy is the fact that the fourth commandment (Exod. 20:8) places the positive command to keep the Sabbath holy before the negative prohibition to cease working. As worship, additional sacrifices were offered (Num. 28:9–10) at the temple, and the special shewbread was to be set out "sabbath after sabbath" to signify Israel's commitment to the covenant (Lev. 24:8). During and after the Babylonian exile, worship became a more prominent part of Sabbath observance. In Jewish homes the benedictions of *kiddush* (Friday evening) and *habdalaha* (Saturday evening) were recited, and there were morning and afternoon services at the synagogue. The joyous character of the Sabbath is reflected in, among other things, the Jewish tradition of eating richly, which derives from its inclusion in the list of "festivals of the Lord" (Lev. 23) the prohibition of fasting, and the forbidding of outward expressions of grief and mourning.

In the prophets, observance of the Sabbath becomes the touchstone for Israel's obedience to its covenant with God. The future of Jerusalem depends on faithful Sabbath keeping (Jer. 17:24–27). One's personal well-being is also at stake (Isa. 56:2–7). Those who honor the day will find joy, riding on the heights of the earth and being fed with the heritage of Jacob (Isa. 58:14). As God once desired to destroy his people in the desert because of their Sabbath desecration (Ezek. 20:12–14), so he now counts this among Israel's present moral failures (Ezek. 22:8) for which there will be purging and dispersion. Amos issues a stern warning to those merchants who endure the Sabbath, anxious only to get on with the selling of grain (8:5).

The consistency of the prophets' call to honor the Sabbath testifies in part to the growing need, especially during the exilic period, to preserve Jewish identity in a pagan environment. In this sense prophetic aims are continuous with those of the Mosaic period. But scholarly consensus finds in the prophetic writings a subtle transformation wherein the Sabbath, formerly a social institution of festivity, rest, and worship, became above all a religious mark of personal and national holiness vis-à-vis the Gentiles.

The New Testament. The Gospels record six cases in which Jesus' action resulted in controversy over the Sabbath, and two more that did not. Jesus faces the accusation that his disciples have broken the Sabbath by picking grain and eating (Matt. 12:1–8). He is interrogated concerning his healing of a man with a withered hand (Matt. 12:9–14), a crippled woman (Luke 13:10–14), a man with dropsy (Luke 14:1–6), a sick man by the pool of Beth-zatha (John 5:1–18), and a blind man (John 9). Neither the healing of Peter's mother-in-law (Mark 1:29–31) nor Jesus' synagogue address in Nazareth seems to have occasioned any opposition. Just how Jesus regarded the Sabbath is a matter of discussion. Some argue that Jesus deliberately broke the Sabbath commandment in order to call attention to his messianic character. Others contend that Jesus violated not the Sabbath commandment but only the casuistry of the Pharisees as contained in the *halachah.* In the final analysis, a comprehensive statement about Jesus' attitude toward the Sabbath would require an investigation into his attitude toward the Law in general.

But even in the face of interpretive difficulties, the particular nature of Jesus' response to these controversies make two things quite clear. First, by his statement "the Son of Man is Lord of the Sabbath" (Matt. 12:8) Jesus claims that the authority of the Sabbath does not exceed his own. Hence, the Son of Man as Lord decides the true meaning of the Sabbath. In two Johannine accounts in particular, the authority by which Jesus' Sabbath healings are performed is linked directly to God the Father, according both to the blind man's (9:33) and Jesus' own witness (5:17). Second, by stressing that the Sabbath was made for humankind and not humankind for the Sabbath (Mark 2:27) Jesus gives an indication as to its true meaning. That is, he places it against the universal horizon of God's intent that it benefit all creation and not just Israel. Jesus' healings on the Sabbath underscore this beneficent character, for "it is lawful to do good on the Sabbath" (Matt. 12:12). By his response to the religious leaders in two Lukan incidents, one gathers the impression that what is ultimately at stake is the health (physical and spiritual) of those healed. Just as naturally as one would lead an ox or donkey to water (13:15) or rescue a child who has fallen into a well on the Sabbath (14:5), Jesus acts, with eschatological urgency, in the interest of life and salvation.

Among the several references to the Sabbath in Acts (1:12; 13:14–44; 15:21; 17:2; 18:4; 20:7) there is little evidence to suggest that the earliest Christian communities deviated from the traditional Sabbath observed on the seventh day. The lone reference to a gathering "On the first day of the week" (20:7) most likely reflects an emerging Christian consensus that the first day was an appropriate day on which to meet for worship and celebrating the Lord's Supper.

In his letters Paul shows concern for certain restrictions placed on his converts (Rom. 14:5; Gal. 4:10; Col. 2:16), among them Sabbath keeping no doubt. In his characteristic refusal to allow such things to become a basis for judging fellow believers, Paul seems, especially if Romans 14:5 refers to Sabbath keeping, a claim not unanimously accepted, to support one's freedom either to observe or not observe the Jewish sabbath, though he evidently continued to observe it for himself (Acts 17:2).

Hebrews anticipates an eschatological "sabbath rest" (*sabbatismos*) that remains for the people of God (4:1–11). The term *sabbatismos* appears nowhere else in the New Testament, and may be the writer's own creation to indicate the superiority of the coming rest to that of the seventh day. Though a superior quality of rest, it is still marked chiefly by the cessation of labor patterned after God's rest on the seventh day.

Craig J. Slane

See also Lord's Day, the.

Bibliography. N. A. Barack, *A History of the Sabbath;* S. Baron, *The Jewish Community;* D. A. Carson, *From Sabbath to Lord's Day;* S. Goldman, *A Guide to the Sabbath;* A. Heschel, *The Sabbath;* P. Jewett, *The Lord's Day.*

Sacrifice. *See* Offerings and Sacrifices.

Sadducees. Jewish group mentioned in three different contexts in the Synoptic Gospels (Mark 12:18 [= Matt. 22:23–34; Luke 20:27]; Matt. 3:7; 16:1–12) and six in Acts (4:1; 5:17; 23:6–8). They always appear as inquisitors or opponents of John the Baptist, Jesus, or the early Christians. Acts 23:8 defines the Sadducees theologically, saying that, in contrast to the Pharisees, they hold there "is no resurrection, and neither angels nor spirits." The Sadducean rejection of the resurrection is the point at issue in Mark 12:18 and parallels. Additional information about them, primarily through the Jewish historian, Josephus, and the rabbinic writings, is scanty and hostile. Rabbinic writings sometimes interchange the term "Sadducee" with "Samaritans" (here meaning "opponents") and "Boethuians." The latter is probably from their connection with the house of Boethus, from which came several high priests during the New Testament period.

It should be noted that the "Herodians" (Matt. 22:16; Mark 3:6; 12:13) are sometimes assumed to be Sadducees. Their name identifies them as members of household-court of the Herods or supporters of the dynasty. It may be assumed that the Sadducees generally supported Herod and his reigning descendants (although Herod executed forty-five of them at the beginning of his reign), but there is no evidence for equating the Herodians and Sadducees.

The name "Sadducee" is closely associated with attempts to determine the origin of this group. Suggestions include linking it with an Old Testament priestly family (Zadok), the Hebrew word for "just" or "righteous" (*ṣdq*) or "fiscal officials" (Gk. *syndikoi*). There are problems with etymologies and all other attempts to identify their origin.

Josephus lists the Sadducees as one of the three sects/groups of Jewish "philosophy" (*Ant* 18.1.2 [11]; cf. 13.5.9 [293]). His first historical reference says John Hyrcanus (135–105 B.C.) came under their influence after his break with the Pharisees. Josephus describes them as argumentative (*Ant* 18.1.4 [16]), "boorish" and "rude" to both each other and aliens (*War* 2.9.14 [166]), few in number but including "men of the highest standing" (*Ant* 18.1.4 [17]). They have "the confidence of the wealthy" but not the populace (*Ant* 13.1.4 [298]). When exercising their office the Sadducees were forced by public opinion to follow "the formulas of the Pharisees" (*Ant* 18.1.4 [17]). Evidently they were more severe in administering punishments than Pharisees (*Ant* 13.10.6 [294]). Like the New Testament, Josephus mentions the Sadducean rejection of the resurrection (*War* 2.9.14 [165]); and twice says they rejected "Fate" (predestination) to dissociate God from evil and to assert the human free choice of good or evil (*War* 2.9.14 [165]; *Ant* 18.1.4 [14]).

Josephus says, "The Pharisees had passed on . . . certain regulations handed down by former generations and not recorded in the Laws of Moses, . . . rejected by the Sadducean group, who hold only those regulations should be considered valid which were written down (in Scripture)" (*Ant* 13.10.6 [297]; cf. *Ant* 18.1.4 [16]). This points toward a major feature of Sadduceanism: rejection of the Pharisaic Oral Law, or "the traditions of the elders." In the centuries after the destruction of Jerusalem by the Babylonians (586 B.C.), the Pharisees compiled and transmitted orally a body of traditional interpretations, adaptations, and additions to Scripture that they believed to be of divine origin. These included ways of applying the Law to various situations—expansion and prescriptions regarding a wide range of levitical ceremonies and regulations. These traditions also included certain theological points, such as resurrection and angels and spirits, which, although not particularly emphasized in the Old Testament, were prominent during the intertestamental period. Although the Sadducees rejected the Pharisaic Oral Law they certainly had their own traditions, interpretations, and procedures.

In Acts 5:17 those with the high priest are identified as "the party of the Sadducees." Josephus depicts the Sadducees as closely associated with the priestly Hasmonean rulers. By the time of the New Testament they appear to be the majority in the Sanhedrin, over which the high priest presided.

Religiously, the Sadducees were literal in handling the Old Testament Law and resisted the "new" ideas and traditions of the Pharisees. Politically and socially, they were open to rapprochement with Hellenistic (Greek) culture and the Roman political system. The Sadducees were essentially secularists, a result of their exclusion of God ("Fate") from human affairs and their conviction that humans can expect nothing beyond this life. In general it seems the Sadducees supported those interpretations and procedures that enhanced the prestige, power, and financial benefit of the priestly temple cult and the aristocracy.

Jesus and the early Christians posed a threat to the Sadducees (John 11:47–50). Jesus' proclamation of the reality of the spiritual realm, his denunciation of the Jewish religion as then practiced, and his wide popular support could have endangered the already precarious position of the Sadducees. Furthermore, Jesus and his followers supported some of the positions of the Pharisees. The Sadducees found particularly objectionable the Christian proclamation that in Jesus the resurrection is a present reality (Acts 4:2).

The Sadducees were inseparably bound to the external political, social, and especially the temple-centered institutions of Judaism. With the destruction of the Jewish state and temple in A.D. 70, they passed into the pages of history.

J. JULIUS SCOTT, JR.

See also PHARISEES.

Bibliography. E. E. Ellis, *NTS* 10 (1963–64): 274ff.; L. L. Grabbe, *Judaism from Cyrus to Hadrian;* A. J. Saldarini, *Pharisees, Scribes, and Sadducees in Palestinian Society;* E. Schürer, *The History of the Jewish People in the Age of Jesus Christ;* M. Simon, *The Jewish Sects at the Time of Jesus;* S. Zeitlin, *The Sadducees and the Pharisees.*

Saints. The word "saint" is derived from a Greek verb (*hagiazō*) whose basic meaning is "to set apart," "sanctify," or "make holy." In the history of the Old Testament religion, the idea of holiness or separateness was inherent in the concept of God. God was unapproachable in the tabernacle or temple by the ordinary individual, being accessible only to the priests and only under carefully specified conditions. His presence (the Shekinah) dwelled in the Holy of Holies or the Most Holy Place, the most remote and inaccessible place in the wilderness tabernacle and later in the Jerusalem temple. Only the high priest was allowed to stand in God's presence in this area, and then only once a year at Yom Kippur (the Day of Atonement).

This sacred place was further separated from the ordinary Jewish worshiper by another room called "the Holy Place," which could be entered only by priests. The intent was to impress upon the people the utter holiness and sacredness of the God they worshiped, as well as the necessity of their being set apart or sanctified as saints in his service. This sense of Jehovah's separateness from the sins of the people and from the pagan idols of the lands in which they dwelled was the heart of Jewish monotheism. Its eventual disregard led to the destruction of the temple and the exile of Israel.

This idea of the separateness of God and his people is carried forward in the New Testament, which was written by Jews (except possibly Luke–Acts) who interpreted God's covenant with Israel through the teachings of Christ. Those who were dedicated to the teachings of Christ were frequently called saints by these writers (e.g., Matt. 27:52; Acts 9:13; 26:10; Rev. 14:12). Six of Paul's letters to churches are addressed to saints (Romans, 1–2 Corinthians, Ephesians, Philippians, and Colossians).

Saints, in the New Testament, are never deceased individuals who have been canonized by the church and given sainthood. They are living individuals who have dedicated themselves to the worship and service of the one true God as revealed through his Son, Jesus Christ. Even the children of such parents are called "sanctified" (1 Cor. 7:14–15). That is, they are considered undefiled by paganism if at least one of their parents is a Christian. All saved are sanctified, but not all sanctified are saved.

On occasion, when discussing the atonement, Paul carefully differentiates between Jewish Christians and Gentile Christians, calling the former saints and the latter believers. It was the saints, the holy people of God in the Old Testament, who brought the Messiah and redemption into the world, eventually extending the blessings to the Gentiles.

This usage may be seen in 1 Corinthians 1:2, which is addressed to "those sanctified in Christ Jesus and called to be holy [saints—Jewish Christians], together with all those [Gentiles] everywhere who call on the name of our Lord Jesus Christ—Lord and ours." The same distinction is made in Ephesians 1:1: "to the saints [Jewish Christians] in Ephesus and the faithful [Gentiles] in Christ Jesus." Colossians is also addressed to "the holy and faithful brothers" in Christ.

Paul addresses the letter to all the Christians in Rome as saints (Rom. 1:7, because Gentiles who, as wild olive branches have been grafted into the stem of Judaism, now share in the full relationship to that plant and are also saints), but the Jewish Christians in Rome, who are to be recipients of a special contribution Paul collected among Gentile churches, are called "the saints" in distinction (Rom. 15:25–33).

It is informative in this regard that Paul refers to this same collection in 2 Corinthians 8:1–4 as a sharing by the Macedonian churches with "the saints," not with the "other" saints. Paul's apprehension over whether the Jerusalem saints would accept such a contribution was based on the fact that Jewish Christians were being asked to accept the offering from Gentile Christians. The entire discussion of the issue in Acts 21 when Paul arrived in Jerusalem makes this clear.

Thus, although Gentile Christians are saints, too, because they were given access to the faith of Abraham and the people of the Old Testament, when redemptive history is discussed the Jews are specially designated the "saints" while the Gentiles are considered believers who were later admitted into this "holy" Jewish nucleus.

John McRay

See also Christians, Names of; Church, the; Holy, Holiness.

Salvation. Of the many Hebrew words used to signify salvation, *yāšaʿ* (to save, help in distress, rescue, deliver, set free) appears most frequently in the Old Testament. Commonly, the deliverance of which the Old Testament speaks is material in nature, though there are important exceptions. In contrast, the employment of *sōtēria* in the New Testament, though it may include material preservation, usually signifies a deliverance with special spiritual significance. In addition to the notion of deliverance the Bible also uses salvation to denote health, well-being, and healing.

Broadly speaking, one might say that salvation is the overriding theme of the entire Bible. But since it is a multidimensional theme with a wide range of meaning, simple definitions are impossible. The biblical writers speak of salvation as a reality with at once spiritual and physical, individual and communal, objective and subjective, eternal and historical dimensions. Since the biblical writers view salvation as a historical reality, the temporal dimensions of past, present, and future further intensify and deepen the concept. Salvation is a process with a beginning and an end. Further, salvation involves the paradox of human freedom and divine election. Despite the complexity of these dimensions, the Bible constantly speaks about salvation in the context of some very simple and concrete relationships—between humans and God, between human beings, and between human beings and nature. God is the main actor throughout, from the deliverance of Noah's family to the great multitude who shout "Salvation belongs to our God, who sits on the throne, and to the Lamb!" (Rev. 7:10).

The Old Testament. In general the Old Testament writers see salvation as a reality more physical than spiritual, more social than individual. Where individuals are singled out it seems to be for the good of the community. For example, the Genesis narrative develops the theme of God's blessing, which though resting on certain individuals, renders them agents for some greater work of God. Joseph's rise to fame in Egypt preserves the lives of his entire family (Gen. 45:4–7). Through Noah's faithfulness God brings salvation to his family as well as animal life (Gen. 7–9). And the blessing of the promise of nationhood and land for Abraham was not only for his descendants but for all families on the earth (Gen. 12:1–3). After 430 years in Egypt, an entire people is delivered through Moses (Exod. 1–12). Through Esther's rise to power the Jewish people are spared annihilation (Esther 7).

Despite the importance of human agency, salvation is attributed above all to God. None but God can save (Isa. 43:14; Hos. 1:7). He is the keeper of his flock (Ezek. 34) and on him alone one waits for a saving word to penetrate the silence (Ps. 62). Idolatry is an illusion, for the salvation of Israel is in the Lord (Jer. 3:23). God is the warrior—not Moses—who triumphs gloriously over Pharaoh's armies at the sea (Exod. 15). Salvation is something to stand and watch, for "The Lord will fight for you; and you need only be still" (Exod. 14:13). "In repentance and rest is your salvation; in quietness and trust is your strength" summons Isaiah (30:15). The content of God's salvation includes personal and national deliverance from one's enemies, deliverance from slavery (Deut. 24:18), ongoing protection and preservation from evil (Ps. 121), escape from death (Ps. 68:19), healing (Ps. 69:29; Jer. 17:14), inheritance of land, descendants, and long life.

Salvation from sin, though not a dominant concern, is by no means absent, especially in the prophets. As much as he is concerned for Israel's national restoration, Ezekiel stresses the need for salvation from uncleanness, iniquity, and idolatry (36:22–32). Here salvation involves the gift of a new heart of flesh and new spirit, which will finally empower his people to keep the commandments, after which comes habitation in the land. In this passage, too, we encounter a common refrain: such salvation, when it comes, will be neither for the sake of Israel nor her deeds, but for God and his glory, which has been profaned and which now must be vindicated among the nations. Isaiah tells of a salvation still on the way, which will be achieved through the vicarious suffering of the Servant (chap. 53) who bears the sin of many. This salvation will last forever (51:6).

The anticipated salvation of the prophetic writings manifests a tension similar to that which pervades the New Testament. While salvation is a fait accompli—God saved Israel from slavery in Egypt unto a covenant relationship with himself—Israel still awaits God's salvation. God had saved Israel in the past, and therefore God can be expected to deliver in the future. Whatever else salvation may be from a biblical perspective, its dimensions of "settled past" and "anticipated future" show it in its widest scope to be an elongated reality covering the entire trajectory of history. This recognition has helped recent biblical scholarship to avoid the earlier pitfall of relegating the role of the Old Testament to that of mere preparation or precursor for the gospel. One cannot escape the fact that for the Jews of the Old Testament salvation was not an abstract concept, but a real and present experience. The psalms are replete with praise for God's salvation, which is experienced as joy (51:12). It is a cup of thanksgiving lifted to God (116:13) and a horn (18:2). Elsewhere salvation is depicted as a torch (Isa. 62:1), a well (Isa. 12:3), and a shield (2 Sam. 22:36).

The New Testament. The advent name "Immanuel," "God with us," signifies momentous progress in the history of salvation. In Matthew's Gospel the angel tells Joseph that Mary's child is conceived of the Holy Spirit, and that he is "to give him the name Jesus, because he will save his people from their sins" (1:21–23). The name "Jesus" (derived from the Hebrew Joshua) itself means salvation. The purpose for the Son of Man's coming is to seek out and save the lost (Luke 19:10). The New Testament continues the Old Testament affirmation that salvation belongs to God alone, but with greater specificity. Now it is God's presence in and to the man Jesus that proves decisive. Peter's certainty of this relation between "Jesus Christ of Nazareth, whom you crucified" and the "God [who raised him] from the dead" moves him to the exclusive confession that salvation belongs only to the name of Jesus Christ (Acts 4:10–12).

In Jesus' teaching salvation is linked to the advance of God's kingdom, which is in turn linked to Jesus' own person. By using God's kingdom as a circumlocution for salvation, Jesus deepens the Old Testament conviction that salvation belongs to God, for the kingdom signifies a sphere of reality in which God reigns sovereign. The disciples themselves responded to Jesus' teaching about the kingdom with the question "Who then can be saved?" (Mark 10:23–26). That Jesus understood himself to be that bringer of God's kingdom is evident in the claim following his synagogue reading, "Today this scripture is fulfilled in your hearing" (Luke 4:21). Salvation belongs to those who follow Jesus, bringer and embodiment of God's kingdom.

Salvation is described as the mystery of God that is now revealed (Eph. 3:9; 6:19), a plan conceived before the foundations of the world (Eph. 1:3–14), a light for revelation to the Gentiles (Luke 2:30–32), a transition from death to life (John 5:24), a message especially for sinners (Mark 2:17), a gift of grace through faith not of works (Eph. 2:8–9), that for which the whole creation groans (Rom. 8:22), the revelation of God's righteousness to faith and for faith (Rom. 1:16–17), the justification that comes through faith (Rom. 4:22–25), reconciliation (2 Cor. 5:18–19), and redemption (Rom. 8:23). In response to Nicodemus's statement, salvation is said to be a spiritual birth, a birth from above without which one cannot enter the kingdom (John 3:1–11). Salvation means death to and freedom from sin (Rom. 6), a new perspective that transcends the human point of view and participation in a new creation (Rom. 5:16–17), peace with God (Rom. 5:1), life as adopted children of God's (Gal. 4:4), baptism into Christ's death (Rom. 6:4), and the reception of the Holy Spirit (Rom. 5, 8).

Salvation encompasses both the physical and spiritual dimensions of life, having relevance for the whole person. On the physical side, entrance into the kingdom requires attention to earthly needs, especially those of the poor. Jesus demands that a wealthy man give his riches to the poor (Mark 10:17–22). The salvation that comes to Zacchaeus's house inspires him to give half his possessions to the poor (Luke 19:8–10). Care for the poor was a regular function of the earliest Christian communities (Acts 9:36; 10:4, 31; 24:17; Gal. 2:10; James 2:1–7). But for Jesus the physical and spiritual dimensions are held very close together. Forgiveness of sins and physical healing frequently coexist, as in the healing of the paralytic (Mark 2:1–12). Other healings done in Jesus' name call attention to the intimate connection (Acts 3:16; 4:7–12) among spirit, mind, and body. In these examples salvation means not only forgiveness of sin but mitigation of its effects.

Salvation also extends beyond the parameters of national Jewish identity. On at least two occasions Jesus corrects (or at least sidesteps) national expectations concerning the kingdom—-once in response to the disciples' question (Acts 1:6–8) and once on the Emmaus road (Luke 24:25–26). Since Jesus' death was for all people (John 11:51), repentance and forgiveness of sins were to be proclaimed to all nations (Luke 24:47). This gospel, says Paul, was given in advance in the form of God's promise to bless all the nations through Abraham (Gal. 3:8).

The objective basis and means of salvation is God's sovereign and gracious choice to be "God with us" in the person of Jesus Christ, who is described as both author and mediator of salvation (Heb. 2:10; 7:25). But the movement of Jesus' life goes through the cross and resurrection. It is therefore "Christ crucified" that is of central importance for salvation (1 Cor. 1:23), for "Christ died for our sins according to the Scriptures" (1 Cor. 15:3) and was handed to death for our trespasses (Rom. 4:25). What Jesus did in our name he also did in our place, giving "his life as a ransom for many" (Matt. 20:28). And if Christ demonstrated his love by dying when we were still sinners, how much more shall we now be saved by his life? (Rom. 5:8–10). So critical is the resurrection to the future hope of salvation that "If Christ has not been raised, your faith is futile; you are still in your sins" (1 Cor. 15:17).

The subjective basis of salvation is personal repentance and faith, often associated closely with water baptism. John the Baptist preached a baptism of repentance for the forgiveness of sins (Matt. 3:2; Mark 1:4), a message echoed by Peter (Acts 2:38) and Paul (Acts 20:21). Jesus said salvation required belief in him (Mark 16:15; John 6:47). Paul enjoined confession with the mouth that "Jesus is Lord" and belief that God raised him from the dead (Rom. 10:8–9). The writer of Hebrews suggests that the hearing of the gospel is of no value unless combined with faith (4:1).

The New Testament articulates salvation in terms of past, present, and future time. In Christ we were elected before the foundation of the world (Eph. 1:4). In hope we were saved (Rom. 8:24). Yet the cross is the power of God for those who are being saved (1 Cor. 1:18). Likewise Paul's readers are admonished to work out their salvation with fear and trembling (Phil. 2:12). And there is yet a salvation that lies waiting to be revealed in the last time (1 Peter 1:5), a redemption for which we groan inwardly (Rom. 8:23). For Paul, the past dimension of salvation is generally conceived as justification, redemption, and reconciliation, while its present dimension is depicted in terms of the Spirit's sanctifying work. Its future dimension is said to be glorification, the culmination of the saving process wherein believers will experience Christ's presence in new and resurrected bodies no longer burdened by the vestiges of sin. William T. Arnold

See also Atonement; Cross, Crucifixion; Death of Christ; Eternal Life, Eternality, Everlasting Life; Faith; Gospel.

Bibliography. D. Bloesch, *The Christian Life and Salvation;* O. Cullmann, *Salvation in History;* E. M. B. Green, *The Meaning of Salvation;* S. Kevan, *Salvation;* H. D. McDonald, *The Atonement of the Death of Christ;* G. G. O'Collins, *ABD,* 5:909–14; U. Simon, *Theology of Salvation;* G. R. Smith, *The Biblical Doctrine of Salvation;* J. R. W. Stott, *The Cross of Christ.*

Samuel, First and Second, Theology of. 1–2 Samuel appears midway through the sequence of the Old Testament books that narrate the flow of Israel's history from the time of the conquest to that of the exile (Joshua–2 Kings). The Books of Samuel are particularly significant for understanding Israel's religious and historical development because they tell of the momentous transition from the period of the judges to that of the monarchy.

Overview of 1–2 Samuel. The early chapters of 1 Samuel depict the historical setting for the rise of kingship in Israel. These chapters include descriptions of Samuel's birth and call to be a prophet (1–3); Israel's defeat by the Philistines and the capture of the ark (4–6); and the role of Samuel as a judge and deliverer (7).

This introductory section of the book is followed by a series of narratives telling how and why kingship was introduced in Israel under the guidance of the prophet Samuel (chaps. 8–12). Here it becomes evident that the kingship in Israel was to be radically different from the kingship of the surrounding nations. It was to be a "covenantal kingship."

Saul's violation of his covenantal responsibilities as king quickly led to his rejection by the word of the Lord through Samuel (chaps. 13–15).

Samuel is then sent to anoint David as king, in place of Saul (chap. 16). Subsequent narratives describe the progressive deterioration of Saul's reign, while at the same time depicting David's gradual rise to the throne (1 Sam. 16–2 Sam. 5). The reign of David is then described both in its grandeur and glory (2 Sam. 6–9), as well as in its weaknesses and failures (chaps. 10–20). The book ends with final reflections on David's reign in the narratives and poems of 2 Samuel 21–24.

Theology and History in 1–2 Samuel. The narratives of 1–2 Samuel are important not only for the light they shed on the historical events that spawned and gave birth to the monarchy in Israel's national life, but also, and perhaps even more important, for the insights they provide on the theological issues that attended this significant development. These theological issues, in turn, have significant implications for the biblical theology of both the Old and New Testaments.

The "Deuteronomic" Perspective. In keeping with the character of all the historical books in the Old Testament, this historiography of 1–2 Samuel is not simply a detached and disinterested presentation of a series of historical occurrences. This is not to suggest that the historiography of 1–2 Samuel is distorted or untrustworthy, for any historiography worthy of the name must utilize some well-defined perspective or point of view in order to select, organize, and disclose the significance of the events of which it speaks. In Jewish tradition the "historical books" have long been known as the "former prophets" (the "prophetic books" are then known as the "latter prophets"). This is an appropriate designation, because the historical books present a "prophetic" and, therefore, trustworthy representation and interpretation of Israel's history.

The events about which they speak are clearly placed in a theological context, and described from a particular "point of view." It is in this "point of view" that the theological orientation of the narrator, as well as the theological significance of the events themselves, is highlighted.

The dominating theological "point of view" in all of the books from Joshua to 2 Kings, including 1–2 Samuel, is that which found its fullest expression in the Sinai covenant. Yahweh had chosen Israel to be a people of his own possession (Exod. 19:1–6). He had delivered them out of Egypt and brought them to Sinai where he entered into covenant with them. There he had given them his Law (the stipulations of the covenant, found in the legal sections of Exodus and Leviticus) sanctioned by blessings for obedience and cursing for disobedience (cf., e.g., Lev. 26). He had led and preserved them through the wilderness period, and then renewed the covenant on the plains of Moab, at the point of transition between the leadership of Moses and that of Joshua, just prior to Israel's entrance into the land of Canaan. This renewal of the covenant is described in detail in Deuteronomy. It is especially the theological perspectives of Deuteronomy, including blessings for obedience to the covenant, and cursing for disobedience (chap. 28), which inform and dominate the theological viewpoint embraced in all the historical books, including 1–2 Samuel.

Divine Sovereignty. It is quite apparent upon reading 1–2 Samuel (which was originally one book) that the unknown author used "The Song of Hannah" (1 Sam. 2:1–10) at the beginning of his narrative and "David's Song of Praise" (2 Sam. 22) and "Last Words" (2 Sam. 23:1–7) at its end to frame the entire book, and in so doing to indicate the theological underpinnings on which the entire presentation rests. These poems are three of the few pericopes in the book that are not narrative in style and thus more adaptable to explicit theological assertions. The poems complement each other in presenting a magnificent God concept.

There is only one God, the Lord God of Israel (1 Sam. 2:2; 2 Sam. 22:32). This God has spoken, and his word is true (2 Sam. 22:31; 23:2). The Lord God of Israel is sovereign over all things (1 Sam. 2:6–10; 2 Sam. 22:33–46). He is a Rock, a place of refuge and security for those who trust in him (1 Sam. 2:2; 2 Sam. 22:2, 3, 32, 47; 23:2).

By means of these introductory and concluding poems, as well as by numerous comments within the body of the book, some made by the narrator and others included in the dialogue of the persons described in the book, all that happens in both individual lives and Israel's national life is placed in the context of divine sovereignty.

In many instances recognition of divine sovereignty is made implicit in the events narrated, rather than conveyed by explicit statement. Note, for example, when Saul's forces were closing in on David in their effort to capture him and "a messenger came to Saul saying, 'Come quickly! The Philistines are raiding the land.' Then Saul broke off his pursuit of David" (1 Sam. 23:26–28). From the standpoint of the narrator this can hardly be viewed as mere coincidence. God was sovereignly ordering events to protect David from the designs of Saul. All of this combines to impress on the reader the conclusion that everything that happens in the lives of the individuals described in the book, as well as everything that happens in the national life of Israel, lies within the sphere of God's sovereign control.

The narrator also makes it clear, however, that divine sovereignty does not mean that God is an impersonal, fatalistic force. On the one hand God is presented as a personal being who responds with grace and mercy to the needs and concerns of his people when they seek him and are truly repentant of their sins; but, on the other hand, he is also depicted as one who reacts in righteous anger and judgment against those who rebel against his commands and show no true repentance. In the final chapter, when Gad, the prophet, gives David three options for punishment after his sin in the matter of the census taking, David says, "Let us fall into the hands of the LORD, for his mercy is great; but do not let me fall into the hands of men" (2 Sam. 24:14). Later in this same chapter we are told that, "When the angel stretched out his hand to destroy Jerusalem, the LORD was grieved because of the calamity and said to the angel who was afflicting the people, 'Enough! Withdraw your hand'" (v. 16). The narrator makes it clear that God is merciful, even in judgment. He is a personal God, not an unmoved mover. This does not mean, however, that he is permissive or lax. When Saul disobeyed the Lord's command to completely destroy the Amalekites and their cattle, and then attempted to justify himself by shifting the blame to his soldiers and arguing that his troops had kept some of the better cattle for sacrifices, the Lord said, "Because you have rejected the word of the LORD, he has rejected you as king" (1 Sam. 15:23).

The narratives also make it abundantly clear, although not according to the neat formulations of systematic theology, that while God's sovereignty extends to all human actions (both good and evil) it does not annul human responsibility, nor does it nullify God's justice or holiness. The narratives suggest that the narrator understands that in whatever way these notions of divine sovereignty and human responsibility may be defined, they are ultimately not inconsistent. God is the sovereign ruler of the universe, including all that comes to pass in human history, yet human beings are consistently held accountable for their actions (cf., e.g., Eli, who is held responsible for the evils practiced at the tabernacle during the time of his priesthood [1 Sam. 2:12–36; 3:11–14]; Saul, who is held responsible for his rejection of the Word of the Lord [1 Sam. 13:13–14; 15:11–26]; David, who is held responsible for his actions in the incident with Bathsheba [2 Sam. 12:7–11]).

Kingship and Covenant. It is within the overarching perspective of God's sovereignty, and men and women's responsibility to respond in faith and obedience to his Word, that Israel's history is described in 1–2 Samuel in connection with the dual themes of kingship and covenant. These two concepts function as the major organizing principles of the book. A number of subthemes are integrated into the structure of 1–2 Samuel by virtue of their relationship to these major themes of kingship and covenant. Among the most significant of these subthemes are: the role of the prophet in relation to the king; the significance of the ark; and the messianic idea and the Davidic covenant.

Organizing the book around the concepts of kingship and covenant yields a fourfold division of its content.

First, kingship as requested by the people was a denial of the covenant (1 Sam. 1–8). When the elders of Israel asked for a king, Samuel was displeased (1 Sam. 8:6). But the Lord told Samuel that even though the request meant that "they have rejected me [the Lord] as their king" (v. 7), nevertheless Samuel was to give them a king (vv. 9, 22). Although Samuel warned the people (vv. 9–18) about what a king like those in all the other nations would be like, they persisted in their demand to be given a king "to lead us and to go out before us and fight our battles" (v. 20). It is clear that the people wanted the wrong kind of a king for the wrong reasons. The Lord was their great King. He had already promised his people security and victory over their enemies as long as they remained faithful to their covenant obligations (Exod. 23:22; 34:11; Deut. 21:1–4). He had demonstrated his faithfulness to this promise as recently as the victory over the Philistines under the leadership of Samuel as reported in 1 Samuel 7. In fact the whole history of the period of the judges reflected in the cycles of oppression, repentance, and restoration demonstrated the reliability of God's covenant faithfulness. But evidently this was not sufficient for the Israelites. They wanted a human ruler, like those of the neighboring nations, to fight their battles and to provide them with a symbol of national unity and security. Unfortunately this desire was, at the same time, a rejection of the Lord who was their King.

Second, kingship as given by Samuel was consistent with the covenant (1 Sam. 9–12). The Lord told Samuel that although the people had sinned in requesting a king (1 Sam. 10:19; 12:17, 19), the time to establish kingship in Israel had arrived (1 Sam. 8:9, 22; 9:16; 10:1). Kingship in itself was not wrong for Israel, and, in fact, had been anticipated in previous revelation (Gen. 17:6; 49:10; Num. 24:17; Deut. 17:14–20). After Samuel had anointed Saul privately (1 Sam. 9:1–10:16), he called all Israel to an assembly at Mizpah (1 Sam. 10:17–27), where he supervised the public selection of Saul by lot and then clearly defined the role and responsibilities of the king in Israel. "Samuel explained to the people the regulations of the kingship. He wrote them down on a scroll and deposited it before the Lord" (1 Sam. 10:25). After Saul led Israel to victory over the Ammonites (1 Sam. 11:1–13) Samuel called for an assembly at Gilgal, where he presided in the inauguration of Saul's reign at a public ceremony of covenant renewal (1 Sam. 11:14–12:25). On this occasion Samuel made it clear that even though human kingship had now been incorporated into the theocracy, in obedience to the command of the Lord (1 Sam. 12:12–15), this in no way annulled the responsibility of either the people or the new king to continue to recognize the Lord as their ultimate Sovereign (1 Sam. 12:20, 24–25). Kingship in Israel was to function in a way that was consistent with the covenant and the continued recognition that the Lord was Israel's great King.

Third, the kingship of Saul failed to correspond to the covenant ideal (1 Sam. 13–31). Saul quickly demonstrated that he was not prepared to submit to the requirements of a covenantal kingship. When the Philistines gathered to attack Israel, Saul did not wait for Samuel as he had been instructed, but offered a sacrifice himself. When Samuel arrived he said, "You acted foolishly. . . . You have not kept he command the Lord your God gave you" (1 Sam. 13:13). Later, after being instructed by Samuel to utterly destroy the Amalekites and everything that belonged to them, Saul disobeyed the word of the prophet and spared their king, Agag, as well as the best of the plunder from the battle (1 Sam. 15:9, 18). On this occasion Samuel confronted him again, and said, "Because you have rejected the word of the Lord, he has rejected you as king" (v. 23). So Saul rebelled against the Lord (v. 23a), and failed to rule in a way consistent with the requirements of a covenantal king.

Fourth, the kingship of David was an imperfect, but true, representation of the covenantal ideal (1 Sam. 16–2 Sam. 24). David's reign is described in great detail in 2 Samuel 2–24. The climax of these narratives is found in 2 Samuel 7, where David is told by Nathan the prophet that "Your house and your kingdom will endure forever before me; your throne will be established forever" (v. 16). This promise of an enduring dynasty for David carries forward the promise made centuries earlier to Abraham, and confirmed to Isaac and Jacob, that through his offspring "all nations of the earth will be blessed" (Gen. 12:3; 26:4; 28:14). Ultimately both of these promises find their roots in the statement of Genesis 3:15 that the offspring of the woman would crush the head of the serpent. It is now made clear that this promised offspring will arise among the descendants of David and will sit on his royal throne.

In view of this promise it is surprising that David, like Saul before him, is not presented in the narratives of 2 Samuel as a king whose reign perfectly conforms to the covenantal ideal. David sinned in treacherous ways with Bathsheba and Uriah (2 Sam. 11). He betrayed his reliance on military might rather than trust in the Lord, when he took the census of his army later in his reign (2 Sam. 24). David is clearly not a perfect example of the covenantal king. Yet while God had rejected Saul and judged him severely, the Lord was merciful to David and promised him an eternal dynasty. The question arises, "Why did God treat these two sinful men so differently?" The answer lies in their attitudes after they had sinned. Saul made excuses and tried to justify his actions (1 Sam. 13:12; 15:15, 21, 24). David confessed his sin and repented: "I have sinned against the LORD" (2 Sam. 12:13); "David was conscience-stricken after he had counted the fighting men, and he said to the LORD, 'I have sinned greatly in what I have done. Now, O LORD, I beg you to take away the guilt of your servant. I have done a very foolish thing'" (2 Sam. 24:10); "I am the one who has sinned and done wrong. These are but sheep. What have they done? Let your hand fall upon me and my family" (2 Sam. 24:17). For this reason David is termed a "man after God's own heart" (1 Sam. 13:14; Acts 13:22). It was David's desire to serve the Lord faithfully, even though his obedience was far from perfect.

David himself describes the covenantal ideal for kingship in words given to him by God. "The God of Israel spoke, the Rock of Israel said to me: 'When one rules over men in righteousness, when he rules in the fear of the God, he is like the light of morning at sunrise on a cloudless morning, like the brightness after rain that brings grass from the earth'" (2 Sam. 23:3–4). Even though David was not perfect, the narrator has previously told us that "David reigned over all Israel, doing what was just and right for all his people" (2 Sam. 8:15). His reign, in spite of its flaws, became the standard by which all the subsequent kings of Israel were measured.

Perhaps the key to understanding the difference between David and Saul is found in 2 Samuel 22:21–32 where David says "I have kept the ways of the LORD" and "I have not turned away from his decrees." One might wonder what these statements could possibly mean, when it is abundantly clear that David's obedience was not perfect and that he "despise[d] the Word of the LORD by doing what [was] evil in his eyes" (2 Sam. 12:9) when he committed murder and adultery. It would appear that David is not claiming that his life was absolutely perfect, but that he had lived with the set purpose of serving the Lord and being faithful to his covenant. David's "righteousness" (2 Sam. 22:21, 25) and his "keeping of the ways of the LORD" (2 Sam. 22:22) were not absolute, but they were substantial. The general pattern of his life reflected covenant faithfulness rather than the reverse. When he sinned, he was quick to repent. David affirms that the Lord shows himself faithful to the faithful (2 Sam. 22:26) and saves the humble (2 Sam. 22:28). He clearly views himself as included among the "faithful" and the "humble." It is in these traits that David truly, although imperfectly, exemplifies the ideal of the covenantal king.

The Role of the Prophet. The narratives of 1–2 Samuel contribute in a significant way to our understanding of the role of the prophet in ancient Israel. The early chapters of 1–2 Samuel tell of Samuel's birth (1–2) and his call to be a prophet (3). These narratives prepare the way for Samuel's role in the establishment of the monarchy. When Samuel was young we are told that "in those days the word of the LORD was rare" (1 Sam. 3:1). As he became a young man we are told that "All Israel . . . recognized that Samuel was attested as a prophet of the LORD" (1 Sam. 3:20). Samuel's prophetic authority was used by the Lord in the anointing of Saul as Israel's first king (1 Sam. 9:1–10:16). Kingship was not autonomous in Israel, but was established by the word of the prophet and limited in its authority. The king was required to submit to both the laws of the Sinai covenant and the word of the prophet. This requirement of subordination to the word of the prophet was clearly spelled out at Saul's inauguration when Samuel told the king and the people that he would continue to teach them "the way that is good and right" (1 Sam. 12:23). When Saul disobeyed the word of the Lord given by Samuel, he was confronted by Samuel and rejected as king (1 Sam. 13, 15). The Lord then sent Samuel to anoint David to replace Saul as king (1 Sam. 16).

From these early narratives in 1–2 Samuel we learn that a pattern was established when kingship was inaugurated in Israel that provided the foundation for the work of all the prophets who would follow Samuel. These individuals were never afraid to call to account the kings of Israel and Judah when they went astray from the covenant. In fact the ministries of many of the prophets seem to be more directly concerned with the kings than with the people of the land. The prophets were the guardians of the theocracy and therefore functioned mainly at its center, the royal court.

The Significance of the Ark. In addition to the narratives that focus primarily on Samuel, Saul, and David there are a group of narratives in 1–2 Samuel that focus on the ark of the covenant (1 Sam. 4–6; 2 Sam. 6). Instructions for the building of the ark are recorded in Exodus 25:10–22. Its lid was made of solid gold and at each end was a golden cherub. The Lord told Moses that he would be present in the space above the lid of the ark between the two cherubim, and from this place he would give Moses commandments for Israel (v. 22). Subsequently, the ark held the two tablets of the Decalogue (Exod. 25:16, 21; 40:20; Deut. 10:5). Because of the close identification of the ark with the presence of God among his people, he is said to be "enthroned between the cherubim" (1 Sam. 4:4; 2 Sam. 6:2), which suggests that the ark was viewed as the throne of the Lord from which he guided and ruled over his people.

Because of the close identification of the ark with God's presence (cf., e.g., the role it played at the crossing of the Jordan [Josh. 3–4) and the fall of Jericho [Josh. 6]) it is not surprising that when the Israelites were defeated by the Philistines (1 Sam. 4) the elders requested that the ark be brought to the battlefield. They thought that this would guarantee God's presence with them and thus ensure victory in battle. To their dismay, they were again defeated, and, worst of all, the ark was captured by the Philistines. From this incident it is clear that God cannot be manipulated by his people, and that his connection with the ark was not automatic or mechanical, but spiritual.

When the Philistines placed the ark in the temple of their god, Dagon, at Ashdod, the next day they found that the image of their deity had fallen to the floor and broken in pieces before the ark of the Lord (1 Sam. 5). In addition a plague of tumors broke out among the people of the city of Ashdod. When the ark was moved to other cities the same tumors appeared among their inhabitants. Eventually the Philistines were forced to send the ark back to Israel where it remained for twenty years in the house of Abinadab in Kiriath Jearim (1 Sam. 6:1–7:2). In these chapters it becomes clear that while the Lord will not permit his people to manipulate the symbol of his presence to gain victory over the Philistines, neither will he permit the Philistines to conclude that because they defeated the Israelites, their god, Dagon, was more powerful than the God of Israel.

The ark remained in obscurity during the reign of Saul. It was not until David was made king that the ark was returned to its rightful place at the political and religious center of the nation. David brought the ark to his capital city, Jerusalem (2 Sam. 6). In so doing he confesses that the nation's ultimate sovereign is the Lord, who sits "enthroned between the cherubim," and that his own kingship is subordinate to divine authority. This is the perspective of a covenantal king.

When, in his later years, David was driven from Jerusalem by the revolution led by his son, Absalom, the ark was brought along by the priests who fled from the city. But David said, "Take the ark of God back into the city. If I find favor in the LORD's eyes, he will bring me back and let me see it and his dwelling place again. But if he says, 'I am not pleased with you,' then I am ready; let him do to me whatever seems good to him" (2 Sam. 15:25). Here David recognizes the true significance of the ark as a symbol of the presence and power of the great King of Israel. He knew that possession of the ark was not an automatic guarantee of the Lord's blessing. He also understood that it was proper for the ark to remain in Jerusalem, because ultimately the Lord was the true Sovereign of the land.

The Messianic Idea and the Davidic Covenant. Perhaps the most significant theological feature of 1–2 Samuel is its contribution to the development of the messianic idea in Scripture by virtue of its association of anointing with kingship (1 Sam. 2:10b; 9:16; 10:1; 16:13), as well as by its provision of a framework for the development of this idea through its presentation of the Davidic covenant (2 Sam. 7; 23:5).

It is striking that in the very beginning of 1 Samuel Hannah speaks with prophetic insight when she proclaims that the Lord "will give strength to his king and exalt the horn of his anointed" (2:10b). This is the first time in Scripture that the king of Israel is referred to as the "anointed of the LORD" or "messiah." In the remainder of 1–2 Samuel the expression "the anointed of the LORD" is applied frequently to both Saul and David (1 Sam. 2:35; 12:3, 5; 16:6; 24:6, 10; 26:9, 11, 16, 23; 2 Sam. 1:14, 16, 21; 19:21; 22:51; 23:1). To say that Saul and David were the "anointed of the LORD" became equivalent to saying they occupied the office of king in Israel. Although the technical sense of "messiah" as an "ideal king of the future" did not emerge until much later in Israel's history, the foundation for its usage lies in the association of anointing with kingship first introduced in 1 Samuel.

Along with the introduction of messianic terminology, 1–2 Samuel is also particularly significant from a theological standpoint because it is here that we find the announcement of the Davidic covenant. The Lord gave David a promise through Nathan the prophet that his dynasty would endure forever (2 Sam. 7:16). In subsequent reflection on this promise David termed it "an everlasting covenant" (2 Sam. 23:5). Psalm 89 elaborates further on the promise, also using the term "covenant" ("I will maintain my love to him forever, and my *covenant* with him will never fail. I will establish his line forever, his throne as long as the heavens endure. . . . I will not violate my *covenant* or alter what my lips have uttered" [vv. 28–29, 34]).

It is this covenant that provides the framework for the flow of redemptive history from the old covenant (the Sinai covenant) to the new covenant. The Davidic covenant is often termed a "promissory covenant" and placed in sequence with the Abrahamic covenant, which also was "promissory" in its basic thrust, and spoke of the coming of a descendant of Abraham in whom all the nations of the earth would be blessed (Gen. 12:3). The Abrahamic and Davidic covenants are also sometimes terms "unconditional" covenants because of their promissory nature, and then set in contrast with the Sinai covenant, which is viewed as a "law covenant" and "conditional" in nature. The terms "promissory" and "unconditional" as applied to the Abrahamic and Davidic covenants and the terms "law" and "conditional" as applied to the Sinai covenant certainly have some validity as indicators of the primary emphasis found in each of these covenants. Yet it must be noticed that the Sinai or "law" covenant is not totally devoid of promise (Judg. 2:1; 1 Sam. 12:22), and the promissory nature of the Abrahamic and Davidic covenants does not mean that they are totally devoid of law or obligation (Gen. 12:1; 17:1; 2 Sam. 7:14–15; 1 Kings 2:4; 8:25; 9:4–5; Ps. 89:30–33). From these texts it is clear that both the Abrahamic and Davidic covenants brought obligations on those to whom the promise was given. In the Davidic covenant it seems clear that the conditionality referred to in the above texts pertains to individual participation in the promised blessings, but not to the certainty of the fulfillment of the promise itself. Here it becomes clear that the Davidic covenant is not only an extension of the Abrahamic promise, but is also intertwined with the Sinai covenant in connection with individual participation in its benefits. Failure to live up to these obligations would invalidate the benefits of the covenant to the person involved, but would not jeopardize the ultimate fulfillment of the promise through the line of Abraham and David.

A look at Israel's subsequent history reveals that David's descendants (not to mention the line of kings in the northern kingdom) failed even more miserably than had David himself to live up to the ideal of the covenantal king. As it became increasingly apparent that these kings were unworthy of the high office to which they were called, the prophets and psalmists of Israel began to speak of a king who would come in the line of David who would be a worthy occupant of his throne. The surprising thing about this future king is that he is not only spoken of as a descendant of David, but he also begins to be spoken of in terms of deity (see, e.g., Pss. 2; 45; 72; 110; Isa. 7:14; 9:6–7; Jer. 23:5–6; 33:15–16; Mic. 5:2). Unblemished covenantal kingship will only be completely realized when the Lord himself enters human history in the person of Jesus to sit on the throne of his father David and to rule in righteousness and justice (Matt. 1; Luke 1:32–33, 67–80; Rev. 22:16). J. Robert Vannoy

See also Covenant; Israel; Prophet, Prophetess, Prophecy.

Bibliography. W. Dumbrell, *JETS* 33/1 (1990): 49–62; R. P. Gordon, *1 & 2 Samuel*; H. Heater, *A Biblical Theology of the Old Testament*, pp. 115–56; R. F. Youngblood, *1, 2 Samuel.*

Sanctification. The generic meaning of sanctification is "the state of proper functioning." To sanctify someone or something is to set that person or thing apart for the use intended by its designer. A pen is "sanctified" when used to write. Eyeglasses are "sanctified" when used to improve sight. In the theological sense, things are sanctified when they are used for the purpose God intends. A human being is sanctified, therefore, when he or she lives according to God's design and purpose.

The Greek word translated "sanctification" (*hagiasmos*) means "holiness." To sanctify, therefore, means "to make holy." In one sense only God is holy (Isa. 6:3). God is separate, distinct, other. No human being or thing shares the holiness of God's essential nature. There is one God. Yet Scripture speaks about holy things. Moreover, God calls human beings to be holy—as holy as he is holy (Lev. 11:44; Matt. 5:48; 1 Peter 1:15–16). Another word for a holy person is "saint" (*hagios*), meaning a sanctified one. The opposite of sanctified is "profane" (Lev. 10:10).

From time to time human beings are commanded to sanctify themselves. For example, God commanded the nation of Israel, "consecrate to me every firstborn male" (Exod. 13:2). God said through Peter, "in your hearts set apart Christ as Lord" (1 Peter 3:15). One sanctifies Christ by responding to unbelievers meaningfully, out of a good conscience and faithful life. God calls his own to set themselves apart for that which he has set them apart. Sanctify, therefore, becomes a synonym for "trust and obey" (Isa. 29:23). Another name for this action is "consecration." To fail to sanctify God has serious consequences (Num. 20:12).

Human beings ultimately cannot sanctify themselves. The Triune God sanctifies. The Father sanctifies (1 Cor. 1:30) by the Spirit (2 Thess. 2:13; 1 Peter 1:2) and in the name of Christ (1 Cor. 6:11). Yet Christian faith is not merely passive. Paul calls for active trust and obedience when he says, "Since we have these promises, dear friends, let us purify ourselves from everything that contaminates body and spirit, *perfecting holiness* out of reverence for God" (2 Cor. 7:1). No one may presume on God's grace in sanctification. Peter reminds believers to be diligent in making their calling and election sure (2 Peter 1:10).

A person or thing can be sanctified in two ways—according to God's creative purpose or according to God's redemptive design. All sanctified in the first sense are used by God in the second sense. Not all God uses in the second sense are sanctified in the first sense.

Sanctification According to God's Creative Design. God created the universe and human beings perfect (i.e., sanctified). Everything and everyone functioned flawlessly until Adam and Eve believed Satan's lie. The fall plunged the human race and the universe into a state of dysfunction (Gen. 3:14–19). Neither was so distorted by the fall so as to obliterate God's original purpose and design completely. Fallen human beings still bear God's image (James 3:9–10). Fallen creation still witnesses to God's existence and attributes (Ps. 19:1–6; Rom. 1:20). Yet both, depending on the analogy employed, are skewed, broken, fallen, dysfunctional, "unsanctified."

The imperfect state of creation is a reminder that God's fully sanctified purpose for it has been disrupted by sin. Evil is the deprivation of the good that God intends for the creation he has designed. The creation groans, awaiting its sanctification when everything will be set right (Rom. 8:21–22; Rev. 20–21).

Human beings, made in God's image, were the pinnacle and focus of his creation. The sanctification of human beings, therefore, is the highest goal of God's work in the universe. God explicitly declared it to be his will (1 Thess. 4:3). He purposed that human beings be "like him" in a way no other created thing is. Human beings are like God in their stewardship over creation (Gen. 1:26–31). Yet this role is dependent on a more fundamentally important likeness to God—moral character. By virtue of God-given discretionary autonomy (faith), human beings may so depend upon God that his moral character (communicable attributes) are displayed.

The unsanctified state of fallen humanity is not caused merely by lack of effort or poor motivation. It constitutes an inherent structural flaw. When Adam sinned, he and his race forfeited that which made it possible for them to function as designed—the presence of God himself. Adam and Eve's prefallen sanctification was not a result of their inherent capabilities. God's indwelling presence was responsible for the manifestation of his attributes in them. Sanctification always requires God's presence. His presence is more than his "being there"—a corollary of his omnipresence. It is his dynamic presence, producing fruit for which he alone is the source. "Indwelling" is not God's way of getting close to us sensually. It is a theological, rather than experiential, reality; it is "experienced" by faith, not by feeling.

Human beings "fall short of God's glory" (Rom. 3:23) because they lack God's presence, which produces glory. "Glory" is always the manifestation of the attributes of God resulting from the presence of God. God's presence was the essential missing factor in Adam and Eve's postfall state. God called out to the fleeing man, "Where are you?" (Gen. 3:9). God was not seeking information. He was clarifying to sinful humanity that his presence was now lost.

God sought Adam and Eve, indicating that restoration of the original purpose would be undertaken by him. Sanctification, therefore, is exclusively the work of God in grace (Lev. 21:8; Ezek. 20:12; Heb. 2:11; Jude 1). Functioning moral likeness to God, lost in the fall, is restored through God's redemption in Christ (Eph. 4:23–24; Col. 3:9–10). Human beings are "made holy" through Christ's work. The blood of Jesus Christ sanctifies (Heb. 13:12) because his substitutionary atonement reversed all of the dysfunctional, as well as legal (i.e., guilt), effects of sin. Human beings are progressively sanctified now through faith in Christ and by the indwelling Spirit (2 Cor. 3:18), while awaiting full sanctification at the resurrection. Believers under both the old and new covenants are sanctified the same way—by grace through faith.

Sanctification According to God's Redemptive Purposes. In addition to designing the goal of creation (functioning human beings in a fittingly perfect environment), God has also designed the means of achieving that goal. He not only wants to make the universe, especially human beings, sanctified. He also uses sanctified (set-apart) means to accomplish his end.

God calls specific people at specific times to be sanctified for a particular role in his redemptive program. God uses all people for his purposes, even those who defy him (Rom. 9:21–22). For example, God used Pharaoh even though he did not let Israel go (Rom. 9:17). God also used Cyrus, a pagan ruler, to discipline Israel (Isa. 45:1). The Scripture, however, is largely the story of how God wants to use willing "vessels." He set apart some to be kings, priests, and prophets. God sanctified Jeremiah even before birth for his prophetic ministry (Jer. 1:5). The Holy Spirit "set apart" Paul and Barnabas for missionary service from among the gathered church (Acts 13:2). Every believer has a "calling" or "vocation" based on "gifting." Just as each Israelite had a role in the corporate life under the old covenant, so the church functions by the ministry of gifted and called individuals. Each one has a gift. The prominence of ministry will vary from person to person. Yet each sanctifies his or her calling through faithfulness.

It is possible, to one's peril, to confuse God's calling to "be redeemed" and God's calling to "be a redemptive agent." The former is a prerequisite for the latter. The latter cannot substitute for the former. Many Israelites were unsanctified personally because they presumed that their calling to be a redemptive nation guaranteed God's sanctifying grace. They disregarded God's Word, lacked faith in God (Heb. 4:2), and became proud of their achievements. Jesus spoke his harshest words against the unsanctified Pharisees (Matt. 23). God judged Israel as a nation by setting them aside as God's channel of blessing for the world (Matt. 21:43)—this but for a time. God is determined to fulfill all of his promises to his redemptive channel (Rom. 11:25–29). God used Israel, nevertheless, as a disobedient people. From a remnant within ethnic Israel, God built his church. Paul confronted an oft-posed question, "How can an elect [i.e., sanctified] nation be lost?" (Rom. 9–11). He reminded his Jewish audience that when God elected Israel to be a redemptive agent (Gen. 12:1–3), he did not guarantee redemption for every Israelite. Paul also warned non-Israelite believers, likewise blessed as redemptive agents (the church), not to confuse privilege with standing when he said, "Do not be arrogant, but be afraid. For if God did not spare the natural branches [Israel], he will not spare you either" (Rom. 11:20b–21).

Jesus Christ: The Sanctifier and Model of Sanctification. The singular means of God's sanctifying grace is Jesus Christ: "We have been made holy through the sacrifice of the body of Jesus Christ once for all" (Heb. 10:10). Christ was qualified to sanctify because he himself had been sanctified through suffering (Heb. 2:10–11). First, Jesus Christ was the only human being since the fall to live a continuously, perfectly sanctified life. He was without sin, therefore, without guilt or dysfunctionality. He was sanctified from the moment of his conception (Matt. 1:18–20; Luke 1:35). He was rightly called the "Holy One of God" (Mark 1:24), sanctified by the Father (John 10:36). In his character, therefore, Jesus Christ was *morally* sanctified. Second, he was *vocationally* sanctified. Christ did what the Father called him to do (John 5:19, 30, 36; 6:38; 8:28–29; 12:49). He accomplished his vocational purpose through time, yet he continually fulfilled his moral purpose. He sanctified himself by fulfilling his unique calling as the Messiah (John 17:19), being declared the Son of God at his resurrection (Rom. 1:4). Jesus Christ, therefore, is the model human being for both moral and vocational sanctification (Phil. 2:5–11).

Just as all forgiveness of sin was provisional until the ministry of the Messiah was complete, so all sanctification was provisional (Heb. 9:13–14; 10:10–12). The incarnation was an indispensable means for sanctifying humanity because it was necessary that the sanctifier be from within humanity (Heb. 2:11). Christ's sacrificial offering of himself to God achieved comprehensive sanctification for all people (Heb. 10:10, 14, 29; 13:12). In addition, the return of Christ will mark the beginning of remade heaven and earth (2 Peter 3:10–13).

Anything that prefigured the work of Christ was holy in a redemptive sense. Something need not be inherently holy to serve a sanctifying purpose. Though God instructed his people to choose animals for sacrifice that were "without spot," this was technically impossible. Only the unblemished Lamb of God was qualified to sanctify the world. Nevertheless, the lambs, bulls, and goats used in the ceremonial sacrifices in the Old Testament were sanctified because they anticipated the one sacrifice for sins forever. Jesus was the fulfillment of the Old Testament offices of prophet, priest, and king. Yet many of these are not numbered among God's faithful. Everything is rendered holy by its proper use. The New Testament emphasis is that everything can be sanctified in a redemptive sense. When the believer glorifies God by thanking God for everything (1 Cor. 10:31; 1 Thess. 5:18), the believer thereby sanctifies everything. Nothing that God has created is unclean in itself. Its misuse renders it unclean.

God has ordained specific means, however, by which the church sets Christ apart. For example, participation in the new covenant "Table of the Lord" sanctifies the believer. Apart from what Christ has done, the exercise of eating bread and drinking wine would be common. God sanctifies a believer through his or her faithful remembrance of Christ's redemptive work according to the command of the Lord. People may so profane the Lord's Supper so as to receive judgment prematurely from God (1 Cor. 11:27–32).

Worship under the old covenant foreshadowed Christ. Israel was ever conscious of the "sanctuary" (*hagion*)—the place where God resided and which he loved (Mal. 2:11). During Israel's captivities, the people were separated from the sanctuary and, hence, alienated from the assurance of God's saving blessings. It was the geographical and spiritual center of the nation's life.

The material used for the earthly sanctuary was made "holy" by virtue of its use. God stipulated strict standards for the sanctuary's construction (Exod. 25–40) and operation (Leviticus). Everything to do with the tabernacle and temple was holy: garments (Exod. 28:2), anointing oil (Exod. 30:25), crown (Exod. 39:30), linen tunic (Lev. 16:4), convocation of the people (Lev. 23:2), water (Num. 5:17), vessels (Num. 31:6), utensils (1 Kings 8:4), ark (2 Chron. 35:3), day (Neh. 8:11), and place (Exod. 28:29; 1 Kings 6:16). The items and procedures had typological significance. Although every typological feature cannot be established with absolute precision, Scripture indicates that the tabernacle and temple, including its priestly service, foreshadowed Christ (Heb. 8:5; 9:23).

The old covenant sanctuaries were merely provisional. Only Christ could take away sin, "perfecting for all time those who are being sanctified" (Heb. 10:14, marginal reading). The Hebrew writer contrasts the earthly sanctuary of Israel with the heavenly sanctuary. It was the latter that Christ entered and opened for all who come to God through him (Heb. 8:1–6; 9:23–26; 10:19–22).

Old and new covenants are linked by Christ. For example, the Sabbath and other designated days were to be kept "holy" (Gen. 2:3; Exod. 20:11; Num. 29:1). Christ is the Sabbath rest for believers (Heb. 4:1–11). Because of the sanctifying ministry of Christ, each day may be lived equally to the glory of God. Even in cases when believers differ in this matter, Paul urges all to live each day for the Lord (Rom. 14:5–12) for he is the "substance" (Col. 2:16–17). God's name is to be sanctified (Ps. 103:1; Isa. 29:23). We sanctify God's name when we worship him properly. Christians are "sanctified in Christ Jesus and called to be holy" (1 Cor. 1:2). Jesus taught us to pray, "Our Father . . . hallowed [sanctified] be your name" (Matt. 6:9). Praying in Jesus' name sanctifies our prayers (John 15:16).

Key Concepts. *God's usual modus operandi is to sanctify common things for his redemptive purposes,* rather than to employ perfect heavenly things (1 Cor. 1:26–31). He sanctified common coats of skin to cover Adam and Eve's nakedness (Gen. 3:21). He sanctified a common man, Abram of Ur, in order to make a great nation (Gen. 12:1–7). He sanctified a common bush in the Sinai desert from which to commission a man to lead Israel out of bondage. Moses stood on "holy ground" (Exod. 3:5), on a "holy mountain" (Ezek. 28:14). God made Jerusalem a "holy city" (Neh. 11:1; Isa. 48:2). In dramatic fashion, God sanctified the common womb of a common virgin girl by which to incarnate his Son. God's presence was with her (Luke 1:28). Jesus sanctified the world by his presence, "tabernacling" with us (John 1:14). God's method is grace. He alone is to be credited.

God's law is holy (Rom. 7:12). Christ sanctified God's Law by fulfilling it (Matt. 5:17). That means Christ fulfilled the ceremonial purpose of the Law by being the antitype of all that it prefigured, and fulfilled the moral demands of the Law by living perfectly according to its standards. The "law of Christ" (Gal. 6:2) is synonymous with the moral demands God places on all humanity. We sanctify God's Law by obeying it. Obedience is not contrary to faith. It is not works-sanctification. Biblical faith is a faith that works (James 2). The New Testament is full of commands, imperatives—laws. God is pleased when the believer does "good works," for he designed them from the beginning (Eph. 2:10).

It is understandable why some downplay or even deny any present usefulness of "law" in the sanctification of believers. They appeal to such verses as, "you are not under law, but under grace" (Rom. 6:14b). They are right that "law" is not the dynamic that sanctifies (Heb. 7:18–19). But the Law was never given for that purpose (Gal. 3:21). Its purpose for unbelievers is to show them how far from the original design they have come. It has an evangelistic purpose (Gal. 3:24). Its purpose for believers, however, is to guide them to where grace is leading them. The old covenant anticipated a fuller application of the Law. God said to Old Testament Israel that he would inaugurate a new covenant in which he would put his Law within them, and write it on their hearts (Jer. 31:33; Heb. 8:10; see Ezek. 36:27). Jesus reiterated, however, the continuing sanctifying function of the moral law, which can never be superseded (Matt. 5:17–20).

Legalism threatens sanctification by distorting the biblical teaching about the Law to the opposite extreme. In short, legalism is substituting law for grace, achievement for faith. The Pharisees followed the Law, having first tinkered with its meaning and application. Yet they would not come to Christ (John 5:39). The Judaizers followed after Paul, preaching a pregospel "gospel" of legalism. Paul flatly condemned it (Gal. 1:6–9; 2:16; 3:11). It is legalism when one obeys in order to glorify self before God or others (John 5:44). Similarly, insisting that forgiveness from unremitted guilt requires more "work" or "penance" from the supplicant is legalism masquerading as humility.

Sanctification is applied justification. By its very nature justification does not have a progressive character. It is God's declaration of righteousness. The focus of justification is the removal of the guilt of sin. The focus of sanctification is the healing of the dysfunctionality of sin. Since all spiritual blessings, justification and sanctification included, are the Christian's the moment he or she is "in Christ" (Eph. 1:3), sanctification is total and final in one sense (Acts 20:32; 26:18; 1 Cor. 6:11). Yet, unlike justification, sanctification also continues until it will be consummated when Jesus Christ returns. For then we will be like him (1 John 3:2)—perfect and complete. Sanctification, therefore, has an initial, progressive, and final phase. A believer's present preoccupation is with progressive sanctification (2 Cor. 3:18, note the present continuous tense, "are being transformed"), by which the child of God lives out the implications of initial sanctification with an eye to the goal of final sanctification. The sanctified life is victorious (Rom. 8:37), though it is lived out in the context of temptation and suffering. God promises the "overcomers" in Revelation 2 and 3 to restore all that was lost in the fall (2:7, 11, 17, 26; 3:5, 12). In sanctification, the believer is simply applying the implications of his or her justification.

The Holy Spirit is the dynamic of sanctification. Jesus said that he had to go away so that the

Holy Spirit would indwell believers (John 14:16–20). The "Holy" Spirit is so named not because he is more holy than the Father and the Son, but because his specific ministry vis-à-vis salvation is sanctification (Rom. 15:16; 1 Thess. 4:3–4; 2 Thess. 2:13; 1 Peter 1:2). The Spirit that inspired the Word of God now uses it to sanctify. Jesus, therefore, prayed concerning his own, "Sanctify them by the truth" (John 17:17). The Holy Spirit is the Spirit of truth (John 16:13). The blessing of the new covenant is the presence of the Spirit (Ezek. 36:27; Gal. 3:14).

The Holy Spirit not only is the restoration of the presence of God in believers; he also equips believers to serve the church and the world. As the fruit of the Spirit are the result of the reproduction of godly character in believers (Gal. 5:22–23), so the gifts of the Spirit (Rom. 12:4–6; 1 Cor. 12, 14) are the means by which believers serve others.

Though God sanctifies by grace, human beings are responsible to appropriate God's grace by faith. Faith is "the" means of sanctifying grace. The Bible indicates that there are other means at the disposal of believers to promote the direct faith—the Word, prayer, the church, and providence. The Word reveals God's will (John 17:17). Prayer allows the believer to apply faith to every area of life. The church is the context in which mutual ministry takes place. Providence is God's superintendence over every detail of life so that a believer will always have a way to grow in grace. Whether abounding or not (Phil. 4:11), whether certain of the outcome or not (Esther 4:11–5:3), the people of God may sanctify each situation knowing that God has allowed it and is present in it. In the case of temptation, the believer knows that there always will be a sanctifying faith response available (1 Cor. 10:13). When God disciplines his children, it is for their good, that they may "share in his holiness" (Heb. 12:10).

God detests sacrifices that are not offered by faith (Ps. 40:6; Heb. 10:5–7). On the other hand, a person is sanctified by presenting to God offerings that he proscribes (1 Sam. 16:5; Job 1:5). In New Testament language, we present ourselves as "living sacrifices" (Rom. 12:1). According to the old covenant, sacrifices are usually slain. Yet in the new covenant a believer dies with Christ in order to live a new holy life in the power of Christ's resurrection and in identification with Christ's suffering (Rom. 6:1–11; Gal. 2:20; Phil. 3:8–10).

A believer grows in sanctification by living according to his or her new identity. Before being "in Christ" the believer was "in Adam" (Rom. 5:12–21). To be "in Adam" is to be spiritually dead. Death means "separation," not "annihilation." A spiritually dead person is separated from God, the Life which alone can make one "godly." While separated from God, the unbeliever develops a working relationship with three related counter-sanctifying influences—the world, the flesh, and the devil. "The world" provides an allure to which "the flesh" readily responds, so that the believer has a topsy-turvy outlook that places created things before the Creator (Rom. 1:23–25). All the while "the devil"—Satan, the liar and slanderer of God—along with those under his sway, give hearty approval.

Faith in the gospel places the believer "in Christ," where everything becomes new (2 Cor. 5:17). Scripture calls all that the "new" believer was outside of Christ the "old man" or "old self." That identity has passed away through faith-solidarity with Christ in his death. The new identity is characterized by faith-solidarity with Christ in his resurrection so that "we might bear fruit to God" (Rom. 7:4b; cf. Rom. 6:1–11; Col. 3:1–4). Formally, the transformation by faith is immediate, but does not automatically result in changed thinking or behavior. The world, the flesh, and the devil still operate in their usual insidious way, but the power of each has been rendered inoperative (Rom. 6:6; Heb. 2:14) for those who live by faith according to their new identity. Faith includes repentance—identifying and forsaking everything that characterizes the "old man." Faith also includes trust—living in the light of everything that characterizes the "new man," even if it doesn't "feel" right. All of this is done in hope, or forward-looking faith—confidence that God will carry out his sanctifying purposes to the end. When Christ returns to complete his work, he will remake the world, resurrect believers, and banish Satan eternally.

Sexual purity is a frequently mentioned application in Scripture of a properly functioning sanctified life (1 Cor. 6:18–20; 1 Thess. 4:3–8). This is so, in part, because marriage is the most revealing context from which to understand Christ's sanctifying purpose for the Church (Eph. 5:25–30). Believers' bodies are sanctified by controlling them in such a way that God's purposes are being fulfilled by them (Rom. 6:19, 22; 12:1–2; 1 Thess. 4:4).

Sanctification has a negative and positive orientation. Negatively, sanctification is the cleansing or purifying from sin (Isa. 66:17; 1 Cor. 6:11; Eph. 5:26; Titus 3:5–6; Heb. 9:13). The laver in God's sanctuary provided a place for those offering sacrifice to God to ritually cleanse themselves. Christ cleanses the sinner once for all. The believer testifies to this through a lifestyle of self-denial (Matt. 16:24). Biblical self-denial is not asceticism—withholding pleasure or causing pain as an inherent means of spiritual growth. It is placing the interests of God before the interests of self. Believers do not deny or ridicule legitimate human desires. These desires, however, need to be continually prioritized according to God's purposes (Matt. 6:33).

Positively, sanctification is the growth in righteous attitudes and behavior. Good deeds (Eph.

2:10), godliness (1 Peter 1:15), Christ-likeness (1 Peter 2:21), and fulfilling the demands of the Law (Rom. 8:4) are all ways of referring to the product of sanctification. The believer "presses on" by laying hold by faith on the promises of God (Phil. 3:12), striving according to his indwelling resources (Col. 1:29).

The initial avenue of spiritual experience is the mind. Faith must have an object. God transforms believers from a worldly perspective and lifestyle by renewing the mind (Rom. 12:2). The Word of God makes us wise (2 Tim. 3:15), for "faith comes from hearing the message, and the message is heard through the word of Christ" (Rom. 10:17). We need the mind of Christ (Phil. 2:5), by which we take every thought captive (2 Cor. 10:5).

The result of sanctification is glory—the manifestation of God's presence. Glory is symbolized by a fire that does not consume (Exod. 3:5), by a visible pillar of cloud and fire hovering above the Holy of Holies (Exod. 40:34–35), by fire and violent quaking accompanying the giving of the Law on Sinai (Exod. 19:18), and by the splendor that will accompany Christ's return to earth (Rev. 19). God's sanctifying presence among people results in the manifestation of his glorious moral attributes. The new covenant brings greater glory than the old (2 Cor. 3). The Spirit occupies the place in the new covenant that the Lord did in the old covenant (2 Cor. 3:17). He progressively grows believers into God's likeness from glory to glory (2 Cor. 3:18). So, whereas sanctification has been accomplished fully and finally in Christ and all those who are in Christ are positively sanctified, the Christian is progressively sanctified through the Spirit's ministry.

The New Testament stresses moral, not ritual sanctification. Christ's atoning work put an end to the ceremonial foreshadowing of Israel's cultic practice. Jesus' reference to the temple altar in Matthew 23:19 was from the perspective of the practice he came to supersede.

A sanctified believer has assurance that he or she is Christ's. The call to sanctification reminds the Christian that he or she cannot presume upon justification. Professing believers are to "pursue" sanctification (Heb. 12:14). Apart from God's sanctifying work in human beings, "no one will see the Lord" (Heb. 12:14). God will judge any person claiming identification with Christ while not actively engaged in pursuing sanctification (Matt. 7:21–23). John bases assurance on a faith that perseveres in sanctification (1 John 2:3–6; 5:2–4). Though sanctification is never complete in this life (1 John 1:8–10), it is not an optional extra tacked on to justification.

BRADFORD A. MULLEN

See also ETHICS; SPIRITUALITY; UNION WITH CHRIST.

Bibliography. D. L. Alexander, ed., *Christian Spirituality;* J. S. Baxter, *Christian Holiness: Restudied and Restated;* G. C. Berkouwer, *Faith and Sanctification;* M. E. Dieter, et al., *Five Views of Sanctification;* S. B. Ferguson *Know Your Christian Life: A Theological Introduction;* D. C. Needham, *Birthright: Christian, Do You Know Who You Are?;* J. I. Packer, *Keep in Step with the Spirit;* W. T. Purkiser, et al., *Exploring Christian Holiness.*

Sanctuary. In the Old Testament the word *miqdāš* (from *qdš*, "holy," implying a distinction between space that is "sacred" versus "profane") commonly refers to the worship "sanctuary" (e.g., Exod. 25:8), where the Israelites offered their various kinds of offerings and sacrifices to the Lord under the supervision of the priesthood. As in English, however, where the word "sanctuary" can sometimes refer to a "refuge," there are two instances where the Lord refers to himself metaphorically as the "sanctuary" (i.e., refuge) of faithful Israelites in distress (Isa. 8:14; Ezek. 11:16). The more abstract term *qōdeš* ("holiness, sacredness") also many times refers concretely to a "holy place" (e.g., Exod. 30:13).

In the New Testament *hagios* (i.e., "holy [place]") means "sanctuary in nine instances, all in the Book of Hebrews. It also occurs three times as an adjective for the temple as the "*holy* place" of Israel (Matt. 24:15; Acts 6:13; 21:28). Other Old Testament and New Testament words may sometimes refer to or can even be translated "sanctuary" in some English versions, but none of them actually mean "sanctuary," strictly speaking.

Although the Hebrew term *miqdāš* can be used of sacred objects within a "sanctuary" (Num. 10:21), it most often refers to open air or housed sanctuaries as whole units, whether they be foreign "sanctuaries" (Isa. 16:12; Ezek. 28:18), multiple Israelite sanctuaries (whether illegitimate, Lev. 26:31; Ezek. 21:2; Amos 7:9, 13, or legitimate, e.g., Josh. 24:26), the tabernacle complex (e.g., Exod. 25:8), the Solomonic temple (e.g., 1 Chron. 22:19; 28:10), the second temple (Neh. 10:39), or the future temple on Mount Zion (e.g., Ezek. 37:26, 28; 44:9–16).

When referring to the tabernacle, *miqdāš* commonly designates the entire worship complex (Exod. 25:8a) as the special sanctified dwelling place of the Lord among his people, in the midst of which was the building known as the "tabernacle" (25:9) and over which they stretched a "tent" (26:7). It can refer to the multiple holy precincts within the tabernacle or temple complex (note the plural "sanctuaries" in Lev. 21:23; Ps. 73:17; Jer. 51:51), the "holy place" where incense was offered (only once, 2 Chron. 26:18), and possibly to "the Most Holy Place" (only once, Lev. 16:33a).

Like *miqdāš*, when *qōdeš* is used of a "holy place" (as opposed to holy people or things) it sometimes refers overall to the entire worship complex (e.g., Exod. 30:13; 36:1; Lev. 10:4; 2 Chron. 29:5, 7; Ps. 74:3; Ezek. 44:27). However, it is also used alone or in various combinations to distinguish between certain holy precincts within the sanctuary, specifically, the area of the court near the altar sometimes referred to as "the holy place" (Lev. 10:17–18), the outer "Holy Place" in the tabernacle or temple building itself (e.g., Exod. 26:33; 1 Kings 8:10; 2 Chron. 5:11; Ezek. 42:14), and the inner "holy place" (Lev. 16:2 [cf. 4:6]) which is the "Most Holy Place"), where the ark of the covenant was located. When these terms are used together in the same context, *miqdāš* tends to signify the whole complex as a unit within which one would find the tent or house structure known as the *qōdeš* and all its various furnishings.

The Lord determined that he would dwell in a sanctuary in the midst of his "kingdom of priests," his "holy nation" (Exod. 19:6; Ps. 68:32–35). They were to stand in awe and fear of this (Lev. 19:30) as when they "trembled" at the Lord's appearance on Mount Sinai (Exod. 19:16). This sanctuary was the primary place where the Lord manifested his presence in the midst of Israel (Exod. 40:34–38) and, therefore, became the preeminent place of worship (Lev. 9:6, 22–24).

The Lord sanctified the sanctuary and with it an officiating "Aaronic priesthood" (Exod. 29:44; Lev. 8:10; Num. 7:1). To the latter he assigned the responsibility of maintaining the sanctity of the Lord's presence in the sanctuary (Lev. 10:10–11, 17; Num. 18:1; Deut. 18:5) lest the people "die in their uncleanness for defiling my dwelling place, which is among them" (Lev. 15:31). However, because he was dealing with a sinful and unclean people who would inevitably defile the sanctuary, the Lord provided for its regular cleansing (see, e.g., the regular sin offering in Lev. 4:1–5:13) as well as the annual cleansing and (re)sanctifying of the defiled sanctuary (Lev. 16:19). Nevertheless, he warned that he would completely abandon his sanctuary if his covenant people abandoned him (1 Kings 9:6–7; 2 Chron. 7:20), a threat he eventually acted upon.

Of course, the New Testament writers were, by and large, fully familiar with the Jerusalem sanctuary complex, but it was the writer of Hebrews who developed the theology of the "sanctuary" motif. He began with the "heavenly sanctuary" (8:22) as the model or "pattern" (8:5) of which the "earthly" and "man-made sanctuary" (9:1, 24) was only a "copy" (9:23–24). In the Old Testament earthly sanctuary there was a tabernacle (tent) or building in which there was an outer room called "the Holy Place" separated by a veil from an inner room called "the Most Holy Place," which only the high priest could enter and even he only once a year. Jesus entered the "holy of holies" of the "heavenly" sanctuary for us (9:25; cf. 8:1–5) when he sacrificed his own body as our High Priest once for all (9:24–25). By this means he, in fact, granted us direct access into the heavenly sanctuary and, indeed, the very presence of God (10:19; cf. 4:14–16). RICHARD E. AVERBECK

See also ALTAR; OFFERINGS AND SACRIFICES; PRIEST, PRIESTHOOD; TABERNACLE; TEMPLE.

Bibliography. G. D. Alles, *The Encyclopedia of Religion,* 13:59–60; D. N. Freedman, *Temples and High Places in Biblical Times,* pp. 21–30; M. Haran, *Temples and Temple-Service in Ancient Israel,* pp. 13–57, 149–204; P. P. Jenson, *Graded Holiness: A Key to the Priestly Conception of the World;* T. E. McComiskey, *TWOT,* 2:786–89; O. Procksch and K. G. Kuhn, *TDNT,* 1:88–115; R. de Vaux, *Ancient Israel,* 2:271–330; D. P. Wright, *The Disposal of Impurity.*

Satan. The Hebrew word *śāṭān* means "an adversary, one who resists." It is translated as "Satan" eighteen times in the Old Testament, fourteen of those occurrences being in Job 1–2, the others in 1 Chronicles 21:1 and Zechariah 3:1–2. There is some dispute as to whether it should be taken as a proper name or a title. In Job and Zechariah the definite article precedes the noun (lit., "the satan" or "the accuser"). Thus some argue it should be a title, while in 1 Chronicles (no article) it should be a proper name. The word is used also of various persons in the Old Testament as "adversaries," including David (1 Sam. 29:4), Rezon of Damascus (1 Kings 11:23, 25), and the angel of the Lord (Num. 22:22, 32).

In the Old Testament, then, Satan is not an evil principle opposing God. In Job "the Satan" is not God's adversary, but Job's. He acts as one of God's subordinates/courtiers to follow his directives. (This view is premised on the idea that there is a difference in this being while he is still in heaven, rather than being cast out and being assigned to the realm of earth.) He does not seem, at this point, to be an adversary of all humans, but rather, of selected people. In Zechariah 3:1, he is a potential accuser; in 1 Chronicles 21:1, one inciting David to evil. Within the Job narrative, Satan acts at God's directive. While 1:12; 2:6–7 point to Satan's causal role in Job's life, later texts like 6:4; 7:14; 9:17 appear to lay blame on God. Thus Satan carries out divine directives.

Not Job's piety, but the connection between his piety and his prosperity was what Satan was questioning. (This is one of the "wisdom" themes of the Old Testament.) He implied that Job's piety was based on self-interest. The tests that followed were meant to demonstrate what that relation was.

"Satan" occurs thirty-six times in the New Testament, eighteen of that number in the Gospels and Acts. The Greek term *satanas* is a loan word from the Hebrew Old Testament, and twenty-eight of the total occurrences are accompanied by the definite article. Often in the Gospel accounts Jesus is in contact with Satan directly or indirectly. He was tempted by Satan (Mark 1:13). In the famous "Beelzebub controversy" Jesus made clear his intention to drive Satan out of people's lives and to destroy his sovereignty (Matt. 12:26; Mark 3:23, 26; Luke 11:18). He liberated a woman "whom Satan (had) kept bound for eighteen long years" (Luke 13:16). Paul spoke of his being sent to turn people "from the power of Satan to God" (Acts 26:18), and that the works of the "lawless one (were) in accordance with the work of Satan," in doing sham miracles, signs, and wonders (2 Thess. 2:9). Christ will come, he wrote, to overthrow that agent of Satan.

While the activity of Satan is carried out in "the world" (i.e., among those who do not acknowledge Christ as Lord), he also works against the followers of Christ. He influenced Peter's thinking about Jesus to the extent that Jesus said to his disciple, "Get behind me, Satan!" (Matt. 16:23). He asked for all the disciples in order to severely test them (Luke 22:31). He "entered" Judas Iscariot (Luke 22:3), and "filled the heart" of Ananias (Acts 5:3). Believers can be tempted by Satan due to a lack of self-control in sexual matters (1 Cor. 7:5), and he can even masquerade as "an angle of light" to accomplish his purposes (2 Cor. 11:14). He tormented Paul by means of "a thorn in (his) flesh" (2 Cor. 12:7). Some people even turn away from their faith to follow Satan (1 Tim. 5:15).

Satan opposes the proclamation of the gospel, snatching away the seed (the word) that was sown in people's hearts (Mark 4:15; Luke 8:12). He also "stopped" Paul from traveling to Thessalonica (1 Thess. 2:18).

Satan is regarded in the New Testament as "master of death and destruction," who carries out God's wrath against sinners. Twice we read of persons "handed over to Satan" for spiritual discipline by the church (1 Cor. 5:1–5; 1 Tim. 1:19–20). This appears to mean that excommunication puts people out into Satan's realm, a sovereignty from which believers have been rescued (Col. 1:13; cf. Heb. 2:14–15). In other cases, Satan attacked the disciples of Jesus by "sifting" them (Luke 22:31), a figure that is enigmatic. It may have meant to test their faith (with the intent of destroying it), or, it may have meant "to separate off the rubbish" (I. H. Marshall). In any case, Satan was up to no good. He was able to "enter" Judas Iscariot (Luke 22:3; cf. John 13:27), resulting in that disciple becoming a betrayer of his Master. Peter's sifting may have brought about his threefold denial of Jesus.

The nascent church in Jerusalem felt the brunt of Satan's attacks. He "filled" Ananias' heart and he lied to the Holy Spirit (Acts 5:3), resulting in his sudden demise. The believers in Smyrna felt the sting of persecution (Rev. 2:9–10). The nations of earth in John's vision were deceived by him (Rev. 20:7–8).

Jesus spoke of seeing Satan "fall like lightning from heaven" (Luke 10:18), a fall not identified but spoken of within the context of demons being cast out—a sign of Satan's loss of authority. In Revelation, amid a war in heaven, Satan was "hurled to the earth" along with his angels/demons (12:9). He, the Accuser, was overcome by One stronger than he. Finally, he is bound, imprisoned in the abyss for one thousand years, then ultimately banished in the fiery lake to suffer eternal torment (20:1–3, 10; cf. Matt. 25:41).

The other common appellation for Satan in the New Testament is "the devil" (*diabolos*), not found in the Old Testament, but thirty-four times here, meaning one who is traducer, a slanderer. The word often translates *satan* in the Septuagint (either as "the satan" or an "adversary"). In the New Testament the "devil" becomes "an evil principle/being standing against God."

In the New Testament the word appears to be used interchangeably with "Satan." Mark refers to "Satan" five times, but never uses "devil." Matthew has three of the former, but six of the latter. The Fourth Gospel has one instance of "Satan" (with none in the Epistles of John), while the "devil" (as Satan) occurs twice in the Gospel and three times in the Epistles.

Jesus would drive out "the prince of this world" by his cross (John 12:31); the latter would have no hold on Christ, for he was without sin (14:30); and Satan stood condemned at the bar of God's judgment (16:11). While the devil has had a career of sinning "from the beginning," the Son of God came to destroy his wicked works (1 John 3:8). Those unable to hear and receive Jesus' words belong to the devil, who is their "father" (John 8:44)—they share a family likeness to him.

Believers need to exercise care about anger, so as "not to give the devil a foothold" (Eph. 4:26). They are to don God's full armor so as to stand against the devil's schemes. With the shield of faith they are to thwart his "flaming arrows" (Eph. 6:11, 16). Ultimate victory comes by "the blood of the Lamb and by the word of their testimony," as the devil is cast down from heaven to the earth (Rev. 12:11). WALTER M. DUNNETT

See also DEMON; EVIL; SIN.

Bibliography. H. Bietenhard, *NIDNTT*, 3:468–72; O. Bocher, *EDNT*, 1:297–98; D. J. A. Clines, *Job 1–20*; W. Foerster, *TDNT*, 2:1–20; E. Lanyton, *Satan, A Portrait;* D. W. Pentecost, *Your Adversary, The Devil;* G. von Rad, *Old Testament Theology.*

Savior. *See* SALVATION.

Scandal. *See* OFFENSE.

Scapegoat. *See* OFFERINGS AND SACRIFICES.

Scripture. *See* BIBLE, AUTHORSHIP OF THE; BIBLE, CANON OF THE; BIBLE, INSPIRATION OF THE.

Scripture, Unity and Diversity of. Study of the nature of the relationship of the sixty-six canonical books of the Bible. The unity of Scripture claims that the Bible presents a noncontradictory and consistent message concerning God and redemptive history. The fact of diversity is observed in comparing the individual authors' presentations of God and history.

Foundational Issues. The foundation of the unity of the Bible is the belief that the sixty-six books of the Bible encode God's self-disclosure of himself and his will to his creation. God's method of conveying this revelation includes the diversity of time, culture, authors, literary genre, and the theological themes that address the special needs in the progress of that revelation.

The self-witness of the Bible to its inspiration demands a commitment to its unity. The ultimate basis for unity is contained in the claim of divine inspiration in 2 Timothy 3:16, that "all Scripture is given by inspiration [*theopneustos*] of God, and is profitable for doctrine, for reproof, for correction, for instruction in righteousness" (KJV). The term "inspiration" renders the Greek word *theopneustos*. This term only occurs here in the New Testament and literally means "God-breathed" (the chosen translation of the NIV). Paul's use of "all" focuses on the already composed Old Testament as well as the developing New Testament. This certainly reflects Jesus' authoritative use of the Old Testament in his teaching recorded in the Gospels. Peter also stresses that Scripture is a divine product and therefore authoritative (2 Peter 1:19–21; 3:15–16). Peter's discussion of earth history in 2 Peter 3 assumes the unity of God's control of history. It is obvious that he would also assume a unity in the biblical record of that control. The statements of Paul and Peter model a belief in the unity of Scripture on a priori grounds.

This approach to the unity of Scripture is often attacked on the basis that it is circular reasoning, using the source (the Bible) as a testimony to itself. Modern liberal scholars claim to reject such a procedure, denying unity by highlighting the diversity of the data within the Bible. We have noted, however, that ultimately our commitment to Scripture is an issue of faith. All ultimate beliefs appeal to a circle of reasoning for their support, even the beliefs of liberal biblical critics. At the same time, while it is not within the purpose of the present article to prove the point, it can be argued vigorously and with intellectual integrity that the phenomena of Scripture support a belief in its unity.

The Unity of Scripture. The Bible has one heart beat. It is an organic unity because an infinite God orchestrated its production. God normally accomplished this task through human instrumentality without violating the integrity of those individuals. Such a process cannot be studied in a test tube; it can only be proclaimed. This is exactly how Peter and Paul described it. Therefore, the organic unity of Scripture is ultimately a theological proposition that reflects a presupposition concerning the nature of God. Although this unity is a deductive proposition, it is inductively illustrated from the phenomena. We do not have a unity of Scripture because we can prove it from the phenomena, but we have phenomenological unity because it exists. The phenomenological study of Scripture serves several purposes: (1) to explicate the beauty of the product of Scripture; (2) to answer the critics who would demean its divine origin and unity; (3) to expose the diversity that is a part of God's plan as represented by its presence in the biblical record.

The unity of Scripture is observed in numerous categories. The normative nature of moral biblical teaching over a period of thousands of years as recorded from Genesis to Revelation is most striking. While the narrative structures make their own contextually specific points, there is a thread of continuity in regard to the larger moral expectations of God. It is as if the Bible reads us rather than us reading the Bible. It is a mirror in which we see ourselves, whether observing the struggles of the first family, the patriarchs, David and the kings, the prophets, or Jesus and the apostles. The Ten Commandments, the Sermon on the Mount, James, and 1 John present a harmonious voice for what constitutes godly character.

The interdependence of the Old Testament and New Testament requires a view of unity. The Old Testament is incomplete without the next chapter, the New Testament. The New Testament is not understandable without the Old Testament as a prolegomena. Jesus as Messiah brings both together and presents not only a unity but provides information for the final chapter—the eschaton. The use of the Old Testament in the Old Testament (e.g., the call narrative of Jer. 1 reflects Deut. 18) and the Old Testament in the New Testament illustrates this interdependence. The naturalness of this relationship is noted in that the New Testament uses the Old Testament as proof texts, showing continuity with the Old Testament in theological assertions, analogies in redemptive history (e.g., Matt. 2:17–18), and typological fulfillment. The use of the Old Testament in the New Testament as direct predictive prophecy is much less frequent than the above categories, but the fact of prophetic fulfillment argues strongly for the unity of the Bible. Prophetic fulfillment within the Old Testament and especially during the earthly messianic era demonstrates God's sovereign control over history and the resultant unity of the redemptive record.

The preaching of John the Baptist and Jesus did not totally take Israel by surprise because it was in concord with the Old Testament prophets. Paul presented promise and fulfillment themes from the perspective that his teaching is identical with the Old Testament promises (cf. Rom. 1:2; 4:14; Gal. 4:18). The Book of Revelation does not contain one formal quote from the Old Testament, yet it cannot be understood without a thorough knowledge of all biblical revelation that preceded it.

The historical and ethnic details illustrate continuity. The genealogies of Jesus rehearse ethnic origins and God's plan. Abraham is still a father model for those who believe when Romans and Galatians are read. Jesus and Paul go to the "Jews first." Paul argues that Israel is still important to God even though the Gentiles are now grafted into his plan (Rom. 9–11). The Book of Revelation ends where Genesis began, in an edenic garden.

A permeating theological continuity exists throughout Scripture. The development of a complete Christian worldview requires an understanding of the biblical story line from Genesis to Revelation. Genesis provides the nesting place for redemptive history. Revelation forecasts the culmination with abundant allusions to Genesis motifs. It is also interesting that the Gospel authored by the apostle John (assuming he also authored Revelation) focuses on the creation motif in its prologue.

The Scriptures present a singular view regarding sin and salvation. The Bible opens in Genesis 1–3 with a narrative on creation, fall, and redemption. The Scriptures then proceed to develop these themes. All subsequent passages depend upon these established motifs until the consummation in the Apocalypse delivers humankind and places them in an eternal utopia like the Garden of Eden. The New Testament illustrates this dependence. The classic text of Romans 3 defines sin by stringing Old Testament quotes together. When Peter engages his own sinfulness, it seems that he does so in Isaianic imagery (cf. Isa. 6:5 with Luke 5:8). From Abraham to Paul, salvation is by faith and faith alone. From Abraham to James, righteousness by faith is functional (a point also noted by Paul in Eph. 2:10; Titus 3:3–8).

The concept of covenant provides a major framework for unity and diversity within the record of God's redemptive work. The Old Testament presents the relationship between God and humankind in terms of a series of covenants. Covenant forms are presented to Adam, Noah, Abraham, and Moses; then the promise of a new covenant appears in the prophets. Old Testament theology forms many of its concepts around covenantal terminology. Common terms such as "know," "lovingkindness," and "love" bear special meaning in many contexts. The statement in Romans 9:13, "Jacob I loved, but Esau I hated," is best understood in terms of an established covenant with Jacob and not with Esau. The New Testament reflects the continuing presence of a covenant consciousness in Zechariah's hymn of praise (Luke 1:67–79) and the Epistle of Hebrews.

The christological continuity of the Testaments is undeniable. The New Testament correlates with the Old Testament concerning Jesus' place of birth, family line, forerunner, suffering, death, and future kingdom. Matthew is so conscious of this correlation that he creates a quotation from the Old Testament on a very broad analogy of Jesus as the rejected one in order to justify Jesus being raised in Nazareth (Matt. 2:23). The baptism of Jesus marks him as the anointed servant of the Lord. Jesus adopts a particularly messianic title—"son of man"—from Daniel 7 as his favorite way of referring to himself. All Bible students wish Luke would have recorded more than a mere reference of Jesus' exposition of himself from the Old Testament (24:25–27; 24:44). The correlation of Jesus with the Passover Lamb at the beginning and end of his earthly ministry presents a most prominent Jewish imagery of salvation.

The Diversity of Scripture. The focus of skepticism in relation to Scripture as a unified divine revelation has been on what it views as irreconcilable diversity within the phenomena of the biblical text. Several issues need to be considered as one evaluates diverse data. One major flaw in evaluating what constitutes unity is to assume that unity means unanimity. The New Testament's record of disagreements between Peter and Paul, Paul and Barnabas, and many other items, does not reflect irreconcilable differences but reveals the struggle of the christological transition. Jesus warned about a variety of tensions that accompany times of transition when he described old and new wine, old and new cloth, family members turning against each other, and many other aspects of conflict over the revelation of God's developing program.

Another problem in evaluating diversity relates, once again, to the matter of presuppositions. An example by analogy is the matter of Luke's record of the Quirinius census at the time of Jesus' birth. If a scholar assumes that the biblical authors are only correct when clear external collaborating evidence is present, then Luke will not be viewed as accurate. If Luke, however, is given the benefit of the doubt as a historian, then one can build a strong case of probability on behalf of his accuracy. The same principle applies when evaluating diverse material in the Bible. If Scripture is viewed for what it claims to be, reasonable explanations for diversity can usually be provided or merely allow the tension to stand. On the other hand, if Scripture is viewed as nothing more than a composite body of literature that records a varied history of religion, no amount of explanation will satisfy.

A failure to accept diversity can often be another problem. The unity and diversity of Scripture must ultimately be described by the evidence in the biblical text. What exists in the text is, by our own evangelical presupposition, what God intended for us to have and it is inerrant. If we fail to assimilate into our overall biblical worldview the diversity God has created, we will miss an important aspect of God's character and plan. Diversity itself is complementary and not contradictory! Therefore, diversity as well as unity must be taken into account. The technical development of exegesis among evangelical biblical scholars over the past several decades provides us with an adequate tool chest to accomplish this task. The work of evangelical scholars in relation to accounting for the diversity that exists in the Synoptic Gospels provides some helpful principles in accounting for other areas of diversity within Scripture.

The old liberal presentation of negative diversity in the Bible was based upon certain controlling presuppositions. Examples include composite authors who were attached to rival sects (e.g., the JEDP theory), assumed antitheses between Jesus and Paul, and discontinuity between the historical Jesus and the kerygmatic Christ (which means the Christ preached by the early church without any necessary connection with what Jesus of Nazareth actually said). This article will cite the more positive examples of diversity, which should be viewed from the human perspective as God-ordained diversity.

The New Testament writers use a great variety of semantic domains to describe the same issues. One striking example occurs between Paul and John's description of gospel proclamation. Paul uses the *euangel-* word-group ("proclaim the gospel/good news") to image his proclamation of the gospel and thereby has made the term "gospel" a household word among Christians. John never uses any form of this term in his Gospel or epistles (the occurrences in Rev. 10:7 and 14:6 are merely good news in general). John utilizes the *martur-* word-group ("witness") and thereby images his proclamation of the gospel as a "witness." Since John's Gospel was probably written after Paul's influential mission, does this mean that he disagreed with Paul? No, he merely chose another term to suit his purposes. Another aspect of semantics concerns the definition a writer gives to a term. Paul views the concept of righteousness almost exclusively as a forensic issue. Most other biblical writers use the terms for righteousness in functional ways, reflecting the evidences of one's legal standing with God. Jesus and Paul and James and Paul do not contradict one another; they merely provide a variety of perspectives upon a larger issue.

Apparent theological diversity provides many difficult areas to explain. How do you resolve the dilemma of the divine will and human responsibility? The "problem of evil" question—"If God is ultimate good, and God has ultimate power, then how can he allow evil to exist?"—challenges each new generation of Christian theologians. The acts of Yahweh in the Old Testament (Josh. 6:15–21), and the teaching of the God-Man (Luke 9:54–55) in the New Testament appear on opposite ends of a continuum to many. How God can hate sin and love sinners, save some and consign others to eternal punishment, defies explanation in the minds of many sensitive people. Yet, these are all expressions of diversity Scripture upholds without providing the reader with a systematic theology footnote to ease the tension. Biblical diversity is not to be rejected or simply explained away. It must be incorporated into our total world and life view. GARY T. MEADORS

See also BIBLE, AUTHORITY OF THE; BIBLE, INSPIRATION OF THE; OLD TESTAMENT IN THE NEW TESTAMENT, THE.

Bibliography. D. L. Baker, *Two Testaments, One Bible;* J. Barr, *The Bible in the Modern World and Fundamentalism;* J. D. G. Dunn, *Unity and Diversity in the New Testament;* W. Eichrodt, *Theology of the Old Testament;* D. P. Fuller, *The Unity of the Bible;* F. Gaebelein, "The Unity of the Bible," in *Revelation and the Bible;* N. Geisler, ed., *Inerrancy;* J. Goldingay, *VT* 34 (1984):153–68; J. Grier, *GTJ* 1ns (1980); C. F. H. Henry, *God, Revelation and Authority,* vol. 4; L. J. Kuyper, *The Scripture Unbroken;* G. Maier, *The End of the Historical-Critical Method;* R. Nash, *The Word of God and the Mind of Man;* J. I. Packer, *JETS* 25 (1982):409–14; V. Poythress, *Symphonic Theology;* H. H. Rowley, *The Unity of the Bible;* F. Schaeffer, *Escape From Reason;* J. Walvoord, ed., *Inspiration and Interpretation.*

Seal. A seal, in biblical times as today, is used to guarantee security or indicate ownership. Ancient seals were often made of wax, embedded with the personalized imprint of their guarantor. The Roman authorities used such a seal to secure Jesus' tomb (Matt. 27:66). A signet ring was also called a seal. It was valued among Israel's booty (Num. 31:50).

The significance of the act of sealing is dependent on the importance of the one doing the sealing. This is why Jezebel falsely authenticated letters she wrote in Ahab's name by affixing them with his seal (1 Kings 21:8). Ahasuerus's solemn decree to annihilate the Jews (Esther 3:12) and then to bless them (8:8, 10) was sealed with his signet ring.

The word "seal" often is used figuratively in the Bible. The divine origin of prophet "books" solemnizes the opening of the seals with which they are securely fastened. They are opened at God's discretion, often announcing doom (Isa. 29:11–12; Dan. 9:24; 12; Rev. 5:1). Also, the Book of Job speaks of the great God who "seals off the light of the stars" (9:7). God providentially uses clouds to block out the otherwise helpful presence of stars. He also seals up transgressions, disposing of them as he wills (Job 14:17; Hos. 13:12). The bridegroom refers to his bride as a sealed (chaste) garden spring (Song of Sol. 4:12). Pledging fidelity, the bridegroom asks his beloved to seal him to herself on the heart and on the arm (8:6). The psalmist asks God to seal his lips to prevent sinful speech (141:3).

The New Testament continues the mostly metaphorical use of "seal." For example, Satan's ineffectiveness is secured by God's sealing of the abyss (Rev. 20:3). Paul sealed a generous offering collected from believers in Macedonia and Achaia by delivering it to the needy church in Jerusalem (Rom. 15:28). Paul described his Corinthian converts as the seal of his apostleship (1 Cor. 9:2). Those who dogged him could not refute his effective ministry in transforming lives (see also 2 Cor. 3:1–3). Testimonies to the truth are sealed to indicate the certainty of the one making the claim (John 3:33). God the Father has staked such a claim on his son, rendering the words of Jesus equivalent in authority to those of the Father (John 6:27–29).

Paul described Abraham's circumcision as a seal, or guarantee, that Abraham was reckoned righteous by God (Rom. 4:11). By commanding this outward observance of the old covenant, God indicated how human beings could demonstrably consecrate themselves by faith to him. The covenant was bilateral in the sense that it needed to be ratified (i.e., sealed) by each individual. God takes covenant-keeping signs and vows seriously. The seal has no effect unless accompanied by faith. A God-ordained sign entered into by faith makes certain the grace that it signifies (Rom. 4:16). "The Lord knows those who are his" and "Everyone who confesses the name of the Lord must turn away from wickedness" (2 Tim. 2:19), the insignias etched into the seal placed on "God's firm foundation," are at the same time a blessing and a warning. The tribulation saints have a seal with God's name protecting them from judgment (Rev. 9:4; 14:1). Throughout eternity all of God's people will bear this mark of identification (Rev. 22:4).

The Holy Spirit seals those who trust in Christ. The Spirit's presence is God's guarantee that believers are owned by him and secure in him. Since the Holy Spirit's task is to apply Christ's work to God's people, he anoints believers "in Christ" the moment they believe (2 Cor. 1:21–22; Eph. 1:13). The Father anointed Christ with the Spirit at his baptism, the inauguration of his messianic ministry (Luke 3:22; 4:18). Similarly, a believer's baptism marks him or her out as God's. A believer is a secure member of God's family, not because he or she is "holding on," but because the Spirit is applying the promises about Christ. His sealing merely comprises the initial down payment that anticipates the future, full redemption of God's "marked possession" (Eph. 1:14; cf. 2 Cor. 5:5). In the meantime, Paul commands Christians not to grieve the Holy Spirit in light of the coming day of redemption (Eph. 4:30). The Christian is marked as a "new self," a "re-creation" of God (Eph. 4:24), indwelt by the Holy Spirit. His work of sealing believers, therefore, implies a moral responsibility. His name, "Holy" Spirit, is not without significance. His sealing separates the believer from the world and from his or her unholy past. It is incongruous for a sealed believer to ignore God's present sanctifying work through the Spirit resulting in practical godliness (Eph. 4:14–6:9).

Bradford A. Mullen

See also Holy Spirit; Redeem, Redemption.

Second Adam. *See* Adam, the Second.

Second Coming of Christ. In Old Testament times the idea that in due course God would send his Messiah (= "Anointed One") made its appearance and this thought continued in the intertestamental period. The term could be applied to Gentiles, such as Cyrus (Isa. 45:1), but its characteristic use was for a great king whom God would send at the end of the world, a deliverer who would set God's people free from their oppressors. The Christians accepted this idea and built on it. They gave it a new twist when they spoke of Jesus as "the Christ," "the Anointed One," and saw him not only as having lived a life on earth here in time but as destined to return to the earth at the end of the age to set up God's final state of things. There was a difference from previous messianic expectations in that Jesus had lived out a life on earth so that the coming to which Christians looked forward was a second coming. And it was important that the one for whose second coming believers looked had already lived on earth and wrought redemption for all who believed in him.

The Teaching of Jesus. The greater part of Jesus' teaching concerned life here and now and the way people should live in the service of God. He drew attention to the fulfillment of Old Testament prophecies (e.g., Luke 4:21; cf. Matt. 12:17–21), and clearly saw himself as sent by the Father to inaugurate the kingdom of God. Some have seen this as "realized eschatology," the view that the present kingdom of God, established in the life and the teaching of Jesus, is the whole story (C. H. Dodd argued for this view). But this perspective overlooks the fact that Jesus certainly looked forward to a future "coming" when this world order would be done away and a completely new state of affairs would be inaugurated.

Thus he warned his hearers that anyone ashamed of him and his teaching would find the Son of Man ashamed of him "when he comes in his Father's glory with the holy angels" (Mark 8:38). This teaching is given as something already accepted and it thus appears to be part of Jesus' teaching from earlier days. There is no point at which he ceases to teach other things and begins to enunciate teaching on his second coming. Right at the beginning Jesus taught that "the kingdom of God is near" (Mark 1:15) and this may be held to imply the second coming for it was when that took place that the kingdom would be set up in its fullness. That he spoke more about his second coming than is recorded seems clear from the question the disciples asked him toward the end of his life: "What will be the sign of your coming and of the end of the age?" (Matt. 24:3). Not much teaching about his return is recorded before this time, but these words show that Jesus had previously taught the disciples that he would come back. All three Synoptists record significant teaching about Jesus' coming again in the Olivet discourse.

The coming will be sudden and unexpected (Matt. 25:13; Luke 12:40), but when it happens it will be like lightning, obvious to all (Matt. 24:27; Luke 17:24). Jesus makes it clear that his coming will take place at a time when people will not be expecting it (Matt. 24:36, 44). His call for watchfulness is important (Matt. 24:42–51), for it indicates that the coming of the Son of Man has decisive importance. Earlier there had been a request that the places of honor in the kingdom should be given to the sons of Zebedee. Jesus did not deny that there would be such places, but said they were for those for whom the Father had prepared them (Matt. 20:20–23). The call for watchfulness is surely related to the coming of the kingdom. When Jesus comes it will be too late to make preparations, so he exhorts his followers to be watchful, ready for his coming, whenever it should be. We should also bear in mind the teaching of the parable of the talents. When the Master returns there will be an accounting of what his people have done with the talents he has given them.

An important part of Jesus' teaching about his second coming is the truth that it will form a strong contrast with his first coming. Then he had been a poor man, despised by religious and secular authorities and indeed probably quite unknown to many people. But when he comes back he will be "coming in clouds with great power and glory" (Mark 13:26). Something of his eminence is to be discerned from the fact that he will "gather his elect from the four winds, from the ends of the earth to the ends of the heavens" (v. 27); he will be seen "sitting at the right hand of the Mighty One and coming on the clouds of heaven" (14:62).

Right to the end of his life Jesus firmly enunciated the idea that he would come again, for at his examination before Caiaphas he said, "you will see the Son of Man sitting at the right hand of the Mighty One and coming on the clouds of heaven" (Mark 14:62). And Luke records Jesus' words just prior to his ascension: "It is not for you to know the times or dates the Father has set by his own authority" and the words of the angels, "This same Jesus, who has been taken from you into heaven, will come back in the same way you have seen him go into heaven" (Acts 1:7, 10). Acts also has a reference to God's having set a day "when he will judge the world with justice by the man he has appointed. He has given proof of this to all men by raising him from the dead" (Acts 17:31). This book does not often refer to the second coming, but the subject is not absent from Luke's second volume.

There is a strong emphasis on judgment at the time of Jesus' return. This is seen first in the separation of the saved from the lost. Thus of two men working in a field and of two women grinding at a hand mill at that time in each case "one will be taken and the other left" (Matt. 24:37–41). This will be seen also in the mourning of "all the nations of the earth" when they "see the Son of Man coming on the clouds of the sky, with power and great glory" (Matt. 24:30; in Luke Jesus speaks on "the day the Son of Man is revealed," Luke 17:30). What is stressed is that worldly people will be carrying on their usual manner of life without regard to their responsibility to God and without realizing their accountability right up to the time of Jesus' second coming. We discern the thought of final judgment also in such teachings of Jesus as the parable of the talents. Always there are the thoughts of human accountability and of final judgment which is to take place following the return of Jesus in triumph at the end of the age.

There is not a great deal about the second coming in the Fourth Gospel, but there is a persistent reference to Jesus' care for his own who will have eternal life and whom he will raise up at the last day (6:39, 40, 44, 54). This is seen also in his coming back to take the disciples to be with him (14:3, 28) and in the words about the disciples seeing him which puzzled them so much (16:16–18, 22). In the concluding verses of this Gospel there is another reference to Jesus' return (21:22–23).

The Parousia. Clearly Christ's second coming meant a great deal to the New Testament writers. Paul, for example, mentions it in most of his letters. He makes a good deal of use of the word *parousia* (14 times), which meant originally "presence" (Phil. 2:12) and thus a "coming to be present" (other ways of referring to the coming see it as an *apokalypsis,* "a revelation," or as an *epiphaneia,* "an appearing"; it is not infrequently referred to as "the day" or "the great day"). It was used of the "coming" of a king or emperor visiting a province and, in some religions, of the manifestation of the deity. In the New Testament it came to be used as a technical term for the second coming of a King. That Jesus first came in lowliness, despised and rejected, a man of sorrows, was important for those early believers. But that he would in due course come back in triumphant majesty was just as important.

The subject of the return of Christ is certainly important as the number of references to it in the New Testament makes amply plain. But there were difficulties in understanding what it meant even in the early church. Thus Paul counsels one group of early Christians not be "unsettled or alarmed" by teaching "that the day of the Lord has already come" (2 Thess. 2:2). If the teaching about it could be so drastically misunderstood in the earliest days of the church we should not be surprised if we find it difficult to fit all that the New Testament says about it into one coherent pattern.

In what is certainly one of his earliest surviving letters, 1 Thessalonians, Paul devotes attention to the problem of believers who had died. Apparently some of the early Christians thought that these people would miss out on the wonders when Christ returns. Paul says that on the contrary, when Jesus returns they will be with him; the living will have no precedence. He goes on to say that the Lord will "come down from heaven, with a loud command, with the voice of the archangel and with the trumpet call of God" (4:16). Clearly Paul is describing a majestic coming, a coming to rule and not as at Christ's first coming, a coming to serve. He goes on to speak of living believers as caught up to meet the coming Lord in the air. Traditionally this has been understood to mean that Paul is speaking of the end of this life as we know it and the ushering in of the final state of affairs.

But some Christians have seen in the words a secret rapture ("rapture" is from the Latin *raptus*, "seized," "carried off"), wherein believers are caught up secretly out of this life and taken to be with the Lord while earthly life goes on without them for the rest of the human race. Pretribulationists hold that there follows a period of tribulation for those remaining on earth (Matt. 24), which will last for a thousand years (Rev. 20:5). Midtribulationists think that the church will experience three and a half years of the tribulation before being raptured (citing Dan. 7:25, etc.). Posttribulationists hold that the church will remain on earth throughout the tribulation and that the return of Christ is after that. It is difficult to resist the conclusion that some have been far too confident in the way they interpret some difficult scriptural passages. That Christ will return at the end of the age, bringing "those who have fallen asleep in him" (1 Thess. 4:14) and that living believers will be caught up to meet the Lord in the air is clearly taught (1 Thess. 4:17). So is the fact that all this will be public and open, for the Lord will come "with a loud command, with the voice of the archangel and with the trumpet call of God" (1 Thess. 4:16). But we must exercise care in the way we go beyond these words and in our attempts to relate them to other scriptural passages. Whichever way we interpret the difficult passages we must bear in mind Jesus' exhortation to his followers to watch (Matt. 24:42).

That the returning Christ will come in majesty is made very clear. He will be "revealed from heaven in blazing fire with his powerful angels" (2 Thess. 1:7). It is "the day he comes to be glorified in his holy people and to be marveled at among all those who have believed" (v. 10). Paul can speak of waiting for "the blessed hope," which he goes on to explain as "the glorious appearing of our great God and Savior, Jesus Christ" (Titus 2:13). There will be "praise, glory and honor when Jesus Christ is revealed" (1 Peter 1:7; cf. "glories," v. 11). In the opening of Revelation we read, "he is coming with the clouds, and every eye will see him" (1:7) and from then on right through the book we are left in no doubt as to the majesty of the Christ whose place is supreme in heaven, but who will come back to this earth.

Final Triumph of Goodness. The return of Christ will usher in the era in which goodness will be triumphant, a truth that is brought out in many ways. Thus throughout the Book of Revelation we are reminded that the power of evil cannot stand up to the might of God. The final triumph of good over evil is brought out in a number of ways, notably in the magnificent vision of the heavenly city and in the vision of the wedding of the Lamb. Sometimes this is emphasized with the thought of the defeat of the forces of evil as when Paul says that Christ will hand over the kingdom to the Father after he has destroyed all opposing powers (1 Cor. 15:24). "The wrath of God" is coming (Col. 3:6), which surely means that that wrath will triumph over all evil. And Paul speaks of "the rebellion" as something that will occur and of "the man of lawlessness" as being "revealed." He goes on to say that "the secret power of lawlessness" is already at work in this world, but that it will be more fully manifested when "the one who now holds it back" is taken out of the way. But the Lord Jesus will destroy the evil power "by the splendor of his coming" (2 Thess. 2:3–12). Believers "are looking forward to a new heaven and a new earth, the home of righteousness" (2 Peter 3:13).

Sometimes the strength of evil, especially in the last days before Jesus' return, is emphasized. "There will be terrible times in the last days" (2 Tim. 3:1) and even among those who profess to be followers of Christ some will abandon the faith and accept "things taught by demons" (1 Tim. 4:1). Paul speaks of "the coming of our Lord Jesus Christ" and says plainly, "that day will not come until the rebellion occurs and the man of lawlessness is revealed" (2 Thess. 2:1–3). There will be scoffers who will say, "Where is this 'coming' he promised?" (2 Peter 3:4). In 1 John there is a warning against "the antichrist" and the writer goes on to speak of "many antichrists" as being present whereby his readers know that it is "the last hour" (1 John 2:18). In Revelation there are some vivid pictures of the evil that will be at the last times. The New Testament writers never underestimate the strength of evil; they encountered it in their own lives as they tried to live out the faith in the face of strenuous opposition, and they were sure that it would continue to the end of time. But they were equally sure that at the return of Christ all evil will be defeated and the kingdom of God finally set up, a kingdom in which righteousness will be supreme.

Unexpectedness of the Day. Though the second coming of Christ is plainly taught in a variety of ways throughout the New Testament it is also made clear that when it comes it will be sudden and unexpected. That day "will come like a thief in the night" (1 Thess. 5:2). So also the risen Lord tells the church at Sardis to wake up lest he come to them "like a thief" (Rev. 3:3). People will be saying "Peace and safety" when destruction suddenly comes (1 Thess. 5:3). Believers are exhorted that they "continue in him, so that when he appears [at the *parousia*] we may be confident and unashamed before him at his coming" (1 John 2:28). Though there will be "signs" that herald the coming, its arrival cannot be calculated accurately and people will still be surprised when Jesus comes.

Sometimes it is said that this will happen soon: "For in just a very little while, 'He who is coming will come and will not delay'" (Heb. 10:37). We should understand "a very little while" in the perspective of eternity. In terms of one short human life the delay is already considerable, but the biblical writer is not thinking in those terms. His "very little while" speaks of what is certain, rather than of what is soon in human terms. That the second coming will be soon is stressed in Revelation (22:7, 12, 20). But it will be "soon" in God's time, not in ours.

Eager Expectation. The awe-inspiring nature of the coming and its unexpectedness should not make believers view it with apprehension. The Corinthian church "eagerly" awaits the day (1 Cor. 1:7). The Ephesians are told that they by the Holy Spirit "were sealed for the day of redemption" (Eph. 4:30). This is an unusual way of referring to Christ's return but there can be no doubt that it is his coming that is in mind. Believers may have assurance as they look forward to that day. Until it comes they "wait for (God's) Son from heaven" (1 Thess. 1:10). Paul can express his trust in Christ and express his conviction "that he is able to guard what I have entrusted to him for that day" (2 Tim. 1:12). There is no need for him to explain which day "that day" is; so central was it to Christian teaching that Paul had no need to define it further. And we should notice his confidence about what will happen on that day. Similarly the writer to the Hebrews looks forward to the coming of "a kingdom that cannot be shaken" (12:28).

Sometimes this is expressed in terms of hope. We have been saved "in hope" (Rom. 8:24), a hope that is not centered on this life (1 Cor. 15:19), but is "stored up" for us in heaven (Col. 1:5). This hope is "held out in the gospel" and it can be spoken of as "Christ in you, the hope of glory" (Col. 1:23, 27). Christ is himself our hope (1 Tim. 1:1). Christians wait for "the blessed hope—the glorious appearing of our great God and Savior, Jesus Christ" (Titus 2:13). Peter speaks of the "living hope" given to Christians and goes on to refer to "the salvation that is ready to be revealed in the last time" (1 Peter 1:3–5). He exhorts his readers: "set your hope fully on the grace to be given you when Jesus Christ is revealed" (1 Peter 1:13). Believers must always be ready to give a reason for the hope that is within them (1 Peter 3:15). In 1 John we find that "When he appears, we shall be like him" and we are told that "Everyone who has this hope in him purifies himself" (3:2–3). Instead of hope the writer may refer to confidence: "Love is made complete among us so that we will have confidence on the day of judgment" (4:17).

Judgment. That the return of Christ leads on to judgment for all is made very clear. This may be expressed in terms of confidence for believers, and there are many passages that speak of their final state. Thus Paul assures the Corinthians that Christ will be "revealed" and that he "will keep you strong to the end, so that you will be blameless on the day of our Lord Jesus Christ" (1 Cor. 1:7–8). That they will be "blameless" indicates that blame will be assessed. A little later Paul has his teaching about Christians building on the foundation Christ laid and his reminder that "the day" will bring judgment. Fire will test everyone's work. What survives the flames will lead to a reward and what does not means loss (1 Cor. 3:11–15). It is said of believers that when Christ appears they will "appear with him in glory" (Col. 3:4), and further, that we wait for the coming of him who "rescues us from the coming wrath" (1 Thess. 1:10). Paul prays for the Thessalonians that their "whole spirit, soul and body be kept blameless at the coming of our Lord Jesus Christ" (1 Thess. 5:23). And that apostle speaks of "the crown of righteousness, which the Lord, the righteous Judge, will award to me on that day," a crown, which he adds, will be given "also to all who have longed for his appearing" (2 Tim. 4:8). Sometimes there is a reference to judgment without specific reference to the coming of Christ, but where this is clearly implied (e.g., 1 Peter 4:5; cf. v. 7).

Paul can use the certainty of the coming of "the day" as a way of motivating believers to be active in the service of their Lord. Thus he prays that the love of the Philippian Christians may abound more and more so that they may have discernment "and may be pure and blameless until the day of Christ" (Phil. 1:10). He asks the Thessalonian believers, "What is our hope, our joy, or the crown in which we will glory in the presence of our Lord Jesus when he comes?" and answers, "Is it not you?" (1 Thess. 2:19).

The Supremacy of Christ. At his first coming Jesus was "despised and rejected by men" (Isa. 53:3), but the New Testament makes it clear that it will not be this way at the second coming. Then the Father will have "put everything under his feet" (1 Cor. 15:27). At that time all his people will be "gathered to him" (2 Thess. 2:1), and they "will be with the Lord forever" (1 Thess. 4:17). This confidence Paul can speak of as "the blessed hope" which he proceeds to explain as "the glorious appearing of our great God and Savior, Jesus Christ" (Titus 2:13). We should understand passages referring to the kingdom here, for the thought is that Christ will be King in that day, as Revelation makes so abundantly clear. The writer to the Hebrews adds an interesting point when he says of the Old Testament saints that God has provided "that only together with us would they be made perfect" (11:40). And Jude adds the thought that "you wait for the mercy of our Lord Jesus Christ to bring you to eternal life" (v. 21). There is, of course, a sense in which believers already have eternal life, but Jude is referring to the sense in which the consummation will be reached only when Jesus returns.

The Millennium. The thought of Jesus' second coming dominates Revelation with its vivid imagery expressing the certainty of his return and the transformation of all things when that happens. There are problems in knowing exactly how the visions are to be interpreted, none more so than in the reference to the binding of Satan for a thousand years and the reign of certain believers with Christ for that period (Rev. 20:1–6). The interpretation of this chapter has divided evangelical Christians. Pre-millennialists hold that Christ will come before the thousand years, post-millennialists that the return of Christ will follow the thousand years, and amillennialists that the thousand years are to be understood symbolically; this period refers to the whole time before the second coming.

LEON L. MORRIS

See also ANTICHRIST; APOCALYPTIC; ARMAGEDDON; JUDGMENT; RESURRECTION; REVELATION, THEOLOGY OF.

Bibliography. G. R. Beasley-Murray, *Jesus and the Kingdom of God;* L. Berkhof, *The Second Coming of Christ;* G. C. Berkouwer, *The Return of Christ;* E. Brunner, *Eternal Hope;* C. H. Dodd, *The Apostolic Preaching and Its Developments;* E. Earle Ellis, *Eschatology in Luke;* J. E. Fison, *The Christian Hope;* T. F. Glasson, *Jesus and the End of the World;* idem, *The Second Advent: The Origin of the New Testament Doctrine;* G. E. Ladd, *The Blessed Hope;* idem, *Crucial Questions about the Kingdom of God;* idem, *The Presence of the Future;* J. Moltmann, *Theology of Hope;* A. L. Moore, *The Parousia in the New Testament;* J. A. T. Robinson, *Jesus and His Coming;* G. Vos, *The Pauline Eschatology.*

Second Death. This phrase is found only in Revelation 2:11, 20:6, 20:14, and 21:8. The Targums use it (Deut. 33:6; Ps. 49:11). Philo uses the term to refer to all miseries arising from sin causing physical death followed by hopelessness in the afterlife (*Rewards and Punishments* 2.419). Revelation 2:10–11 contrasts it with the life given to the faithful. Death is the loss of the only kind of life worthy of the name.

The word used for "eternal punishment" in Matthew 25:46 is *kolasis.* According to Bauer writers during the New Testament period used it only of temporal torture and conscious torment in the afterlife. No other idea for koine Greek is recognized. Moulton and Milligan can find only examples in papyrus where *kolasis* involves the person actually feeling the punishment. It is used elsewhere in the New Testament only in 1 John 4:18, which says fear has torment.

The second death is to be cast into the lake of fire (Rev. 20:14). This is a permanent state (Rev. 14:11), where in anything that would qualify as "life" is forever absent.

PAUL FERGUSON

See also ETERNAL PUNISHMENT; JUDGMENT; LAKE OF FIRE.

Seer. *See* PROPHET, PROPHETESS, PROPHECY.

Self, New. *See* NEW SELF.

Seraph, Seraphim. *See* ANGEL.

Sermon on the Mount. Of the five discourses of Jesus in Matthew, the Sermon on the Mount (chaps. 5–7) is the first, the longest, and the most prominent. Following Matthew's introduction to the person of Jesus (1:1–4:25), the sermon comprises the first words of Jesus to confront the reader and because of the arrangement of the canon, it holds the place of honor in the New Testament. Since the postapostolic age it has attracted more attention than any other section of the Bible and was considered the quintessential expression of Jesus' teachings. The study of its interpretations is the history of the development of theology. Luke's parallel, the Sermon on the Plain (6:17–49), with its 33 verses compared to Matthew's 107 or 109, does not match its detail, organization, complexity of interpretation, and unequivocal demands. Luke locates many parallels to Matthew's Sermon in other episodes of Jesus' life and not his Sermon on the Plain. Where Matthew's Sermon has the Lord's Prayer as part of a general instruction given by Jesus to the disciples (6:9), Luke has the disciples asking Jesus to follow the example of John the Baptist who taught his disciples to pray (11:1). Mark has no similar discourse and his parallels are few (4:21, 24–25; 9:43–48; 11:25).

Matthew and His Sermon on the Mount. Matthew's Sermon on the Mount must be interpreted within the totality of his Gospel and not as an isolated discourse. His penchant for order is evident in the division of the genealogy into three parts each with fourteen persons (1:2–17), the five discourses, and the division of the Gospel into two parts (4:17; 16:21); this indicates that he is arranging and editing preexisting material spoken by Jesus on more than one occasion, a suggestion put forth by Calvin and supported recently by Joachim Jeremias. Such divisions concluding with repetitions (e.g., "when Jesus had finished" [7:28; 11:1]), aided the reader's memory. Matthew is more the editor of sayings collected in the Sermon on the Mount than he is their author.

The dating of the Gospel affects the sermon's interpretation and its place of origin. A date after 70 A.D. means that the evangelist was not an eyewitness but dependent on oral tradition. Indications within the sermon challenge this. Laying gifts before the altar (5:23–24) and swearing by Jerusalem (5:35) reflect a time when Christians were still involved in Jewish cultic life (cf. Acts 3:1). Recent attempts to place the composition of the Sermon on the Mount after 85 to correspond with the Council of Jamnia are unconvincing, as the temple's destruction made its rituals inoperative. Disparaging remarks about Gentiles praying empty phrases (6:7) would hardly fit a situation where they had become the majority (cf. Acts 15:1–29). The world reflected in the Sermon on the Mount was that of Jerusalem in the first half of the first century. Matthew's retention of such severely cruel commands as plucking out one's eye and cutting off one's hand (5:28–29) can only be adequately explained if they originated with Jesus. Such common oriental paradoxical exaggeration, rarely taken literally even by absolutist interpretations, requiring total commitment to the kingdom might escape or offend converts from a non-Jewish background. It is more likely that Luke passed over these sayings than that a later writer like Matthew added them. The sermon most likely was transmitted first orally, as were rabbinic teachings, with repetition devices to aid memory. This oral transmission developed into a fixed body of tradition that Matthew, apart from what he knew directly and remembered, also had at his disposal. References in the list of the apostles to Matthew as a tax collector (10:3), missing in the synoptic parallels (Mark 3:18; Luke 6:15), suggest that the author had heard Jesus. As Jesus with his "but I tell you" (5:22, 28, 32, 34, 39, 44) puts himself in the place of God and makes his words the standard for the judgment (7:24–27), it is possible these sayings were gathered into written collections before being placed into Matthew's Gospel. Behind Matthew's Sermon on the Mount is probably one delivered near Capernaum. References to the temple could reflect discourses given in Judea (5:24; 6:35).

The Place of the Sermon within Matthew's Gospel. Matthew's fivefold division for the sayings of Jesus suggests that the Sermon on the Mount should be interpreted within the totality of the Gospel. All five discourses are directed to the disciples and end with Matthew's characteristic "and when Jesus had finished" (7:28; 11:1; 13:53; 19:1; 26:1), with the last bringing them together with "all these things" (26:1). These further are assumed into 28:20 with Jesus' command to his disciples to teach the Gentiles everything he commanded. Items raised in the sermon appear elsewhere, specifically in Matthew's four other discourses: the apostles and their authority (chap. 10); the kingdom explained in parables (chap. 13); humility as a mark of the community (18:1–19:1); and the end-times (chaps. 24–25).

The Beatitudes with their initiatory "blessed" (5:3–11) prepare for this title given first to the apostles as those who have heard and understood the parables (13:16) and then to Peter who confesses Jesus as Christ (16:17). The sermon's parable of the two houses (7:24–27), a brief apocalypse in its own right, sets the literary tone for the second discourse with its parables (chap. 13), the last of which deals also with the judgment (13:47–50) and anticipates "the little apocalypse" (25:31–46). With the words of Jesus as the basis for the final judgment, the Sermon on the Mount looks ahead to the Gospel's conclusion, which obligates the disciples to teach its words (28:20). The transfiguration with God's command to listen to Jesus (17:5) makes his words superior to those of Moses and Elijah and thus in him the law and the prophets reach their conclusion (5:28). Disciples who are only partially named at the sermon's beginning (4:18, 20; 5:1) are all named in 10:2–4 and appear at the end of the Gospel as the guardians of Jesus' words. Persecution promised in 5:11–12 is spelled out in 10:17–18 and is actualized in Jesus' own suffering (chaps. 26–27). The demand for unalloyed faith (6:25–33, esp. v. 30) is explicated in the discourse on the humility and faith of children (18:1–5). The necessity of forgiveness (18:15–35) is presupposed in loving the enemy (5:38–48). The sermon is a self-contained unit introducing the remainder of Matthew where its themes are further developed.

The Sermon's Speaker, Order, and Message. The sermon introduces Jesus sitting on the mountain (5:1–2), reminding the reader of Moses' giving of the law at Sinai. Jesus opens up his mouth (5:2), assuming the law and prophets into his words and mission (5:17).

The Beatitudes, as the sermon's first words, come not with threats, but describe the new community in christological terms to identify believers with Jesus (5:3–11). They are God's law fulfilled in Jesus and applied to Christians. The community in Christ described in the Beatitudes is a continuation of Israel in which the prophetic word is not annulled but fulfilled and remains in force in him and not as separate legislation (5:17–20). Jesus' coming transformed the Old Testament. Each beatitude describes the new community in Jesus from a different perspective: the poor in spirit, the merciful, the peacemakers, those persecuted for his sake and those persecuted because of righteousness. The Beatitudes anticipate specific behavioral standards for the community (5:21–46). Reconciliation with the estranged brother is required (5:21–26); adultery even of the heart brings condemnation (5:27–30); divorce carries severe consequences (5:31–32); oaths about future undertakings are disallowed (5:33–37); retaliation for alleged wrongs is renounced (5:38–42); and love is extended to one's enemies (5:43–48). Directives for the worshiping community are set down (6:1–18): giving to the needy is to be done in secret (6:1–4); rubrics on prayer include reciting the Lord's Prayer and avoiding long repetitions (6:5–15); and fasting remains part of Christian piety, but must be unannounced (6:16–18). Then follow general directives (6:19–7:12): treasures are to be laid up in heaven (6:19–21); the eye as the body's organ of light must remain uncontaminated (6:22–23); anxiety, the enemy of faith, must be avoided (6:25–34); condemnation of the brother is forbidden (7:1–5); faith believes God answers prayers (7:7–11); and the "Golden Rule" requires the same behavior one desires from others (7:12). The sermon closes with warnings. Those not following the "way," set forth in the sermon, are destined for damnation (7:13–14). False teachers will deceive believers (7:15–20). The parable of the houses describes the final judgment (7:24–27). At the end of the sermon the superior authority of Jesus is recognized by the crowds (7:28–8:1), and later confirmed by the resurrection (28:18). Although the sermon has the form of directives, its central message is that the community of Jesus is reconciled with those within and without. Thus, like God, it renounces retribution (5:43–48).

The Sermon's Audience. The Sermon on the Mount is best understood as instruction (*didachē* [7:28; 28:20]) for believers. Matthew's discourses are intended for the community of baptized believers and individuals as members of this community. Even when the believer prays alone (6:6), he does so as a member of the community in saying "*Our* Father" (6:9). Reconciliation is important for the sake of the community. The Sermon on the Mount defines the church and then describes how it appears in Christ.

Matthew's Sermon on the Mount continues to inform and shape the church's life. It joins believers with Christ and gives unity to his teachings. Its Beatitudes (5:3–11), Lord's Prayer (6:9–13), and Golden Rule (7:12), along with other sections belong to common Christian piety. Differing interpretations have not robbed the Sermon on the Mount of its continued influence.

David P. Scaer

See also Beatitudes; Ethics; Golden Rule; Jesus Christ.

Bibliography. W. D. Davies, *The Setting on the Sermon on the Mount;* W. D. Davies and D. C. Allison, Jr., *A Critical and Exegetical Commentary on the Gospel According to Saint Matthew;* idem, *SJT* 44: 283–309; H. McArthur, *Understanding the Sermon on the Mount;* R. A. Guelich, *Sermon on the Mount;* J. Jeremias, *The Sermon on the Mount;* W. S. Kissenger, *The Sermon on the Mount: A History of Interpretation and Bibliography;* I. A. Massey, *Interpreting the Sermon on the Mount in the Light of the Jewish Tradition as Evidenced in the Palestinian Targums of the Pentateuch.*

Serpent. *See* Satan.

Servant, Service. The words "servant," "service," and "serve," in various forms, occur well over 1,100 times in the New International Version. People are servants of other human beings or servants of God.

In the Old Testament, the Hebrew word for servant, *ʿebed,* contains at least two key ingredients: action (the servant as "worker") and obedience. Servants belonged to other people (Gen. 24:35; Exod. 21:21), and performed a variety of work.

Many persons in the Old Testament are called "servants," among them Abraham (Gen. 26:24), Jacob (Gen. 32:4), Joshua (Josh. 24:29), Ruth (Ruth 3:9), Hannah (1 Sam. 1:11), Samuel (1 Sam. 3:9), Jesse (1 Sam. 17:58), Uriah the Hittite (2 Sam. 11:21), Joab (2 Sam. 14:20), Isaiah (Isa. 20:3), Daniel (Dan. 9:17), Ben-Hadad of Aram (1 Kings 20:32), and Nebuchadnezzar of Babylon (Jer. 25:9). Moses is designated as such about forty times and David more than fifty.

The Book of Isaiah contains the "servant Songs" (42:1–4; 49:1–6; 50:4–9; 52:13–53:12). In them the servant may represent Israel as a whole; Israel after the Spirit; or the mediator of salvation (the Messiah of Israel). Many personal qualities are attributed to the Servant. While often called "Israel," the Servant appears to represent some great individual. Like David, he will rule and establish justice on earth (42:1, 4). But he will also suffer. The suffering, death, and new life of the Servant become exemplified in the New Testament in Christ (Isa. 52:13—Acts 3:13; Isa. 61:1—Acts 4:27; Isa. 53:7–8—Acts 8:32–33; Isa. 53:4–5, 7, 9—1 Peter 2:22–24).

In the New Testament, *doulos* is frequently used to designate a master's slave (one bound to him), but also a follower of Christ (a "bondslave" of Christ). The term points to a relation of absolute dependence, in which the master and the servant stand on opposite sides—the former having a full claim, the latter having a full commitment. The servant can exercise no will or initiative on his or her own.

Doulos is applied to several Old Testament worthies, including Moses (Rev. 15:3) and the prophets (Rev. 10:7). Paul (Titus 1:1) and James (1:1) both refer to themselves as servants of God; Paul also calls himself the "servant of Christ" (Rom. 1:1; Phil. 1:1).

Christ took upon himself the "form of a servant" (Phil. 2:7). Believers have moved from being slaves to sin to become slaves of righteousness (Rom. 6:17–18).

Another common New Testament term, *diakonos,* derives from a verb meaning "to wait at table," "to serve." As the Son of man, Jesus "did not come to be served, but to serve, and to give his life as a ransom for many" (Matt. 20:28; Mark 10:45).

The *diakonos* gives hospitality (Matt. 8:15), distributes food (Acts 6:1), sets a table (John 12:2), does the work of a deacon (1 Tim. 3:10), or exercises spiritual gifts (1 Peter 4:10–11). In the New Testament, the idea of "serving at table" is expanded to encompass "the service of the saints" (1 Cor. 16:15). Paul regarded the collection of money for the church in Jerusalem as a "service" (2 Cor. 8:4; 9:11–13), along with preaching and ministering in spiritual things.

One striking modification of usage from the Old Testament to the New is the occurrence of the word groups *latreia* and *leitourgia.* While the primary use in the Old Testament was cultic, describing the service of the priests and Levites in the sanctuary, the New Testament use is rarely so. The New Testament describes Christ as the High Priest "who serves in the [heavenly] sanctuary" (Heb. 8:10). But more often it describes the worship of one's heart (Acts 24:14b), of serving in the preaching of the gospel (Rom. 1:9), of those who "worship by the Spirit of God" (Phil. 3:3).

WALTER M. DUNNETT

See also SERVANT OF THE LORD; WORSHIP.

Servant of the Lord. God's servants were those who worshiped him and carried out his will, often in important leadership roles. Individuals such as Abraham (Gen. 26:24), Moses (Exod. 14:31; Deut. 34:5), David (2 Sam. 7:5, 8), and Isaiah (20:3) were called God's "servants" as they obediently walked with the Lord. There are several references to "my servants the prophets" (2 Kings 17:13; Jer. 7:25; 26:5), sent by God to call Israel to repentance and renewal of the covenant. Sadly, the prophets were often rejected and sometimes killed (Luke 11:47–51), in spite of the divine word they delivered. In the last half of Isaiah, scholars have identified four servant songs that describe the accomplishments and suffering of one called the servant of the Lord (42:1–7; 49:1–6; 50:4–11; 52:13–53:12). Possibly Isaiah 61:1–3 contains yet another servant song. Although Isaiah sometimes refers to the servant as "Israel," New Testament quotations and allusions clearly relate the ministry of the servant to the first coming of Christ and his atoning death.

The Identity of the Servant. At times it seems quite clear that the servant refers collectively to the nation of Israel. In 41:8–9 the servant is called "Israel" or "Jacob," the "descendants of Abraham my friend." Since the nation often proved to be unresponsive to the word of the Lord, the servant is called "blind" and "deaf" in 42:19. The suffering and affliction caused by Israel's sin (1:5–6) is similar to the experience of the servant in 53:4–5. Sometimes the concept of the "servant" seems to refer to those in Israel who were spiritual, the righteous remnant who remained faithful to the Lord. In 42:5 and 49:8 the servant functions as "a covenant for the people" and is involved in the restoration of the land after the Babylonian exile. Even though the servant is called "Israel" in 49:3, he is distinguished from Israel in verse 5, where the servant brings Israel back to the Lord. Starting with 54:17 and ending with 66:14 there are several references to "the servants" of the Lord, and the plural may be another term for the righteous remnant.

A careful reading of the four servant songs has nonetheless led many scholars to argue that the servant refers to an individual who fulfills in himself all that Israel was meant to be. This individual was the ideal Israel, a righteous and faithful servant who suffered unjustly and died to atone for the sins of humankind. H. H. Rowley has said that by chapter 53 the personification has become a person. The one who "was led like a lamb to the slaughter" died to bear "the sins of many" (vv. 6, 12) and "was assigned a grave with the wicked" (v. 9). This description does not apply very well to a nation or even a part of the nation, but it certainly can apply to an individual. In some respects the servant can be compared with the Davidic messianic king. Both were chosen by God and characterized by righteousness and justice (cf. 9:7; 42:1, 6). The Spirit of God would empower both the king and the servant (11:1–4; 42:1), and ultimately the suffering servant would be highly exalted (cf. 52:13; 53:12) and given the status of a king. The "shoot" or "branch" from the family of Jesse (11:1) is linked with the description of the servant as "a tender shoot" (53:2).

The Work of the Servant. Unlike the nation Israel, the servant of the Lord listened to God's word and spoke words of comfort and healing (42:2–3; 50:4–5). Yet his words were powerful and authoritative, and like a judge he was concerned about establishing justice and righteousness (42:1, 4; 49:2). Twice the servant is called "a light to the Gentiles" (42:6; 49:6), and "light" is clearly paralleled to "salvation." Similarly, the servant is involved in the restoration of the nation Israel (49:5). He is "a covenant for the people" (42:6; 49:8) as the ruler who was promised in the Davidic covenant (2 Sam. 7:16) and the One who would initiate the new covenant. The servant opens the eyes of the blind and frees captives from prison (42:7; cf. 61:1).

The Suffering of the Servant. In order to bring salvation to Israel and the nations, the servant had to die to pay for sin, and this theme of suffering and death becomes increasingly clear as the servant songs unfold. At first we are told only that "he was not falter or be discouraged" (42:4), but then the servant faces strong opposition and appears to have failed (49:4). He was despised and mocked to the point of being spit on, beaten, and otherwise humiliated (49:7; 50:6–7). In the final servant song (52:13–53:12) we learn that the servant was disfigured "beyond human likeness" (52:14) and "poured out his life unto death" as a guilt offering to make atonement for sin (53:10, 12). His vicarious death brought peace and healing to humankind and justification for many (53:5, 11). As the perfect sacrifice for sin, the death of the servant was in accord with God's will and resulted ultimately in victory and exaltation. The one who died now lives to intercede on behalf of believers (53:10, 12).

New Testament Quotations. Although the number of quotations from the servant songs are surprisingly limited in the New Testament, there are several important references to Christ as God's servant (*pais theous*). The longest quotation is found in Matthew 12:18–21, which cites almost all of Isaiah 42:1–4 in connection with Christ's healing of the sick. Matthew 8:17 also refers to Christ's ability to heal the sick and drive out evil spirits as a fulfillment of Isaiah 53:4: "He took up our infirmities and carried our diseases." Paul quotes Isaiah 52:15 in connection with his mission to preach the gospel to the Gentiles (Rom. 15:21), and both Paul and John cite 53:1 with reference to Jewish unbelief (Rom. 10:16; John 12:38). Paul also utilized Isaiah 49:6 as his preaching became "a light for the Gentiles" (Acts 13:47). Of the Gospel writers only Luke uses Isaiah 53 in speaking of Christ's suffering and death: "And he was numbered with the transgressors" (53:12; Luke 22:37). It was also Luke who related Philip's encounter with the Ethiopian eunuch, who was reading Isaiah 53:6–7 (Acts 8:32–33). Answering the eunuch's question, Philip preached "the good news about Jesus" from this passage about the lamb who was sacrificed (Acts 8:34–35).

While encouraging believers who were suffering, Peter cites several verses from Isaiah 53. Christ's submission in the midst of unjust threats is linked to verse 9 (1 Peter 2:22), and the substitutionary nature of Christ's death is derived from verses 4 and 11 (1 Peter 2:24). We have been healed by the wounds Christ suffered on our behalf as the good Shepherd gave his life to rescue the straying sheep (Isa. 53:5–6; 1 Peter 2:25).

New Testament Allusions. The portrayal of Christ as the suffering servant stands behind many other passages. Four times in Acts the word "servant" (*pais*) is applied to Christ in connection with his death (3:13, 26; 4:27, 30). Twice Christ is called the "Righteous One," perhaps an allusion to the "righteous servant" of Isaiah 53:11 (Acts 3:14; 7:52). John the Baptist called Jesus "the Lamb of God" (John 1:29, 36), while on the day of Pentecost Peter spoke of "God's set purpose and foreknowledge" that lay behind Calvary (Acts 2:23). Paul's reference to Christ's being raised for our justification reflects the Greek translation of Isaiah 53:11 (Rom. 4:25), and the same verse may have affected the wording of "the many will be made righteous" (Rom. 5:19). Mark's key reference to the Son of Man as a servant who gave his life "as a ransom for many" (10:45) may also stem from Isaiah 53.

Herbert M. Wolf

See also Isaiah, Theology of; Jesus Christ; Messiah.

See also Jesus Christ, Names and Titles of.

Bibliography. R. T. France, *Tyn Bul* 19 (1968); M. D. Hooker, *Jesus and the Servant;* F. D. Lindsey, *The Servant Songs;* C. R. North, *The Suffering Servant in Deutero-Isaiah;* H. M. Wolf, *Interpreting Isaiah;* W. Zimmerli and J. Jeremias, *The Servant of God.*

Sexuality, Human. ***Foundations.*** This essay is based on the following premises: (1) Those functions founded in the unfallen created order that God proclaimed good (Gen. 1:31) may be seen as normative for matters touching theological ethics. (2) Sin came as a result of the fall, introducing a distortion of the created order and fostering enmity and alienation where none had previously existed. (3) That distortion brought with it not only alienation from God, but also alienation from other human beings (Gen. 4:10–14) and from one's self (Rom. 7:15–24). Sin has also introduced a distortion into all social relationships, including those between men and women (Gen. 3:16). (5) Redemption attempts to remove or rectify the alienation introduced by the fall, restoring humankind to fellowship with God (Rom. 5:12–21; Eph. 2:1–22) and with itself (Isa. 2:1–5; Mic. 4:1–7). (6) The community of the redeemed is charged with modeling in itself the fruits of redemption and with laboring to bring about the redemption of the world.

Accordingly, since narratives of Eden before the fall picture the unsullied created order as God ordained it, they become normative and prescriptive; hence the way that unfallen man interfaced with woman should provide a working model for male/female relationships in the community of the redeemed. Narratives of fallen humanity (such as the stories of Samson's womanizing or Solomon's polygyny) are descriptive and provide information about what *was,* but not always about what *ought* to have been. Jesus, untainted by the fall (Heb. 4:15), lived the only unfallen life since humanity's banishment from Eden. His life, therefore, like the Edenic narratives, becomes normative and thus exemplary and prescriptive in matters of morality. The way that Jesus, the "second Adam," related to women should, like that of unfallen Adam, provide a model for intersexual relationships. As can be demonstrated by the overt parallels between Eden and the New Jerusalem portrayed in Revelation 21–22, the world to come (the eschaton) will be established as a postfallen order with the effects of the fall fully negated. The eschaton and its values, therefore, reflect the end toward which the present redeemed community labors. The values of the eschaton, accordingly, are prescriptive. Commands, teachings, laws, and institutions that are designed to move one from a fallen to a postfallen (redeemed) state or community are redemptive and therefore prescriptive, although care must be taken to distinguish the *spirit* from the *letter* in their application (Mark 9:47).

The Image of God: Male and Female. Although the words "sex" and "gender" are constantly being redefined by modern usage, this article will use the term "sex" to indicate the sum of the structural and functional differences by which the male and female are distinguished, as well as the phenomena or behavior dependent on those differences (adapted from *The Random House Unabridged Dictionary,* 2d ed.). "Gender" will be used to describe the interpretation given sexual distinctions and the roles assigned them in a given social setting. Accordingly, sex will deal with identity as it is determined biologically and genetically, whereas gender will address identity as it is determined socially and environmentally.

From a theological perspective, human sexuality in Scripture is predicated on the pronouncement that the human species is created in the image and likeness of God (Gen. 1:26–28). Many and bitter have been the arguments over the specific meaning of the term "image of God." Basically, the image of God is the essence and substance of theological humanness. By this term is intended that quality which theologically separates human beings from lower animals and which provides some sort of analogous relationship with God, making it possible for humans to communicate and fellowship with him. Further, since Adam transmits it to his progeny (Gen. 5:1–3), it is likewise clear that the image of God (*imago Dei*) was not lost in the fall. After the flood the image of God became a universal standard for punishing antisocial actions (Gen. 9:6; cf. James 3:9). Accordingly, human social ethics are not founded exclusively on a person's organic relationship to other human beings through participation in a common ancestor or a covenant community such as Israel or the church. Instead, they assume a theologically prior dimension whereby a crime against any human being, within or without the community, becomes a blasphemy against him in whose image humanity was fashioned. The combination of these two factors, the organismic and the *imago Dei,* brought about a lack of stratification in Hebraic law when compared with other laws of the ancient Near East. In the Bible a person's life was considered of great value even if his social standing was merely that of a slave (Exod. 21:20–21, 26–27).

The application of the *imago Dei* to human sexuality becomes clearer when Genesis 1:27 is analyzed:

> So God created man in his own image.
> In the image of God he created him.
> Male and female he created them.

The poetic parallelism found in lines 2 and 3 strongly suggests that the term "him" (line 2) bears a close relationship to the word "them" (line 3). It also suggests a strong though unspecified tie between the term "image of God" (line 2) and the words "male and female" (line 3).

If the term "man" (*'ādām*) referred to in Genesis 1:26–28 designates only a male human being, then traditional male-dominated exegesis would be correct in considering only the male as bearing the image of God and, thus, as being fully human. It is crucial, therefore, to recognize that the man (*'ādām*) referred to in Genesis 1:26–28 ("him") represents the human species ("them") made up of male and female, and that they *corporately,* not severally, reflect the image of God. Such an understanding expresses the bisexual (dipolar) nature of corporate human society, and cannot be applied to the male alone. The concomitants, then, of being created in God's image would be shared by both sexes in the charges and provisions given them by God: (1) having joint dominion over creation (Gen. 1:26); (2) working together to increase the human population (Gen. 1:28); and (3) having shared and unimpeded access to available food supplies (Gen. 1:29). These benefits, charges, and responsibilities are shared equally by the two humans and lead to a picture of corporate humankind as God's representatives on earth, somehow displaying God to the lower animals. It is together that they reflect the divine image in which they were created, with no indication that one component of the mix reflects more of that image than the other.

Those who see women as inherently inferior to men often appeal to the specific account of the creation of woman (Gen. 2:18, 20–22) as shedding further light on the relationship that existed between the sexes in their unfallen state: woman, they maintain, is a secondary creation, a mere "helpmeet" to the man. But an unforced analysis of the narrative shows that no sort of inherent inferiority can be derived from it. Woman is made of the same essence and substance as man and can hardly, therefore, be considered inferior. Some have even argued that since the man was made of dirt and the woman from the man, she becomes twice refined and, if anything, superior.

The woman's relationship to the man is described by two words: she is *'ēzer* and *kĕnegdô* (Gen. 2:20). The former term, *'ēzer,* means help. The psalmists' use of the term to describe God (Pss. 46:1; 54:4) demonstrates that the word has in itself no hint of inferiority. Indeed, the verses cited above point to God as one who is strong enough to share his strength with another. The latter term, *kĕnegdô*, is a strange three-part compound composed of *kĕ*, meaning like or as; *neged*, meaning over against, opposite; and *ô*, meaning him. Woman was made because man's being alone was the only thing pronounced "not good" in the creation narrative (2:18). The help for Adam would therefore designate "that which is lacking, necessary for completion" that "helps" Adam become, not simply the male of the species, but a legitimate microcosm of the human race. There is an equality implicit in the latter part of the phrase, which may be roughly approximated as "his corresponding opposite." Woman, accordingly, becomes man's complement or reciprocal, not merely his supplement. Together they make up what may be called theological humanity.

On the other hand, rejecting the superiority of the male does not mean that the sexes were undifferentiated and that the term *'ādām* denotes some sort of androgynous being or "earth creature" from which both man (*'îš*) and woman (*'iššâ*) were formed. This interpretation does not do exegetical justice to the narrative, for the loneliness described in 2:18–20 would be incomprehensible for a sexually undifferentiated creature unaware that he/she was lacking a sexual counterpart. Moreover, as Childs has pointed out, just as *'îš* and *'iššâ* are paralleled in verse 23, so *'ādām* and *'iššâ* are paralleled in verse 25. There is no hint in the narrative that *'ādām* was split into *'îš and 'iššâ* but rather that *'iššâ* was derived from *'ādām*.

Although the man was created first, relationships between the sexes are horizontal, not vertical. Yet *equality* is not *identity*. As Childs notes, to posit equality of essence and substance is not to posit a sameness of function. Sameness would be redundancy, not complementarity. The anatomical differences between the sexes and the ever growing body of literature pointing to substantial psychological distinctions between them demonstrate that their roles in society were designed to be different. A man, for example, is physically incapable of childbearing. Such distinctions are not a product of the fall to be redeemed, therefore, but a part of the created order to be nurtured.

Male/female relationships before the fall are described in Genesis 2:25: although they were naked, they felt no shame. But when sin entered with the fall, resulting in banishment from Eden (Gen. 3:24), shame came with it also; a barrier was erected to the sort of naive innocence that had characterized the relationship previously. Clothing was necessary to cover the nakedness of the man and woman (Gen. 3:7) even though they were man and wife. It was only *after the fall* that God said to the woman, "Your desire will be for your husband, and he will rule over you" (Gen. 3:16). Likewise, it was after the fall that Adam named his wife Eve, using the same naming formula (Gen. 3:20) as he used in naming the animals (2:20), and by its use implying the same authority of a superior over an inferior.

To summarize: the creation texts make it clear that any pattern of absolute male dominance and female inferiority found in the Bible must result from the fall, not from a theology of the created order. The process of redemption taught by the Bible is clear: it seeks to restore humanity, and with it creation (Rom. 8:19–22), from the effects of the fall. If, therefore, man's dominion over woman is a consequence of the fall (Gen. 3:16), one of the ramifications of the gospel would be to abolish institutions such as concubinage that reduce her to a chattel. It would seek to elevate her from any secondary position she may occupy to one of full equality with the man as God's viceregent, with full and unimpeded access to available food supplies (economic resources). Unless, however, one insists that equality means identity, whatever woman's redeemed position may be will not be the same as that held by the man. Instead, the two roles function in a complementary manner, each contributing its unique gifts to the perfecting of a redeemed society.

Intersexual Relationships. If the reason for the creation of woman was to enable the man to become whole and a legitimate microcosm of the human species, then it follows that man/woman relations in a redeemed society would be theologically humanizing. Any exploitive efforts by a member of the redeemed community to reduce another to an object that can be manipulated is therefore wrong. Interpersonal relationships, including intersexual ones, should leave the other party feeling as though he or she has been appreciated even when disagreement is involved.

In Jesus' ministry, no member of either sex was treated as an object, but as a person. Throughout the Gospels it is clear that, whether the woman was a persistent Canaanite (Matt. 15:22–28), a repentant sinner (Luke 7:36–50), or a cripple to be healed on the Sabbath (Luke 13:10–17), Jesus considered them first of all as human beings. His first address was always to their personhood, never to their sex; he shared none of the condescending attitudes assumed by many of his contemporaries. Although some Jewish authorities of the time made specific prohibitions about teaching women, many were numbered among Jesus' disciples.

Models for such relationships are found throughout the life of Jesus although limited space permits only a few to be mentioned here. Perhaps the most striking is his interchange with the Samaritan woman (John 4:5–29), who not only belonged to an ethnic group despised by the Jews but also had an unsavory past. Most people would have reacted to her by pulling away and trying to avoid her, but Jesus did not. Sensing here a life that could be redeemed, he engaged her in dialogue. During the course of their conversation, he led her to see that he was the one who could redeem her from the sins of her past. She left the encounter, not crushed and dehumanized from a harsh polemic or judgmental accusation, but rejoicing because she saw hope for her salvation.

Jesus chides Martha for caring more about her housekeeping than about hearing his teaching (Luke 10:38–42). Yet the words convey not a thundering rebuke, but a gentle remonstrance designed to teach and not to humiliate, motivated not by egotistical considerations but by his love for Martha and his desire to help her. Always, even in rebuke, the concern for the other party as a person permeated his ministry.

Marriage. Christian marriage can be considered a loving, bonded, sexually exclusive relationships that is publicly declared to exist between a man and a woman in a manner recognized by society as licit and proper. Its foundations are laid in Genesis 2:23–24, where the man, seeing the woman, declares her to be "bone of my bones and flesh of my flesh"; she was to be called "woman" *('iššâ)* because "she was taken out of man *('îš)*." Now that he has finally located a fitting counterpart, a man can "leave his father and mother and be united to his wife, and they will become one flesh." The Genesis narrative, considering the union of the man with one of the lower animals unthinkable, sees such a union possible only when woman, created like man in God's own image, becomes the complement that made not only the human species, but also the male person, whole. Just as there is stability in a dipolar human race embracing two sexes, so there is stability in a marital union. Indeed, one may argue that such stability derives from the nuclear family so formed because it is a microcosm of the human species as a whole. If an inquiry be made as to what are the characteristics of that union, the following emerge from the Edenic narrative:

1. It is an *exclusive* union. Sexual activity outside the marital bond violates the Edenic pattern, whether such activity be premarital promiscuity or postmarital adultery.

2. The union is between man and woman; it is *heterosexual,* not *homosexual.*

3. The union is between a single man and a single woman. Because more females are born than males and because the equal access to food supplies that had existed in Eden was corrupted into an economic system dominated by males, most ancient societies allowed polygyny as a means of assuring females economic viability. But the biblical pattern for marriage is described as being "one flesh," a term patterned after expressions used to describe genetic relationships of the closest order (Gen. 29:14; 37:27; 2 Sam. 5:1; 16:11; 19:12–13; 1 Kings 8:19; 2 Kings 20:18; 1 Chron. 11:1; 2 Chron. 6:9; Isa. 39:7; 49:26; 58:7). Since the degree of intimacy and solidarity diminishes as the size of any group increases, it becomes clear that monogamy is premised not only on the example of Adam and Eve as the first married couple, but also on the metaphor "one flesh" and the nature of the relationships implied by it.

4. The relationship is a loving one. The reality on which the metaphor "one flesh" depends requires one to consider the other as though that person were an extension of one's own body. Paul says in Ephesians 5:28, "he who loves his wife loves himself."

5. The union is stable and virtually indissoluble. In the Gospels, Jesus makes an appeal to the Edenic narrative and order of creation theology in order to demonstrate the inappropriateness of casually dissolving a marriage (Matt. 19:4–5; Mark 10:6–8).

Sexual Intimacy. Discussions about sexual intercourse, aside from proscriptions about engaging in it either before or outside marriage, have been considered a taboo in Christian circles. The result has been that many have been left with the impression that the Bible's treatment of the subject is a wholly negative one and that such matters are not to be discussed. Such an attitude cannot be biblically justified. The Bible is very candid—sometimes even shockingly so—on matters of sex.

Apart from the term "one flesh," Genesis 2:24 uses another term denoting marital intimacy: the verb *dābaq,* meaning "adhere to." For example, Shechem's heart was drawn (*dābaq*) to Dinah and he loved her (34:3). Another use of the term is illustrated in Genesis 19:19, where Lot pleads that he be allowed to seek refuge in a city lest the disaster of Sodom cling to (NIV "overtake") him in the mountains. In Deuteronomy 13:17 Israel is not to permit to "stick to their hand" anything that was supposed to be devoted to destruction. In Numbers 36:7, 9, land transactions between tribes are proscribed; every Israelite is to "stick to" (NIV "keep") the land his family inherits. In Deuteronomy and Joshua the word appears as a common term for the intimate love Israel is to have for Yahweh: they are not just to fear and obey but to love and to "stick" (NIV "hold fast") to him (Deut. 4:4; 10:20; 11:22; 13:4; 30:20; Josh. 22:5; 23:8). The books of Samuel and Kings use the word in a similar fashion to denote the Israelites loyal to David (2 Sam. 20:2) and Solomon's devotion to his foreign wives (1 Kings 11:2). In describing a marriage, the word does not expressly portray sexual relations, but speaks to the deep and intimate bonds that give sanction to any functional marriage and that are to undergird sexual activity conducted within it.

The canonization of the Song of Solomon caused some ancient rabbis no end of concern because of its frankly erotic dialogue between a man and a woman, presumably the man's wife. But it is only by the most strained and tortuous exegesis that one can avoid the book's metaphors of sexual intimacy. For example, she calls him "a sachet of myrrh resting between my breasts" (1:13), his left arm cradling her head while his right arm embraces her (2:6). A number of references express fondling that is overtly erotic (7:7–8; cf. 2:16; 4:5). She calls him handsome and proclaims her marriage bed to be fertile (verdant; 1:16). When she looks for him there and cannot find him (3:1), she goes about the city until she locates him; she embraces him and leads him to her mother's bedroom where she had been conceived (3:4). He, on the other hand, proclaims her beautiful (4:1), with breasts that are like twin fawns (4:5; 7:3). She declares herself a wall, with breasts that are like towers (8:10); he likens them to clusters of palm fruit that he intends to gather in his hands (7:7–8). One cannot help being struck by the Edenic tone to this interchange where the partners are candid in their sexuality, yet not ashamed.

Three Hebrew verbs, with their derivative nouns, are commonly used to express sexual intercourse: (1) *šākab,* "to lie with," where emphasis is placed on the position assumed in sexual activity; (2) *bô',* "to go to, into, enter," where emphasis is placed on the act of physically drawing near and, perhaps, penetration of the female by the male; and (3) *yāda',* "to know." The latter term denotes a knowledge that is experiential and not primarily cognitive. Unlike *šākab* and the nouns derived from it that are used to denote sexual relations that are illicit (Lev. 20:11–13, 18, 20; Deut. 27:20–23), the word *yāda'* is never used of human beings having sexual relations with relatives or animals. Like any word, its distinctive meaning at times overlaps its synonyms and so *yāda'* appears one time as a designation for heterosexual rape, although perhaps it may have been used sarcastically (Judg. 19:25). Generally, however, it depicts the act of sexual intercourse as more than physical copulation driven by lust. Instead, the emphasis of this term seems to be on the exchange of intimate, unspoken, nonrational information that takes place in properly contextualized sexual activity. Sexual intercourse thus becomes a vital element in the communication process so essential for any sound marriage. The intimacy, care, and love transmitted in that act, properly contextualized within a marriage, are not only permissible but highly desirable.

In the New Testament Paul, recognizing the value of a healthy sex life for a solid marriage, warns married couples that they should not use the other's sexual desire as a weapon. Instead, the wife should remember that her "body does not belong to her alone but also to her husband. In the same way, the husband's body does not belong to him alone but also to his wife" (1 Cor. 7:3).

Sexual Aberrations. *Homosexuality.* The best evidence for the existence of homosexual shrine prostitutes among the Canaanites comes, not from Canaanite literature, but from the biblical text, which is avowedly polemic in its attitude. It would appear, however, that the male prostitute was found in Judah along with his female counterpart until the purge by Asa. Together, they obviously represented a pagan, and therefore local, influence on the religion of Judah (Deut. 23:17; 1 Kings 14:24; 15:12; 22:46; 2 Kings 23:7). The term "dog" appears to have been used in Scripture to refer to homosexual cult prostitutes (Deut. 23:18). Leviticus uses a strong word "detestable" to describe homosexual practice (18:22; 20:13). Parallel condemnations are found in Romans 1:27 and 1 Corinthians 6:9.

The biblical refutation of homosexuality, however, does not reside in the occasional text that condemns the practice or in stories in which homosexual practice is observed in a negative light, but in the created order itself. Adam's complement is not found in another man (which would be redundancy, not complementarity), but in a woman, his corresponding opposite. Likewise, though not stated, it may be inferred that the same holds true for Eve.

Bestiality. Bestiality, practiced to some extent in every ancient rural society and known from Egyptian, Canaanite, and Hittite sources, is condemned in Scripture (Exod. 22:19; Lev. 20:15–16; Deut. 27:21) for much the same reason as is homosexuality: in the Edenic narrative the possibility of a sexually bonded liaison with an animal is expressly ruled out (Gen. 2:20). Bestiality rejects the human sexual partner God has ordained in favor of an animal that the Edenic narrative has expressly rejected. The pattern ordained by God in Eden is man and woman, not human and animal.

Seduction and Rape. If the initial sexual act is that which consummates the marriage whereby two now become "one flesh," it is reasonable to conclude that this represents a "channelizing" or confinement of all sexual activity to expressions that reinforce the solidarity of the marital union. The generally dim view taken of promiscuity by the Old Testament may then be explained as seeing premarital sexual intercourse to be a potential weakening of the marital union by rendering it less exclusive: that is, the more frequent the person's premarital sexual liaisons, the less exclusive is the initial act of sexual intercourse with one's spouse.

Cases of rape or seduction are uncommon in Scripture. The case of Dinah and Shechem (Gen. 34:1–31) is the first mentioned. Shechem first seduced Dinah and then found he loved her. At that point he attempted to pay Jacob the bride-price to marry the girl. But Simeon and Levi, outraged at the treatment accorded their sister, tricked the males of the town into being circumcised and, while they were still in pain from the operation, slaughtered them. The rape of the Levite's concubine in Gibeah (Judg. 19:1–30) resulted in a civil war wherein the tribe of Benjamin, except for six hundred, was exterminated. Amnon's rape of his half-sister Tamar (2 Sam. 13:11–14) resulted in a blood feud between Amnon and Absalom, Tamar's brother. The consequences were Amnon's murder by order of Absalom (13:28–29).

Laws treating rape or seduction seem to be concerned for the economic well-being of the disadvantaged woman. The classic reference to the seduction of a virgin is Exodus 22:16–17. The seducer must marry the girl and pay the bride-price for virgins. If her father refused to give her to him, then he still had to pay. A woman who was not a virgin was considered "damaged goods" and was therefore less eligible for marriage, presumably commanding a lower bride-price (Exod. 22:17). If she concealed her lack of virginity in order to get a husband or a higher bride-price, she could be tried and, if found guilty, executed (Deut. 22:13-21). Because the girl's marriageability had been severely compromised, the money was probably designed to provide for the girl's livelihood in her father's house.

There is no agreement among commentators as to whether Deuteronomy 22:28–29 treats seduction (and is therefore an expansion of the case in Exod. 22:16–17) or rape. If the New International Version is correct in interpreting the passage as addressing rape, the monetary increase (fixed at fifty shekels) may be seen as a penalty exacted against the offender because he shamed her (v. 29). Whereas the former case (Exod. 22:16–17) would have been subject to conventional divorce procedure (Deut. 24:1–4), an additional provision is made for the woman's economic security in the latter case: the man can never divorce her, whatever she does (Deut. 22:28–29). The concern for the woman is also reflected in the distinctions between the two rape cases described in Deuteronomy 22:23–27: the betrothed woman raped in the city would have been heard if she had cried for help, but the woman raped in the country is presumed to have cried out, whether she did or not. In the latter case, only the man is put to death.

Prostitution. The word "prostitute" in the New International Version most often translates the Hebrew word *zônâ* or the Greek term *pornē*. The Hebrew term, however is much broader than its English counterpart and simply designates a woman who commits fornication. Likewise, the use of the Greek *porneia* in the so-called exceptive clauses in Jesus' divorce pronouncements has been interpreted as a broad term that includes all sorts of illicit sexual conduct (Matt. 5:31–32; 19:8–9). Although sacred prostitution in ancient Israel carried with it penalties that were often severe (Deut. 23:17–18; cf. Gen. 38:21–24), secular prostitution was not expressly forbidden by commandment, law, or penalty except in the case of the high priest's daughter (Lev. 21:9). Yet the general way prostitution is looked down on throughout the Old Testament shows that it was not a socially acceptable practice (cf. the metaphors in Hosea, Jeremiah, and Ezekiel). In the much stricter ethos of the New Testament, those who commit fornication are to suffer punishment for it (Jude 7).

Adultery. Although adultery in the New Testament involved a married partner of either sex, in the Old Testament it was predicated on the woman's marital status: if she was married or "betrothed" the act was adultery, regardless of the man involved. In both Mesopotamian and Hittite laws the husband had the right to prosecute or to drop charges against his wife. The husband has no such explicit option in Hebraic law, nor has the state any expressed right to pardon the subject. The absence of such explicit legal testimony leads one to conclude that, since prosecution in Mesopotamia was a matter of private preference, the offense was considered primarily as a violation of property rights. But in Israel, where the matter fell into the hands of the state to prosecute, the matter was construed primarily as a crime against society, and only secondly against the husband. These two factors—the role of the state in prosecution and the death penalty awarded the guilty parties—point to criminal rather than civil law. The matter is all the clearer when Assyrian and Hittite law affords the husband the right to dispatch both guilty parties on the spot if caught in the act, whereas the executioner in Israel was always the community or state, or its representatives. Accordingly, adultery must be seen as a crime that threatened society, not simply as a tort against the husband.

Ethics for Israel constituted an extension of that ethic designed for the preservation of familial integrity. The family is the microcosm, Israel its analogous macrocosm. Given such an organismic interrelatedness of family and people, and taking into consideration the value placed on wholeness for the larger body, the guarding of the family against forces that threaten its existence no longer seems difficult to explain. To fail to curb adultery in a solidary society would lead to fragmentation, alienation, and ultimately dissolution of the community. With the integrity of the home considered a foundational societal value, the emphasis on the woman's status becomes clear: she is the family member most intimately connected to preserving the harmony and integrity of the nuclear family.

Incest. Incest, like adultery, was punishable by death (Lev. 20:11–12, 14, 17, 19–21). One's father's wife, mother-in-law, and sister (including one's half-sister) are declared forbidden degrees of sexual relationship in Deuteronomy (22:30; 27:20, 22–23), to which Leviticus adds one's mother, granddaughter, aunt (including the wife of one's uncle), daughter-in-law, sister-in-law, his wife's child or grandchild, and the sister of one's wife (18:6–18). That the issue is not the genetic stability of the offspring can be demonstrated by the inclusion of a number of "inlaws" who have no genetic relationship to the perpetrator.

Again, lying behind the laws against incest is the intention to safeguard the solidarity of the family from internal sexually generated tensions. Sexual activity within the home, beside that carried on within the bonds of marriage, introduced the element of rivalry with its concomitant alienation. Those elements are hostile to the solidarity of the home that is valued so highly in the Bible and that is so vital to a healthy society. Evidence for this interpretation may be found in the laws against one's marrying two sisters (Lev. 18:18) or a mother and her daughter (18:17). Incest, therefore, becomes criminal for the same reason as adultery: it fragments the home, and, with it, the community.

Gender Roles. Unfortunately, the acceptability of biblical models in determining a theology of sexuality often turns, not on the validity of the models or the supporting biblical evidence, but on the way in which that theology is actually fleshed out in society. On one pole there are the male supremacists who will insist that, just as woman's creation was somewhat of a divine afterthought, so she is inherently inferior and her gender role must reflect that subservience to the male in all its aspects. At the other extreme are some who would insist that there is no equality without identity and that the woman's role in any redeemed society must be the same as the man's in all respects.

The Edenic model speaks of woman as man's complement, his corresponding opposite, his equal in essence and substance. It was observed earlier in this article that sameness of function would be redundancy, not complementarity, an interpretation supported by the anatomical and psychological differences between the sexes. Accordingly, while the sexes were to be considered as equals, the roles assigned them in the redeemed community would certainly be different. It is because of this that Paul can say, "For as a woman came from man, so also man is born of woman. But everything comes from God" (1 Cor. 11:12). Husbands and wives must live in mutual love and respect (Eph. 5:28–33).

Unfortunately Paul's doctrine of male headship for the family and its concomitant doctrine of wifely submission (1 Cor. 11:3; Eph. 5:22–24; Col. 3:18) has been used as a weapon by some men to command respect from their wives. But if the Ephesians passage is read in the context of the verse that precedes it (5:21: "Submit to one another out of reverence for Christ"), the manner in which any wifely submission is to take place becomes clear. A wife is not to vaunt herself over her husband but is to remember a cardinal rule of Christian conduct and apply it to her marriage: put the other person first! The following context (5:25–27) interprets the way the husband is to respond: he is not to bully or browbeat, nor demand her adulation, but to love her in the way Christ loved the church and to be prepared to surrender his selfish ambitions for her betterment.

Male supremacists have often attempted to interpret Paul's use of the word "head" (Gk. *kephalē*) as representing the Hebrew *rōʾš* and therefore take "head" to mean authority. But a tribal head in Israel was no king; he was the leader of an extended family of which he was a member (Num. 1:4; 17:3; Josh. 22:14). The Hebrew word *rōʾš* carries within it the idea of being first, not of being most powerful. Headship in the Old Testament placed an emphasis on leadership, not authority. True leadership invites others to follow rather than forcing them into submission. It knows when to lay down power as well as when to take it up. It cannot operate unless the other party is willing to be led. It is probably this sort of "subjection" that is spoken of in Titus 2:5.

Radical feminists, on the other hand, have sometimes sought refuge from traditional interpretations of gender roles by urging that Paul's use of *kephalē* means not "authority" but "source" (as in 1 Cor. 11:3). Paul, then, would be saying that, because woman was taken out of man, he is her "source," just as Christ is the "source" of the church and God is the "source" of Christ. But biblical evidence fits this explanation of Paul no better than it does the other extreme. Paul's reference point is Christ as the head of the church; this does not portray the "head" as founder but as representative and leader (Col. 1:18).

It is clear that the truth must lie somewhere between the two extremes cited above. The biblical pattern seems to assume that in any partnership of only two persons, there are bound to be disagreements; some plan of action must be in place to break the tie. In those cases, the options available for the partnership are limited: it can have *one* head, *two* heads, or *no* head. When disagreements occur, a partnership with two heads pulls in two different directions; a partnership with no head would not move in any direction. Paul says that there is to be a head to the partnership and assigns the man to be "head of the woman" as God is the head of Christ. His grounds for this are that man was created first and thereby assumes the responsibilities of the firstborn. The man, accordingly, is charged with resolving such deadlocks as may occur in a marriage, not by brute force of strength or will, but by loving, caring means, emulating Christ's example in his leadership of the church. It has been argued that marriage, by incorporating the two sexes that make up the human species, provides a microcosm of the species, the two elements that together reflect the image of God and make humankind theologically human. Marriage, therefore, should be a humanizing experience, both sociologically and theologically. If the situation becomes dehumanizing, one partner or the other has overstepped his or her boundaries.

By following the prescriptive norms of the Edenic pattern, the redeemed community strives to alleviate the fallen state of society wherein woman assumes a lesser standing. Equality *does not* mean that there are now *two* heads in the marriage, though some have tried to make it this. It *does* mean that now the headship is based on the "one flesh" principle. If the man is the "head," then the woman is the "body" that gives reality to the head; her "submission" cannot be forced but must be given of her own free will to this role arrangement. To put it in other words, the nuclear family is *led,* not forcibly *driven,* by its head. A "head" without a "body" would be monstrous.

Peter's idea of submission is illustrated by Sarah, "who obeyed Abraham and called him her master" (1 Peter 3:6). Sarah was hardly a groveling wife, merely a respectful one. In the next verse Peter adds that husbands, who are usually physically stronger than their wives, are not to bully them but are to "treat them with respect" as fellow Christians.

A sore problem comes with 1 Timothy 2:11–14, where Paul declares to Timothy, bishop of Ephesus, that a woman is not "to teach or to have authority over a man; she must be silent." No consensus on this passage exists among scholars and any attempt to resolve it is fraught with danger. It may be said, however, that it seems quite unlikely that the apostle is issuing a blanket proscription for women under any circumstances, since in Titus 2:3–5 the apostle expressly charges the older women to teach the younger women what is good. Moreover, 1 Timothy 5:1–2 requires that older women be treated as mothers; sons as well as daughters learn from their mothers. It seems no accident that Paul's Epistle to the Ephesians is where the submission of the wife to the husband and the husband's love for the wife is most forcefully articulated. This may point to a situation in Ephesus where women were teaching things that challenged the headship of their husbands and the husbands were responding in a less than loving manner. This, the apostle says, should not happen. The apostolic argument does not turn on whether women make judgments that are better or poorer, more rational or more intuitive than men, but on the rights and responsibilities of the firstborn son of a family ("for Adam was formed first"), the matter of headship. Just as the firstborn son assumes the leadership of the family in his father's absence, so Paul commits leadership to the husband as the one who was "formed first."

Summary and Conclusions. While their roles in the imperfect society of a fallen world may differ, men and women are essentially and qualitatively equal. They are corporately fashioned in the image of God and together make up theological humanity. Relationships between the sexes are designed to humanize, not to dehumanize, and this especially applies to marriage. Roles, though they may differ, must always keep the humanness of both parties in view. Role distinctions are in no way to reflect vertical, or superior-inferior, patterns, but horizontal ones that cultivate parity.

WILLIAM C. WILLIAMS

See also HOMOSEXUALITY; IMMORALITY, SEXUAL; LUST; MARRIAGE; PROSTITUTION.

Bibliography. G. Ch. Aalders, *Genesis;* G. C. Berkouwer, *Man: The Image of God;* G. Belezikian, *Beyond Sex Roles: What the Bible Says about a Woman's Place in Church and Family;* A. Bloom, *Int* 8 (1954): 422–32; G. J. Botterweck, *TDOT,* 5:448–81; John R. Chamberlayne, *Numen* 10 (1963): 153–64; B. S. Childs, *Old Testament Theology in a Canonical Context;* W. G. Cole, *Sex and Love in the Bible;* L. M. Epstein, *Sex Laws and Customs in Judaism;* W. Eichrodt, *Theology of the Old Testament;* A. Gelin, *The Concept of Man in the Bible;* J. B. Hurley, *Man and Woman in Biblical Perspective: A Study in Role Relationships and Authority;* D. Jacobson, *Word and World* 10/2 (1990): 156–60; D. Kidner, *Genesis: An Introduction and Commentary;* G. Larue, *Sex and the Bible;* A. Mickelsen, ed., *Women, Authority and the Bible;* E. Neufeld, *Ancient Hebrew Marriage Laws;* J. B. Payne, *The Theology of the Older Testament;* P. Trible, *JAAR* 41 (1973): 30–48; G. Wallis, *TDOT,* 3:81; C. J. H. Wright, *An Eye for an Eye: The Place of Old Testament Ethics Today;* R. Yaron, *JJS* 17 (1966): 1–11.

Shame. Shame is a consequence of sin. Feelings of guilt and shame are subjective acknowledgments of an objective spiritual reality. Guilt is judicial in character; shame is relational. Though related to guilt, shame emphasizes sin's effect on self-identity. Sinful human beings are traumatized before a holy God, exposed for failure to live up to God's glorious moral purpose. The first response of Adam and Eve to their sinful condition was to hide from God, and consequently from one another (Gen. 3:7–8; cf. 2:25). Christ's unhindered openness to the Father was both a model for life and the means of removing humanity's shame. Christian self-identity is transformed "in him."

The word-group for shame ("disconcerted," "disappointed," "confounded") occurs in the Old Testament most frequently in the Wisdom Literature and in the prophets (especially Isaiah and Jeremiah). David captures the pervasive Old Testament perspective when he says, "Let me not be put to shame, O LORD, for I have cried out to you; let the wicked be put to shame, and lie silent in the grave" (Ps. 31:17). The godly Israelite believed God would remove his or her shame (Ps. 119:31) while expecting God to defeat his or her enemies in the present as he will do it utterly at the judgment (Pss. 35:26; 44:7; 132:18). Some presumed on their elect status, ignoring faith and obedience.

God shamed them and the nation by causing its defeat and dispersion (Isa. 22:18; Jer. 2:26; 7:19; Ezek. 7:18; Dan. 9:7–8). The believing Israelite remnant trusted God through suffering (Isa. 49:23; 54:4). At the final judgment the wicked will be shamed because of their utter defeat (Isa. 47:3) and because of the manifest impotence of their idols (Isa. 42:17; 44:9, 11; Jer. 22:22; Hos. 10:6). Israel, however, will not bear its shame forever (Isa. 45:17; 61:7). Proverbs emphasizes the shame of public humiliation for undisciplined behavior (13:18; 18:13; 25:8), with particular attention to family relationships (12:4; 17:2; 19:26; 29:15).

The New Testament deepens and expands the concept of shame. A disciple of Christ stands with him unashamedly in a world that finds the cross (Heb. 12:2), God's ways (1 Cor. 1:27), and God's persecuted messengers (2 Tim. 1:8, 12) shameful. Those ashamed of him now will find Christ ashamed of them on the day of judgment (Mark 8:38; Luke 9:26). Conversely, God is not ashamed to call the faithful "brothers" of Christ (Heb. 2:11).

Suffering for Christ is identification with Christ, glory not shame (Acts 5:41; 1 Peter 4:16). Paul was not ashamed of the gospel because it is the only antidote for humanity's shame (Rom. 1:16). Ultimately, the Christian who trusts in Christ need not be ashamed of anything (Phil. 1:20; cf. Isa. 28:16; Rom. 9:33; 10:11; 1 Peter 2:6). When one confesses Christ and openly rebels against him, however, the work of Christ is publicly shamed (Heb. 6:6). Christians must be diligent to renounce shameful behavior, though tempting because of its hidden character (2 Cor. 4:2).

Shame is a godly motivator. A virtuous life shames the ungodly, providing a context for evangelism (Titus 2:8; 1 Peter 3:16). A believer's shame for past sin is a spur to forsake sinning (Rom. 6:21), to renounce disobedience (2 Thess. 3:14), and to minister the gospel (2 Cor. 4:2). The prospect of shame at Christ's return is sometimes a necessary inducement to godliness (Rev. 3:18; 16:15). Paul uses the concept of shame most frequently with the immature Corinthian believers, urging them not to shame themselves (1 Cor. 4:14; 6:5; 15:34; 2 Cor. 9:4) or him (2 Cor. 7:14; 10:8).

Shameless people flaunt their unholiness, calloused to God (Zeph. 3:5) and glorying in their shame (Phil. 3:19). Yet no one is shameless ultimately. "Shameless acts" receive the judgment inherent in the act (Rom. 1:27). Also, at the final judgment the nakedness of those not clothed with Christ' righteousness will be exposed (Rev. 3:18; 16:15).

BRADFORD A. MULLEN

See also GUILT; SIN.

Sheol. ***Old Testament.*** The Hebrew word *šĕʾôl*, "Sheol," refers to the grace or the abode of the dead (Ps. 88:3, 5). Through much of the Old Testament period, it was believed that all went one place, whether human or animal (Ps. 49:12, 14, 20), whether righteous or wicked (Eccles. 9:2–3). No one could avoid Sheol (Pss. 49:9; 89:48), which was thought to be down in the lowest parts of the earth (Deut. 32:22; 1 Sam. 28:11–15; Job 26:5; Ps. 86:13; Isa. 7:11; Ezek. 31:14–16, 18).

Unlike this world, Sheol is devoid of love, hate, envy, work, thought, knowledge, and wisdom (Eccles. 9:6, 10). Descriptions are bleak: There is no light (Job 10:21–22; 17:13; Pss. 88:6, 12; 143:3), no remembrance (Pss. 6:5; 88:12; Eccles. 9:5), no praise of God (Pss. 6:5; 30:9; 88:10–12; 115:17; Isa. 38:18)—in fact, no sound at all (Pss. 94:17; 115:17). Its inhabitants are weak, trembling shades (Job 26:5; Ps. 88:10–12; Isa. 14:9–10) who can never hope to escape from its gates (Job 10:21; 17:13–16; Isa. 38:10). Sheol is like a ravenous beast that swallows the living without being sated (Prov. 1:12; 27:20; Isa. 5:14). Some thought the dead were cut off from God (Ps. 88:3–5; Isa. 38:11); while others believed that God's presence reached even to Sheol (Ps. 139:8).

Toward the end of the Old Testament, God revealed that there will be a resurrection of the dead (Isa. 26:19). Sheol will devour no longer; instead God will swallow up Death (Isa. 25:8). The faithful will be rewarded with everlasting life while the rest will experience eternal contempt (Dan. 12:2). This theology developed further in the intertestamental period.

The New Testament. By the time of Jesus, it was common for Jews to believe that the righteous dead go to a place of comfort while the wicked go to Hades ("Hades" normally translates "Sheol" in the LXX), a place of torment (Luke 16:22–23). Similarly, in Christianity, believers who die go immediately to be with the Lord (2 Cor. 5:8; Phil. 1:23). Hades is a hostile place whose gates cannot prevail against the church (Matt. 16:18). In fact, Jesus himself holds the keys of Death and Hades (Rev. 1:18). Death and Hades will ultimately relinquish their dead and be cast into the lake of fire (Rev. 20:13–14).

The fact that theology develops within the Old Testament and between the Old Testament and the New Testament does not mean that the Bible is contradictory or contains errors. It only indicates progressive revelation, that God revealed more of himself and his plan of salvation as time went on. That some Old Testament saints believed in Sheol, while the New Testament teaches clearly about heaven and hell, is nor more of a problem than that the Old Testament contains a system of atonement by animal sacrifice now made obsolete in Christ (Heb. 10:4–10) or that the Old Testament teaches God is one (Deut. 6:4) while the New Testament reveals a Trinity.

WILLIAM B. NELSON, JR.

See also DEATH; HADES; HELL; INTERMEDIATE STATE; PIT.

Sign. *See* MIRACLE.

Sickness. *See* DISEASE; HEAL, HEALTH; SUFFERING.

Sin. Sin is a riddle, a mystery, a reality that eludes definition and comprehension. Perhaps we most often think of sin as wrongdoing or transgression of God's law. Sin includes a failure to do what is right. But sin also offends people; it is violence and lovelessness toward other people, and ultimately, rebellion against God. Further, the Bible teaches that sin involves a condition in which the heart is corrupted and inclined toward evil. The concept of sin is complex, and the terminology large and varied so that it may be best to look at the reality of sin in the Pentateuch first, then reflect theologically.

The History of Sin. In the biblical world sin is, from its first appearance, tragic and mysterious. It is tragic because it represents a fall from the high original status of humankind. Created in God's image, Adam and Eve are good but immature, fine but breakable, like glass dishes. They are without flaw, yet capable of marring themselves. Satan uses a serpent to tempt Eve and Adam, first to question God, then to rebel against him. First, Satan introduces doubts about God's authority and goodness. "Did God really say, 'You must not eat from any tree in the garden'?" (Gen. 3:1). He invites Eve to consider how the fruit of the tree of knowledge is good for food and for knowledge. We see the tendency of sin to begin with a subtle appeal to something attractive and good in itself, to an act that is somehow plausible and directed toward some good end.

Throughout the Bible almost every sin reaches for things with some intrinsic value, such as security, knowledge, peace, pleasure, or a good name. But behind the appeal to something good, sin ultimately involves a raw confrontation between obedience and rebellion. Will Adam and Eve heed their impressions or God's instructions? Will they listen to a creature or the Creator? Will they serve God or themselves? Who will judge what is right, God or humans? Who will see to the results? Ultimately, by taking the position of arbiter between the conflicting counsel of God and the serpent, Eve and Adam have already elevated themselves over God and rebelled against him.

Here too the first sins disclose the essence of later sins. Sin involves the refusal of humankind to accept its God-given position between the Creator and lower creation. It flows from decisions to reject God's way, and to steal, curse, and lie simply because that seems more attractive or reasonable. Here we approach the mystery of sin. Why would the first couple, sinless and without inclination toward sin, choose to rebel? Why would any creature presume to know more or know better than its creator?

Adam and Eve become sinners by a historical act. The principal effects of sin are alienation from God, from others, from oneself, and from creation. They emerge almost at once. Alienation from God lead Adam and Eve to fear and flee from him. Alienation from each other and themselves shows in their shame (awareness of nakedness) and blame shifting. Adam acts out all three alienations at once when, in response to God's questions, he excuses himself by blaming both Eve and God for his sin: "The woman you put here with me—she gave me some fruit" (3:12). The sentence God pronounces upon sin includes grace (3:15) and suggests that he retains sovereign control over his creation even in its rebellion, but it also establishes our alienation from nature in the curse upon childbearing, work, and creation itself (3:14–19). After the curse, God graciously clothes the first couple, but he also expels them from the garden (3:21–24). He graciously permits them to reproduce, but death enters human experience a short time later (4:1, 8; 5:5–31). These events prove the vanity and futility of sin. Adam and Eve seek new freedoms and dignity, but sin robs them of what they have; seeking advantage, they experience great losses.

Genesis and Romans teach that Adam and Eve did not sin for themselves alone, but, from their privileged position as the first, originally sinless couple, act as representatives for the human race. Since then sin, sinfulness, and the consequences of sin have marred all. Every child of Adam enters a race marked by sin, condemnation, and death (Rom. 5:12–21). These traits become theirs both by heritage and, as they grow into accountability, by personal choice, as Cain's slaughter of Abel quickly shows.

In Cain's sin we have an early hint of the virulence and intractability of sin. Whereas Satan prompted Adam and Eve to sin, God himself cannot talk Cain out of it (Gen. 3:1–5; 4:6). While sin was external to Adam and Eve, it appears to spring up spontaneously from within Cain; it is a wild force in him, which he ought to master lest it devour him (4:7). Sin is also becoming more aggravated: it is premeditated, it begins in the setting of worship, and it directly harms a brother, who deserves love. After his sin, far from manifesting guilt or remorse, Cain confesses nothing, refuses to repent, and chides God for the harshness of his punishments (4:5–14). Cain's sin and impenitence foreshadow much of the future course of sin both within and without the Bible.

Genesis 4–11 traces the development of sin. It becomes proud and deliberate (4:23–24), yet the line of Cain, the line of sinners, remains human and fulfills the mandate to fill and subdue the earth. Indeed, perhaps Cain's line does better in the cultural arena, although those who make bronze and iron tools also fashion weapons. Eventually, sin so pervades the world that every inclination of the thoughts of the human heart is only evil all the time (Gen. 6:5; 8:21). Consequently, the Lord purges the earth of evil through the flood. When sin threatens to reassert itself in both direct disobedience and idolatry, God reveals his new intention to restrain sin by confusing human language at Babel: better that humanity be divided than that it stand together in rebellion against God.

Genesis 12–50 illustrates that sin plagues even the people of God, as members of the covenant family manipulate, betray, lie to, and deceive one another. The history Moses recounts also shows that punishment naturally follows, or is built into iniquity. Scheming Rebekah never sees her favorite son again; Jacob tastes the bitterness of deceit through Laban; Jacob's sons suffer for their sin against Joseph. As Proverbs 5:22 says, "The evil deeds of a wicked man ensnare him; the cords of his sin hold him fast."

Exodus reveals that sin not only brings suffering and punishment, but also violates the law of the Lord, Israel's holy redeemer and king. At Sinai Israel learned that sin is transgression of God's law; it is behavior that trespasses onto forbidden territory (Rom. 4:15). The law also labels sin and unmasks it. One can sin without knowing it, but the law makes such ignorance less common. The Mosaic law emphasizes the external character of sin, but the laws that command Israel to love God and forbid it to worship idols or covet show that sin is internal too. Paradoxically, the law sometimes prompts sin, Paul says (Rom. 7:7–13). Upon seeing that something is forbidden, desire to do it rises up. This perverse reaction reminds us that the root of sin is sinfulness and rebellion against God (Rom. 7:7–25).

The sacrifices and rituals for cleansing listed in the Pentateuch remind us of the gravity of sin. Transgressions are more than mistakes. The Bible never dismisses a sin simply because it was done by someone young or ignorant, or because it was done some time ago. Sin pollutes the sinner, and the law requires that the pollution be removed. One chief motive of the penal code is to remove evil from the land (Deut. 13:5, quoted in 1 Cor. 5:13). Sin also offends God, and the law requires atonement through sacrifices, in many of which a victim gives its life blood for an atonement.

The Biblical Terminology of Sin. The vast terminology, within its biblical contexts, suggests that sin has three aspects: disobedience to or breach of law, violation of relationships with people, and rebellion against God, which is the most basic concept. Risking oversimplification, among the most common Hebrew terms, *ḥaṭṭa᾿t* means a missing of a standard, mark, or goal; *pešaᶜ* means the breach of a relationship or rebellion; *ᶜāwōn* means perverseness; *šĕgāgāh* signifies error or mistake; *rešaᶜ* means godlessness, injustice, and wickedness; and *ᶜāmāl,* when it refers to sin, means mischief or oppression. The most common Greek term is *hamartia,* a word often personified in the New Testament, and signifying offenses against laws, people, or God. *Paraptōma* is another general term for offenses or lapses. *Adikia* is a more narrow and legal word, describing unrighteousness and unjust deeds. *Parabasis* signifies trespass or transgression of law; *asebeia* means godlessness or impiety; and *anomia* means lawlessness. The Bible typically describes sin negatively. It is law*less*ness, *dis*obedience, *im*piety, *un*belief, *dis*trust, darkness as opposed to light, a falling away as opposed to standing firm, weakness not strength. It is *un*righteousness, faith*less*ness.

The Biblical Theology of Sin. The historical and prophetic books of the Old Testament illustrate the character of sin under these terms. From Judges to Kings, we see that Israel forsook the Lord who had brought them out of Egypt and established a covenant with them. They followed and worshiped the gods of the nations around them (Judg. 2:10–13). Sometimes they served the Baals with singleness of purpose, filling Jerusalem with idols, and lawlessness reigned (Ahab, Ahaz, and Manasseh). The sin of human sacrifice followed in the reigns of such kings (2 Kings 21:6). The existence of human sacrifice underscores the depth and gravity of sin. People can become so perverted, so self-deceived, that they perform the most unnatural and heartless crimes, thinking them to be worship. Isaiah rightly says they "call evil good and good evil" (5:20). Later the Pharisees, utterly sincere, yet hypocritical because self-deceived, would revive this sin by killing not their children, but their maker, and calling it an act of service to God.

Many kings compounded their sin by rejecting and sometimes persecuting the prophets who pressed God's covenantal claims. Ahaz even spurned God's free offer of deliverance from invasion; he thought he had arranged his own deliverance through an alliance with Assyria and its gods. Not all kings were so crass; many tried to serve the Lord as they chose, in forbidden manners (Jeroboam I, Jehu, and other northern kings). Others attempted to serve God and the Baals at once (Solomon, the final kings of Judah, and many northern kings). The kings in question may have called it diplomacy; the prophets called it adultery.

Other prophets decried the social character of sin: "They sell the righteous for silver, and the needy for a pair of sandals. They trample on the heads of the poor as upon the dust of the ground and deny justice to the oppressed" (Amos 2:6–7). If sin is lack of love for God, it is also hate or indifference toward fellow humans.

The history of Israel illustrates how impenitence compounds sin. Saul magnified his sins by repenting superficially at best (1 Sam. 13:11–12; 15:13–21; 24:16–21). David, by contrast, repented of his sin with Bathsheba, without excuses or reservations (2 Sam. 12:13). Sadly, true repentance was the exception in Israel's history. God prompted Israel to repent by sending adversity—empty stomachs, drought, plague, warfare, and other curses for disobedience—but Israel would not turn back. Later, the Lord wooed Israel with food, clothing, oil, and new wine; he lavished silver and gold on her, but she gave "her lovers" the credit. Because she did not acknowledge that he was the giver, he swore he would remove his gifts (Hos. 2:2–13).

Jesus continued the prophets' work of deepening the concept of sin in two ways. First, he said God requires more than obedience to external norms. People sin by hating, despising, and lusting even if they never act on their desires. People sin if they do the right things for the wrong reasons. Obedience that proceeds from fear of getting caught, or lack of opportunity to act on wicked desires lacks righteousness (Matt. 5:17–48). Second, Jesus' harsh denunciations of sin show that sin cannot be overlooked. It must be confronted, unpleasant as that may be (Matt. 18:15–20; Luke 17:3–4). Otherwise, the sinner dies in his sins (John 8:24; cf. James 5:19–20).

Jesus also explained that sin arises from the heart. Bad trees bear bad fruit, blasphemous words spring from hearts filled with evil, and wicked men demand signs when they have already seen enough to warrant faith (Matt. 7:17–20; 12:33–39). Therefore, evildoing is not simply a matter of choice, rather, "Everyone who sins is a slave to sin" (John 8:34).

But the Christ came not just to explain but to forgive or remove sin. His name is Jesus because he will deliver his people from their sins (Matt. 1:21; Luke 1:77). Thus he was a friend of sinners (Matt. 9:9–13; Luke 15:1–2), bestowed forgiveness of sins, and freed those suffering from its consequences (Mark 2:1–12; Luke 7:36–50). Jesus earned the right to his name and the right to grant forgiveness by shedding his blood on the cross for the remission of sins. The crucifixion is at once the apex of sin and the cure of sin (Acts 2:23–24). That the Son of God had to bear the cross to accomplish redemption shows the gravity of sin. That he rose from the dead demonstrates that sin is defeated. After his resurrection, Jesus sent out his disciples to proclaim the victory and forgiveness of sins through his name (Luke 24:47; John 20:23).

Paul's theology of sin principally appears in Romans 1–8. God is angry because of sins humans commit against him and one another (1:18–32). Unbelief is the root of sin. The failure to glorify or thank God leads to idolatry, foolishness, and degradation (1:21–25). Sometimes he permits sins to develop unimpeded, until every kind of wickedness fills the human breast (1:26–32). Paul's imaginary reader objects to this indictment in several ways (2:1–3:8). Paul replies that while not everyone sins so crudely, everyone violates standards they consider just (2:1–3). If someone professes to belong to the covenant, have knowledge, and so enjoy special standing with God, Paul asks if they live up to the knowledge they have of God's law (2:17–29). Everyone is a sinner, he concludes, and stands silent, guilty, and accountable before God (3:10–21). Paul's sin lists cover the gamut of transgressions, from murder to gossip. Despite his use of the term "flesh" ("sinful nature" in some translations), relatively few sins on the lists are sensual; most concern the mind or the tongue (Rom. 1:28–32; Gal. 5:19–21). Like Jesus, Paul affirms that sin is an internal power, not just an act. It enslaves any whom Christ has not liberated and leads to their death (6:5–23), so that the unbeliever is incapable of pleasing God (8:5–8). Sin continues to grip even the redeemed (7:14–25). But principal deliverance from sin comes through justification by faith in Jesus, so there is no condemnation for those who are in Christ Jesus (3:21–4:25; 8:1–4). The Spirit renews believers and empowers them to work out that deliverance (8:9–27).

Much of the rest of the New Testament restates themes from the Gospels and Paul. James remarks that sin begins with evil desires (1:14; 4:1–4) and leads to death when fully grown (1:15). This and other biblical remarks suggest that iniquity gains some of its power through repetition. When an individual commits a sin, it can become, through repetition, a habit, a vice, and a character trait. When one person imitates the sins of another, wickedness can be institutionalized. Whole governments can become corrupt; whole industries can be based on deception or abuse of others. Societies can wrap themselves in a fabric of deceit. Thus one sinner encourages another and the wrong kind of friendship with the world makes one an enemy of God (James 4:4–6).

The Book of Revelation also reminds us that sin involves more than individual people and acts. In some places Satan reigns (2:13). The dragon, in his futile desire to devour the church, prompts the wicked to persecute it (12:1–17). Both government and religious leaders serve him in his wars against the saints (12:17–13:17). Revelation also depicts the end of sin. A day comes when God will condemn sin (20:11–15). Evildoers will be driven from his presence; the devil, his allies, death, and Hades will be thrown into the lake of fire (20:10–15). Then the new heavens and new earth, free of sin forever, will descend (chaps. 21–22).

What, then, is the essence of sin? Sin has three chief aspects: breach of law, violation of relationships with people and things protected by the law, and rebellion against God. The essence of sin, therefore, is not a substance but a relationship of opposition. Sin opposes God's law and his created beings. Sin hates rather than loves, it doubts or contradicts rather than trusts and affirms, it harms and abuses rather than helps and respects.

But sin is also a condition. The Bible teaches that there are lies and liars, sins and sinners. People can be "filled" (meaning "controlled") by hypocrisy and lawlessness (Matt. 23:28). God "gives some over to sin," allowing them to wallow in every kind of wickedness (Rom. 1:18–32). Paul, speaking of the time before their conversion, told the Ephesians, "You were dead in your transgressions and sins, in which you used to live" (2:1–2).

This said, we have hardly defined sin, and with good reason. Sin is elusive. Sin has no substance, no independent existence. It does not even exist in the sense that love or justice do. It exists only as a parasite of the good or good things. Sin creates nothing; it abuses, perverts, spoils, and destroys the good things God has made. It has no program, no thesis; it only has an antithesis, an opposition. Sometimes wickedness is as senseless as a child who pulls the hair or punches the stomach of another, then honestly confesses, "I don't know why I did that." In some ways sin is an absence rather than a presence: it fails to listen, walks past the needy, and subsists in alienation rather than relation.

Negative as sin is, it hides itself under the appearance of what is good. At the first temptation, sin operated under the guise of claiming good things such as food and knowledge. Even the goal of being like God is good in some ways; after all, God made the first couple in his image. Similarly, when Satan tempted Jesus, the second Adam, he offered things good in themselves: food, knowledge, and rule over the kingdoms of the earth. Sin and temptation continue to appeal to things good and desirable in themselves. Fornication promises bodily pleasure, boasting seeks honor, by breaking promises or vows people hope for release from hardship. Someone can make a persuasive defense for almost every offense.

Yet ultimately, sin is most unreasonable. Why would Adam and Eve, well-cared-for and without propensity toward sin, rebel against God? Why would a creature want to rebel against the Creator? The prophets find Israel's rebellion absurd; even animals know better. "The ox knows his master, the donkey his owner's manger, but Israel does not know, my people do not understand" (Isa. 1:3).

Although negative and irrational, sin is also a power. It crouches at Cain's door, ready to devour him (Gen. 4:7). It compels Paul to do the evil he does not wish (Rom. 7:14–20). It moves and is moved by demonic and societal forces. It enters the heart, so that wickedness wells up spontaneously from within (Matt. 15:17–19). Its stronghold is the all but instinctive tendency to put one's own interests and desires first. From the selfish heart comes rebellion, godlessness, cursing, lies, slander, envy, greed, sensuality, and pride (Matt. 12:34–37; Rom. 1:18–32).

Three factors compound the tragedy of sin. First, it pervades the whole person; no sphere escapes, for the very heart of the sinner is corrupt (Ps. 51:5; Jer. 17:9; Rom. 8:7). Second, evil resides in the heart of the crown of God's creation, the bearer of God's image, the one appointed to rule the world for God. The remarkable capacities of humans to think, plan, persuade, and train others enables wickedness to become clever and strong. Third, sin is proud; hence it resists God and his salvation and offers a counterfeit salvation instead (2 Thess. 2:2–4).

Despite all its dismal qualities, sin makes one contribution. Because God chose to redeem his people from it, sin has been the stimulus for God's demonstration of his amazing patience, grace, and love (Rom. 5:6–8; Gal. 2:17–20; 1 Tim. 1:15–17). So the study of sin need not merely grieve the Christian. From a postresurrection perspective, sin indirectly gives opportunity to praise the creating and redeeming Lord for his gracious deliverance (Rom. 11:33–36).

Daniel Doriani

See also Blasphemy Against the Holy Spirit; Fall, The; Guilt.

Bibliography. G. C. Berkouwer, *Sin;* G. W. Bromiley, *ISBE,* 4:518–25; J. Calvin, *Institutes of the Christian Religion;* C. E. B. Cranfield, *Romans;* D. Kidner, *Genesis;* A. Kuyper, *The Work of the Holy Spirit.*

"Sin unto Death." The expression "sin unto death" (1 John 5:16–17) appears in a context concerning confident, effective prayer (cf. 1 John 3:21–22; 4:17). First John 5:14–15 speaks generally about the confidence that God will answer requests made according to his will. Verses 16–17 speak specifically about the confidence that God will answer intercession for believers who are committing a sin not unto death and give life to them. But no such confidence is available when the sins is unto death. While all unrighteousness is sin, not all sin is unto death. Thus, the comment about sin unto death is something of an afterthought.

But what are the nondeadly and deadly sins? Some answers are unconvincing because they stress remote contexts rather than the immediate context in 1 John. The view that mortal and venial sins are distinguished is anachronistic. In another approach, death is understood as physical, but in 1 John death and life are spiritual (1:1–2; 2:25; 3:14–15; 4:9; 5:11–13). Another view connects 1 John 5:16–17 with the blasphemy against the Holy Spirit (Matt. 12:31–32; Mark 3:28–30), but 1 John says nothing about attributing the miracles of Jesus to Satan's power. Yet another theory sees the sin unto death as apostasy (cf. Heb. 2:3; 6:6; 10:29–31), but 1 John 2:19 indicates that "apostates" were never really in the community to begin with. Thus, another solution must be sought.

The polemic of 1 John views sin very seriously (1:7–10; 2:12; 3:4–5, 8–9; 4:10; 5:18). While believers do sin occasionally (1:7, 9; 2:1; 5:16), they do not persist in ethical disobedience (2:4), social bigotry (2:9; 3:14–17; 4:20–21), or christological heresy (2:18–29; 4:1–3). In this qualified sense they do not sin (3:6, 9; 5:18); in other words, their sin is not deadly (5:16–17). But those who walk in darkness while claiming to be in the light (1:6), who hate believers (2:9), and who deny that Jesus is the Messiah (2:22) are committing deadly sins. Thus, the polemic admits the reality of believers' sinning against the opponents' perfectionistic claims, but it also stresses the ideal of sinlessness. In this setting, the community is commanded to intercede for fellow believers who occasionally sin, but it is not commanded to pray for the deadly sins of those outside the community. DAVID L. TURNER

See also BLASPHEMY AGAINST THE HOLY SPIRIT; SIN.

Bibliography. R. E. Brown, *The Epistles of John;* I. A. Busenitz, *The Master's Seminary Journal* 1 (1990): 17–31; R. Law, *The Tests of Life;* I. H. Marshall, *The Epistles of John;* S. M. Reynolds, *Reformation Review* 20 (1973): 130–39; D. M. Scholer, *Current Issues in Biblical and Pastristic Interpretation,* pp. 230–46; S. S. Smalley, *1, 2, 3, John.*

Sin Offering. *See* OFFERINGS AND SACRIFICES.

Sister. *See* CHRISTIANS, NAMES OF; FAMILY LIFE AND RELATIONS.

Slave, Slavery. State of being subjected to involuntary servitude. It usually included being legally owned as property by another person. Slavery in the biblical world was complex and normally very different than the slavery of the eighteenth- and nineteenth-century Western world.

Slavery in the Ancient Near East. This historical and legal antecedents to slavery in the Old Testament are derived from the nations of the Fertile Crescent, ranging from Babylon to Egypt. The society of the ancient Near Eastern world had three major categories: free, semifree, and slave. All social structures were defined within these categories. Pictorial impressions of war captives suggesting slavery have survived from the fourth millennium B.C. The specific literary evidence, however, is contained in a number of law codes that have survived from Babylonia and Assyria. These documents provide information concerning slavery in the ancient Near East that conditioned the culture in which Israel's ideologies developed. The Ur-Nammu Code (2050 B.C.) is one of the oldest; the Code of Hammurabi (ca. 1700 B.C.) is probably the most well known. The earliest Sumerian terms for slaves indicate that enslaved captives of war from foreign countries constituted the initial category of slaves. Slaves were treated in the legal codes as property, not human beings. If a slave was killed by another, the main concern was to settle on the price for the lost property.

The Old Testament. The Old Testament record of Israel's origin and development demonstrates that they functioned within the cultural milieu of their own time. God's self-disclosure and direction to his elect nation often accommodated existing cultural aspects. While such accommodation reflects God's way of dealing with his creation, it does not necessarily imply his ideal will. Slavery is accepted in the Old Testament as part of the world in which Israel functioned. It is not abolished but regulated. The legal codes for that regulation (Exod. 21; Lev. 25; Deut. 15) and the numerous texts that reflect Israel's development in this domain indicate an increasing humanization of slavery in contrast to the rest of the ancient Near East. The Hebrew slave was more protected than those of other nationalities. The Old Testament raised the status of the slave from property to that of a human being who happened to be owned by another person (Exod. 21:20, 26–27; Job 31:13–15; Eccles. 7:21–22). The fact that Israel was enslaved in Egypt may have influenced this development (Lev. 25:39–43; Deut. 5:15; 15:13–15; Joel 2:29).

The Old Testament provides numerous opportunities for the manumission of slaves. Freedom could be purchased (Lev. 25:48–55). The Hebrew slave was to be released in the Sabbatical and Jubilee year cycles (Exod. 21:2–4; Lev. 25:40-43). Inhumane treatment by masters was grounds for release (Exod. 21:7–11, 26–27; Deut. 21:14). Some were released by the direct command of Yahweh (Jer. 34:8–10).

The terminology for slavery permeated relational metaphors in Israel. It was adopted as a metaphor to image the believer's relationship to Yahweh and is more appropriately translated servant rather than slave (cf. Jer. 2:14). Leaders such as Moses, Joshua, and David were servants of the Lord. All the citizens of Israel were viewed as servants of their earthly king (1 Sam. 17:8). Those who were in subordinate positions to others were referred to as servants without implying formal slavery.

The New Testament. The New Testament in contrast with the Old Testament does not record the origin and development of a national entity. Therefore, its references to slaves and slavery are more coincidental and secondary. The Gospels refer to slaves as part of the fabric of society. The personal slave of a centurion (Matt. 8:5–13) or of a high priest (Matt. 26:51) is a natural part of the narrative. Incidental references to the everyday functions of slaves are numerous. Jesus frequently used slave motifs in his parables because such images were the common stock of his audiences. His mere reference to the social phenomenon neither approved nor condemned its existence.

Paul's epistle to Philemon and his treatment of household codes directly addresses the issue of owner and slave relationships. Paul reflects the dual worlds for which Christians are responsible. He recognizes the legal ownership of Philemon by returning the runaway slave Onesimus (vv. 12–14). He also emphasizes the human relational changes that are the result of believing in Christ. Onesimus now has the status of a brother (v. 16) and thereby deserves to be viewed as such. Paul's statement in verse 16a, "no longer as a slave," does not abolish the legal issue but highlights the new spiritual relationship. The tone of Paul's appeal for Onesimus may well imply his desire that Philemon give Onesimus his freedom, but Paul comes short of demanding this response. It is Philemon's decision.

The household codes that address slaves call for Christian integrity within existing structures, even when these structures have what can be perceived as negative consequences (cf. Eph. 5:22–6:9; Col. 3:18–4:1; 1 Tim. 6:1–2; cf. 1 Peter 2:13–3:7). Paul's instructions to slaves calls for them to fulfill their obligations to human masters as if they were rendering service to Christ. The motive for providing honest and dedicated service is that the Christian witness may be advanced. These texts reflect the missionary mandate Christ gave to the apostles for his church (Matt. 28:18–20). While early Christian teaching contained humanitarian emphases (cf. Matt. 24:45–51; Luke 15:22; 17:7) and has often resulted in social change, there is no social mandate to abolish slavery in these texts. The revolutionary nature of the early church is contained in the concept of being "in Christ." The result of being "in Christ" is, on the one hand, spiritual egalitarianism (Gal. 3:23–25), and on the other, responsible behavior within existing structures.

Christ plays on the concept of servant to image his own mission (Mark 10:45; Luke 22:27). The epistolary literature focuses on the figurative usage of slave. These books frequently use the primary term for slave, *doulos,* as a metaphor of being a servant to God (Rom. 1:1; Phil. 1:1; 2 Tim. 2:24; Titus 1:1; James 1:1; 1 Peter 2:16; 2 Peter 1:1), to fellow believers (2 Cor. 4:5), and even to sin (Rom. 6:20). This is a most striking metaphor because a Greek person linked personal dignity and freedom together. Freedom was power and something about which to be proud. The use of *doulos* to image relationship to God and fellow believers sent a message of commitment and abandonment of autonomy (1 Cor. 7:22; Eph. 6:6; Col. 4:12). GARY T. MEADORS

Bibliography. R. Lyall, *Slaves, Citizens, Sons;* I. Mendelsohn, *IDB,* 4:383–91; N. R. Petersen, *Rediscovering Paul: Philemon and the Sociology of Paul's Narrative World;* J. Pritchard, *Ancient Near Eastern Texts;* E. Schürer, *The History of the Jewish People in the Age of Jesus Christ;* J. E. Stambaugh and D. L. Balch, *The New Testament in Its Social Environment;* W. L. Westermann, *The Slave Systems of Greek and Roman Antiquity.*

Sleep. In the Scriptures the words that designate sleep are used in both a literal and a figurative way. When the word is used literally, as it frequently is, it usually depicts sleep as a simple fact of human experience (Gen. 28:16; Dan. 8:18; Matt. 25:5). Even our sleeping state is not outside the active involvement of God, who neither slumbers nor sleeps (Ps. 121:4). The Lord watches over us while we sleep (Ps. 121:3, 5–6), and the darkness of night is as the light of day to him (Ps. 139:11–12). God uses our sleep on occasion to give us revelatory dreams and guidance (Gen. 20:6–7; Judg. 7:13–15; 1 Kings 3:5; Matt. 1:20; 2:12–13, 22). In the Old Testament, natural sleep is occasionally referred to as a sweet blessing of God (Pss. 4:8; 127:2; Eccles. 5:12).

The word "sleep" is also used metaphorically of spiritual dullness, sloth, or lack of watchfulness. In the Book of Proverbs, laziness, sloth, and sleep are used in a quasi-moral way to depict the irresponsible person who refuses to acknowledge the reasonable demands of human life (6:9–11; 19:15; 20:13; 24:33–34); such a person will suffer the inevitable consequences. In Isaiah 29:10 and frequently in the New Testament (Mark 13:36; Rom. 13:11; Eph. 5:14; 1 Thess. 5:6–9) it is used to describe a spiritual heaviness that must be shaken off in order to remain awake in this evil time. It is often used in this way in an eschatological context, warning us to be alert to the signs of the times.

"Sleep" is also used metaphorically of death. This is common in the Old Testament (Job 7:21; 14:12; Ps. 13:3; Jer. 51:57; Dan. 12:2). The expression "he slept with his fathers" is a fixed formula in reference to death, and is used over thirty-five times in the Old Testament. This expression does not continue into New Testament times, although the metaphorical use of sleep for death does. Six observations can be made about this expression in the New Testament.

First, Jesus is never said to have fallen asleep. There is no softening of what he experienced at the end of his earthly life. Second, unbelievers are never said to fall asleep. They, too, experience death in a stark and crushing way. Death is no pleasant sleep for them, but a final, unending negation. The difference from Jesus is, of course, that the unbeliever dies for his or her own sins, whereas Jesus died for the sins of others and rose again in triumphant life. Third, believers are said to fall asleep at death (1 Cor. 15:6, 18, 20; 1 Thess. 4:13, 15), and in one instance "to fall asleep in Jesus" (1 Thess. 4:14). Although believers are still occasionally said to die, death is described as gain (Phil. 1:21); it has lost its sting (1 Cor. 15:54–57). Death comes attended by blessedness and rest (Rev. 14:13) and a conscious sense of the presence of Christ (2 Cor. 5:8). Death is, in fact, not death anymore, and those who believe in Jesus will never really die, even though they might still experience what used to be called death (John 11:25–26). So the metaphor of sleep is used to emphasize that we have no more to fear from death than we do from falling asleep. Fourth, believers are never said to have fallen asleep in the death of Jesus; rather, we died with him (Col. 2:20; 2 Tim. 2:11) or were crucified with him (Gal. 2:20). It is only because of *Jesus'* death, and our death in him, that death no longer holds any terror, becoming instead a peaceful sleep and a blessedness (Rev. 14:13). Fifth, even when believers are punished by the Lord with temporal death, it is still no longer death but a falling asleep (1 Cor. 11:30). Finally, not only do believers never experience death (in the old way) anymore, although they must go through what is metaphorically called sleep; there are some who will not even experience that—that single generation of believers, who are alive at the second coming of Christ (1 Cor. 15:51), they will not sleep, but will be transformed instantaneously into their new unending life. WALTER A. ELWELL

See also DEATH; THESSALONIANS, FIRST AND SECOND, THEOLOGY OF.

Son, Sonship. *See* ADOPTION; CHRISTIANS, NAMES OF; JESUS CHRIST, NAME AND TITLES OF.

Son of David. *See* JESUS CHRIST, NAME AND TITLES OF.

Son of God. *See* ADOPTION; JESUS CHRIST, NAME AND TITLES OF.

Son of Man. *See* JESUS CHRIST, NAME AND TITLES OF.

Song, New. *See* NEW SONG.

Song of Solomon, Theology of. At first reading it seems impossible to describe a theology of the Song of Songs. After all, the name of God may appear only one time in the book, and that is debated (8:6). Moreover, God is not the only surprising absence in the book; we look in vain for a reference to Israel, the covenant, worship institutions, or anything explicitly religious. How then could Rabbi Akiba call this book the Bible's "Holy of Holies"?

The way chosen by many during the history of interpretation was to suppress the obviously sexual language of human love in the book by allegorizing it. Jewish interpreters, as represented by the Targum of the book (ca. seventh century A.D.), thought that the lover of the Song was Yahweh and the beloved Israel. Thus, when the woman pleads with the king to take her into his chamber (1:4), this has nothing to do with human lovemaking but rather describes the exodus from Egypt, God's bedroom being the land of Palestine. Early Christian interpreters also desexed the Song in this way, but, of course, identified the main characters with Jesus Christ and the church and/or the individual Christians. Hippolytus (ca. A.D. 200) was the first known Christian to allegorize the Song. From fragments of his commentary we learn that he takes the statement in 1:4 to mean that Christ has brought the worthy ones whom he has wedded into the church. The Targum and Hippolytus are just examples of an interpretive tendency that was dominant from early times until the nineteenth century and still is occasionally found today.

The allegorical method, however, lacks any external justification. The Song gives no indication that it should be read in any but a straightforward way. The discovery and publication of formally similar love poetry from modern Arabic literature as well as ancient Egypt and Mesopotamia signaled the end of the allegorical approach to the text, but left the church with a number of questions about the theological meaning of the Song.

The Song serves an important canonical function with its explicit language of love. Allegorization in early times arose from the belief that such a subject was unsuitable for the Holy Scriptures. The church and the synagogue had been influenced by foreign philosophy (Neo-Platonism) to the point where bodily functions were seen in opposition to the things of the Spirit and thus to be avoided. The same attitudes and beliefs that motivated the monastic movement led to the allegorization of the Song. The Song, however, stands against such attempts and tells the church that sexuality within the context of marriage is something God created for the pleasure of his human creatures. Thus, the woman delights in the physical beauty of the man (5:10–16) and vice versa (4:1–15), and this physical attraction culminates in passionate lovemaking (5:1–2). God endowed humans at creation with sexuality as a blessing, not as a curse.

Indeed, the Song must be read in the context of the garden of Eden, where human sexuality is first introduced. The pervasive garden theme in the Song evokes memories of the garden before the fall. Since Adam had no suitable partner, God created Eve, and the man and the woman stood naked in the garden and felt no shame (Gen. 2:25), exulting in one another's "flesh" (Gen. 2:23–24).

This perfect harmony between the male and female tragically ended at the fall. Eve, then Adam, rebelled against God and a horrible distance grew between the sinful human race and their holy God. This separation between the divine and the human had repercussions in the human sphere as well. Now Adam and Eve were naked and they felt shame and fled from one another (Gen. 3:7, 10). The sin of Adam and Eve was not a specifically sexual sin, but the alienation that resulted from the sin is recounted in sexual terms.

The Song of Songs, then, describes a lover and his beloved rejoicing in each other's sexuality in a garden. They feel no shame. The Song is as the story of sexuality redeemed.

Nonetheless, this reading does not exhaust the theological meaning of the Song. When read in the context of the canon as a whole, the book forcefully communicates the intensely intimate relationship that Israel enjoys with God. In many Old Testament Scriptures, marriage is an underlying metaphor for Israel's relationship with God. Unfortunately, due to Israel's lack of trust, the metaphor often appears in a negative context, and Israel is pictured as a whore in its relationship with God (Jer. 2:20; 3:1; Ezek. 16, 23). One of the most memorable scenes in the Old Testament is when God commands his prophet Hosea to marry a prostitute to symbolize his love for a faithless Israel. In spite of the predominantly negative use of the image, we must not lose sight of the fact that Israel was the bride of God, and so as the Song celebrates the intimacy between human lovers, we learn about our relationship with God.

So we come full circle, reaching similar conclusions to the early allegorical approaches to the Song. The difference, though, is obvious. We do not deny the primary and natural reading of the book, which highlights human love, and we do not arbitrarily posit the analogy between the Song's lovers and God and Israel. Rather, we read it in the light of the pervasive marriage metaphor of the Old Testament.

From a New Testament Perspective. The New Testament also uses human relationships as metaphors of the divine-human relationship, and none clearer than marriage. According to Ephesians 5:22–23, the church is the bride of Christ (see also Rev. 19:7; 21:2, 9; 22:17). So Christians should read the Song in the light of Ephesians and rejoice in the intimate relationship that they enjoy with Jesus Christ.

TREMPER LONGMAN III

Bibliography. G. L. Carr, *Song of Solomon;* F. Delitzsch, *Proverbs, Ecclesiastes, Song of Songs;* M. Falk, *Love Lyrics from the Bible;* W. G. Lambert, *JSS* 4 (1959): 1–15; M. H. Popoe, *Song of Songs;* P. Trible, *God and the Rhetoric of Sexuality;* J. B. White, *A Study of the Language of Love in the Song of Songs and Ancient Near Eastern Poetry.*

Soul. ***The Old Testament.*** The Hebrew word so rendered is *nepeš*. It appears 755 times in the Old Testament. The King James Version uses 42 different English terms to translate it. The two most common renderings are "soul" (428 times) and "life" (117 times). It is the synchronic use of *nepes*˙ that determines its meaning rather than the diachronic. Hebrew is inclined to use one and the same word for a variety of functions that are labeled with distinct words in English.

Nepeš in the Old Testament is never the "immortal soul" but simply the life principle or living being. Such is observable in Genesis 1:20, 21, 24, where the qualified (living) *nepeš* refers to animals and is rendered "living creatures." The same Hebrew term is then applied to the creation of humankind in Genesis 2:7, where dust is vitalized by the breath of God and becomes a "living being." Thus, human being shares soul with the animals. It is the breath of God that makes the lifeless dust a "living being"—person.

Frequently in the Old Testament *nepeš* designates the individual (Lev. 17:10; 23:30). In its plural form it indicates a number of individuals such as Abraham's party (Gen. 12:5), the remnant left behind in Judah (Jer. 43:6), and the offspring of Leah (Gen. 46:15).

Nepeš qualified by "dead" means a dead individual, a corpse (Num. 6:6). More significant here is that *nepeš* can mean the corpse of an individual even without the qualification "dead" (Num. 5:2; 6:11). Here *nepeš* is detached from the concept of life and refers to the corpse. Hebrew thought could not conceive of a disembodied *nepeš*.

Frequently *nepeš* takes the place of a personal or reflexive pronoun (Ps. 54:4; Prov. 18:7). Admittedly this movement from the nominal to the pronominal is without an exact borderline. The Revised Standard Version reflects the above understanding of *nepeš* by replacing the King James Version "soul" with such translations as "being," "one," "self," "I/me."

Nepeš is also used to designate parts of the body, primarily to stress their characteristics and functions. It can refer to the throat (Isa. 5:14; Hab. 2:5), noting that it can be parched and dry (Num. 11:6; Jer. 31:12, 25), discerning (Prov. 16:23), hungry (Num. 21:5), and breathing (Jer. 2:24). *Nepeš* also can mean the neck, and the vital function that takes place there, noting that it can be ensnared (1 Sam. 28:9; Ps. 105:18), humbled and endangered (Prov. 18:7), and bowed to the ground (Ps. 44:25). Even while focusing on a single part of the body, by synecodoche the whole person is represented.

Nepeš is often used to express physical needs such as hunger (Deut. 12:20; 1 Sam. 2:16) and thirst (Prov. 25:25). It can be used of excessive desires (gluttony—Prov. 23:2) and of unfulfilled desires (barrenness—1 Sam. 1:15). Volitional/spiritual yearning is also assigned to *nepeš*, such as the desire for God (Ps. 42:1–2), justice (Isa. 26:8–9), evil (Prov. 21:10), and political power (2 Sam. 3:21). Emotions are expressed by *nepeš* so that it feels hate (so used of Yahweh—Isa. 1:14), grief (Jer. 13:17), joy and exultation, disquietude (Ps. 42:5), and unhappiness (1 Sam. 1:15).

Clearly, then, in the Old Testament a mortal is a living soul rather than having a soul. Instead of splitting a person into two or three parts, Hebrew thought sees a unified being, but one that is profoundly complex, a psychophysical being.

The New Testament. The counterpart to *nepeš* in the New Testament is *psychē* (*nepeš* is translated as *psychē* six hundred times in the Septaugint). Compared to *nepeš* in the Old Testament, *psychē* appears relatively infrequently in the New Testament. This may be due to the fact that *nepeš* is used extensively in poetic literature, which is more prevalent in the Old Testament than the New Testament. The Pauline Epistles concentrate more on *sōma* (body) and *pneuma* (spirit) than *psychē*.

This word has a range of meanings similar to *nepeš*. It frequently designates life: one can risk his life (John 13:37; Acts 15:26; Rom. 16:4; Phil. 2:30), give his life (Matt. 20:28), lay down his life (John 10:15, 17–18), forfeit his life (Matt. 16:26), hate his life (Luke 14:26), and have his life demanded of him (Luke 12:20).

Psychē, as its Old Testament counterpart, can indicate the person (Acts 2:41; 27:37). It also serves as the reflexive pronoun designating the self ("I'll say to myself"—Luke 12:19; "as my witness"—2 Cor. 1:23; "share . . . our lives"—1 Thess. 2:8).

Psychē can express emotions such as grief (Matt. 26:38, Mark 14:34), anguish (John 12:27), exultation (Luke 1:46), and pleasure (Matt. 12:18).

The adjectival form "soulish" indicates a person governed by the sensuous nature with subjection to appetite and passion. Such a person is "natural/unspiritual" and cannot receive the gifts of God's Spirit because they make no sense to him (1 Cor. 2:14–15). As in the Old Testament, the soul relates humans to the animal world (1 Cor. 15:42–50) while it is the spirit of people that allows a dynamic relationship with God.

There are passages where *psychē* stands in contrast to the body, and there it seems to refer to an immortal part of man. "Do not be afraid of those who kill the body but cannot kill the soul. Rather, be afraid of the One who can destroy both soul and body in hell" (Matt. 10:28). While Scripture generally addresses humans as unitary beings, there are such passages that seem to allow divisibility within unity. CARL SCHULTZ

See also PERSON, PERSONHOOD; SPIRIT.

Bibliography. W. Dryness, *Themes in Old Testament Theology;* R. H. Gundry, *Somma in Biblical Theology;* R. Jewett, *Paul's Anthropological Terms;* N. Snaith, *The Distinctive Ideas of the Old Testament;* H. W. Wolff, *Anthropology of the Old Testament.*

Speaking in Tongues. *See* HOLY SPIRIT, GIFTS OF .

Spirit. *The Old Testament.* The Hebrew word for "spirit" is *rûaḥ*. It appears 389 times in the Old Testament. Its varied use almost defies analysis, but some emphases are discernible. It is used more often of God (136 times) than of persons or animals (129 times).

Its basic meaning is wind (113 times). The trees of the forest sway before a wind (Isa. 7:2); a wind sweeps over the waters (Gen. 1:2); and the Lord walked in the garden at the breezy time of day (Gen. 3:8). It was an east wind that brought locusts (Exod. 10:13) and a strong east wind that divided the Red Sea and dried it up (Exod. 14:21).

Breath is also a basic meaning of this term. It is the Lord who gives breath to people (Isa. 42:5) and to lifeless bodies (Ezek. 37:9–10—in this chapter there is a wordplay on *rûaḥ*, allowing it to mean wind, breath, spirit; a similar phenomenon is found in John 3:5, 8, where *pneuma* means both wind and spirit). It is also used of bad breath—Job's breath was repulsive to his wife (Job 19:17).

By extension when applied to a person *rûaḥ* comes to mean vital powers or strength. It is the spirit that sustains a person through illness (Prov. 18:14), but the spirit of the troubled person can be crushed (Ps. 34:18). This dynamic force can be impaired or diminished as well as renewed or increased. It was a drink that caused the spirit (strength) of Samson to return and revive him (Judg. 15:18–19) and the coming of the wagons from Egypt that revived Jacob's numb heart (Gen. 45:26–27). Spirit also bespeaks limitations. When taken back, the person returns to dust (Ps. 104:29–30).

The spirit of the Lord is the creative power of life (Ps. 33:6). When it descends on the judges it activates and enables them to do great exploits (Judges 3:10; 14:6). By contrast, there is no spirit in idols of wood and stone. They are inert and have no power to awake and arise (Hab. 2:19).

Rûaḥ can also refer to feelings. The queen of Sheba was left breathless when she saw the wisdom and wealth of Solomon (1 Kings 10:5). She was overcome by astonishment. Eliphaz accuses Job of venting his anger on God (Job 15:13). Ahab was dispirited and sullen because of Naboth's unwillingness to sell his vineyard (1 Kings 21:4). "Shortness" of spirit is impatience, whereas "longness" of spirit is patience (Prov. 14:29). To be proud in spirit is to be arrogant (Eccles. 7:8). The suspicious husband is said to have a (fit) spirit of jealousy (Num. 5:14, 30).

Rûaḥ can also refer to the will. Those whose spirits God had stirred up went up to rebuild the temple (Ezra 1:5). Caleb had a different spirit from the other spies (Num. 14:24) and thus was resolute in his assessment relative to the conquest of the land. The psalmist prays for a steadfast spirit (Ps. 51:10).

Given the distributed uses of *rûaḥ* (standing twice as often for the wind/power of God as it does for the breath/feelings/will of the person), mortals cannot see themselves as independent of God. The *rûaḥ* is living not simply through a surge of vitality, but because of God's initiatives and actions. The link between the anthropological and the divine *rûaḥ* is not always clear and well defined.

The New Testament. *Pneuma* is the New Testament counterpart to the Old Testament *rûaḥ*. While it occasionally means wind (John 3:8) and breath (Matt. 27:50; 2 Thess. 2:8), it is most generally translates "spirit"—an incorporeal, feeling, and intelligent being.

It was Mary's spirit that rejoiced (Luke 1:47). Jesus "grew and became strong; he was filled with wisdom" (Luke 2:40). He was "deeply moved in spirit" when he saw Mary weeping over the death of Lazarus (John 11:33). Apollos was characterized as speaking with "great fervor" (Acts 18:25) and Paul "had no peace of mind" when Titus did not meet him at Troas (2 Cor. 2:13). Jesus pronounced a blessing on the "poor in spirit" (Matt. 5:3).

In the New Testament spirit is also seen as that dimension of human personality whereby relationship with God is possible (Mark 2:8; Acts 7:59; Rom. 1:9; 8:16; 1 Cor. 5:3–5). It is this human spiritual nature that enables continuing conversation with the divine Spirit (Rom. 8:9–17).

Occasionally *pneuma* will be treated in a parallel structure with *psychē*. The terms seem to be one and the same (Luke 1:46–47) and seem to be interchangeable. On the other hand, there are passages that distinguish between the two. Paul speaks of Adam as a "living soul" but of Christ as a "life-giving spirit." The one is oriented to human life and the other to heavenly life.

Flesh and spirit are often juxtaposed. Both can be defiled (2 Cor. 7:1) and both can be holy (1 Cor. 7:34). The flesh (works) and the spirit (fruit) are unalterably opposed to each other (Gal. 5:16–26). Spirit is also contrasted with letter. While the letter kills, the Spirit gives life (2 Cor. 3:6). Spirit is also contrasted with human wisdom (1 Cor. 2:5). Weakness of flesh can prove stronger than the spirit's will to pray (Mark 14:38).

Worship of God in the spirit is acceptable, contrasting with unacceptable worship in the flesh (Phil. 3:3). "God is spirit, and his worshipers must worship in spirit and in truth" (John 4:24).

While God's Spirit is holy, reference is made to unclean, evil, and demonic spirits that are injurious to relationships with God and other humans.

There are a few passages that see the spirit as disembodied (2 Cor. 5:1–5; Heb. 12:23; 1 Peter 3:19). Paul speaks of being absent in body, but present in spirit (Col. 2:5), and James notes that the body without the spirit is dead (James 2:26).

CARL SCHULTZ

See also HOLY SPIRIT; PERSON, PERSONHOOD.

Bibliography. W. Dryness, *Themes in Old Testament Theology;* R. H. Gundry, *Sōma in Biblical Theology;* R. Jewett, *Paul's Anthropological Terms;* A. R. Johnson, *The Vitality of the Individual in the Thought of Ancient Israel;* N. Snaith, *The Distinctive Ideas of the Old Testament;* H. W. Wolff, *Anthropology of the Old Testament.*

Spirit, Holy. *See* HOLY SPIRIT.

Spirit, Evil. *See* DEMON.

Spirits in Prison. The spirits in prison are referred to in 1 Peter 3:19–20, where Peter declares that they disobeyed in the time of Noah and that Christ went and preached to them in prison. This passage has often been identified as one of the most obscure in the entire New Testament. Other passages are often used to interpret this one, but it must be understood in its own literary context and ideological environment.

Verses 19–21 appear in the middle of a christological confession of the death and resurrection of Jesus Christ (v. 18) and his exaltation to the right hand of the Father (v. 22; cf. 1 Tim. 3:16). Verses 19–21 declare his triumphant declaration to the evil spirits, and contrasts them with Noah, who was saved through water—a type of Christian baptism.

Peter used this confession and triumphant journey of Christ to encourage his readers, who were suffering ridicule and persecution as a result of their conversion (1:6; 4:4). In particular it follows 3:13–17, which explains how they should respond to unreasonable abuse, especially when they have been zealous in living an honorable life before their accusers (2:11–3:12). And their participation in the triumph of Christ is assured by their pledge of a good conscience in baptism (v. 21).

This journey of Christ took place after the resurrection rather than between his death and resurrection, since the description follows the resurrection in verse 18, and the relative clause "in which" (*en hō*) refers either to his resurrected spiritual state, or "at that time," that is, after his death and resurrection. Since the very same form of the participle (*poreutheis,* "going," or "traveling") is used in both verse 19 and verse 22, it is most likely that this is a single journey of Christ through the heavens to the right hand of the Father (v. 22).

The distinctive characteristic of these spirits is that they were in prison when Christ traveled to them, since the prepositional phrase is in the attributive position (*tois en phulakē pneumasin,* "the in prison spirits").

That these spirits are the evil angels of Genesis 6:1–4 (or their offspring) is indicated by their being in prison, their disobedience in the time of Noah, their mention in 2 Peter 2:4 and Jude 6, and the New Testament use of the plural noun ("spirits," *pneumasin*) as a reference to evil spirits unless otherwise qualified. This is further supported by contemporary Jewish literature (1 Enoch 6:1–8; 12:1–16:4; 19:1; 2 Baruch 56:12), which describes these evil angels in the same way as the passage in 1 Peter. NORMAN R. ERICSON

See also DESCENT INTO HELL (HADES).

Spirituality. ***Hebrew Spirituality.*** Hebrew spirituality is a life lived within the framework defined by God's saving acts in his history with his people. This sacred history is reflected in the faith of the community and its liturgy, particularly as that was rehearsed in annual commemorations (such as Passover) and centered around the temple and its practices.

The individual appropriated this history and identity, especially in his or her prayer life. The Psalter, for instance, supplied worshipers with prayers to express petitions, praise, thanksgiving, and repentance, just as the Psalter would do for Christians.

Israel's prayer life went beyond the Psalter, though. Intercession, especially for the sins of a people, stretch from Abraham (Gen. 20:7) to Amos (Amos 7:1–6). God is even argued with, particularly to persuade God that the pray-er's cause is just and that God would be benefited if the request were granted (Gen. 18:25; Exod. 32:11–12).

This reflects a conception of God as one who enters into a dialogical relationship with his people. He is concerned for his people's needs, angry at their sins, and even open to a change of mind (Exod. 32:7–14; Num. 14:13–25; 1 Sam. 8:4–22). He can also be absent from and silent to his people (Job 23:8–9; Ps. 30:7; Hab. 1:2), or present to and seen by his people (Pss. 42:2; 84:7).

Much of Hebrew spirituality focuses on God's presence in this life. Though his presence is sometimes dreaded or not always desired (e.g., Job 23:15–17; Ps. 51:9), God's absence is painful to endure (Ps. 51:11). Life is to be lived in the consciousness of God's presence; death (*sheol*) usually means the loss of consciousness, the absence of God, and the cessation of the praise of God (Pss. 6:4–5; 88:3–6; Eccles. 9:5–6, 10).

Those who truly experience life are those who obey God and are penitent and humble in God's presence (Deut. 30:15–20; Ps. 119). For this reason, obedience to the law is central in Hebrew spirituality, for the law of God is virtually the presence of God in his people's midst. The law expresses the mind of God and his intentions for his people, let alone for all of his creatures. Thus, one is to meditate on, study, and keep the law (Deut. 6:4–9); by so doing, the Hebrew was perhaps exercising the equivalent of the Christian way of practicing the presence of God.

Christian Spirituality. In order to appreciate what Christian spirituality is, we must first clarify what it is not. Christian spirituality is not a gnostic renunciation of the created world nor the Platonic flight of the soul from the body. The world is the object of God's love (John 3:16), and we are to glorify God *in* our bodies (Rom. 12:1; 1 Cor. 6:19–20). Furthermore, such attitudes fly in the face of appropriating the Christian doctrine of the creation and the incarnation. Spirituality must be practiced in *this* world, which God made good (Mark 7:19) and which God is in the process of redeeming (Rom. 8:18–25). As in the Old Testament, spirituality does not imply that one is to flee this world to find God, but that one must find God and grow in grace in this world, even discovering avenues (i.e., spiritual disciplines) in and through the physical realm for spiritual growth.

Christian spirituality begins with our redemption in Christ. We are baptized into Christ: We die to sin and the "old man" and we are made alive to God as a new creation (Rom. 6:3–11; 2 Cor. 5:17). True spirituality, then, is not a human self-help program or a means of justifying ourselves (Gal. 2:15–21). It begins with a divine call, rebirth, and conversion (John 3:3–8; Acts 2:38–39) wherein we admit we are helpless to help ourselves in our bondage to sin and enmity with God (Rom. 5:6–11).

With this foundation clearly in mind, Christian spirituality has to do primarily with sanctification. It requires divine grace (first and always) and deliberate human cooperation. It is neither a passive quietism nor a triumphalist activism. (This combination is epitomized by Paul in 1 Cor. 15:10.) So, spirituality has to do with holiness, which is the restoration of the human person to what he or she was created to be. One could say that holiness involves the recovery of wholeness—the integrity of our lives as they are being restored by the Spirit.

This is a process, depicted by several metaphors in Scripture. We are to be trees whose roots are firmly established in Christ planted by streams of nurturing water (Eph. 3:17). We are people of "the Way"—sojourners on a journey (Acts 9:2; 1 Peter 2:11). We are "born again" and meant to grow from infancy to adulthood, sustained on a diet of rich spiritual food (John 3:3; Heb. 5:12–14).

The goal of the process is to be renewed in holiness, righteousness, and knowledge after the likeness of God (Eph. 4:24; Col. 3:10), or, what is the same thing, to become more like Jesus Christ by whose stature our maturity is measured (Eph. 4:13–16). The goal is to acquire a Christian construal of everything. How does one acquire such a Christian construal of everything? The process is similar to that which we have found in Hebrew spirituality. It is formed by what one reads and listens to, the people with whom one associates (hence the importance of the church in Christian spirituality), the activities in which one engages, the way one eats, and so on, but above all it is formed by what one loves. When a Christian mixes the Christian construal with other construals (such as a materialistic conception of the world), then there is a kind of double vision that leads to conflicts, hypocrisy, and the like (see Matt. 6:19–24). We need a single focus—a total devotion to God (Matt. 6:33). This is simplicity, and it requires the grace of God and our response of total sacrifice and the transformation of our minds (Rom. 12:1–2).

Developing and keeping this single focus is accomplished by spiritual disciplines like Bible reading, meditation, prayer, fasting, church attendance, giving things away, and serving others. Initially, this begins by repenting (*metanoia*—turning our spiritual eyes away from our former conceptions of the world to see life from Christ's vantage point), followed by concentrating on, focusing on, conceptualizing, and even imaging Christ's character and God's presence and activity primarily through Scripture reading and prayer in the context of the fellowship of believers. (Recall the Hebrew and later Jewish focus on God's presence and the law.)

These disciplines mold and shape the embodied self. They are activities of mind and body intentionally undertaken to bring our entire person into effective cooperation with God's work. So, they are means to an end—like a balloon angioplasty that opens up our spiritual arteries to receive and circulate divine grace. They put us in a condition whereby God's grace can really work on us. Our minds and bodies are then usable as instruments of righteousness (Rom. 6:12–14; 12:2).

By these disciplines the Christian is not simply copying Jesus Christ as a model (as in Sheldon's *In His Steps*), though "putting on Christ" might mean that the Christian sometimes acts like Christ even if he or she does not yet understand why (Rom. 13:11–14). Nor is one merely accepting the values of Jesus (as in nineteenth-century liberalism). The Christian is learning Christlikeness by sharing Christ's life in an organic way (John 15:1–17; 17:20–24). We share in the life of the risen Christ through the Holy Spirit who indwells us and who groans in us for the completion of our redemption (Rom. 8:22–27). This indwelling is creative and transforming. It has been called "sanctifying" or "habitual" grace because it is not just a momentary help, but a vital source of holiness. Through this work of the indwelling presence of the Spirit of Christ and our response we come to have the "mind of Christ"—Christ's way of seeing the world that becomes "second nature" in us (Phil. 2:1–5). This is coming to "know" Christ—to become like him in his death and to share in the power of his resurrection (Phil. 3:3–11; 1 Peter 4:12–5:11). The result is that obedience to God is "from the heart"; we become "slaves to righteousness" (Rom. 6:17–19). We are now free to serve God and others with self-sacrificial love.

On the way to this conformation to Christ's image we will experience continuing struggle (Rom. 7:15–25); but we also will continually experience God's grace, for through Christ we are "more than conquerors" (Rom. 7:24–25; 8:37), something that should manifest itself in every aspect of the Christian's existence as the one who calls us remains faithful to complete what he began in us (Phil. 1:6). DENNIS L. OKHOLM

See also SANCTIFICATION; UNION WITH CHRIST.

Bibliography. D. Alexander, *Christian Spirituality: Five Views of Sanctification;* D. Allen, *Temptation;* A. Bloom, *Beginning to Pray;* R. Foster, *Celebration of Discipline;* idem, *The Freedom of Simplicity;* T. Kelly, *A Testament of Devotion;* S. Kierkegaard, *Practice in Christianity;* R. C. Roberts, *Spirituality and Human Emotions;* idem, *The Strengths of a Christian;* W. Stringfellow, *The Politics of Spirituality;* D. Willard, *The Spirit of the Disciplines.*

State. *See* GOVERNMENT.

Statute. The statutes of the covenant range from apodictic law (thou shalt not under any circumstances), to casuistic law (if this is the case, then do this), to detailed descriptions of ritual regulations to be observed by the priests and the community. For Israel, everything required by the covenant was a matter of life and blessing, if properly observed, or of death and cursing, if ignored or forsaken. There are no circumstances that allow for the antisocial act of one human being killing another human being with no legal sanction: thou shalt not commit murder.

Ignorance of a given statute was no excuse. Any failure to obey a statute, ordinance, or judgment of the law was a sin. The statutes related to sacrifices for the unwitting sin are a good example of case law. If someone was guilty of an unwitting sin, the sinner performed the sacrifice when he learned of his sin (Lev. 4).

Leviticus 10 provides a good example of ritual law based on a specific case that results in an apodictic statute: Nadab and Abihu had been drinking before they entered the tabernacle to perform their duties. Because they were unable to distinguish "between the holy and the common, and between the unclean and the clean," they died in a blaze of fire before Yahweh. Thus, the everlasting statute through all generation is given. Priests are to drink no wine or strong drink when performing their duties lest they die (vv. 1–11).

Israel understood that the statutes applied to everyone equally, whether native born or resident alien. Uriah the Hittite is a good example of an alien who had joined himself to Yahweh and Israel. His faithful adherence to the statutes related to holy war resulted in his "murder" by David. This incident also illustrates another important point. When an Israelite sinned against another human being, he also sinned against the community and

Yahweh. There was no distinction between public and private morality (Deut. 29:18–21).

A theological problem that continues to haunt us today is taking the promise of God's blessing for observance of all the statutes as an almost magical formula. One tries to evaluate his or her relationship with God in terms of outward circumstances. If everything is fine, one is basking in God's favor. If one is ill or oppressed or poor, one is under God's curse and needs to repent of sin or lack of faith. The Book of Job deals with this issue. The parable of Lazarus and the rich man speaks to it as well. Often our faith in God is in spite of circumstances, not because of them (Luke 16:19–31; cf. Jer. 44). MARK D. MCLEAN

See also COMMAND, COMMANDMENT; LAW.

Stoicism. *See* PHILOSOPHY.

Stranger. *See* FOREIGNER.

Strength. *See* POWER.

Stricism. *See* PHILOSOPHY.

Strong and Weak. The words "strong" and "weak" are often found in conjunction in Paul's writings. The parallelism of the two terms is used to communicate two central principles. First, human weakness allows the power of God to be most preeminently manifested. As Paul says, "For when I am weak, then I am strong" (2 Cor. 12:10b). Second, the two words are used metaphorically to describe the degree of spiritual development in the life of the believer (Rom. 14:1–23; 15:1–8; 1 Cor. 8:7–13; 10:23, 32).

"Weak" and "strong" serve as operative terms that combine such concepts as the kingdom of God, knowledge, love, conscience, freedom, and judgment. Paul's special use of the terms provides a theological context that informs and clarifies them. Those who have an accurate understanding of God and his kingdom and are able to actualize their Christian freedom without a conflict in conscience are "strong." Those who lack clarity and are unsure of how they are supposed to use their freedom in Christ are "weak." Knowledge alone cannot determine our use of Christian liberty; rather, the love of God in Christ must be the guiding factor in how we seek to realize the kingdom of God on earth.

Paul specifically identifies two areas of concern when addressing the strong and the weak: food and holy days. Some have the strength to eat meat; others, "whose faith is weak" (Rom. 14:1), feel that they should eat only vegetables (v. 2). Similarly, the weak are very concerned about observing special holy days, while the strong consider each day alike (v. 5). The weak consider issues like this extremely important in regards to God's kingdom, while the strong do not.

The beliefs and customs of the weak influence their understanding of Christian liberty. Their scrupulosity oversensitizes their consciences. When they look at the antithetical conduct of the strong, they end up in great moral torment (14:14–15). Some weak people start emulating the practices of the strong, yet do so out of fear and doubt (v. 23). This experience of confusion and doubt has serious consequences for the weak. The strong have caused the weak to stumble, and have possibly even destroyed them (v. 20).

A similar situation can be seen centering around meat offered to idols (1 Cor. 8:1–13; 10:23–33). The strong have knowledge that an idol is nothing (vv. 4–6). They have adopted a libertarian approach and believe that "everything is permissible" (10:23). The weak possess no such knowledge, and experience a great moral conflict because of the actions of the strong (8:7–13).

The weak judge the freedom of the strong as impiety; the strong scoff at the convictions of the weak. Such tensions between believers threaten the very unity of the church.

Paul addresses the issue as follows. Because God is the Creator of all things, nothing is unclean in and of itself (Rom. 14:14, 20; 1 Cor. 8:8; 10:26). Food and observance of holy days have nothing at all to do with salvation—they are *adiaphora,* of no spiritual consequence. We are no better off for partaking or abstaining, because these things are of no significance to the kingdom of God. It is for this reason that Paul identifies with the strong (Rom. 14:14; 1 Cor. 8:4–6; 10:25–27, 29–31).

Paul sees that the bottom line issue is the spiritual intentions that lie behind the practices of believers. Both the strong and the weak have failed in this regard. The strong are failing to act out of love and are placing stumbling blocks before the weak that threaten to destroy them spiritually. The weak doubt that God is able to make the strong stand. Both the strong and the weak have usurped the divine prerogative by judging one another (Rom. 14:1, 4, 10–13).

Paul addresses the tensions between the weak and the strong on both the personal and community levels. Believers are not to argue over matters of personal piety (Rom. 14:1). Rather, they should be fully convinced in their own minds and not do anything that conflicts with their consciences (14:5, 14). Their personal convictions about what is permissible need to come from sincere faith, be kept to themselves, and not be made a norm for the whole community (14:22–23).

On the community level, there is to be mutual acceptance and tolerance, because the conduct of both the strong and the weak comes from genuine devotion to God (Rom. 14:6–8). Jesus Christ is the model for actualizing the freedom of believers in the church (vv. 9, 15, 18). We are prohibited from doing anything that might harm or destroy other believers (Rom. 14:13, 15, 20–21; 1 Cor. 8:9–13). Everything we do is to be done in love, for the purpose of mutual edification and peace (Rom. 14:19). WILLIAM A. SIMMONS

See also CORINTHIANS, FIRST AND SECOND, THEOLOGY OF; ETHICS; FREEDOM.

Bibliography. C. E. B. Cranfield, *Romans: A Shorter Commentary;* V. Furnish, *The Love Command in the New Testament;* P. W. Gooch, *NTS* 33/2 (1987): 244–54; idem, *Crux* 13/2 (1976): 10–20; V. Jack, *Christian Brethren Review* 38 (1987): 35–47; R. J. Karris, *CBQ* 35/2 (1973): 155–78; P. S. Minear, *The Obedience of Faith: The Purposes of Paul in the Epistle of Romans;* R. L. Omanson, *BT* 33/1 (1983): 106–14.

Stumbling Block. *See* OFFENSE.

Suffering. The experience of physical pain and/or mental distress. The words and phrases in the Bible expressing this concept are too numerous to list. The Old Testament, intertestamental literature, and the New Testament present two perspectives on human suffering. On the one hand, suffering is the consequence of the flawed nature of creation. In this view human beings—with the exception of the first man and woman—are victims, exposed constantly to the perils of a created order gone away. On the other hand, a person's suffering is the direct consequence of his or her violation of God's laws. The same can be true of a collective.

Suffering as the Consequence of the Flawed Nature of Creation. On account of the disobedience of Eve and then Adam, a wretched legacy has been bequeathed to the human race. God cursed the ground, so that human beings can stay alive only through much toil; the pain of childbirth is greatly increased for all women (Gen. 3:16–19); death and all the suffering attendant upon dying have entered the world (Gen. 2:17).

In this context, the prophets speak about a future time when much of the suffering caused by the flawed creation will be removed for a restored Israel, often with benefits accruing to the nations (Isa. 11:6–9; 25:6–9; 65:17–25; Hos. 2:21; Amos 9:11–15). Isaiah 65:17 actually speaks of the creation of a new heaven and a new earth.

In line with the eschatological promises of the prophets, many intertestamental sources anticipate a time in the future when Israel will be restored to the land in a state of prosperity, sometimes with the help of a messianic figure. Some texts call this the kingdom of God (e.g., Pss. Sol. 17; T. Mos. 10:1). Often there is a differentiation made between this age/world and the age/world to come; the latter follows the resurrection and judgment and is the domain of the righteous alone (4 Ezra; 2 Apoc. Bar.; early rabbinic writings). The age/world to come for the righteous is to be an existence of blessedness, without suffering. In this vein, 1 Enoch 45:4–5 speaks about the transformation of the heaven and the earth, at which time the Elect One, the Messiah, will dwell on earth with the righteous. In many intertestamental texts, Satan is viewed as a contributing cause of the flawed nature of creation and, therefore, the suffering of human beings, so that his removal—and along with him all of his demonic subordinates—is expected at the eschaton (e.g., T. Mos. 10:1; T. Levi 18:12; T. Judah 25:3; T. Zebulon 9:8; T. Dan. 5:10–11; 6:3; 1 Enoch 1; 10:13–16; 54:6; 55; 69:28–29; 90:24; Jub. 23:29; 1QS 4; 11QMelch).

The New Testament continues what is found in the Old Testament and the intertestamental texts. Paul writes that the creation, subject to futility, awaits its liberation from its bondage to destruction, groaning as if in the pangs of childbirth (Rom. 8:19–22). Similarly, in 2 Peter 3:13 and Revelation 21:1, the Isaian concept of the new heaven and new earth finds expression. Paul attributes the tyranny of death, "the last enemy" (1 Cor. 15:26), to the sin of Adam, the effects of which reach to all human beings and are nullified by the death and resurrection of Christ (Rom. 5:12–17; 1 Cor. 15:20–22). The New Testament also assumes that creation is flawed as a result of the activity of Satan and allied spirits, who wreak havoc on human existence (e.g., Mark 9:14–27 = Luke 9:37–43).

Unlike the Old Testament and intertestamental texts, however, the New Testament understands the flawed nature of creation to have been at least partially rectified, inasmuch as the influence of Satan and allied spirits on it has been curtailed through the appearance, death, and resurrection of the Messiah. Jesus understands his healings and exorcisms as an assault on the kingdom of Satan (Matt. 12:25–29 = Mark 3:23–27 = Luke 11:17–22; Luke 10:18–20; John 12:31; 16:11). Paul speaks of the exaltation of Christ over all spiritual beings (Eph. 1:19–22; Col. 2:15), and describes believers as those who have been rescued from the kingdom of darkness and brought into the kingdom of the Son (Col. 1:13; cf. 1 Peter 2:9).

Suffering as the Consequence of Sin. In the Old Testament, the intertestamental literature, and the New Testament, suffering more frequently is causally linked to the sins of the descendants of the first man and woman. God established a moral order in creation, with the result that retributive justice is meted out in life experience. In this worldview, the appearance of suffering in human experience is not random, but has its causal antecedents in an individual's or community's moral decisions. Retributive justice is sometimes conceived as the working out of a moral law imminent in creation, as in the Book of Proverbs. At other times, it is the direct judgment of God manifesting itself through such things as drought, disease, or foreign invasion.

Collective Suffering. In the Old Testament, nations fall under God's judgment for their disregard of God's will. Nineveh faces imminent judgment on account of the collective guilt of its inhabitants; national repentance forestalls the wrath of God (Book of Jonah). The nations of Moab, Edom, and Philistia are singled out for judgment because of their hostile foreign policy toward Judah (Ezek. 25:8–17). Babylon, though the instrument of God's judgment against Judah, is also destined for judgment for its atrocities committed against the nation (Isa. 21; Jer. 50–51).

Israel's covenant at Sinai is a special historical manifestation of the principle of retributive justice. The people are placed conditionally under the Torah: obedience brings blessing, while disobedience brings destruction or exile (Deut. 27–28). In this regard, the Book of Esther stands in contrast to Lamentations. The former is a testimony to God's protection granted to his obedient people against their enemies. "For such a time as this" God raises up Queen Esther to bring deliverance to Israel. On the other hand, Lamentations places the blame for the destruction of Jerusalem squarely on the shoulders of the apostate nation. The Book of Judges, similarly, interprets Israel's suffering through foreign domination as stemming from national disobedience to the law (2:6–23).

Israel's situation differs from that of other nations, for God, on account of the patriarchs, has promised never ultimately to destroy his people, even when they sin (Lev. 26:42; Ps. 106:40–46). This may necessitate, however, that God discipline the nation when disobedient to the Torah, so that at times it may appear that God favors the nations more than Israel.

It could also happen that the sin of a minority or even one individual within Israel could have consequences for the nation. The fate of the nation as a corporate entity is bound up intricately with the moral decisions of its individual members. Achan, for instance, disobeys God, but the whole nation is defeated in battle as a consequence of his disobedience (Josh. 7).

Individual sins also have intergenerational consequences. The sins of a man will adversely affect his descendants: "Yet he [God] does not leave the guilty unpunished; he punishes the children and their children for the sin of the fathers to the third and fourth generations" (Exod. 34:7; cf. also Exod. 20:5; Num. 14:18; Deut. 5:9–10).

The notion that national calamity originates with national sin prevails in the intertestamental literature. The Maccabean crisis was interpreted as resulting from the sin of the nation; Antiochus's persecution was really God's discipline of an unruly people (cf. 1 Macc. 1:64; 2 Macc. 6:13–16; 7:18, 32–33, 37–38; Jub. 23; T. Mos. 8). Similarly, Pompey's intervention in the internal affairs of the Jewish nation, which brought about much suffering and death to some Jews, was understood as precipitated by national sin (cf. Pss. Sol. 2, 8, 17–18). Later, in the context of the destruction of the Jerusalem temple, the deuteronomistic principle that invasion by foreign powers is God's chastisement of Israel for its sins is reiterated (2 Apoc. Bar. 1:5; 78:3–4; 79:2).

A new element in the intertestamental sources is the notion that the judgment of Israel's Gentile oppressors takes place as part of Israel's eschatological vindication (cf. also the Book of Daniel). As in the Old Testament, it is sometimes asserted that, although the Gentile nations are God's instruments of discipline, they are nonetheless in line for similar treatment at the hands of God. In some texts, the deliverance expected on completion of God's discipline of the nation through foreign domination is the eschatological deliverance foretold in the prophets. One Enoch 90, 93, Jubilees 23, and Testament of Moses 8–10, for example see the Antiochean persecution as precipitating the final, eschatological deliverance of God, whereas Psalms of Solomon and 4 Ezra look for messianic deliverance from Roman oppression.

The idea that national suffering is consequent on disobedience to God is continued in the New Testament. Jesus warns that Israel's rejection of the kingdom of God will lead to the visitation of God's wrath on the nation (Matt. 12:38–45 = Luke 11:29–32; Matt. 21:33–46 = Mark 12:1–12 = Luke 20:9–19; Matt. 23:33–38; Luke 13:6–8; 19:41–44). Paul, likewise, believes that the nation is temporarily rejected by God until the fullness of the Gentiles has come in (Rom. 11). Cities are also threatened with judgment on account of their rejection of Jesus or his emissaries (Matt. 11:20–24 = Luke 10:13–15).

Individual Suffering. Apart from an individual's suffering because of his or her belonging to a nation under God's judgment or on account of the sins of a previous generation, the Old Testament (with some exceptions), the intertestamental texts, and the New Testament portray God as dealing with each human being on the principle of retributive justice. When the righteous do suffer, the need for theodicy arises: in order for God to be exonerated from the charge of being unjust, justification for the apparently anomalous situation of the suffering of the righteous must be found.

In the Old Testament, that the principle of retributive justice is operative in the existence of each human being comes to expression most clearly in Proverbs and Psalms. In Proverbs wisdom and the fear of Yahweh are correlated with long life and prosperity; conversely, the wicked and the foolish will die prematurely and be deprived of earthly goods (2:21–22; 3:9–10, 33–34; 5:23; 9:11; 10:3, 16, 24, 27; 11:19, 21, 27–28; 16:31;

24:19–20; 29:25). Likewise, many psalms are premised on the notion that Yahweh blesses those who are righteous—those who desire to obey him and habitually do so—and protects those who take refuge in him. The wicked, on the other hand, he destroys. Psalm 1, for example, compares the man whose delight is in the Torah of Yahweh to a tree planted by streams of water bearing fruit in its season; the wicked, on the other hand, are compared to chaff blown away by the wind.

But the Old Testament also gives evidence of the irregular working out of the principle of retributive justice. Sometimes, the application of the principle is delayed, so that the righteous suffer for a period of time before vindication. At other times, the correlation between righteousness and longevity/prosperity in this life breaks down altogether. Three types of justification are offered in the Old Testament for the suffering of the righteous: eschatological, remedial, and expiatory.

In the Daniel apocalypse, the suffering of those who are "wise" (11:35) is an eschatological necessity. The period of time in which the temple is defiled and the righteous are oppressed is predetermined, established according to the divine timetable. The individual righteous person is at the mercy of the larger historical designs of God. Nonetheless, at the judgment of the dead, God will vindicate those who are martyred, raising them to everlasting life (Dan. 12).

The suffering of the righteous also has a remedial function. God disciplines the righteous individual, taking preventative and corrective measures in order to keep the heart of the righteous from turning away from him. Proverbs 3:11–12 says: "My son, do not despise the LORD's discipline, and do not resent his rebuke, because the LORD disciplines those he loves as a father the son he delights in" (cf. also Ps. 94:12; Dan. 11:35).

In the Servant Songs of Isaiah, the suffering and death of the servant has a vicarious and expiatory purpose (Isa. 53). Although in these texts (Isa. 42, 44, 49, 50, 52–53) the servant is often a collective noun denoting Israel, in Isaiah 53 the servant clearly is an individual who suffers on behalf of the collective, the people. Daniel 11:35 is another example of the suffering of the righteous having an expiatory effect.

In the intertestamental literature the three explanations for the suffering of the righteous found in the Old Testament also appear.

The eschatological argument for the suffering of the righteous figures prominently in many texts. The application of God's retributive justice is postponed, so that the righteous suffer unjustly in this life. The righteous are urged, therefore, to be patient in their suffering and to wait for the eschatological judgment and salvation of God, at which time they will receive the blessing due to them, whereas the wicked, who are often the oppressors of the righteous, will be punished and destroyed (cf. 2 Macc. 6–7; 1 Enoch 102:3–103:15; 104:6–8; 108:3; 2 Enoch 9:1; 50:1–6; 51:3–5; 65:6–11; 66:6; 4 Ezra 7:18; 2 Apoc. Bar. 14:1–19; 15:7–8; 24:1–2; 44:13–14; Wis. 1–5). Often human wickedness and the persecution of the righteous are expected to intensify greatly just prior to the final judgment and salvation of God (cf. Jub. 23; 1 Enoch 100:1–3; 107; Sib. Or. 3.632–51; 1QH 3:29–36; 2 Apoc. Bar. 25–29; 70–71; 4 Ezra 5:1–13; 8:50; 9:1–6; 16:70–73).

Continuing what is found in the Wisdom Literature of the Old Testament, many texts understand the sufferings of the righteous as being remedial: they are one of God's means of preserving the righteous as such, thereby retaining for them the benefits of being righteous in either this life or the next. The attitude of the one afflicted should be that of acceptance and even joy that God would relate to him or her as a father who disciplines his children (cf. Sir. 16:12; 18:13–14; 22:27–23:3; Wis. 3:5; Pss. Sol. 10:1–2; 13:9–10; 14:1; 16:1–11; Jdt. 8:27; 1QH 2:13–14; 9:23–24).

Although the suffering servant seems not to have played a major role in shaping the conceptualities of the extant literature of the intertestamental period, the notion of vicarious suffering and death does crop up now and then, paralleling what is found in Daniel 11:35. The Maccabean martyrs are said to bring God's judgment of the nation to an end (4 Macc. 1:11; 6:29; 17:21; T. Mos. 9:6–10:1), and the Qumran community understood its own suffering as expiatory (1QS 8:3–6; cf. also Sir. 2:4–5). A cornerstone of early rabbinic theology is the view that God manifests his mercy to the righteous in this age, in that he allows their suffering, when received with equanimity, to expiate the guilt generated by previous sins (Sipre Deut. 6:5 [32]; Mek. Bahodesh 10:1–86).

The three explanations for the suffering of the righteous individual found in the Old Testament—eschatological, remedial, expiatory—also occur in the New Testament. In addition, a fourth explanation, unique to it, appears: Paul writes that suffering has the effect of ensuring his dependence on the power of God in his apostolic labors.

In the Beatitudes Jesus teaches that the appearance of the kingdom of God will bring an eschatological reversal, so that the righteous who now suffer will no longer (Matt. 5:3–12; Luke 6:20–26). Jesus also warns his disciples that their suffering will be an eschatological necessity; until the consummation of the kingdom of God, those who follow him and especially those who proclaim him will experience resistance and hostility from those on the outside (or, to use Johannine terminology, "the world"), especially during the period just prior to the end (cf. Matt. 10:19–23 = Luke 12:11; Matt. 20:22–23 = Mark 10:38–39; Matt. 24:9–10 = Mark 13:9–11 = Luke 21:12–18; John 7:6–11; 15:18–25; 17:14). The idea of the eschatological necessity of suffering is also found in the rest of the New Testament (Rom. 8:16–18; Gal. 3:3–4; Phil. 1:27–30; 1 Thess. 1–3; 2 Thess. 1:4–10; Heb. 10:32–34; James 5:11; 1 Peter 2:18–20; 3:13–4:19; Rev. 2:10; 4–22).

The remedial view comes to expression most prominently in the letter to the Hebrews (12:3–13). The author instructs his readers to "endure hardship as discipline; God is treating you as sons" (v. 7), quoting Proverbs 3:11–12 to make the point. The Book of James similarly identifies trials as a means of engendering holiness (1:2–3), as does 1 Peter 1:3–9. Paul also believes that God disciplines believers in order to bring about repentance (1 Cor. 5:1–8; 2 Cor. 11:17–33; 1 Tim. 1:20).

Jesus interprets his death as expiatory and vicarious. At the Last Supper he understands himself as the eschatological Passover lamb (Matt. 26:26–28 = Mark 14:22–24; Luke 22:19–20). He also interprets his impending fate as the fulfillment of the destiny of the suffering servant (Matt. 20:28 = Mark 10:45; Luke 22:37). A presupposition of the message preached by the early church was that Jesus' death was vicarious and expiatory. In two passages outside the Gospels it is explicit that Jesus' death is the fulfillment of the vicarious and expiatory death of the servant (Acts 8:32–33; 1 Peter 2:21–25).

There is a fourth interpretation of the suffering of the righteous individual that comes to expression in the New Testament. Paul interprets his own suffering as a means of ensuring that he be ever conscious of his own weakness, so that he remembers always that the power at work in him is from God and not himself and so that he is not deluded into relying on his own power (2 Cor. 1:8–10; 4:7–12). Similarly, Paul says God sent him a "thorn in the flesh" to keep him from becoming conceited on account of his surpassingly great revelations (2 Cor. 12:7).

The Books of Job and Ecclesiastes. Generally, in the Old Testament, God deals with human beings on the principle of retributive justice. If the righteous do suffer it must be for a reason, which functions as a valid exception to the moral principle that the righteous prosper and the wicked suffer. But there are some cases of the suffering of the righteous impervious to theodicy. That sometimes the righteous suffer for no apparent reason is the thesis of the Book of Job. Job suffers, yet he is righteous. Although his comforters defend the principle of retributive justice and conclude that Job cannot be innocent, as he claims, the reader knows that they are wrong: Job speaks truly about his moral condition. In the end God never explains to Job the point of his suffering (although the reader is aware of Satan's involvement); instead, he asks Job a series of rhetorical questions designed to make the pint that some things are beyond human comprehension. Job is to accept his suffering without questioning god's wisdom or justice.

The Book of Ecclesiastes also questions the causal relation between righteousness and prosperity. In the author's experience, the fates of the righteous and the wicked are opposite of what they should be, which only adds to the meaninglessness of life (7:15; 8:14; but cf. 12:13–14).

BARRY D. SMITH

See also DISCIPLINE; ECCLESIASTES, THEOLOGY OF; JOB, THEOLOGY OF; JUSTICE; PERSECUTION; PROVIDENCE OF GOD.

Bibliography. J. Carmignac, *Revue de Qumran* 3 (1961): 365–86; J. L. Crenshaw, *A Whirlpool of Torment;* idem, *Theodicy in the Old Testament;* C. S. Lewis, *The Problem of Pain;* J. S. Pobee, *Persecution and Martyrdom in the Theology of Paul;* D. Sölle, *Suffering;* J. A. Sanders, *Suffering as Divine Discipline in the Old Testament and Post-Biblical Judaism.*

Sunday. *See* LORD'S DAY, THE.

Synagogue. The synagogue was the place where Jews gathered for instruction and worship in the New Testament period. The Greek word *synagōgē* means "assembly" and can refer simply to the gathering of people itself (James 2:2) or to the building in which they gather (Luke 7:5). The origins of the synagogue are obscure, but they probably extend back at least to the period of Ezra. At the time of the New Testament, synagogues were found throughout the Roman Empire as local centers for the study of the law and for worship. As such, they served a different role in the life of the Jewish people than did the Jerusalem temple, with its focus on the sacrificial cult.

Synagogue services included prayers, the reading of Scripture, and, usually, a sermon explaining the Scripture. The chief administrative officer was the synagogue ruler (Mark 5:22; Luke 13:14; Acts 13:15; 18:8, 17), who was assisted by an executive officer who handled the details of the synagogue service (Luke 4:20). Laypeople were allowed to participate in the services, especially in the reading of the prayers and the Scripture (Luke 4:16–20). Visiting sages could be invited to provide the sermon (Luke 4:21; Acts 13:15). Synagogues were attended by both men and women, as well as by God-fearing Gentiles who were committed to learning more about the God of the Jews (Acts 17:4, 12).

In the New Testament synagogues are occasionally mentioned merely in their role as Jewish institutions. The people at Capernaum, for example, commend to Jesus a certain centurion as one who "loves our nation and has built our synagogue" (Luke 7:5). At the Jerusalem council James notes that "Moses has been preached in every city from the earliest times and is read in the synagogues on every Sabbath" (Acts 15:21). Paul, at his trial before Felix, observes that his accusers "did not find me arguing with anyone at the temple, or stirring up a crowd in the synagogues or anywhere else" in Jerusalem (Acts 24:12). Indeed, in an early letter to Jewish Christians James even refers to their gatherings as "synagogues" (2:2).

Yet for the most part synagogues take on a larger meaning in the New Testament. In particular, synagogues frequently serve as places of God's revelatory activity. At several points the Gospel writers' summaries of Jesus' ministry include preaching or teaching "in their synagogues" (Matt. 4:23; 9:35; Mark 1:39; Luke 4:15; cf. Luke 4:44). Specifically, Jesus teaches in the synagogues at Nazareth (Matt. 13:53–58; Mark 6:1–6; Luke 4:16–30) and Capernaum (Mark 1:21–22; John 6:59), casts out an evil spirit from a man in the synagogue at Capernaum (Mark 1:23–27), heals a man with a withered hand in an unspecified Galilean synagogue (Matt. 12:9–14; Mark 3:1–6; Luke 6:6–11), and heals a woman crippled for eighteen years in another (Luke 13:10–17). Indeed, Luke's account of the Nazareth incident includes a programmatic self-revelation by Jesus of the very nature of his ministry (4:16–21).

A similar situation holds in the Book of Acts. Stephen argues powerfully in the Synagogue of the Freedmen in Jerusalem (6:9–10); Paul preaches in the synagogues of Damascus shortly after his conversion (9:20–22); and Apollos preaches boldly in the synagogue of Ephesus (18:26). Indeed, once he begins his missionary journeys Paul consistently uses the synagogue as his initial platform for preaching the gospel as he moves from one city to the next. As was the case with Jesus' synagogue appearance in Luke 4, so also Luke's account of Paul's teaching in the synagogue at Pisidian Antioch not only contains a prototypical sermon (13:16–46) but also a self-revelatory statement concerning Paul's role as missionary to the Gentiles (13:46–47). Clearly, synagogues are places where both Jews and Gentiles hear the Word of God proclaimed by God's chosen agents.

Yet despite this display of divine power and teaching in the synagogues, the response of those who encounter Jesus and the apostles in them is mixed. To be sure, those in the Capernaum synagogue are amazed at Jesus' actions, recognize his unique authority, and spread the news about him (Mark 1:22, 27–28). But in the Nazareth synagogue an initial amazement turns to offense and Jesus' own amazement at the people's lack of faith (Matt. 13:54–58; Mark 6:2–6; Luke 4:22–23). In Luke's account the people become so furious with Jesus that they try to throw him down the cliff (4:28–29). John's account of Jesus' bread of life discourse in the synagogue at Capernaum ends with a similar turning against Jesus, though not with violence (6:41–42, 52, 60–61, 66). The two synagogue healings occur on the Sabbath and thus raise the question of Jesus' understanding of the Sabbath commandment; after the one healing the synagogue ruler is indignant with Jesus (Luke 13:14), and as a result of the other the Pharisees begin to plot to kill Jesus (Matt. 12:14; Mark 3:6).

Again the situation in Acts is similar. Paul's synagogue preaching frequently results in Jews and Gentiles coming to faith (13:42–44, 48 [Pisidian Antioch]; 14:1 [Iconium]; 17:1–4 [Thessalonica], 10–12 [Berea]; cf. 18:4–8 [Corinth], 20 [Ephesus]). Yet members of the Synagogue of the Freedmen oppose Stephen and bring about his martyrdom (6:9–14); an initial astonishment on the part of the Jews in Damascus turns into a conspiracy to kill Paul (9:21–24); and Jews oppose Paul's synagogue preaching in Pisidian Antioch (13:45), Corinth (18:6), and Ephesus (19:9). Jewish opposition is such that in Corinth and Ephesus Paul is forced to move his teaching outside the synagogue (18:7; 19:9), and in Pisidian Antioch he is even expelled from the region (13:50). In addition, in both Pisidian Antioch and Corinth Paul responds to the opposition by resolving to turn his attention to the Gentiles (13:46; 18:6). Thus, synagogues serve as places where both Jews and Gentiles respond positively to the Word of God, yet also where other Jews oppose it. They therefore serve a certain transition role as the proclamation of the gospel moves from a focus on Jews and God-fearing Gentiles (within the synagogue) to one directed primarily to Gentiles (outside the synagogue).

The opposition that Paul encounters in certain synagogues is consistent with Jesus' warnings that synagogues will be places of persecution. Jesus tells his disciples that they will be delivered to synagogue authorities (Luke 12:11; 21:12), flogged in synagogues (Matt. 10:17; 23:34; Mark 13:9), and even put out of synagogues (John 16:2). The pre-Christian Paul himself travels from synagogue to synagogue in his relentless zeal to imprison, beat, and otherwise punish Christians (Acts 9:2; 22:19; 26:11).

Despite such warnings and instances of persecution, certain synagogue rulers fare well in the New Testament. Jesus responds to Jarius' plea by raising his twelve-year-old daughter from the dead (Matt. 9:18–19, 23–25; Mark 5:21–24, 35–43; Luke 8:40–42, 49–56); the synagogue rulers at Pisidian Antioch invite Paul and Barnabas to preach (Acts 13:15); and Crispus and his household are among the small number of Jews at Corinth who believe in the Lord (Acts 18:8). Yet one synagogue ruler is indignant when Jesus heals a crippled woman on the Sabbath (Luke 13:14), and another, Sosthenes (who may have become a Christian later; cf. 1 Cor. 1:1), is beaten by his fellow Jews at Corinth when their legal maneuvers against Paul fail (Acts 18:17).

Some associated with synagogues do not fare as well as the synagogue rulers. Jesus criticizes those who flaunt their religiosity by seeking recognition in the synagogues for their almsgiving and prayer (Matt. 6:2, 5) and loving the most important seats in the synagogue (Matt. 23:6; Mark 12:39; Luke 11:43; 20:46). These people are variously identified as teachers of the law (Mark 12:39; Luke 20:46), Pharisees (Luke 11:43), teachers of the law and Pharisees (Matt. 23:6), and hypocrites (6:2, 5). Such criticism indicts neither synagogues nor the majority of the Jews who attend them, but it does show how synagogues could be misused by those concerned with self-promotion.

The harshest words concerning synagogues are found in the Book of Revelation. In the letters to the seven churches Jesus twice speaks of the synagogue of Satan (2:9; 3:9). He notes that these people claim to be Jews, but are not; rather, they are liars and are guilty of slander. Such individuals will be responsible for the coming persecution of the church at Smyrna (2:10) and will be brought to fall down before the church at Philadelphia and acknowledge that Jesus has loved it (3:9). Such language seems to be indicative of the widening gulf between Judaism and Christianity by the end of the first century and of the tendency to view the church increasingly in terms formerly associated with the Jews (cf. 1:5–6; 7:3–17; 14:1–5; 21:9–22:5).

JOSEPH L. TRAFTON

See also CHURCH, THE; ISRAEL; JEWS, JUDAISM; PHARISEES.

Bibliography. J. Gutman, ed., *The Synagogue: Studies in Origins, Archaeology, and Architecture;* L. I. Levine, ed., *Ancient Synagogues Revealed;* idem, *The Synagogue in Late Antiquity;* E. M. Meyers and R. Hachili, *ABD,* 6:251–63; S. Safrai, *The Jewish People in the First Century,* 2:908–44.

Tt

Tabernacle. The structure referred to in Scripture as the tabernacle was the center of the worship of Yahweh by the people of Israel from shortly after the exodus until it was replaced by Solomon's temple around 960 B.C. The term "tabernacle" is sometimes used to refer to one part of a larger complex: the tent-like structure that stood within a court enclosed by linen curtains. At other times the term describes the entire complex. The inner structure was comprised of gold-plated planks linked together and standing on edge. They formed three sides of a rectangle, with the fourth closed by a heavy curtain. The whole was draped with several layers of cloth and leather. Here God was understood to be especially present for his people. Even more important, the tabernacle and the sacrificial system connected with it are understood by the Bible to be richly symbolic of truths concerning God and the possibility of human fellowship with him.

The first references to the tabernacle appear in Exodus 25, where Moses begins to receive the instructions for making this structure. These instructions continue through chapter 31. Then, after a three-chapter interlude dealing with the golden calf episode and its aftermath, chapter 35 resumes the story of the tabernacle, reporting how the complex was built. This report repeats the previous instructions almost word for word. The report carries on through chapter 40, where the book reaches its climactic conclusion with God's glory filling the tabernacle.

Part of the significance of the tabernacle is seen through the placement of this block of material in the Book of Exodus. The book contains three segments: chapters 1–15, the account of the deliverance from Egypt, culminating in the Red Sea crossing; chapters 16–24, the account of the journey to Sinai, culminating in the sealing of the covenant; and chapters 25–40, the account of the building of the tabernacle, culminating in its being filled with the glory of God. This literary structure shows that the ultimate need of the people was not for deliverance from physical oppression or from theological darkness, but from alienation from God. Deliverance from bondage and from spiritual darkness are not ends, but means to the end of fellowship with God. This is the significance of the title "tabernacle (or "tent," Heb. ʾōhel) of meeting." Apparently first applied to the interim tent where Moses met God before the tabernacle was complete (33:7), the phrase aptly sums up the function of the tabernacle. Not only does the structure symbolize the presence of God with his people; it also shows how it is that sinful people can come into, and live in, the presence of a holy God.

The incident of the golden calf, which is reported between the instructions for the tabernacle and its building, highlights both the significance and function of the tabernacle. The people recognized they needed divine protection and guidance, especially in the light of Moses' inexplicable failure to return from the mountain (32:1). And they were sure they could not have these unless God was tangibly present with them. The tragedy of the story is that at the very moment they were demanding that Aaron meet their needs, God was giving Moses the instructions that would meet those needs in a much more complete way than Aaron's feeble efforts ever could.

When human needs are met in God's way the results far surpass anything we could conceive on our own. The golden calf could hardly compare to the tabernacle. In the tabernacle there was beauty of design, color, texture, and shape. There was a satisfying diversity in objects and spaces. There was a sense of motion through separate stages from the profane to the sacred. There was a profound, yet evident, symbolism capable of conveying multiple truths to different persons.

Moreover, the impact upon people is profoundly different when our needs are met in God's way. Here, instead of limited gifts and no participation (32:3–4), everyone has something to contribute, whether in talent or material (35:4–10). Here persons give freely, without coercion (35:21, contra 32:2). Here work is done according to Spirit-imparted gifts, not according to rank or appearance (35:30–36:2). And here, instead of further alienation from God (32:9), the glory of God's presence is revealed in the midst of human life (40:35).

Thus, Exodus 32–34 is an integral part of the whole final segment of the book, illustrating by contrast the same truths that chapters 25–31 and 35–40 teach in a positive way.

Beyond a tangible representation of the presence of God, the tabernacle also is intended to teach by visual means the theological principles whereby that presence is possible. It is necessary to exercise care at this point because the Bible does not explain all the visual symbolism, and it is possible to expend too much energy in speculation. However, the main lines are clear enough. The color white, which was especially prominent in the linen curtains of the court, calls attention to the purity of God and the necessary purity of those who would live in his presence. Blue speaks of God's transcendence; purple, of his royalty; and red, of the blood that must be shed if a holy God is ever to live with a sinful human. The accents of gold and silver that occurred throughout the structure speak of the riches of the divine kingdom and its blessings. Possibly the multiple coverings over the Holy Place and the Holy of Holies speak of the security that attends those who live with God.

The most significant symbolism is surely that found in the arrangement of spaces and objects. The court itself speaks of the separation between God and the sinner. It is impossible for us to come into the presence of God in our normal state. This gulf is further reinforced by the veil at the door of the Holy Place, and by the one that closed off the Holy of Holies. It is impossible that good intentions and honest effort can ever bring us to God. We come in the ways he has dictated, or not at all.

Then, how is it possible for us to come into that Presence which is life itself? The tabernacle shows the way. The first object encountered is the altar. Here, in the starkest visual terms, is the representation of the truth that "without the shedding of blood there is no forgiveness" (Heb. 9:22). But the altar raises its own questions: How can a bull or a sheep or a goat die in the place of a person who has been made just a little lower than God himself (Mic. 6:6–8)? For the Old Testament believer, the solution to this enigma was, in many ways, a mystery. Nevertheless, there is no other way to the Holy of Holies than past the altar.

Behind the altar is the laver. Here we are reminded that God is clean. "Clean" describes the essential character of God, who is faithful, upright, merciful, and true. To be unclean is to fail to share that character, and that which does not share God's character cannot exist in his white-hot presence (Isa. 6:5). Thus, it is necessary for those who would come into his presence to be washed and made clean (Ps. 51:7), and the laver represents both that necessity and that possibility.

Inside the Holy Place three objects demand attention. On the right is a table with twelve loaves of bread on it. In pagan temples this is where the gods were believed to sit and eat. But in Israel's tabernacle this is where God was understood to feed his people (Ps. 23:5). He had no need of food (Ps. 50:12–13), but Israel was famished for him (Ps. 107:9; Isa. 65:13). On the left was the lampstand where the light was never permitted to go out. This represented the light that God was to his people in the darkened world of sin (Ps. 27:1). Directly in front of the worshiper at the far end of the space was the altar of incense. Here incense burned day and night, symbolizing both the sacred presence and the prayer of worshipers that can rise to God like sweet perfume at any moment of the day (Ps. 141:2; Rev. 8:3–4). Thus, the objects in the Holy Place were the evidence of the blessings that are for those who live in the presence of God: light, sustenance, and communion.

In all the pagan temples the innermost space was reserved for the idol, the visual expression of the pagan insistence that the divine is clothed with this world, and that this world is the body of the divine. Alone of all the ancient peoples, the Hebrews insisted this is not true. God is not part of this world, and may not be represented by any natural object. So what was in the innermost space of the tabernacle? A box! We usually refer to the object with the A.D. 1611 term "ark," but that is just an archaic word for "box." A box to represent the presence of God? To be sure it was a beautifully ornamented box, with winged figures of some sort molded into its golden top. But for all that, it was still just a box.

Why would the Hebrews use something as mundane as a box to convey the presence of the almighty God? Negatively, a box simply cannot be worshiped as somehow being God. It is neither a human figure nor a natural object. To be sure, some translations have God sitting "upon" the cherubim, but the Hebrew does not use the preposition "upon." Rather, it uses no preposition, or "with respect to"—a clear attempt to avoid even that potential confusion of object and reality. If it is desired to have an object that will remind persons of God's real presence while underscoring the prohibition of images, a box is an excellent choice.

But the ark has positive significance as well. It represents the true basis of divine-human relations. Those relations do not rest upon ritualistic manipulation—magic—as idol-worship assumes. Rather, the basis is covenant, a relationship of mutual commitment whereby grace is responded to in obedience, especially on an ethical plane. Surrender, trust, and obedience are the operative principles, not magical identification. How appropriate that all these truths should be represented in the box in the Holy of Holies. Aaron's rod represents the delivering grace of God, both in the exodus events and in God's selection of the priests as mediators; the manna represents God's sustaining grace; and the tablets of the Ten Commandments summarize the terms of the relationship. The ark tells us that we cannot manipulate the essence of God; we can only remember what he has done for us and relate to him and one another accordingly.

The sad truth is that the human spirit is not able to fulfill the terms of the covenant, no matter how pure the initial intentions may have been. As the Hebrews first broke their covenant with God in less than six weeks, so every human who has ever lived has learned that living for God is not a matter of good intentions. Every one who has ever sought to live for God has discovered that when all has been done, we have fallen far short of God's moral perfection. What then is to be done? The covenant was sworn to with the most solemn oaths. Now it lies broken in the presence of God, calling out for justice. How can God be Justice and Love at the same time? The answer is the "cover" (mercy-seat). The Hebrew word for the nullification of the effects of sin is *kāpar*, "to cover." It is surely not a coincidence that the lid of the box is called "the cover." For this lid not only covers what it is in the box; it is also the place where covering for sin, particularly unconscious sin, is made once a year through sprinkling the blood of a sacrificial animal upon that cover (Lev. 16:11–17). The broken covenant, calling out for the death of those who swore in the name of God that they would be obedient or die, was satisfied by a representive sacrificial death.

But this brings to the fore the question raised by the great altar in the court outside. If the fundamental tenet of the Hebrew faith, God's transcendence, is true, if God cannot be magically manipulated through the creation, then of what ultimate good is the sacrifice of one bull, or, for that matter, tens of thousands of bulls? This seems a hopeless dilemma. God's justice cannot be satisfied magically, but it must be satisfied. God cannot simply ignore it. To do so would be to destroy the whole basis of a world of cause and effect.

This is the dilemma that came to such a dramatic resolution for the persons of the first century A.D., who suddenly realized what the coupling of Jesus Christ's divinity and his unjust death and his glorious resurrection meant. Here was the perfect sacrifice! Here was the one to whom the sacrificial system and the tabernacle pointed. That system and that structure had no magical efficacy in themselves. They were only efficacious in removing sin insofar as they pointed to the One who could indeed die for all. If God could die and then return to life, that death could indeed be in the place of all who would ever live and sin.

This is the vision that captured the writer of the Book of Hebrews and is recorded in chapter 9 of that book. He realized that the tabernacle and the sacrificial system were simply symbolic of an eternal reality. The language used there might suggest that the author thought the earthly tabernacle was a copy of an eternal heavenly one. But to take that position is to miss the point of the passage. The author is saying that the earthly tabernacle and the sacrifices offered there are representative of eternal, spiritual truth: the all-sufficiency of the sacrifice of Christ for all eternity. The tabernacle represents truth, not some other material entity. The author is possibly using the language of Platonic philosophy, but the biblical philosophy of transcendence is diametrically at odds with Plato's insistence that this world is unreal. That the writer of Hebrews knows this is evident in 9:25–26, where he shows that Christ is not being continually sacrificed in some heavenly reality, but that he died once for all here on earth, and so *here* fulfilled what the tabernacle was all about.

JOHN N. OSWALT

See also AARON; ALTAR; ARK; EXODUS, THEOLOGY OF; HEBREWS, THEOLOGY OF; ISRAEL; MOSES; OFFERINGS AND SACRIFICES; PRIEST, PRIESTHOOD; TEMPLE.

Bibliography. P. F. Kiene, *The Tabernacle of God in the Wilderness of Sinai;* M. Levine, *The Tabernacle: Its Structure and Utensils;* S. F. Olford, *The Tabernacle: Camping with God;* S. Ridout, *Lectures on the Tabernacle;* A. B. Simpson, *Christ in the Tabernacle.*

Tabernacles, Feast of. *See* FEASTS AND FESTIVALS OF ISRAEL.

Tammuz. *See* GODS AND GODDESSES, PAGAN.

Teach, Teacher. Although several Hebrew words are translated "teach" in English translations of the Old Testament, two words predominate: *yāră*ᶜ, "to point out," and *lāmad*, "to goad." In the New Testament Greek words more frequently used are *didaskō*, "to teach," *katēcheō*, "to instruct systematically," *mathēteuō*, "to train disciples," *paideuō*, "to train, instruct," *nouthēteō*, "to correct, counsel," *parangellō*, "to command, order," and *paradidō*, "to hand down tradition."

The variety and extent of this biblical vocabulary make it clear that teaching is at the heart of God's plan for redemptive history. God as the ultimate Teacher has mandated in Scripture that teaching occur in two primary contexts, both of which arise from his creative and redemptive acts. God delegates teaching to the family and the redeemed community. Both institutions explain his gracious initiative in redemption and urge a loving, obedient response. God's gracious initiative places his people in covenant relationship with him in which parents teach their children and spiritually gifted leaders of the people of God teach its members. Thus, the following discussion will focus on teaching in the nuclear family and in the extended family, the people of God.

The creation of Adam and Eve signaled the institution of the family (Gen. 1:26–28; 2:18–25; 4:1; 5:1–2). God intended the promises of the Mosaic covenant for parents and their children (Deut. 6:1–2). The fifth commandment underlined the sacred character of the family by commanding children to honor their parents (Exod. 20:12; cf. Deut. 5:16). Cursing one's parents was a capital offense (Exod. 21:15, 17; Deut. 21:18–21; 27:16). The New Testament confirms Old Testament teaching that heterosexual monogamy is the ideal family setting for the teaching of children (Matt. 19:4–6, 19; 1 Cor. 5:1; 6:16; Eph. 5:31; 6:1–3; 1 Peter 3:7).

The Bible repeatedly calls on parents to educate their children concerning the mighty redemptive acts of God and the appropriate response of loyal obedience. Such education should occur in the context of the Passover feast and the consecration of the firstborn (Exod. 13:1–16). In anticipation of entering the promised land, Israel is reminded of God's activity for them and their consequent obligation to obey him and to teach their children to do the same (Deut. 4:1–14, 40; 5:29; 6:1–7, 20–25; 11:19–21). Even after the people were settled in the land, the importance of teaching children was not minimized (Ps. 78:5–8). Proverbs repeatedly enjoins the education of children, with particular stress on sons obeying their fathers and mothers. The New Testament also stresses the teaching role of parents, especially the father (Luke 2:39–52; Rom. 1:30; Eph. 6:1–4; Col. 3:20–21; 1 Tim. 3:4–5, 12; 5:4, 10, 14; 2 Tim. 1:5; 3:2, 15; Titus 1:6; 2:4). The repeated stress of both Old Testament and New Testament on care for widows and orphans indicates that the covenant community is to strengthen the family and, if necessary, serve as a sort of surrogate family setting.

The role of teaching in Israel's family life must be seen in the context of teaching in the Old Testament community. Moses commands parents to teach their children (Exod. 13:9), teaches Israel's elders how to adjudicate civic matters (Exod. 18:20), and assigns responsibility for teaching the law to Aaron and his descendants, the priests and Levites (Lev. 10:11; Deut. 33:10; cf. 2 Chron. 15:3). Upon entering the land, Israel was not to intermarry with its inhabitants because this would result in apostasy (Deut. 7:3–6). Instead, the land's inhabitants were to be eliminated in order to do away with false teaching (Deut. 20:18). David longs for forgiveness and cleansing so that he may teach God's ways to sinners (Ps. 51:6–13). God's covenant with David involved David's sons obeying the laws they were taught (Ps. 132:11). The psalms frequently express longing for a deeper understanding of God's law. Solomon prayed at the dedication of the temple that God in the future would forgive repentant Israel and teach them obedience (1 Kings 8:35–36). Jehoshaphat and Josiah oversaw the teaching of true religion and the overthrow of false religious structures (2 Chron. 17:5–9; 34:33–35:4). After the deportation to Babylon and the return to the land, Ezra and Nehemiah led Israel in studying, obeying, and teaching the law of Moses.

Israel's prophets also have much to say about education. As the archetypical prophet, Moses taught Israel and spoke of a future prophet like himself to whose teaching Israel must give heed (Deut. 18:15–19). The prophets foresee days when all nations will be taught God's ways (Isa. 2:3; 54:13; Mic. 4:2). While Israel has rebelled against God and given their allegiance to false gods, nevertheless, God's power will yet "teach" Israel through judgment and restoration (Jer. 16:14–21). God's chosen Servant will reestablish the law (Isa. 42:1–4) and inaugurate a new covenant that will implant his law in Israel's hearts and supersede the former manner of teaching (Jer. 31:31–34; Ezek. 36:24–27).

In the New Testament Jesus is the Servant of God who inaugurates the new covenant (Matt. 12:17–21; 26:28). His ministry of word and deed and his redemptive sacrifice fulfill the Old Testament prototypes: kings, priests, and prophets. Jesus teaches with divine authority (Matt. 4:23; 5:2; 7:29). His approach to the Old Testament differs from that of Israel's leaders in that his teaching stresses love, justice, and mercy over external matters. After his resurrection and exaltation Jesus sends his apostles forth with the mandate to perpetuate his teachings (Matt. 28:19; John 21:15–17) in the power of the Holy Spirit.

As the Book of Acts makes clear, the earliest Christians took Jesus' mandate seriously as apostolic teaching was featured in their communities. The Spirit sent by Jesus equipped some with the gift of teaching (Rom. 12:7; 1 Cor. 12:28; 14:6, 12, 19, 26; Eph. 4:11; 1 Peter 4:10–11).

The New Testament teaches that those who aspire to leadership in the community have to be competent teachers (1 Tim. 3:2; 2 Tim. 1:13; 2:1, 15; Titus 1:9). God's people are expected to eagerly receive and obey apostolic teaching (Rom. 15:15–16; 1 Cor. 11:2; 2 Thess. 3:6, 14; Heb. 13:7, 17, 22; 2 Peter 3:2).

In the Bible, then, God as Creator and Redeemer teaches his creatures through the agency of two institutions, the family and the covenant community in which families worship God and grow in his grace. This teaching was carried out through the kings, priests, and prophets of the Old Testament theocratic community. These three Old Testament motifs coalesce in Jesus the Messiah, who enables the new covenant community to be taught by spiritually gifted teachers who lead the church. David L. Turner

See also Disciple, Discipleship; Jesus Christ.

Bibliography. W. Barclay, *Train Up a Child: Educational Ideals in the Ancient World;* M. Civil, et al., *ABD,* 2:301–17; J. P. Gammie and L. G. Perdue, eds., *The Sage in Israel and the Ancient Near East;* K. Giles, *Patterns of Ministry among the First Christians;* J. P. Louw and E. A. Nida, eds., *Greek-English Lexicon of the New Testament Based on Semantic Domains,* J. I. H. McDonald, *Kergyma and Didache;* S. Sifrai, *The Jewish People in the First Century,* 2:945–70; K. Wegenast and D. Fürst, *NIDNTT,* 3:759–81; R. C. Worley, *Preaching and Teaching in the Earliest Church;* R. B. Zuck, *BSac* 121 (1964):228–35.

Teaching, Gift of. *See* HOLY SPIRIT, GIFTS OF.

Temple. While the temple certainly has a history and integrity of its own, it was created by extension of the tabernacle and is associated with such diverse topics as a mountain and a city, the cosmos and a person's body, and God's glory and name. The biblical authors from Moses through Ezekiel and Haggai to John of Patmos never describe a complete temple, but offer a vision of what the temple was to be: the locus of the presence of God.

Offering a vision rather than a blueprint for the temple is in keeping with the inherent ambiguity of the concept "temple of the Lord," for how can the transcendent deity be localized in a building? The vision is also in keeping with the function of temple as a symbol. The temple is indeterminate literally and figuratively.

The Preexistence of the Temple. The foundation for temple is laid in the Pentateuch. Already in the patriarchs we find the promise of God's presence: "Do not be afraid, for I am with you, I will bless you" (Gen. 26:24). How and *where* will this presence be mediated?

Although various locales were deemed sacred by virtue of God's presence (Gen. 32:30), patriarchal religion did not put much importance on sacred space or the cultic practices that typify Mosaic Yahwism. Nevertheless, in various forms of foreshadowing, we find the usual lines of continuity with later persons, events, institutions, and practices—Scripture's penchant for typology. Thus "Jerusalem," where centralization of the cult eventually took place, figures prominently in two key texts that address "cultic" issues: in Genesis 22 with the "binding" (sacrifice) of Isaac ("Moriah"; cf. 2 Chron. 3:1) and in Genesis 14 with the tithe paid to Melchizedek.

With Mosaic Yahwism a change in perspective and practice occurs. God appears to the newly created covenantal community, a community formed by the exodus and, now at Sinai (which parallels Jerusalem as a place par excellence for "visions" of God), given an identity, including instructions where Yahweh's presence—with the full implication of both blessing and danger—would be manifest (Exod. 24–26; 33:12–17).

How would God's presence in the covenant community and ceremony be evident? Inevitably certain symbols were necessary (despite the aniconic nature of Mosaic Yahwism; Exod. 20:4). The symbols appeal to the senses, but not simply as "visual aids." The ark, cherubim, and the tent of the meeting become the institutional representations of the Lord's presence among his people. Here, in this *place*, Yahweh appears and makes his will known (Exod. 33:7–11).

The tent of the meeting in the Pentateuch, and the priestly tabernacle, is not, however, a projection (or retrojection!) of the temple, but an independent dwelling reflecting the life of Israel prior to settlement and the centralization of worship. The tent is a "portable temple" of sorts, but not provisional nor simply a pattern; rather, the tent is a unique "dwelling."

With the ritual performances in the tabernacle/temple complex, and the personnel and attendant appurtenances, we come to a theologically significant point about temple practice: coming into the presence of a holy God. In each change of location, vestment, instrument, or ritual act, with their various gradations of importance, the "needs" of the people and the holiness of God come together: I am holy, it is holy, you are (to be) holy.

The extensions and the symbolic associations began early in the canonical literature. As a commentary on the Torah, Deuteronomy expresses the presence of Yahweh in the cult devoid of some simplistic equation of Yahweh's presence constrained by the natural order of cause and effect by utilizing his alter ego, his "name," as the manifestation of his transcendent reality. Even the ark itself is divested of its throne-like setting by its role as the "container" of the tablets of the law (Deut. 10:1–5). Yahweh is not seated on a throne like some dowager duchess.

The paradoxical and symbolic nature of the temple is thus seen as the author(s) construct the parameters of temple theology: the transcendent deity graciously appears before his holy people in the *place* of his choosing, a dwelling symbolically rich by virtue of its ability to generate varied metaphoric associations (fire, cloud, tent, ark, and most especially "name" in the Pentateuch).

The Construction of the Temple. The construction of the temple began with David to serve as, at least on sociopolitical grounds, a "media event" of divine support and favor. David, however, was deterred from completing the task. No doubt sociopolitical forces played their usual role in this. The biblical authors were not oblivious to these explanations (1 Kings 5:13–18), but characteristically pass theological judgment (1 Chron. 22:8–9), or, more important, God himself divulges his feelings on the matter: "Did I ever say . . . 'Why have you not built me a house of cedar'?" (2 Sam. 7:7). God does not *require* an immutable dwelling, but the metaphoric associations are kept open, even those of monarchal justification (i.e., a "house" like the house in which the monarch resides).

The "cedar house" is ultimately built. And in Solomon's great prayer of dedication the paradox of this dwelling is acknowledged once again by his classic statement: "But will God really dwell on earth? The heavens, even the highest heaven, cannot contain you. How much less this temple I have built!" (1 Kings 8:27). The paradox is softened by "quoting" the Deuteronomic "name" formula: "My Name shall be [in this place]" (v. 29). (This terminology underscores the point that the correspondence between God's presence and his "dwelling"—tabernacle or temple—is more "textual" than physical.) But what does the Lord *think* of this structure?

Solomon, like Bezalel before him with the building of the tabernacle, is described as having "wisdom." Unlike Bezalel, however, Solomon sends straightaway for supplies and instructions from Phoenician artisans. Moreover, a labor force is needed to complete the project, a force not unlike what the Israelites experienced in Egypt. Finally, Solomon is portrayed as the central figure in the planning and implementation of the project: "As for this temple that *you* are building . . . " (1 Kings 6:12). No editorial judgment from the author is forthcoming from these contrasts, but the reader is left with the impression that Solomon's project is equivocal before God.

The equivocal nature of the project is supported by the Lord's response to it in 1 Kings 9:3–5. The Lord does hallow the place, but it is still Solomon's doing: "I have *consecrated* this temple which *you* have built" (v. 3). A clear stipulation is also attached: "if you walk *before me*" (v. 4; the sanctity of the place must be preserved, at the very least).

Responses to the Temple. What responses do we find in Scripture to the building of the temple beyond those found in the immediate context of it being built?

Rather than "going up" to the mountain of the house of the Lord to hear the word of the Lord, as in the eschatological visions of Isaiah and Micah (4:1–2), the Babylonians "descend" upon the temple to break down its wall and carry off the temple treasures. After centuries of covenant disloyalty, the Lord withdraws his presence from this *place* (Ezek. 10:18); in fact, he is driven from the temple because of the abominations of the people (Ezek. 8:6). This destruction could be seen as one of the contingencies of history except for the interpretations put upon it; the theologian of Lamentations states the destruction of the temple in unequivocal terms: "The Lord *determined* to tear down the wall of the Daughter of Zion" (2:8). The destruction is purposed by God because the people failed to live *before him*.

Reconstructing the Temple. High on the agenda of the postexilic community was the rebuilding of the temple. Indeed, it was not long before all their troubles—which were many—were attributed to the disrepair, the virtual absence, of the dwelling of God (Hag. 1:3–9). The question must surely be asked: Why? Why, after a stern critique by the prophets, an outmaneuvering in the wisdom tradition, and its abandonment by God and destruction, would the people rebuild this structure?

The most obvious and strongest answer is that the Lord commands its construction (Ezra 1:2). But a further answer lies in the theological sophistication of the biblical authors themselves and in the power of this symbol to go beyond mere structure. The means for rebuilding temple theology are present in the preexilic theology itself, the selfsame theology that so thoroughly critiqued an overly literal-minded approach to the presence of God.

The temple was always symbolic, "textual" even before (and as much as) it was physical. To the extent that the metaphoric associations speak to the reality of our experience(s) before God, the symbol retains its power *as a symbol*. Although Jeremiah held little esteem for the ark/temple, he nevertheless prophesied that God's *throne* would be Jerusalem itself (3:17), and Torah would be written in their hearts (31:31–34). These extensions of the symbol are developed further in the New Testament (Rev. 21:22–27: "I did not see a temple in the city, because the Lord God Almighty and the Lamb are its temple. . . . Nothing impure will ever enter it."). The relativizing of the temple and moral earnestness that we see in Jeremiah were precisely the points of the Deuteronomic theology that influenced the short-lived reforms of Josiah.

The most extensive view of the new temple comes from Ezekiel. The construction of the temple is once again more ideal than real. In Ezekiel's new temple a remarkable event takes place: water flows from the temple (in Jerusalem) with such abundance that it calls to mind the rivers of paradise (see also Ps. 46:4; Rev. 21:6).

The Songs of Zion in the Psalter are particularly rich in their celebration of the temple. With all their "sensuality"—the reader is instructed to "behold" the beauty of the temple; walk about it; clap and shout; smell; bow down; and other sense-oriented activities—the Songs show that one is not to ponder the temple simply as a theological abstraction. The one who enters the temple not only receives spiritual blessings but material ones as well (Ps. 36:7–9).

While we do not find much by way of extensions of this symbol, its paradoxical and metaphoric nature are everywhere testified to in what takes place in the life of the communicant. The most powerful statement of this sort comes in Psalm 73, where the psalmist cries out because his inherited beliefs are at odds with his personal experiences. Everything is "oppressive" (v. 16). "Till I entered the sanctuary of God . . . " and what unfolds is a transformation of his character and his understanding of God. What happens in the sanctuary? It is, as it should be, unspecified. We are simply told at the end of the psalm that "as for me, it is good to be near God. . . . I will tell of all your deeds."

In sum, by building the temple and by extending the metaphoric associations with temple, a continuity between the pre- and postexilic community was established (Ezra 1:7; Hag. 2:9). For all the critique of the temple, in the final analysis, Yahweh takes pleasure in this place and it is a source of delight for those who assemble there (Pss. 43:3–4; 65:4; 84:1).

Jesus, Paul, and Judaism. In Judaism the temple was the religious, cultural, and national center; indeed, the temple was a microcosm of the universe. The power of the temple as a symbol is especially seen in its ability to continue long after the temple building itself was destroyed in A.D. 70.

According to the Gospels, Jesus participated fully in the practices and ethos of the temple. Jesus' birth was announced in the temple (Luke 1:17; 2:27–32), where he was also circumcised and studied with the rabbis as a lad (Luke 2:46). Later, of course, Jesus taught in the temple himself (John 7:14). It is not without significance that while Jesus is teaching in the temple precincts, he says, "If anyone is thirsty, let him come to me" (John 7:37), and the next day offers forgiveness to the woman taken in adultery (John 8:1–11). Blessing and forgiveness, priestly functions, are pronounced by Jesus in the shadow of the temple.

Jesus is not only a communicant and priest of sorts; he is also a prophet. Thus, when the temple practices are compromised, Jesus assails those who jeopardize the sanctity of the temple: "My house will be called a house of prayer. . . . But you have made it a den of robbers" (Mark 11:17). They were not living *before God*. Jesus, while teaching in its precincts, preserves the sanctity of the temple by his ethical admonitions. Even the forgiven woman is told to sin no more (John 8:11; see also John 4:23).

In the cleansing of the temple we also find a development and extension of the metaphoric associations of temple. Jesus employs a wordplay equivocating on the term "body" to break the parochial thinking of his audience (John 2:19). John characteristically points out the error of their literal-mindedness: "But the temple he had spoken of was his body" (John 2:21). Thus, in Jesus' acts and words we see the temple once again as a place of holiness, of danger (words of judgment; Jesus's own death) as well as blessing, and further extensions of the symbol are generated.

Paul also makes the correspondence between the temple and body: "Do you not know that your body is a temple of the Holy Spirit?" (1 Cor. 6:19; see also Rom. 12:1–2). Of course, the believer can be called the temple of God only because Christ himself is the temple and the believer participates *in Christ* (1 Cor. 3:9–17). The believer, like Paul himself, must be (cultically) pure in order to live in God's presence (2 Cor. 2:17). If God can dwell in a holy *place*, by extension, he could dwell in a holy person!

After the destruction of the temple in A.D. 70, temple theology loses none of its living and healing power since the temple was always "beyond" its physical presence. A theology of temple answers the problem of how God's presence is mediated. Specifically, temple theology recognizes the importance of "sacred space." Its analogue is sacred time—Sabbath, festivals, and appointed times of prayer. Humankind is oriented in time and space, thus Sabbath and temple testify to "eternity" beyond the confines of our usual orientation. Sabbath and temple redeem time and space.

Temple theology shows a high degree of theological sophistication—holding ambivalent attitudes/doctrines in tension, part of the mystery of faith, of paradox. Temple theology is most fruitful when it is functioning as a powerful symbol, with the ability to be fully grounded in (sacred) space and yet generate new metaphoric associations—a vision of life in the presence of the Lord. Even though the temple is both protological and eschatological, it is always grounded in the realities of our lives: it is a mere edifice, yet, Behold! Thy God.

ANTHONY J. PETROTTA

See also ALTAR; ISRAEL; OFFERINGS AND SACRIFICES; PRIEST, PRIESTHOOD; TABERNACLE.

Bibliography. B. Childs, *Old Testament Theology in a Canonical Context;* R. E. Clements, *God and Temple;* idem, *Wisdom for a Changing World;* R. H. Gundry, Sōma *in Biblical Theology;* M. Haran, *Temples and Temple Service in Ancient Israel;* A. J. Heschel, *Quest for God;* A. F. Kirkpatrick, *The Book of Psalms;* M. E. Isaacs, *An Approach to the Theology of the Epistle to the Hebrews;* G. Josipovici, *The Book of God;* K. Koch, *The Prophets: The Assyrian Period;* C. Koester, *The Dwelling of God;* H. J. Kraus, *The Theology of the Psalms;* J. D. Levenson, *Sinai and Zion;* J. G. McConville, *Law and Theology in Deuteronomy;* W. McKane, *ZAW* 94 (1982): 251–66; D. H. Madvig, *NIDNTT,* 3; R. Mason, *Preaching the Tradition;* C. Meyers, *Ancient Israelite Religion;* R. W. L. Moberly, *The Old Testament of the Old Testament;* J. Neusner, *Wrong Ways and Right Ways in the Study of Formative Judaism;* W. Nowottny, *The Language Poets Use;* D. A. Renwick, *Paul, the Temple, and the Presence of God;* J. Z. Smith, *To Take Place;* W. R. Smith, *The Prophets of Israel and Their Place in History;* idem, *The Religion of the Semites;* J. Soskice, *Metaphor and Religious Language;* N. T. Wright, *The New Testament and the People of God.*

Temptation, Test. While the number of terms denoting temptation and testing is small, their range of meaning is wide, extending from a secular sense of trying something out to a religious sense of luring toward evil. In the Old Testament the most common terms are *bāḥan* and *nāsâ. Bāḥan* is used in the sense of examining to determine value (Job 7:18; Ps. 139:23). A literal application is to the testing of metal to determine its purity (Job 23:10;

Zech. 13:9). It is also used of the testing of persons. *Nāsâ* exhibits a similar range of meaning. It may mean try in the sense of attempt (Deut. 4:34). In 1 Samuel 17:39 David refuses Saul's armor because he has not tested it. The term is also used of the testing of persons (Gen. 22:1).

Corresponding to the Hebrew *bāḥan* is the Greek *dokimazō* and its cognates. It is used of the testing of buildings (1 Cor. 3:13) and precious metals (1 Peter 1:7), as well as of Christian character (Rom. 5:4; James 1:2–3). But by far the most common term in the New Testament is *peirazō* and its cognates. This verb expresses the idea of trying in the sense of attempting (Acts 9:26; 26:21), but the overwhelming majority of uses denote the testing of persons (Gal. 6:1; Heb. 11:17).

Christian believers are encouraged to test themselves (2 Cor. 13:5). Sometimes the precise objective is stated: to ensure fitness for the Lord's Supper (1 Cor. 11:28) or to distinguish authentic prophetic utterances from unauthentic ones (1 Thess. 5:21; 1 John 4:1). Second Corinthians 13:5 shows that testing can have a negative outcome even though that is not its intended purpose.

At times persons are tested by others to prove their truthfulness (Gen. 42:15), knowledge (1 Kings 10:1), or character (Job 34:36). Jesus is tested by the Pharisees with hostile intent (Matt. 16:1; Mark 10:2). God puts people to the test to disclose their inner quality, testing the heart and the thoughts (Prov. 17:3; Jer. 12:3; 1 Chron. 29:17) so much so that those seeking his approval implore him to do so (Pss. 17:3; 26:2; 139:23). In particular, he tests those exercising a pivotal role in his purposes, such as Abraham (Gen. 22:1) and especially the people of Israel (Exod. 15:25; 16:4; Deut. 8:2; 13:3). Jesus also tested people (John 6:6). Those who emerge successfully from such testing are described as "attested" or "approved" (1 Thess. 2:4; 2 Tim. 2:15). The recognition that God holds the power of testing is expressed in Matthew 6:13. While it is accepted throughout the Bible that God puts people to the test, the form of his involvement is carefully defined.

Positively, the purpose of God's testing is that it might go well with his people and keep them from sinning (Exod. 20:20; Deut. 8:16). When they experience enticement to evil, he is able to deliver them (1 Cor. 10:13; 2 Peter 2:9; Rev. 3:10). Negatively, it is denied that God tempts anyone to evil (James 1:13). God can also be the object of testing, particularly on the part of those who question his will or power. The classic example in the Old Testament is the Israelites in the wilderness, who tested God by doubting his presence with them and care for them (Exod. 17:2, 7). On the other hand, in some instances God invites people to put him to the test so that his power and benevolence may be made clear (Isa. 7:10–12; Mal. 3:10). The picture in the New Testament is no different. It is possible—and dangerous—to test God's tolerance of sin (Acts 5:9; 1 Cor. 10:9; Heb. 3:9) or the scope of his grace (Acts 15:10).

In Jesus' ministry Satan stands out as the great choreographer of temptation, so that he is referred to as the tempter (Matt. 4:3) and the devil (Mark 1:13). His single purpose is to harass the people and destroy the work of God (Acts 5:3; 2 Cor. 2:11; 1 Thess. 3:5; Rev. 2:10; 12:9). But the prime target of his attention is Christ, and in particular, at two critical points in Jesus' saving mission: his baptism and death. Matthew 4:1–11 and Luke 4:1–11 depict Jesus as tempted to deviate from his appointed task by seeking provision, protection, and fake power as Israel had done in the wilderness. But Jesus triumphed where Israel failed. Mark 1:13 describes the same struggle, but in terms suggestive of the temptation in paradise, whose gates Christ reopened by his victory. The climactic test is in Gethsemane, where the incitement to avoid the cross is described as temptation by all the Synoptists (Matt. 26:41; Mark 14:38; Luke 22:46). The language of the "evil inclination" is not prominent in the New Testament in connection with temptation, although the idea is not absent (1 Cor. 5:5; 1 Tim. 1:20; James 1:14–15). Other terms such as "flesh" carry that sense, but in speaking of temptation the New Testament writers appear to prefer apocalyptic over anthropological language.

In general, testing and temptation are facts within God's world and constitute some of the tools through which he is bringing to fulfillment his redemptive purpose. Both trials (as revealing and stimulating character and progress) and temptations (understood as allurements to evil) may minister to the divine purpose, provided the outcome is positive (James 1:12). But there is this important distinction: since temptation embodies incitement to evil, it cannot be God's doing (James 1:13). Hence the tendency of the biblical writers is to say that while God *sustains* his people during testing (Rom. 5:3; Rev. 3:10), he *delivers* them from temptation (1 Cor. 10:13; 2 Peter 2:9). What is true in the private experiences of individuals is also true in the history of salvation in which the testing of Abraham (Gen. 22:1), Israel (Ps. 66:8–12), or Christ (Heb. 2:17–18) contributed to the furtherance of God's saving purpose.

Temptation neither constitutes nor necessarily leads to sin. Temptation could not destroy Christ's sinlessness (Heb. 4:15), and his temptations were entirely like those of all other humans (Heb. 2:17). Still more, succumbing to temptation is never inevitable. The triumph of Christ over the powers of darkness (Matt. 12:28–29; Col. 1:13) means that a way of escape is always open for those united to him (1 Cor. 10:13). When temptation is yielded to, forgiveness is available through Christ (Heb. 2:18; 4:14–16; 1 John 2:1).

Alex R. G. Deasley

See also Endurance; Persecution.

Bibliography. E. Best, *The Temptation and the Passion;* B. Gerhardsson, *The Testing of God's Son;* W. Popkes, *EDNT,* 3:64–67; W. Schneider and C. Brown, *NIDNTT,* 3:798–808; H. Seesemann, *TDNT,* 6:23–36.

Tempter, the. *See* Satan.

Ten Commandments. The portion of Scripture known as the "Ten Commandments" (Exod. 20:3–17; Deut. 5:7–21) is a key segment of the Sinai covenant, which was entered into by God and the people of Israel. This covenant was modeled on the political treaties of that day between a great king and a subject people. In these treaties the king offered certain benefits and, in turn, called for certain behaviors from the people. All these treaties followed the same basic format, which the Sinai covenant, both in Exodus and in its restatement in Deuteronomy, also adheres to closely.

In both Exodus and Deuteronomy, the Ten Commandments are a brief summary of the more detailed covenantal requirements that follow them. These requirements relate to the whole of life: ceremonial, civil, and moral. Many of the commands are very similar to those found in the law codes that have been discovered in the ancient Near East. But it is very significant that the biblical commands have been placed in the context of covenant. In the rest of the ancient law codes, the commands are simply presented as givens, dropped from heaven by the gods. There is no real motive for obeying the commands except the avoidance of punishment. But in the Old Testament, the inclusion of the laws within the covenant puts the motivation on a whole new level. Why should I treat my fellow Israelites in a certain way? Because God has said that is the way in which I can express my covenant loyalty to him. Thus obedience is an expression of grateful appreciation for what God has done for us and what we know he will do. Ethics is not about what will advance one's self-interest, but about maintaining an all-important relationship with God.

A further implication of putting the commandments in the covenant context is the aspect of character. It is apparent from a study of the ancient treaties that many of the stipulations that the kings put upon subject peoples were an expression of the various kings' characters and preferences. Thus, the carrying out of the biblical commandments is a means of learning and replicating the character of God. It is here that the continuing significance of the Ten Commandments is found: they reveal the character and will of the unchanging Creator of the universe. Thus, even though the Sinai covenant is not binding on Christians, the moral truths revealed in it are.

A final important implication of the covenant form is especially significant for the Ten Commandments. In the ancient law codes, the laws are always stated in terms of cases ("If such and such infraction occurs, then such and such a punishment shall be meted out"). There are no statements of absolute prohibition. It is easy to understand why this is the case. A polytheistic setting cannot know of an absolute right or wrong. What is right for one god will be wrong for another. But in the political treaties, since there was only one king to whom the covenanters were professing loyalty, that king could indeed make absolute prohibitions. Thus it is in the biblical covenant that the One God can summarize his stipulations for his people in a series of absolute statements, the Ten Commandments. This shows that the succeeding commands, many of which are stated in terms of cases, are nevertheless based on principles inherent in God's creation, and not simply situationally derived attempts to promote social harmony.

One of the features that marks the Ten Commandments is also typical of the stipulations as a whole. That is the wholistic character of the subject matter. Social behavior and religious behavior are treated together. This is not found elsewhere in the ancient Near East. There is mythological and ritual material, and there are social prescriptions, but the two are never related. The Old Testament insists that the ways in which we treat each other are inseparable from our relationship to God. Ethics are a religious matter, and worship of the true God is the foundation of all nonmanipulative ethics. Thus the first four commandments are primarily in relation to God while the remaining six have to do with human relationships. But it is clear that the four cannot be separated from the six, nor vice-versa.

Although the commandments are, with the exception of the fifth, all prohibitive, they are not negative. They speak about love: love of God and love of others. But what is it to love? If it were necessary to prescribe every loving act and attitude, there would not be enough books in the world. What the commands do is to define the parameters beyond which love cannot exist. This much is then clear: if I love my neighbor I will not steal what belongs to him.

The first commandment is typical of the covenantal stipulations: no other king, or in this case, god, is to be recognized. This feature of the covenants was a marvelous tool for beginning to teach the truth of monotheism. Instead of going into philosophical arguments about unity and origins, God merely tells his people that if they wish to be in covenant with him, they must refuse to recognize any other god. Eventually, having accepted this stipulation and having sought to live it out, they would be in a position to accept Isaiah's insistence that there *are* no other gods (46:9).

The second command has no analogue in the ancient Near Eastern covenants, but its truth was just as vital as the first for God's education of his people. Around the world, religions that have arisen from human reflection agree upon one fundamental principle: the unseen, divine realm is one with, continuous with, the visible world of nature. Above everything else, this principle suggests that it is possible to manipulate the divine world and to appropriate its power through manipulation of the visible world. In short, it pretends to make it possible for humans to take control of their destinies. This principle is everywhere expressed through the practice of idolatry. By making the god or goddess in the shape of something in nature, preferably a human shape, we both express our conviction about reality and create a mechanism for influencing that god or goddess.

Unfortunately, according to the Bible, that principle is absolutely wrong. The one God is not continuous with the natural world, or with anything in it. He created the world and everything in it as something other than himself. To be sure, he is everywhere present in the world, and no part of it can escape his power. But he is not the world and cannot be manipulated by means of any activity in the world.

How is God to teach his people a truth that is at odds with everything they have learned for four hundred years, and at odds with everything the fallen human heart wants to believe? Once again, he does not enter into a philosophical argument. He simply makes it a requirement for a covenantal relationship with himself that they never try to make an idol of him. As with monotheism, when they have lived with the requirement long enough, they will eventually be ready to draw the right conclusions about God's transcendent nature (Isa. 40:21–26).

The third commandment also strikes at the magical view of reality. Because of the principle of continuity, it was common to believe that a person's name was identical with the person himself or herself. Thus, simply by invoking a powerful person's name, and especially a god's name, in connection with something that one wanted to happen, it was possible to make the thing happen. God says that this is a vain, or empty, use of his name. It is an attempt to use his power without submitting to him, or living in trusting relation with him.

Instead of emptying God of significance by an attempt to use his name magically for our own ends, we are called upon to "hallow" his name, that is, to show the true perfection of his character and power by the quality of our lives (Lev. 22:31–33). We cannot manipulate him, but through faith and trust we can receive power from him to live lives of integrity, purity, and love.

The fourth commandment is the only one of the ten that has to do with matters of worship. There is no absolute statement given with regard to worship practices, such as sacrifices, or festivals, or clean and unclean food. Those matters had to do with a particular era, and would serve their purpose and pass away. What this one summary statement regarding worship does treat is a matter of underlying attitude. What does our use of time say about our estimate of who supplies our needs? When we work seven days a week we surely say that our needs are met through our efforts alone. But the commandment requires persons to stop their work one day out of seven and to remind themselves that it is God who supplies our needs every day of the week (Deut. 5:12–15). Furthermore, if God rested after his labors, who are we that we think we can outdo God (Exod. 20:9–11)? The manner or way a Sabbath is kept is not important, but it is important that we consciously set aside one day in seven, filling it with worshipful rest, to remind ourselves to whom all our time belongs.

The fifth commandment is transitional. From one point of view it is the first of the commandments to deal with human relations. But from another point of view it continues the theme of acceptance of dependence that is at the heart of the fourth command. To honor one's parents is fundamental to any healthy personality. It is the best antidote to the foolish arrogance of "the self-made man." It recognizes that someone else gave me life and took care of me when I could not take care of myself. On the other hand, honor implies honesty. It is impossible to honor someone whom we constantly blame for our faults and failures. To honor them recognizes their faults and failures, and forgives. The person who refuses to honor his parents cuts himself off from his roots and almost certainly from his posterity. If a culture is to survive "long in the land" (Exod. 20:12) it must have a glad connection between the generations.

The five remaining commands all have to do with the self in relation to others. As noted above, they specify where the limits are beyond which healthy relations become impossible. We may not abuse the physical life, the sexual life, the possessions, or the reputation of those around us if we are to remain in covenant with God. Nor dare we allow ourselves to think that if we were just in someone else's shoes, enjoying what they possess, we would be happy. These brief statements, hardly more than fifty words in English, speak volumes about the character of the God who made them. They also explain some of the high value that has been put on individual worth in Western thought. To God, the boundaries around an individual's life are sacred. The insistence that all persons are to be able to hold their physical life, their sexual fidelity, their possessions, and their reputation inviolate shows that no one is a faceless molecule in some larger entity. Each one is a distinctive combination of these features, which comprise his or her identity, and they must be guarded for each person.

If we claim to be in relationship with God, we must see persons in the same way he does. Their lives are not ours to take for our purposes. Human sexuality is to be expressed in heterosexual commitment and we may not do anything that would lead someone to break those commitments. There is a boundary drawn around a person's possessions, and we may not cross that boundary to satisfy our own desires. A person's reputation is an extension of himself or herself, and we may not violate it, particularly to make ourselves look better.

What is involved here is a statement about dependence upon God. Those who depend upon themselves make themselves the center of the universe; they have broken the first two commandments. For such persons, anything is permissible in the attempt to supply their needs. Others are either enemies or slaves, in any case to be dominated, used up, and cast aside. But obviously if humans are to live together in any kind of harmony these rapacious instincts must be moderated in some way. Thus human laws. But God seeks to strike at the heart of the issue. If persons can ever realize that they are not the suppliers of their needs, but that God is, and surrender those needs to him, then ethics will move to a new plane.

Some of these commands deserve further comment. As several modern versions indicate, the King James Version's "Thou shalt not kill" is too broad to convey the sense of the Hebrew of the sixth command. The word used is *harag,* which does not refer to killing in general, but to the premeditated murder of one person by another. Thus, it is not proper to build a case against war or capital punishment upon the basis of this verse. These activities may indeed be condemned on biblical grounds, but this verse should only be a tertiary part of the evidence.

It is significant that all of the sexual sins that the Bible prohibits are summarized by the command against adultery. There are very important implications to be drawn from this fact. The clearest is that sexuality is to be expressed only in the context of heterosexual fidelity. It is for this reason that all other expressions of sexuality are condemned in Leviticus 18 and 20 and elsewhere. Without diminishing the seriousness of those aberrations, it is apparent that the most serious sexual sin is to break faith with one's spouse and the spouse of another, a breach of covenant.

The ninth commandment continues the emphasis upon ethical relationships. The command does not confine itself to prohibiting the telling of untruths, but speaks particularly about telling untruths concerning others. Congratulating oneself upon one's honesty is to miss the point of the commandment. Integrity is not for oneself, but for the sake of others; it is that they may live in security, knowing that we will treasure their reputation above our own.

The tenth command is in some ways merely a continuation of the previous four concerning love of one's neighbor. To love one's neighbor is to refuse to surrender to the sin of envy. It is to rejoice in the neighbor's good fortune, knowing that one's own fortune is in the good hands of God. In this sense it is the climax of the previous four commands. They only spoke about not abusing the neighbor. This one speaks about a deeper issue: guarding those springs of desire from which the abuses would arise. If we are to keep the commands not to abuse our neighbors, it will be because we have made a prior surrender of all our wants and needs to the covenant God.

It is at this point that the command begins to assume a larger function than merely the fifth of a series on nonabuse of neighbors. The Pentateuch, if not the entire Bible, is clear that the root of all evil is the human attempt to meet our needs for ourselves. From Genesis 3 on the issue is the same: Will we allow God to satisfy our desires in his way, or will we insist on trying to satisfy them in our own strength? This is where idolatry comes from; it is an attempt to manipulate the divine in order to satisfy the human desires for power, security, comfort, and pleasure. Thus it is that Paul makes the remarkable identification of covetousness with idolatry (Eph. 5:5; see also Isa. 57:13–17, where the same connection is implied).

The covenant is designed as a teaching device: there is only one God who is not a part of this world; he is utterly holy, just, and faithful, and it is he who supplies our needs not we ourselves. Knowing that fact, we do not have to see others as rivals and enemies; instead we can treasure their individuality as God does. But if we give assent to all that and then succumb to the sin of covetousness, believing that happiness consists in getting hold of something that we have seen in the possession of another, we will have missed the whole point of God's instruction and be in dire peril of falling back into the very pit from which we have been lifted. JOHN N. OSWALT

See also EXODUS, THEOLOGY OF; ISRAEL.

Bibliography. W. Barclay, *The Ten Commandments for Today;* J. Davidman, *Smoke on the Mountain;* W. Harrelson, *The Ten Commandments and Human Rights;* G. von Rad, *Old Testament Theology.*

Testimony. The biblical concept of testimony or witness is closely allied with the conventional Old Testament legal sense of testimony given in a court of law. Linguistically, the biblical term principally derives from the Hebrew *yāʿad, ʿûd, ʾānāh* and Greek *marturein* word groups; conceptually, it broadly influences the thought patterns, truth claims, and theology of nearly all of Scripture.

Its validity consists in certifiable, objective facts. In both Testaments, it appears as the primary standard for establishing and testing truth claims. Uncertifiable subjective claims, opinions, and beliefs, on the contrary, appear in Scripture as inadmissible testimony. Even the testimony of one witness is insufficient—for testimony to be acceptable, it must be established by two or three witnesses (Deut. 19:15).

Thus, within Scripture an inseparable bond exists between the message and its historical reliability on the basis of sound testimony. The message is as trustworthy as the events themselves. In the Old Testament, the truth claims have to do mainly with God and the revelation of himself to Israel; in the New Testament, this picture is greatly deepened with the additional revelation of Jesus Christ, and now to all the world.

Testimony in the Old Testament. *Testimony as the Revelation of God.* The idea of testimony is intrinsic to the idea of biblical revelation. The content of biblical revelation, whether general or special, stands as testimony to its Giver. Furthermore, God has unveiled divine truth to people within the matrix of secular history. This means that people were able to verify divine revelation. Paul proclaims that the coming of Jesus and the worldwide spread of the gospel were "not done in a corner" (Acts 26:26). These events were well observed by many. This assessment holds true for most of biblical revelation.

Concerning Old Testament general revelation, the psalmist praises the created order for revealing and bearing witness to God's glory and supremacy (Pss. 8:1–4; 19:1–6; 29; see Job 36:24–33; 37:1–13). The sun/moon and day/night cycles appear as eternally established faithful witnesses, affirming Yahweh as a promise-keeping God (Ps. 89:35–37; Jer. 33:20–21, 25).

Concerning God's special revelation of himself to Old Testament Israel, the Ten Commandments are called the Testimony (Exod. 31:8); as the revelation of God's legislation, they testify to his person and work and to his expectations for Israel. The ark and the tabernacle are also occasionally called the ark of the Testimony (Exod. 25:22; Num. 4:5; Josh. 4:16) and the tabernacle/tent of the Testimony (Exod. 38:21; Num. 10:11; 2 Chron. 24:6). In these instances, testimony more specifically refers to the revelatory self-witness of God to his people. Here, by the ark in the tabernacle, God testifies to his own existence in the act of revealing himself to Moses (Exod. 25:22; 33:9–11; Num. 7:89) and to future generations (Exod. 29:42).

The Old Testament prophets also reveal God's mind and will when testifying against Israel (2 Chron. 24:19; Amos 3:13) and the nations (Zeph. 3:8). All instances of this kind of prophecy in the Old Testament—of which there are many—appear as divine testimony against unrepentant peoples. The content of the prophetic testimony is often directly inspired revelation. Its truth claim lies ultimately in its fulfillment. But the history of prophetic fulfillment also guarantees its reliability.

Testimony and the Lawcourt of God. The seat of justice in Old Testament Israel was the legal assembly, which usually met near the town gate. Here the accuser and defender presented their cases before the town elders, who presided over the assembly as judges. The litigants often called in witnesses to substantiate their cases.

Old Testament writers frequently use the language of the lawcourt to express God's disposition toward various individuals and groups of people. He appears as defender, accuser, and judge. As defender, God is beseeched to take up the cause, to testify on behalf of an aggrieved party. Job, for example, appeals to God to defend him as his witness, advocate, intercessor, and friend (Job 16:19–21). Elsewhere, God defends the cause of the poor, sick, and disenfranchised (Deut. 10:18; Pss. 10:18; 72:4; 82:3; Prov. 23:10), the righteous (Ps. 119:154), and Israel (Jer. 50:34; 51:36). As accuser, God testifies against Israel because of their sin (Ps. 50:7, 21; Isa. 57:16; Hos. 4:1; Mic. 1:2; 6:2; Mal. 2:14); as judge, he reaches a just verdict on the basis of his own testimony (Hos. 12:2; Mic. 6:2, 9–16; Zeph. 3:7–8; Mal. 3:5). But even as accuser and judge, God's gracious love is still in force: "He will not always accuse, nor will he . . . treat us as our sins deserve or repay us according to our iniquities" (Ps. 103:9–10). God's desire for justice establishes a precedent for his people to follow. To defend the cause of the powerless and to testify against injustice reflect knowledge of God's ways and personal obedience to him (Isa. 1:17; Jer. 22:16).

Testimony also appears in the Old Testament as the legal proof of God's trustworthiness. Certain visible evidence existed within Israel attesting to the trustworthiness of God's revelation of himself to them. The Song of Moses (Deut. 31:14–32:44) and the Book of the Law (Deut. 31:26) stand as testimony against Israel; these documents contain God's prediction that Israel will one day rebel against him and turn to idols. Israel's legacy of apostasy verifies the reliability of God's predictions that they would forsake him. More broadly, the fulfillment of these predictions in Israel's history endorses the trustworthiness of God's entire revelation given through Moses.

Testimony appears, moreover, as a visible reminder of God's supremacy. The Transjordan tribes of Reuben, Gad, and Manasseh built a replica of the Lord's altar near the Jordan, not for burnt offerings and sacrifices, but as testimony to Israel that they would remain faithful to God's law given to Moses and that they had a continuing legal right to worship at the Lord's tabernacle even though living outside of the promised land (Josh. 22:27–28). They named the memorial: A Witness Between Us that the LORD is God (v. 34). It stands as visible evidence that Yahweh is supreme. The prophet Isaiah apparently takes up the altar and memorial ideas of Joshua 22 in describing a significant future conversion of Egyptians to the Lord. At that time, they too will have a legal right to worship the sovereign God of Israel at his tabernacle/temple (Isa. 19:19–20).

Furthermore, to invoke God as witness in oaths and binding agreements in the Old Testament implicitly indicates the participant's complete confidence in God as irreproachable, and thus as utterly reliable. For this reason, he is called "the true and faithful witness" (Jer. 42:5).

Testimony as the Proclamation of God as Lord and Savior. In Isaiah 43:8–13, the prophet depicts the nations as forming a legal assembly to proclaim the superiority and saving work of their gods. But their case proves groundless. Their gods are blind and deaf, mere idols made of the commonest materials; their makers are nothing but men. Hence, their message is nothing but a lie (43:10, 12; 44:9–20). The nations ultimately have no case, because they lack any evidence to support their claims (44:11).

In the same assembly, Israel takes the witness stand (43:10, 12; 44:8) to proclaim Yahweh as the Lord and that apart from him there is no savior (43:11). Their case, in contrast, is undeniable. Israel's history proves it. God has historically, time and again, revealed himself to Israel and redeemed them from oppression (43:12). God's revelation of himself to Moses, his giving of the law, his abiding presence in the tabernacle (and temple) and his redemption of Israel from Egypt provide the Israelite witnesses with solid evidence to support their claims. In defending Yahweh, Israel proclaims to the nations God's lordship and that salvation can be found only in him.

Here testimony is equivalent to proclamation. It presents historical evidence attesting to God's unique person, position, and work. It simultaneously is evangelistic: the message of God's saving work in Israel's history becomes itself an offer of salvation to those listening.

Testimony in the New Testament. The New Testament takes up the Old Testament concept of testimony and greatly expands it in light of God's special revelation in Jesus Christ. Here again the content of the testimony is certifiable, objective evidence (John 3:11; Acts 1:21–22; 1 John 1:1–4), and for this reason, it is considered true (John 3:33; 5:32–33; 19:35; 21:24; 3 John 12). The association of Christian witness with suffering and martyrdom, on the other hand, is mostly a post-New Testament Christian development.

Testimony Concerning the Divine Identity of the Earthly Jesus. Biblical and early nonbiblical writings indubitably affirm that Jesus truly lived. But the New Testament explicitly and implicitly testifies that the earthly Jesus considered himself as God incarnate.

John's Gospel, in particular, offers a wealth of Jesus' self-claims concerning his divine identity (see the numerous "I am" sayings). In fact, the entire Gospel ostensibly appears as a legal defense of Jesus' divine sonship. Jesus regarded his personal testimony as valid (8:14), but knowing that, according to Jewish law, appearing as one's own witness without confirmation invalidates the testimony (5:31; 8:13–18), he summoned other witnesses, whose testimony he also considered beyond dispute. Jesus stressed that his miraculous works affirmed his divine status (5:36; 10:25, 38; 14:11; 15:24). He could not have performed them if he were not from God. This unity implies, furthermore, that the Father testifies to his divine identity as well (5:32, 37; 8:17–18). In the same sense, Jesus declares that the Old Testament Scriptures testify about him (5:39), as will the Holy Spirit, whom he will send to his followers from heaven (15:26) and the apostles (15:27). John the Baptist also offers testimony endorsing Jesus' self-claims about his divinity (3:26; 5:32–33): Jesus is the true light through whom all people can be saved (1:7–9), is preexistent (1:15), will baptize with the Spirit (1:32–33), and is the Son of God (1:34).

Jesus as Testimony about God. Scripture uniformly asserts that no one has seen God (John 1:18; 1 Tim. 6:16). God is spirit (John 4:24; 2 Cor. 3:17–18) and invisible (Col. 1:15; 1 Tim. 1:17). Jesus, on the other hand, declares that his purpose for coming into the world was to testify to the truth (John 18:37). According to John 14:6, Jesus is the truth. Only he has seen the Father (John 6:46) and for this reason has come to make God known (John 1:18). Jesus' testimony, therefore, is about God as revealed through him.

Thus, to see Jesus is to see what God is like: "Anyone who has seen me has seen the Father" (John 14:9). Jesus is the image of the invisible God (2 Cor. 4:4; Col. 1:15); he is the exact representation of God's being (Heb. 1:3).

The theological importance of this reality is that Jesus' person, qualities, attitudes, and behavior expressly image the Father's. For Jesus willingly to have given up his life that we might live not only depicts the lowest point of his earthly career and describes the depth of his love for us (Phil. 2:8), but it correspondingly reveals what it means when John says that God is love (1 John 4:8, 16): God so loved the world, that he gave of himself in giving Jesus (John 3:16). Because of the incarnation, we have now received "the knowledge of the glory of God in the face of Christ" (2 Cor. 4:6).

Testimony and the Gospel. The legal sense of testimony as the presentation of evidence plays a decisive role in the New Testament church's propagation of the gospel. In the New Testament, reliable historical evidence is a handmaiden to the theological significance of the gospel message. Eyewitness testimony is of utmost importance. The New Testament church's confidence in the gospel as saving is directly proportional to its confidence in the historical reliability of the gospel events themselves. It would have been untenable for Jewish Christians to use the Old Testament legal procedure for establishing the legitimacy of the gospel via the testimony of multiple witnesses, if all the while knowing that historically the events had not transpired in the way they had so claimed. Jewish opponents of Christianity would, otherwise, have been able to find bonafide witnesses of their own (something historically they were unable to do) to refute the legitimacy of the Christian claims.

The New Testament two types of witness as legal testimony. First, it appears as a literal courtroom defense of Jesus and the gospel. It stems from Jesus' own teaching. Jesus announced to his followers that they will stand trial before Jewish and Gentile authorities as witnesses to them on account of him (Matt. 10:18; Mark 13:9; Luke 21:13; John 15:27; Acts 10:42). In the New Testament, the Book of Acts especially attests to the fulfillment of this promise. Luke recounts numerous occasions when believers appeared in court settings bearing witness to Jesus as savior before Jewish, Greek, and Roman authorities. Second, witness as legal testimony frequently appears as a way of presenting the gospel. In its technical usage, it strictly refers to Jesus' followers who witnessed his entire earthly ministry, from John's baptism to the ascension. They vouched for the certainty of the gospel message from their first-hand knowledge of the events of Jesus' earthly career, and provided able sources for the contents of the Gospels. In a more general sense, it also refers to the way believers appealed to Jesus' life, the Old Testament Scriptures, the Spirit's presence and personal testimony to substantiate the legitimacy of the gospel message.

Furthermore, in the New Testament the historical reliability of Jesus' life, death, and resurrection is intrinsic to the preaching of the gospel. The interrelation between testifying and preaching in the New Testament closely resembles the Old Testament example in Isaiah 43–44. Paul, for instance, while at Corinth "devoted himself exclusively to preaching, testifying to the Jews that Jesus was the Christ" (Acts 18:5). For Paul to present evidence that Jesus was the Messiah was at the same time intended to induce a believing response from his Jewish listeners. Proclamation in the New Testament means bearing witness to the historical reliability of God's saving work in Jesus. The authenticity of the message preached is what grants the message its authority. To preach the gospel to the nations is to challenge them with the fact of Jesus (Matt. 24:14; Mark 13:10; Luke 24:48; Acts 1:8).

Another New Testament form of testifying to Jesus and the gospel is through proper Christian conduct. Jesus tells his disciples (John 13:34–35), "A new command I give you: Love one another. As I have loved you, so you must love one another. By this all men will know that you are my disciples, if you love one another." The command to love is not new (cf. Lev. 19:18; Deut. 6:5). What is new is the revelation of God's love through Jesus. As Jesus bore witness of God's love to the world by his life and death (John 3:16), his followers by loving as he has loved will reveal a Christ-like love to a world that has never seen him. Any inquiry into the reason for this selfless love will encounter the good news of Jesus' saving work—an event historically reliable and theologically certain. Proper Christian conduct, therefore, provides timeless testimony to Jesus' perfect and final expression of God's love.

The Witness of the Spirit as the Testimony of God. According to 1 John 5:6–11, the Spirit's witness appears as God's testimony that Jesus is his Son. The witness the Spirit bears is recognizable outwardly to all people and inwardly to believers. Outwardly, "the signs, wonders and various miracles, and gifts of the Holy Spirit" appear as God's testimony to the salvation first announced by Jesus and then confirmed by eyewitnesses (Heb. 2:3–4). The tangible evidence of the Spirit's presence is displayed both in Jesus' life and in the experience of the church. The Spirit's ministry in the church becomes, in effect, incontrovertible evidence to Judaism (and to the nations) that the church's message about Jesus comes from God. Jesus foretold that the Spirit will testify about him (John 15:26). Inwardly, the Spirit testifies to believers that they are God's children (Rom. 8:16; 1 John 3:24) and have God's testimony about Jesus in their hearts (1 John 5:10).

The forensic language of these New Testament passages is historically and theologically important. The Spirit's witness—yet visible to us even now!—verifies that, historically, Jesus did not receive his divine sonship by adoption. The witness by water and blood (1 John 5:6–7) indicates that Jesus already was God's Son at the time of his water baptism by John and his death on the cross. The Spirit of Truth (John 15:26; 1 John 5:6) affirms this. Therefore, as witnesses the water, blood, and the Spirit unanimously agree that Jesus was God's Son by divine nature, not by divine appointment (1 John 5:8).

The Word of God and the Testimony of Jesus. John's Apocalypse marvelously depicts the unity of God and Jesus in the compound designation "the Word of God and the testimony of Jesus Christ" (1:2, 9; 6:9; 20:4). The separate titles mean the same thing. Both refer to Jesus. John envisions Jesus at the time of his glorious return as "dressed in a robe dipped in blood, and his name is the Word of God" (19:13). God's final word of revelation and redemptive act were consummated in Jesus' passion work. The phrase "the Word of God and the testimony of Jesus" does not refer to a concept but to an event: the incarnation. The historical reality of Jesus' life and passion is central to Christian confession and lies at the heart of the compound designation. Its usage in the book's introduction (1:2) indicates its thematic importance for the entire work. Jesus is the true and enduring witness of God's love (1:5; 3:14). He is the slain Lamb of God who, vindicated by God, presently reigns supreme by his Father's side. Therefore, to believers facing persecution and possible martyrdom for bearing witness to the Word of God and the testimony of Jesus in a human court of law, John reminds them with the Book of Revelation that their ultimate destiny is as assured as the reliability of the message they preach: the Lord Jesus himself will vindicate them in the heavenly lawcourt.

H. Douglas Buckwalter

See also Confess, Confession.

Bibliography. J. Beutler, *EDNT,* 2:389–91; L. Coenen and A. A. Trites, *NIDNTT,* 3:1038–51; H. Strathmann, *TDNT,* 4:474–514; A. A. Trites, *The New Testament Concept of Witness.*

Thankfulness, Thanksgiving. *The Old Testament.* Early in the Old Testament both the language and the concept of thanksgiving are conspicuous by their absence. The Old Testament lacks an independent vocabulary of thanksgiving or gratitude; it uses the verb *yādâ,* and the cognate noun *tôdâ,* both ordinarily translated as "praise," to convey the concept. Even the concept is rare in the Pentateuch. Neither Adam nor Eve thanked God for his creation, and, compared to Abel's gift of the fat portions from the firstborn of his flock, Cain's gift of "some fruit" seems singularly thankless. The families of Isaac and Jacob contended over God's blessing rather than thanking him for it. Ingratitude reached its nadir when, after the exodus, Israel grumbled again and again, rather than thanking God for his deliverance and for food that literally fell from heaven.

Perhaps the laws for thank offerings should be seen against Israel's failures to that point. The thank offering was one type of peace or fellowship offering within the sacrificial system of the Mosaic covenant. Distinct from the sin and guilt offerings, they were a subcategory of peace offering, ordained to express gratitude to the Lord for any deliverance, any act of love (Lev. 7:11–16; Ps. 107:21–22). Even apart from the sacrificial system or the terminology of thanksgiving, wisdom literature encourages gratitude for God's material provision and exposes the folly of greed (Ps. 104:15–28; Eccles. 5:8–6:9).

Thanksgiving is more common in the psalms. About twenty psalms command or invite Israel to sing songs of thanksgiving. "Give thanks to the Lord, for he is good" is a common refrain (106:1; 118:1; 136:1). Some psalms specify a reason, linking thanksgiving with acts of love and worship, exhorting worshipers to glorify God with thanksgiving (69:30), come before him with thanksgiving (95:2), enter his gates with thanksgiving (100:4), sing to the Lord with thanksgiving (147:7). Perhaps surprisingly, many cries for aid and laments conclude with thanksgiving (individual cries for help in 7:17; 28:7; 35:18; 52:9; 54:6; 86:12; communal cries in 79:13; 106:47).

Chronicles and Nehemiah often mention thanksgiving, as both take strong interest in the temple and the offerings and songs that rise from it to God. For example, when David brings the ark of the covenant to Jerusalem, the people sing psalms that call Israel to give thanks again and again (1 Chron. 16:4, 7, 8, 34, 35, 41). David also appointed Levites to thank God morning and evening in the temple (23:30), and he thanked God as his life ended, exhorting the people to join him in giving to the building of Solomon's temple (29:13–20).

Despite the paucity of the language of thanksgiving, gratitude or something akin to it was foundational for covenant life in the Old Testament. The law rested upon gratitude for God's redeeming work. As God said to Israel through Moses, "I am the Lord your God who brought you out of Egypt, out of the land of slavery." By that deliverance, Israel became the Lord's treasured possession. Remembering it, they become his priests, his holy nation.

The New Testament. In the New Testament the vocabulary for thanksgiving and gratitude expands and expressions increase. The verb *eucharisteō* and the cognate noun *eucharistia* together appear about fifty-five times. Several other terms convey the idea, most commonly *charis* (often with *echō, I* have). Thanksgiving is a motive for Christian life and conduct, a general attitude toward both the blessings and trials of life, a central component of prayer, and the context for the proper use of material things.

In the Gospels and Acts thanksgiving most often occurs in prayer over a meal, such as the feeding of the multitudes (Matt. 15:36; Mark 8:6; John 6:11, 23) or at the last supper (Matt. 26:27; Mark 14:23; Luke 22:17, 19). Yet the crowds that surrounded Jesus often repeated Israel's sin at the exodus, by gobbling up the bread Jesus multiplied and enjoying his miracles without expressing gratitude (John 6:22–24).

Paul thanked God for his final meal on the storm-battered boat that took him to Malta (Acts 27:35). Jesus also thanked the Father for hearing his prayer that God hide his secrets from the wise and reveal them to children (Matt. 11:25;

Luke 10:21) and to raise Lazarus (John 11:41). In the worship scenes of Revelation, the heavenly hosts give thanks to God for creating all things (4:9–11) as well as redeeming multitudes of humanity (5:9–14).

The Gospels introduce and the Epistles develop the concept that gratitude for God's deliverance in Christ characterizes the believer. When a sinful woman interrupted a dinner party to anoint Jesus with precious perfume, Jesus told his shocked host that her action sprang from gratitude for forgiveness (Luke 7:40–47). When Jesus healed ten lepers as they walked to the temple, he marveled aloud that only one, a Samaritan, returned to thank him (Luke 7:11–19). Paul agrees that believers should be thankful for every individual provision, and that gratitude for God's saving grace envelops the entire Christian life. Those whom God has brought from death to life should offer their bodies to him as instruments of righteousness (Rom. 6:13). In view of God's mercies, knowing they were bought at a price, they should offer their bodies to God as living sacrifices in general and honor him with purity in particular (Rom. 12:1; 1 Cor. 6:20). Those who have received an unshakeable kingdom from God should be thankful, worship God, and faithfully endure the hardships of persecution (Heb. 12:28 and context).

A general attitude of thanksgiving in both the trials and blessings of life distinguishes the Christian. Paul enjoins his churches to give thanks for all things, in all circumstances (Eph. 5:20; 1 Thess. 5:18), even in suffering (Rom. 5:3–5; James 1:1–4), and to do everything in the name of Jesus out of a spirit of gratitude (Col. 3:17). On the other hand, thanklessness marks godless and wicked men who suppress the truth about God (Rom. 1:18–21).

Believers retain joy and peace especially when, "in everything, by prayer and petition, with thanksgiving [they] present their requests to God" (Phil. 4:6–7). Thanksgiving is a central component of prayer for Paul. He prays that his churches will be thankful (Col. 1:12), and gives thanks in turn for answered prayer, especially for the extension of the gospel and the strength of his churches (2 Cor. 4:15). Paul begins most of his letters (Galatians, 1 Timothy, and Titus being the exceptions) with expressions of thanksgiving to God for the church or individual to which he writes. The thanksgiving usually leads to a prayer, and the two together ordinarily introduce some of Paul's themes for the letter. For example, Paul thanks God for the faith of the Romans (1:8), for his grace given to the Corinthians so that they lack no spiritual gift (1 Cor. 1:4–7), and for the Philippians' partnership in the gospel (1:3–5; see also 1 Thess. 1:2–3; 2 Thess. 1:3–4).

A legalistic asceticism afflicts some false teachers (1 Tim. 4:1–3) and rebels tend toward thanklessness (Rom. 1:21; 2 Tim. 3:2). Believers, on the contrary, give thanks for material things, and consecrate them with prayer (1 Tim. 4:4–5). No food or drink, no created thing is unclean in itself; all are good if used with thanksgiving, to the glory of God (Rom. 14:1–6; 1 Cor. 10:30–31).

The Book of Revelation leads the redeemed to give thanks for the fundamentals. Four living creatures "give glory, honor and thanks to him who sits on the throne" (4:9), twenty-four elders worship him for he has taken his great power and begun to reign (11:17). God's reign entails the final overthrow of evil, for which believers also give thanks (19:1–6), since the doom of God's foes clears the path for the arrival of the new heavens and new earth. DANIEL DORIANI

Theophany. Manifestation of God that is tangible to the human senses. In its most restrictive sense, it is a visible appearance of God in the Old Testament period often, but not always, in human form. Some would also include in this term Christophanies (preincarnate appearances of Christ) and angelophanies (appearances of angels). In the latter category are found the appearances of the angel of the Lord, which some have taken to be Christophanies, reasoning that since the angel of the Lord speaks for God in the first person (Gen. 16:10) and the human addressed often attributes the experience to God directly (Gen. 16:13), the angel must therefore be the Lord or the preincarnate Christ. Yet, though the angel is clearly identified with the Lord, he is distinguished from him (he is called "angel," meaning "messenger"; similar patterns of identification and distinction can be seen in Genesis 19:1, 21; 31:11, 13; Exod. 3:2, 4; Judg. 2:1–5; 6:11–12, 14; 13:3, 6, 8–11, 13, 15–17, 20–23; Zech. 3:1–6; 12:8). In the ancient oriental world, a king's messenger spoke in the name of the king. Any insult rendered him was interpreted as an insult to the king himself (cf. Hanun's treatment of David's embassy, 2 Sam. 10:1–4; 1 Chron. 19:2–6). There seems, therefore, no necessity to posit a theophany for the angel of the Lord. In Joshua 5:13–6:5, the conquest narrative is interrupted by the abrupt appearance of a being who calls himself the "commander of the army of the Lord" (5:14). To interpret this event as an encounter with God or with the preincarnate Christ forces the text. Angels were sent on missions of this kind (Judg. 6:11; 13:3), and some were identified as captains over heavenly armies (Dan. 10:5, 20; 12:1). While there are no indisputable Christophanies in the Old Testament, every theophany wherein God takes on human form foreshadows the incarnation, both in matters of grace and judgment.

Following are a number of what may be considered classic theophanies. The Lord appears to Abraham on his arrival in the land, wherein God promised the land to Abraham and his descendants (Gen. 12:7–9); God reaffirmed his promises of land and progeny when Abraham was ninety-nine years old (Gen. 17:1), and on the Plains of Mamre on his way to destroy Sodom (Gen. 18:1).

God appeared to Jacob in his dream at Bethel (Gen. 28:11–19). It is also clear that in the events at the Jabbok ford, Jacob somehow received a revelation through an encounter with God, although neither a strict reading of the text (Gen. 32:22–32) nor its later interpretation by Hosea (12:3–4) demand a theophany.

God appeared to Moses alone on the mountain (Exod. 19:20; 33:18–34:8). God also appeared to Moses, with Aaron and his sons and the seventy elders (Exod. 24:9–11) and in the transfer of leadership to Joshua (Deut. 31:15).

While he suffered, Job had complained that he sought an audience with God (31:35). At the conclusion of the book the Lord appears in a thunderstorm to deliver two discourses, designed to grant Job's request for a hearing and arguably to supply at least one of the meanings for Job's affliction: God is sovereign.

In a looser sense, God's promise of the land to Abraham (Gen. 15), as well as his commission that Abraham sacrifice Isaac (Gen. 22), could be considered theophanies. Frequently the term, "glory of the LORD," reflects a theophany, as in Exodus 24:16–18; the "pillar of cloud" has a similar function in Exodus 33:9. The Spirit of God or the Spirit of the Lord must be considered theophanous, particularly when it comes upon men, transforming them (1 Sam. 10:6) and equipping them for divine service (1 Sam. 16:13). The Lord appears to people in visions (Gen. 15:1; 46:2; Job 33:15; Ps. 89:19; Dan. 2:19; Acts 9:10; 18:9) and in dreams (Gen. 20:3; 31:24; 1 Kings 3:5; Matt. 2:13) to reveal his plans for them or to unveil mysteries for the future.

The Lord appears in theophanies both to bless and to judge. A frequent introduction for theophanies may be seen in the words, "The LORD came down." Examples may be found in Genesis 11:5, Exodus 34:5, Number 11:25, and Numbers 12:5. Although the most common verb for the manifestation of the glory of the Lord is "appeared" (Lev. 9:23; Num. 14:10; 16:19, 42; 20:6), God's glory also "settled" on Mount Sinai (Exod. 24:16). WILLIAM C. WILLIAMS

See also ANGEL OF THE LORD.

Bibliography. Th. Booij, *Biblia* 65 (1984):1–26; J. Vander Kam, *VT* 23 (1973):129–50; M. G. Kline, *WTJ* 40 (1977):245–80; J. Lust, *VT* 25 (1975):110–15; E. W. Nicholson, *VT* 24 (1974):77–97; idem, *VT* 25 (1975):69–79; K. L. Schmitz, *Faith and Philosophy* 1 (1984):50–70.

Thessalonians, First and Second, Theology of. The epistles of Paul to the Thessalonians are forceful evidence that Paul was no mere armchair theologian. This servant of Jesus Christ had experienced harsh treatment at the hands of both misguided Gentiles and hostile Jews for the sake of Jesus (2 Cor. 11:23–27; 1 Thess. 2:2; cf. Acts 14:4–5, 19). This committed preacher of the gospel was called a god at Lystra, raised a dead man at Troas, and created riots in many places, including Thessalonica (Acts 14:12; 20:10–12; 17:5–9). While some might unfortunately be tempted to view this great apostle to the Gentiles as an authoritarian personality because of some statements in letters he wrote to the Galatians and Corinthians, readers are encouraged to gain a sense of the other side of Paul by studying the Thessalonian correspondence.

Place in the Canon. Hidden near the end of the Pauline corpus are these two precious letters that provide important insight into the mind and heart of Paul. Students of the Bible should be aware that the present order of the New Testament books is not according to their date of writing but according to more theological principles of organization. In the case of the Pauline Epistles, early Christian collators of the New Testament began with Romans heading the corpus as a kind of summation concerning soteriology or salvation. It was followed by 1 and 2 Corinthians and Galatians, which dealt with inadequate responses to the meaning of salvation. These texts in turn were followed by Ephesians, Philippians, and Colossians, which have generally been regarded as the Prison Epistles and which treat various implications of Christology for the life of the church. Sandwiched between these seven letters and those addressed to persons (1–2 Timothy and Philemon) are the Thessalonian epistles.

Almost overlooked, these little letters deal primarily with how eschatological (endtime) issues affect the church. These letters are significant because they may be the earliest preserved documents of the New Testament, having been written shortly after A.D. 50. Their significance, however, has often been lost because the major concern of many Christian theologians has been issues of soteriology (salvation) and because some other interpreters have sought to use these letters along with Daniel and Revelation to build schemes for predicting the end of time. But a careful reading of these letters will provide a greater spectrum, including insights into how the apostle sought to deal with the crucial issues of early community life on the basis of believers' transformation in Christ.

Historical and Literary Issues. These epistles have been the subject of considerable recent scholarly discussion involving a wide variety of issues, such as authorship, order, style, and theological consistency. While some have argued strongly against Pauline authorship of 2 Thessalonians based on matters of style and tone, such arguments when fully reviewed are more speculative than might be apparent at first glance. On the issue of the order of the Thessalonian letters, the case is not as easily settled since an argument can be made both ways concerning the matter of hostility that seems to be in the *past* for 1 Thessalonians (e.g., 1:6; 2:14–16; 3:2–5), but a *current* reality in 2 Thessalonians (1:4–8). Probably there is insufficient information in the letters themselves to determine the case, although the allusion in 2 Thessalonians 2:15 may be to 1 Thessalonians (2 Thess. 2:2 may suggest some fraudulent correspondence arriving between the two legitimate letters).

Concerning any major theological inconsistencies that have been suggested by comparing the two letters, it seems best treated in terms of Paul's reaction or response to eschatological questions raised or perceived in the community. Moreover, suggestions that one or both of these letters were directed against powerful outside forces such as gnostics or Judiazers can hardly be gleaned from these epistles. Such ideas are constructs from outside the letters themselves.

The Setting. First Thessalonians was undoubtedly written from Achaia (probably Corinth) following Paul's hasty departure from Thessalonica and Berea (cf. Acts 17:1–18:1). Paul was relieved by the good report brought by Timothy concerning the situation at Thessalonica (1 Thess. 3:6), and this letter is both a response to their concerns and a general exhortation to authentic living. Together with 1 Corinthians it provides a unique study in contrast. In 1 Corinthians 16:5–12 one has the feeling that none of the missionaries are anxious to go to Corinth whereas Macedonia is quite another matter (1 Cor. 16:5). The same positive view of the Thessalonians is present when one reads that their faith is recognized not only in Macedonia but in *Achaia* and elsewhere (1 Thess. 1:7–8). It is a contest of two cities, both capitals of their respective provinces! Little can be added from 2 Thessalonians except to note that Paul recognized that the community was experiencing hostility from without (1:4–8). The presence of such hostile treatment is confirmed even at the early stage of the Christian mission (Acts 17:5–13). Pain, loss, and suffering are often the seed beds for birthing significant theological reflections and such is clearly the case with Paul's letters to Thessalonica.

Themes of the Letters. Paul's letters provide intriguing studies in the thematic concerns. Such is certainly the case with these Thessalonian epistles.

Paul's Triadic Emphases. Those familiar with the famous faith, hope, and love triad of 1 Corinthians 13 may not realize that Paul frequently employs triadic thinking in his writing or that this famous triad is employed to identify a theological emphasis. The concluding member of the triad provides a signal for the emphasis being made in the work. In the case of 1 Corinthians the theological emphasis falls on authentic living, the second aspect of the salvation triad (justification, sanctification, glorification). The same emphasis on authentic living is present in Romans 5–8, where the discussion is introduced with a similar order (Rom. 5:1, 2, 5). In 1 Thessalonians, however, where the concern is eschatology or hope and endtimes, the order is faith, love, and hope (1:3). The same emphasis is evident in the triad of "turned," "serve," and "wait" (1:9–10).

Hope in this Life. Yet such an emphasis does not mean that Paul is unconcerned with sanctification (see 1 Thess. 3:12–13; 4:3–4, 7; 5:23; 2 Thess. 1:10; 2:13). Because God in Christ has brought a new sense of hope to the world, Paul is able to view the pain and suffering experienced in this world from the ultimate perspective of the resurrection and glorification of Christians (1 Thess. 4:14–17; 2 Thess. 1:10) together with the judgment of evil (1 Thess. 5:2–3; 2 Thess. 1:6–9).

In the light of this ultimate reality, Paul calls on his readers to exemplify in their lives the way of holiness (1 Thess. 4:3–7; 5:23; 2 Thess. 3:13–14) and the marks of love, faithfulness, peace, courage, purity, patience, and diligence (1 Thess. 4:1–7, 9–11; 5:6–22; 2 Thess. 3:6–13).

Imitation. But Paul's exhortations are not meant to be understood as mere words of advice. Having grown up in a multicultural context, he had learned that authentic teaching was rooted in the authentic living of the teacher, whether that teacher was a Jewish rabbi in Jerusalem or a stoic philosopher in Tarsus. Accordingly, Paul employs the technical concept of imitation to challenge his readers to follow or copy his way of life as a significant model (1 Thess. 1:6–7; 2:14; 2 Thess. 3:7–9; cf. Phil. 3:17). But he clearly recognizes that he is not the ultimate model. He himself is copying the model of Christ, and his readers are to copy that model of Christ as well (1 Thess. 2:14–16; cf. Phil. 2:1–18).

Paul's imitation of Christ meant a personal involvement in the lives of his understudies. Thus, in 1 Thessalonians he exemplifies his role by reference to both female (mother, 2:7), and male (father, 2:11) descriptions of his relationship with them. But perhaps the most important description of Paul's relationship with his followers is found in the word-family of *parakalein/paraklēsis* ("comfort," "support," etc.), which describes a personal concern for another's well-being, a theme that becomes a personification of the Spirit's role with believers in John (see *paraklētos* in John 14:16, 26; 15:26; 16:7; cf. also the role of Jesus 1 John 2:1 and by implication "another" in John 14:16). In Thessalonians Paul is in fact assuming the role of an earthly paraclete to the church, his model being that of Christ and the Spirit. So strategic is this idea in 1 Thessalonians that some scholars have pondered whether in principle the entire epistle should be categorized as a "Letter of Consolation."

Hope in the Hereafter. But the theological force in these letters concerns the future expectations of the Thessalonians. Their driving question seems to have been the timing of the Lord's *parousia* ("coming" or "presence"; see 1 Thess. 2:19; 3:13; 4:15; 5:23; 2 Thess. 2:1, 8–9). Christians were dying, just like non-Christians! Funerals were necessary. Where was their hope for a future life with Jesus?

Paul's answer was clear. Death does not end hope because death is not a Christian's final state (1 Thess. 4:13). The answer, as Cullmann has so helpfully articulated, is not some vague Greek immortality theory where the soul takes wings and is absorbed into the divine soul in the manner suggested by Plato. The answer is that the dead will rise (v. 16)! All Christians will thus join in the meeting with Jesus. Those who are still alive will be removed or lifted up from the context of this earth and all will be together with their Lord forever (v. 17).

The concept of removal is defined here in spatial terminology as "snatched away" or "caught up" (*harpazein,* 1 Thess. 4:17). The Latin equivalent, *rapere,* has given birth to English theories of "rapture." Dispensationalist interpreters of the past century sought to program this motif of Thessalonians into their understanding of Revelation. But since there was no precise literal equivalent of the idea in Revelation, they inserted it between chapters 3 and 4 of that book. Whatever view one takes of a rapture, it is important to recognize that Paul's intended purpose here is the comforting of believers in the midst of loss (4:18) with the fact that both dead and living Christians will be safe with Jesus forever.

This text has also given rise to questions concerning the state of the dead between their death and resurrection. Some have proposed theories of "soul sleep." Two matters, however, should be clarified briefly at this point. First, the concept of an immortal "soul" is a Greek idea, which in the theory has been imported into the Christian theology of the resurrection. Second, the concept of "sleep" implies that a person is subject to the element of time when dead. Neither idea is necessarily compatible with Paul's thinking elsewhere or with his use of figurative language here.

The point of his argument is to assure the Thessalonians not to worry about the dead. They are secure in God's hand. But Paul does use the sleep idea here to call them from a lack of involvement to authentic life while they are still alive on earth (cf. 1 Thess. 5:6). And they are not to be surprised by events as they take place because timing is also in God's hand (5:1–4). Yet a timetable is not here provided to readers. Only the warning is given to be prepared for the "descent" of the Lord at a time to be signaled by God (described as the trumpet call, 4:16; and coming unexpectedly as at night or at pregnancy reaching term, 5:2–3).

But such nonprecise expectation theology was apparently not satisfying to some in the church and so Paul in 2 Thessalonians had to remind them not to accept unsubstantiated reports or even a fraudulent letter (today a book?) concerning God's timing for his coming (*parousia,* 2:2). The time had not yet arrived; the signs or conditions were not there! They should not be duped by deluded proclaimers of timing (v. 11). The world would still get worse until evil seemed to be utterly rampant and someone (a man of lawlessness and destruction) would seem to gain complete control and impersonate God (symbolized in the picture of control of the temple, v. 4). They should never forget that God is always in control, restraining evil from exploding (v. 6) until the time he has determined to end the work of Satan (vv. 8–10).

Paul's concern in both epistles then is not in programming the coming of the Lord but in assuring Christians of their ultimate relationship with God and that God is in control of history, not the forces of evil and persecution.

In these early epistles there is little attempt to theologize about Christology or the Trinity. It is merely assumed that God, Jesus, and the Holy Spirit are ultimately one (1 Thess. 1:2–5; 2 Thess. 2:13–16); that the one God is in fact working in Christ Jesus (1 Thess. 2:13–14; 5:18); that the death and resurrection of Jesus are fundamental elements of Christian faith and the basis for Christian hope and authentic Christian living (1 Thess. 1:10; 2:14–16; 4:14).

The spread of the gospel for Paul was directly linked to the authenticity of Christians (1 Thess. 1:8; 2:13–16; 4:11; 5:12–22; 2 Thess. 1:3–4, 11–12). His joy in their examples of Christian integrity is clear (1 Thess. 1:6–7) and his concern for their well-being is evident in his calling of judgment on their persecutors (1 Thess. 1:5–10). Because of his commitment to integrity as the basis for the evangelization of the world, he strongly and repeatedly counseled his followers to persevere in all matters of integrity and goodness and to abstain from all forms of evil and idleness (1 Thess. 2:3–6, 9–11; 3:4–5, 10, 13; 4:1–12; 5:12–23; 2 Thess. 1:3–4, 11; 2:13–15; 3:3–5, 9–10, 12–14). In this concern for them his advice and prayers are beautifully united in a spirit of genuine care for their well-being in Christ.

Gerald L. Borchert

See also Paul the Apostle; Resurrection; Revelation, Theology of; Second Coming of Christ; Sleep.

Bibliography. J. M. Bassler, *Pauline Theology;* G. L. Borchert, *Discovering Thessalonians;* F. F. Bruce, *1 and 2 Thessalonians;* J. Chapa, *NTS* 40 (1994): 150–60; O. Cullmann, *Immortality of the Soul or Resurrection from the Dead;* R. Jewett, *The Thessalonians Correspondence: Pauline Rhetoric and Millenarian Piety;* A. J. Malherbe, *Paul and the Thessalonians: The Philosophical Tradition of Pastoral Care;* I. H. Marshall, *1 and 2 Thessalonians;* L. Morris, *The First and Second Epistles to the Thessalonians;* W. Schmithals, *Paul and the Gnostics;* C. A. Wanamaker, *1 and 2 Thessalonians.*

Thrones. *See* POWERS.

Time. It is debatable whether the Bible contains enough information to formulate a full-scale doctrine of time; nonetheless, the significance of the biblical concept of time is unmistakably the way it uniformly presents God at work in guiding the course of history according to his saving plan. The Hebrew *ʿēt, môʿēd, ʿiddan, zĕmān, yôm a*nd Greek *kairos, chronos, aiōn* are the main biblical time words depicting this divine work.

God as Lord over Time. Time is not fatalistic or capricious, but, according to Scripture, under God's personal direction and control. Time began at creation and becomes the agency through which God continues to unveil his divine purpose for it.

God is transcendent over time. He established the cycle of days and seasons by which time is known and reckoned (Gen. 1:14) and possesses the power to dissolve them according to his eternal purposes (Isa. 60:19–20); moreover, he controls world history, determining in advance the times set for all nations and bringing them to pass (Dan. 2:21; Acts 17:26). But God is not limited by time (Ps. 90:4). It in no sense diminishes his person or work: the eternal God does not grow tired or weary (Isa. 40:28) and his purposes prevail (Prov. 16:4; Isa. 46:10).

Furthermore, God imminently expresses concern for his creation. He reveals himself in history according to the times and dates set by his own authority (Acts 1:7) and will bring about in his own time the consummation of world history in Jesus' return (Eph. 1:9–10; 1 Tim. 6:15).

God as "the First and Last" (Isa. 41:4; 44:6; 48:12), "the Beginning and End" (Rev. 21:6), "the one who is, was, and is to come" (Rev. 1:4, 8), "King of the Ages" (1 Tim. 1:17; Rev. 15:3) further points out his lordship over time.

The New Testament presents Jesus as Lord over time. With the Father, he existed prior to the beginning of time, created all things, and sustains all things (John 1:1–3; Col. 1:16–17; Heb. 1:2–3). He is neither limited by time, nor adversely affected by it: "Jesus Christ is the same yesterday and today and forever" (Heb. 13:8). He too is properly called "the Alpha and Omega, the First and Last, the Beginning and End" (Rev. 22:13).

Humanity as Subject to Time. In contrast to God and Jesus, humanity is limited by time in the cycle of birth, life, and death. Every person bears the marks of time in the aging process and ultimately dies (Job 14:5; Heb. 9:27). The span of life is brief and passing (Ps. 144:4; James 4:14). Even our time on earth—the events/circumstances and length of life—are in God's hands (Ps. 31:15; 139:16).

All people, moreover, will experience the passage of time in life after death. Because of sin, all people face spiritual death, which involves eternal separation from God (Rom. 5:17–21; 6:23). Jesus' death and resurrection brings deliverance from sin and spiritual death, granting eternal life to all who believe (John 3:14–17, 36; 1 John 5:10–13).

Time as Redemptive History. Throughout history God has been carrying out his plan for redeeming a fallen world. The course of time, in effect, appears as redemptive history.

It is true that biblical writers perceive history as cyclical, in that various predictable, recurring sequence of events are inherent to it: the ordliness and seasonal regularity of nature (Pss. 19:1–6; 104:19; Eccles. 1:4–7), the cycle of life (Eccles. 3:1–15) and its wearisomeness (Eccles. 1:8–11), the rise and fall of kings and empires (Dan. 2:21), and the universal inclination toward evil (Judg. 2:6–23; 2 Chron. 36:15–16; Neh. 9:5–37; Rom. 1:18–32).

But they do not perceive history as static. Chronological time is of greatest importance in both Testaments as a way of tracing God's redemptive interventions in history. The most outstanding Old Testament example of this is Israel's redemption from Egypt (Neh. 9:9–25; Ps. 78:12–55; Hos. 11:1); in the New Testament it is the coming of Jesus as Messiah, Savior, and Lord (Acts 3:12–26; 10:34–43; 13:16–41). The revelatory nature of these divine in-breakings dispels any notion that time is merely cyclical, without purpose and value.

Time is meaningfully forward-moving. The covenants God made with Adam, Noah, Abraham, Moses, David, and Jeremiah illustrate that history reveals a progressive unveiling of God's redemptive plan for humanity. Prophetic fulfillment, according to God's appointed times, does so as well. The incarnation supremely exemplifies this: "But when the time had fully come, God sent his Son, born of a woman, born under law, to redeem those under law, that we might receive the full rights of sons" (Gal. 4:4–5; cf. Mark 1:15; Rom. 16:25–26; Eph. 1:10; 1 Tim. 2:6; 1 Peter 1:10–12). Jesus' death was not accidental, but a once for all atoning sacrifice (Rom. 6:10; Heb. 7:27; 9:26; 1 Peter 3:18), occurring exactly when God had intended (Rom. 5:6). In the same way, Jesus' second coming, the goal and end-point of redemptive history, will come to pass at God's appointed time (Mark 13:32; Acts 1:7; 3:21; 1 Tim. 6:14–15).

The Present as the Time of Salvation. The Bible unanimously declares that now is the time of salvation. In the Old Testament, on the basis of Israel's redemption from Egypt, every succeeding generation was to respond in loving obedience to the laws issued at Sinai by God their Savior (Deut. 11; Ps. 95:7–8). The injunction "it is time to seek the LORD" (Hos. 10:12) was to be Israel's perpetual desire.

In the New Testament, Jesus' coming as the Messiah inaugurated "the year of the Lord's favor" (Luke 4:19, 21). The time interval between the incarnation and the second coming appears symbolically as a jubilee year (Luke 4:19/Isa. 61:1–2; cf. Lev. 25:10), a time when salvation has been made available to all people through God's saving work in Jesus. Thus, "now is the time of God's favor, now is the day of salvation" (2 Cor. 6:2); now is the appointed season to declare this divine mystery hidden from ages past (Col. 1:26; Titus 1:3).

The present time holds a sense of urgency for unbelievers and believers. God now commands all people to repent for he has set a time when he will judge the world through Jesus (Acts 17:30–31). The time for repentance, however, is growing shorter (Rev. 2:21; 10:6). Believers are encouraged to make the most of every opportunity in serving God (Eph. 5:16; Col. 4:5) and to mature in faith "as long as it is called Today" to ward off encroaching apostasy (Heb. 3:13).

The End-Times. The end-time period surrounding Jesus' second coming is variously called the last times, last hour, last days, day of the Lord, day of judgment, day of Gods wrath, time of punishment, end of the ages, end of all things. The temporal finality of these expressions highlights the firm New Testament belief that the present course of history will come to an end when Jesus returns. The certainty of the first advent guarantees the certainty of the second (Acts 1:7).

The start of the end-times takes two forms in the New Testament. On the one hand, the messianic age, inaugurated with Christ's first coming, appears as the beginning of the last days according to Peter's use of Joel 2:28 in explaining the charismatic phenomena accompanying the Spirit's outpouring at Pentecost (Acts 2:17). Here the messianic age is equivalent to the end-times. It is a time of great salvation as well as of mounting evil growing to unprecedented proportions as the parousia nears. For this reason, the many antichrists, false teachers, and forms of ungodliness that have already appeared show without contradiction that it is the last hour (1 Tim. 4:1; 2 Tim. 3:1; 1 John 2:18).

On the other hand, although the end is near (Heb. 10:37; James 5:8; Rev. 22:7, 10), it has not yet arrived. Nor has the tumultuous period leading up to it. Because of the unique character of the end-times, it also has an identity not entirely the same as the messianic age. Its events include the fulfillment of the signs portending the end, Christ's return, the setting up of his eternal kingdom, and the last judgment. But even here the time periods partially overlap: the benefits derived from salvation in Christ promised to believers in the coming age (eternal life, perfect Christlikeness, etc.), are, nonetheless, the property of believers to enjoy in part in this age.

Time and Eternity. The Bible does not specify if or in what sense time existed before creation or will exist after Jesus' return. Nor does it specify the relation between time and eternity either as unending time or timelessness.

But how God and humanity relate to time may parallel how time differs from eternity. On the one hand, God is eternal, having no beginning or end (Ps. 102:25–27; Isa. 40:28; Rom. 1:20); he is Lord over time. He is timeless in the sense that as Creator and Lord he is non- or supratemporal, standing outside of or above time (Ps. 90:2, 4). Time is real for God. It becomes the means through which he makes known his enduring love to humankind. On the other, time and humanity are immortal in the sense that both have a starting point and continue on indefinitely. God promises unending life with him to those who believe in Jesus' redeeming work (John 3:16; 1 John 5:13) and unending separation from him to those who spurn it (Matt. 25:46; 2 Thess. 1:6–8).

H. DOUGLAS BUCKWALTER

See also DAY; FULLNESS OF TIME; LAST DAY(S), LATTER DAYS, LAST TIMES.

Bibliography. J. Barr, *Biblical Words for Time;* O. Cullmann, *Christ and Time;* G. Delling, *TDNT,* 3:455–64; 9:581–93; J. Guhrt and H. -C. Hahn, *NIDNTT,* 3:826–50; C. F. H. Henry, *EDT,* pp. 1094–96; E. Jenni, *IDB,* 4:642–49; C. H. Pinnock, *ISBE,* 4:852–53; H. Sasse, *TDNT,* 1:197–209.

Timothy, First and Second, Theology of. The two epistles Paul wrote to Timothy are not usually associated with theology as much as they are with church organization and practice. However, it is significant to notice how many doctrines of the Christian faith are supported by key verses from these epistles. Beginning with bibliology, the crucial passage for the inspiration of all of Scripture is 2 Timothy 3:16–17. It is stated here that all Scripture is inspired or "God-breathed" and for that reason is "useful for teaching, rebuking, correcting and training in righteousness, so that the man of God may be thoroughly equipped for every good work." These verses indicate that anything that goes under the name of "scripture" is God-breathed out, and God-originated, and hence is his Word. As such, it is reliable and trustworthy and must be inerrant. For this reason Paul also writes that we should work hard to present ourselves approved to God, so we do not have to be ashamed, correctly handling the Word as characterized by truthfulness (2 Tim. 2:15). Paul also writes that the sacred writings of Scripture are able to give wisdom and to lead to salvation through faith in Jesus Christ (2 Tim. 3:15). Consequently, the Scriptures for Paul were, as God's Word, the authoritative and inerrant foundation stone upon which all other Christian doctrines and ethics rest.

Theology. Regarding the doctrine of God proper, the two epistles to Timothy contribute mostly to our understanding of the attributes of

God. He is called "the King eternal, immortal, invisible, the only God" (1 Tim. 1:17). His oneness is again declared in 1 Timothy 2:5, where Paul says that "there is one God and one mediator between God and men, the man Christ Jesus." Stressing again some of the same characteristics, Paul describes God as "the blessed and only Ruler, the King of kings and Lord of lords, who alone is immortal and who lives in unapproachable light, whom no one has seen or can see" (1 Tim. 6:15–16a).

With regard to God's work in creation, Paul asserts that "everything God created is good, and nothing is to be rejected if it is received with thanksgiving, because it is consecrated by the word of God and prayer" (1 Tim. 4:4–5). Apparently, there were hypocrites who were forbidding marriage and were advocating abstention from certain foods, things that Paul insists were among the good things created by God to be rightfully enjoyed. In another passage related to creation and in defense of his statement relative to the position of women in the church, Paul points out that "Adam was formed first, then Eve" (1 Tim. 2:13). It is apparent that Paul believed Adam and Eve to be historical figures and that the order in which they were created indicated God's desire for male headship in the family and in the church.

The Doctrine of Sin. In regards to the doctrine of sin, Paul refers to the first sin of Adam and Eve as the origin of all kinds of sinning, from the love of money to the sin of apostasy, which he particularly stresses in 1 and 2 Timothy. He seems to take the blame for the first sin from the shoulders of Eve, and places it squarely on those of Adam. He points out that "Adam was not the one deceived; it was the woman who was deceived and became a sinner" (1 Tim. 2:14). Some believe that Paul is implying that Eve was not able to help herself, but Adam sinned deliberately with his eyes wide open. At any rate, the human race, according to Paul in Romans 5:12–21, fell in its head, Adam, and not in Eve.

In a context in which the apostle is speaking about godliness with contentment as great gain and about the fact that we cannot take anything out of this world with us when we die, he declares that "the love of money is a root of all kinds of evil" and that some have even apostatized from the faith by longing for money (1 Tim. 6:10). Paul does not say that such a love for possessions is the only source or root of all evil, but it is one, and an important one at that. It has caused people to covet first, then to rob and steal, to deceive, to kidnap, to murder, and even to apostatize from Christ.

Another emphasis in these epistles is Paul's stress on the danger of apostasy and falling away from the faith. Whether this is a falling out of grace and a loss of salvation or a falling away from grace of which one was never a part, Paul sees the danger as a very real and serious one, a danger about which he warns Timothy and desires that he will warn others. In the last days, some will fall away from the faith or apostatize (1 Tim. 4:1). Others, according to the apostle, have already left the faith or have lost their way (1 Tim. 6:21). In 2 Timothy 2:17–18, Paul even names two who have done this, Hymenaeus and Philetus, and states the heresy they were preaching. They were saying that the resurrection had already taken place; as a result, they were upsetting the faith of some. Another who may have committed the same sin of apostasy was Demas; because he loved the present world, he deserted Paul (2 Tim. 4:10). It may be noteworthy that it is not said that he deserted Christ, but rather that he deserted the apostle.

Christology. Paul's doctrine of Christ emphasizes both Christ's divine and human natures. Paul's belief in Christ's divinity is seen in his references to Jesus as "Christ Jesus our Lord" (1 Tim. 1:2, 12; 2 Tim. 1:10), and as "our Lord Jesus Christ" (1 Tim. 6:3, 14). On the other hand, Christ's humanity is seen elsewhere in Paul's writings to Timothy. According to 1 Timothy 2:5–6, we have "one mediator between God and men, the man, Christ Jesus." He "appeared in a body" (1 Tim. 3:16) and "descended from David" with a human genealogy (2 Tim. 2:8). In addition to all of this, the three great events in the earthly life of Christ are all referred to briefly in these rather short epistles. Christ's death is referred to in 2 Timothy 2:11, his resurrection in 2 Timothy 2:8, and his ascension in 1 Timothy 3:16. In addition, there is also a reference to his second coming to judge the living and the dead (2 Tim. 4:1).

Pneumatology. It is interesting to note that Paul, who believed strongly in the doctrine of the Trinity and had much to say in other epistles about the Person of the Holy Spirit, did not say much in his epistles to Timothy about him. In both of the letters to Timothy, his salutations mention God the Father and God the Son, but do not include God the Spirit. Paul does refer one time to the Spirit's revelatory work regarding the future, noting that "The Spirit explicitly says" that in the future some will fall away from the faith. Thus, his work on revelation, spoken of in other Pauline epistles, is not overlooked in the pastorals.

However, even though the Person of the Spirit is overlooked in these epistles, his work of sanctification, or separation from sin unto holy living, is not. Even when dealing with this doctrine, Paul stresses more human responsibility with regard to it rather than the Spirit's. This is seen in instructions such as the following: "Everyone who confesses the name of the Lord must turn away from wickedness" (2 Tim. 2:19); "a man should cleanse himself from these things" the secular babblings and the ungodliness and the gangrenous words of the heretics, cited in 2 Timothy 2:16–17; and a youth should "flee the desires of youth, and pursue righteousness, faith, love and peace" (2 Tim. 2:22). It is important to remember that the sanctified life taught in the Bible demands the work of God and the cooperation of the individual Christian. The theology of the Bible includes both the declarations of the Bible relative to God's work and the demands of the Scriptures stating our responsibilities. These latter are the things stressed in 1 and 2 Timothy.

Even in regard to eternal life and spiritual gifts, Paul in these epistles stresses more of the human obligations relative to them than God's declared promises. Note 1 Timothy 6:12, where Paul commands Timothy to take hold of eternal life to which he had been called. Even though Timothy already possessed it, Paul exhorts him to lay hold of it, use it, live in the light of possessing it, and make it real and applicable in his life. In 2 Timothy 1:6, Paul tells Timothy "to fan into flame the gift of God," which was in him by the laying on of Paul's hands. He had been given a gift, but now he had to stir it up or exercise that which had been given to him by the Spirit. The spiritual gift, the *charisma* of God, is not identified here, but is reminiscent of the charismata or other spiritual gifts apportioned out by the Holy Spirit as listed in 1 Corinthians 12. The implication is that what we do not use, we may lose.

Soteriology. The doctrine of salvation is seen from various angles in 1 and 2 Timothy. The universal purview of the atonement provided by God for humankind is seen in several verses. In 1 Timothy 1:15, Paul claims that Christ Jesus came into the world to save sinners, himself being one of the worst. Paul also writes that God desires all humankind to be saved, not just a few (1 Tim. 2:4). In 1 Timothy 4:10, the surprising declaration is made that the living God is the Savior of all humankind, especially of those believing. This latter verse has been interpreted in different ways. One thing is clear: God is not going to save all humankind; for other Scriptures state conditions that must be met before the universally applicable salvation becomes a reality in individual lives. Others have taught that the verse means that God *wants to save* all humankind and provides it for all, but it becomes applicable only for those who continue receiving it. Possibly, the best explanation is that God's salvation is one salvation that includes the many blessings of common grace bestowed upon all and intended to bring all to repentance. Even on this view, the salvation does not become effectual until those blessings are actually appropriated by faith.

Along with this emphasis on human response are certain verses that speak of salvation for those who have been "called . . . to a holy life" by God, "because of his own purpose and grace" (2 Tim. 1:9) and for those who have been chosen that "they too may obtain the salvation that is in Christ Jesus, with eternal glory" (2 Tim. 2:10). In this way, both the free will of man and the sovereignty of God are seen as operative in the salvation of humankind as Paul presents it in 1 and 2 Timothy.

A strong soteriological emphasis in these epistles, which is found elsewhere in the Pauline writings, is that we are not saved by our own good works, but for the *purpose* of good works. The same emphasis found, for example, in Ephesians 2:8–10 and in all of the practical sections of Paul's writings, is stressed heavily in 1 and 2 Timothy. Paul clearly states that God has saved us, "not because of anything we have done, but because of his own purpose and grace" (2 Tim. 1:9). The Agent of this salvation is asserted to be God in 1 Timothy 4:10 and 2 Timothy 1:8–9, and Jesus Christ in 2 Timothy 1:10, where he is called "our Savior."

With this emphasis that humankind cannot save itself, goes the stress also on the fact that our salvation is for the purpose of good works; and this is a major theme in 1 and 2 Timothy. Often, this emphasis takes the form of laws or commands. For example, Paul commands Timothy to "keep this command," probably a reference to the whole Christian way of life (1 Tim. 6:14). Timothy is told to instruct the rich "to be rich in good deeds" (1 Tim. 6:18). In addition, "everyone who confesses the name of the Lord must turn away from wickedness" (2 Tim. 2:19). We are also to cleanse ourselves from empty and worldly chatter so we can be vessels for honor, sanctified and useful to the master, having prepared ourselves for every good work (2 Tim. 2:21). Along with these are commands to "flee the evil desires of youth" and to pursue righteousness, faith, love and peace (2 Tim. 2:22).

While noting Paul's commands to Timothy and Christians in general, it is important to interpret correctly his words relative to law in 1 Timothy 1:8–10. Paul is not ruling out all relevance of the law for righteous people, only, in the idiom of his days toning down the first part of the statement to put greater stress on the latter. The law is not *primarily* for the righteous, but for the unrighteous; however, it still retains a didactic function for believers. The law teaches them how to love Christ and their neighbor. In no way can it be for any sinner a way of salvation from the wrath of God.

There is one rather strange and difficult verse relative to the salvation of women: 1 Timothy 2:15 (NASB)—"But women shall be preserved through the bearing of children if *they* continue in faith and love and sanctity with self-restraint." It is obvious that physical salvation from death in childbirth is not meant here, since godly women do die in childbearing. Spiritual salvation through childbirth is contrary to many other portions of Scripture that never include this as a condition for salvation. It is probably that the definite article with "childbearing" is the important item here, and that the intent of the verse is that the woman will be saved, even though she fell into transgression in the beginning, through *THE Childbearing,* the incarnation of Christ as promised to Eve in Genesis 3:15. The woman's continuance in faith, love, and sanctity with self-restraint are then assumed, by these interpreters, to be evidences of a living faith within the saved woman.

Ecclesiology. First Timothy 2:8–15 gives a number of instructions relative to the respective positions of men and women in public worship. Important themes are those of the leadership of men an the submission of women, and all that those roles may entail. It is important for the theologian to stress that this does not mean that men are superior to women, only that, for the purposes of getting the divine mission of the church (and the family) completed, God has assigned the leadership role to men, as a general rule. Some have taken these to be cultural instructions for Paul's day only; however, it is important to notice that Paul grounds his directions here on Adam's being created first and then Eve and also on Eve's being deceived, not Adam.

Specifically, the men in every place are to lead in prayer (1 Tim. 2:8) and the women are to "learn in quietness and full submissiveness" (1 Tim. 2:11). Paul goes on to say, using the Greek present tense to clarify his injunctions, that he does not allow a woman to continue teaching or to continue exercising authority over a man (1 Tim. 2:12). It goes without saying that there may be times when no qualified men are available. Then Paul permits, in those emergency situations, the women to take charge; but this is not to be the usual or the norm. That the apostle is not forbidding all teaching for women is clear from Paul's favorable reference to Timothy's grandmother Lois and his mother Eunice. As believers (2 Tim. 1:5) who were undoubtably the responsible parties, through their teaching, for Timothy's good knowledge of the Scriptures from childhood (2 Tim. 3:15). Thus, apparently it was all right for the women of a household to teach the children in it.

Furthermore, to these instructions regarding a woman's service in the church, Paul adds some instructions regarding her dress for worship (1 Tim. 2:9–10). She is to adorn herself with proper clothing "modestly and discretely, not (primarily) with braided hair and gold or pearls or costly garments, but rather by means of good works, as befits women making a claim to godliness." In keeping with the manner of speaking of the time, he does not forbid all outward adornment, but desires that a woman's primary attractiveness come from the good words of a godly character.

The officers in the early church organization, according to Paul, were elders or bishops, deacons, and possibly deaconesses. The title "elder" referred to the honor and respect due the office of pastor while the title "bishop" or "overseer" stressed the function of the office. In 1 Timothy 3:1–7, the apostle lists those qualities that should characterize the men appointed to such an office. In keeping with his instructions discussed earlier, these are male in nature. The stipulations for deacons are given in 1 Timothy 3:8–10, 12–13. There is some question as to whether the references to women in verse 11 refer to the wives of the deacons, or to the deaconesses. Since there does not appear to be a word for "deaconess," and the word for "deacon" had to serve for both, there was no clear way here to distinguish deaconesses. (See Rom. 16:1, where the masculine word for "deacon" is used of Phoebe.) Those who believe Paul was addressing another office in the early church point out that he does not single out the wives of the elders or overseers for special instructions. Consequently, why should he insert material relevant to deacons' wives? It is possible, therefore, that he was referring to a third church office in 1 Timothy 3:11, namely, deaconess.

Eschatology. Both of Paul's epistles to Timothy place some emphasis on prophecy and the doctrine of the Lord's second coming. First Timothy 4:1–5 speaks of the great apostasy that will transpire in the latter times. The other more extensive prophetic passage is 2 Timothy 3:1–13, which speaks of the last days as "terrible times" and then lists a number of characteristics of the people who will live in those last days just prior to Christ's return. Again, deception of people living at that time is a primary concern of Paul's.

The second advent of Christ is called by Paul "the appearing of our Lord Jesus Christ" (1 Tim. 6:14). The Greek word used for Christ's "appearing" refers to his glorious second coming to this earth to reign. Two other places where this same word occurs with the same reference are 2 Timothy 4:1 and 8. In 2 Timothy 4:1, Paul solemnly charges Timothy in the presence of God and of Christ Jesus and "in view of his appearing and his kingdom" to do various things. In 2 Timothy 4:8, he declares that there is a reward awaiting him on a future day and for all those who have longed for the Lord's appearing, that is, his glorious return. Paul also reminds Timothy that God will bring about this return when the situation is ripe for it (1 Tim. 6:15), even as he did the first coming, as declared by Paul in Galatians 4:4.

In addition to the above, Paul makes it very clear that the doing of good works by believers is the way to store up treasure for themselves for the future, so that they may lay hold of that which is life indeed (1 Tim. 6:19). He speaks of receiving in the future the crown of righteousness that the Lord, the righteous Judge, will give to him and to all those who love the Lord's appearing (2 Tim. 4:8). WESLEY L. GERIG

See also CHURCH, THE; DEACON, DEACONESS; ELDER; LAYING ON OF HANDS; LEADERSHIP; OVERSEER; PAUL THE APSOTLE; TITUS, THEOLOGY OF.

Bibliography. H. A. Kent, *Pastoral Epistles;* R. C. Lenski, *Interpretation of Colossians, Thessalonians, First and Second Timothy, Titus, Philemon;* W. Lock, *International Critical Commentary: Pastoral Epistles.*

Tithe, Tithing. Giving a portion of one's profit or the spoils of war was known in the ancient world from Greece to China. Gifts were made as religious offerings, or given to a political authority as tribute or tax. Religious and political uses often combined since it was common to associate earthly and divine authority. Donation of a tenth portion, or tithe, was common apparently because most peoples counted in tens, based on ten fingers.

Tithing first appeared in the Bible when Abraham gave one-tenth of the spoils of war to Melchizedek, the priest-king of Salem (Gen. 14:18–20). The writer of Hebrews presumed that tithes were paid to a higher authority and inferred that there was a greater priesthood than Aaron's (Heb. 7:4, 9). Tithing as a tribute to God appeared later in Genesis when Jacob promised to give a tenth to God if he returned home safely (28:22). But these tithes were spontaneous and no details were given.

The Book of Exodus required giving only firstfruits (23:16, 19; 34:26) and is not clear whether the tithe later specified the percent of the total to be given as firstfruits or was a separate gift. Sometimes firstfruits and tithing appear to be identical (Deut. 26:1–14), other times separate (Neh. 12:44).

Tithes were awarded to the Levites for their priestly service because they would not receive land in Canaan (Num. 18:19–21). They, too, gave a tenth of what they received (v. 26).

If a person did not want to give what he produced he could give 120 percent of its value (Lev. 27:31). For livestock, however, there could be no substitute. Animals passed single file under a rod dipped in coloring and every tenth one was marked. Selecting inferior animals was prohibited (vv. 32–33).

Deuteronomy instructed households to bring their tithes to the sanctuary for a joyous sacrificial meal. If it was too far, the offerer was told that the goods could be sold locally and the money used near the sanctuary to buy "anything you wish" including oxen, sheep, wine, or strong drink (Deut. 14:22–26). Every third year tithes remained in the hometown and were given to the Levite, alien, orphan, and widow (vv. 28–29). The offerer had to "say before the Lord" that the tithe had been properly given (26:13–14).Thus tithing taught the people to "revere the LORD" always (14:23), and supported the poor and the priests. Samuel later warned Israel that an earthly king (whom they desired against God's wishes) would require a tenth to sustain his rule (1 Sam. 8:15, 17).

The difference between instructions in Deuteronomy and Numbers led some rabbis to believe that there were two tithes each year, one for the Levite and one to be eaten before the Lord. Yet it is unlikely that the text would institute a second tithe the way it does, without introduction or clarification. Some also believed that the triennial tithe was additional, making a total of three tithes. But it is unlikely that the offerer would have to affirm that such tithe was given properly while saying nothing of the first, or primary tithe.

It is possible that there was only one tithe and that the differences in descriptions were due to changing circumstances. Numbers, written during the period of wandering, instructs the people to give their tithes to the Levites. Deuteronomy, written as Israel entered the land and began a more settled existence, required that tithes be eaten in the sanctuary (where the remaining portion was no doubt left). It seems every third year the tithe was given to the poor.

Tithing indicated Israel's devotion to God, and the people did not always give as they should. Withholding tithes and offerings was regarded as robbing God, but great prosperity was promised if they would obey (Mal. 3:8–12). When the people forsook worship of Yahweh their tithes went to idols (Amos 4:4). Hezekiah oversaw a restoration of obedience to God during which so much was given in tithes and offerings that rooms had to be prepared in the house of the Lord (2 Chron. 31:10–11). Upon return from captivity Nehemiah led another restoration and made sure tithes and offerings were collected (Neh. 12:44) so the Levites would not have to work in the fields (13:10).

Jesus refocused attention on inward attitudes. He criticized some who went so far as to tithe tiny grains of spice—not because they tithed, but because they neglected the weightier matters of the law (Matt. 23:23). He regarded stewardship of finances as an indication of trustworthiness with spiritual things (Luke 16:11), which were more important (Matt. 6:19–20).

Nowhere does the New Testament require Christians to tithe in the sense of giving 10 percent, but it does reiterate many things associated with tithing: those who minister are entitled to receive support (1 Cor. 9:14); the poor and needy should be cared for (1 Cor. 16:1; Gal. 2:10); those who give can trust God, as the source of all that is given (2 Cor. 9:10), to supply their needs (2 Cor. 9:8; Phil. 4:19); and giving should be done joyously (2 Cor. 9:7). The New Testament directs that taxes be paid to the state (Rom. 13:6–7), which replaced Israel's theocracy. Paul's vocabulary and teaching suggest that giving is voluntary and that there is no set percentage. Following the example of Christ, who gave even his life (2 Cor. 8:9), we should cheerfully give as much as we have decided (2 Cor. 9:7) based on how much the Lord has prospered us (1 Cor. 16:2), knowing that we reap in proportion to what we sow (2 Cor. 9:6) and that we will ultimately give account for our deeds (Rom. 14:12). BRIAN K. MORLEY

See also COLLECTION; CONTRIBUTION.

Bibliography. S. R. Driver, *A Critical and Exegetical Commentary on Deuteronomy;* D. L. Feinberg, *ZPEB,* 4:756–58; G. F. Hawthorne, *NIDNTT,* 3:851–55; M. Wischnitzer, *Encyclopedia Judiaca,* 15:1156–62.

Titus, Theology of. The New Testament Epistle to Titus was written, according to 1:1, by Paul. Since 1 Timothy and Titus do not reflect, as a background, any imprisonment at all and since 2 Timothy implies a more serious imprisonment than is reflected by the prison epistles written earlier, many evangelical scholars believe that Paul suffered two imprisonments. The first and less serious is described in Acts 28. Paul may then have been released, during which time, among other things, he revisited Crete and began a church there, leaving Titus in charge. Had Luke, the author of the Book of Acts, added to his book later, he undoubtedly would have described this release and second imprisonment. Since we have nothing describing this period in Paul's life, we have no way of knowing the place from which he sent this letter to Titus or the exact time when it was penned.

The purpose of Paul's writing to Titus, as stated in 1:5, was to give him practical directions for setting in order the things remaining unfinished for the church on the island of Crete. For this reason, it may seem surprising to find as much theological teaching in this brief epistle as there is. Many of the major theological terms are found within this short epistle, terms like election (1:1), salvation (2:11), faith and believing (1:1; 2:2; 3:8), the grace of God (2:11; 3:7), redemption (2:14), regeneration (3:5), and justification (3:7).

Bibliology. Titus 1:2 is a verse often used in defense of the inerrancy of God's Word, the Bible. In it, Paul refers to God as the One "who cannot lie," as One who is free from deceit and is totally truthful and trustworthy. Not only will he not lie, but he *cannot* do so. Hence, his words must be true and dependable. Also, because the Scriptures are God's Word, Paul writes that young men are to live so as not to bring dishonor and reproach upon that Word (2:5). Of course, Paul's implication is that all Christians are to conduct their lives to reflect favorably upon the Word of God, by whose standards they are to be living.

Anthropology. Humankind's original condition, without Christ and salvation, is very carefully described in 3:3. Paul writes, concerning our unsaved state, that "we too were foolish, disobedient, deceived and enslaved by all kinds of passions and pleasures. We lived in malice and envy, being hated, hateful and hating one another." Paul implies that when we are saved by faith in Jesus Christ, we then become free from the bondage of sin so that we can serve God and righteousness by holy living.

Christology. Paul's epistle to Titus contains one of the strongest statements in all of Scripture regarding the divinity of Jesus Christ. There is no question that Paul believed Jesus to be a co-equal and consubstantial member of the divine Trinity. In 2:13, Paul calls Christ Jesus "Our great God and Savior," after which he proceeds to briefly mention his substitutionary atonement for our sins. Jesus was the One who "gave himself for us to redeem us from all wickedness and to purify for himself a people that are his very own, eager to do what is good" (v. 14). Again, the need of the unsaved for redemption or freedom from all of the lawless deeds that they performed in their unsaved state appears. This concept of redemption has as its background the need of ancient slaves for freedom from one master (sin) to become bondservants of another master (righteousness through Jesus Christ). Paul in this manner briefly, but clearly, states both who he believed Christ to be and what Christ has provided for those who would accept it by faith.

Soteriology. Of all the biblical doctrines, for some unknown reason, Paul seems to treat the doctrine of salvation most thoroughly in his Epistle to Titus. The universal *aim* of Christ's atonement is stated in 2:11, where Paul writes that "the grace of God that brings salvation has appeared to all men." In keeping with the facts that God is not willing that any should perish (1 Peter` 3:19) and that hell was prepared for the devil and his angels only (Matt. 24:31), Paul stresses the universal scope of the atonement Christ provided. The *agent* of salvation, in accord with the other pastoral epistles, is said to be "God our Savior" three times (1:3; 2:10; 3:4) and "Jesus Christ our Savior" two times (2:13; 3:6). The entire Godhead, and especially the second Person of the Trinity, were and are directly involved in the salvation of humankind according to Paul.

The *instrument* by which this salvation was provided was Christ's vicarious death on the cross. Jesus Christ "gave himself for us to redeem us from all wickedness and to purify for himself a people that are his very own, eager to do what is good" (2:14). The *motivation* for God's provision of this salvation is clearly said to be his mercy (3:5) and, a little later, his grace or unmerited favor extended to humankind (3:7). Paul makes it crystal clear that salvation is not based on righteous works that we ourselves have done (3:5). The *occa-*

sion of God's saving us is quite clearly our faith in the work that God our Savior did for us (3:8).

The *goals* of our salvation according to Paul in Titus are twofold. *One* is that believers may exhibit their faith by their own good works. This is said in a number of ways. Those who profess to know God must not deny that acquaintance by detestable deeds of disobedience (1:16). As Christians, we must deny ungodliness and worldly passions and live sensible, righteous, and godly lives (2:12). As God's special possessions, we are to be "eager to do what is good" (2:14). Christians are to be "subject to rulers and authorities, . . . obedient, . . . ready to do whatever is good" (3:1). Continuing this theme of good works, Paul encourages Titus to speak confidently "so that those who have trusted in God may be careful to devote themselves to what is good" (3:8). On the negative side, Christians are to "avoid foolish controversies and genealogies and arguments and quarrels about the law" (3:9). Finally, all Christians are to learn "to devote themselves to doing what is good, in order that they may provide for daily necessities and not live unproductive lives" (3:14). As Paul stresses in the practical sections of his other epistles, there is to be a balance in the Christian's life between saving faith and good works, salvation and sanctification. The *other* goal of salvation seen in Titus is that we Christians may have the hope of eternal life (1:2; 2:7).

Ecclesiology. It would appear from Paul's teaching to Titus that the positions of elder (1:5) and bishop or overseer (1:7) were one and the same office in the early days of the church. The former term apparently emphasized the dignity of the office, while the latter stressed the function or duty connected with the position. It is important to note also that Paul commands Titus "to appoint" elders in every city (1:5). Apparently in the early church, it was necessary to do things in more episcopal than congregational fashion, although hints of both forms of church government can be found in the New Testament. Paul lists for Titus those qualities that should characterize men appointed to the position of elder-bishop (1:5–9).

Eschatology. Three times in Titus Paul refers to the hope of the Christian. Twice he calls it "the hope of eternal life" (1:2; 3:7). In 3:7, he adds the idea that we have been made heirs according to that hope. While other New Testament verses stress the present possession of eternal life by the Christian, Paul emphasizes the future consummation of that eternal life with the return of Jesus Christ in glory and power. Along with living proper lives in this present age, Paul gives additional instructions to Christians to continue looking for "the blessed hope—the glorious appearing of our great God and Savior Christ Jesus" (2:13). It is significant that the hope of the church is the revelation of Jesus Christ, when he will return to this earth in power and glory to reign; and it is for this return that the church of Jesus Christ is to continue waiting. WESLEY L. GERIG

See also PAUL THE APSOTLE; TIMOTHY, FIRST AND SECOND, THEOLOGY OF.

Bibliography. H. A. Homer, *Pastoral Epistles;* R. C. Lenski, *Interpretation of Colossians, Thessalonians, First and Second Timothy, Titus, Philemon;* W. Lock, *International Critical Commentary: Pastoral Epistles.*

Touch. Bringing into bodily contact of one thing with another. The Hebrew *nāgā* and Greek *haptō (-omai)* are the main biblical terms for "touch." In addition to the many ordinary uses, they embrace several important theological themes.

The Old Testament. *God's Touch as All-Powerful.* The Old Testament depicts God's supremacy through the image of touch in several ways. Although God created all things by his spoken word (Gen. 1), Genesis 2:7, 21–22 pictures him as personally shaping man and woman from the dust of the earth. Expressions such as God touches "the earth and it melts" (Amos 9:5) and "the mountains, and they smoke" (Pss. 104:32; 144:5) describe his supreme power over the created order. In contrast, idols are powerless. They are insensible, unable to touch: "they have hands, but cannot feel" (Ps. 115:7).

The biblical expression "to lay hands on" can mean to exact vengeance on. God is so pictured in judging Egypt (Exod. 7:4), Israel (Jer. 15:6), and the nations (Ezek. 39:21). Trust in the wicked cannot ward off the touch of a divine scourge (Isa. 28:15; Jer. 14:15). Conversely, whoever touches God's people "touches the apple of his eye" (Zech. 2:8) and will themselves be punished.

Through his divine touch, God turns people to him (1 Sam. 10:26), purifies them from sin (Isa. 6:7; Jer. 1:9), and imparts divine truth through them (Jer. 1:9; Dan. 10:16, 18). Israel is also urged to lay hold of God by learning his ways (Prov. 4:4; Isa. 64:7).

Satan's Touch as Limited by God. God limits Satan's power and freedom to harm people. In Job's case, Satan was unable to touch him beyond what God had permitted (Job 1:12; 2:6).

Touching and Moral Cleanness. Old Testament laws governing ceremonial cleanness prohibit touching unclean things, mainly food (Lev. 11; Deut. 14:1–21), bodily discharges (Lev. 15), and corpses (Num. 19). They had hygienic and religious significance in preventing the spread of disease and in distinguishing Israel from her ancient contemporaries, who had no laws against many of these unclean practices. They ultimately reveal, however, something of God's holy and gracious character and the sinful condition of humanity. On the one hand, God's holiness was severe: upon the threat of immediate death, no one was to touch Mount Sinai while God's glory was upon it (Exod. 19:12) or the sacred furnishings of the tabernacle except Aaron and his sons (Num. 4:15; cf. 2 Sam. 6:6–7). On the other hand, God graciously gave these prohibitions (cf. Lev. 27:34) to provide a way for sinful people to approach him. The link to moral purity is evident in Leviticus 7:21: "if anyone touches something unclean . . . and then eats any of the meat of the fellowship offering . . . , that person must be cut off from his people." These laws helped clarify the terms of purification by which one could come to God and, in turn, God's expectations for the continuing moral cleanness of his people.

The New Testament. The New Testament takes up these same themes of touching, but now expresses them mainly through Jesus Christ.

Jesus' Touch as All-Powerful. All four Gospels present Jesus' touch as all-powerful over nature, sickness, and death. Concerning the created order, Jesus walked on water (Mark 6:45–56 pars.) and twice multiplied enough food with his hands from meager rations to feed thousands of people (Mark 6:30–44 pars.; 8:1–3 par.). Concerning physical healing, Jesus' touch cured people of various infirmities and restored life to the dead. Three Greek expressions are synonomously used: *haptesthai*, "to touch," *kratein tēs cheiros*, "to take by the hand," and *epitithēnai ten cheira*, "to lay the hand upon." Examples include a man with leprosy (Mark 1:41 pars.), Simon's feverish mother-in-law (Matt. 8:15 pars.), many sick people (Mark 6:5, Luke 4:40), two dead children (Mark 5:41 pars.; Luke 7:14), blind men (Matt. 9:29; Mark 9:22–25; John 9:6), a deaf/mute man (Mark 7:33), a boy with an evil spirit (Mark 9:27), a crippled woman (Luke 13:13), and a servant with a severed ear (Luke 22:51). Many were also healed by touching Jesus or his clothes (Mark 3:10 par.; 5:25–34 pars.; 6:56 par.). Through Jesus' name the early church communicated similar miraculous healing powers over sickness and death through touch (Acts 2:43; 3:1–16; 9:17; 19:12).

Touching the Resurrected Jesus as First-Century Christian Apology. The doubt of the disciples that Jesus had risen from the dead and his subsequent appearances to them gave rise to early Christian apology concerning the historicity of Jesus' bodily resurrection. Crucial to this apology was the physical contact the disciples had with the resurrected Jesus: "They came to him, clasped his feet and worshiped him" (Matt. 28:9); "Touch me and see" (Luke 24:39); "Put your finger here; see my hands. Reach out your hand and put it into my side" (John 20:27). It is this Jesus whom "our hands have touched" (1 John 1:1). Physical contact with the resurrected Jesus no doubt formed some of the "many convincing proofs" he had given them before ascending to heaven (Acts 1:3).

Jesus as Touched by Our Sin. In redeeming humanity from sin and spiritual death, Jesus bore in his body our sin, thus bringing its deadly consequences upon himself: "he took up our infirmities and carried our sorrows, . . . he was pierced for our transgressions, he was crushed for our iniquities; the punishment that brought us peace was upon him, and by his wounds we are healed" (Isa. 53:4–5, 11; cf. 2 Cor. 5:21; 1 Peter 2:24; 1 John 3:5).

Satan's Touch as Limited by Jesus Christ. In the New Testament, Satan's power to harm believers is also limited by deity; but in this instance, it is by "the one who was born of God," Jesus Christ (1 John 5:18). Here Jesus' work uniquely parallels Yahweh's.

Touching and Moral Cleanness. The contrast in touch between the giving of the law and the gospel could not be greater. In the first, the obedient are to refrain on the pains of death from coming close to God's presence (Heb. 12:18–21); but in the second, through Christ's blood they enter eternally into God's very presence (vv. 22–24). The appropriate charge to believers, therefore, is to live a holy life befitting this intimate relationship (vv. 14–17, 25–19), which at present is spiritual but will become a physical reality at Jesus' return (cf. Rev. 21:1–22:5). Believers must avoid evil (1 Thess. 4:3; 5:22; 1 Peter 2:11; cf. Col. 2:21; 1 Tim. 4:3) and lay hold of God and Christ through Christ-like living (cf. Matt. 11:12; Luke 16:16). H. Douglas Buckwalter

See also ANTHROPOMORPHISM.

Bibliography. R. Stevenson, *Hasting's Dictionary of Christ and the Gospels,* 2: 736–37; N. Turner, *IDB,* 4: 675; R. Grob, *NIDNTT,* 3: 859–61.

Transfiguration. An event in Jesus' life in which his appearance was radiantly transformed. The transfiguration is recorded in each of the Synoptic Gospels (Matt. 17:1–9; Mark 9:2–10; Luke 9:28–36) and in 2 Peter 1:16–21. The place of this event is "a high mountain" (Matt. 17:1; Mark 9:2). The association with a mountain is also found in Luke 9:28 and 2 Peter 1:18. Several geographical locations have been suggested: Mount Hermon (truly "high," at 9,200 ft.); Mount Carmel (out of the way for the surrounding events); and the traditional site of Mount Tabor (not a "high" mountain and the presence of a Roman garrison stationed on the top in Jesus' day makes this questionable). The biblical writers apparently were not interested in locating exactly *where* this event took place; they were more concerned with *what* took place.

Attempts have been made to interpret the transfiguration as a misplaced resurrection account. There are several reasons why this is unlikely: the title given to Jesus ("Rabbi") in Mark 9:5 and the equation of Jesus with Moses and Elijah (Matt. 17:4; Mark 9:5; Luke 9:33) would be strange addressed to the resurrected Christ; the form of this account is quite different from resurrection accounts; the presence of Peter-James-John as an inner circle occurs in other accounts during the life of Jesus, but not in a resurrection account; and the temporal designations associated with the resurrection are "first day" or "after three days," not "after six days" (Matt. 17:1; Mark 9:2) or "about eight days after" (Luke 9:28). Attempts to interpret the transfiguration as a subjective "vision" (Matt. 17:9 RSV) ignore the fact that this term can be used to describe historical events. The Septuagint does this in Deuteronomy 28:34 and 67. There is nothing in the accounts themselves that suggests that this is anything other than an actual event.

The transfiguration possesses one of the very few chronological connections found in the Gospel traditions outside the passion narrative. These temporal designations tie this event intimately with the events of Caesarea Philippi (Matt. 16:13–28; Mark 8:27–38; Luke 9:18–27). The temporal tie between the transfiguration and the events of Caesarea Philippi extends to how this event is to be interpreted. The words, "This is my Son, whom I love" (Mark 9:7), are a rebuke of Peter's placement of Jesus on the same level as Moses and Elijah ("Let us put up three shelters—one for you, one for Moses and one for Elijah" [Mark 9:5]) as well as a divine confirmation of Jesus' identity given in Peter's confession (Mark 8:29). Whereas the voice at the baptism is directed to Jesus (Mark 1:11), here it directed to the three disciples. "Listen to him" is best interpreted in light of what had taken place at Caesarea Philippi, for Jesus does not speak in the present account. These words are best understood as a rebuke of Peter's unwillingness to accept Jesus' teaching concerning his future passion (Mark 8:31–33).

It is difficult to understand exactly what happened to Jesus during his transfiguration. Unlike Moses, who radiated the divine glory that shone upon him (Exod. 34:29), Jesus' transfiguration comes from within. He is transfigured and his garments as a result become radiant. Some have interpreted this event in light of John 1:14 and Philippians 2:6–9. At the transfiguration the glory of the preincarnate Son of God temporarily broke through the limitations of his humanity; the "kenosis" of the Son was temporarily lifted. In 2 Peter 1:16, however, the transfiguration is interpreted rather as a glimpse of the future glory of the Son of God at his second coming (cf. Matt. 24:30). Still another interpretation is that the transfiguration is a proleptic glimpse of the glory that awaits Jesus at his resurrection (Luke 24:26; Heb. 2:9; 1 Peter 1:21). In light of Mark 8:38 and 2 Peter 1:16 the second interpretation is to be preferred. The presence of Moses and Elijah is probably best interpreted as indicating that Jesus is the fulfillment of the Law (Moses) and the Prophets (Elijah). Luke adds that Moses and Elijah spoke to Jesus of his "departure" or forthcoming death (Luke 9:31). This fits well Luke's own emphasis on Jesus being the fulfillment of the Old Testament Scriptures. The Gospel writers seem also to have understood this account as the fulfillment of Jesus' words with respect to the disciples seeing the kingdom of God coming with power in their lifetime. ROBERT H. STEIN

See also CHRIST, CHRISTOLOGY; JESUS CHRIST.

Bibliography. G. B. Caird, *ET* 67 (1955–56): 291–94; A. Kenny, *CBQ* 19 (1957): 444–52; A. M. Ramsey, *The Glory of God and the Transfiguration of Christ;* T. F. Torrance, *EvQ* 14 (1942): 214–29; J. W. C. Wand, *Transfiguration.*

Transgression. *See* SIN.

Trespass. *See* SIN.

Tribulation. *See* PERSECUTION; SUFFERING.

Triumph. *See* VICTORY.

Truth. In Scripture, truth is characterized by both qualitative and quantitative aspects. In the historical narratives of the Old Testament, truth is identified with personal veracity and historical factuality. Before identifying himself to his brothers, Joseph desires to test them by commanding them to send one of their brothers as a prisoner, to see if there is truth in them (Gen. 42:16). Both Joseph's brothers and Achan claim to be speaking the truth when they confess their respective sins (Gen. 42:21; Josh. 7:20).

Truth is also a quality used to describe utterances that are from the Lord. When Elijah intervenes for the son of the widow of Zarephath, bringing the boy back to life, the boy's mother remarks that now she knows that Elijah is a man of God, and that the word of the LORD in his mouth is truth. Ahab becomes angry with Micaiah, his personal incarcerated prophet, because the latter has given a sarcastic favorable forecast for battle. Ahab responds by saying, "How many times must I make you swear to tell me nothing but the truth in the name of the LORD?" (1 King 22:16; 2 Chron. 18:15).

The Psalter describes truth as a fundamental characteristic of God, a characteristic that the psalmist desires to share. The wicked do not speak truth (5:9), whereas the blameless one speaks truth from the heart (15:2). The psalmists often depict truth as a quality separate from God, and which God serves by virtue of his nature. In many instances, truth appears to be personified. The psalmist tells God to "guide me in your truth" (25:5); the psalmist asks God to "send forth your light and your truth" to lead him

(43:3); the psalmist asks the Lord to "ride forth victoriously in behalf of truth" (45:4). The psalmist desires to walk in God's truth (86:11). Indeed, the sum of God's word is truth.

Proverbs seldom speaks of truth, but when it does it defines it as a virtue that the person of God should practice. Truth is to proceed from one's mouth, and wickedness is an abomination to the lips (8:7); the one who speaks the truth gives honest evidence (12:17); truth is described as a commodity that one should purchase, along with wisdom, instruction, and understanding (23:23).

Jeremiah bemoans the fact that in Judah truth is absent. He tells the people that if they can find a man in Jerusalem who does justice and speaks truth, God will pardon the entire city (5:1). The Lord looks for truth (5:3), but it is notoriously absent from Judah (7:28; 9:3, 5). In Daniel, truth is an eschatological virtue related to the interpretations of the visions that God shows to Daniel. Daniel inquires of the truth of the vision of the four beasts (7:16, 19). The casting down of truth allows the little horn to act and prosper (8:12); the future dealings of the kings of Persia are referred to as the truth (10:21; 11:2). Zechariah commands his readers to speak the truth (8:16), and to love truth and peace (8:19).

The Synoptic Gospels scarcely use the word truth at all, while in John it is an extremely significant term referring to Jesus and his ministry. Jesus, as the Word become flesh, is full of grace and truth (1:14), and is the source of grace and truth (1:17). In contrast to the woman at the well, who felt geographic location of worship was important, Jesus states that the issue is not whether one should worship God in Moriah or Gerizim, but rather one should worship in spirit and in truth. For John, truth is ultimately identified with, and is personified in the person of, Jesus Christ. The ministry of John the Baptist is to bear witness to the truth (5:33). Jesus speaks the truth, and for this the Jews seek to kill him (8:40). This is because the Jews who contended with Jesus were ultimately of their father the devil, who has no truth in him whatsoever (8:44–46).

Jesus describes himself as the way, the truth, and the life, and as such he is the only means to the Father (14:6). Even when Jesus departs, the ministry of truth will continue because the Comforter, who is the Spirit of truth (14:17), will be active both in the church as well as in the world.

For Paul, truth is the message of God that all of humanity has repressed (Rom. 1:18) and exchanged (1:25) for lie, in that they have directed their worship not to the Creator, but to the creation. All unbelievers ultimately do not obey the truth, which is embodied in the law (2:8, 20). In Galatians, truth is synonymous with the gospel, which the Judaizers have perverted by requiring converts to practice law observance (2:5, 14; 4:16; 5:7; cf. Eph. 1:13; Col. 1:5–6).

In addition, Paul also uses truth to speak practically of the believer's deportment in following the Lord. Believers are to speak the truth to one another in a loving manner, as we grow up into submission to our head, namely Christ (Eph. 4:15). The importance of speaking the truth to one another is underscored by the fact that we are members of one another (Eph. 4:25).

In 2 Thessalonians Paul equates the truth with the believers' salvation. Those who perish do so because they are under a wicked deception, and so refuse to love the truth and be saved (2:10). Such people are condemned because they did not believe the truth, but instead had pleasure in unrighteousness (2:12). God's choosing of the Thessalonian believers for salvation came about by means of sanctification by the Spirit as well as belief in the truth. Interestingly, the term "truth" does not appear in 1 Thessalonians.

In the Pastoral Epistles, truth takes on the characteristics of a repository, or official body of beliefs, of which the church is the faithful steward and guardian. Salvation includes, and is likely synonymous with, knowledge of the truth (1 Tim. 2:4). The church of the living God is both the pillar and ground of the truth. Knowledge of and belief in the truth prevents one from becoming entangled in erroneous doctrines, such as the belief that marriage is to be avoided, abstinence from certain foods is to be enjoined, and that godliness is a means of gain (1 Tim. 4:3; 6:5), as well as the belief that the resurrection is past (2 Tim. 2:18). Paul further encourages Timothy to guard the truth, which the Holy Spirit has entrusted to him (2 Tim. 1:14). The Scriptures are themselves the word of truth (2 Tim. 2:15). Individuals who oppose God and naively listen to others (i.e., Jannes and Jambres, Pharaoh's two magicians) never arrive at the truth, and, in fact, actually oppose it (2 Tim. 3:7–8). Paul informs Titus that the knowledge of the truth goes along with the furtherance of faith and with godliness (Titus 1:1). Paul informs both Timothy and Titus that the only alternative to the truth is to believe in myths (2 Tim. 4:4; Titus 1:14).

While the term "truth" appears only sporadically in most of the General Epistles, it appears repeatedly throughout the Johannine epistles. To claim to have fellowship with God, and to walk in darkness, is not to live according to the truth (1 John 1:6). To claim sinlessness for the believer is to practice self-deceit and thus be void of truth (1 John 1:8). The basic message of Christianity is termed "the truth," and believers know the truth, and can discern that no lie is of the truth (1 John 2:4, 21). Believers are to love in both deed and in truth (i.e., "truly"; 1 John 3:18). Believers are of the truth, which no doubt means that they belong to Jesus, who is the truth (1 John 3:19). Likewise, the fact that we are of God allows us to know the spirit (Holy Spirit?)

of truth, and to discern it from the spirit of error (1 John 4:6). The truth abides with us forever (2 John 2), and the Elder rejoices because the elect lady's children follow the truth (2 John 4; cf. also 3 John 4). Further references in 3 John indicate that the Elder refers to Jesus Christ as "the truth" (3 John 3, 4, 8, 12). Interestingly, the term "truth" does not occur in Revelation. ANDREW L. SMITH

Bibliography. S. Aalen, *Studia Evangelica* 2 (1964): 3–24; J. Barr, *The Semantics of Biblical Language;* R. E. Brown, *The Gospel According to St. John;* I. Jepsen, *TDOT,* 1:292–323; L. J. Kuyper, *Interp* 18 (1964): 3–19; E. T. Ramsdell, *JPOS* 31 (1951): 264–73; V. H. Stanton, *Hastings Dictionary of the Bible,* 4:816–20; D. J. Theron, *Ev Q* 26 (1954): 3–18.

Type, Typology. The "type" is perhaps the least understood but most important concept in the hermeneutics of biblical prophecy. Typological prophecy occurs throughout the Bible and can be considered the "normal" way that the prophets, including Jesus, spoke of the future. Failure to take this method of speaking into account can lead to gross distortions of the prophetic message.

Typology is often confused with allegorical interpretations and is sometimes wrongly labeled as "double fulfillment." It also contrasts with what is sometimes called the "literal interpretation."

Allegorism arose in pre-Christian Hellenism as a means whereby early philosophers could explain the immoral and offensive elements of the Greek myths. Scholars such as Metrodorus of Lampascus (331–278 B.C.) and Chrysippus of Soli (280–207 B.C.) used allegory to discern moral and philosophical lessons behind the bawdy stories of the gods and goddesses. Christian thinkers, particularly those of Alexandria, adopted allegorism to demonstrate the presence of Christian theological and spiritual truth in the Old Testament. Clement of Alexandria and Origen, following the trail laid by the Jewish scholar Philo, used incidental parallels and similarities to propound interpretations that were regrettably forced and alien to the text. This hermeneutic dominated Christendom through the medieval period. Books such as the Song of Songs were especially subjected to allegorism (e.g., the implied two lips of 1:2 were taken to represent the law and gospel), but no texts were immune from such treatment. True allegories are rare in the Bible, and when they occur, their allegorical nature is self-evident (e.g., Judg. 9:7–20).

The idea of a "double-fulfillment" of prophecy is closer to the concept of typology, but as a hermeneutical model it is crude and imprecise. The metaphor of two mountains often accompanies the idea of double-fulfillment. The prophet is said to have seen two separate events in the future juxtaposed like two mountains, one in front of the other. The one event was much closer in time than the other, but he saw the two together through "prophetic foreshortening." This model does not explain why the two specific events were juxtaposed by the prophet; why two events rather than three, four, or five are juxtaposed; and what the basis for the "foreshortening" is.

A popular claim in some quarters is that one holds to a "literal" or a "literal where possible" hermeneutic. Those who follow this model frequently look for some single, highly specific fulfillment to a prophecy, whether it be an event in the earthly ministry of Jesus or some alleged fulfillment to come in the "great tribulation" or millennium.

Such interpretations generally face three difficulties. First, they often fail to account for the contextual meaning of a given prophecy both in the historical context of the prophet's own generation and in the literary context of the book in which the prophecy is found. In short, the prophecies are thought to address some far-off situation but are all but irrelevant to the people who first heard them and to the central messages of the books in which they are found. Second, this hermeneutic obscures the fact that every reasonable interpretation of prophecy is to some degree literal and to some degree metaphorical. Third, this hermeneutic is not followed by the New Testament itself, in that it does not demand the literalism allegedly maintained by "single fulfillment" interpretations of prophecy. For example, Jesus did not regard it as a violation of valid interpretation to assert that John the Baptist could fulfill the prophecy that Elijah would come before the Messiah (Matt. 17:11–13; Mark 9:11–13), notwithstanding the fact that John was not "literally" Elijah. Like true allegory, predictions of singular events are rare in the Bible and are marked by explicit and precise language (e.g., 1 Kings 13:2, in which a prophet explicitly predicts that Josiah would profane the altar of Bethel).

The typological interpretation of prophecy asserts that the prophets did not so much make singular predictions as proclaim certain theological themes or patterns and that these themes often have several manifestations or fulfillments in the course of human history. These patterns often have their greatest manifestations in the life of Christ or in the eschaton, but there may be one or more other fulfillments elsewhere in human history, especially in the immediate historical context of the prophet.

This principle of interpretation can best be illustrated from a prophecy of Jesus himself. In Matthew 24–25, Jesus gives the "Olivet Discourse," in which he speaks both of the destruction of the Jerusalem temple (24:2) and of the "end of the age" (24:3). The destruction of Jerusalem in A.D. 70 and the last judgment are juxtaposed under the theological theme of the wrath of God. Some aspects of the prophecy may apply more precisely to A.D. 70 (e.g., 24:17–20) and other aspects to the end of the age (24:27–31), but the text does not attempt to separate the two events chronologically because they are linked conceptually. The signs that precede the wrath of God, not some specific events, are the real focus of the text.

In addition, the typological interpretation of the Olivet Discourse reveals how a text may be applied legitimately to situations other than one or two specific fulfillments. Throughout the discourse, Jesus warns of false messiahs to come. Because the text describes the signs and upheavals that precede the pouring out of God's wrath and not some single, specific event, this need not be taken simply as a prediction about a final Antichrist. All false messiahs are fulfillments of this prophecy, and all are indicators of a troubled time that is a prelude to divine judgment.

As another example, Joel understands the "day of the LORD" (2:31) to be not a single event but a theological concept with multiple fulfillments, or perhaps better, multiple manifestations. The locust plague, a terrible judgment of God on his people, was the day of the Lord, but an apocalyptic invasion yet to come (vv. 1–11, referring to a human, not locust, army) was still another manifestation of the day of the Lord. Even so, the day of the Lord was also salvation for his people, as seen in the restoration of the land (vv. 21–27), the pouring out of the Spirit (vv. 28–32), and the judgment on the nations (3:1–21). Each of these events is a separate manifestation of the day of the Lord and each can be called a "fulfillment." Peter, therefore, can cite the entirety of Joel 2:28–32 as fulfilled on Pentecost Sunday since the pouring out of the Spirit, in Peter's understanding as well as in Joel's, was no less than the day of the Lord. In short, the locust plague that took place in Joel's time, the destruction of Jerusalem by invading troops of men, the pouring out of the Spirit, and the final judgment on the nations are all genuine fulfillments of the idea of the day of the Lord.

Typological interpretation clarifies how a prophecy can have its ultimate fulfillment in Jesus and yet have other fulfillments as well. Perhaps the clearest example here is the series of "Servant Songs" in Isaiah (42:1–4; 49:1–6; 50:4–9; 52:13–53:12). The major concern has always been that of the identity of the servant. At one point, Isaiah explicitly identifies the servant as Israel (49:3), but in 50:4–9 he describes the servant in very individualistic terms and in verse 9 the prophet seems to identify himself, speaking in the first person, as the servant. He ascribes various functions to the servant; the role of taking the gospel to the nations figures prominently (49:5–6). In 52:13–53:12, however, the servant suffers and dies vicariously for the sins of the world but is ultimately vindicated and exalted. There is little need to wonder why the debate about the identity of the servant has raged for so long.

The difficulty of these songs greatly diminishes, however, when one realizes that Isaiah is not speaking of any one individual but of the ideal of the servant of the Lord. That ideal may have its fulfillment corporately (in Israel) or individually (in, for example, the prophets), but the ultimate and complete fulfillment is in Christ himself. Thus, not everyone who might be legitimately called a "servant of the Lord" fulfills every aspect of these prophecies; only the Messiah can atone for the sins of the world. Even so, anyone who with patience endures hardship and persecution for God's sake and carries on with the task of proclaiming God's message to the nations is properly a "servant of the Lord" and fulfills this prophecy. Paul, therefore, can speak of suffering to fill up what is lacking in Christ's afflictions (Col. 1:24). This interpretation, moreover, does not diminish but rather enhances the glory of Christ as the ultimate fulfillment of Servant Songs.

Typology also explains how many of the events in Jesus' life and ministry are fulfillments of Old Testament patterns. Like the nation of Israel, Jesus came out of Egypt (Matt. 2:15), spent forty days in the wilderness (comparable to the forty years of Israel's wandering), and gave his law on a mountain. Jesus individually fulfills the highest ideals of the role of Israel as God's servant and is in a sense the nation of Israel incarnate.

Typology also functions in prophecies about evil. Babylon, for example, is the type of cultural and institutional opposition to God's people. It is a kind of antikingdom of God and figures prominently in Revelation 17–18. It is unnecessary and in fact misleading, however, to ask if Babylon in this text is either "literal" Babylon or Rome, because it is both of those cities but more than either. Any city or civilization, with its institutions, culture, wealth, oppression, and power structure, is a rival to the city of God. These chapters in Revelation therefore speak directly to any believer in any age or culture and are bound neither to the ancient past nor to the prophetic future.

The value of typology is twofold. First, it provides an intelligible hermeneutic for dealing with biblical prophecy. The problems of interpreting prophecies, especially those concerning Christ, have often left the interpreter with the unhappy choice of either ignoring the historical and literary context of a passage in order to point the text toward Christ or of focusing exclusively on the historical situation of the prophet with the implication being that the passage in fact has nothing to say about Christ. Faced with this dilemma, some interpreters take Isaiah 7:14 exclusively as a prophecy of the virgin birth of Christ and employ fairly desperate exegesis to explain why Isaiah would make such a prediction in the context of the Syro-Ephraimite war. Others relate Isaiah 7:14 exclusively to its historical context and in effect say that Matthew was wrong to take it as a prophecy of Christ's birth (Matt. 1:23). In typological exegesis, however, the dilemma is not only avoided but is meaningless.

Second, typology allows for very direct and practical application of prophetic texts to the situations in which God's people find themselves in the real world. Christians need not vex themselves over the identity of the Antichrist and should not suppose that only some future generation will face the trials and persecutions of Antichrist. Martyrs who suffered under Nero or Stalin, for example, faced Antichrist just as surely as anyone ever did or ever will.

Duane A. Garrett

See also Allegory; Old Testament in the New Testament, the; Prophet, Prophetess, Prophecy.

Bibliography. F. F. Bruce, *New Testament Development of Old Testament Themes;* D. A. Garrett, *An Analysis of the Hermeneutics of John Chrysostom's Commentary on Isaiah 1–8 with an English Translation;* L. Goppelt, *Typos: The Typological Interpretation of the Old Testament in the New;* G. Osborne, *The Hermeneutical Spiral.*

Twelve, the. *See* Apostle.

Uu

Uncleanness. *See* CLEAN, UNCLEAN.

Unclean Spirit. *See* DEMON.

Understanding. ***The Old Testament.*** The basic Hebrew word so translated is the verb *bîn* or one of its derivatives, together used some 247 times in the Old Testament. In the Revised Standard Version this root accounts for 89 out of 113 appearances of the word "understanding." Occasionally *lēb* (heart/mind) will be rendered "understanding" in contexts where the rational rather than the emotional is stressed (Job 8:10; 12:24).

Bîn is associated with the Hebrew substantive *bayin*, which means "interval" and, when used as a preposition, "between." Thus, the basic meaning of *bîn* is to separate, to distinguish. It is perceptive insight with the ability to judge.

Understanding is seen as a gift of God (Dan. 2:21) and it is to be prayed for (Ps. 119:34). In answer to the question, "Where shall wisdom or understanding be found?" the response is, "God alone knows" (Job 28:12, 20, 23). It also results from the study of the divine precepts (Ps. 119:104) and careful reflection in the sanctuary (Ps. 73:17). Hearing is no assurance of understanding (Dan. 12:8).

Understanding has a moral character (Job 28:28). This does not, however, preclude the cognitive (Ps. 49:3–4) for understanding is to be gotten (Prov. 4:5, 7), sought (23:23), and learned (4:1). This can be seen in references to the understanding of a foreign language (Isa. 33:19) and Daniel's understanding of all the subjects in which he was interrogated by Nebuchadnezzar (Dan. 1:20). The emphasis of this word goes beyond collection of data, however. Acquired knowledge must be used and used correctly. The injunction is to trust in the Lord rather than to rely on one's understanding (Prov. 3:5).

A person can perceive data with the senses: with the eyes (Job 13:1; 23:8), with the ears (Job 23:5; Prov. 29:19), with the touch (pots can feel the heat—Ps. 58:9), and with the taste (Job 6:30).

Understanding can pertain to arts and crafts (2 Chron. 2:13) or to the administrative functions of the king (2 Chron. 2:12)—even extended to the messianic king (Isa. 11:2). David's understanding as shepherd of his people is extolled (Ps. 78:72). While artisans have made idols according to their understanding (Hos. 13:2), Isaiah challenges the effectiveness of such effort, noting that artisans can create no gods at all (44:17). Daniel possesses apocalyptic understanding (Dan. 9:2, 23; 10:1).

Understanding is associated with wisdom and personified (Prov. 2:3; 7:4; 8:14–31). While some see this as an hypostasis, it is more likely a poetic personification of an abstract principle.

On the one hand, God is the most important object of understanding (Isa. 43:10; Jer. 9:24), but in an intellectual sense he is beyond a person's understanding (Isa. 40:28).

The New Testament. Of the seventeen occurrences of understanding in the Revised Standard Version New Testament, ten are translations of *suniemi* or one of its derivatives. This is the word that the Septuagint uses as a translation of *bîn*. Its meaning is to understand, to gain insight into something.

It can designate a positive quality as when the scribe concurred with Jesus about loving the Lord with "all your understanding" (Mark 12:33) and in Paul's prayer for the Colossians where he couples it with "spiritual wisdom" (Col. 1:9). It can be the means of understanding an important truth (2 Tim. 2:7) or the Lord's will (Eph. 5:17).

There is also a negative quality to this word. Jesus used parables because of his audience's slowness to understand (Matt. 13:13). Even his own disciples did not understand the miracle of loaves and fishes (Mark 6:52). Jesus notes that infants understand God's program better than the intellectuals (Matt. 11:25).

The other significant Greek word rendered "understand" is *noeō* and its derivatives, which refer to rational reflection or inner contemplation. Paul notes the limits of human understanding by noting that the peace of God surpasses it

(Phil. 4:7). The apocalyptic number 666 is a challenge to the person who has understanding (Rev. 13:18). The pagans act as they do because they are "darkened in their understanding" (Eph. 4:18). On the other hand, John affirms that understanding has been made possible by the revelation of Jesus (1 John 5:20).

Understanding, then, involves the cognitive, the spiritual, and the moral. While human efforts are called for, the ability to understand comes from God. The final test of understanding is obedience to God.

CARL SCHULTZ

See also MIND/REASON; WISDOM.

Union with Christ. According to the New Testament, the religious experience of the earliest Christians was derived from and dependent upon Christ. Christian experience is more than an imitation of the life and teaching of Jesus. It is the present experience of the risen Christ indwelling the believer's heart by the Spirit. Both Johannine and Pauline literature refer to this reality by emphasizing the inclusive and corporate personality of Christ.

Usage. Paul more often than any other New Testament author combines the preposition "in" (*en*) with some designation for Christ. The phrase and its cognates occur some two hundred times in Pauline literature. The apostle uses the term in more than one sense, and scholars have attempted to interpret the concept in a variety of ways (e.g., mystical, existential, sacramental, local, eschatological, and ecclesiastical). In places, the words "in Christ" can be understood as just another way of designating a Christian (Eph. 1:1; Phil. 1:1; Col. 1:2; 1 Thess. 4:16). The idea of instrumentality or causality is an alternate usage of the phrase (Rom. 14:14; 2 Cor. 3:14; Gal. 2:17; Phil. 4:13). It is clear, however, that the words "in Christ" also have soteriological meaning for Paul (Rom. 8:1; 2 Cor. 5:19; Eph. 1:20). Being "in Christ" is presented as the only basis for justification and glorification (Col. 1:27). This is not a mysticism of absorption, the losing of human identity in the divine, but rather an intimate communion with God through Christ.

Paul expresses the personal appropriation of the work of Christ by the term "in Christ." It is the apostle's favorite term to describe the personal and dynamic relation of the believer to Christ, and appears in a variety of contexts. The phrase is found eight times in Galatians, thirty-four times in Ephesians, and eighteen times in Colossians. A number of these occurrences have nothing to do with the concept of incorporation, but rather, are instrumental. In Ephesians, for example, the phrase "in Christ" is predominantly used in the instrumental sense, signifying Christ as the channel through whom God works his will, elects, redeems, forgives, blesses, imparts new life, and builds up the church. The formula, however, is sometimes descriptive in character (Rom. 9:1; 1 Cor. 3:1). As such it has the meaning of "being a Christian" (Rom. 16:11; 1 Cor. 7:39; 2 Cor. 12:2; Phil 1:1; Philem. 16), and denotes certain identifiable characteristics that define a Christian. The formula is also applied to relations of those who are in the church (Rom. 16:12; Gal. 3:28; Col. 4:7; 1 Thess. 1:1). Thus, "in Christ" serves as the bond of unity within the fellowship of believers.

There are some occurrences, however, that use the formula "in Christ" in a locative sense, denoting the idea of incorporation (Rom. 8:1; 16:7; 1 Cor. 15:22; 2 Cor. 5:17; Phil. 3:8–9). In this sense, Christ is depicted as the locus of the believer's life. If the preposition (*en*) is interpreted in a local, spatial sense, and *Christos* is understood mystically as the Spirit of the glorified Lord, then close union of Christ and the Christian is meant (2 Cor. 5:17). "In Christ" is an expression of intimate interrelatedness, analogous to the air that is breathed: it is in the person, yet at the same time, the person is in it. Thus, Paul's use of the phrase is similar to his concept of being baptized "into Christ" (Gal. 3:27), with connotations of intimate spiritual communion with Christ. Those who have been baptized into Christ are "in him." There are, however, eschatological dimensions of the phrase that indicate a dynamic influence of Christ on the Christian who is incorporated into him.

Union with Christ is the result of an act of divine grace, the baptism of the Holy Spirit. Baptized into Christ, the believer is incorporated into the body of Christ (1 Cor. 12:13). This new position, "in Christ," is the fulfillment of Jesus' promise to his disciples: "On that day you will realize that I am in my Father, and you are in me, and I am in you" (John 14:20). The phrase "in Christ," thus, has a corporate meaning as well: "those in the community of Christ." Communion with Christ necessarily involves a social dimension, experiencing the shared life of his body. This community is defined by its relation to its representative head. Being "in Christ" is thus new life shared in community with those who are related to Christ.

The heart of Pauline theology is union with Christ (Rom. 8:1; 1 Cor. 6:17; Gal. 2:20). Although often overlooked in favor of an emphasis on justification by faith, Paul's treatment of the spiritual life in Christ is central to the apostle's understanding of religious experience. Communion with Christ is presented as synonymous with salvation, achieved by faith and consummated in love. Christ "for us" must be kept together with Christ "in us." Union with Christ is organically related to both justification and sanctification (Rom. 5:8–10), and as such, life "in Christ" is the essence of Paul's proclamation and experience. The concept, however, is also found in the teaching of

Jesus: "For where two or three come together in my name, there am I with them" (Matt. 18:20); "Remain in me, and I will remain in you. No branch can bear fruit by itself; it must remain in the vine. Neither can you bear fruit unless you remain in me" (John 15:4). Thus, the concept is not unique to Paul, but is implicit in the Gospel sayings of Jesus that stress his solidarity with God's people (Matt. 18:20; Mark 8:38; John 15:1–11).

Paul gives particular emphasis to the "in Christ" theme in his epistle to the Ephesians. This is especially evident in 1:3–14, where the phrase (or a variant) occurs some eleven times. The majority of references in Ephesians posit God as the one acting "in Christ." Those "in Christ" are in the thought and eternal purpose of God (1:3, 4, 9, 11; 2:6, 10; 3:9–11). Saints are elect "in Christ" (1:3–14). Christ is not only the means of election (1:5), but is depicted as the first elect (1:9). Election is made "in Christ," denoting the execution of God's purposes in and through his Son. Inclusion in Christ is to be united to his body. Those "in Christ" become part of God's family (1:5; 2:18). Given the corporate nature of Paul's "in Christ" formula, election "in Christ" entails God's gracious choice of a people, a corporate election relative to the election of the Son. The blessings of redemption are stored by God "in Christ" (1:3, 6, 7, 13). Ephesians also utilizes the phrase to depict the sphere of the Christian's daily life and experience (1:1, 3), and to describe the focal point of God's plan to unite all things (1:10, 2:21)—a unification now in progress for those who are "in Christ" (2:13, 15, 21; 3:6).

Elsewhere, Paul uses the phrase to describe a mode of existence in which the believer identifies with the death and resurrection of Christ (Rom. 6:11); shares in his wisdom and holiness (1 Cor. 1:30); and receives a new life or existence (2 Cor. 5:17). This is expressed in the epistle to the Colossians by relating the theme of Christ's "fullness" to the believer's position "in him" (2:8–15). In Christ, who is the "fullness of the Deity" (v. 9), believers "have been given fullness" (v. 10). They have been circumcised by the "circumcision done by Christ" (v. 11), "buried with him in baptism," and "raised with him through . . . faith" (v. 12). Faith-union with Christ, therefore, makes possible incorporation into a new sphere of existence marked by "fullness," covenant relation, and resurrection life.

For the apostle, to be "in Christ" is the same as having "Christ in me" (Gal. 2:19–20). In fact, the message of "Christ in you" is the revelation of God's "mystery" and the "hope of glory" for believers (Col. 1:27). Through faith and love the believer is united with his Lord. Present by his Spirit, Christ indwells believers and makes possible their adoption as sons and daughters of God (Rom. 8:14–16; Gal. 4:6). The Spirit of Jesus is given the believer and conforms the individual to the image of Christ. Thus, the clue to understanding the concept of fellowship with Christ is found in the phrase "in the Spirit." The New Testament teaches that the Spirit mediates Christ's presence to the believer. Paul develops this connection and identifies being "in Christ" with being "in the Spirit" (Rom. 8:9). The apostle perceives the Christian as existing in the Spirit and having the Spirit within. By making Christ real to the Christian, the Spirit provides the environment within which the believer lives "in Christ."

Union with Christ is the result of an act of divine grace, the baptism of the Holy Spirit. Baptized into Christ (Gal. 3:27), the believer is incorporated into the body of Christ (1 Cor. 12:13). A variety of biblical metaphors describe this union: vine and branches (John 15:1–6); head and body (Eph. 1:22–23; 4:15–16; 5:23); marital relation of Christ and the church (Eph. 5:23–32). The result of identification with Christ is organic union and spiritual life. Although Johannine literature depicts this incorporation as mutual and symmetrically reciprocal, Paul emphasizes the relationship of believers "in Christ" more than the indwelling of Christ in believers. The reverse, however, is the case with Paul's treatment of the Spirit. There is more emphasis on the Christian being indwelt by the Spirit than on the believer in the Spirit. Thus, for Paul, the major agent of indwelling is the Spirit.

Incorporation and the Second Adam. "In Christ" denotes a profound personal identification with Christ that serves as the basis of salvation and new life. This is closely associated with the notion of sharing in Christ's death and resurrection (Rom. 6:1–11; 8:17; Gal. 2:20; Col. 2:12; 3:1). Underlying these meanings is the concept of corporate personality. By faith believers are incorporated into the representative head of the new humanity, the Second Adam. For Paul, union with Christ results in the personal appropriation of the effects of Jesus' life, death, resurrection, and glorification. By sharing in these events, the believer experiences them as living realities. In this way, Christ comes to live in and through a person.

Rather than interpreting this phrase as an isolated mystical experience, it is more appropriate to view it as describing a spiritual reality that interpenetrates all of life and finds corporate expression in the body of Christ. Thus, "dying and rising with Christ" is to be understood objectively as a participation in the historical death and resurrection of Jesus. This reality is expressed by Paul in the parallel drawn between Adam and Christ (Rom. 5:12–21; 1 Cor. 15:21–22). As representatives of old and new humanity, the actions and futures of these "corporate personalities" are paradigmatic for all those who belong to them.

Christ has accomplished his redemptive work "for us" through his suffering, death, and resurrection (Rom. 5:6–8; Gal. 1:4; 3:13). What took place "in Christ" makes possible the relationship of being "in him" (2 Cor. 5:17). The application of both past and future dimensions of his redemptive work to the believer is characterized by the phrase "with Christ." Christians are identified as those who have died and been resurrected with Christ (Rom. 6:5; Col. 2:12–13, 20; 3:1, 3), who sit with him in heaven (Eph. 2:6), and who will appear with him in glory (Col. 3:4). The relation of Christians to Christ is one of faith, not mystical absorption. When the apostles John and Paul speak of being "in Christ," they are referring to solidarity with a corporate personality. Just as humankind is "in Adam," and Israel is God's son (or the Servant of Yahweh), so the New Israel is "in Christ." Those who believe in Christ and are baptized into him are a part of the new humanity; they are incorporated into the corporate personality of Christ. The biblical doctrine of representative humanity is also the basis for understanding the expressions "Christ in you" (Rom. 8:10; 2 Cor. 13:5; Col. 1:27), Christ dwelling in his disciples (Eph. 3:17), and being in or abiding in them (John 14:20; 15:4, 7; 17:23, 26; 1 John 3:24).

Through identification with the crucified and resurrected Savior, the believer dies to the old humanity and is incorporated into the new humanity made possible by the Second Adam. "In Christ" there is a "new creation" (2 Cor. 5:17), the believer having entered an entirely new sphere of existence. Union with Christ thus means to be enlivened by the power of his resurrection, to live in the realm of the Spirit. Christ's presence is directly connected to the eschatological gift of the Spirit. In Christ, the Spirit is at work carrying out God's redemptive purposes. These purposes are summed up by Paul in 2 Corinthians 5:14–21. God has reconciled the world to himself through Christ. Not only through him, but "in him" there is redemption and reconciliation. It is through solidarity with Christ as the Second Adam that humanity has the possibility of a new course (Rom. 5:14; 1 Cor. 15:21–22, 45; Col. 1:18). Paul identifies this new mode of existence with being indwelt by the Spirit of Jesus. The glorified Christ lives in his followers by his Spirit (Rom. 8:9–11; Gal. 4:6). In him, who is the Head of the new humanity, there is life eternal.

In close connection with the Adam-Christ parallel are Paul's references to the "old" and "new" nature (Rom. 6:6; Eph. 4:22–24; Col. 3:9–10). These are terms that not only represent the status of an individual before and after conversion, but also signify the change that has already taken effect in Christ's death (Rom. 6:6—"we know that our old self was crucified with him"). On the cross, the old nature was judged, condemned, and put to death (Rom. 8:3). In identifying with this death, believers have died to the old nature (Rom. 6:2; Col. 3:3), and have been freed from the tyranny of sin. "In Christ," they have been transferred to a new order of existence, that of the "new nature." Thus, "old" and "new" signify more than personal and ethical change, but are also to be understood as terms referring to old and new humanity in the scope of salvation history.

Incorporated into Christ's death, believers have "put off the old nature." Through identification with Christ's resurrection, they have likewise "put on the new nature." Being in solidarity with Christ makes possible the new creation, renewal in the image of the Creator (Col. 3:10). "In Adam," old humanity experiences solidarity with him in sin and death. "In Christ," however, the creation of a new humanity is made possible, which experiences solidarity with him in righteousness and life (Rom. 5:18–21). Thus, just as humankind bears the image of the first Adam by virtue of corporate identification, those who have become incorporated into Christ are recreated in the image of the Second Adam (Eph. 2:10). The corporate nature of this identification is emphasized by Paul in his treatment of the new creation, referring to the whole body of Christ as "the one new man" (Eph. 2:15).

Being "in Christ" is not only the basis of Christian individual and corporate identity, but also serves as the basis of transformed relationships (Gal. 3:26–29). Those "in Christ" are not only Abraham's seed and heirs to the promise (v. 29), they also are meant to manifest a oneness that knows no barriers, whether racial, social, or sexual (v. 28). The concept of being "in Christ" refers not only to the believer's vertical relationships ("sons of God" who "put on Christ," vv. 26–27), but also to the horizontal relationships of daily living ("neither Jew nor Greek, slave nor free, male nor female," v. 28). "All" who respond to Christ "through faith" (v. 26) and are "baptized into Christ" (v. 27) are "one" (v. 28). Incorporation into Christ by identification with his death and resurrection means to become part of a body. To be joined to the corporate Christ is to become part of an organic whole, under his headship (1 Cor. 6:15; 12:12–13; Gal. 3:28; Eph. 1:22–23; 2:14–16; 3:6; 4:4, 12–16; 5:23, 30; Col. 1:18; 2:19; 3:15). The principle of incorporation is also highlighted in Paul's use of the temple metaphor. Christ is the foundation and cornerstone of the temple, while believers are the stones built together into a corporate whole and indwelt by God (1 Cor. 3:16–17, 19; 2 Cor. 6:16; Eph. 2:20–22).

Thus, the nature of the Christian is described by Paul with the formula "in Christ." This meant for the apostle that those who put their faith in Christ identified with him as the head of a new humanity. The phrase is a social concept; to become incorporated into this new humanity is represented as belonging to the church as the true community of God. At the same time, however, Paul's understanding of being "in Christ" involved a personal and intimate relationship with Christ. Although the corporate meaning of the formula is important, this does not preclude the apostle's emphasis on personal faith-union and fellowship with Christ. The theme of incorporation is found outside the Pauline corpus, especially in the Johannine writings (John 14:10–11; 15:4–5, 7; 17:21–23; 1 John 2:5–6, 24, 27; 3:6, 24; 4:4, 12–13, 15; 5:20). These passages speak of a variety of relationships that are represented in terms of a reciprocal indwelling.

Christ-Mysticism and Union with God. Paul's teaching on union with Christ has often been labeled as Christian "mysticism." This is an appropriate term if understood in a qualified sense. Paul viewed communion with God as an act of divine grace, coming not by any spiritual exercises, but by God's self-revelation (Gal. 1:16). Thus, union with Christ is something to accept by faith, not something to achieve by human effort. Neither does being "in Christ" involve the loss of individuality, nor the absorption of the individual into the divine Spirit (Rom. 8:14, 16; Gal. 2:20), but the heightening of individual qualities and characteristics. In addition, being "in Christ" is more than mystical union; it involves a moral union that provides the ethical dynamic for Christian living. This is more than a gospel of ethical example (an impossible ideal), but the indwelling of Christ who provides the motive power to live in obedience to God.

For Paul to be "in Christ" was to be "in the Spirit." Paul distinguishes between Christ and the Spirit, but views the function of the latter as mediating the former to believers. As the operative agent of God in the Christian's life, the Spirit never acts apart from Christ. Thus, although distinct entities, Christ and the Spirit are experienced together, and are the means by which persons come into relation with God. Pauline mysticism, however, is a communal or corporate mysticism. "In Christ" is used in a way that is similar to Paul's understanding of Christians being fellow members of the body of Christ. Incorporation into this body is by faith in Jesus Christ. Having identified with the death and resurrection of Christ, the body is empowered by his Spirit to manifest his presence to the world. The Christian lives in vital union with Christ, expressing corporately the love of Christ personally appropriated by faith.

Union with Christ is union with God. Although Christocentric, Paul's theology is grounded on the premise that "God was in Christ"(2 Cor. 5:19). Fellowship with Christ is fellowship with God (Rom. 8:11; cf. 1 John 1:3). Although union with God is dependent on God's gracious initiative, it also requires a human response (Eph. 2:8). Central to Paul's notion of being "in Christ" is the fact of faith. It is the indispensable condition for salvation, a placing of one's trust in the God revealed in Jesus Christ. This faith is the basis for intimate union with Christ, since it is the self-abandonment of the redeemed to the Redeemer. Faith-union thus finds its focal point in the death and resurrection of Christ. At the same time, being "in Christ" also has eschatological implications. Union with him involves looking beyond the present to the future. Even though the believer experiences communion with Christ, there is a yearning for more intimate knowledge and relationship (Phil. 1:23; 3:10). Present union with Christ is still "absence from the Lord," and hence seeks fulfillment in his future advent or "presence" (*parousia*).

Conclusion. The notion of union with Christ is multidimensional in theological significance. "In Christ," believers identify with his death (Rom. 6:3, 5–11), his burial (Rom. 6:4), his resurrection (Col. 3:1), his ascension (Eph. 2:6), his lordship (2 Tim. 2:12), and his glory (Rom. 8:17). As a result, certain characteristics of Christ's person and work are attributed to those in communion with him. The "in Christ" formula is thus a comprehensive term, tying together soteriological, pneumatological, and ecclesiological dimensions of Christian experience. At the same time, it is a mystical concept, in that union with Christ is experienced "in the Spirit." The phrase also has an ethical dimension, as reflected in the idea of a new humanity made possible in solidarity with the Second Adam. Last but not least, "in Christ" has eschatological significance, in describing the status of the believer, whose life has been transformed by the presence of the kingdom of God experienced in Christ. R. David Rightmire

See also Church, the; New Creation; Salvation; Sanctification; Spirituality.

Bibliography. M. Barth, *Ephesians;* M. Bouttier, *Christianity According to Paul;* E. Best, *One Body in Christ;* F. F. Bruce, *Paul: Apostle of the Heart Set Free;* W. D. Davies, *Paul and Rabbinic Judaism;* J. D. G. Dunn, *Jesus and the Spirit;* A. Fitzmeyer, *Paul and His Theology: A Brief Sketch;* W. Grossouw, *In Christ;* A. M. Hunter, *The Gospel According to St. Paul;* R. N. Longenecker, *Galatians;* idem, *The Ministry and Message of Paul;* C. F. D. Moule, *The Origin of Christology;* P. O'Brien, *Colossians, Philemon;* J. K. S. Reid, *Theology Today* 17 (1960): 353–65; A. Richardson, *An Introduction to the Theology of the New Testament;* H. Ridderbos, *Paul: An Outline of His Theology;* A. Schweitzer, *The Mysticism of Paul the Apostle;* J. S. Stewart, *A Man in Christ;* V. Taylor, *Forgiveness and Reconciliation.*

Unleavened Bread, Feast of. *See* Feasts and Festivals of Israel.

Unpardonable Sin. *See* Blasphemy Against the Holy Spirit.

Upright, Uprightness. "Upright" is the English equivalent most often used for the Hebrew *yāšār.* Literally, *yāšār* pertains to that which is vertically erect (Gen. 37:7; Exod. 36:20) or horizontally level or smooth (Isa. 26:7). It also means straight (Isa. 40:3) or evenly distributed (1 Kings 6:35). Application in theological settings brings to mind the notions of unchanging standards, correctness, genuineness, and forthrightness. From the beginning of the relationship between Israel and God, his nature is reflected as truthful and faithful. Uprightness is a further moral aspect to Israel's perception of God's holy character. Note the coinciding themes in Moses' summary hymn of praise: "He is the Rock, his works are perfect, and all his ways are just. A faithful God who does no wrong, upright and just is he" (Deut. 32:4). To find a straightforward deity was uncommon in antiquity. God possessed rock-solid, upfront integrity that his people never saw waver.

Only a God who was good and upright in character could require the pleasure of total loyalty and close genuine attention to the straight way of the law (Pss. 11:7; 119:7; cf. Neh. 9:13). What pleased Yahweh ethically and morally was that in which Israel was to find its true pleasure. Friendship with God was to walk in an upright way guided by his upright word through the sincerity of an upright heart (Pss. 25:8; 33:4; Hos. 14:9).

Wholeness or integrity of heart is a close counterpart to uprightness. Doing right must find resonance in the very center of one's being. Thus, the kings of Israel and Judah are assessed carefully according to their sincere uprightness in applying the whole law personally and socially (1 Kings 3:6; 9:4; 2 Kings 22:2). The Wisdom books underscore the relation among the goodness of Yahweh, his words, and the reflection of his own character in the heart of the righteous. Purity, honesty, obedience, goodness, and blamelessness are key indications of uprightness. Job's integrity and uprightness (1:1, 8; 2:3) in the midst of dire circumstances bring into bold relief the fear of God that shuns evil in the upright. Crookedness or perversity of heart is the opposite of the character and intentions of the "upright One" (Prov. 3:32; 21:8; 28:10).

Isaiah makes use of the contrast between crooked and straight to illuminate the uprightness of Yahweh, his prophets, and the Messiah (26:7; 40:3–4; cf. Jer. 31:9). The kingdom of God is revealed through unbending moral principles, honor, and rectitude. Yet these are most clearly seen in individual lives, particularly that of the one who was the Branch on whom the Spirit rested.

The Hebrew mind made little distinction between uprightness and righteousness (*ṣedeq*, which literally means to be right: Pss. 11:7; 32:11; 33:1; Isa. 26:7). Ethical expressions of justice and truth are expressions of the faith of those who are in right relationship with God (Pss. 17:1–6, 15; 145:17). The upright walk a straight road, one that is focused on divine standards and the application of livingkindness to all persons.

Perhaps the greatest good offered to the upright was the clear trustworthiness of the relationships for which they were created. Uprightness is reflected in a genuine openness or humility that does not harbor calculated reservations. Created upright, fallen men consistently choose "schemes" (Eccles. 7:29). This may account for the usage of upright in the much debated verse in Habakkuk regarding the upright who "live by faith" (2:4). Though the ethical elements of *yāšār* are intended, the deeper moral content cannot be missed. Pride, the essence of sin, resides and swells in the human heart as it flaunts its lack of dependence on God. In contradistinction, the righteous who "live by faith," that is, in continued faithfulness, do so not by volition or external action but by an internal transformation of their desires. Biblical faith, then, is radical openness to full trust in an upright and holy God. Relational faith must be expressed in upright desires. Moral content always informs total abandonment to God.

The translation of the Hebrew terms for upright into Greek include convenient, equity, just, meet, pleasing, and righteous. The Septuagint translates the terms related to upright as *arestos* (pleasing), *dikaios* (just), *euthus* (straight). The concepts that fund the Old Testament concept of uprightness appear in the New Testament as well. The concept of righteousness is incomplete without this Old Testament concept. Wholeness, blamelessness, and integrity are found in the few passages where upright is in focus.

Although it is difficult to distinguish between righteous and upright (both are found as *dikaios*) in the New Testament, there are indications of a difference. The persons surrounding the birth of the Savior are described by terms that set them apart from the typical first-century Jew. Joseph is just (RSV, Matt. 1:19); Zechariah and Elizabeth are both upright (Luke 1:6), as is Simeon (Luke 2:25). Apparently they were blameless according to the law of God; they revered God and their yieldedness was the context of their witnessing God do extraordinary new things. When it came to the revelation of God himself, it was the upright that he sought to introduce him.

Cornelius, the god-fearing centurion, and Joseph of Arimathea are upright (Luke 23:50; Acts 10:22). In the Pastoral Epistles, the overseers are to be blameless in their character, "upright, holy and disciplined" (Titus 1:8). A similar triad is commanded of all believers. This is the most marked difference between Old Testament and New Testament views of uprightness. No longer an exception, the common Christian will exemplify whole-hearted commitment to God that shows itself in a blameless character. A self-controlled person will express a solid trustworthiness and thereby live "upright and godly lives in this present age" (Titus 2:12). M. William Ury

See also Righteousness.

Bibliography. N. H. Snaith, *The Distinctive Ideas of the Old Testament.*

Urim and Thummim. The terms "Urim" and "Thummim" have traditionally been understood as "light(s)" and "perfection(s)" or as "perfect light." The Urim and Thummim were a means of revelation entrusted to the high priest. No description of them is given. This oracular means apparently consisted of a material object or objects since it was physically stored in the breastpiece of the high priest (Exod. 28:30; Lev. 8:8). Most scholars today think that the Urim and Thummim were a lot oracle, but this is by no means certain.

Besides being mentioned by their full name (Exod. 28:30; Lev. 8:8; Ezra 2:63; Neh. 7:65; in reverse order with possessives, Deut. 33:8), the Urim and Thummim could also be referred to by Urim alone (Num. 27:21; 1 Sam. 28:6). Sometimes the mention of the ephod (on which the breastpiece housing the Urim and Thummim were fastened) includes a reference to the Urim and Thummim (1 Sam. 23:9–12; 30:7–8). Also the verb "inquire of" followed by "the LORD" or "God" when no means of revelation is specified refers to a usage of the Urim and Thummim.

The Urim and Thummim were used at critical moments in the history of God's people when special divine guidance was needed. The civil leader was expected to make use of this means for all important matters for which he needed direction. Although referred to in Ezra 2:63 and Nehemiah 7:65, there is no convincing evidence that the Urim and Thummim were used after the time of David.

The reason for the demise of the Urim and Thummim is not explicitly given. Since the Urim and Thummim, in whatever way they functioned, were a physical means of revelation, it appears that God was taking his people away from the easy certainty inherent in a mechanical means of revelation to the more consistent use of prophecy and the Word alone. This would require the more difficult application of the norms for true and false prophecy (Deut. 13:1–4; 18:20–22) and thus necessitate a faithful teaching priesthood (Deut. 33:10; Mal. 2:7).

Although the lot theory has wide support today, there are significant difficulties with so identifying the Urim and Thummim. It is questionable whether the key evidence, the Greek text of 1 Samuel 14:41, is really to be preferred over the Hebrew text. Also, the vocabulary of lot casting is not used, and the answers contain more information than the casting of lots could yield (e.g., 2 Sam. 5:23–24). This last point suggests the involvement of prophecy and the divine inspiration of the high priest in giving revelation. It can also be noted that the use of the actual object(s) constituting the Urim and Thummim appears to have been self-authenticating. Even in extremely difficult circumstances, the guidance of the Urim and Thummim is followed (Judg. 20:18–28). It could be theorized that a perfect light that miraculously shone from the gem(s) constituting the Urim and Thummim (which belonged to God, Deut. 33:8) gave the needed authentication to the actual answer spoken by the high priest under divine inspiration. In this way the judgment of the Urim, the light, may have been given (Num. 27:21). Such authentication would not have been out of place in Old Testament times when special signs were provided more often.

CORNELIS VAN DAM

See also PRIEST, PRIESTHOOD; REVELATION, IDEA OF.

Bibliography. C. Van Dam, *ISBE,* 4:957–59.

Vv

Vanity. In common parlance "vanity" and "vain" apply to conceited persons with exaggerated self-opinions. While the biblical usage includes this nuance, it describes the world as having as no ultimate meaning, a concept shared with some philosophies. The meanings of emptiness and lacking in reality are already present in the Latin *vanitas,* from which the English word "vanity" is derived. This approaches the chief Old Testament understanding that human life apart from God, even at its best, has no ultimate significance and consequently is valueless. This theme characterizes the Book of Ecclesiastes, which begins with "Vanity of vanities! All is vanity" (1:2 NRSV), words that have become classical in the languages into which the Bible has been translated. In viewing life without God the believer is on the same level as the unbeliever in recognizing the desperateness of life. *Hebel,* the Hebrew for vanity, as its Arabic cognate, suggests a wind or vapor. Man's life is like a breath (Ps. 39:5). The development of vanity as reflecting the despair of human life in Ecclesiastes shows to some commentators that its author was a skeptic, an agnostic, or a rationalist, as its message seemed to contradict the prophetic message that Israel place its hope in God. The tension between hope and hopelessness can be resolved in realizing that the inspired writer is expressing his emotions apart from his life as a believer. It does not suggest that he has gone after other gods, but rather he views life apart from God. Searching for wisdom is no more productive than striving after the wind (1:14, 17). All work (4:8), wealth (2:1–17), and varied experiences (4:7) add nothing to life's meaning. Human life is of equal value with that of animals (3:19–20). Though vanity is the theme of Ecclesiastes, the idea is found elsewhere. It is the despair and frustration in seeing that projected goals are unrealized as with Job (7:3), David (2 Sam. 18:31–33), and Elijah (1 Kings 19:4). Despair is lacking in Jesus, who in the forsakenness of death places his confidence in God (Matt. 27:46). In the Sermon on the Mount he uses the transience of life to engender in Christians confidence as God's children (Matt. 6:25–33). The other biblical usage of vanity condemns idolatrous religions and philosophies as useless. Gentiles or pagans failing to recognize the true God live in the vanity of their minds. Their unbelief is caused by ignorance and hardness of heart (Eph. 4:17–24). The vanity of false worship is of no value, as it fails to see that other religions and philosophies lead only to damnation. Vanity as a despair of value of human life thus destroying confidence in self, abilities, and possessions can be of value if faith is allowed to focus on him with whom true joys are to be found.

DAVID P. SCAER

See also ECCLESIASTES, THEOLOGY OF.

Bibliography. M. V. FOX, *Qohelet and His Contradictions.*

Vengeance. An injured party's desire for retribution or repayment from those who harmed him or to demonstrate his innocence against false accusations. Vengeance demonstrates God's righteousness in compensating the wrong with right. He takes vengeance against the murderers of the helpless (Ps. 94:1–6) and enemies of his people (Joel 3:19–21). The idea of vengeance is incorporated into Israel's moral code, making them as his people accountable for their infractions. Vengeance most frequently translates the Hebrew *nāqam* and is used of God (Isa. 1:24) and human beings (Exod. 20:20–21) in meting out legally deserved punishments. Personal vengeance from a designated family member was required to avenge an unlawful death (Num. 35:19–21). In cases of uncertainty over unintentional death, the perpetrator could find protection from the victim's surviving relatives in the cities of refuge (Num. 35:22–29). As Israel developed from a loose confederation into a kingdom, carrying out vengeance became a state function (Deut. 24:16). The lex talonis, requiring "life for life, eye for eye, tooth for tooth" (Exod. 21:23–25), is widely understood as prohibiting disproportionate punishment. Still basic to this principle is that wrongs had to be avenged. Without the perpetrator's execution the land remained defiled (Deut. 19:11–13). Vengeance reflects a sense of justice in restoring the right. It was also a national function, as Israel retaliated against its neighbors. Samson kills three thousand Philistines for blinding him (Judg. 14–16). God is the avenger of last resort in destroying the Egyptians as Israel's enemies (Exod. 15:1–18; Deut. 32:35–36). Vengeance is approached differently in the New Testament. Government remains as the executor of divine vengeance against law breakers (1 Peter 2:14), but personal vengeance is prohibited. Jesus requires that an ethic of helping one's enemies replace retaliation (Matt. 5:38–48). Similarly Paul forbids returning evil for evil and seeking personal vengeance (Rom. 12:17–21). This apparent dissimilarity lead Marcion in the second century, Schleiermacher in the eighteenth century, and some scholars since then to conclude that the Old Testament religion was inferior to that of the New Testament. Such a view characterizing the Old Testament as absolute demand for vengeance overlooks Joseph's forgiving his brothers (Gen. 45:1–4) and David's sparing the lives of Saul (1 Sam. 26) and later Saul's family (2 Sam. 9:9–13). God does not completely destroy Israel but forgives them, preserving a remnant in spite of their transgressions (Mic. 7:18–20). Divine vengeance in the Old Testament is not to be understood as God's desire for self-gratification in exacting punishment, but as an expression of displeasure over all unrighteousness to restore the original balance (Joel 3:19–21). Vengeance anticipated redemption. The relative seeking revenge was called the *gōel haddām* (Num. 35:19), the avenger or redeemer of blood. This provides a necessary background for understanding Christ's death as satisfying God's vengeance to provide redemption. Divine retributive righteousness seeking revenge against the sinner becomes in Christ redemptive. Forgiveness rather than vengeance is the basis for Christian morality. Vengeance incapable of being placated is reserved for Christ's and the church's enemies who unbelievingly reject its resolution in Christ's death.

David P. Scaer

See also Accursed; Devote, Devoted; Judgment; Justice; Providence of God; Punishment; Worship; Wrath of God.

Bibliography. H. McKeating, *Exp T,* 74:239–45; G. E. Mendenhall, *The Tenth Generation.*

Victory. The number of times the word "victory" occurs in the English Bible depends very much on the particular version one uses. For example, "victory" occurs only eleven times in the Authorized Version, while the Revised Standard Version contains forty-four occurrences of the word. This is because a variety of Greek and Hebrew words are used to communicate the concept.

In its Old Testament use, the concept of victory signifies more than just a military conquest, though it includes that. For many of the writers of the Old Testament, victory is ultimately something that comes from the Lord, and it is the Lord who carries on the fight. The Lord will go with the Israelites in their conquest of Canaan. He will fight against their enemies, and he will give them the victory (Deut. 20:4). Jonathan's role in Israel's victory over the Philistines was possible only because he and God fought together against the enemy (1 Sam. 14:45). David's defeat of Goliath was in fact the Lord's victory wrought for all Israel (1 Sam. 19:5). David's conquest of the Edomites was a victory that the Lord gave to David (2 Sam. 8:6, 14). Similar victories, wrought by the Lord through human agency, are found in the stories of Eleazar, son of Dodo the Ahohite (2 Sam. 23:10, 12) and many others. All ascription of victory must go to the Lord, for his is the greatness, power, glory, and majesty, as well as victory (1 Chron. 29:11). In fact, the prophet Jahaziel on one occasion communicates the word of the Lord to the people of Judah that they need not fight, but simply stand still and see the Lord's salvation (2 Chron. 20:17). So complete is God's sovereignty in victory that he even gives victory to Syria through the agency of Naaman, who is called a mighty man of valor, despite being a leper (cf. the angel of the Lord's similar words to Gideon in Judg. 6:12).

In the Psalter, the psalmist petitions for victory (i.e., salvation, deliverance) through God's co-regent, the Davidic king. Such victory belongs to the king (20:5, 9), even though it comes from the right hand and arm of God (44:3). However, such victory is not guaranteed by simply military superiority (33:17), but comes only from God (cf. 60:5; 98:1–3; 118:15; 144:10; 149:4). Proverbs reminds the reader that, while human preparation is necessary for battle, victory belongs to the Lord (21:31).

The prophets comment very little on the notion of victory. Isaiah reminds the inhabitants of Judah living in the postcaptivity restoration that the victorious Babylonian army completes its conquests only because the Lord gives them nations and kings (41:2). When there is no human agent to intervene, it is the Lord's own arm that brings victory (59:16; 63:5). The Lord, through Jeremiah, promises to avenge himself against arrogant Babylon by sending his own locust-like army to conquer them (Jer. 51:14). Zechariah reminds Judah that the Lord himself, as a warrior who gives victory, will restore Judah, renewing his love and exulting over them with loud singing (12:7).

In the New Testament, the noun form "victory" (*nikos*) occurs only five times, three of which are Old Testament citations. Matthew 12:20, quoting from Isaiah 42:1–4, states that Jesus (the Suffering Servant) will neither break a bruised reed nor quench a smoldering wick, until he brings justice to victory. Paul states that the resurrection will result in victory over death, rather than death having the victory (1 Cor. 15:54–55; cf. Isa. 25:8; Hos. 13:14). For John, the victory that triumphs over the world is our faith, and the one that overcomes the world is the one who believes that Jesus is the Son of God (1 John 5:4–5).

In traditional diatribe style, Paul first asks rhetorically if Israel's unbelief makes God's faithfulness ineffective. Paul rejects such a suggestion outright, instead insisting that even if every man is false, God will be true, insisting that God will triumph in victory when He is judged (Rom. 3:4). Likewise, believers are not to be overcome with evil, but are to have the victory over it (Rom. 12:21). For Paul, life in Christ is similar to a military battle or an athletic contest, in which it is crucial that one triumph. It is crucial that those who run in this race run so as to obtain the prize (1 Cor. 9:24). Paul describes his own life as pressing on toward this same prize, the upward call of God in Christ Jesus (Phil. 3:14). However, believers can be thankful to God, who, in Christ, always leads them in triumph (2 Cor. 2:14). In fact, Christ has already publicly triumphed over the hostile principalities and powers (Col. 2:15).

Revelation makes much of the language of conquest and victory. In each of the letters to the seven churches of Asia Minor there is a reference to him to "overcomes." The Lord will grant to the one who overcomes the following: eating of the tree of life, in the paradise of God (2:7); immunity to the second death (2:11); receipt of the "hidden manna," a white stone with a new name inscribed on it, known only to the person himself (2:17); power over the nations, to rule over them with a rod of iron (2:26–27); being clad in white garments, name not being blotted out of the book of life, and the confession of his name before the Father and the angels (3:5); made a pillar in the temple of God; and three new names: the name of God, the name of the city of God, the new Jerusalem, and the Lord's own new name (3:12); and sitting on the Lord's throne with him (3:21). The Lord himself, on a white horse, rides forth to conquer (6:2). The beast will conquer the people of God temporarily (11:7; 13:7), but they will eventually conquer the beast (15:2). The Lamb, who is King of kings and Lord of lords, will conquer them (17:14). Finally, the Lord promises that for the one who conquers, the Lord will be his God, and he will be God's son (21:7).

Andrew L. Smith

Bibliography. O. Bauernfeind, *TDNT,* 4:942–45; 6:502–15; G. Deling, *TDNT,* 3:159f.; G. von Rad, *Studies in Deuteronomy,* pp. 45–49; E. Stauffer, *TDNT,* 1:134–40; L. E. Toombs, *IDB,* 4:797–801; L. Williamson, *Interp* 22 (1968): 317ff.; Y. Yadin, *The Art of Warfare in Biblical Lands.*

Violence. Old Testament terms that particularly explicate the concept are *ḥāmās, gāzal,* and *ʿāšaq,* (and their derivatives). Primary among these is *ḥāmās.* The main New Testament term is *bia,* although it is used sparingly. An understanding of the phenomenon should not be built on isolated readings of what appear to be narratives of violence.

The term *ḥāmās* first appears in the Pentateuch in Genesis 6:11, 13: "The earth was filled with violence." Although the term is undefined in Genesis 6, acts of violence (murder) have already been encountered (Gen. 4:8, 23). Jacob describes the swords of Simeon and Levi as "weapons of violence" (Gen. 49:5), an apparent reference to their killing the Shechemites (Gen. 34).

Sarah perceived the conception of Ishmael as violence done to her (Gen. 16:5). The Book of the Covenant identifies the act of carrying a false rumor with being a form of verbal violence (Exod. 23:1).

The Former Prophets also link violence with murder in the Gideon narrative, when the narrator refers to the murder of Abimelech's brothers as "violence" (Judg. 9:5, 24). The specific nature of violence remains unspecified in 2 Samuel 22:3, where David celebrates his deliverance from violence by God, although physical violence, including murder, might well be within the scope of the reference.

The Latter Prophets reflect the dual nuance of physical violence and nonphysical violence/ethical violence of the term. Jeremiah's complaint that his message is one of "violence and destruction" (20:8) is of particular interest because it serves as a possible double entendre. On the one hand, Jeremiah's message anticipated the violence of Babylonian destruction; in the context of his complaint, the prophet has just announced to Pashur ben Immer, the priest, that he will go into Babylonian captivity (20:1–6). The subsequent destruction of Jerusalem and the temple by Babylon, lamented by the prophet in Lamentations, is described as violence achieved by Yahweh (Lam. 2:6). Furthermore, proclamation of the message elicited a violent act from Pashur ben Immer toward Jeremiah. On the other hand, from the prophet's perspective, the message itself appears to constitute verbal violence. Elsewhere, Jeremiah portrays taking advantage of the disadvantaged (orphan, widow, and stranger) as violence (Jer. 22:3).

In the dramatic prophetic narration of Ezekiel 8, violence is described as pagan idolatry that had come to characterize Israel (v. 17). Ezekiel 45:9 confronts the "princes of Israel" for violence against their own people; the context takes the term in the direction of heavy taxation of the covenant community (cf. Neh. 5:1–5).

Amos's antithetic woe to Zion and Samaria concerning delaying the day of calamity but bringing near "the seat of violence" (6:3) is ambiguous, but may allude to a reign/rule of violence that contextually refers to oppression of the disadvantaged (cf. 3:9–10; 4:1). Micah's use of the term in 6:12 connotes verbal violence when he links it to "speaking lies" and "deceitful tongues." Three of Habakkuk's six uses of the term refer to violence done to the land (2:8, 17 [2x]). In two of those three uses, violence done to the land is paired with bloodshed (Hab. 2:8, 17). Included in Zephaniah's excoriation of the covenant leaders of his day were the priests, who are accused of doing violence to the Law (3:4). Cultic violence seems to be the object of Yahweh's hatred, according to Malachi 2:16.

The psalms employ the root fourteen times, mostly in unspecified contexts. However, two psalms use the term in the sense of verbal violence (27:12; 35:11)—two uses that seem to share some commonality with Exodus 23:1 and Deuteronomy 19:16. This is a nuance that may also be intended by the dual proverbial use of the observation that the mouth of the wicked conceals violence (Prov. 10:6, 11). Lady Wisdom simply asserts that one who misses her inflicts violence on himself (Prov. 8:36).

From an examination of the term *hāmās* we conclude that it may refer to either physical or nonphysical/ethical violence. However, from among the latter usages, one can further isolate the nuances of verbal violence and cultic violence.

The Pentateuch uses the term *gāzal* to describe violent taking/robbing/plundering—an act that, while it may be viewed as "violent," may or may not involve physical harm. Abraham's wells were "grasped" by Abimelech, without any apparent physical harm to the patriarch (Gen. 21:25).

Similar usage of the term is found in the Former Prophets when Judges 9:25 asserts that the Shechemites "plundered" all who passed by. Perhaps the Judges narrator intones a sense of ethical violence in his description of certain of the Benjaminites who carried away wives from among the dancing maidens (21:23). That the term is sometimes associated with physical harm is demonstrated by its use in 2 Samuel 23:21 (cf. 1 Chron. 11:23).

Several of the Latter Prophets inveigh against various leaders of Israel because they, through legal manipulation or in some situations physical abuse, "plunder" the poor (Isa. 3:14; 10:2; Jer. 22:3; Mic. 2:2; 3:2; Mal. 1:13).

Wisdom use of the term correlates with the indictments of the prophets; one of the words of the wise counseled against plundering the poor because he is poor (Prov. 22:22; cf. Job 20:19; 24:2, 9, 19). Ironically, evil men are "plundered" of sleep unless they are engaged in evil activity (Prov. 4:16).

Conceptually, *ʿāšaq* comes along side *gāzal* in that it often alludes to nonphysical violence. Samuel declared that he had not "defrauded" anyone (1 Sam. 12:2–3); the context appears to refer to activity akin to extortion/bribery, which he declares he had shunned in carrying out his covenant functions.

Hosea accused Ephraim of loving to oppress, a description that is paired with a description of a merchant with false balances (Hos. 12:7). Ezekiel indicates that neighbors have oppressed neighbors for profit by taking (charging) interest (22:12); and the prophet indicts the nation for "oppressing" the alien (22:7). Various pre- and postexilic prophets use the term with a similar nuance of ethical violence.

Verbal violence is, likewise, included in the scope of this term; Israel confessed in Isaiah's day that she was guilty of speaking oppression (Isa. 59:13; cf. Ps. 73:8).

The wisdom slant tends to focus on ethical violence as well. An antithetical proverb juxtaposes oppressing the poor with being gracious to the needy (Prov. 14:31); oppressing the poor for much gain is said to bring poverty (Prov. 22:16). In a context where it is paired with bribery, Qoheleth asserts that "oppression" makes a wise person mad (Eccles. 7:7).

Contextually, *gāzal* and *ʿāšaq* come alongside each other quite literally inasmuch as the terms are paired in several passages. Leviticus 6:2, 4 pair *gāzal* with *ʿāšaq* as "plundering" and "extortion." The context is a continued discussion of the trespass offering, the introduction of which speaks of unintentional sin. That 6:1–7 addresses a trespass offering for intentional sin is evident from the nature of the situations described. Noteworthy is the fact that violent plundering of one's neighbor, whether figurative or literal, is cast as sin against Yahweh.

The two terms are paired again in Leviticus 19:13, where "plundering" and "extortion" appear to be associated with withholding the wages of a hired person until the morning (cf. Deut. 24:14).

Micah charges the officials of his day with coveting fields and "grasping" them (Mic. 2:2a); perhaps this violence was accomplished by means of "extortion" of the household (2:2b). Although none of the terms under examination is used by the narrator, the Ahab/Naboth incident appears to offer a classic narrative illustration of the Micah situation in the extreme. There, the "coveting"/"grasping" went beyond use of extortion as the vehicle. The violence of murder was Ahab's means of "grasping a field" (1 Kings 21).

The psalmist counsels not to trust in "oppression" (*ʿāšaq*) and not to become vain in "robbery" (*gāzal*) (Ps. 62:10). Wisdom literature pairs the terms in much the same way. Qoheleth recognized that officials were characterized by "extortion," (*ʿāšaq*) and that there was "snatching away" (*gāzal*) of justice and righteousness in the provinces of the kingdom (Eccles. 5:8).

The range of meaning exposed by examination of the uses of the primary term, *ḥāmās,* appears to be paradigmatic. inasmuch as the latter two terms mirror the physical/nonphysical (ethical) range, but stop short of the more particular nuances of ethical violence delineated above.

It is noteworthy that terms alluding to and the narrative descriptions of violence in the Gospels, Acts, and Epistles are less common than in the older biblical corpus.

In the much discussed context of Matthew 11:12, Christ is narrated as using two forms of the term *bia* when he observed that the "kingdom of heaven suffers violence, and violent men take it by force" (NASB). There are attempts to read it as a positive assertion. In the context, however, it was the imprisoned, soon to be murdered, Baptist's inquiry concerning Christ that elicited what seems best read as a pejorative evaluation of John's/Christ's opponents and their agenda. So read, the statement emits overtones alluding both to physical and nonphysical violence. Luke's narration of Christ's statement in Luke 16:16 is akin to the Matthew narrative. Other Lucan uses of the term in Acts (2:2; 5:26; 21:25; 27:41) connote violence that either involves or potentially involves some form of physical harm.

JOHN I. LAWLOR

See also JUDGMENT; JUSTICE; PROVIDENCE OF GOD; WAR, HOLY WAR; WRATH OF GOD.

Bibliography. P. C. Craigie, *The Problem of War in the Old Testament;* J. Ellul, *Violence: Reflections from a Christian Perspective;* H. Haag, *TDOT*, 4:478–87.

Virgin Birth. Historically, the Christian belief that Jesus was miraculously conceived through the power of the Holy Spirit, born of the virgin Mary without sexual union with man (Matt. 1:18–25; Luke 1:34–35). This doctrine is to be distinguished from the Roman Catholic belief in the "perpetual virginity" of Mary (i.e., that she remained a virgin throughout her life) and the "immaculate conception" (i.e., that she remained sinless throughout her life), two ideas in tension with the birth narratives themselves.

Four views exist concerning the origin of the New Testament virgin birth stories: (1) a fact of history (traditional Christian view); (2) an error; Christians got it wrong for whatever reason (antagonist view traced to the early second century); (3) a natural phenomenon reexplained supernaturally (modern rationalist view); (4) a myth/legend, a religious idea put into historical form (modern mythical view). Views 3 and 4 assume an antisupernatural bias. View 2 accepts the supernatural but harbors disbelief about Jesus as the Messiah.

This article surveys the theological importance of the virgin birth rather than matters primarily relating to its origin. But the issue of historicity is, nonetheless, indispensable to it, for history in the New Testament is the handmaiden of theology. None of the Gospels were merely doctrinal speculations about the person of Christ but records of actual events of his life, although assuredly preserved for theological reasons. In the case of the virgin birth, its historical integrity holds up well (as the next point shows). This factor weighs heavily against views 2, 3, and 4.

Historical Reality. The birth narratives of Matthew and Luke assume as established fact that the virgin birth indeed happened. But by its very nature, the event is nonrepeatable and therefore cannot be proven. Numerous pieces of evidence, however, strongly recommend it as the only satisfactory explanation of what happened.

The virgin birth is unique. Pre-Christian Jewish tradition never anticipated a virgin birth of the Messiah. It appears that Judaism never understood Isaiah 7:14 as messianic or describing a virgin birth and that Philo, a first-century Jewish scholar, never imagined a literal divine betting in his allegorical understanding of the birth of several Old Testament characters (cf. *On the Cherubim,* 40–52). Pagan parallels are scarcely more fitting. Greek and Egyptian mythology, for example, depict lustful pagan deities begetting male offspring through carnal relations with women. The New Testament accounts, in contrast, mention no father figure. God is not described as procreator or as sexually desiring Mary. The virgin birth is solely a creative work of God through his Holy Spirit. Comparative religions offer no precursor that remotely parallels the special theological features of the New Testament virgin birth stories; it suggests nothing that could have logically and naturally given rise to them.

The unity of the infancy narratives with the main body of the First and Third Gospels supports the belief that their authors considered Jesus' virgin birth as authentic. Luke, for example, indicates in his Gospel preface (1:1–4) that the content of his Gospel (and Acts) is reliable tradition received from his predecessors. He apparently is not recording much that is new. Quite possibly the authenticity of the virgin birth was common knowledge to his readership and thought to be well attested to them when he wrote the preface (v. 4).

Jewish antagonism toward Christianity would have made the truth known if Jesus' birth had happened otherwise. But as second-century Jewish polemic against the virgin birth shows, it had no such independent piece of tradition to appeal to; it was merely a reaction to the broadly accepted tradition of the virgin birth. It seems, furthermore, that Mary and Jesus' brothers would have carefully preserved, after Pentecost, the story of Jesus' birth from distortion of any kind, whether from naturalizing it or giving it legendary form.

Matthew and Luke show considerable restraint to the miraculous in their birth narratives. This reserve is unexpected if the stories were indeed fabrications. One would expect an exaggerated emphasis on the miraculous as the New Testament apocryphal versions of Jesus' birth and childhood in fact do (cf. *Proto-Gospel of James,* 17–21; *Infancy Gospel of Thomas*).

The birth narratives lack Christian interpretation of the virgin birth. Many who deny the historicity of the virgin birth see it as "christianized" legend. But this position fails to account adequately for the primitive Old Testament character of the infancy narratives. The narratives lack specific Christian concepts and christological explanation or reflection, except where compatible with Old Testament messianic expectations. This phenomenon is highly unusual if the narratives were indeed products of Christian legend rather than accounts carefully documenting what happened at the time of Jesus' birth before the christological significance of Jesus was yet known.

The relative silence of the Gospel tradition to the virgin birth probably reveals the true historical situation: Mary and Joseph kept the matter secret in an attempt to ward off possible misunderstanding and ridicule. Though Mark and John have no record of Jesus' birth and say almost nothing about it in their Gospels (Mark 6:3; John 1:13; 6:41–42; 8:41 are probably references to it), their silence does not weigh against it. The plan of their Gospels was apparently to record events witnessed by others, especially the disciples, beginning with Jesus' baptism by John the Baptist.

The supernatural nature of Jesus' birth is compatible with the broader New Testament picture of him—in particular, his resurrection. While Jesus' entrance into the world defied the normal means of conception, his raising from the dead defied the normal permanence of death. His birth is no more cause for amazement than the events associated with his death. Likewise, for Paul, Adam's appearance as the firstborn of the human race directly created by God coincides well with the idea of the virgin birth, where through Jesus as the second Adam, God has made a new and perfect start (1 Cor. 15:20–22, 45–49; Rom. 5:14–19). Knowledge of the virgin birth may explain Paul's unusual use of *ginesthai* ("to come") rather than the customary *gennasthai* ("to be born") in describing Jesus' entrance into the world (Rom. 1:3–4; Gal. 4:4–5; Phil. 2:7).

Finally, the unquestioned support of the early church fathers to the virgin birth (e.g., Ignatius of Antioch, Justin Martyr, Irenaeus, Origen) strongly endorses it as a well-accepted first-century Christian tradition.

It should also be noted at this juncture that the alleged historical discrepancies involving the census of Quirinius, Herod's massacre of the infants, the star and visit of the magi, the appearance of angels, the location of Jesus' parental home, the genealogies, the independent traditions of the two infancy narratives, and Matthew's version as midrash (i.e., a fictitious account developed from Old Testament texts) have reasonable explanations defending their historicity.

The theological value of the virgin birth is that it happened. To strip it of its supernatural character is to make the story nothing more than a moral example or ideal: It humanizes Christ's birth, devalues the redemptive significance of his coming, and makes God untrue in that he never did what was claimed he would do in regard to Jesus' birth. The historicity of the virgin birth, so firmly accepted by Matthew and Luke, forces us to reckon theologically with the importance of Jesus at the highest level possible: that Jesus is God incarnate.

Inbreaking of the Supernatural into the Natural. The birth narratives have as their centerpiece the entrance of the supernatural into ordinary human life. Something is about to happen at God's initiative, unprecedented in the history of the world. It is a new beginning and one that shall endure: The baby to be born "will be great and will be called the Son of the Most High. The Lord God will give him the throne of his father David, and he will reign over the house of Jacob forever; his kingdom will never end" (Luke 1:32–33). As the title "Immanuel" entails, it is the permanent coming of God's presence in the person of his Son.

The reason for this divine intervention is for the redemptive well-being of creation: more specifically, as Jesus' name implies, "to save his people from their sins" (Matt. 1:21). The fact of God's unique presence in Jesus' birth makes unassailable the promise of salvation to Israel and the world. The virgin birth glimpses the extent of God's love for people; of course, how the Son's earthly life ended is necessary to picture its extent fully.

In contrast to the promiscuous stories of Greek mythology in which male offspring appear as by-products of liaisons between the gods and earthly women, the virgin birth as God's creative work in no way compromises or offends his holiness or his supreme lordship over all creation. The virgin birth is the revelation of a holy God through his equally righteous Son.

Revelation of Jesus as the God-Man. The personal union of God and man in Jesus mysteriously took place through the Spirit's generating power in the virginal conception and birth. It is impossible to explain exactly what happened or how it happened. In addition, the birth narratives say little about who Jesus is and what he has come to do in any specific Christian sense. But the christological significance of the virgin birth is clear from the broader context of the New Testament.

Jesus is God's Son not by adoption but by nature: his life was free from sin (2 Cor. 5:21; Heb. 4:15; 1 Peter 2:22; 1 John 3:5) and he showed some self-awareness of his divine equality with God the Father (John 6:38; 8:42; 13:3). The virgin birth intersects Jesus' incarnation with his preexistent glory (cf. Rom. 1:3–4; Phil. 2:5–8). It is not absolutely certain that the virgin birth was the only means God could have used to bring about the incarnation; but that he did so in this way perfectly reveals and preserves the divine integrity of the Father and Son.

The virgin birth also affirms Jesus' true humanity. Born of a woman, he was fully human—liable to all the temptations of a fallen race (Heb. 4:15). Jesus' humanity revealed his (and God's) complete identification with humankind. He became as they were. The nature of Jesus' birth uniquely qualifies him as the One through whom God brings about his new saving work.

Inauguration of God's Final Plan of Redemption. The virgin birth opens a new era of God's saving activity in history. It is not an end in itself. God has inaugurated in Jesus' birth a plan of salvation that will affect the destiny of the human race to the end of time. Through the One who is born of a virgin, God makes salvation universally available: it will be "a light for revelation to the Gentiles and for glory to your people Israel" (Luke 2:32). The saving value of Jesus' birth is realized on the cross. By means of his death and resurrection, God has provided humanity with complete and final deliverance from sin and death. The primary theological thrust, therefore, of the virgin birth is eschatological in the sense that it implicitly envisions as its ultimate goal the consummation of world history in Jesus' second coming.

Humanity, on the other hand, desperately needs divine help. Irretrievably lost in its own sin, it is completely unable to save itself. It stands in need of deliverance from a source outside itself. The virgin birth is just that—the supernatural coming for the sake of and on behalf of the natural. It is the planned gracious rescue from above of an otherwise lost humanity below.

Perfect Expression of Divine Grace. The virgin birth reveals that God cares for his creation in the way he actively carries out a plan for its restoration. This act of divine love, however, is fully undeserved. While the human race was willfully following a self-destructive, sinful course, God intervened to provide a gracious Deliverer in Jesus. This unmerited grace initiated in the virgin birth is finalized on the cross where God through his Son became sin in our stead so that we might have new life in him. The unmerited favor God showed to Mary in choosing her to bear the Messiah parallels the more general unmerited favor he has shown to all people through the Messiah's redemptive work. The biblical history of salvation is not fatalistic or deterministic but a free expression of God's love for the world. In Scripture, salvation is always an act of divine grace.

Fulfillment of Old Testament Scripture. According to Matthew 1:22–23, the virgin birth is understood as a prophetic fulfillment of Isaiah 7:14: "Therefore the Lord himself will give you a sign: The virgin will be with child and will give birth to a son, and will call him Immanuel." Pre-Christian Judaism did not consider the Isaiah passage as messianic or predicting a virgin birth. The Hebrew *ʿalmâ* denotes a young woman, married or single. Although the equivalent passage in the Septuagint (a Jewish, pre-Christian Greek translation of the Hebrew Old Testament) uses *parthenos,* which specifically means virgin, the sense of the passage probably conforms to the more nonspecific Hebrew parallel.

The lack of anticipation of a virginal conception of the Messiah in pre-Christian Jewish literature suggests that the event was apparently fully unexpected. But reading the Septuagint version with the historical situation of Jesus' birth in view provides pointed biblical confirmation of the event. The scriptural connection drawn between these two passages in Matthew marks the virgin birth of Jesus the Messiah as a fulfillment of Old Testament Scripture. It describes the scriptural significance of Jesus' coming: to carry out God's saving work and to involve God personally in doing so.

Pattern of Christian Obedience to God. The birth narratives portray Joseph and Mary as responding obediently to the unexpected and bewildering news from God that a baby is to be born to them without male sexual involvement. Mary humbly submitted to God's will: "I am the Lord's servant. . . . May it be to me as you have said" (Luke 1:38). Joseph willingly shared in Mary's call despite the likelihood of future shame and reproach (Matt. 1:19–25).

In view of the whole Gospel story, their acceptance of God's call unquestionably cost them dearly at times: as the recipients of slander and gossip, in lingering confusion as to when and how Jesus would fulfill what was announced of him, and ultimately Mary's deep grief at seeing Jesus crucified—plus her added difficulties of not (fully) understanding that Jesus was to be raised from the dead or the saving significance of his death until some time after the resurrection.

Faith is the willingness to heed God's call, whatever its demands and costs. The most powerful biblical example of such obedience is with the One virgin-born—for Jesus, his willingness to obey God's call led him to certain death. He knew he was to die, but remained true to what God sent him to do. And as the early church has exemplified in its own life and practice, life in Christ for us should involve no less an unwavering commitment to God.

In summary, the New Testament includes belief in the virgin birth as part of the saving gospel message. It is, however, highly instructive for understanding the biblical nature of salvation. No one is saved by works. It is indisputably a gift of God freely given to a fallen humanity. The virgin birth introduces the perfect and final expression of God's saving love: his Son Jesus, who has come to deliver people from their sin.

H. DOUGLAS BUCKWALTER

See also ISAIAH, THEOLOGY OF; JESUS CHRIST; MIRACLE.

Bibliography. K. Barth, *Church Dogmatics,* 1/2, pp. 172–202; idem, *Dogmatics in Outline;* T. Boslooper, *The Virgin Birth;* R. E. Brown, *The Birth of the Messiah;* idem, *The Virginal Conception and Bodily Resurrection of Jesus;* C. E. B. Cranfield, *SJT* 41 (1988): 177–89; D. Edwards, *The Virgin Birth in History and Faith;* R. T. France, *Gospel Perspective,* 2:201–37; R. H. Fuller, *JSNT* 1 (1978): 37–52; R. G. Gromacki, *The Virgin Birth: Doctrine of Deity;* J. G. Machen, *The Virgin Birth of Christ;* J. Orr, *The Virgin Birth of Christ;* O. Piper, *Int* 18 (1964): 131–48; B. B. Warfield, *The American Journal of Theology* 10 (1906): 21–30; J. S. Wright, *Faith and Thought* 95 (1966–67): 19–29.

Vision(s). Visions occur frequently in the Bible as instruments of supernatural revelation. They are audiovisual means of communication between a heavenly being and an earthly recipient.

The terms used to designate visions in both Testaments have to do with seeing or perceiving. The Old Testament terms for vision (the Hebrew verbs *rā'â* and *ḥāzâ* and their several noun derivatives) mean simply to look at or to see. In the New Testament, *horaō* is one of the Greek verbs for see, observe, or perceive, but its related noun (*horama*) is the common term for "vision."

Revelatory visions portray scenery or dramatic circumstances to the human recipient while the human is awake. The distinction between a vision and a dream has to do with whether the human is awake or asleep; the result is the same. The prophetic use of dreams and visions is summarized in the Lord's dramatic defense of Moses in the face of Aaron and Miriam's revolt: "When a prophet of the LORD is among you, I reveal myself to him in visions, I speak to him in dreams" (Num. 12:6).

Visions are most frequently found in the prophetic portions of the Old Testament. A prophetic work could be titled as a vision (Isa. 1:1; Nah. 1:1), and certain prophecies—Ezekiel, Daniel, Zechariah—developed a greater capacity for visionary revelation. The extensive use of the term in nearly all the Old Testament prophets implies that visions were a normal medium for receiving the divine word. As such, the "vision" of the Old Testament prophets represents not just a visionary drama perceived by the eyes (as in Isa. 6, for example), but also a distinctive worldview or perception of reality that was proclaimed through the prophets. So the prophetic vision may be both a scenic, visual communication and a more general prophetic worldview. Sometimes a prophetic sermon is introduced as a burden (or "oracle," *maśśā,*). But even this is something that the prophet "sees," usually using the term *ḥāzâ* (Hab. 1:1; NIV's "the oracle that Habakkuk the prophet received").

Visions are also central to the biblical literature known as apocalyptic. There are many definitions of apocalyptic and exactly what we mean by the term can only be explained in sweeping generalities. Ezekiel, Daniel, Zechariah, and Revelation are the biblical books that exhibit the traits of apocalyptic material most clearly, though there are other passages in the Bible and other books from the ancient world that have similar features. In these books, God has revealed details of future events to a seer (human recipient), making heavy use of dreams and visions. The seer is permitted to peer into the heavens to witness scenes that determine future events, and the vision is usually explained by an angelic interpreter.

Visions play an important structural role in the Book of Ezekiel. The book is introduced as the "visions of God" (1:1). The opening chapter depicts four living creatures in human form, each accompanied by wheels within wheels. The book is structured around visions of the "glory of God" (1:28; 8:2–4; 10:18–22; 43:1–5), which portray the sacred and holy presence of God, first departing from the Holy City and then returning. The departure of the glory of God was due to the sinfulness of Israel (10:18–22), but his return was in keeping with his promises (43:1–5).

The prophecies of Zechariah contain a series of eight "night visions" (1:7–6:15). Though the interpretation of these chapters is difficult, it is clear that the visions reveal God's intention to deliver the beleaguered restoration community. The first and last visions stress the sovereignty of God, hence surrounding the others in a tenor of certainty. These visions contain an important prediction of the coming of God's servant, "the Branch" (3:8), a term that in biblical thought became synonymous with "Messiah."

As an apocalyptic book, Daniel is also a book of visions. The first six chapters are historical narratives in which the God-given ability to interpret dreams and visions plays an important role (1:17). It was Daniel's vision of the night that saved Daniel and the wisemen of Babylon from the irrational Nebuchadnezzar, who had been frightened by his own bizarre dream (2:1, 19). Daniel was the only "wiseman" in Babylon who could interpret Nebuchadnezzar's second dream (chap. 4) and Belshazzar's encoded message on the wall (chap. 5). The second half of Daniel contains four visions of great theological importance. The visions of chapters 7 and 8 are related to each other. Chapter 7 is both a dream and a vision (vv. 1–2), in which the coming triumphant kingdom of God displaces the four great kingdoms of earth. The vision of chapter 8 presents more details of the experiences of God's people under the rule of the Medo-Persians and Greeks, and is interpreted by Gabriel. The third vision (9:20–27) comes to Daniel as a result of his prayer. The final vision (chaps. 10–12) is about the future attempt to destroy Judaism in 169 B.C.

Besides the Book of Revelation, visions in the New Testament are concentrated in the writings of Luke. Gabriel appeared to announce the births of John (Luke 1:8–20) and Jesus (Luke 1:26–37). Ananias and Paul received visions to prepare Paul for baptism (Acts 9:10–19). Likewise, Peter and Cornelius received visions to prepare them for Peter's ministry among Gentiles (10:3–35). Angelic visions freed Peter from prison (12:9), called Paul to a European ministry (16:9), and encouraged Paul in his ministry at Corinth (18:9). So the visions of Luke–Acts announce God's plans for the immediate future or empower the church for the present.

The Book of Revelation is a record of prophetic visions given to John, who was exiled on the island of Patmos. The book is in the form of a letter (address, 1:4–7, and concluding blessing, 22:21), the main body of which consists of a single, yet highly sectioned, visionary experience (1:9–22:5). The vision was revealed by a heavenly messenger, whose purpose was to point out "the things that must soon take place" (1:1; 22:6). The visions of the book reveal the struggle between God and Satan and their servants in heaven and on earth, in addition to visions of God's care for his people. John's role, as the human recipient, was to hear and see "these things" and to respond with appropriate reverence (22:8).

Throughout the Bible, visions of God and his sovereign lordship are needed in order to propagate his truth among humankind. Where prophetic vision is lacking (NIV's "revelation," Prov. 29:18), proclamation of God's will among his people ceases, and civilization itself is jeopardized.

WILLIAM T. ARNOLD

See also REVELATION, IDEA OF.

Bibliography. R. D. Culver, *TWOT,* 1:274–75.

Vocation. *See* CALL, CALLING.

Ww

Wages. Payment given for services rendered. The semantic field of this term is usually found in economic contexts, where payment means some type of monetary compensation. During earlier periods payments would be made as a result of barter arrangements, where goods (cattle, food, etc.) would be given in exchange for work (Gen. 30:32; 38:16–17). As culture evolved the use of standardized forms and weights of metals such as gold and silver were substituted for goods because of convenience and efficiency. It was not until the Persian period that coins came into common use as currency. The price for service was usually set in advance as a result of an agreement between the employer and employee. The time allotted for work could be as short as a day (Deut. 24:15) or as long as a year (Isa. 16:14).

The Old Testament. The first explicit mention of the term for wage in the Bible occurs in a theological context. After humanity's rebellion against God and the consequent catastrophic judgments of the fall, the deluge, and Babel, God calls Abram to be the bearer of salvation for the world. A threefold promise is made to him, ensuring a relationship with God, descendants, and land. Abram obeys the divine call, leaving Mesopotamia for Canaan, but requires a sign that the promise is to be fulfilled. His aged wife is still childless, the land is occupied, and consequently the relationship with God is threatened. In Genesis 15 God gives the sign by formally ratifying a covenant with Abram guaranteeing both descendants and land. The text is introduced by a formal announcement declaring that there is no need for doubt or fear since God himself will be Abram's shield of protection and his "very large wage" (*śākār*). The oracle stresses that the ultimate reward of the righteous is a relationship with the Lord, a reward acquired through faith and obedience. The final proof for Abram that this relationship is a reality happens when Isaac is born and a plot of burial ground is secured for Sarah's body (Gen. 23).

If the Abram story stresses the goodness of God in rewarding faith and obedience, the ensuing narrative demonstrates what it is like for Israel to serve a hard taskmaster. Jacob has his wages changed ten times by a deceitful Laban, who simply wishes to exploit his son-in-law (Gen. 28–31). This "Mesopotamian exile" is a prelude to Israel's oppressive sojourn in Egypt, where a tyrannical Pharaoh pays her the "wages" of a slave (Exod. 1–3). In both situations God overrules these despots and Israel makes an exodus from each location laden with wealth and riches (Gen. 30:43; Exod. 12:35–36).

When Israel is formally constituted as a nation at Sinai, some of the laws given to her are specifically concerned with wages. In Israelite society the wage-earning class was small, placed on the social scale somewhere between land owners and slaves. Consequently, hired laborers could be classed with the *personae miserabiles,* the widow, orphan, and stranger. Working for wages was often the only way members of this class could support themselves. But they could be easily exploited, and were totally dependent on a daily wage. It was required, therefore, that hired servants receive a wage promptly. If this did not happen, they could have recourse to God, who was passionately concerned about such matters, and it would be reckoned as a sin against the employer (Deut. 24:15, cf. Exod. 22:14). Moreover, the law intended to prevent the Israelite legal system from corruption. Judges had to be persons of integrity. They were not only to refuse to take unjust wages or "bribes" but to hate them (Exod. 18:21). Other wages were regarded as unjust by virtue of the way they were acquired (e.g., through prostitution) and therefore could not be offered to the sanctuary (Deut. 23:19).

The narrative of the conquest relates God's reward to his people, fulfilling the promise of the gift of land. Israel thrives and is prosperous in the land, but there is the constant temptation to assume that the fertility deities of the Canaanites are the ones responsible for making the land productive and the population numerous. Hosea's verdict at a later time is true also of the period of the judges: "She has not acknowledged I was the one who gave her the grain, the new wine and oil, who lavished on her the silver and gold" (2:8). Consequently idolatry is common, which results in material gain becoming the paramount concern of the people, especially the leaders. The moral nadir of this period occurs when Eli is high priest and his sons exploit their position to gratify their material and sensual lusts (1 Sam. 1–2). Samuel's birth means the dawn of a new era in which God will intervene to bring justice, one consequence being that the wealthy will be humbled to the status of hired servants in order to earn a few scraps of food (1 Sam. 2:5). The Elide priesthood is judged harshly, but the new order evolves slowly. Even the new leader, Samuel, has sons who are more concerned with material gain than justice (1 Sam. 8:3). One of the few bright moments during the dark days of the judges is reflected in the story of Ruth, a Moabite widow, who faithfully determines to help her widowed Israelite mother-in-law. She merits the blessing of Boaz, who believes that Yahweh is a good God, who will fully pay her wages (Ruth 2:12).

The experience of kingship is generally negative for Israel. The kings become harsh taskmasters whose reign results in oppressive taxes (1 Sam. 8:11–18, cf. 1 Kings 12:1–17) and the exploitation of workers (Jer. 22:13). Few are the rulers who, like Josiah, protected the powerless from the powerful; the majority are like his son, whose life was obsessed with making a profit through oppression and extortion (Jer. 22:16–17). Forced labor of the corvée becomes a characteristic of oppressive regimes, as does the exploitation of the *personae miserabiles*. Such economic oppression is accompanied by idolatry.

The prophets relate how an idolatrous society quickly became corrupt, as the focus was placed on material gain rather than on a relationship with Yahweh and neighbor. Children, who were regarded as God's reward to his people (Ps. 127:3), could be offered up as sacrifices to a nature god (Mic. 6:7). Amos criticizes the merchants who use dishonest measures to increase their wages, and who cannot wait for the Sabbath to end in order to resume their exploitive businesses (8:5–6). Micah laments that Judah's "leaders judge for a bribe, her priests teach for a price, and her prophets tell fortunes for money" (3:11). A century later the situation is more critical. "From the least to the greatest, all are greedy for gain" (Jer. 6:13; 8:10). The moral consequence is hideous as justice is perverted and people are treated like commodities, especially the *personae miserabiles*. Judah suffers the same fate as her sister, the northern kingdom of Israel, had experienced a few centuries earlier. The Assyrians laid Israel waste as the prophets predicted, and the Babylonians destroyed Judah, demonstrating clearly the principle that the wages for serving a false god are quite different than those obtained from serving Yahweh. Instead of having land, the people live in exile; instead of numerous descendants, the population has been decimated. And the razed temple demonstrates what has happened to the relationship with Yahweh. To use the metaphor of marriage, the people have been divorced from their Divine Husband (Isa. 50:1). In exile the people can be described simply as dead (Ezek. 37).

It is during the exile that Israel hears a new word of hope. She is going to be liberated by a foreign king who will work for Yahweh without a wage (Isa. 45:13). Israel is called to believe that Yahweh is for her even in the midst of judgment. In fact, the time of her hard service of judgment is over; she has paid double for all her sins (Isa. 40:2). She can now come to Yahweh and purchase milk and wine without paying a fee (Isa. 55:1). God is depicted as a shepherd leading his sheep home to Judah from Babylon; the prophet switches the metaphor to describe God as a strong liberator who brings wages to distribute to his people: the wages of grace and salvation (Isa. 40:10–11; 62:11). This is a word of life from death (Ezek. 37) and means not only a return to the land, but an increase in population (Isa. 54) and a restoration of the relationship with the Lord (Isa. 49:14–16; 62:3–5).

During the times of blessing and judgment on Israel, the wisdom tradition contributed its perspective on the issues of wages and reward. Proverbs repeatedly condemns the pursuit of profit for its own sake and stresses the inextricable relation between actions and consequences. A theme in Ecclesiastes is that there is no profit to be made in anything in life (1:3; 2:11, 13; 3:9; 5:15); yet, in contrast to Grecian thought, Ecclesiastes encourages faith instead of moral licence. But the Book of Job is the book that deals principally with the issue of wages or rewards: Satan's accusation against Job is that he serves God for "a good wage" (1:9–11). It is because Job has been so richly blessed that he serves God, says Satan. But an important message of the book is that Lord himself is the believer's reward. Job eventually learns this in his vision of God (38–42).

Toward the end of the Old Testament period, when Israel returned to the land, the people again lost the divine focus as they became preoccupied with material comforts. They were more concerned with their own work than the temple and earned wages only to put them in torn purses (Hag. 1:6). They began to question God's goodness: "It is futile to serve God. What did we gain by carrying out his requirements?" (Mal. 3:14). It is on such a bleak note that the Old Testament ends.

The New Testament. The stress on wages and rewards is an important religious concern in the Judaism of Jesus' time. It forms the background to the Sermon on the Mount, in which Jesus emphasizes that those for whom religion is an external form already have their reward, while the true disciple will receive in secret a wage from God (Matt. 6:1–4, 5–6, 16–18; cf. 5:12, 46). When Jesus commissions the twelve disciples to preach throughout Israel, they are urged not to take money with them; it is expected that they will be paid by those to whom they minister, for "the worker is worth his keep" (Matt. 10:10). In some of his parables Jesus instructed his disciples to be diligent about their calling since a day of judgment would reward the righteous as well as recompense the unrighteous (Matt. 24:45–51; 25:14–30, 31–46).

But overshadowing all of this is Jesus' announcement of the gospel. The poor are richly rewarded because they can now be members of God's kingdom even though they have no money. God's incredible grace is lavished on all who are mired in spiritual debt. The parable of the unforgiving servant demonstrates that all are deeply in debt to God; all debts that human beings owe to each other are trivial in comparison. Consequently God's act of forgiveness should stimulate believers to forgive each other (Matt. 18:21–35). The parable of the workers in the vineyard shows that God is in the business of hiring employees until the very end of the working day. The fact that all receive the same wage teaches that it is a privilege even to work for God. The payment is not calculated on the basis of performance but is purely gracious (Matt. 20:1–16).

In the epistles Paul stresses the importance of wages. Practically, he argues that those who minister the gospel are entitled to a monetary payment, just as people are paid for work done in the secular sphere (1 Cor. 9:7). He himself received similar support on occasion (2 Cor. 11:8). Teaching elders in the churches are to be paid since "the worker deserves his wages" (1 Tim. 5:17–18). Moreover, the gospel affects the working lives of all those who embrace it. Slaves must primarily work for their Lord, not their human master, since it is he who will pay them the wage that really matters (Col. 3:22–25); masters need to remember that unpaid wages scream out to God for justice (James 5:4). On the judgment day all will appear before the throne of Christ to receive "final payment" (Rom. 2:6–8; cf. 1 Cor. 3:8; 2 Cor. 5:10; Rev. 20:11–15).

This practical and sober teaching is balanced by exhilarating good news. There is a radical difference in the human condition apart from and in Christ. Satan is a hard taskmaster, doling out the wages of death for sin (Rom. 6:23), but God is a loving Father who lavishes believers with the gifts of life and adoption and promises an infinitely rich inheritance—all things! (1 Cor. 3:22–23; Eph. 1:5–12). God is immeasurably rich in mercy (Eph. 2:4)! As proof he has offered up Christ as a payment for humanity's sins, and given believers a downpayment of their gracious wage to come in the presence of the Holy Spirit who takes up residence within them (2 Cor. 1:22; 5:5; Eph. 1:14). They now await the time of the full payment of the Spirit without measure, when they will enter the glorious liberty of the children of God (Rom. 8:21), experience the beatific vision, and partake of the divine nature (Rev. 22:4), God himself being their exceeding great reward (Gen. 15:1). All previous experience of the Lord will be regarded as so much hearsay. Until then, believers are encouraged with the promise that "no eye has seen, no ear has heard, no mind has conceived what God has prepared for those who love him" (1 Cor. 2:9). STEPHEN G. DEMPSTER

See also MONEY; REWARD; WEALTH; WORK.

Bibliography. P. Barrios, *IDB,* 4:795; O. Becker, *NIDNTT,* 3:144–45; P. Bottger, *NIDNTT,* 3:134–36; M. Dandamaev, *ABD,* 6:58–65; P. Davies, *IDB,* 4:71–77; G. Goosen, *The Theology of Work;* D. E. Gowan, *Int* 41 (1987): 341–53; N. K. Gottwald, *The Tribes of Yahweh;* H. Hamburger, *IDB,* 4:423–35; B. Malina, *Int* 41 (1987): 354–67; I. Mendelsohn, *BASOR* 143 (1956): 17–22; H. Preisker and E. Wurthwein, *TDNT,* 4:695–728; R. de Vaux, *Ancient Israel: Social Institutions;* H. E. von Waldrow, *CBQ* 32 (1970): 182–204; C. Wiener, *Dictionary of Biblical Theology*, pp. 505–8; C. H. J. Wright, *God's People in God's Land: Family, Land and Property in the Old Testament.*

Walk. The verb "walk" in its literal sense of going along or moving about on foot at a moderate pace is found numerous times in the Gospels. However, this same verb is more often used throughout the Old Testament and the epistles of the New Testament in a metaphorical way. In this sense it means to follow a certain course of life or to conduct oneself in a certain way. Many times the verb translated "walk" is present tense in the Greek of the New Testament, which means that the writer is referring to a continued mode of conduct or behavior. In fact, the infinitive "to walk" can be translated, in a Hebraistic way, "to live." Such a use is common in the Old Testament and the writings of Paul and of John, but is not found in those of Peter or James.

Throughout the New Testament, the verb "walk" is qualified in various ways to ensure that the reader understands what correct Christian living or conduct is and what it is not. Christians are not to continue to walk in darkness (1 John 1:6; 2:11). What John means is that Christians should not continue living in ignorance of divine truth, an ignorance that is associated with sin and its evil results. Along with this, their walk should not be characterized by craftiness and cunning (2 Cor. 4:2) or by such sins as immorality, impurity, passion, evil desire, and greed, sins, the writer says, which used to characterize their continual living before salvation (Col. 3:5–7).

To the contrary, Christian living should be characterized by newness of life (Rom. 6:4), good works (Eph. 2:10), love (Eph. 5:2), wisdom (Col. 4:5), truth (3 John 4), and obedience to the light received from the apostle (1 Thess. 4:10).

The standard of victorious Christian living is stated two different ways by the apostle Paul. His dominant theme in Romans 8 is that the Christian is not to continue walking "according to the sinful nature but according to the Spirit" (v. 4; see also vv. 12–13). The sinful nature in this expression is not bodily, material flesh but that ethical flesh, which refers to the sin dwelling in the Christian, as referred to in Romans 7:17, 20, 21, 23. It is the nature of humankind, apart from the supernatural influences of the Holy Spirit; and this corrupt sinful nature, the core of which is selfishness, must not govern our conduct. In other words, Paul writes that the Christian should not live in accordance with the age to which this world belongs (Eph. 2:2). The mature Christian will walk in accordance with the Holy Spirit's leading (Rom. 8:4) via the Lord's commands given to him in the Scriptures (2 John). This leading is not some ethereal, mystical kind of guidance but comes in the form of clear "Thou shalts" and "Thou shalt nots."

In addition to writing the instruction given above, the New Testament writers do not leave maturing Christians in the dark as to the manner of walking that is expected from them. They are not to keep on walking as the nations or Gentiles outside Christ do (Eph. 4:17). The apostle Paul thereby lets his readers know that he expects a different lifestyle from Christians than from non-Christians. They are not to conduct their lives in an unruly or disorderly fashion, deviating from the prescribed kind of life or rule given by the apostles in the Bible (2 Thess. 3:6, 11). Some Christians in Thessalonica, because of wrong beliefs about the second coming of Christ, had given up their jobs and were sponging off the other church members. Paul reminds the church that this should not be tolerated and that the one who does not work should not be allowed to eat at the expense of the others.

To the contrary, the members of the faith should continue walking decently and properly, as in the daylight (Rom. 13:13), not in carousing, drunkenness, sexual promiscuity, sensuality, strife, or jealousy. The deeds of darkness must be put away and the armor of the light needs to be put on (Rom. 13:12). They should walk worthy of their calling as Christians (Eph. 4:1). They should walk as children of the light who have the lamp of the Bible for their guidance (Eph. 5:8). Furthermore, they should walk, not as unwise but as wise, making the most of the time because the days are evil. They should behave circumspectly and with great care and understanding of what the will of the Lord is (Eph. 5:15–17). In addition, they ought to walk in a manner that is suitable and worthy of God, whose children they are (Eph. 4:1). A Christian should continue walking decently and properly with reference to those outside the church (1 Thess. 4:12). Finally, the Christian should continue behaving in this world, as much as possible, as Christ behaved (1 John 2:6) and as Paul, in his own life, exemplified a pattern of Christian living (Phil. 3:17).

In 2 Corinthians 5:7 Paul described the means of the Christian's walk or behavior which he describes in his epistles. He succinctly says, "We live by faith, not by sight." To walk by faith means to rely on Christ for one's own salvation and to trust that the promises found in the Bible, God's Word, are dependable and will be faithfully fulfilled. Paul also wrote the Galatians that they should continue walking by the Spirit (Gal. 5:16).

From both the Old and New Testament references, it is clear that the metaphorical or figurative use of the English verb, "walk," refers to conduct or behavior which, it is insisted, should support one's verbal testimony. The metaphorical use of the word "walk" in the Bible refers to the way in which an individual lives or conducts his or her life; and regularly, the Christian's walk will be in stark contrast to that of the unbeliever's.

WESLEY L. GERIG

See also ETHICS; SANCTIFICATION; SPIRITUALITY.

War, Holy War. Despite the fact that many nations have used Scripture passages out of context to promote martial ventures, the Old Testament does not glorify or even recommend warfare as a solution to problems. Quite the opposite: Violence is thoroughly condemned.

Lamech and his song of vengeance is an aberration in the history of man (Gen. 4:23–24). The famous heroes of old, men of renown, are not presented in a context of approbation (Gen. 6:4). Violence that filled the earth with pain was one of the major causes of the flood (Gen. 6:11). Nimrod, the mighty warrior and the first military aggressor (10:8–11), is not part of the redemptive line. The land of Nimrod is destined to be ruled by the sword (Mic. 5:6).

Simon and Levi lose their rights among the firstborn because their swords are weapons of violence. Although their massacre (Gen. 34) was for an allegedly moral purpose, it caused them to be scattered in Israel (49:5–7). When Moses killed an Egyptian to help an Israelite, he found that this method only delayed God's deliverance (Exod. 2:12).

David is associated with the successful expansion of his realm by warfare. He cannot, however, build God's temple because he has fought many wars and shed much blood in God's sight

(1 Chron. 22:8). When David sought to carry out a census with a military purpose it very nearly cost him his kingdom (2 Sam. 24).

Wars in the Bible have been discouraged or even stopped by prophets. The prophet Shemaiah would not allow Rehoboam to put down the rebellion of the northern tribes by force of arms (1 Kings 12:22–23). Micaiah refused to be swayed by the unanimous clamor of the war prophets (1 Kings 22).

Israel's leaders are rebuked by the prophet Oded for bringing Judean prisoners of war into the country (2 Chron. 28:11). Judah's leaders are destined for wrath because they sought to expand their borders when Israel was weakened by Assyrian aggression in the north (Hos. 5:10). Their aggression is compared to unscrupulous landowners who move the boundary stones to increase the size of the property.

When war is inevitable, it must be carried out humanely. Nations are not allowed to go beyond the use of reasonable force necessary to achieve their objectives. In the first two chapters of Amos foreign nations are designed for judgment because of their war crimes both against Israelites and against each other. Jehu was authorized by Yahweh to end Ahab's dynasty, but his violence went far beyond his objectives. Thus the house of Jehu is to be punished for the massacre at Jezreel (Hos. 1:4).

The Torah contained rules to ensure wars would be conducted as humanely as possible. Female captives could not be violated. If a man saw a prisoner he wished to marry, her rights and feelings must be respected. She must be given time to mourn her family. If he later grew tired of her, he could not abuse her or sell her for money (Deut. 21:10–14). Before a city was attacked the law required that terms of peace be offered. If peace was accepted the city was not to be destroyed (Deut. 20:11). There were even conservation laws governing destruction of trees in a siege (Deut. 20:19–20).

In the Old Testament era wars were often made unnecessary by miraculous or unusual circumstances. Exodus 14 presents a standard paradigm of biblical deliverance. Moses proclaims to the people, "Stand firm and you will see the deliverance the LORD will bring you today." The Pharaoh's elite chariot corps is destroyed by the waters of the sea without the use of a single human weapon.

Troops besieging Elisha's house are smitten with blindness. The prophet leads them straight into Samaria. When their eyes are opened, the prophet will not allow the king to kill them. After they are fed, they are returned to their master (2 Kings 6:18–22). Later in 2 Kings 7:6 the Aramean armies retreat because Yahweh makes a loud noise. In Hezekiah's time, the Assyrian siege is ended by the angel of death (2 Kings 19:35).

In Jonah 3:8 the Ninevites are not faulted for their idolatry but because of their violence. God makes it clear in Jonah 4 that it is his interest to save lives, not to take them. While it is true that Yahweh will one day punish the godless nations with a sword, it will be in his own good time. It will not be because he is overwhelmed by the anger of the moment. God is not slack concerning his promises but is willing for all to come to repentance (2 Peter 3:9). In Zechariah 1:12–13 even the angel of the Lord loses patience at this slowness and must be comforted.

The hope of the future for the people of God is not in war and conquest. It is when nations stream to the holy mountain to learn about God. It will be a time when weapons are turned into farm implements and war shall be no more (Isa. 2:1–4).

Genocide in the Book of Joshua. The killing of everyone in Jericho and Ai, young and old, men and women in Joshua (6:21; 8:24–25) seems harsh and cruel when taken out of context. It must be remembered that this is a special circumstance carried out only during the initial conquering of the land. It is not a general rule to be applied in every armed conflict.

Israel is forbidden to make an alliance with Canaanites or to give any quarter to them (Exod. 23:32–33; 34:12–15). Yet in Abraham's day no one felt it was strange for the patriarch to have an alliance with Eshcol and Aner (Gen. 14:13). In 15:16 Abraham is told that the sin of the Amorites has not yet reached its full measure. Simon and Levi are rebuked for their slaughter of Canaanites at Shechem (Gen. 34; 49:5–7).

In Genesis 38 Judah leaves his brethren to stay with a Canaanite named Hirah who becomes his friend (vv. 1, 12). Later both he and his son marry Canaanite girls. One of these girls becomes a direct descendant of Christ and the first woman mentioned in the New Testament (Matt. 1:3).

At the end of the period of judges David conquers Jerusalem. Yet he does not kill the Jebusites there or even take their land by force. Instead, he refuses the gift of Arunah, the Jebusite's threshing floor, choosing to pay him for it (2 Sam. 24:18–23). In the period of Solomon when all the Canaanite strongholds are under the authority of Israel, the Canaanites are not killed but are put to forced labor (1 Kings 9:20–21).

All this indicates that special circumstances were prevailing in the initial period of conquest. Leviticus 18 mentions the depraved state of Canaanite society at this time. Heinous sexual perversions were a part of their religion. Child sacrifice was also practiced. Verse 25 indicates that the land was so defiled that it vomited out its inhabitants. All these practices would not only have contaminated pure Mosaic Yahwehism but would have destroyed the fabric of any society's family structure.

Deuteronomy 20:16–18 indicates the Canaanites were to be killed that they may not "teach you to follow all the detestable things they do in worshiping their gods." It is a fact attested by archaeological finding that the immorality mentioned in Leviticus 18 was an integral part of Canaanite worship. One piece of literature depicts the head of the Canaanite pantheon bearing two children by a man's wives. The man is delighted they have been chosen for this purpose. Liturgical markings indicate it was used in worship. This story celebrates the birth of two Canaanite gods called Shachar and Shalim. It appears that the killing of these people was to be done at the outset so as to allow Mosaic morality to gain a foothold in the land.

Practices of Jezebel, Ahab's wife from Sidon, shows what happens when just one Canaanite occupies a place of authority. She attempts to kill all the prophets of the Lord (1 Kings 18:13). She has Naboth killed so Ahab can possess his vineyard. Ahab grew up in a society where the Ten Commandments were an important standard. Jezebel grew up in a context where she heard about a Canaanite goddess smashing a young man's skull because she wanted his bow.

Life is sacred in the Old Testament. Murder is a capital offense in the covenant of Genesis 9:1–7. Yet no physical life can be more important than God's redemptive purpose for the whole world. If Canaanites had been allowed to survive unbridled, they would have slowly and painfully killed their own selves.

It does not seem to have ever been God's purpose to slaughter all the Canaanites at once. The Book of Joshua describes a few dramatic victories for a theological purpose. Exodus 23:29–30, however, indicates it was God's original purpose to drive the Canaanites out "little by little" so the land would not become desolate and wild animals multiply against them. Judges 3:1–4 informs us that Canaanites were left to test the Israelites and to keep them militarily alert. What is seen in Joshua is the rapid crushing of Canaanite capability of being an offensive threat. They were militarily crippled so there would be little chance for them to gain control of Israelite society.

Actually the Book of Joshua plays down the human element in warfare. Joshua categorically denied that the land of Canaan was won with their own sword and bow (Josh. 24:12). Moses before him had told the people that the nations would not be driven out because of Israel's righteousness but because of the wickedness of these nations (Deut. 9:4).

When the Israelites cross Jordan after a supernatural parting of the waters, Joshua seemingly proceeds to do everything a competent military commander should never do. He cripples his entire fighting force for two weeks by subjecting them to the painful act of circumcision (Josh. 5:2). When the army recovered, they celebrated the Passover (5:10). Thereafter Joshua learns he is, after all, not the commander of the forces and must take off his shoes before his superior heavenly leader (5:14).

Israelites have no engineering skills to use in capturing a walled city. Instead they proceed to walk around the city and will use only faith to bring the walls down. After only two cities (Jericho and Ai) are taken they proceed north into hostile territory to Shechem. Here they pause to perform a lengthy, time-consuming consecration service (Josh. 8:30–35).

The message of the Book of Joshua is that the land was not taken by brilliant military strategy, technologically advanced weaponry, or great heroism of mighty warriors. It was solely a supernatural act of the grace of God according to the promise. It was given by the promise and it will be kept by being faithful to the promises of God.

Holy War. The Old Testament speaks of the "wars of Yahweh" (Num. 21:14; 1 Sam. 18:17; 25:28), but does not use the term "holy war." This was introduced into the literature by the German scholar Friedrich Schwally in 1901. It refers to a type of warfare totally devoted to the plans and purposes of the Lord. God not only endorses and directs it but is an active participant.

The first example of this kind of warfare in the Hebrew Bible is found in Exodus 17:8–16. Here the Amalekites are the aggressors. It is learned from Deuteronomy 25:17–19 that they were attacking the stragglers at Israel's rear when they were faint and weary. Although knowledge of the destruction of Egyptians in the Red Sea was widespread, these treacherous people had no qualms about attacking God's people. Therefore, these attacks were an affront to the glory of God.

Moses took the rod of God to the top of a hill. When the rod was raised, Israel prevailed. When Moses put his hands down, Amalek prevailed. At the end of the day the battle was won by Israel because Aaron and Hur kept Moses' hands held high. Moses was commanded by the Lord to record these events on a scroll. Hereafter there would be perpetual warfare between Yahweh and Amalek until they were completely blotted out.

Because this is war devoted to the Lord, it was often preceded by sacrifices, prayer, and some type of religious liturgy. The leader would often remind the troops that Yahweh had already delivered the enemy into their hand and would himself be fighting next to them. In Deuteronomy 20 the priest was to do this (vv. 1–4). In at least one battle the liturgy itself celebrating Yahweh's amazing grace was sufficient to bring about a decisive victory (2 Chron. 20:20–23).

It was not always apparent that the war was actually a holy war. Various means of determining Yahweh's stance in the coming battle were sought such as Urim, dreams, or prophets. If the

Lord did not answer by any of these, it was considered to be an ominous foreboding (1 Sam. 28:5–7) and called for desperate measures. Kings were often very careful to determine if prophetic oracles endorsing the attack were genuine (cf. 1 Kings 22).

Because the war was a holy war, those who comprise the fighting force must also be holy. They were consecrated to the Lord (Josh. 3:5). This would often require extensive inspection and preparations. Everyone was expected to be ritually clean. Even the camp itself must be holy. The Lord must not see anything indecent among them (Deut. 23:9–14). Even the weapons themselves would sometimes be consecrated to the Lord (1 Sam. 21:5; 2 Sam. 1:21).

The mental and emotional state of the army was important. Anyone who was fainthearted and did not put his full trust in Yahweh was sent home. Anyone who might have his mind too much on affairs back home was dismissed (Deut. 20:1–8).

Sometimes kings would attempt to write their own rules of holy war. A case in point would be Saul's requirement that no one could eat until the enemy was completely destroyed (1 Sam. 14:24). Sometimes a battle would be won by bypassing ritual and prescribed routine. Jonathan and his armor bearer spontaneously attacked and routed a seemingly impregnable Philistine garrison in this way (1 Sam. 14:1–23).

These examples indicate that God is not to be manipulated into giving victory because a certain set "recipe" was followed. Hophni and Phineas made the fatal mistake of assuming victory would be guaranteed by bringing a sacred cult object into the camp, namely, the ark of Yahweh (1 Sam. 4). Later Jeremiah's temple sermon denounced the theology that assumed Jerusalem was inviolable because of the presence of the temple there (Jer. 7:8–15).

In 1 Samuel 13 and 15 Saul felt that the ritual sacrifice was more import than listening to God's word (15:22–23). Only faithfulness to the Torah and loyal obedience to Yahweh would insure victory. If the Torah is strictly followed it is promised that the enemy will come out one way and flee seven ways (Deut. 28:1, 7). Wisdom literature observed that "when a man's ways are pleasing to the LORD, he makes even his enemies live at peace with him" (Prov. 16:7).

The high point and conclusion to the battle was the dedication of the booty to the Lord. In total, all out holy war this was completely devoted to the sacred treasury (Josh. 6:18–19). Personal appropriation of things under the ban would cause serious consequences. Achan's transgression caused defeat at Ai (Josh. 7–8). Saul's keeping back some of the spoil caused him to lose the kingdom (1 Sam. 15:23).

David's Wars of Expansion. Early in his career David's military successes incited the wrath of Saul. Women sang of him that he had killed his ten thousands (1 Sam. 18:7) while Saul was only given credit for his thousands. His first success over the giant Goliath was because he came not trusting in weapons but in the name of the Lord (17:45). Early in his life he had learned that simple faith in the Lord gave him victory over the lion and the bear. He brought this way of thinking to his first actual military situation. His viewpoint, which made the difference, was that Israel's forces were actually the army of the living God and thus should be invincible (17:36).

Psalm 60, traditionally considered to be Davidic, affirms that the help of man is worthless. "With God," David says, "we will gain the victory, and he will trample down our enemies." He believed that God raises a victory banner for those who fear him. In faith he could proclaim, "Moab is my washbasin, upon Edom I toss my sandal" (vv. 4–12).

In 2 Samuel 22 David avers that Yahweh is the sum total of his strategic military potential (vv. 1–3). Through the eyes of faith he saw his victory being brought about by the march of the Divine Warrior in the attendant circumstances of storm and earthquake (vv. 8–16). With God's help he believes he is personally capable of astounding feats (v. 30). It is from Yahweh he has learned all his military expertise (v. 35). Only by God's grace has victory been achieved.

No king ever experienced David's victorious results. In direct contrast are Jeroboam II's hollow victory celebrations vaunting victory by his own hand (Amos 6:13–14). David's small empire became a model, illustration, and pattern for the coming triumph of the ideal messianic king who will rule from sea to sea (Zech. 9:9–10). He will rule the nations with a rod of iron (Ps. 2:8–9).

Amos 9:11–15 foretells of the restoration of David's fallen tent. The early New Testament church considered the conversion of the Gentiles as at least a partial fulfillment of this prophecy (Acts 15:15–18). David's empire was never a biblical ideal toward which temporal kings were to strive. Such conquests would only be realized in the messianic era.

Warfare in Wisdom Literature. For waging war guidance is needed; many advisors will bring victory (Prov. 20:18; 24:6). A small city with few people in it can be saved by the wisdom of a poor man (Eccles. 9:14–15). This advice is echoed in the teaching of Christ in Luke 14:31–32. A king who wages war against another must count the cost. So a disciple who follows Christ in the way of the cross must also count his cost.

Secular warfare is risky business. Even with superior resources victory is never assured because time and chance happen to all (Eccles. 9:11). There is, however, safety against capricious fate. The name of the Lord is a strong tower where the righteous can be safe (Prov. 18:10).

One can have many war horses but in the end the battle is the Lord's (Prov. 21:31; Isa. 31:1).

Some weapons are more lethal than military hardware. The teeth of the wicked are like knives and swords (Prov. 30:14). There are those who use their tongue like the thrusts of a sword (Prov. 30:14). James 3:5–6 says that the tongue can set the whole world on fire. There are some tasks more difficult than capturing enemy cities. Controlling your own spirit and winning back an offended brother are examples (Prov. 16:32; 25:28).

Wisdom, power, and warfare are interconnected in Isaiah 51:9–10 with the exodus. In the Wisdom of Solomon, an apocryphal book, wisdom, the Logos, the all-powerful Word, is a fierce warrior. He leaps from heaven's royal throne with a sharp sword to slay the firstborn in Egypt (18:14–16). Following this concept of wisdom and the word, the New Testament identifies the sword of the Spirit as the Word of God (Eph. 6:18). The same theme is found in Hebrews 4:13–14. Here the Word is like a sharp sword penetrating the thoughts and attitudes of the heart.

Eschatological Warfare. Prophets foretold that in the days to come Israel would be given special powers over their enemies. With horns of iron and hoofs of bronze they will break to pieces many nations (Mic. 4:13). The sons of Zion will become like a warrior's sword against the sons of Greece (Zech. 9:13). Sheep of the flock will one day be made like proud war horses (10:3). These predictions are set in a postexilic scenario. Possibly second century B.C. successes of the Maccabees and even recent triumphs of Israeli forces in modern history are partial fulfillments of these events.

Many of the prophets foretold overconfident, empty hopes of nations who felt that Jerusalem would be an easy conquest (Isa. 29:7–8; Ezek. 38–39; Zech. 12–14). Such unrealistic expectations are compared by Isaiah to a hungry man who dreams he is at a banquet. Just when defeat seems assured the Divine Warrior will appear on behalf of his people (Isa. 63:1–5; Rev. 19:11–21).

In this final conflict the battle is conspicuous by its absence. There is no fight! Dramatically the two forces come together. Where one would expect to see the onset of hostilities, there is the simple narrative statement that the enemy leadership is seized. Summarily, with no fanfare, they are simply thrown into the lake of fire (Rev. 19:20). Rank and file are systematically killed with the sword that comes from the mouth of the lone horseman (v. 21).

Warfare in the New Testament. Christ's triumphal entry into Jerusalem celebrated his past and future defeat of the powers of darkness. He fulfills the prophecy of Zechariah 9:9 of the gentle king riding on a donkey (Matt. 21:5). People cry out portions of Psalm 118, saying, "Blessed is he who comes in the name of the Lord" (Mark 11:9–10). Psalm 118 is regarded by many Old Testament scholars as a celebration of a king returning from a military victory.

In Psalm 118:12 the king states his enemies surrounded him like bees. In the name of the Lord he cuts them off. Shouts of victory go up in the tents of the righteous (vv. 12–15). Christ had recently defeated demons (Mark 9) and death (John 11). He had told his disciples he saw Satan fall like lightening from heaven (Luke 10:18).

Upon his triumphal entry the divine warrior goes straight to his temple and cleanses it (Matt. 21:12) of the money makers (Mal. 3:1–4). His subsequent death and resurrection were described by apostle Paul as a military victory over the powers of darkness. He disarmed the powers and authorities. He made a public spectacle of them, triumphing over them by the cross (Col. 2:15). Thereupon victorious, as the conquering king in Psalm 68:18, he ascended on high, he led captives in his train, and he gave gifts to men (Eph. 4:8).

Just before his death Christ foresaw the awful tragedy of the revolts against the Romans and wept over the city (Luke 19:41–44). On the way to the cross he told the women not to weep for him but for themselves and for their children who would be caught up in this awful pogram (Luke 23:27–30). In the Olivet Discourse he warned his disciples to flee when they saw Jerusalem encompassed about with armies (Luke 21:20–24).

His warning of false messiahs coming in his name was probably fulfilled in part by Bar Kosiba, who in A.D. 132 styled himself as "son of the star" (Bar Kochbah). Even the great rabbi Akivah believed he was the messiah. These revolts initiated the trampling of Jerusalem by the Gentiles (Luke 21:8, 24). He foretold that wars and rumors of wars would be commonplace throughout the age (21:9–11).

All this proves to be a model and an illustration of the endtime conflict of the people of God. Christ did not believe the end would come in his day. He believed these things would be the beginning of sorrows (Matt. 24:8). One who reads the Olivet Discourse is like a person watching the landscape and seeing two mountain ranges. They appear to be close together when in fact they may be miles apart.

Destruction of Jerusalem by the Romans of the first century is the close mountains. Far off in the distance is another, high cluster of peaks. This is the final war at the end of the age, which will be attended by a great deal of supernatural phenomena (Luke 21:25–28). It is this endtime generation that will not pass away until all is fulfilled (Matt. 24:34).

The horrors of the final conflict are introduced in the Book of Revelation by four eerie horsemen (6:1–8). The first phase of war is quick, easy conflict with the bow, a long-range weapon. Then comes wholesale slaughter with the red horse.

The black horse introduces famine and rationing. The final horse brings ravaging death to the home front by starvation, disease, and wild animals. These are only the beginning of sorrows.

The arch criminal called the "antichrist" will even have power to wage war against the saints and overcome them (Rev. 13:7; cf. Dan. 7:21–25). The sudden arrival of the Ancient of Days will, however, abruptly terminate his activities. At that time the saints of the most high will be given sovereignty and dominion over the earth (Dan. 7:26–27).

In the meantime the Christian life is metaphorically compared to warfare. Timothy is exhorted to endure hardship as a good soldier of Jesus Christ (2 Tim. 2:3). He is encouraged to fight the good fight of faith and hold on to eternal life (1 Tim. 6:12). This conflict, however, is not against flesh and blood but against the powers of this dark world, against spiritual forces in heavenly realms (Eph. 6:12). Paul warns the Ephesians to put on the whole armor of God into this conflict (6:10–15).

The church at Corinth was told that the weapons we fight with are not the weapons of this world. They have divine power to demolish strongholds. These strategic assets can take into captivity every thought to the obedience of Christ (2 Cor. 10:1–5). PAUL FERGUSON

See also DEVOTE, DEVOTED; DISCIPLINE; JUDGMENT; JUSTICE; PROVIDENCE OF GOD; PUNISHMENT; VENGEANCE; VIOLENCE.

Bibliography. D. Christensen, *Transformations of the War Oracle in Old Testament Prophecy;* R. Gonen, *Weapons and Warfare in Ancient Times;* M. Lind, *Yahweh Is a Warrior;* G. von Rad, *Holy War in Ancient Israel;* Y. Yadin, *The Art of Warfare in Biblical Lands.*

Wash. *See* CLEAN, UNCLEAN.

Watchfulness. Watchfulness suggests a preparedness in order to avoid being taken unaware by an enemy (Ps. 127). It involves fighting carelessness to reach a desired goal (Prov. 8:34; see Neh. 4:9; 7:3). In the New Testament three basic emphases are found: (1) be prepared for the Lord's return; (2) be on guard against temptation; and (3) struggle in prayer.

The Lord's Return. In the Synoptic Gospels Jesus exhorts the disciples to be prepared for the coming of the Son of Man (Mark 13:33–37). He employs a variety of parables and illustrations to paint word portraits of watchfulness (see Matt. 24:32–51). The disciples are even to abstain from sleep because the coming of the Son of Man will be unexpected, like a thief in the night.

Watchfulness characterizes the attitudes of the disciples who await with hope the return of Jesus. Vigilant watchfulness demands alertness and detachment from earthly pleasures and activities (see Luke 21:34–36). The parable of the ten virgins emphasizes the imminence of the parousia (Matt. 25:1–13).

The Pauline epistles echo a similar theme. Paul's eschatological anticipations reflect the vigilance of the Gospels (see 1 Thess. 5:1–7). Believers must resist evil so as not to be taken by surprise at the Lord's coming. Watchfulness implies sobriety, an avoidance of worldly excesses associated with darkness. Beyond that believers must wake from their sleep to prepare for the consummation of their salvation (Rom. 13:11–14).

The Apocalypse urges the church at Sardis to faithful watchfulness (Rev. 3:1) so it will be able to participate in the Lord's triumphal procession.

Guard against Temptation. Vigilant watchfulness for the Lord's return enables the disciples to battle temptation. The Synoptic Gospels picture Jesus' struggle in Gethsemane as an adumbration of the Church's struggle at the end of time. Jesus serves as a model of how to stand against temptation (Matt. 4:1–11). The petition in the Lord's Prayer to be able to stand against temptation points not only toward the eschatological future, but to the daily enablement needed by believers (Matt. 6:9–13).

Both Paul and Peter issue the command to be watchful, to stand against the evil one (see Eph. 6:10–17; 1 Peter 5:8). The church must watch unless savage wolves, influenced by the evil one, overtake the community and lead it astray.

Watch and Pray. The picture of Jesus' stand against the devil's temptation is all the more powerful because of the disciples' failure to do the same. They fail to hear and obey their master's warning to watch and pray so as not to fall into temptation (Matt. 26:41).

Paul urges the church to pray with unfailing perseverance. The actions of watchfulness and prayer are indissolubly united. Prayer is an act of vigilance and vigilance a consequence of prayer (Eph. 6:18–19). Vigilant watchfulness is a manifestation of genuine spiritual life. It keeps the church faithful in avoiding being lulled into false security. DAVID S. DOCKERY

See also SECOND COMING OF CHRIST; TEMPTATION, TEST.

Water. The word "water" is used in a variety of metaphorical ways in Scripture. It is used to symbolize the troublesome times in life that can and do come to human beings, especially God's children (Pss. 32:6; 69:1, 2, 14, 15; Isa. 43:2; Lam. 3:54). In some contexts water stands for enemies who can attack and need to be overcome (2 Sam. 22:17–18; Pss. 18:16–17; 124:4–5; 144:7; Isa. 8:7; Jer. 47:2). In both the Old and New Testaments, the word "water" is used for salvation and eternal life, which God offers humankind through faith in his Son (Isa. 12:3; 55:1; Rev. 21:6; 22:1, 2, 17). In John 4:10–15, part of Jesus' discourse with the Samaritan woman at the well, he speaks metaphorically of his salvation as "living water" and as "a spring of water welling up to eternal life."

Following along this same theme, water sometimes symbolizes the spiritual cleansing that comes with the acceptance of God's offer of salvation (Ezek. 36:25; Eph. 5:26; Heb. 10:22). In fact, in Ephesians 5:26, the "water" that does the cleansing of the bride, the church, is directly tied in with God's Word, of which it is a symbol.

In a very important passage, Jesus identifies the "streams of living water" that flow from within those who believe in him with the Holy Spirit (John 7:37–39). The reception of the Holy Spirit is clearly the special reception that was going to come after Jesus had been glorified at the Father's right hand and happened on the Day of Pentecost as described in Acts 2. Two times in Jeremiah Yahweh is metaphorically identified as "the spring of living water" (Jer. 2:13; 17:13). In both instances Israel is rebuked for having forsaken the Lord for other cisterns that could in no way satisfy their "thirst."

In other passages of Scripture, the following are said metaphorically to be "water": God's help (Isa. 8:6: "the gently flowing waters of Shiloah"); God's judgment (Isa. 28:17: "water will overflow your hiding place"); man's words (Prov. 18:4: "The words of man's mouth are deep waters"); man's purposes (Prov. 20:5: "The purposes of a man's heart are deep waters"); an adulterous woman (Prov. 9:17: "Stolen water is sweet"); and a person's posterity (Isa. 48:1: "Listen to this, O house of Jacob, who are called by the name of Israel and have come forth out of the line [waters] of Judah").

The reference to "water" in John 3:5 has been variously interpreted by scholars. Some have taken the phrase, "being born of water," to mean being born again by means of water baptism. Others have taken the verse to involve a hendiadys and take "water" and "Spirit" together as one reference since water is a symbol of the Holy Spirit in other passages. Still others take the birth by water to be one's natural birth and the birth by the Spirit to be the supernatural birth of being "born again" or regenerated. This seems to be what Nicodemus, in the context, understood Jesus to be saying. In order to enter the kingdom of God one must have two births, each a different kind. After all, water, in its ordinary sense, has a great part to play in the natural birth of a baby. Furthermore, there are too many clear passages and single verses in the Bible that base salvation, entrance into the kingdom of God, and eternal life on faith alone. WESLEY L. GERIG

Wave Offering. *See* OFFERINGS AND SACRIFICES.

Weakness. While the Gospels often use the word "weakness" to describe the many illnesses Jesus healed, the concept of weakness is seldom used in a physical sense in Scripture. In fact, the incarnational theology of the Gospels sets forth the most important spiritual principle. The "infleshing" of the Word means that God's power is most preeminently evidenced in human weakness (1 Cor. 1:25; 2 Cor. 13:4; Heb. 5:2).

The paralleling of divine empowerment and human suffering in the life of Christ commences with his birth and continues through to the cross and the resurrection. Indeed, the cross and resurrection encapsulate the paradox of God's power being evidenced in the midst of human suffering and weakness. Yet the realization of this paradox in the life of Jesus fulfills the Suffering Servant motif of Isaiah and forms the basis of the atonement (Isa. 52:13–53:12; Heb. 4:15).

For Paul the principle of strength in weakness serves as the paradigm for life and ministry. Humankind is weak by nature. Yet weakness is the very point at which God reveals his power and grace (1 Cor. 1:27; 2 Cor. 12:9). Human weakness is not a liability only because it makes room for the power of God (2 Cor. 12:10). Weakness facilitates dependence on God, cultivates the appropriation of grace, and ascribes all glory and credit to God (2 Cor. 12:7–12). For these reasons Paul boasts of his weakness and views it as a sign of true apostleship (2 Cor. 11:30).

The spiritual union between the believer and Christ permits us to experience not only the weakness and the suffering of the cross, but also the power and glory of the resurrection (Rom. 6:1–5; 2 Cor. 13:4). WILLIAM A. SIMMONS

See also STRONG AND WEAK.

Bibliography. R. Bauckham, *Themelios* 7 (1982): 4–6; D. A. Black, *Paul, Apostle of Weakness;* T. Y. Mullins, *JBL* 76 (1957): 299–303; G. G. O'Collins, *CBQ* 33 (1971): 528–37.

Wealth. The most basic English definitions of wealth are "the condition of being happy and prosperous" and "spiritual well-being" (*OED*). But the most common usage probably involves the narrower sense of "abundance of possessions, or of valuable products." A large percentage of Scripture focuses on right and wrong uses of this latter kind of wealth, while always subordinating it to the former.

The Old Testament. All wealth originally formed part of God's good creation, over which humans were given dominion (Gen. 1:26). This responsibility remained after the fall (9:1–3), but sin corrupted the process. God promised to make a great nation of Abraham's offspring, centered around prosperity in the promised land (12:7; 15:18; 17:8; 22:17). The patriarchs themselves were wealthy, as a first token of this blessing from God (24:35; 26:13; 30:43). So too God materially blessed the Israelites in Goshen as a testimony to the Egyptians (47:27). En route to Canaan, however, God very clearly places stipulations on the accumulation of wealth; manna and quail were to be collected so that no one had too little or too much (Exod. 16:16–18; quoted in 2 Cor. 8:15).

The law assumes the inherent worth of private property. It regulates the boundaries of fields (Deut. 19:14) and inheritance rights (21:16). It promises Canaan as a land of abundant resources that the Israelites may enjoy so long as they obey God's laws (Num. 13:27; 14:8; Deut. 6:3). But the law also provides safeguards against theft and covetousness (Exod. 20:15, 17; 22:1–15), forbids usury or "excessive interest" (22:25; Deut. 23:19–20), and includes a variety of constraints against the accumulation of unnecessary wealth. People may not work on the Sabbath; loans must be cancelled in Sabbath and Jubilee years (Lev. 25); tithes and offerings of the best of one's goods must be given to the Lord (Deut. 14:22–29; 25:1–15), creating genuine sacrifices; and generous provisions must be left behind for the poor and alien in the land (Lev. 19:9–10; Deut. 15:4–11; 23:24–25; 24:19–22). One's livelihood may not be taken as security (Deut. 24:6), and wages must be paid on time (19:13). Great quantities of material resources were expended in constructing and furnishing the tabernacle (Exod. 25–30), but the temptations to use wealth for idolatry loomed menacingly near (chap. 32).

God's promises and threats are repeatedly fulfilled from the time of Joshua through the monarchy to the exile and return. When the nation and her leaders obey God, he blesses them with peace and prosperity in the land; when they disobey, conquest and oppression by foreign nations follow. The Book of Ruth illustrates a compassionate rich man (Boaz) properly following the laws of gleaning. David amasses great wealth through military victories; Solomon's comes more from tribute and trade. By not first of all seeking wealth, God grants Solomon greater prosperity than any other ancient monarch (1 Kings 3–4). His palace and God's temple require vast material resources for their erection, but at the expense of the conquered peoples. At the very moment his wealth reaches its zenith, his foreign alliances, reflected in his huge harem, lead him into idolatry (1 Kings 10–11). Later kings more consistently abuse the privileges their wealth grants them, among whom Ahab is probably the worst (1 Kings 21). Ezra–Nehemiah describes the rebuilding of the temple after exile, but this time the needs of the poor are given greater priority (Neh. 5:1–13).

Despite its dangers, wealth has so far been seen as primarily a blessing from God, with poverty often viewed as a curse. The Book of Job offers the most important Old Testament corrective to this notion. God allows Satan to take away Job's great wealth (and health) to test him. Job's friends are convinced that he has sinned, but God vindicates Job against his friends. Psalms and Proverbs therefore continue a two-pronged approach to riches and poverty. Wealth may be a reward for industry or righteousness (Ps. 112; Prov. 12:11; 13:21; 21:5). But it is at least as often the ill-gotten product of wickedness or hostility, in which case it is better to be poor (Ps. 37:16–17; Prov. 15:16–17; 16:8; 17:1). These contrasting emphases caution against absolutizing any one particular proverb; wisdom literature after all provides only generalizations of what is often true, and some statements are descriptive rather than prescriptive. Biblical wisdom also stresses the transience of earthly wealth (Ps. 39:4–6; Prov. 23:4–5; Eccles. 5:8–17) and the future recompense of the oppressed (Ps. 49:10–20). Those who are given much must therefore not trust in their own resources but in God (Ps. 52:7; Prov. 3:9–10) and must use their abundance to help the needy (Ps. 82:3–4; Prov. 29:7). The ideal is to pray for enough possessions to avoid the temptation to steal but not enough to feel independent of God (Prov. 30:8–9).

The prophets continue the theme of offering prosperity for obedience and threatening its removal as a punishment for sin. Yet in view of the wickedness of their audiences, the latter predominates. Foreign nations are lambasted for the arrogance their wealth has engendered (Isa. 14; Ezek. 26, 28). Although Judah and Israel should know better, however, they too selfishly amass property while ignoring God's moral standards (Isa. 5:8–9); they trust in ritual worship rather than true repentance (Jer. 7:5–8); and they extort, rob, and oppress the poor to gain more land (Ezek. 22:29; Mic. 2:2). They boast in their wealth (Hos. 12:8), revel in their affluence (Amos 4:1; Hab. 2:16–17), and cannot wait for the Sabbath to end so they can make more money (Amos 8:5). Their leaders' motives for ministry are largely financial (Mic. 3:11)! Instead, they should "Seek justice, encourage the oppressed. Defend the cause of the fatherless, plead the case of the widow" (Isa. 1:17; cf. Jer. 22:13–17). They should give to God the full amount of tithes and offerings due him (Mal. 3:10). In expectation of just such obedience, the prophets look beyond the coming exile to the restoration of a remnant in the land, whose prosperity will once again be great (Isa. 54–55, 60–66), including much to eat (Joel 2:23–27) and the shared wealth of all the nations (Zech. 14:14).

In short, the Old Testament recognizes wealth as often a blessing from God. But frequently that wealth is tied up with the land or the temple in ways that do not carry over into a New Testament age that knows no one sacred piece of geography or architecture (John 4:24). Even in the Old Testament, the Israelites' wealth was meant to be shared, with the poor in the land and with Gentiles outside, so as to bring people to a knowledge of the Lord. Increased privilege carries increased responsibility. Governments and economic institutions today are not theocracies, but they may still be judged on how they meet the needs of the powerless and dispossessed.

The New Testament. As a carpenter, Jesus probably came from the lower end of the small "middle-class" of the ancient world although by modern standards he would still be considered poor. The same is probably true of his fishermen disciples. Matthew would doubtless have been better off. Joseph of Arimathea is called rich (Matt. 27:57). But the overriding thrust of Jesus' teaching on wealth is to highlight "mammon" (material resources) as a major competitor with God for human allegiance (Matt. 6:19–24; Luke 16:1–13). Wealth is "deceitful" (Mark 4:19) and can distract people from taking care of their spiritual condition, thereby causing them to forfeit eternal life (Mark 8:36). Hence, Jesus comes to announce God's reversal of human standards concerning rich and poor. Luke in particular emphasizes this theme. The rich will be sent away empty (1:53), the poor will be blessed (6:20) and liberated from their oppression (4:16–21). Those who accumulate wealth with no thought for God or the destitute around them will be eternally condemned (12:16–21; 16:19–31).

The right use of money thus forms a crucial part of Jesus' teaching on discipleship. His followers should have special concern for the poor (Luke 14:7–24), give generously of their resources (Matt. 5:42) even when they are meager (Mark 12:43–44), and be content with their daily bread (Matt. 6:11). There are unique occasions in which it remains justifiable to lavish expense on the worship of Christ in ways some people will find wasteful (Mark 14:3–9, with v. 7 quoting Deut. 15:11a), but these should remain the exception and not the norm (cf. Deut. 15:11b). Perhaps the most famous teaching of Jesus on money is his call to the rich young ruler to sell all he had, give it to the poor, and follow him (Mark 10:21; cf. esp. v. 25). Luke's redaction makes it clear this command does not apply to all; it appears as first in a series of three episodes on wealth (Luke 18:18–30; 19:1–10, 11–27). In the second, repentant Zaccheus gives up only half of his possessions; in the third, the faithful servants invest their master's money for kingdom priorities. But it is precisely those who too quickly become complacent by this observation whom God probably would call to give up all!

Not only individuals but Christian communities must come to grips with Jesus' ethic. As a promise to individuals, Matthew 6:33 ("seek first [God's] kingdom and his righteousness, and all these things [food, clothing, and drink] will be given to you as well") would have been frequently disproved. In light of Mark 10:30 and Luke 12:33 it must rather mean that to the extent that God's people collectively obey his commands, which include caring for the poor, then individual needs will be met. God provides enough for all his people to live a decent life; the question is if they will distribute his resources equitably to bring about this state of affairs. Eternal destinies hang in the balance; God will judge people on the basis of how they have cared for the needy in their midst (Matt. 25:31–46). The parable of sheep and goats most likely refers only to needy disciples ("brothers"), but the parable of the good Samaritan generalizes the principle to embrace even one's enemies, including those of entirely different religions and races (Luke 10:25–37).

In the early church, Jesus' disciples begin to put his teachings into practice. While retaining private property and not forcing anyone to participate, they develop a system of communal sharing in which believers sell their goods and redistribute the profits from "each according to his ability" (Acts 11:29) "to anyone as he had need" (2:45)—the identical two clauses that formed the heart of Marx's manifesto! Some have labeled this experiment a mistake that exacerbated the effects of a later famine, but Luke makes it clear that God supported and blessed these arrangements (2:46–47; 5:14). Barnabas provides a positive illustration of donating the proceeds from selling a field to the common pot (4:36); Ananias and Sapphira offer a negative illustration of deceiving the apostles about how much they were donating (5:2).

Acts nevertheless makes clear that physical and spiritual healing take priority over material needs (3:6–10). Philip rebukes Simon Magus for thinking the power of the Holy Spirit could be bought (8:18–20). Paul stresses that he has not coveted anyone's goods but worked to supply his own needs. And he quotes Jesus: "It is more blessed to give than to receive" (20:33–35). Still, his preaching has an impact on how people use their wealth, particularly in Ephesus; believers who no longer buy idols cause such a downturn in the silver business that the merchants riot (19:23–27).

Members of the Pauline churches, particularly in Corinth, are predominantly poor and hence more receptive to the gospel, which seems foolish to persons of power and influence (1 Cor. 1:18–31). This is one of Paul's reasons for not seeking support from the churches to which he ministers (1 Cor. 9), while still accepting such support when it comes unsolicited (Phil. 4:10–19), and encouraging Christians to support others who teach or lead them (Gal. 6:6; 1 Tim. 5:17–18; 2 Tim. 2:6). But remuneration must never be a motive for ministry (1 Tim. 3:8; Titus 1:8) and "the love of money is a root of all kinds of evil" (1 Tim. 6:10; cf. 2 Tim. 3:2). A key theme in several letters is the collection for the poor Christians in Judea, based in part on a sense of indebtedness to the mother church there (Rom. 15:25–27). Support for leaders in ministry and help for the needy of the world thus form the two central purposes for Christian giving.

In 2 Corinthians 8–9, Paul stresses that such giving should be sacrificial (8:1–3), sincere (v. 8), voluntary, and cheerful (9:7). Commitments should be kept (8:10–12), systems of accountability established (8:16–24), and giving in proportion to one's income—a "graduated tithe" (8:12–15; cf. 1 Cor. 16:2b). In the context of this collection appears the first record of a weekly Sunday offering (1 Cor. 16:2a). Christians should take particular care of needy relatives (1 Tim. 5:3–16) and be rich in good needs, sharing rather than trusting in their wealth (1 Tim. 6:17–19). They should pay their taxes (Rom. 13:6–7) and work diligently, avoiding idleness so as not to be a financial burden to anyone else (1 Thess. 4:11; 2 Thess. 3:6–15). Perhaps more than any other writer, Paul gives the lie to the so-called prosperity gospel, by stressing hardships, including economic ones, as standard fare for the believer (1 Cor. 4:8–13; 2 Cor. 6:3–10; 11:23–29).

After reading James, one wonders if it is possible to be both rich and Christian! Current economic states will be reversed (1:9–11); true religion cares for the dispossessed (1:27); God has a preferential option for the poor who love him (2:5); the rich exploit the poor Christians to whom he is writing (2:6–7); indeed they are characterized as affluent, self-indulgent oppressors whose doom is near and certain (5:1–6). Still, there is a small merchant class in James' congregation (4:13–17), and the rich in 1:10 probably are believers. But 2:14–17 makes plain that unless rich Christians use their wealth to help their poorer fellow Christians they cannot claim to have saving faith.

Peter too knows false teachers who are "experts in greed" (2 Peter 2:14) and commands elders not to be eager for money but for service (1 Peter 5:2). Women should not seek beauty from expensive, outward adornment (1 Peter 3:3; cf. 1 Tim. 2:9–10). John echoes James: Claims to have Christ's love without sharing material possessions with the needy prove vacuous (1 John 3:17–18). Jude's false teachers "have rushed for profit" (v. 11). And the end times will be characterized by rich, professing Christians who pitifully refuse to acknowledge their spiritual bankruptcy (Rev. 3:17). Indeed, the Antichrist's empire will rule by economic discrimination against believers (13:17); the lament over the fall of end-time "Babylon" focuses on the destruction of its great luxuries and affluence (chap. 18). But although fallen humanity has used wealth for great evils, God will redeem his originally good purposes in creation in the new heavens and earth when all wealth will be used for godly ends (21:24).

In sum, the New Testament is less positive about wealth than the Old Testament. It creates great temptations, even among God's people, for sin, self-indulgence, and exploitation of the poor. It is possible to be rich and Christian, but only if one is a good steward of that wealth, generous in giving and not worshiping unrighteous mammon. Yet one day, wealth, like the rest of creation, will be restored to its true and perfect place in God's designs to recreate the cosmos.

CRAIG L. BLOMBERG

See also MONEY; REWARD; WAGES; WORK.

Bibliography. J. Ellul, *Money and Power;* G. A. Getz, *A Biblical Theology of Material Possessions;* N. K. Gottwald, *The Tribes of Yahweh;* G. Gutierrez, *A Theology of Liberation;* T. D. Hanks, *God So Loved the Third World;* M. Hengel, *Property and Riches in the Early Church;* R. M. Kidd, *Wealth and Beneficence in the Pastoral Epistles;* P. U. Maynard-Reid, *Poverty and Wealth in James;* R. H. Nash, *Poverty and Wealth;* D. E. Oakman, *Jesus and the Economic Questions of His Day;* R. J. Sider, *Rich Christians in an Age of Hunger;* T. E. Schmidt, *Hostility to Wealth in the Synoptic Gospels;* D. P. Seccombe, *Possessions and the Poor in Luke–Acts;* C. J. Vos, *ISBE,* 4:185–90; R. N. Whybray, *Wealth and Poverty in the Book of Proverbs;* H. G. M. Williamson, *EQ* 57 (1985): 5–22.

Weeks, Feast of. *See* FEAST AND FESTIVALS OF ISRAEL.

Wickedness. *See* SIN.

Widow. Married woman whose husband has died and who remains unmarried. The Hebrew word translated "widow" is *ʾalmānā*, and it occurs fifty-six times in the Old Testament. Two of these cases are probably textual corruptions for the word "palace," which is similar in spelling and sound in the Hebrew (Isa. 13:22; Ezek. 19:7; cf. LXX). The Septaugint virtually always translates *ʾalmānā* with the Greek term for widow, *chēra* (cf. Job 24:21). The same Greek word occurs twenty-six times in the New Testament.

Words that occur in the general semantic field of the term "widow" in the Bible shed light on both her personal experience and social plight. Weeping (Job 27:15; Ps. 78:64), mourning (2 Sam. 14:2), and desolation (Lam. 1:1) describe her personal experience after the loss of her spouse. Poverty (Ruth 1:21; 1 Kings 17:7–12; Job 22:9) and indebtedness (2 Kings 4:1) were all too often descriptive of her financial situation, when the main source of her economic support, her husband, had perished. Indeed, she was frequently placed alongside the orphan and the landless immigrant (Exod. 22:21–22; Deut. 24:17, 19, 20–21) as representative of the poorest of the poor (Job 24:4; 29:12; 31:16; Isa. 10:2) in the social structure of ancient Israel, as well as in the ancient Near East. With minimal, if any, inheritance rights, she was often in a "no-man's land." She had left her family, and with her husband's death the bond between her and his family was tenuous.

The Old Testament. A recent body of influential research has argued that the Hebrew *ʾalmānā* must be distinguished from the English term "widow." It is claimed on the basis of Mesopotamian parallels that the former term referred to a woman whose husband had died and who was left without any economic and social support. Although this is true for the Akkadian *ʾalmattu* (Middle Assyrian Laws #33, #45), there is little basis for this meaning in the Bible. Often Hebrew widows would experience such a plight, but the term *ʾalmānā* itself simply referred to a woman whose mate had died and who had remained single (see 2 Sam. 14:2, 5, where the death of the husband is simply in view, and Lev. 21:14, which classes an *ʾalmānā* with a divorcée in opposition to a virgin). Moreover, in biblical literature there is evidence that some widows managed to support themselves economically (2 Sam. 14; Job 24:3; Prov. 15:25) and in later extrabiblical literature, it can be assumed that the term was used even of the wealthy Judith (Judith 9:4, 10).

Nonetheless, the loss of a husband in ancient Israel was normally a social and economic tragedy. In a generally patriarchal culture, the death of a husband usually meant a type of cultural death as well. Although the denotation of widow referred to a woman whose husband had died, because of the social context the word quickly acquired the connotation of a person living a marginal existence in extreme poverty. The widow reacted with grief to her plight, and probably wore a distinct garb as a sign of her status (Gen. 38:14, 19; 2 Sam. 14:2; cf. Judith 8:5–6; 10:3; 16:8). Disillusionment and bitterness could easily result (Ruth 1:20–21). Her crisis was aggravated if she had no able-bodied children to help her work the land of her dead spouse. To provide for her children, to maintain the estate, and to continue payments on debts accrued by her husband imposed severe burdens. Since she was in an extremely vulnerable economic position, she became the prime target of exploitation. The fact that she was classed with the landless stranger and Levite indicates that she was often unable to keep her husband's land.

In general, the widow's inheritance rights were minimal. Some scholars believe that Israelite widows could inherit land as was the case with their Mesopotamian counterparts. But the evidence is sparse. The general rule was that the land was inalienably connected to the family of the male to whom it was apportioned. The fact that an individual desired to marry the widow of a king did not assume that the woman had inherited her husband's estate; it was simply an attempt to legitimize a claim to royalty (cf. 1 Kings 2:13–18). The fact that widows had land within their possession probably indicated that they held it in trust for their children (1 Kings 17:7–9; 2 Kings 4:1–2; cf. Prov. 15:25). If a widow had male children, the land would pass to her sons when they reached maturity if she was able to maintain the land and the sons survived. If she had only female children, the land would be transferred to them provided they married within the tribe (Num. 27:8–11). If she was childless and of marriageable age (i.e., still able to reproduce), it was the duty of the closest male relative on her husband's side (normally the brother-in-law [Lat. *levir*]) to marry her and provide an heir for the land of her dead husband, and to continue his name in Israel (Deut. 25:5). The story of Judah and Tamar (Gen. 38) is an example of this custom of "levirate" marriage. Later, Deuteronomy 25:5–10 codifies legislation for such unions. The Book of Ruth provides a historical example of the application of the law. If no relative would marry a childless widow, it seemed that she could return to her father's house (Gen. 38:11; cf. Lev. 22:13) and dispose of the land to the husband's family (Ruth 4:1–3).

The distribution of the term "widow" is found approximately one-third of the time in legal texts, one-third in prophetic texts, and one-third in wisdom and historical literature. But the vast majority of the contexts are legal in nature, either dealing with justice (the legal protection of the widow) or injustice (the exploitation of her status). In the former case the Old Testament is replete with legislation that attempted to provide a social security net for the widow: she was not to be exploited (Exod. 22:21–22; Deut. 27:19); she was specifically permitted to glean the fields and vineyards during harvest time (Deut. 24:19–21, cf. Ruth 2); tithes were to be shared with her (Deut. 14:29; 26:12–13); provision was to be made for her at the main religious feasts (Deut. 16:9–15); her garment could not be taken as collateral for a loan (Deut. 24:17); and the levirate institution would not only provide an heir for the land for childless widows, it would help them be integrated back into society. Moreover, the supreme measure by which a ruler in Israel was to be judged was whether such powerless ones were cared for (Ps. 72:4, 12–14; Jer. 22:16).

At the same time, the legislation acknowledged the fact of the vulnerability of the widow and many Old Testament texts indicate that she was victimized repeatedly (Exod. 22:22–23; Isa. 1:23; 10:2; Ezek. 22:7; Mal. 3:5). The prophets were the champions of exploited widows. As far as they were concerned, repentance began with redressing wrongs done to such unfortunate women (Isa. 1:17; Jer. 7:6; 22:3; Zech. 7:10). Wisdom texts encouraged a benevolent attitude toward widows. Job's comforters accused him of heinous crimes, particularly of oppressing the widow (Job 22:9), but he countered with the argument that he never sent away a begging widow without food and he often made her broken heart sing (29:13; 31:16).

Although there are similar concerns for the widow in ancient Near Eastern texts, there does not seem to be the same pervasive and comprehensive attitude toward the powerless. This difference is rooted in theological reasons. When Israel was once in a powerless condition, God had mercy on her and delivered her from the harsh oppression of Egypt. She was thus called to remember her liberation and to imitate her God who was not only the father of the orphan, but the legal defender of the widow (Ps. 68:6) and the guardian of her property (Prov. 15:25). The transcendent "high and holy One," the Lord of Lords, sees the last first in the human social order and describes himself as the judge of the widow (Deut. 10:18; Ps. 146:9; cf. Ps. 113; Isa. 57:15). Yahweh instituted the death penalty for those who committed capital crimes in the earliest legal code (Exod. 21–23); but when people oppressed the widow, he himself directly intervened to execute the exploiters (Exod. 22:24). His prophets were sent as messengers with the directive to his people: "Don't hurt my little ones." Even non-Hebrew widows could trust in Him (Jer. 49:11).

The widow—who was absolutely dependent, whose value was found in "being" and not "doing" and "achieving," who had known both the joy of love and the anguish of loss—perhaps reflected more than others the image of God. After all, proud Babylon symbolized the satanic image in her quest for power. She incarnated pure autonomy with her statement: "I am, and there is none besides me. I will never be a widow or suffer the loss of children" (Isa. 47:8).

The concept of widowhood was also used as a metaphor to describe God's relationship to Israel. When the nation was judged in 586 B.C., a devastated Jerusalem could be described as a widow; her husband, the Lord, having departed, was as good as dead to her (Lam. 1:1; cf. Ezek. 11:22–23). Yet Jeremiah stated that this perspective was distorted: Israel was not a widow, nor Judah deprived of her God, even though the land was contaminated with sin (Jer. 51:5). Isaiah accepted the description of Israel's widowhood, but promised future salvation: "You will forget the shame of your youth and remember no more the reproach of your widowhood. For your Maker is your husband—the LORD Almighty is his name" (54:4–5).

The New Testament. Widows were prominent in the New Testament. It was no accident that one of the poorest of the poor, Anna, was privileged to greet the infant Messiah (Luke 2:36–38). The adult Jesus followed in the footsteps of his prophetic predecessors with his concern for the plight of the widow. He healed a widow's son because of compassion for his mother (Luke 7:11–17); he protested the exploitation of widows (Mark 12:40). He reversed the standards by which people were judged with the parable of the widow's tithe: the widow gave from her poverty while the wealthy merely offered from their abundance (Mark 12:41–42). In another parable, the church was compared with an importunate widow who kept demanding that her case be heard. Similarly, the church must persistently pray for eschatological justice, the redressing of all wrongs against her (Luke 18:1–8).

The early church, the messianic community, defined the essence of true religion as demonstrating compassion to the poor and needy, in particular the widow and the orphan (James 1:27). A special fund was instituted for widows (Acts 6:1–6) and as the church matured, younger widows were urged to remarry while a special class of widows was maintained economically (1 Tim. 5:3–16). By the end of the first century A.D., as Christians were being persecuted by Rome, John wrote to a church whose husband seemed dead and impotent to her grief and need. The church was a widow, while proud Rome boasted: "I sit as a queen; I am not a widow, and I will never mourn" (Rev. 18:7). At the end of history the roles will be reversed, as Rome will become destitute and the church will be united to her resurrected and reigning husband who will wipe every tear from her eyes (Rev. 21:4). In that great day the reproach of the new Israel's widowhood will no longer be remembered, for her husband will appear, whose name is the Lord God of hosts (Isa. 54:5). STEPHEN G. DEMPSTER

See also FAMILY LIFE AND RELATIONS; WOMAN.

Bibliography. G. W. Coats, *CBQ* 34 (1972): 461–66; C. Cohen, *Encyclopedia Judaica,* 16:487–91; E. W. Davies, *VT* 31 (1981): 138–44; 31 (1981): 257–68; G. R. Driver and J. C. Miles, *The Assyrian Laws;* P. S. Hiebert, *Gender and Difference in Ancient Israel;* D. E. Gowan, *Int 41* (1987): 341–53; H. Hoffner, *TDOT,* 1:287–91; J. Kühlewein, *THAT,* 1:169–73; J. Limburg, *The Prophets and the Powerless;* S. Niditch, *HTR* 72 (1979): 143–49; J. H. Otwell, *And Sarah Laughed: The Status of Women in the Old Testament;* R. D. Patterson, *BSac* 130 (1973): 223–34; N. W. Porteous, *Service in Christ;* S. Solle, *DNTT* 3:1073–75; G. Stählin, *TDNT,* 9: 440–65; T. and D. Thompson, *VT* 18 (1968): 79–99; W. C. Trenchard, *Ben Sira's View of Women;* H. E. von Waldow, *CBQ* 32 (1970): 182–204; C. H. J. Wright, *ABD* 2:761–69.

Wife. *See* MARRIAGE.

Will. The created image of God carries with it awesome responsibility and glory. It includes the ability to make meaningful moral choices (Gen. 1:26–27; 2:16–17). By grace, the freedom to use a created will as a moral agent is one of the key biblical distinctions between humans and the rest of the created order. The sovereignty of God is deepened in a radically personal way when creation is climaxed by persons who possess wills that can choose to either obey or disobey, to love or not to love. True sovereignty is neither arbitrary nor coercive; it allows other wills.

The perversion of the fallen will is revealed in the defiant attitude of all who build the blasphemous tower of Babel (Gen. 11:1–9). The story of redemption is founded on God's offer to humanity to return to the fullness of relationship lost in Eden, despite its radical consequences. Not surprisingly, this included a series of moral choices.

The core of sin is the independent use of mind and will to choose what is good or evil (Gen. 3:5, 22). Faith and trust ultimately are tested at the level of intention (Gen. 17:1; cf. 20:5–6). Intention in a certain direction is the basic meaning of the Hebrew term *ʾābâ*. It is intriguing that this term of willing determination is most often found in the negative—"not willing" (Exod. 10:27; Isa. 1:19–20). Its relation to the verb "to hear" (*šamaʿ*) indicates that a preliminary intuition, an ability to comprehend, followed by "hearing," which almost always means making decisive steps toward or against something or someone (Ezek. 3:7).

It is remarkable that love for God has been commanded (Deut. 6:5). True love cannot be coerced. The obvious implication for this central response to Israel's fundamental statement of God's unique nature is the requirement of loyalty based on the ability to choose. The Western mind quickly shifts to a discussion of the parts—heart, soul, and strength. But in the ancient Near East the unified conception of the human being resulted in a complete choice for Yahweh as the only true Lord. The personal attachment of one's being (heart), the direction of one's desires (soul), and the totality of one's devotion (might) have true meaning if there is personal freedom to love God by volitional choice (Deut. 30:15–20; cf. Josh. 23:11; 24:14).

Biblically, the heart (*lēb*) refers primarily to the inner nature of a person, including will, thought, and emotions. Decisions are viewed as a setting of the heart (2 Chron. 11:16; 12:14; Job 34:14). Intention is clearly conjoined with moral responsibility. Both good and evil are revealed prior to actions at the point of one's will (Gen. 6:5; Ps. 78:8). Thus, rebellion, hardness of heart, or the inner resistance of the will to comply with the obligations of the covenant required an inner transformation for peace to be restored. This is clearly indicated in David's prayer for an "undivided" heart for both fear and praise of God (Ps. 86:11–12). Again, at base it is virtually impossible to separate God's will from the human. The reality of continued uncompelled service and sacrifice depends on the gracious action of God.

The willingness of Yahweh to choose (1 Sam. 12:22) his own is responded too often by a misuse of will on Israel's part (Neh. 9:17; Hos.. 5:11; Zech. 7:11–12). God's relationship with his people was restored when they responded to his grace by trying to observe his law with all their hearts. This restored relationship was evidenced by God's desire for and pleasure with freewill offerings (Exod. 35:29; Lev. 23:18). The free movement of the will of each party is evident in Israel's understanding of what brought true pleasure (Ps. 51:15–17). There is a willingness that is pleasurable to God (Mal. 1:8, 13).

An appraisal of the evidence in the Old Testament reveals a primary focus on the will of God. Humanity images God when it deliberately chooses. Covenantal loyalty and commitment are defined by mutual wills and the choice to love even though, as in the case of Israel, one party is eternally superior (Deut. 7:7–9).

The New Testament only deepens the notions of the significance of human choices that the Old Testament initiated. God's sovereign will is affirmed and the gracious gift of human determination within the context of divine comprehension and direction remain intact throughout.

There are two major word groups: (1) inner volitional purposes or decisions (*boulē*), mentally directed intention (*boulema*), and deliberated and free decision of the will (*boulemai*); (2) desire, wish, or will (*thelō*) and will or intention (*thelēma*). These two are used interchangeably for all the Old Testament notions we have observed. It is interesting that *thelō* outstrips *boulomai* in use (207 usages to 37). Freedom of decision in ways not directly related to God are evident throughout the New Testament. Joseph "did not want" (*thelō*) to expose Mary, so he had deliberated or, "had in mind" (*boulomai*), to divorce her. The passages from both word-groups pertaining to human volition underscore the biblical tradition that though God alone comprehends all the data, there is very little evidence for arbitrary and impersonal coercion of human wills. (Luke 7:30, "rejected God's purpose"; 1 Cor. 4:5). God's will or desire is perfect, but it is large enough to incorporate and circumvent human will where necessary (Acts 2:23).

As in every area of human life, Jesus is the supreme example of perfect obedience to the will of God without the diminution of personal choice. The use of will in both John and Luke provides not only christological implications but human ramifications as well. A proper interpretation of the prayer in Gethsemane disallows predetermination without the consent of the Savior (Luke 22:42). Jesus prays, "Father, if you are willing (*boulē*) . . . yet not my will (*thelēma*), but yours be done."

The crucial issues pertaining to human will are revealed here. Divine will is primarily revealed to humans as the desire to offer salvation. Humanity is invited to respond to that will and provision. Once a person chooses the will of God over his or her own desires, much of what transpires is closely related to the cross. If the will of God pertains primarily to the work of redemption, then that will must become the believer's main intention also. The impact of bearing the will of God shows itself in all the ethical and moral choices a believer makes (Matt. 22:37; Mark 12:30; Phil. 2:13; Heb. 13:21) M. WILLIAM URY

See also HEART; PERSON, PERSONHOOD; WILL OF GOD.

Bibliography. A. P. Hayman, *SJT* 37:1 (1984): 13–22.

Will of God. One theme that all parts of Scripture take up in one way or another is the will of God. God's will is as vast as his entire plan for creation, and from the standpoint of objective content, it seems to be settled and unchanging. Old and New Testament writers can thus refer to God's will as if its existence is accepted by all. But though it may seem to have the character of a broad blueprint, in practical applications it is expressed in specific terms. God's will can also be viewed from its active side as his conscious "deciding," "willing," and "choosing" to do something.

The Old Testament. The affirmation that there exists with the God of Israel a will that is resolute and bears on his actions and the life of his people is made in all parts of the Old Testament. The impression created is that he has worked and continues to interact with his creation according to a design. Psalm 135:6 announces that "the LORD does whatever pleases him." His will is also the pattern to be followed in life by his people.

The will of God is not simply a passive plan, the blueprint for his creation. Rather, very often the Old Testament describes God as *accomplishing his will.* In this we glimpse the sovereign control he exerts over nations and individuals as well as the imperturbable certainty that characterizes his will. Broadly speaking, "Our God is in heaven; he does whatever pleases him" (Pss. 115:3; 135:6). More specifically, his will applies to nations (Isa. 48:14) as well as to decisions made about individuals (1 Sam. 2:25). What God has planned (his will), he himself will bring to pass. Consequently, the development in understanding of the will of God in the Old Testament reveals that God in one sense may be seen as the initiator in the execution of his will and that this may involve the events that make up human history. Human history is never regarded as beyond his control. This includes not only the sweeping developments that affect whole nations, but also the specific events that touch individual lives.

For this reason, the people of Israel and individuals are to align their lives with and do the will of God. Psalm 40:8 becomes a programmatic statement in this respect: "I desire to do your will, O my God; your law is within my heart." In this text the psalmist brings together two essential elements in describing the ideal life of obedience to God. God requires certain patterns of behavior in response to his covenant. The law is the articulation of the ethical requirements of God's will. This pattern is also taken up in the "new covenant" passage of Jeremiah 31:31–34: doing God's law (will) is the essence of the appropriate life of response to God's covenant. For God's will to be done, it had first to be known and understood by his people: "Teach me to do your will, for you are my God" (Ps. 143:10). Through Moses, the judges, and the prophets, God made known his will and led the people in applying it in everyday situations. In one case, the application of God's will to a specific situation meant putting away foreign wives (Ezra 10:11). When people take action it is to be done in awareness that God's will is to be the guide and that it cannot be thwarted (Job 42:2): thus before taking action, David said to the people, "If it seems good to you, and if it is the will of the LORD our God, let us . . ." (1 Chron. 13:2).

The concept of God's will is developed specifically along theological lines, in reference to salvation, in the Servant passages in Isaiah. God selected Cyrus to carry out his purpose, which would allow the city of Jerusalem and the temple to be rebuilt (44:28). Here God's will is executed in a historical event; moreover, that act is soteriological for through it God's people experience salvation. The song of the Suffering Servant reveals that "it was the LORD's will to crush him" (53:10). This expression of the will of God, his resolute plan, however, takes its meaning from 42:1–9 and 49:1–7, which make it clear that God's purpose is the deliverance of Israel and the Gentile nations, and that somehow the suffering of the Servant plays a role within this plan. Again, historical events are seen to have saving significance as they develop out of the determined will of God. Finally, the execution of God's salvific will, the "mission" of the redemption of Israel and the nations, is linked to the proclamation of God's efficacious word: "so is my word that goes out from my mouth: It will not return to me empty, but will accomplish what I desire" (55:11). God's will includes the plan of salvation.

The New Testament. The will of God as a superstructure for God's intervention in the affairs of humankind and for all of life was a belief that shaped much of the early church's outlook on theology and life. In addition to the influence of the Old Testament, Jesus' own life, ministry, and teaching undoubtedly provided a formative influence.

Jesus' life and teaching as recorded in the Gospels bear witness to the importance of the concept of the will of God for his understanding of his own place and that of his followers in redemptive history. Jesus modeled for his disciples a life lived in perfect conformity with God's will, and demonstrated that this life did not always take the easy course. The poignant Gethsemane scene, recorded by Matthew, Mark, and Luke (with slight variations), depicts this most clearly. As Jesus prayed to the Father, he acknowledged both the strength of his own will and his commitment to God's: "My Father, if it is possible, may this cup be taken from me. Yet not as I will, but as you will. . . . My Father, if it is not possible for this cup to be taken away unless I drink it, may your will be done" (Matt. 26:39, 42; cf. Mark 14:36; Luke 22:42). Both Jesus and the Gospel writers knew that God's will concerning the Messiah's death was specific. But John especially characterizes the whole of Jesus' ministry in terms of conformity with the will of God. At one point Jesus said to his disciples, "My food is to do the will of him who sent me" (John 4:34). His ministry is described as the outworking of God's will: "I can do nothing on my own. As I hear, I judge; and my judgment is just, because I seek to do not my own will but the will of him who sent me" (5:30 NRSV; cf. 6:38–40).

If Jesus was to do God's will, so were his disciples. The prayer that Jesus taught them made God's will a central concern in the life of discipleship. They were to petition God that his kingdom might come and his will be done on earth as it is in heaven (Matt. 6:10). The coming of the kingdom, God's power in Christ and then, through the Holy Spirit, in his church, would mean the manifestation of God's will on the earthly plane. The implication contained in the petition extends to the conduct of the disciples, as the Sermon on the Mount's context reveals. Thus, the message of the kingdom of God and the concept of God's will are joined together. In fact, kinship with Jesus is demonstrated not by correct doctrine but by doing God's will (Matt 12:50; Mark 3:35). Equally, membership in God's kingdom is demonstrated not by good intentions but by the actual execution of God's will (Matt. 7:21; 21:31; Luke 12:47). Obedience to the will of God challenges and supersedes legalistic obedience to religious rules, which through concretization have become meaningless and even hinder the pursuit of a knowledge of God (John 9:31). Ultimately, the readiness of an individual to acknowledge and then do God's will determines whether that person will be able to apprehend the truth of Jesus (John 7:17).

In the thought of the early church, as represented by Paul and other New Testament writers, the will of God continues to have a prominent place.

God's Will and the Direction of Life. At its most basic level, belief in an all-encompassing will of God means the belief that things are moving in a direction such as Romans 1:9–10 ("I remember you in my prayers at all times; and I pray now at last by God's will the way may be opened for me to come to you"), Romans 15:32 ("so that by God's will I may come to you"), and James 4:15 ("Instead, you ought to say, 'If it is the Lord's will, we will live and do this or that'"). The early Christians held that God's will might supervene in the lives of his people and bring a change to human plans. For God's will cannot be resisted (Rom. 9:19). Consequently, the Christian's aim is to live according to the perfect will of God and to pray according to it (1 John 5:14). In many cases this may exceed the ability of the believer, but the Holy Spirit is capable, who "intercedes for the saints in accordance with God's will" (Rom. 8:27).

God's Will and the Plan of Salvation. Receiving special emphasis is the place of the plan of salvation within God's will. The adoption as children (Eph. 1:5) and inheritance of the blessings of redemption (v. 11) are according to God's counsel and will. The basis of salvation, the crucifixion of God's son Jesus, is explicitly described as the outworking of God's will (Acts 2:23; 4:28; Gal. 1:4). In this way, Jesus' death becomes integral to God's plan, rather than being an unforeseen event to be fit in whatever way possible. Furthermore, the redemptive will of God, which began long ago in the promises to Abraham, has proceeded without change through each stage of the plan (Heb. 6:17). Like Abraham, others played significant roles in the outworking of God's will to save (Acts 13:36); at each point God's will was determinative and could not be circumvented (Luke 7:30). Paul viewed his own call to apostleship, which was to bring salvation to the Gentiles (Titus 1:1), in precisely these terms. Nearly all of his letters emphasize that it was God's will that established him in his ministry (1 Cor. 1:1; 2 Cor. 1:1; Eph. 1:1; Col. 1:1; 2 Tim. 1:1; cf. Gal. 1:1; 1 Tim. 1:1; Titus 1:1).

Does the New Testament teach that it is God's will that all be saved, and therefore none will be lost? Two passages relate God's will to the expansiveness of the salvation plan. First Timothy 2:3–4 states, "God our Savior . . . wills (*thelei*) all men to be saved and to come to a knowledge of the truth." Second Peter 3:9 expresses a similar sentiment: "The Lord . . . does not will (*boulomenos*) anyone to perish but that everyone might come to repentance." It should be emphasized that neither text says that *all* will be saved regardless of their disposition toward the gospel. In the first text, "to come to a knowledge of the truth" is a formula that means to make a rational decision about the gospel, that is, to respond to the gospel message. The second text similarly relates God's will to save the all-inclusive "anyone" to the volitional element involved in repentance. Consequently, while these texts tell us that God's will to save extends to all people, and that he desires to save rather than to condemn, they do not remove the necessary element of the faith-response to the gospel.

The Christian Life as a Continuous Response to God's Will. God's will applies to every part of the church's and believer's lives. Occasionally, *thelema,* meaning "what is acceptable," occurs alone. The strong connection of the term with God's will makes it almost certain that in such cases (Rom. 2:18; James 4:15) it stands as an abbreviation for God's will. Christian living and "doing the will of God" are one and the same and are not to be separated. In general terms, the summary of faithful Christian living, given by the writer of Hebrews, is "doing the will of God": "For you need endurance, so that when you have done the will of God, you may receive what was promised" (10:36 NRSV). John describes the life of faithfulness, which demonstrates true Christianity, similarly as doing the will of God (1 John 2:17). Viewed more specifically, for the slave, being a Christian within the social institution of slavery called for obedience to the master—this was doing the will of God from the heart (Eph. 6:6). Suffering as Christians is an aspect of Christian existence that corresponds to God's will (1 Peter 4:19).

Other specific applications of God's will reveal still more clearly how it is relevant to all areas of human life. First Thessalonians 4:3 states that God's will is "our sanctification," which Paul then goes on to apply in the specific principle "abstain from fornication." Later in the same letter the will of God is said to be thankfulness in all situations (5:18). It is God's will that a Christian's conduct remove any cause for slander by unbelievers (1 Peter 2:15). Doing good deeds and sharing what we have with one another are "acceptable to God," that is, accords with his will (Heb. 13:15–16). Finally, the will of God, which Paul desires his people to know and do in Romans 12:2, is spelled out specifically in terms of mutual service among Christians in the passage that follows. In no case do the specifics or even any combination of them exhaust or fully describe the will of God. They merely show the directions its practical application will take.

The will of God must be done by Christians if they are genuine Christians, but for this to occur two things are required. First, it must be taught and understood. Paul, for one, was chosen by God to know God's will (Acts 22:14). He also endeavored to make all of God's will (counsel) known, both theology and Christian ethics (Acts 20:27). His prayer for believers was that they "be filled with a knowledge of God's will" (Col. 1:9; 4:12). And he admonished foolish believers to make gaining an understanding of God's will their chief aim (Eph. 5:17).

Second, God must equip the believer to be able to execute the divine will in appropriate behavior. Human inability continues to coexist alongside divine sovereignty. This means that God must give the enlightenment necessary for the believer to perceive what the will of God is (Col. 1:9b). But then he must also enable his children in each situation to carry it out to completion: "Now may the God of peace, who brought back from the dead our Lord Jesus . . . make you complete in everything good so that you may do his will, working among us that which is pleasing in his sight" (Heb. 13:20–21 NRSV).

The Will of God and Guidance. Within the church today there are various views about how specifically God's will may be known and followed in matters of life's decisions. In the Old Testament God provided tools (the Urim and Thummim) for discerning his direction in various situations. At times he "spoke," whether in dreams, through the burning bush, or in the "still small voice" that came to Elijah. In the New Testament similar events of guidance are recorded. It becomes clear that the church and individual believers are to seek to know God's will and base their actions on it. But while a general pattern emerges that tells us that God is in control of his church and the whole world and interested in each aspect of his children's lives, we are not told specifically that God will give us a "yes" or "no" to each question we might ask. Much of the biblical teaching about his will pertains to behavior and his plan of salvation. With regard to the first, "seeking" his will means (1) learning what God's Word says about aspects of our response to him and, (2) in concert with the church, determining how that teaching is to be applied in new historical and cultural contexts.

But the mystical element so obvious in Scripture—God's direct guidance in times of need or searching—cannot be ruled out today. We are to seek God with our questions about vocation, but he may direct through the wisdom of church and family leaders, as well as through circumstances. What is normative is difficult to say. But it is certainly incorrect to say that God's will does not apply to the small areas of our lives. It is also incorrect to say that we should expect God to reveal his will always in a specific "yes" or "no" through internal prompting or external signs, or to think that the reality of God's will relieves us of the responsibility of decision making. We are left "in the middle," knowing that we are to seek God's guidance through the Scriptures, prayer, the counsel of Christian leaders, and wise assessment of the options before us and knowing that he promises to guide us, but not being able to limit his means for doing this. PHILIP H. TOWNER

See also ELECT, ELECTION; FOREKNOWLEDGE; PREDESTINATION; PROVIDENCE OF GOD.

Bibliography. G. J. Botterweck, *TDOT,* 5:92–107; G. Friesen, *Decision Making and the Will of God: A Biblical Alternative to the Traditional View;* E. Lohmeyer, *The Lord's Prayer;* D. Müller, *NIDNTT,* 3:1015–23; G. Schrenk, *TDNT,* 1:629–37; 3:46–62; E. Stauffer, *New Testament Theology.*

Wine. *See* ABSTAIN, ABSTINENCE.

Wisdom. The paradigms of Israel's religion—law, prophecy, and wisdom—were not exclusive to Israel but were shared by other ancient Near Eastern cultures. So it was not the form of Israel's religion that made it distinctive, but its content. Wisdom was a common way of thinking in this part of the ancient world. Briefly, it was a way of viewing and approaching life, which involved instructing the young in proper conduct and morality and answering the philosophical questions about life's meaning.

The Old Testament. In the Old Testament wisdom at one level describes skilled arts and artisans, like weavers (Exod. 35:25–26), architects (Exod. 35:30–36:1), and goldsmiths (Jer. 10:9). At a second level, wisdom was keen insight into life and ways of dealing with its problems. Solomon was associated with wisdom in this sense (1 Kings 3:1–15; see also 1 Kings 4:32–34), although the term used was "understanding," which occurs often as a synonym of wisdom. At a fourth level, the terms "wisdom" and "wise" apply to men and women who represent a way of thinking and conduct that is orderly, socially sensitive, and morally upright. Thus, the major thrust of wisdom in the Old Testament was a code of moral conduct. This is especially represented by the Book of Proverbs, which gives instruction on personal behavior from the discipline of children (22:6) to the golden-rule treatment of one's neighbor (24:29). The goal of wisdom was to build an orderly and functional society that reflected the moral requirements of God as set forth in the law of Moses. Although Wisdom Literature has no emphasis on Mosaic Law as a code, the moral propositions of that law nevertheless underwrite the moral code of Wisdom Literature, particularly the books of Proverbs and Ecclesiastes. The closing admonition of Ecclesiastes, only implied in the main body of the book, is to "Fear God and keep his commandments, for this is the whole duty of man" (12:13). The apocryphal book of Ecclesiasticus (Jesus ben Sirach) carries this view to the point of equating wisdom with law. Keeping the law produces wisdom, and wisdom is found in the keeping of the law (15:1; 21:11; 24:23–33).

Certain theological presuppositions undergird the Wisdom Literature of the Old Testament. First, the individual rather than the nation is addressed. In one sense, wisdom is an appropriate theological complement to the law and the prophets, the latter two religious paradigms basically addressing the nation. That is not to overlook the fact, however, that much in the law and prophets applies to individuals. Rather, it is to recognize that God spoke the law to the nation of Israel, and similarly the prophets spoke basically to the nation. It is not reading too much into Wisdom Literature to say that wisdom's way of building the society that reflected Yahweh's will for humankind was to work from the individual up, whereas law and prophecy tended to work from the corporate nation down to the individual.

Second, the view of God put forth by Wisdom Literature was God as Creator rather than God as Redeemer, the latter theological construct characterizing law and prophecy. This is evident in the Lord's redemptive acts of bringing Israel out of Egypt and giving them the land of Canaan. In contrast, wisdom never makes reference to historical events, but rather describes God as Creator of the world. Again, this view is a helpful theological complement to the Redeemer theology of the Torah and Prophets.

Third, wisdom simplifies religion by describing faith as born out of decisions that are either wise or foolish. There are two ways a person may take, and the choices one makes determine one's direction. In Proverbs, wisdom personified stands in public places and calls to those who will listen to follow her precepts (1:20–33; 8:1–31). The disposition that characterizes the wise person is summed up in the phrase the "fear of the Lord." It is this disposition that is the beginning of wisdom, and it also designates the process by which wisdom matures the individual. Not surprisingly, the fear of the Lord also names the end of the process. Sometimes in the Old Testament this phrase is a general term for religion (since the Old Testament has no specific word for religion), and sometimes, as in the Book of Proverbs, the phrase carries a meaning very close to the New Testament concept of faith.

The wisdom books of the Old Testament are Job, Ecclesiastes, and Proverbs. A few psalms fall into the wisdom category (1, 37, 49, 73, 112, 127, 128). The emphasis of this material subdivides into two rubrics, one emphasizing the theological problems of life, such as the suffering of the innocent (Job) and the meaning of life (Ecclesiastes). Scholars sometimes call this rubric higher or reflective wisdom. The other rubric is much more practical (Proverbs), and deals with the issues that touch the individual's life, such as personal industry, integrity, sexual purity, and family relations. This subcategory is sometimes called lower or practical wisdom. The wisdom psalms divide into these categories as well, 37, 49, and 73 representing higher wisdom, and 1, 112, 127, and 128 belonging to the practical category.

The New Testament. In the New Testament the Epistle of James is often considered to incorporate wisdom elements in its practical advice for Christian living. The practical nature of the Beatitudes (Matt. 5:3–12) also puts them in a category akin to wisdom. Luke took note that Jesus "grew in wisdom and stature, and in favor with God and men" (2:52). Perhaps this connotes the practical side of Jesus' teaching, so simple and direct, but it could also include a deeper knowledge of mission and God's purpose of salvation.

Paul compares the wisdom (*sophia*) of men to a "wisdom that has been hidden and that God destined for our glory before time began" (1 Cor. 2:6–7). The "wisdom of men" was human understanding as compared with the "hidden wisdom of God," which was a knowledge of God's plan of salvation through Jesus Christ foreordained before the world began. The ultimate manifestation of wisdom was Jesus Christ. Ultimately God revealed his wisdom in the person of his own Son, Jesus Christ (1 Cor. 1:24, 30).

C. HASSELL BULLOCK

See also MIND/REASON; PROVERBS, THEOLOGY OF; UNDERSTANDING.

Bibliography. C. H. Bullock, *An Introduction to the Old Testament Poetic Books;* J. L. Crenshaw, *Old Testament Wisdom;* J. H. Walton, *Ancient Israelite Literature and Its Cultural Context.*

Witness. *See* TESTIMONY.

Woman. In an age of women's liberation, modern Bible readers have understandably scrutinized Scripture for its teachings on gender. Assessments have alternately found it hopelessly patriarchal and gloriously redemptive. A brief survey can do no more than scratch the surface of key issues and perspectives.

Creation. In the first creation account, God fashions man and woman as fully equal bearers of his image. They jointly receive his blessing and commission to rule the earth (Gen. 1:26–31). In the second account, it is specified that God created the man first, and that he created the woman from the man's rib only after all the animals proved inadequate companions (Gen. 2:18–23). The controversial words, "suitable helper" in verse 18 have traditionally been taken to imply a functional subordination of the woman to the man as part of God's design in creation, but this interpretation is increasingly being rejected. Certainly, the emphasis of Adam's outburst, "bone of my bones and flesh of my flesh" (v. 23) highlights the similarity rather than any differences between these first two human beings.

The Fall. The utter goodness of this primeval human pair (Gen. 1:31) quickly turns into rebellion. The serpent coaxes the woman to eat forbidden fruit, and her husband, in apparently more conscious disobedience (1 Tim. 2:14), follows suit. As a result, God utters a three-part curse on the triad of rebels. To the woman he promises increased pain in childbearing and then adds, "your desire will be for your husband, and he will rule over you" (Gen. 3:16). For those who see hierarchy in Genesis 2, what was intended to be fully harmonious will now deteriorate into seduction and tyranny. For others, here is where relationships of authority and submission first appear. "To love and to cherish" has degenerated into "to desire and to dominate."

Old Testament Culture. Old Testament culture was overwhelmingly patriarchal. Women were valued most for their roles as wives and mothers, as bearers and rearers of children. Because of the importance of having children to preserve the family line and inheritance, barren women were particularly disgraced. On several key occasions, God miraculously intervened to overcome such barrenness (as with Sarah—Gen. 16; and Hannah—1 Sam. 1). Although never condoned, this same desire for progeny could lead to illicit sexual relationships (e.g., Lot's daughters with their father—Gen. 19:30–38; Tamar with Judah—Gen. 38).

Old Testament wives can function as windows to their husband's career and character. David's first wife, Michal, aids his escape from Saul (1 Sam. 19:9–17). Abigail stands out for her intelligence and good judgment (1 Sam. 25:3, 33) and comes to the fore during David's ascendancy to the kingship. Bathsheba, as the victim of David's seduction and adultery (2 Sam. 11), portends the decline of David's family and fortunes.

Yet despite all these androcentric illustrations, the ideal woman of Old Testament times can seem surprisingly modern. The wife of noble character (Prov. 31:10–31) works industriously not only in traditional domestic spheres but in running a business out of her house, purchasing property, making investments, speaking wisely, and ruling her household. Men should value such a prudent wife far above property and wealth (Prov. 19:14; cf. 18:22).

The Old Testament consistently commends women to monogamous marriage and sexual fidelity, based on God's creation ordinance (Gen. 2:24; endorsed again by both Jesus [Matt. 19:5] and Paul [Eph. 5:31]). Song of Songs celebrates the erotic bliss of newlyweds, often from the woman's perspective and initiative. Subsequent faithfulness remains equally crucial (Eccles. 9:9; Mal. 2:14–16). The ordeal for a suspected adulteress seems harsh today (Num. 5:11–31), as does Ezra's edict for the Israelites to divorce their newly but illegally married foreign wives (Ezra 9–10). But the positive side of each of these episodes is the high value placed on sexual and spiritual fidelity. The notion that polygamy was common or condoned in ancient Israel is seriously misguided. Polygamy remained the exception rather than the rule; in twelve of the thirteen Old Testament instances in which it occurred, the husbands were men of great wealth—kings and aristocrats. Few others could afford such luxury! Solomon's many wives clearly led to his ruin (1 Kings 11:1–13); concubines often played more a political than a romantic role (2 Sam. 16).

As in all ages of human history, the Old Testament shows women who were victimized by abuse, rape, and even murder: Dinah (Gen. 34),

Tamar (2 Sam. 13:1–22), Jephthah's daughter (Judg. 11:29–30), and the Levite's concubine (Judg. 19). The latter two atrocities illustrate the depravity of a society in near-anarchy; the former two are each avenged by kinsmen. In other instances, women seduce men (Delilah and Samson—Judg. 16) or unjustly accuse them (Potiphar's wife and Joseph—Gen. 39). God never condones such behavior, but, like evil in general, he often permits it. An overriding and encouraging message of the Old Testament is God's sovereign outworking of his plans in spite of his people's failures.

In the same vein, the queens of God's own people may prove murderous and idolatrous, leading them to ruin (Athaliah—2 Kings 11; Jezebel—1 Kings 21). Or God may use the compassion of pagan royalty to preserve and nurture the savior of his own people (Pharaoh's daughter and Moses—Exod. 2:1–10). Perhaps the paradigm of God's sovereignty through the grace of unlikely heroines is the story of Rahab, the Canaanite prostitute, who believes in the God of the Israelites, protects their spies from her own officials (Josh. 2), and becomes one of the great persons of faith praised in Hebrews 11 (v. 31). Similarly, Ruth the Moabitess epitomizes the foreigner who attaches herself to Israel. Her devotion to her mother-in-law Naomi leads to her covenant-faithfulness to Yahweh and to a surprising proposal of marriage to her redeemer-kinsman Boaz (Ruth 3:9).

Old Testament Legislation. Old Testament laws also send mixed signals. In some places, women are clearly prized as equals to men. Both father and mother deserve equal honor from their children (Exod. 20:12) and share in the trial of a rebellious child (Deut. 21:18–19). In cases of alleged rape, if unable to summon help, the woman is given the benefit of the doubt (Deut. 22:23–27). But women consistently remain under the control of their fathers or husbands (Exod. 21:7; Num. 30:3–15), although in the (unusual) absence of such men may be granted equal rights with them (Num. 27:1–11). Various laws seem to value women less than men. They incur greater uncleanness for menstruation than do men for seminal emissions (Lev. 15:16–33) and for giving birth to female children than for males (Lev. 12:1–5). Male slaves command a higher price than do females (Lev. 27:1–8); the more important sacrifices require male animals only (Num. 15:22–29). In other cases, certain laws simply did not apply to women (Exod. 23:17). Some of these injunctions may be seen as accommodations to the prevailing cultures, but it is hard to explain them all in this fashion.

Widows are consistently presented as a paradigm of the dispossessed. Because they came under no specific man's care, they became the responsibility of the whole community (Exod. 22:22–24).

Old Testament Leadership. Although women were not permitted to be priests, they did on occasion hold other offices or leadership roles in Israel. Deborah was a judge (the "political" leader of her day) and, like Miriam (Exod. 15:20–21) and Huldah (2 Kings 22:11–20), a prophetess (Judg. 4). Jael (Judg. 4) and the anonymous woman of Judges 9:53 proved timely and valiant in battle. Although Athaliah was a wicked queen, Esther, who came to power in Persia under most unusual circumstances, used her position to save her Jewish kinsfolk. The wise women of Tekoa (2 Sam. 14) and of Abel Beth Maacah (2 Sam. 20:14–22) probably were the heads of city councils. Although each of these examples of women in leadership were exceptions and not norms, there is no evidence to support the claim that God used women only when there were no available or willing men.

Jesus and Women. The first-century Jewish world shared many of the cultural assumptions of the Old Testament concerning women. In the Hellenistic world, women at times gained greater wealth, freedom, or privilege. Against these prevailing cultures, Jesus' own teachings and practices stand out as radically liberating. God highly favored Mary with the privilege of bearing and rearing his Son; the most detailed accounts of Christ's birth seem to reflect Mary's (and Elizabeth's) perspective and may well have been transmitted by her (Luke 1–2). Several of the recipients of Jesus' healing were women (Jairus's daughter—Matt. 9:23–26; and the crippled woman—Luke 13:10–17). In two instances their faith is particularly praised (the hemmorhaging woman—Matt. 9:22), even when one is not a Jew but a Syrophoenician (Matt. 15:21–28—anticipating the church's ministry to Gentiles). In another episode, the woman healed was Jewish but still illustrates Jesus' ministry of compassion to the outcasts of society (Simon's mother-in-law [Matt. 8:14–15]), as the third in a series of such miracles (cf. Matt. 8:1–4, 5–13). In the same spirit, Jesus forgives a notoriously sinful woman who demonstrates her repentance through her love, even when she expresses it in culturally suspect ways (Luke 7:36–50). The later, similar actions of Mary of Bethany elicit Jesus' praise in language evocative of the memorializing of Jesus himself in the Lord's Supper (Mark 14:9)!

Women play an important role among Jesus' followers. An unspecified number forms part of the larger company of disciples that regularly follows him on the road and forms his "support team" (Luke 8:1–3; cf. Acts 1:14–15). Jesus specifically praises Mary of Bethany for choosing to "sit at his feet" and learn from him (Luke 10:38–42)—a quasi-technical reference to a disciple being trained by a rabbi and a practice usually denied to women in Jewish circles. Martha's traditional preoccupation for domestic chores receives only censure! Jesus chooses women as the first witnesses to his resurrection (Luke 24:1–12), even though their testimony would have been thrown out of a legal court, and Mary Magdalene becomes the "apostle to the (male) apostles" (John 20:1–2, 18). No woman appears among the company of the Twelve; but it is not clear if this reflects any timeless principle besides a commitment to present the gospel to a given culture in ways which will most likely speed its acceptance.

Jesus' ethics preserve and intensify the strong Old Testament emphasis on sexual propriety (Matt. 5:27–30; 19:1–12), but for the first time make clear that women and men will be judged by identical standards (Matt. 5:32; Mark 10:11–12). Luke frequently pairs episodes in which men and women function in identical ways. Both Elizabeth and Zechariah praise under the Spirit's inspiration (Luke 1:41–45, 67–79). Both Simeon and Anna prophesy that in Christ they have seen Israel's salvation (2:25–38). Male and female cripples receive identical healings (13:10–17; 14:1–6). The parables of the mustard seed and leaven (like the lost sheep and coin), each make the same point but alternate between male and female protagonists (13:18–21; 15:1–10). Clearly Luke wants to highlight God's care for both genders and Jesus' concern to relate to both. The story of Jesus meeting the Samaritan woman perhaps epitomizes his commitment to revolutionizing the lot of the disenfranchised of his day. Despite strong cultural taboos against any social exchange between a Jewish holy man and a sexually promiscuous Samaritan woman, Jesus speaks to this woman in private, affirms her personhood and leads her to faith in himself and to service as an evangelist (John 4:1–42).

Acts. With the arrival of Pentecost comes the fulfillment of Joel's prediction about the egalitarian outpouring of the Spirit (Acts 2:17–21). Women as well as men prophesy. Apart from the ministry of the New Testament writers, Christian prophecy does not supplement or contradict the canon but applies spiritual truth to specific contexts in the lives of God's people. To the extent that contemporary preaching involves this spiritual gift, gifted women must be encouraged to preach. Acts also describes a significant Christian woman teacher, Priscilla, who with her husband Aquila enabled Apollos to learn and disseminate correct doctrine (18:26). Inasmuch as her name more often than not appears before her husband's (cf. vv. 18, 19), she may well have been the more prominent.

Women in Acts continue to receive other spiritual blessings. As in the Gospels, they benefit from miraculous healings (the slave girl—16:16–18) and resurrections (Tabitha—9:36–42). Lydia is the first-mentioned European convert (17:11–15); Paul's willingness to preach to a group of God-fearing women without any men present itself carries on Jesus' tradition of boundary breaking. Damaris, a woman, is among the few to respond favorably to Paul's Areopagus address (17:34).

The Epistles. Just as in the Old Testament women enjoyed many prominent roles save one, the rest of the New Testament reveals women in all positions of spiritual leadership save that of elder or overseer. But their participation in these roles was much more common and accepted than in Old Testament times. Paul calls Phoebe a *diakonos* (probably "deacon") and *prostatis* (most likely "patron") of the church in Cenchreae. First Timothy 3:11 is best understood as containing injunctions for women deacons rather than deacons' wives (it would be incongruous for Paul to be concerned about deacons' wives but not overseers' wives!). Junia(s) in Romans 16:7 is most likely a woman, and she is called "an apostle." This will be in Paul's broader sense of the term as a missionary or church planter.

Chloe in Corinth (1 Cor. 1:11) and Nympha in Colossae (Col. 4:15) are women whose households figure prominently (and the fact that the households are attributed to these women suggest that no male heads are present). The elect ladies of 2 John 1, 13 almost certainly refer to house-churches, although quite possibly hosted by individual Christian women (as more clearly with Nympha). Paul calls Euodia and Syntyche his fellow workers (Phil. 4:2–3) and frequently praises women as co-laborers in ministry (Rom. 16:6, 12). First Timothy 5:2 commands respect for older Christian women. The term used here, *presbytera,* is the feminine form of "elder" (*presbyteros*), but the context and parallel passage in Titus 2:3, which uses a more unambiguous term for "old woman" (*presbytis*), suggests a nontechnical sense. Titus 2:4–5 also insists that older women train younger women in godliness, which includes being good "home-workers."

In the domestic sphere, wives must remain submissive to their husbands, who are the heads of the family (Eph. 5:22–24; Col. 3:18). Attempts to interpret "head" (*kephalē*) and "submit" (*hypotassō*) so as to remove all vestiges of hierarchy or authority (as, e.g., with the respective translations "source" and "defer" prove unconvincing on both lexical and contextual grounds). The command to mutual submission of Ephesians 5:21 becomes incoherent if it is assumed that all Christians must subject themselves to all other believers; this verse is best taken as an introduction to all three examples of submission in 5:22–6:9. But Paul's commands to husbands in 5:25–33 radically redefine their authority particularly in light of similar "domestic codes" of antiquity. The man's headship is now one of greater responsibility rather than privilege. And given the voluntary nature of entering into marriage, individuals not prepared to accept the responsibilities of submission and headship need not marry at all. Indeed the best interpretation of a woman as the "weaker vessel" (1 Peter 3:7) probably has nothing to do with physical or emotional weakness but rather refers to a voluntarily adopted position of greater "vulnerability."

Two passages in the epistles that do not directly refer to women doing anything nevertheless have far-reaching implications. First Corinthians 12:7, 11, makes clear that God's Spirit dispenses his spiritual gifts as he wills, which surely implies "irrespective of gender." This means that Paul envisioned women not only as apostles, prophets, and teachers but speaking in tongues, working miracles, ministering as evangelists, and pastors/shepherds (11:5; 12:8–10; Eph. 4:11), indeed, exercising every other spiritual gift that God may choose to give them. Galatians 3:28 proves even more programmatic, declaring that in Christ, "there is neither Jew nor Greek, slave nor free, male nor female." It cannot be demonstrated from this statement that Paul thereby imagined no timeless role differentiation among women and men; clearly patriarchal rabbinic sources could nevertheless make quite similar claims. But the baptismal context (v. 27) does suggest that Paul had more in mind than merely equal access to salvation. As an initiation rite that included women (unlike Jewish circumcision), baptism publicly affirmed the equal value of women and men in a way that suggests that the church should continue to seek outward, visible forms for demonstrating this equality.

Restrictions on Leadership. Notwithstanding the overwhelming emphasis on liberation, privilege, freedom, and equality for women that characterizes most of the New Testament teaching, three passages stand out as implying certain limits on women in church leadership, perhaps analogous to the relationship of wife and husband in the family. At least they have traditionally been so taken, throughout almost all of church history, corresponding to the general lack of women in the highest or most authoritative positions of ecclesial office (even as women's roles in all other positions of leadership have been more plentiful than the average textbook of church history discloses). Today, however, Christian feminists have seriously challenged the traditional interpretations of all three of these passages.

In 1 Corinthians 11:3–16, Paul commands women to cover their heads (with either veils or long hair) as a sign of respect to their spiritual heads—their husbands. The cultural impropriety of women either unveiled or with short hair (often involving sexually misleading connotations) probably lay behind these commands. But a timeless principle appears as well: "man did not come from woman but woman from man; neither was man created for woman, but woman for man" (vv. 8–9). These observations are immediately qualified with reminders of the mutual interdependence of the genders in Christ (vv. 11–12), but it is not obvious that these verses imply the reversibility of the statements in verses 8–9. Although not immediately germane to the question of church office, the reminder of the relevance of the structure of the family for church life probably provides a foundation for Paul's teaching in the next two passages below.

In 1 Corinthians 14:33b–38 Paul enjoins women to be silent in church. In view of 11:5, this cannot be an absolute prohibition. Many have taken it to be entirely time-bound (due, e.g., to gossiping or noisy or uneducated women), but Paul bases his rationale in the law (v. 34) and says nothing of these cultural phenomena. Others take verses 33b–35 to be a Corinthian slogan that Paul refutes in verses 36–38, but this relatively new interpretation ignores the quite different length, style, and content of all other Corinthian slogans (e.g., 6:12–13; 7:1; 8:1). Inasmuch as twenty of the other twenty-one references to "speak" (*laleo*) in 1 Corinthians 14 refer to tongues, their interpretation, prophecy, or evaluation, it is probably better to see one of these forms of speech in view. Given that the first three of these are spiritual gifts that the immediate context is one of the proper response to prophecy (vv. 29–33a), and that the ultimate responsibility of reevaluating prophecy would have fallen to the (presumably) all male leadership of the Corinthian congregation, it is best to limit Paul's prohibition to speech in the context of the church's authoritative response to prophecy.

The text which is most hotly debated of all is 1 Timothy 2:8–15. Here Paul forbids women "to teach or to have authority over a man" (v. 12) in church (3:15). Again this prohibition cannot be absolute (recall Acts 18:26), and in view of Paul's penchant for hendiadys, or pairs of largely synonymous expressions in 1 Timothy 2 (cf. vv. 1a, 1b, 2a, 2b, 3, 4, 5, 7a, 7b, etc.), it is probable that "teach" and "have authority" are mutually interdefining—Paul is prohibiting "authoritative teaching." In view of the distinction between (apparently) all male overseers and both male and female deacons in 3:1–13, a plausible interpretation of 2:12 is that women may not hold the highest office in a given ecclesial context (perhaps roughly analogous to modern-day senior pastors in congregationally governed churches). Again, egalitarians have regularly proposed some historical background (most notably the presence of heresy in Ephesus—1 Tim. 1:3–7) as the rationale for Paul's mandate, which is then seen as culturally limited in application. But Paul's own explanation appeals instead to the order of creation (1 Tim. 2:13); the explicit evidence of women's roles in the Ephesian heresy elsewhere in the Pastorals is entirely limited to their roles as victims rather than propagators (2 Tim. 3:6–7).

Conclusion. Christianity will doubtless be divided for the foreseeable future over women's roles in the contemporary home and church. The scriptural evidence is sufficiently ambiguous that room must be given for both complementarian and egalitarian perspectives. Charges that one or the other are heretical are unfounded and destructive. Church history does not inspire much confidence that Christian consensus will ultimately be based on exegesis rather than the trends of secular society. But Bible-believing Christians should stand against this tide and seek to ground their views on the best understandings of Scripture possible. Perhaps team-ministry remains the most appropriate model, in which team leaders remain male but in which women are warmly encouraged to participate and exercise pastoral gifts. So too, in the home, if husbands do retain any unique authority, they must exercise it entirely in seeking the well-being of their wives. CRAIG L. BLOMBERG

See also EVE; FAMILY LIFE AND RELATIONS; HEAD, HEADSHIP; MARRIAGE; PERSON, PERSONHOOD; SEXUALITY, HUMAN; WIDOW.

Bibliography. A. Berlin, *Poetics and Interpretation of Biblical Narrative;* G. Bilezikian, *Beyond Sex Roles;* E. Cantarella, *Pandora's Daughters;* D. Dockery, *CTR* 1 (1987): 363–86; R. B. Edwards, *The Case for Women's Ministry;* E. S. Fiorenza, *In Memory of Her;* M. Hayter, *The New Eve in Christ;* J. B. Hurley, *Man and Woman in Biblical Perspective; ISBE,* 4:1089–97; W. C. Kaiser, Jr., *Toward Old Testament Ethics;* R. C. and C. C. Kroeger, *I Suffer Not a Woman;* A. Mickelsen, ed., *Women, Authority and the Bible;* J. Piper and W. Grudem, eds., *Recovering Biblical Manhood and Womanhood;* A. B. Spencer, *Beyond the Curse;* J. Stott, *Issues Facing Christians Today;* L. Swidler, *Biblical Affirmations of Woman;* P. Trible, *Texts of Terror;* R. A. Tucker and W. Liefeld, *Daughters of the Church;* L. Wilshire, *NTS* 34 (1988): 120–34; B. Witherington, *NTS* 27 (1981): 593–604.

Wonder. *See* MIRACLE.

Word (Heb. *dābār;* Gk. *logos* and *rhēma*). The theological meaning of "word" within Scripture spans a wide theological spectrum. From the divine point of view, it consists of God revealing something about himself through his spoken word, which is ultimately and perfectly personified in his Son, Jesus Christ. In a broader sense, it designates Scripture itself. In contrast, the human word mirrors the human condition: it is limited, fallen, and dependent on divine intervention for restoration and sustenance.

The Word of God. *The Old Testament.* The concept of the word of God is a major Old Testament theme. It points out the absolute uniqueness of Israel's religion on the basis of personal contact with Yahweh—the transcendent, sovereign, creator God.

It is the means by which God created all things. Genesis 1 firmly establishes God's supremacy over the whole of creation. God has created all things by his spoken word. The psalmist declares, "By the word of the LORD were the heavens made, their starry host by the breath of his mouth" (33:6); "For he spoke, and it came to be; he commanded, and it stood firm" (v. 9; cf. Ps. 104:7). His word continues to reign supreme over all of creation (Ps. 147:15–18). Creation in turn speaks words of praise to its Creator (Ps. 19:1–4).

It unveils God to his creation. Though fully transcendent and incomparable deity, in giving his word to people, God reveals something of himself to them. Balaam, for example, speaks as "one who hears the words of God, who has knowledge from the Most High" (Num. 24:16; cf. Josh. 24:27; 1 Kings 18:31; Ezek. 3:10–11). God's word is an important instrument of divine revelation; at Shiloh, the Lord continued to reveal himself to Samuel through his word (1 Sam. 3:21). At times God's word nearly appears as synonymous with his person (1 Sam. 15:23, 26; 28:15; Ps. 138:1–2).

Its qualities describe God to his creation. The close connection between God and his word means that the qualities attributed to God's word also describe God's own personal character. In the Old Testament God's word is creative (Ps. 33:6), good (Mic. 2:7), holy (Jer. 23:9), complete (Jer. 26:2), flawless (2 Sam. 22:31; Pss. 12:6; 18:30; Prov. 30:5), all-sufficient (Deut. 8:3; Isa. 50:4; Jer. 15:16), sure (Isa. 31:2; 45:23; Jer. 44:28), right and true (Judg. 13:12, 17; 1 Sam. 3:19; Ps. 33:4; Isa. 55:11), understandable (Deut. 4:10, 12, 36; Neh. 8:12), active (Hos. 6:5), all-powerful (Pss. 68:11–14; 147:15–18), indestructible (Jer. 23:29), supreme (Ps. 17:4), eternal (Ps. 119:89; Isa. 40:8), life-giving (Deut. 32:46–47), wise (Ps. 119:130), and trustworthy (2 Sam. 7:28; 1 Kings 17:16). Therefore, God was understood similarly.

It discloses God's plan for his creation. God discloses his plan for creation through his word. The common Old Testament expression, "the word of the LORD came," indicates the sending and reception of divine prophecy. It occurs once in the Pentateuch (Gen. 15:4), numerous times in the historical books, and many times in the prophets. The sending and reception of God's word are by the Spirit (Zech. 7:12) and often through visions (Num. 24:15–16; 1 Sam. 3:1; 1 Kings 22:19); it is pictured as God reaching out his hand and touching the mouth of the prophet (Jer. 1:9). In times of judgment, God frequently refrained from communicating his word to his people (1 Sam. 3:1; Amos 8:11; also 1 Sam. 28:6; Mic. 3:4, 7). God's word will come to fulfillment according to the divine plan (Ps. 105:19; Lam. 2:17; Ezek. 12:28). God asserts, "I am watching to see that my word is fulfilled" (Jer. 1:12). God's word is in perfect harmony with his will and plan for creation (2 Sam. 7:21; Ps. 103:20–21; Lam. 2:17).

It is known by creation. People knew something of the transcendent God through his word. Balaam "hears the words of God, . . . has knowledge from the Most High, and sees a vision from *the Almighty*" (Num. 24:16). Israel as a nation was the unique recipient of "the words of the living God, the LORD Almighty" (Jer. 23:36). To them, God's word was equivalent to law (Isa. 1:10). Accordingly, God's word demands proper human response; it is to be obeyed (Num. 15:30–31; Deut. 11:18–21; Ezek. 33:32), feared (Exod. 9:20–21; Ezra 9:4; Ps. 119:161; Isa. 66:2, 5), praised (Ps. 56:4, 10), preserved (Jer. 23:36), and proclaimed to others (Deut. 5:5; 1 Sam. 3:31–4:1; Neh. 8:14–15; Jer. 11:6).

It is for the good of creation. God's word at times comes upon creation as judgment, but only as a divine response to disobedience. Its primary objective and appeal was for the well-being of creation. God's word is equivalent to divine rescue. It brings healing (Ps. 107:20; Ezek. 37:4–14) and refreshing (Deut. 32:1–2). To those who reject it, it becomes offensive (Jer. 6:10) and meaningless (Isa. 28:13), and in judgment will come upon them as a raging fire and a hammer that breaks rocks to pieces (Jer. 23:29). But to those who accept it, it gives and sustains life (Deut. 8:3). God's word is like living water, welling up to nourish creation from the Spring on High (Jer. 2:13).

It is supremely authoritative for all of creation. As God is supreme deity, his word bears supreme authority. The expression "the LORD has spoken" (Isa. 24:3) signifies unrivaled authority. It is uncontestable. No power can overturn it or thwart it. God's word is authoritative for *all* of creation.

The New Testament. The New Testament reiterates the Old Testament depiction of the word of God as the divine means of creating and sustaining all things (Heb. 11:3; 2 Peter 3:5–7), as divine revelation (Rom. 3:2; 1 Peter 4:11), and as prophetic speech (Luke 3:2; 2 Peter 1:19). Hebrews 4:12–13 powerfully sums up its supreme authority as "living and active . . . sharper than any double-edged sword," able to expose even the most hidden thoughts before God.

But the New Testament significantly deepens the Old Testament in light of the incarnation. In view of Jesus' life and work, the word of God now especially refers to God's consummate message of salvation to all people, the gospel of Jesus Christ.

Accordingly, the New Testament richly describes the gospel as "the word" (Acts 8:4; 16:6; 1 Cor. 15:2), "word of God" (Acts 6:7; 12:24; Heb. 13:7; 1 Peter 1:23), "word of the Lord" (Acts 8:25; 13:48–49), "word of his [God's] grace" (Acts 20:32), "word of Christ" (Rom. 10:17; Col. 3:16), "word of truth" (Eph. 1:13; Col. 1:5; James 1:18), "word of faith" (Rom. 10:8), and "word of life" (Phil. 2:16).

Similar to its Old Testament uses, the word of God as the gospel is to be kept free of distortion (2 Cor. 4:2) and is to be preached in its fullness (Col. 1:25). It is to be believed (1 Peter 3:1) and obeyed (Acts 6:7; 1 John 2:25). The gospel as the saving message of Jesus Christ is the living and enduring word of God (1 Peter 1:18–23). It is reliable and supremely authoritative, for it is inseparable from the person and character of its Sender—the sovereign, loving, creator God.

Christ. Although the Old Testament never uses the concept of *word* to describe the expected coming of the messiah, the New Testament significantly develops its theological meaning by equating the Old Testament concept of *word of God* with the person and work of Jesus Christ. Whereas extrabiblical concepts may have influenced, to a limited degree, the New Testament formulation of Jesus as the Word, the main influence comes from the Old Testament itself. Exactly when the early church understood Jesus in this way is uncertain, but nothing demands that it was necessarily late (i.e., well toward the end of the first century). For, as John's Gospel especially stresses, all the criteria for making such a connection were present in Jesus' own teaching, work, and self-consciousness.

The first two words of John's Gospel are most instructive in this regard. The phrase *en archē* ("in the beginning") recalls the opening words of the Old Testament in Genesis 1:1. The association is deliberate. It establishes from the Gospel's outset how its author intended the reader to understand Jesus' person and work throughout the remainder of the book. But justification for doing so originates in the life of Jesus himself.

According to Genesis 1 God created all things by his spoken word. The formula, "And God said, 'Let there be,' and it was so" provides the pattern for how God created on each day of creation. God's word is supremely powerful, able to create ex nihilo ("out of nothing").

The opening verses of John's Gospel explicitly link God's creative word to the person and work of the preincarnate Jesus (1:1–3). The evidence for this christological claim comes from Jesus' own ministry. The Fourth Gospel recounts seven sign miracles of Jesus (2:1–11; 4:46–54; 5:1–9; 6:5–14; 6:19–21; 9:1–7; 11:1–44). As "signs" these miracles indicate the importance of what Jesus did in conjunction with understanding him as the preincarnate word of God. Jesus performed these miracles through his *spoken word.* His creating anew expressly images the Father's creating of old. Jesus' words were all-powerful and able to create out of nothing.

The New Testament views the incarnate Jesus as none other than the Old Testament word of God personified (John 1:14a). The incarnation of the Word was a humble coming. Jesus came in the "flesh" (*sarx*) and physically made his abode or "tabernacled" with humanity. The Old Testament closely images this gracious act of divine love. Yahweh also came at his own initiative and "tabernacled" among his people in a humble abode not befitting his divine status (cf. Exod. 25:8; Lev. 26:11–12). To see Jesus is to see God. As "the exact representation of his [God's] being," Jesus sustains "all things by his powerful word" (Heb. 1:3). Jesus' words are life-giving (John 6:63, 68) and to be believed (John 2:22). What he speaks is from the Father (John 12:49–50; 14:10, 24; 17:8). His words will never pass away (Matt. 24:35; Mark 13:31; Luke 21:33) and are all-sufficient (Matt. 7:24, 26; Luke 6:46–49; John 8:51–59; 12:47–48; 15:7), even unto the granting of eternal life (John 5:24). The incarnation personifies God's sending of his saving creative Word: through his Son, God has made something of eternal value out of nothing (cf. John 3:16–18; Rev. 1:2, 9; 20:4).

Moreover, Jesus as the Word of life, the eternal life, had come into *full* human contact with others (John 1:14b; 1 John 1:1–3). The strength of John's high Christology is that it stems from Jesus' earthly life and was demonstrable by eyewitness testimony to it (19:35; 20:30–31; 21:24–25). Luke mentions in his Gospel preface that he uses reliable tradition from "eyewitnesses and servants of the word [i.e., of Jesus' life and work]" (1:2). Jesus also promised to send the Spirit to assist the apostles' accurate recollection and assessment of his life and teaching (John 14:26; 16:14–15; so 2:22).

Thus in connection to the Old Testament picture of *the word of God,* the New Testament understands Jesus as the ultimate means through which God created, revealed, and personified himself to creation. Jesus as the word of God discloses God's saving plan for and to creation, makes God better known to creation, is known firsthand by creation, has come for the saving good of creation, and is equal to the Father as supreme authority over all of creation. To preach the gospel of Jesus Christ is to preach in its fullness the word of God. Therefore, in most fitting description, at the consummation of history, Jesus will return "dressed in a robe dipped in blood, [whose] name is the Word of God" (Rev. 19:13).

Human Words. In both Testaments, human words stand in stark contrast to those of God. Whereas God's words are creative, perfect, and of supreme authority, human words are finite, frail, and fallen. Yet despite the human condition, when controlled by the Holy Spirit, they become as the very words of God.

Human words can be true or false. They are testable (Gen. 42:16, 20), especially in the legal sense of eyewitness testimony (Deut. 19:15–19). Keeping one's word was highly esteemed (Ps. 15:4) and an obligation in making vows and oaths (Num. 30:2; Judg. 11:30, 36); but breaking one's word, especially of promises made to the Lord, was a serious offense holding grave consequences for the offender (cf. Deut. 23:21–23; Eccles. 5:1–7). In view of these Old Testament considerations, for a Gospel writer to profess that his testimony is true, reliable, is a weighty claim (John 21:24; cf. Zech. 8:16–17). In effect, he asserts that its contents are true in the legal, investigative sense and as on oath before God because of its claims about God (cf. John 3:33; 7:28; 8:26).

Words also reflect a person's true character. They show the person for what he or she truly is: "out of the overflow of the heart the mouth speaks" (Matt. 12:34); "it is what comes out of a man that makes him unclean" (Mark 7:15). The righteous speak truth and wisdom to the praise and glory of God (2 Sam. 22:1; Job 33:3; Pss. 15:2; 19:14; Prov. 16:23), but the wicked speak folly and lies (Prov. 12:23) and blaspheme God (2 Kings 19:6) and his Spirit (Matt. 12:31–32).

For this reason, words become sufficient for passing judgment upon those who utter them. On the day of judgment God will hold people accountable for what they have said: "For by your words you will be acquitted and . . . condemned" (Matt. 12:37). In this sense the tongue has the power of life and death (Prov. 18:21): the mouth of a fool will bring him to ruin (Prov. 10:14; 13:3), but the one who controls what he says is wise and virtuous (James 3:1–12).

Under divine control, human words can have eternal value. The Spirit inspires and empowers the words of God's servants as they defend the faith (Luke 12:11–12; cf. Acts 4:8), proclaim the gospel (Eph. 6:19; 1 Thess. 1:5), and instruct and exhort other believers (1 Cor. 14:6, 26; 1 Thess. 4:18; Heb. 13:22). This divine enabling sets apart the Christian message from mere human wisdom or persuasive rhetoric (1 Cor. 1:17; 2:4, 13). The Christian becomes, as it were, "one speaking the very words of God" (1 Peter 4:11; 2 Peter 1:21).

Scripture. The word of God has also come to refer to Scripture itself. In the Old Testament, the words God had given Moses at Sinai became written law (Exod. 24:3; Deut. 4:10–14; 27:3; 31:24–29). The Ten Commandments were called "the word of the covenant" (Exod. 34:27–28); all of God's revelation to Moses was called "the words [book] of the law" (Deut. 28:58; 31:24; Josh. 8:34; 2 Kings 22:13), "word of the LORD" (2 Chron. 34:21), and "word of truth" (Ps. 119:43). With God's powerful display of redeeming Israel from Egypt in view, God gave these decrees, laws, and commands to serve as an abiding written record to his person, presence, and ways before Israel and the nations (Deut. 4:5–8, 32–40). The book of the Law then is none other than the revealed word of God put down into written form. It remained authoritative to Israel. Israel and their descendants were to search, learn, and obey it (Deut. 4:6; Neh. 8:13; Ps. 119:11). As such it becomes the guide for righteous living (Ps. 119:9) and is synonymous with "the Book of the Law" (cf. Deut. 31:24, 26). Psalm 119 has it in view. The Old Testament word of

God as written scripture represents "all the laws that come from your [God's] mouth" (v. 13). By Daniel's time prophetic material was being written down and preserved as well (cf. Dan. 9:2).

By the New Testament era, the word of God as Scripture referred to the entire Old Testament, to the Law of Moses, the Prophets, and the Psalms (cf. Matt. 15:6; Mark 7:13; John 10:35). The idea of Scripture as being "God-breathed" (2 Tim. 3:16) suggests that the entire Old Testament represents God's revealed word and holds supreme authority for faith and practice. At what point the early church began to view some of the New Testament writings in this way is uncertain. But given the church's proclamation of Jesus and of the gospel as the "Word of God" and the early recognized authority of apostolic teaching, many of the New Testament books were probably seen in this way well before the close of the first century.

In summary, on the basis of the word of God, all natural and human reality was created, sustained, redeemed, and will be consummated. As with the Giver, what is Given is unshakable and unstoppable: "my word that goes out from my mouth . . . will not return to me empty, but will accomplish what I desire and achieve the purpose for which I sent it" (Isa. 55:11). God's word as his creative power and revelation is perfect and all-sufficient, especially as it is personified in his Son, Jesus Christ. Our response to God and to his revelation of himself in his Son as preserved in Scripture must therefore be as that of the royal official to Jesus—to take him at his word (John 4:50).

H. Douglas Buckwalter

See also Bible, Authority of the; Bible, Inspiration of the; Jesus Christ, Name and Titles of; John, Theology of.

Bibliography. A. Debrunner, et al., *TDNT,* 4:69–136; H. Haarbeck, et al., *NIDNTT,* 3:1078–1146; D. H. Johnson, *Dictionary of Jesus and the Gospels,* pp. 481–84; E. Linnemann, *Historical Criticism of the Bible,* pp. 81–159; H. D. McDonald, *EDT,* pp. 1185–88; S. Wagner, *TDOT,* 1:228–45.

Work. For contemporary humanity the meaning and character of work have been divorced from religion, being largely shaped by secular ideologies associated with Marxism and capitalism. This is radically different from the biblical concept of work, which is laden with theological significance. The expenditure of physical and mental energy to produce sustenance and culture, the activity that engages most of humanity's population and time (Augustine), has a profoundly religious inspiration and direction in both Testaments. The biblical evidence indicates that human beings must be guided by God's will in their work. Without this guidance, work will ultimately be useless.

The Old Testament. *Creation.* All human work is based on the analogy of God's work in creating the natural world as classically described in Genesis 1–2. God is depicted as effortlessly expending energy to create a world of exquisite beauty from nothing. Material, temporal, and spatial reality are made in a sequence of six days. The text climaxes with a poetic depiction of the creation of humanity, made in the image and likeness of God (Gen. 1:27). This poetic climax, as well as God's survey of his completed creation (1:31), captures something of the ecstatic joy in the Creator's mind evoked by the splendor of his work. On the seventh day, God rests from his work, celebrating his accomplishments.

In this creation text human beings are given a mandate to work, which is intimately related to their identity as the image of God (Gen. 1:26). As image bearers, the human race is to work by ruling and serving the creation. As God has shown his transcendence to the created order through his work, human beings replicate the divine likeness by having dominion over the creation (Gen. 1:26–28). Work has therefore an extremely wide scope, but the theological point is central: human beings are called to *imitatio dei* (imitation of God) through work. It is not to be drudgery but glory. The assumption, of course, is that work will be done in response to the divine will.

Whereas the first creation narrative presents a comprehensive vision of God's activity, the second (2:4–25) focuses on the creation of humanity, God's supreme work. The Creator is depicted as a potter and a builder crafting the human race. A poetic climax also concludes this account, when woman is created (Gen. 2:23). One of the prime tasks God gives Adam and Eve is the cultivation of the earth and the classification of the species of wildlife (Gen. 2:5, 15, 20).

The creation texts confer a sanctity on work. God is involved in work, being its raison d'être. Human beings have the responsibility and privilege of virtually replicating the works of God. The human race co-creates and co-rules with God as it replenishes the earth and exercises dominion over the universe. This attitude is fundamentally different from that found in the ancient Near East. In creation texts associated with Israel's neighbors, the divine work is not something to be admired, as creation emerged from either a struggle between the gods (Mesopotamia) or an act of defilement (Egypt—but cf. the Memphite theology). Work was regarded as a dreary burden. In fact, the gods made the human race as slaves to provide relief from the labor of running the universe (Mesopotamia). Although human beings are regarded as the divine image in some Egyptian texts, they are essentially "the cattle of the god" (Merikare).

The Fall. Sin transformed human work. The judgment of God affects the material world: Adam's efforts to extract a living from it is met by its resistance and his sweat (Gen. 3:17–19). The perspective of humanity has also been altered. The first couple's eyes have been opened to the reality of evil (Gen. 3:7) and closed to the reality of God's works and God's will. That is why they attempt to hide in creation from the Creator; it also explains how their firstborn son, Cain, can destroy God's climactic work, the image of God in the face of his brother (Gen. 4:8).

In the subsequent chapters of Genesis some scholars detect a critique of the first builders of civilization. This analysis is false. Both Cain and Abel have dominion over the earth as farmer and shepherd respectively. God does not prefer one occupation to another; the issue is obedience. Furthermore, the descendants of Cain may be known for their accomplishments in the field of human endeavor—agriculture, metallurgy, music, and art—but that is all they are known for. They have lost themselves in their work, having defined themselves by their achievements. The Cainite genealogy concludes with the dark portrait of Lamech singing his "song of the sword" (Gen. 4:23–24). Early technological skills developed without reference to God produce instruments of death (cf. Isa. 2:4). In the absence of the knowledge of God's works, human effort is directed toward death instead of life.

The main predeluvian human activity is social violence (Gen. 6:11, 13). The creation that had been declared repeatedly "good" at the beginning is now full of corruption and strife. That which once evoked ecstatic joy in the heart of God now wounds him with grief (Gen. 6:6).

At the same time, the Sethite genealogy (chap. 5) concludes with Noah, who is chosen by God to use human effort for the divine purpose. This work must have seemed absurd to his contemporaries, but it provided redemption for creation. Human work, placed not at the service of self but at the service of God, saves. Noah the humble, obedient servant of God contrasts sharply with the heroic warriors of that time.

After the flood, human beings are again given dominion over their natural environment, but the effects of the fall into sin remain. Noah becomes intoxicated with the products of his viticulture, which leads to sexual sin. As a result, slavery is imposed as a curse on the descendants of Ham. The human race uses its capacities and energies to build a huge tower—a monument to human pride and ambition (Gen. 11:1–9). Babel—human work at the service of self—becomes a symbol for chaos and judgment as God sends linguistic confusion to thwart this collective, autonomous venture.

The Patriarchs. God's gracious work in calling Abraham occurs against the backdrop of the failure of human work to achieve salvation (Gen. 12:1–3). Abraham and Sarah represent the beginning of God's new saving work in history, designed to bring a blessing on the entire universe through their seed. Abraham's work is simply to believe and obey, to accept as gifts the new relationship with God as well as the promises of land and descendants. Instead of building a tower to heaven, Abraham and his family are constantly building altars, thereby demonstrating God's dominion over the new land (Gen. 12:7–8; 21:33; 26:25; 28:18).

Egypt. The story of Joseph (Gen. 37–50) describes Israel's entry into Egypt. Devoted to God, Joseph is blessed in everything he does, whether living at home, serving in slavery, or working in prison. This blessing eventually elevates him to the top administrative position in Egypt whereby he is able to use his skill to save not only the Egyptians but many peoples from natural disaster. Joseph is certainly a paradigm for a person who is devoted to God. Primarily a servant of God, he has success in various "callings."

After a significant period of time, the Israelites are oppressed by the Egyptians (Exod. 1–3), who teach them the harsh meaning of slavery as they are forced to build earthly cities for the Pharaoh. Work has been transformed into something demonic, as Israel groans under the backbreaking burden of manual labor. No human effort can provide relief. In such an oppressive situation, Israel experiences liberation through the works of God alone.

Sinai. At Mount Sinai Israel becomes a nation and is given a constitution and law (Exod. 19–24). The divine intent expressed in the Law demonstrates Israel's attitude toward work. Slaves were to be treated with respect and Israelite slaves were to be freed every seven years (Exod. 21:1–11, 26–27). Runaway slaves would be given refuge (Deut. 23:15–16). Property would return to its original owner every fifty years (Lev. 25:8–13). The poor were not to be overlooked in the increase of wealth (Deut. 24:17–22). Wages were to paid equitably and promptly (Deut. 24:14–15). Interest was not to be charged on loans made to Israelites (Exod. 22:25; Deut. 23:19–20). Moreover, collateral for loans had to be returned to poverty-stricken individuals at the end of the day, if this meant deprivation of clothing during the cool night (Exod. 22:26–27).

The major presuppositions for this concern are found in the Decalogue. Exodus states that the Sabbath command is based on the pattern of divine work and rest in Genesis (Exod. 20:8–11). The Israelites are thus to image God in their alternation of work and rest. The parallel command in the Decalogue of Deuteronomy gives a different reason for the observance of the seventh day (Deut. 5:12–15). Israel is to observe the Sabbath by specifically remembering the oppressive Egyptian experience where she was "worked to death." The stress is more on rest as redemption from the tyranny of work. As God delivered Israel from labor with his redemptive work, Israel is to do the same for those who live in her borders every week. Even animals and the land are to experience rest from work.

Sabbatical cycles are not only weekly but yearly. The seventh year is to be a time of rest for the land and release of Israelite slaves (Exod. 23:10–12). A cycle of seven sabbatical years ends in the year of Jubilee, not only a time of rest and liberty, but a time of debt cancellation and the return of property to its original owners (Lev. 25). The divine will clearly places a limit on work, which can easily become harsh and oppressive in a fallen world. While human achievement is important, it must serve the divine purpose. Israel is to be reminded constantly that God is the Lord of people, time, land, and work. When Israel places work under divine lordship, human beings again begin to exercise dominion of the creation as God intended for them.

The results of work are clearly brought within the religious sphere. The law of the tithe is a recognition that the strength to work comes from God alone, as do the rewards of working the land. Moreover, it is also a recognition that the fruits of work must be shared with the less fortunate, particularly the foreigner, the widow, and the orphan (Deut. 14:22–29; 26:12–15).

Israel constructs a tabernacle for the divine presence, to bring as it were, heaven to earth (Exod. 25–40). This symbol of God at the center of life is crucial for human work. When Israel is on the verge of entering the promised land, she is reminded through the Shema (Deut. 6:4–9) to keep God at the center of her existence in all that she does. God's love is not only to be placed between the eyes (i.e., to dominate vision); it is also to be placed on the hands (i.e., to motivate action). The options for possible vocations are unlimited, given these theological principles.

The gift of the land will mean many blessings to the nation, but primarily they will be the ability to build houses, plant vineyards, plow fields, and mine for ore. With God at the center, the work of Israel's hands will overflow with blessing. As well as the blessing, however, there is also the constant danger—to idolize the results of work, prosperity, and consequently assume that human strength alone or the fertility gods of the pagan neighbors are responsible for the abundance (Deut. 8:17; cf. 32:15). This view is fatal for if the doxological center is lost, all of Israel's work will be futile: all their hard work would do you no good, because their land will not produce crops and the trees will not bear their fruit (Lev. 26:20; Deut. 28:33).

Conquest and Kingdom. The promised land is recognized as God's gift to Israel, yet she must work for it. If the nation does not cooperate with God in taking the land, death in the wilderness is the result (Num. 13–14). A generation later, the conquest of Jericho is a dramatic example of trust in God's work (Josh. 6–7). The city is taken on the Sabbath, when Israel encircles it seven times. The walls of the city come crashing down as a result of the divine action. Israel fights but God also fights for her. The entire conquest is a result of God working for Israel (Josh. 11:22). She takes cities that she did not build, vineyards that she did not plant, fields that she did not plow (Josh. 24:13). Israel's response is to use the gift as God's steward. Israel is like a new Adam and Eve entering the paradisical garden.

Psalms. The community at worship also has a vision of human work. Humanity is assigned the task of work by the Creator (104:23). This means taking God-like dominion over the natural order (8). But work that is done without a focus on God is like building a house in vain or guarding a city uselessly (127:1–2). The strength of the strong and mighty is useless without trust in Yahweh (20:7–8; 33:16–19; 147:10–11). Given the transience and impermanence of human life, God must be implored to make any human achievement last (90:12, 16–17).

Wisdom Literature. The primary presupposition of the Wisdom books is that God has made the world according to a certain pattern. Work and the attitude toward work are important themes. Laziness leads to poverty and even death (Prov. 10:4; 21:25). Diligence, on the other hand, results in life (Prov. 13:4; cf. 12:11). The life of crime, a shortcut to prosperity, is condemned as moral suicide (Prov. 1:9–20; 16:8). In everything it is to be remembered that it is the Lord's blessing that produces true wealth; hard work cannot make a person any richer (Prov. 10:22).

While Proverbs presents a positive perspective on work, Ecclesiastes has a more negative outlook. As a result of God's curse on human life, it is virtually impossible to detect God's work. Therefore human work can be characterized as toil. Death introduces an element of futility into human life, even making work seem useless (2:18–20). What can be gained from work if death erases one's accomplishments (3:9)? In spite of all our work, there is nothing we can take with us. We labor trying to take the wind, and what do we get? Grief (5:15). It is also observed that envy and greed supply the motivation for the work of many (4:4; 6:7). If one has a more noble religious inspiration, there can be a certain amount of pleasure: "nothing is better for a man under the sun than to eat and drink and be glad. Then joy will accompany him in his work all the days of the life God has given him under the sun" (8:15).

The Prophets. The prophets possessed great social consciousness. The consequences of selfishness and idolatry are always human oppression, as the powerless become trampled in the mad stampede for wealth. Amos describes the affluent in his days as crushing the poor (2:7), and anxiously waiting for the Sabbath to finish so that they can overcharge their poor customers (8:5).

Micah (2:2) characterizes the rich as seizing fields and homes whenever they want. But God is not a passive onlooker. The prophets announce his judgment, his "strange work" in history (Isa. 28:21). As a result all human effort and work without him as the focus ends up being wasted.

After the exile, the Israelites who returned soon forgot the importance of God. They became preoccupied with their own work and neglected the building of the temple. Consequently their labors suffered (Hag. 1:2–11), as they were not able to provide for themselves (cf. Mal. 3:6–12). After the completion of the temple, Israel became prosperous until the religious focus was lost again (Malachi).

This vision of God's work at the center of human life, and the blessing of human work that results, is magnificently illustrated in the prophets' eschatological vision. At the end of time the temple will be the focus of life as all the nations will travel to Jerusalem. There they will be instructed from Yahweh's Torah and the consequence will be the transformation of human work. Instruments one used for destructive purposes such as war will be changed into ones used for productive purposes like agriculture (Isa. 2:1–4; Mic. 4:1–6). There will be universal shalom and the river of God's life will flow from the temple and heal all the nations (Ezek. 47).

This clearly indicates that the important point in the Old Testament about work is not a particular vocation; any human work is a life-enhancing blessing when it is controlled by God.

The New Testament. John the Baptist was sent to prepare the way for Jesus. In light of God's coming great work to judge and to save, John called people to repentance. This meant that everyone had to change his or her action in the light of the imminent divine action. Those whose professions were notorious for graft and extortion were not told to leave their jobs, but to change their behavior (Luke 3:12–14). The problem was not with the profession but with the human heart.

Jesus is equipped for his work with the power of the Holy Spirit. As the new Adam he is also tested by Satan, where the issues of allegiance and work are repeatedly stressed (Matt. 4:1–11). Will Jesus use his power to make bread from stones in order to satisfy his own hunger? Will he push God to the test to be recognized as his unique messenger? Will he seek power illegitimately to accomplish his mission? The answers are negative. Jesus will only do his Father's will. As such, Jesus, the new Adam—the divine image restored—sets the standard for any human activity. Work must be done in obedience to God's will. If it is not, it becomes quickly corrupted by selfishness (v. 3), the desire for human recognition (v. 6), and power (vv. 8–9).

In order for human beings to be restored to their rightful place as masters of the universe instead of its prisoners, individuals must trust in Jesus Christ, God's work, and not in themselves. Some must leave their professions to become apostles (Mark 1:14–20; 2:13–17). All must abandon an old mode of existence in which the divine will was not central. This means a totally new attitude toward work. All labor must be motivated by love of God and neighbor. Only then will human work be free from anxiety, idolatry, laziness, and lethargy.

Human existence is fraught with anxiety as a result of the competitive struggle to make a living. The disciples of Jesus are to learn from the created order: birds do not have storehouses and grass does not toil, yet God lavishly provides for such creatures not made in his image! Consequently how much more should disciples work without anxiety, knowing that their loving Father will provide also for them. But this means a radical reorienting of priorities. The focus must be placed on doing God's will above everything else (Matt. 6:33). Martha in her frantic preoccupation with domestic preparations has lost the focus; her sister, Mary, has not (Luke 10:38–42).

If anxiety characterizes much of human work, so does idolatry. Work and its products become the end and not the means. Jesus condemns this in unequivocal terms with such statements as, "You cannot serve both God and Money" (Matt. 6:24). This means that if one's work inhibits one from doing the will of God, it must go—it is an idol. Prospective disciples who use their work as an excuse for following Christ are condemned (Luke 14:15–24). Moreover, others who ignore the demands of Christ while accumulating possessions are rich fools. They, too, are doomed (Luke 12:13–21).

Laziness and lethargy are also possible responses to work. Jesus' parable of the talents implies that refusal to use one's gifts and talents for God is an unacceptable response to his grace (Matt. 25:14–30). Discipleship is implied to be a work in itself. Those who abandon Jesus have started plowing and then have looked back (Luke 9:62); they have begun to build a tower and not been able to finish (Luke 14:28–30). Industry, diligence, and foresight are required.

Jesus announces his message of salvation in terms drawn from the work-a-day world. A sower begins to plant seed (Matt. 13:1–9). A merchant discovers a valuable pearl (Matt. 13:45–46). A woman mixes yeast with a bushel of flour (Matt. 13:33). Fishermen cast out their nets and draw them in (Matt. 13:47–50). But most important, God has a job for everyone to do: he is in the business of hiring the unemployed—even at the last hour! Yet everyone is paid the same wage. To be hired is grace, to work is grace, the wage is grace (Matt. 20:1–16). The labor of the law is a back-breaking burden as opposed to the work that Jesus offers (Matt. 11:28–30).

The work that is required of the disciples is to do the will of God. If Jesus did divine works, his disciples can do the same as long as they rely on their master (John 14:12; 15:5). They begin to do these works in the Book of Acts when the church is born. As Jesus was baptized by the Spirit and sent forth as the new Adam, the church is similarly immersed and called forth as a new humanity to do the works of God. Pentecost reverses the curse of Babel. There, as people sang the praises of their own achievements in defiance of God, they could not understand one another as God sent linguistic confusion, which ultimately destroyed their work. At Pentecost, as the Holy Spirit descends, all linguistic barriers are broken down as people hear the mighty works of God in their own languages (Acts 2:11). The result is the building of the city of God, a new society whose members meet each other's material as well as spiritual needs (Acts 2:43–47). Or, to use a different metaphor, this new community is understood to be the actual body of Christ whose function is to do the will of its head (Christ) on the earth through the power of the Holy Spirit (1 Cor. 12–14). As the different body parts work together in harmony, love is demonstrated and the greatest work of God is accomplished (1 Cor. 13).

The dynamic of love for God and each other shapes the church's perspective on its members' occupations and social positions. Everything is evaluated in terms of God's actions in Christ. Criminal behavior is totally unacceptable. Former thieves must start working in order to earn an honest living and help the poor (Eph. 4:28). Similarly, laziness is inadmissible for a Christian (1 Thess. 4:11–12; 2 Thess. 3:6–13). All employees must serve God in their jobs, not just their human employers; and the latter must serve God in the way they treat their employees (Eph. 6:5–9). Slaves and their masters can even be called "brothers" in Christ (Gal. 3:28; Philem. 15–16). The new relationship with each other transforms perceptions of occupations and motives for work. Believers can even be said to be slaves, whose tools are the wash basin and towel (John 13). Hostility and alienation between labor and management are dealt a death blow with the cross (Eph. 2:16). Human beings are being restored to the divine image in order to exercise dominion over the creation (Eph. 4:23–24). Since death has been defeated, no work is done in vain (1 Cor. 15:58).

The New Testament concludes with an unparalleled vision of God alive and active in history, bringing the historical process to consummation. In the Book of Revelation God's deeds are repeatedly celebrated. The cheap imitations of the satanic anti-Trinity (Satan, the beast, and the false prophet) are deceptive and destructive. Babylon, the creation of the latter, where people marked by the image of the beast work for selfish profit, perishes from the earth (Rev. 18). Jerusalem, the creation of God, where people work for their Redeemer and Savior, lasts for eternity. A return to Eden has finally been accomplished, where the new Adams and Eves, crowned with glory and honor, are restored finally to their rightful positions as kings and queens of the new creation, God's resplendent images, who will exercise dominion through service and love (22:1–5).

STEPHEN G. DEMPSTER

See also MONEY; REWARD; WAGES; WEALTH.

Bibliography. J.-M. Aubert, *Theology Digest* 30 (1980): 7–11; B. Birch, *What Does the Lord Require? The Old Testament Call to Social Witness;* J. Ellul, *Cross Currents* 35 (1985): 43–48; G. Goosen, *A Theology of Work;* H.-C. Hahn and F. Thiele, *NIDNTT* 3:1147–59; G. Mendenhall, *Biblical Archaeologist Reader,* pp. 3–24; J. Murray, *Principles of Conduct;* E. Nash, *Modern Churchman* 29 (1986): 23–27; I. G. Nicol, *Scottish Journal of Theology* 33 (1980): 361–73; R. T. Osborn, *Quarterly Review* 5 (1985): 28–43; J. Pritchard, ed., *Ancient Near Eastern Texts Relating to the Old Testament;* G. von Rad, *Wisdom in Israel;* H. C. Shank, *WTJ* 37 (1974): 57–73; J. H. Stek, *Calvin Theological Journal 13* (1978): 133–65; V. Westhelle, *Word and World* 6 (1986): 194–206; R. de Vaux, *Ancient Israel;* H. W. Wolff, *Anthropology of the Old Testament;* M. H. Woudstra, *New Perspectives on the Old Testament,* pp. 88–103; C. J. H. Wright, *An Eye for an Eye: The Place of Old Testament Ethics Today.*

Works of the Law. The term *erga nomou* ("works of the Law") is used by Paul to denote deeds prescribed by the Mosaic Law (Rom. 2:15; 3:20, 27, 28; Gal. 2:16; 3:2, 5, 10). Although not found in the Old Testament or later rabbinic literature, this phrase appears in Qumran literature (*maʿăśê tôrāh,* 4QFlor 1:1–7; cf. 1QS 6:18; 1 QpHab 7:11). At times Paul shortens the phrase and uses *erga,* "works" (Rom. 4:2, 6; 9:11, 32; 11:6), referring to a mode of relationship to the Law and set in contrast to faith in Christ.

Various interpretations of this phrase include: "good works," in the sense of humankind's striving for self-achievement apart from God; observances of Mosaic Law that seek to earn God's favor; and distinctive Jewish identity markers (i.e., circumcision, dietary regulations, and Sabbath observance). Judaism was "nomistic," observing the Law not as a means of justification but as a response to a gracious God, who acts on behalf of his people and requires that they in turn identify themselves as his people by keeping his ordinances (covenantal nomism). In this context, the performance of "works of the law" does not refer to an individual's striving for moral improvement, but to a religious mode of existence, marked out by certain religious practices that demonstrate the individual's covenant relationship. Paul's polemical argument in Galatians, however, is concerned with the inherent legalism of the Judaizers, who required Gentile converts to observe Jewish traditions in order to qualify as members of God's covenant people. Thus, when Paul uses *erga nomou,* he is not just referring to nomistic practices, but to merit-amassing observance of the Law as well.

The nonattainability of righteousness by keeping the Law is attested to by Paul in Philippians 3:4–9. The works of the Law the apostle was "blameless" in performing actually were hindrances to true righteousness, found only in Christ. Any attempt to justify oneself before God based on meritorious action is counted as "loss" or "refuse." Trusting in one's ability to keep the Law is a reliance on the "flesh" (Phil. 3:3) and an attempt to establish one's "own righteousness" (Rom. 10:3). Thus, the cross of Christ, as the sole basis of justification, becomes an "offense," because it repudiates any other means of obtaining righteousness (1 Cor. 1:23; Gal. 5:11; cf. Rom. 9:33). R. DAVID RIGHTMIRE

See also GALATIANS, THEOLOGY OF; GRACE; JUDAIZERS; LAW.

Bibliography. G. Bertram, *TDNT,* 2: 635–55; F. F. Bruce, *Bulletin of the John Rylands Library* 57 (1974–75): 259–79; C. E. B. Cranfield, *Scottish Journal of Theology* 17 (1964): 43–68; W. D. Davies, *Paul and Rabbinic Judaism;* J. D. G. Dunn, *Jesus, Paul and the Law;* J. A. Fitzmyer, *Paul and His Theology;* D. P. Fuller, *WTJ* 38 (1975): 28–42; R. H. Gundry, *Biblica* 66 (1985): 1–38; H. C. Hahn, *NIDNTT,* 3: 1147–51; R. Heiligenthal, *Exegetical Dictionary of the New Testament,* 2:49–50; R. N. Longenecker, *Galatians;* idem, *Paul: Apostle of Liberty;* H. Ridderbos, *Paul: An Outline of His Theology;* E. P. Sanders, *Paul and Palestinian Judaism;* idem, *Paul, the Law, and the Jewish People;* S. Westerholm, *Israel's Law and the Church's Faith: Paul and His Recent Interpreters.*

World. The biblical concept of world falls into five categories: the physical world, the human world, the moral world, the temporal world, and the coming world.

The Physical World. The physical world at its largest extent includes the whole universe, the cosmos (John 1:9; Acts 17:24) or the creation (Rom. 8:20). When biblical writers refer to the world, however, they usually mean the earth itself, not including sun, moon, and stars. No clear Old Testament references appear to the world as a planet, although Isaiah 40:22, "the circle of the earth," is suggestive to some. Many Old Testament uses of world or earth (*ʾereṣ,* in poetry sometimes *tēbēl*) could refer equally to the planet or the ground. When Old Testament writers wanted to refer to the universe, they used an expression like "the heavens and the earth" (Gen. 1:1) or an expansion of that expression (Exod. 20:11; Neh. 9:6).

Scripture affirms first of all that God created the world (Gen. 1:1–2:4; Acts 4:24; 14:15; Rev. 10:6). Because he created it, he owns it and may be addressed as its Lord (Matt. 11:25; Luke 10:21; Acts 17:24). The whole world is full of its Creator's glory (Isa. 6:3). Because God is Creator and Lord of the earth, it holds only secondary value; a believer must not swear by it (Matt. 5:34–35) or accumulate treasure on it (Matt. 6:19).

God designed the world to be fruitful. His creation includes provision for animals as well as for people (Ps. 104:10–22).

God's judgment encompasses the physical world. He flooded it in Noah's time and it lies ready for his judgment at the end (2 Peter 3:7, 10). The world's permanence is only relative. At the end God's angels will gather his chosen ones "from the ends of earth to the ends of heaven" (Mark 13:27 NRSV). Until that time the earth is the arena of God's activity through his people. Christians are to witness to Jesus "to the ends of the earth" (Acts 1:8).

The Human World. The human world includes dry land where people can live, the inhabited earth where they do live, and by metonymy, the people who live there.

The dry land appears in contrast to the sea in Genesis 1:9–10 and Revelation 10:2. Much of this dry land makes up the inhabited earth. The inhabited earth was created with delight by God's wisdom (Prov. 8:27–31). Before Jesus' birth Caesar Augustus attempted to take a census of "the whole world" (really only the Roman Empire; Luke 2:1). The tempter offered Jesus "all the kingdoms" of the inhabited world (Luke 4:5; cf. Matt. 4:8). Jesus predicted that the gospel would be preached to the whole world (Matt. 24:14; 26:13; cf. Rom. 10:18), a prediction so successful that the early church, in its opponents' opinion, upset the whole world (Acts 17:6). The whole world is deceived by the devil (Rev. 12:9) and will experience great trouble before the end (Luke 21:26; Rev. 3:10).

The people of the world are called simply the "world" or the "earth" occasionally in the Old Testament and frequently in the New Testament. "Yahweh will judge the world," or a similar statement, means he will judge the world's inhabitants (Pss. 9:8; 96:13; Isa. 13:11; 26:9). Similar New Testament references to the Christ's or his apostles' authority appear. The Son of Man "has authority on the earth," authority over the people of the world (Matt. 9:6; parallels Mark 2:10; Luke 5:24). The apostles have a derived authority, the power of "binding and loosing" (Matt. 16:19; 18:18).

In the Johannine literature the "world" often means the people of the world. The world did not know the Word (John 1:10), the Lamb who would take away its sin (John 1:29). God loved the world, sending his Son into it to save rather than condemn it (John 3:16–17; cf. 12:47; 1 John 4:9). The Son of God is the "Savior of the world" (John 4:42; 1 John 4:14), giving life to it as the "bread of life" (John 6:33, 51).

The Moral World. The moral world includes people indifferent or hostile to God, the God-hostile environment generally, and in the widest sense, corruption and evil summed up under the general term "the world."

If the people of the world can be spoken of as "the world" in a neutral sense, "the world" can also refer to the subclass of indifferent and hostile people who reject God and his ways. Before the flood nearly all the people of the world became corrupt (Gen. 6:11). In Jesus' time the world hated him (John 7:7) and will hate his followers (John 15:18–19). The world, ungodly people, cannot receive the things of God (John 14:17, 22; 16:8–9; cf. 1 John 3:1) and is not even worthy of the people of faith who live among them (Heb. 11:38).

In the New Testament the world also appears as a hostile environment. Because of the hatred of the world's people, the Son asks the Father to protect his followers rather than remove them from their alien surroundings (John 17:14–16). Paul expresses his indifference to the world by saying he "is crucified" as far as the world is concerned (Gal. 6:14). Seven times in 1 Corinthians 1–3 Paul refers to the world's ignorance of God and its powerlessness to find him without the cross of Christ.

Because of the world's hostility to God, it is full of corruption (2 Peter 1:4) and stands as a symbol of corruption. One cannot be friendly with the evil world and love God at the same time (James 4:4; 1 John 2:15–17). Believers by their faith must "overcome the world" (1 John 5:4–5), killing whatever belongs to their "earthly nature" (Col. 3:5) and denying "worldly passions" (Titus 2:12).

The Temporal and Coming Worlds. Although the Old Testament presents the idea that the present world is temporary (Ps. 102:25–27), the distinction between this world/age and the world/age to come does not appear clearly until the late intertestamental and New Testament periods. By the time of the New Testament, the distinction is clear and frequent.

Satan rules only this world (John 12:31; 14:30; 16:11; 2 Cor. 4:4), not the next one, while Jesus' kingdom is "not of this world" (John 18:36) but belongs to the coming age. Jesus warns that a person may "gain the whole world" (the material things of this passing age) yet lose life in the next (Matt. 16:26; parallels Mark 8:36; Luke 9:25). Paul expresses concern that believers may become so caught up in the affairs of this world that they will experience undue hardship in living for Christ (1 Cor. 7:29–35).

The present world is passing away even now (1 John 2:17). Living in this transient world, one must not love it (2 Tim. 4:10), become conformed to its ways (Rom. 12:2), or fall in love with its godless "wisdom" (1 Cor. 2:6; cf. 3:18–19; James 3:15). Instead one must live a godly life (Titus 2:12), avoiding the snares of the "present evil age" from which Christ's death has set his people free (Gal. 1:4). The believer may look forward to the new world, "a new heaven and a new earth, the home of righteousness" (2 Peter 3:13; cf. Rev. 21:1–5). CARL BRIDGES, JR.

See also AGE, AGES; VICTORY.

Bibliography. H. Sasse, *TDNT,* 1:197–209; 3:867–98.

Worship. If Christianity is the transformation of rebels into worshipers of God, then it is imperative for the Christian to know and understand what constitutes biblical worship. One may always consult *Webster's Dictionary* for the precise meaning of worship (adore, idolize, esteem worthy, reverence, homage, etc.). Yet truly defining worship proves more difficult because it is both an attitude and an act.

Worship Ancient and Modern. Both the Old and New Testaments admit the possibility of false worship, usually associated with idolatrous cults and gross misconduct (Deut. 7:3–6). For example, the Canaanites practiced ritual prostitution and infant sacrifice under the guise of worship to gods like Molech and Baal (Lev. 18:6–30; 20:1–5), while Paul found little had changed in the practice of idolatrous worship in Greek Corinth of the first century A.D. (1 Cor. 6:12–20; 10:14–22). The psalmist recognized the folly of such false worship, noting that those who make idols will be like them (Ps. 115:2–8). The prophets, too, warned against idolatry, a fatal attraction for the people of God (Ezek. 14:3–7). Sadly, the biting sarcasm of these divine messengers, who decried images with plastered eyes that had to be nailed to shelves to prevent them from toppling over, fell on deaf ears—as deaf as those of the idols they had fashioned (Isa. 41:5–7). In the end, of course, these "stumbling blocks" of wood, stone, and precious metal overlay could not save Israel (Isa. 44:17).

The antidote Jesus commended in his discourse with the Samaritan woman remains the best preventive against false worship (John 4:23–24). All true worshipers must worship God in "spirit and in truth." That is, true worship takes place on the inside, in the heart or spirit of the worshiper (cf. Pss. 45:1; 103:1–2). Worship pleasing to God must be unfeigned and transparent, offered with a humble and pure heart (Ps. 24:3–4; Isa. 66:2).

But this is not enough. Worship "in truth" connects the heart or spirit of worship with the truth about God and his work of redemption as revealed in the person of Jesus Christ and the Scriptures. David understood the importance of worshiping in truth and the necessary linkage between "truth" and the Word of God when he wrote, "Teach me your way, O LORD, and I will walk in your truth; give me an undivided heart, that I may fear [i.e., worship] your name" (Ps. 86:11; cf. Ps. 145:18). Here both the Old and New Covenants agree! The true worship of God is essentially internal, a matter of the heart and spirit rooted in the knowledge of and obedience to the revealed Word of God.

The Bible also warns of more insidious forms of false worship, namely, religious syncretism and religious hypocrisy. Religious syncretism is a process of assimilation that incorporates elements of one religion into another. As a result, the basic tenets and character of both religions are fundamentally altered. For the Hebrews during Old Testament times this religious syncretism usually involved the union of Mosiac Yahwism and Canaanite Baalism. The prophet Elijah chided the people for attempting to "waver between two opinions" (1 Kings 18:21), and the subsequent contest on Mount Carmel between the prophet of God and the prophets of Baal demonstrated the superiority of Yahweh's religion. In the New Testament Jesus took issue with those who mixed faith and materialism when he declared, "you cannot serve both God and Money" (Matt. 6:24); Paul continually battled those who preached a different gospel, one that perverted justification by faith in Christ by blending the teachings of Judaism and Christianity (Gal. 3:1–14).

Hypocrisy is a pseudo-pietism that pays "lip-service" to covenant keeping and social justice (Jer. 12:2), and exhibits all the external trappings of true worship of God. However, this worship is "godless," based as it is on rules formulated by human teachers (Isa. 29:13). Additionally, this false piety is also lawlessness, in that it multiplies sacrifices while it tramples the poor (Amos 5:11, 21–24). The impious and insincere nature of this worship is further characterized by a consistent pattern of infidelity to Yahweh's covenant (Jer. 12:10). Much later, Jesus described religious hypocrisy as both "play-acting" (Matt. 6:2, 5, 16) and godlessness (worshipers who were outwardly pious but inwardly profane, Matt. 23:13–29). Nonetheless, their end is the same in either covenant: the pseudo-pious or hypocritical worshiper is rejected and judged severely by almighty God (Jer. 14:11–12; Matt. 23:35).

Worship in the Old Testament. The study of the Old Testament worship is important for at least two reasons. First, the Old Testament Scriptures are part of the Christian canon, which means these documents are valuable for the Christian church as divinely inspired revelation of God and authoritative for the life of the church—at least in theological principle, if not in literal teaching. Second, the life of the Israelite nation depicted in the accounts of the Old Testament provides the pattern for public worship found in both Judaism and Christianity.

The God of Israel. The object of veneration in the Old Testament was the God of creation (Gen. 1:1–2), the God of covenant revelation (Gen. 12:1–3), and the God of redemptive acts in history (Exod. 20:2–3). This God, Yahweh, merited the worship and devotion of the Hebrew people both for who he is and for what he does.

The God of the Old Testament is utterly holy and thus transcendent, inaccessible, mysterious, and inscrutable (Ps. 99:3–9). But if this alone were true about God, why worship such a terrible and awesome deity? Happily, this same God is also the "Holy One among you" (Hos. 11:9), a God who at once dwells "in a high and holy place, but also with him who is contrite and lowly in spirit" (Isa. 57:15). God merits worship because in his imminent presence he is able to answer those who call upon him and forgive their wrongdoings (Ps. 99:8). It was this intimate presence of a holy God that prompted heartfelt praise and worship (Ps. 99:3) and the keen desire for holy living among the people of Israel (Lev. 19:2).

And yet, this were not enough if God was not sovereign in all of his creation. The sovereignty of God indicates his absolute authority and power over all creation for the purpose of accomplishing his divine will. The God of Israel alone rules forever (Exod. 15:18) and accomplishes his sovereign plan among the nations (Isa. 14:24–27). Otherwise the Hebrews would have been little better off than the rest of the nations the Rabshakeh of Assyria chided, "Has the god of any nation ever delivered his land from the hand of the king of Assyria?" (Isa. 36:18). All this, the holiness of God, the holy imminence of God, and the sovereignty of God, make him a unique divine being. For the prophet Isaiah, the uniqueness of God constituted a call to worship the Lord as King and Redeemer of Israel (44:6–8; 45:20–23).

Despite the majesty and perfection of God's person and character, Hebrew worship would have been misplaced if this God were impotent to act, to intervene in the experiences of life on behalf of his worshipers. Hence, the activity of God in human history served as both a basis for Hebrew worship and justification of the worship of the particular God, Yahweh. Among all the deeds of God recorded in the Old Testament two are foundational to the idea of Hebrew worship. First is the activity of God in creating new relationships with Israel (and others) by yoking himself through covenant promise ("I will be your God") and covenant stipulation ("you will be my people") to establish a worshiping community in holiness. The second was the event of the Hebrew exodus from Egypt, God's redemption of Israel (Ps. 77:13, 15) designed to prompt worship on the part of those who witnessed or later heard about Yahweh's dealings with the Egyptians (Exod. 18:10–12).

Hebrew Anthropology. While Hebrew anthropology affirms the individual is comprised of distinguishable physical and spiritual elements, there is no systematic distinction between the material and the immaterial, the physical and the spiritual in the Old Testament. According to the pattern of ancient Hebrew thought, a human being is an indivisible totality or unity. Thus, it is the whole person, not just the immaterial essence of an individual, which blesses the holy name of the Lord in worship (Ps. 103:1).

This understanding of the synthetic nature and constitution of humanity by the ancient Hebrews is remarkably relevant for contemporary Christianity. The holistic emphasis of Hebrew anthropology affirms persons created in the image of God as indivisible unities, thus serving as a potent antidote for the far-reaching (and lethal) effects of Platonic dualism within Western thought. Acknowledging the interrelatedness of the physical and the spiritual dimensions in human beings also helps prevent establishing false dichotomies between the "sacred" and "secular," meaning work, play, and worship are all sacred activities under the rule of a sovereign God. Recognition of the integrative unity of humanness permits a "whole person" response to God in worship, instilling the freedom to worship God with intellect, emotions, personality, senses, and body. Finally, Hebrew anthropology fosters the notion of corporate identity or the sense of belonging to the organic unity of humanity. This means the privatized worship of the individual finds its completion in the public worship of the larger worshiping community (cf. Heb. 10:25).

The Practice of Worship. Worship during the patriarchal period was either an expression of praise and thanksgiving prompted by a theophany (the visible or auditory manifestation of God to human beings) or the act of obedience to some divine directive (e.g., Abram "obeying" the command of God to sojourn in Canaan, Gen. 12:4). Often this expression of worship took the form of altar building (Gen. 33:20) and sometimes combined prayer (Gen. 26:25) or animal sacrifice (Gen. 31:54; 46:1). Other expressions of patriarchal worship included the erection of stone pillars and the pouring of drink offerings (drink offering, Gen. 28:18, 22), taking of vows in response to divine revelation (Gen. 28:20; 31:13), ritual purification (Gen. 35:2), the rite of circumcision as a sign of covenant obedience (Gen. 17:9–14), and prayers of praise and thanksgiving (Gen. 12:8; 13:4), petition (Gen. 24:12; 25:21), and intercession (Gen. 18:22–33; 20:7).

The Book of Job confirms much of this assessment of pre-Mosaic religion among the Hebrews. The date of the literature of Job notwithstanding, the cultural and historical background of Job's testing certainly reflect the patriarchal age. Like the Hebrew patriarchs, Job is cast in the role of priest for his clan as head of the family and offers sacrifices on their behalf (1:5). Confession and repentance (42:6), and petition and intercessory prayer (6:8–9; 42:8–9) were routine practices for Job as a blameless and upright man. Even the internal attitude of worship represented by the "fear of God" (2:3) and the lifestyle response of obedience as seen in Job's oath of clearance (chap. 31) parallel the patriarchal worship experience.

The Mosaic period (ca. 1400–1100 B.C.) is widely recognized as the formative era of Israelite history and worship. Hebrew religious consciousness and worship practice was largely shaped by the dramatic events of the exodus from Egypt. Likewise, the covenant ceremony at Mount Sinai was the vehicle by which God established Israel as his "treasured possession" (Exod. 19:5). The divine law attached to the Sinai treaty became the instrument that both molded and preserved Israel's identity as the people of God and chartered Israel as a theocratic kingdom of priests (Exod. 19:6). Whereas the events of the exodus from Egypt bonded Israel together as a worshiping community, the covenant ceremony at Mount Sinai resulted in a "constitution" that created the nation of Israel (cf. Deut. 4:32–40).

This covenant legislation enacted at Mount Sinai prohibited the Hebrews from attempting to represent Yahweh's likeness with an image (Exod. 20:3–4). The question of the existence of other gods was not an issue. The Hebrews acknowledged the existence of foreign deities. The sole task of the Hebrews was to worship their God, Yahweh, and serve him alone.

The Old Testament celebrates the Passover and exodus as both the supreme act of divine judgment and divine deliverance in Hebrew history (Exod. 6:6; 15:13; Deut. 7:8). As such it furnished the seedbed for the growth and development of the Israelite theological language of redemption. Specifically, the purpose of the Passover animal sacrifice was didactic in that the enactment of the ritual of atonement was designed to instruct the Israelites in the principles of God's holiness and his unique role as Redeemer, human sinfulness, substitutionary death to cover human transgression, and the need for repentance leading to cleansing and renewed fellowship within the community and with Yahweh. The Passover ceremony and the exodus event exalted the covenant God, Yahweh, who redeemed Israel from the foe (Ps. 78:12). They also stood as a perpetual reminder to the successive generations of Hebrews that redemption leads inevitably to the worship of Yahweh (Exod. 15:18).

The legal code forming the stipulations of the Sinai covenant also formally organized Hebrew worship. Mosaic Law legitimized and standardized the media or form and the institutions of Israelite worship of Yahweh. Worship as recitation for the ancient Hebrews included liturgical responses like "Amen!" (1 Chron. 16:36) or "Hallelujah!", singing (Ps. 92:1), prayer (Ps. 5:3), vows and oath taking (Ps. 66:13–19), and the reading and teaching of God's Law (Deut. 31:9–13). Worship as ritual drama for the ancient Hebrews included sacrificial worship (Lev. 1–7), the Sabbath (Exod. 20:8–11), the seasonal festivals (Lev. 23), the pilgrimage festivals (Exod. 23:14–17), incense offerings and libations (Exod. 30:7–9), penitential rites (Lev. 16:29), purification rites (Lev. 12:1–8), the tithe (Lev. 27:30–32), and artistic responses (e.g., music 2 Chron. 5:11–14; dance, Ps. 30:11; and sign and symbol, Exod. 28:6–30).

The exodus event and the covenant pact ratified at Mount Sinai also reshaped Hebrew understanding of time and reordered Hebrew life according to a new religious calendar. The Decalogue command to observe one day in seven as holy to the Lord established the connection between the Sabbath and original creation (Exod. 20:11). The "rest" in God's presence on the Sabbath day typified the goal of redemption in Old Testament revelation: rest in Yahweh's presence in the land of covenant promise.

The divinely ordained covenant prescriptions for holiness in Hebrew life extended beyond the Sabbath to the entire calendar. Six annual festivals and holy days were inaugurated as part of Mosaic legislation, including the Passover (and the Feast of Unleavened Bread), the Fest of Firstfruits, the Feast of Pentecost, the Feast of Trumpets, the Day of Atonement, and the Feast of Tabernacles (Lev. 23). These great religious festivals and holy days corresponded to the major seasons of the agricultural cycle of the land of Palestine so that the Israelites might acknowledge Yahweh as their Provider and Sustainer. Three of the festivals required pilgrimages of all Israelite males to appear before the Lord at the central sanctuary (Passover/Unleavened Bread, Pentecost, and Tabernacles; Exod. 23:17). This assembling of the Hebrews for worship both reinforced the ideals of covenant community and personal piety, as well as reminded the Israelites that their physical and spiritual well-being was solely dependent upon the covenant love of Yahweh (Deut. 30:15–20).

Much of the worship associated with Solomon's temple was simply the transference of the worship practices associated with the tabernacle rituals established by the Mosaic covenant at Mount Sinai. However, biblical scholars have discerned a temple liturgy in Psalm 95 consisting of the entrance (implying preparation, confession, forgiveness, and cleansing), enthusiastic praise, worship proper (getting low before God), and the response of obedience. In addition, this first temple period witnessed the development of the Psalter as the songbook of Israel's private and public worship. According to later rabbinic tradition the psalms were used daily in the temple service accompanying the morning and evening sacrifices. These "proper" psalms included Psalm 24 (day 1), Psalm 48 (day 2), Psalm 82 (day 3), Psalm 94 (day four), Psalm 81 (day 5), Psalm 93 (day 6), and Psalm 92 for the Sabbath. The Hallelujah Psalms (113–118) were used in conjunction with the New Moon, Passover, Pentecost, Tabernacles, and Dedication feasts; while Psalm 7 was included in the Purim liturgy, Psalm 47 was part of the New Year's Celebration, and the Songs of Ascents were associated with the three great pilgrimage festivals (Pss. 120–134). The prominent place of music in temple worship accorded the priestly musical guilds status equivalent to the priests responsible for the sacrificial liturgy.

The Institutions of Worship. The tabernacle was a portable tent-sanctuary ordained by God and constructed by the Israelites under the supervision of Moses. The instructions for the design and fabrication of the structure, as well as the directives for implementing the worship of Yahweh there, were part of the covenant legislation revealed by God to Moses at Mount Sinai (Exod. 25–40). According to Exodus 40:1, 16, the tabernacle was completed in the second year after the exodus from Egypt, a little less than a year after the revelation had been given to Moses at Sinai. The cloud of the glory of the Lord that filled the tent sanctuary then guided the Israelites in the stages of their desert trek to Canaan, the land of covenant promise (Exod. 40:34–38). The three clans of levitical priests—the Kohathites, Gershonites, and Merarites—were responsible for transporting, dismantling, and erecting this "tent of meeting" (Num. 3–4).

The tabernacle was a rectangular wooden-frame structure some 10 cubits wide and 30 cubits wide according to the biblical dimensions (about 15' x 45'). The tent itself was divided into two rooms or compartments by a veil. The other room or Holy Place measured 10 cubits by 20 cubits (about 15' x 30') and contained the lampstand, the table of presence, and the altar of incense. The inner room or Most Holy Place was 10 cubits by 10 cubits (about 15' x 15') and housed the sacred ark of the covenant. The tent shrine was centered in a fenced courtyard some 50 cubits wide and 100 cubits long (about 75' x 150'). Entrance to the sanctuary was from the east court; the bronze laver or basin and the altar of burnt offering were set in the courtyard between the court entrance and the tabernacle proper.

The direct purpose of the tabernacle was to showcase the imminence of God, a habitat where God might live among his people (Exod. 25:8). The indirect purpose of the tabernacle was to afford the Israelites the means by which they might honor Yahweh through carefully prescribed worship rituals orchestrated by the newly established levitical priesthood. The very design and construction of the tabernacle, as well as the prescriptions for the worship liturgy performed there, all reinforced key theological emphases of the Mount Sinai theophany (e.g., the tension between divine immanence and transcendence and the principle of mediation to enter the presence of God). Likewise, the artistry and craftsmanship employed in the design and construction of the tabernacle and its furnishings introduced the use of sign and symbol for inspiring worship and conveying theological education to God's people (especially Yahweh's majesty and holiness).

No organized Hebrew priesthood functioned during the pre-Mosaic period of Israelite history. Rather, the patriarch or elder of the Hebrew family or clan officiated as the priest for that group (Gen. 35:2–5; Job 1:5). The sole exception was Abram's encounter with the priest-king of Salem, Melchizedek (Gen. 14:18–20). The New Testament identifies this enigmatic Old Testament figure as the prototype of the later levitical priesthood and ultimately the prototype of the messianic priesthood fulfilled in Jesus Christ (Heb. 7:1–27; cf. Ps. 110:4).

The Mosaic covenant enacted at Mount Sinai legislated the establishment of a formal Hebrew priesthood to serve God in worship. This priesthood represented the entire Israelite community before the Lord, since they were constituted a kingdom of priests and a holy nation (Exod. 19:5–6). The Hebrew priests were employed in the service of Yahweh full-time and were supported in their ministry by the tithes, offerings, and portions of the sacrificial offerings of the Israelite community (Lev. 7:28–36; Deut. 14:22–29). The period of service for the priesthood was twenty years, from age thirty to age fifty (Num. 4:47). It appears the priests were trained for their duties during a five-year apprenticeship, from age twenty-five to age thirty (Num. 8:24–26). Unlike the other Hebrew tribes, the levitical priesthood received no inheritance of land in Palestine. Instead, the priests and Levites were allotted forty-eight cities in which to live (Num. 35:1–5). The Aaronic priests and Levites were denied territorial rights since the Lord God and service to Israel in his name was their inheritance (Num. 18:20; Deut. 10:9–10).

Only males from the tribe of Levi were permitted to hold priestly office (Num. 3:1–39). Following the prescription of Mosaic Law the Israelite priesthood consisted of two orders or divisions, the priests and the Levites. While the term "Levite" may refer to the entire Hebrew priesthood, technically the priests were descendants of Aaron (Exod. 29:1–37; Lev. 8:1–36). One from among the Aaronic lineage was chosen and ordained high priest for life (Lev. 21:10). Specifically, the Levites were non-Aaronic descendants of Levi who functioned in the service of the sanctuary in subordinate roles. Three clans or subdivisions of Levites are recognized in the Old Testament, taking their names from the three sons of Levi: Gershon, Kohath, and Merari (Num. 3–4).

Duties charged to the Aaronic priesthood basically fell into two categories: superintending sanctuary worship and instructing the people of God in the Law of Moses (Exod. 28:30; Lev. 8:8; Deut. 33:8–10). The high priest supervised sacrificial worship in the sanctuary (Lev. 4:3–21), officiated over the Day of Atonement ceremony (Lev. 16:1–9), and handled the Urim and Thummin, peculiar objects carried in a pouch on the breastplate of the priestly vestments and used for determining the will of God in certain instances (Num. 27:21; Deut. 33:8). The Aaronic priests officiated over sacrificial worship in the sanctuary under the direction of the high priest (Lev. 4–5), led the congregation of Israel in corporate and festival worship (Lev. 23:15–22), transported the ark of the covenant (Deut. 10:8; 31:9), served as religious educators (Deut. 27:14–26) and advisers to civic leaders (Deut. 20:2; Judg. 18:18–19), and were models of covenant obedience and holiness (Lev. 21:1–24).

Originally, the non-Aaronic priests or Levites were designated as assistants to the Aaronic priesthood and porters of the tabernacle, God's portable tent-sanctuary. This levitical assistance included doing the service at the tabernacle, having charge of the sanctuary and its furnishings, and attending to the duties of the Israelites (Num. 3:5–8). Later the levitical duties were reorganized since they were no longer required as porters given the construction of the Jerusalem temple. According to the Chronicler, David was responsible for reassigning the levitical priests to new duties that included assisting the Aaronic priesthood in temple worship, cleaning and maintenance, procuring and storing supplies, and serving as temple musicians (1 Chron. 9:28–32; 23:26–32).

Despite the divine prohibition against his actually building a temple for God, David did make arrangements for its construction, including gathering the necessary materials and supplies to ensure his son Solomon's success in erecting a house for the name of Yahweh (1 Chron. 22:2–19). Solomon began construction of the elaborate edifice in the fourth year of his reign (ca. 966 B.C.) and it was completed seven years later (1 Kings 6:37–38). The magnificent structure was patterned after the tabernacle and replaced that tent-sanctuary as the religious center of Israel, with the levitical priesthood continuing to officiate over the sacrificial and festival worship of Yahweh. Solomon's temple witnessed both the blessing of God's divine presence in the form of the cloud of glory (1 Kings 8:11), and the abasement of divine abandonment as God's glory departed the temple due to Israel's sin of idolatry (Ezek. 10:18). Not long after Ezekiel's vision, Nebuchadnezzar and the Babylonian hordes plundered the treasures of Solomon's temple and reduced Jerusalem and Yahweh's "house" to ashes and rubble in 587 B.C. (2 Kings 25:1–21). All that remained of the splendor of Solomon's temple was the memory.

The sanctuary of the Lord as a symbol of God's presence in the midst of his people was retained in the shift from desert tabernacle to urban temple (1 Kings 8:57). However, new theological emphases surface in Solomon's prayer of dedication, including the temple as the embodiment of the fulfillment of divine promises regarding the Davidic covenant and perpetual dynastic kingship (vv. 14–21), the idea of Yahweh's temple as a house of prayer (vv. 27–54), the temple as both a witness to God's sovereignty over all creation and as a token of Israelite covenant obedience (vv. 41–43, 56–61), and the temple as a tangible reminder of God's transcendence—a God who does not dwell in a house made by human hands (vv. 27–30).

Unfortunately, by the time of Jeremiah the prophet (ca. 627–580 B.C.), this lofty "temple theology" had been forgotten or so corrupted by religious syncretism with surrounding paganism as to be unrecognizable. The temple was no longer a symbol of God's divine presence and a monument to his sovereignty, but was now equated with God's actual presence and considered the ultimate spiritual reality by the Hebrews. The mere association of Yahweh's temple with Jerusalem insured divine protection, security, and covenant blessing in the minds of the people of God. Jeremiah indignantly condemned this misplaced trust in the temple as a talisman or fetish and predicted its eventual destruction (chaps. 7–10).

A second temple dedicated to the worship of Yahweh was erected in Jerusalem after the Babylonian exile at the prompting of the prophets Haggai and Zechariah (Ezra 5:1–2; Hag. 2:9). The rebuilding project commenced in 520 B.C. and was completed sometime in 516 or 515 B.C. The second temple was but a shadow of its predecessor, to such a degree that those who remembered Solomon's temple lamented the inferiority of the new edifice (Ezra 3:12–13). This temple complex was expanded and refurbished in grandiose style by King Herod the Great (begun in 20 B.C. but not completed until A.D. 64, well after Herod's death). It was in this temple that the infant Jesus was dedicated by Joseph and Mary and recognized as Israel's messiah by Simeon and Anna (Luke 2:22–38). In keeping with the emphasis of Solomon's dedication of the first temple, Jesus cleansed the second temple so it might truly be a house of prayer (Mark 11:15–19). Ironically, Jesus' teaching in the temple during his Passion week (including his forecast of the destruction of the temple) incited his rejection as Israel's messiah and sealed his fate for crucifixion as a religious imposter (Mark 14:53–65) and enemy of the state (Mark 15:1–15). Fulfilling Jesus' prophecy (Mark 13:1–8) to the letter, the second temple was completely destroyed in A.D. 70 by the Roman general Titus during the First Jewish War.

The New Testament records indicate that the sacrificial system associated with temple worship remained at the core of the Jewish religious experience, with throngs of Jews from Palestine and beyond overrunning the city during the great pilgrimage festivals. However, the dispersion of Jews across the Mediterranean world under Greek and Roman rule prompted the rise of a competing religious institution, the synagogue. Increasingly the temple became identified with the Hellenized Jewish aristocracy of Jerusalem, sparking the growth of the synagogue among the grassroots population outside the environs of Jerusalem who were attracted to the emphasis on simple personal piety and the spiritual sacrifices of prayer, fasting, and almsgiving.

Theological Implications. The Old Testament anticipates Christian worship in theological principle, in that Hebrew worship: (1) required conscious preparation on the part of the worshiper; (2) encouraged private and family worship as a complement to corporate public worship; (3) demanded the response of the whole person to God as Creator and Redeemer; (4) encouraged congregational worship that was active and participatory; (5) focused on the redemptive acts of God in human history (i.e., the Passover/exodus event); (6) employed symbolism to enhance worship aesthetically and improve worship didactically; (7) observed a liturgical calendar that heightened the worshiper's anticipation of and participation in ritual reenactment; and (8) assumed that a lifestyle of obedience in service to God completed the integrity of worship.

Worship in the New Testament. *The Jewish Roots of Christianity.* The Jewish character of early Christianity may be traced to three primary points of origin, including ethnicity, the Old Testament Scriptures, and the institution of the synagogue.

First, and most obvious, early Christianity was essentially Jewish because the early Christians were Jews. Jesus Christ was a Jew from Nazareth in Galilee (Matt. 1:1), the twelve apostles and the pillars of Christ's church were all Jewish (Mark 3:13–19), the outpouring of the Holy Spirit at Pentecost was largely a Jewish event (Acts 1:15; 2:1–5), and the initial missionary thrust of the church focused on the Jew first (Acts 6:7; 13:5).

Second, the continuity between early Christianity and Judaism may be linked to the Holy Scriptures of Judaism—the Old Testament. The Old Testament was the Bible for the early church. Jesus Christ, by word and deed, demonstrated himself as the fulfillment of the old covenant promises concerning the Messiah made to God's people Israel. Hence, the Old Testament was the source book for early New Testament preaching and the apologetic of early Christianity was essentially one of evincing Jesus as the Christ by appeal to this fulfillment of Old Testament prophecy. The Jewish-Christian authors of the New Testament appealed to the Hebrew Old Testament for instruction, exhortation (Rom. 15:4–6; 1 Cor. 10:1–13), and illustrative examples of faith in God (Heb. 11). In addition, they understood the church of Jesus Christ to be the new Israel (Rom. 4:16–24; 9:11–27; Gal. 3:19–29). Thus, while the Holy Bible contains two covenants, the Old and the New, it is a continuous and single record of divine redemption in human history.

Finally, the antecedents of the form and practice of worship of early Christian worship may be found in the liturgy of the Jewish temple and synagogue.

The Apostolic Church. The Book of Acts indicates that the first church gathered daily for worship in the Jerusalem temple and in the homes of believers, devoting themselves to instruction in the apostles' doctrine, fellowship, prayer, and the Eucharist or Lord's Table (2:42–47). Given their Jewish heritage and the example of Jesus, who worshiped in the synagogues and temple (Luke 4:16; John 10:22–23), it is only natural that the apostolic church retained temple worship and Sabbath keeping along with the development of Christian worship patterns for Sunday, the day of Christ's resurrection (Luke 24:1).

By the time Paul had evangelized Asia Minor and Greece, the church (now decidedly Gentile in composition) met for corporate worship (the breaking of bread or Lord's Table) on the first day of the week or Sunday (Acts 20:7; 1 Cor. 16:2). In addition to the weekly observance of the Lord's Table, the New Testament records indicate worship in the apostolic church also included the singing of psalms, hymns, and spiritual songs (Col. 3:16), prayer (1 Tim. 2:1–2), almsgiving (1 Cor. 16:1–4), the reading and teaching of the Old Testament and apostolic doctrine (1 Tim. 4:11–13), and the manifestation of a variety of spiritual gifts (1 Cor. 12:1–11). In fact, when Paul instructed the church at Corinth on the subject of spiritual gifts and orderly worship he specifically mentioned the hymn, a lesson from Scripture, a word of revelation, and a tongue and its interpretation as a few of the elements comprising Christian worship (1 Cor. 14:26).

Of course, the transition from Judaism to Christianity posed real problems for many Jewish believers in Christ, as did the inclusion of Gentiles in the predominantly Jewish early church (Acts 15:1–29; Gal. 1:11–14). The tensions between form and freedom in worship were also pressing, evidenced by Paul's treatise on spiritual gifts and lay participation in the worship service (1 Cor. 14:26–40). The letters of Paul establish helpful guidelines for resolving these problems associated with the practice of Christian worship; primary among them are the principle of edification or common good of the congregation gathered for worship (1 Cor. 12:7; Eph. 4:12–13), the principle of order and peace governing the form of worship (1 Cor. 14:33, 40), and the principle of a clear conscience and individual accountability before the Lord in certain matters related to personal freedoms and preferences in worship (Rom. 14:1–12).

Basic to the formation, identity, and worship of the apostolic church were the ritual symbols of baptism and the breaking of bread or Lord's Table. The ceremony of baptism symbolized the cleansing from sin effected by Christ's redemption and served as the rite of initiation into the church as the body of Christ (Rom. 6:1–4). As such, Christian baptism holds great significance for worship because it places the believer formally in a worshiping community—the church of Jesus Christ; and it signifies newness of life in Christ and the things of the Holy Spirit who activates Christian worship (Rom. 8:5–6; 1 Cor. 12:11). Much like the Passover meal of the Old Covenant symbolized Israel's redemption in the exodus event, so the Eucharist or Lord's Table depicts Christian redemption because "Christ, our Passover lamb, has been sacrificed" (1 Cor. 5:7). As a living symbol of the Christ-event, the Lord's Table comprises the central element of Christian worship because it represents the fulfillment of Old Testament promises (Luke 2:28–32). As an act of remembrance, it recalls the redemptive work of Jesus Christ (1 Cor. 11:23–26); it symbolizes Christian unity and fellowship (1 Cor. 12:12–31); and it constitutes the church's eschatological hope in the return of Christ and the consummation of his kingdom (Matt. 22:16–18; Acts 1:11; 1 Cor. 11:26). This sense of bonding or unity in covenant community was rehearsed in the apostolic church by means of the fellowship meal or *agapē* feast that accompanied the observance of the Lord's Table (1 Cor. 11:17–22).

Worship in the apostolic church is not without implications for worship and worship renewal in the contemporary Christian church. For instance, if worship recapitulates the Christ-event, then significant attention must be given to the eucharistic aspect of worship and to the value of sign and symbol in instruction and worship (1 Cor. 11:23–26). Likewise, if worship actualizes the church, then the corporate worship experience must balance form and freedom in the structure of worship and provide time for Holy Spirit-prompted lay participation and opportunity for the worship response of meaningful service (1 Cor. 12:4–7). Finally, if worship anticipates the kingdom, then worship has a prophetic function in that it testifies of Christ's triumph over sin and death and engenders hope for the realization of the heavenly worship at the heart of John's apocalyptic vision—the Lamb of God enthroned in the New Jerusalem (Rev. 21:1–5).

The Synagogue and Early Christian Worship. The origins of the Jewish institution known as the synagogue are obscure. It is likely the synagogue evolved from some kind of informal gathering or association of Hebrews during the Babylonian exile. Development continued and perhaps was even spurred by the Torah-based reforms of Ezra and Nehemiah during the mid-fifth century B.C.

The oldest testimony of a diaspora synagogue is an inscription dated to the reign of Ptolemy III Euergetes (247–221 B.C.), found at Schedia in Egypt.

Wherever Jews settled in the diaspora, a synagogue was established. In fact, according to the Jewish historian Josephus, it was difficult to find a place without a synagogue (*Ant* 14.115). More than 150 known ruins of ancient synagogues dot the Mediterranean world from Galilee and Syria, to Asia Minor and Greece, to Italy, Gaul, Spain, North Africa, and Egypt.

The New Testament cites the synagogue as a place of prayer, reading and teaching and preaching of the Old Testament Scriptures, almsgiving, exhortation, and fellowship. New Testament era synagogues were local Jewish congregations scattered throughout Palestine and beyond, and apparently under the jurisdiction of Jerusalem as the religious power center of Judaism (Acts 9:1–2). The synagogue was also the site for judgment and punishment in matters of Jewish law (Mark 13:9; Acts 22:19). Jesus taught, healed, and preached in the synagogues of Palestine, often attacking the abuses associated with the institution—not the institution itself (Mark 1:21; 3:1; Luke 4:16–24).

The Book of Acts indicates the synagogue later became the primary target of early Christian missionary outreach. It seems Jewish Christians constituted themselves within local synagogue congregations for the first several decades of church history, until the Jew-Gentile issue split the two groups (Acts 18:26; 19:8; 22:19; cf. Acts 15:1–35). During New Testament times the synagogue stood alongside the temple as an equivalent religious institution in Judaism. After the destruction of the second temple by the Romans in A.D. 70, the synagogue was considered a full substitute for the temple as the religious institution of Judaism.

Influence on Early Christian Worship. First-century Jewish Christianity rooted in the synagogue tradition had a considerable impact on the development of the early Christian church, specifically in the areas of church architecture, organization, and liturgy.

The influence of synagogue architecture and furnishings on the early Christian church may be seen in the use of the bema or raised platform, including an altar or table (replacing the ark of the Torah in the synagogue) and a pulpit or podium (much like the synagogue lectern used for the Scripture readings and sermon). In addition, seating the worship participants on the platform and arranging the congregation in rows of benches facing the platform are Christian adaptations of synagogue design and practice.

Similarities may also be identified in the functions of the ancient synagogue officers and the officers of the early Christian church. For example, the Christian office of bishop or overseer combined some of the duties of the head of the synagogue (who presided over the worship service), the minister (who often functioned as the synagogue tutor), and the interpreter (who both translated and explained the Scripture lessons and sermon). The concept of spiritual patriarchs or elders in the synagogue congregation carried over into the early church as well. The first deacons of the Christian church were charged with the same commission of the almoners of the ancient Jewish synagogue, gathering and distributing charitable gifts to the needy in the congregation (cf. Acts 6:1–7).

By way of general principle, the influence of the Jewish synagogue on the worship of the early church may be seen in the church's commitment to prayer and instruction in the Scriptures (by means of reading and exposition, cf. Acts 2:42). This development was only natural, given the fact that the early church was essentially Jewish. In addition, the prominent place given to the reading, chanting, and singing of the psalms in early Christian liturgy was borrowed directly from synagogue practice. Thus, much like the Jewish synagogue, the worship of the early Christian church was founded upon praise, prayer, and the exposition of the Scriptures.

Of course, Christian worship continued to develop in distinct worshiping communities through the centuries of church history. Quite naturally the form and practice of Christian liturgy changed over time. Christian worship gradually drifted away from its close ties to Jewish worship, especially as the church became an increasingly "Gentile enterprise." The official schism between the two groups (Judaism and Christianity) occurred in the second century A.D. The intention here is simply to recognize the importance of synagogue worship for the form of worship in the early church and to garner an appreciation for the Jewish roots of the Christian tradition.

Theological Implications. By way of theological principle, the Jewish roots of early Christianity grounded the church of Jesus Christ solidly in the belief of the divine and supernatural origins of the Scriptures, and ordained an apostolic authority in the divine authority of the Old Testament.

By way of worship in the early church, the Jewish Christianity of the first century A.D. facilitated the shift from the theocentric worship characteristic of Judaism to the Christocentric (and even Trinitarian) worship that is the hallmark of Christianity. Second, the church inherited the concept of the centrality of the Scriptures in worship (reading and exposition) from the Jewish synagogue. Third, and significantly given the explosion of spiritual gifts in some segments of the Christian church today, like the Jewish synagogue the early church was primarily a lay institution encouraging extensive lay participation in worship.

However, this shift from Judaism to Jewish Christianity was not without difficulty. Two key issues dominated theological discussion in the early decades of Christianity. In modern terms, the first issue was really one of ethnic and cultural diversity, as the early church debated the implications of the gospel of Jesus Christ for Jew and Gentile (Acts 15:1–35). The compromise solution achieved at the Jerusalem Council later proved ineffective, and to this day the church continues to debate the relationship of "law" and "grace" in the life of the Christian. The second concerned the relationship of Jesus Christ to the primary institutions of Judaism, the priesthood, the temple, and sacrificial worship. Here the author of the Book of Hebrews, by means of typological interpretation, demonstrated Jesus Christ as the greater high priest (chaps. 5, 7), the more perfect temple (chap. 9), and the ultimate sacrifice for sin (chap. 10) to the Jewish Christian recipients of the letter.

Unfortunately, many Jews were unable to accept the harsh teaching that Jesus necessarily abolished the first order (the Old Covenant and its form and practice of worship) to establish a new order of form and practice in worship (Heb. 10:9)—the worship of continual praise and the worship of doing good (Heb. 13:15–16). Likewise, the ever-expanding Gentile church failed to appreciate and nurture the Jewish roots of Christianity and proclaimed itself the "new Israel," further compounding the division between Jew and Gentile. Today in many quarters of the Christian church there is renewed effort to implement Paul's missionary vision—"first for the Jew, then for the Gentile" (Rom. 1:16). ANDREW E. HILL

See also CHURCH, THE; ISRAEL; TABERNACLE; TEMPLE; TYPE, TYPOLOGY.

Bibliography. *ABD* 6:973–79; M. J. Dawn, *Keeping the Sabbath Wholly: Ceasing, Resting, Embracing, Feasting;* W. Dyrness, *Themes in Old Testament Theology;* M. Eliade, *The Sacred and the Profane;* C. D. Erickson, *Participating in Worship: History, Theory, and Practice;* A. J. Heschel, *The Sabbath: Its Meaning for Modern Man;* A. E. Hill, *Enter His Courts with Praise!;* C. Jones, G. Wainwright, and E. Yarnold, *The Study of Liturgy*; R. P. Martin, *Worship in the Early Church*; A. Millgram, *Jewish Worship;* W. O. E. Oesterley, *The Jewish Background of Christian Liturgy;* D. Peterson, *Engaging with God: A Biblical Theology of Worship;* R. N. Schaper, *In His Presence;* M. H. Shepherd, *The Psalms for Christian Worship: A Practical Guide;* A. W. Tozer, *The Best of A. W. Tozer;* R. deVaux, *Ancient Israel: Religious Institutions;* R. E. Webber, *Worship Old and New;* idem, *Worship is a Verb;* W. H. Willimon, *Word, Water, Wine and Bread;* J. F. White, *Introduction to Christian Worship.*

Wrath of God. The Scriptures use various terms to express God's emotions that are in contrast to his love for, pleasure in, and satisfaction with his people. In the Old Testament at least six terms are used to express his negative reactions to humanity, particularly to his covenant people. These terms, all of which express varied shades or degrees of wrath, anger, displeasure, or vexation, are the following: *ʾaph* (to be angry), *zāʿaph* and derivatives (to be wroth, displeased, sad); *ḥêmâh* (indignation, anger, wrath); *kâʿas* (to be angry, wrathful, indignant, vexed, grieved); *ʿebrâh* (rage, wrath); *qâsaph* (to be displeased, angry, wroth); *ʾsaneh* (to hate). In the New Testament there are more than twenty references to the anger, wrath, or vengeance (*orgē*) of God and a few references to indignation and displeasure (*achthŏs*). These terms are to be considered anthropopathic expressions; human terms, however, cannot give the full meaning of the infinite and sovereign God's emotional experiences. As his love is infinitely incomprehensible, so are his displeasure, hate, anger, wrath, and vengeance. There is good reason indeed for the writer to the Hebrews to warn sinful people that it "is a dreadful thing to fall into the hands of the living God" (Heb. 10:31).

In order to understand what the Scriptures reveal concerning the anger and wrath of God, it is necessary to consider his character, the contexts in which they are spoken of, and with whom God is displeased, angry, or wroth.

God is holy; he totally and completely distances himself from sin, evil, corruption, and the resultant filth and guilt. He maintains his purity and rejects, fights against, and destroys that which would offend, attack, or undo his holiness and love. Hence, God's anger and wrath must always be seen in relation to his maintaining and defending his attributes of love and holiness, as well as his righteousness and justice. The emotion or passion that moves God to this maintaining and defending is expressed by the terms "displeasure," "indignation," "anger," and "wrath." A consequence of his wrath is vengeance, punishment, and death.

The wrath of God has been revealed throughout the entire history of humanity. It was implied when Adam was warned he would die if he disbelieved and disobeyed God (Gen. 2:17) and when he revealed that Satan's head would be crushed (Gen. 3:15) because God's loving character, will, and purposes were challenged by Satan and Adam and Eve. God revealed the execution of his wrath when he drove Adam and Eve from Paradise (Gen. 3:24–25). God revealed his displeasure when, placing a curse on Cain, he banished him (Gen. 4:11). When he destroyed the cosmos by the flood God demonstrated the results of his grief and wrath with his image-bearer (Gen. 6–8).

The revelation of God's wrath was clearly demonstrated by means of the plagues of Egypt and the destruction of Pharaoh's army (Exod. 15:7). His anger and wrath also arose against Israel with whom he had covenanted when they worshiped the golden calf (Exod. 32:11), and when they rebelled after hearing the report of ten of the twelve spies (Num. 14:11–12, 23; Heb. 3:10–11; 4:3). Moses warned of the consequences of God's wrath for Israel if as a people they broke the covenant (Deut. 11:17; 29:23, 28); because

God's love was offended they would experience famine, defeat, exile, and death. The Chronicler referred to God's wrath repeatedly because Israel, God's covenant people, ignored, rejected, and spurned his love, his will, and their life with God-given blessings. The psalmists referred to the wrath of God against nations (Pss. 2:5; 59:5, 13; 78:49; 79:6), against personal enemies (Ps. 55:3), against the covenant people for their sin (Pss. 89:46; 92:7; 95:11), and against the psalmists themselves (Ps. 88:7). The prophets likewise prophesied concerning the wrath of God executed upon nations for their hatred of and destruction wreaked on the covenant people (Isa. 13:13; 14:6). The anger of God was demonstrated in the exile of Israel (Isa. 60:11).

The wrath of God that the New Testament speaks of is to be expressed in judgments on a wicked, rebellious covenant people (Matt. 3:7; Luke 3:7), and upon those who refuse to believe in and accept Jesus Christ as the Savior of the world (John 3:36). Paul repeatedly warns about the wrath of God (Rom. 1:18; 2:5), from which people are to be saved (Rom. 5:9). All people are under wrath (Eph. 2:3), and the only way to escape this wrath, which is sure to be in full and fierce force in the judgment day, is to believe in Jesus Christ who bore the curse of the covenant and endured the wrath of God when he was crucified. This same Christ will execute divine wrath and vengeance to its fullest degree in judgment day (Rev. 6:16–17).

GERARD VAN GRONINGEN

See also DISCIPLINE; GOD; JUDGMENT; JUDGMENT, DAY OF; JUSTICE; PROVIDENCE OF GOD; PUNISHMENT; SIN; VENGEANCE.

Bibliography. A. T. Hanson, *The Wrath of the Lamb;* J. B. Payne, *The Theology of the Older Testament;* R. V. G. Tasker, *The Biblical Doctrine of the Wrath of God;* R. White, Jr., *ZPEB,* 5:990–95.

Yy

Yahweh. *See* God, Names of.

Year. *See* Time.

Zz

Zealot. Recent studies seek to distinguish among several features of intertestamental Judaism to which the term "zealot" might be applied. The term could refer to certain persons with fervent devotion to God's Law. The term could also be applied to a general attitude and movement illustrated by Judas of Gamala and Saddok, a Pharisee, who led an abortive revolt against a Roman census in A.D. 6. These leaders promised "that Heaven would be their zealous helper." The Jewish historian Josephus calls the movement, "The Fourth of the Philosophies," and says it agreed with the Pharisees, differing only in their "passion for liberty . . . convinced that God alone is their leader and master"; they were willing to die for this conviction (*Ant* 18.1.4 [23]). The movement could also be called a "violent religious revolutionary" one. Josephus also speaks of "The Zealots" (first in *War* 4.3.9 [161]) as one of several Jewish revolutionary factions, one he says was a coalition of bandits and miscreants, who fought between themselves and against the Romans in the Judeo-Roman war (A.D. 66–70). He names such leaders as Eleazer son of Simon and John of Gischala.

Matthew 10:4; Mark 3:18; Luke 6:15; and Acts 1:13 term one of the apostles "Simon the Zealot." The distinct revolutionary faction developed only later; the title must describe either Simon's pious zeal or participation in the revolutionary spirit.

Some scholars associate Jesus with the zealot movement. The title over the cross, "This is the King of the Jews," may indicate Pilate condemned him as a violent nationalist. The whole of Jesus' teaching and actions indicate to the contrary. A true zealot revolutionary would never advocate, "Love your enemies" (Matt. 5:44), paying taxes to Caesar (Matt. 22:21; Mark 12:17; Luke 20:25), and satisfaction with two swords (Luke 22:38).

J. JULIUS SCOTT, JR.

Bibliography. W. R. Farmer, *Maccabees, Zealots, and Josephus;* M. Hengel, *The Zealots;* R. Horsley, *NovT* 27 (1986): 159–92; M. Smith, *HTR* 64 (1971): 1–19.

Zechariah, Theology of. ***Introduction.*** *Authorship.* The book of Zechariah falls naturally into two parts: chapters 1–8 and 9–14. In the first part we find dates locating the prophecies in the Persian era (late sixth century B.C.), references to Joshua the high priest and Zerubbabel the Davidic governor, encouragement to rebuild the temple, and a mixture of oracles and visions. However, in the second part dates are missing, the leaders are unnamed shepherds, and the rebuilding of the temple has no place. These differences plus distinct stylistic features have led most scholars to see more than one author of this important prophetic work. Zechariah wrote the first eight chapters, but perhaps chapters 9–14 stem from a later anonymous prophet. If so, it is important to emphasize that chapters 9–14 are still fully inspired, just as the anonymous New Testament book, Hebrews, is inspired. Many scholars also connect the second section of Zechariah with Malachi because Zechariah 9–11, Zechariah 12–14, and Malachi all begin with the word "oracle." Alternately, some scholars argue that chapters 9–14 were composed by Zechariah, but at a later time in his life.

Historical Background. In 587 B.C. Nebuchadnezzar, king of Babylon, destroyed Jerusalem and its temple, exiling many of Judah's leaders to Babylon. After a time God raised up Cyrus, the Persian king, to defeat Babylon (539) and to release the Jews from captivity by issuing an edict in 538 allowing them to return to their land. Not only did he liberate them; he returned the temple vessels that Nebuchadnezzar had plundered and gave them permission to rebuild their temple with Persian funds (Ezra 6:3–5).

Rebuilding the Temple. When the Jews returned from Babylon, they followed the restoration program of the earlier prophets, Ezekiel and Jeremiah. The former predicted the rebuilding of the temple (Ezek. 40–48). Both foresaw Judah being led by two rulers: a Zadokite priest (Jer. 33:18; Ezek. 44) and a Davidic prince (Jer. 33:15–17; Ezek. 34:23). Sheshbazzar led the first group of Jews home. Since he was a Davidic descendant (son of the last king of Judah, Jehoiachin) he was qualified to be the first governor. However, he only succeeded in laying the temple's foundation (Ezra 6:16). Zerubbabel, Sheshbazzar's nephew and Jehoiachin's grandson, became the second governor. He assumed leadership during a severe economic crisis. The Lord raised up the prophet Haggai to reveal the cause: neglecting to rebuild the temple (Hag. 1:1–11). At about the same time God inspired Zechariah to prophesy. Together Haggai and Zechariah joined in common cause to encourage Zerubbabel, the Davidic governor, and Joshua, the Zadokite high priest, to complete this important building project (Zech. 4:9).

Theological Themes. *Building for Christ.* Christians emphasize the spiritual world and the second coming of Christ to such an extent that they neglect material needs. The Book of Zechariah shows the importance of this world. It affirms the necessity of human institutions, political structures, and mundane things such as buildings. In order for the Jews to reestablish themselves in the land, they had to rebuild the temple and restore the priesthood; they also had to set up a form of governance.

This provides an example for us today. Although "our citizenship is in heaven" (Phil. 3:20), we still are members of political communities on earth. While we cannot hope to bring the eschatological kingdom of God to earth by our efforts, we can be involved in society as influences for good. Our government is not a theocracy as was that of Zechariah, so we may not be able to fashion our secular and pluralistic governments completely according to Christianity. But we can attempt to make our societies more just.

We are also members of Christian societies: local churches, denominations, and parachurch organizations. We can encourage the building of houses of worship, hospitals, rescue missions, mental health centers, food distribution centers, and shelters for the homeless, the battered, and unwed mothers. In addition we should construct Christian schools, colleges, and theological seminaries for the purpose of training Christian leaders.

Worship. With its emphasis on the temple, the prophecy of Zechariah also speaks to us about the importance of worship. Following the reforms of Josiah (ca. 620 B.C.) the only acceptable place to offer animal sacrifice was Jerusalem. God was pleased when the faithful would entreat his favor there (Zech. 8:20–22). The sacrifices made Jerusalem holy (14:20–21). People were expected to come to Zion for the pilgrim feasts if they wanted to receive heaven's blessings (14:16–17). Not only were there shouts of joy and songs of gladness in the temple (8:19) but there were times of holy silence in the awesome presence of God (2:13). This last part is directly applicable. It is good to worship God both with loud praises and with silent devotion.

Some scholars have discounted the religious value of this book because it is tied so closely to the Jerusalem cult. However, we must be careful not to read Christian biases into the Old Testament. Of course, Jesus spoke of a day when the devout would not need to go to Jerusalem for God would accept all who worshiped "in spirit and truth" (John 4:20–24). And we know that God's presence is not limited to human shrines (Acts 7:48; 17:24). Furthermore, we now that animal sacrifice is now unnecessary on account of our Lord's final sacrifice for sin (Heb. 9–10). Nevertheless, through Moses God had given his people the forms of worship that eventually became established in Jerusalem; these were valid for their time.

Zechariah is still relevant for our time, though, because it highlights the necessity of obedience in worship. Although today we enjoy greater freedom in the ways we approach God than the Old Testament believers did, we still must be careful to worship as God ordains, not in ways entirely of our choosing. Under the Old Covenant, animal sacrifice was required. Under the New Covenant, we must come to God through the sacrifice of his Son. Also, instead of the blood of dead animals, God desires us to offer our bodies as "living sacrifices" (Rom. 12:1) and to offer continually the "sacrifice of praise" (Heb. 13:15). As with the tower of Babel (Gen. 11:1–9), humans are still trying unsuccessfully to reach God through edifices made of false religions or good works. These ways lead to confusion, for Jesus is the only way to the Father (John 14:6).

The Sovereignity of God. Christ is controlled by Israel's God, not by the pagan deities. One of the reasons for the punishment of exile was that the Jews had been participating in the Canaanite fertility cult. They erroneously thought that Baal rode upon the storm cloud bringing rain to the crops. However, it is the Lord who blesses the farmer with showers in response to prayer (Zech. 10:1–2). He also controls history. God scattered his people among the nations; he will bring them back to their land again (10:9–10). Moreover, he will punish the nations who harmed his people (2:8–9; 10:11; 12:9).

Providence. The Persian authorities allowed the rebuilding of the temple but it was not until later, in the time of Nehemiah (445 B.C.), that permission to restore the city walls was granted. Because some of the local peoples opposed the Jews, the returnees were concerned about their security. But God dispelled their fears by promising to encircle Jerusalem with his protective fire and by assuring them of his presence in their midst (2:5). An additional sign of his providence was his commitment to end the economic depression. As a reward for their obedient response in rebuilding the temple, God would bless his people with prosperity (8:9–13).

Satan. In Zechariah 3 we catch a glimpse of a heavenly tribunal in which Joshua, the high priest, stands accused by a figure known as "The Satan" or "The Adversary." The term in Hebrew has the definite article so it should be translated as a title rather than by "Satan," as if it were a proper name. As represented in Zechariah, he is not good, for he is rebuked (3:2). However, at this stage in progressive revelation, he was not understood to be thoroughly evil either, since he is presented as a member of the divine King's court. He is somewhat akin to a prosecuting attorney in modern, Western societies. Similarly, Revelation 12:10 calls him the "accuser of our brothers." God's revelation in the Old Testament is limited; having the benefit of the New Testament our picture of Satan as an entirely wicked spiritual foe, fallen from heaven, is more complete. Nevertheless, Zechariah agrees with the New Testament that we should not be afraid of the enemy of our souls. We must trust God for forgiveness as Joshua did; then we do not need to fear any accusations.

Sin, Sanctification, and Salvation. The book opens with a call to repentance, reminding the people of the sins of their ancestors. The former prophets had risen up to rebuke the previous generation but no repentance followed. Zechariah exhorts the Jews not to repeat the past. Instead God promises that if the people return to him, he will return to them (1:2–6; cf. 7:8–14). Specific sins of idolatry (13:2), pride (of Assyria, 10:11), and lack of compassion (7:9–11) are listed.

The outward evidence of the inward repentance was the willingness of the returnees to start building the temple again. God showed his favor by first removing the guilt of Joshua, the high priest (3:1–5) and then the guilt of the land (3:9). The prophet also sees iniquity and wickedness being transported from Judah to Babylon in the vision of the measuring basket (5:5–11). The second part of the book reveals that toward the end of history, God will open a fountain capable of cleansing from "sin and impurity" (13:1). In that day, the Lord will save his people by bringing them back to their land (8:7; 10:6–10) and by providing for them (9:16).

Ethics. Zechariah highlights the importance of acting justly toward others and treating them with kindness and mercy. We should especially be careful not to mistreat those weaker elements of society: widows, orphans, and resident foreigners (7:9–10). This teaching goes back to Moses (Exod. 22:22; 23:9), is central to the prophets (Isa. 1:16–17; Jer. 7:5–7; Amos 5:15, 24), and is confirmed in the New Testament (Acts 6:1–3; James 1:27).

There is also a warning not to mistreat God's chosen people, the Jews, for they are "the apple of his eye" (Zech. 2:8). The Gentiles will be punished for any harm they inflict on them (2:9). Consequently, Christians must take a stand against anti-Semitism. Today, however, God's people is a more inclusive group comprised of Jews and Gentiles who have believed in Jesus (Rom. 11:13–24). But God has not rejected the Jews (Rom. 11:2) who will one day return to the Lord as a people (Rom. 11:26).

Preparation for the Gospel. Zechariah anticipated the day when the door of salvation would be opened to non-Jews. He predicted that many nations would worship the Lord in Jerusalem. They will take hold of the robe of a Jew and say, "We have heard that God is with you" (8:20–23). Those nations refusing to participate in the festival of tabernacles will be punished (14:16–19). This inclusiveness theme is not unique to Zechariah. Isaiah and Micah also looked to a day when the nations would seek God in Zion (Isa. 2:2–3; Mic. 4:1–2). The Jews were to be a light to the nations (Isa. 42:6; 49:6); they were to be God's witnesses (Isa. 43:12). Foreign peoples, including some of their rulers, would come to the Jews bringing their wealth and acknowledging the God of Israel to be the only deity (Isa. 45:14; 49:7, 22–23).

Although Judaism has not been a missionary religion throughout most of its history, there were those Jews in the second temple period who endeavored to convert Gentiles to Judaism (Matt. 23:15). Those foreigners who responded partly fulfilled Zechariah's prophecy. It was also partly fulfilled in the many pagans who became "God-fearers." These did not fully convert but gave up their idols to worship the one, true God. They could enter the court of the Gentiles in the Jerusalem temple but were forbidden upon pain of death from going beyond the wall of partition between Jews and Gentiles. Christians see an even greater fulfillment of Old Testament prophecy in the finished work of Jesus. The separating wall has been destroyed by the death of Christ so that all may come to God through him, whether Jew or Gentile (Eph. 2:13–16).

Pneumatology. Zechariah teaches us not to rely on our own strength, for God accomplishes his will through the Spirit (4:6). Furthermore, it teaches us to trust in God's Word, which is inspired by the Spirit (7:12).

Messianism. Zechariah contributes to the development of messianism in the Old Testament. Isaiah predicted that a branch would grow out of the stump of Jesse (David's father), who would rule in righteousness and bring about a return to paradise (11:1–9). Zechariah focused his attention on Zerubbabel, the Branch, or descendant of David, who would rebuild the temple (3:8; 4:9; 6:12–13). As mentioned above, the postexilic Jews were following the restoration plan of Ezekiel. He had described paradise-like conditions accompanying the rebuilding of the temple (47:1–12). Because of this and because of Haggai's words, that God was about to overturn the kingdoms of the world and appoint Zerubbabel his signet ring (2:20–23), many hoped that Zerubbabel was the messiah and would usher in the kingdom of God. However, in spite of the fact that crowns are mentioned, only Joshua the priest is crowned (Zech. 6:11). There are hints of restoration of the monarchy—"royal honor" and "throne" (Zech. 6:13)—but nothing comes to fruition. Haggai's prophecy was fulfilled because God did shake the nations by raising up the Persians to free his people. And Zerubbabel did serve as God's signet ring by carrying out divine plans in his capacity as governor of Judah. But he did not become king, and did not bring the kingdom of God to earth.

Zechariah's prophecy was fulfilled because Zerubbabel did complete the temple. The fact that Joshua is crowned but not Zerubbabel, with that one crown being kept in reserve in the temple (6:14), indicates that it was not God's time to introduce the messiah, the Davidic descendant who would reign forever in righteousness. Rather, God was planning to provide spiritual leadership and governance through the priestly line. This is exactly what happened following Zerubbabel when God sent Ezra the priest to the people in 458 B.C.

Eschatology. The second part of Zechariah announces the universal peaceable domain of a humble human king (9:9–10). Zerubbabel was a type of that one who was to come. Zechariah 14:1–9 also testifies that the Lord himself will come to earth to reign over all. Jesus, who is fully man and fully God, inaugurated God's kingdom in his first advent but his reign will not be completely realized until his second coming (1 Cor. 15:24–28). In that day, Jesus will descend to the Mount of Olives (Zech. 14:4; Acts 1:11) in the same way that he ascended, bringing his heavenly host with him (Zech. 14:5; Matt. 25:31).

The two olive trees, or anointed ones, in the Book of Zechariah are clearly Joshua and Zerubbabel (4:3, 11–14). However, John reuses this imagery to disclose the two endtime witnesses of the apocalypse (Rev. 11:1–13).

New Testament Usage. The New Testament quotes Zechariah seventy-one times. Thirty-one of these are in Revelation and twenty-seven in the Gospels. The second half of Zechariah is the source of the more familiar passages cited in the New Testament. For example, Jesus' triumphant entry into Jerusalem on a donkey shows that he is the king whom the prophet foretold (Zech. 9:9–10; Matt. 21:4–5; John 12:14–15). For betraying the Lord, the chief priests paid Judas thirty pieces of silver (Matt. 26:31), which he subsequently cast into the temple (Matt. 27:3–5). Matthew interpreted this to be a fulfillment of the Old Testament (cf. Matt. 27:9, which mentions Jeremiah but is a quote from Zech. 11:12–13). Zechariah 13:7 says, "Strike the shepherd, and the sheep will be scattered." This was fulfilled when the disciples abandoned Jesus during the trial and crucifixion (Matt. 26:31, 56). A double fulfillment is recorded for Zechariah 12:10, which predicts mourning for a pierced one by those who pierced him: first, when Jesus' side was pierced on the cross (John 19:34–37), and second, when Jesus returns at the end of time (Rev. 1:7).

William B. Nelson, Jr.

See also Haggai, Theology of; Israel; Malachi, Theology of; Prophet, Prophetess, Prophecy; Vision(s).

Bibliography. E. Achtmeier, *Nahum-Malachi;* J. G. Baldwin, *Haggai, Zechariah, Malachi;* R. J. Coggins, *Haggai, Zechariah, Malachi;* P. D. Hanson, *The Dawn of Apocalyptic;* R. A. Mason, *The Books of Haggai, Zechariah, and Malachi;* C. L. Meyers and E. M. Meyers, *Haggai, Zechariah* 1–8; D. L. Petersen, *Haggai and Zechariah* 1–8; R. L. Smith, *Micah-Malachi.*

Zephaniah, Theology of. Zephaniah, whose name, translated "Yahweh has hidden/protected," indicating his parents' personal faith, was himself a faithful messenger to God's people. He prophesied during the reign of Josiah (1:1; 640–609 B.C.), the sixteenth king of Judah and one of its few good rulers. Zephaniah's faithfulness to God was challenged as he matured during or after the corrupt reigns of Josiah's grandfather, Manasseh, and his father, Amon. His conscientious Yahwism is clear from his clarion call of judgment. The book perhaps also underscores Zephaniah's piety by showing his genealogy of four generations going back to Hezekiah (1:1), another godly king of Judah, who was also an ancestor of Josiah. Zephaniah's association with these good kings could imply that he shares their godly qualities.

It is unclear when in Josiah's reign Zephaniah prophesied. Since pagan practices are condemned (1:4–9), many suggest a date prior to 621 B.C., the start of Josiah's religious reforms, calling the people back to a true worship of God. This is not necessarily the case, however, since calling for spiritual renewal and its actualization are two different and not necessarily contemporaneous things. These prophecies could come from later in Josiah's reign, calling the people to obey the same call to godliness to which their king had already responded.

There is theological significance in noting the practices condemned by the prophet. In the religious sphere these include apostasy (1:4–5), the worship of foreign gods, and abandoning the only true God. He also bemoans a lack of integrity on the part of civil and religious leaders, who exploit positions of trust for personal gain (3:3–4).

Even more invidious is the apathy of so many. As wine resting on its dregs stagnates (1:12), so many of God's people are lethargic in their faith. They do not in words deny God's existence, but rather deny his power in their actions, claiming him powerless, or at least inactive, in the history of Israel and in their personal lives. This is a supreme insult to the God who formed them as a nation and acted throughout Israel's history to preserve them. Even the angry questioning of God by Habakkuk and Job is preferable to this glacierlike, grinding boredom. As many marriages are ruined by loss of interest, often leading to infidelity, so these two manifestations of trouble are present in the life of the nation that was betrothed to God.

Because of these wrongs, and more, God turns against his people in judgment. Like a cuckold who finally reacts to continued perfidy, so Yahweh reacts against Israel. This time of reaction in judgment, called "the day of the Lord" or "that day," is a theme that unites the prophetic collection (see, e.g., 1:7, 14; 3:11, 16). The "day" is not monolithic, but rather multifaceted. An early conception of it by Israel was as a time of blessing and well-being for them as God's people. God's enemies would be destroyed and those true to him treated well (see Amos 5:18). They soon found that this concept was simultaneously right and wrong. It was correct in that followers of God would be blessed but wrong since just because Israel had entered into a covenant relationhip with God at Sinai, their position as blessed people was not henceforth inviolable. While God was true to his covenant, there were also responsibilities for Israel which, if violated, resulted in judgment and loss of covenant blessing. Blessing was bound to obedience, not to a historical relationship. As Israel's history reminded her, and as we need to preach today, there is no second-generation child of God. Faithful ancestors do not assure including the next generation in the covenant. Only fidelity to the covenant can do that.

The day is not only one of judgment, however, but also and simultaneously a day of hope and blessing. Israel was right. Fortune will follow fidelity, so if the latter were restored, the former would follow. Therefore, in addition to Zephaniah's severe warnings of judgment (1:2–3:8), there are also promises of hope (3:9–20). God is both a God of justice and holiness, exacting judgment upon those who oppose him, and also a God of love and compassion, showing these to his faithful followers. Judah is called to abandon her practices as opponents to benefit from his compassion. Instead of abandoning God, Judah is to return to him (2:3), abandoning apathy and syncretism for humility and right living.

The day of the Lord is also shown as international and not just parochial, since judgment will descend on other nations also (Philistines, 2:4–7; Transjordanian Moabites and Ammonites, 2:8–11; Ethiopians or Egyptians, 2:12; Assyrians, 2:13–15; cf. more generally, 3:6–8). All powers, great or small, are under the power and authority of God. This is in stark and ironic contrast to the denial of this same God by his own people of any power or interest in the world (1:12).

Even more encompassing than the day of the Lord in the structure of Zephaniah is "the Lord" Yahweh himself. His name is not only in the book's opening phrase; it is also its final word, forming an envelope providing the parameters within which Zephaniah's whole message must be viewed. Zephaniah's prophecies in particular, and indeed all of Scripture, are theocentric.

The divine name "Yahweh," used often in Zephaniah, is theologically significant. Anachronistically translated "LORD" in most English versions, it is God's personal, covenant name revealed to his own people (Exod. 6:2–3). Not the universal, impersonal "God," it connotes intimacy, being restricted to those closely related to God. This is doubly significant in these prophecies of judgment and hope. Judgment follows transgressing the intimate relationship into which the people and their ancestors had voluntarily entered. Their judge is not an impersonal unknown, but one with whom they were intimate and had personally wronged. In spite of the wrong, and the punishment God must dispense, he still reveals himself to Judah as Yahweh, their loving covenant God even though he must punish Israel because she has abandoned him. He cannot abandon them or break his covenant. If the people would only hear, the very name by which he presents himself to them in this judgment is an offer of continued love and hope.

DAVID W. BAKER

See also DAY OF THE LORD, GOD, CHRIST; GOD; ISRAEL; PROPHET, PROPHETESS, PROPHECY.

Bibliography. E. Achtemeier, *Nahum–Malachi;* D. W. Baker, *Nahum, Habakkuk, Zephaniah;* J. J. M. Roberts, *Nahum, Habakkuk, and Zephaniah.*

Zion. *See* JERUSALEM.

Scripture Index

Exodus

Leviticus

Numbers

Deuteronomy

Joshua

2 Samuel

1 Kings

1 Chronicles

Psalms

Proverbs

Ecclesiastes

Song of Solomon

Daniel

Hosea

Obadiah

Jonah

Micah

Mark

John

Acts

1 Corinthians

2 Corinthians

Ephesians

Philippians

2 Thessalonians

1 Timothy

Scripture Index

James

Extrabiblical Writings

1 Esdras

2 Esdras

4 Esdras

4 Ezra

Tobit

Wisdom of Solomon

Ecclesiasticus

Baruch

2 Baruch